P9-CFV-611

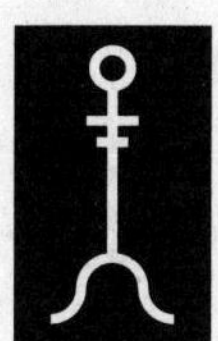

A ROLLING STONE PRESS BOOK

EDITOR

HOLLY GEORGE-WARREN

ASSOCIATE EDITOR

NINA PEARLMAN

ASSISTANT EDITOR

JORDAN N. MAMONE

EDITORIAL ASSISTANT

ANDREW SIMON

EDITORIAL CONTRIBUTORS

ANDREA DANESE, ELIZABETH GALL, MICHELE GARNER, KATHY HUCK, WENDY MITCHELL

WRITERS

Ann Abel
Steve Appleford
Steve Dollar
Paul Evans
Bill Friskics-Warren
Holly George-Warren
Jordan N. Mamone
Steven Mirkin
Wendy Mitchell
Andrea Odintz
Nina Pearlman
Patricia Romanowski
Michael Shore
Andrew Simon
Richard Skanse
Elisabeth Vincentelli

(Contributors from previous editions: Ken Braun, Shawn Dahl, Paul Evans, Jim Farber, Steve Futterman, Elysa Gardner, Nelson George, Holly George-Warren, Jeff Howrey, Ben Hunter, Ira Kaplan, Mark Kemp, Evelyn McDonnell, John Milward, Steven Mirkin, Jon Pareles, Patricia Romanowski, Mitchell Schneider, Michael Shore)

THE Rolling Stone ENCYCLOPEDIA OF ROCK & ROLL

Revised and Updated for the 21st Century

Edited by
Holly George-Warren
and
Patricia Romanowski

Consulting Editor
Jon Pareles

FIRESIDE

A ROLLING STONE PRESS BOOK

New York | London | Toronto | Sydney | Singapore

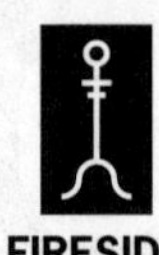

FIRESIDE
Rockefeller Center
1230 Avenue of the Americas
New York, NY 10020

For information about special discounts for bulk purchases,
please contact Simon & Schuster Special Sales:
1-800-456-6798 or business@simonandschuster.com

Designed by Joy O'Meara

Manufactured in the United States of America

3 5 7 9 10 8 6 4 2

Library of Congress Cataloging-in-Publication Data

The Rolling stone encyclopedia of rock & roll /edited by Patricia Romanowski and Holly George-Warren ;
consulting editor, Jon Pareles.—Rev. and updated for the 21st century.
p. cm.
Rev. ed. of: New Rolling stone encyclopedia of rock & roll.
"A Rolling Stone Press book."
Includes discographies.
1. Rock music—Encyclopedias. I. Romanowski, Patricia. II. George-Warren, Holly.
III. Pareles, John. IV. Rolling stone (San Francisco, Calif.) V. New Rolling stone encyclopedia of rock & roll.

ML102.R6 R64 2001

781.66'03—dc21 2001040285

ISBN 0-7432-0120-5

Acknowledgments

Just as this third edition of *The Rolling Stone Encyclopedia of Rock & Roll* has multiplied in word count from the last, so has the size of the team whose efforts have made the book a reality.

First, of course, our gratitude goes to the tireless and talented writers who turned the past five years' worth of rock & roll history into pithy encyclopedia entries: Steve Appleford, Steve Dollar, former *Encyclopedia* contributor Paul Evans, Bill Friskics-Warren, Andrea Odintz, Richard Skanse, and Elisabeth Vincentelli. Other writers contributed as well: last edition vets Michael Shore, Mark Kemp, and Steve Mirkin; former Rolling Stone Press editors Ann Abel and Wendy Mitchell; as well as the most recent Rolling Stone Press staff editors, Andrew Simon, Jordan Mamone, and Nina Pearlman, the three of whom demonstrated diligence and good cheer under the worst of circumstances. Thanks also to the writers who contributed to the previous editions, from which this book was built: Ken Braun, Jim Farber, Steve Futterman, Elysa Gardner, Nelson George, Jeff Howry, Ira Kaplan, Evelyn McDonnell, John Milward, and Mitchell Schneider. My above-mentioned staff at Rolling Stone Press not only wrote entries but helped with editing, fact-checking, proofreading, and photo research. Thanks, too, to Andrea Danese, Elizabeth Gall, and Michele Garner, who contributed editorial expertise to the project. My coeditor, Patricia Romanowski, added her unparalleled editing, writing, and organizational powers to this project—for the third time. Thanks to Jon Pareles for his guidance. And we're very grateful to our team of Rolling Stone Press interns: Joshua Sturtevant, Christopher Cooper, Kim Curry, Marya Garskof, Rachael Shook, Emily Bodenberg, Agata Zak, Heidi Pauken, Becki Heller, Marcie Muscat, and Dana Grayson. Former and current Rolling Stone staffers who helped immensely include John D'Amico, Allison Grochowski, Evan Schlansky, Doug Gottlieb, Lee Berresford, and Omnia Othello Leathers. Thanks, also, to additional fact-checkers Michael Chandler, Stephen Pener, and Carrie Smith.

Without the fine team at Fireside/Simon & Schuster, we couldn't have created the book we envisioned. A thousand kudos to our very supportive editor, Dominick Anfuso, as well as Kristen McGuiness, Nancy Inglis, Suzanne Anderson, Jennifer Love, and J. P. Jones for their editorial expertise. We also appreciate the efforts of our agent, Sarah Lazin, and her staff, Paula Balzer and Dena Koklanaris, as well as those of Rolling Stone's Jann S. Wenner, Kent Brownridge, John Lagana, Fred Woodward, and Evelyn Bernal.

Our thanks to the numerous musicians, their publicists, managers, and record company personnel who helped us get the facts straight. Above-and-beyond honors go to Graham Parker, Jeff Hanna, Spencer Davis, Will Rigby, Ed Sanders, Phoebe Snow, Irwin Chusid, Andy Schwartz, Eric Andersen, Sue Khaury, Cynthia Barry, Lisa Kidd, Gary Lambert, Suzzy Roche, Meryl Wheeler, Steve Chapman, Bruce Duff, Mike Donahue, Daniel Markus, Debbie Rawlings, Michelle Chambers, Mitchell Greenhill, Tim Livingston, Charles Turner, Rick Gershon, Bill Bentley, Gary Stewart, James Austin, David McLees, David Dorn, Harry Weinger, Steve Burton, John Jackson, Brian Gilmore, John Fisher, Risa Morley, Alison Tarnofsky, and Karen Wiessen. Others who went out of their way for us include Robert Warren, David McGee, Anthony DeCurtis, and Michael Hill. Finally, we thank all those readers who made the previous editions such a success. We hope you find rock & roll trivia nirvana with this first edition of the 21st century.

Holly George-Warren
May 2001

The *Encyclopedia* writers acknowledge the following:

SA thanks Holly George-Warren and Andrew Simon, along with that heroic army of RS Press fact-checkers. Also, extra points go to John Doe, Dave Alvin, Craig Rosen, and Lisa Fancher.

SD: Thanks to neighborly Fall completist Steven Joerg for technical assistance and letting me bum smokes (as well as rare vinyl from his golden archive). And thanks again to Holly and the staff of Rolling Stone Press for making this such a congenial and, even, educational experience. I dedicate half of my future *Rock & Roll Jeopardy* winnings to you.

BFW: Thanks to Holly, Patty, and Andrew, especially for your patience toward the end.

AO wishes to thank Holly George-Warren for the opportunity, Patricia Romanowski for the feedback, Andrew Simon and Wendy Mitchell for their hard work and patience, David McGee for his continued guidance, Norma and Mel Odintz for their belief in my goals, and Jeffrey and Benjamin Cohen for their love and support.

EV would like to thank Holly George-Warren and everyone at Rolling Stone Press for their assistance.

Preface
to the First Edition

by Jon Pareles

There's no stopping rock & roll. It is the most vital, unpredictable force in pop culture, and the exception to every rule. Like all important popular art, it can speak to and from the public's heart of hearts even if it has been crafted by the most knowing artisans. And even at its most elaborate it hints at a rebel spirit: the idea that an outsider with something important to say can broadcast it to the world. At its best, rock can be entertainment, good business, and catharsis all at once; at its worst, it's only rock & roll.

It is music that just can't be pinned down, a contradiction any old way you choose it. Rock can be both amateur and professional, innocent and slick, subtle and crass, sincere and contrived, smart and stupid. It is a happy bastard style, claiming a pedigree from jazz, blues, Tin Pan Alley, country, classical music, movies, television, sex, drugs, art, literature, electronics, and out-and-out noise. It is rooted in real emotion; it is also rooted in racism, cynicism, and greed.

Rock accepts everything its detractors say, only to laugh it off. Sure, its basics are stolen, and its ideas are often clichés. Yes, it tends to aim for a lowest common denominator and appeal to base, primal impulses. It is proud to be a commodity, one that brings in billions of dollars, with "artistic" success frequently measured in sales figures. It doesn't even have to be in tune. No matter—rock & roll moves people, in simple and sophisticated ways. And it never takes no for an answer.

The history of rock & roll is a wild tangle, affected by changes in technology, media, demographics, politics, and the economy as well as by the inspirations of packagers and musicians. Rock cheerfully accepts all its roles; it is product and spectacle and art, something for everybody, and its development and documentation are by no means orderly.

In the '50s, pop was infiltrated by rockabilly from Memphis and blues from Chicago and rhythm & blues from New Orleans and doo-wop from city street corners, more like outbreaks of some mysterious contagion—rockin' pneumonia?—than a concerted artistic movement. The music business counterattacked with its own more malleable teen idols and girl groups, but by the early '60s their records were rocking anyway. As baby-boom babies became America's largest population group, the Beatles and other British Invasion bands fed back Little Richard and Chuck Berry and teen-idol pop to an eager audience, and rock took over pop.

During the '60s the music grouped and regrouped into an explosion of genres: folk rock, soul, Motown, psychedelic rock, hard rock, funk, blues rock, jazz rock, progressive rock, country rock, bubblegum. By the '70s, a split had been established between singles buyers (who listened to bouncy AM pop) and album buyers, as genres solidified and subdivided; the early '70s brought heavy metal, Southern rock, fusion, hard funk, singer/songwriters, and classical rock. As rock record buying peaked in the later '70s, disco and punk and reggae arose to reemphasize rhythm and energy, and in the '80s those styles—and all the rest—helped foster new wave, rap, and other genres yet unnamed. After all these years, rock is still wide open.

But one kind of tension shows up in every phase of rock. That's the tension between convention and rebellion—between familiarity and freedom. In the music itself, musicians forge personal statements from a common "commercial" language; imitators become innovators because they can't help leaving fingerprints on the formula. Periodically, when genres become too familiar, new generations of rockers arrive with something tougher and simpler, shaking down the current convention. That tension makes rock an eternal hybrid, testing and absorbing and mutating new ideas as the public listens.

The music business also sees battles between tradition and insurgency, between a pop-star careerism it understands and a rock-rebel goal it doesn't. Rock has always been a collision—and a marriage—of minority culture and majority tastes; new ideas pop out of unlikely places to threaten, then merge with, the mainstream. Virtually every rock genre has come out of nowhere—amateur musicians, independent record labels—to be taken up and marketed by major corporations when the coast is clear. As the music annexes ideas, the music business accepts new approaches.

Rock's most pervasive minority-to-majority connection has been to act out the tug-of-war between black and white culture in America. "If I could find a white man who had the Negro sound and the Negro feel," said Sam Phillips, who discovered Elvis Presley, "I could make a billion dollars." Rock has continually crisscrossed the color line, as each side borrowed the other's secrets and added a few tricks of its own, a constant process of thievery and homage and inexact imitation. In uncountable ways, rock is a metaphor for American culture—a vital, unpredictable mess of individualism and assimilation.

So much for my grand theories (which owe quite a bit to Greil Marcus, Ishmael Reed, Robert Palmer, Robert Christgau, and others). With the information in this *Encyclopedia,* you are welcome to assemble your own thesis, and you'll be able to base it on accurate, objective, salient information. This encyclopedia was designed to tell, as clearly and concisely as possible, the stories of the people who made the music. As in the music, the category of "rock" is open-ended. We have included entries on country, blues, jazz, and even classical musicians who have left a mark on rock music. And since rock's commercial peaks don't always coincide with its artistic ones, we have included unsung (or perhaps unsold) innovators as well as hitmakers, Professor Longhair and Captain Beefheart along with Styx.

Why assemble another rock encyclopedia? Because, frankly, the others are inadequate. *The ROLLING STONE Encyclopedia of Rock & Roll* covers more musicians in more depth than any other rock encyclopedia. In particular, we have made efforts to cover more black music, and more new music, than earlier encyclopedias; and we have made every effort to cut through the inaccuracies—from public-relations mythmaking to moralistic scare tactics—that have surrounded rock from the start. . . . The facts are here.

So many people have been involved in rock that we were forced to make hard decisions about who was best to include in this encyclopedia. The criterion—which, like every critical standard in rock, is ultimately subjective—was that those people included had a direct impact on the music, through popularity or through influence on other musicians. . . . And since this is a biographical volume, not a critical one, the length of an entry is not directly related to a musician's worth. Someone who makes great records and does nothing else in public is likely to receive less space than a band that breaks up every two months; we have chosen to use as few or as many words as it takes to get the story straight. Musicians tend to lead complicated lives, and the entries make sense of them as economically as the facts allow.

Naturally, some bands and musicians are left out; given the inevitable limitations of space, we chose those whom we considered most important. We would appreciate hearing about any sins of omission, but we have tried to err on the permissive side, as rock always does.

To read about these thousands of musicians, finally, is to be astonished at the combinations of creativity, ambition, and recklessness it takes to make it in rock & roll. For every band in this encyclopedia, there are 20 whose records nobody heard, and hundreds that never recorded at all; there are musicians who practice in basements around the world trying to find that certain chemistry. As these entries show, a rock career can be as short as the trajectory of a single hit or as long as the reign of Chuck Berry or the Rolling Stones, and some factors are out of anyone's control. Still, musicians keep trying and keep breaking through—and the glory of rock & roll is that even now, anyone can try it.

Preface
to the Third Edition

by Jon Pareles

When the first edition of *The Rolling Stone Encyclopedia of Rock & Roll* appeared in 1983, popular music was in the middle of an upheaval. Hip-hop was gathering momentum, on its way to revolutionizing not just the way songs are conceived, produced, and performed, but an entire generation's approach to fashion, race relations, and language itself. At the same time, mass-distributed music video was about to transform the image of popular music, market it to an untapped audience, and shape musicians—veterans and newcomers alike—to use and be used by television. Vinyl LPs and singles, the talismans of rock since its birth in the 1950s, were soon to be supplanted by shiny little digital CDs. Punk rock had dropped from mainstream view only to organize at the grass roots, building local audiences and training musicians for a worldwide resurgence. All of these factors would converge in the 1990s in a commercial juggernaut that would vastly enrich recording companies, turn musicians into highly visible icons, and provide countless new avenues for popular music to rebel, disturb, annoy, and sell out—sometimes all at once.

Along the way, the iffy distinctions observers once drew between rock and pop and their subgenres collapsed as even the roughest, nastiest rockers and rappers clamored for their five minutes of MTV. During the 1990s, chart-topping music spent a bipolar decade oscillating between extremes: from the sullen self-loathing of grunge to the the aggression and egomania of gangsta rap, from the surliness of rap-metal to the well-groomed, smiley-faced come-ons of teenypop. A demographic surge of preteens and teenagers, rivaling the baby boom, has been tuned in to every mood swing.

This, the third edition of the *Encyclopedia,* appears during another sea change, one that's less immediately visible but that could reach even further. As the Internet extends to every desktop and living room, the entire structure of popular music and the music business will be affected in ways no one can predict.

Technology has always shaped music, from the moment some primordial ancestor tapped two sticks together or blew across a hollow reed. Rock in particular has been the spawn of musicianship and technology: of microphones, electric guitars, multitrack studios, and synthesizers, and of radios, turntables, tapes, and CDs. Technological change produces musical results, from power chords to drum-machine beats. And music, in turn, constantly demands more from its technology: more flexibility, more fidelity, more push-button possibilities, more distortion.

Business shapes music, too. Popular music has been inextricably tied to the businesses that finance, market, and disseminate it: recording companies, concert promoters, electronic media. And throughout rock history, the careers that are detailed in this *Encyclopedia* have all been connected, to some extent, to the business of selling round hunks of plastic. Countless songs are written and recorded in the hope that they'll sound good enough on the radio to encourage listeners to buy the plastic they are encoded upon.

A handful of large conglomerates and a swarm of independent labels working largely on the fringes have controlled the manufacture and widespread distribution of that plastic. Musicians have had to navigate through a series of gatekeepers: club promoters, label talent scouts, radio and video programmers, and store buyers who largely determine which plastic discs get heard and which fade back into the silence. With music, however, as with other forms of information, the Internet skips past the gatekeepers, and music breaks out of its plastic containers to travel as pure digital information.

Songs now bounce around the Internet (which is to say they travel the world), replicating without commercial controls and raising the fear among the gatekeepers that listeners may stop paying for music entirely. Instead, musicians can reach their fans directly, freed from compromise and the industry's demand for a percentage. Musicians no longer need recording companies and broadcasters to "let" the public hear their music. And the friction between art and commerce that has always made rock so fascinating—that has magnificently honed some music and probably destroyed just as much—is bound to change, with unforeseen results.

One notion at the heart of rock & roll is that the right song with the right sound at the right time is a chance to use the mass media to send a private, even subversive message. The Internet, which has the pervasiveness of mass media but not the uniformity, could alter that ambition. Songwriters may no longer create or record with an eye to broadcasting to the world all at once. Instead, a song might work like an e-mail or a computer virus, spreading from person to person rather than from transmitter to receivers. Musicians may be content to reach a handful of fans, or they may be determined to be heard by huge numbers of people without corporate involvement. The typically steep and narrow career ladder—from local efforts to regional fame to a major-label shot at the big time—could turn into a labyrinth of do-it-yourself choices.

Habits so ingrained they once seemed like laws of nature are likely to crumble as online music reveals its own technological imperatives. One of those habits is treating the album as rock's artistic unit. The four-minute recording time of a 78 rpm disc still shapes our conception of how long a pop song should be. The length of an LP, and then a CD, trained both listeners and musicians to hear an album as a whole. And since the 1960s, most rock careers have been measured in albums, which appear every year or two in a regular cycle of recording and touring. Although singles remain pop's calling cards and sales tools, they're almost invariably attached to albums. This *Encyclopedia,* like its subjects, its writers, and most of its readers, is a product of the album era.

The Internet frees musicians from the need to assemble an album's worth of work at a time, convince a company to release it, then wait while it's manufactured, packaged, and distributed. Instead, musicians can make music available the moment it's finished. If they're willing to live with imperfections, they can offer songs in every stage from demo recording to full studio production, or let each fan assemble an individual version of a live album from an entire tour's worth of recordings. They can still compile full albums, but they can also release one-minute jingles or 90-minute jams. The technical limit to album length is now the capacity of a fan's computer storage: in essence, infinite. Or irrelevant.

The album had already been under siege through the 1990s. Music television and radio stations care about hit songs, not performers' careers, and recording companies have been increasingly impatient with musicians who don't have immediate commercial success. The 1990s were filled with one- or two-hit wonders who saturated the airwaves and then, all of a sudden, seemed to have worn out their welcome permanently, perhaps because they had released albums that surrounded a single or two with obvious filler.

Recording companies also made handsome profits from compilations and soundtrack albums that included hit singles but didn't build an identity for the musicians who made them. They trained listeners to hear the song, not the singer—a return, in a way, to the early years of rock & roll, when the hit song was the point and the album an afterthought. Meanwhile, Internet music swapping has encouraged listeners to chase down one song at a time, not to hear a batch of them in the order and context that a musician creates on an album.

So this *Encyclopedia* could be the summation of the album era, a chance to reconnoiter before the music turns back into a cottage industry and the Internet floodgates burst wide open. Not all the musicians in this book courted the mass market, but even the most unworldly and unprofitable of them had to deal with corporate priorities. That may change, and soon.

In the end, this is a book about individuals: geniuses and hustlers, virtuosos and amateurs, hooligans and do-gooders, hard workers and hangers-on, idealists and phonies. The stories of the musicians and groups here are unpredictable arcs in which inspiration conspires with entrepreneurship, musical skill allies itself with brilliant mistakes, naiveté faces off with cynicism, and listeners hijack finished songs to make them their own.

They are chronicles of friendships, romances, legal entanglements, and the mutable relationships between musicians, their work, and their audience. They are tales about the infinitely variable distance between artistic and commercial success, and about the rewards and the price of those successes. They are cautionary parables and claims of miracles.

Most of all, they testify to the ability of rock and hip-hop to invert all received notions: to create raunchy beauty, crude grace, and lowbrow brilliance. Just when pop seems predictable, when corporate moguls and cultural watchdogs think they've got everything under control, the only sure thing is that the music will shake things up.

Introduction

by Patricia Romanowski

This, the second revision of *The Rolling Stone Encyclopedia of Rock & Roll,* brings up to date our last major revision, published in 1995. We began this project in 1980, when the editors of Rolling Stone Press set out to create an accurate guide to the people and phenomena of rock & roll. Since its original publication in 1983, the *Encyclopedia* has grown from the initial 1,300 entries to approximately 1,800 in 1995, to the nearly 2,000 contained herein. For the first time, the book is devoted entirely to the people who make the music.

Each of the alphabetically arranged entries provides basic biographical information and, where appropriate, a selective or full discography plus group personnel chronology showing as clearly as can be determined the history of personnel changes. This is followed by an essay that not only sums up the subjects' lives and careers but also attempts to place their work in critical and historical perspective.

Approach and Content. In compiling this edition we reviewed the 1,800-plus extant entries and opted to remove three categories of "nonartist" entries: the Grammy Award boxes, the Rock and Roll Hall of Fame boxes, and the entries that consisted of style and genre definitions. Given the rapidly evolving plethora of hyphenated subgenres, attempting to catalogue them all seemed an exercise in futility destined to be outdated upon publication. As a result, we had space to add more artists.

For this edition, we continued our policy of consolidating some artists who were originally listed as solo artists back into the groups with which they came to fame. So, for example, the last time out, we moved Eddie Kendricks and David Ruffin back to the Temptations entry, and Ronnie Spector's solo career is traced in the Ronettes. For this edition, we created a separate solo entry for Brian Setzer, under which we have included the Brian Setzer Orchestra. Because of space limitations, we have continued trying to place related artists and groups (for example, Pearl Jam, Temple of the Dog) under one general entry and been a little stingier than before in spinning group members off into their own solo entries. Extensive cross-referencing throughout will guide readers to the correct entry.

It was with great regret and hard consideration that we again cut entries (listed by title in the appendix and most still available online at RollingStone.com). There were many factors we considered in deciding which entries would be cut, but if there was a single "reason" for making cuts in general, it was simply space. When we decided on cuts, they usually were made to older artists whose impact on subsequent artists was not as dramatic as some of their contemporaries' or to newer artists for whom we had jumped the gun by including them earlier.

Choosing which new artists to include was a difficult decision that involved not only Holly George-Warren, Jon Pareles, and me but our writers and countless other acquaintances. Not surprisingly, each person we consulted—actually everyone we knew—had an opinion and a short list of favorites: hot new bands they were sure would make a big splash and older, unfairly neglected artists. While a third of our choices were obvious and a second third very nearly indisputable, a good third fell onto a list for which any of several other acts could have been chosen. Generally, however, artists who were critically or commercially successful, influential, or otherwise interesting for other, even nonmusical, reasons fared better than those who were not. Conversely, a few little-known artists were so unique they could not be ignored. Other times the inclusion of a given artist in a previous edition dictated making room for a newer artist in the same vein. Or the last edition's subtle overemphasis on certain types of artists and genres at the expense of others called for some balancing in this edition.

As for the length of any given entry, this really is one place—maybe the only place—where size does not matter. There is no reason for John Lennon's current entry to be longer than any of his fellow former Beatles' except that it took more words to tell his and Yoko Ono's story. A subject's so-called "importance" was considered with the same weight we gave other criteria: length of career, influence on other artists and listeners, uniqueness, newsworthy extra-music activities (lawsuits, arrests, benefit work, acting and writing credits, etc.), and the degree to which the subject was representative of a given style, period, or issue. One way in which this volume differs from previous editions is a more selective inclusion of information not directly related to the subject's musical career. When faced with choosing between the ability to add more entries or include more details about an aging rocker's fourth divorce, we opted for the music.

Our Sources. The incredible developments in how we create, access, and share information has changed—and improved—our ability to find the facts. For the last edition, it was the CD-drive anthologization of rock's recorded history that brought us not only some great, overlooked music, but pieces of history that either had passed unwritten or unpreserved. Thanks to anthologies and historic compilations, artists who had hung up their rock & roll shoes decades ago were suddenly back. Interestingly, the Internet revolution has continued that trend, giving listeners access to a greater variety of music than ever before. It has also given longevity to artists whose career paths diverged from the high-speed, high-stakes, roadkill-strewn superhighway to stardom. Ten years ago, the loss of a recording contract or lack of radio play or heavy rotation often spelled the loss of a viable career. No more. The Internet has given "fringe" artists a new way to share their music and allowed major-label veterans a way to continue the dialogue between artist and listener. In addition to music, the Internet has given researchers not only information—most of it quite good, since devoted fans tend to know more about an artist's career than anyone else—but access. In creating their own official Web sites, many artists have provided anyone interested with an insider's perspective, untainted by a journalistic "middleman."

For the purposes of researching and verifying the information here, the mainstream media continues to provide more and, in some cases, better coverage of music today than in the past. Not only are there more publications devoted to music but most of them are increasingly specialized, which, at least theoretically, should result in more accurate reporting. While this does not guarantee factual accuracy (or the ever-present PR concerns of artists and their employers), taken together these publications give researchers and writers a standard by which to judge an item's veracity. For example, while a string of reviews from local newspapers across the country can provide invaluable insight into a group's concert tour, revealing everything from lineup and playlists to audience response, for the correct spellings of musicians' names or the legal particulars of Marilyn Manson's skirmishes with local law enforcement on tour, we would favor accounts from respected, fact-checked national publications. Conversely, obituaries from local newspapers and specialized magazines are generally more complete and accurate than the "abridged" accounts that appear in larger publications. This is particularly true when the artist is less well known or past his or her career peak.

Our second edition was transformed and the entries it contained made more complete thanks to the rise in serious studies, autobiographies, and biographies of groups and individual artists. While few of these proved error-free, they made great contributions, if not by setting the record straight, at least by broadening our understanding of the subjects. Now they have been joined by cable television's steady stream of subject-friendly documentaries: *Behind the Music, A&E Biography,* and *Headliners and Legends* are just three of the series through which performers are rewriting their own stories.

Searchin'. These new waves of information have changed rock history, and for the better, I think. The view of rock and what it means was, until the past decade or so, largely the view of rock critics and what it meant to predominantly middle-class white-boy rock fans grown up. Through artist-dedicated Web pages, fans have brought the DIY ethic that revolutionized the music in the late '70s to history and criticism. Now that everyone is getting into the act, our conception of rock history—and thus of rock itself—changes from a series of snapshots to a richly textured, multihued tapestry of fresh ideas. Somewhere out there someone is writing from around a corner that regular music journalism rarely turns, making connections, arguing points, introducing or resurrecting some song, some fact, some artist, some passion that makes the music real to them.

As we move into the 21st Century, we are witnessing the first wave of artists who are destined to get old before they die. (And these days, even Pete Townshend in his joyously defiant way seems pretty pleased about that.) As they continue to work and to share their thoughts on their pasts, older artists also reshape our views. The *Beatles Anthology* video series and book are good examples of the power of artists to rekindle the imaginations of both longtime fans and new listeners in a way third-person accounts rarely do. Their revelations also provide a humbling reminder that all that is known at any moment is not necessarily all there is to know.

There is no artist's story that could not, with the next wave—the next book, the next interview, the next record, the next day—be suddenly recast and rewritten in triumph or in tragedy. The twists and turns of any artist's life can rarely be foreseen: just ask Tina Turner. In the last edition, we mentioned a few surprising developments—including Sonny Bono's election to Congress and Lisa Marie Presley's marriage to Michael Jackson. With this edition, we are rewriting those stories once again, sometimes sadly. At the same time, we are pondering developments that a decade ago would have sounded like Conan O'Brien predictions for the year 2000: Elvis Costello and Burt Bacharach? A Supremes reunion? Iggy Pop in a kids' movie? The Beatles at #1? Brian Wilson on tour? Prince becoming Prince again? A former Menudo dominating the charts? At this point, the only artist we would never count out or be surprised by is Cher.

Our Method. As we did in the previous editions, we collected information from a broad range of sources in all media: print (newspapers, magazines, books), video (documentaries as well as commercial releases), and CDs, LPs, and singles (as well as their accompanying liner notes). As mentioned before, the other major source this time out was the "official" or highly credible artist- and genre-dedicated Web pages. Again, we made several attempts at contacting each and every artist or group and/or their appointed press representative or manager. We invited those who were included in our previous edition to submit corrections of factual errors to their existing entries and to provide current information, which was then scrupulously fact-checked.

As always, we were very encouraged and happily surprised at the number of responses we received. For the most part, artists who took the time to answer us personally, via post, fax, e-mail, or telephone, graciously pointed out errors and offered verifiable corrections. It is important to note, however, that we refused to disclose the full contents of new or revised entries and did not offer artists the chance to review or approve their entries before publication. While fact-checkers, researchers, writers, and editors may have contacted an artist with specific questions, we never submitted to any artist or artist's representative the full, completed text of his or her entry for further comment.

Any artist or group that could not be traced through an Internet search of national newspapers and Web sites and a thorough review of current record charts and record catalogues, or that was not listed in any industry directory as having a manager, an agent, or other means of contact, and/or whose death could not be verified, was considered as having retired. The *Encyclopedia* never was intended to become a "Where are they now?" collection. However, the temptation to add what we learned of some artists' recent, nonmusical pursuits proved irresistible. For a small minority, however, an artist's name returned to the news only through tragedy or death.

For the artists covered in the new entries, we used these research hunts to collect all the information we needed. These facts were corroborated by other independent sources. In many ways these new entries show the benefit of documenting a piece of history as it happens, while the records are still available, the artists still living (and talking), and the trail still too hot to be overgrown with legend, hype, and rumor.

We kept all of the letters we received from readers after the second edition was published. In every instance, we researched readers' corrections and considered their comments. As it turned out, not all "corrections" were correct, but the approximately 20 percent that were proved invaluable. We like to think of *The Rolling Stone Encyclopedia of Rock & Roll* as a living reference work. We remain open to and welcome all comments, suggestions, information, and corrections. Please address them to: Rolling Stone Press, *Encyclopedia of Rock & Roll,* 1290 Avenue of the Americas, New York, NY 10104.

That said, the history of rock & roll can never totally escape being the history of show business. Never before have artists' images been so painstakingly created and controlled. We have striven—gleefully at times—to scrape away the glitz and slow the spin. Even so, sometimes it is an artist himself who deliberately (and sometimes quite successfully) muddies the truth. When an artist retracts and/or denounces his own quotes and autobiography, writers recount interviews not recorded on paper or tape, and so-called reputable publications exempt their "arts" sections from the rigorous fact-checking standards they routinely apply to the front page, the results can be baffling. While in some areas no source is as valuable as the subject is, we made it a rule to approach "official" information with a healthy skepticism (which, by the way, continues to be very generously rewarded). We have been particularly tough on anyone who claims to be the first, the best, the only, or the latest anything.

In each case, we weighed our sources and our standard references (see later), taking into consideration the reliability of all. In many instances, the truth is quite clear: For our purposes, a chart position is a *Billboard* chart position or, for British charts, those listed in Guinness' *British Hit Singles* and *British Hit Albums;* a gold or platinum record is one so certified by the Recording Industry Association of America; an award is really an award if the organization bestowing it says so in its official publications, Web site, or press releases. Record release dates are based on the copyright date on the actual record or CD or, if that is not available, the date the record entered the charts, the dates of contemporaneous reviews and feature stories about it (usually from Rolling Stone), or discographies that appear in reputable publications (such as *Goldmine*), reliable reference works (*The Rolling Stone Album Guide,* for example, or *The Trouser Press Record Guide*), Internet sources, and books (such as label histories, autobiographies, biographies). Accounts of other important events are based on a wide range of sources, and each source is usually corroborated by at least two other reliable sources.

As always, we encountered the usual problems with accurate birth dates, or, I should say, some artists' birth dates. The first time out, in the early '80s, about 75 percent of our requests for a performer's date of birth were either refused, answered incompletely (day and month but no year), or answered in a way that proved misleading. We are very pleased to report that many artists whose birth dates were not entirely accurate in the first edition later volunteered corrections. (How interesting to note that they all "became" older.) Obviously, by the time the second edition came out, it was clear that the *Encyclopedia* was not going to disappear, and we were touched that so many artists cared enough about our mission to fess up and give us the real dates. Others, however, persist in blurring the truth. In cases where we have sufficient documentation to support another year, we have used it. Where the artist has either refused to offer any date or has given one that stretches credulity, we have calculated it from published accounts that mention the possible dates. Feel free to draw your own conclusions.

Discographies and Chronologies. Generally speaking, most of our discographies are selective, which is to say that we have edited them to give the reader a general picture of an artist or group's recorded history through the inclusion of important releases of original material (as opposed to greatest-hits packages, although we do list some of these selectively); releases that have special critical, commercial, or historical significance; and releases that have been deemed to be representative of the entire oeuvre. Most major artists and those first included in the 1995 edition are complete (except, of course, for those recordings released after this book goes to press). For artists and groups whose careers are considerably longer, the selective discography is almost a given. Before the late '60s, careers were based on singles, not albums. Ironically, however, many popular artists then released two, three, four, maybe even five albums a year. It's interesting to note that in 1964 and 1965 alone the Beatles released more albums than Madonna did in her first decade; Johnny Cash had eight charting LPs out (including some greatest hits and repackages) in 1969; in contrast, Michael Jackson built his entire post-Motown solo career over 22 years on five.

Decisions on what to keep and what to cut were made on a case-by-case basis. To cite one example, it was absolutely necessary that we list every single Beatles album of new original material, though we have not included most of the repackaged greatest-hits releases. In contrast, space alone prohibits listing the full discography of Johnny Cash, while lack of critical, historical, and commercial importance eliminated most of Chubby Checker's, and a paucity of verifiable information and/or product has rendered some doo-wop groups' discographies misleadingly short. Among those releases we have routinely omitted are soundtracks where the artist's input is minimal or not historically significant, Christmas albums, and those that did not chart within the Top 100 albums, as determined by *Billboard.* We omitted most of Elvis Presley's soundtrack releases (due to space considerations and because there was such a wealth of other significant albums to choose from), but we included a handful of extremely successful Christmas albums in other artists' discographies and included soundtracks where they are a crucial part of the artist's work (e.g., Quincy Jones, Tangerine Dream, Curtis Mayfield, Ry Cooder). In the case of group entries, some discographies end up being more complete than historically necessary because group personnel and lineup shifts occur around them, and it's simply easier to fix these changes to album releases than to provide a longer, more complicated explanation in the text. However, the order of facts in the Discographies/Chronologies for artists whose careers began after the mid-'80s will generally reflect the order of events, not who plays on what album.

Rather than be limited by hard-and-fast restrictions, we chose instead to try to craft for each entry a discography that worked with the narrative text to give a full picture of the artist or group, musically, historically, commercially, and critically. To that end, we have also not indicated differences in content between formats except where they are of interest beyond their existence, and then only in the text. Nor have we routinely included Internet-only releases or alternate foreign releases or alternate titles or information regarding dates and labels of reissued product except when the record was too important to cut and information regarding the original release was unavailable or seemed unreliable.

Although these discographies are based on LPs or their equivalents (we refer to both vinyl records and CDs as "albums" and "LPs"), where appropriate, we have also included a limited number of EPs (extended-play recordings), foreign releases (particularly British), and cassette-only releases. Because the *Encyclopedia* is concerned primarily with history, wherever possible the record label given is the one that the work was first released on in the United States. In the interest of saving space, record labels are noted in parentheses following the album title of the first release on that label listed. Thereafter, each album can be assumed to have been released on the same label until indicated otherwise by a new label name following a title. In those instances where foreign releases are included, the label is followed by an abbreviation for the country of release. Alternate formats (EP- and cassette-only releases) are noted following the title, as is the word "soundtrack" where applicable. An "N.A." in the place of the release date or the label signifies that the information was "not available" or impossible to verify with a reasonable degree of certainty.

How to Read These Entries. The artists' entries come in two basic forms: that for a solo artist and that for a group. The solo artist's entry begins with his or her name, followed by his or her given name (if appreciably different from his or her stage name), date of birth, place of birth, date of death, and place of death. Only in cases where there are discrepancies among highly reliable sources are two possibilities offered. This is followed by a discography.

The group entry begins with the group's date and place of formation, followed by a personnel chronology/discography that sets forth for each group member the same basic biographical information provided for solo artists, followed by that member's role in the band. Except for original lineups, all personnel shifts are listed as they occur chronologically in parentheses, with a plus sign (+) indicating an addition to the group and a minus (–) a departure.

The personnel chronology lists only those musicians who have recorded with the group or whose membership is clearly documented in published articles or press releases. Thus most guest or session musicians are not listed, although major ones are mentioned in the entry text. Where the discography is complete, the chronology indicates the approximate order of two main recurrent events in the life of a band: personnel changes and record releases. Generally speaking, the chronology of a successful, well-documented band that began recording in the late '60s will reveal which musicians appeared on a given album. One reason for this is many of those groups released albums frequently enough that there was little lag time between recording and release. Bearing in mind that there are exceptions to every rule, this same claim probably cannot be made as readily for less thoroughly covered acts, such as R&B and disco groups.

While we use album credits as a source of information, there are a number of compelling reasons why following these credits strictly and exclusively would distort the order of events. For one thing, there are many groups for whom personnel listings are incomplete or nonexistent. Second, it is typical for years to elapse between the recording of a given song and its release as a single or on an album. During that time, key personnel events, including deaths, may have occurred. Third, it is more common now than ever to repackage recordings, so that a single album may contain songs recorded by any number of previous lineup configurations (imagine tackling the personnel on a Frank Zappa or Jefferson Airplane/Starship retrospective).

How the chronologies were handled was largely determined by the amount and quality of information available and the group itself. It is an arduous but relatively simple task to construct a chronology for, say, Fleetwood Mac, a group with many widely documented changes over the course of relatively few albums. It is as good as impossible, however, to accurately and fully list the name of every singer who ever appeared with the Drifters. Some groups have endured for decades, yet their true historical significance is restricted to a finite period in time. For these, we have indicated "original lineup" or "best-known lineup." In cases where the space necessary to recount a group's complete chronology was in inverse proportion to its significance, or where a group has developed into the musical equivalent of a temporary employment agency, we have indicated "numerous personnel changes follow," or words to that effect. There are also a handful of cases where only one or several versions of a long-lived group could be determined; there we indicate "lineup ca. late '60s" or "lineup ca. 1994." Regardless of how complete the discography/ chronology section is, it is not intended to replace the discussion of these events in the body of the text. We use this abbreviated format simply because it provides a great amount of information in a small amount of space, makes it easy to see at a glance the basic order of events, saves the basic biographical information from being buried in the text, and gives the writer the option of not having to list in the text releases and personnel changes about which there may not be too much to say at the expense of other, more important occurrences. Virtually all discography and personnel listings are current through spring 2001, though we have continued to include major updates for selected entries through summer 2001.

The Charts. As in the *Encyclopedia's* first edition, chart positions are based on those published weekly in *Billboard* and compiled and published in Joel Whitburn's series of Record Research books. Record Research books are the bible of U.S. chart, label, and title information, and no serious rock fan should be without at least one of these scrupulously researched and dependable tomes. Fortunately, many of these are now available to the general public in bookstores. A wider variety of more specialized titles is available from Record Research Inc., P.O. Box 200, Menomonee Falls, WI 53052–0200; 262–251–5408; www.recordresearch.com

One of the most profound changes in popular music has been the continuing "subgenre-fication" of styles. Today *Billboard* tracks record sales, radio airplay, and club play through more than 30 different charts. For our purposes, we are mainly concerned with the singles and LP charts in three different categories: pop, R&B (rhythm & blues), and C&W (country & western). Through the years, *Billboard* has refined its methods of compiling its charts, most notably in 1991 when it incorporated actual record sales figures and changed the charts' titles to best reflect the current market.

Unless indicated otherwise, every chart position included here should be assumed to be U.S. pop, derived from the "Hot 100" (established in August 1958) for singles, and the "Billboard 200" for albums. "R&B" and "C&W" follow positions from the rhythm & blues and country & western charts or their equivalents. The official chart titles in all three genres, and on all six charts, have changed periodically. For example, through the years the official title of what we consider the R&B singles chart has evolved from "Race Records" in 1945, to "Rhythm & Blues Records" in 1949, to "Hot Soul Singles" in 1973 and "Hot Black Singles" in 1981, before changing to "Hot R&B Singles" in 1990. (In fact, for a period between November 1963 and January 1965, there were no R&B singles charts, and from August to early October 1972, no R&B LPs chart.) In this book, all of these positions are categorized as R&B. In our discussions of music, however, we do make stylistic distinctions between R&B, soul, rap, hip-hop, and black music, although any charting records within these genres would be charted under "R&B." The country charts, which debuted in 1944, contained "C&W" in their titles only between 1949 and 1962; since then, it's been just country, and we use the terms "country" and "C&W" interchangeably.

Discussions of a record's showing on other charts, such as jazz, modern rock, world music, adult contemporary, or New Age, is limited. Where necessary, we have included some British chart positions. These are denoted by "U.K." and apply to pop singles or albums only.

In every instance, the chart position shown is the highest attained by that recording. The year that follows the position is, in almost all cases, the year it debuted on the chart. Discrepancies may arise for those singles for which Record Research's *Top Pop Artists & Singles, 1955–1978* was the main source. For that book, the year given was that in which the record reached its peak, or highest, position. Then it is only a problem in those instances where a record was released at year's end but did not chart until early the next year. In updating the material carried over from the first edition, we have made every effort to revise the chart positions to reflect the "debut" as opposed to the "peak" year. Because a record's natural commercial life cycle is typically short and its fate rendered in mere weeks, the year of debut and the year of peak are usually the same.

Perspective. All that explains how we traced, collected, sifted, and verified our information. Here I'll try to give some idea of how we determined what to do with it.

The ROLLING STONE Encyclopedia of Rock & Roll is a reference work—not a history, not a consumer guide, not an alphabetized collection of critics' musings. The hardest part of this job for all of us was not only consciously putting aside our personal opinions but deliberately separating the prevailing critical line from the facts. For better or worse, however, sometimes it's the historical backdrop and the facts that dictate the critical line, and not the other way around.

As the deservedly esteemed music historian Peter Guralnick advised me nearly 20 years ago, "It isn't necessary to have an opinion about everything." To most hard-core music fans, that may seem unthinkable, but I think he's right. History is not a story that has been told but a story that bears retelling from many different points of view. After rocking this baby for 20 years, I have witnessed the revolutions within the revolution that is rock. Every couple of years brings forth a new generation of listeners, another wave to hear the music and claim it as their own. That might make you feel older, but it can also make you feel somewhat wiser, too. Some of us know that one day Ricky's skintight leather pants, Sean Combs' phat furs, and Marilyn Manson's trash-cum-glam gear will look every bit as fabulous and silly as the same duds once worn by the Lizard King, vintage *Shaft*-era Isaac Hayes, and Alice Cooper in his ingenue days. We may hear the traces of an older, even forgotten artist in the "latest" sound, or see more clearly through the transparent aping that some pass off as "inspiration" and find the real thing. We can save ourselves exasperation over the latest wave of teen groups, for example, because we know what, historically, fate probably has in store for them. We can recognize that snippet of "Pink Moon" in a car commercial and know that not even a voice as obscure as Nick Drake's will be lost for long.

Since this is probably the last edition of the *Encyclopedia* for me, I want to thank all of the editors, writers, researchers, and fact-checkers who have contributed to this since the beginning, particularly my wonderful friend Holly George-Warren. All of these people were incredibly passionate and highly opinionated. And yet they put that aside to answer what I think of as this "higher calling." Speaking as someone who in nearly 30 years still has not entirely recovered from the realization that people actually like the Eagles and does not understand why Laura Nyro is not a household name, I know how hard it is to ignore the writer's and editor's reflexive need to be "right" (although we strive to always be accurate) and to allow even the most familiar stories to tell us how to tell them. That has meant listening anew, allowing for possibilities and improbabilities, and seeing every artist and every record not as we might see them today but within their original contexts, on their own terms, in their own times. In a field where great music, even whole careers, were sparked by hearing a single two-minute-long recording—perhaps even one made 75 years before by someone from the other side of the world—nothing can be discounted. Rock & roll is always unpredictable, improbable, impossible. And yet it stands.

No matter where they came from, the genre they worked in, or how well they fared, every artist here is someone who believed he or she had something to say and had the guts to get up and say it. For that alone, these artists demand and deserve attention and respect. Whether it was worth saying or hearing is almost beside the point. After all, who knows? We cannot determine whether Kiss, or Fabian, or Eminem "deserved" to be heard; we can only tell you what happened once they were.

And that's the story of rock & roll. Whether the revolutions come at 45 per minute or at the speed of light, it's never going to slow down or stop. Best of all, it's your story, too. Read on.

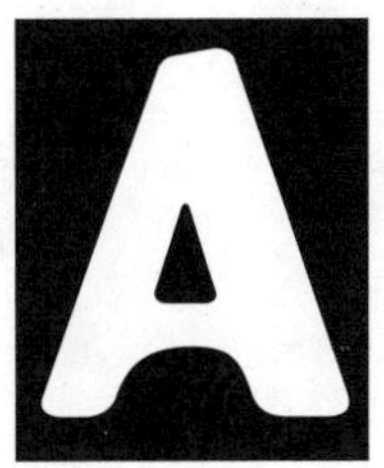

Abba

Formed 1971, Sweden
Benny Andersson (b. Dec. 16, 1946, Stockholm, Swe.), kybds., synth., voc.; Bjorn Ulvaeus (b. Apr. 25, 1945, Gothenburg, Swe.), gtr., voc.; Agnetha "Anna" Fältskog (previously Ulvaeus; b. Apr. 5, 1950, Jönköping, Swe.), voc.; Anni-Frid "Frida" Synni-Lyngstad-Fredriksson-Andersson (b. Nov. 15, 1945, Narvik, Nor.), voc.
1974—*Waterloo* (Atlantic) 1975—*Abba* 1976—*Greatest Hits, vol. 1; Arrival* 1977—*The Album* 1979—*Voulez-Vous; Greatest Hits, vol. 2* 1980—*Super Trouper* 1981—*The Visitors* 1982—*Abba, The Singles, The First Ten Years* 1984—*I Love Abba* 1986—*Abba Live* 1995—*Thank You for the Music* (A&M).
Anni-Frid "Frida" Lyngstad-Frederiksson-Andersson solo: 1982—*Something's Going On* (Atlantic) 1984—*Shine.*
Agnetha Fältskog solo: 1983—*Wrap Your Arms Around Me* (Atlantic) 1985—*Eyes of a Woman* (Epic) 1987—*I Stand Alone* (Atlantic).

Easily the most commercially successful group of the '70s, Abba became the focus of a revival in the early '90s, when its *Abba Gold* topped charts around the world. Abba's wholesome image and buoyant, catchy records made the group international pop stars (Nelson Mandela once declared Abba his favorite pop group) and the second most profitable corporation on the Stockholm stock exchange. Ironically, it was their massive financial success that, according to group members, led to the death and kidnapping threats that prompted their disbanding in 1982.

Though Bjorn Ulvaeus and Benny Andersson's hook-laden singles ("Fernando" and "Money, Money, Money," 1976; "Knowing Me, Knowing You," 1977) often topped European charts, U.S. success was limited to several hit albums and three Top 10 singles: "Waterloo" (#6, 1974), "Dancing Queen" (#1, 1977), and "Take a Chance on Me" (#3, 1978).

Each member was a solo star in Sweden before Abba (an acronym of their first initials) coalesced in 1973. "Waterloo" won the prestigious Eurovision Song Contest in 1974, a year after they began recording in English. Abba tours were limited initially because of the difficulty of re-creating the group's densely layered, richly produced sound live. Nevertheless, Abba mounted its first international tour in 1977 and appeared in the U.S. two years later. Longtime live-in lovers Benny and Anni-Frid (who both have children from teenage marriages) were wed in 1978; they divorced in 1981. Two years earlier, Bjorn and Agnetha's marriage of six years had also ended in divorce. Abba's public image, however, remained harmonious. By then the group had sold an estimated 100 million records worldwide. In 1982 Phil Collins produced Frida's post-Abba solo debut, *Something's Going On,* which featured "I Know There's Something Going On," a Top 20 hit. In 1985 her duet with B.A. Robertson, "Time," was a minor U.K. hit. Andersson and Ulvaeus cowrote with British lyricist Tim Rice the London and Broadway musical *Chess,* from which "One Night in Bangkok" became a #3 hit for Murray Head in 1985. Agnetha "Anna" Fältskog has also released solo albums and had several minor U.K. hits; her "Can't Shake Loose" hit #29 in 1983.

In more recent years, Abba's enduring appeal has manifested itself in the Australian Abba impersonators Bjorn Again, Erasure's #1 U.K. cover EP *Abba-esque*, and the A*Teens, four Stockholm-based singing and dancing youngsters who deal in pimple-pop updates of Bjorn and Benny's most beloved material. Featuring 22 Abba songs, *Mamma Mia!*, created by Andersson and Ulvaeus, became a hit musical in London in 1999, reaching the States in 2001.

ABC

Formed 1980, Sheffield, Eng.
Martin Fry (b. Mar. 9, 1958, Manchester, Eng.), voc.; Mark White (b. Apr. 1, 1961, Sheffield), gtr., kybds.; Mark Lickley, bass; David Robinson, drums; Stephen Singleton (b. Apr. 17, 1959, Sheffield), sax.
1980—(– Lickley; – Robinson; + David Palmer [b. May 29, 1961, Chesterfield, Eng.], drums) 1982—*The Lexicon of Love* (Mercury) 1983—*Beauty Stab* (– Singleton; – Palmer; + Eden, voc., perc; + David Yarritu, kybds., synth.) 1985—*How to Be a . . . Zillionaire!* 1987—*Alphabet City* 1989—*Up* 1990—*Absolutely* 1996—(– White) 1997—(+ various musicians) *Skyscraping* (Deconstruction, U.K.) 1999—*Lexicon of Live* (Blatant, U.K.).

Hailed by the British music press as "purveyors of perfect pop," ABC was actually a highly self-conscious white neosoul group that articulated singer Martin Fry's grandiloquent vision. His mannered vocals recall "Thin White Duke"–era David Bowie, and his songs of romance revisit the worldly fatalism of Roxy Music's Bryan Ferry.

Fry was writing and editing his own music fanzine, *Modern Drugs*, when he interviewed White and Singleton about their electric rock band, Vice Versa. They asked Fry to join them, and he did—changing the group's name to ABC and its direction toward pop. Completed by a rhythm section, the group recorded "Tears Are Not Enough" and released it on their own Neutron Records. A British Top 20 hit in 1981, it was followed over the next six months by three more crafty, melodramatic Top 10 hits—"Poison Arrow," "The Look of Love," and "All of My Heart"—from the lavish Trevor Horn–produced *Lexicon of Love*. Released stateside, the album garnered rave reviews and sold well (#24, 1982); bolstered by lush, evocative videos, "The Look of Love" (#18, 1982) and "Poison Arrow" (#25, 1983) were hit singles, too.

ABC lost most of its U.S. fans with *Beauty Stab* (#69, 1983), a harsher, harder-rocking, guitar-based collection that contained only one charting single: "That Was Then but This Is Now" (#89, 1984). With female percussionist Eden and American keyboardist David Yarritu replacing David Palmer and Stephen Singleton, ABC adopted a cartoonish image and rebounded with *Zillionaire* (#30, 1985), which yielded the yearning pop ballad "Be Near Me" (#9, 1985) and another hit in "(How to Be a) Millionaire" (#20, 1986).

Shortly thereafter, Fry was diagnosed with non-Hodgkin's lymphoma. ABC was off the scene until *Alphabet City* (#48, 1987), which featured the group's biggest hit to date, the Motown tribute "When Smokey Sings" (#5, 1987). Fry dropped out of the music business after the release of *Up*. He made a full recovery from his illness and, by 1997, was back onstage. A new edition of ABC, with Fry the sole remaining original member, recorded two British releases—*Skyscraping* and the live album *Lexicon of Live*—and toured the U.S. in 1999.

Paula Abdul

Born June 19, 1962, Los Angeles, CA
1988—*Forever Your Girl* (Virgin) 1990—*Shut Up and Dance (The Dance Mixes)* 1991—*Spellbound* 1995—*Head Over Heels* 1998—*Greatest* (Virgin, U.K.) 2000—*Greatest Hits* (Virgin).

A true MTV-era success story, Paula Abdul choreographed videos for several popular artists before becoming a pop star herself. Trained as a dancer, Abdul had had little singing experience before recording 1988's *Forever Your Girl*, and her vocals were widely panned. Nonetheless, the album sold 7 million copies domestically, thanks to catchy hooks, perky bubblegum-funk arrangements, and glossy videos that displayed Abdul's true strengths: her stylish, high-energy dance technique and plucky girl-next-door charm.

The second daughter of a French-Canadian mother and a father of Syrian and Brazilian extraction, Abdul began taking dance lessons when she was seven; at 10, she won a scholarship to study tap and jazz dancing. She captained her high school cheerleading squad, and while attending California State, Northridge, joined the Los Angeles Lakers' cheerleaders; she eventually became head Laker girl. Her work was spotted by Jackie Jackson (with whom she later became romantically involved), who asked her to choreograph the Jacksons' 1984 "Torture" video. She also befriended sister Janet Jackson and choreographed all of her *Control* videos (she makes a cameo as Janet's girlfriend in "Nasty"). Abdul's other clients have included the Pointer Sisters, ZZ Top, and Duran Duran, and she has choreographed for television *(The Tracey Ullman Show)* and films, most notably *The Doors* and *American Beauty*.

In the late '80s Abdul signed to Virgin Records. The release of her debut album followed auspiciously on the heels of "Knocked Out," a single that Abdul recorded for a Virgin sampler. That song became popular on R&B radio, but with *Forever Your Girl*, Abdul immediately crossed over into the pop stratosphere, topping the albums chart and producing four #1 singles: 1988's "Straight Up" and, in 1989, "Forever Your Girl," "Cold Hearted," and "Opposites Attract" (with the Wild Pair). Another track, "(It's Just) the Way That You Love Me," went to #3.

Virgin capitalized on Abdul's success by releasing an album of dance remixes of her hit songs in 1990. In 1991 she released *Spellbound*, an LP of new songs—some of them cowritten by Abdul, many written and produced by the New York–based R&B trio the Family Stand. (Other contributors included John Hiatt and Prince.) The album peaked at #1 and spawned the #1 singles "Rush, Rush" (Abdul's first hit ballad) and "The Promise of a New Day," "Blowing Kisses in the Wind" (#6, 1991), "Vibeology" (#16, 1992), and "Will You Marry Me" (#19, 1992). But legal troubles ensued when Yvette Marine, credited as a backup singer on *Forever Your Girl,* sued Virgin, alleging that her voice had been overdubbed on some of the album's lead vocals. In 1993, a jury ruled in Virgin's favor. *Head Over Heels* peaked at #18 on the pop album chart and included "My Love Is for Real" (#28, 1995), which featured backing vocals by Ofra Haza. In the mid- to late '90s Abdul delved into acting, segueing from cameos playing herself on episodes of sitcoms to starring roles in TV movies.

A-Bones: See the Cramps

AC/DC

Formed 1973, Sydney, Austral.
Angus Young (b. Mar. 31, 1951, Glasgow, Scot.), gtr.; Malcolm Young (b. Jan. 6, 1953, Glasgow), gtr.; Dave Evans, voc.
1974—(– Evans; + Bon Scott [b. Ronald Belford, July 9, 1946, Kirriemuir, Scot.; d. Feb. 19, 1980, London, Eng.], voc.; + Phillip Rudd [b. May 19, 1946, Melbourne, Austral.], drums; Mark Evans [b. 1957, Melbourne], bass) 1976—*High Voltage* (Atlantic) 1977—*Let There Be Rock* (– Evans; + Cliff Williams [b. Dec. 14, 1949, Rumford, Eng.], bass) 1978—*Powerage; If You Want Blood, You've Got It* 1979—*Highway to Hell* 1980—(– Scott; + Brian Johnson [b. Oct. 5, 1947, North Shields, Eng.], voc.) *Back in Black* 1981—*Dirty Deeds Done Dirt Cheap; For Those About to Rock We Salute You* 1983—*Flick of the Switch* (– Rudd; + Simon Wright [b. 1963], drums) 1984—*'74 Jailbreak* 1985—*Fly on the Wall* 1986—*Who Made Who* 1988—*Blow Up Your Video* 1989—(– Wright; + Chris Slade, drums) 1990—*The Razors Edge* (Atco) 1992—*Live (Special Collector's Edition); Live* 1995—(– Slade; + Rudd) *Ballbreaker* (Elektra) 1997—*Bonfire* 2000—*Stiff Upper Lip.*

Australian heavy-metal band AC/DC features knickers-clad guitarist Angus Young, who became as famous for mooning audiences regularly as for his gritty blues-based lead guitar and songs about sex, drinking, and damnation. AC/DC's raucous image, constant touring, and raw, juvenile yet amusing lyrics in songs like "Big Balls" and "The Jack" helped make it one of the top hard-rock bands in history. The group has remained a major concert draw, and its albums consistently go platinum despite its never having had a Top 20 single in the U.S.

The Young brothers moved with their family from Scotland to Sydney in 1963. In 1973 they formed the first version of AC/DC, adding vocalist Bon Scott in early 1974, followed by drummer Phillip Rudd and bassist Mark Evans later that year. Their first four albums were produced by ex-Easybeats Harry Vanda and George Young, Angus' older brother. The group had gained a solid reputation in their homeland early on, but it wasn't until 1979 with the platinum *Highway to Hell* (#17, 1979) that they became a presence on the American charts.

Within months of AC/DC's American success, vocalist Scott died from choking on his own vomit after an all-night drinking binge. Two months later he was replaced by ex-Geordie vocalist Brian Johnson, and less than four months after that, *Back in Black* began a yearlong run on the U.S. chart, peaking at #4 (1980), selling over 13 million copies to date, and featuring the double-entendre-ridden "You Shook Me All Night Long." *Dirty Deeds Done Dirt Cheap,* a 1981 reissue of a 1976 Australian LP, went to #3 in the U.S., followed by *For Those About to Rock We Salute You,* the group's first and, to date, only U.S. #1 LP, in late 1981. The less spectacular showings of the gold albums *Flick of the Switch* (#15, 1983) and *Fly on the Wall* (#32, 1985) gave way to the multiplatinum *Who Made Who* (the soundtrack to *Maximum Overdrive*) and *The Razors Edge* (#2, 1990). The latter contains the group's closest thing to a hit single, "Moneytalks" (#23, 1991). In January 1991 three fans were crushed to death at an AC/DC show in Salt Lake City, Utah. In late 1992, the group paid the families of the three deceased teenagers an undisclosed sum, following an out-of-court settlement. Other parties to the settlement included the convention center, the concert's promoter, and the company in charge of security.

AC/DC laid low until 1995, when the Rick Rubin–produced *Ballbreaker* (which also marked the return of drummer Phil Rudd) entered the charts at #4. The bulk of the 5-CD box set *Bonfire,* released in 1997, was made up of live tracks recorded in 1977 and 1979, as well as of a remastered version of *Back in Black.* It marked the first time AC/DC had released material featuring Bon Scott since the singer's death. With older brother George Young (who had worked on such early AC/DC albums as *Let There Be Rock* and *Powerage*) back on board as producer, *Stiff Upper Lip* (#7, 2000) confirmed AC/DC's status as one of the most enduringly popular hard-rock bands on the planet. Wisely sticking to its time-tested formula of no-frills riffing, the band followed the record's release with extensive touring, during which Angus Young wore, as always, a schoolboy uniform. (That outfit has become such a part of rock legend that it was included in Rock Style, an exhibit at New York's Metropolitan Museum of Art, which opened in 1999.) Always a reliable live act, AC/DC once more brought out the big guns—literally, since the band's stage act included cannons that went off during "For Those About to Rock (We Salute You)."

Ace/Paul Carrack

Formed 1972, London, Eng.
Alan "Bam" King (b. Sep. 1946, London), gtr., voc.; Phil Harris (b. July 1948, London), gtr.; Paul Carrack (b. Apr. 1951, Sheffield, Eng.), kybds., voc.; Terry "Tex" Comer (b. Feb. 1949, Burnley, Eng.), bass; Steve Witherington, drums.
1974—(– Witherington; + Chico Greenwood, drums; – Greenwood; + Fran Byrne [b. Mar. 1948, Dublin, Ire.], drums) *Five-A-Side* (Anchor) 1975—*Time for Another* (– Harris; + Jon

Woodhead [b. San Francisco, CA], gtr., voc.) 1977—*No Strings.*
Paul Carrack solo: 1980—*Nightbird* (Vertigo, U.K.) 1982—*Suburban Voodoo* (Epic) 1987—*One Good Reason* (Chrysalis) 1988—*The Carrack Collection* 1989—*Groove Approved* 1996—*Blue Views* (Ark 21) 1997—*Beautiful World* 2000—*Satisfy My Soul* (Compass).

Ace became the best known of London's pub-rock bands when "How Long," written and sung by Paul Carrack, became a #3 U.S. hit in 1975. The group had been founded by Alan King and Phil Harris, and "How Long" was a product of its first recording session. What many listeners believed was a love song actually concerned Terry Comer's temporary departure from the band to work with the Sutherland Brothers and Quiver and his return to Ace. The rest of the group's material failed to match the success of the debut single, and after a 1976 tour with Yes, the group resettled in L.A. and in 1977 disbanded. Carrack, Byrne, and Comer joined Frankie Miller.

Carrack later recorded with Roxy Music, Squeeze (he sings lead on its 1981 hit "Tempted") [see entry], and a short-lived backup band for Carlene Carter. In 1982 he joined Nick Lowe's Noise to Go, and in 1985, Mike + the Mechanics, for which he sang lead on the latter group's Top 10 "Silent Running (On Dangerous Ground)" and on the #1 "Living Years" [see Genesis entry]. In 1987 Carrack's "Don't Shed a Tear" went Top 10. He rejoined Squeeze for its 1993 album, *Some Fantastic Place,* then returned to Mike + the Mechanics for 1995's *Beggar on a Beach of Gold.* In 1997 Carrack finally resumed his solo career with *Blue Views,* which featured the #2 adult-contemporary hit "For Once in Our Lives." His subsequent albums continue to explore his signature brand of blue-eyed soul pop.

Johnny Ace

Born John Alexander Jr., June 29, 1929, Memphis, TN; died Dec. 24, 1954, Houston, TX
1974—*Johnny Ace Memorial Album* (MCA).

Johnny Ace was one of the most popular balladeers of the early '50s but is perhaps most famous for the way he died: He allegedly shot himself while playing Russian roulette. Ace served in the navy during World War II. After his discharge he joined Adolph Duncan's Band as a pianist; he often jammed with B.B. King and Bobby "Blue" Bland in Memphis' famed Beale Streeters. In 1953 he released his first single, "My Song," which became a big R&B hit. Like his subsequent releases, it featured his soothing baritone in a subdued arrangement similar to the style of Nat "King" Cole.

On Christmas Eve 1954 Ace died backstage at Houston's City Auditorium. In recent years some familiar with the details of Ace's death have questioned whether it might have been a murder. One of his biggest pop successes came with the posthumously released Top 20 hit "Pledging My Love" in early 1955. In 1983 Paul Simon invoked the singer's name in "The Late Great Johnny Ace," a song about the assassination of John Lennon.

Roy Acuff

Born Roy Claxton Acuff, Sep. 13 or 15, 1903, Maynardsville, TN; died Nov. 23, 1992, Nashville, TN
1966—*Roy Acuff Sings Hank Williams* (Hickory) 1970—*Best of Roy Acuff* (Capitol); *The Great Roy Acuff; Songs of the Smoky Mountains; The Voice of Country Music; Roy Acuff: Columbia Historic Edition* (Columbia) 1989—*The Best of Roy Acuff* (orig. 1963; Capitol) 1992—*The Essential Roy Acuff 1936–1949* (Legacy).

Singer, songwriter, fiddler, bandleader, music publisher, show-business booster, Roy Acuff was the "King of Country Music" for over 50 years, and continued to perform regularly at the Grand Ole Opry until shortly before his death at the age of 89.

As a teenager he suffered a sunstroke, which prevented him from realizing his ambition to play pro baseball. He took up the fiddle and later joined a traveling medicine show that was passing through his Tennessee mountain hometown—only after he had been assured that he'd work only after sundown. In medicine and tent shows traversing the South he perfected an act that included old-time string-band music, hymns, a few popular contemporary songs, and comedy routines (he was known for the yo-yo he played with onstage). In 1933 he formed the Tennessee Crackerjacks, with whom he performed on Knoxville radio. The next year, the group became the Crazy Tennesseans, and in 1936 they began recording. That same year Acuff recorded his two best-known hits, "Great Speckled Bird" (a million-selling record in 1943) and "Wabash Cannonball."

In 1938 he changed the group's name to the Smoky Mountain Boys. Acuff and the Boys began appearing regularly at Nashville's Grand Ole Opry, and Acuff became one of the Opry's first solo stars. His dry, high-pitched voice became familiar on such hits as "Night Train to Memphis," "Fire Ball Mail," and "Wreck on the Highway." His career sales total exceeds 25 million records. He also appeared in several feature films through the '40s, including *The Grand Ole Opry.*

In 1942 Acuff formed the Acuff-Rose Music Publishing Company with songwriter Fred Rose. Though Acuff continued to record, his success as a music publisher eclipsed that of his later recording career. Acuff-Rose eventually became one of the biggest country music publishing companies in the world, and in the process Acuff and Rose were mentors to many of Nashville's most successful songwriters and performers (Hank Williams, Marty Robbins, Boudleaux Bryant, and others). Such was Acuff's popularity and influence that in 1944 and 1948 he ran for the governorship of Tennessee. He continued to appear at the Opry and traveled the world to entertain troops during both World War II and the Vietnam War.

In 1962 he became the first living musician elected to the

Country Music Hall of Fame. Among his many honors were the Grammy Lifetime Achievement Award (1987) and the National Medal of Art and the Kennedy Lifetime Achievement Award (both 1991). He recorded his last single in 1974. In 1971 his version of "I Saw the Light" from the Nitty Gritty Dirt Band's *Will the Circle Be Unbroken* became his last charting single. In 1983 he moved into a home that was especially constructed for him on the grounds of the Opryland USA amusement park. He died of congestive heart failure.

Adam and the Ants/Adam Ant

Formed 1977, London, Eng.
1978—first recorded lineup: Adam Ant (b. Stuart Goddard, Nov. 3, 1954, London), voc., gtr., piano; David Barbe (a.k.a. Barbarossa, b. Eng.), drums, perc.; Matthew Ashman (b. 1960, London; d. Nov. 21, 1995, London), gtr., piano; Andrew Warren (b. Eng.), bass.
1979—*Dirk Wears White Sox* (Do-It, U.K.) (– Warren; + Leigh Gorman, bass) 1980—(– Ashman; + Marco Pirroni [b. Apr. 27, 1959, London], gtr.; – Barbe; + Terry Lee Miall [b. Nov. 8, 1958, London], drums; + Merrick [b. Chris Hughes, Mar. 3, 1954, London], drums; – Gorman; + Kevin Mooney [b. Eng.], bass) *Kings of the Wild Frontier* (Epic) 1981—(– Mooney; + Gary Tibbs [b. Jan. 25, 1958, London], bass) *Prince Charming* 1990—*Antics in the Forbidden Zone.*
Adam Ant solo: 1982—*Friend or Foe* (Epic) 1983—*Vive Le Rock* 1988—*Manners & Physique* (MCA) 1995—*Wonderful* (Capitol).

The undisputed leaders of Britain's short-lived, fantasy-oriented New Romantic movement of the early '80s, Adam and the Ants were less well appreciated stateside. Using their music as only one facet of an imaginary world, complete with self-promoting mottos like "Antmusic for Sexpeople" and their own vocabulary (fans were Antpeople), these cheeky swashbucklers took England by storm. Late in 1980, foppish postpunkers began to imitate Adam's fashion sense, which combined cartoonish hero images of pirates, Western men, and Native Americans. His unusual music, which featured double-drum rhythms from Burundi and yodeling vocals, produced several British pop singles, including "Ant Music" (#2) and "Dog Eat Dog," (#4) and a #1 LP, *Kings of the Wild Frontier.*

Ant, who had played in various bands since 1976, first came to national attention under the auspices of ex–Sex Pistols manager Malcolm McLaren, who worked on the Ants' debut LP, *Dirk Wears White Sox* (unreleased in the U.S. until 1983). McLaren left in 1980, taking with him Gorman and Barbe, and adding Ashman to form Bow Wow Wow [see entry]. Ant teamed up with ex–Rema Rema guitarist Marco Pirroni, who had played one gig with Siouxsie and the Banshees in 1976. The pair developed the Antpeople image that imbued the songs on *Kings of the Wild Frontier,* the group's U.S. debut. Despite extensive media coverage and a well-publicized American tour, the album sold a disappointing 300,000 copies. In November 1981 *Prince Charming,* which

Adam Ant

was recorded with ex–Roxy Music bassist Gary Tibbs, spent over six months on the British charts, but failed to become a U.S. hit.

The Ants disbanded in 1982. Adam's debut solo effort, a single entitled "Goody Two Shoes," peaked at #1 in England and reached #12 in the U.S., making *Friend or Foe* a Top 20 album. None of his succeeding LPs fared as well, although *Manners & Physique* (produced by former Prince cohort André Cymone) boasted "Room at the Top" (#17, 1990). Adam has also pursued acting; his credits include the films *World Gone Wild* and *Slam Dance,* along with television's *The Equalizer* and *Northern Exposure.* Following a 1993 comeback tour, Ant made several guest live appearances with Nine Inch Nails. This activity predated the modest success of 1995's *Wonderful,* the adult-alternative title track of which peaked at #39 on the U.S. singles chart.

Bryan Adams

Born Bryan Guy Adams, Nov. 5, 1959, Kingston, Can.
1980—*Bryan Adams* (A&M) 1981—*You Want It, You Got It* 1983—*Cuts Like a Knife* 1984—*Reckless* 1986—*Live! Live! Live!* (A&M, Jap.) 1987—*Into the Fire* (A&M) 1991—*Waking Up the Neighbours* 1993—*So Far So Good* 1996—*18 til I Die* 1997—*MTV Unplugged* 1998—*On a Day Like Today* 1999—*The Best of Me* (A&M/Universal, Can.).

With his trademark white T-shirt and blue jeans, Bryan Adams may have looked like a regular guy. But his unerring gift for radio-friendly pop hooks made him the most successful artist exported from Canada in the '80s. Even as critics dismissed his straightforward, anthemic rock as a shallow formularization of Bruce Springsteen, Adams' work received multiple Juno and Grammy awards, as well as three Oscar nominations.

Adams' father was a Canadian diplomat, and Adams attended military schools in England, Austria, Portugal, and Israel. When he was 12 his parents separated, and he lived with his mother in Vancouver, British Columbia. By then he had taught himself to play guitar and decided to make music his career. At 16, he quit school, bought a grand piano with money from his college fund, and joined bands. At age 17 he befriended Jim Valliance, who had written songs for the Canadian band Prism. After two years of writing and recording demo tapes, their partnership produced the 1979 disco-styled Canadian single "Let Me Take You Dancing." The pair sold songs to Bachman-Turner Overdrive, Joe Cocker, and Juice Newton, then landed a publishing deal with A&M Records, which led to Adams' recording contract.

Adams' eponymously titled debut album stiffed, but the followup, *You Want It, You Got It* (#118, 1982), fared better, and Adams opened shows for such bands as the Kinks, Foreigner, and Loverboy. *Cuts Like a Knife* (#8, 1983) was Adams' U.S. breakthrough, producing hits in "Straight From the Heart" (#10, 1983), the title cut (#15, 1983), and "This Time" (#24, 1983); the latter two were accompanied by popular eye-catching videos. *Reckless* (#1, 1984) was even bigger, selling over 5 million copies and yielding such hits as "Run to You" (#6, 1984), "Somebody" (#11, 1985), and "Summer of '69" (#5, 1985), Adams' first hit ballad in "Heaven" (#1, 1985), and "It's Only Love" (#15, 1985), a duet with Tina Turner (with whom Adams toured, and for whom he produced a track on her 1986 *Break Every Rule*). Adams appeared at Live Aid in Philadelphia in 1985, and in 1986 he performed on Amnesty International's Conspiracy of Hope Tour with Sting and U2.

His *Into the Fire* yielded hits in "Heat of the Night" (#6, 1987), "Hearts of Fire" (#26, 1987), and "Victim of Love" (#32, 1987). Adams refused to allow the use of the album's "Only the Strong Survive" in the Tom Cruise film *Top Gun* because he felt the movie glorified war.

After performing at the 1988 Freedomfest in London to honor freed South African apartheid fighter Nelson Mandela, Adams began work on *Waking Up the Neighbours*. Meanwhile, Joe Cocker recorded Adams' "When the Night Comes," and Dion recorded his "Drive All Night"; Adams had a quick cameo in the 1989 Clint Eastwood film *Pink Cadillac* and performed at Roger Waters' 1990 Berlin production of *The Wall*. The release of *Waking Up the Neighbours* (#6, 1991) was preceded by the appearance of "(Everything I Do) I Do It for You" under the credits of the Kevin Costner film *Robin Hood—Prince of Thieves*. The ballad was an instant smash, topping the U.S. pop chart for seven weeks and the U.K. chart for a record-breaking 16 weeks, as well as scoring an Oscar nomination. In February 1992 Adams took issue with his homeland's "Canadian Content" regulations, which restricted airplay of *Neighbours* because Adams cowrote and coproduced the record with an Englishman, Robert John "Mutt" Lange. Adams briefly threatened to boycott the annual Juno Awards, Canada's version of the Grammys, where he ended up winning Entertainer and Producer of the Year awards. A hits collection, *So Far So Good* (#6, 1993), featured the new song "Please Forgive Me" (#7, 1993). This, along with a collaboration with Rod Stewart and Sting for the movie *The Three Musketeers*, "All for Love" (#1, 1993), cemented Adams' status as a pop balladeer. This new image continued with *18 til I Die* (#31, 1996), which included yet another film soundtrack hit, "Have You Ever Really Loved a Woman?" (#1, 1995) from *Don Juan de Marco*, garnering Adams his second Oscar nod. The album also produced the popular love song "Let's Make a Night to Remember." Adams' balladry reached new heights when he recorded a duet with Barbra Streisand for her 1996 movie, *The Mirror Has Two Faces*. "I Finally Found Someone" hit #8 on the pop chart and earned an Academy Award nomination.

The following year, Adams performed a concert for the MTV series *Unplugged* with his band as well as a 16-piece orchestra of students from the Juilliard School of Music. Highlights were quickly released as an album, *MTV Unplugged* (#88, 1997). *On a Day Like Today* (#103, 1998) found Adams duetting with Melanie C., Sporty Spice of the Spice Girls. In 1999 Adams focused on three non-U.S. projects: a second greatest-hits collection, titled *The Best of Me*, which had been rejected by A&M's new parent company in the States, Universal, but sold 4 million copies worldwide; and two collections of black-and-white portraits of women, *Made in Canada* and *Heaven*. The first showcased Adams' photographs of 80 prominent Canadian women (among them Celine Dion, Alanis Morissette, and Joni Mitchell). The book's royalties were donated to the Canadian Breast Cancer Foundation. *Heaven*'s royalties benefited Haven Trust, a London breast-cancer support center.

King Sunny Ade

Born Sunday Francis Adeniyi, Sep. 26, 1946, Ondo, Nigeria
1968—*The Master Guitarist* (African Songs/Serengeti, U.K.) 1976—*The Late General Muritala Mohammed* (Decca); *Sunny Ade Live Play* (Sunny Alade) 1978—*Festac 77* 1980—*Check "E"* 1981—*The Message* 1982—*Ariya Special; Juju Music* (Mango) 1983—*Synchro System; Ajoo* (Makossa) 1984—*Aura* (Island) 1985—*Otito* (Sunny Alade) 1986—*Saviour* 1987—*Return of the Juju King* (Mercury) 1988—*Live! Live Juju!* (Rykodisc) 1989—*Funmilayo* (Sunny Alade) 1994—*Live at the Hollywood Palace* (I.R.S.) 1995—*E Dide (Get Up)* (Mesa) 1998—*Odu* 2000—*Seven Degrees North* (Mesa/V2).

A superstar in his native Nigeria since the late '60s, *juju* bandleader King Sunny Ade was hailed by American critics in 1982 as the next Bob Marley. While Ade, who sings in his native Yoruba tongue, never achieved that level of popularity in the U.S., he and his 20-piece African Beats band did whet American and European appetites for "world music." In addition, Ade helped open the door for other Afro-pop artists, among them fellow Nigerian *juju* stars Ebenezer Obey and Dele Abiodun, Zaire's Tabu Ley Rochereau and Papa Wemba, Senegal's Youssou N'Dour, South Africa's Mahlathini and the Mahotella Queens, and Madagascar's Rossy and Tarika Sammy.

Born into the royal family of Ondo, the youthful Ade horri-

King Sunny Ade

fied his parents by pursuing music, which was considered a profession for commoners. He dropped out of school in 1963 to join semipro bands in the capital of Lagos, playing *juju*, a popular Nigerian guitar music style since the '20s, which had been radically altered by the infusion of electric guitars and Western rock influences. Within a year Ade was a guitarist with a top *juju* outfit, Moses Olaiya's Rhythm Dandies. By 1967 he had formed his own band, the Green Spots (taking off on the name of longtime *juju* king I.K. Dairo's Blue Spots band), and recorded his first single, "Challenge Cup," which celebrated a local soccer team's championship and became a national hit.

By the early '70s Ade's Green Spots had grown into the African Beats, an orchestral ensemble with four or five vocalists, just as many guitarists, a Hawaiian guitarist (inspired by the pedal-steel heard on records by Ade's favorite country singer, Jim Reeves), keyboards or vibraphone (in the '80s, he added synthesizers), bass, trap drums, and a half-dozen or so percussionists, including the talking drum players so central to the distinctive *juju* sound. ("Talking drums" are small hand drums with variable pitch.) Ade's style of *juju* music is a gently hypnotic, polyrhythmic mesh of burbling guitars, sweet harmony vocals, swooping Hawaiian guitar, and throbbing talking drums.

By 1975 Ade was a certified superstar in his homeland; by decade's end, he'd released a half-dozen albums a year, selling around 200,000 copies of each. He set up his own Sunny Alade record label and Ariya nightclub in Lagos. The early '80s found Ade building a substantial European cult following, leading Island Records to sign him for both Europe and North America, where his influence had already been felt on such albums as Talking Heads' *Remain in Light* (1980) and King Crimson's *Discipline* (1981). *Juju Music*, featuring new recordings of tunes from Ade's vast repertoire, got universal rave reviews, as did his first of many U.S. tours; the album sold well enough to graze the bottom of the pop chart (#111, 1983). *Synchro System*, with a harder rhythmic edge and more prominent synthesizers, fared slightly better (#91, 1983), but when *Aura* failed to chart, despite a guest appearance by Stevie Wonder, Island dropped Ade. The African Beats then broke up, amidst dissension and claims of being underpaid (though Ade was reportedly losing money on tours, supporting his large band while playing undersized venues). Back in Lagos, Ade formed a new band, Golden Mercury, retaining his trademark sound and continuing to record and tour internationally, periodically returning to the U.S. Ade's 1995 album, *E Dide (Get Up)*, was his first U.S. studio recording in a decade. It was followed by the Grammy-nominated 1998 release, *Odu*, and 2000's *Seven Degrees North*.

Aerosmith

Formed 1970, Sunapee, NH
Steven Tyler (b. Steve Tallarico, Mar. 26, 1948, New York, NY), voc.; Joe Perry (b. Sep. 10, 1950, Lawrence, MA), gtr.; Brad Whitford (b. Feb. 23, 1952, Winchester, MA), gtr.; Tom Hamilton (b. Dec. 31, 1951, Colorado Springs, CO), bass; Joey Kramer (b. June 21, 1950, New York), drums.
1973—*Aerosmith* (Columbia) 1974—*Get Your Wings* 1975—*Toys in the Attic* 1976—*Rocks* 1977—*Draw the Line* 1978—*Live Bootleg* 1979—*A Night in the Ruts* (– Perry; + Jim Crespo, gtr.) 1980—*Aerosmith's Greatest Hits* (– Whitford; + Rick Dufay, gtr., voc.) 1982—*Rock in a Hard Place* 1984—(– Crespo; – Dufay; + Perry; + Whitford) 1985—*Done With Mirrors* (Geffen); *Classics Live!* (Columbia) 1987—*Classics Live II*; *Permanent Vacation* (Geffen) 1988—*Gems* (Columbia) 1989—*Pump* (Geffen) 1991—*Pandora's Box* (Columbia) 1993—*Get a Grip* (Geffen) 1994—*Big Ones*; *Box of Fire* (Columbia) 1997—*Nine Lives* 1998—*A Little South of Sanity* (Geffen) 2001—*Just Push Play* (Columbia).
The Joe Perry Project: 1980—*Let the Music Do the Talking* (Columbia) 1981—*I've Got the Rock 'n' Rolls Again* 1984—*Once a Rocker Always a Rocker.*
The Whitford/St. Holmes Band: 1981—*Whitford/St. Holmes* (Columbia).

Fronted by Mick Jagger lookalike Steven Tyler and known for its aggressive blues-based style, Aerosmith was the top American hard-rock band of the mid-'70s, despite endless attacks from critics who considered them a poor man's Rolling Stones. But the members' growing drug problems and internal dissension contributed to a commercial decline

Aerosmith: Tom Hamilton, Joey Kramer, Joe Perry, Steven Tyler, Brad Whitford

that began with 1977's *Draw the Line*. Two crucial lineup changes and a few poorly received albums preceded a 1984 reunion of the original lineup and the multiplatinum *Permanent Vacation*, which signaled one of the most spectacular comebacks in rock history. Though now vociferous adherents to the sober lifestyle, Aerosmith forfeited none of their bad-boy image, and their live shows were among the best of their long career. Even critics liked them better the second time around. With its members now over 50, Aerosmith continues to embody classic rock grounded in a late-'70s style—typically, most of their recent hits have been power ballads.

The group was formed in 1970 by Joe Perry, Tom Hamilton, and Tyler, who was then a drummer. The group was completed with drummer Joey Kramer and Brad Whitford; Tyler became lead singer. For the next two years all five members shared a small apartment in Boston and played almost nightly throughout the area, occasionally venturing to New York City. Clive Davis saw them perform at Max's Kansas City in New York and signed them to Columbia. A minor hit and future FM-radio staple from their debut, "Dream On," strengthened their regional following.

Meanwhile, Aerosmith began to tour widely. In 1976 "Dream On" recharted, rising to #6. And by the time of "Walk This Way" (#10, 1977), the band had become headliners. Its phenomenal success was short-lived, however. A series of sold-out tours and platinum albums (including *Aerosmith, Get Your Wings, Toys in the Attic*) peaked in 1976.

By 1977 the group's constant touring and the band members' heavy drug use (Perry and Tyler were nicknamed "the Toxic Twins" for their heroin habits) had begun to take their toll. After months of rest, Aerosmith recorded *Draw the Line* and appeared as the villains in Robert Stigwood's movie *Sgt. Pepper's Lonely Hearts Club Band;* their version of Lennon and McCartney's "Come Together" from the soundtrack was a minor hit. But Aerosmith was unraveling: In 1979 Perry quit, admitting to long-standing personality and musical conflicts with Tyler, his songwriting partner. Jim Crespo took his place. The next year Whitford departed to form the Whitford/St. Holmes band with ex–Ted Nugent sidekick Derek St. Holmes and was replaced by Rick Dufay. Neither Perry's nor Whitford's outside records did particularly well.

Rock in a Hard Place, Aerosmith's first new recording in almost three years and the first without Perry, peaked at #32, as the band was eclipsed by a new breed of young hard rockers. In early 1984 the five original members met backstage at an Aerosmith concert and decided to re-form. *Done With Mirrors,* their first "comeback" LP, sold moderately. The group's reascendence began in earnest when Perry and Tyler appeared with rap duo Run-D.M.C. in a video for the latter's version of the 1977 Aerosmith warhorse "Walk This Way" (#4, 1986). That fall, just as "Walk This Way" was peaking on the chart, *Permanent Vacation* (#11, 1987) was released, with three hit singles and their accompanying videos—"Dude (Looks Like a Lady)" (#14, 1987), "Angel" (#3, 1988), and "Rag Doll" (#17, 1988)—introducing Aerosmith to a new generation.

Aerosmith further consolidated its success with the quadruple-platinum *Pump* (#5, 1989), which boasted "Love in an Elevator" (#5, 1989), "Janie's Got a Gun" (#4, 1989)—the song about incest won 1990's Grammy for Best Rock Performance by a Duo or Group With Vocal—"What It Takes" (#9, 1990), and "The Other Side" (#22, 1990).

In 1991 the group signed a record deal with Sony worth a reported $30 million for four albums and including provisions for 22 percent royalties. Three years later, in summer 1994, the group landed a seven-figure deal from G.P. Putnam's Sons for its group autobiography. With the hit singles "Living on the Edge" (#18, 1993), "Cryin" (#12, 1993), and "Crazy" (#7, 1993), *Get a Grip* hit #1, followed by 1994's double-platinum #6 greatest-hits package, *Big Ones,* continuing Aerosmith's run at the top. *Box of Fire*, a 12-CD compilation of Aerosmith's Columbia output, went gold in early 1995.

Aerosmith got back into rougher waters in 1996. The band started working on the followup to *Get a Grip*—and its first album back on Columbia—but didn't get along with producer Glen Ballard. Ballard left in the middle of the sessions and was replaced by Kevin Shirley. Meanwhile, Joey Kramer's father had died, sending the drummer into such a depression that he had to be replaced by session drummer Steve Ferrone on some tracks. In the midst of it all, the band fired its longtime manager, Tim Collins, who had helped the musicians through sobriety and helmed their '80s comeback. Collins retaliated by suggesting that some of the band members had fallen off the wagon; Tyler was then accused of "not being part of the team" in a letter sent to him by his four bandmates. Tyler denied taking drugs, saying, "I've had no mood-altering substances in 10 years."

When *Nine Lives* finally came out in 1997, it entered the chart at #1. Yet it sold only a disappointing 140,000 copies the week of its release and didn't yield any memorable singles—though "Pink" (#27, 1998) did win Aerosmith another Grammy for Best Rock Performance by a Duo or Group With Vocal in 1999.

The group landed on its feet yet again when "I Don't Want to Miss a Thing" (#1, 1998), its contribution to the soundtrack of *Armageddon* (which starred Tyler's increasingly successful daughter Liv), became a huge hit the following year and was nominated for an Academy Award. In early 2001, Aerosmith was inducted into the Rock and Roll Hall of Fame, just as the band's new album, *Just Push Play* (#2, 2001), yielded the hit single "Jaded" (#7, 2001).

Christina Aguilera

Born Dec. 18, 1980, Staten Island, NY
1999—*Christina Aguilera* (RCA) 2000—*Mi Reflejo; My Kind of Christmas.*

Sexy teen idol Christina Aguilera was one of a handful of former Mouseketeers who, by the turn of the millennium, had graduated from the Disney Channel to MTV.

An army brat, Aguilera spent her early childhood traveling with her family from Texas to Japan to New Jersey. Her parents divorced when she was seven, and Aguilera settled with her mother and sister in Wexford, Pennsylvania. The following year, she appeared on *Star Search* performing the Whitney Houston hit "Greatest Love of All." Four years later, in 1993, Aguilera was a member of *The New Mickey Mouse Club*, along with Britney Spears and future members of 'N Sync.

In 1998, after Disney tapped Aguilera to sing "Reflections" for the animated film *Mulan*, RCA signed the budding star and spent a rumored $1 million for a team of songwriters, producers, voice teachers, and marketing experts. Aguilera's first single, "Genie in a Bottle," came out the following year and topped the pop chart on the strength of its suggestive lyrics and bubblegum pop sound. A chart-topping self-titled album followed. When the video for Aguilera's second single, "What a Girl Wants" (#1, 1999), hit MTV, the teenaged singer's grown-up looks and steamy moves had critics describing her as everything from a "micro-diva" to a "legal Lolita." In late 1999, Aguilera released a holiday single, "The Christmas Song (Chestnuts Roasting on an Open Fire)" (#18, 1999).

Capitalizing on the popularity of the Latin music movement (and her Spanish surname), Aguilera learned enough Spanish to record a Spanish-language album, *Mi Reflejo* (#27, 2000); it was followed closely by a holiday collection, *My Kind of Christmas* (#28, 2000). By late 2000, each of Aguilera's first three albums were on *Billboard*'s Top 200 chart; she had sold more than 8 million copies of her debut album and won a Grammy for Best New Artist. In 2000 her singles included "Come On Over Baby (All I Want Is You)," and in 2001 she duetted with Ricky Martin on "Nobody Wants to Be Lonely" (#13) and appeared in the #1 remake of "Lady Marmalade" with Lil' Kim and others.

a-ha

Formed 1982, Oslo, Nor.
Morten Harket (b. Sep. 14, 1959, Kongsberg, Nor.), voc.; Magne "Mags" Furuholmen (b. Nov. 1, 1962, Oslo), kybds.; Pål Waaktaar (b. Sep. 6, 1961, Oslo), gtr.
1985—*Hunting High and Low* (Warner Bros.) 1986—*Scoundrel Days* 1988—*Stay on These Roads* 1990—*East of the Sun, West of the Moon* 1991—*Headlines and Deadlines: The Hits of a-ha* 1993—*Memorial Beach* 2000—*Minor Earth, Major Sky* (Warner Music, Ger.).

With chiseled Scandinavian good looks and a few pop hooks, a-ha is a Norwegian electropop answer to Duran Duran, as mid-'80s teen idols of the music-video age. It might be argued that Steve Barron, who directed the video for the trio's "Take On Me," and Michael Patterson and Candace Reckinger, who animated the clip, were as important to a-ha's American success as the band members themselves.

A-ha's three members had played in such Scandinavian bands as Spider Empire, Soldier Blue, and Bridges before coming together in the early '80s and moving together to London. The group's first single, "Take On Me" (#1, 1985), got heavy MTV play with its video clip, which blended live action and animation in a romantic adventure starring the handsome Harket as a comic-book hero who comes to life and pulls an unsuspecting young woman into the action. The song propelled *Hunting High and Low* to #15. A-ha would score a few more hits—including "The Sun Also Shines on TV" (#20, 1985) and "Cry Wolf" (#50, 1987)—but its album sales steadily decreased, and *East of the Sun* and *Memorial Beach* failed to chart at all. A-ha remained a steady draw internationally, however, especially in Latin America, where it topped the singles charts no fewer than 14 times, and in 1991 played for record-breaking crowds at Brazil's Rock in Rio concert. In 1987 a-ha wrote and recorded the theme song for the James Bond film *The Liv-*

ing Daylights. In 1995 Harket began a solo career with *Wild Seed* (*Vogts Villa* followed a year later), while Waaktaar and his wife, Lauren Savoy, formed the band Savoy, who released *Mary Is Coming* (1996) and *Lackluster Me* (1997). With "Take On Me" placing high atop such lists as MTV's *100 Greatest Music Videos Ever,* Harket, Furuholman, and Waaktaar reconvened to greet the new millennium with a new Europe-only a-ha album, *Minor Earth, Major Sky.*

Air

Formed 1995, Versailles, Fr.
Nicolas Godin (b. Dec. 25, 1969, Paris, Fr.), kybds., gtr., bass, piano, others; Jean-Benoit Dunckel (b. Sep. 7, 1969, Versailles), kybds., gtr., bass, piano, others.
1998—*Moon Safari* (Source/Caroline) 1999—*Premiers Symptomes* (Source/Astralwerks) 2000—*Original Motion Picture Score for "The Virgin Suicides"* (Record Makers/Source/Astralwerks) 2001—*10,000 Hz Legend* (Record Makers/Source/Virgin).

At a time when its native country had become the new hotbed of electronic music, French duo Air distinguished itself from its more house-music-oriented contemporaries (Daft Punk, Dimitri From Paris) with soft, keyboard-heavy compositions that recalled music from the '60s and '70s. With Jean-Benoit Dunckel having been formally trained in classical music at Paris' Conservatoire, he and his musical partner, Nicolas Godin, often cited classical composers like Debussy and Bach as influences. But their lush melodies also drew inspiration from sources as varied as Ennio Morricone, Brian Wilson, and Moog composer Jean Jacques Perrey.

Godin and Dunckel met during the mid-'80s while attending college in Versailles; they were introduced by Alex Latrobe (later known as the producer Alex Gopher), with whom they formed the indie-rock band Orange. After graduation, they continued to collaborate without Latrobe, recording their first single as Air, "Modular Mix," in 1995 for France's Source label. Three years later Source released Air's full-length debut, *Moon Safari,* which landed the band on countless critics' top-10 lists. In 1999 Air issued an expanded EP, *Premiers Symptomes,* which previously had been released in Europe in 1997 and which collected the band's pre–*Moon Safari* singles. Continually promising a proper followup to *Moon Safari,* Air next composed the soundtrack to *The Virgin Suicides* (#161, 2000) before releasing *10,000 Hz Legend* in 2001. The latter recording featured vocals by Beck and Japan's Buffalo Daughter.

Air Supply

Formed 1976, Melbourne, Austral.
1978—Graham Russell (b. June 1, 1950, Nottingham, Eng.), voc., gtr.; Russell Hitchcock (b. June 15, 1949, Melbourne), voc.; Ralph Cooper (b. Apr. 6, 1951, Coffs Harbour, Austral.), drums; David Moyse (b. Nov. 5, 1957, Adelaide, Austral.), gtr.; David Green (b. Oct. 30, 1949, Melbourne), bass; Rex Goh (b. May 5, 1951, Singapore), gtr.; Frank Esler-Smith (b. June 5, 1948, London, Eng.), kybds.
1980—*Lost in Love* (Arista) 1981—*The One That You Love* 1982—*Now and Forever* 1983—*Greatest Hits* 1985—*Air Supply* 1986—*Hearts in Motion* 1988—(group disbands) 1991—(group re-forms: Russell; Hitchcock; Cooper) *The Earth Is* (Giant) 1993—*The Vanishing Race* 1995—*News From Nowhere* 1997—*Book of Love.*

Air Supply is an Australian group based around the duo of Graham Russell (the main songwriter) and Russell Hitchcock. The group's light pop-rock hits have earned Air Supply several platinum LPs and gold singles worldwide; *Greatest Hits* was quadruple platinum in the U.S., and *The Earth Is,* which failed to chart here, went gold in over 20 countries.

The group originally consisted of lead vocalists Hitchcock and Graham backed by studio musicians. As such, they had several hit singles in Australia, including "Love and Other Bruises" (1976), "Empty Pages" and "Do What You Do" (both 1977), and two gold albums. After forming a band to record their third LP, they came up with one of the U.S.'s biggest hits in 1979, "Lost in Love," (#3, 1979). A string of Top 10 hits followed: "Every Woman in the World" (#5, 1980), "The One That You Love" (#1, 1981), "Even the Nights Are Better" (#6, 1982), and "Making Love Out of Nothing at All" (#2, 1983). To date, the group has sold over 15 million records worldwide.

The group first disbanded in 1988, but Russell and Hitchcock re-formed Air Supply in 1991, including only Cooper from the old lineup. The pair has continued to tour with various backing configurations.

Alabama

Formed 1969 (as Young Country), Fort Payne, AL
Jeff Cook (b. Aug. 27, 1949, Fort Payne), gtr., fiddle, voc.; Randy Owen (b. Dec. 13, 1949, Fort Payne), gtr., voc.; Teddy Gentry (b. Jan. 22, 1952, Fort Payne), bass, voc.
N.A.—*Wild Country* (LSI); *Deuces Wild; Alabama 3* 1973—(+ Rich Scott, drums) 1979—(– Scott; + Mark Herndon [b. May 11, 1955, Springfield, MA], drums) 1980—*My Home's in Alabama* (RCA) 1981—*Feels So Right* 1982—*Mountain Music* 1983—*The Closer You Get* 1984—*Roll On* 1985—*40 Hr. Week; Alabama Christmas* 1986—*Greatest Hits; The Touch* 1987—*Just Us* 1988—*Alabama Live* 1989—*Southern Star* 1990—*Pass It On Down* 1991—*Greatest Hits II* 1992—*American Pride* 1993—*Cheap Seats* 1994—*Greatest Hits III* 1995—*In Pictures* 1997—*Dancin' on the Boulevard* 1998—*For the Record* 1999—*Twentieth Century* 2001—*When It All Goes South.*

The biggest-selling country group of the '80s, Alabama began in 1969 as a trio of cousins: Jeff Cook, Randy Owen, and Teddy Gentry. Then known as Young Country, the band performed on weekends at a local amusement park, Canyonland. In 1973, after moving to Myrtle Beach, South Carolina, the group (with drummer Rich Scott), began playing its own songs in clubs, renaming itself Alabama.

After a few self-produced singles, the group signed with GRT Records in 1977. Its first release, "I Want to Be With You," made the country Top 100, but subsequent releases failed to match even that standing. In 1979 Alabama went to MDJ Records of Dallas, and its first single on the independent label, "I Wanna Come Over," reached #32 on the country chart in 1980, and the followup, "My Home's in Alabama," #17. Alabama's first RCA single, "Tennessee River," hit #1 in 1980. It was the first of 42 country chart-toppers.

To date the group has sold over 65 million records worldwide of its country-pop sound, becoming the first country group to sell quintuple-platinum albums. Of its 16 releases on RCA through 1993, only that year's *Cheap Seats* failed to go gold or platinum—an indication that after nearly 15 years, Alabama's thunder had been stolen by Garth Brooks, Travis Tritt, and other contemporary country acts. Nevertheless, 1993 did see the quartet win the People's Choice award for favorite musical group, and as the decade ended the group had scored several country Top 5 singles. *When It All Goes South* debuted on the country albums chart at #4 (#37 pop) in early 2001.

The Alarm

Formed 1978 (as Seventeen), Rhyl, Wales
Eddie MacDonald (b. Nov. 1, 1959), bass; Mike Peters (b. Michael Peters, Feb. 25, 1959), voc., gtr.; Dave Sharp (b. David Sharp, Jan. 28, 1959), gtr., voc.; Nigel Twist (b. July 18, 1958), drums.
1983—*The Alarm* EP (I.R.S.) 1984—*Declaration* 1985—*Strength* 1987—*Eye of the Hurricane* 1988—*Electric Folklore Live* 1989—*Change* 1990—*Standards* 1991—*Raw* 1998—*The Best of the Alarm and Mike Peters* (EMI, U.K.) 1999—*King Biscuit Flower Hour* (King Biscuit) 2000—*The Alarm 2000 Collection* (21st Century).
Dave Sharp solo: 1991—*Hard Travellin'* (I.R.S.) 1996—*Downtown America* (Dinosaur).
Mike Peters solo: 1994—*Breathe* (Cra, U.K.) 1996—*Feel Free* (Select) 1998—*Rise* (Velvel) 2000—*Flesh & Blood* (21st Century, U.K.) 2001—*The Millenium Gathering*.
Mike Peters with ColourSound: 1999—*ColourSound* (21st Century, U.K.).

The earnest guitar-dominated band the Alarm first came to the attention of American audiences when it opened U2's 1983 tour. Like U2, the Alarm sought to forge a new, idealistic arena rock, one marked by a sense of band-audience communion and punk's galvanizing spirit. Eschewing electronic effects, the Alarm's Mike Peters and Dave Sharp strummed acoustic guitars.

The quartet came together in their native Wales while all were in their teens. Peters and Nigel Twist were part of the Toilets when Eddie MacDonald and Sharp joined them in 1978. Inspired by the Sex Pistols, for a while they called themselves Seventeen. In 1981 they relocated to London, where, after gigging steadily in clubs, they were signed by I.R.S. Records. The following year they became the Alarm. Despite scoring hits on rock-oriented radio with such songs as "Strength" (#61, 1985) and "Rain in the Summertime" (#71, 1987), only one album broke the Top 40, *Strength* (#39, 1985). Sharp released his first solo album, *Hard Travellin'*, in late 1991; the band broke up in 1992.

Peters moved on to a solo career, releasing four albums in five years. The third, *Rise*, was accompanied by an all-request tour, in which fans determined the set list for each concert date via fax and the singer's Web site. At the same time, Peters began a collaboration with Billy Duffy, onetime guitarist for the Cult. Their band, ColourSound, released an eponymously titled album in 1999. To promote an Alarm box set, Peters embarked on the Mike Peters Alarm 2001 Tour, with a lineup (guitarist James Stevenson, bassist Richard Llewellyn, and drummer Steve Grantley) that had performed together in 2000.

Arthur Alexander

Born Arthur Bernard Alexander Jr., May 10, 1940, Florence, AL; died June 9, 1993, Nashville, TN
1962—*You Better Move On* (Dot) 1972—*Arthur Alexander* (Warner Bros.) 1993—*Lonely Just Like Me* (Elektra Nonesuch); *The Ultimate Arthur Alexander* (Razor & Tie) 1994—*Rainbow Road* (Warner Bros.).

Country-soul vocalist Arthur Alexander wrote and recorded the 1962 hit "You Better Move On." He began singing in church as a child, and during his teens belonged to an a cappella group called the Heartstrings. In 1961 he was working a day job as a bellhop and recording occasionally. Early the next year, his song "You Better Move On" hit #24 on the pop chart. Not only was it Alexander's first and most successful single, but the first hit to come out of Rick Hall's Muscle Shoals studios. Dot Records unwisely attempted to market Alexander as a pop singer, and such followup releases as the Barry Mann–Cynthia Weil composition "Where Have You Been (All My Life)" and his own "Anna (Go to Him)" (both 1962) were well sung but commercially unsuccessful.

His records had more impact in England, and his songs were later recorded by the Beatles ("Anna"), the Rolling Stones ("You Better Move On"), Bob Dylan ("Sally Sue Brown"), Elvis Presley ("Burning Love"), and Otis Redding ("Johnny Heartbreak"). In 1972 Alexander's eponymous album on Warner Bros. drew critical kudos but low sales. A few years later he reentered the pop chart with "Every Day I Have to Cry" (#45, 1975), but then he quit the music business, tired, as he said, of "the rip-offs." After 1981 he drove a bus for a Cleveland social-services agency. He remained popular in England, where three of his albums (*Shot of Rhythm and Soul, Soldiers of Love,* and *Arthur Alexander*) were reissued through the '80s. Following the 1991 murder of his eldest son, he returned to music.

Alexander was on the verge of a commercial comeback in 1993, with the release of his first LP in two decades, *Lonely*

Just Like Me. Unanimously praised by critics, the album featured backing by such Muscle Shoals mainstays as guitarist Dan Penn and keyboardist Spooner Oldham. Sadly, just a few months after its release and on the eve of a summer tour, Alexander died of heart failure.

Alice in Chains

Formed 1987, Seattle, WA
Jerry Cantrell (b. Mar. 18, 1966, Tacoma, WA), gtr.; Layne Staley (b. Aug. 22, 1967, Bellevue, WA), voc.; Sean Kinney (b. May 27, 1966, Seattle), drums; Mike Starr (b. Apr. 4, 1966, Honolulu, HI), bass.
1990—*We Die Young* EP (Columbia); *Face Lift* 1991—*Sap* EP 1992—*Dirt* (– Starr; + Mike Inez [b. May 14, 1966, San Fernando, CA], bass) 1993—*Jar of Flies* EP 1995—*Alice in Chains* 1996—*MTV Unplugged* 1999—*Music Bank; Nothing Safe—Best of the Box* 2000—*Live.*
Jerry Cantrell solo: 1998—*Boggy Depot.*
Layne Staley with Mad Season (Staley; Mike McCready, gtr.; Barrett Martin, drums; John Baker Saunders, bass): 1995—*Above* (Columbia).

A metal band with an alternative-rock edge, Alice in Chains was among the biggest to emerge from the grunge scene that spawned Nirvana, Pearl Jam, and Soundgarden. The group's dark, bitter songs, laden with references to drug addiction and death, occupy a musical landscape somewhere between Metallica's dense head bangers and Pearl Jam's grinding anthems. Layne Staley formed Alice N' Chains with an earlier lineup while still in high school. In 1987 he met Jerry Cantrell at the Music Bank, a notorious Seattle warehouse rehearsal space, and the two put together the newly christened Alice in Chains along with Cantrell cohorts Kinney and Starr. By 1989 the group had signed to Columbia Records, where it became the beneficiary of an aggressive promotion campaign that saw the release of a five-song promotional EP, *We Die Young*, and had the group opening for a range of disparate acts, including Iggy Pop and Poison. As a result, by September 1991, *Face Lift* (#42) had sold a half-million copies and featured the Grammy-nominated "Man in the Box." A low-key and mostly acoustic EP, *Sap*, and a track in the Seattle youth culture movie *Singles* kept the band in the public eye between albums.

The group's thematically bleaker sophomore effort, *Dirt* (#6), went platinum in 1992 (eventually selling 3 million copies), and the group's appearance on the following summer's Lollapalooza Tour confirmed its popularity. Reports of drug abuse, however, had begun to plague Staley and the band; a couple of songs from *Dirt*—"Junkhead" and "Angry Chair"—had hinted at mental fatigue and self-destruction. Yet Alice in Chains' success was at an all-time high: In late 1993 *Dirt* went double-platinum, and the following year the acoustic *Jar of Flies* rocketed to #1, the first EP to ever top the *Billboard* album chart. In 1994 Staley hooked up with fellow Seattleites Mike McCready (Pearl Jam), Barrett Martin (Screaming Trees), and John Baker Saunders to play a few gigs under the name Gacy Bunch; the next year they changed their name to Mad Season and released *Above* (#24, 1995), but Staley quit the side project (replaced by Mark Lanegan of Screaming Trees) before its second album.

In 1995 Alice in Chains returned to action with a self-titled album (which debuted at #1), but the quartet failed to tour, owing to internal discord and rumored addictions. Even so, the band reconvened in 1996 for its first public performance in three years to record and release *MTV Unplugged* (#3), which stripped the band's hard-rock sound to an acoustic, unexpectedly melodic core. Nothing new was heard from Alice in Chains until the 1999 release of *Music Bank* (and the excerpted *Nothing Safe—Best of the Box*). Named for the warehouse where the band lived and recorded in its early days, the album was a 48-song collection that mixed two new tracks ("Get Born Again" and "Died") with the band's hits, live recordings, demos, and B sides. Another anthology of sorts, *Live* documented performances from throughout the band's career.

Lee Allen

Born July 2, 1927, Pittsburg, KS; died Oct. 18, 1994, Los Angeles, CA
1958—*Walkin' With Mr. Lee* (Ember).

Although the closest Lee Allen ever came to getting a hit for himself was "Walking With Mr. Lee" (#54, 1958), his tenor saxophone session performances and arrangements were integral to numerous hits by Fats Domino, Little Richard, and others who recorded in New Orleans in the '50s and early '60s. He moved to New Orleans in 1944, where he attended Xavier University on a music and athletic scholarship. By 1948 he was performing professionally with Paul Gayten's band, one of the pioneer New Orleans R&B bands. In 1956 he joined Dave Bartholomew's band, which recorded and toured with Fats Domino during Domino's peak years. At that time Allen also worked as a session musician and arranger; he and baritone saxophonist Alvin "Red" Tyler led New Orleans' most in-demand session ensemble, the Studio Band, which included drummers Earl Palmer and Charles "Hungry" Williams, guitarists Ernest McLean and Justin Adams, pianists Salvador Doucette, Edward Frank, and Allen Toussaint, bassist Frank "Dude" Fields, and trumpeter Melvin Lastie.

Bumps Blackwell hired the Studio Band to back Little Richard on some of his hit records: "Tutti Frutti," "Long Tall Sally," "The Girl Can't Help It," and others. Allen also played behind Shirley and Lee ("Let the Good Times Roll"), Huey Smith and the Clowns ("Rockin' Pneumonia and the Boogie Woogie Flu"), Sam Cooke, Lowell Fulson, Charles Brown, and Jimmy Clanton. In 1957 Allen signed a solo contract with Herald Records. His first single was "Walking With Mr. Lee," a #1 hit in New Orleans, followed by "Tic Toc" and a tour of the U.S. in the late '50s. He then returned to the New Orleans studios to work for $42 per session on hit records that sold millions of copies. He retired in the early '60s but returned in

1982 to tour with the Blasters; he guested on the band's first album.

In 1994 Allen contributed tenor saxophone and vocals to *Crescent City Gold,* an album featuring an aggregation of New Orleans jazz and R&B greats. Later that year Allen died of lung cancer at age 67.

Luther Allison

Born Aug. 17, 1939, Mayflower, AR; died Aug. 13, 1997, Madison, WI
1969—*Love Me Mama* (Delmark) 1972—*Bad News Is Coming* (Gordy) 1974—*Luther's Blues* 1976—*Night Life* 1979—*Gonna Be a Live One Here Tonight* (Rumble) 1993—*Hand Me Down My Moonshine* (Inak, Ger.) 1994—*Soul Fixin' Man* (Alligator); *Serious* (Blind Pig) 1995—*Blue Streak* (Alligator) 1997—*Reckless.*

Luther Allison belongs to a generation of electric blues guitarists who came of age in the '60s. These musicians appealed to both old-line blues audiences and younger, white rock audiences. Born on a cotton plantation, Allison was one of 15 children. Before he was 10 years old, he sang with a gospel group, the Southern Travellers, with whom he toured throughout the South. Circa 1951, he moved with his family to Chicago and began playing guitar. One of his boyhood friends in that city would turn out to be Muddy Waters' son. Allison first performed as a blues guitarist with his elder brother's band, which played Chicago clubs between 1954 and 1957. Luther's own nascent band, the Rolling Stones (later renamed the Four Jivers), lasted for one year.

For the next decade Allison was a mainstay of the Chicago blues scene, often playing behind Freddie King and Magic Sam. He made his first records for Delmark in 1967, the same year he took to the road with his group, the Tornados. In 1968 he toured and recorded for World Pacific with Shakey Jake, and began making annual appearances at the Ann Arbor Blues and Jazz Festival. Hoping to find success in the music business, he moved to California in the late '60s and soon began playing such rock venues as the Fillmore West and, in New York City, the Fillmore East and Max's Kansas City. Dispirited, he returned to Chicago and recorded three albums for Motown's Gordy label and the soundtrack to *Cooley High.*

Allison, who eventually settled near Paris, began extensively touring Europe in the '70s and continued to delight the festival circuit over the next two decades with his lengthy, intense performances. In July 1997, Allison was diagnosed with inoperable lung cancer, succumbing to the illness a few days short of his 58th birthday.

Mose Allison

Born Mose John Allison Jr., Nov. 11, 1927, Tippo, MS
1957—*Back Country Suite* (Prestige) 1983—*Lessons in Living* (Elektra/Musician) 1988—*Ever Since the World Ended* (Blue Note); *Greatest Hits* (Fantasy) 1990—*My Backyard* (Blue Note) 1993—*I Don't Worry About a Thing* (Rhino) 1994—*The Earth Wants You* (Blue Note); *Allison Wonderland—The Mose Allison Anthology* (Rhino); *High Jinks!: The Mose Allison Trilogy* (Columbia) 1997—*Gimcracks and Geegaws* (Blue Note).

Singer/pianist Mose Allison has been popular in jazz circles for over 40 years. Rock musicians know him for his songs—which have been covered by the Who ("A Young Man Blues"), Bonnie Raitt ("Everybody's Cryin' Mercy"), John Mayall ("Parchman Farm"), Van Morrison ("If You Only Knew"), the Clash ("Look Here"), and the Yardbirds ("I'm Not Talking"), among others—and for a sardonic sense of humor as evidenced in his "Your Mind Is on Vacation (But Your Mouth Is Working Overtime)." The son of a stride jazz pianist, Allison began playing at age six. Later, he also took up the trumpet. He absorbed both jazz and country blues, and when he arrived in New York City in 1956, he played piano with "cool" jazzmen Al Cohn, Stan Getz, Gerry Mulligan, and Zoot Sims. Allison's style blended the simplicity of the blues with modernist harmonies. He began to sing in 1957, when he formed his own trio. For decades to come, his understated and laconically cynical songs would be periodically rediscovered by the rock audience. In the '90s, Allison's daughter, Amy, became known for her twangy voice, inspired songwriting, and critically acclaimed alt-country albums.

The Allman Brothers Band

Formed 1969, Jacksonville, FL
Duane Allman (b. Nov. 20, 1946, Nashville, TN; d. Oct. 29, 1971, Macon, GA), gtr.; Gregg Allman (b. Dec. 8, 1947, Nashville), kybds., gtr., voc.; Berry Oakley (b. Apr. 4, 1948, Chicago, IL.; d. Nov. 11, 1972, Macon), bass; Dickey Betts (b. Forrest Richard Betts, Dec. 12, 1943, West Palm Beach, FL), gtr., voc.; Jaimoe, a.k.a. Jai Johanny Johanson (b. John Lee Johnson, July 8, 1944, Ocean Springs, MS), drums; Butch Trucks (b. May 11, 1947, Jacksonville), drums.
1969—*The Allman Brothers Band* (Capricorn) 1970—*Idlewild South* 1971—*At Fillmore East* (– D. Allman) 1972—*Eat a Peach* (+ Chuck Leavell, kybds.; – Oakley; + Lamar Williams [b. 1947; d. Jan. 25, 1983, Los Angeles, CA], bass) 1973—*Brothers and Sisters* 1974—*Beginnings* 1975—*Win, Lose or Draw* 1976—*Wipe the Windows, Check the Oil, Dollar Gas; The Road Goes On Forever* 1979—(– Leavell; – Williams; + Dan Toler, gtr.; + Rook Goldflies, bass) *Enlightened Rogues* 1980—*Reach for the Sky* (Arista) 1981—*Brothers of the Road* (– Johanson; + David Toler, drums) *The Best of the Allman Brothers Band* (Polydor) 1982—(group disbands) 1989—(group re-forms: Gregg Allman; Dickey Betts; Johanson; Butch Trucks; + Warren Haynes, gtr.; + Allen Woody [d. Aug. 26, 2000, New York, NY], bass; + Johnny Neel, kybds.) *Dreams* 1990—*Seven Turns* (Epic); *Live at Ludlow's Garage 1970* (Polydor) (– Neel; + Marc Quiñones, perc.) 1991—*Shades of Two Worlds; Decade of Hits (1969–79)* (Polydor) 1992—*An Evening With*

(Epic) 1994—*Where It All Begins* 1995—*2nd Set* 1996—(– Woody; – Haynes; + Oteil Burbridge, bass; + Jack Pearson, gtr.) 1997—*Fillmore East 2/70* (Grateful Dead) 1998—*Mycology: An Anthology* (550 Music/Epic) 1999—(– Pearson; + Derek Trucks, gtr.) 2000—(– Betts) *Peakin' at the Beacon.*
Duane Allman solo: 1972—*An Anthology* (Capricorn) 1974—*An Anthology, vol. 2.*
Gregg Allman solo: 1974—*Laid Back* (Capricorn) 1975—*The Gregg Allman Tour* 1997—*One More Try: An Anthology* (Chronicles); *Searching for Simplicity* (Sony/550).
The Gregg Allman Band: 1977—*Playin' Up a Storm* 1987—*I'm No Angel* (Epic) 1988—*Just Before the Bullets Fly.*
Dickey Betts solo: 1974—*Highway Call* (Capricorn).
Dickey Betts and Great Southern: 1977—*Dickey Betts and Great Southern* (Arista) 1978—*Atlanta's Burning Down.*
The Dickey Betts Band: 1988—*Pattern Disruptive* (Epic).
Sea Level (Leavell; Jaimoe; Williams): 1977—*Sea Level* (Capricorn) 1978—*Cats on the Coast; On the Edge* (– Jaimoe) 1979—*Long Walk on a Short Pier* 1980—*Ballroom* (Arista).
Chuck Leavell: 1997—*What's in That Bag?* (Capricorn).
Gov't Mule (Haynes; Woody; Matt Abts, drums): 1995—*Gov't Mule* (Foundation) 1996—*Live at the Roseland Ballroom* (Relativity) 1998—*Dose* (Capricorn) 1999—*Live . . . With a Little Help From Our Friends* 2000—*Life Before Insanity.*

The Allman Brothers Band blended strains of Southern music—blues, R&B, country, jazz, and gospel—into a flexible, jam-oriented style that reflected the emergence of the "New South" and set the style for Lynyrd Skynyrd, the Marshall Tucker Band, and countless other Southern rockers. Oddly—or eerily, some would say—the band's unusual string of untimely deaths has been repeated in other Southern-rock bands. Through personal tragedy and turmoil, the Allman Brothers Band has endured and, though lacking the commercial clout of its early-'70s heyday, it remains highly respected and well received by legions of fans.

Brothers Gregg and Duane Allman were living in Daytona Beach, Florida, in 1960, and played in various bands until 1963, when they formed the Escorts, which became the Allman Joys in 1965. After their version of Willie Dixon's "Spoonful" failed as a single, the two brothers and three other band members went to L.A., where they signed with Liberty Records as the Hourglass. They recorded two albums of outside material (*Hourglass,* 1967, and *Power of Love,* 1968) before heading to Muscle Shoals, Alabama, to record at Fame Studios. Liberty rejected the resulting tapes, and Duane and Gregg returned to Florida.

Soon after, the brothers joined the 31st of February, whose drummer was Butch Trucks. After recording an album, Gregg went back to L.A. to make good on the Liberty contract. (A 1973 Bold album called *Duane and Gregg* consisted of tapes made by the 31st of February.) Duane stayed in Jacksonville, where he began playing with the Second Coming, which included Dickey Betts and Berry Oakley, veterans of Tommy Roe and the Romans. But before Duane became an established member of the Second Coming, Fame Studios owner Rick Hall asked him to return to Muscle Shoals to play lead guitar for a Wilson Pickett session. At Duane's suggestion, Pickett recorded Lennon and McCartney's "Hey Jude." Duane became Fame's primary session guitarist, recording over the next year with Aretha Franklin, King Curtis, Percy Sledge, Clarence Carter, and Arthur Conley, and signing with Fame Productions as a solo artist.

At the urging of Atlantic Records vice president Jerry Wexler, Phil Walden bought the Fame contract, with the notion to build a band around Duane for his upstart Capricorn Records. Allman hired Jai Johanny Johanson, a Muscle Shoals drummer who had worked with Otis Redding, Percy Sledge, Joe Tex, and Clifton Chenier. He went back to Florida and reconvened Trucks, Oakley, Betts, and Gregg. Once assembled, the Allman Brothers Band moved to Macon, Georgia, where Walden was launching Capricorn. (In 1991 Trucks said of the group's long tenure with the label: "We had grossed $40 million and woke up one day to realize our own manager [Phil Walden] had cheated us out of every cent.") *The Allman Brothers Band,* the group's debut, was well received only in the South. After its release, Duane continued to play on sessions with Boz Scaggs, Laura Nyro, Otis Rush, Delaney and Bonnie, Ronnie Hawkins, and John Hammond. He appears with Eric Clapton on Derek and the Dominos' *Layla.* (His session work is collected on the two *Anthology* volumes.)

On the strength of the Allman Brothers' growing reputation as a live band, its second album sold well. In March 1971, four shows at New York's Fillmore East were recorded for release as a live double LP set in July. By the time the album reached the Top 10, the Allman Brothers Band was being hailed in print as "America's best rock & roll group." But on October 29, 1971, less than three months after *At Fillmore East*'s release, Duane was killed in a motorcycle accident in Macon. The group played at his funeral and decided to continue without a new guitarist. Three songs on their next LP, *Eat a Peach,* had been recorded before Duane's death, and with live material from the Fillmore East concerts, the double LP was released in February, entered the chart in the Top 10, and rose to #4. In 1972, Oakley was killed in a motorcycle crash three blocks from the site of Duane's accident a year earlier.

Dickey Betts, by then the band's unofficial leader, wrote and sang "Ramblin' Man," the band's first and biggest hit single (#2, 1973); *Brothers and Sisters* went to #1, with Lamar Williams, a childhood friend of Jaimoe's, taking Oakley's place, and Chuck Leavell on keyboards. The first two albums, when reissued as *Beginnings,* more than doubled their original sales. The group returned to the road after two years. In Watkins Glen, New York, 600,000 people gathered in July 1973 for an all-day concert by the Allman Brothers Band, the Grateful Dead, and the Band. There was growing dissension in the group, however, as Gregg and Betts began to disagree over schedules and musical direction. In 1974 they each released a Top 20 solo album (Allman's *Laid Back* and Betts' *Highway Call*), and Allman formed the Gregg Allman Band with Johanson, Leavell, Williams, and others to tour and record *The Gregg Allman Tour.* The subsequent Allman Brothers Band album, *Win, Lose or Draw* (#5, 1975), sold well, but it was four years before the next album of new material; *The Road Goes On Forever,* a compilation, and *Wipe the Windows,* a live collection, were released in 1976. By 1975, Allman was involved in a tumultuous marriage to Cher (they divorced in 1979). They had a son, Elijah Blue, in 1977. Their 1977 LP, *Allman and Woman: Two the Hard Way,* was universally panned.

But the greatest blow to the group occurred in 1976, when Allman testified against Scooter Herring, his personal road manager, charged with dealing narcotics. Herring was subsequently sentenced to 75 years in prison (later reduced to two years on appeal). Allman's action, the others said, betrayed the fraternal loyalty that had sustained them: They vowed never to work with him again.

The members pursued separate but at times intertwining paths. Betts formed Great Southern, duplicating the original Allman Brothers lineup with two guitars, two drums, bass, keyboards, and vocals. Only the group's first album charted in the Top 100. After Allman's disastrous duet LP with Cher, he regrouped the Gregg Allman Band, with no help from any former Brothers, and put out *Playin' Up a Storm* in 1977. The other members also remained active: Trucks studied music at Florida State University for two years and formed an experimental group, Trucks. Leavell, Williams, and Johanson, with guitarist Jimmy Nails, formed the fusion-oriented Sea Level. Later, Leavell returned to session work, notably with the Rolling Stones, with whom he has toured since 1989.

In 1978, the Allman Brothers Band regrouped for the first time. After Allman, Trucks, and Jaimoe joined Betts and Great Southern onstage in New York in 1978, Great Southern guitarist Dan Toler and bassist Rook Goldflies also joined the new Allman Brothers Band. *Enlightened Rogues* (#9, 1979) was certified gold within two weeks of its release. Two years later *Brothers of the Road* gave the group a minor hit single, "Straight From the Heart." The group broke up again in 1980. In 1983 Lamar Williams died of Agent Orange–related cancer. Betts recorded an album with the Dickey Betts Band, and Allman released *I'm No Angel* (#30, 1987) with its #49 title track.

Regrouping yet again in 1989 with core members Allman, Betts, Jaimoe, and Trucks, the Allman Brothers Band took to the road. *Dreams,* a box set, compiles songs from 1966 to 1988. The group's recent albums and performances have attracted a new generation of fans who have come to appreciate the Allman Brothers as the root of much latter-day collegiate jam rock. There was renewed critical respect, as well, especially for Allman's singing and writing. Allman, who finally won his struggles with heroin and alcohol, has also acted, appearing in the film *Rush* and the syndicated TV series *Superboy.*

In 1995 the group was inducted into the Rock and Roll Hall of Fame and released *2nd Set.* It received its first Grammy Award (for Best Rock Instrumental Performance) the next year, for "Jessica." Gregg Allman released his first solo recording in a decade with 1997's *Searching for Simplicity,* which opens with a remake of the Allman Brothers' classic blues "Whipping Post." Allman's solo anthology, *One More Try,* includes only eight previously released songs.

The Allman Brothers Band: Butch Trucks, Dickey Betts, Berry Oakley, Duane Allman, Gregg Allman, Jai Johanny Johanson

A series of personnel changes, and the occasional intramural ruckus, have kept the band in flux. In 1996, Warren Haynes and Allen Woody left to work full-time with their own project, the blues-rock trio Gov't Mule. Guitarist Jack Pearson, who cowrote Gregg Allman's epic "Sailin' 'Cross the Devil's Sea," and bassist Oteil Burbridge (Aquarium Rescue Unit) replaced them. Pearson's departure in 1999 made way for 20-year-old guitarist Derek Trucks, Butch's nephew, to join a band he had been sitting in with for years. In June 2000, Betts was ousted via fax from the band on the eve of a summer tour. Soon thereafter, he put together a new eight-piece band, touring as the Dickey Betts Band.

Herb Alpert

Born Mar. 31, 1935, Los Angeles, CA
1962—*The Lonely Bull* (A&M) 1963—*Herb Alpert's Tijuana Brass, vol. 2* 1964—*South of the Border* 1965—*Whipped Cream & Other Delights; Going Places* 1966—*What Now, My Love; S.R.O.* 1967—*Sounds Like; Herb Alpert's Ninth* 1968—*The Beat of the Brass; Christmas Album* 1969—*Warm; The Brass Are Comin'* 1970—*Greatest Hits* 1971—*Summertime* 1972—*Solid Brass* 1973—*Four Sider* 1974—*You Smile—The Song Begins* 1975—*Coney Island* 1976—*Just You and Me* 1977—*Greatest Hits, vol. 2* 1978—*Main Event Live* (with Hugh Masekela) (Horizon) 1979—*Rise* (A&M) 1980—*Beyond* 1981—*Magic Man* 1982—*Fandango* 1983—*Blow Your Own Horn* 1984—*Bullish* 1985—*Wild Romance* 1987—*Keep Your Eye on Me* 1988—*Under a Spanish Moon* 1989—*My Abstract Heart* 1991—*North on South Street* 1992—*Midnight Sun* 1996—*Second Wind* (Almo Sounds) 1997—*Passion Dance* 1999—*Herb Alpert & Colors.*

Herb Alpert rose to fame in the mid-'60s as the king of South of the Border MOR, or as it was called, "Ameriachi." He has since become a music industry force, both as a performer (he's sold more instrumental records than any artist in history) and as cofounder and vice chairman of A&M Records, which he and Jerry Moss sold to PolyGram in 1990 for a sum reported to be in excess of $500 million.

Alpert was raised in L.A. and began playing trumpet at age eight. After returning from the army he had briefly acted and then recorded as Dore Alpert for RCA. Under the pseudonym Barbara Campbell, Alpert, Lou Adler, and Sam Cooke cowrote a number of Cooke's hits, among them "Only Sixteen" and "Wonderful World." During the late '50s he produced Jan and Dean, and with songwriting partner Lou Adler recorded a cover version of the Hollywood Argyles' "Alley Oop" under the name Dante and the Evergreens.

In 1962 he and Jerry Moss (b. 1946) founded A&M Records. Initially a shoestring operation out of Alpert's garage, A&M eventually became the nation's biggest independent record company, largely on the strength of Alpert's Tijuana Brass hits such as "The Lonely Bull" (#6, 1962), "A Taste of Honey" (#7, 1965), and "The Mexican Shuffle" (#85, 1964), later used in chewing gum commercials as the "Teaberry Shuffle." In 1965 the group had five LPs in the Top 20 and in 1966 sold 13 million records.

Among Alpert's signings for A&M were the Carpenters and Carole King. He returned to the charts in 1979 with the biggest record of his career, "Rise." It was only Alpert's second #1 hit, the other being a rare vocal outing, 1968's "This Guy's in Love With You." His third-biggest hit, "Diamonds" (#5, 1987), was produced by Jimmy Jam and Terry Lewis and featured one of A&M's biggest latter-day coups, Janet Jackson. Alpert launched his own fragrance, called Listen, in 1989. In 1994 Alpert and Moss resumed their record business activity and founded Almo Sounds, the company that would release the trumpet player's post-A&M catalogue. The alternative-rock quartet Garbage was among the new label's early successes; however, the company closed down in 2000. Alpert has also exhibited his paintings throughout Europe, produced for Broadway, and done philanthropic work through his Herb Alpert Foundation. Alpert's wife is singer Lani Hall.

Dave Alvin, Phil Alvin: See the Blasters

Amazing Rhythm Aces

Formed 1974, Knoxville, TN
Russell Smith (b. Howard Russell Smith, Lafayette, TN), gtr., harmonica, voc.; Butch McDade (b. Feb. 24, 1946, TN; d. Nov. 29, 1998, TN), drums, voc.; Jeff Davis (b. TN), bass; Billy Earhart III (b. TN), kybds.; James Hooker (b. TN), kybds., voc.; Barry "Byrd" Burton, gtr., Dobro, mandolin, voc., pedal steel gtr.
1975—*Stacked Deck* (ABC) 1976—*Too Stuffed to Jump; Toucan Do It Too* 1978—*Burning the Ballroom Down* 1979—*Amazing Rhythm Aces* (– Byrd; + Duncan Cameron, gtr., voc.) 1980—*How the Hell Do You Spell Rythum?* (Warner Bros.) 1981—(group disbands) 1995—(group re-forms: Smith; McDade; Davis; Earhart; Hooker; + Danny Parks, gtr., mandolin) *Ride Again* (Breaker) 1996—*Out of the Blue* 1997—(– Parks; + Kelvin Holly, gtr.) 1998—(– McDade; – Holly; + Tony Bowles, gtr.) 1999—*Chock Full of Country Goodness* (Breaker) (– Hooker; + Bryan Owings, drums).

The country-rock Amazing Rhythm Aces were formed as an informal assemblage headed by guitarist/lead singer/main songwriter Russell Smith, who had learned how to sing country blues while working as a teenage disc jockey on a station in his native Lafayette. The group was temporarily sidetracked in the early '70s when several members joined Jesse Winchester's backup band, but they then regrouped. Their debut, *Stacked Deck*, featured a mixture of country, gospel, rock, and bluegrass and yielded a hit single, "Third Rate Romance" (#14, 1975). Despite continuous touring, however, that success was never repeated, even though subsequent efforts like "The End Is Not in Sight" (1976) and "Amazing Grace (Used to Be Her Favorite Song)" (1976) placed in the Top 20 on the country chart. The band has had a turbulent managerial history; in 1979 its album *Amazing Rhythm Aces* appeared first on ABC, then on Columbia when the group's contract changed hands. The Amazing Rhythm Aces broke up in 1981.

Since 1982 Smith has released solo albums. He has written songs for such country artists as Ricky Van Shelton and the title track of rockabilly pioneer Billy Lee Riley's comeback LP, *Blue Collar Blues*. In 1991 he joined the so-called Spinal Tap of country & western, Run C&W (which includes ex-Eagle Bernie Leadon, Jim Photoglo, and Vince Melamed), which performs country versions of '60s soul classics. Earhart joined the Bama Band (Hank Williams Jr.'s backing band) in 1986.

The Aces, abetted by a new guitarist, reconvened in 1995 to record *Ride Again*, a self-released collection of remakes of their most popular material. Following the all-new *Out of the Blue*, the band deemed its reunion "official," though the group was sidelined by the cancer-related death of drummer Butch McDade in 1998. A session drummer was employed for *Chock Full of Country Goodness*. Founding keyboardist James Hooker left in 1999, though the Aces and their Breaker label remained active.

Ambitious Lovers: See DNA/Arto Lindsay

Amboy Dukes: See Ted Nugent

Ambrosia

Formed 1971, Los Angeles, CA
David Pack (b. 1952), gtr., voc.; Joe Puerta (b. 1952), bass,

voc.; Burleigh Drummond (b. 1952), drums, voc.; Christopher North (b. 1952), kybds., voc.
1975—*Ambrosia* (20th Century–Fox) 1976—*Somewhere I've Never Travelled* (Warner Bros.) 1977—(– North) 1978—*Life Beyond L.A.* 1980—*One Eighty* 1982—*Road Island.*

Ambrosia plays pop with classical flourishes and is best known for its late-'70s hit singles. David Pack and Joe Puerta met in high school and were later joined by Burleigh Drummond and Christopher North. Three months later, while helping check a new sound system in the Hollywood Bowl, renowned classical-music engineer Gordon Parry heard them play and arranged for them to perform at UCLA. Parry arranged for Los Angeles Philharmonic conductor Zubin Mehta to attend the performance, and Mehta then invited the group to participate in his All American Dream Concert in the Hollywood Bowl soon thereafter. In 1973 Ambrosia performed in the debut of Leonard Bernstein's *Mass* at the Kennedy Center for the Performing Arts in Washington, DC.

The four members play a total of 72 instruments, and their songs often contain literary allusions such as "Nice, Nice, Very Nice," a line from Kurt Vonnegut's *Cat's Cradle.* The group contributed to the soundtrack of *All This and World War II.* Its hit singles include "Holdin' On to Yesterday" (#17, 1975), "How Much I Feel" (#3, 1978), "Biggest Part of Me" (#3, 1980), and "You're the Only Woman (You & I)" (#13, 1980). Ambrosia broke up in 1984, but the four original members reunited in 1989 and continue to tour. They contributed three new songs to a 1997 best-of anthology.

Amen Corner/Andy Fairweather-Low

Formed 1966, Cardiff, Wales
Andy Fairweather-Low (b. 1948), voc., gtr.; Neil Jones, gtr.; Blue Weaver, organ; Clive Tayler, bass; Dennis Byrn, drums; Allen Jones, baritone sax; Mike Smith, sax.
1968—*Round Amen Corner* (Deram) 1969—*National Welsh Coast Live* (Immediate); *Farewell the Real Magnificent Seven; World of Amen Corner* (Decca) 1975—*Amen Corner and Small Faces* (New World) 1976—*Return of the Magnificent Seven* (Immediate) 1978—*Greatest Hits.*
Andy Fairweather-Low solo: 1974—*Spider Jiving* (A&M) 1975—*La Booga Rooga* 1977—*Be Bop 'n' Holla* 1980—*Mega-Shebang* (Warner Bros.).

Amen Corner was one of the last British Mod bands. Led by Andy Fairweather-Low, it had its first British Top 20 hit in 1967 with "Gin House," an R&B song, and subsequent hits included a cover of the American Breed's "Bend Me, Shape Me" and "High in the Sky," both of which went Top 10 in 1968. The group's only #1 hit came in 1969 with "(If Paradise Is) Half as Nice"; "Hello Suzie" was a Top 5 hit later that year.

After Immediate Records folded at the height of the group's popularity, Amen Corner was overhauled. The two horn players were dropped, and the name was changed to Fairweather. It had a 1970 Top 5 single with "Natural Sinner" but disbanded soon thereafter. Byron played briefly with the Bee Gees, and Weaver worked with the Bee Gees and the Strawbs.

Fairweather-Low went on a sabbatical of several years before beginning a solo career in 1974. He enjoyed a pair of Top 10 U.K. hits—"Reggae Tune" (1974) and "Wide Eyed and Legless" (1975)—although none of his solo albums charted in the U.S. He has appeared on albums by Dave Edmunds, Gerry Rafferty, Richard Thompson, the Who, and Roy Wood, among others. In 1990 he appeared in Roger Waters' production of *The Wall* in Berlin. Fairweather-Low subsequently joined Eric Clapton's backing band.

America

Formed 1969, London, Eng.
Dewey Bunnell (b. Jan. 19, 1952, Yorkshire, Eng.), gtr., voc., drums; Dan Peek (b. Nov. 1, 1950, Panama City, FL), gtr., voc.; Gerry Beckley (b. Sep. 12, 1952, Fort Worth, TX), gtr., voc.
1972—*America* (Warner Bros.); *Homecoming* 1973—*Hat Trick* 1974—*Holiday* 1975—*Hearts; History: America's Greatest Hits* 1976—*Hideaway; Harbor* 1977—*America/Live* (– Peek) 1979—*Silent Letter* (Capitol) 1980—*Alibi* 1982—*View From the Ground* 1983—*Your Move* 1984—*Perspective* 1990—*Encore! More Greatest Hits* (Rhino) 1994—*Hourglass* (American Grammaphone) 1998—*Human Nature.*

With its breezy acoustic guitars, high vocal harmonies, and smooth production, America was one of the most popular U.S. folk-rock groups of the early '70s. Sons of U.S. servicemen stationed in England, America's members were schoolmates in London's Central High when they began composing and performing together. Three years later "A Horse With No Name" hit #1 in March 1972. A string of gold and platinum singles ("I Need You," #9, 1972; "Ventura Highway," #8, 1972; "Tin Man," #4, 1974; "Lonely People," #5, 1975; "Sister Golden Hair," #1, 1975) and albums followed.

After Dan Peek's departure in May 1977, America continued as a duo, but with less success. Peek, who had become a born-again Christian, made some religious records; his 1979 *All Things Are Possible* was nominated for a Grammy. In late 1981 Bunnell and Beckley were the subject of controversy when they toured South Africa, defying the "cultural boycott" the United Nations had instituted to protest the nation's apartheid policies.

Bunnell and Beckley collaborated with Billy Mumy (Will Robinson from TV's *Lost in Space*) and in 1982 America returned to the Top 10 with "You Can Do Magic" from *View From the Ground.* Subsequent albums, however, fared poorly, with *Perspective* (which included songs by Jimmy Webb, among others) peaking at #185. Bunnell and Beckley continue to tour; in 1993 Peek rejoined them as America opened for the Beach Boys. After a 10-year absence from the studio, Bunnell and Beckley returned to record *Hourglass.* In 1998 America signed a multialbum deal with Oxygen Records. That same year the band performed "Ventura Highway" at the inaugural ball for newly elected Minnesota governor/former WWF wrestler Jesse Ventura.

The American Breed

Formed 1966, Chicago, IL
Al Ciner (b. May 14, 1947, Chicago), gtr.; Gary Loizzo (b. Aug. 16, 1945, Chicago), gtr., voc.; Lee Graziano (b. Nov. 9, 1943, Chicago), drums; Charles Colbert (b. Aug. 30, 1944, Chicago), bass; later added Kevin Murphy, kybds.
1967—*American Breed* (Dot) 1968—*Bend Me, Shape Me; Pumpkin, Powder, Scarlet and Green* (Atlantic); *Lonely Side of the City.*

With five hit singles in 1967 and 1968, the American Breed was one of Chicago's top pop bands. Originally called Gary and the Nite Lights, they recorded one unsuccessful single for MGM entitled "I Don't Think You Know Me." After signing with Acta, a Dot subsidiary, they changed their name to the American Breed and rereleased the song, thus beginning a short but successful string of hits including "Step Out of Your Mind" (#24, 1967), "Green Light" (#39, 1968), and the song for which the band is best remembered, "Bend Me, Shape Me" (#1, 1968). Following the American Breed's peak years, Kevin Murphy, along with Andre Fischer (a later member) and Chaka Khan [see entry], founded Rufus in 1972. Fischer later married singer Natalie Cole. Gary Loizzo worked through the late '60s as a jingles singer before establishing his recording studio, Pumpkin Studio, in a Chicago suburb. He has produced records by Styx and Liza Minelli, among others. The American Breed still performs; in 1993 it released an homage to its local baseball team, "Rock With the Sox."

American Music Club

Formed 1983, San Francisco, CA
Mark Eitzel (b. Jan. 30, 1959, Walnut Creek, CA), voc. gtr.; Mark "Vudi" Pankler (b. Sep. 22, 1952, Chicago, IL), gtr.; Dan Pearson (b. May 31, 1959, Walnut Creek), bass, gtr., mandolin, voc.; Brad Johnson, kybds.; Matt Norelli, drums.
1985—*The Restless Stranger* (Grifter) 1987—(– Johnson; – Norelli; + Tom Mallon, gtr., drums, voc.; + Dave Scheff, drums) *Engine* (Grifter/Frontier) 1988—(– Scheff) *California* 1989—(– Mallon; + Mike Simms, drums) *United Kingdom* (Demon, U.K.) 1991—(+ Bruce Kaphan [b. Jan. 7, 1955, San Francisco], pedal steel gtr., kybds.) *Everclear* (Alias) 1993—(– Simms; + Tim Mooney [b. Oct. 6, 1958, Las Vegas, NV], drums) *Mercury* (Reprise) 1994—*San Francisco* 1995—*Hello Amsterdam* EP.
Mark Eitzel solo: 1991—*Songs of Love* (Demon, U.K.) 1996—*60 Silver Watt Lining* (Warner Bros.) 1997—*West* 1998—*Caught in a Trap and I Can't Back Out 'Cause I Love You Too Much, Baby* (Matador) 2001—*The Invisible Man.*

Led by the charismatic songwriter Mark Eitzel, American Music Club became one of the most acclaimed U.S. underground bands of the '80s.

In 1980 Eitzel moved to San Francisco from Columbus, Ohio, with his band Naked Skinnies. After that group dissolved, he formed American Music Club, going through various lineups and becoming infamous for his desperate attempts to either entertain or terrify the audience. Tom Mallon produced and released the band's debut on his Grifter label; later he joined the group. *The Restless Stranger* introduced Eitzel's songs of loneliness and decay, set to AMC's postpunk honky-tonk. *Engine,* featuring such classic downers as "Gary's Song," "Nightwatchman," and "Outside This Bar," revealed emotional and musical depth. *California* confirmed the band as an underground favorite and garnered international attention.

When the band's label, Frontier, signed a licensing deal with BMG it financed what would have been AMC's major-label debut. Bruce Kaphan, who had been playing as a sideman for the band, joined full-time and produced *Everclear,* but the BMG deal collapsed, and AMC parted company with both Frontier and Mallon. While in limbo, the band recorded the partially live *United Kingdom,* named after the only country in which the album was released and where AMC had developed a strong following. In 1991 Eitzel released a solo live record, *Songs of Love,* on the same label.

Everclear was eventually released by the indie Alias to much fanfare (Rolling Stone critics dubbed it album of the year in 1991) but negligible sales. Eitzel's alienation from religion—as a teen, he was born again—fueled songs like "What the Pillar of Salt Held Up" and "Jesus' Hands." Notorious for his often alcohol-induced rages and depressions, the singer became sober around this time. He subsequently returned to drinking, although not to the onstage abuses of yore.

In 1991 AMC's revolving door of drummers settled on the Toiling Midgets' Tim Mooney, who had also played with the band in the mid-'80s (Eitzel moonlighted in the Midgets for a while and sang on their 1992 Matador release *Son*). The band signed with Reprise/Warner Bros. in 1992 after a bidding war. *Mercury,* produced by Mitchell Froom, was a strange major-label debut, full of lush, discordant music and obtuse musings with titles like "What Godzilla Said to God When His Name Wasn't Found in the Book of Life" and "Johnny Mathis' Feet."

The title cut of AMC's 1995 *Hello Amsterdam* EP (the song first appeared on 1994's *San Francisco*) confronted the band's commercial lack of success and proved to be its last gasp. In 1996 Eitzel released his second solo album, *60 Watt Silver Lining,* a jazzy adult-contemporary affair. Eitzel made *West,* a collaboration with R.E.M.'s Peter Buck, in 1997. Recorded with members of Yo La Tengo and Sonic Youth, *Caught in a Trap and I Can't Back Out 'Cause I Love You Too Much, Baby* appeared the following year. Meanwhile, former AMC members Mooney and Pearson formed Clodhopper, a rootsy, banjo-driven outfit that included Pearl Jam's Jeff Ament, and released *Red's Recovery Room* in 1998.

Tori Amos

Born Myra Ellen Amos, Aug. 22, 1963, Newton, NC
1992—*Little Earthquakes* (Atlantic); *Crucify* EP 1994—*Under*

the Pink 1996—*Boys for Pele; Hey Jupiter* EP 1998—*From the Choirgirl Hotel* (Atlantic) 1999—*To Venus and Back* (Atlantic).

After spending her youth studying classical piano, child prodigy Tori Amos' first foray into rock—with her hard-rock band Y Kant Tori Read—was mercifully short. It was a return to her beloved piano and the development of an intimate style of pop songwriting that brought her widespread success.

The youngest of three children of a Methodist minister father and homemaker mother, Amos showed signs of being a gifted musician when she began tinkering on the piano at age two and a half. At five, she began studying classical piano at the prestigious Peabody Institute at Baltimore's Johns Hopkins University. After she insisted on playing her own pop compositions for the school's examination board, her scholarship wasn't renewed. By the time she was 13, Amos was performing her songs at clubs in Washington, DC.

In 1984 Amos moved to L.A. to pursue her dream of becoming a rock star; she also began calling herself Tori. Three years later she signed a deal with Atlantic Records, and in 1988 her band Y Kant Tori Read, which included future Guns n' Roses drummer Matt Sorum, released one self-titled album. Adorned with teased hair and sporting a low-cut corset, Amos appeared on the LP's cover brandishing a saber.

The album's quick failure and a cathartic experience at the piano resulted in many of the extremely personal songs that eventually appeared on Amos's solo debut, *Little Earthquakes*. The most revealing, "Me and a Gun," detailed Amos' experience of being raped by an acquaintance.

With her record company's encouragement, Amos moved to London to perform in that city's small clubs—and to help break her album in a smaller market. By the end of 1992 *Little Earthquakes* had gone gold in Britain; a year later, it went gold in the U.S. as well. *Crucify*, an EP of mostly covers, included a soft, understated "Smells Like Teen Spirit."

With her more ornate platinum followup, *Under the Pink* (#12, 1994), Amos continued to embrace songs about the female experience: "God" questions male authority; "Cornflake Girl" explores what happens when one woman betrays another. *Boys for Pele* debuted in 1996 at #2 and quickly went platinum, despite being her least accessible album to date.

Amos collapsed during a grueling world tour in support of *Boys for Pele*. In 1998 she married Mark Hawley, an engineer working on *From the Choirgirl Hotel* (#5, 1998). That album departed from Amos' "girl with a piano" image with fuller instrumentation and dance-music twiddles, and it included "Jackie's Strength," a ballad in which she compares Jacqueline Kennedy's wedding day with her own. The two-disc set *To Venus and Back* (#12, 1999) comprises one disc of new studio tracks and one disc of live recordings from her 1998 tour.

In 1994 Amos cofounded RAINN, the Rape, Abuse and Incest National Network, which operates a free 24-hour hotline and works with more than 600 crisis centers across the country. She continues to serve as a chairperson on RAINN's board and participates in fund-raisers such as pay-per-view video downloads on the Web, ticket auctions, and benefit concerts.

Eric Andersen

Born Feb. 14, 1943, Pittsburgh, PA
1965—*Today Is the Highway* (Vanguard) 1966—*'Bout Changes & Things* 1967—*'Bout Changes & Things, Take Two* 1968—*More Hits From Tin Can Alley; Avalanche* (Warner Bros.) 1969—*A Country Dream* (Vanguard); *Eric Andersen* (Warner Bros.) 1972—*The Best of Eric Andersen* (Vanguard); *Blue River* (Columbia) 1975—*Be True to You* (Arista) 1976—*Sweet Surprise* 1977—*The Best Songs* 1989—*Ghosts Upon the Road* (Gold Castle) 1991—*Stages: The Lost Album* (Columbia) 1999—*Memory of the Future* (Appleseed); *Violets of Dawn* (Vanguard) 2000—*You Can't Relive the Past* (Appleseed).
With Danko/Fjeld/Andersen: 1991—*Danko/Fjeld/Andersen* (Rykodisc) 1994—*Ridin' on the Blinds.*

Eric Andersen is a critically acclaimed folksinger/songwriter best known for his compositions such as "Thirsty Boots," "Violets of Dawn," "Be True to You," and "Is It Really Love at All." Andersen, who began playing guitar at age eight, attended Hobart College in Geneva, New York. He traveled via freight car to the West Coast in search of a music publishing deal. When nothing developed, he returned East.

While living in Cambridge in 1963, the singer/guitarist became part of the burgeoning folk scene. A brief period of homelessness in Cambridge inspired his later composition "Ghosts Upon the Road." In 1964 he moved to Greenwich Village, where he performed at Gerde's Folk City and the Gaslight Cafe, garnering enthusiastic reviews in the *New York Times* and elsewhere. Several days after his arrival, he had secured a recording contract with Vanguard Records. With the 1965 release of his debut album and his frequent appearances in New York and at the Newport and Cambridge folk festivals, Andersen established himself on the folk circuit.

Though he has never had a hit single, most of his albums have been well received by critics, who praise his poetic, evocative lyrics, particularly on *Blue River*, his best-selling album to date, and *Ghosts Upon the Road*, considered one of the best albums of the '80s. Release of the long-awaited followup to *Blue River* was delayed when the master tapes were lost. They were not found again until 1991, when researchers looking through old tapes for a Paul Revere and the Raiders anthology stumbled across an unmarked reel. The rediscovered recordings were released in 1991 as *Stages* and include appearances by Leon Russell and Joan Baez. Andersen's songs have been recorded by Rick Nelson, Judy Collins, Peter, Paul and Mary, Johnny Cash, Joan Baez, the Grateful Dead, Fairport Convention, and Linda Ronstadt.

Since the '80s, Andersen primarily has made his home in Norway, where he also founded his own record label. His collaborations with the Band's Rick Danko and Norwegian folksinger Jonas Fjeld resulted in a pair of critically acclaimed albums. John Prine produced Andersen's 1999

Eric Andersen

album, *Memory of the Future,* which also included such guests as Danko and Garth Hudson of the Band, Heartbreakers Howie Epstein and Benmont Tench, and Dylan bassist Tony Garnier. Andersen recorded much of his 2000 release, the bluesy *You Can't Relive the Past,* in Mississippi, though four tracks were originally cowritten and recorded with the late Townes Van Zandt in 1986. Lou Reed cowrote and added vocals to the title track. Andersen's prose has appeared in such publications as 1999's *The Rolling Stone Book of the Beats.*

John Anderson

Born John David Anderson, Dec. 13, 1954, Apopka, FL
1980—*John Anderson* (Warner Bros.) 1981—*John Anderson 2; I Just Came Home to Count the Memories* 1982—*Wild & Blue* 1983—*All the People Are Talkin'* 1984—*Eye of a Hurricane; Greatest Hits* 1985—*Tokyo, Oklahoma* 1986—*Countrified* 1988—*Blue Skies Again* (MCA); *10* 1990—*Too Tough to Tame* (Capitol); *Greatest Hits, vol. 2* (Warner Bros.) 1992—*Seminole Wind* (BNA) 1993—*Solid Ground* 1994—*You Can't Keep a Good Memory Down* (MCA); *Christmas Time* (BNA); *Country 'Til I Die* 1995—*Swingin'* 1996—*Greatest Hits; Paradise* 1997—*Takin' the Country Back* (Mercury) 1998—*Super Hits* (BNA); *The Essential John Anderson* 1999—*Backtracks* (Renaissance) 2001—*Nobody's Got It All* (Columbia).

John Anderson's career is an exception to F. Scott Fitzgerald's maxim that there are no second acts in American life. One of the first "New Traditionalist" stars, Anderson enjoyed 22 Top 40 C&W hits between 1982 and 1987, including three #1s ("Wild & Blue" [1982], "Swingin'" [1983], and "Black Sheep" [1983]), before bad management and label changes brought his career to a halt. But in the 1990s Anderson returned, placing five singles in the Top 10, including three more #1s: "Straight Tequila Night" (1991), "Seminole Wind" (1992), and "Money in the Bank" (1993). Rock & roll was Anderson's first love, but listening to Merle Haggard at 14 made him a convert to country. He followed his sister Donna to Nashville in 1972, working on the Opryland construction crew by day and playing clubs with her at night. After a deal with Ace of Hearts Records in 1974 resulted in three unsuccessful singles, he concentrated on songwriting; in 1977 Warner Bros. signed him to a singles deal. Anderson's singing, usually compared to Lefty Frizell, garnered some attention, and in 1978 George Jones covered Anderson's first Top 40 hit, "The Girl at the End of the Bar" (#40 C&W, 1978). It took until 1980 and five Top 40 hits for Warners to release his first album. Anderson won the Country Music Association's Best New Artist award in 1981. Two years later he became one of the earliest New Traditionalist stars to cross over when "Swingin' " hit #43 on the pop chart and the album *Wild & Blue* went to #58.

After four more unhappy years with Warners, Anderson followed producer Jimmy Bowen to MCA. But MCA seemed unsure of how to handle Anderson (only "Somewhere Between Ragged and Right" [#23 C&W, 1987] cracked the Top 30); yet another label change (to Capitol) did not improve matters. In the wake of new stars like Garth Brooks, Anderson seemed like a has-been.

In a strange turn of events, Dire Straits guitarist Mark Knopfler helped Anderson's comeback. After seeing him play, Knopfler took Anderson's case to RCA, which signed him to their new BNA subsidiary. Knopfler then wrote and played on "When It Comes to You" (#2 C&W, 1991) from *Seminole Wind* (#35 pop, #10 C&W, 1992). Anderson followed it up with *Solid Ground* (#75 pop, #12 C&W, 1993);

MCA capitalized on Anderson's commercial renewal with a 1994 anthology, *You Can't Keep a Good Memory Down*. *Paradise* (#40 C&W, 1996), despite guest appearances by Knopfler and the Band's Levon Helm, was something of a commercial disappointment, and after its release, Anderson changed labels once again, moving to Mercury. His first album for the label, 1997's *Takin' the Country Back* revived his career yet again, peaking at #19 C&W, spawning a hit single in "Somebody Slap Me" (#22 C&W, 1997). Moving to Columbia, Anderson released the rootsy *Nobody's Got It All* in 2001.

Laurie Anderson

Born June 5, 1947, Chicago, IL
1982—*Big Science* (Warner Bros.) 1984—*Mister Heartbreak; The United States Live* 1986—*Home of the Brave* 1989—*Strange Angels* 1994—*Bright Red* 1995—*The Ugly One With the Jewels; In Our Sleep* EP 2000—*Talk Normal: The Anthology* (Rhino).

Avant-garde performance artist Laurie Anderson had a British pop hit with her 1981 recording "O Superman" (b/w "Walk the Dog"). Like all her music, "O Superman" was just one aspect of a larger multimedia oeuvre—in this case a seven-hour work in four parts called *United States, I–IV,* which premiered at the Brooklyn Academy of Music early in 1983. (A lavishly illustrated book about the show was published shortly thereafter, as well as the five-record *United States Live.*) With background music performed on various electronic keyboard instruments and woodwinds, and Anderson's speaking and singing voice (sometimes electronically treated), "O Superman" was one of the year's more unusual hits.

Anderson studied violin through her teens, and moved from Chicago to New York in 1967. She earned a B.A. in art history from Barnard College in 1969 and an M.F.A. in sculpture from Columbia University in 1972. She then taught art history and Egyptian architecture at City College. Anderson's works incorporate graphics, sculpture, film, slides, lighting, music, mime, and spoken and printed language. She claims that all her pieces are based on words and their declamation. In 1973 she began performing her works publicly, and by 1976 she was performing in museums, concert halls, and art festivals around the United States and in Europe. "O Superman" sold over 30,000 copies in Europe in 1981, reaching #2 in Britain, and Anderson signed for an album with Warner Bros. The American response to the single was considerably milder.

In 1982 Warner Bros. released her debut album, *Big Science.* Its followup, a collaboration with Peter Gabriel entitled *Mister Heartbreak,* was Anderson's only LP to chart in the Top 100, peaking at #60 in 1984. She composed the musical score for director Jonathan Demme's 1987 film of monologuist Spalding Gray's *Swimming to Cambodia* and, later, Gray's *Monster in a Box* (1991). On *Strange Angels* she abandoned her electronically treated vocals for her regular singing voice. *Bright Red* was inspired by her brush with death while mountain climbing in Tibet in the early '90s. The album, recorded with Brian Eno, also featured Lou Reed, with whom Anderson was romantically involved. The two-disc set *Talk Normal: The Anthology* was released in 2000. Also in 2000, she signed with Nonesuch.

Anderson consistently has toured with various pieces including "Talk Normal" (1987–88), "Speaking Japanese" (1989), "Empty Places" (1990), "Voices From the Beyond" (1991), "Stories From the Nerve Bible" (1993), which appears on *The Ugly One With the Jewels,* and "The Speed of Darkness" (1997–98). In addition, she has also collaborated with Interval Research Corporation, a research and development lab, on new creative tools, such as the Talking Stick. Among her books are *The Package: A Mystery* (1971), *Transportation* (1974), *Notebook* (1977), *Words in Reverse* (1979), *Home of the Brave* (1986), *Empty Places* (1991), *Stories From the Nerve Bible* (1994), and *Laurie Anderson* (2000), which offers the first major career retrospective of her visual work.

The Angels

Formed 1961, Orange, NJ
Barbara Allbut (b. Sep. 24, 1940, Orange), voc.; Phyllis "Jiggs" Allbut Meister (b. Sep. 24, 1942, Orange), voc.; Linda Jansen (b. Hillside, NJ), voc.
1962—(– Jansen; + Peggy Santiglia McCannon [b. May 4, 1944, Bellview, NJ], voc.) 1963—*My Boyfriend's Back* (Smash); *A Halo to You.*

The Angels were one of the most successful of the early-'60s girl groups. Originally known as the Starlets, they were formed when Barbara and Jiggs Allbut, who had sung together in high school, began doing backup vocal work in New York with Linda Jansen. After they were signed to Caprice, Jiggs dropped out of college and Barbara (who arranged the group's early records) ended her studies at the Juilliard School of Music. Shortly before their first release, " 'Til," they drew the name Blue Angels out of a hat, then dropped the *Blue.* Their debut single went to #14 in 1961; after their second, "Cry Baby Cry" (#38, 1962), lead vocalist Jansen left and was replaced by Peggy Santiglia, who had sung commercial jingles and appeared on Broadway in *Do Re Mi.*

Several more singles failed to click until the Angels released the million-selling "My Boyfriend's Back" (#1 pop, #2 R&B, 1963), cowritten by producer Richard Gottehrer. After a few minor followups—"I Adore Him" (#25, 1963), "Thank You and Goodnight" (#84, 1963), and "Wow Wow Wee (He's the Boy for Me)" (#41, 1964)—the group faded from the limelight. They provided backup vocals for other singers, including Jackie Wilson and Lou Christie ("Lightnin' Strikes"), and continued to record. They broke up in 1969, then re-formed in the early '70s as the oldies craze created a new audience for their appearances. They cut their last major-label single for Polydor in 1974, "Papa's Side of the Bed."

The Animals: John Steel, Dave Rowberry, Eric Burdon, Chas Chandler, Hilton Valentine

The Animals

Formed 1962, Newcastle upon Tyne, Eng.
Alan Price (b. Apr. 19, 1942, County Durham, Eng.), kybds.; Eric Burdon (b. May 11, 1941, Newcastle upon Tyne), voc.; Bryan "Chas" Chandler (b. Dec. 18, 1938, Newcastle upon Tyne; d. July 17, 1996, London, Eng.), bass; John Steel (b. Feb. 4, 1941, Gateshead, Eng.), drums; Hilton Valentine (b. May 21, 1943, North Shields, Eng.), gtr.
1964—*The Animals* (MGM) 1965—*The Animals on Tour; Animal Tracks* (– Price; + Dave Rowberry [b. Dec. 27, 1943, Newcastle upon Tyne], kybds.) 1966—*The Best of the Animals; Animalization; Animalism* (– Steel; + Barry Jenkins [b. Dec. 22, 1944, Leicester, Eng.], drums) late 1966—(group disbands) 1968—(Burdon forms Eric Burdon and the New Animals: Burdon; Jenkins; + Johnny Weider [b. Apr. 21, 1947, Shepherd's Bush, Eng.], gtr.; + Vic Briggs [b. Feb. 14, 1945, Twickenham, Eng.], gtr.; + Danny McCulloch [b. July 18, 1945, London], gtr.; + Zoot Money, kybds., voc.)
1967—*Eric Is Here; Best of Eric Burdon and the Animals, vol. 2; Winds of Change* 1968—*The Twain Shall Meet; Every One of Us* (– McCulloch; – Briggs; + Andrew Somers [a.k.a. Andy Summers, b. Dec. 31, 1942, Blackpool, Eng.], gtr.) 1969—*Love Is; The Greatest Hits of Eric Burdon and the Animals* (group disbands) 1977—(original lineup re-forms) *Before We Were So Rudely Interrupted* (United Artists) 1983—*Ark* (I.R.S.) 1984—*Rip It to Shreds: Greatest Hits Live.*

Of the original British Invasion bands, the Animals were the most clearly influenced by black American R&B rather than blues. Originally the Alan Price Combo (formed in 1958), they became the Animals shortly after the addition of lead vocalist Eric Burdon in 1962. By 1964, under the wing of U.K. producer Mickie Most, they had recorded their second single, "House of the Rising Sun," a #1 hit on both sides of the Atlantic in summer 1964.

More hits followed through 1966: "Don't Let Me Be Misunderstood" (#15, 1965), "We Gotta Get Out of This Place" (#13, 1965), and "It's My Life" (#23, 1965). In late 1965 Price left the band (the result of tension between him and Burdon) for a solo career. That, and frequent drug use by members, shook up the band somewhat, but Price was replaced by Dave Rowberry, and the Animals had another hit ("Inside-Looking Out," #34, 1966) before John Steel left. With Barry Jenkins (formerly of the Nashville Teens) replacing Steel, the group had several more hits ("Don't Bring Me Down," #12, 1966; "See See Rider," #10, 1966), but by the end of the year Hilton Valentine left to pursue a solo career, and Chas Chandler became a successful manager (the Animals, Jimi Hendrix, and Slade). Steel became Chandler's assistant.

Now billed Eric Burdon and the Animals, the band endorsed psychedelia with "San Franciscan Nights" (#9, 1967), "Monterey" (#15, 1968), and "Sky Pilot" (#14, 1968). The Animals fell apart, but a year and a half later Burdon formed Eric Burdon and the New Animals, with a lineup that briefly included future Police guitarist Andy Summers, before embarking on an intermittently successful solo career [see entry].

The original Animals reunited for a Christmas show at City Hall in Newcastle in 1968. In 1969 Valentine recorded a solo album entitled *All in Your Head.* The original band reunited in 1976 to record a one-shot LP, *Before We Were So Rudely Interrupted.* In 1983 they reunited once more. The Animals recorded *Ark* and mounted a tour (captured on *Rip It to Shreds*) before the band members again went their separate ways. In 1992 an Animals lineup that included Vic Briggs (who had become a Sikh and recorded under the name Vikram S. Khalsa) and Barry Jenkins performed in Moscow's Red Square. In 1994 the Animals were inducted into the Rock and Roll Hall of Fame. Chandler died of a heart attack in 1996.

Paul Anka

Born July 30, 1941, Ottawa, Can.
1960—*Paul Anka Sings His Big 15* (ABC); *Paul Anka Sings His*

Big 15, vol. 2; Anka at the Copa; Young, Alive and in Love (RCA); *Let's Sit This One Out; Diana and Other Hits; Paul Anka's 21 Golden Hits; Goodnight My Love; Life Goes On; Paul Anka* (Buddah) 1972—*Jubilation* (United Artists) 1975—*Feelings; Times of Your Life; The Painter; The Music Man; Listen to Your Heart* (RCA); *Paul Anka—His Best; Both Sides of Love; Walk a Fine Line* (Columbia) 1989—*30th Anniversary Collection* (Rhino) 1996—*Amigos* (Columbia).

Disparaged by critics for his often overwrought vocal style on songs such as "Puppy Love," Paul Anka was unique among late-'50s teen idols in that he was also a successful songwriter. After his string of early hits tapered off in 1962, Anka concentrated on composing film scores *(The Longest Day)* and writing and performing more adult-oriented works, like the English lyrics to the French song that became Frank Sinatra's theme song, "My Way."

The son of a Lebanese restaurateur, Anka began performing at age 10, singing and doing impersonations. Four years later Anka's father paid for a trip to Hollywood, where, in September 1956, the 15-year-old recorded "I Confess" (backed by the Cadets) for Modern. Anka returned to Canada and later, though underage, worked a nightclub in Gloucester, Massachusetts. In 1957 he won a contest for saving soup-can labels. First prize was a trip to New York City, and in May of that year Anka auditioned for ABC with "Diana," a song he had written about a girl he knew. Within a year, "Diana" was a #1 hit.

Throughout his career, Anka composed many of his hits, including "You Are My Destiny" (#7, 1958), "Crazy Love" (#15, 1958), "Lonely Boy" (#1, 1959), "Hello Young Lovers" (#23, 1960), "Put Your Head on My Shoulder" (#2, 1959), and "Puppy Love" (#2, 1960), the latter two about his relationship with Annette Funicello. In 1962 he purchased all of his masters from ABC and signed with RCA. Although his Top 20 hits ended temporarily in 1962, he continued to write and record in French, German, and Italian and remained a top concert draw around the globe. Like many of his teen-idol contemporaries, Anka briefly essayed an acting career; his film credits include *Girls Town* (1959), *Look in Any Window* (1961), and *The Longest Day* (1962), for which he also wrote the theme song.

In 1970 he signed with Buddah, and four years later Anka's controversial "(You're) Having My Baby," a duet with his protégée Odia Coates, became his first #1 since 1959. Due in part to outcry against the song's seemingly sexist tone, Anka substitutes "our baby" for "my baby" in concert. In 1983 he made his last foray into the Top 40 with "Hold Me 'Til the Mornin' Comes." He has become a fixture on the Las Vegas–Lake Tahoe circuit, where he is extremely successful. Over 400 of his compositions have been recorded, including "It Don't Matter Anymore" (Buddy Holly), "My Way" (Frank Sinatra), and "She's a Lady" (Tom Jones). He wrote the *Tonight Show* theme (originally entitled "It's Really Love," and written for and recorded by Funicello). His "Times of Your Life" became the signature song for Kodak films in the mid-'70s. He has amassed worldwide record sales in excess of 100 million copies.

Annette: See Annette Funicello

Anthrax

Formed 1981, New York, NY
Scott Ian (b. Dec. 31, 1963, Queens, NY), gtr.; Dan Spitz (b. Jan. 28, 1963, Queens), gtr.; Dan Lilker (b. Oct. 18, 1964, Queens), bass; Charles Benante (b. Nov. 27, 1962, Bronx, NY), drums; Neil Turbin, voc.
1984—*Fistful of Metal* (Caroline/Megaforce) (– Turbin; – Lilker; + Joey BellaDonna [b. Oct. 30, 1960, Oswego, NY], voc.; + Frank Bello [b. Sep. 7, 1965, Bronx], bass) 1985—*Armed and Dangerous; Spreading the Disease* (Island) 1987—*Among the Living; I'm the Man* EP 1988—*State of Euphoria* 1990—*Persistence of Time* 1991—*Attack of the Killer B's* 1992—(– BellaDonna; + John Bush [b. Aug. 24, 1963, Los Angeles, CA], voc.) 1993—*Sound of White Noise* (Elektra) 1994—*Live—Island Years* (Island) 1995—*Stomp 442* (Elektra) (– Spitz) 1998—*Vol. 8—The Threat Is Real* (Ignition/Tommy Boy) 1999—*Return of the Killer A's* (BMG/Beyond).

Anthrax began as an average posthardcore thrash band but eventually developed its own distinct sound by blending rap's street sense with heavy metal's brute force. The band hit a career height in 1991 when it joined forces with rap group Public Enemy for a recording and video of the latter's rallying cry, "Bring the Noise." Two years later the band inked a reported $10 million, five-album deal with Elektra.

Anthrax hit New York City's postpunk metal scene in 1981 when Bayside, Queens, native Scott Ian, still in his teens, formed the band along with friends Neil Turbin and former Overkill guitarist Dan Spitz. The group literally began following managers Johnny and Marsha Zazula, heads of the independent metal label Megaforce Records, around the city. Eventually the couple signed the band and began directing its career. By album number three, Anthrax had landed on Island, and its cult following had begun to expand. The group's 1987 EP, *I'm the Man,* sold platinum and hinted at Anthrax's growing social consciousness in songs such as "Indians" and "One World."

One of the few heavy-metal-oriented bands to get consistently high critical marks, Anthrax—along with Metallica and Megadeth—redefined the metal genre in the '80s, stressing anger, speed, and emotional intensity over big hair and power ballads. The band flirted with funk and rap rhythms, a sound that peaked with "Bring the Noise." Anthrax adjusted its style after replacing longtime lead singer Joey BellaDonna with L.A. native and ex–Armored Saint singer John Bush in 1992. Bush, a more traditional, smooth-voiced vocalist, gave the group a slicker sound, though the basic speed-metal foundation remained. The band signed a much-publicized $10 million contract with Elektra, but left the label after just two albums.

By 1995's *Stomp 442,* lead guitarist Spitz had departed the group, which remained as a four-piece. Drummer Charlie Benante began dabbling on lead guitar during the recording.

Anthrax: Dan Spitz, Frankie Bello, Scott Ian, Charlie Benante, John Bush

Guitarist Scott Ian was arrested in 1998 (though the charges were later dropped) after breaking into a New York Yankees training facility.

Vol. 8—The Threat Is Real (#118, 1998) included guest appearances by the likes of Pantera's Phil Anselmo and Dimebag Darrell, joining forces to celebrate the return of hard, hard rock at the end of the '90s. The most popular songs from the band's first two decades were gathered for *Return of the Killer A's* in 1999, setting in motion plans for both singers BellaDonna and Bush to lead an Anthrax tour in 2000. BellaDonna withdrew from the tour shortly before it began.

Aphex Twin

Born Richard David James, Aug. 18, 1971, Cornwall, Eng.
1991—*Analogue Bubblebath* EP (with Schizophrenia) (Mighty Force, U.K.) 1992—*Digeridoo* EP (R&S, Bel.); *Selected Ambient Works 85–92* 1994—*Selected Ambient Works, vol. 2* (Sire/Warp) 1995—*. . . I Care Because You Do; Donkey Rhubarb* EP 1996—*Richard D. James Album* 1997—*Come to Daddy* EP.
As AFX: 1991—*Analog Bubblebath, vol. 2* EP (Rabbit City).
As Caustic Window: 1992—*Joyrex J4* EP (RePhLeX, U.K.); *Joyrex J5* EP 1993—*Joyrex J9* EP.
As Polygon Window: 1993—*Surfing on Sine Waves* (TVT/Wax Trax!/Warp).
As Mike & Rich: 1996—*Expert Knob Twiddlers* (with Michael Paradinas) (RePhLeX, U.K.).

Aphex Twin is perhaps the best known of the many monikers used by Richard D. James, one of the more creative minds in '90s electronica. James, who has recorded as AFX, Polygon Window, Caustic Window, and several others, is equally capable of both Eno-esque ambient pieces and headache-inducing techno. He will juxtapose melodies played by computer-generated string instruments with frantic, machinized beat patterns that make sense only to him. More an avant-garde composer than a creator of dance-floor hits, he has spent most of his extremely prolific career ignoring commercial trends.

James began his unique approach to music making early on. As a child, he conducted sound experiments on the strings and hammers of his family piano; by age 14, he had recorded his first compositions. During the late '80s, he DJ'd at raves in Cornwall before moving to London, where he attended college for one year before dropping out to focus on his music. His first release came in 1991 with the *Analogue Bubblebath* EP, recorded with Tom Middleton (known as Schizophrenia). His second EP, *Analog Bubblebath, vol. 2*—a solo James effort under the name AFX—followed the same year; it contained the single "Digeridoo" (#55, U.K.), which foreshadowed the advent of drum-and-bass. After putting out a series of singles as Caustic Window on his own RePhLeX imprint, James released his first full-length album as Aphex Twin, *Selected Ambient Works 85–92,* in 1992. Hailing the album as an ambient masterpiece comparable to work by the Orb and Brian Eno, critics similarly applauded *Selected Ambient Works, vol. 2,* which followed two years later and went to #11 in the U.K.

His next Aphex Twin full-length, *. . . I Care Because You Do,* saw James seeking a middle ground between his ambient and hardcore techno compositions. The result placed him more in line with minimalist composers like Philip Glass, who attempted to re-create one of the album's songs with a live orchestra on his *Donkey Rhubarb* EP. The *Richard D. James Album* continued its namesake's marriage of drifting melodies and frenzied beats, as did the *Come to Daddy* EP (#36, U.K.) and 1999's "Windowlicker" (#16, U.K.) single. James spent 2000 writing the score to the independent short film *Flex.*

Fiona Apple

Born Fiona Apple McAfee-Maggart, Sep. 13, 1977, New York, NY
1996—*Tidal* (Work/Clean Slate/Sony) 1999—*When the Pawn Hits the Conflicts He Thinks Like a King What He Knows Throws the Blows When He Goes to the Fight and He'll Win the Whole Thing 'Fore He Enters the Ring There's No Body to Batter When Your Mind Is Your Might So When You Go Solo, You Hold Your Own Hand and Remember That Depth Is the Greatest of Heights and If You Know Where You Stand, Then You Know Where to Land and If You Fall It Won't Matter, 'Cuz You'll Know That You're Right* (Clean Slate/Epic/Sony).

A late-'90s overnight sensation, Fiona Apple was cast as the antidote to packaged pop divettes like Britney Spears and Christina Aguilera. Considering her angst-ridden lyrics and her propensity to shock interviewers, some critics classed her among such provocateurs as Alanis Morissette and Sinéad O'Connor; others, listening to her jazz-tinged, full-throated, accomplished debut, compared her to Laura Nyro and Nina Simone.

Her parents, actor Brandon Maggart and singer/dancer/chef Diane McAfee, never married and separated when Fiona was four years old. Her father relocated to L.A.; Fiona grew up in Manhattan with her mother and older sister. Teaching herself piano (and starting psychotherapy) at eight, Fiona was drawn to the Beatles, Jimi Hendrix, Joan Armatrading, and jazz standards. The primary influence she claims was the poet Maya Angelou; Apple herself wrote poetry and journals as a girl, then, at 11, began combining music and lyrics. Moving to L.A. at 16, Apple completed high school through independent study and recorded a three-song demo. She passed a tape along to a friend who baby-sat for Kathryn Schenker, the publicist for Sting and Lenny Kravitz, among others. Impressed by Fiona's precocious talent, Schenker alerted Wallflowers manager Andy Slater, who landed the singer a record contract in early 1996.

Tidal, featuring Apple's melodically and rhythmically intricate songs, strong piano work, and achingly confessional lyrics, along with Slater's inventive production work, drew nearly unalloyed raves. Yet Apple was controversial, speaking openly about her rape at age 12 (the basis for the song "Sullen Girl") and appearing in her underwear for the video for "Criminal" (#21 pop, 1997). The video was interpreted alternately as either self-exploitation or a cryptic denunciation of such exploitation. Accorded Best New Artist in a Video honors at the 1997 MTV Video Awards, Apple, in an obscenity-laced acceptance speech, derided the star-making machinery of show biz and its deleterious effects on adolescents, a maneuver that was mocked by some and praised by others. Musically, with gems like the Modern Rock hit "Shadowboxer" making her case, Apple was unassailable; in media terms, however, she'd become known as a "loose cannon."

In 1999 Apple chose a 90-word "poem" as a title for her followup to the double-platinum-selling *Tidal. When the Pawn . . .* (#13, 1999) showed influences ranging from the late Beatles to bossa nova, and yielded the Modern Rock hit "Fast as You Can."

The Archies

Formed 1968, Riverdale, NY
"Archie" (Ron Dante, b. Carmine Granito, Aug. 22, 1945, Staten Island, NY), voc.; Toni Wine, voc.; Ellie Greenwich (b. 1940, Brooklyn, NY), voc.; Andy Kim (b. Andrew Joachim, Dec. 5, 1946, Montreal, Can.), voc.; Tony Passalacqua, voc.
1968—*The Archies* (Calendar) 1969—*Everything's Archie* (RCA); *Jingle Jangle* 1970—*Sunshine* (Kirshner); *The Archies Greatest Hits* 1993—*The Archies* (Sony).

The Archies were a make-believe group based on the comic book and mid-'60s cartoon series of the same name. "Sugar, Sugar," cowritten by Jeff Barry and Andy Kim, was a #1 hit and the biggest-selling single of 1969, with 6 million copies sold worldwide. Songwriter Barry produced the Archies: studio musicians (among them Hugh McCracken, Dave Appell, and Bobby Bloom) were hired to provide the cartoon series' soundtrack. The singing Archie, voiced by Ron Dante, led his group, which included songwriters Ellie Greenwich and Andy Kim, through a number of hits, including "Bang-Shang-a-Lang" (#2, 1968), "Jingle Jangle" (#10, 1969), and "Who's Your Baby" (#40, 1970).

Dante later produced several Barry Manilow hits and records by Cher and Pat Benatar. In 1971 he became editor of the literary magazine *Paris Review.* He continued to work as a composer through the '90s. Among his most familiar recent "performances" is the "You deserve a break today" theme from McDonald's commercials. Andy Kim went on to a successful pop career, with a number of Top 40 singles, among them "Baby I Love You" (#9, 1969) and "Rock Me Gently" (#1, 1974).

Argent/Rod Argent

Formed 1969, England
Rod Argent (b. June 14, 1941, St. Albans, Eng.), kybds., voc.; Jim Rodford (b. July 7, 1941, Eng.), bass; Robert Henrit (b. May 2, 1944, Broxbourne, Eng.), drums; Russ Ballard (b. Oct. 31, 1945, Waltham Cross, Eng.), gtr., voc.
1970—*Argent* (Epic) 1971—*Ring of Hands* 1972—*All Together Now* 1973—*In Deep* 1974—*Nexus* (– Ballard; + John Grimaldi [b. May 25, 1955, St. Albans], gtr., cello, mandolin, violin; + John Verity [b. July 3, 1949, Bradford, Eng.], gtr., voc., bass) *Encore* 1975—*Circus Counterpoint; Anthology: A Collection of Greatest Hits.*
Russ Ballard solo: 1974—*Russ Ballard* (Epic) 1976—*Winning* 1978—*At the Third Stroke* 1980—*Barnet Dogs* 1981—*Into the Fire* 1984—*Russ Ballard* (EMI) 1985—*The Fire Still Burns.*
Rod Argent solo: 1991—*Red House* (Relativity).

After the Zombies broke up in 1967, keyboardist Rod Argent started his own band just in time to capitalize on the Zombies' postmortem hit, "Time of the Season" (#3, 1969). Argent had heavier rhythms than the Zombies, while continuing that band's penchant for minor keys and obscure lyrics. Although their debut album was their most consistent, the group peaked commercially with "Hold Your Head Up" (#5, 1972), and "Liar" and "God Gave Rock & Roll to You" became FM-radio staples. In 1974 songwriter Ballard left, and after expanding to a quintet, Argent folded in mid-1976. In recent years, the group has re-formed to perform for charities.

Ballard and Argent went on to solo careers, although Ballard was more successful as a songwriter (Redbone's "Come and Get Your Love," Three Dog Night's "Liar," Rainbow's "Since You've Been Gone," Ace Frehley's "New York Groove," Santana's "Winning," Hot Chocolate's "So You Win Again") and producer (Roger Daltrey, Leo Sayer) than as a performer. John Verity, Jim Rodford, and Robert Henrit formed Phoenix, which recorded briefly for Columbia. By 1978 Rodford had joined the Kinks; six years later Henrit joined him as Mick Avory's replacement.

Through the years Rod Argent has worked as a pianist, composer, record producer, and arranger. He played piano on the Who's "Who Are You," coproduced Nanci Griffith's *Late Night Grand Hotel*, and has scored music for BBC Television. His musical *Masquerade* was staged in London in 1982, and he was the keyboardist for the London productions of two Andrew Lloyd Webber musicals, *Starlight Express* and *Cats*. He released a series of U.K. solo albums in the late '70s and '80s: *Moving Home, Siren Songs*, and *Red House* (which was released in the U.S. as well). In 1994 Argent coproduced and played keyboards on Jules Shear's *Healing Bones*. He has since become a classical pianist; his 1998 solo effort, *Classically Speaking*, mixed original compositions with works by Chopin, Greig, and Ravel. In 2001 he reunited with Zombie mate Colin Blunstone for *Out of the Shadows*.

Joan Armatrading

Born Dec. 9, 1950, St. Kitts, West Indies
1974—*Whatever's for Us* (A&M) 1975—*Back to the Night* 1976—*Joan Armatrading* 1977—*Show Some Emotion* 1978—*To the Limit* 1979—*How Cruel; Steppin' Out* 1980—*Me, Myself, I* 1981—*Walk Under Ladders* 1983—*The Key; Track Record* 1985—*Secret Secrets* 1986—*Sleight of Hand* 1988—*The Shouting Stage* 1990—*Heart and Flowers* 1991—*The Very Best of Joan Armatrading* 1992—*Square the Circle* 1995—*What's Inside* (RCA).

Joan Armatrading's synthesis of folk, reggae, soul, and rock has made her a critical and cult favorite in America, where *Me, Myself, I* (#28, 1980) and *The Key* (#32, 1983) were successful. In Europe, particularly in the U.K., she is a major star. She left the West Indies and moved to England with her family while still a child. She began her professional career in 1972 in collaboration with lyricist Pam Nestor (born April 28, 1948, Guyana), but by the mid-'70s the two had parted.

A distinctive vocalist and lyricist, Armatrading has worked with producers Gus Dudgeon, Glyn Johns, Richard Gottehrer, and Steve Lillywhite, but generally does her own arranging; she produced *Heart and Flowers*. Her backup bands have included alumni of Fairport Convention and Little Feat, and guitarist Albert Lee. Except for a sole charting single, "Drop the Pilot" (#78, 1983), from *The Key*, Armatrading has had relatively little commercial success in the States. In comparison, her albums have consistently charted in the U.K. Top 30, with *Show Some Emotion, Me, Myself, I, Walk Under Ladders*, and *The Key* going Top 10. In 1994, she parted ways with her longtime label, A&M Records, and signed to RCA, which released *What's Inside* the following year.

Arrested Development

Formed 1988, Atlanta, GA
Speech (b. Todd Thomas, Oct. 25, 1968, Milwaukee, WI), voc.; Headliner (b. Tim Barnwell, July 26, 1967, NJ), DJ; Rasa Don (b. Donald Jones, Nov. 22, 1968, NJ), voc., drums; Aerle Taree (b. Jan. 10, 1973, WI), voc., dancer, stylist; Montsho Eshe (b. Dec. 23, 1974, GA), dancer, choreographer; Baba Oje (b. May 15, 1932, Laurie, MS), spiritual adviser; Dionne Farris (b. Bordentown, NJ), voc.
1992—*3 Years, 5 Months & 2 Days in the Life of . . .* (Chrysalis) 1993—*Unplugged* 1994—(– Taree; – Farris; + Ajile, voc., dancer; + Kwesi, DJ, voc.; + Nadirah, voc.) *Zingalamaduni* 1998—*The Best of Arrested Development*.
Speech solo: 1996—*Speech* (Chrysalis/EMI) 1999—*Hoopla* (TVT).
Dionne Farris solo: 1994—*Wild Seed—Wild Flower* (Columbia).

Arrested Development took the light, funky sound of the Native Tongues school of hip-hop (De La Soul, Queen Latifah), blended in the folk-blues instrumentation of their native South (harmonica, acoustic guitars), added uplifting, gospel-tinged lyrics, and became one of the most successful crossover acts in rap. On the strength of its first single, "Tennessee" (#6 pop, #1 R&B), the group's 1992 debut album shot to #13 (#3 R&B).

Born in Milwaukee and raised part-time in Ripley, Tennessee, Todd Thomas grew up listening to a wide range of artists, from Kiss to Parliament/Funkadelic. His father owned a disco, but by high school he was a budding DJ who listened exclusively to hip-hop. In 1987 he moved to Georgia to study at the Art Institute of Atlanta. There he met Tim Barnwell, a New Jersey native raised in the coastal Georgia city of Savannah. After an initial, unsuccessful attempt at gangsta rap under the name Disciples of a Lyrical Rebellion, Thomas and Barnwell, who started going by the names Speech and DJ Headliner, reexamined their motives for wanting to make music. In 1988 they discovered the political fire-and-brimstone sound of Public Enemy and decided to change direction. Rejecting gangsta-rap expressions like "nigga," "bitch," and "ho," the two incorporated their Christian values into politically and philosophically charged songs that celebrated African-American culture and history. Inspired by Speech's belief that the black community needed spiritual rebirth, they renamed the group Arrested Development.

With the addition of drummer Rasa Don, the group's

music became softer and funkier. By the time of its 1992 signing to Chrysalis, Arrested Development had expanded into a coed and multigenerational group, including "extended family" members Aerle Taree, Speech's cousin and designer of the group's clothing; dancer/choreographer Montsho Eshe; and elder spiritual advisor Baba Oje.

The group's platinum-selling debut was a critical as well as commercial success. The album produced two other hits: "People Everyday" (#8 pop, #2 R&B, 1992) and "Mr. Wendal" (#6, 1992). "Tennessee" featured the singer Dionne Farris, another "extended member" who ultimately left the group and had her own Top 10 single, "I Know," in 1995. The non-LP single "Revolution," recorded for Spike Lee's film *Malcolm X,* reached #90 (#49 R&B, 1992). In 1993 Arrested Development's performance on MTV's *Unplugged* (#38 R&B) was issued on CD, and the group participated in the third annual Lollapalooza Tour. Taree departed and three new members joined for the summer 1994 release, *Zingalamaduni,* which means "beehive of culture" in Swahili. That album was met mostly by ambivalence from critics and disappointing sales. *Zingalamaduni* eventually went gold, but by 1996 the band had officially split up.

The solo career of Speech has at least earned the attention of critics, if not fans. His 1996 self-titled solo debut album failed to chart at all, and the single "Like Marvin Gaye Said (What's Going On)" peaked at #59 R&B. He continued to write a column for the *Milwaukee Community Journal,* his mother's newspaper, and lectured on college campuses. In 1999 Speech released *Hoopla* on TVT, using strings for the first time and focusing on lyrics that were less political and more personal (though it included a version of Bob Marley's "Redemption Song"). That same year, Arrested Development reunited in Atlanta for its first concert in five years and in 2000 began recording a new album, tentatively entitled *The Heroes of the Harvest.*

Arrow

Born Alphonsus Cassel, Nov. 16, 1954, Montserrat, West Indies
1974—*On Target* (Arrow) 1977—*Positively Jumpy* 1983—*Hot Hot Hot* (Arrow/Chrysalis) 1985—*Soca Savage* (London) 1987—*Best of Arrow, vol. 1* (Arrow) 1988—*Knock Dem Dead* (Mango/Island) 1989—*Massive* (Arrow); *Ola Soca* (Mango/Island) 1990—*Soca Dance Party* 1991—*Zombie Soca* (Arrow) 1992—*Best of Arrow, vol. 2; Modely De Bam Bam* 1993—*Outrageous* 1995—*Phat* 1997—*Ride De Riddim* 1998—*Turbulence* 1999—*Best of Arrow; Hot Soca Hot.*

A founding father and leading purveyor of soca, a Trinidad-based blend of soul music and calypso, Arrow is best known in the U.S. for having written "Hot, Hot, Hot"—an international hit for the singer in 1983, but an American hit only as it was covered in 1987 by Buster Poindexter (David Johansen's lounge-lizard alter ego).

The youngest of nine children, Arrow listened to American R&B on the radio while growing up in Montserrat. He began composing calypso songs at a young age, earning the island-wide title of "calypso king" in a 1971 competition. He retained the title for four years and in 1974 started releasing albums on his own label while supporting himself by selling insurance and running a men's clothing store. In 1983, with numerous LPs already to his credit, Arrow signed with Chrysalis Records. Subsequent singles such as 1984's "Long Time" and 1988's "Groove Master" proved popular in British and American dance clubs, but the singer's ebullient melodies and seductive rhythms never made him a big star outside the Caribbean. Having switched labels repeatedly throughout the '80s, Arrow returned to releasing his own albums in 1991. He continues to draw crowds at calypso and reggae festivals.

Art Ensemble of Chicago

Formed 1969, Paris, Fr.
Roscoe Mitchell (b. 1940, Chicago, IL), saxes, flutes, reeds, misc.; Lester Bowie (b. 1941, Fredrick, MD; d. Nov. 9, 1999, New York, NY), trumpet, misc.; Malachi Favors, a.k.a. Magoustous (b. 1937, Lexington, MS), bass, perc., misc.; Joseph Jarman (b. 1941, Pine Bluff, AR), saxes, flute, reeds, misc.
1969—*People in Sorrow* (Nessa); *Reese and the Smooth Ones* (BYG); *A Jackson in Your House; Message to Our Folks; Tutankhamun* (Freedom) 1970—(+ Don Moye, a.k.a. Dougoufana Famoudou [b. 1946, Rochester, NY], drums, perc.) *Certain Blacks* (Nessa) 1971—*Home* (Galloway); *Art Ensemble With Fontella Bass* (America); *Phase One* (Prestige) 1972—*Baptizum* (Atlantic); *Live at Mandel Hall* (Delmark/Trio) 1973—*Fanfare for the Warriors* (Atlantic) 1974—*Kabbalaba Live at Montreux* (AECO); *Spiritual* (Black Lion) 1978—*Nice Guys* (ECM) 1979—*Live in Berlin* 1980—*Full Force; Urban Bushmen* 1981—*Among the People* 1984—*The Third Decade; The Complete Live in Japan, vols. 1–2* (DIW); *Naked* 1987—*Ancient to the Future, vol. 1* 1989—*Art Ensemble of Soweto; Alternate Express* 1990—*Dreaming of the Masters Suite; Live at the Eighth Tokyo Music Joy* 1992—*America–South Africa* (as the Art Ensemble of Soweto) (Columbia); *Thelonious Sphere Monk* (DIW) 1998—(– Jarman) *Coming Home Jamaica* (Atlantic).

The Art Ensemble of Chicago was arguably the most innovative jazz group to emerge in the '70s. Its compositions and collective improvisations draw from all sorts of world musics, traditional and avant-garde jazz, rhythm & blues, African music, 20th-century European art music, even rock & roll, gospel, martial music, jug-band music, and the natural sounds of human and animal voices. The quintet has been known to employ 500 instruments in a concert, which might also include a slide show, dance, or vaudeville shtick. No matter the format, they adhere to their motto: "Great Black Music—Ancient to the Future."

The Ensemble evolved from collective jazz experiments in Chicago in the early and mid-'60s. Roscoe Mitchell and Malachi Favors first played together in Muhal Richard Abrams' Experimental Band in 1961. Along with Abrams, the two were charter members of the Association for the Advancement of Creative Music, founded in 1965 with such jazz experimentalists as Anthony Braxton and the future members of Air (not the French duo of the same name). Lester Bowie (who had played R&B with Little Milton and Albert King) was also an AACM member. In 1968 the Roscoe Mitchell Art Ensemble (including Mitchell, Bowie, Favors, and drummer Phillip Wilson) began gigging and earned a local reputation for both their music and their integration of music and conceptual theater.

Before the end of 1968, Wilson had joined the Paul Butterfield Blues Band. The Ensemble continued without a drummer, but the addition of Joseph Jarman (who had studied under John Cage and Indian classical musicians) kept it a quartet. In 1969 the players moved to Paris, and over the next two years, they recorded 11 albums and three film scores, performed hundreds of concerts, and met drummer Don Moye (who joined the group in 1970). They returned to the U.S. in 1971 to tour. Atlantic signed the Art Ensemble in 1972, but it took a grant from the National Endowment for the Arts to finance the group's second Atlantic album. Since then the Ensemble has recorded for large and small labels including its own AECO Records.

Each of the members has recorded solo and with other musicians, including Anthony Braxton, Henry Threadgill, and Jack DeJohnette. Abrams and singer Fontella Bass (who had a #1 soul hit with "Rescue Me" in 1965; Bowie and Bass were married at this time) have performed frequently with the Art Ensemble.

Although the late 1980s and 1990s saw the band recording in a variety of different settings (*Dreaming of the Masters* is a collaboration with pianist Cecil Taylor; *America–South Africa* is a collaboration with an African vocal choir), band members' side projects cut into the Ensemble's visibility. Bowie led the popular Brass Fantasy, Mitchell composed and played with his own new music groups, and Moye played in the all-star Leaders band with Lester Bowie.

While in London, on tour with Brass Fantasy, Bowie fell ill. Subsequently diagnosed with liver cancer, he died in 1999.

Art of Noise

Formed 1983, London, Eng.
Anne Dudley (b. May 7, 1956), kybds., voc.; Jonathan "J.J." Jeczalik (b. May 11, 1955), kybds., voc.; Paul Morley, kybds., voc.; Gary Langan, various instruments.
1983—*Into Battle With the Art of Noise* EP (ZTT/Island); *Art of Noise* 1984—*(Who's Afraid of?) The Art of Noise* (Island) 1986—*In Visible Silence* (China/Chrysalis); *Re-works of the Art of Noise* 1988—*The Best of the Art of Noise [Blue Cover]* (China) 1989—*Below the Waste* 1990—*Ambient Collection: Remix Collection* (Alex) (group disbands) 1992—*Best of the Art of Noise [Pink Cover]* (Discovery); *Best of Art of Noise [#1]* (Alex) 1993—*Best of Art of Noise [#2]; Best of Art of Noise [#3]* 1996—*Drum & Bass Collection* (Discovery) 1997—*State of the Art; Fon Mixes* (group re-forms: Morley; Dudley; + Trevor Horn [b. July 15, 1949, Hertfordshire, Eng.], kybds.; + Lol Creme [b. Lawrence Creme, Sep. 19, 1947, Manchester, Eng.], gtr.) 1999—*Seduction of Claude Debussy* (ZTT/Universal).

With its name culled from an Italian Futurist manifesto, Art of Noise approached pop from a distinctly postmodern slant. Using the studio as their tool, these three producers/programmers/arrangers were virtually anonymous; star power, when called for, was imported. Dudley, formely a producer for Paul McCartney and Frankie Goes to Hollywood, joined up with Jeczalik and Langan as part of Trevor Horn's innovative production team in the early '80s. Under Horn's auspices, Art of Noise was formed to fashion state-of-the-art dance instrumentals. "Beat Box" and "Close (to the Edit)"—with their audacious and influential mixture of treated musical textures, found sounds, and overdriven disco rhythms—became popular on both sides of the Atlantic.

Breaking away from Horn, Art of Noise recruited rock & roll guitar pioneer Duane Eddy to update his 1960 hit "Peter Gunn" (#50, 1986); the song won a 1986 Grammy for Best Rock Instrumental Performance. The video for "Paranoimia" (#34, 1986) incorporated computer-generated TV character Max Headroom; Art of Noise also contributed to the *Headroom* television series. Eschewing any pretense of aesthetic purity, the group began doing considerable advertising work for Revlon, Swatch, and Barclays' Bank, among others. In July 1986 Art of Noise toured for the first time, appearing in the U.S., Japan, and at a solitary British performance. The next year the group worked on the soundtrack to the film adaptation of *Dragnet*. A remake of Prince's "Kiss" (#31, 1988) featuring '60s pop icon Tom Jones helped revive Jones' career. Other left-of-center recordings followed, including "Yebo" (#63 U.K., 1989), which featured South African singers Mahlathini and the Mahotella Queens. By the turn of the decade the three were concentrating on individual projects, and Art of Noise dissolved. Throughout the '90s, the group enjoyed a kind of vicarious fame, its music frequently sampled by other artists and its sound recognized as seminal by hip-hoppers, minimalist composers, and ambient musicians. Paul Morley and Anne Dudley reunited in 1999 to release, along with Trevor Horn and Lol Creme of 10cc, *The Seduction of Claude Debussy*, an homage to the 19th Century French composer. Mixing dance versions of Debussy's music with lush orchestration, Art of Noise drew parallels between the classical music innovator and their own pioneering.

Peter Asher: See Peter and Gordon

Ashford and Simpson

Nickolas Ashford (b. May 4, 1943, Fairfield, SC), voc.; Valerie Simpson (b. Aug. 26, 1948, Bronx, NY), voc., kybds.
1973—*Keep It Comin'* (Tamla); *Gimme Something Real* (Warner Bros.) 1974—*I Wanna Be Selfish* 1976—*Come As You Are* 1977—*Send It* 1978—*Is It Still Good to Ya?* 1979—*Stay Free* 1980—*Musical Affair* 1981—*Performance* 1982—*Street Opera* 1983—*High-Rise* (Capitol) 1984—*Solid* 1986—*Real Love* 1989—*Love or Physical* 1996—*Been Found* (Hopsack and Silk).

Valerie Simpson solo: 1971—*Exposed* (Tamla) 1972—*Valerie Simpson.*

During the late '60s, writer/performer/producers Nickolas Ashford and Valerie Simpson wrote and produced some of Motown's greatest hits, and since the early '70s they've also become successful performers. The son of a construction worker, Ashford grew up in Willow Run, Michigan, where he sang in the church choir as a child. He spent one semester at Eastern Michigan College before dropping out. Against his parents' wishes, he left home and moved to Harlem with only $57. He worked as a busboy and began attending the White Rock Baptist Church in Harlem, where in 1964 he met Simpson, then 17 years old. She had recently graduated high school and was studying music at Chatham Square School.

They began writing songs together (the first bunch of which they sold for $64). Two years later, when Ray Charles had a hit with their "Let's Go Get Stoned," they signed on with Berry Gordy's Motown organization as staff writers and producers. They created a series of romantic duets, including Marvin Gaye and Tammi Terrell's "Ain't No Mountain High Enough" and "You're All I Need to Get By," and Diana Ross' "Reach Out (and Touch Somebody's Hand)." While neither of Simpson's Ashford-produced solo albums sold well, the pair were anxious to concentrate on performing (which Gordy discouraged) and recorded *Keep It Comin'* just before leaving Motown in 1973 for Warner Bros. They married in 1974. Their early R&B hit singles included "So, So Satisfied" (#27, 1977) and "Is It Still Good to Ya?" (#12, 1978), and 1979's "Found a Cure" was their first 45 to make the pop Top 40. They had to wait six years for their next one, "Solid," which reached #12 in 1985 and topped the R&B chart. Two other R&B hits followed: "Outta the World" (#4, 1985) and "Count Your Blessings" (#4, 1986). *Send It, Is It Still Good to Ya?* and *Stay Free* have been certified gold. The duo's most recent studio album, *Been Found,* features esteemed poet Maya Angelou on seven of its 11 songs. Ashford and Simpson also continue to tour and work frequently as independent writers and producers; their clients include Diana Ross *(The Boss),* Gladys Knight and the Pips *(About Love),* and Whitney Houston ("I'm Every Woman"). The latter song, contained on *The Bodyguard* soundtrack, hit #5 in 1993.

Asia

Formed 1981, Los Angeles, CA
Carl Palmer (b. Mar. 20, 1947, Birmingham, Eng.), drums; John Wetton (b. July 12, 1949, Derby, Eng.), bass, voc.; Steve Howe (b. Apr. 8, 1947, London, Eng.), gtr.; Geoffrey Downes (b. Eng.), kybds.
1982—*Asia* (Geffen) 1983—*Alpha* (– Wetton; + Greg Lake [b. Nov. 10, 1948, Bournemouth, Eng.], bass, voc.) 1985—(– Howe; + Mandy Meyer, gtr.; – Lake; + Wetton; – Meyer; + Pat Thrall [b. San Francisco, CA], gtr.) *Astra Then & Now* 1992—*Asia: Live in Moscow* (Rhino) (– Thrall; + Howe; + Downes; + Palmer; + John Payne, voc., bass; + Al Pitrelli, gtr.); *Aqua* (Pyramid) 1994—*Aria* (Mayhem) 1996—*Arena* (Resurgence); *Archiva 1 & 2* 1997—*Anthology* (Snapper); *Live in Köln* (Blueprint); *Live in Osaka; Live in Philadelphia* 1999—*Axioms* (Snapper); *Live at the Town & Country Club* (Resurgence); *Live Acoustic* 2000—*The Very Best of Asia: Heat of the Moment 1982–1990* (Geffen) 2001—*Aura* (Recognition, U.K.).

The first supergroup of the '80s, Asia was composed of famous musicians whose earlier work in major rock groups virtually guaranteed their success. Carl Palmer had been a member of Emerson, Lake and Palmer; Steve Howe and Geoffrey Downes had both belonged to Yes, and Downes had worked with the Buggles; John Wetton had been bassist for King Crimson, U.K., Family, and Roxy Music. Greg Lake, who briefly replaced Wetton, was also an ELP alumnus. Despite widespread critical revulsion and a cool reception in its native U.K., the group was embraced by AOR radio programmers and fans of bombastic arena rock.

The group's quadruple-platinum debut LP, *Asia,* held the #1 spot for over two months in 1982 and launched two hits: "Heat of the Moment" (#4, 1982) and "Only Time Will Tell" (#17, 1982). *Alpha* (#6, 1983), with the #10 1983 hit "Don't Cry," was also certified platinum. At its commercial peak, Asia performed live from the Budokan Theatre in Tokyo, Japan, in a satellite telecast, *Asia in Asia,* that was seen by 20 million viewers. But *Astra* (#67, 1985) proved markedly less popular than its predecessors. Howe was replaced by ex-Krokus guitarist Mandy Meyer, and in 1986 Asia disbanded until 1990, when it re-formed with guitarist Pat Thrall (formerly of Automatic Man and the Pat Travers Band) in the spot originally held by Howe. By 1992 Howe was back in with Downes, Palmer, John Payne, and Al Pitrelli to record *Aqua* (Simon Phillips, Anthony Glynne, and Nigel Glockler also contributed).

When Downes and Payne regrouped with Pitrelli to record Asia's 1994 album, *Aria,* both Howe and Palmer were gone again. By the time of the band's 1996 album *Arena,* Downes and Payne were the only constant members, performing together on occasion as an acoustic duo. Between 1996 and 2000, Asia released numerous collections of demos, live performances, and hits packages on small labels. In early 2001, the band reemerged yet again with an album of new material, *Aura,* and an all-star cast of prog-rock musicians cranking out more of the same arena-style rock that had initially put Asia on the map.

Asleep at the Wheel

Formed 1970, Paw Paw, WV
Original lineup: Ray Benson (b. Ray Benson Seifert, Mar. 16, 1951, Philadelphia, PA), gtr., voc.; Leroy Preston, drums, gtr.; Lucky Oceans (b. Reuben Gosfield), pedal steel gtr.
1973—*Comin' Right at Ya* (United Artists) 1974—*Asleep at the Wheel* (Epic) 1975—*Fathers and Sons Texas Gold* (Capitol)

1976—*Wheelin' and Dealin' Texas Country* (United Artists) 1977—*The Wheel* (Capitol) 1978—*Collision Course Served Live Framed* (MCA) 1981—*American Band 3* (Capitol) 1985—*Asleep at the Wheel* (MCA) 1987—*Asleep at the Wheel: 10* (Epic) 1988—*Western Standard Time Keepin' Me Up Nights* (Arista) 1992—*Route 66* (Liberty); *Greatest Hits (Live and Kickin')* (Arista); *The Swingin' Best of Asleep at the Wheel* (Epic) 1993—(lineup: Benson, gtr., voc.; Tim Alexander, piano, accordion, voc; Cindy Cashdollar, Hawaiian steel gtr.; Mike Francis [b. June 25, 1951, Yuma, AZ], sax; Ricky Turpin, fiddle, electric mandolin, voc.; David Earl Miller, bass; Tommy Beavers, drums) *Tribute to the Music of Bob Wills and the Texas Playboys* (Liberty) 1997—*Back to the Future Now* (Lucky Dog) 1999—*Ride With Bob* (DreamWorks).

For over three decades Asleep at the Wheel has been steadfastly dedicated to reviving, with slight modernization, the Western swing pioneered by Bob Wills in the '30s and '40s, a hybrid of country, big-band jazz, Cajun fiddling, and be-bop. With frequent personnel changes (there have been more than 80 lineup changes over the past 30 years), Asleep at the Wheel has become a dependable attraction in country and roots-rock circles. The group was founded by three Easterners: lead guitarist/vocalist Ray Benson, rhythm guitarist/vocalist/songwriter Leroy Preston, and pedal steel guitarist Lucky Oceans; female singer Chris O'Connell joined for the debut album. At first they mixed satiric originals with Western swing standards, to the incomprehension of their early record companies. Today the Grammy-winning group is acknowledged as the leading practitioner and champion of Western Swing.

After a few years in San Francisco, Asleep at the Wheel resettled in Austin, Texas, in 1974. The following year the group signed with Capitol and began to reach the country market with such deadpan songs as "The Letter That Johnny Walker Read" (#10 C&W, 1975) and versions of "Bump Bounce Boogie" (#31 C&W, 1975) and "Nothin' Takes the Place of You" (#35 C&W, 1976). Each of its Capitol releases since 1976 garnered at least one Grammy nomination; the group snagged its first in 1978 when its version of Count Basie's "One O'Clock Jump" won for Best Country Instrumental Performance. (The band has since won a total of seven Grammys.)

Though the group's recordings have sold only moderately, Asleep at the Wheel has retained a strong live following. For the critically acclaimed 1993 Bob Wills tribute album, Benson—the group's sole remaining founding member and leader—assembled such artists as Dolly Parton, Vince Gill, Chet Atkins, Garth Brooks, Huey Lewis, Lyle Lovett, and Merle Haggard, who were joined by Texas Playboys Eldon Shamblin and Johnny Gimble and Asleep alumni Lucky Oceans, Chris O'Connell, and Floyd Domino. "Red Wing" from the Wills tribute album won the 1993 Grammy for Best Country Instrumental Performance. Another Wills tribute, *Ride With Bob* (#24 C&W, 1999), featured yet more guests, ranging from Lyle Lovett to Tim McGraw to the Dixie Chicks.

The Association

Formed 1965, Los Angeles, CA
Jules Alexander (b. Sep. 25, 1943, Chattanooga, TN), gtr., voc.; Terry Kirkman (b. Dec. 12, 1941, Salinas, KS), kybds., voc.; Brian Cole (b. Sep. 8, 1942, Tacoma, WA; d. Aug. 2, 1972, Los Angeles), bass, voc.; Ted Bluechel Jr. (b. Dec. 2, 1942, San Pedro, CA), drums; Jim Yester (b. Nov. 24, 1939, Birmingham, AL), gtr., voc.; Russ Giguere (b. Oct. 18, 1943, Portsmouth, NH), gtr., voc.
1962—*And Then . . . Along Comes the Association* (Valiant) 1967—*Renaissance* (– Alexander; + Larry Ramos [b. Apr. 19, 1942, Kauai, HI], gtr., voc., harm.); *Insight Out* (Warner Bros.) 1968—*Birthday; Greatest Hits* 1969—(+ Alexander) *Goodbye Columbus* soundtrack; *The Association* 1970—*"Live"* (– Giguere; + Richard Thompson [b. San Diego, CA], gtr., voc.) 1971—*Stop Your Motor Waterbeds in Trinidad!* (CBS) 1981—(group re-forms with surviving original members) 1986—*Songs That Made Them Famous* (Pair).

A primarily soft-rock and ballad band, the Association sold over 15 million records in the '60s. The group first formed when Terry Kirkman, who had played in several bands, including Frank Zappa's Mothers of Invention, and Jules Alexander recruited Brian Cole and Jim Yester (whose brother Jerry was a member of the Lovin' Spoonful). Russ Giguere and Ted Bluechel joined soon after, and following six months of rehearsal the band debuted in Pasadena.

The hits, most written by various group members, began in 1966 with the group's first single, "Along Comes Mary" (which some listeners believed was an ode to marijuana), and continued with the more romantic songs for which the Association is best remembered: "Cherish" (#1, 1966), "Windy" (#1, 1967), "Never My Love" (#2, 1967), and "Everything That Touches You" (#10, 1968). Its singles, including the theme song from the movie *Goodbye Columbus* (1969), continued to chart but never again reached the Top 30. After an unsuccessful try at progressive rock from 1969 through 1973, the group faded from the charts and began working nightclubs. Several members (Ramos, Bluechel, Yester) released a single in 1975, but the Association attracted no further notice until early 1981, when all of the band's original surviving members (Cole died in 1972 of a heroin overdose) made a comeback attempt. Giguere and Ramos continued to tour with other musicians under the Association name into the '90s. In 1990 BMI designated "Never My Love" (along with the Beatles' "Yesterday") one of the most often played songs in history.

Chet Atkins

Born Chester Atkins, June 20, 1924, Luttrell, TN; died June 30, 2001, Nashville, TN
1951—*Chet Atkins Plays Guitar* (RCA) 1958—*Chet Atkins at Home* 1960—*Mister Guitar* 1962—*Back Home Hymns* 1963—*The Pops Goes Country* 1964—*Best of Chet Atkins* 1965—*My Favorite Guitars* 1966—*Chet Atkins Picks on the Beatles* 1969—*Solid Gold '69* 1970—*Me and Jerry* (with

Jerry Reed) 1971—*For the Good Times* 1974—*The Atkins-Travis Travelin' Show* (with Merle Travis) 1976—*Chester and Lester* (with Les Paul) 1983—*Work It Out With Chet Atkins* (Columbia) 1985—*Stay Tuned* 1989—*Chet Atkins, C.G.P.* 1990—*Neck and Neck* (with Mark Knopfler) 1992—*Sneakin' Around* (with Jerry Reed); *The RCA Years: 1947–1981* (RCA) 1994—*Read My Licks* (Columbia) 1996—*Almost Alone* 1997—*The Day Finger Pickers Took Over the World* (Sony) 1999—*Reflections* (Sugar Hill); *Country Pickin'* (RCA).

With more than 35 million copies of his 75-plus original releases sold, Grammy Lifetime Achievement Award winner Chet Atkins was one of the most successful guitarists in history; as a country music producer, he was largely responsible for the pop-oriented "Nashville Sound" of the '60s.

Raised in poverty, Atkins received musical training from his evangelical-singer father and an older half brother. He took up the guitar at age nine, and counted among his influences Les Paul, Django Reinhardt, and Merle Travis (Atkins' finger-picking style is a modification of Travis' technique). Beginning professionally in his teens playing fiddle for Archie Campbell, by the late '40s he had switched exclusively to guitar, performed at the Grand Ole Opry, and recorded as a sessionman and a solo artist. In the late '50s he became vice president in charge of RCA's Nashville operations and as such was involved as both a player and producer in the development of Eddy Arnold, Perry Como, Elvis Presley, and Roy Orbison. Later he expanded country music's horizons by helping introduce black country singer Charley Pride and encouraging the "outlaw" movement of Waylon Jennings and Willie Nelson.

As a producer at RCA from 1957 through the mid-'70s, Atkins established the Nashville Sound, string-laden and embellished with pop-style backup choruses. Traditionalists balked, but Atkins insisted that the style, augmented by his use of innovative studio technique (echo, reverb, tremolo guitars), brought country music into the pop mainstream. Admired by such diverse musicians as Paul McCartney, Leo Kottke, Earl Klugh, and George Benson, Atkins' guitar style was characterized by versatility. He recorded 12 duet albums featuring the likes of Les Paul, Doc Watson, Jerry Reed, and Mark Knopfler. He also performed with sitar player Ravi Shankar, the Atlanta Symphony, and Arthur Fiedler and the Boston Pops. As designer of a series of Chet Atkins Signature Guitars, he consistently maintained an interest in the technical side of guitar-playing.

In 1973 Atkins became, at 49, the youngest inductee into the Country Music Hall of Fame; a year later, he released an autobiography, *Country Gentleman,* its title Atkins' longtime nickname (on his albums he bills himself "C.G.P."—"Certified Guitar Player," a title he coined). In the '80s, backing off from producing, the guitarist enjoyed a performing renaissance: He toured with folksy pundit Garrison Keillor and continued to put out critically acclaimed albums with other guitarists. In 1991, South Street, in the heart of Nashville's Music Row, was renamed Chet Atkins Place. And in 1997, he received the Century Award, *Billboard*'s highest honor. Atkins died of cancer at age 77.

Atlanta Rhythm Section/ARS

Formed 1971, Doraville, GA
Barry Bailey (b. June 12, 1948, Decatur, GA), gtr.; Rodney Justo, voc.; Paul Goddard (b. June 23, 1945, Rome, GA), bass; Robert Nix, drums; J.R. Cobb (b. Feb. 5, 1944, Birmingham, AL), gtr.; Dean Daughtry (b. Sep. 8, 1946, Kinston, AL), kybds.
1972—*Atlanta Rhythm Section* (MCA) (– Justo; + Ronnie Hammond [b. Macon, GA], voc.) 1973—*Back Up Against the Wall* 1974—*Third Annual Pipe Dream* (Polydor) 1975—*Dog Days* 1976—*Red Tape* 1977—*A Rock and Roll Alternative* 1978—*Champagne Jam* (MCA) (– Nix; + Roy Yeager [b. Feb. 4, 1946, Greenwood, MS], drums) 1979—*Are You Ready!; Underdog* 1980—*The Boys From Doraville* 1981—*Quinella* (Columbia) (group disbands) 1989—(group re-forms as ARS) *Truth in a Structured Form* (Imagine/CBS) 1991—*The Best of ARS* (Polydor) 1997—*Partly Plugged* (Platinum Entertainment) 1999—*Eufaula.*

Comprised of former sessionmen, the Atlanta Rhythm Section smoothed out Southern rock's rough edges with studio sophistication. J.R. Cobb, Dean Daughtry, and producer/manager Buddy Buie had been members of the Classics IV. Daughtry, Rodney Justo, and Don Nix had also been in the Candymen, a group that at one time included Bobby Goldsboro, had backed Roy Orbison, and recorded two LPs (*The Candymen,* 1967, and *Bring You Candypower,* 1968). They met the other Section members while working together on a Roy Orbison session in 1970 and soon after formed the group, adding lead vocalist Justo for their debut LP. He was soon replaced by Ronnie Hammond, a former recording engineer. Though hampered by the lack of a distinctive frontman or a group identity and only moderate sales, the Atlanta Rhythm Section became established through frequent touring in the late '70s. Beginning in 1977 the group had a string of hit singles that included "So in to You" (#7, 1977), "Imaginary Lover" (#7, 1978), "I'm Not Gonna Let It Bother Me Tonight" (#14, 1978), "Do It or Die" (#19, 1979), and a remake of the Classics IV hit "Spooky" (#17, 1979). *A Rock and Roll Alternative* and *Underdog* have been certified gold and *Champagne Jam,* platinum, but after *Quinella* peaked at #70 with only one charting single ("Alien" [#29, 1981]), the band members drifted apart.

A loose aggregation comprised of Buie, Hammond, Bailey, Daughtry, and a revolving door of other musicians re-formed as ARS in 1989 and performed sporadically over the next decade. *Truth in a Structured Form* (1989), an attempt to update the band's trademark sound, flopped. *Partly Plugged* (1997) found a revamped Atlanta Rhythm Section using its original name again and celebrating its 25th aniverary by running through 11 of its hits and three new songs. *Eufaula* (1999) is an all-new studio recording.

Brian Auger

Born July 18, 1939, London, Eng.
1967—*Open* (Marmalade) 1968—*Definitely What* 1969—*Streetnoise* 1970—*Befour* (RCA) 1971—*Brian Auger's*

Oblivion Express; A Better Land 1972—*Second Wind* 1974—*Closer to It* 1975—*Straight Ahead; Live Oblivion, vols. 1 and 2; Genesis* (early Steampacket recordings) (Polydor); *This Is* (Metronome); *Reinforcements* (RCA) 1977—*Happiness Heartaches* (Warner Bros.); *Best of Brian Auger* (RCA) 1978—*Encore Here and Now* (Grudge) 1989—*Planet Earth Calling* (Dunhill/Garland) 2000—*Voices of Other Times* (Miramar).

British keyboardist Brian Auger helped lay the groundwork for fusion with his jazz-rock hybrids in the '60s and early '70s. In 1964 he abandoned pure jazz and upright piano for R&B and a Hammond organ. He soon formed the Brian Auger Trinity with bassist Rick Brown and drummer Mickey Waller. Within a few months he was asked to join a new group, Steampacket, which included vocalists Long John Baldry, Rod Stewart, and ex-model Julie Driscoll. Each had a spotlight segment during the group's live shows, which also featured jazzy R&B instrumentals highlighting Auger's keyboards. In mid-1966 Auger left, and the group dissolved.

Auger then reorganized Trinity with bassist Dave Ambrose (b. Dec. 11, 1946, London), drummer Clive Thacker (b. Feb. 13, 1940, Enfield, Eng.), guitarist Gary Boyle (b. Bihar, India), and Driscoll. In 1969 they had hits in Europe ("Save Me") and England (a cover of Dylan's "This Wheel's on Fire"). Subsequent singles floundered, however, and during a 1969 U.S. tour Driscoll quit the group. She later married pianist Keith Tippetts and continues to record occasionally under the name Julie Tippetts. Further hampered by contractual and management problems, Trinity broke up in mid-1970 after releasing *Befour,* and Auger reemerged late in the year with the four-piece Oblivion Express (at one time including drummer Robbie McIntosh, who later joined the Average White Band), a jazz-rock band that released several influential albums but failed to crack the U.S. market in a big way. The group's latter-day vocalist was Alex Ligertwood, later of Santana. By 1977 Auger was playing synthesizers as well, and the following year he did a reunion album with Julie Driscoll Tippets, *Encore.* As the '70s closed Auger was without a recording contract and living in California. He wrote "Happiness Is Just Around the Bend," a minor 1974 hit for the Main Ingredient.

Since then Auger has remained active, releasing albums in Europe and, to a lesser extent, America. In 1990 he teamed up with singer Eric Burdon and continues to tour the globe. A live CD recorded in California, *Access All Areas,* was issued in Europe in 1993. In 1995 a new Oblivion Express was conceived. The lineup on *Voices of Other Times* includes Auger's daughter, Savannah, on vocals, and his son, Karma, on drums.

Frankie Avalon

Born Francis Avallone, Sep. 18, 1939, Philadelphia, PA
1959—*Swingin' on a Rainbow* (Chancellor) 1995—*The Best of Frankie Avalon* (Varèse Sarabande).

Teen idol Frankie Avalon was originally a trumpet-playing prodigy when, at age 18, he joined a group called Rocco and the Saints (which then included neighbor Bobby Rydell). He began making appearances on local television, and in 1958 his debut single, "DeDe Dinah," was #7. Through the late '50s and up until 1960, Avalon had six Top 10 hits: "Ginger Bread" (#9, 1958), "Bobby Sox to Stockings" (#8, 1959), "A Boy Without a Girl" (#10, 1959), "Just Ask Your Heart" (#7, 1959), "Venus" (#1, 1959), and "Why" (#1, 1960). He was a regular on Dick Clark's *American Bandstand,* appeared in several beach-party movies with Annette Funicello (including *Beach Blanket Bingo*), and also appeared in *Disc Jockey Jamboree* (1957), *Guns of the Timberland* (1960), and *The Carpetbaggers* (1962).

By the '70s he was appearing regularly on the resort club circuit and occasionally had TV roles on such shows as *Love, American Style.* His 1976 disco remake of "Venus" peaked at #46. In 1987 he and Funicello coproduced and costarred in *Back to the Beach;* the pair's Back to the Beach concert tour (1989/90) was well received. They also released a Christmas single, "Together We Can Make a Merry Christmas," and made a number of guest appearances. Avalon continues to tour solo and with Bobby Rydell and Fabian as one of the "Boys of *Bandstand.*"

Average White Band

Formed 1972, Scotland
Alan Gorrie (b. July 19, 1946, Perth, Scot.), bass, voc.; Onnie McIntyre (b. Sep. 25, 1945, Lennox Town, Scot.), gtr., voc.; Roger Ball (b. June 4, 1944, Dundee, Scot.), kybds., saxes; Malcolm "Molly" Duncan (b. Aug. 24, 1945, Montrose, Scot.), tenor sax; Robbie McIntosh (b. 1950, Scot.; d. Sep. 23, 1974, Los Angeles, CA), drums; Hamish Stuart (b. Oct. 8, 1949, Glasgow, Scot.), gtr., voc.
1973—*Show Your Hand* (MCA) 1974—*AWB* (Atlantic) (– McIntosh; + Steve Ferrone [b. Apr. 25, 1950, Brighton, Eng.], drums) 1975—*Cut the Cake; Put It Where You Want It* (MCA) 1976—*Soul Searching* (Atlantic); *Person to Person* 1977—*Benny and Us* 1978—*Warmer Communications* 1979—*Feel No Fret* (Arista); *Volume VIII* (Atlantic) 1989—(group re-forms: Gorrie; McIntyre; Ball; + Alex Ligertwood, voc.; + Eliot Lewis, bass, kybds., gtr., voc.) *Aftershock* (Track) 1996—(– Ligertwood; + Pete Abbot, drums) *Soul Tattoo* (Foundation) 1997—(– Ball; + Fred Vigdor, kybds., sax).

The Average White Band's derivative but convincing funk crossed the Atlantic and the color line, heralding the arrival of disco in the mid-'70s. Each of the members had been active in various English and Scottish bands before Alan Gorrie founded the group. Robbie McIntosh had been with Brian Auger's Oblivion Express; Roger Ball and Malcolm Duncan had been members of the Dundee Horns. After opening for Eric Clapton at his January 1973 Rainbow Theatre comeback concert, they released an unnoticed debut album. The next year they began abbreviating the band name as AWB, and a 1974 album produced by Arif Mardin yielded a Grammy Award–winning disco hit, "Pick Up the Pieces" (#1, 1975). The group was shaken by drummer McIntosh's death from accidental heroin poisoning at a Hollywood party but regrouped for a second gold album, *Cut the Cake* (which it dedicated to McIntosh). *Put It Where You Want It* is a rerelease of their debut album. *Benny and Us* featured soul singer Ben E. King.

After 1975, AWB began recording together less often while its members worked as sidemen, including backup work for Chaka Khan in 1978. Gorrie, Ferrone, and Stuart recorded as Easy Pieces, with Renee Geyer. Ferrone later played drums for Duran Duran, and Stuart joined Paul McCartney's band for *Flowers in the Dirt* and his subsequent tour. In 1989, Gorrie, McIntyre, and Ball enlisted vocalist Alex Ligertwood and re-formed the AWB. The group continued to perform (and to a lesser extent, record) in the '90s. Meanwhile, in 2000, the Hamish Stuart Band released the album *Sooner or Later.*

Kevin Ayers

Born Aug. 16, 1945, Herne Bay, Eng.
1970—*Joy of a Toy* (Harvest) 1971—*Shooting at the Moon* 1972—*Whatevershebringswesing* 1973—*Bananamour* 1974—*Confessions of Dr. Dream* (Island); *June 1st, 1974* (with John Cale, Brian Eno, and Nico) 1975—*Sweet Deceiver* 1976—*Old Ditties* 1977—*Yes We Have No Mañanas* 1978—*Rainbow Takeaway.*

Cheerfully eccentric Kevin Ayers has been active in British progressive rock since 1963, when he and some friends from Canterbury founded the Wilde Flowers. In 1966 Ayers and drummer Robert Wyatt left to start Soft Machine [see entry]. He played bass with the group until 1968, then began his ongoing solo career. Singing in a deep bass voice and making quiet jokes about moons and bananas—his specialty is pataphysical humor, the British equivalent of Zen koans—Ayers has played alongside Mike Oldfield (who first recorded on Ayers' albums), Steve Hillage, John Cale, Brian Eno, and Andy Summers. He spends most of his time at his estate on the island of Ibiza and continues to tour and release European albums every few years.

Roy Ayers

Born Sep. 10, 1940, Los Angeles, CA
1963—*West Coast Vibes* (United Artists) 1967—*Virgo Vibes* (Atlantic) 1968—*Stoned Soul Picnic* 1969—*Daddy Bug and Friends* 1970—Vibrant (Alex) 1971—*Roy Ayers: Ubiquity* (Polydor) 1972—*He's Coming; Live at the Montreux Jazz Festival* (Verve) 1973—*Virgo Red* (Polydor) 1974—*Change Up the Groove* 1975—*A Tear to a Smile; Red, Black and Green* 1976—*Mystic Voyage; Vibrations; Everybody Loves the Sunshine* 1977—*Lifeline* (Polydor); *Crystal Reflections* (Muse) 1978—*Let's Do It* (Polydor); *You Send Me; Step Into Our Life* 1979—*Fever; Love Fantasy* 1980—*No Stranger to Love; Prime Time* 1981—*Africa, Center of the World* 1982—*Feelin' Good* 1983—*Drivin' On Up; Silver Vibrations* (Uno Melodic) 1984—*In the Dark* (Columbia) 1985—*You Might Be Surprised* 1987—*I'm the One (for Your Love Tonight)* 1990—*Wake Up* (Ichiban) 1991—*Searchin'* (Ronnie Scott's) 1992—*Double Trouble* (Uno Melodic) 1995—*Vibrant* (Alex); *Evolution: The Polydor Anthology* (Polydor); *Good Vibrations* (Ronnie Scott's); *Vibesman Live at Ronnie Scott's; Naste* (Groovetown) 1996—*Essential Groove Live* (Ronnie Scott's) 1998—*Spoken Word* (AFI); *Lots of Love* (Charly); *Fast Money—Ronnie Scott's* (Castle).

Vibraphonist Roy Ayers crossed over from jazz to funk and found commercial success in the mid-'70s with what he called "disco jazz." He then was rediscovered in the '90s as one of the precursors of acid-jazz. He learned piano at an early age; at five, his playing impressed Lionel Hampton, who gave him a pair of mallets. Ayers began playing vibes professionally with West Coast bands in the late '50s. In 1965 he formed his own quartet but disbanded it when Herbie Mann invited him to join his band. He recorded and toured with Mann from 1966 to 1970, and Mann produced Ayers' first three solo albums.

Around 1970 Ayers began experimenting with electronics and rock rhythms. He was probably the first vibraphonist to electrify his instrument and certainly the first to employ such devices as the wah-wah pedal and effects like fuzztone. In 1970 he formed the Roy Ayers Ubiquity, a fully electrified ensemble that fused jazz, rock, Latin pop, and R&B. Guest soloists with Ubiquity have included drummer Billy Cobham, flutist Hubert Laws, guitarist George Benson, trombonist Wayne Henderson of the Crusaders, vocalist Dee Dee Bridgewater, R&B composer and vocalist Edwin Birdsong, and Nigerian saxophonist Fela Anikulapo Kuti, with whom he toured Nigeria in 1979, resulting in the 1981 LP *Africa, Center of the World.* His albums from this period earned him a loyal audience among jazz and R&B fans.

Beginning in 1976, Ayers' records hit the charts after receiving radio and disco play; "Running Away," which became a dance-club classic, made the R&B Top 20 in 1977. "The Freaky Deaky" inspired a dance step of the same name in 1978. Ayers broke up Ubiquity that year and formed a recording partnership with Henderson on the album *Step Into Our Life;* they had a minor hit with "Heat of the Beat" (#59 R&B, 1978).

In 1981 Ayers formed his own label, Uno Melodic, to release other artists' work that he produced. Throughout the next decade Ayers continued to have hits, including "In the Dark" (#35 R&B, 1984), "Slip 'n Slide" (#49 R&B, 1985), and "Hot" (#20 R&B, 1986), and remained popular in Great Britain. In 1987 Ayers recorded with Whitney Houston on her "Love Will Save the Day."

By the '90s, Ayers had become a seminal influence on the burgeoning acid-jazz scene, particularly in the U.K. Such hip-hop artists as Big Daddy Kane, A Tribe Called Quest, Brand Nubian, Monie Love, and Mary J. Blige sampled Ayers' '70s recordings; his 1976 song "Everybody Loves the Sunshine" was an especially popular sample. This brought him even more visibility, as did his appearance on *Jazzmatazz,* the hip-hop/jazz project produced by Guru of GangStarr.

Aztec Camera

Formed 1980, East Kilbride, Scot.
Roddy Frame (b. Jan. 29, 1964, East Kilbride), voc., gtr., most other instruments in studio; Campbell Owens, bass; Dave Mulholland, drums.
1983—*High Land, Hard Rain* (Sire) 1984—*Oblivious* EP (– Owens; – Mulholland); *Knife; Still On Fire* EP (WEA) 1985—*Backwards and Forwards* EP (Sire) 1987—*Love* 1988—*Somewhere in My Heart* EP (WEA) 1990—*Stray* (Sire) 1993—*Dreamland* 1994—*Covers & Rare* (Alex) 1995—*New, Live, and Rare* (WEA); *Live on the Test* (Windsong); *Frestonia* (Reprise); *Old Grey Whistle Test Series—Live* (Alex) 1999—*The Best of Aztec Camera* (WEA International).
Roddy Frame solo: 1998—*North Star* (Sony International).

This one-man band arrived on the heels of punk. Roddy Frame had started writing songs at 15. He formed Aztec Camera a year later as a vehicle for his highly individual style of folky pop. Initially signed to the Glasgow independent label Postcard, Aztec Camera soon moved to the much higher profile English indie Rough Trade. A flurry of attention in Great Britain piqued Sire's interest. Before the release of *High Land, Hard Rain,* however, the group's original bassist Campbell Owens and drummer Dave Mulholland departed. Aztec Camera has since consisted of Frame with various backup musicians.

Frame's songs never charted well in the U.S., but his penchant for hook-drenched melodies and clever wordplay made him a critic's darling. Aztec Camera's debut fared better in Britain, with modest hits including "Oblivious" and "Walk Out to Winter." The second album, produced by Dire Straits' Mark Knopfler, offered more of the same. Frame fell out of critical favor with 1987's *Love,* an ill-conceived attempt to marry his singer/songwriter pop with Philadelphia soul. Despite that, the album achieved platinum status internationally and in Europe spun off four hit singles, including "Somewhere in My Heart."

He reclaimed his critical reputation with *Stray.* On 1993's *Dreamland,* Frame collaborated on two songs with Ryuichi Sakamoto. In 1995 four albums were released under the Aztec Camera banner, most of them live recordings, but also including *Frestonia,* a collection of new studio tracks that continued Frame's exploration of classic pop. Nothing else was heard from Frame until 1998, when his first official solo album, *North Star,* was released in England.

Babes in Toyland

Formed 1987, Minneapolis, MN
First recorded lineup: Michelle Leon (b. Feb. 11, 1969, Newark, NJ), bass; Katherine "Kat" Bjelland (b. Dec. 9, 1963, Salem, OR), voc., gtr.; Lori Barbero (b. Nov. 27, 1960, Minneapolis), drums.
1990—*Spanking Machine* (Twin/Tone) 1991—*To Mother* 1992—(– Leon; + Maureen Herman [b. July 25, 1966, Philadelphia, PA], bass) *Fontanelle* (Reprise) 1993—*Painkillers* EP 1995—*Nemesisters* 2000—*Lived* (Almantone, U.K.).

Babes in Toyland, one of the first all-female bands to come out of the early-'90s grunge scene, featured Kat Bjelland's distinctive and demanding vocals. Defying expectations by wearing baby-doll dresses while venting a deep rage, Bjelland and her band opened doors for such groups as Hole and Bikini Kill.

In 1987 Bjelland moved from San Francisco, where she had played with L7's Jennifer Finch and Hole's Courtney Love in a band called Sugar Baby Doll, to Minneapolis, then an indie-rock hotbed. Babes' original all-girl lineup included Barbero, who had never drummed before, bassist Chris Holetz, and singer Cindy Russell; Holetz and Russell left after one year and Leon joined.

Babes released their first single on an independent label in 1989 and already had a following by the time *Spanking Machine* was released a year later. They toured Europe that fall with Sonic Youth. Originally released only in Europe, *To Mother,* a seven-song disc, spent 12 weeks on top of the U.K.

Babes in Toyland: Kat Bjelland, Lori Barbero, Maureen Herman

indie charts. That and frequent touring, including the Reading Festival, secured Babes in Toyland's European following. Leon left Babes in early 1992 after her boyfriend, roadie Joe Cole, was shot and killed when he and his roommate, Henry Rollins, were attacked by robbers. She was replaced by Maureen Herman. Babes' major-label debut, *Fontanelle*, was produced by Sonic Youth's Lee Ranaldo and featured a cover photo by noted artist Cindy Sherman. In 1993 Babes first broke through to American audiences after being the only female-led band on that summer's Lollapalooza Tour and having their video for "Bruised Violet" plugged by MTV's *Beavis and Butt-head*. *Painkillers* featured that track and a live CBGB performance.

Nemesisters was Babes' most "polished" record yet, including an eclectic mix of covers: Eric Carmen's "All by Myself," Billie Holiday's "Deep Song," and Sister Sledge's "We Are Family." The record nevertheless failed to earn the trio the critical or commercial acceptance of their all-female counterparts L7 and Hole. Herman left the group in June 1996 to pursue a writing career (she later started her own multimedia company). Bjelland and Barbero soldiered on with different bass players, including Leon, before calling it quits in 1997. The three women reunited in 1998 to play on *Songs of the Witchblade*, a Bjelland-produced soundtrack to the comic book *The Witchblade*.

The Babys/John Waite/Bad English

Formed in 1975, London, Eng.
John Waite (b. July 4, 1955, Lancaster, Eng.), bass, voc.; Wally Stocker (b. Mar. 17, 1954, London), gtr., voc.; Mike Corby (b. July 3, 1955, Eng.), voc., kybds., gtr.; Tony Brock (b. Mar. 31, 1954, Bournemouth, Eng.), drums, voc.
1976—*The Babys* (Chrysalis) 1977—*Broken Heart* (– Corby) 1978—*Head First* (+ Jonathan Cain [b. Feb. 26, 1950, Chicago, IL], kybds.; + Ricky Phillips, bass) 1980—*Union Jacks; On the Edge* (– Cain) 1981—*Anthology* 1997—*The Best of the Babys* (EMI).
John Waite solo: 1982—*Ignition* (Chrysalis) 1984—*No Brakes* (EMI) 1985—*Mask of Smiles* 1987—*Rover's Return* 1992—*Essentials* (Chrysalis) 1995—*Temple Bar* (Imago) 1996—*Falling Backwards* (EMI) 1997—*When You Were Mine* (Pure).
Bad English, formed 1988: Waite; Cain; Phillips; + Neal Schon (b. Feb. 27, 1954, San Mateo, CA), gtr.; + Deen Castronovo, drums.
1989—*Bad English* (Epic) 1991—*Backlash* (– Schon; – Castronovo).

Power pop with a veneer of youthful vibrancy made the Babys a hot act on FM rock radio in the late '70s. Formed in London as a teen-oriented act, the group signed with Chrysalis in late 1976 on the strength of one of the first video demos. Conceived by producer Mike Mansfield, it showed off the members' looks, gleaming smiles, and wardrobes. The Babys appeared on several American television programs in 1977 to support their debut (produced by Bob Ezrin) and, aided by massive advertising, had such hits as "Isn't It Time" (#13, 1977). As the '70s drew to a close, the Babys experimented with a more synthesizer-oriented style on *Head First* and 1980's *Union Jacks*, which bore two moderate hits, "Back on My Feet Again" (#33, 1980) and "Turn and Walk Away" (#42, 1980). Jonathan Cain joined Journey in early 1981, and the Babys disbanded.

Chrysalis released lead singer John Waite's solo debut, *Ignition*, in 1982, and the album's "Change" went to #54. *No Brakes* became a Top 10 LP on the strength of "Missing You" (#1, 1984). "Every Step of the Way" (#25, 1985) was Waite's last Top 30 single; his fourth album, *Rover's Return*, stalled at #77.

Two years later Waite reemerged, fronting Bad English, which featured two ex-Babys, Jonathan Cain and Ricky Phillips, and included Cain's ex-Journey mate, Neal Schon, and drummer Deen Castronovo. The group's eponymously titled debut struck platinum, peaking at #21 in 1989 and boasting two Top 10 hits: "When I See You Smile" (#1) and "Price of Love" (#5). The group's second effort did not repeat the success, and after its release, Schon quit the group; he and Castronovo joined Hardline, and Castronovo later joined up with Paul Rodgers for his Muddy Waters tribute record. Cain began pursuing a solo career while John Waite continued his with 1995's *Temple Bar*. The late '90s found Schon, Cain, and Castronovo back together again in a new version of Journey [see entry].

Bachman-Turner Overdrive/BTO

Formed 1972, Winnipeg, Can.
Randy Bachman (b. Sep. 27, 1943, Winnipeg), gtr., voc.; Tim Bachman (b. Winnipeg), gtr.; Robbie Bachman (b. Robin Bachman, Feb. 18, 1953, Winnipeg), drums; C.F. (Fred) Turner (b. Oct. 16, 1943, Winnipeg), bass, voc.
1973—*Bachman-Turner Overdrive* (Mercury); *Bachman-Turner Overdrive 2* (– T. Bachman; + Blair Thornton [b. July 23, 1950], gtr.) 1974—*Not Fragile* 1975—*Four Wheel Drive; Head On* 1976—*Best of Bachman-Turner Overdrive* 1977—*Freeways* (– Randy Bachman; + Jim Clench, bass, voc.) 1978—*Street Action; Rock 'n' Roll Nights* (+ Randy Bachman; + T. Bachman; + Gary Peterson, drums; – Robbie Bachman) 1984—*Bachman-Turner Overdrive* (Compleat) 1993—*Bachman-Turner Overdrive: The Anthology* (PolyGram) (– Randy Bachman; + Robbie Bachman; + Randy Murray [b. Dec. 9, 1955, Calgary, Can.], gtr.) 1996—*Trial by Fire* (CMC) 1998—*Bachman-Turner Overdrive* (King Biscuit Flower Hour).

Bachman-Turner Overdrive parlayed workmanlike heavy metal, a blue-collar image, and nonstop touring into over 7 million records sold in the U.S. by 1977. The group—in various personnel combinations—has retained an impressive following in its homeland, where Randy Bachman is a respected guitar hero and successful solo artist.

Guess Who founders Chad Allan and Randy Bachman had left that group in 1966 and 1970 respectively [see entry]. After Bachman made a solo album (*Axe*, 1970), he teamed up with Allan and younger brother Robbie Bachman in Brave Belt. After two albums (*Brave Belt I* and *Brave Belt II*), Tim Bachman and vocalist/bassist Fred Turner replaced Allan, and Brave Belt became Bachman-Turner Overdrive, named in part after the truckers' magazine *Overdrive.*

Twenty-five record companies rejected the band before Mercury released its 1973 debut album. Extensive touring netted BTO several hit singles, including "Let It Ride" (#23, 1974), "Takin' Care of Business" (#12, 1974), "You Ain't Seen Nothing Yet" (#1, 1974), "Roll On Down the Highway" (#14, 1975), "Hey You" (#21, 1975), and "Take It Like a Man" (#33, 1976). (Live recordings from 1974 resurfaced on a King Biscuit Flower Hour CD in 1998.) In 1975 Tim Bachman left to become a producer. That year Warner Bros. rereleased *Brave Belt II* under the title *As Brave Belt.* With Randy Bachman's departure in 1977 for a solo career (he released *Survivor* and later formed Ironhorse, which recorded two LPs, *Ironhorse* and *Everything Is Grey*), BTO's momentum slowed considerably, although the group did release two more LPs.

The group disbanded for the first time in 1979 or 1980, but regrouped several times through the '80s to tour under the names Bachman-Turner Overdrive and BTO (sometimes with Turner, sometimes without) while brother Robbie Bachman performed under the BTO moniker (again, not always with Turner along). The ensuing confusion caused Randy to file suit against his ex–band mates' brother Robbie, Turner, and Thornton for rights to the band's logo. Randy Bachman left for good in 1993, leaving the band to Robbie. The new lineup released 1996's *Trial by Fire,* which included a mix of rerecorded Bachman-Turner Overdrive songs and a handful of new ones.

Randy Bachman tours occasionally with the reconstituted Guess Who (the latest reunion occurred in 2000) and also records as a solo artist. Nineteen-ninety-three's *Any Road* (Sony, Canada), his first solo album of the decade, featured guest appearances by the guitarist's protégé from their early days in Winnipeg, Neil Young, on "Prairie Town," and by the Cowboy Junkies' Margo Timmins. Young also showed up on Bachman's 2000 album *Merge* (True North, Canada). By the late '90s he was working as a songwriter for hire, commuting between his Canadian home, London, and Nashville. His son, Tal Bachman, released a self-titled album on Columbia in 1999.

Backstreet Boys

Formed 1993, Orlando, FL
Nick Carter (b. Jan. 28, 1980, Jamestown, NY), voc.; Howie Dorough (b. Howard Dwaine, Aug. 22, 1973, Orlando), voc; Brian Littrell (b. Feb. 20, 1975, Lexington, KY), voc.; Alexander James "A.J." McLean (b. Jan. 9, 1978, West Palm Beach, FL), voc.; Kevin Scott Richardson (b. Oct. 3, 1971, Lexington), voc.
1996—*Backstreet Boys* (Jive, U.K.) 1997—*Backstreet's Back; Backstreet Boys* (Jive) 1999—*Millennium* 2000—*Black & Blue.*

After sweeping the European charts, it took almost two years for the Florida vocal group Backstreet Boys to bring its teen-friendly music and arena-ready choreographed moves back to its home country. Selling over 55 million records worldwide in three years, the group embodied the late-'90s pop explosion.

High school friends A.J. McLean and Howie Dorough met Nick Carter at local acting auditions in Orlando. Shortly thereafter, they hooked up with Kentucky native Kevin Richardson, who was singing in shows at Disney World; Richardson got his cousin Brian Littrell, with whom he used to sing back home, to relocate to Florida, and the five named themselves Backstreet Boys, using the name of an Orlando flea market. They were spotted by manager Lou Pearlman, who handed the group's daily care over to former New Kids

Backstreet Boys: Kevin Richardson, Howie Dorough, Brian Littrell, Nick Carter, A.J. McLean

on the Block road manager Johnny Wright and his wife, Donna. They started performing around local malls, theme parks, and schools, with Carter, Littrell, and McLean emerging as the main lead singers.

Backstreet Boys signed to Jive Records in 1994, but their first Jive single, "We've Got It Goin' On" (#69, 1995), flopped in an American market still in grunge's waning grip. The song did a lot better everywhere else in the world, though, hitting #1 in Germany, for instance; the Boys' self-titled debut, released in the spring of 1996 everywhere but the U.S., sold over 11 million copies worldwide.

The Florida group finally made its full-length American debut with the 14-million-selling *Backstreet Boys* (#4, 1997), whose bulk was made up of the band's foreign release including a cover of P.M. Dawn's "Set Adrift on Memory Bliss" with a smattering of extra tracks. The group's label and managing company focused their marketing campaign on teen and preteen girls, distributing free tapes at cheerleading camps and placing them in JC Penney makeup cases. This time the strategy worked, and, with the extra help of a musical climate more open to bubblegum R&B, the group rocketed to the top of the pop charts with several singles, including the 2-million-selling "Quit Playing Games (With My Heart)" (#2, 1997), "Everybody (Backstreet's Back)" (#4, 1998), and "I'll Never Break Your Heart" (#35, 1998). The group was also nominated for a Grammy for Best New Artist. In May 1998 it filed a lawsuit for back touring and recording revenues against Pearlman and the two associates he'd hired. (The suit was eventually settled out of court with Pearlman receiving one-sixth of the band's earnings.) The band was also angry that Pearlman had been working with the nascent boy band 'N Sync. At about the same time, Littrell had open-heart surgery to correct a congenital defect.

Recorded mostly in Stockholm, 1999's *Millennium* confirmed Backstreet Boys as the reigning boy band. Featuring some songs cowritten by the singers, the album debuted at #1, selling a record-breaking 1,134,000 copies the week of its release (it has sold over 13 million copies to date). It generated the hit singles "All I Have to Give" (#5, 1999), "I Want It That Way" (#6, 1999), and "Larger Than Life" (#25, 1999), and was nominated for five Grammys, including Best Album. The Millennium Tour sold out all its dates in less than a day, confirming the Backstreet Boys' phenomenal popularity. Also that year the group entered into a promotional campaign for Burger King, which distributed miniature plastic figures of each Boy.

With the group's top position endangered by the rise of rival boy band 'N Sync, it returned with the single "Shape of My Heart" (#9, 2000) and the album *Black & Blue* (#1, 2000), which included two songs written by the Boys themselves. *Black & Blue* sold 5 million copies worldwide in its first week but topped the chart for only two weeks—an accomplishment for anybody, but a letdown for the Boys, and not nearly as successful as 'N Sync's simultaneous release. The Boys postponed their summer 2001 North American tour so that McLean could enter a treatment program for depression, anxiety, and alcohol abuse.

Bad Brains

Formed 1979, Washington, DC
HR (b. Paul D. Hudson, Feb. 11, 1956, London, Eng.), voc.; Dr. Know (b. Gary Wayne Miller, Sep. 15, 1958, Washington, DC), gtr.; Darryl Aaron Jenifer (b. Oct. 22, 1960, Washington, DC), bass; Earl Hudson (b. Dec. 17, 1957, AL), drums.
1982—*Bad Brains* (ROIR); *Bad Brains* EP (Alternative Tentacles); *I and I Survive/Destroy Babylon* EP (Important) 1983—*Rock for Light* (PVC) 1986—*I Against I* (SST) 1988—*Live* 1989—*Attitude: The ROIR Session* (ROIR/Important); *Quickness* (Caroline) 1990—*The Youth Are Getting Restless: Live in Amsterdam* 1991—*Spirit Electricity* (SST) 1993—*Rise* (Epic) (– HR; – E. Hudson; + Israel Joseph-I [b. Dexter Pinto, Feb. 6, 1971, Trinidad], voc.; + Mackie Jayson [b. May 27, 1963, New York, NY], drums) 1995—*God of Love* (Maverick) (– Joseph-I; – Jayson; + HR; + E. Hudson) 1996—*Black Dots* (Caroline) 1997—*Omega Sessions* (Victory).

The members of Bad Brains started out playing '70s jazz-rock fusion, but took a sharp turn when they began breaking up their live sets into reggae and punk. Together with Black Flag and the Dead Kennedys, the band became pioneers of punk's hardcore fringe, influencing nearly every subsequent hardcore or quasi-hardcore outfit, including the earliest incarnation of the Beastie Boys. As an all-black rock band, they also inspired Living Colour and the entire New York City Black Rock Coalition of the '80s.

By 1977 guitarist Gary Miller (a.k.a. Dr. Know) had grown tired of his fusion noodling and looked to the Sex Pistols and Bob Marley for fresh inspiration. He and his mates viewed punk and reggae as complementary (both musically and politically) and believed that if punk and reggae acts could share the same stages in the U.K. they could share one band's set list in the U.S.

Bad Brains' single "Pay to Cum" remains a classic of the hardcore genre. Unfortunately, the band's music was never well documented on record; "Pay to Cum" was available only in its rare single form and on the band's self-titled ROIR cassette (since reissued on LP and CD). Ric Ocasek produced 1983's *Rock for Light,* which mingled two reggae tracks amidst the hardcore.

The long-awaited *I Against I* was an all-rock explosion, leaning more toward heavy metal than punk. It left the band fragmented, with HR and Earl Hudson wanting to do more reggae and Dr. Know and Darryl Jenifer preferring the new hard-rock direction. After years of coming and going, both HR and Hudson left again in 1989 (the two have recorded several reggae albums under HR's name since 1985's *It's About Luv* on Olive Tree). Chuck Mosely of Faith No More briefly assumed vocals but appeared on no albums. Bad Brains recruited Trinidadian-born singer Israel Joseph-I and Mackie Jayson on drums to replace HR and released *Rise.*

In 1995 HR and Hudson returned and the band released *God of Love.* That same year, the band was booked to tour with the Beastie Boys and seemed poised to finally reach beyond its lingering cult following. But on the tour's first night in Montreal, HR brutally attacked manager Anthony Countey and was arrested (he was released later that same night). The band regrouped in time to participate on the tour's final dates, but HR was arrested on a subsequent club tour after allegedly attacking a fan in Lawrence, Kansas, with a microphone stand (charges were later dropped). Bad Brains split up again, seemingly for good. But in 1999 the quartet reunited once more as the Soul Brains, a name HR reportedly chose to separate the band from the bad vibes of the past. The reunited band toured throughout 2000 and began recording in Woodstock, New York, with tentative plans to release a new album the following year.

Bad Company

Formed 1973, England
Paul Rodgers (b. Dec. 17, 1949, Middlesborough, Eng.), voc.; Mick Ralphs (b. Mar. 31, 1944, Hereford, Eng.), gtr.; Simon Kirke (b. July 28, 1949, London, Eng.), drums; Boz Burrell (b. Raymond Burrell, Aug. 1, 1946, Holbeach, Eng.), bass.
1974—*Bad Company* (Swan Song) 1975—*Straight Shooter* 1976—*Run With the Pack* 1977—*Burnin' Sky* 1979—*Desolation Angels* 1982—*Rough Diamonds* (group disbands) 1986—(group re-forms: Ralphs; Kirke; + Brian Howe, voc.) *10 From 6* (Atlantic); *Fame and Fortune* 1988—*Dangerous Age* 1990—*Holy Water* (Atco) 1992—*Here Comes Trouble* 1993—(+ Rick Wills, bass; + Dave Colwell, gtr.) *The Best of Bad Company Live . . . What You Hear Is What You Get* 1995—(– Howe; + Robert Hart, voc.) *Company of Strangers* (Elektra) 1996—*Stories Told & Untold* 1999—(– Wills; – Colwell; – Hart; + Rodgers; + Burrell) *The "Original" Bad Co. Anthology.*
Paul Rodgers solo: 1983—*Cut Loose* (Atlantic) 1993—*Muddy Waters Blues* (Victory); *The Hendrix Set* EP 1996—*Live* 1997—*Now* (Velvel) 2000—*Electric* (CMC International).
Paul Rodgers with the Firm: 1985—*The Firm* (Atlantic) 1986—*Mean Business.*
Paul Rodgers with the Law: 1991—*The Law* (Atlantic).

The members of Bad Company were stars before their first concert in March 1974. Paul Rodgers and Simon Kirke had been members of Free, Mick Ralphs had been Ian Hunter's main sidekick in Mott the Hoople, and Boz Burrell had played with King Crimson [see entries]. Their self-titled debut album, recorded in only 10 days with a minimum of overdubs in Ronnie Lane's mobile studio, eclipsed all that by going #1 worldwide with the single "Can't Get Enough." The album from which it came also hit #1 and to date has sold more than 5 million copies.

Playing sparse, elemental hard rock dominated by Rodgers' husky vocals and Ralphs' power chords, the original Bad Company sold more than 12 million records worldwide. Its 1975 release, *Straight Shooter,* yielded the Top 10 single "Feel Like Makin' Love" (#10, 1975) while *Run With the Pack* was the group's third consecutive album to go platinum.

On *Desolation Angels* (which included the Rodgers-penned hit "Rock and Roll Fantasy," #13, 1979), Bad Company added synthesizers and strings. Indicative of its increasingly sporadic activities, three years elapsed between *Angels* and *Rough Diamonds,* which seemed an anachronism upon its 1982 release. The group disbanded that year, with Rodgers releasing a solo LP in 1983, then forming yet another supergroup, the Firm, with Jimmy Page, bassist/keyboardist Tony Franklin, and drummer Chris Slade.

The Firm never came close to matching the level of success its two principals had enjoyed with their previous groups. After two LPs, the quartet broke up in 1986, just as Ralphs and Kirke were putting Bad Company back together. Former Ted Nugent vocalist Brian Howe stood in for Rodgers. The group stuck closely to the original lineup's riffy blues-rock formula, but its first album, *Fame and Fortune,* disappeared from the chart after just nine weeks. However, *Dangerous Age* eventually went gold, while *Holy Water* went platinum and produced a Top 20 power ballad, "If You Needed Somebody." *Here Comes Trouble* also sold in excess of 1 million copies and gave the group two more Top 40 hits. In 1993 Bad Company expanded into a quintet, adding journeyman bassist Rick Wills (Frampton's Camel, Roxy Music, Foreigner) and rhythm guitarist Dave Colwell, and celebrated its 20th anniversary with a live greatest-hits album. Rodgers, meanwhile, struggled to find musical direction. The Law, a hard-rock duo with drummer Kenney Jones, couldn't get arrested, and the singer returned to a solo career, first releasing two curious tribute albums, one interpreting the music of Muddy Waters, the other a live set of Jimi Hendrix tunes featuring Neal Schon on guitar.

In the fall of 1998 Rodgers and Burrell joined Ralphs and Kirke for a reunion of the original lineup. The group contributed four new songs, including the single "Hey, Hey," to the 2-CD set *The "Original" Bad Co. Anthology,* then embarked on a farewell tour in 1999. Rodgers has announced that he would resume his solo career afterward, when he is not playing as part of the original Bad Company.

Bad English: See the Babys

Badfinger

Formed 1968, England
Pete Ham (b. Apr. 27, 1947, Swansea, Wales; d. Apr. 23, 1975, Weybridge, Eng.), voc., gtr., piano; Tom Evans (b. June 5, 1947, Liverpool, Eng.; d. Nov. 23, 1983), voc., gtr., bass; Mike Gibbins (b. Mar. 12, 1949, Swansea), drums; Ron Griffiths, bass.
1968—(– Griffiths; + Joey Molland [b. June 21, 1947, Liverpool], voc., gtr., kybds.) 1970—*Magic Christian Music* (Apple); *No Dice* 1971—*Straight Up* 1973—*Ass* 1974—*Badfinger* (Warner Bros.); *Wish You Were Here* (– Molland; + Bob Jackson, kybds.) 1975—(– Ham; group disbands) 1978—(group re-forms: Molland; Evans; + Joe Tanzin, gtr.; + Kenny Harck, drums; – Tanzin; – Harck) 1979—*Airwaves* (Elektra) 1981—(+ Tony Kaye, kybds.; + Glenn Sherba, gtr.; + Richard Bryans, drums) *Say No More* (Radio) 1989—*The Best of Badfinger, vol. 2* (Rhino) 1990—*Day After Day* (Rykodisc).
Joey Molland solo: 1983—*After the Pearl* (Earthtone) 1992—*The Pilgrim* (Rykodisc).

Pete Ham solo: 1997—*7 Park Avenue* (Rykodisc) 1999—*Golders Green.*

Badfinger was a popular British pop-rock band in the early '70s. Originally called the Iveys, the group signed with Apple Records in late 1968 after its demo tape found its way into Paul McCartney's hands. In 1969 McCartney supervised the quartet's soundtrack work on the Ringo Starr–Peter Sellers film, *The Magic Christian,* for which he wrote "Come and Get It," Badfinger's first hit (#7, 1970).

During the early '70s Badfinger had three more hit singles: "No Matter What" (#8, 1970), "Day After Day" (#4, 1972), and "Baby Blue" (#14, 1972). Pete Ham and Tom Evans' "Without You," covered by Harry Nilsson on *Nilsson Schmilsson,* became a #1 single in February 1972; in 1994 it was a hit again, this time for Mariah Carey. The group frequently backed the ex-Beatles on tours and records, appearing at George Harrison's 1971's benefit concert for Bangladesh and on his album *All Things Must Pass,* on John Lennon's *Imagine,* and on Ringo Starr's "It Don't Come Easy."

After its fourth album, 1973's *Ass,* sold disappointingly, Badfinger moved to Warner Bros. the following year for a reported $3 million advance. It proved a disastrous relationship. The group's second album for its new label, *Wish You Were Here,* was selling a brisk 25,000 copies a week when Warners, claiming (erroneously, it would turn out) that $600,000 in a band escrow account was missing, pulled the album from stores. In frustration over management problems, Molland quit. A despondent Ham, the leader and chief songwriter, hanged himself in his London home on April 23, 1975. Badfinger collapsed. Soon thereafter, Molland formed a group called Natural Gas in L.A. with former Humble Pie drummer Jerry Shirley; Evans returned to England to join the Dodgers. By 1978 Molland was installing carpets for a living, while Evans was a pipefitter. Together they revived Badfinger, releasing *Airwaves* in 1979 and *Say No More* in 1981. Each produced a minor hit in "Love Is Gonna Come at Last" and "Hold On," respectively. Business problems continued to haunt the group, which didn't see royalties from its days with Apple Records until 1985. Tragically by then Evans had committed suicide in the same manner as Ham. Molland and drummer Gibbins, now both living in America, still tour as Badfinger; Molland also has recorded several solo albums. The late '90s saw a renewed interest in the group's records, and a documentary film, *Badfinger,* appeared in 1997. The '90s Ham solo releases consist of demos from the '60s and '70s.

Erykah Badu

Born Erica Wright, Feb. 26, 1972, Dallas, TX
1997—*Baduizm* (Kedar/Universal); *Live* 2000—*Mama's Gun* (Motown/Universal).

Along with D'Angelo and Mary J. Blige, singer Erykah Badu championed the hip-hop/soul movement of the '90s. Her smooth voice, trademark head wrap, and majestic demeanor manifest sentiments of black pride, self-love, and female liberation. Badu's collaborations with the Roots, as well as with jazz bassist Ron Carter, trumpeter Roy Hargrove, and funk vibraphonist Roy Ayers, signify her strong ties to the new and old schools of black music.

The daughter of professional actress Kolleen Wright, Badu began playing piano around the age of seven. She graduated from Dallas' Booker T. Washington High School, an arts-oriented magnet school, and studied theater at Grambling State University in Louisiana. After performing locally and cutting a demo with her cousin, Badu opened a concert for D'Angelo and impressed D'Angelo manager Kedar Massenburg. Massenburg soon signed Badu to a solo deal for Universal and began transforming her demo into *Baduizm* (#2 pop, #1 R&B), which yielded the hits "On & On" (#12 pop, #1 R&B, 1997) and "Next Lifetime" (#61 pop, #1 R&B, 1997). An album that many critics would argue saved R&B music from complete dilution, *Baduizm*'s integration of jazzy instrumentation, hip-hop beats, and soaring vocals quickly solidified Badu as torchbearer for soul music and won her two Grammys: Best Female R&B Vocal Performance and Best R&B Album. Badu's next album, November 1997's *Live* (#4 pop, #1 R&B), brought her acclaimed live performances to the masses and yielded "Tyrone" (#62 pop, #1 R&B, 1997), an anthem about a woman's scorn for an oft-apathetic boyfriend.

In 1999 Badu plied her acting skills, appearing in *The Cider House Rules,* which was nominated for a Best Picture Oscar. She also recorded a couple of successful songs with her Roots counterparts: the Grammy Award–winning "You Got Me" (#39 pop, #11 R&B, 1999) and "Southern Girl" (#76 pop, #24 R&B, 1999) with human beat-box Rahzel. For her next album, *Mama's Gun* (#11 pop, #3 R&B), a soulful journey into the genres of rock and reggae, Badu enlisted Roots drummer Ahmir-Khalib "?uestlove" Thompson for several tracks. The album yielded another hit, "Bag Lady" (#6 pop, #1 R&B, 2000).

Joan Baez

Born Jan. 9, 1941, Staten Island, NY
1960—*Joan Baez* (Vanguard) 1961—*Joan Baez, vol. 2* 1962—*Joan Baez in Concert* 1963—*Joan Baez in Concert 2* 1964—*Joan Baez 5* 1965—*Farewell, Angelina* 1966—*Noel; Portrait* 1967—*Joan* 1968—*Baptism; Any Day Now* 1969—*David's Album* 1970—*One Day at a Time; First Ten Years* 1971—*Blessed Are . . .* 1972—*Carry It On; Come From the Shadows* (A&M); *The Joan Baez Ballad Book* (Vanguard) 1973—*Where Are You Now, My Son?; Hits/Greatest and Others* 1974—*Gracias a la Vida (Here's to Life)* (A&M) 1975—*Diamonds and Rust; Live in Japan* (Vanguard) 1976—*Love Song Album; From Every Stage* (A&M); *Gulf Winds* 1977—*Blowing Away* (Portrait); *Best of Joan* (A&M) 1979—*Honest Lullaby* (Portrait); *Country Music* (Vanguard) 1987—*Recently* (Gold Castle) 1989—*Diamonds and Rust in the Bullring; Speaking of Dreams* 1992—*Play Me Backwards* (Virgin) 1993—*Rare, Live and Classic* (Vanguard) 1995—*Ring Them Bells* (Guardian) 1997—*Gone From Danger.*

Joan Baez

Singer/songwriter Joan Baez was the perfect symbol of the early-'60s folk revival: young, sincere, technically gifted, and equally committed to traditional songs and social action. Though her biggest-selling album, *Diamonds and Rust,* was released in 1975, in the late '70s she found it increasingly difficult to be both commercial and socially conscious. During most of the '80s she all but ceased recording, concentrating instead on her political, humanitarian activities, only to revive her singing career in the '90s, as she connected with a new generation of (mostly female) singer/songwriters.

The daughter of a Mexican-American physicist father and Scottish drama teacher mother, Baez and her two sisters had traveled widely before her parents settled in Southern California by her early teens. A Quaker, Baez became involved with political issues while attending Boston University in the mid-'50s. Baez emerged from the 1959 Newport Folk Festival acclaimed for the purity of her three-octave voice. In the early '60s, she released several influential albums of sparsely arranged traditional folk material, and—largely through her association with the anthemic "We Shall Overcome"—she became a voice of the early-'60s civil rights movement.

Baez also played an important role in the rise of Bob Dylan by recording his songs and sharing concert bills with him in the early '60s. From 1963 until 1965, when their personal relationship disintegrated, Baez and Dylan were virtually inseparable. Nearly a decade later their romance provided the subject matter for Baez's hit "Diamonds and Rust." By 1975 the two were reconciled, and they sang duets in Dylan's Rolling Thunder Revue, captured on the fall 1976 TV special *Hard Rain.* Baez also appeared in Dylan's 1978 feature film, *Renaldo and Clara.*

By 1965 politics had become Baez's main concern. In that year, she founded in Carmel, California, the Institute for the Study of Nonviolence, signaling her increasing preoccupation with U.S. involvement in Vietnam. She later founded the Humanitas International Human Rights Committee (which she closed in 1992). In 1968 she married student protest leader David Harris, who was jailed for draft evasion a year later, fueling Baez's antiwar fervor (reflected in *David's Album* and *One Day at a Time*). The marriage ended in 1974, five years after the birth of their son, Gabriel. Baez's career suffered under the burden of her political commitment. At the height of her antiwar activities, she devoted the second side of *Where Are You Now, My Son?* to a quasi-documentary account of a U.S. bombing raid of Hanoi. But in the early '70s, she also made some of the most commercial music of her career, including her #3 rendition of the Band's "The Night They Drove Old Dixie Down" (a gold single in 1971) and *Diamonds and Rust.* Her voice had become lower and richer than in her folk phase.

Baez has remained politically active. In 1973 she was a vocal opponent of the coup in Chile and of the assassination of Socialist president Salvador Allende. In August 1981 Baez toured Latin America and was met with bomb threats and harassment. Later in the year, she met with U.S. government officials in Washington, DC, to discuss human rights in South America. A 90-minute TV special on the tour was scheduled for 1982 but was not shown. She has toured on behalf of Amnesty International, appeared at the Live Aid concert in 1985, and has since extended her activism to fighting on behalf of gay and prisoners' rights. In 2000 she participated in the Honor the Earth Tour organized by the Indigo Girls.

After venturing into uncharted pop territory on 1989's *Speaking of Dreams* (which featured a Spanish version of "My Way" and guest appearances by Jackson Browne, Paul Simon, and the Gipsy Kings), Baez reverted to classic folk mode and regular touring in the '90s. Her 1992 album, *Play Me Backwards,* was nominated for a Grammy for Best Contemporary Folk Recording, and on its followup, 1997's *Gone From Danger,* she interpreted songs written by a new generation of writers who in turn had been heavily influenced by her. Several of those singers and songwriters, such as Dar Williams, the Indigo Girls, Mary Chapin Carpenter, and Tish Hinojosa, joined Baez onstage at New York's Bottom Line nightclub for the shows that comprised the live *Ring Them Bells.* In 2000 she received a lifetime achievement award at the British Folk Awards.

Anita Baker

Born Dec. 20, 1957, Detroit, MI
1983—*The Songstress* (Beverly Glen) 1986—*Rapture* (Elektra) 1988—*Giving You the Best That I've Got* 1990—*Compositions* 1994—*Rhythm of Love.*

With the success of singer Anita Baker's *Rapture,* a new musical appellation came into being: "Quiet Storm." Baker's elegant, smoldering approach to R&B was a marked return to traditional vocalizing. In her controlled passion, Baker was reminiscent of one of her idols, jazz-pop singer Nancy Wilson.

After singing in church choirs as a child, Baker began her

professional career with the Detroit band Chapter 8, which released an eponymously titled album on Ariola in 1980. After moving to L.A. she recorded her first solo album, *The Songstress,* which yielded the #5 R&B hit "Angel" and won Baker the first of seven Grammy Awards to date. Despite legal difficulties from her former record label, Baker moved on to Elektra. *Rapture,* with its pop single "Sweet Love" (#8), was an immediate and influential hit, ultimately selling more than 6 million copies. Baker helped write some of *Rapture*'s most popular tunes, including "Sweet Love" and "Watch Your Step"; as executive producer, she also collaborated on production and arranging. Her next album, *Giving You the Best That I've Got,* went to #1, its title track single climbing to #3. *Compositions,* recorded live in the studio and featuring Baker's own songs, played up her jazz sensibilities. Despite spawning no hit singles, it still went platinum. In the years between *Compositions* and *Rhythm of Love* (#3 pop, #1 R&B, 1994), Baker sang with Frank Sinatra on his 1993 Reprise album, *Duets,* and gave birth to two sons.

Ginger Baker

Born Peter Baker, Aug. 19, 1939, Lewisham, Eng.
Ginger Baker's Air Force: 1970—*Air Force* (Atco); *Air Force 2.*
Ginger Baker solo: 1972—*Fela Ransome-Kuti and Africa '70 With Ginger Baker* (Signpost); *Stratavarious* (Polydor); *Ginger Baker at His Best* 1977—*Eleven Sides of Baker* (Sire) 1980—*Kuti and Africa* 1986—*Horses and Trees* (Celluloid) 1990—*Middle Passage* (Island/Axiom) 1992—*Unseen Rain* (Day Eight Music) 1998—*Do What You Like* (Chronicles/Polygram).
Baker-Gurvitz Army: 1975—*Baker-Gurvitz Army* (Janus); *Elysian Encounter* (Atco) 1976—*Hearts On Fire.*
With Masters of Reality: 1990—*Masters of Reality* (Delicious Vinyl/Island) 1993—*Sunrise on the Sufferbus* (Chrysalis).
BBM: (Baker, drums, perc.; Jack Bruce, bass, cello, voc.; Gary Moore, gtr., voc.) 1994—*Around the Next Dream* (Virgin).
The Ginger Baker Trio: 1994—*Going Back Home* (Atlantic) 1996—*Falling Off the Roof.*
With the DJ Q20 and James Carter: 1999—*Coward of the County* (Atlantic).

In the adulation that outlasted Cream [see entry], Ginger Baker was touted as a great drummer. "Toad," his lengthy live showcase, paved the way for a decade of heavy-metal drum solos, and he was one of the first rock drummers to incorporate third world rhythms into his style. He has since expanded his palette even further to incorporate jazz.

As a teenager Baker played with traditional jazz bands, but he got his first taste of R&B with Alexis Korner's Blues Incorporated when Charlie Watts left the group to join the fledgling Rolling Stones in 1962. A year later Baker and two other group members, singer Graham Bond and bassist Jack Bruce, formed the Graham Bond Organisation. He and Bruce remained until forming Cream with Eric Clapton in mid-1966. Over the course of two-plus years, Cream became a supergroup. After Cream split up in November 1968, Baker joined the short-lived Blind Faith [see entry].

Ginger Baker's Air Force debuted in January 1970. The percussion-dominated group was loosely structured, both in arrangements and personnel, which in various permutations included Stevie Winwood, Rick Grech, Bond, Denny Laine, and Remi Kabaka, one of three full-time drummers. Another drummer, Phil Seaman, and the members of Air Force encouraged Baker's growing interest in African music, and in 1971 he moved to Lagos, Nigeria, to build the first 16-track studio in West Africa. For the next few years he played with local talent, formed the group Salt, and ran his recording studio. Paul McCartney recorded *Band on the Run* there in 1973, by which time Baker had been musically inactive for many months. In 1974 he reemerged with the Baker-Gurvitz Army, which recorded three jazz-rock albums before disbanding in the late '70s. By then Baker was reportedly spending a lot of his time playing polo.

In the early '80s Baker moved to Milan, Italy, where he signed with CGD Records, formed a band with American musicians, and set up a drum school in a small mountain village. But mostly he ran an olive farm and tended to his health, for he'd only recently kicked a 21-year heroin addiction. In 1986 producer Bill Laswell coaxed the drummer to play on Public Image Ltd.'s *Album.* Baker relocated to California, then to Denver, Colorado, and recorded several LPs with Laswell behind the board and occasionally on bass. Baker has also teamed up with Masters of Reality for two albums to date, and in 1994 he released *Around the Next Dream* with Bruce and Gary Moore (Thin Lizzy). In 1993 Cream was inducted into the Rock and Roll Hall of Fame; at the ceremony, Baker, Clapton, and Bruce reunited for the first time since 1968 to perform some Cream songs.

In the mid- to late '90s, Baker began pushing his exploration of jazz further. In 1994 he formed the Ginger Baker Trio with bassist Charlie Haden and guitarist Bill Frisell and released *Going Back Home,* followed by *Falling Off the Roof* two years later. Baker also initiated the formation of the DJ Q20 (Denver Jazz Quintet-to-Octet) in 1995. Unfortunately, the group's recording sessions were interrupted by Baker's undergoing shoulder surgery. The album, *Coward of the County,* finally came out in 1999, around the time Baker relocated again, this time to South Africa.

LaVern Baker

Born Dolores Williams, Nov. 11, 1929, Chicago, IL; died Mar. 10, 1997, New York, NY
1958—*LaVern Baker Sings Bessie Smith* (Atlantic) 1970—*Let Me Belong to You* (Brunswick) 1971—*LaVern Baker: Her Greatest Recordings* (Atco) 1991—*LaVern Baker: Soul On Fire* (Rhino); *LaVern Baker: Live in Hollywood '91* 1992—*Woke Up This Mornin'* (DRG).

A major R&B vocalist during the '50s, LaVern Baker saw her career decline in the early '60s before she essentially retired. Her triumphant return to recording and performing in the late '80s is one of the rare happy endings in the history of early R&B. Baker first sang gospel as a little girl but was familiar with more secular styles; her aunt Merline Baker was better known as Memphis Minnie, a blues singer and guitarist. The singer got her first professional experience working at Chicago's Club DeLisa, where she appeared in the mid-'40s as Little Miss Sharecropper. She was soon signed by Columbia, but her recordings for that label were unsuccessful, as were her efforts for King beginning in 1952. Her luck changed with the emerging Atlantic label in 1953, where she cut tunes like "Tweedle Dee," "Bop-Ting-a-Ling," and "Play It Fair."

Ahmet Ertegun and Herb Abramson, who produced most of her sessions, started getting her stronger material in 1956. Rocking items like "Jim Dandy," "Jim Dandy Got Married," and "Voodoo Voodoo" established her as a major international R&B star in the late '50s, although her sales were perpetually hampered by white acts' cover versions. (At one point, the competition was so fierce that Baker fired off a letter to her Detroit congressman. All she got back was publicity.) Her only big pop hit came in 1959 with the ballad "I Cried a Tear" (#6), which featured King Curtis on sax. The followup, "I Waited Too Long," reached only #33. Although continuing to score minor hits through the early '60s ("Tiny Tim," "Shake a Hand," "Bumble Bee," "You're the Boss," "Saved," "See See Rider"), by the time she switched to Brunswick in 1963, her career was waning.

In 1969 Baker developed a case of pneumonia during a tour entertaining troops in Vietnam, forcing her to seek treatment in the Philippines. Nearly two decades passed before she journeyed back to the States from Subic Bay, where she had run a nightclub. The occasion was Atlantic Records' 40th-anniversary celebration in New York City in 1988. Shortly thereafter, she replaced Ruth Brown on Broadway in *Black and Blue,* and in 1990 she was given the Rhythm & Blues Foundation's Career Achievement Award. In 1990 she was inducted into the Rock and Roll Hall of Fame. Baker, a diabetic whose health worsened as the decade progressed, continued to perform to help pay for her medical expenses. She died in 1997.

John Baldry

Born Jan. 12, 1941, East Maddon-Doveshire, Eng.
1966—*Looking for Long John* (United Artists) 1971—*It Ain't Easy* (Warner Bros.); *Long John's Blues* 1972 *Everything Stops for Tea* 1974—*Heartaches (Golden Hour)* (Pye) 1976—*Baldry's Out* (EMI); *Welcome to Club Casablanca* (Casablanca) 1977—*Good to Be Alive* 1980—*Long John Baldry* 1981—*Rock With the Best* (Capitol, Can.) 1982—*Best of Long John Baldry* (EMI) 1991—*It Still Ain't Easy* (Stony Plain, Can.) 1996—*Right to Sing the Blues.*

Although sustained commercial success has eluded him, blues vocalist John Baldry's influence in the '60s on future British superstars was considerable. He grew up in the English countryside and began playing guitar at age 15. He played in Dixieland bands before becoming a solo performer on the English folk-club circuit. After touring Europe with Ramblin' Jack Elliott between 1957 and 1961, he turned to the blues and R&B.

Baldry (nicknamed Long John because of his six-foot-seven frame) came to prominence in Britain's early-'60s blues-rock scene. He played in Alexis Korner's Blues Incorporated (which at times included Jack Bruce, Ginger Baker, Mick Jagger, and Charlie Watts) until 1962, when he toured Germany with a jazz band for a few months.

Upon his return to England, he joined the Cyril Davies R&B All-Stars, and when Davies died in January 1964 from leukemia, Baldry recruited some of the All-Stars to start his own band, the Hoochie Coochie Men, which included Rod Stewart. The following year Baldry formed Steampacket with Stewart, Brian Auger, Julie Driscoll, drummer Mickey Waller (later with Jeff Beck), and guitarist Vic Briggs (later with the Animals). In 1966 he formed Bluesology; its roster included keyboardist Reg Dwight, who would later change his name to Elton John.

Beginning in 1967 Baldry had several hit pop ballads in the U.K. ("Let the Heartaches Begin," #1, 1967; "Mexico," #15, 1968), but he turned to blues and rock in 1971 and recorded *It Ain't Easy.* Former protégés John and Stewart each produced one side of the disc, which yielded a U.S. Top 100 single, "Don't Try to Lay No Boogie-Woogie on the King of Rock 'n' Roll." After spending a couple of months in a mental institution in 1976, Baldry released an LP titled *Baldry's Out.* Through the late '70s, Baldry toured the U.S. and Canada. He became a Canadian citizen in 1980, and, as of this writing, resides in Vancouver. Still active musically, Baldry is also often heard on commercial voiceovers. He has become something of a star to the kiddie set as the voice of Captain Robotnick, sworn enemy of the popular cartoon hero Sonic the Hedgehog. In 1998 Baldry was nominated for his first Grammy; he was recognized for narrating *The Original Story of Winnie the Pooh,* which appeared on a Disney read-along tape for preschoolers.

Marty Balin: See the Jefferson Airplane

Hank Ballard

Born Nov. 18, 1936, Detroit, MI
1992—*Naked in the Rain* (After Hours) 1993—*Sexy Ways: The Best of Hank Ballard and the Midnighters* (Rhino) 1998—*From Love to Tears* (Pool Party).

Hank Ballard earned distinction as a rock pioneer by laying sexually explicit lyrics over raw gospel-derived rhythms. With his backup group the Midnighters, he recorded several successful sides for the King label in the early '50s. In his best year, 1954, he had three R&B Top 10 hits with the "Annie" trilogy—"Work With Me, Annie," "Annie Had a Baby," and "Annie's Aunt Fanny"—each of which sold over a million copies internationally despite being widely banned from the airwaves. They made Ballard a top draw on the R&B circuit, although he did not have another major hit until "Teardrops on My Letter" in 1958.

While recording "Teardrops," he quickly composed a B-side novelty dance tune called "The Twist." In 1960 Chubby Checker's slicker version became one of early rock's best-selling singles. Ballard and the Midnighters had two hits in 1960, "Finger Poppin' Time" (#7) and "Let's Go, Let's Go, Let's Go" (#6). In 1963 he embarked on a solo career. By then his fortunes had waned, and he returned to playing soul clubs. Befitting a man whose biggest successes were risqué records, Ballard tried to promote his 1974 song "Let's Go Streaking" by recording it in the nude. Ballard, who continued to perform in clubs well into the '90s, was inducted into the Rock and Roll Hall of Fame in 1990, three months after his wife and manager, Theresa McNeil, was killed in a hit-and-run accident. He released an album of new material in 1998.

Afrika Bambaataa

Born Kevin Donovan, Apr. 10, 1960, Bronx, NY
1983—*Don't Stop . . . Planet Rock (The Remix EP)* (Tommy Boy) 1988—*The Light* (EMI) 1991—*1990–2000 The Decade of Darkness* 1993—*Time Zone* (Planet Rock) 1994—*12 Mixes* (ZYX) 1996—*Lost Generation* (Hot Production) 1999—*Afrika Bambaataa vs. Danmass: Electro Funk Express* (Dust II Dust).

Afrika Bambaataa was an important rap-music pioneer who, much like Grandmaster Flash, became a forgotten elder statesman as rap evolved. Bambaataa, who took his name (which means "affectionate leader") from a movie about Zulu warriors, quit the notorious Black Spades street gang in the mid-'70s and formed Zulu Nation, a music-oriented "youth organization." Among the members who became minor rap luminaries were DJs Red Alert, Jazzy Jay, and Whiz Kid, as well as Afrika Islam, who went on to work with Ice-T.

Bambaataa became a popular DJ on the nascent South Bronx rap scene, where his encyclopedic knowledge of funk grooves earned him the nickname "Master of Records." He formed two rap crews: the Jazzy 5 (with MCs Ice, Mr. Freeze, Master D.E.E., and AJ Les) and Soulsonic Force (Mr. Biggs [Ellis Williams], Pow Wow [Robert Darrell Allen], and Emcee G.L.O.B.E. [John B. Miller]). Each made its debut 12-inch single in 1980: Jazzy 5's "Jazzy Sensation" and Soulsonic Force's "Zulu Nation Throwdown," both classic proto-hip-hop party anthems, with round-robin rapping backed by live bands playing slinky funk vamps.

In 1982 Bambaataa and Soulsonic Force dropped the live band to go high-tech. Producer Arthur Baker (who had worked on "Jazzy Sensation") and synthesizer player John Robie provided electronic "beat-box" rhythm and an eerie keyboard hook modeled on "TransEurope Express" by Kraftwerk, whose robotic trance music had long been popular with inner-city youth. The result was "Planet Rock," a pop hit (#48, 1982) that went gold and spawned an entire school of "electro-boogie" rap and dance music.

While Bambaataa continued to exert some influence on rap music, "Planet Rock" turned out to be his only hit. Bambaataa's groundbreaking tracks that failed to chart include 1982's "Looking for the Perfect Beat" (sampled in Duice's 1993 rap-dance hit "Dazzey Duks" [#12]); 1983's "Renegades of Funk" (on which G.L.O.B.E. pioneered the rapid-fire "poppin' " style of rap later popularized by Big Daddy Kane and Das EFX); 1984's "World Destruction" by Time Zone, a rap-rock fusion unit featuring Bambaataa, ex–Sex Pistol John Lydon, and bassist/producer Bill Laswell; and 1984's "Unity," which Bambaataa recorded with rap forebear James Brown. Even Bambaataa's and Soulsonic Force's appearance in the 1984 rap movie *Beat Street* brought problems: Emcee G.L.O.B.E. and Pow Wow were arrested for their roles in a 1979 Manhattan bank holdup, when a policeman watching the movie recognized Pow Wow from the bank surveillance video. G.L.O.B.E. and Pow Wow were later put on probation and received community service sentences for convictions on conspiracy to commit bank robbery.

Bambaataa has remained active if not commercially successful. *The Light* featured guests George Clinton, Sly and Robbie, Boy George, and UB40. *Decade of Darkness* collected dance-oriented tracks produced for an Italian label. Bambaataa formed his own label to release the *Time Zone* compilation. The rise of "turntablism" as its own subgenre and the ratification of "electronica" as an industry-certified trend in the late '90s brought Bambaataa renewed recognition well beyond the hip-hop community. Each year brings a new batch of remixes on multiple dance and import labels, and updates of his signature hit. *Lost Generation* sports "Planet Rock '96," and the millennium would not have been complete without the release of "Planet Rock 2000."

Bananarama/Shakespear's Sister

Formed late 1981, London, Eng.
Sarah Dallin (b. Dec. 17, 1960, Bristol, Eng.), voc.; Keren Woodward (b. Apr. 2, 1961, Bristol), voc.; Siobhan Fahey (b. Sep. 10, 1960, Ire.), voc.
1983—*Deep Sea Skiving* (London) 1984—*Bananarama* 1986—*True Confessions* 1987—*Wow!* 1988—(– Fahey; + Jacqui O'Sullivan, voc.) *The Greatest Hits Collection* 1991—*Pop Life* 1992—(– O'Sullivan) *Please Yourself* 1996—*Ultra Violet* (Curb).
Shakespear's Sister: Fahey, voc.; Marcella Detroit (b. Marcella Levy, June 21, ca. 1954, Detroit, MI), voc., gtr.
1989—*Sacred Heart* (ffrr-PolyGram) 1992—*Hormonally Yours* (London).
Marcella Detroit solo: 1994—*Jewel* (London).

Bananarama was one of the most successful British girl groups in pop history despite the original trio's inability to play instruments and refusal to do concert tours. Musically, Bananarama (the name combines the late-'60s kids' show *The Banana Splits* and Roxy Music's "Pyjamarama") presented fluffy pop tunes and a girly image that won fans and sold records.

Woodward and Dallin were childhood friends. Dallin met Fahey at the London College of Fashion, and the three began singing at friends' parties. Bananarama's first single was produced by ex–Sex Pistols drummer Paul Cook. The trio sang backup on Fun Boy Three's "It Ain't What You Do, It's the Way That You Do It," and the guys returned the favor on Bananarama's first U.K. hit, "He Was Really Sayin' Somethin'," which was a minor 1965 hit for Motown's Velvelettes. *Deep Sea Skiving* collected Bananarama's earliest singles. *Bananarama* was produced and cowritten by Swain and Jolley (Spandau Ballet, Alison Moyet) and gave the group its first U.S. hit, "Cruel Summer" (#9, 1984). The song was big in England a year before it broke in the U.S.; the band always had greater success at home (although the British press hated the trio). "Robert De Niro's Waiting," Bananarama's second single, got little airplay in the States.

Bananarama switched producers to Stock/Aitken/Waterman (Kylie Minogue, Rick Astley) while recording *True Confessions* (#15, 1986), and the team (who produced two of the album's tracks) delivered the smash cover of Shocking Blue's 1970 #1 hit "Venus" (#1, 1986). S/A/W produced *Wow!*, which featured "Love in the First Degree" and "I Heard a Rumour" (#4, 1987) (used in the Fat Boys movie *Disorderlies*).

In 1987 Fahey married the Eurythmics' Dave Stewart and a few months later left Bananarama. She was replaced on *Pop Life* by Jacqui O'Sullivan, formerly of the Shilelagh Sisters. That album was produced primarily by ex–Killing Joke bassist Youth and included a cover of the Doobie Brothers' "Long Train Running." O'Sullivan left the group in mid-1991, and Bananarama continued as a duo, releasing 1992's *Please Yourself* before being dropped from its record label the following year.

Fahey formed Shakespear's Sister with Marcella Detroit, who in the '70s toured with Eric Clapton and cowrote "Lay Down Sally." Shakespear's Sister's first single, "You're History," made it clear that Fahey was eager to leave Bananarama behind. The band's name came from a Smiths song, which was itself inspired by a Virginia Woolf essay lamenting the lack of credit given to female artists. Although its records have been self-consciously artsy and strange, Shakespear's Sister had a major pop hit with a song from its second album, the ballad "Stay" (#4, 1992).

Shakespear's Sister called it quits in 1993, and Detroit released her solo debut, *Jewel*, the following year. In 1996 Dallin and Woodward resurfaced with a new Bananarama album, *Ultra Violet*. The duo continues to perform, mostly overseas, and according to U.K. sources, has a new album in the works.

The Band

Formed 1967, Woodstock, NY
James Robbie Robertson (b. July 5, 1944, Toronto, Can.), gtr.; Richard Manuel (b. Apr. 3, 1945, Stratford, Can.; d. Mar. 4, 1986, Winter Park, FL), piano, voc.; Garth Hudson (b. Aug. 2, ca. 1943, London, Can.), organ, sax; Rick Danko (b. Dec. 29, 1942, Simcoe, Can., d. Dec. 10, 1999, Woodstock, NY), bass, viola, voc.; Levon Helm (b. May 26, 1940, Marvell, AR), drums, voc., mandolin.
1968—*Music From Big Pink* (Capitol) 1969—*The Band* 1970—*Stage Fright* 1971—*Cahoots* 1972—*Rock of Ages* 1973—*Moondog Matinee* 1975—*Northern Lights—Southern Cross* 1976—*The Best of the Band* (group disbands) 1977—*Islands* 1978—*The Last Waltz* (Warner Bros.); *Anthology* (Capitol) 1993—(group re-forms: Helm; Danko; Hudson; + Jim Weider, gtr.; + Randy Ciarlante, drums, voc.; + Richard Bell, kybds.) *Jericho* (Pyramid) 1994—*Across the Great Divide* (Capitol) 1995—*Live at Watkins Glen* 1996—*High on the Hog* (Pyramid) 1998—*Jubilation* (River North) 2000—*Greatest Hits* (Capitol).
Robbie Robertson solo: 1987—*Robbie Robertson* (Geffen) 1991—*Storyville* 1998—*Contact From the Underworld of Red Boy* (Capitol).
Robbie Robertson and the Red Road Ensemble: 1994—*Music for "The Native Americans"* (Capitol).
Levon Helm solo: 1977—*Levon Helm and the RCO All-Stars* (ABC) 1978—*Levon Helm* 1980—*American Son* (MCA) 1982—*Levon Helm* (Capitol).
Rick Danko solo: 1977—*Rick Danko* (Arista) 1997—*In Concert* (Woodstock) 1999—*Live on Breeze Hill* (Breeze Hill).
Danko/Fjeld/Andersen: 1991—*Danko/Fjeld/Andersen* (Rykodisc) 1994—*Riding on the Blinds*.
Jim Weider solo: 1999—*Big Foot* (Paras Recording).

With its rock-ribbed, austerely precise arrangements and a catalogue of songs that linked American folklore to primal myths, the Band—four Canadians and a Southerner—made music that was both earthy and mystical, still unsurpassed in its depth and originality. The group had been playing together for most of a decade before it recorded its first album in 1968. Beginning with Levon Helm, the five members joined rockabilly singer Ronnie Hawkins' Hawks one by one, and by 1960 the future Band members had all been with Hawkins on and off, an association that continued until 1963. They then began working on their own, variously as Levon and the Hawks, or the Crackers, or the Canadian Squires. Singer John Hammond heard them in a Canadian club in 1964 and asked them to perform and record with him in New York, Chicago, and Texas.

Once active in Greenwich Village, the group attracted Bob Dylan's attention. Helm and Robbie Robertson were in the electrified backup band at Dylan's controversial Forest Hills, New York, concert of August 28, 1965. Despite a falling-out between Dylan and Helm, Dylan hired the Hawks—with drummer Mickey Jones in lieu of Helm—for his 1965–66 world tour, inaugurating a longtime collaboration.

After Dylan's 1966 motorcycle accident, the group settled near the suddenly reclusive star in the Woodstock, New York, area. Helm rejoined, and while recording extensively with Dylan (the much-bootlegged sessions were released in 1975 as *The Basement Tapes*), they began working on their own material, most of it written by Robertson and Richard Manuel. Recorded in a basement studio in the group's house (Big Pink) in West Saugerties, the material made up the Band's debut album. With its unflashy sound and enigmatic lyrics, *Music From Big Pink* was a revolutionary album.

The group moved to Hollywood, but its second album, *The Band*, was a celebration of rural life and the past. It was the group's masterpiece and commercial breakthrough, and the quintet undertook its first headlining tour to support it.

The Band: Rick Danko, Levon Helm, Richard Manuel, Garth Hudson, Robbie Robertson

Robertson was emerging as chief songwriter as well as producer, and his impressions of the road inspired the Band's third album, *Stage Fright*. After 1971's *Cahoots* (with an appearance by Van Morrison), the Band recorded a double live LP, *Rock of Ages*, followed in 1973 by a tribute to early rock & roll (*Moondog Matinee*, named after Alan Freed's radio show).

With the exception of a joint appearance in 1969 at the Isle of Wight Festival in Britain, the Band rarely worked with Dylan in the early '70s. But shortly after the Band played before a crowd of nearly 600,000 at the 1993 Watkins Glen rock festival with the Grateful Dead and the Allman Brothers Band (documented on a 1995 live album), the group joined Dylan in the studio for his *Planet Waves*. The next year, they toured together and produced the live album *Before the Flood*. The Band's output continued to slow through the '70s. In November 1975 the group released its first new material in four years, *Northern Lights—Southern Cross*, followed two years later by *Islands*. Robertson produced an album for Neil Diamond, *Beautiful Noise*, in 1976. After 16 years together, the Band called it quits with a gala concert on Thanksgiving Day 1976. The Band and guests (including Dylan, Morrison, Neil Young, Muddy Waters, Joni Mitchell, and Neil Diamond) performed at San Francisco's Winterland (the site of its first concert as the Band in 1969) for *The Last Waltz*, filmed by Martin Scorsese.

After the breakup, Helm continued to record and tour with the RCO All-Stars, an aggregation that included Dr. John, Paul Butterfield, Steve Cropper, Duck Dunn, and Booker T. Jones; the Cate Brothers; and Danko. He made his acting debut in 1980 in *Coal Miner's Daughter* and has since appeared in several other films. Robertson starred in and composed part of the score for 1980's *Carny* and wrote music for Scorsese's *The King of Comedy* before releasing his first solo album in 1987. *Robbie Robertson*, produced by Daniel Lanois, received tremendous media attention and went gold; 1991's *Storyville*, however, fared poorly. In 1994 Robertson, whose mother was of Mohawk Indian descent, composed the soundtrack to a six-hour television documentary, *The Native Americans*, which featured American Indian musicians collectively dubbed the Red Road Ensemble. He continued to explore Native American music—with a trip-hop twist—on the adventurous *Contact From the Underworld of Red Boy*. Danko, too, recorded on his own, releasing his solo debut in 1977 and a pair of albums with singer/songwriter Eric Andersen and Norwegian folksinger Jonas Fjeld in the '90s.

The Band regrouped in 1983 with guitarist Jimmy Weider replacing Robertson, who'd declined an invitation to join. On March 4, 1986, following an appearance at the Cheek to Cheek Lounge in Winter Park, Florida, Manuel returned to his room and hanged himself with a belt. His body contained traces of cocaine and alcohol. The three remaining originals carried on with a variety of backing musicians. In 1993 they released the Band's first album of new material in 16 years, *Jericho*, which included interpretations of Bruce Springsteen's "Atlantic City" and Bob Dylan's "Blind Willie McTell," as well as their own compositions.

In 1994 the Band was inducted into the Rock and Roll Hall of Fame. Robertson turned out for the ceremony, but Helm stayed home. As he made abundantly clear in his 1993 autobiography, *This Wheel's on Fire*, the drummer bitterly resented Robertson for allegedly having claimed sole writing credit for collaborative efforts. *Across the Great Divide*, a three-disc box set, was released the same year.

With the same lineup as for *Jericho*—Helm, Danko, Hudson, Weider, Randy Ciarlante on vocals and drums, and Richard Bell on keyboards—the Band released *High on the Hog* in 1996, followed by *Jubilation* (featuring guests Eric Clapton and John Hiatt) two years later. In 1996 Danko was found guilty of colluding to smuggle heroin into Japan (after legal wrangling, he was eventually released from custody and left Japan). Hudson and Weider both sat in with Danko for his 1999 outing, *Live on Breeze Hill,* but on December 10 of that year, three weeks shy of his 57th birthday, Danko died in his sleep at his home in Woodstock, New York. He had returned home from a tour earlier that week and had been recording songs for what would have been his first new solo studio album in 22 years.

In 2000 Capitol began to reissue the Band's original albums, all embellished with extensive bonus tracks and outtakes.

The Bangles

Formed 1981, Los Angeles, CA
Susanna Hoffs (b. Jan. 17, 1959, Los Angeles), gtr., voc.; Debbi Peterson (b. Aug. 22, 1961, Los Angeles), drums, voc.; Vicki Peterson (b. Jan. 11, 1958, Los Angeles), gtr., voc.; Annette Zilinskas (b. Nov. 6, 1964, Van Nuys, CA), bass, voc.
1982—*Bangles* EP (Faulty Products) 1984—(– Zilinskas; + Michael Steele [b. June 2, 1955, Pasadena, CA], bass, voc.) *All Over the Place* (Columbia) 1985—*Different Light* 1988—*Everything* 1990—*Greatest Hits* 1998—*Super Hits* (Sony).
Susanna Hoffs solo: 1991—*When You're a Boy* (Columbia) 1996—*Susanna Hoffs* (London).
Debbi Peterson with Kindred Spirit: 1994—*Kindred Spirit* (I.R.S.).
Vicki Peterson with the Continental Drifters: 1994—*Continental Drifters* (Monkey Hill) 1999—*Vermilion* (Razor & Tie) 2001—*Better Day.*

The Bangles wanted to be an all-girl Beatles from California: four pop stars who played competently, wrote good songs, and had distinct personalities. The group formed when a "band members wanted" ad in an L.A. newspaper led Hoffs to the Peterson sisters. The group first called themselves the Colours, followed by the Supersonic Bangs, which they shortened to the Bangs. When a group with prior claim to that moniker showed up, they became the Bangles. Early on, the group was heralded as part of L.A.'s "paisley underground," a constellation of folky psychedelic bands that included the Rain Parade and the Dream Syndicate. After establishing a reputation through a self-released single and live shows, the band signed a management deal with I.R.S. Records head Miles Copeland.

In 1983 the Bangles signed to Columbia. Bass player Zilinskas quit and joined Blood on the Saddle; she was replaced by Michael Steele, who had once sung for the Runaways. Veteran power-pop producer David Kahne produced *All Over the Place,* which featured such classic Bangles songs as "Hero Takes a Fall" and Kimberley Rew's (Soft Boys, Katrina and the Waves) "Going Down to Liverpool." The record initially sold a respectable 150,000 copies and earned critical praise. After seeing the video for "Hero Takes a Fall," Prince became a fan of the Bangles, particularly of Hoffs. He gave them the song "Manic Monday" (#2, 1986), written under the pseudonym Christopher; the single paved the way for the breakthrough success of *Different Light* (#2, 1986). The Kahne-produced album included "Walk Like an Egyptian" (#1, 1986), Jules Shear's "If She Knew What She Wants" (#29, 1986), "Walking Down Your Street" (#11, 1987), and a cover of Alex Chilton's "September Gurls." In 1987 the Bangles' version of Paul Simon's "Hazy Shade of Winter" from the *Less Than Zero* soundtrack became their second #1.

Everything (#15, 1988) yielded the hits "In Your Room" (#5, 1988) and "Eternal Flame" (#1, 1989). The group's plan to share songwriting, vocals, and fame had been steadily eroded by the media's focus on Hoffs, especially in light of her feature role in the largely forgotten 1987 film *The All-nighter,* which her mother, Tamar Hoffs, cowrote, directed, and produced. The other Bangles resented the star treatment and the musical direction in which it pushed the band. In late 1989 the group broke up.

Hoffs' first solo album (produced by Kahne) featured songs by or cowritten with such diverse figures as Diane Warren, Cyndi Lauper, and Juliana Hatfield. A version of David Bowie's "Boys Keep Swinging" (with the Who's John Entwistle on bass) gave the album its title, *When You're a Boy.* Vicki Peterson began collaborating with Susan Cowsill; they billed themselves as the Psycho Sisters and played clubs backed by the Continental Drifters (which the two eventually joined), and also sang backup for Giant Sand. In 1994 Peterson joined the Go-Go's' reunion tour, filling in for Charlotte Caffey, who was pregnant. Debbi Peterson formed the band Kindred Spirit, which released a self-titled album on I.R.S. in 1994.

Hoffs released her second solo album in 1996. The record included hidden bonus covers of Stealers Wheel's "Stuck in the Middle With You" and Lulu's "To Sir With Love." Hoffs and Debbi Peterson began writing together again in 1998, and the entire group reunited in 1999 to record "Get the Girl" for the movie *Austin Powers: The Spy Who Shagged Me.* In June 1999 the Bangles sang with the Los Angeles Philharmonic, conducted by George Martin, in a tribute to the Beatles at the Hollywood Bowl. The following year the band began recording a new album and in September 2000 embarked on a brief tour.

The Barbarians

Formed 1963, Provincetown, MA
Jerry Causi, bass; Jeff Morris, gtr.; Bruce Benson, gtr.; Moulty (b. Victor Moulton, Feb. 24, 1945, Greenfield, MA), drums.
N.A.—*The Barbarians* (Laurie) 1979—*The Barbarians* (Rhino).

A classic mid-'60s protopunk garage band, the Barbarians boasted a drummer named Moulty who had a hook for a left hand (the result of an accident with a homemade pipe bomb when he was 14). He sang many of the band's songs, including the autobiographical "Moulty" (#90, 1966), in which he implored, "Don't turn away," and spoke of meeting "a girl, a real girl." Members of Levon and the Hawks (later known as the Band) backed Moulty on that track. The group had a minor hit with "Are You a Boy or Are You a Girl" (#55, 1965), a reference to the band's prepsychedelic long hair. The Barbarians appeared in the mid-'60s documentary *The T.A.M.I.*

Show. Moulty now operates a cleaning service and is involved in real estate in Massachusetts. In the mid-'90's he formed a new Barbarians lineup that included two of his sons.

Barclay James Harvest

Formed 1967, Oldham, Eng.
Stewart "Wooly" Wolstenholme (b. Apr. 15, 1947, Oldham), kybds., voc.; Melvyn John Pritchard (b. Jan. 20, 1948, Oldham), drums; John Lees (b. Jan. 13, 1947, Oldham), gtr., voc.; Les Holroyd (b. Mar. 12, 1948, Bolton, Eng.), bass, voc.
1970—*Barclay James Harvest* (Capitol) 1971—*Once Again* (Sire) 1972—*Early Morning Onward* (EMI); *Barclay James Harvest* (Sire) 1973—*Baby James Harvest* (Capitol) 1974—*Live* (Polydor); *Everyone Is Everybody Else* 1975—*Time Honoured Ghosts* 1976—*Octoberon* (MCA) 1977—*Gone to Earth* 1978—*Live Tapes* (Polydor); *XXI* 1979—*Best Of, vol. 2* (Harvest) (– Wolstenholme) 1980—*Eyes of the Universe* (Polydor) 1992—*Best of Barclay James Harvest* 1993—*Caught in the Light.*

This English art-rock band has developed a loyal cult following in its homeland, though only one album, 1976's *Octoberon,* has ever charted in the U.S. With a remarkably consistent personnel record for a veteran band that's never been financially successful, BJH has carried on for more than 25 years. Like the nascent Pink Floyd, with whom it is often compared, BJH was a hard-rock group with classical overtones when it signed to EMI/Parlophone in 1968. The group turned a frequently heard criticism—"poor man's Moody Blues"—into a song title on its 1977 LP *Gone to Earth.*

Barclay James Harvest was formed by art-school classmates John Lees and Stewart "Woolly" Wolstenholme. Beginning in 1970 EMI released its albums on a subsidiary label, Harvest, which was named after the promising BJH. But the promise never panned out, leaving BJH as a minor British attraction supported by an enthusiastic but limited cult. It released a number of albums in the '80s, but none in the U.S. Cofounder Wolstenholme left the group in 1979 and recorded a 1980 solo album, *Maestro.*

Barenaked Ladies

Formed 1988, Toronto, Can.
Steven Page (b. June 22, 1970, North York, Can.), voc., gtr.; Ed Robertson (b. Oct. 25, 1970), gtr., voc.; Jim Creeggan (b. Feb. 12, 1970, Toronto), bass; Tyler Stewart (b. Sep. 21, 1967, Toronto), drums; Andrew Creeggan, kybds.
1992—*Gordon* (Sire/Reprise) 1994—*Maybe You Should Drive* (– A. Creeggan) 1996—*Born on a Pirate Ship* (+ Kevin Hearn [b. July 3, 1969, Grinsby, Can.], kybds.) 1997—*Rock Spectacle* 1998—*Stunt* 2000—*Maroon.*

After a decade of mainstream success in their native Canada, the Barenaked Ladies finally hit big in America with their fifth album, *Stunt,* and its #1 smash, "One Week." A deliberately silly hybrid of pop and "rap," the song and its accompanying video were unavoidable during the summer of 1998, establishing the Ladies as the biggest Canadian crossover act since Alanis Morissette and Sarah McLachlan.

Cofrontmen and childhood friends Steven Page and Ed Robertson began writing music together after attending a summer music camp in 1988. After a couple of years performing in Toronto as a duo, Page and Robertson were joined by Tyler Stewart and brothers Jim and Andrew Creeggan, and in 1991 the band released an independent EP, *The Yellow Tape.* They were quickly signed to Sire/Reprise, which issued the band's debut album, *Gordon,* in 1992. The set reprised the hit "Be My Yoko Ono" from *The Yellow Tape* and also featured the Canadian hits "Brian Wilson" and "If I Had $1,000,000." Subsequent releases, *Maybe You Should Drive* (1994) and *Born on a Pirate Ship* (1996), didn't sell nearly as well, but produced enough Canadian hits to keep them on the pop radar. In 1997 the live album *Rock Spectacle* provided the group its first hint at U.S. success; although it only made it to #108 on the album chart, two of the album's songs cracked the Hot 100—the bittersweet "The Old Apartment" (#88) and "Brian Wilson" (#68). When *Stunt* was released the following summer, it debuted at #3.

Just before *Stunt* hit big, keyboardist Keven Hearn (who had joined in 1996, two years after Andrew Creeggan's departure) was diagnosed with leukemia. (His treatments seemed to put the disease in remission.) In 2000, Barenaked Ladies released *Maroon* (#5). Although it didn't produce a hit on the level of "One Week," the song "Pinch Me" climbed to #15.

The Bar-Kays

Formed mid-'60s, Memphis, TN
Original lineup: Jimmy King (b. 1949; d. Dec. 10, 1967, Madison, WI), gtr.; Ron Caldwell (b. 1948; d. Dec. 10, 1967, Madison), organ; Phalin Jones (b. 1949; d. Dec. 10, 1967, Madison), sax; Carl Cunningham (b. 1949; d. Dec. 10, 1967, Madison), drums; Ben Cauley, trumpet; James Alexander, bass.
1967—*Soul Finger* (Volt) 1969—*Gotta Groove* (Stax) 1982—*Night Cruisin'* (Mercury) 1984—*Dangerous* 1985—*Banging the Wall* 1987—*Contagious* 1989—*Bar-Kays: Animal* 1994—*48 Hours* (Basix) 1996—*Best of Bar-Kays* (Curb).

The Bar-Kays were part of the Stax-Volt roster in the mid-'60s and had one big hit, "Soul Finger" (#17), in 1967. The band's career seemed finished when four members died in the icy plane crash that also killed Otis Redding in 1967. Bassist James Alexander, who'd missed the flight, and trumpeter Ben Cauley, the only passenger to survive the accident, re-formed the group in late 1968, although Cauley quit soon after. For many years Alexander and a changing roster of Bar-Kays consistently placed singles on the R&B chart and enjoyed the occasional pop hit, such as "Shake Your Rump to the Funk" (#23, 1976). The '80s saw five R&B Top 10s for the group: "Boogie Body Land" (#7, 1980), "Hit and Run" (#5, 1981), "Do It (Let Me See You Shake)" (#9, 1982), "Freakshow on the Dance Floor" (#2, 1984) (from the hip-hop film *Breakin'*), and "Certified True" (#9, 1987).

Regarded as one of soul's premier backing bands, the Bar-Kays worked in the early '70s with such artists as the Staple Singers, Albert King, Carla Thomas, Johnnie Taylor, and Isaac Hayes. They backed the latter on his Grammy Award–winning "Shaft" in 1971. Several excellent R&B musicians have passed through the Bar-Kays' ranks, including vocalist Vernon Burch and drummer Willie Hall, who went on to play in Hayes' band for several years and then joined the revamped Booker T. and the MG's in 1975. Since 1987 the Bar-Kays lineup has remained fairly stable, with vocalist Larry Dodson and Alexander still at the helm.

Syd Barrett

Born Roger Keith Barrett, Jan. 6, 1946, Cambridge, Eng.
1970—*The Madcap Laughs* (Harvest); *Barrett* (Capitol)
1987—*Peel Sessions* (Harvest) 1989—*Opel* (Capitol)
1994—*Crazy Diamond—The Complete Syd Barret* (EMI); *Octopus* (Cleopatra).

British singer/songwriter/guitarist Syd Barrett was an art-school student in London when he founded and named Pink Floyd [see entry] in 1964. He wrote "See Emily Play" and "Piper at the Gates of Dawn" for the group, and his acid-inspired lyrics were the quintessence of London's 1967 Summer of Love. Barrett was dismissed from the band in April 1968 because of his drug-induced personality problems; David Gilmour replaced him after covering for him when he began missing shows. Barrett released two intriguing but poor-selling solo albums in 1970. He appeared on John Peel's BBC radio show (released on album in 1987) and did a couple of gigs with a loose-knit band called Stars. He has basically been living in Cambridge as a recluse since 1972, and in recent years has suffered from declining health. Pink Floyd dedicated a popular 1975 song, "Shine On, You Crazy Diamond," to its eccentric founder. Barrett's surreal songwriting and atmospheric sound has influenced such artists as Robyn Hitchcock and Julian Cope. As of 2000, Barrett, an insulin-dependent diabetic, was reportedly almost totally blind due to complications from the disease.

Syd Barrett

Basehead

Formed Apr. 1990, Washington, DC
Michael Ivey (b. Feb. 5, 1968, Pittsburgh, PA), voc., gtr., kybds., bass, perc.; Brian Hendrix (b. July 29, 1968, Pittsburgh), drums, perc.; DJ Unique (b. Paul Howard), DJ.
1991—*Play With Toys* (Emigre) (– Howard; + Keith Lofton [b. May 9, 1967, Washington, DC], gtr.; + Bill Conway [b. Nov. 29, 1967, Washington, DC], bass; + Clarence "Citizen Cope" Greenwood [b. May 20, 1965, Washington, DC], DJ) 1993—*Not in Kansas Anymore* (Imago) 1996—*Faith.*

Featuring a scratching DJ and spoken-sung vocals by group leader Michael Ivey, Basehead defied simple categorization. Ivey mumbled or sleepily crooned his wryly ironic lyrics over quirky, quietly rockish arrangements in a hip-hop/college rock hybrid critics termed "slacker rap," while comparing Ivey to Lou Reed, Tom Waits, and Sly Stone.

A middle-class black kid who grew up learning guitar, Ivey formed high school bands with fellow Pittsburgh native Brian Hendrix, then complained about the lack of guitar parts in their keyboard-dominated R&B covers. While studying film at Howard University, Ivey (who made his directing debut with the video "Do You Wanna Fuck [or What]?" from *Not in Kansas Anymore*) recorded *Play With Toys* almost exclusively himself. The album signaled its offbeat genre crossing by opening with Ivey, as "Jethro and the Graham Crackers," performing a hillbilly version of James Brown's "Sex Machine" to the sound of audience catcalls.

The tiny West Coast label Emigre released 3,000 copies of *Play With Toys* to considerable college-radio play and rave reviews. Ivey recruited friends from Howard for a 1991 tour with "alternative rap" acts Me Phi Me, Disposable Heroes of Hiphoprisy, and Divine Styler. The Basehead band also played on three tracks of the *Kansas* album, which backed Ivey's deadpan takes on racial and sexual politics with a somewhat harder sound. In 1996 Basehead released *Faith.* Guitarist Keith Lofton, working as Lazy K, released a solo effort, *Life in One Day* (Mutant Sound System), the next year.

Basia

Born Basia Trzetrzelewska, Sep. 30, 1956, Jaworzno, Pol.
1987—*Time and Tide* (Epic) 1989—*London Warsaw New York* 1991—*Brave New Hope* EP 1994—*The Sweetest Illusion* 1995—*Basia on Broadway* 1998—*Clear Horizon: The Best of Basia* (Sony).

The Polish-born Basia crossed the Iron Curtain in the '80s to become an international pop singer and fixture on "jazz-lite" stations everywhere. Born in the industrial city of Jaworzno, she first performed with the all-female group Ali Babki in 1975, touring the Soviet bloc for two years. In 1979 she moved to Chicago to sing with a cover band in a Polish-American club. Two years later she was in London, singing for the jazz-funk group Bronze. She then joined Matt Bianco, a threesome whose hit record, *Whose Side Are You On?*, featured a smooth pop blend of jazz and Latin styles. In 1985 Basia left Matt Bianco to go solo, taking keyboardist Danny White with her as cowriter. Her first album, the platinum *Time and Tide* (#36, 1988), yielded the pop hits "Time and Tide" (#26, 1988) and "New Day for You" (#53, 1989). She continued to explore soul, samba, swing, and bossa nova on *London Warsaw New York* (#20, 1990), a platinum album that featured the single "Cruising for Bruising" (#29, 1990). *The Sweetest Illusion* (1994) included more Latin-tinged material, including the salsa-styled "An Olive Tree."

The Sweetest Illusion didn't sell nearly as well as its predecessors, and the singer followed it up with the 1995 live set, *Basia on Broadway*. Culled from dates during Basia's engagement at New York City's Neil Simon Theatre, the album consists of hits and new material; one track features saxophonist Jay Beckenstein from the MOR jazz combo Spyro Gyra. Basia's 1998 best-of includes four songs previously unreleased in the U.S.

Bauhaus/Peter Murphy/ Love and Rockets

Formed 1979, Northampton, Eng.
Peter Murphy (b. July 11, 1957, Northampton), voc.; Daniel Ash (b. July 31, 1957, Northampton), gtr., voc., sax, kybds., bass; David J (a.k.a. David Jay, b. David J. Haskins, Apr. 24, 1957, Northampton), bass, voc., kybds., gtr.; Kevin Haskins (b. July 19, 1960, Northampton), drums, kybds.
1980—*In the Flat Field* (4AD, U.K.) 1981—*Mask* (Beggars Banquet, U.K.) 1982—*The Sky's Gone Out* (A&M) 1983—*Burning From the Inside* (group disbands) 1989—*Swing the Heartache: The BBC Sessions* (Beggars Banquet/RCA) 1998—(group re-forms) *Crackle* (Beggars Banquet) 1999—*Gotham* (Metropolis).
Peter Murphy solo: 1986—*Should the World Fail to Fall Apart* (Beggars Banquet, U.K.) 1988—*Love Hysteria* (Beggars Banquet/RCA) 1990—*Deep* 1992—*Holy Smoke* 1995—*Cascade* (Beggars Banquet/Atlantic) 2000—*Wild Birds: 1985–1995.*
Tones on Tail, formed 1981, Eng.: Ash; Glenn Campling, bass, voc.
1983—(+ Haskins) 1985—(group disbands) 1986—*"Pop"* (Beggars Banquet/PVC) 1987—*Night Music* 1990—*Tones on Tail* (Beggars Banquet/RCA) 1998—*Everything!* (Beggars Banquet).
Love and Rockets, formed 1985, Eng.: Ash; Haskins; J.
1985—*Seventh Dream of Teenage Heaven* (Beggars Banquet, U.K.) 1986—*Express* (Beggars Banquet/RCA) 1987—*Earth-Sun-Moon* 1989—*Love and Rockets* 1994—*Hot Trip to Heaven* (American) 1996—*Sweet F.A.* 1998—*Lift* (Red Ant).
David J solo: 1990—*Songs From Another Season* (Beggars Banquet/RCA) 1992—*Urban Urbane* (MCA).
Daniel Ash solo: 1991—*Coming Down* (Beggars Banquet/RCA) 1992—*Foolish Thing Desire* (Beggars Banquet/Columbia).

Resembling a convention of the undead and playing songs distinguished by spare, atmospheric guitars, sonorous, death-rattle vocals, and deliberate tempos, Bauhaus was the progenitor of gothic rock. Its founding members have gone on to pursue various other projects in the realm of underground rock.

In 1978 brothers David and Kevin Haskins formed the Craze with Daniel Ash, an old school friend. With the addition of vocalist Peter Murphy they became Bauhaus 1919, named after the German architectural group whose credo was "Less is more." The "1919" was dropped for their 1979 debut single, "Bela Lugosi's Dead," an eight-minute epic later heard in the 1983 David Bowie film, *The Hunger*.

An appearance on BBC radio DJ John Peel's show led to a record contract. Bauhaus became an underground success in Britain, and made the U.K. chart with "Kick in the Eye" (#59, 1981) and *Mask* (#30, 1981). *The Sky's Gone Out* (1982) was its American debut. That year the band released its biggest U.K. hit, a cover of David Bowie's "Ziggy Stardust" (#15). Bauhaus' influence was also felt in the Batcave, a popular London club that took its musical and sartorial cues from the band. *Burning From the Inside*, more a compilation of solo songs than a band project (Murphy was ill and missed most of the sessions), foreshadowed Bauhaus' breakup later that year.

Murphy joined Japan's Mick Karn in the experimental Dali's Car; they recorded one album in 1984. In 1985 he launched a solo career. Collaborating with keyboardist/producer Paul Stratham, Murphy toned down the more excessive, arty elements of Bauhaus and emphasized his Bowie-esque vocals. He had a minor hit with 1990's "Cuts You Up" (#55), from the album *Deep* (#44, 1990).

Ash, along with Bauhaus roadie Glenn Campling, originally began Tones on Tail as a side project in 1981. When Bauhaus split, Kevin Haskins signed on. They released several U.K. EPs and singles plus an album, all of which have been compiled on several U.S. releases. After a 1984 American tour, Ash and Haskins dissolved the band. David J joined the Jazz Butcher, but left after the 1984 album *A Scandal in Bohemia*. He also released a string of U.K. solo albums in the early to mid-'80s. With their careers stalled, the members of Bauhaus planned to reunite in 1985. When Murphy demurred at the last minute, the other three decided to re-form as Love and Rockets (the name comes from the underground comic book series by Los Angelenos Gilbert and Jaime Hernandez). A more danceable version of Bauhaus' atmospherics, their initial release, 1985's *Seventh Dream of Teenage Heaven,* went unreleased in the U.S. until 1988, but their U.K. hit cover of the Temptations' "Ball of Confusion" was included in their U.S. debut, *Express* (#72, 1986); they broke into the mainstream in 1989 with *Love and Rockets* (#14) and the Top 10 single "So Alive" (#3).

In the early '90s, Ash issued his solo debut and J resumed his solo recording, this time on an American label. Love and Rockets came under the sway of the acid house/techno sound rampant in England and returned to the studio in 1994. This new inspiration is evident on the resultant *Hot Trip to Heaven,* especially in the 14-minute ambient "Body and Soul" and in "Ugly," featuring Middle Eastern–inflected vocals by Natacha Atlas of Trans-Global Underground. *Sweet F.A.* and *Lift* continued to mix contemporary techno with guitar-based gloom. Their careers cooling once more, Murphy, Ash, J, and Haskins resurrected Bauhaus for a successful tour in 1998, by which time goth rock had become the subject of numerous nostalgic theme nights at American dance clubs. *Crackle* is a best-of that includes several rarities. *Gotham* is a two-disc live set taped at New York's Hammerstein Ballroom.

Bay City Rollers

Formed 1970, Edinburgh, Scot.
Alan Longmuir (b. June 20, 1953, Edinburgh), bass; Eric Faulkner (b. Oct. 21, 1955, Edinburgh), gtr.; Derek Longmuir (b. Mar. 19, 1955, Edinburgh), drums; Leslie McKeown (b. Nov. 12, 1955, Edinburgh), voc.; Stuart "Woody" Wood (b. Feb. 25, 1957, Edinburgh), gtr., bass.
1975—*Bay City Rollers* (Arista) 1976—*Rock 'n' Roll Love Letter Dedication* (– A. Longmuir; + Ian Mitchell [b. Aug. 22, 1958], gtr.; – Mitchell; + Pat McGlynn [b. Mar. 31, 1958, Edinburgh], gtr.) 1977—*Greatest Hits* (– McGlynn) 1978—*Strangers in the Wild* (– McKeown; + Duncan Faure, voc.) 1982–2000—(various reunions, spinoffs, and partial re-formations).

Though the Bay City Rollers were initially hyped as the "new Beatles," the Rollers actually were cute young musicians who were vigorously promoted to a market of teenagers. Probably the most successful act ever to emerge from Scotland, the group scored its first English hit in 1971. Through the next few years, under the guidance of mentor/manager Tam Paton (who named the group by arbitrarily sticking a pin in a U.S. map and hitting Bay City, Michigan), the Bay City Rollers slowly expanded their predominantly female audience. Clad in tartan uniforms, they eventually inspired a genuine outbreak of teenage frenzy reminiscent of Beatlemania. Rollermania spread to the U.S. briefly in early 1976 with the group's first stateside concerts and a late-1975 #1 single, "Saturday Night." The Rollers' close-knit, wholesome image was tarnished somewhat in the late '70s with the disclosures that they had all regularly taken Valium to help them cope with the rigors of superstardom and life on the road and that Faulkner and Mitchell had been treated for overdoses in apparent suicide attempts. (In 1993 Faulkner claimed that his OD was accidental.)

By the early '80s they were a quartet playing bars in the U.S., still wearing their tartan plaid. In an unforeseen turn of events, demand for the reconstituted band was on the rise, particularly in Japan. Years of partial reunion tours and spin-off acts ensued. Alan Longmuir, Faulkner, Wood, and a drummer named Kass toured the U.S. in 1993. In 2000 Wood, who has released several albums of Celtic mood music, was reportedly working on a new album with McKeown. In March of that year, Derek Longmuir pleaded guilty to possessing child pornography. In addition, Courtney Love, who had purchased the rights to Caroline Sullivan's Rollers memoir *Bye Bye Baby,* was planning to direct a film about the group's fall from grace.

The Beach Boys

Formed 1961, Hawthorne, CA
Brian Wilson (b. June 20, 1942, Hawthorne), voc., bass, piano; Dennis Wilson (b. Dec. 4, 1944, Hawthorne; d. Dec. 28, 1983, Marina Del Rey, CA), voc., drums; Carl Wilson (b. Dec. 21, 1946, Hawthorne; d. Feb. 6, 1998, Los Angeles, CA), voc., gtr.; Mike Love (b. Mar. 15, 1941, Los Angeles), voc., misc., perc.; Al (Alan) Jardine (b. Sep. 3, 1942, Lima, OH), voc., gtr.
1962—(– Jardine; + David Marks [b. Newcastle, PA], gtr.) *Surfin' Safari* (Capitol) 1963—*Surfin' USA* (– Marks; + Jardine); *Surfer Girl; Shut Down; Little Deuce Coupe* 1964—*Shut Down, vol. 2; All Summer Long; The Beach Boys' Christmas Album; The Beach Boys' Concert* 1965—(+ Bruce Johnston [b. June 24, 1944, Chicago, IL], gtr., voc.) *The Beach Boys Today; Summer Days (and Summer Nights!!); The Beach Boys' Party!* 1966—*Pet Sounds; Best of the Beach Boys, vol. 1;* 1967—*Best of the Beach Boys, vol. 2; Smiley Smile; The Beach Boys Deluxe Set; Wild Honey* 1968—*Friends; Best of the Beach Boys, vol. 3; Stack o' Tracks* 1969—*20/20; Close Up* 1970—*Sunflower* (Brother/Reprise) 1971—*Surf's Up* (+ Blondie Chaplin [b. S.A.], gtr., voc.) 1972—(– Johnston; + Ricky Fataar [b. S.A.], drums, voc.) *Carl and the Passions/So Tough; Holland* (Reprise) 1973—*The Beach Boys in Concert* (Brother/Reprise) 1974—(– Fataar; – Chaplin) *Endless Summer* (Capitol) 1975—*Spirit of America; Good Vibrations: Best of the Beach Boys* (Brother/Reprise) 1976—*15 Big Ones; Beach Boys '69 (The Beach Boys Live in London)* (Capitol) 1977—*Love You* (Brother/Reprise) 1978—*M.I.U. Album* (+ Johnston) 1979—*L.A. (Light Album)* (Caribou) 1980—*Keepin' the Summer Alive;* 1981—*Ten Years of Harmony* (– C. Wilson) 1982—(+ C. Wilson) *Sunshine Dream* (Capitol) (– B. Wilson) 1983–(– D. Wilson) 1985—(+ B. Wilson) *The Beach Boys '85* (Caribou) 1986—*Made in U.S.A.* (Capitol) 1988—(– B. Wilson) 1989—*Still Cruisin'* (Capitol) 1992—*Summer in Paradise*

(Brother) 1993—*Good Vibrations: Thirty Years of the Beach Boys* (Capitol) 1995—*The "Smile" Era* 1996—*Stars and Stripes, vol. 1* (River North) 1997—*Pet Sounds—The Pet Sounds Sessions Produced by Brian Wilson* (Capitol) 1998—(– C. Wilson; – Jardine) *The Beach Boys: Endless Harmony Soundtrack* 1999—*20 Good Vibrations: The Greatest Hits, vol. 1; 20 More Good Vibrations: The Greatest Hits, vol. 2; Best of the Brother Years: Greatest Hits, vol. 3 (1970–1986).*
Mike Love solo: 1981—*Looking Back With Love* (Boardwalk).
Brian Wilson solo: 1988—*Brian Wilson* (Sire) 1995—*I Just Wasn't Made for These Times* soundtrack (MCA); *Orange Crate Art* (Warner Bros.) 1998—*Imagination* (Giant) 2000—*Live at the Roxy Theatre* (Brimel Records).
Carl Wilson solo: 1981—*Carl Wilson* (Caribou) 1983—*What You Do to Me.*
Dennis Wilson solo: 1977—*Pacific Ocean Blue* (Caribou/Epic).

In their early '60s hits the Beach Boys virtually invented California rock. Brian Wilson's songs celebrated an idealized California teenhood—surfing, driving, dating—and his productions were a glossy, perfectionistic, ultra-smooth blend of guitars and vocal harmonies, with their experiments concealed. While the Beach Boys attempted more grown-up topics and more obvious progressivism in the late '60s, they survived into the late '90s as America's premier nostalgia act. Through the years, the Beach Boys have not only been "America's band" but arguably one of the greatest American rock bands ever. The Beach Boys have sold well over 65 million records worldwide.

The three Wilson brothers were encouraged by their parents, Murray and Audree, to try music and sports. Brian was a varsity baseball player at suburban Hawthorne High when he began to work seriously on music. His first band included brothers Dennis and Carl (who was expelled from Hawthorne High for going to the bathroom without permission), cousin Mike Love, and friend Al Jardine. As the Pendletones, Kenny and the Cadets (Brian was "Kenny"), or Carl and the Passions, the group played local gigs. At Dennis' suggestion, Love and Brian wrote "Surfin'," which became a regional hit on the soon defunct Candix label in December 1961 while the group was calling itself the Beach Boys. Like most of their early songs, "Surfin' " used Chuck Berry guitar licks with vocal harmonies (arranged by Brian) recalling '50s pop groups like the Four Freshmen, which Brian studied closely.

Murray Wilson, who was later revealed to have been psychologically and physically abusive to his sons, managed their band and got them a contract with Capitol. The hits began: "Surfin' Safari" (#14, 1962); "Surfin' U.S.A." (#3, 1963), a note-for-note copy of Berry's "Sweet Little Sixteen" with new lyrics; and "Surfer Girl" (#7, 1963), all of which launched and capitalized on the "surf music" fad, although only Dennis surfed regularly. "Surfer Girl" marked Brian's emergence as a producer, with its complex vocal harmonies and sophisticated pop chords. An admirer of producer Phil Spector, Brian would continue to refine his skills and become perhaps one of the greatest record producers in rock.

The years 1963–1965 established the Beach Boys' legacy: "Little Deuce Coupe" (#15, 1963), "Be True to Your School" (#6, 1963), and "Fun, Fun, Fun" (#5,1964), written by Brian and Love in a taxi to the Salt Lake City airport; "I Get Around" (#1, 1964); "Dance, Dance, Dance" (#8, 1964); "Help Me, Rhonda" (#1, 1965); "California Girls" (#3, 1965); and such ballads as "In My Room" (#23, 1963) and "Don't Worry, Baby" (#24, 1964). Early in 1965 Brian Wilson suffered a nervous breakdown and decided to quit touring, though he continued writing, recording, and producing.

Pet Sounds, which was released in March 1966, and included "Caroline, No" (#23), "Wouldn't It Be Nice" (#8, 1966), and "God Only Knows" (#39, 1966), hit #10 but sold comparatively poorly. (In fact, it was not certified gold until the 30th anniversary of its release, in 1996.) Nonetheless, it stands as one of the most important works in the Beach Boys oeuvre, for it ushered in the era of studio experimentation, predating the Beatles' *Sgt. Pepper's Lonely Hearts Club Band* and rivaling even Spector in terms of sophistication. With the passage of time, the importance of *Pet Sounds* has only grown. Paul McCartney and Beatles producer George Martin have acknowledged that it was the inspiration for *Sgt. Pepper,* and the album's 30th anniversary was celebrated in 1997 (a year late) with the release of a four-CD box set that included tracks stripped of vocals and vocal tracks without instrumentation. At the same time grunge indie label Sub Pop released a single containing three previously unreleased tracks: a stereo mix of "I Just Wasn't Made for These Times," a vocal-only version of "Wouldn't It Be Nice," and the stereo backing track for "Here Today." (All three tracks are also contained in the *Pet Sounds* box.)

The highlight of the Beach Boys' borderline psychedelic period was "Good Vibrations" (#1, 1966) (from *Wild Honey*), Wilson's production masterpiece. It took six months and cost $16,000 to make, with several distinct sections and such exotic instruments as Jew's harp, sleighbells, harpsichord, and theremin. Meanwhile, Brian's ambitions, neuroses, and drug intake were increasing throughout the '60s. He and Van Dyke Parks began collaborating on *Smile* in late 1966, but after a mysterious fire at the studio where they were working, Wilson reportedly destroyed most of the tapes in a fit of paranoia. Several songs have surfaced since; the Wilson-Parks "Heroes and Villains" (#12, 1967) appeared on *Smiley Smile,* and the melancholy, beautiful title cut of 1971's *Surf's Up* was also a *Smile* composition. The *Smile* debacle, and *Smiley Smile,* marked the end of Brian's reign as the Beach Boys' sole producer.

Beginning with *Wild Honey* (#24, 1967), other group members shared writing and production, along with Bruce Johnston, who had joined the touring Beach Boys after Brian retired from the road in late 1964. (Johnston replaced Glen Campbell after a brief stint.) Johnston has been associated on and off with the Beach Boys, primarily as producer, ever since. The Beach Boys' late-'60s touring band also included Daryl Dragon (later the Captain of the Captain and Tennille) on keyboards; Blondie Chaplin (later a sideman with the Rolling Stones and others) on guitar, bass, and vocals; and Ricky Fataar (later of Joe Walsh's band) on drums. In 1968 the

The Beach Boys: Al Jardine, Dennis Wilson, Brian Wilson, Carl Wilson, Mike Love

Beach Boys became the first major American rock band to play behind the Iron Curtain when they performed in Czechoslovakia. Increasingly, Carl played a larger role in directing the group. His was the lead voice on "Good Vibrations," "Surf's Up," "Wild Honey" (#31, 1967), "Darlin' " (#19, 1967), and "Friends" (#47, 1968), among others.

Beginning in 1970 and for the next 18 years, the Beach Boys released their records on their own Brother label, a custom imprint of Warner/Reprise. Their first album under the deal, *Sunflower* (#151, 1970), inaugurated a five-year performance hiatus for Brian, although he tried one live show in early 1970 at the Whisky-a-Go-Go in L.A. The group's hugely popular oldies-dominated live shows reinforced in the public's mind the image of a group whose creative past was behind it. In fact, however, *20/20* (#68, 1969), *Sunflower,* and its more successful followup, *Surf's Up* (#29, 1971) contained some of the group's more adventurous and interesting work: the lower charting but important singles "Do It Again" (#20, 1968), "I Can Hear Music" (#24, 1969), "Add Some Music to Your Day" (#64, 1970), "Long Promised Road" (#89, 1971), and the intriguing album cuts "This Whole World" and " 'Til I Die."

In 1972 the Beach Boys decided to record in Holland, but after relocating their families learned there were no adequate studio facilities. They had a studio broken down, shipped, and reconstructed in a converted barn, where over six months they recorded *Holland.* Reprise initially rejected the album for a lack of what the company considered a solid hit single, so Brian Wilson and Van Dyke Parks provided "Sail On Sailor" (written by Brian and several others in addition to Parks). With a rare lead vocal by Blondie Chaplin, the single hit #79 when released in 1973, but rose to #49 when rereleased in 1975. *Holland* also contained "The Trader," yet another of Carl's more introspective, mature works, and Al Jardine's "California Saga (On My Way to Sunny Californ-i-a)" (#84, 1973). Aside from a critically acclaimed double live album, *The Beach Boys in Concert* (#25, 1973), the group's next five charting releases would be repackages and greatest-hits compilations, including *Endless Summer* (#1, 1974) and *Spirit of America* (#8, 1975). Another stellar live collection, *Beach Boys '69 (The Beach Boys Live in London)* came out in 1976 (#75).

Meanwhile, efforts continued to coax Brian out of his Bel Air mansion, which included a sandbox as well as a recording studio. In the late '60s he had briefly run a West Hollywood health food store, the Radiant Radish, and in 1972 he produced an album by his wife, Marilyn, and her sister Diane Powell, as Spring (or American Spring). In 1976, after a much-publicized rehabilitation, Brian rejoined the band for *15 Big Ones* (#8, 1976). It included oldie remakes (Chuck Berry's "Rock and Roll Music," which went to #5 and was the Beach Boys' only Top 10 hit from late 1966 through mid-1988) and Brian Wilson originals such as "It's O.K." (#29, 1976), with backing tracks Brian had recorded with ELO founder Roy Wood's group Wizzard.

In 1977 open personality clashes (primarily between Dennis Wilson and Mike Love) jeopardized the band's future as it switched labels and moved over to CBS; eventually Love's brothers Stan and Steve were removed from the Beach Boys' management organization. Steve Love was later sentenced to prison for embezzling nearly $1 million from the group. Johnston was back as coproducer for *L.A. (Light Album);* in the mid-'70s he had left the band to concentrate on songwriting (including Barry Manilow's hit "I Write the Songs") and make a solo album, *Going Public* (1977). *Love You* (#53, 1977) contained another overlooked gem, "Honkin' Down the Highway" along with Brian's surreal tribute to the king of late-night TV, "Johnny Carson." Chartwise, the late '70s were a low time for the group: Neither *M.I.U. Album* (1978) nor *L.A. (Light Album)* (1979) charted. A flop single from *M.I.U.* was rereleased in 1981 and provided the group's first nonmedley Top 20 hit since 1976 in a #18 remake of the Dell-Vikings' "Come Go With Me."

The '80s proved a tumultuous decade for the group. Carl Wilson quit in 1981 to concentrate on his solo career. He, more than the others, seemed to resist the band's increasingly nostalgic appeal. But after his return the following year, the Beach Boys continued being known more as an oldies-but-goodies act, albeit an extraordinarily successful one. In 1983 they unwittingly became the center of controversy when Secretary of the Interior James Watt banned them from performing a Fourth of July concert at the Washington Monument. Public opinion was solidly against Watt, who later resigned, and the group was personally invited to play the Washington Monument the next summer by First Lady Nancy Reagan. Nineteen eighty-three marked Brian's return to the stage with the group, but also the death of Dennis. On December 28 the hard-living drummer drowned while swimming off his boat in Marina Del Rey, California. With the help of President Ronald Reagan, special permission was granted so that Dennis' body could be buried at sea. Brian had since come and gone from the group. The Beach Boys enjoyed their third #1 hit, their biggest-selling single ever, "Kokomo" (1988), from the hit film *Cocktail,* without him. Brian's long-awaited first solo album came out that year. Coproduced by his long-time therapist, Dr. Eugene Landy (whose license to practice therapy was later revoked), *Brian Wilson* elicited glowing reviews but sold poorly. The Beach Boys were inducted into the Rock and Roll Hall of Fame in 1988.

As of 1993 Brian was a touring Beach Boy again. Later Mike Love sued Brian, his cowriter Todd Gold, and Landy, claiming he had been defamed in Wilson's autobiography, *Wouldn't It Be Nice?: My Own Story.* The case was settled out of court in early 1994. In 1995 Brian and Love settled a long-running legal dispute over songwriting credit and royalties for Love. Wilson paid Love $5 million and Love has writing credit on such songs as "Wouldn't It Be Nice" and "California Girls." That same year, Brian Wilson and his estranged daughter Carnie reconciled their differences and contributed "Fantasy Is Reality/Bells of Madness" to Rob Wasserman's *Trios* LP.

The period from the mid-'90s through the turn of the century brought dramatic changes within the group, including what appears to be, at this writing, the end of the Beach Boys as we know them. They made their biggest impression on the country chart, where their *Stars and Stripes, vol. 1* (#12 C&W, 1996) featured "duets" with the group and country stars. In 1995 Brian was the subject of producer Don Was' documentary *I Just Wasn't Made for These Times;* he also released a second solo album, *Orange Crate Art,* and remarried. In 1997 he provided some production work, songwriting, and background singing for his daughters Carnie and Wendy's album *The Wilsons.* His third solo album, *Imagination* (#88, 1998), was warmly received upon its release, and Wilson returned to performing. By then he had relocated to Illinois, and in a series of candid interviews gave the impression of someone happy and comfortable at last. "My music isn't going to save the world," he said when *Imagination* was released. "But I think it's going to save souls, certain people in the world. It pleases me to be able to do that. It feels good." He began touring in 1999. For his 2000 tour, he performed *Pet Sounds* accompanied by a symphony orchestra; a live album was released from that tour in 2001. In June 2000, Brian was inducted into the Songwriters' Hall of Fame. In 2001 he and *Pet Sounds* were the recipients of a star-studded tribute (with guests Elton John, Paul Simon, and Billy Joel, among others), televised on TNT.

Ironically, as Brian Wilson seemed to be coming back into his own, the Beach Boys were enduring perhaps the most difficult times of their long career. In 1997 Carl Wilson was diagnosed with lung cancer, which later developed into brain cancer. He continued to tour with the group as his health would permit, sometimes even performing sitting in a chair. However, by fall 1997 he retired (he was replaced by David Marks, an original member who quit the group in 1963 but continued receiving about $20,000 a year in royalties). Carl died on February 6, 1998, in L.A., at age 51.

Shortly after Carl's passing, Al Jardine quit the group, leaving only Love, Johnston, and Marks (who, ironically, had been replaced by Jardine back in 1964). The trio toured as the Beach Boys, with added musicians, while Jardine emerged with his Beach Boys Family and Friends (later renamed Al Jardine's Family and Friends Beach Band after Brother Records International, the corporate entity that is the Beach Boys, got an injunction against his using the Beach Boys name), which included two of his sons and Carnie and Wendy Wilson. Love and Jardine feuded bitterly in the press and in court, but much of this was overshadowed by an ongoing celebration of the Beach Boys legacy, in a documentary (VH1's *The Beach Boys: Endless Harmony*), a made-for-TV miniseries *(The Beach Boys: An American Family),* and three simultaneously released greatest-hits packages. In 2001 the group received a Lifetime Achievement Award Grammy.

Beastie Boys

Formed 1981, New York, NY
MCA (b. Adam Yauch, Aug. 5, 1965, New York), voc., bass; Mike D (b. Michael Diamond, Nov. 20, 1966, New York), voc., drums; John Berry, gtr.; Kate Schellenbach (b. Jan. 5, 1966, New York), drums.
1982—*Polly Wog Stew* EP (Rat Cage) (– Berry; – Schellenbach; + King Ad-Rock [b. Adam Horovitz, Oct. 31, 1967, New York], voc., gtr.) 1985—*Rock Hard* EP (Def Jam) 1986—*Licensed to Ill* (Def Jam-Columbia) 1989—*Paul's Boutique* (Capitol) 1992—*Check Your Head* (Grand Royal/Capitol) 1994—*Some Old Bullshit; Ill Communication; Sure Shot* EP 1995—*Root Down* EP; *Aglio E Olio* EP 1996—*The In Sound From Way Out!* 1998—*Hello Nasty; Love American Style* EP 1999—*Beastie Boys Anthology: The Sounds of Science.*
BS2000 (Ad-Rock with Amery "AWOL" Smith): 1997—*BS2000* (Grand Royal) 2001—*Simply Mortified.*

The Beastie Boys were the first white group to offer a successful send-up of rap. After emerging from New York's hardcore punk underground of the early '80s, the group crossed over into the mainstream in 1986 with its first full-length album, *Licensed to Ill,* the first rap album to hit #1. Featuring "(You Gotta) Fight for Your Right (to Party)" (#7) and "Brass Monkey" (#48 pop, #83 R&B, 1987), the album sold 720,000 copies in six weeks, becoming one of Columbia's fastest-selling debuts ever. By the late '80s, the Beastie Boys' sound had begun to mature, expanding into spaced-out funk and psychedelia, yet retaining its adolescent charm and hit-making sensibility.

At 14, Adam Horovitz, son of playwright Israel Horovitz, joined the hardcore band the Young and the Useless. His friends Adam Yauch and Mike Diamond, children of wealthy New York families, had formed the four-piece hardcore band the Beastie Boys along with Kate Schellenbach, later of the group Luscious Jackson, and John Berry. By 1982 the Beasties had released a 7-inch EP, *Polly Wog Stew,* on the independent label Rat Cage. Horovitz joined shortly thereafter.

The Beasties' first attempt at rap came with the 1983 12-inch spoof, "Cookie Puss," based on a crank call they made to

The Beastie Boys: Mike D, Ad-Rock, MCA

the Carvel ice cream company. It wasn't until the trio teamed up with friend Rick Rubin—who would start the Def Jam label in his college dorm room the next year—that the Beasties began taking rap seriously. The marriage was perfect, producer Rubin working into the group's bratty raps samples with appropriately white, upper-middle-class references: Led Zeppelin, heavy-metal guitar, and the theme to TV's *Mr. Ed.*

With thumbs-up from Rubin's then-partner, Russell Simmons, head of Rush Productions and manager of Run-D.M.C., the Beasties were signed to Def Jam in 1985. That same year they appeared in one of rap's first movies, *Krush Groove,* with the single "She's on It." They also opened for Madonna's Virgin Tour, during which they shouted obscenities to the audiences and got booed in return. In 1986 the trio toured with Run-D.M.C.'s violence-plagued Raisin' Hell Tour.

Nineteen-eighty-seven was a watershed year for the Beasties. The success of "Fight for Your Right" led to the trio headlining their own tour, which was plagued by lawsuits, arrests, blame for violence and vandalism, and accusations of sexism and obscenity. In 1988 they appeared in Run-D.M.C.'s movie, *Tougher Than Leather.* The Beastie Boys broke with Rubin and Def Jam over financial and personal differences, and moved to L.A., where they met producers the Dust Brothers (John King and Mike Simpson). Together they created the long-awaited second album, *Paul's Boutique* (#14, 1989), whose release on Capitol came three years after the Beasties' debut—partially due to a bitter legal dispute with Rubin. The band made an artistic leap on the record, turning their obnoxious, white, bourgeois take on rap into a funky, album-long sound collage. The record produced the Top 40 song "Hey Ladies" (#36), but sold far less than *Licensed to Ill.*

It would be another three years until their third LP, *Check Your Head* (#10, 1992), an eclectic album on which the Beastie Boys picked up their instruments again, was released on their own Capitol-distributed Grand Royal label. The record marked the first appearance of longtime sidemen DJ Hurricane and keyboardist Money Mark (a.k.a. Mark Ramos Nishita). It broke the Top 10 in a week, even though it jumps stylistically from funk to rap to hardcore. In 1994 the Beasties released a compilation of their early hardcore singles and EPs as *Some Old Bullshit* (#46), followed by a new album, *Ill Communication* (#1 pop, #2 R&B, 1994), which continued in the eclectic (and successful) vein of *Check Your Head* and debuted at the top of the albums chart. That summer, the Beastie Boys joined Smashing Pumpkins, the Breeders, George Clinton, and other big names for Lollapalooza '94 (as Luscious Jackson played on the second stage).

It would be four more years before the Beastie Boys released another full album of new material. Meanwhile, they demonstrated a lingering fondness for hardcore punk on the *Aglio E Olio* EP (1995), and collected old and new jazzy, soul-influenced instrumental tracks on *The In Sound From Way Out!* (#45, 1996).

Yauch had been responsible for some of the Beasties' wildest behavior (with girls, drugs, and egg-throwing), but in the '90s embraced Buddhism and organized the annual star-studded Tibetan Freedom Concert, which demanded independence for Tibet. Diamond assumed hands-on management of Grand Royal, which branched off into a short-lived magazine of the same name, and co-owned a clothing company called X-Large. In the late '80s Horovitz dabbled in acting, married actor Ione Skye, and created the side project BS2000, releasing *Simply Mortified* in 2001.

After the hit Spike Jonze–directed video for "Sabotage," the director and the Beasties began discussing doing a feature film. When those ideas fell through, the band began work on a new album. *Hello Nasty* (1998) debuted at #1 with 22 tracks of hip-hop, rock, soul, bossa nova, opera, salsa, and cutting-edge turntablism by Mixmaster Mike (replacing DJ Hurricane). The band toured that same year. The first single, "Intergalactic," was accompanied by a video directed by Nathaniel Hornblower, a "Swiss independent filmmaker" (actually Yauch in lederhosen and a fake beard). Another tour scheduled for 2000—to include coheadliner Rage Against the Machine—was canceled after Diamond was seriously injured in a bicycle accident.

The Beat/The Nerves

The Beat, formed 1979, Los Angeles, CA
Paul Collins (b. New York, NY), gtr., voc.; Steve Huff, bass; Mike Ruiz, drums; Larry Whitman, gtr.
1979—*The Beat* (Columbia) 1982—*The Kids Are the Same*
1983—(– Whitman; – Ruiz; + Jay Dee Daugherty, drums; + Jimmy Ripp, gtr.) *To Beat or Not to Beat* EP (Passport).
The Nerves, formed 1976, San Francisco, CA: Collins, drums; Peter Case (b. Apr. 5, 1954, Buffalo, NY), bass; Jack Lee, gtr., voc.
1976—*Nerves* EP (Nerves).

The power pop Paul Collins produced with the Nerves and with his own band, the Beat, has been compared to the Hollies and Byrds for its soaring harmonies and spare, gritty guitars.

The Nerves were part of the early San Francisco new-wave scene; they are best known for the original version of "Hangin' on the Telephone," covered by Blondie in 1978. They broke up in 1978; bassist Peter Case went on to form the Plimsouls, songwriter Jack Lee attempted a solo career, and Collins moved to L.A. There he met bassist Steve Huff through a classified ad; the two began to write songs and record them at Huff's home studio. The resulting tape attracted drummer Mike Ruiz, who brought in Larry Whitman.

In 1979 the Beat opened for Eddie Money at Bill Graham's Kabuki Theater in San Francisco. Graham became the new band's manager and secured a contract with Columbia later that year. While the Beat's energetic, concise songs were popular on college radio, the quartet never had a national hit. Columbia dropped the group in 1982. The next year, Collins returned with a new Beat, backed by former members of the Patti Smith Group and Tom Verlaine's solo band. In the early '90s, Collins, then living in New York, began recording and touring with his Paul Collins Band, with whom he has released several live and import titles.

The Beat (English): See the English Beat; Fine Young Cannibals

The Beatles

Formed 1959, Liverpool, Eng.
John Lennon (b. John Winston Lennon, Oct. 9, 1940, Liverpool; d. Dec. 8, 1980, New York, NY), gtr., voc., harm., kybds.; Paul McCartney (b. James Paul McCartney, June 18, 1942, Liverpool), bass, voc., gtr., kybds.; George Harrison (b. Feb. 25, 1943, Liverpool), gtr., voc., sitar; Stu Sutcliffe (b. Stuart Fergusson Victor Sutcliffe, June 23, 1940, Edinburgh, Scot.; d. Apr. 10, 1962, Hamburg, Ger.), bass; Pete Best (b. 1941, Eng.), drums.
1961—(– Sutcliffe) 1962—(– Best; + Ringo Starr [b. Richard Starkey Jr., July 7, 1940, Liverpool], drums, perc., voc., misc.)
1963—*Please Please Me* (Parlophone, U.K.); *With the Beatles; Introducing . . . The Beatles* (Vee-Jay) 1964—*Meet the Beatles* (Capitol); *The Beatles' Second Album; A Hard Day's Night* (United Artists); *Something New* (Capitol); *The Beatles' Story; Beatles '65* 1965—*The Early Beatles; Beatles VI; Help!; Rubber Soul* 1966—*Yesterday . . . and Today; Revolver* 1967—*Sgt. Pepper's Lonely Hearts Club Band; Magical Mystery Tour* 1968—*The Beatles* (a.k.a. the White Album) (Apple) 1969—*Yellow Submarine* (Capitol); *Abbey Road* (Apple) 1970—*Hey Jude; Let It Be* 1973—*The Beatles 1962–1966* (Capitol); *The Beatles 1967–1970* 1976—*Rock 'n' Roll Music* 1977—*At the Hollywood Bowl; Beatles Live! At the Star-Club in Hamburg, Germany, 1962* (Lingasong); *Love Songs* (Capitol) 1980—*Rarities* 1982—*Reel Music; 20 Greatest Hits* 1988—*Past Masters, vol. 1; Past Masters, vol. 2* 1994—*Live at the BBC* (Apple) 1995—*Anthology 1* 1996—*Anthology 2; Anthology 3* 2000—*1* (Apple/Capitol).

The impact of the Beatles—not only on rock & roll but on all of Western culture—is simply incalculable. As musicians they proved that rock & roll could embrace a limitless variety of harmonies, structures, and sounds; virtually every rock experiment has some precedent on Beatles records. As a unit they were a musically synergistic combination: Paul McCartney's melodic bass lines, Ringo Starr's slaphappy no-rolls drumming, George Harrison's rockabilly-style guitar leads, John Lennon's assertive rhythm guitar—and their four fervent voices. One of the first rock groups to write most of its own material, they inaugurated the era of self-contained bands and forever centralized pop. And as personalities, they defined and incarnated '60s style: smart, idealistic, playful, irreverent, eclectic. Their music, from the not-so-simple love songs they started with to their later perfectionistic studio extravaganzas, set new standards for both commercial and artistic success in pop. Although many of their sales and attendance records have since been surpassed, no group has so radically transformed the sound and significance of rock & roll. At the dawn of the 21st century, a chart-topping collection of their #1 hits, *1*, was well on its way to becoming one of the best-selling albums of all time.

Lennon was performing with his amateur skiffle group the Quarrymen at a church picnic on July 6, 1957, in the Liverpool suburb of Woolton when he met McCartney, whom he later invited to join his group; soon they were writing songs together, such as "The One After 909." By the year's end McCartney had convinced Lennon to let Harrison join their group, the name of which was changed to Johnny and the Moondogs in 1958. In 1960 an art-school friend of Lennon's, Stu Sutcliffe, became their bassist. Sutcliffe couldn't play a note but had recently sold one of his paintings for a considerable sum, which the group, now rechristened the Silver Beetles (from which "Silver" was dropped a few months later, and "Beetles" amended to "Beatles"), used to upgrade its equipment. Tommy Moore was their drummer until Pete Best replaced him in August 1960. Once Best had joined, the band made its first of four trips to Hamburg, Germany. In December Harrison was deported back to England for being underage and lacking a work permit, but by then their 30-set weeks on the stages of Hamburg beer houses had honed and strengthened their repertoire (mostly Chuck Berry, Little Richard, Carl Perkins, and Buddy Holly covers), and on February 21, 1961, they debuted at the Cavern club on Mathew Street in Liverpool, beginning a string of nearly 300 performances there over the next couple of years.

In April 1961 they again went to Hamburg, where Sutcliffe (the first of the Beatles to wear his hair in the long, shaggy style that came to be known as the Beatle haircut) left the group to become a painter, while McCartney switched from rhythm guitar to bass. The Beatles returned to Liverpool as a quartet in July. Sutcliffe died from a brain hemorrhage in Hamburg less than a year later.

The Beatles had been playing regularly to packed houses

at the Cavern when they were spotted on November 9 by Brian Epstein (b. Sep. 19, 1934, Liverpool). After being discharged from the British Army on medical grounds, Epstein had attended the Royal Academy of Dramatic Art in London for a year before returning to Liverpool to manage his father's record store.

The request he received for a German import single entitled "My Bonnie" (which the Beatles had recorded a few months earlier in Hamburg, backing singer Tony Sheridan and billed as the Beat Boys) convinced him to check out the group. Epstein was surprised to discover not only that the Beatles weren't German but that they were one of the most popular local bands in Liverpool. Within two months he became their manager. Epstein cleaned up their act, eventually replacing black leather jackets, tight jeans, and pompadours with collarless gray Pierre Cardin suits and mildly androgynous haircuts.

Epstein tried landing the Beatles a record contract, but nearly every label in Europe rejected the group. In May 1962, however, producer George Martin (b. Jan. 3, 1926, North London, Eng.) signed the group to EMI's Parlophone subsidiary. Pete Best, then considered the group's undisputed sex symbol, was asked to leave the group on August 16, 1962, and Ringo Starr, drummer with a popular Liverpool group, Rory Storme and the Hurricanes, was added, just in time for the group's first recording session. On September 11 the Beatles cut two originals, "Love Me Do" b/w "P.S. I Love You," which became their first U.K. Top 20 hit in October. In early 1963 "Please Please Me" went to #2, and they recorded an album of the same name in one 10-hour session on February 11, 1963. With the success of their third English single, "From Me to You" (#1), the British record industry coined the term "Merseybeat" (after the river that runs through Liverpool) for groups such as the Beatles and Gerry and the Pacemakers, Billy J. Kramer and the Dakotas, and the Searchers. By midyear the Beatles were given billing over Roy Orbison on a national tour, and the hysterical outbreaks of Beatlemania had begun. Following their first tour of Europe in October, they moved to London with Epstein. Constantly mobbed by screaming fans, the Beatles required police protection almost any time they were seen in public. Late in the year "She Loves You" became the biggest-selling single in British history (in the years since, only six other singles have sold more copies there). In November 1963 the group performed before the Queen Mother at the Royal Command Variety Performance.

EMI's American label, Capitol, had not released the group's 1963 records (which Martin licensed to independents like Vee-Jay and Swan with little success) but was finally persuaded to release its fourth single, "I Want to Hold Your Hand," and *Meet the Beatles* (identical to the Beatles' second British album, *With the Beatles*) in January 1964 and to invest $50,000 in promotion for the then unknown British act. The album and the single became the Beatles' first U.S. chart-toppers. On February 7 screaming mobs met them at New York City's Kennedy Airport, and more than 70 million people watched each of their appearances on *The Ed Sullivan Show* on February 9 and 16. In April 1964 "Can't Buy Me Love" became the first record to top American and British charts simultaneously, and that same month the Beatles held the top five positions on *Billboard* singles chart ("Can't Buy Me Love," "Twist and Shout," "She Loves You," "I Want to Hold Your Hand," "Please Please Me").

Their first movie, *A Hard Day's Night* (directed by Richard Lester), opened in America in August; it grossed $1.3 million in its first week. The band was aggressively merchandised—Beatle wigs, Beatle clothes, Beatle dolls, lunch boxes, a cartoon series—from which, because of Epstein's ineptitude at business, the band made surprisingly little money. The Beatles also opened the American market to such British Invasion groups as the Dave Clark Five, the Rolling Stones, and the Kinks.

By 1965 Lennon and McCartney rarely wrote songs together, although by contractual and personal agreement songs by either of them were credited to both. The Beatles toured Europe, North America, the Far East, and Australia that year. Their second movie, *Help!* (also directed by Lester), was filmed in England, Austria, and the Bahamas in the spring and opened in the U.S. in August. On August 15 they performed to 55,600 fans at New York's Shea Stadium, setting a record for largest concert audience. McCartney's "Yesterday" (#1, 1965) would become one of the most often covered songs ever written. In June the Queen of England had announced that the Beatles would be awarded the MBE (Member of the Order of the British Empire). The announcement sparked some controversy—some MBE holders returned their medals—but on October 26, 1965, the ceremony took place at Buckingham Palace. (Lennon returned his medal in 1969 as an antiwar gesture. Interestingly, even

The Beatles: (top) Paul McCartney, Ringo Starr, (bottom) George Harrison, John Lennon

though he rejected the medal, the honor itself cannot be returned; Lennon technically remained an MBE.)

With 1965's *Rubber Soul*, the Beatles' ambitions began to extend beyond love songs and pop formulas. Their success led adults to consider them, along with Bob Dylan, spokesmen for youth culture, and their lyrics grew more poetic and somewhat more political. In summer 1966 controversy erupted when a remark Lennon had made to a British newspaper reporter months before was widely reported in the U.S. The quote—"Christianity will go. It will vanish and shrink. I needn't argue with that; I'm right and will be proved right. We're more popular than Jesus now"—incited denunciations and Beatles record bonfires. The anti-Beatles backlash was particularly intense in the U.S., where the group was set to begin a tour just two weeks after the controversy erupted, and included death threats against the group. Largely out of concern for the safety of his fellow band members, Lennon apologized at a Chicago press conference.

The Beatles gave up touring after an August 29, 1966, concert at San Francisco's Candlestick Park and made the rest of their music in the studio, where they had begun to experiment with exotic instrumentation ("Norwegian Wood," 1965, had featured sitar) and tape abstractions such as the reversed tracks on "Rain." "Strawberry Fields Forever," part of a double-sided single released in February 1967 to fill the unusually long gap between albums, featured an astonishing display of electronically altered sounds and hinted at what was to come. With "Taxman" and "Love You To" on *Revolver,* Harrison began to emerge as a songwriter.

It took four months and $75,000 to record *Sgt. Pepper's Lonely Hearts Club Band* using a then state-of-the-art four-track tape recorder and building each cut layer by layer. Released in June 1967, it was hailed as serious art for its "concept" and its range of styles and sounds, a lexicon of pop and electronic noises; such songs as "Lucy in the Sky With Diamonds" and "A Day in the Life" were carefully examined for hidden meanings. The album spent 15 weeks at #1 (longer than any of their others) and has sold over 8 million copies. On June 25, 1967, the Beatles recorded their new single, "All You Need Is Love," before an international television audience of 400 million, as part of a broadcast called *Our World.* On August 27, 1967—while the four were in Wales beginning their six-month involvement with Transcendental Meditation and the Maharishi Mahesh Yogi (which took them to India for two months in early 1968)—Epstein died alone in his London flat from an overdose of sleeping pills, later ruled accidental. Shaken by Epstein's death, the Beatles retrenched under McCartney's leadership in the fall and filmed *Magical Mystery Tour,* which was aired by BBC-TV on December 26, 1967, and later released in the U.S. as a feature film. Although the telefilm was panned by British critics, fans, and Queen Elizabeth herself, the soundtrack album contained their most cryptic work yet in "I Am the Walrus," a Lennon composition.

As the Beatles' late-1967 single "Hello Goodbye" went to #1 in both the U.S. and Britain, the group launched the Apple clothes boutique in London. McCartney called the retail effort "Western communism"; the boutique closed in July 1968. Like their next effort, Apple Corps Ltd. (formed in January 1968 and including Apple Records, which signed James Taylor, Mary Hopkin, and Badfinger), it was plagued by mismanagement. In July the group faced its last hysterical crowds at the premiere of *Yellow Submarine,* an animated film by Czech avant-garde designer and artist Heinz Edelmann featuring four new Beatles songs; a revised soundtrack featuring nine extra songs was released in 1999 (#15). In August they released McCartney's "Hey Jude" (#1), backed by Lennon's "Revolution" (#12), which sold over 6 million copies before the end of 1968—their most popular single. Meanwhile, the group had been working on the double album *The Beatles* (frequently called the White Album), which showed their divergent directions. The rifts were artistic—Lennon moving toward brutal confessionals, McCartney leaning toward pop melodies, Harrison immersed in Eastern spirituality—and personal, as Lennon drew closer to his wife-to-be, Yoko Ono. Lennon and Ono's *Two Virgins* (with its full frontal and back nude cover photos) was released the same month as *The Beatles* and stirred up so much outrage that the LP had to be sold wrapped in brown paper. (*The Beatles* went to #1, *Two Virgins* peaked at #124.)

The Beatles attempted to smooth over their differences in early 1969 at filmed recording sessions. When the project fell apart hundreds of hours of studio time later, no one could face editing the tapes (a project that eventually fell to record producer Phil Spector), and "Get Back" (#1, 1969) was the only immediate release. Released in spring 1970, *Let It Be* is essentially a documentary of their breakup, including an impromptu January 30, 1969, rooftop concert at Apple Corps headquarters, their last public performance as the Beatles.

By spring 1969 Apple was losing thousands of pounds each week. Over McCartney's objections, the other three brought in manager Allen Klein to straighten things out; one of his first actions was to package nonalbum singles as *Hey Jude.* With money matters temporarily out of mind, the four joined forces in July and August 1969 to record *Abbey Road,* featuring an extended suite as well as more hits, including Harrison's much-covered "Something" (#3, 1969). While its release that fall spurred a "Paul Is Dead" rumor based on clues supposedly left throughout their work, *Abbey Road* became the Beatles' best-selling album, at 9 million copies. Meanwhile, internal bickering persisted. In September Lennon told the others, "I'm leaving the group. I've had enough. I want a divorce." But he was persuaded to keep quiet while their business affairs were untangled. On April 10, 1970, McCartney released his first solo album and publicly announced the end of the Beatles. At the same time, *Let It Be* finally surfaced, becoming the group's 14th #1 album (a postbreakup compilation would become their 15th in 1973) and yielding the Beatles' 18th and 19th chart-topping singles, "Let It Be" and "The Long and Winding Road."

Throughout the '70s, as repackages of Beatles music continued to sell, the four were hounded by bids and pleas for a reunion. Lennon's murder by a mentally disturbed fan on December 8, 1980, ended those speculations. In 1988 the Beatles were inducted into the Rock and Roll Hall of Fame.

McCartney, citing business conflicts with the two other surviving members, did not attend. Relations between him and Harrison, in particular, had been strained for some time.

In January 1994 *Goldmine* magazine reported that McCartney, Harrison, and Starr had begun recording music for a long-rumored Beatles documentary the previous August, with more secret sessions scheduled. There were other signs that the three band members were on the mend—when Lennon was inducted to the Rock and Roll Hall of Fame as a solo artist in 1994, for instance, McCartney did the honors (McCartney himself was inducted in 1999). Later in 1994 *Live at the BBC* was released, featuring 56 songs the Beatles performed on the British radio between 1962 and 1965. It debuted at #1 in the U.K.; in the U.S., it debuted and peaked at #3.

The Beatles Anthology, the long-awaited six-hour television special, was broadcast over three nights in November 1995, coinciding with the release of the George Martin–compiled double-CD *Anthology 1* (#1), which featured alternate takes, demos, and rare tracks, and premiered the first new song by John, Paul, George, and Ringo since 1970. "Free as a Bird" (#6, 1995), a demo recorded by Lennon in 1977, was completed by the other three and produced by Jeff Lynne; it became the Beatles 34th Top 10 single. Lennon's lyrics didn't extend much beyond the title, and so Harrison and McCartney collaborated on lyrics for a new bridge. Two additional double CDs, *Anthology 2* and *3* (both #1), followed in 1996, as well as an extended videotape version of the documentary. *Anthology 2*'s "Real Love" (again a Lennon demo, from 1979, with modern additions by the others) reached #11 and became the group's 23rd gold single (the most of any group).

The Liverpool juggernaut continued to roll on in 2000: the Beatles became the highest certified act of all time, with over 113 million albums sold; a coffeetable book, *The Beatles Anthology*, topped the *New York Times* bestseller list; and *1*, a collection of the band's #1 hit songs, became its 19th chart-topping album. By early 2001, it had sold over 20 million copies worldwide, vying for the greatest-selling album of all time.

[See also: George Harrison; John Lennon and Yoko Ono; Paul McCartney; Ringo Starr.]

The Beau Brummels

Formed 1964, San Francisco, CA
Sal Valentino (b. Sal Spampinato, Sep. 8, 1942, San Francisco), voc.; Ron Elliott (b. Oct. 21, 1943, Healdsburg, CA), gtr., voc.; Declan Mulligan (b. County Tipperary, Ire.), bass; John Petersen (b. Jan. 8, 1942, Rudyard, MI), drums; Ron Meagher (b. Oct. 2, 1941, Oakland, CA), gtr., bass.
1965—(– Mulligan) *Introducing the Beau Brummels* (Autumn) (– Petersen) 1966—*Beau Brummels '66* (Warner Bros.) 1967—*Triangle* 1968—*Bradley's Barn* (group disbands) 1974—(group re-forms: Valentino; Elliott; Meagher; Petersen; + Dan Levitt, gtr.) 1975—*The Beau Brummels; The Best of the Beau Brummels* (Rhino) 1994—*Autumn of Their Years.*

The Beau Brummels were the first nationally successful rock act to emerge from San Francisco; they were also the first American rock band influenced by the Beatles to have a hit. With the exception of their Irish-born bassist, Declan Mulligan (who quit the group before their hits began and later sued for a piece of their earnings), all the members were Bay Area high school graduates. Their early performances featured covers of Beatles and Rolling Stones songs as well as Ron Elliott's originals. San Francisco disc jockey Tom Donahue signed them to his Autumn Records. Their first release, "Laugh, Laugh" (produced by Sylvester Stewart, who later reached fame as Sly Stone), went to #15 in 1965, only a few months after they had played their first live show together. Their next single, "Just a Little" (#8), was their only Top 10 hit. None of their subsequent releases—"You Tell Me Why," "Don't Talk to Strangers," "Good Time Music" (1965), or "One Too Many Mornings" (1966)—entered the Top 30.

In 1965 Autumn went out of business, and the group's contract was sold to Warner Bros. It failed to regain commercial favor but produced interesting failures, including 1967's progressive *Triangle* (recorded after Petersen had left to join Harper's Bizarre [see entry]) and one of the first country-rock albums, *Bradley's Barn* (recorded in Nashville in 1968 by Valentino and Elliott). Neither LP sold well, and by the end of 1968 the Beau Brummels moniker was retired. Valentino then recorded a couple of singles for Warner Bros. before assembling Stoneground. Elliott released a solo album called *The Candlestick Maker* in 1969 and then took a lengthy sabbatical before resurfacing with a group called Pan in the early '70s. In 1974 the original Beau Brummels regrouped, augmented by guitarist Dan Levitt. They released *The Beau Brummels*, but the LP met with little success and the group disbanded. In the years since, versions of the Beau Brummels have included Valentino, Elliott, and Mulligan, in various combinations. The 1994 album *Autumn of Their Years* includes material recorded from 1964 to 1966.

Beausoleil

Formed 1976, Louisiana
Tommy Alesi (b. July 15, 1951, San Diego, CA), drums;
Jimmy Breaux (b. Nov. 18, 1967, Breaux Bridge, LA), accordion;
David Doucet (b. July 6, 1957, Lafayette, LA), gtr., voc.;
Michael Doucet (b. Feb. 14, 1951, Lafayette), fiddle, voc.;
Al Tharp (b. Feb. 8, 1950, Indianapolis, IN), bass, banjo, voc.;
Billy Ware (b. John William Ware, Apr. 26, 1954, Mobile, AL), perc.
1977—*The Spirit of Cajun Music* (Rounder) 1980—*Zydeco Gris Gris* 1981—*Parlez Nous à Boire* (Arhoolie) 1986—*Bayou Boogie* (Rounder); *Belizaire the Cajun* soundtrack (Arhoolie); *Allons à Lafayette* 1987—*Hot Chili Mama* 1989—*Live! From the Left Coast* (Rounder); *Bayou Cadillac* 1990—*Déjà Vu* 1991—*Cajun Conja* (RNA/Rhino) 1992—*Bayou Deluxe: The Best of Michael Doucet & Beausoleil* (Forward/Rhino) 1993—*La Danse de la Vie* 1994—*L'echo* 1995—*Vintage Beausoleil* 1997—*L'amour ou la Folie; Best of Beausoleil* 1999—*Cajunization.*

The premier Cajun band, Beausoleil has moved comfortably between traditional Cajun music and rock and jazz influences. The group is best known for its work on two 1986 soundtracks, *The Big Easy* and *Belizaire the Cajun*.

In the mid-'70s Beausoleil's founder, Michael Doucet, fronted Coteau, known as the "Cajun Grateful Dead." Funded by a NEA grant, he tracked down early Cajun music. The original Beausoleil (the name of an Acadian settlement in Nova Scotia) was a trio: Doucet, mandolin/guitar player Kenneth Richard, and Coteau member Bessyl Duhon on accordion and fiddle. But Doucet employed French folk musicians on Beausoleil's 1976 debut, recorded and released in France. In 1977 a new Beausoleil included his brother David on guitar and Duhon on accordion (later replaced by Pat Breaux, who was then replaced by his brother Jimmy) and signed with Arhoolie Records. *The Spirit of Cajun Music,* their American debut, is an eclectic mix of blues, ballads, standards, and traditional music.

The members of Beausoleil are regulars on the folk festival circuit and *The Prairie Home Companion* National Public Radio show. They shared the stage with the Grateful Dead in 1990, and for their 1991 album *Cajun Conja* they were joined by one of Doucet's heroes, guitarist Richard Thompson. Beausoleil also came to the attention of a wider mainstream audience when it backed Mary Chapin Carpenter on her Grammy-winning "Down at the Twist and Shout" (1991).

The band won its own Grammy in 1997, when *L'Amour ou la Folie (Love or Folly)* received the Best Traditional Folk Album award. While Beausoleil has expanded its musical palate, adding Latin flavors to 1999's *Cajunization,* Doucet has also recorded with the more traditionally Arcadian Savoy-Doucet Cajun Band.

The Beautiful South

Formed 1988, Hull, Eng.
Paul Heaton (b. May 9, 1962, Birkenhead, Eng.), voc.; Dave Hemingway (b. Sep. 20, 1960, Hull), voc.; Dave Rotheray (b. Feb. 9, 1963, Hull), gtr.; Sean Welch (b. Apr. 12, 1965, Enfield, Eng.), bass; Briana Corrigan (b. May 30, Antrim, Eng.), voc.; Dave Stead (b. Oct. 15, 1966, Huddersfield, Eng.), drums.
1989—*Welcome to the Beautiful South* (Go! Discs/Elektra) 1990—*Choke* 1992—*0898* 1993—(– Corrigan; + Jacqueline Abbott [b. Nov. 10, 1973, Merseyside], voc.) 1994—*Miaow* (Go! Discs) 1995—*Best Of: Carry On Up the Charts* (Go! Discs/PolyGram) 1996—*Blue Is the Colour* (Go! Discs) 1999—*Quench* (PolyGram) 2000—*Painting It Red* (Ark 21) (– Abbott).

When the British pop band the Housemartins [see Fatboy Slim/The Housemartins entry] dissolved in the late '80s, frontman Paul Heaton and drummer Dave Hemingway formed the Beautiful South; its name, a barb aimed at the posh southern region of the country, is as drenched in irony as its lyrical sentiments. The Beautiful South's juxtaposing of sweet vocals and sunny hooks with acerbic lyrics evoked the group from whose ashes it rose, while it replaced the Housemartins' jangly guitar arrangements with jazzier textures. Fleshing out their previous band's music, both Heaton and Hemingway sang in the Beautiful South, as did ex–Anthill Runaways vocalist Briana Corrigan (replaced in 1993 by Jacqueline Abbott, who, in turn, left in 2000). Their lush orchestrations gained the band several U.K. hits, starting as early as its first single, "Song for Whoever" (#2, 1989). Lyricist Heaton's caustic wit drew mixed reviews from critics, some of whom found him too clever—or bitter—for his own good. The British public, however, seemed not to care: The band's greatest-hits collection, *Carry On Up the Charts,* still ranks as one of the fastest-selling albums in U.K. history. Although Beautiful South albums continued to sell well in the U.K. into the 21st century, the band never made more than a passing impression in America.

Be-Bop Deluxe

Formed 1972, England
Bill Nelson (b. Dec. 18, 1948, Wakefield, Eng.), gtr., voc., kybds.; Robert Bryan (b. Eng.), bass; Nicholas Chatterton-Dew (b. Eng.), drums; Ian Parking (b. Eng.), gtr.; Richard Brown (b. Eng.), kybds.
1974—(group disbands; re-forms: Nelson; + Milton Reame-James, kybds.; + Paul Jeffreys, bass; + Simon Fox, drums) *Axe Victim* (Harvest) (– Reame-James; – Jeffreys; + Charles Tumahai, bass) 1975—*Futurama* (+ Andrew Clark, kybds.) 1976—*Sunburst Finish; Modern Music* 1977—*Live in the Air Age* 1978—*Drastic Plastic* 1979—*The Best and the Rest of Be-Bop Deluxe.*

Bill Nelson was an accomplished guitarist by his late teens; he began his professional career in his early 20s. With a Yorkshire-based group, Gentle Revolution, he recorded two locally distributed albums. On his own he recorded a home-produced LP entitled *Northern Dream* in 1971. He put together Be-Bop Deluxe, styled after David Bowie's science-fiction rock efforts, in early 1972. Though a modest success in England, the band failed to attract large audiences in America, and Nelson retired its name in 1979. His next group, Bill Nelson's Red Noise, produced the LP *Sound-on-Sound* in 1979 LP. Since then Nelson, who is also an accomplished producer, has maintained a staggeringly prolific solo career, though many of his largely experimental, soundtrack-like records—some all-instrumental, some with vocals—remained unreleased in the U.S. until 1989, when his complicated import catalogue become available domestically. *Quit Dreaming and Get on the Beam,* his 1981 double LP, hit the English Top 10. He continues to record, both on his own and with other artists, with remarkable frequency.

Beck

Born Beck Hansen, July 8, 1970, Los Angeles, CA
1993—*Golden Feelings* (Sonic Enemy) 1994—*A Western*

Harvest Field by Moonlight EP (Fingerpaint); *Stereopathetic Soulmanure* (Flipside); *Mellow Gold* (DGC); *One Foot in the Grave* (K) 1996—*Odelay* (DGC) 1998—*Mutations* 1999—*Midnite Vultures* (Interscope).

Beck took the lo-fi sound of DIY indie rock to the top of the charts in 1994 with his oddball folk-rap hit "Loser." But his avant-pop musical palette extends well beyond the beats and samples of that hit, including everything from feedback and other sources of noise to toy instruments and found sounds. His disjointed, surreal lyrics have often been compared to *Highway 61 Revisited*–era Bob Dylan.

Beck was born in L.A. to bohemian parents. His mother, Bibbe, was raised amid New York's Andy Warhol Factory art scene of the '60s and in the '90s was part of the underground L.A. punk-drag band Black Fag. His father was a bluegrass street musician. During his childhood, Beck was shuttled back and forth between his mother in L.A. and his paternal grandparents in Kansas. His grandfather, Al Hansen, was a pioneer in the avant-garde Fluxus movement, and in 1998, Beck helped put together a traveling art exhibition that paired his visual artwork with his late grandfather's. During his teens he discovered the music of Sonic Youth and Pussy Galore. After hearing a record by Mississippi John Hurt at a friend's house, however, he began playing his own postpunk brand of acoustic country blues.

In 1989 Beck took a bus to New York City, where he caught the tail end of the ill-fated East Village antifolk scene.

Beck

After running out of money, Beck moved back to L.A., where he started performing in arty Silverlake coffeeshops along with other underground acts such as Ethyl Meatplow and That Dog. He was approached during this period by Bongload Records owner Tom Rothrock, whose casual recording sessions with Beck produced "Loser." The single came out on Bongload and became so popular on L.A.'s alternative radio station KROQ that it led to a bidding war among the major labels. DGC signed Beck to an unusual deal whereby the songwriter could continue recording for tiny indie labels. "Loser" reached #10 and its album, the critically acclaimed *Mellow Gold* (#13, 1994), sold 500,000 copies. A second single, "Beercan," reached only #27 on *Billboard*'s Modern Rock Chart, and Beck seemed in danger of being lumped in with novelty acts.

Stereopathetic Soulmanure, another critical success, failed to sell as big because it was released on the tiny L.A. label Flipside. *One Foot in the Grave*, released on the Olympia, Washington, label K later that year, showed Beck's songwriting was becoming stronger and more focused than ever.

It was *Odelay* (#16, 1996) that really put Beck on the map. The platinum album pushed his earlier sound-pastiche experiments further, earned album-of-the-year nods from publications including ROLLING STONE, *Spin*, and the *Village Voice*, and won Beck two Grammys: Best Alternative Music Performance for the album, and Best Rock Male Vocal Performance for "Where It's At." Beck toured for two full years with a full band, DJ, and horn section and earned a reputation as an impressive live performer.

Beck's next album, *Mutations* (#13, 1998), offered considerably quieter, stripped-down fare, reminiscent of the folky *One Foot in the Grave*. Intended for release on the indie label Bongload, which had released the 12-inch of "Loser," it was released on DGC instead. With the pop-culture-meets-soul *Midnite Vultures* (#34, 1999), Beck returned to his sonic-collage making. The album, which he produced himself (except for two tracks he coproduced with the Dust Brothers, who also coproduced *Odelay*), featured Stax-Volt horns on "Sexx Laws" and the falsetto soul workout "Debra," which was written during the *Odelay* sessions and had become a live staple. Both albums garnered critical praise (with *Vultures* earning two Grammy nominations), went gold.

Jeff Beck

Born June 24, 1944, Surrey, Eng.
Jeff Beck Group, formed 1967, Eng.: Beck, gtr.; Rod Stewart (b. Jan. 10, 1945, London, Eng.), voc.; Ron Wood (b. June 1, 1946, Hillingdon, Eng.), bass; Aynsley Dunbar (b. 1946, Liverpool, Eng.), drums.
1967—(– Dunbar; + Mickey Waller, drums) 1968—(+ Nicky Hopkins [b. Feb. 24, 1944, London; d. Sep. 6, 1994, Nashville, TN], kybds.) *Truth* (Epic) (– Waller; + Tony Newman, drums) 1969—*Beck-Ola* 1971—(new group: Max Middleton, kybds.; Cozy Powell [b. Dec. 29, 1947, Cirencester, Eng.], drums; Clive

Chaman, bass; Bobby Tench, voc.) *Rough and Ready* 1972—*The Jeff Beck Group* (new lineup: Tim Bogert, bass; Carmine Appice, drums) 1973—*Beck, Bogert and Appice.*
Jeff Beck solo: 1975—*Blow by Blow; Truth/Beck-Ola* 1976—*Wired* 1977—*Jeff Beck With the Jan Hammer Group—Live* 1980—*There and Back* 1985—*Flash* 1989—*Jeff Beck's Guitar Shop With Terry Bozzio and Tony Hymas* 1991—*Beckology* 1993—*Crazy Legs* (with the Big Town Playboys) 1999—*Who Else!* 2000—*You Had It Coming.*

One of the most influential lead guitarists in rock, Jeff Beck has helped shape blues rock, psychedelia, and heavy metal. Beck's groups have been short-lived, and he has probably been handicapped by the fact that he doesn't sing, but his aggressive style—encompassing screaming, bent sustained notes, distortion and feedback, and crisply articulated fast passagework—has been more important than his material.

After attending Wimbledon Art College in London, Beck backed Lord Sutch before replacing Eric Clapton in the Yardbirds [see entry]. He established his reputation with that band, but he left in late 1966 and after a short sabbatical released a version of "Love Is Blue," played deliberately out of tune because he loathed the song. In 1967 he founded the Jeff Beck Group with Ron Wood and Rod Stewart; the band's reworkings of blues-based material laid the groundwork for '70s heavy metal. Clashing temperaments broke up the group after two acclaimed LPs and several U.S. tours. Stewart and Wood went on to join the Faces [see the Small Faces/the Faces entry], and Stewart continued to use drummer Mickey Waller on his solo albums until 1974. Beck was planning to form a band with Vanilla Fudge members Tim Bogert and Carmine Appice when he was sidelined for 18 months with a fractured skull he sustained in a car crash. (A car aficionado, Beck has been in three crashes and was once sidelined for months after getting his thumb trapped under a car.) When he recovered, Bogert and Appice were busy in Cactus, so Beck assembled a second Jeff Beck Group and put out two albums of Memphis funk laced with heavy metal. When Cactus broke up in late 1972, Beck, Bogert, and Appice returned Beck to a power trio format, but weak vocals hampered the band, and it dissolved in early 1974.

Beck then went into the first of many periods of hibernation. In 1975 he reemerged in an all-instrumental format, playing jazzy tunes. He toured as coheadliner with the Mahavishnu Orchestra and started an on-again, off-again collaboration with former Mahavishnu keyboardist Jan Hammer in 1976 with *Wired* (#16). During the later '70s Beck reportedly spent most of his time on his 70-acre estate outside London. He and Hammer worked together on the 1980 album *There and Back,* but Hammer did not join Beck for his 1980 tour, the guitarist's first in over four years. In 1981 Beck appeared at Amnesty International's Secret Policeman's Ball, and in 1985 he toured Japan. *Flash,* which includes Beck's sole charting single, "People Get Ready" (#48, 1985), with Rod Stewart on vocals, and the Grammy-winning "Escape," written by Hammer, peaked at #39. Four years later *Jeff Beck's Guitar Shop With Terry Bozzio and Tony Hymas* (#49, 1989) garnered the Grammy for Best Rock Instrumental Performance. *Crazy Legs,* an homage to Gene Vincent's Blue Caps and rockabilly guitar legend Cliff Gallup, met with mixed reviews.

During the '80s and '90s Beck turned up on recordings by artists including Mick Jagger, Malcolm McLaren, Roger Waters, and Jon Bon Jovi. He finally recorded an album of new material (all instrumental) in 1999. On *Who Else!,* the guitarist got support from longtime collaborators Hammer (on one song) and Hymas and explored a more electronic environment; a tour followed. The same year Beck was nominated for two Grammys: "A Day in the Life," his contribution to George Martin's album *In My Life,* was nominated for Best Pop Instrumental Performance, while the guitarist's own "What Mama Said" was nominated for Best Rock Instrumental Performance. Beck spent much of 1999 touring, then returned to the studio with his road band to record *You Had It Coming.*

The Bee Gees

Formed 1958, Brisbane, Austral.
Barry Gibb (b. Sep. 1, 1947, Manchester, Eng.), voc., gtr.; Robin Gibb (b. Dec. 22, 1949, Isle of Man, Eng.), voc.; Maurice Gibb (b. Dec. 22, 1949, Isle of Man), voc., bass, kybds.
1967—*Bee Gees First* (Atco) 1968—*Horizontal; Rare Precious and Beautiful; Rare Precious and Beautiful, vol. 2; Idea* 1969—*Odessa; Best of Bee Gees* 1970—(– R. Gibb) *Cucumber Castle* (Atco); (+ R. Gibb) *Sound of Love* (Polydor) 1971—*2 Years On* (Atco); *Trafalgar* 1972—*To Whom It May Concern* 1973—*Life in a Tin Can* (RSO); *The Best of the Bee Gees, vol. 2* 1974—*Mr. Natural* 1975—*Main Course* 1976—*Children of the World; Bee Gees Gold* 1977—*Here at Last . . . Live; Saturday Night Fever* soundtrack (with others) 1979—*Spirits Having Flown; Bee Gees Greatest* 1981—*Living Eyes* 1983—*Staying Alive* 1987—*E-S-P* (Warner Bros.) 1989—*One* 1990—*Tales From the Brothers Gibb: A History in Song, 1967–1990* (Polydor) 1991—*High Civilization* (Warner Bros.) 1993—*Size Isn't Everything* (Polydor) 1997—*Still Waters* 1998—*One Night Only* 1999—*Tomorrow the World* (Magnum) 2001—*This Is Where I Came In* (Universal).

In a career now in its fourth decade, the Bee Gees have sold over 120 million albums worldwide. At several points throughout their career, Barry, Maurice, and Robin Gibb have borne commercial dry spells, and critics have chronically dismissed them. However, with the passage of time, their legacy is less defined by the phenomenal disco crossover success of their *Saturday Night Fever* era than by their enduring pop appeal and the modern standards they created ("To Love Somebody," "Words," "How Can You Mend a Broken Heart"). If anything, the Bee Gees' versatility and undiminished knack for creating hits have earned the group a belated if sometimes grudging critical respect.

The three Gibb brothers (Barry and fraternal twins Robin and Maurice), sons of English bandleader Hugh Gibb, started performing in 1955. They moved with their parents to Bris-

The Bee Gees: Maurice Gibb, Barry Gibb, Robin Gibb

bane in 1958 and worked talent shows and other amateur outlets, singing sets of Everly Brothers songs and an occasional Barry Gibb composition, by this time calling themselves the Bee Gees. They signed with Australia's Festival Records in 1962 and released a dozen singles and two albums in the next five years. Then as now, close high harmonies were the Bee Gees' trademark, and the Gibbs wrote their own material.

They hosted a weekly Australian TV show, but their records went unnoticed until 1967, when "Spicks and Specks" hit #1 after the Bee Gees had relocated to England. There they expanded to a quintet with drummer Colin Peterson and Vince Melouney (both Australians) and found themselves a new manager, Robert Stigwood, then employed by the Beatles' NEMS Enterprises. Their first Northern Hemisphere single, "New York Mining Disaster 1941," was a hit in both the U.K. and the U.S. (#14, 1967), and was followed by a string of equally popular ballads: "To Love Somebody" (#17, 1967), "Holiday" (#16, 1967), "Massachusetts" (#11, 1967), "Words" (#15, 1968), "I've Got to Get a Message to You" (#8, 1968), and "I Started a Joke" (#6, 1969). Their clean-cut neo-Edwardian image and English-accented three-part harmonies were a variation on the Beatles' approach, although the Bee Gees leaned toward ornate orchestration and sentimentality as opposed to American-style straight-ahead rock.

Cracks in their facade began to show in 1969, when the nonfamily members left the group and reports of excessive lifestyles and fighting among the brothers surfaced. From mid-1969 to late 1970 Robin tried a solo career and had a #2 U.K. hit, "Saved by the Bell." Meanwhile, Barry and Maurice (then married to singer Lulu) recorded *Cucumber Castle* as a duo and cut some singles individually. The trio reunited for two more hit ballads—the gold "Lonely Days" (#3, 1970) and "How Can You Mend a Broken Heart" (#1, 1971)—before bottoming out with a string of flops between 1971 and 1975. Stigwood effected a turnabout by recruiting producer Arif Mardin, who steered them to the funk-plus-falsetto combination that brought them their third round of hits. *Main Course* (#14, 1976), including "Jive Talkin' " (#1, 1975) and "Nights on Broadway" (#7, 1975), caught disco on the upswing and gave the Bee Gees their first platinum album.

In 1976 Stigwood's RSO label broke away from its parent company, Atlantic, rendering Mardin unavailable to the Bee Gees. Engineer Karl Richardson and arranger Albhy Galuten took over as producers, and the group continued to record with Miami rhythm sections for hits such as "You Should Be Dancing" (#1, 1976) and a ballad, "Love So Right" (#3, 1976), which recalled the Philly-Motown influence. By this point, the brothers had relocated to Miami. Stigwood, meanwhile, had produced the film versions of *Jesus Christ Superstar* and *Tommy,* and asked the Bee Gees for four or five songs he could use in the soundtrack of a John Travolta vehicle about the mid-1970s Brooklyn disco scene, *Saturday Night Fever.* The soundtrack album, a virtual best-of-disco, included Bee Gees chart-toppers "Stayin' Alive," "Night Fever," and "How Deep Is Your Love," hit #1, stayed on the album chart for over two years, and eventually sold 30 million copies worldwide. Barry, with Galutan and Richardson, also wrote and produced hits for Yvonne Elliman, Samantha Sang, Tavares, Frankie Valli, and younger brother Andy Gibb [see entry] as well as the title tune for the film version of the Broadway hit *Grease.*

In 1978, with *Saturday Night Fever* still high on the charts, the Bee Gees started Music for UNICEF, donating the royalties from a new song and recruiting other hitmakers to do the same. They also appeared in Stigwood's movie fiasco *Sgt. Pepper's Lonely Hearts Club Band* and continued to record. After *Saturday Night Fever,* even the platinum *Spirits Having Flown* (#1, 1979) with three #1 hits—"Too Much Heaven," "Tragedy," and "Love You Inside Out"—seemed anticlimactic. As of 1979, the Bee Gees had made five platinum albums and more than 20 hit singles.

Along with such phenomenal commercial success came a critical backlash. While the intense antidisco sentiment certainly played a role, the fact that one literally could not turn on a radio without hearing a Bee Gees track did not help. Their career then entered another dry season. In October 1980 the Bee Gees filed a $200 million suit against Stigwood, claiming mismanagement. Meanwhile, Barry produced and sang duets with Barbra Streisand on *Guilty* (1980). The lawsuit was settled out of court, with mutual public apologies, in May 1981. *Living Eyes* (#41, 1981) was the Bee Gees' last album for RSO. They composed the soundtrack to *Saturday Night Fever*'s dismal sequel, *Stayin' Alive;* the soundtrack went to #6 and platinum and included "Woman in You" (#24, 1983). Barry also wrote and produced an album for Dionne Warwick, *Heartbreaker.* With his brothers he cowrote Diana Ross' "Chain Reaction" and the Kenny Rogers–Dolly Parton hit "Islands in the Stream."

In 1987 the Brothers Gibb again joined forces and refired their singing career with *E-S-P*, which included "You Win Again" (#75, 1987). While these records appeared commercial disappointments in comparison to previous chart showings, in fact this was the case only in the U.S. *E-S-P* went to #1 in Germany and the Top 5 in the U.K. Thus began another phase of the Bee Gees' history, in which their singles and albums would top the charts practically everywhere but the U.S.

In March 1988, their younger brother Andy Gibb died of myocarditis, a heart condition, at age 30. He had a long history of addiction to drugs and alcohol, and his surviving brothers were devastated by the loss. They retired for a time, and Maurice suffered a brief relapse of his alcoholism. They returned with *One* (German Top 5, U.K. Top 30) featuring the trio's highest-charting single of the '80s in its title track (#7, 1989), followed by *High Civilization* (1991), which did not even chart in the U.S. but hit #2 in Germany and the U.K. Top 30.

In 1997 the Bee Gees were inducted into the Rock and Roll Hall of Fame. They also released *Still Waters* (#11, 1997), which produced the minor hits "Alone" (#28, 1997) and "Still Waters (Run Deep)" (#57, 1997). A live album, *One Night Only* (#72, 1998), was the soundtrack to a live concert, which was filmed. *Tomorrow the World* and *This Is Where I Came In* (#33, 2001) followed. The group has twice received Britain's Ivor Novello Trust for Outstanding Contribution to British Music (1988, 1997) and the BRIT Award (1997), all in recognition of their outstanding contribution to British music. In 1994 they were inducted into the Songwriters' Hall of Fame.

Adrian Belew

Born Robert Steven Belew, Dec. 23, 1949, Covington, KY
1982—*Lone Rhino* (Island) 1983—*Twang Bar King* 1986—*Desire Caught by the Tail* 1987—*The Bears* (Primitive Man) 1988—*Rise and Shine* 1989—*Mr. Music Head* (Atlantic) 1990—*Young Lions* 1991—*Desire of the Rhino King* (Island) 1992—*Inner Revolution* (Atlantic) 1994—*Here* (Plan 9/Caroline) 1995—*Acoustic Adrian Belew* (Discipline); *Experimental Guitar Series, vol. 1* (Adrian Belew Presents) 1997—*The Guitar as Orchestra* (Discipline); *Op Zop Too Wah* (Passenger) 1998—*Belew Prints* (Adrian Belew Presents); *Salad Days* (Thirsty Ear) 2000—*Coming Attractions.*

A wizard of sonic manipulation and texture, Belew has been the guitarist of choice for the art-rock crowd, playing with Frank Zappa, Talking Heads, David Bowie, Laurie Anderson, and Nine Inch Nails [see entries]. He has also fronted a version of King Crimson and sustained a lower-profile career as a solo artist.

In his hometown of Cincinnati, Belew was originally a rock drummer before developing his prowess on guitar. He was working the mid-American club circuit with his band Sweetheart when Zappa happened to attend a Nashville performance and tapped Belew for his band. Belew toured and recorded with Zappa (*Sheik Yerbouti*, 1979). After touring with David Bowie (captured on 1978's *Stage;* he also appears on 1979's *Lodger*), Belew recorded with Talking Heads (*Remain in Light*, 1980). Belew's startling work—e.g., his careening solo on "The Great Curve"—immediately established him as a sought-after player. Belew toured briefly with the first expanded edition of Talking Heads and can be heard on their live 1982 album *The Name of This Band Is Talking Heads.* Belew later worked with Talking Heads Chris Frantz and Tina Weymouth on their band Tom Tom Club's first album.

In 1981 Belew joined Robert Fripp, Bill Bruford, and Tony Levin in a latter-day King Crimson. Belew's virtuosic playing—which by now included a whole lexicon of electronically produced animal sounds—as well as his urgent singing of his own caustic lyrics helped make this one of the most popular and respected Crimson lineups. Belew recorded *Discipline* (1981), *Beat* (1982), and *Three of a Perfect Pair* (1984) with the band before they broke up in 1984. He also made guest appearances on Laurie Anderson's *Mister Heartbreak* (1984) and *Home of the Brave* (1986) and on Paul Simon's *Graceland* (1986).

With the Bears—a short-lived band he helped form in 1985—and in his subsequent career as a solo artist, Belew displayed his ease with pop songwriting and singing. *Mr. Music Head* yielded the minor hit "Oh Daddy" (#58, 1989), a humorous look at the vicissitudes of a middle-aged rocker, which Belew sang with his 11-year-old daughter, Audie. *Inner Revolution* both paid homage to, and affectionately deconstructed, the sound of the Beatles. He joined David Bowie on his 1989 Sound + Vision career retrospective tour. In 1994 Belew's guitar playing was featured on the industrial band Nine Inch Nails' album *The Downward Spiral.* Belew's own album of that year, *Here,* recorded at his home in Cincinnati, showcased his vocals and multi-instrumental expertise; Belew played all the instruments and produced. Throughout the '90s and into the new century, Belew continued his guitar explorations, either acoustically or, more typically, employing a full range of techno-heavy effects—an approach best summed up by the title of his 1997 release *The Guitar as Orchestra.*

Archie Bell and the Drells

Formed mid-'60s, Houston, TX
Archie Bell (b. Sep. 1, 1944, Henderson, TX); Huey "Billy" Butler; Joe Cross; James Wise.
1968—*Tighten Up* (Atlantic) 1969—(– Butler; – Cross; + Willie Parnell; + Lee Bell) *There's Gonna Be a Showdown* 1977—*Dance Your Troubles Away* (Philadelphia International); *Hard Not to Like It.*
Archie Bell solo: 1981—*I Never Had It So Good* (Becket).

Archie Bell and his group had the nation dancing in 1968 with the strutting "Tighten Up" (#1 pop, #1 R&B), which featured a choked guitar phrase. The Drells were frequently produced by noted Philadelphia soul stylist Bunny Sigler, although their followup hit, the Top 10 "I Can't Stop Dancing" in late 1968, was produced by the then-emerging black music titans Kenny Gamble and Leon Huff. They scored another Top 30 success in early 1969, "There's Gonna Be a Showdown," but have since reached only a loyal black audience; in 1970 they released a #33 R&B version of "Wrap It Up," a minor hit for the Fabulous Thunderbirds in 1986. "Let's Groove (Part 1)" was a Top 10 R&B hit in 1976. In the late '70s Archie Bell and the Drells recorded extensively for the Philadelphia International label, releasing a discofied version of "Tighten Up." By 1981 Bell was recording solo for the Becket label.

William Bell

Born William Yarborough, July 16, 1939, Memphis, TN
1967—*The Soul of a Bell* (Stax) 1968—*Tribute to a King; Duets* 1969—*Bound to Happen* 1971—*Wow . . . William Bell* 1973—*Phases of Reality* 1974—*Relating* 1977—*Coming Back for More* (Mercury); *It's Time You Took Another Listen* 1983—*Survivor* (Kat Family) 1985—*Passion* (Wilbe) 1989—*On a Roll* 1990—*The Best of William Bell* (Stax) 1992—*Bedtime Stories* (Wilbe); *A Little Something Extra* (Stax).

A soul singer of great subtlety, William Bell was one of the principal architects of the Memphis Sound. Starting off with Rufus Thomas' band in 1953 and recording with the Del Rios vocal quartet in 1957, Bell became an early writer and performer for the Stax/Volt label. Going solo in 1961, the next year he released "You Don't Miss Your Water," its stark power exemplifying the Stax style that provided counterpoint to Motown's pop approach. Sidelined by two years in the army, Bell reemerged in the mid-'60s with songs that fared respectably on the R&B charts: "Everybody Loves a Winner" (#18, 1967) and "A Tribute to a King" (#16, 1968). The latter, an homage to Otis Redding, made clear, however, that Bell had been eclipsed commercially by such other classic soul talents as Redding, Sam and Dave, and Wilson Pickett.

A 1968 R&B Top 10, "I Forgot to Be Your Lover," and duets with Judy Clay ("Private Number," "My Baby Specializes") highlighted Bell's skills as a balladeer, and the singer has continued crafting sophisticated soul. In 1969 Bell moved to Atlanta and founded his own Peachtree label; with 1976 and his signing to Mercury came the refreshing success of "Trying to Love Two," a #1 R&B hit.

Throughout the 1980s, on Kat Family and his own Wilbe label, Bell continued a low-profile career. In 1997 he received the Pioneer Award from the Rhythm & Blues Foundation. He continues to perform. As a writer and as an elegant singer of romantic tumult, Bell remains a seminal artist.

Bell Biv DeVoe

Formed 1988, Boston, MA
Michael Bivins (b. Aug. 10, 1968, Boston), voc.; Ricky Bell (b. Sep. 18, 1967, Boston), voc.; Ronnie DeVoe (b. Nov. 17, 1967, Boston), voc.
1990—*Poison* (MCA) 1991—*WBBD-Bootcity! The Remix Album* 1993—*Hootie Mack.*

As members of the teenage R&B vocal group New Edition [see entry], Ricky Bell, Michael Bivins, and Ronnie DeVoe kept fairly low profiles, leaving the limelight to singers Ralph Tresvant and Bobby Brown, and later Johnny Gill. But when Brown went solo in 1986, Bell, Bivins, and DeVoe began thinking about pursuing their own separate paths together. Two years later—with some prodding from prominent hip-hop producers Jimmy Jam and Terry Lewis—Bell Biv DeVoe was born, and the fierce, provocative pop funk it eventually unleashed on the charts marked a dramatic departure from New Edition's wholesome image.

On New Edition's last studio album, 1988's *Heartbreak,* Bell, Bivins, and DeVoe had worked with Jam and Lewis, who had crafted for them a harder-edged, more urban sound. As a subsequent tour wrapped, the producers approached the three singers with the idea for Bell Biv DeVoe. The trio then enlisted various hip-hop savants—including Public Enemy producers Hank and Keith Shocklee—to write and produce material for its debut album. Released in 1990, *Poison* featured streetsmart, rap-tinged arrangements and sexually suggestive lyrics. Its title track, a slamming slice of misogyny, topped the R&B chart and became a #3 pop hit. The album itself shot to #5 pop and #1 R&B that year and included "Do Me!" (#3 pop, #4 R&B), "B.B.D. (I Thought It Was Me)" (#1 R&B), and "When Will I See You Smile Again?" (#3 R&B).

In 1991 the group had a #9 R&B single, "She's Dope!" Later that year Bell Biv DeVoe released *WBBD-Bootcity! The Remix Album* (#18 pop and R&B). In 1992 the trio reappeared on the singles chart with "Gangsta" (#21 pop, #22 R&B, 1993), an unlikely collaboration with smooth soul singer Luther Vandross. Bell Biv DeVoe released its third album, *Hootie Mack,* in 1993 (#19 pop, #6 R&B), which yielded the single "Something in Your Eyes" (#38 pop, #6 R&B, 1993).

Regina Belle

Born Regina Edna Belle, July 15, 1963, Englewood, NJ
1987—*All by Myself* (Columbia) 1989—*Stay With Me* 1993—*Passion* 1995—*Reachin' Back* 1997—*Baby Come to Me: The Best of Regina Belle* 1998—*Believe in Me* (MCA).

A contemporary soul singer with roots in gospel and jazz, Regina Belle had several R&B hits in the late '80s before her 1992 #1 pop duet with Peabo Bryson, "A Whole New World (Aladdin's Theme)"—the theme song from the Walt Disney animated film *Aladdin* that won three Grammys as well as an Oscar. Born to a gospel-loving mother and a father who was an R&B enthusiast, Belle began singing in church as a child, and was influenced early on by the work of Billie Holiday, Nancy Wilson, and Phyllis Hyman. During high school, Belle studied opera at the Manhattan School of Music. Then, while majoring in accounting and history at Rutgers University, she sang with a jazz ensemble.

In 1985 she began singing backup for the Manhattans and soon signed to that band's label, Columbia. Belle's debut album, *All by Myself,* yielded the #2 R&B hit "Show Me the Way," as well as favorable comparisons to Anita Baker and

Sade. *Stay With Me* became a #1 R&B album and topped the singles chart for that genre with "Baby Come to Me" and "Make It Like It Was." Also in 1989, Belle teamed up with James "J.T." Taylor, of Kool and the Gang, on "All I Want Is Forever," a #2 R&B hit featured in the movie *Tap. Reachin' Back,* a collection of '70s R&B covers, produced the #29 R&B single "Love T.K.O.," a version of the 1980 Teddy Pendergrass soul classic.

Belle and Sebastian

Formed 1996, Glasgow, Scot.
Stuart Murdoch, voc., gtr.; Stuart David, bass, voc.; Chris Geddes, kybds.; Sarah Martin, violin; Stevie Jackson, gtr., voc.; Richard Colburn, drums; Isobel Campbell, cello, voc.
1996—*Tigermilk* (Electric Honey); *If You're Feeling Sinister* (Jeepster) 1997—*Dog on Wheels* EP; *Lazy Line Painter Jane* EP; *3..6..9..Seconds of Light* EP 1998—(+ Mick Cooke, trumpet) *The Boy With the Arab Strap* (Matador) 2000—*Fold Your Hands Child, You Walk Like a Peasant* (– David).
Campbell solo as Gentle Waves: 1999—*The Green Fields of Foreverland* (Jeepster) 2000—*Swansong for You.*
David with Looper: 1999—*Up a Tree* (Sub Pop) 2000—*The Geometrid.*

Scotland's Belle and Sebastian were one of indie rock's most celebrated groups during the '90s. Critics applauded the band's soft, unobtrusive folk rock, while fans connected with the group's lyrics, which perfectly capture a misfit's cynicism, confusion, and pain. Notorious for their media-shyness—they often use snapshots of friends for press photos, while reluctant frontman Stuart Murdoch refused to conduct interviews until 2000—Belle and Sebastian have nevertheless achieved a surprising amount of commercial success, particularly in the U.K.

Murdoch and bassist Stuart David started playing together in January 1996, recruiting the band's remaining members—including Mick Cooke, who switched from part-time to full-time status in 1998—soon thereafter. Naming the group after a novel by Madame Cécile Aubry (and its resultant French children's television series) about a boy and his dog, the octet recorded a few demos that were chosen for release by the local Stow College music business course, which had a policy of producing one record every year for the college label Electric Honey Records. The label released 1,000 vinyl copies of an album's worth of recordings entitled *Tigermilk.* The pressings sold out so quickly and became such a commodity that collectors paid up to £400 for a copy. (It was eventually rereleased on CD in 1999.)

After signing to U.K. label Jeepster that same year, Belle and Sebastian released *If You're Feeling Sinister.* That same year the octet released a series of EPs: *Dog on Wheels* (#59 U.K.), *Lazy Line Painter Jane* (#41 U.K.), and *3..6..9..Seconds of Light* (#32 U.K.), all three of which were repackaged as the *Lazy Line Painter Jane Box Set* in 2000. The band's next album and first for U.S. label Matador, *The Boy With the Arab Strap* (#12 U.K.), was followed by the band's first full-scale tour of the States. Two years passed before the Glaswegians released a new album of original material, *Fold Your Hands Child, You Walk Like a Peasant,* which entered the U.S. pop charts at #80 and at #10 in the U.K. In the meantime, the band won a 1999 BRIT Award for Best Newcomer. Cellist Isobel Campbell also released two albums of solo material under the name Gentle Waves, while Stuart David recorded two albums as Looper with his wife, Karn, and brother Ronnie Black. In 2000 David left Belle and Sebastian to focus full-time on Looper.

Jesse Belvin

Born Dec. 15, 1933, Texarkana, AR; died Feb. 6, 1960, Los Angeles, CA
1975—*Yesterdays* (RCA) 1990—*Jesse Belvin: The Blues Balladeer* (Specialty) 1991—*Goodnight, My Love* (Flair/Virgin).

Jesse Belvin's untimely death came just as the singer was achieving success commensurate with his influence on West Coast black vocal music in the '50s. He began his career as a 16-year-old vocalist for Big Jay McNeely's band. After a stint in the army, he formed a vocal duo with Marvin Phillips—Jesse and Marvin—and scored an R&B Top 10 hit with "Dream Girl" in 1953. Over the next eight years, he served as unofficial leader of L.A.'s doo-wop groups, coaching them, writing and arranging their material, and using his influence with the city's independent companies to get them recorded. His biggest songwriting success was with "Earth Angel," a million-seller for the Penguins in 1955. He also sang with the Cliques, the Sharptones, Three Dots and a Dash, and the Sheiks. The Cliques had a 1956 hit with his "The Girl in My Dreams."

Belvin recorded as a solo artist for numerous labels, including Specialty, Knight, and Modern/Kent, but not until the mid-'50s did his soft, careful enunciation and tasteful ballads enjoy some success. "Goodnight My Love" hit the R&B Top 10 in 1956. In 1958 Belvin was signed to RCA; in 1959 "Guess Who" went #7 R&B. Nine months later he died in an auto accident.

Belly: See Throwing Muses/Belly

Pat Benatar

Born Patricia Andrzejewski, Jan. 10, 1953, Brooklyn, NY
1979—*In the Heat of the Night* (Chrysalis) 1980—*Crimes of Passion* 1981—*Precious Time* 1982—*Get Nervous* 1983—*Live From Earth* 1984—*Tropico* 1985—*Seven the Hard Way* 1988—*Wide Awake in Dreamland* 1989—*Best Shots* 1991—*True Love* 1993—*Gravity's Rainbow* 1997—*Innamorata* (CMC International) 1998—*8-15-80* 1999—*Synchronistic Wanderings: Recorded Anthology 1979–1999* (Chrysalis/Capitol) 2001—*Extended Version* (BMG Special).

Pat Benatar was the most successful female hard-rock singer of the '80s. She grew up on Long Island, where at age

17 she began vocal training in preparation for study at the Juilliard School of Music. She soon rebelled against the rigorous training and ended her studies. After turning 18, she married Dennis Benatar, a GI stationed in Richmond, Virginia. There she worked as a bank clerk before taking a job as a singing waitress. In 1975 the couple returned to New York; they later divorced.

Benatar began working Manhattan's cabaret circuit in 1975 with a chanteuse style derived from Barbra Streisand and Diana Ross. At Catch a Rising Star, she attracted the attention of club owner Rick Newman, who became her manager. By 1978 she had switched to a more aggressive rock approach, and after being rejected by several labels was signed to Chrysalis.

Benatar's debut went platinum (the first of six) on the strength of the #23 single "Heartbreaker." Her 1980 followup, *Crimes of Passion,* sold over 4 million, yielding two hit singles, "Hit Me With Your Best Shot" (#9, 1980) and "Treat Me Right" (#18, 1981). *Precious Time* (also multiplatinum), boasted "Promises in the Dark" (#38, 1981) and "Fire and Ice" (#17, 1981).

Benatar's early sex-kitten image—which she later stated had been thrust upon her—belied the singer's choice of assertive, tough-girl lyrics and take-no-crap delivery. In 1982 she married her guitarist and musical director, Neil Giraldo, with whom she wrote most of her songs. Her streak of hits continued with "Shadows of the Night" (#13, 1982), "Little Too Late" (#20, 1983), "Love Is a Battlefield" (#5, 1983), and "We Belong" (#5, 1984). She returned to recording after the birth of her first daughter, Haley, with "Invincible" (#10, 1985), "Sex as a Weapon" (#28, 1985), and "All Fired Up" (#19, 1988). Something of a stylistic departure, *True Love,* a collection of blues recordings, produced no hits. Two years later, Benatar was back with *Gravity's Rainbow,* which failed to chart.

The disappointing response to her comeback, along with the birth of her second daughter, Hana, in 1994 and the absorption of her longtime label, Chrysalis, by EMI in 1995, caused an extended break in Benatar's recording career. She left Chrysalis and recorded 1997's largely acoustic *Innamorata* for CMC International, a label that focuses on artists who had their heyday in the '70s and '80s. (The label also released a recording of a 1980 Benatar concert.) In addition to joining new labelmates Styx on a summer tour that year, she performed two dates of the first Lilith Fair. In 1999 Benatar and Giraldo were given carte blanche to select songs for the three-disc hits collection *Synchronistic Wanderings,* distributed by Chrysalis' new parent company. The box set includes eight previously unreleased tracks, including an early cover of Roy Orbison's "Crying." In 2000 the couple began recording a new album for Sony's Portrait label and had turned their attention to encouraging their teenage daughter Haley's band, GLO.

Tony Bennett

Born Anthony Dominick Benedetto, Aug. 3, 1926, Queens, NY
1957—*The Beat of My Heart* (Columbia) 1959—*Basie Swings, Bennett Sings* (Roulette) 1962—*I Left My Heart in San Francisco* (Columbia); *Tony Bennett at Carnegie Hall* 1964—*When Lights Are Low* 1966—*The Movie Song Album* 1975—*The Tony Bennett/Bill Evans Album* (Fantasy) 1976—*The Rodgers and Hart Songbook* (DRG); *Together Again* (with Bill Evans) 1986—*The Art of Excellence* (Columbia) 1987—*Jazz; Bennett/Berlin* 1990—*Astoria: Portrait of the Artist* 1991—*Forty Years: The Artistry of Tony Bennett* 1992—*Perfectly Frank* 1993—*Steppin' Out* 1994—*Tony Bennett—MTV Unplugged* 1995—*Here's to the Ladies* 1997—*On Holiday (A Tribute to Billie Holiday)* 1998—*The Playground* 1999—*Bennett Sings Ellington Hot & Cool* 2000—*Ultimate Tony Bennett.*

The epitome of cool, Tony Bennett is second only to Frank Sinatra as an interpreter of classic jazz-inflected American song. Careful articulation, a sure sense of swing, and an air of restrained bemusement characterize his style. Originally popular in the late '50s, Bennett enjoyed a remarkable resurgence in the early '90s.

His mother American, his father an Italian grocer, Benedetto worked as a singing waiter in his teens. After performing with the U.S. Army's entertainment corps in World War II and then appearing on Arthur Godfrey's talent show, he was discovered, under the stage name Joe Bari, while performing with Pearl Bailey in 1949. Bob Hope then enlisted him to open shows at New York's Paramount Theater and changed his name to Tony Bennett. In 1950, following an audition with Mitch Miller, he was signed to Columbia Records. His first hit, "Because of You" (#1, 1951) remained on the charts for 32 weeks. His next single, Hank Williams' "Cold, Cold Heart," was the first notable pop cover of a country tune. Both featured the Percy Faith Orchestra, who provided the lush backdrop for most of the 24 Top 40 charters he earned before 1964. Among those hits were "Rags to Riches" (#1, 1953), "Stranger in Paradise" (#2, 1953), and "There'll Be No Teardrops Tonight" (#7, 1954). During that period, his *Basie Swings, Bennett Sings* served as a blueprint for later forays into jazz singing; in 1956 he formed an alliance with Ralph Sharon, the pianist and musical director who would become Bennett's lifelong collaborator. In 1962 Bennett sold out Carnegie Hall and recorded his first Grammy Award winner and subsequent trademark, "I Left My Heart in San Francisco" (#19, 1962).

But Bennett was primarily an album artist. Given occasionally to the experimental—1957's *The Beat of My Heart* highlighted percussion as the primary instrumentation—he achieved equal aesthetic triumphs with the polished pop of *The Movie Song Album* (#18, 1966) and the straight-ahead jazz of *When Lights Are Low* (#79, 1964), a tribute to the King Cole Trio. Critics reserved special praise for his work with Bill Evans, a pianist whose elegant minimalism matched Bennett's own.

Yet after his '60s heyday came a fallow spell. Bennett continued to appear in concert, but from 1978 to 1985 he didn't record. In the late '70s he formed an independent label, which fared poorly commercially, and his contract with Columbia was not renewed. While other vocalists of the prerock era had expanded their repertoire to include songs by younger composers, Bennett adamantly refused such a manuever, continuing to record material by the Gershwins, Rodgers and Hart, Cole Porter, and the like. And his career stalled. He concentrated instead on painting and began exhibiting in Paris, London, and New York.

In 1986 Bennett re-signed with Columbia. *The Art of Excellence* featured "Everybody Has the Blues," a duet with Ray Charles. *Bennett/Berlin* was a critically lauded set of Irving Berlin standards performed with Dizzy Gillespie, Dexter Gordon, and George Benson. But it was with 1992's *Perfectly Frank* (#102), an homage to Bennett's favorite singer, Frank Sinatra, that his revival began in earnest. The album won a Grammy, as did *Steppin' Out* (#128, 1993), a collection of songs made famous by Fred Astaire. The singer's son, Danny Bennett, who had managed his father since 1979, capitalized on the newfound popularity, engineering a campaign that saw Bennett appearing in a cameo role on television's youth-oriented *The Simpsons* in 1991. Paul Shaffer, musical director for *Late Night With David Letterman*, became Bennett's champion; by appearing on that television show, the singer furthered his exposure to a younger demographic. With the release of *Forty Years: The Artistry of Tony Bennett*, a four-disc retrospective, Bennett's stature was confirmed, while his hipness quotient intensified with his appearance, alongside Flea and Anthony Kiedis of the Red Hot Chili Peppers, as a presenter at the 1993 MTV Music Video Awards. In 1994 *Tony Bennett—MTV Unplugged* (#48), including duets with k.d. lang and Elvis Costello, gained Bennett two more Grammys, including Album of the Year.

In 1996 Rizzoli International published *What My Heart Has Seen*, a collection of Bennett's paintings. In addition to graduating from New York City's High School of Industrial Arts, Bennett has been tutored by artists such as John Barnicoat, Everett Kinstler, and Basil Baylin. His body of artwork includes portraits of idols such as Frank Sinatra, Ella Fitzgerald, and Duke Ellington. In 1998 he published his autobiography, *The Good Life*.

George Benson

Born Mar. 22, 1943, Pittsburgh, PA
1964—*The New Boss Guitar* (Original Jazz Classics) 1965—*Benson Burner* (Columbia) 1966—*It's Uptown; The George Benson Cookbook* 1967—*Giblet Gravy* (Verve/MGM) 1968—*Shape of Things to Come* (A&M) 1969—*The Other Side of Abbey Road* 1971—*Beyond the Blue Horizon* (CTI) 1972—*White Rabbit* (Columbia) 1973—*Body Talk* (CTI) 1974—*Bad Benson* (Columbia) 1976—*Benson and Farrell* (with Joe Farrell) (CTI) 1977—*George Benson in Concert—Carnegie Hall; Breezin'* (Warner Bros.); *In Flight* 1978—*Weekend in L.A.* 1979—*Livin' Inside Your Love* 1980—*Give Me the Night* 1981—*The George Benson Collection* 1983—*In Your Eyes* 1985—*20/20* 1986—*While the City Sleeps* 1987—*Collaboration* (with Earl Klugh) 1988—*Twice the Love* 1989—*Tenderly* 1990—*Big Boss Band Featuring the Count Basie Orchestra* 1991—*Midnight Moods* (Telstar) 1993—*Love Remembers* (Warner Bros.) 1994—*Vol. 21—Verve Jazz Masters* (Verve) 1995—*Best of George Benson* (Warner Bros.) 1996—*That's Right* (GRP) 1997—*Talkin' Verve* (Verve); *Best of—Instrumentals* (Warner Bros.) 1998—*Standing Together* (GRP) 2000—*Absolute Benson: The George Benson Anthology* (Rhino).

Jazz guitarist/vocalist George Benson's breakthrough came in 1976 when *Breezin'* brought him into the pop mainstream; from 1976 through 1983, he racked up seven Top 40 singles. His jazz-pop formula has since been updated by the likes of Earl Klugh and Kenny G, while Benson himself continues to release expert mellow fare—jazz- and blues-based pop material with a consistent melodic emphasis.

Benson won a singing contest when he was four years old and later performed on radio as Little Georgie Benson. He took up the guitar at age eight but worked as a vocalist with numerous Pittsburgh R&B bands before playing guitar in public at age 15. Soon after, he began playing sessions outside Pittsburgh. With his groups the Altairs and George Benson and His All-Stars, he recorded for Amy Records. By the late '50s he had given up singing to concentrate solely on the guitar. In 1965 he moved to New York and met his main influence, Wes Montgomery; John Hammond signed him to Columbia. Though his mainstream jazz albums on Columbia, A&M, and CTI helped him establish a reputation, sales were never outstanding.

In late 1975 Benson signed with Warner Bros., where for the first time in his recording career he was encouraged to sing. *Breezin'*, winner of three Grammys in 1976, featured Leon Russell's "This Masquerade," the first song in history to reach #1 on the jazz, R&B, and pop charts. His success continued throughout the late '70s and early '80s (all six Warners albums of the period are platinum sellers). Understated pop funk with vocals modeled on Stevie Wonder and Donny Hathaway, his hits included "On Broadway" (#7, 1978), "Give Me the Night" (#4, 1980), and "Turn Your Love Around" (#5, 1981).

Benson's sales have remained consistent, but his life hasn't been without tumult. Becoming a Jehovah's Witness in the early '80s, he credited his conversion for his good fortune. However, one of his sons was killed in a 1991 bar fight. In 1988 CTI Records was awarded $3.2 million in a judgment against Warner Bros. Records; Warners, a jury ruled, owed the money in damages for breaching an agreement with Benson. During this period, Benson reaffirmed his jazz roots with live work with Dizzy Gillespie, Freddie Hubbard, and Lionel Hampton. In 1989 *Tenderly*, with pianist McCoy Tyner, reached the #1 jazz spot; in 1990 *Big Boss Band* featured a vital partnership with the Count Basie Orchestra. In 1993 Benson, an eight-time Grammy winner, again proved his hitmaking currency when his *Love Remembers* supplanted Kenny G's *Breathless* as the #1 Contemporary Jazz album. In 1998 his *Standing Together* featured MDRC, a band including Benson's son Robert. The release incorporated Caribbean and hip-hop elements.

Brook Benton

Born Benjamin Franklin Peay, Sep. 19, 1931, Lugoff, SC; died Apr. 9, 1988, New York, NY
1960—*The Two of Us* (with Dinah Washington) (Mercury) 1961—*Brook Benton's Golden Hits; The Boll Weevil Song and 11 Other Great Hits; If You Believe* 1962—*Singin' the Blues* 1963—*Brook Benton's Golden Hits, vol. 2* 1967—*Laura, What's He Got That I Ain't Got* (Reprise) 1969—*Do Your Own Thing* (Cotillion) 1970—*Brook Benton Today; Home Style* 1971—*The Gospel Truth* 1973—*Something for Everyone* (MGM) 1975—*Brook Benton Sings a Love Story* (RCA) 1976—*This Is Brook Benton* (All Platinum) 1977—*Making Love Is Good for You* (Olde Worlde) 1986—*The Brook Benton Anthology* (Rhino).

One of a handful of black singers who wrote their own material in the early '60s, Brook Benton had four gold records and 16 Top 20 hits over a lengthy and resilient career. Benton's hits feature his smooth baritone (in a style he learned from Nat "King" Cole and Billy Eckstine) and lush string backing. In the early '50s he sang with Bill Landford and the Golden Gate gospel quartets. By the middle of the '50s Benton had begun recording pop songs for Epic and then Vik Records, for whom he had a minor 1958 hit, "A Million Miles From Nowhere."

Collaborations with songwriter Clyde Otis and arranger Belford Hendricks produced 1958 hits for Nat "King" Cole ("Looking Back") and Clyde McPhatter ("A Lover's Question"). In 1959 Otis helped get Benton a contract with Mercury, and Benton began four years of success for the label, beginning with four Benton/Otis/Hendricks compositions: "It's Just a Matter of Time" (#3), "Endlessly" (#12), "Thank You Pretty Baby" (#16), and "So Many Ways" (#6).

Benton's early-'60s hits included two duets with Dinah Washington, "Baby (You've Got What It Takes)" (#5, 1960) and "A Rockin' Good Way" (#7, 1960), as well as the folk-tinged "The Boll Weevil Song" (#2, 1961) and "Frankie and Johnny" (#20, 1961). Other hits included more standard soul-pop fare like "Think Twice" (#11, 1961), "Revenge" (#15, 1961), "Lie to Me" (#13, 1962), "Shadrack" (#19, 1962), and "Hotel Happiness" (#3, 1963). Thereafter his Mercury releases fared noticeably poorer on the charts. He recorded for RCA (1965–67) and Reprise (1967–68) with meager results.

In 1970 he had one more big pop hit with a stirring version of Tony Joe White's "Rainy Night in Georgia" (#4 pop, #1 R&B, 1970) on Cotillion. As the decade progressed, he recorded for MGM, Brut, Stax, All Platinum, and Olde Worlde. He died at age 56 from pneumonia.

Berlin

Formed 1979, Los Angeles, CA
John Crawford (b. Jan. 17, 1957, Palo Alto, CA), bass, voc.; Rob Brill (b. Jan. 21, 1956, Babylon, NY), drums; Terri Nunn (b. June 26, 1959, Baldwin Hills, CA), voc.
1983—*Pleasure Victim* (Geffen) 1984—*Love Life* 1986—*Count Three & Pray* 1989—*Best of Berlin 1979–1988* 2000—*Berlin Live: Sacred and Profane* (Time Bomb).

While best known for the Giorgio Moroder–produced "Take My Breath Away" (#1, 1986) from the *Top Gun* soundtrack, Berlin's real raison d'être is probably better divined from the title of its panting, quasi-pornographic song "Sex (I'm a . . .)" (#62, 1983). A vehicle for teen actress (in *Lou Grant*)-turned-singer Terri Nunn, Berlin combined her moaning boy-toy image with the rhythm section of John Crawford and Rob Brill (three different groups of musicians backed them on album). The resulting slick synth pop and a steamy video brought *Pleasure Victim* (#30, 1983) some commercial success. *Love Life* (#28, 1984) successfully repeated the debut album's formula. *Count Three & Pray* (#61, 1986) featured cameos by Ted Nugent, David Gilmour, and Elliot Easton. While the *Top Gun* track soared, the rest of the album sputtered, and when Nunn left in 1987, Berlin called it quits. Crawford went on to form the Big F in 1989.

In 1990, Berlin found themselves back on the charts in England, as "Take My Breath Away" was used in a series of car commercials, reissued, and reached #3. The group reunited in 1999 and performed a show of both old and new material, which was recorded and released in 2000 as *Berlin Live: Sacred and Profane.*

Chuck Berry

Born Charles Edward Anderson Berry, Oct. 18, 1926, San Jose, CA
1958—*After School Session* (Chess); *One Dozen Berrys* 1959—*Chuck Berry Is on Top* 1960—*New Juke Box Hits* 1964—*Chuck Berry Greatest Hits* 1965—*Chuck Berry in London* 1967—*Golden Hits* (Mercury); *Chuck Berry's Golden Decade* (Chess) 1972—*The London Sessions* 1973—*Golden Decade, vol. 2* 1974—*Golden Decade, vol. 3* 1975—*Chuck Berry '75* 1979—*Motorvatin'* (Atlantic); *Rockit* (Atco) 1982—*The Great Twenty-eight* (Chess) 1986—*Rock 'n' Roll Rarities* (Chess/MCA) 1987—*Hail! Hail! Rock 'n' Roll* (MCA) 1988—*The Chess Box* (Chess/MCA) 1990—*Missing Berries: Rarities, vol. 3* 1996—*The Best of Chuck Berry* (MCA) 1997—*His Best, vol. 1* (Chess); *His Best, vol. 2* 1999—*Best of Chuck Berry: 20th Century Masters* (MCA) 2000—*The Anthology* (Chess).

The archetypal rock & roller, Chuck Berry melded the blues, country, and a witty, defiant teen outlook into songs that have influenced virtually every rock musician in his wake. In his best work—about 40 songs (including "Round and Round," "Carol," "Brown Eyed Handsome Man," "Roll Over Beethoven," "Back in the U.S.A.," "Little Queenie"), recorded mostly in the mid- and late '50s—Berry matched some of the most resonant and witty lyrics in pop to music with a blues bottom and a country top, trademarking the results with his signature double-string guitar lick. On awarding Berry the prestigious Kennedy Center Honors Award in December

Chuck Berry

2000, President Bill Clinton hailed him as "one of the 20th Century's most influential musicians."

Berry learned guitar as a teenager. From 1944 to 1947 he was in reform school for attempted robbery; upon release he worked on the assembly line at a General Motors Fisher body plant and studied hairdressing and cosmetology at night school. In 1952 he formed a trio with drummer Ebby Harding and pianist Johnnie Johnson, his keyboardist on and off for the next three decades. By 1955 the trio had become a top St. Louis–area club band, and Berry was supplementing his salary as a beautician with regular gigs. He met Muddy Waters in Chicago in May 1955, and Waters introduced him to Leonard Chess. Berry played Chess a demo tape that included "Ida Red"; Chess renamed it "Maybellene," and sent it to disc jockey Alan Freed (who got a cowriting credit in the deal), and Berry had his first Top 10 hit.

Through 1958 Berry had a string of hits. "School Day" (#3 pop, #1 R&B, 1957), "Rock & Roll Music" (#8 pop, #6 R&B, 1957), "Sweet Little Sixteen" (#2 pop, #1 R&B, 1958), and "Johnny B. Goode" (#8 pop, #5 R&B, 1958) were the biggest. With his famous "duckwalk," Berry was a mainstay on the mid-'50s concert circuit. He also appeared in such films as *Rock, Rock, Rock* (1956), *Mister Rock and Roll* (1957), and *Go, Johnny, Go* (1959).

Late in 1959 Berry was charged with violating the Mann Act: He had brought a 14-year-old Spanish-speaking Apache prostitute from Texas to check hats in his St. Louis nightclub, and after he fired her she complained to the police. Following a blatantly racist first trial was disallowed, he was found guilty at a second. Berry spent two years in federal prison in Indiana, leaving him embittered.

By the time he was released in 1964, the British Invasion was underway, replete with Berry's songs on early albums by the Beatles and Rolling Stones. He recorded a few more classics—including "Nadine" and "No Particular Place to Go"—although it has been speculated that they were written before his jail term. Since then he has written and recorded only sporadically, although he had a million-seller with "My Ding-a-Ling" (#1, 1972), and 1979's *Rockit* was a creditable effort. He appeared in the 1979 film *American Hot Wax*. Through it all, Berry continued to tour internationally, often with pickup bands.

In January 1986 Berry was among the first round of inductees into the Rock and Roll Hall of Fame. The following year he published the at-times sexually and scatalogically explicit *Chuck Berry: The Autobiography* and was the subject of a documentary/tribute film, *Hail! Hail! Rock 'n' Roll*, for which his best-known disciple, Keith Richards of the Rolling Stones, organized a backing band.

When not on the road, Berry lives in Wentzville, Missouri, where he owns the amusement complex Berry Park. Problems with the law and the Internal Revenue Service have plagued him through the years. Shortly before a June 1979 performance for Jimmy Carter at the White House, the IRS charged Berry with income tax evasion, and he served a 100-day prison term in 1979. In 1988 in New York City, he paid a $250 fine to settle a $5 million lawsuit from a woman he allegedly punched in the mouth. In 1990 police raided his home and, finding 62 grams of marijuana and videotapes of women—one of whom was apparently a minor—using the restroom in a Berry Park restaurant, filed felony drug and child-abuse charges against Berry. In order to have the child-abuse charges dropped, Berry agreed to plead guilty to one misdemeanor count of marijuana possession. Berry was given a six-month suspended jail sentence, placed on two years' unsupervised probation, and ordered to donate $5,000 to a local hospital.

As of this writing, Berry was still touring the world, sometimes with fellow classic rockers such as Jerry Lee Lewis and Little Richard.

Jello Biafra: See the Dead Kennedys

The B-52's

Formed Oct. 1976, Athens, GA
Cindy Wilson (b. Feb. 28, 1957, Athens), voc., perc., gtr.; Keith Strickland (b. Oct. 26, 1953, Athens), drums, gtr., kybds.; Fred Schneider III (b. July 1, 1956, Newark, NJ), voc., toy piano; Ricky Wilson (b. Mar. 19, 1953, Athens; d. Oct. 12, 1985), gtr., kybds.; Kate Pierson (b. Apr. 27, 1948, Weehawken, NJ), voc., kybds.
1979—*The B-52's* (Warner Bros.) 1980—*Wild Planet; Party Mix* EP 1982—*Mesopotamia* EP 1983—*Whammy!* 1985—(– R. Wilson) 1986—*Bouncing Off the Satellites* 1989—*Cosmic Thing* (Reprise) 1990—(– C. Wilson) 1992—*Good Stuff* 1994—(+ C. Wilson) 1998—*Time Capsule—Songs for a Future Generation.*
Fred Schneider solo: 1991—*Fred Schneider and the Shake*

Society (Reprise) (as Fred Schneider and the Shake Society) 1996—*Just . . . Fred.*

Initially, the gleefully eccentric party music of the B-52's—stripped-down, off-kilter funk, topped by chirpy vocals and lyrics crammed with '50s and '60s trivia—garnered such a large following at dance clubs and colleges that the band's debut album sold 500,000 copies despite minimal airplay. Named for the tall bouffant hairdos worn onstage by the two female members, the group claims that it originated in a jam session under the influence of tropical drinks. Fred Schneider, Kate Pierson, and Keith Strickland had minimal previous performing experience; the Wilson siblings had none. The B-52's debuted at a Valentine's Day party in 1977 in the college town of Athens, Georgia; they originally performed with taped guitar and drum parts, but they preferred the sound when someone accidentally pulled the plug on the tape recorder.

Their first "official" gig was at Max's Kansas City. They soon attracted a New York cult, partly thanks to their stage image: miniskirts, go-go boots, toy instruments, and demonstrations of such dance steps as the Camel Walk and the Shy Tuna. They pressed 2,000 copies of the single "Rock Lobster," which sold out rapidly, before signing in early 1979 to Warner Bros. Their debut album sold steadily as the band toured the U.S. and Europe. *Wild Planet,* which hit #18 in 1980, was even more successful, and songs from it reappeared in remixed, more danceable versions on the *Party Mix* EP. For 1982's *Mesopotamia* EP, the B-52's collaborated with producer David Byrne of Talking Heads, who brought in backup musicians to broaden the sound. *Whammy!* was a Top 30 LP, boosted by the singles "Legal Tender" and "Song for a Future Generation." The accompanying videos captured the group's trademark retro American style. Drummer Ricky Wilson's death from AIDS in 1985 made it impossible for the group to tour or promote *Bouncing Off the Satellites.*

Nearly four years passed before the B-52's returned with their most successful release, the double-platinum *Cosmic Thing* (#4, 1989). With Keith Strickland moving from drums to lead guitar, the B-52's seemed to strike the perfect balance between their stylistic idiosyncrasies and a four-on-the-floor drive with "Love Shack" (#3, 1990); other hit singles from the Don Was– and Nile Rodgers–produced LP included "Roam" (#3, 1990) and "Deadbeat Club" (#30, 1990). In 1990 Cindy Wilson started a family and left the group (Julee Cruise filled in on tour), which continued as a trio on *Good Stuff* (#16, 1992). Concurrently Kate Pierson appeared on Iggy Pop's hit single "Candy." (She had previously sung on R.E.M.'s "Shiny Happy People.") Calling themselves the B.C. 52's, the band recorded "(Meet) the Flintstones" (#33) for the 1994 film version of *The Flintstones.* Cindy Wilson returned for the ensuing concert appearances.

Time Capsule contained songs spanning two decades of the B-52's' existence, as well as two new tracks. A tour with the Pretenders followed. Schneider, who had previously recorded a campy, cheerfully smutty album with the Shake Society (its delightful single "Monster" warned of what lurked inside Fred's pants), released his second solo album in 1996. *Just . . . Fred,* produced by ex–Big Black noise master Steve Albini, was a radical departure, featuring aggressive surfabilly backing by members of such indie grind-punks as the Didjits, the Jon Spencer Blues Explosion, and Tar.

Big Audio Dynamite/B.A.D. II/Big Audio

Formed 1984, London, Eng.
Mick Jones (b. Michael Jones, June 26, 1955, London), voc., gtr.; Don Letts, kybds.; Leo "E-Zee Kill" Williams, bass; Greg Roberts, drums; Dan Donovan, kybds.
1985—*This Is Big Audio Dynamite* (Columbia) 1986—*No. 10 Upping St.* 1988—*Tighten Up Vol. 88* 1989—*Megatop Phoenix.*
As B.A.D. II: 1991—(– Letts; – Williams; – Roberts; – Donovan; + Gary Stonadge [b. Nov. 24, 1962, Southampton, Eng.], bass; Nick Hawkins [b. Feb. 3, 1965, Luton, Eng.], gtr.; Chris Kavanagh [b. June 4, 1964, Woolwich, Eng.], drums; DJ Zonka [b. Michael Custance, July 4, 1962, London], DJ) *The Globe.*
As Big Audio: 1994—(+ Andre Shapps, kybds.) *Higher Power* (Columbia).
As Big Audio Dynamite (again): 1995—*F-Punk* (Radioactive); *Planet B.A.D.: Greatest Hits* (Sony) 1999—*Super Hits.*

With Big Audio Dynamite, Mick Jones took the mixing of styles he had experimented with in the Clash to adventurous extremes, creating a rock-reggae-house-hip-hop fusion ahead of its time. B.A.D. was one of the first British bands to sample and mix club and rock music, prefiguring such groups as EMF and the Farm.

Just over a year after he was kicked out of the Clash by Joe Strummer and Paul Simonon [see the Clash entry] because they wanted the band to return to its "punk roots," Jones bounced back with an unlikely combo featuring filmmaker/DJ Don Letts and former Basement 5 bassist Leo Williams. The group played a series of dates in 1984 in France, opening for U2 and the Alarm, before adding keyboardist Dan Donovan. On *This Is Big Audio Dynamite,* B.A.D. programmed a swirl of sound effects and audio vérité collage, including a running motif of dialogue from such movies as *A Fistful of Dollars.* Jones sang about the kind of political issues he had in the Clash on such songs as "Medicine Show," "E=MC2," and "The Bottom Line," but the emphasis was on dancing and rocking. B.A.D. polished its hybrid further on *No. 10 Upping St.,* which was produced and written by Jones with his old Clash mate Joe Strummer and featured the college radio hit "C'mon Every Beatbox."

Tighten Up Vol. 88, featuring the single "Just Play Music," had barely been released when Jones caught chicken pox in 1988 from his daughter and nearly died. He spent nine months recuperating. The acid-house–inspired *Megatop Phoenix* was a spiritual rebirth for Jones; the album was dedicated to his grandmother, whose death in 1989 was even more traumatic to the singer than his own brush with mortality. Jones had found in the rave scene a musical movement whose energy reminded him of punk. Unfortunately, the rest of the band wasn't as interested in the new style, and they and Jones subsequently parted ways. Letts, Williams, and Roberts formed Screaming Target, while Donovan joined Sisters of Mercy.

Jones formed B.A.D. II in 1990 with three young musicians who shared his passion for raves and soccer, including former Sigue Sigue Sputnik drummer Chris Kavanagh. (Though DJ Zonka guested on 1991's *The Globe*, he didn't become an official member of the group until after its release.) In England they released an eight-song disc called *Kool-Aid*, as well as a live album, *Ally Pally Paradiso*, that was packaged like a bootleg DJ record, white label and all.

On *The Globe* B.A.D. II explored systems, techno, and ambient music. The album also featured an acoustic ballad, an orchestral reprise, and the single "Rush" (#32), a techno rocker that sampled the Who's "Baba O'Riley." The song was released as a B side to "Should I Stay or Should I Go?" when the Jones-penned Clash tune became a #1 U.K. single in 1991 after being used in a Levi's ad. Touring heavily behind the album, including opening for U2 on the U.S. Zoo TV Tour and playing with PiL on the 1992 MTV 120 Minutes Tour, B.A.D. II mixed rock-concert staging with a clubby environment, playing extended versions of songs and highlighting DJ Zonka's role. With the same lineup (plus keyboardist/coproducer Andre Shapps), the band returned as Big Audio in 1994, releasing *Higher Power*. The album also featured noted producer Arthur Baker ("Planet Rock") on one track.

In 1995 Jones and company reassumed their original Big Audio Dynamite moniker, jumped record labels, and released *F-Punk*, an album that infused the group's beat-wise sound with Clash-like guitar punk. The record also included a cover of David Bowie's "Suffragette City." The same year, Sony issued *Planet B.A.D.*, a hits collection spanning the band's entire career.

Big Black/Rapeman/Shellac

Formed 1982, Chicago, IL
Steve Albini, gtr., voc., bass, kybds.
1982—*Lungs* EP (Ruthless) 1983—(+ Santiago Durango, gtr., voc.; + Jeff Pezatti, bass, voc.; + Pat Byrne, drums) *Bulldozer* EP (Ruthless/Fever) (– Byrne) 1985—*Racer-X* EP (Homestead) (– Pezatti; + Dave Riley, bass, voc.) 1986—*Atomizer* 1987—*Headache* EP (Touch and Go); *Songs About Fucking* 1992—*Pigpile*.
Rapeman, formed 1988, Chicago: Albini, gtr., voc.; David Wm. Sims, bass; Rey Washam, drums.
1988—*Budd* EP (Touch and Go) 1989—*Two Nuns and a Pack Mule*.
Arsenal, formed 1988, Chicago: Durango, gtr., voc., bass, kybds.
1989—*Manipulator* EP (Touch and Go) 1990—(+ Pierre Kezdy, bass) *Factory Smog Is a Sign of Progress* EP.
Shellac, formed 1992, Chicago: Albini; Robert Weston IV, bass, voc.; Todd Trainer, drums.
1994—*At Action Park* (Touch and Go) 1997—*The Futurist* (no label) 1998—*Terraform* (Touch and Go) 2000—*1000 Hurts*.

Steve Albini is an independent-rock renaissance man. The outspoken producer, guitarist, lyricist, writer, and DIY music advocate first emerged in Chicago in the early '80s while still a journalism student at Northwestern. Big Black began as a solo project. As the band developed, it became notable for imposing the physical impact of American hardcore and the unconventional racket of post–no wave noise onto the stern melodicism of early English art punks like Wire, Gang of Four, and PiL. Albini's subsequent groups, Rapeman and Shellac, refined the approach with technical precision and a flirtation with the chunky riffs of '70s hard rock. A strong critic of slick pop, the CD format, managers, and major-label business practices, Albini has paved the way for countless other musical free-thinkers. In the '90s, he became a prominent engineer; his visceral, naturalistic recording techniques bombarded the mainstream on records by Nirvana, PJ Harvey, and Jimmy Page and Robert Plant.

The six-song *Lungs* developmentally sketches Big Black's 1982 beginnings. The basic formula—numbing drum machine, trebly guitar, hoarse vocals, and sensationalistic lyrics—is laid out but more closely resembles anemic new wave than raging fury. Albini's project expanded with the addition of Jeff Pezatti and Santiago Durango of Naked Raygun, a group who, along with Big Black, helped define Chicago postpunk. Future Urge Overkill drummer Pat Byrne briefly joined them on the more forceful *Bulldozer*. *Racer-X* introduces a less rinky-dink, massively effective drum machine and increased violence in the guitar department. The lineup stabilized for Big Black's first full-length LP, 1986's *Atomizer*. Low in the mix, Albini shrieks and growls stories from the Midwest's underbelly, unflinchingly detailing brutal sex ("Fists of Love"), arson ("Kerosene"), and child molestation ("Jordan, Minnesota"). Bassist Dave Riley's fractured funk edge brightens the Herculean beats, ultradistorted guitar leads, and punctuations of feedback. The trio ruled the American and European undergrounds as the *Headache* EP and the precise, tightly wound *Songs About Fucking* capped off Big Black's career. (The live *Pigpile*, also released as a box set, coincided with Touch and Go Records' reissues of the group's catalogue.) Durango recorded two shadowy EPs as Arsenal, married British pop singer Cath Carrol, and became a lawyer for the likes of Albini and infamous cock-rock sculptor Cynthia Plaster Caster. In the early '90s Riley had a brief tenure with Chicago's Bull.

In 1988 Albini founded Rapeman with Rey Washam and David Wm. Sims, formerly of Texas' Scratch Acid. *Two Nuns and a Pack Mule* is less abstract and alien than Big Black; its superbly executed power crunch predates grunge irony with in-joke lyrics and tributes to Golden Earring and ZZ Top. After the group's dissolution, Washam drummed with a succession of acts, Sims formed the Jesus Lizard, and Albini concentrated on his studio. His most recent endeavor, the heavier, more minimalistic Shellac, features ex–Breaking Circus/Rifle Sport drummer Todd Trainer and ex–Volcano Suns bassist/engineer Bob Weston. They record and tour sporadically, on their own terms, crafting meticulously loud albums full of odd time signatures, economical rhythms, and trademark guitar clang.

The Big Bopper

Born Jiles Perry "J.P." Richardson, Oct. 24, 1930, Sabine Pass, TX; died Feb. 3, 1959, near Clear Lake, IA
1989—*Hellooo Baby!: The Best of the Big Bopper, 1954–1959* (Rhino).

The Big Bopper, a disc jockey moonlighting as a pop star, was killed in a plane crash with Buddy Holly and Ritchie Valens, leaving as his legacy the line "Oh baby that's-a what I like!"

Richardson began working as a disc jockey at KTRM, Beaumont, Texas, while still attending high school, calling himself the "Big Bopper." Except for a two-year hitch in the army (as a radio communications instructor), he worked at KTRM the rest of his life. He began writing songs during his army years, and in 1957 he sent a demo of original material to a Houston record producer, who brought him to the attention of Mercury Records. He cut two country & western singles for Mercury under his real name and a novelty record called "The Purple People Eater Meets the Witch-Doctor" as the Big Bopper. The flip side was a rockabilly original called "Chantilly Lace," which became the international hit of 1958.

He followed "Chantilly Lace" with two modest singles, "Little Red Riding Hood" and "The Big Bopper's Wedding," and developed a stage show based on his radio persona. Buddy Holly, a longtime West Texas friend, invited him to accompany a Midwestern tour in the winter of 1959. On February 3, 1959, between concert stops in Mason City, Iowa, and Fargo, North Dakota, the tour plane flew into a snowstorm and crashed, killing all on board.

Richardson left little in the way of recordings. As a songwriter, however, he returned to the charts a year after his death with "Running Bear," which he'd written for Johnny Preston.

Big Brother and the Holding Company

Formed 1965, San Francisco, CA
Peter Albin (b. June 6, 1944, San Francisco), bass, gtr., voc.; Sam Andrew (b. Dec. 18, 1941, Taft, CA), gtr., piano, sax, voc.; James Gurley (b. Dec. 22, 1939, Detroit, MI), gtr.; David Getz (b. Jan. 24, 1940, Brooklyn, NY), drums, piano, voc.; Janis Joplin (b. Jan. 19, 1943, Port Arthur, TX; d. Oct. 4, 1970, Hollywood, CA), voc.
1967—*Big Brother and the Holding Company* (Mainstream) 1968—*Cheap Thrills* (Columbia) (– Joplin; – Andrew) 1970—(+ David Shallock, bass; + Nick Gravenites [b. Chicago, IL], voc.) *Be a Brother* (– Gurley; – Shallock; – Gravenites; + Andrew; + Michael Pendergrass, gtr.; + Kathy McDonald, voc.; + Mike Finnigan, kybds.) 1971—*How Hard It Is* 1972—(group disbands) 1973—*Joplin's Greatest Hits* 1982—*Farewell Song* 1984—*Cheaper Thrills* (Edsel) 1985—*Big Brother and the Holding Company Live* (Capitol) 1986—(group re-forms: Albin; Andrew; Gurley; Getz; + various vocalists) *Joseph's Coat* (Edsel) 1993—*Janis* (Sony) 1997—(– Gurley; – Albin; + Tom Finch, gtr.) 1998—*Do What You Love* (Cheap Thrills).

While Big Brother and the Holding Company are remembered as Janis Joplin's band, they were active before Joplin joined them and after she left. Leader Peter Albin (a country-blues guitarist who had played with future founders of the Grateful Dead Jerry Garcia and Ron McKernan) met Sam Andrew, Big Brother's musical director, who had a jazz and classical background and had played rock & roll professionally. They approached James Gurley (who had taught himself to play guitar on hallucinogenic sojourns through the California desert), and the three began playing open jam sessions hosted by entrepreneur Chet Helms in 1965. Helms encouraged them to form a group, found them a drummer, and set up their first gig, at the Trips Festival of January 1966. In the festival audience was art historian and amateur musician David Getz, who soon replaced the original drummer. Big Brother and the Holding Company became the house band at the Avalon Ballroom, playing a progressive style of instrumental rock. Feeling a need for a strong vocalist, Helms recalled having heard Joplin before, and contacted her in Austin, Texas. She returned to San Francisco to join the band in June 1966.

The Holding Company was clearly blues influenced, and Joplin had listened intensively to Bessie Smith, Ma Rainey, and Big Mama Thornton. Joplin's voice and presence, and the band's devil-may-care intensity, made them a whole greater than the sum of its parts—and a Bay Area sensation. Their debut album spread their reputation, and their appearance at the Monterey Pop Festival in June 1967 thrust them into the national spotlight. New manager Albert Grossman brought them to Columbia Records, which issued their legacy, *Cheap Thrills*. The album went to #1 with the help of "Piece of My Heart" (#12, 1968). Numerous observers convinced Joplin that she could use a more precise backing band, and at the end of 1968 she and Andrew left the group [see Janis Joplin entry]. After a year, Big Brother returned as a loose assemblage of four to eight musicians, which might include Gravenites (ex–Electric Flag), Kathy McDonald (a backup vocalist for Ike and Tina Turner, Joe Cocker, and Leon Russell), or no lead singer at all. Albin and Andrew were the only regular members (at times only Andrew). In 1972 Big Brother disbanded; the group re-formed in 1986. By the early '90s they were recording and performing in Europe and on the West Coast. *Do What You Love* features vocalist Lisa Battle.

Big Country

Formed 1982, Dunfermline, Scot.
Stuart Adamson (b. Apr. 11, 1958, Manchester, Eng.), voc., gtr.; Mark Brzezicki (b. June 21, 1957, Slough, Eng.), drums; Tony Butler (b. Feb. 2, 1957, London, Eng.), bass; Bruce Watson

(b. Mar. 11, 1961, Timmins, Ontario, Can.), gtr.
1983—*The Crossing* (Mercury) 1984—*Wonderland* EP; *Steeltown* 1986—*The Seer* 1988—*Peace in Our Time* (Reprise) 1990—*Through a Big Country: Greatest Hits* (Mercury, U.K.) 1991—*No Place Like Home* (Vertigo, U.K.) 1993—*The Buffalo Skinners* (Fox/RCA) 1994—*The Best of Big Country* (Mercury) 1995—*Live: Without the Aid of a Safety Net* (Compulsion, U.K.); *Why the Long Face* (Castle, U.K.) 1996—*Eclectic* 1997—*King Biscuit Flower Hour: Big Country* (King Biscuit); *Brighton Rock* (Snapper, U.K.) 1998—*Kings of Emotion* (Recall, U.K.); *Greatest Hits Live* (Disky, U.K.).
The Skids: 1995—*Best of the Skids: Sweet Suburbia* (Caroline).

In the early '80s Big Country was among a sprinkling of bands that favored guitars over synthesizers and earnest idealism over irony. Like their contemporaries in U2 and the Alarm, the members of Big Country were inspired by punk's energy and its emphasis on connecting with the audience.

Lead singer Stuart Adamson launched his rock career by playing guitar in a self-styled punk quartet called the Skids, who released three albums between 1977 and 1980 and had a #10 hit in England with the 1979 single "Into the Valley." Believing that the band was not living up to its initial ideals of professional and artistic integrity, Adamson decided to form his own band in Scotland. Big Country's first incarnation featured Adamson on vocals and guitar, plus four local Scottish musicians, among them guitarist Bruce Watson. Adamson and Watson eventually parted company with the other three and hooked up with London sessionmen Mark Brzezicki and Tony Butler, who had previously played in a trio with Pete Townshend's brother Simon, a childhood friend of Butler's.

After a series of sessions with producer Chris Thomas, Big Country decided to enlist U2 producer Steve Lillywhite for its debut album. The resulting effort, 1983's *The Crossing*, emphasized the young band's penchant for passionate, often anthemic songs and Celtic-flavored arrangements that were at once fierce and folky. ROLLING STONE made note of Adamson's "unconventional guitar playing, which at times recalls such traditional instruments as bagpipes or fiddles"—a feature that was a highlight of Big Country's first and biggest hit, "In a Big Country" (#17, 1983). The following year the EP *Wonderland* and the album *Steeltown* were also well received. After that, the band's recordings faltered critically and commercially in the U.S., though a series of largely live albums still consistently reached the U.K. Top 30. The band folded in 1997.

Big Daddy Kane

Born Antonio M. Hardy, Sep. 10, 1968, Brooklyn, NY
1988—*Long Live the Kane* (Cold Chillin') 1989—*It's a Big Daddy Thing* 1990—*Taste of Chocolate* 1991—*Prince of Darkness* 1993—*Looks Like a Job for Big Daddy Kane* 1994—*Daddy's Home* (MCA) 1998—*Veteranz Day* (Blackheart) 2001—*The Very Best of Big Daddy Kane* (Rhino).

With his suave good looks and hard, smooth vocal delivery, Big Daddy Kane became rap's first niche-marketed sex symbol. In addition to his own albums, videos, and performances, he has written hits for other artists and posed nude in *Playgirl* magazine (June 1991) and for Madonna's 1992 book, *Sex*. He has been described as the Barry White of rap.

Kane grew up in the tough Bedford-Stuyvesant neighborhood of Brooklyn. As a child, he listened to his mother's records by artists such as Evelyn "Champagne" King; later, he discovered his own favorites in White and Otis Redding. In junior high Kane was introduced to the two worlds he would soon join: the rap world and the Five Percent Nation, an elitist black Muslim sect popular among the hip-hop community. By high school, he had begun writing poetry and looking up to the pioneering rap of Melle Mel, Grandmaster Caz, and Kool Moe Dee.

As his wordplay improved, Kane was asked to write material for the Juice Crew and Kurtis Blow. By 1988 his songs had been covered by Biz Markie ("Vapors" [#80 R&B, 1988] and the notorious "Pickin' Boogers") and Roxanne Shanté ("Have a Nice Day" and "Go On Girl"). After touring as Shanté's DJ, Kane decided to try rapping.

For his first album, produced by Marley Marl, the songs Kane wrote for himself proved as wide-ranging as those he'd written for others. The macho posturing on "Raw" became his calling card, with the rest of the album ranging from the romantic ("The Day You're Mine") to the cool and funky ("Ain't No Half-Steppin' "). Kane's subsequent albums relied on a similar recipe. *Taste of Chocolate* (#37 pop, #10 R&B, 1990) provided another career highlight, as two generations of romantic vocalists were brought together when Kane duetted with White. Although he has received consistent critical kudos, Kane has also been criticized for promoting homophobia and sexism. In the '90s he acted in movies, appearing in Mario Van Peebles' *Posse* and Robert Townsend's *Meteor Man*. His 1994 album, *Daddy's Home* (#26 R&B), included a guest appearance by Ol' Dirty Bastard of the Wu-Tang Clan. And he returned to the studio once again for 1998's *Veteranz Day* (#62 R&B).

Big Star/Alex Chilton

Formed 1971, Memphis, TN
Alex Chilton (b. Dec. 28, 1950, Memphis), voc., gtr.; Chris Bell (b. Jan. 12, 1951, Memphis; d. Dec. 27, 1978, Memphis), voc., gtr.; Andy Hummel (b. Jan. 26, 1951, Memphis), bass; Jody Stephens (b. Oct. 4, 1952, Memphis), drums.
1972—*#1 Record* (Ardent) 1973—(– Bell) 1974—*Radio City* 1978—*Third* (a.k.a. *Sister Lovers*) (PVC) (– Hummel) 1992—*Big Star Live* (Rykodisc) 1993—(+ Jonathan Auer, gtr., voc.; + Ken Stringfellow, gtr., bass) *Columbia: Live at Missouri University* (Zoo) 1999—*Nobody Can Dance* (Norton).
Alex Chilton solo: 1977—*Singer Not the Song* EP (Ork) 1979—*Like Flies on Sherbert* (Peabody) 1982—*Live in London* (Line) 1985—*Feudalist Tarts* EP (Big Time) 1986—*No Sex* EP 1987—*High Priest* 1990—*Black List* (New Rose)

1991—*19 Years: A Collection of Alex Chilton* (Rhino) 1994—*Clichés* (Ardent) 1995—*A Man Called Destruction* 1996—*1970* 1997—*Top 30* (Last Call) 2000—*Set* (Bar/None). Chris Bell solo: 1992—*I Am the Cosmos* (Rykodisc).

Big Star's combination of Beatles-style melody, Who-like punch, and Byrdsy harmonies defined power pop before the term (or an audience for it) existed. In less than four years, Big Star created a seminal body of work that never stopped inspiring succeeding generations of rockers, from the power-pop revivalists of the late '70s to alternative rockers at the end of the century. Despite commercial failure, Big Star has acquired near-mythic status through such songs as "September Gurls" and the continuing solo work and mystique of its chief singer/songwriter, Alex Chilton. Paid homage to by the Replacements ("Alex Chilton" from 1987's *Pleased to Meet Me*), Big Star has influenced a number of artists, such as Georgia's R.E.M., Scotland's Teenage Fanclub, and New Zealand's Chills.

The band was formed in Memphis by singer/songwriter Chris Bell; Alex Chilton, who'd been a hitmaker in the Box Tops [see entry], was recruited soon after. Following the release of the band's richly textured debut, *#1 Record*, Bell left the group. Drummer Jody Stephens and bassist Andy Hummel stayed on, and, with Chilton at the helm, the band recorded the more stripped-down *Radio City*, which included Chilton's "September Gurls" (covered by the Bangles in 1982). Though both albums garnered critical raves, neither sold well and the band fizzled. The dark and haunting *Third* (a.k.a. *Sister Lovers*; the LP was never titled at its completion), more of a Chilton solo effort, was not officially issued in the U.S. for years.

Bell, whose solo recordings were posthumously released in 1992, was killed in a car accident in 1978. Chilton moved to New York, formed a band that included future dB Chris Stamey, and recorded an EP. He made the adventurous *Like Flies on Sherbert* in Memphis with *Third*'s producer Jim Dickinson. Then after producing recordings by the Cramps [see entry] and swampabilly band Panther Burns, Chilton disappeared from the scene. He reemerged in New Orleans in the mid-'80s, playing mostly cover songs in clubs. His music of this period, recorded on *Feudalist Tarts, No Sex,* and *High Priest,* veered more toward R&B. Usually with a trio, he continued to tour the U.S. and European club circuit into the '90s, mixing his original songs with an eclectic selection of covers. He recorded several of the jazz songs and standards of his live shows on *Clichés* (1994). *A Man Called Destruction* consists of Chilton originals and R&B-tinged obscurities. New product continues to trickle out, mostly reissues and rarities. The album *1970* is a historical footnote, catching Chilton at Ardent shortly after the breakup of the Box Tops and a few months before he cofounded Big Star. The singer was unable to secure a record deal he liked, and the album was lost for 26 years. *Set* is a latter-day studio recording that breaks no new ground, mingling New Orleans jukebox classics with novelties like "You've Got a Booger Bear Under There."

In 1993 students at the University of Missouri coaxed Chilton and drummer Jody Stephens (by then projects director at Ardent Records, Big Star's label during the '70s) to reunite for a campus concert. With bassist Andy Hummel long retired from music, Jon Auer and Ken Stringfellow of the Posies were recruited to round out the quartet. Released in 1993, *Columbia: Live at Missouri University* chronicles the sloppy but spirited set that draws from all three Big Star LPs. Big Star sporadically performed together through the following year. The band has infrequently reunited since. In 1998 *That '70s Show* adopted the music from "In the Street" as its title theme. A post-Hummel live album, *Nobody Can Dance*, surfaced the following year.

Big Youth

Born Manley Buchanan, ca. 1949, Kingston, Jam.
1973—*Screaming Target* (Trojan, U.K.) 1976—*Natty Cultural Dread; Hit the Road Jack* 1977—*Reggae Phenomenon* (Big Youth, U.K.) 1978—*Dreadlocks Dread* (Klik, U.K.); *Isiah, First Prophet of Old* 1979—*Everyday Skank (Best of)* (Trojan, U.K.) 1982—*Some Great Big Youth* (Heartbeat) 1983—*The Chanting Dread Inna Fine Style* 1984—*Live at Reggae Sunsplash* (Sunsplash) 1985—*A Luta Continua* (Heartbeat) 1988—*Manifestation* 1990—*Jamming in the House of Dread* cassette (ROIR) 1997—*Higher Grounds* (Jet Star) 2000—*Tell It Black* (Recall, U.K.).

A cabbie turned disc jockey, Big Youth was Jamaica's most popular "toaster" (a disc jockey who ad libs over instrumental tracks) in the '70s. His early records featured rhymes, doggerel, and scat singing over previously released tunes by other artists remixed to cut out the original vocals and bring out the bass and drums. His style influenced the early rappers, who adapted his Caribbean methods to the inner city. Like his first hit, "Ace 90 Skank" (1972), his songs frequently dealt with current events: When a heavyweight boxing championship was fought in Kingston in 1973, Youth took to the airwaves with "George Foreman" and "Foreman and Frazier."

Big Youth later adopted Rastafarianism as his religion, and his songs took on weightier topics, as in "House of Dreadlocks" and "Natty Cultural Dread." He also began writing his own music, recording with a band and singing in a high, breathy croon rather than toasting. "When Revolution Come," produced by Prince Buster, was his first of many Jamaican chart-toppers in the mid-'70s. He performs periodically in the U.S. and Great Britain, and appears at the annual Reggae Sunsplash festival.

Bikini Kill

Formed Oct. 1990, Olympia, WA
Tobi Vail (b. July 20, 1969, Auburn, WA), drums; Kathleen Hanna (b. Kathleen Hanna-Dando, June 9, 1969, Portland, OR), voc.; Billy Boredom (b. William F. Karren, Mar. 10, 1965, Memphis, TN), gtr.; Kathi Wilcox (b. Nov. 19, 1969, Vancouver, WA), bass.

1992—*Bikini Kill* EP (Kill Rock Stars) 1993—*Yeah Yeah Yeah Yeah* (split album with Huggy Bear's *Our Troubled Youth*); *Pussy Whipped* 1996—*Reject All American* 1998—*Singles*.
Julie Ruin: 1998—*Julie Ruin* (Kill Rock Stars).
Le Tigre, formed 1999, New York, NY: 2000—*Le Tigre* (Mr. Lady).

Proclaiming themselves riot grrrls and calling for "Revolution Girl Style Now," Bikini Kill pioneered both a musical and a feminist movement in the early '90s. Hanna, Vail, and Wilcox met at Evergreen College in Olympia, Washington. In their feminist fanzine *Bikini Kill* they articulated an agenda for young women in and outside of music; the band put those ideas to practice. (Ironically, the zine first coined the "girl power" slogan, later co-opted by England's bubblegum pop band the Spice Girls.) Bikini Kill earned a reputation in the punk underground for confronting certain standards of that genre; for example, asking people to slam at the side of the stage, so that women would not get pushed out of the front, and inviting women to take the mike and talk about sexual abuse. A former stripper, Hanna (who inspired Nirvana's first hit by spray-painting "Smells Like Teen Spirit" on Kurt Cobain's bedroom wall) challenges the sexual expectations of her audience by pulling her shirt off or writing "Kill Me" across her stomach or chest.

In 1991 Bikini Kill circulated a tape, *Revolution Girl Style Now,* that introduced their fiery style. Some of the same songs appear in new versions, produced by Fugazi's Ian Mackaye, on their debut EP, which features the call-to-arms "Double Dare Ya" and the wrenching "Feels Blind." The Olympia-based indie Kill Rock Stars (Bikini Kill refused to work with majors) released *Yeah Yeah Yeah Yeah,* an album backed with British riot grrrl band Huggy Bear's *Our Troubled Youth,* in a joint venture with the U.K. label Catcall on International Women's Day.

Huggy Bear and Bikini Kill toured England together in spring 1993, generating a wave of international interest in riot grrrl and a storm of controversy in the British press. That fall, Joan Jett produced a Bikini Kill single featuring the anthem "Rebel Girl"; Jett and the band toured together the next year. On *Pussy Whipped,* Bikini Kill returned to a rawer sound; this album included songs by Vail and Wilcox as well as Hanna. All three also wrote tracks for the group's last studio album, the more accessible *Reject All American*.

On the 1995 Lollapalooza Tour, Hanna made headlines not for her riot grrrl politics but for her riotous scuffle with Hole frontwoman Courtney Love. The two longtime rivals came to blows backstage, and though accounts of the fisticuffs vary, Love was later charged with assault in the fourth degree and received a suspended one-year sentence.

Bikini Kill disbanded in 1998 (the same year a posthumous singles compilation was released), but in 1998 Hanna released a home-recorded, electronica-influenced solo album under the name Julie Ruin. Hanna then left the Pacific Northwest to form the New York–based trio Le Tigre with 'zine editor Johanna Fateman and videographer Sadie Benning. Their self-titled debut album borrowed from Bikini Kill's punk, softened with synth-pop flourishes and girl group influences. The politics were as potent as ever, though, as Le Tigre's songs name-dropped feminists from Gertrude Stein to Yoko Ono and questioned whether filmmaker John Cassavetes was a misogynist.

Birdsongs of the Mesozoic: See Mission of Burma

The Birthday Party: See Nick Cave and the Bad Seeds

Elvin Bishop

Born Oct. 21, 1942, Tulsa, OK
1969—*Elvin Bishop* (Fillmore) 1970—*Feel It* (Columbia/Epic) 1971—*Rock My Soul; Applejack* 1972—*Crabshaw Rising: The Best of Elvin Bishop; Let It Flow* (Capricorn) 1975—*Juke Joint Jump* 1976—*Struttin' My Stuff; Hometown Boy Makes Good* 1977—*Live! Raisin' Hell* 1978—*Hog Heaven* 1979—*The Best of Elvin Bishop* 1988—*Big Fun* (Alligator) 1991—*Don't Let the Bossman Get You Down!* 1994—*Tulsa Shuffle: The Best of Elvin Bishop* (Legacy) 1995—*Ace in the Hole* (Alligator) 1998—*The Skin I'm In* 2000—*That's My Partner!*

Although Elvin Bishop's good-humored blues rock was well received live, the ex–Paul Butterfield guitarist didn't establish his solo recording career until his 1976 smash hit single "Fooled Around and Fell in Love"—sung by Mickey Thomas, who went on to join Jefferson Starship.

Bishop met Paul Butterfield at the University of Chicago. Though Bishop had just started playing guitar, he and Butterfield began jamming together at parties; Bishop also played the Chicago folk circuit by himself. Eventually he and Butterfield jammed with Muddy Waters, Howlin' Wolf, and other leading South Side bluesmen. One winter, when times were especially hard, Bishop was jailed for stealing a preacher's coat from a restaurant. He moved to New York, where he worked breaking toys (for manufacturers' discounts) at a department store but returned to Chicago to join Butterfield's first Blues Band [see entry]. After 1967's *The Resurrection of Pigboy Crabshaw,* Bishop left the Blues Band to form his own group, settling in Mill Valley, California. He brought with him a Boston folk trio: Jo, Janice and Mary. Jo Baker was the only one to remain with the group. Bishop also jammed with Al Kooper at the Fillmore when Mike Bloomfield was ill. Bishop signed with Bill Graham's Fillmore Records and made several albums.

Dickey Betts of the Allman Brothers Band then persuaded Capricorn's Phil Walden to sign Bishop. His first few Capricorn LPs sold fairly well, yielding near-hits in "Travelin' Shoes" and "Sure Feels Good." His breakthrough finally came with *Struttin' My Stuff* and its #3 single, "Fooled Around and Fell in Love." Bishop hasn't had a real hit since, but he continues to tour the West Coast and record every so often. Nineteen-eighty-eight's *Big Fun* was his first U.S. release in nearly

10 years (a 1981 LP, *Is You Is or Is You Ain't My Baby,* came out in Germany); *Don't Let the Bossman Get You Down!,* a mix of Bishop originals and old blues, was hailed as a delightful return to form. For *That's My Partner!,* Bishop teamed up with one of his mentors, guitarist Little Smokey Smothers.

Biz Markie

Born Marcel Hall, Apr. 8, 1964, New York, NY
1988—*Goin' Off* (Cold Chillin') 1989—*The Biz Never Sleeps* 1991—*I Need a Haircut* 1993—*All Samples Cleared!* 1994—*Biz's Baddest Beats.*

The class clown of New York hip-hop, Biz Markie proved himself as adept at goofily sincere crooning and lowbrow comedy as rapping. A rap link to the Coasters of "Charlie Brown" and "Yakety Yak," he is also known for losing the first rap-sampling lawsuit to be decided by a judge.

Born in Harlem and reared on Long Island, Biz got his start on the early-'80s downtown-Manhattan rap scene in such clubs as the Roxy and the Funhouse. In 1985 he met producer Marley Marl (L.L. Cool J, Big Daddy Kane) and made his first demo recordings. His debut album, *Goin' Off* (#90 pop, #19 R&B, 1988), had such club hits as "Vapors" (#80 R&B, 1988), "Make the Music With Your Mouth, Biz" (a showcase for his human beat-box skills), and the grossout comedy classic "Pickin' Boogers."

Biz Markie's triumph came with *The Biz Never Sleeps* (#66 pop, #9 R&B, 1989), which featured a Top 10 pop crossover hit in "Just a Friend" (#9, 1990)—a disarmingly abject expression of romantic betrayal in which Biz rapped the verses and sang the pleading chorus in passionate, off-key fashion.

But his next album brought disaster: *I Need a Haircut* (with a cover showing a chainsaw being put to Biz's head) included "Alone Again"—built on an unauthorized sample of the piano figure underpinning Gilbert O'Sullivan's 1972 #1 pop hit, "Alone Again (Naturally)." O'Sullivan sued, and in a landmark court case, the presiding judge ruled against Biz Markie, ordering Warner Bros. to remove all copies of *Haircut* worldwide. The album (#113 pop, #44 R&B, 1991) quickly went out of print, and labels began making greater efforts to clear permission before using copyrighted material. Markie covered himself, and kept his sense of humor, with *All Samples Cleared!*—appearing on the cover as an angry judge handing down a sentence on himself. The Beastie Boys, long outspoken fans of Markie, put him on the bill of their second Tibetan Freedom Concert in 1997 in New York City, and he appeared on their 1998 album, *Hello Nasty.* That year he also joined jazz clarinetist Don Byron on his *Nu Blaxploitation* album, recorded live at the downtown-Manhattan avant-garde club the Knitting Factory.

Björk/The Sugarcubes

Formed 1986, Reykjavík, Iceland
Björk Gudmundsdóttir (b. Nov. 21, 1965, Reykjavík), voc.; Einar Örn Benediktsson (b. Oct. 29, 1962, Copenhagen, Den.), voc., trumpet; Thór Eldon Jonsson (b. June 2, 1962, Reykjavík), gtr.; Einar Mellax, kybds.; Bragi Ólafsson (b. Aug. 11, 1962, Reykjavík), bass; Sigtryggur "Siggi" Baldursson (b. Oct. 2, 1962, Stavanger, Nor.), drums.
1988—*Life's Too Good* (Elektra) (– Mellax; + Margret "Magga" Ornolfsdottir [b. Nov. 21, 1967, Reykjavík], kybds.) 1989—*Here Today, Tomorrow, Next Week!* 1992—*Stick Around for Joy.*
Björk solo: 1993—*Debut* (Elektra) 1995—*Post* 1997—*Telegram; Homogenic* 2000—*Selmasongs—Music From the Motion Picture "Dancer in the Dark."*

The biggest rock band to emerge from Iceland, the Sugarcubes drew notice for their offbeat songs and singer Björk Gudmundsdóttir, an elfin womanchild with a powerful, keening voice.

Björk, whose stepfather had been in an Icelandic rock band, recorded her first album at age 11, and later joined Theyr, a legendary Icelandic hard-rock band whose drummer was Siggi Baldursson. Einar Örn Benediktsson launched Gramm Records, and with Bragi Ólafsson formed punk band Purrkur Pillnikk, whose debut EP reached Iceland's Top 20 in 1981. In 1982 Theyr recorded with Jaz Coleman and Youth of British punk band Killing Joke (who'd suddenly turned up in Iceland fearful of an impending apocalypse), while Purrkur Pillnikk toured with British punk band the Fall (which had done some recording in Iceland, where it had a strong cult following).

In 1984 Björk, Einar, Siggi, and keyboardist Einar Mellax formed KUKL (Icelandic for "witch"), an atonal, theatrical rock band that toured England and Europe and released some singles on a label run by the British anarchic-punk band Crass. KUKL became the Sugarcubes, who formed the company Bad Taste (encompassing record label, art gallery, bookstore, publishing house, and radio station). *Life's Too Good* (#54, 1988) got rave reviews in England and the U.S., where MTV aired the video for the hypnotic, incantatory "Birthday."

In 1989 Björk's ex-husband Thór (with whom she had a son, Sindri) married new keyboardist Magga Ornolfsdottir, while Ólaffson and Örn also were wed (the first openly gay marriage in rock history). *Here Today, Tomorrow, Next Week!* (#70, 1989), with fussier arrangements featuring strings and horns, was panned by critics. Björk and Baldursson then worked on *Gling Glo,* a Bad Taste album of jazzed-up '50s Icelandic pop songs. The Sugarcubes played for French President François Mitterrand during a 1991 summit meeting in Reykjavík, before recording *Stick Around for Joy* (#95, 1992). A year later Björk ventured outside the Sugarcubes to record her first U.S. solo album, *Debut* (#61, 1993), with producer/composer Nellee Hooper of British soul/jazz collective Soul II Soul. It yielded the single "Human Behavior," which reached #2 on the Modern Rock chart.

Björk's next solo album, *Post* (#32, 1995), featured a pair of tracks cowritten and produced by trip-hop artist Tricky, with whom she had a brief affair. She was later briefly engaged to drum-and-bass star Goldie. Björk made headlines in 1996 when she attacked a reporter in the Bangkok airport for trying to ambush her and her young son with a live TV interview. Later that year, an obsessed fan tried to send her a letter bomb (which was intercepted), as well as a videotape of his own suicide.

Fearing for her life as well as her son's, Björk considered retiring from the public life after the incident. She bounded back within a year with two new releases, beginning with *Telegram* (#66, 1997), a remix album of songs from *Post*. Later that year Björk released *Homogenic* (#28, 1997), which marked her first turn as coproducer (with Mark Bell). Soon afterward, she returned to her hometown of Reykjavík after four years of living in London.

Björk (who had made her film debut in 1986's *The Juniper Tree*) had a lead role in Danish director Lars von Trier's musical *Dancer in the Dark*, which won the Palme d'Or award for Best Film at the Cannes Film Festival. Björk's portrayal of a factory worker aspiring to a role in a local production of *The Sound of Music* while confronting impending blindness earned her an award for Best Actress at the festival, but she immediately vowed never to act again, choosing to focus entirely on music. *Selmasongs*, her soundtrack to the film, debuted at #41.

Clint Black

Born Feb. 4, 1962, Long Branch, NJ
1989—*Killin' Time* (RCA) 1990—*Put Yourself in My Shoes* 1992—*The Hard Way* 1993—*No Time to Kill* 1994—*One Emotion* 1995—*Looking for Christmas* 1996—*The Greatest Hits* 1997—*Nothin' but the Taillights* 1999—*D'lectrified*.

With his husky, expressive voice and matinee-idol looks, Clint Black was one of the dominant forces in '90s country music. Between 1989 and late 1999, he sold over 12 million albums and had a dozen #1 C&W singles, including "A Better Man" (1989), "Loving Blind" (1991), "When My Ship Comes In" (1993), and "Like the Rain" (1996).

Born in New Jersey (where his father was working on a pipeline), Black grew up near Houston. His father, a Cole Porter fan, originally wanted to name his son after the songwriter. He resisted the urge, and Clint was spared the name Cole Black. Part of a musical family, Black started playing harmonica at 13; by 15 he had taught himself guitar, had started writing songs, and was performing everything from Merle Haggard to Yes with one of his three brothers in the Full House Band. He dropped out of high school in 1979 and spent the next eight years working in construction, writing songs, and playing clubs.

Black met Hayden Nicholas, his main songwriting collaborator, at a club in 1987. Nicholas joined Black's band, and the two soon began work on a demo. Their break came later that year when ZZ Top producer and manager Bill Ham met Black, was impressed, and got him a deal with RCA.

"A Better Man" was the first C&W debut single to top the chart in 14 years. *Killin' Time* (#31 pop, #1 C&W, 1989) contained three other #1 C&W singles: "Killin' Time" (1989), "Nobody's Home" (1989), and "Walkin' Away" (1990). It held the #1 spot on the C&W chart for eight months, sold over 3 million copies, and won four Academy of Country Music Awards. Black, who, unlike other country acts, toured with his studio band, also became a major concert attraction.

Put Yourself in My Shoes (#18 pop, #1 C&W, 1990) proved that Black was no fluke, with two #1 C&W hits, "Where Are You Now" (1991) and "Loving Blind" (1991). Black was named Best Male Vocalist of 1990 by the Country Music Association. He recorded a duet with legendary King of the Cowboys Roy Rogers, "Hold On Partner" (#42 C&W, 1991).

Black's marriage to *Knots Landing* star Lisa Hartman in 1991 and his messy break with manager Bill Ham in 1992 led to some speculation that Black was losing touch with his "roots." But the rueful, melancholy album *The Hard Way* (#8 pop, #2 C&W, 1992) proved otherwise. The following year's *No Time to Kill* included a hit duet with Wynonna Judd, "A Bad Goodbye" (#2 C&W, 1993), and backing vocals from Kenny Loggins and former Eagle Timothy B. Schmit. In 1994 Black released his fifth album, *One Emotion* (#8 C&W), which yielded several C&W Top 10 singles, including the #1 "A Good Run of Bad Luck."

Black followed up the next year with a holiday-themed album, *Looking for Christmas*, which reached only #25 on the C&W charts. *The Greatest Hits* (#2 C&W, 1996) returned Black to platinum status and included three new songs, including the chart-topping "Like the Rain" (1996). *Nothin' but the Taillights* (#4 C&W, 1997) was another hit but included only one charting single, "Still Holding On" (#11 C&W, 1997), a duet with Martina McBride. While there were no new albums forthcoming in 1998, Black was active, appearing on the Eagles tribute album, *Common Thread*, and the soundtrack of the animated film *The Prince of Egypt*. He returned with his own material on 1999's *D'lectrified*.

Frank Black: See Pixies

The Black Crowes

Formed 1988, Atlanta, GA
Chris Robinson (b. Dec. 20, 1966, Atlanta), voc.; Rich Robinson (b. May 24, 1969, Atlanta), gtr.; Jeff Cease, gtr.; Johnny Colt (b. May 1, 1968, Cherry Point, NC), bass; Steve Gorman (b. Aug. 17, 1965, Hopkinsville, KY), drums.
1990—*Shake Your Money Maker* (Def American) (– Cease; + Marc Ford [b. Apr. 13, 1966, Los Angeles, CA], gtr.) 1992—*The Southern Harmony and Musical Companion* 1994—(+ Eddie Harsch [b. May 27, 1957, Toronto, Can.], kybds.) *Amorica* (American) 1996—*Three Snakes and One Charm* 1997—(– Ford; – Colt; + Sven Pipien [b. May 30, 1967, Hannover, Ger.], bass) 1998—*Sho' Nuff* 1999—*By Your Side* (Columbia) (+ Audley Freed [b. Oct. 5, 1962, VA], gtr.) 2000—*Live at the Greek* (with Jimmy Page); *A Tribute to a Work in Progress: Greatest Hits 1990–1999* (Musicmaker.com) (– Pipien) 2001—*Lions* (V2).

With members not much older than the trends they revived, the Black Crowes had the look (long hair, velvet flares, fur-trimmed vests, impossibly skinny physiques) and the bluesy, boozy, two-guitar rock sound of the early-'70s Rolling Stones and Faces. The Robinson brothers' father, Stan, was a one-time singer who had a pop hit in 1959 with "Boom-a-Dip-Dip." He discouraged his sons from becoming professional musicians, but by 1984 they had formed the band Mr. Crowe's Garden (named for a favorite childhood fairy tale). This group evolved into the Black Crowes, with Chris dropping out of college along the way. Their debut album, *Shake Your Money Maker* (#4, 1990), sold a million copies and won them Best New American Band in the ROLLING STONE readers and critics polls. In true album-rock throwback fashion, its singles were only minor hits: "Jealous Again" (#75, 1990), "She Talks to Angels" (#30, 1991), and a cover of Otis Redding's "Hard to Handle" (#26, 1991).

In March 1991 the Black Crowes were fired from their opening-act slot on ZZ Top's Miller Beer–sponsored tour after Chris Robinson, onstage in Atlanta, made sarcastic remarks about commercialism. That May the Crowes launched their own tour and three shows into it fired opening act Maggie's Dream, after hearing that band in a Miller Beer radio ad. Also in May, Chris Robinson was arrested for assault and disturbing the peace after a postshow argument with a female customer at a Denver convenience store. Before pleading no contest three months later (he got six months' probation and a $53 fine), he collapsed of malnutrition and exhaustion during a British tour. Upon his recovery, the Crowes played Moscow on the Monsters of Rock Tour of the Soviet Union.

With new guitarist Marc Ford (from L.A. band Burning Tree), the Crowes acted on their pro-marijuana rhetoric by playing the April 1992 Great Atlanta Pot Festival, staged by the National Organization to Reform Marijuana Laws (NORML). Two months later the band's second album (named for an antebellum hymnal) entered the *Billboard* pop albums chart at #1; again its singles were only minor hits: "Remedy" (#48, 1992) and "Thorn in My Pride" (#80, 1992). In February 1993 the band played a free show in Houston, with its own handpicked security, to make up for a show the previous October, at which, the band felt, security guards had roughed up fans. The next month the band ended a Louisville, Kentucky, show after one song, ostensibly because of a backstage fracas between its road crew and plainclothes narcotics officers. The band's security chief and merchandising supervisor were charged with assault and resisting arrest. The band's 1994 album, *Amorica,* reached #11, but again yielded no hit singles. *Amorica's* original cover, depicting a closeup of a woman's bikini underwear with pubic hair showing, was changed after some chains refused to carry the album.

The making of the band's 1996 release, *Three Snakes and One Charm* (#15), was fraught with tension. The group returned to Atlanta to record the effort but was distracted by a lawsuit brought by a former manager (the case was later thrown out of court). During the next year, guitarist Ford was fired and original bassist Johnny Colt quit (he was replaced by Sven Pipien, a friend of the band's from Atlanta). A career-spanning box set, *Sho' Nuff,* came out in 1998. And in 1999, the group resurfaced on a new label, Columbia, and an album, *By Your Side* (#26), that was greeted as a return to rollicking form. The single "Kicking My Heart Around" reached #3. Later that year, the band joined former Led Zeppelin guitarist Jimmy Page for concerts at L.A.'s Greek Theatre, which were documented on the 2000 release *Live at the Greek.* The artists also toured to support the recording. On New Year's Eve 2001, Chris Robinson was in the news again, when he wed 21-year-old actress Kate Hudson, the daughter of actress Goldie Hawn and singer/songwriter Bill Hudson, who had starred as the groupie Penny Lane in director Cameron Crowe's autobiographical '70s rock saga, *Almost Famous.* The band's 2001 album, *Lions,* debuted in the Top 20.

Black Flag/Henry Rollins/Greg Ginn

Formed 1977, Hermosa Beach, CA
Greg Ginn (a.k.a. Dale Nixon, b. ca. 1953), gtr., bass; Chuck Dukowski (b. Gary McDaniel), bass; Keith Morris (a.k.a. Johnny "Bob" Goldstein), voc.; Brian Migdol, drums.
1978—*Nervous Breakdown* EP (SST) (– Morris; – Migdol; + Chavo Pederast [b. Ron Reyes], voc.; + Robo [b. Roberto Valverde, Colombia], drums) 1980—*Jealous Again* 1981—(– Pederast; + Dez Cadena, gtr., voc.; + Henry Rollins [b. Henry Garfield, Feb. 13, 1961, Washington, DC], voc.) *Damaged* (– Robo; + Emil Johnson, drums) 1982—(– Johnson; + Chuck Biscuits [b. Apr. 17, CA], drums, voc.) 1983—*Everything Went Black* (– Biscuits; + Bill Stevenson [b. ca. 1964], drums; – Cadena; – Dukowski) 1984—*The First Four Years; My War* (+ Kira Roessler, bass) *Family Man; Slip It In* 1985—*Loose Nut; In My Head; The Process of Weeding Out* EP 1986—(– Stevenson; + Anthony Martinez, drums) *Who's Got the 10 1/2?* (– Roessler; + C'el Revuelta, bass) 1987—*Wasted . . . Again.*
Henry Rollins solo: 1987—*Hot Animal Machine* (Texas Hotel); *Big Ugly Mouth* 1988—*Sweat Box* 1989—*Live at McCabe's* 1990—*Human Butt* (1/4 Stick) 1993—*The Boxed Life* (Imago) 1994—*Get in the Van* 1996—*Everything; Black Coffee Blues* 1998—*Think Tank* (DreamWorks) 1999—*Eric the Pilot.*
Rollins as Henrietta Collins and the Wifebeating Childhaters: 1987—*Drive By Shooting* EP (Texas Hotel).
Rollins with Rollins Band: 1988—*Life Time* (Texas Hotel) 1989—*Do It* EP; *Hard Volume* 1990—*Turned On* (1/4 Stick) 1992—*The End of Silence* (Imago) 1994—*Weight* 1997—*Come In and Burn* (DreamWorks) 1999—*Insert Band Here* (BMG/Buddah) 2000—*Get Some, Go Again* (DreamWorks).
Rollins with Wartime: 1990—*Fast Food for Thought* EP (Chrysalis).
Greg Ginn solo: 1993—*Getting Even* (Cruz); *Dick* 1994—*Let It Burn (Because I Don't Live There Anymore).*
Ginn with Gone: 1986—*"Let's Get Real, Real Gone for a Change"*

(SST); *Gone II—But Never Too Gone!* 1994—*The Criminal Mind.*
Ginn as Poindexter Stewart: 1993—*College Rock* EP (SST).

Black Flag became America's premier hardcore punk band in the early '80s. With its uncompromising DIY ethic, constant low-budget touring, and angry, driving songs, the group provided the blueprint for subsequent postpunk bands.

Guitarist Greg Ginn formed the group in 1977, two years after he graduated from UCLA with a degree in economics. He and bassist Chuck Dukowski cofounded SST Records so they could get the group's music into the hands of its small but rabid audience. With its roster of other critically acclaimed bands, including Minutemen, Hüsker Dü, Sonic Youth, and Meat Puppets, SST became the most respected American indie of the '80s.

Black Flag's early songs were marked by Ginn's scorching rhythm and tangled lead guitar work, Dukowski's guttural bass playing, and a succession of wailing vocalists. The band's first single, "Wasted," reflected the nihilistic angst of Black Flag's suburban, middle-class, "party-hearty" surroundings, with a theme that popped up repeatedly in later songs such as "TV Party" (from *Damaged*) and "Annihilate This Week" *(Loose Nut)*.

When singer Keith Morris left to form the Circle Jerks, Black Flag went through several vocalists before locking in with Henry Rollins, a Washington, DC, punk who had jumped onstage with the band during a New York performance. MCA refused to release the group's first full-length album, *Damaged*, but after Ginn released it himself on SST—to overwhelmingly favorable critical response—a bitter legal dispute ensued with MCA-distributed Unicorn Records. For two years Black Flag was forbidden to use its name or logo. When Unicorn went bankrupt, Ginn came out of the struggle vowing never to deal with other labels, especially the majors.

In its most prolific period—1984 to 1986—Black Flag released more than one LP per year, in addition to its continuous touring. In 1986 Ginn formed a side trio, Gone (which released three albums), and soon dissolved Black Flag. He has since focused on running SST, although he returned to music in 1993, releasing solo albums under his own name, the pseudonym Poindexter Stewart, and with a new version of Gone.

While it was Ginn who composed all of Black Flag's music and the majority of its lyrics, Rollins' career got the greatest boost from his former band's momentum. With the demise of Black Flag, Rollins immediately formed his own Rollins Band, taking Gone's Andrew Weiss and Sim Cain with him, while enlisting DC guitarist Chris Haskett. Soundman Theo Van Rock was credited as a full member. The Rollins Band recorded several albums and gained a wide following that intensified after its appearance on the 1991 Lollapalooza Tour and with the release of *The End of Silence*. *Weight* was even nominated for a Grammy, and in 1997, *Come In and Burn* reached #89 on the *Billboard* Top 200. By the release of 2000's *Get Some, Go Again*, the original Rollins Band had moved on, replaced by the members of Mother Superior, an L.A.-based trio, which provided a more straight-ahead hard-rock canvas for Rollins' shouted vocals. In 1998, Rollins collaborated with Bone Thugs-N-Harmony, Flesh-N-Bone, Flea, and Tom Morello of Rage Against the Machine on a remake of the 1970 Edwin Starr hit "War" for the soundtrack to *Small Soldiers*.

Rollins remains equally busy as a spoken-word artist, releasing numerous spoken-word recordings and videos. He has written a number of books published by his own press, 2.13.61, which has released books by other authors, including Iggy Pop. Rollins is also a working actor, both narrating TV commercials (the Gap, Nike, GMC trucks) and winning roles in serious films alongside the likes of Al Pacino *(Heat)* or in lighter family fare *(Jack Frost)*.

Ritchie Blackmore/Rainbow

Formed 1975, Los Angeles, CA
Ritchie Blackmore (b. Apr. 14, 1945, Weston-super-Mare, Eng.), gtr.; Ronnie James Dio (b. Ronald Padavona, July 10, 1949, Portsmouth, NH), voc.; Gary Driscoll, drums; Craig Gruber, bass; Mickey Lee Soule, kybds.
1975—*Ritchie Blackmore's Rainbow* (Polydor) (– Driscoll; – Gruber; – Soule; + Cozy Powell [b. Dec. 29, 1947, Cirencester, Eng.], drums; + Tony Carey [b. Oct. 16, 1953], kybds.; + Jim Bain, bass) 1976—*Rainbow Rising* 1977—*Onstage* (– Carey; – Bain; + Bob Daisley, bass; + David Stone, kybds.) 1978—*Long Live Rock 'n' Roll* (– Dio; – Daisley; – Stone) 1979—(+ Roger Glover [b. Nov. 30, 1945, Brecon, S. Wales], bass; + Don Airey, kybds.; + Graham Bonnet, voc.) *Down to Earth* (– Bonnet; – Powell; + Joe Lynn Turner, voc.; + Bob Rondinelli, drums) 1981—*Difficult to Cure* (– Airey; + David Rosenthal, kybds.) *Jealous Lover* 1982—*Straight Between the Eyes* (Mercury) 1983—*Bent out of Shape* 1986—*Finyl Vinyl.*
Blackmore's Night, formed 1997: Blackmore, gtr., mandolin; Candice Night, voc., pennywhistle.
1998—*Shadow of the Moon* (Edel) 1999—*Under a Violet Moon* (Platinum Entertainment).

Hard-rock guitarist Ritchie Blackmore began studying classical guitar at age 11, then switched to rock in his teens. He became a session player and worked with Screaming Lord Sutch before cofounding Deep Purple in 1968. Associates claim that Blackmore is often arrogant and belligerent, and after Purple had peaked, he left in 1975 amid rumors of dissension. He founded his own band, made up mostly of members of the upstate New York band Elf (which had frequently opened for Deep Purple), and it was billed alternately as Rainbow or Ritchie Blackmore's Rainbow.

The frequently changing lineup included vocalists Ronnie James Dio (who later replaced Ozzy Osbourne in Black Sabbath and found success on his own) and Graham Bonnet (briefly a member of Deep Purple after singer Ian Gillan split in 1973), keyboardist Tony Carey (marginally successful in the mid-'80s both under his own name and as Planet P), and drummer Cozy Powell (formerly of the Jeff Beck Group and later with Sabbath, the Michael Schenker Band, and others). Ex–Deep Purple bassist Roger Glover joined Blackmore in 1979, and with vocalist Joe Lynn Turner and Blackmore he cowrote Rainbow's Top 40 hit "Stone Cold."

Rainbow dissolved two years later when Blackmore, Glover, and the other three members of the "classic" Purple lineup got back together. Turner, after releasing a solo album in 1985, joined Purple in 1990 but was replaced (by Ian Gillan, whom he'd replaced) in 1993. Shortly thereafter, Blackmore quit. A new Rainbow, which released a 1995 European album, toured the U.S. in 1997. By the decade's close, Blackmore was devoting his time to Blackmore's Night, a largely acoustic, medieval-style duo with vocalist Candice Night and various support casts. *Shadow of the Moon* features flute by Jethro Tull's Ian Anderson. The band has enjoyed great success in Japan and in New Age circles.

Black Oak Arkansas

Formed 1969, Los Angeles, CA
Jim "Dandy" Mangrum (b. Mar. 30, 1948, Black Oak, AR), voc.; Ricky Reynolds (b. Oct. 29, 1948, Manilan, AR), gtr.; Harvey Jett, gtr.; Stan Knight (b. Feb. 12, 1949, Little Rock, AR), gtr.; Pat Daugherty (b. Nov. 11, 1947, Jonesboro, AR), bass; Wayne Evans, drums.
1969—*The Knowbody Else* (Stax) 1971—*Black Oak Arkansas* (Atco) 1972—*Keep the Faith; If an Angel Came to See You, Would You Make Her Feel at Home?* 1973—*Raunch 'n' Roll/Live* (– Evans; + Tommy Aldridge, drums); *High on the Hog* (Atlantic) 1974—*Street Party* (– Jett; + Jimmy Henderson [b. May 20, 1954, Jackson, MS, gtr.]) *Hot and Nasty* 1975—*Ain't Life Grand; X-Rated* (MCA) 1976—(numerous lineup changes) *Balls of Fire; Live! Mutha* (Atco); *10 Year Overnight Success* (MCA) 1977—*Race With the Devil* (Capricorn); *Best Of; I'd Rather Be Sailing* 1980—(group disbands) 1984—(group re-forms: Mangrum; Reynolds; + various lineups) 1986—*The Black Attack Is Back* (Heavy Metal America) 1999—(+ Daugherty, bass; + Rocky Athas, gtr.; + Johnnie Bolin, drums) *The Wild Bunch* (Dead Line/Cleopatra).
Jim Dandy solo: 1984—*Ready as Hell* (Heavy Metal America).

Black Oak Arkansas was a Southern heavy-metal group whose boogie philosophy and long-haired, bare-chested frontman, Jim Dandy Mangrum, were briefly popular in the early to mid-'70s. All of the band's original members grew up in rural Arkansas near the small town of Black Oak. They were in a juvenile gang before becoming a band. (In a 1976 press release they boast of having stolen a P.A. system.) They toured the South as Knowbody Else and released one album on Stax before moving to L.A. in 1969 and changing their name to Black Oak Arkansas. They soon signed with Atlantic, the first of several labels for which they recorded.

With almost constant touring, they eventually built up an enthusiastic following, composed mainly of young fans who appreciated the group's down-home Dixie boogie and quasi-mystical lyrics. In 1970 they made their national debut, but big-time success eluded them until *High on the Hog* (1973) and *Raunch 'n' Roll/Live* (1973) went gold. They also had a #25 hit with "Jim Dandy," which featured Dandy exchanging double entendres with a female singer, a sometime group member named Ruby Starr. By the mid-'70s the group was a huge draw on the U.S. concert circuit. The group sustained numerous personnel changes, and by 1977 Mangrum was the only original member of the band left. He later cited "despotic management" and the rigors of the road for driving the band apart. After recovering from a heart attack, Mangrum recorded a 1984 solo album with original Black Oak guitarist Ricky Reynolds. Several touring versions of the band existed in the '80s and '90s. Daugherty rejoined in time for Black Oak's 1999 studio effort.

Black Sabbath

Formed 1967, Birmingham, Eng.
Ozzy Osbourne (b. John Michael Osbourne, Dec. 3, 1948, Birmingham), voc.; Terry "Geezer" Butler (b. Terence Michael Joseph Butler, July 17, 1949, Birmingham), bass; Tony Iommi (b. Anthony Frank Iommi, Feb. 19, 1948, Birmingham), gtr.; Bill Ward (b. William Ward, May 5, 1948, Birmingham), drums.
1970—*Black Sabbath* (Warner Bros.) 1971—*Paranoid; Master of Reality* 1972—*Volume 4* 1973—*Sabbath, Bloody Sabbath* 1975—*Sabotage* 1976—*We Sold Our Soul for Rock 'n' Roll; Technical Ecstasy* 1978—*Never Say Die* 1979—(– Osbourne; + Ronnie James Dio [b. Ronald Padavona, July 10, 1949, Portsmouth, NH], voc.) 1980—*Heaven and Hell* (– Ward; + Vinnie Appice [b. Staten Island, NY], drums) 1981—*Mob Rules* 1982—(– Dio; – Appice; + Dave Donato, voc.; + Ward) 1983—*Live Evil* (– Donato; + Ian Gillan [b. Aug. 19, 1945, Hounslow, Eng.], voc.) *Born Again* 1984—(– Gillan) 1985—(– Ward; – Butler; + Glenn Hughes [b. Aug. 21, 1952, Penkridge, Eng.], voc.; + Geoff Nichols [b. Birmingham], kybds.; + Dave Spitz [b. New York, NY], bass; + Eric Singer [b. Cleveland, OH], drums) *Seventh Star* 1987—(– Spitz; – Hughes; + Bob Daisley, bass; + Tony Martin [b. 1957], voc.; – Singer; + Bev Bevan [b. Nov. 25, 1946, Birmingham], drums) *The Eternal Idol* (– Bevan; – Daisley) 1989—(+ Cozy Powell [b. Dec. 29, 1947, Cirenchester, Eng.; d. Apr. 5, 1998, Bristol, Eng.], drums; + Spitz) *The Headless Cross* (I.R.S.) (– Nichols; + Lawrence Cottle, bass; – Cottle) 1990—(+ Neil Murray, bass; – Murray; + Nichols) *TYR* (– Powell; – Martin; + Appice; + Butler; + Dio) 1992—*Dehumanizer* (Reprise) 1993—(– Dio; – Appice; + Butler; + Martin; + Bob Rondinelli, drums) 1994—*Cross Purposes* (I.R.S.) (– Rondinelli; + Ward) 1995—(– Butler; – Ward; + Murray; + Powell) *Forbidden* (Capitol) 1996—(– Powell) 1997—(– Martin; – Murray; + Osbourne; + Butler; + Mike Bordin [b. Nov. 27, 1962, San Francisco, CA], drums; – Bordin; + Ward) 1998—*Reunion* (Epic).
Tony Iommi solo: 2000—*Iommi* (Priority).

Mixing equal parts bone-crushing volume, catatonic tempos, and ominous pronouncements of gloom and doom delivered in Ozzy Osbourne's keening voice, Black Sabbath was the heavy-metal king of the '70s. Despised by rock critics and ignored by radio programmers, the group sold over 8 million albums before Osbourne departed for a solo career in 1979 [see entry]. The band's original lineup reunited for a two-year tour in 1997.

The four original members, schoolmates from a working-class district of industrial Birmingham, first joined forces as the Polka Tulk Blues Company, a blues band. They quickly changed their name to Earth, then, in 1969, to Black Sabbath; the name came from the title of a song written by bassist Geezer Butler, a fan of occult novelist Dennis Wheatley. It may also have been an homage to a Boris Karloff film. The quartet's eponymously titled 1970 debut, recorded in two days, went to #8 in England and #23 in the U.S. A single, "Paranoid," released in advance of the album of the same name, reached #4 in the U.K. later that year; it was the group's only Top 20 hit.

The single didn't make the U.S. Top 40, but the *Paranoid* LP, issued in early 1971, eventually sold 4 million copies despite virtually no airplay. Beginning in December 1970 Sabbath toured the States relentlessly. Despite the band members' intense drug and alcohol abuse, the constant road work paid off, and by 1974 Black Sabbath was considered peerless among heavy-metal acts, its first five LPs all having sold at least a million copies apiece in America alone.

In spite of their name, the crosses erected onstage, and songs dealing with apocalypse, death, and destruction, the band members insisted their interest in the black arts was nothing more than innocuous curiosity (the sort that led Ozzy Osbourne to sit through *eight* showings of *The Exorcist*), and in time Black Sabbath's princes-of-darkness image faded. Eventually, so did its record sales. Aside from a platinum best-of, *We Sold Our Soul for Rock 'n' Roll* (1976), not one of three LPs from 1975 to 1978 went gold. Osbourne, racked by drug use and excessive drinking, quit the band briefly in late 1977 (ex–Savoy Brown–Fleetwood Mac vocalist Dave Walker filled his shoes for some live dates). In January 1979 he was fired. Ronnie James Dio, formerly of Ritchie Blackmore's Rainbow, replaced Osbourne.

Although Dio could belt with the best of them, Sabbath would never be the same. Its first album with Dio, *Heaven and Hell* (1980), went platinum; its second, *Mob Rules* (1981), gold. But thereafter, the group's LPs sold fewer and fewer copies, as Black Sabbath went through one personnel change after another. Ill health forced Bill Ward out of the band in 1980; Carmine Appice's brother Vinnie took his place. Friction between Iommi and Dio led the singer to quit angrily in 1982; he took Appice with him to start his own band, Dio. Vocalists over the years have included Dave Donato; Deep Purple singer Ian Gillan; Glenn Hughes, another ex-member of Purple; Tony Martin; and Dio again.

By 1986's *Seventh Star*, only Iommi remained from the original lineup. He had to wince when Geezer Butler teamed up with the phenomenally successful Osbourne in 1988, though the bassist did return to the fold three years later. Despite bitterness expressed in the press between Osbourne and Iommi, the original foursome reunited in 1985 at the Live Aid concert in Philadelphia, and again in 1992, at the end of what was supposedly Osbourne's last tour. Throughout 1993 word had it that Osbourne, Iommi, Butler, and Ward would tour, but by year's end Osbourne had backed out, allegedly over money. The indefatigable Tony Iommi went right back to work with Butler, rehiring vocalist Tony Martin and adding former Rainbow drummer Rob Rondinelli. That lineup proved as unstable as the previous one, with drummers coming, going, and returning over the following years. Despite hiring Body Count's Ernie C to produce 1995's *Forbidden* (and inviting guest vocalist Ice-T to sing on a track), Black Sabbath seemed increasingly out of touch with the times, and at the end of the Forbidden Tour, the band unofficially went on hiatus.

But not for long, as Iommi, Butler, and Osbourne reunited to headline Ozzfest 1997. Ward was not invited (he was replaced by Faith No More's Mike Bordin), but he did participate in two shows in the band's hometown of Birmingham, England, in December 1997. The resulting live album, *Reunion* (#11, 1998), also featured two new studio tracks, including the single "Psycho Man." The album went platinum in the U.S., and the live version of "Iron Man" earned the band its first Grammy for Best Metal Performance—nearly 30 years after the song was originally released. The ensuing tour lasted two years and ended in December 1999. (Ward, who suffered a heart attack in May 1998 before the European tour kicked off, rejoined the group in December 1998; Appice sat in for him while he recuperated). Tony Iommi released his first solo album in 2000; a prestigious roster of guest singers (Osbourne, Billy Corgan, Henry Rollins, Dave Grohl) handled the vocals. Among metalheads, Iommi is something of a guitar god, due in part to the fact that he plays spectacularly despite having lost the tips of two right fingers in a welding accident at age 17. His hero was the great jazz guitarist Django Reinhardt, who also lost two fingers and yet continued to play. In mid-2001 it was announced that all original members were writing material for a new Black Sabbath album.

Black Star/Mos Def/Talib Kweli

Formed 1996, Brooklyn, NY
Mos Def (b. Dante Smith, Dec. 11, Brooklyn), voc.; Talib Kweli (b. Talib Kweli Green, Oct. 3, Brooklyn), voc.
1998—*Mos Def & Talib Kweli Are Black Star* (Rawkus).
Mos Def solo: 1999—*Black on Both Sides* (Rawkus).
Talib Kweli & Hi Tek: 2000—*Reflection Eternal—Train of Thought* (Rawkus).

During a time when the success of Sean Combs, Jay-Z, and Master P seemed to pull the curtain over socially conscious rap music, Black Star summoned the spirit of the Native Tongues movement and brought organic hip-hop back to the mainstream. Combining B-boy sensibility and African-American academics, the duo consisting of Mos Def and Talib Kweli began spreading its message of racial and social transcendentalism at the Lyricist Lounge—an underground, open-mike forum for unsigned MCs in New York.

Mos Def first presented his rhythmically precise flow onstage at the Lyricist Lounge in 1992, along with artists like Mobb Deep, Foxy Brown, and the Notorious B.I.G. Mos Def and Kweli also came together at the club, and after appearing individually on various compilations and 12-inch singles, formed Black Star—the name deriving from Marcus Garvey's Black Star Line of boat service to Africa. Their debut album, *Mos Def & Talib Kweli Are Black Star* (#53 pop, #13 R&B, 1998), was filled with poetry about self-determination and political injustice. In the ensuing two years, both Mos Def and Kweli received critical acclaim for their solo releases. In 2000, the two members of Black Star also founded the Hip-Hop for Respect Foundation (HHFRF), a nonprofit organization dedicated to motivating the entertainment industry to become more involved in philanthropy. To raise money for HHFRF, Mos Def and Kweli enlisted a roster of artists including RZA, De La Soul, Pras, and Rah Digga to create a maxi-single that paid tribute to the killing of West African immigrant Amadou Diallo, who was gunned down by four New York City police officers outside his home in the Bronx in 1999. At the end of 2000, Mos Def performed in Manhattan with his Jack Johnson side project, which featured Parliament-Funkadelic's Bernie Worrell and Living Colour's Doug Wimbish and Will Calhoun.

Black Uhuru

Formed 1974, Kingston, Jam.
Don Carlos (b. Euvin Spencer, June 29, 1952, Kingston), voc.; Rudolph "Garth" Dennis (b. Dec. 2, 1949, Kingston), voc.; Derrick "Duckie" Simpson (b. June 24, 1950, Kingston), voc.
1977—(– Carlos; – Dennis; + Errol Nelson, voc.; + Michael Rose [b. July 11, 1957, Kingston], voc.) *Love Crisis* (Prince Jammy's) (– Nelson) 1978—(+ Sandra "Puma" Jones [b. Oct. 5, 1953, SC; d. Jan. 28, 1990], voc.) 1979—*Showcase* (Taxi) 1980—*Sinsemilla* (Mango) 1981—*Red* 1982—*Tear It Up; Chill Out* 1983—*The Dub Factor; Anthem* 1985—*Reggae Greats* (– Rose; + Delroy "Junior" Reid, voc.) 1986—*Brutal* (RAS); *Brutal Dub* 1987—(– Jones; + Olafunke [b. Janet Reid, Jam.], voc.) *Positive* 1988—*Positive Dub* 1990—(– Olafunke; – Reid; + Carlos; + Dennis) *Now* (Mesa); *Now Dub* 1991—*Iron Storm* 1992—*Iron Storm Dub* 1993—*Mystical Truth; Mystical Truth Dub; Liberation: The Island Anthology* (Island) 1994—*Strongg* (Rhino); *Strongg Dub* 1997—*Portraits* (RAS) 1998—*Unification* (Five Star General) (– Carlos; – Dennis; + Jenifah Nyah Connally, voc.; + Andrew Bees, voc.) 2000—*Ultimate Collection* (Uni/Hip-o).

Although its lineup has changed often over a 27-year career ("Duckie" Simpson is the only constant), Black Uhuru has remained true to its fierce Rastafarian politics and haunting vocal harmonies. The group's most popular period coincided with Michael Rose's membership, when the vocal group was backed by Jamaica's finest instrumentalists, with songs made distinctive by "Puma" Jones' descant and melodies that suggest Hebrew cantillation.

The original (and mid-'90s) Uhuru (Swahili for "freedom") was formed by Duckie Simpson with Garth Dennis and Don Carlos. They played clubs around Jamaica but failed to attract much local attention despite their Top Cat single "Folk Songs." Dennis and Carlos quit soon after (Dennis to join the Wailing Souls), and Simpson brought Errol Nelson and Rose to Uhuru. Their next singles, "Natural Mystic" and "King Selassie," found their way to England in 1977, and U.K. distributor Count Shelly issued their first album there.

Nelson left the group to join the Jayes, and Simpson and Rose recorded some singles as a duo. After cutting a couple of songs with producer Lee "Scratch" Perry, they teamed with drummer Sly Dunbar (an old friend of Rose) and his partner Robbie Shakespeare. Uhuru's "Observe Life" was the first single Sly and Robbie produced and the first issued on their Taxi label. Simpson and Rose were then joined by Sandra "Puma" Jones, a Southern-born American with a master's degree from Columbia University who had come to Jamaica as a social worker. Her only professional experience had been as a dancer and backup singer with Ras Michael and the Sons of Negus. With Sly and Robbie the trio recorded its best-known singles, "General Penitentiary," "Guess Who's Coming to Dinner," "Plastic Smile," "Abortion" (which was anti- and was banned in Jamaica), and "Shine Eye Gal." *Showcase* followed. After its release, New York City radio station WLIB sponsored Uhuru's first appearance outside Jamaica, a concert at Hunter College, and Island Records signed the group to its Mango subsidiary. *Sinsemilla* (Black Uhuru's American debut) and *Red* were recorded in Jamaica with Sly and Robbie and their Taxi All-Stars (Keith Richards added his guitar to the former).

Rose's move to New York at the time of 1982's *Chill Out* was reflected in the album's urban subject matter. Island tried to build on its success by remixing *Anthem* for American listeners. Although it won a Grammy for Best Reggae Album, Rose was unhappy with the band's direction and left soon afterward; he has remained active, releasing numerous singles and albums, including *Proud* (1990), *Be Yourself* (1996), and *Bonanza* (1999).

Junior Reid replaced Rose on *Brutal,* and dance-music specialist Arthur Baker joined Sly and Robbie in the production booth. Jones left before the recording of *Positive* (she died of cancer in 1990) and was briefly replaced by Janet Reid. In late 1987 original members Dennis and Carlos joined Simpson onstage during a Jamaican awards show. They decided to make this impromptu reunion permanent, recording the Grammy-nominated *Now.* Ice-T added contemporary hip-hop elements to "Tip of the Iceberg" on 1992's *Iron Storm.*

By 1995, old animosities (mostly over money) were reignited and Uhuru split yet again. But Dennis and Carlos continued to tour using the Black Uhuru name and in 1997 were taken to court by Simpson, who claimed the exclusive right to the Black Uhuru trademark. Simpson prevailed, and he premiered the latest version of Black Uhuru, with Jenifah Nyah Connally and Andrew Bees, on March 21, 1998, in Negril, Jamaica.

Rubén Blades

Born July 16, 1948, Panama City, Panama
1979—*Bohemio y Poeta* (Fania) 1980—*Maestra Vida, Primera*

Parte; Maestra Vida, Segunda Parte 1982—*El Que la Hace la Paga* 1984—*Mucho Mejor; Buscando America* (Elektra) 1985—*Escenas* 1986—*Crossover Dreams; Doble Filo* (Fania) 1987—*Agua de Luna* (Elektra) 1988—*Antecedente; Nothing but the Truth* 1990—*Y Son del Solar . . . Live!* 1991—*Caminando* (Sony Discos International) 1992—*Amor y Control* 1996—*La Rosa de los Vientos* 1999—*Tiempos.*

Panamanian singer Rubén Blades is as much a political activist as he is a singer and actor. As one of the premier performers of salsa music, he is an innovator who has broadened the genre's appeal far beyond its Latin-American base.

Son of a police officer and an actress mother, Blades was influenced as a child by his maternal grandmother, a Rosicrucian vegetarian who exposed him early to American films. Rock & roll also affected him; when he joined his brother's band in 1963, he sang in English. The Canal Zone riots of 1964, however, checked his romance with stateside culture, and he began delving into salsa, the Afro-Cuban music powered by horns and percussion. While playing with local bands, he worked on a law degree at the University of Panama; he took time off to make an album in New York City with Latin musician Pete Rodriguez but returned to finish his studies.

In 1974, after a stint as an attorney for the Bank of Panama, Blades moved to New York. Four years later he became the songwriter/vocalist for the Willie Colon Combo. The pair released *Siembra,* one of salsa's most popular albums, and for Fania, the major salsa label, Colon produced Blades' first records. In 1982 Blades formed his own band, Seis del Solar. Signing him as its first Latin artist, Elektra released *Buscando America,* an album that stirred controversy among salsa purists for its use of synthesizers and rock-inflected instrumentation. In addition, its lyrics, inspired by Blades' friend, Colombian author Gabriel García Márquez *(One Hundred Years of Solitude),* were somber, poetic, and political, a sharp departure from salsa's traditionally escapist themes. With 1985 came *Escenas,* featuring a duet with Linda Ronstadt; throughout the '80s Blades continued to record for both Fania and Elektra, for the latter releasing *Nothing but the Truth,* his English-language singing debut.

Blades had also been busy at other pursuits. Immediately after his Elektra debut, Blades enrolled at Harvard, where he earned a master's degree in international law. In 1985 he starred in the salsa film *Crossover Dreams,* drawing notice for his acting and, in the process, helping to raise the profile of salsa. Subsequent roles in forgettable fare *(Critical Condition, Fatal Beauty)* didn't seem to affect his acting career, and he regained credibility with television roles and parts in such films as *Waiting for Salazar, The Milagro Beanfield War, Mo' Better Blues,* and *The Two Jakes.* For the movies *When the Mountains Tremble, Caminos Verdes,* and *Q&A,* Blades composed scores.

All along, Blades remained active in politics. In 1992 he launched Papa Egoro, a Panamanian political party dedicated to social justice. The next year, he announced his temporary retirement from music and acting in order to pursue the Panamanian presidency in 1994; he lost that race.

As the '90s progressed, Blades continued to expand artistically, starring in Paul Simon's 1998 Broadway musical *The Capeman,* receiving a Grammy (his third) for *La Rosa de los Vientos,* and in 1999 releasing *Tiempos,* considered by some critics to be his finest work.

Blake Babies: See Juliana Hatfield

Bobby "Blue" Bland

Born Robert Calvin Brooks, Jan. 27, 1930, Rosemark, TN
1960—*Barefoot Rock and You Got Me* (Duke) 1961—*Two Steps From the Blues* 1962—*Here's the Man* 1963—*Call on Me* 1964—*Ain't Nothing You Can Do* 1968—*Touch of the Blues* 1972—*The Best of Bobby Bland* (MCA) 1973—*His California Album* (ABC) 1974—*Dreamer; B.B. King and Bobby Bland/Together for the First Time . . . Live* (with B.B. King); *Ain't Nothing You Can Do* (MCA); *Here's the Man; The Soul of the Man; The Best of Bobby Bland, vol. 2* 1975—*Get On Down With Bobby Bland* 1976—*Bobby Bland and B.B. King/Together Again . . . Live* (with B.B. King) 1977—*Reflections in Blue* 1978—*Come Fly With Me* 1979—*I Feel Good, I Feel Fine* 1980—*Sweet Vibrations* 1981—*Try Me, I'm Real* 1982—*Here We Go Again; Introspective Early Years* 1985—*Members Only* (Malaco) 1986—*After All* 1987—*Blues You Can Use; First Class Blues* 1989—*Midnight Run* 1991—*Portrait of the Blues* 1992—*I Pity the Fool/The Duke Recordings, vol. 1* 1993—*Years of Tears* 1994—*Turn On Your Love Light/The Duke Recordings, vol. 2* (MCA) 1995—*Sad Street* (Malaco) 1997—*Just One More Step* (601) 1998—*Live on Beale Street* (Malaco); *Memphis Monday Morning; Greatest Hits vol. 1* (Duke/Peacock); *Greatest Hits vol. 2* (MCA).

Bobby "Blue" Bland is one of the patriarchs of modern soul singing, his distinctively grainy vocal style drawing on gospel and blues. Raised in Memphis, he joined a gospel ensemble, the Miniatures, in the late '40s. He later met guitarist B.B. King and joined the Beale Streeters, an informal group of Memphis blues musicians that included King, Johnny Ace, Roscoe Gordon, and Willie Nix. But not until 1954 (after working as King's chauffeur) did he land his first recording contract, when an executive of Duke Records heard him sing at a Houston talent show.

His first successful single, "It's My Life, Baby," was released in 1955. He played one-nighters around the country accompanied by his band, led by tenor saxophonist Bill Harvey and trumpeter/arranger Joe Scott. Members of the band, under the pseudonym Deadric Malone, wrote or cowrote most of Bland's material. His band was bigger and brassier than most current blues bands, and anticipated the rich sound of '60s soul music while harking back to big-band jazz.

Since 1957, when "Farther Up the Road" was a #5 R&B hit, Bland has had over 30 R&B Top 20 singles, including "I'll Take Care of You" (#2, 1959), "I Pity the Fool" (#1, 1961), "Don't Cry No More" (#2, 1961), "Turn On Your Love Light" (#2, 1961), and "That's the Way Love Is" (#1, 1963).

Most of Bland's records enjoyed only modest success in

the pop market; only three singles ever made the pop Top 30. In the mid-'60s Bland adopted a slicker, more upbeat style, but his career stalled until Duke Records was taken over by ABC-Dunhill in 1972. Dunhill paired him with producer Steve Barri (the Four Tops), who guided Bland back to a bluesier vocal style while giving him contemporary material by Leon Russell and Gerry Goffin, as well as new material by Deadric Malone. *His California Album* and *Dreamer* introduced him to white audiences and proved to be the most popular LPs of his career.

While he never achieved the wide recognition of B.B. King (with whom he toured and collaborated on two LPs, *Together* and *Together Again*), he had a considerable influence on modern soul music. He continues to record and tour internationally. In 1992 he was inducted into the Rock and Roll Hall of Fame. In 1997 he was the recipient of the Recording Academy's coveted Lifetime Achievement Grammy. In 1998 he received a Lifetime Achievement Award from the Blues Foundation. He remains a vital performer.

The Blasters

Formed 1979, Downey, CA
Phil Alvin (b. Mar. 6, 1953, Los Angeles, CA), gtr., voc.; Dave Alvin (b. Nov. 11, 1955, Los Angeles), gtr.; John Bazz (b. July 6, 1952), bass; Bill Bateman (b. Dec. 16, 1951, Orange, CA), drums; Gene Taylor (b. July 2, 1952, Tyler, TX), piano.
1980—*American Music* (Rollin' Rock) 1981—*The Blasters* (Slash/Warner) 1982—*Over There: Live at the Venue, London* EP 1983—*Non Fiction* 1985—*Hard Line* 1990—*The Blasters Collection.*
Phil Alvin solo: 1986—*Un "Sung Stories"* (Slash) 1994—*County Fair 2000* (HighTone).
Dave Alvin solo: 1987—*Romeo's Escape* (Epic) 1991—*Blue Blvd* (HighTone) 1993—*Museum of Heart* 1994—*King of California* 1996—*Interstate City: Dave Alvin and the Guilty Men Live* 1998—*Blackjack David* 2000—*Public Domain—Songs From the Wild Land.*

The Blasters led the early-'80s American roots music revival, performing styles from rockabilly and country to blues and R&B. Brothers Phil and Dave Alvin (whose father was a labor organizer) grew up in the L.A. suburb of Downey listening to the music of Big Joe Turner, T-Bone Walker, Jimmy Reed, and Elvis Presley. The brothers played in various bands and in 1979 they formed the Blasters, named after bluesman Jimmy McCracklin's Blues Blasters.

The group struggled for gigs around L.A. until championed in 1980 by the likes of X's John Doe, rockabilly pioneer "Wildman" Ray Campi, and the Go-Go's. (The Blasters would perform a similar service to East L.A.'s Los Lobos in the early '80s.) When the Blasters' first album, *American Music,* caused a buzz on the underground scene, the L.A. punk label Slash signed the band. The following year *The Blasters* reached #36 on the album chart. By then, the Alvins' longtime hero, New Orleans R&B saxophonist Lee Allen, was a full-time member (along with fellow saxman Steve Berlin), which he remained until his death in 1995.

After a live EP in 1982, the Blasters tried to branch out on the critically acclaimed *Non Fiction,* with songs that broke from the rockabilly mold and explored themes of working-class alienation. For *Hard Line* the Blasters attempted a commercial crossover, enlisting John Mellencamp, who wrote and produced one song ("Colored Lights"), Los Lobos' David Hidalgo, and Elvis Presley's former early backup singers, the Jordanaires. But the band's momentum was soon shaken after a combative performance in Montreal by the abrupt departure of songwriter/guitarist Dave Alvin, who immediately joined X [see entry]. (He had already appeared on an album by X's short-lived acoustic-country alter ego, the Knitters.) He was with X for two years, long enough to appear on the band's 1987 album, *See How We Are* (for which he wrote "4th of July"), before focusing on a solo career. Alvin's replacements in the Blasters included, among others, Hollywood Fats (until his death in 1987) and then Smokey Hormel (Tom Waits, Beck). In the years since, the band continued to tour sporadically while Phil Alvin returned to graduate school, where he took a master's degree in mathematics and artificial intelligence, later pursuing a Ph.D. in these subjects at UCLA.

By the mid-'80s, Dave Alvin had become active in L.A.'s burgeoning spoken-word performance scene, appearing on three spoken-word compilation albums and eventually publishing two books of his poetry. For director Allison Anders' *(Gas, Food, Lodging)* first film, *Border Radio,* Dave made a cameo appearance and composed the soundtrack music, released by Enigma Records in 1987. (Some of that same music surfaced again in Oliver Stone's *Wall Street.*) Alvin also wrote and produced music for John Waters' *Cry-Baby* (1990).

Phil Alvin has also maintained an active, if less visible, solo career, beginning with *Un "Sung Stories,"* a traditionalist album that features the very untraditionalist Sun Ra's Arkestra on three songs. With original bassist John Bazz, Phil enlisted the newest version of the Blasters for some tracks on his 1994 solo album and ensuing performances. (The entire original lineup did one reunion show at an L.A. benefit in the early '90s, but Dave has otherwise been steadfast in his refusal to rejoin—even on a part-time basis—the band he helped create.)

Dave Alvin's solo career began with 1987's *Romeo's Escape,* which mixed new compositions with older songs originally written for the Blasters and X. But it was with 1994's *King of California* and, later, *Blackjack David* that critics finally began praising Alvin's once-ragged vocals as much as his already acclaimed songwriting. In addition to releasing several solo albums, Dave joined the Pleasure Barons, a Who's Who of roots-oriented players (led by the late Country Dick Montana of the Beat Farmers) that at various times included John Doe, Mojo Nixon, and postpunk country singer Rosie Flores. (The band released one live recording.) He also has produced several albums, among them rockabilly legend Sonny Burgess' *Tennessee Border* (1992), three albums by the Derailers, and a 1994 Merle Haggard tribute, *Tulare Dust,* to which he also contributed a track. In 2000 Alvin reunited with Doe and Exene Cervenka in the Knitters for selected club shows, while continuing his solo career on the road, and in 2001 Alvin won Best Traditional Folk Album for his *Public Domain*.

Carla Bley

Born Carla Borg, May 11, 1938, Oakland, CA
1972—*Escalator Over the Hill* (JCOA) 1974—*Tropic Appetites* (Watt) 1975—*13 and 3/4* 1977—*Dinner Music* 1978—*European Tour 1977* 1979—*Musique Mecanique* 1981—*Social Studies* (ECM) 1982—*Carla Bley Live!* 1984—*Heavy Heart* (Watt) 1985—*I Hate to Sing; Night-Glo* 1988—*Duets* 1989—*Fleur Carnivore* 1991—*The Very Big Carla Bley Band* 1993—*Go Together* 1994—*Big Band Theory* 1995—*Songs With Legs* 1996—*The Carla Bley Big Band Goes to Church* 1998—*Fancy Chamber Music* 1999—*Are We There Yet?* 2000—*Carla Bley 4 x 4.*

Composer Carla Bley has experimented with free jazz, punk rock, big bands, orchestras, and forms and groupings of her own. But while many of her pieces are tricky and eccentric, they are rarely less than tuneful, and her gift for bittersweet parody has earned her comparisons with Kurt Weill. Bley plays keyboards and sax, but she is best known for her tunes, her arrangements, and the bands she has conducted.

The daughter of a piano teacher and choir director, she began composing at age nine. After she moved to New York in the late '50s, her works were performed by pianists George Russell and Paul Bley (whom she married) and later by vibraphonist Gary Burton (who has done an entire album of Bley's pieces entitled *Dreams So Real*) and Charlie Haden's Liberation Music Orchestra (which reunited in 1982). She began performing in 1964, when she and her second husband, trumpeter Michael Mantler, formed the Jazz Composers Orchestra, which featured Cecil Taylor, Pharoah Sanders, and others.

With lyricist Paul Haines, she began working on *Escalator Over the Hill* in 1968. To record it she assembled an unlikely assortment of musicians including Linda Ronstadt, Jack Bruce, John McLaughlin, Gato Barbieri, and Don Cherry and Charlie Haden from Ornette Coleman's quartet. Since then she has continued to use both jazz and rock musicians. *Tropic Appetites* featured singer Julie Tippets (who as Julie Driscoll was part of Brian Auger's Trinity). *Dinner Music* used R&B session players Stuff, and Nick Mason's *Fictitious Sports* (1981), which was released under Pink Floyd drummer Mason's name, used her band along with British progressive rockers, including Chris Spedding. In 1975, for six months, she played alongside Mick Taylor in the Jack Bruce Band. In 1977 she formed the Carla Bley Band, which has included NRBQ pianist Terry Adams, Soft Machine bassist Hugh Hopper, Mothers of Invention keyboardist Don Preston, and Modern Lovers drummer D. Sharpe. Bley has been active in the dissemination of new music, beginning in 1964, when she was a charter member of the Jazz Composers Guild (with Cecil Taylor, Sun Ra, and others), a cooperative to promote avant-garde music. In 1966 Bley and Mantler founded JCOA (Jazz Composers Orchestra Association) Records. Six years later, they began the New Music Distribution Service, which (until its demise in 1990) handled hundreds of small independent jazz, classical, and rock labels, including Bley and Mantler's own Watt Records. Mantler moved back to Europe in 1991, divesting himself of Watt Records; Karen Mantler, his daughter with Bley, was one of Watt's original recording artists. She now records for Virgin/EMI in addition to playing organ in her mother's band.

Through the '80s and '90s, Bley's output and workload increased. She contributed arrangements to *Ballad of the Fallen* and *Dreamkeeper* by Charlie Haden's Liberation Orchestra and three Hal Willner projects: *Lost in the Stars, That's the Way I Feel Now,* and *Amacord Nino Rota*. She also played on the Golden Palominos' *Drunk With Passion* and *Vision of Excess*. In addition to making duet recordings with bassist Steve Swallow *(Duets, Go Together)*, Bley continued to experiment with ensembles of various sizes. In 1995, her *Big Band Theory* was nominated for a Grammy for Best Jazz Big Band Album; at the end of the '90s, she assembled 4 x 4, a group consisting of four horns and a four-piece rhythm section. As ever, her stylistic range remains virtually encyclopedic and her audience international.

Mary J. Blige

Born Mary Jane Blige, Jan. 11, 1971, Bronx, NY
1992—*What's the 411?* (Uptown/MCA) 1993—*What's the 411? The Remixes* 1994—*My Life* (MCA) 1997—*Share My World* 1998—*Tour* 1999—*Mary.*

In 1992 Mary J. Blige became a top pop diva by appealing to older fans with her soul sensibility and maintaining youthful credibility with her hip-hop savvy. Blige was born in the Bronx but spent her early years in Savannah, Georgia, where she sang in a Pentecostal church. Her family moved to suburban Yonkers, New York, where Blige continued to sing. Her first demo (recorded at a karaoke studio in a shopping mall) was a version of Anita Baker's "Caught Up in the Rapture," which eventually got her signed by Andre Harrell to Uptown Records.

Blige's debut, *What's the 411?* (#6 pop, #1 R&B, 1992), mixed her affinity for classic soul (she covered Chaka Khan's "Sweet Thing") with a contemporary urban edge. The album includes cameos by rappers Grand Puba, Heavy D., C.L. Smooth, De La Soul's P.A. Pasemaster Mase, and EPMD's Erick Sermon. Blige first charted with "You Remind Me" (#29 pop, #1 R&B, 1992), from the film *Strictly Business,* but her debut album's single "Real Love" (#7 pop, #1 R&B, 1992) made Blige one of the biggest crossover artists of the year. It also helped earn her the tag "queen of hip-hop soul." In 1993 a remix album of *What's the 411?* was released and the "Sweet Thing" single peaked at #28 on the pop charts. Blige's 1994 album, *My Life,* reached #7 (#1 R&B) and yielded a #6 single, "Be Happy."

In 1995 Blige and the Wu-Tang Clan's Method Man [see Wu-Tang Clan entry] had a Grammy-winning smash hit with a medley of Ashford and Simpson songs, "I'll Be There for You/You're All I Need to Get By" (#3 pop, #1 R&B). The track was mixed by frequent Blige collaborator and budding hip-hop kingpin Sean Combs [see entry]. In 1996 Blige's "Not Gon' Cry" (#2 pop, #1 R&B) was featured in the film adaption of the Terry McMillan novel *Waiting to Exhale*. The single also appeared on *Share My World* (#1 pop, #1 R&B, 1997). The album yielded seven R&B hits, including "It's On" (#8), featuring R. Kelly, and found Blige's music stressing the soul side of her hip-hop/soul hybrid.

In 1999 Blige sang on the R&B hits of Kirk Franklin and George Michael and released *Mary*, her sixth and most pop-leaning album. Focusing less on hard times and heartache than its predecessors, the record features uplifting music and explores themes of spirituality and self-worth. It also sports a sweeping supporting cast, including everyone from Aretha Franklin and Babyface to Eric Clapton and Elton John. "All That I Can Say" (#6 R&B) was written and produced by hip-hop diva Lauryn Hill [see the Fugees entry]; "Sincerity" (#72 R&B), a track showcasing rappers Nas and DMX [see entries], was left off the album at the last minute. In interviews Blige has said that the projected second volume of *Mary* will be a more hip-hop-oriented affair.

Blind Faith

Formed 1969, London, Eng.
Steve Winwood (b. May 12, 1948, Birmingham, Eng.), kybds., gtr., voc.; Eric Clapton (b. Mar. 30, 1945, Ripley, Eng.), gtr., voc.; Ginger Baker (b. Peter Baker, Aug. 19, 1939, Lewisham, Eng.), drums; Rick Grech (b. Nov. 1, 1946, Bordeaux, Fr.; d. Mar. 17, 1990), bass, violin.
1969—*Blind Faith* (Atco).

Blind Faith's already famous personnel stayed together for one album and one arena-circuit tour before splitting up. Eric Clapton and Ginger Baker had been two thirds of Cream [see entry], and Steve Winwood had led (and would return to) Traffic [see entry]. Rick Grech was from Family [see entry], which had been considerably more popular in Britain than in the U.S. The first rock "supergroup" debuted before 100,000 fans in London's Hyde Park on June 7, 1969, and began a sold-out American tour in July before its one and only album had been released. The LP was recorded in such haste that side two consisted of just two songs, one of them a 15-minute jam entitled "Do What You Like." Nevertheless, *Blind Faith* did include two classics: Winwood's "Can't Find My Way Home" and Clapton's "Presence of the Lord." Its jacket, featuring a prepubescent nude girl, was deemed controversial in the U.S. and was replaced by a photograph of the band. (A later U.S. reissue bore the original cover.)

Clapton and Winwood went on to highly successful solo careers. Grech's post–Blind Faith résumé included Baker's Air Force, Traffic, the Crickets, and KGB, a mid-'70s supergroup (far less super than Blind Faith, however) that included Mike Bloomfield, Carmine Appice, and Barry Goldberg. Grech died in 1990 of a brain hemorrhage.

Blink-182

Formed 1992, Poway, CA
Tom Delonge (b. Dec. 13, 1975), voc., gtr.; Mark Hoppus (b. Markus Allen Hoppus, Mar. 15, 1972, Ridgecrest, CA), voc., bass; Scott Raynor, drums.
1993—*Fly Swatter* EP (Rapido) 1994—*Buddha* (Kung Fu) 1995—*Cheshire Cat* (Cargo) 1996—*Wasting Time* EP (Rapido) 1997—*Dude Ranch* (Cargo) 1998—*Dick Lips* EP (– Raynor; + Travis Barker [b. Travis Landon Barker, Nov. 14, 1975], drums) 1999—*Enema of the State* (MCA) 2000—*The Mark, Tom and Travis Show* 2001—*Take Off Your Pants and Jacket.*

Blink-182 continued the unexpected '90s journey of pop-punk into the mainstream. The trio emerged from Southern Californian skate-punk culture with a high-energy stage show heavy with slapstick and fart jokes. But like the slightly older Green Day, closer study revealed hook-filled rock songs obsessed with breakup and loneliness, even occasionally delving into such topics as teen suicide ("Adam's Song").

Mark Hoppus grew up in the California desert town of Ridgecrest before moving to Washington, DC, when his parents divorced. A fan of the Cure and the Descendents, Hoppus played bass in a high school garage band. Meanwhile, Tom Delonge grew up riding skateboards near San Diego and picked up his first guitar at church camp. They met in 1991 while Hoppus was attending college near San Diego, and with drummer Scott Raynor they later formed a band, at first simply called Blink. When an Irish band with the same name threatened a lawsuit, it was changed to Blink-182.

Early shows featured wet T-shirt and wet pants contests. The band slowly built a young, devoted following with indie recordings and an endless series of performances at various clubs and festivals. Major labels took notice in 1997 with the fast-selling indie release *Dude Ranch* (#67), which included the modern rock hit "Dammit (Growing Up)" (#11). Raynor was then fired from the band and replaced by Travis Barker (Aquabats). The band signed to MCA, releasing the Top 10 triple-platinum album *Enema of the State* (#9, 1999). It included the hits "All the Small Things" (#6) and "What's My Age Again" (#58). Band members also appeared briefly in the teen comedy *American Pie*. The band's next release was a live album, *The Mark, Tom and Travis Show* (#8, 2000), which yielded one single, "Man Overboard," that had only moderate success. *Take Off Your Pants and Jacket* (#1, 2001) took Blink-182 to the top of the album chart for the first time.

Blodwyn Pig

Formed 1968, England
Original lineup: Mick Abrahams (b. Apr. 7, 1943, Luton, Eng.), gtr., voc.; Jack Lancaster, saxes, flute; Andy Pyle, bass; Ron Berg, drums.

1969—*Ahead Rings Out* (A&M) 1970—*Getting to This* 1993—(lineup: Abrahams; Dave Lennox, kybds.; Graham Walker, drums; Mike Summerland, bass) *Lies* (Viceroy).

Mick Abrahams quit Jethro Tull [see entry] after one album to form Blodwyn Pig. A blues guitarist in the British style of Eric Clapton and Peter Green, he made Blodwyn Pig more blues-based than Jethro Tull. Like Ian Anderson, Jack Lancaster was influenced by Rahsaan Roland Kirk and played alto and soprano sax simultaneously a la Rahsaan. Pig's debut album was a distinctly British meeting of rock, blues, and jazz. Abrahams left the group after recording the second album (another U.K. Top 10), while the remaining members of Pig enlisted guitarist Peter Banks (formerly of Yes) and guitarist/vocalist Larry Wallis (later of UFO) to take his place. The second lineup never recorded, and they disbanded in December 1970.

In 1970 Abrahams formed Womnet, which never recorded; the following year he formed the Mick Abrahams Band, which continued in a blues vein with a hint of country. This group recorded two albums in 1971 and 1972. Disillusioned with the music business, Abrahams quit and drove a truck, all the while playing sessions and recording an instructional guitar record, *Have Fun Learning Guitar With Mick Abrahams* (1974). In 1974 Abrahams, Lancaster, and Pyle hooked up with former Jethro Tull drummer Clive Bunker in place of Ron Berg, but nothing came of it, and Blodwyn Pig broke up again. Lancaster went on to become a producer.

In 1988 Abrahams, also a financial consultant, once again re-formed Blodwyn Pig, with Bunker, Pyle, and Bruce Boardman, Bernie Hetherington, and Dick Heckstall-Smith (Graham Bond, John Mayall, Colosseum). Originally put together for a single appearance at a friend's club, this group, with a few changes, continued playing live into the '90s. They recorded *All Said and Done*, which was released only in Europe in 1991. Blodwyn Pig saw its next U.S. release in 1993. Pyle has put in time with Savoy Brown, the Kinks, and Chicken; Berg, too, was a member of Savoy Brown, as well as Network.

Blondie

Formed 1974, New York, NY

Deborah Harry (b. July 1, 1945, Miami, FL), voc.; Chris Stein (b. Jan. 5, 1950, Brooklyn, NY), gtr., voc.; Billy O'Connor, drums; Fred Smith (b. Apr. 10, 1948, New York), bass.

1975—(– O'Connor; – Smith; + Clem Burke [b. Nov. 24, 1955, New York], drums; + Gary Valentine [b. Dec. 24], bass; + Jimmy Destri [b. Apr. 13, 1954], kybds.) 1976—*Blondie* (Private Stock) (– Valentine) 1977—*Plastic Letters* (+ Frank Infante, bass, gtr.; + Nigel Harrison [b. Apr. 24, 1951, Stockport, Eng.], bass; Infante switched to guitar) (Chrysalis) 1978—*Parallel Lines* 1979—*Eat to the Beat* 1980—*Autoamerican* 1981—*The Best of Blondie* 1982—*The Hunter* (group disbands) 1994—*The Platinum Collection* (Chrysalis/EMI) 1995—*Remixed Remade Remodeled* 1998—(group re-forms: Harry; Stein; Burke; Destri; + Leigh Fox, bass; + Paul Carbonara, gtr.) 1999—*No Exit* (Beyond); *Live.*

Deborah Harry solo: 1981—*KooKoo* (Chrysalis) 1986—*Rockbird* (Geffen) 1989—*Def, Dumb & Blonde* (Sire) 1993—*Debravation.*

Jimmy Destri solo: 1982—*Heart on a Wall* (Chrysalis).

Checquered Past (Burke and Harrison with Steve Jones, others): 1984—*Checquered Past* (EMI, U.K.).

Blondie started as an ironic update of trashy '60s pop. By the end of the '70s it was far and away the most adventurous and commercially successful survivor of the New York punk scene, with three platinum albums *(Parallel Lines, Eat to the Beat,* and *Autoamerican)* and an international recognition factor for bleached-blond lead singer Deborah Harry, new wave's answer to Marilyn Monroe. Blondie's repertoire, most of it written by Harry and boyfriend Chris Stein, was always on the melodic side of punk and grew increasingly eclectic, trademarked mostly by Harry's deadpan delivery.

Born in Miami, Harry was adopted at age three months by Richard and Catherine Harry. She grew up in Hawthorne, New Jersey, and after graduating from high school moved to Manhattan. Harry joined a folk-rock band, the Wind in the Willows, which released one album for Capitol in 1968; she worked as a beautician, a Playboy bunny, and a barmaid at Max's Kansas City. In the mid-'70s she became the third lead singer of a glitter-rock band, the Stilettoes, which also included future Television bassist Fred Smith. Stein, a graduate of New York's School of Visual Arts, joined the band in October 1973, and he and Harry reshaped it, first as Angel and the Snakes, then as Blondie.

By 1975 the band was appearing regularly at CBGB, home of the burgeoning punk underground. Its first single, "X Offender," was independently produced by Richard Gottehrer and Marty Thau, who sold it to Private Stock. The label released Blondie's debut, also produced by Gottehrer, in December 1976. The group expanded its cult following to the West Coast with shows at L.A.'s Whisky-a-Go-Go in February 1977 and opened for Iggy Pop on a national tour. A few months later, they made their British concert debut. In July Gary Valentine (who wrote "[I'm Always Touched by Your] Presence Dear," a 1978 U.K. Top 10 hit) left the band to form his own trio, Gary Valentine and the Know, which broke up in spring 1980. In early 1978 Blondie's "Denis" hit #2 in the U.K.

After one album for Private Stock and some legal wrangling, Blondie signed with Chrysalis in October 1977. Mike Chapman, a veteran of glitter pop, produced *Parallel Lines,* which slowly made its way into the Top 10, breaking first in markets outside the U.S. The disco-style "Heart of Glass" hit #1 in April 1979 and established the group with a platinum album. Blondie maintained its popularity and dabbled in black-originated styles, collaborating with Eurodisco producer Giorgio Moroder for the *American Gigolo* soundtrack ("Call Me," #1, 1980), covering the reggae tune "The Tide Is High" (#1, 1980), and writing a rap song, "Rapture" (#1, 1981),

Blondie: Chris Stein, Frank Infante, Deborah Harry, Nigel Harrison, Jimmy Destri, Clem Burke

on *Autoamerican* (#7, 1980). Harry also did the rounds as a celebrity, including an endorsement of Gloria Vanderbilt designer jeans in 1980.

As the group's success continued, there were reports that Stein and Harry were asserting more control; by 1981 some Blondie backing tracks were played by session musicians under Stein's direction. Burke produced the New York band Colors, and Destri released a solo album, *Heart on a Wall,* in 1982. In 1981 Harry released her solo *KooKoo* (#25). Produced under the direction of Chic's Bernard Edwards and Nile Rodgers, *KooKoo* went gold.

Harry also began acting, appearing off-Broadway in *Teaneck Tanzi: The Venus Flytrap* (1983), in the films *Union City* (1979), *Videodrome* (1982), and John Waters' *Hairspray* (1988), in the television series *Wiseguy,* and in Showtime's *Body Bags.*

Early in 1982 Infante brought suit against the group, claiming they were out to destroy his career by excluding him from group meetings, rehearsals, and recording sessions. The suit was settled out of court and Infante remained in the band. However, by late 1982, following a disastrous tour (Blondie was never known as a great live act), the group quietly disbanded.

Harry and Stein's planned vacation from the music business stretched to a couple of years after he was felled by a rare genetic illness called pemphigus. By 1987, their romantic relationship had ended. Harry's comeback momentum was again stalled in the mid-'80s by legal problems with the group's label, Chrysalis. *Rockbird* (#97, 1986) drew critical raves, but neither it nor her subsequent releases have approached Blondie's in sales or acclaim, although she has had major hits in the U.K. ("French Kissin' in the U.S.A.," #8, 1986, and "I Want That Man," #13, 1989). She sang a duet with Iggy Pop, "Well, Did You Evah!," on the AIDS benefit album *Red Hot + Blue.* Harry collaborated with New York underground group the Jazz Passengers and appeared on their 1996 album *Individually Twisted* (32 Records).

Harrison and Burke joined a group called Checquered Past, which included ex–Sex Pistol Steve Jones. Later Harrison supervised the music for several feature films, including *Repo Man,* before becoming an A&R man for Capitol and Interscope. In the early '90s Burke became one of the Romantics and worked as a session musician with the Plimsouls, Dramarama, and Mark Owen. Stein continued producing acts for his Animal Records label, and Destri began producing.

In 1998 Harry, Burke, Stein, and Destri reunited and recorded *No Exit* (#18, 1999), Blondie's seventh studio album. *No Exit,* which contains an appearance by rapper Coolio on the title cut and yielded the poppy "Maria" (#82), helped ring in a new generation of Blondie fans. In early 1999 the band launched a U.S. tour—its first in over 15 years—and became inspired to record a live album. Meanwhile, ex-members Infante and Harrison filed a lawsuit in the summer of 1998 over the use of the Blondie name and due royalties. In a separate legal case, Blondie sued former label EMI for breach of contract, claiming that EMI refused to pay the group proper royalties for albums recorded from 1977 to 1982—a payment plan agreed upon in 1996. These lawsuits remained unresolved as of this writing.

Bloodstone

Formed 1962, Kansas City, MO
Willis Draffen Jr. (b. Kansas City), voc., gtr.; Charles Love, voc., gtr.; Charles McCormick, bass, voc.; Harry Williams Jr. (b. Tupelo, MS), perc., voc.; Roger Durham (b. 1946; d. 1973), perc., voc.
1973—*Natural High* (London); *Unreal* (– Durham) 1974—*I Need Time; Riddle of the Sphinx* 1975—*Train Ride to Hollywood* 1976—*Do You Wanna Do a Thing?; Lullaby of Broadway* (Decca) 1979—*Don't Stop* (Tamla) 1981—(– McCormick; + Ron Wilson [b. Los Angeles, CA], kybds., voc.; + Ronald Bell [b. CA], perc., voc.) 1982—*We Go a Long Way Back* (T-Neck) 1985—*Greatest Hits* (CBS).

Bloodstone's pop music blended soul vocal harmonies with funk and Hendrix-inspired guitar flash. The five original members were high school classmates in Kansas City, where they formed an a cappella group, the Sinceres, in 1962. In 1968 they spent a year as a nightclub act in Las Vegas, then moved on to L.A. There they decided to learn to play instruments themselves. They reappeared as Bloodstone in 1971, with a succession of drummers (including Edward Summers, Darryl Clifton, and Melvin Webb) as associate members. On the advice of their manager, they moved to England, where in 1972 they teamed up with English producer Mike Vernon (John Mayall, Ten Years After, Savoy Brown) for their first five albums. Bloodstone's first single, "Natural High," went gold, reaching #4 on the R&B chart and #10 pop in

1973. The group followed it with a series of soul hits, including "Never Let You Go" (#7 R&B, 1973), "Outside Woman" (#34 pop, #2 R&B, 1974), "That's Not How It Goes" (#22 R&B, 1974), "My Little Lady" (#4 R&B, 1975), "Give Me Your Heart" (#18 R&B, 1975), and "Do You Wanna Do a Thing" (#19 R&B, 1976).

In 1975 Bloodstone produced and appeared in a feature movie entitled *Train Ride to Hollywood,* for which it also wrote the soundtrack. Among the songs covered in this musical comedy were "Toot Toot Tootsie" and "As Time Goes By," and like all of the band's albums since *Unreal,* the soundtrack also contained versions of oldies like "Sh-Boom" and "Yakety Yak."

Blood, Sweat and Tears

Formed 1967, New York, NY
Al Kooper (b. Feb. 5, 1944, Brooklyn, NY), kybds., voc.; Steve Katz (b. May 9, 1945, New York), gtr., voc.; Fred Lipsius (b. Nov. 19, 1944, New York), alto sax, piano; Jim Fielder (b. Oct. 4, 1947, Denton, TX), bass; Bobby Colomby (b. Dec. 20, 1944, New York), drums; Dick Halligan (b. Aug. 29, 1943, Troy, NY), kybds., trombone, flute; Randy Brecker (b. Nov. 27, 1945, Philadelphia, PA), trumpet, fluegelhorn; Jerry Weiss (b. May 1, 1946, New York), trumpet, fluegelhorn.
1968—*Child Is Father to the Man* (Columbia) (– Kooper; – Brecker; – Weiss; + Chuck Winfield [b. Feb. 5, 1943, Monessen, PA], trumpet, fluegelhorn; + Lew Soloff [b. Feb. 20, 1944, Brooklyn], trumpet, fluegelhorn; + Jerry Hyman [b. May 19, 1947, New York], trombone; + David Clayton-Thomas [b. Sep. 13, 1941, Surrey, Eng.], voc.) *Blood, Sweat & Tears* 1970—*Blood, Sweat & Tears 3* (– Hyman; + Dave Bargeron [b. Sep. 6, 1942, MA], trombone, tuba, trumpet) 1971—*B,S&T; 4* 1972—*Greatest Hits* (– Lipsius; – Halligan; – Clayton-Thomas; + Bobby Doyle [b. Houston, TX], voc; + Lou Marini Jr. [b. Charleston, SC], saxes, flute; + Georg Wadenius [b. Swe.], gtr.; + Larry Willis [b. New York], kybds.; – Doyle; + Jerry Fisher [b. 1943, Dekalb, TX], voc.) *New Blood* (– Katz; – Winfield; + Tom Malone, trumpet, fluegelhorn, trombone, saxes) 1973—*No Sweat* (– Fielder; – Soloff; – Marini; – Malone; + Ron McClure, bass; + Tony Klatka, trumpet; + Bill Tillman, saxes, flute, clarinet; + Jerry LaCroix, voc., sax, flute, harmonica) 1974—*Mirror Image* (– LaCroix; – Fisher; + Clayton-Thomas; + Joe Giorgianni, trumpet, fluegelhorn) 1975—*New City* (– Wadenius; – McClure; – Giorgianni; + Danny Trifan, bass; + Mike Stern, gtr.; + Forrest Buchtell, trumpet; + Don Alias, perc.) 1976—*More Than Ever* (– Colomby; – Alias; + Roy McCurdy, drums) 1977—*Brand New Day* (ABC) 1980—(lineup continues to fluctuate, with only Clayton-Thomas remaining) *Nuclear Blues* 1991—*Live & Improvised* (Columbia).

Founder Al Kooper conceived Blood, Sweat and Tears as an experiment in expanding the size and scope of the rock band with touches of jazz, blues, classical, and folk music. When Kooper was forced out of the band soon after its eclectic debut, *Child Is Father to the Man,* BS&T became increasingly identified as a "jazz-rock" group, although its music was essentially easy-listening R&B or rock with the addition of brass.

Kooper formed BS&T after leaving the Blues Project in 1967 [see entry]. The nucleus of the original band was Steve Katz, also of the Blues Project; Jim Fielder, who had played with the Mothers of Invention and Buffalo Springfield; and Bobby Colomby, who had drummed behind folksingers Odetta and Eric Andersen. The horn players were recruited from New York jazz and studio bands. *Child Is Father* featured songs by Harry Nilsson, Tim Buckley, Randy Newman, Gerry Goffin, and Carole King, along with Kooper originals and arrangements by Fred Lipsius for brass, strings, and studio effects. The band nearly broke up when Kooper, Randy Brecker, and Jerry Weiss left (Brecker to join the Thad Jones–Mel Lewis Band). Regrouping under Katz and Colomby, and fronted by David Clayton-Thomas (who had sung with a Canadian blues band, the Bossmen), BS&T entered a period of immense popularity. *Blood, Sweat & Tears* featured arrangements of music by French composer Erik Satie and jazz singer Billie Holiday, as well as by Laura Nyro, Steve Winwood, and others. It was the #1 album for seven weeks in 1969, sold over 3 million copies, and spawned three gold singles: "You've Made Me So Very Happy," "Spinning Wheel," and "And When I Die," each of which hit #2.

In 1970 the U.S. State Department sent the band on a goodwill tour of Yugoslavia, Romania, and Poland. *Blood, Sweat & Tears 3* duplicated the *Blood, Sweat & Tears* mix of styles and was almost as popular. The album went to #1, and two singles, "Hi-De-Ho" and "Lucretia MacEvil," hit the Top 30. But interest in the group began to wane, and *4,* which contained almost all original material, barely made the Top 10. In 1971 "Go Down Gamblin' " was its last hit. By the time Clayton-Thomas left for a solo career in 1972, BS&T's place on the charts had been filled by similarly styled bands such as Chicago, Chase, and Ides of March. Katz left the next year, first to join the short-lived American Flyer and then to an A&R position at Mercury Records.

BS&T became regulars in Las Vegas, with ever-changing personnel recruited largely from big bands like Maynard Ferguson's, Woody Herman's, and Doc Severinsen's. Vocalist Jerry LaCroix appeared between his tenures with Edgar Winter's White Trash and Rare Earth, while guitarist Mike Stern later played with Miles Davis' early-'80s band. Clayton-Thomas' return in 1974 briefly boosted BS&T's popularity, but Columbia dropped the group, and Colomby, the last original member, left in 1976. He continued to influence BS&T as producer of *Brand New Day* and, with Clayton-Thomas, as co-owner of the band's name and catalogue. He then moved on to a career in A&R for several labels, as well as TV reporting. Since 1975 the live act has been billed as Blood, Sweat and Tears Featuring David Clayton-Thomas.

Luka Bloom

Born Barry Moore, May 23, 1955, Newbridge, Ire.
1988—*Luka Bloom* (Mystery, U.K.) 1990—*Riverside* (Reprise)

1992—*The Acoustic Motorbike* 1994—*Turf* 1999—*Salty Heaven* (Shanachie).

The kid brother of Irish folk star Christy Moore, Barry Moore chose a professional alias that combined the surname of a character from James Joyce's *Ulysses* with a reference to the protagonist of a Suzanne Vega song. Likewise, the themes addressed in Luka Bloom's music, a Celtic-flavored folk-rock hybrid driven by the singer's vigorous "electro-acoustic" guitar work, have revealed a fascination with both Irish and American culture.

The youngest of six children, Bloom began touring European folk clubs in the mid-'70s. Chronic tendinitis eventually forced him to develop a guitar style that relied more on strumming than finger-picking. After recording three albums as Barry Moore (now out of print), playing briefly in a rock band called Red Square, and spending time in New York City, the singer moved to Washington, DC, in 1988, having renamed himself Luka Bloom. He soon landed a regular gig at a Greenwich Village pub as well, and spent several months commuting to New York once a week. That experience, and subsequent stints opening for Hothouse Flowers and the Pogues on their American tours, influenced the writing on his sparsely produced major-label debut album. Released in 1990, *Riverside* featured song titles like "Dreams in America" and "An Irishman in Chinatown." Bloom returned to his native country, where he wrote and recorded *The Acoustic Motorbike*, which includes a lyrical cover of New York–based rapper L.L. Cool J's "I Need Love." For *Turf* Bloom re-created the sound of his live performances by recording the album in a studio set up with a stage, P.A., and lights, and for four songs, even an audience (although no one was allowed to clap). In 1995, at the age of 40, Bloom began taking singing lessons, sessions he maintained for two years while he started work on *Salty Heaven*. Unlike his previous efforts, this album was lushly produced and featured string arrangements and keyboard playing by Rod Argent of the Zombies and Argent.

Michael Bloomfield

Born July 28, 1944, Chicago, IL; died Feb. 15, 1981, San Francisco, CA
1968—*Super Session* (with Al Kooper, Stephen Stills) (Columbia) 1969—*It's Not Killing Me; The Live Adventures of Mike Bloomfield and Al Kooper* (with Al Kooper) 1973—*Try It Before You Buy It; Triumvirate* 1976—*Mill Valley Session* (Polydor) 1977—*If You Love These Blues, Play 'Em As You Please* (Guitar Player); *Analine* (Takoma); *Count Talent and the Originals* (Clouds); *Michael Bloomfield* (Takoma) 1980—*Between the Hard Place and the Ground* 1981—*Cruisin' for a Bruisin'; Living in the Fast Lane* (Waterhouse) 1983—*Bloomfield* (Columbia) 1994—*Don't Say That I Ain't Your Man!: Essential Blues 1964–1969* (Legacy).

As a teenager living on Chicago's North Shore, Michael Bloomfield ventured downtown to seek out the patriarchs of

Michael Bloomfield

Chicago blues—Muddy Waters, Albert King, and others—and learned their guitar techniques firsthand. Playing Chicago blues and folk clubs with singer Nick Gravenites and harmonica player Charlie Musselwhite in the early '60s, he attracted the attention of Paul Butterfield, whose band he joined in 1965 [see entry]. Bloomfield played electric guitar on Dylan's "Like a Rolling Stone" and later that year on *Highway 61 Revisited*.

He left the Butterfield band after recording a second album with them and formed the Electric Flag with Gravenites, but quit after their first album [see entry]. Thereafter he devoted himself mainly to studio work and solo ventures, including *Super Session* with Al Kooper and *Triumvirate* with John Hammond Jr. (John Paul Hammond) and Dr. John (Mac Rebennack). Bloomfield's last shot at stardom came in 1975 with KGB, an attempt by MCA Records to create a supergroup with Bloomfield, keyboardist Barry Goldberg, bassist Rick Grech, drummer Carmine Appice, and singer Ray Kennedy. After one album, Bloomfield abandoned the group and the corporate music world. He supported himself by scoring pornographic movies. His previous movie soundtrack credits included *Medium Cool, Steelyard Blues,* and *Andy Warhol's Bad*. In 1975 he returned to recording solo albums, releasing eight in the six years before his death from an accidental drug overdose. *If You Love These Blues, Play 'Em As You Please*, a blues guitar "sampler" produced by *Guitar Player* magazine, was nominated for a Grammy Award in 1977.

Kurtis Blow

Born Kurt Walker, Aug. 9, 1959, New York, NY
1980—*Kurtis Blow* (Mercury) 1981—*Deuce* 1982—*Tough* 1983—*Party Time?* 1984—*Ego Trip* 1985—*America* 1986—*Kingdom Blow* 1988—*Back by Popular Demand* 1994—*The Best of Kurtis Blow.*

Kurtis Blow's "The Breaks" (#87 pop, #4 R&B, 1980) was one of the first records to popularize rap outside the form's native New York City. A graduate of Fiorello H. LaGuardia High School of Music & Art and Performing Arts, Blow was a disco DJ before he made records. He started out working at a Harlem disco in 1976, blatantly copping rhymed lines from an originator of rap, DJ Hollywood (Anthony Holloway). Later he worked with one of the masters of instrumental track editing, Grandmaster Flash (Joseph Saddler). In 1979, while he was working on his first single, "Christmas Rappin'," the Sugar Hill Gang's "Rapper's Delight" rocketed up the charts; a Mercury A&R rep heard what Blow was up to and signed him to an initial two-single deal. "Christmas Rappin' " was released at the end of the year and became—with "Rapper's Delight" and the Fatback Band's "King Tim III"—one of the first rap records on the market. It sold almost 400,000 copies; "The Breaks" sold over 600,000 copies nationwide. By the end of 1980, Blow was performing around the country with his partner Davy D (David Reeves) at the turntables. In 1981 he toured Europe.

Blow's subsequent albums varied little. He was admired by a number of young rappers, including Run (Joe Simmons) of Run-D.M.C., who as a teenager had worked for Blow. Run-D.M.C. repaid him by doing a guest rap on *Ego Trip*'s "8 Million Stories." By the time of 1988's *Back by Popular Demand,* Blow's lighthearted style was passé. In the early '90s, Blow began promoting and performing at rap shows featuring the genre's pioneers.

In 1995 he was hired as a DJ for an L.A. radio station, and in 1997 he produced a three-volume anthology for Rhino Records titled *Kurtis Blow Presents the History of Rap,* which gathered highlights of hip-hop's growth. The rapper also returned to the R&B singles chart in 1997 with a remake of "The Breaks" (#58 R&B) with newcomer Nadanuf. Blow gave acting a shot in the summer of 2000 and starred in *Echo Park*—a musical about rap music's formative years—at New York City's Apollo Theatre.

Blue Cheer

Formed 1967, Boston, MA
Dickie Peterson (b. 1948, Grand Forks, ND), voc., bass; Paul Whaley, drums; Bruce "Leigh" Stephens, gtr.
1968—*Vincebus Eruptum* (Philips); *Outside Inside* (– L. Stephens; + Randy Holden, gtr.) 1969—*New! Improved!* (– Whaley; – Holden; + Norman Mayell [b. 1942, Chicago, IL], drums; + Bruce Stephens [b. 1946], voc., gtr.; + Ralph Burns Kellogg, kybds.) *Blue Cheer* 1970—(– B. Stephens; + Gary Yoder, gtr.) *The Original Human Beings* 1971—*Oh! Pleasant Hope* (group disbands) 1985—(group re-forms: Peterson; Whaley; + Tony Rainier, gtr.) 1986—*Louder Than God: The Best of Blue Cheer* (Rhino) 1989—*The Beast Is Back* (Megaforce) (– Whaley).

Blue Cheer appeared in spring 1968 with a thunderously loud remake of Eddie Cochran's "Summertime Blues" that many regard as the first true heavy-metal record. One of the first hard-rock power trios, the group was named for an especially high-quality strain of LSD. Its manager, Gut, was an ex–Hell's Angel.

After moving to San Francisco, the band was taken under the wing of an enthusiastic DJ, Abe "Voco" Kesh of underground KMPX-FM. He aired a three-song tape of Blue Cheer, leading to a contract with Philips Records. "Summertime Blues" reached #14, while the trio's first album, *Vincebus Eruptum,* hit #11 and remains something of a heavy-metal landmark. None of the group's subsequent five albums had nearly the same impact, however, and in 1971 Peterson, the lone original member left, broke up the band.

Leigh Stephens, who now raises Thoroughbreds in California, recorded two solo albums, another with the band Silver Metre, and two more with Bruce Stephens; he too has released a solo album, 1982's *Watch That First Step.* Peterson has twice put together new versions of Blue Cheer, in 1979 and 1985. The second attempt, which included Whaley and guitarist Tony Rainier, son of an original Blue Cheer roadie, produced an album, *The Beast Is Back.* With Peterson still at the helm but Whaley gone, Blue Cheer has put out two more LPs in Europe.

Blue Öyster Cult

Formed 1969, Long Island, NY
Eric Bloom (b. Dec. 1, 1944), gtr., voc.; Albert Bouchard (b. May 24, 1947, Watertown, NY), drums, voc.; Joe Bouchard (b. Nov. 9, 1948, Watertown), bass, voc.; Allen Lanier (b. June 25, 1946), kybds., synth., gtr.; Donald "Buck Dharma" Roeser (b. Nov. 12, 1947), lead gtr.
1972—*Blue Öyster Cult* (Columbia) 1973—*Tyranny and Mutation* 1974—*Secret Treaties* 1975—*On Your Feet or on Your Knees* 1976—*Agents of Fortune* 1977—*Spectres* 1978—*Some Enchanted Evening* 1979—*Mirrors* 1980—*Cultosaurus Erectus* 1981—*Fire of Unknown Origin* (– A. Bouchard; + Rick Downey, drums) 1982—*Extraterrestrial Live* 1983—*Revolution by Night* 1985—(– Downey; + Tommy Zvoncheck, kybds.; + Jimmy Wilcox, drums) 1986—*Club Ninja* (– Lanier; – J. Bouchard; – Zvoncheck; – Wilcox; + Jon Rogers, bass) 1987—(+ Ron Riddle, drums) 1988—*Imaginos* 1990—*Career of Evil: The Metal Years* 1991—(– Riddle; + Chuck Bürgi, drums) 1994—*Cult Classic* (Herald) 1995—*Workshop of the Telescopes* (Columbia) (– Rogers; + Danny Miranda, bass; – Bürgi) 1997—(+ Bobby Rondinelli, drums) 1998—*Heaven Forbid* (CMC); *Super Hits* (Columbia) 2000—*Don't Fear the Reaper: The Best Of.*
Buck Dharma solo: 1982—*Flat Out* (Portrait).

Semisatiric exponents of the high-decibel apocalypse, Blue Öyster Cult forged an unlikely alliance between teen tastes and critical appeal and were a major heavy-metal band from the mid-'70s through the '80s. The group goes back to 1967, when future rock critic R. Meltzer and future Cult producer Sandy Pearlman, students at the State University of New York at Stony Brook, decided to organize a band. Along with Allen Lanier, Donald Roeser, and Albert Bouchard, they formed Soft White Underbelly (a name the Cult still uses for club dates). Vocalist Meltzer was replaced by Les Bronstein, with whom they recorded one unreleased LP for Elektra, and several vocalists followed before Eric Bloom joined in 1969. With Bloom, the group's name changed to Oaxaca. By then, Bouchard's brother Joe had joined the band. They recorded another unreleased LP before changing the group's name from the Stalk-Forrest Group to Blue Öyster Cult.

They signed with Columbia in late 1971, and their debut album was released a few months later. There followed several years of extensive touring as Alice Cooper's opening act. Their show—featuring lasers, flash pots, and Buck Dharma's guitar solos—built a small but loyal following that paved the way for their 1976 commercial breakthrough with the platinum LP *Agents of Fortune* and its #12 hit single "(Don't Fear) the Reaper," a Buck Dharma composition. *Agents* also featured vocals and songwriting from Patti Smith, who was then Lanier's girlfriend. The Cult's performances have been captured on three live LPs: *On Your Feet or on Your Knees* (their second gold album), *Some Enchanted Evening,* and *Extraterrestrial Live.*

The band's dark imagery is symbolized by its logo, the ancient symbol of Cronos, the Titan god who ate his son the Grim Reaper. A good deal of BÖC's success and image can be credited to its longtime manager and occasional songwriter and producer Pearlman. The group has also enjoyed the support of rock writers like Meltzer, who has also written songs for the band. In 1980 it coheadlined with Black Sabbath on the Black and Blue Tour.

Although "Burnin' for You" was a Top 40 hit and frequently aired video clip, the album it came from, *Fire of Unknown Origin,* was the group's last gold record. Subsequent studio albums—*Revolution by Night, Club Ninja,* and *Imaginos*—came less frequently and had decreasing commercial impact. Dropped by Columbia in 1987, the group disbanded, then promptly got back together in 1988—though by *Cult Classics* (which featured rerecorded versions of BÖC's chestnuts) the Bouchard brothers had left. Anchored by the core of Bloom, Lanier, and Buck Dharma, BÖC would spend a decade touring but unable to record a proper full-length studio album. The band finally secured a new U.S. label and released *Heaven Forbid,* on which science-fiction author John Shirley contributed lyrics to several songs.

Blue Ridge Rangers: See Creedence Clearwater Revival

Blues Image

Formed 1966, Tampa, FL
Malcolm Jones (b. Cardiff, Wales), bass; Mike Pinera (b. Sep. 29, 1948, Tampa), gtr.; Joe Lala (b. Tampa), drums, perc.; Manuel Bertematti, drums.
1968—(+ Frank "Skip" Konte [b. Canon City, OK], kybds.)
1969—*Blues Image* (Atco) 1970—*Open; Red, White, and Blues Image.*

Tampa-based Blues Image was one of the first groups to experiment with Latin-tinged rock and is best remembered for its 1970 #4 hit, "Ride Captain Ride." *Open* contained Blues Image's lone smash hit. The quintet disbanded two years later, with some of the members joining Manna in 1972. Lead guitarist Mike Pinera's career itinerary took him to Iron Butterfly [see entry], Ramatam, the New Cactus Band, and Thee Image. After releasing solo albums in 1978 and 1979, *Isla* and *Forever,* he played behind Alice Cooper [see entry]. Conga player Joe Lala became an in-demand session player; among those he's backed are Stephen Stills in Manassas; Crosby, Stills, Nash and Young; Neil Young; Jackson Browne; Joe Walsh; and the Souther-Hillman Furay Band.

Blues Incorporated: See Alexis Korner

Blues Magoos

Formed 1964, Bronx, NY
Ralph Scala (b. Dec. 12, 1947, IL), kybds., voc.; Ronnie Gilbert (b. Apr. 25, 1946, Bronx), bass, voc.; Peppy Castro (b. Emil Thielhelm, June 16, 1949), gtr., voc.; Geoff Daking (b. Dec. 8, 1947, DE), drums; Mike Esposito (b. 1943, DE), gtr.
1966—*Psychedelic Lollipop* (Mercury) 1967—*Electric Comic Book Basic Blues Magoos* (group disbands) 1969—(group re-forms: Castro; Eric Kaz [b. 1946, Brooklyn, NY], kybds.; Roger Eaton, bass; Richie Dickon, perc.) *Never Goin' Back to Georgia* (ABC) 1970—(– Eaton; + various) *Gulf Coast Bound* 1992—*Kaleidoscope Compendium: The Best of the Blues Magoos* (Mercury).

A lightweight blues-rock band known to wear bell-bottoms trimmed with neon-filled plastic tubes, the Blues Magoos were popular at the height of psychedelia. They signed with Mercury in mid-1966 and released *Psychedelic Lollipop* (#21), which featured the gold single "(We Ain't Got) Nothin' Yet" (#5, 1967). They played the Fillmores and opened tours for Herman's Hermits and the Who. In 1969, a few months after they disbanded, Castro put together a halfhearted new version of the band (which included Eric Kaz) before joining the Broadway cast of *Hair.* He later played in the soft-rock group Barnaby Bye with brothers Billy and Bobby Alessi, as well as Wiggy Bits and Balance. The latter band had a #22 hit in 1981, "Breaking Away."

The Blues Project

Formed 1965, New York, NY
Danny Kalb, gtr., voc.; Roy Blumenfeld, drums; Andy Kulberg (b. 1944, Buffalo, NY), bass, flute; Steve Katz (b. May 9, 1945,

New York), gtr., harmonica, voc.; Tommy Flanders, voc.; Al Kooper (b. Feb. 5, 1944, Brooklyn, NY), kybds., voc.
1966—*Live at the Cafe Au Go Go* (Verve/Forecast) (– Flanders) *Projections* 1967—*Live at Town Hall* (group disbands) 1968—*Planned Obsolescence* 1969—*Best of the Blues Project* (group re-forms: Kalb; Blumenfeld; + Don Kretmar, bass, sax); *Lazarus* (Capitol) 1972—(+ Flanders; + David Cohen [b. 1942, Brooklyn], piano; + Bill Lussenden, gtr.) *Blues Project* (group disbands) 1973—(group re-forms: Kalb; Blumenfeld; Kulberg; Katz; Kooper) *Reunion in Central Park* (MCA) 1989—*The Best of the Blues Project: "No Time Like the Right Time"* (Rhino).

The Blues Project, along with the Paul Butterfield Blues Band, helped start the blues revival of the late '60s. The group was formed in early 1965 with folk, bluegrass, and pop musicians. Danny Kalb, formerly one of Dave Van Ronk's Ragtime Jug Stompers, and Roy Blumenfeld, a jazz fan, had discussed playing folk and country blues on electric instruments and drums. Blumenfeld brought in Andy Kulberg, who had studied modern jazz theory at the New York University School of Music, and Kalb rounded up guitarist Artie Traum and folksinger Tommy Flanders. Traum dropped out during rehearsals, and Steve Katz, who had played with the Ragtime Jug Stompers and Jim Kweskin's Even Dozen Jug Band, replaced him. The final addition was keyboardist Al Kooper (one of the Royal Teens), fresh from Bob Dylan's *Highway 61 Revisited* sessions. The group made its debut at Greenwich Village's Cafe Au Go Go in summer 1965, toured the East Coast, traveled to San Francisco in spring 1966, then played campus shows all the way back to New York.

They made their debut album in May 1966. Flanders then left for a solo career and recorded *Moonstone Verve* in 1969. The Project continued as a quintet, which did three open-air concerts in Central Park in the summer of 1966 and gigs as backup band for Chuck Berry.

Projections yielded the FM standbys "I Can't Keep From Crying" and the instrumental "Flute Thing," but the Blues Project's popularity was limited to New York and scattered college towns. Chief arranger and songwriter Kooper left the group after a second live album had been recorded in the summer of 1967, Kalb mysteriously disappeared, and the group soon disbanded. Katz joined Kooper in Blood, Sweat and Tears [see entry]; Kalb later returned to session work; and Kulberg and Blumenfeld went to California to form Seatrain. *Planned Obsolescence* was pieced together from recordings the Project had made as a quintet in 1967.

Kalb revived the Blues Project in 1971. Blumenfeld joined him and brought in Seatrain alumnus Kretmar. *Lazarus* sold no better than previous Project releases. The eponymously titled followup found Flanders again singing with the group, which now included pianist David Cohen, once of Country Joe and the Fish, and guitarist Bill Lussenden. The next year, Kooper reunited the original lineup—minus Flanders—for a concert in Central Park, documented on the live *Reunion*. There have been periodic reunion concerts since, continuing up into the early '90s. Kulberg and guitarist Chris Michie collaborated on soundtrack music for PBS documentaries, independent feature films, TV commercials, and such shows as *Starsky and Hutch*. Kulberg, who settled in San Francisco, also won a local drama critics award for his 1985 stage musical, *The Dead End Kid*. Kalb continues to live in New York City, where he performs sporadically and teaches guitar.

Blues Traveler

Formed 1987, Princeton, NJ
John Popper (b. Mar. 29, 1967, Cleveland, OH), voc., harmonica; Chandler Kinchla (b. May 29, 1969, Hamilton, Can.), gtr.; Brendan Hill (b. Mar. 27, 1970, London, Eng.), drums; Bobby Sheehan (b. June 12, 1968, NJ; d. Aug. 20, 1999, New Orleans, LA), bass.
1990—*Blues Traveler* (A&M) 1991—*Travelers & Thieves* 1993—*Save His Soul* 1994—*four* 1996—*Live From the Fall* 1997—*Straight On Till Morning* 1999—(– Sheehan) 2000—(+ Tad Kinchla [b. Feb. 21, 1973, Princeton], bass; + Ben Wilson [b. Nov. 17, 1967, Chicago, IL], kybds.).
John Popper solo: 1999—*Zygote* (A&M) 2001—*Bridge*.

Like Phish and Widespread Panic, Blues Traveler emerged in the early '90s as part of a new vanguard of jam bands in the tradition of the Grateful Dead and the Allman Brothers. Early on, the band's reputation was built on relentless touring, marathon sets, and the explosive harmonica solos of oversized frontman John Popper.

Blues Traveler came together in Princeton, where the Cleveland-born Popper formed the Blues Band with fellow high school students Brendan Hill, Bobby Sheehan, and Chan Kinchla. After graduation, the quartet moved to New York City, where they adopted the name Blues Traveler and became fixtures on the area club circuit. Famed concert promoter Bill Graham agreed to manage them and helped them secure a contract with A&M in 1989. Relentless touring helped push the band's self-titled debut to #136 in early 1991. *Travelers & Thieves,* released later that year and featuring a guest turn by Gregg Allman on the epic jam "Mountain Cry," went to #125.

In 1992, Popper founded the H.O.R.D.E. (Horizons of Rock Developing Everywhere) festival as a means to unite with like-minded, jam-oriented bands for outdoor summer shows. The H.O.R.D.E. fest would soon rival the alternative Lollapalooza festival, attracting an eclectic array of performers ranging from Beck to Neil Young. Blues Traveler's own touring momentum was slowed temporarily in 1992 when Popper was injured in a motorcycle accident, but they soon returned to the road with the frontman performing in a wheelchair.

After the success of *Save His Soul* (#72, 1993), A&M began to focus on the still-unconquered radio market. "Run-Around," the bouncy first single from *four* (#8, 1995), introduced Blues Traveler to the mainstream. The song went to #8, set up a second hit single ("Hook," which went to #23), and helped push sales of *four* over the 6-million mark. "Run-Around" also earned the band a Grammy in 1995 for Best Rock Performance by a Duo or Group with Vocal.

Wary of alienating its veteran fans, Blues Traveler chased

four with *Live From the Fall* (#46, 1996), a double-disc live set that bypassed the two hits in favor of lengthy jams. Their next studio album, 1997's *Straight On Till Morning,* went to #11 but stalled at platinum.

In the summer of 1999, the then dangerously overweight Popper was hospitalized for chest pains and had to undergo emergency angioplasty. He survived, began a strict diet and exercise regimen, and was fit to tour behind his first solo album, *Zygote,* in the fall. He and the band were dealt a heavier blow, though, when Bobby Sheehan died of an accidental drug overdose that August. In the midst of their mourning, the remaining band members decided to carry on, with Chan Kinchla's younger brother Tad coming on board to play bass and a fifth member, Ben Wilson, joining on keyboards. While working on a new studio album for release in 2001, the band released a four-song, downloadable EP, *Decisions of the Sky—A Traveler's Tale of Sun and Storm,* on its Web site.

Blur

Formed 1989, Colchester, Eng.
Damon Albarn (b. May 23, 1968, London, Eng.), voc.; Graham Coxon (b. Mar. 12, 1969, Rinteln, Ger.), gtr.; Alex James (b. Nov. 21, 1968, Bournemouth, Eng.), bass; Dave Rowntree (b. May 8, 1964, Colchester), drums.
1991—*Leisure* (SBK/Food) 1993—*Modern Life Is Rubbish* 1994—*Parklife* 1995—*The Great Escape* (Virgin/Food/Parlophone) 1997—*Blur* (Virgin) 1999—*13* (Virgin/Food) 2000—*Blur: The Best Of.*
Graham Coxon solo: 1998—*The Sky Is Too High* (Caroline) 2000—*The Golden D.*

Early on, Blur epitomized the Brit-pop movement of the '90s. Frontman Damon Albarn's lyrics recalled the wry character sketches of the Kinks' Ray Davies, and the band affected an unabashedly British pop sound on its first four albums. By the end of the decade, however, Blur had refashioned itself in the mold of American bands Pavement and Sonic Youth.

Albarn, the son of an author/art professor and a theatrical stage designer, met guitarist Graham Coxon, a self-taught musician whose father played in an army band, in school in Colchester in 1980. The pair collaborated on some demos before heading off to different art colleges—Albarn to study acting, Coxon to pursue art. They met up again at a party on behalf of Albarn's band Circus, which featured drummer Dave Rowntree, a classically trained percussionist. Coxon introduced Albarn to his school friend Alex James, and when Circus folded, the four began recording demos and performing club gigs in late 1989 under the name Seymour (after a J.D. Salinger character). EMI-distributed Food Records signed them in 1990, whereupon they changed their name to Blur and debuted with the Top 50 British single "She's So High." "There's No Other Way" fared even better, and *Leisure,* released a year later, went to #2 on the U.K. album chart. The followup, *Modern Life Is Rubbish,* peaked at #17, but 1994's chart-topping *Parklife,* featuring the hit "Girls and Boys," cemented Blur as British superstars and won the band four BRIT Awards, including Best Group and Best Album. By the time Blur released 1995's *The Great Escape,* it was locked in a battle of the bands with a new contender to the Brit-pop throne, working-class heroes Oasis. The U.K. press made front-page news out of each band's bid for #1 with their new singles, and Blur's "Country House" beat out Oasis' "Roll With It" by a narrow margin. It was the #1 Oasis album *(What's the Story) Morning Glory,* however, that "won" in the end—earning the Manchester band bragging rights as the biggest new band in the U.K. and significant stateside success, while *The Great Escape* stalled on the U.S. chart at #150.

Blur's U.S. breakthrough came in 1997 with "Song 2," a hard-rock blitzkrieg from its self-titled fifth album (#61, 1997). The song's exuberant "woo-hoo!" chorus made it a favorite at sporting events, though the band turned down the U.S. military's bid to use it at the unveiling of the new Stealth bomber. *Blur* was heavily informed by the group's love of American lo-fi rockers Pavement and bore little in common with the clean, theatrical pop sound on which it had built their British following. They went even further off the track with the William Orbit–produced *13* (#80, 1999), though the album kicked off with a lush ballad, "Tender." Albarn had recently split with girlfriend Justine Frischmann of Elastica, and many of *13*'s songs were mined from the ashes of their eight-year relationship.

Despite a handful of side projects (two lo-fi solo albums by Coxon, and Albarn's score [in collaboration with Michael Nyman] to the movie *Ravenous*), Blur came out of its first decade in one piece.

The Bobbettes

Formed 1956, New York, NY
Helen Gathers (b. 1944), voc.; Laura Webb (b. 1943), voc.; Reather Dixon (b. 1945), voc.; Emma Pought (b. 1944), voc.; Janice Pought (b. 1945), voc.
1961—(– Gathers).

Conspicuously absent from many histories of rock & roll are the Bobbettes, the first female vocal group to have a #1 R&B hit and a pop Top 10 hit (#6), 1957's "Mr. Lee." What makes this feat even more noteworthy is that the young women were all between the ages of 11 and 14, and they not only sang but wrote it as well, along with 10 other songs they recorded.

The girls began singing together at Harlem amateur nights (including the famed Apollo Theatre) with three other girls under the name the Harlem Queens in 1955. Within two years, they had a manager, three fewer members, a new name, and their first hit. The song was written about one of their fifth-grade schoolteachers, Mr. Lee, whom they did not like, a fact made quite clear by their 1960 hit "I Shot Mr. Lee." Although their debut hit was their only pop Top 40 entry, they continued to record consistently through 1966, and sporadically through 1974. They also provided backup vocals for Clyde McPhatter, the Five Keys, and Ivory Joe Hunter. Although several later singles grazed the lower reaches of the chart—"Have Mercy, Baby" and "Dance With Me, Georgie" (both 1960) and "I Don't Like It Like That, Part 1" (1961)—the quintet was no doubt hampered by frequently label-hopping (eight from 1957 to 1962). They sang backup on Johnny Thunder's #4 1962 hit "Loop De Loop" and "Love That Bomb" for the film *Dr. Strangelove*, but except for the enduring interest and respect of doo-wop aficionados, their later releases went unnoticed.

BoDeans

Formed 1983, Waukesha, WI
Samuel Llanas (b. Feb. 8, 1961, Waukesha), voc., gtr.; Kurt Neumann (b. Oct. 9, 1961, Waukesha), gtr., voc., mandolin.
1985—(+ Guy Hoffman [b. May 20, 1954, Milwaukee, WI], drums) 1986—(+ Bob Griffin [b. Dec. 4, 1959, Waukesha], bass) *Love & Hope & Sex & Dreams* (Slash) 1987—(– Hoffman) 1988—*Outside Looking In* 1989—(+ Michael Ramos [b. Nov. 18, 1958, Houston, TX], kybds.) *Home* 1991—(+ Rafael "Danny" Gayol [b. July 13, 1958, Mexico City, Mex.], drums) *Black and White* 1993—(– Gayol) *Go Slow Down* 1995—*Joe Dirt Car* (– Ramos; + Nick Kitsos [b. June 22, 1961], drums) 1996—*Blend.*
Sam Llanas with Absinthe: 1998—*A Good Day to Die* (Llanas).
Kurt Neumann: 2000—*Shy Dog* (Oarfin).

The title of BoDeans' debut album, *Love & Hope & Sex & Dreams,* alludes to the Rolling Stones song "Shattered," and to promote it, Llanas, Neumann, Griffin, and Hoffman went by the stage names Sammy, Beau, Bob, and Guy BoDean, a la the Ramones. Both bands have strongly influenced BoDeans' bracing guitar rock; the band's wistful pop sensibility, however, is evocative of Buddy Holly and the Everly Brothers. Chief songwriters Sam Llanas and Kurt Neumann, whose plangent harmonies are a key feature of the band's sound, met in high school in Waukesha, Wisconsin. In Milwaukee they hooked up with drummer Guy Hoffman, who left the band in 1987. Subsequent drummers have included Bo Conlon (on the road), Danny Gayol (on *Black and White* and the double-disc live set *Joe Dirt Car*), honorary BoDean Kenny Aronoff of John Mellencamp fame (on *Home, Go Slow Down,* and on the road), and Nick Kitsos (on *Blend*). Keyboardist Susan Julian also toured with the band briefly and appeared on *Home.*

Throughout most of their career, BoDeans won critical praise and amassed a loyal cult following. The group had a taste of Top 40 popularity when the producers of the hit television series *Party of Five* selected the catchy "Closer to Free," from *Go Slow Down,* as the show's theme song; the weekly exposure caused the tune to rise to #16 on the pop singles chart in 1996. The band hoped that history would repeat itself with its cover of the Beatles' "I've Just Seen a Face," the theme to Jennifer Love Hewitt's *Party of Five* spinoff, *Time of Your Life* (1997), but neither the series nor the song caught on.

While continuing to tour together as BoDeans, the founding members recorded side projects in the late '90s. Llanas formed the band Absinthe with former BoDeans drummer Hoffman and guitarist/bassist Jim Eannelli; BoDeans drummer Kitsos appeared on Absinthe's self-released 1998 album as well. Oarfin Records released Neumann's solo disc, *Shy Dog,* in 2000.

Body Count: See Ice-T

Angela Bofill

Born 1954, New York, NY
1978—*Angie* (GRP) 1979—*Angel of the Night* 1981—*Something About You* (Arista) 1983—*Too Tough; Teaser* 1988—*Intuition* (Capitol/EMI) 1993—*I Wanna Love Somebody* (Jive) 1996—*Love in Slow Motion* (Cachet/Shanachie).

Pop-jazz singer Angela Bofill grew up in the Bronx, the daughter of a French-Cuban father (a former bandleader) and a Puerto Rican mother. At age 10 she began studying piano and viola, and a few years later began writing her own songs. In high school she sang in the All-City Chorus and after hours with a group called the Puerto Rican Supremes. By graduation day she was singing on the Latino club circuit with the Group, Ricardo Morrero's popular salsa band. Meanwhile she studied voice (she has a four-octave range) at the Hartford Conservatory and the Manhattan School of Music. She developed an interest in jazz through friendships with Herbie Hancock, Joe Zawinul, and Flora Purim. After earning her music degree she was hired by the Dance Theater of Harlem as a singer, dancer, composer, and arranger. She also wrote and performed a jazz suite premiered at the Brooklyn Academy of Music and sang with jazz masters Dizzy Gillespie and Cannonball Adderley and with the reggae group Inner Circle.

Through flutist Dave Valentin of the Group, she met Dave Grusin and Larry Rosen of GRP Records, who signed her to a seven-year contract in 1978. Her debut was a best-selling jazz album and a promising soul and pop debut. "This Time I'll Be Sweeter" made #23 on the R&B singles charts. Her second album moved her closer to widespread popularity, charting at #10 R&B.

It was two years before she made another record. In the interim she settled a royalty dispute with GRP by transferring her contract to Arista. She also toured North America, South America, and Asia. Her 1981 album was produced by Narada Michael Walden. She produced half of *Too Tough* herself.

Marc Bolan: See T. Rex

Tommy Bolin

Born 1951, Sioux City, IA; died Dec. 4, 1976, Miami, FL
1975—*Teaser* (Nemperor) 1976—*Private Eyes* (Columbia) 1989—*The Ultimate . . .* (Geffen).

Guitarist/songwriter Tommy Bolin played in several hard-rock bands before dying of a drug overdose in 1976. Bolin dropped out of high school in Sioux City in 1968 and drifted to Denver. There he joined Zephyr, a quintet fronted by a woman singer named Candy Givens. Its eponymously titled debut album cracked the Top 50 in 1969. Next Bolin played in a group called Energy.

In 1971 Joe Walsh left the James Gang. Two years later, when his replacement, Dominic Troiano, quit the band, Walsh recommended Bolin. In addition to playing guitar, Bolin wrote much of the material on *Bang* (1973) and *Miami* (1974). Though best known for hard rock, he was a versatile musician, playing jazz-rock fusion on Billy Cobham's 1973 LP *Spectrum.* Bolin went from the James Gang to filling Ritchie Blackmore's shoes in Deep Purple in 1975. For the next two years he recorded both with that group (*Come Taste the Band* contained seven of his songs) and on his own: His first solo album, *Teaser,* came out in 1975. Bolin also appears on Deep Purple's *Last Concert in Japan* (a 1977 U.K. release) and *When We Rock, We Rock, and When We Roll, We Roll* (1978). After Purple disbanded in summer 1976, the guitarist returned to his solo career. *Private Eyes* came out shortly before Bolin's death. His body was found in a Miami hotel room.

Michael Bolton

Born Michael Bolotin, Feb. 26, 1953, New Haven, CT
1983—*Michael Bolton* (Columbia) 1985—*Everybody's Crazy* 1987—*The Hunger* 1989—*Soul Provider* 1991—*Time, Love and Tenderness* 1992—*Timeless (The Classics)* 1993—*The One Thing* 1995—*Greatest Hits 1985–1995* 1996—*This Is the Time—The Christmas Album* 1997—*All That Matters* 1998—*My Secret Passion: The Arias* (Sony Classical) 1999—*Timeless (The Classics), vol. 2* (Columbia).

Not since Barry Manilow has a singer/songwriter at once inspired such enduring enthusiasm among fans and such chronic irritation among critics as Michael Bolton. Crooning love ballads to a largely female adult-contemporary audience, Bolton reached his pop peak in the late '80s and early '90s.

Bolton became infatuated with soul music at an early age, listening to records by Ray Charles and Marvin Gaye. He took up the saxophone at seven, began playing guitar at 11, and by his early teens was singing with the Nomads, a local bar band. The Nomads were signed to Epic Records when Bolton was 15 but were dropped after two singles. Two more record deals later—one as a solo artist, one with a hard-rock outfit called Blackjack—Bolton was still struggling, now with a wife and three children to support.

In 1982 he signed a solo deal with Columbia. Bolton's eponymously titled first album for the label peaked at #89 in 1983; that same year, though, Laura Branigan took a song he had cowritten, "How Am I Supposed to Live Without You," to #12. Soon afterward, superstars as diverse as Barbra Streisand, Kenny Rogers, and Kiss recorded Bolton's tunes, while he established relationships with such successful songwriters as Diane Warren, Eric Kaz, and Barry Mann and Cynthia Weil, who would later contribute and collaborate on material for Bolton's own albums. In 1987 the singer cracked pop's Top 20 with "That's What Love Is All About" (#19), cowritten by Kaz. The following year, Bolton reached #11 with a cover of Otis Redding's "(Sittin' on) The Dock of the Bay," which Redding's widow pronounced her favorite rendition of the song. Bolton's next album, *Soul Provider,* shot to #3, and included Bolton's own #1 version of Branigan's hit. In 1990 two other tracks, "How Can We Be Lovers" and "When I'm Back on My Feet Again," made #3 and #7 respectively. The next year's *Time, Love and Tenderness* topped the charts and generated hit singles with the title track (#7) and a #1 rendering of Percy Sledge's "When a Man Loves a Woman." The album's #4 single "Love Is a Wonderful Thing," which Bolton cowrote with Andrew Goldmark, caused some trouble for the singer. In 1994 a federal jury found that his song borrowed significantly from the Isley Brothers' 1966 composition of the same name, and ordered that the Isleys receive 66 percent of the single's royalties, an amount estimated at $5.4 million.

In 1992 Bolton released an album of covers, *Timeless (The Classics),* which followed its predecessor to #1 and produced a #11 single with the Bee Gees' "To Love Somebody." Also that year, the singer scored a #12 duet with saxophonist Kenny G, "Missing You Now." *The One Thing* peaked at #3 and yielded the #6 hit "Said I Loved You . . . But I Lied." By this time, Bolton had divorced and was regularly pictured in the tabloids with glamorous girlfriends, including actresses Ashley Judd and Nicolette Sheridan.

After releasing a greatest-hits compilation, Bolton sought unconventional collaborations, teaming up with both country star Wynonna (Judd's sister) and opera legend Placido Domingo for duets on *This Is the Time—The Christmas Album* (#11, 1996). (He also embarked on a tour with Wynonna in 1998.) More changes followed in 1997 and 1998, amidst the release of two albums back-to-back, the pop *All That Matters* and the classical *My Secret Passion: The Arias.* The former included an Oscar-nominated, #1 Adult Contemporary hit "Go the Distance" (#24, 1997) from the Disney animated film *Hercules,* while the latter was a more surprising move. Inspired by performing a duet with Luciano Pavarotti at a benefit concert, Bolton studied opera for two years, an interest that culminated in a classical album that received lukewarm reviews.

In addition to Bolton's musical change of pace, 1997 saw the publication of the singer's children's book, *The Secret of the Lost Kingdom,* and a major change in physical appearance when he cut his trademark long blond hair short for the first time in 30 years. In 1999 Bolton returned to the tried and true with another album of covers, *Timeless (The Classics), vol. 2,* which includes a version of Marvin Gaye's "Sexual Healing."

Graham Bond

Born Oct. 28, 1937, Romford, Eng.; died May 8, 1974, London, Eng.
1965—*The Sound of '65* (Columbia, U.K.) 1966—*There's a Bond Between Us* 1968—*Mighty Graham Bond* (Pulsar, U.K.); *Love Is the Law Solid Bond* (Warner Bros.) 1970—*Solid Bond* 1971—*Holy Magick* (Vertigo, U.K.) 1972—*This Is Graham Bond* (Philips, U.K.) 1974—*We Put Our Magick on You* (Mercury).

Along with Alexis Korner and John Mayall, Graham Bond was a pioneer of British R&B. Initially a jazz musician, Bond earned his early reputation in the late '50s playing alto sax with the Don Rendell Quintet. He left Rendell in 1962 to join Korner's R&B-rock band, Blues Incorporated. His discovery of the electric organ as a blues instrument led him to quit the group in 1963 and, with drummer Ginger Baker and bass player Jack Bruce, to form the Graham Bond Organisation, to which guitarist John McLaughlin was later added. When McLaughlin left the band in 1964 to join Brian Auger's Trinity, Bond replaced him with saxophonist Dick Heckstall-Smith, also late of Blues Incorporated. After Bruce's 1965 departure for Mayall's Blues Breakers, Bond employed a succession of bassists. In late summer Baker left, emerging three months later with Bruce and Eric Clapton in Cream. Shortly thereafter the Graham Bond Organisation collapsed. An album of the group's work was released in the U.K. in 1984.

Bond tried working as a solo act but was forced to take on session work. After reuniting with Ginger Baker in 1970 in Baker's short lived supergroup Air Force, Bond collaborated with lyricist Pete Brown on *Two Heads Are Better Than One* (1972).

He married British singer Diane Stewart, with whom he shared a fascination for the occult (he claimed to be the son of renowned Satanist Aleister Crowley). Together they formed Holy Magick. After that marriage failed, Bond formed Magus in 1973 with British folksinger Carolanne Pegg. The group broke up within the year because of Bond's financial mismanagement. He also had drug problems. After suffering a nervous breakdown, Bond spent a month in the hospital in 1973. At the time that he died, he had been trying to revive his career. His body was discovered under the wheels of a stationary train.

Gary "U.S." Bonds

Born Gary Anderson, June 6, 1939, Jacksonville, FL
1960—*Dance Till Quarter to Three* (Legrand); *Twist Up Calypso* 1961—*Greatest Hits of Gary U.S. Bonds* 1981—*Dedication* (EMI) 1982—*On the Line Certified Soul* (Rhino) 1990—*Best of Gary U.S. Bonds.*

An early-'60s hitmaker with a rough, expressive voice, Gary "U.S." Bonds had his career revived in 1981 by fan Bruce Springsteen. As a young street-corner doo-wop singer named Gary Anderson, Bonds caught the attention of Norfolk, Virginia, music business jack-of-all-trades Frank Guida, who signed him to his Legrand Records. With Guida as producer, they released some of the most exuberant R&B singles of the day. Their first national release in late 1960, "New Orleans," was credited by Guida to one "Gary U.S. Bonds"; Anderson was not consulted. When the single became a hit, Anderson found himself with a new identity. For the next two years Bonds had a string of hits—"School Is Out" (#5, 1961), "Dear Lady Twist" (#9, 1962), "Twist, Twist Senora" (#9, 1962)—that peaked with the May 1961 release of his #1 hit "Quarter to Three." Though Bonds recorded for Legrand through the mid-'60s, his last chart single of the decade was "Copy Cat" in 1962.

Bonds doggedly continued playing one-nighters as a lounge act until 1978, when Bruce Springsteen—of whom Bonds had never heard—showed up and jammed with him. Springsteen (who often climaxed his concerts with "Quarter to Three") later proposed making a comeback album. *Dedication,* produced by Springsteen's guitarist Steve Van Zandt, was a hit in 1981, and the Springsteen-penned "This Little Girl Is Mine" was a #11 single that same year—Bonds' first hit in nearly 20 years. A 45 produced by Springsteen and Van Zandt, "Out of Work," hit #21 in 1982. Bonds remains active on the touring circuit.

Bone Thugs-N-Harmony

Formed 1992, Cleveland, OH
Layzie Bone (b. Steven Howse), voc.; Krayzie Bone (b. Anthony "Ant" Henderson), voc.; Wish Bone (b. Byron McCane), voc.; Bizzy Bone (b. Charles Scruggs), voc.; Flesh-N-Bone (b. Stanley Howse), voc.
1994—*Creepin' on ah Come Up* EP (Ruthless) 1995—*E. 1999 Eternal* 1996—(– Flesh-N-Bone) 1997—*The Art of War* 2000—*BTNHResurrection* (Ruthless/Epic).
Flesh-N-Bone solo: 1996—*T.H.U.G.S.—Trues Humbly United Gatherin' Souls* (Mo Thugs).
Krayzie Bone solo: 2000—*Thug on Da Line* (Loud).

Childhood friends (Steven and Stanley Howse are brothers) who grew up in Cleveland, Ohio's impoverished Northeast Side, the members of Bone Thugs-N-Harmony were self-professed teenage drug dealers who adopted their group identity—pairing nicknames with the surname Bone—in 1992 as an act of fraternal solidarity. After Layzie Bone was shot (nonfatally) in the head, the group decided to turn one of its chief leisure activities, rapping, into a new profession. In late 1993, the group took a Greyhound bus to L.A., and four months later won a telephone audition with former N.W.A member and Ruthless Records head Eazy-E. Nothing came of the call, but when the group learned that the rapper was performing in Cleveland, it returned home and met Eazy-E backstage after a show. Immediately impressed by the group's blend of street-corner harmonies and hardcore rap, he signed the act and produced its double-platinum debut 1994 EP, *Creepin' on ah Come Up* (#12 pop, #2 R&B). Eazy-E died of complications from AIDS the following March, and the following August Bone Thugs-N-Harmony's first full-length album, *E. 1999 Eternal* (#1 pop, #1 R&B, 1995), was released, selling more than 4 million copies. Its Grammy-winning track, "Tha Crossroads" (#1 pop, #1 R&B, 1996), became an unintentional elegy for the group's mentor and the fastest-rising single since the Beatles' "Can't Buy Me Love" in 1964, reaching the top in two weeks. Subsequently, the group released *The Art of War* (#1 pop and R&B, 1997), a quadruple-platinum double disc, and *BTNHResurrection* (#2 pop, #1 R&B, 2000).

The Bongos

Formed 1980, Hoboken, NJ
Richard Barone (b. Oct. 1, 1960, Tampa, FL), gtr., voc.; Frank Giannini (b. Aug 6, 1959, Morristown, NJ), drums, voc.; Rob Norris (b. Apr. 1, 1955, New York, NY), bass, voc.
1982—*Drums Along the Hudson* (PVC) (+ James Mastro [b. James Mastrodimos, Dec. 9, 1960, Springfield, OH], gtr., voc.) 1983—*Numbers With Wings* EP (RCA) 1985—*Beat Hotel.*
Richard Barone/James Mastro: 1983—*Nuts and Bolts* (Passport).
Richard Barone solo: 1987—*Cool Blue Halo* (Passport) 1990—*Primal Dream* 1993—*Clouds Over Eden* (Mesa) 1997—*Between Heaven and Cello* (Line, Ger.) 2000—*The Big Three.*
James Mastro with the Health and Happiness Show: 1993—*Tonic* (Bar/None) 1995—*Instant Living* 1999—*Sad and Sexy* (Cropduster).

Hoboken, formally a sleepy Hudson port town best known as Frank Sinatra's birthplace, became a major pop center in the early '80s, spurred by the fresh, literate, guitar-based pop of the Bongos. Although they were formed after the breakup of an early Hoboken band, the Bongos were initially popular in England, where they released several singles and took part in a "New York in London" concert with the Bush Tetras, Raybeats, Fleshtones, and dB's, recorded and later released as *Start Swimming.*

Drums Along the Hudson, a compilation of their British singles, was released to rapturous reviews. James Mastro, who had played in Richard Lloyd's post-Television band, was added to flesh out the live sound and stayed on. A 1982 tour with the B-52's brought them to the attention of RCA, who released an EP, *Numbers With Wings,* and *Beat Hotel,* but the records fizzled commercially. Mastro departed and was briefly replaced by ex-Voidoid Ivan Julian before the band called it quits.

Barone recorded the live *Cool Blue Halo* (1987), trying out a cello-based chamber-pop sound. In *Primal Dream* (1990) and *Clouds Over Eden* (1993) he expanded that sound in a studio context. He continues to record for a German label. James Mastro also used strings in his first solo project, Strange Cave. In 1991 he formed the Health and Happiness Show (named after a Hank Williams radio program) with former Feelies and Richard Lloyd drummer Vincent Denunzio. The group has released three albums of neo-rootsy rock. In 1992 Razor & Tie reissued the Bongos' catalogue.

Bon Jovi/Jon Bon Jovi

Formed 1983, New Jersey
Jon Bon Jovi (b. John Francis Bongiovi Jr., Mar. 2, 1962, Perth Amboy, NJ), voc.; Richie Sambora (b. Richard Stephen Sambora, July 11, 1959, Perth Amboy), gtr.; David Bryan (b. David Bryan Rashbaum, Feb. 7, 1962, Edison, NJ), kybds.; Alec John Such (b. Nov. 14, 1956, Yonkers, NY), bass; Tico Torres (b. Hector Torres, Oct. 7, 1953, New York, NY), drums.
1984—*Bon Jovi* (Mercury) 1985—*7800° Fahrenheit* 1986—*Slippery When Wet* 1988—*New Jersey* 1992—*Keep the Faith* (Jambco) 1994—*Cross Road: 14 Classic Grooves* (Mercury) (– Such; + Hugh McDonald [b. Philadelphia, PA], bass) 1995—*These Days* 2000—*Crush* (Island/Def Jam) 2001—*One Wild Night: Live 1985–2001.*
Jon Bon Jovi solo: 1990—*Blaze of Glory (Young Guns II)* soundtrack (Mercury) 1997—*Destination Anywhere.*
Richie Sambora solo: 1991—*Stranger in This Town* (Mercury) 1998—*Undiscovered Soul.*
David Bryan solo: 1992—*Netherworld* (Moonstone) 2000—*Lunar Eclipse* (Rounder).

Like an American Def Leppard, Bon Jovi used good looks and good hooks, toned-down aggression, and pumped-up production to forge the pop-metal alloy that made it one of the dominant mainstream rock bands of the late '80s.

As a working-class teenager, John Bongiovi showed little interest in school, preferring to sing with his friend David Rashbaum in local bands. Cousin Tony Bongiovi, owner of New York City's Power Station recording studio, let John sweep floors there and record demos with such musicians as Aldo Nova and members of Bruce Springsteen's E Street Band. The nucleus of the Bon Jovi band played clubs to support local radio play for one demo, "Runaway." PolyGram won a record label bidding war (reportedly signing only John Bongiovi, with the rest of the band as his employees) and had Bongiovi de-ethnicize the spelling of his last name (Rashbaum dropped his surname, too). After seeing Bon Jovi at a New Jersey club, Sambora auditioned and replaced Dave Sabo (later of Skid Row).

Bon Jovi's self-titled debut album (#43, 1984) yielded hits in "Runaway" (#39, 1984) and "She Don't Know Me" (#48, 1984). Tony Bongiovi then sued the band, claiming he had helped develop its sound; Jon called his cousin's influence "slim to none" but settled out of court. *7800° Fahrenheit* (#37, 1985) went gold, with minor hit singles in "Only Lonely" (#54, 1985) and "In and Out of Love" (#69, 1985).

Bon Jovi then made two crucial marketing moves: bringing in composer Desmond Child (former leader of the '70s New York club band Rouge, he also wrote for Aerosmith, Cher, and Kiss) as a song doctor, and basing the next album's content on the opinions of New York and New Jersey teenagers for whom they played tapes of over 30 possible songs. The resulting selections formed *Slippery When Wet* (#1, 1986), which sold over 12 million copies, with the help of straightforward performance videos that showcased the videogenic band. Hit singles included "You Give Love a Bad Name" (#1, 1986), the anthemic "Livin' on a Prayer" (#1,

1986)—both of which Child cowrote—and "Wanted Dead or Alive" (#7, 1987).

The *Slippery* formula was followed for *New Jersey* (#1, 1988), which sold over 7 million copies and contained the hits "Bad Medicine" (#1, 1988), "Born to Be My Baby" (#3, 1988), "I'll Be There for You" (#1, 1989), "Lay Your Hands on Me" (#7, 1989), and "Living in Sin" (#9, 1989). In the midst of a 1989 tour Jon Bon Jovi married his high school sweetheart Dorothea Hurley in Las Vegas (they have two children). Sambora went out with Cher for a while, and Bon Jovi backed her on some tracks of her 1989 *Heart of Stone* album. In 1994 Sambora married actress Heather Locklear. Later in 1993 Bon Jovi played the Soviet Union in the Moscow Music Peace Festival—arranged as part of a community-service sentence on Bon Jovi's manager Doc McGhee, who in 1988 had pleaded guilty to drug-smuggling charges from a 1982 arrest.

After 18 months of touring, the band members went separate ways. Jon Bon Jovi's *Blaze of Glory* (#3, 1990)—for the movie soundtrack of the Western *Young Guns II* (in which he had a bit part), recorded with Jeff Beck, Elton John, Little Richard, and others—yielded hits in the title track (#1, 1990) and "Miracle" (#12, 1990) and earned Oscar and Grammy nominations. Bon Jovi ended a year of breakup rumors with a Tokyo concert on December 31, 1991. The band then recorded *Keep the Faith* (#5, 1992), which had hit singles in the title track (#27, 1993) and "Bed of Roses" (#10, 1993). Bon Jovi's 1994 anthology, *Cross Road* (#8), yielded the hit single "Always" (#4, 1994).

In 1995 the band released *These Days* (#9), which yielded one Top 40 hit, "This Ain't a Love Song" (#14). After a full-scale world tour, the band went on hiatus. Jon Bon Jovi took a role in the 1995 film *Moonlight and Valentino* (and continued to act throughout the '90s, also appearing in Ed Burns' *No Looking Back* and the World War II submarine adventure *U-571*). He also released his first official, nonsoundtrack solo album, *Destination Anywhere* (#31, 1997). In 1998 Sambora released his second solo album, *Undiscovered Soul*. The band regrouped in 1999 to record a track, "Real Life," for the *EdTV* soundtrack, and the following year released *Crush* (#9, 2000), with the hit single "It's My Life" (#33, 2000).

Karla Bonoff

Born Dec. 27, 1952, Los Angeles, CA
1977—*Karla Bonoff* (Columbia) 1979—*Restless Nights* 1981—*Wild Heart of the Young* 1988—*New World* (Gold Castle) 1999—*All My Life: The Best of Karla Bonoff* (Legacy).

Songwriter Karla Bonoff has written some of Linda Ronstadt's most effective ballads, including "Someone to Lay Down Beside Me." Bonoff began playing Monday-night hoots at the Troubadour folk club near her family's West L.A. home when she was 16. After briefly attending UCLA in the late '60s, she was part of Bryndle, a short-lived group that included Wendy Waldman and Andrew Gold. The band recorded an unreleased album for A&M. A few years later, Bonoff was introduced to Ronstadt by Bryndle's bassist (and longtime Bonoff associate) Kenny Edwards. Ronstadt included "Lose Again," "Someone to Lay Down Beside Me," and "If He's Ever Near" on her album *Hasten Down the Wind*. Bonoff's first solo album was released in late 1977. It sold respectably, but she was mercilessly compared to Ronstadt, and she took two years to assemble a second album.

Wild Heart of the Young yielded a Top 20 hit in "Personally" (#19, 1982), but Bonoff then retreated behind the scenes and focused on composing. Her songs were recorded by Bonnie Raitt and Nicolette Larson; Bonoff briefly returned to recording to contribute tracks for the '80s films *About Last Night . . .* and *Footloose*. In 1990 she wrote three songs for Ronstadt's *Cry Like a Rainstorm, Howl Like the Wind;* one of them, "All My Life," won Ronstadt and Aaron Neville a Grammy for Best Pop Vocal Duo. In 1993 Wynonna Judd topped the country charts with a recording of Bonoff's "Tell Me Why" (for which Bonoff also played guitar and sang backup). The following year Bonoff contributed two songs to the soundtrack of the film *8 Seconds*. In 1995, 25 years after the band's ill-fated association with A&M, a rekindled Bryndle released its self-titled debut album. Bonoff continues to perform with the band as well as on her own.

The Bonzo Dog Band

Formed 1965, London, Eng.
Roger Ruskin Spear (b. June 29, 1943, Wormwood Scrubbs, Eng.), kazoos, Jew's harp, various other musical and nonmusical toys; Rodney Slater (b. Nov. 8, 1944, Lincolnshire, Eng.), saxes; Vivian Stanshall (b. Mar. 21, 1943, Shillingford, Eng.; d. Mar. 5, 1995, London), voc., trumpet, ukulele; Neil Innes (b. Dec. 9, 1944, Essex, Eng.), voc., gtr., kybds.; Vernon Dudley Bohay-Nowell (b. July 29, 1932, Plymouth, Eng.), gtr.; "Legs" Larry Smith (b. Jan. 18, 1944, Oxford, Eng.), drums; Sam Spoons (b. Martin Stafford Ash, Feb. 8, 1942, Bridgewater, Eng.), perc.
1967—*Gorilla* (Liberty) 1968—(– Bohay; – Nowell; – Spoons; + Dennis Cowan [b. May 6, 1947, London], bass) *Urban Spaceman* 1969—*Tadpoles* 1970—*Keynsham* (United Artists) (group disbands) 1971—(group re-forms: Stanshall; Innes; Cowan; + Bubs White, gtr.; + Andy Roberts, gtr., fiddle; + Dave Richards, bass; + Dick Parry, flute; + Hughie Flint [b. Mar. 15, 1942, Eng.], drums) 1972—*Let's Make Up and Be Friendly* 1990—*Best of the Bonzo Dog Band* (Rhino); *Bestiality of the Bonzo Dog Doo-Dah Band* (Liberty).

Originally the Bonzo Dog Dada Band, the group was the brainchild of art-college classmates Roger Spear and Rodney Slater, and its express purpose was to do to music—especially the jazz and popular music of the '20s and '30s—what Dadaists Marcel Duchamp and Tristan Tzara had respectively done to art and poetry: give it a good kick in the pants. Early versions of the group contained about 30 members, mostly fellow art students. By the time they began performing in pubs in 1965—the Dada in their name changed to Doo-Dah—they had been reduced to fewer than a dozen. Within a year they were playing clubs and had broadened their act to include parodies of musical styles, surrealistic sight gags, and comic skits in the punning, non-sequitur style of the popular British TV comedy series *The Goon*

Show. Their stage setup was cluttered with Spear's collection of useless gadgets, machines, mannequins, and robots.

They cut two singles for Parlophone before signing with Liberty in 1967. *Gorilla* included gag advertisements and radio interviews sandwiched between parodies of Prohibition-era jazz, Tony Bennett, Rodgers and Hammerstein, and Elvis Presley (most of the material written by Viv Stanshall or Neil Innes). It was Innes' interest in electronic music, rock, and drugs that lent subsequent LPs the psychedelic touches epitomized by "I'm the Urban Spaceman," a Top 5 1968 British hit written by Innes and produced by one Apollo C. Vermouth, a.k.a. Paul McCartney. The Bonzos appeared in *Magical Mystery Tour,* singing a Presley takeoff titled "Death Cab for Cutie."

Despite growing popularity, the Bonzos broke up in 1970. Larry Smith, Vernon Bohay-Nowell, and Sam Spoons joined Bob Kerr's Whoopee Band, an outfit similar to the early Bonzos. Slater quit show business to become a government social worker. Innes and Cowan formed a group called World and made an album called *Lucky Planet* before Innes briefly joined McGuinness Flint. Stanshall, with Dennis Cowan, Spear, and former Bonzo roadie "Borneo" Fred Munt (as percussionist and saxophonist), formed the Big Grunt. Spear left to put together the Kinetic Wardrobe, in which he was backed by a band of robots. He toured Britain and the Continent opening for the Who in the early '70s. Stanshall led several other groups—the Human Beans, Gerry Atric and His Aging Orchestra, Viv and His Gargantuan Chums—boasting Eric Clapton and Keith Moon and John Entwistle of the Who as sidemen on occasional singles.

In 1971 Stanshall, Innes, and Cowan revived the Bonzo Dog Band—or at least the name—for one album, *Let's Make Up and Be Friendly.* In spite of contributions from Smith and Spear, old Bonzo fans did not take well to the new band, which ultimately split up. Spear returned to his Kinetic Wardrobe. Smith toured twice in 1974, supporting Elton John and Eric Clapton. Innes has released solo albums (including 1973's *How Sweet to Be an Idiot*) and worked primarily as a composer for British television, most notably *Monty Python's Flying Circus* and *Rutland Weekend Television* with Python's Eric Idle. In 1977 he and Idle wrote, directed, and performed in *The Rutles,* a television special spoofing the Beatles. Innes played the John Lennon character, Ron Nasty.

Stanshall's voice graced a number of commercials. He also announced on Mike Oldfield's *Tubular Bells,* David Bowie's *Peter and the Wolf,* and his own BBC show, *Viv Stanshall's Radio Flashes.* He released several solo albums and contributed lyrics to Steve Winwood's first two solo LPs. In 1991 he staged a show, *Rawlinson Dogends,* at London's Bloomsbury Theatre. Included in the backing band were ex-Bonzos Spear and Slater. Bonzo's final single, recorded during a one-off 1987 reunion, was finally released a year later. Stanshall died in a fire at his London home in 1995.

Boogie Down Productions: See KRS-ONE

James Booker

Born Dec. 17, 1939, New Orleans, LA; died Nov. 8, 1983, New Orleans
1976—*Junco Partners* (Island, U.K.) 1981—*New Orleans Piano Wizard: Live!* (Rounder) 1982—*Classified Resurrection of the Bayou Maharajah; Spiders on the Keys.*

Although James Booker had only one hit, his keyboards on hits by Joe Tex, Fats Domino, Bobby Bland, Lloyd Price, and Junior Parker and his unpredictable temperament made him a New Orleans legend. A child piano prodigy, the son of a minister and brother of gospel singer Betty Jean Booker, he made his first recordings for Imperial Records, working with Dave Bartholomew, when he was 14. He also recorded for the Ace and Duke labels and toured with Joe Tex, Shirley and Lee, Huey Smith's Clowns (impersonating the road-weary Smith), and the Dovells.

In the late '50s Booker's already high value as a session musician rose when he became the first notable New Orleans R&B musician to play the organ. His R&B organ instrumental "Gonzo" hit #3 on the national R&B chart and made the pop Top 50 in 1960. He continued to work as a session musician and sideman with B.B. King, Little Richard, and Wilson Pickett, among others, into the mid-'60s, when he was sidelined by drug problems and a jail term. He began working again around 1968, most notably with Fats Domino, Dr. John, Ringo Starr, and the Doobie Brothers. He toured Europe in 1977 (the Rounder live album was recorded in Zurich that year), then returned to regular engagements in New Orleans. The Clash covered his "Junco Partner" on its 1980 album *Sadinista!* In 1983 Booker died of a heart attack.

Booker T. and the MG's

Formed 1961, Memphis, TN
Booker T. Jones (b. Nov. 12, 1944, Memphis), organ; Lewis Steinberg (b. Sep. 13, 1933), bass; Al Jackson (b. Nov. 27, 1935, Memphis; d. Oct. 1, 1975, Memphis), drums; Steve Cropper (b. Oct. 21, 1941, Willow Springs, MO), gtr.
1962—*Green Onions* (Stax) 1963—(– Steinberg; + Donald "Duck" Dunn [b. Nov. 24, 1941, Memphis], bass) 1966—*And Now, Booker T. and the MG's* 1967—*Hip Hug-Her; Back to Back* 1968—*The Best of Booker T. and the MG's* (Atlantic); *Doin' Our Thing* (Stax); *Soul Limbo; Uptight* soundtrack 1969—*The Booker T. Set* 1970—*McLemore Avenue* 1971—*Melting Pot* 1973—*Star Collection* (Warner Bros.) 1974—*Greatest Hits* 1975—*Memphis Sound* 1976—*Union Extended; Time Is Tight* (– Jackson; + Willie Hall [b. Aug. 8, 1950], drums) 1977—*Universal Language* (Asylum) 1992—(lineup: Dunn; Cropper; Jones; + Steve Jordan, drums) 1994—(+ James Gadson, drums) *That's the Way It Should Be* (Columbia) (– Jordan; – Gadson; + Steve Potts [b. Nov. 12, 1953, Memphis], drums).
Steve Cropper solo: 1969—*Jammed Together* (Stax) 1970—*With a Little Help From My Friends* (Volt) 1982—*Night After Night* (MCA).

As the rhythm section of the Stax Records house band, Booker T. and the MG's were principal architects of the lean, punchy Stax sound. Though they had some instrumental hits on their own, they did invaluable backup work on hits by other Stax and Atlantic performers like Otis Redding, Sam and Dave, Wilson Pickett, Albert King, Eddie Floyd, and Rufus and Carla Thomas. Booker T. Jones was a teenage multi-instrumental prodigy who joined the Stax organization in 1960 as a saxophonist. Jamming with Mar-Keys guitarist Steve Cropper led to the formation of the MG's (Memphis Group) and to the recording of "Green Onions." The single went to #3 (and gold) in 1962. Several minor hits followed, including "Hip Hug-Her" (#37, 1967), a cover version of the Rascals' "Groovin' " (#21, 1968), "Soul-Limbo," (#17, 1968), and two 1969 film soundtrack hits, "Hang 'Em High" (#9) and "Time Is Tight" (#6). The best-known version of the band was comprised of Jones, Cropper, Jackson, and Dunn. Having written much of the MG's' material, Cropper also has credits on Wilson Pickett's "In the Midnight Hour," Eddie Floyd's "Knock on Wood," Sam and Dave's "Soul Man," Otis Redding's "(Sittin' on) The Dock of the Bay," and at least 20 other Stax-Volt hits. He produced, among others, Redding. In 1969 he opened his own Memphis studio, TMI. Among his extra-MG's projects were *Jammed Together* with Albert King and Roebuck Staples, and a solo album, *With a Little Help From My Friends,* with Leon Russell, Buddy Miles, Jim Keltner, Carl Radle, the Bar-Kays, the Memphis Horns, and the MG's. In 1975, with the MG's disbanded, Cropper moved to L.A., where he resumed his session career by playing with Rod Stewart, Art Garfunkel, and Sammy Hagar.

The MG's proper were a very informal assemblage and played together only intermittently, partly due to Jones' frequent absences while completing his music major at Indiana University. Often limited to working only when Jones was available on weekends and vacations, the group eventually broke up in 1971. Soon afterward Jones began working as a producer (for Rita Coolidge, Bill Withers, Willie Nelson [on *Stardust*], among others), as a session player, and as a solo vocal performer. Jackson also returned to session work, notably for Al Green. In 1973 he joined Dunn in a short-lived MG's reunion. A reunion album was in the planning stages two years later when Jackson was shot and killed in his home by a burglar. Former Bar-Kays drummer Willie Hall took his place in reunion sessions with Jones, Cropper, and Dunn between 1975 and 1978. In 1977 Jones, Cropper, and Dunn toured with Levon Helm's RCO All Stars. Since then Cropper and Dunn have been active as freelance musicians and producers, joining the Blues Brothers in 1978, while Jones has worked on his solo career. He had a disco hit with his 1982 A&M single "Don't Stop Your Love."

Through the '80s the members were actively involved in dozens of projects. Cropper continued producing such artists as John Prine, Poco, Jeff Beck, Tower of Power, and José Feliciano. Through the late '80s and early '90s, Cropper, Dunn, and Potts also worked a side job as the Blues Brothers Band.

The MG's reunited for a 1990 tour, with Anton Fig (session musician and member of Paul Shaffer's band on David Letterman's late-night TV talk show) on drums. The group was inducted into the Rock and Roll Hall of Fame in 1992. That year they were the house band for the Bob Dylan tribute show at Madison Square Garden. In 1993 they played backup for Neil Young's tour. Following their induction, the members began playing together and finding an enthusiastic audience. They decided to reconvene on a more permanent basis. In 1994 they released their first album in 17 years, *That's the Way It Should Be,* with drummer Steve Jordan (who'd preceded Fig in the Letterman band and had played with Keith Richards). The MG's remain a sporadically active live attraction, now featuring the late Al Jackson's nephew, Steve Potts, on drums.

The Boomtown Rats/Bob Geldof

Formed 1975, Dun Laoghaire, Ire.

Bob Geldof (b. Oct. 5, 1954, Dublin, Ire.), voc.; Johnny Fingers (b. Ire.), kybds.; Pete Briquette (b. Ire.), bass; Simon Crowe (b. Ire.), drums; Gerry Cott (b. Ire.), gtr.; Garry Roberts (b. Ire.), gtr.

1977—*The Boomtown Rats* (Mercury) 1979—*A Tonic for the Troops* (Columbia); *The Fine Art of Surfacing* 1981—(– Cott) *Mondo Bongo* 1983—*Ratrospective* 1985—*In the Long Grass* 1997—*Great Songs of Indifference: The Best of Bob Geldof & the Boomtown Rats.*

Bob Geldof solo: 1986—*Deep in the Heart of Nowhere* (Atlantic) 1988—*The Vegetarians of Love* 1993—*The Happy Club* (Polydor).

Irish new wavers, the Boomtown Rats were full-fledged pop stars in Britain and Europe while being virtually ignored in the U.S., where none of their four albums even cracked the Top 100. By the mid-'80s, the group was overshadowed by the high-profile humanitarian activities of its lead singer, Bob Geldof, who was nominated for a Nobel Peace Prize, before putting his music career on indefinite hold.

Originally called the Nightlife Thugs, they changed their name to the Boomtown Rats after a gang in Woody Guthrie's *Bound for Glory.* They moved to London (and into a communal house in Chessington) in 1976. Their stage show attracted attention for Johnny Fingers, who was known for wearing pajamas, and the Mick Jagger–David Bowie posturings of frontman Bob Geldof (who had previously worked as a meat worker, bulldozer operator, photographer, and *Melody Maker* correspondent).

While most of London's punk bands were sneering at rich, selfish rock stars, Geldof announced his ambition to become one. The first Rats single, "Looking After No. 1," hit #11 in England in August 1977 (the first new-wave single to be playlisted by the BBC), and the media discovered Geldof's willingness to utter controversial opinions on virtually any subject. The Rats' first album (recorded in Germany and released in England in late 1977) did well in the U.K. With *A Tonic for the Troops* ("She's So Modern") the group established a pattern of critical raves but poor sales in the U.S. In Britain its success continued; by early 1981 the Rats had nine consecutive Top 15 singles, among them two #1s: "Rat Trap" (1978) and "I Don't Like Mondays" (1979). The latter became a controversial, minor U.S. hit (#73, 1980). It was based on the case of a 17-year-old San Diego girl named Brenda Spencer, who randomly shot 11 passersby (killing two) on Monday, January 29, 1979, and explained her actions by saying, "I don't like Mondays." The single was banned by some radio stations and prompted a lawsuit by the girl's parents, who claimed it created adverse pretrial publicity.

The '80s found the Rats continuing to tour internationally and release records, such as 1981's *Mondo Bongo* and the reggae single "Banana Republic." It was their last British Top 10 single, although through 1984 a number of records charted, including "The Elephant's Graveyard," "Never in a Million Years," "House on Fire," "Tonight," and "Drag Me Down."

In 1982 Geldof played the lead role of Pink in a film of Pink Floyd's *The Wall.* Moved by news coverage of the Ethiopian famine, Geldof and Ultravox's Midge Ure cowrote "Do They Know It's Christmas," which was recorded in a single 24-hour session by an ad hoc group called Band Aid that included Boy George, Paul McCartney, George Michael, Phil Collins, Paul Young, Sting, and members of Duran Duran, Spandau Ballet, U2, and Kool and the Gang. Within 10 days the song sold over 2 million copies, hitting #1 on the U.K. chart in 1984. (It went to #3 in December of the following year, and remained the biggest-selling single in the history of British pop until surpassed by Elton John's 1997 tribute to Princess Diana, "Candle in the Wind 1997.") All proceeds went directly to famine relief, and in January 1985 Geldof toured Africa to see for himself that the food was being distributed. Later that month, he addressed the group of American performers gathered by Michael Jackson, Quincy Jones, and Lionel Richie to record a similar benefit record, "We Are the World," under the group name U.S.A. for Africa. U.S.A. for Africa—which included Bob Dylan, Bruce Springsteen, Ray Charles, Tina Turner, Diana Ross, the Jacksons, Cyndi Lauper, Paul Simon, Stevie Wonder, Willie Nelson, Huey Lewis, and Geldof—raised $40 million. Geldof later remarked, " 'We Are the World' sounds too much like the Pepsi generation." In a characteristically blunt appraisal of the resulting rash of benefit records, Geldof described them as artistically "awful."

On July 13, 1985, over 1.5 billion people tuned in to watch Live Aid, a 16-hour-long star-studded concert that was broadcast via satellite from London's Wembley Stadium and Philadelphia's JFK Stadium. Among the performers were Madonna, Paul McCartney, Queen, Phil Collins, David Bowie, Led Zeppelin (with Phil Collins and Tony Thompson sitting in for the deceased John Bonham), Power Station (with Michael des Barres), Duran Duran, U2, Judas Priest, Black Sabbath, and the Boomtown Rats. All told, the shows and the resulting album raised about $120 million. In November of that year, Columbia Records canceled the Boomtown Rats' U.S. record deal. The group broke up in 1986. Geldof went on to become a familiar face, pictured with Mother Teresa and other world leaders. In June 1986 Queen Elizabeth II awarded him with an honorary knighthood, making him Bob Geldof, KBE (Knight Commander of the British Empire); because he is an Irish citizen he is not, as has been published, referred to as Sir Bob. That year saw the publication of his critically well-received, best-selling autobiography, *Is That It?* (He has said that he accepted the offer to write his book only because the advance covered his debts.) Geldof, who often admitted that becoming an institution overnight has at times overwhelmed him, stated in 1990, "I never said we were going to stop world poverty or world hunger. [The function] was to raise the issue to the top of the political agenda, and we did that." Geldof remains involved in world affairs; most recently, he lobbied for the debt relief of poor countries.

Geldof's recording career has been on hold since the release of his last solo album in 1993—as a recording artist, wide commercial appeal had always eluded him anyway. He was chairman of Planet 24 Productions, which produced, among others, the popular U.K. morning television program *The Big Breakfast.* He later cashed in his stake in Planet 24 for £5 million. Since 1998 he's also been a DJ on the London radio station XFM. Geldof's name was in the news when his wife, television personality Paula Yates, left him for INXS' singer Michael Hutchence in 1995. Geldof and Yates were divorced the following year. Paula Yates died in September 2000, leaving behind the three daughters she had with Geldof and Tiger Lily, her daughter by Hutchence (who died in 1997). In 2000 Geldof, who had custody of his daughters at the time of Yates' death, was awarded temporary custody of Tiger Lily.

Debby Boone

Born Sep. 22, 1956, Hackensack, NJ
1977—*You Light Up My Life* (Curb/Warner Bros.) 1978—*Midstream* 1979—*The Promise* 1980—*Love Has No Reason* 1990—*The Best Of* (Curb).

Debby Boone had one of the longest-running #1 hit singles—10 weeks—with "You Light Up My Life" in 1977. One of singer Pat Boone's four daughters, Debby began performing with her sisters in 1969 as the Boone Girls. They toured with their father and recorded for the Lamb & Lion label. In 1977 producer Mike Curb persuaded Debby to record solo. The song he chose for her, "You Light Up My Life," the theme song from a movie, won an Oscar for Best Song and resulted in Boone winning three Grammy Awards, including that year's Best New Artist.

Boone retired to start a family; she married Gabriel Ferrer, the son of singer Rosemary Clooney and actor José Ferrer. She wrote an autobiography that chronicled her teenage "rebelliousness" and her life with Christ, titled *Debby Boone . . . So Far.* She returned to performing in 1982, when she starred in the play *Seven Brides for Seven Brothers,* a hit around the country, which closed within weeks of its Broadway debut. Boone's recent musical work is in the contemporary Christian and children's music veins. In 1990 she starred in a revival of *The Sound of Music.* Later in the decade she exorcized her inner bad girl by playing Rizzo in the stage production of *Grease* and by portraying a hired killer on an episode of the short-lived television show *Baywatch Nights*.

Pat Boone

Born Charles Eugene Boone, June 1, 1934, Jacksonville, FL
1962—*Pat Boone's Golden Hits* (Dot) 1990—*Greatest Hits* (Curb) 1997—*In a Metal Mood: No More Mr. Nice Guy* (Hip-O).

Singer Pat Boone was easily the most commercially successful of the white '50s teen idols, with a string of 38 Top 40 hits, among them several cleaned-up, hit cover versions that outsold the arguably superior versions by the original artists: Little Richard's "Tutti Frutti" (#12, 1956) and "Long Tall Sally" (#8, 1956), Ivory Joe Hunter's "I Almost Lost My Mind" (#1, 1956), the Five Keys' "Gee Whittakers!" (#19, 1955), and Joe Turner's "Chains of Love" (#10, 1956).

Boone claims to be a descendant of early American frontier hero Daniel Boone. He attended high school in Nashville, where he lettered in three varsity sports, served as student body president, and was elected the school's most popular boy. Following his graduation, he married country & western star Red Foley's daughter, Shirley. In the early '50s he attended David Lipscomb College in Nashville before transferring to North Texas State. There he won a local talent show, which led to an appearance on the Ted Mack program and then Arthur Godfrey's amateur hour, where Boone became a regular for a year. By mid-decade he had begun recording some mildly successful singles for Nashville's Republic Records. In February 1955 he released his first single for Dot Records, "Two Hearts, Two Kisses." By the end of the year he had his first of dozens of hits for the label, a relaxed cover of Fats Domino's "Ain't That a Shame," which hit #1.

Over the next seven years Boone made 54 chart appearances, including many two-sided hits, and became one of the all-time biggest-selling pop singers. His Top 10 hits for Dot included "At My Front Door (Crazy Little Mama)" (#7, 1955), "I'll Be Home" (#4, 1956), "Friendly Persuasion" (#5, 1956), "Don't Forbid Me" (#1, 1957), "Why Baby Why" (#5, 1957), "Love Letters in the Sand" (#1, 1957), "April Love" (#1, 1957), "A Wonderful Time Up There" (#4, 1958), "Moody River" (#1, 1961), and "Speedy Gonzales" (#6, 1962). At his peak he was considered a rock & roller—a parent-approved alternative to Elvis, Jerry Lee Lewis, and Chuck Berry in white buck shoes. He starred in 15 films, including *Bernardine* and *April Love* (both 1957) and *State Fair* (1962). From 1957 to 1960 he had his own television series, *The Pat Boone–Chevy Showroom* on ABC.

Boone did not have another Top 40 single after 1962, but he continued to record for Dot through the late '60s, then for a series of other labels, including Capitol, MGM, Motown, and Warner Bros. subsidiary Curb (on which he released covers of "Oh Boy!" and "Rip It Up" in 1981), until the early '80s. His later recording projects included "Let Me Live," which become the anthem for the antichoice movement.

At the height of his popularity, Boone became an author, penning a series of tomes full of wholesome teen advice: *Twixt Twelve and Twenty; Between You, Me and the Gatepost;* and *The Care and Feeding of Parents.* In 1981 he published *Pray to Win.* He has also performed with Shirley and their four daughters, Cherry, Lindy, Debby, and Laury. In 1977 Debby became a star in her own right, and Cherry later revealed her problems with an eating disorder, which she discussed in her book *Starving for Attention.*

Pat, who began hosting a nationally broadcasted Christian radio program in 1983, is also active in a number of charitable and religious causes, including the Easter Seals Society. The Israeli Tourism Department made him Christian Ambassador to Israel, and he has written and recorded music encouraging better Christian-Jewish relations. In 1994 he appeared in the title role of a Branson, Missouri, production of *The Will Rogers Follies.*

Three years later Boone, 62 at the time, resurfaced on the album chart sporting black leather, a dog collar, a deep tan, and temporary tattoos. The jovial *In a Metal Mood* (#125), on which he imposed big-band arrangements on songs by Led Zeppelin, Metallica, and Van Halen, caused a minor media stir. He was subsequently dismissed from his Trinity Broadcasting Network program *Gospel America.*

Boston

Formed 1975, Boston, MA
Tom Scholz (b. Mar. 10, 1947, Toledo, OH), gtr., kybds.; Brad Delp (b. June 12, 1951, Boston), voc., gtr.; Barry Goudreau (b. Nov. 29, 1951, Boston), gtr.; Fran Sheehan (b. Mar. 26, 1949, Boston), bass; Sib Hashian (b. Aug. 17, 1949, Boston), drums.
1976—*Boston* (Epic) 1978—*Don't Look Back*
Early 1980s—(– Goudreau; – Sheehan; – Hashian) 1986—*Third Stage* (MCA) (group disbands, Scholz leads various lineups) 1994—*Walk On* 1995—(+ Delp).
Barry Goudreau solo: 1980—*Barry Goudreau* (Portait) 1984—(with Orion the Hunter) *Orion the Hunter.*
RTZ (Goudreau and Brad Delp): 1992—*Return to Zero* (Giant).

In 1976 sonic-rock group Boston had the fastest-selling debut album in rock. *Boston* was a slightly altered version of tapes guitarist Tom Scholz had made in his 12-track basement studio, characterized by what he calls "power guitars, harmony vocals, and double-guitar leads." Scholz had a master's degree in mechanical engineering from MIT and was a senior product designer for Polaroid Corporation who made music during his off-hours. Eventually the tapes attracted the interest of Epic Records, which signed Scholz and a band of local musicians, Boston. Upon signing, the band recut some tracks on the West Coast with producer John Boylan, but its 1976 debut was essentially Scholz's basement tapes. It sold 11 million copies and spawned three Top 40 singles—"More Than a Feeling" (#5, 1976), "Long Time" (#22, 1977), and "Peace of Mind" (#38, 1977). Boston went almost directly to the arena circuit on tour.

Two years later *Don't Look Back* (#1, 1978) presented the Boston formula virtually unchanged and sold a comparatively disappointing 6 million copies. Less-than-sellout concert crowds suggested that audience interest was flagging. This time the group took eight years to record a followup. Barry Goudreau, who'd released a solo album in 1980, quit in 1982 to form Orion the Hunter, which issued a Top 60 LP in 1984.

By the time *Third Stage* appeared in 1986, only Scholz and singer Brad Delp remained. The loss of the others hardly mattered, as Delp's soaring vocals and Scholz's guitar defined the Boston sound. The album lodged at #1 for four weeks and produced hit singles in "Amanda" (#1, 1986), "We're Ready" (#9, 1986), and "Can't Cha Say (You Believe in Me)/Still in Love" (#20, 1987). And then another long wait, during which Scholz fended off lawsuits. In 1989 Goudreau sued Scholz for allegedly damaging his musical career; the two reached an out-of-court settlement. The following year Scholz won his seven-year legal battle against CBS, which had sued him for allegedly reneging on his contract with the label. Scholz countersued, claiming the company owed him millions in back royalties. A jury sided with the guitarist, and CBS was ordered to release his money.

In addition to selling millions of records, Scholz invented the Rockman, a paperback-sized guitar amplifier with headphones. Shortly after winning the CBS suit, he built a new studio and began work on Boston's fourth album. Released in 1994, *Walk On* included only Scholz from the original lineup.

In 1991 Delp and Goudreau formed a short-lived band called RTZ and released *Return to Zero,* which featured the single "Until Your Love Comes Back Around" (#26, 1992). By 1995 Delp had rejoined Scholz in a new, dual-vocalist incarnation of Boston. The band's 1997 *Greatest Hits* (#47) collection includes three new songs, among them a rock arrangement of "The Star-Spangled Banner." As of 1998 Goudreau was backing bluesy singer Lisa Guyer.

David Bowie

Born David Robert Jones, Jan. 8, 1947, London, Eng.
1967—*The World of David Bowie* (Deram, U.K.) 1970—*Man of Words, Man of Music* (Mercury); *The Man Who Sold the World* 1971—*Hunky Dory* (RCA) 1972—*The Rise and Fall of Ziggy Stardust and the Spiders From Mars* 1973—*Aladdin Sane; Pin Ups; Images 1966–67* (London) 1974—*Diamond Dogs* (RCA); *David Live* 1975—*Young Americans* 1976—*Station to Station; ChangesOneBowie* 1977—*Low; "Heroes"* 1978—*Stage* 1979—*Lodger* 1980—*Scary Monsters* 1981—*ChangesTwoBowie; Christiane F* soundtrack 1982—*Cat People* soundtrack; *Bertolt Brecht's Baal* 1983—*Let's Dance* (EMI); *Golden Years* (RCA); *Ziggy Stardust/The Motion Picture* 1984—*Fame and Fashion; Tonight* (EMI) 1987—*Never Let Me Down* 1989—*Sound + Vision* (Rykodisc) 1990—*ChangesBowie* 1993—*Black Tie White Noise* (Savage) 1994—*Sound + Vision* with CD-ROM (Rykodisc) 1995—*Outside* (Virgin); *Buddha of Suburbia* soundtrack 1997—*Earthling* 1999—*Hours* . . . .

Tin Machine, formed 1989, Switz.: Bowie; Reeves Gabrels (b. June 4, 1956, Staten Island, NY), gtr.; Hunt Sales (b. Mar. 2, 1954, Detroit, MI), drums; Tony Sales (b. Sep. 26, 1951, Cleveland, OH), bass.
1989—*Tin Machine* (EMI) 1991—*Tin Machine II* (Victory).

A consummate musical chameleon, David Bowie created a career in the '60s and '70s that featured his many guises: folksinger, androgyne, alien, decadent, blue-eyed soul man, modern rock star—each one spawning a league of imitators. His late-'70s collaborations with Brian Eno made Bowie one of the few older stars to be taken seriously by the new wave. In the '80s, *Let's Dance* (#1, 1983), his entrée into the mainstream, was followed by attempts to keep up with current trends. In the '90s, this meant embracing grunge, industrial rock, rap, and dance music. While these experiments were greeted with varying degrees of artistic and commercial success, Bowie remains one of the more restless and venturesome classic rock survivors.

David Jones took up the saxophone at age 13, and when he left Bromley Technical High School (where a friend permanently paralyzed Jones' left pupil in a fight) to work as a commercial artist three years later, he had started playing in bands (the Konrads, the King Bees, David Jones and the Buzz). Three of Jones' early bands—the King Bees, the Manish Boys (featuring session guitarist Jimmy Page), and Davey Jones and the Lower Third—each recorded a single. In 1966, after changing his name to David Bowie (after the knife) to avoid confusion with the Monkees' Davy Jones, he recorded three singles for Pye Records, then signed in 1967 with Deram, issuing several singles and *The World of David Bowie* (most of the songs from that album, and others from that time, are collected on *Images*).

On these early records, Bowie appears in the singer/songwriter mold; rock star seemed to be just another role for him. In 1967 he spent a few weeks at a Buddhist monastery in Scotland, then apprenticed in Lindsay Kemp's mime troupe. He started his own troupe, Feathers, in 1968. American-born Angela Barnett met Bowie in London's Speakeasy and married him on March 20, 1970. Son Zowie (now Joey) was born in June 1971; the couple divorced acrimoniously in 1980. After Feathers broke up, Bowie helped start the experimental Beckenham Arts Lab in 1969. To finance the project, he signed with Mercury. *Man of Words, Man of Music* included "Space Oddity," its release timed for the U.S. moon landing. It became a European hit that year but did not make the U.S. charts until its rerelease in 1973, when it reached #15.

Marc Bolan, an old friend, was beginning his rise as a glitter-rocker in T. Rex and introduced Bowie to his producer, Tony Visconti. Bowie mimed at some T. Rex concerts, and Bolan played guitar on Bowie's "Karma Man" and "The Prettiest Star." Bowie, Visconti, guitarist Mick Ronson, and drummer John Cambridge toured briefly as Hype. Ronson eventually recruited drummer Michael "Woody" Woodmansey, and with Visconti on bass they recorded *The Man Who Sold the World,* which included "All the Madmen," inspired by Bowie's institutionalized brother, Terry. *Hunky Dory* (#93, 1972), Bowie's tribute to the New York City of Andy Warhol, the Velvet Underground, and Bob Dylan, included his ostensible theme song, "Changes" (#66, 1972, rereleased 1974, #41).

Bowie started changing his image in late 1971. He told *Melody Maker* he was gay in January 1972 and started work on a new theatrical production. Enter Ziggy Stardust, Bowie's projection of a doomed messianic rock star. Bowie became Ziggy; Ronson, Woodmansey, and bassist Trevor Bolder became Ziggy's band, the Spiders From Mars. *The Rise and Fall of Ziggy Stardust and the Spiders From Mars* (#75, 1972) and the rerelease of *Man of Words* as *Space Oddity* (#16, 1972) made Bowie the star he was portraying. The live show, with Bowie wearing futuristic costumes, makeup, and bright orange hair (at a time when the rock-star uniform was jeans), was a sensation in London and New York. It took *Aladdin Sane* (#17, 1973) to break Bowie in the U.S. Bolan and other British glitter-rock performers barely made the Atlantic crossing, but Bowie emerged a star. He produced albums for Lou Reed (*Transformer* and its hit "Walk on the Wild Side") and Iggy and the Stooges *(Raw Power)* and wrote and produced Mott the Hoople's glitter anthem "All the Young Dudes."

In 1973 Bowie announced his retirement from live performing, disbanded the Spiders, and sailed to Paris to record *Pin Ups* (#23, 1973), a collection of covers of mid-'60s British rock. That same year, the 1980 Floor Show, an invitation-only concert with Bowie and guests Marianne Faithfull and the Troggs, was taped for broadcast on the TV program *The Midnight Special.* Meanwhile, Bowie worked on a musical adaptation of George Orwell's *1984* but was denied the rights by Orwell's widow. He rewrote the material as *Diamond Dogs* (#5, 1974) and returned to the stage with an extravagant American tour. Midway though the tour, Bowie entered Philadelphia's Sigma Sound Studios (then the capital of black music) and recorded the tracks that would become *Young Americans* (#9, 1975). The session had a major effect on Bowie, as his sound and show were revised. Bowie scrapped the dancers, sets, and costumes for a spare stage and baggy Oxford trousers; he cut his hair and colored it a more natural blond. His new band, led by former James Brown sideman Carlos Alomar, added soul standards (e.g., Eddie Floyd's "Knock on Wood") to his repertoire. *David Live* (#8, 1974), also recorded in Philadelphia, chronicles this incarnation.

"Fame," cowritten by Bowie, John Lennon, and Alomar, was Bowie's first American #1 single (1975). Bowie moved to L.A. and became a fixture of American pop culture. He also played the title role in Nicolas Roeg's *The Man Who Fell to Earth* (1976). *Station to Station* (#3, 1976), another album of "plastic soul" recorded with the *Young Americans* band, portrayed Bowie as the Thin White Duke (also the title of his unpublished autobiography). His highest charting album, *Station to Station* contained his second Top 10 single, "Golden Years" (#10, 1975). Bowie complained life had become predictable and left L.A. He returned to the U.K. for the

David Bowie

first time in three years before settling in Berlin, where he lived in semiseclusion, painting, studying art, and recording with Brian Eno. His work with Eno—*Low* (#11, 1977), *"Heroes"* (#35, 1977), *Lodger* (#20, 1979)—was distinguished by its appropriation of avant-garde electronic music and the "cut-up" technique made famous by author William Burroughs. Composer Philip Glass wrote a symphony incorporating music from *Low* in 1993.

Bowie revitalized Iggy Pop's career by producing *The Idiot* and *Lust for Life* (both 1977) and toured Europe and America unannounced as Pop's pianist. He narrated Eugene Ormandy and the Philadelphia Orchestra's recording of Prokofiev's *Peter and the Wolf* and spent the rest of 1977 acting with Marlene Dietrich and Kim Novak in *Just a Gigolo.* The next year, he embarked on a massive world tour. A second live album, *Stage* (#44, 1978), was recorded on the U.S. leg of the tour. Work on *Lodger* was begun in New York, continued in Switzerland, and completed in Berlin.

Bowie settled in New York to record the paranoiac *Scary Monsters* (#12, 1980), updating "Space Oddity" in "Ashes to Ashes." One of the first stars to understand the potential of video, he produced some innovative clips for songs from *Lodger* and *Scary Monsters.* After *Scary Monsters,* Bowie turned his attention away from his recording career. In 1980 he played the title role in *The Elephant Man,* appearing in Denver, in Chicago, and on Broadway. He collaborated with Queen on 1981's "Under Pressure" and provided lyrics and vocals for "Cat People (Putting Out Fire)" (#67, 1982), Giorgio Moroder's title tune for the soundtrack of Paul Schrader's remake of *Cat People*. His music was used on the soundtrack of *Christiane F* (1982) (he also appeared in the film). Also that year, Bowie starred in the BBC-TV production of Brecht's *Baal*, and as a 150-year-old vampire in the movie *The Hunger*.

In 1983 Bowie signed one of the most lucrative contracts in history and moved from RCA to EMI. *Let's Dance* (#4, 1983), his first album in three years, returned him to the top of the charts. Produced by Nile Rodgers with Stevie Ray Vaughan on guitar, the album was a slick revision of Bowie's soul-man posture. It contained three Top 20 singles—"Let's Dance" (#1, 1983), "China Girl" (#10, 1983), and "Modern Love" (#14, 1983)—which were supported with another set of innovative videos; the sold-out Serious Moonlight Tour followed. Bowie's career seemed to be revitalized.

What first seemed like a return to form actually ushered in a period of mediocrity. Without Nile Rodgers' production savvy, Bowie's material sounded increasingly forced and hollow; his attention alternated between albums and film roles. *Tonight* (#11, 1984) had only one hit, "Blue Jean" (#8, 1984). Bowie and Mick Jagger dueted on a cover of Martha and the Vandellas' "Dancing in the Street" (#7, 1985) for Live Aid. Although *Never Let Me Down* (#34, 1987), with Peter Frampton on guitar, was roundly criticized, it made the charts with "Day In, Day Out" (#21, 1987) and the title song (#27, 1987). Bowie hit the road with another stadium extravaganza, the Glass Spiders Tour; it was recorded for an ABC-TV special.

Bowie had scarcely better luck in his acting career: *Into the Night* (1985), *Absolute Beginners* (1986)—a Julien Temple musical featuring some Bowie songs—*Labyrinth* (1986), *The Linguini Incident* (1992), and *Twin Peaks—Fire Walk With Me* (1992) were neither critical nor commercial successes.

Bowie set about reissuing his earlier albums on CD. *Sound + Vision* (#97, 1989), a greatest-hits collection, revived interest in Bowie's career; the set list for the accompanying tour was partially based on fan response to special phone lines requesting favorite Bowie songs. Bowie claimed it would be the last time he performed those songs live. Later reissues, with previously unreleased bonus tracks, brought the Ziggy-era Bowie back onto the charts.

Bowie formed Tin Machine in 1989. The band included Bowie discovery Reeves Gabrels on guitar and Hunt and Tony Sales, who had worked with Bowie on Iggy Pop's *Lust for Life* album and tour in the '70s. Although Bowie claimed that the band was a democracy, Tin Machine was perceived as Bowie's next project. The group debuted with a series of club dates in New York and L.A. Tin Machine's eponymous album (#28, 1989) was a rougher, more guitar-oriented collection than any of Bowie's previous albums. A second album, *Tin Machine II* (#126, 1991), lacked the novelty of the debut and was quickly forgotten.

In 1992 Bowie married Somalian supermodel Iman. *Black Tie White Noise* (#39, 1993), which Bowie called his wedding present to his wife, received generally positive reviews but failed to excite the public. For a followup, Bowie reunited with Brian Eno to create *Outside—The Nathan Adler Diaries: A Hyper Cycle*, a concept album of sorts that did not create much in the way of sales, although Bowie did tour the States with Trent Reznor's Nine Inch Nails opening. *The Buddha in Suburbia* is the music from the British television show of the same name; Lenny Kravitz appears on guitar.

Bowie celebrated his 50th birthday in January 1997 with a sold-out gig at Madison Square Garden, where he was joined onstage by Lou Reed, the Cure's Robert Smith, Smashing Pumpkins' Billy Corgan, Frank Black, the Foo Fighters, and Sonic Youth.

In early 1997 Bowie was again on the cutting edge—this time in the financial world. In a complicated transaction that was definitely a first, something called Bowie Bonds were offered for sale. These asset-backed bonds (in this case the assets are the royalites on Bowie's songs recorded prior to 1990) allowed Bowie to collect $55 million. The sale of the bonds came on the eve of the release of *Earthling*, which incorporated the recently hip musical stylings of drum-and-bass into a basically rock sound. By the end of the year a Reznor remix of the last song on the CD, "I'm Afraid of Americans," was receiving video and radio airplay. Into the edgy song (cowritten with Eno) Reznor inserted some keyboard and guitar textures and an urgent rap by Ice Cube. *Hours . . .* (1999) was not a particularly well-received album but was notable for expanding Bowie's early and enthusiastic advocacy of the Internet. The entire album was available for download weeks before its official release and contained a song available only online.

Bow Wow Wow

Formed 1980, London, Eng.
Annabella Lwin (b. Myant Myant Aye, ca. 1966, Rangoon, Burma), voc.; Matthew Ashman (b. 1960, London; d. Nov. 21, 1995, London), gtr.; Dave Barbarossa (b. Eng.), drums; Leigh Gorman (b. Eng.), bass.
1981—*See Jungle! See Jungle! Go Join Your Gang Yeah! City All Over! Go Ape Crazy!* (RCA) 1982—*Last of the Mohicans; I Want Candy; 12 Original Recordings* (Capitol) 1983—*When the Going Gets Tough, the Tough Get Going* (RCA) (group disbands) 1997—(group re-forms: Lwin; Gorman; + Dave Calhoun, gtr.; + Eshan Khadaroo, drums).
Annabella Lwin solo: 1986—*Fever* (RCA).

After manager/entrepreneur Malcolm McLaren assembled the Sex Pistols, he followed up with Bow Wow Wow. He discovered Annabella Lwin (from a reportedly aristocratic Burmese family, she had arrived in England a refugee at the age of five) when she was 14, working in a dry cleaner's. Although she didn't sing, she had the look, and he installed her in front of Matthew Ashman, Dave Barbarossa, and Leigh Gorman, whom he had separated from Adam and the Ants. The key to the group's sound was Barbarossa's percussion, a pounding tom-tom beat derived from Burundi ritual music (and the essence of Adam's Antmusic). With Annabella's girlish squeal, Bow Wow Wow's songs (mostly written by McLaren and the instrumentalists) were a heady concoction of African rhythms, Balinese chants, surf instrumentals, and New Romantic pop melodies.

EMI released "C30, C60, C90 Go!" in fall 1980, and the song entered the U.K. Top 30 despite EMI's refusal to promote it because it allegedly advocated home taping. The group's next release was one of the first commercial recordings to be released on tape but not on vinyl. *Your Cassette Pet* was a 20-minute, eight-song cassette packaged to resemble a pack of Marlboro cigarettes and became the first tape to place on the British singles chart. Songs like "Sexy Eiffel Towers" helped to win headlines suggesting that McLaren was promoting child pornography. EMI dropped Bow Wow Wow after issuing its second single, "W.O.R.K.," in 1981.

"W.O.R.K." became a best-selling import single in the U.S., and Bow Wow Wow signed with RCA. Just before a planned U.S. tour, Annabella's mother instigated a Scotland Yard investigation of alleged exploitation of a minor for immoral purposes. A magistrate granted permission to leave England only when McLaren and RCA promised not to publish a photograph of Annabella as the nude woman of Manet's painting *Déjeuner sur l'Herbe* or to promote her as a "sex kitten." A 1982 EP, containing the minor hit "I Want Candy," produced by Joan Jett's producer/manager Kenny Laguna, used the *Déjeuner sur l'Herbe* photo on its jacket after all. Later albums moved away from the Burundi beat and toward heavy metal. Bow Wow Wow eventually booted Lwin from the group; she recorded one solo LP in the mid-'80s that went nowhere. After a hiatus from show business, she returned in summer 1994 with a single, "Car Sex." Guitarist Matthew Ashman surfaced in 1988 with the Chiefs of Relief, a band that included former Sex Pistols drummer Paul Cook. In the '90s, Ashman worked as a session player before he succumbed to complications arising from diabetes. Barbarossa found mid-'90s success with the electronic pop band Republica. In 1997 Gorman and Lwin enlisted two new recruits for a revived Bow Wow Wow, which toured the U.S. and issued a live/remix album.

The Box Tops

Formed 1967, Memphis, TN
Alex Chilton (b. Dec. 28, 1950, Memphis), voc.; Bill Cunningham (b. Jan. 23, 1950, Memphis), kybds., bass; Gary Talley (b. Aug. 17, 1947), gtr., bass; John Evans, organ; Danny Smythe, drums.
1967—*The Box Tops "The Letter"/"Neon Rainbow"* (Bell) 1968—*Cry Like a Baby* (Stateside) (– Evans; – Smythe; + Tom Boggs [b. July 16, 1947, Wynn, AK], drums; + Rick Allen [b. Jan. 28, 1946, Little Rock, AK], organ, bass) *Super Hits; Non-Stop* 1969—*Dimensions* 1970—*1970* (Ardent); *The Best of the Box Tops: Soul Deep* (Arista) (– Cunningham; + Swain Scharfer, piano; + Harold Cloud, bass) (group disbands) 1982—*Greatest Hits* (Rhino) 1998—(original group reunites) *Tear Off!* (Last Call).

The Box Tops came out of Memphis in the late '60s with a string of blue-eyed soul hits. Young Alex Chilton's raw lead vocals sparked million-selling singles "The Letter" (#1, 1967) and "Cry Like a Baby" (#2, 1968). Their success was partially due to producer/writer Dan Penn, who later released a solo album that was a Box Tops soundalike. As was later evidenced by Chilton's recordings with Big Star [see entry], the gravelly delivery Penn had him employ on Box Tops records was not Chilton's natural voice. (Chilton later attributed the sound to lack of sleep and too much booze.)

The band toured infrequently, and its lineup was unstable: John Evans and Danny Smythe quit the group at the height of its success to return to college and avoid the draft. After several albums for Bell and minor hits like "Sweet Cream Ladies" (#28, 1969), the Box Tops disbanded in 1970, and Chilton soon joined Big Star. Guitarist Talley has remained in music as a country and R&B sessionman in Memphis. Into the late '90s, Chilton occasionally performed with the Box Tops for oldies shows. The five original Box Tops reunited in Memphis to make *Tear Off!* (1998), an album bolstered by the Memphis Horns and a selection of vintage tunes previously unrecorded by the band, plus the obligatory remake of "The Letter."

Tommy Boyce and Bobby Hart

Formed 1964, Los Angeles, CA
Tommy Boyce (b. Sep. 29, 1939, Charlottesville, VA; d. Nov. 23, 1994, Nashville, TN); Bobby Hart (b. Feb. 18, 1939, Phoenix, AZ).
1967—*Test Patterns* (A&M) 1968—*I Wonder What She's Doing Tonite; Which One's Boyce and Which One's Hart?; It's All Happening on the Inside* 1995—*The Songs of Tommy Boyce and Bobby Hart* (Varèse Sarabande).

One of the top songwriting teams of the mid-'60s, Boyce and Hart teamed up to write "Last Train to Clarksville," "Valleri," and "(I'm Not Your) Steppin' Stone" for the Monkees and songs for Paul Revere and the Raiders. They began working together in the early '60s and their "Come a Little Bit Closer," a hit in 1964 for Jay and the Americans, led to a songwriting contract with Screen Gems. They wrote most of the material for the made-for-TV Monkees. In May 1967 they began recording as a duo and a few months later enjoyed pop success with "I Wonder What She's Doing Tonite" (#8, 1967) and "Alice Long (You're Still My Favorite Girlfriend)" (#27, 1968). They toured nightclubs through the late '60s. In 1975 they teamed up with ex-Monkees Davy Jones and Mickey Dolenz for an album and tour.

In the late '70s Boyce moved to London for a while and produced hits for British '50s revivalist bands Showaddywaddy and Darts. On November 23, 1994, Boyce shot himself at his Nashville, Tennessee, home.

Hart, with Austin Roberts, wrote the country hit "Over You" by Lane Brody (it was heard in the film *Tender Mercies* and was nominated for an Academy Award in 1983); in 1985 he cowrote New Edition's R&B hit "My Secret," and in 1988 cowrote Robbie Nevil's hit "Dominoes." The duo has to its credit more than 300 compositions and sales of more than 42 million records.

Eddie Boyd

Born Nov. 25, 1914, Coahoma County, MS; died July 13, 1994, Helsinki, Fin.
1967—*Eddie Boyd and His Blues Band* (Decca) 1968—*7936 South Rhodes* (Epic); *Eddie Boyd Live* (Storyville) 1974—*Legacy of the Blues, vol. 10* (GNP).

Guitarist/keyboardist/singer Eddie Boyd was responsible for the 1952 #1 R&B hit "Five Long Years." Half brother of Memphis Slim and first cousin of Muddy Waters, Boyd was born on a plantation in Coahoma County, Mississippi, where he worked until he ran away from home in 1928. He taught himself to play the guitar and keyboards and began touring the Mississippi bar and juke-joint circuit during the early '30s. In 1936 he moved to Memphis, where he worked in Beale Street bars.

In 1937 he formed his first group, the Dixie Rhythm Boys, with whom he toured Tennessee and Arkansas before moving to Chicago in 1941. Quickly embraced by the South Side blues circles, he worked through the mid-'40s with Memphis Slim, Sonny Boy Williamson, and his cousin Waters. He made his first recordings (with Williamson) for the Victor/Bluebird label around 1943 and recorded for several labels over the years, including Chess Records from 1952 to 1957. He gave Chess two R&B Top 10 hits—"24 Hours" and "Third Degree"—in 1953.

By the start of the '60s Boyd was recording for small independent labels, but a blues and R&B resurgence led him to Decca in 1965. From the mid-'60s on, he frequently toured Europe with rock artists like John Mayall and recorded for various European labels. He lived in London, Paris, Finland, and other foreign locations. By 1971 he had made Helsinki his permanent home. He remained active both in recording and club work (which included occasional trips back to the U.S.) until shortly before his death.

Boy George: See Culture Club

Boyz II Men

Formed 1988, Philadelphia, PA
Wanya "Squirt" Morris (b. July 29, 1974), voc.; Michael "Bass" McCary (b. Dec. 16, 1972), voc.; Shawn "Slim" Stockman (b. Sep. 26, 1973), voc.; Nathan "Alex Vanderpool" Morris (b. June 18, 1972), voc.
1991—*Cooleyhighharmony* (Motown) 1993—*Christmas Interpretations* 1994—*II* 1995—*The Remix Collection* 1997—*Evolution* 2000—*Nathan Michael Shawn Wanya* (Universal).

The teenage hip-hop/harmony quartet Boyz II Men became an overnight sensation in 1991 upon release of its 3-million-selling debut album. With nostalgic nods to '50s, '60s, and '70s vocal groups—from Frankie Lymon and the Teenagers to the Temptations to the O'Jays—the Boyz' first hit, "Motownphilly," climbed to #3 on the pop chart (#4 R&B). The group's musical and visual style was described in ROLLING STONE as "distinctive, nonthreatening, and video friendly."

The group met and began singing its sugary sweet harmonies together at the High School for the Creative and Performing Arts in Philadelphia. In 1989 they gained an important fan in Michael Bivins (of New Edition and Bell Biv DeVoe), who helped them land a record deal. The quartet's massive success in turn helped breathe new life into Motown Records, which had fared poorly through the '80s.

Cooleyhighharmony is divided into a dance side and a ballads side. Followup singles from the album included "It's So Hard to Say Goodbye to Yesterday" (#2 pop, #1 R&B, 1991) and "Uhh Ahh" (#16 pop, #1 R&B, 1991). In 1992 the group toured with Hammer. The group returned in 1994 with the 7-million-selling smash *II* (#1 pop and R&B, 1994) and became the third act in the rock era to succeed itself on the singles chart at #1 (after Elvis Presley and the Beatles), with the hits "I'll Make Love to You" and "On Bended Knee."

By 1997 the group's members founded the Stonecreek Recordings label. That year the label released the debut by Uncle Sam, which included songwriting and backing vocals by Boyz II Men. The group also released its next album of new material, *Evolution* (#1 pop and R&B, 1997), which spawned two hit singles, "4 Seasons of Loneliness" (#1 pop, #2 R&B, 1997) and "A Song for Mama" (#7 pop, #1 R&B, 1997). A Spanish-language version of the album was also released. Boyz II Men enjoyed a hit single with 1999's "I Will Get There" (#32 pop, #23 R&B), from the soundtrack to the children's animated feature *The Prince of Egypt*.

The group left Motown for Universal, and in 2000 returned with *Nathan Michael Shawn Wanya*, but one of the biggest-selling R&B acts of the '90s found itself on a new musical landscape populated by the likes of 'N Sync and the Backstreet Boys—male vocal groups trading in the same multipart harmonies and weepy ballads the Boyz once rode to the top of the charts.

Billy Bragg

Born Steven William Bragg, Dec. 20, 1957, Barking, Essex, Eng.
1986—*Talking With the Taxman About Poetry* (Elektra) 1987—*Back to Basics* 1988—*Help Save the Youth of America; Workers Playtime* 1990—*The Internationale* EP 1991—*Don't Try This at Home* 1996—*William Bloke* 1998—*Mermaid Avenue* (with Wilco) 1999—*Reaching to the Converted* (Rhino) 2000—*Mermaid Avenue, vol. 2* (with Wilco) (WEA/Elektra).

Billy Bragg is a true working-class hero: an irrepressible socialist troubadour whose anthems of love and politics have transcended the usual ghettoizations of folk and punk troublemakers. The singer, songwriter, and guitarist got his inimitable Cockney accent growing up in an industrial suburb of London. He left school at 16 and became a punk rocker, forming his first band, Riff Raff, with childhood friend Wiggy in

1977. They released a few singles and one EP before disbanding in 1981. Discouraged, Bragg joined the army, but bought his way out after three months.

He began playing solo gigs around England before signing with a tiny British indie. Bragg's debut, *Life's a Riot With Spy vs. Spy,* went to #30 on the U.K. charts in 1984. (His first three British records were compiled for U.S. release on *Back to Basics.*) It featured "A New England," whose chorus of "I don't want to change the world . . . I'm just looking for another girl" introduced Bragg's continuing effort to balance a political call-to-arms with the search for loving arms. (In 1985 Kirsty MacColl made "A New England" a #7 U.K. hit.) Bragg has called Thatcherism in general and the British miners' strike in particular the catalyst for his political conversion; he played several benefits for miners in 1984–85.

With *Brewing Up With Billy Bragg,* the "Big-Nosed Bard of Barking" began to reach college-radio audiences in the U.S. and garner international press. *Talking With the Taxman About Poetry,* featuring such classic tunes as "Levi Stubbs' Tears," solidified his standing as a moving and witty songwriter. In 1986 Bragg helped found Red Wedge, a collective of musicians that toured the U.K. to promote the British Labour Party. He has also toured extensively in the U.S., as well as the Soviet bloc and Latin America, supporting the causes of such political groups as ACT UP, Committee in Solidarity with the People of El Salvador, and Democratic Socialists of America. Live, Bragg is both an endearing entertainer and an effective speechmaker.

In 1988 Bragg had a #1 U.K. hit with a cover of the Beatles' "She's Leaving Home," a duet he recorded with Cara Tivey for a benefit album (although it was probably airplay of "With a Little Help From My Friends" by Wet Wet Wet, the other side of the single, that propelled sales). In 1989 he reactivated the label Utility to nurture new acts and released *The Internationale,* a seven-track disc whose liberation songs showed that the singer didn't consider leftist politics buried beneath the Berlin Wall's rubble. Bragg also began pursuing more commercial musical directions, releasing a dance track ("Won't Talk About It") with Beats International on the 1990 album *Let Them Eat Bingo,* and recording *Don't Try This at Home* with a band, full production, and such guests as Kirsty MacColl, R.E.M.'s Peter Buck, and ex-Smiths guitarist Johnny Marr. The track "Sexuality," a dance hit in England, was a celebration of active and diverse lovemaking in the age of AIDS.

Bragg became a father in 1993, at which point he cut back on touring and recording, although he did write music for several films, including *Mad Love.* He also emerged as a social and political commentator in the popular British press, airing his leftist views on BBC Radio and in the music magazine *New Musical Express.* In 1996 Bragg returned to the studio and released *William Bloke,* an uncharacteristically humorless album dominated by brooding ballads.

Meanwhile, Woody Guthrie's daughter Nora asked Bragg to set some of her father's unrecorded lyrics to music, for which the Englishman enlisted the help of American roots rockers Wilco [see entry]. Wry, sexy, and above all fun, the critically acclaimed album that resulted, *Mermaid Avenue,* breathed new life into Guthrie's legacy and helped introduce his music to a new generation of listeners. The album—its title is a reference to the Coney Island street on which Guthrie lived when he wrote the lyrics—also featured cameos from singer Natalie Merchant and blues guitarist Corey Harris. (A second volume of tracks was released in 2000.)

In 1999 Bragg assembled *Reaching to the Converted,* a collection of odds and ends, all of them previously unavailable in the U.S. The album included Bragg's smash version of "She's Leaving Home," plus covers of "Walk Away Renee," the McGarrigle sisters' "Heart Like a Wheel," and the Smiths' "Jeane."

Brand Nubian/Grand Puba

Formed 1990, New Rochelle, NY
Lord Jamar (b. Lorenzo DeChalus, Sep. 17, 1968, Bronx, NY), voc.; Sadat X (b. Derek Murphy, Dec. 29, 1968, New York, NY), voc.; Grand Puba Maxwell (b. Maxwell Dixon, Mar. 4, 1966, Bronx), voc.; DJ Alamo, DJ.
1990—*One for All* (Elektra) (– Maxwell; – Alamo; + Sincere Allah [b. Terence Perry, June 5, 1970, New Rochelle], voc.) 1993—*In God We Trust* (– Allah) 1994—*Everything Is Everything* 1998—*Foundation.*
Grand Puba solo: 1992—*Reel to Reel* (Elektra) 1995—*2000.*
Sadat X solo: 1996—*Wild Cowboys* (Loud/RCA).

Brand Nubian arrived on the hip-hop scene of the early '90s as one of the more outspoken advocates of the Five Percent Nation, an Islamic offshoot that considers whites "devils" and maintains that only 5 percent of the black population will serve as enlightened spiritual leaders. The group's didactic lyrics mostly center on Islamic themes.

Founded by Grand Puba Maxwell, who had rapped with the nonreligious group Masters of Ceremony in the late '80s, Brand Nubian mixes supple, laid-back rhythms with the singsong delivery of Puba and Lord Jamar. When the former departed in the fall of 1991 for a solo career, taking DJ Alamo with him, Jamar took over as lead rapper.

Aside from receiving positive critical notice, *One for All* reached #34 on the R&B chart (#130 pop, 1991) and produced the minor R&B hit singles "Wake Up" (#92, 1991) and "Slow Down" (#63, 1991), which borrowed a sample from Edie Brickell and New Bohemians' "What I Am." *In God We Trust* (#12 pop, #4 R&B, 1993) fared much better and included the hit "Punks Jump Up to Get Beat Down" (#42 R&B, 1992), which reached #2 on *Billboard*'s rap singles chart. *Everything Is Everything* followed in 1994 with an increasing emphasis on the glorification of money and cars. Four years passed before Brand Nubian returned with *Foundation* and music that maintained the Nation of Islam philosophy but had grown more reflective with age. Guests on the album included Busta Rhymes and Common.

Grand Puba's solo debut, *Reel to Reel* (#28 pop, #14 R&B, 1992), though stylistically similar to Brand Nubian's music, featured less of the Five Percenter doctrine. Puba's single

"360° (What Goes Around)" (#68 pop, #30 R&B, 1992) took its main sample from Gladys Knight and the Pips' "Don't Burn Down the Bridge." Puba also appeared on Sadat X's solo debut, 1996's *Wild Cowboys,* a concept album that compared the Old West with the Bronx today.

Brandy

Born Rayana Norwood, Feb. 11, 1979, McComb, MS
1994—*Brandy* (Atlantic) 1998—*Never S-a-y Never.*

Guided by parents who moved from Mississippi to California when she was four, the pop vocalist and actress known as Brandy was raised to be a show-business kid (as was her younger brother Willie Norwood Jr., who performs as the singer Ray-J). Schooled in a church youth choir directed by her father, Brandy got her first professional break at age 12, when she joined the R&B group Immature as a backup singer. Two years later, she signed a recording contract with Atlantic, which released her debut, *Brandy* (#20 pop, #6 R&B, 1994). The album sold more than 4 million copies, yielding the hit singles "I Wanna Be Down" (#6 pop, #1 R&B, 1994) and "Baby" (#4 pop, #1 R&B, 1995) that dressed up Brandy's wholesome adolescent diva image—reminiscent of a younger Whitney Houston—in smooth, pop-soul production that gave her gospel-inspired vibrato room to roar. Two Grammy nominations followed, as did another hit, "Sittin' Up in My Room" (#12 pop, #2 R&B, 1995), from the film soundtrack *Waiting to Exhale.* "Missing You," featuring Brandy along with Tamia, Gladys Knight, and Chaka Khan (#25 pop, #10 R&B, 1996), from the film *Set It Off,* was also a hit.

Brandy's spirited homegirl-next-door persona translated quickly to TV, where the sitcom *Moesha* was developed for her, debuted in 1996, and became the first hit for the fledgling UPN (United Paramount Network). The show revolved around the experiences of Brandy as a smart, responsible teenage girl growing up in a middle-class home in South Central L.A. Brandy also won the lead in ABC's version of *Rodgers and Hammerstein's Cinderella* in 1997. The following year *Never S-a-y Never* (#2 pop, #2 R&B, 1998) was released, featuring six songs that she had cowritten. These included the huge hit "The Boy Is Mine" (#1 pop, #1 R&B, 1998), a duet with Monica [see entry], which earned the duo a Grammy for Best Rhythm & Blues Performance by a Duo or Group with Vocal. The song's video implied there was a rivalry between the two, but Brandy and Monica denied this. Later that year, Brandy made her big-screen debut in the teen slasher sequel *I Still Know What You Did Last Summer,* in which she added some mild spice to her image: She exposed her navel, uttered a swear word, and had her first Hollywood make-out scene.

Laura Branigan

Born July 3, 1957, Brewster, NY
1982—*Branigan* (Atlantic) 1983—*Branigan 2* 1984—*Self Control* 1985—*Hold Me* 1987—*Touch* 1990—*Laura Branigan* 1993—*Over My Heart* 1995—*The Best of Branigan.*

In 1982 Laura Branigan's "Gloria" peaked at #2 on the pop chart and began a run of hits that, for a few years, made Branigan's plaintive alto a radio staple. After singing in her choir, performing in high school musical productions, and recording an album with a hippie rock band called Meadow, Branigan attended the American Academy of Dramatic Arts in Manhattan, then found work touring Europe as a backup singer in Leonard Cohen's band. Eventually, she came to the attention of Sid Bernstein, who had promoted the Beatles' first U.S. appearance and managed the Rascals and the Bay City Rollers. Bernstein helped Branigan land an audition with Atlantic Records chairman Ahmet Ertegun, who signed the singer to his label.

Branigan, her solo debut, featured "Gloria," originally an Italian song, which had been rewritten with English lyrics. The following year, *Branigan 2* solidified her success with two more hit singles: "Solitaire" (#7, 1983) and the Michael Bolton–copenned "How Am I Supposed to Live Without You" (#12, 1983). In 1984 the title track to a third album, Self Control, gave Branigan her last Top 10 song to date (#4). In the mid- to late '80s, Branigan focused on acting, landing starring roles in two minor films. On her 1993 album, *Over My Heart,* Branigan sang some of the songs' lyrics in Spanish and in a South African dialect. Her 1995 greatest-hits package featured a cover of Donna Summer's "Dim All the Lights."

Brave Combo

Formed 1979, Denton, TX
Lyle Atkinson, bass, tuba; Dave Cameron, drums; Carl Finch (b. Nov. 29, 1951, Texarkana, AK), gtr., kybds., accordion; Tim Walsh, sax, clarinet, flute.
1981—*Music for Squares* (Four Dots) 1982—*Originals* cassette; *Urban Grown-ups* 1983—(– Cameron; – Walsh; + Mitch Marine, drums; + Jeffrey Barnes [b. July 27, 1951, Fremont, OH], horns) *World Dance Music* 1985—(– Atkinson, + Bubba Hernandez [b. Cenobio Xavier Hernandez, Nov. 28, 1958, San Antonio, TX], bass) 1987—*Polkatharsis* (Rounder); *Musical Varieties* 1988—*Humansville* 1990—*A Night on Earth* 1991—*Eejhanaika* 1992—(– Marine; + Phil Hernandez [b. Feb. 5, 1971, Buffalo, NY], drums; + Joe Cripps [b. Jan. 5, 1965, Little Rock, AK], perc.); *It's Christmastime, Man* 1993—(+ Danny O'Brien [b. July 12, 1966, Lakenheath, Eng.], trumpet) *No, No, No, Cha Cha Cha* 1995—*Polkas for a Gloomy World* 1996—*Mood Swing Music; Kiss of Fire* (with Lauren Asnelli) (Watermelon) 1997—(+ Alan Emert, drums) *Group Dance Epidemic* (Rounder) 1998—*Polka Party With Brave Combo: Live & Wild!* (Easydisc) 1999—*Polkasonic* (Cleveland International) 2000—*The Process* (Rounder).

The brainchild of University of North Texas art student and accordionist Carl Finch, Brave Combo was formed with a singular purpose: to destroy people's misconceptions about what's cool to like in music. A potent mixture of polka and other genres—conjunto, salsa, merengue, cha cha, ska, zydeco, and rumba, among others—played with superior musicianship, Brave Combo's witty, adventurous albums have made them critical and cult heroes, influencing bands such as 3 Mustaphas 3 and Camper Van Beethoven.

Originally releasing albums on its own Four Dots label, the band forged an alliance with Rounder Records in 1986 to widen its audience. After an initial tour of mental institutions, Brave Combo had its music heard on the National Public Radio shows *Prairie Home Companion* and *Fresh Air,* in the movie *True Stories* (directed by David Byrne), at the Macy's Thanksgiving Day Parade, and at festivals around the world. Finch has also produced the recordings of other artists, ranging from conjunto legend Santiago Jiménez to singer/songwriter Sara Hickman, and backed up cult artist Tiny Tim on his final album, *Girl,* in 1996. *Kiss of Fire* was a special collaboration between Lauren Agnelli (ex–Washington Squares) and Brave Combo, under suggestion of Carl Finch, to re-create "the feeling of an old Parisian cabaret show." In 1999 *Polkasonic* won a Grammy for Best Polka Album.

Toni Braxton

Born Oct. 7, 1968, Severn, MD
1993—*Toni Braxton* (LaFace) 1996—*Secrets* 2000—*The Heat.*

One of a new generation of R&B stars to emerge in the '90s, and a flagship artist for the Atlanta-based LaFace Records production team of Kenneth "Babyface" Edmonds and Antonio "L.A." Reid, vocalist Toni Braxton rocketed to success with her self-titled #1 pop and R&B 1993 debut. It sold more than 8 million copies, scored a half-dozen hit singles—"Another Sad Love Song" (#7 pop, #2 R&B, 1993), "Breathe Again" (#3 pop, #4 R&B, 1993), "Seven Whole Days" (#1 R&B, 1993), "You Mean the World to Me" (#7 pop, #3 R&B, 1994), "I Belong to You" (#28 pop, #6 R&B, 1994), and "How Many Ways" (#35 pop, #11 R&B, 1994)—and won the artist three Grammy Awards, including one for Best New Artist.

The daughter of a Maryland Pentecostal minister, Braxton studied piano and joined her siblings in church choirs. Once she reached high school, Braxton convinced her strict parents to let her sing in a band, which they later forced her to quit. In the late '80s, she formed a singing group with her sisters. As the Braxtons, they recorded a 1990 single for Arista that was little heard but did catch the ears of Edmonds and Reid, who were taken with Toni Braxton's smoky alto and gave her a contract in 1991. (Her sisters, who would later record an album as the Braxtons, toured with Braxton as backup vocalists.) Braxton's second album, *Secrets* (#2 pop, #1 R&B), was released in 1996, producing a #1 Grammy-winning single, "You're Making Me High." Other hits followed: "Unbreak My Heart" (#1 pop and R&B, 1996) and "I Love Me Some Him" b/w "I Don't Want To" (#19 pop, #9 R&B, 1997). The album sold nearly as well as her debut, eventually pushing total sales of both recordings to more than 16 million copies combined. Despite this and a major tour with smooth jazz saxophonist Kenny G., Braxton filed for bankruptcy in 1998, reporting a $3.9 million debt. That September, she started a four-month stint as Belle in Disney's Broadway musical *Beauty and the Beast.* Her relationship with pro football player Curtis Martin ended, but she found new romance with Keri Lewis of the R&B group Mint Condition. In 2000 Braxton released *The Heat* (#2 pop, #1 R&B), which sold 2 million copies and was driven by the single "He Wasn't Man Enough" (#2 pop, #1 R&B, 2000), which won a Grammy for Best Female R&B Vocal Performance. Other singles from the album were "Just Be a Man About It" (#32 pop, #6 R&B, 2000) and "Spanish Guitar" (#75 R&B, 2000).

Bread

Formed 1969, Los Angeles, CA
David Gates (b. Dec. 11, 1940, Tulsa, OK), voc., gtr., kybds.; James Griffin (b. Memphis, TN), voc., gtr.; Robb Royer, kybds.
1969—*Bread* (Elektra) (+ Mike Botts [b. Sacramento, CA], drums) 1970—*On the Waters* 1971—*Manna* (– Royer; + Larry Knechtel [b. Bell, CA], kybds.) 1972—*Baby I'm-a Want You; Guitar Man* 1973—*The Best of Bread* 1974—*The Best of Bread, vol. 2* 1977—*Lost Without Your Love* 1996—*Retrospective* (Rhino).
David Gates solo: 1973—*First* (Elektra) 1975—*Never Let Her Go* 1979—*Goodbye Girl* 1994—*Love Is Always Seventeen* (Discovery).
Black Tie (James Griffin): 1986—*When the Night Falls* (Bench).
The Remingtons (James Griffin): 1991—*Blue Frontier* (BNA) 1993—*Aim for the Heart.*

Bread's mellow pop rock was an early-'70s model for the "adult contemporary" sound. Led by guitarist and songwriter David Gates, the nucleus of Bread was made up of studio players who had been working as Pleasure Faire before they made their first album for Elektra in 1969. Their second album gained them the first of several gold singles, "Make It With You," a #1 hit in the summer of 1970. Buoyed by its success, they permanently added drummer Mike Botts (studio musician Jim Gordon had handled percussion on their first album) to play live concerts. Hits like "It Don't Matter to Me" (#10, 1970), "If" (#4, 1971), "Baby, I'm-a Want You" (#3, 1971), "Everything I Own" (#5, 1972), and "Guitar Man" (#11, 1972) continued until the group broke up in 1973. After three years together Bread had earned six gold albums. Thereafter, Gates had hit singles with "Never Let Her Go" (#29, 1975) and "Goodbye Girl" (#15, 1978). Bread re-formed in late 1976 to release its seventh gold album and a single, "Lost Without Your Love" (#9, 1977), and disbanded once again.

Gates and Griffin's legal battle over the rights to the Bread name dragged on from the late '70s to 1984, during which time a judge prohibited the group from recording, performing, or collecting royalties until the case was resolved. In 1994 Gates released his first album in more than 13 years. He remains active in music, usually working out of his home studio and performing his own and Bread songs at solo shows.

Gates, Griffin, Botts, and Knechtel re-formed Bread in 1997 for a 25th-anniversary tour.

Griffin teamed up with Billy Swan and ex-Eagles Randy Meisner in Black Tie, then founded the Remingtons, who released two country albums in the early '90s. Knechtel retired from music but returned to recording (including a 1979 New Age album, *Mountain Moods*) and touring (with Elvis Costello). Botts has written commercial jingles and children's music.

The Breeders: See Pixies

Edie Brickell and New Bohemians

Formed 1985, Dallas, TX
Edie Brickell (b. Mar. 10, 1966, Oak Cliff, TX), voc., gtr.; Kenny Withrow (b. Apr. 13, 1965), gtr.; Brad Houser (b. Sep. 7, 1960), bass; Wes Burt-Martin (b. May 28, 1964), gtr.; Matt Chamberlain (b. Apr. 17, 1967, San Pedro, CA), drums; John Bush, perc.
1988—*Shooting Rubberbands at the Stars* (Geffen) 1990—*Ghost of a Dog*.
Edie Brickell solo: 1994—*Picture Perfect Morning* (Geffen).

Edie Brickell and New Bohemians' relaxed, improvisational blend of rock, jazz, folk, and reggae suited its bohemian image. The band's 1988 debut single, "What I Am," was a #7 pop hit. Frontwoman Brickell made a reluctant star, shy and a bit awkward, especially onstage; but her endearingly offbeat soprano, with its subtle jazz inflections, charmed critics and fans alike, as did the trippy ingenuity of her lyrics, which drew on subjects ranging from the tragic Andy Warhol protégée Edie Sedgwick to the need for simplicity in expression addressed by "What I Am."

Brickell joined New Bohemians in 1985, after catching the band's gig in a Dallas bar. An art student at the city's Southern Methodist University, Brickell had dabbled in songwriting but was intimidated by the prospect of singing live. That night, though, a shot of Jack Daniel's gave her the courage to join the band onstage for an improvised jam. A couple of weeks later, Brickell and local guitarist Kenny Withrow were enlisted as full-time band members.

The group quickly developed a strong following and was signed to Geffen Records in late 1986. Recording sessions were plagued by delays and tensions between the band and producer Pat Moran. *Shooting Rubberbands at the Stars* was finally released in fall of 1988. Supported by the success of "What I Am" and the second single, "Circle" (#48, 1989), the album reached #4 and was named one of the best albums of the year by ROLLING STONE. A second effort, *Ghost of a Dog*, peaked at #32 and yielded no major hit singles, but a romantic relationship with Paul Simon kept Brickell's name in the press. Brickell married Simon in May 1992 and gave birth to their son in December; their daughter was born in 1995. The band had dissolved, and Brickell went solo, writing and performing acoustic guitar on all the songs for *Picture Perfect Morning* (1994), which was produced by her husband and Roy Halee and featured such guests as Dr. John, Barry White, and Art and Cyril Neville. Since then, she has chosen a quiet family life over the spotlight. New Bohemians drummer Matt Chamberlain carved out a successful niche for himself as a session player; he has recorded with such artists as Tori Amos, Fiona Apple, Melissa Etheridge, Peter Gabriel, Macy Gray, and Chris Isaak.

Brinsley Schwarz

Formed 1970, England
Brinsley Schwarz, gtr., voc., sax; Nick Lowe (b. Mar. 25, 1949, Woodbridge, Eng.), bass, voc., gtr.; Billy Rankin, drums; Bob Andrews (b. June 20, 1949), kybds., bass, voc.
1970—*Brinsley Schwarz* (Capitol); *Despite It All* (Liberty, U.K.) (+ Ian Gomm [b. Mar. 17, 1947, London, Eng.], gtr.) 1972—*Silver Pistol* (U.A., U.K.); *Nervous on the Road* 1973—*Please Don't Ever Change* 1974—*New Favourites; Original Golden Greats* 1978—*15 Thoughts of Brinsley Schwarz*
1979–*Brinsley Schwarz* (Capitol).

Brinsley Schwarz was not successful outside the early-'70s English pub circuit, but the later successes of its members have given the group semilegendary status.

Overzealous promotion almost nipped the band in the bud when a planeload of U.K. journalists was flown to the States to witness its Fillmore East debut and returned with tales of overpromotion that hounded the band until its death. Brinsley Schwarz's good-time aura and country-flavored rock—a back-to-basics attitude in the wake of psychedelia—attracted ardent followers in England, but major success eluded it. The group's last album, *New Favourites,* was produced in 1974 by Dave Edmunds. After its release, Nick Lowe [see entry] teamed up with Edmunds to form Rockpile, but not before he and Ian Gomm cowrote "Cruel to Be Kind," which eventually became Lowe's biggest U.S. hit (#12, 1979). Gomm himself scored an American hit in 1979 with "Hold On" (#18). Bob Andrews and Brinsley Schwarz earned subsequent kudos in the Rumour, primarily backing Graham Parker and later Garland Jeffreys. In 1979 Capitol released a Brinsley Schwarz double-album compilation.

David Bromberg

Born Sep. 19, 1945, Philadelphia, PA
1972—*David Bromberg* (Columbia); *Demon in Disguise* 1974—*Wanted Dead or Alive* 1975—*Midnight on the Water* 1976—*How Late'll Ya Play 'Til?* (Fantasy) 1977—*Best: Out of the Blues* (Columbia); *Reckless Abandon* (Fantasy) 1978—*Bandit in a Bathing Suit; My Own House* 1980—*You Should See the Rest of the Band* 1989—*Sideman Serenade* (Rounder).

As a virtuoso on guitar, mandolin, fiddle, and other stringed instruments, David Bromberg was a folk-rock mainstay through the '70s. He grew up in Tarrytown, New York, and studied at Columbia University before becoming part of the mid-'60s Greenwich Village folk scene. He began playing sessions regularly in the late '60s and has since appeared on more than 90 albums, including ones by Bob Dylan, Ringo Starr, Tom Paxton, Chubby Checker, Sha Na Na, Carly Simon, and Phoebe Snow. Bromberg's eclecticism embraces blues, jazz, rock, bluegrass, country, and old-timey traditional music. He began releasing solo albums in 1972. By 1976 he had formed the David Bromberg Band, which toured extensively worldwide. In 1978 and 1979 he toured with fellow Fantasy Records artist Ralph McTell. But in mid-1980, following the accidental death of a band member, Bromberg retired from performing in order to spend more time with his family and began studying the craft of violin making in Chicago. He continues to play the occasional gig and has also become a leading collector and international dealer of violins.

The Brooklyn Bridge

Formed 1968, Long Island, NY
Johnny Maestro (b. John Mastrangelo, May 7, 1939, Brooklyn, NY), voc.; Fred Ferrara (b. 1945), voc.; Mike Gregorio (b. 1947), voc.; Les Cauchi (b. 1945), voc.; Tom Sullivan (b. 1946), musical director; Carolyn Woods (b. 1947), organ; Jim Rosica (b. 1947), bass; Jim Macioce (b. 1947), gtr.; Artie Cantanzarita (b. 1949), drums; Shelly Davis (b. 1950), trumpet, kybds.; Joe Ruvio (b. 1947), sax.
1969—*Brooklyn Bridge* (Buddah); *The Second Brooklyn Bridge.*

The Del-Satins, a longstanding vocal quartet with which Johnny Maestro (formerly of the Crests) sang, and the Rhythm Method, a seven-piece band led by Tom Sullivan, joined forces to become the Brooklyn Bridge after they met as rivals in a Long Island talent contest in 1968. They had their first hit with a Jim Webb song originally recorded by the 5th Dimension, "Worst That Could Happen" (#3, 1969). "Blessed Is the Rain," "Your Husband—My Wife," and "Welcome Me Love" (all 1969) grazed the Top 40. The group charted its last single in 1970 but continued to record. By 1975, when they signed with Private Stock, the group had been trimmed to a quintet with Maestro still leading. They continued playing throughout the New York–New Jersey metropolitan area and appearing at nostalgia shows. In the '90s Maestro and Ferrara (an ex–Del Satin) continued to live on Long Island and play with revised lineups of the Brooklyn Bridge.

Garth Brooks

Born Troyal Garth Brooks, Feb. 7, 1962, Tulsa, OK
1989—*Garth Brooks* (Capitol) 1990—*No Fences* 1991—*Ropin' the Wind* 1992—*Beyond the Season* (Liberty); *The Chase* (Capitol) 1993—*In Pieces* 1994—*The Hits* 1995—*Fresh Horses* 1997—*Sevens* 1998—*Double Live; The Limited Series* 1999—*Garth Brooks in . . . the Life of Chris Gaines; Garth Brooks & the Magic of Christmas.*

The most stunning success story of the early-'90s contemporary country music boom was that of Garth Brooks. Blending rock and country influences, he is a singer/songwriter whose style owes as much to the influence of James Taylor as it does to George Jones. In performance, Brooks' high-energy stage show reflects his admiration for theatrical rock bands such as Queen and Kiss. Having sold more than 100 million albums since 1989, Brooks has easily outdistanced his competition, becoming the top-selling solo artist in history. By 1992, Brooks was a household name, and he represented a new breed of straight-talking country music heroes, defending homosexuals in song ("We Shall Be Free" from 1992's *The Chase*) and talking to Barbara Walters on national television about his past marital infidelity.

Brooks' mother had been a singer before marrying his father, a working-class draftsman. Both parents had children by former spouses; Brooks was the younger of two they had together. Brooks learned to play guitar and sing with his mother and joined a band during high school. His primary interest was sports, though, and he attended Oklahoma State University on a track scholarship. Only after graduating did Brooks devote himself to music. He briefly moved to Nashville in 1985 but found little luck there. After moving back to Oklahoma, marrying, and saving some money, Brooks decided to give Nashville another try. His persistence paid off when a Capitol Records talent scout spotted the singer in a club and signed him.

Released in 1989, Brooks' self-titled debut album peaked at #2 on the country albums chart and spawned four Top 10 country singles: "Much Too Young (To Feel This Damn Old)" (#8 C&W, 1989), "If Tomorrow Never Comes" (#1 C&W, 1989), "Not Counting You" (#2 C&W, 1990), and "The Dance" (#1 C&W, 1990). *No Fences* outdid its predecessor, reaching #1 on the country chart and #3 on pop and generating four #1 country hits: "Friends in Low Places" (1990), "Unanswered Prayers" (1990), "Two of a Kind, Workin' on a Full House" (1991), and "The Thunder Rolls" (1991). The video for the last single got flak from Country Music Television and the Nashville Network for its graphic depiction of domestic violence, a subject Brooks addressed in the song. But VH1 supported Brooks, thus heightening his crossover appeal to pop audiences, and *No Fences* became the biggest-selling country album of all time.

Brooks' winning streak continued with 1991's *Ropin' the Wind,* the first album in history to enter both Billboard's pop and country albums charts at #1. This time, there were three chart-topping country singles—a cover of Billy Joel's "Shameless" (1991) and 1992's "What's She Doing Now" and "The River"—as well as "Rodeo" (#3 C&W, 1991) and "Papa Loved Mama" (#3 C&W, 1992). Later in 1992 a Christmas album, *Beyond the Season,* shot to #2 on the pop and country albums charts. Before the year was out, the singer topped both those charts again with *The Chase,* which yielded "We Shall Be Free" (#12 C&W, 1992), "Somewhere Other Than the Night" (#1 C&W, 1992), "Learning to Live Again" (#2 C&W, 1993), and "That Summer" (#1 C&W, 1993).

Brooks' *In Pieces* surprised no one by debuting at #1 on the pop and country charts, and produced two 1993 #1 country singles: "Ain't Going Down (Till the Sun Comes Up)" and "American Honky-Tonk Bar Association." *The Hits* peaked at #1 on both pop and country charts in 1994. Hit singles of 1994 included "Standing Outside the Fire" (#3 C&W) and "One Night a Day" (#7 C&W). With such a massive sales record, the same success was expected of 1995's *Fresh Horses,* which included the #1 country singles "She's Every Woman" and "The Beaches of Cheyenne," as well as "It's Midnight Cinderella" (#5), "The Change" (#19), and a cover of Aerosmith's "The Fever" (#23). *Fresh Horses* was no slouch at #2 on the pop albums chart with 4 million copies sold, but the fact that it didn't quite hit the top slot and sold millions less than its predecessors made the driven Brooks consider the disc a disappointment. Although he'd said in interviews that he'd quit the music business when his fans stopped buying his albums, this setback wasn't nearly enough to push him into retirement. Still, when he was named Favorite Artist of the Year at the 1996 American Music Awards, he declined the honor, saying he didn't feel he deserved it.

In 1997 Brooks returned with a new album, *Sevens* (#1 pop and country), and a strong marketing campaign. Preceded by a free concert for 250,000 people in New York's Central Park in August 1997, which was broadcast live on HBO, the original release of *Sevens* was a limited-edition run of 777,777 copies offered as collectibles. The ploy worked, the special-edition copies sold out in a week, and the disc was well on its way to outselling *Fresh Horses. Sevens* contained its share of country hits: the #2 songs "In Another's Eyes," a duet with Trisha Yearwood, and "She's Gonna Make It," plus the #1 tracks "Longneck Bottle" and "Two Piña Coladas." The following year, Brooks' label continued its savvy marketing efforts, first broadcasting a live-via-satellite concert to Wal-Marts nationwide to promote his live album, then releasing a box set, *The Limited Series,* containing his first six studio albums, each with a previously unreleased track, then discontinuing the manufacture of those six individual discs. The label's plan was for each title to be reissued, with higher-quality sound, on the 10th anniversary of its original release; meanwhile, the only available option was the higher-priced compilation.

Satisfied that his career was back on track, Brooks moved on to an elaborate multimedia project that entailed the creation of an alter ego. Taking on the persona of Chris Gaines, a fictional Australian alternative-rock star with a goatee, Brooks recorded an album with producer Don Was that posed as Gaines' greatest hits and encompassed styles from new wave to R&B. The concept album, as well as two TV specials, served as an introduction to a supposed future film, *The Lamb,* in which Brooks would star as Gaines. A daring idea (albeit subject to ridicule by critics), the Chris Gaines album peaked at #2 on the pop chart, selling 1.1 million copies (though country fans shunned it).

The Brothers Johnson

Formed 1976, Los Angeles, CA
George Johnson (b. May 17, 1953, Los Angeles), gtr., voc.; Louis Johnson (b. Apr. 13, 1955, Los Angeles), bass, voc.
1976—*Look Out for #1* (A&M) 1977—*Right on Time* 1978—*Blam!* 1980—*Light Up the Night* 1981—*Winners* 1982—*Blast! (The Latest and the Greatest)* 1984—*Out of Control* 1988—*Kick It to the Curb.*
Louis Johnson solo: 1981—*Passage* (A&M).

George and Louis Johnson began playing music together when they were seven and eight years old, respectively. They put together their first group, the Johnson Three + 1, with older brother Tommy on drums and cousin Alex Weir (later a member of the Brothers Johnson Band) on rhythm guitar. They worked their way up from school dances to opening L.A. shows for such acts as the Dells, David Ruffin, and Bill Medley, among others. Bobby Womack produced their first single, "Testify." George had just graduated from high school when Billy Preston invited him to join his band, the God Squad, as lead guitarist. When Preston's bass player abruptly left in the middle of a tour, George persuaded Preston to hire Louis. In their two years with Preston, the Johnsons contributed several songs to his albums, including his 1974 hit single "Struttin' " (#22 pop, #11 R&B).

The brothers left Preston in 1975 and spent almost a year writing songs, rehearsing, and recording demo tapes. That same year Quincy Jones hired the Johnsons for a tour of Japan. He later recorded four Johnson compositions on his *Mellow Madness* (#16, 1975) and, having signed the duo to an A&M recording contract of their own, produced their first four albums. *Look Out for #1* sold over a million copies, with two hit singles, "I'll Be Good to You" (#3 pop, #1 R&B, 1976) and "Get the Funk Out Ma Face" (#30 pop, #4 R&B, 1976). *Right on Time* went gold three days after its release and platinum three months later. "Strawberry Letter 23" (a Shuggie Otis song) was a hit single (#5 pop, #1 R&B, 1977) and "Q," the Brothers' tribute to Jones, was awarded the 1977 Grammy for Best Instrumental. With the eight-piece Brothers Johnson Band, George and Louis toured the U.S., Europe, and Japan in 1977.

A departure from the nonstop dance format of their first two albums, *Blam!* contained the Johnsons' first ballad and "Ride-O-Rocket," a song written for them by Ashford and Simpson. The U.S. tour in support of that album took them to 80 cities. After a year's vacation, they returned to the charts in 1980 with *Light Up the Night* (#5 pop, #1 R&B) and its hit single "Stomp!" (#7 pop, #1 R&B). Their first self-produced album, 1981's *Winners,* was their first LP to sell fewer than a million copies, but it did deliver a #11 R&B single, "The Real Thing." Their last R&B Top 20 hits were "Welcome to the Club" (1982) and "You Keep Me Coming Back" (1984).

In 1989 the Brothers Johnson appealed to A&M principals Jerry Moss and Herb Alpert to release them from their contract, which they did. In 1997 "Strawberry Letter 23" was resurrected by director Quentin Tarantino, who featured the tune in his high-profile film *Jackie Brown.* As of 2000 George Johnson was touring under the Brothers Johnson name—though his retired brother Louis was nowhere to be seen.

Arthur Brown

Born June 24, 1942, Whitby, Eng.
1968—*The Crazy World of Arthur Brown* (Atlantic) 1972—*Galactic Zoo Dossier* (Polydor) 1973—*Kingdom Come* (Track, U.K.); *The Journey* (Polydor) 1975—*Dance With Arthur Brown* (Gull).

The eccentric Arthur Brown had one U.S. hit, "Fire" (#2, 1968). A trailblazer of theatrical rock, he capped his performances by igniting what appeared to be his hair (actually a metal helmet) and so became the rage in London during the summer of 1967. Pete Townshend gave him a record deal with the Who's Track label, but Brown proved unable to repeat his initial success. By 1969 his band, the Crazy World of Arthur Brown (which included drummer Carl Palmer, later of Emerson, Lake and Palmer and Asia, and keyboardist Vincent Crane of Atomic Rooster), had broken up.

Brown subsequently attempted several comebacks. From 1970 to 1974 he fronted Kingdom Come, an electronic rock band (and one of the first to employ a drum machine). After departing that group he toured the Middle East and upon returning to England studied meditation. He played a small role in the Who's *Tommy* movie in 1975. The Who connection continues to this day: In 1989 Pete Townshend convened the Who to cut "Fire" for his solo LP *The Iron Man.*

Brown moved to Austin, Texas, in 1980 and toured occasionally with a group he called the Even Crazier World of Arthur Brown. He's recorded a number of albums for small labels, including *Brown, Black, and Blues* (Blue Wave Records), with former Mothers of Invention drummer Jimmy Carl Black, then Brown's partner in a housepainting company.

Bobby Brown

Born Robert Baresford Brown, Feb. 5, 1969, Boston, MA
1986—*King of Stage* (MCA) 1988—*Don't Be Cruel* 1989—*Dance! . . . Ya Know It!* 1992—*Bobby* 1993—*Remixes in the Key of B* 1997—*Forever* 2000—*Greatest Hits.*

After leaving the popular kiddie-funk vocal group New Edition in 1986, Bobby Brown found even greater success as a solo artist. The singer's bad-boy charisma and sexually charged dance moves thrilled female fans, and the hook-ridden songs and buoyant New Jack Swing arrangements on his albums suited his breezily confident delivery to a tee.

Brown's first solo album, 1986's *King of Stage,* produced the #1 R&B hit "Girlfriend," but his pop crossover came with 1988's *Don't Be Cruel.* Brown enlisted the fledgling writer/producers who would soon emerge as giants in the hip-hop and R&B communities: Antonio "L.A." Reid and Kenneth "Babyface" Edmonds helped craft most of the album's material, and Teddy Riley collaborated with Brown on the singer's first #1 pop single, "My Prerogative" (1988). The album also topped the pop chart, and Brown enjoyed five more Top 10 pop hits in 1988 and 1989: "Don't Be Cruel" (#8 pop, #1 R&B, 1988), "Roni" (#3 pop, 1989), "Every Little Step" (#3 pop, #1 R&B, 1989), "On Our Own" (#2 pop, #12 R&B, 1989), and "Rock Wit'cha" (#7 pop, #3 R&B, 1989). A remix album, *Dance! . . . Ya Know It!,* reached #9 on the pop chart and #7 on R&B. In 1990 Brown had another #1 pop single, a duet with Glenn Medeiros called "She Ain't Worth It."

Meanwhile, rumors of drug abuse were tainting Brown's good fortune. When he married pop superstar Whitney Houston in 1992, cynics assumed that both singers were trying to alleviate image problems. (It had been rumored that Houston was a lesbian.) Houston appeared on Brown's 1992 album, *Bobby,* on the duet "Something in Common." *Bobby* became a #2 pop album and topped the R&B chart; it also spawned the hits "Humpin' Around" (#3 pop, #1 R&B, 1992) and "Good Enough" (#7 pop, #5 R&B, 1992). In 1993 Houston and Brown—who had fathered three children with a previous girlfriend—welcomed a daughter, Bobbi.

After participating in a 1996 New Edition reunion tour and its accompanying '96 album, *Home Again,* Brown released *Forever* (#61 pop, #15 R&B) in 1997. But it was for his numerous run-ins with the law that Brown remained in the public eye: He was arrested in 1995 for allegedly assaulting a tourist at a Disney World nightclub (the charges were later dropped); the following year he received two years probation for kicking a security guard at a West Hollywood hotel. In 1998 Brown spent five days in jail on a drunk-driving charge. Two years later, he returned to the slammer for 75 days, this time for violating his probation from the drunk-driving conviction.

Charles Brown

Born Sep. 13, 1922, Texas City, TX; died Jan. 21, 1999, Oakland, CA
1952—*Mood Music* (Aladdin) 1961—*Sings Christmas Songs* (King) 1962—*Million Sellers* (Imperial) 1963—*The Boss of the Blues* (Mainstream) 1964—*Great Charles Brown Will Grip Your Heart* (King) 1965—*Ballads My Way* (Mainstream) 1971—*Blues n' Brown* (Jewel) 1975—*Charles Brown* (Bulldog) 1979—*Sunny Land* (Route 66) 1986—*One More for the Road* (Blueside) 1990—*All My Life* (Bullseye Blues) 1992—*Driftin' Blues: The Best of Charles Brown* (EMI); *Someone to Love* (Bullseye Blues) 1993—*Song for Christmas/Driftin' Blues* 1994—*Just a Lucky So and So; Cool Christmas Blues* (Rounder) 1995—*Walkin' in Circles* (Night Train); *These Blues* (Verve) 1996—*Honeydripper* 1998—*So Goes Love* 1999—*In a Grand Style.*

A highly influential singer of the prerock era, Charles Brown was a master of "ballad blues," the smooth, jazz-inflected vocal music whose better-known exponent was Nat "King" Cole. Prompted by his uncle and grandmother to study the raw blues of Big Maceo and Leroy Carr and the sophisticated style of Art Tatum, Brown learned to play the piano as a child. He graduated with a degree in chemistry, and his first job was teaching high school chemistry; he also worked in a chemical factory.

His musical career began with a move to L.A. in 1943, when he filled the pianist's spot in Johnny Moore's Three

Blazers. He first recorded in 1945 when, after winning a talent contest for playing Rachmaninoff, he was given studio time by Philo Records. His "Driftin' Blues," released as a single by Three Blazers, introduced his sound—so smoky and elegant that it became known as "cocktail blues," despite its bleak undercurrents. Its vocals also revealed Brown's influences—Robert Johnson, Louis Jordan, and Frank Sinatra among them.

In 1948 Brown went solo and throughout the early '50s penned wistful R&B hits: "Trouble Blues" (#1, 1949), "Black Night" (#1, 1951), "Seven Long Days" (#2, 1951), "Hard Times" (#7, 1952). He recorded his classic "Merry Christmas Baby" (covered in the '60s by Otis Redding and Elvis Presley, and in the '80s by Bruce Springsteen) in 1947, and in 1960 he released "Please Come Home for Christmas," which entered the Christmas charts for 10 consecutive seasons and was later recorded by the Eagles. These holiday songs are perhaps his best known. In 1962 Sam Cooke refashioned Brown's "I Want to Go Home" into "Bring It On Home to Me," one of Cooke's biggest hits. While Brown continued to perform in small venues, he also supported himself by working as a janitor. He enjoyed a career renaissance through the '90s that began when he toured with Bonnie Raitt in 1990. He remains best known as a songwriter whose compositions have been recorded by B.B. King, Fats Domino, and Bruce Springsteen, and as a stylist on whom the early Ray Charles, among numerous others, patterned his singing technique. Brown died of congestive heart failure in 1999; singer and minister Solomon Burke presided at the funeral.

Clarence "Gatemouth" Brown

Born Apr. 18, 1924, Vinton, LA
1974—*Clarence "Gatemouth" Brown Sings Louis Jordan* (Black and Blue) 1975—*Gate's on the Heat* (Barclay); *Down South in Bayou Country* 1976—*Bogalusa Boogie Man* 1978—*Blackjack* (Music Is Medicine) 1979—*San Antonio Ballbuster* (Charly) 1982—*Alright Again!* (Rounder) 1983—*One More Mile; The Original Peacock Recordings* 1986—*Real Life; Pressure Cooker* (Alligator) 1989—*Standing My Ground* 1991—*No Looking Back* 1993—*Just Got Lucky* (Evidence) 1995—*The Man* (Verve) 1996—*Long Way Home* 1997—*Gate Swings* 1999—*American Music, Texas Style* (Blue Thumb).

Although blues singer/guitarist Clarence "Gatemouth" Brown has had only one chart single during his career, his mix of blues and country marks him as a Texas original. Born in Louisiana, he grew up in Orange, Texas. His father was a musician who taught him to play the guitar when he was five; by age 10 he could play the fiddle and mandolin as well, and in ensuing years he picked up the drums, bass, and harmonica. Nicknamed by a teacher for his big voice, "Gatemouth" Brown began singing at an early age.

In the early '40s he was a drummer for the Brown Skin Models. After serving in the Army Corps of Engineers, he returned to show business after World War II, working in big bands in San Antonio. He made his solo debut in 1945 when he sat in for an ill T-Bone Walker. That show introduced him to club owner Don Robey, who signed him to a management contract that bound him for the next 20 years. Robey sent Brown to L.A. in 1947 to record for Aladdin Records. In 1949 Brown was the first to record for Robey's own company, Peacock Records; that same year he cut "Mary Is Fine," his only hit. Either under his own name or as D. Malone, Robey took songwriter's credit on many of Brown's compositions; Brown's bitter "You Got Money" was written about Robey. Between 1947 and 1960 Brown recorded more than 50 sides for Peacock, including "Pale Dry Boogie" and "Okie Dokie Stomp."

He spent most of the '50s leading two bands, a 23-piece black orchestra and a smaller group of white musicians. This arrangement allowed him to play both all-black clubs and white establishments. His style combined elements of country, jazz, blues, and Cajun music, and has influenced guitarists as diverse as Albert Collins, Frank Zappa, Roy Buchanan, and Guitar Slim.

Brown broke free of Robey sometime between 1959 and 1964. He continued touring and recording (for several labels, including Chess) and worked for a while as a deputy sheriff in New Mexico. By 1971 he was performing again and building a following in Europe, especially in France, where he enjoyed great popularity and recorded for French companies such as Black and Blue, Barclay, and Blue Star. He appeared at numerous jazz festivals throughout the years. His half brother, James "Widemouth" Brown, was also a singer and died in 1971.

After a U.S. State Department–sponsored tour of East Africa, Brown settled in New Orleans and recorded his first domestically released album, *Blackjack*. In 1979 he recorded *Makin' Music* with country star Roy Clark. *Alright Again!* won a Best Blues Grammy in 1982. Brown continued touring extensively and, in 1988, again sponsored by the State Department, played Honduras and Nicaragua.

As of 2000, Brown has been nominated for seven Grammys. He has also received various W.C. Handy Awards and a Pioneer Award from the Rhythm & Blues Foundation. He was inducted into the Blues Foundation Hall of Fame in 1999. His recent work explores the union of roots music and big band sounds.

Dennis Brown

Born Feb. 1, 1957, Kingston, Jam.; died July 1, 1999, Kingston
1972—*Super Reggae and Soul Hits* (Trojan) 1975—*Just Dennis* 1978—*Visions of Dennis Brown* (Lightning); *Westbound Train* (Third World) 1979—*Words of Wisdom* (Laser); *Live at Montreux; Wolf and Leopards* 1980—*Spellbound* 1981—*Foul Play* (A&M) 1982—*Love Has Found a Way* 1989—*Visions* (Shanachie); *Words of Wisdom* 1990—*Slow Down* 1991—*Over Proof; Victory Is Mine* (RAS) 1992—*Blazing* (Shanachie); *Friends for Life* 1993—*Cosmic Force* (Heartbeat) 1994—*Light My Fire* 1995—*Temperature Rising* (VP); *Nothing*

Like This (RAS) 1996—*Milk and Honey; Could It Be* (VP) 1999—*Tribulation* (Heartbeat); *Stone Cold World* (VP); *Bless Me Jah* (RAS) 2000—*May Your Food Basket Never Empty; Let Me Be the One* (VP).
With Gregory Isaacs: 1984—*Judge Not* (Shanachie) 1989—*No Contest* (Music Works) 1994—*Blood Brothers* (RAS).

The most prominent exponent of the romantic style of reggae known as "lovers rock," singer Dennis Brown began his career in Jamaican and other West Indian tourist clubs when he was nine. In his teen years, he became a protégé of Jamaican bandleader and producer Bryon Lee, and by the mid-'60s he was recording regularly for such producers as Coxsone Dodd, Derrick Harriot, and Joe Gibbs. He had a string of Jamaican hits in the late '60s and '70s—including "No Man Is an Island" (1968), "Silhouettes" (1968), "Baby Don't Do It" (1971), "Look of Love" (1971), "Things in Life" (1972), and "Money in My Pocket" (1972)—mostly conventional pop love songs set to reggae rhythms. In 1979 he rerecorded "Money in My Pocket" for issue in the U.K.; it reached #14 on the British charts and launched Brown's international popularity. That year he toured Europe, and in 1980 he signed with A&M, his first major label. He toured North America, poised to reach the pop market with such numbers as "Foul Play" and "If I Ruled the World," both of which were given some airplay on black stations. This period also yielded two modest pop chart hits in the U.K., "Love Has Found Its Way" (#47, 1982) and "Halfway Up Halfway Down" (#56, 1982).

In 1983 Brown tried to expand his American following by recording with KC and the Sunshine Band but ended up alienating the fans he had. His collaborations with Gregory Isaacs, however, reestablished his credibility. He remained popular in Jamaica, working with producers King Jammy and Gussie Clark. In America, Brown signed with the world music specialist Shanachie in 1987 and appeared on the Reggae Sunsplash Tour in 1991. Brown succumbed to respiratory ailments in 1999; a memorial celebration featuring numerous reggae luminaries was held on the one-year anniversary of his death. Brown's posthumously released *Let Me Be the One* (2000) was nominated for a Grammy, as was 1995's *Light My Fire*.

Foxy Brown

Born Inga Fung Marchand, Sep. 6, 1979, Brooklyn, NY
1996—*Ill Na Na* (Violator/Def Jam) 1999—*Chyna Doll* (Def Jam) 2001—*Broken Silence*.
With the Firm (Nas Escobar, AZ, and Nature): 1997—*The Album* (Aftermath/Interscope).

Taking her stage name and a strong dose of attitude from a tough, streetwise heroine played by Pam Grier in a '70s "blaxploitation" film, Foxy Brown began attracting notice as a guest rapper on hip-hop hits before she was 17. She performed on tracks by Jay-Z, Nas, Toni Braxton, and L.L. Cool J, whose producers invited her to rap over "I Shot Ya" after she won a 1994 talent show in her native Brooklyn. Brown's accomplishments as a guest artist prompted a major-label bidding war, and in 1996 her debut album, *Ill Na Na* (#7 pop, #2 R&B), was released with the hits "Get Me Home" (#42 pop, #10 R&B, 1996) and "I'll Be" (#7 pop, #5 R&B, 1997). The album flaunted Brown's provocative sexuality, a sometimes controversial stance she shared with another ribald, luxury-obsessed female MC, estranged friend Lil' Kim. The next year, Brown joined fellow rap artists Nas, AZ, and Nature in the hip-hop supergroup the Firm, which released *The Album* (#1 pop, #1 R&B, 1997). She was also featured as part of the R&B/hip-hop Smokin' Grooves summer package tour. In 1999 Brown's second album, *Chyna Doll* (#1 pop, #1 R&B), was released, boasting blunt, autobiographical lyrics on such tracks as "I Can't" (#61 R&B, 1997). *Broken Silence* addressed the difficulties Brown had faced following her stardom in the '90s.

James Brown

Born May 3, 1928 or 1933, Barnwell, SC
1959—*Try Me; Please, Please, Please* (King) 1960—*Think* 1961—*The Amazing James Brown* 1962—*Shout and Shimmy; James Brown and His Famous Flames Tour the U.S.A.* 1963—*Live at the Apollo; Prisoner of Love* 1964—*Pure Dynamite!; Showtime* (Smash); *Out of Sight; Grits and Soul* 1965—*Papa's Got a Brand New Bag* (King); *James Brown Plays James Brown; Today and Yesterday* (Smash) 1966—*I Got You (I Feel Good)* (King); *James Brown Plays New Breed* (Smash); *It's a Man's Man's Man's World* (King); *Handful of Soul* (Smash); *Mighty Instrumentals* (King) 1967—*The James Brown Show* (Smash); *James Brown Sings Raw Soul* (King); *Live at the Garden; Plays the Real Thing* (Smash); *Cold Sweat* (King) 1968—*I Can't Stand Myself (When You Touch Me); Live at the Apollo, vol. 2; I Got the Feelin'* (Polydor); *James Brown Plays Nothing but Soul* (King); *James Brown Sings Out of Sight* (Polydor); *James Brown Presents His Show of Tomorrow* (King) 1969—*Say It Loud, I'm Black and I'm Proud; Getting' Down to It; It's a Mother; The Popcorn; Excitement* 1970—*Ain't It Funky; Soul on Top; It's a New Day So Let a Man Come In* (Polydor); *Sex Machine; Hey America* (King) 1971—*Sho Is Funky Down Here; Hot Pants* (Polydor); *Revolution of the Mind—Live at the Apollo, vol. 3; Super Bad* (King) 1972—*There It Is* (Polydor); *Get on the Good Foot* 1973—*Black Caesar; Slaughter's Big Rip-Off* 1974—*Hell; The Payback* 1975—*Reality; Sex Machine Today; Everybody's Doin' the Hustle and Dead on the Double Bump* 1976—*Get Up Offa That Thing; Bodyheat; Hot* 1977—*Mutha's Nature* 1978—*Jam/1980's; Take a Look at Those Cakes; Fabulous James Brown* (HRB) 1979—*The Original Disco Man* (Polydor); *Mister Dynamite; This Is* (Philips) 1980—*People* (Polydor); *Hot on the One* 1981—*Nonstop!; The Third Coming; Live in New York* (Audio Fidelity); *Special* (Polydor) 1982—*Mean on the Scene* (Audio Fidelity) 1983—*Bring It On!* (Augusta Sound) 1985—*Live in Concert* (Sugar Hill); *Dead on the Heavy Funk* (Polydor) 1986—*Gravity* (Scotti Bros.); *In the Jungle Groove* (Polydor) 1988—*I'm Real* (with Full Force) (Scotti Bros.) 1989—*Roots of a Revolution* (Polydor) 1990—*Messing With the Blues* 1991—*Star Time; Love Over-Due* (Scotti Bros.) 1992—*Love Power Peace* (Polydor); *Spank* (PolyGram); *Universal James* (RCA) 1993—*Soul Pride: The Instrumentals*

(1960–1969) (PolyGram) 1995—*Live* (Summit); *Living in America* (Scotti Bros.); *Live at the Apollo 1995* 1996—*JB40* (Chronicles); *Foundations of Funk: A Brand New Bag: 1964–1969; Funk Power: A Brand New Thang* 1998—*I'm Back* (PGD/PolyGram) 1999—*On Stage* (Charly); *Live at Chastain Park.*

"Soul Brother Number One," James Brown was perhaps the best known and clearly the most successful black artist of the '60s and early '70s; his polyrhythmic funk vamps virtually reshaped dance music. With some 800 songs in his repertoire, the astonishingly prolific Brown has influenced a wide range of contemporary artists from every genre—rock, soul, jazz, R&B, and hip-hop. And his adamant refusal to conform to anyone's vision other than his own bolstered his icon status.

Brown was born into poverty in the rural South around the time of the Depression (some records give his birth date as 1928; he claims it is 1933). As a child, he picked cotton, shined shoes, danced for pennies in the streets of Augusta, Georgia, and stole. Convicted of armed robbery at age 16, he spent three years in a juvenile detention institution. While incarcerated, Brown made the acquaintance of Bobby Byrd, who performed with his family gospel group at the institution. Byrd's family eventually helped obtain Brown's release by taking the youngster in and getting him a job. Brown tried semiprofessional sports, first as a boxer, then as a baseball pitcher, but a leg injury ruined his chances of going pro. In the meantime, Byrd and Brown had put together a gospel group, which performed under a succession of different names at the Mount Zion Baptist Church, in Toccoa, Georgia, and at auditoriums in the area. Byrd and Brown sang duets, with three or four other members singing background vocals and harmonies. After seeing a rock & roll show featuring Hank Ballard and the Midnighters, Fats Domino, and others, Brown and Byrd left gospel music behind, transforming the group (Johnny Terry, Sylvester Keels, and Floyd Scott) into the Flames. Each Flame sang, danced, and played an instrument or two—Brown's were piano and drums. Byrd also played keyboards and shared vocals; he would remain Brown's sideman off and on during the next three-plus decades.

From a base in Macon, Georgia, the Flames had been touring the South for two years when Ralph Bass, head of Federal Records, signed them in 1956. Their first single, "Please, Please, Please," a big hit in Georgia and adjacent states, eventually sold a million copies. Subsequent releases in the same gospel-influenced yet distinctly rougher R&B style made Brown a regional star until "Try Me" became a national hit in 1958, charting #1 in R&B, #48 in pop.

By this time, Brown had become the de facto leader of the group, now called the Famous Flames. Guided by Universal Attractions director Ben Bart, Brown created the James Brown Revue, complete with opening acts, his own emcee, and a stage band—the James Brown Band. The show was precisely choreographed, with Brown pumping his hips, twisting on one foot, and doing splits as the troupe executed their own intricate steps. Night after night, he would feign collapse and be helped from the stage, only to stop, throw off the cape, and start all over again. Despite its predictability, the gimmick never lost its power to bring fans to their feet. Sweating off a purported seven pounds a night, and breaking box-office records in every major black venue in America, Brown earned the nickname "Mr. Dynamite" and the title "The Hardest Working Man in Show Business."

As Brown's band became one of the tightest in the field, Brown wanted to showcase them on his recordings. Federal, however, refused to let him use them in the studio, so he arranged for the band to record for another company as Nat Kendrick and the Swans. The resulting instrumental hit, "Mashed Potatoes," persuaded Federal's parent company, King, to take over Brown's contract and to sign up the James Brown Band both for Brown's sessions and as a separate act. From then on, Brown concentrated on pared-down, jump-and-shout dance music ("Think," "Night Train"). If a new song made the concert crowd dance, he would record it that night, often in one take.

Simultaneously, Brown was sending such raw, emotive R&B ballads as "Bewildered" (#8 R&B, #40 pop, 1961), "I Don't Mind" (#4 R&B, #47 pop, 1961), and "Lost Someone" (#2 R&B, #48 pop, 1961) up the charts. Brown's *Live at the Apollo,* recorded in Harlem in 1962 and patterned after Ray Charles' live *In Person,* sold a million copies, unprecedented for a black music album. In 1963, frustrated by King's failure to reach into the white market, Brown and Bart formed Fair Deal Productions. "Out of Sight," which Fair Deal released through Smash Records, hit #1 R&B, #24 pop.

Brown's revised contract with King in 1965 gave him complete artistic control. He revamped his band under the leadership of Nat Jones, and with his "Papa's Got a Brand New Bag," became a world-class force in popular music. Disposing of the conventional verse and chorus structure, eliminating even chord progressions, he distilled his sound to its essence: rhythm and, more specifically, "the 1." "Brand New Bag" topped the R&B chart, as did "I Got You (I Feel Good)" and "It's a Man's, Man's, Man's World." After Alfred "Pee Wee" Ellis replaced Jones as bandleader, Brown continued to score with "Cold Sweat," "I Got the Feelin'," "Say It Loud, I'm Black and I'm Proud," "Give It Up or Turn It A-Loose," and "Mother Popcorn"—which were all Top 20 (many of them Top 10) pop hits. Concurrently, he recorded instrumental albums (a total of 11 between 1961 and 1971) that never attained great commercial success but, featuring his organ and piano work, continued his rhythmic explorations (tracks from the best of these can be found on the 1993 anthology, *Soul Pride*).

The late '60s found James Brown a cultural hero, "Soul Brother Number One." As a black man of wealth, independence, and influence, he was a symbol of self-determination and triumph over racism. He took that responsibility seriously. Songs such as "Say It Loud," "Don't Be a Drop-Out," and "I Don't Want Nobody to Give Me Nothing (Open Up the Door I'll Get It Myself)" contained direct social messages. He sponsored programs for ghetto youth, spoke at high schools, invested in black businesses, performed for troops in Vietnam, and went on television after the April 4, 1968, assassination of Martin Luther King Jr. to plead for calm—a service for which he was ceremoniously thanked by Vice President

James Brown

Hubert Humphrey. In Boston, where he was scheduled to perform after rioting had broken out in several cities, city authorities feared violence. Brown's decision to televise the concert live locally was credited with helping to maintain the peace.

In late 1969 Brown faced the mutiny of his celebrated '60s band, which included saxophonist Maceo Parker and trombonist Fred Wesley. Brown enlisted hot young instrumentalists who, with his nurturing, continued to develop the sound that would be called funk. The youngbloods, who as the new band were dubbed the JBs, included brothers William "Bootsy" and Phelps "Catfish" Collins, whose distinctive bass and lead guitar playing, respectively, ushered in a new sound in soul music. The Collinses left after a year, later joining George Clinton's Parliament/Funkadelic organization [see entry]. Key '60s band members saxophonist St. Clair Pinckney and guitarist Jimmy Nolan, as well as Parker and Wesley, eventually returned, but the only consistent member was drummer John "Jabo" Starks, who originally joined in 1965.

The JBs were then led by Wesley, who with Brown began creating music that was even less formal than before; as the instrumental sections dug into funk grooves, Brown, dubbing himself "Minister of New New Super Heavy Funk," mixed sociopolitical messages and stream-of-consciousness phrasing with an undeniable beat.

Brown had been managing himself since the death of his manager in the late '60s, and in 1971 he had signed with an international record company, Polydor, and sold it his entire back catalogue. His records—"Hot Pants" (#15, 1971), "Make It Funky" (#68, 1971), "Talking Loud and Saying Nothing" (#27, 1972), "Get on the Good Foot" (#18, 1972), "The Payback" (#26, 1974), "My Thang" (#29, 1974), and "Papa Don't Take No Mess" (#31, 1974)—continued to sell by the millions. Though R&B chart-toppers, they increasingly failed to crack the pop Top 20, on which softer rock, highly polished R&B ballads, and the first hints of disco dominated.

Around 1975 Brown's popularity began to wane. Because of financial difficulties, Brown was forced to sell his three black radio stations and his jet. The Internal Revenue Service claimed he owed $4.5 million in back taxes; a manager said Brown was part of a payola scandal; Brown's son Teddy had died in a car crash in 1973; and his second marriage ended. Young record buyers favored heirs like the Ohio Players, Kool and the Gang, and the Parliafunkadelicment Thang (which now employed Wesley and Parker).

He was welcomed to Africa and Japan as a star, and at home he continued to work. When disco peaked in the late '70s, he promoted himself as "The Original Disco Man," which he was. When "It's Too Funky in Here" reached #15, it was called a "comeback." With a cameo role in the 1980 movie *The Blues Brothers,* Brown introduced his soul-church preaching to a new generation. Returning to American stages that year, he drew much of his audience from the white punk-funk faction, for whom he was the essence of polyrhythmic minimalism. In 1980 he recorded "Rapp Payback (Where Iz Moses?)," an homage to his earlier singles "Brother Rapp" and "The Payback," which prefigured the enormous influence he would come to have on the incipient rap scene. The single, a British dance hit (#39 U.K., 1981), helped activate a James Brown resurgence there. Finding himself label-less in the early '80s, Brown recorded the album *Bring It On!* for his own Augusta Sound label.

In 1984 Brown joined with rapper Afrika Bambaataa on "Unity," released on New York rap label Tommy Boy. By this time, his music had been claimed as the virtual basis for hip-hop beats; among others, Kool Moe Dee and Eric B. & Rakim scored hits by sampling Brown's rhythms, and his 1969 recording "Funky Drummer" (featuring drummer Clyde Stubblefield) began appearing in myriad versions on rap and pop records. The rappers also borrowed poses from Brown's persona—street-savvy, self-contained, defiant. With Brown inducted as a charter member into the Rock and Roll Hall of Fame in 1986, his revival was bolstered by "Living in America," the theme song to *Rocky IV.* Recorded at the request of director Sylvester Stallone, the single (#4, 1986), included on the album *Gravity* (with guest stars Alison Moyet and Steve Winwood), won a Grammy in 1987 for Best R&B Performance. In 1989 Brown (with writer Bruce Tucker) published an autobiography, *James Brown: The Godfather of Soul.*

In 1988, however, Brown's career ground to a halt. When his fourth wife, Adrienne, reported beatings, Brown was charged with assault with intent to murder and aggravated assault and battery. He surrendered to Aiken County, South Carolina, authorities near his 60-acre home in May and was released on bond. Then followed a year of bizarre legal troubles during which Adrienne, after her own arrest for alleged possession of PCP, first announced that she would file for legal separation, then relented and also withdrew the assault charges. Adrienne was arrested again for PCP possession and for arson. In September, as rumors circulated about his own PCP abuse and problems with the IRS, Brown allegedly threatened a group of people with a shotgun and then engaged in an interstate car chase with police that ended in his receiving a six-year sentence in a work-release program.

Paroled in 1991 after serving two years of his sentence—during which he was visited by the Reverend Al Sharpton, Jesse Jackson, and Republican stalwart Lee Atwater but ignored by the music industry and most of his old friends—Brown returned to work with a pay-per-view television concert and a new album. With *Star Time*, a four-CD retrospective (later chosen by ROLLING STONE as Reissue of the Year), the best of Brown's catalogue was freshly available, and the singer's stature was unassailable.

The late '90s were difficult for Brown personally. His wife died in January 1996, two days after undergoing cosmetic surgery. Two years later, the singer—then in his 60s—was arrested for possession of drugs and firearms. He continued making music, however, releasing *I'm Back* in 1998, his first studio album in four years.

Roy Brown

Born Sep. 10, 1925, New Orleans, LA; died May 25, 1981, Los Angeles, CA
N.A.—*The Blues Are All Brown* (Bluesday); *Roy Brown Sings 24 Hits* (King); *Roy Brown and Wynonie Harris* 1973—*Hard Times* (Bluesway) 1976—*Hard Luck Blues* (King) 1978—*Good Rocking Tonight* (Route 66); *Laughing but Crying* 1979—*Cheapest Price in Town* (Faith) 1982—*Good Rockin' Tonight* (Quicksilver).

Blues shouter Roy Brown had a major impact on early rock & roll. He wrote and recorded the jump-blues "Good Rocking Tonight" in 1947, and it became a #13 R&B hit the following year; Elvis Presley recorded it at one of his 1954 Sun Records sessions and also had a hit. Throughout the late '40s and '50s, Brown enjoyed over a dozen Top 10 R&B hits, including " 'Long About Midnight" (#1, 1948), "Boogie at Midnight" (#3, 1949), "Cadillac Baby" (#6, 1950), and "Hard Luck Blues" (#1, 1950).

Brown's big-band backups helped shape the New Orleans sound (Fats Domino, Allen Toussaint); his stage shows with his band, the Mighty Men, foreshadowed modern rock theatrics. B.B. King, Bobby "Blue" Bland, and others have cited Brown's singing as an influence. Brown was still playing frequent club dates when he died of a heart attack in 1981. Three years later Robert Plant and the Honeydrippers had a Top 25 hit with Brown's "Rockin' at Midnight."

Ruth Brown

Born Jan. 30, 1928, Portsmouth, VA
1959—*Late Date With Ruth Brown* (Atlantic); *Miss Rhythm Along Comes Ruth* (Philips); *Gospel Time* (Lection) 1976—*Sugar Babe* (President) 1982—*The Soul Survives* (Flair) 1988—*Have a Good Time* (Fantasy) 1989—*Blues on Broadway; Miss Rhythm (Greatest Hits and More)* (Rhino) 1993—*The Songs of My Life* (Fantasy) 1996—*Rockin' in Rhythm: The Best of Ruth Brown* (Rhino) 1997—*R+B=Ruth Brown* (Bullseye Blues) 1999—*A Good Day for the Blues.*

Known as "Miss Rhythm," Ruth Brown was, arguably, the biggest female R&B star of the '50s, briefly rivaling Dinah Washington as the era's leading black woman singer. In its early days, her label Atlantic Records was known as "the House That Ruth Built." As a teenager she sang in her church choir, then worked with jazz big bands in the '40s. She signed with the fledgling Atlantic in 1948 and recorded more than 80 songs for the label before 1962, making her its most prolific and best-selling act of that period. At first her hits were confined to the R&B charts, which she topped with "Teardrops From My Eyes" (1950), "5–10–15 Hours" (1952), "(Mama) He Treats Your Daughter Mean" (1953, recorded with a band led by Ray Charles), and "Oh What a Dream" and "Mambo Baby" (both 1954). In 1956 she began performing in disc jockey Alan Freed's rock & roll shows and attracting a white youth audience. "Lucky Lips"—written by Jerry Leiber and Mike Stoller—made #25 on the pop chart in 1957, followed the next year by "This Little Girl's Gone Rockin' " (#24 pop). Her last R&B Top 10 hit, "Don't Deceive Me," appeared in early 1960.

In 1961 Brown left Atlantic for Philips. She had a couple of minor hits on that label, then retired. In the '70s she reemerged to record for Cobblestone and President, and, later, Fantasy, where her records featured jazz and blues stylings. Brown costarred in the 1986 off-Broadway musical *Staggerlee*, and in 1989 earned a Tony Award for her role in Broadway's *Black and Blue*. She appeared in the John Waters film *Hairspray* (1988). She was inducted into the Rock and Roll Hall of Fame in 1993.

One of the many stories in her award-winning autobiography, *Miss Rhythm*, (1996), traces her long battle to recover decades-old royalties from Atlantic Records. That situation led to the establishment of the Rhythm & Blues Foundation, which is supported by recording companies and issues grants to pioneering performers.

Highlights of the 1997 album *R+B=Ruth Brown* include two duets: "I'm Gonna Move to the Outskirts of Town" with Bonnie Raitt and "False Friend Blues," a reunion with Amos Milburn who had backed Brown on her very first demo. In 1999 she won a Blues Foundation Lifetime Achievement Award. *A Good Day for the Blues* was nominated for a Grammy.

Jackson Browne

Born Oct. 9, 1948, Heidelberg, W. Ger.
1972—*Jackson Browne* (Asylum) 1973—*For Everyman* 1974—*Late for the Sky* 1976—*The Pretender* 1978—*Running on Empty* 1980—*Hold Out* 1983—*Lawyers in Love* 1986—*Lives in the Balance* 1989—*World in Motion* (Elektra) 1993—*I'm Alive* 1996—*Looking East* 1997—*The Next Voice You Hear: The Best of Jackson Browne.*

Singer/songwriter Jackson Browne's introverted, finely observed songs made him one of the most influential West

Jackson Browne

Coast songwriters. Browne's first songs infused domestic sagas with a sense of romantic doom, making lovers into heroes. In the '80s Browne focused more sharply on the sociopolitical, but in 1993 returned to more personal themes with *I'm Alive*.

Browne's family moved to Southern California when he was young, and in his late teens he played guitar with an embryonic version of the Nitty Gritty Dirt Band, which later performed his songs. He spent the winters of 1967 and 1968 in Greenwich Village, where he backed Tim Buckley and Nico; she did an early cover of Browne's "These Days." By 1969 he had begun to establish a reputation as a songwriter, and in the next few years Tom Rush, the Byrds, Bonnie Raitt, Linda Ronstadt, and others performed his songs, and he toured as an opening act for Laura Nyro and Joni Mitchell. Browne's solo debut album produced a hit with "Doctor My Eyes" (#8, 1972) and eventually went gold. He cowrote the Eagles' first hit, "Take It Easy."

With each album Browne's following grew. *Jackson Browne* (#53, 1972) went gold; *For Everyman* (#43, 1973) and *Late for the Sky* (#14, 1974) went platinum. *The Pretender* became his first Top 10 album; its sense of despair derived in part from the suicide of his first wife, Phyllis, in 1976, two and a half years after the birth of their son, Ethan. A 1977 tour produced *Running on Empty* (#3, 1978), a live concept album about touring featuring new material recorded onstage, in hotel rooms, and on the tour bus, including hits in the title track and a remake of "Stay" (#20, 1978). *Hold Out* (1980) went to #1 in its first week of release. Browne's 1983 album, *Lawyers in Love* (#8), introduced many of the sociopolitical themes he would continue to explore in *Lives in the Balance* (#23, 1986) and *World in Motion* (#45, 1989). Though *Lawyers*, boosted by the Top 20 title track, hit #8, it did not go platinum.

In 1993 Browne returned to matters of the heart with *I'm Alive* (#40), on which he worked with long-time collaborator and coproducer Scott Thurston (Don Was also produced two tracks). The album generated unusually careful media scrutiny, coming as it did after Browne's highly publicized breakup with actress Daryl Hannah. Browne took a three-year leave from the studio before coming back with *Looking East* (#36, 1996), on which he blended his political voice with his more introspective outlook. The album failed to generate much interest, though, and the following year Browne commemorated his quarter-century of recording with the release of a best-of collection.

Browne continues to tour internationally and has been active in numerous organizations devoted to social change, including MUSE (Musicians United for Safe Energy), Amnesty International, and the Christic Institute. He has produced albums for Warren Zevon, his former guitarist David Lindley, Native American poet John Trudell, and high school friend Greg Copeland, as well as Nicaraguan group Guardabarranco. He has collaborated with fellow West Coast songwriters, including J.D. Souther, Lowell George, Valerie Carter, and the Eagles.

Brownsville Station

Formed 1969, Ann Arbor, MI
Cub Koda (b. Michael Koda, Oct. 1, 1948, Detroit, MI; d. July 1, 2000, Detroit), gtr., voc.; Michael Lutz, gtr., voc.; T.J. Cronley, drums; Tony Driggins, bass.
1970—*No B.S.* (Warner Bros.) 1972—(– Cronley; + Henry Weck, drums) *A Night on the Town* (Big Tree) 1973—(– Driggins; Lutz switches to bass) *Yeah* 1974—*School Punks* 1975—(+ Bruce Nazarian, gtr., bass, voc.) *Motor City Connection* 1977—*Brownsville Station* (Private Stock) 1979—*Air Special* (Epic) 1993—*Smokin' in the Boys' Room: The Best of Brownsville Station* (Rhino).
Cub Koda solo: 1993—*Welcome to My Job—The Cub Koda Collection, 1963–1993* (Blue Wave) 1994—*Abba Dabba Dabba—A Bananza of Hits* (Schoolkids') 1997—*Box Lunch* (J-Bird) 2000—*Noise Monkeys*.

Brownsville Station was formed by Michael Lutz and Cub Koda through a chance meeting at a local music store. The band spent most of its 10 years together earning a reputation as an energetic live rock act on the arena circuit. Its 1973 hit single "Smokin' in the Boys' Room" reached #3 in January 1974. Like much of their material, "Smokin' " was written by Koda. After the group disbanded in June 1979, Koda began a solo career; distancing himself from Brownsville's big rock sound, his albums mixed lo-fi rockabilly, blues, and R&B. In addition, Koda became a respected music journalist, writing liner notes for more than 60 CD collections, contributing to *Goldmine*, and coauthoring the book *Blues for Dummies*. Koda died in 2000 of complications from kidney failure.

Koda's former band mates are still involved in music. Lutz teaches and writes music, and played with Ted Nugent in the '80s and '90s. Henry Weck co-owns a recording studio. In

1985 Mötley Crüe made its commercial breakthrough with a Top 20 cover of "Smokin' in the Boys' Room."

Jack Bruce

Born John Symon Asher Bruce, May 14, 1943, Glasgow, Scot.
1969—*Songs for a Tailor* (Atco) 1970—*Things We Like* 1971—*Harmony Row* 1972—*Jack Bruce at His Best* (Polydor) 1974—*Out of the Storm* (RSO) 1977—*How's Tricks* 1980—*I've Always Wanted to Do This* (Epic) 1982—*Truce* (Chrysalis) 1989—*Willpower* (Polydor); *A Question of Time* (Epic) 1993—*Somethin Els* (CMP) 1994—*Cities of the Heart* 1995—*Monkjack* 1996—*The Jack Bruce Collector's Edition* 2001—*Shadows in the Air* (Sanctuary).
With BBM (Bruce, bass, cello, voc.; Ginger Baker [b. Peter Baker, Aug. 19, 1939, Lewisham, Eng.], drums, perc.; Gary Moore [b. Apr. 4, 1952, Belfast, Ire.], gtr., voc.): 1994—*Around the Next Dream* (Virgin).

The punchy bass riffs and urgent tenor vocals Jack Bruce lent to Cream were widely imitated by the heavy-metal bands that followed. Although Bruce's virtuosity and arty inclinations led him to make jazzy, complex music after he left Cream, he has returned periodically to hard rock.

At age 17 he won a scholarship to the Royal Scottish Academy of Music for cello and composition but dropped out after three months to play jazz in Glasgow. He moved to London in his late teens and played with British R&B pioneers Alexis Korner and Graham Bond. In 1965 he left the Graham Bond Organisation, whose drummer was Ginger Baker, for John Mayall's Bluesbreakers, a band that included guitarist Eric Clapton. After a brief stint in Manfred Mann, Bruce joined Clapton and Baker in forming Cream in 1966 [see entries]. The three virtually invented a hard-rock trio style—complete with extended improvisations in which Bruce's bass chased Clapton's guitar—before breaking up in 1968. Most of Cream's hit singles were written by Bruce and lyricist Pete Brown.

After Cream's breakup Bruce divided his efforts between fusion, hard rock, and an ambitious, eccentric folk-rock–classical hybrid style of songwriting he tried on *Songs for a Tailor, Harmony Row,* and *Out of the Storm.* Among the songs on those albums, "Theme for an Imaginary Western" became a hit for Mountain. Bruce's first post-Cream group, Jack Bruce and Friends, included jazz guitarist Larry Coryell and Jimi Hendrix Experience drummer Mitch Mitchell. In 1970 and 1971 Bruce was a member of the Tony Williams Lifetime [see entry], the pioneering fusion band that also included guitarist John McLaughlin. Bruce's *Things We Like* was a jam session with McLaughlin, Dick Heckstall-Smith, and other British progressive jazzmen; Bruce also appeared (as vocalist) with McLaughlin on Carla Bley's 1972 *Escalator Over the Hill,* and in 1979 he toured with McLaughlin and Mahavishnu Orchestra alumni Billy Cobham and Stu Goldberg.

On the hard-rock side, Bruce put together a power trio with Mountain's Leslie West and Corky Laing, which released albums in 1972, 1973, and 1974 [see Mountain entry]. He appeared on Frank Zappa's *Apostrophe (')* in 1974, and in 1975 he fronted the Jack Bruce Band, with keyboardist Bley and former Rolling Stones guitarist Mick Taylor, on a tour of Europe; they did not record. The 1980 version of Jack Bruce and Friends included drummer Cobham, ex–Humble Pie guitarist Clem Clempson, and erstwhile Bruce Springsteen pianist David Sancious. In 1981 Bruce joined another power trio, B.L.T., led by Robin Trower; and in 1982 Bruce and Trower collaborated on *Truce.* Bruce kept a low profile through the rest of the '80s, reportedly battling drug and alcohol problems.

Following a European tour with a 13-piece Latin–jazz-rock orchestra, Bruce recorded *A Question of Time,* which mirrored his growing interest in world music and reunited him with Cream drummer Ginger Baker. *Somethin Els* (with lyrics by Peter Brown) featured Eric Clapton, Dick Heckstall-Smith, and Clem Clempson, while *Cities of the Heart,* recorded live at a 1993 show, featured Baker, Clempson, and former P-Funk/Talking Heads keyboardist Bernie Worrell. In 1994 Bruce and Gary Moore (who was a replacement guitarist on a Bruce tour) recorded *Around the Next Dream* with Baker, and then Bruce put down his bass to team up with Worrell on 1995's *Monkjack,* a collection of jazz compositions for piano and organ.

Eclectic as always, Bruce joined Peter Frampton, Procol Harum's Gary Brooker, and Bad Company's Simon Kirke for a tour as Ringo Starr's backing band, the All-Starrs, in 1997; he was an All-Starr again in 2000. His 2001 album, *Shadows in the Air,* featured guests Vernon Reid, Dr. John, and Clapton.

Bill Bruford

Born William Scott Bruford, May 17, 1949, Sevenoaks, Kent, Eng.
1978—*Feels Good to Me* (Polydor) 1997—*If Summer Had Its Ghosts* (Discipline Global Mobile).
With Bruford, formed 1979: Bruford, drums, kybds., perc.; Dave Stewart, kybds.; Alan Holdsworth, gtr.; Jeff Berlin, bass.
1979—*One of a Kind* (Polydor) (– Holdsworth; + John Clark, gtr.) 1980—*The Bruford Tapes; Gradually Going Tornado* 1986—*Master Strokes* (EG).
Earthworks, formed 1986: Bruford, drums, electronic drums, perc., kybds.; Iain Ballamy, sax, kybds.; Django Bates, kybds., trumpet, E-flat tenor horn; Mick Hutton, bass.
1987—*Earthworks* (EG) (– Hutton; + Tim Harries, bass) 1989—*Dig?* 1991—*All Heaven Broke Loose* 1994—*Stamping Ground Live* 1997—*Heavenly Bodies* (Virgin U.K./Venture).
Bruford Levin Upper Extremities, formed 1998, Woodstock, NY: Bruford, drums, perc.; Tony Levin, bass, Chapman Stick; David Torn, gtr.; Chris Botti, trumpet.
1998—*Upper Extremities* (Papa Bear) 2000—*B.L.U.E. Nights.*
Earthworks: 1999—(group re-forms: Bruford, drums; Patrick Clahar, sax; Steve Hamilton, piano; Mark Hodgson, bass) 1999—*A Part, and Yet Apart* (DGM) 2001—*The Sound of Surprise.*

After distinguishing himself with Yes, King Crimson, and Genesis, Bill Bruford became a jazz-rock bandleader and made fusion music with the same crisp angularity and tasteful smarts that marked his drumming. Bruford supported his more adventurous work by returning periodically to the big-rock arena, with U.K. in 1979, a re-formed Crimson in 1981, fellow ex–Yes-men Jon Anderson, Rick Wakeman, and Steve Howe in 1989, and a full Yes reunion in 1991 [see entries].

After Crimson disbanded in 1974 Bruford took sundry odd jobs: on the obscure 1975 all-star album *Flash Fearless vs. the Zorg Women* (with Alice Cooper, the Who's John Entwistle, and Jim Dandy Mangrum of Black Oak Arkansas, among others); on 1975 albums by Yes' Chris Squire *(Fish Out of Water)* and Steve Howe *(Beginnings)* and British folk rocker Roy Harper *(HQ)*; and on 1976 albums by American progressive rockers Pavlov's Dog *(At the Sound of the Bell)* and space rockers Absolute Elsewhere *(In Search of Ancient Gods)*. In 1976 Bruford toured with Genesis—at the request of drummer Phil Collins, who was replacing departed frontman/vocalist Peter Gabriel—then formed the British jazz-rock band National Health with ex-Hatfield and the North keyboardist Dave Stewart. In 1977 Bruford recruited Stewart, ex–Soft Machine/Tony Williams Lifetime/Gong guitarist Allan Holdsworth (a major influence on Eddie Van Halen), and Americans Jeff Berlin (bass) and Annette Peacock (vocals), to record *Feels Good to Me*. Rather than play drum solos, Bruford, who wrote all the songs, played the serpentine melodies on vibes.

After guesting on Peacock's 1978 album *X-Dreams*, Bruford formed U.K., with ex-Crimson band mate John Wetton on bass and vocals, ex–Roxy Music/Frank Zappa keyboardist/violinist Eddie Jobson, and Holdsworth. Bruford left after one album and tour to form his eponymous jazz-rock band, dissolving it only when Robert Fripp re-formed King Crimson in 1981. In that band Bruford played electronic drum pads, made by English inventor Dave Simmons, which were fed with sampled or synthesized sounds. When Crimson disbanded again, the Simmons drums keyed the approach of Earthworks, in which Bruford tapped out repeated keyboardlike melodies and chordal harmonies to back the boppish lines of Iain Ballamy and Django Bates (two rising stars of the British jazz scene who were half Bruford's age). In between Crimson and Earthworks, Bruford recorded two solo albums with ex–Yes/Moody Blues keyboardist Patrick Moraz (1983's *Music for Piano and Drums*, 1985's *Flags*); in 1987 he recorded *(Clouds About Mercury)* and toured with ECM guitarist David Torn, and played drums and percussion with the New Percussion Group of Amsterdam on the album *Go Between*.

In the '90s, Bruford joined Jon Anderson and Steve Howe on 1993's *Symphonic Music of Yes*, and played on Steve Hackett's 1997 *Watcher of the Skies: Genesis Revisited*. Upper Extremities, his jazz-rock side project with Crimson bassist Tony Levin, featured the Miles Davis–inspired trumpet playing of Chris Botti (who later worked with Sting). But Bruford also traded his signature metallic rimshot for a softer wooden snare on *If Summer Had Its Ghosts* (featuring Ralph Towner of Oregon and jazz bassist Eddie Gomez), then sat out the 1999–2000 edition of King Crimson [see entry] to lead the new all-acoustic Earthworks.

Peabo Bryson

Born Apr. 13, 1951, Greenville, SC
1976—*Peabo* (Bang) 1977—*Reaching for the Sky* (Capitol) 1978—*Crosswinds* 1979—*We're the Best of Friends* (with Natalie Cole) 1980—*Paradise; Live and More* (with Roberta Flack) (Atlantic) 1981—*I Am Love* (Capitol); *Turn the Hands of Time* 1982—*Don't Play With Fire* 1983—*Born to Love* (with Roberta Flack) 1984—*Straight From the Heart* (Elektra); *The Peabo Bryson Collection* (Capitol) 1985—*Take No Prisoners* (Elektra) 1988—*Positive* 1991—*Can You Stop the Rain* (Columbia) 1994—*Peabo Bryson* 1997—*Peace on Earth* (Angel) 1999—*Unconditional Love* (Private Music/Windham Hill) 2000—*Super Hits* (Columbia).

Peabo Bryson grew up on a farm in South Carolina, sang in a church choir, and joined his first group, Al Freeman and the Upsetters, as a harmony singer at age 14. His first professional group was Mose Dillard and the Tex-Town Display, with whom he sang from 1968 to 1973, touring the U.S., the Caribbean, and Vietnam. The group recorded on the Curtom and Bang labels. Bang president Eddie Biscoe encouraged Bryson to write and sing his own material, and in 1970 he signed a solo contract with Bang and moved to Atlanta, where he worked as a staff producer before recording his solo debut album. He had his first hit as guest vocalist with Michael Zager's Moon Band, whose "Do It With Feeling" made the R&B Top 30 in 1976. On his own he placed three singles in the R&B Top 30: "Underground Music" (#22 R&B, 1976), "Just Another Day" (#27 R&B, 1977), and "I Can Make It Better" (#23 R&B, 1977).

He signed with Capitol in 1977, and his next album, *Reaching for the Sky*, included R&B hit singles in the title song (#6, 1978) and "Feel the Fire" (#13, 1978). *Crosswinds* boasted a #2 R&B single, "I'm So Into You" (1978). In 1979 Bryson toured with Natalie Cole; their studio collaborations yielded an album, *We're the Best of Friends*, and two R&B hit singles: "Gimme Some Time" (#8 R&B, 1979) and "What You Won't Do for Love" (#16 R&B, 1980). Later in 1980, after charting R&B Top 20 with Michael McDonald's "Minute by Minute," he joined Roberta Flack for a concert tour and a live album that gave the duo a hit R&B single, "Make the World Stand Still" (#13 R&B, 1980). In 1983 the pair had a bigger hit with "Tonight, I Celebrate My Love" (#16 pop, #5 R&B) from *Born to Love* (#25 pop, #8 R&B, 1983).

The next year Bryson's "If Ever You're in My Arms Again" (#10 pop, #6 R&B, 1984) became the first of a series of crossover hits, culminating in two hit duets from Disney animated films *Beauty and the Beast* ("Beauty and the Beast" with Celine Dion, #9 pop, 1992) and *Aladdin* ("A Whole New World [Aladdin's Theme]" with Regina Belle, #1 pop, #21 R&B, 1992); both earned Oscars for Best Song. Bryson's recordings have appeared on the classical (*The King and I*, with Lea Salonga) and contemporary jazz (Kenny G's *Breathless*, featuring Bryson singing "By the Time This Night Is Over") charts. But by the end of the '90s, Bryson's smooth style had lost a bit of its appeal. After a 1997 Christmas album, the singer found himself without a record label. He then signed with Private Music/Windham Hill, which released *Unconditional Love* (#75 R&B) in 1999. Despite its relative lack of commercial success, the album yielded two Grammy-nominated songs, the title track and "Did You Ever Know."

Roy Buchanan

Born Sep. 23, 1939, Ozark, AR; died Aug. 14, 1988, Fairfax, VA
1972—*Roy Buchanan* (Polydor) 1973—*Roy Buchanan Second Album* 1974—*That's What I Am Here For; In the Beginning* 1975—*Rescue Me; Live Stock* 1976—*A Street Called Straight* (Atlantic) 1977—*Loading Zone* 1978—*You're Not Alone* 1980—*My Babe* (Waterhouse) 1985—*When a Guitar Plays the Blues* (Alligator) 1986—*Dancing on the Edge* 1988—*Hot Wires* 1992—*Sweet Dreams: The Anthology* (Polydor) 1993—*Guitar on Fire: The Atlantic Sessions* (Rhino).

Blues guitarist Roy Buchanan was considered a musician's musician in the '70s for his impeccable Telecaster leads. Among his fans were Jeff Beck, Eric Clapton, and Robbie Robertson. The son of a Pentecostal preacher, Buchanan grew up in Pixley, California, and was a proficient guitarist by age nine. At 15 he ran away to L.A. and came under the tutelage of R&B great Johnny Otis. The guitarist toured and recorded with rockabilly star Dale Hawkins ("Suzy Q") for three years before joining Ronnie Hawkins. He moved to the Washington, DC, area, and in the mid-'60s did East Coast session work. In 1968 he formed the Soundmasters and worked clubs on the Eastern Seaboard regularly for the next several years.

A 1971 ROLLING STONE article inspired some interest in Buchanan, as did a PBS documentary called *The Best Unknown Guitarist in the World*. He claimed the Rolling Stones had asked him to replace Brian Jones in 1969, but he had turned them down. In 1972 Buchanan signed his first solo recording contract. He toured and released albums steadily to a cult audience throughout his life, which ended in a Virginia jail cell. An intoxicated Buchanan was arrested on the street by police responding to a phone call from his wife. When deputies went to check on him an hour later, they found the 48-year-old father of seven hanging by his own shirt.

Lindsey Buckingham: See Fleetwood Mac

The Buckinghams

Formed 1965, Chicago, IL
Carl Giammarese (b. Aug. 21, 1947, Chicago), gtr.; Dennis Tufano (b. Sep. 11, 1946, Chicago), gtr., harmonica; Nick Fortune (b. Nicholas Fortuna, May 1, 1946, Chicago), bass; Jon-Jon Poulos (b. Mar. 31, 1947, Chicago; d. Mar. 26, 1980), drums; Dennis Miccolis, kybds.
1967—*Kind of a Drag* (U.S.A.) (– Miccolis; + Marty Grebb [b. Sep. 2, 1946, Chicago], kybds.) *Time and Charges* (Columbia) 1968—*Portraits; In One Ear and Gone Tomorrow* 1969—*Greatest Hits* (– Grebb; + John Turner, kybds.) 1970—(group disbands) 1980—(group re-forms: Tufano; Giammarese; Fortuna; + John Cammelot, kybds.; + Tom Scheckel [b. Nov. 19, 1954, Chicago], drums) 1985—(– Tufano) *A Matter of Time* (Red) 1991—*Mercy, Mercy, Mercy: A Collection* (Legacy).

In 1967 the Buckinghams' rock-with-horns sound made them a staple of Top 40 radio, with five Top 20 hits. The group came together in 1965 when Carl Giammarese and Nick Fortune of the Centuries teamed up with Dennis Tufano and Jon-Jon Poulos of the Pulsations. Adding Dennis Miccolis on keyboards, the new Pulsations auditioned for a Chicago variety show, *All Time Hits*. Informed that the program's producers were looking for a British-style group, they changed their name to the Buckinghams and passed the audition. Four singles on two local labels failed to chart, but "Kind of a Drag"—with its polite horns and cheesy organ—rocketed to #1 in February 1967. The group signed with Columbia Records, which paired it with producer/manager James Guercio. Through the end of the year, the Buckinghams monopolized the airwaves with "Lawdy Miss Clawdy" (#41), "Don't You Care" (#6), "Mercy, Mercy, Mercy" (#5), "Hey Baby (They're Playing Our Song)" (#12), and "Susan" (#11). But as predicted by the title of a 1968 Buckinghams LP, *In One Ear and Gone Tomorrow*, the quintet's appeal mysteriously vanished. It broke up in 1970, by which time producer Guercio was perfecting the brass-rock sound with the group Chicago. Tufano and Giammarese recorded as a duet for Ode Records in 1973, while keyboardist Marty Grebb formed the Fabulous Rhinestones. Poulos died of a drug overdose in 1980 at age 32. That year Tufano, Giammarese, and Fortune revived the band, and they have continued to play the oldies circuit. By 1985 Tufano had departed to pursue acting.

Jeff Buckley

Born Jeffrey Scott Buckley, Nov. 17, 1966, Anaheim, CA; died May 29, 1997, Memphis, TN
1993—*Live at Sin-é* EP (Columbia) 1994—*Grace* 1998—*Sketches for My Sweetheart the Drunk* 2000—*Mystery White Boy*.

Possessed of a striking, multioctave voice and a passion for high drama in his performances, Jeff Buckley emerged out of New York's avant-garde music scene in 1994 with *Grace*, an album that would garner him international critical acclaim and a devoted cult fan base. Three years later, just shy of his 31st birthday and the recording of his second album, he drowned in a freak accident.

Throughout his life, Buckley was haunted by the shadow

of a famous father he never really knew, singer/songwriter Tim Buckley [see entry] (who also died young, of a heroin overdose at age 28). Buckley met his father only once, spending a week with him when he was eight. He was closer to his stepfather Ron Moorhead, an auto mechanic who helped inspire Buckley's pursuit of music by giving him his first Led Zeppelin album. Growing up in Southern California, Buckley was known as Scotty Moorhead until his mother, Mary Guibert, divorced her second husband.

After performing in a handful of cover bands throughout high school and attending the Los Angeles Musicians Institute, Buckley moved to New York City in 1990. He went back to L.A. after seven months, then returned to somewhat reluctantly participate in a Tim Buckley tribute concert at Brooklyn's St. Ann's Church in 1991; his buzz-winning performance led to a relocation to New York in 1992 and a short stint performing in the band Gods and Monsters with former Captain Beefheart guitarist Gary Lucas. He soon left the group to focus on a solo career and took up residence at the tiny cafe Sin-é in the East Village. His eclectic performances—which revealed as much of an affinity for Edith Piaf as Zeppelin—led to a contract with Columbia Records in 1993. *Live at Sin-é,* a four-song EP, was released while Buckley assembled a band to record his full-length debut, *Grace* (#149, 1994).

Featuring Buckley originals such as "Last Goodbye" as well as a cover of Leonard Cohen's "Hallelujah," *Grace* sold only modestly but was warmly received by critics. He would tour behind the album for nearly three years. In mid-1996 Buckley began recording demos for his second album—to be titled *My Sweetheart the Drunk*—with producer Tom Verlaine (of Television fame). He intended to record the album itself with *Grace* producer Andy Wallace in Memphis, Tennessee, where Buckley had recently relocated. On May 29, 1997—the night he was expecting his band to arrive from New York—Buckley and a friend were en route to a rehearsal space when they decided to take a break alongside the bank of the Wolf River channel of the Mississippi River. After Buckley waded into the water fully clothed and began swimming, he was sucked under by a wake created by a passing boat; his body was spotted six days later by a riverboat passenger.

Following his death, Buckley's mother began to work closely with Columbia on all affairs concerning his posthumous releases. The first was *Sketches for My Sweetheart the Drunk* (#64, 1998), a double-disc set featuring the Verlaine-produced studio sessions and a selection of unfinished songs that Buckley had recently recorded on four-track. The live album *Mystery White Boy* followed in 2000, along with the DVD/VHS release *Jeff Buckley—Live in Chicago.*

Tim Buckley

Born Feb. 14, 1947, Washington, DC; died June 29, 1975, Santa Monica, CA
1967—*Tim Buckley* (Elektra); *Goodbye and Hello* 1969—*Happy Sad* 1970—*Blue Afternoon* (Straight); *Lorca* (Elektra) 1971—*Starsailor* (Warner Bros.) 1972—*Greetings From L.A.* 1974—*Look at the Fool* (DiscReet); *Sefronia* 1990—*Dream Letter (Live in London, 1968)* (Retro) 2001—*Morning Glory: The Tim Buckley Anthology* (Rhino).

Tim Buckley was a highly respected singer/songwriter throughout the late '60s. His professional career began in the early '60s when he played frequently with bassist Jim Fielder (later of Buffalo Springfield and Blood, Sweat and Tears) and attracted the attention of Frank Zappa's manager Herb Cohen, who got him a deal with Elektra in 1966. (Buckley later signed with Cohen's Straight Records.) His second album, *Goodbye and Hello,* was produced by the Lovin' Spoonful's Jerry Yester.

Buckley began exploring avant-garde jazz and later recorded in Swahili. After several label switches, he tried funky, danceable material in the mid-'70s, without success. On June 29, 1975, Buckley died of a heroin and morphine overdose; according to a coroner's inquest testimony, he had snorted what he believed was cocaine. The man who owned the house where he died was later convicted of involuntary manslaughter. Buckley's son, Jeff, who barely knew his father, launched his own career in the early '90s and also tragically died young.

Buckwheat Zydeco

Born Stanley Dural Jr., Nov. 14, 1947, Lafayette, LA
1980—*Take It Easy Baby* (Blues Unlimited) 1983—*100% Fortified Zydeco* (Black Top) 1984—*Turning Point* (Rounder) 1985—*Waitin' for My YaYa* 1987—*Zydeco Party; On a Night Like This* (Island) 1988—*Taking It Home* 1990—*Where*

Buckwheat Zydeco

There's Smoke There's Fire 1992—*On Track* (Charisma) 1993—*Menagerie: The Essential Zydeco Collection* (Island) 1995—*Five Card Stud* 1997—*Trouble* (Atlantic) 1999—*The Buckwheat Zydeco Story: A 20-Year Party* (Tomorrow) 2001—*Down Home Live!*

Born in the heart of the bayou, Buckwheat Zydeco blends a love for Creole culture with an ability to rock out, a combination that has made him a popular exponent of zydeco. Playing organ and piano since the age of nine (he was nicknamed after a *Little Rascals* character—a moniker he considers racist but has stuck with), he led his own R&B band, Buckwheat and the Hitchhikers, in 1971. From 1976 to 1978 he played keyboards with zydeco master Clifton Chenier, which inspired in him a newfound appreciation of his ethnic roots and led him to play the accordion.

In 1979 Buckwheat formed Ils Sont Partis and released a string of well-received independent releases. *On a Night Like This,* which featured Buckwheat's interpretations of songs by Bob Dylan, the Blasters, and Booker T. and the MG's, as well as his own compositions, was embraced by critics and nominated for a Grammy. Further widening his popularity, Buckwheat has opened shows for U2 and Robert Cray, toured with Eric Clapton (who played on *Taking It Home*), and worked with Keith Richards (he appears on the Stone's *Talk Is Cheap*) and Los Lobos' David Hidalgo (who produced *Where There's Smoke There's Fire*). Buckwheat's music has been featured in the films *The Big Easy, The Waterboy,* and *Casual Sex?*

True to his heritage, Buckwheat forbids his music to be classified as "Cajun" and speaks frequently about the racism that kept zydeco music off the air for years while its white counterpart (Cajun) was popularized. In 1999 he formed his own Tomorrow Recordings label, reissuing *Trouble,* his 1997 album for Atlantic. He also released *The Buckwheat Zydeco Story: A 20-Year Party,* a multilabel anthology that spans his entire career, and *Down Home Live!*

Buffalo Springfield

Formed 1966, Los Angeles, CA

Neil Young (b. Nov. 12, 1945, Toronto, Can.), voc., gtr.; Stephen Stills (b. Jan. 3, 1945, Dallas, TX), voc., gtr.; Richie Furay (b. May 9, 1944, Dayton, OH), voc., gtr.; Dewey Martin (b. Sep. 30, 1942, Chesterville, Can.), voc., drums; Bruce Palmer (b. 1946, Liverpool, Can.), bass.

1967—*Buffalo Springfield* (Atco); *Stampede* (unreleased) (– Palmer; + Ken Koblun, bass; – Koblun; + Jim Fielder [b. Oct. 4, 1947, Denton, TX], bass; – Young; + Doug Hastings, gtr.) *Buffalo Springfield Again* (Atco) (– Fielder; – Hastings; + Young; + Jim Messina [b. Dec. 5, 1947, Maywood, CA], bass) 1968—*Last Time Around* 1969—*Retrospective* 1973—*Buffalo Springfield* 2001—*Boxed Set* (Rhino/Reprise Archives).

During its brief and stormy lifetime, Buffalo Springfield broke ground for what became country rock. After the band's dissolution, several members found success in Poco; Crosby, Stills, Nash and Young; Loggins and Messina; and as solo artists.

Buffalo Springfield: Richie Furay, Dewey Martin, Neil Young, Stephen Stills, Bruce Palmer

Furay and Stills had played together, as had Canadians Young and Palmer, before the four hooked up in L.A. in 1966 to form Buffalo Springfield (named after a steamroller). Originally called the Herd, they added Martin on drums and vocals.

After a stint as the house band at the Whisky-a-Go-Go and touring with the Byrds, Springfield inked a deal with Atlantic and released its first album in 1967. Stills' "For What It's Worth" (#7, 1967) gave the group its biggest hit. By the time of its second album, Springfield was a major group coming apart at the seams. After Palmer was deported (following a drug bust) and producer Jim Messina was added on bass, and amid persistent squabbling between Stills and Young (who quit in May 1967, only to rejoin four months later), the group disbanded in May 1968. When *Last Time Around* was released later that year, each of the members was on his own. Martin kept the band's name alive with hired musicians and then had an abortive solo career. Stills and Young were successful in the '70s with CSN&Y [see entry] and solo work. Short-term bassist Jim Fielder joined Blood, Sweat and Tears [see entry], while Messina and Furay formed Poco [see entry] with pedal-steel guitarist Rusty Young, who had played on Springfield's final album; Messina went on to the duo Loggins and Messina [see entry]. Later in the '80s, Furay became a pastor for a Christian fellowship. In 1997 Buffalo Springfield was inducted into the Rock and Roll Hall of Fame; Young did not attend the ceremony. The long-awaited Buffalo Springfield box set was finally released in 2001.

Jimmy Buffett

Born Dec. 25, 1946, Pascagoula, MS
1970—*Down to Earth* (Barnaby) 1973—*A White Sport Coat and a Pink Crustacean* (Dunhill) 1974—*Living and Dying in 3/4 Time; A-1-A* 1975—*Rancho Deluxe* (United Artists) 1976—*Havana Day-dreamin'* (ABC); *High Cumberland Jubilee* (Barnaby) 1977—*Changes in Latitudes, Changes in Attitudes* (ABC) 1978—*Live; Son of a Son of a Sailor; You Had to Be There* 1979—*Volcano* (MCA); *Before the Salt* (Barnaby) 1981—*Coconut Telegraph* (MCA); *Somewhere Over China* 1983—*One Particular Harbour* 1984—*Riddles in the Sand* 1985—*Last Mango in Paris; Songs You Know by Heart—Jimmy Buffett's Greatest Hit(s)* 1986—*Floridays* 1988—*Hot Water* 1989—*Off to See the Lizard* 1990—*Feeding Frenzy* 1992—*Boats Beaches Bars & Ballads* (Margaritaville) 1993—*Before the Beach; Margaritaville Cafe Late Night Menu* 1994—*Fruitcakes* 1995—*Barometer Soup* 1996—*Banana Wind; Christmas Island* 1998—*Don't Stop the Carnival* (Island) 1999—*Beach House on the Moon* (Margaritaville); *Buffett Live, Tuesdays, Thursdays, Saturdays* (Mailboat).

Singer/songwriter Jimmy Buffett is known for humorous chronicles of a laid-back seafaring life; his philosophical outlook is encapsulated in tunes like "Why Don't We Get Drunk (and Screw)" and "My Head Hurts, My Feet Stink and I Don't Love Jesus." In addition to releasing popular albums, Buffett has built a small Florida-based financial empire, written several best-selling books, and become a leading environmentalist.

Raised in the Deep South, Buffett attended Auburn University and then the University of Southern Mississippi, majoring in journalism (he later worked as a *Billboard* reporter). He moved to Nashville in the late '60s, intent on becoming a country singer. His first album, 1970's *Down to Earth,* sold 324 copies. Barnaby Records then temporarily misplaced the master tape of his second album before its release. By 1972 Buffett had left both Nashville and a failed marriage, moving to Key West. There he helped to support himself by smuggling a little marijuana from the Caribbean. He signed to ABC-Dunhill, and his 1973 release, *A White Sport Coat and a Pink Crustacean,* found Buffett developing his drunken-sailor persona. Although he'd had a Top 30 hit with 1974's "Come Monday," Buffett's commercial breakthrough came in 1977 with the platinum *Changes in Latitudes, Changes in Attitudes* (#12) and its hit single, "Margaritaville" (#8).

During that period Buffett toured infrequently, spending most of his time living on his 50-foot ketch *Euphoria II.* He frequently docked at Montserrat, where his 1979 LP *Volcano* was recorded. He formed the first version of his Coral Reefer Band in 1975. Buffett scored and acted in the 1974 film *Rancho Deluxe,* and appeared in the 1977 movie *FM.* His 1981 *Coconut Telegraph* album inspired a fan-club newsletter of the same name, which has maintained a worldwide subscriber base of "Parrot Heads"—Buffett's fans rival the Grateful Dead's in their enthusiasm for their hero.

The 1985 compilation *Songs You Know by Heart* (subtitled *Jimmy Buffet's Greatest Hit[s]* in self-mocking reference to the fact that "Margaritaville" was his only major pop hit) sold 2 million copies; 1992's *Boats Beaches Bars & Ballads* also went platinum. By that time Buffett had established a Margaritaville empire, including a record label and Margaritaville Store and Cafe outlets in Key West, New Orleans, Orlando, and Charleston. He wrote three best-selling books: *Tales From Margaritaville,* a collection of short stories; the novel *Where Is Joe Merchant?;* and the memoir *A Pirate Looks at Fifty,* which made Buffett only the sixth author ever to top both the fiction and nonfiction lists. He has also coauthored two children's books, *The Jolly Mon* and *Trouble Dolls,* with his daughter, Savannah Jane. In 1993, 1994, and 1995 *Forbes* magazine included Buffett on its list of highest-paid entertainers. The singer spends some of his time and money on various charities, especially the ones supporting environmental issues—he crusades on behalf of Florida's endangered manatees and created the SFC Charitable Foundation in 1995. Buffett continued to pick up steam all through the '90s, performing to sell-out crowds, his albums becoming more successful than ever—he hit the Top 10 with *Fruitcakes* (#5, 1994), *Barometer Soup* (#6, 1995), *Banana Wind* (#4, 1996), and *Beach House on the Moon* (#8, 1999). Secure in his success, Buffett collaborated with Herman Wouk on a musical adaptation of Wouk's novel *Don't Stop the Carnival.* The show briefly ran in Miami in 1997, and Buffett released an album of songs from that production the following year. In 1999 Buffett, ever the entrepreneur, launched his own independent label, Mailboat Records (the first release was a live album recorded in Nantucket), and Radio Margaritaville, an online radio station.

The Buggles

Formed 1979, England
Trevor Horn (b. July 15, 1949, Hertfordshire, Eng.), bass, voc.; Geoffrey Downes (b. Eng.), kybds.
1980—*Age of Plastic* (Island) 1982—*Adventures in Modern Recording* (Epic).

The electropop "Video Killed the Radio Star," written by Horn, Downes, and Bruce Wooley, was a huge international hit in 1979, #1 in the U.K. and in the Top 40 in the U.S. On August 1, 1981, it was the first video ever aired by MTV and soon proved itself a piece of musical prophesy.

Keyboardist Downes and vocalist Horn viewed themselves more as producers than rock stars. Following "Video Killed the Radio Star," the duo had three more U.K. hits, including "The Plastic Age" in 1980. After producing Yes' *Tormato,* they shocked the music world by joining the band in March 1980 [see Yes entry]. They appeared on *Drama* and Yes' 1980–81 tour. Following Yes' 1981 breakup, Downes joined Asia [see entry]. Horn went on to become a successful producer for many hit groups, including Frankie Goes to Hollywood and ABC, as well as Band Aid's "Do They Know It's Christmas."

Eric Burdon

Born May 11, 1941, Newcastle upon Tyne, Eng.
Eric Burdon and War: 1970—*Eric Burdon Declares War* (Polydor) 1971—*The Black Man's Burdon* (MGM) 1976—*Love Is All Around* (ABC).
Eric Burdon solo: 1971—*Guilty* (MGM) 1974—*Ring of Fire* (Capitol); *Sun Secrets* 1975—*Stop* 1978—*Survivor* (Polydor) 1988—*Wicked Man* (GNP).
Eric Burdon/Brian Auger Band: 1993—*Access All Areas* (SPV, Eur.).

Eric Burdon's rudely emotive vocals kept him on the charts through the British Invasion (as frontman for the Animals), psychedelia (as a solo act), and early-'70s funk (with War). He grew up in working-class Newcastle and went to art school, where he studied graphics and photography and was introduced to blues records. Unable to find a job, he became a musician and joined the Alan Price Combo in 1962, which became the Animals [see entry]. With their success, Burdon took to drinking, womanizing, and shooting his mouth off, experiences that no doubt shaped a later song entitled "Good Times."

By 1967 Burdon had been converted to flower power. He traded his denims for a Nehru jacket and moved to California. After the 1969 double album, *Love Is,* Burdon announced his retirement. In late 1969 Burdon heard a funk band called Night Shift; they became War and backed him on his 1970 hit "Spill the Wine" (#3) and their debut album, *Eric Burdon Declares War.* After a second album together, Burdon became exhausted on a 1971 European tour, and War went on without him [see War entry].

Since then Burdon has remained active, recording solo albums and making an album with blues legend Jimmy Witherspoon *(Guilty)* in 1971 and an Animals reunion album, *Before We Were So Rudely Interrupted,* in 1977. ABC put out material recorded in 1970 by Burdon and War on a 1976 album, *Love Is All Around.* During the late '70s Burdon appeared in several European movies, and in 1981 he starred in and composed the soundtrack for a German film titled *Come Back.* In 1983 the original Animals lineup re-formed for an album and tour, and three years later Burdon published his autobiography, *I Used to Be an Animal, but I'm All Right Now.*

In 1990 Burdon formed a touring band with ex-Doors guitarist Robbie Krieger and appeared in the TV show *China Beach.* In 1991 Burdon formed a band with veteran British jazz-rock keyboardist Brian Auger; they released a 1993 album, *Access All Areas,* recorded live in California and released only in Europe. Burdon's name turned up in the press that year after he made repeated, ultimately unsuccessful, requests that Scotland Yard investigate the death of his friend Jimi Hendrix. The '90s saw Burdon touring as the leader of both the I-Band and the New Animals.

Solomon Burke

Born 1936, Philadelphia, PA
1962—*Solomon Burke* (Apollo); *Solomon Burke's Greatest Hits* (Atlantic) 1963—*If You Need Me* 1964—*Rock 'n Soul* 1965—*The Best of Solomon Burke* 1967—*King Solomon* 1968—*I Wish I Knew* 1969—*Proud Mary* (Bell) 1971—*Electronic Magnetism* (MGM) 1972—*Cool Breeze* soundtrack; *We're Almost Home* 1973—*Get Up and Do Something* 1974—*I Have a Dream* (ABC/Dunhill) 1975—*Music to Make Love By* (Chess) 1977—*Back to My Roots; Greatest Hits* (Atlantic) 1981—*Take Me, Shake Me* (Savoy); *Sidewalks, Fences and Walls* (Infinity) 1984—*Soul Alive!* (Rounder) 1986—*A Change Is Gonna Come* 1989—*The Best of Solomon Burke* (Atlantic) 1992—*Home in Your Heart: The Best of Solomon Burke* (Rhino/Atlantic) 1993—*Soul of the Blues* (Black Top) 1994—*Solomon Burke Live at the House of Blues* 1997—*The Definition of Soul* (Pointblank/Virgin).

With his big, powerful voice and fervent but controlled emotionality, Solomon Burke was a pioneer of soul music in the early '60s. By the age of nine he was a preacher and choir soloist for his family's Philadelphia church, the House of God for All People. At 12 he began hosting his own gospel radio show, Solomon's Temple, and touring the gospel circuits billed as the "Wonder Boy Preacher." In 1955 he began recording both religious and secular music for Apollo and Singular before signing with Atlantic in 1960.

At Atlantic Burke made some of the first soul records by setting his gospel "preaching" style in song forms borrowed from R&B, rock & roll, and other secular music. His second Atlantic release, "Just Out of Reach (of My Two Open Arms)," was a country & western song, and it became his first hit when it reached #7 R&B in 1961. Burke called his big-beat dance songs "rock 'n' soul music" and won crossover popularity with "Cry to Me" (#44 pop, #5 R&B, 1962), "If You Need Me" (#37 pop, #2 R&B, 1963), "You're Good for Me" (#49 pop, #8 R&B, 1963), "Got to Get You off My Mind" (#22 pop, #1 R&B, 1965), and "Tonight's the Night" (#28 pop, #2 R&B, 1965). He had two more R&B Top 20 records on Atlantic, including "Keep a Light in the Window" and "Take Me (Just as I Am)" in 1967. He was a primary influence on Mick Jagger, who covered Burke's "You Can Make It If You Try," "Everybody Needs Somebody to Love," and "Cry to Me" on early Rolling Stones albums. Burke was also covered by Otis Redding ("Down in the Valley").

In 1969 he moved to Bell and hit with a cover of John Fogerty's "Proud Mary" (#45 pop, #15 R&B, 1969). In the '70s Burke recorded with uneven results for MGM, Dunhill, and Chess, but did enjoy a couple of R&B hits, including "Midnight and You" (#14 R&B, 1974) and "You and Your Baby Blues" (#19 R&B, 1975). In 1981 he toured with the Soul Clan, which included Don Covay, Wilson Pickett, Ben E. King, and

Joe Tex. That year he also returned to his gospel roots, releasing the Grammy-nominated *Take Me, Shake Me.* He made his film debut in *The Big Easy* (1987). For a time, Burke owned a West Coast chain of mortuaries (several of his kids remain in the family business). He is the father of 21 and a great-grandfather. He continues to tour and record while remaining active in the church. Burke was inducted into the Rock and Roll Hall of Fame in 2001.

T Bone Burnett

Born John Henry Burnett, Jan. 14, 1948, St. Louis, MO
1972—*The B-52 Band & the Fabulous Skylarks* (UNI) 1980—*Truth Decay* (Takoma) 1982—*Trap Door* EP (Warner) 1983—*Proof Through the Night* 1984—*Behind the Trap Door* EP (Demon, U.K.) 1986—*T Bone Burnett* (Dot) 1988—*The Talking Animals* (Columbia) 1992—*The Criminal Under My Own Hat.*

T Bone Burnett is a critically acclaimed singer/songwriter whose own projects have been eclipsed by his work as a producer for such artists as Elvis Costello, Roy Orbison, the BoDeans, Los Lobos, Counting Crows, Jimmie Dale Gilmore, Gillian Welch, and the Wallflowers.

Burnett grew up in Fort Worth, Texas, where he absorbed the area's rich tradition of blues, Tex-Mex, and R&B. Foreshadowing his later fame, Burnett opened his own studio and opted for producing blues records over attending college. By the early '70s Burnett had relocated to L.A., where he produced a record for Delbert McClinton and Glen Clark and recorded his first solo album.

After teaming up with singer/songwriter and Bob Dylan crony Bob Neuwirth and moving to the East Coast, Burnett found himself in the right place at the right time. Recruiting musicians for his Rolling Thunder Revue in 1975, Dylan tapped Burnett to be one of his guitarists. When the tour ended, Burnett and two other Rolling Thunder members, Dave Mansfield and Steve Soles, formed the Alpha Band. After three eccentric, eclectic, but unsuccessful albums (1977's *Alpha Band* and *Spark in the Dark* and 1978's *Statue Makers of Hollywood*), the Alpha Band split up and Burnett went solo.

Burnett, who reportedly influenced Dylan's conversion to Christianity, weaves themes of personal religiosity throughout his work. His nimble wordplay and highly crafted songwriting caught the attention of the rock community if not the public; Pete Townshend and Richard Thompson were among the guest musicians on *Proof Through the Night.* Despite critical kudos and vocal support from rock heavyweights—Mark Knopfler and Bono are avid Burnett admirers—Burnett has remained more a cult figure. None of his own albums has ever gone gold.

As a producer, though, Burnett is responsible for some of the most highly regarded albums of the late '80s and '90s. Burnett's flair for roots rock comes through on Los Lobos' first two albums, *. . . And a Time to Dance* and *How Will the Wolf Survive?;* the BoDeans' debut, *Love & Hope & Sex & Dreams;* and Marshall Crenshaw's *Downtown.* On Elvis Costello's *King of America,* Burnett revamped Costello's sound by mating him with American musicians and emphasizing an earthier approach. During this period, Burnett also produced a contemporary Christian singer named Leslie Phillips, who soon after changed her name to Sam Phillips and turned to secular music making. Burnett continued producing her and, in 1989, they married. Two years before Roy Orbison's death, Burnett produced the music for the all-star collaborative video that featured Orbison with Bruce Springsteen, Jackson Browne, k.d. lang, Tom Waits, and a host of acolytes. His other production credits include Costello's *Spike;* Counting Crows' 1993 debut, *August and Everything After;* Sam Phillips' *Martinis & Bikinis* and *Omnipop (It's Only a Flesh Wound Lambchop);* Bruce Cockburn's *Dart to the Heart;* Jimmie Dale Gilmore's *Braver New World;* and Gillian Welch's *Revival.* Next to the Counting Crows album, Burnett's most commercially successful producing project was the Wallflowers' 1996 effort, *Bringing Down the Horse,* an album that went multiplatinum, collected two Grammys, and made Bob Dylan's son Jakob a star in his own right.

In 1997 Burnett wrote new music for Sam Shepard's play *Tooth of Crime (Second Dance)* and is planning to release the soundtrack on Nonesuch in 2001 along with a new solo album. He also scored and produced the Depression-era-themed soundtrack to the Coen brothers' film *O Brother, Where Art Thou?* (2000). The LP, featuring Emmylou Harris, Ralph Stanley, Alison Krauss, and others, became a Top 20 album (#13). He had previously produced soundtracks for the films *Stealing Beauty* (1996) and *The Horse Whisperer* (1998). Burnett directed a special all-star concert version of the soundtrack at Nashville's Ryman Auditorium, which was filmed by documentary filmmaker D.A. Pennebaker (Bob Dylan's *Don't Look Back*); plans were in the works for the concert's release on CD and video.

Billy Burnette

Born May 8, 1953, Memphis, TN
1971—*Billy Burnette* (Columbia/Entrance) 1979—*Billy Burnette* (Polydor); *Between Friends* 1980—*Billy Burnette* (Columbia) 1981—*Gimme You* 1993—*Coming Home* (Capricorn) 2000—*Are You With Me Baby* (Freefalls Entertainment).
Bekka and Billy: 1997—*Bekka and Billy* (Almo Sounds).

Son of Dorsey Burnette, nephew of Johnny Burnette, and cousin of Rocky Burnette, Billy Burnette moved from Memphis to L.A., where he made his recording debut at age seven with "Hey Daddy." His second record, "Just Because We're Kids," was written by Dr. Seuss (Theodor Seuss Geisel), produced by Herb Alpert, and released on A&M Records when he was 11 years old. During his early teen years he recorded for Warner Bros., made TV appearances, and—at age 13—toured the Far East with the Brenda Lee show. He moved to Memphis in 1972, where he started playing guitar and writing songs; the next year he began an apprenticeship with producer Chips Moman (Elvis Presley, Aretha Franklin), who produced his first solo album. He also toured with Roger Miller.

Burnette spent most of the '70s leading his father's band, playing guitar, and singing with Delaney Bramlett. His songs have been recorded by Charlie Rich, Loretta Lynn, Conway Twitty, Irma Thomas, Ray Charles, Jerry Lee Lewis, the Everly Brothers, Charley Pride, Glen Campbell, Gary Stewart, Tammy Wynette, and Levon Helm. He made two country albums in 1979, but it was not until after his father died that year that he began playing rock & roll. His first Columbia album contained remakes of "Tear It Up" and "Honey Hush," two rockabilly numbers made famous by his father's Rock 'n' Roll Trio.

In 1987 Burnette joined Fleetwood Mac, replacing Lindsey Buckingham; he appears on *Behind the Mask*. He left the group in January 1993, shortly before the release of his Capricorn debut, *Coming Home*, but returned to Fleetwood Mac for its 1994 tour. In 1997 Burnette and Bekka Bramlett (the daughter of Delaney and Bonnie Bramlett, who replaced Stevie Nicks in Fleetwood Mac's mid-'90s lineup) collaborated on the *Bekka and Billy* album. In 2000 Burnette re-emerged as a solo act with *Are You With Me Baby*.

Dorsey Burnette

Born Dec. 28, 1932, Memphis, TN; died Aug. 19, 1979, Canoga Park, CA
1963—*Dorsey Burnette* (Capitol) N.A.—*Dorsey Burnette* (Dot); *Dorsey Burnette's Greatest Hits* (Era); *Tall Oak Tree* 1977—*Things I Treasure* (Calliope).

Dorsey Burnette played bass in brother Johnny Burnette's pioneering rockabilly group, the Rock 'n' Roll Trio. Following their brief fling with stardom in 1955–56, he moved with his brother from Memphis to L.A. They wrote a number of successful tunes for Rick Nelson ("Believe What You Say," "It's Late"), and each enjoyed moderate solo success in the early '60s. Dorsey's hits on Era Records included "Tall Oak Tree" (#23, 1960). From 1968 until his death in 1979 from a heart attack, he was a popular mainstream country artist, charting 10 C&W singles. In 1973, after some 20 years in the music business, he was named the year's most promising newcomer by the Academy of Country Music. He died six years later.

Johnny Burnette

Born Mar. 25, 1934, Memphis, TN; died Aug. 1, 1964, Clear Lake, CA
1975—*The Very Best of Johnny Burnette* (United Artists) 1976—*Tear It Up* (Solid Smoke) 1979—*Stars of Rock 'n' Roll, vol. 1* (MCA) 1981—*Johnny Burnette's Rock and Roll Trio and Their Rockin' Friends From Memphis* (Rock-a-billy).

With his brother Dorsey, Johnny Burnette was a mid-'50s rockabilly pioneer and had some solo success in the early '60s. A guitarist/singer/songwriter, with Dorsey he put together the Rock 'n' Roll Trio along with guitarist Paul Burlison (who released his first solo album in 1981 on a small Memphis label). They had a couple of minor hits like "Train Kept a-Rollin'," distinguished by Burlison's breakthrough fuzz guitar riff, but disbanded in late 1957.

Johnny and Dorsey moved to L.A., where they cowrote several hits for Rick Nelson, among others. In 1958 Johnny got a solo contract with Liberty Records, for which he cleaned up his sound and image. He had the biggest hit of his career in November 1960 as a teen idol with the million-selling "You're Sixteen" (#8). With a couple of lesser hits in 1961, Johnny had his last taste of rock glory. He was plotting a comeback when he drowned in a boating accident in 1964.

Rocky Burnette

Born June 12, 1953, Memphis, TN
1979—*Son of Rock 'n' Roll* (EMI) 1980—*Rocky Burnette*.

After 26 years in the shadow of his father, Johnny, and uncle Dorsey Burnette, Rocky—the self-proclaimed "Son of Rock 'n' Roll"—came into his own with a #8 hit single, "Tired of Toein' the Line." He began writing songs in his early teens and at age 14, three years after his father's death, became a songwriter with the Acuff-Rose publishing company. His songs were recorded by several minor country singers. After finishing college, where he studied film and religion, Rocky made some unreleased recordings for Curb Records. In January 1979, broke after leaving Curb, he traded the rights to a couple of his songs for the studio time to record "Clowns From Outer Space," which he sent to EMI in London. EMI released it as a single. Its B side, "Tired of Toein' the Line," was written in less than half an hour. EMI put it on the A side. It hit first in Europe and Australia, making the British chart in 1979, before crossing to America the following year. To date, that was his first and last hit, although he had a single, "Three Flags," that appeared on the lower reaches of the country chart in 1990. More recently Rocky Burnette has toured with longtime family associate Paul Burlison, who originally served as the guitarist in Johnny Burnette's Rock 'n' Roll Trio back in the '50s.

Burning Spear

Born Winston Rodney, Mar. 1, 1945, St. Ann's Parish, Jam.
1975—*Marcus Garvey* (Island) 1976—*Garvey's Ghost* (Mango); *Man in the Hills* 1977—*Dry and Heavy; Live* (Island) 1979—*Harder Than the Best* 1980—*Hail H.I.M.* (Tammi) 1981—*Social Living* 1982—*Farover* (Heartbeat) 1983—*Fittest of the Fittest* 1984—*Resistance; Reggae Greats* (Mango) 1986—*People of the World* (Slash) 1988—*Mistress Music* 1989—*Live in Paris: Zenith '88* 1990—*Mek We Dweet* (Mango); *100th Anniversary* 1992—*Jah Kingdom; The Original* (Sonicsoul) 1993—*The World Should Know* (Heartbeat) 1994— *Living Dub, vol. 1; Living Dub, vol. 2;*

Burning Spear

Love and Peace: Burning Spear Live 1995—*Rasta Business* 1996—*Chant Down Babylon* (Island) 1997—*Living Dub, vol. 3* (Heartbeat); *Appointment With His Majesty* 1999—*Calling Rastafari; Living Dub, vol. 4.*

In a career remarkable for its consistency of both quality and subject matter, Winston Rodney, a.k.a. Burning Spear, concerns himself with oppression—black Jamaicans' heritage of slavery—and mystical transcendence through Rastafarianism. His stark, hypnotic reggae is for the most part far removed from thoughts of love or sex or marijuana, the staples of pop reggae.

Rodney, Burning Spear's sole member since 1977, was born in St. Ann's Parish, the same neighborhood in which Bob Marley and '30s black leader Marcus Garvey were born, and continues to live in the northern hill region of Jamaica. He formed Burning Spear with bass vocalist Rupert Willington in the late '60s. (Burning Spear was the name given to Kenyan leader Jomo Kenyatta.) In 1969 the two cut their first single for Clement "Sir Coxsone" Dodd. Second tenor Delroy Hines joined soon after, and Spear became a vocal trio in the popular Jamaican style, with a repertoire based on traditional songs and chants dating from slave times. They were not particularly popular, and between 1971 and 1974 the group virtually disappeared.

In 1974, however, a runaway hit single on Lawrence "Jack Ruby" Lindo's Fox label, "Marcus Garvey," was heard all over Jamaica, followed by "Slavery Days." Dodd released three five-year-old singles—"Swell Headed," "Foggy Road," and "Ethiopians Live It Out"—and Britons as well as Jamaicans snapped them up, along with other singles and two import albums, *Burning Spear* and *Rocking Time.*

Marcus Garvey and its dub remix, *Garvey's Ghost* (which featured guitarist Earl "Chinna" Smith, bassist Robbie Shakespeare, drummer Leroy "Horsemouth" Wallace, and keyboardist Tyrone Downie), were released in the U.S. When Willington and Hines left Burning Spear in 1977, Rodney continued to record solo. He appeared in the film *Rockers* (made in 1977, released in the U.S. in 1980) in concert footage, and in an interview in the documentary *Reggae Sunsplash* (1980). While Rodney's brand of traditional reggae has fallen out of favor in his homeland, he tours the U.S. regularly with his own highly regarded band. By the '90s, Rodney's persistence had paid off, as Burning Spear returned to reggae's forefront with a series of albums recorded for the Heartbeat label, including the popular Living Dub series and *Calling Rastafari,* which was awarded the 1999 Grammy for Best Reggae Album.

Rodney still lives in Jamaica, where he teaches cultural history at the Marcus Garvey Youth Club, which he founded.

Bush

Formed 1992, London, Eng.
Gavin Rossdale (b. Oct. 30, 1967, London), voc., gtr.; Nigel Pulsford (b. Apr. 11, 1964, Newport, Wales), gtr.; Dave Parsons (b. July 2, 1965, Uxbridge, Eng.), bass; Robin Goodridge (b. Sep. 10, 1965, Crawley, Eng.), drums.
1994—*Sixteen Stone* (Trauma/Interscope) 1996—*Razorblade Suitcase* 1997—*Deconstructed* 1999—*The Science of Things.*

Propelled by a steady stream of hook-laden hit singles and frontman Gavin Rossdale's pinup good looks, Bush emerged as one of the most successful modern-rock acts of the mid-'90s. The band's 1994 debut album, *Sixteen Stone,* sold nearly 6 million copies in the U.S., despite the band being widely dismissed by critics and virtually ignored in its native England.

The son of a doctor, Rossdale grew up in an upper-class section of North London. An early interest in soccer (he tried out for London's Chelsea team as a teenager) gave way to music shortly after he graduated from high school, when he threw himself into the city's club culture and wound up fronting a number of unsuccessful bands in the mid-'80s. Discouraged, he moved to L.A. in 1991 and found work as a music video production assistant, but he was back in London within six months and in 1992 connected with guitarist Nigel Pulsford, a veteran of the indie band King Blank. A shared love of the Pixies brought them together under the name Future Primitive, which evolved into Bush with the addition of drummer Robin Goodridge and bassist Dave Parsons, an alum of Transvision Vamp.

Unable to secure an English record deal, Bush signed with the Disney-owned Hollywood Records in the States, though that deal fell through shortly after the completion of its first album. It was picked up by the Interscope-distributed Trauma, which released *Sixteen Stone* in late 1994. The album climbed all the way to #4 the following year and spawned five successive Modern Rock radio hits—"Everything Zen," "Little Things," "Comedown," "Glycerine," and "Machinehead." In the span of a year, Bush had graduated from opening club gigs to headlining arenas. Curiously, while *Sixteen Stone* was selling millions of copies in the U.S., Bush's grunge-inspired guitar rock hardly registered on the British radar amid the prevailing sounds of Brit pop and electronica. Meanwhile, American critics promptly wrote the band off as grunge carpetbaggers, particularly indebted to Nirvana. The band's decision to record its second album with producer Steve Albini—who had been at the helm on Nirvana's *In Utero*—didn't help deflect the comparisons. Nevertheless, *Razorblade Suitcase* (1996) debuted at #1 and went triple platinum on the strength of the singles "Swallowed" (#27 Hot 100 Airplay) and "Greedy Fly" (#41 Hot 100 Airplay). The following year, Bush released *Deconstructed* (#36), a collection of remixes by the likes of Tricky, Goldie, and Jack Dangers of Meat Beat Manifesto.

Although Rossdale's budding romantic relationship with No Doubt frontwoman Gwen Stefani helped keep him in the spotlight, Bush's momentum was somewhat slowed by a $40 million breach-of-contract lawsuit filed against it by Trauma in early 1999. The label claimed that the band was withholding its third studio album and shopping around for a new deal. The matter was resolved after a few months with the band signing a new multiyear contract with the label. Bush premiered some of its new material to an enthusiastic crowd at Woodstock '99, but when *The Science of Things* was finally released in late 1999, the gold album peaked at #11. The moderately electronica-tinged lead single, "The Chemicals Between Us," went to #67.

Kate Bush

Born July 30, 1958, Bexleyheath, Eng.
1978—*The Kick Inside* (Capitol); *On Stage* (EMI America); *Lionheart* 1980—*Never for Ever* 1982—*The Dreaming* 1983—*Kate Bush* EP 1985—*The Hounds of Love* 1986—*The Whole Story* 1989—*The Sensual World* (Columbia) 1993—*The Red Shoes* 1999—*This Woman's Work: Anthology 1979–90* (EMI, U.K.).

British singer/songwriter Kate Bush's idiosyncratic style has proved immensely popular in her homeland and around the world. Her debut single, "Wuthering Heights," hit #1 in the U.K. a month after its release in January 1978 and went on to become the year's best-selling single there and in Australia (only Abba was more popular in Western Europe). But except for "Running Up That Hill" (#30, 1985), Bush has yet to achieve the same broad popularity in the U.S., though her albums, particularly her later, more mature works, have been critically well received. Nonetheless, she has proved a major influence on artists such as Sinéad O'Connor, Jane Siberry, Björk, Tori Amos, and Dolores O'Riordan of the Cranberries.

Bush was something of an art-rock prodigy. The daughter of a British physician, Bush began playing the piano at the age of 11. She had been writing songs for two years when family friends told Dave Gilmour of Pink Floyd about the 16-year-old's four-octave range and interest in the supernatural. Gilmour financed the demo tape that got her signed to EMI. Because of her age and developing talent, she spent the next two years studying music, dance, and mime and writing the songs for her first album, recorded in 1977 under the supervision of Gilmour and producer Andrew Powell (Pink Floyd, Alan Parsons, Cockney Rebel). The album was preceded by the release of "Wuthering Heights." The song's runaway success also spurred sales of the Emily Brontë novel. Pat Benatar covered the song on *Crimes of Passion*.

The Kick Inside went to the U.K. Top 10, and two singles—"The Man With the Child in His Eyes" (#85, 1987) and "Wow," from *Lionheart*—made the Top 20. Bush's double EP of concert recordings also cracked the Top 10. She sang on Peter Gabriel's eponymous 1980 album, and her elaborately theatrical self-produced *The Dreaming*, which entered the U.K. chart at #3, shows his influence. Soon thereafter she constructed a state-of-the-art studio in her home, where she records. A known perfectionist, Bush uses the studio as an instrument, much the way Brian Wilson did, and her recordings evince a range of influences and styles, from Celtic to Middle Eastern music, and a mastery of rock and pop idioms, from lavish ballads to hard rockers.

Her next release, *The Hounds of Love* (#30 U.S., #1 U.K., 1985) featured her biggest U.S. single, "Running Up That Hill," as well as two other U.K. Top 20 singles, "Cloudbusting" and the title track. Her 1986 retrospective album and video, *The Whole Story*, was another #1 U.K. hit. With *The Sensual World*, Bush returned to literature for her inspiration, namely James Joyce's Molly Bloom, on whose soliloquies in *Ulysses* Bush based the title track's concept. *This Woman's Work* is a box set.

After a four-year hiatus, Bush returned with the ambitious (some critics thought confused) *The Red Shoes*, its title taken from the 1948 Michael Powell film (which was based on a Hans Christian Andersen tale) about a young ballerina. Bush, who had long been directing her own evocative videos, wrote, directed, and costarred (with performance artist–mime master Lindsay Kemp and actress Miranda Richardson) in her own 50-minute film. After six years without any solo activity, Bush started work on a new album in 1999; as of this writing, it had not yet been released.

The Bush Tetras

Formed 1979, New York, NY
Pat Place (b. 1954, Chicago, IL), gtr.; Laura Kennedy (b. May 30, 1957, Cleveland, OH), bass; Dee Pop (b. Dimitri Papadopoulous, Mar. 14, 1956, Queens, NY), drums; Cynthia Sley (b. May 3, 1957, Cleveland), voc., perc.
1980—*Too Many Creeps* EP (99) 1981—*Rituals* EP (Stiff) 1983—*Wild Things* cassette (ROIR) (– Kennedy; – Pop)

1989—*Better Late Than Never, 1980–1983* cassette 1995—*Boom in the Night* 1997—*Tetrafied: Rare and Unreleased Recordings* (2.13.61) (+ Kennedy; + Pop); *Beauty Lies* (Tim/Kerr/Mercury).

Emerging from Cleveland's new-wave and New York's no-wave scenes, the Bush Tetras mixed funk, noise, and no-nonsense urban-jungle lyrics. In 1977 James Chance [see entry] enlisted Pat Place for his incipient Contortions. Although she had no musical experience, she played bass, then slide guitar (as a Contortion and sometime member of James White and the Blacks) and developed her atonal slide style. Laura Kennedy and Cynthia Sley, classmates at the Cleveland Institute of Art, were in a performing arts group associated with Pere Ubu and Johnny and the Dicks. Kennedy moved to New York in 1977 to make films. Through a Cleveland acquaintance, Contortion Adele Bertei, she also worked as a roadie for the Contortions. When that band broke up in 1979, she joined rehearsals with Bertei, Place, Pop, and guitarist Jimmy Uliano. Bertei and Uliano dropped out after several months (Bertei went on to form the Bloods) and were replaced by lyricist and intoner Sley, who had been in New York since 1979 designing clothes for Lydia Lunch and Judy Nylon.

The Bush Tetras debuted in New York in early 1980. Their first record, a three-song EP, featured the club hit "Too Many Creeps." It was followed by a four-song EP, *Rituals*, produced by Topper Headon of the Clash; it appeared on national disco charts early in 1982. The band's other releases from that time include a 1983 live cassette and a 1989 anthology (*Boom in the Night* from 1995 is essentially the 1989 anthology). In 1983 the band lost momentum as members began dropping out. By the mid-'80s, Sley had formed a new band, Mad Orphan (the name later changed to the Lovelies), with her husband, ex-Voidoid Ivan Julian (the couple later split). In the '90s Sley started the all-women band 1-800-BOXX before calling it quits. Pop formed the group Floor Kiss with his then-wife, ex–John Cale vocalist Deerfrance, later playing drums with a succession of outfits. Kennedy left the music business, and Place turned up in the '90s, playing guitar behind spoken-word artist Maggie Estep.

The Bush Tetras briefly reunited in 1992 to play a handful of shows, then again in 1995. At that point the original lineup decided to record its first proper full-length album. Preceded by a single, "Page 18" b/w "Find a Lie," produced by Henry Rollins, *Beauty Lies* (which was produced by Nona Hendryx) failed to recapture the band's original energy. The Bush Tetras went their separate ways again in 1998, continuing to pursue an assortment of musical projects.

Jerry Butler

Born Dec. 8, 1939, Sunflower, MS
1962—*Moon River* (Vee-Jay) 1964—*Delicious Together* (with Betty Everett) 1967—*Mr. Dream Merchant* (Mercury) 1968—*Jerry Butler's Golden Hits Live; The Soul Goes On* 1969—*The Ice Man Cometh; Ice on Ice* 1970—*The Best of Jerry Butler; You and Me* 1971—*Jerry Butler Sings Assorted Sounds; Gene & Jerry—One & One* (with Gene Chandler); *The Sagittarius Movement* 1972—*The Spice of Life* 1973—*The Power of Love* 1974—*Sweet Sixteen* 1976—*Love's on the Menu* (Motown) 1977—*Suite for the Single Girl; Thelma & Jerry* (with Thelma Houston); *It All Comes Out in My Song* 1978—*The Soul Goes On* (Mercury) 1979—*Nothing Says I Love You Like I Love You* (Philadelphia International) 1980—*The Best Love I Ever Had* 1982—*Ice and Hot* (Fountain) 1987—*The Best of Jerry Butler* (Rhino) 1992—*The Iceman: The Mercury Years* (PolyGram) 1993—*Time and Faith* (Ichiban) 1994—*Simply Beautiful* (Navarre).

A distinctive soul singer for over four decades, Jerry Butler has a smooth but soulful style that has earned him his "Iceman" sobriquet. He and childhood friend Curtis Mayfield defined Chicago soul with the Impressions. Butler, who had a gospel background, moved with his family from Sunflower, Mississippi, to Chicago in 1942. By the time he and Mayfield put together Jerry Butler and the Impressions [see entry] in 1957, Butler was perfecting a delicate, hesitant delivery. The Impressions had their first hit with "For Your Precious Love" (#11 pop, #3 R&B, 1958), cowritten by Butler. Butler went solo shortly thereafter but worked with Mayfield as songwriter and producer for several more years. The team scored its first post-Impressions hit in 1960 with Mayfield's "He Will Break Your Heart" (#7).

Specializing in mellow ballads, Butler continued to score occasional hits. He was the first artist to record "Moon River," the theme song to the popular 1961 film *Breakfast at Tiffany's*. Although it is Butler's version that appears in the film (and which went to #11 pop, #14 R&B, 1961), Andy Williams was asked to sing on the Academy Awards telecast. Butler also worked with Hal David and Burt Bacharach and scored a hit with "Make It Easy on Yourself" (#20 pop, #18 R&B, 1962). In 1964 he had a pair of hits with Betty Everett [see entry], "Let It Be Me" (#5 pop, #5 R&B) and "Smile" (#42 pop, #42 R&B).

Butler seemed destined to be a middle-of-the-road balladeer, but a move to Philadelphia in 1967 and a series of recordings with writer/producers Kenny Gamble and Leon Huff redefined his style. His two albums with that production team, *The Ice Man Cometh* (#29 pop, #2 R&B, 1969) and *Ice on Ice* (#41 pop, #4 R&B, 1969), were among the most highly acclaimed soul works of the period. Other hits from this collaboration include "Never Give You Up" (#20 pop, #4 R&B, 1968), "Hey, Western Union Man" (#16 pop, #1 R&B, 1968), "Are You Happy" (#39 pop, #9 R&B, 1968), "Only the Strong Survive" (#4 pop, #1 R&B, 1969), "Moody Woman" (#24 pop, #3 R&B, 1969), and "What's the Use of Breaking Up" (#20 pop, #4 R&B, 1969). In 1971 Butler and Gene Chandler recorded together. That same year, "Ain't Understanding Mellow," a duet with Brenda Lee Eager, hit #21 pop, #3 R&B. Later in the decade he teamed with Thelma Houston. Butler continued performing, and in 1979 he reunited with Gamble and Huff for *Nothing Says I Love You Like I Love You* and its followup, *The Best Love I Ever Had*. In 1980 he founded Fountain Records.

Butler, who has always had an interest in politics, first won an elected office in Chicago in 1985. By 2001, he was serving his fourth four-year term as a Cook County (Chicago) Commissioner. He was inducted with the Impressions into the Rock and Roll Hall of Fame in 1991 and received the Rhythm & Blues Foundation's Pioneer Award in 1994 (he subsequently was elected chairman of its board). In 2000 he published his memoir, *Only the Strong Survive: Memoirs of a Soul Survivor* (cowritten with Earl Smith). He continues to perform.

Paul Butterfield Blues Band/ Paul Butterfield

Formed 1963, Chicago, IL
Paul Butterfield (b. Dec. 17, 1942, Chicago; d. May 4, 1987, North Hollywood, CA), voc., harmonica; Jerome Arnold, bass; Sam Lay, drums; Elvin Bishop (b. Oct. 21, 1942, Tulsa, OK), gtr; Mark Naftalin, kybds.; Mike Bloomfield (b. July 28, 1944, Chicago; d. Feb. 15, 1981, San Francisco, CA), gtr.
1965—*The Paul Butterfield Blues Band* (Elektra) (– Lay; + Billy Davenport, drums) 1966—*East-West* (– Bloomfield) 1967—*The Resurrection of Pigboy Crabshaw* (– Bishop; + various members) 1968—*In My Own Dream* 1969—*Keep on Moving* 1971—*Sometimes I Just Feel Like Smilin'* 1972—(group disbands) *Golden Butter—The Best of the Paul Butterfield Blues Band; Offer You Can't Refuse* (Red Lightnin').
Paul Butterfield's Better Days, formed 1972, Woodstock, NY: Butterfield; Billy Rich, bass; Amos Garrett, gtr.; Geoff Muldaur, voc.; Christopher Parker, drums; Ronnie Barron, kybds.
1973—*Better Days* (Bearsville); *It All Comes Back* 1976—*Put It in Your Ear* 1981—*North-South.*
Paul Butterfield solo: 1986—*The Legendary Paul Butterfield Rides Again* (Amherst).

Paul Butterfield, a white singer and harmonica player who apprenticed with black bluesmen, helped spur the American blues revival of the '60s. The teenage Butterfield ventured into Chicago's South Side clubs, eventually working his way into onstage jams with Howlin' Wolf, Buddy Guy, Otis Rush, Little Walter, Magic Sam, and other blues legends. Butterfield played with University of Chicago classmate Elvin Bishop in bar bands named the Salt and Pepper Shakers and the South Side Olympic Blues Team. In 1963 he formed the Paul Butterfield Blues Band with two former members of Howlin' Wolf's band, Jerome Arnold and Sam Lay, later adding Bishop, Mark Naftalin, and lead guitarist Mike Bloomfield. The group built a strong local following, and its debut album was released in 1965. At that year's Newport Folk Festival, after playing its own set, the Butterfield band backed Bob Dylan for his controversial premiere electric performance. *East-West* featured extended jams and showed the influences of jazz and Indian music. Bloomfield left to form Electric Flag; Bishop moved to lead guitar.

By 1967 Butterfield had begun the first of many experiments, adding a brass section (including David Sanborn on alto saxophone) and changing his orientation from blues to R&B. He played on Muddy Waters' 1969 album, *Fathers and Sons,* and after disbanding the Blues Band in 1972, moved to Woodstock, New York. There he formed Butterfield's Better Days with Amos Garrett, Geoff Muldaur, and Ronnie Barron.

Butterfield made an appearance at the Band's Last Waltz concert in 1976, and during the late '70s he toured with Levon Helm's RCO All Stars and with ex-Band bassist Rick Danko in the Danko-Butterfield Band. In early 1980, while recording *North-South* in Memphis, Butterfield was stricken with a perforated intestine and peritonitis, which forced him to undergo three major operations over the next several years. Butterfield's next—and last—album, *The Legendary Paul Butterfield Rides Again,* came out in 1986, one year before the 44-year-old musician, an alcoholic, was found dead in his apartment.

Butthole Surfers

Formed 1981, San Antonio, TX
Gibby Haynes (b. Gibson Haynes, ca. 1957), voc.; Paul Leary (b. ca. 1958), gtr.
1983—*Butthole Surfers* (Alternative Tentacles) (+ King Coffey, drums; + Theresa Nervosa, drums) 1984—*Live PCPPEP* 1985—*Psychic . . . Powerless . . . Another Man's Sac* (Touch and Go); *Cream Corn From the Socket of Davis* EP 1986—*Rembrandt Pussyhorse* (+ Jeff Pinkus, bass) 1987—*Locust Abortion Technician* 1988—*Hairway to Steven* 1989—*Double Live* (Latino Bugger Veil); *Widowermaker!* (Touch and Go) (– Nervosa) 1990—*"The Hurdy Gurdy Man"* EP (Rough Trade) 1991—*Piouhgd* 1993—*Independent Worm Saloon* (Capitol) 1995—*The Hole Truth and Nothing Butt* 1996—*Electriclarryland.*

Butthole Surfers are perhaps the most perversely confrontational and calculatedly outrageous American postpunk band. Their stage shows have included everything from backdrop projections of auto accidents and sex-change operations to androgynous nude dancers, crude pyrotechnics, and the incessant grossout shenanigans of singer Gibby Haynes. (At an early show he removed the dress he was wearing during a performance and—depending on who tells the story—either simulated sex or had sex with one of the band's dancers.) Though the Butthole Surfers' music combines the noisy, avant-garde tendencies of late '70s no wave with the throbbing, distorted drive of hardcore, much of it is informed by classic, psychedelic rock.

Haynes, whose father hosted a children's TV show in Dallas under the name Mr. Peppermint, met Paul Leary in 1977 while attending San Antonio's Trinity College. Four years later, Haynes, then doing graduate work in accounting, and Leary, son of the business school's dean, formed a band. They became Butthole Surfers when an announcer mistook one of their song titles for their band name. In San Francisco in 1981, the Surfers met the Dead Kennedys' Jello Biafra, who signed them to his Alternative Tentacles label. The band's self-titled first album contained the legendary dada-hardcore anthem "The Shah Sleeps in Lee Harvey's Grave."

Butthole Surfers: King Coffey, Paul Leary, Jeff Pinkus, Gibby Haynes, Theresa Nervosa

Between 1982 and 1985 the Surfers went through a succession of bass players and drummers. They toured constantly, perfecting their bizarre show by adding dancers, sometimes two drummers, and cultivating a hard-core cultish Deadhead-style following. Membership stabilized with the addition of King Coffey on drums in 1983. In 1985 the group signed with Touch and Go, soon becoming the label's best-selling band, and its music got even weirder and more depraved. Haynes' gut-wrenching sleaze and pseudo-Satanic ranting hit an all-time low on such songs as "Lady Sniff" *(Psychic . . . Powerless . . .)* and "Sweet Loaf" (*Locust Abortion Technician*'s spoof of Black Sabbath's "Sweet Leaf"), while Leary's inventive lead guitar chugged and meandered around newly added instrumentation such as acoustic guitars, piano, organ, violin, and strange effects, like speeded-up and slowed-down vocals, and tape manipulations. *Rembrandt Pussyhorse* stands as one of the most "out" psychedelic albums of the postpunk era, featuring snaky, Middle Eastern–style instrumentation and drones, twisted folk melodies, avant-garde improvisation, industrial noise and feedback, and gastrointestinal sounds. Haynes' attempts to shock include deranged laughter, *Exorcist*-like growls, and lyrics such as "There's a creep in the cellar that I'm gonna let in . . . and he really freaks me out when he peels off his skin." After appearing on the first Lollapalooza Tour in 1991, the Surfers signed with Capitol. Two years later the band released its major-label debut, the slightly more accessible *Independent Worm Saloon,* produced by former Led Zeppelin bassist John Paul Jones. In 1993 Haynes also formed a side band with actor Johnny Depp called P.

The Butthole Surfers' music has received radically mixed reviews, with underground observers generally applauding the envelope-pushing experimentations, and many mainstream rock critics put off by the band's constant arty attempts to shock. Through it all, the group is among the few '80s fringe acts to rise from independent to major-label status with its core audience and sound intact.

In 1996 the more streamlined sound of *Electriclarryland* (#31) was rewarded with sales of more than 625,000 copies and a high-profile gig on *Late Night With David Letterman.* And with the accessible single "Pepper," the band had the #1 song on *Billboard*'s Modern Rock Tracks chart, ahead of Smashing Pumpkins, Stone Temple Pilots, and Everclear. But this sudden brush with pop success was followed by a few years of legal troubles. Butthole Surfers recorded a followup in 1997 called *After the Astronaut,* but became enraged when Capitol provided copies to critics before it was finished. Legal wrangling to exit Capitol left that album unreleased, and the band was unable to record again until a departure was negotiated. By 1999, the band had moved to the Surfdog label, an imprint of Disney's Hollywood Records, and began reworking *After the Astronaut.* After an ugly break with Touch and Go, the Surfers' back catalogue was reissued on the band's own Latino Bugger Veil label.

The Buzzcocks

Formed 1975, Manchester, Eng.
Howard Devoto (b. Howard Trafford), voc.; Steve Diggle, gtr., bass; John Maher, drums; Pete Shelley (b. Peter McNeish, Apr. 17, 1955), voc., gtr.
1977—*Spiral Scratch* (New Hormones) (– Devoto; + Garth Smith, bass) 1978—(– Smith; + Steve Garvey, bass) *Another Music in a Different Kitchen* (UA/I.R.S.); *Love Bites* 1979—*Singles Going Steady* (I.R.S.); *A Different Kind of Tension* 1981—(group disbands) 1993—(group re-forms: Shelley; Diggle; + Tony Barber, bass; + Phil Barker, drums) *Trade Test Transmissions* (Caroline) 1996—*French* (I.R.S.); *All Set* 1999—*Modern* (Go-Kart) 2000—*Time's Up* (Mute).

The Buzzcocks were a successful U.K. new-wave singles band during the late '70s, combining Beatlesque romance and melodicism with a buzzsaw guitar attack and blistering punk-rock tempos. They came together at Bolton Institute in 1975 and made frequent London club appearances the following year. Their first recordings, including the four-song EP called *Spiral Scratch* (widely credited as Britain's first independent-label punk recording), were made with visionary early group leader Howard Devoto. When Devoto left the group in 1977 to form Magazine [see entry], Diggle switched from bass to guitar, and Garth Smith joined. Pete Shelley (who himself left the group in February 1981) became chief vocalist and songwriter. During their second U.S. tour in 1980, they picked up an enthusiastic coterie of followers, but their record sales were disappointing. In mid-1980, displeased with its lack of international success, the group disbanded. Shelley had a British hit on his own with "Homosapien," a sharp turn from the trademark Buzzcocks sound to synth-and-sequencer dance music.

In 1989 Shelley, Diggle, Garvey, and Maher reunited for a U.S. tour. By then, the Buzzcocks were seen as a core influence on modern British pop (as illustrated by the hit remake of their "Ever Fallen in Love" by Fine Young Cannibals in 1987). Four years later, with a new rhythm section—and with Nirvana's Kurt Cobain having told the rock press they were an inspiration—the Buzzcocks recorded a well-received comeback album, *Trade Test Transmissions,* and toured the U.S. It was the beginning of a renewed career, followed by a 23-cut live set, *French,* and the studio album *All Set*—both released in 1996. Though the band failed to tap into the popularity of Green Day and other young acts playing in a style the Buzzcocks helped invent, the quartet returned again in 1999 with *Modern.*

The Byrds

Formed 1964, Los Angeles, CA
Roger McGuinn (b. James Joseph McGuinn III, July 13, 1942, Chicago, IL), gtr., voc.; Chris Hillman (b. Dec. 4, 1942, Los Angeles), bass, voc.; Gene Clark (b. Harold Eugene Clark, Nov. 17, 1941, Tipton, MO; d. May 24, 1991, Sherman Oaks, CA), voc., tambourine, gtr.; David Crosby (b. David Van Cortland, Aug. 14, 1941, Los Angeles), gtr., voc.; Michael Clarke (b. June 3, 1944, New York, NY; d. Dec. 19, 1993, Treasure Island, FL), drums.
1965—*Mr. Tambourine Man* (Columbia) 1966—*Turn! Turn! Turn!* (– Clark) *Fifth Dimension* 1967—*Younger Than Yesterday; Greatest Hits* (– Crosby; – Clarke) 1968—*The Notorious Bird Brothers* (+ Kevin Kelley [b. 1945, CA], drums; + Gram Parsons [b. Ingram Cecil Connor III, Nov. 5, 1946, Winter Haven, FL; d. Sep. 19, 1973, Yucca Valley, CA], gtr., voc.); *Sweetheart of the Rodeo* (– Parsons; – Kelley; – Hillman; + Clarence White [b. June 6, 1944, Lewiston, ME; d. July 14, 1973, Palmdale, CA], gtr., voc.; + Gene Parsons [b. Apr. 9, 1944], drums; + John York, bass) 1969—*Dr. Byrds and Mr. Hyde; The Ballad of Easy Rider* (– York; + Skip Battin [b. Feb. 2, 1934, Gallipolis, OH], bass, voc.) 1970—*Untitled* 1971—*Byrdmaniax* 1972—*Farther Along* (– Gene Parsons; – Battin; + John Guerin, bass; + temporary drummers Daryl Dragon [b. Aug. 27, 1942, Los Angeles], Jim Moon) *Best of the Byrds—Greatest Hits, vol. 2* 1973—(group disbands; original group reunites for one-shot album) *The Byrds* (Asylum); *Preflyte* (Columbia) 1980—*Singles 1965–67* 1990—*The Byrds* 2000—*Live at the Fillmore—February 1969* (Columbia/Legacy).
Roger (Jim) McGuinn solo: 1973—*Roger McGuinn* (Columbia) 1974—*Peace on You* 1975—*Roger McGuinn and Band* 1976—*Cardiff Rose* 1977—*Thunderbyrd* 1991—*Back From Rio* (Arista) 1992—*Born to Rock & Roll* (Columbia) 1996—*Live From Mars* (Hollywood).
McGuinn, Clark, and Hillman: 1979—*McGuinn, Clark, and Hillman* (Capitol).
McGuinn and Hillman: 1980—*City.*
Gene Clark solo: 1967—*Echoes* (Columbia); *Gene Clark With the Gosdin Brothers* 1969—*Fantastic Expedition* (A&M); *Through the Morning* 1972—*White Light; Roadmaster* (Edsel, U.K.) 1974—*No Other* (Line) 1987—*Firebyrd* (Takoma); *So Rebellious a Lover* (with Carla Olson) (Razor & Tie) 1992—*Silhouetted in Light* (Edsel, U.K.) 1997—*American Dreamer* (Raven, Austral.) 1998—*Flying High* (A&M).
David Crosby solo: See Crosby, Stills, Nash and Young entry.
Chris Hillman solo: See Flying Burrito Brothers entry.
Gram Parsons solo: See entry.

The Byrds, led by Roger McGuinn, pioneered folk rock and later country rock. With their high harmonies, ringing guitars, and obsession with studio technique, they also became the sonic model for many rock bands, including the Eagles, Tom Petty, and the latter-day Fleetwood Mac.

The band was formed in summer 1964 as the Jet Set and toyed with the name Beefeaters before settling on the Byrds, misspelled à la the Beatles. A few months later, the Byrds were touted as "L.A.'s answer to London." After signing with Columbia in November 1964 they recorded demos released years later as *Preflyte.* In January 1965 they met Bob Dylan who provided their first hit, the #1 "Mr. Tambourine Man." The single had Dylan's lyrics, a guitar hook, chorus harmonies, and a rock rhythm section: folk rock. *Mr. Tambourine Man,* released in June 1965, went to #6.

In 1966 the Byrds had a major hit with the anthemic "Turn! Turn! Turn!"—a Bible passage set to music by Pete Seeger. But the Byrds failed to achieve such commercial success for the rest of their existence. By the time *Fifth Dimension* was released in summer 1966, Gene Clark had left to embark on a solo career. His departure, plus their somewhat avant-garde LP, marked the start of the Byrds' "space rock" phase. The hit single "Eight Miles High" (#14, 1966) from *Fifth Dimension* solidified their new style. It was also one of the first records to be widely banned because of supposedly drug-oriented lyrics.

Tensions within the band increased and occasionally erupted into onstage fisticuffs. The group managed to stay together long enough to see 1967's *Younger Than Yesterday* released and to record the countryish followup, *The Notorious Byrd Brothers,* but by the time the later album hit stores in January 1968, Crosby and drummer Michael Clarke were both gone. Crosby went on to superstardom with Crosby, Stills, Nash and Young, while Clarke joined the Dillard and Clark group. McGuinn and Hillman soldiered on with new drummer Kevin Kelley and International Submarine Band singer/songwriter/guitarist Gram Parsons. Parsons took the Byrds even further into country territory; *Sweetheart of the Rodeo,* recorded in Nashville and released in the fall of 1968, remains a cornerstone of the country-rock movement that spawned groups like the Eagles and Poco in the '70s and Uncle Tupelo in the '90s.

By October 1968 McGuinn was the only original Byrd remaining, as Parsons and Hillman left to continue their country experiments with the Flying Burrito Brothers. He kept the patchwork Byrds alive through 1973 with a series of partners, most notably guitarist Clarence White, a session veteran of several previous Byrds albums. The various combos toured steadily and put out a series of mildly successful albums, including the double live and studio set *Untitled,* which contained "Chestnut Mare," one of McGuinn's signature tunes. After 1972's *Farther Along,* however, McGuinn disbanded the group to record a reunion album with Crosby, Clark, Hillman, and Clarke in 1973. Simply titled *The Byrds,* the album flopped and the name was laid to rest.

McGuinn subsequently embarked on a low-key solo career. In late 1975 and early 1976 he was prominently featured in Dylan's Rolling Thunder Revue. With fellow Revue trouper Mick Ronson producing, he recorded *Cardiff Rose.* In early 1977 he assembled a new band, wryly dubbed Thunderbyrd, and recorded an album of the same name. By late in the year he was playing occasional dates in tandem with Clark, and the alliance soon expanded to include Hillman as well. In 1979 the three recorded their self-titled debut disc and enjoyed some pop success with "Don't You Write Her Off" (#33, 1979). In 1980 McGuinn and Hillman returned with *City,* before the band gradually fragmented, and McGuinn took up his solo career again. It was more than 10 years before he released another LP. *Back From Rio,* with assistance from admirers such as Tom Petty and Elvis Costello, reached #44.

The same month the LP charted, January 1991, the Byrds were inducted into the Rock and Roll Hall of Fame. McGuinn, Hillman, and Crosby had been at odds with Michael Clarke and Gene Clark for touring using the Byrds name. To prevent them from doing so, in 1989 McGuinn, Hillman, and Crosby had played three dates to establish their legal right to the name. A year later they recorded four songs for inclusion on the four-CD *The Byrds* anthology. Four months after the Hall of Fame ceremonies, Gene Clark died at age 46; in 1993 Michael Clarke died of liver failure.

Beginning in 1996, Columbia/Legacy began a lavish Byrds reissue series, eventually re-releasing the entire catalogue (minus the reunion album, which had been recorded for Asylum) embellished with multiple bonus tracks, including an entire disc's worth of unissued recordings with *Untitled.* Along with the reissues came the previously unreleased *Live at the Fillmore—February 1969.* McGuinn, meanwhile, directed his energies toward recording solo versions of obscure folk songs, which he made available as MP3s on the Internet as part of his "Folk Den" Web site.

David Byrne

Born May 14, 1952, Dumbarton, Scot.
1981—*The Complete Score From the Broadway Production of "The Catherine Wheel"* (Sire) 1985—*Music for "The Knee Plays"* (ECM) 1986—*Sounds From "True Stories"* (Sire) 1988—*Married to the Mob* soundtrack (Reprise) 1989—*Rei Momo* (Luaka Bop/Sire) 1991—*The Forest* 1992—*Uh-Oh* 1994—*David Byrne* 1997—*Feelings* 2001—*Look Into the Eyeball* (Luaka Bop/Virgin).
With Brian Eno: 1981—*My Life in the Bush of Ghosts* (Sire).
With Ryuichi Sakamoto and Cong Su: 1988—*The Last Emperor* soundtrack (Virgin Movie Music).

In his work outside Talking Heads [see entry], David Byrne has explored electronics, performance art, and world music. Byrne was born in Scotland but raised in Baltimore where his father was an electronics engineer. Coming from a working-class environment, Byrne felt alienated from the many wealthy students he encountered as an art student at the Rhode Island School of Design. He dropped out after one year but stayed in Providence, playing one-man shows with a ukulele and eventually forming the Artistics (a.k.a. the Autistics) and then Talking Heads.

Byrne's first project outside the Heads, *My Life in the Bush of Ghosts,* was a collaboration with Heads producer Brian Eno. The resulting collage of electronic music, vocal tapes, and African and other third world rhythms was widely acclaimed as groundbreaking. It ran into controversy when Muslims objected to the track "Qu'ran" for its use of religious text; it was replaced with "Very Very Hungry." This was the first of many times Byrne has been accused by detractors of colonialist appropriation.

Byrne next turned to theatrical collaborations, writing music for the Twyla Tharp dance piece *The Catherine Wheel.* For *Knee Plays,* a section of Robert Wilson's epic *CIVIL warS,* Byrne incorporated text and music based on New Orleans brass bands. In 1986 he wrote, directed, and starred in the film *True Stories,* a series of vignettes about American eccentrics. He produced and wrote the majority of the songs for the film soundtrack (not the same as the Talking Heads album) and performed two of them. He also composed the soundtrack for the Jonathan Demme film *Married to the Mob* (1988). With Ryuichi Sakamoto and Cong Su, he won an Oscar for the soundtrack to *The Last Emperor* (1988). Byrne has also written soundtracks for two movies by Philip Haas.

In 1988 Byrne's conversion to world music led him to form Luaka Bop Records, which has released, along with Byrne's records, music by Brazilian, Cuban, and Asian artists, as well as the U.K. avant-dance band A.R. Kane and the L.A. rockers Geggy Tah. He also made Cuban records available in the U.S. for the first time since the 1961 boycott. Byrne collaborated with a number of Latin musicians on the Steve Lillywhite–produced *Rei Momo,* particularly percussionist Milton Cardona, arranger Angel Fernandez, and songwriters Willie Colon and Johnny Pacheco. He was again accused of white privilege when Colon said in *Billboard* that Byrne had exploited musicians starved for validation. Byrne included many of the album's performers in his 14-piece band on the Rei Momo world tour.

Byrne's film *Ilé Aiyé (The House of Life),* a documentary about Yoruban dance-music rituals, kicked off the *Alive From Off Center* series on PBS in summer 1989. He worked with Robert Wilson again on 1991's *The Forest,* a composition for a full orchestra. *Uh-Oh* featured more conventional rock songs, with Byrne using the same band on every track—although that band included Meters bassist George Porter Jr., Latin percussionists Hector Rosado and Cafe, and Miami drummer Oscar Salas. A concert film, *Between the Teeth,* documented the tour.

Byrne formed an all-new band with a more stripped-down sound (Todd Turkisher on drums, Paul Socolow on bass, and Mauro Refosco on mallet instruments and percussion) for *David Byrne,* which marked a return to the wry, affectless writing style he perfected with Talking Heads. In 1996 Byrne, citing "wrongful use," filed a lawsuit against the members of his former band and Radioactive Records head (and Heads ex-manager) Gary Kurfirst to halt the release of a new, Byrne-less album, *No Talking Just Head,* and to prevent the musicians' use of the name Heads for a tour. The suit was settled out of court, and plans for both album and tour proceeded. Two years later, Byrne recorded *Feelings,* which featured collaborations with the British dance-music group Morcheeba and members of Devo. The subsequent tour featured the English avant-classical string group Balanescu Quartet. In the fall of 1998 the singer began a half-year stint as host of the PBS music program *Sessions at West 54th.* In 1999 he collaborated with the Belgian dance troupe Ultima Vez, composing music for director Wim Vandekeybus's *In Spite of Wishing and Wanting. Look Into the Eyeball* boasted a variety of influences, including Philly soul, and featured a Byrne composition written in Spanish.

Cabaret Voltaire

Formed 1973, Sheffield, Eng.
Stephen Mallinder (b. Sheffield), voc., bass, perc.; Richard H. Kirk (b. Sheffield), gtr., kybds., wind instruments; Christopher R. Watson, kybds., tape machines.
1978—*Extended Play* EP (Rough Trade, U.K.) 1979—*Mix Up* 1980—*Live at the YMCA 27-10-79; Three Mantras; The Voice of America; 1974–1976* cassette (Industrial, U.K.) 1981—*3 Crépuscule Tracks* (Rough Trade); *Live at the Lyceum* cassette; *Red Mecca* (– Watson) 1982—*2 X 45; Hail! Live in Japan* 1983—*The Crackdown* (Some Bizarre-Virgin, U.K.); *Johnny YesNo* (Doublevision, U.K.) 1984—*Micro-Phonies* (Some Bizarre-Virgin, U.K.) 1985—*Drinking Gasoline* (Caroline); *The Arm of the Lord* 1986—*The Drain Train* EP (Mute) 1987—*The Golden Moments of Cabaret Voltaire* (Rough Trade, U.K.); *Code* (EMI Manhattan) 1988—*Eight Crépuscule Tracks* (Giant) 1990—*Listen Up With Cabaret Voltaire* (Mute-Restless); *The Living Legends; Groovy, Laidback and Nasty* (Parlophone, U.K.) 1992—*Plasticity* (Instinct, U.K.); *"International Language"* 1994—*The Conversation* 1999—*BBC Recordings 1984–86* (Pilot).

Cabaret Voltaire was one of the earliest electronic industrial-dance groups. Along with Throbbing Gristle and Psychic TV, the trio had a profound influence on the techno, ambient, and industrial styles that came to prominence in the late '80s and early '90s.

Little is known about the members of Cabaret Voltaire, except that in the early '70s, seven teenagers came together in the industrial city of Sheffield, England, and began making tapes of noises to play at parties for laughs. The group was soon whittled down to just Stephen Mallinder, Richard Kirk, and Christopher Watson, who hooked up with the music department at Sheffield Haddam University and gained access to a synthesizer, tape recorders, and other instruments.

Inspired by the dada art movement, the ambient work of Brian Eno, and its industrial environment, Cabaret Voltaire blended the sounds of everyday objects with the textures of musical instruments to create aural collages of noise, beats, and disembodied vocals. They named themselves after the dadaist club formed in Zurich in 1917 by Hugo Ball.

Cabaret Voltaire's early recordings are harsh and abrasive; its first EP contains a distorted version of Lou Reed's "Here She Comes Now." As the group matured during its prolific early-'80s period, it became increasingly interested in Middle Eastern sounds and more accessible dance music; it hit an artistic peak with 1982's *2 X 45*.

Watson left the group in 1981 to work in television, and later showed up with the avant-garde Hafler Trio. By the mid-'80s Cabaret Voltaire's music had become slicker, though the group never scored a major hit. In the late '80s it had begun flirting with house music, releasing 12 different mixes of the 1989 single "Hypnotized." In the early '90s Cabaret Voltaire returned to the more ambient sounds of its earlier days, and then disappeared from the scene as mysteriously as the group entered it. Its most recent album of new material was 1994's *The Conversation,* followed six years later by the archival *BBC Recordings 1984–86.*

The Cadillacs

Formed 1953, New York, NY
Lineup ca. 1954: Earl Carroll (b. Nov. 2, 1937, New York), lead voc.; Robert Phillips (b. 1935, New York), voc.; La Verne Drake (b. 1938, New York), voc.; Johnny "Gus" Willingham (b. 1937, New York), voc.; James "Poppa" Clark, voc.
1990—*The Best of the Cadillacs* (Rhino).

A distinguished '50s R&B group whose legend has grown appreciably over the years, the Cadillacs considered uptempo numbers like "Speedo" (sometimes spelled "Speedoo") (#17 pop, 1956; #3 R&B, 1955) their forte, although latter-day fans often prefer their slow ballads.

Originally called the Carnations, the Cadillacs came together in 1953 after a series of informal sing-along sessions in Harlem. A short time later they met manager Esther Navaroo, who persuaded them to change their name to the Cadillacs and helped them record "Gloria," a song she had written. (Navaroo received writer's credit for many of the group's releases; it was later revealed that some songs had been written by the group members.) Their stage show included flamboyant attire and tight choreography, a precursor of and influence on the Motown style, not surprising since the Temptations and the Four Tops fell under the tutelage of the Cadillacs' choreographer, Cholly Atkins.

In late 1955 the group released "Speedo," about its happy-go-lucky singer Earl Carroll. The record employed fast scat harmonies and became one of the Cadillacs' few hits, along with "Peek-a-Boo" (#28, 1959) and "What You Bet" (#30 R&B, 1961). Other releases included "Zoom," "Woe Is Me," and "Rudolph the Red-Nosed Reindeer" (1956). In 1957 the group splintered into two singing groups, both calling themselves the Cadillacs. The group that included Carroll released "Jay Walker," "Please Mr. Johnson" (both 1959), and several other singles through 1961. Through 1963 both groups of Cadillacs released records to dwindling public interest.

In 1961 Earl Carroll left to replace Cornell Gunter in the Coasters, with whom he toured through the '70s. Three years later Carroll's new group released "Speedo's Back in Town," a tribute to Speedo recorded live at the Apollo. The Cadillacs continued to run through the '60s. In the early '80s the group re-formed with original members Carroll and Phillips.

J.J. Cale

Born Jean Jacques Cale, Dec. 5, 1938, Oklahoma City, OK
1972—*Naturally* (Shelter); *Really* 1974—*Okie* 1976—*Troubadour* 1979—*Number 5* 1981—*Shades* 1982—*Grasshopper* (Mercury) 1983—*#8* 1990—*Travelog* (Silvertone) 1992—*Number 10* 1994—*Closer to You* (Virgin) 1996—*Guitar Man* 1997—*Anyway the Wind Blows—Anthology* (PolyGram) 1998—*Very Best of J.J. Cale.*

Self-described "semiretired," reclusive singer/songwriter J.J. Cale's songs have been covered by artists ranging from Johnny Cash to Captain Beefheart. But his trademark sinuous, bluesy guitar lines and mumbly, near-whispered vocals have been popularized by Dire Straits and Eric Clapton; the latter's versions of "After Midnight" and "Cocaine" have become radio hits.

Cale took up the guitar at age 10. After playing in a succession of Tulsa, Oklahoma, bands (one group included Leon Russell) during high school, he went on the road in 1959 and played in the Grand Ole Opry road company. By the early '60s, he was back in Tulsa playing with Russell, and in 1964 the two moved to L.A. with fellow Oklahoma native Carl Radle (later of Derek and the Dominos). Cale hooked up with Delaney and Bonnie, and by 1965 he was recording on his own, including the first release of "After Midnight." He left Delaney and Bonnie and in 1967 returned to Tulsa.

Radle passed on some of Cale's homemade demo tapes to Denny Cordell, and Cale became one of the first signings of Cordell and Russell's Shelter Records in 1969. Following Clapton's 1970 success with "After Midnight" (#18), Cale recorded *Naturally* in 1972, from which "Crazy Mama" went to #22. "Magnolia," also on that album, was later covered by Poco and José Feliciano. Throughout the '70s, Cale recorded and toured at a leisurely pace. Cale moved to Mercury Records in 1982, releasing two albums, *Grasshopper* (#149, 1982) and *#8* (1983). Disappointed by their sales, he asked to be released from his contract. He spent the next six years living in a mobile home outside L.A., emerging only for an annual tour.

Cale released two albums on Silvertone, a U.K.-based independent label, *Travelog* (#131, 1990) and *Number 10* (1992). He also produced John Hammond's *Got Love If You Want It* (1992) and *Trouble No More* (1994). *Closer to You* (1994) and *Guitar Man* (1996) continued Cale's trademark laid-back bluesy songwriting.

John Cale

Born Mar. 9, 1942, Cwmamman, Garnant, South Wales
1969—*Vintage Violence* (Columbia) 1971—*Church of Anthrax* 1972—*The Academy in Peril* (Reprise) 1973—*Paris 1919* 1974—*Fear* (Island); *June 1, 1974* 1975—*Slow Dazzle; Helen of Troy* 1977—*Guts* 1980—*Sabotage/Live* (I.R.S.) 1981—*Honi Soit* (A&M) 1982—*Music for a New Society* (Ze/Island/Passport); 1984—*Caribbean Sunset* (Ze/Island); *John Cale Comes Alive* 1985—*Artificial Intelligence* (Beggars Banquet) 1989—*Land* (Island); *Words for the Dying* (Opal) 1990—*Wrong Way Up; Songs for Drella* (with Lou Reed) (Sire); *HN* (Mango) 1991—*Even Cowgirls Get the Blues* (ROIR) 1992—*Fragments of a Rainy Season* (Rykodisc); *Paris S'eveille* (Crepuscule) 1993—*23 Pieces for La Naissance de L'Amour* 1994—*Seducing Down the Door: A John Cale Collection* (Rhino) 1996—*Island Anthology* (Island); *Walking on Locusts* (Hannibal) 1997—*Eat/Kiss—Music From the Films of Andy Warhol* 1998—*Dance Music* (Detour); *Nico* (Elektra/Asylum) 1999—*Close Watch* (Polygram International).

John Cale has brought an avant-garde ear to rock & roll ever since he founded the Velvet Underground with Lou Reed in 1966. His work shows a fascination with opposites: lyricism

John Cale

and noise, subtlety and bluntness, hypnotic repetition and sudden change. Even as a student of classical music, he was an extremist: During a recital at the Guildhall School of Music, London, where he was studying theory and composition, he demolished a piano. Cale studied in Britain with composer Humphrey Searle, came to America in 1963 to work with Iannis Xenakis and Aaron Copland under the auspices of a Leonard Bernstein Fellowship, then settled in New York with such radical composers as John Cage and La Monte Young. That year Cale was one of a group of pianists to perform Erik Satie's nearly 19-hour-long "Vexations." Through his association with the Lower Manhattan art community, Cale met Reed, who directed him toward electric instruments and rock & roll and helped conceive the Velvet Underground [see entry], for whom Cale played keyboards, bass, and electric viola.

After two Velvets albums *(The Velvet Underground and Nico* and *White Light/White Heat),* Cale left in 1968 for a solo career. In the early '70s he worked as an A&R man for Warner Bros. and Elektra, and as a consultant for Columbia, remixing albums by Barbra Streisand and Paul Revere and the Raiders in quadrophonic sound. On his solo albums of the decade, he used elegant pop (*Paris 1919,* with Little Feat's Lowell George), hard rock *(Fear),* Phil Spector/Brian Wilson gloss *(Slow Dazzle),* minimalism *(Church of Anthrax,* with fellow La Monte Young pupil Terry Riley), full orchestra *(The Academy in Peril),* and punk *(Sabotage).* Lyrically, he displayed equal daring; delivered in a strong baritone, his work ranged from musings about terrorism, espionage, and states of psychological extremity to love songs. His '70s tours, generally featuring guitarist Chris Spedding, were often acts of disturbing theater (recorded at New York's CBGB, *Even Cowgirls Get the Blues* captured the punk ambience of the period); at one point Cale chopped up a chicken onstage, causing his band members to walk out.

By the next decade Cale had established himself as a producer/collaborator on some 80 albums, ranging from the debut efforts of Iggy Pop and the Stooges, Patti Smith, Jonathan Richman's Modern Lovers, and Squeeze to four albums by former Velvets singer Nico; he also had worked with Brian Eno, Kevin Ayers, Kate and Anna McGarrigle, Nick Drake, and Mike Heron and scored soundtracks for Andy Warhol's *Heat* and Roger Corman's *Caged Heat.* While commercial success continued to elude him, he was lauded as one of punk's godfathers, a status he contended against with characteristic irony: His primary interest remained classical music. As the '80s waned he continued producing (Happy Mondays), scoring (the soundtrack for Jonathan Demme's *Something Wild* with Laurie Anderson and David Byrne), and releasing solo work as various as the almost-pop of *Wrong Way Up* to "The Falklands Suite," an orchestration of Dylan Thomas poetry that highlighted *Words for the Dying.*

By 1993 Cale had come full circle: Having, two years earlier, collaborated with Lou Reed on *Songs for Drella,* a tribute to Velvet Underground mentor Andy Warhol, he teamed with the Velvets on a reunion tour.

On his own, he continued to innovate, releasing in 1996, with help from David Byrne and Velvets drummer Maureen Tucker, *Walking on Locusts,* featuring a moving tribute to Velvets guitarist Sterling Morrison, and, in 1998, *Nico,* an elegy for Velvets chanteuse Nico.

Cameo

Formed 1974, New York, NY
Larry Blackmon (b. New York), drums, bass, voc.; Tomi Jenkins, voc.; Nathan Leftenant, trumpet, voc.
1977—*Cardiac Arrest* (Chocolate City) 1978—*We All Know Who We Are* 1979—*Ugly Ego; Secret Omen* 1980—*Cameosis; Feel Me* 1981—*Knights of the Sound Table* 1982—*Alligator Woman* (Atlanta Artists) 1983—*Style* 1984—*She's Strange* 1985—*Single Life* 1986—*Word Up!* 1988—*Machismo* 1990—*Real Men . . . Wear Black* 1992—*Emotional Violence* (Reprise) 1993—*The Best of Cameo* (Mercury) 1994—*In the Face of Funk* (Way 2 Funky) 1996—*The Best of Cameo, vol. 2* (Mercury); *Nasty* (Intersound) 1998—*Ballads Collection* (PolyGram); *Greatest Hits* 1999—*12" Collection & More* 2000—*Sexy Sweet Thing* (Universal/Private Eye).

The brainchild of multi-instrumentalist and songwriter Larry Blackmon, the group Cameo is a confusingly complex net of personal and financial entanglements. By the early '70s the Juilliard-trained Blackmon became leader of the dozen or so musicians and in 1974 changed their name from the New York City Players to Cameo. Viewed as a minor-league Funkadelic (with whom Cameo shared a label and for whom they frequently opened), they were moderately successful, with three Top 10 R&B hits: "I Just Want to Be" (#3 R&B, 1979), "Sparkle" (#10 R&B, 1979), and "Shake Your Pants" (#8 R&B, 1980).

Unhappy with how the band was being treated, and finding the North inhospitable to African-Americans, in 1981 Blackmon moved operations to Atlanta, where he started his Atlanta Artists label. The early albums were unsuccessful, and to save money, the personnel of the band—always a mystery, since Blackmon withheld credit from some musicians—was reduced to a core band of Blackmon, Tomi Jenkins, and Nathan Leftenant. This version of the band produced the spare, ominous, stalking funk of "She's Strange" (#47 pop, #1 R&B, 1984), "Word Up" (#6 pop, #1 R&B, 1986), "Candy" (#21 pop, #1 R&B, 1986), and "Back and Forth" (#50 pop, #3 R&B, 1987).

Stardom gave the always voluble Blackmon license to make outrageous statements, dismissing Steve Winwood and Peter Gabriel as false funk, calling Kool and the Gang plagiarists, and chastising rap musicians for irresponsible attitudes. Cameo also made a striking visual impression, with geometric haircuts and Jean-Paul Gaultier–designed clothes (with Blackmon's oversize red leather codpiece the center of attention). In 1987 Cameo collaborated with Miles Davis on "In the Night."

Blackmon has made a name for himself as a producer; his credits include Bobby Brown's debut. In 1991 he was named vice president of A&R at Warner-Reprise Records, though by 1994 that relationship had ended. By that time, Blackmon and Cameo were no longer reaching the top of the charts but remained a dependable touring attraction (documented on the live *Nasty*). Will Smith introduced a new generation of listeners to Cameo when he featured the band on his 1997 album, *Big Willie Style*.

Glen Campbell

Born Apr. 22, 1936, Billstown, AR
1967—*Gentle on My Mind* (Capitol); *By the Time I Get to Phoenix* 1968—*Hey Little One; A New Place in the Sun; Bobbie Gentry and Glen Campbell* (with Bobbie Gentry); *Wichita Lineman; That Christmas Feeling* 1969—*Galveston; Glen Campbell Live* 1970—*Try a Little Kindness* 1971—*Glen Campbell's Greatest Hits; The Last Time I Saw Her* 1975—*Arkansas; Rhinestone Cowboy* 1976—*The Best of Glen Campbell; Bloodline* 1977—*Southern Nights* 1978—*Basic* 1979—*Highwayman* 1980—*Somethin' 'Bout You Baby I Like* 1981—*It's the World Gone Crazy* 1984—*Old Home Town* (Atlantic America) 1987—*Still Within the Sound of My Voice* (MCA); *The Very Best of Glen Campbell* (Capitol) 1988—*Light Years* (MCA) 1990—*Walkin' in the Sun* (Capitol Nashville); *Greatest Country Hits* (Curb); *Classics Collection* (Capitol Nashville) 1991—*Unconditional Love; Show Me Your Way* 1992—*Wings of Victory* 1993—*Somebody Like That* (Liberty).

Glen Campbell has been a critically respected mainstream country-pop star for more than two decades. A subtle, adept interpreter (as evidenced in such Jimmy Webb compositions as "Wichita Lineman"), Campbell has also been well received by contemporary Christian audiences.

Campbell was one of 12 children in a family where everyone played the guitar and sang. He got his first guitar at age four and left home as a teenager to tour with an uncle, a musician named Dick Bill. In 1960 Campbell moved to L.A., where he became known in country and rock circles and supported himself with session work for Frank Sinatra, Rick Nelson, Johnny Cash, Dean Martin, the Mamas and the Papas, Gene Clark, and several of Phil Spector's groups. In 1965 he played bass or guitar (sources differ) with the Beach Boys for eight months following Brian Wilson's decision not to appear with the band.

Campbell signed with Capitol in 1962 and recorded with occasional and minor success; his 1965 cover of Donovan's "Universal Soldier" entered the Top 50. In 1967 he hit with John Hartford's "Gentle on My Mind" (#39) and became a regular guest on the Smothers Brothers' variety program. His other '60s hits included the Jimmy Webb compositions "By the Time I Get to Phoenix" (#11, 1967), "Wichita Lineman" (#3, 1968), and "Galveston" (#4, 1969). From January 1969 to June 1972 Campbell hosted his own variety show, *The Glen Campbell Goodtime Hour*. His later hits include "Rhinestone Cowboy" (#1, 1975), Allen Toussaint's "Southern Nights" (#1, 1977), and "Country Boy (You Got Your Feet in L.A.)" (#11, 1976). Over the years, he has also worked in movies (*True Grit* with John Wayne, *Norwood*) and has made countless appearances on television, including the syndicated series *The Glen Campbell Music Show* (1982–83).

Though Campbell's appearances in the pop Top 40 became rare, he toured relentlessly and remained a strong presence on the country and gospel charts during the '80s and '90s. He also spoke freely in interviews about his 1981 baptism. In 1991 he launched a long-running tour that featured John Hartford, Jim Stafford, and Nicolette Larson. The following year he voiced Chanticleer the Rooster in the animated feature film *Rock-a-Doodle*. In 1994 he published his autobiography, *Rhinestone Cowboy*. Campbell recently resumed touring after a five-year stint at his own Glen Campbell Goodtime Theatre in Branson, Missouri. He continues to record occasional gospel and Christmas albums. He is also a frequent performer on the golf course, often with his somewhat unlikely pal Alice Cooper.

Milton Campbell: See Little Milton

Camper Van Beethoven/Cracker

Formed 1984, Santa Cruz, CA
David Lowery (b. Sep. 10, 1960, San Antonio, TX), gtr., voc., drums; Victor Krummenacher (b. Apr. 7, 1965, Riverside, CA), bass, voc.; Chris Molla, gtr., voc., drums; Jonathan Segal (b. Sep. 3, 1963, Marseilles, Fr.), violin, kybds., mandolin, noise,

voc.; Greg Lisher (b. Nov. 29, 1963, Santa Cruz), gtr.
1985—*Telephone Free Landslide Victory* (Independent Projects/Rough Trade) 1986—*II & III* (Pitch a Tent/Rough Trade); *Camper Van Beethoven* (+ Chris Pedersen [b. Aug. 16, 1960, San Diego, CA], drums) 1987—*Vampire Can Mating Oven* EP (– Molla) 1988—*Our Beloved Revolutionary Sweetheart* (Virgin) 1989—*Key Lime Pie* (– Segal; + Morgan Fichter, violin) 2000—*Camper Van Beethoven Are Dead. Long Live Camper Van Beethoven* (Pitch-A-Tent).
Cracker, formed 1990, Richmond, VA: Lowery; Johnny Hickman, voc., gtr.; Davey Faragher, voc., bass; Michael Urbano, drums; Phil Jones, drums, perc.
1992—*Cracker* (Virgin) 1993—*Kerosene Hat* 1996—*Golden Age* (– Faragher; – Urbano; – Jones; + Bob Rupe, bass; + Charlie Quintana, drums) 1998—*Gentleman's Blues* (– Quintana) 2000—*Garage D' Or.*

Camper Van Beethoven introduced an eclectic, often humorous blend of hippie psychedelia, avant-garde improvisation, country-western shadings, pseudo-ethnic sounds, and a hardcore punch to the mid-'80s postpunk scene. What saved the group from novelty status was its genuine talent for making interesting, adventurous music. After its breakup, Lowery went on to greater commercial success in his band Cracker.

Born in San Antonio, Texas, and raised in cities around the globe as an air force brat, CVB leader David Lowery ultimately landed as a teenager in Redlands, California (just outside of L.A.). By 1983 Lowery was studying mathematics at UC Santa Cruz and had begun playing with his first band, Sitting Duck, which experimented with ethnic sounds by way of TV shows and advertisements, and played alongside thrashy punk and psychedelic rock & roll. The earliest version of Camper Van Beethoven grew out of Sitting Duck and included Lowery, Krummenacher, Molla, and guitarist David McDaniel (who actually named the band shortly before leaving). It wasn't until the next year, however, that the Campers began following their eclectic muse in earnest. Lowery had returned to college in Santa Cruz and was soon followed by Krummenacher and Molla. There they met up with local guitarist Greg Lisher and composition student Jonathan Segal.

The band's first album, *Telephone Free Landslide Victory,* on the arty L.A.-based label Independent Projects, produced the humorous "Take the Skinheads Bowling," which became a cult favorite among college students. The album also featured a slowed-down, violin-drenched version of Black Flag's first single, "Wasted." The album was followed by a string of equally offbeat collections of songs—which featured titles like "ZZ Top Goes to Egypt" and "Joe Stalin's Cadillac"—on which the Campers experimented with everything from Beatlesque tape manipulation and Arabic-like drones to absurdist lyrics and offbeat covers (such as Ringo Starr's "Photograph" and Pink Floyd's "Interstellar Overdrive"). In 1987 the group recorded with the eccentric guitarist Eugene Chadbourne—calling themselves Camper Van Chadbourne—for the tiny indie label Fundamentalist Records. Virgin signed the band in 1988, releasing the more accessible (yet still very offbeat) *Our Beloved Revolutionary Sweetheart* and *Key Lime Pie.*

In 1988 Krummenacher, Lisher, and Pedersen took the band's arty quality to their side project, Monks of Doom, and Segal recorded a solo album. Camper Van Beethoven parted ways in 1989, and Lowery took the hooky pop side of the band into his group Cracker. With guitarist and Redlands friend Johnny Hickman, Lowery relocated to Richmond, Virginia, to make music. Coming immediately after Camper's far-out *Key Lime Pie,* the feisty roots-rock sound of Cracker initially earned derision from alternative circles, as it discarded Camper's violins and strange polyrhythms.

After the first, self-titled album won airplay on college radio with the typically cynical anthem "Teen Angst (What the World Needs Now)," Cracker's followup, *Kerosene Hat* (#59, 1993), yielded the modern-rock radio hit "Low." It helped propel the album to sales above 1 million. After playing to larger audiences, Cracker reconvened for *Golden Age* (#63, 1996), which failed to repeat the same lasting commercial success of *Kerosene Hat.* While *Gentleman's Blues* (#182, 1998) continued that trend, Lowery became busy as a producer, recording both new pop acts and hardcore bands in his Richmond studio, and coproducing the Counting Crows' *This Desert Life.*

In 2000 Lowery released both a Cracker retrospective, *Garage D' Or,* and another retrospective called *Camper Van Beethoven Are Dead. Long Live Camper Van Beethoven.* The members of both bands then toured together in a roadshow that included sets by Cracker and solo artists Krummenacher, Segal, and Lisher.

Can

Formed 1968, Cologne, W. Ger.
Irmin Schmidt (b. May 29, 1937, Berlin, Ger.), kybds., voc.; Michael Karoli (b. Apr. 29, 1948, Straubing, Ger.), gtr., violin, voc.; Holger Czukay (b. Mar. 24, 1938, Danzig, Ger.), bass, voc., electronics; Jaki Liebezeit (b. May 26, 1938, Dresden, Ger.), drums, reeds, voc.; Malcolm Mooney, voc.; David Johnson, flute, electronics.
1968—(– Johnson) 1969—*Monster Movie* (United Artists, U.K.) (– Mooney; + Kenji "Damo" Suzuki [b. Jan. 16, 1950, Jap.], voc.) 1970—*Soundtracks* 1971—*Tago Mago* 1972—*Ege Bamyasi* (United Artists) 1973—*Future Days* (– Suzuki) 1974—*Limited Edition* (United Artists, U.K.); *Soon Over Babaluma* 1975—*Landed* (Virgin, U.K.) 1976—*Unlimited Edition* (Caroline, U.K.); *Flow Motion* (Virgin, U.K.); *Opener: 1971–1974* (Sunset, U.K.) 1977—(+ Rosko Gee, bass; + Reebop Kwaku Baah [b. 1944, Lagos, Nigeria; d. 1982, Swe.], perc.) *Saw Delight* (Virgin, U.K.) (– Czukay) 1978—*Cannibalism* (United Artists, U.K.); *Out of Reach* (Peters Int'l) 1979—(+ Czukay) Can (Laser, U.K.) (group disbands) 1980—*Cannibalism 1* (Spoon, Ger.) 1981—*Incandescence 1969–1977* (Virgin, U.K.); *Delay 1968* (Spoon, Ger.) 1986—(group re-forms: Schmidt; Karoli; Czukay; Liebezeit; Mooney) 1988—*Rite Time* (Mercury, U.K.) 1990—*Cannibalism 2* (Spoon-Mute); *Cannibalism 3* 1991—(– Czukay) 1999—*Can Box.*

European art-rock band Can was one of the first groups to use electronic "treatments" of instruments, and it pioneered an exploratory postpsychedelic-rock style that would later influence Amon Duul, Ash Ra Temple, and the generations of new-wave, techno, experimental postrock, and ambient artists that followed. Can's sound was based on repetitive, trance-inducing rhythms overlaid with atmospheric noise and sudden bursts of distorted electronic effects, with instruments often unrecognizable in the mix.

The debut *Monster Movie* finds the approach still rather primitive. But when vocalist Malcolm Mooney was taken ill and replaced by Kenji "Damo" Suzuki—who the group discovered singing on the streets of Munich—Irmin Schmidt and Holger Czukay began making full use of their studies with German avant-garde composer Karlheinz Stockhausen. Can expanded its frontiers and sounded more assured on *Tago Mago, Ege Bamyasi, Future Days,* and *Soon Over Babaluma.* The music was natural for films; the ensemble scored part of Jerzy Skolimowski's *Deep End. Soundtracks* collects these and similar commissioned efforts.

In 1976 Can enjoyed a few hit singles abroad with "I Want More" and a version of "Silent Night." With the addition of ex-Traffic members Rosko Gee and Reebop Kwaku Baah, the players' sound got funkier on the well-received *Saw Delight.*

Can soon went into limbo, with various members splitting off for solo and collaboration LPs. The most prolific was Czukay, whose works include the Brian Eno–ish *Movies* (1980), *On the Way to the Peak of Normal* (1982), *Der Osten Ist Rot* (1984), *Rome Remains Rome* (1987), and *Radio Wave Surfer* (1991). Czukay has also worked with Rolf Dammers (*Canaxis,* 1982), Eurythmics, David Sylvian (1988's *Plight and Premonition,* 1989's *Flux + Mutability*), and Jah Wobble (1981's *How Much Are They* EP with Liebezeit and 1983's *Snake Charmer* with the Edge).

In 1986 the post-Johnson lineup reunited to record *Rite Time.* In 1991, without Czukay, the band contributed a track to the Wim Wenders film *Until the End of the World* and went back on hiatus. Despite numerous requests to reunite and its immense influence on modern independent acts as varied as England's Stereolab, America's Tortoise, and Finland's Circle, Can has refused to formally regroup. In 1997 Mute Records released *Sacrilege,* on which artists ranging from Sonic Youth to A Guy Called Gerald remixed Can's classic material. In 1999 the label unveiled a retrospective box set alongside domestic reissues of Can's entire catalogue.

C + C Music Factory

Formed Oct. 1990, New York, NY
Robert Clivillés (b. Aug. 30, 1964, New York), drums, perc., bass; David Cole (b. June 3, 1962, Johnson City, TN; d. Jan. 24, 1995, New York), kybds., bass, voc.; Zelma Davis (b. Aug. 2, 1970, Republic of Liberia), voc.; Freedom Williams (b. Feb. 13, 1966, Brooklyn, NY), voc.
1991—*Gonna Make You Sweat* (Columbia) 1994—*Anything Goes!* 1995—*Ultimate—Greatest Remixes* (Sony Music) 1996—*In the Groove* 2000—*Super Hits* (Sony/Columbia).
Clivillés and Cole: 1992—*Greatest Remixes, vol. 1* (Columbia).
Freedom Williams solo: 1993—*Freedom* (Columbia).

In the early '90s as the creative team guiding C + C Music Factory, Robert Clivillés and David Cole personified the reemergence of the producer/songwriter as star in pop music. They also endured clashes with artists who felt that their work within this dance-pop collective hadn't been properly acknowledged.

Clivillés and Cole met in the mid-'80s at a Manhattan nightclub where Clivillés DJ'd while Cole played live keyboards. Before long, they were remixing club hits for the likes of Janet Jackson ("Pleasure Principle"), Natalie Cole ("Pink Cadillac"), and Fleetwood Mac ("Big Love"). The duo next set its sights on making original recordings, using keyboards and a computer to write and arrange material, then recruiting performers to lay down vocals. Their breakthrough came when they assembled the R&B trio Seduction, whose debut album, *Nothing Matters Without Love* (#36, 1989), produced several hit singles, including "You're My One and Only (True Love)" (#23 pop, #56 R&B, 1989) and "Two to Make It Right" (#2 R&B, 1989).

With C + C Music Factory, Clivillés and Cole brought their own involvement to the fore. The outfit's 1991 debut album, *Gonna Make You Sweat,* hit #2 on the pop chart and yielded a #1 title track (on the pop and R&B charts) and the #3 single "Here We Go, Let's Rock & Roll" (#7 R&B). The album featured singers Martha Wash and Deborah Cooper and rapper Freedom Williams; but these vocalists were only briefly mentioned in the LP's production notes and liner material. Furthermore, Wash, whose booming soprano had also been the uncredited voice of Seduction and the dance group Black Box (she sang with the Weather Girls [see entry] and Two Tons O'Fun, as well) was conspicuously absent in C + C's popular videos, in which the more lithe, attractive Zelma Davis lip-synched to her vocals.

In 1991 Wash filed two lawsuits against Clivillés and Cole, one charging that she hadn't received ample credit for *Sweat,* the other protesting her deceptive exclusion from the videos. While still hashing it out with her lawyers, the producers worked with Mariah Carey on her single "Make It Happen" and, in 1992, released a followup album, as Clivillés and Cole. *Greatest Remixes, vol. 1* (#87, 1992) spawned the #4 single "Things That Make You Go Hmmm. . . ." and the dance-club smash "A Deeper Love" (#44), which the team would later produce for Aretha Franklin. Later that year, Williams also sued the team, claiming they had misled him about solo opportunities and withheld royalties (part of Wash's claim, too).

Williams did strike out on his own, releasing *Freedom* in 1993. Wash settled her differences with Clivillés and Cole, though, and in 1994 C + C Music Factory resurfaced with *Anything Goes!* featuring Wash, Davis, and the Latin hip-hop/R&B threesome Trilogy. That same year Clivillés and Cole won a Grammy for their production work with Whitney Houston on the soundtrack to *The Bodyguard.*

In early 1995 Cole died of complications from spinal meningitis at the age of 32. Columbia and its parent label,

Sony Music, released three repackaged hit collections under the name C + C Music Factory after Cole's death. Clivillés continued to work behind the scenes, producing several cuts on Wash's second solo album in 1995.

Canned Heat

Formed 1966, Los Angeles, CA
Bob "Bear" Hite (b. Feb. 26, 1945, Torrance, CA; d. Apr. 5, 1981, Venice, CA), voc., harmonica; Alan "Blind Owl" Wilson (b. July 4, 1943, Boston, MA; d. Sep. 3, 1970, Topanga, CA), gtr., harmonica, voc.; Henry Vestine (b. Dec. 24, 1944, Washington, DC; d. Oct. 20, 1997, Paris, Fr.), gtr.; Frank Cook, drums; Larry Taylor (b. Samuel Taylor, June 26, 1942, Brooklyn, NY), bass.
1967—*Canned Heat* (Liberty) 1968—(– Cook; + Adolpho "Fito" de la Parra [b. Feb. 8, 1946, Mexico City, Mex.], drums) *Boogie With Canned Heat; Living the Blues* 1969—(– Vestine; + Harvey Mandel [b. Mar. 11, 1945, Detroit, MI], gtr.) *Hallelujah* 1970—*Vintage Heat* (Janus); *The Canned Heat Cookbook/Best Of* (Liberty); *Hooker 'n' Heat* (with John Lee Hooker); *Live in Europe* (– Wilson; – Taylor; – Mandel; + Vestine, gtr.; + Antonio de la Barreda, bass) *Future Blues* 1971—*Live at the Topanga Corral* (Wand) 1972—*Historical Figures and Ancient Heads* (United Artists) (– Barreda; + Richard Hite, bass) 1973—*New Age* 1974—*One More River to Cross* (Atlantic) 1975—*The Very Best of Canned Heat* (United Artists) 1978—*Human Condition* (Takoma) 1981—(– B. Hite) *Hooker 'n' Heat Live* (Rhino) 1984—(+ James Thornbury, slide gtr., harmonica, voc.) 1987—*The Best of Canned Heat* (EMI) 1990—*Reheated* (Chameleon) 1992—*Burnin' Live* (Aim) 1994—(lineup: de la Parra; Vestine; Thornbury; + Junior Watson, gtr., voc.; + Ron Shumake, bass, voc.) *Uncanned (The Best of Canned Heat)* (EMI) (+ Taylor; + Mandel) 1995—*Internal Combustion* (River Road/Two Goats) (– Taylor; – Mandel) 1997—(– Vestine) *Canned Heat Blues Band* (Ruf/Platinum) 2000—*Boogie 2000; The Boogie House Tapes (Vintage Collection 1966–1976).*

Canned Heat was rare among the American blues-loving bands of the late '60s and early '70s: The group had a few hits. As one critic noted, the musicians were more popularizers than purists. The 1981 death of cofounder Bob Hite essentially ended Canned Heat's most visible period, but the players have always persevered. They endured Al Wilson's death in 1970 and weathered dozens of personnel shifts (the above chronology lists only the most important ones). Canned Heat has continued under the leadership of Fito de la Parra.

The original Canned Heat evolved out of a jug band that was formed in 1965. Record-collecting blues fanatics Alan Wilson and Bob Hite (nicknamed "Bear" because of his 300-pound frame) changed the group's focus to electric boogie. Though its debut, *Canned Heat,* sold respectably, its appearance at the Monterey Pop Festival that year attracted more attention. Its second album spawned a #16 hit, Wilson's "On the Road Again," and the band toured Europe. "Going Up the Country" gave it a #11 hit in 1969, and it played the Woodstock Festival in August.

The following year was a watershed, with a worldwide hit cover of Wilbert Harrison's "Let's Work Together" and an appearance at the Bath Festival in England. But the drug overdose death of Wilson (who was partly blind and subject to severe depression) in late 1970 proved to be a setback from which the band never fully recovered. Larry Taylor and guitarist Harvey Mandel joined John Mayall's band. (Later Mandel would be considered to replace Mick Taylor in the Rolling Stones; he would record a number of albums, as both an artist and a session musician.) The remaining members, with replacements, soldiered on. Prior to Wilson's death, they had backed bluesman John Lee Hooker on *Hooker 'n' Heat;* in 1989 a latter-day incarnation assisted him again on *The Healer.* In 1973 the band backed Clarence "Gatemouth" Brown and Memphis Slim on French albums released on the Barclay label.

Canned Heat's electric blues fell out of fashion; by the early '80s the band was playing the California bar circuit. Sometime after Hite's death (he suffered a fatal heart attack) the group drifted, and while 1990's *Reheated* revived interest, Canned Heat has not made a commercial comeback, though it remains a steadily working band. In the early '90s guitarist Mandel rejoined the group for some live dates, and original members Taylor, Mandel, and Henry Vestine appear on 1994's *Internal Combustion.* They departed sometime afterward. Since then, Canned Heat has recorded two more albums with longtime manager/producer Skip Taylor. In 1999, several years after the death of Vestine, de la Parra and his new recruits made five trips to Europe and played a number of festivals in the U.S. The drummer also finished his tell-all book about the band, *Living the Blues.*

Freddy Cannon

Born Frederick Anthony Picariello, Dec. 4, 1939, Lynn, MA
1961—*The Explosive Freddy Cannon* (Swan) 1962—*Freddy Cannon Sings Happy Shades of Blue; Freddy Cannon's Solid Gold Hits; Freddy Cannon at Palisades Park* 1964—*Freddy Cannon Steps Out* 1965—*Freddy Cannon* (Warner Bros.) 1966—*Freddy Cannon's Greatest Hits; Action!* 1982—*14 Booming Hits* (Rhino).

A major star in the early '60s, singer/guitarist/songwriter Freddy Cannon broke big with two million-sellers: "Tallahassee Lassie" (#6, 1959) and an updated version of a 1922 jazz hit, "Way Down Yonder in New Orleans" (#3, 1960). Cannon was discovered in 1957 by a Boston disc jockey; two years later he recorded "Tallahassee Lassie," a song his mother had written.

He toured internationally during the mid-'60s, scoring minor hits regularly. His only other big hit, the Chuck Barris–penned "Palisades Park," was #3 in 1962. That same year he was featured in the British film *Just for Fun.* In 1965 he had a Top 20 hit with "Action," the theme song from the TV series *Where the Action Is.* He remained a major performer in the U.K. years after his star had faded in America. In 1960 *The Explosive Freddy Cannon* became the first LP by an American artist to go to #1 in England. In the '70s he became a promotion man for Buddah Records, but he returned to the charts in 1981 with "Let's Put the Fun Back in Rock 'n' Roll," backed by the Belmonts. He continues to perform.

Captain and Tennille

Daryl Dragon (a.k.a. the "Captain," b. Aug. 27, 1942, Los Angeles, CA), kybds.; Toni Tennille (b. Catheryn Antoinette Tennille, May 8, 1943, Montgomery, AL), voc.
1975—*Love Will Keep Us Together* (A&M) 1976—*Song of Joy* 1977—*Come in From the Rain; The Captain and Tennille's Greatest Hits* 1978—*Dream* 1979—*Make Your Move* (Casablanca) 1980—*Keeping Our Love Warm.*
Toni Tennille solo: 1984—*More Than You Know* (Mirage) 1987—*All of Me* (Gaia) 1992—*Never Let Me Go* (Bay Cities) 1998—*Tenille Sings Big Band* (Honest).

The Captain and Tennille are a husband-and-wife pop duo who debuted on the pop charts with the top-selling single of 1975, a bouncy version of Neil Sedaka's "Love Will Keep Us Together." The single sold over 2.5 million copies and was awarded a Grammy for Record of the Year.

Toni Tennille began singing with her three sisters in their hometown of Montgomery, Alabama. Her father had sung professionally in the '30s, and her mother was a local television talk-show host. Tennille studied classical piano for nine years, and in 1964 she moved with her family to L.A., where she joined the South Coast Repertory Theater. There she cowrote a rock musical entitled *Mother Earth,* and during the play's run she met Daryl Dragon, a keyboard player in the house band. The son of conductor Carmen Dragon, Daryl plays synthesizer, organ, piano, and vibes, as well as bass. Before he met Tennille, he had also worked with the Beach Boys. When Tennille's play closed in 1971, after three performances, he hired her to tour as a keyboard player with the Beach Boys' band. They were married on November 11, 1975.

In 1974 the two financed and produced a Tenille-penned single, "The Way I Want to Touch You," which was first a regional hit. "Love Will Keep Us Together" followed, and upon its rerelease in 1975, "The Way I Want to Touch You" went to #4. Other hit singles included "Lonely Night (Angel Face)" (#3, 1976), "Muskrat Love" (#4, 1976), a cover version of Smokey Robinson's "Shop Around" (#4, 1976), "Can't Stop Dancin' " (#13, 1977), "You Never Done It Like That" (#10, 1978), and "Do That to Me One More Time" (#1, 1979). From mid-1977 on, the duo's misses outnumbered their hits; still they managed to sell over 23 million records throughout their career. During that time Tennille provided backup vocals for Pink Floyd's *The Wall* and Elton John's "Don't Let the Sun Go Down on Me."

They hosted their own prime-time series on ABC in 1976–77, and in the early '80s Tennille hosted a daytime talk show. The couple moved to Nevada, where Dragon works in his home studio, produces records and film scores, and works on an Internet enterprise. Tennille recorded four albums of standards, made guest appearances on television, and has performed on the musical stage. The duo occasionally performs as Captain and Tennille.

Captain Beefheart and the Magic Band

Formed 1964, California
Captain Beefheart (b. Don Glen Vliet, Jan. 15, 1941, Glendale, CA), voc., harmonica, saxes, bass clarinet, musette.
The Magic Band: Alex "St. Clair[e]" Snouffer, gtr., drums; Doug Moon, gtr.; Jerry Handley, bass; Vic Mortensen, drums (– Mortensen; + Rich Hepner, gtr.; – Hepner; + Paul Blakely, drums; – Blakely; + John French [a.k.a. Drumbo], drums; – Moon; + Ry Cooder [b. Mar. 15, 1947, Los Angeles, CA], gtr.).
1967—*Safe as Milk* (Buddah) (– Cooder; + Jeff Cotton, gtr.) 1968—*Mirror Man; Strictly Personal* (Blue Thumb) (– Snouffer; – Handley; + Antennae Jimmy Semens [b. Jeff Cotton], gtr.; + Zoot Horn Rollo [b. Bill Harkleroad], gtr.; + Rockette Morton [b. Mark Boston], bass; + the Mascara Snake [b. Victor Hayden], bass clarinet; + Moon, gtr. on "China Pig") 1969—*Trout Mask Replica* (Straight/Warner Bros.) (– Cotton; – Moon; – Hayden; + Ed Marimba [b. Arthur Tripp III], drums, marimba, perc.) 1970—*Lick My Decals Off, Baby* (+ Winged Eel Fingerling [b. Elliot Ingber], gtr.) 1972—*The Spotlight Kid* (Reprise) (– French; – Ingber; + Orejon [b. Roy Estrada], bass) *Clear Spot* (– Estrada; + Snouffer, gtr.; + Mark Marcellino, kybds.) 1974—*Unconditionally Guaranteed* (Mercury) (all new lineup: Dean Smith, gtr.; Ira Ingber, bass; Gene Pello, drums; Ty Grimes, perc.; Michael Smotherman, kybds.; Jimmy Caravan, kybds.) *Bluejeans and Moonbeams* (all new lineup: Bruce Lambourne Fowler, trombone, air bass; Richard Redus, gtr., bass, accordion; Robert Arthur Williams, drums; Jeff Morris Teper, gtr.; Eric Drew Feldman, kybds., bass, synth.) 1978—*Shiny Beast (Bat Chain Puller)* (Warner Bros.) (– Redus; + Gary Lucas, gtr., French horn; + John French, gtr., bass, drums, marimba, perc.) 1980—*Doc at the Radar Station* (Virgin) (– French; – Williams; + Richard Snyder, bass; + Cliff Martinez, drums) 1982—*Ice Cream for Crow* (Virgin/Epic) (original 1964 lineup) 1984—*The Legendary A&M Sessions* (A&M) 1992—*I May Be Hungry but I Sure Ain't Weird* (Sequel) 1999—*The Mirror Man Sessions* (Buddah); *Grow Fins: Rarities* 1965–82 (Revenant); *The Dust Blows Forward: An Anthology* (Rhino).

The irregular rhythms, grating harmonies, and earthy, surreal lyrics of Captain Beefheart's songs and his blues-inflected seven-and-a-half-octave vocals (or, depending on who you believe, three-octave; the voice is impressive no matter what) suggest a near-chaotic improvised blend of Delta blues, avant-garde jazz, 20th-century classical music, and rock & roll. Actually, Beefheart's repertoire is a sort of modern chamber music for rock band, since he plans every note and teaches the band their parts by ear. Because it breaks so many of rock's conventions at once, Beefheart's music has always been more influential than popular, leaving its mark

Captain Beefheart

on Tom Waits, Sonic Youth, and other avant-garde rock performers.

A child-prodigy sculptor, Don Vliet (who reportedly had his name legally changed to Don Van Vliet by 1964) was noticed at age four by Portuguese sculptor Augustinio Rodriguez, who featured Vliet and his clay animals on his weekly television show for the next eight years. When Vliet was 13, his parents declined their son's scholarship to study art in Europe and moved the family to the California desert communities of Mojave, then Lancaster, where Vliet met the young Frank Zappa. Vliet learned to play harmonica and saxophone and played one show with local R&B band the Omens (who promptly kicked him out) before enrolling in Antelope Valley College in 1959. After one semester, he dropped out and went to Cucamonga, California, with Zappa, intending to form a band, the Soots, and make a film, *Captain Beefheart Meets the Grunt People.* Both projects fell through, and while Zappa went to Los Angeles to form the Mothers of Invention, Vliet returned to Lancaster and, adopting the Beefheart stage name, formed the first Magic Band in 1964.

A&M signed the group in 1964 and released its version of "Diddy Wah Diddy," which sold enough locally for A&M to commission an album. Label president Jerry Moss rejected the Van Vliet originals as "too negative." After the first in an endless series of Magic Band personnel changes, Beefheart redid the songs and recorded some new ones, on *Safe As Milk,* which attracted enough interest for the band to tour Europe. Shortly before a scheduled appearance at the 1967 Monterey Pop Festival, guitarist Ry Cooder's abrupt departure forced the group to cancel.

Mirror Man was recorded in November 1967, but Buddah didn't release it until 1970, after Beefheart had left the label. *Strictly Personal* was recorded in 1968, but radically remixed by producer Bob Krasnow and released on his own Blue Thumb label as the band toured Europe. Van Vliet, disgusted, retired to the San Fernando Valley until Zappa, now in charge of his own Straight Records, promised him complete artistic control over his next recordings. After allegedly composing 28 songs in eight and a half hours (John "Drumbo" French, who transcribed Beefheart's piano parts for the band, says it was more like 60 to 80 hours over several months), Beefheart formed a new Magic Band and recorded *Trout Mask Replica* over the next year. That album and 1970's *Lick My Decals Off, Baby* brought Beefheart critical acclaim and, along with his appearance on Zappa's *Hot Rats* (1969), enough interest for a national tour. The next two albums, marginally more commercial-sounding, reached the lower echelons of the pop charts.

After a two-year hiatus, Van Vliet signed with Mercury and released two openly conventional pop-blues albums, then toured with and dissolved another Magic Band (Harkleroad, Boston, and Tripp formed Mallard, which released two mid-'70s albums; French went on to record *O Solo Drumbo,* plus albums with Richard Thompson and Henry Kaiser, among others). For a short time, Beefheart appeared as a vocalist with Zappa and the Mothers of Invention, including songs on 1975's *Bongo Fury.* In 1978 Warner Bros. re-signed him and released *Shiny Beast (Bat Chain Puller),* hailed by critics as a return to *Trout Mask* form; Beefheart toured a somewhat more receptive new-wave circuit. Virgin sued to keep Beefheart on its roster (it had British rights to Beefheart since his Mercury period) and won ownership of *Doc at the Radar Station* and *Ice Cream for Crow.*

Beefheart's 1980 American and European tours, including a November 1980 appearance on *Saturday Night Live,* were his most successful to date. But after the release of *Ice Cream for Crow,* Van Vliet left the music business and retired to the trailer in the Mojave where he'd lived since the mid-'70s with his wife, Jan (he later moved to a house in the Northern California coastal town of Trinidad). Van Vliet devoted himself to painting and in 1985, with the help of New York postmodern painter and Beefheart fan Julian Schnabel, began exhibiting his semiabstract, primitivist canvases (some of which have adorned his album covers) at galleries in America and Europe, some of them selling for as much as $25,000. The only "new" Beefheart music to emerge was previously unreleased live and studio tracks on such reissues as *Safe as Milk* (1999), and anthologies like *I May Be Hungry, The Dust Blows Forward,* and especially the five-disc *Grow Fins* (which also had copious, revelatory liner notes by French detailing the band's little-known history). While there was no official word on Van Vliet's health, he looked and sounded very weak in a 1994 short documentary, *Some Yo-Yo Stuff,* by rock photographer and video director Anton Corbijn.

Mariah Carey

Born Mar. 27, 1970, Long Island, NY
1990—*Mariah Carey* (Columbia) 1991—*Emotions* 1992—

MTV Unplugged EP 1993—*Music Box* 1994—*Merry Christmas* 1995—*Daydream* 1997—*Butterfly* 1998—*#1's* 1999—*Rainbow* 2001—*All That Glitters* soundtrack (Virgin).

With a stunning seven-octave voice that she put through stratospheric gymnastics, Mariah Carey became an overnight star. Her vocal prowess and range drew comparisons to Minnie Riperton and Yma Sumac, but most often to her contemporary Whitney Houston. Yet unlike Houston, Carey cowrote or coproduced her own gospel-inflected, dance-pop songs and ardent ballads. These have found immense popularity: Carey is the best-selling female artist of all time, with more than 140 million albums and singles sold worldwide. She was the only artist to have scored a #1 hit in every year of the '90s, and (at this writing) has had more #1 hits for more weeks at #1 than any other artist in history. In October 1999 she surpassed the Beatles' long-running record of 59 weeks at #1.

Carey was born to a black Venezuelan aeronautics engineer father and an Irish-American opera singer mother who also worked as a voice coach. The couple divorced when Mariah was three, and she moved with her mother to successive towns in suburban Long Island, New York. At 17 she moved to New York City and pursued a career in music while supporting herself as the self-professed "world's worst waitress."

Carey befriended keyboardist Ben Margulies, with whom she began writing songs, and landed backup singing jobs. One, with minor late-'80s dance-music singer Brenda K. Starr, proved crucial when Starr met Columbia Records chief Tommy Mottola at a party and gave him a demo tape of Carey's songs. Mottola reportedly played the tape in his car on his way home, and doubled back to the party to seek out Carey. He signed her and made her career development a top priority. Carey's debut album (#4, 1990) yielded #1 hit singles in "Vision of Love" (1990), "Love Takes Time" (1990), "Someday" (1991), and "I Don't Wanna Cry" (1991), and brought her Grammy Awards in 1991 for Best New Artist and Best Female Vocalist. *Emotions* (#1, 1991) continued Carey's roll, with such hits as the title track (#1, 1991), "Can't Let Go" (#2, 1991), and "Make It Happen" (#5, 1992). *Unplugged* produced a hit cover of the Jackson 5's "I'll Be There" (#1, 1992), which also led to a solo recording deal for Trey Lorenz, the backup singer featured on the single with Carey.

In June 1993 Carey married Mottola, a man 20 years her senior. She then released *Music Box* (#1, 1993), which promptly yielded the #1 hits "Dreamlover" and "Hero." In fall 1993 she embarked on her first concert tour, for which she received mixed reviews. Her 1994 Christmas album spawned the hit "All I Want for Christmas Is You."

Carey achieved a milestone with the 1995 release of *Daydream,* which debuted at #1. The first single, "Fantasy," debuted at the top as well. With *Daydream,* Carey became the first female artist in history to have three albums that each sold more than 8 million copies. The second single, "One Sweet Day," a duet with the Philadelphia R&B vocal group Boyz II Men, also hit #1, holding the spot for a record-setting 16 weeks. A third single, "Always Be My Baby," followed suit, completing the hat trick.

Carey and Mottola divorced in 1997. She released *Butterfly* (#1, 1997), which asserted a stronger hip-hop flavor and yielded the #1 hits "Honey" (with rappers Ma$e and the Lox) and "My All." *#1's* collected Carey's 13 chart-topping singles, with four new tracks, including "When You Believe" (from *The Prince of Egypt*), a duet with Whitney Houston.

The 1999 release of the multiplatinum *Rainbow* (#2, 2000), which produced a #1 single in "Heartbreaker," capped a decade in which Carey was its biggest-selling female artist. Musically, the singer continued to embrace hip-hop elements, emphasizing samples and inviting such rap stars as Jay-Z, Missy Elliott, Da Brat, and Snoop Dogg to make guest vocal appearances. In early 2001 Carey signed a multirecord, multimillion-dollar deal with Virgin. It was announced her first Virgin release would be the soundtrack to the film *All That Glitters,* in which Carey played the lead.

Belinda Carlisle: See the Go-Go's

Eric Carmen: See the Raspberries

Kim Carnes

Born July 20, 1945, Los Angeles, CA
1972—*Rest on Me* (A&M) 1975—*Kim Carnes* 1976—*Sailin'* 1979—*St. Vincent's Court* (EMI) 1980—*Romance Dance* 1981—*Mistaken Identity* 1982—*Voyeur; The Best of You* (A&M) 1983—*Cafe Racers* (EMI) 1985—*Barking at Airplanes* 1986—*Light House* 1988—*A View From the House* (MCA) 1993—*Gypsy Honeymoon: The Best of Kim Carnes* (EMI).

Singer/songwriter Kim Carnes recorded the top-selling single of 1981, "Bette Davis Eyes." Carnes grew up in suburban L.A. By her early 20s, she was working the city's nightclubs, singing mainly ballads; she was also a member of the New Christy Minstrels. Ballads composed the bulk of several of her albums (including *Sailin',* produced by Jerry Wexler) from the '70s. Her songs, some of which were cowritten with her husband, Dave Ellingson (who is also a member of her backup band), have been covered by Frank Sinatra, Rita Coolidge, Anne Murray, and Barbra Streisand. The couple's biggest break came when Kenny Rogers recorded their songs on 1980's *Gideon.* That same year Carnes duetted with Rogers on his hit "Don't Fall in Love With a Dreamer."

In 1978 she signed with Rogers' label, EMI, and gradually began recording rock-oriented material. She had a #10 hit in 1980 with a cover of Smokey Robinson's "More Love." But album sales remained sluggish until 1981's *Mistaken Identity* and its single, a Donna Weiss/Jackie DeShannon composition, "Bette Davis Eyes" (#1, 1981), which won a Grammy for Record of the Year. Later hits include "Draw of the Cards" (#28, 1981), "Voyeur" (#29, 1982), "What About Me?" (#15, 1984) with Kenny Rogers and James Ingram, and "Crazy in the Night (Barking at Airplanes)" (#15, 1985). Carnes has since become a Nashville-based songwriter, whose work has been covered by various country artists.

Mary Chapin Carpenter

Born Feb. 21, 1958, Princeton, NJ
1987—*Hometown Girl* (Columbia) 1989—*State of the Heart* 1990—*Shooting Straight in the Dark* 1992—*Come On Come On* 1994—*Stones in the Road* 1996—*A Place in the World* 1999—*Party Doll and Other Favorites* 2001—*time*sex*love*.*

An Ivy League–educated singer/songwriter from the Northeast with a reflective, literate style of lyric writing, Mary Chapin Carpenter has always stopped short of mocking the sequined outfits, big hair, and simple romanticism often associated with country divas. Accordingly, Carpenter's music—which incorporates folk and rock textures as well as country—has been embraced by both Nashville and fans of progressive pop.

Carpenter grew up mostly in Princeton, listening to records by Woody Guthrie, the Beatles, and Judy Collins and playing her mother's acoustic guitar. After she graduated from high school in Washington, DC, where her family had moved, her father, a publishing executive, encouraged her to attend an open-mike session at a local bar. Though reluctant at first, the singer soon began performing live on a regular basis, while studying at Brown University, where she earned a degree in American civilization. Carpenter spent weekends and summers performing a mixture of radio hits and rootsy standards in bars. After graduating, she decided to focus more on her own material and moved back to Washington, DC, where she won several local music awards and became a favorite on the local club circuit. In the mid-'80s Carpenter landed a deal with Columbia Records.

Carpenter's debut album was released on Columbia in 1987. The articulate country-folk songs on *Hometown Girl* impressed critics, but it was her sophomore album, 1989's *State of the Heart,* that proved Carpenter's commercial potential, spawning two Top 10 country hits: "Never Had It So Good" (#8) and, in 1990, "Quittin' Time" (#7). The Academy of Country Music named Carpenter 1989's Best New Female Vocalist.

The '90s saw Carpenter's star rise even higher. Her 1990 album, *Shooting Straight in the Dark,* yielded the #1 country single "Down at the Twist and Shout," a hit that won her a 1991 Grammy for Best Female Country Vocal Performance. *Come On Come On* (1992) reached #6 on the country albums charts, producing seven hit singles and earning the singer another Grammy, for a cheekily sexy track called "I Feel Lucky." That single peaked at #4 on the C&W chart, as did "Passionate Kisses" (written by Lucinda Williams [see entry]), for which Carpenter won her third Best Female Country Vocal Performance Grammy. "He Thinks He'll Keep Her" reached #1 C&W. Carpenter's *Stones in the Road* (1994) featured such guest musicians as country artists Lee Roy Parnell and Trisha Yearwood, folkie Shawn Colvin, Heartbreaker Benmont Tench, saxophonist Branford Marsalis, onetime R.E.M. producer Don Dixon (on bass), and drummer Kenny Aronoff. The album continued Carpenter's awards streak, netting her fourth consecutive best female country vocal award for "Shut Up and Kiss Me" and that year's Best Country Album Grammy for *Stones in the Road.*

Carpenter started exploring another creative outlet when she wrote her own essays for the *Stones in the Road* tour book in 1995. Her ability to write nonfiction prose, along with her social activism, led her to contribute an essay to *A Voice of Our Own: Leading American Women Celebrate the Right to Vote,* a 1996 book that also featured the writings of First Ladies Rosalynn Carter and Hillary Rodham Clinton, among others. Carpenter became a bona fide author with the publication of a children's book, *Dreamland,* the same year; it was based on a lullaby she'd written and recorded for a compilation album. The musician didn't forsake the recording world for publishing, however; she also released her sixth album, *A Place in the World* (#20 pop), in 1996. The album produced more country hits in the Grammy-nominated "Let Me Into Your Heart" (#11) and "I Want to Be Your Girlfriend" (#35).

Carpenter published a second children's book, *Halley Came to Jackson*—also based on one of her songs—in 1998. *Party Doll and Other Favorites,* featuring greatest hits, live cuts, and rare tracks from compilations, peaked at #4 on the country album chart in 1999. She returned with her first album of new material in five years with *time*sex*love** in 2001.

The Carpenters

Richard Carpenter (b. Oct. 15, 1946, New Haven, CT), voc., kybds.; Karen Carpenter (b. Mar. 2, 1950, New Haven; d. Feb. 4, 1983, Los Angeles, CA), voc., drums.
1969—*Ticket to Ride* (A&M) 1970—*Close to You* 1971—*Carpenters* 1972—*A Song for You* 1973—*Now and Then; The Singles 1969–1973* 1975—*Horizon* 1976—*A Kind of Hush* 1977—*Passage* 1978—*Christmas Portrait* 1981—*Made in America* 1983—*Voice of the Heart* 1985—*Yesterday Once More* 1989—*Lovelines* 1991—*Once From the Top.*
Richard Carpenter solo: 1987—*Time* (A&M) 1998—*Pianist, Arranger, Composer, Conductor.*
Karen Carpenter solo: 1996—*Karen Carpenter* (A&M).

A popular brother-and-sister team, the Carpenters sold millions of hit records in the early '70s. Richard started taking piano lessons at age 12 and studied classical piano at Yale before the family relocated to Downey, California, in 1963. Richard studied at USC and Cal State at Long Beach. He formed his first group in 1965, a jazz-pop instrumental trio that included younger sister Karen on drums and their friend Wes Jacobs (who later abandoned pop for a seat in the Detroit Symphony) on bass and tuba. The group won a battle of the bands at the Hollywood Bowl and subsequently signed with RCA. Four sides were recorded, but after label executives deemed them not commercially viable, they were never released. In late 1966 the trio broke up. Richard and Karen recruited four Cal State students into the vocal harmony-oriented band Spectrum. They played various Southern California venues to less than ecstatic response and disbanded.

The Carpenter siblings' densely layered, pop-oriented demo tapes eventually caught the attention of Herb Alpert, who signed them to A&M in 1969. They released their first album that November. Originally titled *Offering*, it was ignored until it was repackaged as *Ticket to Ride*, on the strength of the moderate success of their Beatles-cover single. *Close to You*'s title track, a Burt Bacharach tune, sold more than a million copies and went to #1 in the U.S. and several other countries. Their hits continued: "We've Only Just Begun" (#2, 1970), "For All We Know" (#3, 1971; it won an Oscar for Best Song in 1970), "Rainy Days and Mondays" (#2, 1971), "Superstar" (#2, 1971; written by Leon Russell), "It's Going to Take Some Time" (#12, 1972), "Hurting Each Other" (#2, 1972), "Goodbye to Love" (#7, 1972), "Sing" (#3, 1973), "Yesterday Once More" (#2, 1973), "Top of the World" (#1, 1973), "Won't Last a Day Without You" (#11, 1974), "Please Mr. Postman" (#1, 1975), and "Only Yesterday" (#4, 1975).

The 1973 LP *The Singles 1969–1973* was a bestseller, and the Carpenters were three-time Grammy winners. They hosted a short-lived variety series, *Make Your Own Kind of Music*, on NBC in 1971. At the request of President Nixon, they performed at a White House state dinner honoring West German Chancellor Willy Brandt on May 1, 1973. They toured internationally through the mid-'70s. Their 1976 tour of Japan was, at the time, the biggest-grossing concert ever in that country. From 1976 to 1980 the pair hosted five ABC television specials. Through the late '70s the Carpenters were noticeably absent from the charts, but returned to the Top 20 in 1981 with "Touch Me When We're Dancing."

On February 4, 1983, Karen Carpenter died in her parents' home of cardiac arrest, resulting from her long struggle with anorexia nervosa. Her story was presented in the highly rated made-for-television movie *The Karen Carpenter Story* in 1988. The posthumous LP *Lovelines* drew critical notice for its inclusion of four tracks Karen had recorded for an unreleased 1980 solo album. Richard's solo effort, *Time*, featured duets with Dionne Warwick and Dusty Springfield yet failed to chart. The followup merely features easy-listening, instrumental revisions of various Carpenters songs.

With time, the duo's saccharine image has receded somewhat, and Karen Carpenter is acknowledged by women rock musicians, including Chrissie Hynde and Madonna, as a pioneer. Sonic Youth, Sheryl Crow, Matthew Sweet, Cracker, and the Cranberries were among the fourteen acts who contributed to the 1994 Carpenters tribute album *If I Were a Carpenter*. Around the same time that fall, the Karen and Richard Carpenter Performing Arts Center at Cal State University opened in Long Beach, California. Karen Carpenter's eponymous solo debut, recorded in 1979 and 1980 but unreleased until 1996, continued to keep her memory alive. The somewhat mature—but hardly edgy—album found her experimenting with disco and mildly suggestive lyrics.

Paul Carrack: See Ace; Squeeze; Mike + the Mechanics in Genesis entry

Joe "King" Carrasco and the Crowns

Formed 1979, Texas
Joe "King" Carrasco (b. Joseph Teutsch, Dumas, TX), gtr., voc.
1980—*Joe "King" Carrasco and the Crowns* (Hannibal) 1981—*Party Safari* 1982—*Synapse Gap (Mundo Total)* (MCA) 1983—*Party Weekend* 1984—*Tales From the Crypt (The Basement Tapes 1979)* cassette (ROIR) 1989—*Tex-Mex Rock-Roll* (tape-only reissue of Joe "King" Carrasco and El Molino's eponymously titled 1978 album) 1990—*Royal, Loyal & Live* (Rio's Royal Texacali).
Joe King Carrasco y Las Coronas: 1987—*Bandido Rock* (Rounder).

Calling his music "nuevo wavo," Joe Carrasco blends garage rock (Sam the Sham), Tex-Mex (Doug Sahm), Chicano polkas, and new-wavish intensity into speedy, good-humored party music. Carrasco started playing in West Texas rock & roll bands before he was a teenager. By 1973, when he settled in Austin, he had played with bands such as Salaman, a mariachi outfit, and Shorty y los Corvettes, who had a couple of local Spanish hits. His Chicano colleagues dubbed him "King" Carrasco.

In 1976 he formed his own band, El Molino, with local trumpeter Charlie McBurney, keyboardist Augie Meyers, and saxophonist Rocky Morales. El Molino was popular in Austin and San Antonio, where it recorded *Tex-Mex Rock-Roll* on Carrasco's Lisa label in 1978. The album found a cult audience in New York and London (Elvis Costello was an early admirer). Carrasco had no takers when he took the album to L.A. in search of a distribution deal, but he moved to the city's Mexican barrio and wrote songs with Sir Douglas Quintet drummer Johnny Perez.

Returning to Austin in 1979, he met Kris Cummings, Mike Navarro, and bassist Brad Kizer. Cummings had studied piano in New Orleans with Huey "Piano" Smith and Professor Longhair, but Carrasco gave her the Farfisa organ that defined the Crowns' trashy sound. They went to New York in late 1979, where their partylike shows, bolstered by Carrasco's antics (wearing cape and crown, leaping from the stage during guitar solos, and wandering as far as his 60-foot cord allowed), won the enthusiastic support of clubgoers and the music press.

They returned to Austin heroes in the spring of 1980 and later that year signed to Stiff Records. Despite some critical kudos, a small loyal following, and a reputation as an exciting live act, Carrasco never achieved widespread popularity. He continued to perform into the '90s.

Jim Carroll

Born Aug. 1, 1950, New York, NY
1980—*Catholic Boy* (Atco) 1982—*Dry Dreams* 1983—

I Write Your Name (Atlantic) 1991—*Praying Mantis* (Giant) 1993—*The Best of the Jim Carroll Band: A World Without Gravity* (Rhino) 1998—*Pools of Mercury* (Mercury).

Poet, novelist, and former heroin addict Jim Carroll followed his friend Patti Smith into rock & roll with unexpected results: an almost-charting single, "People Who Died." After two more albums of music, he resumed writing poetry, and his first album of the '90s, *Praying Mantis,* is one of the earliest full-length spoken-word releases.

Carroll was a prodigy; his first collection of poetry was published when he was 16. In 1970 selections from *The Basketball Diaries,* his teenage journal of high school, hustling, and heroin, appeared in *Paris Review* (the complete journal was first published in 1978). A later poetry collection, *Living at the Movies,* was rumored to have been nominated for a Pulitzer Prize (it was not). In 1974 Carroll moved to Northern California, where he kicked his drug habit and, along with a San Francisco band, began performing rock & roll in area clubs.

On a visit to New York in 1979, he played his demo tape for Earl McGrath, then president of Rolling Stones Records, who arranged a record deal with Atco and produced *Catholic Boy.* The album featured "People Who Died," a powerful invocation of friends fallen victim to drugs and street life, and drew critical raves. His next two albums were not as well received, and Carroll dismissed his band (which, for *Dry Dreams,* had included Lenny Kaye) to concentrate on his writing.

Since then he has had four additional books published (*The Book of Nods,* 1986; *Forced Entries: The Downtown Diaries, 1971–1973,* 1987; *Fear of Dreaming: The Selected Poems of Jim Carroll,* 1993; *Void of Course: Poems 1994–1997,* 1998), written lyrics for Blue Öyster Cult and Boz Scaggs, and occasionally acted. In 1995 he rerecorded "Catholic Boy" with Pearl Jam for the soundtrack to *The Basketball Diaries,* a film by music video director Scott Kalvert that updated Carroll's memoir to the '90s with lead Leonardo DiCaprio.

Though his singing appearances remain rare and he most often appears publicly to read from his work, Carroll returned to music with 1998's *Pools of Mercury.* The album (his first music album without the Jim Carroll Band) mixed spoken-word and ambient tracks with straight-up rock & roll and featured musicians Lenny Kaye and Robert Roth.

The Cars

Formed 1976, Boston, MA

Ric Ocasek (b. Richard Otcasek, Mar. 23, 1949, Baltimore, MD), voc., gtr.; Ben Orr (b. Benjamin Orzechowski, Sep. 8, 1947, Cleveland, OH; d. Oct. 3, 2000, Atlanta, GA), bass, voc.; Elliot Easton (b. Elliot Shapiro, Dec. 18, 1953, Brooklyn, NY), gtr.; Greg Hawkes, kybds.; David Robinson (b. Apr. 2, 1953, Boston), drums.

1978—*The Cars* (Elektra) 1979—*Candy-O* 1980—*Panorama* 1981—*Shake It Up* 1984—*Heartbeat City* 1985—*Greatest Hits* 1987—*Door to Door* 1995—*The Cars Anthology: Just What I Needed* (Atlantic) 1999—*The Cars (Deluxe Edition)* (Rhino).

Ric Ocasek solo: 1983—*Beatitude* (Geffen) 1986—*This Side of Paradise* 1991—*Fireball Zone* (Reprise) 1993—*Quick Change World* 1996—*Getchertikitz* (Sound Effects) 1997—*Troublizing* (Columbia).

Ben Orr solo: 1986—*The Lace* (Elektra).

Greg Hawkes solo: 1983—*Niagara Falls* (Passport).

Elliot Easton solo: 1985—*Change No Change* (Elektra).

Ric Ocasek's artful pop songs drove the Cars, the new-wave band with the fastest, most consistent success. Their debut and second albums sold more than 6 million copies worldwide, and each album since (except their final group effort, *Door to Door*) has sold over a million copies. Although the group initially got the critics' nod for Ocasek's coolly detached stance and the smoothly burnished keyboard- and guitar-laced hooks, in retrospect the Cars were essentially the new-wave model of a Top 40 hit machine. That their off-center pop sensibility found expression in a series of original and frequently aired music videos (especially "You Might Think") made them, for a time, one of America's top bands.

Ocasek and Ben Orr had been partners for nearly a decade before starting the Cars. Ocasek took up the guitar at 10 and immediately began to write songs; he started working as a musician after he'd dropped out of Antioch College and Bowling Green State University. He met Orr—who as a teenager had fronted the house band on a TV rock show, *Upbeat*—in Cleveland, where Orr worked in a studio as a producer and session musician. After working together in various bands in Cleveland, New York City, Woodstock, and Ann Arbor, they settled in Cambridge, Massachusetts, in the late '70s.

As part of a folk trio, Milkwood, they released an album on Paramount in 1972, with Hawkes as session keyboardist. Ocasek and Orr continued to form bands, while Hawkes worked with Martin Mull and the Boston group Orphan, and wrote music with progressive rockers Happy the Man. In 1974 Easton joined Cap'n Swing, Ocasek and Orr's band at the time, which became popular in Boston but broke up when no recording contract was forthcoming. Hawkes rejoined, and Robinson, formerly of Jonathan Richman's Modern Lovers, DMZ, and L.A.'s the Pop, completed the Cars in late 1976.

After intensive rehearsals in Ocasek's basement, the Cars made some demo tapes, including "Just What I Needed," which became a top requested song on Boston radio station WBCN. Recorded in just two weeks, *The Cars* yielded three chart singles—"Just What I Needed" (#27, 1978), "My Best Friend's Girl" (#35, 1978), and "Good Times Roll" (#41, 1979)—and went platinum, staying on the charts so persistently that the release of *Candy-O,* recorded early in 1979, was delayed. By 1979 the Cars were on the arena circuit; with "Let's Go" (#14, 1979) and "It's All I Can Do" (#41, 1979), *Candy-O* went platinum in two months. On *Panorama,* the Cars toyed with dissonance and odd meters; it

The Cars: Greg Hawkes, Elliot Easton, Ben Orr, Ric Ocasek, David Robinson

went platinum with "Touch and Go" (#37, 1980), while their debut, *The Cars,* remained on the charts.

In 1981 the Cars also bought Intermedia Studios in Boston and remodeled it as Syncro Sound, where they recorded parts of *Shake It Up*. That album, with singles "Shake It Up" (#4, 1981) and "Since You're Gone" (#41, 1981), also went platinum. Ocasek, Orr, and Hawkes started solo albums in 1982.

Three years later *Heartbeat City* launched the hit singles "You Might Think" (#7, 1984), "Magic" (#12, 1984), "Drive" (#3, 1984), and "Hello Again" (#20, 1984). "Drive," which was used as background music to film clips documenting the famine stricken of Africa during the Live Aid concert and telecast, recharted in the U.K.; Ocasek donated the resulting royalties to the Band Aid Trust. The video for the song starred model Paulina Porizkova, whom Ocasek wed in 1989. The couple's sons, Jonathan and Oliver Orion, were born in 1993 and 1998, respectively.

The Cars' last Top 20 hits were "Tonight She Comes" (#7, 1985) and "You Are the Girl" (#17, 1987). The latter comes from *Door to Door,* an album recorded as the group was unraveling due to personal conflicts. Ocasek later described it as "a substandard album"; it peaked at #26. A couple of greatest-hits collections were released after the group's 1988 demise, notably the two-CD set *The Cars (Deluxe Edition),* which included demo versions of early hits and five previously unreleased songs. Throughout the Cars' career Ocasek and Orr shared lead vocals, with Orr singing "My Best Friend's Girl," "Just What I Needed," "Drive," "Let's Go," and "Candy-O." Of the group members' solo efforts, theirs were by far the most popular. Each had a hit single: Ocasek, "Emotion in Motion" (#15, 1986), and Orr, "Stay the Night" (#24, 1987).

Although Ocasek went on to record several more solo albums, including 1997's *Troublizing,* which featured Greg Hawkes on keyboards, Smashing Pumpkins' Billy Corgan, Hole's (and later Smashing Pumpkins') Melissa Auf Der Maur, and Bad Religion's Brian Baker, he largely concentrated on his producing career. His '90s credits include Weezer's eponymous debut album, Hole's cover of Fleetwood Mac's "Gold Dust Woman" for *The Crow: City of Angels* soundtrack, as well as albums for cult favorites Black 47, Guided by Voices, and Jonathan Richman.

Orr formed a band called ORR in the mid-'90s. He died in 2000 after battling pancreatic cancer. Guitarist Easton played in the band the Tiki Gods for a time, did session work with Jerry Lee Lewis and Brian Wilson, toured with ex–Creedence Clearwater Revival members Stu Cook and Doug Clifford in Creedence Clearwater Revisited, and worked as a producer. Hawkes contributed keyboards to most of Ocasek's solo albums.

Carlene Carter

Born Rebecca Carlene Smith, Sep. 26, 1955, Nashville, TN
1978—*Carlene Carter* (Warner Bros.) 1979—*Two Sides to Every Woman* 1980—*Musical Shapes* 1981—*Blue Nun* 1983—*C'est C Bon* (Epic) 1990—*I Fell in Love* (Reprise) 1993—*Little Love Letters* (Giant) 1995—*Little Acts of Treason.*

A third-generation member of America's preeminent country music family, Carlene Carter is the granddaughter of Mother Maybelle Carter of the Carter Family, and daughter of June Carter Cash and '50s country star Carl Smith. Since she began recording in the late '70s, Carlene Carter evolved from a twangy rocker to a successful country singer/songwriter in the early '90s.

Carter spent her early years in Nashville; her parents divorced and her mother married Johnny Cash when Carlene was 12. As a child, she often traveled with her mother, aunts, and grandmother, who toured as Mother Maybelle and the Carter Sisters. Carter learned to play the piano at six and the guitar at 10, and began singing onstage during her family's shows. After two brief teenage marriages, during which she had two children, Carter appeared sporadically as a member of the Carter Family revue.

In 1978 Carter recorded her first, self-titled album in England, backed by Graham Parker's band, the Rumour. A collection of upbeat, piano-based pop songs, *Carlene Carter* received some favorable notices but flopped. Her second album, *Two Sides to Every Woman,* recorded with New York session players, rocked harder, but lacked personality—though Carter herself certainly did not. At a performance in a New York club to support the album, she introduced one of its racier songs with the comment, "If this song doesn't put the cunt back in country, nothing will." Unbeknownst to her, her stepfather and mother were in the audience. The comment briefly caused a family riff, and earned Carter a *Playboy* award, for Quote of the Year.

In the late '70s Carter married her third husband, British singer/songwriter/producer Nick Lowe [see entry], whose band mates in Rockpile, Dave Edmunds and Billy Bremner, joined him in backing her on her raucous country-rock breakthrough album *Musical Shapes* (#139, 1980). Though still far from a commercial success, the album won critical raves and broadened Carter's audience.

Disappointing followup albums, *Blue Nun* and *C'est C Bon,* as well as personal problems (an ectopic pregnancy that almost killed her and the breakup of her marriage to Lowe), put Carter out of commission in the mid-'80s. The party lifestyle had also taken its toll, and Carter temporarily quit the music business. In 1986 she began touring with the Johnny Cash and June Carter Cash revue. Stating, "It was time to learn about my heritage," Carter dug into her country roots wholeheartedly for the first time, and after two years of performing with her family, she returned to Nashville drug- and alcohol-free and eager to commence her solo career.

In 1990 Carter hit country chart pay dirt with *I Fell in Love* (#19 C&W), an album ranging from progressive country rock to traditional Appalachian folk and produced by Tom Petty bassist Howie Epstein. The album yielded several C&W hit singles: the title track (#3 C&W, 1990), "Come On Back" (#3 C&W, 1990), "The Sweetest Thing" (#25 C&W, 1991), and "One Love" (#33 C&W, 1991). *Little Love Letters* (#35 C&W, 1993), again produced by Epstein, with whom Carter was living, featured Heartbreaker keyboardist Benmont Tench, as well as guitarists John Jorgenson, Albert Lee, and NRBQ's Al Anderson, who toured with Carter. Anderson and Carter cowrote the album's #3 C&W hit, "Every Little Thing." *Little Acts of Treason* (#65 C&W, 1995) did not fare as well, and Carter has kept a low profile since.

Clarence Carter

Born Jan. 14, 1936, Montgomery, AL
1968—*This Is Clarence Carter* (Atlantic); *The Dynamic Clarence Carter* 1969—*Testifyin'* 1970—*Patches* 1971—*The Best of Clarence Carter* 1973—*Sixty Minutes With Clarence Carter* (Fame); *Real* (ABC) 1975—*Loneliness and Temptation* 1976—*Heart Full of Song* 1981—*Let's Burn* (Venture) 1985—*Messin' With My Mind* (Ichiban) 1986—*Dr. CC* 1987—*Hooked on Love* 1988—*Touch of Blues* 1990—*Between a Rock and a Hard Place* 1992—*Snatching It Back: The Best of Clarence Carter* (Rhino/Atlantic); *Have You Met Clarence Carter . . . Yet?* (Ichiban) 1996—*Carter's Corner* (Cee Gee).

Blind singer/guitarist Clarence Carter is best known for his late-'60s hit singles: "Slip Away" and "Patches." His career began as part of Clarence and Calvin and the C and C Boys on the Duke label. In 1965 they joined Rick Hall's Fame Records. Calvin Scott had a car accident shortly afterward and retired, but Carter stayed with Fame, recording solo efforts and playing on sessions. As guitarist of the Mellow Men, he backed Otis Redding, Joe Tex, Solomon Burke, and Gene Chandler. In 1968 he met Candi Staton, whom he later married. Staton had hits as a soul ballad singer in the early '70s and as a disco star in the late '70s. (They divorced after a few years.) Carter had nine R&B hits before he crossed over to the pop chart with 1968's "Slip Away" (#6 pop, #2 R&B) and "Too Weak to Fight" (#13 pop, #3 R&B). He followed up in 1969 with "Snatching It Back" (#4 R&B), "The Feeling Is Right" (#9 R&B), and "Doin' Our Thing" (#9 R&B). His 1970 story song "Patches" (#4 pop, #2 R&B) was hailed as an instant classic. Carter signed with ABC in the mid-'70s, but the hits stopped coming for a while. Carter has continued to tour and record. His last hit was from *Dr. CC,* "Strokin'," a song sufficiently ribald to preclude radio play. Nonetheless, it sold 1.5 million copies.

The Carter Family

Formed 1926, Maces Spring, VA
Alvin Pleasant Carter (b. Apr. 15, 1891, Maces Spring; d. Nov. 7, 1960, Maces Spring), voc.; Sara Dougherty Carter (b. July 21, 1898, Wise County, VA; d. Jan. 9, 1979), voc., gtr., Autoharp, banjo; Maybelle Addington Carter (b. May 10, 1909, Nickelsville, VA; d. Oct. 23, 1978), voc., gtr., Autoharp, banjo.
1961—*The Famous Carter Family* (Harmony) 1963—*Great Original Recordings by the Carter Family* 1964—*Keep on the Sunny Side* (Columbia) 1965—*The Best of the Carter Family* 1967—*An Historic Reunion* 1991—*The Carter Family* (MCA) 1993—*Anchored in Love: Their Complete Victor Recordings 1927–1928* (Rounder); *My Clinch Mountain Home: Their Complete Victor Recordings 1928–1929* 1996—*Sunshine in the Shadows: Their Complete Victor Recordings 1931–1932.*

The Carter Family pioneered modern country music by setting folk songs to string-band backup, and were one of the most popular groups in America from 1926 until they disbanded in 1943. After that, A.P. performed sporadically with his children, and Maybelle continued to tour with her daughters through the '50s and '60s. Their songs, which included such standards as "Wildwood Flower," "Wabash

Cannonball," "I'm Thinking Tonight of My Blue Eyes," "Will the Circle Be Unbroken," and their radio program theme song, "Keep on the Sunny Side," were immensely popular; the 78 rpm version of "Wildwood Flower" sold more than a million copies.

The group formed in 1926 when A.P. Carter and his wife, Sara Dougherty, were joined by A.P.'s brother Ezra's wife (and Sara's cousin), Maybelle. Each had performed with friends and neighbors and as a group for about a year before they auditioned in Bristol, Tennessee, for Ralph Peer, who had been sent by the Victor label to record local musicians (Jimmie Rodgers was "discovered" by Peer on the same day). The Carter Family was soon recording quite frequently, although it wasn't until they had left Virginia some years later that any of them could stop working day jobs. In 1928 they recorded their biggest hit, "Wildwood Flower."

In 1936 A.P. and Sara were divorced, but the group continued to perform and record and in 1938 moved to Del Rio, Texas, where for the next three years they were regulars on radio station XERA. They then moved to Charlotte, North Carolina, to work for WBT, but shortly after their arrival, A.P. and Sara decided to retire. The original Carter Family had their last radio shows around 1939. The next year Maybelle began working with her daughters June, Helen, and Anita as Mother Maybelle Carter and the Carter Sisters. Meanwhile A.P. and several of his children had formed another group, with whom he performed until his death in 1960. After A.P. died, Maybelle and her daughters adopted the Carter Family name.

The family's influence on latter-day singers and songwriters derives not only from their songs and recordings but also from Maybelle Carter's unique acoustic guitar techniques, particularly what has become known as the "chicken-scratch," or the "Carter" style, which is widely imitated by folksingers. Maybelle and Sara reunited at the 1967 Newport Folk Festival to record *An Historic Reunion.* Throughout the '60s, Maybelle performed with her daughters in her son-in-law Johnny Cash's revue and later on his television program. She sang the title track on the Nitty Gritty Dirt Band's *Will the Circle Be Unbroken* in 1971. With the exception of Maybelle's three daughters and of June's daughter, Carlene Carter [see entry], none of the second- and third-generation Carters have achieved wide recognition, although many of them remained active in country music as performers and session musicians. June and Anita Carter each recorded solo albums; June's 1999 album, *Press On,* was released by an independent alternative-rock label. Helen Carter died on June 2, 1998, and Anita Carter died on July 29, 1999.

Peter Case

Born Apr. 5, 1954, Buffalo, NY
With the Plimsouls (Lou Ramirez, drums; Dave Pahoa, bass; Eddie Munoz, gtr.): 1980—*Zero Hour* EP (Beat) 1981—*The Plimsouls* (Planet) 1983—*Everywhere at Once* (Geffen) 1988—*One Night in America* (Fan Club) 1992—*The Plimsouls . . . Plus* (Rhino) 1998—(– Ramirez; + Clem Burke [b. Nov. 24, 1955, New York, NY], drums) *Kool Trash* (Shaky City).
Peter Case solo: 1986—*Peter Case* (Geffen) 1989—*The Man With the Blue Postmodern Fragmented Neotraditionalist Guitar* 1992—*Six Pack of Love* 1994—*Peter Case Sings Like Hell* (Vanguard) 1995—*Torn Again* 1998—*Full Service No Waiting* 2000—*Flying Saucer Blues.*

Singer/songwriter Peter Case began his career in punk-rock bands but in the mid-'80s went solo and became a folk-rock troubadour. The son of two teachers, Case dropped out of school in 10th grade, got his GED, and studied at State University of New York at Buffalo. One winter he boarded a Greyhound bus, eventually winding up in San Francisco, where he busked on street corners and in coffeehouses, sometimes accompanying Beat poet Allen Ginsberg.

In 1976 Case cofounded seminal West Coast punk band the Nerves with Paul Collins (later of the [American] Beat [see entry]), for whom he played bass. By 1978 he had moved to L.A. and formed the Plimsouls, a power-pop band popular in the local club scene. After a successful indie EP, Elektra subsidiary Planet signed the group, but when *The Plimsouls* stiffed, it dropped them. The band then released the independent 12-inch "A Million Miles Away," a college-radio hit that brought the band its second major-label deal. *Everywhere at Once* included that single and a number of other catchy tunes but failed to deliver on sales, despite the band's cameo in the teen flick *Valley Girl.*

In 1984 Case dissolved the Plimsouls, became a born-again Christian, and started playing solo shows. One night he saw singer/songwriter Victoria Williams performing in a restaurant; the two formed the Incredibly Strung Out Band and married in April 1985 (they divorced in 1989). The critically praised *Peter Case,* produced by T Bone Burnett and Mitchell Froom, included the college-radio hit "Steel Strings." Case supported the album by opening arenas for Jackson Browne.

Case's second solo album also pleased critics with its strong melodies and writerly lyrics; it included contributions from David Lindley, Jim Keltner, and Los Lobos' David Hidalgo. *Six Pack of Love* saw Case return to his more rocking roots. In 1993 he formed a band including ex-Plimsoul Eddie Munoz. The following year, Case released on Vanguard a collection of folk-blues songs, which he recorded live to two-track in a living-room studio set up by producer Marvin Etzioni (Lone Justice, Toad the Wet Sprocket).

Case has since settled into a groove with Vanguard, releasing three more "rock & roll folksinger" (his term) albums; each of these records features urgent melodies, spare, acoustic-based arrangements, and vivid originals about characters living on society's margins. In 1996 Case also reunited with the Plimsouls for a few live dates, with former Blondie drummer Clem Burke sitting in for Ramirez. The group subsequently released *Kool Trash,* a studio album that mines much the same vein as their '80s power-pop efforts.

Johnny Cash

Born Feb. 26, 1932, Kingsland, AR
1957—*With His Hot and Blue Guitar* (Sun) 1958—*Songs That Made Him Famous* 1959—*Fabulous Johnny Cash* (Columbia) 1960—*Ride This Train* 1962—*Sound of Johnny Cash* 1963—*Ring of Fire* 1964—*Keep on the Sunny Side; I Walk the Line* 1965—*Orange Blossom Special* 1968—*The Holy Land; At Folsom Prison* 1969—*Jackson; At San Quentin* 1970—*Johnny Cash Show* 1971—*A Man in Black* 1973—*Gospel Road; Sunday Morning Coming Down; America* 1974—*Five Feet High and Rising; Ragged Old Flag* 1975—*Look at Them Beans* 1977—*Last Gunfighter Ballad* 1980—*Rockabilly Blues* 1982—*The Survivors* (with Jerry Lee Lewis, Carl Perkins); *The Adventures of Johnny Cash* 1985—*Rainbow* 1986—*Believe in Him* (Word) 1987—*Johnny Cash Is Coming to Town* (Mercury); *The Vintage Years (1955–1963)* (Rhino) 1988—*Water From the Wells of Home* (Mercury) 1990—*The Sun Years* (Rhino) 1991—*The Mystery of Life* (Mercury) 1992—*The Essential Johnny Cash (1955–1983)* (Columbia/Legacy) 1994—*American Recordings* (American/Warner Bros.) 1996—*Unchained* 1998—*VH1 Storytellers: Johnny Cash and Willie Nelson* (with Willie Nelson) 2000—*Love God Murder* (Sony Legacy); *American III: Solitary Man* (American/Columbia).

Country music patriarch Johnny Cash, the "Man in Black," has walked the line between rock and country since his early days as a rockabilly singer. His songs' characteristic marching bass lines have influenced Waylon Jennings and others, while his deep, quavery baritone growl has become a trademark. A preeminent songwriter, Cash has been courted over the years by rock's elite, beginning with Dylan in the '60s. In 1994 Cash returned to the spotlight, boosted by the support of a whole new generation of fans—many of them alternative-rock aficionados—with the release of the stark (just vocals and acoustic guitar) *American Recordings*. Ill health slowed Cash down in the late '90s but did not stop his creative output.

The son of Southern Baptist sharecroppers, Cash began playing the guitar and writing songs at age 12. During high school, he performed frequently on radio station KLCN in Blytheville, Arkansas. Cash moved to Detroit in his late teens and worked there until he joined the air force as a radio operator in Germany. He left the air force and married Vivian Liberto in 1954; the couple settled in Memphis, where Cash worked as an appliance salesman and attended radio announcers' school.

With the Tennessee Two—guitarist Luther Perkins and bassist Marshall Grant—he began recording for Sam Phillips' Sun label in 1955. The trio recorded "Cry, Cry, Cry" (#14 C&W, 1955), and followed it with "Folsom Prison Blues" (#5 C&W, 1956). Later in 1956 came Cash's most enduring hit, the million-seller "I Walk the Line" (#17, 1956). At Sun, he was also part of an impromptu gospel sing-along with label mates Elvis Presley, Carl Perkins, and Jerry Lee Lewis that was widely bootlegged as *The Million Dollar Quartet* and finally released commercially in 1981 (on the U.K. label Charly).

Johnny Cash

Cash moved near Ventura, California, in 1958, signed with Columbia, and began a nine-year period of alcohol and drug abuse. He released a number of successful country and pop hits, among them "Ring of Fire" (#1 pop, #1 C&W, 1963), written by June Carter of the Carter Family and Merle Kilgore. By then, he had left his family and moved to New York's Greenwich Village. Late in 1965 Cash was arrested by customs officials for trying to smuggle amphetamines in his guitar case across the Mexican border. He got a suspended sentence and was fined. After a serious auto accident and a near fatal overdose, his wife divorced him. By then Cash had moved to Nashville, where he became friends with Waylon Jennings. Together they spent what both have described as a drug-crazed year and a half.

But in Nashville, Cash began a liaison with June Carter, who helped him get rid of his drug habit by 1967 and reconverted him to fundamentalist Christianity. By the time Cash and Carter married in early 1968, they had been working together regularly. They had hit duets with "Jackson" (#2 C&W, 1967), "Long-Legged Guitar Pickin' Man" (#6 C&W, 1967), and versions of Bob Dylan's "It Ain't Me, Babe" (#58 pop, #4 C&W, 1964) and Tim Hardin's "If I Were a Carpenter" (#36 pop, #2 C&W, 1970).

Cash's 1968 live album, *At Folsom Prison* (#13), became a million-seller in 1968. Bob Dylan invited him to sing a duet ("Girl From the North Country") and write liner notes for *Nashville Skyline*, and Dylan appeared in the first segment of ABC-TV's *The Johnny Cash Show* in June 1969. The highly rated series, which lasted two years, developed a reputation as an eclectic showcase of contemporary American music, with guests ranging from Louis Armstrong to Carl Perkins to Bob Dylan. Cash had a 1969 hit with Shel Silverstein's "A Boy Named Sue" (#2), a track from *Johnny Cash at San Quentin;* his best-selling album, the live LP was #1 for four weeks.

In 1970 Cash performed at the Nixon White House. He and June Carter traveled to Israel in 1971 to make a documentary, *Gospel Road.* Cash continued to tour and make hits through the '70s, including "A Thing Called Love" (#2 C&W, 1972) and "One Piece at a Time" (#1 C&W, 1976). He also became active in benefit work, particularly on behalf of prisoners, Native American rights, and evangelist Billy Graham's organization.

In 1982 Cash regrouped with fellow surviving Million Dollar Quartet members Carl Perkins and Jerry Lee Lewis to record *The Survivors.* Three years later Cash hooked up with three other compadres—Kris Kristofferson, Waylon Jennings, and Willie Nelson—to form the Highwaymen, releasing *Highwayman* in 1985. The Highwaymen performed together sporadically throughout the late '80s and '90s, recording *Highwayman 2* in 1990 and *Highwaymen: The Road Goes On Forever* (produced by Don Was) in 1995.

Cash's 25-year relationship with Columbia Records ended in the mid-'80s, and in 1986 he began a somewhat desultory liaison with Nashville's branch of Mercury Records. By the late '80s, his long streak of country hits had ended, and Cash complained to an interviewer that he'd been "purged" from Nashville, replaced by contemporary "hat acts." He continued to perform constantly, however, usually with a package tour that included his wife and her sisters Helen and Anita Carter, as well as Johnny and June's son, John Carter Cash (other Cash and Carter siblings would sometimes show up too). Throughout these years, Cash turned to acting, in a slew of Western-themed movies and TV shows. He also suffered from health problems and underwent heart surgery as well as drug treatment for an addiction to painkillers.

Already a member of the Nashville Songwriter's Hall of Fame (Cash has more than 400 songs to his credit) and the Country Music Hall of Fame, Cash was inducted into the Rock and Roll Hall of Fame in 1992. Also that year came the release of the critically acclaimed box set *The Essential Johnny Cash.* In 1993 he began his return to the forefront with a guest vocal turn on U2's *Zooropa;* he sang lead vocals on the darkly haunting track "The Wanderer." The following year, Cash was toasted by alt-rock audiences with the release of *American Recordings,* on the label by the same name, known for its rap and rock artists. Label chief Rick Rubin's production emphasized Cash's brooding, deep vocals, backed by his own simple, but rhythmic acoustic guitar. Featuring, among Cash's own compositions, covers of such artists as Nick Lowe, Leonard Cohen, and Tom Waits, the album's songs veered from Cash's "Redemption" to satanic-rocker Glenn Danzig's "Thirteen." Appearing solo or backed by guitar, bass, and drums, Cash performed in several intimate venues crawling with hipsters. Though the album only reached #110 on the pop charts (#29 C&W), it received airplay on alternative-rock and college radio stations, garnering critical raves.

In 1996 Cash released another well-received album, *Unchained,* on which he was backed by Tom Petty and the Heartbreakers and covered edgy songs by the likes of Beck and Soundgarden. The album won the Best Country Album Grammy, and Cash also garnered a Lifetime Achievement Award Grammy. Then, after experiencing dizziness and tremors in 1997, Cash was diagnosed with the degenerative nervous disorder Shy-Drager syndrome. He retired from the road and began treatments for his illness. In 1999 he was the subject of a televised tribute (featuring Dylan, U2, Springsteen, and others) and made his first public appearance since his diagnosis. In 2000 Cash's health seemed better, and his doctors were beginning to question if they'd made the right diagnosis. Cash released another critically acclaimed album, *American III: Solitary Man,* which won a Grammy for Best Contemporary Folk Recording. (It also brought him back to Columbia, which had begun distributing the American label.)

Rosanne Cash

Born May 24, 1955, Memphis, TN
1980—*Right or Wrong* (Columbia) 1981—*Seven Year Ache* 1982—*Somewhere in the Stars* 1985—*Rhythm and Romance* 1987—*King's Record Shop* 1989—*Hits 1979–1989* 1990—*Interiors* 1993—*The Wheel* 1996—*10 Song Demo* (Capitol) 2001—*The Rules of Travel.*

The oldest daughter of country music star Johnny Cash and Vivian Liberto, Rosanne Cash began her recording career with a sound that blended Nashville C&W and California country rock. By the '90s, after scoring numerous country hits and divorcing country producer/singer/songwriter Rodney Crowell, she had developed into an eloquent and introspective singer/songwriter, whose troubled personal life was reflected in evocative, pain-wracked compositions.

Though born in Memphis, Cash grew up in Ventura, California, where her parents had moved in 1958; the two divorced in 1966. The day after graduating from high school, she joined her father's touring revue as a wardrobe assistant and later became a backup singer. After three years with the Johnny Cash show, she moved to London in 1976, returning home in 1977 to attend Vanderbilt University in Nashville. Then she moved to Hollywood and enrolled in the Lee Strasberg Theater Institute the next year. She took time off in January 1978 to record a demo produced by Rodney Crowell [see entry], attracting the attention of the German-based Ariola label. She went to Munich to record an album, and although it was never released in the U.S. it persuaded the Nashville branch of Columbia Records to sign her.

Cash and Crowell married in 1979. For a while she played with Crowell's band, the Cherry Bombs, before Columbia released her debut U.S. album, *Right or Wrong,* which sold surprisingly well despite her inability to tour; she was pregnant. Her 1981 followup, *Seven Year Ache,* drew critical raves, solid sales, and yielded a #1 country hit with the title tune (two other tracks from the LP hit #1 as well).

Cash continued to score on the country charts: "Ain't No Money" (#4 C&W, 1982), "I Don't Know Why You Don't Want Me" (#1 C&W, 1985), "Never Be You" (#1 C&W, 1985), "Hold On" (#5 C&W, 1986), "Second to No One" (#5 C&W, 1986). By the mid-'80s, though, childbearing had curtailed her touring (she and Crowell have three daughters), and a cocaine dependence landed her in rehab. She sprang back, however, with the eclectic *King's Record Shop* (#6 C&W, 1987), which featured a remake of her father's "Tennessee Flat Top Box" (#1 C&W, 1987) and marked a healing of her strained relationship with her dad. The album also yielded #1 C&W hits in John Hiatt's "The Way We Make a Broken Heart," "If You Change Your Mind," and "Runaway Train." A longtime Beatles fan, Cash took the group's "I Don't Want to Spoil the Party" to the top of the country charts in 1989.

Self-produced, *Interiors* (#23 C&W, 1990) was Cash's first album without Crowell at the helm. Her brutally dark take on intimate relationships was reflected throughout and made clear the marital problems that had been hinted at on earlier albums, both in her own songs and those contributed by her husband. Cash began touring the singer/songwriter circuit in the '90s, and as her songs became more personal and her music's sound more stripped down, her country hits stopped coming. In 1992 her marriage ended in divorce. Its painful aftermath and her own self-actualization were the themes of her critically acclaimed album *The Wheel* (#37 C&W, 1993). Cash's interest in Jungian psychology was apparent in her compositions as well. Always highly critical of the Nashville country star lifestyle, Cash relocated to New York City and began a relationship with guitarist/songwriter/producer John Leventhal (Shawn Colvin), with whom she began collaborating and touring; the couple married in 1995.

After moving to Capitol Records, Cash released the spare *10 Song Demo* in 1996. Produced by Leventhal, it featured Cash singing her introspective songs, for the most part backed only by her acoustic guitar or piano. That same year, a book of Cash short stories, *Bodies of Water,* was published to favorable reviews. She has since published a children's book, *Penelope Jane: A Fairy's Tale* (in 2000), and edited a book of prose, *Songs Without Rhymes,* by such songwriters as David Byrne and Suzanne Vega. In early 2001 she returned with her first new album of songs in five years, entitled *The Rules of Travel.*

David Cassidy

Born Apr. 12, 1950, New York, NY
1972—*Cherish* (Bell); *Rock Me Baby* 1974—*Cassidy Live* 1975—*The Higher They Climb* (RCA) 1976—*Home Is Where the Heart Is* 1990—*David Cassidy* (Enigma) 1992—*Didn't You Used to Be* (Scotti Bros.) 1998—*Old Trick, New Dog* (Slamajama).

Early-'70s teen idol and actor David Cassidy is the son of actor Jack Cassidy and actress Evelyn Ward. He moved to Hollywood in 1957 with his mother when his parents divorced. (His father then married actress Shirley Jones, who played Cassidy's mother in the television series *The Partridge Family.*) During his teens, he played guitar and drums, wrote songs, and acted; his credits include Allan Sherman's Broadway production *Fig Leaves Are Falling* and guest shots on television's *Bonanza* and *Marcus Welby, M.D.*

In fall 1970 he began a four-year run as Keith Partridge on *The Partridge Family* (inspired by the Cowsills). The Partridge Family's premiere single, "I Think I Love You" (released before the TV series debuted), sold nearly 6 million copies. Several hits followed. Cassidy received royalties from the sales of *Partridge Family* coloring books, lunch boxes, dolls, comic books, postcards, clothes, books, records, and the show itself [see entry].

His solo recording career began in 1971 with a Top 10 remake of the Association's "Cherish." His several world tours inspired mass hysteria; Cassidy began to disclaim the teen-idol role after a 14-year-old fan named Bernadette Wheeler suffered a fatal heart attack at a London show in May 1974. That year he quit the TV series and in 1975 signed a long-term contract with RCA.

Cassidy's subsequent efforts did little to establish credibility with more mature listeners in the United States. Across the Atlantic, in the U.K., it was quite a different story, with Cassidy claiming 10 Top 20 singles there between 1972 and 1985, including two chart-toppers ("How Can I Be Sure" and "Daydreamer" b/w "The Puppy Song"). In 1976 he and Mick Ronson cut a single entitled "Gettin' It On in the Streets" and were supposed to record an album and form a band; none of it ever came to pass.

During 1978–79 he returned to television in a police drama, *David Cassidy—Man Undercover,* but he never abandoned music. He starred in 1983 in *Joseph and the Amazing Technicolor Dreamcoat* on Broadway, and in 1987 he took over Cliff Richard's role in Dave Clark's London musical *Time.* In 1990 he launched a comeback effort that resulted in his first U.S. Top 30 appearance since 1972, "Lyin' to Myself" (#27, 1990). Seemingly resigned to *The Partridge Family* legacy (the show found new audiences in syndication and on Nickelodeon), he titled a recent effort *Didn't You Used to Be* and had another ex-Partridge, comedian/disc jockey Danny Bonaduce, open some of his shows. In 1993 he opened in the New York production of *Blood Brothers,* a dramatic musical costarring Petula Clark and his half-brother Shaun Cassidy. His autobiography, *Come On, Get Happy,* was published in 1994. Cassidy remains active in both music and the theater and has headlined in Las Vegas. In early 2000 NBC aired the made-for-television movie *The David Cassidy Story.*

Shaun Cassidy

Born Sep. 27, 1959, Hollywood, CA
1977—*Shaun Cassidy* (Warner Bros./Curb); *Born Late* 1978—*Under Wraps* 1979—*Room Service; That's Rock 'n' Roll—Shaun Cassidy Live* 1980—*Wasp.*

Following in the footsteps of his half brother David Cassidy, Shaun Cassidy was a teen idol in the late '70s. The son of actor Jack Cassidy and actress Shirley Jones, he grew up in Beverly Hills and formed his first rock band at age 11, just after he began writing his own songs. Signed by Mike Curb to the Warner/Curb label in 1975, Cassidy had his first success in Europe, where his photos saturated the teen magazines. His debut single—"Morning Girl," released in January 1976—went Top 20 in most of Europe. His second single, a cover of Eric Carmen's "That's Rock 'n' Roll," expanded his appeal to Australia and later went gold in the U.S. in a 1977 release.

He starred in *The Hardy Boys Mysteries* TV series from 1977 to 1979. His first U.S. single, a cover of the Crystals' 1963 hit "Da Doo Ron Ron," was released in May 1977 and hit #1; his simultaneously released debut album, *Shaun Cassidy*, went platinum. "Hey Deanie," another Carmen song, hit #7 in 1978, but followups sank. Like half brother David before him, Shaun tried with little success to make the transition to a serious rocker; his 1980 *Wasp* was produced by Todd Rundgren and featured versions of songs by David Bowie, Ian Hunter, Peter Townshend, and David Byrne.

He concentrated on acting. Among his television credits are the 1979 television movie *Like Normal People*, the 1980 series *Breaking Away*, and, later in the decade, the soap *General Hospital*. In 1993 he played David Cassidy's twin in the Broadway production of *Blood Brothers*. Cassidy also created, wrote, and produced several television shows, among them the horror-themed *American Gothic* (CBS, 1995) and the action series *Roar* (Fox, 1997).

Jimmy Castor

Born June 22, 1943, New York, NY
N.A.—*Hey Leroy* (Smash) 1972—*It's Just Begun* (RCA); *Phase Two* 1973—*Dimension 3* 1974—*The Everything Man* (Atlantic) 1975—*Super Sound* (Atco); *Butt of Course* 1976—*E Man Groovin'*.

Singer/songwriter/saxophonist Jimmy Castor is best known for "Troglodyte (Cave Man)," a 1972 funk novelty hit, but his career stretches back to the '50s. He assembled his first group, Jimmy Castor and the Juniors (Johnny Williams, Orton Graves, Al Casey Jr.), around 1955. Their "I Promise to Remember" (a Castor original) was a modest New York hit in 1956, but later that year Frankie Lymon and the Teenagers' cover version was a national hit. Castor, a friend of the Teenagers, was asked to sub for Lymon on occasion.

After graduating from New York's High School of Music and Art, Castor dropped out of the music business to study accounting at City College of New York. He reentered the music business in 1962, when he played the sax on Dave "Baby" Cortez's Top 10 hit "Rinky Dink." He then recorded solo for the Winley, Clown, Jet-Set, and Decca labels before forming the Jimmy Castor Bunch (percussionist Leonard Fridie Jr., bassist Douglas Gibson, guitarist Harry Jensen, drummer Robert Manigault, and keyboardist Gerry Thomas) in the mid-'60s. The Bunch recorded for Compass and Capitol before "Hey, Leroy, Your Mama's Callin' You" (#31 pop, 1967; #16 R&B, 1966) was recorded for Smash. "Troglodyte" (#6 pop, #4 R&B, 1972) is Castor's biggest hit to date. Castor left RCA for Atlantic and returned to the Top 20 with a sequel to "Troglodyte," "The Bertha Butt Boogie" (#16 pop, #22 R&B, 1975). His other hits on Atlantic were "Potential" (#25 R&B, 1975), "King Kong, Part 1" (#23 R&B, 1975), and "Space Age" (#28 R&B, 1977).

Through the early '80s, Castor continued to record solo, his singles peaking at the nether points of the R&B chart. In 1988 he had an R&B Top 30 hit in a duet with Joyce Sims, "Love Makes a Woman." In the early '90s Castor became a Teenager when he joined the two surviving group members and two other singers in a re-formed lineup of that group.

Nick Cave and the Bad Seeds/ The Birthday Party

The Birthday Party, formed 1976 (as the Boys Next Door), Melbourne, Austral.
Nick Cave (b. Nicholas Edward Cave, Sep. 22, 1957, Warracknabeal, Austral.), voc., gtr.; Mick Harvey (b. Sep. 29, 1958, Rochester, Austral.), gtr., drums, kybds., bass; Tracy Pew (b. 1958; d. Nov. 7, 1986), bass; Phil Calvert, drums.
1978—(+ Rowland S. Howard [b. Oct. 24, 1959, Melbourne], gtr., voc.) 1979—*Door Door* (Mushroom, Austral.); *Hee-Haw* EP (Missing Link, Austral.) 1980—*The Birthday Party* 1981—*Prayers On Fire* (Thermidor/4AD) 1982—*Junkyard* (4AD, U.K.) (– Calvert) 1983—*The Bad Seed* EP; *Mutiny!* EP (Mute) (– Harvey) 1985—*It's Still Living* (Missing Link, Austral.); *A Collection . . .* 1991—*The Peel Sessions Album* (Strange Fruit) 1992—*Hits* (4AD) 1993—(group disbands) 1999—*Live 1981–82*.
Nick Cave and the Bad Seeds, formed Sep. 1983, London, Eng.: Cave; Harvey; Barry Adamson (b. June 1, 1958, Manchester, Eng.), bass, kybds., gtr., voc., drums; Blixa Bargeld (b. Christian Emmerich, Jan. 12, 1959, Berlin, Ger.), gtr., piano, voc.
1984—*From Her to Eternity* (Mute) 1985—*The Firstborn Is Dead* (Mute) (+ Thomas Wydler [b. Oct. 9, 1959, Zurich, Switz.], drums, trombone, voc.) 1986—*Kicking Against the Pricks; Your Funeral . . . My Trial* (– Adamson; + Roland Wolf [d. ca. 1994], kybds.; + Kid Congo Powers [b. Brian Tristan, Mar. 27, 1961, La Puente, CA], gtr., voc.) 1988—*Tender Prey* 1989—(– Wolf) 1990—*The Good Son* (– Powers; + Martyn P. Casey [b. July 10, 1960, Chesterfield, Eng.], bass, voc.; + Conway Savage [b. July 27, 1960, Foster, Austral.], kybds., voc.) 1992—*Henry's Dream* 1993—*Live Seeds* 1994—(+ Warren Ellis, violin, accordion; + Jim Sclavunos, drums) *Let Love In* 1996—*Murder Ballads* 1997—*The Boatman's Call* 1998—*The Best of Nick Cave and the Bad Seeds* 2001—*No More Shall We Part*.
These Immortal Souls, formed 1987, London: R. Howard; Harry Howard (b. Oct. 10, 1961, Melbourne), bass; Genevieve McGuckin, kybds.; Epic Soundtracks (b. Kevin Paul

Godley, Mar. 23, 1959, Croydon, Eng.; d. Nov. 6, 1997, London), drums, piano.
1987—*Get Lost (Don't Lie)* (Mute) 1992—*I'm Never Gonna Die Again.*
Rowland S. Howard solo: 1999—*Teenage Snuff Film* (Reliant, Austral.).

The Birthday Party combined overdriven, postpunk guitar cacophony with Delta blues influences and the alternately morose and ranting vocals of Nick Cave. After the group imploded in 1983, an entire generation of Australian, English, and American noisemongers began roaming the earth. Since then, the Birthday Party's members, most notably singer/songwriter Cave, have formed an orbit of bands that share both personnel and a dramatically dark sensibility.

The Birthday Party had its beginnings in Melbourne, Australia, where the teenage Cave—a former petty thief and misfit in his hometown—had met Mick Harvey at boarding school. In the mid-'70s the pair formed the Boys Next Door, who released several records in their homeland. Constrained by the provincial Melbourne scene, the band set off for England in 1980, when it changed its name to the Birthday Party. An Australian album from that year was credited to both names. The musicians' intense, assaultive live act and appearances on early supporter John Peel's BBC-1 radio program led to a contract with the U.K. indie label 4AD. In 1982 they released their signature album, *Junkyard.* Around that time, bassist Tracy Pew (who died from epilepsy-related causes in 1986) was arrested on drug charges; former Magazine bassist Barry Adamson and guitarist Rowland S. Howard's brother, Harry, were among his temporary fill-in replacements. By the end of the year, Pew had returned and drummer Phil Calvert was gone; the latter briefly joined the Psychedelic Furs.

The Birthday Party's violent, sacrilegious subject matter ("Dead Joe," "Big-Jesus-Trash-Can," "The Six Strings That Drew Blood") and dark, brooding attitude caused the U.K. press to somewhat erroneously associate the group with the gothic-rock scene. In 1982 Cave, Harvey, Rowland Howard, and Pew moved to Berlin and recorded another EP, *The Bad Seed.* (They also collaborated with Lydia Lunch [see entry] on her *Honeymoon in Red* album.) The followup EP, *Mutiny!,* proved to be the Birthday Party's final release together. The band unraveled after Harvey quit in 1983.

Cave returned to London. He formed the Bad Seeds with Adamson, Harvey, and Einstürzende Neubauten [see entry] frontman Blixa Bargeld. (Numerous guests have drifted in and out of the ensemble ever since.) A more refined, controlled version of the Birthday Party, the Bad Seeds retained the earlier group's intensity, but Cave added a Leonard Cohen–style romantic gloom. He also unveiled an Elvis obsession, with a cover of "In the Ghetto" on *From Her to Eternity;* both *The Firstborn Is Dead* and its initial single "Tupelo" (1985) directly concern Presley. Cave showed his range on 1986's *Kicking Against the Pricks,* convincingly covering Leadbelly, gospel, Hendrix, and "By the Time I Get to Phoenix." The same year, the Bad Seeds released a double EP of mostly original material, *Your Funeral . . . My Trial.* Several lineup changes ensued, and Cramps guitarist Kid Congo Powers filled out the sound on *Tender Prey.*

In the late '80s Cave took time off from music to pursue his literary ambitions. *King Ink,* a collection of song lyrics, plays, and prose pieces, was published in England in 1988 and eventually made its way to the U.S.; a novel, *And the Ass Saw the Angel,* hit the shelves the next year. The Southern Gothic fable, filled with Cave's scatologically religious imagery, received generally favorable notices.

The Good Son (1990) was recorded in Brazil with largely acoustic instrumentation; the album has a quiet, mournful intensity. *Henry's Dream* and *Let Love In* focus largely on Cave's richly narrative compositions. The subdued playing on 1996's *Murder Ballads* contrasts its harsh, gruesome theme. This collection of death-obsessed originals and covers boasts duets with Polly Jean Harvey and fluffy pop star Kylie Minogue. *The Boatman's Call* eases off on the overbearing grimness of its predecessor. On *No More Shall We Part,* Cave continues his exploration of death experience and the twists and turns of the human heart.

Once the Birthday Party had split, Rowland S. Howard, Harry Howard, and Harvey joined their old Melbourne friend Simon Bonney, who since the late '70s had been leading the group Crime and the City Solution. Accompanied by ex–Swell Maps drummer Epic Soundtracks, they played on several of that band's mid-'80s releases. In 1987 the Howards and Soundtracks left to form the sinister, noirish These Immortal Souls. Rowland Howard, who has also made records with Nikki Sudden, Lydia Lunch, and Einstürzende Neubauten, issued his solo debut in 1999.

Over the years, Cave, Bargeld, and Harvey have dabbled in film scores, crafting the soundtracks to *Ghosts . . . of the Civil Dead* (1989) and *To Have and to Hold* (1996). Cave also acted in 1992's *Johnny Suede* (alongside Brad Pitt) and in a number of Wim Wenders movies.

Peter Cetera: See Chicago

Chad and Jeremy

Formed ca. 1963, London, Eng.
Chad Stuart (b. Dec. 10, 1943, Eng.), voc., gtr., piano, sitar, tamboura, tablas, banjo, flute; Jeremy Clyde (b. Mar. 22, 1944, Eng.), voc., gtr.
1964—*Yesterday's Gone* (World Artists) 1965—*Chad and Jeremy Sing for You; Before and After* (Columbia); *I Don't Want to Lose You Baby* 1966—*The Best of Chad and Jeremy* (Capitol); *More Chad and Jeremy; Distant Shores* (Columbia) 1967—*Of Cabbages and Kings* 1968—*The Ark* 1992—*Painted Dayglow Smile* (Legacy Rock Artifacts Series) 1993—*Yesterday's Gone—A Golden Classics Collection* (Collectables).

Chad and Jeremy's innocuous soft-rock hits kept them on the charts from 1964 through 1966. Sons of affluent British families, both were well educated (Eton and the Sorbonne, respectively). They met while studying at the Central School of Drama in London, where they began singing folk-based material. In 1964 one of their first singles, "Yesterday's Gone," went to #21 in the U.S.

The pair soon moved to Hollywood and began to rival Peter and Gordon as the world's top folk-rock duo. Chart hits like "A Summer Song" (#7, 1964) and "Distant Shores" (#30, 1966) combined with frequent television appearances *(Hullabaloo, The Hollywood Palace)* kept them in the public eye. They broke up in late 1966, when Jeremy departed to act in a London stage musical. The two later regrouped and recorded *Of Cabbages and Kings,* one of the first "concept albums," and *The Ark.* They ended their partnership in November 1967. Thereafter Clyde resumed his acting career: He has appeared on the London stage, in movies, and in a television miniseries. Stuart served as musical director for *The Smothers Brothers Comedy Hour* and worked as a musical-comedy composer.

Chairmen of the Board

Formed 1969, Detroit, MI
Original lineup: General Norman Johnson (b. May 23, 1943), voc.; Danny Woods (b. Apr. 10, 1944), voc.; Harrison Kennedy (b. Ontario, Can.), voc.; Eddie Curtis, voc.
1970—*Give Me Just a Little More Time* (Invictus); *In Session* 1972—*Bittersweet* 1973—*Greatest Hits* 1990—*Greatest Hits* (HDH/Fantasy) 1995—*Success* (Surfside).

The Chairmen of the Board is a soul vocal group whose biggest hit was the Holland/Dozier/Holland–produced "Give Me Just a Little More Time" (#3, 1970). The group's leader and main songwriter, General Norman Johnson, grew up in Norfolk, Virginia, where he sang in church choirs as a child. By age 12 he had formed his first group, the Humdingers. During his senior year of high school (1961), Johnson and his group the Showmen recorded his salute to rock & roll, "It Will Stand," for Minit Records.

After several more singles for Minit and later Swan, Johnson left the group to sign with ex-Motown producers Holland/Dozier/Holland's Invictus label. There the Chairmen of the Board was formed, with Johnson; another Showman, Danny Woods; Harrison Kennedy of the Canadian group Stone Soul Children; and Eddie Curtis, an alumnus of Lee Andrews and the Hearts and Huey Smith and the Clowns. Their debut single, "Give Me Just a Little More Time," was followed by several minor hits and "Pay to the Piper" (#13) in 1970. They briefly disbanded the next year but regrouped in 1972. Now billed as General Johnson and the Chairmen of the Board, a trio of Johnson, Woods, and saxman Ken Knox, continues to play and enjoy self-released, local hits in the Southeast. Several of Johnson's songs have been hits for other performers, including Honey Cone ("Want Ads," "Stick Up," "One Monkey Don't Stop No Show"), Freda Payne ("Bring the Boys Home"), and Clarence Carter ("Patches"). In 1994 Johnson and Joey Ramone duetted on "Rockaway Beach" for the album *Godchildren of Soul.*

The Chambers Brothers

Formed ca. 1961, Los Angeles, CA
George E. Chambers (b. Sep. 26, 1931, Flora, MS), voc., bass; Willie Chambers (b. Mar. 3, 1938, MS), voc., gtr.; Lester Chambers (b. Apr. 13, 1940, MS), voc., harmonica; Joe Chambers (b. Aug. 24, 1942, Scott County, MS), voc., gtr.
1965—(+ Brian Keenan [b. Jan. 28, ca. 1944, New York, NY; d. ca. mid-'80s], drums) *People Get Ready* (Vault) 1966—*Chambers Brothers Now* 1968—*Shout!; The Time Has Come* (Columbia); *A New Time, A New Day* 1969—*Love, Peace and Happiness* 1970—*Chambers Brothers Live at Fillmore East; Feelin' the Blues* (Vault) 1971—*A New Generation* (Columbia); *The Chambers Brothers' Greatest Hits* 1972—*Oh My God!* 1973—*Best of the Chambers Brothers* (Fantasy) 1974—*Unbonded* (Avco) 1975—*Right Move.*

Black gospel/funk/psychedelic innovators, the Chambers Brothers had an enthusiastic following in the late '60s. The four brothers grew up in a poverty-stricken Mississippi sharecropping family and first sang together at the Mount Calvary Baptist Church in Lee County. George, the eldest, was drafted into the army in 1952. Once discharged, he gravitated to south L.A. and was eventually joined by his brothers. They began performing around Southern California as a gospel and folk quartet in 1961.

After their first New York dates in 1965, they became an interracial group with the addition of drummer Brian Keenan and moved toward rock. The group attracted national attention at the 1965 Newport Folk Festival and worked both the psychedelic ballrooms (the Fillmores, Electric Circus) and soul venues like New York's Apollo Theatre. They signed with Columbia in 1967, and the title track from their first album for that label, "Time Has Come Today," became a major hit (#11, 1968). They charted with several more singles, including "I Can't Turn You Loose" (#37, 1968), and LPs *(A New Time, A New Day* and *Love, Peace and Happiness)* over the next few years.

The original group broke up in early 1972, with drummer Keenan joining Genya Ravan's band. The Chambers Brothers reunited in 1974 for *Unbonded.* They continue an on-again, off-again career. In 1980 they supported Maria Muldaur on her *Gospel Nights* and made commercials for Levi Strauss. Early in 1980 Lester relocated to New York (where he formed a band with ex–Electric Flag bassist Harvey Brooks), and several of the brothers worked on solo careers. Willie and Joe became session players, George sang gospel, and all the brothers belong to an extended-family gospel choir called the Chambers Family Singers. Keenan went on to run his own Connecticut recording studio; in the mid-'80s, he died of an apparent heart attack.

The Champs

Formed 1957, Los Angeles, CA
Original lineup: Dave Burgess (b. Lancaster, CA), gtr.; Dale Norris (b. Springfield, MA), gtr.; Chuck Rio (b. Rankin, TX), sax; Gen Alden (b. Cisco, TX), drums; Bobby Morris (b. Tulsa, OK), bass.
1960—*Everybody's Rockin'* (Challenge) 1994—*Greatest Hits—Tequila* (Curb).

The Champs were West Coast sessionmen whose first single, the instrumental "Tequila" (written by Rio), stayed on the charts for 19 weeks, reached #1, eventually sold more than 6 million copies worldwide, and won a Grammy Award for the best R&B record of 1958. Subsequent hits—"Too Much Tequila" (#30, 1960), "Limbo Rock" (#40, 1962), and "Tequila Twist" (#99, 1962)—failed to match the success of "Tequila." Over the years the group underwent numerous personnel changes, including a brief membership by guitarist/vocalist Delaney Bramlett (later of Delaney and Bonnie), before disbanding in 1965. Two other ex-Champs, Jimmy Seals and Dash Crofts, went on to form the Dawnbreakers before they reemerged in 1970 as Seals and Crofts [see entry].

James Chance

Born James Siegfried, Apr. 20, 1953, Milwaukee, WI
1979—*Buy the Contortions* (with the Contortions) (Ze); *Grutzi Elvis* EP; *Off-White* (with James White and the Blacks) 1980—*Live aux Bains Douches* (with the Contortions) (Invisible, Fr.) 1981—*Live in New York* (with the Contortions) (ROIR); *Sax Maniac* (with James White and the Blacks) (Animal/Chrysalis); 1982—*Flaming Demonics* (Ze) 1991—*Soul Exorcism* (with the Contortions) (ROIR) 1995—*Lost Chance.*

In the late '70s and early '80s, James Chance's "punk funk"—an edgy, atonal fusion, incorporating funk, free-form jazz, and punk intensity—was a pervasive strain in New York City dance music, with former band mates showing up in many New York dance groups. While Chance is not well known to many of today's music fans, his influence can be felt in the in-your-face aggression of Limp Bizkit and the skronky freedom of David S. Ware and the Boredoms' avant-garde music.

Growing up in suburban Milwaukee, Siegfried started studying piano in the first grade. In high school he became interested in jazz and at age 19 took up the alto sax. He attended the Wisconsin Conservatory of Music but dropped out less than a semester short of receiving his degree. He went to New York in 1976 and studied for a short time with avant-garde saxophonist David Murray.

In 1977 Chance formed the Contortions, whose most famous lineup comprised organist Adele Bertei, guitarist Jody Harris, bassist George Scott III, slide guitarist Pat Place, and drummer Don Christensen. Like Captain Beefheart, he arranged and demonstrated to his musicians the instrumental parts of every song. Contortions concerts—the first of which were given in fall 1977—could be violent experiences: Chance was notorious for diving from the stage and engaging in fisticuffs with spectators.

The first Contortions recordings were the four tracks they contributed to a Brian Eno–produced *No New York* anthology (Antilles/Island). In 1979 the Contortions dissolved and Chance formed James White and the Blacks. During the recording of *Off-White*, the Blacks included all the original Contortions except Bertei, who occasionally performed with them as a guest, along with Lydia Lunch and Voidoid Robert Quine. That group also dissolved; Bertei formed the Bloods and Place the Bush Tetras [see entry], while Scott joined Lunch in 8 Eyed Spy, later reuniting with Harris and Christensen in the Raybeats. Chance collaborated with Arto Lindsay (DNA, Lounge Lizards), Bradley Field (Teenage Jesus and the Jerks), and George Scott on a Diego Cortez film soundtrack, *Grutzi Elvis*. (Scott died in 1980 of a heroin overdose.) Chance continued to perform in New York, backed by pickup bands until he relocated in 1980 to Paris, the base from which he toured Europe. The reception and respect accorded him there far exceeded what he received in America. Throughout the '80s, Chance returned periodically to New York, where he played with musicians like trombonist Joseph Bowie (of the Black Arts Group, later founder of Defunkt), avant-garde reedman Henry Threadgill, and guitarists Bern Nix (Ornette Coleman) and Tomas Donker (the Dance).

In 1994 Henry Rollins' label, Infinite Zero, reissued Chance/White's early LPs. Chance moved back to New York and returned to live performances. By the end of the decade, he was fronting Convulsion Cabaret, a punk "supergroup" with Billy Ficca (Television) and Walter Stedding. He also performs as James Chance and His Sardonic Sinfonics. In addition, newer Contortions lineups continue to perform. Most of the '79 band reunited in 1995 and again in 2001.

Gene Chandler

Born Eugene Dixon, July 6, 1937, Chicago, IL
1962—*Duke of Earl* (Vee-Jay) 1964—*Just Be True* (Constellation); *Greatest Hits* 1965—*Live! On Stage* 1966—*The Duke of Soul* (Checker) 1967—*The Girl Don't Care* (Brunswick) 1968—*There Was a Time* 1969—*The Two Sides of Gene Chandler* 1970—*The Gene Chandler Situation* (Mercury) 1971—*One & One* (with Jerry Butler) 1978—*Get Down* (Chi-Sound) 1979—*When You're #1* (20th Century) 1980—*Gene Chandler '80* 1981—*Here's to Love* (Chi-Sound) 1982—*I'll Make the Living If You Make the Loving Worthwhile* 1984—*Stroll On With the Duke* (Solid Smoke); *The Duke of Soul* (Chess) 1985—*Your Love Looks Good on Me* (Fastfire).

A fixture in Chicago soul for over 30 years, balladeer Gene Chandler was raised on the tough South Side and sang doo-wop in street-corner groups before joining the army in 1957. After his discharge in 1960 he joined Chicago's Dukays, who had a minor hit late in 1961 with "The Girl Is a Devil." A&R man Carl Davis, who had discovered the Dukays, renamed Eugene Dixon after Davis' favorite actor, Jeff Chandler, and produced his solo debut, a backward glance at doo-wop style called "Duke of Earl" (#1 pop, #1 R&B, 1962). The single sold a million copies within a month of its November 1961 release.

Chandler's string of hits lasted until the early '70s. The best of them were written and arranged by Curtis Mayfield, including "Just Be True" (#19, 1964), "You Can't Hurt Me No More" (#92, 1965), "Nothing Can Stop Me" (#18, 1965), and "What Now" (#40, 1965). The hits slowed after that, though he made several memorable records including his 1968 collaboration with Barbara Acklin, "From the Teacher to the Preacher" (#57), followed by "Groovy Situation" (#12, 1970).

Chandler gave up touring to concentrate on songwriting and production, bought Bamboo Records, and moved it to Chicago. There he produced hits, including Mel and Tim's 1969 "Backfield in Motion," and continued to record throughout the '70s, including a soul hit with Jerry Butler. He also founded Mr. Chand Records and worked for A&M as a producer from 1974 to 1977. In 1976 Chandler was convicted of selling 388 grams of heroin; he served a four-month sentence. A #53 disco hit, "Get Down," returned Chandler to the pop chart in 1979; it went to #11 in the U.K. Similarly, "Does She Have a Friend for Me" attracted scant interest stateside but became a Top 30 hit in England. Chandler continues to perform.

The Chantels

Formed 1956, New York, NY
Arlene Smith (b. Oct. 5, 1941, New York), voc.; Lois Harris, voc.; Sonia Goring, voc.; Jackie Landry (d. Dec. 23, 1997), voc.; Rene Minus, voc.
1958—*We Are the Chantels* (End) 1959—(– Smith; – Harris; + Annette Smith) 1990—*The Best of the Chantels* (Rhino).

The Chantels were one of the first and most popular of the girl groups. The five girls (all between 14 and 17) had been singing together in their Bronx parochial school choir since childhood. Led by Arlene Smith, the group was named after Saint Francis de Chantelle School, the rival school of their own alma mater, Saint Anthony of Padua. Richard Barrett of the Valentines produced their first singles ("He's Gone," "The Plea"), both Smith compositions that failed to hit. However, in 1958 the Chantels had their biggest success with another Smith song, "Maybe" (#15 pop, #2 R&B), which sold over a million copies. The Chantels' version hit #116 when rereleased in 1969; Janis Joplin covered it that year.

After several more singles—none of them major hits—End dropped them in 1959 and they moved to Carlton Records. By then Smith had quit to pursue a solo career, Harris was in college, and the following Chantels records were often recorded using other singers, including producer Barrett. Nonetheless, "Look in My Eyes" (#14 pop, #6 R&B, 1961) and "Well, I Told You" (#29, 1961) were hits before the group disbanded in 1970.

Smith, who has also worked as a schoolteacher, later attended the Juilliard School of Music. In the early '70s she re-formed the Chantels with new members. The original Chantels reunited for several one-off performances in the '90s, including the 1996 Rhythm & Blues Foundation Awards in Hollywood. The current incarnation, active since 1996, consists of Harris, Goring, and Minus plus new singer Ami Ortiz. Landry was a member until she succumbed to breast cancer in 1997. Smith is now a solo artist.

Harry Chapin

Born Dec. 7, 1942, New York, NY; died July 16, 1981, Jericho, NY
1972—*Heads and Tales* (Elektra); *Sniper and Other Love Songs* 1973—*Short Stories* 1974—*Verities and Balderdash* 1975—*Portrait Gallery* 1976—*On the Road to Kingdom Come; Harry Chapin's Greatest Stories Live* 1977—*Dance Band on the Titanic* 1978—*Living Room Suite* 1979—*Legends of the Lost and Found* 1980—*Sequel* (Boardwalk) 1985—*Anthology of Harry Chapin.*

Although singer/songwriter Harry Chapin initially came to fame with his story songs, his true legacy is that of an anti-hunger activist who, years before such public activism became common, was performing over half of his 200 concert dates each year for charitable causes.

The son of a jazz drummer, Chapin sang in the Brooklyn Heights Boys Choir, and in his teens he played guitar, banjo, and trumpet in a band with his brothers. After a stint at the Air Force Academy, Chapin spent a semester at Cornell University. He and his brothers began working in Greenwich Village clubs and making documentary films. (A documentary he made with Jim Jacobs in the late '60s called *Legendary Champions* was nominated for an Academy Award.) His brothers left the country in 1964 to escape the draft, and Chapin continued in filmmaking.

He formed his own band, including a cello player, in 1971. Chapin's debut album, *Heads and Tales,* was released in February 1972 and stayed on the charts for over half a year, peaking at #60 when "Taxi" became a Top 20 single. His 1973 album, *Short Stories,* produced another solid hit, "W.O.L.D." (#36). *Verities and Balderdash* became Chapin's first gold album in 1974 on the strength of his #1 "Cat's in the Cradle." His subsequent albums sold respectably through the end of the '70s. His *The Night That Made America Famous* ran on Broadway for 75 performances and was nominated for two Tony Awards.

Chapin's later backup band included his brother Steve (piano and vocals), who also produced Harry's 1977 LP *Dance Band on the Titanic.* Another Chapin brother, Tom, has carried on a career of his own as a singer/songwriter and a children's artist.

Chapin was an active lobbyist for various causes and a benefactor of Long Island arts organizations. In 1975 he founded World Hunger Year (WHY) and became a familiar figure on Capitol Hill and other centers of government as he worked tirelessly against hunger. The next year he served as a delegate to the Democratic National Convention and was named one of the Jaycees' 10 Most Outstanding Young Men in America.

Chapin died in a car crash on the Long Island Expressway while driving to a benefit performance. By then he had raised over $5 million for charity. In 1987 he was honored at an all-star Carnegie Hall tribute during which his widow, Sandy (who continues his work), accepted a posthumously awarded Special Congressional Gold Medal on his behalf. An album documenting the event—with performers including Bruce Springsteen, Richie Havens, and Judy Collins—titled *Tribute* was released in 1990.

Marshall Chapman

Born Jan. 7, 1949, Spartanburg, SC
1977—*Me, I'm Feeling Free* (Epic) 1978—*Jaded Virgin* 1979—*Marshall* 1982—*Take It On Home* (Rounder) 1987—*Dirty Linen* (Tall Girl/Line Import) 1991—*Inside Job* (Tall Girl) 1995—*It's About Time . . . Recorded Live at the Tennessee State Prison for Women* (Margaritaville/Island) 1996—*Love Slave.*

Singer/songwriter/guitarist Marshall Chapman, of an aristocratic Southern family, was schooled at Nashville's Vanderbilt University, where she studied French and fine arts and started jamming with country, blues, and rock musicians. Around 1973, after living in France and Boston, she moved back to Nashville. There she waited tables and wrote songs, waiting for the opportunity to sing in local bars. She won the admiration of country stars like Tompall Glaser, Linda Hargrove, Jessi Colter, and Waylon Jennings.

In 1976 she went to L.A., where she was signed by Epic/CBS. Her debut album consisted predominantly of country-flavored songs. "Somewhere South of Macon" got airplay on country stations before it was decided that some of its lines were too sexually suggestive. Other songs—most often "A Woman's Heart (Is a Handy Place to Be)"—were covered by performers such as Colter, Crystal Gayle, Glaser, Olivia Newton-John, and the Earl Scruggs Revue. In concert, however, she fronted a rock & roll trio and drew rock crowds. Despite critical praise, Chapman's records did not sell, and once her third one was released, Epic dropped her. She continued to perform and record with her band, the Love Slaves, and her material was covered by Emmylou Harris, Ronnie Milsap, Conway Twitty, and Jimmy Buffett. *It's About Time . . .*, her first effort for Jimmy Buffett's Margaritaville label, was recorded on Halloween Eve, 1994, at the Tennessee State Prison for Women. *Love Slave* is a studio release. In the late 1990s she collaborated with songwriter Matraca Berg on a musical theater work based on the writing of Southern novelist Lee Smith.

Tracy Chapman

Born Mar. 20, 1964, Cleveland, OH
1988—*Tracy Chapman* (Elektra) 1989—*Crossroads* 1992—*Matters of the Heart* 1995—*New Beginning* 2000—*Telling Stories.*

Quiet and publicity shy, Tracy Chapman at first seemed an unlikely candidate for stardom. Add to that the fact that singer/songwriter Chapman delivered mostly spare, sobering folk-rock songs, and you have perhaps the most astonishing pop music success story of the late '80s and '90s. With her 1988 self-titled debut album, Chapman topped the album charts and entered the ranks of rock's most respected songwriters and live performers. Though her mainstream popularity hasn't remained consistent over the years, she resurfaced in 1996 with the blues-rock smash "Give Me One Reason" and continues to have a dedicated following.

Growing up in a predominantly black working-class neighborhood, Chapman was close to her older sister and single mother and shared their love of music; their tastes ranged from Mahalia Jackson to Neil Diamond. At an early age, she began writing songs and teaching herself to play the guitar. A minority placement scholarship enabled Chapman to attend Wooster, a prestigious prep school; there she became interested in folk-influenced rock music. She then attended Tufts University, majoring in anthropology and African studies while singing and playing guitar at coffeehouses and recording demos at the campus radio station. After hearing her play, Chapman's classmate Brian Koppelman, the son of music industry honcho Charles Koppelman, recommended her to his father. In 1986 Chapman signed a management deal with Charles Koppelman's SBK Publishing; in addition to hooking her up with manager Elliot Roberts (Joni Mitchell, Neil Young), Koppelman helped secure her a contract with Elektra Records.

Produced by David Kershenbaum (Joan Baez, Joe Jackson), Chapman's Elektra debut set her socially conscious songs and rich, emotive alto against sparse acoustic arrangements. Released in spring 1988, the album was critically praised, and Chapman began opening shows for 10,000 Maniacs. By that summer, after a stunning solo performance at a star-studded 70th-birthday tribute to Nelson Mandela at England's Wembley Stadium, Chapman began headlining. The album's sales soared, and one single, "Fast Car," reached #6. ("Talkin' 'Bout a Revolution" and "Baby Can I Hold You" followed, at #75 and #48, respectively.) In September Chapman began a six-week international tour with Bruce Springsteen, Sting, Peter Gabriel, and Youssou N'Dour on behalf of Amnesty International. Accompanying herself with only a guitar and rarely addressing the audience, Chapman acquitted herself commendably, though some found her reticence off-putting.

After capping off the year with three Grammys, including Best New Artist, Chapman released *Crossroads*. Dealing with topics ranging from spirituality to racism in a bluntly realistic manner, the album was hardly a departure. Despite reaching #9, it proved less commercially successful than its predecessor. Infamous by now for her shyness and reluctance to deal with the press, Chapman withdrew for a few years, returning in 1992 with *Matters of the Heart*, which got mixed reviews and peaked at #53. Her career appeared to be petering out when she released the elegantly melodic and eloquently written *New Beginning* (#4) in 1995. The following year, "Give Me One Reason," an uncharacteristically simple, sultry love song, leaped to #3 on the pop chart, eventually propelling the album to triple-platinum sales. The single also earned Chapman her fourth Grammy, this one for Best Rock Song of 1996, and was a crowd pleaser on the first Lilith Fair tour in 1997. She returned with *Telling Stories* (#33, 2000); the title track, subtitled "There Is Fiction in the Space Between," rose to #8 on the Adult Contemporary chart, showing that even after several years out of the public eye, Chapman's soulful acoustic compositions were all that mattered to her fans.

The Charlatans

Formed 1964, San Francisco, CA
George Hunter, voc.; Mike Wilhelm, gtr.; Richard Olson, bass; Michael Ferguson, piano; Sam Linde, drums.
N.A.—(– Linde; + Dan Hicks [b. Dec. 9, 1941, Little Rock, AR], drums) 1967—(– Ferguson; + Patrick Gogerty, piano; + Terry Wilson, drums; Hicks switched to gtr.) 1968—(– Hicks; – Hunter; – Gogerty; + Darrel DeVore, piano) 1969—*The Charlatans* (Philips).

As the original Haight-Ashbury band, the Charlatans remained true to the area's bohemian ethic. They were an amateur group, conceived by draftsman/designer George Hunter, whose main talent was a sense of rock's visual possibilities. Outfitted in Victorian and Old West costumes, they first played for three months at the Red Dog Saloon in Virginia City, Nevada, in the summer of 1965, before returning to the Haight. For this show, Ferguson designed what is generally considered to be the first rock poster ever. Soon they were sharing bills with the Jefferson Airplane and the Grateful Dead (then called the Warlocks) at the Fillmore, Avalon, and other Bay Area venues.

The Charlatans' repertoire remained essentially unchanged throughout their brief career: folk, blues, ballads, and jug-band tunes. MGM signed them, then sold the group to Kama Sutra. They recorded one unreleased album for that label (Kama Sutra did release an unsuccessful single over the group's objections). Reduced to a quartet (Hunter departed in early 1968, as did Dan Hicks to form his Hot Licks [see entry]), the Charlatans finally released their first album in 1969 before disbanding.

Bobby Charles

Born Robert Charles Guidry, Feb. 21, 1938, Abbeville, LA
1972—*Bobby Charles* (Bearsville) 1995—*Wish You Were Here Right Now* (Stony Plain) 1998—*Secrets of the Heart.*

Bobby Charles, discovered by Leonard Chess during a mid-'50s talent search, contributed to the creation of South Louisiana swamp-pop music, a mixture of traditional Cajun, Creole, C&W, and New Orleans R&B. He recorded several sides in New Orleans that garnered some attention when Chess released them in the late '50s; their impact with other artists was more substantial. Several of the songs (among them "See You Later Alligator," "I Don't Know Why I Love You but I Do") were covered by Bill Haley and Clarence "Frogman" Henry respectively. With Fats Domino and Dave Bartholomew, Charles wrote Domino's classic hit "Walkin' to New Orleans."

Charles toured with the Platters, Little Richard, Chuck Berry, and B.B. King before retiring from personal appearances in the early '60s. Throughout the decade, though, he recorded for several labels and did promotional work for Chess Records. By the early '70s he was living in Woodstock, New York, where Albert Grossman signed him to Bearsville Records. His much-ballyhooed comeback album, *Bobby Charles,* included guest appearances by the Band, Dr. John, and other notables, but despite an excellent single—"Small Town Talk" (later covered by Rick Danko of the Band)—the LP failed to find a market, and Charles was soon dropped. He appeared on two Paul Butterfield albums (including *Better Days,* from 1973) and made a rare live appearance at the Band's Last Waltz concert, Thanksgiving Day, 1976. That same year, two of his compositions were covered on Joe Cocker's *Sting Ray. Wish You Were Here Right Now,* issued in 1995, marked Charles first domestic album in 24 years. *Secrets of the Heart,* which contains a birthday salute to Fats Domino, proved that Charles' comeback was more than just a one-off affair.

Ray Charles

Born Ray Charles Robinson, Sep. 23, 1930, Albany, GA
1957—*Ray Charles* (Atlantic) 1958—*The Great Ray Charles* 1959—*What'd I Say; Genius of Ray Charles* 1962—*Story, vol. 1; Story, vol. 2; Modern Sounds in Country and Western Music* (ABC); *Modern Sounds in Country and Western Music 2* 1963—*Story, vol. 3* (Atlantic); *The Greatest Ray Charles* 1964—*Have a Smile With Me* (HMV); *Great Hits* (Atlantic) 1966—*Crying Time* (ABC-Paramount) 1967—*A Man and His Soul* 1973—*Ray Charles Live* (Atlantic) 1977—*True to Life* 1983—*Wish You Were Here Tonight* (Columbia) 1984—*Do I Ever Cross Your Mind; Friendship* 1985—*The Spirit of Christmas* 1986—*From the Pages of My Mind* 1987—*Ray Charles Live (1958–59); His Greatest Hits (1960–1971), vol. 1* (DCC); *His Greatest Hits (1960–72), vol. 2* 1988—*Greatest Country & Western Hits (1962–65); Greatest Hits (1960–67), vol. 1* (Rhino); *Greatest Hits (1960–72), vol. 2; Just Between Us* (Columbia) 1989—*Anthology* (Rhino); *Seven Spanish Angels and Other Hits* (Columbia) 1990—*Would You Believe?* (Warner Bros.) 1991—*Ray Charles 1954–66* (Time Life Music); *The Birth of Soul—The Complete Atlantic Rhythm & Blues Recordings, 1952–59* (Atlantic) 1993—*My World* (Warner Bros.) 1994—*Blues + Jazz* (Rhino) 1996—*Strong Love Affair* (Qwest).
With Milt Jackson: 1958—*Soul Brothers* (Atlantic) 1962—*Soul Meeting* 1989—*Soul Brothers/Soul Meeting.*
With Cleo Laine: 1976—*Porgy and Bess* (RCA).

Singer/composer/pianist Ray Charles virtually invented soul music by bringing together the fervor of gospel, the secular lyrics and narratives of blues and country, the big-band

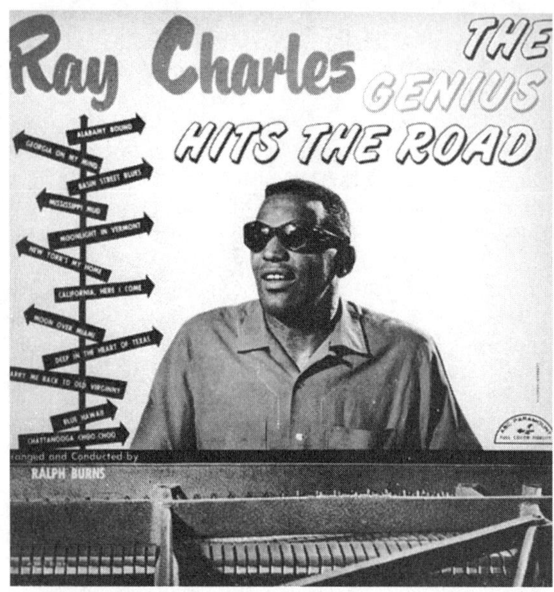

Ray Charles

arrangements of jazz, and the rhythms and improvisational possibilities from all of them, making music that was both sophisticated and spontaneous.

He was raised in Greenville, Florida, and started playing the piano before he was five; at six he contracted glaucoma, which went untreated and eventually left him blind. He studied composition (writing music in braille) and learned to play the alto saxophone, clarinet, trumpet, and organ while attending the St. Augustine School for the Deaf and the Blind from 1937 to 1945. His father died when he was 10, his mother five years later, and he left school to work in dance bands around Florida, dropping his last name to avoid confusion with boxer Sugar Ray Robinson. In 1947, with $600 worth of savings, he moved to Seattle and worked as a Nat "King" Cole–style crooner.

Charles made his first single, "Confession Blues," in L.A. and recorded for several independent West Coast labels until he scored a Top 10 R&B hit in 1951 with "Baby Let Me Hold Your Hand" and began a national tour with blues singer Lowell Fulson. Late in 1953 he went to New Orleans and became a pianist and arranger for Guitar Slim (Eddie Jones). Guitar Slim's "The Things That I Used to Do," arranged by Charles and featuring him on piano, sold a million copies, and when Charles returned to recording—leading and arranging for his own band—the earthier style carried over to his own work. Atlantic signed him in 1954, and he made a few conventional recordings in New York; he also assembled a band for label mate Ruth Brown.

"I've Got a Woman," with a seven-piece band fronted by Charles' pounding gospel piano and a new raspy, exuberant vocal sound, became his first national hit (#2 R&B, 1955). Through the decade he appeared regularly on the charts as he synthesized more and more styles and was nicknamed the "Genius." He recorded with Milt Jackson of the Modern Jazz Quartet, sang standards with strings, and expanded his band to a full-scale revue, complete with horns and gospel-style backup singers, the Raelettes.

"What'd I Say" (#6 pop, #1 R&B, 1959), a wild blues/gospel/Latin mix, became Charles' first million-seller. In late 1959 he signed to ABC-Paramount Records and moved into the pop market with "Georgia on My Mind" (#1, 1960) and "Hit the Road, Jack" (#1, 1961). *Modern Sounds in Country and Western Music* (1962), which included Charles' versions of songs by Hank Williams, Floyd Tillman, and other country songwriters, sold more than a million copies, as did its single, "I Can't Stop Loving You" (#1, 1962).

In 1965 Charles was arrested for possession of heroin and revealed that he had been using it since he was 16. He cleaned up in a California sanatorium and spent a year away from performing. In 1966 he made his motion-picture debut in *Ballad in Blue* (also known as *Blues for Lovers*). In it, Charles (playing himself) befriends a blind boy in London; he also performed two of his best-known songs, "What'd I Say" and "I Got a Woman." While his singing remained influential through the '60s (especially for Steve Winwood and Joe Cocker) and he kept making hits—including Ashford and Simpson's "Let's Go Get Stoned" (#31, 1966)—his taste was moving away from rock, although he did appear on Aretha Franklin's *Live at Fillmore West* (1971).

His albums from the mid-'60s onward have downplayed gospel and blues in favor of jazz standards, pop songs, and show tunes, although his singing remains distinctive. Charles made custom-label deals with ABC (Tangerine Records) and later Atlantic (Crossover), for whom he recorded an album a year. In 1978 he published his autobiography (cowritten with David Ritz), *Brother Ray;* it became a national bestseller. The following year, his version of "Georgia on My Mind" was named the official song of the State of Georgia. It was later used as the theme song for the hit television series *Designing Women.* Charles also appeared in the movie *The Blues Brothers* (1980); he subsequently made guest appearances on the television series *St. Elsewhere* and *Who's the Boss.*

In 1982 he recorded another country album, *Wish You Were Here Tonight;* two years later, he released *Friendship* (#75, 1985), which included duets with 10 country artists, including Hank Williams Jr., the Oak Ridge Boys, Mickey Gilley, Merle Haggard, Johnny Cash, and Willie Nelson. In 1993 *My World* reached #145; as of this writing, that was his last album of new material to make the pop albums chart. Still, as a performer, he shows no signs of slowing down. Ironically, Charles became best known to younger listeners through a series of diet Pepsi ads ("You Got the Right One, Baby, Uh-huh!"), which began airing in 1990. He also was featured prominently on USA for Africa's 1985 hit, "We Are the World," in which his vocal interplay with Bruce Springsteen was a prime example of his trademark call-and-response style. In 1986 Charles was not only a recipient of the Kennedy Center Honors but one of the first inductees into the Rock and Roll Hall of Fame. As of this writing, he has collected a dozen performance Grammy Awards (he also received the 1988 Lifetime Achievement Award), most recently for 1993's "A Song for You," named by President Clinton as his favorite song. In 1993 Clinton presented Charles with a National Medal of the Arts. Charles has received similar awards from countries around the world.

Throughout his career, Charles has been active in a range of political and humanitarian causes. He provided financial support for the Reverend Martin Luther King Jr. and the civil rights movement; he is also a staunch supporter of Israel. In 1984 he performed his version of "America the Beautiful" at the Republican National Convention. Three years later, he formed the (Ray Charles) Robinson Foundation for Hearing Disorders, with a $1 million personal endowment.

Cheap Trick

Formed 1974, Rockford, IL
Robin Zander (b. Jan. 23, 1952 or 1953, Loves Park, IL), voc.; Tom Petersson (b. Tom Peterson, May 9, 1950, Rockford), bass; Rick Nielsen (b. Dec. 22, 1946, Rockford), gtr.; Bun E. Carlos (b. Brad Carlson, June 12, 1951, Rockford), drums.
1977—*Cheap Trick* (Epic); *In Color* 1978—*Heaven Tonight* 1979—*At Budokan; Dream Police* 1980—*Found All the Parts* EP; *All Shook Up* (– Petersson; + Pete Comita [b. Italy], bass) 1981—(– Comita; + Jon Brant [b. Feb. 20, 1954], bass) 1982—*One on One* 1983—*Next Position Please* 1985—*Standing on the Edge* 1986—*The Doctor* 1987—(– Brant; + Petersson) 1988—*Lap of Luxury* 1990—*Busted* 1991—*The Greatest Hits* 1994—*Woke Up With a Monster* (Warner Bros.); *Budokan II (Live)* (Epic) 1996—*Sex America Cheap Trick* (Epic/Legacy) 1997—*Cheap Trick* (Red Ant) 1998—*At Budokan: The Complete Concert* (Epic/Legacy) 1999—*Music for Hangovers* (Cheap Trick Unlimited) 2000—*Authorized Greatest Hits* (Epic/Legacy) 2001—*Silver* (Cheap Trick Unlimited).
Robin Zander solo: 1993—*Robin Zander* (Interscope).

The aggressively marketed, hard-touring, self-caricaturing rock group Cheap Trick worked its way up to platinum sales with a blend of Beatles-style pop and a cartoonish stage act, which played Rick Nielsen's exaggerated mugging and guitar gymnastics against Robin Zander's teen-idol looks and rich, powerful voice.

In 1961 Nielsen, then in his teens, began playing locally in Rockford, Illinois, utilizing his ever-increasing collection of rare and valuable guitars. His band, the Phaetons, became the Boyz, then the Grim Reapers, and finally Fuse in 1967 with the addition of bassist Tom Petersson. One album for Epic in 1968 was generally ignored. Frustrated, Fuse, which by then included college dropout Bun E. Carlos on drums, moved to Philadelphia in 1971. As Sick Man of Europe, they enlisted ex-Nazz vocalist Robert "Stewkey" Antoni, but the group soon disbanded. After a year in Europe, Nielsen and Petersson returned to Rockford, reunited with Carlos, and a few months later asked folkie vocalist Zander to join the

Cheap Trick: Robin Zander, Tom Petersson, Rick Nielsen, Bun E. Carlos

group they named Cheap Trick. Midwestern booking agent Ken Adamany, who'd played in one of Steve Miller's high school bands, became their manager. Adamany encouraged them to develop their stage show, and Cheap Trick toured incessantly over the next several years, playing an average of 250 shows a year, opening for Kiss, the Kinks, Santana, Boston, and others.

Cheap Trick's early releases were only moderately successful in the U.S.; its 1977 debut sold 150,000 copies, while *In Color* and *Heaven Tonight* failed to crack the Top 40. In Japan, however, all three had gone gold, and the group's initial tour there in early 1978 met with hysteria reminiscent of Beatlemania. During that visit Cheap Trick recorded *At Budokan,* which went triple platinum in the States largely on the strength of their single "I Want You to Want Me" (#7, 1979), a song that had originally appeared on *In Color.*

By the time *Dream Police* (#6) was released in fall 1979, the band was headlining arenas and stadiums. *All Shook Up* (#24, 1980), produced by George Martin, went gold in late 1980 but was considered a disappointment, producing no Top 40 singles. The band contributed "Everything Works If You Let It" (#44, 1980) to the *Roadie* soundtrack that year, and Nielsen and Carlos played on John Lennon and Yoko Ono's recording sessions for *Double Fantasy.* (They appear on *The Lost Lennon Tapes* and "I'm Losing You.")

As the '80s dawned, the group's activities slowed considerably. In 1981 Epic rejected an LP, and after a flurry of lawsuits and countersuits, Cheap Trick began recording *One on One.* Petersson departed in 1980 to form a group with his wife, Dagmar, as vocalist. He recorded an LP in 1982, but Epic refused to release it. Pete Comita replaced him, but was himself replaced by Jon Brant before the recording of *One on One* (#39, 1982), which included two minor hits, "If You Want

My Love" (#45, 1982) and "She's Tight" (#65, 1982), and eventually went gold.

Cheap Trick's fortunes began to wane with the release of *Next Position Please* (#61, 1983), produced by Todd Rundgren. Neither it nor the group's next two albums went gold, although 1985's *Standing on the Edge* (#35) contained its strongest material since *Heaven Tonight*. *The Doctor* (#115, 1986) didn't even crack the Top 100, and the quartet's future seemed in jeopardy.

Petersson rejoined in 1987, and in 1988 *Lap of Luxury* (#16) was a surprise hit. The hard-rock ballad "The Flame" gave the group its first #1 single, a version of "Don't Be Cruel" (#4) became the first Elvis Presley cover to hit the Top 10 since the singer's death, and "Ghost Town" reached #33. Just as inexplicably, the band's next album, *Busted* (#48, 1990), stiffed. "Can't Stop Fallin' Into Love" (#12) did go Top 20. Aside from a solo album from Zander, and a duet he recorded with Heart's Ann Wilson, "Surrender to Me" (#6, 1988), Cheap Trick maintained a low profile until 1994's *Woke Up With a Monster* (#123, 1994), its first and only album for Warner Bros. In 1996 Epic/Legacy anthologized the band's music with a four-CD box set, *Sex America Cheap Trick*. But Cheap Trick was not yet finished. The band enjoyed yet another triumphant return, in 1997, when it went back to the basics, releasing its 14th album of new material on the indie label Red Ant. The album received such a warm reception from the alternative-rock set that Cheap Trick applied its old creative marketing flair by staging a series of club gigs in which the band performed each of its first three albums from start to finish on three consecutive evenings. *Music for Hangovers* is a live album compiled from the series. By the end of the millennium Cheap Trick was still performing more than 200 shows a year. In 2000 Petersson collaborated on an album with Ken Coomer of Wilco and Robert Reynolds of the Mavericks. *Swag* (the band's name as well) was released in conjunction with a brief tour by Swag in 2001.

Chubby Checker

Born Ernest Evans, Oct. 3, 1941, Andrews, SC
1960—*Twist With Chubby Checker* (Cameo/Parkway) 1961—*For Twisters Only; Let's Twist Again; Your Twist Party* 1962—*Teen Twisters Only; All the Hits* 1982—*The Change Has Come* (MCA) 1994—*Texas Twist* (TEEC).
With the Fat Boys: 1988—*Coming Back Hard Again* (Tin Pan Apple).

Although Chubby Checker didn't invent the Twist, the dance craze was his ticket to stardom. Written and recorded as a B side by R&B singer Hank Ballard, Checker's version of "The Twist" went to #1 in September 1960, stayed on the chart for four months, dropped off, and returned to #1 early in 1962. It is the only rock & roll record to enjoy two stays at #1 more than a year apart.

The young Ernest Evans worked as a chicken plucker in a local poultry shop while in high school. On the job he would frequently entertain customers by singing songs and telling jokes. Evans' boss put him in touch with Philadelphia's Cameo-Parkway label, which signed him in 1959. Shortly thereafter—at the suggestion of Dick Clark's wife—he became "Chubby Checker" (in emulation of the similarly built Fats Domino). His first single, "The Class," released in the summer of 1959, featured Checker doing vocal impersonations, but it was only a minor hit, and subsequent singles were even less successful.

Then "The Twist" hit. After it, Checker promoted several less successful dance crazes: the Hucklebuck, the Fly, the Mess Around, the Pony, the Limbo—even Freddie and the Dreamers' the Freddie. His Top 10 hits included "Pony Time" (#1, 1961), "Let's Twist Again" (#8, 1961), "The Fly" (#7, 1961), "Slow Twistin' " (#3, 1962), "Limbo Rock" (#2, 1962), and "Popeye the Hitchhiker" (#10, 1962). In December 1963 Checker married Dutch-born Catharina Lodders, Miss World 1962; he wrote "Loddy Lo" for her. His hits ended in 1965, and Checker became a mainstay on the nightclub circuit. He recorded for Buddah in 1969 and for Chalmac in 1971, with regular appearances as part of rock revival shows and a featured spot in the film *Let the Good Times Roll*. His early-'80s work for MCA moved toward disco, with some success ("Running" [#91, 1982], "Harder Than Diamond" [#104, 1982]), but in 1988 Checker hit the Top 40 for the first time in 25 years with a rap version of "The Twist," featuring the Fat Boys. The song went to #2 in the U.K. After self-releasing *Texas Twist* in 1994, Checker was recruited by K-tel's Bare Bones imprint, which in 1998 reissued his Halloween-themed dance single "Doin' the Zombie." Checker continues to perform frequently; having marketed a line of beef jerky and the Twist-a-Sizer weight-loss machine, he also dabbles in the food and exercise industries.

The Chemical Brothers

Formed 1992, Manchester, Eng.
Tom Rowlands (Jan. 11, 1971, Oxfordshire, Eng.), producer; Ed Simons (June 9, 1970, London, Eng.), producer.
1995—*Exit Planet Dust* (Astralwerks) 1996—*Live at the Social, vol. 1* (Heavenly, U.K.) 1997—*Dig Your Own Hole* (Astralwerks) 1998—*Brothers Gonna Work It Out* 1999—*Surrender.*

Layering rock, samples, and a strong psychedelic streak on their guest-studded albums, the Chemical Brothers successfully made the transition from the DJ booth to the recording studio in the late '90s.

Two former history students at Manchester University, Tom Rowlands (who at the time was in a group called Ariel) and Ed Simons started DJ'ing together in 1992. That year the duo self-released their first single, "Song to the Siren," under the name the Dust Brothers. They sent it to DJ Andrew Weatherall, who reissued it on his label, Junior Boy's Own. In 1994 the duo released another pair of EPs, *14th Century Sky* and *My Mercury Youth*. They became in-demand DJs, holding a residency (to be immortalized later on *Live at the Social*) at London's popular Heavenly Social club, and accumulated remix jobs for the likes of Leftfield, Primal

Scream, and the Charlatans U.K. After changing their name to the Chemical Brothers (at the request of the preexisting Los Angeles–based production team the Dust Brothers, made famous for its work with Beck and the Beastie Boys), Rowlands and Simons finally released their debut album in 1995. *Exit Planet Dust* was a heady fusion of big beat (the bass-pumping, hook-filled dance-floor style they had pioneered along with Fatboy Slim), electro, hip-hop, and catchy pop melodies anchored by guest singers Beth Orton and the Charlatans' Tim Burgess.

After successfully touring America, the Chemical Brothers released the hit single "Setting Sun" (#80 pop, 1997; #1, U.K.), which featured vocals by Oasis' Noel Gallagher. It was followed by the album *Dig Your Own Hole* (#14, 1997), which went gold. Its opening track, "Block Rockin' Beats," was another U.K. chart-topper and a U.S. modern-rock hit; it also won a Grammy for Best Rock Instrumental. In addition to Gallagher, guests included the American neo-psychedelic rock band Mercury Rev. Along with Prodigy's *The Fat of the Land, Dig* embodied the "summer of electronica," the first time America began embracing the dance-floor sounds that had been ruling the U.K. for more than a decade. After the release of the mix CD *Brothers Gonna Work It Out* in 1998, Rowlands and Simons came back with *Surrender* (#32, 1999), which was overall more quiet and experimental than their previous efforts and featured the single "Hey Boy Hey Girl" (#3, U.K.). Once again Gallagher was on board for a guest appearance; other vocalists included Mazzy Star's Hope Sandoval, Primal Scream's Bobby Gillespie, and New Order's Bernard Sumner.

Clifton Chenier

Born June 25, 1925, Opelousas, LA; died Dec. 12, 1987, Lafayette, LA
1965—*Louisiana Blues & Zydeco* (Arhoolie) 1966—*Bon Ton Roulet* 1967—*Black Snake Blues* 1970—*King of the Bayous* 1971—*Bayou Blues* (Specialty) 1972—*Live* (Arhoolie) 1974—*Out West* 1976—*Bogalusa Boogie* 1978—*And His Red Hot Louisiana Band; Cajun Swamp Music Live* (Tomato) 1980—*Classic Clifton* (Arhoolie) 1983—*I'm Here!* (Alligator) 1993—*Zydeco Dynamite: The Clifton Chenier Anthology* (Rhino).

Clifton Chenier was the undisputed king of zydeco music, the rousing black Creole party music that, influenced by Cajun music, mixes blues, French folk tunes, country, New Orleans R&B, and rock & roll. Wearing a jeweled crown and flashing his gold tooth onstage, Chenier pumped his chrome-studded accordion and sang in Creole French and English; he also played the harmonica, piano, and organ.

He grew up as a sugar cane cutter and weekend musician in such places as New Iberia, Louisiana, where he met his wife, Margaret, in 1945. In 1946 he followed his brother Cleveland to Lake Charles, Louisiana, for a job at an oil refinery, where he worked until 1954. The brothers began playing at parties as a duet, with Clifton on accordion and Cleveland on "rub board," a piece of corrugated steel played with beer-can openers like a washboard. In 1954 Chenier made his first recordings at radio station KAOK in Lake Charles for Elko Records, and a year later recorded his more R&B-style material at Specialty, including the R&B hit "Ay 'Tit Fille (Hey Little Girl)" (originally "Ay Tete Fee") and "Boppin' the Rock."

Chenier became a full-time musician, performed on both coasts, and in 1958 moved to Houston. In 1964 he began to record for the folk-oriented Arhoolie label and had a number of regional Gulf Coast hits, including "Louisiana Blues" and "Black Gal." He appeared in 1966 at the Berkeley Blues Festival and continued to appear regularly on the West Coast and more infrequently in the East. He earned a Grammy Award for *I'm Here* in 1984.

He was featured in the 1974 documentary *Hot Pepper* by Les Blank, and inspired a generation of zydeco accordionists, including Rockin' Dopsie, Rockin' Sidney, Queen Ida, Buckwheat Zydeco, and his son, C.J. Chenier. Chenier had suffered from diabetes since 1979, one reason his recorded output slowed during his last decade. Upon his death, C.J., who had come into his own as a zydeco singer and musician, took over the Red Hot Louisiana Band.

Cher

Born Cherilyn Sarkasian LaPier, May 20, 1946, El Centro, CA
1965—*All I Really Want to Do* (Imperial) 1966—*Cher* 1967—*With Love, Cher* 1968—*Backstage* 1969—*3614 Jackson Highway* (Atco) 1971—*Cher* (Kapp) 1972—*Foxy Lady* 1973—*Half-Breed* (MCA) 1974—*Dark Lady* 1975—*Stars* (Warner Bros.) 1976—*I'd Rather Believe in You* 1977—*Allman and Woman: Two the Hard Way* (with Gregg Allman) 1979—*Take Me Home* (Casablanca) 1980—*Black Rose* 1982—*I Paralyze* (Columbia) 1987—*Cher* 1989—*Heart of Stone* 1991—*Love Hurts* 1996—*It's a Man's World* (Reprise) 1998—*Believe* (Warner Bros.) 1999—*If I Could Turn Back Time: Cher's Greatest Hits* (Geffen).

In a long career that's well into its fourth decade, Cher has reinvented herself a number of times: as a hippie rock singer, a wisecracking TV comedienne, as a forthright film star, a middle-aged sex symbol, a fitness guru, and most recently a dance-club diva.

Cher dropped out of school and left home at 16, moving to Hollywood to be an actress. In 1963 she sang in sessions for producer Phil Spector and met Sonny Bono. Her musical and romantic partnership with Bono lasted until 1975 [see Sonny and Cher entry]. After their bitter split, Cher hosted her own TV variety show, which lasted one year. She had been having an affair with record producer David Geffen but married guitarist Gregg Allman five days after her divorce from Bono. That 1975 marriage produced a son, Elijah Blue, and an album, the critically reviled *Allman and Woman: Two the Hard Way*. The couple divorced in 1979. Cher became famous for her relationships with younger rockers, including a late-'70s romance with Kiss' Gene Simmons and an early-'90s relationship with Bon Jovi guitarist Richie Sambora.

In 1979 Cher had her first hit since her breakup with Bono

with the disco hit *Take Me Home* (#25, 1979) and its title track (#8, 1979). In 1980 she formed the hard-rock band Black Rose with her boyfriend Les Dudek (who had previously played with Steve Miller and Boz Scaggs), but critics buried them. Cher returned to playing Las Vegas and Atlantic City, where she has always been popular; her casino stints also led her to the infamous Sun City resort in South Africa.

Cher made her Broadway debut in Robert Altman's *Come Back to the 5 and Dime, Jimmy Dean, Jimmy Dean* in 1982. She starred in the movie of the play also, a role that finally broke down the Hollywood doors she had been knocking on for years. (In 1969 she had starred in the ill-fated film entitled *Chastity.*) In the next decade she landed featured roles in *Silkwood, Mask, The Witches of Eastwick, Suspect, Moonstruck,* and *Mermaids;* she won an Oscar for best actress for her performance in *Moonstruck.*

In 1987 Cher returned to recording and had a gold record with *Cher* (#32, 1987), which featured the singles "I Found Someone" (#10, 1987) and "We All Sleep Alone" (#14, 1988). Sonny and Cher last performed together singing an impromptu version of "I Got You Babe" on *Late Night With David Letterman* in February 1988. In 1989 her duet with Peter Cetera from the *Chances Are* soundtrack, "After All" (#6, 1989), became a hit. *Heart of Stone* (#10, 1989) went double platinum with the singles "If I Could Turn Back Time" (#3, 1989), "Just Like Jesse James" (#8, 1989), and "Heart of Stone" (#20, 1989). Cher's cover of Betty Everett's "The Shoop Shoop Song (It's in His Kiss)" (#33, 1990) was featured in *Mermaids.* In 1993 Cher recorded "I Got You Babe," her 1965 hit with Sonny, backed by MTV cartoon characters Beavis and Butt-head for *The Beavis and Butt-head Experience* album.

Always obsessed with her appearance, Cher has released exercise videos, a diet guide, perfume, and a line of skin-care products. (She has denied reports that she has had numerous cosmetic surgical procedures.) Since playing the mother of a physically deformed child in *Mask,* Cher has been active in a charity benefiting children with craniofacial problems.

In 1996 Cher released *It's a Man's World* (#64), her first studio album in five years. The single "One by One" (#5, 1996) became a big club hit; one of the song's remixes featured rapper Melle Mel, formerly of the groundbreaking hip-hop crew Grandmaster Flash and the Furious Five. *It's a Man's World* employed a half-dozen producers and included songs written by James Brown, Don Henley, the Walker Brothers, Paul Brady, and Trevor Horn, among others.

On January 8, 1998, Cher's former husband and singing partner, Sonny Bono, then a Republican congressman from California, died in a skiing accident at Lake Tahoe. Cher delivered a tearful eulogy at Bono's funeral. Her autobiography, *The First Time* (with Jeff Coplon), got surprisingly little attention. Cher's subsequent album, *Believe* (#7, 1998), went platinum. The record's electronically enhanced title track (#1, 1998) was an international dance smash, her biggest hit ever. In 1999 Cher acted alongside Dame Maggie Smith, Dame Judi Dench, and Lady Joan Plowright in *Tea With Mussolini,* a film directed by Franco Zeffirelli.

Neneh Cherry

Born Neneh Mariann Karlsson, Mar. 10, 1964, Stockholm, Swe.
1989—*Raw Like Sushi* (Virgin) 1992—*Homebrew* 1996—*Man* (Hut, U.K.).

Throwing punches like a tomboy homegirl, dropping beats and wisdom like a cosmo boho, or prancing like an African queen, Neneh Cherry plays an intelligently crafted version of post-rap dance pop. The daughter of artist Moki Cherry and West African percussionist Ahmadu Jah, Cherry was raised by her mother and stepfather Don Cherry, a pioneering jazz trumpeter, and grew up shuttling between Stockholm and New York.

Cherry dropped out of school at 14. The following year she went to Africa with her biological father. In 1980 she joined the Cherries in London, where she found through the burgeoning punk scene a new, tough identity. She sang backup for the ska band the Nails and briefly performed with the seminal all-girl group the Slits. After being raped on a street late one night, Cherry moved back to New York. But friends convinced her to return to London to sing and play percussion with Rip Rig + Panic, a group whose mixture of punk, funk, jazz, and soul coincided with her own musical interests.

Cherry recorded three albums with Rip Rig + Panic (*God,* 1981; *I Am Cold,* 1982; *Attitude,* 1983). At 18 she married drummer Bruce Smith and had her first child. The couple split within three years, and Cherry began singing with RR+P spinoff Float Up C.P. She also started rapping at a London club, where she was spotted by a talent scout. Her first single, "Stop the War," was about the Falkland Islands.

Cherry began dating and working with a composer and musician named Cameron McVey, who cowrote *Raw Like Sushi* (#40, 1989) and, under the name Booga Bear, coproduced several songs. The album received critical accolades for its pop melodies, positive messages, and fusion of hip-hop with jazz and rock stylings; in retrospect, *Raw* was probably the first "alternative rap" album. The hit "Buffalo Stance" (#3, 1989) introduced Cherry's tough street smarts, followed by "Kisses on the Wind" (#8, 1989). The birth of Cherry's second baby shortly before the album's release added to her image as a strong, mature sex symbol; she memorably appeared shimmying and fully pregnant on the British TV show *Top of the Pops.*

A few months after the album's release, Cherry collapsed backstage at the MTV Music Awards, possibly with Lyme disease. For the next few years, her only artistic foray was recording "I've Got You Under My Skin" for the *Red Hot + Blue* AIDS benefit album. She and McVey married and moved to the converted schoolhouse in Sweden in which Cherry had grown up. There they began writing and recording *Homebrew.* The album was more thoughtful, less in-your-face than Cherry's debut, although the opening track, "Sassy" (featuring Gang Starr rapper Guru), showed the singer's braggadocio was intact. *Homebrew* prospered mostly on alternative and college radio, where the Michael Stipe duet "Trout" was popular, and the "Buddy X" video became a staple on MTV.

In 1994 Cherry recorded a duet with Youssou N'Dour, "7 Seconds." The single was a hit in Europe, and it later appeared, along with a version of Marvin Gaye's "Trouble Man," on Cherry's 1996 album, *Man*. Coproduced by Cherry and McVey, with help from Geoff Barrow (half of the trip-hop duo Portishead), the record has yet to be released in the States. Cherry has also appeared on Tricky's *Nearly God* (1996). Her half brother, Eagle-Eye Cherry, released his debut album, *Desireless,* in 1998.

Vic Chesnutt

Born Nov. 12, 1964, Jacksonville, FL
1990—*Little* (Texas Hotel) 1992—*West of Rome* 1994—*Drunk* 1995—*Is the Actor Happy?* 1996—*About to Choke* (Capitol) 1998—*The Salesman and Bernadette* (Capricorn).
brute: 1995—*Nine High a Pallet* (Capricorn).
Vic Chesnutt and Mr. and Mrs. Keneipp: 2000—*Merriment* (Backburner).

Vic Chesnutt began his career as a protégé of R.E.M.'s Michael Stipe, only to emerge as one of the most incisive and revered singer/songwriters of his generation. Chesnutt, who has been wheelchair-bound since a near-fatal auto accident in 1983, met Stipe when the R.E.M. lead singer came to hear him play at a club in Athens, Georgia. Stipe proceeded to help Chesnutt land a record deal and to produce his first two albums.

Little (1990) was basically a solo acoustic affair spotlighting Chesnutt's creaky tenor, wry phrasing, and sense of humor. It also established him as a gifted, if often dour, miniaturist and garnered him a spot on a nationwide tour opening for Bob Mould, late of Hüsker Dü. Chesnutt's second album, *West of Rome* (1992), was sonically more ambitious, fleshing out his acerbic, rock- and soul-inflected originals with piano, cello, drums, and his wife Tina's bass. The sessions were captured on film in *Speed Racer: Welcome to the World of Vic Chesnutt,* a documentary by New York filmmaker Peter Sillen. Eventually airing on PBS, *Speed Racer* premiered at the 1994 Sundance Film Festival. *Drunk,* a predictably loose album that Chesnutt made with some friends while on a bender, also came out that year.

In 1995 Chesnutt recorded *Nine High a Pallet* with members of the Athens jam band Widespread Panic. Released under the group name brute, the record leaned toward generic country rock, but its crunchier, Neil Young–inspired numbers anticipated Chesnutt's next solo album, *Is the Actor Happy?* His most streamlined, and fully realized, record to date, *Is the Actor Happy?* also featured a duet with Stipe. Meanwhile, Chesnutt's reputation as a songwriter had grown beyond that of a cult hero. In 1996 a circle of his admirers, including Madonna, Garbage, and Live, paid tribute to him by recording *Sweet Relief II: Gravity of the Situation,* an album consisting entirely of covers of Chesnutt originals. Proceeds from the record went to a fund that helps musicians who are experiencing medical and financial hardships. Chesnutt subsequently toured as an opening act for Live and made his big-screen debut in the critically acclaimed feature film *Sling Blade.*

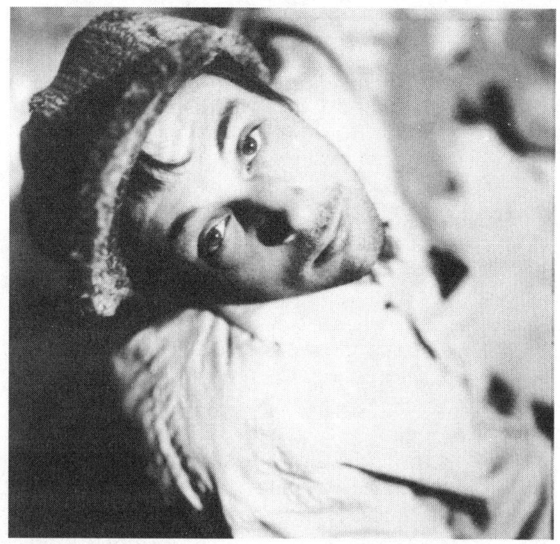

Vic Chesnutt

In 1996 Capitol released Chesnutt's long-awaited major-label debut, *About to Choke.* But the album fared better with critics than at the cash register, prompting Chesnutt and Capitol to dissolve their partnership after the singer embarked on extensive U.S. and European tours. Chesnutt then teamed with Nashville's mood-twang ensemble Lambchop for *The Salesman and Bernadette,* a whimsical, groove-rich album that sounds like it could have been made at Muscle Shoals during the late '60s.

Chic/Nile Rodgers/Bernard Edwards

Formed 1976, Bronx, NY
Bernard Edwards (b. Oct. 31, 1952, Greenville, NC; d. Apr. 18, 1996, Tokyo, Jap.), bass; Nile Rodgers (b. Sep. 19, 1952), gtr.; Norma Jean Wright, voc.; Tony Thompson, drums; Alfa Anderson (b. Sep. 7, 1946), voc.
1977—*Chic* (Atlantic) (– Wright; + Luci Martin [b. Jan 10, 1955], voc.) 1978—*C'est Chic* 1979—*Risque; Les Plus Grands Succes de Chic—Chic's Greatest Hits* 1980—*Real People* 1981—*Take It Off* 1982—*Tongue in Chic* 1983—*Believer* 1991—*Dance, Dance, Dance: The Best of Chic* (Atlantic/Rhino) (group re-forms) 1992—*The Best of Chic, vol. 2* (– Thompson; + Sterling Campbell, drums; + Sylver Logan Sharp, voc.; + Jenn Thomas, voc.) *Chic-ism* (Warner Bros.) 1996—*Chic Freak and More Treats* 1999—*Live at the Budokan* (Sumthing Else Music Works).
Bernard Edwards solo: 1983—*Glad to Be Here* (Warner Bros.).
Nile Rodgers solo: 1983—*Adventures in the Land of the Good Groove* (Warner Bros.) 1985—*B-Movie Matinee* 1986—(as Outloud) *Out Loud.*

Boasting a series of gold and platinum hit singles that began with 1977's #1 "Dance, Dance, Dance (Yowsah, Yowsah,

Yowsah)," Chic's stripped-down, not-quite-mechanical groove made them the premier black disco group of the late '70s and early '80s. In addition, cofounders Nile Rodgers and Bernard Edwards produced, wrote, or played on records by many other performers and became two of the most influential contemporary black writers and producers.

Edwards and Rodgers met in the Bronx while working at various gigs around New York in 1970. Over the next six years, they worked in soul and R&B groups; former Black Panther Rodgers played for the Apollo Theatre's house band. Soon after meeting former Patti LaBelle drummer Tony Thompson, they formed a rock-fusion power trio called Big Apple Band, aiming to become the black version of Kiss. They changed their name to Chic in the wake of Walter Murphy and the Big Apple Band's disco hit "A Fifth of Beethoven."

Frustrated by its inability to land a record deal, the band teamed with vocalists Alfa Anderson (who had sung on *The Wiz* soundtrack) and Norma Jean Wright to make disco records. Several record companies rejected the original demo tape of "Dance, Dance, Dance" before Atlantic took it in late 1977. In less than a month, the single, powered by Rodgers' distinctive rhythm guitar, sold a million copies and reached #6. Their second album, *C'est Chic* (with the 6-million-selling #1 song "Le Freak," the all-time top-selling single for Atlantic Records), and its followup, *Risque*, were both certified platinum. "Dance, Dance, Dance" (#1, 1977), "I Want Your Love" (#7, 1979), and "Good Times" (#1, 1979) were gold singles. "Good Times" (specifically its ominous yet playful bass line) inspired two hits: the Sugar Hill Gang's "Rapper's Delight," based on the instrumental track, and Queen's "Another One Bites the Dust."

In 1983, after releasing *Believer,* Chic disbanded, only to reassemble nearly a decade later. In 1992, with Rodgers and Edwards at their core but with a new drummer and new singers, Chic re-formed and signed with Warner Bros. In a version that included Steve Winwood, Sister Sledge, and Slash of Guns n' Roses, they toured Japan in 1996 and 1997 with great success. It was on the 1996 tour that Bernard Edwards died suddenly of pneumonia.

Rodgers has released two solo albums; Edwards, one (none was a hit). In 1989, with Tony Thompson, Edwards formed the band the Distance and recorded their album. But it was as producers, both as a team and individually, that Rodgers and Edwards made the greatest impact. Sister Sledge's *We Are Family* (1979) established them as studio purveyors of a streamlined sound (the title song earned Rodgers his first Grammy nomination for best songwriter); they went on to collaborate on albums, including Diana Ross' highly successful *Diana,* Debbie Harry's *KooKoo,* Sheila and B. Devotion's self-titled LP, and a soundtrack, *Soup for One.*

On his own, Edwards produced such artists as Power Station (with Robert Palmer and Tony Thompson), ABC, Jody Watley, Rod Stewart, Gladys Knight, and Kenny Loggins, his most noteworthy effort being Robert Palmer's *Riptide* and its 1986 #1 single "Addicted to Love." Rodgers has been even more prolific, producing more than 50 records between 1981 and 1993. He, too, has worked with a tremendous variety of musicians, among them Peter Gabriel, Eric Clapton, the Stray Cats, Ric Ocasek, Duran Duran, and David Lee Roth. Especially with his more notable productions—David Bowie's *Let's Dance* (Bowie's best-selling album), Madonna's *Like a Virgin,* Mick Jagger's *She's the Boss,* and the B-52's' *Cosmic Thing*—he lent a new sonic clarity to contemporary music without sacrificing any of its power. In the late '90s, Rodgers founded his own record label, Sumthing Else Music Works. In 1992 he received a Lifetime Achievement Award Grammy.

The Chic sound reemerged at the turn of the century, with their songs sampled by artists ranging from Will Smith to Sean Combs to Notorious B.I.G.

Chicago/Peter Cetera

Formed 1967, Chicago, IL
Terry Kath (b. Jan. 31, 1946, Chicago; d. Jan. 28, 1978, Los Angeles, CA), gtr., voc.; Peter Cetera (b. Sep. 13, 1944, Chicago), bass, voc.; Robert Lamm (b. Oct. 13, 1944, Brooklyn, NY), kybds., voc.; Walter Parazaider (b. Mar. 14, 1945, Chicago), saxes, clarinet; Danny Seraphine (b. Aug. 28, 1948, Chicago), drums; James Pankow (b. Aug. 20, 1947, St. Louis, MO), trombone; Lee Loughnane (b. Oct. 21, 1946, Chicago), trumpet.
1969—*Chicago Transit Authority* (Columbia) 1970—*Chicago II* 1971—*Chicago III; Chicago at Carnegie Hall* 1972—*Chicago V* 1973—*Chicago VI* 1974—*Chicago VII* (+ Laudir De Oliveira [b. Brazil], perc.) 1975—*Chicago VIII; Chicago IX* 1976—*Chicago X* 1977—*Chicago XI* 1978—(– Kath; + Donnie Dacus, gtr.) *Hot Streets* 1979—*Chicago XIII* (– De Oliveira; – Dacus; + Chris Pinnick, gtr.) 1980—*Chicago XIV* 1981—*Chicago's Greatest Hits, vol. 2* (– Pinnick; + Bill Champlin [b. May 21, 1947, Oakland, CA], voc., kybds., gtr.) 1982—*Chicago 16* (Warner Bros./Full Moon) 1983—*If You Leave Me Now* (Columbia) 1984—*Chicago 17* (Warner Bros./Full Moon) (– Cetera; + Jason Scheff, bass, voc.) 1986—*Chicago 18* (Warner Bros.) 1988—(+ DaWayne Bailey, gtr.) *Chicago 19* (Reprise) 1989—*Chicago's Greatest Hits 1982–89* (– Seraphine; + Tris Imboden, drums) 1991—*Twenty 1; Group Portrait* (Columbia/Legacy) 1995—(– Bailey; + Keith Howland [b. Aug. 14, 1964, Silver Spring, MD], gtr.) *Night & Day (Big Band)* (Giant) 1997—*The Heart of Chicago 1967–1997* (Reprise) 1998—*The Heart of Chicago 1967–1998, vol. II; Chicago 25—The Christmas Album* (Chicago).
Peter Cetera solo: 1981—*Peter Cetera* (Warner Bros.) 1986—*Solitude/Solitaire* 1988—*One More Story* 1992—*World Falling Down* 1995—*One Clear Voice* (River North) 1997—*You're the Inspiration: A Collection.*

Chicago followed the lead of Blood, Sweat and Tears and the Electric Flag by grafting a horn section onto a rock band. For over a quarter of a century, Chicago has produced 20 Top 10 hits and 15 platinum or multiplatinum albums and sold more than 100 million records.

School friends Terry Kath and Walter Parazaider formed the band in 1967 and named it the Big Thing. After they were joined by James William Guercio, who had worked with the Buckinghams and Blood, Sweat and Tears as a Columbia staff producer, they changed their name to the Chicago Transit Authority. The band's 1969 debut, *Chicago Transit Authority,* like BS&T's, was an ambitious jumble of jazz and rock, including protesters' chants from the 1968 Chicago Democratic convention.

Under Guercio's guidance and pressure from the city of Chicago, Chicago shortened its name and moved toward MOR pop with a string of hits ("Does Anybody Really Know What Time It Is?" #7, 1970; "Colour My World," #75, 1971; "Saturday in the Park," #3, 1972; "Feeling Stronger Every Day," #10, 1973; "Wishing You Were Here," #11, 1974, and many others) that made the group a constant presence on AM radio and kept its albums in the gold and platinum range. Several band members made cameo appearances in the Guercio-produced and -directed 1973 film *Electra Glide in Blue.*

In 1974 the group's unofficial leader, keyboardist Robert Lamm, made a solo album, *Skinny Boy.* Despite its moniker, Chicago worked out of L.A. (Guercio's base) from the late '60s on. In the later '70s the group's appeal began to flag. In 1977 they left Guercio, who had founded his own Caribou studio. Kath died of an accidental self-inflicted gunshot wound (some sources claim he was playing Russian roulette) in 1978; he was replaced by Donnie Dacus, formerly with Stephen Stills and Boz Scaggs. In 1979 Chicago played several benefits for presidential candidate Jerry Brown. Columbia, which had sold millions of Chicago records, dropped the group from its roster in 1981; ironically, with Warners, the group started a second-phase streak of hits: "Hard to Say I'm Sorry" (#1, 1982), "Hard Habit to Break" (#3, 1984), "You're the Inspiration" (#3, 1984), "Will You Still Love Me?" (#3, 1986), "I Don't Wanna Live Without Your Love" (#3, 1988), "Look Away" (#1, 1988), "You're Not Alone" (#10, 1989), and "What Kind of Man Would I Be?" (#5, 1989).

The Stone of Sisyphus, the group's less ballad-oriented 1993 album, remains unreleased in the U.S.; it marked the end of Chicago's contract with Warner Bros. *Night & Day* (#90, 1995) was an experiment in updated big-band stylings. In 1995 Chicago secured the rights to its Columbia catalogue, which it has since reissued on its own label. *The Heart of Chicago,* a career-spanning 1997 compilation of hits, peaked at #55; its 1998 sequel hit #154. The band's seasonal, self-released *Chicago 25* reached #47 in 1998.

Cetera released a self-titled solo album in 1981. He left the group in 1985 (and was replaced by Jason Scheff, son of longtime Elvis Presley bassist Jerry Scheff) for what began as a promising solo career with "Glory of Love" (#1, 1986), "The Next Time I Fall" (a duet with Amy Grant, #1, 1986), "One Good Woman" (#4, 1988), and "After All" (a duet with Cher, #6, 1989). Nonetheless, none of his albums went Top 20; only one, *Solitude/Solitaire,* was certified gold, and *World Falling Down* peaked at #163. *One Clear Voice* contains "(I Wanna Take) Forever Tonight" (#86, 1995), a duet with television star Crystal Bernard *(Wings).* In 1997 Cetera and the R&B vocal group Az Yet charted with revisions of "Hard to Say I'm Sorry" (#8 pop, #20 R&B) and "You're the Inspiration" (#77 pop). *You're the Inspiration* (#134, 1997) contains hits alongside rerecordings of Chicago-era material. In 1987 Cetera produced ex-Abba vocalist Agnetha Fältskog's solo album, *I Stand Alone,* and sang a duet with her on "I Wasn't the One (Who Said Goodbye)."

Chicken Shack

Formed 1967, London, Eng.
Stan Webb, gtr., voc.; Andy Sylvester, bass; Christine Perfect (b. July 12, 1943, Birmingham, Eng.), piano, voc.; Dave Bidwell, drums.
1968—*Forty Blue Fingers, Freshly Packed and Ready to Serve* (Blue Horizon); *OK, Ken?* 1969—(– Perfect; + Paul Raymond, kybds.) *Hundred Ton Chicken; Accept* 1970—(– Sylvester; – Bidwell; – Raymond; + Hughie Flint, drums; + John Glascock, bass) 1971—(– Flint; + Paul Hancox, drums) 1972—*Imagination Lady* (London) (– Glascock; + Bob Daisley, bass; + Chris Mercer, reeds; + Tony Ashton, piano) 1973—*Unlucky Boy* (group disbands) 1974—*Goodbye* (Nova) 1978—(– Webb; + Robbie Blunt, gtr.; + Ed Spevock, drums; + Dave Winthrop, sax; + Paul Martinez, bass) *The Creeper* (Ariola).

Chicken Shack was a leading band of the late-'60s British blues revival, but it is best remembered for pianist/singer Christine Perfect, who later became better known as Christine McVie of Fleetwood Mac. Stan Webb, Andy Sylvester, and Perfect played together in a Birmingham band, the Shades of Blue, in 1965. That band broke up when Perfect completed art college and moved to London. She later met up with Webb and Sylvester, and they regrouped as Chicken Shack, adding Bidwell. They made their U.K. debut at the Windsor Blues Festival in August 1967. There Perfect met her future husband, John McVie of Fleetwood Mac.

Chicken Shack's rendition of the Etta James blues "I'd Rather Go Blind" reached the U.K. Top 20 in May 1969, but in August Perfect left the group. A year later, after recording a solo album, she joined Fleetwood Mac [see entry]. Chicken Shack had a U.K. Top 30 hit with "Tears in the Wind" before Sylvester, Dave Bidwell, and Paul Raymond dropped out, later to join Savoy Brown.

Subsequent personnel under Webb's leadership included Hughie Flint (cofounder of McGuinness Flint), Paul Hancox (formerly of Wayne Fontana and the Mindbenders), Chris Mercer (veteran of numerous British blues sessions), Tony Ashton (of Family and Paice, Ashton and Lord), and Bob Daisley (who later joined Ritchie Blackmore's Rainbow and Ozzy Osbourne). Webb disbanded Chicken Shack in 1973. After brief stints with Savoy Brown and his own Broken Glass (which cut one album for Capitol in 1975), he revived Chicken Shack with Robbie Blunt and Paul Martinez, who went on to play with Robert Plant after the demise of Led Zeppelin.

The Chieftains

Formed 1963, Dublin, Ire.
Paddy Moloney (b. 1938, Dublin), uilleann pipes, tin whistle; Sean Potts (b. 1930), tin whistle, bodhran; Michael Tubridy (b. 1935), flute, concertina, whistle; Martin Fay (b. 1936, Dublin), fiddle; David Fallon, bodhran.
1964—*Chieftains 1* (Claddagh) 1969—(– Fallon; + Peadar Mercier [b. 1914], bodhran, bones; Sean Keane [b. 1946, Dublin], fiddle, whistle) *Chieftains 2* 1971—(+ Derek Bell [b. 1935, Belfast, Ire.], harp, dulcimer, oboe) *Chieftains 3* 1973—*Chieftains 4* 1975—(+ Ronnie McShane, bones) *Chieftains 5* 1976—(– Mercier; + Kevin Conneff [b. Dublin], bodhran) *6 Bonaparte's Retreat* 1977—*Chieftains Live* (Island) 1978—*7* (Columbia); *8* 1980—(– Tubridy; – Potts; + Matt Molloy [b. Ballaghadereen, Co. Roscommon, Ire.], flute) *9 Boil the Breakfast Early* 1981—*10 Cotton Eyed Joe* (Shanachie) 1985—*In China* 1987—*Celtic Wedding* (BMG Classics/RCA) 1989—*A Chieftains Celebration* 1991—*"Reel Music"/The Filmscores* (RCA Victor); *The Bells of Dublin* 1992—*An Irish Evening: Live at the Grand Opera House, Belfast; Another Country* 1993—*The Celtic Harp* 1995—*The Long Black Veil* 1996—*Film Cuts; Santiago* 1998—*Celtic Wedding: Music of Britta; Fire in the Kitchen* 1999—*Tears of Stone* 2000—*Water From the Well.*
With James Galway: 1987—*In Ireland* (BMG Classics/RCA) 1991—*Over the Sea to Skye* (RCA Victor).
With Van Morrison: 1988—*Irish Heartbeat* (Mercury).

The Chieftains are indisputably the world's leading proponents of traditional Irish music. As such, their appeal has extended well beyond Ireland's folk community, engendering international praise and collaborations with a wide range of musicians, from leading symphony orchestras to major rock artists. The five original Chieftains—including current members Paddy Moloney, initially the group's sole producer/arranger and still its leader, and fiddler Martin Fay—met in the late '50s while playing in Ceoltoiri Caulann, a folk ensemble. As the Chieftains, they aimed to lend their classical training to skilled interpretations of Celtic music, using traditional instruments like the tin whistle, uilleann pipes, and bodhran drum. In the decade following the group's 1964 debut, it put out albums sporadically—*Chieftains 2* didn't materialize until 1969—and made some personnel changes as its members tried to maintain their day jobs.

The Chieftains finally became a full-time act in 1975 and commemorated it by selling out London's Royal Albert Hall and providing the Oscar-winning soundtrack for Stanley Kubrick's film *Barry Lyndon*. In 1979 they played before 1.3 million people at an outdoor Mass in Dublin, as the supporting act for Pope John Paul II. The following year they released their ninth studio album, *9 Boil the Breakfast Early*, which introduced vocals to their music, courtesy of bodhran player Kevin Conneff. *10 Cotton Eyed Joe* found the Chieftains diversifying further, experimenting with American country textures. In 1983 they were among the first Western acts to play China, performing with a Chinese folk orchestra. Appearances with prominent North American symphonies, including the Boston Pops, followed.

In 1987 the group recorded the first of two traditional albums with Irish classical flutist James Galway. The following year saw a similar collaboration with Van Morrison [see entry]. Morrison also appeared, alongside singer/songwriter Nanci Griffith [see entry] and others, on *A Chieftains Celebration*. That year the Irish government made the Chieftains national musical ambassadors. The group's '90s accomplishments include *The Bells of Dublin* (1991), featuring such folk and rock luminaries as Griffith, Elvis Costello, Jackson Browne, and Rickie Lee Jones; *An Irish Evening* (1992), recorded live at Belfast's Grand Opera House with Griffith and Roger Daltrey; and *Another Country* (1992), a collaboration with C&W stars including Willie Nelson and Emmylou Harris. The latter recordings won Grammys for Best Contemporary Folk Album and Best Traditional Folk Album, respectively.

The Long Black Veil (#22, 1995) includes contributions from Sinéad O'Connor, Marianne Faithfull, Ry Cooder, Mark Knopfler, Sting, and the Rolling Stones. The record went gold, and its version of Van Morrison's "Have I Told You Lately That I Love You" beat out Mariah Carey and Michael Jackson to win a 1995 Grammy for Best Pop Vocal Collaboration. *Santiago,* released in 1996, won a Grammy for Best World Music Album. *Tears of Stone* (1999), a concept album about women and love, features guest performances from Bonnie Raitt, Joni Mitchell, Joan Osborne, and others. Recorded live and in the studio at locations throughout Ireland, *Water From the Well* consists entirely of traditional Celtic music.

The Chiffons

Formed 1960, Bronx, NY
Barbara Lee (b. May 16, 1947, Bronx; d. May 15, 1992), voc.; Patricia Bennett (b. Apr. 7, 1947, Bronx), voc.; Judy Craig (b. 1946, Bronx), lead voc.
1962—(+ Sylvia Peterson [b. Sep. 30, 1946, Bronx], voc.) 1963—*He's So Fine* (Laurie) 1966—*Sweet Talkin' Guy* 1992—(– Lee) 1994—(+ Connie Haynes).

A black female vocal group, the Chiffons had several international hits in the early '60s. Barbara Lee, Patricia Bennett, and Judy Craig met and began singing together in high school. In 1960 manager/songwriter Ronald Mack got them a contract with Big Deal Records. After one small hit that year, a cover of the Shirelles' "Tonight's the Night," they were not heard from again until 1962, when fourth member Sylvia Peterson joined. Their three-year string of hits included the Mack-penned "He's So Fine" (#1, 1963), which George Harrison was convicted of having unintentionally plagiarized in 1976 with his 1970 hit "My Sweet Lord." (In 1975 the Chiffons recorded their version of "My Sweet Lord.")

Other hits for the Chiffons included "One Fine Day" (#5, 1963), "Nobody Knows What's Going On" (#49, 1965), and "Sweet Talkin' Guy" (#10, 1966). In 1963 the group also recorded two songs as the Four Pennies ("My Block" and "When the Boy's Happy"). After 1966 the group ceased to appear on the charts in the U.S., but a 1972 rerelease of "Sweet Talkin' Guy" went to #4 in the U.K. Lee died of a heart attack in 1992. The soundtrack to the 1997 film *One Fine Day* contained the Chiffons' track of the same name. The group continues to perform both with and without Craig, who first left the group in the '70s.

The Chi-Lites

Formed 1960, Chicago, IL
Marshall Thompson (b. Apr. 1941, Chicago), voc.; Creadel Jones (b. 1939, St. Louis, MO), voc.; Robert Lester (b. 1942, McComb, MS), voc.; Eugene Record (b. Dec. 23, 1940, Chicago), voc.; Clarence Johnson, voc.
1964—(– Johnson) 1968—*Give It Away* (Brunswick) 1971—*Give More Power to the People* 1972—*A Lonely Man* 1973—*A Letter to Myself; The Chi-Lites* (– Jones; + Stan Anderson, voc.) 1974—*Toby* 1975—*Half a Love; Chi-Lites Greatest Hits, vol. 2* (– Record; + David Scott, voc.; + Danny Johnson, voc.) 1976—*Happy Being Lonely* 1977—*The Fantastic Chi-Lites* (Mercury) (– Johnson; + Vandy Hampton, voc.) 1980—(original lineup re-forms: Thompson; Lester; Jones; Record) *Heavenly Body* (Chi-Sound) 1981—*Me and You* 1983—*Bottom's Up* (Larc) (– Jones) 1990—*Just Say You Love Me* (Ichiban) 1992—*The Chi-Lites Greatest Hits* (Rhino) 1998—*Help Wanted* (Copper Sun).

The Chi-Lites' yearning ballads, featuring falsetto vocals and close harmonies, made them a leading soul vocal group of the early '70s. Originally known as Marshall and the Hi-Lites (later Chi-Lites), the quintet performed around Chicago and recorded for local labels. Former cabdriver Eugene Record became lead singer and eventually their songwriter and producer as well. The Chi-Lites signed with Chicago-based, nationally distributed Brunswick in 1968 and had a few soul hits before Record's "Have You Seen Her" (#3, 1971), cowritten with Barbara Acklin, became a pop hit. "Oh Girl" (#1, 1972) also sold in the millions and was later covered by Paul Young. The Chi-Lites had 11 Top 20 R&B hits between 1969 and 1974. In 1976 they were embroiled in the Brunswick label's tax evasion problems. Record went solo, recording for Warner Bros., while the Chi-Lites switched to Mercury, with meager results. Record returned in 1980, and with the group recording on his own Chi-Sound label, the Chi-Lites hit the R&B Top 20 with "Hot on a Thing" in 1982 and "Bottom's Up" in 1983. Creadel Jones retired, not permanently, however, in 1983. Record has been in and out of the group several times, and there have been several personnel changes that are not included in the chronology above. A core of Lester and Thompson were still performing as of the late '90s.

The Chills

Formed Oct. 1980, Dunedin, N.Z.
Martin Phillipps (b. July 2, 1963, N.Z.), gtr., voc.; Peter Gutteridge (b. May 19, 1961, N.Z.), gtr., voc.; Alan Haig (b. Aug. 5, 1961, N.Z.), drums; Jane Dodd (b. Sep. 9, 1962, N.Z.), bass; Rachel Phillipps (b. June 17, 1965, N.Z.), kybds.
1981—(– Gutteridge; – Dodd; – Rachel Phillipps; + Fraser Batts [b. Apr. 14, 1964, N.Z.], kybds., gtr.; + Terry Moore [b. Oct. 27, 1961, Eng.], bass) 1982—*Dunedin Double* EP (Flying Nun, N.Z.) (– Batts; – Haig; + Martyn Bull [b. Mar. 6, 1961, N.Z.; d. July 18, 1983, N.Z.] 1983—(+ Peter Allison [b. June 7, 1960, N.Z.], kybds.; + David Kilgour [b. Sep. 6, 1961, N.Z.], gtr., voc.) June 1983—(– Bull; – Kilgour; + Haig, drums) Nov. 1983—(– Moore; + Martin Kean [b. June 17, 1961], bass) 1984—(– Kean; + Moore, bass) 1985—*The Lost EP* (Flying Nun) 1986—(– Moore; – Allison; – Haig; + Caroline Easther [b. Nov. 30, 1958, N.Z.], drums; + Andrew Todd [b. Dec. 15, 1958, N.Z.], kybds.; + Justin Harwood [b. July 6, 1965, N.Z.], bass) *Kaleidoscope World* (Creation) 1987—*Brave Words* (Flying Nun) 1988—(– Easther; + James Stephenson [b. May 17, 1970], drums) 1990—*Submarine Bells* (Slash/Warner Bros.) (– Todd; – Harwood; + Moore; + Gillian Dempster [b. Apr. 26, 1970, N.Z.], kybds.) 1992—(– Stephenson; – Dempster; + Steven Schayer [b. Feb. 12, 1965, U.S.], gtr.; + Earl Robertson [b. Apr. 15, 1962, U.S.], drums; + Lisa Mednick [b. June 27, 1957, U.S.], kybds.) *Soft Bomb* Sep. 1992—(– Robertson; + Craig Mason [b. July 28, 1961, N.Z.], drums) 1996—(– Mednick; + Dominic Blaazar [b. Feb. 25, 1963, Jam.], kybds.; + Steven Shaw [b. May 5, 1965, N.Z.], bass; – Mason; + Jonathan Armstrong [b. Nov. 11, 1968, N.Z.], drums) *Sunburnt* (Flying Nun).
Martin Phillipps solo: 1999—*Sketchbook: vol. 1.*

Antipodean isolation bred a unique musical scene in New Zealand in the '80s, when bands like the Clean, Tall Dwarfs, the Bats, Straitjacket Fits, the Verlaines, and the Jean Paul Sartre Experience created postpunk singer/songwriter music. The Chills were the first of several Kiwi bands to be signed by American labels; in 1992 the band, always a volatile unit, exploded under the pressure of being an international act.

Martin Phillipps began playing music at 15 when he joined the Same, one of Dunedin's first punk bands. He started the Chills in 1980 with ex-Clean guitarist Peter Gutteridge (later of Snapper). Gutteridge soon left the group, thus starting the endless cycle of personnel changes that saw 14 Chills lineups in 12 years. In March 1982 the band recorded three songs for the *Dunedin Double* EP, the debut compilation from Flying Nun, the record company that soon became synonymous with the sound of the South Island.

In May '82 the Chills recorded their first single, "Rolling Moon," and the following month drummer Martyn Bull was diagnosed with leukemia. The band took a brief hiatus, then resumed under the moniker Time Flies, with the Clean's David Kilgour. That lineup lasted only a few months. In July 1983 Bull died, a traumatic event in Phillipps' life, which he later commemorated on the single "I Love My Leather Jacket."

Later in 1983 Phillipps re-formed the band with an eighth lineup and the name a Wrinkle in Time, but soon reverted to the Chills. In 1984 the band released its second and third singles, "Pink Frost" and "Doledrums," and recorded *The Lost EP.* The next year the Chills' ninth lineup made its first overseas trip to England. They were well received by the press there and promoted by influential disc jockey John Peel. On returning to New Zealand, however, the band broke up again.

In 1986 the British label Creation issued *Kaleidoscope World,* a collection of singles. The Chills finally released their first album, *Brave Words,* the following year. They played the New Music Seminar in New York that summer and spent the fall in Europe negotiating a record deal and touring. In 1988 the eleventh version of the Chills toured the U.S., then relocated to Europe.

The Chills signed to Slash and recorded *Submarine Bells* in 1989. The album was released in 1990 to critical acclaim, but the single "Heavenly Pop Hit" failed to live up to its title. The band collapsed again that summer, and after going through several more lineups, Phillipps recorded *Soft Bomb* basically as a solo effort, accompanied by longtime Chill Terry Moore. The album was wanly received, and at the end of a bitter U.S. tour, Phillipps announced the Chills' demise at a New York show.

But, in keeping with the band's on-again, off-again past, things weren't over yet. Instead of launching his solo career outright, Phillipps opted for a compromise. The next album, 1996's *Sunburnt,* was credited to Martin Phillipps and the Chills and included XTC members as guests. In addition to the name change, the sound was a bit more spare than lush older tunes like "Heavenly Pop Hit."

While the fate of the Chills as a proper group was continually debated as the band marked its 20th anniversary in 2000, Phillipps worked with members of the Clean in the New Zealand supergroup the Pop Art Toasters. He toured alone in 1999 to promote his solo album, *Sketchbook,* a compilation of home recordings and unreleased material written from 1988 to 1995.

Alex Chilton: See Big Star

Charlie Christian

Born 1919, Dallas, TX; died Mar. 2, 1942, New York, NY
1972—*Solo Flight—The Genius of Charlie Christian* (Columbia) 1987—*The Genius of the Electric Guitar.*

As the musician who took the guitar out of the rhythm section and made it a lead instrument, Charlie Christian had a profound influence on both jazz and rock & roll.

Christian's recording career spanned only three years. He was discovered playing in a jazz band in Oklahoma City by John Hammond in 1939. Benny Goodman brought him to New York to play with his sextet and his orchestra, and it was with Goodman that Christian revolutionized jazz guitar. The newly introduced electrified guitar gave the instrument an authoritative volume and tonal range it had never had before, and Christian's innovative single-string picking technique made the guitar a solo voice equal to the trumpet and the saxophone. Additionally, as one of the participants in after-hours jam sessions with Thelonious Monk, Dizzy Gillespie, and Kenny Clarke, Christian was one of the originators of bebop, which became the dominant force in jazz after his death. He developed tuberculosis in 1940 and was hospitalized in the summer of 1941. He spent the last six months of his life in the hospital.

Lou Christie

Born Lugee Alfredo Giovanni Sacco, Feb. 19, 1943, Glen Willard, PA
1963—*Lou Christie* (Roulette) 1966—*Lightnin' Strikes* (MGM); *Lou Christie Painter of Hits; Lou Christie Strikes Again* 1969—*I'm Gonna Make You Mine* (Buddah); *This Is Lou Christie* (Marble Arch) 1971—*Paint America Love* (Buddah) 1974—*Lou Christie* (Three Brothers) 1988—*EnLightn'ment Strikes: The Best of Lou Christie* (Rhino) 1989—*Rhapsody in the Rain* (PolyGram) 1997—*Pledging My Love* (Varèse Sarabande).

Singer Lou Christie had two big hits in 1963—"The Gypsy Cried" (#24) and "Two Faces Have I" (#6)—in the quavery falsetto style popularized by Del Shannon and Frankie Valli. Three years later he returned to the charts with "Lightnin' Strikes" (#1, 1966).

In Pennsylvania the young singer won a scholarship to Moon Township High School, where he studied classical music and vocal technique and also sang with a group called the Classics. From 1959 to 1962 he recorded with various local acts for several small Pittsburgh labels, adopted the stage name of Lou Christie, and in October 1962 recorded "The Gypsy Cried." The first of several songs cowritten with Twyla Herbert (a mystic 20 years Christie's senior who claimed she could foresee his future and predict his hits), it was a big local hit and was subsequently picked up for national distribution by Roulette Records. By then Christie had moved to New York, where he found frequent session work as a background vocalist. Shortly after the release of "Two Faces Have I" (#6, 1963), he served two years in the army. After his discharge in 1966, he signed with MGM and returned with the lushly produced "Lightnin' Strikes," which sold over 2 million copies.

His followups included "Rhapsody in the Rain" (#16, 1966), a fairly sexually explicit song for its time. Christie subsequently recorded for Colpix and Columbia before signing to Buddah in 1969. "I'm Gonna Make You Mine" (#10, 1969) was a hit in the U.S., Europe, and the U.K. Christie experienced problems with drugs in the early '70s, and after cleaning up in London, he held a range of jobs, including offshore oil driller, ranch hand, and carnival barker. In the late '70s he returned to New York, where he has done background vocal work. He continues to tour today. *Pledging My Love* is his first new studio album in over 20 years.

The Church

Formed 1980, Sydney, Austral.
Steven Kilbey (b. Sep. 13, ca. 1959, Welwyn Garden City, Eng.), bass, voc.; Marty Willson-Piper (b. May 7, ca. 1959, Stockport,

Eng.), gtr., voc.; Peter Koppes (b. ca. 1959, Austral.), gtr., voc.; Richard Ploog (b. ca. 1959, Austral.), drums.
1981—*Of Skins and Heart* (Parlophone, Austral.) 1982—*The Blurred Crusade* (Carrere, Austral.) 1983—*Seance* 1984—*Remote Luxury* (Warner Bros.) 1985—*Heyday* 1988—*Starfish* (Arista) 1990—*Gold Afternoon Fix* (– Ploog; + Jay Dee Daugherty [b. Mar. 22, 1956, Santa Barbara, CA], drums) 1992—*Priest = Aura* (– Daugherty; – Koppes) 1994—*Sometime Anywhere* 1996—*Magician Among the Spirits* (Thirsty Ear) 1998—*Hologram of Baal* (+ Koppes) 1999—*Box of Birds; Under the Milky Way—Best of the Church* (Buddha Records/BMG).

This Australian quartet initially rehashed the jangly, psychedelic side of the Byrds, though by the mid-'80s the Church had forged its own style of guitar pop with willfully obscure lyrics. Principal songwriter Steven Kilbey is a private man who grew up consumed by rock music, listening to rare, import-only albums alone in his bedroom. In 1980 Kilbey formed the Church with friends Marty Willson-Piper and Peter Koppes, who shared his passion for music. Drummer Richard Ploog was added a year later. After much success among underground and alternative-rock audiences in Australia and abroad, the Church gained a larger, AOR-oriented audience when Arista signed the band to a U.S. deal in 1987. Often lumped together with R.E.M., the group finally reached the pop charts with its first Arista release, 1988's *Starfish* (#41), and subsequent single, "Under the Milky Way" (#24).

Ploog left after 1990's *Gold Afternoon Fix,* replaced by former Patti Smith Group drummer Jay Dee Daugherty for 1992's *Priest = Aura.* In 1992 Koppes also quit. By 1993, only Kilbey and Willson-Piper remained. Since 1987, Kilbey, Willson-Piper, and Koppes have each released several solo albums; Kilbey also collaborated with Go-Between G.W. McLennan for the 1991 album *Jack Frost* and 1995's *Snow Job.*

In 1998 the band released *Hologram of Baal,* the first 7,500 copies of which included a free bonus disc devoted to an hour-long instrumental titled "Bastard Universe." The release precipitated the Church's first U.S. tour as a full band in eight years. Band members pursued various solo projects, and Kilbey kept busy publishing books of poetry and producing albums for other artists. In 1999 the band regrouped for *Box of Birds,* a loving collection of new recordings of covers of such artists as Hawkwind ("Silver Machine"), Ultravox ("Hiroshima Mon Amour"), David Bowie ("All the Young Dudes"), and Neil Young ("Cortez the Killer").

Cibo Matto

Formed 1994, New York, NY
Yuka Honda (b. Jap.), kybds.; Miho Hatori (b. Jap.), voc.
1996—*Viva! La Woman* (Warner Bros.) 1997—*Super Relax* EP 1999—(+ Sean Lennon [b. Oct. 9, 1975, New York], gtr., bass; + Timo Ellis [b. June 7, 1970], drums; + Duma Love, perc.) *Stereotype A.*
Butter 08 (Hatori; Honda; Russell Simins, drums; Mike Mills, bass; Rick Lee, guitar): 1996—*Butter* (Grand Royal).

Centered around two female Japanese musicians, Cibo Matto grew out of New York's cultural and musical melting pot in the mid-'90s. Miho Hatori and Yuka Honda met in the East Village in 1994. Hatori had just moved there from Japan (where she was in a group called Kimidori) the previous year, but Honda had been there since 1987, playing with such local luminaries as the Brooklyn Funk Essentials and John Zorn. The two women started working together in the noise combo Laitoh Lychee ("frozen lychee") before switching to Cibo Matto ("food crazy" in Italian). Honda programmed and triggered a small sampler; Hatori wrote lyrics in fractured English and sang. Cibo Matto regularly played New York clubs and in 1995 released a vinyl single, "Birthday Cake" b/w "Know Your Chicken," the first in a series of songs centered around food that made up the bulk of 1996's *Viva! La Woman.* Produced by Mitchell Froom and Tchad Blake (Suzanne Vega), the critically acclaimed album was an offbeat, giddy mix of sampled beats, Ennio Morricone–influenced atmospheres, funk, and pop, with songs covering the entire culinary palette from "Artichoke" and "Beef Jerky" to "White Pepper Ice Cream."

The group did not rest on its laurels and started filling out its sound on the 1997 EP *Super Relax,* which included a cover of Antonio Carlos Jobim's "Águas de Marҫo." That evolution continued on *Stereotype A* (#171, 1999). Honda handled the producing duties, while frequent collaborators such as her then-boyfriend Sean Lennon (on bass and guitar) and drummer Timo Ellis became permanent members. The group's sound expanded as well, jumping from hip-hop to hard rock, from bossa nova to funk. When performing live, the band's lineup would often swell with rotating guests like guitarist Marc Ribot or bassist Sebastian Steinberg (formerly of Soul Coughing).

Honda and Hatori have made guest appearances on records by Arto Lindsay and Yoko Ono, and they play with graphic designer Mike Mills, the Jon Spencer Blues Explosion's Russell Simins, and Skeleton Key's Rick Lee, the latter two occasional Cibo Matto collaborators in the band Butter 08, which released the more rockist *Butter* in 1996.

Cinderella

Formed 1983, Philadelphia, PA
Eric Brittingham (b. May 8), bass; Tom Keifer (b. Jan. 26), gtr., kybds., voc.; Jeff LeBar (b. Mar. 18), gtr.; Tony Destra, drums.
1986—(– Destra; + Jody Cortez, drums) *Night Songs* (Mercury) (– Cortez; + Fred Coury, drums) 1988—*Long Cold Winter* 1990—*Heartbreak Station* 1994—*Still Climbing* 1997—*Once Upon a . . .* 1999—*Live at the Key Club* (Dead Line).

In 1986 Cinderella was a heavy-metal band when heavy metal was not cool, headlined arenas when metal became cool, and remained a heavy-metal band long enough to capitalize on its late-'90s revival. Their teased coiffures, leather 'n' lace costumes, and thudding blues-based music heard on the multiplatinum albums *Night Songs* (#3, 1986) and *Long Cold Winter* (#10, 1988) and Top 20 singles "Nobody's Fool" (#13, 1986), "Don't Know What You Got (Till It's Gone)" (#12, 1988), and "Coming Home" (#20, 1989) can be seen as the advance wave of the metallic invasion that produced Guns n' Roses, Poison, et al.

Cinderella was formed by Philadelphia bar-band veterans Tom Keifer and Eric Brittingham. Jeff LeBar, who sometimes played the same clubs as the nascent band, thought they needed a guitarist and volunteered. They chose the name Cinderella for its lack of heavy-metal connotations, but the band did have a Prince Charming, in the form of Jon Bon Jovi. He saw them at a club in 1985 and recommended them to his label, Mercury, which signed them the next year. Drummer Fred Coury joined while they recorded *Night Songs*. Produced by Andy Johns, the album has a slick, aggressive sound, topped off by Keifer's throat-shredding vocals. The band supported it and its followup, the bluesy, ballad-laden *Long Cold Winter,* with near-constant touring, opening for Bon Jovi, David Lee Roth, Judas Priest, and AC/DC and playing before a crowd of over 100,000 at England's Castle Donnington festival in 1987.

Heartbreak Station (#19, 1990), led by the ballad "Shelter Me" (#38, 1990), was a surprising turn toward a softer sound. Embellished with horns, gospel singers, and strings arranged by ex–Led Zeppelin John Paul Jones, it gave the band entrée to MTV and classic-rock formats and secured its headliner status. Like so many other metal bands, Cinderella sounded irrelevant in the wake of Nirvana and grunge. *Still Climbing* (1994) sank without a trace, a fate that also befell the greatest-hits collection *Once Upon a . . .* (1997). A live album released in 1999 by the indie metal-specialist label Dead Line garnered some interest, and the band found itself signed to a major label deal in 2000 and, back on the road, touring with Poison, Dokken, and Slaughter.

Circle Jerks

Formed 1980, Los Angeles, CA
Keith Morris, voc.; Greg Hetson, gtr.; Roger (Dowding) Rogerson, bass; Lucky Lehrer, drums.
1980—*Group Sex* (Frontier) 1982—*Wild in the Streets* (Faulty Products) (– Lehrer; + John Ingram, drums) 1983—*Golden Shower of Hits* (LAX) (– Rogerson; – Ingram; + Zander Schloss, bass; + Keith Clark, drums) 1985—*Wönderful* (Combat Core) 1987—*VI* (Relativity) 1992—*Gig* 1995—*Oddities, Abnormalities and Curiosities* (Mercury).

This unruly L.A. hardcore band became a popular live attraction, particularly among skateboarders and slam dancers, and were key players in creating the influential '80s Southern California punk scene. Like Black Flag, X, and the Germs, the Circle Jerks played punk when it was far more likely to attract the ire of L.A. police than major-label interest. Lead singer Keith Morris had the whine and scowl of Johnny Rotten, and the group's music was basic loud, speedy, three-chord punk.

Morris was also the original singer for Black Flag [see entry]. After that group's first EP (*Nervous Breakdown,* 1978), Morris quit Black Flag and teamed up with former Redd Kross guitarist Greg Hetson in a garage in Hawthorne, soon forming the Circle Jerks. The group recorded its first album in 1980 and the next year appeared in the L.A. punk documentary *The Decline of Western Civilization.*

Wild in the Streets was originally released on Faulty Products, the label of Police manager Miles Copeland. *Golden Shower of Hits* contains a humorous hardcore medley in which the group desecrates '70s AM pop gems like "Afternoon Delight," "(You're) Having My Baby," and "Love Will Keep Us Together." The group changed rhythm sections for *Wönderful,* which was marked by a more heavy-metal sound. *VI* continued in the direction of its predecessor. The Circle Jerks performed into the '90s, releasing *Gig,* an anthology of live recordings, in 1992.

By then Hetson was also playing guitar in Bad Religion, while bassist Zander Schloss moonlighted as a guitarist for both Joe Strummer and Thelonious Monster. But the rise of pop-punk act Green Day suddenly had the Circle Jerks courted by major labels. Mercury released 1995's *Oddities, Abnormalities and Curiosities,* the band's first studio album in eight years. The album included a cover of the Soft Boys' "I Wanna Destroy You" (with guest vocals by former teen pop star Debbie Gibson). Four weeks into a tour, the band split up. Hetson returned to Bad Religion, and Schloss joined the Low & Sweet Orchestra, releasing *Goodbye to All That* in 1996. Morris was sidelined in the late '90s by diabetes but returned in 2000 leading a new band, Midget Handjob, which released a debut album on Epitaph.

Eric Clapton

Born Eric Clapp, Mar. 30, 1945, Ripley, Eng.
1970—*Eric Clapton* (Atco) 1972—*History of Eric Clapton; Eric Clapton at His Best* (Polydor) 1973—*Eric Clapton's Rainbow Concert* (RSO) 1974—*461 Ocean Boulevard* 1975—*There's One in Every Crowd; E.C. Was Here; The Best of E.C.* (Polydor) 1976—*No Reason to Cry* (RSO) 1977—*Slowhand* 1978—*Backless* 1980—*Just One Night* 1981—*Another Ticket* 1982—*Time Pieces I* 1983—*Money and Cigarettes* (Duck/Warner Bros.); *Time Pieces II* 1985—*Behind the Sun* 1986—*August* 1988—*Crossroads* (Polydor) 1989—*Homeboy* soundtrack (Virgin); *Journeyman* (Duck/Warner Bros.) 1991—*24 Nights* 1992—*Rush* soundtrack (Reprise); *Unplugged* (Duck/Warner Bros.) 1994—*From the Cradle* (Reprise) 1995—*The Cream of Clapton* (Polydor) 1996—*Crossroads 2: Live in the Seventies* 1998—*Pilgrim* (Duck/Reprise) 2001—*Reptile* (Reprise).
With Derek and the Dominos: 1970—*Layla and Other Assorted Love Songs* 1973—*Derek and the Dominos in Concert* 1990—*The Layla Sessions—20th Anniversary Edition* (Polydor).
With Simon Climie (as T.D.F.): 1997—*Retail Therapy* (Warner Bros.).
With B.B. King: 2000—*Riding With the King* (Duck/Reprise).

Eric Clapton

In the Yardbirds, Cream, Blind Faith, Derek and the Dominos, and his own bands, guitarist Eric Clapton has continually redefined his own version of the blues. Raised by his grandparents after his mother abandoned him at an early age, Clapton grew up a self-confessed "nasty kid." He studied stained-glass design at Kingston Art School and started playing the guitar at 15 and joining groups two years later. He stayed with his first band, the early British R&B outfit the Roosters (which included Tom McGuinness, later of Manfred Mann and McGuinness Flint), from January to August 1963 and frequently jammed in London clubs with, among others, future members of the Rolling Stones. The guitarist put in a seven-gig stint with a Top 40 band, Casey Jones and the Engineers, in September 1963. He joined the Yardbirds [see entry] in late 1963 and stayed with them until March 1965, when they began to leave behind power blues for psychedelic pop.

Upon leaving the Yardbirds, Clapton did construction work until John Mayall [see entry] asked him to join his Bluesbreakers in spring 1965. With Mayall, he contributed to several LPs while perfecting the blues runs that drew a cult of worshipers (the slogan CLAPTON IS GOD became a popular graffito in London). Also with Mayall he participated in a studio band called Powerhouse (which included Jack Bruce and Steve Winwood); they contributed three cuts to a 1966 Elektra anthology, *What's Shakin'*. Clapton left the Bluesbreakers in July 1966 and cut a few tracks with Jimmy Page, then with bassist Jack Bruce and drummer Ginger Baker he formed Cream [see entry].

Clapton perfected his virtuoso style, and Cream's concerts featured lengthy solo excursions, which Clapton often performed with his back to the crowd. During his tenure with Cream, Clapton contributed lead fills to the Beatles' "While My Guitar Gently Weeps" and appeared on Frank Zappa's *We're Only in It for the Money*.

When Cream broke up in November 1968, Clapton formed the short-lived supergroup Blind Faith with Baker, Winwood, and Rick Grech [see entry]. During their only U.S. tour, Clapton embraced Christianity, which he has given up and reaffirmed periodically ever since. As a corrective to Blind Faith's fan worship, Clapton began jamming with tour openers Delaney and Bonnie, then joined their band as an unbilled (but hardly unnoticed) sideman. Clapton's 1969 activities also included a brief fling with John Lennon's Plastic Ono Band *(Live Peace in Toronto)*.

He moved to New York in late 1969 and continued to work with Delaney and Bonnie through early 1970. With several members of the Bramletts' band, and friends like Leon Russell and Stephen Stills, whose solo albums Clapton played on, he recorded his first solo album, *Eric Clapton*, which yielded a U.S. #18 hit, the J.J. Cale song "After Midnight." The album marked Clapton's emergence as a strong lead vocalist, a role he continued to fill after forming Derek and the Dominos with bassist Carl Radle, drummer Jim Gordon, and keyboardist Bobby Whitlock, all former Delaney and Bonnie sidemen. The Dominos' only studio album, the two-record *Layla* (#16, 1970), was a guitar *tour de force* sparked by the contributions of guest artist Duane Allman. The title track, an instant FM standard (and a Top 10 hit two years later), was a tale of unrequited love inspired by Pattie Boyd Harrison (wife of ex-Beatle George), whom Clapton eventually married in 1979; they divorced in 1989. Clapton toured on and off with the Dominos through late 1971, but the group collapsed due to personal conflicts, most, Clapton later claimed, drug- or alcohol-induced. Over the following two decades, Derek and the Dominos would prove to be one of the most star-crossed groups in rock: Allman died in a motorcycle crash in October 1971; Radle died of alcohol poisoning in 1981; Gordon was convicted of murdering his mother and imprisoned in 1984.

Clapton sat in on albums by Dr. John and Harrison, who enticed Clapton to play at the benefit concert for Bangladesh in August 1971. Depressed and burdened by a heroin habit, Clapton retreated to the isolation of his Surrey, England, home for most of 1971 and 1972. With the aid of Pete Townshend, he began his comeback with a concert at London's Rainbow Theatre in January 1973. Supported by Townshend, Winwood, Ron Wood, Jim Capaldi, and others, Clapton released tapes from the ragged concert in a September 1973 LP. By the time *461 Ocean Boulevard* (#1, 1974) was released, he had kicked heroin for good.

In the '70s Clapton became a dependable hitmaker with the easygoing, more commercial style he introduced on *461*—a relaxed shuffle that, like J.J. Cale's, hinted at gospel, honky-tonk, and reggae while retaining a blues feeling but not necessarily the blues structure. Playing fewer and shorter guitar solos, he emphasized his vocals—often paired with harmonies by Yvonne Elliman or Marcy Levy—over his guitar virtuosity. He had hits with his cover of Bob Marley's "I Shot the Sheriff" (#1, 1974) and originals "Lay Down Sally" (#3, 1978) and "Promises" (#9, 1979). His albums regularly sold in gold quantities; *Slowhand* and *Backless* were certified platinum.

He had a Top 10 hit in 1981 with "I Can't Stand It," from *Another Ticket* (#7), and later that year formed his own label, Duck Records. During the early '80s he made frequent appearances at major benefit concerts. In that decade Clapton's singles veered closer to balladry than blues, producing a string of hits, including "I've Got a Rock 'n' Roll Heart" (#18, 1983) and "Forever Man" (#26, 1985).

In 1985 he separated from his wife, Pattie, and went into rehabilitation to overcome the alcoholism that had replaced his heroin addiction over a decade earlier. The next year Italian actress Lori Del Santo gave birth to Clapton's son, Conor.

Clapton continued to tour and record; *24 Nights* captured Clapton's 1990–91 concert series at London's Royal Albert Hall, which since 1987 has become an annual event. Guests on the album include Jimmie Vaughan, Phil Collins, Buddy Guy, Albert Collins, and Robert Cray. He had spent the better part of the past two years on the road, and in August 1990 his agent and two members of his road crew died in the same helicopter crash that claimed Stevie Ray Vaughan. On March 20, 1991, four-and-a-half-year-old Conor died after falling 50 stories through a window in his mother's Manhattan apartment. A maintenance worker had left it open by mistake. Clapton was staying at a hotel just blocks from the apartment when the tragedy occurred. The following year Clapton made public service announcements warning parents to protect their children by installing gates over windows and staircases.

After a period of seclusion, Clapton began to work again, writing music for *Rush*, a film about drug addiction. In March 1992, almost a year after Conor's death, Clapton taped a segment for MTV's *Unplugged* series, the soundtrack of which peaked at #2 in 1992 and included a reworking of "Layla" (#12, 1993) and "Tears in Heaven" (#2, 1993), the latter written for his son. That year he was nominated for nine Grammy Awards and won six, including Record of the Year, Song of the Year, and Best Pop Vocal Performance, Male, for "Tears in Heaven." In early 1993 Clapton and his former cohorts in Cream, Jack Bruce and Ginger Baker, reunited to perform three songs at the group's Rock and Roll Hall of Fame induction. Clapton was inducted as a solo artist in 2000. In 1994 Clapton released an album of pure electric blues, *From the Cradle*, which topped the charts and won a Grammy for Best Traditional Blues Album. The double-platinum album became the best-selling traditional blues recording in history.

Two years later he returned with another career milestone. The single "Change the World," produced by R&B mastermind Kenny "Babyface" Edmonds for the soundtrack to the John Travolta film *Phenomenon*, became Clapton's highest-debuting single, hitting #9 in its first week (it peaked at #5 pop, #54 R&B, and #1 Adult Contemporary). The guitarist also dabbled in electronica, recording with keyboardist Simon Climie as the duo T.D.F. The 1997 release *Retail Therapy* was little more than a curiosity. The next year Climie also collaborated on *Pilgrim*, Clapton's first studio album of mostly original material since 1989. With its focus on slick, R&B-flavored pop, the album got mixed reviews from critics but charted well (#4) and produced a hit in the ballad "My Father's Eyes" (#26 pop, #2 Adult Contemporary). Another track, "She's Gone," reached #19. The subsequent tour was sponsored by luxury car manufacturer Lexus, which employed Clapton for a 30-second commercial performing "Layla" as pop-up script called attention to similarities—such as "effortless shifting"—between Clapton and the car. On June 24, 1999, Clapton auctioned off 100 of his guitars at Christie's with the proceeds going to support the Crossroads Centre on Antigua, a drug and alcohol rehabilitation facility that he founded in 1998.

In 2000 Clapton joined forces with one of his heroes, blues guitar legend B.B. King, to record *Riding With the King*, which featured several vintage King numbers and which won a Grammy for Best Traditional Blues Album. *Reptile* (#5, 2001) returned Clapton to the rock sound of his early solo career. He announced his subsequent 2001 tour would be his last.

The Dave Clark Five

Formed 1961, Tottenham, Eng.
Dave Clark (b. Dec. 15, 1942, Tottenham), drums, voc.; Mike Smith (b. Dec. 6, 1943, London, Eng.), piano, voc.; Rick Huxley (b. Aug. 5, 1942, Dartford, Eng.), gtr.; Lenny Davidson (b. May 30, 1944, Enfield, Eng.), gtr.; Denis Payton (b. Aug. 11, 1943, London), sax.
1964—*Glad All Over* (Epic); *American Tour; The Dave Clark Five Return* 1965—*Coast to Coast; Having a Wild Weekend; I Like It Like That* 1966—*The Dave Clark Five's Greatest Hits; Try Too Hard; Satisfied With You; More Greatest Hits* 1967—*5 by 5; You Got What It Takes* 1968—*Everybody Knows* (Columbia); *Weekend in London* (Epic) 1971—*Good Old Rock 'n' Roll* 1993—*The History of the Dave Clark Five* (Hollywood).

The Dave Clark Five, a British Invasion phenomenon, was formed in 1961 by members of the Tottenham Hotspurs soccer team in suburban London because they needed to raise funds to travel to Holland for a match. Photogenic leader Dave Clark, a former film stuntman, had never played the drums but quickly learned; he soon became the group's chief songwriter, producer, and manager as well.

The quintet's sound differed strikingly from its British Invasion counterparts. On songs like "Glad All Over" and especially "Anyway You Want It," the DC5 was probably the *loudest* U.K. act until the arrival of the Who. Denis Payton's sax underpinned a dense, churning rhythm section, while Clark's crackling snare-drum triplets punctuated the mix. And in Mike Smith the DC5 possessed a truly outstanding (and greatly overlooked) soul shouter.

"Glad All Over" (#6, 1964) was the first in a string of 17 Top 40 hits in just three years. The group's Top 10s included "Bits and Pieces" (#4), "Can't You See That She's Mine" (#4), and the ballad "Because" (#3) in 1964; "I Like It Like That" (#7), "Catch Us If You Can" (#4), and "Over and Over" (#1) in 1965; and "You Got What It Takes" (#7) in 1967. The DC5 was the second British act after the Beatles to appear on the *Ed Sullivan Show;* its 18 appearances on that show eclipsed both the Fab Four and the Rolling Stones. Clark and company also followed the Beatles into film, appearing (with the Animals) in *Get Yourself a College Girl* (1964) and *Having a Wild Weekend* (1965).

By 1968, the group's U.S. hits had dried up, although the Dave Clark Five continued to score hits in Britain through 1970, the year the band split up. Smith and Clark continued to put out records under the name Dave Clark and Friends for another three years. Smith then made an album with onetime Manfred Mann vocalist Mike D'Abo in 1975. He later got into commercial jingle writing and session work, and appeared on the original album to *Evita.* In 1990 he recorded an album of '50s American rock standards as well as originals.

Clark wrote and produced the 1986 musical *Time,* which starred Cliff Richard and, later, David Cassidy. An accompanying album of music from the stage production featured Richard, Freddie Mercury, Stevie Wonder, and others. Clark, a savvy businessman, has owned the DC5's original masters from the beginning. When he put together the 1993 double-CD retrospective, it marked the first time the DC5 catalogue was made available in 20 years. Over its career, the Dave Clark Five has sold over 50 million records worldwide.

Petula Clark

Born Nov. 15, 1932, Epsom, Eng.
1965—*Downtown* (Warner Bros.) 1967—*These Are My Songs* 1968—*Petula Clark's Greatest Hits, vol. 1* 1995—*Blue Lady: The Nashville Sessions* (Varèse Sarabande) 1998—*Here for You.*

British pop singer Petula Clark is best known in America for mid-'60s hits such as "Downtown" and "Don't Sleep in the Subway" but has also carried on a varied career in Europe. She began singing professionally at age eight; by nine she was a regular on radio shows; at 11, she hosted her own radio show, *Pet's Parlour.* Along with other child stars Julie Andrews and Anthony Newley, she performed for British troops during World War II.

She was 12 when she made her film debut in *A Medal for the General.* By the early '50s, she was a major star in the U.K., with over 20 movie credits. In 1954 "The Little Shoemaker" (#12, U.K.) became her first hit, followed by "Majorca" and others. She got her first #1 in the U.K. with 1961's "Sailor," followed by her first million-seller, "Romeo" (#3 U.K., 1961). That same year she married Vogue Records publicity director Claud Wolff, who became her manager. They moved to France, and she became popular there with such hits as "Chariot" and "Monsieur," also a big seller in Germany. Her string of English hits continued throughout the early '60s—"My Friend the Sea," "Ya Ya Twist," "Casanova"—and she cracked the American market with "Downtown" (#1, 1965), which won a Grammy Award in 1964.

Clark toured U.S. nightclubs for the next few years and managed followup hits like "I Know a Place" (#3, 1965), "My Love" (#1, 1966), and "I Couldn't Live Without Your Love" (#9, 1966). Although she cut down her personal appearances to raise her family, there were a few more hits like "Don't Sleep in the Subway" (#5, 1967), "The Other Man's Grass Is Always Greener" (#31, 1967), and "Kiss Me Goodbye" (#15, 1968). *Blue Lady,* issued in 1995, unearths previously unreleased material recorded in 1975, overseen by famed Nashville producer Chips Moman.

In the late '60s, she revived her acting career, starring in the films *Goodbye, Mr. Chips* and *Finian's Rainbow.* She has also performed on the British stage, in *The Sound of Music* (1981) and *Someone Like You* (1990), which she cowrote with Fay Weldon. She made her Broadway debut in 1993 in *Blood Brothers,* which costarred David Cassidy and his half brother Shaun Cassidy. From the late '90s through 2000, Clark toured the U.S. playing Norma Desmond in Andrew Lloyd Webber's *Sunset Boulevard;* she also appeared in the musical during its 1995–97 U.K. run.

In late 1988, Clark returned to the upper reaches of the pop charts when a remix of "Downtown," entitled "Downtown '88," became a Top 10 U.K. hit. Ten years later Queen Elizabeth named Clark a Commander of the Order of the British Empire, one of the U.K.'s highest honors. *Here for You* contains an assortment of standards and show tunes.

Stanley Clarke

Born June 30, 1951, Philadelphia, PA
1973—*Children of Forever* (Polydor) 1974—*Stanley Clarke* (Epic) 1975—*Journey to Love* 1976—*School Days* 1978—*Modern Man* (Nemperor) 1979—*I Wanna Play for You* 1980—*Fuse One* (IMS); *Rocks, Pebbles and Sand* (Epic) 1981—*The Clarke/Duke Project* (with George Duke) 1982—*Let Me Know You* (Columbia) 1983—*The Clarke/Duke Project II* (with George Duke) 1984—*Time Exposure* (Epic) 1985—*Find Out!* 1986—*Hideaway* 1988—*Project* (CBS); *If This Bass Could Only Talk* (Portrait) 1989—*3* (with George Duke) (Epic) 1992—*Passenger 157* 1993—*East River Drive* 1994—*Live at the Greek; Live in Montreaux* (Jazz Door) 1995—*Rite of Strings* (Gai Saber); *At the Movies* (Epic Soundtrax) 1997—*The Bass-ic Collection.*

Stanley Clarke earned a considerable reputation as a jazz bassist before entering the rock market with Return to Forever and switching to electric bass. His trademark on acoustic bass is precise upper-register vamping; on the electric, a metallic plunk.

Clarke studied at the Philadelphia Academy of Music before moving to New York in 1970. He soon worked with Art Blakey, Gil Evans, the Thad Jones–Mel Lewis Orchestra, and Chick Corea [see entry], whom he met in Philadelphia in 1971. Clarke also played in a group led by saxophonist Stan Getz; the vaguely Brazilian-style material Corea furnished for Getz became the repertoire for a Corea quintet with Clarke, reedman Joe Farrell, singer Flora Purim, and percussionist Airto Moreira on the 1972 Corea albums *Return to Forever* and *Light as a Feather.*

Corea and Clarke, both Scientologists, kept the name Return to Forever for their group. They formed an electrified band with drummer Lenny White and guitarist Bill Connors—soon replaced by Al DiMeola—which grew increasingly bombastic and popular. In 1976 Clarke and DiMeola both left to pursue solo careers. Clarke had already begun releasing his own fusion albums including 1975's *Journey to Love* with guest Jeff Beck.

At the end of the '70s, he released the half-studio, half-live double album *I Wanna Play for You* and joined Rolling Stones Ron Wood and Keith Richards for a North American tour as the New Barbarians. He teamed up with keyboardist George Duke (who had appeared on previous Clarke LPs) as the Clarke/Duke Project in 1981, and had a hit with the ballad "Sweet Baby." He also recorded with Corea, White, and Chaka Khan on the acoustic jazz session *Echoes of an Era.* In 1983 Clarke joined Corea, White, and DiMeola on a Return to Forever reunion tour.

Clarke has worked as a producer and played on albums by Santana, Aretha Franklin, and Quincy Jones, among others; he also appeared on Paul McCartney's *Tug of War* (1982).

In the late '80s Clarke turned to composing for television and films. He began by writing for TV pilots, movies of the week, and *Pee-wee's Playhouse;* by the '90s, he graduated to feature films, scoring, among others, the Tina Turner biopic, *What's Love Got to Do With It,* and John Singleton's *Boyz N the Hood* and *Poetic Justice.* In 1989 Clarke played in the band Animal Logic with former Police drummer Stewart Copeland. He also continued playing jazz, with 1988's *If This Bass Could Only Talk* and 1995's acoustic *The Rite of Strings,* featuring Jean-Luc Ponty and Al DiMeola, illustrating his constantly evolving technique. In 1997 he formed Basic Music Co. (BMC), an entertainment company with a record label, an instructional video company, and a management firm for film composers.

The Clash

Formed 1976, London, Eng.
Mick Jones (b. Michael Jones, June 26, 1955, London), gtr., voc.; Paul Simonon (b. Dec. 15, 1955, London), bass; Tory Crimes (b. Terry Chimes, London), drums; Joe Strummer (b. John Graham Mellor, Aug. 21, 1952, Ankara, Tur.), voc., gtr.
1977—*The Clash* (CBS, U.K.) (– Crimes; + Nicky "Topper" Headon [b. May 30, 1955, Bromley, Eng.], drums) 1978—*Give 'Em Enough Rope* (Epic) 1979—*The Clash; London Calling* 1980—*Black Market Clash* EP; *Sandinista!* 1982—*Combat Rock* (– Headon; + Crimes, drums) 1985—(– Jones; – Crimes; + Vince White [b. ca. 1961], gtr.; + Nick Sheppard [b. ca. 1961], gtr.; + Pete Howard, drums) *Cut the Crap* 1988—*The Story of the Clash, vol. 1* 1991—*Clash on Broadway* 1999—*The Clash Live: From Here to Eternity.*
Havana 3 A.M. (Simonon, bass.; Gary Myrick, gtr.; Nigel Dixon, voc.): 1991—*Havana 3 A.M.* (I.R.S.).
Joe Strummer solo: 1987—*Walker* (Virgin Movie Music) 1989—*Earthquake Weather* (Epic) 1999—*Rock Art and the X-Ray Style* (Epitaph) 2001—*Global A Go-Go.*

The Clash took the raw anger of British punk and worked it into a political and aesthetic agenda. Outstripping all of their peers in terms of length and depth of career, they were rebels with a cause—with many causes, from anti-Thatcherism to racial unity to the Sandinistas. Their music was roots-based but future-visionary; their experiments with funk, reggae, and rap never took them far from a three-minute pop song. Hyped as "the only band that matters," the Clash fell apart just as it broke through to an American audience. By then it had shown that punk was not just a flash-in-the-pan explosion and had delivered an arsenal of unforgettable rock songs.

The Clash was very much dependent on the band chemistry between its four longest-time members: Strummer, Jones, Simonon, and Headon. Primary songwriter Strummer, the son of a British diplomat, grew up in a boarding school. He quit school while still in his teens and in 1974 formed the 101ers, a pub-rock band named either for the address of the building where they squatted or the number of the torture room in the George Orwell novel *1984.*

Jones and Simonon are both from working-class Brixton. The gangling, handsome Simonon was attending art school when he met Jones. He had never played an instrument until he heard the Sex Pistols; he then acquired a bass and joined Jones' band, the London SS, which in its 11-month existence included Tory Crimes and Topper Headon (as well as future Generation X/Sigue Sigue Sputnik bassist Tony James). Seeing the Pistols induced Strummer (a name he got when he strummed "Johnny B. Goode" on a ukulele as a busker in London subway stations) to leave the 101ers, which included guitarist Keith Levene, soon after they recorded the single "Keys to Your Heart." Strummer and Levene then joined Jones, Simonon, and Crimes in their new group, named the Clash by Jones because it was the word that seemed to appear most often in newspaper headlines.

The Clash played its first, unannounced gig opening for the Sex Pistols in summer 1976 as a quintet. They opened for the Pistols on their Anarchy in the U.K. Tour after Levene quit. (He eventually joined Public Image Ltd.) The Clash was managed by Malcolm McLaren associate Bernard Rhodes, who helped the band articulate its political mission. Where the Sex Pistols were nihilists, the Clash were protesters, with songs about racism, police brutality, and disenfranchisement. They mixed rock with reggae, the music of Britain's oppressed Jamaicans; one of their early singles was a cover of Junior Murvin's "Police and Thieves." Throughout its career, the Clash was active in several political causes and performed benefit concerts for Rock Against Racism.

In February 1977 British CBS Records signed the Clash for a reported $200,000 advance. Their debut album was released that spring and entered the British charts at #12. Columbia considered the album too crude for American release (although the import sold 100,000 copies, making it the biggest-selling import album of that time). In response, the Clash recorded "Complete Control" with Jamaican producer Lee "Scratch" Perry.

Crimes quit the group in late 1976. Headon, who had been drumming with Pat Travers in Europe since his stint in the London SS, accompanied the group on its first national headlining tour. The White Riot Tour, named after the current Clash single, ended at a London concert where the audience ripped the seats out of the floor. It was the first in a series of confrontations between the Clash and the police, especially in Britain, where the group members were arrested on charges ranging from petty theft to illegal possession of firearms (for shooting prize pigeons).

In October 1978 the Clash's stormy relationship with Rhodes took a turn for the worse and the band fired the manager, only to rehire him years later. They worked with journalist Caroline Coon and Kosmo Vinyl, among others, in between times.

One of the four songs on an EP entitled *Cost of Living,* a cover of the Bobby Fuller–Sonny Curtis "I Fought the Law," was the first Clash record released in the U.S. At Columbia's behest, American producer Sandy Pearlman, best known for his work with Blue Öyster Cult, produced *Give 'Em Enough Rope,* which reached #2 on the British charts but failed to crack the American Top 200.

The Clash launched its Pearl Harbour Tour of America in February 1979. They also persuaded Columbia to release their first album, which in its American version contained only 10 of the original 14 tracks. A bonus 45 and EP selections dating as far back as two years made up the rest. The album eventually went gold. The Clash toured the U.S. again that fall, with Mickey Gallagher, of Ian Dury's Blockheads, on keyboards.

London Calling (#27, 1980), with its eclectic collection of pop styles, was both an artistic and commercial breakthrough. Produced by Guy Stevens (who had worked with Mott the Hoople) and supplemented by a brass section and Gallagher, the album went gold thanks to a hit single penned by Jones, "Train in Vain (Stand by Me)" (#23, 1980). Beginning with *London Calling,* the Clash insisted that its records sell at lower than standard prices, a laudable position, considering that *London Calling* is a double LP and album prices were rising sharply then due in part to the oil crisis.

In 1980 the semidocumentary film *Rude Boy* was released. It wove a fictional story about a fan (played by Ray Gange) around actual footage of Clash shows and backstage scenes, filmed during the previous 18 months. That year Jones also produced an album by his then-girlfriend, singer Ellen Foley.

The Clash recorded *Sandinista!* in New York, producing it themselves. The triple-LP package was a deliberately anticommercial gesture. It sold for less than most double albums, and Columbia took the lost profits out of the group's royalties and tour support funds. The sprawling, often-experimental album was chosen by a poll of *Village Voice* critics as album of the year, and *Sandinista!* (#24, 1981) was the first Clash album to sell more copies in the U.S. than in the U.K.

In December 1981, as the band was beginning to record their next album, Headon was arrested for heroin possession. In April 1982, just as *Combat Rock* was about to be released, Strummer disappeared, to be found a month later in Paris. (Some accounts say the vanishing act was a publicity stunt engineered by Rhodes.) Upon Strummer's return, Headon left the group, reputedly because of "political differ-

The Clash: Mick Jones, Paul Simonon, Topper Headon, Joe Strummer

ences," although Strummer later revealed that the problem was the drummer's drug use; he was replaced by Crimes for the Clash's U.K. tour. Ironically, Headon wrote "Rock the Casbah" (#8, 1982), which became an early MTV staple, the Clash's biggest hit, and in 1999 provided the distinctive sample for Will Smith's "Will2K." In July 1982 Headon was arrested in London for receiving stolen property.

Combat Rock (#7, 1982), produced by Glyn Johns, continued the Clash's forays into funk and rap. One song featured Beat poet Allen Ginsberg. The album went platinum; the single "Should I Stay or Should I Go" was a Top 50 hit that summer. In fall 1982 the Clash toured the U.S. with the Who, playing for its biggest audiences yet. In spring 1983 they headlined at the US Festival in California, with Pete Howard on drums.

That fall Simonon and Strummer kicked Jones out of the band, replacing him with two guitarists, Vince White and Nick Sheppard. Jones went on to form Big Audio Dynamite [see entry]. *Cut the Crap* was poorly received by critics and fans; the new Clash was a feeble imitation of its old self, and the band soon called it quits.

Strummer briefly reunited with Jones to work on B.A.D.'s second album. He pursued film work with director Alex Cox, writing "Love Kills," the theme song for *Sid & Nancy;* starring in *Straight to Hell* and contributing to the soundtrack; and scoring *Walker.* Forming the short-lived combo Latino Rockabilly War (including ex–Circle Jerk guitarist Zander Schloss), Strummer recorded the B side of the soundtrack for *Permanent Record,* a 1988 film about teen suicide. In 1988 Strummer toured as the rhythm guitarist for the Pogues [see entry]; he later produced their 1990 album, *Hell's Ditch,* and filled in for erstwhile frontman Shane MacGowan following its release. In 1989 he appeared in Jim Jarmusch's film *Mystery Train* and released the poorly received solo album *Earthquake Weather.*

Strummer was something of a recluse during the '90s but became somewhat more active as the decade wore on—and as ska-punk bands like Rancid and Sublime refocused attention on the Clash. In 1996 Strummer and Rat Scabies of the Damned formed Electric Dog House and contributed a track to the benefit album, *Generations I: A Punk Look at Human Rights.* Strummer also scored the music for the movie *Grosse Pointe Blank* and appeared on the animated TV show *South Park* and its *Chef Aid* soundtrack. In 1999 Strummer formed the Mescaleros and released *Rock Art and the X-Ray Style,* an album that fused hip-hop, dub, punk, and rockabilly and featured reggae star Horace Andy on one track. The follow-up, *Global A Go-Go,* continued in the same vein.

Simonon formed the roots-oriented Havana 3 A.M. with longtime L.A. scenester Gary Myrick; they recorded one album. He has mostly pursued his painting since the band's demise. Headon released a solo album in England in 1987 but later that year was sentenced by a London court to 15 months in jail for supplying heroin to a friend who died of an overdose.

The Story of the Clash, vol. 1 and *Clash on Broadway* compiled Clash songs. In 1991 the Clash had their biggest British hit ever when "Should I Stay or Should I Go" was released, after being featured in a Levi's commercial. It went to #1 in the U.K. In 1998 Strummer oversaw the creation of *Burning London,* a Clash tribute album featuring covers of the band's songs by Rancid, Afghan Whigs, Ice Cube, Moby, and others. A much-anticipated live album drawn from the Clash's punk heyday surfaced the following year. On June 16, 2000, the band's best-known lineup—Strummer, Jones, Simonon, and Headon—were scheduled to reunite for the first time since 1985 to perform as part of a tribute to the late Ian Dury at London's Brixton Academy. However, Strummer withdrew less than two weeks before the tribute.

The Classics IV

Formed mid-1960s, Jacksonville, FL
J.R. Cobb (b. Feb. 5, 1944, Birmingham, AL), gtr.; Dennis Yost, voc.; Kim Venable, drums; Joe Wilson, bass; Wally Eaton, gtr. (– Wilson; + Dean Daughtry [b. Sep. 8, 1946, Kinston, AL], bass).
1975—*The Very Best of Classics IV* (United Artists).

The Classics IV made several major soft-pop hits, including "Spooky" (#3, 1968), "Stormy" (#5, 1968), and "Traces" (#2, 1969), featuring lead vocalist Dennis Yost. J.R. Cobb, producer/writer Buddy Buie, and Dean Daughtry went on to studio work and in 1974 formed the Atlanta Rhythm Section [see entry].

Johnny Clegg

Born Oct. 31, 1953, Rochdale, Eng.
With Juluka, formed 1976, Johannesburg, S.A.: Clegg, gtr., voc.; Sipho Mchunu (b. 1951, Kuanskop, S.A.), voc., gtr., perc.
1979—*Universal Men* (Priority) 1981—*African Litany* (+ Gary Van Zyl [b. Riversdale, S.A.], bass; + Scorpion Madondo [b. S.A.], sax, flute) 1982—*Ubhule Bemvelo* 1983—*Scatterlings* (Warner Bros.) (+ Derek De Beer [b. S.A.], drums; + Cyril Mnculwane [b. S.A.], kybds.; + Glenda Millar, kybds.) *Work for All* 1984—*Musa Ukungilandela; The International Tracks; Stand Your Ground* 1986—*The Good Hope Concerts* 1991—*The Best of Juluka* (Rhythm Safari) 1996—*A Johnny Clegg & Juluka Collection* (Putumayo).
With Savuka, formed 1986, Johannesburg, S.A.: Clegg, gtr., voc.; Dudu Zulu (b. Mntowaziwayo Ndlovu, Dec. 25, 1957, S.A.; d. May 4, 1992, S.A.), voc., perc.; De Beer, drums; Keith Hutchinson (b. S.A.), kybds., sax, voc.; Solly Letwaba (b. S.A.), bass; Steve Mavuso (b. S.A.), kybds., voc.; Mandisa Dlanga (b. S.A.), voc.
1987—*Third World Child* (Capitol) 1988—*Shadow Man* 1990—*Cruel, Crazy, Beautiful World* (– Zulu; – Dlanga) 1993—*Heat, Dust & Dreams* 1994—*In My African Dream* (Rhythm Safari) 2000—*Anthology* (Valley Entertainment).

One of the most politically charged "world music" artists to emerge from Africa in the '80s, Johnny Clegg fell so deeply in love with Zulu tribal culture that he not only fused it with Western-based music, he actually became an honorary Zulu tribesman. He was arrested and harassed for flouting South Africa's apartheid system to play music with blacks, yet managed to garner international acclaim.

Clegg took after both of his parents: his mother was a cabaret singer and his father was a journalist who admired black culture and abhorred apartheid. Born in England, he moved with his family to South Africa at the age of six. As a teenager, Clegg was frequently arrested for hanging out in Zulu bars, listening to the music he preferred. He later lectured on Zulu anthropology at the University of the Witwatersrand in Johannesburg.

He left academic life in the mid-'70s to pursue a career in music. In Johannesburg he befriended migrant gardener/street musician Sipho Mchunu, who taught him traditional Zulu music. The two formed a duo, Johnny and Sipho, which was renamed Juluka (Zulu for "sweat"), and played *mbaqanga* music with political lyrics, gradually integrating Western funk, soul, and reggae elements. Juluka gained a large, interracial South African audience and found some success internationally, especially with 1983's *Scatterlings*. After Mchunu returned to his family's farm in Zululand in 1985, Clegg formed a fully electric, more rock-oriented update of Juluka, called Savuka (Zulu for "we have arisen"), which included Juluka drummer Derek De Beer. Ironically, Clegg was expelled from the musicians union in his native Britain for performing in South Africa.

Despite its never having had a U.S. hit single, Savuka enjoyed a high enough international profile to be invited on the 1988 Amnesty International Conspiracy of Hope Tour, with Bruce Springsteen, Sting, Peter Gabriel, and others. *Cruel, Crazy, Beautiful World* (1990) included songs inspired by the assassination of Clegg's friend, antiapartheid activist David Webster. In 1992 Savuka percussionist Dudu Zulu—with whom Clegg performed the acrobatic, crowd-pleasing Zulu dances known as Indlamu—was murdered during factional warfare between different Zulu tribes. Clegg's next album, *Heat, Dust & Dreams*, featuring many non–South African guest musicians, included "The Crossing," a tribute to Dudu Zulu.

Juluka reunited in 1996 to perform at the National Festival of the Arts, South Africa's leading cultural event, and subsequently toured the U.S., newly incorporating hip-hop influences into its synthesis of sounds. The retrospective *A Johnny Clegg & Juluka Collection* was released that year. *Anthology* followed in 2000.

The Reverend James Cleveland

Born Dec. 23, 1932, Chicago, IL; died Feb. 9, 1991, Los Angeles, CA
1961—*This Sunday in Person: James Cleveland With the Angelic Gospel Choir* (Savoy) 1962—*Rev. James Cleveland With the Angelic Choir, vol. 2* 1963—*Peace Be Still: Rev. James Cleveland and the Angelic Choir, vol. 3* 1968—*Songs of Dedication* 1970—*I Stood on the Banks of Jordan: Rev. James Cleveland With the Angelic Choir, vol. 4* 1973—*In the Ghetto: Rev. James Cleveland and the Southern California Community Choir; Give It to Me: Rev. James Cleveland and the Southern California Community Choir* 1978—*Tomorrow* (with the Charles Fold Singers) 1979—*Lord Let Me Be an Instrument: James Cleveland With the Charles Fold Singers, vol. 4* (with the Charles Fold Singers) 1980—*James Cleveland Sings With the World's Greatest Choirs* 1982—*It's a New Day; 20th Anniversary Album; Where Is Your Faith* 1983—*This Too Will Pass: James Cleveland, Charles Fold and the Charles Fold Singers* 1990—*Jesus Is the Best Thing That Ever Happened to Me* (with the Charles Fold Singers); *Touch Me* (with the Charles Fold Singers).

The Reverend Cleveland was a dominant force in gospel music, through numerous releases and the work of his Gospel Music Workshop Convention. As the leader of the Southern California Community Choir, Cleveland helped to expand the musical base of gospel music and to integrate jazz and pop rhythms and arrangements into spiritual material. The pop gospel of Andrae Crouch and Edwin Hawkins are offshoots of Cleveland's pioneering efforts. Cleveland's foghorn vocal style, ridiculed by some when he started singing in the '50s, earned him the title "Gospel's Louis Armstrong."

His recordings of "Peace Be Still," "Lord Remember Me," "Father, I Stretch My Hands to Thee," and "The Love of God" are gospel standards. His 1972 double-platinum album with Aretha Franklin, *Amazing Grace*, is interesting not just because of the music but for the fact that Franklin's father, the Reverend C.L. Franklin, gave the Reverend Cleveland the opportunity to arrange for Detroit's New Bethel Baptist Church choir when Cleveland was only 26. Cleveland also appeared on Elton John's *Blue Moves* LP in 1976. In 1968 Cleveland organized the interdenominational Gospel Music Workshop Convention, which brought together top gospel musicians with churchgoers and showcased new artists. In the early '80s the organization boasted over 25,000 members and 250 chapters; a decade later the membership had more than doubled. The GMWC played an important role in gaining exposure for gospel music outside churches. Cleveland died of heart failure in 1991.

Jimmy Cliff

Born James Chambers, Apr. 1, 1948, St. James, Jam.
1967—*Hard Road to Travel* (Island, U.K.) 1968—*Jimmy Cliff* 1970—*Wonderful World, Beautiful People* (A&M) 1971—*Another Cycle* (Island, U.K.) 1972—*The Harder They Come* soundtrack (with various artists) (Mango) 1973—*Unlimited* (Warner Bros.) 1974—*Struggling Man* (Island); *House of Exile* (EMI, U.K.); *Music Maker* (Warner Bros.) 1975—*Brave Warrior* (EMI, U.K.); *Follow My Mind* (Warner Bros.) 1976—*In Concert—The Best of Jimmy Cliff* 1978—*Give Thanx* 1980—*I Am the Living* 1981—*Give the People What They Want* 1982—*Special* (Columbia) 1984—*The Power and the Glory* 1985—*Cliff Hanger* 1988—*Hanging Fire; The Best of Jimmy Cliff* (Mango) 1990—*Images* (Cliff Sounds and Films) 1993—

Struggling Man (Mango) 1999—*The Ultimate Collection* (Hip-O); *Humanitarian* (Eureka).

As the star of the groundbreaking film *The Harder They Come* and its soundtrack album, Jimmy Cliff was one of the first reggae stars to be heard outside of Jamaica. Although he remains active and is popular in Europe and Africa, he never achieved the international stardom of Bob Marley. Like Ivan, the character he plays in *The Harder They Come*, Cliff left his country home for the city when he was barely a teenager. He arrived in Kingston in 1962; within the year he had recorded his first record, a single called "Daisy Got Me Crazy." In the following months he cut a half-dozen tracks for various disc jockeys to play over their "sound systems." In 1962 he had a hit produced by Leslie Kong, "Dearest Beverly." Cliff's second collaboration with Kong, "Hurricane Hattie," went to #1 on the island, followed by "My Lucky Day," "King of Kings," and "Miss Jamaica." As a vocalist for Byron Lee's Dragonaires, he toured the Americas in 1964; at the New York World's Fair, Cliff met Chris Blackwell of Island Records, who signed him and enticed him to move to London in 1965.

Cliff worked at first as a backup singer. By divesting himself of his Jamaican patois, assuming the style of a cosmopolitan and the repertoire of a jet-setting troubadour, he developed a following in France and Scandinavia, and in 1967 "Give and Take" hit the British charts. The following year he traveled to Brazil as Jamaica's representative at an international music festival. His song "Waterfall" won a festival prize and became a South American hit. "Wonderful World, Beautiful People" was an international bestseller in 1969, a Top 10 hit in the U.K., and one of the first reggae tunes widely heard outside of Jamaica.

Jimmy Cliff

In 1969 Desmond Dekker recorded Cliff's "The Song We Used to Sing." Cliff was best known at this time as a songwriter. (Bob Dylan described his "Vietnam" as "the best protest song ever written.") He wrote "You Can Get It If You Really Want" for Dekker, and the Pioneers had a hit with his "Let Your Yeah Be Yeah." Cliff returned to Jamaica at the end of 1969 and recorded "Many Rivers to Cross," which inspired Jamaican filmmaker Percy Henzell to offer him the lead in *The Harder They Come*.

After the film, Cliff became a major star in Europe, Africa, and Latin America. "Under the Sun, Moon and Stars," "Struggling Man," and "House of Exile" were international hits between 1973 and 1975. In the attempt to expand his following, he left Island in 1973, signing with EMI in the U.K. and Warner Bros. in the U.S. But instead of reaching new fans, he almost lost those he had. In Jamaica he was denounced for abandoning his musical, religious, and national roots.

A Muslim—Cliff converted from Rastafarianism in 1973—he is welcomed in Africa and the Middle East. African religion, culture, history, and music became recurrent themes in his songs and were the focus of a film he made in 1980, *Bongo Man*.

In 1982 Cliff switched labels (moving to Columbia) and returned to Jamaica. There he recorded *Special* (#186, 1982) and coheadlined the World Music Festival in an effort to win back his Jamaican fans. Cliff recorded parts of two albums, *The Power and the Glory* and *Cliff Hanger*, with Kool and the Gang, the latter winning the Grammy for Best Reggae Recording in 1985. That year Bruce Springsteen covered his song "Trapped" on the *USA for Africa* benefit album.

An appearance in the 1986 movie *Club Paradise*, with Robin Williams and Peter O'Toole, was accompanied by seven songs on the soundtrack, including "Seven Day Weekend," a duet with Elvis Costello. None of the above helped Cliff gain American listeners. He formed his own production company, Cliff Sounds and Films, in 1990 and released *Images* that year. *Humanitarian* (1999), which includes covers of the Beatles and Carole King, consists of synth-heavy sessions with such famed reggae players as Sly Dunbar, Judy Mowatt, and Ansel Collins. That year Cliff toured with the Dave Matthews Band.

Climax Blues Band

Formed 1968, Stafford, Eng.
Original lineup: Colin Richard Francis Cooper (b. Oct. 7, 1939, Stafford), sax, harmonica, clarinet, gtr., voc.; Peter John Haycock (b. Apr. 4, 1952, Stafford), gtr., voc.; Arthur Wood (b. Stafford), kybds.; Derek Holt (b. Jan. 26, 1949, Stafford), bass, gtr., kybds., voc.; George Newsome (b. Aug. 14, 1947, Stafford), drums, harmonica.
1968—*Climax Chicago Blues Band* (Sire, U.K.); *The Climax Blues Band Plays On* (Sire) 1970—*A Lot of Bottle* 1972—*Tightly Knit; Rich Man* 1973—*FM Live* 1974—*Sense of Direction* 1975—*Stamp Album* 1976—*Gold Plated* 1978—*Shine On* 1979—*Real to Reel* 1980—*Flying the Flag* (Warner Bros.)

1981—*Lucky for Some* 1983—*Sample and Hold* (Virgin) 1988—*Drastic Steps* (Clay, U.K.) 1995—*Blues From the Attic* (Griffin).

While its name reveals its British blues revival beginnings, the Climax Blues Band became a dependable AOR outfit that reached the Top 40 every few years, with a sound trademarked by shared lead vocals from Peter Haycock and Colin Cooper and Cooper's saxophone playing. The group toured Europe and North America frequently, taking time off to cut its annual album through the '70s. Since then it has released albums with decreasing frequency.

CBB recorded each of its first two albums in less than three days. At first, it was a derivative blues band distinguished mainly by its youthful lineup; Haycock was only 16 when the band got started. By 1973, when the group first received extensive FM radio airplay in the U.S. with "Rich Man," it had already moved toward pop songwriting and production. Climax's first U.S. tour that same year yielded *FM Live* (#37, 1973), recorded in New York during an Academy of Music concert broadcast over WNEW-FM. Its first self-produced album, *Gold Plated,* became CBB's biggest seller on the strength of "Couldn't Get It Right" (#3, 1977), and 1980's *Flying the Flag* featured the MOR ballad "I Love You" (#12, 1981). By the time of 1983's *Sample and Hold,* the group's name was carried by Haycock, Cooper, and keyboardist George Glover, along with studio musicians.

Through its lengthy tenure, the group (in which Cooper is presently the only original member) has kept a low profile and a reputation for professionalism and a good live act. In 1997 a former CBB keyboardist, Peter Filleul, organized a free concert on the Caribbean island of Montserrat, the volcano-devastated U.K. colony. The gig, which coincided with a big-name benefit in London, featured several original CBB alumni.

Patsy Cline

Born Virginia Patterson Hensley, Sep. 8, 1932, Winchester, VA; died Mar. 5, 1963, Camden, TN
1973—*Greatest Hits* (MCA) 1989—*Walkin' Dreams: Her First Recordings, vol. 1* (Rhino); *Hungry for Love: Her First Recordings, vol. 2; Rockin' Side: Her First Recordings, vol. 3* 1991—*The Patsy Cline Collection* (MCA) 1993—*Walkin' After Midnight* (Rhino) 1994—*The Patsy Cline Classics Collection* (Curb) 1996—*The Birth of a Star* (Razor & Tie) 1997—*Live at the Cimarron Ballroom* (MCA Nashville).

Country singer Patsy Cline's career was in full swing, with pop Top 40 hits and national concert tours, when she was killed in a plane crash at the age of 30. Her honeyed soprano has been emulated not only by country singers like Loretta Lynn and Dolly Parton but also by pop singers like Linda Ronstadt.

Cline took up the piano at age eight but didn't begin singing until her teens. In 1948 she won a trip to Nashville through an audition; nine years later she appeared on TV on *Arthur Godfrey's Talent Scouts* and was spotted by Owen Bradley of Decca Records. Her first record, "Walkin' After Midnight," was both a country hit (#3) and a pop hit (#12) in 1957.

She was soon one of country music's biggest stars. Despite her numerous country hits, she sought a broader audience and refused to be saddled with a hillbilly or cowgirl image. Under Bradley's direction, she came to embody the smooth, sophisticated new Nashville sound. "I Fall to Pieces" was a pop hit (#12) in 1961, followed later that year by "Crazy" (#9 pop, #2 country), a song written by a then little-known writer named Willie Nelson. She had another pop Top 20 hit with "She's Got You" (#14) in 1962.

On March 5, 1963, Cline was returning from a Kansas City, Missouri, show when the single-engine plane her manager was piloting crashed. Over 25,000 people attended her funeral. In 1973 Cline became the first woman solo artist elected to the Country Music Hall of Fame. Actress Jessica Lange played the singer in the 1985 biopic *Sweet Dreams;* its soundtrack climbed to #29 on the U.S. LP chart. Cline's memory remained alive in the '90s, thanks to a flood of reissues, box sets, unreleased live albums, anthologies, and radio-session compilations. At least five musical plays about the singer's life, including *A Closer Walk With Patsy Cline* and *Always . . . Patsy Cline,* were presented in North America and Europe. As of 1999, her *Greatest Hits* collection (MCA, 1973) had sold over 7 million copies.

George Clinton/Parliament/Funkadelic

Born July 22, 1940, Kannapolis, NC
1982—*Computer Games* (Capitol) 1983—*You Shouldn't-Nuf Bit Fish* 1985—*Some of My Best Jokes Are Friends* 1986—*R&B Skeletons in the Closet; The Best of George Clinton; The Mothership Connection (Live From Houston)* 1989—*The Cinderella Theory* (Paisley Park/Warner Bros.) 1993—*Hey Man . . . Smell My Finger* 1996—*T.A.P.O.A.F.O.M. [The Awesome Power of a Fully Operational Mothership]* (Sony/550); *Greatest Funkin' Hits* (Capitol) 1997—*Live and Kickin'* (Intersound) 1998—*Dope Dogs* (Dogone) 2000—*George Clinton's Greatest Hits* (The Right Stuff/Capitol).
Parliament (Clinton, voc.; Bernie Worrell [Apr. 19, 1944, NJ], kybds.; Bootsy Collins [b. William Collins, Oct. 26, 1951, Cincinnati, OH], bass; Eddie Hazel [b. Apr. 10, 1950], gtr.; Raymond "Tiki" Fulwood [b. May 23, 1944], drums; Gary Shider, gtr.; "Junie" Morrison, kybds.).
1970—*Osmium* (Invictus) 1974—*Up for the Down Stroke* (Casablanca) 1975—*Chocolate City* 1976—*Mothership Connection; The Clones of Dr. Funkenstein* 1977—*Live—P. Funk Earth Tour; Funkentelechy vs. the Placebo Syndrome* 1978—*Motor-Booty Affair* 1979—*Gloryhallastoopid (or Pin the Tale on the Funky)* 1980—*Trombipulation* 1984—*Parliament's Greatest Hits* 1996—*Live 1976–1993* (Sequel) 1997—*Early Years* (Deep Beats) 1999—*12" Collection & More* (PolyGram); *20th Century Masters—The Millennium Collection: The Best of Parliament; First Thang* (Fantasy).

Funkadelic: 1970—*Funkadelic* (Westbound); *Free Your Mind and Your Ass Will Follow* 1971—*Maggot Brain* 1972—*America Eats Its Young* 1973—*Cosmic Slop* 1974—*Standing on the Verge of Getting It On* 1975—*Let's Take It to the Stage; Funkadelic's Greatest Hits* 1976—*Tales of Kidd Funkadelic; Hardcore Jollies* (Warner Bros.) 1977—*Best of the Funkadelic Early Years* (Westbound) 1978—*One Nation Under a Groove* (Warner Bros.) 1979—*Uncle Jam Wants You* 1981—*Connections and Disconnections* (LAX); *The Electric Spanking of War Babies* (Warner Bros.).
P-Funk All-Stars: 1983—*Urban Dancefloor Guerrillas* (Uncle Jam/CBS Associated) 1995—*Hydraulic Funk.*
Incorporated Thang Band: 1988—*Lifestyles of the Roach and Famous* (Warner Bros.).

Since 1955, George Clinton (a.k.a. Dr. Funkenstein, a.k.a. the Maggot Overlord, a.k.a. Uncle Jam) has headed a loose aggregation of musicians known variously as "The Mothership Connection," his "Parliafunkadelicment Thang," or "P-Funk All-Stars." Composed of members of two main groups, Parliament and Funkadelic, and various offshoot bands, the organization made some of black pop's most adventurous—and often popular—music of the '70s. Since then, Clinton's zany presence was being felt in the music of a wide range of postdisco and postpunk artists, from Prince to Public Enemy, Dr. Dre, and the Red Hot Chili Peppers. Clinton's music mixes funk polyrhythms, psychedelic guitar, jazzy horns, vocal-group harmonies, and often scatological imagery. His lengthy concerts are unpredictable, characterized by extended, improvised jams, and sometimes compared in scope to those of the Grateful Dead. One of his many quotable mottoes is: "Free your ass and your mind will follow."

As a teenager in Plainfield, New Jersey, Clinton straightened hair working in a local barbershop, where he also founded a vocal group called the Parliaments. They struggled through the '50s and most of the '60s, by which time Clinton had moved to Detroit to work as a staff writer for Motown. In 1967 the Parliaments had a major hit with Clinton's "(I Wanna) Testify" (#20 pop, #3 R&B), a straight love song. The Parliaments' next charted single, "All Your Goodies Are Gone" (#21 R&B), suggested Clinton's future direction. Hanging out with Detroit hippies and listening to local hard-rock bands like the MC5 and the Stooges influenced Clinton's approach to music, and he began to contemplate making a radical change in the Parliaments' sound.

At the same time in 1967, a legal battle over the Parliament name ensued, so Clinton and the group's singers began recording with their backup band as Funkadelic for Westbound Records in 1968. After winning the lawsuit, Clinton would record Parliament (the "s" was dropped) and Funkadelic separately. Initially Parliament was more commercially oriented and Funkadelic more experimental and gritty, though as time went on these distinctions blurred.

Early Funkadelic albums built a cult audience. Parliament/Funkadelic concert appearances featured Clinton jumping out of a coffin, musicians running around in diapers, smoking marijuana, and simulating sex acts. On both Parliament and Funkadelic albums, Clinton wrote about the dark realities of funk—which he had elevated to a philosophy—utilizing negative imagery from the Process Church of Final Judgment and clear-eyed wit; he wrote for denizens of "Chocolate City" surrounded by "vanilla suburbs."

Parliament's 1974 hit on Casablanca, "Up for the Down Stroke" (#63 pop, #10 R&B), introduced Clinton's concepts to a wider audience and helped Funkadelic get signed to Warner Bros. Over the years, the group attracted top R&B instrumentalists, including bassist Bootsy Collins (ex–James Brown), guitarists Eddie Hazel and Gary Shider, keyboardist Bernie Worrell, keyboardist Junie Morrison (ex–Ohio Players), and reedmen Fred Wesley and Maceo Parker (ex–James Brown). Parliament's *Mothership Connection* and gold single "Tear the Roof Off the Sucker" (#15 pop, #5 R&B) made Clinton and company a major concert attraction. With a weird, lengthy stage show that included a spaceship descending onstage from a huge denim cap, the P-Funk crew rivaled Earth, Wind & Fire as black America's favorite band. From 1976 to 1981, Clinton's salesmanship and success landed recording contracts for many P-Funk offshoots: Bootsy's (Collins) Rubber Band [see Bootsy Collins entry], Eddie Hazel, the Horny Horns, Parlet, Bernie Worrell, the Brides of Funkenstein, Phillippe Wynne, Junie Morrison, and Zapp [see entry].

Parliament's "Flash Light" (#16 pop, #1 R&B)—in which Worrell introduced the synthesized bass lines later imitated by many funk and new-wave bands—and the platinum *Funkentelechy vs. the Placebo Syndrome* in 1977; "Aqua Boogie" (#1 R&B) in 1978; and Funkadelic's funk anthem "One Nation Under a Groove—Part I" (#28 pop, #1 R&B) in 1978 were Clinton's commercial peaks in the '70s.

Beginning in 1980, internal strife and legal problems temporarily sapped Clinton's P-Funk tribe of its energy and key performers. And while P-Funk's sound got absorbed into mainstream funk and hip-hop, Clinton's many projects became entangled. Drummer Jerome Brailey left P-Funk to start his own group, Mutiny, which pointedly devoted its first album to imprecations against the "Mamaship." Other ex-sidemen actually recorded as Funkadelic, although their album (the poorly received *Connections and Disconnections*) carried a sticker to the effect that Clinton was not involved. After Warner Bros. refused to release *The Electric Spanking of War Babies* (with guest Sly Stone) as a double album, Clinton cut it to a single LP and began proceedings to end his Warners contract. He recorded two singles, "Hydraulic Pump—Part I" and "One of Those Summers," with the P-Funk All-Stars on an independent label, Hump Records. Then he reemerged with a name that was not in litigation—his own—on a George Clinton solo album, *Computer Games* (1982), which included P-Funk's core members and the hit single "Atomic Dog" (#1 R&B, 1983).

In 1983 Clinton began a six-year sabbatical from the pop limelight, during which time his music showed up (both in spirit and as samples) in rap and hip-hop (as well as on albums of Clinton's collected works); "Atomic Dog" became

George Clinton

one of the most-requested dance-floor songs. In 1985 he produced the Red Hot Chili Peppers' second album, *Freaky Styley*. Clinton returned to music making in 1989 with *The Cinderella Theory* (featuring guests Chuck D and Flavor Flav) on Prince's Paisley Park label and regrouped the P-Funk All-Stars for concerts. In 1993 he and P-Funk performed at President Clinton's Youth Inaugural Ball. Later that year he released *Hey Man... Smell My Finger* (with an all-star lineup of guests including rappers Ice Cube and Yo-Yo and members of the Chili Peppers), and, though the album was not a commercial smash (peaking at #145), it appeared as though Clinton's career was back on the upswing. In the summer of 1994, he appeared on the Lollapalooza Tour. In 1997 the Parliament/Funkadelic conglomeration was inducted into the Rock and Roll Hall of Fame.

A followup album, *T.A.P.O.A.F.O.M. [The Awesome Power of a Fully Operational Mothership]*, reunited Clinton in the studio with Worrell, Collins, and other original P-Funk sidemen for the first time in more than a decade. The record peaked at #121 in 1996 and was followed that same year by *Greatest Funkin' Hits* (#138), which gathered modern remixes of his work and included such guests as Coolio, Digital Underground, and Ice Cube. Two years later Clinton returned with a concept album about dogs and the drug war called *Dope Dogs*.

The Clovers

Formed 1946, Washington, DC
Lineup ca. 1950: John "Buddy" Bailey (b. ca. 1930, Washington, DC; d. 1994), voc.; Matthew McQuater (d. Dec. 19, 2000), voc.; Harold "Hal" Lucas Jr. (b. ca. 1923; d. Jan. 6, 1994, Washington, DC), voc.; Harold Winley, bass voc.; Bill Harris (d. 1988), gtr. 1953—(– Bailey; + Charlie White [b. ca. 1930, Washington, DC; d. ca. late '90s], voc.) 1954—(– White; + Billy Mitchell, voc.).
1975—*Their Greatest Recordings—The Early Years* (Atco)
1991—*Down in the Alley* (Rhino); *The Best of the Clovers—Love Potion No. 9* (EMI).

Emerging out of the Washington, DC, area, the Clovers were the most successful R&B group of the '50s. They were an important force in the fusion of big-beat R&B with gospel-style vocals, which laid the groundwork for soul music a decade later. With the Top 30 success of "Love, Love, Love" in 1956, the Clovers became one of the first black vocal groups to arrive on the pop chart.

The group was formed in a Washington, DC, high school by Harold Lucas in the late '40s. Then known as the Four Clovers, they were singing at a local nightspot, the Rose Club, when they were discovered by record-store owner Lou Krefetz, who became their manager and got them a contract with Atlantic Records in 1950. By then the group's lineup had settled into that outlined above. Label president Ahmet Ertegun wrote their first of many R&B hits in 1951, including two R&B #1s, "Don't You Know I Love You" and "Fool, Fool, Fool." Through 1952 they continued their hitting streak with "One Mint Julep," "Ting-A-Ling," "Hey Miss Fannie," and "I Played the Fool." They were also a top draw at black nightclubs.

Their string of R&B hits continued through the early '50s with "Crawlin'," "Good Lovin' " (1953), "Lovey Dovey," "I've Got My Eyes on You," "Your Cash Ain't Nothing but Trash" (1954), "Blue Velvet" (later covered by Bobby Vinton), "Devil or Angel" (later covered by Bobby Vee), and "Nip Jip" (1955). In late 1952 Bailey joined the army; his replacement, Charles White, had sung with the Dominoes and the Checkers. In April 1954 he left for the Playboys, and Billy Mitchell replaced him. In 1956 the Clovers had another R&B hit with "From the Bottom of My Heart."

Ironically, however, the historic appearance of "Love, Love, Love" in the pop listings marked the beginning of the Clovers' commercial decline. After moving to United Artists in 1959, they had their last major hit with Leiber and Stoller's "Love Potion No. 9" (#23 R&B). In 1961 the group disbanded, and for a time two groups of Clovers (one led by Bailey and Winley, another by Lucas) and their innumerable variations performed and recorded through the years. Lucas had only stopped touring approximately two years before he died in early 1994. In 1988 he and the other founding members received the Rhythm & Blues Foundation's Pioneer Award.

The Coasters/The Robins

Formed 1955, Los Angeles, CA
Carl Gardner (b. Apr. 29, 1928, Tyler, TX), tenor voc.; Leon Hughes, tenor voc.; Billy Guy (b. June 20, 1936, Ittasca, TX), baritone voc.; Bobby Nunn (b. Sep. 20, 1925, Birmingham, AL; d. Nov. 5, 1986, Los Angeles), bass voc.
1956—*The Coasters* (Atco) (– Nunn; – Hughes; + Will "Dub"

Jones [b. May 14, 1928, Shreveport, LA; d. Jan. 16, 2000, Long Beach, CA], bass voc.; + Cornell, or Cornelius, Gunter [b. Nov. 14, 1938, Los Angeles; d. Feb. 26, 1990, Las Vegas, NV], tenor voc.) 1958—*Greatest Hits* 1959—*One by One* 1960—*Coast Along* 1961—(– Gunter; + Earl "Speedo" [also spelled "Speedoo"] Carroll [b. Nov. 2, 1937, New York, NY], tenor voc.) 1962—*Greatest Recordings* 1965—(– Jones; + Ronnie Bright [b. Oct. 18, 1938], tenor voc.; – Guy; + Jimmy Norman, baritone voc.) 1971—*Their Greatest Recordings—The Early Years* 1974—*On Broadway* (King) 1978—*20 Great Originals* (Atlantic) 1992—*50 Coastin' Classics: The Coasters Anthology* (Rhino/Atlantic) 1994—*The Very Best of the Coasters* (Rhino).

The Coasters' comic vocals plus the writing and production of Jerry Leiber and Mike Stoller resulted in a string of wisecracking doo-wop hits in the late '50s. They were among the first black singing groups to truly cross over and be considered a rock & roll act, and their catalogue includes not only their famous humorous hit singles but social protest (1959's "What About Us"), one of the first great rock anthems ("That Is Rock and Roll"), and a wealth of future cover hits for artists ranging from Elvis Presley ("Girls, Girls, Girls") to Leon Russell ("Young Blood").

The group originated in the late '40s as an L.A. vocal quartet, the Robins. Protégés of Johnny Otis, they recorded for Savoy Records, hitting #1 on the R&B chart in 1950 with "Double Crossing Blues," which featured Little Esther Phillips. They began their association with Leiber and Stoller when they moved from Crown Records to RCA in 1953. When Leiber and Stoller founded Spark Records in 1954, the Robins became the label's most successful act, hitting on the West Coast with "Riot in Cell Block No. 9," "Framed," "The Hatchet Man," and "Smokey Joe's Cafe." The latter song attracted Atlantic Records, which bought the Robins' catalogue in 1955 and contracted Leiber and Stoller as independent producers.

At that point the Robins split into two groups: Carl Gardner and Bobby Nunn stayed with Leiber and Stoller, while the other Robins went on to record for Whippet Records. Billy Guy and Leon Hughes joined Gardner and Nunn to become the Coasters (so-named because of their West Coast origins). Their first single, "Down in Mexico," made the R&B Top 10 in 1956. Its double-sided followup, "Searchin' " b/w "Young Blood," went to #1 on the R&B chart and #3 on the pop chart in 1957; it was the first of the Coasters' four gold records. The group, together with Leiber and Stoller, moved to New York. After yet another personnel change—the addition of Cornell (a.k.a. Cornelius) Gunter from the Flairs—the Coasters returned to the charts with "Yakety Yak" (#1, 1958), "Charlie Brown" (#2, 1959), "Along Came Jones" (#9, 1959), and "Poison Ivy" (#7, 1959). Their backup group often featured King Curtis on sax and Mickey Baker or Adolph Jacobs on guitar. By decade's end, the Coasters were America's most popular black rock & roll group.

Four more Coasters records made the Top 40 in 1960 and 1961, and (joined by Earl "Speedo" Carroll, formerly of the Cadillacs, and Ronnie Bright, the featured vocalist on Johnny Cymbal's "Mr. Bass Man") they continued to record for Atco until 1966. Their last chart appearance was in 1971, with a Leiber-and-Stoller reproduced "Love Potion No. 9" (#76). They last worked with Leiber and Stoller in 1973, and in 1976 they released their last single, a version of "If I Had a Hammer." Since then, Nunn, Gardner, and Hughes individually, and Guy and Jones together, at one time or another all led groups billed as the Coasters.

In 1988 Gardner, Guy, Jones, and Gunter (with Tom Palmer) performed at the Atlantic Records' 40th-anniversary concert in New York City. In 1987 the Coasters were inducted into the Rock and Roll Hall of Fame. Gunter was murdered in Las Vegas in early 1990. Ten years earlier, latter-day member Nathaniel Wilson disappeared from Las Vegas; his dismembered body was recovered in California a month later. Nunn died of a heart attack in 1986.

Billy Cobham

Born May 16, 1944, Panama
1973—*Spectrum* (Atlantic) 1974—*Shabazz; Crosswinds; Total Eclipse* 1975—*A Funky Thide of Sings* 1976—*Life and Times* 1977—*Alivemutherforya* (Columbia); *Magic; Inner Conflicts* (Atlantic); *Simplicity of Expression* (Columbia) 1979—*B.C.* 1980—*Cobham Meets Richard Davis* (Tobacco Road); *Flight Time* (Inakustik); *The Best of Billy Cobham* (Columbia) 1981—*Stratus* (Inakustik) 1982—*Smokin'* (Elektra); *Observations; Observatory* 1985—*Consortium* (MOOD); *Warning* (GRP) 1986—*Power Play* 1987—*Picture This* 1988—*Billy's Best Hits* 1990—*No Filters* (Tiptoe) 1993—*The Traveler* (Evidence) 1996—*Incoming* (Musidisc) 1997—*Paradox* (Tiptoe) 1998—*Mississippi Nights Live* (Wenlock); *Billy Cobham/George Duke Live* (Atlantic) 1999—*Focused* (Cleopatra); *By Design; Nordic.*

Recording with Miles Davis and then starring with the Mahavishnu Orchestra in the '70s, drummer Billy Cobham was a key figure in the development of jazz-rock fusion.

Learning to play the timbales by age three, Cobham moved with his mother from Panama to New York when he was about seven to join his pianist father. In 1959 he enrolled at the High School of Music and Art. After serving in the armed forces, he worked in the city's jazz circles, playing with the Billy Taylor Trio and the New York Jazz Sextet in the late '60s. In 1968 he earned his first session credit, George Benson's *Giblet Gravy,* followed by two albums with Horace Silver. He has since played on numerous recordings, backing James Brown, Quincy Jones, Carlos Santana, Carly Simon, Sam and Dave, and Larry Coryell, among others. In 1969, after stints with Stanley Turrentine and Kenny Burrell, he joined the Miles Davis band that virtually invented jazz rock; ultimately, he played on eight Davis albums, including the landmark *Bitches Brew.* Concurrently, with Michael and Randy Brecker, he founded the jazz-rock group Dreams, which recorded two albums before disbanding in 1970.

In 1971 Cobham joined fellow Davis alumnus John McLaughlin in his Mahavishnu Orchestra, staying with the pioneering fusion group until the end of 1973 [see entry]. He then went solo, recording *Spectrum* with such guests as jazz bassist Ron Carter and saxophonist Joe Farrell and rock guitarist Tommy Bolin; the album and its two successors made the pop Top 40. In 1974 Cobham assembled a band called Spectrum including keyboardist George Duke, guitarist John Scofield (who later joined Miles Davis), and ex-Santana bassist Doug Rauch (later replaced by Alphonso Johnson). By 1976 the group had become the Billy Cobham–George Duke Band.

In 1979 and 1980 he worked extensively as part of Jack Bruce's band, followed by a year's stint with Grateful Dead guitarist Bob Weir's Midnites. In the mid-'70s he produced albums for Airto and pianist David Sancious. Throughout the decade Cobham's solo albums, either in a small-group format or with more extensive lineups, continued to mine the jazz-rock vein.

Cobham settled ultimately in Zurich, Switzerland, continuing to record solo projects during the '80s. Still an influential percussionist, Cobham found a new forum in the drum clinic. In the '90s he toured with ex–Dixie Dregs keyboardist T. Lavitz in Jazz Is Dead, an ensemble that specialized in jazz interpretations of Grateful Dead songs. Becoming a renowned lecturer about jazz, he also premiered, in 2000, a multimedia project: a DVD, recorded with the London Jazz Orchestra, that enables musicians to play along with Cobham compositions.

Eddie Cochran

Born Oct. 3, 1938, Oklahoma City, OK; died Apr. 17, 1960, London, Eng.
1960—*Eddie Cochran* (Liberty) 1962—*Cherished Memories; Memorial Album; Singing to My Baby* 1963—*Never to Be Forgotten* 1964—*My Way* 1970—*C'mon Everybody* (Sunset); *10th Anniversary Album* (Liberty) 1972—*Legendary Masters* (United Artists) 1990—*Greatest Hits* (Curb).

In his brief career, Eddie Cochran made a lasting imprint on rock with songs like "Summertime Blues." Born in Oklahoma, he was raised in Minnesota until 1949, when he moved with his family to Bell Gardens, California. By then he had taught himself to play blues guitar. He and guitarist Hank Cochran (no relation) began recording as the Cochran Brothers in 1955.

The following year Eddie and Hank split up, and Cochran began writing songs with Jerry Capeheart, whom he'd met while buying guitar strings at a local music shop. While the two were recording background music for a low-budget film, the producer, Boris Petroff, enlisted him to sing his song "Twenty Flight Rock" in another movie he was making: *The Girl Can't Help It,* with Jayne Mansfield. Liberty Records signed him soon after.

His first hit was 1957's "Sittin' in the Balcony" (#18). A year later Cochran and Capehart's good-humored anthem of teen boredom, "Summertime Blues," made the Top 10. It has since revisited the charts in versions by the Who and Blue Cheer. Two more hits, "C'mon Everybody" (#35, 1958) and "Somethin' Else" (#58, 1959), established him as a star, especially in England.

Cochran toured steadily, backed by the Kelly Four (bassist Connie Smith, who was later replaced by Dave Schrieber; drummer Gene Ridgio; and a series of pianists and saxophonists). He was an exceptionally talented guitarist, an energetic stage performer, and an early master of studio overdubbing; he played and sang all the parts on both "C'mon Everybody" and "Summertime Blues." Cochran was 21 when he died on April 17, 1960, in an auto accident en route to the London airport. His hit single at the time was "Three Steps to Heaven," which went to #1 in the U.K. Injured in the crash were Gene Vincent and Cochran's fiancée, Sharon Sheeley, cowriter of "Somethin' Else" and composer of Rick Nelson's 1958 #1 smash "Poor Little Fool." Cochran and Nelson both entered the Rock and Roll Hall of Fame posthumously in 1987.

Bruce Cockburn

Born May 27, 1945, Ottawa, Can.
1970—*Bruce Cockburn* (True North, Can.) 1971—*High Winds, White Sky* 1972—*Sunwheel Dance* 1973—*Night Vision* 1974—*Salt, Sun & Time* 1975—*Joy Will Find a Way* 1976—*In the Falling Dark* (Island) 1977—*Circles in the Stream* 1978—*Further Adventures Of* 1979—*Dancing in the Dragon's Jaws* (Millennium) 1980—*Humans* 1981—*Inner City Front; Mummy Dust* (or *Resumé*) (True North, Can.) 1983—*The Trouble With Normal* (Columbia) 1984—*Stealing Fire* (Gold Mountain) 1986—*World of Wonders* (MCA) 1987—*Waiting for a Miracle* (True North, Can.) 1989—*Big Circumstance* (Gold Castle) 1990—*Bruce Cockburn Live* (True North, Can.) 1991—*Nothing but a Burning Light* (Columbia) 1993—*Christmas* 1994—*Dart to the Heart* 1997—*The Charity of Night* (Rykodisc) 1998—*You Pay Your Money and You Take Your Chance—Live* EP 1999—*Breakfast in New Orleans, Dinner in Timbuktu.*

Singer/songwriter Bruce Cockburn has been a major star in his homeland since his debut album in 1970, garnering 10 Juno awards, two Canadian platinum records, and 13 gold. A virtuoso guitarist, Cockburn has progressed from folk-style songs to his own blend of jazz, reggae, and rock, and most recently Latin and Afro-pop. His lyrics have ranged from hippie-ish mysticism to openly fundamentalist Christianity, although Cockburn told *Musician* magazine in 1986: "Personally, I think the whole moral majority, hard-right, virulent anticommunist thinking that's centered around America First is pathological and dangerous. . . . [O]ne of the reasons I stopped making such a public issue of being a Christian has to do with not wanting to be identified with that version of fundamentalism." Since the mid-'80s, his work has become increasingly political.

In his late teens, Cockburn traveled through Europe as a street musician, then studied at Boston's Berklee School of Music for three years before returning to Ottawa to play the organ in a Top 40 cover band and harmonica in a blues band. He made his recording debut in 1970 as a soloist; his first two albums, *Bruce Cockburn* and *High Winds, White Sky,* were released in Canada on True North and appeared in the U.S. on Epic, but his next four appeared only in Canada. There he began to win wide acclaim. In 1976 he signed with Island and made forays into the U.S.; his first Millennium album included his first and, to date, only U.S. hit, "Wondering Where the Lions Are" (#21, 1980).

With 1980's *Humans,* Cockburn's work began focusing on political and humanitarian issues, inspired not only by his religious beliefs but by fact-finding trips to strife-torn areas around the globe. He is perhaps best known to U.S. audiences through his 1984 single "If I Had a Rocket Launcher," which, although it peaked at #88, was an oft-seen video on MTV. *Mummy Dust,* alternately titled *Resumé,* summed up his first 10 albums.

Cockburn remained faithful to his social and political activism through the '90s, and he performed at President Clinton's inauguration in 1993. But while critics applaud his eclecticism and craft, his albums have only rarely broken in the Top 100 in the U.S., where he is mostly known as a "musician's musician." Indeed, 1997's *The Charity of Night* featured an array of prestigious guests such as Bob Weir, Rob Wasserman, Ani DiFranco, Bonnie Raitt, and Maria Muldaur, while 1999's *Breakfast in New Orleans, Dinner in Timbuktu* included Lucinda Williams and Margo Timmins (of Cowboy Junkies).

Joe Cocker

Born John Robert Cocker, May 20, 1944, Sheffield, Eng.
1969—*With a Little Help From My Friends* (A&M); *Joe Cocker!* 1970—*Mad Dogs and Englishmen* 1972—*Joe Cocker* 1974—*I Can Stand a Little Rain* 1975—*Jamaica Say You Will* 1976—*Sting Ray; Live in L.A.* 1977—*Greatest Hits* 1978—*Luxury You Can Afford* 1982—*Sheffield Steel* (Island) 1984—*Civilized Man* (Capitol) 1986—*Cocker* 1987—*Unchain My Heart; Classics Volume 4* (A&M) 1989—*One Night of Sin* (Capitol) 1990—*Joe Cocker Live* 1992—*Night Calls* 1993—*The Best of Joe Cocker* 1994—*Have a Little Faith* (550 Music) 1995—*The Long Voyage Home* (A&M) 1996—*Organic* (550 Music) 1998—*Across From Midnight* (CMC International) 1999—*The Anthology* (A&M) 2000—*Best Of—The Millennium Collection; No Ordinary World* (Eagle).

British white-soul singer Joe Cocker parlayed Ray Charles–ish vocals and an eccentric stage presence into a string of late-'60s hits only to suffer from his excesses in drugs and alcohol by the mid-'70s. In the '80s and '90s, however, he went from tragic figure to well-respected interpreter, and his gritty, powerful voice remains one of the most distinctive in rock & roll.

Cocker attended Sheffield Central Technical School and worked as a gas fitter for the East Midlands Gas Board. In 1959 he joined his first group, the Cavaliers, playing drums and harmonica. He moved to lead vocals in 1961, and the band changed its name to Vance Arnold (Cocker) and the Avengers. They released regional singles and toured locally with the Hollies and the Rolling Stones. Decca offered Cocker a contract in 1964, and he took a six-month leave of absence from the gas company. Cocker's version of the Beatles' "I'll Cry Instead" (which he hated so much that he refused to sing it onstage) and an English tour opening for Manfred Mann were ignored, and he went back to his day job.

The following year Cocker and keyboardist Chris Stainton assembled the Grease Band with guitarists Henry McCullough and Alan Spenner and two other musicians. They played Motown covers in northern England pubs until 1967, when producer Denny Cordell became Cocker's manager and persuaded him and the band to move to London. A Cocker-Stainton song, "Marjorine," became a minor British hit, and after some exposure in London, Cocker and the Grease Band recorded *With a Little Help From My Friends* in 1968 with guests Jimmy Page, Steve Winwood, and others. The title track, one of many cover versions Cocker would record over his career, went to #1 in England and #68 in the U.S. His explosive performance of the song at Woodstock was a festival highlight, and his habit of wildly flailing his arms as he sang became as much a rock archetype as Pete Townshend's windmill. When Cocker sang Traffic's "Feelin' Alright" on *The Ed Sullivan Show* in 1969, the program's producer hid him behind a group of dancers—shades of Elvis Presley and his wiggling hips.

During the U.S. tour, Cocker met Leon Russell, who wrote "Delta Lady" and coproduced *Joe Cocker!,* the Grease Band's swan song. Russell also pulled together the assemblage of musicians, hangers-on, and animals for the boisterous Mad Dogs and Englishmen tour Cocker made in 1970, resulting in a #2 live double album that yielded a pair of hits—"The Letter" (#7, 1970) and "Cry Me a River" (#11, 1970)—and a film. But the tour left Cocker broke and ill. On a 1972 tour, with Stainton again leading the band, Cocker was often too drunk to remember lyrics and to hold down food, although material from that tour was released in 1976 as *Live in L.A.* Cocker toured Britain and then Australia, where he was arrested for possession of marijuana.

At the height of his troubles, Cocker had one of the biggest hits of his career, the achingly tender modern standard "You Are So Beautiful" (#5, 1975), written by Billy Preston. He recorded regularly throughout the '70s, but without much success. In 1976 he sang on TV's *Saturday Night Live,* with comedian John Belushi doing a deadly accurate parody behind him. Given Cocker's state at the time, it seemed more cruel than funny.

Cocker's career turned around in 1982. A duet with Jennifer Warnes, "Up Where We Belong," from the movie *An Officer and a Gentleman,* hit #1. Since then, several other Cocker songs have graced films, including his version of Randy Newman's "You Can Leave Your Hat On" (*9½ Weeks,* 1986) and "When the Night Comes" (*An Innocent Man,* 1990). The latter, a dramatic hard-rock ballad cowritten by Bryan Adams, hit #11 in 1990.

Cocker, who moved to Colorado in 1991, continues to

record and tour—sometimes accompanied by old friend Chris Stainton—and remains a popular live attraction in Europe. His 1994 album, *Have a Little Faith,* hit the U.K. Top 10, and at the request of his German label he revisited several songs from his own catalogue, including "You Are So Beautiful" and "Delta Lady," on 1996's Don Was–produced *Organic.*

Cocteau Twins

Formed 1981, Grangemouth, Scot.
Robin Guthrie (b. Jan. 4, 1962, Grangemouth), gtr., various instr.; Elizabeth Fraser (b. Aug. 29, 1963, Grangemouth), voc.; Will Heggie, bass.
1982—*Garlands* (4AD); *Lullabies* EP 1983—(– Heggie) *Head Over Heels; Peppermint Pig* EP; *Sunburst and Snowblind* EP 1984—(+ Simon Raymonde [b. Apr. 3, 1962, London, Eng.], bass, kybds.) *Pearly-Dewdrops' Drop* EP; *The Spangle Maker* EP; *Treasure* 1985—*Aikea-Guinea* EP; *Tiny Dynamine* EP; *Echoes in a Shallow Bay* EP 1986—(– Raymonde) *Victorialand* (+ Raymonde); *Love's Easy Tears* EP; *The Moon and the Melodies; The Pink Opaque* 1988—*Blue Bell Knoll* (4AD/Capitol) 1990—*Iceblink Luck* EP; *Heaven or Las Vegas* 1993—*Four-Calendar Café* (Capitol) 1995—*Otherness* EP; *Twinlights* EP 1996—*Milk & Kisses* 1999—*BBC Sessions* (Rykodisc).

One of contemporary pop's more distinctive and prolific acts, Cocteau Twins have maintained an avid cult following since the early '80s. While their singles have only occasionally entered the Top 40 in England (though they've topped the U.K.'s independent charts without fail), and have never done so in the U.S., the band is appreciated by many critics and progressive pop fans for its lush, dreamy sound, which centers on Elizabeth Fraser's ethereal vocals and composer/producer/multi-instrumentalist Robin Guthrie's inventive use of modern musical devices like tape loops, echo boxes, and drum machines. Fraser and Guthrie are partners outside the studio as well; longtime lovers, they had a daughter together in 1989.

The couple met in 1979, when Guthrie spotted Fraser dancing in a pub. At the time, he and bassist Will Heggie were forming a band, and after hearing Fraser sing, they recruited her, completing the Cocteaus' original lineup. In 1982 the trio signed with the British label 4AD and released its debut album, *Garlands,* which drew wide praise and attracted the interest of influential BBC Radio 1 DJ John Peel. Heggie quit the band soon afterward, though, leaving Fraser and Guthrie to record their second album, *Head Over Heels,* as a duo. Also in 1983 Guthrie and Fraser were involved in This Mortal Coil, for which they recorded Tim Buckley's "Song to the Siren" on the album *It'll End in Tears* (4AD).

The Twins became a threesome again later that year, with the addition of bassist Simon Raymonde (ex–Drowning Craze), who would eventually play an active role in writing, arranging, and producing the band's songs. He also participated in some of the 1983–84 sessions for This Mortal Coil. (Fraser also emerged as more of a creative contributor as time went on.) In the years that followed, Cocteau Twins put out several albums and/or EPs a year. They moved to Capitol for the 1993 release, *Four-Calendar Café,* which they supported in 1994 with their first world tour in four years. The group used a four-piece backing band for the first time and also made their debut appearance on U.S. television, performing on *The Tonight Show With Jay Leno.*

In 1995 Cocteau Twins issued a pair of EPs, *Twinlights,* a largely acoustic affair, and *Otherness,* which explored more ambient terrain. *Milk & Kisses* reprised some of the material from those two EPs and included lyrics drawn from Fraser's daily journal. The album is less impressionistic than much of the group's catalogue and is perhaps their most song-based effort to date. The trio also wrote a tune for the *Judge Dredd* soundtrack before calling it quits in 1996 (Fraser and Guthrie had already split up as a couple). Guthrie and Raymonde formed the Bella Union record label while Fraser went on to work with Massive Attack and Craig Armstrong and to sign a solo deal with the Blanco Y Negro label.

David Allan Coe

Born Sep. 6, 1939, Akron, OH
1970—*Penitentiary Blues* (SSS) 1974—*Mysterious Rhinestone Cowboy* (Columbia); *Mysterious Rhinestone Cowboy Rides Again* 1976—*Once Upon a Rhyme; Long-Haired Redneck* 1977—*David Allan Coe Rides Again; Tattoo* 1978—*The Family Album* 1979—*Human Emotions* 1980—*I've Got Something to Say* 1981—*Invictus Means Unconquered* 1982—*D.A.C.* 1983—*Castles in the Sand* 1984—*For the Record: The First 10 Years* 1989—*Crazy Daddy* 1990—*1990 Songs for Sale* (DAC) 1994—*Standing Too Close to the Flame; Granny's Off Her Rocker* 1996—*Living on the Edge* 1997—*Live! If That Ain't Country . . .* (Lucky Dog/Columbia) 1999—*Recommended for Airplay.*

Singer/songwriter David Allan Coe is the composer of country hits like Tanya Tucker's "Would You Lay With Me (in a Field of Stone)" and Johnny Paycheck's "Take This Job and Shove It." Coe's life is the stuff of outlaw legends. Orphaned at age nine, he was arrested the next year for stealing a car. After spending several years in an Ohio reformatory, he was released on parole, only to be arrested again for possession of obscene material (a comic book). He was sentenced to the Ohio State Correctional Facility. (He later falsely claimed to have fatally stabbed a fellow convict, for which he spent three months on death row before Ohio abolished the death penalty. None of it ever happened.) In the early '90s, without a record label, Coe admitted some regret over his past "outlaw" image.

By the time he was finally released in 1967, he had been writing songs for 14 years. Encouraged by fellow prisoner Screamin' Jay Hawkins, Coe pursued his music career and with singer Hugh X. Lewis' help met music publisher Audie Ashworth and producer Shelby Singleton, who helped get Coe a contract with his Plantation label; Coe later signed with Columbia. Coe's albums sold respectably through the

'70s and early '80s, though his greatest success has been as a songwriter of hits for other artists. In 1976 he was featured in a PBS documentary, *The Mysterious Rhinestone Cowboy,* so titled because of the mask Coe wore onstage in his early days. Only his 1983 album, *Castles in the Sand,* hit the pop chart, at #183, but he scored a #1 country hit with "The Ride" (about a singer's encounter with Hank Williams' ghost) and "Mona Lisa Lost Her Smile." He has also appeared in several films, among them *The Last Days of Frank and Jesse James* (with Willie Nelson, Waylon Jennings, Johnny Cash, and Kris Kristofferson).

Coe, who never stopped touring and recording even when he was without a record label, underwent a resurgence in the late '90s. He was signed to Sony's new alternative-country imprint and was embraced by a new generation of performers, who identified with his bad-boy image. In 2000 he opened Kid Rock's summer tour and collaborated with Dallas metal band Pantera. Coe ran into controversy again with the CD reissue of *Underground* and *Nothing Sacred,* a pair of X-rated albums brimming with racist, sexist, and homophobic material that he sold through biker magazines in the early '80s. Despite refusing to put his name on the CD, Coe sells it on his own Web site.

Leonard Cohen

Born Sep. 21, 1934, Montreal, Can.
1968—*Songs of Leonard Cohen* (Columbia) 1969—*Songs From a Room* 1971—*Songs of Love and Hate* 1972—*McCabe and Mrs. Miller* soundtrack (CBS) 1973—*Live Songs* (Columbia) 1974—*New Skin for the Old Ceremony* 1975—*Best of Leonard Cohen* 1977—*Death of a Ladies' Man* 1979—*Recent Songs* 1984—*Various Positions* (PVC) 1988—*I'm Your Man* (Columbia) 1992—*The Future* 1994—*Cohen Live* 1998—*Live Songs* (Sony International).

Singer/songwriter Leonard Cohen was a noted poet and novelist before turning to music in the '60s. His songs have been widely covered by Judy Collins ("Suzanne," "Famous Blue Raincoat") and Aaron Neville ("Bird on a Wire"), among others, and in Europe his aura of quasi-suicidal romantic despair has won him acclaim as an heir of Jacques Brel.

Cohen studied English literature at Montreal's McGill University and later at Columbia University in New York, and published his first book of poems, *Let Us Compare Mythologies,* in 1956. In 1957 he recited his poetry to jazz piano backup, Beat-style. Cohen tried and failed to sell songs in the late '50s, and continued to write poems as well as two novels, *The Favorite Game* (1963) and *Beautiful Losers* (1966).

He set some poems from his 1966 collection, *Parasites of Heaven,* to simple chord progressions; Judy Collins recorded one of them, "Suzanne," for her album *In My Life,* and she brought Cohen onstage at a 1967 Central Park concert. Cohen performed at the 1967 Newport Folk Festival, and his debut album came out early in 1968. Songs from that album later appeared on the soundtrack of Robert Altman's *McCabe and Mrs. Miller.*

After his second album, which included "Bird on a Wire" and "Famous Blue Raincoat," Cohen began extensive touring of the U.S. and Europe and appeared in 1970 at the Isle of Wight festival. Although he entertained Israeli troops in 1973, he cut back on touring after 1971's *Songs of Love and Hate.* Cohen lived on a Greek island in the mid-'70s and continued to write poems, prose, and songs. In 1976 he resumed touring, and in 1977 he collaborated with producer Phil Spector on *Death of a Ladies' Man,* which also included backing vocals by Bob Dylan. He pronounced the finished album mix a "catastrophe," and on *Recent Songs* he returned to a more conventional folk-pop style. *Various Positions* evinced Cohen's fascination with religious themes.

With Cohen's dry, flat baritone intoning his hard-bitten, topical poems over sleek, modern-sounding tracks, *I'm Your Man* suddenly made him hip and prompted a 1991 tribute album, *I'm Your Fan,* with Cohen songs recorded by such college-radio stars as R.E.M., Nick Cave, Lloyd Cole, and others. *The Future* has been Cohen's best-seller to date; its anthemic "Democracy" was performed by Don Henley at MTV's January 1993 Inaugural Ball for President-elect Bill Clinton. Two years later another tribute album, *Tower of Song: The Songs of Leonard Cohen,* featured versions of his compositions by Bono, Elton John, Willie Nelson, and others.

Cohen has published many other books, including *The Spice-Box of Earth* (1961), *Flowers for Hitler* (1964), *Selected Poems, 1956–1968* (1968), *The Energy of Slaves* (1972), *Death*

Leonard Cohen

of a Lady's Man (1978), *Book of Mercy* (1984), and *Stranger Music* (1993). His interest in film is strong, too: his 1984 short feature, "I Am a Hotel," received Academy Award consideration. A student of Buddhism since the early '70s, Cohen made his home between 1993 and mid-1999 in the Mount Baldy Zen Center, a monastery near L.A.

Marc Cohn

Born July 5, 1959, Cleveland, OH
1991—*Marc Cohn* (Atlantic) 1993—*The Rainy Season* 1998—*Burning the Daze.*

Singer/keyboardist Marc Cohn writes songs that fuse the influences of '60s soul music and '70s singer/songwriter pop. On the strength of his self-titled debut album, he earned the 1991 Grammy for Best New Artist.

Cohn grew up in Cleveland, where he listened to Van Morrison, Jackson Browne, James Taylor, and the Band. He taught himself to play the piano while attending Oberlin College and performed solo in L.A. clubs before moving to New York in the '80s and founding a 14-piece band, the Supreme Court. Discovered by Carly Simon, the blues-based outfit played at Caroline Kennedy's 1986 wedding but broke up after only five performances.

Cohn then began concentrating on songwriting, eventually landing a contract with Atlantic. Producing his own debut, he scored a #13 hit in 1991 with "Walking in Memphis," an homage to that city's blues players and its most famous former resident, Elvis Presley. The song was covered by numerous performers, among them Tom Jones. *The Rainy Season,* bluesier and more somber than its predecessor, featured David Crosby, Graham Nash, Bonnie Raitt, and Heartbreaker Benmont Tench. *Burning the Daze,* released after a five-year hiatus, again showcased thoughtful songwriting that provoked comparisons to the Band and Bruce Springsteen.

Natalie Cole

Born Feb. 6, 1950, Los Angeles, CA
1975—*Inseparable* (Capitol) 1976—*Natalie* 1977—*Thankful* 1978—*Natalie . . . Live!* 1979—*We're the Best of Friends* (with Peabo Bryson) 1980—*Don't Look Back* 1981—*Happy Love* 1983—*I'm Ready* (Epic) 1984—*The Natalie Cole Collection* (Capitol) 1985—*Dangerous* (Modern) 1987—*Everlasting* (Manhattan) 1989—*Good to Be Back* (EMI) 1991—*Unforgettable With Love* (Elektra) 1993—*Take a Look* 1994—*Holly & Ivy* 1996—*Stardust* 1999—*Snowfall on the Sahara; The Magic of Christmas* (with the London Symphony Orchestra) 2000—*Greatest Hits, vol. I.*

When Natalie Cole debuted in 1975, she was hailed as the next Aretha Franklin, and *Inseparable* brought her a gold record and two Grammys, including that year's Best New Artist. But by 1983 a decade-long drug problem forced her career into a downward spiral from which she did not reemerge commercially until 1987. An early-'90s "duet" with her late father (made possible by electronic editing) brought her biggest success yet.

The second of Nat "King" Cole's five children, Natalie grew up in the exclusive Hollywood enclave known as Hancock Park. Her father died of lung cancer when she was 15, and she moved east several years later to attend the University of Massachusetts at Amherst, where she began singing in local clubs with a group called Black Magic and earned a degree in child psychology. Although she was arrested for possession of heroin in Canada in 1973 and continued to have problems with alcohol and cocaine through the following decade, Cole launched an initially dazzling career. She met her first husband, songwriter Marvin Yancy (they married in 1976), when he and his partner Chuck Jackson coproduced *Inseparable.* Her critically acclaimed debut included "This Will Be" (#6 pop, #1 R&B, 1975) and "Inseparable" (#32 pop, #1 R&B, 1976).

She subsequently released a top-selling album nearly every year throughout the '70s and made consistent appearances on the singles chart: "Sophisticated Lady" (#25 pop, #1 R&B, 1976), "I've Got Love on My Mind" (#5 pop, #1 R&B, 1977), and "Our Love" (#10 pop, #1 R&B, 1978). In 1978 she hosted *The Natalie Cole Special* on prime-time TV. The next year she teamed up with Peabo Bryson for an album and two R&B Top 20 singles, "Gimme Some Time" and "What You Won't Do for Love." Despite her auspicious beginning and a strong run on the R&B chart, it would be about nine years before her next pop Top 20 hits: 1987's "Jump Start" (#13 pop, #2 R&B) and "I Live for Your Love" (#13 pop, #4 R&B), and a cover of Springsteen's "Pink Cadillac" (#5 pop, #9 R&B, 1988) from her first commercial comeback, *Everlasting* (#42, 1987). Two duets with Ray Parker Jr., "I Don't Think That a Man Should Sleep Alone" (#5 R&B) and "Over You" (#5 pop, #10 R&B), were also released in 1987. In 1989 she scored another hit with "Miss You Like Crazy" (#7) and married her second husband, Andre Fischer, a producer and former member of the group Rufus.

Cole, who spoke openly of growing up in her father's shadow and in 1983 appeared on Johnny Mathis' Cole tribute album *(Unforgettable—A Tribute to Nat "King" Cole),* swept the Grammy Awards in 1992 with her quintuple-platinum #1 album *Unforgettable With Love,* a tribute to her father. On it she not only recorded a number of his best-known songs but, in a feat of technical wizardry, produced a duet and video of her "singing with" him on the title track. (Hank Williams Jr. did the same thing in 1992 using old recordings of his father for "There's a Tear in My Bear.") That album garnered six Grammys, including Record of the Year, Album of the Year, and Song of the Year (for "Unforgettable").

In 1993 she made her acting debut in the acclaimed TV series *I'll Fly Away* and released *Take a Look,* another collection of pop standards from a range of artists, among them Billie Holiday, Carmen McRae, and her father. "Take a Look" from that album reached #68 in 1993 and earned her yet another Grammy, for Best Jazz Vocal Performance.

In 1996 the singer released another collection of standards, *Stardust* (#20 pop, #11 R&B), which included a new "collaboration" with her father on "When I Fall in Love." She returned to her pop and R&B roots with *Snowfall on the Sahara* (#163 pop, #64 R&B, 1999), cowriting the title track with Peter Wolf and covering Bob Dylan's "Gotta Serve Somebody." In the fall of 2000 Cole published her autobiography, *Angel on My Shoulder,* in which she frankly detailed her addiction to cocaine and heroin; she also played herself from age 35 on in the TV biopic *Livin' for Love: The Natalie Cole Story.*

Paula Cole

Born Apr. 5, 1968, Rockport, MA
1994—*Harbinger* (Imago) 1996—*This Fire* (Warner Bros.) 1999—*Amen.*

Singer, songwriter, and pianist Paula Cole gained fame as part of the Lilith Fair sisterhood of women musicians who topped the charts and packed arenas in the late '90s, bringing the singer/songwriter genre back into the pop spotlight after some 20 years in the wings. Cole's wry single about a failing marriage, "Where Have All the Cowboys Gone?" (#8, 1997), catapulted her to stardom and won the singer a Grammy for Best New Artist.

Raised in the small town of Rockport, Massachusetts, Cole played an active role in chorus and school musicals at an early age. By high school, the cheerleader, junior prom queen, and three-time class president excelled in academics and, with the blessings of her artist mother and biology professor father, attended the prestigious Berklee College of Music in Boston. There, suffering from depression, she began writing dark, introspective songs in a style influenced by arty singer/songwriters like Kate Bush. (One of those songs, "Bethlehem"—about growing up in repressed, upper-middle-class white culture—wound up on her debut album, *Harbinger.*)

After graduating from Berklee, Cole moved to San Francisco, continued writing songs at a furious pace, and in 1993 signed to Imago Records. Prior to its release, *Harbinger* landed in the hands of Peter Gabriel, who had worked with Kate Bush and liked Cole's album so much that he asked her to sing on his 1993–94 Secret World tour. Inspired by Gabriel's onstage dynamic, Cole began performing her own songs with a thespian's sense of gesture and movement.

In 1995, after Imago's demise, Cole moved to Warner Bros. and recorded her second album, *This Fire,* which she produced herself. Released in October 1996, the album yielded the 1997 single "Cowboys," which helped to finally propel the album to #20. By the time Cole appeared on the summer 1997 Lilith Fair Tour, her star had risen. Eventually selling 2 million copies, *This Fire* wound up with seven Grammy nominations (including one for Best Producer, the first time in Grammy history that a woman had been nominated for such). By early 1998, the album's second single, "I Don't Want to Wait," reached #11, helped along by its inclusion in the popular TV series *Dawson's Creek.*

In 1999 Cole returned with another self-produced album, *Amen* (#97), a more R&B-flavored recording, which sold only modestly.

Ornette Coleman

Born Mar. 19, 1930, Fort Worth, TX
1958—*Something Else!* (Contemporary) 1959—*Tomorrow Is the Question; Twins* (Atlantic); *The Shape of Jazz to Come; Change of the Century* 1960—*This Is Our Music; Free Jazz* 1961—*Jazzlore: Ornette Coleman, vol. 29; Ornette!; Ornette on Tenor* 1962—*Town Hall Concert* (Blue Note); *Town Hall Concert 1962* (ESP) 1965—*The Great London Concert* (Freedom); *At the Golden Circle, vols. 1 and 2* (Blue Note) 1966—*Empty Foxhole; Who's Crazy* (Affinity) 1967—*Saints and Soldiers* (RCA); *The Music of Ornette Coleman: Forms and . . .* (Bluebird) 1968—*New York Is Now!; Love Call* (Blue Note) 1969—*Crisis* (Impulse!); *Ornette at 12* 1970—*Friends and Neighbors* (Flying Dutchman); *The Art of the Improvisers* (Atlantic) 1971—*Science Fiction* (Columbia); *Broken Shadows* 1972—*Skies of America* 1976—*Body Meta* (Artist's House) 1977—*Dancing in Your Head* (Horizon); *Soapsuds, Soapsuds* 1979—*Of Human Feelings* (Antilles); *Broken Shadows* (Columbia) 1985—*Opening the Caravan of Dreams* (Caravan of Dreams); *Prime Design/Time Design* 1986—*Song X* (with Pat Metheny) (Geffen) 1987—*In All Languages* 1988—*Virgin Beauty* (CBS Portrait) 1993—*Beauty Is a Rare Thing* (Atlantic/Rhino) 1995—*Tone Dialing* (Harmolodic) 1996—*Colors: Live From Leipzig* (PolyGram); *Hidden Man; Three Women* (Harmolodic).

Ornette Coleman's bluesy, playful music revolutionized jazz in the '60s by ignoring regular harmonies and rhythms. In the '70s he formalized his "harmolodic" theory and applied it to rock instrumentation with his group, Prime Time, pioneering a powerful and increasingly influential jazz-rock-funk-ethnic-music fusion. In the late '90s, he enjoyed a considerable revival of interest.

Coleman taught himself to play alto sax in his early teens. At 16, he switched to tenor sax and began playing in R&B and jazz bands around the South. His unorthodox notions of music were already meeting resistance (he switched back to alto sax when three members of the audience in Baton Rouge threw his tenor sax over a cliff), and he got used to getting fired. In 1950 he wrote an unpublished book in which he theorized that melody "has nothing to do with harmony or chords or key centers."

In 1952 he went to L.A. with the Pee Wee Crayton Band. He returned to Fort Worth after Crayton fired him, then returned to L.A. in 1954. The L.A. jazz community ignored him for most of the decade. In 1958 he formed his first band with trumpeter Don Cherry, bassist Charlie Haden, and drummer Billy Higgins and established a mode of playing in which, as he explained, "no one player has the lead; anyone can come out with it at any time."

In 1959 the Coleman quartet went to New York, where their engagements and recordings developed the concept of "free jazz." For *Free Jazz,* a collective improvisation, Coleman employed a "double quartet" (drummers Higgins and Ed Blackwell, trumpeters Cherry and Freddie Hubbard, bassists Haden and Scott LaFaro, and reedmen Coleman and Eric Dolphy).

Coleman withdrew from the public between 1962 and 1965, during which time he taught himself to play the trumpet and violin. When he resumed performing, he introduced compositions for these instruments and for wind quintets, larger chamber orchestras, and vocalists. He rarely performed with a regular band, although he continued to collaborate with Haden, Cherry, Higgins, Blackwell, and tenor saxophonist Dewey Redman. (In the late '70s Cherry, Haden, Redman, and Blackwell formed Old and New Dreams, playing their own music and occasional new Coleman tunes.) He also played with saxophonist Pharoah Sanders, drummer Elvin Jones, and Yoko Ono, whose 1968 performance with Coleman's band is documented on her 1970 *Yoko Ono/Plastic Ono Band.*

A Guggenheim fellowship allowed him to compose *Skies of America,* a long work for orchestra that he debuted at 1972's Newport in New York Festival and recorded later that year with the London Symphony Orchestra. *Skies of America* introduced his theory of "harmolody," in which harmonies, rhythms, and melodies function independently.

Coleman went to Morocco in 1973 to record with the Master Musicians of Joujouka (a short selection was included on *Dancing in Your Head*), and in New York and Paris, he became interested in the guitar and electrified instruments and started working with guitarist James Blood Ulmer. He rehearsed a new band, Prime Time—electric guitarists Bern Nix and Charles Ellerbee, electric bassist Jamaaladeen Tacuma, and drummers Ronald Shannon Jackson and his son Denardo Coleman—for two years before recording *Dancing in Your Head* in Paris and introducing them at the 1977 Newport in New York Festival.

Prime Time's music incorporated rock and funk rhythms and melodic fragments that recall Joujouka and R&B among its harmolodic possibilities; Coleman stated that he considered it dance music. The band's instrumentation—especially in latter-day lineups—suggested a double rock band version of Coleman's double quintets. In the early '80s ex–Prime Time members Ulmer and Jackson started their own harmolodic rock-funk bands, and Coleman returned to public performances, touring the U.S. and Europe in 1982.

Song X, a 1986 collaboration with guitarist Pat Metheny (who had covered Coleman tunes on his own recordings), was a critical success; later that year the two men toured together with a band that included Charlie Haden, Jack DeJohnette, and Denardo Coleman. Denardo, who had made his recording debut with his father when he was 10, was now both a drummer in Ornette's band and his business manager.

In 1987—to celebrate the 30th anniversary of the formation of the original quartet—Coleman released *In All Languages,* pairing a reunited version of the 1957 acoustic group and a 1987 electric band both covering the same material. *Virgin Beauty* featured a guest appearance by Grateful Dead guitarist Jerry Garcia, a longtime Coleman admirer. Coleman participated in the formation of the Caravan of Dreams, an arts center that opened in his hometown of Fort Worth, Texas. An affiliated record label released Coleman's next few recordings.

Coleman continued writing for all manner of instrumentation and size; later editions of Prime Time mixed acoustic and electric instruments. In 1993 Coleman's monumental Atlantic recordings were released in an acclaimed CD box set, *Beauty Is a Rare Thing.*

In 1997 Coleman was inducted into the American Academy of Arts and Letters. Also that year New York's Lincoln Center hosted a festival of his work featuring a performance of *Skies of America* by the New York Philharmonic and the surviving members of Prime Time; concurrently, a long Coleman composition, "? Civilization," received its world premiere in Paris.

Albert Collins

Born Oct. 1, 1932, Leona, TX; died Nov. 24, 1993, Las Vegas, NV

1965—*The Cool Sound of Albert Collins* (TCF Hall) 1969—*Truckin' With Albert Collins* (Blue Thumb); *Love Can Be Found Anywhere (Even in a Guitar)* (Imperial); *Trash Talkin'* 1970—*The Complete Albert Collins* 1972—*There's Gotta Be a Change* (Tumbleweed) 1978—*Ice Pickin'* (Alligator) 1980—*Frostbite* 1981—*Frozen Alive!* 1983—*Don't Lose Your Cool* 1984—*Live in Japan* 1985—*Showdown!* (with Robert Cray and Johnny Copeland) 1986—*Cold Snap* 1991—*Iceman* (Pointblank/Charisma); *The Complete Imperial Recordings* (EMI) 1993—*Collins Mix* (Pointblank/Charisma).

Guitarist/singer/songwriter Albert Collins' hard-rocking Texas shuffle blues and his gregarious showmanship have made him one of the most popular contemporary bluesmen. Jimi Hendrix once called him "one of the best guitarists in the world," and six of his albums have been nominated for Grammy Awards; in 1986 *Showdown!,* recorded with Robert Cray (who had played in Collins' backing band) and Johnny Copeland, won for Best Traditional Blues Recording.

The son of sharecroppers, Collins grew up in rural Texas before moving to Houston's Third Ward ghetto at age nine. He studied the piano in school, and a cousin gave him a cheap electric guitar and taught him the unusual minor-key tuning that remains a distinctive aspect of his sound. Another cousin, Sam "Lightnin' " Hopkins, was a primary influence on his single-string guitar technique.

Collins began working the Houston blues-club circuit in 1948, playing with Clarence "Gatemouth" Brown. The following year he formed his own band, the Rhythm Rockers, and fronted them until 1951, when he joined Piney Brown's band. After leaving Brown in 1954, he became a pickup guitarist, performing and occasionally recording with Johnny "Guitar" Watson, Little Richard, and Willie Mae Thornton,

Albert Collins

among others. A 1958 session resulted in his first record, "The Freeze," an instrumental that introduced Collins' "cool sound"—the highly amplified, sustained treble notes of his guitar set against three horns, keyboard (piano or, more often, organ), bass, and drums. Over the next five years he recorded more than a dozen such instrumentals, including "Defrost," "Thaw-Out," "Sno-Cone," and "Hot 'n' Cold." Several were regional hits. "Frosty" reportedly sold a million copies in 1962 without placing on national charts.

Sometime around 1968, blues scholar Bob Hite of Canned Heat discovered Collins playing in a Houston lounge and brought him to the attention of Imperial Records, which awarded him a contract. Collins moved to L.A., where for the next two years he recorded three albums, produced by members of Canned Heat. These were also the first on which he sang. The Canned Heat connection attracted young, white blues fans, and Collins frequently played West Coast rock venues, including the Fillmore West.

In 1971 Collins was the first artist signed to producer Bill Szymczyk's Tumbleweed label, and there he recorded his sole charting R&B single, "Get Your Business Straight" (#46, 1972). But Tumbleweed folded two years later, and he did not record again until 1978. With his band the Icebreakers, he recorded *Ice Pickin'*, which was named Best Blues Album of 1979 by several American and European journals and nominated for a Grammy Award. From then on, through a series of releases on Alligator, he continued to rack up Grammy nominations and solidify his reputation as "the Master of the Telecaster." In the late '80s, he appeared to be on the verge of a mainstream breakthrough. At the insistence of George Thorogood, Collins appeared at Live Aid in Philadelphia in 1985. He appeared in a wine-cooler ad with blues-singing wanna-be Bruce Willis and had a cameo in the film *Adventures in Babysitting.*

Throughout his career Collins guested on albums by artists as diverse as David Bowie *(Labyrinth)*, John Lee Hooker *(Mr. Lucky; Boom, Boom)*, Branford Marsalis *(Super Models in Deep Conversation)*, and John Zorn *(Spillane)*. He received several W.C. Handy Awards as well. At 61, Collins died at his home of cancer.

Bootsy Collins

Born William Collins, Oct. 26, 1951, Cincinnati, OH
1976—*Stretchin' Out in Bootsy's Rubber Band* (Warner Bros.) 1977—*Ahh . . . the Name Is Bootsy, Baby!* 1978—*Bootsy? Player of the Year* 1979—*This Boot Is Made for Fonk-N* 1980—*Ultra Wave* 1982—*The One Giveth and the Count Taketh Away* 1988—*What's Bootsy Doin'?* (Columbia) 1990—*Jungle Bass* (Zillitron) 1994—*Back in the Day: The Best of Bootsy* (Warner Bros.); *Blasters of the Universe* (Rykodisc) 1995—*Keepin' Dah Funk "Alive" 4–1995* 1998—*Fresh Outta 'P' University* (Private I/WEA).
With Zillatron (Collins; Bernie Worrell, kybds.; Buckethead, gtr.): 1994—*Zillatron: Lord of the Harvest* (Rykodisc).

As Parliament-Funkadelic's bassist and songwriter, Collins has attracted a personal following to challenge George Clinton's. Already given to spontaneous reproduction, it was natural for P-Funk to spawn Bootsy's Rubber Band. While Bootsy's records have sold better than the parent group's, Collins continues to play with P-Funk on occasion, in addition to his work with other musicians [see George Clinton entry].

Collins worked as a session musician for King Records in his hometown of Cincinnati until James Brown recruited the 16-year-old and his group, the Pacemakers, into his JBs in 1969. Two years later Collins left Brown, and after doing sessions with the Spinners and Johnnie Taylor—and turning down the Spinners' invitation to join them—he joined P-Funk. He became Clinton's right-hand man, contributing music and lyrics to many of P-Funk's best-known songs and helping to formulate the band's doctrine of "silly seriousness." When Clinton negotiated Funkadelic's contract with Warner Bros. in 1976, a solo contract for Collins was part of the deal.

Collins put together Bootsy's Rubber Band from musicians outside the P-Funk family. Guitarist Phelps "Catfish" Collins (Bootsy's elder brother) and drummer Frankie "Kash" Waddy had been Pacemakers and JBs; saxophonist Maceo Parker and trombonist Fred Wesley had been JB stalwarts until Collins lured them to the Rubber Band; others had been members of the Complete Strangers, a Cincinnati band Collins had sponsored: singers Gary "Mudbone" Cooper, Leslyn Bailey, and Robert "Peanuts" Johnson; keyboardist Frederick "Flintstone" Allen (later replaced by Joel "Razor Sharp" Johnson); and trumpeters Rick Gardner and Richard "Kush" Griffith. The Rubber Band became part of P-Funk; its horn section, the Horny Horns, became an integral part of

Bootsy Collins

every P-Funk session; and Clinton brainchildren like the Brides of Funkenstein sang with the Rubber Band.

With Clinton collaborating with Collins on material and production, Bootsy's albums were very much in the P-Funk mold: irrepressibly rhythmic, ironic, at once earthy and spacey. The ostensible difference was in their intended audiences. While P-Funk was aimed at older teenage American youths, Bootsy wrote for the "geepies"—kids six to 12 years old who could respond to songs of Collins' alter egos like Casper the Friendly Ghost and Bootzilla. He advocated abstinence from drugs and liquor (if not prepubertal sex) and projected an aura of childlike optimism.

His second and third albums went gold (*Player of the Year* went to #16 pop and #1 R&B), and he had 10 R&B Top 30 singles in five years: "Stretchin' Out (in a Rubber Band)" (#18, 1976), "I'd Rather Be With You" (#25, 1976), "The Pinocchio Theory" (#6, 1977), "Can't Stay Away" (#19, 1977), "Bootzilla" (#1, 1978), "Hollywood Squares" (#17, 1978), "Jam Fan (Hot)" (#13, 1979), "Mug Push" (#25, 1980), "Take a Lickin' and Keep On Kickin' " (#29, 1982), and "Body Slam!" (#12, 1982).

Aside from his work with the Rubber Band and P-Funk, Collins has produced, arranged, and written songs for other acts. He arranged Johnnie Taylor's 1976 gold hit, "Disco Lady." He produced albums by Zapp and the Sweat Band in 1980 and by Godmoma in 1981. He has also collaborated on songs with Sly Stewart and James Brown. Collins was not heard from again for six years until *What's Bootsy Doin'?* (#58 R&B, 1988). In the interim he had recorded with an array of artists, including Keith Richards, Bill Laswell, the Last Poets, Buddy Miles, and Wilbert Longmire. He recorded and performed with Deee-Lite and appeared on the record and in the video for their hit "Groove Is in the Heart." In 1994 he appeared in Ice Cube's video for "Bop Gun."

The year 1994 also saw the release of three Bootsy albums (one a best-of) and what appeared to be a resurgence. Resplendent in his freaky wardrobe, Bootsy talked openly about the toll performing and drugs had taken before his hiatus. "I got so tired of living up to that Bootsy character," he told ROLLING STONE in 1994. "I'd become a so-called star, and I just didn't know how to handle it." In 1997 Collins was inducted into the Rock and Roll Hall of Fame as a member of Parliament-Funkadelic. The following year he released *Fresh Outta 'P' University,* which includes an appearance by rapper MC Lyte. Bootsy also appeared alongside his JBs and P-Funk brethren for an interactive "thrill ride" on funk music for Seattle's Experience Music Project (EMP) museum.

Judy Collins

Born May 1, 1939, Seattle, WA
1961—*A Maid of Constant Sorrow* (Elektra) 1962—*Golden Apples of the Sun* 1964—*Judy Collins #3; The Judy Collins Concert* 1965—*Judy Collins' Fifth Album* 1966—*In My Life* 1967—*Wildflowers* 1968—*Who Knows Where the Time Goes* 1969—*Recollections* 1970—*Whales and Nightingales; Living* 1972—*Colors of the Day: The Best of Judy Collins* 1973—*True Stories and Other Dreams* 1975—*Judith* 1976—*Bread and Roses* 1977—*So Early in Spring: The First Fifteen Years* 1979—*Hard Times for Lovers* 1980—*Running for My Life* 1982—*Times of Our Lives* 1984—*Home Again* 1985—*Amazing Grace* (Telstar) 1987—*Trust Your Heart* (Gold Castle) 1989—*Sanity and Grace; Innervoices* (with Richard Stolzman) (RCA) 1990—*Fires of Eden* (Columbia) 1993—*Judy Sings Dylan . . . Just Like a Woman* (Geffen) 1995—*Shameless* (Atlantic) 1997—*Forever . . . The Judy Collins Anthology* (Elektra); *Christmas at the Biltmore Estate* 1998—*Both Sides Now* (Intersound) 2000—*Live at Wolf Trap* (Wildflower); *All on a Wintry Night* 2001—*The Best of Judy Collins* (Rhino).

Judy Collins, who describes herself as an "interpretive singer," was a major force in '60s folk rock, and her cover versions provided exposure for such then-unknown songwriters as Joni Mitchell, Leonard Cohen, Sandy Denny, and Randy Newman. Her later repertoire incorporated show tunes, pop standards, and cabaret material. Collins' clear, unwavering soprano has been equally effective on "Both Sides Now" (#8, 1968) and "Send in the Clowns" (#36, 1975; #18, 1977).

Inspired by her father, Chuck Collins, a blind bandleader and radio personality in the Rocky Mountain area, she began classical piano training at five and made her public debut at 13 with the Denver Symphony. Collins attended college in Jacksonville, Illinois, and then the University of Colorado.

She became interested in traditional folk music and began playing regularly in local coffeehouses before moving to Chicago around 1960. By then she had married college lecturer Peter Taylor (they were divorced in 1966). Shortly after moving to Chicago, her debut album, *A Maid of Constant Sorrow,* was released.

She began steady club work and met politically conscious folksinger/songwriters with whom she frequently performed at civil rights rallies. Her later political concerns would include ecology, endangered species, and reproductive rights. *Judy Collins #3* and *The Judy Collins Concert* found her moving away from traditional ballads and focusing on protest material written by Bob Dylan, Tom Paxton, and Phil Ochs.

With *In My Life,* she abandoned the sparse production of her early folk-oriented efforts for the often idiosyncratic experiments of producer Joshua Rifkin, who later spurred the Scott Joplin revival with his piano ragtime recordings. On *Wildflowers,* she debuted as a songwriter. For the gold *Who Knows Where the Time Goes,* her backing ensemble included Stephen Stills on guitar. The alliance prompted a brief affair, which Stills later documented in the Crosby, Stills and Nash hit "Suite: Judy Blue Eyes."

In 1969 she played Solveig in the New York Shakespeare Festival's production of Ibsen's *Peer Gynt.* Two years later *Whales and Nightingales* went gold with a #15 single: an unaccompanied choral version of "Amazing Grace." In 1974 Collins codirected the documentary *Antonia: A Portrait of the Woman,* about a former music teacher turned conductor; it was nominated for an Academy Award.

In 1975 she released one of her best-selling LPs, *Judith,* which produced a major European hit, "Send in the Clowns" (from Stephen Sondheim's *A Little Night Music*). Despite the help of veteran producer Jerry Wexler, *Bread and Roses* did not go gold, and she maintained a very low profile for the next two and a half years. The title track of *Hard Times for Lovers* would be her last U.S. hit single (#66, 1979).

Collins published her autobiography, *Trust Your Heart,* in 1987, wherein she detailed her battle with alcoholism. (The singer's private life would be shaken again in 1992 when her son Clark, who also had alcohol problems, committed suicide.) Her previous book, *Amazing Grace,* concerned her experiences with spirituality. She recorded 1989's *Innervoices* with classical clarinetist Richard Stolzman. In 1992 presidential candidate Bill Clinton revealed that his daughter, Chelsea, was named for Collins' recording of "Chelsea Morning" and that her *Colors of the Day* was his favorite album of all time. Collins released an album of Bob Dylan songs in 1993. In 1995 she released an album and her first novel, both titled *Shameless* (some of the songs borrowed lines and characters from the novel). The 1997 anthology *Forever* included four new songs, one of which was a collaboration with the Gin Blossoms' Jesse Valenzuela. The year 1998 brought another volume of her autobiography, *Singing Lessons: A Memoir of Love, Loss, Hope, and Healing.* Collins, who maintains a regular touring schedule, has also started her own label, Wildflower.

Paul Collins: See the Beat

Phil Collins: See Genesis

Color Me Badd

Formed 1987, Oklahoma City, OK
Bryan Abrams (b. Nov. 16, 1969, Oklahoma City), voc.; Mark Calderon (b. Sep. 27, 1970, Oklahoma City), voc.; Sam Watters (b. July 23, 1970, Oklahoma City), voc.; Kevin "KT" Thornton (b. June 17, 1969, Oklahoma City), voc.
1991—*C.M.B.* (Giant) 1993—*Time and Chance* 1996—*Now & Forever* 1998—*Awakening* (Columbia).

Color Me Badd was part of an early-'90s revival of R&B vocal groups that also included Boyz II Men and En Vogue. The multiracial quartet's 1991 debut sold 4 million copies and spawned the racy hip-hop doo-wop hit "I Wanna Sex You Up" (#2).

All four members attended Northwest Classen High School in Oklahoma City, where they would sing the doo-wop featured in Levi's 501 Blues commercials filmed in the hallways between classes. In time, the group discovered the '60s R&B vocal harmonies of the Dells, the Temptations, and the Four Tops.

In 1987 Kool and the Gang's Robert Bell heard Color Me Badd and helped the group relocate to New York and find a manager. The quartet landed a deal with Giant Records in 1991 and released *C.M.B.,* which peaked at #3 and produced four additional hits: "I Adore Mi Amor" (#1, 1991), "All 4 Love" (#1, 1991), "Thinkin' Back" (#16, 1992), and "Slow Motion" (#18, 1992). Their sophomore release, *Time and Chance* (#56 pop, #20 R&B, 1993), produced by Jimmy Jam and Terry Lewis and DJ Pooh (Ice Cube), didn't bring the hits, with only the title track charting (#24 pop, #9 R&B, 1993). Likewise, their 1996 followup, *Now & Forever,* spawned only one hit, "The Earth, the Sun, the Rain" (#21 pop). The album was certainly a disappointment in the U.S. (#113 pop, #39 R&B), yet it strengthened CMB's following in Southeast Asia and Japan, where the album topped the charts.

The group's fourth album, *Awakening,* didn't even make the U.S. charts, although the single "Remember When" peaked at #48 pop. Nevertheless, Color Me Badd decided to share its "wealth" from the album to honor the victims of the 1995 bombing of the federal building in their hometown of Oklahoma City. The group recorded an alternate version of "Remember When" with local musicians and students and donated the proceeds to a memorial fund.

Shawn Colvin

Born Shawna Lee Colvin, Jan. 10, 1958, Vermillion, SD
1989—*Steady On* (Columbia) 1992—*Fat City* 1994—*Cover Girl* 1995—*Live '88* (Plump) 1996—*A Few Small Repairs*

(Columbia) 1998—*Holiday Songs and Lullabies* 2001—*Whole New You.*

When folk-pop artist Shawn Colvin made her recording debut in the late '80s, her graceful melodies, reflective lyrics, and achingly pure soprano led some critics to compare the singer/songwriter to her idol, Joni Mitchell. Fittingly, it was through the help of Suzanne Vega—another heir to Mitchell's cerebral tradition—that Colvin finally landed a major-label contract after years of impressing audiences on the Northeast U.S. club circuit. In 1996 Colvin finally reached mass success with the Grammy-winning *A Few Small Repairs.*

One of four children, Colvin taught herself to play her brother's guitar when she was 10. Though her inclination was toward folk music, the aspiring singer found herself dabbling in various genres in different regions; she played with a rock band in Illinois and a country-swing outfit in Texas, and did Springsteen covers in California. Eventually Colvin decided to follow her own muse. Settling in New York, she began performing in Greenwich Village, at first covering the work of other local folk artists. Then one of Colvin's own compositions, "I Don't Know Why," earned her an appearance at a folk revue at the Bottom Line, where Vega was also on the bill. The song proved popular with college radio stations in Boston. Meanwhile, Colvin collaborated on material with songwriter/guitarist John Leventhal, who became her romantic partner as well.

In the late '80s Vega enlisted Colvin for backup vocals on the single "Luka," which became Vega's breakthrough hit. Colvin toured Europe with Vega and secured her own deal with Columbia Records. Her debut, *Steady On,* was produced and cowritten by Leventhal, and included a support vocal from Vega. Despite peaking at only #111 on the pop chart, the album won Colvin a Grammy for Best Contemporary Folk Recording. Her second effort, *Fat City,* was recorded in the wake of a personal and professional estrangement from Leventhal. Produced by Larry Klein, the album featured guest appearances by Richard Thompson and Bruce Hornsby (she has toured with both), and Klein's then-wife, Joni Mitchell.

In 1993 Colvin married Thompson's tour manager, Simon Tassano, and the couple soon moved to Austin, Texas. For 1994's *Cover Girl,* Colvin recorded songs by Tom Waits, Bob Dylan, Sting, and others. The following year she and Tassano divorced, and Colvin began working on her next album of original material, with Leventhal back as her cowriter and producer. Released in 1996, *A Few Small Repairs* (#39) was a strong collection of songs about disillusionment. The first single, "Get Out of This House," was surprisingly upbeat and helped give the album its first round of critical attention. The single earned a Grammy nomination for Best Female Vocal Performance, while the disc was nominated for Album of the Year in 1997. The Grammy ceremony one year later marked a series of changes for Colvin professionally and personally: she had married Mario Erwin, an advertising photographer, the previous year; at 40, she was pregnant with her first child; and the same album's second single, the deceptively troubled character study "Sunny Came Home," won awards for both Record of the Year and Song of the Year. This made Colvin 1997's long-persevering success story. Not only was she a critics' darling, she was a hit with the public, too: "Sunny Came Home" was a Top 10 hit (#7, 1997) and reached #1 on the Adult Contemporary chart.

At the height of her popularity, Colvin worked throughout her pregnancy, embarking on a U.S. club tour and playing a few dates of Lilith Fair, as she also had the previous summer. Just weeks before her due date, she headed into the studio to record *Holiday Songs and Lullabies,* inspired by a book of lullabies illustrated by Maurice Sendak (of *Where the Wild Things Are* fame) she'd had as a child. The CD booklet featured some of Sendak's illustrations from the book. In July 1998 Colvin's daughter, Caledonia, was born. In early 2001 Colvin released the much-anticipated *Whole New You.*

Sean Combs

Born Nov. 4, 1969, New York, NY
1997—*No Way Out* (Bad Boy) 1999—*Forever* 2001—*The Saga Continues. . . .*

Sean Combs' rise in the world of rap could hardly have been more dramatic. After dropping out of college, he became the head of A&R at Uptown Records; in 1993 he was president of his own record company, Bad Boy Entertainment. From there Combs went on to become not only one of the biggest and most controversial producers, songwriters, and performers of the '90s, but also an insatiable entrepreneur and owner of, among other things, his own clothing line and film production company. His career was jeopardized, however, due to criminal proceedings brought against him surrounding a New York nightclub shooting in late 1999; his acquittal was followerd by Combs' announcement in March 2001 that he was changing his stage name from Puff Daddy to P. Diddy.

Combs first started promoting hip-hop events during the late '80s while attending Howard University in Washington, DC. Upon the recommendation of rapper Heavy D, Combs began interning at Uptown Records. After just a few months on the job, he became the label's director of A&R, producing records by R&B megastars Jodeci and Mary J. Blige [see entries]. Combs came under attack, though, when nine people were trampled at a benefit concert that he and Heavy D organized at the City College of New York in December 1991. An investigation into whether the two men failed to provide enough security for the overbooked event ensued, as did enough bad press to lead Uptown to fire Combs. A civil suit brought by a woman injured during the melee was later settled out of court.

By 1994, Combs was back on top after negotiating a deal with Arista Records to form Bad Boy Entertainment, installing himself as president and his mother, Janice, as owner. Combs then signed Craig Mack, the Notorious B.I.G. [see entry], and Faith Evans and produced gold or platinum records by each. Bad Boy was on its way to becoming one of the most prolific and successful urban music labels of the '90s. In the process, Combs also produced records by outside artists ranging from Mariah Carey and Aretha Franklin to TLC and Boyz II Men. Combs didn't just oversee the projects he produced; he performed on virtually all of them as well. In 1996 he won the ASCAP award for Songwriter of the Year.

Controversy, however, seemed to follow Combs wherever he went. His detractors claimed that the records he made diluted hip-hop by relying too heavily on rock and pop samples. Then West Coast rapper Tupac Shakur [see entry] accused Combs of involvement in a 1994 shooting in which he was injured. The fracas was an outgrowth of an ongoing rivalry pitting Shakur and Death Row Records owner Suge Knight against Combs and the Notorious B.I.G. (Shakur was gunned down by unidentified killers in 1996, and B.I.G. died in much the same way the following year.)

In 1997, recording under the name Puff Daddy, Combs released his long-awaited solo debut, *No Way Out* (#1 pop and R&B). The record went gold in its first week and has sold more than 7 million copies to date. It also produced several runaway hit singles, including "Can't Nobody Hold Me Down" (#1 pop and R&B, 1997) and "I'll Be Missing You" (#1 pop and R&B, 1997). The former featured rapper Ma$e and sampled "The Message" by Grandmaster Flash. The latter, a touching farewell to the Notorious B.I.G., included Faith Evans on backing vocals and sampled "Every Breath You Take" by the Police. In 1998 "I'll Be Missing You" also won a Grammy Award for Best Rap Performance by a Duo or Group, while *No Way Out* earned Combs the Grammy for Best Rap Album. Combs' followup, *Forever* (#2 pop, #1 R&B, 1999), found his limited skills as a rapper improving, yet it went only platinum, a major disappointment compared to its blockbuster predecessor.

Meanwhile, Combs found himself under suspicion again, this time over a December 27, 1999, altercation at a Manhattan club in which three people were shot and seriously injured. Combs and his girlfriend at the time, singer/actor Jennifer Lopez [see entry], as well as two members of Combs' entourage, were arrested over the incident. Authorities released Lopez, but Combs and his bodyguard were charged with criminal weapons possession, while Combs protégé Jamal "Shyne" Barrow faced charges of attempted murder. Combs was later indicted for bribery for allegedly offering his chauffeur $50,000 and jewelry to claim that the gun found in Combs' car the night of the shooting belonged to him. In March 2001 a New York Supreme Court jury found Combs and his bodyguard not guilty of all charges. Barrow was found not guilty of attempted murder and intentional assault but was convicted on counts of criminal possession of a weapon and assault. A few months after his announcement regarding his impending name change, Combs released *The Saga Continues . . .*, debuting at #2 on the pop chart, as P. Diddy and the Bad Boy Family.

Commander Cody and His Lost Planet Airmen

Formed 1967, Ann Arbor, MI
Commander Cody (b. George Frayne, July 19, 1944, Ann Arbor), voc., piano; John Tichy (b. St. Louis, MO), gtr., voc.; Andy Stein (b. New York, NY), fiddle, sax, trombone; Billy C. Farlow (b. Decatur, AL), voc., gtr.; Rick Higginbotham, gtr.; Stan Davis, pedal steel gtr.; Bill Kirchen (b. Ann Arbor), gtr., voc.
1971—(+ Lance Dickerson, drums; + Bruce Barlow, bass) *Lost in the Ozone* (Paramount) 1972—*Hot Licks, Cold Steel and Truckers Favorites* 1973—*Country Casanova* 1974—*Live From Deep in the Heart of Texas* 1975—*Commander Cody and His Lost Planet Airmen* (Warner Bros.); *Tales From the Ozone* 1976—*We've Got a Live One Here!* 1977—*Rock 'n' Roll Again* (Arista) 1978—*Flying Dreams* 1980—*Lose It Tonite* (Peter Pan) 1986—*Let's Rock* (Blind Pig) 1988—*Commander Cody Returns From Outer Space* (Edsel); *Sleazy Roadside Stories* (Relix Indie C&W) 1990—*Aces High; Too Much Fun—The Best of Commander Cody* (MCA) 1993—*Lost in Space* (Relix) 1994—*Worst Case Scenario* (Rounder) 1995—*Relix's Best Of* (Relix) 1996—*The Tour From Hell—1973* (Aim) 2000—*Live at Gilley's* (Q/Atlantic). 2000—(lineup: Frayne; Mark Emmerick, gtr.; Brad Higgins, pedal steel gtr.; Rick Mullen, bass; Steve Barbuto, drums).
Bill Kirchen solo: 1994—*Tombstone Every Mile* (Black Top) 1996—*Have Love, Will Travel* 1997—*Hot Rod Lincoln Live!* (Hightone) 1999—*Raise a Ruckus.*

Behind their hard-drinking, deep-toking image, Commander Cody's various bands have always played a virtuosic, revved-up assortment of boogie-woogie, Western swing, country, and rockabilly. Frayne grew up in Brooklyn and studied sculpture and painting at the University of Michigan; during summers he was a lifeguard at Long Island's Jones Beach, where he performed with an all-lifeguard band, Lorenzo Lightfoot A.C. and Blues Band. After graduating, Frayne and some college friends formed the Lost Planet Airmen, which played around the Michigan and Wisconsin area while Frayne taught art for a year at Wisconsin State University. Frayne christened his onstage persona after Commando Cody, Sky Marshal of the Universe, from a 1952 film, *The Lost Planet Airmen.*

When the band lineup stabilized, they moved to San Francisco in 1969 and earned a local following. Their debut album, *Lost in the Ozone,* mixed originals like "Seeds and Stems" and oldies, notably a hit remake of Tex Ritter's "Hot Rod Lincoln" (#9, 1972). The followup, *Hot Licks, Cold Steel and Truckers Favorites,* was recorded on four tracks for a mere $5,000. They toured through the early '70s and had two more minor novelty hits—"Beat Me Daddy Eight to the Bar" and Ritter's "Smoke Smoke Smoke"—before leaving Paramount to sign with Warner Bros.

The making of the band's Warners debut album was chronicled in Geoffrey Stokes' book *Starmaking Machinery.* The album included Cody's last U.S. hit, "Don't Let Go." After a 1976 European tour, the Airmen disbanded. The rhythm section of Lance Dickerson and Bruce Barlow joined Roger McGuinn's Thunderbyrd. Cody recorded two albums with singer Nicolette Larson, then toured backed by former band mate Bill Kirchen and his group the Moonlighters in 1979. Kirchen went on to gain a cult following for his solo endeavors, experiencing a renaissance of sorts in the mid-'90s as he became associated with the Americana genre. In addition to appearing on Nick Lowe's *Party of One* and *The Impossible Bird* albums and touring with him in 1995, Kirchen has released a string of critically acclaimed solo records.

Commander Cody, who moved back to New York state in 1997, continues to record and tour with an ever-changing lineup of Lost Planet Airmen. Frayne has also found acclaim as a painter; his art has been exhibited in galleries around the world, and he published some of his paintings in the 1979 book *StarArt*.

The Commodores/Lionel Richie

Formed 1968, Tuskegee, AL
Lionel Richie Jr. (b. June 20, 1949, Tuskegee), voc., piano; Milan Williams (b. 1949, MS), kybds., trombone, gtr.; Ronald LaPread (b. 1950, AL), bass, trumpet; Walter "Clyde" Orange (b. Dec. 9, 1946, FL), drums; William King Jr. (b. Jan. 29, 1949, AL), horns; Thomas McClary (b. 1950, FL), gtr.
1974—*Machine Gun* (Motown) 1975—*Caught in the Act; Movin' On* 1976—*Hot on the Tracks* 1977—*Commodores; Commodores Live* 1978—*Natural High; Greatest Hits; Platinum Tour* 1979—*Midnight Magic* 1980—*Heroes* 1981—*In the Pocket* 1982—*All the Great Hits* (– Richie) 1983—*Commodores Anthology* (+ James Dean "J.D." Nicholas [b. Apr. 11, 1952, Paddington, Eng.], voc., kybds.; – McClary) *Commodores 13* 1985—*Nightshift* 1986—(– LaPread) *United* (Polydor) 1988—*Rock Solid* (– Williams) 1992—*Commodores Hits, vol. I* (Commodore Records); *Commodores Hits, vol. II* 1993—*Commodores XX—No Tricks* 1995—*Anthology Series: The Best of the Commodores* (Motown) 1997—*Ultimate Collection; Commodores Live!*
Lionel Richie solo: 1982—*Lionel Richie* (Motown) 1983—*Can't Slow Down* 1986—*Dancing on the Ceiling* 1992—*Back to Front* 1996—*Louder Than Words* (Mercury) 1998—*Time* 2001—*Renaissance* (Island/Def Jam).

The Commodores began as a pop-and-funk sextet, a funky party band whose music was heavily influenced by Sly and the Family Stone and the Bar-Kays. During their second, most commercially successful phase, the Commodores became a popular ballad group led by singer/songwriter Lionel Richie. Following Richie's departure, the group began a third phase, marked by the Grammy-winning memorial tribute "Nightshift." In its latest incarnation, the group is a trio based around cofounders Walter Orange and William King and latter-day member James Dean "J.D." Nicholas.

The six original group members met at a Tuskegee Institute talent show when they were all freshmen. With drummer Walter Orange, the only one with prior professional experience, handling vocals, the group began performing as the Mystics. They later picked the name Commodores out of a dictionary by placing a finger on the page. In the summer of 1969 they traveled via van to Harlem, seeking summer employment. Soon after their arrival, their equipment was stolen, then sold back to them. Undaunted, they landed a gig at Small's Paradise, where they met a local businessman they knew, Benny Ashburn, who became their manager. They signed to Atlantic Records and released one single produced by Jerry "Swamp Dogg" Williams, which did not chart.

In 1971 the group signed to Motown and for the first two years worked as the opening act for the Jackson 5. Because the group refused to conform to the polished Motown style, the Commodores did not record until 1974, when they were teamed up with producer/arranger James Carmichael, who produced all their albums until 1983.

On the first three albums, the Commodores' sound was dominated by a hard funk, which inspired one reviewer to describe them as "black music's answer to heavy metal." The group had several early hits, including "Machine Gun" (#22 pop, #7 R&B, 1974), "I Feel Sanctified" (#75 pop, #12 R&B, 1974), "Slippery When Wet" (#19 pop, #1 R&B, 1975), "Fancy Dancer" (#39 pop, #9 R&B, 1977), and "Brick House" (#5 pop, #4 R&B, 1977). Although each of the group members wrote, Richie eventually became the Commodores' main songwriter, and by 1977 his ballads were taking center stage; "Just to Be Close to You," "Sweet Love," and "Easy" were all Top 10 pop hits.

By 1978, when the group appeared in the disco movie *Thank God It's Friday*, the Commodores were moving swiftly toward crossover pop stardom, largely on the strength of Richie tunes like "Three Times a Lady" (#1 pop, #1 R&B, 1978), a platinum single that firmly established the Commodores as the premier black pop group. "Sail On" and "Still" were Top 5 pop ballads in 1979.

The Commodores: Thomas McClary, Walter Orange, Ronald LaPread, Milan Williams, William King, Lionel Richie

Richie began to pursue outside projects. He wrote "Lady (You Bring Me Up)" (#8 pop, #5 R&B) and produced "Share Your Love" for Kenny Rogers. He also wrote and performed a duet with Diana Ross on another #1 hit, the title song from the movie *Endless Love.* In 1982 Richie released his solo debut, *Lionel Richie* (#3 pop, #1 R&B), featuring his Top 5 hit "Truly." Earlier that year Ashburn died of a heart attack in New Jersey, and Richie departed for a solo career. He was followed a year later by McClary. In the meantime James Dean "J.D." Nicholas came aboard, and two years later the group had a #3 pop, #1 R&B hit with Orange's tribute to Marvin Gaye and Jackie Wilson, "Nightshift." The song won a Grammy, but the Top 15 album of the same title was the Commodores' last of new material for Motown.

They moved to Polydor for two albums, but by then LaPread and Williams had departed, leaving the core membership of Orange, King, and Nicholas. The three cofounded Commodore Records and began releasing greatest-hits packages that featured Orange and Nicholas on all lead vocals. In the U.S. to date, the group has been awarded three platinum albums. Worldwide, the Commodores have sold over 40 million records.

In the meantime, Lionel Richie's spectacular solo success eclipsed even the Commodores at their commercial peak. His self-titled debut peaked at #3 on the pop chart and #1 R&B, followed a year later by the #1 *Can't Slow Down,* which won the 1984 Grammy for Album of the Year and contained the hit singles "All Night Long (All Night)" (#1 pop, #1 R&B, 1983), "Running With the Night" (#7 pop, #6 R&B, 1983), "Hello" (#1 pop and R&B, 1984), "Stuck on You" (#3 pop, #8 R&B, 1984), and "Penny Lover" (#8 pop and R&B, 1984). It was said to be the biggest-selling album in the history of Motown Records.

In 1985 Richie cowrote "We Are the World" with Michael Jackson, which was recorded for the benefit project USA for Africa, and the next year Richie won an Oscar for the #1 song "Say You, Say Me" from the film *White Nights.* The streak continued with his third solo effort, *Dancing on the Ceiling* (#1 pop, #6 R&B, 1986), which featured the #2 title track, "Love Will Conquer All" (#9 pop, #2 R&B, 1986), "Ballerina Girl" (#7 pop, #5 R&B, 1987), and "Se La" (#20 pop, #12 R&B, 1987). These three albums alone were certified for U.S. sales of over 18 million copies. In addition, Richie had strong followings in the U.K., Canada, and throughout Europe.

In the late '80s and early '90s Richie faced some hardships that put his recording career on hold, including a messy divorce, surgery to remove a polyp on his throat, and the death of his father. The singer rebounded in 1992 with *Back to Front* (#19 pop, #7 R&B), a greatest-hits package that included some of his work with the Commodores as well as brand-new songs such as "Do It to Me" (#21 pop, #1 R&B, 1992) and "My Destiny" (#56 R&B, 1992). After yet another break from recording, Richie reentered the pop, R&B, and Adult Contemporary charts with 1996's *Louder Than Words* (#28 pop, #15 R&B), which yielded "Don't Wanna Lose You" (#39 pop, #17 R&B) and "Ordinary Girl" (#101 pop, #76 R&B). He followed up *Louder Than Words* with 1998's *Time* (#152 pop, #77 R&B) and 2001's *Renaissance.* He has won a number of awards, including the Oscar and four Grammys.

Concrete Blonde

Formed 1981, Los Angeles, CA
Johnette Napolitano (b. Sep. 22, 1957, Hollywood, CA), voc., bass; Jim Mankey (b. May 23, 1955, PA), gtr.; Harry Rushakoff (b. Nov. 17, 1959, Chicago, IL), drums.
1986—*Concrete Blonde* (I.R.S.) 1989—*Free* (– Rushakoff; + Alan Bloch, bass) 1990—*Bloodletting* (– Bloch; + Paul Thompson [b. May 13, 1951, Jarrow, Eng.], drums) 1991—(– Thompson) 1992—(+ Rushakoff) *Walking in London* 1993—(+ Thompson) *Mexican Moon* 1996—*Recollection: The Best of Concrete Blonde* 1997—(– Rushakoff) *Concrete Blonde y Los Illegals* (Ark 21).

Concrete Blonde got its start playing the same early-'80s L.A. club circuit that spawned X, Wall of Voodoo, and the Go-Go's. Though Blonde took a while to settle on a record deal and didn't enjoy a successful single until 1990, it has ultimately proven among the most resilient bands to emerge from that L.A. scene. The lean rock textures and dark, edgy lyricism of Concrete Blonde's music may not have made its members household names, but it has earned the band an enduring level of credibility and respect among critics and fans.

Singer Johnette Napolitano met guitarist Jim Mankey while both were working at Leon Russell's L.A. studio. After Russell relocated to Nashville, Napolitano and Mankey began working on their own songs in a studio owned by Mankey's brother Earle (a founding member of the band Sparks, with whom Jim also played). Calling itself the Dreamers, the duo set out in search of a drummer and a bassist. By 1984 Napolitano herself had assumed bass duties. As Dream 6, the band released an EP on a French independent label that year (Capitol reissued the EP in 1993). Dream 6 was courted by several major labels, but its demands for complete artistic control put off many record company executives. Finally, in 1987, after signing to I.R.S. Records, Concrete Blonde—a name suggested by a fellow I.R.S. artist, R.E.M.'s Michael Stipe—released its debut album, with Harry Rushakoff on drums.

Ex–Roxy Music drummer Paul Thompson took over for Rushakoff on the band's sophomore album and on its third LP, *Bloodletting* (#49, 1990), which yielded a Top 20 hit with the lovelorn "Joey." Rushakoff reappeared on a less commercially successful fourth album, *Walking in London* (#73, 1991), and he and Thompson both played on *Mexican Moon* (#67, 1993). The album's "Heal It Up" became popular on "modern rock" radio formats, but in early 1994 Napolitano decided that she'd had enough and left the band, which resulted in its demise.

In 1995 Napolitano teamed with fellow punk veteran Holly Vincent to record an album titled *Vowel Movement,* on which both women played all the instruments and sang. The same year Napolitano formed a new band, Pretty & Twisted, with ex–Wall of Voodoo guitarist Marc Moreland and drummer Danny Montgomery; she produced the group's lone, self-titled album. She also recorded vocals for a track on the 1996 Heads album, a short-lived project by the three remaining members of Talking Heads [see entry], and toured with them, taking on David Byrne's parts on the band's older material.

In 1997 Napolitano reestablished her partnership with Mankey when the pair collaborated on an album with East L.A. bilingual rock group Los Illegals. The same year Napolitano produced an album for Maria Fatal, an L.A. Chicano band that then opened for her on solo club dates. She recorded a solo album, *The Sound of a Woman,* for Island Records in 1998, but when Island founder Chris Blackwell departed, the label dropped her from its roster and didn't release the disc. In 1999 Napolitano focused on studying Mexican art and began to showcase her work at galleries while still performing occasional live gigs.

Con Funk Shun

Formed 1968, Vallejo, CA
Michael Cooper, gtrs., perc., synth., voc.; Karl Fuller, trumpet, voc.; Paul Harrell, saxes, flute, voc.; Cedric Martin, bass, voc.; Louis McCall, drums, voc.; Felton Pilate, trombone, gtr., synth., voc.; Danny Thomas, kybds., voc.
1976—*Con Funk Shun* (Mercury) 1977—*Secrets* 1978—*Loveshine* 1979—*Candy* 1980—*Spirit of Love; Touch* 1981—*Con Funk Shun 7* 1982—*To the Max* 1983—*Fever* 1985—*Electric Lady* 1986—*Burnin' Love* 1992—*The Best of Con Funk Shun* 1996—*The Best of Con Funk Shun, vol. 2.*

This Memphis soul band had been together almost 10 years when it placed "Ffun" at the top of the national R&B chart in 1977. In 1968 high school classmates Michael Cooper and Louis McCall formed the group, calling it Project Soul, and established its current lineup within a year. In the early '70s Project Soul relocated to Memphis, backed the Stax Records group the Soul Children (and in that capacity appeared in the 1973 movie *Wattstax*), and contributed to other Stax sessions. In 1972 the group changed its name to Con Funk Shun. After several local hits on Memphis labels, Mercury signed it in 1976. Con Funk Shun made its first appearance on the R&B chart with "Sho Feels Good to Me" (#66) the following year.

The success of "Ffun" (#23) made *Secrets* the first of four gold albums. It was followed by the Top 20 R&B hits "Shake and Dance With Me" (#5 R&B, 1978), "Chase Me" (#4 R&B, 1979), "Got to Be Enough" (#8 R&B, 1980), "Too Tight" (#8 R&B, 1980), "Bad Lady" (#19 R&B, 1981), "Ms. Got-the-Body" (#15 R&B, 1983), "Baby, I'm Hooked (Right Into Your Love)" (#5 R&B, 1983), "Electric Lady" (#4 R&B, 1985), "I'm Leaving Baby" (#12 R&B, 1985), and "Burnin' Love" (#8 R&B, 1986). In 1987 after the release of *Burnin' Love,* Con Funk Shun disbanded. Cooper went on to a solo career, while Felton Pilate has worked with rapper Hammer.

Harry Connick Jr.

Born Sep. 11, 1967, New Orleans, LA
1978—*11* (Columbia) 1987—*Harry Connick Jr.* 1988—*20* 1989—*When Harry Met Sally . . .* soundtrack 1990—*We Are in Love; Lofty's Roach Soufflé* 1991—*Blue Light, Red Light* 1992—*25* 1993—*When My Heart Finds Christmas* 1994—*Imagination; She* 1995—*Whisper Your Name* 1995—*Star Turtle* 1996—*All of Me* 1997—*To See You* 1999—*Come by Me.*

A throwback to the prerock entertainment era, singer/pianist Harry Connick Jr. revives the elegance of classic American singers like Frank Sinatra. Flaunting his retro taste for Tin Pan Alley–style show business and jazz piano exotica, Connick garnered mixed critical reviews but took the country by storm in the late '80s.

The son of New Orleans' chief district attorney, five-year-old Harry played "The Star-Spangled Banner" at his father's inauguration. Due to his father's clout, Harry Jr. was able to attend nightclub performances while still a child. He became friendly with the legendary New Orleans pianist James Booker, who gave the boy lessons at home. As an adolescent, Connick studied at the New Orleans Center for the Creative Arts with Branford and Wynton Marsalis' father, Ellis. At age 11, Connick recorded his first album for Columbia.

Connick's 1987 eponymous album was an instrumental project that showcased his facility as a jazz and New Orleans–style pianist. Named for his age at the time of its release, *20* featured Connick's vocals on a few tracks. His amiable performance style, clean-cut looks, and reverence for the show-biz tradition of the '40s and '50s attracted media attention and fostered a growing cult following. Full-fledged stardom followed Connick's appearance on the soundtrack to the hit film *When Harry Met Sally. . . .* From this point on, Connick the singer and Connick the jazz pianist would be compartmentalized, with singing getting the lion's share of attention.

Mounting an extravagant tour in 1990, which saw him fronting a big band, Connick struck some as an incarnation of the young Sinatra, albeit without the undercurrent of arrogant menace. Singing in a light, self-consciously off-the-cuff manner reminiscent of Sinatra and Bobby Darin, playing New Orleans piano, and bounding about the stage and through the audience with tireless enthusiasm, Connick drew raves from critics and fans apparently starved for old-fashioned entertainment. But Connick wasn't peddling a nostalgia act. On *We Are in Love,* Connick wrote original songs; *Lofty's Roach Soufflé,* a jazz piano trio recording, contained Connick's instrumental compositions. For a nonrock act, Connick's sales are staggering: three of his albums have gone platinum, two others are gold.

Unsurprisingly, Connick began appearing in films, acquitting himself in featured roles (*Memphis Belle, Little Man Tate, Hope Floats,* the voice of the town beatnik in the children's animated *Iron Giant*). He also appeared on the 1990 Academy Awards telecast to sing the nominated theme from *The Godfather, Part III.* In 1993 his wholesome image was barely scratched after he was arrested at New York's Kennedy International Airport for trying to take a gun onto a plane; charges were later dismissed.

By the mid-'90s, Connick had established a career on many fronts—as film actor (a role in the blockbuster *Independence Day*), jazz aficionado (he founded his own Columbia-distributed label, Noptee), and recording artist idiosyncratic enough to veer from big band and funk to the conceptual novelty of *Star Turtle*, an album that featured the singer communing with a turtle from outer space. Neither the album nor Connick's concert incarnation as a rock star was warmly received. With subsequent albums, Connick returned to the swing and ballads he is best known for.

The Contours

Formed 1958, Detroit, MI
Billy Gordon, voc.; Billy Hoggs, voc.; Joe Billingslea, voc.; Sylvester Potts, voc.; Hubert Johnson (b. Jan. 14, 1941; d. July 11, 1981), voc.; Huey Davis, voc., gtr.
1981—*Do You Love Me?* (Motown) 1999—*The Very Best of the Contours.*

Hoarse screams over feverish dance beats characterized the Contours' string of hits in the mid-'60s. Originally a quartet formed in 1958 by Billy Gordon, Billy Hoggs, Joe Billingslea, and Sylvester Potts, the Contours were unknown even in their hometown of Detroit until joined by Hubert Johnson. He had them sing for his cousin Jackie Wilson, and in turn Wilson presented them to Motown owner Berry Gordy Jr. They cut their first record, "Whole Lotta Woman," in 1961; when it flopped, Gordy prepared to drop them. Wilson persuaded Gordy to give them another chance. That chance was a Gordy composition, "Do You Love Me?"—originally intended for the Temptations—which the Contours took to the top of the R&B chart in 1962 (#3 pop). The song was later covered many times, notably by the Dave Clark Five.

While the Contours never repeated the success of the million-selling "Do You Love Me?" they did follow it with five more clear-the-floor-'cause-I-gotta-dance numbers: "Shake Sherry" (#21 R&B, 1963), "Can You Jerk Like Me?" (#15 R&B, 1965), "The Day When She Needed Me" (#37 R&B, 1965), "First I Look at the Purse" (#12 R&B, 1965), and "Just a Little Misunderstanding" (#18 R&B, 1966). Their last chart hit, "It's So Hard Being a Loser" (#35 R&B, 1967), was a ballad. One later member of the Contours was future Temptation Dennis Edwards.

In 1988 "Do You Love Me?" reached #11 after being featured in the film *Dirty Dancing*. The Contours, who include originals members Billingslea and Potts (Johnson committed suicide in 1981), joined the subsequent *Dirty Dancing* tour. They continue to perform.

Ry Cooder

Born Ryland Peter Cooder, Mar. 15, 1947, Los Angeles, CA
1970—*Ry Cooder* (Reprise) 1972—*Into the Purple Valley; Boomer's Story* 1974—*Paradise and Lunch* 1976—*Chicken Skin Music* 1977—*Showtime* (Warner Bros.) 1978—*Jazz* 1979—*Bop Till You Drop* 1980—*The Long Riders* soundtrack; *Borderline* 1981—*The Border* soundtrack (Backstreet) 1982—*The Slide Area* (Warner Bros.) 1984—*Paris, Texas* soundtrack 1985—*Alamo Bay* (Slash) 1986—*Blue City* (Warner Bros.); *Crossroads* 1987—*Get Rhythm* 1989—*Johnny Handsome* 1993—*A Meeting by the River* (with V.M. Bhatt) (Water Lily Acoustics); *Geronimo* soundtrack (Columbia) 1994—*Trespass* soundtrack (Sire/Warner Bros.); *Talking Timbuktu* (with Ali Zarka Touré) (Hannibal) 1995—*Music by Ry Cooder* (Warner Bros.) 1997—*The End of Violence* soundtrack (Outpost); *Buena Vista Social Club* (with Buena Vista Social Club) (World Circuit/Nonesuch) 1998—*Primary Colors* soundtrack (MCA).

Ry Cooder is a virtuoso on fretted instruments—slide guitar, mandolin, Mexican tiple, banjo, Middle Eastern saz—who crossbreeds his own sense of syncopation with vernacular musics. As a fan/musicologist, he has sought out local styles such as calypso, Hawaiian slack-key guitar, Tex-Mex, gospel, country, vaudeville "coon songs," and most recently, with the Buena Vista Social Club, prerevolutionary Cuban music. He records with L.A. session players and various "ethnic" musicians in and out of their own contexts.

Cooder began playing the guitar when he was three years old. He has had a glass eye since he was four, when he accidentally stuck a knife in his left eye. In the early '60s Cooder became active in Southern California blues and folk circles, and in 1963 he played in an unsuccessful group with vocalist Jackie DeShannon. With Taj Mahal, another musical archivist, he started the Rising Sons in 1966. He also appears on Mahal's debut album. Cooder was a busy session player in the late '60s, working for Gordon Lightfoot and on numerous commercials. He was a member of Captain Beefheart's Magic Band and appeared on Beefheart's *Safe As Milk* (1967), although he quit just before Beefheart was scheduled to play the Monterey Pop Festival. He also sat in on Little Feat's 1971 debut LP.

Cooder appeared on the soundtracks of *Candy* (1968) and *Performance* (1970, with Mick Jagger) and claims to have recorded extensively on the Rolling Stones' *Let It Bleed*. Although he is credited only for the mandolin on "Love in Vain," he claims to have provided the main riff for the Stones' "Honky Tonk Women."

Since 1969, when he got a solo contract, Cooder has cut down on session work to concentrate on his yearly albums. His general strategy is to rework obscure songs (mostly pre-'60s) in his own lunging, syncopated style laced with elements from outside rock. He has championed the music of Bahamian guitarist Joseph Spence (a major influence), and he later produced an album by the Gabby Pahinui Hawaiian Band. On 1974's *Paradise and Lunch*, he recorded a duet with jazz pianist Earl "Fatha" Hines, and following *Chicken Skin Music* (1976), he toured with a band that included Mexican accordionist Flaco Jiménez and a Tex-Mex rhythm section alongside gospel-style singers Bobby King, Eldridge King, and Terry Evans (documented on the live *Showtime*).

Jazz actually contained early-jazz ragtime and vaudeville songs. Cooder played a onetime concert at Carnegie Hall with an orchestral group and tap dancers for its unveiling. *Bop Till You Drop, Borderline,* and *The Slide Area* turned toward '50s and '60s R&B. *Bop* was the first major-label digitally recorded album; the next two albums (and attendant tours) featured songwriter John Hiatt. Cooder also provided soundtracks for *Blue Collar* (1979), *The Long Riders* (1980), *Southern Comfort* (1981), *The Border* (1982), *Paris, Texas* (1983), *Streets of Fire* (1984), *Cocktail* (1988), *Steel Magnolias* (1989), *Geronimo* (1993), *The End of Violence* (1997), and *Primary Colors* (1998). Selections from his film scores were collected on the double-disc anthology *Music by Ry Cooder.*

Cooder played only a few session dates in the '70s, behind Randy Newman *(Good Old Boys* and *Sail Away),* Arlo Guthrie, and Van Dyke Parks. He joined Nick Lowe, Jim Keltner, and John Hiatt in Little Village, a group whose self-titled debut appeared in early 1992. He recorded with V.M. Bhatt, an Indian musician whom he had not met before recording the critically acclaimed *A Meeting by the River.* Cooder's critically acclaimed and commercially successful *Talking Timbuktu* featured Ali Zarka Touré, a West African guitar master, hit #1 on the World Music chart and remained there 25 weeks straight, setting a record for that chart. It won a Grammy for Best World Music Album in 1995.

In 1996 Cooder traveled to Havana, Cuba, to record an album with Cuban and African musicians for the English label World Circuit. When the African musicians couldn't make the trip, Cooder put together an all-star ensemble of Cuban musicians, most in their 70s or 80s, and recorded *Buena Vista Social Club* (#178, 1998), a celebration of traditional Cuban music forms such as the *bolero* and the *son* (a precursor to salsa). Licensed in America by Nonesuch, the album topped *Billboard*'s Latin chart, won a Grammy in 1998 for Best Tropical Latin Performance, and inspired an Oscar-nominated documentary by filmmaker Wim Wenders. Cooder also produced solo albums by two of the BVSC's star players, pianist Ruben Gonzalez and singer Ibrahim Ferrer.

Sam Cooke

Born Jan. 22, 1931, Clarksdale, MS; died Dec. 11, 1964, Los Angeles, CA
1960—*Cookes Tour* (RCA); *Hits of the 50's; Sam Cooke* 1961—*My Kind of Blues; Twistin' the Night Away* 1962—*Best of Sam Cooke, vol. 1; Mr. Soul* 1963—*Night Beat* 1964—*Soul Stirrers* (London); *Ain't That Good News* (RCA); *At the Copa* 1965—*Shake; Best of Sam Cooke, vol. 2; Try a Little Love* 1966—*Unforgettable Sam Cooke* 1968—*Man Who Invented Soul* 1969—*The Gospel Soul of Sam Cooke With the Soul Stirrers, vol. 1* (Specialty) 1975—*Sam Cooke Interprets Billie Holiday* (RCA) 1976—*Forever* 1985—*One Night Stand: Sam Cooke Live at the Harlem Square Club, 1963* 1986—*The Man and His Music* 1991—*Sam Cooke With the Soul Stirrers* (Specialty) 2000—*The Man Who Invented Soul* (BMG/RCA).

Songwriter and performer Sam Cooke merged gospel music and secular themes and provided the early foundation of soul music. Cooke's pure, clear vocals were widely imitated, and his suave, sophisticated image set the style of soul crooners for the next decades.

Sam Cooke

One of eight sons of a Baptist minister, Cooke grew up in Chicago and was a top gospel artist by 1951. As a teenager, he became lead vocalist of the Soul Stirrers (which later included Johnnie Taylor), with whom he toured and recorded for nearly six years. Cooke's phrasing and urban enunciation were distinctive from the start.

Hoping not to offend his gospel fans, he released his pop debut, "Lovable" (1956), as Dale Cooke, but Specialty dropped him for deserting the Soul Stirrers. He released his own "You Send Me" the following year, and the 1.7-million-selling #1 song was the first of many hits. In the next two years his several hits—"Only Sixteen" (#28, 1959), "Everybody Likes to Cha Cha" (#31, 1959)—concentrated on light ballads and novelty items. He signed to RCA in 1960 and began writing bluesier, gospel-inflected tunes.

Beginning with his reworking of "Chain Gang" (#2) in August 1960, Cooke was a mainstay in the Top 40 through 1965, with "Wonderful World" (#12, 1960), "Sad Mood" (#29, 1961), "Twistin' the Night Away" (#9, 1962), "Bring It On Home to Me" (#13, 1962), "Another Saturday Night" (#10, 1963), and "Shake" (#7, 1965).

His shooting death on December 11, 1964, tarnished his image. Bertha Franklin, the manager of the Hacienda motel in L.A., claimed she killed the singer in self-defense after he'd tried to rape a 22-year-old woman, then turned on Franklin. The coroner ruled it a justifiable homicide. There still remain questions about the circumstances surrounding Cooke's murder.

Two months after his death his song "Shake" peaked at #7 on the singles chart. Cooke's hits have been covered widely by rock and soul singers; "Shake," for instance, was interpreted by Otis Redding and Rod Stewart. The posthumously released "A Change Is Gonna Come" hit #31 in 1965. It represented a return to Cooke's roots, placing him back in the spiritual setting from which he had first emerged just nine years earlier. Cooke's material continues to be widely covered by rock and soul performers.

Cooke was also a groundbreaking independent black-music capitalist. He owned his own record label (Sar/Derby), music publishing concern (Kags Music), and management firm. His influence can be heard in the work of artists as varied as Michael Jackson and the Heptones, but it is most profoundly felt in the singing of Redding, Stewart, and Al Green. Cooke was one of the first inductees into the Rock and Roll Hall of Fame in 1986; three years later the Soul Stirrers entered separately.

Rita Coolidge

Born May 1, 1945, Lafayette, TN
1971—*Rita Coolidge* (A&M); *Nice Feelin'* 1972—*Lady's Not for Sale* 1974—*Fall Into Spring* 1975—*It's Only Love* 1977—*Anytime . . . Anywhere* 1978—*Love Me Again* 1979—*Natural Act* (with Kris Kristofferson); *Satisfied* 1981—*Greatest Hits; Heartbreak Radio* (with Kris Kristofferson) 1992—*Love Lessons* (Caliber) 1995—*Cherokee* (Concept Records) 1996—*Out of the Blues* (Beacon Records) 1998—*Thinkin' About You* (404 Music) 2000—*Best Of—The Millennium Collection* (A&M).
Walela: 1997—*Walela* (Triloka) 2000—*Unbearable Love.*

Former backup singer Rita Coolidge became a hitmaking soloist in the late '70s and early '80s. The daughter of a Baptist minister and a Cherokee Indian, she sang in church choirs as a child. In her late teens, she briefly attended Florida State University before moving to Memphis, where she did radio jingles. She cut a locally successful hit single, then moved to L.A.

By 1969 she was recording and touring regularly as part of Delaney and Bonnie and Friends, and she joined much of that same troupe on Joe Cocker's Mad Dogs and Englishmen tour, where her featured rendition of "Superstar" was a highlight. (Leon Russell wrote Cocker's "Delta Lady" about Coolidge.) She continued backup work in the early '70s for Eric Clapton, Stephen Stills, Boz Scaggs, Graham Nash, Marc Benno (who later joined Coolidge's backup band, the Dixie Flyers), and Dave Mason. (Her sister Priscilla recorded with her husband and producer, Booker T. Jones of Booker T. and the MG's.)

In 1971 Coolidge met Kris Kristofferson [see entry], whom she married two years later. By then her first solo album had been released to little response. In 1977 *Anytime . . . Anywhere* went platinum on the strength of three hit singles: Jackie Wilson's "Higher and Higher" (#2, 1977), Boz Scaggs' "We're All Alone" (#7, 1977), and the Temptations' "The Way You Do the Things You Do" (#20, 1978). She frequently toured with Kristofferson, whose growing movie career provided her with cameo roles in *Pat Garrett and Billy the Kid, Convoy,* and *A Star Is Born.* They also collaborated on 1979's *Natural Act,* released shortly before their divorce in 1980, and collected two Grammys for best country duo.

In the '80s Coolidge scored with "All Time High" (#36, 1983) from the soundtrack to the James Bond thriller *Octopussy.* Although she hasn't enjoyed any hits since, the singer has remained visible. She was one of the original VJs on the video music channel VH1; sang a duet with former Pink Floyd leader Roger Waters on his *Amused to Death* solo album; and continued to record. *Love Lessons* featured duets with country star Lee Greenwood, her sister Priscilla, and Bonnie Bramlett.

In the '90s, Coolidge became increasingly involved in Native American culture and issues. With Priscilla and Priscilla's daughter Laura Satterfield, she formed the trio Walela, whose debut features a version of "Amazing Grace" sung in Cherokee.

Coolio

Born Artis Leon Ivey Jr., Aug. 1, 1963, Los Angeles, CA
1994—*It Takes a Thief* (Tommy Boy) 1995—*Gangsta's Paradise* 1997—*My Soul.*
With WC and the MAAD Circle: 1991—*Ain't a Damn Thang Changed* (Priority).

Drawing on real-life experiences (as a teen he ran with members of the L.A. Crips) and using a can't-miss sample (Stevie Wonder's 1976 song "Pastime Paradise") rapper Coolio had a worldwide hit in 1995 with his haunting, cautionary anthem, "Gangsta's Paradise." Originally featured on the soundtrack to the Michelle Pfeiffer film *Dangerous Minds* and later included on his second album (also called *Gangsta's Paradise*), the song hit the top of the charts in both the U.S. and the U.K., won Coolio a Best Rap Solo Performance Grammy, and was *Billboard*'s #1 single of 1995. Coolio first achieved fame the previous year with his platinum debut, *It Takes a Thief* (#8 pop, #5 R&B, 1994), and it's #3 crossover pop single "Fantastic Voyage." Prior to that he had recorded an album with WC and the MAAD Circle (1991's *Ain't a Damn Thang Changed*).

Raised by his mother in Compton, California, Coolio was a bookworm and star student early on (skipping the sixth grade), but he began hanging out with gang members as a teen to keep from getting beaten up. Not long after he began rapping in high school, he spent 10 months in jail on a larceny charge (he was arrested for trying to cash a stolen money order but maintained he was innocent). He was addicted to crack by the time he was 20, but he went straight after a stint as a firefighter with the California Department of Forestry.

Coolio strived for a positive message in his music, drawing on his past for cautionary tales like "Gangsta's Paradise" ("Tell me why are we so blind to see/That the ones we hurt are you and me") rather than songs glorifying crime and violence. In the late '90s, however, he made headlines several times for incidents that belied his clean image. In 1997 Coolio and several members of his group 40 Thievz were charged with committing theft and assault in Germany, and he spent 10 days in jail in 1999 after pleading guilty to felony possession of a firearm.

After 1997's *My Soul* (#39), which featured the #12 hit "C U When U Get There," Coolio left Tommy Boy and spent the next few years concentrating on his acting career. He seemed primed for a comeback at the end of the decade, guesting on Blondie's own 1999 comeback album *No Exit* and signing a deal with Allied Artists Records with plans to release a new album, *Coolio.com,* by the end of the year. It had yet to be released at the time of this writing in mid-2001.

Alice Cooper

Born Vincent Furnier, Feb. 4, 1948, Detroit, MI
The group that was formed in the mid-'60s in Phoenix, AZ: Glen Buxton (b. Nov. 10, 1947, Akron, OH; d. Oct. 19, 1997, Clarion, IA), gtr.; Michael Bruce (b. Mar. 16, 1948), gtr., kybds.; Dennis Dunaway (b. Dec. 9, 1948, Cottage Grove, OR), bass; Neal Smith (b. Sep. 23, 1947, Akron, OH), drums.
1969—*Pretties for You* (Straight) 1970—*Easy Action* 1971—*Love It to Death* (Warner Bros.); *Killer* 1972—*School's Out* 1973—*Billion Dollar Babies* 1974—*Muscle of Love; Alice Cooper's Greatest Hits* (group disbands; Cooper goes solo with backing musicians.) 1975—*Welcome to My Nightmare* (Atlantic) 1976—*Alice Cooper Goes to Hell* (Warner Bros.) 1977—*Lace and Whiskey; The Alice Cooper Show* 1978—*From the Inside* 1980—*Flush the Fashion* 1981—*Special Forces* 1982—*Zipper Catches Skin* 1983—*DaDa* 1986—*Constrictor* (MCA) 1987—*Raise Your Fist and Yell* 1989—*Trash* (Epic) 1991—*Hey Stoopid* 1994—*The Last Temptation* 1997—*Fistful of Alice* (Capitol) 1999—*The Life and Crimes of Alice Cooper* (Rhino) 2000—*Brutal Planet* (Spitfire).

Between '50s showman Screamin' Jay Hawkins emerging from a coffin and Kiss' Gene Simmons spitting "blood" in the mid-'70s, no one defined shock rock like Alice Cooper. Cooper used violent (and vile) theatrics—simulated executions, the chopping up of baby dolls, and draping himself with a live boa constrictor—and explicit lyrics to become a controversial yet hugely popular figure in the early and mid-'70s. After a decade of fluctuating record sales, Cooper returned to platinum with the #20 1989 LP *Trash.* Though he is respected by a new generation of hard-rock fans, he never reached this kind of popularity again.

Vincent Furnier, son of a preacher, assembled his hard-rocking band in Phoenix. They were first known as the Earwigs, then the Spiders, and finally the Nazz (not to be confused with Todd Rundgren's band). They moved en masse to L.A. in 1968. Billing themselves as Alice Cooper (who, according to a Ouija board, was a 17th-century witch reincarnated as Furnier), they established themselves on the Southern California bar circuit with a bizarre stage show and a reputation as the worst band in L.A. Frank Zappa's Straight Records released their first two albums, which sold poorly and, with tour costs, left them $100,000 in debt.

The band members moved to Detroit, where they lived for several months in a single hotel room before the release of their major-label debut and breakthrough album, *Love It to Death.* Joining Cooper's taboo-defying lyrics to powerful hard rock, the album became the first in a string of gold and platinum releases and included "Eighteen" (#21, 1971). Subsequent hit singles included "School's Out" (#7, 1972), "Elected" (#26, 1972), "Hello Hooray" (#35, 1973), and "No More Mr. Nice Guy" (#25, 1973). *Killer* (#21, 1971), *School's Out* (#2, 1972), and *Billion Dollar Babies* (#1, 1973) are all platinum.

In 1973 Surrealist master Salvador Dalí filmed the singer, wearing diamond necklaces and tiara, as he bit the head off a small replica of the Venus de Milo for a holographic work. With such widespread success, even amid the gruesome stage sets and macabre makeup, Cooper seemed less threatening.

The band broke up in 1974 and Cooper began using such musicians as ex–Lou Reed guitarists Dick Wagner and Steve Hunter. (In 1977 former band members Bruce, Dunaway, and Smith formed Billion Dollar Babies and recorded one unsuccessful album.) *Alice Cooper—The Nightmare,* an April 1975 prime-time TV special, seemed to indicate Cooper's acceptance as a mainstream entertainer, as did a handful of appearances on *The Hollywood Squares.* His then-current hit, "Only Women Bleed" (#12, 1975), was a ballad, as were two subsequent hits: "I Never Cry" (#12, 1976) and "You and Me" (#9, 1977).

In 1978 Cooper committed himself to a psychiatric hospital for treatment of alcoholism, an experience chronicled on *From the Inside,* which includes some lyrics by Elton John's songwriting partner Bernie Taupin and the hit "How You Gonna See Me Now" (#12, 1978). Neither the hard-rocking *Flush the Fashion* nor *Special Forces* was especially successful, and Cooper took a hiatus. He returned in 1986 with *Constrictor,* followed by *Raise Your Fist and Yell,* both deep in the heavy-metal vein. The Nightmare Returns Tour and MTV Halloween special brought Cooper's violent, twisted onstage fantasies to a new generation, and he closed the '80s with the platinum *Trash* and "Poison" (#7, 1989), his first Top 20 single in more than a decade.

Cooper, for whom Alice is such a character that he speaks of him in the third person in interviews, has also appeared in several films: *Prince of Darkness* (1988), *Freddy's Dead: The Final Nightmare* (1991), and most notably *Wayne's World* (1992). For *The Decline of Western Civilization, Part II—The Metal Years,* he rerecorded "Under My Wheels" with Guns n' Roses' Axl Rose, Slash, and Izzy Stradlin. Prominent among Cooper's legion of second-generation fans are Steve Vai, Nikki Sixx, Joe Satriani, and Slash, all of whom guested on

Alice Cooper

Hey Stoopid; Soundgarden's singer, Chris Cornell, was on *The Last Temptation,* while Sammy Hagar and Rob Zombie appeared on the live recording *A Fistful of Alice.*

His career flagging in the late '90s, Cooper moved away from the power ballads that had marked his '80s records and reunited with producer Bob Ezrin (who had worked on *Love It to Death, Killer,* and *School's Out,* among others) on the indie release *Brutal Planet,* a science-fiction concept album. But despite the return of a guillotine (a mainstay of his '70s shows) as an accessory on the Live From the Brutal Planet Tour, Cooper seems mild compared to the likes of Slipknot or Marilyn Manson, who arguably were directly inspired by him. Not only does he now play family-friendly places such as state fairs but he also opened a restaurant, Alice Cooper'stown, in Phoenix.

Julian Cope/The Teardrop Explodes

Born Oct. 21, 1957, Deri, Wales
The Teardrop Explodes, formed 1978, Liverpool, Eng.:
Cope, voc, bass; Michael Finkler, gtr.; Paul Simpson, kybds.; Gary Dwyer, drums; (– Simpson; + Dave Balfe; – Finkler; + Alan Gill).
1980—*Kilimanjaro* (Mercury) 1981—*Wilder* 1990—*Everyone Wants to Shag the Teardrop Explodes* (Fontana).
Julian Cope solo: 1984—*World Shut Your Mouth* (Mercury); *Fried* 1986—*Julian Cope* EP (Island) 1987—*Saint Julian; Eve's Volcano* EP 1988—*My Nation Underground* 1990—*Skellington* (CopeCo-Zippo); *Droolian* (MoFoCo-Zippo) 1991—*Peggy Suicide* (Island) 1992—*Floored Genius: The Best of Julian Cope and the Teardrop Explodes 1979–91; Jehovah Kill* 1994—*Autogeddon* (American); *Floored Genius, vol. 2* (Dutch East); *Head On* (Ma-Gog) 1995—*20 Mothers* (Autogeddon) 1996—*Interpreter* (Cooking Vinyl) 1997—*Rite2* (Head Heritage, U.K.); *The Followers of Saint Julian* (Island Masters) 1999—*Leper Skin* (PolyGram International).

As the singer of the neopsychedelic Liverpool band the Teardrop Explodes, Julian Cope was a wildly eccentric frontman whose lyrics were often maddeningly inscrutable and stage manner unpredictable. While attending college in Liverpool, Cope discovered punk and joined the Teardrops in 1978, earning U.K. pop hits ("Reward," "Treason," and "Passionate Friend") in the early '80s. He left the band in 1983 during the recording sessions for what would have been the group's third album (eventually released unfinished in 1990 as *Everyone Wants to Shag the Teardrop Explodes*). Cope then continued on an even more bizarre career path.

Prior to the Teardrops, Cope had played in two short-lived bands with future Echo and the Bunnymen singer Ian McCulloch. Shortly after the Teardrops imploded, his solo career began on a rough note when he intentionally jabbed himself in the stomach with a microphone stand onstage at London's Hammersmith Palais. Cope became well known for his experimentation with psychedelic drugs, which began during his days with the Teardrop Explodes and led some observers to liken him to two of his musical heroes, the acid casualties Syd Barrett and Roky Erickson. Mercury dropped Cope after his second album and refused to release his completed third one, *Skellington* (which later came out independently and included a song called "Out of My Mind on Dope and Speed").

In 1987, after moving to Island Records, Cope got his first slight crack at mainstream acceptance with "World Shut Your Mouth" (#84), from his most critically acclaimed album *Saint Julian* (#105, 1987). Cope's mental state continued to be an issue. In 1990, during a three-year hiatus from music, he appeared at London's anti–Poll Tax demonstration disguised as an alien named Mr. Sqwubbsy. The oddball double-length album *Peggy Suicide,* was a resounding artistic success, though its theme—an ambitious but confused political/environmental statement—was as convoluted as anything the singer had previously done. By 1992, it appeared as if Cope's fans had grown weary of his eccentricities. Follow-

Julian Cope

ing a compilation of solo and Teardrops material, Cope released *Jehovah Kill* to critical indifference and much less media attention. *Autogeddon* completed Cope's musical trilogy that began with *Peggy Suicide* and *Jehovah Kill*—this time with a theme on the evils of the automobile.

By 1995, Cope may have been appearing in public with half his head shaved, but he was also living quietly in the village of Wiltshire as a husband and father, releasing *20 Mothers* that same year. He had given up psychedelics a decade earlier at the request of his mother-in-law. In 1996 Cope authored *Krautrocksampler* (published by his own Head Heritage imprint), a book that pays tribute to German electronic music by the likes of Can, Faust, Kraftwerk, and Tangerine Dream. In 1999 he published a book on Neolithic archaeology and embarked on a lecture tour on the same topic wearing three-inch platform boots. In 2000 Cope was dabbling in "glambient" with a band called Queen Elizabeth and "false metal" with Brain Donor.

Stewart Copeland: See the Police

Chick Corea

Born Armando Anthony Corea, June 12, 1941, Chelsea, MA
1966—*Tones for Jones Bones* (Vortex) 1968—*Now He Sings, Now He Sobs* (Solid State) 1969—*Is* 1970—*The Song of Singing* (Blue Note); *Circulus; Circling In; A.R.C.* (ECM) 1971—*Circle, Paris Concert; Piano Improvisations, vol. 1; Piano Improvisations, vol. 2* 1972—*Inner Space* (Atlantic); *Crystal Silence* (with Gary Burton) (ECM); *Return to Forever* 1975—*Chick Corea* (Blue Note) 1976—*The Leprechaun* (Polydor); *My Spanish Heart* 1977—*Musicmagic* (Columbia) 1978—*Mad Hatter* (Polydor); *Friends; Secret Agent* 1979—*Delphi 1* 1980—*Tap Step* (Warner) 1981—*Three Quartets* 1982—*Trio Music* (ECM); *Touchstone* (Warner) 1983—*Again and Again* (Elektra/Musician) 1984—*Children's Songs* (ECM) 1985—*Chick Corea Works; Voyage; Septet* 1986—*The Chick Corea Elektric Band* (GRP) 1987—*Trio Music Live in Europe* (ECM) 1987—*Light Years* (GRP) 1988—*Eye of the Beholder* 1989—*Chick Corea Akoustic Band* 1990—*Inside Out* 1991—*Alive; Beneath the Mask* 1992—*Play* (with Bobby McFerrin) (Blue Note) 1993—*Paint the World* (GRP) 1994—*Expressions* 1995—*Time Warp* 1996—*The Mozart Sessions* (with Bobby McFerrin) (Sony Classical) 1997—*Remembering Bud Powell* (Stretch); *Native Sense* (with Gary Burton) 1999—*Corea Concerto* (Sony Classical).
With Return to Forever: 1973—*Light as a Feather* (Polydor); *Hymn of the Seventh Galaxy* 1974—*Where Have I Known You Before* 1975—*No Mystery* 1976—*The Romantic Warrior* (Columbia) 1996—*Music Forever & Beyond* (with John McLaughlin, Herbie Hancock, Blue Mitchell) (GRP); *Return to the 7th Galaxy* (Verve).
With Origin: 1998—*Live at the Blue Note; A Week at the Blue Note* 1999—*Change.*

Chick Corea established himself as a major, influential jazz keyboardist, including a three-year stint with Miles Davis, before turning to rock fusion with Return to Forever. In the late '70s he returned to acoustic piano. Corea's distinctively brittle and precise tone on the piano has been widely imitated.

The son of a musician, Corea began studying classical piano at four and played with his father's band. As a teenager, he also played with a Latin band. He briefly attended Columbia University and the Juilliard School of Music but quit to go professional. Corea's first major job was with Mongo Santamaria in 1962, followed by work with Blue Mitchell, Stan Getz, Herbie Mann, and Sarah Vaughan. In 1968 Miles Davis Quintet drummer Tony Williams invited him to sit in for an ailing Herbie Hancock, and Corea wound up working for Davis for three years. At Davis' behest, he began playing the electric Fender Rhodes piano, appearing on *Filles de Kilimanjaro* and the landmark jazz-rock albums *In a Silent Way* and *Bitches Brew.*

Corea formed the avant-garde Circle with bassist Dave Holland, drummer Barry Atschul, and reedman Anthony Braxton in 1971. Circle recorded three albums, while Corea recorded two solo sessions. Corea was introduced to Scientology, which led him to adopt the idea of "communication"—in practice, playing simpler music. He then formed Return to Forever with fellow Scientologist Stanley Clarke [see entry], whom Corea met during a brief stint with saxophonist Joe Henderson. Corea had written some of the group's initial material for a Stan Getz band (on Getz's album *Captain Marvel*) that included Clarke, percussionist Airto Moreira, and drummer Tony Williams. When Corea recorded the material on his own, Joe Farrell replaced Getz, Moreira played both drums and percussion, and Moreira's wife, Flora Purim, sang. The result was a Corea album called *Return to Forever,* followed by *Light as a Feather.* The two albums contained melodic pop jazz, full of buoyant melodies and quasi-Latin rhythms.

When Moreira and Purim left to start their own group, Fingers, in 1973, Farrell went back to session work and Corea and Clarke revamped Return to Forever with drummer Lenny White and guitarist Bill Connors. Openly modeled on the Mahavishnu Orchestra (Corea had performed with Mahavishnu John McLaughlin in Davis' band), the new group made bombastic use of electric instruments, including Corea's synthesizers. After guitarist Al DiMeola replaced Connors, Return to Forever reached a peak of popularity on the rock circuit. Clarke and DiMeola went solo in 1976, and Corea briefly expanded Return to Forever to a 13-piece ensemble before retiring the group name. Corea, Clarke, White, and DiMeola did a reunion tour in 1983.

During the late '70s and through the '80s, Corea played mostly acoustic piano as half of a duo with fellow pop refugee Herbie Hancock [see entry] and with various acoustic groups that have included drummer Steve Gadd, bassist Eddie Gomez, Henderson, Farrell, Moran, and others, including a trio reuniting him with bassist Miroslav Vitous and drummer Roy Haynes, who had recorded earlier on *Now He Sings, Now He Sobs.* He also recorded solo albums and duets with vibraharpist Gary Burton and wrote a monthly column for *Contemporary Keyboard* magazine.

The Chick Corea Elektric Band formed in 1985 with two top-rated L.A. musicians, bassist John Patitucci and drummer Dave Weckl; guitarist Frank Gambale and others have joined over the years. In order to accommodate his fusion/traditional jazz mind-split, Corea formed the Akoustic Band in 1989 with Patitucci and Weckl. This trio performed jazz standards as well as Corea originals, including a reworking of his classic "Spain." Patitucci and Weckl left the Elektric Band in 1993 and were replaced by bassist Jimmy Earl and drummer Gary Novak.

Corea started his own label, Stretch Records (a subsidiary of GRP), in 1992 to record like-minded musicians including Patitucci and guitarist Robben Ford. That same year he teamed with vocalist Bobby McFerrin on the Grammy-winning *Play;* five years later he formed a new sextet, Origin, to showcase his acoustic piano work. In 1999, with the London Philharmonic Orchestra and members of Origin, he recorded the Grammy-winning Corea *Concerto,* drawing on his passion for Mozart.

Cornershop

Formed 1992, Preston, Eng.
Tjinder Singh (b. Tjinder Singh Nurpuri, Feb. 8, 1968, New Cross, Eng.), voc., gtr.; Ben Ayres (b. Benedict Ayres, Apr. 30, 1968, St. John's, Can.), tamboura, kybds., gtr.; David D. Chambers (b. 1969, Lincoln, Eng.), drums; Avtar Singh (b. Avtar Singh Nurpuri, May 11, 1965, Punjab, India), gtr.; Anthony Saffery, harmonium, kybds., sitar.
1993—*Lock Stock & Double-Barrel* EP (Wiiija) 1995—*Hold On It Hurts; Woman's Gotta Have It* (Luaka Bop) (– A. Singh; – Chambers; + Peter Bengry, perc.; + Nick Simms, drums) 1997—*When I Was Born for the 7th Time.*
Clinton: 1999—*Disco & the Half Way to Discontent* (Luaka Bop/Astralwerks).

London-based Cornershop began its career as concerned with social activism as it was with pop music. The band mixed alternative rock and British dance beats with traditional Indian music (and occasional lyrics in Punjabi), and in 1997 enjoyed the modern rock hit "Brimful of Asha," a tribute to Indian film singer Asha Bhosle.

Tjinder Singh was born in the U.K. to an immigrant family from northern India. He grew up in Wolverhampton, in the center of England, where he was frequently confronted about his ethnicity. While a teenager, he learned to play Indian instruments and discovered American R&B. He attended Preston University, where he met Ben Ayres and formed a band called General Havoc. Both explored Western and Eastern instruments and evolved into Cornershop (after the stereotype that all British Asians run "cornershops") with drummer David Chambers, guitarist Avtar Singh, and multi-instrumentalist Anthony Saffery. Cornershop was signed to the Wiiija label, but the band was still largely a vehicle for social issues, burning posters of Morrissey onstage and outside his label's offices in the early '90s, when the singer seemed to adopt a near-skinhead look and recorded the allegedly racist songs "Asian Rut" and "Bengali in Platforms."

Cornershop released several EPs before issuing the 1995 album, *Hold On It Hurts.* David Byrne signed the band in the U.S. to his Luaka Bop label, releasing *Woman's Gotta Have It* in 1995—the same year Tjinder Singh was assaulted in London for having a non-Indian girlfriend. Two years later came *When I Was Born for the 7th Time* (#144), which included "Brimful of Asha" and "Good to Be on the Road Back Home." When not touring, Saffery kept his job as a social worker, and T. Singh and Ayres formed a dance music side project called Clinton, releasing *Disco & the Half Way to Discontent* in 1999.

Larry Coryell

Born Apr. 2, 1943, Galveston, TX
1967—*Out of Sight & Sound* (as Free Spirits) (ABC) 1968—*Larry Coryell* (Vanguard) 1969—*Lady Coryell; Coryell* 1970—*Spaces* 1971—*Live at the Village Gate; Fairyland* (Mega); *Barefoot Boy* (Flying Dutchman) 1972—*Offering; Introducing Larry Coryell and the 11th House* (Vanguard) 1973—*The Real Great Escape* 1974—*At Montreux; Restful Mind; Level One* (as Eleventh House) (Arista); *Planet End*

1975—*The Other Side of Larry Coryell* (Vanguard) 1976—*Aspects; The Lion and the Ram* (Arista); *Twin House* (with Philip Catherine) (Atlantic); *Two for the Road* (with Steve Khan) (Arista) 1977—*Back Together Again* (with Alphonse Mouzon) (Atlantic); *Live in Europe* (LC) 1978—*Difference* (EGG); *Standing Ovation* (Mood); *European Impressions* (Arista); *Splendid* (with Philip Catherine) (Elektra); *Larry Coryell and Eleventh House at Montreux* (Vanguard) 1979—*Return; Free Smile* (Arista) 1981—*Bolero* (Evidence) 1982—*Larry Coryell–Michael Urbaniak Duo* (Keynote) 1983—*A Quiet Day in Spring* (Steeple Chase) 1984—*Comin' Home* (Muse); *L'Oiseau de Feu/Petrouchka* (Philips); *Just Like Being Born* (Flying Fish) 1985—*Equipoise* (Muse); *Together* (Concord Jazz) 1986—*Le Sacre du Printemps* (Philips) 1987—*Toku Do* (Muse) 1989—*American Odyssey* (DRG); *The Dragon Gate* (Shanachie); *Shining Hour* (Muse) 1990—*Coryell Plays Ravel and Gershwin* (Soundscreen) 1991—*12 Frets to One Octave* (Shanachie) 1992—*Live From Bahia* (CTI) 1993—*Fallen Angel* 1994—*I'll Be Over You* 1996—*Sketches of Coryell* (Shanachie) 1997—*Spaces Revisited* 1996—*Major Jazz Minor Blues* (32 Jazz); *Cause and Effect* (Tone Center) 1999—*Monk, 'Trane, Miles and Me* (High Note); *Private Concert* (Acoustic Music) 2000—*Coryells* (Chesky); *New High* (High Note).

Guitarist Larry Coryell's penchant for high volume and fast fingerwork led him to jazz rock early. Coryell played piano as a child, switching to guitar in his teens. After studying journalism at the University of Washington, he moved to New York City in 1965, where he worked with drummer Chico Hamilton in 1966 and cofounded an early jazz-rock band, the Free Spirits. In 1967 he joined vibraphonist Gary Burton's band; two years later he recorded "Memphis Underground" with flutist Herbie Mann.

Coryell began leading his own bands in 1969. He toured Europe and the U.S. that year with a band that included ex–Cream bassist Jack Bruce, ex–Jimi Hendrix Experience drummer Mitch Mitchell, and Coryell's longtime keyboardist Mike Mandel. In 1970 he joined John McLaughlin, Billy Cobham, Chick Corea, and future Weather Report bassist Miroslav Vitous on *Spaces. Barefoot Boy* (1971) was a virtual tribute to Hendrix.

Coryell formed a variety of bands in the '70s, including the Mahavishnu Orchestra–styled Eleventh House, and later toured playing solo acoustic guitar and in a duo with ex–Focus guitarist Philip Catherine or session guitarist Steve Khan. Although he returned briefly to the electric fusion format, Coryell mainly concentrated on acoustic guitar. Aside from continued duets with Catherine, Coryell played in tandem with Al DiMeola, John McLaughlin, John Scofield, and others.

Coryell's leanings toward traditional jazz surfaced during the late '80s and '90s. Coryell toured and recorded in acoustic quartet settings with such jazz heavyweights as bassists Buster Williams and George Mraz, pianists Stanley Cowell and Kenny Barron, and drummers Beaver Harris and Billy Hart. He recorded *Live From Bahia* in Brazil with drummer Billy Cobham, saxophonist Donald Harrison, trumpeter Marcio Montarroyos, and vocalist Dori Caymmi. The album was a blend of samba, rhumba, rock, and funk, with African and Caribbean rhythms. In 1993 Coryell shifted direction once again, recording *Larry Coryell and the Fallen Angels*, using horns and synthesizers. Eclecticism remains Coryell's signature. He has recorded works by Stravinsky and Rimsky-Korsakov, explored Brazilian music, and with his two guitar-playing sons, Murali and Julian, formed a trio, the Coryells.

Elvis Costello

Born Declan Patrick McManus, Aug. 25, 1954, London, Eng.
1977—*My Aim Is True* (Columbia) 1978—*This Year's Model* 1979—*Armed Forces* 1980—*Get Happy!!; Taking Liberties* 1981—*Trust; Almost Blue* 1982—*Imperial Bedroom* 1983—*Punch the Clock* 1984—*Goodbye Cruel World* 1985—*The Best of Elvis Costello and the Attractions* 1986—*King of America; Blood and Chocolate* 1989—*Spike* (Warner Bros.) 1990—*Girls Girls Girls* (Columbia) 1991—*Mighty Like a Rose* (Warner Bros.) 1993—*The Juliet Letters; 2½ Years* (Rykodisc) 1994—*Brutal Youth* (Warner Bros.); *The Very Best of Elvis Costello and the Attractions* (Rykodisc) 1995—*Kojak Variety* (Warner Bros.) 1996—*All This Useless Beauty* 1997—*Extreme Honey—The Very Best of the Warner Brothers Years* 1998—*Painted From Memory* (with Burt Bacharach) (Mercury).

Elvis Costello arrived as part of a late-'70s new wave of singer/songwriters, who reinvigorated the literate, lyrical traditions of Bob Dylan and Van Morrison with the raw energy and sass that were principal ethics of punk. Early in his career, Costello listed "revenge and guilt" as his primary motivations, but what really counted was the construction of his songs, which set densely layered wordplays in an ever-expanding repertoire of styles. Since Costello's melodic instincts were as sure as his gifts as a lyricist, his musical experiments generally drew kudos, enhancing his reputation as a quintessential critics' favorite. (Rock singer David Lee Roth once remarked that critics liked the bespectacled, nerdy Costello so much because they all looked liked him.) Granted, some members of the pop intelligentsia never forgave Costello for moving beyond the brash minimalist urgency of his first few albums; but it's just this progress that has allowed the singer to remain a relevant, respected artist.

Costello's father was a successful big-band singer and trumpet player. While attending Catholic school in working-class London, Costello tried playing violin and several other instruments before discovering the guitar at 15, at which point he was already interested in songwriting. Soon after, he moved to Liverpool to live with his mother, who'd divorced his father. In the early '70s, he and his high school sweetheart married and had a son, settling in London. There, Costello continued to write, record demos, and perform (sometimes under the name D.C. Costello, his mother's maiden name), while supporting his family as a computer operator. In 1975 he quit his job, became a roadie for Brinsley Schwarz, and got friendly with their bass player, Nick Lowe.

Elvis Costello

Stiff Records signed Costello in 1976 on the advice of staff producer Lowe; one of the label's owners, Jake Riviera, became his manager and rechristened him Elvis Costello.

Costello's debut single, "Less Than Zero," was released in April 1977 and was included on *My Aim Is True*, which Lowe produced. Soon Top 20 in England, *Aim* (#32 U.S.) made Costello a major British cult star and attracted critical kudos in the U.S. Costello then assembled the Attractions: keyboardist Steve "Nieve" Nason, drummer Pete Thomas, and bassist Bruce Thomas. Bolstered by his new cohorts on *This Year's Model* (#30, 1978), he rocked harder, while maintaining his distinctively wounded, clipped vocal delivery. Meanwhile, his "angry young man" image was amplified by punk-friendly habits like onstage rudeness, brief sets, and an aversion to the press. In late 1978 Costello left his wife and young son, only to return to them a year later. His next release, the Top 10 *Armed Forces* (originally titled *Emotional Facism*), repeatedly equated love affairs with military maneuvers ("Oliver's Army"). By then Costello's style encompassed lush, Beatlesque arrangements and more diverse influences.

While he toured the U.S. to promote *Armed Forces* in 1979, Costello's onstage contrariness and dark moods—sometimes induced by drinking—reached alarming proportions. In Columbus, Ohio, that March, a minor but much-publicized conflict with American singers Bonnie Bramlett and Stephen Stills occurred in a hotel bar after Costello reportedly referred to Ray Charles as a "blind, ignorant nigger." Besides tainting his work with the Rock Against Racism organization, this outburst brought the wrath of the previously supportive press. Costello lay low for a while, producing the Specials' 1979 debut and appearing at the Concert for Kampuchea.

Trust (#28, 1981) brought Costello back to frontline duty, and his subsequent American tour revealed an uncharacteristically polite and reserved stage manner, as if experience had mellowed the performer, who was still in his mid-20s. His touring partners were Squeeze, a critically acclaimed pop band whose 1981 LP *East Side Story* Costello coproduced. Later that same year Costello released *Almost Blue* (#50), an album of country & western covers recorded in Nashville that got mixed reviews. (A C&W aficionado, Costello later re-covered a version of his "Stranger in the House" with George Jones, while Costello's own songs have been covered by Dave Edmunds and Linda Ronstadt.)

Imperial Bedroom (#30, 1982), in contrast, earned raves. Full of wry, elegant, haunted ballads, the album marked Costello's most sophisticated pop craftsmanship yet, garnering comparisons to such prerock bards as Cole Porter and Rodgers and Hart. With 1983's *Punch the Clock* (#24), Costello continued to move beyond the punk minimalism of his early work, serving up soulful, accessible pop ("Everyday I Write the Book," a Top 40 U.S. hit) and serious balladry (the politically astute "Shipbuilding"). While less consistent, 1984's *Goodbye Cruel World* (#35) also found him diversifying in this vein.

Costello's personal life was also undergoing changes. Estranged again from his wife, he struck up a relationship with the Pogues' bassist Caitlin O'Riordan while the Irish band toured with him in the fall of 1984. (Costello also produced the Pogues' 1985 album, *Rum, Sodomy & the Lash*.) Costello divorced his wife in 1985 and married O'Riordan in 1986. Also in 1986, Costello temporarily traded in the Attractions for a pickup band he called the Confederates—former Elvis Presley musicians guitarist James Burton, drummer Ronnie Tutt, and bassist Jerry Scheff—who appeared with him on all but one cut (on which the Attractions appeared) on the lushly melodic *King of America* (#39). Later that year, Costello reenlisted the Attractions for the more raucous *Blood and Chocolate* (#84). The tour to promote both these albums alternated between sets featuring the Attractions, the Confederates, and Costello performing solo, acoustically. In addition, Costello designed the Spinning Songbook, a device through which audience members could "choose," by luck of the draw, songs from his vast repertoire.

In 1987 Costello cowrote a bunch of songs with Paul McCartney, several of which materialized two years later on *Spike* (#32). Costello's 1989 album—which also included support from Roger McGuinn, Chrissie Hynde, and the Dirty Dozen Brass Band—produced a Top 20 hit in the McCartney-Costello collaboration "Veronica" (#19, 1989) and went gold. Some critics found *Spike* inconsistent, though, preferring the subsequent collection *Girls Girls Girls*, on which Costello chronicled his career thus far with his own favorite material.

Like *Spike*, 1991's *Mighty Like a Rose* (#55) was made without the Attractions, and was perceived as lacking focus. In 1993, though, Costello found a new sense of direction in perhaps his most ambitious project yet: *The Juliet Letters* (#125), a song cycle he wrote and performed with the string players in England's Brodsky Quartet, inspired by an article about letters sent to Shakespeare's character Juliet Capulet, received by a Veronese academic. The album and subsequent tour drew wild praise from some, while baffling or putting off others. Meanwhile, in the '90s, Rykodisc began releasing the early Costello albums on compact disc, with extra tracks consisting of live and previously unreleased recordings.

In 1994 Costello reunited with the Attractions for *Brutal Youth* (which also featured Nick Lowe); the maturely rocking results garnered almost unanimous acclaim, and the album climbed to #34. That summer, Costello began touring with the Attractions, marking a reconciliation between Costello and bassist Bruce Thomas, whose published memoirs had enraged the singer. In 1995 Costello was back on his own (with some help from Attractions drummer Pete Thomas and a handful of studio musicians) with *Kojak Variety* (#102), a cover album featuring songs by Screamin' Jay Hawkins and Bob Dylan, among others. The following year he covered himself on *All This Useless Beauty* (#53), which highlighted several original Costello songs that had been recorded by other artists.

Also in 1996 the cynical Costello surprised critics and fans by collaborating with '60s love-song composer Burt Bacharach for the soundtrack to the film *Grace of My Heart*. Their cowritten effort, "God Give Me Strength," was featured in the movie, nominated for a Grammy, and paved the way for the duo to write enough songs to record their own album, *Painted From Memory* (1998). A track from that album, "I Still Have That Other Girl," won the pair a Grammy for Best Pop Collaboration With Vocals. Costello and Bacharach became so well known as artistic partners that they appeared together in a cameo as themselves in the comedy *Austin Powers: The Spy Who Shagged Me* in 1999. Costello lightened up enough to appear as himself in the Spice Girls movie *Spice World* (1997) and the '80s nostalgia flick *200 Cigarettes* (1999). The artist continues to tour, sometimes as a duo with Attractions keyboardist Nieve. He has recorded with his son Matthew and Supergrass drummer Danny Goffrey. In the late '90s and 2000, he contributed original songs to movie soundtracks and returned to dabbling in classical music: He played on classical saxophonist John Harle's 1997 album *Terror & Magnificence* and in 2000 produced songs for Swedish mezzo-soprano Anne Sofie von Otter.

James Cotton

Born July 1, 1935, Tunica, MS
1967—*The James Cotton Blues Band* (Verve) 1968—*Pure Cotton; Cotton in Your Ears; Cut You Loose!* (Vanguard) 1971—*Taking Care of Business* 1974—*100% Cotton* (Buddah) 1975—*High Energy* 1975—*Superharp Live and on the Move* 1980—*Take Me Back* (Blind Pig) 1984—*High Compression* (Alligator) 1986—*Live From Chicago* 1987—*Live at Antone's* (Antones) 1990—*Mighty Long Time* 1994—*Living the Blues* (PolyGram/Verve) 1995—*The Best of the Verve Years* 1996—*Deep in the Blues* 1999—*Superharps* (with Charlie Musselwhite, Billy Branch, and Sugar Ray Norcia) (Telarc) 2000—*Fire Down Under the Hill.*

A blues harmonica player, Cotton has played for years with Muddy Waters and frequently contributed to the records of rockers such as Johnny Winter. He has also led his own band, supporting himself on club dates and recording sporadically.

Cotton began playing blues harmonica after meeting Sonny Boy Williamson (Aleck "Rice" Miller). He left home at nine to seek out Williamson, whom he had heard on radio station KFFA in West Helena, Arkansas; he spent the next six years playing with him. For two years after that he was with Howlin' Wolf and then formed his own band with Willie Nix before joining Muddy Waters, with whom he worked for 12 years. In 1966 he left Waters to form his own band. Over the next few years he worked with several rock acts, including Paul Butterfield, Janis Joplin, Steve Miller, Boz Scaggs, Johnny Winter, Edgar Winter, Elvin Bishop, and the J. Geils Band's Peter Wolf. He has also recorded with Howlin' Wolf, Otis Spann, Big Mama Thornton, and Muddy Waters (he appeared on the latter's Hard Again Tour in the late '70s).

In the '80s Cotton was nominated for three Grammy Awards and won several W.C. Handy International Blues Awards. He has continued to tour and record in the '90s, appearing with numerous rock acts, including the Grateful Dead. *Living the Blues* features Dr. John and Jerry Garcia, along with blues artists Lucky Peterson and John Primer. *Deep in the Blues* won Cotton a W.C. Handy Award and a 1997 Grammy for Best Traditional Blues Album.

John Cougar: See John Mellencamp

The Count Five

Formed ca. 1965, San Jose, CA
Ken Ellner (b. 1948, Brooklyn, NY), voc.; John "Mouse" Michalski (b. 1948, Cleveland, OH), gtr.; Sean Byrne (b. 1947, Dublin, Ire.), gtr.; Roy Chaney (b. 1948, Indianapolis, IN), bass; Craig "Butch" Atkinson (b. 1947), drums.
1966—*Psychotic Reaction* (Double Shot).

A psychedelic garage band, the Count Five scored one major hit, "Psychotic Reaction" (#5, 1966). They emerged from the same California Bay Area bar circuit that spawned the Syndicate of Sound ("Little Girl") and the Golliwogs (later Creedence Clearwater Revival). In 1966 they signed with the L.A.-based Double Shot label. Followups to "Psychotic Reaction" failed to make national impact, although the band remained popular for a while regionally. Byrne continued his music career in his homeland, joining two fairly obscure groups, Public Foot the Roman and later Legover.

Counting Crows

Formed 1989, San Francisco, CA
Adam Duritz (b. Aug. 1, 1964, Baltimore, MD), voc., kybds.; David Bryson (b. Nov. 5, 1961), gtr.; Charlie Gillingham (b. Jan. 12, 1960, Torrance, CA), kybds., accordion; Matt Malley (b. July 4, 1963), bass, gtr.; Steve Bowman (b. Jan. 14, 1967), drums.
1993—*August and Everything After* (DGC) (+ Dan Vickrey [b. Aug. 26, 1966, Walnut Creek, CA], gtr.) 1994—(– Bowman;

+ Ben Mize [b. Feb. 2, 1971], drums) 1996—*Recovering the Satellites* 1998—*Across a Wire: Live in New York* 1999—(+ David Immergluck, gtr., mandolin, pedal steel gtr.) *This Desert Life* (Desert Life).

Released in the fall of 1993—smack in the middle of the alternative grunge boom—the Counting Crows' debut album *August and Everything After* sounded like a blast from rock's more organic, rootsier past. Dreadlocked frontman Adam Duritz managed to simultaneously draw comparisons to Bob Dylan and Van Morrison with his literate songwriting and soulful vocals, while the band's music seemed tapped from the same Americana wellspring that nourished the Band. The album spawned a handful of Modern Rock hit singles—"Mr. Jones" (#2, 1993) and "Round Here" (#7, 1994)—climbed to #4, and went on to sell 7 million copies as the band seemed to connect with fans of both alternative and classic rock.

Duritz and guitarist David Bryson met in 1989 and started writing songs together; the following year they began performing under the Counting Crows banner as an acoustic duo in the San Francisco Bay Area. They expanded into a band the following year with the addition of bassist Matt Malley, drummer Steve Bowman, and multi-instrumentalist Charlie Gillingham, and recorded a demo that eventually netted the band a record deal.

After recording *August and Everything After* with producer T Bone Burnett (but prior to the album's release), Counting Crows performed at the 1993 Rock and Roll Hall of Fame Induction Ceremony, representing absent inductee Van Morrison. The debut album was released later that year and began its 93-week chart run at the beginning of 1994, a year that found them opening for the Rolling Stones. That same year Duritz cowrote and recorded a duet, "Going Back to Georgia," with Texas folk-country singer Nanci Griffith for her *Flyer* album. Counting Crows—now featuring additional guitarist Dan Vickrey and new drummer Ben Mize—began recording its second album, *Recovering the Satellites*, at the end of 1995. It debuted at #1 in the fall of 1996, eventually going double platinum behind the Modern Rock hits "Angels of the Silences" (#3, 1996), "A Long December" (#5, 1996), "Daylight Fading" (#26, 1997), and "Have You Seen Me Lately?" (#34, 1997).

In 1998 Counting Crows released a double live album, *Across a Wire: Live in New York* (#19), with one disc spotlighting an intimate performance for VH1's *Storytellers* and the second a more uptempo set recorded for MTV's *Live From the 10 Spot*. Produced by Cracker frontman David Lowery, *This Desert Life* debuted at #8 in 1999 and spawned the #28 hit "Hanginaround."

Country Joe and the Fish

Formed 1965, San Francisco, CA
Country Joe McDonald (b. Jan. 1, 1942, Washington, DC), voc., gtr.; Chicken Hirsch (b. 1940, CA), drums; Bruce Barthol (b. 1947, Berkeley, CA), bass; Barry Melton (b. 1947, Brooklyn, NY), gtr.; David Cohen (b. 1942, Brooklyn), gtr., kybds.
1967—*Electric Music for the Mind and Body* (Vanguard); *I-Feel-Like-I'm-Fixin'-to-Die* 1968—*Together* 1969—*Here We Go Again; Greatest Hits* 1970—(group disbands) *C.J. Fish* 1971—*Life and Times of Country Joe and the Fish (From Haight-Ashbury to Woodstock)* 1973—*The Best of Country Joe McDonald and the Fish* 1976—*The Essential Country Joe McDonald* 1977—*Reunion* (Fantasy) 1980—*Collector's Items: The First 3 EP's* (Rag Baby) 1987—*The Collected Country Joe and the Fish* (Vanguard).
Country Joe McDonald solo: 1969—*Thinking of Woody Guthrie* (Vanguard); *Tonight I'm Singing Just for You* 1970—*Hold On, It's Coming; Quiet Days at Clichy* 1971—*War, War, War* 1972—*Incredible! Live!* 1973—*The Paris Sessions* 1974—*Country Joe* 1975—*Essential Country Joe; Paradise With an Ocean View* (Fantasy) 1976—*Love Is a Fire* 1977—*Goodbye Blues* 1978—*Rock and Roll Music From the Planet Earth* 1979—*Leisure Suite* 1981—*On My Own* (Rag Baby); *Into the Fray* 1982—*Animal Tracks* 1983—*Child's Play* 1984—*Peace on Earth* 1986—*Vietnam Experience* 1991—*Superstitious Blues* (Rykodisc) 1996—*Carry On* (Shanachie).

Country Joe and the Fish were one of the most overtly political bands to emerge from San Francisco's late-'60s folk-turned-psychedelic scene. Joe McDonald (named after Stalin by left-leaning parents) wrote his first song, "I Seen a Rocket," as a campaign song for a friend's high school class presidency attempt. At age 17 he joined the navy for three years. After a year at Los Angeles City College he moved to Berkeley and wrote protest songs while occasionally publishing a magazine, *Et Tu, Brute*.

McDonald made his first record, *The Goodbye Blues*, in 1964 with Blair Hardman. He then joined the Berkeley String Quartet and the Instant Action Jug Band, which included Barry Melton. The two started Country Joe and the Fish in 1965 to make a series of political EPs for Takoma, including the first appearance of the notorious "F-U-C-K" cheer ("Gimme an F!" etc.).

The group started as a loose-knit jug band but switched to electric instruments late in 1966. As the Summer of Love loomed, the Fish were signed to Vanguard and settled into a stable lineup for two years. The "Feel-Like-I'm-Fixin'-to-Die Rag," a black-humored electric shuffle about the Vietnam War, brought them notoriety with their second album; the "F-U-C-K" cheer was changed to "F-I-S-H."

The band appeared at the Monterey Pop Festival (and in the film of it), and at Woodstock, McDonald, solo, led nearly 500,000 people in the cheer. The Fish continued to tour and record, but by 1969, they were getting fewer bookings after their arrest in Worcester, Massachusetts, for inciting an audience to lewd behavior (the cheer). The group began to unravel, although McDonald and Melton (who also had a 1969 marijuana bust) kept a lineup together to appear in the 1971 film *Zachariah*. The Fish disbanded in 1970. McDonald tried some film scores and continued his solo career, sometimes in tandem with Melton, who released his own solo album in

1971, *Bright Sun Is Shining.* Melton became a public defender in Mendocino County, north of San Francisco. He ran unsuccessfully for a city judgeship in Mendocino in 1992.

McDonald continued to tour and in late 1975 signed with Fantasy and recorded *Paradise With an Ocean View.* The Fish regrouped for 1977's *Reunion,* but McDonald was solo again for *Rock and Roll Music From the Planet Earth.* In the '80s McDonald began releasing albums on his own Rag Baby label. Though still a pacifist, he also became a champion of Vietnam veterans' causes. From the '90s through 2000 he worked to erect memorials in the notoriously antiwar Bay Area. *Vietnam Experience* is a thematic concept work featuring a new version of the "Feel-Like-I'm-Fixin'-to-Die Rag." Both *Superstitious Blues* and *Carry On* are studio albums that boast guest guitar by Jerry Garcia. In 1998 McDonald went to England and recorded *Eat Flowers and Kiss Babies,* a collaboration with the indie-psych band the Bevis Frond.

Wayne/Jayne County

Born Wayne Rogers, July 13, 1947, Dallas, GA
1978—*The Electric Chairs* (Safari, U.K.); *Storm the Gates of Heaven* 1979—*Things Your Mother Never Told You* 1980—*Rock 'n' Roll Resurrection* 1986—*Private Oyster* (Revolver, U.K.) 1995—*Deviation* (Royalty); *Rock 'n' Roll Cleopatra.*

Rock & roll's most famous transsexual, Jayne County started out as rock & roll's most famous transvestite, Wayne County. His life in the spotlight began when he moved to New York from his native Georgia in the late '60s. County appeared playing a female role opposite Patti Smith in an off-Broadway production of *Femme Fatale* before tackling the role of Florence Nightingale in *World—Birth of a Nation.* In 1970 Andy Warhol cast County in his show *Pork,* with which County traveled to England. David Bowie was impressed and signed County to his Mainman management company.

On returning to New York, County's first band, Queen Elizabeth, began performing in lower Manhattan clubs like Max's Kansas City, where groups like the New York Dolls were forging a new union between camp and rock & roll. Queen Elizabeth's drummer, Jerry Nolan, was a late addition to the Dolls' lineup and later a member of the Heartbreakers. County's stage wardrobe consisted of skimpy pink dresses, fishnet stockings, heavy makeup, and a platinum-blond wig, but in spite of the sexual spoofs, County's performances were more rock & roll show than drag show.

In 1975, after being dropped by Mainman, County cut an album for ESP-Disk; its release was delayed, and then the tracks were lost in a fire. His vinyl debut was three tracks on the double-album compilation *Max's Kansas City.* He formed the Electric Chairs in 1977 and toured Britain that year. In 1978 the Electric Chairs were signed up by a German label, Safari, and released their first album. County disappeared for some time after that, reemerging in 1980 after starting the hormone treatment for a sex-change operation (County never had the final operation). *Rock 'n' Roll Resurrection* was a live set that included "Cream in My Jeans," "(If You Don't Want to Fuck Me, Baby), Fuck Off!," and "Bad in Bed." By the late '80s County, who had spent several years in Germany, was living in London, England. She had recorded several European solo releases and was planning to forsake music for a religious college, to study Biblical archaeology. In the '90s, County resurfaced and became a fixture on the glam rock and drag/transexual scenes. Her autobiography, *Man Enough to Be a Woman,* was published in 1996 (it had appeared the previous year in England). A new, domestic studio album, *Deviation,* and a career-spanning anthology, *Rock 'n' Roll Cleopatra,* coincided with the book. County's latest effort is a remix single entitled "Fuck Off 2000."

Don Covay

Born Mar. 1938, Orangeburg, SC
1964—*Mercy* (Atlantic) 1966—*Seesaw* 1969—*The House of Blue Lights* (with the Jefferson Lemon Blues Band) 1970—*Different Strokes for Different Folks* (with the Jefferson Lemon Blues Band) (Janus) 1973—*Super Dude I* (Mercury) 1974—*Hot Blood* 1976—*Travelin' in Heavy Traffic* (Philadelphia International) 1992—*Checkin' in With Don Covay* (Mercury) 2000—*Adlib* (Cannonball).

As a soul singer with a high gospel-inspired voice, Covay had a handful of hits in the '60s and '70s, but is best known for a songwriting catalogue that includes Aretha Franklin's "Seesaw" and "Chain of Fools." The son of a Baptist minister who moved the family to Washington when Covay was a child, he sang with the family gospel quartet the Cherry-Keys. When he was 17, he joined the Rainbows, who had already had a local hit, "Mary Lee." His solo career got underway two years later when he opened a Washington concert for Little Richard, who named him Pretty Boy and took him to Atlantic Records. Atlantic issued Covay's first Pretty Boy disc, "Bip Bop Bip," in 1957.

Covay recorded under his own name and with his group, the Goodtimers, for Sue, Columbia, Epic, RCA, Arnold, Cameo, Parkway, Landa, and Rosemart, placing four singles on the pop chart—including "Pony Time" (#60, 1961) and "Mercy Mercy" (#35, 1964)—before Atlantic reacquired him in 1965. With Atlantic he scored his first soul hit, "Please Do Something" (#21, 1965). "Seesaw" was both an R&B hit (#5, 1965) and a pop hit (#44). Covay continued to record for Atlantic until 1971, when he signed with Janus. In 1972 he joined Mercury, both as an artist and A&R director. He returned to the charts in 1973 with "I Was Checkin' Out, She Was Checkin' In" (#29 pop, #6 R&B) and followed it the next year with "It's Better to Have (and Don't Need)" (#21 R&B). In 1981 he toured with Wilson Pickett and Solomon Burke in a package called the Soul Clan. Covay, who suffered a major stroke in 1992, was the subject of a critically acclaimed tribute album, *Back to the Streets: Celebrating the Music of Don Covay,* in 1993. By 2000 the R&B great had recovered enough to release his first new album in 25 years, *Adlib.* Credited to Don Covay and Friends, the record features Huey Lewis, Paul Rodgers, Wilson Pickett, and numerous other guests.

Cowboy Junkies

Formed 1985, Toronto, Can.
Michael Timmins (b. Apr. 21, 1959, Montreal, Can.), gtr.; Alan Anton (b. Alan Alizojvodic, June 22, 1959, Montreal), bass; Margo Timmins (b. Jan. 27, 1961, Montreal), voc.; Peter Timmins (b. Oct. 29, 1965, Montreal) drums.
1986—*Whites Off Earth Now!* (Latent; reissued by RCA in 1990) 1988—*The Trinity Session* (RCA) 1990—*The Caution Horses* 1992—*Black-Eyed Man* 1993—*Pale Sun, Crescent Moon* 1995—*200 More Miles: Live Performances 1985–1994* 1996—*Studio: Selected Studio Recordings 1986–1995; Lay It Down* (Geffen) 1998—*Miles From Our Home* 1999—*Rarities, B-Sides and Slow, Sad Waltzes* (Latent) 2000—*Waltz Across America* 2001—*Open* (Zoë/Rounder).

The Cowboy Junkies play slow, pensive country- and blues-based songs rendered unearthly by Margo Timmins' angelic drawl. The band is based around its sibling trio and an old musical partnership between Michael Timmins and Alan Anton, childhood friends who moved to New York and then London to play in punk bands in the early '80s. When neither situation worked out, Michael moved back to Toronto and began jamming with his brother; soon they were joined by Anton and Margo. They chose their name and the title of their first album specifically to provoke attention. It worked; the self-released debut and the band's local following won them a deal with RCA.

The Trinity Session, recorded in a 14-hour session in an old church on a shoestring budget, became a sensation on college radio, helped by some video play and Lou Reed's endorsement of their version of the Velvet Underground's "Sweet Jane." The album also included covers of Hank Williams' "I'm So Lonesome I Could Cry," Patsy Cline's "Walking After Midnight," and a reworking of "Blue Moon."

On *The Caution Horses,* Michael wrote more songs and proved that his obsession with country music had trained his ear for lyric twists and simple melodies. The album was recorded live, but in a professional studio.

On *Black-Eyed Man,* Michael continued to develop his narrative style in a country vein, writing about "Southern Rain" and murder in a trailer park. Townes Van Zandt wrote two songs for the album, and "Crescent Moon," the opening track of the band's 1993 album, was dedicated to the Texas singer/songwriter. That album's literary pretensions—two tracks quoted William Faulkner and Gabriel García Márquez—were balanced by a cover of Dinosaur Jr's "The Post."

Lay It Down was the group's first album for Geffen and their first to enlist an outside producer, John Keane (R.E.M., Indigo Girls); it also yielded the Modern Rock hit "A Common Disaster." *Miles From Our Home,* recorded in London with producer John Leckie (Radiohead, the Verve), featured songs that reflected on the death of Van Zandt and the Timmins' 94-year-old grandfather. In 1999 the group revived their Latent imprint and released a collection of odds and ends, including covers of songs written by Bob Dylan and the Grateful Dead.

The Cowsills

Formed mid-'60s, Newport, RI
Barbara Cowsill (b. 1929; d. Jan. 31, 1985); Bill Cowsill (b. Jan. 9, 1948, Newport); Bob Cowsill (b. Aug. 26, 1950, Newport); Dick Cowsill (b. Aug. 26, 1950, Newport); Paul Cowsill (b. Nov. 11, 1952, Newport); Barry Cowsill (b. Sep. 14, 1954, Newport); John Cowsill (b. Mar. 2, 1956, Newport); Susan Cowsill (b. May 20, 1960, Newport).
1967—*The Cowsills* (MGM) 1968—*We Can Fly; Captain Sad and His Ship of Fools* 1969—*The Best of the Cowsills; The Cowsills in Concert* 1971—*On My Side* (London).

This musical family from Rhode Island provided the inspiration for TV's *The Partridge Family.* Under father William "Bud" Cowsill's direction, the Cowsill kids and mom played the New York City clubs regularly in the mid-'60s, attracting the attention of MGM, which released their debut album in November 1967. By early 1968 they had had their first hit single, "The Rain, the Park, & Other Things" (#2). Lots of touring, network TV appearances, and a few more hits, including the theme from the rock musical *Hair* (#2, 1969), preceded their disbandment in early 1970. Mother Barbara died in 1985; three of the brothers and Susan reunited to tour and record demos five years later.

In the '90s Barry Cowsill worked as a solo artist. Bill Cowsill formed the band Blue Shadows, which released several albums in Canada. In 1991 Susan Cowsill and ex-Bangle Vicki Peterson formed the L.A.-based Psycho Sisters. The duo performed together and sang with such artists as Giant Sand, Steve Wynn, and the Continental Drifters, the latter of whom they would eventually join. Susan Cowsill married fellow Drifter Peter Holsapple (ex-dB's); they split up in 2000. Bob, John, Susan, and Paul revived the Cowsills in 1994 and contributed a new track to the compilation *Yellow Pills, Volume One. Global,* their 1998 comeback album, was released only through the Internet. Various Cowsill siblings occasionally reunite to perform together.

Kevin Coyne

Born Jan. 27, 1944, Derby, Eng.
1972—*Case History* (Dandelion, U.K.) 1973—*Marjory Razorblade* (Virgin) 1974—*Blame It on the Night* 1975—*Matching Head and Feet* 1976—*Heartburn; In Living Black and White* 1978—*Dynamite Daze; Millionaires and Teddy Bears; Beautiful Extremes* 1979—*Babble* (with Dagmar Krause) 1980—*Bursting Bubbles* 1982—*Pointing the Finger* 1982—*Politicz; Dandelion Years* 1983—*Beautiful Extremes Etcetera; Legless in Manila* (Rough Trade) 1990—*Peel Sessions* (Strange Fruit).

British songwriter Kevin Coyne released several albums in the '70s, but his unconventional song formats and abrasive vocal style have proven commercially unsuccessful. Born and raised in England, he attended art school in the early '60s. In 1965 he began working as a social therapist in a psychiatric hospital in Preston, England, and his experiences were the subject of several of his songs. After appearing sporadically in Preston clubs, he moved to London in 1969.

In 1972 Coyne abandoned social work for a musical career. He was already known as lead vocalist with the group Siren, which recorded two albums for Dandelion. His first solo effort, *Case History,* was released on Dandelion in the U.K. and has since become a collector's item. He signed with Virgin in 1973 and drew critical kudos for his double set *Marjory Razorblade,* which was reduced to a single disc for U.S. release. Throughout the mid-'70s he continued to record regularly and generally kept his own band together. His strongest backing aggregation played on 1976's *Heartburn* and the following year's double live set, *In Living Black and White.* Group personnel included Zoot Money (keyboards and vocals) and Andy Summers (guitar), who joined the Police shortly thereafter. Coyne has also written and appeared in several theatrical productions. He is also a painter and artist. Throughout the '80s and '90s he has released numerous albums on small labels in the U.K. and Germany. These include 1992's *Burning Head,* a limited-edition CD, and 1995's *The Adventures of Crazy Frank,* which formed the basis of an improvised musical about English comic Frank Randle. Coyne continues to tour and record, often with his sons, Robert and Eugene.

Cracker: See Camper Van Beethoven

The Cramps

Formed 1975, New York, NY
Lux Interior (b. Erick Lee Purkhiser, Oct. 21, 1946, Akron, OH), voc.; Poison Ivy Rorschach (b. Christine Marlana Wallace, Feb. 20, 1953, Sacramento, CA), gtr.; Bryan Gregory (b. 1955, Detroit, MI; d. Jan. 10, 2001, Anaheim, CA), gtr.; Pam "Balam" Gregory (b. Detroit), drums.
1975—(– Pam Gregory; + Miriam Linna [b. Oct. 16, 1955, Sudpury, Can.], drums) 1977—(– Linna; + Nick Knox [b. Nicholas George Stephanoff], drums) 1979—*Gravest Hits* EP (I.R.S.) 1980—*Songs the Lord Taught Us* (– Bryan Gregory + Kid Congo Powers [b. Brian Tristan, Mar. 27, 1961, La Puente, CA], gtr.) 1981—*Psychedelic Jungle* 1983—*Smell of Female* EP (Enigma) (– Powers) 1984—*Bad Music for Bad People* (I.R.S.) 1986—*A Date With Elvis* (Big Beat, Austral.) 1987—(+ Candy Del Mar, bass) *Rockin' n' Reelin' in Auckland New Zealand* (Vengeance) 1990—*Stay Sick!* (Enigma); *Creature From the Black Leather Lagoon* EP (– Del Mar + Slim Chance, bass; + Jim Sclavunos, drums) 1991—*Look Mom, No Head!* (Restless) 1994—(– Sclavunos, + Harry Drumdini, drums) *Flamejob* (Warner Bros.) 1997—*Big Beat From Badsville* (Epitaph).

The Cramps: Poison Ivy, Lux Interior, Slim Chance, Harry Drumdini

The Cramps combine rockabilly, psychedelia, sex, and B-movie sleaze into a thick, swampy stew. They were conceived in Cleveland, by Erick Purkhiser (who took the name Lux Interior) and Christine Wallace (Poison Ivy Rorschach), who had met in Sacramento and moved together to Lux's native Ohio. Lux and Ivy moved to New York in 1975, and started the Cramps after enlisting brother and sister Bryan Gregory and Pam "Balam" the following year. Aspiring journalist Miriam Linna, who'd known Lux and Ivy in Ohio, replaced Balam on drums after a few months. With their energetic two-guitar, no-bass attack and Lux's energetic, slightly deranged stage presence, the Cramps quickly became mainstays of the CBGB scene. Linna left in 1977 to join Nervus Rex (she has since played with the Zantees and the A-Bones, and founded *Kicks* magazine and Norton Records with fellow A-Bone Billy Miller), and was replaced by drummer Nick Knox.

With this lineup, the band went to Ardent studios in Memphis to record its Alex Chilton–produced 1977 singles "Surfin' Bird" b/w "The Way I Walk" and "Human Fly" b/w "Domino." In 1979 they combined them, along with "Lonesome Town," also from the Chilton sessions, for an EP, *Gravest Hits.* Signed to I.R.S., with Chilton again producing, they released *Songs the Lord Taught Us,* its echoey psychobilly powering originals ("T.V. Set"), '50s classics (Johnny Burnette's "Tear It Up"), and oddities ("Strychnine"). These recordings, as well as the band's wild performances, earned them a rabid cult following, including a fan club, Legion of the Cramped (one of its founders was future Smiths frontman, Morrissey).

In May 1980 Bryan Gregory left the band under mysterious circumstances; soon after, he released a single with Beast and unsuccessfully sought to become an actor. Reportedly, his post-Cramps occupations ranged from coven warlock to sex-shop entrepreneur to tattoo artist. He died of heart failure in 2001. After the Cramps relocated to L.A., Gregory was replaced by then–Gun Club guitarist and founding member Kid Congo Powers, who played on the aptly named, self-produced *Psychedelic Jungle* (1981).

By late 1981, the band filed a $1.1 million suit against I.R.S. charging the company and its owner, Miles Copeland, with thwarting their industry growth. The case was settled out of court, details untold, but effectively releasing the band from the label. With the exception of the 1983 live EP, *Smell of Female* (released within a week after the case was settled), and the *Bad Music for Bad People* compilation, the Cramps' recordings were not released domestically until 1990. With only Lux and Ivy remaining, the Cramps toured extensively, using a revolving cast of (usually female) guitarists and, in later years, bass players. Cramps albums emphasized the band's sexual obsessions, with songs that could be offensive were it not for their good-humored tastelessness.

In 1991 Lux and Ivy, with help from Iggy Pop, released *Look Mom, No Head!,* and toured Europe and the States, with bassist Slim Chance and former Teenage Jesus and sometime Bad Seed drummer Jim Sclavunos. With Harry Drumdini replacing Sclavunos, the band recorded two albums, *Flamejob* (1994) and *Big Beat From Badsville* (1997). While neither album was a big seller, the Cramps remain a popular touring unit.

The Cranberries

Formed 1990, Limerick, Ire.
Dolores O'Riordan (b. Sep. 6, 1971, Limerick), voc.; Noel Hogan (b. Dec. 25, 1971, Limerick), gtr.; Mike Hogan (b. Apr. 29, 1973, Limerick), bass; Fergal Lawler (b. Mar. 4, 1971, Limerick), drums.
1993—*Everybody Else Is Doing It, So Why Can't We?* (Island) 1994—*No Need to Argue* 1996—*To the Faithful Departed* 1999—*Bury the Hatchet* (PolyGram).

The Celtic-tinged music of the Cranberries combines the vocal strength of their chanteuse Dolores O'Riordan with a simple acoustic guitar–driven sound. In the mid-'90s the band became Ireland's most successful musical export since U2 when the band's atmospheric pop single "Linger" hit the U.S. Top 10. Embroiled in infighting, the band has struggled to duplicate its early success.

In 1990 brothers Mike and Noel Hogan formed a band with drummer Fergal Lawler called the Cranberry Saw Us. They soon recruited O'Riordan, who had been writing songs since she was 12. After listening to guitarist Noel Hogan's instrumental demos, O'Riordan quickly composed the lyrics and melody to "Linger."

Following their signing with Island Records, the Cranberries had a falling-out with their original manager/producer Pearse Gilmore. In 1992, replacing Gilmore with a new manager and a new producer, they recorded their debut album, *Everybody Else Is Doing It, So Why Can't We?* (#18, 1993). The Cranberries' U.S. tour included an appearance at Woodstock '94; that performance and heavy MTV rotation of the "Linger" video help propel the single to #8. *No Need to Argue* (#6, 1994) produced more hit singles, including "Zombie" and "Ode to My Family," and was certified gold or platinum in more than 25 countries.

In the wake of international success, the Cranberries fell prey to dissension, which was fueled by O'Riordan's increased profile as the band's frontperson. The recording of *To the Faithful Departed* (#4, 1996) was reportedly acrimonious, and the accompanying tour had to be curtailed; the Cranberries then decided to take off several months before recording *Bury the Hatchet* (#13, 1999). While *No Need to Argue* and especially *To the Faithful Departed* attempted to mix rock and social commentary, *Bury the Hatchet* was a return to the band's more introspective pop side.

Robert Cray

Born Aug. 1, 1953, Columbus, GA
1980—*Who's Been Talkin'* (Tomato) 1983—*Bad Influence* (HighTone) 1985—*False Accusations* 1986—*Strong Persuader* (Mercury) 1988—*Don't Be Afraid of the Dark* 1990—*Midnight Stroll; Too Many Cooks* (Tomato) 1992—*I Was Warned* (Mercury) 1993—*Shame + a Sin* 1995—*Some Rainy Morning* 1997—*Sweet Potato Pie* 1999—*Take Your Shoes Off* (Rykodisc) 2001—*Shoulda Been Home.*
With Albert Collins and Johnny Copeland: 1985—*Showdown!* (Alligator).

In the '80s guitarist and singer Robert Cray revitalized the audience for contemporary blues. With a lean style owing much to Albert Collins, Cray is also capable of Jimi Hendrix–like pyrotechnics; a player of unarguable conviction, he has managed to evade the myopia of the "blues purist" by incorporating funk, R&B, and jazz touches. With Cray displaying a passion for soulful vocalists like O.V. Wright, his lyrics also introduce an emotion that was rare in the blues: remorse.

Of middle-class background, Cray learned the blues secondhand, through his parents' collection of Otis Rush, Buddy Guy, and Chicago blues records, as well as gospel and R&B classics. By 1974 the Robert Cray Band (then featuring bassist Richard Cousins and drummer Tom Murphy) had established itself on the Pacific Northwest blues scene; in 1978 Cray appeared in *Animal House,* playing in the movie's fictional band. Also that year, he signed with Tomato, which released his debut two years later.

Due in part to Tomato dissolving, *Who's Been Talkin'* died commercially, but *Bad Influence* and *False Accusations* brought Cray a growing following among musicians (Eric

Clapton later covered "Bad Influence"). The latter album was Cray's breakthrough, a Top 200 release. *Strong Persuader* fared even better, entering the Top 20 and winning a Grammy. *Don't Be Afraid of the Dark* confirmed Cray's maturity.

While hailed as a songwriter of emotionally complex material, Cray continued to draw notice chiefly for his guitar work: He played with Clapton and Keith Richards in the Chuck Berry documentary *Hail! Hail! Rock 'n' Roll,* and with Steve Cropper at a 1992 Guitar Legends concert in Spain. Backed by the Memphis Horns, *Midnight Stroll* and *I Was Warned* showed the guitarist and a new lineup of players moving even further from their blues base. While trying out gospel- and Stax-inflected numbers, Cray ensured nonetheless that the music retained its grit. His critical stature remained high: Since 1998, each of his albums has been nominated for Grammy Awards.

Cream

Formed 1966, England
Eric Clapton (b. Mar. 30, 1945, Ripley, Eng.), gtr., voc.; Jack Bruce (b. May 14, 1943, Glasgow, Scot.), bass, harmonica, voc.; Ginger Baker (b. Peter Baker, Aug. 19, 1939, Lewisham, Eng.), drums, voc.
1966—*Fresh Cream* (Atco) 1967—*Disraeli Gears* 1968—*Wheels of Fire* 1969—*Goodbye; The Best of Cream* 1970—*Live Cream* 1972—*Live Cream, vol. 2; Off the Top* (Polydor) 1975—*The Best of Cream Live* 1983—*Strange Brew: The Very Best of Cream.*

Cream was the prototypical blues-rock power trio. In a mere three years, it sold 15 million records, played to SRO crowds throughout the U.S. and Europe, and redefined the instrumentalist's role in rock. Cream formed in mid-1966 when drummer Ginger Baker left Graham Bond's Organisation, bassist Jack Bruce (formerly of Bond's band) left Manfred Mann, and Eric Clapton, already a famous guitarist in the U.K., left John Mayall's Bluesbreakers.

Debuting at the 1966 Windsor Jazz and Blues Festival, Cream established its enduring legend on the high-volume blues jamming and extended solos of its live shows. Its studio work, however, tended toward more sophisticated original rock material, most of it written by Bruce with lyricist Pete Brown. Cream's U.S. hit singles included "Sunshine of Your Love" (#5, 1968), "White Room" (#6, 1968), and a live version of the Robert Johnson country blues "Crossroads" (#28, 1969). *Wheels of Fire,* made up of a live LP and a studio LP (both recorded in the U.S.), was #1 for four weeks in summer 1968, just as the group was coming apart.

Tension within the band led to a quick breakup. Cream gave its farewell concert, which was filmed as *Goodbye Cream,* on November 26, 1968, at London's Royal Albert Hall. After patching together the *Goodbye* LP—which featured "Badge," cowritten by Clapton and George Harrison—Clapton and Baker subsequently formed Blind Faith [see entry], and Bruce went solo [see entry]. Clapton and Baker soon also went on to solo careers [see entries]. In 1993 the trio was inducted into the Rock and Roll Hall of Fame; Clapton, Baker, and Bruce reunited to perform three songs at the ceremonies.

Cream: Ginger Baker, Eric Clapton, Jack Bruce

Creed

Formed 1995, Tallahassee, FL
Scott Stapp (b. Aug. 8, 1973, Orlando, FL), voc., gtr.; Mark Tremonti (b. Apr. 18, 1973, Detroit, MI), gtr; Scott Phillips (b. Feb. 22, 1973, GA), drums; Brian Marshall (b. Apr. 24, 1973, MS), bass.
1997—*My Own Prison* (Blue Collar Records; Wind-Up) 1999—*Human Clay* 2000—(– Marshall).

Creed emerged from the same North Florida club circuit that spawned fellow chart-champions Matchbox Twenty. Led by singer Scott Stapp, Creed's mainstream rock sound was heavily influenced by the Doors, Pearl Jam, and the Christian psalms Stapp's father once forced him to copy down as punishment. On the band's multimillion-selling debut album, *My Own Prison* (#26), Stapp's dramatic baritone tackled themes of unity, tolerance, and his own spiritual crises.

The son of a Pentecostal preacher, Stapp grew up in a devoutly Christian home where rock & roll was not tolerated. Soon after leaving home, he quit his prelaw studies at Florida State University and drifted from job to job, even living in his car for a time. In Tallahassee, Stapp reunited with high school friend Mark Tremonti, who had been playing guitar for 10 years. They recruited drummer Scott Phillips and bassist Brian Marshall and began playing club shows, drawing on lyrics that Stapp had already been writing.

The band spent $6,000 to record an album that was independently released in April 1997 on Blue Collar Records. The album had sold 6,000 CDs when Creed signed to the BMG-distributed Wind-Up Records, which had the band back in the studio to refine the album's sound. *My Own Prison* eventually sold 4 million copies, becoming the best-selling hard-rock album in 1998. "One" (#70) and the title song became rock-radio hits.

Though pointedly not a Christian pop band, Creed has attracted a large following partly for its music's existential and theological content. The debut was followed in 1999 by the heavier *Human Clay* (#1), which included the hit "Higher" and "With Arms Wide Open" (#1, 2000), which won a 2000 Grammy for Best Rock Song. Creed produced the soundtrack for *Scream 3,* which included a new Creed song, "Is This the End?" and "What If" from *Human Clay.* The band also performed "Riders on the Storm" on 2000's *Stoned Immaculate* tribute to the Doors. By now the band endured the open disdain of critics and such contemporaries as Limp Bizkit and Blink-182. Marshall left the band in August 2000 after criticizing Pearl Jam on a Seattle radio show. He was temporarily replaced on a subsequent tour by singer/guitarist Brett Hestla (Virgos Merlot).

Creedence Clearwater Revival

Formed 1959, El Cerrito, CA
John Fogerty (b. May 28, 1945, Berkeley, CA), gtr., voc., harmonica, sax, piano; Tom Fogerty (b. Nov. 9, 1941, Berkeley; d. Sep. 6, 1990, Scottsdale, AZ), gtr.; Stu Cook (b. Apr. 25, 1945, Oakland, CA), bass; Doug "Cosmo" Clifford (b. Apr. 24, 1945, Palo Alto, CA), drums.
1968—*Creedence Clearwater Revival* (Fantasy) 1969—*Bayou Country; Green River; Willie and the Poor Boys* 1970—*Cosmo's Factory; Pendulum* 1971—(– Tom Fogerty) 1972—*Mardi Gras; Creedence Gold* 1973—*More Creedence Gold; Live in Europe* 1976—*Chronicle* 1980—*Live at Albert Hall* 1986—*Chronicle Vol. 2*
John Fogerty solo: 1973—*The Blue Ridge Rangers* (Fantasy) 1975—*John Fogerty* (Asylum) 1985—*Centerfield* (Warner Bros.) 1986—*Eye of the Zombie* 1997—*Blue Moon Swamp* 1998—*Premonition* (Reprise).
Tom Fogerty solo: 1972—*Tom Fogerty* (Fantasy) 1973—*Excalibur* 1974—*Zephyr National* 1975—*Myopia* 1981—*Deal It Out.*
Tom Fogerty with Ruby: 1976—*Ruby* (Alchemy) 1977—*Rock and Roll Madness* 1985—*Precious Gems* (Fantasy).
Sidekicks (Tom Fogerty with Randy Oda): 1991—*Rainbow Carousel* (Fantasy).

John Fogerty's fervent vocals and modernized rockabilly songs built on his classic guitar riffs made Creedence Clearwater Revival the preeminent American singles band of the late '60s and early '70s. The Fogerty brothers were raised in Berkeley, where John studied piano and at the age of 12 got his first guitar. He met Cook and Clifford at the El Cerrito junior high school they all attended. They began playing together, and by 1959 were performing at local dances as Tommy Fogerty and the Blue Velvets. In 1964 the quartet signed to San Francisco–based Fantasy Records, where Tom had been working as a packing and shipping clerk. The label renamed them the Golliwogs and began putting out singles. "Brown-Eyed Girl" sold 10,000 copies in 1965, but the followups were flops. Greater success came after they adopted the CCR moniker in 1967.

Several Fogerty compositions appeared on *Creedence Clearwater Revival,* but cover versions of Dale Hawkins' "Suzie Q" and Screamin' Jay Hawkins' "I Put a Spell on You" were the group's first hit singles. With the release of *Bayou Country* it became the most popular rock band in America. Beginning with the two-sided gold hit "Proud Mary" (#2, 1969) b/w "Born on the Bayou," Creedence dominated Top 40 radio for two years without disappointing the anticommercial element of the rock audience.

CCR's rough-hewn rockers often dealt with political and cultural issues, and the quartet appeared at the Woodstock Festival. Creedence had seven major hit singles in 1969 and 1970, including "Bad Moon Rising" (#2, 1969), "Green River" (#2, 1969), "Fortunate Son" (#14, 1969), "Down on the Corner" (#3, 1969), "Travelin' Band" (#2, 1970), "Up Around the Bend" (#4, 1970), and "Lookin' Out My Back Door" (#2, 1970).

Although Creedence's success continued after *Cosmo's Factory,* it was the group's artistic peak. Internal dissension, primarily the result of John Fogerty's dominant role, began to pull the band apart in the early '70s. Tom left in January 1971, one month after the release of the pivotal *Pendulum,* which became the group's fifth platinum album. The band carried on as a trio, touring worldwide; *Live in Europe* was the recorded result. CCR's final album, *Mardi Gras,* gave Cook and Clifford an equal share of the songwriting and lead vocals. It was the band's first album not to go platinum. Creedence disbanded in October 1972, and Fantasy has subsequently released a number of albums, including a live recording of a 1970 Oakland concert, which upon original release was erroneously titled *Live at Albert Hall* (it was later retitled *The Concert*).

Creedence Clearwater Revival: Tom Fogerty, Doug Clifford, Stu Cook, John Fogerty

Tom Fogerty released a number of albums on his own and with his band Ruby, and worked occasionally in the early '70s with organist Merle Saunders and Grateful Dead guitarist Jerry Garcia. He moved to Arizona in the mid-'80s and died there from respiratory failure brought on by AIDS in 1990 at age 48. Clifford released a solo album in 1972 of '50s-style rock & roll. Thereafter, he and Cook provided the rhythm section for Doug Sahm on his 1974 LP and the Don Harrison Band after 1976. In the mid-'80s Cook joined country group Southern Pacific, which had several hits.

Not surprisingly, John Fogerty's solo pursuits have attracted the greatest attention. Immediately after the breakup he released a bluegrass/country album, *The Blue Ridge Rangers,* on which he played all the instruments. Two songs, the Hank Williams classic "Jambalaya (On the Bayou)" and "Hearts of Stone," made the Top 40. Nearly three years passed before his next LP, another one-man show titled *John Fogerty.* It sold poorly, and his next album, to be called *Hoodoo,* was rejected by Asylum Records. Fogerty and his family retired to a farm in rural Oregon. Except for two brief Creedence reunions he was not heard from for 10 years.

He emerged with *Centerfield* (#1, 1985), a typically simple, tuneful collection that sold 2 million copies and produced hit singles in "The Old Man Down the Road" (#10, 1985), "Rock and Roll Girls" (#20, 1985), and "Centerfield" (#44, 1985). "Old Man" and another song from the album, "Zanz Kant Danz," landed Fogerty in legal trouble however. The latter, a thinly veiled attack against Fantasy owner Saul Zaentz ("Zanz can't dance but he'll steal your money"), led Zaentz to sue for $142 million, not only over that song, but over "Old Man": Fantasy claimed the song plagiarized the music of the 1970 CCR B side "Run Through the Jungle." In 1988 a jury ruled in Fogerty's favor; six years later the Supreme Court ordered Fantasy to reimburse Fogerty for over $1 million in lawyers' fees.

For years Fogerty refused to perform CCR songs live; he'd had to surrender his artist's royalties on them to get out of his Fantasy contract in the '70s. But during a July 4, 1987, concert for Vietnam veterans in Washington, DC, he broke his boycott, singing eight Creedence classics. He then dropped out of sight again, surfacing only for the annual Rock and Roll Hall of Fame induction ceremonies; in 1993 his own turn came when CCR were inducted into the hall. Fogerty refused to perform with Cook and Clifford that evening.

After a decade remission, Fogerty released *Blue Moon Swamp* (#37, 1997); inspired by several trips to the Mississippi Delta, the album had taken over four years to make. It went on to win a Grammy for Best Rock Album, while the single "Southern Streamline" hit #67 on the C&W chart. Fogerty followed up the release with an extensive U.S. tour on which he played many CCR classics such as "Proud Mary" and "Fortunate Son" along with his new material; the live album *Premonition* (#29) was released the following year.

In 1995 Cook and Clifford started touring as Creedence Clearwater Revisited. Fogerty sued and won a temporary injunction barring them from using that name, but his former bandmates ultimately prevailed in the case.

Marshall Crenshaw

Born Marshall Howard Crenshaw, Nov. 11, 1953, Detroit, MI

1982—*Marshall Crenshaw* (Warner Bros.) 1983—*Field Day* 1985—*Downtown* 1987—*Mary Jean & 9 Others* 1989—*Good Evening* 1991—*Life's Too Short* (Paradox/MCA) 1994—*My Truck Is My Home* (Razor & Tie) 1996—*Miracle of Science* 1998—*The Nine Volt Years: Battery Powered Home Demos & Curios (1979–198?)* 1999—*#447.*

As he did in his portrayal of John Lennon in the traveling '70s stage show *Beatlemania* and as Buddy Holly in the 1987 film *La Bamba,* Marshall Crenshaw has breathed new life into old pop forms. His solidly crafted rootsy albums have been praised for their tunefulness, spirit, and romantic lyrics.

Crenshaw grew up in a musical family (his brother, Robert Crenshaw, has drummed in his band) in suburban Detroit, where he listened to '60s AM rock radio and rockabilly. He began playing guitar when he was six. After high school he performed in oldies bands until he moved to L.A. and got the role in *Beatlemania.* He quit after two years and moved to New York City in 1980, where he gigged around town and won praise for his original tunes and solid musicianship. His debut, released to much acclaim, contains his biggest hit to date, "Someday, Someway" (#36).

Crenshaw's songs have been covered by Bette Midler, the Nitty Gritty Dirt Band, Robert Gordon, Freedy Johnston, Kelly Willis, Marti Jones, and the Gin Blossoms. In the U.K., Owen Paul took the Crenshaw B side "My Favorite Waste of Time" to #3. A music aficionado, Crenshaw has recorded songs by Richard Thompson, John Hiatt, Bobby Fuller, the Isley Brothers, and Chris Knox. By *Good Evening,* his lack of commercial success had eroded his relationship with Warner, and he was barely writing songs; in one last (unsuccessful) bid for stardom, he recorded a Diane Warren tune, then moved to MCA.

Crenshaw's acting career includes an appearance in *Peggy Sue Got Married.* He turned down the lead in the London stage production of *Buddy,* however, because he considered the show blindly nostalgic. Enlisting fellow pop-culture trivia buffs, Crenshaw oversaw and wrote reviews for *Hollywood Rock: A Guide to Rock 'n' Roll in the Movies* (1994). He issued *My Truck Is My Home,* a live album, the same year.

In 1996 Crenshaw released the self-produced *Miracle of Science,* most of it recorded at his home studio. Along with original material, the set included covers of songs by Ray Price, Billy Fury, Dobie Gray, and ex–Hüsker Dü drummer Grant Hart. Crenshaw also recorded the theme song to the 1996 TV sitcom *Men Behaving Badly.* Since then he has released a collection of demos and rarities and a new studio album, *#447.*

Jim Croce

Born Jan. 10, 1943, Philadelphia, PA; died Sep. 20, 1973, Natchitoches, LA
1969—*Approaching Day* (Capitol); *Croce* 1972—*You Don't Mess Around With Jim* (ABC) 1973—*Life and Times; I Got a Name* 1974—*Photographs and Memories: His Greatest Hits* (21 Records/Atlantic); *The Faces I've Been* (Lifesong) 1977—*Time in a Bottle: Jim Croce's Greatest Love Songs* (21 Records/Atlantic).

Singer/songwriter Croce had several early-'70s hits before he died in a plane crash. Croce began playing guitar professionally at 18, when he entered Villanova University. There he hosted a folk and blues show on campus radio and played in local bands. After graduation he did construction work and had to alter his guitar technique after breaking a finger with a sledge hammer. By 1967 he was living in New York and playing the coffeehouse circuit. He and his wife, Ingrid, released *Approaching Day* on Capitol that year. When it failed to chart, he returned to club work and drove trucks.

In 1971 he submitted some songs to producer Tommy West, an old college chum. With partner Terry Cashman, West helped Croce cut *You Don't Mess Around With Jim.* Released in early 1972, it produced two hit singles, "Operator" (#17, 1972) and the title track (#8, 1972). *Life and Times* and "Bad, Bad Leroy Brown" (#1, 1973) followed. He was killed when his chartered plane crashed into a tree soon after takeoff on September 20, 1973, in Louisiana. Among the five other victims of the crash was his longtime guitarist Maury Muehleisen. (Croce, in fact, had supported Muehleisen on his own Capitol album, *Gingerbread.*)

I Got a Name, completed before Croce's death and released in late 1973, went gold, as did its #10 title track and "Time in a Bottle" (#1, 1973). Within months of Croce's death, three of his LPs were in the Top 20: *Life and Times, I Got a Name,* and *You Don't Mess Around with Jim.* The latter reigned at #1 for five weeks in early 1974. As of this writing, the singer's widow Ingrid owns a San Diego club called Croce's, where his son A.J. performs.

Steve Cropper: See Booker T. and the MG's

Crosby, Stills, Nash and Young

Formed 1968, Los Angeles, CA
David Crosby (b. David Van Cortland Crosby, Aug. 14, 1941, Los Angeles), gtr., voc.; Stephen Stills (b. Stephen Arthur Stills, Jan. 3, 1945, Dallas, TX), gtr., kybds., bass, voc.; Graham Nash (b. Graham William Nash, Feb. 2, 1942, Salford, Eng.), gtr., kybds., voc.; Neil Young (b. Neil Percival Kenneth Ragland Young, Nov. 12, 1945, Toronto, Can.), gtr., voc.
1969—*Crosby, Stills and Nash* (Atlantic) 1977—*CSN* 1980—*Replay* 1982—*Daylight Again* 1983—*Allies* 1990—*Live It Up* 1991—*CSN* 1994—*After the Storm.*
Crosby, Stills, Nash and Young: 1970—*Déjà Vu* (Atlantic) 1971—*Four Way Street* 1974—*So Far* 1988—*American Dream* 1999—*Looking Forward* (Reprise).
Crosby and Nash: 1972—*Graham Nash/David Crosby* (Atlantic) 1975—*Wind on the Water* (ABC) 1976—*Whistling Down the Wire* 1977—*Crosby-Nash Live* 1978—*The Best of Crosby/Nash.*
David Crosby solo: 1971—*If I Could Only Remember My Name* (Atlantic) 1989—*Oh Yes I Can* (A&M) 1993—*Thousand Roads* (Atlantic) 1994—*It's All Coming Back to Me Now.*
Graham Nash solo: 1971—*Songs for Beginners* (Atlantic) 1973—*Wild Tales* 1980—*Earth and Sky* (EMI) 1986—*Innocent Eyes* (Atlantic).
Stephen Stills solo: 1970—*Stephen Stills* (Atlantic) 1971—*Stephen Stills 2* 1972—*Manassas* (with Manassas) 1973—*Manassas Down the Road* (with Manassas) 1975—*Stills* (Columbia); *Stephen Stills Live* (Atlantic) 1976—*Illegal Stills* (Columbia); *Still Stills: The Best of Stephen Stills* (Atlantic) 1978—*Thoroughfare Gap* (Columbia) 1984—*Right by You* (Atlantic) 1991—*Stills Alone* (Vision).
The Stills-Young Band (with Neil Young): 1976—*Long May You Run* (Reprise).

The close, high harmonies and soft-rock songs of David Crosby, Stephen Stills, and Graham Nash, sometimes joined by Neil Young, sold millions of albums and were widely imitated throughout the '70s. The members were as volatile as their songs were dulcet, and since 1970 have continually split up and regrouped. Crosby, Stills and Nash—all singer/songwriter/guitarists—had already recorded before their debut LP, *Crosby, Stills and Nash,* was released in 1969: Crosby with the Byrds [see entry], Stills and Young with Buffalo Springfield [see entry], and Nash with the Hollies [see entry].

Crosby had worked as a solo performer before joining the Byrds in 1964. In 1967 he quit because of differences with leader Roger "Jim" McGuinn, among them McGuinn's refusal to allow onto *Notorious Byrd Bros.* Crosby's "Triad," a song about a menage à trois that the Jefferson Airplane recorded on *Crown of Creation;* Crosby sang it on *Four Way Street* (and the Byrds' recording of it eventually surfaced on the 1990 Byrds box set). Crosby began preparation for a solo album, which eventually appeared in 1971 as *If I Could Only Remember My Name.* He also produced Joni Mitchell's debut album in 1968; Mitchell's "Woodstock" later became a hit for Crosby, Stills, Nash and Young.

Young had quit Buffalo Springfield on the eve of the 1967 Monterey Pop Festival, and Crosby sat in for him at that concert. After the Springfield broke up in May 1968, Stills and Crosby began jamming together and were soon joined by Nash. Nash, who had been dissatisfied with the Hollies—they had refused to record his "Marrakesh Express" and "Lady of the Island"—joined Crosby and Stills. The three first sang together at a party in the L.A. home of Cass Elliot of the Mamas and the Papas.

Recorded early in 1969, *Crosby, Stills and Nash* was an immediate hit, with singles "Marrakesh Express" (#28) and

Stills' "Suite: Judy Blue Eyes" (#21) (about Judy Collins). At the helm was Stills, playing nearly every instrument on the album, a feat that earned him the nickname Captain Manyhands. Although the trio's harmonies were less than perfect outside the recording studio, Crosby, Stills, Nash and Young began touring in midyear (Young joined them in summer 1969; Stills had originally asked John Sebastian, formerly of the Lovin' Spoonful, to round out the group). Their second live appearance was before half a million people at the Woodstock Festival in August 1969.

The quartet's first album, *Déjà Vu,* took two months to make and had advance orders for 2 million copies—it eventually went on to sell over 7 million—and included three hit singles: "Woodstock" (#11, 1970), "Teach Your Children" (#16, 1970), and "Our House" (#30, 1970). A few weeks after *Déjà Vu's* release, the National Guard shot and killed four students during an antiwar demonstration at Kent State University. In response, Young wrote "Ohio," which the group recorded and released as a single (#14, 1970). They toured that summer, but by the time the double live album *Four Way Street* was released, they had disbanded. The planned next album, *Human Highway,* was started in 1973 but was left unfinished. Young later recorded a single and produced a motion picture of the same title. Released in 1982, it failed to find a distributor, but came out on video in 1995.

Crosby and Nash released solo and duo albums in the early '70s and toured together, while Young returned to his solo career, and Stills started his. Stills' solo debut, which included "Love the One You're With" (#4, 1971), featured guest guitarists Eric Clapton and Jimi Hendrix. In 1974 the quartet toured together for the first time since 1970; Young traveled separately. Stills and Young made a duet album, *Long May You Run,* in 1976, but Young suddenly left Stills mid-tour.

In 1977 Crosby, Stills and Nash regrouped for the quadruple-platinum *CSN,* which included "Just a Song Before I Go" (#7, 1977). The next summer they toured as an acoustic trio, and in the fall of 1979 they performed at the antinuclear benefit concerts sponsored by Musicians United for Safe Energy (MUSE). In 1980 the British-born Nash was granted American citizenship. In 1982 the trio released *Daylight Again,* for which Stills wrote most of the songs, and toured arenas once more. *Daylight* was a Top 10 LP and boasted two Top 20 singles, "Wasted on the Way" (#9) and "Southern Cross" (#18).

In 1985 Crosby—who'd already had a number of run-ins with the law and been charged with drug and weapons possession —was sentenced to prison for nine months after leaving the drug rehabilitation program he was allowed to enter instead of serving a five-year prison sentence for possessing cocaine and carrying a gun. He appeared with Stills, Nash and Young at Live Aid while out on appeal bond. Shortly after his release from prison in 1986, he wrote a compelling account of his long-term drug abuse entitled *Long Time Gone,* which was published in 1990. The four reunited to record *American Dream* (#16, 1989), after which Young refused to tour with his ex–band mates. The trio's next release, *CSN*—a reissue with unreleased tracks—did not crack the Top 100.

By the '90s, Young's solo status as "Godfather of Grunge" had been established. Nash had been successful with Nash Editions, specializing in digital fine-art printing, as a photographer, and as a host of his own cable television talk show. Crosby had received a liver transplant in 1994 shortly after the release of *After the Storm.* In 1995 he reunited with a son, James Raymond, whom the child's mother had given up for adoption in 1962; as CPR, David and Raymond have recorded three albums. By the decade's end, Crosby had also achieved notoriety as the sperm donor for celebrity lesbian mothers Melissa Etheridge and Julie Cypher.

In 1999, largely at the instigation of Stephen Stills, CSN&Y re-formed to record *Looking Forward.* Earlier that year, Nash had broken both legs in a boating accident, but the group's spirits and creativity were sufficiently high for the album to garner critical praise. It was followed by the band's first tour since 1974, a heavily hyped cross-country trek entitled the CSNY2K Tour that featured studio veteran Jim Keltner on drums and Donald "Duck" Dunn of Booker T. and the MG's on bass.

Christopher Cross

Born Christopher Geppert, ca. 1951, San Antonio, TX
1980—*Christopher Cross* (Warner Bros.) 1983—*Another Page* 1985—*Every Turn of the World* 1988—*Back of My Mind* (Reprise) 1992—*Rendezvous* (Ariola/BMG, Ger.) 1995—*Window* (Rhythm Safari) 1998—*Walking in Avalon* (CMC International) 1999—*Red Room.*

Christopher Cross was reared an army brat in Texas. By his late teens he was fronting a copy band in Texas clubs that, in 1972, was ranked Austin's leading cover band. Cross kept writing his own songs as well, and was finally signed by Warner Bros. in fall 1978. When his debut LP was released two years later, it went quadruple platinum and yielded four Top 20 hits: "Sailing" (#1); "Ride Like the Wind" (#2), which featured backing vocals by Michael McDonald of the Doobie Brothers; "Never Be the Same" (#15); and "Say You'll Be Mine" (#20). *Christopher Cross* also featured backing vocals by Nicolette Larson and Valerie Carter.

In 1981 Cross won five Grammy Awards, including Best Record, Best Album, and Best Song. His debut LP was still going strong on the chart in late 1981. In the fall of that year Cross had another massive hit with "Arthur's Theme (The Best That You Can Do)" (from the hit film *Arthur*), a song cowritten by Cross, Peter Allen, Burt Bacharach, and Carole Bayer Sager. It received an Academy Award for Best Original Song. His star soon faded: *Every Turn of the World* (#127, 1985) met mediocre sales, and yielded only a minor hit single in "Charm the Snake" (#68, 1985); *Back of My Mind* featured McDonald on backing vocals again, but still flopped.

Many die-hard fans consider the European-only *Rendezvous* to be Cross' finest work. *Window,* from 1995, is the result of an attempted American comeback. The double-CD *Walking in Avalon* contains a studio album and a live disc of greatest hits. The new songs were also issued separately as *Red Room.*

Sheryl Crow

Born Feb. 11, 1962, Kennett, MO
1993—*Tuesday Night Music Club* (A&M) 1996—*Sheryl Crow* 1998—*The Globe Sessions* 1999—*Sheryl Crow and Friends: Live From Central Park.*

Once a backup singer for Michael Jackson and Don Henley, Sheryl Crow gained mass popularity as a solo artist almost a year after the release of her 1993 debut album, *Tuesday Night Music Club.* Two more well-received records brought her respect for her rootsy pop rock.

Crow grew up in a rural farming community in Missouri. Exposed to music all her life—her parents were amateur musicians who often played in big bands in Memphis, Tennessee—she started singing in rock groups at 16. After receiving a degree in classical piano from the University of Missouri, Crow taught music at a St. Louis elementary school. Then, in 1986, the aspiring singer/songwriter moved to L.A. to pursue a career in the music business. Her first big gig was singing backup on Michael Jackson's 1987–88 Bad tour. She was also a backup singer for Don Henley, George Harrison, Joe Cocker, Stevie Wonder, and Rod Stewart.

In 1991 Crow signed with A&M. She recorded a self-titled debut album the next year but then convinced the record company to scrap it because of its slick production. She replaced it with the rawer *Tuesday Night Music Club* (#3, 1994), which was recorded with a loose-knit group of musicians that gathered on Tuesday nights at producer Bill Bottrell's L.A. studio. The supportive atmosphere encouraged Crow to focus her writing on her personal experiences: The album's "What I Can Do for You" discusses sexual harassment, and "No One Said It Would Be Easy" deals with a relationship's dissolution. The often-boozy evenings also produced more lighthearted songs, including "Leaving Las Vegas," a group collaboration written on the first Tuesday get-together, and "All I Wanna Do" (#2, 1994). The latter received a Grammy as 1994's Record of the Year; Crow also received the Best New Artist and Best Female Pop Vocal Performance awards that year. Bolstered by that song's huge success and Crow's constant touring (she played 542 shows between September 1993 and December 1995), the album went on to sell 9 million copies worldwide.

But while Crow was receiving critical accolades and commercial success, she also had a bitter falling-out with the members of the Tuesday Night Music Club, who accused her of trying to take sole credit for what they felt had been a collaborative effort.

Crow addressed her critics head-on by writing and recording most of her next album, symbolically named *Sheryl Crow* (#6, 1996), on her own. Yet controversy struck again almost immediately. In "Love Is a Good Thing," the singer wrote about children killing each other "with a gun they bought at a Wal-Mart discount store," leading the chain to pull the record from its stores in protest. In spite of that, the album showed that its predecessor was no fluke: A critical success, it also went on to sell 6 million copies with the help of the singles "If It Makes You Happy" (#10, 1996) and "Everyday Is a Winding Road" (#11, 1997). Crow, who had relocated from L.A. to New York, then released the confessional *The Globe Sessions* (#5, 1998) and its flagship single "My Favorite Mistake" (#20, 1998).

Testifying to the respect in which she is held by her peers, the "friends" on the 1999 live recording *Sheryl Crow and Friends* included Keith Richards, Eric Clapton, Chrissie Hynde, and Stevie Nicks (the latter of whom Crow has produced).

Crowded House

Formed July 1985, Melbourne, Austral.
Neil Finn (b. May 27, 1958, Te Awamutu, N.Z.), voc., gtr.; Paul Hester (b. Jan. 8, 1959, Melbourne), drums; Nick Seymour (b. Dec. 9, 1958, Benella, Austral.), bass.
1986—*Crowded House* (Capitol) 1988—*Temple of Low Men* 1989—*I Feel Possessed* EP 1991—(+ Tim Finn [b. June 25, 1952, Te Awamutu], kybds., voc.) *Woodface* 1993—(– Tim Finn; + Mark Hart [b. July 2, 1953, Fort Scott, KS], kybds.) *Together Alone* 1995—(– Hester) 1996—*The Recurring Dream—The Very Best of Crowded House* 2000—*Afterglow.*
Neil and Tim Finn: 1996—*Finn Brothers* (Discovery).
Neil Finn solo: 1998—*Try Whistling This* (Work Group/Sony).
Tim Finn solo: 2000—*Say It Is So* (Periscope Recordings).

Formed by two ex-members of the eccentric, cult-favored pop outfit Split Enz, Crowded House quickly eclipsed that band's popularity, thanks to a debut album of buoyant, impeccably crafted guitar pop. With their radiant melodies and breezy wit, the songs written by Crowded House's singer/guitarist Neil Finn invited references to the work of such smart-pop icons as Squeeze, the Kinks, and the Beatles.

Finn got his start playing in Split Enz [see entry], which was fronted by his big brother Tim, as a teenager. After the group's demise—precipitated by Tim's decision to pursue a solo career—Neil decided to form a band with Paul Hester, a drummer who had joined the latter-day Enz. After enlisting bassist Nick Seymour, the trio Crowded House released its eponymous debut album in 1986, to widespread acclaim. Commercial success wasn't immediate, but the album spawned two Top 10 hits in 1987, the wistful ballad "Don't Dream It's Over" (#2) and the more upbeat "Something So Strong" (#7). A moodier sophomore album, 1988's *Temple of Low Men* (#40), got some good notices but sold poorly.

In 1991 Crowded House resurfaced as a quartet: Tim Finn joined as keyboardist and vocalist/songwriter for *Woodface.* The album did well on the Modern Rock charts, but again yielded no pop hits; after touring with the group that year, the elder Finn returned to his critically praised (but commercially less distinguished) solo career. Crowded House remained a four-piece band, though, replacing Tim with American musician Mark Hart for 1993's *Together Alone.*

During a 1996 tour and just a few weeks before the release of the band's greatest-hits collection, Neil, citing a lack of creative inspiration, disbanded the group. More than 100,000 fans attended Crowded House's televised farewell concert in Sydney, Australia, in November of that year; Hester, who had quit touring in 1995, returned to make the gig a reunion, and Tim joined the others for an encore.

At that time, Neil and Tim had recently released their own collaboration, *Finn Brothers*. Each brother went on to record a solo effort as well. Neil continued to tour on his own, while Tim dabbled in a side project called alt and composed music for a touring tap-dance show called *Steel City* in 1998. Hester became the drummer for the Australian group the Largest Living Things, and co-ran a recording studio and a cafe; Seymour played with the Melbourne-based band Deadstar; and Hart joined the re-formed Supertramp.

Rodney Crowell

Born Aug. 7, 1950, Houston, TX
1978—*Ain't Living Long Like This* (Warner Bros.) 1980—*But What Will the Neighbors Think* 1981—*Rodney Crowell* 1986—*Street Language* (Columbia) 1988—*Diamonds & Dirt* 1989—*Keys to the Highway; The Rodney Crowell Collection* (Warner Bros.) 1992—*Life Is Messy* (Columbia) 1993—*Greatest Hits* 1994—*Let the Picture Paint Itself* (MCA) 1995—*Jewel of the South* 2001—*The Houston Kid* (Sugar Hill).

Rodney Crowell is a country-rock singer/songwriter best known for his production work and his compositions performed by other singers, particularly Rosanne Cash, to whom he was married for 13 years. Crowell's performance of his own confessional songs, many of which were inspired by his rocky marrige to Cash, have earned him more critical acclaim than country- or pop-chart success.

He began drumming in his father's Houston rockabilly band when he was 11 years old, and he played with garage rock & roll bands in his high school and college years before moving to Nashville in the early '70s. Jerry Reed got him a staff songwriting job and recorded several of his songs.

In 1975 Crowell joined Emmylou Harris' Hot Band as backup singer and guitarist, and Harris subsequently recorded more than a dozen Crowell originals ("Leaving Louisiana in the Broad Daylight," "Amarillo"). In 1978 Crowell left the Hot Band to make his recording debut, produced by Harris' then-husband, Brian Ahern; guest musicians included Willie Nelson, Ry Cooder, and Mac Rebennack (Dr. John). The album sold fewer than 20,000 copies, but two years later the title song hit #1 on the country charts twice, in separate versions by Waylon Jennings and the Oak Ridge Boys. Other Crowell interpreters have included Carlene Carter, Willie Nelson, the Dirt Band, Bob Seger, Alan Jackson, Trisha Yearwood, Jimmy Buffett, and Foghat.

In 1979 Crowell began producing Rosanne Cash [see entry], whom he married later that year. He had a hit of his own in 1980 with "Ashes by Now," which made the pop Top 40. In addition to his own albums and his wife's '80s LPs, he has produced albums by Guy Clark, Bobby Bare, Carl Perkins, Johnny Cash, Jerry Lee Lewis, and Jim Lauderdale, among others. In 1985, along with his wife, he ended a cocaine dependence.

Crowell finally attained country chart success with his 1988's *Diamonds & Dirt,* which netted him five #1 C&W singles, including a duet with Rosanne Cash, "It's Such a Small World" (his first-ever Top 10 country single). Crowell became the first country artist to have five self-penned #1 C&W hits from one album. His increasingly confessional songs, many of whose lyrics reflected the tumultuous state of his marriage, turned up on his wife's albums as well as his own. *Keys to the Highway* (1989) was a moving testament to his father, who had died just prior to the album's recording.

In 1992 Crowell and Cash divorced, resulting in many of the songs on *Life Is Messy.* The album featured such guest artists as Linda Ronstadt and Steve Winwood. Crowell left Columbia for MCA in 1994, releasing the more upbeat *Let the Picture Paint Itself.* He recorded *Jewel of the South* for MCA the following year, but departed soon after and returned to Warner Bros. He left that label before completing an album, however, convinced the project he had in mind—a loosely autobiographical song cycle inspired by his Houston roots—wouldn't fit in with the boundaries of mainstream country radio. He ended up financing *The Houston Kid* on his own and releasing it in early 2001 on the independent label Sugar Hill. The critically well-received set features a guest appearance by Johnny Cash on "I Walk the Line (Revisited)."

The Crows

Formed ca. 1951, New York, NY
Daniel "Sonny" Norton (d. 1972), lead voc.; William Davis (d. N.A.), baritone voc.; Harold Major (d. N.A.), tenor voc.; Jerry Wittick (d. N.A.), tenor voc.; Gerald Hamilton (d. ca. '60s), bass voc.
1952—(– Wittick; + Mark Jackson, gtr., tenor voc.).

The Crows' 1954 pop hit "Gee" (#14 pop, #6 R&B) was one of the first records by a black group to cross over into the pop market. The group, which perfected its sound on Harlem street corners, released two flop sides with singer Viola Watkins ("Seven Lonely Days" b/w "No Help Wanted") for the newly formed Rama Records in 1953. Under the guidance of label head George Goldner, the group next recorded William Davis' "Gee," the Crows' only pop hit. Its success prompted Goldner to launch a subsidiary label, Gee, in 1956 (its roster included Frankie Lymon and the Cleftones). The flip side of "Gee," "I Love You So," was a Top 50 hit for the Chantels in 1958. After a quick succession of failed singles (including 1954's "Mambo Shevitz"), Davis joined the Continentals, and the Crows disbanded. There are no surviving original members.

Arthur "Big Boy" Crudup

Born 1905, Forrest, MS; died Mar. 28, 1974, Nassawadox, VA
1968—*Look on Yonder's Wall* (Delmark) 1969—*Mean Ole Frisco* (Trip) 1970—*Crudup's Mood* (Delmark) 1971—*Father of Rock 'n' Roll* (RCA) 1974—*Roebuck Man* (Liberty).

Bluesman Arthur "Big Boy" Crudup wrote "That's All Right, Mama"—one of the first songs Elvis Presley recorded and his first hit—and other rock standards, including "My Baby Left Me" and "Rock Me Mama." Crudup grew up in the Deep South, where he sang in church as a child. In the late '30s he joined a gospel group called the Harmonizing Four and moved with them to Chicago. In 1939 he began playing the guitar and the blues. A year later he was discovered by Okeh and Bluebird Records talent scout Lester Melrose, who helped Crudup get a record deal, but also took advantage of his client's naiveté and never paid him royalties. Crudup stayed with Melrose until 1947, when he realized that he was being cheated. Melrose sold Crudup's contract to RCA, but Crudup recorded only sporadically, and often on other labels under the name Elmore Jones or Percy Crudup (his son's name).

Crudup recorded through the mid-'50s until he quit in disgust. "I just give it up," he said later. He was retired from music, digging and selling sweet potatoes, when during the '60s Philadelphia blues promoter Dick Waterman took an interest in him and his business problems. Waterman began working with the American Guild of Artists and Composers in an attempt to collect some of the royalties Melrose (by then deceased) had withheld from Crudup. Waterman eventually collected $60,000 from BMI and reached a settlement with the music publisher Hill and Range.

Crudup resumed his music career in 1968 and toured the U.S. and Europe until his death from a heart attack in 1974. During his lifetime he had supported a family of 13 children, only four of whom were actually his.

The Crusaders

Formed 1954 as the Jazz Crusaders, Houston, TX
Wilton Felder (b. Aug. 31, 1940, Houston), tenor sax, bass; Joe Sample (b. Feb. 1, 1939, Houston), kybds.; Nesbert "Stix" Hooper (b. ca. 1939, Houston), drums; Wayne Henderson (b. Sep. 24, 1939, Houston), trombone.
1961—*Freedom Sounds* (Pacific Jazz); *Looking Ahead* 1962—*Young Rabbits* (Blue Note); *The Jazz Crusaders at the Lighthouse* (Pacific Jazz) 1963—*Tough Talk; Heat Wave* 1965—*Chile Con Soul* 1966—*Live at the Lighthouse '66; The Festival Album; Talk That Talk* 1967—*Uh Huh* 1968—*Powerhouse* 1969—*Give Peace a Chance* (Liberty) 1971—(+ Larry Carlton [b. Mar. 2, 1948, Torrance, CA], gtr.) *Pass the Plate* (Chisa) 1972—*Crusaders 1* (Blue Thumb); *The 2nd Crusade* (Chisa) 1973—*Unsung Heroes* (Blue Thumb); *The Crusaders at Their Best* (Motown); *Hollywood* 1974—*Scratch* (MCA); *Southern Comfort* (Blue Thumb/MCA) 1975—*Chain Reaction* (– Henderson) 1976—(+ Robert "Pops" Popwell [b. Atlanta, GA], bass) *Those Southern Knights; The Best of the Crusaders* 1977—*Free as the Wind* (– Carlton); *Live: Midnight Triangle* 1978—*Images* (– Popwell) 1979—*Vocal Album; Street Life* 1980—*Rhapsody and Blues; Ghetto Blaster; Standing Tall* 1981—*Live in Japan* (GRP); *Royal Jam* (MCA) 1982—*Ongaku Kai: Live in Japan* (Crusaders) 1983—(– Hooper; + Leon "Ndugu" Chancler, drums) *Vocal Tape* 1986—*The Good and the Bad Times; Life in the Modern World* 1991—(+ Marcus Miller, bass, synth.) *Healing the Wounds* (GRP) 1992—(group disbands) *The Golden Years* 1995—*Soul Shadows* (Alex); *And Beyond* (Music Club); *A.C.* (MCA); *Good Times; Mr. Cool; Mulholland Nights; New Moves; Way It Goes; Zalal'e Mini (Take It Easy);* (Henderson and Felder re-form as the Jazz Crusaders) *Happy Again* (Sin-Drome) 1996—*Way Back Home* (Blue Thumb/MCA); *Louisiana Hot Sauce* (Sin-Drome).
Wilton Felder solo: 1978—*We All Have a Star* (ABC) 1980—*Inherit the Wind* (MCA) 1985—*Secrets* 1991—*Nocturnal Moods* (Par) 1992—*Forever Always.*
Nesbert Hooper solo (as Stix Hooper): 1979—*The World Within* (MCA).
Joe Sample solo: 1978—*Rainbow Seeker* (MCA); *Carmel* (ABC/Blue Thumb) 1981—*Voices in the Rain* (MCA) 1983—*The Hunter* 1985—*Oasis* 1986—*Swing Street Cafe* 1987—*Roles* 1989—*Spellbound* (Warner Bros.) 1990—*Ashes to Ashes* 1991—*Collection* (GRP) 1993—*Invitation* (Warner Bros.) 1994—*Did You Feel That?* 1996—*Old Places Old Faces* 1999—*The Song Lives On* (with Lalah Hathaway) (GRP/PRA).

After 15 years of playing under the name of the Jazz Crusaders and being overlooked by pop, jazz, and soul audiences, in the '70s the Crusaders became one of pop music's hottest instrumental bands, as well as in-demand session players. Wilton Felder, Joe Sample, and Nesbert Hooper first played together in their Houston high school marching band. They then formed the Swingsters, a bebop jazz and Texas-style R&B group. While attending Texas Southern University, they met Wayne Henderson and, with two other students, formed the Modern Jazz Sextet (a tuxedoed outfit modeled on the Modern Jazz Quartet). In 1958 the four future Crusaders moved to L.A., where as the Nighthawks, they backed Jackie DeShannon at one point and played dance clubs as far away as Las Vegas until 1961, when they returned to jazz. As the Jazz Crusaders, they landed a record contract from World Pacific Jazz and during the next decade built a modest following. In 1969, frustrated by lack of recognition, the quartet took a year off.

When they reemerged as the Crusaders, their music had changed to a blend of funk vamps and riffs, terse solos, and dance rhythms. Their singles began placing in the R&B Top 40—"Put It Where You Want It" (#39, 1972), "Don't Let It Get You Down" (#31, 1973), "Keep That Same Old Feeling" (#21, 1976), and "Street Life" (#17, 1979), sung by Randy Crawford—and the pop Top 100. Most of their '70s albums went gold, and in 1975 they became the only instrumental band chosen by the Rolling Stones as an opening act. As studio players, the Crusaders backed Steely Dan, Curtis Mayfield, Joni Mitchell, Ray Charles, Van Morrison, Joan Baez, B.B. King, and Barry White, among others. Other vocalists who have appeared on their albums include Joe Cocker and jazz great Nancy Wilson.

In 1971 Carlton became the first new full-fledged member in over 15 years. Felder played both bass and sax in recording sessions until Popwell's induction in 1976. Henderson left in 1975 to work in production; Carlton left for a solo career in 1976. With Popwell's departure, the band was back to the three founders; this core remained constant until Hooper's departure in 1983, when Leon "Ndugu" Chancler joined as drummer. (The chronology above tracks only the comings and going of key members.) In 1986 the Crusaders celebrated their 30th anniversary with *The Good and Bad Times*. For 1991's *Healing the Wounds* the group included Sample, Felder, and Marcus Miller on bass and synthesizer. While the Crusaders officially dissolved soon after that album, Henderson and Felder reappeared in 1995 and revived the original name, the Jazz Crusaders for *Happy Again*.

The Crystals

Formed 1961, Brooklyn, NY
Original lineup: Dee Dee Kennibrew (b. Delores Henry, 1945, Brooklyn), voc.; Dolores "La La" Brooks (b. 1946, Brooklyn), voc.; Mary Thomas (b. 1946, Brooklyn), voc.; Barbara Alston (b. 1945, Brooklyn), voc.; Patricia Wright (b. 1945, Brooklyn), voc.
1963—*He's a Rebel* (Philles) 1992—*The Best of the Crystals* (Abkco).

One of producer Phil Spector's first successful groups, the Crystals had a sultry image. The group was formed by Brooklyn schoolgirls. In 1961 they met Spector while auditioning in New York, and they became the first act signed to his Philles Records. Their first two releases—"There's No Other (Like My Baby)" (#20, 1961) (the B side of "Oh Yeah Maybe Baby") and Barry Mann and Cynthia Weil's "Uptown" (#13, 1962)—were hits, but their third, "He Hit Me (And It Felt Like a Kiss)," was denied airplay when radio programmers objected to the violent implications of its title and lyrics ("He hit me and I was glad . . .").

The group's only #1 hit, Gene Pitney's "He's a Rebel," was not recorded by the Crystals but by a group of L.A. session singers, the Blossoms, fronted by Darlene Love [see entry], who also sang on the followup, "He's Sure the Boy I Love" (#11, 1963). The original Crystals were featured on the 1963 hits "Da Doo Ron Ron" (#3) and "Then He Kissed Me" (#6). But their 1964 releases—"Little Boy" and "All Grown Up"—were unsuccessful, and Spector lost interest in them. They bought their contract back from him and signed with United Artists, but their Motown-influenced singles also failed to hit.

Kennibrew has kept the Crystals active. Gretchen Gale and Marilyn Byers have accompanied her since the mid-'80s.

The Cult

Formed 1983, Brixton, London, Eng.
Ian Astbury (b. Ian Lindsay, May 14, 1962, Heswell, Merseyside, Eng.), voc.; Billy Duffy (b. William H. Duffy, May 12, 1959, Manchester, Eng.), gtr.; Jamie Stewart, bass; Nigel Preston (b. 1959; d. May 7, 1992), drums.
1984—*Dreamtime* (Beggars Banquet) 1985—(– Preston) *Love* (Sire) (+ Les Warner [b. Feb. 13, 1961], drums) 1987—*Electric* 1989—*Sonic Temple* (– Stewart; – Warner; + Matt Sorum [b. Nov. 19, 1960, CA], drums) 1990—(– Sorum) 1991—*Ceremony* (+ Craig Adams [b. Apr. 4, 1962, Otley, Yorkshire, Eng.], bass; + Scott Garrett [b. Mar. 14, 1966, Washington, DC], drums) 1994—*The Cult* 1999—(– Garrett; – Adams; + Sorum; + Martyn Lenoble [b. Apr. 14, 1969, Neth.], bass) 2000—*The Cult: The Best of Rare Cult* (– Lenoble).
Holy Barbarians (Astbury, voc.; Matt Garret, bass; Patrick Sugg, gtr., voc.; Scott Garrett, drums): 1996—*Cream*.
Ian Astbury solo: 2000—*Spirit Light Speed* (Beggars Banquet).

When the Cult first surfaced on the British indie label Beggars Banquet in the early '80s, its music attempted to bridge the gap between heavy metal and goth-style punk. It wasn't until the group decided to claim the heavy-metal tag in earnest, however, that it finally found its signature sound, which combines the pseudo-mysticism of the Doors and Led Zeppelin with the hard-rock crunch of AC/DC. For some listeners, the Cult is a brilliant parody; for others, it is the real thing.

Ian Astbury, son of a merchant navy man, formed Southern Death Cult in Bradford, England, in 1981. Two years later he recruited ex–Theatre of Hate guitarist Billy Duffy, a Manchester native who had played in a pre-Smiths combo with Morrissey, and changed the group's name to simply the Cult.

Although the lineup was rounded out on *Dreamtime* by bassist Jamie Stewart and drummer Nigel Preston, the group's roster was never etched in stone. Preston was replaced by Les Warner. Thereafter, the Cult underwent a succession of drummers, both onstage and in the studio, including Mickey Curry, Big Country's Mark Brzezicki, and future Guns n' Roses drummer Matt Sorum. Over the years, Warner would resurface now and again. By *Ceremony*, both Stewart and Warner were gone for good, and the band's official lineup was back down to original members Astbury and Duffy, soon joined by Craig Adams and Scott Garrett.

The dreamy, layered, almost experimental music on the Cult's 1984 debut kept the band obscure. The group's 1985 major-label debut, *Love*, however, reached #87 and spawned two U.K. Top 20 singles, "She Sells Sanctuary" and "Rain." With producer Rick Rubin (Beastie Boys, Run-D.M.C.) behind the mixing board for *Electric* (#38, 1987), the Cult was propelled out of cultdom and into the lucrative heavy-metal arena. The band's subsequent albums fared much better: The platinum-selling *Sonic Temple* reached #10 in 1989, with the singles "Edie (Ciao Baby)" (#93, 1989), a tribute to the late Andy Warhol star/model Edie Sedgwick, and "Fire Woman" (#46, 1989). On *Ceremony* (#25, 1991) Astbury continued his Native American/Robert Bly bonding philosophy in songs such as "Wild Hearted Son" (containing an Indian dance chant), the environmentalist "Earth Mofo," and "Indian."

After a three-year hiatus, Astbury and Duffy returned with a new version of the band for *The Cult* (#69, 1994), an album closer in sound and spirit to *Love*, but the album was met with mixed reviews while interest in the band had seemingly diminished in the grunge era. While touring behind the album, the Cult broke apart once again when Astbury abruptly quit after a 1995 show in Rio de Janiero. The singer reemerged in 1996 with a new band called Holy Barbarians (including Garrett), which released one album, *Cream*. Astbury also would release a solo album in 2000. But by 1999, the Cult had re-formed once again (this time including Sorum and ex–Porno for Pyros bassist Martyn Lenoble), playing its most popular material to sold-out audiences.

Culture Club/Boy George

Formed 1981, London, Eng.
Boy George (b. George Alan O'Dowd, June 14, 1961, Bexley, Eng.), voc.; Roy Hay (b. Aug. 12, 1961, Southend-on-Sea, Eng.), gtr., kybds.; Mikey Craig (b. Feb. 15, 1960, London), bass; Jon Moss (b. Jonathan Aubrey Moss, Sep. 11, 1957, London), drums.
1982—*Kissing to Be Clever* (Virgin) 1983—*Colour by Numbers* 1984—*Waking Up With the House On Fire* 1986—*From Luxury to Heartache* (Virgin/Epic) 1993—*At Worst . . . The Best of Boy George and Culture Club* (SBK) 1998—*VH1 Storytellers/Greatest Moments* (Virgin).
Boy George solo: 1987—*Sold* (Virgin) 1989—*High Hat* 1991—*The Martyr Mantras* 1995—*Cheapness & Beauty* (EMI) 1999—*Unrecoupable One Man Bandit* (Nu Gruv/Finetune).

Led by soulful tenor and ever-quotable androgyne Boy George, Culture Club took its blue-eyed soul to the top of the charts. An exponent of London's postpunk New Romantic club scene, which saw disaffected youths sporting flamboyant clothes and makeup, Boy George charmed with his disarming playfulness and basically wholesome wit. Culture Club's music, ridden with sensual rhythms and irresistible hooks, proved equally accessible. George's decidedly feminine makeup, long braided locks, and penchant for long, dresslike tunics clearly stood out amid the other acts in heavy rotation on the then-nascent MTV, where for a time Culture Club was a staple. But after two huge albums, the band and its frontman began a downward spiral that culminated in one of the biggest pop star drug scandals of the 1980s.

George appeared briefly in the Malcolm McLaren–managed pop outfit Bow Wow Wow before meeting bassist Mikey Craig. The two enlisted drummer Jon Moss, who had played with Adam and the Ants and the Damned, and guitarist/keyboardist Roy Hay. Culture Club had its first major hit with the reggae-laced 1982 single "Do You Really Want to Hurt Me," which went to #1 in England and #2 in the U.S. The group's debut album reached America in early 1983, yielding two more Top 10 singles that year, "Time (Clock of the Heart)" (#2, 1983) and "I'll Tumble 4 Ya" (#9, 1983). A second album, 1983's *Colour by Numbers*, shot to #2 and spawned the hits "Church of the Poison Mind" (#10, 1983), "Karma Chameleon" (#1, 1983), "Miss Me Blind" (#5, 1984), and "It's a Miracle" (#13, 1984). Culture Club won the 1983 Grammy for Best New Artist.

A disappointing third album, which contained the simplistic single "The War Song" (#13 U.S., #2 U.K.) followed, and before long rumors were circulating that George was addicted to heroin. Pressured by police raids, the singer publicly revealed his drug habit in July 1986, months after the release of Culture Club's fourth and final album. George was arrested on possession charges, and sought treatment with Dr. Meg Patterson, who had helped Eric Clapton and Pete Townshend overcome dependencies. Once weaned off heroin, however, George turned to prescription narcotics. Later that year two of his friends died of drug overdoses—one, musician Michael Rudetsky, at George's home.

After being cleared of charges implicating him in Rudetsky's death, George successfully completed another drug rehabilitation program. Several solo albums followed, producing dance hits in Europe (including a reggae-inflected cover of Bread's "Everything I Own"), but George failed to reemerge significantly on the U.S. pop chart until his cover of Dave Berry's 1964 British hit "The Crying Game" was featured in the 1992 film of the same name. Buoyed by the movie's success, the single reached #15.

In 1995 George released a new solo album and a telling autobiography, *Take It Like a Man*, in which he wrote openly about his homosexuality and revealed that he'd had a romantic relationship with drummer Moss during the band's heyday. (Moss later married and maintained that he was heterosexual.) George became a successful DJ on the London club scene and ran a small, independent, British dance-music label called More Protein Records. Then in 1998, Culture Club reunited for a nostalgia tour with other '80s acts; the band's first comeback performance was a taping of *VH1 Storytellers*, which was recorded as half of a new double-disc set. George released another solo album the following year.

The Cure

Formed 1976, Crawley, Eng.
Robert Smith (b. Apr. 21, 1959, Blackpool, Eng.), gtr., voc.; Michael Dempsey, bass, voc.; Laurence "Lol" Tolhurst (b. Feb. 3, 1959), drums.
1979—*Three Imaginary Boys* (Fiction, U.K.); *Boys Don't Cry* (– Dempsey; + Simon Gallup [b. June 1, 1960, Surrey, Eng.], bass; + Mathieu Hartley, kybds.) 1980—*Seventeen Seconds* (– Hartley) 1981—*Faith; Carnage Visors* cassette (Fiction); *. . . Happily Ever After* (Fiction/A&M) 1982—*Pornography* 1983—*The Walk* EP (Fiction/Sire); *Japanese Whispers* 1984—*The Top; Concert: The Cure Live* (Fiction); (+ Porl Thompson [b. Nov. 8, 1957, London, Eng.], gtr.; + Boris Williams [b. Apr. 24, 1957, Versailles, Fr.], drums) 1985—*The Head on the Door* (Elektra) 1986—*Quadpus* EP; *Standing on a Beach: The Singles; Staring at the Sea: The Singles* 1987—*Kiss Me, Kiss Me, Kiss Me* 1988—*The Peel Sessions* EP (Strange Fruit/Dutch East India) (+ Roger O'Donnell, kybds.) 1989—

Disintegration (Elektra) (– Tolhurst) *Entreat* (Fiction) (– O'Donnell; + Perry Bamonte [b. Sep. 6, 1960, London], kybds.) 1990—*Pictures of You* EP (Elektra); *Integration; Mixed Up* (Elektra) 1992—*Wish* 1993—*Show; Paris* (– Thompson) 1994—(– Williams) 1994–1995—(+ O'Donnell; + Jason Cooper, drums) 1996—*Wild Mood Swings* (Fiction/Elektra) 1997—*Galore* (Elektra) 2000—*Bloodflowers* (Fiction/Elektra).
Robert Smith with the Glove (with Steve Severin, bass): 1983—*Blue Sunshine* (Polydor).

Dubbed the "masters of mope rock," the Cure rose from Britain's late-'70s punk scene to become one of the biggest-selling "underground" acts of the '80s. Frontman Robert Smith, who has been described as the "messiah of melancholy" and the "guru of gloom," is known for wearing death-white facial makeup, crimson lipstick, and teased black hair; he is rivaled only by Morrissey as a heartthrob for the discontented. The Cure's goth-pop style is characterized by self-obsessed lyrics, minor-key melodies, and Smith's vexatious whine.

Robert Smith grew up in working-class Crawley, Sussex, a suburb of London. He recalls his childhood years as difficult, a time of run-ins with his parents and the law. At 17 he formed the Easy Cure with childhood friends Laurence Tolhurst and Michael Dempsey as a sort of catharsis for his feelings of frustration. The group's music has remained therapeutic for Smith.

The Cure made its initial splash in the U.K. with the 1979 single "Killing an Arab," which stirred controversy when it reappeared on the mid-'80s retrospective *Standing on a Beach: The Singles*. Some U.S. radio DJs used the song, which was inspired by Albert Camus' *The Stranger*, to advance anti-Arab sentiments; the group included a disclaimer with subsequent pressings stating that the song "decries the existence of all prejudice and consequent violence."

While the Cure toured in 1979 as the support act to Siouxsie and the Banshees, the headliner's guitarist quit the band. Smith was recruited to fill in on the tour, beginning an active collaboration with the Banshees. He ultimately devoted much of 1983–84 as a full-time member of the band, recording both the live *Nocturne* and a studio album, *Hyaena*. In 1983, he also joined Banshees bassist Steve Severin for a side project called the Glove, releasing one album, *Blue Sunshine*.

When Smith once again devoted himself to the Cure, the music evolved from the sparse punk pop of that song and other early singles ("Boys Don't Cry," "Jumping Someone Else's Train," "The Lovecats") to the dirgy, moody music of *Faith* and *Seventeen Seconds*, to the more focused hits on the later albums *Kiss Me, Kiss Me, Kiss Me, Disintegration*, and *Wish*.

While the Cure had been a top hitmaking indie band in the U.K. since the early '80s, it wasn't until the release of *Standing on a Beach* (and its CD-only counterpart, *Staring at the Sea*) (#48, 1986) that the band moved beyond its cult status in the U.S. The double-album *Kiss Me, Kiss Me, Kiss Me* (#35) debuted in June 1987, spawning the minor hits "Why Can't I Be You?" (#54, 1987), "Just Like Heaven" (#40, 1987),

The Cure: Simon Gallup, Perry Bamonte, Boris Williams, Robert Smith

and "Hot Hot Hot!!!" (#65, 1988). In 1989 *Disintegration* reached #12 and included the group's biggest hit yet, "Love Song" (#2). *Wish* is the band's most successful album to date, reaching #2 and including the surprisingly upbeat "Friday I'm in Love" (#18). The subsequent tour was documented on record and a film, both titled *Show* (an additional live collection, *Paris*, culled from the same tour was also released in 1993).

In 1996 the Cure released *Wild Mood Swings* (#12), which attempted to broaden the band's sound to include a track of Latin-flavored pop, earning mostly negative reviews, and with "The 13th" (#44) its highest-charting single. Another best-of, *Galore* (#32), followed in 1997. Then, in 2000, Smith unveiled the band's best-reviewed album in years, *Bloodflowers*. That same year, Smith launched a world tour by announcing that it would be the band's last. But the bandleader soon began to hedge on that promise, saying all the subsequent attention and sudden acclaim made him strangely . . . happy.

Cypress Hill

Formed 1988, Los Angeles, CA
B-Real (b. Louis Freese, June 2, 1970, Los Angeles), voc.; Sen Dog (b. Senen Reyes, Nov. 20, 1965, Havana, Cuba), voc.; DJ

Muggs (b. Lawrence Muggerud, Jan. 28, 1968, Queens, NY), DJ.
1991—*Cypress Hill* (Ruffhouse/Columbia) 1993—*Black Sunday* 1994—(+ Eric Bobo [b. Aug. 27, New York, NY], perc.) 1995—*Cypress Hill III: Temples of Boom* 1996—(– Sen Dog) *Unreleased & Revamped* EP ca. 1997–98—(+ Sen Dog) 1998—*IV* 1999—*Los Grandes Éxitos en Español* 2000—*Skull & Bones; Body Parts* EP; *Live at the Fillmore.*
DJ Muggs solo: 1997—*Muggs Presents . . . Soul Assassins Chapter 1* (Ruffhouse/Columbia) 2000—*Muggs Presents Soul Assassins II* (Ruffnation).
B-Real with the Psycho Realm: 1997—*The Psycho Realm* (Ruffhouse/Columbia) 2000—*A War Story* (Meanstreet).
Sen Dog with SX-10: 1998—*Get Wood Sampler* (Flip) 2000—*Mad Dog American* (Latin Thug/X-Ray).

A Latino rap trio based near South Central L.A., Cypress Hill made a controversial name for itself in the early '90s by speaking out in favor of marijuana legalization. The trio's songs—characterized by smooth and funky bass-heavy rhythms, a nasal vocal delivery reminiscent of the Beastie Boys, and hard-hitting musical mixes filled with screaming sirens and car alarms—feature constant references to pot ("cheeba," "blunts," "buddha") and guns. Lyrics also tap into B-Real's experiences growing up surrounded by gangs and crime, including his own days selling drugs and being hit with a .22-caliber bullet during a deal gone bad (an incident later recounted in 1993's "Lick a Shot").

In 1986 Cuban-born Sen Dog and his younger brother, rapper Mellow Man Ace, formed a group called DVX, which included homeboys B-Real and Muggs. Pioneers of the Latin lingo style, "Spanglish," they became a trio and renamed the group for a neighborhood street when Ace departed for a solo career.

Cypress Hill's self-titled debut reached #31 pop and #4 R&B in 1992 and remained on the pop chart for 89 weeks. It contained the controversial single "How I Could Just Kill a Man" (#77, 1992) b/w "The Phuncky Feel One" (#94, 1992). Their highly successful followup, the pessimistic *Black Sunday* (#1 pop, #1 R&B, 1993), gave the group a Top 20 single via "Insane in the Brain" (#19 pop, #27 R&B, 1993). *Cypress Hill III: Temples of Boom* (#3 pop, #3 R&B, 1995) leaned more on live players and sold respectably but failed to spawn a signature hit single. ("Boom Biddy Bye Bye" got only as far as #87 pop, #73 R&B). That failure initially seemed to spell the end of Cypress Hill: Sen Dog quit in 1996, while Muggs focused on a critically praised solo album, *Muggs Presents . . . Soul Assassins* (#20 pop, #6 R&B, 1997), an all-star gathering that included B-Real, Dr. Dre, Wyclef Jean, and KRS-ONE. Sen Dog formed an alternative rock band called SX-10, and was temporarily replaced for live Cypress performances by rapper Shag G. The *Unreleased & Revamped* EP reached #21 pop, #15 R&B in 1996.

Sen Dog returned in time for Cypress Hill's *IV* (#11 pop, #15 R&B, 1998), followed a year later by *Los Grandes Éxitos en Español,* which collected Spanish versions of Cypress hits, as translated with the help of Mellow Man Ace. By then percussionist Eric Bobo (the son of noted Latin percussionist Willie Bobo), who had joined in 1994, was a full member of the group. Cypress Hill experienced a commercial comeback with the two-disc *Skull & Bones* (#5 pop, #4 R&B, 2000). Half the album was dedicated to straight-ahead hip-hop, with the other half mixing rap and metal guitars, spawning two versions of their song "Superstar," one rap, the other rock.

Billy Ray Cyrus

Born Aug. 25, 1961, Flatwoods, KY
1992—*Some Gave All* (Mercury) 1993—*It Won't Be the Last* 1994—*Storm in the Heartland* 1996—*Trail of Tears* 1997—*The Best of Billy Ray Cyrus: Cover to Cover* 1998—*Shot Full of Love* 2000—*Southern Rain* (Monument).

Not since white rapper Vanilla Ice has an entertainer become so hot so fast, or inspired as much derisive backlash, as country singer Billy Ray Cyrus did in 1992. Cyrus' ticket to superstardom was a catchy #1 country single called "Achy Breaky Heart," (#4 pop, 1992) penned by Don Von Tress, which propelled the singer's debut album *Some Gave All* to the top of both the pop and country charts. The album sold over 9 million copies, and Cyrus eclipsed Garth Brooks—for a while, anyway—as contemporary country's biggest crossover star. For years, he looked to be a one-hit wonder, though eventually, he enjoyed a more modest degree of success.

Cyrus began playing guitar at 20, forming a band called Sly Dog. He moved to L.A. soon afterward to pursue a recording contract. He wound up selling cars instead and eventually moved back East to Huntington, West Virginia. Cyrus was signed to Mercury in 1990, and recorded *Some Gave All* with the members of a re-formed Sly Dog. The "Achy Breaky Heart" single and video premiered in early 1992, and Mercury promoted them with dance-club contests that made "the Achy-Breaky" a national line dance craze. But Cyrus' music, much of which he wrote, was dismissed as fluff by critics and by several of his Nashville peers. The singer's good ole boy simplicity and macho good looks earned him an unfortunate reputation as a dumb hunk. In a nod to his skeptics, Cyrus called his 1993 sophomore album *It Won't Be the Last* (and it wasn't). The album was actually better received than its predecessor, but it didn't spawn any monster hits on the order of "Achy Breaky." Neither did 1994's *Storm in the Heartland.*

Cyrus took a more roots-oriented approach to *Trail of Tears* (#125, 1996), but ironically, it was his greatest-hits collection (#23 C&W, 1997) that sparked a country comeback. "It's All the Same to Me," a new track off the album, hit #19 on the country singles chart. In late 1998, he released *Shot Full of Love* (#32 C&W) and had another country hit, the #3 "Busy Man." Yet Cyrus' redemption was short-lived: His longtime label, Mercury, dropped him in 1999. Afterward, Cyrus turned his attention to acting, scoring roles in the TV movies *Mullholland Drive* (a failed David Lynch series pilot) and *Doc,* as well as the feature films *Radical Jack* and *Wish You Were Dead.*

Dick Dale

Born Richard Monsour, May 4, 1937, Boston, MA
1962—*Surfer's Choice* (Deltone) 1963—*King of the Surf Guitar* (Capitol); *Checkered Flag* 1964—*Mr. Eliminator; Summer Surf* 1984—*The Tigers Loose* (Balboa) 1986—*Greatest Hits* (Crescendo) 1989—*King of the Surf Guitar: The Best of Dick Dale and His Del-Tones* (Rhino) 1993—*Tribal Thunder* (HighTone) 1994—*Unknown Territory* 1996—*Calling Up Spirits* (Beggars Banquet) 1997—*Better Shred Than Dead: The Dick Dale Anthology* (Rhino) 2000—*Spacial Disorientation* (Dick Dale).

Guitarist Dick Dale's 1961 West Coast hit "Let's Go Trippin' " (#60 pop), released two months before the Beach Boys' "Surfin'," is considered the harbinger of the '60s surf-music craze. Billed as the "King of the Surf Guitar," Dale pioneered a musical genre that Beach Boy Brian Wilson and others would later bring to fruition. His twangy, heavily reverbed tone on the 1962 "Misirlou" (which, like "Trippin'," the Beach Boys covered on their early LPs) influenced Beach Boy Carl Wilson and many other California guitarists; his signature staccato slide down the strings was copied by the Chantays to open their surf instrumental classic "Pipeline." Dale said he created this style to mirror the feeling of surfing, which he'd first discovered as a teenager, when his family moved from Boston to Southern California.

"Misirlou" had originally been a Greek pop standard in the '40s; Dale, whose father was Lebanese, often worked Middle Eastern melodies into his music (even recording "Hava Nagila" on the flip side of one early single), translating mandolin-style rapid double-picking to his highly amplified Fender Stratocaster. The left-handed Dale played his Strat upside-down; he later claimed the young Jimi Hendrix often came to see him perform at the Rendezvous Ballroom in Balboa. Dale developed a close relationship with the Fender company: He was the first to road-test its portable reverb unit, and he designed the Showman amplifier with Leo Fender.

Dale and his band the Del-Tones were so popular in Southern California's Huntington Beach/Balboa area that he felt no need to tour nationally. Though he appeared on TV's *Ed Sullivan Show* in 1963, Dale never reaped the commercial rewards of the surf boom; his only other appearance on the chart came in 1963 with "The Scavenger." By 1965, disillusioned with the music business, he retired. The following year doctors found six cancerous tumors in his intestines; he was told he had only months to live, but he survived surgery. He re-formed the Del-Tones in 1970 and continued performing around Southern California with different versions of the group (ranging from seven to 12 pieces) through the '80s. Dale rerecorded many of his best-known tunes on the 1986 *Greatest Hits,* and recorded *The Tigers Loose* [*sic*] live in Huntington Beach.

Dale's comeback began with a guest appearance in the 1987 Frankie Avalon–Annette Funicello movie *Back to the Beach* (he had appeared in several of their '60s beach-party epics), in which he and Stevie Ray Vaughan performed "Pipeline." Their version was nominated for a Best Rock Instrumental Grammy. He returned in earnest in 1993, with critics acclaiming the speed-metal ferocity of *Tribal Thunder,* which added a Native American feel to Dale's Bedouin-surf mix, prompted the first nationwide tour of his career, and even brought him to MTV with his first music video, "Nitro." Dale gained even more prominence via his "Misirlou," which opened the hit film *Pulp Fiction* (1994). *Calling Up Spirits* (1996) was similar in inspiration to *Tribal Thunder.* Dale continues to record and perform, to the delight of fans who call themselves Dick Heads.

Roger Daltrey: See the Who

The Damned

Formed 1976, England
Brian James (b. Brian Robertson, Feb. 18, 1955, Eng.), gtr.; Captain Sensible (b. Raymond Ian Burns, Apr. 24, 1954, Eng.), bass, gtr.; Rat Scabies (b. Chris Millar, July 30, 1955, Surrey, Eng.), drums; Dave Vanian (b. David Letts, Oct. 12, 1958, Eng.), voc.
1977—*Damned, Damned, Damned* (Stiff, U.K.) (– Scabies; + Lu Edmonds [b. Robert Edmonds, Sep. 24, 1957], gtr.; + Jon Moss [b. Sep. 11, 1957, London, Eng.], drums) *Music for Pleasure* 1978—(– James; – Edmonds; + Alistair Ward a.k.a. Algy [b. July 7, 1959], bass) (group disbands) (group re-forms: Scabies; Sensible; Vanian; + Henry Badowski [b. Sep. 5, 1958], bass; – Badowski; + Ward) 1979—*Machine Gun Etiquette* (Chiswick, U.K.) 1980—(– Ward; + Paul Gray [b. Aug. 1, 1958], bass, voc.) *The Black Album* (I.R.S.) 1981—(+ Roman Jugg [b. July 25, 1957], kybds., gtr.) 1982—*Strawberries* (Bronze, U.K.) 1983—(– Gray) 1984—(– Sensible; + Bryn Merrick [b. Oct. 12, 1958], bass) 1985—*Phantasmagoria* (MCA) 1986—*Anything* 1987—*The Light at the End of the Tunnel* 1988—(+ Sensible) 1989—(– Jugg; – Merrick) *Final Damnation* (Restless) 1993—*Tales From the Damned* (Cleopatra) (+ Kris Dollimore, gtr.; + Alan Lee Shaw, gtr.; + Moose [b. Jason Harris], bass) 1995—(– Dollimore; – Shaw; – Moose; – Scabies) 1996—(+ Gray, bass; – Gray; + Patricia Morrison [b. Patricia Rainone, bass; + Garrie Dreadful, drums; + Monty the Moron, kybds.) *Not of This Earth; Fiendish Shadows* 1999—(– Dreadful; + Spike, drums; – Spike; + Pinch [b. Andrew Pinching], drums).
Captain Sensible solo: 1984—*A Day in the Life of Captain Sensible* (A&M).

The Damned were the first British punk band to record, to chart, and to tour America. Their history goes back to early 1975, when Brian James joined Mick Jones in the London S.S., a punk group whose members included Paul Simonon and Terry Chimes (a.k.a. Tory Crimes), who later formed the Clash with Jones; Tony James, who went on to Chelsea and Generation X; and Rat Scabies, with whom Brian James joined Nick Kent's Subterraneans. When Kent returned to writing for the *New Musical Express,* James, Sensible, and Scabies stayed together as the Masters of the Backside. They were managed by Malcolm McLaren (who later managed the Sex Pistols), and their singer was Chrissie Hynde, who later formed the Pretenders [see entry]. Scabies enlisted Vanian, a gravedigger, into the group after overhearing him sing, "I Love the Dead" at his sister's funeral.

The four first performed in London in July 1976. They were notorious for their stage act, with Sensible dressed in a tutu and prodding front-row spectators with his bass, Scabies bounding from behind his drums to exchange blows with onlookers, and Vanian as Dracula in a black cape. Stiff Records signed them in September, and in October they released a single, "New Rose," one month before the Sex Pistols' first record. Early in 1977 they released their first album (produced by Nick Lowe, as was "New Rose") and played clubs in New York, L.A., and San Francisco.

Their second album (produced by Nick Mason of Pink Floyd) got a poor reception. Scabies left to form a group with Patti Smith pianist Richard Sohl and former Clash/future Public Image Ltd. guitarist Keith Levene. He was replaced by Jon Moss for a tour of Britain with the Dead Boys, but by April 1978 the Damned had fallen apart. James formed Tanz der Youth, Moss and second guitarist Lu went to the Edge, and Sensible formed King. Moss would later turn up in Adam and the Ants [see entry] and Culture Club [see entry].

In late 1978 Scabies, Sensible, and Vanian got together again, after joining to play a one-off date with Lemmy of Motörhead. With bassist Henry Badowski of King, they toured Britain as the Doomed—James owned the name "the Damned" and only later relinquished it. Their new records were the most popular of their four years: "Love Song" hit #20 on the U.K. singles chart, and "Smash It Up" made the Top 40. Later in the year, they returned to the U.S., and in 1980, after Ward had been replaced by Paul Gray, formerly of Eddie and the Hot Rods, they cut their first American-released album. In 1982 Captain Sensible released a solo album in the U.K., *Women and Captains First* (A&M), which included the hit single "Wot" (#26 U.K.). His U.S. solo debut album, *A Day in the Life of Captain Sensible* contained tracks from his first two albums, which were not released here. James and Dead Boys vocalist Stiv Bators formed the Lords of the New Church [see the Dead Boys entry].

In 1984 Captain Sensible left the band, and Merrick joined. The group's next few singles went Top 40 in the U.K.: "Grimly Fiendish," "The Shadow of Love," and "Is It a Dream" (1985); "Anything" (1986); "Gigolo" and a cover of Love's "Alone Again Or" (1987). The biggest single of the Damned's career was 1986's "Eloise," which went to #3 in their homeland. In the summer of 1989 the group made its farewell concert tour—only to reunite several times through the '90s. Tension erupted between Vanian and Scabies over creative control of 1996's *Not of This Earth,* and Scabies was not a part of the band's 1998 U.S. tour. On the other hand, Captain Sensible did return to the Damned fold. Since 1996 he and Vanian have anchored the band's lineup, which also includes former Gun Club and Sisters of Mercy (and Vanian's wife) Patricia Morrison on bass.

Since the late '80s Vanian has fronted the Phantom Chords, a side project that performs a variety of tunes from the '30s through the '60s. In 2000 Brian James formed Mad for the Racket with MC5 guitarist Wayne Kramer; their debut album, *The Racketeers,* featured Stewart Copeland, Clem Burke, and Duff McKagan.

Damn Yankees

Formed Apr. 1989, New York, NY
Ted Nugent (b. Dec. 13, 1948, Detroit, MI), gtr., voc.; Jack Blades (b. Apr. 24, 1954, Palm, CA), bass, voc.; Tommy Shaw (b. Sep. 11, 1953, Montgomery, AL), gtr., voc.; Michael Cartellone (b. June 7, 1962, Cleveland, OH), drums.
1990—*Damn Yankees* (Warner Bros.) 1992—*Don't Tread.*

Damn Yankees was the most successful of a spate of late-'80s groups formed by aging rock stars such as Bad English (vocalist John Waite with ex-Journey guitarist Neal Schon) and the Firm (ex–Led Zeppelin guitarist Jimmy Page with ex–Bad Company vocalist Paul Rodgers). Damn Yankees added Ted Nugent's trademark metallic crunch to the polished AOR melodicism of Styx and Night Ranger (of "Sister Christian" fame), the respective former bands of Tommy Shaw and Jack Blades.

Nugent and Shaw met at a record-label convention in 1988, began casually jamming and composing together, then recruited Blades. They later maintained that Damn Yankees was not the record-company-boardroom-product it seemed and, in fact, they were turned down by every major label at their first New York City audition.

They finally landed a deal with Warner Bros., and the group's debut album (#13, 1990) went platinum, thanks largely to the anthemic power-ballad "High Enough" (#3, 1990). *Don't Tread* (#22, 1992) yielded the chart single "Where You Goin' Now" (#20, 1992). Nugent, meanwhile, became famous—or infamous—for his outspoken espousal of guns and bow-hunting (which he practiced himself to feed his family) and his verbal attacks on such animal-rights advocates as k.d. lang and Chrissie Hynde [see Ted Nugent entry]. When the group took a hiatus in 1993, Shaw and Blades continued as an eponymous act, and released *Hallucination* (1995).

D'Angelo

Born Michael D'Angelo Archer, Feb. 11, 1974, Richmond, VA
1995—*Brown Sugar* (EMI) 2000—*Voodoo* (Virgin).

Comparing D'Angelo to Prince is almost unavoidable: Both are multitalented, sexy soul-singers studied in the art of the groove. Along with Maxwell, D'Angelo emerged in the '90s as one of the few male vocalist/songwriters to perfect the hybrid of hip-hop and R&B.

The son of a Baptist preacher, D'Angelo began experimenting with keyboards around the age of three. In addition to playing church music on Sundays, D'Angelo spent much of his childhood mimicking artists such as Stevie Wonder, George Clinton, James Brown, and Prince. At 17, D'Angelo rocked the crowd on *Amateur Night at the Apollo* with an energetic rendition of Johnny Gill's "Rub You the Right Way"

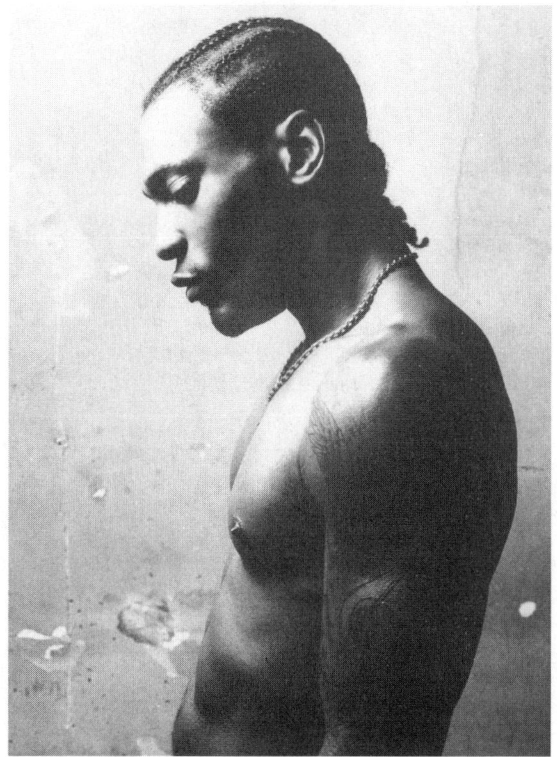

D'Angelo

and won $500—most of which he used to purchase a four-track recorder. At his mother's house he began writing and recording much of the material that would constitute *Brown Sugar* (#22 pop, #4 R&B, 1995)—a collection of afro-tantric grooves that feature D'Angelo playing virtually all of the instruments. The title track "Brown Sugar" (#27 pop, #5 R&B, 1995), "Cruisin' " (#53 pop, #10 R&B, 1995), and "Lady" (#10 pop, #2 R&B, 1996) all enjoyed chart success and radio rotation.

D'Angelo disappeared from the pop limelight for a few years in the late '90s, making scattered cameos on albums by Lauryn Hill, the Roots, and Method Man. D'Angelo resurfaced with the highly anticipated *Voodoo* (#1 pop and R&B, 2000), featuring appearances by Roots drummer Ahmir-Khalib "?uestlove" Thompson and jazzmen Charlie Hunter and Roy Hargrove. Merging the worlds of hip-hop, jazz, and down-home funk, *Voodoo* yielded the hit "Untitled (How Does It Feel)" (#25 pop, #2 R&B, 2000).

The Charlie Daniels Band

Charlie Daniels, born 1937, Wilmington, NC
1970—*Charlie Daniels* (Capitol); *Te John, Grease, and Wolfman* (Kama Sutra) 1972—*Honey in the Rock* 1974—*Way Down Yonder; Fire on the Mountain* 1975—*Nightrider* 1976—*Saddle Tramp* (Epic); *Volunteer Jam* (Capricorn) 1977—*High*

Lonesome; Midnight Wind (Epic) 1978—*Volunteer Jam III and IV* 1979—*Million Mile Reflections* 1980—*Full Moon; Volunteer Jam VI* 1981—*Volunteer Jam VII* 1982—*Windows* 1983—*A Decade of Hits* 1985—*Me and the Boys* 1987—*Powder Keg* 1988—*Homesick Heroes* 1990—*Simple Man; Christmas Time Down South* 1991—*Renegade* 1993—*All-Time Greatest Hits; America, I Believe in You* (Liberty) 1994—*The Door* (Sparrow); *Super Hits* (Epic) 1995—*Same Ol' Me* (Capitol Nashville) 1996—*Steel Witness* (Sparrow); *The Roots Remain* (Epic) 1997—*Blues Hat* (Blue Hat); *By the Light of the Moon* (Sony Wonder) 1998—*Fiddle Fire—25 Years of the Charlie Daniels Band* (Blue Hat) 1999—*Tailgate Party; Volunteer Jam/Classic Live Performances, vol. 1; Volunteer Jam/Classic Live Performances, vol. 2* 2000—*Road Dogs.*

Sessionman-turned-bandleader Charlie Daniels worked his way up to platinum sales with heavy touring, an instinct for quasi-political novelty singles and an eclectic repertoire that touched on boogie, bluegrass, country, blues, hard rock, and a touch of Tex-Mex.

The son of a North Carolina lumberman, guitarist and fiddler, Daniels turned pro at 21 when he formed the Jaguars. For the next decade (except for five weeks when he worked in a Denver junkyard), he played in Southern bars and roadhouses. In 1964 a song he cowrote, "It Hurts Me," became the B side of Elvis Presley's double-sided Top 30 hit "Kissin' Cousins." Daniels disbanded the Jaguars and in 1967 settled in Nashville, where he became a session musician, playing guitar, fiddle, bass, and banjo on albums by Bob Dylan, Ringo Starr, Leonard Cohen, Pete Seeger, and numerous country sessions. His songs were covered by Tammy Wynette, Gary Stewart, and others. He also worked as a producer, most notably on four albums by the Youngbloods.

In 1971 he started the Charlie Daniels Band, modeled after the Allman Brothers Band, with two drummers and twin lead guitars. *Honey in the Rock* included the talking-bluegrass novelty "Uneasy Rider," a 1973 Top 10 hit. The band played nearly 200 shows a year and built a loyal following in the South and West. *Nightrider* included the definitive rebel rouser "The South's Gonna Do It" (#29, 1975). Daniels began his annual Volunteer Jam concerts in 1974 in Nashville, and several have been recorded for live albums.

In 1975 Daniels moved to Epic for a reported $3 million contract, recorded *Saddle Tramp,* then realigned his band with three new members. He continued a grueling tour schedule (including benefits in 1976 for presidential candidate Jimmy Carter; he later performed at Carter's inaugural ball) and recorded albums. His multimillion-selling breakthrough, *Million Mile Reflections,* yielded "The Devil Went Down to Georgia" (#3, 1979), for which Daniels received the Best Country Vocal Grammy Award.

Daniels' music often has a politically conservative edge. During the Iranian hostage crisis, he had a hit with "In America" (#15 pop, #13 C&W, 1980); two years later his version of Dan Daley's "Still in Saigon," concerning the traumas of a Vietnam vet, was a Top 25 hit. The title cut of Daniels' 1990 *Simple Man* (#2 C&W) called for the lynching of drug dealers,

Charlie Daniels

and for rapists and child abusers to be left in swamps to be gnawed to death by alligators and snakes. Daniels often expands on these themes in articles running on his own Web site. In 1993 he switched to Nashville's Liberty Records, with another patriotic anthem in the title cut of *America, I Believe in You.* The following year, Daniels released his first gospel recording. Entitled *The Door,* it featured a songwriting collaboration between Daniels and Steven Curtis Chapman; *Steel Witness* followed in 1996.

In 1997 Daniels created his own label, Blue Hat, which was available only in Wal-Mart stores before securing national distribution. Since 1998 he has been taking his Volunteer Jam on the road, touring with like-minded groups such as the Marshall Tucker Band and Little Feat. He also paid tribute to Southern rock on 1999's *Tailgate Party,* covering songs by Lynyrd Skynyrd and Stevie Ray Vaughan.

Danny and the Juniors

Formed 1957, Philadelphia, PA
Danny Rapp (b. May 10, 1941; d. Apr. 5, 1983, AZ), lead voc.; Joe Terranova (b. Jan. 30, 1941), baritone voc.; Frank Maffei, second tenor voc.; Dave White (b. David White Tricker), first tenor voc.
1958—*Rock and Roll Is Here to Stay* (Singular) 1992—*Rockin' With Danny and the Juniors* (MCA).

A harmony group, Danny and the Juniors are best remembered for their 1958 #1 hit "At the Hop." The foursome, all from Philadelphia, came together in high school as the Juvenairs and were subsequently discovered by music entrepreneur Artie Singer, who became their manager. Together they wrote "At the Hop" and recorded it for the local Singular label. ABC-Paramount picked it up, and it went gold on both sides of the Atlantic. The group toured frequently over the next few years (often as part of disc jockey Alan Freed's revue) and scored a few minor hits, notably the Top 20 followup "Rock and Roll Is Here to Stay" (1958). By the beginning of the '60s the Juniors had switched to the Swan label, where they last charted in early 1963. David White Tricker released a solo album on Bell Records in 1971 under his full name. Rapp committed suicide in 1983. Original members Terranova and Maffei continue to perform with Danny and the Juniors on the oldies concert circuit.

Danzig

Formed 1986, Los Angeles, CA
Glenn Danzig (b. June 23, 1955, Lodi, NJ), voc.; John Christ (b. Feb. 19, 1965, Baltimore, MD), gtr.; Eerie Von (b. Aug. 25, 1964, Lodi), bass; Chuck Biscuits (b. Apr. 17, CA), drums.
1988—*Danzig* (Def American) 1990—*Danzig II—Lucifuge* 1992—*Danzig III: How The Gods Kill* 1993—*Thralldemonsweatlive* EP 1994—*Danzig 4* (American) (– Biscuits; + Joey Castillo [b. Mar. 30, 1966, Gardenia, CA], drums) 1995—(– Von; – Christ; + Tommy Victor, gtr.; + Josh Lazie, bass) 1996—*Blackacidevil* (Hollywood) 1999—*6:66 Satan's Child* (Evilive/E-Magine) 2000—*Sacrifice* EP (– Lazie, + Howie Pyro, bass).

Before there was Marilyn Manson and before there was Limp Bizkit (although after Alice Cooper), Danzig embodied everything about heavy metal that parents fear: Satanic, profane, antiauthoritarian music played by people who are no doubt proud of their "cult" status. Stentorian, muscular, multitattooed vocalist Glenn Danzig was a member of the Misfits, part of the late-'70s New York punk scene. Though now cited as an influence by many metal bands, the Misfits never escaped the hardcore ghetto and dissolved. In 1982 Danzig formed Samhain with Eerie Von, a drummer turned bassist. The addition four years later of Chuck Biscuits and John Christ completed the quartet.

In 1986, Rick Rubin signed Danzig to his Def American label. While critics consider Danzig's music more meaty, varied, and compelling than other metal, stardom eluded the band, although its third LP, *Danzig III—How the Gods Kill*, peaked at #24 in 1992.

In 1994, Danzig garnered attention via *Thralldemonsweatlive*'s live version of "Mother" (#43, 1994) which got a thumbs-up from MTV's Beavis and Butthead. That same year, a song penned by Danzig, "Thirteen," was featured on Johnny Cash's *American Recordings*. Near the year's end, the band's new album, *Danzig 4*, entered the charts at #29.

In 1996 Danzig shuffled the band's lineup, adding ex-Prong guitarist Tommy Victor and bassist Josh Lazie to the returning Castillo, and left Rubin and Def American for Hollywood Records. But the Disney-owned imprint's *Blackacidevil* (1996) sank without a trace.

Danzig next took a three-year recording hiatus, but his songs appeared on the soundtracks for the *X Files* (1996) and *The Crow: Salvation* (1998). He returned in 1999 with *6:66 Satan's Child*, released on his own Evilive label, followed by a world tour, during which he recorded a live album. Danzig returned to the studio in 2000 to record a seventh studio album, with former D-Generation bassist Howie Pyro replacing Lazie.

Terence Trent D'Arby

Born Terence Trent Darby, Mar. 15, 1962, New York, NY
1987—*Introducing the Hardline According to Terence Trent D'Arby* (Columbia) 1989—*Terence Trent D'Arby's Neither Fish nor Flesh* 1993—*Terence Trent D'Arby's Symphony or Damn (Exploring the Tension Inside the Sweetness)* 1995—*TTD Vibrator.*

American-born, British-based rock & soul singer Terence Trent D'Arby has a voice so flexible that it has been compared to Sam Cooke, Smokey Robinson, Al Green, even Roberta Flack. A media manipulator from day one, D'Arby proclaimed his first album among "the most brilliant debuts from any artist in the past 10 years" before its 1987 release. Reaction to D'Arby's braggadocio and widely publicized "discrepancies" in his early bio was cool. Yet few critics or R&B aficionados failed to note the encyclopedic references to '60s rock and soul in his style.

Born into a musical Manhattan family—his father played guitar and was a rock & roll fan before becoming a Pentecostal minister—D'Arby (then known as Terry Darby) spent his teen years in DeLand, Florida, where he sang with the DeLand High School Modernaires. He also was an avid boxer.

After studying journalism at the University of Central Florida for a year, he quit to join the army in 1980 so he could continue boxing as a Golden Gloves contender. When he refused paratrooper training, the Army assigned Darby to a supply clerk post in the Third Armored Division in Germany (Elvis Presley's old unit). His interest in Frankfurt's nightlife and renewed desire to sing coincided with an increasing frustration with military life. Shortly after joining the nine-piece, pop-soul combo Touch (in 1989 IMP-Polydor released an album of the group's music, *The Touch With Terence Trent D'Arby: Early Works*), Darby went AWOL. He turned himself in just before his solo signing to Columbia.

In October 1987, D'Arby (with new spelling) released his first single from *Hardline* (#4, 1987), "If You Let Me Stay" (#68); it wasn't until the following January that the handsome, androgynous singer hit #1 with "Wishing Well," whose blend of rock and funk drew comparisons to Prince. His subsequent hit was the romantic "Sign Your Name" (#4, 1988), released in May.

Two years after D'Arby's debut, the more experimental *Neither Fish nor Flesh* met with critical kudos but was a commercial flop, yielding no hit singles and reaching only #61. Four years later D'Arby returned with 1993's *Symphony or Damn* (#119), which fared even worse, though it did manage to score a Top 100 single, "Delicate" (#74). In 1995, he released *TTD's Vibrator*, a typically eclectic blend of soul and funk, with hard rock, gospel, and Latin flavors. Its commercial failure led D'Arby to threaten to retire as a performer and turn toward work behind the scenes as a producer.

Bobby Darin

Born Walden Robert Cassotto, May 14, 1936, Bronx, NY; died Dec. 20, 1973, Los Angeles, CA
1959—*That's All* (Atco) 1960—*This Is Darin; Darin at the Copa* 1961—*The Bobby Darin Story; Two of a Kind: Bobby Darin With Johnny Mercer* 1967—*If I Were a Carpenter* (Atlantic) 1972—*Bobby Darin* (Motown) 1974—*Darin 1936–1974* 1989—*Capitol Collector's Series* (Capitol) 1991—*Splish Splash: The Best of Bobby Darin, vol. 1* (Atco); *Mack the Knife: The Best of Bobby Darin, vol. 2.* 1995—*As Long as I'm Singing: The Bobby Darin Collection* (Rhino).

Although Bobby Darin began his career as one of the most popular '50s teen idols, he viewed himself as a serious singer, musician, and songwriter. Darin briefly attended Manhattan's Hunter College before dropping out to pursue a music career. He wrote some songs for Don Kirshner's Aldon Music and landed an Atco recording contract in 1957. His records met with little success until label president Ahmet Ertegun produced "Splish Splash," a song that Darin had written in 12 minutes. (He eventually wrote over 75 songs.) Reaching #3 in 1958, it sold over 100,000 copies in less than a month. Three more gold singles followed: "Queen of the Hop" (#9, 1958), his own "Dream Lover" (#2, 1959), and "Mack the Knife" (#15, 1959), for which Darin won two Grammy Awards. Darin was also extremely successful in the U.K., where "Dream Lover" went to #1.

"Beyond the Sea," a remake of a 1945 French hit "La Mer," clearly indicated the direction Darin was headed. Its swinging, big band–style arrangements sounded more at home in Vegas than on *American Bandstand,* and in fact, Darin moved quickly onto the nightclub circuit, with appearances at the Copacabana in New York and the Sahara and Flamingo hotels in Las Vegas. The year 1960's "Clementine" (#21), "Won't You Come Home Bill Bailey" (#19), and "Artificial Flowers" (#20) were all in this more "adult" vein.

Brash, outspoken, and ambitious (he said he wanted to be "bigger than Sinatra"), Darin was, by many accounts, a man in a hurry. He suggested that this was because he was certain he would die at an early age from a congenital heart defect. He went to Hollywood and made several movies, beginning in 1960 with *Come September* (he later married his leading lady, Sandra Dee) and 1963's *Capt. Newman, M.D.,* for which he received an Oscar nomination. He appeared in approximately eight more films, including *State Fair* (1962).

Darin later scored hits with "You Must Have Been a Beautiful Baby" (#5, 1961), "Irresistible You" (#15, 1961), "What'd I Say" (#24, 1962), his own "Things" (#3, 1962), "You're the Reason I'm Living" (#3, 1963), and "18 Yellow Roses" (#10, 1963). A string of nonhit singles led to Darin's 1965 move to folk-rock material by writers like Randy Newman and Tim Hardin, whose "If I Were a Carpenter" (#8, 1966) provided Darin with his first Top 10 single since 1961 and last major hit. (Ironically, Hardin's sole, albeit minor, hit single, "Simple Song of Freedom," was written by Darin.)

He continued to appear in Las Vegas and on TV through the mid-'60s and worked extensively for Robert Kennedy during his 1968 presidential campaign. Darin claimed to have had a mystical-religious experience at Kennedy's funeral service that prompted him to stop working, sell his possessions, and retreat to a mobile home at Big Sur, California. He had also discovered that the woman he believed was his sister was actually his mother. After more than a year of contemplation he reemerged, blue-jeaned and mustachioed, to start his own short-lived label, Direction Records.

Working in a soft-rock vein, he cut an unsuccessful politically oriented album called *Born Walden Robert Cassotto.* The early '70s found Darin signed to Motown and playing Las Vegas again. His Motown releases were commercially unsuccessful (allegedly, the label still has a number of unreleased tracks), and critics consider them the nadir of his career. He married legal secretary Andrea Joy Yeager in June 1972 (he had divorced Dee in 1967). He died during heart surgery to repair a faulty heart valve in 1973. He was inducted into the Rock and Roll Hall of Fame in 1990.

Das Fürlines

Formed 1985, Black Forest, Ger.
Wendy Wild (b. Aug. 31, 1956; d. Oct. 26, 1996, New York, NY), voc., banjo, gtr.; Holly Hemlock (b. Oct. 10, 1956), gtr., voc.; Liz Luv (b. Aug. 24, 1960), bass; Deb O'Nair (b. May 7, 1957), kybds., voc.; Rachel Schnitzel (b. Mar. 11, 1958), drums., voc.
1985—*Das Fürlines Go Hog Wild* (Palooka) 1986—*Lost in the Translation* 1987—*Das Fürlines Live at Paddles* 1988—*The Angry Years* 1992—*Bratwurst, Bierhalls & Bustiers: The Box Set.*

One of the most compelling and sensually alluring live bands on the New York postpunk scene, the five-girl Das Fürlines pioneered the punk-polka genre, making their initial splash with *Go Hog Wild,* a sloppy but inspired set of the sort of adrenalized polka that would become the group's signature.

Not much is known about the quintet's early days in its homeland, the Black Forest region of Germany. Soon after its formation, though, the band relocated to New York and quickly assimilated into the East Village postpunk music scene. The fetching fivesome—Wendy Wild, Holly Hemlock, Liz Luv, Deb O'Nair, and Rachel Schnitzel—became renowned for their elaborate costumes and frenetic performances, which included a storytelling segment and chicken-polka-dancing contests. Though Das Fürlines seemed the toast of the town—featured on such TV shows as *Entertainment Tonight* and *Andy Warhol's 15 Minutes*—a record deal eluded them. Impatiently, they released their debut, *Das Fürlines Go Hog Wild,* on their own vanity label. The promise suggested by such *Hog Wild* cuts as "Polka Palooka" and "Honk 'n' Holler" was more than realized on the frankly sexual second LP, *Lost in the Translation,* on which the comely lasses did breathy polka versions of "Funkytown" ("Polkatown"), "The Immigrant Song," and "Magic Carpet Ride" ("Hofbrau Haus"). With 1987's *Live at Paddles,* the Fürlines transferred the musky heat of their infamous live performances to vinyl. *The Angry Years,* an ambitious concept album based on the self-help classic *Women Who Love Too Much,* sums up the group's erotic command, personal exhaustion, and gluttony into a brilliant rock & roll statement.

The group split up after a 1988 U.S. tour (each Fürline had been horribly betrayed by her mate while on the road, causing irreparable rifts among them). The Das Fürlines' contribution to 20th-century American culture is expertly documented on *Bratwurst, Bierhalls & Bustiers,* a four-CD collection of B sides, rare singles, G-strings, outtakes, and spoken-word recipes. The carefully annotated track listings and liner notes written by their fan-club president, Bebe Dahl, provides each band member's vital statistics and preferences of all sorts. (The band's work can also be found on various polka anthologies.) The group reunited for a few performances in the early '90s, to raise funds for lead singer Wendy Wild's medical bills. Wild succumbed to breast cancer in 1996.

Cyril Davies

Born 1932, Eng.; died Jan. 7, 1964, Eng.
1970—*The Legendary Cyril Davies* (Folklore, U.K.).

Cyril Davies was a catalyst of the early-'60s British R&B scene. He began his professional career in the early '50s as a banjoist in traditional jazz bands and later moved into skiffle, which led him to blues and R&B in the late '50s. By then Davies was concentrating on singing and playing blues harmonica. He and Alexis Korner opened a series of blues clubs in London's Soho district and jammed with visiting blues performers like Sonny Terry, Brownie McGhee, Memphis Slim, and Muddy Waters.

In the early '60s Korner and Davies went electric and in 1961 cofounded Blues Incorporated, which proved an important breeding ground for future stars like Mick Jagger, Charlie Watts, and Brian Jones (Rolling Stones), and Jack Bruce and Ginger Baker (Cream). Blues Incorporated was the house favorite at London's Marquee Club by the end of 1962, but Davies left the group to form his Cyril Davies All-Stars. Guitarist Jeff Beck, keyboardist Nicky Hopkins, and drummer Mickey Waller were all, at some time, members of the All-Stars, and the group's live performances and recordings inspired a cult following. After Davies died of leukemia, All-Stars vocalist Long John Baldry shaped his Hoochie Coochie Men from the remains of Davies' band.

Dave and Ray Davies: See the Kinks

The Reverend Gary Davis

Born Apr. 30, 1896, Laurens, SC; died May 5, 1972, Hammonton, NJ
N.A.—*Pure Religion* (Prestige); *The Guitar and Banjo of Rev. Gary Davis* 1972—*When I Die I'll Live Again* (Fantasy) 1973—*O, Glory* (Adelphi); *A Little More Faith* (Prestige) 1990—*Reverend Gary Davis at Newport* (Vanguard) 1992—*From Blues to Gospel* (Biograph) 1993—*Blues and Ragtime* (Shanachie) 2001—*Demons and Angels.*

Influential in both blues and folk, the Reverend Gary Davis' percussive finger-picked guitar style lives through the work of Ry Cooder, Taj Mahal, and Jorma Kaukonen. Davis was born into a poor family. He suffered from ulcerated eyes, was partially blind throughout his youth and totally blind by age 30. When he was five, he taught himself to play the harmonica, and during the next two years he learned banjo and guitar. At 19 Davis enrolled in a school for the blind in Spartanburg, South Carolina.

He jammed the blues with Sonny Terry, Blind Boy Fuller, Big Red, and others, spending the '20s as an itinerant musician in the Carolinas. By the close of that decade, though, Davis had decided the blues was the "Devil's music." He was ordained in 1933 at the Free Baptist Connection Church in Washington, North Carolina, and soon became a popular gospel singer on the revival circuit. In 1935 he was discovered by a talent scout for the New York "race" label Perfect Records, for whom he recorded religious songs. He lived as a street singer for the next three decades in Harlem, recording occasionally (the most noteworthy sessions in 1956 and 1957), and subsisting off his small royalties, music lessons, and passing the plate whenever he had a congregation. He emerged in 1959 at the Newport Folk Festival, then toured America and England and moved his family to Jamaica, Queens. Davis died of a heart attack in 1972.

Mac Davis

Born Jan. 21, 1942, Lubbock, TX
1971—*I Believe in Music* (Columbia) 1972—*Baby Don't Get Hooked on Me* 1973—*Mac Davis* 1974—*Song Painter; Stop and Smell the Roses* 1975—*All the Love in the World; Burnin' Thing* 1976—*Forever Lovers* 1977—*Thunder in the Afternoon* 1978—*Fantasy* 1979—*Greatest Hits* 1980—*It's Hard to Be Humble* 1981—*Midnight Crazy* (Casablanca) 1982—*Forty 82* 1984—*Soft Talk* 1985—*Till I Made It With You* 1994—*Will Write Songs for Food* (Sony) 1995—*A Man Don't Cry* 2000—*The Best of Mac Davis* (Razor & Tie).

Mac Davis is a country-pop singer/songwriter whose songs, recorded by himself and by others, have sold millions of records. His father bought him his first guitar at age nine, but it wasn't until after a year at Emory University in Atlanta and after working in Atlanta's probation department that he formed his first rock band.

In the early '60s Davis became Vee-Jay Records' Southern regional sales manager; four and a half years later he worked for Liberty Records. Liberty later sent him to Hollywood to work in its music publishing division. There he sold several of his tunes to major artists: "In the Ghetto," "Memories," and "Don't Cry Daddy" (Elvis Presley); "Friend, Lover,

Woman, Wife" (O.C. Smith); "Watching Scotty Grow" (Bobby Goldsboro); "Something's Burning" (Kenny Rogers and the First Edition).

Since he first recorded it, "I Believe in Music" has sold millions of copies in cover versions by over 50 artists. In 1972 a #1 hit, "Baby Don't Get Hooked on Me," started a streak that continued through the mid-'70s with "Rock and Roll (I Gave You the Best Years of My Life)" (#15, 1975), "One Hell of a Woman" (#11, 1974), and "Stop and Smell the Roses" (#9, 1974). In December 1974 he began hosting his own television variety program, *The Mac Davis Show.*

Later recordings—"Burnin' Thing" (1975), "Forever Lovers" (1976), "It's Hard to Be Humble," "Texas in My Rear View Mirror" (1980)—were less successful.

Davis made his film debut in 1979, costarring with Nick Nolte as a quarterback in *North Dallas Forty.* He later starred in the romantic comedy *Cheaper to Keep Her.* In 1981 he signed a personal performance contract at the MGM Grand Hotel in Las Vegas. While he put recording on hold for the latter half of the '80s, Davis became a fixture on TV talk shows. In 1992 he made his Broadway debut playing the title character in *Will Rogers Follies.* The following year Dolly Parton recorded Davis' "Slow Dancing with the Moon" as the title track of a new album, which also included another Davis composition, "Full Circle."

Miles Davis

Born Miles Dewey Davis, May 25, 1926, Alton, IL; died Sep. 28, 1991, Santa Monica, CA

1945—*First Miles* (Savoy) 1949—*Birth of the Cool* (Capitol) 1951—*And Horns* (Original Jazz); *Blue Period* (Prestige); *Conception* (Original Jazz); *The New Sounds of Miles Davis* (Prestige); *Diggin'; Dig; Collector's Items* 1952—*Live at the Barrel, vol. 2* 1953—*Miles Davis Plays the Compositions of Al Cohn; Miles Davis Featuring Sonny Rollins; Blue Haze* (Original Jazz) 1954—*Miles Davis Quintet* (Prestige); *Miles Davis and the Modern Jazz Giants; Bags Groove* (Original Jazz); *Walkin'* 1955—*Green Haze* (Prestige); *The Musings of Miles* (Original Jazz); *Odyssey* (Prestige); *Milt and Miles; Miles Davis and Milt Jackson Quintet/Sextet* (Original Jazz); *Circle in the Round* (Columbia); *Round About Midnight; Cookin'* (Original Jazz); *The New Miles Davis Quintet* (Prestige); *Miles; Miles Davis and Horns 51–53* (Original Jazz); *Miles and Monk at Newport* (Columbia) 1956—*Workin'* (Original Jazz); *Steamin'; Relaxin'; Cookin' With the Miles Davis Quintet* (DCC) 1957—*Miles Ahead* (Columbia) 1958—*Milestones; Porgy and Bess* 1959—*Kind of Blue; Sketches of Spain* 1960—*Directions; Friday at the Blackhawk; Friday at the Blackhawk, vol. 2* (CBS) 1961—*Friday and Saturday Nights in Person* (Columbia); *Miles Davis in Person, vol. 1; Miles Davis in Person, vol. 2; In Person: Saturday Night at the Blackhawk; At Carnegie Hall; Miles in St. Louis* (VGM); *In Person at the Blackhawk* (CBS); *Someday My Prince Will Come* (Columbia) 1962—*Quiet Nights; Sorcerer; Miles at Antibes* (CBS) 1963—*Seven Steps to Heaven* (Columbia) 1964—*Four and More; My Funny Valentine; Miles in Tokyo; Miles in Berlin* (CBS); *In Europe* 1965—*E.S.P.* (Columbia); *Live at the Plugged Nickel* (CBS) 1966—*Miles Smiles* (Columbia); *In Berlin* 1967—*Nefertiti; Water Babies* 1968—*Miles in the Sky; Filles de Kilimanjaro* 1969—*In a Silent Way; Bitches Brew; Big Fun* 1970—*Live-Evil; A Tribute to Jack Johnson; Black Beauty: Miles Davis at Fillmore West; Live at the Fillmore* 1972—*On the Corner; Miles Davis in Europe; In Concert* 1974—*Big Fun; Get Up With It; Dark Magus* (Tristar) 1975—*Pangaea* (Columbia); *Agharta* 1981—*The Man With the Horn; We Want Miles* 1982—*Star People; New Quintet* 1983—*Decoy* 1985—*Aura; You're Under Arrest* 1986—*Tutu* (Warner Bros.); *Miles Davis and the Jazz Giants* (Prestige) 1987—*Music From Siesta* (Warner Bros.) 1988—*Live Around the World* 1989—*Miles in Montreux* (Jazz Door); *Amandla* (Warner Bros.) 1990—*Dingo; Hot Spot* (Antilles) 1991—*Doo-Bop* (Warner Bros.); *Miles & Quincy Live at Montreux.*

Miles Davis played a crucial and inevitably controversial role in every major development in jazz since the mid-'40s, and no other jazz musician has had so profound an effect on rock. He was the most widely recognized jazz musician of his era, an outspoken social critic and an arbiter of style—in attitude and fashion—as well as music.

Davis was raised in an upper-middle-class black home in an integrated East St. Louis neighborhood. His father was a dentist; his mother, a onetime music teacher. In 1941 he began playing semiprofessionally with St. Louis jazz bands. Four years later, his father sent him to study at New York's Juilliard School of Music. Immediately upon arriving in New York City, Davis sought out alto saxophonist Charlie Parker, whom he had met the year before in St. Louis. He became Parker's roommate and protégé, playing in his quintet on the 1945 Savoy sessions, the definitive recordings of the bebop movement. He dropped out of Juilliard and played with Benny Carter, Billy Eckstine, Charles Mingus, and Oscar Pettiford as well as with Parker.

As a trumpeter Davis was far from virtuosic, but he more than made up for his technical limitations by emphasizing his strengths: his ear for ensemble sound, unique phrasing, and a distinctive haunted tone. He started moving away from speedy bop and toward something more introspective. His direction was defined by his collaboration with Gil Evans on the *Birth of the Cool* sessions in 1949 and early '50, playing with a nine-piece band that included Max Roach, John Lewis, Lee Konitz, and Gerry Mulligan using meticulous arrangements by Evans, Mulligan, Lewis, Davis, and Johnny Carisi.

By 1949 Davis had become a heroin addict. He continued to perform and record over the next four years, but his addiction kept his career in low gear until he cleaned up in 1954. The following year, he formed a group with drummer Philly Joe Jones, bassist Paul Chambers, pianist Red Garland and, in his first major exposure, tenor saxophonist John Coltrane. The Miles Davis Quintet quickly established itself as the premier jazz group of the decade.

Between 1958 and 1963 the personnel in Davis' groups—

quintets, sextets, and small orchestras—shifted constantly and included pianists Bill Evans and Wynton Kelly, saxophonists Cannonball Adderley, Sonny Stitt, and Hank Mobley, and drummer Jimmy Cobb. Continuing the experiments begun with *Birth of the Cool,* Davis' work moved toward greater complexity—as on his orchestral collaborations with Gil Evans (*Miles Ahead,* 1957; *Porgy and Bess,* 1958; *Sketches of Spain,* 1959; *Quiet Nights,* 1962)—and greater simplicity, as on *Kind of Blue* (1959), where he dispensed with chords as the basis for improvisation in favor of modal scales and tone centers.

In 1963 Davis formed a quintet with bassist Ron Carter, pianist Herbie Hancock [see entry], drummer Tony Williams [see entry], and saxophonist George Coleman, who was replaced by Wayne Shorter in 1965. This group stayed together until 1968. In that time, it exerted as much influence on the jazz of the '60s as the first Davis quintet had on the jazz of the '50s. Davis and his sidemen—especially Shorter—wrote a body of original material for the quintet.

In 1968 Davis began the process that eventually brought him to a fusion of jazz and rock. With *Miles in the Sky,* the quintet introduced electric instruments (piano, bass, and George Benson's guitar on one piece) and the steady beat of rock drumming to their sound. With *Filles de Kilimanjaro,* on which Chick Corea [see entry] substituted on some tracks for Hancock, and Dave Holland replaced Carter, the rock influence became more pronounced. *In a Silent Way* featured three keyboardists—Hancock, Corea, and composer Joe Zawinul, on electric pianos and organs—and guitarist John McLaughlin [see Mahavishnu Orchestra entry] in addition to Williams, Shorter, Holland, and Davis. For his next recording sessions he put together what he called "the best damn rock & roll band in the world"—Shorter, McLaughlin, Holland, Corea, and Zawinul, plus organist Larry Young, bassist Harvey Brooks, bass clarinetist Bennie Maupin, and percussionists Jack DeJohnette, Lenny White, Don Alias, and Jim Riley—and, with no rehearsals and virtually no instructions, let them jam. The result was the historic *Bitches Brew,* a two-LP set that sold over 400,000 copies.

In the three years following *Brew*'s release, Davis amassed a rock star–level following and performed in packed concert halls in America, Europe, and Japan. As his sidemen (who in the early '70s included pianist Keith Jarrett and percussionists Billy Cobham and Airto Moreira) ventured out on their own, in such bands as Weather Report [see entry] and the Mahavishnu Orchestra [see entry], jazz-rock fusion became one of the dominant new forms.

A car crash that broke both his legs in 1972 put a temporary stop to Davis' activity and marked the beginning of his growing reclusiveness. The recordings he made between 1972 and 1975 advanced the ideas presented on *Bitches Brew,* extracting the percussive qualities of tuned instruments, making greater use of electronics and high-powered amplification, and deemphasizing solos in favor of ensemble funk. His sidemen in the mid-'70s included bassist Michael Henderson, guitarists Reggie Lucas and Pete Cosey, drummers Al Foster and Mtume, and saxophonists Sonny Fortune and Dave Liebman. *Agharta,* recorded live in Japan in 1975, was his last album of new material for five years. He spent much of that time recuperating from a hip ailment. With the encouragement of his new wife, actress Cicely Tyson, he reemerged in 1981 with a new album and concert appearances. While many old supporters were disappointed by his newly acquired pop clichés (including some vocals), *The Man With the Horn* was his most popular release since *Bitches Brew* and marked his return to live concerts. *We Want Miles* was a live set; *Star People* reenlisted Gil Evans as arranger along with Davis' '80s sextet: Mike Stern or John Scofield on guitar, Marcus Miller or Tom Barney on electric bass, Bill Evans on saxophone, Al Foster on drums, and Mino Cinelu on percussion.

Davis' music took increasingly commercial turns; he recorded material by Cyndi Lauper and the rock band Scritti Politti (Davis guested on the group's *Provision*), later experimenting with hip-hop and go go rhythms. Critics generally lambasted the lukewarm funk of Davis' new music, but the trumpeter had reached new heights of popularity, his concerts selling out all over the world and his recordings even making dents in the pop charts. Davis continued to surround himself with young musicians; among them, saxophonists Kenny Garrett and Bob Berg, and keyboardist Joey DeFrancesco.

Tutu, Davis' first recording for Warner Bros. after ending his 30-year tenure with Columbia, was a purely studio-created project with Davis' horn the only "live" instrument. *Aura* (recorded in 1985) had Davis in front of Danish arranger Palle Mikkelborg's big band for pieces that harkened back to the protofusion experiments of the late '60s.

In 1985 Davis contributed to the antiapartheid *Sun City* recording, and the next year he and his band appeared at the televised Amnesty International Concert at Giants Stadium. Davis devoted increasing time to visual art—his paintings were exhibited in galleries and a book devoted to them was published. In 1988 Davis' marriage to Tyson ended, and Gil Evans, his close friend and musical associate, died; the long-rumored adaptation of *Tosca* that the two had been discussing for years never came to fruition.

Davis' quest for increased public recognition led him to TV and film. He appeared on *Miami Vice,* made commercials for a New York jazz radio station, and had a featured role in the 1990 film *Dingo.* Davis also worked on the soundtracks for *Siesta, The Hot Spot,* and *Scrooged* (in which he played a street musician). In 1989 Davis' controversial autobiography (cowritten with poet Quincy Troupe) was published. While detailing Davis' drug problem and romantic involvements, the book was noticeably skimpy in its praise for important Davis collaborators. In 1990 Davis received the Grammy Award for Lifetime Achievement.

In failing health, Davis began to look backward for the first time in his career. The summer before his death Davis participated in a career retrospective—something he had always studiously avoided—held at La Villette in Paris. Joining Davis and his current band were important Davis-associated instrumentalists including Jackie McLean, John McLaughlin, Chick Corea, Herbie Hancock, and Wayne Shorter. Shortly after that concert, Davis performed at the Montreux Jazz Festival with a big band led by Quincy Jones, re-creating the legendary Davis–Gil Evans collaborations.

Davis died in September 1991, reportedly suffering from pneumonia, respiratory failure, and a stroke. The posthumously released *Doo-Bop,* a jazz/hip-hop collaborative project with rapper Easy Mo Bee, proved that Davis continued experimenting to the end.

Spencer Davis Group

Formed 1963, Birmingham, Eng.
Original lineup: Spencer Davis (b. July 17, 1942, Swansea, Wales), voc., gtr., harmonica; Pete York (b. Aug. 15, 1942, Middlesborough, Eng.), drums; Steve Winwood (b. May 12, 1948, Birmingham), voc., gtr., kybds.; Muff Winwood (b. Mervyn Winwood, June 14, 1943, Birmingham), bass.
1965—*1st Album* (Fontana, U.K.) 1966—*Second Album; Autumn '66* 1967—*Gimme Some Lovin'* (United Artists); *I'm a Man* (– S. Winwood; – M. Winwood; + Eddie Hardin, drums, voc.; + Phil Sawyer, gtr.; – York; + Nigel Olsson, drums; – Hardin; + Dee Murray [d. Jan. 14, 1992, Atlanta, GA], bass) 1968—*The Very Best of the Spencer Davis Group; Spencer Davis Greatest Hits; With Their New Face On* 1969—*Heavies* 1973—*Gluggo* (Vertigo) 1974—*Living on a Back Street* (Mercury) 1987—*The Best of the Spencer Davis Group* (Rhino).
Spencer Davis solo: 1972—*Mousetrap* (United Artists) 1984—*Crossfire* (Allegiance).
World Classic Rockers (with Spencer Davis): 1999—*Live* (WCR).

The Spencer Davis Group was a British R&B-influenced rock band best known for introducing Stevie Winwood [see entry] to the pop audience with "Gimme Some Lovin' " and "I'm a Man." Various Spencer Davis groups continued to record into the '70s.

Davis was a lecturer on German at the University of Birmingham who moonlighted as a musician. In 1963 he met drummer Pete York and persuaded brothers Steve and Muff Winwood to leave their trad-jazz band. They toured England and parts of the Continent, then moved to London and released "Keep On Running" in 1965. "Gimme Some Lovin' " (written by Davis and the Winwood brothers) went to #7 on early 1967; two months later "I'm a Man" (by Steve Winwood, Davis, and J. Miller) went to #10. Both were driving, repetitive songs that featured young Steve Winwood's lead vocals.

In 1967 Steve Winwood left to form Traffic, and his brother Muff moved into producing and A&R work. His credits include producing Dire Straits, Sparks, Squeeze, and the Bay City Rollers. After a few personnel changes, Davis was joined by Nigel Olsson and Dee Murray, who in 1969 went on to join Elton John's band. At that point, Davis ended the group.

From 1969 to 1972 Davis performed in acoustic duos with Alun Davies (later with Cat Stevens) and Peter Jameson, with whom he recorded two bluegrass-influenced albums. He re-formed the Spencer Davis Group with York in 1972, but their albums were ignored. By the late '70s Davis was working as an independent producer and as a publicist for Island Records. In 1970 he moved to the United States, where he has worked in various capacities in the record business. His solo album *Crossfire* featured such guests as Dusty Springfield and Booker T. Jones. In 1984 he toured the world with his own band, then with Brian Auger and Chris Farlowe. Later in the decade he opened shows for Hall and Oates, among others, and he guested on the television series *Married With Children.*

Although he heads his own management firm in L.A., Davis finds time to perform over 200 dates a year. From 1993 to 1995 he toured with Mike Pinera, Peter Rivera, and Jerry Corbetta in a group called the Classic Rock Allstars, then left it to reunite with drummer York and embark on a world tour with the Spencer Davis Group (which also included Miller Anderson, Colin Modgkinson, and keyboardist Zoot Money). In 1997 Davis formed the World Classic Rockers with the Eagles' Randy Meisner and Steppenwolf's Nick St. Nicholas and Michael Monarch. Both the Spencer Davis Group and the World Classic Rockers are currently active.

Tyrone Davis

Born May 4, 1938, Greenville, MS
1969—*Can I Change My Mind* (Dakar) 1970—*Turn Back the Hands of Time* 1972—*I Had It All the Time; It's All in the Game; Tyrone Davis' Greatest Hits* 1973—*Without You in My Life* 1976—*Love and Touch* (Columbia) 1977—*Let's Be Closer Together* 1978—*I Can't Go On This Way* 1979—*In the Mood With Tyrone Davis* 1980—*I Just Can't Keep On Going* 1981—*Everything in Place* 1982—*The Best of Tyrone Davis; Tyrone Davis* (Highrise) 1991—*I'll Always Love You* (Ichiban) 1992—*The Best of Tyrone Davis* (Rhino); *Something's Mighty Wrong; The Best of the Future Years* 1994—*You Stay on My Mind* 1997—*Pleasing You* (Malaco).

Romantic mid-tempo ballads like 1969's "Can I Change My Mind" made Davis one of the top black singers of the '70s. He spent his early years in Mississippi, then at age 14 moved with his family to Saginaw, Michigan. Five years later he went to work in a Chicago steel factory, and there he began to get involved with the local music scene, making friends with Otis Rush, Freddie King, Mighty Joe Young, and Otis Clay. Through Clay he met producer Howard Burrage, who named him Tyrone the Wonder Boy and recorded him for the Four Brothers and Hit Sound labels.

After Burrage died, Davis continued to record but without major success until 1968's "Can I Change My Mind" (#5 pop). Its brassy flourishes, relaxed rhythms, and aggressive horns perfectly complemented Davis' style. More hits followed: "Is It Something You've Got" in spring 1969, and his biggest song, "Turn Back the Hands of Time" (#3, 1970). Davis' later releases ("I'll Be Right Here," "Let Me Back In," "Could I Forget You") were essentially MOR soul. In the mid-'70s he left Dakar for Columbia Records, where he enjoyed a number of R&B hits, including "In the Mood," "Give It Up

(Turn It Loose)," and "Get On Up (Disco)." Davis continues to record and tour.

Taylor Dayne

Born Leslie Wunderman, Mar. 7, 1963, Baldwin, NY
1988—*Tell It to My Heart* (Arista) 1989—*Can't Fight Fate* 1993—*Soul Dancing* 1995—*Greatest Hits* 1998—*Naked Without You* (Platinum Productions/Intersound).

Unlike most female dance-pop divas, big-voiced Taylor Dayne is a white Jewish girl from Long Island. In 1985 fellow Baldwinian Dee Snider of Twisted Sister suggested that Leslie Wunderman change her name to something more glamorous. By that time, she had sung with various high school and local bands, recorded two unsuccessful singles under the name "Leslee," and studied music and singing.

As Taylor Dayne, she was discovered singing in Russian-American clubs in Brooklyn's Brighton Beach. Her debut album hit #21, thanks to its title track (#7, 1987). The album yielded such other disco-ish hits as "Prove Your Love" (#7, 1988), "I'll Always Love You" (#3, 1988), and "Don't Rush Me"(#2, 1988). *Can't Fight Fate* (#25, 1989), on which Dayne tried to sound more mature, included "With Every Beat of My Heart" (#5, 1989), "Love Will Lead You Back" (#1, 1990), "I'll Be Your Shelter" (#4, 1990), and "Heart of Stone" (#12, 1990). Dayne wrote much of the music for *Soul Dancing* (#51), which also contained a remake of disco heavyweight Barry White's "Can't Get Enough of Your Love" (#20). Arista repackaged these and others for *Greatest Hits.* She pursued acting and appeared in feature films *(Love Affair),* in theater *(Archie and Mehitabel),* and on television *(Martial Law, Rude Awakening).* Dayne returned to recording in 1998 with *Naked Without You.* Released on the Atlanta-based Intersound, a label strongly associated with black gospel music, the album included a bonus disc of remixes.

The dB's

Formed 1978, New York, NY
Will Rigby (b. Mar. 17, 1956, Winston-Salem, NC), drums, voc.; Peter Holsapple (b. Feb. 19, 1956, Greenwich, CT), gtr., organ, voc.; Gene Holder (b. July 10, 1954, Philadelphia, PA), bass, gtr.; Chris Stamey (b. Dec. 6, 1954, Chapel Hill, NC), gtr., organ, voc.
1981—*Stands for deciBels* (Albion, U.K); *Repercussion* 1983—(– Stamey) 1984—(+ Rick Wagner, bass) *Like This* (Bearsville) (– Wagner; + Jeff Beninato, bass) 1987—*The Sound of Music* (I.R.S.) (– Holder; + Eric Peterson, gtr.) 1993—*Ride the Wild Tom Tom* (Rhino) 1994—*Paris Avenue* (Monkey Hill).
Chris Stamey solo: 1983—*It's a Wonderful Life* (dB) 1984—*Instant Excitement* EP (Coyote) 1986—*Christmas Time* 1987—*It's Alright* (Coyote/A&M) 1991—*Fireworks* (Rhino).
Peter Holsapple and Chris Stamey: 1991—*Mavericks* (Rhino).
Peter Holsapple solo: *Out of My Way* (Monkey Hill).
Peter Holsapple with Continental Drifters: 1994—*Continental Drifters* (Monkey Hill) 1999—*Vermilion* (Razor & Tie) 2001—*Better Day.*
Will Rigby solo: 1985—*Sidekick Phenomenon* (Egon) 1996—*Untitled* EP (Hello).

Ironic pop-rockers, the dB's met at elementary school in Winston-Salem, North Carolina. Peter Holsapple and Chris Stamey brought their first group together in 1972, and as members of Rittenhouse Square they recorded an album for an independent label the next year. In 1975 Will Rigby joined a group that Stamey formed at the University of North Carolina, Chapel Hill, called Sneakers. The band released an EP, Mitch Easter joined on guitar, and the group traveled to New York to play Max's Kansas City in 1976 before breaking up. (A Sneakers LP, *In the Red,* came out posthumously in 1978; in 1992 a Sneakers anthology, *Racket,* was released.)

In early 1977 Stamey moved to New York, where he played with Alex Chilton's band, and did a one-off project with Television guitarist Richard Lloyd. He recorded a Chilton-produced single for Ork Records and set up his own label, Car Records. Rigby and Gene Holder moved to New York, and as Chris Stamey and the dB's, the trio began playing locally in June 1978 and released a single, "If and When"; Holsapple joined the group that fall.

The dB's were favorites of the New York club scene and rock press, but U.S. record companies shied away. Their first two albums were originally released only in Britain by the U.K. label Albion. Stamey left to pursue a solo career in 1983. Finally, the band scored a deal with a U.S. label, Bearsville, but its recording career was legally stalled for three years after label chief Albert Grossman died intestate, not long after the release of *Like This.* In the meantime, Holder moved from bass to guitar, and a succession of new players began coming in. The band opened for R.E.M. [see entry] on its 1984 and 1987 U.S. tours. Eventually, the dB's signed to I.R.S., releasing *The Sound of Music* (#171, 1987). They toured for the next six months, and I.R.S. rereleased their Albion albums in 1989, not long after the dB's had unofficially called it quits. (*Ride the Wild Tom Tom* and *Paris Avenue* are compilations of early and late demos, respectively.)

Holsapple then played keyboards and guitar on R.E.M.'s Green tour, and also guested on *Out of Time.* He later recorded *Mavericks* with Chris Stamey, and joined the Continental Drifters, a roots-rock combo that also included former member of the Cowsills Susan Cowsill (to whom Holsapple was married for several years), Vicki Peterson of the Bangles [see entry], and ex–Dream Syndicate [see entry] bassist Mark Walton, among others. Holsapple also toured as a sideman with Hootie and the Blowfish [see entry], appearing on the group's *Fairweather Johnson* (1996), *Musical Chairs* (1998), and *Scattered, Smothered & Covered* (2000). As a sideman, Holsapple has contributed to many other artists' recordings, including John Hiatt, Nanci Griffith, Indigo Girls, and the Troggs.

Stamey released several solo albums and toured sporadically. He also guested on recordings by the Golden Palominos, Matthew Sweet, and Freedy Johnston, among others.

Beginning in the late '90s, he worked mainly as a producer, including albums by Alejandro Escovedo and Whiskeytown.

Rigby went on to make a solo album and play drums with such artists as Matthew Sweet, Kelly Willis, Cheri Knight, and Steve Earle, whose band, the Dukes, Rigby joined following the recording of Earle's 2000 album *Transcendental Blues*. Since the late '80s, Holder has worked as a producer for such artists as Freedy Johnston and Yo La Tengo.

The Dead Boys

Formed 1976, Cleveland, OH
Cheetah Chrome (b. Gene Connor), gtr.; Stiv Bators (b. Stivin Bator, Oct. 22, 1949, Cleveland; d. June 4, 1990, Paris, Fr.), voc.; Jimmy Zero, gtr.; Jeff Magnum, bass; Johnny Blitz, drums.
1977—*Young, Loud and Snotty* (Sire) 1978—*We Have Come for Your Children* 1981—*Night of the Living Dead Boys* (Bomp) 1998—*All This and More.*
Stiv Bators solo: 1980—*Disconnected* (Bomp).
Lords of the New Church, formed early '70s: Stiv Bator, voc.; Brian James, gtr.; Dave Tregunna, bass; Nick Turner, drums. 1982—*Lords of the New Church* (I.R.S.) 1983—*Is Nothing Sacred?* 1984—*The Method to Our Madness* 1985—*Killer Lords* 1988—*Live at the Spit* (Illegal).

The Dead Boys, Cleveland natives (Chrome and Blitz had played in the seminal Rocket from the Tombs), emigrated to New York when the Bowery scene first gained national attention in 1976. Managed by CBGB's owner, Hilly Kristal, they were adopted by scenemakers for their raucous, impish brand of punk, fully captured by the title of their debut album if not exactly by the music on it. Genya Ravan's production couldn't hide the fact that, for all their highjinks, the Boys had little to offer musically, making them the American counterparts to England's the Damned.

After Johnny Blitz was seriously injured in a mugging, the band regrouped for the Felix Pappalardi–produced *We Have Come for Your Children,* then dissolved. Bators, who released several solo singles on Bomp and had an album released on Lolita in France in 1983 *(The Church and the New Creatures),* did an album with Sham 69 members as the Wanderers. He then hooked up with ex-Damned Brian James; calling themselves the Lords of the New Church they combined '70s punk with '80s apocalyptics to create a postpunk sound. The band fell apart in the mid-'80s. On June 4, 1990, Bators was struck by a bus on a Paris street and died later that night. He'd been recording there with a new band featuring ex-members of Hanoi Rocks, Sigue Sigue Sputnik, and other groups, and had reportedly planned to include Cheetah Chrome in the sessions and on a subsequent U.S. tour.

The Dead Kennedys/Jello Biafra

Formed 1978, San Francisco, CA
Jello Biafra (b. Eric Boucher, June 17, 1958, Boulder, CO), voc.; East Bay Ray (b. Raymond John Pepperell), gtr.; Klaus Fluoride (b. Geoffrey Lyall), bass; Ted (b. Bruce Slesinger), drums.
1980—*Fresh Fruit for Rotting Vegetables* (I.R.S.) 1981—(– Ted; + D.H. Peligro [b. Derron Henley], drums) *In God We Trust, Inc.* EP (Alternative Tentacles) 1982—*Plastic Surgery Disasters* 1985—*Frankenchrist* 1986—*Bedtime for Democracy* 1987—*Give Me Convenience or Give Me Death.*
Jello Biafra solo: 1987—*No More Cocoons* (Alternative Tentacles) 1989—*High Priest of Harmful Matter* 1991—*I Blow Minds for a Living* 1994—*Beyond the Valley of the Gift Police* 1998—*If Evolution Is Outlawed, Only Outlaws Will Evolve.*
Jello Biafra with D.O.A.: 1989—*Last Scream of the Missing Neighbors* (Alternative Tentacles).
Jello Biafra with Lard: 1989—*The Power of Lard* EP (Alternative Tentacles) 1990—*The Last Temptation of Reid* 1997—*Pure Chewing Satisfaction* 2000—*70's Rock Must Die* EP.
Jello Biafra with Tumor Circus: 1991—*Tumor Circus* (Alternative Tentacles).
Jello Biafra with NOMEANSNO: 1991—*The Sky Is Falling and I Want My Mommy* (Alternative Tentacles).
Jello Biafra with Mojo Nixon: 1994—*Prairie Home Invasion* (Alternative Tentacles).
Jello Biafra with the No WTO Combo: 2000—*Live From the Battle in Seattle* (Alternative Tentacles).

Formed in the volatile San Francisco punk scene of the late '70s, the Dead Kennedys became one of the West Coast's most visible punk bands, pioneering hardcore. Fueled by a cutting political preoccupation, lead singer Jello Biafra's quavering vocals conveyed the excess that marked such songs as "Drug Me" and "California Über Alles." Biafra and company directed diatribes against the Moral Majority, creeping U.S. imperialism and fascism, and their perceptions of a plastic suburban lifestyle. The band's rapid-fire instrumental overkill attracted punk fans in the U.S. and abroad; they even matched the Sex Pistols on their home turf, going to #36 in England with the airplay-banned "Too Drunk to Fuck." Biafra, the son of a psychiatric social worker, ran for mayor of San Francisco in 1979; one of his campaign planks was that businessmen wear clown suits downtown. The Dead Kennedys formed their own record label, Alternative Tentacles, which in 1982 released a compilation album, *Let Them Eat Jellybeans,* consisting of tracks by various unsigned American bands.

The DKs' *Frankenchrist* album made free-speech history when, on April 15, 1986, Biafra's apartment was raided by nine cops; the singer and others associated with Alternative Tentacles were soon charged in an L.A. courtroom with distributing pornography ("harmful matter") to minors under the nation's revised obscenity laws; the album included the H.R. Giger painting, *Landscape #XX,* which featured genitalia and sex acts in a surreal, assembly-line setting. The case ended in a hung jury and was dismissed. Former L.A. deputy city attorney Michael Guarino later admitted the case was "a comedy of errors." But the drawn-out legal battle put such a strain on the Kennedys that they split up after *Bedtime for Democracy.* Biafra took full ownership of the label after the band dissolved in 1986. *Give Me Convenience or Give Me Death* collects the band's more accessible material. The

Dead Kennedys made the news again in 1993 when a box of reissues of their first album were mixed up with a package of Christian radio broadcast CDs, and inadvertently shipped to Christian stations around the country.

Biafra has persisted with his political ranting—which often revolves around free speech issues—on his spoken-word albums, college-lecture tours, and occasional collaborations with other artists. Among those collaborations was the band Lard (including Al Jourgenson and other members of Ministry). Biafra also appeared on the Offspring's *Ixnay on the Hombre.* In 1994 he was beaten and his knee permanently damaged by "fundamentalist punks" at the Berkeley 924 Gilman club, once the home turf of Green Day. Mostly, he tends to the business of running Alternative Tentacles, which continues to put out music by button-pushing rock bands. Klaus Fluoride formed the politically charged acoustic band Five Year Plan, and East Bay Ray plays with hard rockers Skrapyard and a surf instrumental band—with East Bay Ray and Fluoride—called Jumbo Shrimp.

Running the label has often been a struggle. In 1997 a federal judge ordered Biafra and Alternative Tentacles to pay $2.2 million to the Philadelphia Fraternal Order of Police after the label printed a photograph of police on the back of a Crucifucks album. The singer also was found liable for failing to promote the Dead Kennedys' catalogue (when he refused to license "Holiday in Cambodia" for a Levi's commercial) and for paying insufficient royalties to his former bandmates; a jury awarded East Bay Ray, Fluoride, and Peligro about $220,000 in damages. In a countersuit filed by Biafra, a jury ruled in his favor that Ray had mismanaged the business partnership and had to pay Biafra $5,000. The ruling also stated that Decay Music, not the individual songwriters, owns the band's work and that the partnership can now make decisions based on a majority vote.

In 2000 Biafra toured as part of the Spitfire spoken word tour, founded by Nirvana's Krist Novoselic, and he ran in the New York state primary for the Green Party's presidential nomination. Alternative Tentacles released a live recording by the No WTO Combo, featuring Biafra, Novoselic, and Soundgarden guitarist Kim Thayil, in a protest of policies of the World Trade Organization.

DeBarge/Chico DeBarge

Formed 1978, Grand Rapids, MI
Bunny DeBarge (b. Mar. 15, 1955, Grand Rapids), voc.; El DeBarge (b. Eldra DeBarge, June 4, 1961, Grand Rapids), voc., kybds.; Marty DeBarge (b. Mark DeBarge, June 19, 1959, Grand Rapids), voc.; Randy DeBarge (b. Aug. 6, 1958,Grand Rapids), voc.
1981—*The DeBarges* (Gordy) 1982—(+ James DeBarge [b. Aug. 22, 1963, Grand Rapids], voc.) *All This Love* 1983—*In a Special Way* 1985—*Rhythm of the Night* 1986—*Greatest Hits* (Motown) 1988—(– El DeBarge; – Bunny DeBarge) *Bad Boys* (Striped Horse) 1997—*The Ultimate Collection* (Motown).
Bunny DeBarge solo: 1987—*In Love* (Motown).
El DeBarge solo: 1986—*El DeBarge* (Gordy) 1989—*Gemini* (Motown) 1992—*In the Storm* (Warner Bros.) 1994—*Heart, Mind and Soul* (Reprise).
Chico DeBarge (b. Jonathan DeBarge, 1966, Grand Rapids) solo: 1986—*Chico DeBarge* (Motown) 1997—*Long Time No See* (Kedar/Universal) 1999—*The Game* (Motown).

At its peak in the mid-'80s, the family act DeBarge was touted as a fledgling pop-soul dynasty and often compared to the Jacksons. El DeBarge was singled out a la Michael Jackson for his superb singing and dancing skills. The Jackson association continued; Jermaine Jackson was instrumental in the group's signing to Motown's Gordy Records subsidiary, and in 1984 James DeBarge and Janet Jackson eloped (within seven months they filed for an annulment).

DeBarge landed its first record deal as a quartet, four of 10 siblings raised by a black mother and a white father. The family was religious, and the group members began singing in church. In the late '70s they set their sights on pop and moved to Hollywood in pursuit of a contract with Motown Records. (Two older brothers, Bobby and Tommy DeBarge, already played in a Motown band called Switch.) In 1979 brothers El, Marty, and Randy DeBarge and sister Bunny were signed to Gordy. The vocal group released its debut, *The DeBarges,* in 1981, establishing its penchant for creamy love songs. Two gold albums followed, 1982's *All This Love* (with brother James added to the lineup) and 1983's *In a Special Way.*

DeBarge's most successful album was 1985's *Rhythm of the Night.* The catchy title track became a #3 single, and "Who's Holding Donna Now" went to #6. El then left DeBarge; his biggest solo hit was 1986's "Who's Johnny" (#3), from the *Short Circuit* soundtrack. Meanwhile, El's brothers switched to Striped Horse Records, while Bunny stayed on at Motown, releasing the solo album, *In Love.*

Another brother, Chico (who had never been part of the group), joined Motown in 1986 and released a harder-edged funk album, featuring "Talk to Me" (#21 pop, #7 R&B, 1986). Unfortunately, Chico got press for more dubious accomplishments: He and brother Bobby were arrested and convicted on cocaine-trafficking charges in 1988. El himself served jail time in 1987, after failing to complete a sentence he'd received after allegedly hitting a woman who had rejected his advances. The sentence involved performing a benefit concert.

By the early '90s, the group's collective star, and El's individual one, had fallen, thanks to legal problems and what was generally perceived as a lack of creative progress. By late 1994, El DeBarge showed signs of a comeback with the Babyface production *Heart, Mind and Soul,* which received critical praise.

In the late '90s, Chico carved out his own niche as a soul singer. After serving five years and eight months in prison, he attracted a following with the release of the appropriately titled *Long Time No See* (#86 pop, #14 R&B, 1997), featuring "No Guarantee" (#18 R&B, 1998). Meanwhile, El collaborated with the jazz quartet Fourplay on a 1998 cover of Marvin Gaye's "Sexual Healing" (#56 R&B) and with producer/arranger Quincy Jones on a 1999 duet with Siedah Garrett,

"I'm Yours" (#73 R&B). Both El and Chico played on and contributed to the production of R&B singer Grenique's debut album in 1999, the same year that Chico returned to Motown with *The Game*.

Joey Dee and the Starliters

Formed 1958, Passaic, NJ
Joey Dee (b. Joseph DiNicola, June 11, 1940, Passaic), voc.; Carlton Latimor, organ; Willie Davis, drums; Larry Vernieri (d. Dec. 7, 1999), voc., dancer; David Brigati, voc., dancer.
1961—*Doin' the Twist at the Peppermint Lounge* (Roulette) 1962—*Hey, Let's Twist!*.
Joey Dee solo: N.A.—*Joey Dee* (Roulette); *Dance, Dance, Dance.*

In 1960 Joey Dee and the Starliters (sometimes misspelled "Starlighters") were the house band at New York's famed Peppermint Lounge. When Dee noticed that everyone there was gyrating to Chubby Checker's "The Twist," he and R&B producer Henry Glover decided to personalize the dance fad, and they came up with the "Peppermint Twist." Released in late 1961, the song was a #1 smash and landed the group cameo roles in two quickie fad films, *Hey Let's Twist* and *Two Tickets to Paris*. The group scored a few more hits ("Hey Let's Twist," "Shout," "What Kind of Love Is This," "Hot Pastrami with Mashed Potatoes") before sinking back into lounge-band anonymity in late 1963.

By then, however, the Starliters featured three of the four future Young Rascals: Felix Cavaliere, Gene Cornish, and Eddie Brigati (whose brother David had been with Dee from the beginning). A psychedelic twist: In 1966 the group included Jimi Hendrix. And a showbiz twist: An earlier version of the group had actor-to-be Joe Pesci on guitar and backing vocals. In 1987 Dee established the Foundation for the Love of Rock 'n' Roll—later renamed the National Music Foundation—which tried to find health insurance and a retirement community for needy musicians. Dee continues to perform. By the '90s, Dee's act included his wife Lois and son Ronnie, and played cruise liners and Atlantic City resorts. Brigati is a popular backup singer and part of the all-star New York Rock and Soul Revue.

Deee-Lite

Formed 1986, New York, NY
Lady Miss Kier (b. Kier Kirby, Youngstown, OH), voc.; Super DJ Dmitry (b. Dmitry Brill, ca. 1964, Kirovograd, Ukraine), DJ; Jungle DJ Towa Towa (b. Towa Tei, Tokyo, Jap.), DJ.
1990—*World Clique* (Elektra) 1992—*Infinity Within* 1994—(– DJ Towa Towa; + DJ Ani, DJ, bass) *Dew Drops in the Garden* 1996—*Sampladelic Relics and Dancefloor Oddities.*
Towa Tei solo: 1995—*Future Listening* (Elektra) 1998—*Sound Museum.*

Deee-Lite combines techno, ambient, house, rap, and funk with a sense of style that borrows equally from '60s psychedelia and '70s kitsch. After four years of notoriety on New York's hip underground club scene, the trio scored mainstream success with its infectious dance hit "Groove Is in the Heart" (#4, 1990).

Kier Kirby and her three sisters and brother grew up in various spots across the eastern U.S., including Pittsburgh. Her mother, an urban planner and political activist, divorced her father, a food manufacturer, when Kier was seven, and remarried a former Navy commander. At 18 Kier moved to New York to study textile design at the Fashion Institute of Technology but dropped out after becoming disillusioned with the program. In 1982 she met Dmitry Brill, a classically trained Ukrainian émigré who had discovered pop music early on, learning "Stairway to Heaven" on guitar at age 12. With a mutual interest in dance music, the two began writing songs together, and formed Deee-Lite, named for Cole Porter's "It's Delovely," in 1986. One year later, they added Towa Tei, a club DJ who had recently moved from Japan.

Deee-Lite became a hot ticket among New York's club culture, attracting large, multiracial, pansexual crowds to shows in which the trio would dress outrageously and throw flowers from the stage. Elektra signed the group and released *World Clique* in 1990 to commercial and critical success; the album reached #20 and sold a half-million copies, fueled by the catchy "Groove Is in the Heart," which featured such guests as bassist Bootsy Collins, Q-Tip (of A Tribe Called Quest), and saxman Maceo Parker. In addition to that breakthrough track, *World Clique* contained the minor hit, "Power of Love" (#47). Deee-Lite's visual style and sex appeal won the group plenty of photo spreads in music and fashion magazines. The trio followed up two years later with *Infinity Within* (#67, 1992), whose songs carried more obvious political messages—touching on the environment, voting, and safe sex. The 1994 album *Dew Drops in the Garden* was coproduced by a new collaborator, DJ Ani (DJ Towa Towa went on sabbatical). At this point, Deee-Lite wholeheartedly embraced rave culture, headlining Ravestock (Friday night to early Saturday morning) at Woodstock '94 (the Orb, Aphex Twin, and Orbital also performed). As the band's commercial fortunes faded, Deee-Lite released the 1996 remix album *Sampladelic Relics and Dancefloor Oddities* and broke up.

The breakup only drove its members deeper into the club culture from whence they came. Both Towa and Dmitry continued spinning. Kier moved to London and became a DJ herself on the thriving U.K. jungle/drum-and-bass scene. She also appeared on "Accelerate," a song from Jonny L's *Magnetic* album, and in 1999 announced plans for a solo album. But the most prolific recording artist of the trio has been DJ Towa, back to calling himself Towa Tei, who released *Future Listening* (1995) and *Sound Museum* (1998), an album rich with old-school funk and reggae, with such guest vocalists as Kylie Minogue and Biz Markie, and a samba-infected take on Hall and Oates' "Private Eyes."

Deep Purple

Formed 1968, Hertford, Eng.
Rod Evans (b. 1945, Edinburgh, Scot.), voc.; Nick Simper

(b. 1946, London, Eng.), bass; Jon Lord (b. June 9, 1941, Leicester, Eng.), kybds.; Ritchie Blackmore (b. Apr. 14, 1945, Weston-super-Mare, Eng.), gtr.; Ian Paice (b. June 29, 1948, Nottingham, Eng.), drums.
1968—*Shades of Deep Purple* (Tetragrammaton); *Book of Taliesyn* 1969—*Deep Purple* (– Evans; + Ian Gillan [b. Aug. 19, 1945, London], voc.; – Simper; + Roger Glover [b. Nov. 30, 1945, Brecon, S. Wales], bass) 1970—*Concerto for Group and Orchestra* (Warner Bros.); *Deep Purple in Rock* 1971—*Fireball* 1972—*Machine Head; Purple Passages; Made in Japan* 1973—*Who Do We Think We Are!* (– Glover; + Glenn Hughes [b. Penkridge, Eng.], bass; – Gillan; + David Coverdale [b. Sep. 22, 1949, Saltburn, Eng.], voc.) 1974—*Burn; Stormbringer* 1975—(– Blackmore; + Tommy Bolin [b. 1951, Sioux City, IA; d. Dec. 4, 1976, Miami, FL], gtr.) *Come Taste the Band* (– Bolin) *24 Carat Purple* 1976—*Made in Europe* 1978—*When We Rock, We Rock and When We Roll, We Roll; Powerhouse* (Purple, U.K.) 1980—*Deepest Purple* (Warner Bros.) 1982—*In Concert* (Portrait) 1984—(group re-forms: Blackmore; Gillan; Glover; Lord; Paice) *Perfect Strangers* (Mercury) 1986—*Nobody's Perfect* 1989—(– Gillan; + Joe Lynn Turner, voc.) 1990—*Slaves and Masters* (RCA) 1992—*Knocking at Your Back Door: The Best of Deep Purple in the '80s* (Mercury) 1993—(lineup: Gillan; Blackmore; Glover; Paice; Lord) *The Battle Rages On* (Giant) (– Gillan; numerous personnel changes) 1996—*Purpendicular* (CMC) 1998—*Abandon; Shades (1968–1998)* (Rhino).
Roger Glover solo: 1974—*The Butterfly Ball and the Grasshopper's Feast* (Oyster).

Deep Purple shifted halfway through its career from rock with pseudo-classical keyboard flourishes to guitar-dominated heavy metal; in the latter, vastly popular phase, it was listed as loudest rock band by the *Guinness Book of World Records*. In the wake of a highly publicized regrouping of the classic lineup, Deep Purple has emerged as one of the longest-lived (with a few interruptions) U.K. hard-rock/metal outfits and a showcase for some of the most successful hard-rock stars of the '70s, '80s, and '90s, including guitarist Ritchie Blackmore and singer David Coverdale.

After woodshedding in Hertfordshire, England, Deep Purple had its first success with an American hit, a version of Joe South's "Hush" (#4, 1968), followed by Neil Diamond's "Kentucky Woman" (#38, 1968). The group's popularity couldn't keep its label, Tetragrammaton, from going under after the band's 1968 tour. In 1969, with a new lineup including Ian Gillan, who had sung in *Jesus Christ Superstar*, Deep Purple recorded Lord's *Concerto for Group and Orchestra*, but after it failed to sell, Ritchie Blackmore began to dominate the band. His simple repeated guitar riffs helped make Deep Purple one of the most successful groups of the early '70s, but his personality clashes with other band members, particularly Gillan, precipitated several personnel shifts in between.

In Rock and *Fireball* attracted attention, and *Machine Head* made the U.S. Top 10 (#7), thus adding to the band's success in England, Europe, Japan, and Australia. One year after *Machine Head* was released, "Smoke on the Water"—about the band's near-disastrous Montreux concert with Frank Zappa—became a #4 hit single, and the album returned to the Top 10, eventually selling over 2 million copies. By late 1974, Deep Purple had sold nearly 15 million albums. But the band had begun to fall apart. Gillan left for a solo career in 1973. He released a number of albums in the U.K. In 1975 he formed the Ian Gillan Band and after it dissolved in 1983, joined Black Sabbath. Roger Glover followed Gillan, moving on to session and production work (for Judas Priest, Elf, Nazareth, Ian Gillan, Spencer Davis, Michael Schenker of UFO, Barbi Benton, and Blackmore's Rainbow). Gillan's replacement, David Coverdale, sang on *Burn* and *Stormbringer*. He would find greater fame, however, in the '80s with Whitesnake [see entry] and his collaboration with Jimmy Page. Jon Lord recorded a British solo album, *Gemini Suite* (1974). Blackmore left in 1975 to form Ritchie Blackmore's Rainbow [see entry]. He was replaced by Tommy Bolin, with whom the group recorded one LP, *Come Taste the Band*, before announcing its retirement in 1976.

In 1980 a bogus reincarnation of Deep Purple led by original vocalist Evans popped up on the West Coast bar circuit. Blackmore and Glover took legal action to prohibit Evans from using the name. In 1984 they reclaimed the name for themselves, reuniting for their first new LP since 1976, the Top 20, platinum *Perfect Strangers*, which included "Knocking at Your Back Door." Despite being welcomed warmly by its fans, Deep Purple was plagued by personal tensions, and Gillan again departed in 1989. He pursued a solo career, only to return again for 1994's *The Battle Rages On*, but left again shortly thereafter.

Def Leppard

Formed 1977, Sheffield, Eng.
Joe Elliott (b. Aug. 1, 1959, Sheffield), voc.; Pete Willis (b. Feb. 16, 1960, Eng.), gtr.; Rick Savage (b. Dec. 2, 1960, Sheffield), bass; Rick Allen (b. Nov. 1, 1963, Sheffield), drums; Steve Clark (b. Apr. 23, 1960, Sheffield; d. Jan. 8, 1991, London, Eng.), gtr.
1980—*On Through the Night* (Mercury) 1981—*High 'n' Dry* (– Willis; + Phil Collen [b. Dec. 8, 1957], gtr.) 1983—*Pyromania* 1987—*Hysteria* 1991—(– Clark) 1992—*Adrenalize* (+ Vivian Campbell [b. Aug. 25, 1962, Belfast, N. Ire.], gtr.) 1993—*Retro Active* 1995—*Vault—Greatest Hits 1985–1990* 1996—*Slang* 1999—*Euphoria.*

In the beginning a chart-breaking debut album, tours with more established heavy-metal bands, and pinup good looks made Def Leppard one of the leaders of the '80s British heavy-metal renaissance. The members, barely out of their teens when their first album debuted, soon became one of the most consistently successful pop-metal groups of the decade and beyond, becoming, as one *Goldmine* article put it, "The Heavy Metal Band You Can Bring Home to Mother."

Pete Willis and Rick Savage started the group in Sheffield in 1977. Joe Elliott had coined the name Deaf Leopard before joining them; Willis and Savage changed the spelling. As a quartet with a since-forgotten drummer, Def Leppard built a local pub following, and in 1978, after being joined by Steve Clark and hiring a temporary drummer, the group produced its first record, an EP called *Getcha Rocks Off,* released on its own Bludgeon Riffola label. The record got airplay on the BBC and sold 24,000 copies.

The members' self-made success and precociousness (Elliott, the group's eldest member, was 19, and Rick Allen, who became their permanent drummer after playing with several professional Sheffield bands, was 15) brought them the attention of the British rock press. AC/DC manager Peter Mensch added them to his roster and got them a contract with Mercury. Their first album was a hit in the U.K. and reached #51 in the U.S. The group toured Britain with Sammy Hagar and AC/DC, played the 1980 Reading Festival, and first toured the U.S. opening for Ted Nugent, Pat Travers, Judas Priest, and AC/DC. A second U.S. tour, with Blackfoot, Ozzy Osbourne, and Rainbow, coupled with heavy coverage in the U.S. metal press, created a growing American audience.

The group's second album, *High 'n' Dry* was the first of a string of platinum and multiplatinum LPs, hitting #38 in 1981 and selling over 2 million copies. (It was remixed and released in 1984 with two more tracks, a remixed "Bringin' on the Heartbreak" and "Me and My Wine.") By early 1982 the group had reentered the studio to record *Pyromania,* which would eventually sell a phenomenal 10 million copies. Midway through the recording, founding guitarist Pete Willis was fired for alcoholism and replaced by Phil Collen, formerly of Girl. At the same time co-lead guitarist Steve Clark was beginning a slide into the extreme alcohol addiction that would eventually kill him.

Shortly after *Pyromania*'s release, the band embarked on its first world tour. MTV, undeniably a factor in the band's U.S. success, began airing "Bringin' on the Heartbreak," and within the next few years virtually all the band's videos (beginning with *Pyromania*'s "Rock of Ages," "Photograph," and "Foolin' ") would go into heavy rotation. When producer Mutt Lange, with whom the group had recorded since its major-label debut, was unavailable to work on their next album, Def Leppard turned to Jim Steinman, most famous for his work with Meat Loaf. When Steinman proved incompatible, *High 'n' Dry* engineer Nigel Green stepped in. Just one month later, drummer Rick Allen lost his left arm in a New Year's Eve car accident after he attempted to pass another driver at high speed. Surgeons reattached the limb, but after infection set in, it was amputated. Def Leppard's future was in doubt, but by the spring of 1985 Allen was learning to play drums again with the help of a specially adapted Simmons kit. (For a while he performed with special electronic equipment, using prerecorded tapes of his drumming for some parts, then returned to a regular acoustic kit with customized foot pads in 1995.) The band continued recording, but when Lange heard the tapes, he suggested the band scrap them and start again. In August 1986 Allen performed for the first time since his accident on the European Monsters of Rock Tour.

In early 1987 the band finally completed work on the long-awaited *Hysteria,* which spun off six Top 20 singles: "Animal" (#19, 1987; and their first Top 40 hit in the U.K.), "Hysteria" (#10, 1988), "Pour Some Sugar on Me" (#2, 1988), "Love Bites" (#1, 1988), "Armageddon It" (#3, 1988), and "Rocket" (#12, 1989). Though longtime fans and some critics found it disappointingly poppish, on the verge of bubblegum, that change in direction no doubt contributed to it selling over 16 million copies worldwide and topping the U.S. LPs chart for six weeks.

Tragedy struck the group again when on January 8, 1991, guitarist Steve Clark died of a fatal mixture of drugs and alcohol. Beginning in 1982, he had undergone treatment for his alcoholism several times. His addiction was so disabling that Phil Collen had done most of the leads on *Hysteria,* and later the group forced Clark to take a lengthy sabbatical. Once in 1989, after being found comatose in a gutter, he was admitted to a psychiatric hospital, but he seemed beyond help. The group continued recording and even made the video for "Let's Get Rocked" as a foursome.

Clark's replacement, Vivian Campbell, who had previously played with Ronnie James Dio and Whitesnake, joined in 1992, weeks after the release of *Adrenalize.* Another #1 LP, *Adrenalize* spawned a flurry of hit singles: "Have You Ever Needed Someone So Bad" (#12, 1992), "Let's Get Rocked" (#15, 1992), "Make Love Like a Man" (#36, 1992), and "Stand Up (Kick Love Into Motion)" (#34, 1992). *Retro Active* (#9, 1993), a platinum collection of B sides, rarities, and covers, yielded the hit singles "Two Steps Behind" (#32, 1994) (also on the *Last Action Hero* soundtrack) and "Miss You in a Heartbeat" (#39, 1994). The album also included one Mick Ronson song, "Only After Dark." As the band wanted to explore new directions on its next studio album, it decided to release a greatest-hits collection before embarking on the next stage of its career; *Vault* (#15, 1995) went on to sell close to 2 million copies. Unfortunately its successor, *Slang,* which added industrial and even touches of soul to the musical mix, did not fare as well and peaked at #14. The band retreated to its classic '80s pop-metal style on *Euphoria* (#11, 1999).

The DeFranco Family

Formed 1973, Port Colborne, Can.
Benny DeFranco (b. July 11, 1954, Port Colborne), voc.; Nino DeFranco (b. Oct. 19, 1956, Port Colborne), voc.; Marisa DeFranco (b. July 23, 1955, Port Colborne), voc.; Merlina DeFranco (b. July 20, 1957, Port Colborne), voc.; Tony DeFranco (b. Aug. 31, 1959, Port Colborne), voc.
1973—*Heartbeat—It's a Lovebeat* (20th Century–Fox) 1974—*Save the Last Dance for Me.*

Modeled after wholesome family acts like the Osmonds, the Cowsills, and the Jackson 5, the Canadian-born DeFranco Family was sponsored by Laufer Publications (publishers of *Tiger Beat* and *Fave* magazines), which managed the group and distributed fan-club material featuring 10-year-old lead singer Tony DeFranco. "Heartbeat—It's a Lovebeat" sold 2.5

million copies in 1973, becoming the year's top single. The next year, the family charted two more singles: "Abra-Ca-Dabra" (#32) and a remake of the Drifters' classic "Save the Last Dance for Me" (#18). But the family's career was ultimately distinguished by its brevity.

Desmond Dekker

Born Desmond Dacres, July 16, 1941, Kingston, Jam.
1969—*The Israelites* (Uni) 1970—*You Can Get It* (Trojan) 1974—*Double Dekker* 1978—*Sweet 16 Hits* 1980—*Black and Dekker* (Stiff) 1981—*Compass Point* 1992—*Rockin' Steady: The Best of Desmond Dekker* (Rhino); *Music Like Dirt* (Trojan) 1994—*Action!* (Lagoon) 1995—*King of Kings* (Trojan) 1996—*Moving Out* 1997—*Intensified* (Lagoon) 1998—*Writing on the Wall* (Trojan) 2000—*Halfway to Paradise; Desmond Dekker* (Recall).

Desmond Dekker was one of the pioneers of reggae and the creator of one of the genre's best-known songs, 1969's "The Israelites." As a teenager in Jamaica, he worked in the same welding shop as Bob Marley, who encouraged him to audition for producer Leslie "King" Kong. Kong helped Dekker put together a group, the Aces, and produced their first record, "Honour Thy Father and Mother," in 1963. Eventually a #1 hit in Jamaica, it was followed by a score of Caribbean hits that won Dekker the title "King of the Bluebeat" and the annual Golden Trophy (awarded to Jamaica's top singer) five times between 1963 and 1969.

In 1964 Chris Blackwell released "Honour Thy Father and Mother" in Britain on his Island label. Dekker's first U.K. Top 20 hit was a 1967 single on Pyramid, "007 (Shanty Town)," later featured on the soundtrack of *The Harder They Come* (1972). Dekker's only U.S. hit, "The Israelites" (#9 pop, 1969), personalized imagery from the Biblical Exodus story. It sold over a million copies worldwide, reaching #1 in Britain. (Twenty years later, it was featured prominently in the Gus Van Sant film *Drugstore Cowboy,* starring Matt Dillon.)

A handful of British hits followed "The Israelites," including "It Miek" (#7, 1969) and "You Can Get It If You Really Want" (#2, 1970), written for him by Jimmy Cliff. A reissue of "The Israelites" returned him to the British Top 10 in 1975. "Sing a Little Song" made the Top 20 later that year. Dekker didn't record again until 1980, when Stiff Records signed him at the height of the ska and rock-steady revival. His comeback album, *Black and Dekker,* featured one of the original rock-steady groups, the Pioneers, and Graham Parker's band the Rumour in supporting roles. Its followup, *Compass Point,* was produced by singer Robert Palmer.

In 1984 Dekker was declared bankrupt by a British court. He claimed that his former manager had withheld funds. Things looked up for Dekker, however, when a 1990 British TV ad for Maxell Tapes used the melody of "The Israelites" for its jingle, and the song was reissued once again. Dekker capitalized on his renewed fame, spending the '90s touring and recording.

Delaney and Bonnie

Bonnie Bramlett, born Nov. 8, 1944, Acton, IL; Delaney Bramlett, born July 1, 1939, Pontotoc County, MS
1969—*Accept No Substitute: The Original Delaney and Bonnie* (Elektra); *Home* (Stax) 1970—*On Tour With Eric Clapton* (Atco); *To Bonnie From Delaney* 1971—*Motel Shot; Genesis* (GNP-Crescendo) 1972—*D and B Together* (Columbia) 1973—*The Best of Delaney and Bonnie* (Atco) 1990—*The Best of Delaney and Bonnie* (Rhino).
Bonnie Bramlett solo: 1973—*Sweet Bonnie Bramlett* (Columbia) 1975—*It's Time* (Capricorn) 1976—*Lady's Choice* 1978—*Memories.*
Delaney Bramlett solo: 1972—*Something's Coming* (Columbia) 1973—*Mobius Strip* 1975—*Giving Birth to a Song* (MGM) 1977—*Delaney and Friends—Class Reunion* (Prodigal) 1998—*Sounds From Home* (DK/Zane).

This husband-and-wife duo's best songs fused gospel, country, funk, and rock, but the pair was overshadowed by its Friends, a backup crew that occasionally included Eric Clapton, Leon Russell, Dave Mason, and George Harrison. The couple met in L.A. in 1967. Bonnie Lynn had worked as a bewigged, blackfaced Ikette with Ike and Tina Turner in the mid-'60s; Delaney had fallen in with a group of Southwestern musicians, including Russell and J.J. Cale, contacts that netted him a brief stint with the Champs and then a steady job with the Shindogs, house band for ABC's *Shindig.* The Shindogs were moonlighting at an L.A. bowling alley when Bramlett met Lynn; a week later they married.

Although the group's first album went largely unnoticed, Blind Faith offered Delaney and Bonnie an opening slot on its 1969 tour. Clapton began riding in the couple's tour bus, which turned into a rolling jam session. After Blind Faith disbanded, Clapton began to perform regularly with the duo, assuming a low-key, sideman-only stance.

Clapton brought Delaney and Bonnie to England, where Harrison, Mason, and others came onstage for shows that resulted in Delaney and Bonnie's best-selling album, *On Tour With Eric Clapton* (#29, 1970). The entourage briefly participated in John Lennon's Plastic Ono Band in late 1969 and toured Europe with Clapton. They returned to America as headliners in 1970, but their drawing power plummeted when Clapton left, and Leon Russell then hired most of the Friends to tour with Joe Cocker's Mad Dogs and Englishmen. The Bramletts canceled their tour.

They appeared on Clapton's solo debut in 1970, produced by Delaney, and continued to record their own albums, which included two major hits, "Never Ending Song of Love" (#13, 1971) and Dave Mason's "Only You Know and I Know" (#20, 1971).

In 1972 they signed with Columbia and made their last album, *Together,* before their marriage dissolved. Delaney made two solo LPs for Columbia to fulfill contractual obligations *(Something's Coming* and *Mobius Strip)* as well as 1975's *Giving Birth to a Song* on MGM and 1977's *Class Reunion* for Motown's Prodigal label. Bonnie, backed by the uncredited Average White Band, made one album for Columbia

(Sweet Bonnie Bramlett) before signing with Capricorn. While touring with Stephen Stills in 1979, she punched Elvis Costello in a Columbus, Ohio, bar when he called Ray Charles "a blind, ignorant nigger." She later had a recurrent acting role in the hit '90s TV sitcom *Roseanne*. She had by then changed her surname to Sheridan.

Delaney overcame alcoholism at his Rock and Roll Ranch in Shadow Hills, California, became a born-again Christian, and recorded commercial jingles. In 1993 Delaney and Bonnie's daughter Bekka Bramlett briefly replaced Stevie Nicks in Fleetwood Mac. In the late '90s Delaney recorded and toured with his wife, Kim Carmel Bramlett.

De La Soul

Formed 1985, Amityville, NY
Posdnuos (b. Kelvin Mercer, Aug. 17, 1969, Bronx, NY), voc.; Trugoy the Dove (b. David Jolicoeur, Sep. 21, 1968, Brooklyn, NY), voc.; Maseo (b. Vincent Mason, Mar. 24, 1970, Brooklyn), DJ, voc.
1989—*Three Feet High and Rising* (Tommy Boy) 1991—*De La Soul Is Dead* 1993—*Buhlōōne Mindstate* 1996—*Stakes Is High* 2000—*Art Official Intelligence (Mosaic Thump).*

De La Soul made rap history as the first group to go against the hip-hop grain of macho braggadocio, hectoring social comment, and mammoth beats, all while winning respect and acclaim from inside and outside of the hip-hop community. With its middle-class suburban Long Island roots, light rhythms, laid-back raps, thoughtfully irreverent lyrics, esoteric sampling, and quasihippie attitude, De La Soul paved the way for a steady stream of gently adventurous "alternative" rap groups (A Tribe Called Quest, P.M. Dawn, Basehead, and Digable Planets).

De La Soul began as three high school friends whose stage names reflected their sense of whimsical in-jokery: through backward spelling David Jolicoeur became "Trugoy the Dove" (*yogurt,* his favorite food, spelled backwards); Kelvin Mercer derived "Posdnuos" (his nickname as a high school DJ, "Sound-Sop"). Their first demo, "Plug Tunin'," attracted the attention of Paul "Prince Paul" Houston, of local rap group Stetsasonic. He played the tape for colleagues on New York's rap scene, and soon De La Soul signed with Tommy Boy. Houston produced the group's debut album, a mock-game show soundtrack that introduced such De La terms as "the D.A.I.S.Y. Age (Da Inner Sound, Y'all)." De La Soul were labeled "hippies"—a term at which the group bridled—but also hailed as ingenious revolutionaries. The album brimmed with off-center inventiveness, its samples taken not from the usual James Brown rhythm tracks but from TV shows and obscure recordings, many from De La Soul's parents' collections. "Transmitting Live From Mars" set a sample from a French-lesson record atop a sample from the 1968 Turtles hit "You Showed Me." The former Turtles filed a $1.7 million lawsuit, charging their music was sampled without their permission; the case was settled out of court for an undisclosed sum. *Three Feet* (#24 pop, #1 R&B, 1989) yielded a hit single in "Me Myself and I" (#34 pop, #1 R&B, 1989), set to a sample of Funkadelic's 1979 "(not just) Knee Deep." De La Soul then formed "Native Tongues," a loose alliance with A Tribe Called Quest, the Jungle Brothers, Queen Latifah, Monie Love, and Black Sheep.

De La Soul's second album was an obvious reaction to the perception that its debut, however innovative, was "soft." Titled *De La Soul Is Dead* (#26 pop, #24 R&B, 1991), it took a darker, more serious tone with songs about drug abuse ("My Brother's a Basehead"), incest ("Millie Pulled a Pistol on Santa"), and the vicissitudes of fame ("Ring Ring Ring [Ha Ha Hey]" [#22 R&B, 1991]). Critical and commercial reaction to the album was mixed. De La Soul came back strong in late 1993, however, with *Buhlōōne Mindstate* (#40 pop, #9 R&B), hailed as a return to the group's quirky, groundbreaking form. A more conventional effort, the 1996 album *Stakes Is High* found the group stuck in neutral. Three singles—"The Bizness" (#53 R&B), "Stakes Is High" (#70 R&B), and "Itsoweezee (Hot)" (#60 R&B)—failed to stir sustained interest. De La Soul wasn't dead, however, as the trio returned to the studio for a 2000 release, *Art Official Intelligence (Mosaic Thump)*. Guest artists include Chaka Khan, the Beastie Boys, Busta Rhymes, and Redman.

The Delfonics

Formed 1964, Philadelphia, PA
William Hart (b. Jan. 17, 1945, Washington, DC), lead voc.; Wilbert Hart (b. Oct. 19, 1947, Philadelphia), baritone voc.; Ricky Johnson, bass voc.; Richard Daniels, tenor voc.
1965—(– Daniels; – Johnson; + Randy Cain III [b. Herbert Randal, May 2, 1945, Philadelphia], tenor voc.) 1968—*La La Means I Love You* (Philly Groove) 1969—*The Sound of Sexy Soul; The Delfonics Super Hits* 1970—*The Delfonics* 1972—*Tell Me This Is a Dream* 1973—(– Cain; + Major Harris [b. Richmond, VA], tenor voc.) 1974—*Alive and Kicking* (– Harris; + John Johnson, voc.) 1975—*Let It Be Me* (Sounds Superb) 1997—*La-La Means I Love You: The Definitive Collection* (Arista).

The Delfonics' late-'60s MOR soul hits were among producer Thom Bell's earliest works and set standards for elegant black pop. Originally the Orphonics, the group formed in the mid-'60s around chief songwriter William Hart in a Philadelphia high school. Their high-pitched harmony style shone on medium-tempo ballads like "He Don't Really Love You," a local hit in 1967, shortly after they'd signed with manager Stan Watson, who persuaded them to call themselves the Delfonics. They worked East Coast clubs until early 1968, when Watson formed the Philly Groove label and brought in budding producer Thom Bell.

Their first collaboration with Bell, "La-La Means I Love You" (a phrase Hart picked up from his young son), was an instant #4 smash in spring 1968. Bell also worked on subsequent Delfonics hits ("I'm Sorry," "Break Your Promise," "Ready or Not, Here I Come," "You Get Yours and I'll Get

Mine" and their 1970 Top 10 landmark "Didn't I [Blow Your Mind This Time]").

R&B veteran Major Harris ("One Monkey Don't Stop No Show") joined the group in 1973, when Cain retired due to illness; he left the following year. In 1975 Harris had a solo hit with "Time Won't Let Me Wait" (#5 pop, #1 R&B, 1975). Although no charting singles followed 1974's "Lying to Myself," the group continued to perform.

Harris, the Hart brothers, and Cain eventually regrouped. In the early '90s Wilbur Hart left and formed his own version of the Delfonics. Throughout the decade the Fugees, Prince, and Missy Elliott covered Delfonics songs, while vocal acts like Boyz II Men cited them as a primary influence. Thanks to praise from director Quentin Tarantino, who used "Didn't I" in his 1997 film *Jackie Brown,* a younger audience embraced the group's music.

The Del-Lords: See the Dictators

The Dells

Formed 1952, Harvey, IL
Marvin Junior (b. Jan. 31, 1936, Harrell, AK), first tenor voc.; Michael "Mickey" McGill (b. Feb. 17, 1937, Chicago, IL), baritone voc.; Johnny Funches (b. ca. 1937; d. Jan. 23, 1998), lead voc.; Chuck Barksdale (b. June 11, 1935, Chicago), bass voc.; Verne Allison (b. Laverne Allison, June 22, 1936, Chicago), tenor voc.; Lucius McGill (b. 1935, Chicago), tenor voc.
1955—(– L. McGill) 1958—(– Funches; + Johnny Carter [b. June 2, 1934, Chicago], lead voc.) 1968—*There Is* (Cadet) 1969—*The Dells Greatest Hits* 1970—*Like It Is* 1972—*Freedom Means* 1973—*Give Your Baby a Standing Ovation* 1974—*The Mighty Mighty Dells; The Dells vs. the Dramatics* (Chess/MCA) 1975—*No Way Back* (Mercury); *The Dells Greatest Hits, vol. 2* (Cadet) 1976—*They Said It Couldn't Be Done* (Mercury) 1977—*Love Connection* 1980—*I Touched a Dream* (20th Century–Fox) 1981—*Whatever Turns You On* 1984—*One Step Closer; The Dells* (Chess) 1988—*The Second Time* (Urgent/Ichiban) 1992—*On Their Corner: Best of the Dells* (MCA); *I Salute You* (Philadelphia International) 1994—*You Gotta Have Soul: vol. 2* (Vee-Jay) 1996—*Bring Back Love: Classic Dells Soul* (Chess) 1998—*Oh, What a Night! The Great Ballads* 2000—*Reminiscing* (Volt).

The Dells are a black vocal group that has been together nearly 50 years and whose story and perseverance inspired filmmaker Robert Townshend's *The Five Heartbeats.* The original members began singing together as freshmen at Thornton Township High School in the Chicago suburb of Harvey. A street-corner a cappella doo-wop group, they called themselves the El Rays and picked up their style from records by the Clovers and the Dominoes. Harvey Fuqua of the Moonglows took them as protégés, and within months the El Rays were including Michael McGill's and Marvin Junior's originals in their club sets.

In late 1953 they recorded their first single for Chess, the a cappella "Darling Dear, I Know" b/w "Christine." The resulting $36 in royalties sent the group back to the street-corners, but the quintet continued to record for Chess until 1955, when, billing itself as the Dells, it switched to Vee-Jay Records. Their second release for that label, "Oh, What a Night," became a Top 10 R&B hit. Barksdale did not sing on this single, since he had left the group to join Otis Williams and the Charms; he soon rejoined the Dells.

En route to a gig in 1958, the group had an auto accident that left McGill in the hospital for six months, forced Funches to retire, and put the band out of commission for nearly two years. In 1959 Funches was replaced by ex-Flamingo falsetto Johnny Carter.

The early '60s found the Dells slowly regrouping and label-hopping between Vee-Jay and Chess. By mid-decade they had become a contemporary soul group a la the Temptations and the Impressions; they hit the pop chart in 1968 with three Top 20 hits: "There Is" (#20), "Always Together" (#18), and their biggest hit, "Stay in My Corner" (#10 pop, #1 R&B). Hits in 1969 included a medley of "I Can Sing a Rainbow"/"Love Is Blue" (#22) and a Top 10 remake of "Oh, What a Night." They hit occasionally in the early '70s ("Give Your Baby a Standing Ovation," "The Love We Had [Stays on My Mind]"). All told, the Dells have had 30 R&B Top 40 and eight pop Top 40 hits.

Through the years the group has backed countless singers, including Jerry Butler, Dinah Washington, and Barbara Lewis (they sang on her 1963 hit "Hello Stranger"). Although pop hits have eluded them for decades, the Dells have recorded consistently and remain a live attraction. Their 1992 LP, *I Salute You,* was produced by Kenny Gamble and Leon Huff. "The Heart Is the House of Love" (#13 R&B, 1991) was included on the *Five Heartbeats* soundtrack. Signed to the newly reactivated Volt imprint of Stax, the Dells released *Reminiscing* in 2000.

The Del-Vikings/Dell Vikings

Formed 1956, Pittsburgh, PA
Clarence Quick (b. Brooklyn, NY), voc.; Dave Lerchey (b. New Albany, IN), voc.; Norman Wright (b. Oct. 21, 1937, Philadelphia, PA), voc.; Don Jackson, voc.; Corinthian "Kripp" Johnson [b. Cambridge, MA; d. June 22, 1990], voc.
1957—(– Jackson; + Donald "Gus" Backus [b. Southampton, NY], voc.) (numerous personnel changes follow).

One of rock's first racially integrated groups, the Del-Vikings were a vocal quintet that came together at a Pittsburgh Air Force base and scored two Top 10 hits in 1957, "Come Go with Me" (#5) and "Whispering Bells" (#9). The group first recorded for Luniverse (owned by Dickie Goodman of the "Flying Saucer" novelty hits) in 1956 with little success. The following year, after adding Kripp Johnson, it recorded the R&B-tinged million-seller "Come Go With Me." The group toured widely, and in mid-1957 scored again with "Whispering Bells."

But after that, ex–Del-Viking Kripp Johnson formed his

own group of Del-Vikings and added a second "l" to their name, thus sparking confusion that has plagued rock historians ever since. Among these new Dell Vikings was Chuck Jackson, who had soul hits in the '60s ("I Don't Want to Cry," "Any Day Now," "Tell Him I'm Not Home") and '70s ("Needing You"). Under threat of legal action, this group then recorded as the Versatiles. The first group, with some personnel shifts, continued to tour and record, breaking up in the mid-'60s, then regrouping in 1970. In the '70s Johnson, Lerchey, Wright, and others were touring internationally. Despite a dizzying sequence of personnel changes, the Del-Vikings continue and as late as 1991 had released a new single, "My Heart" b/w "Rock & Roll Remembered."

Iris DeMent

Born Iris Luella DeMent, Jan. 5, 1961, Paragould, AR
1992—*Infamous Angel* (Philo/Rounder) 1994—*My Life* (Warner Bros.) 1996—*The Way I Should.*

Iris DeMent's spare, unaffected blend of country and folk music couldn't have been more out of sync with the ironic shrug that greeted the early '90s—or more welcome.

The youngest of 14 children, DeMent was only three years old when her parents' farm went belly up and they moved the family to a suburb of L.A. DeMent's father, who found work as a gardener and janitor, played the fiddle; her mama sang in the Pentecostal church the family attended. Iris grew up singing old-time country and gospel but also listened to the records of Bob Dylan, Joni Mitchell, and Aretha Franklin. She dropped out of high school at 17 to see the country, working odd jobs and obtaining her GED. While living in Topeka, Kansas, she took a course in creative writing that inspired her to try her hand at songwriting and, after moving to Kansas City, Missouri, in 1986, started playing open-mike nights at local clubs.

After DeMent moved to Nashville, songwriter/producer Jim Rooney helped her obtain a deal with folk label Rounder Records. Rooney also produced DeMent's debut, *Infamous Angel* (1992), a mostly autobiographical bluegrass- and gospel-inflected affair that got a big boost from singer/songwriter John Prine, whose liner notes gave the record a resounding endorsement. Ultimately, however, it was the devastating catch in DeMent's Ozark twang, her strong populist leanings, and her writerly command of narrative and detail that had critics scurrying for superlatives.

Critical praise for *Infamous Angel,* plus a duet performance of the song "Let the Mystery Be" by Natalie Merchant and David Byrne on *MTV's Unplugged,* led to a contract with Warner Bros. The label promptly reissued her debut and booked DeMent on tours with Prine, Nanci Griffith, and country hitmaker Mary Chapin Carpenter. The exposure also earned DeMent an invitation to perform at the Presidential Inauguration of fellow Arkansan Bill Clinton. "Our Town," a song from *Infamous Angel,* later appeared on the final episode of the TV series *Northern Exposure.*

DeMent's second album, *My Life* (1994), was another stripped-down record produced by Rooney, and it drew even more raves than its predecessor. But in place of the fond memories of home and sense of wonder that marked DeMent's debut, *My Life* conveyed mostly doubt and loss, especially the gut-wrenching "No Time to Cry," a song subsequently recorded by Merle Haggard that found DeMent confronting the recent death of her father. This personal searching turned political on DeMent's next album, *The Way I Should* (1996). Unlike her first two records, the album received mixed reviews, due on the one hand to Randy Scruggs' somewhat heavy-handed, country-rock production, and on the other to the often strident, preachy tone of DeMent's lyrics.

In the late '90s DeMent appeared on various tribute albums and as a guest vocalist on recordings by Prine and Steve Earle, among others. In 2001 DeMent made her acting debut in the movie *Songcatcher,* which won the Special Jury Prize for Ensemble Cast at the Sundance Film Festival.

Sandy Denny

Born Jan. 6, 1947, Wimbledon, Eng.; died Apr. 21, 1978, London, Eng.
1968—*All Our Own Work* (Pickwick) 1970—*Fotheringay* (A&M); *Sandy Denny* (Saga) 1971—*The Northstar Grassman and the Ravens* (A&M) 1972—*Sandy; Rock On* 1973—*Like an Old Fashioned Waltz* (Island) 1977—*Sandy Denny* (Nova); *Rendezvous* (Island) 1985—*Who Knows Where the Time Goes?* (Hannibal) 1987—*The Best of Sandy Denny* 1991—*Sandy Denny and the Strawbs* (Rykodisc) 2000—*No More Sad Refrains: The Anthology* (A&M).

Sandy Denny's smoky alto made her one of England's most popular singer/songwriters of the early '70s, both as a member of the electric folk group Fairport Convention [see entry] and on her own. She studied classical piano, and while working as a nurse after graduating high school, she learned guitar. She later enrolled in Kensington Art School (classmates included Jimmy Page, Eric Clapton, and John Renbourn) and began frequenting London's folk pubs and coffeehouses. Denny jammed with the then-struggling Simon and Garfunkel, who encouraged her to start performing regularly.

By the mid-'60s she was playing London folk clubs and had recorded one privately distributed LP. During 1967, she belonged to the nascent Strawbs [see entry] (later an art-rock aggregate but then a country-folk group) for six months, recording one unreleased album. She also wrote "Who Knows Where the Time Goes?," later the title track of a gold album by Judy Collins. In May 1968 Denny joined Fairport Convention, with whom she recorded three albums. She quit the group in December 1969, following the release of its landmark *Liege and Lief.*

Denny hesitantly announced a solo career and formed Fotheringay (named after a song on *Fairport Convention*) with American guitarist Jerry Donahue, bassist Pat Donaldson, guitarist Trevor Lucas (whom she married in 1973), and drummer Gerry Conway. Though Fotheringay was moderately successful, the group disbanded late in 1970 before completing a second album.

Denny, voted top British female vocalist in the 1970 and 1971 *Melody Maker* polls, started her solo career in earnest, touring Europe, the U.S., and Britain frequently over the next few years, usually backed by Fairport and Fotheringay alumni. In 1972 she joined the Bunch, a casual aggregation of electrified folkies (including Richard Thompson and Fairport percussionist Dave Mattacks), and recorded an album of rock oldies, *Rock On*. She also contributed vocals to Led Zeppelin's "The Battle of Evermore."

Around the time of *Like an Old-Fashioned Waltz*, Denny rejoined Fairport Convention, although she had already played a low-key support role in the group's 1973 tour. (Lucas and Donahue had preceded her into the group.) Though she contributed to 1975's *Rising for the Moon*, the reunion never quite clicked, and Denny and Lucas left Fairport in February 1976. She released *Rendezvous* in May 1977 and died the next year from head injuries sustained in a fall down a flight of stairs in her home. In 1989 Lucas died of a heart attack.

John Denver

Born John Henry Deutschendorf Jr., Dec. 31, 1943, Roswell, NM; died Oct. 12, 1997, Monterey Bay, CA

1969—*Rhymes and Reasons* (RCA) 1970—*Whose Garden Was This; Take Me to Tomorrow* 1971—*Poems, Prayers and Promises; Aerie* 1972—*Rocky Mountain High* 1973—*John Denver's Greatest Hits; Farewell Andromeda* 1974—*Back Home Again; A John Denver Songbook; Beginnings With the Mitchell Trio* (Mercury) 1975—*An Evening With John Denver* (RCA); *Windsong; Rocky Mountain Christmas* 1976—*Spirit; Rocky Mountain Christmas* 1977—*I Want to Live; John Denver's Greatest Hits, vol. 2* 1979—*John Denver; John Denver and the Muppets: A Christmas Together* 1980—*Autograph* 1981—*Some Days Are Diamonds* 1982—*Seasons of the Heart* 1983—*It's About Time* 1985—*Dreamland Express* 1986—*One World* 1990—*The Flower That Shattered the Stone* (American Grammaphone); *Christmas, Like a Lullaby* (Windstar) 1991—*Different Directions* 1995—*The Wildlife Concert* (Legacy) 1996—*Reflections: Songs of Love & Life* (RCA) 1997—*The Best of John Denver Live* (Legacy) 1998—*Greatest Country Hits* (RCA); *The Best of John Denver* (Madacy); *Forever, John* (RCA).

Through the '70s, country-pop singer/songwriter John Denver was one of the most successful recording artists in the world. Of his albums, 12 are gold and four are platinum, and in the mid-'70s he had a string of gold singles.

Denver was raised in an Air Force family and lived in various Southern and Southwestern towns. In his early teens his grandmother gave him a 1910 Gibson acoustic guitar. He enrolled at Texas Tech in 1961, majoring in architecture and playing in local clubs. In 1964 he dropped out of college and moved to L.A., and after he adopted Denver as his stage name, he replaced Chad Mitchell in the Chad Mitchell Trio in 1965. The Trio, a major draw on the early-'60s hootenanny circuit, was $40,000 in debt upon Denver's arrival, which he later helped it pay back. The group recorded for Mercury (which later repackaged the results under Denver's name as *Beginnings*) and toured widely. At a 1966 Trio concert at Gustavus Adolphus College in Minnesota, Denver met sophomore Ann Martell, who married him the next year (they would divorce in 1983).

Rhymes and Reasons included "Leaving on a Jet Plane," a #1 hit that year for Peter, Paul and Mary; Denver shared their producer, Milt Okun. His own rise began with the million-selling "Take Me Home, Country Roads" (#2, 1971). After he had moved to Aspen, Colorado, *Rocky Mountain High* sold over a million copies. The #1 "Annie's Song" (written for his wife) and "Sunshine on My Shoulders," plus "Back Home Again" (#5) made Denver the best-selling pop musician of 1974. *Greatest Hits* sold over 10 million copies worldwide and stayed in the Top 100 for two years. The governor of Colorado proclaimed John Denver the state's poet laureate.

While the hits continued—"Thank God I'm a Country Boy" (#1, 1975), "I'm Sorry" (#1, 1975)—Denver tried TV and film appearances, with variety specials, dramatic roles, and a screen debut costarring with George Burns in 1977's *Oh, God!* He started Windsong Records (distributed by RCA) in 1976, and signed the Starland Vocal Band ("Afternoon Delight," #1, 1976), whose Bill and Taffy Danoff had written "Take Me Home . . ." with him.

Denver did volunteer work for ecological causes, the ERA, and space exploration (he was a board member of the National Space Institute) and against nuclear power. In 1984 he made the first of several tours of the then–Soviet Union; he recorded a special version of "Let Us Begin (What Are We Making Weapons For?)," from *One World*, in Moscow with Soviet singer Alexandre Gradsky. In 1987 he returned to the USSR, where he performed a benefit concert for victims of the Chernobyl nuclear power plant disaster.

From the mid-'80s until his death in 1997, Denver never regained a commercial foothold (1985's *Dreamland Express* reached only #90, 1990's *The Flower That Shattered the Stone*, only #185); he had a brief return to prominence in late summer 1993, when he was arrested for drunk driving in Aspen, Colorado. The following year he was arrested on similar charges. A second marriage ended in divorce in 1991. As his musical career waned, Denver devoted more attention to humanitarian causes and his first love, flying. In 1993 Denver became the first nonclassical musician given the Albert Schweitzer Music Award, for lifetime humanitarianism. In 1994 he published *Take Me Home: An Autobiography*. A pilot for over 20 years, Denver died on October 12, 1997, when the experimental plane he was flying suddenly dove into Monterey Bay, killing him instantly. After his death, some of those close to him revealed that Denver had suffered bouts of depression and insecurity throughout his life. His ashes were spread throughout his beloved Rocky Mountains.

Depeche Mode

Formed 1980, Basildon, Eng.
Vince Clarke (b. July 3, 1960, South Woodford, Eng.), kybds.; Andrew Fletcher (b. July 8, 1961, Nottingham, Eng.), kybds.; Dave Gahan (b. David Gahan, May 9, 1962, Epping, Eng.), voc.; Martin Gore (b. July 23, 1961, Basildon), gtr., kybds., voc.
1981—*Speak and Spell* (Mute) (– Clarke) 1982—*A Broken Frame* (+ Alan Wilder [b. June 1, 1959, London, Eng.], drums, kybds., voc.) 1983—*Construction Time Again* 1984—*People Are People; Some Great Reward* 1985—*Catching Up With Depeche Mode* 1986—*Black Celebration* 1987—*Music for the Masses* 1989—*101* 1990—*Violator* 1993—*Songs of Faith and Devotion* 1995—(– Wilder) 1997—*Ultra* 1998—*The Singles 86–98* 1999—*The Singles 81–85* (Reprise) 2001—*Exciter.*

Perhaps the quintessential '80s electropop band, Depeche Mode—the name was inspired by a French fashion magazine—parlayed a fascination with synthesizers into huge success on the British charts (where all its albums went Top 10) and eventually on the U.S. pop chart. Whereas a more traditional four-piece rock band might feature three members playing instruments and the fourth singing and perhaps playing guitar or bass, the lineup of this British group was thus described in a 1993 press release: "Dave (Gahan) is the singer, Martin (Gore) the songwriter, Alan (Wilder) the musician, and Andrew (Fletcher) the coordinator." Though Depeche Mode's stark, synthetic sound and often moody, provocative lyrics buck classic pop convention, the hooks that distinguish its most popular songs are among postmodern rock's most ingratiating. For a time, the group did share an unfortunate trait with numerous conventional rock bands, however: a troubled, drug-addicted lead singer.

When the group's original members united in 1980, in a working-class suburb of London called Basildon, they gravitated toward synthesizers and drum machines in part because they were easy to carry around and didn't require amplifiers. In fact, they took the train to their early gigs in local pubs. The group's recording career began auspiciously: 1981's dance beat–ridden *Speak and Spell* (#10 U.K.) became one of the year's best-selling albums in England. Shortly after its release, though, principal songwriter Vince Clarke left. He eventually formed the techno-driven bands Yazoo and, later, Erasure [see entry].

But Depeche Mode bounced right back with 1982's *A Broken Frame* (#8 U.K.), on which Gore assumed chief songwriting duties; soon after, Alan Wilder, who had toured with the band earlier, joined as a full-time member. Two years later the band released the critically and commercially groundbreaking *Some Great Reward* (#5 U.K.), whose content ranged from the bitter and shocking "Blasphemous Rumours" to "People Are People," a catchy plea for tolerance that went to #13 in the U.S., where Depeche Mode had previously been considered an obscure alternative act.

In spite of its success on the American tour circuit, where they were selling out arenas, Depeche Mode didn't have another U.S. hit until "Personal Jesus" (#28, 1990), its first gold single. *Violator* (#7, 1990), the album that single introduced, yielded the group's first Top 10 single, "Enjoy the Silence" (#8, 1990). *Songs of Faith and Devotion* (1993) was heralded by critics as a bold foray into warmer musical textures and more spiritual imagery. It also entered the American pop album chart at #1, boding well for Depeche Mode's future on both sides of the Atlantic.

However, after another successful tour, that promising future was in doubt. Gore and Fletcher were physically exhausted from the band's 18 months on the road, Wilder had become disenchanted and left the group (he later formed the largely instrumental project Recoil), and most disturbingly, Gahan slashed his wrists in a suicide attempt in August 1995. The now-trio had already begun to record its next album when Gahan took a near-lethal overdose of heroin and cocaine in May 1996; he actually flatlined for a few minutes. Soon after regaining consciousness, the singer was arrested for drug possession and sentenced to rehab. He emerged from the program clean and sober, and later spoke frankly in interviews about how he had believed he had to live the pain of Depeche Mode's songs to perform them (although Gore wrote the lyrics).

The group released *Ultra* in 1997 and enjoyed a resurgence: The album went to #5 in the U.S, and the singles "Barrel of a Gun" and "It's No Good" were popular Modern Rock tracks (#11 and #4, respectively, on that chart). The band declined to tour in consideration of Gahan's still-new sobriety. They did return to the stage to support *The Singles 86–98* (#38) the following year.

Derek and the Dominos: See Eric Clapton

Rick Derringer

Born Rick Zehringer, Aug. 5, 1947, Union City, IN
With the McCoys: 1965—*Hang On Sloopy* (Bang) 1966—*You Make Me Feel So Good* 1968—*Infinite McCoys* (Mercury); *Human Ball* 1970—*Outside Stuff* 1974—*Rick Derringer and the McCoys.*
Solo: 1973—*All American Boy* (Blue Sky) 1975—*Spring Fever* (Blue Sky) 1976—*Derringer* 1977—*Sweet Evil; Live* 1978—*If I Weren't So Romantic, I'd Shoot You* 1979—*Guitars and Women* 1980—*Face to Face* 1983—*Good Dirty Fun* (Passport) 1993—*Back to the Blues* (Blues Bureau Int'l) 1994—*Electra Blues* 1998—*Blues Deluxe* 2000—*Jackhammer Blues.*

A teen star with the '60s prototype garage band, the McCoys ("Hang On Sloopy"), singer/guitarist Rick Derringer joined Johnny and Edgar Winter for several successful albums in the early '70s. He has conducted an uneven solo career since.

Rick Zehringer formed the McCoys at age 13 after he and his younger brother, drummer Randy, persuaded the kid next door to buy a bass. Producer/songwriter Bert Berns brought them to New York, where they recorded "Hang On Sloopy." In mid-1965 that song became the McCoys' only #1 hit. "Fever" hit #7 later that year.

A few minor hits followed, and in the late '60s Zehringer produced a couple of psychedelic blues-rock albums for the group. By 1969, the McCoys were the house band at Steve Paul's club, the Scene, in New York. Paul soon became their manager and introduced them to Johnny Winter. After changing his name to Derringer, Rick produced and played on several Winter albums (including *Johnny Winter And* and the gold *Johnny Winter And Live*). When Johnny quit touring to kick a heroin habit in late 1971, Derringer joined Johnny's brother Edgar Winter and his band White Trash for a seven-month tour (he appears on *Roadwork*). Derringer then produced Edgar's *They Only Come Out at Night* and the #1 instrumental single "Frankenstein." By December 1973 he was back on the road with Edgar and cobilled as a feature attraction.

Derringer's first solo album, *All American Boy* (#25, 1973), featured his best-known composition, "Rock and Roll Hoochie Coo" (previously recorded by both Winters), which went to #15 as a single. In 1973 he produced Johnny Winter's "comeback" LP, *Still Alive and Well*. He continued studio work with Johnny *(Saints and Sinners)* and Edgar throughout the '70s. In addition, he played guitar on sessions with Steely Dan, Alice Cooper, Bette Midler, Todd Rundgren, and many others.

Derringer's unsuccessful second solo album prompted the 1976 formation of a group called Derringer, featuring second guitarist Danny Johnson and a rhythm section consisting of Carmine Appice's brother Vinnie on drums and bassist Kenny Aaronson. The group produced four albums *(Derringer, Sweet Evil, If I Weren't So Romantic, I'd Shoot You,* and *Derringer Live)* and toured constantly through the late '70s, opening for Blue Öyster Cult, Aerosmith, and Foghat. But the group never clicked, and Rick ended the decade playing East Coast clubs with makeshift pickup bands that for a while included guitarist Neil Giraldo and drummer Myron Grombacher, who later joined Pat Benatar's band. After *Good Dirty Fun,* Derringer would not release another album for 10 years.

Behind the scenes through the '80s, Derringer produced demos for Cyndi Lauper's first solo album; produced and played on singles and albums by "Weird" Al Yankovic (from 1983's "I Love Rocky Road" to 1990's *UHF*); and sang on and produced a single for professional wrestler Hulk Hogan ("Real American") and a version of "Rock and Roll Hoochie Koo" by Wrestlemania.

Back to the Blues (1993) kicked off a series of more subdued, rootsier albums. Derringer also continued to tour and to collaborate with Edgar Winter. As of 2000 he was experimenting with contemporary Christian stylings.

Desert Rose Band: See the Flying Burrito Brothers

Jackie DeShannon

Born Aug. 21, 1944, Hazel, KY
1968—*Laurel Canyon* (Imperial) 1969—*Put a Little Love in Your Heart* 1972—*Jackie* (Atlantic) 1974—*Your Baby Is a Lady* 1975—*New Arrangement* (Columbia) 1978—*You're the Only Dancer* (Amherst); *Songs* (Capitol) 1991—*The Best of Jackie DeShannon* (Rhino) 2000—*You Know Me* (Varèse Sarabande).

Singer/songwriter Jackie DeShannon is one of the most important songwriters of her time, and many of her songs, made hits by other artists, are classics: from Brenda Lee's "Dum Dum" (1961), the Byrds' "Don't Doubt Yourself, Babe" (1965), the Searchers' "Needles and Pins" and "When You Walk in the Room" (both 1964), and Kim Carnes "Bette Davis Eyes" (1981). In the course of a career that has spanned more than four decades, DeShannon recorded in a wide range of pop styles, from folk to standards.

Born into a musical Kentucky family, she had her own local radio show by age 11 and scored a regional hit when she moved with her family to Chicago. She landed on the West Coast in 1960. There she sang backed by a group called the Nighthawks, which eventually evolved into the Crusaders.

DeShannon's first songwriting success came in the early '60s with hits for Brenda Lee (including "Dum Dum," #4, 1961) and the Searchers ("When You Walk in the Room," #35, 1964; a minor hit for DeShannon as well). In 1965 the Byrds included her "Don't Doubt Yourself, Babe" on *Mr. Tambourine Man*. DeShannon began recording in 1960, though, as she later remarked, her record company tolerated rather than encouraged her. In 1963 she and Ry Cooder formed a short-lived and unrecorded band. In 1964 she opened for the Beatles during their first American tour. Later that year, she met Jimmy Page in England, and they wrote several songs in early 1965 that were recorded by Marianne Faithfull (for whom Jackie penned the British hit "Come Stay With Me"). Page plays on her "Don't Turn Your Back on Me." DeShannon's single of Burt Bacharach's "What the World Needs Now Is Love" was a #7 hit in 1965 and earned four Grammy nominations. Her next hit was the 4-million-selling "Put a Little Love in Your Heart" (#4) in 1969.

In the early '70s DeShannon recorded *Your Baby Is a Lady* and *Jackie* in a slick country-soul style, but neither LP sold well. She also sang background vocals on some Van Morrison sessions; Morrison later produced some of her sessions. She switched to Columbia in 1975 for *New Arrangement,* which also sold poorly. In 1977 DeShannon released an album on the small Amherst label. Her songwriting prowess was still being recognized into the '80s: Bruce Springsteen has performed "When You Walk in the Room" in concert, and DeShannon and Donna Weiss cowrote Kim Carnes' 1981 international hit, "Bette Davis Eyes," which won a Grammy for Song of the Year.

DeShannon, who for a time also headed a production company, Raider Music and Film, returned to the studio with 2000's *You Know Me,* her first new album in roughly two decades.

Destiny's Child: Kelly Rowland, Beyoncé Knowles, Michelle Williams

Destiny's Child

Formed 1989, Houston, TX
Beyoncé Knowles (b. Sep. 4, 1981, Houston), lead voc.; Kelly Rowland (b. Kelendria Rowland, Feb. 11, 1981, Houston), voc.; LeToya Luckett (b. Mar. 11, 1981, Houston), voc.; LaTavia Roberson (b. Nov. 1, 1981, Houston), voc.
1998—*Destiny's Child* (Columbia) 1999—*The Writing's on the Wall* 2000—(– Luckett; – Roberson; + Farrah Franklin [b. May 3, 1981, Houston], voc.; + Michelle Williams [b. Tenetria Michelle Williams, July 23, 1980, Houston], voc.) (– Franklin) 2001—*Survivor.*

Destiny's Child emerged from a pack of late-'90s girl groups with a formula that was fresh yet surprisingly familiar. An enterprise based on childhood friendship and dreams of stardom, Destiny's Child were a new-generation Supremes (tapes of whose performances they studied as part of being, in their words, "divas in training") in more ways than one. However, despite a flurry of personnel changes (complete with lawsuits alleging conflict of interest on the part of the group's manager, Beyoncé Knowles' father, Mathew Knowles), Destiny's Child emerged a winner, with a string of hit singles and over 7 million albums sold in the U.S.

The four original members—Knowles, Kelly Rowland, LeToya Luckett, and LaTavia Roberson—first joined forces in 1989 when they were all around nine years old. After a few years of name changes (GirlsTyme, Somethin' Fresh, Cliché, and Da Dolls) and a shattering loss on *Star Search,* the group signed a deal with Elektra and writer/producer Darryl Simmons in 1994. By then the girls had become Da Dolls, and Knowles' father, a medical equipment salesman, was their manager. (In 1992 Rowland's mother agreed to let her reside with the Knowles family.) Simmons never completed the group's first album, and Elektra canceled their contract in 1995. Despite having virtually no prior experience in show business, Mathew Knowles landed the girls a deal with Columbia in 1997.

Now known as Destiny's Child, the quartet hit platinum with its eponymous debut album (#67 pop, #14 R&B, 1998), which featured a Wyclef Jean–remixed "No, No, No" (#3 pop, #1 R&B, 1997). Released in summer 1999, *The Writing's on the Wall* (#6 pop, #2 R&B) was the group's breakthrough, spinning off "Bills, Bills, Bills" (#1 pop, #1 R&B, 1999), "Bug a Boo" (#33 pop, #15 R&B, 1999), "Say My Name" (#1 pop, #1 R&B, 1999), and "Jumpin', Jumpin' " (#3 pop, #8 R&B, 2000).

Media coverage of the still-teen foursome focused on the girls' wholesome Christian values and the role of Knowles' parents (her mother Tina, a Houston salon owner, is their stylist and designs their wardrobe) in guiding the group. But the fairy tale soon turned soap opera after Roberson and Luckett, upon reaching age 18 in late 1999, informed Mathew Knowles that they were terminating their management contracts with him and seeking independent management. By early 2000 the pair was out of the group, replaced by Tenetria Williams (a former backup singer for Monica) and Farrah Franklin (a singer/actress who had been a dancer in one of the group's early videos). When Mathew Knowles suggested that Tenetria sounded too ethnic, Williams began using her middle name, Michelle. In March 2000 Roberson and Luckett sued, accusing Mathew Knowles of "greed, insistence on control, self-dealing, and promotion of his daughter's interest at the expense of the plaintiffs." The pair also charged that they were not aware that they were officially out of the group until they saw the "Say My Name" video with Williams and Franklin in their places. (As of this writing, the lawsuit remains unresolved, and Roberson, Luckett, and a third singer have formed Angel and signed with Arista.)

Within five months, however, Franklin was dismissed after allegedly missing performances. Now a trio, Destiny's Child opened for Christina Aguilera during her summer 2000 tour, and the group's "Independent Women, Part 1," from the *Charlie's Angels* soundtrack became a #1 pop and R&B smash that fall. Of five nominations, the group won two Grammy Awards for "Say My Name": Best R&B Performance by a Duo or Group With Vocal and Best R&B Song (the group members, including Roberson and Luckett, are cowriters). Group members, particularly Knowles, also write and produce some of Destiny's Child's material. Both Knowles and Rowland have worked on outside projects with other artists and indicate that they see Destiny's Child as a stepping stone to possible solo careers.The double-platinum *Survivor* (#1, 2001) continued the group's winning streak with its #1 title track and "Bootylicious" (#7 pop, #17 R&B).

Devo

Formed 1972, Akron, OH
Jerry Casale, bass, voc.; Mark Mothersbaugh, voc., kybds., gtr.; Bob "Bob I" Mothersbaugh, gtr., voc.; Bob "Bob II" Casale, kybds. gtr., voc.; Alan Myers, drums.
1978—*Q: Are We Not Men? A: We Are Devo!* (Warner Bros.) 1979—*Duty Now for the Future* 1980—*Freedom of Choice* 1981—*Devo Live* EP; *New Traditionalists* 1982—*Oh No! It's Devo* 1984—*Shout* (– Myers; + David Kendrick, drums) 1987—*Now It Can Be Told* (Enigma); *Devo E-Z Listening Disc* (Rykodisc) 1988—*Total Devo* (Enigma) 1989—*Smooth Noodle Maps* 1990—*Greatest Hits* (Warner Bros.); *Greatest Misses; Hardcore, vol. 1* (Rykodisc) 1991—*Hardcore, vol. 2* 1992—*Live: The Mongoloid Years* 1996—*Adventures of the Smart Patrol: Soundtrack From the Inscape CD-ROM Game* (Discovery) 1997—*New Traditionalists CD-ROM* (Warner Bros.) 2000—*Devo: Pioneers Who Got Scalped* (Rhino).

Sporting an original tongue-in-cheek world view proclaiming man to be in a state of genetic and cultural "de-evolution," Devo made the unlikely step from novelty act to real contender—an ironic new wave version of Kiss, whose marketing was as important as its music. The group exploited film and video from the beginning of its career, yet was never sufficiently pop-oriented to earn much play on MTV. Indeed, when Devo proved unable to follow up its one big hit, 1980's "Whip It," the group faded from view, and its smart-alecky view of America as a happy-faced toxic-waste dump eventually found expression in the (dysfunctional) sitcom world of *The Simpsons*.

The details of the members' pre-Devo existence were intentionally obscured as part of their automatonlike image. (They always performed in uniform, favoring futuristic yet sturdy ensembles that featured yellow reactor-attendant suits, overturned red flowerpots for hats, and roller-derby style protective gear.) Mark Mothersbaugh and Jerry Casale met while studying art at Kent State University. Neither was musical, so to build their band, the two recruited their "Bob I" and "Bob II" brothers and drummer Alan Myers and produced a 10-minute video clip entitled *The Truth About De-Evolution*, which won a prize at the Ann Arbor Film Festival in 1975. They followed up with club dates.

In summer 1977 Devo released its first single, "Jocko Homo" b/w "Mongoloid," on its own Booji Boy Records. The infantile robot Booji was the group's corporate mascot, and was often featured in videos and concerts. Devo's cutting-edge status was confirmed when David Bowie introduced the band at its New York debut, at Max's Kansas City. In early 1978 its second single, a syncopated version of the Rolling Stones' "Satisfaction," increased the band's growing cult and garnered the group a record deal with Warner Bros.

Q: Are We Not Men? A: We Are Devo!, produced by Brian Eno, was released in fall 1978, and the group hit the road in earnest. *Freedom of Choice* provided Devo's 1980 commercial breakthrough by eventually going platinum with the million-selling single, "Whip It." Devo continued to revive rock chestnuts with noteworthy success. The group covered Johnny Rivers' "Secret Agent Man" in 1980 and received substantial airplay in mid-1981 with a hiccuppy rendition of Lee Dorsey's "Working in the Coalmine." The group also changed its identity: Clad in leisure suits and crooning born-again lounge music, Devo occasionally opened its own concerts disguised as Dove, the Band of Love.

Neither *New Traditionalists* nor *Oh No! It's Devo* produced a hit single. (Devo's last charting single was "Theme from *Doctor Detroit*" [#59, 1983], for the Dan Aykroyd comedy film.) The band lost its Warner Bros. contract and disappeared for four years. Mark Mothersbaugh began composing and producing music for commercials and television shows, including CBS' *Pee Wee's Playhouse*, Nickelodeon's *Rugrats*, and MTV's *Liquid Television*. He also scored the '90s videogame *Crash Bandicoot* (and three unreleased Devo tunes ended up on the videogame *Interstate '82*).

With Alan Myers replaced by David Kendrick, Devo re-formed for *Total Devo* (1988), which barely charted. A subsequent tour of small halls and large clubs, with no expen-

Devo: Bob Mothersbaugh, Bob Casale, Mark Mothersbaugh, Alan Myers, Jerry Casale

sive high-tech theatrics, yielded the live album *Now It Can Be Told.* Devo's next studio album, *Smooth Noodle Maps,* failed to chart at all, and the band once again vanished—just as its songs began being covered by alternative-rock bands (Nirvana with "Turnaround"; Soundgarden and Superchunk with "Girl U Want"). In 1992 two bands—L.A.'s Clawhammer and Chicago's Honeywagon—emerged, playing nothing but Devo songs (echoing the 1980 Rhino collection *KROQ Devotees Album*). By then Rykodisc had begun issuing archival live and studio Devo tracks, including the *E-Z Listening Disc* (originally available only through Devo's fan club), on which the band recorded Muzak versions of its own songs.

Devo reunited in 1991 for a 30-city European tour, and again for several dates on the 1996 and 1997 Lollapalooza tours. Jerry Casale continued to direct the occasional music video, such as the Foo Fighters' "I'll Stick Around." Mark Mothersbaugh and Bob Casale produced 2000's *Heroes & Villains,* an album of music inspired by Cartoon Network's *Powerpuff Girls,* with Devo's "Go Monkey Go" plus tracks by David Byrne, Frank Black, and Shonen Knife.

Neil Diamond

Born Jan. 24, 1941, Brooklyn, NY
1966—*The Feel of Neil Diamond* (Bang) 1967—*Just for You* 1968—*Neil Diamond's Greatest Hits; Velvet Gloves and Spit* (Uni) 1969—*Brother Love's Traveling Salvation Show; Touching You, Touching Me* 1970—*Neil Diamond Gold; Tap Root Manuscript; Shilo* (Bang) 1971—*Do It!; Stones* (Uni) 1972—*Moods; Hot August Night* (MCA) 1973—*Double Gold* (Bang); *Rainbow* (MCA); *Jonathan Livingston Seagull* (Columbia) 1974—*His 12 Greatest Hits* (MCA); *Serenade* (Columbia) 1976—*Beautiful Noise; And the Singer Sings His Song* (MCA) 1977—*Love at the Greek* (Columbia); *I'm Glad You're Here With Me Tonight* 1978—*You Don't Bring Me Flowers* 1979—*September Morn* 1980—*The Jazz Singer* soundtrack (Capitol) 1981—*On the Way to the Sky* (Columbia) 1982—*12 Greatest Hits, vol. 2; Heartlight* 1983—*Classics—The Early Years* 1984—*Primitive* 1985—*Love Songs* (MCA) 1986—*Headed for the Future* (Columbia) 1987—*Hot August Night II* 1988—*The Best Years of Our Lives* 1991—*Lovescape* 1992—*The Greatest Hits 196\6–1992; Glory Road—1968 to 1972* (MCA); *The Christmas Album* (Columbia) 1993—*Up on the Roof—Songs From the Brill Building* 1994—*Live in America* 1996—*Tennessee Moon; In My Lifetime* 1998—*The Movie Album: As Time Goes By.*

Pop songwriter Neil Diamond, a veteran of the Brill Building song factory, became one of the best-selling MOR performers of the '70s. Singing his own melodramatic quasi-gospel songs in a portentous baritone, he has sold over 92 million records worldwide, amassing over 35 Top 40 singles and 18 platinum albums.

Diamond recorded his first single soon after graduating from Brooklyn's Erasmus Hall High School. He attended NYU as a premedical student on a fencing scholarship until 1962, when he dropped out and began hawking songs to Broadway publishers, one of whom soon hired him as a $50-a-week staff songwriter. Diamond worked for various publishers, including Don Kirshner's Aldon Music, where he wrote the Monkees' #1 1967 hit "I'm a Believer." Fellow songwriters Jeff Barry and Ellie Greenwich helped him sign with Bang Records in 1965, for whom he recorded a string of Top 20 hits: "Cherry, Cherry" (#6, 1966), "I Got the Feeling" (#16, 1966), "You Got to Me" (#18, 1967), "Girl, You'll Be a Woman Soon" (#10, 1967), "Thank the Lord for the Night Time" (#13, 1967), and "Kentucky Woman" (#22, 1967).

Bang lost interest after Diamond began looking for significance with songs like "Shilo." He moved to California in 1966, where Uni Records promised him full artistic control. His Uni (later MCA) debut, *Velvet Gloves and Spit,* sold poorly, but subsequent singles—"Brother Love's Traveling Salvation Show" (#22, 1969), "Sweet Caroline" (#4, 1969), "Cracklin' Rosie" (#1, 1970), and "Song Sung Blue" (#1, 1972)—established him as a major star. He toured the U.S., Europe, and Australia in 1972 and placed two albums in the U.S. Top 5: *Moods* and the live *Hot August Night* (which also became Australia's best-selling album at the time; 3 million sales in a country of 14 million people). He also played a 20-performance one-man show on Broadway in 1972.

The following year Diamond signed with Columbia for a record-breaking $5 million; his first album for his new label, the soundtrack to *Jonathan Livingston Seagull,* grossed more money than the film itself. He returned to touring in February 1976 and appeared in the Band's *Last Waltz* concert on Thanksgiving Day. Band guitarist Robbie Robertson produced Diamond's *Beautiful Noise,* a tribute to Diamond's '60s songwriting days. It was his 11th album in a row to go gold.

NBC aired a TV special of Diamond in concert on February 24, 1977; subsequent television specials proved popular with viewers. In 1980 he starred in a poorly received remake of *The Jazz Singer.* Nonetheless, his soundtrack LP for that film went platinum five times over, yielding Top 10 singles in "Love on the Rocks," "America," and "Hello Again." *Heartlight* was another Top 5 album, and the title track (#5, 1982) became a long-running staple of "lite FM" adult-contemporary radio. *Primitive* (#35, 1984), *Headed for the Future* (#20, 1986), *Hot August Night* (#59, 1987), and *The Best Years of Our Lives* (#46, 1989) all went gold. *Lovescape* (#44, 1991) included a duet with Kim Carnes, "Hooked on the Memory of You," Diamond's first duet since his chart-topping 1978 "You Don't Bring Me Flowers" with Barbra Streisand. *Up on the Roof* found Diamond singing the Brill Building pop of his early days; critics panned the album but gave glowing reviews to Diamond's subsequent tour, which as always, was attended by intensely devoted throngs. Meanwhile, Diamond continues to collect royalties for the many cover versions of his songs, including Deep Purple's "Kentucky Woman," UB40's chart-topping '80s version of "Red, Red Wine," and Urge Overkill's "Girl, You'll Be a Woman Soon," from the 1994 *Pulp Fiction* soundtrack.

In 1996 Diamond made a somewhat radical departure into country with *Tennessee Moon* (#14 pop, #3 C&W). The same year Columbia released the 70-song *In My Lifetime,* a career-spanning box set. *The Movie Album* (#31 pop, 1998) contains Diamond's renditions of 20 famous songs from classic motion pictures.

Manu Dibango

Born Feb. 10, 1934, Douala, Cameroon
1972—*Soul Makossa* (Atlantic) 1973—*Makossa Man; O Boso* (London) 1975—*Makossa Music* (Creole) 1976—*Manu '76* (Decca); *Super Kumba* 1978—*Afrovision* (Island); *Sin Explosion* (Decca) 1980—*Gone Clear* (Island); *Reggae Makossa* 1981—*Ambassador* (Mango) 1983—*Melodies Africanes, vols. 1 & 2* (Sonodisc) 1984—*Deadline* (RCA) 1985—*Electric Africa* (Celluloid) 1986—*Afrijazzy* 1990—*Trois Kilos de Cafe* 1990—*Polysonik* (Soundwave) 1994—*Wakafrika* (Giant); *Live '91* (Stern's Music); *Seventies* (Sonodisc); *Tropical Garden* 1995—*Negropolitaines, vol. 2* (Melodie) 1996—*Bao Bao* (M.I.L. Miltime); *Lamastabtani* (Celluloid) 2000—*Abele Dance.*

Manu Dibango's "Soul Makossa" was one of the first African pop songs to catch on in America. Dibango moved from Cameroon to Europe at age 15 and studied piano and music theory in Paris and Brussels. At age 20 he took up the saxophone and over the next 15 years maintained a career as a jazz and R&B musician in Europe. In the late '60s Dibango returned to Africa, settling in Kinshasa, Zaire. There he assembled a band composed of African, European, and Caribbean musicians to play an array of Western instruments (horns, keyboards, electric guitars, and basses) and traditional African instruments on music that drew on jazz, R&B, calypso, Cuban, rock, and traditional and modern African forms.

Beginning in the early '70s, he and his bands toured and recorded in Europe and Africa. "Soul Makossa," recorded in France by La Société Française du Son in 1972 and released in the U.S. the following year, reached #35 pop and #21 R&B on the American singles chart. In 1974 Dibango toured the U.S. He traveled to the West Indies in 1980 and 1981, and there recorded with reggae musicians Sly Dunbar and Robbie Shakespeare.

Dibango returned to France in 1983 and recorded the solo piano compositions released as *Melodies Africanes, vols. 1 & 2.* He collaborated with Herbie Hancock and New York avant-funk producer/bassist Bill Laswell on *Deadline* and *Electric Africa.* Laswell also produced a remake of "Soul Makossa" on *Afrijazzy.*

Trois Kilos de Cafe, Dibango's autobiography, was published in 1990, the same year he also released an identically titled retrospective album containing rerecorded versions of his past work. In 1991, leading the Soul Makossa Gang, Dibango continued to keep his sound contemporary. Adding to the African music sung in what Dibango calls the "Negropolitan" languages, the band included the English raps of MC Mello.

Wakafrika (1995) continued Dibango's move toward internationalism. A collection of what Dibango called "African classics" (including "Soul Makossa"), it featured guest appearances by western musicians such as Sinéad O'Connor and Peter Gabriel, and African expats such as Angelique Kidjo and Papa Wemba.

Dibango continues to tour and makes the occasional guest appearance on other acts' records, but his own time in the studio has been limited. He appears on Zap Mama's 1999 album *A Ma Zone* and produced an album for South Africa's Mahotella Queens.

The Dickies

Formed 1977, Los Angeles, CA
Chuck Wagon (d. 1981), kybds.; Stan Lee (b. Sep. 24, 1956), gtr.; Billy Club, bass; Leonard Graves Phillips, voc.; Karlos Kaballero, drums; Jonathan Melvoin (b. Dec. 6, 1961; d. July 12, 1996, New York, NY), drums; Enoch Hain, gtr.; Charlie Alexander, bass; Lorenzo Buhne, bass; Cliff Martinez, drums.
1979—*The Incredible Shrinking Dickies* (A&M); *Dawn of the Dickies* 1983—(– Wagon) *Stukas Over Disneyland* (PVC) 1986—*We Aren't the World!* (ROIR) 1988—*Killer Clowns From Outer Space* EP (Enigma) 1989—*Great Dictations* (A&M); *Second Coming* (Enigma) 1991—*Live in London: Locked 'n' Loaded* (Taang!) 1994—*Idjit Savant* (Triple X) 1998—*Dogs From the Hare that Bit Us* (Relativity) 1999—*Still Live Even If You Don't Want It* (ROIR).

The Dickies are best known for their covers of "classic" rock tunes, which they speed up to comic proportions. Their repertoire includes "Nights in White Satin," "Eve of Destruction," the Banana Splits television cartoon theme song, "Communication Breakdown," "Hair," and Black Sabbath's "Paranoid." The San Fernando Valley group was one of L.A.'s most popular punk bands in the late '70s, although A&M was undoubtedly disappointed that their local following never expanded nationally. Alongside their twisted covers, they have penned such originals as "(I'm Stuck in a Pagoda) With Tricia Toyota" and "Rondo (The Midget's Revenge)"; tunes like "I'm a Chollo" and "Goin' Homo" proved that there were no limits to how low the Dickies would sink for a laugh. In 1988 their perennial B-movie sensibility landed one of their tracks in the movie *Killer Clowns From Outer Space.* The band has gone through a number of personnel changes, including the 1981 suicide of keyboardist Chuck Wagon, with Lee and Phillips remaining the band's core.

In 1994, just as Green Day and the Offspring were taking Dickies-inspired pop punk to the bank, the band released *Idjit Savant,* an album of typically cartoonish originals and covers. *Dogs From the Hare That Bit Us* (1998) was nothing but covers, including disposable fare from the catalogues of Uriah Heep, Iron Butterfly, and the Knack. The version of the Human Beinz' "Nobody But Me" that appeared on the album was featured on the *BASEketball* soundtrack. In 1999 the Dickies toured the U.S. with their SoCal punk spawn the Offspring.

The Dictators

Formed 1974, Bronx, NY
Handsome Dick Manitoba (b. Richard Blum, Jan. 29, 1954), voc; Ross "the Boss" Funicello (b. Jan. 3, 1954, Bronx), gtr., voc.;

Scott "Top Ten" Kempner (b. Feb. 6, 1954, Bronx), gtr., voc.; Andy "Adny" Shernoff (b. Apr. 19, 1952, Bronx), kybds., bass, voc.; Stu Boy King, drums.
1975—*Go Girl Crazy!* (Epic) (– King; + Ritchie Teeter [b. Mar. 16, 1951, Long Island, NY], drums; + Mark Mendoza [b. July 13, 1956, Long Island], bass) 1977—*Manifest Destiny* (Elektra) (– Mendoza) 1978—*Bloodbrothers* (Asylum) 1981—*Fuck 'Em If They Can't Take a Joke* (ROIR) 1990—(– Teeter; + Frank Funaro, drums) 1997—(– Funaro; + J.P. Patterson, drums) 1998—*Live New York New York.*
Del-Lords: 1984—*Frontier Days* (Enigma) 1986—*Johnny Comes Marching Home* 1988—*Based on a True Story* 1989—*Howlin' at the Halloween Moon* (Restless) 1990—*Lovers Who Wander* (Enigma) 1999—*Get Tough: The Best of the Del-Lords* (Restless).
Manitoba's Wild Kingdom: 1990—*. . . And You?* (Popular Metaphysics/MCA).
The Spinatras (Ross "the Boss" Funicello, gtr; Brian Corley, voc.; Richie Fazio, drums; Ron Giordano, bass): 2000—*@midnight.com* (CMC International).

Loved by some, hated by many more, and misunderstood and/or ignored by the rest, the Dictators straddled heavy metal and punk rock with a slapstick sense of humor. In the early '70s Andy "Adny" Shernoff was editing a mimeographed rock fanzine, *Teenage Wasteland Gazette*, an influence on *Creem* and a forerunner of *Punk* magazine. With virtually no musical experience, he gave up writing to form the Dictators with Scott Kempner and Ross "the Boss" Funicello; the latter had been in a unit called Total Crud. Manitoba, who began as their roadie, soon became their vocalist and frontman.

Though their music was much closer to brazenly amateurish heavy metal than punk, the Dictators were mainstays in the early days at Manhattan's CBGB. In 1976 Manitoba was nearly killed when, after heckling transvestite rocker (now transsexual) Wayne/Jayne County at CBGB, County hit him over the head with a microphone stand. Despite, or because of, such antics, their debut (recorded with Blue Öyster Cult's producer Sandy Pearlman) was a critical success, but sold only 6,000 copies.

They broke up in late 1978, Teeter resurfacing in a New York band called VHF a year later. Ross "the Boss" went to San Francisco in 1979 and formed Shakin' Street, which released one LP for Columbia in 1980; in 1982 he formed a heavy-metal band called Manowar. Mendoza joined the briefly, incredibly popular Twisted Sister, as did Teeter at one point. Shernoff has been involved in off-Broadway theatrical productions and has produced many records for New York bands. Kempner formed the Del-Lords, and Manitoba and Shernoff belonged to Manitoba's Wild Kingdom, which by 1990 also included Ross "the Boss" Funicello.

Despite all these offshoots, the Dictators themselves never really went away. They started playing reunion shows as early as 1980, and the 1998 CD reissue of their 1981 live album *Fuck 'Em If They Can't Take a Joke* (under the name *Live New York New York*) included extra tracks recorded in the early '80s. They also performed as part of CBGB's 20th-anniversary celebration in 1994. In 1996 the band released a single, "I Am Right" with Del-Lord's drummer Frank Funaro on board. Funaro played in the Dictators from 1990 to 1997, when he was replaced by Manitoba's Wild Kingdom's J.P. Patterson. The Dictators also contributed a new song, "What's Up With That?," to the *Boys Don't Cry* soundtrack in 1999. As of late 2000 the band was recording a new album.

Bo Diddley

Born Ellas Otha Bates, later changed to McDaniel, Dec. 30, 1928, McComb, MS
1962—*Bo Diddley* (Checker) 1963—*Bo Diddley Is a Gunslinger; Bo Diddley Rides Again* (Pye, U.K.) 1964—*Two Great Guitars* (with Chuck Berry) (Chess); *Hey Good Looking* 1965—*Let Me Pass* 1974—*Big Bad Bo* (Checker) 1975—*Another Dimension* 1976—*20th Anniversary* (RCA) 1983—*His Greatest Sides* (Chess) 1986—*The Super Super Blues Band: With Bo Diddley, Muddy Waters, and Little Walter* (Chess); *Superblues: Bo Diddley, Muddy Waters, and Little Walter* 1989—*Breaking Through the B.S.* (Triple X) 1990—*The Chess Box* (Chess/MCA) 1992—*This Should Not Be* (Triple X) 1994—*Promises* 1996—*A Man Amongst Men* (Code Blue/Atlantic) 1997—*His Best* (Chess).

Bo Diddley's syncopated "hambone" beat—CHINK-a-CHINK-a-CHINK, a-CHINK-CHINK—is a cornerstone of rock & roll songs, from Diddley's own "Who Do You Love," "Mona," "Bo Diddley," and "I'm a Man" to the Who's "Magic Bus," Bruce Springsteen's "She's the One," and the Pretenders' "Cuban Slide." Still a popular live act, Diddley has been on the road for more than five decades.

Adopted by a Mississippi sharecropping family, he moved with them to the South Side of Chicago. As a child, he began studying violin under Professor O.W. Frederick at the Ebenezer Baptist Church. In grammar school he acquired his Bo Diddley nickname (a "diddley bow" is a one-stringed African guitar). By the time he entered Foster Vocational School in his early teens, he had switched to the guitar and regularly played on Chicago's Maxwell Street when he was not in school, where he learned to make violins and guitars. (He also built his first rectangular guitar at age 15.) After several years of performing on streetcorners, he played at the 708 Club in 1951 and became a regular South Side performer for the next four years.

In July 1955 Leonard Chess signed Diddley to his Checker label. Diddley's first single, "Bo Diddley," was an immediate #1 R&B success. "I'm a Man" (1955, later recorded by the Yardbirds and others) also fared well on the R&B chart. His biggest pop success came in 1959, when "Say Man" (#3 R&B) hit the Top 20 late in the year. He had a lesser hit in 1962 with the rollicking "You Can't Judge a Book by the Cover" (#48 pop, #21 R&B).

Diddley toured steadily through the late '50s and early '60s, playing rock package tours and one-nighters at R&B venues. The band that recorded with him in the mid-'50s included drummers Clifton James and Frank Kirkland, pianist Otis Spann, Bo's half sister "The Duchess" on guitar and vocals, and Diddley's eternal sidekick, bassist and maracas shaker Jerome Green (who also provided call-and-response repartee on "Hey Bo Diddley" and "Bring It to Jerome").

Diddley's legacy was enhanced considerably during the mid-'60s, when many of his songs were covered by British Invasion groups like the Rolling Stones. In 1964 the Animals paid tribute to him in an album track entitled "The Story of Bo Diddley." Through the years, his material has also been recorded by countless other artists.

Diddley has recorded erratically since the early '60s, with a catalogue that even includes surfing albums *(Surfin' With Bo Diddley)*. In the mid-'60s he recorded traditional blues with Little Walter and Muddy Waters on *Superblues* (reissued in 1986). In the early '70s Diddley continued to tour frequently, concentrating on Europe. One such outing was documented in *Let the Good Times Roll*. Around the same time, he also appeared in D.A. Pennebaker's *Keep On Rockin'*. In 1976 RCA released *20th Anniversary of Rock 'n' Roll*, a tribute to Diddley that featured over 20 artists. Diddley opened several dates for the Clash on their 1979 U.S. tour. He made cameo appearances in George Thorogood's video "Bad to the Bone" (1982) and played a pawnbroker in the Dan Aykroyd–Eddie Murphy movie, *Trading Places*. In 1998 he appeared in *Blues Brothers 2000*. He tried recording over electro-funk grooves on 1992's *This Should Not Be;* critics agreed with the album's title.

Despite a lack of commercial success, Bo Diddley's stature as a founding father of rock & roll is undiminished. He was inducted into the Rock and Roll Hall of Fame in 1987. In 1996 he released his first major-label album in two decades, *A Man Amongst Men*, with guest artists including Ron Wood, Keith Richards, and the Shirelles. That album was nominated for a 1997 Grammy in the Best Contemporary Blues Album category. The following year, he received the National Recording Arts and Sciences Lifetime Achievement Award. He is also the recipient of the Rhythm & Blues Foundation Lifetime Achievement Award.

Ani DiFranco

Born Sep. 23, 1970, Buffalo, NY
1990—*Ani DiFranco* (Righteous Babe) 1991—*Not So Soft* 1992—*Imperfectly* 1993—*Puddle Dive; Like I Said* 1994—*Out of Range* 1995—*Not a Pretty Girl* 1996—*Dilate; More Joy, Less Shame* EP 1997—*Living in Clip* 1998—*Little Plastic Castle* 1999—*Up Up Up Up Up Up; To the Teeth* 2000—*Swing Set* EP 2001—*Revelling/Reckoning.*
With Utah Phillips: 1996—*The Past Didn't Go Anywhere* 1999—*Fellow Workers.*

Singer/songwriter Ani DiFranco pioneered the do-it-yourself (DIY) ethic of the '90s. Even when her albums started charting in the Top 100, she turned down major-label offers and released her work on her own Righteous Babe Records instead. DiFranco's personal punk- and funk-influenced folk music—and its often politically charged lyrics—has gained DiFranco a loyal fan base and made her DIY enterprise a smashing success.

Ani DiFranco

DiFranco started singing and playing acoustic guitar in bars around her hometown before she was 10; by 15, she was writing her own songs—as well as living on her own. In 1990 she started Righteous Babe in order to produce her first album, which she sold from the trunk of her car while touring the country's colleges. Proudly feminist and openly bisexual, the singer soon gained a devoted, primarily female fan base and had cracked the Top 100 by her eighth release, *Dilate* (#87, 1996). At this point, Righteous Babe—which by now had moved operations from DiFranco's living room to an actual office space—had sold 200,000 copies of her releases. By 1999, its sales equaled 2 million, including two Top 30 releases—*Little Plastic Castle* (#22, 1998) and *Up Up Up Up Up Up* (#29, 1999). *To the Teeth* (#76) featured appearances by Prince and Maceo Parker. She has also collaborated with activist folksinger Utah Phillips on two albums and produced a recording by Janis Ian.

Digable Planets

Formed 1989, New York, NY
Butterfly (b. Ishmael Butler, July 3, 1969, Seattle, WA), voc.; Ladybug (b. Katrina Lust), voc.; Squibble the Termite (b. Michael Gabredikan), DJ.
1992—(– Lust; – Gabredikan; + Doodlebug [b. Craig Irving, Feb. 20, 1967, Philadelphia, PA], voc.; + Ladybug, a.k.a. Mecca, [b. Mary Ann Vieira, July 25, 1973, Washington, DC], voc.)
1993—*Reachin' (a new refutation of time and space)* (Elektra)
1994—*Blowout Comb.*

Digable Planets were the most successful group to emerge from the 1993 "jazz rap" movement—in which middle-class black bohemians, acutely aware of their cultural heritage

Digable Planets: Doodlebug, Ladybug, Butterfly

and far less angry-sounding than inner-city hard-core rappers, revived a style that went back to the late-'60s Last Poets. Digable Planets briefly crossed over to the pop charts in spring 1993 with the single "Rebirth of Slick (Cool Like Dat)" (#15 pop, #8 R&B), which featured sampled horn riffs from a record by hard-bop jazz great Art Blakey and his Jazz Messengers.

The first version of the group met at City College of New York; according to founder Butterfly, the group name came from the belief that "each person is a planet," and the individual members' names from admiration for the selfless, community orientation of some insect species. Butterfly recruited Doodlebug from the New York City rap/poetry collective Dread Poets Society; Doodlebug brought along his friend, Mecca, who became the second Ladybug. Butterfly's father had exposed him to Blue Note jazz as a youth; Doodlebug's father had been a member of the Black Panthers; Ladybug's parents were Brazilian.

Digable Planets emerged from a "hip bop" scene that had been fermenting since at least 1989, when Spike Lee had recruited Gang Starr, which was already mixing jazz samples into its records, to record "Jazz Thing" for his film *Mo' Better Blues.* Following such jazz-rap hybrids as A Tribe Called Quest and Us3, Digable Planets released the mellow *Reachin'* (#15 pop, #5 R&B, 1993). In addition to the Blakey horns in "Rebirth of Slick," the album included samples from Sonny Rollins, Eddie Harris, the Last Poets, and the Crusaders (as well as K.C. and the Sunshine Band and Curtis Mayfield), and lyrics saluting jazz legends, existentialist authors, Nikki Giovanni, and Jimi Hendrix. *Blowout Comb* (#32 pop, #13 R&B) and its attendant singles failed to match the success of the debut. Although they have since performed at least one reunion gig, Digable Planets became inactive in the mid-'90s, and Doodlebug went solo under the name Cee Knowledge.

Digital Underground

Formed 1988, Oakland, CA
Shock-G/Humpty Hump (b. Greg Jacobs, Aug. 25, 1963, Queens, NY), voc.; Money B. (b. Ronald Brooks, Sep. 22, 1969, Oakland), voc.; DJ Fuze (b. David Scott, Syracuse, NY), DJ.
1990—*Sex Packets* (Tommy Boy) 1990—*This Is an E.P. Release* EP 1991—*Sons of the P* 1993—*The Body-Hat Syndrome* 1996—*Future Rhythm* (Critique) (+ Erika "Shay" Sulpacal, voc.; + Eric Baker, gtr.) 1998—*Who Got the Gravy?* (Jake/Interscope) (– DJ Fuze) 1999—*Lost Files* (Lil Butta).
Raw Fusion (Money B. and DJ Fuze): 1991—*Live From the Styleetron* (Hollywood) 1994—*Hoochiefied Funk.*
Money B. solo: 2000—*Talkin' Dirty* (Bobby Beats).

Digital Underground strives to be the Parliament/Funkadelic of rap. Like P-Funk's George Clinton, D.U. mastermind Shock-G wears colorful costumes onstage and assumes a variety of zany alter egos in the music, most memorably with the chronically congested character in Groucho glasses known as "Humpty Hump." Also like P-Funk, the group is an umbrella organization: With its core membership based in the Bay Area, Digital Underground uses a revolving-door crew of musicians from around the country, some of whom are pseudonymously credited.

Shock-G is the child of a television producer mother and computer executive father. As a boy, he was shuttled between Florida, New York, Pennsylvania, and California. In the late '70s he dropped out of high school and got involved in street life—pimping, selling drugs, and stealing cars. He eventually returned to school, earning his high school diploma and taking college courses in music. In 1987 he put together the first version of Digital Underground in Oakland and scored a #1 hit in the Netherlands with his self-released single, "Underwater Rimes."

In 1990 the current lineup released its debut album, *Sex Packets* (#24 pop, #8 R&B, 1990), which sold a million copies on the strength of a #11 pop single, "Humpty Dance," rapped by Shock-G's alter ego, Humpty Hump. The album was praised for its clever lyrics and inventive mixes. The gold followup, *This Is an E.P. Release*, reached #29 on the pop chart and featured rapper 2Pac (Tupac Shakur). Shakur went on to a successful, if troubled, career as a solo artist and actor [see entry] until his murder in 1996.

D.U.'s *Sons of the P* (#44 pop, #23 R&B, 1991) (P standing for P-Funk) featured George Clinton and included the single "Kiss You Back," which barely made the Top 40. *The Body-Hat Syndrome* (#79 pop, #16 R&B) continued their socio-political commentary of previous albums (i.e., proposing the use of a mind condom—a Body Hat—for protection from the power structure). After a three-year break, the group returned in 1996 with *Future Rhythm* (#113), which showed a continued preference for songs about sex, drugs, and politics but disappeared from the charts after only three weeks. The 1998 followup, *Who Got the Gravy?*, included such old-school guests as KRS-ONE, Biz Markie, and Big Punisher. In 2000 Money B. released the solo album *Talkin' Dirty*.

The Dillards

Formed 1962, Salem, MO
Rodney Dillard (b. May 18, 1942, Salem), voc., gtr., synth., Dobro; Doug Dillard (b. Mar. 6, 1937, Salem), banjo; Mitchell Jayne (b. May 7, 1930, Salem), bass; Dean Webb (b. Mar. 28, 1937, Independence, MO), mandolin.
1963—*Back Porch Bluegrass* (Elektra) 1964—*Live . . . Almost!* (+ Byron Berline [b. July 6, 1944, Caldwell, KS], fiddle) 1965—*Pickin' and Fiddlin'* (– D. Dillard; + Herb Pederson, banjo; – Berline) 1968—*Wheatstraw Suite* (– Berline) 1969—(+ Herb Pederson, banjo) 1970—(+ Paul York, drums) *Copperfields* 1972—(– Pederson; + Billy Ray Latham, banjo) *Roots and Branches* (Anthem) 1973—*Tribute to the American Duck* (Poppy) 1974—(– Jayne; + Jeff Gilkinson, bass) 1976—*Best of the Dillards* 1977—*The Dillards Versus Incredible L.A. Time Machine* (Flying Fish) 1979—*Mountain Rock* (Crystal Clear); *Decade Waltz* (Flying Fish) 1980—*Homecoming and Family Reunion* 1985—*Rodney Dillard at Silver Dollar City* 1988—(group disbands) 1990—(group re-forms: R. Dillard; D. Dillard; Jayne; Webb) *Let It Fly* (Vanguard) 1992—*Take Me Along for the Ride.*
Dillard and Clark (Doug Dillard; Gene Clark; others): 1969—*Fantastic Expedition* (A&M) 1970—*Through the Morning, Through the Night.*
Doug Dillard and Band: 1968—*The Banjo Album* (Together) 1973—*Dueling Banjos; You Don't Need a Reason to Sing* 1976—*Heaven* (Flying Fish) 1979—*Jack Rabbit!* 1986—*What's That?* 1989—*Heartbreak Hotel.*
Dillard-Hartford-Dillard (Dillard brothers with John Hartford): 1976—*Glitter Grass From the Nashwood Hollyville Strings* (Flying Fish) 1980—*Permanent Wave.*
Herb Pederson solo: 1976—*Southwest* (Epic) 1977—*Sandman* 1984—*Lonesome Feeling* (Sugar Hill).

A bluegrass band from the Ozarks that went electric, the Dillards helped pave the way for country rock, the bluegrass revival, and newgrass. The original quartet left Missouri for Hollywood in 1962. The Dillards were cast to play a hillbilly band, the Darling Family, on the *Andy Griffith Show* and were signed by Elektra. Their 1963 debut, *Back Porch Bluegrass*, included "Duelin' Banjos," which Eric Weissberg later popularized in the 1972 film *Deliverance*. Their repertoire grew to include Bob Dylan songs as well as traditional bluegrass, and on a 1965 tour with the Byrds the Dillards reportedly helped Roger McGuinn arrange vocal harmonies on *Mr. Tambourine Man*. By then their lineup included national fiddling champion Byron Berline.

In 1965 Doug Dillard left the Dillards; he played on *Gene Clark With the Gosdin Brothers* and in 1968 formed the Dillard-Clark Expedition. The Expedition's first album lineup included Bernie Leadon, later of the Flying Burrito Brothers and the Eagles; they toured with another ex-Byrd, drummer Michael Clarke, who then joined the Burrito Brothers. Berline joined the group for its second album, but the Expedition disbanded in 1969. Doug Dillard recorded solo albums in the early '70s and has continued to work as a studio musician. In 1976 the Dillard brothers recorded the first of two albums with their former neighbor John Hartford, and Doug continued to record with his band through the late '80s.

Meanwhile, Rodney maintained the Dillards band name and released increasingly electric albums with a shifting band through the '70s and '80s. By 1987, he was the sole remaining original member, and the next year, the group broke up, but not for long. In 1989 the original quartet reunited, an event captured on the video *A Night in the Ozarks*. Pederson produced their reunion effort, *Let It Fly*.

Dinosaur Jr

Formed 1984, Amherst, MA
J Mascis (b. Joseph D. Mascis, Dec. 10, 1965), gtr., voc., drums, bass; Lou Barlow (b. July 17, 1966, Dayton, OH), bass, voc., tapes; Murph (b. Emmett "Patrick" J. Murphy, Dec. 21, 1964), drums.
1985—*Dinosaur* (Homestead) 1987—*You're Living All Over Me* (SST) 1988—*Bug* 1989—*Just Like Heaven* EP (– Barlow; + various guests) 1991—*The Wagon* EP (Blanco y Negro, U.K.) 1991—*Green Mind* (Sire) 1992—(+ Mike Johnson [b. Michael Allen Johnson, Aug. 27, 1965], bass) *Whatever's Cool With Me* EP 1993—*Where You Been* 1994—(– Murph) *Without a Sound* 1997—*Hand It Over* 2000—*The BBC Sessions* (BBC, U.K.).

J Mascis solo: 1996—*Martin + Me* (Reprise/Warner) 2000—*More Light* (as J Mascis + the Fog) (Artemis).
Mike Johnson solo: 1994—*Where Am I?* (Up) 1996—*Year of Mondays* (TAG/Atlantic) 1998—*I Feel Alright* (Up).

Dinosaur Jr was the vehicle for J Mascis' grungy lead guitar style, ragged vocals, and inward-looking song lyrics—a combination owing as much to Neil Young as to the postpunk fury of such early-'80s alternative pioneers as Hüsker Dü.

From early on, Mascis was known for his lethargic, nontalkative demeanor and reclusive lifestyle, and has often been described as a "slacker." After his hardcore band Deep Wound broke up in 1983, Mascis and bassist Lou Barlow formed Dinosaur in the liberal environment of their hometown, the five-college city of Amherst, Massachusetts. At the time, Mascis played drums. When former All White Jury drummer Patrick "Murph" Murphy joined, Mascis moved to guitar. The band recorded one album for the East Coast independent label Homestead before signing to the West Coast independent SST in 1987. Meanwhile, the attention the band received for its growing cult status got it into legal hot water with another group that called itself the Dinosaurs. When that group (consisting of former members of such '60s bands as Jefferson Airplane and Country Joe and the Fish) sued, Mascis and company were forced to change the name; they chose to simply add "Jr."

Bug included the underground smash single "Freak Scene." In 1989 the band scored another underground hit with an unlikely cover of the Cure's "Just Like Heaven." Barlow departed and concentrated on his band, Sebadoh (who later recorded on Sub Pop). Dinosaur Jr went through a revolving-door period upon landing its Sire contract, with temporary members including the Screaming Trees' Van Connor and Gumball's Don Fleming; Mascis, meanwhile, also sat in on drums with other bands, including hometown buddies Gobblehoof.

On Dinosaur Jr's major label debut, *Green Mind*, Mascis played nearly everything himself. The album was met with mixed reactions in underground circles, and the band found itself overshadowed on a subsequent tour by opening act Nirvana, then on the verge of a popular explosion. After new bassist Mike Johnson joined, the band put out an EP, *Whatever's Cool With Me*, and followed up with the full-length *Where You Been* (#50, 1993). That album was greeted with massive critical success. In 1993 Dinosaur Jr appeared on the summer's Lollapalooza Tour. Murph left in 1994, so Mascis was back to playing the drums, etc., himself on *Without a Sound* (#44, 1994), but, unfortunately, he concentrated on his singing rather than on his fretboard.

The next year, Mascis began a solo career, releasing *Martin + Me*. He also contributed two Brian Wilsonesque songs to the 1996 Allison Anders film *Grace of My Heart*. In 1996 Mascis played drums and bass on Johnson's understated, brooding second solo album, *Year of Mondays*. Another Dinosaur Jr album, *Hand It Over*, was released that same year. Despite a return to the band's noisy guitar attack, and the production help of My Bloody Valentine guitarist Kevin Shields, the album peaked at #188 on the pop album chart. Soon thereafter, the band split up. Mascis' new backing ensemble, the Fog, has included guitarist/bassist Ron Asheton of the Stooges and bassist Mike Watt of the Minutemen.

Dion and the Belmonts/Dion DiMucci

Formed 1958, Bronx, NY
Dion (b. Dion DiMucci, July 18, 1939, Bronx), lead voc.; Fred Milano (b. Aug. 22, 1939, Bronx), second tenor voc.; Carlo Mastrangelo (b. Oct. 5, 1938, Bronx), baritone voc.; Angelo D'Aleo (b. Feb. 3, 1940, Bronx), first tenor voc.
1959—*Presenting Dion and the Belmonts* (Laurie) 1991—*A Teenager in Love: The Best of Dion and the Belmonts* (EMI/Capitol) 2000—*Drip Drop* (Sony).
Dion DiMucci solo: 1961—*Runaround Sue* 1962—*Lovers Who Wander* 1963—*Ruby Baby* (Columbia); *Dion Sings to Sandy (and All His Other Girls)* (Laurie) 1968—*Dion* 1969—*Sit Down Old Friend* (Warner Bros.) 1971—*You're Not Alone; Sanctuary* 1972—*Suite for Late Summer* 1973—*Reunion* 1976—*Streetheart* 1977—*Dion's Greatest Hits* (Columbia) 1978—*Return of the Wanderer* (Lifesong) 1984—*24 Original Classics* (Arista) 1989—*Yo Frankie!* 1991—*Bronx Blues: The Columbia Recordings (1962–1965)* (Sony/Columbia) 1992—*Dream On Fire* (Vision) 1997—*The Road I'm On: A Retrospective* (Sony/Columbia) 1999—*Déjà Nu* (Collectables) 2000—*King of the New York Streets* (The Right Stuff/EMI).

Easily the suavest of New York City's late-'50s white teen idols, Dion DiMucci broke from that clean-cut pack with an engagingly cool, streetwise swagger epitomized by "The Wanderer." Through the years, he has boldly essayed new musical directions with mixed results, yet endured as an influence on rock singers ranging from Billy Joel to Lou Reed.

He started singing at age five and picked up a guitar a few years later. As a teenager he began singing on streetcorners. He also began dabbling in drugs and eventually developed a heroin habit that he didn't kick until 1968. Shortly after dropping out of high school, Dion recorded a demo as a Valentine's Day present for his mother. It reached the producers of the *Teen Club* TV show out of Philadelphia, where Dion made his performing debut in 1954.

Recording his vocals separately over those of a backing group called the Timberlanes, he released "The Chosen Few," and in early 1958 Dion rounded up some neighborhood friends and dubbed them the Belmonts after Belmont Avenue, a street near the Bronx's Italian Arthur Avenue area. Their second single, "I Wonder Why," skirted the Top 20. "No One Knows" and "Don't Pity Me" followed, but the big break came in the spring of 1959, when "A Teenager in Love" (#5) became an international hit. The next year "Where or When" climbed to #3.

The group toured frequently, often on package tours with other stars; in February 1959 Dion passed up a ride on the chartered plane that later crashed, killing Buddy Holly, Ritchie Valens, and the Big Bopper. At the height of the group's success Dion felt confined, and his drug dependency worsened. (When "Where or When" peaked, he was in a hospital detoxifying.)

By early 1960 Dion was recording solo, backed by the uncredited Del-Satins. He hit the Top 10 with "Runaround Sue" (#1), "The Wanderer" (#2), "Lovers Who Wander" (#3), and "Little Diane" (#8) in 1962; and "Ruby Baby" (#2), "Drip Drop" (#6), and "Donna the Prima Donna" (#6) in 1963. By then he was recording for Columbia. In 1964 Dion went into near seclusion, releasing a string of unsuccessful covers ("Johnny B. Goode," "Spoonful"). He reappeared in 1965 for another round with the Belmonts (who'd remained active after 1960, achieving moderate success with "Tell Me Why" and "Come On Little Angel"). Together they released "Mr. Movin' Man" and "Berimbau" and an album for ABC.

In early 1968 he moved with his wife, Susan (the real "Runaround Sue," whom he married in 1963) and their daughter to Miami, where, with the help of his father-in-law, he finally kicked heroin. (The couple had two more daughters.) Later that year he recorded "Abraham, Martin and John," a #4 hit ballad tribute to Lincoln, King, and Kennedy; the flop followup was a cover of Jimi Hendrix's "Purple Haze."

Dion spent the next few years on the coffeehouse circuit. His Warner Bros. debut, *Sit Down Old Friend,* featured just his voice and acoustic guitar on eight songs. He also released the nonalbum single, the antidrug "Your Own Backyard." Both that folky album and the lusher *Suite for Late Summer* failed to sell, and Dion reunited with the Belmonts. The group played Madison Square Garden in mid-1972, as documented on the *Reunion* LP. Dion then briefly reentered the show-biz mainstream, frequently guesting on TV variety shows like *Cher.* The transfusion also helped the Belmonts, whose *Cigars Acapella Candy* sold respectably. In the mid-'70s Dion recorded with Phil Spector, but their collaboration, *Born to Be With You,* was released only in the U.K.

Dion attempted to update with *Streetheart* in 1976. He recorded five albums of Christian music; in 1988 he published his candid autobiography *The Wanderer: Dion's Story.* The next year he was inducted into the Rock and Roll Hall of Fame, and recorded *Yo Frankie!,* produced by Dave Edmunds and featuring such guests as Lou Reed, in whose songs Dion's influence had long been apparent. In the mid-'90s for some dates, he formed the Little Kings with Scott Kempner of the Dictators and Del-Lords, Mike Mesaros of the Smithereens, and Frank Funaro of the Del-Lords and Cracker. *Déjà Nu* is a collection of new songs written in the style of his earlier material and recorded, according to the Wanderer himself, "with the same techniques and equipment" used on his early classics. Dion continues to perform.

Celine Dion

Born Mar. 30, 1968, Charlemagne, Quebec, Can.
1987—*Incognito* (CBS) 1990—*Union* (Epic) 1991—*Dion Chante Plamondon* (CBS) 1992—*Celine Dion* (Epic) 1993—*The Colour of My Love* (550 Music/Epic) 1994—*A L'Olympia* (Sony) 1995—*D'eux* (a.k.a. *The French Album*) (Sony) 1996—*Falling Into You* (550 Music/Epic); *Live à Paris* (Sony) 1997—*Let's Talk About Love* (550 Music/Sony) 1998—*S'il Suffisait D'Aimer* (Sony); *These Are Special Times* 1999—*Au Cœur du Stade; All the Way . . . A Decade of Song* 2000—*The Collectors Series, Volume One.*

Canadian singer Celine Dion was one of the most commercially successful artists of the '90s. The 14th and youngest child of a musical family, Dion starting singing in her parents' bar when she was five. At age 12, she sent a demo of a French song she'd written to manager Rene Angelil. Though Angelil ignored the recording until prompted by one of Dion's brothers, he devoted himself to managing Dion immediately upon hearing her sing, even mortgaging his house to pay for her first album.

Following some local and European success, Dion dedicated herself to achieving stardom in America. She reached her goal almost instantaneously: Her 1990 single "Where Does My Heart Beat Now" went to #4; her next Top 10 single, the theme song to the animated film *Beauty and the Beast* (a duet with Peabo Bryson), went to #9 and won her both a Grammy and an Oscar. She received two more Grammys (Best Pop Album and Album of the Year) for her first #1 album, *Falling Into You.* But she will perhaps be best remembered for her #1 single "My Heart Will Go On (Love Theme From *Titanic*)" from the *Titanic* soundtrack. It also earned an Oscar for Best Original Song. In 1994, at 26, Dion married her then-51-year-old manager; after Angelil was diagnosed with skin and throat cancer in 1999, Dion released a greatest-hits collection, *All the Way . . . A Decade of Song* (#1, 1999), and then temporarily retired to focus on her family. She gave birth to her first child, a son, in 2001.

Dire Straits

Formed 1977, London, Eng.
Mark Knopfler (b. Aug. 12, 1949, Glasgow, Scot.), gtr., voc.; David Knopfler (b. 1951, Glasgow), gtr.; John Illsley (b. June 24, 1949, Leicester, Eng.), bass; Pick Withers, drums.
1978—*Dire Straits* (Warner Bros.) 1979—*Communiqué* 1980—(– D. Knopfler) *Making Movies* 1982—(+ Hal Lindes, gtr.; + Alan Clark, kybds.) *Love Over Gold* 1983—(– Withers; + Terry Williams, drums) *Twisting by the Pool* EP 1984—*Alchemy: Dire Straits Live* 1985—(+ Guy Fletcher, kybds.) *Brothers in Arms* 1988—*Money for Nothing* 1991—*On Every Street* 1993—*On the Night* 1995—*Live at the BBC* (Winsong) 1998—*Sultans of Swing—The Very Best of Dire Straits* (Warner Bros.).
The Notting Hillbillies: 1990—*Missing . . . Presumed Having a Good Time* (Warner Bros.).
Mark Knopfler and Chet Atkins: 1990—*Neck and Neck* (Columbia).
Mark Knopfler: 1993—*Screenplaying (Music From Local Hero, Cal, The Princess Bride, Last Exit to Brooklyn)* (Warner Bros.) 1996—*Golden Heart* 1998—*Wag the Dog* soundtrack

(PolyGram) 1999—*Metroland* soundtrack 2000—*Sailing to Philadelphia* (Warner Bros.).

British songwriter/vocalist/guitarist Mark Knopfler led Dire Straits to international success with a series of albums full of virtuoso-calibre musicianship and the finely developed songcraft that made some of his best story songs (such as "Romeo and Juliet") irresistible. A touch of wry humor ("Money for Nothing"), a lack of pretentiousness, and a knack for creating groove-driven songs also helped make Dire Straits one of the most successful groups of the mid- to late '80s.

The group's debut album introduced Knopfler's minor-key Dylanesque songs and his limpid mixture of J.J. Cale's and Albert King's guitar styles; the Dire Straits trademark is a dialogue between Knopfler's vocals and guitar lines, as heard in the group's first hit "Sultans of Swing" (#4, 1979).

Mark and David Knopfler, sons of an architect, both learned guitar in their teens. Mark became a rock critic at the *Yorkshire Evening Post* while working for an English degree. He then taught problem students at Loughton College and an adult extension course, worked in South London pub bands, and wrote some songs.

By early 1977 Mark was teaching literature part-time and jamming with David (then a social worker) and David's roommate, John Illsley, a timber broker who was pursuing a sociology degree at the University of London. In July 1977, after rehearsing with studio drummer Pick Withers, the group made a five-track demo tape that included "Sultans of Swing." Critic and DJ Charlie Gillett played "Sultans" on his BBC radio show, "Honky Tonkin'," and listeners and record companies responded.

After opening for Talking Heads on a 1978 U.K. tour, the group spent 12 days and about $25,000 to record *Dire Straits* (#2, 1979), which eventually sold 3 million copies in the U.S. and approximately 11 million copies worldwide as "Sultans of Swing" became a hit (#4, 1979). Jerry Wexler and Barry Beckett produced the 8-million-selling (again, worldwide) *Communiqué* (#11, 1979).

During sessions for *Making Movies* in July 1980, David Knopfler left, and Bruce Springsteen's E Street Band pianist Roy Bittan sat in. For the ensuing tour, Dire Straits added Hal Lindes and Alan Clark to play the longer selections from *Making Movies* (#19, 1980). It included the minor hit and MTV favorite "Skateaway" (#58, 1980). *Love Over Gold* (#19, 1982), with no singles-length cuts, went gold and topped the U.K. chart. Later, Withers departed and was replaced by ex-Rockpile drummer Terry Williams. Tommy Mandel also joined.

Following an EP (*Twisting by the Pool,* whose title track went to #14 U.K., 1983) and a live collection (*Alchemy,* which went to #3 U.K., 1984) came the group's biggest commercial success: the 26-million-selling, worldwide smash *Brothers in Arms* (#1 pop, #1 U.K., 1985). Featuring three hit singles: "Money for Nothing" (#1, 1985)—on which Sting makes a cameo appearance and sings "I want my MTV"—"Walk of Life" (#7, 1985), and "So Far Away" (#19, 1986). In 1987 *Brothers in Arms* passed the 3-million sales mark in the U.K., becoming one of the best-selling LPs in that nation's history. By then, Knopfler had had his hand in a number of outside projects, including producing Aztec Camera's *Knife* and Bob Dylan's *Infidels,* writing one of Tina Turner's comeback hits, "Private Dancer," and scoring a handful of films (*Local Hero* [1983], *Cal* [1984], *Comfort and Joy* [1984], *The Princess Bride* [1987], and *Last Exit to Brooklyn* [1989]). Knopfler's film music was anthologized on 1993's *Screenplaying.*

With *Brothers* still riding the charts on both sides of the Atlantic, Knopfler continued pursuing his own projects, appearing on Joan Armatrading's *The Shouting Stage,* coproducing Randy Newman's *Land of Dreams,* and recording with his idol, country guitar master Chet Atkins. (To date, Knopfler and Atkins have won three Grammys for their duet recordings.) In 1988, following appearances at Nelson Mandela's 70th Birthday Party concert at Wembley and Knopfler's touring with Eric Clapton, Dire Straits went on a two-year hiatus.

Knopfler returned to recording with Guy Fletcher and the Notting Hillbillies, a side project with Brendan Croker, Paul Franklin, Ed Bicknell, and Steve Phillips. The group's debut album, *Missing . . . Presumed Having a Good Time,* was a phenomenal hit in the U.K., where it entered the chart at #2. It was not nearly as successful in the U.S., peaking at #52, despite an appearance on *Saturday Night Live.* Meanwhile, *Money for Nothing,* a Dire Straits greatest-hits compilation, went platinum, peaking at #62 in the U.S. but topping the charts in 28 other countries.

Given the group's high profile in the mid-'80s and the six years that had elapsed between new albums, the platinum *On Every Street* (#12, 1991) was expected to generate great interest. That was not the case in the U.S., where their tour (captured on 1993's *On the Night*) was not a hot ticket and no hit single emerged. As critics have pointed out, however, *Brothers in Arms* was perhaps a fluke, a departure from the group's usual more laid-back style.

In 1996, a year after quietly closing the book on Dire Straits, Knopfler released his first non-soundtrack solo album, *Golden Heart* (#105). He returned to film scoring in 1998 with *Wag the Dog* (which spawned a single with the title track) and 1999's *Metroland.* In February of 2000, Knopfler made the Queen of England's New Year's Honors List and a month later was given an OBE (Order of the British Empire) medal, awarded for outstanding contributions to country, at Buckingham Palace. The year also found him working on the soundtrack to the Robert Duvall/Michael Keaton film *Road to Glory.* His second solo album proper, *Sailing to Philadelphia,* was released in 2000.

Disposable Heroes of HipHoprisy/Spearhead

Formed 1990, Oakland, CA
Michael Franti (b. Apr. 21, 1967, Oakland), voc.; Rono Tse (b. Dec. 8, 1966, Hong Kong), perc., electronics.

1992—*Hypocrisy Is the Greatest Luxury* (Island).
Spearhead: 1994—*Home* (Capitol) 1997—*Chocolate Supa Highway* 2001—*Stay Human* (Six Degrees).

This highly political rap group was formed by two ex-members of the Bay Area interracial punk-rock band the Beatnigs, who'd recorded for Dead Kennedys frontman Jello Biafra's Alternative Tentacles label. Rapper Michael Franti, who stands six-feet-six, had been a University of San Francisco basketball star; percussionist Rono Tse played his own homemade instruments (made from tire rims, grinders, chains, and fire extinguishers, as well as electronic drums) and danced during shows.

The Disposable Heroes formed after the 1989 Persian Gulf War, debuting on Island with the double-A-sided single "Television Is the Drug of the Nation"/"Winter of the Long Hot Summer." Their next single, "Language of Violence," was the first significant rap track to attack homophobia and set Franti apart from the mainstream of rappers, who either condemned homosexuality or let gay-bashing pass unremarked.

On its critically acclaimed debut album the group preached tolerance and attacked prejudice amidst a wide variety of musical settings, ranging from the jazzy to the industrial. The Disposable Heroes opened tours for U2, Public Enemy, and Arrested Development, and in summer 1991 they landed a spot on the first Lollapalooza package tour of alternative rock and rap groups. In 1993 the duo appeared with author William S. Burroughs on an album of his readings called *Spare Ass Annie and Other Tales*. At the end of the year the group announced an indefinite hiatus, with Franti to record a solo album, and Tse to produce Asian-flavored hiphop through his Vitamin C production company. In 1994 Franti's new group Spearhead released *Home*, coproduced by Joe "The Butcher" Nicolo (Schoolly D, Kriss Kross).

Spearhead released a second album, *Chocolate Supa Highway* in 1997, and the group became one of the signature acts on the Smokin' Groove summer tours of the late '90s—a variation on the Lollapalooza formula that focused on alternative hip-hop acts. Franti also explored spoken-word performances and scoring for movies, and was one of 36 American artists who participated in a 1999 cultural-exchange festival in Havana, Cuba, organized by Music Bridges. Spearhead's *Stay Human* was influenced by Franti's work as an opponent of the death penalty.

Divinyls

Formed 1981, Sydney, Austral.
Christina Amphlett (b. Oct. 25, ca. 1960, Geelong, Victoria, Austral.), voc.; Mark McEntee (b. July 16, ca. 1961, Perth, Austral.), gtr.; Bjarre Ohlin, gtr., kybds.; Rick Grossman, bass; Richard Harvey, drums.
1982—*Monkey Grip* EP (WEA, Austral.) 1983—*Desperate* (Chrysalis) 1985—*What a Life!* 1988—*Temperamental* (– Ohlin; – Grossman; – Harvey) 1991—*Divinyls* (Virgin); *Essential Divinyls* (Chrysalis) 1996—*Underworld* (RCA).

Critically acclaimed upon their emergence as a sort of Australian answer to the Pretenders, Divinyls never hit it big in the U.S. until a decade later. By then the band consisted solely of the singer, Christina Amphlett, and her cowriter, guitarist Mark McEntee.

Amphlett left school at age 17 to travel alone to Europe, spending time in Paris and, in Barcelona, Spain, getting jailed for street singing. Back in Sydney, she joined a church choir (purely "to develop the top range of my voice," she later said). During one choir performance her stool fell over and got tangled in her microphone chord, so she dragged the stool across the stage while singing. McEntee, who was in the audience that night, introduced himself, and the pair began writing songs together and soon formed a band. Amphlett gained instant notoriety with her snarling, nasal voice and trashy onstage look—dumpy schoolgirl uniforms worn over torn fishnet stockings—and her pouty-lipped, heavy-lidded makeup.

Monkey Grip, released in Australia only, contained several songs from a film of the same name in which Amphlett had a costarring role. Three songs from that EP—"Boys in Town," "Only Lonely," and "Elsie"—turned up on *Desperate*. Despite critical acclaim for *Desperate*, the band did not catch on commercially, finding the most success with *What a Life!* (#91, 1985), which yielded a minor hit single in "Pleasure and Pain" (#76, 1986).

Chrysalis dropped Divinyls after *Temperamental*, the band dissolved, and Amphlett and McEntee—who say their relationship has always been purely professional and platonic—moved to Paris, where they lived in the sleazy Pigalle area and wrote songs. Their demo tapes eventually led to the eponymous album (#15, 1991) that was their biggest hit, thanks to "I Touch Myself" (#4, 1991), a slick double-entendre ode to masturbation and/or romance. Amphlett and McEntee toured using hired musicians as backup. Record label entanglements contributed to the delay in releasing *Underworld* (1996), which featured tracks recorded with and produced by guitarist Charley Drayton (of Keith Richards' X-Pensive Winos).

Dixie Chicks

Formed 1989, Dallas, TX
Martie Seidel (b. Martha Elenor Erwin, Oct. 12, 1969, York, PA), fiddle, mandolin, voc.; Emily Robison (b. Emily Burns Erwin, Aug. 16, 1972, Pittsfield, MA), gtr., banjo, Dobro, voc.; Laura Lynch (b. Nov. 18, 1958, Dell City, TX), voc., bass, gtr.; Robin Lynn Macy (b. Nov. 27, 1958, Sunnyvale, CA), voc., gtr.
1990—*Thank Heavens for Dale Evans* (Crystal Clear Sound) 1992—*Little Ol' Cowgirl* (– Macy) 1993—*Shouldn't a Told You That* 1995—(– Lynch; + Natalie Maines [b. Oct. 14, 1974, Lubbock, TX], voc., gtr.) 1998—*Wide Open Spaces* (Monument/Sony) 1999—*Fly*.
Robin Macy with Domestic Science Club: 1993—*Domestic Science Club* (Discovery) 1996—*Three Women* (Crystal Clear Sound).

Robin Macy with Big Twang: 2000—*Pastures of Plenty* (Big Twang).

The Dixie Chicks were ready when success came knocking in the late '90s in the form of their two back-to-back, multi-platinum, Grammy-winning country albums *Wide Open Spaces* and *Fly.* Although singer Natalie Maines was relatively new to the group, sisters Martie Seidel and Emily Robison each had 10 years of Dixie Chicks touring and recording experience behind them. Martie and Emily Erwin were both born in the Northeast but moved with their parents and older sister to Dallas. Each began playing violin at an early age—Martie at five, Emily at seven—and soon after picked up mandolin and banjo, respectively. In 1984, they began performing with the teenage bluegrass band Blue Night Express, a five-year gig that led to opening spots for the likes of Ricky Skaggs and Martie's second-place finish at the 1987 national Old Time Fiddlers Convention. It was on the bluegrass circuit that the sisters met Robin Macy, a math teacher then playing in the Dallas-based group Danger in the Air, and Laura Lynch. Macy and Lynch were each a decade older than the Erwins, but they meshed musically and performed together for the first time on a downtown Dallas street corner in 1989. They returned the following day and were soon drawing big enough crowds to warrant a move to indoor clubs and a band name; "Dixie Chicks" was derived from the Little Feat song "Dixie Chicken."

In their Dale Evans–style cowgirl attire, the Dixie Chicks may have looked like a novelty act, but their seasoned musical chops and a tireless grassroots work ethic earned them considerable regional—and in select circles, national—acclaim. They made their Grand Ole Opry debut in 1991 and performed at President Bill Clinton's 1993 inauguration in Washington, DC. They recorded three independent albums together (1990's *Thank Heavens for Dale Evans,* 1992's *Little Ol' Cowgirl,* and 1993's *Shouldn't a Told You That*). Macy left after the second album over creative differences. She went on to record two albums with singers Sara Hickman and Patty Mitchell Lege as the Domestic Science Club, then moved to Kansas, where she joined the bluegrass group Big Twang.

The Dixie Chicks pressed on and landed a demo deal with Sony Nashville in 1995. It was then that the Erwin sisters decided that the sound (and success) they longed for would require a dramatic change in attitude, and saw their future potential in Lubbock-born Natalie Maines, the daughter of Lloyd Maines, an established Texas producer and veteran steel guitarist with the Joe Ely Band and Jerry Jeff Walker. After asking Lynch to step down, they brought Maines into the fold and spent another two years on the club circuit retooling their act, ditching the cowgirl Western swing shtick in favor of a more rock & roll, honky-tonk edge. Lynch wished them well, retired from music, and married a cattle rancher (and Texas State Lottery winner).

Released in early 1998, the Dixie Chicks' *Wide Open Spaces* marked a new beginning. The album topped the country chart, went to #4 on the pop chart, and spawned a handful of country radio hits, including three #1s: the title track, "You Were Mine," and "There's Your Trouble." Although the album featured only one Chicks composition (the ballad "You Were Mine"), the group members were widely praised for playing their own instruments on the album. The album sold more than 10 million copies, and the trio graduated from honky-tonks to stadiums while touring with the George Strait Country Music Festival (and reaching an audience outside the country sphere as part of Sarah McLachlan's Lilith Fair). In May 1999, Emily married singer/songwriter Charlie Robison. That year both Maines and Seidel underwent divorces. (Maines married actor Adrian Pasdar in June 2000.)

In September 1999, with *Wide Open Spaces* still positioned at #3 on the country chart, the Dixie Chicks released *Fly;* it sold more than 300,000 copies its first week in stores, debuting at the top of both the pop and country charts. In addition to the Top 5 country hits "Cowboy Take Me Away" and "Without You," the album also featured the controversial gold single "Goodbye Earl," a comic *Thelma & Louise*–style domestic abuse revenge fantasy.

The Dixie Cups

Formed 1964, New Orleans, LA
Barbara Ann Hawkins (b. 1943, New Orleans), voc.; Rosa Lee Hawkins (b. 1946, New Orleans), voc.; Joan Marie Johnson (b. 1945, New Orleans), voc.
1964—*Chapel of Love* (Red Bird).

The Dixie Cups were a black girl group that hit the top of the chart in 1964 with "Chapel of Love," a song that producer Phil Spector (with Jeff Barry and Ellie Greenwich) had originally written for the Ronettes. The trio—the Hawkins sisters and their cousin—first sang together in the grade school chorus. By 1963 the three had decided to pursue a career in music, and they began singing locally as the Meltones. Within a year, Joe Jones, a successful singer in his own right (notably, the Top 5 1960 release "You Talk Too Much"), became their manager. He groomed them for five months and then took them to New York, where producers/songwriters Jerry Leiber and Mike Stoller signed them to their fledgling Red Bird Records.

Their initial release, "Chapel of Love," proved to be their biggest hit, although they enjoyed subsequent success with such efforts as "People Say" (#12, 1964), "You Should Have Seen the Way He Looked at Me" (#39, 1964), "Iko Iko" (#20, 1965; later a minor hit for Dr. John and the Belle-Stars) and "Little Bell" (#51, 1965), the last of their hits. Red Bird Records went under in 1966; the Dixie Cups then switched to ABC-Paramount and later temporarily retired from show business.

In 1974 the Hawkins sisters moved from New York back to New Orleans, where they pursued successful modeling careers. They resumed touring (with Dale Mickle replacing Johnson).

Dixie Dregs

Formed 1973, Florida
Steve Morse (b. July 28, 1954, Hamilton, OH), gtr.; Andy West

(b. Feb. 6, 1954, Newport, RI), bass; Rod Morgenstein (b. Apr. 19, 1957, New York, NY), drums; Steve Davidowski, kybds.; Allen Sloan (b. Miami Beach, FL), electric violin.
1977—*Free Fall* (Capricorn) (– Davidowski; + Mark Parrish, kybds.) 1978—*What If* (– Parrish; + T Lavitz, kybds.) 1979—*Night of the Living Dregs* 1980—*Dregs of the Earth* (Arista) (– Sloan; + Mark O'Conner [b. Aug. 4, 1962, Seattle, WA], violin, gtr.) 1981—*Unsung Heroes* 1982—*Industry Standard* (group disbands) 1992—(group re-forms: Morse; Morgenstein; Lavitz; Sloan; + David LaRue, bass) *Bring 'Em Back Alive* (Capricorn) (– Sloan; + Jerry Goodman, violin) 1994—*Full Circle* 2000—(+ Sloan) *California Screamin'* (Zebra).
Steve Morse Band: 1984—*The Introduction* (Elektra/Musician) 1985—*Stand Up* 1989—*High Tension Wires* (as Steve Morse solo) (MCA) 1991—*Southern Steel* 1992—*Coast to Coast* 1995—*Structural Damage* (Windham Hill) 1996—*Stressfest* 2000—*Major Impacts* (Magna Carta).
T Lavitz solo: 1986—*Storytime* (Passport) 1987—*From the West* 1989— . . . *And the Bad Habitz* (Intima) 1991—*Mood Swing* (Nova) 1996—*Gossip* (Wild Cat).

A strictly instrumental band of virtuosi, the Dixie Dregs began as a jazz-rock fusion band modeled after the Mahavishnu Orchestra. They have since forged their own unique style of fusion, one that combines stunning technical prowess with flash, wit, and soul. A highlight of their 1992 live album, for example, found them sandwiching a history-of-rock medley that ranged from "Freebird" to "My Sharona" into their own "Take It Off the Top." They have been nominated for five Grammy Awards.

Steve Morse and Andy West had played together since they were 10th-grade classmates in Augusta, Georgia, putting together a conventional rock & roll band called Dixie Grit. Dixie Grit broke up when Morse was accepted into the University of Miami's School of Music, although he didn't have a high school diploma (having been expelled after refusing to cut his hair). At Miami, he studied in the jazz department with Jaco Pastorious, Pat Metheny, and Narada Michael Walden. There he met Allen Sloan and Rod Morgenstein. Sloan was a classically trained violinist who had played with the Miami Philharmonic and only recently had become interested in pop music. Morgenstein was a jazz drummer. Morse, Sloan, and Morgenstein began playing together, and at Morse's urging West enrolled at the university and joined the group. Their first album, *The Great Spectacular,* was recorded and produced as a course project. Upon graduation in 1975, they moved to Augusta, and began their professional careers.

After the Dregs opened a Nashville show for Sea Level in 1976, Chuck Leavell persuaded Capricorn Records to sign them. Before the end of the year, Mark Parrish—an original member of Dixie Grit—replaced Steve Davidowski. In turn he was replaced by T Lavitz in time for the Dregs' appearance at the 1978 Montreux Jazz Festival in Switzerland. Morse let the group's style become increasingly eclectic; Mark O'Conner (a three-time national champion fiddler) brought a more traditional old-time playing style. *Industry Standard* was the first Dregs (the group dropped the "Dixie" for *Unsung Heroes*) album to feature vocal performances; guest vocalists included Alex Ligertwood (Santana) and Doobie Brother Patrick Simmons.

After *Industry Standard,* the group members went their separate ways. Morse, acknowledged as one of the most important guitarists of the past two decades, released several albums with his Steve Morse Band, as well as one proper solo album. He also played with Kansas, appearing on *Power* (1986) and *In the Spirit of Things* (1988). He has been named Best Overall Guitarist five times in *Guitar Player* magazine's readers' poll. Morgenstein, who was a member of Morse's band, went on to join Winger [see entry]. Lavitz released his own solo albums and worked with a number of other groups, including Widespread Panic, the Bluesbusters, Jefferson Starship, and Billy Cobham's band. Lavitz and Morgenstein also play in Jazz Is Dead, whose two late-'90s albums feature fusion interpretations of Grateful Dead material.

The Dixie Dregs reunited in 1992 for a series of shows that produced *Bring 'Em Back Alive.* West, who was a computer programmer, did not join the reunion, and shortly after it began, Sloan returned to his work as an anesthesiologist. His replacement, Jerry Goodman, had belonged to the Mahavishnu Orchestra. West's replacement, Dave LaRue, is also from Morse's band. *Full Circle* and the Dixie Dregs' supporting tour were met with critical acclaim. Sloan returned to play alongside Goodman on 2000's *California Screamin'.*

The Dixie Hummingbirds

Formed 1928, Greenville, SC
James L. Davis, tenor voc.; Barney Gipson, lead tenor voc.; Barney Parks, baritone voc.; J.B. Matterson, bass voc.
1929—(– Matterson; + Fred Owens, bass voc.) 1930s—(– Owens; + various bass singers) 1939—(+ Jimmy Bryant, bass voc.; – Gipson; + Ira Tucker, lead tenor voc.; – Bryant; + William Bobo [d. 1976], bass voc.) 1944—(– Parks; + Beachy Thompson (b. 1915; d. 1994), baritone voc.) Early 1950s—James Walker [b. ca. 1926, Mileston, MS; d. Oct. 30, 1992, Philadelphia, PA], second lead tenor voc.; + Howard Carroll, gtr.) 1977—*Dixie Hummingbirds Live* (Peacock) 1979—*Golden Flight; Gospel at Its Best; We Love You Like a Rock* 1984—(– Davis) 1987—(+ Paul Owen, voc.) 1992—(– Walker).

The Dixie Hummingbirds were the leading Southern black gospel quartet for over 50 years, a seminal force in the development of that genre and in the parallel development of soul music. Clyde McPhatter, Bobby Bland, and Jackie Wilson are only some of the singers influenced by lead Hummingbird Ira Tucker. Even James Brown's sex-machine calisthenics have some precedent in the Hummingbirds' fervid performances.

The quartet was founded by James Davis and became prominent in the Carolinas during the '30s, making its first record for Decca in 1939. That same year the group was joined by two singers from Spartanburg, South Carolina—Tucker, formerly of the Gospel Carriers, and William Bobo, a

The Dixie Hummingbirds

member of the Heavenly Gospel Singers—when it bettered the Carriers and the Heavenlies in a singing competition.

In 1942 the Hummingbirds moved to Philadelphia and began broadcasting regularly on radio and touring the Northeast gospel circuit. John Hammond began to book them into New York cafes and nightclubs beginning in 1942. In 1945 they began recording for the Apollo and Gotham labels, and in 1952 they signed with Peacock, recording such gospel classics as "Jesus Walked the Water," "In the Morning," and "I Just Can't Help It."

In the early '50s, the Hummingbirds became a sextet with the additions of second lead tenor James Walker and guitarist Howard Carroll; the great Claude Jeter of the Swan Silvertones also joined the group briefly during the '50s.

The Dixie Hummingbirds performed at the Newport Folk Festival in 1966. The '70s found them embracing contemporary pop styles with mixed results. They backed Paul Simon in the studio, and on their *We Love You Like a Rock* covered Simon's "Loves Me Like a Rock" and Stevie Wonder's "Jesus Children of America" (which featured Wonder's keyboards). "Loves Me Like a Rock" was awarded a Grammy for Best Gospel Performance in 1973. While William Bobo had died in 1976, and James L. Davis finally retired in 1984, Tucker and Walker kept the group going into the late '80s.

Willie Dixon

Born July 1, 1915, Vicksburg, MS; died Jan. 29, 1992, Burbank, CA
1970—*I Am the Blues* (Columbia) 1973—*Willie Dixon—Catalyst* (Ovation) 1988—*The Chess Box* (Chess/MCA) 1988—*Hidden Charms* (Bug/Capitol) 1995—*The Original Wang Dang Doodle* (Chess).

Willie Dixon was an important link between the blues and rock & roll, and he wrote scores of blues classics in the '50s. Growing up in Mississippi, he composed poetry and sang in church before moving with his family to Chicago permanently in 1937. A big man (often weighing 250 pounds), the young Dixon won the city's Golden Gloves championship for his weight class in 1938. But his interest switched to music soon after, when he was introduced to the washtub bass. Dixon soon graduated to a four-string upright and later to a Fender electric. His walking bass lines played a major role in defining the postwar urban blues.

By the early '50s Dixon was selling his songs for $30 apiece and was thus cheated out of thousands of dollars in royalties. He was a prolific composer, and his catalogue includes "You Shook Me," "Little Red Rooster," "Back Door Man," "Bring It On Home," "I'm Your Hoochie Coochie Man," "The Seventh Son," "I Just Wanna Make Love to You," "Wang Dang Doodle," "You Can't Judge a Book by Its Cover," "Spoonful," "I Can't Quit You Baby," and others. They were covered by such rock bands as Led Zeppelin, the Doors, Foghat, Cream, the Allman Brothers, and many others.

Dixon's own recording career, which began in the early '50s, has been relatively unsuccessful. For a while he was the bass player in the house band at Chess Records and regularly backed Chuck Berry, Bo Diddley, Muddy Waters, and others, arranging and later producing them, in addition to Howlin' Wolf, Elmore James, Otis Rush, to name a few. In between takes he'd sell his own songs and act as the business intermediary between black artists and the Polish-born Chess brothers.

Dixon remained sporadically active, touring Europe (where he was revered) almost annually since 1960. He played some U.S. dates in 1975 and 1976 with his tour band the Chicago Blues All-Stars. The 1987 settlement of a long-running dispute with Led Zeppelin over the group's failure to credit Dixon as writer of "Whole Lotta Love" (which was largely based on his "You Need Love") led to his forming the Blues Heaven Foundation, a preservation society for blues music and culture that also worked to secure copyrights and royalties for other artists. His final recording, "Dustin' off the Bass," was included on Rob Wasserman's GRP album *Trios* (1994), and teamed him with Wasserman and former Chuck Berry drummer Al Duncan. One year after Dixon's death (he'd earlier lost part of his right leg to diabetes), Blues Heaven, with the help of John Mellencamp, managed to buy the original Chess Records studios in Chicago.

DMX

Born Earl Simmons, Dec. 18, ca. 1970, Baltimore, MD
1998—*It's Dark and Hell Is Hot* (Def Jam); *Flesh of My Flesh, Blood of My Blood* 1999—*. . . And Then There Was X.*

Hailing from the School Street Projects of Yonkers, New York, DMX (short for Dark Man X) became one of the most wildly successful hardcore rappers of the late '90s, crossing over to a mainstream rock audience with gritty, uncompromising lyrics that translated raw street drama into compellingly personal narratives which lived up to his name.

DMX's career began in 1992 with an abortive stint on Columbia, which failed to yield a release. Six years later he appeared on hits by Mic Geronimo, Mase, Onyx, and the Lox, as well as his own "Get at Me Dog" (#39 pop, #19 R&B). His debut album, *It's Dark and Hell Is Hot*, topped the pop and R&B charts upon its release in 1998. Summer tour plans were interrupted when DMX was arrested on rape charges filed by an exotic dancer. He posted bail and rejoined the tour, and was cleared of the charges in August. He then was cast in the gangsta rap drama *Belly*, the filmmaking debut of video director Hype Williams.

In early 1999 *Flesh of My Flesh, Blood of My Blood* reached #1 pop and R&B in its first week, marking the first time a recording artist had his first two albums top the charts within a single year. Despite his success—selling a combined 6 million copies of his first two albums—DMX was hounded by legal problems throughout the year, arrested at various times on weapons charges, as well as for obscenity and assault (as of this writing, the charges had not yet been brought before the courts). He was questioned in a Denver stabbing case, but not charged. In late 1999 DMX's third album, *. . . And Then There Was X*, was released, again debuting at #1. In 2001 DMX was incarcerated at the Erie County Correctional Facility for driving with a suspended license and possession of marijuana. He was allowed to leave jail briefly to attend the premiere of *Exit Wounds*, in which he costarred with Steven Segal.

DNA/Arto Lindsay

Formed 1977, New York, NY
Arto Lindsay (b. May 28, 1953, Richmond, VA), gtr., voc.; Ikue Ile Mori (b. Dec. 17, 1953, Tokyo, Jap.), drums; Robin Crutchfield, kybds., voc.
1978—(– Crutchfield; + Tim Wright, bass, gtr.) 1982—*A Taste of DNA* (American Clavé) 1993—*Last Live at CBGB's* (Avant, Jap.).
Ambitious Lovers (Arto Lindsay, gtr., voc; Peter Scherer, kybds.): 1984—*Envy* (Editions EG) 1988—*Greed* (Virgin) 1991—*Lust* (Elektra).
Arto Lindsay solo: 1995—*Arto Lindsay* (Knitting Factory); *Aggregates 1-26* 1996—*Subtle Body* (Bar/None); *Mundo Civilizado; Hyper Civilizado* (Gramavision) 1998—*Noon Chill* (Bar/None) 1999—*Prize* (Righteous Babe).
Ikue Mori solo: 1992—*Death Praxis* (Tzadik) 1995—*Hex Kitchen* 1996—*Garden* 1997—*Painted Desert* (Avant, Jap.) 1998—*B-side* (Tzadik) 2000—*One Hundred Aspects of the Moon*.

DNA was a leader in New York's "no wave" movement. Radically challenging rock conventions, its tightly structured songs, some of them under 30 seconds long, used neither fixed rhythms nor standard harmonies, and the three instrumental parts were usually independent and clashing. Chief writer Arto Lindsay's untuned guitar—he became known as the "sultan of skronk"—was emblematic both of the band's aesthetic adventurousness and the "downtown" sensibility Lindsay carried on in his work after DNA's demise.

Lindsay arrived in New York in 1975, having spent most of his life in a Brazilian village where his missionary father had built a school. While working as a messenger for the *Village Voice*, he played guitar for the first time when he jammed with James Chance and other "no wave" pioneers in 1977. Out of those sessions emerged the Contortions (Chance's group), Teenage Jesus and the Jerks (Lydia Lunch), and Mars. Lindsay wrote lyrics for Mars and would have joined them as drummer had he not decided to form a band with Ikue Ile Mori and Robin Crutchfield. Mori had just that year arrived from Tokyo. Through Teenage Jesus she met Lindsay, whose unorthodox guitar playing inspired her to try the drums.

DNA debuted with a 1978 single, "Little Ants" b/w "You and You" on the Lust/Unlust label, shortly before contributing four tracks to the "no wave" compilation *No New York*, produced by Brian Eno. At the end of 1978 Crutchfield left to form Dark Day and was replaced by Tim Wright, previously a member of Cleveland's Pere Ubu. Under his influence, DNA's music became even more turbulent and concise before the band broke up in 1981.

In addition to playing with DNA, each member worked with other musicians. Mori played violin, viola, and cello on *John Gavanti*, an inversion of Mozart's *Don Giovanni* featuring members of Mars. Wright played bass on David Byrne and Brian Eno's *My Life in the Bush of Ghosts* (1981).

Lindsay has achieved the largest measure of success. A founder of the "fake jazz" group the Lounge Lizards, he played with them until 1981. He also recorded with James Chance, Kip Hanrahan, and Seth Tillet. He has worked with the Toykillers and Ambitious Lovers; the latter, a duo with keyboardist Peter Scherer, released three albums titled after mortal sins and scored a minor dance hit with a 1991 cover of Jorge Ben's "Umbabarauma."

Mainly, Lindsay's role has been that of an avant-garde presence. He played on *Better an Old Demon Than a New God*, a 1984 album presented by poet John Giorno that showcased musicians with literary leanings. In the late '80s, as curator of the Kitchen, a New York haven for experimentalism, he hosted a new-music series that featured jazz, rap, Latin, and industrial sounds. In 1992 he introduced a new band, Arto. With Melvin Gibbs on bass, Marc Ribot on guitar, Bernie Worrell on keyboards, and Lindsay on vocals and guitar, its sound ranged from psychedelic to Brazilian to funk to noise. Since 1996, his solo albums have fused bossa nova and electronic music; during the decade he also became one of the most celebrated producers on the Brazilian music scene.

Ikue Mori, oftentimes collaborating with experimentalists like Fred Frith and John Zorn, continued working throughout the '90s.

Dr. Dre: See N.W.A

Dr. Feelgood

Formed 1971, Canvey Island, Eng.
Lee Brilleaux (b. Lee Green, 1953, Durban, S.A.; d. Apr. 7, 1994, Canvey Island), voc., harmonica, slide gtr.; John B. Sparks, bass; Wilko Johnson [b. John Wilkinson, 1947], gtr.; John "the Figure" Martin [b. 1947], drums.
1975—*Malpractice* (Columbia) 1977—*Sneakin' Suspicion* (– Johnson; + John Mayo, gtr.) 1981—(– Mayo; + Johnny Guitar, gtr.) 1982—(– Sparks; – Martin; + Buzz Barwell, drums; + Pat McMullen, bass) 1983—(– McMullen; + Paul Mitchell; – Guitar; + Gordon Russell, gtr.; numerous personnel changes follow).

British R&B revivalist Dr. Feelgood was one of the leading bands of the British back-to-basics movement of the mid-'70s. Lee Brilleaux, John B. Sparks, and Wilko Johnson hailed from Canvey Island. They drifted around England and made the rounds of pub bands together and separately before forming Dr. Feelgood in 1971. Johnson brought in John Martin, previously a member of Finian's Rainbow. They took their name from a minor early-'60s British hit by Johnny Kidd and the Pirates (not the Aretha Franklin song of the same title) and assembled a repertoire of Johnson originals and standards by Willie Dixon, Bo Diddley, Huey "Piano" Smith, Leiber and Stoller, and other (mostly black) R&B and rock & roll patriarchs.

Dr. Feelgood signed a United Artists (U.K.) contract in 1974. Its acclaimed debut album, *Down by the Jetty,* was recorded in mono, most of it in one take, with piano and saxes courtesy of Brinsley Schwarz and Bob Andrews of the Schwarz group. A growing concert following and enthusiastic support from people like Pete Townshend boosted its second album, *Malpractice,* into the U.K. Top 20 and a single, "She's a Wind Up," into the Top 40. Dr. Feelgood toured the United States in 1976 but never found a foothold; *Malpractice* and *Sneakin' Suspicion* were its only albums released here.

In 1977 Johnson left to form the Solid Senders; he later joined Ian Dury and the Blockheads. Henry McCullough stepped in for him on Dr. Feelgood's 1977 British tour, but John Mayo had replaced him by the time the group recorded *Be Seeing You* with producer Nick Lowe. "Milk and Alcohol" hit the British Top 10 in 1979, and "As Long as the Price Is Right" reached #40 later in the year.

By 1982 Brilleaux was the only original member left. He continued recording and touring with a succession of musicians. With his death from cancer at age 41, Dr. Feelgood was no more. Its last album, *Down at the Doctor's,* was recorded at Brilleaux's Dr. Feelgood Music Bar in Canvey Island, three months before he died.

Dr. Hook (and the Medicine Show)

Formed 1968, Union City, NJ
Ray Sawyer (b. Feb. 1, 1937, Chickasaw, AL), voc., gtr.; Dennis Locorriere (b. June 13, 1949, Union City), voc., gtr.; William Francis (b. Jan. 16, 1942, Mobile, AL), kybds., perc.; George Cummings (b. July 28, 1938, Meridian, MS), pedal steel gtr.; John "Jay" David (b. Aug. 8, 1942, Union City), drums.
1971—*Dr. Hook and the Medicine Show* (Columbia) (+ Richard Elswit [b. July 6, 1945, New York, NY], gtr.; + Jance Garfat [b. Mar. 3, 1944, CA], bass) 1972—*Sloppy Seconds* 1973—*Belly Up* (– David; + John Wolters [d. June 16, 1997, San Francisco, CA], drums) 1974—*Fried Face* 1975—*Ballad of Lucy Jordan; Bankrupt* (Capitol) (– Cummings) 1976—*A Little Bit More* (+ Bob "Willard" Henke, gtr.) 1977—*Makin' Love and Music; Street People* (Columbia); *Revisited* 1978—*Pleasure and Pain* (Capitol) 1979—*Sometimes You Win* 1980—*Greatest Hits; Rising* (Casablanca) 1982—*Players in the Dark.*

Dr. Hook and the Medicine Show are slapstick purveyors of parody rock, whose "Sylvia's Mother" was taken straight by Top 40 listeners and became the first of 10 Top 40 hits in the '70s and '80s. The group began performing professionally in New Jersey, doing cover versions. During those years, the two frontmen—ex–Jersey folkie Dennis Locorriere and Ray Sawyer, who wears an eyepatch (hence, Dr. Hook) since having lost an eye after a 1967 car crash—developed a repertoire spiced with off-color material.

Their manager, Ron Haffkine, discovered them while looking for backup musicians to perform *Playboy* cartoonist humorist, songwriter, and children's book author Shel Silverstein's material in the movie *Who Is Harry Kellerman and Why Is He Saying All Those Terrible Things About Me?* (1971). The group played "Last Morning" on the soundtrack and also appeared in the movie. After several months of rehearsal Dr. Hook went to California to record another batch of Silverstein's tunes. The group's debut LP featured "Sylvia's Mother" (#5, 1972), which sold 3.5 million copies worldwide but proved to be a mixed blessing. Its lilting style, a too-subtle parody of pop, left the public ill-prepared for the manic, unkempt group behind it. *Sloppy Seconds* was also written by Silverstein and gave the group another Top 10 hit, "The Cover of Rolling Stone" (#6, 1973), which took a satirical look at the rock culture—and landed Dr. Hook on the cover of ROLLING STONE. By the time of *Belly Up,* the band members were writing their own material, but with less success. By 1974 Dr. Hook had filed for bankruptcy and switched to Capitol. The group had hit in 1976 with Sam Cooke's "Only Sixteen" (#6) and "A Little Bit More" (#11). The next few years brought several more hits: "Sharing the Night Together" (#6, 1978), "When You're in Love with a Beautiful Woman" (#6, 1979), "Better Love Next Time" (#12, 1979), "Sexy Eyes" (#5, 1980), and "Baby Makes Her Blue Jeans Talk" (#25, 1982).

By late 1979 Dr. Hook had amassed 35 gold and platinum albums in Australia and Scandinavia, where the group remained a popular attraction until its breakup in 1985. Three years later Sawyer (who'd recorded a solo country album in 1977) revived the name and has been touring the U.S. and overseas ever since. Drummer John Wolters died of liver cancer in 1997. Locorriere resurfaced in the late '80s as a backup singer on Randy Travis' *Always & Forever.* In 2000 his solo album was released in the U.K.

Dr. John

Born Malcolm "Mac" Rebennack, Nov. 20, 1942, New Orleans, LA
1968—*Gris-Gris* (Atco) 1969—*Babylon* 1970—*Remedies* 1971—*The Sun, Moon & Herbs* 1972—*Dr. John's Gumbo* 1973—*In the Right Place; Triumverate* (with Mike Bloomfield and John Paul Hammond) (Columbia) 1974—*Desitively Bonnaroo* 1975—*Cut Me While I'm Hot* (DJM); *Hollywood Be Thy Name* (United Artists) 1978—*Tango Palace* 1979—*City Lights* (Horizon) 1980—*Take Me Back to New Orleans* (with Chris Barber) (Black Lion) 1981—*Dr. John Plays Mac Rebennack* (Clean Cuts) 1983—*The Brightest Smile in Town* 1987—*The Ultimate Dr. John* (Warner Bros.) 1989—*In a Sentimental Mood* 1990—*Bluesianna Triangle* 1991—*Bluesianna 2* (Windham Hill); *On a Mardi Gras Day* (with Chris Barber) (Great Southern) 1992—*Going Back to New Orleans* 1993—*Mos' Scocious: The Dr. John Anthology* (Rhino) 1994—*Television* (GRP/MCA) 1995—*Afterglow* (Blue Thumb); *The Very Best of Dr. John* (Rhino) 1998—*Anutha Zone* (Pointblank/Virgin).

Combining New Orleans funk, glitter, and voodoo charm, pianist Dr. John was an energetic frontman in the early '70s ("Right Place, Wrong Time") and a behind-the-scenes mover before and since.

Rebennack got his first taste of show biz through his mother, a model who got young Malcolm's face on Ivory Soap boxes; his father ran a record store. By his early teens he was an accomplished pianist and guitarist. From hanging around his dad's store and at Cosimo Matassa's studio, he got to know local musicians.

By the mid-'50s he was doing session work with Professor Longhair, Frankie Ford, and Joe Tex. He also helped form the black artists' cooperative AFO (All for One) Records, and he was the first white man on the roster. By the start of the '60s he had graduated to producing and arranging sessions for others (Lee Allen, Red Tyler, Earl Palmer) and recording some on his own (notably 1959's "Storm Warning" on Rex Records). Rebennack's reputation was based on his guitar and keyboard playing, but a hand wound suffered in a 1961 barroom gunfight forced him to take up bass with a Dixieland band.

In the mid-'60s Rebennack moved to L.A. and became a session regular, notably for producer Phil Spector. He played in various unsuccessful, wildly named bands like the Zu Zu Band (with Jessie Hill) and Morgus and the Three Ghouls. He also developed an interest in voodoo, to which he had been introduced by a mystical voodoo artist named Prince Lala in the '50s at AFO. In 1968 Rebennack unveiled his new public persona of Dr. John Creaux the Night Tripper (later shortened to Dr. John) after a New Orleans crony, Ronnie Barron, decided not to front the act. With New Orleans associates (Hill as Dr. Poo Pah Doo and Harold Battiste as Dr. Battiste of Scorpio of bass clef), he recorded *Gris-Gris* for Atlantic in 1968. As indicated by the song titles—"I Walk on Gilded Splinters," "Gris Gris Gumbo Ya Ya," "Croker Courtbouillion"—it was a brew of traditional Creole chants, mystical imagery, and traces of psychedelia, an influence underscored by Rebennack's onstage wardrobe (brightly colored robes, feathered headdresses, and a Mardi Gras–style retinue of dancers and singers).

Dr. John slowly acquired a loyal cult following, including Eric Clapton and Mick Jagger, who played on *The Sun, Moon & Herbs*. He moved to the more accessible regions of funk (backed by the Meters) on *In the Right Place* (#24, 1973). Produced by Allen Toussaint (who also played in Dr. John's band on a 1973 tour and who produced *Desitively Bonnaroo*) "Right Place, Wrong Time" (#9) was his biggest hit, followed a few months later by "Such a Night" (#42). In 1973 Dr. John also worked in Triumvirate, a short-lived trio with Mike Bloomfield and John Hammond Jr. (John Paul Hammond). He appeared in the Band's 1978 farewell concert film, *The Last Waltz*. In 1981 he released the first of several solo piano LPs, *Dr. John Plays Mac Rebennack*.

In the late '80s, Dr. John began reaching back to his New Orleans roots—while also subtly mainstreaming his appeal. His 1989 *In a Sentimental Mood* collected old blues and saloon standards, and earned him his first Grammy, for his duet with Rickie Lee Jones on "Makin' Whoopee!" *Bluesianna Triangle* detoured into jazz, with drummer Art Blakey and saxophonist David "Fathead" Newman, while *Goin' Back to New Orleans*—with a cast of New Orleans all-stars featuring Al Hirt, Pete Fountain, Danny Barker, Alvin "Red" Tyler, and the Neville Brothers—won him another Grammy. By that time his gruff baritone voice had become familiar to millions through a succession of TV commercial jingles. In 1991 rap group P.M. Dawn sampled from one of Dr. John's oldest tracks, "I Walk on Gilded Splinters"; two years later Beck sampled the same track for his folk-rap slacker anthem, "Loser." In 1993 Dr. John published his autobiography, *Under a Hoodoo Moon*. *Anutha Zone* (1998) features a range of guests, notably members of the U.K. space-rock band Spiritualized.

Bill Doggett

Born Feb. 6, 1916, Philadelphia, PA; died Nov. 13, 2000, New York, NY
N.A.—*Everybody Dance to the Honky Tonk* (King); *Hot Doggett*; *A Salute to Ellington*.

Pianist/organist Bill Doggett had a #2 hit in 1956 with the instrumental "Honky Tonk." He recorded for King beginning in 1952 and toured roadhouses throughout the decade with a band (including guitarist Billy Butler and saxophonist Clifford Scott, who later enjoyed moderate success as a solo act) that was renowned for its boogie-woogie groove.

Doggett had worked with several jazz bands in the '30s and '40s, including a stint with Louis Jordan's Tympani 5. He followed up "Honky Tonk" with "Slow Walk," which nearly cracked the Top 20 in late 1956 after Doggett's appearance on *American Bandstand*. Doggett continued to place singles on both the pop and R&B charts over the next five years and to record jazz with artists such as Illinois Jacquet.

Thomas Dolby

Born Thomas Morgan Robertson, Oct. 14, 1958, Cairo, Egypt
1982—*The Golden Age of Wireless* (Capitol) 1983—*Blinded by Science* EP (EMI/Harvest) 1984—*The Flat Earth* 1988—*Aliens Ate My Buick* (EMI/Manhattan) 1992—*Astronauts & Heretics* (Giant) 1994—*Retrospectacle* (Capitol/EMI); *Gate to the Mind's Eye* (Giant).

Best known for his first hit, "She Blinded Me With Science," Thomas Robertson is the son of a prominent British archeologist. He got his "Dolby" nickname (after the British laboratory that created the noise-reduction system for audiotapes) from schoolmates impressed by his avid interest in electronics.

Dolby taught himself guitar, piano, and computer programming. After spending time singing in Parisian subways and playing cocktail piano in London clubs, Dolby built his own synthesizers and PA systems, which he used while working as a soundman for such British postpunk bands as the Fall and the Members. In 1979 he cofounded the Camera Club with Bruce Woolley; a year later he joined Lene Lovich's band and wrote her 1981 hit "New Toy." Dolby then played keyboards and synthesizer on Foreigner's *4,* Joan Armatrading's *Walk Under Ladders,* Def Leppard's *Pyromania,* and Malcolm McLaren's *Duck Rock.* He also wrote and produced Whodini's "Magic's Wand," one of the first million-selling 12-inch rap singles.

Dolby's debut, *The Golden Age of Wireless* (#13, 1982), yielded a minor hit in "Europa and the Pirate Twins" (#67, 1983). The followup EP (#20, 1983) featured the comical synth-dance hit "She Blinded Me With Science" (#5, 1983), with guest vocals by British eccentric Magnus Pike, who also starred in the song's Dolby-directed video. In addition, Dolby directed *Live Wireless,* a long-form tour document, and the video for the manically funky "Hyperactive" (#62, 1984) from *The Flat Earth* (#35, 1984)—which also included a reverently gentle cover of Dan Hicks and His Hot Licks' "I Scare Myself."

As a producer, Dolby worked on George Clinton's *Some of My Best Jokes Are Friends* (1984), Joni Mitchell's *Dog Eat Dog* (1986), three albums for British band Prefab Sprout, and two tracks on Israeli singer Ofra Haza's *Wind* (1989). Dolby also composed and recorded film scores for *Fever Pitch* (1985), *Gothic* (1986), and *Howard the Duck* (1986). In 1986 Dolby Labs sued him for copyright infringement, eventually letting him use "Dolby" only with "Thomas."

In 1988 Dolby—living in L.A., married to actress Kathleen Beller (Kirby Colby of *Dynasty*), and backed by a full band—released *Aliens Ate My Buick* (#70, 1988), for which George Clinton cowrote the track "Hot Sauce." It failed to produce a hit single, as did 1992's *Astronauts & Heretics,* which featured such guests as Jerry Garcia and Bob Weir of the Grateful Dead, Eddie Van Halen, and Ofra Haza. Dolby formed the high-tech firm Headspace, which in 1993 introduced the interactive virtual-reality music program, *The Virtual String Quartet.* Along those lines, Dolby released *Gate to the Mind's Eye* in 1994, a soundtrack to a video compilation of computer graphics and animation. In 1999 Dolby launched a new concern, Beatnik, aimed at providing Web surfers with music remix technology they could use from their home computers.

Fats Domino

Born Antoine Domino, Feb. 26, 1928, New Orleans, LA
1956—*Fats Domino—Rock and Rollin'* (Imperial); *This Is Fats Domino* 1957—*Here Stands Fats Domino* 1958—*Fabulous Mr. D* 1959—*Let's Play Fats Domino* 1960—*Fats Domino Sings* 1961—*I Miss You So* 1962—*Twistin' the Stomp* 1963—*Just Domino* 1966—*Getaway With Fats Domino* (ABC) 1968—*Fats Is Back* (Reprise) 1970—*Fats* 1972—*Legendary Masters Series* (United Artists) 1990—*They Call Me the Fat Man—Antoine "Fats Domino": The Legendary Imperial Recordings* (EMI) 1993—*Christmas Is a Special Day* (The Right Stuff/EMI).

With 65 million record sales to his credit, New Orleans singer and pianist Fats Domino outsold every '50s rock & roll pioneer except Elvis Presley. Born into a musical family, Antoine Domino began playing piano at nine and a year later was playing for pennies in honky-tonks like the Hideaway Club, where bandleader Bill Diamond accurately nicknamed him Fats. At 14 Domino quit school to work in a bedspring factory so he could play the bars at night. Soon he was playing alongside such New Orleans legends as Professor Longhair and Amos Milburn. He also heard the stride and boogie-woogie piano techniques of Fats Waller and Albert Ammons. He mastered the classic New Orleans R&B piano style—easy-rolling left-hand patterns anchoring right-hand arpeggios. By the age of 20 he was married and a father, had survived a near-fatal car crash, and had almost lost his hand in a factory accident.

In the mid-'40s Domino joined trumpeter Dave Bartholomew's band. It was soon apparent, however, that Domino was more than a sideman, and Bartholomew helped arrange his contract with Imperial and became his producer. Their first session in 1949 produced "The Fat Man," which eventually sold a million and whetted the national appetite for the "New Orleans sound." Domino and Bartholomew cowrote most of Domino's material.

By the time the rock & roll boom began in the mid-'50s, Fats was already an established R&B hitmaker ("Goin' Home," 1952; "Going to the River," 1953), his records regularly selling between half a million and a million copies apiece. His pounding piano style was easily adapted to the nascent rock sound, although he proved less personally magnetic than contemporaries like Elvis Presley, Chuck Berry, Jerry Lee Lewis, or Little Richard, all of whom recorded Domino material. Domino's big breakthrough came in mid-1955, when the Top 10 "Ain't That a Shame" (quickly covered by Pat Boone and revived in the late '70s by Cheap Trick) established his identity with white teenagers. For the next five years Domino struck solid gold with "I'm in Love Again" (#3), "Blueberry Hill" (#2), and "Blue Monday" (#5) in 1956; "I'm Walkin' " (#4, 1957); "Whole Lotta Loving" (#6, 1958); and

Fats Domino

many others. He eventually collected 23 gold singles. His last million-seller came in 1960 with "Walkin' to New Orleans." He left Imperial for ABC in 1963 and subsequently switched to Mercury, Warner Bros., Atlantic, and Broadmoor, all with less success.

In 1968 Domino revived public interest in his ongoing career with his rollicking cover of the Beatles' "Lady Madonna." The Beatles consistently sang the Fat Man's praises, noting that "Birthday" on *The Beatles* did little more than sort through the old Domino-Bartholomew bag of riffs and tricks. Through the mid-'70s Fats played six to eight months a year. In 1980 he performed at the Montreux Jazz Festival. Domino continues to record and tour periodically. In 1993 he released his first major-label album in 25 years, *Christmas Is a Special Day,* to critical acclaim but only middling sales. In 1998 he received a National Medal of the Arts from President Bill Clinton. He has lived for many years in a palatial home in New Orleans. Domino has eight children, all of whom have first names beginning with the letter A.

Lonnie Donegan

Born Anthony Donegan, Apr. 29, 1931, Glasgow, Scot.
1961—*More Tops With Lonnie* (Pye, U.K.) 1962—*Golden Age of Donegan* (Golden Guinea, U.K.) 1968—*Showcase* (Marble Arch, U.K.) 1969—*Lonnie Donegan Rides Again* 1978—*Puttin' on the Style* (United Artists, U.K.) 1989—*Lonnie Donegan* (LaserLight) 1994—*More Than Pie in the Sky* (Bear Family, Ger.).

Banjoist Lonnie Donegan was one of the first British artists to enter the American Top 20, and his 1956 success with "Rock Island Line" inspired a generation of young Britons in the late-'50s English skiffle craze. Anthony Donegan's father was a violinist in the National Scottish Orchestra, and by the age of 13 Donegan was playing the drums. At 17 he became a Dixieland jazz convert, switched to the guitar, and played in an amateur jazz band before entering Britain's National Service. He picked up the banjo while working as a drummer with the Wolverines Jazz Band. Once discharged he moved to London and became banjoist and guitarist with the Ken Colyer Jazz Band, which in 1952 recorded one of the first jazz discs cut in England. By then Donegan had adopted the name Lonnie, in honor of his idol Lonnie Johnson.

In 1953 Colyer's band was renamed Chris Barber's band; the following year they recorded *New Orleans Joys,* which contained a version of "Rock Island Line" featuring Donegan's vocals. It became an international sensation, selling 3 million and launching Donegan's solo career as the "King of Skiffle" and one of England's top entertainers of the late '50s. Donegan's followup, "Lost John," didn't crack the American Top 20; his only other U.S. hit was "Does Your Chewing Gum Lose Its Flavor (on the Bedpost Overnight)" in 1961. "Lost John" went to #2 on the U.K. chart, beginning Donegan's six-year domination of the English hit parade, during which he enjoyed 17 Top 10 hits. In lieu of a fan club he formed a folk music appreciation society. Adam Faith (who later produced some of Donegan's sessions) and the nascent Beatles played at one of the society's 1958 membership drives in Liverpool. By 1963 Beatlemania had eclipsed skiffle, although Donegan continued to tour.

In 1974 Donegan toured the U.S. as an opening act for Tom Jones. He settled in Lake Tahoe and began hanging out on the fringe of the rock crowd. At a backstage party following a Wings concert in 1976, an impromptu jam with Faith, Elton John, Ringo Starr, and Leo Sayer led to the idea of an all-star Donegan reunion LP—*Puttin' on the Style*—which also featured Ron Wood, Rory Gallagher, Brian May of Queen, Albert Lee, Gary Brooker (Procol Harum), Mick Ralphs (Mott the Hoople, Bad Company), and other Donegan fans.

Donegan subsequently recorded two countryish albums, including one with Doug Kershaw. In 1981, the year he celebrated the silver anniversary of "Rock Island Line," he underwent heart surgery for chronic cardiac problems. Although a resident of California, Donegan continues to tour the U.K. regularly, where he is revered as the father of skiffle. In 2000 he received an MBE (Member of the Order of the British Empire).

Donovan

Born Donovan Leitch, May 10, 1946, Glasgow, Scot.
1965—*Catch the Wind* (Hickory); *Fairytale* 1966—*Sunshine Superman* (Epic) 1967—*Mellow Yellow; For Little Ones; Wear Your Love Like Heaven; A Gift From a Flower to a Garden* 1968—*Donovan in Concert; The Hurdy Gurdy Man* 1969—*Donovan's Greatest Hits; Barabajagal* 1970—*Open Road* 1973—*Cosmic Wheels; Essence to Essence* 1974—*7-Tease*

1976—*Slow Down World* 1977—*Donovan* (Arista) 1991—*The Classics Live* (Great Northern Arts) 1992—*Troubadour: The Definitive Collection, 1964–1976* (Epic/Legacy) 1996—*Sutras* (American).

Though for many years in the '70s and '80s, Donovan's flowery philosophy was considered passé, his compositions ("Catch the Wind," "Sunshine Superman," "Season of the Witch," "Mellow Yellow") still stand as novel examples of folk-rock hippie mysticism.

Donovan Leitch grew up in the Gorbals section of Glasgow. His family moved to the outskirts of London when he was 10; at 15 he completed the British equivalent of secondary school and enrolled in college but stayed only a year. At age 18 he began recording his songs. Talent scouts from the British rock TV program *Ready Steady Go* heard the demos, and in early 1965 Donovan became a regular on the show. His debut single, "Catch the Wind," hit the Top 25 in mid-1965; like its followups—"Colours" and "Universal Soldier"—the song was almost entirely acoustic. Donovan made his U.S. performing debut at the 1965 Newport Folk Festival.

With producer Mickie Most (with whom he worked until 1969), he left Hickory for Epic. Folklike refrains and exotic instrumentation (sitars, flutes, cellos, harps) kept Donovan's singles in the Top 40. His biggest hit, "Sunshine Superman," hit #1 in 1966 on both sides of the Atlantic. "Mellow Yellow" quickly reached #2 later that year. Some claimed its lyrics referred to smoking banana peels, but Donovan later claimed the song's subject was an electric dildo. Subsequent hits included 1967's "Epistle to Dippy" (#19) and "There Is a Mountain" (#11). By the time of 1968's "Wear Your Love Like Heaven" (#23, later the ad jingle for Love cosmetics) and "Jennifer Juniper" (#26, written for Jenny Boyd, the future Mrs. Mick Fleetwood), Leitch's wardrobe had changed to love beads and flowing robes.

In 1967 Donovan traveled to India to study with the Maharishi Mahesh Yogi. Shortly thereafter he publicly renounced all drug use and requested that his followers substitute meditation for getting stoned. A few more hits followed—"Hurdy Gurdy Man" (#5, 1968), "Atlantis" (#7, 1969), and "Goo Goo Barabajagal (Love Is Hot)" with the Jeff Beck Group (#36, 1969)—but after 1970 no one paid much attention.

Donovan

After a period of seclusion in Ireland, Donovan starred in and wrote the music for the 1972 German film *The Pied Piper*. He also scored *If It's Tuesday This Must Be Belgium*, then a full-length animation feature, *Tangled Details*, and Franco Zeffirelli's *Brother Sun, Sister Moon* in 1973. Following his sparsely attended 1971 U.S. tour, Donovan didn't perform in public until 1974, when he completed *7-Tease*, a conceptual LP about a young hippie and his search for inner peace.

The next year, *7-Tease* toured as a theatrical stage revue. In 1976 Donovan toured U.S. clubs in support of *Slow Down World*. He has published one book of poetry, *Dry Songs and Scribbles*. He essentially retired from recording, though he did release two albums in Germany. In 1983 Jerry Wexler produced *Lady of the Stars*.

Though Donovan sporadically performed in U.S. clubs beginning in the late '80s, his name seemed to appear most often in the U.S. press as a footnote in items about his children. Daughter Ione Skye became an actress; her film credits include *River's Edge*. Son Donovan Leitch Jr. was the "it" boy of 1993/94, a model, actor, and singer in his group Nancy Boy. In the early '90s, Happy Mondays helped rekindle a U.K. Donovan revival of sorts, and he toured there with them in 1992. Two years later he appeared at a memorial concert in England commemorating the 25th anniversary of Rolling Stone Brian Jones' death. (Donovan is married to one of Jones' former girlfriends, Linda Lawrence, and raised Jones' son Julian.)

In 1996 the 50-year-old attempted a comeback with the Rick Rubin–produced *Sutras*, which, as the title alludes, still held on to his '60s mysticism. But in the age of shock rock, this album of mellow pop failed to chart.

The Doobie Brothers

Formed 1970, San Jose, CA
Tom Johnston (b. Aug. 15, 1948, Visalia, CA), gtr., voc.; John Hartman (b. Falls Church, VA), drums; Patrick Simmons (b. Oct. 19, 1948, Aberdeen, WA), gtr., voc.; Dave Shogren (b. San Francisco, CA), bass.
1971—*The Doobie Brothers* (Warner Bros.) (– Shogren; + Tiran Porter [b. Los Angeles, CA], bass; + Michael Hossack [b. Oct. 17, 1946, Paterson, NJ], drums) 1972—*Toulouse Street* 1973—*The Captain and Me* (– Hossack; + Keith Knudsen [b. Feb. 18, 1948, LeMars, IA], drums) 1974—*What Once Were Vices Are Now Habits* (+ Jeff "Skunk" Baxter [b. Washington, DC], gtr.) 1975—*Stampede* (+ Michael McDonald [b. Feb. 12, 1952, St. Louis, MO], kybds., voc.) 1976—*Takin' It to the Streets; The Best of the Doobie Brothers* 1977—*Livin' on the Fault Line* (– Johnston) 1978—*Minute by Minute* 1979—

(– Hartman; – Baxter; + John McFee [b. Santa Cruz, CA], gtr.; + Chet McCracken [b. Seattle, WA], drums; + Cornelius Bumpus, sax, kybds.) 1980—*One Step Closer; The Best of the Doobies, vol. 2* 1982—(group disbands) 1983—*The Doobie Brothers Farewell Tour* 1988—(group re-forms: Johnston; Simmons; Hartman; Porter; Hossack; + Bobby LaKind [d. Dec. 24, 1992], perc.) 1989—*Cycles* (Capitol) 1991—*Brotherhood* 1993—(– Hartman; – Porter; + Knudsen; + McFee) 1996—*Rockin' Down the Highway: The Wildlife Concert* (Legacy) 1999—*Long Train Runnin'* (Warner Bros.); *The Best of the Doobie Brothers Live* (Legacy) 2000—*Sibling Rivalry* (Pyramid).
Tom Johnston solo: 1979—*Everything You've Heard Is True* (Warner Bros.) 1981—*Still Feels Good.*
Pat Simmons solo: 1983—*Arcade* (Elektra).
Michael McDonald solo: see entry.

Fans of the Doobie Brothers' first incarnation as a California country-boogie band had little use for the band's second, even more popular sound: an intricate jazz-inflected white funk. Tom Johnston, who fronted the early Doobies, met John Hartman through Skip Spence of Moby Grape, a group Johnston and Hartman hoped to emulate. They first played together in the short-lived group Pud with bassist Gregg Murphy. When Pud disbanded in 1969, Hartman and Johnston began jamming with local semipro musician Dave Shogren and later with Pat Simmons. They built up an avid following among California Hell's Angels by playing open jam sessions on Sunday afternoons, and dubbed themselves the Doobie Brothers ("doobie" was then popular California slang for a marijuana cigarette).

Warner Bros. A&R man Ted Templeman signed them and produced all their albums through 1980. Their debut LP failed to expand their audience much beyond their local following. With the addition of Michael Hossack and Tiran Porter, the group recorded *Toulouse Street,* which established the formula for its first hits: a strong beat, high harmonies, and repetition of a single phrase like "Listen to the music." The second and third Doobies albums were both million-sellers, the latter certified double platinum and containing such hits as "Long Train Runnin' " (#8, 1973) and "China Grove" (#15, 1973).

The transformation of Steely Dan into a studio-based duo sent Jeff "Skunk" Baxter, who'd done session work on *What Were Once Vices . . . ,* into the Doobies full-time. "Black Water," originally a B side, became the group's first #1 in 1975. Johnston quit touring because of a stomach ailment and was replaced by another Steely Dan alumnus, Michael McDonald. Baxter and McDonald revamped the Doobies' old songs in concert, and McDonald wrote most of their new material, shifting the group toward its later amalgam of funk and pop. McDonald's burry tenor replaced high harmonies as the band's trademark. Johnston rejoined in 1976, but left the next year to try a solo career; he has made two solo albums, *Everything You've Heard Is True* and *Still Feels Good.*

The multimillion sales of *Minute by Minute* (#1, 1978) established McDonald as the clear leader of the band. He sang lead on the Doobies' other #1, "What a Fool Believes." After a 1978 tour of Japan, Baxter left to do session work; he has also produced albums by Livingston Taylor and Carla Thomas. Hartman quit the music business to tend to his California horse ranch. More than a year of auditions enlisted ex–Clover guitarist John McFee and former session drummer (America, Hank Williams Jr., Helen Reddy) Hugh McCracken. Sax player/vocalist Cornelius Bumpus, who'd been in a late version of Moby Grape, also joined. For a 1980 tour, the Doobies were clearly McDonald's backup band; that lineup included session drummer Andy Newmark. The group disbanded in fall 1982 after a farewell tour. Soon afterward McDonald *(If That's What It Takes)* and Simmons *(Arcade)* released their first solo LPs. Not surprisingly, McDonald's distinctive voice made him an instant star on his own [see entry].

In 1987 the Doobies reunited around Johnston for a series of concerts; two years later he, Simmons, Hartman, Porter, Hossack, and percussionist Bobby LaKind (formerly a Doobies lighting man) returned to the band's original sound with the gold *Cycles* (#17) and the Top 10 single "The Doctor." A 1991 release, *Brotherhood,* didn't fare nearly as well, and after a tour, the group claimed to have called it a day. But in 1994, it undertook a major summer tour with a lineup of Johnston, Simmons, Hossack, Knudsen, and McFee; LaKind died of cancer in 1992. McFee joined the popular country group Southern Pacific, which included Stu Cook of Creedence Clearwater Revival. In 1996 the band released *Rockin' Down the Highway: The Wildlife Concert,* with proceeds going to the Wildlife Conservation Society, and in 1998 it joined the concert bill for Farm Aid. In 2000 the same lineup from the 1994 summer tour released the studio album *Sibling Rivalry.*

The Doors

Formed 1965, Los Angeles, CA
Jim Morrison (b. Dec. 8, 1943, Melbourne, FL; d. July 3, 1971, Paris, Fr.), voc.; Ray Manzarek (b. Feb. 12, 1935, Chicago, IL), kybds.; Robby Krieger (b. Jan. 8, 1946, Los Angeles), gtr.; John Densmore (b. Dec. 1, 1944, Los Angeles), drums.
1967—*The Doors* (Elektra); *Strange Days* 1968—*Waiting for the Sun* 1969—*The Soft Parade* 1970—*Morrison Hotel/Hard Rock Cafe; Absolutely Live; 13* 1971—*L.A. Woman* (– Morrison); *Other Voices* 1972—*Weird Scenes Inside the Gold Mine; Full Circle* 1973—*The Best of the Doors* 1978—*An American Prayer—Jim Morrison* 1980—*The Doors Greatest Hits* 1983—*Alive, She Cried* 1985—*Classics* 1987—*Live at the Hollywood Bowl* 1991—*Greatest Hits; The Doors* soundtrack; *In Concert* 1997—*Box Set* 1999—*The Complete Studio Recordings* 2000—*Essential Rarities; The Bright Midnight Sampler* (Bright Midnight) 2001—*Live in Detroit; No One Here Gets Out Alive.*
Robby Krieger solo: 1981—*Robby Krieger and Friends* (Capitol) 1983—*Versions* (Passport) 1988—*No Habla* (I.R.S.) 2000—*Cinematix* (Oglio).
Robby Krieger Organization: 1995—*RKO Live* (One Way).

The Doors: John Densmore, Robby Krieger, Ray Manzarek, Jim Morrison

Ray Manzarek solo: 1975—*The Whole Thing Started With Rock & Roll Now It's Out of Control* (Mercury); *The Golden Scarab.*

Sex, death, reptiles, charisma, and a unique variant of the electric blues gave the Doors an aura of profundity that not only survived but has grown during the 30 years since Jim Morrison's death. By themselves, Morrison's lyrics read like adolescent posturings, but with his sexually charged delivery, Ray Manzarek's dry organ, and Robby Krieger's jazzy guitar, they became eerie, powerful, almost shamanistic invocations that hinted at a familiarity with darker forces, and, in Morrison's case, an obsession with excess and death. At its best, the Doors' music—"Light My Fire," "L.A. Woman"—has come to evoke a noirish view of '60s California that contrasts sharply with the era's prevailing folky, trippy style.

Morrison and Manzarek, acquaintances from the UCLA Graduate School of Film, conceived the group at a 1965 meeting on a Southern California beach. After Morrison recited one of his poems, "Moonlight Drive," Manzarek—who had studied classical piano as a child and played in Rick and the Ravens, a UCLA blues band—suggested they collaborate on songs. Manzarek's brothers, Rick and Jim, served as guitarists until Manzarek met John Densmore, who brought in Robby Krieger; both had been members of the Psychedelic Rangers. Morrison christened the band the Doors, from William Blake via Aldous Huxley's book on mescaline, *The Doors of Perception.*

The Doors soon recorded a demo tape, and in the summer of 1966 they began working as the house band at the Whisky-a-Go-Go, a gig that ended four months later when they were fired for performing the explicitly Oedipal "The End," one of Morrison's many songs that included dramatic recitations. By then Jac Holzman of Elektra Records had been convinced by Arthur Lee of Love to sign the band.

An edited version of Krieger's "Light My Fire" from the Doors' debut album (#2, 1967) became a #1 hit in 1967, while "progressive" FM radio played (and analyzed) "The End." Morrison's image as the embodiment of dark psychological impulses was established quickly, even as he was being featured in such teen magazines as *16. Strange Days* (#3, 1967) and *Waiting for the Sun* (#1, 1968) both included hit singles and became best-selling albums. *Waiting for the Sun* also marked the first appearance of Morrison's mythic alter ego, the Lizard King, in a poem printed inside the record jacket entitled "The Celebration of the Lizard King." Though part of the poem was used as lyrics for "Not to Touch the Earth," a complete "Celebration" didn't appear on record until *Absolutely Live* (#8, 1970).

It was impossible to tell whether Morrison's Lizard King persona was a parody of a pop star or simply inspired exhibitionism, but it earned him considerable notoriety. In December 1967 he was arrested for public obscenity at a concert in New Haven, and in August 1968 he was arrested for disorderly conduct aboard an airplane en route to Phoenix. Not until his March 1969 arrest in Miami for exhibiting "lewd and lascivious behavior by exposing his private parts and by simulating masturbation and oral copulation" onstage did Morrison's behavior adversely affect the band. Court proceedings kept the singer in Miami most of the year although the prosecution could produce neither eyewitnesses nor photos of Morrison performing the acts. Charges were dropped, but public furor (which inspired a short-lived Rally for Decency movement), concert promoters' fear of similar incidents, and Morrison's own mixed feelings about celebrity resulted in erratic concert schedules thereafter.

The Soft Parade (#6, 1969), far more elaborately produced than the Doors' other albums, met with a mixed reception from fans, but it too had a #3 hit single, "Touch Me." Morrison began to devote more attention to projects outside the band: writing poetry, collaborating on a screenplay with poet Michael McClure, and directing a film, *A Feast of Friends* (he had also made films to accompany "Break On Through" and the 1968 single "The Unknown Soldier"). Simon & Schuster published *The Lords and the New Creatures* in 1971; an earlier book, *An American Prayer,* was privately printed in 1970 but not made widely available until 1978, when the surviving Doors regrouped and set Morrison's recitation of the poem to music. In 1989 *Wilderness: The Lost Writings of Jim Morrison* was published. Although Morrison expressed to friends and associates his wish to be remembered as a poet, overall his writings have found few fans among critics. By then some felt, especially after "Touch Me," that the band had sold out, and Morrison's dangerous persona was more often ridiculed than not. Critic Lester Bangs once tagged him "Bozo Dionysus."

Soon after *L.A. Woman* (#9, 1971) was recorded, Morrison took an extended leave of absence from the group. Obviously physically and emotionally drained, he moved to Paris, where he hoped to write and where he and his wife, Pamela Courson Morrison, lived in seclusion. He died of heart failure in his bathtub in 1971 at age 27. Partly because news of his death was not made public until days after his burial in Paris' Père-Lachaise cemetery, some still refuse to believe Morrison is dead. His wife, one of the few people who saw Morrison's corpse, died in Hollywood of a heroin overdose on April 25, 1974.

The Doors continued to record throughout 1973 as a trio, but after two albums it seemed they had exhausted the possibilities of a band without a commanding lead singer. Manzarek had hoped to reconstitute the group with Iggy Pop, whose avowed chief influence was Morrison, but plans fell through. After the Doors broke up, Manzarek recorded two solo albums, and one with a short-lived group called Nite City. He produced the first four albums by L.A.'s X, and in 1983 he collaborated with composer Philip Glass on a rock version of Carl Orff's modern cantata, *Carmina Burana*. Krieger and Densmore formed the Butts Band, which lasted three years and recorded two albums. In 1972 a Doors greatest-hits collection, *Weird Scenes Inside the Gold Mine* was released, hit #55, and went gold. Krieger released his first solo album in 1981 and toured in 1982.

Ironically, the group's best years began in 1980, nine years after Morrison's death. With the release of the Danny Sugerman–Jerry Hopkins biography of Morrison, *No One Here Gets Out Alive*, sales of the Doors' music and the already large Jim Morrison cult—spurred by his many admirers and imitators in new-wave bands—grew even more. Record sales for 1980 alone topped all previous figures; as one ROLLING STONE magazine cover line put it: "He's Hot, He's Sexy, He's Dead." And that was just the beginning. The 1983 release of *Alive, She Cried*, followed by MTV's airing of Doors videos, introduced Morrison and the band to a new generation, and Oliver Stone's 1991 film biography of the group, starring Val Kilmer as Morrison, was a critical and commercial success. The group was inducted into the Rock and Roll Hall of Fame in 1993. Pearl Jam's Eddie Vedder filled in for Morrison for the Doors' performance at the ceremonies.

The Morrison cult continues to grow, particularly among the young. In 1990 his graffiti-covered headstone was stolen; in 1993, on what would have been his 50th birthday, hundreds of mourners—many not even born before he died—traveled from around the world to pay tribute. Because of the destruction these visitors often wreak on the cemetery during their pilgrimages, many Parisians petitioned to move Morrison's grave when its 30-year lease expired in 2001; French officials, however, opted to leave Morrison's remains in their resting place.

A box set with material chosen by the band was released in 1997. Emphasizing live (the set starts off with the notorious version of "Five to One" recorded at the March '69 Miami concert) and lesser-known tracks ("Albinoni's Adagio in G Minor," a 25-minute free-form jam called "Rock Is Dead"), the four-disc set includes "Orange County Suite," a "Free as a Bird"–style song—i.e., new instrumental tracks were dubbed onto an old Morrison vocal. His vocals were resurrected yet again in 2000, when Fatboy Slim sampled Morrison's reading of "Bird of Prey" for a track on his album *Halfway Between the Gutter and the Stars*. That same year, VH1 taped an episode of its *Storytellers* series in which the Cult's Ian Astbury, Creed singer Scott Stapp, Stone Temple Pilot's Scott Weiland, Days of the New frontman Travis Meeks, and Perry Farrell took turns covering Doors songs. The singers were backed by the surviving members of the Doors; it was the first time the three had played together since their induction into the Rock and Roll Hall of Fame. The episode aired around the same time Elektra released *Stoned Immaculate: The Music of the Doors*, which featured Krieger, Manzarek, and Densmore participating in their own tribute album.

Capitalizing on the continual interest in the band, the Doors launched an Internet-based label, Bright Midnight Records, which released *The Bright Midnight Sampler* at the end of 2000. *The Doors Live in Detroit* and *No One Here Gets Out Alive*—a radio interview with the remaining Doors members that originally aired in 1980—followed in 2001.

Lee Dorsey

Born Dec. 24, 1924, New Orleans, LA; died Dec. 1, 1986, New Orleans
1966—*The New Lee Dorsey* (Amy) 1970—*Yes We Can* (Polydor) 1978—*Night People* (ABC) 1985—*Holy Cow!* (Arista).

New Orleans singer Lee Dorsey's dry voice fronted Allen Toussaint's songs ("Working in a Coal Mine," "Holy Cow") for over a decade. Dorsey had been a boxer and a Marine before signing with the Fury label at the start of the '60s. In late 1961 "Ya Ya" (later covered by John Lennon and others) hit #7. "Do Re Mi" did well (#27) three months later, but Dorsey's promising start was cut short by the collapse of his record company. He met Toussaint, who put him back on the charts in late 1965 with "Ride Your Pony," a moderate hit. The next year marked the zenith of Dorsey's career. His Amy Records releases included "Get Out of My Life Woman"; the loping Top 10 smash "Working in a Coal Mine" (a minor hit for Devo in 1981); and "Holy Cow" (later covered by the Band on *Moondog Matinee*), which rose to #23. Dorsey had two minor hits in 1967 ("My Old Car," "Go Go Girl"), then faded from view.

In 1969 he had another minor hit, "Everything I Do Gonna Be Funky." The following year Dorsey and Toussaint recorded *Yes We Can* ("Yes We Can Can") was later a hit for the Pointer Sisters) for Polydor Records. Dorsey remained active—mostly in New Orleans—throughout the '70s and made a guest appearance on the debut album by Southside Johnny and the Asbury Jukes. He signed with ABC Records in December 1977, and Toussaint wrote and produced all the songs on 1978's *Night People*. But ABC was sold, and Dorsey again found himself professionally adrift. In 1980 the Clash hired him to open a U.S. tour, and in 1985—and despite failing health—he performed at the annual Jazz and Heritage Festival in New Orleans. He died approximately a year and a half later after a battle with emphysema.

Doug E. Fresh

Born Douglas Davis, Sep. 17, 1966, New York, NY
1986—*Oh, My God!* (Reality) 1988—*The World's Greatest Entertainer* 1989—*Summertime* EP 1992—*Doin' What I Gotta Do* (Bust It) 1995—*Play* (Gee Street) 1996—*I-ight (Alright)* EP.

Doug E. Fresh's claim to fame as the "original human beat box" precedes his musical reputation. His vocal simulation of drums, computer blips, and telephone ringing briefly encouraged a few other rappers in the mid-'80s; by the '90s the technique had become a dated novelty.

Doug Davis' initial version of Doug E. Fresh and the Get Fresh Crew consisted of Ricky D. (who soon left to chart his own career as Slick Rick [see entry]) and the double-DJ team of Barry Bee and Chill Will. But Rick stayed long enough to appear on the group's first smash single, "The Show" (#4 R&B), in 1985, before the debut album was released. By the time *Oh, My God!* came out the next year, Davis had found religion. Subsequent singles failed to catch fire as "The Show" had, although "All the Way to Heaven" went to #19 R&B. "Lovin' Ev'ry Minute of It" reached only #38, and "Play This Only at Night" failed even to make it into the Top 40. Doug E. Fresh scored a minor comeback in 1988 with "Keep Risin' to the Top" (#17 R&B), from *The World's Greatest Entertainer.*

While Doug E. Fresh was no longer seen as a cutting edge hip-hop artist in the era of gangsta rap, his albums at least continued to land on the nether reaches of the R&B chart: 1992's *Doin' What I Gotta Do* made it to #47, and 1995's *Play* reached #81. By the end of the '90s, the old-school rapper was recruited into a traveling roadshow headed by Prince. Doug E. Fresh closed the decade by appearing on one of Prince's many timely new renditions of his "1999."

Carl Douglas

Born Jamaica
1974—*Kung Fu Fighting and Other Great Love Songs* (20th Century–Fox) 1995—*Kung Fu Fighting: The Best of Carl Douglas* (Hot) 2000—*Soul of the Kung Fu Fighter* (Castle).

A 4,000-year-old Chinese martial art and a reggae-tinged disco beat provided Carl Douglas the inspiration for his gold hit record, "Kung Fu Fighting." Douglas, a Jamaican raised in the United States and England, got into the record business while studying engineering in London in the early '60s.

His British-based career as a singer and composer was undistinguished (the soundtrack to the 1972 movie *Embassy* was his major accomplishment) until he cut "Kung Fu Fighting." The song hit first in England, where it made #1 in August 1974. By October it had reached that position on American R&B charts, soon hitting #1 on the pop charts too. It inspired a dance step, the Kung Fu. Douglas appeared only once more on American charts—with a followup, "Dance the Kung Fu," in 1975 (#48 pop, #8 R&B)—but he continued to have hits in England, where "Run Back" made the Top 30 in 1977. Since then, little has been heard from Douglas. "Kung Fu Fighting" was covered in concert by Robyn Hitchcock and the Egyptians in 1993.

The Dovells

Formed 1959, Philadelphia, PA
Original lineup: Len Barry (b. Leonard Borisoff, Dec. 6, 1942, Philadelphia), lead voc.; Arnie Satin (b. Arnie Silver, May 11, 1943), baritone voc.; Jerry Summers (b. Jerry Gross, Dec. 29, 1942), first tenor voc.; Mike Dennis (b. Mike Freda, June 3, 1943), second tenor voc.; Danny Brooks (b. John Mealey, Apr. 1, 1942; d. early 1970s), bass voc.; Mark Stevens (b. Mark Gordesky), tenor voc.
1961—*Bristol Stomp* (Parkway) 1962—*All the Hits for Your Hully Gully Party* 1963—*You Can't Sit Down; Biggest Hits* (Wyncote).

The Dovells were an early-'60s white doo-wop group, formed by students of Philadelphia's Overbrook High School (thus, their first name, the Brooktones). As the Dovells, the group's string of dance hits began in late 1961 with the #2 hit, "Bristol Stomp." Their 1962 hits included "Do the New Continental" (#37), "Bristol Twistin' Annie" (#27), and "Hully Gully Baby" (#25). They reached #3 in 1963 with "You Can't Sit Down." But subsequent releases on Cameo Parkway went nowhere. In their heyday, the Dovells frequently toured as part of Dick Clark's road revue.

In 1965 lead singer Len Barry had several hits, the biggest being "1-2-3," produced by Leon Huff. Barry was known for his wild, manic stage manner, modeled after James Brown's. When the hits stopped coming, he toned down his style and hit the supper-club circuit. The Dovells continued to tour and record through 1974. The 1968 novelty hit, "Here Comes the Judge," was recorded by Dennis and Summers, with a female lead singer, as the Magistrates. Stevens, Summers, and various singers continue to perform as the Dovells. In the '90s they appeared at both of President Bill Clinton's inaugural balls, joined by Clinton himself on sax. The Dovells reunited with Barry twice in 1991.

Nick Drake

Born June 18, 1948, Burma; died Nov. 25, 1974, Birmingham, Eng.
1969—*Five Leaves Left* (Island) 1970—*Bryter Layter* 1972—*Pink Moon* 1979—*Fruit Tree: The Complete Works of Nick Drake* 1994—*Way to Blue.*

Since Nick Drake's death, his eerie, jazz-tinged folk music has had an ever-growing cult following. Born to British parents, Drake spent his first two years on the Indian subcontinent before moving to the English village of Tanworth-in-Arden. He played saxophone and clarinet in school but turned to the guitar at age 16. Two years later he began writing his own songs. He was a student at Cambridge Univer-

Nick Drake

sity in 1968, when Ashley Hutchings of Fairport Convention heard him performing at London's Roundhouse. Hutchings introduced him to Joe Boyd, who managed Fairport, John Martyn, and other leaders of the British folk revival. Boyd immediately signed Drake to Island Records and put him on Witchseason concert bills. In 1970 Elton John was hired as a session vocalist to record Drake's songs to use as demos to entice established singers to covet Drake's compositions.

Drake was a shy, awkward performer and remained aloof from the public and press. By all accounts his isolation and confusion, results of severe mental illness that at times would leave him catatonic and requiring hospitalizations, grew more severe. By the end of 1970 he had stopped doing concerts. He lived for a short while in Paris at the behest of Françoise Hardy (who never released the recordings she made of his songs) and then settled in Hampstead, where he became increasingly reclusive, allowing the company of only his close friends John and Beverly Martyn. He recorded *Pink Moon* totally unaccompanied, submitted the tapes to Island by mail, and entered a psychiatric rest home. When he left the home months later, vowing never to sing another song, he got a job as a computer programmer. In 1973 he began writing songs again. Drake had recorded four when he died in bed at his parents' home in 1974, the victim of an overdose of antidepressant medication. Suicide was considered probable by the coroner, but Drake's friends and family disagreed. *Fruit Tree* is a box set containing his three albums plus the four songs recorded in 1973. In 2000 Drake's music reached a much larger audience than during his lifetime after Volkswagen used his "Pink Moon" in a car commercial, which greatly spurred sales of his recordings. This music also turned up on a few film soundtracks and became the subject of tributes performed by such artists as Duncan Sheik. Drake's original albums were remastered and repackaged on CD in late 2000.

The Dream Academy

Formed 1983, London, Eng.
Gilbert Gabriel (b. Nov. 16, 1956, Paddington, London), kybds.; Nick Laird-Clowes (b. Feb. 5, 1957, London), voc., gtr.; Kate St. John (b. Oct. 2, 1957, London), voc., oboe, sax.
1985—*The Dream Academy* (Warner Bros.) 1987—*Remembrance Days* (Reprise) 1990—*A Different Kind of Weather.*
Nick Laird-Clowes solo, as Trashmonk: 1999—*Mona Lisa Overdrive* (Creation).
Kate St. John solo: 1995—*Indescribable Night* (Gyroscope) 1997—*Second Sight* (Thirsty Ear).
Kate St. John with Channel Light Vessel: 1994—*Automatic* (Gyroscope) 1996—*Excellent Spirits.*

In the mid-'80s the Dream Academy was among a wave of British acts whose elegant, arty reexamination of psychedelic textures foreshadowed the retro-mania that would consume guitar rock a few years later. In fact, the Academy's self-titled debut album was produced by Pink Floyd's David Gilmour. That album's hit single, 1985's "Life in a Northern Town" (#7), was an unabashedly nostalgic ballad, littered with references to John F. Kennedy and the Beatles.

The three band members were all children of the '60s and had been inspired by what they viewed as pop music's textural eclecticism and daring during that decade's later part. But even as he dressed in velvet suits with Nehru collars, Academy singer/guitarist Nick Laird-Clowes—who shared songwriting duties with keyboardist Gilbert Gabriel—insisted that the band's delicate, diversely textured songs were more contemporary than some of its critics maintained. In any case, the trio released two more albums that generally echoed the first in terms of their arrangements and production values, but neither was commercially successful.

St. John later joined Van Morrison's touring revue and married American singer/songwriter Sid Griffin (ex–Long Ryders). She became a sought-after session musician for such artists as Julian Cope and Blur, formed an avant-garde instrumentalist collective with Roger Eno, among others, and recorded two solo albums in the late '90s. Gabriel formed the band the Color of Love; after releasing two singles under that name in the mid-'90s, the group started fresh with the moniker Futura. Laird-Clowes, who'd found spiritual enlightenment at a Tibetan Buddhist monastery in the Himalayas, dabbled in songwriting, cowriting a track with Gilmour for the 1994 Pink Floyd album *The Division Bell.* He returned to recording in the late '90s, having been signed to a six-album deal with England's Creation Records. His first release, *Mona Lisa Overdrive,* was released under the pseudonym Trashmonk in 1999. In addition, he successfully sued Dario G, who had sampled the "Life in a Northern Town" 's chorus on the 1998 dance hit "Sunchyme"; he won 80 percent of that song's royalties.

The Dream Syndicate/Steve Wynn

Formed 1981, Los Angeles, CA
Steve Wynn (b. Feb. 21, 1960, Santa Monica, CA), gtr., voc.; Karl Precoda (b. ca. 1961), gtr.; Kendra Smith (b. Mar. 14, 1960, San Diego), bass; Dennis Duck (b. Mar. 25, 1953), drums.
1982—*The Dream Syndicate* EP (Down There); *The Days of Wine and Roses* (Ruby) 1983—*Tell Me When It's Over* EP (Rough Trade) (– Smith; + Dave Provost, bass) 1984—*Medicine Show* (A&M); *This Is Not the New Dream Syndicate Album . . . Live!* EP (– Precoda; + Paul Cutler [b. Aug. 5, 1954, Phoenix, AZ], gtr.; – Provost; + Mark Walton [b. Aug. 9, 1959, Fairfield, CA], bass) 1986—*Out of the Grey* (Big Time) 1987—*50 in a 25 Zone* EP 1988—*Ghost Stories* (Enigma) 1989—*Live at Raji's* (Restless) 1992—*Tell Me When It's Over: The Best of Dream Syndicate (1982–1988)* (Rhino) 1993—*3 1/2: The Lost Tapes (1985–1988)* (Normal/Atavistic) 1995—*The Day Before Wine and Roses: Live at KPFK.*
Steve Wynn solo: 1990—*Kerosene Man* (RNA/Rhino) 1992—*Dazzling Display* 1994—*Fluorescent; Take Your Flunky and Dangle* (Normal/Innerstate) 1996—*Melting in the Dark* (Zero Hour); *The Suitcase Sessions* (Normal, Ger.) 1998—*Sweetness and Light* (Zero Hour) 1999—*My Midnight; Pick of the Litter* (Glitterhouse, Ger.) 2001—*Here Come the Miracles* (Innerstate).
Steve Wynn with Danny and Dusty: 1985—*The Lost Weekend* (A&M).
Steve Wynn with Gutterball: 1993—*Gutterball* (Mute) 1995—*Weasel* (Brakeout/Enemy); *Turnyor Hedinkov* (Normal).
Kendra Smith solo: 1992—*Kendra Smith Presents the Guild of Temporal Adventures* (Fiasco) 1995—*Five Ways of Disappearing* (4AD).
Kendra Smith with Opal: 1985—*Northern Line* EP (One Big Guitar) 1987—*Happy Nightmare Baby* (SST) 1989—*Early Recordings* (Rough Trade).

The Dream Syndicate put L.A.'s early-'80s "paisley underground" on the national music map. The group blended Steve Wynn's Dylanesque poetizing with a potpourri of '60s instrumental influences, including feedback-drenched psychedelia, a Velvet Underground drone, and flat-out, Stooges-like rock attacks.

Steve Wynn met Kendra Smith at the University of California's Davis campus in 1981. Within a year, the two moved to L.A. and formed the Dream Syndicate with Karl Precoda and Dennis Duck. The group's self-released debut EP attracted the attention of L.A.'s thriving underground music scene, but it was the full-length *Days of Wine and Roses* that earned the Syndicate a national following. By the time *Medicine Show* appeared on A&M in 1984, Smith had quit the band and Wynn had let his hair grow out and had the band sounding a lot closer to Jim Morrison than to the Velvets. The group's hometown supporters cried "sellout," but the album was highly praised in some corners for its continued commitment to rock & roll. The next year, Wynn recorded *The Lost Weekend* as part of Danny and Dusty, a side project with Dan Stuart of Green on Red.

The Dream Syndicate regrouped for its 1986 comeback, *Out of the Grey,* which moved closer to a Neil Young–inspired cow-punk sound. Among the new members was former 45 Grave guitarist Paul Cutler, whose fiery lead work and use of various kitchen utensils along the guitar strings brought new intensity to the band's stage show. Wynn and company went so far as to recruit former Young producer Elliot Mazer for their bare-bones followup, *Ghost Stories. Live at Raji's,* which was recorded in early 1989 at a favorite L.A. punk-rock dive, spelled the end of the Dream Syndicate.

Wynn immediately embarked on a solo career, recruiting a host of musicians to help out on his highly personal *Kerosene Man,* followed by the critically acclaimed *Dazzling Display.* In 1993 Wynn's garagey supergroup Gutterball (also featuring Johnny Hott and Bryan Harvey, formerly of House of Freaks; Stephen McCarthy, ex–Long Ryders; and Bob Rupe, formerly of the Silos) released its self-titled debut, but the next year Wynn returned to his solo work, and by 1995 had left L.A. for New York. His 1996 album *Melting in the Dark* was a hard-rocking collaboration with Boston's Come. And he was joined by an alt-rock all-star band (Hott, Come guitarist Chris Brokaw, Pere Ubu bassist Tony Maimone, keyboardist Joe McGinty of the Psychedelic Furs, among others) for 1999's *My Midnight.*

Meanwhile, Kendra Smith joined David Roback in Opal (which later evolved into Mazzy Star) long enough to appear on two EPs and 1987's *Happy Nightmare Baby* (SST). She then relocated to a solar-powered homestead in rural Northern California, and despite deep reservations with the music industry, she eventually released the acclaimed *Five Ways of Disappearing,* an atmospheric solo album built on haunting pump organ and acoustic guitar.

Interest in the Dream Syndicate continued in the '90s, with the release of two albums of unreleased tracks and a live radio performance. And in 1996 *Out of the Grey* was reissued by Normal/Atavistic with bonus tracks.

The Drifters/Clyde McPhatter

Formed 1953, New York, NY
Clyde McPhatter (b. Clyde Lensley McPhatter, Nov. 15, 1933, Durham, NC; d. June 13, 1972, Bronx, NY), lead voc.; David "Little David" Baughan (b. New York; d. 1970), tenor voc.; William Anderson, tenor voc.; David Baldwin, baritone voc.; James Johnson, bass voc.

1953—(– Baughan; – Anderson; – Baldwin; – Johnson; + Billy Pinkney [b. Aug. 15, 1925, Dalzell, SC], tenor voc.; + Andrew "Bubba" Thrasher [b. Wetumpka, AL], baritone voc.; + Gerhart "Gay" Thrasher [b. Wetumpka], tenor voc.; + Willie Ferbee, bass voc.; – Ferbee; Pinkney moves to bass voc.) 1954—(– McPhatter; + Baughan, lead voc.; 1955—(– Baughan; + Johnny Moore [b. 1934, Selma, AL; d. Dec. 30, 1998, London], tenor voc.) 1956—(– A. Thrasher; – Pinkney; + "Carnation" Charlie Hughes, baritone voc.; + Tommy Evans [b. 1927, New York; d. 1981], bass voc.) 1957—(– Moore; – Hughes; + Bobby Hendricks [b. 1937, Columbus, OH], lead voc.; + Jimmy Millinder, baritone voc.) 1958—(group disbands; new lineup: Charlie Thomas, tenor voc.; Ben E. King [b. Benjamin Earl Nelson, Sep. 23, 1938, Henderson, NC], tenor voc.; Dock [a.k.a. Doc] Green [b. Oct. 8, 1934; d. Mar. 10, 1989, New York], baritone voc.; Elsbeary Hobbs, bass) 1959—(+ Johnny Lee Williams, tenor voc.) 1960—(– King; + James Poindexter, tenor voc; – Poindexter; + Rudy Lewis [d. 1964], tenor voc.; – Hobbs; + William Van Dyke, bass voc.; – Van Dyke; + George Grant, bass voc.; – Grant; + Tommy Evans, bass voc.) 1962—(– Green; + Gene Pearson [b. Sep. 15, 1935, Brooklyn, NY; d. Apr. 6, 2000, Silver Springs, MD], baritone voc.) 1963—(– Evans; + Johnny Terry, bass voc.; + J. Moore, voc.) 1964—(– Lewis) 1966—(– Terry; + Dan Danbridge, bass voc.; – Danbridge; + William Brent, bass voc.; – Pearson; + Rick Sheppard, baritone voc.) 1967—(numerous personnel changes follow) 1968—*The Drifters' Golden Hits* (Atlantic) 1988—*Let the Boogie Woogie Roll: Greatest Hits 1953–1958; 1959–1965 All-Time Greatest Hits and More* 1994—(lineup: Charlie Thomas, lead voc.; Barry Hobbs [d. May 31, 1996], bass voc.; Terry King, voc.)
Clyde McPhatter solo: 1991—*Deep Sea Ball: The Best of Clyde McPhatter* (Atlantic).

The Drifters helped create soul music by bringing gospel-styled vocals to secular material. Literally scores of singers (like Clyde McPhatter and Ben E. King) worked with this durable institution. After McPhatter left Billy Ward and His Dominoes [see entry], Atlantic Records' Ahmet Ertegun encouraged the singer to put together his own vocal group. According to an early press release and rock lore, the Drifters' name came from the fact that the original members had drifted from one group to another. The truth is that several members of the first lineup were discovered by McPhatter singing with the Mount Lebanon Singers at the Mount Lebanon Church in Harlem. In fact, they chose to name themselves after a bird called the drifter. Clyde McPhatter, already known to the record-buying public, propelled the group to immediate success. He was among the first to apply the emotional fervency of gospel to pop songs about romance, a stylistic keystone in the creation of modern R&B and soul. At its peak, the first set of Drifters was an extremely popular and influential live act, not only for its stellar vocals but for its flashy choreography. After a string of hits—"Money Honey" (#1 R&B, 1953), later covered by Elvis Presley; "Such a Night" (#2 R&B, 1954); "Honey Love" (#21 pop, #1 R&B, 1954); "White Christmas" (#80 pop, #2 R&B, 1954); "Whatcha Gonna Do" (#2 R&B, 1955)—McPhatter was drafted into the army in late 1954.

Following McPhatter's departure, lead vocals fell briefly to "Little" David Baughan before Bill Pinkney discovered Johnny Moore singing in Cleveland. Although McPhatter and Ben E. King are most often recalled as the group's important lead singers, Moore proved the longest-lasting and enduring of the three vocalists. Moore-led singles of this period include "Hypnotized" and "Fools Fall in Love," but they were not enough to buoy the flagging group. Other personnel changes occurred, hits became rarer, and Moore and Hughes were drafted in 1957. Group morale was at an all-time low, and so when manager George Treadwell, who owned the group's name, heard a young, new group called the Crowns at the Apollo Theatre one night, he fired the entire Drifters lineup and christened his discoveries the new Drifters.

This lineup, which featured three lead tenors and included Ben E. King, proved even more successful than the original group. The Drifters were assigned to producer/writers Mike Leiber and Jerry Stoller, and their first release, "There Goes My Baby," was a #2 hit in 1959. The lushly produced song's style—incorporating orchestral strings, a gentle Latin rhythm, and King's yearning, romantic lead—became the Drifters' calling card. King was featured on "This Magic Moment" (#16 pop, #4 R&B, 1960), "Save the Last Dance for Me" (#1 pop, #1 R&B, 1960), and "I Count the Tears" (#17 pop, #6 R&B, 1961), but shortly after "Save the Last Dance for Me" hit in October 1960, he left for a solo career [see entry].

Over the next two years, leads on Drifters hits would be split among Rudy Lewis ("Some Kind of Wonderful" [#32 pop, #6 R&B, 1961], "Please Stay" [#14 pop, #13 R&B, 1961], "Up on the Roof" [#5 pop, #4 R&B, 1962], and "On Broadway" [#9 pop, #7 R&B, 1963], Charlie Thomas ("Sweets for My Sweet" [#16 pop, #10 R&B, 1961]), and Johnny Moore ("I'll Take You Home" [#25 pop, #24 R&B, 1963] and "Under the Boardwalk" [#4 pop, #4 R&B, 1964]). During the two years following the recording of 1961's "Some Kind of Wonderful," additional backing vocals on record were provided by a quartet consisting of Dionne and Dede Warwick, their aunt, Cissy Houston (mother of Whitney), and Doris Troy (of "Just One Look" fame). Lewis died suddenly in 1964; his last-released single was "Vaya con Dios." From 1964 on, Moore dominated the Drifters' hits, which although produced by Bert Berns (as was "Under the Boardwalk") retained the sound of the Leiber and Stoller hits and gave the group a consistency regardless of who was in the lineup. The Drifters kept placing R&B chart hits ("I've Got Sand in My Shoes," "Saturday Night at the Movies") through the '60s while playing the club circuit. Although the group never had another major U.S. hit after that, a reissue of their 1965 single "Come On Over to My Place" went to #9 in the U.K., where the group has enjoyed a large, loyal following since 1960 when "Dance With Me" went to #17 there.

When the Drifters' Atlantic contract expired in 1972, Moore, with a new lineup, moved to England, where they signed with the Bell label and released a string of U.K. Top 10 hits: "Like Sister and Brother" (#7, 1973), "Kissin' in the Back Row of the Movies" (#2, 1974), "Down on the Beach Tonight" (#7, 1974), "There Goes My First Love" (#3, 1975), "Can I Take You Home Little Girl" (#10, 1975), and "You're More Than a Number in My Little Red Book" (#5, 1976).

At the same time, here in America and elsewhere in the world, any number of Drifters aggregations could be found performing in nightclubs. The group's many members have included at least one past or future Swallow, Carol, Raven, Diamond, DuDropper, Turban, Ink Spot, Cadillac, Cleftone, Domino, Royal Joker, or Temptation. One version of the group was founded by Pinkney, included the Thrashers and Ferbee (of the '53-era group), and called itself the Original Drifters.

McPhatter emerged from his two years in the service in 1955 to relaunch his solo career. With Atlantic Records' full support, he quickly charted with a duet with Ruth Brown ("Love Has Joined Us Together" [#8, 1955]). His other hits included "Treasure of Love" (#16 pop, #1 R&B, 1956), "Without Love (There Is Nothing)" (#19 pop, #4 R&B, 1957), "Just to Hold My Hand" (#26 pop, #6 R&B, 1957), "A Lover's Question" (#6 pop, #1 R&B, 1958), "Come What May" (#3 R&B, 1958), "Since You've Been Gone" (#38 pop, # 14 R&B, 1959), "Ta Ta" (#23 pop, #7 R&B, 1960), "Lover Please" (#7 pop, 1962), and the #1 R&B hit, "Long Lonely Nights" (1957).

Although McPhatter had a few more hits after leaving Atlantic, he never regained a commercial foothold after the mid-'60s. He lived in England for a couple of years in the late '60s, but in 1972 succumbed to a heart attack after years of alcoholism. He was inducted into the Rock and Roll Hall of Fame in 1987; the Drifters were inducted in 1988.

Duran Duran

Formed 1978, Birmingham, Eng.
Nick Rhodes (b. Nicholas Bates, June 8, 1962, Birmingham), kybds.; John Taylor (b. June 20, 1960, Birmingham), bass, gtr.; Stephen Duffy, voc., gtr.; Simon Colley, bass, clarinet.
1978—(– Duffy; – Colley; + Andy Wickett, voc.; + Roger Taylor [b. Apr. 26, 1960, Birmingham], drums) 1979—(– Wickett; + John Curtis, gtr.; + various vocalists) 1980—(– Curtis; + Andy Taylor [b. Feb. 16, 1961, Dolver-Hampton, Eng.], gtr., synth.; + Simon Le Bon [b. Oct. 27, 1958, Bushey, Eng.], voc.) 1981—*Duran Duran* (Harvest) 1982—*Rio; Carnival* EP 1983—*Seven and the Ragged Tiger* (Capitol) 1984—*Arena* (– R. Taylor; – A. Taylor) 1986—*Notorious* 1988—*Big Thing* 1989—*Decade* (+ Warren Cuccurullo [b. Dec. 8, 1956], gtr.; + Sterling Campbell, drums) 1990—*Liberty* (– Campbell) 1993—*Duran Duran (The Wedding Album)* 1995—*Thank You* 1996—(– J. Taylor) 1997—*Medazzaland* 1998—*Greatest* 2000—*Pop Trash* (Hollywood) 2001—(– Cuccurullo; + J. Taylor; + A. Taylor; + R. Taylor).
Arcadia (Le Bon; Rhodes; R. Taylor): 1985—*So Red the Rose* (Capitol).
Andy Taylor solo: 1987—*Thunder* (MCA) 1990—*Dangerous* (A&M, U.K.).
The Power Station (A. Taylor; J. Taylor; Robert Palmer [b. Alan Palmer, Jan. 19, 1949, Batley, Eng.], voc.; Tony Thompson, drums): 1985—*The Power Station* (Capitol) 1996—(– J. Taylor) 1997—*Living in Fear* (Angel/Guardian).
John Taylor solo: 1996—*Feelings Are Good and Other Lies* (B5).

Duran Duran was one of several British New Romantic bands—that being a fashion-conscious merger of new wave and disco. The movement itself never really caught on in the U.S., but Duran Duran, thanks in part to provocative videos that soon became an MTV staple, quickly became one of the biggest acts of the mid-'80s, with nine Top 10 hits, three platinum albums, and a string of sold-out concert tours.

Named after a character in Roger Vadim's sex-kitten sci-fi movie *Barbarella,* Duran Duran began as Nick Rhodes, John Taylor, vocalist Stephen Duffy (who eventually went solo and formed the Lilac Time), bassist Simon Colley, and a drum machine. Following numerous lineup changes, Andy Taylor (none of the Taylors in the band are related) joined them when he answered an ad in *Melody Maker.* Simon Le Bon met the group through a friend of his who worked at Duran Duran's preferred hangout the Rum Runner, a club at which Rhodes had been a DJ. The band's debut single, "Planet Earth," was a hit in Europe in 1981; "Hungry Like the Wolf" (#3), "Rio" (#14), "Is There Something I Should Know" (#4), and "Union of the Snake" (#3) broke the U.S. charts in 1983. Lead singer Le Bon became a popular pinup boy among British and U.S. teens, and the group achieved notoriety for its videos, particularly Godley and Creme's "Girls on Film," which featured female models in various stages of undress. (Andy Warhol once remarked that he masturbated to Duran Duran videos.) The clip was banned by BBC-TV and, in the U.S., by MTV. *Seven and the Ragged Tiger,* which included the hits "New Moon on Monday" (#10, 1984) and "The Reflex" (#1, 1984), went to #1 in the U.K., hit #4 stateside, and was later certified double platinum.

The next album, the live *Arena,* also hit #4. It included a studio single "The Wild Boys" (#2, 1984) and a concert version of "Save a Prayer" (#16, 1985). In spring 1985 the group's title theme song to the James Bond film *A View to a Kill* became its second #1 hit. By then Duran Duran had become almost as familiar to readers of fashion magazines and society columns as to rock fans. Both Nick Rhodes (in 1984) and Simon Le Bon (in 1985) married models, and the latter made international news when his racing boat capsized in 1985. During interviews in the '90s, Duran Duran's members spoke frankly about their glory years being full of emotional turmoil, drug abuse, and a general loss of creative and financial control.

The strain took its toll, as during the year and a half that followed "A View to a Kill," John Taylor and Andy Taylor joined with singer Robert Palmer and Chic drummer Tony Thompson to form the Power Station, which had two of the biggest hits of spring 1985, "Some Like It Hot" (#6) and "Get It On" (#9), the latter a retread of the T. Rex classic "Bang a Gong (Get It On)." Meanwhile, Rhodes, Le Bon, and Roger Taylor formed Arcadia, and in late 1985 had a #6 hit with "Election Day," which included narration by Grace Jones.

The followup single, "Goodbye Is Forever," peaked at #33, and the album, *So Red the Rose* (#23), was certified platinum.

That summer Duran Duran appeared together at the U.S. Live Aid concert, but did not release a new studio album until *Notorious* (#12), which arrived late in 1986. Earlier that year, Roger Taylor announced he was taking a year off from the group; he did not return until 2001. That spring Andy Taylor left to pursue a solo career; he had a Top 30 hit earlier in '86 with "Take It Easy." John Taylor's "I Do What I Do" was also a 1986 Top 30 single, but he remained with Duran Duran through 1996. *Notorious* spawned "Notorious" (#2, 1987) and "Skin Trade" (#39, 1987). *Big Thing* featured "I Don't Want Your Love" (#4, 1988) and "All She Wants Is" (#22, 1989).

Although Duran Duran continued to make interesting videos, its commercial hold started to slip. The greatest-hits *Decade* peaked at #67, and *Liberty* did not enter the Top 40 and contained no substantial hits. *Duran Duran* (#7, 1993), released after the addition of former Missing Persons guitarist Warren Cuccurullo, marked a comeback with the singles "Ordinary World" (#3, 1993) and "Come Undone" (#7, 1993).

The 1995 followup, *Thank You* (#19), an album of covers, included a stab at Grandmaster Flash and the Furious Five's "White Lines (Don't Do It)." The two groups joined forces for a performance on *The Late Show With David Letterman*. Roger Taylor guested on Duran Duran's version of Lou Reed's "Perfect Day." The next year John Taylor left to form the one-album, hard-rock supergroup Neurotic Outsiders with ex–Sex Pistols guitarist Steve Jones and members of Guns n' Roses. He bailed out on a Power Station reunion shortly before the project unveiled its 1997 sophomore album, *Living in Fear*. He subsequently resumed his solo career, appeared in films, and led a band called Terroristen.

Le Bon, Rhodes, and Cuccurullo completed 1997's *Medazzaland* (#58), which included the single "Electric Barbarella" (#52). The following year they parted ways with Capitol/EMI, their label of 18 years, and signed a multialbum deal with Hollywood Records. The first fruit of that union, *Pop Trash*, hit stores in spring 2000. Since its inception, Duran Duran has sold over 60 million records worldwide. It was announced in mid-2001 that the original lineup had reformed to record an album for a 2002 release.

Ian Dury

Born May 12, 1942, Upminster, Eng.; died Mar. 27, 2000, London, Eng.
1975—*Handsome* (Dawn, U.K.) 1977—*New Boots and Panties!!* (Stiff) 1978—*Wotabunch* (Warner Bros.) 1979—*Do It Yourself* (Stiff) 1980—*Laughter* 1981—*Lord Upminster* (Polydor); *Juke Box Dury* (Stiff) 1992—*Sex & Drugs & Rock & Roll: The Best of Ian Dury and the Blockheads* (Rhino); *Bus Driver's Prayer & Other* (Demon, U.K.) 1998—*Mr. Love Pants* (CNR).

Though his Cockney accent eluded American audiences, Ian Dury became a superstar in Great Britain with a good-natured mix of pop, funk, reggae, music hall, and general boisterousness.

Stricken by polio at the age of seven, Dury spent two years in the hospital and several more in a school for the physically disabled. He studied at the Royal College of Art and taught painting at the Canterbury Art College. In 1970 he formed his first group, Kilburn and the High Roads, a band specializing in '50s rock & roll spiced with bebop jazz. The High Roads established themselves on the pub circuit, and in 1973 Dury quit teaching.

The group's songs won the support of some influential British critics, among them Charlie Gillett, who became the High Roads' manager. They cut an album for Raft Records, a subsidiary of Warner Bros., but Warners blocked its release until 1978. They released an album on Dawn, a Pye label, before disbanding in 1975. Dury and High Roads pianist/guitarist Chaz Jankel continued to write songs together. Under Dury's name they recorded *New Boots and Panties!!* with session musicians and former High Roaders such as saxophonist Davey Payne. Then, invited to join the Live Stiffs package tour of Britain in the fall of 1977, Dury and Jankel assembled the Blockheads: Payne, bassist Norman Watt Roy, drummer Charley Charles, pianist Mickey Gallagher, and guitarist John Turnbull. *New Boots* eventually sold over a million copies worldwide, staying on the British chart for almost two years: "What a Waste" reached #9 in 1978, and a later single, "Hit Me With Your Rhythm Stick," hit #1.

In 1978 Arista released *New Boots* in America. Sales were unimpressive, and Arista dropped the contract. Back home, *Do It Yourself* entered the charts at #2 on its mid-1979 release, and "Reasons to Be Cheerful (Part 3)" went to #3. The Blockheads' 1979 tour of Britain included an appearance at the Concerts for Kampuchea. When the tour ended, Jankel left the band; he was replaced by Wilko Johnson, formerly of Dr. Feelgood. After signing with Polydor, Dury reunited with Jankel, who traveled with him to the Bahamas to record *Lord Upminster* with Sly Dunbar and Robbie Shakespeare. Included on that album was a single, "Spasticus Autisticus," written for the United Nations Year of the Disabled but rejected.

Dury recorded less frequently, turning his attention to acting and writing music for British television programs and commercials. He has acted on stage, on television, and in film (including in *The Cook, the Thief, His Wife and Her Lover*, 1989). With Gallagher he wrote *Apples*, a musical in which he also starred, and he also hosted the U.K. late-night program *Metro*.

In May 1998, as he celebrated his 56th birthday, Dury disclosed to the public that he had been battling colon cancer for several years. He gave countless interviews about his illness, aiming to offer hope to other cancer patients, and he also continued to make many appearances for UNICEF and a variety of other charities. He seemed to have renewed energy, and in 1998 the re-formed Blockheads released *Mr. Love Pants* and toured England for the first time since the early '80s. Dury died in March 2000 at the age of 57. Just six weeks before his death he had performed with the Blockheads at London's Palladium.

Bob Dylan

Bob Dylan

Born Robert Allen Zimmerman, May 24, 1941, Duluth, MN
1962—*Bob Dylan* (Columbia) 1963—*The Freewheelin' Bob Dylan* 1964—*The Times They Are a-Changin'; Another Side of Bob Dylan* 1965—*Bringing It All Back Home; Highway 61 Revisited* 1966—*Blonde on Blonde* 1967—*Bob Dylan's Greatest Hits; John Wesley Harding* 1969—*Nashville Skyline* 1970—*Self Portrait; New Morning* 1971—*Bob Dylan's Greatest Hits, vol. 2* 1973—*Pat Garrett & Billy the Kid; Dylan* 1974—*Planet Waves* (Asylum); *Before the Flood* 1975—*Blood on the Tracks* (Columbia); *The Basement Tapes* 1976—*Desire; Hard Rain* 1978—*Bob Dylan at Budokan; Street Legal* 1979—*Slow Train Coming* 1980—*Saved* 1981—*Shot of Love* 1983—*Infidels* 1984—*Real Live* 1985—*Empire Burlesque; Biograph* 1986—*Knocked Out Loaded* 1988—*Down in the Groove* 1989—*Oh Mercy; Dylan & the Dead* (with the Grateful Dead) 1990—*Under the Red Sky* 1991—*The Bootleg Series, vols. 1–3 (Rare & Unreleased) 1961–1991* 1992—*Good As I Been to You* 1993—*The 30th Anniversary Concert Celebration* (with other artists); *World Gone Wrong* 1994—*Dylan's Greatest Hits, vol. 3* 1995—*Unplugged* 1997—*Time Out of Mind* 1998—*The Bootleg Series, vol. 4: Bob Dylan LIVE 1966: The "Royal Albert Hall" Concert* 2000—*The Essential Bob Dylan.*

For over 40 years, Bob Dylan has remained the most influential American musician rock has ever produced and unquestionably the most important of the '60s. Inscrutable and unpredictable, Dylan has been both deified and denounced for every shift of interest, while whole schools of musicians took up his ideas. His lyrics—the first in rock to be seriously regarded as literature—became so well known that politicians from Jimmy Carter to Václav Havel have cited them as an influence. By personalizing folk songs, Dylan reinvented the singer/songwriter genre; by performing his allusive, poetic songs in his nasal, spontaneous vocal style with an electric band, he enlarged pop's range and vocabulary while creating a widely imitated sound. By recording with Nashville veterans, he reconnected rock and country, hinting at the country rock of the '70s. In the '80s and '90s, although he has at times seemed to flounder, he still has the ability to challenge, infuriate, and surprise listeners.

Robert Zimmerman's family moved to Hibbing, Minnesota, from Duluth when he was six. After taking up guitar and harmonica, he formed the Golden Chords while he was a freshman in high school. He enrolled at the arts college of the University of Minnesota in 1959; during his three semesters there, he began to perform solo at coffeehouses as Bob Dylan (after Dylan Thomas; he legally changed his name in August 1962).

Dylan moved to New York City in January 1961, saying he wanted to meet Woody Guthrie, who was by then hospitalized with Huntington's chorea. Dylan visited his idol frequently. That April he played New York's Gerdes' Folk City as the opener for bluesman John Lee Hooker, with a set of Guthrie-style ballads and his own lyrics set to traditional tunes. A *New York Times* review by Robert Shelton alerted A&R man John Hammond, who signed Dylan to Columbia and produced his first album.

Although *Bob Dylan* included only two originals ("Talking New York" and "Song to Woody"), Dylan stirred up the Greenwich Village folk scene with his caustic humor and gift for writing deeply resonant topical songs. *The Freewheelin' Bob Dylan* (#22, 1963) included the soon-to-be folk standard "Blowin' in the Wind" (a hit for Peter, Paul and Mary), "A Hard Rain's a-Gonna Fall," and "Masters of War," protest songs on a par with Guthrie's and Pete Seeger's. Joan Baez, already established as a "protest singer," recorded Dylan's songs and brought him on tour; in summer 1963 they became lovers.

By 1964, Dylan was playing 200 concerts a year. *The Times They Are a-Changin'* (#20, 1964) mixed protest songs ("With God on Our Side") and more personal lyrics ("One Too Many Mornings"). He met the Beatles at Kennedy Airport and reportedly introduced them to marijuana. *Another Side of Bob Dylan* (#43, 1964), recorded in summer 1964, concentrated on personal songs and imagistic free associations such as "Chimes of Freedom"; Dylan repudiated his protest phase with "My Back Pages." In late 1964 Columbia A&R man Jim Dickson introduced Dylan to Jim (later Roger) McGuinn, to whom Dylan gave "Mr. Tambourine Man," which became the Byrds' first hit in 1965, kicking off folk rock. Meanwhile, the Dylan-Baez liaison fell apart, and Dylan met 25-year-old ex-model Shirley Noznisky, a.k.a. Sara Lowndes, whom he married in 1965.

With *Bringing It All Back Home* (#6), released early in 1965, Dylan surprised listeners for the first of many times by turning his back on folk purism; for half the album he was backed by a rock & roll band. On July 25, 1965, he played the Newport Folk Festival (where two years earlier he had been the cynosure of the folksingers) backed by the Paul Butterfield Blues Band, and was booed. The next month, he played the Forest Hills (Queens, New York) tennis stadium with a band that included Levon Helm and Robbie Robertson, which accompanied him on a tour and later became the Band [see entry]. "Like a Rolling Stone" (#2, 1965) became Dylan's first major hit.

The music Dylan made in 1965 and 1966 revolutionized rock. The intensity of his performances and his live-in-the-studio albums—*Highway 61 Revisited* (#3, 1965), *Blonde on Blonde* (#9, 1966)—were a revelation. His lyrics were analyzed, debated, and quoted like no pop before them. With rage and slangy playfulness, Dylan chewed up and spat out literary and folk traditions in a wild, inspired doggerel. He didn't explain; he gave off-the-wall interviews and press conferences in which he'd spin contradictory fables about his background and intentions. D.A. Pennebaker's documentary of Dylan's British tour, *Don't Look Back,* shows some of the hysteria that came to surround him and the cool detachment with which he would always regard his celebrity. As "Rainy Day Women #12 & 35" went to #2 in April 1966, Dylan's worldwide record sales topped 10 million, and more than 150 other groups or artists across a wide range of genres had recorded at least one of his songs.

On July 29, 1966, Dylan smashed up his Triumph 55 motorcycle while riding near his Woodstock, New York, home. With several broken neck vertebrae, a concussion, and lacerations of the face and scalp, he was reportedly in critical condition for a week and bedridden for a month, with aftereffects including amnesia and mild paralysis. Though the extent of Dylan's injuries was later questioned by biographers, he did spend nine months in seclusion. As he recovered, he and the Band recorded the songs that were widely bootlegged—and legitimately released in 1975—as *The Basement Tapes* (#7), whose droll, enigmatic, steeped-in-Americana sound would be continued by the Band on their own.

In 1968 Dylan made his public reentry with the quiet *John Wesley Harding* (#2), which ignored the baroque psychedelia in vogue since the Beatles' 1967 *Sgt. Pepper;* Dylan wrote new enigmas into such folkish ballads as "All Along the Watchtower." On January 20, 1968, he returned to the stage, performing three songs at a Woody Guthrie memorial concert, and in May 1969 he released the overtly countryish *Nashville Skyline* (#3), featuring "Lay Lady Lay" (#7, 1969) and "Girl From the North Country," with a guest vocal by Johnny Cash and a new, mellower voice.

Dylan's early-'70s acts seemed less portentous. His 1970 *Self Portrait* (#4) included songs by other writers and live takes from a 1969 Isle of Wight concert with the Band. Widely criticized, Dylan went back into the studio and rush released the mild, countryish *New Morning* (#7, 1970). By mid-1970 Dylan had moved to 94 MacDougal Street in Greenwich Village; on June 9, he received an honorary doctorate in music from Princeton.

George Harrison, with whom Dylan cowrote "I'd Have You Anytime," "If Not for You," and a few other songs that summer, persuaded Dylan to appear at the benefit Concert for Bangladesh; Leon Russell, who also performed, produced Dylan's single "Watching the River Flow." That year he also released his first protest song since the mid-'60s, "George Jackson." In 1971 *Tarantula,* a collection of writings from the mid-'60s, was published to an unenthusiastic reception.

Dylan sang at the Band concert that resulted in *Rock of Ages* (1972) but didn't appear on the album; he sat in on albums by Doug Sahm, Steve Goodman, McGuinn, and others. Late in 1972 he played Alias and wrote a score for Sam Peckinpah's *Pat Garrett & Billy the Kid* (#16, 1973), including "Knockin' on Heaven's Door" (#12, 1973). *Writings and Drawings by Bob Dylan,* a collection of lyrics and liner notes up to *New Morning,* was published in 1973. Between Columbia contracts, Dylan moved to Malibu in 1973 and made a handshake deal with David Geffen's Asylum label, which released *Planet Waves* (#1, 1974); Columbia retaliated with *Dylan* (#17, 1973), a collection of embarrassing outtakes from *Self Portrait.* Dylan and the Band played 39 shows in 21 cities, selling out 651,000 seats for a 1974 tour; the last three dates in L.A. were recorded for *Before the Flood* (#3, 1974).

Dylan scrapped an early version of *Blood on the Tracks,* recut the songs with local Minneapolis players, and the result hit #1 in 1975. He cowrote some of the songs on the platinum *Desire* (#1, 1976) with producer Jacques Levy; before making that LP, Dylan had returned to some Greenwich Village hangouts. A series of jams at the Other End led to the notion of a communal tour, and in October bassist Rob Stoner began rehearsing the large, shifting entourage (including Baez and such Village regulars as Ramblin' Jack Elliott and Bobby Neuwirth) that became the Rolling Thunder Revue, which toured on and off—with guests including Allen Ginsberg, Joni Mitchell, Mick Ronson, McGuinn, and Arlo Guthrie—until spring 1976. The Revue started with surprise concerts at small halls (the first in Plymouth, Massachusetts, for an audience of 200) and worked up to outdoor stadiums like the one in Fort Collins, Colorado, where NBC-TV filmed *Hard Rain.* The troupe played two benefits for convicted murderer Rubin "Hurricane" Carter (subject of Dylan's "Hurricane"), which, after expenses, raised no money. Dylan's efforts helped Carter get a retrial, but he was convicted and one of the witnesses, Patty Valentine, sued Dylan over his use of her name in "Hurricane."

In 1976 Dylan appeared in the Band's farewell concert, *The Last Waltz,* which was filmed by Martin Scorsese. His wife, Sara Lowndes, filed for divorce in March 1977. She received custody of their five children: Maria (Sara's daughter by a previous marriage whom Dylan had adopted), Jesse, Anna, Samuel, and Jakob. (It was revealed in 2001 that in 1986 Dylan had secretly married backup singer Carolyn Dennis, six months after she gave birth to the couple's daughter, Desiree Gabrielle Dennis-Dylan. The couple divorced in 1992.)

In 1978 Dylan took a $2 million loss on *Renaldo and Clara,* a four-hour film including footage of the Rolling Thunder tour and starring himself and Joan Baez. He embarked on an extensive tour (New Zealand, Australia, Europe, the U.S., and Japan, where he recorded *Live at Budokan*), redoing his old songs with some of the trappings of a Las Vegas lounge act.

In 1979 Dylan announced that he was a born-again Christian, having been introduced to its fundamentalist teachings by McGuinn, the Alpha Band (an outgrowth of Rolling Thunder), and Debby Boone. The platinum *Slow Train Coming,* overtly God-fearing, rose to #3; "You Gotta Serve Somebody" (#24, 1979) netted Dylan his first Grammy (for Best Rock Vocal Performance, Male). His West Coast tour late in 1979 featured only his born-again material; *Saved* (#24, 1980) and *Shot of Love* (#33, 1981) continued that message. In late 1981 he embarked on a 22-city U.S. tour; in 1982 amid rumors he had repudiated his born-again Christianity, Dylan traveled to Israel. *Infidels* (#20, 1983), recorded with a band that included Mark Knopfler, Mick Taylor, and reggae greats Sly and Robbie, answered no questions. Despite its title, the album was more churlish than religious, although Dylan did admit that "Neighborhood Bully" was about Arab-Israeli relations.

Biograph (#33, 1985), a five-disc retrospective with 18 previously unreleased tracks, helped put Dylan's long career in perspective, but *Empire Burlesque* (#33), released the same year, puzzled listeners with its backup singers and cluttered production by dance-music specialist Arthur Baker. A tour with Tom Petty and the Heartbreakers in 1986 supported the sloppy, cryptic *Knocked Out Loaded* (#53). Dylan then toured in 1987 with the Grateful Dead as his backup band, yielding the concert album, *Dylan & the Dead* (#37, 1989). Dylan delayed release of *Down in the Groove* (#61, 1988) twice in six months. The final product, with guests including Eric Clapton, Steve Jones (Sex Pistols), rappers Full Force, and members of the Dead sounded tentative and unfocused. But as "Lucky," one-fifth of the Traveling Wilburys [see entry], Dylan appeared to genuinely enjoy participating in a group project.

Dylan was inducted into the Rock and Roll Hall of Fame in 1989 and later that year released his best received album of the '80s, *Oh Mercy* (#30). Produced by Daniel Lanois (U2, Robbie Robertson) in New Orleans, it was a coherent collection of songs, and Dylan sounded reenergized and engaged. But as he had throughout his career, Dylan defied expectations. On his Never Ending Tour, started in 1988, Dylan recast his songs, at times throwing them away with offhand performances. His appearance on the *L'Chaim—To Life* telethon led to rumors he had joined a Hasidic sect. *Under the Red Sky* (#38, 1990), the followup to *Oh Mercy,* was almost universally panned.

In 1990 Dylan was named a *Commandeur dans l'Ordre des Arts et des Lettres,* France's highest cultural honor. At the 1991 Grammy ceremony, where he was given a Lifetime Achievement Award, Dylan's whimsical acceptance "speech" and sloppy, almost unintelligible performance of "Masters of War" (the Gulf War had recently raged), left some fans scratching their heads, while others applauded his pugnacious attitude. Dylan opened up the vaults for *The Bootleg Series, vols. 1–3 (Rare & Unreleased)* (#49, 1991), its 58 outtakes, live tracks, and demos, which proved his prolific virtuosity.

On October 16, 1992, Columbia marked the 30th anniversary of Dylan's first album with Bobfest, an all-star concert at New York's Madison Square Garden featuring more than 30 artists, including Neil Young, Pearl Jam's Eddie Vedder, Tom Petty, George Harrison, Eric Clapton, Johnny Cash, Lou Reed, and Dylan himself. Broadcast live on pay-per-view, it was released as an album and video the next year. As if to bring his career full circle, Dylan then recorded two folkish solo guitar and vocal albums: *Good As I Been to You* (#51, 1992) and *World Gone Wrong* (#70, 1993).

In the mid-'90s Dylan revived his live concerts by assembling one of the best bands of his career—he stopped throwing away his songs, instead playing both countryish rock and acoustic string-band versions of his best compositions. He made a triumphant appearance at Woodstock '94, though he had snubbed the 1969 festival. In late 1994 Dylan performed on *MTV's Unplugged,* with his new band augmented by Pearl Jam's producer Brendan O'Brien on keyboards (highlights were released on the 1995 *Unplugged* album [#23]).

Hooking up again with producer Lanois, Dylan recorded Delta deep-blues songs for 1997's *Time Out of Mind,* which debuted (and peaked) on the *Billboard* chart at #10, becoming his highest-charting release in nearly 20 years. The same year, Dylan found himself on the road touring and crossing paths with his son Jakob Dylan's band the Wallflowers [see entry].

Other highlights of the year for Dylan included performing before Pope John Paul II in Bologna, Italy, the inaugural release on his Egyptian Records label *(The Songs of Jimmie Rodgers—A Tribute),* and receiving the Kennedy Center Lifetime Achievement Award from President Bill Clinton at the White House. That year he had a brush with death when he suffered a serious heart infection that landed him in the hospital for a few tense days. In 1998 he picked up three Grammys for *Time Out of Mind* (Album of the Year, Best Contemporary Folk Album, and Best Male Rock Vocal Performance for the track "Cold Irons Bound"), and released *The Bootleg Series, vol. 4: Bob Dylan LIVE 1966: The "Royal Albert Hall" Concert.* His *Time Out of Mind* song "To Make You Feel My Love" turned into a #1 country smash by Garth Brooks. In 2000 Dylan received the prestigious Polar Prize from the Royal Swedish Academy of Music. He also wrote and performed a new song, "Things Have Changed," for the soundtrack of *Wonder Boys* (it was also included on *The Essential Bob Dylan* double-disc anthology later that year). The song went on to receive a Grammy Award and his first-ever Oscar. As of this writing, a new album was scheduled for release in fall 2001.

Sheila E.

Born Sheila Escovedo, Dec. 12, 1957, Oakland, CA
1984—*The Glamorous Life* (Warner Bros.) 1985—*Sheila E. in Romance 1600* 1987—*Sheila E.* 1991—*Sex Cymbal* 2001—*Writes of Passage* (Vista).

A gifted drummer and percussionist, Sheila E. also proved herself at home fronting a band, once her friendship with Prince gave her the chance to do so. In fact, she became the only one of his many female protégées to find anything more than the most fleeting musical success.

Sheila's father Pete Escovedo was a popular Bay Area Latin percussionist, who played with Santana and his own Latin band, Azteca. She picked up percussion herself as a child, but with several brothers also following their father's footsteps (one of whom, Peto, would play with '70s funk band Con Funk Shun), she did not get to perform with her father's band until she was a teenager. An immediate hit with Azteca, she soon quit high school to join the band full-time, also recording two mid-'70s albums with her father. She became an in-demand studio percussionist, recording and touring with Diana Ross, Herbie Hancock, Lionel Richie, and Marvin Gaye in the late '70s and early '80s. In 1978, while touring with jazz-fusion keyboardist George Duke, she met Prince, who had just recorded his first album. They became fast friends (though never lovers, she would later insist), but did not work together until 1984, when she sang a duet with him on "Erotic City," the B side of his #1 pop hit "Let's Go Crazy." Prince convinced her to become a solo act, renaming her and restyling her in his typical scanty-paisley fashion.

Her debut album, *The Glamorous Life* (#28, 1984) yielded a #7 pop hit in the title track, a Latin take on Prince's pop-savvy funk rock; the poppier "Belle of St. Mark" reached #34. *Sheila E. in Romance 1600* (#50, 1985) contained "A Love Bizarre," a duet with Prince (#11, 1985), also heard in the rap movie *Krush Groove*. Her third album (#56, 1987), which featured many family members, yielded only a minor hit single in "Hold Me" (#68, 1987); Sheila put her solo career on hold to join Prince's band, the Revolution, on drums, for the world tour documented in his *Sign o' the Times* album and film. A collapsed lung suffered after recording 1991's *Sex Cymbal* kept her from touring to support it; the album, topping at #146, flopped.

Though the percussionist continued to tour throughout the rest of the decade, her highest-profile appearance was as the bandleader on basketball great Earvin "Magic" Johnson's short-lived late-night talk show, *The Magic Hour*, in 1998. She returned with a jazz-fusion effort, *Writes of Passage*, in 2001.

The Eagles/Don Henley/Glenn Frey

Formed 1971, Los Angeles, CA
Don Henley (b. July 22, 1947, Gilmer, TX), drums, voc.; Glenn Frey (b. Nov. 6, 1948, Detroit, MI), gtr., piano, voc.; Bernie Leadon (b. July 19, 1947, Minneapolis, MN), gtr., banjo,

mandolin, voc.; Randy Meisner (b. Mar. 8, 1946, Scottsbluff, NE), bass, gtr., voc.
1972—*Eagles* (Asylum) 1973—*Desperado* 1974—(+ Don Felder [b. Sep. 21, 1947, Gainesville, FL], gtr., voc.) *On the Border* 1975—*One of These Nights* 1976—*Eagles: Their Greatest Hits, 1971-1975* (– Leadon; + Joe Walsh [b. Nov. 20, 1947, Wichita, KS], gtr., voc.) *Hotel California* 1977—(– *Meisner*; + Timothy B. Schmit [b. Oct. 30, 1947, Sacramento, CA], bass, voc.) 1979—*The Long Run* 1980—*Live* 1982—*Eagles Greatest Hits, vol. 2* 1994—(group re-forms: Frey; Henley; Walsh; Felder; Schmit) *Hell Freezes Over* (Geffen) 2000—*Eagles 1972–1999: Selected Works* (Elektra/Asylum).
Don Henley solo: 1982—*I Can't Stand Still* (Asylum) 1984—*Building the Perfect Beast* (Geffen) 1989—*The End of the Innocence* 1995—*Actual Miles: Henley's Greatest Hits* 2000—*Inside Job* (Warner Bros.).
Glenn Frey solo: 1982—*No Fun Aloud* (Asylum) 1984—*The Allnighter* (MCA) 1988—*Soul Searchin'* 1992—*Strange Weather* 1993—*Live* 1995—*Solo Collection* 2000—*The Best of Glenn Frey Millennium Collection.*
Timothy B. Schmit solo: 1984—*Playin' It Cool* (Asylum) 1987—*Timothy B* (MCA) 1990—*Tell Me the Truth.*
Don Felder solo: 1983—*Airborne* (Elektra).
Randy Meisner solo: 1980—*One More Song* (Epic) 1982—*Randy Meisner.*

With over 100 million in record sales, the Eagles epitomized commercial Southern California rock in the '70s, and their appeal continues undiminished three decades later. As of early 2001, *Their Greatest Hits, 1971–1975*—a 1976 best-of that was the first album ever certified platinum—is the best-selling album of all time, its 27 million copies outstripping the previous champ, Michael Jackson's *Thriller.* The group's well-crafted songs merged countryish vocal harmonies with hard-rock guitars, and lyrics that were alternately yearning ("One of These Nights," "Best of My Love") and romantically jaded ("Life in the Fast Lane," "Hotel California"). During the band's hugely successful career, it had an increasingly indolent recording schedule until its breakup in the fall of 1980. Subsequently, each of the members pursued a solo career, with Henley's the most successful commercially and critically. In the '90s, the band's sound was frequently cited as an influence by young country stars, many of whom contributed tracks to the album *Common Thread: The Songs of the Eagles* (#3, 1993), which won Album of the Year at the 1994 Country Music Awards. That same year, the Eagles revival culminated in the band's reunion tour and album.

The group originally coalesced from L.A.'s country-rock community. Before producer John Boylan assembled them as Linda Ronstadt's backup band on her album *Silk Purse* (1970), the four original Eagles were already experienced professionals. Leadon had played in the Dillard and Clark Expedition and the Flying Burrito Brothers; Meisner, with Poco [see entry] and Rick Nelson's Stone Canyon Band. Frey had played with various Detroit rock bands (including Bob Seger's) and Longbranch Pennywhistle (with J.D. Souther, a sometime songwriting partner), and Henley had been with a transplanted Texas group, Shiloh. After working with Ronstadt, Henley and Frey decided to form the Eagles, recruiting Leadon and Meisner.

The Eagles: Glenn Frey, Don Henley, Timothy B. Schmit, Don Felder, Joe Walsh

Intending to take the country rock of the Byrds and Burritos a step further toward hard rock, the Eagles recorded their first album with producer Glyn Johns in England. "Take It Easy" (#12, 1972), written by Frey and Jackson Browne, went gold shortly after its release, as did their debut album. (Another single, "Witchy Woman," reached #9 that year.) *Desperado* was a concept album with enough of a plot line to encourage rumors of a movie version. The LP yielded no major pop hits, but its title track, a ballad penned by Henley and Frey, has become a classic rock standard, covered by Linda Ronstadt, among others. With *On the Border,* the Eagles changed producers, bringing in Bill Szymczyk (who worked on all subsequent albums through 1982's *Greatest Hits, vol. 2*) and adding Felder, who had recorded with Flow in Gainesville, Florida (and who once gave guitar lessons to another Gainesville native, Tom Petty), then became a session guitarist and studio engineer in New York, Boston, and L.A.

The increased emphasis on rock attracted more listeners—mid-'70s hits included "Best of My Love" (#1, 1975), "One of These Nights" (#1, 1975), "Lyin' Eyes" (#2, 1975), and "Take It to the Limit" (#4, 1975)—but alienated Leadon. After *One of These Nights,* Leadon left to form the Bernie Leadon–Michael Georgiades Band, which released *Natural Progressions* in 1977. (Leadon went on to become a Nashville session musician, and in the '90s formed Run-C&W, a jokester group who played a blend of country and R&B.)

Leadon was replaced by Joe Walsh, who had established himself with the James Gang [see entry] and on his own. His Eagles debut, *Hotel California,* was their third consecutive #1 album (the second was their record-breaking 1976 greatest-hits compilation). "New Kid in Town" (#1, 1976), the title cut (#1, 1977), and "Life in the Fast Lane" (#11, 1977) spurred sales of more than 15 million copies worldwide.

Meisner left in 1977, replaced by Schmit, who had similarly replaced him in Poco. Meisner has released two solo albums, *Randy Meisner* (1978) and *One More Song* (1980). (In 1981, he toured with the Silveradoes; later, in 1990, Meisner reemerged in the group Black Tie, alongside Billy Swan and Bread's James Griffin.) Henley and Frey sang backup on *One More Song,* and in the late '70s they also appeared on albums by Bob Seger and Randy Newman. In 1981 Henley duetted with Stevie Nicks on the #6 single "Leather and Lace." Between outside projects and legal entanglements, it took the Eagles two years and $1 million to make the multiplatinum LP *The Long Run,* their last album of all-new material. Parting hit singles included "Heartache Tonight" (#1, 1979), "The Long Run" (#8, 1980), and "I Can't Tell You Why" (#8, 1980).

Walsh continued to release solo albums [see entry], though his biggest single to date has been 1978's cheeky "Life's Been Good" (#12). Felder and Schmit also put out their own albums and contributed songs to film soundtracks. Schmit's second LP, *Timothy B,* included "Boys Night Out" (#25, 1987).

In 1982 Don Henley and Glenn Frey both embarked on solo careers. Frey charted with "The One You Love" (#15, 1982) and "Sexy Girl" (#20, 1984) before a movie proved his ticket into the Top 10: "The Heat Is On," featured in *Beverly Hills Cop,* shot to #2 in 1985. Frey followed this success by becoming an actor, making a guest appearance as a drug dealer on the popular TV series *Miami Vice.* The episode was based on a track from his album *The Allnighter,* "Smuggler's Blues," which consequently reached #12 (1985). Later in 1985, Frey's "You Belong to the City" hit #2. While still dabbling in acting with roles in the short-lived TV series *South of Sunset,* the movie *Jerry Maguire,* and a guest spot on the Don Johnson post–*Miami Vice* series *Nash Bridges* in the '90s, Frey also cofounded a music label, Mission Records, in 1997.

Ultimately, though, Henley was the ex-Eagle who garnered the greatest chart success, and the most critical acclaim as well. His "Dirty Laundry" (from his first solo effort, *I Can't Stand Still*) made it to #3, but the 1985 album *Building the Perfect Beast* was to be his true arrival as solo hitmaker and respected singer/songwriter. The kickoff single, "The Boys of Summer," went to #5—supported by an evocative black-and-white video that fast became an MTV favorite—and earned Henley a Grammy for Best Rock Vocal Performance, Male; the hits "All She Wants to Do Is Dance" (#9, 1985) and "Sunset Grill" (#22, 1985) followed. A third album, *The End of the Innocence,* produced a #8 title track, and the additional singles "The Last Worthless Evening" and "The Heart of the Matter," which both hit #21. The LP won Henley another Grammy, in the same category as before. In the early '90s, he sought release from his Geffen Records contract, initiating a long and bitter legal dispute. After participating in the release of a solo best-of album in 1995, Henley was freed from his contract. Five years later, he released a studio album of all-new material, *Inside Job* (coproduced by former Tom Petty and the Heartbreakers drummer Stan Lynch), and embarked on a solo tour to support it. Henley had married for the first time in May 1995 and had three children before releasing *Inside Job.* This life-altering change for the longtime bachelor resulted in a new theme in his songwriting; several of *Inside Job*'s tracks were clearly about marriage and family, including the gentle ballad "Taking You Home" (#58 pop, #1 Adult Contemporary, 2000). Much of the rest of the album, however, still explored Henley's cynicism toward the business world and the media.

In 1990 Henley founded the Walden Woods Project, dedicated to preserving historic lands around Walden Pond in Concord, Massachusetts (where Henry David Thoreau and others reflected and wrote), from corporate development. Among the singer's various fund-raising means were holding charity concerts, featuring other top rock artists, and donating proceeds from some of his own recordings, including a reggae version of the *Guys and Dolls* standard "Sit Down You're Rocking the Boat" (1993). In 1993 the Walden Woods Project got a big boost from *Common Thread: The Songs of the Eagles,* coorganized by Henley and featuring Clint Black, Trisha Yearwood, Travis Tritt, and others.

In 1994, after years of fielding off reunion rumors, Henley, Frey, Walsh, Felder, and Schmit—who had appeared together in the video for Tritt's version of "Take It Easy"—hit the road for a massively successful tour, the third-highest grossing concert tour of that year. The tour went on hiatus toward the end of 1994, due to Frey's gastrointestinal surgery, but it continued in 1995. In November 1994, the band released *Hell Freezes Over,* which featured four new songs, including the singles "Get Over It" (#31, 1994), "Love Will Keep Us Alive" (#1 Adult Contemporary, 1994), "Learn to Be Still" (#15 Adult Contemporary, 1995), and 11 of the old hits culled from the band's 1994 live appearance on MTV. Within months the reunion LP had sold more than 10 million copies and gone to #1 on the pop album chart.

In 1998 the Eagles were inducted into the Rock and Roll Hall of Fame. All seven members of the band performed together for the first time at the induction ceremony. The core members of the group—the ones who had recorded and toured together in the mid-'90s—reunited again for a few concerts at the end of 1999, including a New Year's Eve show in L.A. A four-CD retrospective set, *Eagles 1972–1999: Selected Works* (#109, 2000), was released in November 2000.

Snooks Eaglin

Born Fird Eaglin Jr., Jan. 21, 1936, New Orleans, LA
1958—*Blues From New Orleans, vol. 1* (Storyville); *Country Boy Down in New Orleans* (Arhoolie); *New Orleans Street Singer* (Folkways) 1960—*Possum Up a Simmon Tree* (Arhoolie)

1961—*Message From New Orleans* (Heritage); *That's All Right* (Bluesville) 1971—*Legacy of the Blues* 1973—*Rural* (Fantasy) 1978—*Down Yonder* (GNP/Crescendo) 1987—*Baby, You Can Get Your Gun!* (Black Top) 1988—*Portraits in Blues, vol. 1* (Storyville); *Out of Nowhere* (Black Top); *New Orleans 1960–1961* (Sundown) 1989—*Snooks Eaglin* (Black Top) 1992—*Teasin' You* 1995—*Soul's Edge; Complete Imperial Recordings* (Capitol) 1997—*Live in Japan* (Black Top).

Blind blues guitarist/singer Snooks Eaglin has long been a fixture on the New Orleans R&B circuit. His nickname borrowed from that of an old-time mischief-making radio character, Eaglin's singing style recalls Ray Charles' while displaying his own signature wit. Blinded by complications from surgery for glaucoma when he was 19 months old, Eaglin began playing guitar at age six. A Crescent City street singer in the '50s who also played clubs with Sugar Boy Crawford, Allen Toussaint, and Dave Bartholomew, Eaglin began recording country blues for Folkways in 1958. In the '60s he backed up Professor Longhair after releasing, on Imperial, perhaps the strongest of his own recordings, with Bartholomew producing.

While Eaglin remains largely unknown outside Louisiana, his virtuosic guitar work, huge repertoire (he reportedly knows over 2,500 songs), and often humorous versions of New Orleans standards have gained him a cult following and a reputation as a "human jukebox." Fats Domino's rhythm section has appeared on his Black Top albums and bassist George Porter Jr. (the Meters) has played with Eaglin in the '90s.

Steve Earle

Born Jan. 17, 1955, Fort Monroe, VA
1986—*Guitar Town* (MCA) 1987—*Exit 0; Early Tracks* (Epic) 1988—*Copperhead Road* (Uni/MCA) 1990—*Shut Up and Die Like an Aviator* (MCA) 1991—*The Hard Way* 1993—*Essential Steve Earle* 1995—*Train a Comin'* (Winter Harvest) 1996—*Ain't Ever Satisfied: The Steve Earle Collection* (Hip-O/MCA); *I Feel Alright* (E-Squared/Warner Bros.) 1997—*Johnny Too Bad* EP; *El Corazón* 2000—*Transcendental Blues* (E-Squared/Artemis).
With the Del McCoury Band: 1999—*The Mountain* (E-Squared).

At the start of his career as an opening act for both George Jones and the Replacements, and through his songs—which incorporate the populism of Hank Williams and Bruce Springsteen—Steve Earle bridged country and rock. In the late '80s and through the mid-'90s, however, Earle's personal problems—including his addiction to heroin—temporarily sidetracked what had been a promising career.

Son of an air traffic controller, Earle was raised in South Texas, where he spent a rebellious adolescence as a long-haired Vietnam War opponent with country music sympathies. Leaving home at 16, he married at 19 the first of his five wives, and moved, nearly penniless, to Nashville. Befriending such older proponents of country's "outlaw" movement as Townes Van Zandt and Guy Clark, he wrote songs for Johnny Lee and Patty Loveless and almost managed to place one of his songs on an Elvis Presley album. At age 31 Earle released his critically acclaimed debut, *Guitar Town*. With his backup band the Dukes recalling the twangy style of Duane Eddy, he assailed Reaganomics and championed society's outsiders, appearing at Farm Aid II and allying himself with Fearless Hearts, a relief group for homeless children. *Exit O* was also well received; *Copperhead Road* scored #56 on the pop chart, but that year Earle, as a result of an altercation with a Dallas security guard, was fined $500 and given a one-year unsupervised probation. The tougher guitar sound and darker lyrics of *The Hard Way* reflected his legal problems; again critics lauded his work, but it fared considerably less well than its predecessor.

In late 1993, after a long hiatus from the studio, Earle began recording demos for a new album, but without a record contract at the time, he showed little sign of soon reclaiming his earlier success. In 1994 Earle was arrested in Nashville for possession of narcotics and sentenced to almost a year in jail. After his release, Earle released the acoustic *Train a Comin'* on the Nashville indie label Winter Harvest. Boasting such guest vocalists as Emmylou Harris and Nanci Griffith and stalwart picking from Peter Rowan, Norman Blake, and Roy Huskey Jr., the album included covers of songs by Van Zandt, the Beatles, and the reggae harmony group the Melodians.

Train a Comin' garnered great reviews and sold well for an indie, but it was with the swaggering *I Feel Alright* that Earle returned with a vengeance. "Because I've been to hell and now I'm back again," he snarled on the title track, a hard-won manifesto. The album, his first of entirely new material in five years, found Earle facing and besting his demons. It also launched the E-Squared record label, an imprint that Earle operates with partner Jack Emerson, and marked the debut of the Twangtrust, the production team of Earle and Ray Kennedy whose credits include albums by Lucinda Williams, Cheri Knight, and Marah.

In 1996 Earle contributed a song about the human and social costs of the death penalty, "Ellis Unit One," to the movie *Dead Man Walking*. He has since emerged as a major voice in the campaign to abolish capital punishment. In 1997 Earle released *El Corazón*, a critically acclaimed album encompassing country, blues, folk, and rock. One of the record's tracks also featured a collaboration with the bluegrass group the Del McCoury Band, presaging Earle's headlong foray (with the McCourys) into the idiom, *The Mountain* (1999). In 2000 Earle released *Transcendental Blues* and in 2001 published a volume of short stories, *Doghouse Roses*.

Earth, Wind & Fire

Formed 1969, Chicago, IL
Maurice White (b. Dec. 19, 1944, Memphis. TN), voc., kalimba, drums; Verdine White (b. July 25, 1951), bass; Donald Whitehead, kybds.; Wade Flemons, electric piano; Michael Beale,

gtr.; Phillard Williams, perc.; Chester Washington, horns; Leslie Drayton, horns; Alex Thomas, horns; Sherry Scott, voc. 1970—*Earth, Wind & Fire* (Warner Bros.) 1971—*The Need of Love* (group disbands; new group: M. White; V. White; + Philip Bailey [b. May 8, 1951, Denver, CO], voc., perc.; + Larry Dunn [b. June 19, 1953, CO], kybds., synth.; + Jessica Cleaves [b. 1943], voc.; + Roland Bautista, gtr.; + Roland Laws, reeds) 1972—*Last Days and Time* (Columbia) (– Laws; – Bautista; – Cleaves; + Johnny Graham [b. Aug. 3, 1951, KY], gtr.; + Al McKay [b. Feb. 2, 1948, LA], gtr., perc.; + Andrew Woolfolk [b. Oct. 11, 1950, TX], sax, flute; + Ralph Johnson [b. July 4, 1951, CA], drums) 1973—*Head to the Sky* 1974—*Open Our Eyes; Another Time* (Warner Bros.) (+ F. White [b. Jan. 13, 1955, Chicago], drums) 1975—*That's the Way of the World; Gratitude* (– F. White) 1976—*Spirit* 1977—*All 'n All* 1978—*The Best of, vol. 1* (ARC) *1979—I Am* 1980—*Faces* (– McKay; + Bautista) 1981—*Raise!* 1983—*Powerlight* (Columbia); *Electric Universe* (– Bautista; + Sheldon Reynolds, gtr., kybds., voc.) 1987—*Touch the World* 1988—*The Best of Earth, Wind and Fire, vol. 2* 1990—*Heritage* 1993—(+ Gary Bias, sax; + Ray Brown, trumpet; + Reggie Young, trombone) *Millennium* (Reprise) 1996—*Greatest Hits Live* (Pyramid) 1997—(– Dunn; – Graham; – Woolfolk; – Bias; + Scott Mayo, sax; + Morris Pleasure, voc., kybds.; + Sonny Emory, drums, voc.) *In the Name of Love* 1998—*Greatest Hits.*

Innovative yet popular, precise yet sensual, calculated yet galvanizing, Earth, Wind & Fire changed the sound of black pop in the '70s—their encyclopedic sound topping Latin-funk rhythms with gospel harmonies, unerring horns, Philip Bailey's sweet falsetto, and various exotic ingredients chosen by leader and producer Maurice White. Unlike their ideological rivals, the down and dirty but equally eclectic Parliament/Funkadelic, EW&F have always preached clean, uplifting messages.

Maurice White is the son of a doctor and the grandson of a New Orleans honky-tonk pianist. After attending the Chicago Conservatory, between 1963 and 1967 he was a studio drummer at Chess Records, where he recorded with the Impressions, Muddy Waters, Billy Stewart ("Summertime"), and Fontella Bass ("Rescue Me") among others. From 1967 to 1969 he worked with the Ramsey Lewis Trio ("Wade in the Water"); he later wrote and produced Lewis' 1975 hit "Sun Goddess." While with the trio, he took up kalimba, the African thumb piano, which became an EW&F trademark. White moved to L.A. in late 1969 and formed the first Earth, Wind & Fire (White's astrological chart has no water signs), who recorded for Capitol as the Salty Peppers. Warners signed the group for two moderately successful albums, but after 18 months, White hired a new, younger band, retaining only his brother Verdine on bass.

Earth, Wind & Fire: Larry Dunn, Ralph Johnson, Philip Bailey, Maurice White, Al McKay, Fred White, Verdine White, Johnny Graham, Andrew Woolfolk

The band's second Columbia LP, *Head to the Sky,* went to #27 pop and #2 R&B in 1973, starting a string of gold and, later, platinum albums. In 1975 *That's the Way of the World* (a soundtrack) yielded the Grammy-winning "Shining Star" (#1 pop and R&B, 1975). The band moved up to the arena circuit with elaborate stage shows that included such mystical trappings as pyramids and disappearing acts. (Effects for the 1978 national tour were designed by magician Doug Henning.) Although White's longtime coproducer Charles Stepney died in 1976, EW&F continued to sell. *All 'n All* became their fifth platinum album, and they won two Grammys in 1978. They were a highpoint of Robert Stigwood's 1978 movie *Sgt. Pepper's Lonely Hearts Club Band,* and their version of the Beatles' "Got to Get You Into My Life" went to #9 pop and #1 R&B.

White began to do outside production in 1975 and worked on albums by the Emotions *(Rejoice,* 1977), Ramsey Lewis (*Sun Goddess,* 1975), and Deniece Williams (*This Is Niecy,* 1976). He did composing and production work on Valerie Carter's *Just a Stone's Throw Away* (1977). EW&F's 1979 album, *I Am,* featured the Emotions on "Boogie Wonderland" (#6 pop, #2 R&B, 1979). In 1980 the group toured Europe and South America; 1981's *Raise!* (#5 pop, #1 R&B) featured the Top 5 hit "Let's Groove." While *Touch the World* (#33 pop, #3 R&B) went gold, *Powerlight* (#12 pop, #4 R&B, 1983) yielded their last major hit single, "Fall in Love With Me" (#17 pop, #4 R&B, 1983). Singer Philip Bailey also enjoyed success with his solo career, including a hit duet with Phil Collins, "Easy Lover" (#2 pop, #3 R&B, 1985), and a Grammy-winning gospel LP, *Triumph!* (1986). Since their inception, Earth, Wind & Fire have sold over 19 million albums.

Heritage (#70 pop, #19 R&B, 1990) featured guest rapper M.C. Hammer. For *Millennium* (#39 pop, #8 R&B, 1997) the group returned to Warner Bros. Records. *Greatest Hits Live* (#75 R&B, 1996) documents Maurice's final performances with the band during a mid-'90s Japanese tour. While EW&F continued to perform without their bandleader, Maurice built a recording studio and produced a number of jazz projects, including the *Urban Knights* albums, which have featured Grover Washington Jr., among others. He also founded his own record label, Kalimba Records.

In 2000, during the week leading up to EW&F's induction

into the Rock and Roll Hall of Fame, Maurice ended speculation as to why he quit the stage by revealing that he had been diagnosed with Parkinson's disease. Despite the neurological disorder, Maurice still functions as a producer, vocalist, and songwriter for the band, and played a major role in 1997's *In the Name of Love* (#50 R&B).

Sheena Easton

Born Sheena Shirley Orr, Apr. 27, 1959, Bellshill, Scot.
1981—*Sheena Easton* (EMI); *You Could Have Been With Me* 1982—*Madness, Money and Music* 1983—*Best Kept Secret* 1984—*A Private Heaven* 1985—*Do You* 1987—*No Sound but a Heart* 1988—*The Lover in Me* (MCA) 1989—*The Best of Sheena Easton* (EMI) 1991—*What Comes Naturally* (MCA) 1993—*No Strings* 1995—*My Cherie* (MCA).

Sheena Easton became a pop star in 1981 with a vocal style and image suggesting a new-wave version of easy-rock singers Marie Osmond and Olivia Newton-John. Easton attended the Royal Scottish Academy of Drama and Art and graduated in June 1979 qualified to teach, but instead she began a singing career. (While in school, she had frequently moonlighted in local nightclubs and pubs.) She successfully auditioned for EMI Records in May 1979 and received national exposure when the BBC-TV show *Big Time* documented her grooming for stardom. Her first single, "Modern Girl," was released in February 1980 and hit the Top 10 in England; that November she performed for Queen Elizabeth at the Royal Variety Show.

Easton's American breakthrough came in the spring of 1981, when "Morning Train" stayed at #1 on the U.S. singles chart for two weeks. Its success propelled the reissued "Modern Girl" up to #18, and at one point Easton had the distinction of having two singles in the Top 10. Her hits continued with the theme song from the James Bond film *For Your Eyes Only* (#4, 1981) and "When He Shines" (#30, 1982) from her second album, *You Could Have Been With Me*. She has also received gold records in Japan and Canada, and a Grammy in 1982 for Best New Artist. In 1985 she won a second Grammy, Best Mexican/American Performance, for a duet with Luis Miguel, "Me Gustas Tal Como Eres"; the year before she had released the Spanish-only album *Todo Me Recuerda a Ti*.

Easton revamped her wholesome image with *A Private Heaven* (#15, 1984), which included the tough-talking hit single "Strut" (#7, 1984) and "Sugar Walls" (#9, 1984), a highly suggestive track written for her by Prince. She would duet with Prince on his 1987 hit "U Got the Look." She played Don Johnson's wife in several episodes of *Miami Vice* (1987). In the '90s she appeared in movies *(Indecent Proposal)*, on Broadway *(The Man of La Mancha, Grease)*, and on television *(Jack's Place, The Highlander)*. She designed a line of ceramic angels and did a number of voice-overs for animated features (including 1996's *All Dogs Go to Heaven 2*). In 2000, after recording several Japanese import albums and playing opposite David Cassidy in the Las Vegas musical show *At the Copa*, she announced plans to remodel herself into a retro-styled disco diva.

The Easybeats/Flash and the Pan

Formed 1963, Sydney, Austral.
George Young (b. Nov. 6, 1947, Glasgow, Scot.), gtr.; Gordon Fleet (b. Aug. 16, 1945, Bootle, Eng.), drums; Dick Diamonde (b. Dec. 28, 1947, Hilversum, Neth.), bass; Harry Vanda (b. Harry Vandenberg, Mar. 22, 1947, The Hague, Neth.), gtr.; Stevie Wright (b. Dec. 20, 1948, Leeds, Eng.), voc.
1967—*Friday on My Mind* (United Artists); *Good Friday* 1968—*Falling off the Edge of the World; Vigil* 1970—*Friends* 1985—*The Best of the Easybeats* (Rhino).
Flash and the Pan (Vanda, Young): 1979—*Flash and the Pan* (Epic) 1980—*Lights in the Night* 1982—*Headlines*.

The Easybeats, whose members all emigrated to Australia with their families, were the '60s Australian rock band that launched producer/songwriters Harry Vanda and George Young. The group established itself as Australia's leading pop band in 1965 with "She's So Fine," the first of four chart-toppers Down Under. In 1966 the Easybeats returned to England and began recording with producer Shel Talmy (the Kinks, the Who), an association that resulted in the worldwide hit "Friday on My Mind" (#16, 1967). After their initial success, Vanda and Young kept the Easybeats name for a few years and had some moderately successful U.K. hits before officially disbanding in 1969 and forming a production company back in Australia. As Happy's Whiskey Sour they had a British hit with "Shot in the Head," and as the Marcus Hook Roll Band they recorded "Natural Man" in 1972. They produced Stevie Wright's solo debut, *Hard Road*, and oversaw the early career of Young's brothers Angus and Malcolm's band, AC/DC. Vanda and Young also concocted three studio albums that enjoyed some European success as Flash and the Pan. In 1988 the pair produced AC/DC's *Blow Up Your Video*.

Eazy-E: See N.W.A

Echo and the Bunnymen

Formed 1978, Liverpool, Eng.
Ian McCulloch (b. May 5, 1959, Liverpool), voc; Les Pattinson (b. Apr. 18, 1958, Merseyside, Eng.), bass; Will Sergeant (Apr. 12, 1958, Liverpool), gtr.
1979—(+ Pete De Freitas [b. Aug. 2, 1961, Port of Spain, Trinidad; d. June 15, 1989, Liverpool], drums) 1980—*Crocodiles* (Sire) 1981—*Heaven Up Here* 1983—*Porcupine* 1984—*Ocean Rain* 1986—*Songs to Learn and Sing* (– De Freitas; + Blair Cunningham [b. Oct. 11, 1957, New York, NY], drums; – Cunningham; + De Freitas) 1987—*Echo and the Bunnymen* 1989—(– McCulloch; + Noel Burke [b. Belfast, N. Ire.], voc.; – De Freitas; + Damon Reece, drums) 1990—*Reverberation* 1997—(group re-forms: McCulloch, Sergeant,

Pattinson; + Michael Lee, drums) *Evergreen* (London) 1999—(– Lee; – Pattinson) *What Are You Going to Do With Your Life* (PolyGram Int.) 2001—*Flowers* (SpinArt); *Echo & the Bunnymen: Crystal Days 1979–1999* (Rhino).
Ian McCulloch solo: 1989—*Candleland* (Sire) 1992—*Mysterio*.
Electrafixion, formed 1994: McCulloch; Sergeant; Tony McGuigan, drums; Jules Phillips, bass 1995—*Burned* (Sire).

The standard-bearers of Liverpool's neopsychedelic movement, Echo and the Bunnymen's moody, atmospheric music combined punk's energy and edge with the Doors' poetic theatricality. Self-consciously literary, outspoken, and sometimes arrogant (singer Ian McCulloch was known as "Mac the Mouth"), they never matched their popularity in Europe in the United States. Their influence can be seen in the attitudes and guitar textures of such '90s English bands as Suede.

The Bunnymen were formed when McCulloch was kicked out of an early version of the Teardrop Explodes. (He had earlier played with Teardrop leader Julian Cope [see entry] in the seminal Liverpool punk band the Crucial Three.) Recruiting fellow Doors fan Will Sergeant and Sergeant's friend, Les Pattinson, they were originally a trio backed by Echo, a drum machine. An independently released 1979 single, "Pictures on My Wall" b/w "Read It in Books" led to a contract with Sire. Before going into the studio to record "Rescue," Echo was replaced with the flesh-and-blood drummer Pete De Freitas. This all-human version of the band released *Crocodiles* (#17 U.K., 1980). Early press focused on the strength of the band's songwriting, unadorned sound, and McCulloch's teased, nearly vertical nest of hair.

Heaven Up Here (#10 U.K., 1981) was a darker album, more interested in textures than songs. It reached the bottom of the U.S. charts (#184) but was again widely praised in the press and topped many British polls. *Porcupine* (#137, 1983), which hit #2 in the U.K., signaled a new direction for the band, as did the singles "The Back of Love" (#19 U.K., 1982) and "The Cutter" (#8 U.K., 1983). Augmented by sitarist/violinist Shankar, the music took on an Eastern tint, with modal strings and droning bagpipes. *Ocean Rain* (#87, 1984), the band's first entry into the U.S. Top 100 albums chart, continued this direction, with a full string section in evidence on the quieter, melodic "The Killing Moon" (#9 U.K., 1984).

The band toured during most of 1985, but tensions arose the following year while it prepared to record *Echo and the Bunnymen* (#4 U.K., 1987). De Freitas left the band, only to return later (Haircut 100 drummer Blair Cunningham filled in during his absence). The band also had to rerecord the album. A quieter, reflective work, it was the Bunnymen's U.S. best-seller, peaking at #51 in 1987. That year, working with Doors keyboardist Ray Manzarek, Echo recorded a cover of "People Are Strange" for the 1987 movie *The Lost Boys*. In 1988, following a tour with New Order, McCulloch left to pursue a solo career, releasing *Candleland* (#18 U.K., 1989) and *Mysterio* (#46 U.K., 1992), neither of which matched the group's earlier success.

The band soldiered on, choosing St. Vitas Dance singer Noel Burke from thousands of audition tapes. In June 1989, during rehearsals for Echo's first post-McCulloch album, De Freitas was killed in a motorcycle accident. He was replaced by Damon Reece on the Geoff Emerick–produced *Reverberation* (1990), which failed to make the U.K. or U.S. charts.

McCulloch was publicly offended by the new Bunnymen lineup and did not speak to his former band mates for four years. But a failed collaboration with former Smiths' guitarist Johnny Marr reignited his desire to work with a band, which led to McCulloch's forming Electrafixion with Sergeant in 1994. They released one album *Burned* (1995), which was followed by a tour. While the album was not commercially successful, it did lead to a Bunnymen reunion in 1997. With Page and Plant drummer Michael Lee replacing De Freitas, the revived Bunnymen released *Evergreen* (1997). Following the band's tour, Pattinson, who had become a successful businessman, decided he had enough of the rock & roll life and quit the Bunnymen, leaving Sergeant and McCullough to continue the band as a duo with hired hands backing them up.

Duane Eddy

Born Apr. 26, 1938, Corning, NY
1958—*Have "Twangy" Guitar Will Travel* (Jamie) 1959—*Especially for You; The Twang's the Thing* 1960—*$1,000,000 Dollars Worth of Twang* 1962—*$1,000,000 Dollars Worth of Twang, vol. 2; Twistin' and Twangin'* (RCA) 1965—*The Best of Duane Eddy* 1970—*Twangy Guitar* (London) 1987—*Duane Eddy* (Capitol) 1993—*Twang Thang: The Duane Eddy Anthology* (Rhino) 1999—*Deep in the Heart of Twangsville* (Bear, Ger.).

Guitarist Duane Eddy had a string of instrumental hits ("Rebel Rouser," #6, 1958; "Peter Gunn," #27, 1960) that invariably featured a staccato signature riff labeled the "twangy" guitar sound. His work has influenced numerous guitarists (the Ventures, Shadows, George Harrison), especially in England.

Eddy began playing the guitar at age five. In 1951 he moved with his family to Phoenix. Shortly after dropping out of Coolidge High School at 16, he got a series of steady jobs working with local dance groups, and he acquired the custom-made Chet Atkins-model Gretsch guitar he still plays. In 1957 Phoenix DJ/producer/entrepreneur Lee Hazlewood became his mentor, and Eddy started touring with Dick Clark's Caravan of Stars. The Hazlewood-produced "Rebel Rouser" (on Clark's Jamie label) began a six-year streak of nearly 20 hits, among them "Ramrod" (#27, 1958), "Cannonball" (#15, 1958), and "Forty Miles of Bad Road" (#9, 1959). Though Eddy and Hazlewood parted company in 1961, they later reunited for comeback attempts.

Eddy switched to RCA in 1962 and had a hit with "Dance With the Guitar Man" (#12, 1962), followed by "Deep in the Heart of Texas" and "The Ballad of Palladin" (#33, 1962). He signed with Colpix in 1965 and released LPs like *Duane Does Dylan* and *Duane a Go-Go*. The various back-to-the-roots movements of the '70s (especially the rockabilly revival) rekindled interest in Eddy, who occasionally performs at oldies shows in the U.S. but concentrates primarily in the U.K., where he had a #9 hit in 1975, "Play Me Like You Play Your Guitar."

Eddy's early backup group, the Rebels, included guitarist Al Casey, saxophonist Steve Douglas, and pianist Larry Knechtel, later with Bread. At the height of his success, Eddy made his film debut in *Because They're Young* (1960), scoring a #4 hit with the theme song. He occasionally worked as a producer in the '70s, including a solo LP by Phil Everly (*Star Spangled Springer,* 1973). Eddy moved to California in the late '60s and then to Lake Tahoe, Nevada, in 1976. His 1977 comeback single on Asylum, "You Are My Sunshine," was produced by Hazlewood and included vocals by Willie Nelson and Waylon Jennings. Jennings' wife, Jessi Colter, was married to Eddy from 1966 to 1969.

In 1986 Eddy was introduced to a new generation of fans through British avant-dance group Art of Noise, who enlisted him to play on its industrial-disco version of "Peter Gunn" (#50, 1986). The following year, *Duane Eddy*—his first major-label album in over 15 years—was released; Jeff Lynne, Paul McCartney, George Harrison, and Ry Cooder all helped produce it. In 1994, a year after Rhino released the box set collection *Twang Thang,* Eddy was inducted into the Rock and Roll Hall of Fame.

Dave Edmunds

Born Apr. 15, 1943, Cardiff, Wales
1972—*Rockpile* (MAM) 1975—*Subtle as a Flying Mallet* (RCA) 1977—*Get It* (Swan Song) 1978—*Tracks on Wax 4* 1979—*Repeat When Necessary* 1981—*Twangin'; The Best of Dave Edmunds* 1982—*D.E. 7th* (Columbia) 1983—*Information* 1984—*Riff Raff* 1987—*I Hear You Rockin'* 1990—*Closer to the Flame* (Capitol) 1993—*The Dave Edmunds Anthology 1968–90* (Rhino) 1994—*Plugged In* (Pyramid) 2000—*Hand Picked Musical Fantasies* (Handpicked).

Guitarist/singer/producer/songwriter Dave Edmunds, an active fan of American rockabilly, spurred Britain's pub-rock movement, cofounded Rockpile, and has sustained a solo career for more than two decades.

Like many of his contemporaries, Edmunds was a rock & roll fan and soon found himself picking out the guitar parts played by James Burton on Rick Nelson's records, Chet Atkins on Everly Brothers hits, and Scotty Moore on early Elvis sides. During the early '60s he played in several British blues-rock bands before forming Love Sculpture in 1967 with bassist John Williams and drummer Bob Jones (the group later included drummer Terry Williams, also of Rockpile and, later, Dire Straits). They played rocked-up versions of light-classical pieces by Bizet and Khachaturian, whose "Sabre Dance" gave them a Top 5 U.K. hit in 1968. They toured the U.S. for six weeks before disbanding the next year.

Back in his native Wales, Edmunds built the 8-track Rockfield Studio in Monmouthshire and taught himself how to re-create Sam Phillips' Sun Records slap echo and Phil Spector's Wall of Sound. He spent the early '70s in the studio producing himself (including a 1971 hit remake of Smiley Lewis' 1955 hit "I Hear You Knockin' " and an album called *Rockpile*) and others, including the Flamin' Groovies, Del Shannon, and pub rockers Deke Leonard, Ducks Deluxe, and, later, Brinsley Schwarz and Graham Parker. When he produced Brinsley Schwarz's last LP in 1974, he met bassist Nick Lowe, later of Rockpile, the fiercely rocking band the two shared and led for their own albums.

In 1975 Edmunds costarred in and scored most of the film *Stardust,* and he also released *Subtle as a Flying Mallet,* for which Lowe wrote songs and played bass. After 1977's *Get It,* Edmunds toured regularly with Rockpile. Most of his albums have consisted primarily of covers. *Repeat When Necessary* premiered songs by Elvis Costello ("Girls Talk," a minor hit in America, but a gold U.K. hit) and Graham Parker ("Crawling From the Wreckage"), and contained the uptempo "Queen of Hearts." Though a Top 20 British hit, he could not get Atlantic to release it in the States. Two years later country-pop vocalist Juice Newton took the song to #2 in a near-identical version.

Rockpile broke up acrimoniously in 1981, shortly after releasing its only album under the Rockpile moniker, *Seconds of Pleasure.* Edmunds resumed his solo career. (Williams later drummed on some of his records, and guitarist Billy Bremner, the fourth member of Rockpile, joined Edmunds' 1983 touring band.) *Twangin'* produced a minor hit single with a cover of John Fogerty's "Almost Saturday Night," and "The Race Is On" introduced the Stray Cats, a Long Island neo-rockabilly group for whom Edmunds later produced multimillion-selling albums.

D.E. 7th, his first Columbia release, included the raveup "From Small Things (Big Things One Day Come)," written for Edmunds by Bruce Springsteen. *Information,* one of Edmunds' most successful U.S. LPs, featured two songs written and produced by the Electric Light Orchestra's Jeff Lynne. One of them, "Slipping Away," paired Edmunds' traditional sound with synthesizers, electronically processed vocals, and a drum machine, and became a Top 40 hit in 1983. Lynne stayed on to produce all of the unsuccessful *Riff Raff,* after which Edmunds returned to his roots-rock bent. He has continued to work as a producer, with the Everly Brothers and the reunited Stray Cats, and played guitar on the three tracks of the soundtrack to Paul McCartney's 1984 film *Give My Regards to Broad Street.* His other production credits include the Fabulous Thunderbirds *(Tuff Enuff),* k.d. lang *(Angel With a Lariat),* and Dion DiMucci *(Yo Frankie).* In the '90s he toured and recorded with Ringo Starr's All-Starr Band, supplied music to two Nike ads, and donated a tune to the 1995 film *This Little Girl of Mine.* In 2000 he self-released a new album and survived a triple bypass.

Bernard Edwards: See Chic

808 State

Formed 1988, Manchester, Eng.
Graham Massey (b. Aug. 4, 1960, Eng.), programmer, engineer,

kybds.; Andrew Barker (b. Mar. 9, 1968, Eng.), DJ; Darren Partington (b. Nov. 1, 1969, Eng.), DJ; Martin Price (b. Mar. 26, 1955, Farnworth, Lancaster, Eng.), programmer, engineer, kybds.; Gerald Simpson (b. Feb. 16, 1964, Manchester), programmer, engineer, kybds.
1988—*Newbuild* EP (Creed, U.K.) 1989—*Quadrastate* EP (– Simpson); *808:90* (ZTT, U.K.); *The EP of Dance* EP 1990—*Utd. State 90* (ZTT/Tommy Boy) 1991—*Ex:el* 1993—(– Price) *Gorgeous* 1996—*Don Solaris* 1998—*Thermo Kings* (Cleopatra).

Of the many techno-dance outfits to spring from Manchester in the late '80s, 808 State was the one most committed to emphasizing the "groove" over technical expertise. The group played a major role in developing the techno-rave sound.

808 State grew out of Manchester's legendary Eastern Bloc record shop, where store owner Martin Price also operated his independent label, Creed. It was there that Graham Massey, a former member of the experimental unit Biting Tongues, met the local DJ duo of Darren Partington and Andrew Barker, who were trying to land a deal with Price's label. The four men, along with another local musician, Gerald Simpson, wound up recording together as 808 State (fittingly named after a drum machine). Their first collaboration was the 1988 EP *Newbuild,* which was quickly followed by remixing gigs for such acts as the Inspiral Carpets. In 1989 they performed the British club smash "Pacific State"; Simpson left soon after to form his own project, A Guy Called Gerald.

The next year 808 State released its U.S. debut, *Utd. State 90,* which included "Pacific State" and another dance club favorite, "Cubik." The critically acclaimed followup, *Ex:el,* featured guest vocalists Bernard Sumner of New Order ("Spanish Heart") and Björk Gudmundsdottir, then of the Sugarcubes ("Ooops" and "Qmart"). 808 State's subsequent U.S. tour consisted of a handful of rave appearances.

In 1992 Price left to produce a succession of British rap acts and form the label Sun Text. Later that year, 808 State released *Gorgeous,* and has since produced dance remixes for other artists, including David Bowie, Soundgarden, and the British rapper MC Tunes. In 1996 the experimental *Don Solaris* included sampled bits of wind instruments and guitars, and featured such guest vocalists as M. Doughty of Soul Coughing and James Dean Bradfield of Manic Street Preachers. *Thermo Kings* is a remix of *Don Solaris.*

Einstürzende Neubauten

Formed Apr. 1, 1980, Berlin, Ger.
Blixa Bargeld (b. Christian Emmerich, Jan. 12, 1959, Berlin), voc., gtr., perc., bass; N.U. Unruh (b. Andrew Chudy, June 9, 1957, New York, NY), perc., voc., drums; Beate Bartel, perc.; Gudrun Gut, perc.
1980—(– Bartel; – Gut) 1981—(+ F. M. Einheit [b. Frank Martin Strauss, Dec. 18, 1958, Dortmund, Ger.], drums, perc., kybds.) 1981—*Kollaps* (Zick Zack, Ger.) 1982—(+ Mark Chung [b. June 3, 1957, Leeds, Eng.], bass, perc.; + Alex Hacke [a.k.a. Alexander Von Borsig, b. Oct. 11, 1965, Berlin], gtr., bass, voc., perc., kybds.) 1983—*Drawings of Patient O.T.* (Some Bizarre, U.K.) 1984—*Strategies Against Architecture* (Mute, U.K.) 1985—*½ Mensch* (Some Bizarre/Rough Trade) 1987—*Fuenf auf der Nach Oben Offenen Richterskala* (Some Bizarre/Relativity) 1989—*Haus der Luege* (Some Bizarre/Rough Trade) 1991—*Strategies Against Architecture II* (Mute); *Die Hamletmaschine* (Our Choice, Ger.) 1993—*Interim* EP (Mute); *Tabula Rasa* (– Chung) 1995—(– Einheit) 1996—*Ende Neu* (nothing/Interscope); *Faustmusik* (Our Choice, Ger.) 1997—(+ Jochen Arbeit, gtr.; + Rudolph Moser, drums, perc.) 2000—*Silence Is Sexy* (Mute).

Generally acknowledged as the world's first "industrial" band, Germany's Einstürzende Neubauten—which translates to "collapsing new buildings"—is essentially an avant-garde conceptual/performance-art collective. These hardhat dadaists make their postmodern, neotribal statement with howling vocals and "instruments" that include power tools and large metal industrial objects beaten with hammers, chains, and pipes.

Neubauten's earliest manifestations were in such hit-and-run art statements as Blixa Bargeld and expatriate American N.U. Unruh appearing half-naked, beating on the sides of a hole in a Berlin Autobahn overpass. The Neubauten name took on chillingly prophetic overtones when, a few months after its formation, Berlin's newly constructed, American-built congress hall caved in. The group's earliest, largely freeform recordings—German-issued singles and EPs compiled on *80–83*—mixed atavistic, guttural vocals with distorted guitar and bass drones, and thunderous metal percussion.

With the addition of F. M. Einheit—who brought in power drills, jackhammers, amplified air-conditioning ducts, and giant industrial springs—and later, guitarist Alexander Hacke and bassist Mark Chung, Einstürzende Neubauten expanded its sonic range, exerted ever-finer control over its noise elements, and gradually grew closer to conventional rock-band approaches. The group integrated its first actual chord progression into the title track of *Drawings of Patient O.T.;* the cassette-only live album *2 X 4* found Bargeld at times singing plaintively in a near Middle Eastern style; *½ Mensch* ("Half-Man") ranged from Bargeld's multitracked a cappella vocal workouts, to soft balladlike interludes and even some off-kilter dance beats; *Fuenf auf der Nach Oben Offenen Richterskala* ("Five on the Open-Ended Richter Scale"), recorded after a brief breakup, was uncharacteristically quiet and restrained. In 1993 Neubauten released its most accessible album to date, *Tabula Rasa,* recorded during the Persian Gulf War and including the crackling sounds of burning oil (taped before Iraqis ignited the Kuwaiti oil fields).

The following year brought the import-only *Die Hamletmaschine,* inspired by avant-garde director Heiner Müller's theatrical production. And in 1996 *Ende Neu* was recorded for longtime fan and Nine Inch Nails frontman Trent Reznor's nothing label. The album featured strings and a chorus that established a quieter tone alongside the usual industrial rattlings. *Faustmusik*, released the same year, was music written to accompany a production of German author Werner Schwab's *Faust: My Thorax: My Helmet*.

The band enjoyed a rare, and well-received, 1998 American tour before returning to the studio for an atypically titled 2000 release *Silence Is Sexy*. Neubauten followed up with another U.S. tour.

Outside the group, Bargeld has worked with Nick Cave and the Bad Seeds [see entry], and Hacke with Crime and the City Solution; Einheit formed Berlin's experimental theater-music outfit Stein (Stone), using the sonic properties of friction between rocks and concrete.

Elastica

Formed 1992, England
Justine Frischmann (b. Sep. 16, 1969, London), voc., gtr.; Donna Matthews (b. Dec. 2, 1971, Newport, Wales), gtr., voc.; Justin Welch (b. Dec. 4, 1972, Nuneaton, Eng.), drums; Annie Holland (b. Aug. 26, 1965, London), bass.
1994—*Line Up* EP (Deceptive, U.K.) 1995—*Elastica* (Geffen) (– Holland) 1997—(– Matthews) 1999—(+ Paul Jones [b. Oct. 23, 1965, Billericay, Eng.], gtr.; + Mew [b. Sharon Mew, July 5, 1969, Beccles, Eng.], kybds., voc.; + Dave Bush [b. June 4, 1959, Taplovo, Eng.], kybds.; + Holland) *6-Track EP* (Deceptive, U.K.) 2000—*The Menace* (Atlantic).

Elastica stood among Britain's most promising bands in the mid-'90s, performing crisp, edgy pop with roots reaching deep into punk's earliest days. Catchy songs like "Connection" and "Stutter" quickly earned fans both at home and in the U.S. But a variety of problems delayed a followup, so by the time Elastica reemerged with its second album five years later, the band had endured lineup changes, scrapped recordings, the collapse of the alternative-rock boom, and the end of its U.S. record deal.

Singer/guitarist Justine Frischmann was briefly a member of the London Suede [see entry], while dating the band's singer, Brett Anderson. She quit Suede to study architecture at the University of London and soon formed her own band with drummer Justin Welch (another ex-Suede member). They auditioned other players and began playing the British club circuit as Elastica. The band signed to Deceptive Records in late 1993. Between then and 1995, Elastica released the singles "Stutter," "Line Up," "Connection," and "Waking Up"—all hits in England.

Elastica was sued by the song publishers of Wire and the Stranglers—complaining that Elastica's "Connection" was near-identical to Wire's "Three Girl Rhumba," while the band's "Waking Up" stole a key riff from the Stranglers' "No More Heroes." Elastica settled out of court in time for the 1995 release of a self-titled debut (#66 U.S., #1 U.K.). In America, where the band was signed to Geffen, Elastica enjoyed hits with singles "Connection" (#53) and "Stutter" (#67). Heavy touring finally led to bassist Annie Holland quitting from exhaustion in 1995. Then Matthews quit amid stalled efforts to record a followup album.

Frischmann recruited guitarist Paul Jones and keyboardist Mew. Holland returned in 1999. Elastica soon released *6-Track EP*, which gathered various tracks recorded over the previous years, including a demo called "Nothing Stays the Same" by the now-absent Matthews, plus tracks recorded by the newest lineup of the band. Among the new songs was a collaboration with the Fall's Mark E. Smith called "How He Wrote Elastica Man." The new lineup made its public debut at the 1999 Reading Festival. *The Menace* was finally released the following year (on Deceptive in the U.K., on Atlantic in the U.S.), and featured a blend of pop-punk with occasional flashes of modern electronic influences.

The Electric Flag

Formed 1967, San Francisco, CA
Michael Bloomfield (b. July 28, 1944, Chicago, IL; d. Feb. 15, 1981, San Francisco), gtr.; Buddy Miles (b. Sep. 5, 1946, Omaha, NE), drums, voc.; Barry Goldberg, kybds.; Nick Gravenites (b. Chicago), voc.; Harvey Brooks, bass; Peter Strazza, tenor sax; Marcus Doubleday, trumpet; Herbie Rich, baritone sax.
1968—*A Long Time Comin'* (Columbia) (– Bloomfield) 1969—*The Electric Flag* 1974—(group re-forms: Bloomfield; Miles; Goldberg; Gravenites; Roger "Jellyroll" Troy, bass, voc.) *The Band Kept Playing* (Atlantic).

The short-lived Electric Flag intended to combine blues, rock, soul, jazz, and country; it ended up sparking the rock-with-brass trend of Blood, Sweat and Tears and Chicago. Michael Bloomfield [see entry] started the band in 1967 after leaving the Paul Butterfield Blues Band, and he brought Nick Gravenites with him. Goldberg had played with Mitch Ryder and came to the Flag after the breakup of the Goldberg-Miller Blues Band (with Steve Miller), bringing Strazza with him. The rest had session backgrounds: Buddy Miles [see entry] in R&B, drumming for Otis Redding and Wilson Pickett; Harvey Brooks as the folk rockers' bassist with Bob Dylan, Judy Collins, Phil Ochs, and Eric Andersen, as well as the Doors; Marcus Doubleday from early-'60s work with the Drifters, Jan and Dean, and Bobby Vinton.

Based in San Francisco, the Electric Flag debuted at the Monterey Pop Festival in June 1967, and its first album made the Top 40. But ego conflicts among the members soon undermined them, and the band lasted only 18 months. Bloomfield quit after the debut album, leaving Miles as leader for the Flag's remaining months. Before the breakup, they'd recorded enough material for a second album. The Buddy Miles Express was modeled after the Flag, but Miles left it to join Jimi Hendrix's Band of Gypsies. Gravenites turned to songwriting, then joined Big Brother and the Holding Company. The rest returned to work as sidemen.

In 1974 Bloomfield, Miles, Gravenites, and Goldberg (joined by Roger "Jellyroll" Troy) reunited for a two-album deal. The first, produced by Jerry Wexler, re-created the old sound with Dr. John's Bonaroo Brass and the Muscle Shoals

Horns. But the band's third incarnation broke up before recording a second album.

The Electric Light Orchestra

Formed 1971, Birmingham, Eng.
Roy Wood (b. Ulysses Adrian Wood, Nov. 8, 1946, Birmingham), gtr., voc.; Jeff Lynne (b. Dec. 30, 1947, Birmingham), gtr., voc., synth.; Bev Bevan (b. Beverly Bevan, Nov. 25, 1946, Birmingham), drums; Rick Price (b. Birmingham), bass.
1972—*No Answer/ELO* (United Artists) (– Wood; – Price; + Richard Tandy [b. Mar. 26, 1948, Birmingham], kybds., gtr.; + Michael D'Albuquerque [b. June 24, 1947, London, Eng.], bass; + Mike Edwards, cello; + Colin Walker, cello; + Wilf Gibson [b. Feb. 28, 1945, Dilston, Eng.], violin) 1973—*ELO II* (– Walker; – Gibson; + Hugh McDowell [b. July 31, 1953, London], cello; + Mik Kaminsky [b. Sep. 2, 1951, Harrogate, Eng.], violin) *On the Third Day* (Jet) 1974— (– D' Albuquerque; – Edwards; + Kelly Groucutt [b. Sep. 8, 1945, Coseley, Eng.], bass, voc.; + Melvyn Gale [b. Jan. 15, 1952, London], cello; – Groucutt; – Gale) *Eldorado* 1975—*Face the Music* 1976—*Olé ELO; A New World Record* (Jet) 1977—*Out of the Blue* (– Gale; – Kaminski; – McDowell) 1979—*Discovery; Greatest Hits* 1981—*Time* 1983—*Secret Messages* (– Bevan) 1985—(+ Bevan) 1986—*Balance of Power* (CBS Associated) 1990—(group re-forms as ELO II: Bevan; Groucutt; Kaminski; + Eric Troyer, kybds., voc.; + Phil Bates, gtr., voc.) *Afterglow* (Epic) 1991—*Electric Light Orchestra Part Two* (Scotti Brothers) 1992—*Performing ELO's Greatest Hits Live* (with the Moscow Symphony Orchestra) 1994—*Moment of Truth* (Edel) 1995—*Strange Magic: The Best of Electric Light Orchestra* (Epic/Legacy); *ELO's Greatest Hits, vol. 2* (Epic) 1996—*The Gold Collection* (EMI Gold) 1997—*Light Years: The Very Best of Electric Light Orchestra* (Epic) 1998—*Greatest Hits Live, vol. 2: Encore Collection* (BMG Special) 2000—*Flashback* (Epic/Legacy) 2001—*Zoom* (Epic).
Jeff Lynne solo: 1990—*Armchair Theatre* (Reprise).

The Electric Light Orchestra became a major arena and stadium draw in the mid- and late '70s on the strength of Beatles-like orchestral pop—"Can't Get It Out of My Head" (#9, 1974), "Telephone Line" (#7, 1977), "Evil Woman" (#10, 1975)—and elaborate staging. Formed in 1971 as an offshoot of the Move by leader Roy Wood (who left after ELO's first LP to form Wizzard), drummer Bev Bevan, guitarist/songwriter Jeff Lynne, and bassist Rick Price, ELO initially sought to explore classically tinged orchestral rock. The band has fashioned a series of multimillion-selling LPs and radio hits by sweetening futuristic electronic effects with rich strings, synthesizers, keyboards, and occasional horns. ELO remains based in England, although their greatest success has been in America.

The Electric Light Orchestra has a history of facelessness such that even the most ardent fans generally can't name more than one or two band members (up until 1986 or so, original members Lynne and Bevan were the backbone, with studio assistance from longtime member and multi-instrumentalist Richard Tandy). Wood left the group in 1972, before its first hit, a version of Chuck Berry's "Roll Over Beethoven" (#43, 1973), complete with chugging cellos sending up the opening strains of the Fifth Symphony (they occasionally use fragments of Grieg and others as well).

After Wood quit, Lynne brought the band to the U.S. in 1973 for a 40-date debut tour that was marred by technical problems in miking the cellos (a radical addition to the live rock format). *On the Third Day* (#52, 1973) produced a moderate hit with "Showdown" (#53, 1973). *Eldorado* (#16, 1974), a pseudo-concept album, gave ELO a major hit with "Can't Get It Out of My Head." *Face the Music* (#8, 1975) went gold on the strength of "Evil Woman" (#10, 1975) and "Strange Magic" (#14, 1976). Each subsequent album, including *Xanadu,* went at least gold, and five (*A New World Record, Out of the Blue, Discovery, Greatest Hits,* and the *Xanadu* soundtrack) are platinum. In 1977 ELO's records and tours grossed over $10 million, and *A New World Record* (#5, 1976) eventually sold 5 million copies worldwide.

By the late '70s, ELO was recording for its own label, Jet, whose distribution switch to CBS led ELO to sue the old distributor, United Artists, claiming it had flooded the market with millions of defective copies of the platinum double LP *Out of the Blue* (#4, 1977). ELO's most elaborate tour was in 1978, when it traveled with a laser-equipped "spaceship" (some said it looked like a giant glowing hamburger) that opened with the group playing inside. The Orchestra's live shows were also enhanced by taped backing tracks, and it was accused on more than one occasion of lip-synching the supposed "live parts." (Interestingly, in another decade this practice would be very common.) In 1979 ELO stayed off the road completely (the first time it hadn't toured since 1972). *Discovery* (#5, 1979) went platinum nonetheless, yielding two hits with "Shine a Little Love" (#8, 1979) and "Don't Bring Me Down" (#4, 1979). In 1980 Lynne contributed an album side's worth of songs to the Olivia Newton-John movie *Xanadu* soundtrack (#4, 1980). Three of those songs, "I'm Alive" (#16, 1980), "All Over the World" (#13, 1980), and "Xanadu" (#8, 1980) were hits.

ELO toured the U.S. in late 1981 to promote its latest album, *Time.* Certified gold, *Time* (#16, 1981) featured the hit single "Hold On Tight" (#10, 1981). Still, it marked the start of ELO's commercial decline. Although it hit #1 in the U.K., *Time* didn't help draw U.S. fans to concert halls. Although each boasted a Top 20 single, neither *Secret Messages* (#36, 1983, contains "Rock 'n' Roll Is King" [#19, 1983]) and *Balance of Power* (#49, 1986, contains "Calling America" [#18, 1986]) revived mass interest. Between the release of these two, Bevan briefly joined Black Sabbath. By 1986 ELO was essentially the trio of Lynne, Bevan, and Tandy.

In the meantime, Lynne had become a sought-after record producer (Dave Edmunds' *Information*) and over the next few years would amass some impressive credits: George Harrison's *Cloud Nine,* Roy Orbison's *Mystery Girl,* Tom Petty's *Full Moon Fever,* among others. In 1988 he joined Harrison, Petty, Orbison, and Bob Dylan in the Traveling Wilburys [see entry]. His 1990 solo album was a U.K. Top 30 hit, but barely scraped onto the U.S. albums chart.

In 1991 a new, Bevan-led, Lynne-less version of the group (now known as ELO II or Electric Light Orchestra, Part II) released an eponymously titled album. The following year that group recorded a live greatest-hits album with the Moscow Symphony Orchestra. ELO II continued to tour. In early 2001 Lynne released his own new Electric Light Orchestra album, *Zoom,* which he wrote, produced, and performed himself, with assistance from some of the celebrity musicians he had worked with over the years, including Ringo Starr and George Harrison.

The Electric Prunes

Formed 1965, Los Angeles, CA
James Lowe, Autoharp, harmonica, voc.; Mark Tulin, bass, kybds.; Ken Williams, gtr.; Preston Ritter, drums; Weasel Spagnola, gtr., voc.
1967—*Electric Prunes* (Reprise) (– Ritter; + Quint, drums) *Underground* (group disbands; new lineup: John Herren [b. Elk City, OK], kybds.; Mark Kincaid [b. Topeka, KS], gtr., voc.; Ron Morgan, gtr.; Brett Wade [b. Vancouver, Can.], bass, flute, voc.; Richard Whetstone [b. Hutchinson, KS], drums, voc.) *Mass in F Minor* 1968—*Release of an Oath: The Kol Nidre* (– Herren) 1969—*Just Good Old Rock 'n' Roll.*

The Electric Prunes were actually two separate groups. The original was one of the first psychedelic bands from L.A. The Prunes signed to Reprise in 1966 and had a national hit with the reverb-heavy "I Had Too Much to Dream (Last Night)" (#11, 1966). They followed up with "Get Me to the World on Time" (#27) in 1967. For reasons unknown, the group disbanded, and a totally new band calling itself the Electric Prunes emerged in 1967 with *Mass in F Minor* and *Release of an Oath* in 1968, both the creations of writer/arranger David Axelrod. Their fifth LP, *Just Good Old Rock 'n' Roll,* was an attempt to return to roots music but was unsuccessful. The Electric Prunes again disbanded, this time for good.

Eleventh Dream Day

Formed 1983, Chicago, IL
Janet Beveridge Bean (b. Feb. 10, 1964, Louisville, KY), drums, voc.; Rick Rizzo (b. July 4, 1957), gtr., voc.; Shu Shubat, bass.
1985—(– Shubat; + Douglas McCombs [b. Jan. 9, 1962], bass; + Baird Figi, gtr.) 1987—*Eleventh Dream Day* EP (Amoeba) 1988—*Prairie School Freakout* 1989—*Beet* (Atlantic) 1991—*Lived to Tell* (– Figi; + Matthew "Wink" O'Bannon [b. July 22, 1956], gtr.) 1993—*El Moodio* 1994—*Ursa Major* (Atavistic) 1997—(– O'Bannon) *Eighth* (Thrill Jockey) 2000—*The Stalled Parade.*
Freakwater, formed 1983, Louisville, KY: Bean, gtr., voc.; Catherine Irwin, gtr., voc.; Dave Gay, bass.
1989—*Freakwater* (Amoeba) 1991—*Dancing Underwater* 1993—*Feels Like the Third Time* (Thrill Jockey) 1995—*Old Paint* 1998—*Springtime* 1999—*Endtime.*

Eleventh Dream Day is one of the Midwest's most enduring alternative bands, having latched onto Neil Young's mordant guitar aesthetic years before it was hip. Janet Beveridge Bean and Rick Rizzo met in 1981 when he was a student at the University of Kentucky at Lexington and she was a teenaged drummer. Rizzo had just discovered punk rock and taught himself to play guitar via the songbook of Young's album *Zuma.*

The couple (who married in the fall of 1988) moved to Chicago and formed Eleventh Dream Day with bassist Shu Shubat. In spring 1985 Shubat left and was replaced by Douglas McCombs; guitarist/songwriter Baird Figi also joined around this time, giving the band its Television-style twin-guitar sound. The band's first independent records introduced its flat, Americanist narratives (mostly penned by Rizzo) shot through with twisted guitar and an earnest country twang. *Prairie School Freakout,* recorded in one night with a worn-out, buzzing amp, caught the attention of Atlantic, which signed the band.

Beet, produced by Gary Waleik of Boston alt-rock band Big Dipper, was a modest major-label debut that spent five months on the college-radio charts. On *Lived to Tell,* Bean wrote and sang several of the best tracks. It was a solid, well-received album, but the band suffered a setback when, while touring to promote it, Figi quit the band. He was replaced by Matthew O'Bannon, Eleventh Dream Day's roadie and an old friend. The Jim Rondinelli–produced *El Moodio* featured the Rizzo-Bean duet "Makin' Like a Rug" and a cameo by guitarist Tara Key, of punk-pop combo Antietam. (Rizzo and Bean guested on Key's 1993 album *Bourbon County.*)

Atlantic dropped Eleventh Dream Day from its roster after *El Moodio* failed to sell well. Turning to producer John McEntire (who plays with McCombs in the "postrock" combo Tortoise [see entry]), the group released *Ursa Major,* a record that's less country and more experimental than its predecessors. *Eighth* continued in this vein, incorporating more guitar feedback into the mix. In 2000 Rizzo and Key released an album of instrumentals, *Dark Edson Tiger.*

Before Bean moved to Chicago, she had been playing country songs with her friend Catherine Ann Irwin. The two, along with Chicagoan Dave Gay on bass and a parade of sidemen on banjo, fiddle, and steel guitar, have continued to collaborate as Freakwater. The two women's unvarnished mountain harmonies and Irwin's incisive originals made the band one of the brightest lights of the '90s alt-country movement.

Missy "Misdemeanor" Elliott

Born Melissa Elliott, July 1, 1971, Portsmouth, VA
1997—*Supa Dupa Fly* (EastWest) 1999—*Da Real World* (The Gold Mind) 2001—*Miss E . . . So Addictive.*

One of the most influential artists in pop and R&B of the late '90s, Missy "Misdemeanor" Elliott established a formidable presence both behind the scenes (as a songwriter and/or producer for Whitney Houston, Mariah Carey, SWV, Lil' Kim,

Jodeci, and Aaliyah, among others) and as a solo artist who toyed with a larger-than-life image in spoofy videos and outrageous costumes.

In the early '90s, Elliott formed the group Sista, taking a cue from the pioneering all-female rap group Salt-n-Pepa. After winning a string of high school talent shows, Sista garnered a contract with Elektra, via Jodeci member DeVante Swing's Swing Mob records. The group recorded an album that was never released, and Sista disbanded. Elliott, meanwhile, began writing and producing tracks for Jodeci [see entry] with friend Tim "Timbaland" Mosley. The pair enjoyed multiplatinum success working with teenage diva Aaliyah ("Are You That Somebody"), and though she was in demand as a producer and guest vocalist, Elliott got her shot at a solo career when she signed as a solo artist to Elektra's EastWest subsidiary in 1996. The arrangement included a production deal for her own company, the Gold Mind. Her debut album, *Supa Dupa Fly* (#3 pop, #1 R&B, 1997), quickly established Elliott as a colorful personality and a distinctive vocalist whose trademark was a contagiously playful sense of humor. The album's success was driven by several singles: "Sock It 2 Me" (#12 pop, #4 R&B, 1997) (with a B side, "The Rain [Supa Dupa Fly]," featuring a sample from Ann Peebles's Memphis soul classic "I Can't Stand the Rain"); "Beep Me 911" (#13 R&B, 1998); and "Hit 'Em wit da Hee" (#61 R&B, 1998). During summer 1998, Elliott toured as part of Lilith Fair (the first hiphop artist to do so), and the following year released *Da Real World* (#10 pop, #1 R&B, 1999). The first two singles "She's a Bitch" (#90 pop, #30 R&B, 1999) and "All n My Grill" (#64 pop, #16 R&B, 1999) charted respectably, but "Hot Boyz" (#5 pop, #1 R&B, 1999), with guest raps from Nas, Eve and Q-Tip, became ubiquitous. *Miss E . . . So Addictive* launched the hit "Get Ur Freak On" (#7 pop, #3 R&B).

Ramblin' Jack Elliott

Born Elliott Charles Adnopoz, Aug. 1, 1931, New York, NY
1962—*Ramblin' Jack Elliott Sings Woody Guthrie and Jimmie Rodgers* (Monitor) 1968—*Young Brigham* (Reprise) 1976—*The Essential Ramblin' Jack Elliott* (Vanguard) 1989—*Hard Travelin'* (Fantasy) 1995—*Me & Bobby McGee* (Rounder); *South Coast* (Red House) 1996—*Ramblin' Jack* (Topic) 1997—*Kerouac's Last Dream* (Appleseed); *America* (with Derrol Adams) (A World of Music) 1998—*Friends of Mine* (Hightone) 1999—*The Long Ride; Early Sessions* (Tradition) 2000—*Best of the Vanguard Years* (Vanguard); *The Ballad of Ramblin' Jack* soundtrack.

Brooklyn-born Ramblin' Jack Elliott is one of the last roaming cowboy-troubadours, a distinction he earned by wandering in the West with Woody Guthrie shortly before the latter was hospitalized with terminal Huntington's chorea.

Elliott left home in 1946 to join the rodeo in Chicago, beginning years of traveling that provided the stories he told onstage. As early as 1953 Elliott was performing regularly in Greenwich Village's Washington Square Park, helping to lay groundwork for the early-'60s folk boom. In the late '50s he settled on the moniker "Ramblin' Jack" (after calling himself "Buck Elliott" for a while). He toured England and Europe for several years, jamming with traditional folk artists like Peggy Seeger and Ewan McColl and with British R&B stalwart Long John Baldry. He often performed Guthrie compositions ("Pretty Boy Floyd") and such flat-picking showcases as "Black Snake Moan."

Upon returning to the U.S. in 1961 Elliott found himself an old hand in the burgeoning folk renaissance, and his Vanguard debut album was received enthusiastically. Bob Dylan, also a Guthrie fan, was heavily influenced by Elliott, who recorded several Dylan songs in the '60s (claiming once that Dylan wrote "Don't Think Twice, It's All Right" for him). He was also part of Dylan's 1975 Rolling Thunder entourage.

Elliott recorded consistently through the '60s and '70s. In 1968 he performed at a star-studded memorial concert for Guthrie at Carnegie Hall. His best work can be found on compilations like Vanguard's *Essential Jack Elliott* and Folkways' *Songs to Grow On* (all Guthrie material). Although he didn't record any albums in the '80s (1989's *Hard Travelin'* was a single-disc reissue of two early-'60s albums for the Prestige label, *Sings the Songs of Woody Guthrie* and *Ramblin' Jack Elliott*), the latter-half of the '90s found him enjoying a career resurgence. His 1995 album, *South Coast,* won a Grammy for Best Traditional Folk Album. In 1998 Elliott released another Grammy-nominated set, *Friends of Mine,* which featured collaborations with John Prine, Tom Waits, Emmylou Harris, Nanci Griffith, Arlo Guthrie, Jerry Jeff Walker, Bob Weir, Guy Clark, Peter Rowan, and Rosalie Sorrels. The following year's *The Long Ride* (also nominated for a Grammy) featured Dave Van Ronk, Dave Alvin (of the Blasters), Tom Russell, and Maria Muldaur. In 1999 he received the National Medal of Arts at the White House, and the following year was the subject of a documentary filmed by his daughter Aiyana. *The Ballad of Ramblin' Jack* premiered at the 2000 Sundance Film Festival and won a Special Jury Prize for Artistic Achievement in Documentary Film.

Joe Ely

Born Feb. 9, 1947, Amarillo, TX
1977—*Joe Ely* (MCA) 1978—*Honky Tonk Masquerade* 1979—*Down on the Drag* 1980—*Live Shots* 1981—*Musta Notta Gotta Lotta* 1984—*High Res* 1987—*Lord of the Highway* (HighTone) 1988—*Dig All Night* 1990—*Live at Liberty Lunch* (MCA) 1992—*Love and Danger* 1995—*Letter to Laredo* 1998—*Twistin' in the Wind* 2000—*Live @ Antones* (Rounder).
With the Flatlanders: 1990—*More a Legend Than a Band* (Rounder).
With Los Super Seven: 1998—*Los Super Seven* (RCA).

Joe Ely's band and his songs are rooted in the traditions of his native West Texas—honky-tonk, C&W, R&B, rockabilly, Western swing, and Tex-Mex. Outside of the Lubbock and Austin, Texas, club circuit, most of his early support came from the rock press until the Clash introduced him to their fans in 1980.

Ely began playing in rock & roll bands in his hometown of Lubbock at age 13. When he was 16, he dropped out of school to wander from Texas to California, Tennessee, New York, Europe, New Mexico, and back to Texas. He worked as a fruit picker, a circus hand, a janitor, a dishwasher, and an itinerant musician. On return trips to Lubbock, he played in bands with Jimmie Dale Gilmore [see entry], with whom he would collaborate off and on for the next three decades. Their best-known group effort, the Flatlanders (which also included noted Lubbock songwriter Butch Hancock), played old-timey country music and recorded an album in 1972 that was not widely released until 1990.

Back in Lubbock in 1974, Ely formed his own band with guitarist Jesse Taylor, steel guitarist Lloyd Maines, bassist Gregg Wright, and drummer Steve Keeton. They became local favorites, then began traveling the state honky-tonk circuit. In 1977 MCA signed Ely, and producer Chip Young took him and his band to Nashville to cut his first album. By then, Ely's repertoire included 300 songs, most his own or written by Gilmore or Hancock.

Ely's second album, the critically acclaimed *Honky Tonk Masquerade,* featured accordionist Ponty Bone and was even more multifarious than the first. *Down on the Drag,* produced by Bob Johnston (Bob Dylan, Aretha Franklin, Johnny Cash), focused his image as a tough-skinned-but-gentlehearted singer/songwriter but was no more appealing to radio programmers.

Ely picked up some valuable fans among musicians, however. Merle Haggard took him on a tour of Britain in 1979, and the next year the Clash asked him to open their Texas shows. The Clash's Joe Strummer invited him along for the rest of their American tour and back to England with them: *Live Shots* was recorded at Clash concerts in England. Due to low sales, Ely was dropped by MCA in the mid-'80s, and began recording for independent HighTone. MCA re-signed him in 1990, however, and promptly released *Live at Liberty Lunch* (#57 C&W), which documented an Ely performance at one of Austin's best clubs. With *Love and Danger,* Ely continued to forge his own sound from Texan raw materials, recording his own material as well as two songs by fellow Lonestar State songwriter Robert Earl Keen and a contribution from ex-Blaster Dave Alvin.

Letter to Laredo, a collection of ranchero-flavored story songs (highlighted by Tom Russell's cockfight ballad "Gallo del Cielo"), introduced flamenco guitarist Teyé to the Joe Ely Band and featured background vocals by Bruce Springsteen. *Twistin' in the Wind* (#55 C&W) continued in the same vein, but its disappointing sales resulted in Ely being dropped by MCA a second time. Nevertheless, 1998 proved a fruitful year for Ely. As part of the Tex-Mex supergroup Los Super Seven (which also included Freddy Fender and members of Los Lobos), he shared a Grammy Award for Best Mexican-American Music Performance. He also reteamed with Gilmore and Hancock to record "South Wind of Summer," the first new Flatlanders song in about 25 years, for the soundtrack to *The Horse Whisperer.* A newfound enthusiasm for writing together led to the trio's first-ever national tour in the spring of 2000 and talk of a possible new album. In the meantime, Ely released his third live album, *Live @ Antones,* that summer.

Emerson, Lake and Palmer

Formed 1970, England
Keith Emerson (b. Nov. 1, 1944, Todmorden, Eng.), kybds.; Greg Lake (b. Nov. 10, 1948, Bournemouth, Eng.), bass, gtr., voc.; Carl Palmer (b. Mar. 20, 1947, Birmingham, Eng.), drums, perc.
1970—*Emerson, Lake and Palmer* (Cotillion) 1971—*Tarkus; Pictures at an Exhibition* 1972—*Trilogy* 1973—*Brain Salad Surgery* (Manticore) 1974—*Welcome Back, My Friends, to the Show That Never Ends—Ladies and Gentlemen, Emerson, Lake and Palmer* 1977—*Works, vol. I* (Atlantic); *Works, vol. II* 1978—*Love Beach* 1979—*Emerson, Lake and Palmer in Concert* 1980—*Best of Emerson, Lake and Palmer* 1986—(group re-forms: Emerson; Lake; + Cozy Powell [b. Dec. 29, 1947, Cirencester, Eng.], drums) *Emerson, Lake and Powell* (Polydor) (– Powell) 1987—(+ Palmer; – Palmer) 1988—(+ Robert Barry, gtr.) *To the Power of Three* (as 3) (Geffen) (– Barry) 1992—(+ Palmer) *Black Moon* (Victory) 1993—*Live at the Royal Albert Hall; The Return of the Manticore* 1994—*In the Hot Seat* 1997—*Greatest Hits Live* (King Biscuit Flower Hour) 1998—*Then & Now* (Eagle Entertainment).
Greg Lake solo: 1981—*Greg Lake* (Chrysalis).

Emerson, Lake and Palmer ushered in the classical-flavored progressive rock of the early '70s. With Greg Lake's predominantly acoustic ballads becoming hit singles and Keith Emerson's keyboard excesses supplying pretensions, the trio was enormously popular in its time, although it never regained momentum after a 1975–77 hiatus.

The group was formed after Emerson, then leading the Nice [see entry], and Lake, formerly of King Crimson [see entry], jammed at the Fillmore West in 1969 while both were touring with their respective bands. Emerson had studied classical piano and later dabbled in jazz; he made his professional debut at 19 with British R&B singer Gary Farr and the T-Bones. Two years later he joined the VIPs, some of whose members later surfaced in Spooky Tooth; and in early 1967 he joined American soul singer P.P. Arnold's band, then headquartered in Europe. Emerson formed the Nice in 1967, and broke up the band to work with Lake, whose background included work with various local bands from the age of 12 (the Shame, the Gods, and later, King Crimson).

After plans to work with Jimi Hendrix Experience drummer Mitch Mitchell fell through, in June 1970 Emerson and Lake decided on Carl Palmer, a veteran of Chris Farlowe, Arthur Brown, and Atomic Rooster. ELP debuted on August 25; just four days later the trio appeared at the 1970 Isle of Wight Festival, playing Emerson's transcription of Mussorgsky's *Pictures at an Exhibition,* which later became the band's third album. Its debut LP, recorded in October 1970, went gold on the strength of Lake's "Lucky Man" (#48, 1971). FM radio play and flamboyantly bombastic concerts—with Emerson's electric keyboards flashing lights and whirling around; Palmer's $25,000 percussion set including xylophone, tympani, and gong as well as an elevator platform, and the usual lights and smoke—cemented the group's following.

Each of ELP's first nine albums went gold. *Trilogy,* which reached #5, contained the trio's highest-charting single, Lake's gentle "From the Beginning" (#39, 1972). In 1973 the group formed its own Manticore Records, which released albums by Italy's Premiata Forneria Marconi (P.F.M.) and sometime Lake lyricist Pete Sinfield, along with ELP's *Brain Salad Surgery* (which included the FM staple "Still . . . You Turn Me On"). ELP's 1973–74 world tour required 36 tons of equipment, including a quadraphonic sound system, lasers, and other paraphernalia, and was documented on the triple live set *Welcome Back, My Friends, to the Show That Never Ends.*

With 6 million in sales behind them, ELP took a two-year break, ending it in 1977 with the release of *Works, volume I* and, later that same year, *volume II.* Though advertised as ELP albums, both albums consisted largely of solo pieces, such as Lake's "C'est la Vie" and "I Believe in Father Christmas." A 1977 world tour called for an entourage of 115 people, including full orchestra and choir, but had to be drastically reduced when ticket sales didn't materialize. Shortly after the late-1978 release of *Love Beach,* the group's only LP to that point not to make the Top 40, ELP announced its breakup.

Of the three, Palmer enjoyed the most successful post-ELP career, joining the progressive-pop supergroup Asia in 1981 [see entry]. Emerson was sporadically active; he scored the 1981 thriller film *Nighthawks* and issued a little-heard album of Christmas music in 1988, while Lake revived the solo career begun during the group's hiatus. He released an eponymously titled album in 1981, toured the U.S., and briefly took John Wetton's spot in Asia for a Far East tour.

Having witnessed fellow progressive rockers Yes' mid-'80s commercial revival, Emerson and Lake put ELP back together in 1985—only this time the *P* stood for veteran drummer Cozy Powell; Palmer wasn't interested in rejoining at the time. This lineup's lone album produced one memorable song, the single "Touch & Go" (#60, 1986). Following a U.S. tour, Powell left. This time when invited, Palmer accepted, but when rehearsals for a new ELP album proved unproductive, Emerson and Lake recorded instead as "3" with a California guitarist named Robert Barry. This configuration's 1988 LP, *To the Power of Three,* attracted little attention.

Emerson, Lake and Palmer tried once again, and came up with *Black Moon,* released in 1992 on the Victory label. Despite dismal sales, ELP discovered a vast audience for its live show: A nine-month 1992–93 world tour took the group to America, Europe, and South America. *The Return of the Manticore* box set featured new studio recordings of "Pictures at an Exhibition" as well as tracks from each member's pre-ELP days: the Nice's "Hang On to a Dream," King Crimson's "21st Century Schizoid Man," and Arthur Brown's "Fire."

At the end of 1993, the band started to work on a new album with producer Keith Olsen (Fleetwood Mac, Pat Benatar), but the sessions had to be interrupted when Keith Emerson developed nerve problems in his right arm. The album, *In the Hot Seat,* had to be pieced together, since Emerson couldn't play, and it was an artistic and commercial failure. After the guitarist had recovered, the band resumed touring—which had always been their greatest strength anyway, as exemplified by the several live albums they have released over the years. The latest, *Then & Now,* is a 2-CD set combining a show taped at the 1974 California Jam concert and material from the 1997–1998 tour. In 1998 Palmer joined a re-formed Asia, officially belonging to both bands.

EMF

Formed Oct. 1989, Cinderford, Eng.
James Atkin (b. Mar. 28, 1967, Cinderford), voc.; Ian Dench (b. Aug. 7, 1964, Cinderford), gtr.; Derran "Derry" Brownson (b. Nov. 10, 1970, Cinderford), kybds.; Zachary Foley (b. Dec. 9, 1970, Cinderford), bass; Mark Decloedt (b. June 26, 1967, Cinderford), drums.
1991—*Schubert Dip* (EMI) 1992—*Unexplained* EP; *Stigma* 1995—*Cha Cha Cha* (Parlophone).

EMF emerged from the sleepy, rural Gloucester area in the West of England in spring 1991 with "Unbelievable," an international rock-dance smash that leapt to the top of the charts.

All five members had played in local bands before meeting at keyboardist Derry Brownson's Cinderford clothing store, Kix. Two months after forming, EMF played its first gig; band members later claimed the name stood for "Epsom Mad Funkers," not the oft-speculated "Ecstasy Mother Fuckers" which gave the mistaken impression the group was part of England's rave scene. The group added techno elements to its rock sound only after discovering a cheap Casio sampler/sequencer in a local store.

EMF gradually built a reputation in England, busing in fans from its native Forest of Dean area to London for club gigs. EMI signed the group in spring 1990; by the end of the year "Unbelievable" was a smash British hit, and it later went to #1 on the American pop charts, while EMF's debut album (#12, 1991)—titled with a pun on the classical composer and on the British candy sherbet dipùalso—yielded a lesser hit in "Lies" (#18, 1991). The track drew the ire of Yoko Ono because it included a sample of Mark David Chapman, John Lennon's killer, reciting the lyrics to Lennon's tune "Watching the Wheels." The band paid $15,000 in an out-of-court settlement and deleted Chapman's voice from future editions of the song. While Tom Jones added "Unbelievable" to his stage show, *Stigma* failed to chart or yield a hit single.

The band returned in 1995 with *Cha Cha Cha,* which failed to generate any renewed commercial interest, effectively ending EMF's career.

Eminem

Born Marshall Bruce Mathers III, Oct. 17, 1974, St. Joseph, MO
1997—*Infinite* (Web Entertainment) 1998—*The Slim Shady EP* 1999—*The Slim Shady LP* (Aftermath/Interscope) 2000—*The Marshall Mathers LP.*

From Elvis Presley to N.W.A to Marilyn Manson, many a rock and rap artist has flirted with and even flaunted controversy—but never with the uniform gusto and unapologetic panache of Eminem. On his 1999 major-label debut, *The Slim Shady LP* (#2 pop, #1 R&B), the Detroit-based white rapper spared nobody his verbal crosshairs, including not only his detractors but himself; Kim, his wife and the mother of his daughter; and his *own* mother (who later ended up filing a defamation of character lawsuit against him). The following year's doubly venomous *The Marshall Mathers LP* (#1 pop, #1 R&B) raised/lowered the bar even more, drawing intense protest from gay, lesbian, religious, and women's groups, even as it became the fastest-selling rap album of all time and topped many critics' year-end best-of lists.

Eminem was born Marshall Bruce Mathers III just outside of Kansas City, Missouri. He never knew his father and was raised along with a younger half-brother by his mother, Debbie Mathers-Briggs, who moved the family to a predominately black neighborhood on the East side of Detroit when Mathers was 11. Although he was bullied and harassed by other kids on a regular basis, Mathers found a handful of friends who recognized his rhyming skills, and after failing ninth grade three years in a row, he dropped out of school and began competing in local freestyle throw-downs with his crew, the Dirty Dozen.

He released his first solo album, *Infinite*, on the local Web Entertainment label in 1996. It failed to garner much attention, but the followup, 1998's *The Slim Shady EP*, so impressed N.W.A alum and rap icon Dr. Dre that he signed Eminem to his Interscope imprint, Aftermath. The EP was expanded into the Dre-coproduced *The Slim Shady LP*, which debuted on the pop chart at #3 in February 1999 and went on to sell 3 million copies and win Eminem a Grammy for Best Rap Album. Like the EP before it, the album showcased Eminem's maniacal double ego Slim Shady—a homicidal comedian through whom Mathers enacted his most outrageous and perverse revenge fantasies. The catchy lead single "My Name Is" (#18 R&B) was a huge crossover success, climbing to #36 on the Hot 100 and eventually winning a Grammy for Best Rap Solo Performance. Meanwhile, moral watchdogs loudly protested darker fare on the album like " '97 Bonnie and Clyde," in which Eminem sings lovingly to his baby daughter while enroute to dump her murdered mother in a body of water.

The combination of Eminem's unique, behind-the-beat nasal flow (many critics and artists, both black and white, hailed him as one of the best MCs in the world), crossover appeal, and willingness to attack and offend anything in his way without prejudice quickly established the young rapper as a seemingly unstoppable phenomenon—a fact further proven when *The Marshall Mathers LP* debuted at the top of the chart in 2000 with close to 1.7 million copies sold its first week in stores.

The monster crossover hit came with "The Real Slim Shady" (#4 pop, #11 R&B, 2000), while the Gay and Lesbian Alliance Against Defamation (GLADD) led the protest charge, extremely alarmed over a recurring theme of hateful homophobia throughout the album. The debate peaked when openly gay rocker—and outspoken Eminem fan—Elton John performed with the rapper at the 2001 Grammy Awards ceremony (where Eminem won his second Best Rap Album but lost Album of the Year to Steely Dan). Together, Eminem and John performed the song "Stan," a cautionary tale about a disturbed fan taking Eminem's violent Slim Shady fantasies too seriously. The album version of "Stan" drew its disarmingly pretty chorus from the song "Thank You" by English singer/songwriter Dido, whose own career subsequently took off due to the exposure.

In the midst of all his critical and commercial success and the controversy stirred up over his lyrics, Eminem was besieged by lawsuits and run-ins with the law. In addition to his mother's defamation suit, Mathers was also sued by his estranged wife (the girlfriend he "killed" in " '97 Bonnie & Clyde" and again in "Kim" from *The Marshall Mathers LP*). The couple later reconciled and his wife dropped the suit, but the pair eventually divorced in 2001. Meanwhile, Mathers pleaded guilty to charges of carrying a concealed weapon in a criminal case stemming from a June 2000 incident in which he allegedly assaulted a man outside of a nightclub for kissing his wife. He received two years' probation.

The Emotions

Formed 1968, Chicago, IL
Wanda Hutchinson (b. Dec. 17, 1951, Chicago), voc.; Sheila Hutchinson (b. Jan. 17, 1953, voc.); Jeanette Hutchinson (b. 1951, Chicago), voc.
1969—*So I Can Love You* (Stax) 1970—(+ Theresa Davis [b. Aug. 22, 1950, Chicago], voc.) *Untouched* 1976—*Flowers* (Columbia) 1977—(– J. Hutchinson; + Pamela Hutchinson [b. 1958, Chicago], voc.) *Sunshine* (Stax) (+ J. Hutchinson); *Rejoice* (Columbia) 1979—*Come Into Our World* 1981—*New Affair* 1984—*Sincerely* (Red Label) 1985—*If I Only Knew* (Motown) 1996—*Best of My Love: Best of the Emotions* (Columbia Legacy).

A gospel-turned-soul family group in the Staples tradition, the Emotions have been entertaining black audiences since they could walk. Their biggest successes (like the #1 "Best of My Love") came in the late '70s under the guidance of Maurice White of Earth, Wind & Fire (with whom they recorded EW&F's 1979 hit "Boogie Wonderland").

Father/manager (and occasional guitarist and vocalist) Joe had his three oldest daughters performing in church as tots. Beginning in 1961 they traveled the gospel circuit as the Heavenly (later the Hutchinson) Sunbeams and occasionally toured with Mahalia Jackson. While attending Chicago's Parker High School in the mid-'60s, they became the Three

Ribbons and a Bow (Papa Joe was the "beau") and began concentrating on more secular material, cutting an unsuccessful series of singles for several Midwestern labels, including Vee-Jay. While touring, they met the Staples, who helped them acquire a contract with Stax-Volt in 1968.

Rechristened the Emotions, the group enjoyed substantial R&B success and made occasional modest pop inroads—"So I Can Love You" (#39 pop, #3 R&B, 1969), "Show Me How" (#52 pop, #13 R&B, 1971)—through the early '70s. They appeared in the 1973 film *Wattstax* and toured with the Jackson 5, Sly and the Family Stone, B.B. King, Stevie Wonder, Bobby "Blue" Bland, and others.

When Stax folded in 1975, the Emotions signed with Maurice White's Kalimba Productions and thus got on the Columbia roster. White wrote the title track and produced their gold debut for the label, *Flowers* (which prominently featured Wanda's material and lead vocals), as well as the platinum followup, *Rejoice* (#7, 1977). They enjoyed hit singles with "I Don't Wanna Lose Your Love" (#51 pop, #13 R&B, 1976) and the Grammy-winning disco favorite "Best of My Love," and toured with Earth, Wind & Fire in 1976. Other hits were "Don't Ask My Neighbors" (#44 pop, #7 R&B, 1977) and "Smile" (#6 R&B, 1978). By the late '70s they were writing the bulk of their material themselves. The group recorded briefly for Motown before fizzling out

The English Beat

Formed 1978, Birmingham, Eng.
Andy Cox (b. Jan. 25, 1956, Birmingham), gtr.; Everett Morton (b. Apr. 5, 1951, St. Kitts), drums; David Steele (b. Sep. 8, 1960, Isle of Wight, Eng.), bass; Dave Wakeling (b. Feb. 19, 1956, Birmingham), gtr., voc.
1979—(+ Ranking Roger [b. Roger Charlery, Feb. 21, 1961, Birmingham], voc.; + Saxa [b. ca. 1930, Jam.], sax)
1980—*I Just Can't Stop It* (Sire) 1981—*Wha'ppen* 1982—*Special Beat Service* (I.R.S.) 1983—*What Is Beat?* 1991—*The Beat Goes On* 1995—*b.p.m.—The Very Best of the English Beat (Arista).*
General Public (Wakeling; Roger): 1984—*. . . All the Rage* (I.R.S.) 1986—*Hand to Mouth* 1995—*Rub It Better* (Epic).
Ranking Roger solo: 1988—*Radical Departure* (I.R.S.).
Dave Wakeling solo: 1991—*No Warning* (I.R.S.).

The English Beat (known simply as the Beat everywhere except the U.S., where an L.A. power-pop band also went by that name) originated in the British ska revival of the late '70s. Since the band's breakup in 1983, members of the group have gone on to fame as founders of Fine Young Cannibals.

The three white members of the multiracial Beat, Dave Wakeling, Andy Cox, and David Steele, began playing together in 1978. Reggae and other Jamaican rhythms tempered their punk-rock repertoire when they were joined by Everett Morton, a black West Indian who had drummed for Joan Armatrading. The quartet played its first gig at a Birmingham club in March 1979, opening for a punk group whose black drummer was Ranking Roger; soon after Roger began "toasting" (chanting over the songs) at its gigs and later joined the Beat as second vocalist.

The Specials released the Beat's debut record, a cover of Smokey Robinson's "Tears of a Clown" on their 2-Tone label in late 1979. For that recording session, the group enlisted Saxa, a 50-year-old Jamaican saxophonist who had played with the Beatles in their Liverpool years and with such ska stars as Prince Buster, Desmond Dekker, and Laurel Aitken. When the single went to #6 in the U.K., Saxa joined the Beat.

The group formed its own label, Go Feet; its first two releases, "Hands Off . . . She's Mine" and "Mirror in the Bathroom," made the U.K. Top 10, and the third, "Best Friend," made the Top 30. After recording a debut album, the Beat toured Europe accompanied by David "Blockhead" Wright, who became an unofficial member. The group returned to Birmingham to find *I Just Can't Stop It* at #3, U.K. Billed as the English Beat, it toured the U.S. in fall 1980, opening for the Pretenders and Talking Heads, and returned to tour as headliners in 1981 and '82. In Britain *Wha'ppen* (1981) went to #2, and "Too Nice to Talk To" hit #7, while "Drowning" and "Doors to Your Heart" made the Top 40.

Special Beat Service (#39, 1982) was the English Beat's first album to sell well in America, with the track "Save It for Later" receiving FM airplay. Shortly after its release, Saxa announced that he would no longer tour with the group. The remainder of the band split acrimoniously a year later. Cox and Steele went on to form Fine Young Cannibals [see entry], while Wakeling and Roger became General Public.

General Public recorded two albums, *. . . All the Rage* (1984) and *Hand to Mouth* (1986), which, even with the help of the Clash's Mick Jones (on *Rage*) and Saxa (on *Hand*), failed to make the U.K. or U.S. charts. The group disbanded in 1988, but regrouped in 1994 to record *Rub It Better.* Roger released a solo LP, 1988's *Radical Departure,* and with the Specials' Neville Staples toured as Special Beat in 1990.

Wakeling left the music business in 1989 after sessions for an album, *The Happiest Man in the World,* fell apart (an album, *No Warning,* was released in 1991). He moved to L.A., where he worked for Greenpeace, and sometimes joined Special Beat for Southern California dates. In 1999, billed as "the English Beat's Dave Wakeling," Wakeling opened for Hootie and the Blowfish, who had been covering his "Save It for Later." He has continued to play occasionally under that name. He also formed the Free Radicals. Plans for a revue featuring members of the Beat, General Public, and Fine Young Cannibals have yet to bear fruit.

Brian Eno

Born Brian Peter George St. John le Baptiste de la Salle Eno, May 15, 1948, Woodbridge, Eng.
1973—*No Pussyfooting* (with Robert Fripp) (Antilles); *Here Come the Warm Jets* 1974—*June 1st, 1974* (with John Cale, Nico, and Kevin Ayers); *Taking Tiger Mountain (by Strategy)* 1975—*Another Green World; Evening Star* (with Robert Fripp); *Discreet*

Music (Obscure) 1977—*Before and After Science* (Island); *Cluster and Eno* 1978—*Music for Films* (EG); *After the Heat* (with Moebius and Roedelius) (Sky); *Ambient 1: Music for Airports* (Editions EG) 1980—*Fourth World, vol. 1 Possible Musics* (with Jon Hassell); *The Plateaux of Mirror* (with Roger Eno and Harold Budd); *Ambient 3: Days of Radiance* (with Laraaji) 1981—*My Life in the Bush of Ghosts* (with David Byrne) (Sire); *Music for Airplay* (Editions EG) 1982 *Ambient 4: On Land* 1983—*Music for Films, vol. 2; Apollo: Atmospheres & Soundtracks* (with Daniel Lanois and Roger Eno) 1984—*Begegnungen* (Gyroscope); *The Pearl* (with Daniel Lanois and Harold Budd) 1985—*Hybrid* (with Michael Brook and Daniel Lanois); *Voices* (with Roger Eno); *Thursday Afternoon; Begegnungen II* 1986—*More Blank than Frank* (Polydor); *Desert Island Selection* 1990—*Wrong Way Up* (with John Cale) (Opal/Warner Bros.) 1991—*My Squelchy Life* 1992—*Nerve Net* (Warner Bros.); *The Shutov Assembly* (Opal); *Robert Sheckley's In a Land of Clear Colors* (Alex) 1993—*Neroli* (Gyroscope/Caroline); *Brian Eno II* (Virgin) 1994—*Brian Eno;* Familiar (Gyroscope); *Headcandy* (Ion) 1997—*The Drop* (Thirsty Ear) 1999—*Sonora Portraits* (Materiali Sonori, It.).

Self-described "nonmusician" and studio experimentalist Brian Eno has greatly influenced an encyclopedia of styles—from art rock to punk to world music to techno. A founding member of Roxy Music, he went on to work as a solo artist and a producer/collaborator with U2, Talking Heads, David Bowie, Robert Fripp, and others. His series of ambient music records (by himself and with such composers as Jon Hassell, Harold Budd, and Laraaji) feature an atmospheric instrumental sound that found expression in both New Age and minimalist work. An aesthetic breakthrough, his tape-delay system, developed for Robert Fripp as "Frippertronics," insisted on the conscious use of recording technology as a method of composition and paved the way for the "sampling" used extensively in rap and techno.

The son of a postman and a Belgian emigrant, Eno first heard rock & roll at age seven in the R&B records his older sister got from American servicemen stationed at a nearby air force base. An art-school alumnus, Eno was influenced by contemporary composers John Tilbury and Cornelius Cardew and such minimalists as La Monte Young and Terry Riley; he also participated occasionally in a rock band called Maxwell Demon. In 1971 he helped start Roxy Music [see entry]; their synthesizer player and eccentric visual centerpiece, he electronically "treated" the band's other instruments. After working on *Roxy Music* and *For Your Pleasure,* he departed in 1973 due to friction with songwriter Bryan Ferry.

After *No Pussyfooting* (with Robert Fripp), Eno put out two records of free-associative, noisily inventive songs—*Here Come the Warm Jets* and *Taking Tiger Mountain by Strategy*—and produced the Portsmouth Sinfonia, an orchestra of quasi-competent musicians playing discordant versions of light classics. His 1974 solo tour ended when he was hospitalized for a collapsed lung, although he appeared on two concert albums: *June 1st, 1974* (with Kevin Ayers, John Cale, and Nico) and *801 Live* (801 was a group led by Roxy Music guitarist Phil Manzanera).

Although Eno dabbles on all sorts of instruments, he is most accomplished on tape recorder, of which he owns dozens, and is fascinated by the happy accidents of the recording process. He created a deck of tarotlike cards called Oblique Strategies ("Emphasize the flaws"; "Use another color"), and has used them to make artistic decisions.

In 1975 Eno started Obscure Records to release his tapes and works by other composers. His many collaborations of the decade included *Evening Star* with Robert Fripp; an album by Robert Calvert of Hawkwind; a David Bowie trilogy *(Low, "Heroes",* and *Lodger);* albums with the German synthesizer band Cluster. His concurrent production work included Talking Heads *(More Songs About Buildings and Food; Fear of Music; Remain in Light);* debuts for Ultravox *(Ultravox!)* and Devo *(Q: Are We Not Men? A: We Are Devo!);* and a no-wave compilation featuring DNA, Mars, the Contortions, and Teenage Jesus and the Jerks, entitled *No New York.*

Under his own name, Eno has recorded ambient music albums (*Discreet Music, Music for Films,* and *Music for Airports,* which was broadcast for a while at New York's LaGuardia Airport); pop albums (*Before and After Science* and, with John Cale, *Wrong Way Up);* and a Top 30 album (*My Life in the Bush of Ghosts,* which lent a techno edge to the fast-developing genre of world music).

In 1980 Eno began a partnership with producer Daniel Lanois that proved as fruitful as his alliances with Fripp and Talking Heads. Working on *Voices* with Eno's brother, Roger, and *The Plateaux of Mirror* with minimalist composer Harold Budd, the pair forged a path into unexplored sonic territory. They went on to craft a new sound for U2, producing the Irish quartet's albums *The Unforgettable Fire* and *The Joshua Tree.* For Eno, long regarded as a cult figure, this was an uncharacteristically high-profile enterprise; his collaboration on U2's *Achtung Baby* and *Zooropa* saw him moving the rock band in a quasi-ambient direction and also employing industrial noise touches.

By the 1990s, Eno was an established voice in a range of contemporary musics. In *Low Symphony,* composer Philip Glass spun off themes and variations of Bowie's *Low,* a work indelibly marked by Eno's stamp; the ambient techno bands like the Orb and Irresistible Force owed an obvious debt to Eno. He has also long been interested in other media, his video installations having been exhibited at the Venice Biennale and the Pompidou Centre in Paris, and his 1996 autobiography, *A Year (With Swollen Appendices)* having provided an index of his omnivorous interests. He has also developed computer software that facilitates his interest in self-evolving compositions. As composer, producer, keyboardist, and singer, he is responsible less for a new sound in pop than for a new way of thinking about music—as an atmosphere, rather than a statement, an experiment in sound, rather than a virtuosic expression. Combining the cerebral qualities of European high culture with the technological outlook of a futurist, he has also been responsible for an aesthetic movement that incorporates both Western and Third World sounds.

John Entwistle: See the Who

En Vogue

Formed July 18, 1988, Oakland, CA
Cindy Herron (b. Sep. 26, 1965, San Francisco, CA), voc.; Maxine Jones (b. Jan. 16, 1966, Paterson, NJ), voc.; Terry Ellis (b. Sep. 5, 1966, Houston, TX), voc.; Dawn Robinson (b. Nov. 28, 1968, New London, CT), voc.
1990—*Born to Sing* (Atlantic) 1991—*Remix to Sing* (EastWest) 1992—*Funky Divas* 1993—*Runaway Love* EP 1997—(– Robinson) *EV3* (Elektra/Asylum) 1999—*Best of En Vogue* (WEA) 2000—*Masterpiece Theater.*
Terry Ellis solo: 1995—*Southern Gal* (East/West).
Dawn Robinson with Lucy Pearl: 2000—*Lucy Pearl* (Pookie).

With its tight four-part harmonies, provocative choreography, shared leads, and retro glamour, En Vogue revived the R&B girl-group tradition. Cindy Herron, Maxine Jones, Terry Ellis, and Dawn Robinson barely knew one another before auditioning for a group being assembled by Bay Area producers Denzil Foster and Thomas McElroy, whose previous credits included Timex Social Club ("Rumors"), Club Nouveau ("Lean on Me"), and Tony! Toni! Toné!. They envisioned rejuvenating R&B with hip-hop rhythms, and their New Jack Swing grooves raised En Vogue above the slew of contemporary girl groups (e.g., Sweet Sensation, Exposé).

En Vogue, then just Vogue, sang two songs on *FM²*, Foster and McElroy's Quincy Jones–style concept album. The quartet recorded *Born to Sing* (#21) in fall 1989. After its release the following spring, the album went platinum, led by the single "Hold On" (#2). En Vogue was nominated for a Grammy and toured with Freddie Jackson and Hammer.

That was just a prelude to En Vogue's stunning success with the multiplatinum *Funky Divas* (#8, 1992), whose Foster and McElroy–produced mix of pop, R&B, rock, rap, and reggae included the hit singles "My Lovin' (You're Never Gonna Get It)" (#2, 1992) and "Free Your Mind" (#8, 1992). *Runaway Love* (#49 pop, #16 R&B, 1993) featured new versions of tracks from *Funky Divas,* as well as "Whatta Man," where the women provided the chorus to raps by Salt-n-Pepa.

The group's music and vocals were widely praised by critics, but En Vogue's visual style also played a role. Like its stylistic predecessor, the Supremes, En Vogue performed in chic designer costumes connoting a sexy elegance. In concert the group pays tribute to divas like Aretha, Chaka Khan, and Patti LaBelle. Their glamour has paid off well in the video age; Spike Lee directed their Diet Coke commercial.

Part of En Vogue's image is its unity: Members trade off star vocal turns and cultivate a mystique of separate-but-equal personalities. They profess sister-like affection, and although Cindy Herron, a former Miss Black California, has acted since age 11 (including a role in the film *Juice*), only one of the singers has flirted with a solo career since En Vogue's formation. Not long after the release of *Runaway Love,* though, the group took a three-year sabbatical, in part due to conflict among the four members and between the women and their managers. Herron and Jones each gave birth to a child, while Ellis made a critically acclaimed solo album, *Southern Gal* (1995), that didn't sell particularly well.

Most significantly, Robinson left the group to sign a solo deal with Dr. Dre's Aftermath Records [see N.W.A entry]. Herron, Jones, and Ellis carried on as trio, releasing *EV3* (#8), an album that featured Robinson on several tracks, including lead vocals on the platinum single "Don't Let Go (Love)" (#2, 1996). The album yielded two other pop hits, "Whatever" (#16, 1997), a song written and produced by Babyface, and "Too Gone, Too Long" (#33, 1997), a Diane Warren power ballad. "No Fool No More" (#57, 1998) appeared in the Frankie Lymon biopic *Why Do Fools Fall in Love.* In 2000 En Vogue released *Masterpiece Theater;* Robinson resurfaced as a member of Lucy Pearl, a trio that also included former members of A Tribe Called Quest (DJ Ali Shaheed Muhammad) and Tony! Toni! Toné! (Raphael Saadiq).

Enya

Born Eithne Ni Bhraonain, May 17, 1961, Gweedore, County Donegal, Ire.
1986—*Enya* (Atlantic) 1987—*The Celts* (Warner Bros.) 1988—*Watermark* (Geffen) 1991—*Shepherd Moons* (Reprise) 1995—*The Memory of Trees* 1997—*Paint the Sky With Stars: The Best of Enya* 2000—*A Day Without Rain.*

Enya began her professional career playing keyboards in the successful Irish family act Clannad but eventually achieved greater fame as a solo artist. Combining elements of classical, New Age, and traditional Irish folk music, and lending her ethereal voice to lyrics that incorporated both English and

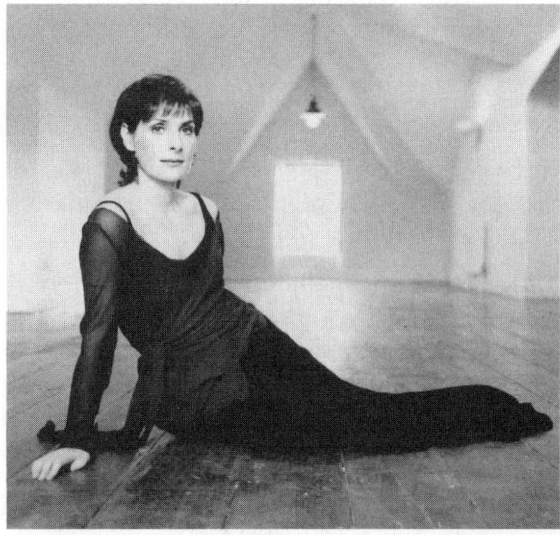

Enya

Gaelic (and sometimes Latin), Enya has produced melodic, gently haunting material that has been better received by New Age–disdaining critics and pop fans than anyone could have expected, making her the second best-selling Irish artist after U2.

One of nine children born to a couple of musicians (her father led the Slieve Foy Band, a noted Irish show band) in a Gaelic-speaking household, Enya received classical piano training during her youth. She joined the group Clannad (Gaelic for "family") in 1979, three years after it was formed by a few of her brothers, sisters, and uncles. In 1982 Enya quit the band—whose theme music for a variety of television shows had by then landed it on the pop charts—in hopes of pursuing what she saw as a more personal, less conventional musical vision. Enya's 1986 debut, composed of music she had originally written for a BBC-TV documentary series, *The Celts* (which was released as a soundtrack), garnered little attention. But its texturally similar successor, 1988's *Watermark* (#25), yielded a #1 single in the U.K., "Orinoco Flow (Sail Away)," which reached #24 in the U.S. and sold 3 million copies worldwide. Enya wrote the melodies and played all of the instruments on her recordings, while former Clannad manager Nicky Ryan served as her producer/arranger, and his wife Roma Ryan contributed lyrics. In 1991 Enya topped the success of *Watermark* with her third album, *Shepherd Moons,* which went to #17 on the U.S. pop chart.

The Memory of Trees (#9, 1995) was Enya's third consecutive album to go multiplatinum in the U.S. With the release of her mostly greatest-hits album, *Paint the Sky With Stars,* in 1997, the singer—who was notorious for not touring and rarely giving interviews—performed on late-night talk shows and spoke with the media about her music, though her personal life remained a mystery. She also played for the Queen of England, the King of Denmark, and the Pope in the late '90s. Though the general public may never hear Enya live in concert, her unique, ethereal sound has been used to evoke a spiritual mood in several films, including *L.A. Story, Far and Away,* and *The Age of Innocence.* The platinum *A Day Without Rain* reached #17 in 2001.

EPMD

Formed 1986, Brentwood, NY
Erick Sermon (a.k.a. E Double E, b. Nov. 25, 1968, Bayshore, NY), voc.; Parrish Smith (a.k.a. PMD, b. May 13, 1968, Smithtown, NY), voc., programmer.
1988—*Strictly Business* (Fresh) 1989—*Unfinished Business* 1991—*Business as Usual* (Def Jam) 1992—*Business Never Personal* (RAL/Def Jam) 1997—*Back in Business* 1999—*Out of Business.*
Erick Sermon solo: 1993—*No Pressure* (Def Jam).
Erick Sermon with Def Squad (Sermon; Redman, voc.; Keith Murray, voc.): 1998—*El Nine O* (Def Jam).
PMD solo: 1994—*Shadé Business* (Def Jam).

Once described as "the rap equivalent of a rock & roll garage band," EPMD (stands for "Erick and Parrish Making Dollars") got into the hip-hop business not to spout its political agenda, but to have fun and get paid.

Erick Sermon and Parrish Smith grew up together on Long Island, home to rappers Eric B. and Rakim, De La Soul, and Public Enemy's Flavor Flav. In 1987, while on a college break, Smith (who played tight end for Southern Connecticut State University's football team) recorded with Sermon the duo's raps, which they had first performed together the previous year. EPMD immediately released the songs as a 12-inch single ("It's My Thing" b/w "You're a Customer") on Sleeping Bag (a subsidiary of independent Fresh Records), which sold 500,000 copies. Within six weeks of its release, *Strictly Business* had topped the R&B LPs chart (#1, 1988) and gone gold. Hits included "You Gots to Chill" (#22 R&B, 1988) and "Strictly Business" (#25 R&B, 1988).

EPMD's initial sound blended suburban angst with the hardcore edge of their inner-city rap brethren. The group's self-produced raw, bass-heavy rhythm tracks were fortified liberally by sampled loops (Steve Miller's "Fly Like an Eagle," Bob Marley's "I Shot the Sheriff"). Critics pegged Sermon's slurred vocal delivery as everything from "cotton-mouthed" to sounding like he was "rapping through a mouthful of marbles."

As its title suggests, *Unfinished Business* offered more of the same. By the early '90s, with the vast popularity of gangsta rap, EPMD acknowledged the style by injecting *Business as Usual* with a harder edge, and it paid off. The album went to #36 on the pop chart and scored hits with "Gold Digger" (#14 R&B, 1991) and "Rampage" (#30 R&B, 1992), the latter a collaboration with L.L. Cool J. In 1992 the duo released *Business Never Personal* (#14 pop, #5 R&B), which contained the hit "Crossover" (#42 pop, #14 R&B, 1992). Sermon and Smith formed a production team, working with K-Solo, Das EFX, and Redman, and put together the Hit Squad package tour.

In early 1993 EPMD called it quits, according to *Billboard,* reportedly over financial disagreements so severe that one member of the duo allegedly hired people to break into the other's home to resolve the matter. Both Sermon and Smith then launched independent careers that included Sermon's Def Squad posse of acts (Redman, K-Solo, and Keith Murray) and the management of Das EFX and other acts via Smith's Shuma Entertainment. Sermon's *No Pressure* (#16 pop, #2 R&B, 1993) charted with the single "Stay Real" (#92 pop, #52 R&B). Smith (now just PMD after his moniker, Parrish Mad Deep) continued to stay in the business with *Shadé Business* (#12 R&B, 1994). Sermon also joined Redman and Murray for a Def Squad album, 1998's *El Nine O.*

The MC duo reunited as EPMD to record 1997's *Back in Business* (#4 R&B), which featured a more stripped-down sound and earned mixed reviews. It was followed two years later by *Out of Business* (#13 pop). By 1999, both had also become devout Christians. And that same year, Sermon launched his own Def Squad label (in a deal with Dreamworks/Universal), debuting with Dave Hollister's *Ghetto Hymns.* He also worked as a producer on new discs by Redman and Murray.

Erasure/Yaz

Yaz: Formed 1982, London, Eng.
Vince Clarke (b. July 3, 1960, South Woodford, Eng.), kybds.; Alison Moyet (b. Genevieve Alison-Jane Moyet, June 18, 1961, Basildon, Essex, Eng.), voc.
1982—*Upstairs at Eric's* (Sire) 1983—*You and Me Both* 1999—*The Best of Yaz* (Warner Bros.).
Erasure, formed 1985, London: Clarke, synth.; Andy Bell (b. Apr. 25, 1964, Peterborough, Eng.), voc.
1986—*Wonderland* (Sire) 1987—*Circus; The Two Ring Circus* 1988—*The Innocents; Crackers International* EP 1989—*Wild!* 1991—*Chorus* 1992—*Abba-esque* (Mute); *Pop!—The First 20 Hits* (Sire) 1994—*I Say I Say I Say* (Mute/Elektra) 1995—*Erasure* (Elektra) 1997—*Cowboy* (Maverick).

After rising to prominence in England as one half of the techno-pop duo Yazoo, songwriter and synthesizer ace Vince Clarke formed Erasure, another two-man electronic music outfit that found him paired with a distinctive, charismatic singer. As the voice of Erasure, Andy Bell became the flamboyant foil to Clarke's shy-wizard persona. Bell was one of the first openly gay pop entertainers—he chose not to change the gender of pronouns in the band's cover versions of Ike and Tina Turner's "River Deep, Mountain High" and Abba's "Gimme Gimme Gimme (A Man After Midnight)"; his gender-bending theatricality defined Erasure's live performances as much as his high-pitched voice and the danceable, synth-drunk songs that he and Clarke collaborated on established the band's overall sound.

An original member of Depeche Mode, Clarke left that group early on to form Yazoo (known as Yaz in the U.S.) with vocalist Alison Moyet [see entry]. Yazoo released two critically acclaimed albums, 1982's *Upstairs at Eric's* (#2 U.K.) and 1983's *You and Me Both* (#1 U.K.), that were successful in England but never surpassed cult-favorite status in America. When Moyet decided to embark on a solo career, Clarke teamed up briefly with Irish singer Feargal Sharkey in the Assembly. Then, in 1985, Clarke placed a blind ad for a vocalist in a British music paper; Bell responded and was selected from more than 40 applicants.

Erasure's first album, 1986's *Wonderland* (#71 U.K.), was a commercial failure that led some critics and Yazoo fans to compare Bell's voice unfavorably with Moyet's warm, husky alto. *The Circus* was better received and reached #6 on the English charts—thus vindicating Bell, whose creative input was greater on the sophomore effort. The following year, a third album, *The Innocents,* hit the top of the U.K. charts (as did the next three LPs), and two of its singles—"Chains of Love" and "A Little Respect"—nearly entered the U.S. Top 10, peaking at #12 and #14, respectively.

Erasure's only other Top 40 song to date was 1994's "Always" (#20), but the band continued to attract attention throughout most of the '90s for its outrageous stage shows, which featured Bell in gaudy drag costumes, paying homage to everyone from Tammy Wynette to Judy Garland. In 1992 Erasure paid tribute to a group of Swedish songbirds with *Abba-esque,* an Abba tribute EP. Later that year, Clarke and Bell released a compilation of their "first 20 hits," most of which deserved to be classified as such in England—where many of their albums hit the top slot—more than in the States. The duo continued to record and tour together, their contrast in personalities oddly contributing to Erasure's longevity: Clarke has said that he and Bell have never had an argument.

Eric B. and Rakim

Formed 1985, New York, NY
Eric B. (b. Eric Barrier, Nov. 8, ca. 1965, Elmhurst, NY), DJ; Rakim (b. William Griffin Jr., Jan. 28, ca. 1968, Long Island, NY), voc.
1987—*Paid in Full* (4th & Broadway/Island) 1988—*Follow the Leader* (Uni) 1990—*Let the Rhythm Hit 'Em* (MCA) 1992—*Don't Sweat the Technique.*
Eric B. solo: 1995—*Eric B.* (Nine).
Rakim solo: 1997—*18th Letter/Book of Life* (Uptown/Universal) 1999—*The Master* (PolyGram).

Hip-hop trailblazers Eric B. and Rakim's first single, "Eric B. Is President" (#48, 1986), sparked early debate on the legality of unauthorized, uncredited sampling when James Brown sued to prevent the duo's use of a fragment of his music. It also established Brown's back catalog as a hip musical mining ground for a new generation of hip-hop programmers.

With Rakim's relaxed vocal delivery ("Microphone Fiend," "Paid in Full") and rhymes that have been described as "existential," together with Eric B.'s deft turntable manipulation, the duo became one of the most acclaimed hip-hop acts of the late '80s. The two met in 1985 when Eric Barrier was working as a DJ at New York City radio station WBLS and looking for an MC to rap over his turntable work. A year later they released "Eric B. Is President" (#48 R&B, 1986) on the independent Harlem label Zakia.

Paid in Full (#58 pop, #8 R&B) appeared in 1987 with a new mix of the single, as well as songs such as "I Know You Got Soul" (#64 R&B, 1987) and "I Ain't No Joke" (#38 R&B, 1987). The duo's subsequent three albums reached the Top 40, with *Follow the Leader* peaking at #22, *Let the Rhythm Hit 'Em* at #32, and *Don't Sweat the Technique* at #22. In 1991 Eric B. and Rakim scored another hit with the theme to *House Party 2,* "What's on Your Mind" (#34 R&B). The duo, who were never close friends, parted ways after *Don't Sweat the Technique,* but not before running into another legal dispute over their sampling of Funkadelic's "No Head, No Backstage Pass," from *Follow the Leader*'s "Lyrics of Fury."

In 1995 Eric B. released a self-titled debut solo album, but spent most of the '90s as a producer and executive for Street Life Records. After suffering years of legal wrangling and label mishaps, Rakim finally reemerged in 1997 with the acclaimed *18th Letter/Book of Life* (#4 pop, #1 R&B, 1997)—a two-disc set split between new material and classic Eric B. and Rakim cuts. That same year, Rakim performed a duet with Mobb Deep for the *Hoodlum* soundtrack. The rapper returned two years later with *The Master,* which eschewed ghetto stories for a more mystical approach.

Roky Erickson/13th Floor Elevators

Born Roger Kynard Erickson, July 15, 1947, Dallas, TX
1980—*Roky Erickson and the Aliens* (CBS, U.K.) 1981—*The Evil One* (415) 1985—*Fire in My Bones* (Texas Archive Recordings) 1986—*Don't Slander Me* (Pink Dust); *Gremlins Have Pictures* 1987—*I Think of Demons* (Edsel, U.K.) 1990—*Reverend of Karmic Youth* (Skyclad) 1991—*You're Gonna Miss Me: The Best of Roky Erickson* (Restless) 1992—*Love to See You Bleed* (Swordfish); *Mad Dog* 1995—*All That May Do My Rhyme* (Trance Syndicate); *Roky Erickson & Evilhook Wildlife* (Sympathy for the Record Industry) 1999—*Never Say Goodbye* (Emperor Jones) 2000—*Hide Behind the Sun* (Aim); *Live at the Ritz* (New Rose, Fr.); *Beauty & the Beast* (Sympathy for the Record Industry).
With the 13th Floor Elevators, formed 1965, Austin, TX: Erickson, voc.; Tommy Hall, jug; Benny Thurman, bass; John Ike Walton, drums; Stacy Sutherland (d. 1977, TX), gtr. 1967—*The Psychedelic Sounds of the 13th Floor Elevators* (International Artists) (– Thurman; – Walton; + Danny Thomas, drums; + Danny Galindo, bass) 1967—*Easter Everywhere* 1968—*Thirteenth Floor Elevators Live; Bull of the Woods* 1987—*Elevator Tracks* (Texas Archive Recordings).

Roky Erickson made his mark in the '60s Texas-based psychedelic band the 13th Floor Elevators, whose garage classic "You're Gonna Miss Me" (#56, 1966) was the closest the group got to a hit single. The Elevators disbanded in 1969 after Erickson was arrested on charges of marijuana possession. He spent three years in Rusk State Hospital for the criminally insane. Since the 1970s, Erickson, who sings in a high, soaring tenor voice, has had an erratic solo career and endured schizophrenia.

The son of an architect and amateur opera singer, Erickson took up piano at five and guitar at 12. Not long after quitting Travis High School, he wrote "You're Gonna Miss Me," the protopunk tune that was originally recorded by Erickson's combo, the Spades, in 1965. The song caught the attention of jug player/lyricist Tommy Hall, who asked Erickson to join the 13th Floor Elevators, the band Hall had founded with the purpose of spreading psychedelia. After the Elevators rerecorded and released "You're Gonna Miss Me," they got a deal with International Artists; their debut album *Psychedelic Sounds* sold 140,000 copies. The band released other singles and albums but had started getting harassed by police for their heavy marijuana and LSD use. In 1969 Erickson was busted for possession of a small quantity of marijuana, pleaded not guilty by reason of insanity, and was sentenced to Rusk, where he was diagnosed as schizophrenic, subjected to electroshock therapy, and treated with Thorazine and other powerful psychotropic medications. While inside, he also formed a band with fellow inmates called the Missing Links.

By 1973 Erickson was out of the hospital and performing again. He wrote the first in a series of songs based on horror themes, including "I Walk With a Zombie," and recorded "Red Temple Prayer (Two-Headed Dog)," which had a profound influence on punk but did not chart. Due to ill-advised management, publishing, and legal decisions, numerous unauthorized releases of his music, from which he has not received royalties, have circulated since the early '80s. In 1982 Erickson signed an affidavit proclaiming himself "inhabited" by a Martian; two years later he stopped recording, and in 1987 he ceased performing.

By the early '90s, Erickson was living on $200 monthly Social Security checks and help from friends. In January 1990 he was arrested on mail theft charges, which were later dropped. Also in 1990 a group of high-profile bands including R.E.M., ZZ Top, and the Butthole Surfers appeared on the album *Where the Pyramid Meets the Eye: A Tribute to Roky Erickson* (Sire). Three years later, in 1993, Erickson reemerged in a brief performance at the Austin Music Awards, and reentered the studio later that year, recording six new songs, with assistance from Austin guitarists Charlie Sexton and Paul Leary (Butthole Surfers). Following the release of a vinyl single at the end of 1994, a new album called *All That May Do My Rhyme* was released on Butthole Surfers drummer King Coffey's Trance Syndicate label in 1995. It was Erickson's first collection of new songs in more than a decade. At the same time, Henry Rollins published *Openers II: The Lyrics of Roky Erickson* through his 2.13.61 Publications. *Never Say Goodbye* gathered previously unreleased lo-fi demos (including six tracks recorded by his mother while he was at Rusk) in 1999. And in early 2000 Erickson returned with *Hide Behind the Sun.*

Alejandro Escovedo: See Rank and File

Esquerita

Born Eskew Reeder Jr. or Esquerita Milochi, New Orleans, LA; died 1986, New York, NY
1987—*Vintage Voola* (Norton) 1990—*Esquerita* (Capitol).

Esquerita was one of the most original, colorful, and mysterious figures in rock & roll, a pianist and singer whose look and style most likely influenced Little Richard's. Little is known of Esquerita's life, and the veracity of some of his claims is hard to establish. Still, there is no denying that he was among, if not the first to combine a pumping piano style, falsetto screams and whoops, and racy lyrics into some very wild early rock & roll records. Visually as well, it would seem that Esquerita originated the flamboyant mannerisms and piled-high pompadour later adopted by Little Richard, who was still recording gospel records when his and Esquerita's paths first crossed. Among his releases—all of which have become highly valued collectors' items—were "Oh Baby," "Rockin' the Joint," "I Need You," "Batty Over Hattie," and "Esquerita Voola." He wrote Jim Lowe's 1956 #1 hit "The Green Door," but Esquerita himself never even made the Top 100 singles chart. Esquerita eventually moved to New York City, where he performed on occasion. He died of AIDS in 1986.

David Essex

Born David Albert Cook, July 23, 1947, London, Eng.
1973—*Rock On* (Columbia) 1974—*David Essex* 1975—*All the Fun of the Fair* 1976—*Out on the Street* 1979—*Imperial Wizard* (Mercury) 1980—*Hot Love* 1981—*Be-Bop the Future* 1995—*Living in England* (Cleveland International).

In the mid-'70s English pop star David Essex inspired teenybopper hysteria in his homeland. While he was able to overcome that image there and establish himself as an actor while continuing to chart singles, here in America, he is best known for his 1974 gold single "Rock On."

Essex grew up in London's East End, and at 14 he started playing the drums with a succession of amateur bands; by the time he graduated from high school he had become a lead singer. In the late-'60s theater columnist-turned-manager Derek Bowman put Essex through voice and dance training and then helped him land a role in the London production of *The Fantasticks.* He moved on to rave reviews as Jesus Christ in *Godspell,* which opened in November 1971 in London. Soon he was a teen pop idol. Essex had a hand in writing most of his U.K. hits ("Lamplight," "Gonna Make You a Star," "Hold Me Close," and "Rock On"). Most were produced by former commercial jingles writer Jeff Wayne.

In late 1974 Essex toured Britain, where young fans greeted him with hysteria. Essex made two films based on the rags-to-riches-to-rags theme of rock stardom: *That'll Be the Day* (1973), in which he costarred with Ringo Starr and Keith Moon of the Who, and *Stardust* (1975), in which he shared billing with Starr and Dave Edmunds. He sang Paul McCartney's "Yesterday" in *All This and World War II,* but was forced to turn down a role in the Who's *Tommy* because of shooting conflicts with *Stardust.* None of these films had much impact in the U.S., but "Rock On" garnered a Grammy nomination.

His reputation as a teenybopper singer proved unshakable in the late '70s despite attempts to attract a more mature audience (e.g., *Out on the Street*). He played Che Guevara in the British stage production of *Evita* in 1978 and has since had several more hit singles in Britain. He starred in the film *Silver Dream Machine,* appeared in *Childe Byron,* and starred in the musical *Mutiny,* based on *Mutiny on the Bounty.* Among his U.K. Top 10 hits are "Rollin' Stone" (1975), "Oh What a Circus" (1978), "Silver Dream Machine (Part 1)" (1980), and "A Winter's Tale" (1982), "Tahiti" (1983). In 1989 "Rock On" was revived in America via teen idol Michael Damian's #1 cover version. Essex continues to perform and release albums, primarily in the U.K. Throughout the '90s he occasionally worked on musical productions and scores for ice ballet. In 1999 the Queen presented him with an OBE for his charity services in Africa.

Gloria Estefan

Born Gloria Fajardo, Sep. 1, 1957, Havana, Cuba
With Miami Sound Machine, formed 1975, Miami, FL: (Estefan, voc.; Enrique "Kiki" Garcia, drums; Juan Marcos Avila, bass; Emilio Estefan Jr., kybds., perc.; Raul Murciano, sax, kybds.; Merci Murciano, voc.): 1982—(– M. Murciano) 1984—*Eyes of Innocence* (Epic) 1985—*Primitive Love* 1987—*Let It Loose.*
Gloria Estefan solo: 1989—*Cuts Both Ways* (Epic) 1991—*Into the Light* 1992—*Greatest Hits* 1993—*Mi Tierra* 1994—*Hold Me, Thrill Me, Kiss Me* 1995—*Abriendo Puertas; Christmas Through Your Eyes* 1996—*Destiny* 1998—*Gloria!* 1999—*20th Anniversary* 2000—*Alma Caribeña* 2001—*Greatest Hits, vol. 2.*

Gloria Estefan rose out of Miami's Cuban community to become a top-selling international pop star, first with the dance band Miami Sound Machine and then with her own ballads. She moved to Miami in 1959 when her father, a bodyguard to Cuban president Fulgencio Batista, fled the Castro-led revolution. She spent her early life nursing her father, who was stricken with multiple sclerosis after serving in Vietnam; she sang for hours in her bedroom to release her emotions.

In October 1975 Gloria Fajardo and her cousin Merci Murciano auditioned for keyboardist Emilio Estefan's wedding band, the Miami Latin Boys. They passed, and the rechristened Miami Sound Machine became one of the most popular groups in Miami, playing a mix of disco-pop and

Gloria Estefan

salsa. (Merci left the band in a dispute in 1982.) In 1978 Emilio and Gloria married, and the following year Miami Sound Machine released the first of several Spanish-language albums for CBS's Hispanic label. It became popular in Latin markets in the U.S. and overseas, but the band didn't cross over until Estefan sang in English on *Eyes of Innocence;* in 1984 "Dr. Beat" became a top dance hit in Europe.

In 1985 Miami Sound Machine released its first all-English album. *Primitive Love* (#21, 1985) went triple platinum, with three Top 10 hits: "Conga" (#10, 1985), "Bad Boy" (#8, 1986), and "Words Get in the Way" (#5, 1986). Most of the songs were written, arranged, and performed by "the Three Jerks," Joe Galdo, Rafael Vigil, and Lawrence Dermer. At this point Miami Sound Machine became two bands: the studio group and the touring band, which included original members Kiki Garcia and Marcos Avila. Gloria was the common denominator. (Emilio had moved from keyboards to management.)

The band was billed as Gloria Estefan and the Miami Sound Machine on their triple-platinum *Let It Loose* (#6, 1987), which included the hits "Rhythm Is Gonna Get You" (#5, 1987), "Can't Stay Away From You" (#6, 1987), "Anything for You" (#1, 1988), and "1-2-3" (#3, 1988). It was Estefan's last record with the Miami Sound Machine; remaining original member Garcia left after the band's 1988 tour. Estefan wrote most of the lyrics and some of the music on her solo debut, *Cuts Both Ways* (#8, 1989), which yielded her second #1 hit, "Don't Wanna Lose You" (1989), as well as "Here We Are" (#6, 1989).

On March 20, 1990, while traveling between shows on a snowy Pennsylvania highway, Estefan's tour bus was hit by a tractor-trailer. Her husband and son were slightly injured, but one of Estefan's vertebrae was broken. She recovered from surgery that included inserting eight-inch metal rods in her back. In 1991 her song about the accident, "Coming Out of the Dark," went #1; the double-platinum *Into the Light* (#5) also yielded the hits "Can't Forget You" (#43, 1991) and "Live for Loving You" (#22, 1991), which were especially popular on adult contemporary radio formats. In 1993 Estefan paid tribute to her Latin roots with her first solo all-Spanish album, *Mi Tierra* (#27), which features cameos from such stars of Cuban music as Nestor Torres, Luis Enrique, Israel (Cachao) Lopez, Paquito D'Rivera, Arturo Sandoval, and Tito Puente. *Hold Me, Thrill Me, Kiss Me* (#9, 1994) yielded the hit singles "Turn the Beat Around" (#13, 1994) and "Everlasting Love" (#27, 1995).

Abriendo Puertas (1995), a dance record that mined grooves from all over the African diaspora, was Estefan's second Spanish-language LP in two years. Since then she has worked mainly in an adult contemporary vein. "Reach" (#42, 1996), a billowy ballad cowritten by Diane Warren, was one of the songs selected for the 1996 Olympic Games in Atlanta. The single also appeared on *Destiny,* along with "You'll Be Mine (Party Time)" (#70, 1996) and "I'm Not Giving You Up" (#40, 1996). *Gloria!* (#23, 1998) produced two more hits, "Heaven's What I Feel" (#27, 1998) and "Don't Let This Moment End" (#76, 1998). In 1999, she made her acting debut in *Music of the Heart.* Her next album, 2000's *Alma Caribeña* (which translated as "Caribbean Soul"), was a Spanish-language LP that featured several Latin styles. It was certified gold and received 2000's Best Latin Tropical Album Grammy.

"Sleepy" John Estes

Born Jan. 25, 1904, Ripley, TN; died June 5, 1977, Brownsville, TN
1963—*The Legend of Sleepy John Estes* (Delmark) 1967—*1929–40* (Folkways) 1974—*Down South Blues, 1935–1940* (MCA).

An important first-generation bluesman, "Sleepy" John Estes lost the sight of one eye as a child and became completely blind by 1950. When Estes was 12, his sharecropper father gave him his first guitar. By the time he was 20 he was playing local house parties. Shortly thereafter he moved to Memphis, where he performed on Beale Street with mandolinist Yank Rachell. He supported himself by working the late shift at a trainyard, where his tendency to doze off (later discovered to be a result of blood-pressure problems) earned him his nickname. In the '30s Estes moved to Chicago with harmonica player Hammie Nixon. Over the next few years he worked as a street musician and occasionally as a medicine-show barker, hawking swamp root for Dr. Grimm's Traveling Menagerie.

In 1941 Estes and Nixon recorded blues for Bluebird: "Someday, Baby" and "Drop Down, Mama." He subsequently returned to Brownsville, Tennessee, and remained an obscure performer until the late '50s, when filmmaker Ralph Blumenthal (who was making a documentary on black migration to the North) rediscovered him. The new attention got Estes a contract with the Chicago-based Delmark label. By 1964 he had gone on his first European tour and appeared at the Newport Folk Festival. Estes' LP *Broke and Hungry* included a guest spot by guitarist Mike Bloomfield, and Estes later played and sang on Ry Cooder's LP *Boomer's Story.* Around the same time, Joy of Cooking had a minor pop hit with the Estes-penned "Going to Brownsville" (1971). Estes died of a stroke in 1977 while preparing to embark on a European tour.

Melissa Etheridge

Born May 29, 1961, Leavenworth, KS
1988—*Melissa Etheridge* (Island) 1989—*Brave and Crazy* 1992—*Never Enough* 1993—*Yes I Am* 1995—*Your Little Secret* 1999—*Breakdown* 2001—*Skin.*

Melissa Etheridge's raw, raspy voice and gritty delivery have inspired comparisons to everyone from Janis Joplin to Bruce Springsteen. Her fervid, percussive guitar work drives the confrontational and often hard-bitten love songs that earned the singer/songwriter a solid core following, encompassing fans of both alternative and album-oriented rock. She broke through to mass popularity with her 1993 album, *Yes I Am.*

Melissa Etheridge

A self-taught musician, Etheridge got her first guitar when she was eight and began writing songs shortly afterward. She started performing at 12, in a country group, and played in various bar bands through her teens. After attending Boston's Berklee College of Music, Etheridge moved to the L.A. area, where she performed in clubs. In 1986 Island Records founder Chris Blackwell spotted her and offered her a contract. Etheridge's first recording gig involved contributing songs to the soundtrack of a film called *Weeds*. Then, working with drummer Craig Krampf, who was eventually replaced by Fritz Lewak, and bassist Kevin McCormick (Lewak and McCormick remained in her band through *Yes I Am*), the singer released her debut album in 1988. *Melissa Etheridge* spawned a pair of singles, "Bring Me Some Water" and "Like the Way I Do"; though neither entered the Top 40, both were well received by album-oriented rock radio. The album went gold, as did its successor, 1989's *Brave and Crazy*. Etheridge's third LP, 1992's gold *Never Enough*, yielded the song "Ain't It Heavy," which failed to chart significantly but earned the singer a Grammy (on her fourth nomination) for Best Rock Vocal Performance, Female. In 1993 Etheridge publicly declared that she was a lesbian; that same year, she released a fourth album, *Yes I Am* (#16). The disc, produced by Hugh Padgham (the Police, Phil Collins), resulted in several hits—including "Come to My Window" (#25, 1994), "I'm the Only One" (#8 pop; #1 Adult Contemporary, 1994), and "If I Wanted To"(#16, 1995)—and spent 138 weeks on the LP chart.

Because of both her increasing success and her coming out, the public grew curious about Etheridge's personal life; she revealed that she was in a long-term relationship with director Julie Cypher, who had once been married to actor Lou Diamond Phillips. In 1995 Etheridge released *Your Little Secret* (#6), coproduced by Padgham and featuring the singles "I Want to Come Over" (#22, 1996) and "Nowhere to Go" (#40, 1996). She embarked on nearly a year of touring worldwide in support of the album.

Etheridge intrigued the public once again in 1996 with the announcement that she and Cypher were expecting a baby. Cypher gave birth to the couple's daughter, Bailey, in February 1997. Aside from occasional performances and benefit appearances, Etheridge opted for the longest break from recording and touring in her career to spend time with her family. In November 1998 Cypher gave birth to their son, Beckett. The following year Etheridge emerged with *Breakdown*, an album of new material coproduced by her guitarist and sometime cowriter since *Your Little Secret*, John Shanks. Though not a hit, it offered the noncharting single "Angels Would Fall" as well as "Scarecrow," a tribute to Matthew Shepard, the gay college student who was murdered in Wyoming. Etheridge and Cypher had another coming out of sorts in the media in January 2000, when they divulged in a ROLLING STONE cover story that musician David Crosby was the biological father of both of their children (via artificial insemination). The women have since announced their breakup.

Eurythmics

Formed 1980, London, Eng.
Annie Lennox (b. Dec. 25, 1954, Aberdeen, Scot.), voc., flute; Dave Stewart (b. David A. Stewart, Sep. 9, 1952, Sunderland, Eng.), gtr., kybds.
1981—*In the Garden* (RCA, U.K.) 1983—*Sweet Dreams (Are Made of This)* (RCA); *Touch* 1984—*1984: For the Love of Big Brother* soundtrack 1985—*Be Yourself Tonight* 1986—*Revenge* 1987—*Savage* 1989—*We Too Are One* (Arista) 1991—*Greatest Hits* 1993—*Live 1983–1989* 1999—*Peace*.
Dave Stewart solo: 1990—*Lily Was Here* (Arista); *Dave Stewart and the Spiritual Cowboys* 1995—*Greetings From the Gutter* (EastWest) 1998—*Sly-Fi* (N2K).
Annie Lennox solo: 1992—*Diva* (Arista) 1995—*Medusa*.

Eurythmics were perhaps the greatest of the early-'80s British synth-pop bands, mixing a cynically business- and image-conscious approach with a sometimes soulful, mournful sound. Although Dave Stewart's studio wizardry provided the band's foundation, Annie Lennox's theatrical appearance and beautiful, icy wail ultimately were the duo's calling cards.

Lennox grew up in Aberdeen, Scotland, the only daughter of a bagpipe-playing shipyard worker. Her piano- and flute-playing skills won her a scholarship to the Royal Academy of Music in London, but she quit on the eve of finals, disgusted with the school's pretensions. She spent three years working odd jobs in London and playing with a folk-rock band, a jazz-rock group, and a cabaret duo. A friend introduced her to Dave Stewart.

Stewart came from an upper-middle-class family in Northern England. By the early '70s his band Longdancer was signed to Elton John's Rocket Records but never accomplished anything. He then played in a variety of groups, which ranged from soul to medieval music. When he met Lennox he was writing music with a recluse named Peet Coombes.

Lennox and Stewart immediately began a musical and romantic partnership. With Coombes they formed a band called Catch, which shortly became the Tourists. The Tourists' three albums (*The Tourists*, 1979; *Reality Effect*, 1979; *Luminous Basement*, 1980) mixed folk, psychedelia, and new wave. A cover of the Dusty Springfield hit "I Only Want to Be With You" was a big hit in England (#4 U.K., 1979), but barely made it into the U.S. Hot 100 (#83, 1980).

When the band disintegrated in late 1980, so did Lennox and Stewart's romance. They continued to work together, however, and named their partnership after Eurythmics, a system of music instruction developed in the 1890s that emphasizes physical response. Their debut was recorded in Germany and featured Blondie drummer Clem Burke, members of Can and DAF, and Marcus Stockhausen, son of the avant-garde composer. Despite good reviews, it was weakly supported by their label.

Lennox and Stewart were committed to making the Eurythmics a solid business and artistic venture, however. In a makeshift studio that Stewart set up, they recorded *Sweet Dreams (Are Made of This)* (#15, 1983), using an 8-track recorder and synthesizers. Though the first British single, "Love Is a Stranger," attracted some attention in clubs, it was the title track (#1) that propelled the band to stardom.

As the singer for the Tourists, Lennox was a platinum blonde often called the British Blondie. Sick of that dolly image, Lennox wore an orange crewcut and a man's suit in the Eurythmics' early work. When the band performed at the 1984 Grammys, she dressed like Elvis. In the video for "Who's That Girl?" she plays a chanteuse who leaves a club with her butch alter-ego; at the end, she-Annie kisses he-Annie.

Touch (#7, 1983) yielded "Here Comes the Rain Again" (#4, 1984), but Eurythmics' next release, the soundtrack for *1984* (the film based on George Orwell's novel), was a disappointment. The film's director complained on a televised awards show that he had been forced to use the band's music, and the single "Sexcrime (Nineteen Eighty-four)" was widely misinterpreted. Lennox suffered another public humiliation when she married a Hare Krishna and divorced him a year later. But *Be Yourself Tonight* (#9, 1985) returned the band to the public grace, showcasing Lennox's soulful vocals in a duet with Aretha Franklin, "Sisters Are Doin' It for Themselves" (#18, 1985). The album also yielded the hit single "Would I Lie to You" (#5, 1985). On *Revenge* (#12, 1986), the Eurythmics went for an arena-rock sound and produced their last Top 20 single, "Missionary Man" (#14, 1986).

In 1987 Stewart married singer Siobhan Fahey, formerly of Bananarama and later half of the duo Shakespear's Sister. Many critics considered the Eurythmics to have run out of steam on *We Too Are One* (#34, 1989), so it was not surprising when Lennox announced that she was taking a couple years off from music to work for a homeless charity. She had delivered a stillborn baby in 1988 and wanted to devote time to her family (she is married to filmmaker Uri Fruchtmann, with whom she's since had two children). In 1992 she released *Diva* (#23, 1992), a platinum-selling solo album that received three Grammy nominations. Stewart, meanwhile, had already released one soundtrack album, *Lily Was Here*, and put together the band Spiritual Cowboys, which included drummer Martin Chambers (Pretenders). He has also produced records for Daryl Hall, Tom Petty, Mick Jagger, and Bob Dylan. In 1995 Stewart released his first real solo album, *Greetings From the Gutter*, a modern Ziggy Stardust–like opus with a funky backing band (Bootsy Collins is on bass). A pop-rock followup, *Sly-Fi*, appeared in 1998.

Lennox and Stewart hadn't spoken with each other for four years when she called in 1997 to inform him of the death of their former Tourists bandmate, Peet Coombes. The conversation got the duo talking again; later, while rehearsing for an acoustic performance at a party for a mutual friend, they began writing new material together. *Peace* (1999), the album that grew out of those sessions, was the first new Eurythmics LP in 10 years and found Lennox's supple, powerful alto fully intact. It also eschewed the catchy, electro-pop of the duo's '80s heyday in favor of lushly orchestrated ballads focusing on the pair's musical and prior romantic partnership. After the record's release, Stewart and Lennox played a series of dates, most of them in Europe, the proceeds of which went to Amnesty International and Greenpeace. There was no indication that the Eurythmics' reunion would be permanent.

Everclear

Formed 1992, Portland, OR
Art Alexakis (b. Apr. 12, 1962, Los Angeles, CA), voc., gtr.; Scott Cuthbert, drums; Craig Aloysius Montoya (b. Sep. 14, 1970, Spokane, WA), bass.
1993—*Nervous and Weird* EP (Tim/Kerr); *World of Noise*
1994—(– Cuthbert; + Greg Eklund [b. Apr. 18, 1970, Jacksonville, FL], drums) 1995—*Sparkle and Fade* (Capitol)
1997—*So Much for the Afterglow* 2000—*Songs From an American Movie Volume One: Learning How to Smile; Songs From an American Movie Volume Two: Good Time for a Bad Attitude.*

By alternative-rock standards, Everclear frontman Art Alexakis was an old man—33 years old—when his band's major label debut *Sparkle and Fade* was released in 1995, and his career took off into high gear. But having already logged years of performing locally and kicking a near-fatal, decade-long drug addiction, he quickly made up for lost time.

Raised by his mother in an L.A. housing project, Alexakis

grew up poor and began abusing hard drugs; by 13 he was on heroin. His addiction continued despite both his older brother and a girlfriend dying of overdoses. He finally kicked the habit after nearly dying himself from an overdose at 22.

He played in a handful of L.A. bands during the '80s and cut an album with the San Francisco group Colorfinger before relocating to Portland, Oregon, where he formed Everclear with bassist Craig Montoya and drummer Scott Cuthbert. The band recorded a $400 EP, *Nervous and Weird* (1993), which was expanded into their debut album, *World of Noise*, later that year. Both were released by Portland indie label Tim/Kerr, though Capitol reissued *World of Noise* after signing Everclear in 1994. Greg Eklund replaced Cuthbert the same year.

Fueled by heavy touring and the modern-rock hits "Heroin Girl," "Santa Monica," and "Heartspark Dollarsign," 1995's *Sparkle and Fade* went platinum and climbed to #25. The momentum continued with 1997's double-platinum *So Much for the Afterglow* (#33), and in 2000 the group went for broke by releasing two albums (based on Alexakis' divorce) within the span of six months: the pop-leaning *Songs From an American Movie Volume One: Learning How to Smile* (#9) and the more hard-rock-oriented *Songs From an American Movie Volume Two: Good Time for a Bad Attitude* (#66). The former featured the #11 hit single, "Wonderful."

Betty Everett

Born Nov. 23, 1939, Greenwood, MS
1964—*Delicious Together* (with Jerry Butler) (Vee-Jay) 1974—*Love Rhymes* (Fantasy); *There'll Come a Time* (MCA) 1975—*Happy Endings* (Fantasy) 1976—*It's in His Kiss* (DJM).

Soul vocalist Betty Everett had a decade's worth of hits in the '60s and '70s. She played piano and sang in church as a child before moving with her family to Chicago at age 17. Everett's career peaked with the pop novelty "The Shoop Shoop Song (It's in His Kiss)" (#6, 1964) and a duet with Jerry Butler, "Let It Be Me" (#5, 1964), the Everly Brothers hit. Lesser hits included "You're No Good," "I Can't Hear You," and "Getting Mighty Crowded." A minor 1964 hit, "Smile," was a duet with Jerry Butler.

Vee-Jay's mid-'60s collapse brought her to a change in labels. After a hitless tenure with ABC-Paramount, Everett made a modest 1969 comeback on Uni with "There'll Come a Time," "I Can't Say No to You," and "It's Been a Long Time." By 1970, she was recording for Fantasy ("I Got to Tell Somebody," 1971). Everett achieved respectable soul sales over the next couple of years with albums like *Love Rhymes* and *Happy Endings*. By then she was taking advantage of her prestigious standing in Europe with regular continental tours. She more or less retired in 1980. In 1991 Cher took "The Shoop Shoop Song" to #33 on the American singles charts. Five years later Everett was honored by the Rhythm and Blues Foundation; she and Butler reunited to sing "Let It Be Me" for the occasion.

Everlast/House of Pain

Everlast, born Erik Schrody, Aug. 18, 1969, Valley Stream, NY
1990—*Forever Everlasting* (Warner Bros.) 1998—*Whitey Ford Sings the Blues* (Tommy Boy) 1999—*Today* EP.
House of Pain, formed 1990, Los Angeles, CA: Everlast, voc.; Danny Boy (b. Daniel O'Connor, Dec. 12, 1968, Los Angeles), voc.; DJ Lethal (b. Leor DiMant, Dec. 18, 1972, Latvia), DJ.
1992—*House of Pain* (Tommy Boy) 1994—*Same As It Ever Was* 1996—*Truth Crushed to Earth Shall Rise Again.*

Not merely a white rap group, House of Pain was the first Irish-American rap group. Its bios were sent out on green paper; the group's logo was a shamrock with the words "fine malt lyrics"; the group's debut album (#14, 1992) included such tracks as "Top o' the Mornin' to Ya" and "Shamrocks and Shenanigans" (#65, 1992). Everlast wore a green Boston Celtics basketball jersey in the video for House of Pain's biggest hit, "Jump Around" (#3, 1992) which—like Kris Kross' contemporaneous hit "Jump"—grafted shouted vocal hooks onto dissonant, Public Enemy–derived mixes brimming with big, bumptious beats and grating, high-pitched whistles and wheezes.

Everlast and Danny Boy first met at Taft High School in L.A., where rapper Ice Cube was a student; Everlast later worked with Ice-T's Rhyme Syndicate before forming House of Pain with Danny Boy and Latvian emigré, DJ Lethal. House of Pain's debut album was coproduced by DJ Muggs of hardcore L.A. rap group Cypress Hill. Muggs also produced *Same As It Ever Was* (#12, 1994).

In March 1993 Everlast was arrested at New York's Kennedy Airport for gun possession, when an unregistered (unloaded) pistol was found in his luggage. He eventually plea-bargained the charge down to a community-service sentence. The *Truth* album sank without a trace, and House of Pain dissolved. DJ Lethal eventually joined Limp Bizkit [see entry], while Everlast, who had released a low-profile solo album in pre–House of Pain days, made a splash with the folk/hip-hop fusion of *Whitey Ford Sings the Blues* (#9 pop, 1998) and its talkin' blues single, "What It's Like" (#13, 1998). Everlast, who suffered a massive heart attack the day he finished recording *Whitey* (an artificial valve was installed during coronary bypass surgery), would go on to join the list of guest stars on Carlos Santana's hit 1999 album, *Supernatural*. In 1999, Danny Boy formed the L.A.-based techno/hip-hop duo XSupermodels with rapper Eric Gregory.

Everly Brothers

Don Everly (b. Feb. 1, 1937, Brownie, KY), gtr., voc.; Phil Everly (b. Jan. 19, 1939, Brownie), gtr., voc.
1958—*The Everly Brothers* (Cadence); *Songs Our Daddy Taught Us* 1960—*The Fabulous Style of the Everly Brothers; It's Everly Time* (Warner Bros.); *A Date With the Everly Brothers* 1963—*Sing Great Country Hits* 1964—*The Very Best of the Everly Brothers* 1967—*The Everly Brothers Sing* 1968—*Roots* 1972—*Stories We Could Tell* (RCA) 1973—*Pass the Chicken*

and Listen 1984—*Reunion Concert* (Passport); *EB 84* (Mercury) 1985—*Cadence Classics (Their 20 Greatest Hits)* (Rhino); *All They Had to Do Is Dream* 1988—*Some Hearts* (Mercury) 1990—*All-Time Greatest Hits* (Curb); *The Best of the Everly Brothers: Rare Solo Classics* 1994—*Walk Right Back: The Everly Brothers on Warner Bros., 1960–63* (Warner Bros.); *The Mercury Years* (Mercury); *Heartaches and Harmonies* (Rhino) 2000—*All-Time Original Hits.*
Don Everly solo: 1970—*Don Everly* (Ode) 1974—*Sunset Towers* 1976—*Brother Juke Box* (Hickory).
Phil Everly solo: 1973—*Star Spangled Springer* (RCA) 1975—*Phil's Diner* (Pye) 1976—*Mystic Line* 1979—*Phil Everly* (Elektra).

The Everly Brothers are the most important vocal duo in rock. The enduring influence of the brothers' close, understated yet expressive harmonies is evident in the work of such British Invasion bands as the Beatles and the Hollies and of folk-oriented acts, such as Simon and Garfunkel, not to mention countless solo artists, among them Dave Edmunds, Gram Parsons, Emmylou Harris, and Linda Ronstadt. Most of the Everlys' hit singles, which merged Nashville's clean instrumental country style with innocuous teenage themes, cut a course to the right of contemporary country-rock hybrids like rockabilly. Their indisputable mastery is revealed in their ballads, among them "Let It Be Me."

They were the children of Midwestern country stars Ike and Margaret Everly. They toured with their parents around the South and Midwest and performed on the family radio show (a taped sample of which appears on *Roots*) throughout their childhoods. In the summer of 1955, still teenagers, they left for Nashville, where they were soon hired by Roy Acuff's publishing company as songwriters. Don had a minor success when his "Thou Shalt Not Steal" became a hit for Kitty Wells. The brothers also recorded a country single entitled "Keep On Loving Me" for Columbia before signing with Cadence in 1957. Songwriters Felice and Boudleaux Bryant gave them "Bye Bye Love," which 30 acts had previously rejected. It was an international hit (#2 U.S., 1957), topped the country chart, and established an Everlys style with close country harmonies over a rocking beat.

The Everlys toured internationally with a small combo over the next few years, sporting matching suits and haircuts and leaving fans to identify each brother by the color of his hair (Don's was darker). Their heyday lasted through 1962, by which time they were at Warner Bros., with cumulative record sales of $35 million. In their three years with Cadence (which they left in a dispute over royalties) they averaged a Top 10 hit every four months, including four #1 hits: "Wake Up Little Susie," "All I Have to Do Is Dream," "Cathy's Clown," and "Bird Dog."

Some of their most successful records—"Till I Kissed You" (#4, 1959), "When Will I Be Loved" (#8, 1960)—were written by Don or Phil Everly. Their best-selling single, "Cathy's Clown" (sales of which exceeded 2 million), came after their switch to Warner Bros., but their success with the new label was short-lived. In June 1962 their string of hits ended with "That's Old-Fashioned" (#9, 1962). They remained major stars in England, but their careers slowed markedly in the U.S. despite continued releases on Warner Bros. ("Bowling Green," #40, 1967) and, beginning in 1972, RCA (where they moved shortly after hosting a summer TV series on CBS). Their latter-day backup band was led by keyboardist Warren Zevon and included future L.A. studio guitarist Waddy Wachtel.

By then the brothers' personal lives had gone through serious upheavals. Both were addicted to speed for a while, and Don was hospitalized for a nervous breakdown. Their relationship became increasingly acrimonious until it blew up at the John Wayne Theater at Knott's Berry Farm in Buena Park, California, on July 14, 1973. Phil smashed his guitar and stalked off stage, leaving Don to announce the duo's obvious breakup. Subsequent solo attempts by both were largely unsuccessful.

In 1983 the Everlys returned to the spotlight. Phil's duet with Cliff Richard, "She Means Nothing to Me," reached the British Top 10 in the spring. That September the brothers reunited onstage at London's Royal Albert Hall for a triumphant concert that was chronicled on *Reunion Concert* and in a video documentary that was widely aired. In 1984 they released *EB 84* (#38, 1984), produced by longtime fan Dave Edmunds. "On the Wings of a Nightingale," penned by another admirer, Paul McCartney (who'd mentioned the pair in his "Let 'Em In"), went to #50 in the U.S. and #41 in England. Edmunds also produced 1986's *Born Yesterday,* which came out the same month that the duo was inducted into the Rock and Roll Hall of Fame. The Everlys continued to perform into 2000. They have inspired several musicals, including 1998's biographical *Bye Bye Love: The Everly Brothers Musical,* which ran in Nashville, and 2000's *Dream, Dream, Dream,* which played Atlantic City.

Everything But the Girl

Formed 1981, England
Tracey Thorn (b. Sep. 26, 1962, Hertfordshire, Eng.), voc.; Ben Watt (b. Dec. 6, 1962, London, Eng.), gtr., kybds.
1984—*Eden* (Blanco y Negro, U.K.); *Everything But the Girl* (Blanco y Negro/Sire) 1985—*Love Not Money* 1986—*Baby, the Stars Shine Bright* 1988—*Idlewild* 1990—*The Language of Life* (Atlantic) 1991—*Worldwide* 1992—*Acoustic* 1994—*Amplified Heart* 1996—*Walking Wounded* 1999—*Tempermental.*

Everything But the Girl makes melodic, literate, and scrupulously crafted pop that often draws on prerock traditions, incorporating elements of jazz, theatrical music, and early-'60s rock & roll. In the mid-'90s, the duo began a successful foray into electronica and dance music.

Watt (who is the chief composer) and vocalist Thorn first met at Hull University. Before joining with Watt, Thorn made two albums as a member of the Marine Girls. In 1982 the duo (who took their name from a local store whose slogan claimed they could supply "everything but the girl") recorded a version of Cole Porter's "Night and Day." Thorn then cut a mini album, *A Distant Shore*, and Watt released his *North Marine Drive*.

Everything But the Girl first charted in Britain with "Each and Everyone" (#28 U.K., 1984); a cover of "I Don't Want to Talk About It" by Danny Whitten (Crazy Horse guitarist who died in 1972) became its biggest hit (#3 U.K.) in 1988.

Signing with Atlantic, Everything But the Girl went for the full L.A. studio treatment on *The Language of Life*. With Tommy LiPuma producing, a host of first-call session musicians, and a guest appearance by jazz saxophonist Stan Getz, *The Language of Life* made the U.S. charts (#77, 1990) and a popular single, "Driving," was culled from it.

Despite its accomplishments, the group was stranded by a sound that was too light for rock airplay yet too sophisticated for "lite" airplay. Neither the followup album, *Worldwide*, nor *Acoustic* (an "unplugged" project that concentrated on covers, including Thorn's rendition of Springsteen's "Tougher Than the Rest") had the commercial impact of *Language of Life*. Shortly before the duo embarked on an acoustic tour of the U.S. in support of the album, Watt was hospitalized with the rare, life-threatening autoimmune disease, Churg Strauss Syndrome. He spent three months in a hospital bed recovering and would later write about his battle in the 1997 book *Patient: The True Story of a Rare Illness*.

In 1994 Everything But The Girl released *Amplified Heart*, a quiet acoustic-leaning affair that produced a surprise club hit when a house remix of the song "Missing" spent an unprecedented year on the Billboard Hot 100 singles chart (peaking at #2 in 1995). The success of the remix, coupled with Thorn's collaboration on the 1994 Massive Attack album *Protection*, propelled Everything But the Girl into the full-on embrace of drum-and-bass and ambient electronica that marked 1996's widely acclaimed *Walking Wounded* (#37) and 1999's *Tempermental*. The later album's more assured take on the genre was no accident; Watt spent the three years between albums perfecting his DJ skills on the club circuit.

Exposé

Formed 1986, Miami, FL
Jeanette Jurado (b. Nov. 14, 1966, Los Angeles, CA), voc.; Ann Curless (b. Oct. 7, 1965, New York, NY), voc.; Gioia Carmen Bruno (b. Italy, June 11, 1965), voc.
1987—*Exposure* (Arista) 1989—*What You Don't Know* 1992—(– Bruno; + Kelly Moneymaker [b. June 4, 1965, Fairbanks, AK], voc.) *Exposé* 1995—*Greatest Hits.*

The phenomenally successful vocal trio Exposé began as a project of Miami pop svengali Lewis Martinee. But by their third album, the three women were trying to assert themselves as artists. Martinee wrote and recorded the single "Point of No Return" with Ale Lorenzo, Laurie Miller, and Sandee Casanas, whom he dubbed Exposé in 1985. The song became a dance hit, followed by 1986's "Exposed to Love," and the group began work on an album. Before its completion, Martinee replaced all three members—reports conflict as to whether the women quit or were fired (perhaps, it has been suggested, for not looking the part). Martinee hired Jurado, Curless, and Bruno to be the new Exposé.

With its Latin-tinged dance grooves, the multiplatinum *Exposure* (#16, 1987) broke the Beatles' record for most Top 10 hits from a debut album with "Come Go With Me" (#5 pop, #14 R&B, 1987), a rerecorded "Point of No Return" (#5, 1987), "Let Me Be the One" (#7 pop, #29 R&B, 1987), and the ballad "Seasons Change" (#1 pop, #27 R&B, 1987). The gold *What You Don't Know* (#33, 1989) followed this success with the singles "What You Don't Know" (#8, 1989), "Tell Me Why" (#9, 1989), "When I Looked at Him" (#10, 1989), and "Your Baby Never Looked Good in Blue" (#17, 1990).

On its third album, Exposé replaced Bruno, who was having throat problems, with the L.A.-based Kelly Moneymaker, who had performed with Todd Rundgren and Wayne Newton. The trio branched away from Martinee on *Exposé*, using four songs written by hitmaker Diane Warren (including "As Long As I Can Dream," written with Roy Orbison) and working with producers Steve Thompson and Michael Barbiero (Madonna, Guns n' Roses) on several tracks. That album includes the hit "I'll Never Get Over You (Getting Over Me)" (#8, 1993). Subsequent singles didn't fare as well and, by the mid-'90s, the trio had faded from the limelight.

Extreme

Formed 1985, Boston, MA
Pat Badger (b. July 22, 1967, Boston), bass; Nuno Bettencourt (b. Sep. 20, 1966, Azores, Port.), gtr.; Gary Cherone (b. July 26, 1961, Malden, MA), voc.; Paul Geary (b. July 24, 1961, Medford, MA), drums.
1989—*Extreme* (A&M) 1990—*Extreme II: Pornograffitti* 1992—*III Sides to Every Story* 1994—(– Geary; + Mike Mangini, drums) 1995—*Waiting for the Punchline.*
Nuno Bettencourt solo: 1997—*Schizophonic.*

Extreme's metal funk is more in line with fellow Bostonians Aerosmith, and Nuno Bettencourt is considered one of the premier hard-rock guitarists, but the group is best known for the acoustic ballad "More Than Words" (#1, 1991). That uncharacteristically soft single made the band's second album, *Pornograffiti* (#10, 1990), a Top 10 double-platinum hit.

Gary Cherone and Paul Geary were part of the Dream, an early-'80s Boston band. When the group broke up, Cherone began writing songs with Bettencourt, a Portuguese-born guitarist who had lived in Boston since he was four. Bettencourt brought in Badger, and the new band began to build a strong local following. A&M Records signed the band in 1987; in 1989 Extreme released its self-titled debut (#80).

That album stalled at the lower end of the Hot 100, and *Pornograffitti* threatened to do the same until "More Than Words" attracted a mainstream audience. The band kept its metal credentials by touring with ZZ Top, while a second ballad, "Hole Hearted" (#4, 1991), returned the band to the Top 10. Seemingly unwilling to give up either style, Extreme released *III Sides* (#10, 1992), an ambitious project divided into three suites: the aggressive "Yours," the introspective "Mine," and a 22-minute orchestral piece, "The Truth." The album, particularly the final three songs recorded at Abbey Road Studios with a 70-piece orchestra, demonstrated the band's eclecticism and willingness to experiment.

Extreme's next album, *Waiting for the Punchline* (#40, 1995), returned the band to its original, stripped-down sound. But without a hit single, the album sold disappointingly, and in 1996 the group decided to call it a day.

Singer Gary Cherone joined Van Halen [see entry] in 1997, when that band's reunion with David Lee Roth failed to take hold. Nuno Bettencourt took the solo route, releasing one album, 1997's *Schizophonic.*

Fabian

Born Fabian Anthony Forte, Feb. 6, 1943, Philadelphia, PA
1959—*Hold That Tiger!* (Chancellor); *Fabulous Fabian* 1995—*The Best of Fabian* (Varèse Vintage).

Fabian was marketed alongside several other late-'50s Philadelphia teen idols, including Frankie Avalon and Bobby Rydell. From 1959 to 1960 his Top 10 hits included "Turn Me Loose" (#9, 1959), his signature song, "Tiger" (#3, 1959), and an Elvis Presley imitation, "Hound Dog Man" (#9, 1959), the theme from his first feature film in 1959.

He then turned to acting. In 1960 he starred with John Wayne in *North to Alaska* and in 1966 was featured in *Fireball 500*. Since the early '70s, Fabian has occasionally appeared on TV sitcoms such as *Laverne and Shirley* and *Blossom*. In 1974, before '50s acts were in great demand on the oldies circuit, Fabian posed nude for a woman's magazine, a move that he publicly regretted; he claimed he looked "fat and stupid." In 1977 he was involved in a program under the auspices of California governor Jerry Brown to encourage citizen volunteers to work with mental patients.

Besides touring on his own, Fabian also performs as part of a package, the Golden Boys (or the Boys of Bandstand) with Avalon and Rydell. The 1980 film *The Idolmaker* is said to have been based on Fabian's first manager, Bob Marcucci, who discovered the teenager and manufactured him in the image of Rick Nelson. Fabian also works as a television producer. In addition to appearing in occasional films and commercials, he has guest-starred on numerous network and cable shows throughout the '80s and '90s, including *The Facts of Life, Blossom,* and *Murphy Brown*. He has also hosted Fabian's Celebrity Golf Tournament, which raises money for veterans' causes.

The Fabulous Thunderbirds

Formed 1974, Austin, TX
Jimmie Vaughan (b. Mar. 20, 1951, Dallas, TX), gtr.; Kim Wilson (b. Jan. 6, 1951, Detroit, MI), voc., harmonica; Keith Ferguson (b. July 23, 1946, Houston, TX), bass; Mike Buck (b. June 1, 1952), drums.
1979—*The Fabulous Thunderbirds* (Takoma) 1980—(– Buck; + Fran Christina [b. Feb. 1, 1951, Westerly, RI], drums) *What's the Word?* (Chrysalis) 1981—*Butt Rockin'* 1982—*T-Bird Rhythm* 1986—(– Ferguson; + Preston Hubbard [b. Mar. 15, 1953, Providence, RI], bass) *Tuff Enuff* (Columbia) 1987—*Hot Number* (Epic) 1989—*Powerful Stuff* 1990—(– Vaughan; + Michael "Duke" Robillard, gtr.; + Doug "the Kid" Bangham, gtr.) 1991—*Walk That Walk, Talk That Talk; The Essential Fabulous Thunderbirds Collection* (Chrysalis) 1992—*Hot Stuff: The Greatest Hits* (Epic) 1995—(– Hubbard; + Mark Carrino, bass; – Robillard; – Bangham; + David "Kid" Ramos, gtr.; + Gene Taylor, kybds.) *Roll of the Dice* (Private Music) (– Carrino; + Willie J. Campbell, bass) 1996—*Different Tacos!* (Country Town Music) 1997—(– Christina; + Jimi Bott, drums); *High Water* (Highstreet) 2000—*Girls Go Wild* (Benchmark).

The Vaughan Brothers (Jimmie Vaughan; Stevie Ray Vaughan, gtr., voc.): 1990—*Family Style* (Epic).
Jimmie Vaughan solo: 1994—*Strange Pleasure* (Epic) 1998—*Out There.*
Kim Wilson solo: 1993—*Tigerman* (Antone's) 1994—*That's Life* (Discovery) 1997—*My Blues* (Blue Collar).

Blues stalwarts the Fabulous Thunderbirds hit their commercial peak in the mid-'80s. Known for their relentless touring, the members were archetypal roots musicians, lean and energetic in style.

Starting in 1963, guitarist Jimmie Vaughan, older brother of Stevie Ray Vaughan, played Hendrix and Clapton covers in Dallas bands such as the Swinging Pendulums and the Chessmen before founding the Fabulous Thunderbirds. With vocalist Lou Ann Barton and drummer Otis Lewis departing shortly after the band's 1974 beginning, Vaughan solidified the lineup with bassist Keith Ferguson (who'd declined an offer to join ZZ Top), drummer Mike Buck, and singer/harmonica player Kim Wilson, who became chief songwriter.

With a self-titled debut blueprinting their no-frills approach, the Fabulous Thunderbirds went on to gain overseas exposure and a new-wave following by opening for Rockpile in 1980 (Rockpile bassist Nick Lowe produced the T-Birds' fourth album). Replacing Buck with Roomful of Blues drummer Fran Christina, they continued live work, but spent the next four years without a record contract. In 1986 came their big break: Signed to Columbia, the Fabulous Thunderbirds opened shows for the Rolling Stones and Santana, and with the Top 10 "Tuff Enuff" (produced by Dave Edmunds, Lowe's former partner in Rockpile), gained a mainstream audience. *Hot Number* (#49, 1987) also fared well; by then, however, only Vaughan and Wilson remained of the original members.

In 1990 Vaughan left to record with his brother, effectively ending the original Thunderbirds. Vaughan released his solo debut, *Strange Pleasure,* in 1994, followed four years later by *Out There.* Meanwhile, with Wilson at the helm, a reconstituted Thunderbirds carried on, featuring New England–based guitarists Duke Robillard, a jazz and blues player who'd founded Roomful of Blues, and the more rock-oriented Kid Bangham. The group finally fizzled, with Kim Wilson going solo. His albums *Tigerman* (1993) and *That's Life* (1994) were very much in the T-Birds' vein.

In 1995 Wilson assembled a new Thunderbirds lineup—now featuring Christina, guitarist David "Kid" Ramos, former Blasters keyboardist Gene Taylor, and bassist Mark Carrino—and cut the Danny Kortchmar–produced *Roll of the Dice* for Private Music. Although that lineup remained more or less intact (minus Christina and Carrino) as the "official" touring Thunderbirds, 1997's *High Water* was recorded by Wilson backed only by studio multi-instrumentalists Kortchmar and Steve Jordan. Wilson released his third solo album, *My Blues,* the same year. The 1996 Thunderbirds album, *Different Tacos!,* was an odds and sods collection of early live recordings and studio outtakes. *Girls Go Wild* is a repackage of the 1979 album with three additional tracks.

Donald Fagen: See Steely Dan

Fairport Convention/Fairport

Formed 1967, London, Eng.
Judy Dyble, piano, voc.; Richard Thompson (b. Apr. 3, 1949, London), gtr., voc.; Simon Nicol (b. Oct. 10, 1950, London), gtr., banjo, dulcimer, bass, viola, voc.; Ashley "Tyger" Hutchings (b. Jan. 1945, London), bass, voc., gtr.; Martin Lamble (b. 1950, Eng.; d. Aug. 1969, London), drums; Iain Matthews (b. Ian Matthew MacDonald, June 1946, Lincolnshire, Eng.), voc., perc., gtr.
1968—*Fairport Convention* (Polydor) (– Dyble; + Sandy Denny [b. Jan. 6, 1947, London; d. Apr. 21, 1978, London], gtr., voc., kybds.) *What We Did on Our Holidays* (Island) (– Matthews) *Heyday* 1969—(– Lamble; + Dave Swarbrick [b. Apr. 5, 1947, London], voc., violin, mandolin) *Unhalfbricking* (+ Dave Mattacks [b. 1948, London], drums, voc., kybds.) *Liege and Lief* (– Denny; – Hutchings; + David Pegg [b. Nov. 2, 1947, Birmingham, Eng.], gtr., viola, voc.) 1970—*Full House* 1971—*Angel Delight* (A&M) (– Thompson; – Nicol; + Roger Hill [b. Eng.], gtr., mandolin) 1972—*Babbacombe Lee* (– Hill; – Mattacks; + Tom Farnell, drums; + David Rea, gtr.; – Farnell; – Rea; + Trevor Lucas [b. Dec. 25, 1943, Bungaree, Austral.; d. Feb. 4, 1989, Sydney, Austral.], gtr.; + Jerry Donahue [b. Sep. 24, 1946, New York, NY], gtr., voc.; + Mattacks) *The History of Fairport Convention* (Island) 1973—*Rosie* 1974—*Nine* (A&M) (+ Denny) *Live Convention (A Moveable Feast)* (Island) (– Mattacks; + Paul Warren, drums; – Warren; + Bruce Rowland [b. Eng.], drums) 1975—*Rising for the Moon* 1976—(– Denny; – Lucas; – Donahue; – Mattacks) *Fairport Chronicles* (A&M); *Live at the L.A. Troubadour; Gottle o' Geer* 1985—(group re-forms: Pegg; Nicol; Mattacks; + Martin Allcock, bass, gtr., bouzouki; Ric Sanders [b. Dec. 8, 1952, Eng.], violin) 1986—*Gladys' Leap* (Varrick) 1987—*Expletive Delighted; In Real Time* (Island) 1989—*Red & Gold* (Rough Trade) 1990—*The Five Seasons* 1992—*25th Anniversary Box Set—Live at Cropredy* (Woodworm, U.K.) 1995—*The Jewel in the Crown* (Green Linnet) 1996—*Old New Borrowed Blue* 1997—(– Allcock; + Chris Leslie [b. Dec. 15, 1956, Eng.], violin, mandolin, bouzouki, voc.) 1998—*The Cropredy Box—30th Anniversary Box Set Live* (Woodworm, U.K.); *Who Knows Where the Time Goes* (Green Linnet) (– Mattacks; + Gerry Conway [b. Sep. 11, 1947, Eng.], drums) 2000—*The Wood and the Wire* (Compass).

Fairport Convention seeded Britain's folk-rock movement, and most British musicians who've tried to play Celtic folk material on modern instruments have some connection with Fairport or its many offshoots. The group's repertoire included traditional British songs rearranged for electric instruments, songs by Bob Dylan and other current songwriters, and originals by Richard Thompson and Iain Matthews (both founders) and Sandy Denny. As the Bunch, Fairport and friends also recorded an album of '50s and '60s rock classics entitled *Rock On.* Their eclecticism inspired their imitators and descendants.

The original Fairport Convention—at first called the Ethnic Shuffle Orchestra—included folk-club veterans who were also Byrds fans, and was named after Simon Nicol's house in Muswell Hill, London. From the beginning, the lineup was unstable. Judy Dyble left in 1968 to form Trader Horne and later Penguin Dust; her replacement, Sandy Denny, had sung with the Strawbs before their first album. Matthews left after *What We Did on Our Holidays* (in the U.S., *Fairport Convention)* to form the country-pop band Matthews Southern Comfort ("Woodstock," 1971) and to record solo and with the short-lived Plainsong [see Iain Matthews entry]. Lamble was killed in an equipment-van crash right before *Unhalfbricking*'s release.

Fairport had its first European hit with *Unhalfbricking*'s "Si Tu Dois Partir," a French translation of Dylan's "If You Gotta Go, Go Now." Denny, whose song "Who Knows Where the Time Goes" was covered by Judy Collins, left to form Fotheringay with husband Trevor Lucas and Jerry Donahue [see Sandy Denny entry]; in 1973 the three rejoined Fairport. *A Moveable Feast* was a live set from Denny's second stint with the band. By then Thompson had started a solo career [see entry], and fiddler Dave Swarbrick had joined Fairport. Swarbrick led the group in its later years, and it toured internationally. By 1976 the band had dropped "Convention" from its name; and by 1979 Fairport had given up, due to financial problems, constantly shifting lineup, and Swarbrick's hearing impairment. Pegg joined Jethro Tull; Swarbrick recorded solo albums. Nicol and Mattacks toured with Richard and Linda Thompson (who had sung with the Bunch as Linda Peters) in 1982. Mattacks became a respected session drummer whose credits include Paul McCartney, Elton John, Mark Knopfler, and XTC. More recently he has recorded and toured with Mary Chapin Carpenter and Richard Thompson solo.

Fairport has been a going concern again since 1985. The members have chosen not to include another female singer, feeling that Denny was "irreplaceable." (She died in 1978 after falling down a flight of stairs.) They do perform with guest singers on rare occasions. The lineup with Ric Sanders (Soft Machine, sessions with Jethro Tull and Gerry Rafferty) and Martin Allcock produced several albums and toured the world from 1985 to 1995.

Pegg left Jethro Tull in 1995 to concentrate on Fairport and on the running of Woodworm Records and Studio. Since then, Fairport has existed as two internationally touring bands—the standard quintet and an acoustic four-piece without a drummer (on *Old New Borrowed Blue).* Their star-studded, annual Cropredy Festival, held in August in the village of Cropredy in Oxfordshire, has become one of Europe's largest folk events, drawing crowds of 20,000 to 25,000. Many Fairport live albums (including the two box sets) were recorded at the festivals.

In 1997 Allcock was replaced by Chris Leslie (Whippersnapper, the Albion Band, tours with Ian Anderson and All About Eve). The following year Gerry Conway, who had played on Fairport spinoffs and solo projects, replaced Mattacks.

Marianne Faithfull

Born Dec. 29, 1946, London, Eng.
1965—*Come My Way* (Decca) 1966—*Faithful Forever* (London) 1977—*Faithless* (NEMS) 1979—*Broken English* (Island) 1981—*Dangerous Acquaintances* 1983—*A Child's Adventure* 1987—*Strange Weather* 1990—*Blazing Away* 1994—*Faithfull: A Collection of Her Best Recordings* 1995—*A Secret Life* 1997—*20th Century Blues* (RCA Victor) 1998—*The Seven Deadly Sins; A Perfect Stranger: The Island Anthology* (Island) 2000—*Vagabond Ways* (Instinct).

Marianne Faithfull first appeared on the British pop scene as the angel-faced, sweet-voiced singer of "As Tears Go By" (#22 U.S., #9 U.K.) in 1964, when she was 18. The song was written for her by Rolling Stones Mick Jagger and Keith Richards, and although she had three more hits independent of the Stones—"Come and Stay With Me" (#26 U.S., #4 U.K.), "This Little Bird" (#32 U.S., #6 U.K.), and "Summer Nights" (#24 U.S., #10 U.K.), all in 1965—she became better known as Jagger's girlfriend than as a singer. After leaving the spotlight for close to a decade, Faithfull made a striking comeback with 1979's *Broken English,* which established her as a songwriter and interpreter in her own right.

Faithfull is the daughter of a London University lecturer in Renaissance studies and an Austrian baroness descended from Leopold von Sacher-Masoch (from whose name "masochism" is derived). She attended St. Joseph's Convent School in Reading until she was 17. At 18 she married London art dealer John Dunbar, through whom she met Jagger. She and Dunbar were separated after the birth of their son, Nicholas, in 1965, and divorced in 1970.

During the late '60s Faithfull became pregnant by Jagger (she miscarried) and was later heavily involved in drug use (she was hospitalized following an overdose on the Australian movie set of *Ned Kelly,* in which she was to costar with Jagger). Although she abandoned her recording career

Marianne Faithfull

after 1966, she contributed lyrics (uncredited) to the Rolling Stones' "Sister Morphine." Her major activity after 1966 was acting: with Alain Delon in a 1968 French film, *The Girl on the Motorcycle;* in Chekhov's *Three Sisters* at the Royal Court Theatre, London, in 1969; and as Ophelia opposite Nicol Williamson in a 1970 film production of *Hamlet.*

Following her breakup with Jagger in 1970 and her widely publicized eight-month commitment to a hospital to cure her heroin addiction, Faithfull withdrew from public life, reappearing only briefly in 1974 on a David Bowie television special. In 1977 she recorded her first album in over 10 years, and although it received little notice, it led to her signing with Island Records in 1979. Her Island debut, *Broken English*—marked by stark instrumentation, venomous lyrics, and Faithfull's raspy vocals—was barely recognizable as the work of the woman who sang "As Tears Go By." It was followed by four more critically acclaimed albums for Island. *Strange Weather* occasioned Faithfull's limited return to live performance; on *Blazing Away,* she was backed by Dr. John, and Band member Garth Hudson, along with her guitarist and cocomposer, Barry Reynolds. She also acted in the films *Turn of the Screw* (1992) and *Shopping* (1993), and published an autobiography entitled *Faithfull* (cowritten with David Dalton) in 1994. A compilation album of the same name featured the Patti Smith–penned "Ghost Dance," on which the singer was backed by the Rolling Stones' Charlie Watts and Ron Wood. The following year she released *A Secret Life,* on which she collaborated with *Twin Peaks* composer Angelo Badalamenti.

Resuming her acting career, Faithfull appeared onstage in a 1989 production of Kurt Weill's *Seven Deadly Sins* in New York, Chicago, and Berlin, and in the Brecht-Weill *Threepenny Opera* in Dublin in 1991. After relocating to Ireland in 1993, she spent the latter part of the '90s exploring the Weimar songbook and consolidating her image as a world-weary chanteuse. A pair of live albums commemorated this evolution: *20th Century Blues* (which focused on Brecht-Weill material but also included songs by Noel Coward and Harry Nilsson) and *The Seven Deadly Sins,* recorded with the Vienna Radio Symphony. Faithfull returned to the studio on 2000's *Vagabond Ways.* The album was a mix of original material—some of which she cowrote with Daniel Lanois and longtime accomplice Reynolds—and covers, including "Incarceration of a Flower Child," a song written by Pink Floyd's Roger Waters in 1968, which had never been recorded before.

Faith No More

Formed 1982, San Francisco, CA
Chuck Mosely, voc.; James "Jim" Martin (b. July 21, 1961, Oakland, CA), gtr.; Roddy Bottum (b. July 1, 1963, Los Angeles, CA), kybds.; Billy Gould (b. Apr. 23, 1963, Los Angeles), bass; Michael "Mike" Bordin (b. Nov. 27, 1962, San Francisco), drums.
1985—*We Care a Lot* (Mordam) 1987—*Introduce Yourself* (Slash/Reprise) (– Mosely; + Michael "Mike" Patton [b. Jan. 27, 1967, Eureka, CA], voc.) 1989—*The Real Thing* 1990—*You Fat Bastard: Live at Brixton Academy* 1992—*Angel Dust* 1993—*Songs to Make Love To* EP 1995—*King for a Day/Fool for a Lifetime* (– Martin; + Trey Spruance, gtr.) 1997—*Album of the Year* (– Spruance; + Jon Hudson, gtr.) 1998—*Who Cares a Lot.*

Most fans who bought Faith No More's #9 1990 hit single "Epic" had no idea the group had been around for eight years and had begun life as a postpunk hardcore-thrash band.

Bassist Billy Gould and keyboardist Roddy Bottum had both played on the Los Angeles punk-rock scene of the late '70s, before moving to San Francisco to attend college. Through a classified ad placed by drummer Mike Bordin, they formed Faith No More, recruiting guitarist Jim Martin from a local thrash band with future Metallica bassist Cliff Burton. At club gigs they let audience members be vocalists; Chuck Mosely, who often wore a dress, was among the most frequent volunteers, and eventually joined the band. "We Care a Lot"—a sardonic thrash-funk answer to "We Are the World"—got college-radio play, and some MTV play for its video, leading to a deal with Warner Bros.–distributed Slash Records. Mosely was kicked out after two albums and two European tours, because of his "unpredictable behavior."

With an album's worth of new music written, Faith No More auditioned new vocalists and quickly selected Mike Patton, from the bizarrely theatrical Mr. Bungle. Patton wrote lyrics to match Faith No More's new tunes for *The Real Thing* (#11, 1990), which sold over a million copies, thanks largely to "Epic" (#9, 1990), an anthemic mix of funk-rap verses and hard-rock choruses. On tour, Patton sometimes wore leisure suits or monster masks, while the band played surprising but seemingly sincere covers of New Kids on the Block's "Right Stuff," Madonna's "Vogue," and the Commodores' easy-listening classic "Easy."

In 1991 Patton recorded an album with Mr. Bungle, and Faith No More contributed "The Perfect Crime" to the soundtrack of the film sequel *Bill & Ted's Bogus Journey,* in which Jim Martin had a bit part. *Angel Dust* (#10, 1992) failed to yield a hit single, while *Songs to Make Love To* included the band's covers of "Easy" and the Dead Kennedys' "Let's Lynch the Landlord." Martin was replaced by Mr. Bungle guitarist Trey Spruance for *King for a Day/Fool for a Lifetime,* a genre-shuffle that added Portuguese balladry and soulful crooning to the band's militantly eclectic agenda. The group's final studio release, *Album of the Year* (#41, 1997), saw another new guitarist, Jon Hudson, step in for Spruance. A greatest hits package, *Who Cares a Lot,* recapped Faith No More's career, which officially ended in 2000 when its members finally called it quits.

Patton recorded a third Mr. Bungle release in 1999, while Bottum achieved fresh commercial success with his own side project Imperial Teen, which formed in 1996. "Yoo Hoo," from that group's second album, *What Is Not to Love* (1998), found steady rotation on modern-rock radio, where its catchy chorus played as quirky novelty.

Falco

Born Johann Holzel, Feb. 19, 1957, Vienna, Austria; died Feb. 6, 1998, Santo Domingo, Dominican Republic
1982—*Einzelhaft* (A&M) 1984—*Junger Roemer* 1986—*Falco 3; Emotional* (Sire) 1988—*Wiener Blut* 1992—*The Remix Hit Collection* 1998—*Out of the Dark (Into the Light)* (EMI Electrola).

Falco was Austria's most successful international pop artist on the basis of two unlikely singles: 1983's "Der Kommissar," a driving technopop ditty on which he rapped in German, and the #1 camp classic Mozart tribute "Rock Me Amadeus," from his 1986 album *Falco 3.* Although he had never reclaimed his '80s fame in the U.S. by the time of his death, he remained a success in his homeland. An estimated 10,000 mourners—from family members and fellow musicians to politicians and fans—attended his funeral.

Young Johann Holzel's parents had wanted him to become a doctor, but he dashed those hopes when, after graduating from school, he moved to West Berlin and began singing in a jazz-rock outfit. Taking the moniker Falco from East German ski jumper Falko Weissflog, he returned to Vienna in the late '70s, where he played bass guitar in a punk band called Drahdiwaberl before landing a contract as a solo artist.

While Falco's version of "Der Kommissar" was a dance-club favorite in the U.S., it was an English-language cover by After the Fire that became the hit, topping at #5 in 1983. Though best known for his cheekier material (including "Vienna Calling," which reached #18 in the U.S. in 1986), and for prancing around dressed as a punk Mozart in the popular video for "Rock Me Amadeus," Falco addressed serious matters in some of his songs. "Jeanny," also from *Falco 3,* was a controversial tale of prostitution that narrowly escaped censorship in Germany, and "The Sound of Musik" took aim at Austria's controversial president Kurt Waldheim, who was alleged to have been a Nazi.

Two weeks before his 41st birthday, Falco was killed in a car accident. News of his death sparked a resurgence of his music throughout Europe. He had completed recording *Out of the Dark (Into the Light)* shortly before, and the album quickly went to #1 in Austria and #5 in Germany. In addition, various retrospectives released overseas—two volumes of *Greatest Hits* as well as a *Best Of* collection—sold enormously well in those countries.

The Fall

Formed 1977, Manchester, Eng.
Mark E. Smith (b. Mark Edward Smith, Mar. 5, 1957, Manchester), voc., kybds., harmonica; Martin Bramah, gtr.; Una Baines, kybds.; Tony Friel, bass; Karl Burns, drums.
1978—(– Friel; – Baines; + Marc Riley, bass, gtr., kybds.; + Yvonne Pawlett, kybds.) 1979—*Live at the Witch Trials* (I.R.S./A&M) (– Bramah; – Pawlett; – Burns; + Craig Scanlon [b. Dec. 7, 1960, Manchester], gtr.; + Steven Hanley [b. Steven Patrick Hanley, May 20, 1959, Ire.], bass; + Mike Leigh, drums) 1979—*Dragnet* (Step Forward, U.K.) 1980—*Totale's Turns (It's Now or Never)* (Rough Trade, U.K.) (– Leigh; + Paul Hanley [b. Manchester], drums, gtr., kybds.) 1980—*Grotesque (After the Gramme)* 1981—*Slates* EP; *77—Early Years—77-79* (Rough Trade) (– P. Hanley; + K. Burns) 1982—*Room to Live (Undiluteable Slang Truth)* (Kamera, U.K.); *A Part of America Therein, 1981* (Cottage) (+ P. Hanley) *Hex Enduction Hour* (– Riley; + Brix Smith [b. Laura Elise Smith, CA], gtr., voc.) 1983—*Perverted by Language* (Rough Trade, U.K.) 1984—*The Wonderful and Frightening World of . . .* (Beggars Banquet, U.K.); *Call for Escape Route* EP (– P. Hanley; + Simon Rogers, kybds., bass) 1985—*Hip Priests and Kamerads* (Situation Two, U.K.) 1986—*The Fall* EP (Jem-PVC); *This Nation's Saving Grace* (– Burns; + Simon Wolstencroft [b. Jan. 19, 1963, Altrincham, Eng.], drums); *Bend Sinister* (Beggar's Banquet, U.K.) (+ Marcia Schofield [b. 1963, Brooklyn, NY], kybds.) 1987—*The Fall In: Palace of Swords Reversed* (Rough Trade, U.K.) 1988—*The Frenz Experiment* (RCA); *I Am Kurious, Oranj* 1989—*Seminal Live* (RCA) (– B. Smith; – Rogers; + Bramah) 1990—*Extricate* (Fontana/Polygram); *458489 A Sides* (RCA); *458489 B Sides* (– Schofield; + Dave Bush [b. June 4, 1959, Taplow, Eng.], kybds.) 1991—*Shift-Work* (Cog Sinister, U.K.) (– Bramah) 1992—*Code: Selfish* 1993—*The Infotainment Scan* (Matador) (+ Burns) 1994—*Middle Class Revolt* 1995—(+ B. Smith) *Cerebral Caustic* (Cog Sinister/Permanent, U.K.) (– Bush; + Julia Nagle, kybds.) *The Twenty-Seven Points* (– Scanlon) 1996—*The Light User Syndrome* (Jet, U.K.) (– B. Smith) 1997—*Levitate* (Artful, U.K.) (+ Tommy Crooks, gtr.; – Wolstencroft) 1998—(– Hanley; – Burns; – Crooks; + Tom Head, drums; + Neville Wilding, gtr., voc.; + Karen Leatham, bass; + Adam Halal, bass; + S. Hitchcock, string arrangements) 1999—*The Marshall Suite* (– Leatham) 2000—*The Unutterable* (Eagle, U.K.)
Mark E. Smith solo: 1998—*The Post Nearly Man* (Artful, U.K.).

Through ongoing personnel and label shifts (not all of them listed above), and with an audience that's international in scope yet cultish in size, the Fall has held fast to a dour, distinctive sound, becoming the longest-lived and most prolific band to emerge from England's late-'70s punk-rock movement. Sole constant Mark E. Smith is a white-rap progenitor who delivers caustic commentary on British life in a distinctively accented, sneering sing-speech (sometimes turning his back on audiences to read handwritten lyric sheets). The Fall's music, rooted in rockabilly and skiffle, hinges on abrasive, twangy guitars and nagging, rackety rhythms.

Named after the Camus novel, the Fall followed the Buzzcocks out of the grimy Northern England industrial city of Manchester, recording *Live at the Witch Trials* in one day. By *Grotesque* and *Slates,* the Fall's scraggly dissonance had grown thicker and, at times, more bright and tuneful. The hooky 1981 single "Totally Wired" became something of a new-wave anthem.

On a 1983 tour Mark E. Smith met Brix Smith at a Chicago show; she married him and replaced Marc Riley as second guitarist (she also led her own band, the Adult Net), honing the Fall's sound in a poppier direction. Mark E. Smith, a frequent critic of clerical hypocrisy (going back to *Dragnet*'s "Spectre vs. Rector"), wrote a musical play about papal politics called *Hey! Luciani*, which was mounted in London in 1985/86; the Fall recorded the title song as a single.

The Frenz Experiment's faithful cover of the Kinks' "Victoria" was a hit single in the U.K. and got some video play on MTV in America; the disco-influenced "Hit the North" seemed to presage the imminent explosion of Manchester's "rave" scene (of which inveterate antitrendy Smith wanted no part). *I am Kurious, Oranj*, based on a Smith fantasy about William of Orange, was the score for a ballet by avant-garde choreographer Michael Clark. Brix Smith dissolved her marriage to Mark E. Smith and left the Fall in 1990. New keyboardist Dave Bush pushed the group's sound toward dub-reggae and techno-dance styles.

Nothing about the Fall, save Smith's rattlesome presence, remained fixed, however. Throughout the '90s, the band's mercurial lineups were rarely the same between tours and albums, which, despite a brief liasion with U.S.-based Matador Records, were recorded for British labels. Brix Smith returned to the group for a tour supporting the 1994 release *Middle Class Revolt* and helped to rejuvenate rock elements on *Cerebral Caustic*, the live *The Twenty-Seven Points* (both 1995), and *The Light User Syndrome* (1996), before departing again in the middle of a tour. Keyboardist Julia Nagle arrived during the same period, replacing the departed Bush, and became the only latter-day member of the group to outlast the decade. She also became Smith's significant other, and led the group toward more electronic experimentalism. Longtime members Steve Hanley and Burns, and guitarist Tommy Crooks (who joined for 1997's *Levitate)*, quit the Fall after a rancorous 1998 U.S. tour that resulted in Smith facing domestic violence charges after an alleged hotel room altercation with Nagle. The meltdown occurred with an ironic timing Fall fans could truly appreciate. Even as the band appeared to be in smithereens, Smith had been declared the winner of the New Musical Express's Godlike Genius Award.

Undaunted, Smith shortly recruited a new roster for the Fall, and in 1999 released *The Marshall Suite*, followed the next year by *The Unutterable*.

Georgie Fame

Born Clive Powell, June 26, 1943, Lancashire, Eng.
1965—*Yeh, Yeh* (Imperial) 1966—*Get Away* 1968—*The Ballad of Bonnie and Clyde* (Epic) 1971—*Fame and Price* (with Alan Price) (Columbia).

Georgie Fame is best known in the U.S. for his 1968 novelty hit "The Ballad of Bonnie and Clyde," and as an R&B/jazz singer and keyboardist in Britain. Clive Powell played keyboards in Eddie Cochran's band during his last tour, before English impresario Larry Parnes steered him to a 1960 job with Billy Fury's band, the Blue Flames. Parnes also suggested the name change to Georgie Fame. In 1962 Fame left Fury and took along the Blue Flames. By the mid-'60s Fame was playing jazzy R&B; guitarist John McLaughlin was in the band for a short time. In late 1963 his expanded group (including Cream's Ginger Baker) released two instrumental singles followed by its influential 1964 set, *Rhythm and Blues at the Flamingo*.

In 1965 Fame had a #1 U.K. hit, "Yeh Yeh," which also slipped into the U.S. Top 30. He had another U.K. #1 in 1966 with "Get Away." When Fame disbanded the Blue Flames later that year, the lineup included future Jimi Hendrix Experience drummer Mitch Mitchell. Fame's first solo LP, *Sound Venture* (Columbia), was MOR jazz; the next year he played an Albert Hall concert with Count Basie. His ragtime novelty hit, 1968's "Bonnie and Clyde," hit #7 in the U.S. From 1971 to 1973 he teamed up with former Animals keyboardist Alan Price; they had a #11 U.K. hit in 1971, "Rosetta." Fame also recorded an LP, *Shorty*, in the early '70s with his group. In 1974 Fame reincarnated the Blue Flames (including Colin Green) and released an album of R&B ballads, *Georgie Fame*. In the '80s he turned to writing for the stage, and produced musical tributes to Hoagy Carmichael (1981) and George Gershwin (1986). He toured and recorded with Van Morrison through the '80s and '90s. With Ben Sidran the duo created the 1996 album *Tell Me Something*, a tribute to Mose Allison. Fame has released several more solo albums, which feature jazzier material. He currently has several floating bands including an Australian incarnation of the Blue Flames and Three Line Whip, which includes his sons Tristan and James.

Family

Formed 1967, Leicester, Eng.
Roger Chapman (b. Apr. 8, 1944, Leicester), voc.; Rob Townsend (b. July 7, 1947, Leicester), drums; Rick Grech (b. Nov. 1, 1946, Bordeaux, Fr.; d. Mar. 17, 1990), bass, violin, voc.; Jim King (b. ca. 1945, Eng.), sax, flute; Charlie Whitney (b. June 4, 1944, Eng.), gtr., voc.
1968—*Music in a Doll's House* (Reprise) 1969—*Family Entertainment* (– Grech; – King; + John "Poli" Palmer [b. May 25, 1943, Eng.], perc., flute, piano; + John Weider [b. Apr. 21, 1947, Eng.], bass, violin) 1970—*A Song for Me; Anyway* (United Artists) (– Weider; + John Wetton [b. July 12, 1949, Derby, Eng.], bass, voc.) 1971—*Fearless* (– Wetton; + Jim Cregan, bass, gtr.) 1972—*Band Stand* (– Palmer; + Tony Ashton, kybds., voc.) 1973—*It's Only a Movie* (– Townsend) 1974—*Best of Family* (Reprise).

Although Family's wildly eclectic progressive rock made it a hitmaker in England, the group remained relatively unknown in the U.S. Family featured the often grating, goatish vibrato singing of Roger Chapman and a repertoire by Chapman and Charlie Whitney, tempered in later years by the jazzy flute and vibraphone of John "Poli" Palmer. The group started in Leicester in 1962 as the Farinas, which included Chapman, Whitney, King, and, later, Grech. They turned into the pinstripe-suited Roaring Sixties, and finally settled on the Family name at the suggestion of Kim Fowley.

Traffic's Dave Mason (with Jimmy Miller) coproduced its debut. The group's harder-rocking followup, *Family Entertainment,* prompted a U.S. tour. Unfortunately, the day before it was to start, Rick Grech quit to join Blind Faith [see entry], and Family's debut performance at the Fillmore East ended in a fistfight between Chapman and promoter Bill Graham. A few days later Chapman lost both his voice and his visa, and Family returned to England. The band's appearance at the 1970 Rotterdam Festival was filmed in *Stomping Ground,* and it was featured in Jenny Fabian's novel *Groupie.* Family's reputation continued to grow at home, with hit singles *Anyway*'s "In My Own Time" (#4 U.K., 1971) and *Band Stand*'s "Burlesque" (#13 U.K., 1972).

Family opened for Elton John in 1972, but never found a U.S. audience despite FM airplay for *Fearless* and *Band Stand. It's Only a Movie,* the group's final album, was released in Britain on its own Raft label in 1973. That fall, Family played a farewell tour of England, including a final gig in Leicester. Chapman and Whitney founded Streetwalkers; Chapman recorded some solo albums and appears on Mike Oldfield's *Islands.* Cregan later joined Rod Stewart's band, and Palmer went into session work, appearing on albums by Pete Townshend of the Who. Ashton and Townsend joined the U.K. group Medicine Head, then Townsend drummed for Kevin Ayers' band in the '70s, and Dave Kelly's group in the early '80s.

Fanny

Formed 1970, California
June Millington (b. 1949, Manila, Philippines), gtr., voc.; Alice de Buhr (b. 1950, Mason City, IA), drums; Addie Clement, gtr.; Jean Millington (b. 1950, Manila, Philippines), bass, voc.
1970—(– Clement; + Nicole "Nicky" Barclay [b. Apr. 21, 1951, Washington, DC], kybds.) *Fanny* (Reprise) 1971—*Charity Ball* 1972—*Fanny Hill* 1973—*Mother's Pride* 1974—(– June Millington; – de Ruhr; + Patti Quatro [b. Detroit], bass; + Brie Brandt-Howard, drums) 1975—*Rock and Roll Survivors* (Casablanca) 2001—*Fanny Live* (Slick Music).
Nicky Barclay solo: 1976—*Diamond in a Junkyard* (Ariola).
Jean Millington and June Millington: 1978—*Ladies on the Stage* (United Aritsts).
June Millington solo: 1981—*Heartsong* (Olivia).

The members of Fanny were true rock & roll pioneers, forming one of the first all-female hard-rock groups. The band's nucleus was the Philippine-born Millington sisters, who moved to Sacramento, California, when their father, a Navy man, was transferred in 1961. They formed their first quartet, the Sveltes, with girlfriends in high school. They played in a series of local bands for five years, under different names, and were performing at the Troubadour in L.A. when record producer Richard Perry's secretary discovered them.

After her boss got them signed to Warner Bros., the group changed its name to Fanny. According to June Millington, "We didn't really think of it [the name] as a butt, a sexual term. We felt it was like a woman's spirit watching over us." Nonetheless, the group's record company launched promotional campaigns that exploited the sexual aspect, including bumper stickers urging people to "Get Behind Fanny" and ads that showed the women from the back.

Perry produced the group's first three albums, and Fanny also backed up Barbra Streisand on her 1970 LP *Stoney End. Charity Ball* yielded their first chart single with its title cut. Perhaps their most fully realized effort was *Fanny Hill,* recorded at the Beatles' Apple studios in London. The group's hardest-rocking release, 1973's *Mother's Pride,* was produced by Todd Rundgren.

Around the same time, Fanny toured extensively (including several dates with Jethro Tull), performing its rock opera, *Rock and Roll Survivors.* Bassist Patti Quatro, Suzy Quatro's elder sister, replaced June Millington, and original Svelte Brie Howard joined. Ironically, the group broke up shortly after scoring its highest-charting single, "Butter Boy," from the last album. Later that year Jean convinced June to return to music, and together they formed the L.A. All-Stars. They were on the verge of signing a record contract but refused when they learned that one of its conditions was that they be called Fanny again.

June became deeply involved in the women's music movement, producing records for Cris Williamson and Holly Near, among others. She recorded with another all-female rock group, Isis, in the mid-'70s, and she has recorded solo. In 1987 she cofounded the Institute for the Musical Arts, a studio and performance space in Bodega, California. By 1979, Jean Millington was married to ex–David Bowie guitarist Earl Slick, playing club dates, and recording and producing for Olivia Records. The sisters recently reunited in a band called the Slammin' Babes.

Keyboardist and chief songwriter Nicky Barclay, who had been included in Joe Cocker's Mad Dogs and Englishmen, went on to form her own group called Good News in 1976 and released an Ariola-American LP, *Diamond in a Junkyard.* She also played on Keith Moon's solo album *Two Sides of the Moon.*

Richard and Mimi Fariña

Richard Fariña (b. 1937, Brooklyn, NY; d. Apr. 30, 1966, Carmel, CA), dulcimer, voc.; Mimi Fariña (b. Mimi Baez, Apr. 30, 1945, New York, NY; d. July 18, 2001, Mill Valley, CA), gtr., voc.
1965—*Celebrations for a Grey Day* (Vanguard) 1966—*Reflections in a Crystal Wind* 1968—*Richard Fariña; Memories* 1971—*The Best of Richard and Mimi Fariña; Mimi Fariña and Tom Jans* (A&M)

The Fariñas were an American husband-and-wife folk duo whose promising career ended with Richard's death in 1966. Richard was born to Irish and Cuban parents. Although his parents had immigrated to the United States in the '20s, Fariña spent extended periods during his youth in Cuba as well as in Brooklyn and Northern Ireland. While living in Northern Ireland in the mid-'50s, he became actively involved with the IRA and the British government had him deported. He later moved to Cuba and supported Castro. In 1959 he moved to Greenwich Village and began performing; he was briefly married to folksinger Carolyn Hester.

In 1963 he wed Joan Baez's younger sister, Mimi, in Paris. The couple moved to California, where they began working as a duo. They recorded three albums for Vanguard in the mid-'60s. The second, *Reflections in a Crystal Wind*, was one of the earliest fusions of folk material with a rock rhythm section. Material from all three was later included on Vanguard's *Best of Richard and Mimi Fariña*. Throughout, Fariña maintained his literary career, writing plays, magazine articles, and *Been Down So Long It Looks Like Up to Me*, a novel concerned with the cultural transition from the beatniks to the hippies. He was returning home from a promotional party for the book when he died in a motorcycle crash in 1966 on his wife's 21st birthday. The book was subsequently reprinted.

Mimi withdrew from the public eye for a few years, but she subsequently worked as both a singer and an actress (notably as a member of the Committee). As the '60s closed, she performed and recorded with her sister, Joan. In the early '70s she helped establish Bread and Roses, a charitable organization that provides entertainment for prisoners, hospital patients, and institutionalized people. She died of cancer in 2001.

Chris Farlowe

Born John Henry Deighton, Oct. 13, 1940, London, Eng. 1967—*The Fabulous Chris Farlowe* (CBS, U.K.) 1968—*Paint It Farlowe* (Immediate, U.K.) 1970—*From Here to Mama Rosa* (with the Hill) (Polydor) 1985—*Out of the Blue* (Polydor, U.K.) 1988—*Born Again* 1996—*As Time Goes By* (KEG/Out of Time, U.K.) 1998—*The Voice* (Citadel/Out of Time, U.K.) 2000—*Glory Bound* (Delicious/Out of Time, U.K.).

A minor English R&B figure in the early '60s, vocalist Chris Farlowe's records sold poorly until mid-decade, when Mick Jagger gave him his first major U.K. hit with a Jagger-Richards composition, "Out of Time."

John Deighton began playing the guitar at age 13 and soon formed the John Henry Skiffle Group, which won the All-English Skiffle Championship. By 1962 he was calling himself Chris Farlowe and singing R&B at London's Flamingo Club with his Thunderbirds. Their early recordings included "Buzz with the Fuzz" and "Stormy Monday Blues" (which Farlowe released under the alias Little Joe Cook).

But it was only after Jagger (who sang occasional backup vocals on Farlowe's records) became his patron that the Thunderbirds sustained any serious impact. "Out of Time" hit #1 in July 1966, but later that year Farlowe disbanded the Thunderbirds, only to re-form the group the following year (with Carl Palmer on drums). Other band members included guitarist Albert Lee, keyboardist Pete Solley, and keyboardist Dave Greenslade, later of Colosseum. In 1970 Farlowe formed a new group, the Hill, which recorded one album. That same year he joined Greenslade in Colosseum. When that group broke up in November 1971, Farlowe lent his services to Atomic Rooster for two LPs.

Concurrently he worked on various solo projects, including a 1970 stint with a band called the Hill. In 1972 Farlowe retired from music to run his Nazi war memorabilia shop in North London. In 1975 he attempted a last-ditch comeback by reissuing "Out of Time" and an LP, *The Chris Farlowe Band Live*. He again retired, but resurfaced in 1985 with *Out of the Blue*. Three years later Farlowe came out with *Born Again* and sang on Jimmy Page's first solo album, *Outrider*. Through the '90s Farlowe's name appeared on numerous import releases. He embarked on a solo tour of Europe in 2001. Colosseum reunited, toured, and recorded an album in 1996.

Fatboy Slim/The Housemartins

Fatboy Slim, born Quentin Cook, July 31, 1963, Bromley, Eng. 1996—*Better Living Through Chemistry* (Astralwerks/Skint) 1998—*You've Come a Long Way, Baby* 2000—*On the Floor at the Boutique; Halfway Between the Gutter and the Stars.*
The Housemartins, formed 1984, Hull, Eng.: Paul Heaton (b. May 9, 1962, Merseyside, Eng.), voc., gtr; Stan Cullimore (b. Apr. 6, 1962, Hull, Eng.), gtr.; Ted Key, bass; Hugh Whitaker, drums. 1985—(– Key; + Cook, bass) 1986—*London 0 Hull 4* (Elektra) (– Whitaker; + Dave Hemingway [b. Sep. 20, 1960, Hull], drums) 1987—*The People Who Grinned Themselves to Death* 1988—*Now That's What I Call Quite Good!* (Go! Discs, U.K.).

Recording under the alias Fatboy Slim, British DJ/producer Norman Cook was one of the major pioneers of big beat; he ranks second only to the Chemical Brothers in terms of breaking the genre in the States. Cook samples from a wide range of music—house, funk, even rock—to create electronic music specifically designed for dancing. This emphasis on hedonism over experimentalism caused many techno purists to scorn Fatboy Slim, though it granted him immense success both at home and in America.

Cook, who was christened Quentin, started DJ'ing at age 15. In 1985 he changed his name to Norman and joined the British pop band the Housemartins, replacing departing bassist and founding member Ted Key. The Housemartins were known for their socially conscious, no-frills image and scathing sarcasm. Their 1986 and 1987 albums yielded several Top 20 pop hits, including "Caravan of Love" (#1 U.K., 1986) and "Happy Hour" (#3 U.K., 1986).

Following the band's split in 1988, Housemartins frontman Paul Heaton and drummer Dave Hemingway formed the Beautiful South [see entry]; Cook, meanwhile, returned to his dance-music roots with Beats International, which scored a #1 hit in the U.K. with its 1990 single "Dub Be Good to Me." Cook also recorded under numerous other monikers, including Pizzaman, Freakpower, and Mighty Dub Katz—who all charted in the U.K.—before embarking on his Fatboy Slim project. He made a minor splash in America with 1996's *Better Living Through Chemistry* and its single, "Going Out of My Head," which drew its defining guitar sample from Yvonne Elliman's remake of the Who's "I Can't Explain." But it was 1998's *You've Come a Long Way, Baby* that transformed Cook into an international star with its inescapable hits "The Rockafeller Skank" and "Praise You," the latter of which stayed on the U.S. pop chart for 20 weeks in 1999. Cook veered away from big beat for his next venture, *Halfway Between the Gutter and the Stars,* on which he worked with live vocalists (including R&B singer Macy Gray) for the first time.

Charlie Feathers

Born June 12, 1932, Holly Springs, MS; died Aug. 29, 1998, Memphis, TN
1973—*Good Rockin' Tonight/Live in Memphis* (Edsel, U.K.) 1978—*Rockabilly Man* (Charly) 1979—*Live in Memphis* (Barrelhouse); *Charlie Feathers, vol.1* (Feathers); *Charlie Feathers; That Rockabilly Cat* (Edsel) 1982—*Honky Tonk Man* (New Rose) 1984—*Rockabilly Kings* (Polydor) 1986—*Legendary '56 Demo Sessions* (Zu-Zazz) 1987—*Jungle Fever* (Kay); *The New Jungle Fever* (New Rose, Fr.); *Wild Wild Party* (Rockstar) 1988—*The Living Legend, vol. 2* (Redita) 1991—*Rock-a-Billy* (Zu-Zazz); *Charlie Feathers* (Elektra/Nonesuch) 1993—*Uh Huh Honey* (Norton); 1995—*Tip Top Daddy* (Norton); *Rock 'n' Roll* (Star) 1998—*Get With It* (Revenant).

Although rockabilly pioneer Charlie Feathers never achieved commercial success, he was present at the creation of the form. Feathers himself hinted that a mysterious, undisclosed "conspiracy" denied him mainstream fame; he has since become a cult legend.

Raised on a farm, Feathers quit school after the third grade, learned guitar from a black sharecropper, and worked on oil pipelines in Illinois and Texas as a teen. Moving to Memphis at 18, he contracted spinal meningitis and spent months bedridden, listening to the radio. Upon recuperating he concentrated on music. Feathers later claimed that he spent a great deal of time in the mid-'50s at Sam Phillips' Sun studios, arranging some of Elvis Presley's early material. Though most of Feathers' assertions have been unsubstantiated, he did cowrite Presley's "I Forgot to Remember to Forget" (#1 C&W, 1955). That year, his own debut single on Flip, "I've Been Deceived," showed the influence of Hank Williams, and from then until 1959, he recorded for Sun and smaller labels (King, Kay, and Walmay among them). Such singles as "Tongue-Tied Jill" and "Get With It" did little on the charts, but Feathers persevered, playing local roadhouses until gaining, in 1977, a gig at London's Rainbow Theatre that drew raves from rockabilly revivalists.

In the late '70s Feathers got the financial backing to start his own short-lived record label, Feathers, upon which he released a couple of albums and several singles. Frequently comic in tone, his work was often straightforwardly country. However, with the critical praise that attended 1991's *Charlie Feathers* (his only major label release), 1995's *Tip Top Daddy* (an unearthed collection of stellar unissued demos), and 1998's *Get With It* (a definitive collection of early singles), Feathers will be remembered essentially as a great, early, if not widely known, rocker. He died in 1998, following complications from a stroke.

The Feelies

Formed 1976, Haledon, NJ
Bill Million (b. William Clayton, ca. 1953, Haledon), gtr., voc.; Glenn Mercer (b. ca. 1955, Haledon), gtr., voc.; John J., bass; Dave Weckerman (b. ca. 1950), drums.
1977—(– J.; – Weckerman; + Keith Clayton [b. Keith DeNunzio, Apr. 27, 1958, Reading, PA], bass; + Vinny D. [b. Vincent DeNunzio, Aug. 15, 1956, Reading], drums) 1978—(– D.; + Anton Fier [a.k.a. Andy Fisher] [b. June 20, 1956, Cleveland, OH], drums) 1980—*Crazy Rhythms* (Stiff) 1986—(– Fier; – Clayton; + Stanley Demeski [b. ca. 1960], drums; + Brenda Sauter [b. ca. 1959], bass, violin; + Weckerman, perc.) *The Good Earth* (Coyote); *No One Knows* EP 1988—*Only Life* (Coyote/A&M) 1991—*Time for a Witness* (A&M).

With their quirky rhythms, frantically strummed guitars, pop melodies, and enigmatic lyrics, the Feelies epitomized New York postpunk. They stubbornly rejected a commercial recording career after one album and disappeared for several years, reappearing in the late '80s with their twin-guitar sound intact and gaining a stronghold in the American indie-rock scene.

Glenn Mercer and Bill Million, the group's songwriters, met at high school in Haledon, New Jersey, where several years later the Feelies made their live debut. After a lineup change, they began playing New York's new-wave venues and quickly earned a place in the vanguard of that city's rock experimentalists; in 1978 the *Village Voice* named them the best underground band in New York. That fall, Vinny D. left to play with Richard Lloyd (Television) and was replaced by Anton Fier.

Adamant about producing their own records, the Feelies did not sign a long-term recording contract until 1980, although they did record a single, "Fa Ce La," for the English independent label Rough Trade in 1979. *Crazy Rhythms* introduced the band as four nerds making intricate and intense white noise; songs included "The Boy With the Perpetual Nervousness" and a cover of the Beatles' "Everybody's Got Something to Hide (Except Me and My Monkey)."

Frustrated and disappointed by Stiff's demands for a hit single, the band fizzled. Fier went on to work with Pere Ubu [see entry] and form the Golden Palominos. Mercer and Million wrote the soundtrack for the punk coming-of-age film *Smithereens* in 1982. They played in several different New Jersey bands, including the Weckerman-led Yung Wu (who released an album in 1987), the Trypes (who released a 1984 EP), and Beatles and Velvet Underground cover bands. It was the instrumental group the Willies, with Weckerman, Brenda Sauter, and Stan Demeski, that led to the reactivation of the Feelies in 1983. As in the past, the Feelies played sporadically, mostly on holidays.

Their second album, *The Good Earth* (coproduced by R.E.M.'s Peter Buck), introduced a kinder, gentler group, with a more reflective, acoustic tone. Live, the Feelies built their songs into a frenzied crescendo culminating in the album track "Slipping (Into Something)," with Mercer shaking feedback out of his electric guitar, Million strumming his acoustic at a breakneck pace, and the two percussionists egging the whole thing on. That fall the Feelies appeared as the band playing the high school reunion in Jonathan Demme's *Something Wild*.

The Feelies' subsequent albums echoed the progression of their live shows, each more manic than the next, with Mercer increasingly taking a leading role. On *Only Life*, their major-label debut, they finally gave in to their longtime Velvets fetish with a cover of "What Goes On." The Feelies have never been musical innovators as much as performance perfectionists, wearing their influences on their sleeves with their frequent covers of Neil Young, Patti Smith, the Monkees, and Modern Lovers, among others. On *Time for a Witness*, those borrowings were dramatically overstated, each song sounding like someone else's, culminating in a cover of the Stooges' "Real Cool Time."

The Feelies broke up shortly after their last album. Demeski went on to play with Luna, while Mercer and Weckerman formed the group Wake Ooloo, recording three LPs for the Pravda label before disbanding in 1998. The two men subsequently formed a new band called Sunburst.

José Feliciano

Born Sep. 10, 1945, Lares, P.R.
1968—*Feliciano!* (RCA); *Souled* 1969—*Feliciano/10 to 23; Alive, Alive-O!* 1970—*Fireworks* 1971—*Encore! Jose Feliciano's Finest Performances; Jose Feliciano* 1972—*Jose Feliciano Sings* 1973—*Compartments* 1974—*And the Feeling's Good* 1975—*Just Wanna Rock 'n' Roll* 1976—*Sweet Soul Music* (Private Stock) 1981—*Jose Feliciano* (Motown) 1983—*Romance in the Night* 1988—*All Time Greatest Hits* (RCA) 1989—*I'm Never Gonna Change* (EMI) 1992—*Latin Street '92* (Capitol/EMI Latin) 1997—*On Second Thought* (32 Jazz); *Americano* (Rodven/PolyGram Latino) 1998—*Señor Bolero*.

José Feliciano reached worldwide popularity with his flamenco-flavored versions of pop hits such as "Light My Fire" (#3, 1968). Born blind, Feliciano was the second of 12 children of a poor Puerto Rican farmer; he grew up in New York's Spanish Harlem. Feliciano was introduced to the accordion and the guitar as a child. He first performed at the Bronx's El Teatro Puerto Rico. At 17 he dropped out of high school and began playing Greenwich Village clubs and coffeehouses like the Cafe Id (where he met his first wife and manager, Hilda Perez) and Gerde's Folk City (where he was discovered).

The next year, he released his first single, "Everybody Do the Click," and album, *The Voice and Guitar of Jose Feliciano*, and appeared at the Newport Folk Festival. Initially most of his releases were in Spanish, intended for the Latin market (in 1966, he played before 100,000 in Buenos Aires). In 1968 his cover of the Doors' "Light My Fire" hit the Top 5, nearly equaling the success of the original version. It went gold, as did *Feliciano!* (#2, 1968). He followed up with minor hits ("Hi Heel Sneakers," #25) and released a controversial rendition of "The Star Spangled Banner," recorded live at the fifth game of the 1968 World Series. He won the Best New Artist Grammy of 1968.

One of the first Western singers to appear behind the Iron Curtain, he tours frequently. Besides guitar, Feliciano also plays bass, banjo, keyboards, timbales, mandolin, and harmonica. His occasional compositions ("Rain," "Destiny") have been covered by Anne Murray and Blue Swede. He has also been a frequent guest on television shows *(Kung Fu* and *McMillan and Wife)*. Feliciano contributed to the soundtrack of the early-'70s film *MacKenna's Gold*. He signed with Motown in 1980, and his label debut, *Jose Feliciano*, was produced by Berry Gordy Jr. and Suzee Ikeda. He recorded two more LPs for Motown, both for its Spanish-language division.

Subsequent U.S. success has been meager, although in the early '70s he recorded with Joni Mitchell ("Free Man in Paris"). His last charting English-language single was the theme song to the television series *Chico and the Man* (#96, 1974). Nevertheless, he has three gold albums in the U.S., but over 40 gold and platinum citations from around the world. He has recorded nearly as many Spanish-language records as English, and he has won Grammys in both language categories. An East Harlem public school was renamed the José Feliciano Performing Arts School in his honor. In the early '90s Feliciano wrote music for Ray Bradbury's play *The Wonderful Ice Cream Suit*. In 1994 he released a dance single, "Goin' Krazy," using the name JF. Having become a father figure to the emerging global Latin pop audience, Feliciano toured extensively during the decade and performed on several television specials. He briefly appeared in the 1995 Coen Brothers film *Fargo*.

Freddy Fender

Born Baldemar Huerta, June 4, 1937, San Benito, TX
1974—*Before the Next Teardrop Falls* (ABC/Dot) 1975—*Are You Ready for Freddy* 1976—*Rock 'n' Country; If You're Ever in Texas* 1977—*Best of Freddy Fender* 1991—*The Freddy Fender Collection* (Reprise) 1993—*Canciones de Mi Barrio* (Arhoolie) 1996—*The Best of Freddy Fender* (MCA).

Freddy Fender is a Tex-Mex country rocker who specializes in the polka-waltz style called *conjunto* and is known for his tearful, choked-up singing in Spanish and English. After recording nine Top 10 C&W hits in the '70s, he found a new audience as lead singer of the all-star Texas Tornados [see entry].

Fender began playing the guitar and singing in amateur contests as a child. He joined the Marines at 16, and upon his return home in the mid-'50s began performing rockabilly tunes in Spanish, billed as El Bebop Kid. At one Corpus Christi nightclub he was the victim of an after-hours fight that left his nose permanently crooked and a deep knife scar in his neck. In 1957 two early recordings—Spanish versions of English-language hits first recorded by Elvis Presley ("Don't Be Cruel") and Harry Belafonte ("Jamaica Farewell")—became big sellers in Mexico and South America, earning him the nickname the Mexican Elvis.

In 1959 he signed to Imperial, changed his surname to Fender (inspired by the guitar), and cut "Holy One" and the original version of "Wasted Days and Wasted Nights," which sold 100,000 copies. On Friday, May 13, 1960, shortly after the release of yet another moderate hit, "Crazy, Crazy, Baby," Fender was arrested for possession of two marijuana cigarettes in Baton Rouge, Louisiana. Sentenced to five years in prison, he subsequently served 30 months in the Angola State Prison.

Upon his release he played bars in New Orleans and in San Benito, Texas, from 1963 until 1968. By 1975, he had released more than 100 records on regional labels, and in early 1974 he met producer Huey Meaux, who masterminded Fender's 1975 national pop breakthrough, "Before the Next Teardrop Falls" (#1). Before the end of the year he'd placed two more 45s in the Top 20: "Wasted Days and Wasted Nights" (#8) and "Secret Love" (#20). Fender's subsequent releases kept him before country audiences. He also acted in the films *Short Eyes* (1977) and *The Milagro Beanfield War* (1987).

In the mid-'80s Fender, who holds a degree in sociology, completed treatment for drug and alcohol dependency. In early 2001 he announced that he was being evaluated by medical professionals for possible kidney and liver transplants due to his chronic health conditions hepatitis C and diabetes, which had resulted in his requiring kidney dialysis.

Bryan Ferry: See Roxy Music

The Fifth Dimension

Formed 1966, Los Angeles, CA

LaMonte McLemore (b. Sep. 17, 1940, St. Louis, MO), voc.; Marilyn McCoo (b. Sep. 30, 1943, Jersey City, NJ), voc.; Ron Townson (b. Jan. 20, 1941, St. Louis; d. Aug. 2, 2001, Las Vegas, NV), voc.; Florence LaRue Gordon (b. Feb. 4, 1944, Philadelphia, PA), voc.; Billy Davis Jr. (b. June 26, 1940, St. Louis), voc.

1967—*Up, Up and Away* (Soul City) 1968—*The Magic Garden; Stoned Soul Picnic* 1969—*The Age of Aquarius* 1970—*Portrait* (Bell) 1971—*Love's Lines, Angles and Rhymes; The Fifth Dimension Live; Reflections* 1972—*Greatest Hits on Earth* 1975—*Earthbound* (ABC) 1986—*Anthology* (Rhino) 1997—*Up-Up and Away: The Definitive Collection* (Arista).

Marilyn McCoo and Billy Davis Jr.: 1976—*I Hope We Get to Love in Time* (ABC) 1977—*The Two of Us* 1978—*Marilyn and Billy* (Columbia).

The Fifth Dimension had a string of pop-soul hits in the late '60s and early '70s (seven gold LPs, five gold singles), which introduced songs by Laura Nyro and Jim Webb. Both the Fifth Dimension and the Friends of Distinction were offshoots of a vocal group, the Hi-Fi's, formed by Marilyn McCoo and LaMonte McLemore. McCoo, who had won the Grand Talent Award in the Miss Bronze California pageant, was working as a fashion model, and McLemore (a onetime minor-league baseball player) was photographing her when they decided to start the Hi-Fi's with Floyd Butler and Harry Elston, who later formed the Friends of Distinction. The Hi-Fi's toured with Ray Charles' revue before breaking up. McCoo then recruited Florence LaRue, who had also won a Grand Talent Award, and they brought in McLemore's fellow St. Louis–born Angeleno, Ron Townson. Billy Davis Jr. was singing with his own group, the Saint Gospel Singers, when McLemore, his cousin, invited him to join.

As the Versatiles, they signed with Johnny Rivers' Soul City label. After a minor West Coast hit, "I'll Be Loving You Forever," Rivers persuaded them to change their name. Their manager suggested the Fifth Dimension. The quintet's first hit was a cover of the Mamas and the Papas' "Go Where You Wanna Go" (#16, 1967), but its pop dominance began with its first Jim Webb song, "Up, Up and Away" (#7, 1967), which received four Grammys. In 1968 the Fifth Dimension made hits of Laura Nyro's "Stoned Soul Picnic" (#3) and "Sweet Blindness" (#13); in 1969 the group had its biggest seller with a medley from *Hair*, "Aquarius/Let the Sunshine In" (#1, 1969), which sold nearly 2 million copies. Another Nyro composition, "Wedding Bell Blues," topped the chart later that year. The group apparently took the song to heart, for McCoo and Davis married, as did LaRue and manager Marc Gordon.

In the early '70s the Fifth Dimension moved toward easy-listening ballads, with occasional hits, including "(Last Night) I Didn't Get to Sleep at All" (#8, 1972). The act began to play the nightclub and television circuits; it also appeared at the Nixon White House. McCoo and Davis left to work as a duo in late 1975; their 1976 album *I Hope We Get to Love in Time* included the #1 hit "You Don't Have to Be a Star." By 1980 she was cohosting the TV show *Solid Gold*.

The remains of the Fifth Dimension, meanwhile, reunited with Webb in 1975 for the unsuccessful *Earthbound;* LaRue and McLemore continue to tour, with Greg Walker, Phyllis Battle, and Willie Williams (who replaced Townson in 1998). In the '90s the group starred in a national tour of the popular Fats Waller musical *Ain't Misbehavin'*. In 1991 the Fifth Dimension became the Original Fifth Dimension for a one-off reunion tour with Davis and McCoo. In 1996 McCoo, who sang solo and acted through the '80s and '90s, made her Broadway debut in *Showboat*. Later in the decade she and Davis wrote and performed several touring musical shows, including a Duke Ellington tribute.

Fine Young Cannibals

Formed 1983, Birmingham, Eng.

Andy Cox (b. Jan. 25, 1960, Birmingham), gtr.; David Steele (b. Sep. 8, 1960, Isle of Wight, Eng.), bass, kybds; Roland Gift (b. Apr. 28, 1961, Birmingham), voc.

1985—*Fine Young Cannibals* (I.R.S.) 1989—*The Raw and the Cooked* 1990—*The Raw and the Remix* (I.R.S.-MCA) 1996—*The Finest.*

When the English Beat [see entry] broke up in 1983, two of the group's founders, Andy Cox and David Steele, continued as Fine Young Cannibals, recruiting the handsome, half-white, half-Caribbean actor/singer Roland Gift as frontman. With Cox and Steele's market-tested blend of ska rhythms, dance beats, and pop hooks, and Gift's quavering, American soul–influenced falsetto and striking, video-friendly face, the Cannibals attained the chart success their predecessor never knew.

Taking the name from an obscure 1960 film, *All the Fine Young Cannibals,* the trio released its first album in 1985 and became familiar to MTV viewers through "Johnny Come Home" and a humorous, overstated remake of Elvis Presley's "Suspicious Minds." The Cannibals gained even more visibility with their updated version of the Buzzcocks' "Ever Fallen in Love," done for the Jonathan Demme film *Something Wild.* When director Barry Levinson heard the music, he asked the group to write some material for his film *Tin Men,* and the resulting tunes made up most of the "raw" side of the group's followup, *The Raw and the Cooked.*

That album shot to #1 and remained there for most of the summer of 1989. It ultimately sold more than 2 million copies, producing two #1 hits ("Good Thing" and "She Drives Me Crazy"); a third single, "Don't Look Back," reached #11, and two others made it into the Top 100.

At home, the British trio was just as well known for its politics, regularly attacking Margaret Thatcher's Conservative government. In 1990 the Cannibals even returned two BRIT Awards, after criticizing the ceremony as a "photo opportunity" for Thatcher's government.

Throughout, Gift was attracting film offers. After the entire band appeared in *Tin Men,* the singer landed starring roles in *Sammy and Rosie Get Laid* and *Scandal;* he also appeared in a stage performance of *Romeo and Juliet.* With Gift becoming increasingly involved with his acting, Cox and Steele did a remixed version of *The Raw and the Cooked.* Plans for a third album, to be titled *The Finest,* were left stillborn. But three tracks (including "The Flame") from that abandoned album surfaced on a best-of collection of the same name in 1996. Gift essentially walked away from both music and acting throughout the '90s, preferring the company of old friends in the neighborhood pub. But in 1999 he reemerged with two high-profile performances at the Edinburgh Festival.

Tim Finn: See Crowded House; Split Enz

The Fireballs

Formed 1957, Raton, NM
Chuck Tharp (b. Feb. 3, 1941), voc.; Stan Lark (b. July 27, 1940), bass; Eric Budd (b. Oct. 23, 1938), drums; George Tomsco (b. Apr. 24, 1940), gtr.; Dan Trammell (b. July 14, 1940), gtr.
1959—(– Trammell) 1960—(– Tharp; + Jimmy Gilmer [b. 1940, LaGrange, IL], voc., piano) 1962—(– Budd; + Doug Roberts [d. Nov. 18, 1981], drums) 1963—*Sugar Shack* (Dot).

Jimmy Gilmer and the Fireballs had the biggest hit of 1963 with the million-selling "Sugar Shack." Gilmer began singing as a youngster, and in 1951 he moved with his family to Amarillo, Texas, where he studied piano for four years at the Musical Arts Conservatory. While studying engineering at Amarillo College in 1957, he formed his first pop band. In 1960 he replaced Chuck Tharp as singer of the Fireballs, a group of high school friends that had placed two instrumentals in the Top 40, "Torquay" (#39, 1959) and "Bulldog" (#24, 1960). Gilmer was introduced to the band by Buddy Holly's producer Norman Petty at his Clovis, New Mexico, recording studio.

With Gilmer on piano and vocals, their first release, "Quite a Party," made the Top 30. "Sugar Shack," credited to Jimmy Gilmer and the Fireballs, and featuring a distinctive-sounding keyboard called a Solovox, held the #1 spot on the chart for over a month. Another 1963 single, "Daisy Petal Pickin'," hit #15. By mid-decade, however, Gilmer and the Fireballs had gone their separate ways. Gilmer had little subsequent success, while the Fireballs returned to the chart in 1968 with a rocked-up version of a Tom Paxton song, "Bottle of Wine" (#9).

Firefall

Formed ca. 1974, Boulder, CO
Rick Roberts (b. 1950, FL), gtr., voc.; Jock Bartley (b. KS), gtr., voc.; Mark Andes (b. Feb. 19, 1948, Philadelphia, PA), bass; Larry Burnett (b. Washington, DC), gtr., voc.; Michael Clarke (b. June 3, 1944, New York, NY; d. Dec. 19, 1993, Treasure Island, FL), drums.
1976—*Firefall* (Atlantic) 1977—*Luna Sea* 1978—*Élan* 1980—*Undertow; Clouds Across the Sun* 1983—*Break of Dawn* 1984—*Mirror of the World* 1992—*Firefall's Greatest Hits* (Rhino) 1994—*Messenger* (Redstone).

With its lightweight blend of acoustic guitars, high harmonies, and pop-flavored country rock, Firefall jumped onto the national scene with one of 1976's biggest hits, "You Are the Woman" (#9, 1976). The band's chief writer and leader, guitarist Rick Roberts, sang on the Byrds' *Untitled* before joining the Burrito Brothers (which then included another ex-Byrd, drummer Michael Clarke), where he stayed until 1972. Roberts then released a couple of solo albums (*Windmills,* 1972, and *She Is a Song,* 1973) while trying to establish himself in L.A. music circles.

He eventually retreated to Boulder, where he formed Firefall in mid-decade, recruiting ex-Spirit and Jo Jo Gunne bassist Mark Andes. With Washington, DC, singer/songwriter Larry Burnett, he wrote most of the material for the group's gold debut, *Firefall.* Its second LP, which also went gold, contained "Just Remember I Love You" (#11, 1977). The following year's *Élan* continued Firefall's streak, going platinum, thanks to Roberts' "Strange Way" (#11, 1978). Two more Top 40 hits followed in the early '80s, "Headed for a Fall" (#35, 1980) and "Staying With It" (#37, 1981), but thereafter Firefall faded from the airwaves. The group's 1984 album, *Mirror of the World,* failed to even chart. Ten years later a new Firefall, led by original guitarist/singer Jock Bartley, released *Messenger* on the independent Redstone label.

fIREHOSE: See Minutemen

The Firm: See Jimmy Page

First Edition: See Kenny Rogers

Wild Man Fischer

Born 1945, Los Angeles, CA
1969—*An Evening With Wild Man Fischer* (Bizarre) 1977—*Wildmania* (Rhino) 1981—*Pronounced Normal* 1984—*Nothing Scary.*
Wild Man Fischer Meets Smegma: 1997—*Sings Popular Songs* (Birdman).

A man who got his start on street corners singing made-to-order compositions for a dime, Larry "Wild Man" Fischer was a well-known eccentric on the L.A. rock fringe in the late '60s. A former mental patient, he met Frank Zappa, who produced *An Evening With Wild Man Fischer* for Bizarre Records in 1969. Fischer spent a good deal of the early '70s roaming the country, singing for his widely scattered band of cult followers.

In 1975 he released his first record in six years, a single promoting a record store, "Go to Rhino Records." He came to record the song because, according to store owner Richard Foos, the Rhino Records store was the only one Fischer could hang around in without being thrown out. When the single sold 2,000 copies, Foos and Harold Bronson decided to start Rhino Records, which has since grown to become a major source of reissues and obscurities. The label's first LP release was Fischer's *Wildmania,* which reconfirmed the singer's out-to-lunch status; he once told a *Los Angeles Times* reporter that he lives "all over." On August 3, 1982, Wild Man Fischer "quit" show business. The next day he was "back in" show business. He currently lives a very private life somewhere near Hollywood. *Sings Popular Songs* (the jacket of which misspells Fischer's surname) contains sessions from 1975, recorded with the charmingly named West Coast noise collective Smegma.

Fishbone

Formed 1979, Los Angeles, CA
John "Norwood" Fisher (b. Sep. 12, 1965, Los Angeles), bass, voc.; Phillip Dwight "Fish" Fisher (b. July 16, 1967, Los Angeles), drums; Kendall Rey Jones (b. Sep. 9, 1965, Los Angeles), gtr., voc.; Angelo Christopher Moore (b. Nov. 5, 1965, Los Angeles), voc., sax; Christopher Gordon Dowd (b. Sep. 20, 1965, Las Vegas, NV), trombone, kybds., voc.; Walter Adam Kibby II (b. Nov. 13, 1964, Columbus, OH), trumpet.
1985—*Fishbone* EP (Columbia) 1986—*In Your Face* 1987—*It's a Wonderful Life (Gonna Have a Good Time)* EP 1988—*Truth and Soul* 1990—*Bonin' in the Boneyard* EP (+ John Bigham [b. Mar. 3, 1959, Chicago, IL], gtr., kybds.) 1991—*The Reality of My Surroundings* 1993—*Give a Monkey a Brain and He'll Swear He's the Center of the Universe* (– Jones) 1996—*Fishbone 101: Nuttasaurusmeg, Fossil Fuelin' the Fonkay; Chim Chim's Badass Revenge* (Rowdy).
As Fishbone & the Familyhood Experience: 2000—(– Dowd; – P. Fisher; + Tracey E. "Spacey T" Singleton III [b. June 6, 1957], gtr., voc.; + John Drewey McKnight [b. Aug. 9, 1968], kybds., horns, voc.; + John Steward [b. Dec. 2, 1961], drums, voc.) *The Psychotic Friends Nuttwerx* (Hollywood).

Fishbone's mélange of ska, funk, punk, and metal was born when residents of South Central L.A. were bussed to the San Fernando Valley for junior high school. Dropped into foreign territory, the Fisher brothers, Jones, Dowd, and Kibby banded together with Valley resident Moore and expressed the tensions of integration through music. Combining homeboy and Valley boy tastes (they cite Funkadelic and Rush as equal influences), Fishbone confront and transcend racial barriers, yet the career hurdles these black rockers have faced compared to the success of their white-funk peers (Red Hot Chili Peppers) indicate the depths of such divisions.

Fishbone played under a variety of names, including Hot Ice, Megatron, and Counterattack, before recording its debut EP. *Fishbone* is a fierce, hardcore record on which the band members flex their credentials as both able social commentators and avid partiers. Producer David Kahne slicked up Fishbone's sound on *In Your Face,* but the record still lives up to its title. Kahne also produced *It's a Wonderful Life,* a collection of twisted Christmas carols, and *Truth and Soul,* which featured a metallic version of "Freddie's Dead." In 1988 Fishbone backed Little Richard on "Rock Island Line," a track on the Woody Guthrie and Lead Belly tribute *Folkways: A Vision Shared.* In an odder pairing yet, Fishbone backed Annette Funicello singing the '60s hit "Jamaican Ska" in the beach party spoof *Back to the Beach.*

Bonin', a collection of studio tomfoolery, including an X-rated version of the title track, was produced by the Jungle Brothers. Fishbone spent more than a year making *The Reality of My Surroundings,* producing it mostly alone, with assistance from Kahne. (The band reportedly fought with Columbia for its independence and was resentful of Kahne's control.) The album was the band's biggest, featuring "Everyday Sunshine" and "Sunless Saturday," both favored by the alt-rock crowd. The video for "Sunless Saturday" was directed by Spike Lee. Having never received much radio play, Fishbone has relied on critical acceptance and infamous live shows, where the musicians thrash and mosh like hyperkinetic punks, to build their following.

The concurrent release of Fishbone's fourth album and its slot on the main stage of Lollapalooza '93 boded well for the band's future (*Give a Monkey a Brain* broke the Top 100). This breakthrough was marred, however, when Norwood Fisher was arrested with four others for trying to kidnap ex-Fishbone guitarist Kendall Jones off a California street in April 1993. Jones had left the band in March, reportedly obsessed with the apocalypse and denouncing Fishbone as "demonic." Fisher said he was trying to take Jones to psychiatric experts. Jones claimed he left the band over philosophical differences. Fisher was later acquitted of the kidnapping charges, and in early 1994 the band (minus Jones) began touring again.

Give a Monkey a Brain didn't sell well enough for Columbia, and the label dropped Fishbone from its roster. The group countered with the caustic *Chim Chim's Badass Revenge* (1996), a Dallas Austin–produced album that likened the record industry to the institution of slavery. Then, just as the third-wave ska revival led by No Doubt and Mighty Mighty Bosstones seemed to have passed Fishbone by, the group, now recording under the name Fishbone & the Familyhood Experience, released *The Psychotic Friends Nuttwerx* (2000). The album owes a stylistic debt to the music of Sly and the Family Stone, even to the point of including a cover of Sly's "Everybody Is a Star." It also boasts a dazzling supporting cast, including Blowfly, George Clinton, Rick James, Perry Farrell, Donny Osmond, No Doubt's Gwen Stefani, and members of the Red Hot Chili Peppers.

The "5" Royales

Formed late 1940s, Winston-Salem, NC
As the Royal Sons Gospel Group: Johnny Tanner (b. ca. 1927), tenor voc.; Lowman Pauling (b. c. 1927; d. Dec. 26, 1973, New York, NY), baritone voc., bass voc., gtr.; Clarence Pauling (a.k.a. Clarence Paul [b. Mar. 29, 1928, Winston-Salem; d. May 6, 1995, Los Angeles, CA]), voc.; Otto Jeffries, bass voc.; William Samuels, voc.
ca. 1950—(– C. Pauling; + Obadiah Carter [d. July 1994, Winston-Salem], tenor voc., baritone voc.; + Jimmy Moore, tenor voc., baritone voc.; + Johnny Holmes, voc.) 1953—(– Jeffries; + Eugene Tanner [d. Dec. 29, 1994, Winston-Salem], voc.)
1960—(– L. Pauling) 1994—*Monkey Hips and Rice: The "5" Royales Anthology* (Rhino).

The "5" Royales were originally a gospel group called the Royal Sons Gospel Group (then Quintet). They emerged in 1953 with two R&B #1 hits on the Apollo label, "Baby Don't Do It" and "Help Me Somebody," both of which were written by lead guitarist Lowman Pauling. Inexplicably, there were at times six members of the "5" Royales.

They enjoyed their first pop success in 1957, when "Think" hit #66. Their most famous song, "Dedicated to the One I Love," another Pauling original, peaked at #81 in 1961 (it had been released with even less success in 1957). "Dedicated to the One I Love" would hit the Top 5 twice in cover versions by the Shirelles (1961) and the Mamas and the Papas (1967). Later releases (with little mass-market impact) came out on ABC, Home of the Blues, Vee-Jay, and Smash, through 1965, and the group broke up.

Original Royal Son Clarence Pauling, going under the name Clarence Paul, became an influential writer, producer, and A&R man for Motown, working with, among others, Stevie Wonder and Marvin Gaye. All the other members have since retired; Lowman Pauling died in 1974. The "5" Royales are among the few groups of their era who have yet to reunite.

The Five Satins

Formed 1955, New Haven, CT
Best-known lineup: Freddie Parris (b. Mar. 26, 1936), lead voc.; Lou Peebles, voc.; Ed Martin, voc.; Stanley Dortch, voc.; Jim Freeman, voc.
1990—*In the Still of the Night* (Relic) 1995—*Lost Treasures*.

The Five Satins were one of the best-known doo-wop vocal groups of the '50s. They evolved from lead singer Freddie Parris' high school group, the Scarlets. By 1956 he'd organized a new group, christened it the Five Satins, and used a two-track machine to record "In the Still of the Night" in the basement of an East Haven Catholic church. Originally released in 1956 on the Standard label, it was later leased to Ember Records and became a #24 hit that October. (The song had some chart success when reissued in 1960 and 1961 and has become an R&B ballad standard. It has been estimated to have sold 15 to 20 million copies and is a perennial winner in oldies-station listeners' polls.)

Soon after the single's release, Parris returned to the army. The Satins had recorded while he was on leave and continued to record with sporadic success. "To the Aisle" (with Bill Baker on lead vocals) hit #25 in 1957. Out of the Satins' many releases, only "Shadows" and "I'll Be Seeing You" reached the lower rungs of the Hot 100 as 1960 began. They sang a cappella re-creations of the latter tune and "In the Still of the Night" in the 1973 film *Let the Good Times Roll*. Upon his discharge in 1958, Parris re-formed the group.

The Five Satins were featured on Dick Clark's *American Bandstand* and on many of his road revues in the late '50s. They also toured Europe, where they built up a following. In 1970 the group appeared in the film *Been Down So Long It Looks Like Up to Me*. By the early '70s they were a staple item on rock revival shows. In 1974, with Parris still underpinning the harmonies, they signed with Kirshner Records and released "Two Different Worlds." The group had an R&B Top 40 hit, "Everybody Stand Up and Clap Your Hands," in 1976 under the name Black Satin. The following year the group appeared on Southside Johnny and the Asbury Jukes' "First Night" from *This Time It's for Real*.

Onetime member Willie Wright went on to become a successful disc jockey in Connecticut. The many labels for which the Five Satins have recorded include Red Bird, Cub, Chancellor, Warner Bros., Roulette, and Mama Sadie. By 1982 the group was recording for Elektra and experiencing limited success on the pop chart (#71) with "Memories of Days Gone

By," a medley of classic doo-wop hits. Parris and company continue to perform and record.

Roberta Flack

Born Feb. 10, 1939, Asheville, NC
1969—*First Take* (Atlantic) 1970—*Chapter Two* 1971—*Quiet Fire* 1972—*Roberta Flack and Donny Hathaway* 1973—*Killing Me Softly* 1975—*Feel Like Makin' Love* 1977—*Blue Lights in the Basement* 1978—*Roberta Flack* 1980—*Roberta Flack Featuring Donny Hathaway; Live and More* (with Peabo Bryson) 1982—*I'm the One* 1983—*Born to Love* (with Peabo Bryson) (Capitol) 1989—*Oasis* (Atlantic) 1991—*Set the Night to Music* 1993—*Softly with These Songs: The Best of Roberta Flack* 1994—*Roberta.*

Roberta Flack's clear, reserved vocals have given her a string of ballad hits. The daughter of a church organist, she entered Howard University in Washington, DC, on a full music scholarship at age 15. While working toward her degree in music, she was the first black student teacher at an all-white school in Chevy Chase, Maryland, then after graduation taught at another all-white school in Farmville, North Carolina. Eventually she returned to Washington, where she taught in several junior high schools and began singing in local clubs. Four years later, she left teaching for good.

In 1968 she was discovered by musician Les McCann. That November she signed with Atlantic, and a few months later recorded her entire debut album in less than 10 hours. Entitled *First Take,* it sold well; by 1971 Flack had toured Europe and Ghana, as well as the U.S. Her first hit single was a duet with Donny Hathaway, "You've Got a Friend" (#29, 1971), which she followed with a Carole King–Gerry Goffin composition, "Will You Love Me Tomorrow." Meanwhile, the Clint Eastwood movie *Play Misty for Me* was released with a song from Flack's debut album, "The First Time Ever I Saw Your Face," on the soundtrack. It became a #1 hit in 1972, and returned the three-year-old *First Take* to the LP chart; it reigned at #1 for five weeks that spring. Another Flack-Hathaway duet, "Where Is the Love" (#5, 1972), followed. After two more #1 hits, "Killing Me Softly With His Song" (1973) and "Feel Like Makin' Love" (1974), Flack cut back her performing to concentrate on recording and to pursue outside interests, including educational programs for disadvantaged youth.

She reemerged in late 1977 with *Blue Lights in the Basement,* which contained "The Closer I Get to You" (#2, 1978); by then she had been awarded four gold records in three years. Hathaway's death in 1979 interrupted the recording of *Roberta Flack Featuring Donny Hathaway;* the album included "You Are My Heaven" and "Back Together Again." In 1980 Flack toured and recorded a live album with vocalist Peabo Bryson *(Live & More);* they collaborated again in 1983 with *Born to Love,* which featured "Tonight, I Celebrate My Love" (#16). In 1981 she composed and produced her first soundtrack, for *Bustin' Loose.* The following year, Flack charted one of her last pop hit singles of the decade, "Making Love" (#13, 1982); "Oasis," a #1 R&B hit from the album of the same name did not chart on pop. But in 1991 Flack returned to the pop charts when the title track to *Set the Night to Music,* a duet with Maxi Priest, went to #6.

Throughout the '80s she performed around the world, including many dates with symphony orchestras and several shows with Miles Davis. She contributed "Goodbye Sadness" to Yoko Ono's tribute album to John Lennon, *Every Man Has a Woman Who Loves Him.* She remains fairly active; 1994's *Roberta* was nominated for a Grammy. In 1996 the Fugees had a hit with their version of "Killing Me Softly." The group made several public appearances with Flack; they even took her to perform at an awards ceremony in Europe.

The Flaming Lips

Formed 1983, Oklahoma City, OK
Wayne Coyne (b. Jan. 13, 1961, Pittsburgh, PA), gtr., voc.; Mark Coyne, voc.; Michael Ivins (b. Mar. 17, 1963, Omaha, NE), bass, kybds., gtr., voc.; various early drummers.
1984—(+ Richard English, drums, gtr., voc.) *The Flaming Lips* EP (Lovely Sorts of Death) 1985—(– M. Coyne) 1986—*Hear It Is* (Restless) 1987—*Oh My Gawd!!!* 1988—*Telepathic Surgery* (– English) 1989—(+ Jonathan Donahue, a.k.a. Dingus, gtr.; + Nathan Roberts, drums) 1990—*In a Priest Driven Ambulance (With Silver Sunshine Stares); Unconsciously Screamin'* EP (Atavistic) 1992—*Hit to Death in the Future Head* (Warner Bros.) (– Donahue; – Roberts; + Ronald Jones [b. Nov. 26, 1970, Angeles, Philippines], gtr.; + Steven Drozd [b. June 11, 1969, Houston, TX], drums, kybds., gtr., voc.) 1993—*Transmissions From the Satellite Heart* 1995—*Clouds Taste Metallic* 1996—(– Jones) 1997—*Zaireeka* 1998—*1984–1990* (Restless) 1999—*The Soft Bulletin* (Warner Bros.).

Oklahoma City's Flaming Lips are one of the most enduring acts of the '80s' American indie-rock explosion. They scored a surprise hit single/video when "She Don't Use Jelly" climbed to #54 in 1994. More important, a loyal following has embraced the group's tuneful, hooky approach to quirky psychedelia and whimsical sound exploration.

The Lips debuted on a self-released EP from 1984. Vocalist Mark Coyne left to be married the following year. Their Restless Records catalogue taints mildly dissonant college rock with acid-fried guitar and lyrical excesses ("Jesus Shootin' Heroin," "Drug Machine"). *In a Priest Driven Ambulance* marks the arrival of abstract-noise guitarist Jonathan Donahue, who later left to pursue Mercury Rev. Warner Bros. signed the Lips in the early '90s, and they began dousing their albums with orchestras, crazed overdubs, and samples. Guitar wizard Ronald Jones and drummer Steven Drozd joined frontman Wayne Coyne and cofounding bassist Michael Ivins for the increasingly accessible *Transmissions From the Satellite Heart* (#108, 1995) and *Clouds Taste Metallic.*

Disheartened by Jones' 1996 departure, the trio changed direction, conducting "parking lot experiments" in which the audience triggered prerecorded sound sources (e.g., fleets of boomboxes or car stereos). These interactive spectacles led to 1997's critically lauded *Zaireeka*—four CDs, designed to be played simultaneously, individually, or in the listener's preferred sequence and/or combination. *The Soft Bulletin* (1999) organizes the studio trickery and mellow drone pop into more manageable songform.

The Flamingos

Formed 1951, Chicago, IL
Earl Lewis, voc.; Zeke Carey (b. Ezekial J. Carey, Jan. 24, 1933, Bluefield, VA; d. Dec. 24, 1999, Washington, DC), voc.; Jake Carey (b. Sep. 9, 1926, Pulaski, VA; d. 1997), voc.; Johnny Carter (b. June 2, 1934, Chicago), voc.; Sollie McElroy (b. July 16, 1933, Gulfport, MS; d. Jan. 15, 1995), voc.; Paul Wilson (b. Jan. 6, 1935, Chicago; d. May 1988), voc.
1955—(– McElroy; + Nate Nelson [b. Apr. 10, 1932, Chicago; d. Apr. 10, 1984], voc.) 1956—(– Carter; – Z. Carey) (group disbands) 1957—(group re-forms: + Tommy Hunt [b. June 18, 1933, Pittsburgh, PA], voc.) 1958—(+ Z. Carey; + Terry Johnson [b. Nov. 12, 1935, Baltimore, MD], voc.) 1961—(– Hunt) 1984—*Flamingos* (Chess) 1990—*Best of the Flamingos* (Rhino).

Vocal-group aficionados consider the Flamingos one of the, if not the, best of their era. Their cool yet dramatic singing and elegant harmonies were unparalleled, and this smooth, mature style influenced later groups such as the Four Tops and the Temptations. They are also remembered for their one major pop success (1959's "I Only Have Eyes for You") and for their contributions of talent to other noted black acts. The group began singing on Chicago's South Side. Early recordings on the Chance label revealed influences ranging from Christian gospel and Jewish hymns to the clean harmonies of the Four Freshmen on such releases as Johnny Carter's "Golden Teardrops." Lead vocalist Sollie McElroy was replaced by Nate Nelson, who subsequently joined the Platters. McElroy joined the Moroccos, another Chicago group, in 1955. He died of cancer-related complications in early 1995.

The Flamingos (who were also known as the Five Flamingos) followed with a variety of sentimental songs aimed at the white market. They remained also-rans until 1956, when "I'll Be Home" hit the R&B Top 10. (Although the song was credited to Fats Washington and New Orleans record distributor Stan Lewis, Nate Nelson subsequently claimed to have written all but the opening line.) Typical of the times, a white artist—Pat Boone—had a bigger pop hit with his cover version. Their crossover break came in 1959 with the languid "I Only Have Eyes for You" (#11 pop, #3 R&B).

For the next two years, the Flamingos had several minor hits on the End label, among them "I Was Such a Fool" and "Nobody Loves Me Like You" in 1960; and "Time Was" in 1961. They scored occasional soul hits through the early '70s with such releases as "Boogaloo Party" (#22 R&B, 1966) and "Buffalo Soldier" (#28 R&B, 1970). Other labels with which the group has been associated include Parrot, Decca, and, beginning in 1972, Ronze. Onetime member Johnny Carter joined the Dells, while another, Tommy Hunt, became a minor soul star ("Human," #48, 1961). Cousins Zeke and Jake Carey continued to lead a group of Flamingos into the late '90s. The Flamingos were inducted into the Rock and Roll Hall of Fame in 2001.

The Flamin' Groovies

Formed 1965, San Francisco, CA
Cyril Jordan (b. 1948, San Francisco), gtr., Mellotron, voc.; Roy Loney (b. Apr. 13, 1946, San Francisco), voc., gtr.; George Alexander (b. May 18, 1946, San Mateo, CA), bass, voc., harmonica; Tim Lynch (b. July 18, 1946, San Francisco), gtr.
1966—(+ Ron Greco, drums; – Greco; + Danny Mihm [b. San Francisco], drums) 1969—*Supersnazz* (Epic) 1970—*Flamingo* (Kama Sutra) 1971—*Teenage Head* (– Lynch; + James Farrell, gtr., voc.; – Loney; + Chris Wilson [b. Sep. 10, 1952, Waltham, MA], voc., gtr., harmonica) 1973—(– Mihm; + Terry Rae, drums; – Rae; + David Wright, drums) 1976—*Shake Some Action* (Sire); *Still Shakin'* (Buddah) (– Farrell; + Mike Wilhelm, gtr.) 1978—*The Flamin' Groovies Now* (Sire) 1979—*Jumping in the Night* 1983—*Bucketful of Brains* (Voxx) (– Wilson; – Wilhelm; – Wright; + Jack Johnson, gtr.; + Paul Zahl, drums) 1986—*One Night Stand* (ABC, U.K.) 1989—*Groovies' Greatest Grooves* (Sire) 1996—*Supersneakers* (Sundazed) 1997—*In Person!* (Norton) 1999—*Absolutely the Best* (Varèse Sarabande).

While the three-minute pop-rock song has gone in and out of fashion, the Flamin' Groovies have stuck to the form since the mid-'60s despite marginal commercial success. They formed in the Bay Area during the tail end of the British Invasion but were overshadowed by psychedelic jam bands on the San Francisco scene. The group was briefly known as the Chosen Few and then the Lost and Found before becoming the Flamin' Groovies.

In 1969 the group made its own EP, *Sneakers,* which sold 2,000 copies and led the Flamin' Groovies to be signed by Epic (it was reissued with 10 additional live tracks in 1996 as *Supersneakers).* Their major-label debut, *Supersnazz,* was popular only in the Midwest. The Groovies toured the Midwest, then returned to San Francisco, where it booked concerts at what had been Bill Graham's Fillmore West. That venture ended when the group's business manager disappeared with the receipts.

The band moved to New York and made *Flamingo* and *Teenage Head,* but in 1971 founding member Tim Lynch was arrested for drug offenses and draft evasion. Roy Loney, the group's main songwriter, quit; he reemerged in the late '70s with his own group, the Phantom Movers. The Groovies moved to England in 1972, released two singles, and returned to San Francisco.

Greg Shaw, editor of *Bomp* magazine, helped finance a single, "You Tore Me Down," and in 1976 pop revivalist Dave Edmunds (whom the band had met in Britain) produced the Groovies' major-label comeback, *Shake Some Action.* While the band toured Europe with the Ramones, Buddah released old tapes as *Still Shakin'.* Edmunds also produced *Now,* and the band continued to tour as the '80s began, though it did the bulk of its performing and recording in Europe, Australia, and New Zealand. The Groovies were particularly popular in France.

Jordan continues to play regularly, joining a reunion show of the Beau Brummels [see entry] in 2000, for instance. After the Phantom Movers, Loney released solo records and played with the Longshots and the Fondellas.

The Flatlanders: See Joe Ely; Jimmie Dale Gilmore

Béla Fleck/the Flecktones

Béla Fleck, July 10, 1958, New York, NY
1979—*Crossing the Tracks* (Rounder) 1981—*Fiddle Tunes for Banjo* 1982—*Natural Bridge* 1984—*Double Time; Deviation* (with New Grass Revival) 1986—*Inroads* 1987—*Daybreak* 1988—*Places; Drive* 1995—*Tales From the Acoustic Planet* (Warner Bros.) 1999—*The Bluegrass Sessions—Tales From the Acoustic Planet, vol. 2.*
With the Flecktones, formed 1990, Nashville, TN: Fleck, banjo; Howard Levy, harmonica, kybds.; Victor Lemonte Wooten, bass; Roy "Future Man" Wooten, Synth-axe Drumitar)
1990—*Béla Fleck and the Flecktones* (Warner) 1991—*Flight of the Cosmic Hippo* 1992—*UFO TOFU* 1993—(– Levy) *Three Flew Over the Cuckoo's Nest* 1996—*Live Art* 1998—*Left of Cool* 1999—*Greatest Hits of the 20th Century* 2000—*Outbound* (Columbia).

While he has yet to spur a full-scale revival of the five-string banjo, Béla Fleck nevertheless played the key role in modernizing the instrument. In his hands the instrument rises out of its traditional bluegrass context to enter the world of contemporary fusion music.

Named for Hungarian composer Béla Bartók, Fleck was turned on to the banjo the way any New Yorker growing up in the rock era might have been—through TV's *Beverly Hillbillies* theme and the 1972 hit single "Dueling Banjos." At age 14 Fleck began playing the banjo while studying guitar and music theory at the New York High School of Music and Art. Fleck's private banjo teachers included renowned players Erik Darling and Tony Trischka.

After graduation Fleck relocated to Boston to join the bluegrass band Tasty Licks. He moved to Kentucky in 1979 and helped form the group Spectrum; Fleck's first solo album, *Crossing the Tracks,* followed that year. In 1982 Fleck joined the New Grass Revival, a forward-thinking outfit whose eclecticism expanded and subverted bluegrass music. "Seven by Seven," a Fleck composition from the 1986 album *New Grass Revival* (Capitol), was nominated for a Grammy. By the time New Grass Revival split, Fleck's reputation as the banjo's most daring practitioner was nearly a point of fact.

In 1989 Fleck participated in a sort of bluegrass supergroup, composed of New Grass Revival mandolinist Sam Bush, Mark O'Connor on fiddle, Edgar Meyer on bass, and Jerry Douglas on Dobro, releasing *Strength in Numbers* (MCA). A stylistically diverse amalgamation of musical concepts, the album relied heavily on classical compositions as well as traditional bluegrass ideas.

Pulling together three musicians whose unconventional approach to their instruments matched his own, Fleck formed the Flecktones in 1990. The virtuosic playing of Howard Levy on harmonica, Victor Wooten on bass, and his brother Roy "Future Man" on his invention, the Drumitar, a guitar-shaped drum synthesizer, garnered as much attention as Fleck's technically flawless, wildly imaginative picking. With a sound that drew upon jazz, funk, world music, and rock while hinting at country roots, the Flecktones became popular with both jazz and rock audiences. After Levy left the band in 1993, the Flecktones carried on as a trio. Bruce Hornsby and Branford Marsalis were among the guests who performed on *Three Flew Over the Cuckoo's Nest.* With *Left of Cool* (#191, 1998), the group introduced vocals to its music, relying on guest singers Dave Matthews and Amy Grant. The album's "Almost 12" won a Grammy for Best Instrumental Composition. The Flecktones' Columbia debut, *Outbound,* featured guest appearances by Shawn Colvin, Yes vocalist Jon Anderson, guitarist Adrian Belew, and B3 organist John Medeski of Medeski, Martin and Wood.

Outside of the Flecktones, Fleck continues to explore new musical territories through both his solo career and additional collaborations, including his 1996 teaming with Indian and Chinese musicians Vishwa Mohan Bhatt and Jie-Bing Chen for the Grammy-nominated world music effort *Tabula Rasa* (Water Lily Acoustics).

Fleetwood Mac/Christine McVie/Stevie Nicks/Lindsey Buckingham/Bob Welch, et al.

Formed 1967, London, Eng.
Peter Green (b. Peter Greenbaum, Oct. 29, 1946, London), gtr., voc.; Mick Fleetwood (b. June 24, 1947, Redruth, Eng.), drums; John McVie (b. Nov. 26, 1945, London), bass; Jeremy Spencer (b. July 4, 1948, West Hartlepool, Eng.), gtr., voc.
1968—*Fleetwood Mac* (Blue Horizon) (+ Danny Kirwan [b. May 13, 1950, London], gtr., voc.) 1969—*English Rose* (Epic); *Then Play On* (Reprise) 1970—(– Green) *Kiln House* (– Spencer; + Christine Perfect/McVie [b. July 12, 1943, Birmingham, Eng.], kybds., voc.) 1971—*Fleetwood Mac in Chicago* (Blue Horizon); *Future Games* (Reprise) (+ Bob Welch [b. July 31, 1946, Los Angeles, CA], gtr., voc.) 1972—*Bare Trees* (– Kirwan; + Bob Weston, gtr.; + Dave Walker, voc., gtr.) 1973—*Penguin* (– Walker); *Mystery to Me* (– Weston) 1974—*Heroes Are Hard to Find* (– Welch; + Lindsey Buckingham [b. Oct. 3, 1947, Palo Alto, CA], gtr., voc.; + Stevie Nicks [b. Stephanie Nicks, May 26, 1948, Phoenix, AZ], voc.)
1975—*Fleetwood Mac* 1977—*Rumours* 1979—*Tusk*

1980—*Live* 1982—*Mirage* 1987—*Tango in the Night* (– Buckingham; + Billy Burnette [b. May 8, 1953, Memphis, TN], gtr., voc.; + Rick Vito [b. Oct. 13, 1949, Darby, PA], gtr., voc.) 1988—*Greatest Hits* 1990—*Behind the Mask* 1991— (– Vito) 1992—*25 Years . . . The Chain* 1993—(– Burnette; – Nicks; + Bekka Bramlett [b. Apr. 19, 1968, Westwood, CA], voc.; + Dave Mason [b. May 10, 1946, Worcester, Eng.], gtr., voc.) 1995—*Time* (Warner Bros.) (group disbands) 1996— (group re-forms: Fleetwood; J. McVie; Nicks; Buckingham; C. McVie) 1997—*The Dance* (Reprise).
Mick Fleetwood solo: 1981—*The Visitor* (RCA).
Mick Fleetwood's Zoo: 1992—*Shakin' the Cage* (Warner Bros.).
Christine McVie solo: 1976—*The Legendary Christine Perfect Album* (Sire) 1984—*Christine McVie* (Warner Bros.).
Stevie Nicks solo: 1981—*Bella Donna* (Modern) 1983—*The Wild Heart* 1985—*Rock a Little* 1989—*The Other Side of the Mirror* 1991—*Time Space—The Best of Stevie Nicks* 1994—*Street Angel* 1998—*Enchanted* (Atlantic) 2001—*Trouble in Shangri-La* (Reprise).
Lindsay Buckingham solo: 1981—*Law and Order* (Asylum) 1984—*Go Insane* (Elektra) 1992—*Out of the Cradle* (Reprise).
Bob Welch solo: 1977—*French Kiss* (Capitol) 1979—*Three Hearts; The Other One* 1980—*Man Overboard.*
Bob Welch with Paris: 1975—*Paris* (Capitol) 1976—*Big Towne, 2061.*
Peter Green solo: 1970—*In the End of the Game* (Reprise) 1980—*Little Dreamer* (Sail) 1997—*The Peter Green Splinter Group* (Artisan/DNA) 1998—*The Robert Johnson Songbook; Blues for Dhyana* (Culture Press) 1999—*Destiny Road* (Artisan/DNA) 2000—*Hot Foot Powder* (with Nigel Watson).
Jeremy Spencer solo: 1973—*Jeremy Spencer and the Children of God* (CBS) 1979—*Flee* (Atlantic).

Whoever named Fleetwood Mac was either lucky or prescient. The only thing about the group that hasn't changed since it formed in 1967 is the rhythm section of Mick Fleetwood and John McVie. Through the '70s, the band's personnel and style shifted with nearly every recording as Fleetwood Mac metamorphosed from a traditionalist British blues band to the maker of one of the best-selling pop albums ever, *Rumours*. From that album's release in 1977 into the present, Fleetwood Mac has survived additional, theoretically key, personnel changes and remained through the mid-'90s a dominant commercial force.

Peter Green's Fleetwood Mac was formed by ex–John Mayall's Bluesbreakers [see entry] Green, McVie, and Fleetwood along with Elmore James enthusiast Jeremy Spencer. McVie had been a charter member of the Bluesbreakers in 1963, Fleetwood had joined in 1965, and Green had replaced Eric Clapton in 1966. With its repertoire of blues classics and Green's blues-style originals, the group's debut at the British Jazz and Blues Festival in August 1967 netted it a record contract. Fleetwood Mac was popular in Britain immediately, and its debut album stayed near the top of the British chart for 13 months. The quartet had hits in the U.K. through 1970, including "Black Magic Woman" and the instrumental "Albatross" (which was #1 in 1968 and reached #4 when rereleased in 1973). America, however, largely ignored Fleetwood Mac; its first U.S. tour had the group third-billed behind Jethro Tull and Joe Cocker, neither of whom was as popular in Britain.

Fleetwood Mac: Lindsey Buckingham, John McVie, Christine McVie, Stevie Nicks, Mick Fleetwood

Green and Spencer recorded *Fleetwood Mac* in Chicago with Willie Dixon, Otis Spann, and other blues patriarchs in 1969 (the LP wasn't released until 1971), yet the group was already moving away from the all-blues format. In May 1970 Green abruptly left the group to follow his ascetic religious beliefs. He stayed out of the music business until the mid-'70s, when he made two solo LPs. His departure put an end to Fleetwood Mac's blues leanings; Danny Kirwan and Christine Perfect moved the band toward leaner, more melodic rock. Perfect, who had sung with Spencer Davis in folk and jazz outfits before joining British blues-rockers Chicken Shack [see entry] in 1968, had performed uncredited on parts of *Then Play On,* but contractual obligations to Chicken Shack kept her from joining Fleetwood Mac officially until 1971; by then she had married McVie.

Early in 1971 Spencer disappeared in L.A. and turned up as a member of a religious cult, the Children of God (later the title of a Spencer solo effort). Fleetwood Mac went through a confused period. Bob Welch joined, supplementing Kirwan's and Christine McVie's songwriting. Next Kirwan was fired and replaced by Bob Weston and Dave Walker, both of whom soon departed. Manager Clifford Davis then formed a group around Weston and Walker, called it Fleetwood Mac, and sent it on a U.S. tour. An injunction filed by the real Fleetwood Mac forced the bogus band to desist (they then formed the group Stretch), but protracted legal complications kept Fleetwood Mac from touring for most of 1974. From then until around the time of the *Tusk* tour in 1979–80, the band managed itself, with Mick Fleetwood taking most of the responsibility.

The group relocated to California in 1974. After Welch left

to form the power trio Paris in 1975, Fleetwood Mac finally found its best-selling lineup. Producer Keith Olsen played an album he'd engineered, *Buckingham-Nicks* (Polydor), for Fleetwood and the McVies as a demo for his studio; Fleetwood Mac hired not only Olsen but the duo of Lindsey Buckingham and Stevie Nicks, who had played together in the Bay Area acid-rock group Fritz from 1968 until 1972, before recording with Olsen. Fleetwood Mac now had three songwriters, Buckingham's studio craft, and an onstage focal point in Nicks, who became a late-'70s sex symbol as *Fleetwood Mac* (#1, 1975) racked up 5 million in sales. The McVies divorced in 1976, and Buckingham and Nicks separated soon after, but the tensions of the two years between albums helped shape the songs on *Rumours* (#1, 1977), which would sell over 17 million copies, win the Grammy for Album of the Year, and contained the 1977 hits "Go Your Own Way" (#10), "Dreams" (#1), "Don't Stop" (#3), and "You Make Loving Fun" (#9).

After touring the biggest venues around the world—with Nicks, who was prone to throat nodes, always in danger of losing her voice—Fleetwood Mac took another two years and approximately $1 million to make *Tusk* (#4, 1979), an ambitious, frequently experimental project that couldn't match its predecessors' popularity, although it still turned a modest profit and spun off a couple of hits: "Tusk" (#8, 1979) and "Sara" (#7, 1979). Buckingham and Mac engineer Richard Dashut also produced hit singles for John Stewart and Bob Welch. As with many bands that have overspent in the studio, Fleetwood Mac's next effort was a live double album (#14, 1980).

In 1980 Fleetwood and Dashut visited Ghana to record *The Visitor* with African musicians, and Nicks began work on her first solo LP, *Bella Donna,* which hit #1 and went quadruple platinum with three Top 20 singles: "Stop Draggin' My Heart Around" (a duet with Tom Petty), "Leather and Lace" (a duet with Don Henley), and "Edge of Seventeen (Just Like the White Winged Dove)." Late 1981 saw the release of Buckingham's solo LP, *Law and Order* (#32, 1981) and his Top 10 single "Trouble."

Fleetwood Mac's first collection of new material in three years, *Mirage* (#1), was less overtly experimental and featured the 1982 hit singles "Hold Me" (written by Christine McVie about her relationship with Beach Boy Dennis Wilson) (#4), "Gypsy" (#12), and "Love in Store" (#22). The following year Nicks released her second solo effort, *The Wild Heart,* which contained "Stand Back" (#5). Unlike Buckingham's critically lauded but only moderately popular solo releases, Nicks' were hugely popular, with her third release, *Rock a Little* ("Talk to Me"), charting at #12. In 1984 Christine McVie released two hit singles, "Got a Hold on Me" (#10) and "Love Will Show Us How" (#30), and Buckingham released his critically acclaimed *Go Insane.* Under the stress of several factors—among them each member having his or her own management team, Buckingham's increasing authority in the studio, Nicks' ascent to solo stardom and chemical dependency (treated during a 1987 stint at the Betty Ford Clinic), Fleetwood's bankruptcy—the group took a hiatus, not coming back together again until 1985, when it began work on *Tango in the Night.* Long dissatisfied with his position in the group, Buckingham officially left the group after deciding not to tour with it to support the album. His replacements, Billy Burnette [see entry], who was a member of Fleetwood's informal side group Zoo, and Rick Vito, toured instead. While the group was at work on *Tango,* Nicks was also recording, working, and touring behind *Rock a Little.* Released in the spring in 1987, *Tango* quickly moved into the Top 10, bolstered by the Top 20 hits "Little Lies," "Seven Wonders," and "Everywhere."

Behind the Mask (#18, 1990), Fleetwood Mac's first studio album not to go platinum since 1975, came out in 1990, around which time Christine McVie and Nicks both announced they would remain in the group but no longer tour. Later that year the drummer's best-selling memoirs, *Fleetwood: My Life and Adventures in Fleetwood Mac,* was published.

In early 1991 Vito left the group, followed two years later by Burnette. In January 1993 Buckingham joined Fleetwood, the McVies, and Nicks to perform Bill Clinton's campaign anthem, "Don't Stop," at his presidential inaugural gala. The next month Nicks announced her departure from the group; in 1994 she released *Street Angel* (#45, 1994), her first album of new material in four years.

Two new members joined Fleetwood Mac in fall 1993: Dave Mason [see entry] and Bekka Bramlett (the daughter of Delaney and Bonnie Bramlett, with whom Mason had toured before Bekka was born). Bramlett had also sung with the Zoo. After releasing *Time* (1995) to disappointing response, the group dissolved.

A year later, the *Rumours* edition of Fleetwood Mac reunited to record *The Dance* (#1, 1997), a live document of an MTV concert that featured the band's greatest hits as well as four new songs. The album's release coincided with a worldwide tour—its first in 15 years—that found Fleetwood Mac's popularity undiminished as it marked the 20th anniversary of *Rumours.* In 1998 the band was inducted into the Rock and Roll Hall of Fame, where it played an acoustic set that Buckingham insisted would be its swan song. Ironically, founding member Peter Green performed as well—but with fellow inductees Santana. Taking stock of Nicks' solo highlights, *Enchanted,* a three-disc box set, was also released. Her 2001 release, *Trouble in Shangri-La,* returned her to the Top 10. Even Green enjoyed a comeback, forming the Peter Green Splinter Group and releasing a series of late-'90s albums devoted to the blues. By 2000, Fleetwood Mac had sold more than 100 million copies of its albums—including 25 million for *Rumours* alone—making it one of the most popular rock bands in history.

The Fleetwoods

Formed 1958, Olympia, WA
Gary Troxel (b. Nov. 28, 1939, Centralia, WA), voc.; Barbara Laine Ellis (b. Feb. 20, 1940, Olympia), voc.; Gretchen Diane Christopher (b. Feb. 29, 1940, Olympia), voc.
1990—*Best of the Fleetwoods* (Rhino).

The Fleetwoods were unique among vocal groups in that their angelic, mellow style proved popular not only with the predominantly white pop audience but with R&B fans as well. Their debut single, "Come Softly to Me," hit #1 on the pop chart, then crossed over to #5 R&B in 1959. The three high school friends were known originally as Two Girls and a Guy. They had several other hits, including "Tragedy" (#12, 1959), and a second #1 hit, the DeWayne Blackwell composition "Mr. Blue," in 1959, but broke up in 1963 after releasing a cover of Jesse Belvin's "Goodnight My Love" (#32, 1963). The trio reunited occasionally through the years. By the '90s Christopher had become the sole remnant of the original lineup.

The Fleshtones

Formed 1976, Queens, NY
Peter Zaremba (b. Sep. 16, 1954, Queens), voc., organ, harmonica, perc.; Keith Streng (b. Sep. 18, 1955, Queens), gtr.; Jan Marek Pakulski (b. Aug. 22, 1956, Lewiston, ME), bass; Lenny Calderone (b. ca. 1955, New York, NY), drums.
1979—(– Calderone; + Bill Milhizer [b. Sep. 21, ca. 1948, Troy, NY], drums) 1980—*Up Front* (I.R.S.) 1982—*Roman Gods; Blast Off* (ROIR) (+ Gordon Spaeth [b. Sep. 21, ca. 1950, New York], sax, organ, harmonica) 1983—*Hexbreaker* (I.R.S.) (– Pakulski; + Robert Burke Warren [b. Mar. 29, 1965, Quantico, VA], bass) 1987—*Fleshtones Vs. Reality* (Emergo) 1988—(– Warren; + Fred Smith, bass) 1989—(– Smith; + Andy Shernoff [b. Apr. 19, 1952, Bronx, NY], bass) 1990—(– Shernoff; + Ken Fox [b. Feb. 19, 1965, Toronto, Can.], bass) 1992—*Powerstance* (Ichiban) 1994—*The Angry Years* (Impossible, Sp.); *Beautiful Light* (Ichiban) 1995—*Laboratory of Sound* 1997—*Hitsburg, USA* (Telstar) 1998—*More Than Skin Deep* (Ichiban) 1999—*Hitsburg Revisited* (Telstar).

Pigeonholed as garage-rock revivalists, the Fleshtones mix the hallmarks of that genre—fuzz-guitar and fuzz-bass riffs, Farfisa organ, "sha-la-la" backing vocals—with elements of rockabilly, surf rock, and Stax-Volt soul into their exuberant retro-raveup rock.

Shortly after forming in 1976, the Fleshtones began playing at CBGB and Max's Kansas City, winning fans on Manhattan's burgeoning punk-rock scene with their spirited shows. Their 1978 debut single, "American Beat" b/w "Critical List," on New York independent label Red Star Records (home of Suicide, among other acts), led to a deal with I.R.S. Records, which released the group's debut EP, *Up Front*. The Fleshtones' first full-length album, *Roman Gods*, was well received by critics but sold in only cult-sized numbers. *Blast Off* collected earlier tracks recorded with original drummer Lenny Calderone. During the mid-'80s, frontman Peter Zaremba moonlighted as the host of MTV's *The Cutting Edge*, an I.R.S.-sponsored show that was an important outlet for the emerging indie-rock movement.

While their audience never grew beyond cult status, the Fleshtones kept recording and touring, gaining enough of an international profile to inspire Spain's Impossible Records label to release the 1994 compilation *The Angry Years*. The band spawned spinoff acts—including Peter Zaremba's Love Delegation and Keith Streng's Full Time Men—but has remained intact, recording for a variety of labels.

Flipper

Formed 1979, San Francisco, CA
Will Shatter (b. Russell Wilkinson, 1956; d. Dec. 9, 1987, San Francisco), voc., bass; Ricky Williams (b. ca. 1955, Palo Alto, CA; d. Nov. 21, 1992, San Francisco), voc.; Ted Falconi (b. Laurence Falconi, Sep. 2, 1947, Bryn Mawr, PA), gtr.; Steve DePace (b. Jan. 29, 1957, San Francisco), drums.
1979—(– Williams; + Bruce Lose [a.k.a. Bruce Loose, b. Bruce Calderwood, June 6, 1959, Fresno, CA], bass, voc.) 1982—*Album—Generic Flipper* (Subterranean) 1984—*Gone Fishin'; Blow'n Chunks* (ROIR) 1986—*Public Flipper Ltd.* (Subterranean) 1987—*Sex Bomb Baby* (– Shatter) 1992—(+ John Dougherty [b. Apr. 20, 1961, Oakland, CA; d. Oct. 31, 1997], bass) *American Grafishy* (Def American).

Flipper emerged from San Francisco in the early '80s as one of America's most powerful and distinctive postpunk bands. Opting for slow-paced noise dirges that, despite their tempo and volume, could never be mistaken for heavy metal, Flipper influenced many Seattle "grunge" bands, including Nirvana. Flipper's sometimes topical ("Love Canal") or philosophical ("Life" rejected nihilism by declaring "Life's the only thing worth living for!") lyrics also set it apart.

Will Shatter and Steve DePace had played together in the Bay Area punk band Negative Trend before forming Flipper with guitarist Ted Falconi and the infamous Ricky Williams. Early on, Williams was replaced by Bruce Lose (sometimes spelled "Loose"), who traded bass and lead vocals onstage with Shatter. Lose was already notorious in local punk clubs for inventing the Worm, a postpogo dance in which he threw himself on the floor and flailed about, trying to knock people over. With a sardonic onstage attitude, Flipper quickly drew a large cult following and recorded its first single, "Love Canal" b/w "Ha Ha Ha," in 1980. Flipper's debut album included "Life," and the seven-minute classic "Sex Bomb"—in which Shatter periodically screamed a single line ("She's a sex bomb, baby, yeah!")—while the band ground out one monolithic, bass-heavy riff.

Flipper carried on in this fashion until December 9, 1987, when Shatter died of an accidental heroin overdose. Three years later Flipper regrouped, with Falconi's old friend John Dougherty on bass. Soon after American Records' Rick Rubin—who had once covered Flipper songs in the New York band Hose—called seeking a demo of new songs. He not only signed Flipper but reissued its first album in 1992. The band toured Europe and the U.S. after the 1992 release of *American Grafishy*. Original vocalist Williams, who spent the '80s singing for the Sleepers and the Toiling Midgets, died that year of respiratory complications. Doughtery suffered a fatal overdose on Halloween 1997. In 2000 the remaining trio recorded tracks for tributes to Nirvana and Metallica.

Flo and Eddie: See the Turtles

A Flock of Seagulls

Formed 1980, Liverpool, Eng.
Mike Score (b. Nov. 5, 1957, Liverpool), voc., kybds.; Ali Score (b. Alistair Score, Aug. 8, 1956, Liverpool), drums; Paul Reynolds (b. Aug. 4, 1962, Liverpool), gtr.; Frank Maudsley (b. Nov. 10, 1959, Liverpool), bass.
1982—*A Flock of Seagulls* (Jive/Arista) 1983—*Listen* 1984—*The Story of a Young Heart* (– Reynolds; + Gary Steadnin [b. U.S.], gtr.; + Chris Chryssaphis [b. U.S.], kybds.) 1986—*Dream Come True* 1991—*The Best of A Flock of Seagulls* 1995—*The Light at the End of the World* (SAVA) 1999—*Greatest Hits Remixed* (Cleopatra).

One of the first post–new wave pop bands of the MTV era, A Flock of Seagulls crafted a few techno-rock hits, but is perhaps better-remembered for frontman Mike Score's bizarre "waterfall" haircut—an exaggerated pompadour that cascaded his peroxide-blond locks forward in a long, thin point hanging down to his nose. Score, in fact, was a former hairdresser with no real musical training when he, salon assistant Frank Maudsley, and Score's brother Ali first formed the band. They made their recording debut with a British EP on Bebop Deluxe guitarist Bill Nelson's Cocteau label; the jet-paced single "Telecommunication" failed to chart in America, but its mix of Eurodisco sequencer beats and sleek dance-rock rhythms found a home in new wave rock-disco dance clubs. The band's self-titled debut album (#10, 1982) yielded hits in the upbeat "I Ran (So Far Away)" (#9, 1982) and "Space Age Love Song" (#30, 1982), which codified A Flock of Seagulls' ballad technique—wrapping simple, yearning love songs in pillowy, billowy layers of string synthesizers and plangent guitar chords that seemed to zoom off into infinity. The group, which got constant MTV play, tried to affect a half-baked sci-fi aura in its videos, with Score's hair the inevitable focus.

Listen (#16, 1983) yielded only one hit single, the lovely ballad "Wishing (If I Had a Photograph of You)" (#26, 1983), while *Story of a Young Heart* peaked at #66 (1984), with its single "The More You Live, The More You Love" hitting only #56 (1984). The band eventually replaced departed guitarist Paul Reynolds with a pair of American musicians and gave it one last try with *Dream Come True*, which failed to chart at all. Ever resilient, Score—at this stage the sole remaining original member—formed a new version of the group for 1989 and toured the U.S. The singer moved to Florida in 1993, where another version of the band recorded the independent release *The Light at the End of the World* (1995).

Eddie Floyd

Born June 25, 1935, Montgomery, AL
1967—*Knock on Wood* (Stax) 1968—*I've Never Found a Girl* 1970—*California Girl* 1973—*Baby Lay Your Head Down (Gently on My Bed)* 1974—*Soul Street* 1977—*Experience* (Malaco) 1986—*Try Me* (Seasaint) 1988—*Flashback* (Wilbe) 1993—*Rare Stamps* (Stax).

R&B singer and songwriter Eddie Floyd was in his teens when he moved to Detroit, where his uncle Robert West founded the LuPine and Flick labels, two early rivals of Berry Gordy Jr.'s fledgling Motown empire. He had sung in a number of vocal harmony groups before cofounding the Falcons, initially a racially integrated group, in 1956. West arranged the group's deal with Mercury, but they recorded without success, and in 1957, a personnel shuffle resulted in their gaining a new lead singer, Joe (brother of the Four Tops' Levi) Stubbs. Their 1959 hit, "You're So Fine" was a Top 20 pop hit.

Following a few less successful singles, Stubbs left and was replaced by Wilson Pickett, with whom the Falcons recorded "I Found a Love" (complete with backing vocals by another LuPine group, the Primettes, which included future Supremes Mary Wilson and Diana Ross). This version of the Falcons disbanded in 1963, although other groups of singers going under the Falcons name continued to record.

Over the next few years, Floyd released singles on LuPine, Atlantic, and Safice, which he partly owned, before he moved to Washington, DC, and began commuting to Memphis, where he wrote songs for Stax. He cowrote "Knock on Wood" with Steve Cropper for Otis Redding, but when the label released Floyd's demo version, it went to #28 in 1966. (According to Floyd, the song has been covered over 60 times, including a #1 hit disco version by Amii Stewart in 1979.) Later hits included 1967's "Raise Your Hand," 1968's "I've Never Found a Girl," and "Bring It On Home to Me" (#17) and "California Girl" in 1970. He also wrote for others, including "Comfort Me" for Carla Thomas, whom he also produced; "Don't Mess With Cupid" for Otis Redding; "Someone's Watching Over You" for Solomon Burke; and "634-5789" for Wilson Pickett.

Floyd occasionally toured the U.S. and Europe as part of the Stax Revue, but the financially beleaguered label took his career under with it. In 1977 he put out a disco record on Malaco called *Experience*, but he, like so many other singers of his generation, was displaced on the charts by disco. In 1989 he reunited with several Stax/Atlantic artists for President George H. Bush's inaugural ball. He continues to perform around the world, often as a guest vocalist with the successful Blues Brothers Band. In 1996 Floyd received a Pioneer Award from the Rhythm & Blues Foundation.

The Flying Burrito Brothers

Formed 1968, Los Angeles, CA
Gram Parsons (b. Ingram Cecil Connor III, Nov. 5, 1946, Winter Haven, FL; d. Sep. 19, 1973, Yucca Valley, CA), gtr., voc., kybds.; Chris Hillman (b. Dec. 4, 1942, Los Angeles), bass, gtr., voc.; Sneeky Pete Kleinow (b. ca. 1935, South Bend, IN), pedal steel gtr.; Chris Ethridge, bass.
1969—*The Gilded Palace of Sin* (A&M) (+ Michael Clarke [b. June 3, 1944, New York, NY; d. Dec. 19, 1993, Treasure Island, FL],

drums, harmonica; – Ethridge; + Bernie Leadon [b. July 19, 1947, Minneapolis, MN], gtr., voc., banjo, Dobro) 1970—*Burrito Deluxe* (– Parsons; + Rick Roberts [b. 1950, FL], gtr., voc.) 1971—*Flying Burrito Brothers* (– Kleinow; + Al Perkins, pedal steel gtr.; – Leadon); *Last of the Red Hot Burritos* (+ Byron Berline, fiddle; + Roger Bush, bass; + Kenny Wertz, gtr.) 1972—(– Hillman; – Perkins; – Clarke; + Alan Munde, banjo, gtr.; + Don Beck, pedal steel gtr.; + Erik Dalton, drums) 1974—*Close Up the Honky Tonks* (group re-forms: Kleinow; Ethridge; + Floyd "Gib" Gilbeau, voc., gtr., fiddle; + Joel Scott Hill, bass, voc.; + Gene Parsons, drums) 1975—*Hot Burrito* (Arista); *Flying Again* (Columbia) (– Ethridge) 1976—(+ Skip Battin [b. Feb. 2, 1934, Gallipolis, OH], bass) *Sleepless Nights* (A&M); *Airborne* (Columbia) 1988—*Farther Along: The Best of the Flying Burrito Brothers* (A&M) 1997—(group re-forms: John Beland, gtr., voc.; Gary Kubal, drums; Wayne Bridge, steel gtr.; Larry Patton, gtr., voc.) *California Jukebox* (Ether) 1999—*Sons of the Golden West* (BMG/Arista) 2000—*Hot Burritos! The Flying Burrito Bros. Anthology 1969–1972* (A&M/Universal).
Gram Parsons solo: see entry.
Chris Hillman solo: 1982—*Morning Sky* (Sugar Hill) 1984—*Desert Rose*.
Chris Hillman with the Desert Rose Band: 1987—*The Desert Rose Band* (Curb) 1988—*Running* 1990—*Pages of Life* 1991—*A Dozen Roses; True Love*.

When Gram Parsons led the Flying Burrito Brothers, his emotive, haunting songs and the band's classic C&W-based virtuosity set the standard for California country rock. After he left, followed by cofounder Chris Hillman, the band quickly devolved into an uninspired follower of the style it had started. Eventually, ex-Burritos went on to greater commercial success in the Eagles, Firefall, and the Desert Rose Band.

Parsons had joined Chris Hillman in the Byrds [see entry] for *Sweetheart of the Rodeo* before the two started the Burritos in L.A. As the lineup gelled (four different drummers played on the band's first album), they recruited ex-Byrd Michael Clarke as drummer. The first album, *The Gilded Palace of Sin* (#164, 1969) only sold about 40,000 copies. The band developed a rabid local following, however, including members of the Rolling Stones (recording in L.A. at the time), who arranged for the group to play at Altamont.

Parsons, who began spending most of his time with Keith Richards, had already lost interest in the Burritos by the recording of the second album. In 1970 Parsons left the band for a solo career [see entry] and was replaced by Rick Roberts, who'd recorded with the Byrds. When Bernie Leadon left to join the nascent Eagles [see entry] and Hillman and Al Perkins were recruited by Stephen Stills for Manassas, Roberts became de facto leader. After Manassas, Hillman joined the Souther-Hillman-Furay Band for two LPs, released a couple of solo albums, and started his own group, the Desert Rose Band, which scored several C&W hits.

Roberts recruited members of bluegrass-rockers Country Gazette for a 1973 European tour (when *Live in Amsterdam* was made), but disbanded the Burritos late in 1973. Roberts then left to form Firefall [see entry]. In 1975 Kleinow and Ethridge revived the name with ex–Canned Heat bassist Joel Scott Hill and fiddler "Gib" Gilbeau, but Ethridge left in 1976. Various aggregations of Burritos (minus any original members) periodically make recordings and hit the honky-tonk club circuit.

The Flying Lizards

Formed 1978, Ireland
David Cunningham, kybds., gtr., perc., etc.; Deborah Evans, voc.
1980—*Flying Lizards* (Virgin) 1981—(– Evans; + various personnel) *Fourth Wall* (Virgin, U.K.) 1984—*Top Ten* (Statik, U.K.).

As the Flying Lizards, conceptual artist David Cunningham and session vocalist Deborah Evans enjoyed novelty hits with their radically rearranged, disinterested versions of Barrett Strong's "Money" and Eddie Cochran's "Summertime Blues."

Irish art-school student Cunningham performed with a 13-piece band, Les Cochons Chic. He made a minimalist solo album, *Grey Scale*, in the late '70s. In 1978 he conceived the Flying Lizards and put out "Summertime Blues," which attracted some attention in Britain. The followup, "Money," had its signature riff played on an upright piano with rubber toys, sheet music, cassettes, and telephone directories inside. The song was recorded for approximately $14 in a home studio. "Money" (#50, U.S., #5 U.K., 1979) picked up substantial U.S. airplay and prompted Virgin to ask for an album, which also included a Brecht-Weill song and more Cunningham instrumentals. The floating lineup on the more experimental *Fourth Wall* features guitarist Robert Fripp, vocalist Patti Palladin, and sax player Peter Gordon.

Cunningham later worked with the Pop Group, the Modettes, the Electric Chairs, and This Heat. He returned to experimental music and work in theater and film. In 1984 he revived the Flying Lizards to issue *Top Ten*, which dismantled songs by Jimi Hendrix, Little Richard, and Leonard Cohen, among others. Since then Cunningham has released numerous solo albums; his Piano Records label has been active since 1976. As of 2001 a Flying Lizards retrospective CD was awaiting release.

Focus

Formed 1969, Amsterdam, Neth.
Thijs Van Leer (b. Mar. 31, 1948, Amsterdam), organ, flute, voc.; Martin Dresden, bass; Hans Cleuver, drums.
1970—(+ Jan Akkerman [b. Dec. 24, 1946, Amsterdam], gtr.) 1971—*In and Out of Focus* (Sire) (– Cleuver; + Pierre Van der Linden [b. Feb. 19, 1946, Neth.], drums; – Dresden; + Cyril Havermanns, bass) *Moving Waves* (– Havermanns; + Bert Ruiter [b. Nov. 26, 1946], bass) 1972—*Focus Three* 1973—*Live at Rainbow* (– Van der Linden; + Colin Allen, drums, perc.) 1974—*Hamburger Concerto* (Atco); *Ship of Memories* (Harvest) 1975—*Mother Focus* (– Allen); *Dutch Masters* 1976—(+ Van der Linden; – Akkerman; – Van der Linden; + Philip Catherine

[b. London], gtr.; + Steve Smith, drums; + Eef Albers, gtr.) 1978—*Focus Con Proby* (with P.J. Proby) (Harvest).
Jan Akkerman solo: 1973—*Profile* (Sire) 1974—*Tabernakel* (Atco) 1977—*Eli* 1978—*Jan Akkerman* (Atlantic).

The progressive-rock band Focus became a major draw in Europe playing extended songs with tinges of classical melody from flutist Thijs Van Leer and pyrotechnical solos by guitarist Jan Akkerman. In the U.S. Focus is remembered for a yodeling novelty single, "Hocus Pocus" (#9, 1973).

Classically trained Jan Akkerman became known in the Netherlands as a member of Brainbox, which also included drummer Pierre Van der Linden. Meanwhile, Thijs Van Leer, a classically trained keyboardist and flutist, formed Focus in 1969 as a trio; its first gig was as a pit band for the Dutch production of *Hair.* In 1970 Akkerman joined in order to try making more complex music than Brainbox's. Focus' debut album was modestly successful in Europe, and the followup included "Hocus Pocus," which became an international hit. The band considered it a joke but wound up stuck with it as a signature song.

Focus had its second and last U.S. chart showing with "Sylvia" (1973), then returned to more ambitious compositions on *Focus 3,* which went gold, as had *Moving Waves.* In the early '70s Focus was a headlining band in the U.S. and Europe. After 1974's *Hamburger Concerto,* the group turned to more concise four-minute pop songs on 1975's *Mother Focus.* Akkerman left in 1976 to continue his concurrent solo career; he was replaced by guitarist Philip Catherine in the group's waning years. Future Journey drummer Steve Smith was briefly a member in 1978. *Focus Con Proby* featured British pop star P.J. Proby.

After Focus' peak, Akkerman released a string of solo albums, and Van Leer released the three-volume *Introspection, Nice to Have Met You,* and *O My Love.* A latter-day Focus led by Akkerman and Van Leer existed in the '80s. The original group re-formed for a Dutch television special around 1990.

Dan Fogelberg

Born Aug. 13, 1951, Peoria, IL
1972—*Home Free* (Columbia) 1974—*Souvenirs* (Full Moon/Epic) 1975—*Captured Angel* 1977—*Netherlands* 1978—*Twin Sons of Different Mothers* (with Tim Weisberg) 1979—*Phoenix* 1981—*The Innocent Age* 1982—*Greatest Hits* 1984—*Windows and Walls* 1985—*High Country Snows* 1987—*Exiles* 1990—*The Wild Places* 1991—*Dan Fogelberg Live—Greetings From the West* 1993—*River of Souls* 1995—*No Resemblance Whatsoever* (with Tim Weisberg) (Giant) 1997—*Portrait: The Music of Dan Fogelberg From 1972–1997* 1999—*The First Christmas Morning* (Chicago) 2000—*Something Old, New, Borrowed . . . and Some Blues.*

Singer/songwriter Dan Fogelberg studied piano for a few years, began playing the guitar, and was composing at age 14. During the two years he studied art at the University of Illinois in Champaign, he also played campus coffeehouses, where he met Irving Azoff, ex-student and manager of local bands like REO Speedwagon. In 1971 Fogelberg dropped out of school, moved to L.A., and signed with Columbia. *Home Free* went largely unnoticed, but his second album, *Souvenirs* (produced by Joe Walsh), went double platinum on the strength of "Part of the Plan" (#31, 1975).

In the early '70s Fogelberg was active in West Coast music circles, guesting on LPs by Jackson Browne, Roger McGuinn, and Randy Newman. Uncomfortable with the starmaker lifestyle, he left California in late 1974. In 1976 his backup group, Fool's Gold, released a self-titled LP that featured its own single, "Rain, Oh Rain."

Eventually settling in Boulder, Colorado, Fogelberg continued his string of platinum albums with *Captured Angel* (#23, 1975); *Netherlands* (#13, 1977); *Twin Sons of Different Mothers* (#8, 1978), a collaboration with jazz-pop flutist Tim Weisberg; *Phoenix* (#3, 1979); and *The Innocent Age* (#6, 1981), a double-album song cycle lamenting the passage of childhood. He appeared on the soundtrack of *Urban Cowboy* in 1980, the same year he made his first live TV appearance.

Although the singer/songwriter genre was in noticeable decline by the early '80s, Fogelberg bucked the trend with *The Innocent Age.* Four singles from that album, "Hard to Say," "Leader of the Band," "Run for the Roses," and "Same Old Lang Syne," reached the Top 20. His last big hit was 1984's "Language of Love" (#13), an uncharacteristically hard rocker. From there, however, Fogelberg changed gear, recording bluegrass with guest stars Doc Watson, Ricky Skaggs, and David Grisman on *High Country Snows.* It was his first album in more than a decade to sell fewer than 500,000 copies. None of his four subsequent albums has matched his former sales, but Fogelberg still commands an audience. *River of Souls* marked another departure, incorporating South African singers, Brazilian rhythms, and other world-music elements, but it peaked at #164.

In 1995 Fogelberg teamed up with Weisberg for a followup to their 1978 collaboration. The box set, *Portrait,* included five previously unreleased songs, one of which, "Song for a Carpenter," he recorded with the Chieftains in 1983. Subsequent releases have included a Christmas album and a live collection. In the summer of 2000, Fogelberg undertook a solo acoustic tour.

John Fogerty: See Creedence Clearwater Revival

Foghat

Formed 1971, London, Eng.
"Lonesome" Dave Peverett (b. Apr. 16, 1943, Dulwich, Eng.; d. Feb. 7, 2000, Orlando, FL), gtr., voc.; Roger Earl (b. 1949, Eng.), drums; Rod Price (b. Eng.), gtr.; Tony Stevens (b. Sep. 12, 1949, Eng.), bass.

1972—*Foghat* (Bearsville) 1973—*Foghat* 1974—*Energized; Rock and Roll Outlaws* (– Stevens; + Nick Jameson [b. MO], bass, kybds., synth.) 1975—*Fool for the City* (– Jameson; + Craig MacGregor [b. CT], bass) 1976—*Night Shift* 1977—*Live* 1978—*Stone Blue* 1979—*Boogie Motel* 1980—*Tight Shoes* (– Price; + Erik Cartwright, gtr.) 1981—*Girls to Chat and Boys to Bounce* 1982—*In the Mood for Something Rude* 1983—*Zig-Zag Walk* 1988—*Best of Foghat* (Rhino) 1992—*Best of Foghat, vol. 2* 1994—*Return of the Boogie Men* (Atlantic) 1998—*Road Cases* (Plum).

In the '70s Foghat's basic blues-based boogie and extensive U.S. touring brought it a loyal audience and gold and platinum albums *(Rock and Roll Outlaws, Fool for the City, Night Shift,* plus four others). "Lonesome" Dave Peverett founded Foghat along the lines of his previous band, Savoy Brown [see entry]. (Tony Stevens and Roger Earl had also been in Savoy Brown.) After three years of heavy touring—the group averaged eight months per year on the road—cofounder Stevens was replaced by Nick Jameson, who had helped mix Foghat's first albums. While he was in the band, Jameson was also producer, and he oversaw its first hit single, "Slow Ride" (#20, 1976).

Jameson left in 1976 for a solo career and other production work. By then the band was based on Long Island and recruited replacements in the U.S. In 1977 Foghat hosted a benefit concert for the New York Public Library's blues collection, with guests Muddy Waters and John Lee Hooker. Foghat's late-'70s albums yielded three hits: "Stone Blue" (#36, 1978), "Third-Time Lucky" (#23, 1979), and a live version of "I Just Want to Make Love to You" (#33, 1977).

In 1993 Peverett, Price, Stevens, and Earl re-formed the original Foghat lineup for a tour and a new studio album, *Return of the Boogie Men.* The band toured regularly until Peverett's death of complications from cancer in 2000.

Ben Folds Five

Formed 1994, Chapel Hill, NC
Ben Folds (b. Sep. 12, 1966, Greensboro, NC), voc., piano; Robert Sledge (b. Mar. 9, 1968, Greensboro), bass, voc.; Darren Jessee (b. Apr. 8, 1971, Houston, TX), drums.
1995—*Ben Folds Five* (Caroline) 1997—*Whatever and Ever Amen* (Sony/550 Music) 1998—*Naked Baby Photos* (Caroline) 1999—*The Unauthorized Biography of Reinhold Messner* (Sony/550 Music).
Ben Folds solo: 2001—*Rockin' the Suburbs* (Sony/550 Music).

Bombastic, piano-driven pop songcraft, an aversion to guitars, and a breakthrough song about the lonely aftermath of a teenage abortion: These are but three of the quirks that made Ben Folds Five—three guys calling themselves a quintet—one of the '90s' most unlikely alternative-rock success stories. Centered around Ben Folds and his baby grand piano, the trio emerged at the tail end of the grunge era with a highly melodic, guitar-free sound reminiscent of Elton John's rock & roll days, spiked with the wry lyrical wit of prime Randy Newman and an exuberant, punkish verve.

Folds, who served as the group's frontman and main songwriter, began taking piano lessons at age nine while growing up in Winston-Salem, North Carolina. He landed a scholarship to study jazz at the University of Miami, but soon left the school to follow his muse to Nashville and New York before ultimately returning home. It was on the Chapel Hill local scene that he met and teamed up with drummer Darren Jessee and bassist Robert Sledge.

The group was signed to the independent Caroline label on the strength of an indie single, "Jackson Cannery." That song kicked off their self-titled 1995 debut, a tuneful showcase of the band's Tin Pan Alley–derived power pop and Folds' knack for offsetting sly sarcasm with bittersweet character portraits. The album earned rave reviews, as did the band's hyperactive live act, which Folds would bring to a climax by plucking the strings of his baby grand by hand or by playing the keys with his feet. A major label bidding war ensued, leading to the trio's move to Sony/550 Music.

The group's major-label debut, *Whatever and Ever Amen* (#42, 1997), continued in much the same vein as its predecessor, featuring such typically wry (and frequently acerbic) fare as "Song for the Dumped" and "Battle of Who Could Care Less." But it was "Brick" (#19, 1998), Folds' melancholy, autobiographical ballad about a young couple dealing with the emotional landslide of an abortion, that propelled the album to gold status in the U.S.

A month and a half after "Brick" debuted on the singles chart, the group fulfilled its commitment to Caroline with the early tracks and demos collection *Naked Baby Photos* (#94, 1998). In stark contrast to the rough, unfinished edges of that set, *The Unauthorized Biography of Reinhold Messner* (#35, 1999) found the group embracing strings and horns (but still not guitars) for a lushly orchestrated, full-on concept album (albeit not one about the real Messner, historically known as the first man to scale Mount Everest sans extra oxygen. The band claimed their association with the name came from a fake ID Jessee used as a teenager.)

In 2000 Folds appeared in a series of Priceline.com commercials with actor William Shatner and guested on Rickie Lee Jones' covers album, *It's Like This.* The group also contributed a cover of Steely Dan's "Barrytown" to the soundtrack of the Jim Carrey comedy *Me, Myself and Irene,* as well as "Lonely Christmas Eve" to Carrey's *How the Grinch Stole Christmas.* Feeling that the group had run its course, however, the trio scrapped plans for a new album and announced their amicable breakup in November. Jessee and Sledge each began assembling new bands, while Folds began work on his first solo album, *Rockin' the Suburbs.*

Wayne Fontana and the Mindbenders

Formed 1963, Manchester, Eng.
Wayne Fontana (b. Glynn Geoffrey Ellis, Oct. 28, 1945, Manchester), voc.; Bob Lang (b. Jan. 10, 1946, Manchester), bass; Eric Stewart (b. Jan. 20, 1945, Manchester), gtr.; Ric Rothwell (b. Mar. 11, 1944, Manchester), drums; Graham Gouldman (b. May 10, 1946, Manchester), bass.

1965—*Wayne Fontana and the Mindbenders* (Fontana); *The Game of Love* 1966—*Eric, Rick, Wayne, Bob; The Mindbenders* 1967—*With Woman in Mind; A Groovy Kind of Love* 1995—*The Best of Wayne Fontana and the Mindbenders.* Wayne Fontana solo: 1966—*Wayne One* (Fontana).

Wayne Fontana and the Mindbenders' contribution to the British Invasion was "Game of Love" (#1, 1965), and the Mindbenders minus Fontana followed up with "A Groovy Kind of Love" (#2, 1966).

Glynn Ellis started out in a school skiffle group, the Velfins. By 1963 he was playing in a Manchester pub band, the Jets, while working as an apprentice telephone engineer. Ellis arranged to have the Jets play for a Fontana Records talent scout at Manchester's Oasis Club, but only Ellis and bassist Bob Lang showed up for the audition. They recruited some musician friends from the audience and landed a contract, with Ellis becoming Wayne Fontana at a Philips/Fontana Records executive's behest. They started recording R&B covers in 1963 and began to score British hits in 1964 with a version of Major Lance's "Um, Um, Um, Um, Um, Um."

In 1965 "Game of Love" became an international hit, but after one more hit, "It's Just a Little Bit Too Late" (#45, 1965), Fontana decided on a solo career. He had a few U.K. hits—"Pamela, Pamela" and "Come On Home"—before moving into cabaret and nostalgia-rock revues, including a major English tour in 1979.

The Mindbenders had two U.S. hits on their own, "A Groovy Kind of Love" and "Ashes to Ashes," and they appeared in *To Sir with Love* before breaking up in the late '60s.

Gouldman—whose songs were British Invasion hits for Herman's Hermits, the Yardbirds, and others—and Stewart founded a group called Hotlegs, and then 10cc [see entry], in the '70s.

Foo Fighters

Formed 1994, Seattle, WA
David Grohl (b. Jan. 16, 1969, Warren, OH), voc., gtr., drums, bass; Pat Smear (b. Georg Ruthenberg, Aug. 5, 1959, Los Angeles, CA), gtr.; Nate Mendel (b. Dec. 21, 1969, Seattle), bass; William Goldsmith (b. July 4, 1972), drums.
1995—*Foo Fighters* (Roswell/Capitol) 1996—*Big Me* EP 1997—*The Colour and the Shape* (– Goldsmith; + Taylor Hawkins [b. Feb. 17, 1972, Laguna Beach, CA], drums; – Smear; + Franz Stahl [b. Oct. 30, 1962], gtr.) 1998—(– Stahl; + Chris Shiflett [b. May 6, 1971, Los Angeles], gtr.) 1999—*There Is Nothing Left to Lose* (RCA).

The Foo Fighters were the first and most substantial success to emerge from the ashes of Nirvana [see entry], but the band's roots were in the years of personal recordings made by leader Dave Grohl. The former Nirvana drummer had played guitar and written songs since he was a Washington, DC, teenager, while also playing drums in several hardcore bands. At age 17, Grohl became the drummer for the veteran punk act Scream. In 1990 he joined Nirvana, but continued to work on his own material during breaks from the road and studio. After finishing Nirvana's *Nevermind,* Grohl returned to DC to record several tracks, which were released on the cassette-only *Pocketwatch.* Plans for another cassette release were shelved with Kurt Cobain's 1994 suicide.

Later that year Grohl entered a studio with friend and producer Barrett Jones to record what would become the first Foo Fighters album. Grohl played all the instruments himself (with the exception of the song "X-Static," which featured guitar by Greg Dulli of the Afghan Whigs). Though he had written and sung just one Nirvana song (the B-side "Marigold"), Grohl demonstrated a flair for pop hooks amid driving guitar rock. (The name Foo Fighters came from what American World War II pilots called unidentified fireballs spotted over Germany.) Grohl signed with Capitol and formed a band in time for a 1995 tour, recruiting bassist Nate Mendel and drummer William Goldsmith (both of Sunny Day Real Estate). Pat Smear, the former Germs guitarist who had joined Nirvana for its final tour, also joined.

Foo Fighters (#23) was released in 1995 and spawned the Modern Rock hits "This Is a Call," "I'll Stick Around," and "Big Me" (#13 pop; also #175 pop album as a seven-track EP in 1996). Goldsmith quit during the making of *The Colour and the Shape* (#10, 1996), the first Foo Fighters album recorded as a band, and was replaced by Taylor Hawkins (Alanis Morissette). The album included the Modern Rock hits "Monkey Wrench," "My Hero," and "Everlong." Smear quit and was briefly replaced by Franz Stahl (Scream), and then Chris Shiflett (No Use for a Name). Grohl relocated to Virginia and recorded *There Is Nothing Left to Lose* (#10, 1999) in his basement; the album included "Learn to Fly" (#19, 1999).

Steve Forbert

Born 1955, Meridian, MS
1978—*Alive on Arrival* (Nemperor) 1979—*Jackrabbit Slim* 1980—*Little Stevie Orbit* 1982—*Steve Forbert* 1988—*Streets of This Town* (Geffen) 1992—*The American in Me* 1993—*What Kinda Guy? The Best of Steve Forbert* (Columbia/Legacy) 1995—*Mission of the Crossroad Palms* (Giant) 1996—*Rocking Horse Head* 2000—*Evergreen Boy* (Koch) 2001—*Young Guitar Days* (Relentless/Nashville-Rolling Tide).

Folk-rock singer/songwriter Steve Forbert learned guitar at age 11 and later played in a variety of semipro rock bands on through college. At age 21, he quit his job as a truckdriver and moved to New York, where he began singing for spare change in Grand Central Terminal. Forbert worked his way up through the Manhattan clubs before landing a contract with Nemperor in 1978. His debut album, *Alive on Arrival,* was well received, and its followup, *Jackrabbit Slim* (#20, 1979), yielded a #11 single, "Romeo's Tune" (allegedly dedicated to the late Supreme Florence Ballard).

Little Stevie Orbit and *Steve Forbert* were neither critical nor commercial hits. In 1985 Forbert moved to Nashville, and he has continued to perform and record. His 1988 album, *Streets of This Town,* was produced by Gary Tallent. Forbert retains a sizable following and the respect of many critics for his finely crafted songs.

Frankie Ford

Born Francis Guzzo, Aug. 4, 1939, Gretna, LA
1959—*On a Sea Cruise* (Ace) 1984—*New Orleans Dynamo* (Ace, U.K.) 1959—*Hot & Lonely* 1998—*Sea Cruise: The Very Best of Frankie Ford* (Music Club).

Frankie Ford was a white singer and pianist whose "Sea Cruise" (#14, 1959) remains one of the best New Orleans rockers of all time. To date the record has sold more than 30 million copies worldwide.

Ford, who appeared on *Ted Mack's Amateur Hour* at age eight, was marketed in the late '50s as Ace Records' attempt at a teen idol. The "Sea Cruise" track was made by Huey "Piano" Smith and the Clowns; Smith's vocals were erased and Ford's overdubbed, as was the case with the less popular followup, "Alimony." Ford's touring band included Mac Rebennack, later better known as Dr. John, on guitar. The singer had minor hits in 1960 ("You Talk Too Much" and "Time After Time") and 1961 ("Seventeen"). He was drafted in 1962. After his discharge, he returned to recording—with the Paula and ABC labels, as well as his own, Briarmeade—but he has supported himself primarily by performing in oldies package shows. He continues to play 200 nights a year. Ford has also comanaged several other oldies acts, including the Dixie Cups and Johnny Preston.

Lita Ford

Born Rosanna Ford, Sep. 23, 1959, London, Eng.
1983—*Out for Blood* (Mercury) 1984—*Dancin' on the Edge* 1988—*Lita* (RCA) 1990—*Stiletto* 1991—*Dangerous Curves* 1992—*The Best of Lita Ford* 1993—*Greatest Hits* 1995—*Black* (ZYX) 2000—*Lita Live* (Cleopatra).

After the Runaways [see entry] broke up, guitarist and singer Lita Ford pursued a solo career as a hard-rock artist, counterbalancing her blond bombshell image by flexing her metal muscularity. She has found rare acceptance in that male world: She was the first woman in 20 years to be inducted into *Circus* magazine's Hall of Fame and was the first woman ever on the cover of *Hit Parader.*

Inspired by Jimi Hendrix, Ford led a power trio on her first two albums. Neither did well, and in 1986 she changed labels, managers, and producers. Ford hit it big with the platinum pop metal of *Lita* (#29, 1988), which was produced by glam master Mike Chapman and featured "Kiss Me Deadly" (#12, 1988), "Can't Catch Me" (cowritten with Motörhead's Lemmy), and "Close My Eyes Forever" (#8, 1989), a duet with Ozzy Osbourne. Sales were helped by her videos, in which she looked like a gas-station calendar girl come to life. Ford's subsequent records failed to sell as well. In 1992 she was a member of the house band for Howie Mandel's CBS show *Howie.*

In 1994 Ford and three other former Runaways sued PolyGram Records and their ex-manager Kim Fowley for breach of contract and unpaid royalties. In 1995 Ford released *Black,* a less hard-rocking album produced by the Robb Brothers (Lemonheads, Buffalo Tom). Ford is no longer a factor on the charts, but her influence, solo and as a member of the Runaways, remains evident in the music of such all-female, metal-leaning bands as L7.

Julia Fordham

Born Aug. 10, 1962, Portsmouth, Eng.
1988—*Julia Fordham* (Virgin) 1989—*Porcelain* 1991—*Swept* 1994—*Falling Forward* 1997—*East West* 1999—*The Julia Fordham Collection.*

In the late '80s Julia Fordham was among a new crop of female singer/songwriters whose folk-influenced, intellectually ambitious pop traced its lineage to the earlier work of Joni Mitchell and Joan Armatrading. Her sultry alto and delicate, jazz-inflected songs about love and other social dilemmas have endeared her to fans of both alternative pop and adult contemporary music, giving her a cult following in the U.S. as well as mainstream success in Europe and Japan.

Fordham grew up on the southern coast of England, got her first guitar at six, eventually began performing in local pubs with her older brother, and quit school at 15 to pursue a music career. In her late teens, Fordham moved to London, where she hooked up with pop singer Mari Wilson and recorded an album as part of a beehive-hairdo-sporting group called Mari Wilson and the Wilsations. After two years as a Wilsation, Fordham found work backing singer Kim Wilde, then decided to parlay the songwriting she'd been doing since early adolescence into more serious artistic pursuits.

Fordham released a self-titled solo album in 1988, featuring two semisuccessful singles, "Happy Ever After" (#27 U.K., 1988) and "Where Does the Time Go?" (#41 U.K., 1989). After a sophomore album, 1989's *Porcelain* (#74, 1990; #13 U.K., 1989), Fordham became a familiar presence on VH1. Like its predecessor, *Porcelain* embellished a mellow pop-jazz with touches of African folk and Brazilian samba. A third album, *Swept,* proved less successful. Fordham returned in 1994 with a less controlled delivery on *Falling Forward,* singing with abandon on "Caged Bird" and the gospel-tinged "Hope, Prayer & Time." She displayed a barer, acoustic sound on 1997's *East West,* and played several dates on the Lilith Fair tour in 1998. The following year saw the release of a best-of album, *The Julia Fordham Collection,* which included a couple of new songs as well as a reworking of "Where Does the Time Go?" as a duet with Curtis Stigers.

Foreigner

Formed 1976, New York, NY
Mick Jones (b. Dec. 27, 1944, London, Eng.), gtr., voc.; Ian McDonald (b. June 25, 1946, London), flute, kybds., reeds, gtr.,

voc.; Al Greenwood (b. Oct. 20, 1951, New York), kybds., synth.; Lou Gramm (b. May 2, 1950, Rochester, NY), voc.; Ed Gagliardi (b. Feb. 13, 1952), bass; Dennis Elliott (b. Aug. 18, 1950, Eng.), drums.
1977—*Foreigner* (Atlantic) 1978—*Double Vision* (– Gagliardi; + Rick Wills [b. Dec. 5, 1947, Eng.], bass) 1979—*Head Games* 1980—(– McDonald; – Greenwood) 1981—*4* 1982—*Records* 1984—*Agent Provocateur* 1987—*Inside Information* (– Gramm) 1991—(+ Johnny Edwards, voc.) *Unusual Heat* 1992—*The Very Best . . . and Beyond* (– Edwards; – Wills; – Elliott; + Gramm; + Bruce Turgon [b. Apr. 25, 1952, Rochester, NY], bass, voc.; + Jeff Jacobs [b. May 23, 1962], kybds., voc.; + Mark Schulman [b. Sep. 4, 1961], drums) 1993—*Classic Hits Live* (Atlantic) 1995—*Mr. Moonlight* (Rhythm Safari) (– Schulman; + Ron Wikso [b. Nov. 18, 1959, Dover, DE], drums) 1998—(– Wikso; + Brian Tichy [b. Aug. 18, 1968, NJ], drums) 2000—*Jukebox Heroes: The Foreigner Anthology* (Rhino/Atlantic Remasters) (– Tichy; + Schulman).
Lou Gramm solo: 1987—*Ready or Not* (Atlantic) 1989—*Long Hard Look.*
Mick Jones solo: 1989—*Mick Jones* (Atlantic).

Despite accusations of formulaic commercialism, Foreigner's heavy metal with keyboard flourishes has racked up sales of over 30 million records worldwide to date.

The band is led by British journeyman rocker Mick Jones, who played in the '60s with Nero and the Gladiators, a Shadows-like group that had several hits in England, including "Hall of the Mountain King." He worked with French rock singer Johnny Hallyday, then with a latter-day version of Spooky Tooth. Jones had worked as an A&R man in New York before joining the Leslie West Band. A year later he decided to form his own band. In early 1976 he met ex–King Crimson multi-instrumentalist Ian McDonald at recording sessions for

Foreigner: (top) Lou Gramm, Mick Jones, (bottom) Rick Wills, Dennis Elliott

Ian Lloyd, former lead singer of Stories. A few months later Jones and McDonald formed Foreigner with four unknown musicians, including lead vocalist Lou Gramm, founder and lead singer of Black Sheep, a Free and Bad Company cover band in upstate New York.

The group's 1977 debut sold more than 4 million copies in the U.S. and stayed in the Top 20 for a year, on the strength of "Feels Like the First Time" (#4, 1977), "Cold as Ice" (#6, 1977), and "Long, Long Way From Home" (#20, 1978). *Double Vision* (#3, 1978), which sold 5 million records, spawned "Hot Blooded" (#3, 1978) and a #2 hit with the title track. Late in the year Foreigner headlined the Reading, England, music festival. *Head Games* (#5) with "Dirty White Boy" (#12) and "Head Games" (#14) hit in 1979 and went double platinum. In 1980 the group became a quartet, with Rick Wills (formerly of Frampton's Camel, Small Faces, and Roxy Music) on bass. Gagliardi and Greenwood went on to form the much-ignored Spys.

Foreigner's next album, *4* (#1, 1981), was its biggest ever, racking up six million in sales. It provided two Top 10 singles: "Urgent" (#4), which featured Junior Walker on sax, and a rare ballad, "Waiting for a Girl Like You" (#2). *Agent Provocateur* (#4, 1985) went double platinum, yielding the #1 pop hit "I Want to Know What Love Is," an epic piece of AOR-gospel on which Gramm was backed by Jennifer Holliday and the New Jersey Mass Choir. The album spawned another hit in "That Was Yesterday" (#12, 1985). *Inside Information* (#15, 1987) also went platinum, spawning the hit "Say You Will" (#6, 1987). Sometime between in the late '80s Gramm "officially" went solo; reliable sources differ, because he initially planned to have a parallel solo career while remaining in Foreigner. He had hits with "Midnight Blue" (#5, 1987) and "Just Between You and Me" (#6, 1989) before forming Shadow King, which went nowhere. Jones' solo album reached only #184 and had no hit singles. In 1989 Jones and Billy Joel coproduced the latter's hit *Storm Front.* Through it all, Gramm and Jones were sniping at each other in the press. Jones brought singer Johnny Edwards aboard for 1991's *Unusual Heat,* Foreigner's first album not to crack the album Top 100.

In 1992 the pair reconciled and the group returned with a lineup that (with the exception of the drum seat) has remained stable ever since. As of this writing, the group has released only one album of new material, 1995's *Mr. Moonlight* (#136). In 1997, on the eve of a tour of Japan and Australia, Gramm was diagnosed with a benign but life-threatening brain tumor. He took off 1998 for treatment and recuperation, and by 1999, Foreigner was back on the concert trail.

Robert Forster: See the Go-Betweens

The Foundations

Formed 1967, London, Eng.
Peter Macbeth (b. Feb. 2, 1943, London), bass; Alan Warner (b. Apr. 21, 1947, London), gtr.; Clem Curtis (b. Nov. 28, 1940, Trinidad), voc.; Eric Allan Dale (b. Mar. 4, 1936, West Indies),

trombone; Tony Gomez (b. Dec. 13, 1948, Sri Lanka), organ; Pat Burke (b. Oct. 9, 1937, Jam.), sax, flute; Mike Elliot (b. Aug. 6, 1929, Jam.), sax; Tim Harris (b. Jan. 14, 1948, London), drums.
1967—*Baby Now That I've Found You* (Uni) 1968—(– Curtis; + Colin Young [b. Sep. 12, 1944, Barbados], voc.) 1969—*Build Me Up Buttercup; Digging the Foundations.*

The Foundations were a mid-'60s pop band that had two major hits: the Motown-ish "Baby Now That I've Found You" and "Build Me Up Buttercup." In London the group became the house band at the Butterfly Club in Westbourne Grove. Record store owner Barry Class became the Foundations' manager and introduced them to songwriter Tony Macauley, who got them a record deal and then wrote and produced their hits.

Their debut single, "Baby Now That I've Found You" (#11, 1968), went gold. A minor hit, "Back on My Feet Again," followed before "Build Me Up Buttercup" (cowritten by Macauley and former Manfred Mann vocalist Mike d'Abo) hit #3 in early 1969. Followups like "In the Bad, Bad Old Days" and "My Little Chickadee" failed to hit, and the group split up in 1970, although the name was used by a British cabaret act (with little relation to the original group) for several years in the early '70s.

The Four Seasons

Formed 1956, Newark, NJ
Frankie Valli (b. Francis Casteluccio, May 3, 1937, Newark), voc.; Tommy DeVito (b. June 19, 1936, Belleville, NJ), gtr.; Nick DeVito, gtr.; Hank Majewski (d. 1969), bass.
1960—(– N. DeVito; + Bob Gaudio [b. Nov. 17, 1942, Bronx, NY], kybds.; – Majewski; + Nick Massi [b. Nicholas Macioci, Sep. 19, 1927, Newark; d. Dec. 24, 2000, West Orange, NJ], bass) 1963—*Sherry* (Vee-Jay); *Greetings; Big Girls Don't Cry; Ain't That a Shame* 1964—*Stay; Dawn* (Philips); *Rag Doll* 1965—(– Massi; + Joe Long, bass; numerous personnel changes follow) *Entertain You; Gold Vault Hits; Working My Way Back to You* 1966—*Second Vault; Looking Back* 1968—*Seasoned Hits* (Fontana) 1969—*Genuine Imitation Life Gazette; Big Ones* 1970—(– T. DeVito) 1972—*Chameleon* (Mowest) 1973—(+ Gerry Polci [b. 1954, Passaic, NJ], drums, voc.) 1974—(– Gaudio; + Don Ciccone [b. Feb. 28, 1946, NY], gtr.) 1975—*Who Loves You* (Warner Bros.) 1977—*Helicon* 1980—(group re-forms: Valli; Gaudio; Ciccone; Polci; + Jerry Corbetta [b. Sep. 23, 1947, Denver, CO], kybds.; + Larry Lingle [b. Apr. 4, 1949, KS], gtr.) 1981—*Reunited Live* 1985—*Streetfighter* 1987—*Frankie Valli and the Four Seasons—25th Anniversary Collection* 1988—*Anthology* (Rhino) 1990—*Rarities, vol. 1; Rarities, vol. 2; 20 Greatest Hits: Live* (Curb); *Greatest Hits, vol. 1; Greatest Hits, vol. 2* (Rhino) 1992—*Hope + Glory* (Curb) 1995—*Oh What a Night.*
Frankie Valli solo: 1975—*Inside You* (Motown); *Close Up* (Private Stock) 1976—*Story* 1978—*Frankie Valli Is the Word* (Warner Bros.) 1979—*Very Best of Frankie Valli* (MCA) 1981—*Heaven Above Me; The Very Best of Frankie Valli* (Warner Bros.).

During their nearly 40-year career, Frankie Valli and the Four Seasons have sold over 100 million records, making them the most long-lived and successful white doo-wop group. Lead singer Valli (whose three-octave range and falsetto are the group's trademark) has also maintained a successful solo career.

Valli, sometimes billed under his real name and later as Valley (after Texas Jean Valley, a country singer who had encouraged him as a child), began singing in his mid-teens with the Newark vocal groups the Romans and the Varietones. The Varietones, which included Hank Majewski and the DeVito brothers, eventually became the Four Lovers. The Lovers' "You're the Apple of My Eye," a tune songwriter Otis Blackwell gave them in exchange for their not recording his "Don't Be Cruel" (which he then gave to Elvis Presley), was a hit in 1956, and they appeared on *The Ed Sullivan Show.*

The Four Lovers became the Four Seasons (named after a Jersey cocktail lounge) with the addition of Bob Gaudio, formerly of the Royal Teens and composer of their hit "Short Shorts." As the group's chief songwriter, Gaudio changed the Four Seasons' repertoire and sound, which were later refined by producer Bob Crewe. After a single, "Bermuda," flopped, they again became the Four Lovers and returned to the clubs. They also served as Crewe's production group, arranging, performing, and providing instrumental and vocal backing in singles Crewe produced for other singers. This arrangement continued until 1962, when Valli, desperate over the group's lack of success, nearly quit the band. Then the group recorded a song by Gaudio, "Sherry." After the song was featured on *American Bandstand,* the Four Lovers became the Four Seasons once again, and within months "Sherry" hit #1.

The followup, "Big Girls Don't Cry," also went to #1, and over the next five years (until Valli's first solo hit, "I Can't Take My Eyes Off of You" in 1967), the Four Seasons had 50 hits, including "Santa Claus Is Coming to Town" (in an arrangement later imitated by Bruce Springsteen) (#23, 1962); "Walk Like a Man" (#1), "Ain't That a Shame" (#22), and "Candy Girl" (#3) in 1963; "Dawn" (#3), "Girl Come Running" (#30), "Let's Hang On" (#3), and "Working My Way Back to You" (#9) in 1965; "Opus 17 (Don't Worry 'bout Me)" (#12), "I've Got You Under My Skin" (#9), and "Tell It to the Rain" (#10) in 1966; "Beggin' " (#16), "C'mon Marianne" (#9), and "Watch the Flowers Grow" (#30) in 1967.

The group left Vee-Jay over a royalty dispute in 1964, and by 1965 was recording for Philips, continuing its string of hits, which ended abruptly with its excursion into psychedelia, *Genuine Imitation Life Gazette.* (It had also recorded several singles, including a cover of Dylan's "Don't Think Twice" in 1965 under the pseudonym the Wonder Who.) As the '60s closed, the group's popularity waned. By the time it signed to Motown's Mowest subsidiary, in 1971, Valli and Gaudio were the only original members left, and a $1.4 million debt had taken its toll.

In 1972 Crewe, whose independent label had folded, joined the group at Mowest. But even with the Crew-Gaudio-Valli team intact, none of its singles hit. The release of a 1972 LP, *The Night,* was canceled, and the group toured supporting the Four Tops and the Vandellas. Valli's 10-year-old hearing problem (diagnosed as otosclerosis, excessive calcium deposits in the ear) became critical. (Faced with the possibility of going deaf, Valli underwent surgery in 1976.) Meanwhile, Gaudio retired from performing to concentrate on writing and producing. In 1973 one Gerald Zelmanowitz testified before a Senate subcommittee that the Four Seasons had ties to organized crime, a charge he later retracted.

Valli signed a solo contract with Private Stock in 1974 and soon had several hits, including "My Eyes Adored You" (#1, 1975), "Swearin' to God" (#6, 1975), and a cover of Ruby and the Romantics' "Our Day Will Come" (#11, 1975). The Four Seasons had almost ceased to exist, but in 1975 they made a comeback with one of their biggest-selling singles, "Who Loves You" (#3), followed the next year by "December 1963 (Oh What a Night)" (#1, 1976). Shortly before a 1977 tour, Valli announced—with some bitterness—that he would never work with the Four Seasons again, although he and Gaudio have retained co-ownership of the group and its name. But despite Valli's solo success ("Grease" hit #1 and sold over 7 million copies), the Four Seasons re-formed in 1980 with Gaudio, Valli, guitarist Don Ciccone (former lead singer of the Critters and a Season since 1974), keyboardist Jerry Corbetta (ex-lead singer of Sugarloaf), guitarist Larry Lingle, and drummer Gerry Polci (who had been singing with the group since 1973).

In 1984 Valli and Gaudio formed FBI Records, and the Four Seasons teamed with the Beach Boys for the single "East Meets West." Valli has appeared in the films *Eternity* and *Modern Love.* In 1990 the original members were inducted into the Rock and Roll Hall of Fame. Thanks to the 1994 film *Forrest Gump,* the Four Seasons' "December 1963 (Oh What a Night)" reentered the Hot 100 and became the longest-running single in the chart's history, with over 50 weeks total. The group, which now fluctuates around Valli (Gaudio no longer performs live), remains successful on the oldies circuit.

The Four Tops

Formed 1954, Detroit, MI

Levi Stubbs (b. Levi Stubbles, Detroit), voc.; Renaldo "Obie" Benson (b. Detroit), voc.; Lawrence Payton (b. Mar. 2, 1938, Detroit; d. June 20, 1997, Southfield, MI), voc.; Abdul "Duke" Fakir (b. Dec. 26, 1935, Detroit), voc.

1965—*Four Tops* (Motown); *Second Album* 1966—*On Top; Live* 1967—*Reach Out; On Broadway; Greatest Hits* 1968—*Yesterday's Dreams* 1969—*Four Tops Now; Soul Spin* 1970—*Still Waters Run Deep; Changing Times; The Magnificent Seven* (with the Supremes) 1971—*Greatest Hits, vol. 2; The Return of the Magnificent Seven* (with the Supremes) 1972—*Dynamite* (with the Supremes); *Nature Planned It; Keeper of the Castle* (Dunhill) 1973—*Four Tops Story* (Motown); *Main Street People* (Dunhill) 1981—*Tonight* (Casablanca) 1982—*One More Mountain* 1983—*Back Where I Belong* (Motown) 1985—*Magic* 1988—*Indestructible* (Arista) 1989—*Anthology* (Motown) 1993—*Until You Love Someone: More of the Best (1965–1970)* (Rhino) 1995—*Christmas Here With You* (Motown) 1997—(– Payton; + Theo Peoples, voc.) *The Ultimate Collection.*

One of Motown's most consistent hitmakers and its longest-lived original lineup, the Four Tops have charted with scores of upbeat love songs featuring Levi Stubbs' rough-hewn lead vocals. In 1994 they celebrated four decades together, without a single change in personnel. The four members met at a party in Detroit and soon began calling themselves the Four Aims. They were signed to Chess Records in 1956 and soon changed their name to the Four Tops to avoid confusion with the Ames Brothers. The single "Kiss Me Baby" b/w "Could It Be You" was the first of a string of supper-club–style flops that lasted for seven years on a series of labels (Red Top, Riverside, and Columbia). All the while, the group performed in top clubs.

By 1964, they had joined up with old friend Berry Gordy Jr., the founder of Motown Records. Gordy had them cut the unreleased *Breaking Through* for his experimental Workshop Jazz subsidiary. Later that year they were finally directed toward contemporary soul. Under the wing of Motown's top production and writing team, Holland-Dozier-Holland, the Four Tops were launched with "Baby I Need Your Loving," which went to #11 in 1964. Over the next eight years they made almost 30 appearances on the chart, and Levi Stubbs (whose brother Joe sang in the Falcons) became an international star and a major influence on other singers from the '60s to the present (in 1986 Billy Bragg had a U.K. hit with "Levi Stubbs Tears").

The group's 1965 hits included "Ask the Lonely" (#24),

The Four Tops: (top) Lawrence Payton, Renaldo Benson, (bottom) Levi Stubbs, Abdul Fakir

"Same Old Song" (#5), and "I Can't Help Myself (Sugar Pie, Honey Bunch)," which was #1. "Reach Out I'll Be There" hit the top of the pop chart in October 1966. The quartet followed up with "Standing in the Shadows of Love" (#6, 1967).

Like other top Motown acts, the Four Tops also became popular in major nightclubs around the world. Even in their hit-making prime, the Tops had less athletic choreography than the Temptations, for example, and the group was equally comfortable handling standards, show tunes, and big ballads. Like virtually all of Motown's first-tier acts, the Tops sought the longevity and stability of a career built equally on live appearances and records. In 1967 they scaled the charts with "Bernadette" (#4) and "Seven Rooms of Gloom" (#14); but when Holland-Dozier-Holland left Motown in 1967 to form their own label, the group's chart successes dwindled. In fact, two of the Four Tops' bigger hits from 1968 were covers: the Left Banke's "Walk Away Renee" (#14) and Tim Hardin's "If I Were a Carpenter" (#20). While many historians view HDH's departure as an irreparable blow to the group, in fact, the Tops cut a number of adventurous and successful singles under the guidance of other Motown staff producers, including "River Deep, Mountain High" with the Jean Terrell–led Supremes (#14 pop, #7 R&B, 1970), and "Still Water (Love)" (#11 pop, #4 R&B, 1970). In addition, Obie Benson cowrote Marvin Gaye's "What's Goin' On."

In 1972 the group left Motown for ABC/Dunhill, where it quickly recorded a couple of million-sellers: "Keeper of the Castle" (#10) and in 1973 "Ain't No Woman Like the One I've Got" (#4). It proved to be only a brief pop chart resurgence, though the group continued to hit the R&B Top 20, with "Seven Lonely Nights" and "Catfish." The Tops continued to tour the world, performing to packed houses. In 1981 the group moved to Casablanca Records and released the comeback hit, "When She Was My Girl" (#11 pop, #1 R&B). Two years later the Tops were back at Motown, and after performing in a "battle of the bands" with the Temptations on the Motown 25th-anniversary television special, embarked on the first of several coheadlining tours with that group, billed as T'n'T. The first tour ran nearly three years, went around the world, and included a sold-out stint on Broadway.

In 1986 Stubbs provided the voice for the man-eating plant Audrey II in the film *Little Shop of Horrors;* in 1985 the group had its last Motown hit: "Sexy Ways" (#21 R&B). Like many older Motown artists, the Four Tops sought another label, and in 1988 they signed with Arista. "Indestructible" (#35 pop, #66 R&B) marked another resurgence in the band's career, especially in the U.K., where their "Loco in Acapulco," from the soundtrack of the Phil Collins film *Buster,* was a Top 10 hit. Chartwise, the Four Tops had become one of the most popular American acts in the U.K., where a remix of "Reach Out I'll Be There" hit #11 in 1988, and the saloon standard "It's All in the Game" had gone to #5 in 1970.

In 1989 the group appeared on Aretha Franklin's *Through the Storm,* and in 1990 Stevie Wonder inducted the Tops into the Rock and Roll Hall of Fame. They returned to Motown in the '90s and recorded a Christmas album, but tragedy struck in 1997 when Lawrence Payton, the architect of the Tops' harmonies, died of liver cancer. The remaining members eventually recruited Theo Peoples, a former member of the Temptations [see entry]. They continue to perform. In 2000 Stubbs claimed that the group had completed an album with the help of former Motown writer Norman Whitfield, but as of mid-2001 it had not been released.

Kim Fowley

Born July 21, 1939, Los Angeles, CA
1967—*Love Is Alive and Well* (Tower/Capitol) 1968—*Born to Be Wild* (Imperial) 1969—*Outrageous; Good Clean Fun* 1972—*I'm Bad* (Capitol) 1973—*International Heroes* 1975—*The Incredible Kim Fowley* (Original Sound) 1977—*Living in the Streets* (Sonet) 1978—*Visions of the Future* (Capitol); *Sunset Boulevard* (PVC) 1979—*Animal God of the Streets; Snake Document Masquerade* (Island) 1980—*Hollywood Confidential* 1981—*Son of Frankenstein* (a.k.a. *Bad News From the Underworld)* (Moxie) 1988—*Automatic* (Secret) 1992—*Hotel Insomnia* (Marilyn, Sp.) 1993—*White Negroes in Deutschland* 1995—*Kings of Saturday Night* (with Ben Vaughan) (Sector 2); *Let the Madness In* (Receiver, U.K.) 1997—*Outlaw Superman* (Bacchus Archives) 1998—*The Trip of a Lifetime* (Resurgence); *Michigan Babylon* (Detroit Electric) 1999—*Underground Animal* (Bacchus Archives).

Songwriter, producer, writer, manager, publisher, consultant, and general scenemaker and rock & roll renaissance man Kim Fowley is the son of actor Douglas Fowley (Doc on *Wyatt Earp)* and stepgrandson of composer Rudolf Friml. In 1957 he met Brian Wilson and began writing songs; he made local news by singing with three members of a black vocal group, the Jayhawks. Since then Fowley has demonstrated an ear for new talent and a knack for gimmicky novelty singles.

In 1959, working as a disc jockey in Boise, Idaho, he produced the first sessions for Paul Revere and the Raiders ("Like, Long Hair" on Gardena). In the early '60s he assembled the Murmaids and produced their version of David Gates' "Popsicles and Icicles" (#3, 1964). He also produced the Hollywood Argyles' "Alley Oop" (#1, 1960); "Nutrocker," based on Tchaikovsky's music, for B. Bumble and the Stingers (#23, 1962); and the Rivingtons' "Papa-Oom-Mow-Mow" (#48, 1962).

In London in the mid-'60s, Fowley appeared on the TV show *Ready, Steady, Go* in 1966. He also produced sessions for Slade, Family, Dave Mason and Jim Capaldi of Traffic, and Soft Machine. Back in L.A., he sang on the Mothers of Invention's *Freak Out.* He also produced records by the Seeds and the Fraternity of Man ("Don't Bogart That Joint"). Fowler then produced Gene Vincent's 1969 comeback, *I'm Back and I'm Proud;* part of Warren Zevon's 1969 *Wanted Dead or Alive;* two albums for Helen Reddy; and Jonathan Richman and the Modern Lovers. In addition he wrote or cowrote songs recorded by the Beach Boys, the Byrds, Doug Sahm's Sir Douglas Quintet, Them, Leo Kottke, and Cat Stevens. He has published countless rock songs and recorded sporadically on his own, both under his own name and as "groups" including the Renegades ("Charge!").

In the late '70s Fowley assembled the teenage band the Runaways, who included Joan Jett and Lita Ford; he cowrote their "Cherry Bomb." In 1987, long after the original group had come apart, Fowley unsuccessfully launched another group with the same name (which he owns), and he later assembled a similar all-female rock band, the Orchids. Several of his poetry books have been published. Throughout the '90s he has satisfied his cult following with a stream of archival and new oddities, most of which are imports. In 1995 Fowley claimed to be 125 years old and announced that he'd been dead for 13 years.

Peter Frampton

Born Apr. 22, 1950, Beckenham, Eng.
1972—*Wind of Change* (A&M) 1973—*Frampton's Camel* 1974—*Something's Happening* 1975—*Frampton* 1976—*Frampton Comes Alive!* 1977—*I'm in You* 1979—*Where I Should Be* 1981—*Breaking All the Rules* 1982—*The Art of Control* 1986—*Premonition* (Atlantic) 1989—*When All the Pieces Fit* 1992—*Shine On: A Collection* (A&M) 1994—*Peter Frampton* (Relativity) 1995—*Frampton Comes Alive II* (El Dorado/I.R.S.) 1998—*The Very Best of Peter Frampton* (A&M) 2000—*Live in Detroit* (CMC International); *Anthology* (Universal).

After years as the moderately successful lead guitarist and singer in a string of British bands—the Herd, Humble Pie, and his own Frampton's Camel—Peter Frampton's nearly continuous U.S. touring paid off in 1976 when his live set *Frampton Comes Alive!* hit #1, sold over 6 million copies, and was briefly ranked among the 10 best-selling albums ever.

Frampton made his professional debut at age 10 and joined the Herd at 16. The band had several U.K. teenybopper hits, including "From the Underworld" and "Paradise Lost" in 1967, and "I Don't Want Our Loving to Die" in 1968. Frampton was named "Face of 1968" by several British magazines. He left the Herd in 1969 to establish a reputation as a more serious musician, and formed Humble Pie [see entry] with ex–Small Face Steve Marriott and ex–Spooky Tooth bassist Greg Ridley. He wrote and sang part of Humble Pie's early repertoire but left in 1971 to pursue his own career.

After a stint of session work (George Harrison's *All Things Must Pass,* Harry Nilsson's *Son of Schmilsson),* Frampton recorded a solo debut with assistance from Ringo Starr, Billy Preston, and others. He formed Frampton's Camel with ex–Spooky Tooth Mike Kellie, Rick Wills (later of Roxy Music, the reunited Small Faces, Foreigner, and Bad Company), and Mike Gallagher in 1973 in order to tour the U.S. Frampton released an album a year and continued touring, making some inroads on FM radio, until the double-record *Frampton Comes Alive!* (#1, 1976), recorded at Winterland in San Francisco with a band composed of guitarist/keyboardist Bob Mayo, bassist Stanley Sheldon, and drummer John Siomos. The album included the best of Frampton's solo compositions and yielded three 1976 hit singles: "Show Me the Way" (#6), "Baby I Love Your Way" (#12), and "Do You Feel Like We Do" (#10). It would eventually sell about 18 million copies worldwide. By year's end Frampton had grossed nearly $70 million in concert fees and royalties.

The followup album, *I'm in You* (#2, 1977), had a #2 hit with the title cut, a gushy ballad, although its other singles didn't reach the Top 10. Frampton made his movie debut in Robert Stigwood's 1978 debacle, *Sgt. Pepper's Lonely Hearts Club Band,* but even before the movie was released there were rumors that he had succumbed to depression and heavy drinking. In June 1978 he suffered a concussion, muscle damage, and broken bones in a car crash in the Bahamas. Later that year his relationship with longtime girlfriend Penny McCall ended. By the late '70s, Frampton had returned to touring 10,000-seaters, although *Where I Should Be* went gold and produced a Top 20 hit, "I Can't Stand It No More" (#14, 1979).

Four albums in the '80s on A&M and Atlantic failed to catch fire; Frampton began playing on others' records again. David Bowie, once a student of Frampton's art-teacher father, asked the guitarist to play on his 1987 *Never Let Me Down* LP and subsequent Glass Spiders Tour. Next Frampton started collaborating with his former Humble Pie cohort Steve Marriott, but their plans died in the house fire that claimed Marriott's life in 1991. *Peter Frampton,* his first album of new songs in five years, was a typically tuneful collection that showcased his lyrical guitar solos. But the stage remains Frampton's natural element, and his next two albums would be live ones, including *Frampton Comes Alive II,* a followup to his most famous recording.

In 2000 Frampton contributed to Cameron Crowe's movie *Almost Famous* by writing two songs, serving as "authenticity adviser," and playing the small part of Humble Pie's manager. (Crowe had written the liner notes for *Frampton Comes Alive.)* That same year, the guitarist, who now lives in Cincinnati, contributed two songs to Disney's *Tigger Mania* and launched Framptone, a company that markets gadgets such as the Talk Box, immortalized in "Show Me the Way."

Connie Francis

Born Concetta Maria Franconero, Dec. 12, 1938, Newark, NJ
1958—*Who's Sorry Now* (MGM) 1986—*The Very Best of Connie Francis* (Polydor) 1987—*The Very Best of Connie Francis, vol. 2* 1993—*White Sox, Pink Lipsticks . . . and Stupid Cupid* (Bear Family, Ger.) 1996—*Live At Trump's Castle* (Click/Legacy); *Souvenirs* (Polydor/Chronicles); *Swinging Connie Francis* (Audiophile) 1997—*Where the Boys Are, Connie in Hollywood* (Rhino).

During the period between 1958 and the Beatles' emergence in spring 1964, singer Connie Francis had 35 Top 40 hits, including three #1s: "Everybody's Somebody's Fool" and "My Heart Has a Mind of Its Own" in 1960, and "Don't Break the Heart That Loves You" in 1962. Popular in Italy, Germany, Japan, France, and Spain, where she records in the native languages, Francis has had over 50 U.S. chart singles (and 25 in the U.K.), more hits than any other female vocalist except Aretha Franklin. Although she came up with, performed with, and got lumped in with the late-'50s teen idols, her international success and a catalogue that ranges from country music (1964's *Connie Sings Great Country Favorites* with Hank Williams Jr.) to Jewish, Irish, Spanish, Italian, and Latin compilations, places her in a class by herself.

Concetta Franconero debuted at age four playing "Anchors Aweigh" on accordion; by age 10 she began appearing on a local television show. By 11 she had appeared on several New York children's programs, and shortly after her 12th birthday sang "Daddy's Little Girl" on Arthur Godfrey's TV talent show. It was Godfrey who suggested that she change her name, which she did, though never legally. While still in her teens she recorded many demos, finally landing a deal with MGM in 1955. After a year and half of releasing flop singles, and with her contract in jeopardy, her father, a former dock worker, suggested she record an uptempo version of one of his favorites, a 1923 tune called "Who's Sorry Now." It was a #4 hit in early 1958, and she later had hits with other oldies like "Among My Souvenirs" (#7, 1960) and "Together" (#6, 1961), both of which were written in 1928.

Over the next five years, Francis had 25 records in the Top 100. Some of her bestsellers included "Stupid Cupid" (#14, 1958), "My Happiness" (#2, 1959), "Lipstick on Your Collar" (#5, 1959), "Mama" (#8, 1960), and "Vacation" (#9, 1962), the last of which she cowrote. Francis appeared in four films: *Where the Boys Are, Follow the Boys, Looking for Love,* and *When the Boys Meet the Girls.* She also sang the theme for *Where the Boys Are* (#4, 1961) and appeared in Brylcreem hair-cream commercials: "A little dab'll do ya!"

Francis' big hits ended with the beginning of Beatlemania, though she had several minor successes through the end of the decade and continued to perform to sold-out crowds around the world. In December 1960, she became the youngest performer to ever headline at the Copacabana. Surgery to correct a problem with her nose resulted in her inability to sing in air-conditioned rooms, and she sang with great difficulty. She made her return to live performing in November 1974 at the Westbury Music Fair on Long Island. After the performance, a man entered her hotel room and beat and raped her. She later sued the Howard Johnson's motel for negligence and was awarded $3,055,000 in damages.

It would be several more years before she recovered from the traumatic assault. She stopped performing and underwent two and a half years of psychiatric treatment. There were frequent reports in the press of battles between her and her father, who had long been instrumental in her career. Her only brother, George, was murdered in 1981. She underwent three additional operations on her nose, and approximately seven years after her farewell live performance Francis made a triumphant return to the Westbury Music Fair. In 1984 she published her autobiography, *Who's Sorry Now?,* a revealing account of the early rock & roll scene, including her romance with singer Bobby Darin. *Swinging Connie Francis* contains covers of '30s jazz standards.

Frankie Goes to Hollywood

Formed 1980, Liverpool, Eng.
Holly Johnson (b. William Johnson, Feb. 19, 1960, Khartoum, Sudan), voc.; Paul Rutherford (b. Dec. 8, 1959, Liverpool), voc.; Nasher Nash (b. Brian Nash, May 20, 1963), gtr.; Mark O'Toole (b. Jan. 6, 1964, Liverpool), bass; Peter Gill (b. Mar. 8, 1964, Liverpool), drums.
1984—*Welcome to the Pleasuredome* (ZTT/Island) 1986—*Liverpool* 1994—*Bang! . . . The Greatest Hits of Frankie Goes to Hollywood* (Atlantic).
Holly Johnson solo: 1989—*Blast* (Uni) 1990—*Hallelujah* EP (MCA) 1991—*Dreams That Money Can't Buy* 1999—*Soulstream* (Pleasuredome, U.K.).

In pop music, controversy can be the mother of ascension. After Frankie Goes to Hollywood's sexually suggestive debut single, 1984's "Relax," was banned by the BBC—along with its accompanying video, set in a gay bar—it shot to the top of the British charts, where it remained for five weeks. And just as producer Trevor Horn's techno-savvy ingenuity had parlayed the mediocre hook propelling "Relax" into an insidious dance track, a promotion blitz engineered by ex-journalist Paul Morley turned the Liverpudlian quintet into an omnipresent phenomenon. Most memorable were the "Frankie Say . . ." T-shirts, as cheekily unabashed in their admonitions on sex and politics as singer Holly Johnson was about his homosexuality.

Frankiemania seemed destined to cross the Atlantic, but the amused fascination with which Americans observed the hoopla didn't translate into huge sales. The group's second smash U.K. single, "Two Tribes," a tepid but danceable anti–Cold War chant, peaked just outside the Top 40 here, despite a popular video in which Reagan and Chernenko lookalikes duked it out in a boxing ring. "Relax" reemerged as a U.S. single, hitting #10 in early 1985. After that, though, Frankie's 1984 debut album, *Welcome to the Pleasuredome,* spawned no more megahits at home or abroad. A subsequent album flopped, and by the end of the band's tour to support it in 1987, Frankie had broken up.

After a legal battle with ZTT Records and beginning a solo career, Johnson discovered in the early '90s that he was HIV-positive—a diagnosis that quickly developed into AIDS—and, after a year-long bout with depression, became a spokesman for AIDS awareness. In 1994 he published a frank and catty autobiography, *A Bone in My Flute,* and released a single, "Legendary Children." Encouraged by new treatments, as well as the enduring love of his longtime partner, art dealer Wolfgang Kuhle, Johnson continued to pursue his creative interests. He exhibited his paintings in a London art gallery in 1996; another exhibition of his artwork was held in Liverpool in 2000. He also established a home studio and record label in order to record and release a 1999 solo album, *Soulstream.* The disc included a new version of the Frankie ballad "The Power of Love," and a song called "Disco Heaven," about the friends Johnson has lost to AIDS. He directed a video for the latter, which featured an appearance by Boy George.

Aretha Franklin

Born Mar. 25, 1942, Memphis, TN
1956—*The Gospel Sound of Aretha Franklin* (Checker) 1961—*Aretha* (Columbia) 1962—*The Electrifying Aretha Franklin; The Tender, the Moving, the Swinging Aretha Franklin* 1963—*Laughing on the Outside* 1964—*Songs of Faith* (Checker); *Unforgettable: A Tribute to Dinah Washington* (Columbia); *Runnin' Out of Fools* 1965—*Yeah!!; Once in a Lifetime* (Harmony) 1966—*Soul Sister* (Columbia) 1967—*Take It Like You Give It; Greatest Hits, vol. 1; Lee Cross (CBS); I Never Loved a Man (the Way I Love You)* (Atlantic); *Take a Look* (Columbia); *Aretha Arrives* (Atlantic) 1968—*Lady Soul; Aretha Now; Aretha in Paris; Greatest Hits, vol. 2* (Columbia); *Queen of Soul* (Harmony) 1969—*Aretha Franklin: Live!* (Hallmark); *Soul '69* (Atlantic); *Aretha's Gold; I Say a Little Prayer* 1970—*Don't Play That Song; This Girl's in Love With You; Spirit in the Dark; Sweet Bitter Love* (Columbia) 1971—*Live at Fillmore West* (Atlantic); *Greatest Hits* 1972—*Young, Gifted and Black; Amazing Grace* 1973—*Hey Now Hey (The Other Side of the Sky); The First Twelve Sides* (Columbia); *The Best of Aretha Franklin* (Atlantic) 1974—*Let Me in Your Life; With Everything I Feel in Me* 1975—*You; Two Originals* 1976—*Sparkle; Ten Years of Gold* 1977—*Satisfaction; Sweet Passion; Most Beautiful Songs* 1978—*Almighty Fire* 1979—*La Diva* 1980—*Aretha Sings the Blues* (Columbia) 1981—*Love All the Hurt Away* 1982—*Jump to It; Sweet Bitter Love* 1983—*Get It Right* (Arista) 1983—*Aretha's Jazz* (Atlantic) 1984—*Never Grow Old* (Chess) 1985—*Who's Zoomin' Who* (Arista); *30 Greatest Hits* (Atlantic); *First Lady of Soul* (Stylus) 1986—*Aretha* (Arista); *Soul Survivor* (Blue Moon) 1987—*After Hours* (Columbia); *One Lord, One Faith, One Baptism* (Arista) 1989—*Through the Storm* (Arista); *After Hours* (Columbia) 1991—*What You See Is What You Sweat* (Arista) 1992—*Jazz to Soul* (Columbia/Legacy) 1994—*Aretha's Greatest Hits (1980–1994)* (Arista); *The Very Best of Aretha Franklin, vol. 1* (Rhino); *The Very Best of Aretha Franklin, vol. 2* 1997—*Love Songs; The Early Years* (Legacy) 1998—*The Delta Meets Detroit: Aretha's Blues* (Rhino); *A Rose Is Still a Rose* (Arista); *You Grow Closer* (Uni/Gospocentric); *I Dreamed a Dream* (Rhino) 1999—*Amazing Grace: The Complete Recordings* (Arista) 2000—*Atlantic Singles* (Rhino); *Aretha Gospel* (Chess).

Aretha Franklin is not only the definitive female soul singer of the '60s, but one of the most influential and important voices in the history of popular music. She fused the leaps and swoops of the gospel music she grew up on with the sensuality of R&B, the innovation of jazz, and the precision of pop. After she hit her artistic and commercial stride in 1967, she made over a dozen million-selling singles, and since then has recorded 20 #1 R&B hits. She moved toward the pop mainstream with fitful success in the '70s, but in the late '80s experienced a resurgence in popularity, and continues to record in a less ecstatic, perhaps more mature style.

Franklin's father, the Reverend C.L. Franklin, was the pastor of Detroit's 4,500-member New Bethel Baptist Church and a nationally known gospel singer ("the Man with the Million-Dollar Voice"). Her mother, Barbara, who was also a

Aretha Franklin

gospel singer, deserted the family when Aretha was six and died four years later. Aretha and her sisters, Carolyn and Erma, sang regularly at their father's church, and Aretha's first recordings were made there when she was 14. The Franklins were among the most prominent black families in Detroit. Many future stars, including Smokey Robinson, knew the family, and in the '50s Berry Gordy Jr. tried to sign Aretha to his fledgling Motown label. Reverend Franklin refused.

The teenaged Aretha toured the gospel circuit with her father, and she was befriended by Clara Ward (according to some sources, the Reverend Franklin's lover), Mahalia Jackson, James Cleveland, and Sam Cooke. Cooke, who had only recently crossed over from recording gospel to pop, was an inspiration to the young singer, encouraging her to sign with the label he recorded for, RCA. In fact, Aretha nearly did, until she was signed by legendary talent scout John Hammond to Columbia. She moved to New York, and at first found acceptance in the R&B market with "Today I Sing the Blues" (#10 R&B, 1960), "Won't Be Long" (#7 R&B, 1961), and "Operation Heartbreak" (#6 R&B, 1961), but in six years and 10 albums, she had only one pop hit: "Rock-a-bye Your Baby With a Dixie Melody" (#37 pop, 1961). As reissues have focused new attention on Franklin's Columbia years, they have proven not to have been wasted entirely. She recorded several original songs ("Without the One You Love," "I'll Keep On Smiling," "Land of Dreams," "I Still Can't Forget") and a critically lauded tribute to her late friend Dinah Washington, as well as a 1962 version of "Try a Little Tenderness" that is said to have inspired Otis Redding to record it.

In 1966 she signed with Atlantic. With the help of producer Jerry Wexler, arranger Arif Mardin, and engineer Tom Dowd, Franklin began to make the records that would reshape soul music. Her first session (and the only one recorded at Muscle Shoals, in Alabama) yielded "I Never Loved a Man (the Way I Love You)" (#9 pop, #1 R&B, 1967) and heralded a phenomenal three years in which she sold in the millions with "Respect" (#1 pop and R&B, 1967), "Baby I Love You" (#4 pop, #1 R&B, 1967), "Chain of Fools" (#2 pop, #1 R&B, 1968), "Since You've Been Gone" (#5 pop, #1 R&B, 1968), "Think" (#7 pop, #1 R&B, 1968), "The House That Jack Built" (#6 pop, #2 R&B, 1968), "I Say a Little Prayer" (#10 pop, #3 R&B, 1968), "See Saw" (#14 pop, #9 R&B, 1968), "The Weight" (#19 pop, #3 R&B, 1969), "Share Your Love With Me" (#13 pop, #1 R&B, 1969), "Eleanor Rigby" (#17 pop, #5 R&B, 1969), "Call Me" (#13 pop, #1 R&B, 1970), and "Spirit in the Dark" (#23 pop, #3 R&B, 1970).

Franklin's material ranged from R&B numbers by Otis Redding ("Respect"), Don Covay ("See Saw" [with Steve Cropper], "Chain of Fools"), and Ronnie Shannon ("I Never Loved a Man") to pop fare by Carole King and Gerry Goffin ("[You Make Me Feel Like] a Natural Woman"), Lennon and McCartney ("Eleanor Rigby"), Burt Bacharach and Hal David ("I Say a Little Prayer"). She also recorded many of her own songs, cowritten with her first husband and then-manager Ted White ("Dr. Feelgood," "Since You've Been Gone [Sweet Sweet Baby]," "Think"), or her sister Carolyn ("Save Me" [with King Curtis]), who received solo songwriting credit for "Ain't No Way." Most of Franklin's '60s sessions were recorded with the Muscle Shoals Sound Rhythm Section, who, after the first session, were imported to New York City, or with a band led by saxophonist King Curtis. Franklin herself was responsible for the vocal arrangements, whose gospel-style call-and-response choruses often featured her sister Carolyn as well as the Sweet Inspirations [see entry].

By 1968 Franklin reigned throughout America and Europe as "Lady Soul"—a symbol of black pride. She was presented an award by Martin Luther King Jr. (to whose cause her father had been a major financial supporter), and appeared on the cover of *Time*, the accompanying profile of which would be her last major interview for many years. As *Time* reported (and other sources have since concurred), Franklin's personal life was quite turbulent. Throughout her career, Franklin has remained an enigmatic figure, alternately outspoken and reclusive, and much of her personal life has been shrouded in secrecy. She had married White in 1961. She already had two sons, Clarence and Edward, born before her 17th birthday. With White, she gave birth to Teddy Jr., a guitarist in her band since the '80s. Her marriage to White ended in 1969, by which time he had struck her in public on one occasion and shot her new production manager on another. Franklin herself was arrested in 1968 for reckless driving and again in 1969 for disorderly conduct. Also in 1969 her father was arrested for possession of marijuana. He hosted a controversial conference for a black separatist group that ended in a violent confrontation with Detroit police that left one officer dead and several other people wounded. During this time his daughter Aretha was rumored to be drinking heavily.

The hits continued (giving her more million-sellers than any other woman in recording history)—"Don't Play That Song" (#11 pop, #1 R&B, 1970), "Bridge Over Troubled Water" (#6 pop, #1 R&B, 1971), "Spanish Harlem" (#2 pop, #1 R&B, 1971), "Rock Steady" (#9 pop, #2 R&B, 1971), "Day Dreaming" (#5 pop, #1 R&B, 1972), and "Until You Come Back to Me (That's What I'm Gonna Do)" (#3 pop, #1 R&B, 1973). In the early '70s she gave birth to her fourth son, Kecalf, and in 1978 she married actor Glynn Turman. During this time Franklin seemed to be searching, sometimes aimlessly, for direction. But this period was not without its high points: *Spirit in the Dark*, *Live at the Fillmore West*, and *Young, Gifted, and Black* were all critically acclaimed. The pure gospel *Amazing Gospel* (recorded live in L.A. with her father officiating and the Reverend James Cleveland at the piano and conducting the choir) would be her last album with Wexler. During her last years with Atlantic she moved from producer to producer: Quincy Jones *(Hey Now Hey)*, Curtis Mayfield (*Sparkle*, which included "Something He Can Feel," a 1992 Top 10 hit for En Vogue and Franklin's last Top 40 pop hit for nearly six years), Lamont Dozier *(Sweet Passion)*, Van McCoy *(La Diva)*. Her concerts became Las Vegas–style extravaganzas, and she soon established a reputation for her idiosyncratic (some would say ill-advised) costume choices. She also began showing signs of the unpredictability that would dog her career, particularly after a bad experience while flying resulted in a phobia that curtailed her touring.

In 1980 Franklin left Atlantic, signed with Arista, and positioned herself as the grande dame of pop. Her cameo appearance (she sang "Respect" and "Think") in *The Blues Brothers* movie that year has been cited as the beginning of a new phase. Her first two Arista albums were produced by Arif Mardin, and each included an old soul standard as well as glossier MOR material. "Love All the Hurt Away," a collaboration with George Benson, went to #6 on the R&B chart in 1981. Her version of Sam and Dave's "Hold On, I'm Comin' " earned a Grammy for Best R&B Vocal Performance, Female. With the Luther Vandross–produced *Jump to It*, she reestablished herself as a hitmaker when the title tune hit #1 R&B and #24 pop in 1982. Vandross was also behind the board for *Get It Right*.

But the momentum of her commercial comeback was halted by a series of personal tragedies, beginning with the 1979 attack on her father, in which he was shot by burglars in his Detroit home. He began to recover from his injuries but then lapsed into a coma state from which he did not emerge before his death in 1984. In 1982 Franklin moved back to the Detroit area, where she still lives. Two years later, she and Turman divorced. The year after her father's death, Franklin came fully back into the public eye with *Who's Zoomin' Who* (#13, 1985), a Narada Michael Walden–produced work that spun off three hit singles: the Grammy-winning "Freeway of Love" (#3 pop, #1 R&B, 1985), the title track (#7 pop, #2 R&B, 1985), and a Top 20 duet with the Eurythmics, "Sisters Are Doin' It for Themselves." The album, which included guest performances by Clarence Clemons, Dizzy Gillespie, Carlos Santana, Peter Wolf, and most of Tom Petty's Heartbreakers, as well as backing vocals by sister Carolyn and Sylvester, among others, became her highest-charting album since 1972. The hits' accompanying videos were heavily played on MTV, and Franklin found the pop crossover success that had once eluded her. Its followup, *Aretha,* included the Top 30 "Jimmy Lee" (#2 R&B, 1986) and a version of "Jumpin' Jack Flash," produced by and featuring Keith Richards, as well as her Grammy-winning #1 duet with George Michael, "I Knew You Were Waiting (for Me)" (1987).

Subsequent albums were less popular. Her critically acclaimed *One Lord, One Faith, One Baptism* marked a return to gospel and featured Mavis Staples and the Reverend Jesse Jackson. It earned Franklin her 15th Grammy, for Best Female Soul Gospel Performance. Despite its hit title track (a duet with Elton John; #16 pop, #17 R&B, 1989), *Through the Storm* peaked at #55, and 1991's *What You See Is What You Sweat* made the lowest showing of any new album in her career. It contained a #13 R&B cover of Sly and the Family Stone's "Everyday People."

In 1987 Franklin became the first woman inducted into the Rock and Roll Hall of Fame. In 1988 Franklin's sister Carolyn died of cancer; around the same period her brother and manager, Cecil, also died. She appeared with Frank Sinatra on his *Duets* album and in 1993 starred in her own television special, *Duets,* which featured her singing with a number of current pop stars, including Bonnie Raitt, Elton John, Smokey Robinson, George Michael, and Rod Stewart. She appeared at the inaugural celebration for President Bill Clinton, where her rendition of "I Dreamed a Dream" (from *Les Miserables*) barely got more attention than her wearing a fur coat (for which she offered no apologies). "A Deeper Love" (#63 pop, #30 R&B, 1994), from the *Sister Act 2* soundtrack, was written and produced by Robert Clivilles and David Cole of C + C Music Factory. "Willing to Forgive" was another Top 20 R&B hit that year. In 1994 Franklin received a Grammy Award for Lifetime Achievement.

In 1996 Franklin signed a three-album deal with Arista for a reported $10 million. The next year, she was accepted into the Juilliard School of Music to study classical piano, and she recorded a new version of "Respect" for the movie *Blues Brothers 2000,* in which she reprised her role as a restaurant owner. She also formed a record label, World Class Records, primarily to release gospel music. In 1998 she delivered her 49th album, *A Rose Is Still a Rose,* a career-revitalizing collaboration with current stars such as the Fugees' Lauryn Hill and producers Sean Combs and Jermaine Dupri.

In 1999 her highly anticipated autobiography, *Aretha: From These Roots* (written with David Ritz), was released. Franklin then entered the new century by selecting, with the White House Millennium Council, "Respect" to be included in a time capsule to preserve significant cultural achievements for future generations.

Erma Franklin (born 1939) and Carolyn Franklin (born 1945; died April 25, 1988, Bloomfield Hills, MI) were professional singers for as long as their better-known sister. After many years on the gospel circuit, Erma began recording soul and pop material in the mid-'60s. Her 1967 Shout release, "Piece of My Heart" (#10, R&B), preceded Janis Joplin's version by several months. She recorded for the Brunswick label in the late '60s and early '70s. Carolyn sang backup for many of Atlantic's stars in the '60s. She later recorded as a solo artist for RCA.

Michael Franks

Born Sep. 18, 1944, La Jolla, CA
1973—*Michael Franks* (Brut) 1976—*The Art of Tea* (Reprise) 1977—*Sleeping Gypsy* (Warner Bros.) 1978—*Birchfield Nines* 1979—*Tiger in the Rain* 1980—*One Bad Habit* 1982—*Objects of Desire* 1983—*Passionfruit* 1985—*Skin Dive* 1987—*The Camera Never Lies* 1989—*Previously Unavailable* (DRG) 1990—*Blue Pacific* (Reprise) 1993—*Dragonfly Summer* 1995—*Abandoned Garden* (Warner Bros.) 1998—*The Best of Michael Franks: A Backward Glance* 1999—*Barefoot on the Beach* (Windham Hill).

Songwriter Michael Franks has been recording his own droll, laid-back pop-jazz tunes since 1973, with occasional pop recognition. His songs have been covered by Melissa Manchester, Manhattan Transfer, and the Carpenters, and he has written for Rod Stewart and Barbra Streisand.

Franks played folk and rock in high school in La Jolla, and he majored in contemporary literature at UCLA while working part-time as a musician. In the late '60s he completed a master's degree in contemporary culture at the University of Montreal. While in Canada he opened shows for Gordon Lightfoot and worked with Carnival, later Lighthouse.

In the early '70s Franks taught undergraduate music courses and worked toward a Ph.D. at UCLA and Berkeley. His doctoral dissertation was entitled "Contemporary Songwriting and How It Relates to Society." He scored two films in 1971, *Count Your Bullets* and *Zandy's Bride.* In 1972 Sonny Terry and Brownie McGhee recorded three of his songs, with Franks backing them on mandolin and banjo, on their *Sonny & Brownie.* Buddah/Brut signed him in 1972, and his "Can't Seem to Shake This Rock 'n' Roll" received some airplay. He toured the U.S. opening for comedian Robert Klein in 1973.

After scoring another film in England, Franks returned to California and took on a research project for Warner Bros. Pictures that led to his Reprise signing. His albums have featured well-known backing musicians—the Crusaders on *The Art of Tea,* which included the minor hit "Popsicle Toes" (#43, 1976); Brazilian musicians on *Sleeping Gypsy*—and have earned him a cult following.

In the '80s, Franks adopted a cooler sound, which eventually found favor in the rising "light jazz" and adult contemporary radio formats. Despite this, he has yet to enjoy any broad chart success, although his entire catalogue remains in print and "Your Secret's Safe With Me" got some exposure via its video on VH1. Franks is known for the varied and respected company he keeps on his records, which have featured Astrud Gilberto (on *Passionfruit),* Patti Austin, Flora

Purim, the Brecker Brothers, David Sanborn, Joe Sample, Larry Carlton, Luther Vandross, Art Garfunkel, Earl Klugh, and Steve Jordan, among many others. *Dragonfly Summer* includes guest appearances by Dan Hicks and Peggy Lee. Following a greatest-hits summary of his years with Warner Bros., Franks released his debut for Windham Hill in 1999.

Freakwater: See Eleventh Dream Day

John Fred and His Playboy Band

Formed late '50s, Baton Rouge, LA
John Fred (b. May 8, 1941, Baton Rouge), voc., harmonica; Charlie Spinosa (b. Dec. 29, 1948, Baton Rouge), trumpet; Ronnie Goodson (b. Feb. 2, 1945, Miami, FL), trumpet; Andrew Bernard (b. 1945, New Orleans, LA), sax; James O'Rourke (b. Mar. 14, 1947, Fall River, MA), gtr.; Harold Cowart (b. June 12, 1944, Baton Rouge), bass; Joe Micelli (b. July 9, 1946, Baton Rouge), drums; Tommy Dee (b. Thomas De Generes, Nov. 3, 1946, Baton Rouge), organ.
1965—*John Fred and His Playboys* (Paula) 1966—*34:40 of John Fred and His Playboys* 1967—*Agnes English* 1969—*Permanently Stated* 1970—*Love in My Soul* (Uni).

John Fred and His Playboy Band were an R&B-inspired rock band best known for its 1968 hit, the 3-million-seller "Judy in Disguise (with Glasses)." Led by John Fred, a former all-American basketball player at Louisiana State University, who began recording in 1958 with "Shirley" on Montel Records, the group established itself in Louisiana and Texas clubs in the early '60s. Its lone hit (which was also the group's 16th single), "Judy in Disguise" (a wordplay on the Beatles' "Lucy in the Sky With Diamonds"), hit #1 in January 1968; the 45's success propelled *Agnes English* to the lower rungs of the album chart. But followups like "Hey Hey Bunny" (#57, 1968) didn't come close to matching "Judy," and the group broke up the next year. Fred formed another Playboy Band in the mid-'70s before going to work for R.C.S. Records in Baton Rouge, where he coproduced a 1979 LP for Irma Thomas. In the late '80s Fred found a second career singing commercial jingles (winning a Clio Award for one of them), and later revived the Playboy Band to play the oldies circuit.

Freddie and the Dreamers

Formed 1960, Manchester, Eng.
Freddie Garrity (b. Nov. 14, 1936), voc., gtr.; Derek Quinn (b. May 24, 1942), gtr., harmonica; Roy Crewsdon (b. May 29, 1941), gtr., piano, drums; Pete Birrell (b. May 9, 1941), bass; Bernie Dwyer (b. Sep. 11, 1940), drums.
1964—*You Were Made for Me* 1965—*Freddie and the Dreamers* (Mercury); *Do the Freddie* 1966—*Freddie and the Dreamers* 1992—*The Best of Freddie and the Dreamers* (EMI).

Freddie and the Dreamers, all born in Manchester, were the buffoons of the British Invasion. The group was formed by ex-milkman Freddie Garrity, who had previously worked in a '50s skiffle band. A bespectacled young man with a slight resemblance to Buddy Holly, Freddie looked silly and nerdish, and—while the band played deadpan foils—gave forth with a cackling laugh and exaggerated dancing that included fairly acrobatic mid-air splits. In 1962, after successfully auditioning for the BBC, they rose to prominence in England and signed with Columbia. Their first single, a cover of James Ray's "If You've Gotta Make a Fool of Somebody," hit the British Top 5. Over the next few years they enjoyed a half-dozen U.K. hits, including "You Were Made for Me" (#3 U.K.) and "I Understand" (#5 U.K.).

"I'm Telling You Now," originally released in England in 1963, went to #1 in the U.S. in spring 1965, spurred by the group's touring and appearances on the *Shindig!* and *Hullabaloo* television shows. Another American hit, "Do the Freddie" (#18, 1965), sparked a momentary dance craze in emulation of Freddie's arm and leg waving. The group was featured in such films as *Seaside Swingers, Just for You,* and *Cuckoo Patrol.* Their U.S. hits ended in 1966. The band played cabarets and clubs until breaking up in 1968. Garrity and Pete Birrell thereafter hosted their own children's TV series in England called *The Little Big Time.* The Dreamers re-formed in 1976, with only Garrity remaining from the original lineup, and they remained active in supper clubs and cabarets into the '90s.

Free

Formed 1968, London, Eng.
Paul Rodgers (b. Dec. 12, 1949, Middleborough, Eng.), voc.; Paul Kossoff (b. Sep. 14, 1950, London; d. Mar. 19, 1976, New York, NY), gtr.; Andy Fraser (b. Aug. 7, 1952, London), bass; Simon Kirke (b. July 28, 1949, Shrewsbury, Eng.), drums.
1969—*Tons of Sobs* (A&M) 1970—*Free; Fire and Water; Highway* 1971—(group disbands) *Free Live* 1972—(group re-forms) *Free at Last* (– Kossoff; – Fraser; + Tetsu Yamauchi [b. Oct. 21, 1947, Fukuoka, Jap.], bass; + John "Rabbit" Bundrick, kybds.; + Kossoff; – Kossoff) 1973—*Heartbreaker* (group disbands) 1975—*Best of Free* 1993—*Molten Gold: The Anthology.*

Free distilled British blues down to riffs, silences, and Paul Rodgers' ornately anguished vocals—most memorably in "All Right Now" (#4, 1970). The style the group established was made more ponderous and commercially successful by Bad Company, Foreigner, and other '70s hard-rock bands.

Free started in the London pubs when Simon Kirke and Paul Kossoff, then in the blues band Black Cat Bones, heard Rodgers singing with Brown Sugar. The three enlisted 16-year-old Andy Fraser from John Mayall's Bluesbreakers, and they got the name Free from Alexis Korner. The quartet failed to make inroads with its first two albums and a U.S. tour opening for Blind Faith in 1969, but *Fire and Water,* which include "All Right Now," signaled that Free had honed its approach. Yet just months after the success of "All Right Now," in mid-1971, the group split up. Kossoff and Kirke joined bassist Tetsu Yamauchi (later with the Faces) and session keyboardist John "Rabbit" Bundrick for one album, *Kossoff, Kirke, Tetsu and Rabbit;* Rodgers formed a group called Peace; and Fraser started Toby. By 1972, the original Free had re-formed for *Free at Last*. Personal problems and drug use—especially Kossoff's—took a toll on the band, and it broke up for good in early 1973. Fraser joined guitarist Chris Spedding in Sharks for one album; Kossoff started Back Street Crawler (later Crawler), but died of a drug-induced heart attack in 1976 on an airplane en route to New York. Rodgers and Kirke were joined by Yamauchi and Bundrick for 1973's *Heartbreaker*, then retired the Free name to start Bad Company [see entry]. Yamauchi replaced Ronnie Lane in the Faces, while Bundrick has added keyboards to the Who. In the mid-'80s Rodgers joined Jimmy Page [see entry] in the Firm; he later formed the Law with Kenney Jones of the Faces. The singer has since released several solo albums. In the late '90s and 2000 Kirke was backing Ringo Starr.

Glenn Frey: See the Eagles

Kinky Friedman

Born Richard Friedman, Oct. 31, 1944, Chicago, IL
1973—*Sold American* (Vanguard) 1975—*Kinky Friedman* (ABC) 1976—*Lasso From El Paso* (Epic) 1983—*Under the Double Ego* (Sunrise) 1993—*Old Testaments and New Revelations* (Fruit of the Tune) 1995—*From One Good American to Another* 2000—*Classic Snatches From Europe* (Sphincter).

Country songwriter and sometime leader of the Texas Jewboys, Kinky Friedman drawls his way through tunes like "High on Jesus," "Asshole From El Paso," "Ride 'em Jewboy," and "They Ain't Makin' Jews Like Jesus Anymore." Born in Chicago but raised in Texas, Richard Friedman studied psychology at the University of Texas, then joined the Peace Corps; he claims to have instructed Borneo natives in throwing the Frisbee. Back in Texas, at a farm called Rio Duckworth, he started King Arthur and the Carrots, whose songs like "Beach Party Boo" and "Schwinn Twenty-four," and Friedman's penchant for gaudy stage outfits, attracted the attention of Austin patrons like Kris Kristofferson and Commander Cody.

Friedman began making albums in 1973, with the support over the years of Waylon Jennings (who produced "Carryin' the Torch"), Ringo Starr, Billy Swan, and Bob Dylan, who invited Kinky to appear with the Rolling Thunder Revue, which provided some live cuts for Friedman's *Lasso From El Paso*. Friedman has appeared at Nashville's Grand Ole Opry but is apparently too vulgar for the mainstream country audience. Friedman takes pride in offending the politically correct crowd as well; he was named "Male Chauvinist of the Year" by the National Organization for Women in 1974 for his song "Get Your Biscuits in the Oven and Your Buns in Bed."

Friedman moved to New York in 1979 and frequently headlined at the Lone Star Cafe. In 1986 he published his first mystery novel: *Greenwich Killing Time*. He has since written 12 others: *A Case of Lone Star* (1987), *When the Cat's Away* (1989), *Frequent Flyer* (1990), *Musical Chairs* (1991), *Elvis, Jesus & Coca-Cola* (1993), *Armadillos & Old Lace* (1994), *God Bless John Wayne* (1995), *The Love Song of J. Edgar Hoover* (1996), *Roadkill* (1997), *Blast From the Past* (1998), *Spanking Watson* (1999), and *The Mile High Club* (2000). Friedman is not only the author of his books, but their protagonist as well. His books are bestsellers in England, Australia, and Germany. He returned to Texas in 1985, and the following year made an unsuccessful bid for Kerrville, Texas, justice of the peace. During the campaign, Friedman revealed that he had harbored his friend Abbie Hoffman at his ranch when the radical was being sought as a fugitive from justice in the mid-'70s.

The compilation *Old Testaments and New Revelations* sold more than 100,000 copies. *From One Good American to Another* collected songs from a couple of radio broadcasts (one recorded at New York's Electric Ladyland Studio in 1974), a 1979 session featuring Dr. John, and a new song, "God Bless John Wayne (People Who Read People Magazine)." In 1998 Friedman called in some of his famous friends—including Willie Nelson, Lyle Lovett, and Tom Waits—and issued the tribute album *Pearls in the Snow—The Songs of Kinky Friedman* on his own label, Kinkajou Records. Friedman continues to perform, although he considers himself primarily a novelist today. (As he wrote in re-

Kinky Friedman

sponse to the *Encyclopedia* researcher: "I've finally found a lifestyle that doesn't require my presence.")

The Friends of Distinction

Formed 1967, Los Angeles, CA
Harry Elston (b. Nov. 4, 1938, Dallas, TX), voc.; Floyd Butler (b. June 5, 1941, San Diego, CA), voc.; Jessica Cleaves (b. Dec. 10, 1948, Beverly Hills, CA), voc.; Barbara Love (b. July 24, 1941, Los Angeles), voc.
1969—*Grazin'* (RCA); *Highly Distinct* 1970—*Real Friends; Whatever* 1971—*Friends and People.*

Black MOR pop vocal group the Friends of Distinction are best remembered for their 1969 "Grazin' in the Grass" (#3). The group was formed around chief composer Harry Elston, who had worked with Ray Charles, as did Floyd Butler and future Fifth Dimension members Marilyn McCoo and LaMonte McLemore under the name the Hi-Fi's. That group disbanded after a short tour with Charles, and after the Friends of Distinction came together, ex-football-star-turned-Hollywood-actor Jim Brown became the group's financial backer. It signed with RCA in 1968.

By early 1969 "Grazin' " had hit the Top 5. Lesser hits—"Going in Circles" (#15, 1969) and "Let Yourself Go" (#63, 1969)—followed. "Love or Let Me Be Lonely" was their last big hit (#6, 1970). In 1971 Barbara Love (daughter of West Coast disc jockey Reuben Brown) left the group, which soon disbanded. Jessica Cleaves went on to join Earth, Wind & Fire.

Robert Fripp

Born May 16, 1946, Wimbourne, Eng.
1973—*No Pussyfooting* (with Brian Eno) (Island, U.K.) 1975—*Evening Star* (with Brian Eno) 1979—*Exposure* (Polydor, U.K.) 1980—*God Save the Queen/Under Heavy Manners* (Polydor) 1981—*Let the Power Fall* (Editions EG); *The League of Gentlemen* 1982—*I Advance Masked* (with Andy Summers) (A&M) 1984—*Bewitched* (with Andy Summers) 1985—*God Save the King* 1986—*Robert Fripp and the League of Crafty Guitarists Live!; The Lady or the Tiger* (with Toyah Wilcox) (Editions EG) 1990—*Robert Fripp and the League of Crafty Guitarists Live II* 1991—*Show of Hands* (with the League of Crafty Guitarists); *Kneeling at the Shrine* 1993—*Kings; The First Day* (with David Sylvian) (Virgin) 1994—*The Bridge Between* (the Robert Fripp String Quartet) (Discipline); *1994: Soundscapes—Live in Argentina; Damage* (with David Sylvian) (Virgin) 1995—*Intergalactic Boogie Express: Live in Europe 1991* (with the League of Crafty Guitarists) (Discipline); *A Blessing of Tears: 1995 Soundscapes, vol. II, Live in California* 1996—*That Which Passes: 1995 Soundscapes, vol. III; Radiophonics: 1995 Soundscapes, vol. I* (Discipline, U.K.) 1998—*The Gates of Paradise; November Suite: Soundscapes—Live at Green Park Station.*

Guitarist, composer, and producer Robert Fripp has been at the forefront of progressive rock and new wave, and his pioneering use of electronics helped usher in ambient music. Founder of King Crimson [see entry], solo artist, and musical theoretician, he grounds his conceptual approach on a highly distinctive blend of rigorous technique and metaphysical discipline.

Starting off with the League of Gentlemen, a band of accompanists for visiting American singers, Fripp first recorded with Giles, Giles and Fripp. Their one album, *The Cheerful Insanity of Giles, Giles and Fripp* (1968), set forth the experimental approach King Crimson would expand from 1969 to 1975. Along with those of Yes and Emerson, Lake and Palmer, Crimson's eight albums, featuring a variety of highly technical players, typified the fusion of classical music elements and theatrical attack that hallmarked progressive rock.

Concurrently, Fripp teamed up with Brian Eno (for *No Pussyfooting* and *Evening Star)* and developed "Frippertronics," a method of tape-looped solo guitar improvisation that produces layers of sound. In 1974 Fripp also took up the teachings of J.G. Bennett, a proponent of the mystical philosophers Gurdjieff and P.D. Ouspensky. The result was an intensification of Fripp's conviction that music is an expression of spiritual aspiration, a link between the human and the divine.

Disbanding King Crimson before its final, live album came out, Fripp produced jazz records for a group called Centipede. He then briefly retired, declaring his intention to act henceforth as "a small, self-sufficient, mobile, intelligent unit." Lending his signature guitar to David Bowie's "*Heroes,"* he returned to performance in 1977 and went on to produce Peter Gabriel's second album and Daryl Hall's 1980 solo LP, *Sacred Songs.*

Exposure was Fripp's solo debut. With vocals by Hall, Gabriel, Terre Roche, and Peter Hammill, it showed him working relatively closely within the pop-song format. Re-forming King Crimson with guitarist Adrian Belew in 1981, he also collaborated in the early '80s with Police guitarist Andy Summers on *I Advance Masked* and *Bewitched.* As the decade progressed, either under his own name or the League of Gentlemen, Fripp continued innovating—from the "Frippertronics"-driven *Let the Power Fall* to the Crimson-like *The League of Gentlemen.*

Furthering his theoretical interests, Fripp founded Guitar Craft in the mid-'80s: A tutorial in his worldview, it offered guitar instruction and philosophical discussion. *The League of Crafty Guitarists Live!* and *Show of Hands,* featuring his students' acoustic playing, showcased the school's approach. With his wife, singer and actress Toyah Wilcox, Fripp put out *The Lady or the Tiger* in 1986, a spoken-word album with musical backing; *Kneeling at the Shrine,* with Toyah fronting a new Fripp outfit, Sunday All Over the World, followed in 1991. Two years later, *The First Day* found Fripp pairing with David Sylvian. One of his more orthodox song-oriented outings, it made clear that his guitar style, for all its electronic modification, remained irrevocably melodic.

In the mid-'90s Fripp formed his own record label, Discipline Global Mobile, to release work by himself, other artists he admires, such as California Guitar Trio and Bill Nelson, and King Crimson spinoffs Projeckt One (Fripp, bassists Tony Levin and Trey Gunn, and drummer Bill Bruford) and Projeckt Two (Fripp, Belew, Gunn). In 1997 Fripp and his former management, publishing, and record company, Editions EG, settled a seven-year legal dispute over alleged nonpayment of royalties and other abuses.

Bill Frisell

Born William Frisell, Mar. 18, 1951, Baltimore, MD
1983—*In Line* (ECM) 1985—*Rambler* 1988—*Lookout for Hope; Works* 1989—*Before We Were Born* (Elektra/Musician) 1990—*Is That You?* 1991—*Where in the World?* 1993—*Have a Little Faith* (Elektra/Nonesuch) 1994—*This Land* 1995—*High Sign/One Week; Go West* 1996—*Quartet* 1997—*Nashville* 1998—*Gone, Just Like a Train* 1999—*Good Dog, Happy Man;* 2000—*Ghost Town* (Nonesuch) 2001—*Blues Dream.*
With Vernon Reid: 1986—*Smash & Scatteration* (Rykodisc).
With Fred Hersch: 1998—*Songs We Know* (Nonesuch).
With Burt Bacharach and Elvis Costello: 1999—*The Sweetest Punch* (Decca).

Bill Frisell first emerged as one of rock's leading improvisational guitar players, a trained jazz musician who initially played primarily with the downtown New York avant-garde scene (although he is now based in Seattle). He has over the years become a bandleader and composer of considerable note. Frisell's music encompasses rock, jazz, country, and blues with great humor, passion, and insight.

Frisell grew up in Denver, the son of a tuba- and bass-playing father. He initially played clarinet and saxophone, but switched to guitar while studying music at the University of Northern Colorado. He also plays banjo, bass, and ukulele. In 1977 he got a degree in arranging and composition from Berklee College of Music; the next year he moved to New York.

Counting Jimi Hendrix and jazz guitarists Wes Montgomery and Jim Hall among his influences, Frisell has played in a number of collaborative ensembles, including Power Tools with Ronald Shannon Jackson and Melvin Gibbs, Naked City with John Zorn, the Paul Bley Quartet, and the Paul Motian Trio. He has played on nearly 100 albums, including Hal Wilner's tributes to Nino Rota, Charles Mingus, and Walt Disney. He has also worked with Marianne Faithfull, Jan Garbarek, John Scofield, Marc Johnson's Bass Desires, Don Byron, and Caetano Veloso.

Frisell's first album, *In Line,* showcases solo work and duets with bassist Arild Andersen. On *Rambler,* he plays with such out-jazz musicians as trumpeter Kenny Wheeler and Motian. On *Lookout for Hope,* Frisell debuted the Bill Frisell Band, featuring cellist Hank Roberts, bassist Kermit Driscoll, and drummer Joey Baron; the quartet also plays on *Where in the World? Is That You?* was recorded with Wayne Horvitz. *Have a Little Faith* is a collection of covers that includes songs by John Philip Sousa, Sonny Rollins, Charles Ives, Bob Dylan, and Madonna.

In 1995 Frisell released *The High Sign/One Week* and *Go West,* albums comprised of music that he composed for three silent Buster Keaton films. *Quartet* featured trumpet player Ron Miles, violinist Eyvind Kang, and trombonist Curtis Fowlkes. *Nashville,* recorded with members of Alison Krauss' bluegrass band Union Station and singer-songwriter Robin Holcomb, was voted "Album of the Year" in *Downbeat*'s 1998 critics poll. The jazz magazine also named Frisell "Guitarist of the Year" in both 1998 and 1999. *The Sweetest Punch* features Elvis Costello, Cassandra Wilson, and a seven-piece band performing Frisell's arrangements of the songs that appeared on Costello and Burt Bacharach's *Painted From Memory.* Frisell also appears with Bono, Brian Eno, Daniel Lanois, and others on the soundtrack to the Wim Wenders film *Million Dollar Hotel* (2000). He composed and recorded the original soundtrack to Gus Van Sant's remake of *Psycho* (2000).

Fred Frith: See Henry Cow

Lefty Frizzell

Born William Orville Frizzell, Mar. 21, 1928, Corsicana, TX; died July 19, 1975, Nashville, TN
1966—*Lefty Frizzell's Greatest Hits* (Columbia) 1982—*Columbia Historic Edition* 1984—*Lefty Frizzell: His Life—His Music* (Down Home Music) 1991—*The Best of Lefty Frizzell* (Rhino).

Singer Lefty Frizzell was one of the legends of honky-tonk country music; his original vocal style and literate songwriting influenced such C&W artists as Merle Haggard, Willie Nelson, Randy Travis, and Dwight Yoakam.

At age 12, Frizzell had a spot on a children's radio program, and by 16 he was a professional musician. His main musical model was the plaintive vocal style of Jimmie Rodgers, "the Singing Brakeman"; Frizzell's own nickname came from his abilities as a fighter. A demo of Frizzell's song "If You've Got the Money I've Got the Time" brought him to the attention of Columbia Records, which signed him in the early '50s. In the years 1950–54, Frizzell had 15 Top 10 country hits, including the classics "Always Late (With Your Kisses)" (#1, 1951), "Mom and Dad's Waltz" (#2, 1951), "I Want to Be With You Always" (#1, 1951), "Travellin' Blues" (#6, 1951), and "Run 'Em Off" (#8, 1954). Top Nashville piano session man Floyd Cramer was a mainstay in Frizzell's band.

Frizzell became disillusioned by the music industry, however, and was plagued by a drinking problem that would continue until his death. By the late '50s, his hits were scarce (his classic 1959 version of "The Long Black Veil" hit #6 on the C&W chart), and by the early '60s he was all but forgotten. "Saginaw, Michigan" (#1 C&W, 1964) was Frizzell's last major hit. He was in the midst of a comeback when he died from a stroke at age 47. Two years after his death in 1975, the Frizzell tribute album, *To Lefty From Willie,* was released by Willie Nelson. Dwight Yoakam, one of many New Traditionalist Frizzell fans, recorded "Always Late (With Your Kisses)" on his 1987 album *Hillbilly Deluxe.*

Fugazi

Formed 1987, Arlington, VA
Ian MacKaye (b. ca. 1963), gtr., voc.; Guy Picciotto (b. ca. 1966), gtr., voc.; Joe Lally (b. ca. 1964), bass; Brendan Canty (b. ca. 1967), drums.
1988—*Fugazi* EP (Dischord) 1989—*Margin Walker* EP 1990—*Repeater* 1991—*Steady Diet of Nothing* 1993—*In On the Kill Taker* 1995—*Red Medicine* 1998—*End Hits* 1999—*Instrument* soundtrack.

Of all the bands to rise from the '80s American independent hardcore punk scene, Fugazi has remained truest to the DIY ethos, releasing albums on its own successful Dischord label. The band also steadfastly shuns mainstream attention and offers from major record labels. Inspired by the early work of hometown hardcore heroes Bad Brains, Fugazi's sound is a progression on the loud-fast aesthetic practiced by founding member Ian Mackaye's former bands, Embrace and the legendary Minor Threat.

Ian MacKaye started Dischord in the Arlington, Virginia, house he moved into after graduating from Washington, DC's Wilson High School in 1980. (Dischord later moved to a basement office beneath a dry cleaners.) He formed the label to put out records by his first band, the Teen Idles, followed by his next group, Minor Threat, which, along with Black Flag, was one of the most highly regarded hardcore punk bands. Dischord ultimately grew into a major underground force and has sold more than 2 million records since its inception. It released only DC-based acts, including Youth Brigade and the early Henry Rollins punk outfit S.O.A. When Minor Threat broke up in 1983, MacKaye moved on to the short-lived Embrace before teaming up with Happy Go Licky members Guy Picciotto and Brendan Canty in 1987 to form Fugazi. Joe Lally, a native of Rockville, Maryland, had worked as a roadie for one of the Dischord bands before joining Fugazi on bass. The band took its name from the Vietnam War–era acronym for "Fucked Up, Got Ambushed, Zipped In."

Despite the quartet's firm status as an independent entity, with relatively little promotion Fugazi has managed to amass a huge following, consistently packing large venues and selling about 150,000 copies of each album. Fugazi takes a decidedly pragmatic approach to rock & roll, eschewing the excessive rock-star lifestyle. The band keeps its album and concert prices low (for years, its CDs were priced at $8 each and admission to its all-ages shows was $5), renounces drugs and alcohol (Minor Threat inadvertently spawned the "straight-edge" hardcore movement of the mid-'80s via the lyrics to such songs as "Out of Step" and "Straight Edge"), refuses extravagant catering spreads backstage, uses only reputable, "alternative" promoters, and discourages the hardcore rituals of slam dancing and stage diving at shows. On album, Fugazi retains the attitude and angst inherent in the hardcore punk rock of its predecessors, but has slowed the tempos and added dense, metal-like instrumental foundations and the precise syncopations of reggae and the Police. *In On the Kill Taker* was Fugazi's first album to appear on the charts, peaking at #153 in 1993. Fugazi returned to the pop chart with *Red Medicine* (#126, 1995) and *End Hits* (#138, 1998).

By 1997, Lally had launched his own small label, Tolotta. And in 1999 Fugazi was the subject of *Instrument,* a film that documented 11 years of collected band footage on and off stage. A soundtrack album included previously unreleased tracks and new instrumental music recorded especially for the film.

The Fugees/Lauryn Hill/Wyclef Jean/Pras

Formed East Orange, NJ, ca. 1992
Lauryn Hill (b. May 26, 1975, South Orange, NJ), voc.; Nelust Wyclef Jean (b. Oct. 17, 1970, Haiti), voc., gtr., kybds.; Prakazrel "Pras" Michel (b. Oct. 19, 1972, Brooklyn, NY), voc.
1994—*Blunted on Reality* (Ruffhouse/Columbia) 1996—*The Score; Bootleg Versions.*
Wyclef Jean solo: 1997—*Wyclef Jean Presents the Carnival Featuring Refugee Allstars* (Ruffhouse/Columbia) 2000—*The Ecleftic: 2 Sides II a Book* (Columbia).
Lauryn Hill solo: 1998—*The Miseducation of Lauryn Hill* (Ruffhouse/Columbia).
Pras Michel solo: 1998—*Ghetto Supastar* (Ruffhouse/Columbia).

Invoking the spirit of Bob Marley, avant-garde hip-hoppers the Fugees reinvented rap with their genre-blending recordings. With traces of reggae, folk, rock, soul, country, and Creole, the music of the Fugees symbolizes the interconnectedness of the African diaspora.

Vocalist Lauryn Hill grew up in the suburban environs of South Orange, New Jersey, in a household stocked with Curtis Mayfield, Stevie Wonder, Aretha Franklin, and Gladys Knight records. Hill was introduced to Pras Michel through a mutual high school friend, and the two came up with the idea for a rap group that would rhyme in different languages. Calling themselves Tranzlator Crew, Hill, Michel, and another female vocalist recorded some songs in a West Orange, New Jersey, studio. Michel's cousin, multi-instrumentalist Wyclef Jean, decided to stop by the studio and check out his relative's new group. Jean soon replaced the other female vocalist as the third member of Tranzlator Crew, and the trio of Hill, Michel, and Jean began hanging out regularly and exchanging musical ideas in the basement of Jean's uncle's house across town in East Orange.

Renaming the group the Fugees, the trio began auditioning for label representatives and caught the ear of Ruffhouse cofounder Chris Schwartz. Ruffhouse, which also discovered Latino rap group Cypress Hill, signed the group and released the mediocre debut, *Blunted on Reality* (#62 R&B, 1994). Except for the folky "Vocab" (#91 R&B, 1995) and the dancehall groove of the "Nappy Heads" remix (#49 pop, #52 R&B, 1994), *Blunted on Reality* failed to showcase the trio's talents.

The group really found its voice on the followup *The Score* (#1 pop, #1 R&B, 1996). Brimming with postcolonial discourse and a gumbo of Afrocentric rhythms, the album exploded into the pop music world. Hill's evocative take on Roberta Flack's 1973 hit "Killing Me Softly" (#2 pop, #1 R&B, 1996) was incessantly played on pop, R&B, hip-hop, and Adult Contemporary radio and won a Grammy for Best R&B Performance by a Duo or Group with Vocal. Other prominent songs like "Fu-Gee-La" (#29 pop, #13 R&B, 1995), "Ready or Not" (#22 R&B, 1996), and a cover of Bob Marley's "No Woman, No Cry" (#38 pop, #58 R&B, 1996) helped *The Score* win the Best Rap Album Grammy as well. *The Score* eventually sold more than 17 million copies, making the Fugees the biggest-selling rap group up to that time.

Following 1996's *Bootleg Versions* (#50 R&B), a collection of remixed and unreleased tracks, the group split up, reportedly so members could pursue solo careers. The first to release an album, Jean emphasized his Haitian roots with *Carnival* (#16 pop, #4 R&B, 1997). Its "We Trying to Stay Alive" (#45 pop, #14 R&B, 1997), "Guantanamera" (#23 R&B, 1997), and "Gone Till November" (#7 pop, #9 R&B, 1998) all achieved chart success, while "Jaspora" and "Yelé" feature Jean rapping and singing in the Haitian patois. After producing a number of R&B and hip-hop recordings, including Destiny's Child's "No, No, No (Part 2)" (#3 pop, #1 R&B, 1997) and Pras's "Ghetto Supastar (That Is What You Are)" (#15 pop, #8 R&B, 1998), Jean recorded *The Ecleftic: 2 Sides II a Book* (#9 pop, #3 R&B, 2000).

Though Pras' album *Ghetto Supastar* (#55 pop, #35 R&B, 1998) made some noise, it was Hill's *The Miseducation of Lauryn Hill* (#1 pop, #1 R&B, 1998) that dominated 1998's pop-music headlines, distinguishing the songstress from her Fugee counterparts. Her romantic involvement with Rohan Marley (Bob Marley's son) and the birth of the couple's first child was reflected in such hits as "Doo Wop (That Thing)" (#1 pop, #2 R&B, 1998), "Nothing Even Matters" (#25 R&B, 1999), "To Zion" (#77 R&B, 1999), and "Everything Is Everything" (#35 pop, #14 R&B, 1999). Her "Lost Ones" (#27 R&B, 1998) and "Ex-Factor" (#7 R&B, 1999) helped inflame the rumor that the end of a love affair between Hill and Jean led to the Fugees' breakup. Hill swept 1999's Grammy Awards show, winning five awards: Album of the Year, Best R&B Album, Best New Artist, Best Female R&B Vocal Performance, and Best R&B Song. *The Miseducation of Lauryn Hill* later stirred controversy when four musicians on the album claimed that they helped write and produce certain songs that were credited only to Hill. In February 2001 Hill settled the legal dispute by paying the musicians an undisclosed sum of money. Since high school, Hill has also pursued acting, appearing in the daytime soap *As the World Turns* as well as 1993's *Sister Act 2: Back in the Habit.*

The Fugs

Formed 1965, New York, NY
Ed Sanders (b. Aug. 17, 1939, Kansas City, MO), voc., gtr.; Tuli Kupferberg (b. Sep. 28, 1923, New York), voc.; Ken Weaver (b. Galveston, TX), voc., drums.
1965—*The Village Fugs* (Broadside/Folkways) 1966—*The Fugs* (ESP) 1967—*Virgin Fugs* 1968—*Tenderness Junction* (Reprise); *It Crawled Into My Hand, Honest* 1969—*The Belle of Avenue A* (group disbands) 1970—*Golden Filth: Live At the Fillmore East* 1984—(group re-forms: Sanders; Kupferberg; Weaver; + Steve Taylor, gtr., voc.; + Coby Batty [b. Nov. 25, 1955], voc., drums; + Scott Petito [b. July 17, 1958], bass, gtr., kybds.) *Refuse to Be Burnt-Out* (Olufsen & New Rose) 1985—*No More Slavery* 1986—*Star Peace* 1988—*Fugs Live in Woodstock* 1992—*Songs From a Portable Forest* (Gazell) 1994—*Fugs Live From the '60s* (Ace) 1995—*The Real Woodstock Festival.*
Ed Sanders solo: 1970—*Sanders Truckstop* (Reprise) 1972—*Beer Cans on the Moon* 1992—*Songs in Ancient Greek* (Olufsen) 1996—*American Bard.*
Tuli Kupferberg solo: 1987—*Tuli and Friends* (Shimmy Disc).

These perverse post-Beatnik poets were too pointedly topical and obscene for mass consumption, but the Fugs were the most relentless comic satirists of the hippie era. Their targets included sexual repression, rock, politics, and the foibles of humanity in general.

Ed Sanders had graduated from New York University in 1960 with a B.A. in ancient Greek; in 1961 he marched on the Pentagon. He was a published poet who briefly ran the Peace Eye bookstore and published the literary magazine *Fuck You.* Tuli Kupferberg, a lanky, hirsute, perennially bedraggled-looking figure whom Beat poet Allen Ginsberg immortalized in *Howl* as "the person who jumped off the Brooklyn Bridge and survived," was also a published poet, and a graduate of Brooklyn College.

With Ken Weaver and an ever-changing roster of backing musicians—including Peter Stampfel and Steve Weber of the Holy Modal Rounders, guitarists Vinny Leary, Pete Kearney, and Ken Pine, bassists John Anderson and Charles Larkey, and drummer Bob Mason—they became a long-running off-off Broadway rock-theater phenomenon in Greenwich Village, with audiences often walking out on their scathingly profane, put-down-riddled theater-of-outrageous-absurdity performances.

After more than 900 shows at the Players Theater and the Bridge Theater, they began touring the United States. In the fall of 1968 they toured Europe, at one point trying unsuccessfully to get into then-troubled Czechoslovakia in order to lie down in front of invading Russian tanks as a protest against the invasion.

In the early '70s Sanders released solo albums on Reprise, *Sanders' Truckstop* and *Beer Cans on the Moon,* and reported on the Charles Manson trial for the underground press; he later wrote a best-selling book about the murder case and the trial, *The Family.* A collection of his poems, *Thirsting for Peace in a Raging Century,* won an American Book Award in 1988. A CD, *Songs in Ancient Greek,* was released in 1992. In 2000 he began publishing his eight-volume *America, A History in Verse.*

During the '60s Kupferberg published a number of books, including *1001 Ways to Make Love* and *1001 Ways to Beat the Draft.* He went on to become an established political cartoonist, whose work has been seen in more than 100 publications. He became the director of Revolting Theater, and performed at colleges and New York venues, as well as gigging with his band, Tuli and the Fuxxons. For a number of years he has produced a cable program on New York City's public access channels.

The band regrouped in 1984 for a reunion concert and remained together into the 21st century, touring and releasing records.

The Bobby Fuller Four

Formed mid-'60s, El Paso, TX
Bobby Fuller (b. Oct. 22, 1943, Baytown, TX; d. July 18, 1966, Los Angeles, CA), gtr., voc.; Randy Fuller, bass; DeWayne Quirico, drums; Jim Reese, gtr.
1965—*The Bobby Fuller Four* (Mustang) 1966—*KRLA King of the Wheels* 1987—*The Best of the Bobby Fuller Four (1965–1966)* (Rhino).

"I Fought the Law" established the Bobby Fuller Four for a half-year of stardom in 1966. The group, all Texans, established a reputation in El Paso, then moved to L.A. "Let Her Dance" became popular in the Southwest in 1965, and "I Fought the Law"—written by a member of Buddy Holly's Crickets, Sonny Curtis—reached #9 in 1966. (The Clash later covered it on *The Clash.)* A Buddy Holly cover, "Love's Made a Fool of You" (#26, 1966), was a followup hit.

In July 1966 Bobby Fuller died under mysterious circumstances in his car parked in front of his Hollywood home. The fact that he had been beaten up and had ingested gasoline was not released to the public at the time. Although the police ruled his death a suicide, friends speculated that he was murdered, possibly by mobsters. Afterward, the Randy Fuller Four continued, but without success.

Jesse "Lone Cat" Fuller

Born Mar. 12, 1896, Jonesboro, GA; died Jan. 29, 1976, Oakland, CA
1963—*San Francisco Bay Blues* (Prestige) 1993—*Jazz, Folk Songs, Spirituals & Blues* (Fantasy).

Jesse Fuller was a country-bluesman, a one-man band, and the composer of "San Francisco Bay Blues." Fuller never knew his father, and the man his mother lived with often brutally mistreated him. By age five Fuller had learned to play a homemade stringed mouth bow. After living with his mother's relatives a few years, he left home at 10 and began traveling around the South and Midwest, working odd jobs and playing the blues.

In the early '20s Fuller was discovered outside Universal Film Studios shining shoes. He was given bit parts in *The Thief of Bagdad, East of Suez,* and other movies, for which he was paid $7.50 a day. During his middle age, he worked a succession of jobs, including cowherding, broom making, and car washing. He remained committed to music, however, and in the late '30s debuted on radio station KNX (Oakland) singing "John Henry."

In 1951 Fuller decided to devote himself entirely to his music, and over the next decade he built a small cult following. He often used a one-man-band setup he had devised that allowed him to play guitar, harmonica, hi-hat with castanets, and his own invention, the footdella (a piano–string bass operated with a foot pedal). He wrote "San Francisco Bay Blues" in 1954, and five years later appeared at the Monterey Jazz Festival. Fuller became popular in Europe and England, and toured the U.S. regularly throughout the '60s. It wasn't until the mid-'50s that he began recording, cutting his early tracks for Prestige (later reissued on Fantasy). In 1976 he died of heart disease.

Lowell Fulson

Born Mar. 31, 1921, Choctaw Indian territory, OK; died Mar. 6, 1999, Long Beach, CA
1966—*Tramp* (Kent) 1969—*Now* (United) 1972—*On a Heavy Bag* (Jewel) 1973—*I've Got the Blues* 1975—*Lowell Fulson* (Arhoolie); *The Ol' Blues Singer* (Granite) 1977—*Hung Down Head* (Chess); *Blues Masters* 1978—*Lovemaker* (Big Town) 1983—*One More Blues* (Evidence) 1988—*It's a Good Day* (Rounder) 1992—*Hold On* (Bullseye Blues) 1995—*Them Update Blues* 1997—*My First Recordings* (Arhoolie); *The Complete Chess Masters* (MCA).

A journeyman R&B performer whose recording career spans four decades, Fulson hit the pop chart in the mid-'60s. He is best known, however, as a songwriter, several of whose compositions have become modern blues classics.

Of Native American and African descent, Fulson (not Fulsom, as is often written) grew up in Tulsa, where many of his relatives played stringed instruments. He left home around age 17 to join a traveling country & western string band. In 1940 he moved to Texas, where he played with the popular Texas Alexander. Shortly thereafter he was drafted and served in the Pacific, where he often entertained fellow soldiers.

A few months after his discharge in late 1945, Fulson moved to California. In 1946 he began recording in Oakland, concentrating on dance-hall blues numbers he had learned during his time with Alexander. His R&B hits began in 1948 with "Three O'Clock Blues" (a.k.a. "Three O'Clock in the Morning"), "You Know That I Love You," and "Come Back Baby" for Downbeat. They continued on the Swingtime label in 1950 and 1951 with "Every Day I Have the Blues" (#5 R&B, 1950), "Blue Shadows" (#1 R&B, 1950), and "Lonesome Christmas" (#7 R&B, 1950).

By the mid-'50s Fulson was recording for Chess/Checker, notably "Reconsider Baby" (#3 R&B, 1954), now a blues standard. His brief pop success began in 1965, when "Black Nights" (#11 R&B, 1965), on the Kent label, became a minor hit, followed two years later by "Make a Little Love" (#20 R&B, 1967), and his most successful release, "Tramp" (#5 R&B, 1967), which almost cracked the pop Top 50. Otis Redding and Carla Thomas subsequently had hits with Fulson's songs. In 1960 Fulson married Guitar Slim's widow, Sadie; she died in 1992. In 1993 he was inducted into the Rhythm & Blues Hall of Fame; during his life, he received five W.C. Handy Awards. Fulson continued to tour and perform around the world until 1997, when declining health caused him to scale back on his shows. He died in 1999. His final studio work, 1995's *Them Update Blues,* was nominated for a Grammy for Best Traditional Blues Album.

Fun Boy Three: See the Specials

Annette Funicello

Born Oct. 22, 1942, Utica, NY
1959—*Annette* (Buena Vista) 1960—*Annette Sings Anka; Hawaiiannette; Italianette* 1961—*Dance Annette* 1962—*Annette Funicello; Annette—The Story of My Teens . . . and Sixteen Songs That Tell It* 1993—*Annette: A Musical Reunion With America's Girl Next Door* (Disney)

Annette Funicello was the first female rock singer who needed only one name, for she was indeed America's girl next door. The first to admit she is not a great singer, Funicello experienced something of a musical revival in the '80s when L.A. disc jockey Rodney Bingenheimer began playing her old records, and since then an array of rockers, from the B-52's Fred Schneider to Redd Kross have noted her influence.

Walt Disney discovered her at a dance-school recital in Burbank, California, and immediately cast her as the last of 24 children for his new kid's TV show, *The Mickey Mouse Club.* Early in the show's original run, from fall 1955 to early 1959 (it was shown in syndication through the '70s), Annette emerged as the most popular Mouseketeer, and when the show was canceled she alone remained under contract to Disney. There she costarred in such films as *Babes in Toyland* (1961) and *The Monkey's Uncle* (1965), the title theme of which she recorded with the Beach Boys. She also guested on numerous television series through the '80s.

Pairing Annette with songwriters Richard and Robert Sherman, Disney launched her recording career with a series of catchy but innocent hits: "Tall Paul" (#7, 1959), "First Name Initial" (#20, 1959), and "Pineapple Princess" (#11, 1960). She became a regular on Dick Clark's shows and soon befriended other teen idols, including Paul Anka, with whom she fell in love. He wrote "Puppy Love" and "Put Your Head on My Shoulder" for her. Annette made her biggest contribution to teen culture, however, in a series of beach-party films costarring Frankie Avalon: *Beach Party* (1963), *Muscle Beach Party, Bikini Beach, Pajama Party* (all 1964), and *Beach Blanket Bingo* (1965).

She retired from show business after marrying in 1965, although she made rare television appearances (and in 1968 had a cameo role in the Monkees' surrealistic *Head*) and in the mid-'70s was the spokesperson for Skippy peanut butter. In 1987, while filming *Back to the Beach* with longtime friend Avalon, Funicello noticed the first symptoms of multiple sclerosis. She and Avalon toured the country through 1988, and in 1992 she publicly announced that she was suffering from MS. She has since become a spokesperson for others with the illness and founded the Annette Funicello Fund for Neurological Disorders. In 1994 she published her well-received autobiography, *A Dream Is a Wish Your Heart Makes: My Story* (cowritten with Patricia Romanowski). The following year, the book was the basis for a made-for-TV movie of the same name in which Annette and her real-life family appear briefly. In years since, Funicello has been largely out of the pubic eye.

Funkadelic: See George Clinton

Harvey Fuqua: See the Moonglows

Richie Furay: See Poco

Kenny G

Born Kenneth Gorelick, June 5, 1956, Seattle, WA
1982—*Kenny G* (Arista) 1984—*G Force* 1985—*Gravity* 1986—*Duotones* 1988—*Silhouette* 1989—*Live* 1992—*Breathless* 1994—*Miracles: The Holiday Album* 1996—*The Moment* 1997—*Greatest Hits* 1999—*Classics in the Key of G; Faith: A Holiday Album.*

President Bill Clinton spoke for a lot of Americans in the early '90s when he called Kenny G one of his favorite jazz musicians. Most jazz purists have dismissed the saxophonist—Kenny G, that is—as a purveyor of soulless fluff that appeals primarily to fans of sentimental pop and New Age music. Nonetheless, Kenny G's instantly recognizable, smooth, mellow "contemporary jazz" style has made him one of the most commercially successful instrumental recording artists in history, selling more than 30 million albums worldwide.

Kenny G took up the saxophone as a child, after seeing the instrument played by a soloist on *The Ed Sullivan Show.* Although he started on alto sax and learned to play tenor as well, the soprano sax eventually became his signature instrument. At 17, he played in Barry White's Love Unlimited Orchestra, and in the mid-'70s he became the only white musician in a Seattle-based funk outfit called Cold, Bold, and Together. After graduating magna cum laude from the University of Washington, with a degree in accounting, Kenny G spent a few years playing in Oregon's Jeff Lorber Fusion Band, then signed with Arista Records as a solo act in the early '80s.

The musician's first three albums sold respectably for instrumentals, but it was his fourth, 1986's *Duotones,* that proved the charm, reaching #6 on the pop chart and spawning the #4 single "Songbird." *Silhouette* followed its predecessor into the Top 10 (#8, 1988), and includes a couple of singles that did well on the R&B and Adult Contemporary charts, notably "We've Saved the Best for Last," on which Smokey Robinson sang. *Breathless* (#2 pop, #2 R&B, #1 Contemporary Jazz, 1992) featured vocals by Peabo Bryson and Aaron Neville, plus the single "Forever in Love," which won a Grammy for Best Instrumental Composition. Kenny G has also recorded with R&B divas Aretha Franklin, Whitney Houston, Dionne Warwick, Natalie Cole, and Toni Braxton, as well as with his even more critically reviled peer Michael Bolton. In 1993 the saxophonist was the only nonsinging pop star to appear on Frank Sinatra's *Duets* album. The following year's *Miracles: The Holiday Album* became one of the best-selling Christmas discs of all time, while 1996's *The Moment* went double platinum and hit #2 on the pop albums chart and #1 on the Top Contemporary Jazz Albums chart. In late 1997, he set the record for the longest-held note—45 minutes and 47 seconds—scoring a place in the *Guinness Book of World Records.* The 1999 album *Classics in the Key of G* was a collection of jazz standards such as "Round Midnight" and "In a Sentimental Mood."

Peter Gabriel

Born Feb. 13, 1950, Cobham, Eng.
1977—*Peter Gabriel* (Atco) 1978—*Peter Gabriel* (Atlantic)

1980—*Peter Gabriel* 1982—*Peter Gabriel (Security)* (Geffen) 1983—*Peter Gabriel Plays Live* 1985—*Birdy* soundtrack 1986—*So* 1989—*Passion: Music for the Last Temptation of Christ* 1990—*Shaking the Tree: Sixteen Golden Greats* 1992—*Us* 1994—*Secret World Live* 1999—*Ovo: Millennium Show* (Real World/Virgin) 2001—*Up* (Geffen).

As frontman for the British progressive-rock band Genesis [see entry], Peter Gabriel cowrote, sang, and acted out elaborate story songs, wearing masks and costumes. Since leaving Genesis in 1975 to begin a solo career, Gabriel has revealed a new array of guises, including soundtrack composer, social activist, world-music aficionado and benefactor, music-video innovator, and multimedia artist.

Gabriel's first solo album was an eponymously titled effort, as were his next three. (The idea, he once explained, was to suggest issues, as one would for a magazine.) The first and second LPs drew attention for the respective singles "Solsbury Hill" and "D.I.Y." The third, produced by Steve Lillywhite, yielded "Games Without Frontiers" (#48, 1980) and showed Gabriel striving to break rock conventions: For instance, drummers Jerry Marotta and Phil Collins (Gabriel's former Genesis bandmate) were prohibited from using cymbals.

Gabriel's fourth album, subtitled *Security* (1982), was the singer's first to go gold; it also gave him his first Top 40 single with "Shock the Monkey." That same year, Gabriel financed the World of Music, Arts, and Dance (WOMAD) Festival, designed to bring African and Far Eastern music—which had increasingly influenced his work—to Western ears. To offset the festival's debt, he staged a Genesis reunion concert and released a WOMAD album, featuring cuts by himself, Robert Fripp (the producer of his second LP), and Pete Townshend alongside ethnic-music sources. The WOMAD Festival became an annual event, and the organization eventually spawned an education program and record label.

In 1984 Gabriel was tapped to score Alan Parker's film *Birdy;* the singer consequently won the Grand Jury Prize at Cannes. In 1985 he founded Real World Inc., aimed at developing cross-cultural projects in technology and the arts. The following year, he started the United Nations University for Peace, intended to fund an international human-rights computer network, and set up Real World Studios, a recording complex near Bath, England, where artists including Van Morrison and New Order have since worked. (A Real World record label, dedicated to exposing ethnic music from around the world, was established in 1989.)

The year 1986 also saw Gabriel's commercial breakthrough. *So,* coproduced with Daniel Lanois, reached #2 and produced the funky, chart-topping "Sledgehammer," which Gabriel accompanied with a groundbreaking video full of provocative live-action-animation images. A video for "Big Time" (#8, 1987) followed suit. Other singles included "In Your Eyes" (#26, 1986) and "Don't Give Up" (#72, 1987), a duet with Kate Bush.

Gabriel joined U2, Sting, and others for a 1986 tour on behalf of Amnesty International. A 1988 Amnesty tour followed, with Gabriel, Sting, Bruce Springsteen, Tracy Chapman, and

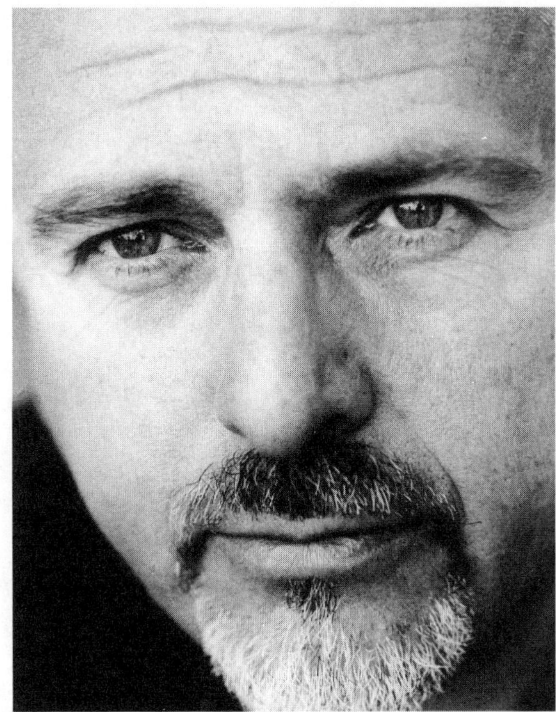

Peter Gabriel

Youssou N'Dour (who had sung on *So*). Also in 1988, Gabriel performed "Biko," his tribute to South African civil-rights martyr Steven Biko (from 1980's *Peter Gabriel*) at a Nelson Mandela tribute at London's Wembley Stadium, and composed music for Martin Scorsese's controversial adaptation of *The Last Temptation of Christ.* The 1989 soundtrack album won a Grammy for Best New Age Performance.

Gabriel's next studio album, 1992's *Us,* was inspired by his mid-'80s divorce from childhood sweetheart Jill Moore and the breakup of a subsequent relationship with actress Rosanna Arquette. The album reached #2 and generated "Digging in the Dirt" (#52, 1992) and "Steam" (#32, 1992). In 1993 Gabriel enlisted an international roster including Sinéad O'Connor, Crowded House, James, and P.M. Dawn for a WOMAD tour. The 1994 double CD *Secret World Live* was recorded during two Italian concerts in 1993.

Also in 1994 the musician added another branch to his corporation, called Real World Multi Media, to use technology as another creative outlet. The division published its first CD-ROM, "Xplora 1," an interactive look into Gabriel's various projects, that year. A followup, "Eve," featuring Gabriel's music and the work of several visual artists, was released in 1997. The musician helped develop an attraction for the London Millennium Dome, which opened on New Year's Day 2000. Although by this time Gabriel seemed to be more involved in the aspects of his Real World organization than performing himself, he did appear on N'Dour's 2000 album, *Joko,* and is said to be working on a followup album to *Us.*

Rory Gallagher

Born Mar. 2, 1949, Ballyshannon, Ire.; died June 14, 1995, London, Eng.
1971—*Rory Gallagher* (Atco) 1972—*Deuce* (Polydor); *Live!* 1973—*Blueprint; Tattoo* 1974—*Irish Tour '74; In the Beginning* (Emerald Gem) 1975—*Against the Grain* (Chrysalis); *Sinner . . . and Saint* (Polydor) 1976—*The Story So Far; Calling Card* (Chrysalis); *The Best Years* (Polydor) 1978—*Photo Finish* (Chrysalis) 1979—*Top Priority* 1980—*Stage Struck* 1982—*Jinx* 1987—*Defender* (I.R.S.) 1990—*Fresh Evidence* 1999—*BBC Sessions* (BMG/Buddah).
With Taste: 1969—*Taste* (Atco).

Blues guitarist Rory Gallagher grew up in Cork, Ireland and got his first guitar at age nine. He played in pickup bands until leaving school at age 15 and toured in the early '60s with the Fontana Showband. By the time the group broke up in 1965, it was called the Impact. Gallagher then began working regularly in Hamburg, Germany, and in Ireland with bassist Charlie McCracken and ex-Them drummer John Wilson in a power trio he called Taste. The band moved to London in 1969 and released the first of several guitar showcase LPs, which met with some enthusiasm in the U.K. and Europe. Taste specialized in hard-rocking versions of blues and country chestnuts like "Sugar Mama." The group broke up in 1971, and Gallagher began leading small bands under his own name.

Bucking all trends, he subsequently conducted a moderately successful solo career, with increasing emphasis on his own blues-rock material. Gallagher played on Muddy Waters' *The London Sessions* (1972) and on the star-studded 1978 comeback LP by English skiffle star Lonnie Donegan. He regularly tours in the U.S., Britain, and Europe; a 1974 Irish tour was the subject of a documentary by director Tony Palmer. Gallagher died of complications following a liver transplant.

Gang of Four

Formed 1977, Leeds, Eng.
Jon King (June 8, 1955, London, Eng.), voc., melodica; Hugo Burnham (b. Mar. 25, 1956, London), drums; Andy Gill (b. Jan. 1, 1956, Manchester, Eng.), gtr.; Dave Allen (Dec. 23, 1955, Cambria, Eng.), bass.
1978—*Damaged Goods* EP (Fast Product, U.K.) 1980—*Entertainment!* (Warner Bros.) 1981—*Solid Gold* (– Allen; + Sara Lee) 1982—*Another Day, Another Dollar* EP; *Songs of the Free* (– Burnham) 1983—*Hard* 1984—*At the Palace* (Phonogram, U.K.) (group disbands) 1990—*A Brief History of the 20th Century* (Warner Bros.) (group re-forms: King; Gill) 1991—*Mall* (Polydor) 1995—*Shrinkwrapped* (Castle) 1998—*100 Flowers Bloom* (Rhino).

The English-born Gang of Four played dissonant, dub-reggae-influenced, atonal funk with political lyrics. The band was extremely influential in the U.K. and a solid concert draw in the U.S. The group started at art school in Leeds in 1977, naming itself after a Chinese Communist political faction associated with Mao Tse-Tung's widow. Gang of Four released its debut EP, *Damaged Goods,* on the independent Fast Product label. Touring and the record, which became a hit at rock discos, brought the quartet a contract with EMI in Britain and, after a self-financed tour, with Warner Bros. in the U.S., which began a jumbled release schedule. (*Entertainment!* was released in Britain in October 1979 and in the U.S. in May 1980, for example.)

In the middle of the U.S. tour supporting *Solid Gold,* bassist Dave Allen quit; he was replaced on tour by Busta "Cherry" Jones, who had performed with Talking Heads and Chris Spedding. Later in 1981 bassist Sara Lee, who had been a member of the League of Gentlemen with Robert Fripp, joined the Gang of Four as a fulltime member. On its 1982 tour, the Gang of Four appeared as a five-piece group with vocalist Edi Reader. Although its music had apparently been too raw for U.S. radio, the group received extensive play in clubs for such danceable British hits as "At Home, He's a Tourist," "Damaged Goods," and "I Love a Man in Uniform."

In 1983 King and Gill fired Burnham and used a drum machine on *Hard,* ironically attacked by critics as sounding too soft. Drummer Stephen Goulding of Graham Parker and the Rumour was added for a tour, while Burnham became a record industry A&R executive (after stints at Island and Imago, he landed at Quincy Jones' Qwest label). Citing musical differences, King and Gill disbanded Gang of Four in 1984; Allen and Burnham played an encore at a London farewell show.

Dave Allen went on to form Shriekback (with ex-XTC and League of Gentlemen keyboardist Barry Andrews) [see entry], King Swamp, and Low Pop Suicide. In addition, Allen founded the independent label World Domination; in 1994, that label released Allen's first solo album, *The Elastic Purejoy.*

Andy Gill produced the Red Hot Chili Peppers' debut album and worked on film soundtracks. (Allen and Jon King cowrote the music for 1984's *The Karate Kid.*) King formed two bands, Mechanic Preachers and King Butcher, before he and Gill re-formed Gang of Four for the critically well-received *Mall* (1991). The group—dubbed by critics the Gang of Two—also released *Shrinkwrapped* (1995), and toured as a four-piece that included Curve drummer Steve Monti, before moving on to other endeavors. A 1998 compilaton, *100 Flowers Bloom,* put the band's history in context.

Gang Starr

Formed 1988, Brooklyn, NY
The Guru Keith E. (b. Keith Elam, July 17, 1966, Boston, MA), voc.; DJ Premier (b. Chris Martin, Mar. 21, 1969, Prairie View, TX), DJ.
1989—*No More Mr. Nice Guy* (Wild Pitch) 1991—*Step in the Arena* (Chrysalis) 1992—*Daily Operation* 1994—*Hard to Earn* 1998—*Moment of Truth* (Noo Trybe/Virgin) 1999—*Full Clip: A Decade of Gang Starr.*
Guru solo: 1993—*Jazzmatazz* (Chrysalis) 1995—*Jazzmatazz*

Gang Starr: Guru, DJ Premier

II: The New Reality; Guru Presents Ill Kid Records (Payday/ London) 2000—*Guru's Jazzmatazz: Street Soul* (Virgin).

Gang Starr's music honors hip-hop's jazz roots. Indeed, the duo's biggest break came when director Spike Lee brought them together with saxophonist Branford Marsalis to collaborate on a piece for the film *Mo' Better Blues.*

Keith Elam (his Guru moniker stands for "Gifted Unlimited Rhymes Universal") formed the initial version of Gang Starr in his native Boston, where his father was the city's first black judge. Elam rebelled against his upbringing and moved to New York in 1983 to seek a career in music, but not before studying business at Morehouse College in Atlanta. In the mid-'80s Elam heard a demo tape by Chris Martin, a DJ from Brooklyn who was then studying computer science at Prairie View A&M University in Texas. When Martin returned to New York, the two moved into a Brooklyn apartment and began jamming.

Gang Starr's first album featured the songs "Positivity" and "Jazz Music," which pointed in the direction the duo would explore further on later albums. Gang Starr's major-label debut, *Step in the Arena,* reached #19, R&B. After the release of *Daily Operation,* Elam announced plans to do a solo project of jazz/hip-hop fusion music as Guru, featuring noted jazzmen Courtney Pine, Marsalis, and others. The resulting album, *Jazzmatazz* (#94), came out in 1993. A 1995 sequel, *Jazzmatazz II: The New Reality* (#71 pop, #16 R&B, 1995), added soul to the mix and featured Donald Byrd, Meshell Ndegéocello, and Chaka Khan. And a third chapter in 2000, *Guru's Jazzmatazz: Street Soul,* gathered Macy Gray, Herbie Hancock, the Roots, Isaac Hayes, and others. Meanwhile, Premier set up shop as a busy producer, working with the likes of KRS-ONE, Jay-Z, Big Daddy Kane, Heavy D., and the Notorious B.I.G. He also announced plans for his own solo project.

The duo reconvened for 1994's *Hard to Earn* (#25 pop, #2 R&B, 1994) and 1998's *Moment of Truth* (#6 pop, #1 R&B), which finally brought Gang Starr some mainstream success and its first gold album.

The Gap Band

Formed early 1970s, Los Angeles, CA
Ronnie Wilson, voc., trumpet, kybds.; Charles Wilson, lead voc., kybds.; Robert Wilson, bass, voc.; + other musicians.
1974—*Magician's Holiday* (Shelter) 1977—*The Gap Band* (Tattoo) 1979—*The Gap Band II* (Mercury) 1980—*The Gap Band III* 1982—*Gap Band IV* (Total Experience) 1983—*Gap Band V—Jammin'* 1985—*Gap Gold/Best of the Gap Band; Gap Band VI* 1986—*Gap Band VII; The 12" Collection* (Mercury) 1987—*Straight From the Heart* (Total Experience) 1989—*Round Trip* (Capitol) 1994—*Best Of* (Mercury); *Testimony* (Rhino) 1995—*Ain't Nothin' But a Party* 1999—*Y2K: Funkin' Till 2000 Comz* (Big Trax/Private I/Island/Mercury).
Charlie Wilson solo: 1992—*You Turn My Life Around* (Bon Ami) 2000—*Bridging the Gap* (Major Hits/Universal).

As the Gap Band, the three Wilson brothers, natives of Tulsa, Oklahoma, became one of the most popular funk bands of the '80s. Their father was a Pentecostal minister and their mother a pianist, and every Sunday the boys sang before their father's sermon. When they started the band in the early '70s, they named themselves using the first initials of three neighborhood streets—Greenwood, Archer, and Pine—to form Gap.

By 1974 they had met Leon Russell, who signed them to his Shelter Records, where they cut one album. They also performed as Russell's backup band for several years. In the mid-'70s the Wilsons moved to Los Angeles, where they recorded one gospel-styled single, "This Place Called Heaven," for A&M. They then moved to RCA-distributed Tattoo Records and cut a self-titled album that attracted some attention.

The Gap Band signed to Mercury Records, and "Shake," "Steppin' (Out)," and "I Don't Believe You Want to Get Up and Dance (Oops, Up Side Your Head)," all R&B Top 10 hits, brought it to national prominence. Then "Burn Rubber (Why You Wanna Hurt Me)" (#1 R&B, 1980) and "Yearning for Your Love" (#5 R&B, 1981) from the platinum *III* (#16, 1981) established the group as a major act. Another platinum album, *Gap Band IV* (#14) contained two 1982 #1 R&B singles: "Early in the Morning" and "Outstanding"; "You Dropped a Bomb on Me" peaked at #2 (#31 pop).

The Gap Band continued with more R&B hits, including "Party Train" (#3 R&B, 1983), "Jam the Motha' " (#16 R&B, 1983), "Beep a Freak" (#2 R&B, 1984), "I Found My Baby" (#8 R&B, 1985), "Going in Circles" (#2 R&B, 1986), "Big Fun" (#8 R&B, 1986), "I'm Gonna Git You Sucka" (#14 R&B, 1988), "All of My Love" (#1 R&B, 1989), "Addicted to Your Love" (#8 R&B, 1990), and "We Can Make It Alright" (#18 R&B, 1990). The group's only other album to enter the Top 40 was the gold *Gap Band V—Jammin'* (#28, 1983). *The Gap Band II* has also been certified gold.

In 1990 Charles worked with Dave Stewart on the soundtrack of *Rooftops;* the film was a box-office flop. Later he toured with Eurythmics, and cowrote two songs on that group's *We Too Are One* ("Revival" and "Your Love Is Precious"). He has also appeared on records by Ray Charles, Quincy Jones, Snoop Dogg, Zapp, and Mint Condition. He later released his solo debut, *You Turn My Life Around* (#42 R&B, 1992). However, he never left the Gap Band, which continues to tour and record. Despite a lack of recent chart success, the trio became newly revered thanks to the mid- to late-'90s hip-hop-inspired, old-school funk revival.

Garbage

Formed 1993, Madison, WI
Shirley Manson (b. Aug. 26, 1966, Edinburgh, Scot.), voc., gtr.; Butch Vig (b. Aug. 2, 1956, Viroqua, WI), drums; Duke Erikson (b. Jan. 15, 1951, NE), gtr., kybds., bass; Steve Marker (b. March 16, 1959, Minneapolis, MN), gtr., bass.
1995—*Garbage* (Almo Sounds) 1998—*Version 2.0.*

In the age of video, many a band has owed its success to MTV. But Garbage may well be the first to owe its formation, at least in a roundabout way, to the channel. The band formed in 1993 as a trio composed of guitarists Steve Marker and Duke Erikson and drummer Butch Vig. Each had been a producer, with Vig achieving fame for manning the boards for Nirvana's *Nevermind* and the Smashing Pumpkins' *Siamese Dream,* among others. Vig and Marker co-owned Smart Studios in Madison, Wisconsin (where both had attended college), while Vig and Erikson had previously played together in the '80s indie bands Spooner and Firetown. As the new trio began writing and recording, they caught the video for the song "Suffocate Me" by the Scottish band Angelfish on MTV's *120 Minutes.* Intrigued by the sound and presence of the band's fiery redheaded frontwoman, Shirley Manson, they contacted her in her native Edinburgh and invited her to Madison for an audition. Unhappy with her situation in Angelfish (an offshoot of Goodbye Mr. Mackenzie, for whom she had previously played keyboards and sang backup), Manson obliged.

With Manson joining on lead vocals and additional guitar, Garbage began work on its debut album in late 1994, fashioning an edgy but melodic electropop sound underscored by layers of crunchy guitars, samples, and rhythmic loops. Although Vig's reputation as a superstar producer was responsible for much of the advance press interest in Garbage, the outspoken, photogenic Manson would quickly emerge as the media focal point and star of the band. Released in late 1995, the group's self-titled debut climbed to #20 and spawned the #24 pop hit "Stupid Girl" and the #1 Modern Rock hit "#1 Crush" ("Vow," "Queer," and "Only Happy When It Rains" also charted). The album earned them multiple Grammy nominations, including Best New Artist, but they walked away from the awards show empty-handed. Nevertheless, continued radio, video, and print exposure, coupled with a two-year touring schedule, pushed the album's sales past double platinum, paving the way for the #13 chart debut of their second album, 1998's *Version 2.0.* That album went platinum behind the Modern Rock hits "Special" and "Push It." The following year, Garbage recorded the theme song to the 1999 James Bond movie, *The World Is Not Enough.*

In late 2000, the band shelved plans for a B sides compilation in order to concentrate on recording the followup to *Version 2.0,* which was tentatively entitled *Beautiful Garbage* and scheduled for a summer 2001 release.

Jerry Garcia: See the Grateful Dead

Art Garfunkel

Born Nov. 5, 1941, New York, NY
1973—*Angel Clare* (Columbia) 1975—*Breakaway* 1977—*Watermark* 1979—*Fate for Breakfast* 1981—*Scissors Cut* 1988—*Lefty* 1993—*Up 'Til Now* (Sony) 1997—*Songs From a Parent to a Child.*

Art Garfunkel contributed high harmonies, some lead vocals, coproduction, and arranging ideas to Simon and Garfunkel's string of folk-pop hits in the late '60s [see entry]. The duo disbanded in 1970, partially due to Garfunkel's growing interest in film. He has released occasional solo albums since. The two reunited to sing for half a million fans at a September 1981 concert in New York's Central Park and have played together onstage several times in the '90s.

Garfunkel met Paul Simon in grade school in Queens. The two had a teenybopper hit record, "Hey Schoolgirl" (#49, 1958), as Tom and Jerry. Garfunkel also recorded a few unsuccessful sides on his own as "Arty Garr" for the Octavia and Warwick labels in the early '60s. But he had been seriously studying architecture and mathematics at Columbia University before deciding to join Simon in a professional music career.

Garfunkel's first film, *Catch-22,* was shot in 1969 as he and Simon drifted apart, and Garfunkel appeared in *Carnal Knowledge* (1971) and in Nicolas Roeg's *Bad Timing/A Sensual Obsession* (1980). He didn't revive his recording career until 1973, with the lavishly orchestrated *Angel Clare* (#5), which included the first of his solo hit singles, Jimmy Webb's "All I Know" (#9, 1973). His other appearances in the Top 40 in the '70s included "I Only Have Eyes for You" (#18, 1975) and "Breakaway" (#39, 1976). Garfunkel is particularly fond of moody, romantic ballads. His 1975 LP, *Breakaway,* included a studio reunion with Simon for "My Little Town," which became a Top 10 hit. In 1978 Garfunkel teamed up with Simon and James Taylor for a Top 20 version of Sam Cooke's "(What a) Wonderful World"; he also undertook his first U.S. solo tour.

Garfunkel seemed to fade from view in the '80s, but 1993

saw the release of *Up 'Til Now,* which hit the stores around the same time as Garfunkel's acclaimed onstage reunion with his former partner at the Paramount Theater at Madison Square Garden for a 23-concert run. Garfunkel also returned to the big screen that year, costarring in director Jennifer Lynch's controversial film *Boxing Helena.* He has also embarked on several walking campaigns: He crossed Japan by foot in the early '80s and traversed America in 40 intervals between 1984 to 1996. As of 2000 he was making his way across Europe.

Leif Garrett

Born Nov. 8, 1961, Hollywood, CA
1977—*Leif Garrett* (Atlantic) 1978—*Feel the Need* (Scotti Brothers) 1979—*Same Goes for You* 1980—*Can't Explain* 1981—*My Movie of You* 1998—*The Leif Garrett Collection* (Rock 'n' Roll).

Leif Garrett was a mid-'70s television teen idol. He began his recording career at age 16 with a self-titled collection of rock oldies that included "Surfin' U.S.A." (#20, 1977). It became the first of several moderate hits, followed by remakes of Dion's "Runaround Sue" (#13, 1978) and "The Wanderer" (#49, 1978). He made his film debut as a child in the 1969 film *Bob and Carol and Ted and Alice.* Among his other film credits are the *Walking Tall* movies; he briefly had his own television series, *Three for the Road* (1975). The biggest hit of Garrett's career came in 1979, when "I Was Made for Dancin' " hit the Top 10 in both the U.S. and the U.K.

Having spent years in obscurity, Garrett resurfaced in 1999 and discussed the pitfalls of teen stardom and drug addiction on VH1's popular *Behind the Music* series. The show reunited him with his old friend Roland Winkler, who was paralyzed in a 1979 car crash in which Garrett was driving while intoxicated. Garrett also guested on *The Crybaby,* the 1999 album by arty sludge-metal kings the Melvins. He then formed a band called Godspeed and became friendly with shock rocker Marilyn Manson.

Marvin Gaye

Born Marvin Pentz Gay Jr., Apr. 2, 1939, Washington, DC; died Apr. 1, 1984, Los Angeles, CA
1961—*Soulful Mood* (Tamla) 1963—*That Stubborn Kinda Fellow* 1964—*Together* (with Mary Wells) 1965—*How Sweet It Is* 1966—*Greatest Hits; United* (with Tammi Terrell) 1967—*Greatest Hits, vol. 2* 1968—*You're All I Need to Get By; Marvin Gaye and His Girls* (Terrell, Wells, Kim Weston) 1969—*M.P.G.* 1970—*Superhits* 1971—*What's Going On* 1972—*Hits of Marvin Gaye; Trouble Man* soundtrack 1973—*Let's Get It On* 1974—*Anthology; Live* 1976—*The Best of Marvin Gaye* 1978—*Here, My Dear* 1981—*In Our Lifetime* 1982—*Midnight Love* (Columbia) 1985—*Dream of a Lifetime; Romantically Yours* 1990—*The Marvin Gaye Collection* (Tamla/Motown) 1991—*The Last Concert Tour* (Giant) 1993—*Seek and You Shall Find: More of the Best (1963–1981)* (Rhino) 1994—*The Marvin Gaye Classic Collection* (Motown); *The Norman Whitfeld Sessions* 1995—*The Master 1961–1984* 1997—*Vulnerable* 1999—*The Best of Marvin Gaye, the Millennium Collection, vol. 1: The '60s* (MCA) 2000—*The Best of Marvin Gaye, the Millennium Collection, vol. 2: The '70s.*

With a career that exemplified the maturation of romantic black pop into a sophisticated form spanning social and sexual politics, Marvin Gaye was one of the most consistent and enigmatic of the Motown hitmakers. Certainly among the most gifted composers and singers, with a mellifluous tenor and a three-octave vocal range, he was also moody—avoiding TV, rarely performing live, and sometimes not showing up for the few concerts he did schedule. From "How Sweet It Is (To Be Loved by You)" to "Heard It Through the Grapevine," from "What's Going On" to "Sexual Healing," Gaye sang some of the most memorable black pop of the '60s, '70s, and '80s. He was nominated for eight Grammys before winning one in 1983. His life ended tragically one year later—and one day before his 45th birthday—when he was shot to death by his father, an Apostolic preacher, after a violent argument. In many respects, Gaye was, as his friend, the cowriter of "Sexual Healing," and author David Ritz titled his biography of him, a divided soul.

Gaye started singing at age three in church and was soon playing the organ as well. After a stint in the Air Force, he returned to DC and started singing in streetcorner doo-wop groups, including a top local group, the Rainbows. He formed his own group, the Marquees, in 1957. Under the auspices of supporter Bo Diddley, they cut "Wyatt Earp" for the Okeh label. In 1958 Harvey Fuqua heard the group and enlisted it to become the latest version of his ever-changing backing ensemble, the Moonglows [see entry]. As such, Gaye was heard on "Mama Loocie" and other songs for the Chess label in 1959.

Marvin Gaye

By 1961, the group was touring widely. Detroit impresario Berry Gordy Jr. heard the group and quickly signed Gaye to his fledgling Motown organization later that year. Soon after, Gaye married Gordy's sister Anna. Gaye's first duties with the label were as a session drummer (he played on all the early hits by Smokey Robinson and the Miracles).

Gaye got his first hit with his fourth release, "Stubborn Kind of Fellow," in 1962. Over the next 10 years, working with nearly every producer at Motown (including the team of Holland-Dozier-Holland, Smokey Robinson, and Norman Whitfield), he enjoyed over 20 big hits. Although he specialized in midtempo ballads, he also had dance hits: "Hitch Hike" (#30, 1963), the 12-bar blues "Can I Get a Witness" (#22, 1963), which became a virtual anthem among the British mods), and "Baby Don't You Do It" (#27, 1964). But by and large he favored romantic, sometimes sensual ballads. He felt that his desire to move into a more mainstream, sophisticated style was hindered by Motown's emphasis on hits. For a performer as unenthusiastic about some of his material as Gaye later claimed to be, he gave almost every song he ever recorded an inspired reading. His Top 10 hits included "Pride and Joy" (#10, 1963), "I'll Be Doggone" (#8, 1965), "Ain't That Peculiar" (#8, 1965), and "How Sweet It Is to Be Loved by You" (#6, 1965). Among his 39 Top 40 singles of the period were also such unlikely hits as "Try It Baby" (#15, 1964, with background vocals by the Temptations), "You're a Wonderful One" (#15, 1964, with backing vocals by the Supremes), "One More Heartache" (#29, 1966), "Chained" (#32, 1968), and "You" (#34, 1968).

Beginning in 1964 Gaye was teamed with Mary Wells [see entry] for a couple of hits, "Once Upon a Time" (#19, 1964) and "What's the Matter With You" (#17, 1964), and with Kim Weston for "It Takes Two" (#17, 1967). But his greatest duets were with Tammi Terrell: "Ain't No Mountain High Enough" (#19, 1967), "Your Precious Love" (#5, 1967), "Ain't Nothing Like the Real Thing" (#8, 1968), and "You're All I Need to Get By" (#7, 1968), all penned and produced by Nicholas Ashford and Valerie Simpson. In a 1967 concert Terrell collapsed into Gaye's arms onstage, the first sign of the brain tumor that killed her three years later. Although, contrary to popular belief, Gaye and Terrell were not romantically involved (she was involved with Temptation David Ruffin), he was deeply affected by her illness and death. Shortly thereafter Gaye had his biggest solo hit of the '60s with a dejected, paranoid reading of Norman Whitfield and Barrett Strong's "I Heard It Through the Grapevine" (#1, 1968), a song that had already been given a fiery treatment by another Motown act, Gladys Knight and the Pips.

The second, quite distinct phase of Gaye's career—and black popular music—began in 1971 with *What's Going On*. Along with Stevie Wonder, Gaye was one of the first Motown artists to gain complete artistic control of his records. *What's Going On* was a self-composed and -produced song cycle that could rightfully be called a concept album. Berry Gordy Jr., who still maintains that he didn't understand the record, was reluctant to release it. Gaye was vindicated when the album hit #6 and spun off three Top 10 singles: "What's Going On" (#2, 1971), "Inner City Blues (Make Me Wanna Holler)" (#9, 1971), and "Mercy Mercy Me (the Ecology)" (#4, 1971) were impassioned, timeless statements on Vietnam, civil rights, and the state of the world. "What's Going On" has been covered many times in the ensuing years, including a Top 20 version by Cyndi Lauper in 1986.

In 1972 Gaye scored the 20th Century–Fox film *Trouble Man,* and the dark, minimalist title track gave him yet another Top 10 hit (#7, 1973). By 1973, he had shifted his attention to pure eroticism with *Let's Get It On,* the title track of which went to #1. His late-1973 album with Diana Ross, *Diana and Marvin,* produced three fairly successful singles: "You're a Special Part of Me" (#12, 1973), "Don't Knock My Love" (#46, 1974), and "My Mistake (Was to Love You)" (#19, 1974), but this project was one of many things Gaye did with Motown that he felt were forced upon him.

Gaye's rocky marriage of 14 years to Anna Gordy Gaye was the subject of *Here, My Dear* as the '70s closed, with Gaye still reeling from the divorce settlement. He filed for bankruptcy, and his ex-wife later considered suing him for invasion of privacy over the content of *Here, My Dear.* (The album had been precipitated by court hearings in 1976, when a judge instructed Gaye to make good on overdue alimony payments by recording an album and giving his wife $600,000 in royalties.) With Gordy he fathered a son, Marvin Gaye III. He married his second wife, Janice, in 1977 and that year had a #1 hit, "Got to Give It Up, Pt. 1." They had two children: Nona, who has since become a recording artist in her own right, and Frankie. Janice was Gaye's muse, but he was also obsessed with her, and the relationship was tumultuous.

Under pressure from the Internal Revenue Service, Gaye moved to Europe to record his 1981 release, *In Our Lifetime,* which concentrated on his philosophies of love, art, and death. The next year, he left Motown for Columbia. His first album for the label, *Midnight Love,* sold 2 million copies and included the hit "Sexual Healing," which won a Grammy for Best Male R&B Vocal Performance. He sang live on the Grammy broadcast and, in 1983, in concert at Radio City Music Hall. During his Sexual Healing Tour, Gaye closed the show singing his hit in a silk robe, often stripping down to bikini underwear. Fan reaction was mixed. Also in 1983 he appeared in one of the more memorable segments of Motown's 25th-anniversary television special, obviously somewhat disoriented but riveting nonetheless. His a cappella version of "The Star-Spangled Banner," performed before the 1983 NBA All-Star game that year, became an instant bootlegged classic and is included on *The Marvin Gaye Collection.*

Gaye's comeback was one for the record books. But even with the recognition he longed for, Gaye was depressed, and his cocaine abuse was escalating, despite several attempts to clean up. He returned to the U.S. and moved into his parents' home—where he often quarreled with his father, with whom he'd been at odds since his teenage years. As Gaye later confessed to David Ritz, his internal life was marked by what Gaye viewed as an irreconcilable conflict between good (as represented by his strict religious upbringing) and evil (sex, drugs). In early 1984 Gaye reportedly threatened suicide several times and had become paranoid and irrational. Following a Sunday morning shouting match in his parents' home, Gaye's father shot him to death at point-blank range, he later claimed, in self-defense. Gaye's father was charged with and convicted of involuntary manslaughter. He was found to have a brain tumor, and was given a six-year suspended prison sentence.

After his death Motown and Columbia collaborated to produce *Dream of a Lifetime* and *Romantically Yours,* both based on unfinished recordings from the *Sexual Healing* sessions; among the tracks on the first album were the ribald, "Savage in the Sack" and "Masochistic Beauty," and some questioned whether Gaye had intended to release them at all. Since then, Gaye's work has been repackaged in a steady stream of new compilations. In addition, his work has been the subject of several tribute projects. In 1987 Gaye was inducted into the Rock and Roll Hall of Fame.

Gloria Gaynor

Born Gloria Fowles, Sep. 7, 1949, Newark, NJ
1975—*Never Can Say Goodbye* (MGM); *Experience Gloria Gaynor* 1976—*I've Got You* (Polydor) 1977—*Glorious* 1978—*Gloria Gaynor's Park Avenue Sound* 1979—*Love Tracks; I Have a Right* 1982—*Gloria Gaynor* (Atlantic) 1984—*I Am What I Am* (CBS) 1986—*The Power* (Stylus, U.K.) 1988—*Gloria Gaynor's Greatest Hits* (Polydor) 1990—*Gloria Gaynor 90* (New Music, It.) 1992—*Love Affair* (Polydor) 1998—*I Will Survive—The Anthology.*

Gloria Gaynor is a singer who is best known for her anthemic late-'70s disco hit "I Will Survive." One of six children, she grew up listening to records by Nat "King" Cole and Sarah Vaughan. Following high school, she worked as an accountant but quit to join a band in Canada. She soon found herself back in Jersey, however, working day jobs until one night at a club a friend persuaded her to sing with the band. The group, the Soul Satisfiers, took her on tour for a year and a half. She then formed her own band and went to New York, where she signed to Columbia Records.

Gaynor's first single, "Honey Bee," was a disco hit in 1973, but Columbia soon lost interest. She signed to MGM, and *Never Can Say Goodbye* was a hit in early 1975. One of the first LPs specifically programmed for dancing, the title cut (an earlier hit for Isaac Hayes and then the Jackson 5) hit #9. She followed up with a less successful cover of another Motown hit, the Four Tops' "Reach Out I'll Be There," before a string of less popular singles. But five years later "I Will Survive" hit #1 on the pop chart (#4 R&B); *Love Tracks* (#4, 1979) went platinum.

Gaynor's last big hit was "I Am What I Am" (from the play *La Cage Aux Folles*), which hit #13 in the U.K. but made it only to #82 here. She became a born-again Christian in 1982 and put years of drug use and drinking behind her. Her 1997 autobiography is entitled *I Will Survive.* She continues to record and tour; she has performed before President Bill Clinton and Pope John Paul II and remains popular in Europe. In addition to recording import albums that mix neo-disco and gospel, she has released several American singles including 2000's Giorgio Moroder collaboration, "Last Night."

J. Geils Band

Formed 1967, Boston, MA
Jerome Geils (b. Feb. 20, 1946, New York, NY), gtr.; Peter Wolf (b. Peter Blankfield, Mar. 7, 1946, Bronx, NY), voc.; Magic Dick (b. Dick Salwitz, May 13, 1945, New London, CT), harmonica; Danny Klein (b. May 13, 1946, New York), bass; Stephen Jo Bladd (b. July 13, 1942, Boston), drums.
1968—(+ Seth Justman [b. Jan. 27, 1951, Washington, DC], kybds., voc.) 1971—*The J. Geils Band* (Atlantic) 1972—*The Morning After; Full House* 1973—*Bloodshot; Ladies Invited* 1974—*Nightmares (and Other Tales From the Vinyl Jungle)* 1975—*Hot Line* 1976—*Blow Your Face Out* 1977—*Monkey Island* 1978—*Sanctuary* (EMI America) 1980—*Love Stinks* 1981—*Freeze-Frame* 1982—*Showtime!* 1983—(– Wolf) 1984—*You're Gettin' Even While I'm Gettin' Odd* 1985—*Flashback: Best of the J. Geils Band* (EMI America) 1993—*The J. Geils Band Anthology: Houseparty* (Rhino) 1999—lineup: Geils; Wolf; Magic Dick; Klein; Justman; Sim Cain, drums.
Peter Wolf solo: 1984—*Lights Out* (EMI America) 1987—*Come As You Are* 1990—*Up to No Good* (MCA) 1996—*Long Line* (Reprise) 1998—*Fool's Parade* (Mercury).
Bluestime (Geils; Magic Dick; Michael "Mudcat" Ward, bass; Steve Ramsay, drums; Jerry Miller, gtr.): 1994—*Bluestime* (Rounder) 1996—*Little Car Blues.*

The J. Geils Band merged its collectors' dedication to blues, doo-wop, and R&B with enough pop know-how to keep the group contemporary. The band was named after guitarist J. (Jerome) Geils, but its lyricist and onstage focus was singer Peter Wolf. A high school dropout who learned to jive-talk on Bronx street corners, Wolf moved to Boston before he was 20 and earned a passable reputation as a painter before becoming a disc jockey on Boston's WBCN-FM, where he called himself Woofuh Goofuh. He joined the Hallucinations, which included drummer and fellow doo-wop collector Stephen Jo Bladd, and by 1967 the group was playing covers of R&B, blues, and '50s rock & roll, from John Lee Hooker to the Miracles. Meanwhile, Geils, bassist Klein, and harpist Magic Dick were working as an acoustic trio called the J. Geils Blues Band. After the Hallucinations broke up in 1967, Bladd and Wolf joined the J. Geils Band, which by then had gone electric.

While other fledgling bands were going psychedelic, this group acted like greasers, and its showmanship and taste in obscure covers earned it a following in New England. Justman, who later became the band's producer and composer, was an organist who had moved north from Atlantic City to attend Boston University; he joined in 1968.

The band toured almost constantly in the early '70s, while occasionally reaching the Top 40 with such songs as

"Looking for a Love" (#39, 1971), the reggae-style "Give It to Me" (#30, 1973, making its album, *Bloodshot,* gold), and "Must of Got Lost" (#12, 1974). In 1977 the Geils band briefly called itself Geils and released *Monkey Island,* the group's first self-produced effort. In 1979 Wolf's five-year marriage to actress Faye Dunaway ended in divorce.

After nine LPs with Atlantic, the band switched to EMI America in 1978 for *Sanctuary,* its first gold disc in five years. In 1980 the J. Geils Band conducted its most extensive tour ever (U.S., Japan, Europe) to support *Love Stinks.* The album introduced Justman's synthesizer work and went gold. *Freeze-Frame* (#1, 1981), with the hits "Centerfold" (#1, 1981), "Freeze-Frame" (#4, 1982), and "Angel in Blue" (#40, 1982), was the band's best-selling album to date. One factor in the group's success was a series of catchy videos that captured Wolf's cool hipster charm ("Love Stinks," "Centerfold").

But tension had been brewing between the songwriting team of Wolf and Justman. When the group turned down material the singer had been writing with R&B legend Don Covay and Michael Jonzun of the Jonzun Crew, Wolf left—reluctantly—for a solo career in 1983. His *Lights Out,* coproduced by Jonzun, produced two Top 40 hits the following year, "Lights Out" (#12) and "I Need You Tonight" (#36), and the title track to 1987's *Come As You Are* reached #15. A third LP, in 1990, disappeared, and Wolf along with it. He spent a few years focusing on painting, and began to play live again in 1993. In 1996 he released *Long Line,* which was followed by *Fool's Parade* a couple of years later. That critically acclaimed album was heavily influenced by '60s Memphis soul and sported liner notes by famed Elvis Presley biographer Peter Guralnick.

Meanwhile, Wolf's former band mates broke up after releasing one unsuccessful album with Justman on lead vocals, 1984's *You're Gettin' Even While I'm Gettin' Odd.* In 1993 Geils (now calling himself Jay) and Magic Dick formed Bluestime, and released a pair of straightforward blues albums in 1994 and 1996.

Surprisingly—since Wolf had left in such an acrimonious atmosphere—in the spring of 1999 the J. Geils Band announced a reunion tour. The original lineup (minus Stephen Jo Bladd, replaced by touring drummer Sim Cain) got back together, and in 2000 there was even talk of a new J. Geils Band studio album, though as of mid-2001 it had not come to pass.

Bob Geldof: See the Boomtown Rats

Generation X: See Billy Idol

Genesis

Formed 1966, Godalming, Eng.
Tony Banks (b. Mar. 27, 1950, East Hoathly, Eng.), kybds.; Michael Rutherford (b. Oct. 2, 1950, Guildford, Eng.), gtr., bass, voc.; Peter Gabriel (b. Feb. 13, 1950, Woking, Eng.), voc.; Anthony Phillips (b. Dec. 1951, Putney, Eng.), gtr.; Chris Stewart, drums.
1968—(– Stewart; + John Silver, drums) 1969—*From Genesis to Revelation* (Decca, U.K.) (– Silver; + John Mayhew, drums) 1970—*Trespass* (Charisma, U.K.) (– Phillips; – Mayhew; + Phil Collins [b. Jan. 31, 1951, London], drums, voc.; + Steve Hackett [b. Feb. 12, 1950, London], gtr.) 1971—*Nursery Cryme* 1972—*Foxtrot* 1973—*Genesis Live; Selling England by the Pound* 1974—*The Lamb Lies Down on Broadway* (Atco) (– Gabriel) 1976—*A Trick of the Tail; The Best of Genesis* (Buddah) 1977—*Wind & Wuthering* (Atco); *Seconds Out* (Atlantic) (– Hackett) 1978—*. . . And Then There Were Three . . .* 1980—*Duke* 1981—*Abacab* 1982—*Three Sides Live* 1983—*Genesis* 1986—*Invisible Touch* 1991—*We Can't Dance* 1992—*Live/The Way We Walk, vol. 1: The Shorts* 1993—*Live/The Way We Walk, vol. 2: The Longs* (– Collins; + Ray Wilson, voc.) 1997—*Calling All Stations* 1998—*Genesis Archives Volume 1: 1967–1975* 2000—*Genesis Archives Volume 2: 1976–9.*
Phil Collins solo: 1981—*Face Value* (Atlantic) 1982—*Hello, I Must Be Going!* 1985—*No Jacket Required* 1989—*. . . But Seriously* 1990—*Serious Hits Live!* 1993—*Both Sides* 1996—*Dance Into the Light* 1998—*Hits* 1999—*A Hot Night in Paris; Tarzan: An Original Walt Disney Records Soundtrack* (Universal/Walt Disney).
Tony Banks solo: 1979—*A Curious Feeling* (Charisma) 1983—*The Fugitive* 1983—*The Wicked Lady* (Atlantic) 1986—*Quicksilver* 1989—*Bankstatement.*
Mike Rutherford solo: 1979—*Smallcreep's Day* (Atlantic) 1982—*Acting Very Strange.*
Mike + the Mechanics, formed 1985: Rutherford, gtr., bass; Paul Carrack (b. Apr. 22, 1951, Sheffield, Eng.), voc., kybds.; Paul Young (b. June 17, 1947, Manchester, Eng., d. July 15, 2000, Altrinchem, Eng.), voc.; Adrian Lee (b. Sep. 9, 1947, London), kybds.; Peter Van Hook (b. June 4, 1950, London), drums.
1985—*Mike + the Mechanics* (Atlantic) 1988—*The Living Years* 1991—*Word of Mouth* 1995—*Beggar on a Beach of Gold.*
Steve Hackett solo: 1976—*Voyage of the Acolyte* (Chrysalis) 1978—*Please Don't Touch* 1979—*Spectral Mornings* (Charisma, U.K.) 1980—*Defector* 1981—*Cured* (Virgin/Epic) 1997—*Watcher of the Skies: Genesis Revisited* (EMD/Angel).
Peter Gabriel solo: See entry.

The long career of Genesis breaks down neatly into two contrasting eras: For the first half Genesis was a cult band fronted by theatrical vocalist Peter Gabriel [see entry], playing majestic art rock that set the style for such American acts as Kansas and Styx—story songs set to complex, richly textured music with hints of classical pomp. After Gabriel left, drummer Phil Collins took over as lead singer—proving himself a more down-to-earth frontman—and the band's audience expanded exponentially, as Genesis streamlined its music into romantic pop songs and abandoned costume drama for laser lightshows. By the mid-'80s, Genesis was one of the world's most popular bands.

After Gabriel and Tony Banks played together in a band called Garden Wall, they formed a "songwriter's collective" with Mike Rutherford and Anthony Phillips while all four were students at Charterhouse, an exclusive British secondary school. In late 1967 British record mogul Jonathan King suggested the name Genesis and got the group a contract that resulted in the poppish 13-song *From Genesis to Revelation* (1968), which was not released in the U.S. until 1974.

Upon graduating, the four members lived together in an English country cottage and rehearsed for several months before playing their first gig in September 1969. They developed an elaborate stage show—Gabriel had a series of costume changes, including a bat and a flower—and with the adroit drumming of Phil Collins (formerly with Flaming Youth), their songs grew into extended suites on *Nursery Cryme, Foxtrot,* and *Selling England by the Pound.* They gained a large following in England and a dedicated cult in the United States. In 1974 Genesis' theatricality peaked with a two-LP set and attendant live show, *The Lamb Lies Down on Broadway,* in which Gabriel played Rael, who suffered various metamorphoses in a surreal Manhattan.

Gabriel left Genesis after *Lamb* for a solo career, and the group took 18 months to adjust. It auditioned over 400 singers before deciding Collins could take over; on tour, the trio employed a second drummer so that Collins could roam the stage. Genesis dispensed with costumes and continued to perform older material, which was credited to the whole group. *A Trick of the Tail* and *Wind & Wuthering* expanded the band's cult (the latter included Genesis' first hit single, "Your Own Special Way" [#62, 1977]), and . . . *And Then There Were Three* . . . , with somewhat shorter songs, became its first gold album in 1978 (the LP later went platinum).

Genesis began to score U.S. Top 40 hit singles with "Follow You, Follow Me" (#23, 1978) from . . . *And Then There Were Three* . . . and "Misunderstanding" (#14, 1980) from *Duke,* in which the trio turned their narrative skills to love songs. For *Abacab,* Genesis incorporated some new-wave concision; the album (#7, 1981) sold 2 million copies, and the title song (#26, 1981) and "No Reply at All" (#29, 1981) were hits. The latter featured the Earth, Wind & Fire horn section, which also appeared on Collins' 2-million-selling solo debut, *Face Value* (#7, 1981). That album yielded the Top 20 hits "I Missed Again" (#19, 1981) and "In the Air Tonight" (#19, 1981).

Collins' second solo album, *Hello, I Must Be Going!* (1982), was a Top 10 hit and featured a cover of the Supremes' "You Can't Hurry Love" (#10, 1982). The group's *Genesis* (#9, 1983) spawned "That's All" (#6, 1983) and "Illegal Alien" (#44, 1984). In 1984 Collins produced ex–Earth, Wind & Fire vocalist Philip Bailey's *Chinese Wall* album and dueted with him on the hit single "Easy Lover" (#2, 1984). The next year Collins earned an Oscar nomination and won a Grammy for his movie love theme "Against All Odds (Take a Look at Me Now)" (#1, 1984), and hit #1 with "Separate Lives" (a duet with Marilyn Martin) from the film *White Nights.* His own 1985 album *No Jacket Required* hit #1 faster than Michael Jackson's *Thriller* had, with such hits as "One More Night" (#1, 1985), "Sussudio" (#1, 1985), "Don't Lose My Number" (#4, 1985), and "Take Me Home" (#7, 1986). For the July 13, 1985, Live Aid concert, Collins performed on his own in London that morning, then flew via the Concorde to the Philadelphia show to perform there solo later that day, as well as play drums in the Led Zeppelin reunion with Robert Plant and Jimmy Page. Also in 1985, Mike Rutherford launched Mike + the Mechanics, whose debut album (#26, 1985) produced hit singles with "Silent Running" (#6, 1985) and "All I Need Is a Miracle" (#5, 1986). *The Living Years* (#13, 1988) yielded a #1 hit in the title track, which was inspired by the death of Rutherford's father.

Genesis returned to the charts with *Invisible Touch* (#3, 1986), containing the title track (#1, 1986), "Throwing It All Away" (#4, 1986), and "Land of Confusion" (#4, 1986). The viciously satirical video for the latter featured England's Spitting Image puppets of Ronald Reagan, Margaret Thatcher, and others. "Tonight, Tonight, Tonight" (#3, 1987) was featured in TV commercials for Michelob beer, which also sponsored Genesis' 1987 tour (the Michelob campaign, which also used Eric Clapton's "After Midnight," was later satirized in Neil Young's "This Note's for You" video).

In 1988 Collins, who had acted professionally as a child, starred in the movie *Buster* (he'd made his big-screen debut as an extra in the Beatles' *A Hard Day's Night*); the soundtrack produced #1 hits for Collins in a cover of the Mindbenders' 1966 hit "Groovy Kind of Love" and "Two Hearts," cowritten with Lamont Dozier of the famed Holland-Dozier-Holland Motown team. His *But Seriously* (#1, 1989), an attempt to confront social issues, certified Collins as an "adult contemporary" superstar, with "Another Day in Paradise" (#1, 1989), "I Wish It Would Rain Down" (#3, 1990), "Do You Remember?" (#4, 1990), and "Something Happened on the Way to Heaven" (#4, 1990).

The hits continued for Genesis into the '90s, as *We Can't Dance* (#4, 1991) produced "No Son of Mine" (#12, 1991), "Hold On My Heart" (#12, 1992), and "I Can't Dance" (#7, 1992). The album was Collins' last studio effort with the group. He announced his departure in 1996, the same year his album *Dance Into the Light* was released. It hit #23, but failed to produce any Top 40 singles. Collins diversified in 1999, recording a live album of greatest hits arranged for a 20-piece big band and lending his vocal and songwriting skills to the soundtrack for Disney's animated *Tarzan.* (He won an Oscar for Best Original Song, for "You'll Be in My Heart.") Genesis continued, returning to the studio in 1997 with a new singer, 28-year-old Scotsman Ray Wilson, formerly of Stiltskin. *Calling All Stations* (#54, 1997) was touted as a slight return to the band's progressive-rock roots but lacked the commercial appeal of the Collins-era catalogue.

Gentle Giant

Formed 1970, England
Derek Shulman (b. Feb. 2, 1947, Glasgow, Scot.), voc., sax; Ray Shulman (b. Dec. 8, 1949, Glasgow), voc., bass, violin, perc.; Phil Shulman (b. Aug. 27, 1937, Glasgow), sax; Kerry Minnear

(b. Apr. 2, 1948), voc., kybds.; Gary Green (b. Nov. 20, 1950), voc., gtr.; Martin Smith, drums; Malcolm Mortimer, drums.
1970—*Gentle Giant* (Vertigo) 1971—(– Mortimer) *Acquiring the Taste* 1972—(– Smith; + John Weathers, drums, voc.) *Three Friends* (Columbia) 1973—*Octopus* (– P. Shulman); *In a Glass House* (WWA, U.K.) 1974—*The Power and the Glory* (Capitol) 1975—*Free Hand; A Giant Step* (Vertigo, U.K.) 1976—*Interview* (Capitol); *Playing the Fool* 1977—*The Missing Piece; Pretentious* 1978—*Giant for a Day* 1980—*Civilian* (Columbia).

Merging medieval madrigals and Béla Bartók's dissonances with rock dynamics, Gentle Giant was one of the most dauntingly complex of '70s British progressive-rock bands. It formed from the remains of an obscure late-'60s British pop band called Simon Dupree and the Big Sound, which included all three Shulman brothers (Derek was Simon Dupree). The Big Sound had one U.K. Top 10 hit, "Kites," in 1967.

John Weathers had been with Graham Bond and the Grease Band before joining the Shulmans; Gary Green had played with blues and jazz bands; and Kerry Minnear had studied at the Royal Academy of Music. With Gentle Giant the Shulmans moved in the direction of King Crimson and Jethro Tull, though they often used dissonant counterpoint far more intricately than either of them. At first they had only a small European cult. The political concept album *The Power and the Glory* finally broke them in America. *The Missing Piece* flirted with shorter, harder-rocking song structures, and the group simplified its music, to little commercial avail, in the late '70s. For a short time the group was managed by radio consultant Lee Abrams, who produced its final LP, *Civilian*.

After the band's breakup, Derek Shulman moved to New York and became a powerful A&R executive with PolyGram Records (he signed Bon Jovi). Ray Shulman produced records by the Sugarcubes, the Sundays, and Ian McCulloch; in 2000 he was making music for computer games, while brother Phil was running a gift shop.

Bobbie Gentry

Born Roberta Lee Streeter, July 27, 1944, Chickasaw County, MS
1967—*Ode to Billy Joe* (Capitol) 1968—*The Delta Sweete; Bobby Gentry and Glen Campbell* (with Glen Campbell) 1969—*Touch 'Em with Love; Bobbie Gentry's Greatest* 1970—*Fancy* 1990—*Greatest Hits* (Curb).

Bobbie Gentry came to national prominence in 1967 with the first—and biggest—hit of her career, the enigmatic ballad "Ode to Billy Joe." From childhood, Gentry was determined to be a music star, and she wrote her first song at age seven on a piano. By her teens she had moved to California, where she attended UCLA (majoring in philosophy) and the L.A. Conservatory of Music. She worked as a secretary, occasionally performing in clubs at night, and then briefly as a Las Vegas showgirl before cutting her debut disc in 1967. "Ode to Billy Joe" hit #1, as did the album of the same name that year. A triple Grammy winner, "Ode" went on to sell 3 million copies internationally. The ballad provided the groundwork for a movie of the same title in 1976.

Gentry's later career never matched the success of her debut, although she was a star in England and hosted a British TV series, *The Bobbie Gentry Show,* in the early '70s. In America her late-'60s releases generally stalled in the middle rungs of the pop chart, except for a 1970 duet with Glen Campbell on the Everly Brothers' "All I Have to Do Is Dream" (#27). By the mid-'70s she was a staple on the Vegas-Reno circuit. She was briefly married to country singer Jim Stafford at the end of the decade. Gentry has since retired from music.

The Gentrys

Formed 1963, Memphis, TN
Larry Raspberry, gtr., voc.; Larry Wall, drums; Jimmy Johnson, trumpet, organ; Bobby Fisher, sax, gtr., piano; Pat Neal, bass; Bruce Bowles, voc.; Jimmy Hart, voc.
1965—*Keep On Dancing* (MGM) 1970—*The Gentrys* (Sun).

The Gentrys were a Memphis garage band whose biggest hit was 1965's "Keep On Dancing." They formed in 1963 to play sock hops and were soon winning local talent contests and battles of the bands. In 1964, after appearing on *Ted Mack's Original Amateur Hour,* they were signed to the local Youngstown label, and their first release, "Sometimes," was a regional hit. Their followup, "Keep On Dancing" (allegedly cut in an amazing 35 minutes), was leased to MGM and hit #4 in October 1965. Their 1966 releases, "Spread It On Thick" and "Everyday I Have to Cry," failed to crack the Top 40.

The group broke up in 1970, but Hart took over singing lead, and with a new group of musicians recorded three minor hits: "Why Should I Cry," "Cinnamon Girl," and "Wild World" on Sun. In the early '70s the Bay City Rollers revived "Keep On Dancing."

In 1973 Gentrys leader Larry Raspberry started Alamo, which recorded one album, then the Highsteppers, who recorded for Stax. He continues to perform and as of 2000 he was still leading a version of the Gentrys. Wall worked in record promotion. Jimmy Hart is a well-known professional wrestling manager for, among others, Hulk Hogan. With the help of late-period Gentry John Maguire and Hogan's wife, the pair wrote and performed the Hulkster's 1995 album *American Made.* Hart occasionally performs solo, as well.

Georgia Satellites

Formed 1979 (as Keith and the Satellites); lineup solidified in 1983, Atlanta, GA
Dan Baird (b. Dec. 12, 1953, CA), gtr., voc.; Mauro Megellan, drums; Rick Price (b. Aug. 15, 1951, Atlanta), bass; Rick Richards (b. Mar. 30, 1954, Jasper, GA), gtr.
1986—*The Georgia Satellites* (Elektra) 1988—*Open All Night*

1989—*In the Land of Salvation and Sin* 1991—(group disbands) 1993—(group re-forms: Richards, Price, + Joey Huffman, kybds.; + Billy Pitts, drums) *Let It Rock* 1997—*Shaken Not Stirred* (3NM).
Dan Baird solo: 1992—*Love Songs for the Hearing Impaired* (American) 1996—*Buffalo Nickel.*
The Yayhoos: Baird; Keith Christopher, voc., bass; Eric "Roscoe" Ambel (b. Aug. 20, 1957, Aurora, IL), gtr., voc.; Terry Anderson, drums, voc.
2001—*Fear Not the Obvious* (Bloodshot).

A latter-day boogie band, the Georgia Satellites proffered bare-bones, full-tilt rock & roll, served up with a silly grin and lust in their hearts. They had a Top 10 single, "Keep Your Hands to Yourself" (#2, 1986), from their eponymous debut (#5, 1986).

Formed in Atlanta in 1979 as Keith and the Satellites with Richards and Baird along with Keith Christopher from local new-wave unit the Brains ("Money Changes Everything"), they honed their sound (called "hick AC/DC" by some record execs) during a residency at Hedgen's Rock 'n' Roll Tavern. In 1983, now known as the Satellites (Christopher left early on), the band shopped around a six-song demo with no success and called it quits the following year.

Making Waves, a British indie label, heard the tape and offered to finance a U.K. tour, releasing the tape as *Keeping the Faith* (1985). Richards and Baird recruited two other former Brains, Magellan and Price, and took the label up on its offer. The tour fell through, but the band persevered, moving to Nashville where it was discovered by Elektra.

Unable to match their debut single and album's success (a cover of "Hippy Hippy Shake" included on the soundtrack of *Cocktail* [1988] hit #45), the Georgia Satellites split again in 1991. After the breakup, Price played on Paul Westerberg's *14 Songs* (1993); Richards joined Izzy Stradlin's post–Guns n' Roses band, the Ju Ju Hounds; Baird released two solo albums, *Love Songs for the Hearing Impaired* (1992) and *Buffalo Nickel* (1996) and performed with the Yayhoos.

After a 1992 reunion show, Richards and Price decided to give the Satellites another try, releasing *Let It Rock* in 1993 and *Shaken Not Stirred* in 1997.

Gerry and the Pacemakers

Formed 1959, Liverpool, Eng.
Gerry Marsden (b. Sep. 24, 1942, Liverpool), voc., gtr.; Les Maguire (b. Dec. 27, 1941, Wallasey, Eng.), piano; John Chadwick (b. May 11, 1943, Liverpool), bass; Freddie Marsden (b. Oct. 23, 1940, Liverpool), drums.
1964—*Don't Let the Sun Catch You Crying* (Laurie); *Gerry and the Pacemakers' Second Album* 1965—*Ferry Cross the Mersey* (United Artists) 1991—*The Best of Gerry and the Pacemakers, the Definitive Collection* (EMI America).

Gerry and the Pacemakers were on the pop end of Liverpool's mid-'60s Merseybeat trend. They built up a following in Liverpool clubs like the Cavern and in the Hamburg, Germany, clubs. In 1962 they became the second group—after the Beatles—to be signed by manager Brian Epstein. Produced by George Martin, their first three records hit #1 on the British chart: "How Do You Do It?" (which the Beatles had also recorded), "I Like It," and "You'll Never Walk Alone." "How Do You Do It?" was one of their biggest U.S. hits (#9) in 1964. They scored Top 10 successes in the U.S. that year with the ballad "Don't Let the Sun Catch You Crying" and in 1965 with "Ferry Cross the Mersey." That year they starred in a movie of the same name, which featured nine original songs by leader Gerry Marsden.

By 1966, however, their releases ceased having much impact on U.S. charts, and the group disbanded a year later. Marsden began a marginally successful cabaret career, scoring minor U.K. hits like "Please Let Them Be" and "Gilbert Green" and acting on stage and TV, where he hosted a children's show, *The Sooty and Sweep Show,* for several years. In 1973 he re-formed the Pacemakers for a nostalgia tour of America, and ever since has performed all over the world.

In 1985 Marsden sang lead on a new version of "You'll Never Walk Alone," credited to "Crowd," intended to raise money for victims of a fire at a British soccer stadium. It went to #1, making him the only British artist ever to top the chart twice with different renditions of the same song. He nearly repeated that feat four years later with a new "Ferry Cross the Mersey" that included Paul McCartney and Frankie Goes to Hollywood's Holly Johnson. Once again the cause was soccer related: Proceeds from the record benefited families of fans who'd been crushed to death by unruly crowds during a match. It, too, made #1, seven spots higher than the original 1964 version.

The Geto Boys

Formed 1986 (as the Ghetto Boys), Houston, TX
Scarface (b. Brad Jordan, Nov. 9, 1969, Houston), voc.; Willie D (b. William Dennis, Nov. 1, 1966, Houston), voc.; Bushwick Bill (b. Richard Stephen Shaw, Dec. 8, 1966, Kingston, Jam.), voc.; Ready Red (b. Collins Leysath), DJ.
1988—*Making Trouble* (Rap-a-Lot) 1989—*Grip It! On That Other Level* 1990—*Geto Boys* (Def American) 1991—*We Can't Be Stopped* (Rap-a-Lot) 1992—(– Willie D; + Big Mike [b. Mike Barnett, Sep. 27, 1971, New Orleans, LA], voc.) *Uncut Dope* 1993—*Till Death Do Us Part* 1996—*The Resurrection* 1998—*Da Good Da Bad & Da Ugly.*
Scarface solo: 1991—*Mr. Scarface Is Back* (Rap-a-Lot) 1993—*The World Is Yours* 1994—*Diary* 1997—*The Untouchable* 1998—*My Homies.*
Bushwick Bill solo: 1992—*Little Big Man* (Rap-a-Lot).
Willie D solo: 1992—*I'm Goin' Out Lika Soldier* (Rap-a-Lot) 1989—*Controversy* 1994—*Play Wicha Mama.*
Willie D with Sho: 1993—*Trouble Man* (Wise Up/Wrap).

The Geto Boys ignited a firestorm of controversy with their first major-label release, a gangsta rap album containing an unprecedented level of explicit violence and pathology.

When Geffen, then-distributor of Def American releases, refused to handle the record (and its lyrics of murder and necrophilia), it started a fierce debate within the music industry about whether record companies should refuse certain albums.

At 22, James "Li'l J" Smith brought together the members of the Geto Boys for his new label, Rap-a-Lot Records. Smith wanted to kick off his label with a group that would represent his old neighborhood, the Fifth Ward, a violent Houston, Texas, ghetto. Smith hand-picked the members: Willie D, a Fifth Ward native who once served time for robbing a Texaco station; Scarface, a multi-instrumentalist (piano, violin, guitar, drums) raised in a more middle-class section of Houston on as much rock & roll (Led Zeppelin, Blue Öyster Cult) as R&B; and Bushwick Bill, a four-foot-six dwarf born on the island of Jamaica and raised in the Bushwick section of Brooklyn, New York.

After two albums for Rap-a-Lot, the group signed with Def American (which later became American Recordings), then the label of death-metal band Slayer and shock comic Andrew "Dice" Clay. Geffen's refusal to distribute the Geto Boys' album led to accusations that the company operated under a double standard, profiting from the homophobia, racism, and misogyny of white artists such as "Dice" Clay, while refusing to release similar material by an African-American rap group. Virgin agreed to distribute the album, but the Geto Boys, disgruntled by the ordeal, returned to Rap-a-Lot. Their postcontroversy album, *We Can't Be Stopped,* shot to #24, higher than any previous release. Its single, "Mind Playing Tricks on Me" (#23 pop, #10 R&B, 1991), was based on the childhood feelings of Scarface, a suicide-prone manic-depressive who spent two of his teenage years in a mental ward.

Outside of the Geto Boys, the members are not friends. Indeed, each of the original rappers has done his own albums, and Willie D left the group permanently in 1992. Still, that same year the Geto Boys returned with *Uncut Dope,* with Big Mike Barnett replacing Willie D. In 1993 *Till Death Do Us Part* reached #1 on the R&B chart.

The Geto Boys have had several brushes with tragedy. In May 1991 Bushwick Bill lost his eye when his 17-year-old girlfriend shot him; drunk and depressed, he had talked her into shooting him by threatening to kill the couple's child if she didn't. In January 1993 Scarface was wounded and a friend of his killed by an off-duty cop during a gang-related fight outside a Shreveport, Louisiana, Waffle House. And in 1997, Bushwick Bill was indicted after allegedly trying to shoot his own brother; charges were later dropped when the brother refused to cooperate with prosecutors.

With 1996's *The Resurrection* (#6 pop, #1 R&B), the original trio unexpectedly reunited to demonstrate its lasting drawing power. The album attracted the usual controversy by mixing political themes with gangsta imagery, while viciously firing back at such vocal critics as Republican Senator Bob Dole. There was also critical acclaim for the Geto Boys' growing musical sophistication, incorporating G-Funk and Parliament-style grooves. The album included a new version of War's "The World Is a Ghetto (#82 pop, #37 R&B). The trio's popularity continued on 1998's *Da Good Da Bad & Da Ugly* (#26 pop, #5 R&B). In 2000 Def Jam Records created a new label imprint to be headed by Scarface and called Def Jam South.

Andy Gibb

Born Mar. 5, 1958, Brisbane, Austral.; died Mar. 10, 1988, Oxford, Eng.
1977—*Flowing Rivers* (RSO) 1978—*Shadow Dancing* 1980—*Andy Gibbs' Greatest Hits; After Dark.*

Pop singer Andy Gibb was the younger brother of the Bee Gees (who often contributed songs, harmonies, and production to his albums). He began a successful solo career in the late '70s with three #1 hits: "I Just Want to Be Your Everything" and "(Love Is) Thicker Than Water" in 1977, and "Shadow Dancing" in 1978.

By the time the elder Gibb brothers were getting their international career rolling in the late '60s, young Andy was already playing in amateur bands of his own. Following his brothers, he first established himself in Australia in the mid-'70s with tours and singles like "Words and Music." He then signed with Bee Gees manager Robert Stigwood, on whose RSO Records his first album was recorded under the tutelage of brother Barry. Brother Maurice supervised the platinum *Shadow Dancing,* which in addition to the title cut contained the hits "An Everlasting Love" (#5, 1978) and "(Our Love) Don't Throw It All Away."

Three Top 20 hits followed in 1980, but Gibb's sales began to slack off the following year. His personal life, too, took a nosedive. In 1982 he was fired as host of the popular syndicated TV show *Solid Gold* after one year and was let go from Broadway's *Joseph and the Amazing Technicolor Dreamcoat* for missing performances. By 1985, Gibb was at the Betty Ford Clinic undergoing treatment for substance abuse, and two years later he filed for bankruptcy. The singer's fortunes began to look up somewhat when he signed with Island Records in January 1988, but while recording the album in England, Gibb died suddenly of myocarditis, inflammation of the heart.

Debbie Gibson

Born Deborah Gibson, Aug. 31, 1970, Merrick, NY
1987—*Out of the Blue* (Atlantic) 1989—*Electric Youth* 1990—*Anything Is Possible* 1993—*Body Mind Soul* 1995—*Think With Your Heart* (SBK/EMI) 1996—*Greatest Hits* (Atlantic) 1997—*Deborah* (Espiritu) 2001—*M.Y.O.B.* (Golden Egg).

In 1987 fresh-faced teenager Debbie Gibson emerged from her suburban Long Island home studio with a wholesome image and a knack for writing innocent poppy tunes young music fans could relate to. Having begun piano studies as a toddler, Gibson won a local songwriting contest at 12 and was signed to Atlantic Records four years later on the basis of her demo. Although categorized as bubblegum, the singles "Only in My Dreams" and "Shake Your Love"—both from *Out of the Blue,* which went to #7—boasted hooks that suggested a savvy songwriter in the making. Both songs peaked at #4 in 1987, and were followed into the Top 10 by the album's title track (#3) and the #1 ballad "Foolish Beat" in 1988, which put Gibson into the *Guinness Book of World Records* as the youngest person to ever write, record, and produce a #1 single.

Electric Youth did well initially, reaching #1 and charting two Top 40 singles (the title track at #11, "No More Rhyme" at #17) but by then, even fans seemed to have tired of Gibson the goody-goody wunderkind, who lived at home, was managed by her mom, and preached against sexual promiscuity and drug use. (In 1989 rock satirist Mojo Nixon released "Debbie Gibson Is Pregnant With My Two-Headed Love Child.") *Anything Is Possible* (#41, 1990) went gold but didn't make the Top 40. After a sabbatical, during which she appeared as Eponine in the Broadway company of *Les Misérables,* Gibson attempted a comeback with *Body Mind Soul.* The 1993 LP tried to present the 22-year-old singer in a more mature, even sensual light. The video for the single "Losin' Myself" (#86, 1993) featured her in slinky lingerie, while the song "Shock Your Mama" slyly poked fun at her squeaky clean image. The album only reached #109, though, and the following year Gibson lost her record contract.

In July 1993 she played Sandy in the London stage production of *Grease.* In 1995 she surprised rock fans by dueting with the punk band the Circle Jerks on a recorded cover of the Soft Boys' "I Wanna Destroy You"; she even appeared with the band at New York's famed CBGB to perform the song. The same year, she went to another musical extreme with her EMI album, *Think With Your Heart,* which featured mostly ballads recorded live with a 44-piece orchestra.

When EMI folded, the budding entrepreneur—now known as Deborah—formed her own label, Espiritu, and returned to dance music with the 1997 album *Deborah,* which included a remake of "Only in My Dreams." But musical theater proved to be the best match for Gibson's talents, and throughout the 1990s she went on to appear as Rizzo in a U.S. national tour of *Grease,* the title roles in local productions of *Funny Girl* and *Gypsy,* Belle in Broadway's *Beauty and the Beast,* and the Narrator in a U.S. national tour of *Joseph and the Amazing Technicolor Dreamcoat.* She also attempted to embark on a film career, with two independently made comedies, *Wedding Band* and *My Girlfriend's Boyfriend,* which eventually were released on video. Gibson also had a sitcom pilot in development with Norman Lear in 2000; she would star as Maggie Bloom, an aspiring Broadway actress. The same year, she released a dance single, "What You Want," performed live at clubs and fairs, and began recording another album.

Jerry Gilmer and the Fireballs: See the Fireballs

Jimmie Dale Gilmore

Born May 6, 1945, Amarillo, TX
1988—*Fair and Square* (HighTone) 1989—*Jimmie Dale Gilmore* 1991—*After Awhile* (American Explorer/Elektra/Nonesuch) 1993—*Spinning Around the Sun* (Elektra) 1996—*Braver Newer World* 2000—*One Endless Night* (Windcharger Music/Rounder).
The Flatlanders, formed 1972: Gilmore; Joe Ely (b. Feb. 9, 1947, Amarillo, TX), voc., harmonica, Dobro, gtr.; Butch Hancock (b. July 12, 1945, Lubbock, TX), voc., gtr.; Tommy Hancock, fiddle; Syl Rice, string bass; Tony Pearson, mandolin; Steve Wesson, musical saw.
1972—*More a Legend Than a Band* (Plantation).
With Butch Hancock: 1993—*Two Roads* (Caroline).

Texas singer/songwriter Jimmie Dale Gilmore's distinctive high, plaintive voice, intriguing, esoteric lyrics, and traditional country & western sound have put him in the forefront of a looseknit group of mavericks who play a roots-based music that's been dubbed "Western beat." Having recorded his first album in 1972 as a member of Lubbock, Texas, country group, the Flatlanders, Gilmore has continuously collaborated over the years with ex–band mates Butch Hancock and Joe Ely. Several of Gilmore's songs, including "Dallas" and "Tonight I Think I'm Gonna Go Downtown," have been covered by such artists as David Byrne, 10,000 Maniacs, and Nanci Griffith.

Gilmore, who was named after "Singing Brakeman" Jim-

Jimmie Dale Gilmore

mie Rodgers, took up guitar as a teen, after first playing fiddle and trombone. Developing a repertoire of traditional country songs, he began providing music at poker parties in his hometown of Lubbock. His first demo recordings were financed in 1965 by Buddy Holly's father. By then a budding songwriter, Gilmore began forming bands: first, the T. Nickel House Band, which included Joe Ely on bass, then the Hub City Movers.

After a stint living in Austin, Gilmore returned to Lubbock in 1972 and formed the Flatlanders with Ely, Hancock, mandolinist Tony Pearson, fiddler Tommy Hancock, and musical-saw player Steve Wesson. That March the group was invited to record an album in Nashville for a small label, which released the recordings only on 8-track. The Flatlanders fizzled soon after (though there have been occasional reunions ever since), and Gilmore, who'd been a philosophy student at Texas Tech, moved to Denver and joined a spiritual sect headed by Indian guru Maharaji Ji. After five years, Gilmore left the group and returned to Austin in 1980, where he began performing his own material, as well as songs written by Butch Hancock, with whom he frequently played. After eight years, he recorded his first solo album, 1988's *Fair and Square,* for the independent label HighTone. *Jimmie Dale Gilmore* followed the next year. He was "discovered" playing at a 1989 folk festival in Cambridge, England by 10,000 Maniacs' singer/songwriter Natalie Merchant and Elektra executive David Bither, who signed Gilmore to the label. Both 1991's *After Awhile* and *Spinning Around the Sun* (#62 C&W, 1993) earned Gilmore rave reviews, including twice being chosen Best Country Artist in ROLLING STONE's annual critics poll. In 1994 Gilmore recorded two songs with Mudhoney for a Sub Pop single and duetted with Willie Nelson on the benefit album, *Red, Hot and Country.* Teaming with producer T Bone Burnett for 1996's *Braver Newer World,* Gilmore simultaneously experimented with a more atmospheric and rock & roll sound somewhat reminiscent of a futuristic Roy Orbison album.

In 1998 the Flatlanders reunited to record "South Wind of Summer" for the soundtrack to *The Horse Whisperer.* It was their first studio collaboration in 26 years, and sparked a desire among Gilmore, Ely, and Butch Hancock to write more songs together for a possible new album. The group embarked on a national tour in the spring of 2000, which coincided with the release of a new Gilmore solo set, *One Endless Night.* The album marked a return to folkier material for the singer, being composed mostly of covers by his favorite songwriters (including Butch Hancock, John Hiatt, Townes Van Zandt, and Jerry Garcia).

Gipsy Kings

Formed 1976 as Los Reyes, Arles, Fr.

Nicolas Reyes, voc., gtr.; Andre Reyes, gtr.; Tonino Baliardo, gtr.; Maurice Victor "Diego" Baliardo, gtr.; Jacques "Paco" Baliardo, gtr.; Djeloul "Chico" Bouchikhi, gtr.

1982—*Allegria* (CBS France) 1983—*Luna de Fuego* 1988—*Gipsy Kings* (Elektra) 1989—*Mosaique* 1991—(– Bouchikhi; + Francois "Canut" Reyes, gtr.) *Este Mundo* 1992—*Live* 1993—(+ Patchai Reyes, voc., gtr.) *Love & Liberté* (Nonesuch) 1995—*The Best of the Gipsy Kings* 1996—*Tierra Gitana* 1997—(+ Georges "Baule" Reyes, gtr., voc.) *Compas* 1998—*Cantos de Amor* 2000—*Volare! The Very Best of the Gipsy Kings.*

Among the more unlikely sounds to emanate from the airwaves in 1989 were the frenetic flamenco chords and *gitane* shouts of the Gipsy Kings. One of the first real manifestations of the new interest in world music, this group comprised primarily of actual French Gypsies caused a brief sensation blending exotica with familiar European MOR like "Volare" and "My Way."

The Gipsy Kings grew out of the family group, Los Reyes, led by father José—a renowned flamenco singer—with sons Andre and Nicolas and brother-in-law, Bouchikhi. When José Reyes died, flamenco guitar virtuoso Tonino Baliardo joined, and the group changed its name to the Gipsy Kings. Sticking to a traditional Gypsy sound on early recordings, the acoustic-based unit gained attention only after modernizing its sound at the behest of producer and manager Claude Martinez. (The group continued to sing in *gitane,* a dialect mixing French, Spanish, and Catalan.)

Their 1988 album *Gipsy Kings* became a hit throughout Europe and yielded two hit singles, "Bamboleo" and "Djobi Djoba." After its U.S. release, *Gipsy Kings* (#57)—helped by the fern bar ubiquity of "Bamboleo"—stayed 42 weeks on the *Billboard* chart, going platinum. (The Gipsy Kings have sold more than 13 million records worldwide.) While neither *Mosaique* (#95, 1989) nor *Este Mundo* (#120, 1991) achieved the American recognition of their predecessor, the Gipsy

Gipsy Kings: Paco Baliardo, Andre Reyes, Diego Baliardo, Canut Reyes, Nicolas Reyes, Tonino Baliardo

Kings remain a popular international live act and have maintained a strong presence on the world music charts. *Tierra Gitana,* released in 1996, peaked at #143 on the pop chart, but 1997's *Compas* fared better, hitting #97. The group has survived numerous lineup changes over the years, with various Reyeses and Baliardos leaving and coming on board between albums and tours. Djeloul "Chico" Bouchikhi left the Gipsy Kings in 1991 and founded a new group, Chico and the Gypsies, shortly thereafter.

Philip Glass

Born Jan. 31, 1937, Baltimore, MD
1972—*Music With Changing Parts* (Chatham Square); *Solo Music* (Shandar) 1973—*Music in Similar Motion/Music in Fifths* (Chatham Square) 1974—*Music in Twelve Parts—Parts 1 & 2* (Elektra); *Strung Out for Amplified Violin* (Music Observations) 1975—*Mad Rush/Dressed Like an Egg* (Soho News) 1976—*Dance Nos. 1 & 5* (Tomato) 1979—*Einstein on the Beach* (CBS Masterworks) 1981—*Soho News* (Soho News) 1982—*Glassworks* (Columbia) 1983—*The Photographer* (CBS Masterworks); *Koyaanisqatsi* (Antilles/Island) 1984—*Satyagraha* (CBS Masterworks) 1985—*Mishima* (Nonesuch) 1986—*Songs From Liquid Days* (Columbia); *The Olympian* 1987—*DancePieces* (CBS Masterworks); *Akhnaten* (Atlantic) 1988—*Powaqqatsi* (Nonesuch) 1989—*1000 Airplanes on the Roof* (Virgin); *Solo Piano* (Columbia); *Mad Rush/Metamorphosis/Wichita/Vortex/Sutra* (CBS Masterworks); *The Thin Blue Line; Music in Twelve Parts* (Virgin) 1990—*Passages* (Private) 1992—*Music From the Screens* (Point) 1993—*"Low" Symphony; Violin Concerto* (Deutsche Grammophon, Ger.); *Itaipu/the Canyon* (Sony Classical); *Hydrogen Jukebox* (Nonesuch); *Glass Organ Works* (Catalyst); *Essential Philip Glass* (Sony Masterworks); *Anima Mundi* (Nonesuch) 1994—*Two Pages/Contrary Motion/Music in Fifths/Music in Similar Motion* 1995—*Kronos Quartet Performs Philip Glass; La Belle et la Bête* 1996—*The Secret Agent* 1997—*"Heroes" Symphony* (Point); *Kundun* (Nonesuch) 1999—*The CIVIL warS; Dracula* 2000—*Symphony No.3* 2001—*Symphony No. 5 (Choral) Requiem, Bardo, and Nirmanakaya.*

With his operas, orchestral works, dance pieces, and film scores, Philip Glass is the quintessential postmodernist composer. Bridging high and popular art, he uses Western and world music, minimalism and high-volume amplification, and has influenced ambient and New Age music.

Glass studied flute as a child and piano at the University of Chicago, where he also studied philosophy and mathematics. In the late '50s he earned a master's degree in composition at New York's Juilliard School of Music. A 1964 Fulbright grant sent him to Paris to study with Nadia Boulanger. There, a job transcribing Indian music with Ravi Shankar and a fascination with Eastern structures led him to repudiate his earlier work and the 12-tone music of purist contemporary classical composers.

After hitchhiking through Africa and India, Glass returned to New York in 1967 and began composing according to principles soon termed minimalist: The music involved repeated rhythmic cycles of notes and, over the years, incorporated counterpoint and harmony. To play it, Glass formed the Philip Glass Ensemble, which toured art galleries and, as early as 1974, rock clubs including Max's Kansas City. He supported himself as a carpenter, furniture mover, and taxi driver. While initially refusing to publish his music so that the Ensemble could get more jobs playing live, Glass formed Chatham Square Productions in 1971 to record his works. He made substantial impact overseas—David Bowie and Brian Eno were among his early fans—and Virgin U.K. signed him in 1974.

Glass and scenarist Robert Wilson collaborated in 1976 on the first of his "portrait operas," *Einstein on the Beach,* a four-and-a-half-hour opera that toured Europe and played the Metropolitan Opera House. After Virgin released an album of short pieces, *North Star,* in 1977, Glass began gigging at both Carnegie Hall and rock clubs.

From the late '70s onward, much of Glass' energy went into theater works, including *Satyagraha* (its Sanskrit libretto was taken from the *Bhagavad Gita*) and *Akhnaten* (examining the myth of a pharaoh). He collaborated again with Wilson on *CIVIL warS,* whose intended 1984 performance was canceled due to lack of funds. In 1984 as well, he composed *The Juniper Tree,* an opera based on a Grimms fairy tale, and music for the 23rd Olympics. In the mid- and late '80s, among his other stage works were *A Descent Into the Maelstrom* with choreographer Molissa Finley, and the operas *The Fall of the House of Usher, 1000 Airplanes on the Roof,* and *The Making of Representative for Planet 8.* He also scored two documentaries, *Koyaanisqatsi* and *Powaqqatsi,* the feature film *Mishima,* and plays for the Mabou Mines company.

For his recordings, Glass signed in 1981 the first exclusive composer's contract with CBS Masterworks since Aaron Copland and released his most popular instrumental album, *Glassworks,* a collection of orchestral and ensemble pieces. *The Photographer,* a music-theater work, included a song with lyrics by David Byrne of Talking Heads. In 1983 Glass collaborated with ex-Doors keyboardist Ray Manzarek on a version of Carl Orff's "Carmina Burana." *Songs From Liquid Days* (1986), with lyrics by Paul Simon, Laurie Anderson, Suzanne Vega, and David Byrne, became his best-selling album. In 1990 Glass collaborated with Allen Ginsberg on *Hydrogen Jukebox,* an interpretation of Ginsberg's poems. In 1993 the composer released the *"Low" Symphony,* based on David Bowie's 1977 *Low* album, formed a new record label, Point, and signed an agreement with Nonesuch that would allow the company to record Glass's new material, remake several of his classics, and release CDs of his earliest pieces.

The late '90s proved to be one of Glass' most prolific periods. He scored Martin Scorsese's *Kundun,* wrote music for *The Truman Show,* and composed an opera, *The Voyage,* commemorating Columbus' arrival in America. By the end of the decade, he had completed two symphonies.

Gary Glitter

Born Paul Francis Gadd, May 8, 1940, Banbury, Eng.
1972—*Glitter* (Bell) 1991—*Greatest Hits* (Rhino).

Gary Glitter was at the forefront of the English glam-rock phase, along with David Bowie, T. Rex, and Slade. He had several hits in Britain with a distinctive sound (later revived by Adam and the Ants), featuring heavy drumming, handclaps, echo guitar, and football-cheer choruses, but only minor chart success in America.

In 1960 Paul Gadd began releasing ballads as Paul Raven. He toured with clean-teen British idol Cliff Richard, Tommy Steele, and Billy Fury. His "Paul Raven" rendition of Burt Bacharach's "Walk On By" became a big hit in the Middle East in 1961. He began working with writer/producer Mike Leander in 1965; the association continued into the '70s.

Gadd sang on the soundtrack to *Jesus Christ Superstar* in 1970 and, under the name Paul Monday, recorded a version of the Beatles' "Here Comes the Sun." But like his earlier records, it went nowhere. After considering such monikers as Terry Tinsel and Horace Hydrogen, he and Leander settled on the Gary Glitter identity in 1971.

Unashamedly climbing onto the glitter-rock bandwagon, Gary Glitter burst onto the English scene in 1972 and by midyear was inspiring regular crowd hysteria. "Rock and Roll Part II" hit #2 in England and became his only U.S. Top 10 entry (though it remains an anthem of choice at sporting events). Over the next two years he reeled off a string of hits, many of which topped the U.K. chart: "I Didn't Know I Loved You (Till I Saw You Rock 'n' Roll)," "Do You Wanna Touch Me?" (later a #20 hit for Joan Jett), "Hello, Hello, I'm Back Again," "I'm the Leader of the Gang," and "I Love You Love Me" in 1973, and "Always Yours," "Oh Yes You're Beautiful," "Love Like You and Me," and "Remember Me This Way" in 1974.

As the decade progressed, Glitter moved dangerously closer to self-parody. By the first of his highly publicized and short-lived "retirements" in 1976, he could boast of 13 consecutive English hits. Through his glory years he was perpetually backed by the Glitter Band wearing stacked heels and playing bejeweled, oddly shaped guitars. Led by Peter Oxendale (piano) and Gerry Shephard (guitar), the Glitter Band began making records on its own in the mid-'70s, including some disco-ish U.K. hits and a 1979 Oxendale and Shephard album, *Put Your Money Where Your Mouth Is* (Nemperor).

In October 1980 Glitter was in London bankruptcy court trying to work out a deal to pay off his nearly half-million pounds in back taxes. Not coincidentally, he returned to the road the following month. He also tried to raise some of the money by auctioning off his extravagant stage wardrobe. Since then Glitter has turned up in the news (an accidental overdose of sleeping pills in 1986), on British TV (a talk segment on a late-night program called *Night Network*), on the U.K. chart ("Another Rock and Roll Christmas" [#7, 1984] went gold), and on successful, annual Christmas tours.

In November 1997 he was arrested for amassing pornographic images of minors on his computer. Shortly thereafter, a married, 32-year-old former fan, alleged that Glitter had sexually assaulted her when she was 14 years old; in November 1999 the singer was cleared of the eight sexual assault charges. However, he pleaded guilty to collecting child pornography and served two months in jail. He retired from performing and publicly apologized for his actions. In June 2000 he was seen sailing off the southern coast of Spain.

The Go-Betweens

Formed Brisbane, Austral., 1977
Robert Forster (b. June 29, 1957, Brisbane), voc., gtr.; Grant McLennan (b. Feb. 12, 1958, Rock Hampton, Austral.), voc., gtr., bass; Lindy Morrison (b. Nov. 2, 1951, Austral.), drums.
1982—*Send Me a Lullabye* (Rough Trade, U.K.) 1983—*Before Hollywood* 1984—(+ Robert Vickers [b. Nov. 2, 1958, Austral.], bass) *Spring Hill Fair* (Sire, U.K.) 1985—*Metal and Shells* (PVC) 1986—*Liberty Belle and the Black Diamond Express* (Big Time) 1987—(+ Amanda Brown [b. Nov. 17, 1965, Austral.], violin, oboe, voc., kybds.) *Tallulah* (Beggars Banquet) 1988—(– Vickers, + John Willsteed [b. Feb. 13, 1957, Austral.], bass) *16 Lovers Lane* (Beggars Banquet/Capitol) 1990—*1978–1990* (group disbands) 1999—*The Lost Album '78–'79* (Jetset); *Bellavista Terrace: Best of the Go-Betweens* (Beggars Banquet) 2000—(group re-forms: Forster; McLennan) *The Friends of Rachel Worth* (Jetset).
Robert Forster solo: 1990—*Danger in the Past* (Beggars Banquet, U.K.) 1993—*Calling From a Country Phone* 1994—*I Had a New York Girlfriend* 1996—*Warm Nights*.
G.W. McLennan solo: 1991—*Watershed* (Beggars Banquet) 1993—*Fireboy* 1995—*Horsebreaker Star* (Beggars Banquet/Atlantic) 1997—*In Your Bright Ray*.

During their 12 years together, the Go-Betweens released a string of exquisitely crafted, heady pop albums that received cult and critical acclaim but never broke through commercially. The band was formed by Brisbane University students McLennan and Forster, who were inspired by '60s folk and '70s punk. The two developed complementary songwriting and singing styles, with McLennan's extroverted minstrelsy balancing Forster's poetic odes. Both wrote about strange people, strange situations, and strange love, loading gentle, moody melodies with intense emotion.

After a string of Australian and British singles, the Go-Betweens moved to London in 1982. With the 1983 addition of bassist Robert Vickers, McLennan moved from bass to guitar. Despite successful tours, laudatory reviews, and at last, a major U.S. record company, success eluded the band. In 1987 they returned to Australia, leaving Vickers in New York. The rich pop album *16 Lovers Lane* was the band's swansong.

Returning to Australia, Morrison and Brown formed the group Cleopatra Wong. Forster and McLennan released solo albums, with McLennan gaining some radio airplay with his Atlantic release, *Horsebreaker Star*. McLennan also recorded with the Church's Steve Kilbey, releasing a pair of albums under the name Jack Frost. Vickers went on to play with the

New York band the Mad Scene, appearing on two of the group's records.

Forster and McLennan toured together as an acoustic duo in 1999, playing a series of dates in Europe, Australia, and the U.S. Their performances coincided with the release of two new Go-Betweens compilations: *The Lost Album '78–'79,* a collection of early tracks that included the group's first two indie singles, and *Bellavista Terrace,* an anthology of material culled from five of the band's six '80s albums. While they were out on road, Forster and McLennan also began writing songs together for a new Go-Betweens album: *The Friends of Rachel Worth* was recorded in Portland, Oregon, with members of Sleater-Kinney and other guests. Its release in 2000 was followed by a Go-Betweens tour with Forster and McLennan backed by a rhythm section.

The Go-Go's

Formed 1978, Hollywood, CA
Belinda Carlisle (b. Aug. 17, 1958, Hollywood), voc.; Charlotte Caffey (b. Oct. 21, 1953, Santa Monica, CA), gtr.; Jane Wiedlin (b. May 20, 1958, Oconomowoc, WI), gtr.; Margot Olaverra, bass; Elissa Bello, drums.
1979—(– Bello; + Gina Schock [b. Aug. 31, 1957, Baltimore, MD], drums) 1980—(– Olaverra; + Kathy Valentine [b. Jan. 7, 1959, Austin, TX], bass) 1981—*Beauty and the Beat* (I.R.S.) 1982—*Vacation* 1984—*Talk Show* (– Wiedlin; group disbands) 1990—*Greatest* (group re-forms: Carlisle; Wiedlin; Caffey; Schock; Valentine) 1994—*Return to the Valley of the Go-Go's* 2001—*God Bless the Go-Go's* (Beyond).
Belinda Carlisle solo: 1986—*Belinda* (I.R.S.) 1987—*Heaven on Earth* (MCA) 1989—*Runaway Horses* 1991—*Live Your Life Be Free* 1993—*Real* (Virgin) 1997—*A Woman & a Man* (ARK 21).
Jane Wiedlin solo: 1985—*Jane Wiedlin* (I.R.S.) 1988—*Fur* (EMI-Manhattan) 1990—*Tangled* (EMI).
Jane Wiedlin with froSTed: 1996—*Cold* (DGC).
The Graces: 1989—*Perfect View* (A&M).
House of Shock: 1988—*House of Shock* (Capitol).

The Go-Go's began as a comically inept all-girl punk novelty act, but within a few years they had made a #1 debut album that yielded two Top 20 hit singles ("Our Lips Are Sealed" and the gold "We Got the Beat") and were selling out arenas on tour.

Belinda Carlisle, who had been a cheerleader in high school, nearly became a member of the seminal L.A. punk band the Germs. With Jane Wiedlin, another L.A. punk scene regular, she began playing guitar. A more experienced guitarist, Charlotte Caffey, soon joined them, and they recruited a rhythm section in the inexperienced Olaverra and Bello.

The group debuted as the Go-Go's at Hollywood's punk club the Masque, with a 1½-song set. Though onlookers considered them another hilariously daring bunch of amateurs, they began rehearsing in earnest and soon recruited Gina Schock, a serious and adept drummer who'd toured briefly with cult-film star Edie Massey and her Eggs. By that time the Go-Go's had been playing the punk circuit for nearly a year, their sound gradually growing from punk to a Blondie-ish bouncy pop rock.

They went to England, where they attracted the attention of British ska-rockers Madness, who had the Go-Go's open a tour there. The British independent label Stiff recorded a Go-Go's single, and "We Got the Beat" became a minor hit in new-wave dance clubs in Britain and America. In early 1980 Olaverra was asked to leave due to her punk style and attitude; the rest of the group thought they wouldn't get a U.S. record deal if they didn't sound poppier. She was replaced by Kathy Valentine, who had played guitar

The Go-Go's: Kathy Valentine, Jane Wiedlin, Gina Schock, Charlotte Caffey, Belinda Carlisle

briefly with British all-female heavy-metal band Girlschool and L.A. punk band the Textones. She joined the Go-Go's after a four-day crash course in bass and the band's repertoire.

The first Go-Go's album was produced by girl-group veteran Richard Gottehrer and Rob Freeman, both of whom had worked on Blondie's first album. By spring 1982, *Beauty and the Beat* was #1, and "We Got the Beat" and "Our Lips Are Sealed" (the latter cowritten by Wiedlin and her lover Terry Hall of Britain's Specials and Fun Boy Three) were long-running hits. *Vacation* (#8, 1982) was slightly less popular but yielded a summertime Top 10 hit single in the title cut. *Talk Show* was a lesser hit (#18, 1984) that spawned hit singles in "Head Over Heels" (#11, 1984) and "Turn to You" (#32, 1984), but Wiedlin left the group soon after, prompting its dissolution. The women revealed years later that nearly nonstop touring and the party lifestyle that often went with it had taken its toll on the band; Caffey has spoken openly about kicking her heroin addiction. Schock underwent open-heart surgery.

Carlisle launched a successful post–Go-Go's solo career with *Belinda* (#13, 1986), on which Caffey and Wiedlin also appeared. It went gold and yielded a hit single in "Mad About You" (#3, 1986). *Heaven on Earth* (#13, 1987) went platinum, yielding Carlisle's biggest hits, "Heaven Is a Place on Earth" (#1, 1987) and "I Get Weak" (#2, 1987), plus another Top 10 hit in "Circle in the Sand" (#7, 1987). *Live Your Life Be Free,* however, flopped, as did albums by Wiedlin (*Fur* did produce a hit single in "Rush Hour" [#9, 1988]), who became an ardent animal rights activist. Caffey, with Meredith Brooks (who later had a solo hit with the song "Bitch") and Gia Ciambotti, recorded one album as the Graces, before the Go-Go's reunited for a tour to promote a 1990 best-of collection. Four years later, they reunited again, this time to record some new material for the compilation *Return to the Valley of the Go-Go's.* After the album's release, the band embarked on a lengthy tour, with ex-Bangles guitarist Vicki Peterson subbing for Caffey, who was pregnant with her daughter by partner Jeff MacDonald of the band Redd Kross.

Disillusioned after being on the road, the members returned to their individual projects. Valentine and Schock formed the Delphines with Dominique Davalos; Wiedlin fronted froSTed, whose 1996 album, *Cold,* featured four songs that she cowrote with Caffey. Caffey wrote songs for and with other artists (including Courtney Love) as well as arranged and "consulted" on albums (including Jewel's debut). Carlisle returned to her home with her husband, film producer Morgan Mason (son of actor James Mason), and their son in Europe, where she's continued to have a successful solo career. Then, in 1999, the quintet got together to write a movie treatment about their lives with the band. Invigorated by the team effort, they decided to play two weeks of concert dates on the West Coast and in the southwestern U.S. They also recorded a live album, which they planned to sell themselves on an official Web site. While each member still maintained her own career—including Wiedlin doing voiceovers for cartoons and playing occasional gigs with Caffey in Twisted & Jaded, and Schock performing in the band K-Five and writing music for movies, TV, and commercials—the group remained reunited this time, collaborating on songs, touring across the U.S. in 2000, and recording an album of new material, *God Bless the Go-Go's.*

Andrew Gold

Born Aug. 2, 1951, Burbank, CA
1975—*Andrew Gold* (Asylum) 1977—*What's Wrong With This Picture?* (Elektra/Asylum) 1978—*All This and Heaven Too* 1980—*Whirlwind* 1996—*. . . Since 1951* (Pony Canyon, Jap.); *Halloween Howls* (Rhino) 1997—*Thank You for Being a Friend—The Best of Andrew Gold.*
Wax UK (with Graham Gouldman): 1986—*Magnetic Heaven* (RCA) 1987—*American English* 1989—*A Hundred Thousand in Fresh Notes* 1992—*What Else Can We Do?* (Caroline).

A studio musician, guitarist, and arranger who was instrumental in Linda Ronstadt's pop breakthrough, Andrew Gold went solo and had a hit of his own with "Lonely Boy" (#7, 1977). Gold is the son of soundtrack composer Ernest Gold *(Exodus)* and singer Marni Nixon, who dubbed vocals for nonsinging stars in *West Side Story, My Fair Lady,* and other Hollywood musicals. In the late '60s Andrew cofounded Bryndle with Karla Bonoff, Wendy Waldman, and ex–Stone Poney Kenny Edwards, and met his producer-to-be, Chuck Plotkin. The group recorded one unreleased album for A&M.

When Bryndle broke up, Gold and Edwards started the Rangers; a demo tape reached Edwards' former employer Linda Ronstadt, who hired them both for her backing band. Gold became her arranger through 1977 and worked on albums including *Heart Like a Wheel* and its hit single "You're No Good," on which Gold played most of the instruments. He made his first solo album in 1975 and opened shows for Ronstadt while continuing to play in her backup band. In 1977 *What's Wrong With This Picture?* yielded "Lonely Boy." *All This and Heaven Too* included "Thank You for Being a Friend" (#25, 1978), which later became the theme song of the popular TV series *The Golden Girls.*

Gold's songs have been covered by Leo Sayer, Judy Collins, the James Gang, Cliff Richard, and Ronstadt; he has played sessions for Wendy Waldman, Carly Simon, Art Garfunkel, Loudon Wainwright III, James Taylor, Maria Muldaur, Karla Bonoff, John David Souther, and Eric Carmen. He has produced Bonoff, Nicolette Larson, Rita Coolidge, Moon Martin, Stephen Bishop, and others. Under the name Wax (later changed to Wax UK), he and 10cc's Graham Gouldman made four albums *(American English; Magnetic Heaven; A Hundred Thousand in Fresh Notes;* and *What Else Can We Do?*). *Magnetic Heaven* included a hit single, "Right Between the Eyes" (#43, 1986). A followup, "Bridge to Your Heart," went to #12 in the U.K. Bryndle re-formed in the mid-'90s and recorded an album in 1995. Gold also sang the theme to the popular '90s television comedy *Mad About You.* His 1996 effort *Halloween Howls* is aimed at children.

Golden Earring

Formed 1961, The Hague, Neth.
1970 lineup: George Kooymans (b. Mar. 11, 1948, The Hague), gtr., voc.; Rinus Gerritsen (b. Marinus Gerritsen, Aug. 9, 1946, The Hague), bass, kybds., harmonica; Barry Hay (b. Aug. 16, 1948, Saizabad, Neth.), voc., flute, sax; Cesar Zuiderwijk (b. July 18, 1950, The Hague), drums.
1964—*Just Earring* (Polydor) 1972—*Together* 1973—*Hearing Earring* (Track) 1974—*Moontan* (MCA) 1975—*Switch* 1976—*To the Hilt* 1977—*Golden Earring Live* 1979—*Grab It for a Second; No Promises, No Debts* (Polydor) 1980—*Long Blond Animal* 1982—*Cut* (21) 1984—*N.E.W.S.; Something Heavy Going Down—Live From the Twilight Zone* 1986—*The Hole* 1989—*Keeper of the Flame* (Jaws/CNR) 1991—*Bloody Buccaneers* (First Quake/Columbia, Neth.) 1992—*The Naked Truth* 1994—*Face It* (Columbia) 1995—*Love Sweat* 1997—*Naked II* (CNR, Neth.) 1999—*Paradise in Distress; Last Blast of the Century.*

A Dutch group that began in 1961, Golden Earring was huge in its homeland and a minor act every place else until "Radar Love" hit #13 in 1974. By then the band had experimented with a range of styles before settling on the hard-rock approach that's brought it into the U.S. Top 40 only twice in its career. Nonetheless, Golden Earring remains the Netherlands' most successful and longest-lived rock export.

The group's original lineup in the mid-'60s included longtime mainstays George Kooymans and Rinus Gerritsen. As schoolboys, they had their first hit in 1964 with the bubblegumish "Please Go." It was the first of nearly 20 Dutch hits. By 1968, the maturing band had tired of the pop format and shifted to hard rock. Attempts to break into the U.S. and U.K. markets were largely unsuccessful, and its first U.S. tour in 1968 went unnoticed. In 1972, shortly after the group enjoyed a big hit in Europe with "Back Home," the Who (whose live histrionics the group openly imitated during its concerts) hired Golden Earring to open for a European tour and signed the group to its Track label. *Hearing Earring* (1973) was a compilation of previous Dutch releases and preceded a breakthrough tour of British college campuses.

Moontan spawned "Radar Love," and Golden Earring briefly became widely known in the U.S., where it opened stadium shows for the Doobie Brothers and Santana. But immediate followup success to "Radar" proved elusive, and through the decade, later LPs never reached the U.S. Top 100, although the group continued to score European hits. In addition to his activities with Earring, Kooymans produced records by other artists, including the 1979 European hit remake of "Come On" by the young Dutch group New Adventures.

In 1982 Golden Earring returned to the U.S. chart with the hit single and stylish video "Twilight Zone" (#10) from *Cut* (#24), but the group's three mid-'80s LPs that followed never made the Top 100. Each member has released solo LPs, all European.

In 1993, Zuiderwijk led a group of 1,000 drummers who performed on pontoons in the harbor of Rotterdam, Holland; Golden Earring joined them for an ultrapercussive "Radar Love." The band remains active and successful in Europe. *The Naked Truth* and *Naked II* contain acoustic hits, covers, and new originals.

Golden Smog: See the Jayhawks

Daevid Allen/Gong

Daevid Allen (b. Jan. 13, 1938, Melbourne, Austral.), gtr.:
1971—*Banana Moon* (BYG Actuel) 1976—*Good Morning* (Virgin) 1977—*Now Is the Happiest Time of Your Life* (Affinity) 1979—*N'existe Pas* (Charly) 1980—*Divided Alien Playbox 80* 1983—*Alien in New York* 1984—*The Death of Rock and Other Entrances* (Shanghai) 1986—*Don't Stop* 1987—*Trial by Headline* (Demi Monde) 1989—*The Owl and the Tree* 1990—*Australia Aquaria; Stroking the Tail of the Bird* 1991—*The Seven Drones* (Voiceprint); *Jewel in the Lotus* 1992—*Live at the Witchwood* 1992—*Who's Afraid* (Shimmy Disc) 1993—*Twelve Selves* (Voiceprint) 1994—*Live 1963* 1996—*Dreamin' a Dream* 1997—*Glissando Spirit; Divided Alien Clockwork Band Live at Squat Theater New York August 1980.*
Gong, formed 1970, Paris, Fr.: Daevid Allen, voc.; Gilli Smyth (b. Fr.), voc.; Didier Malherbe, sax, flute; Rachid Houari, drums, tabla; Burton Greene, piano, piano harp; Dieter Gewissler; Carl Freeman; Barre Phillips, bass; Tasmin Smyth, voc.
1970—*Magick Brother, Mystick Sister* (BYG Actuel) (– Houari; – Greene; – Gewissler; – Freeman; – Phillips; – T. Smyth; + Christian Tritsch, bass, gtr.; + Pip Pyle, drums; + Daniel Lalou, horns, perc.; + Gerry Fields, violin) 1971—*Continental Circus* (BYG Actuel); *Camembert Electrique* (– Pyle; + Laurie Allan [b. Eng.], drums; + Francis Moze, bass; + Steve Hillage [b. Eng.], gtr.; + Tim Blake [b. Eng.], synth.) 1973—*Radio Gnome Invisible: The Flying Teapot* (Virgin) (– Tritsch; – L. Allan; + Mike Howlett [b. Eng.], bass; + Pierre Moerlen [b. Colmar, Fr.], drums, perc.; + Mireille Bauer [b. Fr.], perc.) *Radio Gnome Invisible Part II: Angel's Egg* 1974—*You* (– D. Allen; – Hillage; – Blake; + Benoit Moerlen [b. Colmar, Fr.], kybds., perc.) 1976—*Shamal* (+ Allan Holdsworth [b. Eng.], gtr.; + Patrice Lemoine, kybds.; + Francis Moze, bass) 1977—(+ Mino Cinelu, perc.) *Gazeuse!* (Polydor); *Live Etc.* (– Holdsworth; + D. Allen); *Gong Est Mort* (Tapioca) (– D. Allen) 1978—*Expresso II* (Polydor) 1979—*Downwind* (Arista); *Time Is the Key* (Arista, U.K.); *Pierre Moerlen's Gong Live; Expresso* (Arista) 1981—*Leave It Open* 1987—*Breakthrough* (Pierre Moerlen's Gong disbands; Gong re-forms via Daevid Allen's Gongmaison: D. Allen; Malherbe; Graham Clarke, violin, gtr.; Keith Missile [b. Keith Bailey], bass) 1989—*Gong Maison* (Demi Monde) (+ Pyle; + Shyamal Maitra, perc.) 1992—*Shapeshifter* (Celluloid) (– Missile; + Howlett; + G. Smyth; + Blake; + Steffi Sharpstrings, gtr.) 1995—*The 25th Birthday Concert* (Voiceprint) 1996—*Live at Sheffield 1974* (New Rose Blues) 1998—*Family Jewels* (Outermusic); *Live in Paris* (Bataclan); *Paragong Live 1973* (GAS); *Live on TV 1990* (DEM) (– Missile; – Blake; – Sharpstrings; – Clarke; – Pyle;

+ Theo Travis, sax; + Chris Taylor, drums) 2000—*Zero to Infinity* (Snapper Music).

Gong started out as a European posthippie band with its own mythology of Pothead Pixies and UFOs and an unpredictable mixture of rock, folk, jazz, and synthesizers. Eventually, after numerous personnel changes and offshoots (some called Gong), the band moved into more conventional jazz rock.

The group's founder and leader is Daevid Allen, who had arrived in England from Australia in 1961. While attending Canterbury College of Art in 1966, he joined the original Soft Machine. Following the group's first European tour, Allen was refused reentry to the U.K. He then returned to France, where he lived and wrote poetry through 1969. By then he was playing regularly with vocalist Gilli Smyth, with whom he cut two LPs in 1969, *Magick Brother, Mystick Sister* and *Banana Moon*.

By 1970, the duo had expanded into the group Gong; drummer Pip Pyle quickly returned to England to join Canterbury jazz-rock group Hatfield and the North (and later National Health), and was replaced by Laurie Allan (no relation to Daevid). Band members took fanciful stage names, such as Shakti Yoni (Smyth), Bloomdido Bad de Grasse (saxman Didier Malherbe), and Hi T. Moonweed (synthesizer player Tim Blake). Daevid Allen began dropping in and out of the group in 1972, but after his departure in 1974 he contributed to *You*, which, coupled with earlier releases *Flying Teapot* and *Angel's Egg*, completed his "Radio Gnome Invisible" trilogy about the imaginary planet Gong.

Allen later recorded several LPs for Virgin and occasionally performed, sometimes billed as Gong. His 1976 LP *Good Morning* featured backup from the Spanish group Euterpe. By 1977, he was working with the New York avant-garde outfit Material [see Bill Laswell/Material entry] for *About Time*. In 1979 Allen released *N'existe Pas* and then led the first Gong-related group to play the United States. During the late '70s he lived in Woodstock, New York, and did solo tours (backed by tape collages), billed as the Divided Alien Clockwork Band.

Following Allen's exit from Gong proper, the leadership was assumed by percussionist Pierre Moerlen, who had joined the group in 1973 for *Angel's Egg*. Moerlen's father was the Strasbourg Cathedral organist and taught at the Strasbourg Conservatory, where Pierre studied from 1967 until 1972. Under Moerlen's influence, the group began to specialize in percussion-heavy jazz rock. His rotating cast of sidemen included such guitarists as Steve Hillage (who had departed by 1976 for a fairly successful solo career that included *L*, produced by Todd Rundgren), ex–Rolling Stone Mick Taylor (on whose 1979 solo debut Moerlen guested), and Allan Holdsworth (Tony Williams' Lifetime, Bill Bruford, and his own solo ventures), as well as keyboardists Mike Oldfield and Moerlen's brother Benoit. Of the original group, Didier Malherbe remained.

In 1977 Moerlen's group reunited with Allen to record *Gong Est Mort*. Afterward, Allen went back to his solo work; in 1992 he recorded with New York postpunk artist/producer Kramer the album *Who's Afraid*, which was released on Kramer's Shimmy Disc label. In 1980 Moerlen finally led his version of Gong Stateside for some concerts; in subsequent years he had to compete with other Gong incarnations led by numerous band alumni (Allen's Planet Gong, Gongmaison, and New York Gong, Gilli Smyth's Mother Gong et al.), before his own edition of the group finally drifted apart.

The '90s saw Allen continuing on as a solo act, and convening several reunions with assorted original, previous, and new members, for tours (including U.S. jaunts in 1996 and 1999) and albums. Hillage has made electronic recordings under the name System 7. The new millennium brought a new Gong and *Zero to Infinity*, billed as "part five of the Radio Gnome Trilogy" (its liner notes declaring *Shapeshifter* part four).

Steve Goodman

Born July 25, 1948, Chicago, IL; died Sep. 20, 1984, Seattle, WA
1971—*Steve Goodman* (Buddah) 1973—*Somebody Else's Troubles* 1975—*Jessie's Jig and Other Favorites* (Asylum) 1976—*Words We Can Dance To* 1978—*Say It in Private* 1979—*High and Outside* 1980—*Hot Spot* 1982—*Artistic Hair* (Red Pajamas) 1983—*Affordable Art* 1984—*Santa Ana Winds* 1995—*No Big Surprise: The Steve Goodman Anthology.*

Singer/songwriter Steve Goodman is best remembered as the author of Arlo Guthrie's 1972 hit "The City of New Orleans," a modern train song. Through the '70s he released a series of folk albums.

Goodman enrolled in 1964 at the University of Illinois to study political science; in summer 1967 he went to New York and played in the parks for spare change for several months until he moved back to Chicago, where he began attending Lake Forest College. In 1969 he gave up academics for music and started performing in Chicago folk clubs.

Despite critical acclaim, Goodman's recordings never sold particularly well, and by 1973 he was still living in a $145-a-month apartment several blocks from Wrigley Field. *Somebody Else's Troubles* featured Bob Dylan (as Robert Milkwood Thomas) on piano on the title track. Goodman toured through the early '70s, but was ultimately best remembered for "City of New Orleans," which he wrote about his experiences while campaigning for Edmund Muskie. His songs have since been covered by David Allan Coe, John Denver, Joan Baez, and others.

Goodman, who'd been suffering from leukemia since the early '70s, succumbed to kidney and liver failure in 1984 at age 36 after undergoing a bone-marrow transplant. A year after his death, a *Tribute to Steve Goodman* came out on Red Pajamas, the label he had founded shortly before his death. Among the performers on the two-record set were longtime friends John Prine, Arlo Guthrie, and Bonnie Raitt.

Goo Goo Dolls

Formed 1985, Buffalo, NY
Johnny Rzeznik (b. Dec. 5, 1965, Buffalo), gtr., voc.; Robby Takac (b. Sep. 30, 1964, Buffalo), bass; George Tutuska (b. Oct. 10, 1967, Washington, DC), drums.
1987—*Goo Goo Dolls* (Celluloid/Mercenary) 1989—*Jed* (Enigma/Death) 1991—*Hold Me Up* (Metal Blade/Warner Bros.) 1993—*Superstar Car Wash* 1995—*A Boy Named Goo* (– Tutuska; + Mike Malinin [b. Oct. 10, 1967, Washington, DC], drums) 1998—*Dizzy Up the Girl* (Warner Bros.) 2001—*What I Learned About Ego, Opinion, Art & Commerce* (1987–2000).

Originally a garage band with a strong taste for the melodic thrash championed by mid-'80s contemporaries the Replacements and Soul Asylum, the Goo Goo Dolls were a frequently jokey and loud outfit that evolved over the course of a decade into polished purveyors of mall-friendly power balladry. Thanks to his touch with acoustically sweetened ballads, and his casually videogenic appeal, lead singer Johnny Rzeznik even became a bit of a scruffy-chic idol. Such was not always the case. The band, with bassist Robby Takac and drummer George Tutuska, initially formed in Buffalo, New York, as a group called the Sex Maggots. When a club owner complained about the name, the musicians picked Goo Goo Dolls from an ad in *True Detective* magazine. The band gigged locally, and released its self-titled debut in 1987. The album *Jed* followed two years later, boasting a collaboration with guest vocalist Lance Diamond, a crooner-for-hire who sang on a version of Creedence Clearwater Revival's "Down on the Corner."

Diamond also appeared on *Hold Me Up,* which won attention on college radio, and also marked the first Goo Goo Dolls album to be distributed by Warner Bros., through a deal with the band's label, Metal Blade. *Superstar Car Wash* won the band critical regard and featured a song, "We Are the Normal," cowritten with Replacements frontman Paul Westerberg. But it took the 1995 release *A Boy Named Goo* (#27, 1995) to make the group a commercial success. Produced by Lou Giordano (Hüsker Dü, Sugar), the album took off after an L.A. rock station put the acoustic-flavored ballad "Name" (#5, 1995) into heavy rotation. Despite the breakthrough, and constant touring, the Goo Goo Dolls experienced turbulence. Tutuska was fired before the album's release and replaced by former Minor Threat drummer Mike Malinin, and in 1996 the band sued Metal Blade over royalties. Both Metal Blade and Warner Bros. filed countersuits. The case was settled, and the band signed directly to Warner Bros. The group's career stalled during this period but was rejuvenated with the ballad "Iris" (#9, 1998), which appeared on the *City of Angels* movie soundtrack. The song spent most of a year on *Billboard*'s airplay charts, and was nominated for three Grammys. That September the band released *Dizzy Up the Girl* (#15, 1998), with the hits "Slide" (#8, 1998) and "Black Balloon" (#16, 1999).

Robert Gordon

Born 1947, Washington, DC
1977—*Robert Gordon With Link Wray* (Private Stock) 1978—*Fresh Fish Special* 1979—*Rock Billy Boogie* (RCA) 1980—*Bad Boy* 1981—*Are You Gonna Be the One* 1982—*Too Fast to Live, Too Young to Die* 1994—*All for the Love of Rock & Roll* (Viceroy) 1995—*Red Hot (1977–1981)* (Razor & Tie) 1997—*Robert Gordon* (Llist).

Singer Robert Gordon emerged from the New York new-wave scene in 1976 looking and sounding every bit the rockabilly revivalist he has always claimed not to be.

Gordon grew up in the DC suburb of Bethesda, Maryland, where he began singing at an early age; he joined his first band at 14, the Confidentials (which, with some personnel changes, became the Newports). By age 17, he was appearing in nightclubs. After a stint in the service, he moved New York City, where, around 1976–77, he formed Tuff Darts. He appeared with that group on *Live at CBGB's,* but departed soon after.

Gordon's debut album, *Robert Gordon With Link Wray,* featured his childhood hero Link Wray on guitar. "Red Hot" was a minor hit in 1977, and the pair toured Europe and the U.S. that year. *Fresh Fish Special* featured Bruce Springsteen's "Fire," which was written especially for Gordon and later became a hit for the Pointer Sisters. In December 1978 Gordon signed with RCA and in 1979 released *Rock Billy Boogie.* In 1980 Gordon's fifth album, featuring three songs by Marshall Crenshaw, was released. With its emphasis on a more contemporary pop sound, the LP was a decisive change from the rockabilly of his previous albums. Gordon had a minor hit with Crenshaw's "Someday, Someway" in 1981. Gordon has continued to record. His self-titled album from 1997 exhibits an old-time country influence.

Lesley Gore

Born May 2, 1946, New York, NY
1963—*I'll Cry If I Want To* (Mercury) 1964—*Lesley Gore Sings of Mixed-up Hearts; Boys, Boys, Boys; Girl Talk* 1965—*Golden Hits of Lesley Gore* 1966—*Lesley Gore Sings All About Love* 1967—*California Nights* 1968—*Lesley Gore Golden Hits, vol. 2* 1972—*Someplace Else Now* (Mowest) 1976—*Love Me by Name* (A&M) 1986—*The Lesley Gore Anthology* (Rhino) 1998—*Sunshine, Lollipops & Rainbows: The Best of Leslie Gore.*

As a teenager, Lesley Gore wrote and sang a series of pop weepers; after her hits ended, she moved into acting and songwriting. Her father was a swimsuit manufacturer who sent her to the Dwight Preparatory School for Girls in Englewood, New Jersey. During her senior year, she was discovered by Quincy Jones, who got her a deal with Mercury and produced her recordings through 1967. As she turned 17, they released her song "It's My Party," which went to #1 in June 1963.

At year's end, she had three more Top 5 smashes—"Judy's Turn to Cry," "She's a Fool," and the ballad she performed in the filmed *T.A.M.I. Show,* "You Don't Own Me" (later recorded by Joan Jett). The latter title expressed an undeniably feminist viewpoint virtually unheard before on the pop chart. Subsequent hits included "That's the Way Boys Are" (#12, 1964), "Maybe I Know" (#12, 1964), "Sunshine, Lollipops and Rainbows" (#13, 1965), and "California Nights" (#16, 1967).

Throughout her peak years, Gore studied at least part-time at Sarah Lawrence College, and she graduated in 1968 after her hits had stopped in 1967 (her last chart record was 1967's "Brink of Disaster"). After moving to California, she worked with independent producer Bob Crewe on a series of unsuccessful releases. She tried acting—in films like *Girls on the Beach* and *Ski Party* and TV fare like *Batman.* Largely out of sight for several years, she made several club appearances in 1970 and 1971, and in 1972 she signed with Motown subsidiary Mowest. The result of that pairing, 1972's *Someplace Else Now,* sold poorly. In late 1974 she switched to A&M and was reunited with Quincy Jones for *Love Me by Name.* Again, sales were disappointing here, but the album was well received in England.

In 1980 Gore contributed lyrics to the Oscar-nominated "Out Here on My Own" from the *Fame* soundtrack, which featured music by her brother, Michael. In the latter '80s she recorded "Since I Don't Have You" b/w "It's Only Make Believe," which featured Lou Christie. She continues to perform, often in Atlantic City.

Larry Graham/Graham Central Station

Born Aug. 14, 1946, Beaumont, TX
1974—*Graham Central Station* (Warner Bros.); *Release Yourself* 1975—*Ain't No Bout-A-Doubt It* 1976—*Mirror* 1977—*Now Do U Wanta Dance* 1978—*My Radio Sure Sounds Good to Me* 1979—*Star Walk.*
Larry Graham solo: 1980—*One in a Million You* (Warner Bros.) 1981—*Just Be My Lady* 1982—*Sooner or Later* 1983—*Victory* 1999—*GCS 2000* (NPG).

As bassist for Sly and the Family Stone, Larry Graham updated James Brown's percussive bass lines into a style that set the groove for the progressive funk of the '70s. After leaving Sly, he led Graham Central Station and developed a new image as a ballad singer.

Graham moved with his family to Oakland, California, at age two. By his teens he could play guitar, bass, harmonica, and drums; he also had a three-octave-plus vocal range. At 15 he began playing guitar with his cocktail lounge singer/pianist mother in her Dell Graham Trio. When they were reduced to a duo, Graham switched to bass. After four years, he quit to attend college for a year and a half, while working as a backup musician for John Lee Hooker, Jimmy Reed, the Drifters, and Jackie Wilson.

In 1967 Graham joined Sly and the Family Stone and stayed with the group until late 1972. He then took a local group called Hot Chocolate (not the Hot Chocolate of "Emma" and "You Sexy Thing" fame) and, with the addition of ex–Billy Preston keyboardist Robert Sam, formed the original Graham Central Station. Its debut album, *Graham Central Station,* sold over a quarter-million copies and yielded a minor pop hit, "Can You Handle It," in 1974. *Release Yourself* featured another small hit, "Feel the Need." GCS's third LP, *Ain't No Bout-A-Doubt It,* went gold four months after its release, with "Your Love" reaching the Top Forty.

Graham wrote every selection on the group's fourth release, *Mirror,* a progressive funk outing. In early 1977 the group released *Now Do U Wanta Dance* (with its Top 10 R&B title track), but neither it nor *My Radio Sure Sounds Good to Me* (which marked the addition of Graham's wife, Tina, as vocalist) attracted the hoped-for pop crossover success. *Star Walk* was the last group effort.

By the end of 1980, Graham was billed on his own and singing ballads. *One in a Million You* hit #26 on the pop chart, and the title track was a #9 single. In 1981 Graham produced and played nearly all the instruments on *Just Be My Lady,* which included a #4 R&B title track. Later R&B Top 30 singles include "Don't Stop When You're Hot" and "Sooner or Later" (both 1982), and a mildly successful duet with Aretha Franklin, "If You Need My Love Tonight" (1987).

In the early '90s Graham led a nine-piece band, Psychedelic Psoul, which backed comedian (and guitar player) Eddie Murphy for a series of live shows (including one at the Montreux Jazz Festival) featuring Murphy's original material. In 1992 a revived Graham Central Station embarked on a national tour. GCS stayed on the road thanks to a rabid Japanese following and to the support of Prince, who used the group as a regular support act for his Jam of the Year tour. Original drummer Gaylord Birch, who was in on the reunion, succumbed to cancer in 1996. Boasting several original members, *GCS 2000* also features personnel from the Family Stone and the New Power Generation, along with Chaka Khan and Prince himself, who released the album on his NPG label and coproduced it at Paisley Park Studios.

Grand Funk Railroad

Formed 1968, Flint, MI
Mark Farner (b. Sep. 29, 1948, Flint), gtr., voc.; Mel Schacher (b. Apr. 3, 1951, Owosso, MI), bass; Don Brewer (b. Sep. 3, 1948, Flint), drums.
1969—*On Time* (Capitol) 1970—*Grand Funk; Closer to Home; Live Album* 1971—*Survival; E Pluribus Funk* 1972—*Mark, Don and Mel, 1966–1971* (+ Craig Frost [b. Apr. 20, 1948, Flint], kybds.); *Phoenix* 1973—*We're an American Band* 1974—*Shinin' On; All the Girls in the World—Beware!!* 1975—*Caught in the Act; Born to Die* 1976—*Good Singin', Good Playin'* (MCA); *Grand Funk Hits* (Capitol) (group disbands) 1981—(group re-forms: Farner; Brewer; + Dennis Bellinger [b. Flint], bass) *Grand Funk Lives* (Full Moon/Warner Bros.) 1983—*What's Funk* (group disbands) 1991—*Grand Funk Railroad* (Capitol); *More of the Best* (Rhino) 1996—(group re-forms: Farner; Schacher; Brewer) 1999—*Thirty Years of Funk: 1969–1999* (Capitol).
Mark Farner solo: 1977—*Mark Farner* (Atlantic) 1978—*No Frills.*

Grand Funk Railroad (a.k.a. Grand Funk), the most commercially successful American heavy-metal band from 1970 until it disbanded in 1976, established the '70s success formula: continuous touring. Unanimously reviled or ignored by critics and initially by radio programmers, the group nonetheless amassed 11 gold or platinum albums, sold over 20 million LPs overall, and regularly set attendance records at arenas and stadiums. A prototypical "people's band," Grand Funk was a simplified model of blues-rock power trios like Cream and the Jimi Hendrix Experience. The members were all millionaires within two years of their debut.

Mark Farner began playing guitar at age 15 after a broken finger and bad knees ended his football career. After his high school expelled him in his senior year, he started playing full-time in semipro bands and, briefly, with Terry Knight and the Pack, a group that had a minor hit with "I (Who Have Nothing)" in 1966. The group also included drummer Don Brewer.

In late 1968 Farner and Brewer hooked up with bassist Mel Schacher, ex–? and the Mysterians; they made Knight, a former Detroit radio deejay, their manager and gave him complete business and artistic control. His first order of business was to name the trio Grand Funk Railroad. The band's first date was in Buffalo, New York, in March 1969; the following July the musicians played (for free) for 125,000 people at the Atlanta Pop Festival. While the music consisted mostly of power chords, the group's onstage writhing and sweating made up in energy what it lacked in finesse. Capitol Records witnessed the legendary set and signed Grand Funk immediately.

With Knight producing, Grand Funk released its debut, *On Time,* that fall. Two years later the trio had one gold and five platinum LPs. Farner wrote and sang most of the early material, though Brewer later took the lead vocals on a few tunes. In Grand Funk's best year, 1970, it supposedly sold more than any other group in America. The next year, the band broke the Beatles' ticket sales record at New York's Shea Stadium, selling out a two-day stand in 72 hours and grossing over $300,000.

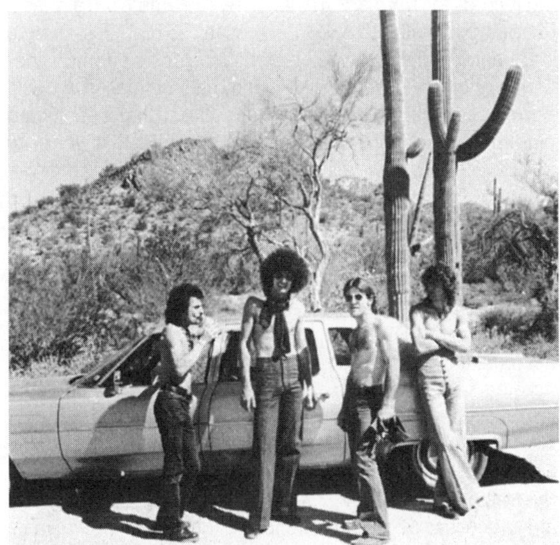

Grand Funk Railroad: Mel Schacher, Don Brewer, Mark Farner, Craig Frost

An undeniably triumphant moment, it marked the end of the honeymoon between Knight and the band. On March 27, 1972, Grand Funk terminated its relationship with Knight; he responded with $60 million in lawsuits. The band lost momentum while courts straightened out the mess, but with attorney John Eastman (Linda McCartney's father) handling its affairs, GFR eventually ditched Knight by buying him out.

Grand Funk's first post-Knight LP, *Phoenix,* introduced a fourth member, organist Craig Frost (who later joined Bob Seger's Silver Bullet Band). In 1973 Todd Rundgren produced the platinum *We're an American Band,* the title track of which was the group's first big AM hit (#1). Rundgren also produced Grand Funk's 10th LP, *Shinin' On,* which yielded another #1 single, a remake of Little Eva's "The Loco-Motion." The band continued to tour in 1975, as documented in *Caught in the Act,* but interest within the group was lagging. It scored two more pop hits that year: "Some Kind of Wonderful" (#3) and "Bad Time" (#4). The 1975 LP *Born to Die,* was to be Grand Funk's last, but when Frank Zappa agreed to produce, the four members stayed together for *Good Singin', Good Playin'.*

The group broke up in 1976 and returned to Michigan. Brewer and Schacher formed Flint, which released one album locally before disbanding. By the late '70s, Brewer had moved to Boca Raton, Florida. Farner spent his time with his wife and two children on his 1,500-acre farm in upstate Michigan and opened an alternative-energy store. He released two solo LPs—*Mark Farner* in 1977 and *No Frills* in 1978—and toured on occasion. In 1981 Farner and Brewer reunited for *Grand Funk Lives,* which picked up some AOR airplay with a remake of the Animals' "We Gotta Get Out of This Place." After a second album, 1983's *What's Funk?,* Grand Funk split up yet again, with Brewer joining former bandmate Craig Frost in Bob Seger's Silver Bullet Band. Farner, meanwhile, had become a born-again Christian. In 1988 a song of his, "Isn't It Amazing," hit #2 on the Inspirational chart.

In 1997, for the first time in 20 years, the original trio reunited onstage, launching a world tour with a tri-city concert event that benefitted the Bosnian-American Relief Fund, a charity that provided aid to the war-torn region. In 1997 the band released a live album, *Bosnia. Pollstar* magazine named Grand Funk one of 1998's 100 biggest-grossing tours, but following the release of a 30th-anniversary box set, Farner announced that he would resume his solo career.

Grandmaster Flash and the Furious Five

Formed 1977, Bronx, NY
Grandmaster Flash (b. Joseph Saddler, Jan. 1, 1958, Barbados), DJ; Cowboy (b. Keith Wiggins, Sep. 20, 1969; d. Sep. 8, 1989), voc.; Melle Mel (b. Melvin Glover), voc.; Kid Creole (b. Nathaniel Glover), voc.; Mr. Ness (b. Eddie Morris), voc.; Rahiem (b. Guy Williams), voc.

1982—*The Message* (Sugarhill) 1983—*Greatest Messages* 1988—*On the Strength* (Elektra).
Grandmaster Melle Mel and the Furious Five: 1984—*Work Party* (Sugarhill) 1985—*Stepping Off* 1997—*Right Now* (Str8 Game).
Grandmaster Flash solo: 1985—*They Said It Couldn't Be Done* (Elektra) 1986—*The Source* 1987—*Ba-Dop-Boom-Bang*.
Grandmaster Flash/The Furious Five/Grandmaster Melle Mel: 1989—*The Greatest Hits* (Sugarhill) 1994—*Message From Beat Street: The Best of Grandmaster Flash, Melle Mel, & the Furious Five* (Rhino) 1996—*The Adventures of Grandmaster Flash, Melle Mel, & the Furious Five: More of the Best*.

Disco DJ Grandmaster Flash and his rap group the Furious Five were the premier DJ-rap team of the early '80s. Flash began spinning records at Bronx block parties, gym dances, and parks when he was 18. Within a year, he was working at local discos while studying electronics at technical school by day. He developed an idiosyncratic style that involved "cutting" (segueing between tracks precisely on the beat), "back-spinning" (turning records manually to make the needle repeat brief lengths of groove), and "phasing" (manipulating turntable speeds) to create aural montages. Strictly a spinner, he began working with rappers around 1977, first with Kurtis Blow and then with the Furious Five, who had mastered a routine of trading and blending lines and had introduced choreography to their act.

Flash and the Five were popular throughout New York by 1978, but they did not record until 1979, after the Sugar Hill Gang's "Rapper's Delight" showed that rap records could be hits. Flash and the Five recorded "Superrappin' " for Harlem-based Enjoy Records in 1979, before signing with Sugarhill Records the next year. Their first Sugarhill release, "Freedom" (#19 R&B, 1980), sold over 50,000 copies; it was followed by "Birthday Party" (#36 R&B, 1981).

These records' appeal was not limited to New York, and in 1980 Flash and the Five toured the nation. "The Adventures of Grandmaster Flash on the Wheels of Steel" (#55 R&B, 1981) was the first record to capture the urban "cutting" technique pioneered by Flash; it incorporated snatches of Chic's "Good Times," Blondie's "Rapture," and Queen's "Another One Bites the Dust." "The Message" (#4 R&B, 1982), a groundbreaking rap in its haunting depiction of ghetto life, was one of the most powerful and controversial songs of 1982, although it sounds tame compared to the gangsta rap that would follow.

During recording of the group's anticocaine single, "White Lines," in 1983, Flash and Melle Mel had a falling-out. The next year there were two Furious Fives performing, though both had lost the power and dazzle of the original group. Flash eventually dropped the Furious Five from his name but continued making solo albums through the '80s. In 1987 Melle Mel, Flash, and the Furious Five reunited for a charity concert hosted by Paul Simon at Madison Square Garden; the result was another album, 1988's *On the Strength*. Popular indifference soon led to another breakup. Flash reemerged in 1994 as coproducer of Public Enemy DJ Terminator's X's *Super Bad* album. The group reunited again in 1994 for a rap oldies package show that also included Kurtis Blow, Whodini, and Run-D.M.C. In 1995 Grandmaster Flash and Melle Mel joined Duran Duran in the studio for a new version of "White Lines (Don't Do It)." In 1997 Grandmaster Melle Mel and Scorpio released an album called *Right Now* and included a remake of Jean Knight's 1971 disco hit "Mr. Big Stuff." Flash closed the '90s as musical director and DJ of HBO's *The Chris Rock Show*.

Amy Grant

Born Nov. 25, 1960, Augusta, GA
1976—*Amy Grant* (Word) 1979—*My Father's Eyes* 1980—*Never Alone* 1981—*Amy Grant in Concert* 1981—*Amy Grant in Concert, vol. 2* 1982—*Age to Age* 1983—*A Christmas Album* 1984—*Straight Ahead* (Myrrh/A&M) 1985—*Unguarded* 1986—*The Collection* 1988—*Lead Me On* 1991—*Heart in Motion* 1992—*Home for Christmas* 1994—*House of Love* 1997—*Behind the Eyes* 1999—*A Christmas to Remember* (Interscope).

Singer/songwriter Amy Grant charted an ascent to pop stardom in the '80s and early '90s that would make her one of the most successful crossover artists in Christian music. With bouncy, hummable songs that became less overtly spiritual on each new album, and with videos that emphasized her wholesome good looks, Grant communicated the message that, as she told a reporter in 1991, "Christians can be sexy."

Grant grew up in Nashville and began playing the guitar while in summer camp, inspired by a friend who played John Denver songs. As a high school freshman, Grant was lured to a Bible-study meeting by her older sister's boyfriend; not long afterward, at 15, she landed a deal with Word Records, a Christian label. For a while, the young singer balanced studies at prep school and then Vanderbilt University with making records for Word's Myrrh label. By the time Word signed a distribution deal with A&M Records in the mid-'80s, Grant's star had already risen on the Christian-music circuit. Nineteen eighty-five's *Unguarded* marked her official arrival as a pop artist, cracking the Top 40 on the album charts and going platinum. Grant showed up at the Grammys that year—to accept one of five awards she's won in the gospel category—wearing a leopard-skin-print jacket and no shoes. In 1986 she recorded a duet with Chicago's Peter Cetera, the very secular #1 love song "The Next Time I Fall." The video also became popular on MTV, which had previously dismissed Grant as a Christian artist.

As Grant's visibility increased, so did skepticism among her more conservative observers in the Christian music community. But accusations of "selling out" to pop trends didn't faze the singer, who maintained that her songs had never been spiritually didactic and her music had always drawn on accessible pop textures. *Heart in Motion* (#10, 1991) included the #1 single "Baby Baby." Although the song's accompanying video showed Grant frolicking chastely with a male model, she and her husband at the time, songwriter and Nashville Network talk-show host Gary Chapman, cowrote the song for Millie, the second of their three children. "Every

Heartbeat" and "That's What Love Is For," also from *Motion*, went to #2 and #7, respectively. In 1992 Grant's *Home for Christmas* peaked at #2, and the following year she began an annual tradition of performing a "Tennessee Christmas" concert in Nashville, which she and coperformer Michael W. Smith took on the road starting in 1997.

Grant further surprised the Christian music community by the confessional singer/songwriter approach on her next album, 1997's *Behind the Eyes* (#8 pop). She wrote many of the songs on an acoustic guitar, alone in a secluded cabin not far from her home. The production was sparse, the lyrics often melancholy; listeners speculated that Grant wasn't as happy as her picture-perfect life seemed. After a couple of singles shot up the Adult Contemporary chart ("Takes a Little Time" went to #4, "Like I Love You" to #15), the underlying reason for her despair became apparent when she separated from Chapman, her husband of 16 years, in December 1998. Hoping it was a temporary situation, her fans were shocked when the couple divorced a few months later and Grant soon began dating friend and country-music star Vince Gill, who also recently had divorced after a long marriage. (The pair had known each other for several years, even recording a duet together, the title track to Grant's 1994 album *House of Love*.) Grant released a third holiday album, *A Christmas to Remember*, and taped a corresponding television special in 1999. Around the same time, she made her acting debut in the leading role of a TV movie. Grant and Gill married in March 2000.

Eddy Grant

Born Edmond Montague Grant, Mar. 5, 1948, Plaisance, Guyana, West Indies
1979—*Living on the Front Line* (Epic); *Walking on Sunshine* 1982—*Killer on the Rampage* 1984—*Going for Broke* 1986—*Born Tough* 1990—*File Under Rock* (Enigma); *Barefoot Soldier* 1993—*Soca Baptism* (Ice).

With his dreadlocks and gravelly voice, Eddy Grant may have looked like a Rastafarian reggae artist, but in fact was a pop-savvy, business-conscious straight arrow and something of a one-man music industry.

Grant's family moved to Britain while he was a youngster. By age 19, he was fronting an interracial British pop-rock band, the Equals, who scored a minor transatlantic hit in 1968 with "Baby, Come Back" (#32). In 1972 Grant left the Equals to form a production company and open a recording studio. He released his debut album on his own Ice Records label, setting his career pattern by playing every instrument himself, and merging reggae, funk, soul, rock, and pop elements. *Walking on Sunshine* (#20 U.K., 1979) hit big in England with the danceable title track and "Living on the Frontline" (#11 U.K., 1979), a protest song about South Africa. In 1982 Grant moved back to the Caribbean, relocating his home and studio to Barbados, and found massive U.S. success with *Killer on the Rampage* (#10, 1983), which contained a #2 smash hit in the funk-rock anthem "Electric Avenue." The reggae-rock ballad "I Don't Wanna Dance" was a minor followup hit (#53, 1983). *Going for Broke* (#64, 1984) yielded his last U.S. hit, "Romancing the Stone" (#26, 1984), written for but not included in the hit film of the same name. By the early '90s, Grant was still reportedly wealthy enough to bid unsuccessfully for control of the late Bob Marley's $16-million estate.

The Grass Roots

Formed 1966, Los Angeles, CA
Warren Entner (b. July 7, 1944, Boston, MA), gtr., voc., kybds.; Creed Bratton (b. Feb. 8, 1943, Sacramento, CA), gtr., banjo, sitar; Ricky Coonce (b. Aug. 1, 1947, Los Angeles), drums; Rob Grill (b. Nov. 30, 1944, Los Angeles), bass, voc.
1967—*Let's Live for Today* (Dunhill) 1969—*Lovin' Thing* (– Bratton; + Dennis Provisor [b. Nov. 5, ca. 1950, Los Angeles], organ) *Leaving It All Behind* 1971—*Their 16 Greatest Hits* 1972—(– Coonce; – Provisor; + Reed Kailing, gtr.; + Virgil Webber, gtr.; + Joel Larson, drums) 1975—*The Grass Roots* (Haven) (– Grill) 1982—*Powers of the Night* (MCA) 1996—*All Time Greatest Hits*.

The Grass Roots were a major American singles band during the late '60s and early '70s. The group was formed when pop producer/writers P.F. Sloan and Steve Barri, who had recorded the 1966 hit "Where Were You When I Needed You" (#28) under the name the Grass Roots, decided to continue recording and drafted an L.A. bar band, the Thirteenth Floor, to play on the records. Barri and Sloan continued to work together. The group that recorded the 1967 hits "Let's Live for Today" (#12) (a remake of an Italian hit by the Rokes) and "Things I Should Have Said" (#23) became the Grass Roots.

The group had several major hits, including the gold "Midnight Confessions" (#5, 1968), "I'd Wait a Million Years" (#15, 1969), "Heaven Knows" (#24, 1969), "The River Is Wide" (#31, 1969), "Temptation Eyes" (#15, 1971), "Sooner or Later" (#9, 1971), and "Two Divided by Love" (#16, 1971). After 1972's "The Runaway" (#39), the hits dried up, and the Grass Roots returned to small clubs. By the mid-'70s, the band was recording for the small Haven Records, where it managed one moderate comeback hit, "Mamacita" (#71, 1975).

Bassist/vocalist Rob Grill's 1980 solo LP, *Uprooted*, featured Mick Fleetwood and Lindsey Buckingham of Fleetwood Mac. He began touring as Rob Grill and the Grass Roots in 1981 before releasing *Powers of the Night* the following year. He and the "group" make the rounds of the oldies circuit to this day. Guitarist Warren Entner, meanwhile, got into the business end of the entertainment industry, managing the hard-rock acts Quiet Riot, Faith No More, L7, the Deftones, and Rage Against the Machine. He also was the executive producer of the 1983 film *Pirates of Penzance*.

Grateful Dead

Formed 1965, San Francisco, CA
Jerry Garcia (b. Jerome John Garcia, Aug. 1, 1942, San Francisco; d. Aug. 9, 1995, Forest Knolls, CA), gtr., voc.; Bob

Weir (b. Robert Hall, Oct. 16, 1947, San Francisco), gtr., voc.; Ron "Pigpen" McKernan (b. Sep. 8, 1945, San Bruno, CA; d. Mar. 8, 1973, San Francisco), kybds., harmonica, voc.; Phil Lesh (b. Philip Chapman, Mar. 15, 1940, Berkeley, CA), bass, voc.; Bill Kreutzmann, a.k.a. Bill Sommers, (b. Apr. 7, 1946, Palo Alto, CA.), drums.
1967—*The Grateful Dead* (Warner Bros.) (+ Mickey Hart [b. ca. 1950, Long Island, NY], drums, perc.) 1968—*Anthem of the Sun* (+ Tom Constanten, kybds.) 1969—*Aoxomoxoa* 1970—*Live Dead* (– Constanten); *Workingman's Dead; American Beauty* (– Hart) 1971—*Grateful Dead* (Skull and Roses) 1972—*Europe '72* (– Pigpen; + Keith Godchaux [b. July 14, 1948, San Francisco; d. July 23, 1980, Marin County, CA], kybds.; + Donna Godchaux [b. Aug. 22, 1947, San Francisco], voc.) 1973—*History of the Grateful Dead* (Bear's Choice); *Wake of the Flood* (Grateful Dead) 1974—*Grateful Dead From the Mars Hotel; Skeletons From the Closet* (Warner Bros.) (+ Hart) 1975—*Blues for Allah* (Grateful Dead) 1976—*Steal Your Face* (Grateful Dead/United Artists) 1977—*Terrapin Station* (Arista); *What a Long Strange Trip It's Been: The Best of the Grateful Dead* (Warner Bros.) 1978—*Shakedown Street* (Arista) 1979—(– K. Godchaux; – D. Godchaux; + Brent Mydland [b. 1953, Munich, Ger.; d. July 26, 1990, Lafayette, CA], kybds.) 1980—*Go to Heaven* 1981—*Reckoning; Dead Set* 1987—*In the Dark* 1989—*Built to Last; Dylan & the Dead* (Columbia) 1990—*Without a Net* (Arista) (+ Vince Welnick [b. Feb. 22, 1952, Phoenix, AZ], kybds.) 1991—*One From the Vault* (Grateful Dead); *Infrared Roses* 1992—*Two From the Vault* 1995—*Hundred Year Hall* (Grateful Dead/Arista) 1996—*Dozin' at the Knick* (Arista) 1997—*Fallout From the Phil Zone* 1997—*Fillmore East 2-11-69* (Grateful Dead); *Live at Fillmore East* (Arista); *Capital Centre, Landover. . . .* (Grateful Dead) 2000—*Dead in a Deck (Built to Last)* (Arista) 2001—*The Golden Road 1965–1972* (Rhino).
Jerry Garcia solo: 1972—*Garcia* (Warner Bros.); *Hooteroll* (with Howard Wales) (Douglas) 1973—*Live at the Keystone* (Fantasy) 1974—*(Compliments of) Garcia* (Round) 1975—*Old & in the Way* 1976—*Reflections* 1978—*Cats Under the Stars* (Arista) 1982—*Run for the Roses* 1988—*Almost Acoustic* (Grateful Dead); *Keystone Encores, vols. 1 and 2* (Fantasy) 1991—*Jerry Garcia/David Grisman* (Acoustic Disc); *Jerry Garcia Band* (Arista) 1993—*Not for Kids Only* (with David Grisman) (Acoustic Disc) 1996—*Shady Grove* (with David Grisman) 1997—*How Sweet It Is* (Arista) 1998—*So What* (Acoustic Disc) 2000—*The Pizza Tapes.*
Bob Weir solo: 1972—*Ace* (Warner Bros.) 1976—*Kingfish* (Round) 1977—*Kingfish Live 'n' Kickin'* (Jet) 1978—*Heaven Help the Fool* (Arista) 1981—*Bobby and the Midnites* 1984—*Where the Beat Meets the Street* (Columbia).
Mickey Hart solo: 1972—*Rolling Thunder* (Warner Bros.) 1976—*Diga Rhythm Band* (Round) 1987—*Apocalypse Now Sessions: The Rhythm Devils Play River Music* (Passport) 1989—*Music to Be Born By* (Rykodisc) 1990—*At the Edge* 1991—*Planet Drum; Honor the Earth* 1996—*Mickey Hart's Mystery Box* 1998—*Supralingua* (Grateful Dead) 2000—*Spirit Into Sound: The Magic of Music* (Arista).
Phil Lesh (with Ned Lagin): 1975—*Seastones* (Round).
The Other Ones: 1999—*The Strange Remain* (Grateful Dead).

Psychedelic pioneers, the Grateful Dead was probably the most improvisatory of all major rock groups. From the late '60s until the 1995 death of leader Jerry Garcia, the Dead played long, freeform concerts that touched down on their own country-, blues-, and folk-tinged rock songs, and on a wide range of country, blues, and rock cover versions. Although Grateful Dead albums tended to sell a dependable 250,000 copies, the group had but one Top 10 single: "Touch of Grey."

The band concentrated on live shows rather than the recording process and by the '90s was consistently among the top-grossing tour attractions in all of rock. Nearly as famous as the band itself were the legions of "Deadheads"—predominantly white 18- to 24-year-olds who have lovingly preserved the era that spawned the Dead by emulating their Summer of Love predecessors' philosophy and that period's accoutrements: tie-dye clothing, hallucinogenic drugs, and the Dead's music. These fans supported the band with an almost religious fervor, following the group around the country and providing a synergy between band and audience that was unique in rock. In true psychedelic style, the Grateful Dead preferred the moment to the artifact—but to keep those moments coming, the Dead evolved into a far-flung and smoothly run corporate enterprise that, for all its hippie trimmings, drew admiring profiles in the financial and mainstream press.

Lead guitarist Jerry Garcia took up guitar at 15, spent nine months in the Army in 1959, then moved to Palo Alto, where he began his long-standing friendship with Robert Hunter, who later became the Dead's lyricist. In 1962 he bought a banjo and began playing in folk and bluegrass bands, and by 1964 he was a member of Mother McCree's Uptown Jug Champions, along with Bob Weir, Pigpen, and longtime associates Bob Matthews (who engineered Dead albums and formed the Alembic Electronics equipment

The Grateful Dead: Mickey Hart, Phil Lesh, Jerry Garcia, Brent Mydland, Bill Kreutzmann, Bob Weir

company) and John Dawson (later of New Riders of the Purple Sage).

In 1965 the band became the Warlocks: Garcia, Weir, Pigpen, Bill Kreutzmann, and Phil Lesh, a former electronic-music composer. With electric instruments, the Warlocks debuted in July 1965 and soon became the house band at Ken Kesey's Acid Tests, a series of public LSD parties and multimedia events held before the drug had been outlawed. LSD chemist Owsley Stanley bankrolled the Grateful Dead—a name from an Egyptian prayer that Garcia spotted in a dictionary—and later supervised construction of the band's massive, state-of-the-art sound system. The Dead lived communally at 710 Ashbury Street in San Francisco in 1966–67 and played numerous free concerts; by 1967's Summer of Love, they were regulars at the Avalon and Carousel ballrooms and the Fillmore West.

MGM signed the band in 1966, and it made some mediocre recordings. The Dead's legitimate recording career began when Warner Bros. signed it. While its 1967 debut album featured zippy three-minute songs, *Anthem of the Sun* (#87, 1968) and *Aoxomoxoa* (#73, 1969) featured extended suites and studio experiments that left the band $100,000 in debt to Warner Bros., mostly for studio time, by the end of the '60s. Meanwhile, the Dead's reputation had spread, and they appeared at the Monterey Pop Festival in 1967 and Woodstock in 1969.

As the '70s began, the Dead recouped its Warner debt with three comparatively inexpensive albums—*Live Dead* (#64, 1970) (recorded in concert), *Workingman's Dead* (#27, 1970), and *American Beauty* (#30, 1970). The former featured extended psychedelic explorations, such as the classic "Dark Star," while in sharp contrast the latter two found the Dead writing concise countryish songs and working out clear-cut, well-rehearsed arrangements. *Workingman's Dead* (including "Uncle John's Band" [#69, 1970] and "Casey Jones") and *American Beauty* (including "Truckin' " [#64, 1971], "Ripple," and "Box of Rain") received considerable FM radio airplay, sold respectably, and provided much of the Dead's concert repertoire.

With a nationwide following, the Dead expanded its touring schedule and started various solo and side projects (aside from the band members' own works, many Dead members also appeared on the half-dozen-plus albums Dead lyricist Robert Hunter began releasing in 1973). The group worked its way up to a 23-ton sound system and a large traveling entourage of road crew, family, friends, and hangers-on—most of whom would later become staff employees complete with health-insurance and other benefits, as the Dead evolved into an efficient and highly profitable corporation. The Dead finished out its Warners contract with a string of live albums including 1971's *Grateful Dead* (#25) (which introduced more concert staples such as "Bertha" and "Wharf Rat"). In 1973 the Dead played for over half a million people in Watkins Glen, New York, on a bill with the Band and the Allman Brothers. By then the group had formed its own Grateful Dead Records and a subsidiary, Round, for nonband efforts.

Europe '72 (#24, 1972) was the last album to feature keyboardist Pigpen, a heavy drinker who died in 1973 of liver disease. Keith Godchaux, who had played piano with Dave Mason, joined the band and brought along his wife, Donna, as background vocalist. The pair toured and recorded with the Dead until 1979, when they were asked to leave and were replaced by pianist Brent Mydland. The following year, Keith Godchaux was killed in a car crash in Marin County.

In 1974 the Dead temporarily disbanded while members pursued outside projects, but the group resumed touring in 1976. After signing with Arista, the group began to use non-Dead producers for the first time: Keith Olsen (Fleetwood Mac) for *Terrapin Station* (#28, 1977) and Little Feat's Lowell George for *Shakedown Street* (#41, 1978). In 1978 the band played three concerts at the foot of the Great Pyramid in Egypt, which were recorded but not released. *Go to Heaven* (#23, 1980) yielded "Alabama Getaway" (#68, 1980), like "Truckin' " and "Uncle John's Band," a minor hit single. The Dead's main support continued to be its touring six months each year. The band celebrated its 15th anniversary with the release of two more live albums, including the mostly acoustic *Reckoning* (#43, 1981).

The band took a hiatus from recording until 1987, during which time the Dead toured with Bob Dylan (one tour was recorded for the album *Dylan and the Dead*) (#37, 1989), while Garcia's health and personal habits made disturbing headlines: In January 1985 he was arrested for heroin possession in San Francisco's Golden Gate Park; in July 1986, 15 months after being in a drug treatment program and while touring with Dylan, Garcia collapsed into a five-day, near-fatal diabetic coma brought on by drug use. Once he recovered, the Dead made a triumphant return with *In the Dark* (#6, 1987), their first Top 10 album, yielding "Touch of Grey" (#9, 1987). Two years later, however, trouble suddenly began following the Dead and its normally mellow army of Deadheads on tour. In April 1989 there were 55 arrests (mostly for drugs and disturbing the peace) and violent encounters with police at two Pittsburgh shows; and 70 arrests and reports of vandalism by Dead fans at three Irvine, California, shows. In October 1989 a college student died of a broken neck outside a Dead show at the New Jersey Meadowlands (his death was never explained, but an investigation cleared security guards of guilt); in December of that year a 19-year-old fan high on LSD died while in police custody for public intoxication at the L.A. Forum (the autopsy reported neck-compression during restraint, but police were cleared of any wrongdoing). As a result, the Dead recorded public service announcements imploring fans to act responsibly.

In July 1990 Mydland died of an overdose of injected cocaine and morphine. He was replaced by Vince Welnick, formerly of San Francisco's the Tubes; Bruce Hornsby, a Dead fan, sometimes sat in on piano during concerts as well. Welnick was not on the two *From the Vault* albums, which issued old tapes of legendary Dead shows (from 1968 in L.A. and San Francisco, and from the latter in 1974). In September 1992 the bearish, chain-smoking Garcia was hospitalized with diabetes, an enlarged heart, and fluid in the lungs. The Dead was forced to postpone a tour until the end of the year;

doctors put Garcia on a strict diet, exercise, and no-smoking regimen. The Dead returned to the road with a slimmer, fitter Garcia in mid-December 1992 with a series of Bay Area concerts.

That same year Garcia—whose paintings, often pastel watercolors, had been exhibited internationally—unveiled a line of designer silk neckties bearing his artwork. By then the massive catalogue of Dead merchandise also included skis and snowboards as well as T-shirts and even a line of toddler wear. The Dead's tours in 1994–95 earned the band $52 million. In 1995 the Dead were inducted into the Rock and Roll Hall of Fame.

On July 9, 1995, Jerry Garcia played his last show with the Grateful Dead. One month later, he died in his sleep at Serenity Knolls, a rehabilitation center where he'd been combating his long-standing heroin addiction. The cause of death was reported as a heart attack. Shortly thereafter, flags flew at half-mast at the San Francisco City Hall to mark the passing of an era. Garcia was survived by four daughters and his third wife, Deborah Koons Garcia, whom he had married the year before. Four months later, the band officially retired.

The music, however, continued. After Garcia's death, archival material, notably in the form of *Dick's Picks,* live sets chosen by super-fan Dick Latvala, was released in abundance. And the band's members, in various conglomerations, resumed playing: Bob Weir with his band, Ratdog, Phil Lesh with Phil Lesh and Friends. In 1998, as the Other Ones, Weir, Lesh, Hart, and Hornsby headlined the Furthur Festival, reviving for many fans the Deadhead spirit.

During their tenure with the Dead, the main members had worked at a number of side projects. Garcia's included session work with Jefferson Airplane and Crosby, Stills, Nash and Young. He formed New Riders of the Purple Sage in 1969 as a side project [see entry]. From 1970 to 1973 he played occasional gigs with Bay Area keyboardist Merl Saunders (captured on the Keystone albums), and he kept up his bluegrass banjo skills with *Old & In the Way,* which also featured Peter Rowan (Sectarian), Vassar Clements, and David Grisman. Garcia recorded his first solo album, *Garcia,* in 1972; the cover shows his right hand, which has been missing its third finger since a childhood accident. Garcia joined organist Howard Wales on *Hooteroll,* and he toured and recorded with various Jerry Garcia bands in the '70s and '80s, before recording with David Grisman (who'd played mandolin on *American Beauty*) for two acoustic albums. His last project was an album of children's music, *Not for Kids Only* (Acoustic Disc), released in 1993.

Weir's first solo effort was 1972's *Ace,* which featured most of the Dead backing him. During the Dead's sabbatical he formed Kingfish with ex–New Rider Dave Torbert; in the early '80s Weir toured and recorded with Bobby and the Midnites, including drummer Billy Cobham (Mahavishnu Orchestra), bassist Alphonso Johnson (Weather Report), and guitarist Bobby Cochran (Steppenwolf). In 1991 Weir and his sister Wendy published *Panther Dream,* a children's book and companion audiocassette aimed at raising awareness of endangered rainforests—a cause the Dead had been supporting for several years through its Rex Foundation. In 1999 Weir completed a musical on the life of baseball legend Satchel Paige and continued working on digitizing the Dead song archives.

Phil Lesh teamed with electronic music composer Ned Lagin to record the atonal, aleatoric *Seastones.* Dead drummer Mickey Hart explored world music through his solo albums, with the Diga Rhythm Band, the Rhythm Devils (Hart and Kreutzmann composed incidental percussion music for the soundtrack of the film *Apocalypse Now*), and by producing albums by musicians from Africa, Asia, and South and Central America on Rykodisc. In 1991 Hart helped arrange a U.S. tour by the Gyuto Monks of Tibet. He also toured with his band, Planet Drum. By 2000, he'd written a book, *Spirit Into Sound: The Magic of Music,* and formed a new ensemble, the Mickey Hart Band.

Dobie Gray

Born Leonard Victor Ainsworth, July 26, 1942, Brookshire, TX
1973—*Drift Away* (Decca) 1975—*New Ray of Sunshine* (Capricorn) 1978—*Midnight Diamond* (Infinity) 1979—*Dobie Gray* 1981—*Welcome Home* (Robox) 1996—*Drift Away: His Very Best* (Razor & Tie).

Following a brief but successful mid-'60s pop career, singer Dobie Gray turned to country soul. Gray was born to sharecroppers with eight children. By the early '60s, he had moved to the West Coast to become a singer. Through a radio ad, he met Sonny Bono, who helped him get started. Gray had a minor hit, "Look at Me" (1963), but his next single, "The 'In' Crowd," was the biggest hit of his early period (#13, 1965), and a gold record. "See You at the 'Go-Go,' " which followed, stalled on the lower rungs of the chart.

By the late '60s, Gray had enrolled in prelaw classes and started acting. He appeared in a New York production of *The Beard,* Jean Genet's *The Balcony,* and the L.A. production of *Hair.* Despite his success in theater, Gray returned to music and through 1969 and 1970 he worked with the group Pollution. While cutting demos for songwriter Paul Williams, he met Williams' brother, Mentor, with whom he worked as a staff writer for A&M Records.

In 1973 Gray released *Drift Away,* the first of three MCA albums produced by Mentor Williams. The title track (written by Williams and later covered by Rod Stewart, among others) sold 1.5 million copies and hit #5. Late that summer Gray followed up with "Loving Arms," which sold over 100,000 copies. In 1975 (the same year he signed with Capricorn for the disco-tinged *New Ray of Sunshine*), Gray began playing benefit concerts for presidential candidate Jimmy Carter; in January 1977 he sang at Carter's inaugural-eve ceremonies. Gray continues to record and perform.

Macy Gray

Born Natalie Renee McIntyre, Sep. 9, 1970, Canton, OH
1999—*On How Life Is* (Epic) 2001—*The Id.*

One of the more unusual vocalists to emerge in the late '90s, Macy Gray claims a high-pitched voice undercut by an earthy rasp. Though it embarrassed her as a child growing up in a working-class black neighborhood in Canton, Ohio, it would later win her acclaim as an inheritor of such classic R&B and blues divas as Tina Turner and Billie Holiday. At 17, Gray (her stage name is an homage to a beloved family neighbor) moved to L.A., where she attended film school at the University of Southern California. There, she began singing jazz standards in local bars. In 1994 she recorded an album for Atlantic Records that was never released. She persevered, hosting open-mike performances after hours at a coffeehouse frequented by members of alternative hip-hop acts the Roots, Black Eyed Peas, and others. Experimenting with her own sound, a mix of old-school R&B, hip-hop, and funk, Gray—by now a single mother of three children—won a deal with Epic Records in 1998 and began recording her debut with producer/manager Andrew Slater (Fiona Apple, the Wallflowers). The triple-platinum *On How Life Is* (#4 pop, #9 R&B, 1999) yielded the hit single "I Try" (#5, 2000), which won a Grammy for Best Female Pop Vocal Performance.

Al Green

Born Al Greene, Apr. 13, 1946, Forrest City, AK
1970—*Green Is Blues* (Hi); *Gets Next to You* 1972—*Let's Stay Together; I'm Still in Love With You* 1973—*Call Me; Living for You* 1974—*Explores Your Mind* 1975—*Al Green Is Love; Greatest Hits* 1976—*Full of Fire; Have a Good Time* 1977—*The Belle Album; Greatest Hits, vol. 2* 1978—*Love Ritual; Truth and Time* 1980—*The Lord Will Make a Way* (Myrrh) 1981—*Higher Plane* 1982—*Precious Lord* 1983—*I'll Rise Again; Al Green Sings the Gospel* (Motown) 1985—*He Is the Light* (A&M) 1986—*Trust in God* (Motown) 1987—*Soul Survivor* 1989—*Love Ritual: Rare and Previously Unreleased 1968–76* (MCA); *I Get Joy* (A&M) 1991—*One in a Million* (Word/Epic) 1992—*Love Is Reality* 1995—*Your Heart's in Good Hands* (MCA) 1997—*Anthology* (The Right Stuff/Capitol).

To a greater extent than even his predecessors Sam Cooke and Otis Redding, Al Green embodies both the sacred and the profane in soul music. He was one of the most popular vocalists in the '70s, selling over 20 million records. His wildly improvisational, ecstatic cries and moans came directly from gospel music, and in the late '70s he returned to the Baptist church as a preacher. He continues to record albums in a pop-gospel style (to date he has earned eight gospel Grammys) with close ties to the Memphis soul music that made him famous.

Green (who dropped the third "e" from his surname when he went solo) was born to a large family of sharecroppers. When he was nine, he and his brothers formed a gospel quartet, the Greene Brothers. They toured the gospel circuits in the South and after the family moved to Grand Rapids, Michigan, three years later. Green's father dismissed him from the quartet after he caught him listening to the "profane music" of Jackie Wilson. At 16 he formed a pop group, Al Greene and the Creations, with high school friends. Two members of the Creations, Palmer James and Curtis Rogers, founded a record company, Hot Line Music Journal, for which the group—renamed Al Greene and the Soul Mates—cut "Back Up Train" in 1967. The single went to #5 on the national R&B chart. Followups failed, however, and the group broke up.

Green met Willie Mitchell in Midland, Texas, in 1969. Mitchell was a bandleader, a producer, and a vice president of Hi Records of Memphis, to which he signed Green. He also became Green's producer and songwriting partner for the next eight years. *Green Is Blues* introduced the sound that would distinguish all the records Green made with Mitchell: simple but emphatic backbeats riding subdued horns and strings, and Green's voice floating untethered over the instruments.

His second album contained Green's first solo hits—"You Say It" (#28 R&B, 1970), "Right Now, Right Now" (#23 R&B, 1970), and "I Can't Get Next to You" (#11 R&B, 1970)—and his first gold single, "Tired of Being Alone" (#11 pop, #7 R&B, 1971), which he wrote. That began a three-year string of gold singles, most of them written by Green, Mitchell, and Jackson: "Let's Stay Together" (#1 pop, #1 R&B, 1971), "Look What You Done for Me" (#4 pop, #2 R&B, 1972), "I'm Still in Love With You" (#3 pop, #1 R&B, 1972), "You Ought to Be With Me" (#3 pop, #1 R&B, 1972), "Call Me (Come Back Home)" (#10 pop, #2 R&B, 1973), "Here I Am (Come and Take Me)" (#10 pop, #2 R&B, 1973), "Sha La La (Make Me Happy)" (#7 pop, #2 R&B, 1974), and "L-O-V-E (Love)" (#13 pop, #1 R&B, 1975).

In October 1974 Green was hospitalized with second-degree burns on his back, arm, and stomach. A former girlfriend, Mrs. Mary Woodson of New Jersey, had poured boiling grits on him while he was bathing in his Memphis home and then killed herself with his gun. The incident apparently triggered a spiritual crisis in Green, and he announced his intention to go into the ministry. In 1976 he purchased a church

Al Green

building in Memphis and was ordained pastor of the Full Gospel Tabernacle.

He did not, however, give up his pop career, and he preached at his church only when he was not on tour. His records continued to place regularly on the R&B chart and occasionally on the pop chart. In 1977 he built himself a studio and, with *Belle*, began producing his own records, maintaining the style and standards he had set with Mitchell. But during a 1979 concert in Cincinnati, he fell off the stage and narrowly escaped serious injury. He considered the incident a warning from God. For a time thereafter, his public appearances were limited to religious services in churches around the country, where he both sang and preached.

His '80s recordings, distributed by Myrrh, a gospel label, contain only religious songs, both standard hymns and Green's originals, in a style that mixes Memphis soul with gospel. In 1982 he did a stint on Broadway, costarring with Patti LaBelle in Vinnette Carroll's gospel musical *Your Arms Too Short to Box With God*. Talking Heads scored one of their biggest pop hits with a cover of Green's "Take Me to the River," and Green himself duetted with Annie Lennox of Eurythmics on the Jackie DeShannon classic "Put a Little Love in Your Heart," for the soundtrack of the 1988 film *Scrooged*. In 1992 Green signed a new deal with BMG Records and returned to the Memphis soul sound of his roots with *Don't Look Back*, which featured production help from David Steele and Andy Cox (Fine Young Cannibals) and Arthur Baker (Afrika Bambaataa's "Planet Rock" and other early-'80s dance hits). MCA released the album in the U.S. under the title *Your Heart's in Good Hands* in 1995. The year before, Green duetted with Lyle Lovett on Willie Nelson's "Funny How Time Slips Away" for *Rhythm, Country, and Blues*, a collection of duets that teamed up well-known artists in each of these fields. That collaboration netted him a Grammy. Green's box set, *Anthology*, includes not only the hits and other album cuts, but his onstage sermonizing and interview snippets. In 1995 Green was inducted into the Rock and Roll Hall of Fame. He sang "Funny How Time Slips Away" with Willie Nelson at the induction ceremony.

Today, Green performs both gospel and soul material in concert. Most recently, he has had an ongoing role in the TV series *Ally McBeal*, where he plays an evanescent character who moves in and out of McBeal's subconsciousness. In fall 2000 HarperCollins released his autobiography, *Take Me to the River*.

Norman Greenbaum

Born Nov. 20, 1942, Malden, MA
1969—*Spirit in the Sky* (Reprise) 1970—*Back Home Again* 1972—*Petaluma* 1995—*Spirit in the Sky: The Best of Norman Greenbaum* (Varèse Vintage).

In 1970 folksinger/songwriter Norman Greenbaum's electrified jug-band stomp "Spirit in the Sky" sold 2 million copies. After playing local coffeehouses while attending Boston University, he had moved to the West Coast in the mid-'60s and formed Dr. West's Medicine Show and Junk Band, a psychedelic jug band that had a minor hit, "The Eggplant That Ate Chicago" (#52, 1966) before disbanding in 1967. Greenbaum then formed several other unsuccessful groups before embarking on his solo career in 1968. Working with producer and cowriter Eric Jacobson, he released a couple of unsuccessful singles from his Reprise debut, *Spirit in the Sky*, before the title track hit #3 on the American chart. Greenbaum's followups ("Canned Ham," 1970; "California Earthquake," 1971) never hit.

When *Petaluma* was released in 1972, he was largely out of the public eye, spending most of his time running a goat dairy on a farm near Petaluma, California. In 1983 the singer began dabbling in management and concert production. In 1986 British glam-pop band Doctor and the Medics recorded a hit cover of "Spirit in the Sky." The song has since become a popular cover for contemporary Christian artists. Greenbaum continues to work on songs at his home in Northern California.

Green Day

Formed 1989, Berkeley, CA
Billie Joe Armstrong (b. Feb. 17, 1972, CA), voc. gtr.; Mike Dirnt (b. Mike Pritchard, May 4, 1972, CA), bass; John Kiffmeyer, drums.
1990—*39/Smooth* (Lookout) 1992—(– Kiffmeyer; + Tre Cool [b. Frank Edwin Wright III, Dec. 9, 1972, Ger.], drums) *Kerplunk* 1994—*Dookie* (Reprise) 1995—*Insomniac* 1997—*Nimrod* 2000—*Warning*.

Punk revivalists in style, this raucous trio achieved triple-platinum status with their major-label debut, *Dookie*. Although Green Day's taut, three-minute, guitar-driven songs ably revive the fierceness of the group's stylistic progenitors (the Who, the Clash, and the Sex Pistols), punk's original aim—to annoy, outrage, shock—is not Green Day's thing.

Friends since age 10, Billie Joe Armstrong and Mike Dirnt grew up in Rodeo, California. They formed their first real band, Sweet Children, at 14. When they were 17, the pair first recorded as Green Day, signing with the punk label Lookout and releasing the 1989 EP *1,000 Hours* with drummer John Kiffmeyer. The next year, the group recorded its first full-length album, *39/Smooth*, in a day. Two more EPs followed, with Kiffmeyer leaving to focus on his studies and Tre Cool, with whom Armstrong had played in a band called the Lookouts, taking over on drums for 1992's *Kerplunk*. With a solid fan base built on the nurturing, all-ages hardcore scene in Berkeley, the group signed with Reprise in April 1993. Its 1994 release, *Dookie*, proclaimed the next generation of punk, hitting #4 on the album chart, buoyed by the band's effervescent presence on MTV and at Lollapalooza and Woodstock '94. The album won a 1994 Grammy Award for Best Alternative Music Performance and sold 10 million copies worldwide. The 1995 followup *Insomniac* sold nearly 3 million copies and charted at #2, but failed to repeat the success of the band's major-label debut. *Nimrod* (#10, 1997) sold a million copies but won fresh exposure for the group, largely on the strength of the ballad "Good Riddance (Time of Your Life)." In 2000, Green Day released *Warning* (#4), a more introspective, even folk-influenced record that showed the group stretching artistically.

Professor Griff: See Public Enemy

Nanci Griffith

Born Nanci Caroline Griffith, July 6, 1953, Seguin, TX
1978—*There's a Light Beyond These Woods* (B.F. Deal) 1982—*Poet in My Window* (Featherbed) 1985—*Once in a Very Blue Moon* (Philo/Rounder) 1986—*Last of the True Believers* 1987—*Lone Star State of Mind* (MCA) 1988—*Little Love Affairs; One Fair Summer Evening* 1989—*Storms* 1991—*Late Night Grande Hotel* 1993—*Other Voices, Other Rooms* (Elektra) 1994—Flyer 1997—*Blue Roses From the Moons* 1998—*Other Voices, Too (A Trip Back to Bountiful)* 1999—*The Dust Bowl Symphony.*

Chronicling the lives of everyday people in a sweet voice and a direct, realistic style, singer/songwriter Nanci Griffith's brand of contemporary folk music—"folkabilly," as she calls it—draws on both country textures and Southern literary tradition. (She has written short stories and novels.) A gifted interpreter, Griffith is equally well regarded for her covers of songs by a range of artists, from Woody Guthrie to Lyle Lovett, as well as having her own songs covered by the likes of Kathy Mattea and Suzy Bogguss.

As a child, Griffith was exposed to a variety of jazz, country, and folk records; folk singer Carolyn Hester was a particular favorite. Griffith began playing guitar and singing in bars when she was 14 and continued while studying at the University of Texas. After graduating and working briefly as a kindergarten teacher, she began recording for independent labels. By the mid-'80s, her graceful soprano had attracted the attention of MCA Records.

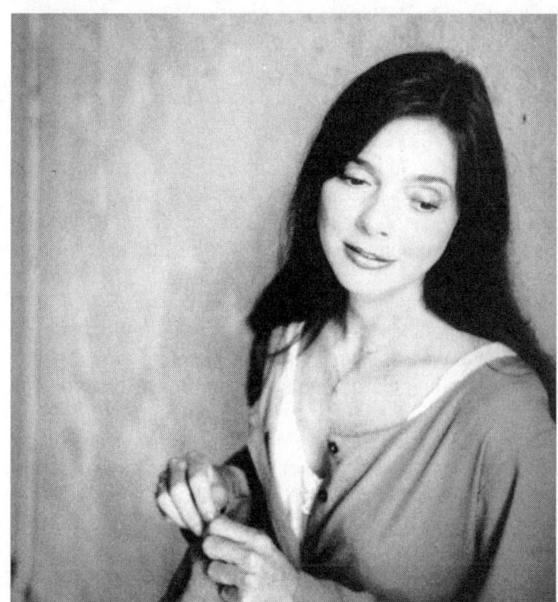

Nanci Griffith

Her MCA debut, *Lone Star State of Mind,* included a rendition of Julie Gold's "From a Distance," which Griffith wanted to release as a single: MCA refused, and in 1990 Bette Midler had a smash hit with the song. (Griffith's version did become a #1 single in Ireland, where she's enormously popular.) Griffith's frustration with MCA worsened, and she eventually defected to Elektra Records. *Other Voices, Other Rooms* (the title of Truman Capote's first book), an assortment of songs by influential folk artists, featured such guest musicians as Bob Dylan, John Prine, and Emmylou Harris, peaked on the charts at #54 in 1993, and won the Grammy for Best Contemporary Folk Album that year.

After undergoing radiation treatment for breast cancer in 1997, Griffith recorded a sequel to that album, *Other Voices, Too (A Trip Back to Bountiful)* (#85, 1998), in which she took a supporting role on several tracks to showcase the singing of her numerous guest vocalists. In addition, she oversaw a book about the recording of both albums, *Nanci Griffith's Other Voices: A Personal History of Folk Music,* published in 1998. In 1999 Griffith went in a classical direction with two projects: an album of new arrangements performed with the London Symphony Orchestra *(Dust Bowl Symphony),* and playing several of her songs live as part of *This Heart,* an original modern dance piece by Paul Vasterling, leader of the Nashville Ballet. She also awaited the publication of one of her novels, *Two of a Kind Heart.* Despite widespread support from fans and peers, to date Griffith has not found a niche on commercial radio.

Grin: See Nils Lofgren

The Guess Who

Formed 1962, Winnipeg, Can.
Chad Allan (b. Allan Kobel, ca. 1945), voc., gtr.; Bob Ashley, piano; Randy Bachman (b. Sep. 27, 1943, Winnipeg), gtr., voc.; Garry Peterson (b. May 26, 1945), drums; Jim Kale (b. Aug. 11, 1943, Winnipeg), bass.
1965—(– Ashley; + Burton Cummings [b. Dec. 31, 1947, Winnipeg], kybds., voc.) *Shakin' All Over* (Scepter) 1966—(– Allan; + Bruce Dekker, voc.; – Dekker) 1969—*Wheatfield Soul* (RCA); *Canned Wheat Packed by the Guess Who* 1970—*American Woman* (– Bachman; + Greg Leskiw [b. Aug. 5, 1947], gtr.; + Kurt Winter [b. Apr. 2, 1946], gtr.) *Share the Land* 1971—*So Long, Bannatyne; Best of* 1972—*Rockin'* (– Leskiw; + Don McDougall [b. Nov. 5, 1947], gtr.) *Live at the Paramount* (– Kale; + Bill Wallace [b. May 18, 1949], bass, voc.) 1973—*#10; Best of, vol. 2* 1974—*Artificial Paradise; Road Food* (– Winter; – D. McDougall; + Domenic Troiano [b. ca.

1945, Modugno, It.], gtr., voc.) *Flavours* 1975—*Power in the Music; Born in Canada* (group disbands) 1977—*The Greatest of the Guess Who* (RCA) 1979—(group re-forms: Kale; D. McDougall; + Allan McDougall, voc.; + Vince Masters, drums; + David Inglis, gtr.; + David Parasz, horns) *All This for a Song* (Hilltak) (numerous personnel changes follow) 1997—*The Ultimate Collection* (RCA) 1999—(classic lineup re-forms: Bachman; Kale; Cummings; Peterson; D. McDougall) 2000—(– Kale; + Wallace).
Burton Cummings solo: 1976—*Burton Cummings* (Portrait) 1977—*My Own Way to Rock* 1981—*Sweet Sweet* (Alfa).

The Guess Who was Canada's premier singles band through the early '70s. The group, whose members were all born in Winnipeg, dates back to 1962, when buddies Chad Allan and Randy Bachman formed Allan and the Silvertones, later the Reflections, and then (to avoid confusion with a Detroit group) Chad Allan and the Expression. In 1965 the group changed its name to the Guess Who and had a surprise hit with a cover of Johnny Kidd and the Pirates' "Shakin' All Over" (#22, 1965). Its record company saw in the Guess Who's name an opportunity to imply that the band was actually a famous British group incognito. The group toured the United States as part of Dick Clark's Caravan of Stars Revue. That summer Burton Cummings joined, and when Allan left in 1966, he became the band's lead vocalist and focal point.

In 1968 the Guess Who landed a regular spot on the CBC-TV show *Where It's At,* hosted by ex-leader Allan. The group had minor success in Canada, but was unable to crack the U.S. market until producer Jack Richardson mortgaged his house to pay for the quartet to record in New York in September 1968. Richardson produced the first gold Guess Who single in the U.S., "These Eyes" (#6, 1969). The band's second RCA LP, *Canned Wheat,* boasted two hits—"Laughing" (#10, 1969) and "Undun" (#22, 1969).

In 1970 the Guess Who's record sales totaled $5 million, largely on the strength of its third album, *American Woman.* The fuzz guitar–propelled title track (#1) and "No Time" (#5) were U.S. hits. The Guess Who performed at the White House with Prince Charles and Princess Anne in attendance; First Lady Pat Nixon, undoubtedly briefed as to "American Woman"'s scathing anti-U.S. sentiment, requested that the band delete the song from its set.

While at the height of success, Cummings and Bachman were feuding bitterly; the guitarist, having recently converted to the Mormon faith, found the band's hedonistic lifestyle offensive. In July he departed, first for a brief collaboration with Allan as Brave Belt, then without Allan as Bachman-Turner Overdrive [see entry]. The Guess Who replaced him with two guitarists and continued its singles success with "Share the Land" (#10, 1970), "Hand Me Down World" (#17, 1970), "Rain Dance" (#19, 1971), and "Albert Flasher" (#29, 1971). But two years passed before the band's next Top 40 hit, by which time former James Gang guitarist Dominic Troiano was a member. A novelty tribute to disc jockey Wolfman Jack, "Clap for the Wolfman," made the Top 10, and another single, "Dancin' Fool," cracked the Top 30. Nevertheless, the group disbanded the next year.

Cummings had a hit on his first solo album with "Stand Tall" (#10, 1976). His 1981 album *Sweet Sweet* included a Top 40 hit, "You Saved My Soul." He continues to release Canadian albums. Cummings and Randy Bachman eventually made amends, and in 1983 the original group got back together for an album and concert video. Four years later the two toured together. Meanwhile, an everchanging Jim Kale–led lineup has continued to tour as the Guess Who since 1979, often with Kale as the sole '60s survivor. As of 1989, drummer Garry Peterson was also on the payroll. The Kale-led Guess Who has released several marginal albums on small labels such as Hilltak and El Mocambo.

In 1999, partially inspired by the U.S. chart success of Lenny Kravitz' take on "American Woman" (#49), the band's classic '60s lineup (plus '70s vet Don McDougall on rhythm guitar) reunited. Kale bowed out before an extensive Canadian tour; another '70s alumnus, Bill Wallace, replaced him. The group also performed with Kravitz at Canada's MuchMusic Awards.

Guided by Voices

Formed ca. 1985, Dayton, OH
Robert Pollard Jr. (b. Oct. 31, 1957, Dayton), voc., gtr. (with numerous personnel changes).
1987—*Devil Between My Toes* (Schwa); *Sandbox* (Halo) 1989—*Self-Inflicted Aerial Nostalgia* 1990—*Same Place the Fly Got Smashed* (Rocket #9) 1992—*Propeller* (Rockathon) 1993—*Vampire on Titus* (Scat) 1994—*Bee Thousand* (Scat/Matador); *Crying Your Knife Away* (Lo-Fi) 1995—*Alien Lanes* (Matador); *Box* (Scat) 1996—*Jellyfish Reflector* (Jellyfish); *Under the Bushes Under the Stars* (Matador) 1997—*Mag Earwig!; Tonics and Twisted Chasers* (Rockathon) 1999—*Do the Collapse* (TVT) 2000—*Suitcase: Failed Experiments and Trashed Aircraft* (Fading Captain Series #6) 2001—*Isolation Drills* (TVT).

Dayton, Ohio's Guided by Voices had been releasing records for years before being discovered by the growing '90s alternative-rock scene. Core member singer/guitarist Robert Pollard, a one-time school teacher, led a revolving cast of players through extremes in melody and noise, making the band a champion of lo-fi indie rock, which evolved by decade's end into an accessible big-rock sound.

Pollard was still teaching fourth grade when he first began spending his summers on musical experiments with drummer Kevin Fennell and guitarist Mitch Mitchell. Calling the band Guided by Voices, the musicians began recording mainly as a hobby, and played to mostly unreceptive local barroom audiences. Early independent releases collected eccentric, lo-fi tracks that were sometimes almost comically brief. By 1992's *Propeller* (on the band's own Rockathon label), the group had essentially broken up. Guided by Voices then regrouped to sign with Ohio-based Scat Records, releasing 1994's *Bee Thousand* to a fast-growing alt-rock following. In 1994, after 14 years, Pollard finally quit his teaching job.

The band reached an even larger audience after it signed to Matador, which released 1995's 28-track *Alien Lanes. Under the Bushes Under the Stars* (1996) was the band's first album cut in a professional recording studio, coproduced by Steve Albini and Kim Deal (Breeders, Pixies). Pollard had branched out into solo projects, including releases under the names Nightwalker and Lexo & the Leapers. With 1999's *Do the Collapse* (produced by Ric Ocasek), Guided by Voices introduced a more accessible rock sound, with conventional guitar solos and more polished production values.

Guitar Slim

Born Eddie Jones, Dec. 10, 1926, Greenwood, MS; died Feb. 7, 1959, New York, NY
1954—*Things That I Used to Do* (Specialty) 1987—*The Atco Sessions* (Atlantic) 1991—*Sufferin' Mind* (Speciality).

Blues guitarist/singer Eddie "Guitar Slim" Jones' "Things That I Used to Do" was one of the top R&B records of 1954, selling a million copies. The song (now a blues standard) fused gospel and the blues, and featured Jones' electric guitar as well as the piano of a then largely unknown Ray Charles.

Jones began singing in church choirs as a child. While still in his teens, he formed a trio with pianist Huey "Piano" Smith and later began working solo. He recorded for Imperial and JB between 1951 and 1952. He served in the U.S. Army in Korea in the early '50s. An electric guitar pioneer, Jones was also a flashy dresser and a famed showman, known for playing hot in-concert solos while wandering as far as his 200-foot extension cord would allow. He died of pneumonia at the age of 32 and is buried (with his gold-top Gibson Les Paul guitar) in Thibodaux, Louisiana. His son has performed under the name Guitar Slim Jr.

The first known "Guitar Slim," incidentally, was a blues musician from Texas, Norman Green (born July 25, 1907; died September 28, 1975), who had minor hits, including "Fifth Street Alley Blues" and "Old Folks Boogie."

Guns n' Roses

Formed 1985, Los Angeles, CA
Axl Rose (b. William Bailey, Feb. 6, 1962, Lafayette, IN), voc.; Slash (b. Saul Hudson, July 23, 1965, Stoke-on-Trent, Eng.), gtr.; Duff McKagan (b. Michael McKagan, Feb. 5, 1964, Seattle, WA), bass; Steve Adler (b. 1965, OH), drums; Izzy Stradlin (b. Jeff Isbell, Apr. 8, 1962, Lafayette, IN) gtr.
1986—*Live?! *@ Like a Suicide* EP (Uzi/Suicide) 1987—*Appetite for Destruction* (Geffen) 1988—*GN'R Lies* 1990—(– Adler; + Matt Sorum [b. Nov. 19, 1960, Long Beach, CA], drums; + Dizzy Reed [b. Darren Reed, June 18, 1963, Hinsdale, IL], kybds.) 1991—*Use Your Illusion I; Use Your Illusion II* (– Stradlin; + Gilby Clarke [b. Aug. 17, 1962, Cleveland, OH], gtr.) 1993—*The Spaghetti Incident?* (– Slash; – McKagan; – Sorum; – Clarke; + Buckethead, gtr.; + Robin Finck, gtr.; + Paul Tobias, gtr.; + Tommy Stinson [b. Oct. 6, 1966, San Diego, CA], bass; + Chris Pittman, kybds.; + Brian "Brain" Mantia, drums) 1999—*Live Era '87–'93* 2001—*Chinese Democracy* (Interscope).
Izzy Stradlin with the JuJu Hounds: Stradlin, gtr., voc.; Jimmy Ashhurst, bass; Charlie "Chalo" Quintana, drums; Rick Richards (b. Mar. 30, 1954, Jasper, GA), gtr.
1992—*Izzy Stradlin & the JuJu Hounds* (Geffen).
Duff McKagan solo: 1993—*Believe in Me* (Geffen).
Gilby Clarke solo: 1994—*Pawn Shop Guitars* (Virgin).
Slash with Snakepit: Slash, gtr.; Sorum, drums; Clarke, gtr.; Mike Inez, bass; Eric Dover, voc.
1995—*It's Five O'Clock Somewhere* (Geffen) 2000—*Ain't Life Grand* (Koch) (– Inez; + Johnny Blackout, bass).

With *Appetite for Destruction,* the biggest-selling debut in history, Guns n' Roses gained stardom in the late '80s with '70s-derived hard rock and a hedonistic rebelliousness that recalled the early Rolling Stones. Combining heavy-metal technique with punk attitude, the band provoked charges of multifarious bigotry but leavened their outrage with songs that bespoke the inchoate emotions of hard rock's primarily young, white male audience.

Raised in a working-class Indiana family, high school dropout Axl Rose had, by age 20, compiled a police record that included charges for public intoxication, criminal trespass, and contributing to the delinquency of a minor. An ELO and Queen fan, the singer became friends with guitarist Izzy Stradlin, and the two joined forces in L.A. in the early '80s to form a band. Crafting their name from those of two groups they'd played in, Hollywood Rose and L.A. Guns, they formed Guns n' Roses with English-born biracial guitarist Slash, whose parents, both in the music industry, had moved to L.A. when he was 11. With bassist Duff McKagan, whose own past included stealing a purported 133 automobiles, and drummer Steve Adler, the Gunners accrued notoriety (alluding to the band's heroin and alcohol abuse, their posters featured the legend "Addicted: Only the Strong Survive").

After independently releasing an EP, Guns n' Roses signed with Geffen in 1986, and, with producer Mike Clink (Heart, Eddie Money), put out *Appetite for Destruction.* Opening for Aerosmith, the band built a live following; and in September 1988, with wide MTV exposure given "Sweet Child o' Mine" (#1, 1988) and "Welcome to the Jungle" (#7, 1988), the album reached #1; it stayed there for five weeks and on the charts for nearly three years.

Next came *GN'R Lies,* a Top 5 album that combined tracks from the EP with new songs, notably "Used to Love Her," with its chorus of ". . . but I had to kill her," and "One in a Million," its lyrics disparaging "faggots," "immigrants," and "niggers." Controversy ensued and would not let up. In 1988 two fans died in crowd disturbances at England's Monsters of Rock Festival, and, while opening select dates for the Rolling Stones' 1989 tour garnered G n' R a larger audience, Slash shocked television viewers with an obscenity-laden

Guns n' Roses: Axl Rose, Duff McKagan, Matt Sorum, Slash

speech at the American Music Awards the following year. Concurrently, reports surfaced of heroin use by Rose, Stradlin, and Adler, and Adler was fired for not straightening out.

In 1990 the band performed at Farm Aid IV and contributed a cover of Bob Dylan's "Knockin' on Heaven's Door" to the *Days of Thunder* soundtrack and an original, "Civil War," to *Nobody's Child,* a project to benefit Romanian orphans; Slash and McKagan played on Iggy Pop's *Brick by Brick* and Slash recorded with Dylan, Michael Jackson, Lenny Kravitz, and on a tribute album for Les Paul. But with Matt Sorum, formerly of the Cult, brought in on drums and with new keyboardist Dizzy Reed, 1990 was a year of regrouping.

The following year brought even greater success if no less turmoil. G n' R embarked on its first headlining world tour and released "You Could Be Mine" (#29, 1991) from the *Terminator 2* soundtrack. But Rose's marriage to Erin Everly, daughter of Don Everly of the Everly Brothers, ended after three weeks amidst allegations of physical abuse, and Rose, after allegedly attacking a camera-wielding fan at a St. Louis concert, was charged with four misdemeanor counts of assault and one of property damage. Rose pleaded not guilty and remained unrepentant about an ensuing riot that left 60 people hospitalized, the band's equipment destroyed or stolen, and the hall sustaining over $200,000 in damages.

With Rose embarked on psychotherapy (during which he maintained discovery of sexual abuse at age two by his father), 1991 saw the simultaneous release of *Use Your Illusion I* and *Use Your Illusion II,* both shipping platinum. Due to tension with Rose, Stradlin then left and formed the JuJu Hounds with bassist Jimmy Ashhurst, drummer Charlie "Chalo" Quintana, and ex–Georgia Satellites guitarist Rick Richards (Stradlin's replacement was Gilby Clarke of Candy and Kills for Thrills). The band then set off on a 28-month tour. Among 1992's highlights were an MTV Vanguard Award for the group's body of work and an appearance in April at the Freddie Mercury Tribute, an AIDS benefit that via satellite drew the largest concert audience in history. In 1993 G n' R released *The Spaghetti Incident?,* an album of covers that paid homage to the band's punk roots. Among the tracks was one penned by Charles Manson, for which the band was heavily criticized. By 1994, rumors were proliferating that the band had broken up. Clarke released a solo album, *Pawn Shop Guitars,* and at the year's end Slash recorded a solo album with Snakepit, featuring Sorum and Clarke, Mike Inez of Alice in Chains, and Jellyfish guitarist Eric Dover on lead vocals.

None of these solo projects attracted G n' R-size audiences, and G n' R itself was falling apart. Slash was convinced to sign over rights to the Guns n' Roses name to Rose, later to the guitarist's regret. Clarke was fired. And Slash quit over creative differences with Rose, who insisted on introducing industrial and electronic elements into the G n' R sound. As the years dragged on, McKagan and Sorum eventually left. Rose seemed to go into seclusion, but was reportedly writing and recording, and at various points tried to recruit Moby and Youth as postmodern producers. Both declined, and Rose recorded with producer Roy Thomas Baker and a revolving cast of musicians. Finally, in 1999, a new, industrial-flavored song called "Oh My God" appeared on the *End of Days* film soundtrack. Then in late 2000, Rose's management promised a 2001 release for the long-delayed *Chinese Democracy.* That was followed by a New Year's Eve concert in Las Vegas where a handful of new songs and a new lineup of Guns n' Roses was first introduced: guitarists Buckethead, Robin Finck (Nine Inch Nails), and Paul Tobias; bassist Tommy Stinson (Replacements); keyboardist Chris Pittman; and drummer Brian "Brain" Mantia. The only holdover from the past was keyboardist Dizzy Reed, who first appeared on *GN'R Lies.* After another appearance at the Rock in Rio festival in Brazil, the new G n' R continued touring.

Guru: See Gang Starr

Arlo Guthrie

Born July 10, 1947, Coney Island, NY
1967—*Alice's Restaurant* (Reprise) 1968—*Arlo* 1969—*Running Down the Road; Alice's Restaurant* soundtrack (United Artists) 1970—*Washington County* 1972—*Hobo's Lullaby* (Reprise) 1973—*Last of the Brooklyn Cowboys* 1974—*Arlo Guthrie* 1975—*Together in Concert* (with Pete Seeger) 1976—*Amigo* 1977—*The Best of* (Warner Bros.) 1978—*One Night* 1979—*Outlasting the Blues* 1981—*Power of Love* 1986—*Someday* (Rising Son) 1991—*All Over the World* 1992—*Son of the Wind* 1994—*More Together Again* (with Pete Seeger) 1996—*Alice's Restaurant—The Massacree Revisited; Mystic Journey.*

Folksinger Arlo Guthrie became popular in the late '60s when his tall-tale "Alice's Restaurant" became an underground favorite and later a movie in which he appeared. His biggest pop hit was Steve Goodman's "City of New Orleans," and he is still a regular attraction on the folk circuit.

One of several children born to folksinger Woody and Marjorie Guthrie, Arlo grew up among musicians. At age three he danced and played the harmonica for Lead Belly. Pete Seeger was also a frequent guest. Arlo's mother taught him guitar at age six. He attended private schools in Brooklyn and then in Stockbridge, Massachusetts, the setting of "Alice's Restaurant." He attended college in Billings, Montana, but soon returned to New York to pursue a music career.

By late 1965, Guthrie was a regular on the East Coast coffeehouse circuit, and in 1967 he toured Japan with Judy Collins. His debut LP was released shortly after his appearance at the Newport Folk Festival, which included the 18-minute "Alice's Restaurant." As the '60s closed, he continued to build a following, and he appeared at Woodstock in August 1969. Guthrie's career picked up noticeably in the early '70s with *Washington County* and *Hobo's Lullaby,* which included the #18 hit, "The City of New Orleans" (1972). Subsequent LPs have been well received, although his record sales have dropped off; he has been less interested in elaborate pop productions.

In 1977 Guthrie converted to Catholicism. During the late '70s he regularly toured the U.S. and Europe backed by Shenandoah, with whom he also recorded. Throughout the decade he often performed and recorded with Pete Seeger *(Together in Concert),* and he was an activist for numerous causes, including the antinuclear and ecological movements. In the late '80s Guthrie began acquiring his entire recording catalogue from Warner Bros. and reissuing it on his own Rising Son label. In 1992 Rising Son produced the Grammy-nominated *Woody's 20 Grow Big Songs,* an album and book set of the elder Guthrie's children's songs recorded by Arlo, his brother Joady, his sister Nora, and their children. That same year, Arlo also bought the Trinity Church in Housatonic, Massachusetts, which had been prominent in the "Alice's Restaurant" story; the edifice became the home of Rising Son Records, and the Guthrie Center, a nonprofit community service charity. It also served as the place of recording for the live, 30th-anniversary edition of *Alice's.*

In the mid-'90s Guthrie portrayed recurring guest characters on several TV shows including USA's *Renegade* and ABC's *The Byrds of Paradise* and *Relativity.* In 1995 he collaborated with artist Alice Brock on the kids' book *Mooses Come Walking. Mystic Journey,* coproduced by Arlo and his son Abe, was Guthrie's first new studio album in a decade. In 1998 he began rearranging his music for symphony performances.

Woody Guthrie

Born Woodrow Wilson Guthrie, July 14, 1912, Okemah, OK; died Oct. 3, 1967, Queens, NY
1967—*This Land Is Your Land* (Folkways) 1977—*A Legendary Performer* (RCA) 1988—*The Greatest Songs of Woody Guthrie* (Vanguard) 1993—*Songs to Grow on for Mother and Child* (Smithsonian Folkways) 1997—*This Land Is Your Land* (Rounder) 1999—*The Asch Recordings, vols. 1–4* (Smithsonian Folkways).

In the '30s and '40s Woody Guthrie reinvented the American folk ballad as a vehicle for social comment and protest, laying the groundwork for Bob Dylan and numerous other rock singer/songwriters with such neotraditional songs as "This Land Is Your Land," "Pastures of Plenty," "So Long, It's Been Good to Know You," and nearly a thousand others.

Guthrie's father was a singer, banjo player, and sometime

Woody Guthrie

professional boxer. Woody left home at 16 and roamed through Texas and Louisiana, working as a newsboy, sign painter, spittoon washer, farm laborer, and at other menial jobs; he also sang in the streets. While visiting his uncle Jeff Guthrie in Pampa, Texas, in 1929, he learned to play guitar. During the Depression, Guthrie rode the rails as a hobo until around 1937, when he settled in L.A. and hosted a radio show on KFVD for a dollar a day.

Guthrie's politics moved leftward, and at the start of World War II he relocated to New York. There he met the Weavers and Pete Seeger. He briefly embraced communism, although he was denied membership in the U.S. Communist party because he refused to renounce his religion, but he did write a column for a communist newspaper, *The People's Daily World.*

Although these leanings did not endear Guthrie to the U.S. government, his anti-Hitler songs did; his guitar had a sign on it saying, "This Machine Kills Fascists." From 1943 to 1945 Guthrie was with the U.S. merchant marine in the U.K., Italy, and Africa. In 1945 he married Marjorie Greenblatt Mazia, and together they had four children: Cathy (who was killed in a fire at age four), Nora, Joady, and Arlo.

Although Guthrie's songs traveled widely, he didn't record until 1940, when Alan Lomax taped several hours of talking and singing for the Library of Congress. Those sessions were later released on commercial labels including RCA *(Woody Guthrie—A Legendary Performer* and *Dust Bowl Ballads)* and Elektra. He also recorded with Lead Belly and Sonny Terry, but his recordings had little impact by themselves.

During his years of riding the rails, Guthrie developed a drinking problem. In 1952 he was diagnosed as alcoholic and confined to a mental institution before his problem was correctly diagnosed as Huntington's chorea, a genetically transmitted degenerative disorder of the nervous system from which Guthrie's mother had died. The disease kept him largely inactive and hospitalized during the last decade of his life.

Guthrie's fame has steadily increased over the years. Bob Dylan, who had traveled to New York to visit Guthrie in the hospital, sang his idol's praises early on, and Guthrie's son, Arlo, has also carried on the family name as a singer/songwriter. Pete Seeger, whose relationship with Woody dates back to the '30s, organized a series of memorial concerts for the singer in the late '60s. Two of those concerts—at Carnegie Hall in 1968 and the Hollywood Bowl in 1970—were recorded and released as albums featuring Dylan, Tom Paxton, Joan Baez, Judy Collins, Richie Havens, and Country Joe McDonald. In 1976 Guthrie's autobiography, *Bound for Glory* (published in 1943), was made into a motion picture with David Carradine playing Guthrie. That same year, Guthrie's previously unpublished prose work, *Seeds of Man,* was published. In 1988 he was inducted into the Rock and Roll Hall of Fame. Billy Bragg and Wilco introduced a new generation to Guthrie with their collaboration on *Mermaid Avenue, vols. 1 and 2.* Released in 1998 and 2000, the albums featured Guthrie lyrics set to new music by Bragg and Wilco.

Buddy Guy

Born George Guy, July 30, 1936, Lettsworth, LA
1967—*Left My Blues in San Francisco* (Chess) 1968—*A Man and the Blues* (Vanguard); *This Is Buddy Guy* 1972—*Hold That Plane* 1981—*Stone Crazy!* (Alligator) 1991—*Damn Right, I've Got the Blues* (Silvertone) 1992—*The Very Best of Buddy Guy* (Rhino); *The Complete Chess Studio Recordings* (Chess/MCA); *My Time After Awhile* (Vanguard) 1993—*Feels Like Rain* (Silvertone) 1994—*Slippin' In* 1996—*Buddy Guy Live: The Real Deal* (with G.E. Smith & the Saturday Night Live Band) (Silvertone) 1997—*Buddy's Blues* (MCA) 1998—*As Good As It Gets* (Vanguard); *Heavy Love* (Silvertone) 1999—*Buddy's Baddest: The Best of Buddy Guy* 2000—*Buddy Guy: 1979–82 Complete JSP Recordings* (JSP, U.K.) 2001—*Sweet Tea.*
With Junior Wells: 1970—*I Was Walking Through the Woods* (Chess) 1972—*Buddy Guy & Junior Wells Play the Blues* (Atlantic) 1981—*Drinkin' TNT 'n' Smokin' Dynamite* (Blind Pig) 1991—*Alone & Acoustic* (Alligator) 1992—*Live in Montreux* (Evidence) 1998—*Last Time Around—Live at Legends* (Silvertone).

Eric Clapton once described him as the best guitar player alive. In fact, it's been through the support of his many famous and respected admirers that blues master Buddy Guy has come to the attention of rock audiences, from touring with the Rolling Stones in 1970 to soliciting guest appearances from Clapton, Jeff Beck, and Mark Knopfler for *Damn Right, I've Got the Blues,* the Grammy-winning 1991 album that both reestablished his stature in the music community and marked his greatest commercial success to date.

Buddy Guy

Guy began playing his instrument as a teenager, inspired by such Southern blues greats as Lightnin' Slim and Guitar Slim. The young guitarist left Baton Rouge in 1957 to test his chops in Chicago, the urban capital of the electric blues. Guy was on the verge of starving when a merciful stranger led him to the 708 Club and persuaded that evening's performer, Otis Rush, to allow him to sit in. Guy's impromptu performance earned him a steady gig at the club, and he was soon playing regularly at other local venues. His fierce, visceral style caught the ear of venerable composer/bassist Willie Dixon, who helped Guy land a contract with the noted blues label Chess Records. Though Guy was originally signed by Leonard Chess as a singer, he became a house guitarist for the company, playing on records by such legendary artists as Muddy Waters and Howlin' Wolf in addition to making radiant recordings on his own. (Waters was an early Guy supporter, having caught his show at the 708 Club.)

Since Guy's arrangement with Chess prevented him from getting credit for his work with artists on other labels, he eventually switched to Vanguard. Some of his most memorable work on Vanguard was done in collaboration with the great harmonica player Junior Wells [see entry], who Guy first met in a Chicago club and with whom he maintained a close association until Wells' death of cancer in early 1998. (The duo's last concert, recorded in 1993, was released as *Last Time Around—Live at Legends.*) Some of Guy's most acclaimed solo albums have been recorded live, including the Alligator release *Stone Crazy!,* one of his personal favorites, which captures a 1978 performance in France.

Although many of Guy's fans insist that he is best appreciated in concert, his recordings through the '90s have proved critical and popular favorites. Among them are three star-studded Grammy-winning albums: 1991's *Damn Right, I've Got the Blues,* 1993's *Feels Like Rain* (featuring Bonnie Raitt, Paul Rodgers, John Mayall, and Travis Tritt), and 1994's *Slippin' In* (with the Double Trouble rhythm section, pianist Johnnie Johnson, and guitarist David Grissom). *Heavy Love* (1998) features Jonny Lang and Steve Cropper. In 1993 Guy received *Billboard*'s Century Award. He tours constantly, appearing at blues clubs and festivals around the world. Guy owns a Chicago club called Buddy Guy's Legends, where he can be found both performing and enjoying the playing of other acts when he's in town.

Guy/Teddy Riley

Formed 1985, New York, NY
Teddy Riley (b. Oct. 8, 1966, Harlem, NY), various instr.; Aaron Hall (b. Aug. 10, 1964, Bronx, NY), voc.; Timmy Gatling, voc., dancer.
1987—*Guy* (Uptown/MCA) 1990—(– Gatling; + Damion Hall [b. Albert Damion Hall June 6, 1968, Brooklyn, NY], voc., choreography) *The Future* (MCA) 1999—(group re-forms) *Guy III.*
Aaron Hall solo: 1993—*The Truth* (Silas/MCA).
Damion Hall solo: 1994—*Straight to the Point* (Silas/MCA).
Teddy Riley with Blackstreet: 1994—*Blackstreet* (Interscope) 1996—*Another Level* 1999—*Finally.*

In the late '80s, while barely out of his teens, Teddy Riley fathered New Jack Swing, a contemporary strain of R&B that wed traditional soul singing to the hip-hop beats that drove rap music. Though Riley first became recognized for his work with Guy, a trio he formed with friends, the wunderkind quickly became one of the most sought-after writer/producers in the R&B community, lending his distinctive talents to hot young artists like Keith Sweat and Bobby Brown and established stars such as James Ingram and Michael Jackson.

Riley took up keyboards and percussion as a young child, and was playing piano in Harlem clubs by age 10. He began jamming with local funk musicians at 12 and performed with a couple of bands before putting together Guy with Aaron Hall, a church-trained singer, and Timmy Gatling. The group's eponymous debut generated the R&B hit "Groove Me" (#4, 1988). Gatling quit shortly after its release, and was replaced by Hall's brother Damion, a singer/dancer/choreographer. Riley scored Guy singles for the film soundtracks to *Do the Right Thing* ("Mr. Fantasy") and *New Jack City* ("New Jack City"). The group's sophomore LP, *The Future* (#16 pop, #1 R&B, 1990), yielded three R&B Top 10 singles in 1991: "Let's Chill" (#3), "Do Me Right" (#2), and "D-O-G Me Out" (#8).

Guy split up soon afterward, with the Hall brothers pursuing solo careers and Riley developing his own production company and continuing his collaborations with major artists. He worked extensively on Michael Jackson's *Dangerous* album, and with the fledgling hip-hop acts Wreckx-N-Effect, Kool Moe Dee, and SWV. In 1994 Riley formed Blackstreet with Chauncey "Black" Hannibal, Dave Hollister, and Levi Little; as a pledge of allegiance to the group, each member had the band's name tattooed on his arm. *Blackstreet,* the band's debut, yielded four singles: "Booti Call" (#34 pop, #14 R&B, 1994), "Before I Let You Go" (#7 pop, #2 R&B, 1994), "Joy" (#43 pop, #12 R&B, 1995), and "Tonight's the Night" (#80 pop, #27 R&B, 1995). But it was the followup, 1996's *Another Level* (#3 pop, #1 R&B), that produced its signature hit "No Diggity" (#1 pop and R&B), which rode the charts for six months. The group also charted with "Fix" (#58 pop, #17 R&B), and guested on hits by Jay-Z ("The City Is Mine") and Janet Jackson (the 1998 R&B chart-topper "I Get Lonely"). "Take Me There," a track recorded with Mya for the soundtrack to *The RugRats Movie,* reached #14 in late 1998. The group's third album, *Finally,* was released in 1999, as was a Guy reunion, *Guy III.*

Sammy Hagar

Born Oct. 13, 1947, Monterey, CA
1976—*Nine on a Ten Scale* (Capitol) 1977—*Sammy Hagar* 1978—*Musical Chairs; All Night Long* 1979—*Street Machine* 1980—*Danger Zone; Loud and Clear* 1982—*Standing Hampton* (Geffen); *Three Lock Box; Rematch* (Capitol) 1984—*VOA* (Geffen) 1987—*Sammy Hagar* 1994—*Unboxed* 1997—*Marching to Mars* (Track Factory/MCA) 1999—*Red Voodoo* (with the Waboritas).

Best known as the successor to Van Halen frontman David Lee Roth, whom he replaced in 1985, Sammy Hagar entered the rock market as the lead vocalist of Montrose [see entry]. He went solo in 1975 and again in the mid-'90s upon his exit from Van Halen [see entry]. Years of touring as an arena-show opening act made him a midlevel star.

As a teenager, he considered following his father into the boxing ring, but by age 19 he was supporting himself as a musician in Southern California bar bands. After seven years of beer-joint one-nighters, he joined Montrose, with whom he would remain for two years, in 1973. A cover of Van Morrison's "Flamingos Fly" garnered AOR airplay for Hagar's first solo disc. His career gained real momentum in 1977, when he formed his own band with Montrose alumni Bill Church (bass), Alan Fitzgerald (keyboards), and Dennis Carmasi (who replaced original drummer Scott Matthews and was later replaced by Chuck Ruff). Guitarist David Lewark (later replaced by Gary Pihl) also joined them. The Sammy Hagar Band's late-'70s releases sold in the 100,000-to-200,000 range. *Three Lock Box*'s "Your Love Is Driving Me Crazy" (#13, 1982) cracked the Top 20, and *VOA* (#32, 1984) went platinum, yielding the hit "I Can't Drive 55" (#26, 1984), an anthemic protest against the lowering of highway speed limits. Two years after joining Van Halen, Hagar released an eponymous solo album (#14, 1987), which produced the hit single "Give to Live" (#23, 1987).

In 1996 Hagar left Van Halen. The Van Halen brothers maintain that Hagar quit the group; Hagar claims that he was fired. Riding a wave of headlines about the split, Hagar struck out on his own again with 1997's bitter *Marching to Mars* (#18) and 1999's more lighthearted, party-and-booze-themed *Red Voodoo* (#22). The latter features backing by the Waboritas, a band named after a mixed drink invented by the singer. Hagar also runs a club, the Cabo Wabo Cantina in Cabo San Lucas, Mexico, and markets his own line of tequila, Cabo Wabo Reposado.

Nina Hagen

Born Katherina Hagen, Mar. 11, 1955, East Berlin, Ger.
1980—*Nina Hagen Band* EP (Columbia) 1982—*Nunsexmonkrock* 1983—*Fearless* 1985—*Nina Hagen in Ekstasy* 1988—*Punk Wedding* EP (Amok, Can.) 1989—*Nina Hagen* (Mercury, Ger.) 1991—*Street* (Polydor) 1993—*Revolution Ballroom* (Phonogram, Ger.) 1995—*Freu(D)euch* (RCA, Ger.) 1996—*Bee Happy; 14 Friendly Abductions: The*

Best of Nina Hagen (Columbia/Legacy) 2000—*Return of the Mother* (Orbit, Ger.).

Singing about God and flying saucers in an operatic punk howl, Nina Hagen is one of the most eccentric artists rock has known, and she provides a vital link in the chain connecting prepunk conceptual artist Yoko Ono with postpunk performance artist Diamanda Galas. Hagen was born into an artistic family in Communist Germany. She sang for her first band in 1972, performing blues and Janis Joplin and Tina Turner covers—an emotive vocal training that shaped her own work. She studied music in school in 1973. One of her early bands, Automobil, did performances that combined the formats of a rock concert and a dance-music club, long before British raves.

Hagen renounced her Eastern bloc citizenship and moved to West Berlin in 1976, when her stepfather, a dissident songwriter, was exiled. Already known west of the Berlin Wall, Hagen immediately signed with CBS in Germany. She spent time in London, working with the Slits and discovering punk. She formed a band with other Germans, and their first album, *Nina Hagen Band,* became a European smash. Hagen ignored her success and moved to Holland to hang with Herman Brood, with whom she appeared in the film *Cha Cha,* along with singer Lene Lovich. She became infamous for such antics as demonstrating masturbation techniques on Austrian TV. In 1979 she was contractually obligated to rejoin her band, and *Unbehagen,* their second album, immediately went gold in Germany.

Hagen's debut American release features two tracks each from her first two albums, including "African Reggae" and German versions of the Tubes' "White Punks on Dope" and Lovich's "Lucky Number." She recorded *Nunsexmonkrock* in New York with a band including Paul Shaffer and Chris Spedding; she sang in English but, with her voice wildly changing pitches and tone, she evoked Babylon. Hagen's religious interests took on a new thematic twist after she claimed to have seen a UFO in Malibu in 1981: The deities in her songs rode in flying saucers on *Fearless.* The dance-music album was produced by Giorgio Moroder and Keith Forsey and featured the club hit "New York New York" and the Red Hot Chili Peppers rapping on "What It Is."

Nina Hagen in Ekstasy mixed dance, punk, and metal sounds; the album includes covers of "My Way" and Norman Greenbaum's "Spirit in the Sky." Unable to land even a novelty hit, Hagen stopped recording for CBS. In 1987 the singer's marriage to a teenage fan became a cause célèbre, something she celebrated on her Canadian EP *Punk Wedding. Nina Hagen* featured "Viva Las Vegas," a cover of Joplin's "Move Over," and "Ave Maria."

Hagen's '90s recordings have had little impact outside her native Germany, despite the fact that *Revolution Ballroom* (1993) was produced by former Roxy Music guitarist Phil Manzanera. Hagen has, however, appeared in a number of feature films, including *Portrait of a Woman Drinker* and Pedro Almodovar's *Pepi, Luci, Bom.* Toward the end of the decade, she also played high-profile gigs in New York, L.A., and San Francisco, during which, among other things, she revealed her growing involvement with Hindu mysticism. In 1999 the colorful diva's career was the subject of German filmmaker Peter Sempel's documentary *Nina Hagen: Punk + Glory.*

Merle Haggard

Born Apr. 6, 1937, Bakersfield, CA
1967—*Branded Man* (Capitol) 1969—*Sing Me Back Home* 1970—*Okie From Muskogee* 1970—*The Fightin' Side of Me* 1972—*The Best of Merle Haggard* 1977—*Songs I'll Always Sing; A Working Man Can't Get Nowhere Today* 1981—*Songs for the Mama That Tried* (MCA); *Big City* (Epic) 1983—*Poncho and Lefty* (with Willie Nelson); *Going Where the Lonely Go* 1985—*Kern River* 1986—*A Friend in California* 1987—*Walking the Line* (with George Jones and Willie Nelson); *Seashores of Old Mexico* (with Willie Nelson) 1990—*Blue Jungle* (Curb) 1994—*1994* 1995—*The Lonesome Fugitive: The Merle Haggard Anthology (1963–1977)* (Razor & Tie) 1996—*1996* (Curb); *Down Every Road: 1962–1994* (Capitol) 1999—*For the Record: 43 Legendary Hits* (BNA) 2000—*If I Could Only Fly* (Anti/Epitaph); *New Light Through Old Windows* (7-N Music).

One of country music's most gifted and prolific songwriters, Merle Haggard symbolizes the American workingman—dignified, downtrodden, and not unlikely to visit the neighborhood bar—of whom he often sings. He is also a staunch upholder of musical traditions, particularly Western swing, and he leads one of country music's most improvisatory bands. Though an outspoken critic of the Nashville star system, Haggard was inducted into the Country Music Hall of Fame in 1994; that same year he was feted with two simultaneous tribute albums, one consisting of country superstars, the other a group of rootsy country mavericks. Haggard himself fits equally into both camps.

Haggard was born to a family of transplanted Oklahomans who were living in a converted boxcar in California. When he was nine, his father died of a brain tumor. He quit school in the eighth grade and hopped a freight train at age 14. Through the end of his teens, he mostly roamed the Southwest. Haggard had been in and out of reformatories—from which he frequently escaped—by the age of 14 for such petty crimes as car theft. A 20-year-old married father, he was arrested for breaking into a cafe (drunk, he thought the booming business was closed) and spent nearly three years in San Quentin. He was paroled in 1960. (In 1972 then–California governor Ronald Reagan expunged Haggard's criminal record, granting him a full pardon.)

After prison, Haggard went back to Bakersfield and worked for his brother digging ditches. He started playing lead guitar in a local country band, and by 1962, when he went to Las Vegas to back singer Wynn Stewart, Haggard had decided to make music his career.

In 1963 he formed an enduring partnership with Lewis Talley and Fuzzy Owens, the owners of Tally Records, an independent label in the Bakersfield area for which Haggard made his early recordings. In 1963 Haggard's first release sold only 200 copies, but his second, "Sing Me a Sad Song," made #19 on the *Billboard* country chart. He recorded with Tally through 1965, and Owens remains one of Haggard's close associates. But after Haggard's third solo single "(All My Friends Are Gonna Be) Strangers" hit the C&W Top 10, he was signed by Capitol.

Haggard formed his own backing group, the Strangers, with whom he began touring an average of about 200 nights a year. (The Strangers released their first album of instrumentals in 1970.) After Haggard's first marriage ended in divorce, he married Buck Owens' ex-wife, singer Bonnie Owens. He had previously recorded with her for Tally, but their duet career began in earnest with their first joint Capitol LP, *Just Between the Two of Us* (#4 C&W, 1965). They shared hit records, tours, and awards until their divorce in 1978. (A few years later, Owens returned to touring and recording as a backup singer with Haggard.)

In 1966 "Swinging Doors" and "The Bottle Let Me Down" hit the Top 5 on the country chart, and later in the year "The Fugitive" became his first country #1. He has amassed more than 100 country chart singles since—including 38 #1 hits—and had at least one Top 5 country hit every year between 1966 and 1987. Among his biggest hits are "Mama Tried," "Sing Me Back Home," "Hungry Eyes," "It's Not Love (But It's Not Bad)," "Everybody's Had the Blues," "If We Make It Through December," "It's All in the Movies," and "Big City." Of the hundreds of songs he's written, many have become country standards (his "Today I Started Loving You Again" has been recorded by more than 400 artists). Haggard became a controversial figure during the Vietnam War era by extolling the virtues of patriotism in "The Fightin' Side of Me" and "Okie From Muskogee."

But Haggard was more a traditionalist than a hard-line conservative. His many recordings—more than 65 albums since 1963—include a tribute to Western swing pioneer Bob Wills *(A Tribute to the Best Damn Fiddle Player in the World);* a gospel tribute, *The Land of Many Churches,* which included backing from the Carter Family; *I Love Dixie Blues,* a 1973 tribute to Dixieland jazz recorded in New Orleans; and *Same Train, a Different Time,* in honor of his first idol, Jimmie Rodgers. He played at the White House in 1973 for President Nixon and his family, and later for the Reagans at their California ranch. His music was part of the *Apollo 16* mission to the moon, per the crew's request.

In 1978 he married one of his backup singers, Leona Williams; that marriage also ended in divorce. (Briefly married for a fourth time, he married again in the early '90s. He has two young children with his fifth wife, and, with his first, three grown children, two of whom have pursued country-music careers.) In 1981 Haggard published an autobiography (cowritten with Peggy Russell), *Sing Me Back Home.*

An occasional actor as well as singer, he appeared on TV in *The Waltons* and *Centennial.* He made his movie debut in 1968's *Killer Three* and was featured the next year in *From Nashville With Music.* In 1980 he made a cameo appearance in *Bronco Billy,* singing a duet with Clint Eastwood, "Bar Room Buddies" (#1 C&W, 1980). In addition to Bonnie Owens and Leona Williams, Haggard has also recorded duets with both George Jones and Willie Nelson.

Haggard's hits began to wind down in the late '80s as the new "hat acts" began to monopolize the country chart. After 25 years on the road, Haggard curtailed touring to an extent, spending more time on his ranch near Lake Shasta. Just after the release of his first album in four years, *1994,* Arista/Nashville issued *Mama's Hungry Eyes: A Tribute to Merle Haggard,* with tracks by Clint Black, Brooks and Dunn, Alan Jackson, Vince Gill, and Alabama, among others. Concurrently, the independent, California-based label Hightone released *Tulare Dust: A Songwriters' Tribute to Merle Haggard,* with contributions from Lucinda Williams, Dwight Yoakam, Joe Ely, John Doe (X), Dave Alvin (the Blasters), Billy Joe Shaver, and others. In October 1994 he was inducted into the Country Music Hall of Fame.

While the music industry lauded Haggard with awards, tribute albums, and lavish reissues (the most expansive being 1996's career-spanning, four-disc Capitol box set, *Down Every Road*), Haggard felt he was given short shift by his label, Curb. After both his *1994* and *1996* albums were issued with near identical, nondescript cover art and released with virtually no promotion, Haggard left Curb Records. His 1999 autobiography, *Merle Haggard's House of Memories: For the Record,* was accompanied in stores by a double-disc collection of rerecorded versions of his greatest hits, *For the Record: 43 Legendary Hits.* A handful of the songs featured Haggard dueting with the varied likes of Willie Nelson, Brooks and Dunn, and pop singer Jewel; his new version of his 1984 #1 hit "That's the Way Love Goes" with Jewel reached #56 on the country singles chart.

If that collaboration raised eyebrows, it was nothing compared to his signing in 2000 to the independent Anti Records, distributed by punk label Epitaph. His Anti debut, *If I Could Only Fly,* received widespread critical acclaim and peaked at #26 on the C&W chart. Also in 2000, Haggard recorded a pair of gospel albums, *Cabin in the Hills* and *Two Old Friends* (with Albert E. Brumley Jr.), which he sold exclusively on his Web site and in Wal-Mart stores.

Haircut 100

Formed 1980, Beckenham, Eng.
Nick Heyward (b. May 20, 1961, Beckenham), voc.; Les Nemes (b. Dec. 5, 1960, Croydon, Eng.), bass; Graham Jones (b. July 8, 1961, Bridlington, Eng.), gtr.; "Memphis" Blair Cunningham (b. Oct. 11, 1957, New York, NY), drums; Phil Smith (b. May 1, 1959, Redbridge, Eng.), gtr.; Mark Fox (b. Feb. 13, 1958), perc., voc.
1982—*Pelican West* (Arista) 1983—(– Heyward) *Paint and Paint* (Polydor, U.K.) 1998—*Nick Heyward & Haircut One Hundred Greatest Hits* (BMG/Camden, U.K.).
Nick Heyward solo: 1983—*North of a Miracle* (Arista) 1987—*Postcards From Home* 1989—*I Love You Avenue* (Reprise)

1994—*From Monday to Sunday* (Epic) 1997—*World's End* (Creation, U.K.) 1998—*The Apple Bed* (Big Deal).

Though it claims but one U.S. Top 40 hit, 1982's "Love Plus One," Haircut 100's name still evokes an early-'80s wave of pretty English boys making fluffy dance pop and ingratiating bubblegum soul. Haircut 100 did enjoy greater (albeit short-lived) success in its native U.K., where the quintet's debut album, *Pelican West* (#2 U.K., 1982), spawned the hits "Favourite Shirts (Boy Meets Girl)" (#4 U.K., 1981) and "Fantastic Day" (#9 U.K., 1982) in addition to "Love Plus One" (#3, 1982). Critics praised the group for its savvy incorporation of Latin rhythms and jazz-funk textures, but scoffed at Nick Heyward's fey vocals and the band's meticulous, preening image. Heyward—also the group's songwriter—soon decided to pursue a solo career, and percussionist Mark Fox took over lead vocals for Haircut's followup LP, *Paint and Paint*, which never reached American shores and failed to chart in England. The group split up shortly afterward. Heyward made pleasurable, more contemplative pop albums on his own and settled down as a husband and father, while drummer "Memphis" Blair Cunningham played in one of the Pretenders' numerous lineups.

Bill Haley

Born July 6, 1925, Highland Park, MI; died Feb. 9, 1981, Harlingen, TX
1955—*Rock Around the Clock* (Decca) 1968—*Greatest Hits* (MCA) 1974—*Golden Hits.*

Bill Haley emerged from country music with "Rock Around the Clock," a rockabilly song that made him a teen idol. He cut his first record, "Candy Kisses," when he was 18, then hit the road for four years as a singer and guitarist with various country & western bands. In 1948 he became a disc jockey at WPWA in Chester, Pennsylvania. Calling himself the Ramblin' Yodeler, he put together a band, the Four Aces of Western Swing, to perform regularly on his radio show. With another group—first called the Down Homers, then the Saddlemen—he recorded country songs that quickly disappeared into obscurity. In 1950 they were signed to a Philadelphia label, Essex, and recorded a handful of country sides before covering Jackie Brenston's 1951 R&B hit, "Rocket 88." That record sold only 10,000 copies, but the song convinced Haley that high-energy music that kids could sing along to, clap to, and dance to—something like black R&B—would prove popular.

In 1952 he dropped his cowboy image altogether, changed the group's name to Bill Haley and His Comets, and covered another R&B hit, "Rock the Joint," which sold 75,000 copies. A Haley original, "Crazy Man Crazy," was covered by one Ralph Marterie and given extensive airplay, but Haley's own more rambunctious version was the one sought in record shops, and in 1953 it became the first rock & roll record to make the *Billboard* pop chart.

In 1954 Haley left Essex and signed with Decca under producer Milt Gabler. His first record for his new label was a song written by Jimmy DeKnight and his manager, Dave Myers, and originally recorded in 1952 by Sunny Dae: "Rock Around the Clock." It sold only moderately when first released in spring 1954, but its followup, a cover of Joe Turner's "Shake, Rattle and Roll," hit the Top 10 both in the U.K. and in the U.S., eventually selling a million copies. When "Rock Around the Clock" was rereleased in 1955 it rose to #1. The song was included on the soundtrack of *Blackboard Jungle,* a 1955 movie about juvenile delinquents, and it led viewers to identify the balding Haley as a young rebel. Throughout 1955 and 1956 he was the most popular rock & roll performer in the world, and within those two years he had 12 U.S. Top 40 records, including "See You Later Alligator," "Burn That Candle," "Dim, Dim the Lights," "Razzle-Dazzle," and "R-O-C-K."

In Britain, where authentic rock & rollers were scarcer than in America, he was even more popular: His visit there in February 1957 met with wild enthusiasm. But already his star was descending in America. High exposure (he starred in two Hollywood movies, *Rock Around the Clock* and *Don't Knock the Rock*) revealed him to be a pudgy, rather stiff, hardly rebellious family man. His last Top 40 hit was "Skinny Minnie" in 1958. While he never attempted to modernize his sound or his image, Haley continued to work as a nostalgia act, especially in Britain and Germany, where he was always treated as a star ("Rock Around the Clock" reentered the U.K. pop chart seven times, most recently in 1974). In 1969 and through the early '70s, Bill Haley and His Comets traveled with the Rock 'n' Roll Revival Shows promoted by Richard Nader and documented in a 1973 movie, *Let the Good Times Roll.* By the time of Haley's death from a heart attack, he had sold an estimated 60 million records; "Rock Around the Clock" alone has sold over 22 million copies worldwide. He was among the first inductees into the Rock and Roll Hall of Fame, in 1986. The Comets, meanwhile, continue to perform.

Daryl Hall and John Oates

Formed 1969, Philadelphia, PA
Daryl Hall (b. Oct. 11, 1949, Pottstown, PA), voc.; John Oates (b. Apr. 7, 1949, New York, NY), gtr., voc.
1972—*Whole Oates* (Atlantic) 1973—*Abandoned Luncheonette* 1974—*War Babies* 1975—*Daryl Hall John Oates* (RCA) 1976—*Bigger Than Both of Us* 1977—*No Goodbyes* (Atlantic); *Beauty on a Back Street* (RCA) 1978—*Along the Red Ledge; Live Time* 1979—*X-Static* 1980—*Voices* 1981—*Private Eyes* 1982—*H_2O* 1983—*Rock 'n Soul Part 1* 1984—*Big Bam Boom* 1985—*Live at the Apollo With David Ruffin and Eddie Kendrick* 1988—*Ooh Yeah!* (Arista) 1990—*Change of Season* 1997—*Marigold Sky* (Push).
Daryl Hall solo: 1980—*Sacred Songs* (RCA) 1986—*Three Hearts in the Happy Ending Machine* 1993—*Soul Alone* (Epic) 1996—*Can't Stop Dreaming* (Push).

Daryl Hall and John Oates' blend of rock and R&B kept them on the singles chart throughout the '70s and '80s. They are

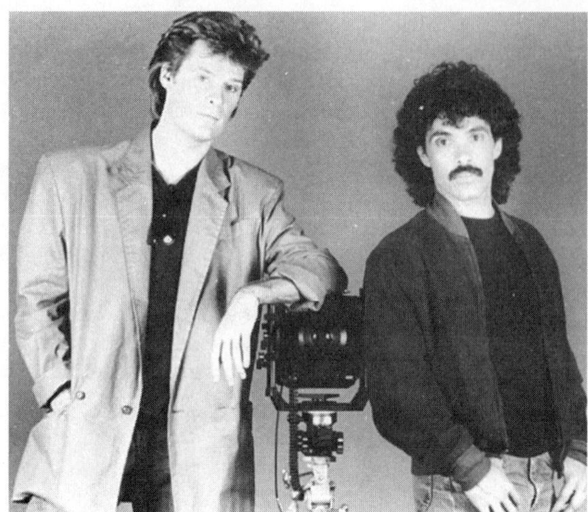
Daryl Hall and John Oates

the #1 charting duo in rock & roll history. Both were raised in Philadelphia suburbs. At age four Oates had moved to Pennsylvania from New York. He began playing guitar at age eight. Hall studied voice and piano. As teens, the two frequented Philadelphia ghettos, where they joined doo-wop groups. In 1967 Hall recorded a single with Kenny Gamble and the Romeos (which included future producers Gamble, Leon Huff, and Thom Bell). He met Oates later that year when his group, the Temptones, and Oates' group, the Masters, competed in a battle of the bands at Philadelphia's Adelphi Ballroom; they shared a freight elevator while escaping a gang fight. At Temple University Oates earned a degree in journalism, and Hall studied music but dropped out in his senior year.

Hall formed Gulliver, a group that recorded one LP on Elektra in 1969, and Oates joined before it disbanded. Oates then traveled to Europe, and Hall became a studio musician, singing backup for the Delfonics, the Stylistics, and the Intruders. Upon Oates' return, the two decided to team up. In 1972 they signed with Atlantic Records and released their Arif Mardin–produced debut, *Whole Oates,* a folky album that attracted little attention. Their next LP, the R&B-oriented *Abandoned Luncheonette* (also produced by Mardin), yielded "She's Gone," a flop for Hall and Oates but a #1 R&B hit for Tavares six months later. In 1974 the two recorded *War Babies,* a concept LP, with producer Todd Rundgren. A drastic departure from their earlier efforts, the LP sold 100,000 copies in the New York area. Citing a lack of hit singles and stylistic inconsistency, Atlantic dropped them, but in 1976 the rereleased version of "She's Gone" made #7.

Their RCA debut *(Daryl Hall John Oates)* contained "Sara Smile," a #4 hit cowritten by Hall for his frequent collaborator/girlfriend Sara Allen (whose sister Janna Allen cowrote "Kiss on My List," "Private Eyes," and other Hall and Oates songs; she died of leukemia in 1993). With the release of 1976's *Bigger Than Both of Us,* the two previous albums went gold. *Bigger* eventually became their first platinum LP and contained their first #1 single, "Rich Girl."

Hall, the more prolific writer of the two, began working with Robert Fripp on a solo LP, *Sacred Songs,* which RCA refused to release until 1980. He also sang on Fripp's *Exposure.* Yet apart from the Top 20 "It's a Laugh" from *Along the Red Ledge,* and "Wait for Me" from *X-Static* the duo hit a late-'70s commercial slump. Hall and Oates retrenched and decided to produce their next LP themselves. The result, 1980's platinum *Voices,* returned them to the singles chart with a vengeance: "How Does It Feel to Be Back" (#30), "Kiss on My List" (#1), a cover of the Righteous Brothers' "You've Lost That Loving Feeling" (#12), and "You Make My Dreams" (#5). The following year's *Private Eyes* was similarly successful; the title cut and "I Can't Go for That (No Can Do)" were both #1, while "Did It in a Minute" went Top 10. *H_2O* yielded still more hits with "Maneater" (#1), "Family Man" (#6), and "One on One" (#7). Even the two new songs included on a best-of LP, the double-platinum *Rock 'n Soul Part 1,* cracked the Top 10: "Say It Isn't So" (#2, 1983) and "Adult Education" (#8, 1984). *Big Bam Boom* incorporated a marked hip-hop influence and produced Hall and Oates' sixth and last #1 hit, "Out of Touch," as well as "Method of Modern Love" (#5, 1985), "Some Things Are Better Left Unsaid" (#18, 1985), and "Possession Obsession" (#30, 1985). After a live LP recorded at Harlem's Apollo Theatre with former Temptations Eddie Kendricks (or Kendrick, as he was sometimes billed) and David Ruffin, Hall and Oates took a three-year sabbatical, during which time Hall released a second solo album, *Three Hearts in the Happy Ending Machine.* Its "Dreamtime" went Top 5 in 1986.

Hall and Oates resumed recording in 1988, but this third career phase was noticeably less successful. Their two albums, *Ooh Yeah!* and *Change of Season,* contained only one hit apiece: "Everything Your Heart Desires" (#3, 1988) and "So Close" (#11, 1990). After a long hiatus, during which Hall released two solo efforts, the pair signed to BMG-affiliated Push Records and released the commercially unspectacular *Marigold Sky* (#95, 1997). The single "Promise Ain't Enough" did however climb to #6 on the Adult Contemporary chart.

Tom T. Hall

Born Thomas Hall, May 25, 1936, Olive Hill, KY
1968—*Ballad of Forty Dollars and His Other Great Songs* (Mercury) 1971—*In Search of a Song* 1972—*We All Got Together And . . . ; The Storyteller* 1973—*The Rhymer and Other Five and Dimers; For the People in the Last Hard Town* 1974—*Songs of Fox Hollow for Children of All Ages* 1976—*The Magnificent Music Machine* 1982—*The Storyteller and the Banjoman* (Columbia) 1995—*Storyteller, Poet, Philosopher* (Mercury) 1996—*Songs From Sopchoppy* 1997—*Homegrown.*

If any writer understood that the key to the durable country song was in the tale told, it is Tom T. Hall, dubbed "the Storyteller." His songs place a premium on narrative, best exemplified by Hall's most popular tune, "Harper Valley P.T.A."

By the time he was nine years old Hall was already writing songs. As a teenager he played guitar in a bluegrass band

and eventually landed a job as a disc jockey. Upon returning from the army in 1961 he enrolled at Roanoke College in Virginia where he studied literature, while continuing to write songs. Hall met with quick acclaim; Dave Dudley, Bobby Bare, and Burl Ives cut his songs.

By 1964, Hall had moved to Nashville, where he began a recording career of his own. His first single, "I Washed My Face in the Morning Dew" (1967), hit the C&W Top 40. The next year Hall's "Harper Valley P.T.A." (as recorded by Jeannie C. Riley) went to #1 on the pop chart and sold 6 million records. As with all of the songs he originally wrote for other artists, Hall has never recorded "Harper Valley P.T.A." himself.

Hall's most acclaimed songs of the '70s, including "The Year That Clayton Delaney Died" and "(Old Dogs, Children and) Watermelon Wine," relate vivid, detailed stories made all the more powerful for their economy of means. In 1973 Hall had his biggest pop hit, "I Love" (#12, #1 C&W). Hall's "I Can't Dance" was also recorded by Gram Parsons, and Leo Kottke cut the ironic "Pamela Brown." In 1978 Hall was inducted into the Nashville Songwriters' Hall of Fame.

All told, Hall has recorded nearly 30 albums, including a pair of bluegrass albums, *The Magnificent Music Machine* and *The Storyteller and the Banjoman,* which featured Bill Monroe and Earl Scruggs, respectively. Notable anthologies include the *Storyteller, Poet, Philosopher* box set and a collection of his country songs for children. Meanwhile, his songs are still being recorded by both mainstream acts (Alan Jackson, Billy Ray Cyrus) and others outside the Nashville establishment (Whiskeytown and Joe Henry, as featured on Sire Record's 1998 tribute album *Real: The Tom T. Hall Project*).

As of this writing, Hall has published nine books, including the novels *The Laughing Man of Woodmont Coves* and *What a Book! A Novel; The Songwriter's Handbook,* an artist's guide; and short story collections.

Hammer

Born Stanley Kirk Burrell, Mar. 30, 1963, Oakland, CA
As M.C. Hammer: 1988—*Feel My Power* (Bust It); *Let's Get It Started* (Capitol) 1990—*Please Hammer Don't Hurt 'Em* 1995—*V Inside Out* (Giant) 1996—*Greatest Hits* (Capitol) 1998—*Family Affair* (Oaktown).
As Hammer: 1991—*Too Legit to Quit* 1994—*The Funky Headhunter* (Giant).

Savvy entrepreneur, showman extraordinaire, product pitchman, inspiration for both a doll and a Saturday morning cartoon, and African-American role model, M.C. Hammer appeared to be the rap incarnation of James Brown after the release of his #1 pop album, *Please Hammer Don't Hurt 'Em.* His massive success proved short-lived, however.

Growing up in the rougher precincts of Oakland, Stanley Kirk Burrell had two interests: performing and baseball. Combining them, he'd dance in the parking lot of the Oakland Coliseum, home of the baseball A's. Discovered there by the team's owner, Charlie Finley, Burrell was hired as a bat boy and soon became the team's unofficial mascot. The players nicknamed him Little Hammer because he resembled home-run king "Hammerin' " Hank Aaron. Two players, Mike Davis and Dwayne Murphy, gave more, each investing $20,000 in Hammer's Bustin' Records, started after an abortive attempt to break into pro ball and a three-year hitch in the Navy.

Hammer's first single, "Ring 'Em," sold by Hammer and his wife, became a #1 Bay Area hit. His debut album, *Feel My Power,* coproduced by Con Funk Shun producer Felton Pilate, sold 60,000 copies. Spotted in the audience at a club by a Capitol Records exec, who "didn't know who he was, but knew he was somebody," the label found out soon enough, handing Hammer a multialbum deal and a $750,000 advance. His first Capitol release, *Let's Get It Started,* a revamped version of *Power,* eventually sold 2 million copies.

Recorded on the back of his tour bus for less than $10,000, *Please Hammer Don't Hurt 'Em* sold more than 10 million copies, holding the #1 position for a record-shattering 21 weeks. It included the hits "U Can't Touch This" (#8, 1990) and "Pray" (#2, 1990). Buttressed by an elaborate, 30-member stage show, Hammer became a household word, appearing in Pepsi ads, heavy MTV rotation, and his own kids' cartoon, *Hammerman.* He also branched out, into management (Oaktown's 3.5.7), horse racing, and his own Help the Children Foundation. This kind of success breeds controversy, and some rappers publicly "dissed" Hammer's mainstream style and extravagant clothes (billowy harem-style pants), calling him a sellout. In 1990 Rick James sued Hammer over the sampling of "Super Freak" in "U Can't Touch This." Settling out of court, James was given cowriter credit.

For *Too Legit to Quit,* Hammer dropped the "M.C." from his name and saw his audience drop with it. Selling a more-than-respectable 3 million copies, *Too Legit* was a disappointment, despite its #5 title track, "2 Legit 2 Quit." A planned world tour was canceled midway, and Hammer's career hasn't been the same since. After a last-gasp hit with "Addams Groove," the theme to *The Addams Family* movie, Hammer returned in 1994 with a new label (Irving Azoff's Giant Records) and a gangsta rap persona. *The Funky Headhunter* only reached #12 and barely made platinum. Losing the gangsta costumes and reattaching the M.C. to his name didn't help *V Inside Out* (1995). Peaking at #119 and falling out of sight after only three weeks, the album effectively put an end to Hammer's career. He declared bankruptcy in 1997, and another album, *Family Affair,* was released.

Peter Hammill: See Van der Graaf Generator

John Hammond

Born Nov. 13, 1942, New York, NY
1962—*John Hammond* (Vanguard) 1964—*Big City Blues; Country Blues* 1965—*So Many Roads* 1967—*Mirrors; I Can*

Tell (Atlantic) 1968—*Sooner or Later* 1969—*Southern Fried* 1970—*The Best of John Hammond* (Vanguard); *Source Point* (Columbia) 1971—*Dustin Hoffman as Little Big Man* soundtrack 1972—*I'm Satisfied* 1973—*Triumvirate* (with Michael Bloomfield and Dr. John) 1975—*Can't Beat the Kid* (Capricorn) 1976—*John Hammond: Solo* (Vanguard) 1978—*Footwork* 1979—*Hot Tracks* 1980—*Mileage* (Sonet) 1982—*Frogs for Snakes* (Rounder) 1984—*John Hammond Live in Greece* (Lyra, Gr.) 1988—*Nobody But You* (Flying Fish) 1992—*Got Love If You Want It* (Pointblank/Charisma) 1994—*Trouble No More* (Pointblank/Virgin) 1995—*Found True Love* 1998—*Long As I Have You* 2001—*Wicked Grin.*

Blues singer John Paul Hammond is the son of talent scout/producer John Hammond. He studied art and sculpture in his youth and he became interested in country and Delta blues. While attending Antioch College in Yellow Springs, Ohio, Hammond learned guitar and harmonica and started singing.

His professional career began in L.A. in 1962, when he recorded an acoustic blues album for Vanguard. He continued to record regularly for Vanguard in the early '60s. In late 1963 he met some musicians who had once backed rockabilly singer Ronnie Hawkins in a Toronto bar. Hammond enticed the group, Levon and the Hawks (who would later become the Band), to come with him to New York. They backed Hammond until they were lured away by Bob Dylan (a discovery of Hammond's father). In the mid-'60s his backing band included, briefly, Jimi Hendrix.

Hammond played clubs regularly in the late '60s. He played many small concert venues (the Fillmores, Matrix Ballroom) as well. He performed on the 1971 soundtrack of the Dustin Hoffman film *Little Big Man.* The following year he recorded an album with bluesman Larry Johnson for the Biograph label. In 1973 he recorded for Columbia as part of a short-lived supergroup called Triumvirate, which also included Dr. John and Mike Bloomfield. By the late '70s, he was still playing clubs and touring internationally (he released a live album recorded in Greece in 1984). While staying true to the blues, Hammond has recorded in a variety of settings, often with name backing: Robbie Robertson, Garth Hudson, and Levon Helm of the Band, and Mike Bloomfield (on piano) on the mid-'60s albums *So Many Roads* and *Mirrors;* Robertson, the Band's Rick Danko, and Rolling Stone Bill Wyman on *I Can Tell;* Duane Allman on *Southern Fried;* blues pianist Roosevelt Sykes on *Footwork;* J.J. Cale and John Lee Hooker on *Got Love If You Want It;* Cale and blues singer Charles Brown on *Trouble No More;* and Duke Robillard and Charlie Musselwhite on *Found True Love.* Following the self-produced *Long As I Have You,* Hammond released *Wicked Grin,* an album consisting primarily of Tom Waits covers and produced by Waits himself.

Herbie Hancock

Born Apr. 12, 1940, Chicago, IL
1962—*Takin' Off* (Blue Note) 1963—*My Point of View; Inventions and Dimensions* 1964—*Empyrean Isles* 1965—*Maiden Voyage* 1966—*Blow-Up* soundtrack (MGM) 1968—*Hancock* (Blue Note); *Speak Like a Child* 1969—*The Prisoner; Fat Albert Rotunda* (Warner Bros.) 1970—*Mwandishi* 1971—*Crossings* 1972—*Sextant* (Columbia) 1973—*Headhunters* 1974—*Dedication; Thrust* (Warner Bros.); *Death Wish* soundtrack (One Way) 1975—*In Concert, vol. 2* (CTI); *Flood* (Columbia); *Love Me by Name* (A&M); *Manchild* 1976—*Live in Japan* (Columbia/Sony, Jap.); *Secrets* (Columbia); *Happy the Man* (Arista); *Kawaida* (DJM) 1977—*Herbie Hancock Trio; V.S.O.P.* (Columbia); *Tempest in the Colosseum* (Columbia/Sony); *Sunlight* 1978—*An Evening With* (Columbia, U.K.); *Direct Step* (Columbia); *The Piano Corea/Hancock* (Polydor); *Feets Don't Fail Me Now* (Columbia) 1979—*Live Under the Sky; In Concert* (CBS) 1980—*Monster* (Columbia); *Mr. Hands* 1982—*Herbie Hancock Quartet; Double Rainbow; By All Means* (MPS); *Magic Windows* (Columbia) 1982—*Lite Me Up* 1983—*Future Shock* 1984—*Sound-System* 1985—*Village Life* (Columbia) 1986—*Jazz Africa* (Verve); *Third Plane* (Carerre) 1988—*Perfect Machine* (Columbia); *Songs for My Father* (Blue Note) 1994—*Dis Is Da Drum* (Mercury); *Jamming* (ROYAL CO.); *A Tribute to Miles* (Qwest) 1995—*Jammin' With Herbie* (Prime Cuts); *Canteloupe Island* (Blue Note); *New Standard* (Verve) 1996—*In Concert* (Tristar); *Living Jazz* (Graphix Zone) 1997—*1+1* (PolyGram) 1998—*Gershwin's World; Return of the Headhunters* (Verve).

Keyboardist Herbie Hancock came to prominence as the pianist in Miles Davis' landmark mid-'60s quintet, a unit that went from refined postbop chamber jazz to pioneering electric fusion. The latter spurred Hancock on to a funk-fusion direction of his own. Once he established himself commercially, however, Hancock divided his time between funk and his harmonically adventurous, impressionistic acoustic jazz.

Although he had studied music, Hancock was working toward a B.A. in engineering at Grinnell College. In 1963 he came to New York and worked with jazz trumpeter Donald Byrd, at whose instigation Hancock recorded his first solo LP. His "Watermelon Man" was a pop-jazz crossover hit for Mongo Santamaria. From 1963 to 1968, Hancock worked with Miles Davis; he also recorded solo albums and played on many sessions for Blue Note Records. After scoring Michelangelo Antonioni's film *Blow-Up,* he left Davis and began pursuing fusion with the 1970 album *Mwandishi.*

Hancock's breakthrough came with *Headhunters,* for which he formed the band of the same name, later explaining, "Rather than work with jazz musicians who could play funk, I worked with funk musicians who could play jazz." That album yielded the crossover hit "Chameleon" (#42 pop, #18 R&B, 1974). *Thrust, Manchild,* and the *Death Wish* film soundtrack also sold well, as did *Fat Albert Rotunda,* his soundtrack to a Bill Cosby cartoon TV special. In 1976 Hancock briefly diverged from his electric-funk course to form V.S.O.P. (Very Special Onetime Performance), an acoustic jazz group with Tony Williams, Weather Report's Wayne Shorter, bassist Ron Carter, and trumpeter Freddie Hubbard, playing in the early Blue Note–Miles Davis mode. They con-

Herbie Hancock

ducted a successful tour and recorded an album, and have since reconvened.

Shortly thereafter, Hancock converted to Nicheran Shoshu Buddhism and two years later undertook an acoustic-piano duo tour with Chick Corea. In 1979 *Feets Don't Fail Me Now* was another commercial success, as was *Monster* in 1980. In 1981 V.S.O.P. toured and recorded as a quartet, minus Shorter and with trumpeter Wynton Marsalis replacing Hubbard. In 1982 Hancock produced Wynton Marsalis' Columbia Records debut; Hancock would later tour with brothers Wynton and Branford Marsalis.

The unexpected success of *Future Shock* and its single, "Rockit" (#71, 1983), gave Hancock even greater visibility. As produced by Bill Laswell, "Rockit" incorporated funk rhythms and hip-hop "scratching." The accompanying video (directed by Godley and Creme) won five MTV Video Music Awards in 1984. Hancock also established a career scoring films, including *A Soldier's Story* (1984), *Round Midnight* (1986), Richard Pryor's *Jo Jo Dancer Your Life Is Calling* (1986), and *Colors* (1988). Hancock won an Oscar for the *Round Midnight* soundtrack.

Though he ventures outside the genre, Hancock never leaves jazz far behind. In 1992, Hancock organized a Tribute to Miles [Davis] tour, which included Tony Williams, Wayne Shorter, Ron Carter, and Wallace Roney. Hancock continues working in a piano trio context, displaying what is perhaps the most influential piano style among today's post-Marsalis players. Later in the '90s Hancock founded Rhythm of Life, a foundation that offers arts and music classes to disenfranchised youth in San Francisco. In 1997 he was appointed artistic director of a $1.2-million jazz performance and education program sponsored by the Music Center of L.A. County and the Washington-based Thelonious Monk Institute of Jazz. In 1998 *Gershwin's World*, featuring Stevie Wonder and Joni Mitchell, won Hancock a Grammy Award. The next year, he began hosting *Future Wave*, a television program about music technology for BET on Jazz.

Hanson

Formed 1992, Tulsa, OK
Taylor Hanson (b. Mar. 14, 1983, Tulsa), voc., kybds.; Isaac Hanson (b. Clarke Isaac Hanson, Nov. 17, 1980, Tulsa), gtr., voc.; Zac Hanson (b. Zachary Hanson, Oct. 22, 1985, Arlington, VA), drums, voc.
1997—*Middle of Nowhere* (Mercury); *Snowed In* 1998—*3 Car Garage: Indie Recordings '95–'96; Live From Albertane* 2000—*This Time Around* (Island).

The brothers Hanson—Taylor, Isaac, and Zac—were the first of a seemingly endless wave of teen pop acts that came to dominate the charts at the tail end of the '90s. After its release in 1997, Hanson's infectious debut single, "MMMBop," rocketed to #1 in 27 countries and pushed *Middle of Nowhere* to worldwide sales of more than 8 million. By the time the boys released their second studio album, 2000's *This Time Around*, however, they learned how fickle the teen audience can be: A year later, it had yet to go platinum in America.

Three of six siblings in Tulsa, Oklahoma, the Hanson brothers were all home-schooled by their mother. After they took up their instruments, their family room jams eventually led to a stint of state fair–type performances and a pair of self-released recordings, a 1995 album, *Boomerang*, and a 1996 EP, *MMMBop*. The title track on the latter landed them a deal with Mercury in 1996, and the group commenced recording its major label debut in L.A. with help from established industry professionals like songwriter Desmond Child and hip producers Stephen Lironi (Black Grape) and the Dust Brothers (Beck, Beastie Boys). Despite all the hired hands, Taylor, Isaac, and Zac—just 14, 16, and 11, respectively, at the time—played their own instruments and wrote or cowrote every song on the album.

The Middle of Nowhere (#2, 1997) was an immediate success, quickly going quadruple platinum and sparking crowds of screaming teen and preteen girls at the group's appearances. Critics were kind to the album, too, recognizing the boys' sharp melodic sensibilities and often comparing precocious lead singer Taylor to the young Michael Jackson, "Little" Stevie Wonder, and the teenage Stevie Winwood of the Spencer Davis Group (underscored by Hanson's straight-up cover of "Gimme Some Lovin' " during their live shows). Mercury fed the frenzy by rapidly releasing three more Hanson albums over the course of the following 18 months: a Christmas set, *Snowed In* (#7, 1997), the live *Live From Albertane* (#32, 1998), and a compilation of songs from their two self-released recordings entitled *3 Car Garage: The Indie Recordings '95–'96* (#6, 1998).

Hanson would take three years before releasing a proper followup to *Middle of Nowhere*, however, and in the interim, the Backstreet Boys, 'N Sync, and Britney Spears had achieved fame on a level that made Hansonmania seem positively modest by comparison. Hanson's return with the more mature, rock-oriented *This Time Around* (featuring guest jams by Blues Traveler harpist John Popper and teen guitarist Jonny Lang) found the group largely out of sync with its teenybopper audience. The title track made it to #20, while the album climbed no higher than #19. In early 2001 the brothers began working on a new album in their home studio in Tulsa, collaborating on the projected first single with Matthew Sweet.

Happy Mondays/Black Grape

Formed 1980, Manchester, Eng.
Bez (b. Mark Berry, Apr. 18, 1964, Manchester), perc., dancer; Paul Davis (b. Mar. 7, 1966, Manchester), kybds.; Mark Day (b. Dec. 29, 1961, Manchester), gtr.; Paul Ryder (b. Apr. 24, 1964, Manchester), bass; Shaun Ryder (b. Shaun William George Ryder, Aug. 23, 1962, Manchester), voc.; Gary Whelan (b. Feb. 12, 1966, Manchester), drums.
1987—*Squirrel and G-Man Twenty Four Hour Party People Plastic Face Carnt Smile (White Out)* (Factory, U.K.) 1988—*Bummed* 1989—*Madchester, Rave On* 1990—*Pills 'n' Thrills and Bellyaches* (Elektra) 1991—*Live* 1992—*Yes, Please* 1993—*Double Easy: The U.S. Singles* (group disbands) 1999—(group re-forms: S. Ryder; P. Ryder; Bez; Whelan; + P. Wagstaff, gtr.; + Nuts, voc.).
Black Grape, formed 1993, Manchester: Bez, Shaun Ryder, Kermit (b. Paul Leveridge) voc.; Jed Lynch, drums; Wags (b. Paul Wagstaff) gtr.; Psycho (b. Carl McCarthy), voc.; Danny Saber, bass, kybds.
1995—*It's Great When You're Straight . . . Yeah!* (Radioactive) (– Bez) 1998—*Stupid, Stupid, Stupid* (group disbands).

Ecstasy-drenched and spacy, Happy Mondays dominated the British clubs and charts in the late '80s with their definitive acid-house grooves. Led by the outspoken Shaun Ryder and featuring Bez, a dancer, Happy Mondays practically invented the U.K. rave scene (along with the Stone Roses) and had an almost exclusively British following until 1990, when *Pills 'n' Thrills and Bellyaches* (#89) caught on in the States.

Formed by Ryder and his bass-playing brother, Paul, Happy Mondays played Manchester's Hacienda Club before signing to Factory Records. After the band toured with New Order, Bernard Sumner produced its second single "Freaky Dancin'." Happy Mondays' debut album, *Squirrel and G-Man . . .*, which John Cale produced in 10 days, included the singles "Tart Tart" and "24 Hour Party People" and established the acid-house sound—bass- and drum-heavy extended dance mixes with touches of '60s psychedelia and '70s R&B.

When Elektra released their second album, 1988's *Bummed*, in the U.S. in 1989, it stiffed. Among other problems, the band seemed too stoned to play its first stateside gig. But fueled by "Step On" (#9 Modern Rock, 1990) and the infectious " 'Step On' Remix '91" (#57, 1991), *Pills 'n' Thrills and Bellyaches* (#89, 1991) broke out in clubs. The album also featured a tribute to their '60s idol, "Donovan," (the Ryder brothers later became romantically linked with the singer's daughters, Astrella and Oriel). A live album, *Live*, followed. Produced by Chris Frantz and Tina Weymouth, *Yes, Please*, along with "Cut 'Em Loose Bruce," again hit in clubs and on modern-music radio, but not with mainstream listeners. In 1993 the band split up.

Shaun Ryder made a surprising return in 1995 with Black Grape. The new band added rap and funk influences to the Monday's raves and immediately entered the British charts with the single "Reverend Black Grape" and the album *It's Great When You're Straight . . . Yeah!* (#1, U.K.). While the title may have reflected a new sobriety for Ryder, his past still haunted him, and the band was originally denied entry to the U.S. due to prior offenses in the U.K. When the band was finally allowed into the States in 1996, it had lost Kermit (who could not tour due to illness but continued to work with the band) and Bez. Whatever momentum the band had was lost, and the record sold only 36,000 copies in America. Another British Top 10 single, "Fat Neck" (1996), recorded with former Smiths guitarist Johnny Marr, failed to shore up the band, and by early 1998, Ryder had parted ways with the rest of Black Grape, save producer Danny Saber. The band's next album, 1998's *Stupid, Stupid, Stupid* (released in the U.K. in late 1997), sold disappointingly on both sides of the Atlantic, and in 1998, Ryder threw in the towel. Just a year later, however, a new, postrehab Happy Mondays (sans original members Day and Davis) re-formed, including Black Grape's Paul Wagstaff (see chronology above for personnel) for a U.K. tour. They also released "The Boys Are Back in Town, Pt. 1," a cover of Thin Lizzy's 1976 rock anthem.

Tim Hardin

Born Dec. 23, 1941, Eugene, OR; died Dec. 29, 1980, Los Angeles, CA
1966—*Tim Hardin I* (MGM) 1967—*Tim Hardin II* 1968—*Tim Hardin III Live in Concert* (Verve) 1969—*Tim Hardin IV; Suite for Susan Moore and Damion—We Are—One, One, All in One* (Columbia) 1970—*The Best of Tim Hardin* (Verve) 1971—*Bird on a Wire* (Columbia) 1973—*Painted Head; Archetypes* (MGM); *Nine* (Antilles) 1981—*Reason to Believe: The Best of Tim Hardin* (Polydor) 1994—*Hang On to a Dream: The Verve Recordings* (Polygram Chronicles) 1996—*Simple Songs of Freedom: The Tim Hardin Collection* (Legacy).

Singer/songwriter Tim Hardin came to prominence during the folk-blues revival in the early '60s. He enjoyed critical acclaim for his smoky voice but had little commercial success on his own; others recorded his songs "If I Were a Carpenter" and "Reason to Believe."

Hardin traced his lineage back to the 19th-century Western outlaw John Wesley Hardin. He quit high school in 1959 and joined the Marines for two years, then enrolled in the American Academy of Dramatic Art in New York, but dropped out after a week. He moved to Cambridge, Massachusetts, and began performing in the folk clubs around Harvard.

Hardin's first tapes were recorded in 1962 but weren't released until 1967, as his third album. He returned to New York in 1963 and became an influential figure in Greenwich Village folk circles, blending strains of folk, blues, and jazz and playing with a group when most folkies were strictly soloists. He began to receive national attention in 1966, the year he performed at the Newport Folk Festival, and *Tim Hardin I* picked up critical accolades. About this time, Bob Dylan named him the country's greatest living songwriter.

His songs included "If I Were a Carpenter" (covered by Johnny Cash and June Carter, Bobby Darin, the Four Tops, Bob Seger, and Robert Plant, among others), "Reason to Believe" (covered by Peter, Paul and Mary, and Rod Stewart), and "Misty Roses." In the mid-'60s he was a regular attraction on the college campus circuits both in the U.S. and in Europe. By the late '60s, Hardin had settled into the rural artists' community in Woodstock, New York, and curtailed his performances. In 1969 he enjoyed his only Top 50 single with Bobby Darin's "Simple Song of Freedom." Hardin's *Bird on a Wire* LP used other writers' material; its studio band included future members of East-West folk-fusion band Oregon and jazz-rockers Weather Report.

In 1974 Hardin moved to southern England with his family and played regularly in English clubs. After a year, he moved back to L.A. His death in his L.A. apartment at age 39 was attributed to a heroin overdose.

John Wesley Harding

Born Wesley Harding Stace, Oct. 22, 1965, Hastings, Eng.
1988—*It Happened One Night* (Demon, U.K.) 1989—*God Made Me Do It: The Christmas EP* (Sire) 1990—*Here Comes the Groom* 1991—*The Name Above the Title* 1992—*Why We Fight* 1996—*John Wesley Harding's New Deal* (Forward/Rhino) 1998—*Awake* (Zero Hour) 1999—*Trad Arr Jones* 2000—*The Confessions of St. Ace* (Malt/Hollywood).

John Wesley Harding took his stage name from Bob Dylan's 1968 album, but critics more often compare the handsome singer/songwriter to such Dylan heirs as Elvis Costello and Billy Bragg, punk and postpunk artists who combine trenchant wit and melodic savvy with folk rock's confessional style.

The son of two musically inclined schoolteachers—his mother had been an opera singer, his father, a jazz pianist—Harding sang and played guitar in pubs as a teenager, then pursued a Ph.D. in political and social theory at Cambridge University before deciding to make music his career in 1988. He quickly landed a deal with the U.K. label Demon Records and released the live album *It Happened One Night* (its title, like *Here Comes the Groom, The Name Above the Title,* and *Why We Fight,* an homage to film director Frank Capra) before signing to Sire. While his Sire debut LP—which featured members of Costello's band, the Attractions—drew praise for its catchy tunes and literate lyrics and spawned a successful video for the single "The Devil in Me," some detractors accused the singer of wearing his influences on his sleeve.

Bruce Springsteen asked Harding to be one of his rare opening acts in 1995, and Harding soon began recording for a series of smaller labels, including Zero Hour, which released his 1999 tribute to traditional folk musician Nic Jones. Country-rock guitarists Jimmie Dale Gilmore and Steve Earle guested on his 2000 album, *The Confessions of St. Ace* (a take on his original surname). Harding has maintained a loyal cult following, promoting his albums with solo acoustic performances.

Ben Harper/Ben Harper and the Innocent Criminals

Born Oct. 28, 1969, Pomona, CA
1994—*Welcome to the Cruel World* (Virgin) 1995—*Fight for Your Mind* 1997—(+ the Innocent Criminals: Juan Nelson [b. Aug., 24, 1958, Cincinnati, OH], bass; Dean Butterworth

Ben Harper and the Innocent Criminals

[b. Sep. 9, 1966, Rochdale, Eng.], drums) *The Will to Live* 1999—(+ David Leach [b. Feb. 4, 1962, Irvington, NJ], perc.)—*Burn to Shine* 2001—*Live From Mars.*

Folk, blues, hard rock, country, jazz, and reggae are just a few of the genres that singer, songwriter, and guitarist Ben Harper has delved into throughout his career. His eclecticism has made him hard to categorize, and he's performed alongside all types of other performers (as a participant in the H.O.R.D.E. festival, as well as guesting on albums by artists as diverse as John Lee Hooker and Beth Orton). Born into a musical family, Harper picked up the guitar at an early age and began performing publicly at age 12. Shortly after appearing alongside Taj Mahal at a concert in 1992, Harper signed a contract with Virgin. His first album, *Welcome to the Cruel World,* introduced Harper as a folk-rocker with a soft, evocative voice and politically charged lyrics. Songs like "How Many Miles Must We March," "Like a King," and "I'll Rise" (with lyrics by Maya Angelou) demonstrate his Woody Guthrie–like propensity to write simply structured songs with sociopolitical messages. *Fight for Your Mind* (1995) features Harper's precocious capabilities on the Weissenborn (a hollow-necked, lap steel guitar), while *The Will to Live* (#89, 1997) and *Burn to Shine* (#67, 1999) highlight his move toward a more electric, amplified sound.

Roy Harper

Born June 12, 1941, Manchester, Eng.
1969—*Folkjokeopus* (World Pacific) 1970—*Flat Baroque and Berserk* (Harvest) 1971—*Stormcock* 1973—*Life Mask* 1974—*Valentine; Flashes From the Archives of Oblivion* 1975—*When an Old Cricketer Leaves the Crease* 1977—*One of Those Days in England* 1978—*Roy Harper 1970–75* 1980—*The Unknown Soldier* (Harvest) 1985—*Whatever Happened to Jugula* (PVC) 1991—*Once* (Awareness/I.R.S.) 1995—*Unhinged* (Griffin Music) 1998—*The Dream Society* (Science Friction) 2000—*The Green Man* 2001—*Hats Off* (The Right Stuff).

Folksinger, songwriter, and guitarist Roy Harper is best known to American rock fans as the subject of Led Zeppelin's "Hats Off to Harper," from its third LP. But in folk circles, and particularly in England, Harper is well known for his eccentric songs.

At age 15 he quit school and after a while joined the Royal Air Force. In an attempt to obtain a discharge, Harper pretended to be mentally ill; following his 1959 discharge he was committed to a mental institution. After his release 15 weeks later he wrote poems and songs in the streets of Blackpool. In 1964 he moved to London, and a year later began performing in clubs, part of a circle that included Jimmy Page, John Paul Jones, and Ronnie Lane. He also performed frequently in London's Hyde Park.

Harper recorded his first LP, *The Sophisticated Beggar,* for a British indie label. Beginning in 1971 with *Stormcock,* Jimmy Page began appearing on Harper's LPs. Among other musicians who have backed Harper are Pink Floyd's David Gilmour, Paul and Linda McCartney, and drummer Bill Bruford. That same year, however, Harper was hospitalized with a strange illness he claims to have contracted while giving a lamb mouth-to-mouth resuscitation (actually, it was a rare congenital circulatory disorder known as multiple pulmonary arterio-venus fistula). In 1972 he made his film debut in the British *Made.*

Those unfamiliar with Harper's solo work have probably heard his voice: He sang lead on Pink Floyd's "Have a Cigar" from 1975's *Wish You Were Here.* Many of his '80s and early-'90s albums are imports (the discography above is partial), though Science Friction has since reissued a large chunk of his catalogue. *The Unknown Soldier* (1980) included "You," a duet with Kate Bush, who later appeared on *Once* (1991). She has also covered Harper's "Another Day."

In the early '90s Harper performed with his musically likeminded son, Nick, who subsequently played with Squeeze and embarked on a solo career. *The Dream Society* (1998), which features Jethro Tull's Ian Anderson, marked the elder Harper's return to touring and recording after a brief, self-imposed hiatus.

Harper's Bizarre

Formed 1963, San Francisco, CA
Ted Templeman (b. Oct. 24, 1944), lead voc.; Dick Scoppettone (b. July 5, 1945), voc., gtr.; Eddie James (b. Santa Cruz, CA), voc., gtr.; Dick Yount (b. Jan. 9, 1943, Santa Cruz, CA), voc., bass, gtr., drums.
1966—(+ John Peterson [b. Jan. 8, 1945, San Francisco], voc., drums) 1967—*Feelin' Groovy* (Warner Bros.); *Anything Goes* 1968—*The Secret Life of Harper's Bizarre* 1969—*Harper's Bizarre 4* 1970—*Best of Harper's Bizarre* 1976—*As Time Goes By* (Forest Bay).

A pop-rock group from prepsychedelic San Francisco, Harper's Bizarre had one big hit with Paul Simon's "The 59th Street Bridge Song (Feelin' Groovy)" (#13, 1967), a tune that Simon had originally offered to the Cyrkle. The group began by playing surf music in local bars, calling itself the Tikis. As such, they made their first records in the mid-'60s for the San Francisco–based Autumn Records. When Autumn went under, the Tikis became Harper's Bizarre in 1966, picked up John Peterson from another Autumn band, the Beau Brummels, and got signed to Warner Bros. Having by this time abandoned surf music for pop rock, they cut *Feelin' Groovy* with arrangements by Leon Russell. Specializing in five-part harmonies, the group revived several standards, like Cole Porter's "Anything Goes" (#43, 1967), Glenn Miller's "Chattanooga Choo Choo" (#45, 1967), and Johnny Horton's "Battle of New Orleans" (#95, 1968).

Harper's Bizarre disbanded in 1970 after recording four albums for Warner Bros. Lead singer Ted Templeman stayed on with the label and became one of its top in-house A&R men and producers (Van Morrison, the Doobie Brothers, Van Halen, among others). Templeman also produced a 1974 album by the re-formed Beau Brummels, which included his old Harper's Bizarre mate, John Peterson.

Slim Harpo

Born James Moore, Jan. 11, 1924, Lobdell, LA; died Jan. 31, 1970, Baton Rouge, LA
1965—*A Long Drink of the Blues* (Stateside) 1976—*Blues Hangover* (Flyright) 1980—*Got Love If You Want It* 1989—*The Best of Slim Harpo* (Rhino).

Slim Harpo was a blues singer, songwriter, guitarist, and harp player who wrote "I'm a King Bee," an early Rolling Stones showpiece.

One of at least four children, Harpo grew up in Port Allen, Louisiana. His parents died while he was still a child, and he quit school to support his siblings. At age 18 he moved to New Orleans to work as a longshoreman, and later went to Baton Rouge to work as a contractor. In the early '40s he played bars and clubs as Harmonica Slim.

Harpo met guitarist Lightnin' Slim, with whom he toured and performed (Lightnin' appears on "Rainin' in My Heart" and "I'm a King Bee") over the next 20 years. He eventually owned his own trucking business but continued to work in clubs, often with Lightnin' Slim. He had a hit in 1961 with "Rainin' in My Heart" (#34) and in 1966 with the sly, sexual "Baby, Scratch My Back" (#16 pop, #1 R&B). He toured rock clubs through the late '60s. Harpo died of a heart attack.

Don "Sugarcane" Harris/ Don and Dewey

Born June 18, 1938, Pasadena, CA; died Nov. 30, 1999, Los Angeles, CA
N.A.—*Keep on Driving* (Musidisc) 1970—*Fiddler on the Rock* (Polydor); *Sugarcane* (Epic) 1973—*Cup Full of Dreams; Sugarcane's Got the Blues* (BASF).
Don and Dewey (with Terry Dewey): N.A.—*Don & Dewey* (Specialty) 1974—*They're Rockin' Till Midnight* 1991—*Jungle Hop.*

He played guitar, harmonica, and piano, but R&B veteran Don "Sugarcane" Harris was best known for his blues-rock electric violin. As half of the '50s duo Don and Dewey, he cowrote "Farmer John" (covered by Neil Young on his *Ragged Glory*) and "Big Boy Pete." The pair cowrote its best-known song, "I'm Leaving It All Up to You." Harris then went on to play with Johnny Otis, Little Richard, Frank Zappa, John Mayall, and Tupelo Chain Sex (with Dewey Terry).

The son of carnival performers, Harris studied classical violin with L.C. Robinson from 1944 to 1954. In the mid-'50s he graduated from Manual Arts High School in L.A. He formed the Squires in 1956, and they played local bars for many months until Harris teamed with Dewey Terry to form Don and Dewey.

They recorded for Specialty Records in the late '50s and toured the West Coast as part of the Johnny Otis show. Otis nicknamed Harris "Sugarcane," reportedly in reference to his reputation as a ladies' man. Harris later recorded with Otis' band for Epic in 1969 *(Cuttin' Up)* and toured with his show before he and Dewey reunited in 1975. They played together sporadically until Harris' health declined in 1998.

After his original pairing with Dewey had disintegrated in the early '60s, Harris toured and recorded with Little Richard. In 1970 he hooked up with Frank Zappa, with whom he played violin and sang, most notably on *Hot Rats* and *Weasels Ripped My Flesh.* (Zappa has said that Don and Dewey's single "Soul Motion" b/w "Stretchin' Out" on Rush Records was one of the all-time great R&B records; both sides featured Harris' kinetic electric-violin work.) Harris also toured and recorded with John Mayall in 1970 and 1971, working concurrently throughout as an occasional solo act in L.A. clubs. In 1970 he began his solo recording career. He died of natural causes in 1999.

Terry also remained active in music, producing and playing on some of Harris' albums, playing with Johnny Otis, and releasing several solo albums.

Emmylou Harris

Born Apr. 2, 1947, Birmingham, AL
1970—*Gliding Bird* (Jubilee) 1975—*Pieces of the Sky* (Reprise) 1976—*Elite Hotel* 1977—*Luxury Liner* (Warner Bros.) 1978—*Quarter Moon in a Ten Cent Town; Profile: The Best of Emmylou Harris* 1979—*Blue Kentucky Girl* 1980—*Roses in the Snow; Light of the Stable* 1981—*Evangeline* 1982—*Cimarron* 1983—*White Shoes* 1984—*Profile: The Best of Emmylou Harris, vol. 2* 1985—*The Ballad of Sally Rose* 1986—*Thirteen* 1987—*Angel Band* 1989—*Bluebird* (Reprise) 1990—*Duets; Brand New Dance* 1992—*At the Ryman* 1993—*Cowgirl's Prayer* (Asylum) 1994—*Songs of the West* (Warner Bros.) 1995—*Wrecking Ball* (Asylum) 1996—*Portraits* (Warner Bros.) 1998—*Spyboy* (Eminent) 2000—*Red Dirt Girl* (Nonesuch) 2001—*Anthology: The Warner/Reprise Years* (Warner Archives/Reprise/Rhino).
With Dolly Parton and Linda Ronstadt: 1987—*Trio* (Warner Bros.) 1999—*Trio II* (Asylum).
With Linda Ronstadt: 1999—*Western Wall: The Tucson Sessions* (Asylum).

During the '70s Emmylou Harris' clear, plaintive soprano made her a country hitmaker, and the neotraditionalist arrangements on her records appealed to rock & folk fans as well. A prolific performer, Harris has continued to garner attention and praise for her work, which has been enriched by superb supporting and collaborating musicians, and has included covers of material by song bards ranging from Gram Parsons to Bruce Springsteen to Lucinda Williams.

Harris grew up in a Virginia suburb of Washington. In high school she was a cheerleader, beauty pageant queen, and class valedictorian; she also played alto sax in the marching band. In 1965 she enrolled at the University of North Carolina at Greensboro and played there with a folk duo, but moved to Greenwich Village a year and a half later,

Emmylou Harris

where she played clubs and sat in with Jerry Jeff Walker and David Bromberg. She also recorded an unsuccessful album for the small Jubilee label. In 1970, after a short time in Nashville, she returned to her parents' house in Washington, DC, where she eventually found a band and began gigging locally.

After one DC club performance, Harris met the Flying Burrito Brothers; impressed by her voice, they recommended her to ex-member Gram Parsons [see entry], who was looking for a female duet partner for his upcoming debut solo recording. Parsons became a huge influence on Harris, introducing her to the music of such classic country greats as the Louvin Brothers. The two collaborated (on two Parsons albums and on a Fallen Angels tour) until Parsons' fatal overdose in September 1973. Devastated by Parsons' death, she later wrote a song about him, "Boulder to Birmingham," and over the years kept his music alive by recording his songs.

Harris subsequently formed a new group, including some former Parsons sidemen, and signed with Warner Bros. On 1975's *Pieces of the Sky,* she was backed by Elvis Presley's former sidemen Ron Tutt, James Burton, and Glen D. Hardin. Harris' touring group, dubbed the Hot Band, included songwriter Rodney Crowell [see entry] on guitar and harmony vocals, bassist Emory Gordy Jr., and pedal steel guitarist Hank DeVito. Guitarist Albert Lee and mandolinist/guitarist Ricky Skaggs [see entry] also played with Harris.

In 1975 her remake of the Louvin Brothers' "If I Could Only Win Your Love" topped the country chart; subsequent C&W hits included "Together Again" (#1, 1976), "One of These Days" (#3, 1976), "Sweet Dreams" (#1, 1976), "(You Never Can Tell) C'est La Vie" (#6, 1977), "Making Believe" (#8, 1977), and "To Daddy" (#3, 1977). *Elite Hotel* and *Luxury Liner* also attracted some rock fans, and she appeared in studio footage for the Band's 1976 documentary *The Last Waltz,* singing Robbie Robertson's "Evangeline." In 1980 she teamed with Roy Orbison for "That Lovin' You Feelin' Again," a #55 pop single that year (also featured on the soundtrack of the film *Roadie*).

In 1977 Harris married producer Brian Ahern, who had played a large role in shaping her early hits (and whose other credits included Anne Murray and Crowell). She began focusing on pure country material, and *Blue Kentucky Girl* won a Grammy for Best Female Country Vocal Performance. There were more C&W hits: "Two More Bottles of Wine" (#1, 1978), a cover of the Drifters' "Save the Last Dance for Me" (#4, 1979), and "Blue Kentucky Girl" (#6, 1979).

By 1982, Harris had eight gold albums. The early '80s also brought numerous top country singles: "Beneath Still Waters" (#1, 1980), "Wayfaring Stranger" (#7, 1980), a cover of the Chordettes' "Mister Sandman" (#10, 1981), a duet with Don Williams, "If I Needed You" (#3, 1981), "Tennessee Rose" (#9, 1982), "Born to Run" (#3, 1982), "(Lost His Love) On Our Last Date" (#1, 1983), "I'm Movin' On" (#5, 1983), "In My Dreams" (#9, 1984), and "Pledging My Love" (#9, 1984).

Harris' marriage to Ahern ended in 1983, and she relocated to Nashville. In 1985 she released *The Ballad of Sally Rose,* a loosely autobiographical "country opera," to great acclaim. Harris cowrote and coproduced the album with her second husband, the Grammy-winning songwriter Paul Kennerley. In 1987 Harris' long-anticipated collaboration with Dolly Parton and Linda Ronstadt (who had both appeared on *Sally Rose*) finally came to fruition with *Trio.* It went platinum, reached #6 on the pop chart, and yielded C&W smashes with a version of the Phil Spector–penned 1958 #1 Teddy Bears hit "To Know Him Is to Love Him" (#1, 1987), "Telling Me Lies" (#3, 1987), "Those Memories of You" (#5, 1987), and "Wildflowers" (#6, 1988).

Harris' other 1988 hits included "We Believe in Happy Endings" (#1), with Earl Thomas Conley, and "Heartbreak Hill" (#8). In 1990 she had a #24 pop album, a compilation of previously released *Duets* pairing her with everyone from Gram Parsons to George Jones and Willie Nelson. She then replaced her longtime Hot Band with an acoustic aggregation, the Nash Ramblers. In 1991 Harris recorded *At the Ryman* live at the Grand Ole Opry's venerable auditorium. Her 1993 album, *Cowgirl's Prayer,* reached only #34 on the country charts but was a critical favorite.

Harris essentially cut her ties to the Nashville hit mill when she released her 1995 album, *Wrecking Ball.* She has always pushed country music's boundaries, but nothing in her catalogue anticipated such a departure. Produced by Daniel Lanois and recorded mainly with rock musicians, including U2 drummer Larry Mullen Jr., the album features unvarnished, otherworldly renditions of songs written by Bob Dylan, Jimi Hendrix, Steve Earle, and other lesser-known artists. Critics hailed the project as a triumph of innovation even as it alienated fans of Harris' more country-sounding work. It won the 1995 Grammy for Best Contemporary Folk Album.

In 1998 Harris signed with Eminent Records, a Nashville independent label, and released *Spyboy,* a live set featuring her touring band of the same name. Harris and guitarist Buddy Miller coproduced the album, which functions as something of a career retrospective. In 1999 Harris, Parton, and Ronstadt released their long-awaited *Trio II* album. The record's version of Neil Young's "After the Gold Rush" won a Grammy for Best Country Collaboration With Vocals. Harris and Ronstadt teamed up for a haunting duo record, *Western Wall: The Tucson Sessions,* later in the year. Harris executive produced and sang on *Return of the Grievous Angel: A Tribute to Gram Parsons,* released by Almo Sounds in 1999. The record featured covers of Parsons' songs by Elvis Costello, Beck, and Sheryl Crow, among others. In 1999 Harris won the prestigious Billboard Century Award. Her 2000 release, *Red Dirt Girl,* continued in the same vein of *Wrecking Ball,* but was composed of Harris originals. The album won a Grammy for Best Contemporary Folk Recording.

Wynonie Harris

Born Aug. 24, 1915, Omaha, NE; died June 14, 1969, Los Angeles, CA
N.A.—*Good Rockin' Blues* (King); *Good Rockin' Tonight; Party After Hours* (Aladdin) 1993—*Women, Whiskey & Fish Tails* (Ace) 1994—*Bloodshot Eyes* (Rhino).

Wynonie Harris was a big-band blues shouter whose style was a major influence on early rock & roll.

Harris dropped out of Creighton University in Omaha and began working as a comedian and dancer in the '30s. After teaching himself to play the drums, in the late '30s and early '40s he led his own local combo. When he moved to L.A. in the early '40s, he quit drumming and worked as a club emcee for a while; he also appeared as a dancer in the film *Hit Parade of 1943.*

In 1944 Harris became a vocalist with Lucky Millinder's band, with whom he cut his first records that year for Decca (and, a few years later, for King Records) and toured major ballrooms throughout America. He continued recording with jazz bands in the mid-'40s (Jack McVea, Oscar Pettiford, Illinois Jacquet, and others). He also worked with Johnny Otis, who influenced him toward a pop-tinged R&B style. While recording for King Records, Harris had his biggest successes with "Good Morning Judge," "Lovin' Machine," "All She Wants to Do Is Rock," and his mid-'50s British hit, "Bloodshot Eyes." Harris also covered Roy Brown's "Good Rockin' Tonight," later an Elvis Presley hit. He toured widely throughout the late '40s with such traveling bands as the Lionel Hampton Orchestra, Dud Bascomb, and Big Joe Turner.

Harris continued club work, often as part of package shows, into the early '50s, cutting records for Cincinnati-based King Records and New York's Apollo label. In the mid-'50s he opened a cafe in Brooklyn and in 1963 went to L.A. and did the same. He was working as a bartender when he died of cancer at age 54. Harris had attempted several comebacks in the interim. In the early '60s he recorded for Atco and Roulette in New York and for Chicago-based Cadet. For one of his last public performances, in 1967, he played Harlem's venerable Apollo Theatre.

George Harrison

Born Feb. 25, 1943, Liverpool, Eng.
1968—*Wonderwall Music* (Apple) 1969—*Electronic Sounds* (Zapple) 1970—*All Things Must Pass* (Apple) 1972—*Concert for Bangla Desh* 1973—*Living in the Material World* 1974—*Dark Horse* 1975—*Extra Texture (Read All About It)* 1976—*33 ⅓* (Dark Horse); *The Best of George Harrison* (Capitol) 1979—*George Harrison* (Dark Horse) 1981—*Somewhere in England* 1982—*Gone Troppo* 1987—*Cloud Nine* 1989—*Best of Dark Horse 1976–1989* 1992—*Live in Japan.*

George Harrison played lead guitar and wrote occasional songs for the Beatles; he also was the group's only convert to Eastern religion. Since the Beatles broke up, he has had an uneven solo career.

Born into a working-class family, Harrison attended Dovedale Primary School, three years behind John Lennon. In 1954 he entered Liverpool Institute, a grade behind Paul McCartney. In 1956, at the height of Britain's skiffle craze, Harrison formed his first group, the Rebels. He started jamming occasionally with his new acquaintance McCartney, and in 1958 McCartney introduced him to Lennon. Soon all three were playing in the Quarrymen, who later became the Silver Beetles and then the Beatles.

Besides playing lead guitar, Harrison sang backup vocals and an occasional lead ("Roll Over Beethoven," "If I Needed Someone," "I'm Happy Just to Dance With You") in the Beatles. In the mid-'60s he was one of the first rock musicians to experiment with Indian and Far Eastern instruments; he studied with Bengali master sitarist Ravi Shankar. Harrison first played sitar on 1965's "Norwegian Wood" and later on "Within You Without You," "The Inner Light," and other songs. Harrison wrote songs as early as 1963 ("Don't Bother Me"), but it was difficult for him to get the group to record his material, one of the problems that led to the Beatles' breakup. Harrison's compositions include "I Need You," "You Like Me Too Much," "Taxman," "Love You To," "Piggies," "Savoy Truffle," "While My Guitar Gently Weeps," "Here Comes the Sun," and "Something" (#3, 1969), the only Harrison song to become a hit single for the Beatles.

After the Beatles officially disbanded in early 1970, Harrison continued his solo career, which he'd begun in November 1968 with the electronic sound collage soundtrack *Wonderwall Music.* In November 1970 he released his three-record set *All Things Must Pass* (#1), produced by Phil Spector and featuring guests such as Eric Clapton and Traffic's Dave Mason, which included the #1 hit single "My Sweet Lord." (A 1976 lawsuit successfully established that Harrison "unknowingly" plagiarized the song's melodic structure from the early-'60s hit by the Chiffons, "He's So Fine.") In late summer 1971 Harrison sponsored and hosted two benefit concerts at New York's Madison Square Garden for the people of Bangladesh. With guests including Ringo Starr, Eric Clapton, Leon Russell, and Bob Dylan, the concerts, the documentary film, and the Grammy-winning three-record set, *Concert for Bangla Desh,* were a resounding success, although funds raised by the proceedings were impounded during a nine-year audit of Apple by the IRS. (In 1981 a check for $8.8 million was finally sent through UNICEF; $2 million had been sent in 1972 before the audit began.) Harrison's song about the plight of the refugees, "Bangla Desh," hit the pop Top 25 in late 1971. *Living in the Material World* produced a #1 hit in 1973, "Give Me Love (Give Me Peace on Earth)."

In 1974 Harrison formed his own Dark Horse Records (with distribution via Warner Bros.), releasing a gold album of the same name late in the year (the title track of which hit #15 as a single), and touring America to support it. The sales of *Extra Texture (Read All About It),* were disappointing, a trend that continued unabated with *33 ⅓* and *George Harrison.* A tribute to the slain Lennon, "All Those Years Ago," went #2 in 1981. Starr and Paul and Linda McCartney also appear on the record. *Gone Troppo* was a commercial flop, and Harrison stopped recording for several years, to concentrate on gardening, auto-racing, and other pursuits.

Harrison began producing albums in the late '60s by Apple Records protégés Jackie Lomax, Billy Preston, and Badfinger; he also participated in sessions by artists signed to his Dark Horse label in the mid-'70s. He has been regularly involved with members of the Monty Python comedy group axis as executive producer of film projects, including *The Life of Brian* and *Time Bandits.* Harrison also appeared in the Python Beatles parody film, *All You Need Is Cash,* as a reporter. In 1979 he privately published an autobiography, *I Me Mine* (a mass market edition was published in 1982).

Harrison ended a five-year hiatus from recording with *Cloud Nine* (#8, 1987), which went platinum and yielded the #1 hit single "Got My Mind Set on You" (a cover of an oldie recorded by Rudy Clark). The album, produced by Jeff Lynne of Electric Light Orchestra, spawned a Top 25 hit in "When We Was Fab," an evocation of the Beatles' cello-driven "I Am the Walrus" sound, which had been so influential on ELO. Harrison went on to join Lynne in the Traveling Wilburys [see entry]. In 1992, with his old friend Eric Clapton, Harrison embarked on his first tour in 18 years; that April Harrison played his first-ever U.K. solo concert (which also served to raise awareness of the Maharishi Mahesh Yogi's new Natural Law party, then seeking seats in British Parliament).

He met his first wife, model Pattie Boyd (born Mar. 17, 1945), in early 1964 on the set of the Beatles film *A Hard Day's Night* (in which she briefly appeared). They were married on January 21, 1966, but their marriage began coming apart a few years later, and they separated and eventually divorced in 1977. Boyd later married guitarist Eric Clapton and was the subject of Clapton's "Layla." Harrison married Olivia Arias in England in September 1978, a month after their son, Dhani, was born.

After touring in the early '90s, Harrison mostly stayed out of the news. He joined Ringo Starr and Paul McCartney for 1995's "new" Beatles songs "Free as a Bird" and "Real Love." He and Starr attended Linda McCartney's funeral in June 1998. It was the first time the surviving Beatles had made a public appearance together in almost three decades. That same year, Harrison announced that he was battling throat cancer. Then, on December 30, 1999, Michael Abram, a mentally ill former heroin addict, stabbed and nearly killed Harrison after breaking into his Friar Park estate in Oxfordshire; Harrison was saved by his wife, Olivia, who managed to hit the assailant over the head with a poker and a table lamp.

His solo career on hold since *Cloud Nine,* he remastered *All Things Must Pass* for a January 2001 reissue; the five extra tracks included "My Sweet Lord 2000," which featured his son, Dhani, with whom Harrison had been reportedly working on a new studio album. In mid-2001 Harrison underwent further treatment for cancer; this followed previous treatment for throat and lung cancer.

Wilbert Harrison

Born Jan. 6, 1929, Charlotte, NC; died Oct. 26, 1994, Spencer, NC
1962—*Battle of the Giants* (Joy); *Kansas City* (Sphere) 1969—*Let's Work Together* (Sue) 1971—*Wilbert Harrison* (Buddah) 1989—*Classic R&B Hits* (Grudge) 1992—*Kansas City* (Relic).

Jump-blues singer Wilbert Harrison had two major pop hits a decade apart: "Kansas City" in 1959 and "Let's Work Together" in 1969. Harrison began recording in the early '50s with "This Woman of Mine" on Rockin. He recorded for DeLuxe and Savoy without notable success. In 1959 Fury Records released "Kansas City," a version of Leiber and Stoller's "K.C. Lovin' " (written in 1952) that went to #1. The song was later recorded by the Beatles.

Harrison recorded through the '60s for numerous labels (Seahorn, Neptune, Doc, Port, Vest) until "Let's Work Together," on Sue, went to #32; it was later covered by Canned Heat, Roxy Music's Bryan Ferry, Dwight Yoakam, and the Kentucky Headhunters. "My Heart Is Yours," on SSS International, went to #98 in 1971, and he recorded through the '70s for Buddah, Hotline, Brunswick, and Wet Soul. For much of his career, Harrison—unable to afford sidemen—performed live as a one-man band. He released several albums in the past two decades, virtually all now out of print. He died of a stroke at age 65.

Deborah Harry: See Blondie

Mickey Hart: See the Grateful Dead

John Hartford

Born Dec. 30, 1937, New York, NY; died June 4, 2001, Nashville, TN
1967—*Looks at Life* (RCA); *Earthwords and Music* 1968—*The*

Love Album; Housing Project; Gentle on My Mind and Other Originals 1969—*John Hartford* 1970—*Iron Mountain Depot* 1971—*Aero-Plain* (Warner Bros.) 1972—*Morning Bugle* 1975—*Tennessee Jubilee* (Flying Fish) 1976—*Mark Twang; Nobody Knows What You Do* 1977—*Dillard, Hartford, Dillard* (with Doug and Rod Dillard); *All in the Name of Love* 1978—*Heading Down Into the Mystery Below* 1979—*Slumberin' on the Cumberland* 1981—*You and Me at Home; Catalogue* 1984—*Gum Tree Canoe* 1987—*Me Oh My, How the Time Does Fly: A John Hartford Anthology* 1989—*Down on the River* 1991—*Hartford and Hartford* 1992—*Cadillac Rag* (Small Dog a Barkin') 1993—*Goin' Back to Dixie* 1994—*The Walls We Bounce Off Of* 1995—*Old Sport* 1996—*No End of Love; Wild Hog in the Red Brush* (Rounder) 1998—*Speed of the Old Long Bow* 1999—*Good Old Boys* 2000—*Live From Mountain Stage* (Blue Plate).

Singer, songwriter, and banjoist Hartford wrote "Gentle on My Mind" for Glen Campbell and recorded folk and bluegrass solo albums.

Best known for his banjo work but also adept at guitar and fiddle, Hartford was raised in St. Louis, where his father was a doctor and his mother a painter. He studied art at Washington University in St. Louis, and before moving to Nashville in the mid-'60s he worked as a sign painter, a commercial artist, a riverboat deckhand (he later became a licensed river pilot), and a disc jockey. His session work slowly picked up, and by the end of the '60s he had participated in the Byrds' *Sweetheart of the Rodeo.* Hartford continued studio gigs through the early '70s. In 1966 he signed with RCA, for which he eventually recorded eight albums.

But his biggest success came as a writer, notably "Gentle on My Mind," which, in addition to Campbell's Grammy-winning hit, has been covered more than 300 times, and has sold over 15 million copies internationally. It was originally a minor country hit for Hartford in 1967. Among his other compositions are "California Earthquake" and "Natural to Be Gone."

Hartford had his most extensive exposure in the late '60s as a regular on the *Smothers Brothers Comedy Hour,* which was followed by a stint on Glen Campbell's weekly television musical-variety show. At the start of the '70s he hosted his own syndicated show, *Something Else.* He switched from RCA to Warner Bros. in mid-1971, releasing his debut for the label, the David Bromberg–produced *Aero-Plain* (featuring guitarist Norman Blake, dobro player Tut Taylor, and fiddler Vassar Clements). Then he switched to the small Flying Fish label, and 1976's *Mark Twang* won a Grammy in the Ethnic-Traditional category—Hartford has gotten several nominations in the Traditional Folk category.

For decades, Hartford performed year-round, usually as a one-man band (he also toured with Campbell). He started slowing down in the late '90s, weakened by cancer and anemia but continued to record regularly, either solo or with a cast of regular collaborators that included his son Jamie. In 2000 he contributed two fiddle pieces to the soundtrack of the Coen brothers' movie *O Brother, Where Art Thou?* His long battle with cancer ended in June 2001.

PJ Harvey

Formed July 1991, Yeovil, Eng.
PJ Harvey (b. Polly Jean Harvey, Oct. 9, 1969, Yeovil), voc., gtr.; Rob Ellis (b. Feb. 13, 1962, Bristol, Eng.), drums; Stephen Vaughan (b. June 22, 1962, Wolverhampton, Eng.), bass.
1992—*Dry* (Island) 1993—*Rid of Me; 4-Track Demos.*
PJ Harvey solo: 1995—*To Bring You My Love* 1998—*Is This Desire?* 2000—*Stories From the City, Stories From the Sea.*
With John Parish: 1996—*Dance Hall at Louse Point.*

Led by the talented guitarist, songwriter, and singer Polly Jean Harvey, the postpunk power trio PJ Harvey came from small-town England in 1991 and took London by storm with its raw, dynamic rock and Harvey's evocative/provocative female-centric lyrics. Harvey formed the band with two friends in Yeovil and recorded its debut for less than $5,000. After creating a buzz in London and two chart-topping singles, PJ Harvey released *Dry* on the U.K. indie label Too Pure (Island Records released the album in the U.S.). In hypnotic tunes like "Dress," "Happy and Bleeding," and "Sheela-Na-Gig," Harvey sang about discovering, reviling, and reveling in her body. The tomboyish Harvey's discomfort with her femininity fueled her lyrics and image. *Dry*'s album cover features the androgynous artist skinny and bare-chested.

Harvey, who grew up on a sheep farm, quickly developed a reputation for being a publicity-shy recluse and reportedly had a near nervous breakdown in 1992, after playing the mammoth Reading Festival. Recovered, she took her career in hand and chose iconoclastic Chicago-based producer

PJ Harvey

Steve Albini to produce the band's second album. *Rid of Me* sounded appropriately noisy and difficult. Harvey's lyrics mocked efforts to control her sexuality and art, taunting lovers on "Rid of Me" and "Legs" and declaring her stature over cock-rockers on "50 Ft. Queenie." Press-friendly now, Harvey disappointed many fans by denouncing feminism in interviews, although listeners found consolation in lyrics that seemed to contradict her stance. Harvey turned down a chance to play 1993's Lollapalooza. Her own American tour revealed a confident performer who was adding touches of a campy glam to her trademark austere appearance.

The tour also indicated that Harvey was having trouble with her band, and in August 1993, Ellis departed. The demos for *Rid of Me*, released as *4-Track Demos*, verified criticism that Albini had buried Harvey's powerful vocals and barely touched the range of her aural ideas. The album included several new tracks, including the irresistible "Reeling."

Harvey completely dispensed with her band for 1995's *To Bring You My Love* (#40), a bluesy collection of songs that she produced with Flood (U2) and guitarist John Parish. Bassist Mick Harvey (ex–Birthday Party) and guitarist Joe Gore were among the guests who played on the critically acclaimed album.

In 1996 Harvey and Parish released *Dance Hall at Louse Point*, an album for which Harvey wrote and sang lyrics to Parish's music. The exception was an irony-drenched cover of Peggy Lee's Leiber/Stoller-penned 1969 hit "Is That All There Is?" Released as a single, the song also appeared on the soundtrack album for the film *Basquiat*, a movie depicting the life of the late graffiti artist.

Harvey duetted with Nick Cave on his *Murder Ballads* album (1996). The collaboration also led to a brief, heated romance, the dissolution of which Cave brooded over on *The Boatman's Call* (1997). Harvey and Flood coproduced *Is This Desire*? (#54, 1998). Built upon a bed of understated electrobeats, the album's songs found Harvey ruminating on the meaning of passion. She also sang on Tricky's *Angels With Dirty Faces* and made her acting debut, playing Mary Magdalene, in the film *The Book of Life*. The critically acclaimed *Stories From the City, Stories From the Sea* was much more upbeat than Harvey's usual fare.

Juliana Hatfield

Born July 27, 1967, Wiscasset, ME
With Blake Babies, formed 1986, Boston, MA: Hatfield, voc., bass; John Strohm (b. Mar. 23, 1967, Bloomington, IN), voc., gtr.; Freda Boner (b. Sep. 3, 1967, Nashville, TN), drums.
1987—*Nicely, Nicely* (Chewbud) 1989—*Earwig* (Mammoth) 1990—*Sunburn* 1991—*Rosy Jack World* EP 1993—*Innocence and Experience* 2001—*God Bless the Blake Babies* (Zoë/Rounder).
Juliana Hatfield solo: 1992—*Hey Babe* (Mammoth) 1993—*Become What You Are* (Mammoth/Atlantic) 1995—*Only Everything* 1997—*Please Do Not Disturb* EP (Bar/None) 1998—*Bed* (Zoë/Rounder) 2000—*Beautiful Creature; Juliana's Pony: Total System Failure.*

With her sweet voice juxtaposed against assertive guitar playing and introspective songwriting, Juliana Hatfield garnered attention on the college rock scene, first with the band Blake Babies, and even more so as a solo artist.

One of three children of a physician father and a *Boston Globe* fashion editor mother, Hatfield, deeply affected at age 11 by her parents' divorce, later drew on memories of adolescent unhappiness for her lyrics. Starting piano lessons from her mother at age six, Hatfield played Police and Rush covers in a high school group called the Squids before gravitating toward the Velvet Underground and X. While studying voice at Boston's Berklee College of Music, she met guitarist John Strohm and drummer Freda Boner. Switching to bass, she joined them to found Blake Babies, whose six-year career and three recordings established them as college-radio stars. Seeking a harder sound, Hatfield departed in 1990; Strohm and Boner formed the band Antenna. Strohm later formed Velo-Deluxe. In 2000 the trio reunited to record *God Bless the Blake Babies*. Upon the album's release, the Blake Babies embarked on a national tour.

In 1990 Hatfield contributed lyrics to the debut album of former Bangles singer Susanna Hoffs; she also sang and played on the Lemonheads' *It's a Shame About Ray*. (Her complicated romantic relationship with Lemonhead singer Evan Dando became fodder for alt-rock gossip columns.)

Dando and John Wesley Harding appeared on Hatfield's own solo debut, the critically acclaimed *Hey Babe*, which showcased Hatfield's return to playing guitar. In 1992 she formed the Juliana Hatfield Three with bassist Dean Fisher and ex–Bullet LaVolta drummer Todd Philips; with songs about self-mutilation, anorexia, and familial tension set to pop melodies and heavy guitar, *Become What You Are* gave voice to blank-generation tension. *Only Everything* continued in the same vein two years later, but Hatfield left Mammoth after the label failed to release the followup, *God's Foot*.

Juliana Hatfield

She left the finished (and unreleased) album behind and moved on with a one-off EP for Bar/None before recording a trio of albums for Zoë.

With the entertainment media fascinated by Hatfield (1992 photo layouts in *Sassy* and *Vogue*), the singer also revealed a penchant for confessional, confrontational statements, asserting in interviews that she was still a virgin at age 25 and that women are genetically determined to be lesser guitarists than men. But her Zoë albums, beginning with *Bed*, found her showcasing edgier lyrics and a renewed passion for distorted guitar solos. *Beautiful Creature* and *Total System Failure* were released simultaneously, with the former's focus on introspective ballads balanced by the significantly louder, hard-rock alter ego of the latter. *Total System Failure* was credited to Juliana's Pony, a new trio composed of Hatfield on guitar, Mikey Welsh on bass, and Zephan Courtney on drums.

Donny Hathaway

Born Oct. 1, 1945, Chicago, IL; died Jan. 13, 1979, New York, NY
1970—*Everything Is Everything* (Atco) 1971—*Donny Hathaway* 1972—*Donny Hathaway Live; Roberta Flack and Donny Hathaway* (Atlantic); *Come Back Charleston Blue* soundtrack (Atco) 1973—*Extension of a Man* (Atlantic) 1978—*The Best of Donny Hathaway* (Atco) 1979—*Roberta Flack Featuring Donny Hathaway* (Atlantic) 1980—*Donny Hathaway in Performance* 1990—*Donny Hathaway Collection.*

A singer/songwriter/keyboardist best known for his duets with Roberta Flack, Donny Hathaway fused R&B, gospel, jazz, classical, and rock strains in a modestly successful solo career. He was raised in St. Louis by his grandmother, Martha Pitts, a professional gospel singer. From the age of three, Hathaway accompanied her on tours, billed as the Nation's Youngest Gospel Singer. He attended Howard University in Washington, DC, on a fine-arts scholarship.

One classmate was Roberta Flack, and in the early '70s, shortly after Flack started her solo career, the two began singing together. Their hits included Carole King's "You've Got a Friend" (#29, 1971) and "Where Is the Love" (#5, 1972), which established them as a duo. *Roberta Flack and Donny Hathaway* was a gold album, but due to personal problems both the partnership and Hathaway's solo career were put on hold for several years. When they reunited in 1978, they had their biggest hit, the gold single "The Closer I Get to You" (#2, 1978). Hathaway was working on *Roberta Flack Featuring Donny Hathaway* when he died after falling from his 15th-floor hotel room of the Essex House. (The police called it suicide; close friends refused to believe it.) The LP, released posthumously, hit #25 and went gold; a single, "You Are My Heaven," reached #47.

At the time of his death, Hathaway had released five solo albums in addition to his discs with Flack. He had recorded briefly for Curtom Records with June Conquest as June and Donnie, and got his first solo contract with Atlantic in 1970 under the patronage of King Curtis. Hathaway enjoyed R&B chart success in the early '70s with singles like "The Ghetto, Part 1" (#23 R&B, 1970), "Little Ghetto Boy" (#25 R&B, 1972), "Giving Up" (#21 R&B, 1972), "I Love You More Than You'll Ever Know" (#20 R&B, 1972), and "Love, Love, Love" (#16 R&B, 1973).

Concurrently, Hathaway worked as a producer and composer for others, including Aretha Franklin, Jerry Butler, and the Staple Singers. He also did freelance production work for Chess, Uni, Kapp, and Stax, and served as arranger for Curtom Records and band director for the Impressions. Quincy Jones hired Hathaway to score the 1972 film *Come Back Charleston Blue*. He also sang the theme song for the television series *Maude*. By the mid-'70s, he had formed his own independent production company. Hathaway's daughter Lalah came out with her debut album in 1990.

Richie Havens

Born Jan. 21, 1941, Brooklyn, NY
1965—*Richie Havens Record* (Douglas) 1966—*Electric Havens* 1967—*Mixed Bag* (Verve) 1968—*Something Else Again* 1969—*Richard D. Havens 1983* 1970—*Stonehenge* (Stormy Forest) 1971—*Alarm Clock; "The Great Blind Degree"* 1972—*Richie Havens on Stage* 1973—*Richie Havens Portfolio* 1974—*Mixed Bag II* (Polydor) 1976—*The End of the Beginning* (A&M) 1977—*Mirage* 1979—*Connections* (Elektra/Asylum) 1987—*Simple Things* (RBI); *Richie Havens Sings the Beatles and Dylan* (Rykodisc); *Collection* 1991—*Now* (Solar/Epic) 1993—*Résumé: The Best of Richie Havens* (Rhino) 1994—*Cuts to the Chase* (Forward).

Richie Havens, a black folksinger with a percussive, strummed guitar style, enjoyed his greatest popularity during the late '60s. He was born and raised in the Bedford-Stuyvesant ghetto, the eldest of nine children in a family headed by a pianist father. As a youth, he sang for spare change on streetcorners. By age 14 he was singing with the McCrea Gospel Singers in Brooklyn, and three years later he dropped out of high school to pursue a music career. He worked his way into Greenwich Village folk circles in the early '60s.

After recording two albums for the Douglas International–Transatlantic label, Havens started touring clubs throughout the U.S. in 1967, and he became a familiar act on the outdoor festival circuit, playing at the Newport Folk Festival (1966), the Monterey Jazz Festival (1967), the Miami Pop Festival (1968), the Isle of Wight Festival (1969), and Woodstock (1969). Despite such massive exposure, Havens never really transformed his concert audiences into record consumers. Signed to Verve in 1966, he jumped from there to MGM, A&M, Elektra, and others.

His repertoire has featured songs by Lennon-McCartney, Van Morrison, Bob Dylan, and James Taylor. His only chart success was with his cover of George Harrison's "Here Comes the Sun" (#16, 1971). Havens continued to be a reliable club and concert performer throughout the '70s. Late in the decade he conducted extensive tours of the Middle East and Europe. In 1979 he released his 15th album and Elektra

Records debut, *Connections.* As an actor, his film credits include *Catch My Soul* (1974) and Richard Pryor's *Greased Lightning* (1977). He was also featured in the 1972 stage presentation of the Who's *Tommy.*

Throughout the '80s and '90s, Havens' slightly hoarse voice became familiar to television viewers through the dozens of commercial jingles he sang, for everything from Amtrak, to McDonald's, to Cotton Incorporated. In 1990 he cofounded the Natural Guard, a national organization that helps children learn to protect the environment. In 1999 he published a book of memoirs entitled *They Can't Hide Us Anymore.*

Dale Hawkins

Born Aug. 22, 1938, Goldmine, LA
1958—*Susie Q* 1969—*L.A., Memphis and Tyler, Texas* (Bell) 1976—*Dale Hawkins* (Chess) 1995—*Oh! Susie Q—The Best of Dale Hawkins* 1997—*Daredevil* (Norton) 1999—*Wildcat Tamer* (Mystic/Lightyear).

A rockabilly original, singer, guitarist, and bandleader Dale Hawkins was an important influence on such later rockers as John Fogerty, whose Creedence Clearwater Revival had a #11 hit in 1968 with Hawkins' "Suzie Q."

Hawkins signed with Chess in the mid-'50s and recorded for its Checker subsidiary for the next several years. He enjoyed his most rewarding year in 1957, when "Suzie Q" climbed to #27 on the pop chart. Hawkins followed up with more modest releases like "La Do-Dada" (#32, 1958), "A House, a Car and a Wedding Ring" (#88, 1958), "Class Cutter Yeah Yeah" (#52, 1959), and uncharted singles like "My Babe" and "Liza Jane." James Burton (who claims to have been coauthor of "Suzie Q"), Scotty Moore (of Elvis Presley's band), and Roy Buchanan were among the guitarists in Hawkins' band.

After touring the U.S. several times, Hawkins left Chess in 1961 and in the next few years recorded, with little impact on the market, for such labels as Tilt, Zonk, Atlantic, Roulette, and ABC-Paramount. By the mid-'60s, he was living in Tyler, Texas, and producing pop hits by the Five Americans ("Western Union," "Do It Again a Little Bit Slower") and Bruce Channel ("Hey Baby"). At the close of the '60s, Hawkins revitalized his recording career with an album recorded in Nashville with Box Tops producer Dan Penn. In the '70s he produced Rio Grande. *Wildcat Tamer,* from 1999, was Hawkins' first new release in 30 years. It includes an updated "Suzie Q."

Edwin Hawkins Singers

Formed 1967, Oakland, CA
1969—*Let Us Go Into the House of the Lord* (Pavillion) 1969—*Oh Happy Day* (Buddah); *More Happy Days* 1971—*Children (Get Together)* 1972—*I'd Like to Teach the World to Sing* 1973—*New World* 1974—*Live* 1983—*Mass Choir* (Mercury) 1985—*The Best of the Edwin Hawkins Singers* (Savoy) 1989—*Imagine Heaven* (Lection) 1990—*Music and Arts Seminar Chicago Mass Choir* 1991—*Face to Face* (Lection/PolyGram) 1992—*Oh Happy Day Reunion* (Intersound) 1993—*If You Love Me* 1994—*Kings & Kingdoms* 1997—*The Best of the Edwin Hawkins Singers* (Capitol).

The Edwin Hawkins Singers had one of the most successful gospel pop hits ever in 1969 with "Oh Happy Day" (#4) and returned to the Top 10 the following year backing Melanie on "Lay Down (Candles in the Rain)" (#6). The group's arranger, director, and pianist, Edwin Hawkins (born August 1943, in Oakland), was a student at Berkeley in 1967 when he and an associate, Betty Watson, organized the large choir to represent their Oakland church, the Ephesian Church of God in Christ, at a Pentecostal Youth Congress in Washington, DC. The group was originally called the Northern California State Youth Choir.

By 1969, the group was 46 members strong and backed by keyboards, drums, and electric bass. To help raise money to finance a trip to the National Youth Congress in Cleveland that year, the choir recorded an album in a San Francisco church on an old two-track stereo machine. It included a fiery reading of the gospel standard "Oh Happy Day," which a local disc jockey started airing. By the spring of 1969, the single was a Top 10 hit; Buddah picked up the LP, *Let Us Go Into the House of the Lord,* for national distribution.

Featured on the album was vocalist Dorothy Morrison (born in Longview, Texas, in 1945), who went on to some prominence as a solo gospel artist, including an appearance at the 1969 Big Sur Folk Festival. Other featured soloists in the Hawkins group included Elaine Kelly ("To My Father's House") and Margarette Branch ("I'm Going Through").

After contributing to Melanie's hit and touring Europe in 1970, the group quickly faded from prominence, partly because the personnel kept changing, and keeping such a large retinue active proved prohibitively expensive. But they remain a respected gospel force, especially in the Bay Area, touring as recently as 1999. Various core members of the choir, including Edwin Hawkins and Grammy-winning vocalist Tremaine Hawkins, have also been active on their own.

Ronnie Hawkins

Born Jan. 10, 1935, Huntsville, AR
1963—*The Best of Ronnie Hawkins* (Roulette) 1970—*Ronnie Hawkins* (Cotillion) 1971—*The Hawk* 1972—*Rock and Roll Resurrection* (Monument) 1974—*The Giant of Rock 'n' Roll* 1990—*Best of Ronnie Hawkins and the Hawks* (Rhino).

A 40-year veteran of roadhouse rock & roll, Ronnie Hawkins is best known as the man who assembled the Band. He formed his first group in 1952 while attending the University of Arkansas and shortly thereafter cut his first record, a cover of an Eddy Arnold tune, for a local label. In the mid-'50s, before moving to Memphis, he played piano behind Carl Perkins and Conway Twitty.

After a stint in the army, Hawkins went to Canada for the first time in 1958. For the next four years he alternated between club work there and one-nighter tours of Southern honky-tonks. In that period, he met the four Canadians and one American who later became known as the Band (Levon Helm, like Hawkins, was a transplanted Arkansan). They joined his band, the Hawks, and accompanied him on his auto tours through the South and Canada before leaving him to back John Hammond Jr. in 1964. (A year later they became Bob Dylan's backing band, and by 1968 they were on their own.) Among other onetime Hawks were guitarists Roy Buchanan, Duane Allman, and Dominic Troiano.

Hawkins recorded extensively for the Roulette label in the late '50s and early '60s. In 1959 he enjoyed two American chart hits, "Mary Lou" (#26) and "Forty Days" (#45). But rockabilly was on its way out by the time Hawkins got his recording career under way. In 1962 he settled in Toronto and became proprietor and featured attraction at the Hawk's Nest Bar. His records were hits in Canada, especially his 1963 recording of Bo Diddley's "Who Do You Love."

By the mid-'60s, Hawkins was recording for his own Hawk label in Canada. He performed regularly on the rock ballroom circuit in the late '60s, and in 1969 he signed with Atlantic/Cotillion. *Ronnie Hawkins* was recorded in Alabama with the Muscle Shoals Rhythm Section, and it produced his last American chart single, "Down in the Alley" (#75, 1970).

In 1976 Hawkins appeared at the Band's farewell concert, documented in Martin Scorsese's film *The Last Waltz*. He also joined the group during the 1989 destruction of the Berlin Wall. He continues to perform in clubs. In 1992 he played President Bill Clinton's inaugural party. In 1995 he compiled *Let It Rock!*, a CD that paired new recordings with tracks by Jerry Lee Lewis and Carl Perkins.

Screamin' Jay Hawkins

Born Jalacy J. Hawkins, July 18, 1929, Cleveland, OH; died Feb. 12, 2000, Neuilly-sur-Sein, Fr.
1957—*At Home With* (Epic) 1961—*I Put a Spell on You* 1970—*Screamin' Jay Hawkins* (Philips) 1990—*Voodoo Jive: The Best of Screamin' Jay Hawkins* (Rhino) 1991—*Cow Fingers and Mosquito Pie* (Legacy) 1993—*Stone Crazy* (Bizarre/Rhino) 1995—*Somthin' Funny Goin' On* (Bizarre/Straight) 1999—*Portrait of a Maniac* (Aim) 2000—*The Best of Screamin' Jay Hawkins/Voodoo Jive* (Rhino).

A show-biz eccentric, Screamin' Jay Hawkins was known more for his flamboyant dress and onstage shenanigans than for his singing or piano and sax playing. His calling card, the wild and chilling "I Put a Spell on You"—a ballad that took a voodoo turn after Hawkins got drunk in the recording studio—was never a chart hit. Nonetheless, it is a rock & roll classic, covered by artists ranging from Nina Simone to Creedence Clearwater Revival and sampled by the Notorious B.I.G. for 1997's "Kick in the Door."

Hawkins, one of eight illegitimate children, was turned over to an orphanage by his mother and raised (or adopted) by a Blackfoot Indian family. He took piano lessons as a young child and by his early teen years was performing for tips in neighborhood bars. Inspired by singers such as Paul Robeson and Enrico Caruso, Hawkins studied opera at the Ohio Conservatory of Music. He was a Golden Gloves champion by 1943, continued boxing through the close of the decade, and in 1949 he won the middleweight championship of Alaska. Hawkins went into the service near the end of World War II. He emerged from the service planning to continue studying opera but turned to R&B around 1951 as a way to make a living. His first gig was working as a pianist and singer with a band led by guitarist Tiny Grimes, with whom he toured and recorded (his first single, "Why Did You Waste My Time," 1951) in the early '50s, and he recorded with the Leroy Kirkland Band in 1954. He also toured U.S. clubs that year with Fats Domino's revue.

In 1955 Hawkins began his solo career. Adopting the "Screamin' " moniker to fit his unrestrained, rocking R&B, he started working clubs, earning a reputation for energetic showmanship that bordered on lunacy; as part of Alan Freed's package tours, Hawkins would be carried offstage in a (sometimes flaming) coffin.

His recorded efforts had far less impact. Aside from a few exceptional recordings like "I Put a Spell on You" (1956), "Alligator Wine" (1958), and "Feast of the Mau Mau" (1967), his records have virtually been ignored. Nonetheless he has recorded extensively over the years for numerous labels, including Okeh, Mercury, Roulette, Decca, RCA, and Bizarre/Straight.

In the early '60s Hawkins lived, performed, and recorded mainly in Hawaii and England, returning to the continental U.S. in mid-decade to play the club circuit. In the early '70s he worked out of New York, frequently performing at the Apollo Theatre in Harlem. In the mid-'70s he toured Europe extensively with the Rhythm and Blues Roots of Rock & Roll troupe. Through the '80s, Hawkins remained active playing club dates. In 1982 Hawkins opened U.S. shows for Nick Lowe; 10 years later, he was doing his campy act—coffin and all—on TV talk shows, to promote Rhino's *Voodoo Jive* set, and the newly recorded *Stone Crazy,* which found him sounding as energetically bizarre as ever. He continued performing the rest of his life, and never lost his fondness for props: In 1999 he was performing in Paris with a toilet onstage for his "Constipation Blues."

Hawkins appeared in several films, notably the rock flicks *Mister Rock 'n' Roll* (1957) and *American Hot Wax* (1978), as well as *Mystery Train* (1989) and *A Rage in Harlem* (1991). He was awarded the Rhythm & Blues Foundation's Pioneer Award in 1998.

Hawkins died of multiple organ failure following surgery for an aneurysm, in France, where he had lived since 1993. He had been married six times and had countless extramarital liaisons. Shortly before his death, he had expressed a desire to find and contact the 57 children he believed to be his. After his death, a Web site was set up so that possible mothers and children could contact the estate.

Hawkwind

Formed 1969, London, Eng.
Original members (as Group X/Hawkwind Zoo): Terry Ollis, drums; Nik Turner (b. Oxford, Eng.), sax, voc., flute; Dave Brock (b. Isleworth, Eng.), gtr., voc., synth.; Dikmik (b. Michael Davis, Richmond, Eng.), electronics, kybds.; John Harrison, bass; Mick Slattery, gtr. (dozens of personnel changes follow; the major ones are listed below).
1970—(– Slattery; + Huw Lloyd Langton, gtr.) 1972—*Hawkwind* (United Artists) (– Langton; – Harrison; + Dave Anderson; bass; + Robert Calvert [b. Pretoria, S.A.; d. 1988], voc., gtr.; + Del Dettmar, electronics) 1972—*In Search of Space* (– Anderson; – Ollis; + Ian Kilmister, a.k.a. Lemmy [b. Dec. 24, 1945, Stoke-on-Trent, Eng.], bass) *Doremi Fasol Latido* 1973—*Space Ritual/Alive in Liverpool and London* (– Dikmik) 1974—(– Calvert; + Alan Powell, drums) *Hall of the Mountain Grill* 1975—(– Dettmar; – Kilmister; + Paul Rudolph, gtr.; + Simon House, violin, Mellotron, kybds.) *Warrior on the Edge of Time* (Atco) (+ Calvert) 1976—*Roadhawks* (United Artists, U.K.); *Astounding Sounds—Amazing Music* (Charisma, U.K.); *Masters of the Universe* (United Artists, U.K.) 1977—*Quark Strangeness and Charm* (Warner/Sire) 1978—(– Turner; – Powell; – Rudolph; – House) *Hawklords 25 Years On* (Charisma, U.K.) (+ Harvey Bainbridge, bass; – Calvert) 1978—(group disbands) 1979—*PXR 5* (Charisma) (group re-forms.) 1980—*Repeat Performance* (Charisma, U.K.); *Live '79* (Bronze, U.K.); *Levitation* (U.K.) 1987—*Live Chronicles* (Profile) 1989—*The Xenon Codex* (Profile) 1990—*Space Bandits* (Road Racer) 1991—*Palace Springs* 1992—*Out & Intake* (Griffin Music); *Electric Teepee; Hawklords Live; California Brainstorm* (Iloki); *The Psychedelic Warlords* (Cleopatra) 1993—*Lord of Light* 1994—*It Is the Business of the Future to Be Dangerous* (Griffin Music) 1995—*Alien 4* 1997—*Distant Horizons* (Emergency Broadcast System, U.K.) 1999—*Epoch Eclipse—30 Year Anthology* (EMI, U.K.).

An English psychedelic rock band, Hawkwind (a.k.a. Hawklords, Hawkwind Zoo, etc.) has been a cult act since its inception, touring and often playing for free (one of its most memorable appearances was outside the gates of the Isle of Wight Festival in 1970). The motley crew, whose one constant remains guitarist Dave Brock, was originally called Group X, then Hawkwind Zoo, then Hawkwind, and its first public performance—a 10-minute set at All Saints Hall in Notting Hill Gate—attracted a booking agent. United Artists signed Hawkwind in November 1969.

With the 1972 addition of South African–born lyricist (and sometimes vocalist) Robert Calvert, the group's material improved. That year the quasi-psychedelic *In Search of Space* sold over 100,000 copies in Britain alone. Part of a live 1972 concert was taped, and from it sprang the prepunk, heavy-metal "Silver Machine," a #3 British hit. Hawkwind's most successful album ever was the double LP *Space Ritual,* which cracked the English Top 10 in 1973. That year the band's hit-bound single "Urban Guerilla" was pulled from distribution by UA because of a coincidental outbreak of terrorist bombings in London.

The group toured the U.S. for the first time in late 1973, with a revue including a seminude dancer, Stacia. It made a couple of subsequent trips to the States in 1974 to support *Hall of the Mountain Grill,* but late in the year Indiana police impounded all of the group's equipment, claiming it owed $8,000 in back taxes, and Hawkwind returned to England.

Undaunted, by spring 1975 Hawkwind was back in America for its fourth tour, to support *Warrior on the Edge of Time.* Bassist Ian "Lemmy" Kilmister was arrested by Canadian customs officials for possession of amphetamine sulphate (initially presumed to be cocaine) and jailed. Not wishing to jeopardize yet another U.S. tour, the band fired him; he later formed the punk-metal band Motörhead [see entry], which was named after the flip side of Hawkwind's 1975 single "Kings of Speed."

Hawkwind played to much acclaim at the Reading Festival in August 1975; soon thereafter longtime collaborator and science-fiction author Michael Moorcock released *New World's Fair* with instrumental backing from the band. Moorcock and coauthor Michael Butterworth featured the group in their 1976 novel, *The Time of the Hawklords* (which inspired the group's name change a few years later).

With lyricist Calvert back in the fold (during his mid-decade absence he released two solo albums: *Captain Lockheed and the Starfighters* [1974] and *Lucky Leif and the Longships* [1975], the latter produced by Brian Eno), the group reshuffled its lineup once again and by 1978 (after a brief tenure as the Sonic Assassins) had changed its name to the Hawklords. Around the same time, Simon House (with Hawkwind since April 1974) left to join David Bowie's band. With linchpin Brock (who by the late '70s had a 10-acre farm in Devon) still dominating the band, Hawkwind continued with moderate English success through the end of the '70s.

By that point, the musicians had developed such a loyal cult that they were often compared to the Grateful Dead. Following an ill-fated tenure with RCA in the early '80s, they all but disappeared on this side of the Atlantic until the '90s. Ironically, they were playing large festivals and arenas at home and all over Europe, including many free and benefit shows. Some long-departed members, including Lemmy, reunited for a tour in the early '80s. They returned for a short concert tour of the U.S. in 1989; *Space Bandits* received an unusual amount of media attention here.

In 1990 Hawkwind added a female singer, Bridget Wishart, and began experimenting with dance music, which made converts of a few drug-crazed ravers. In recent years, the American cult of Hawkwind has grown thanks to touring and to the collective's influence on the noise, electronic, stoner-metal, and neo-psychedelic/space-rock undergrounds. In 2000 "Silver Machine" was used in a British Mazda commercial. The same year, the bulk of Hawkwind's 1969 through 1976 personnel assembled as a massive "Hawkestra" for a three-hour performance at London's Brixton Academy (the venue has also hosted all-night Hawkwind gigs).

Over the years, the group's output has been widely anthologized and reanthologized. Nik Turner continues to perform as a solo artist. Robert Calvert died of a heart attack in 1988, shortly before one of Hawkwind's many reunions.

Isaac Hayes

Born Aug. 20, 1942, Covington, TN
1967—*Presenting Isaac Hayes* (Enterprise) 1969—*Hot Buttered Soul* 1970—*The Isaac Hayes Movement; To Be Continued;* 1971—*Shaft* soundtrack; *Black Moses* 1973—*Joy; Live at the Sahara Tahoe* 1975—*Chocolate Chip* (HBS); *Disco Connection* 1976—*Juicy Fruit (Disco Freak)* 1977—*A Man and a Woman* (with Dionne Warwick); *New Horizon* (Polydor) 1978—*Hotbed* (Stax); *For the Sake of Love* (Polydor) 1979—*Don't Let Go; Royal Rappin's* (with Millie Jackson) 1980—*And Once Again* 1981—*Lifetime Thing* 1986—*U Turn* (Columbia); *Best of Isaac Hayes, vol. 1* (Stax); *Best of Isaac Hayes, vol. 2* 1988—*Love Attack* (Columbia) 1991—*Greatest Hit Singles* (Stax) 1995—*Branded* (Pointblank); *Raw & Refined; Greatest Hits* (Stax) 2000—*Ultimate Collection* (Uni/Hip-O).

As a songwriter, arranger, producer, pianist, and vocalist for Stax-Volt Records in the '60s and early '70s, Isaac Hayes played an essential part in the making of Memphis soul. In the early '70s he also laid the groundwork for disco. He has since been credited as the "Original Rapper," although his influence was first evident in the sexy, seductive bedroom rapping of Barry White and Marvin Gaye.

Hayes was raised by his sharecropper grandparents, and by the age of five was singing in church. By his teens, he and his grandparents had moved to Memphis, where he learned to play sax and piano. He began singing in local clubs with his own band, Sir Isaac and the Doo-Dads, and cut his first records for local labels in 1962. Around the same time, he started playing sax with the Mar-Keys, and his association with the group led to studio work with Stax Records that turned into a formal relationship in 1964, when he was hired to play on Otis Redding sessions.

In the mid-'60s Hayes became more active as keyboardist in the Stax house band, and at Stax he developed a songwriting partnership with lyricist David Porter. Among their more than 200 collaborations were such hits as "Soul Man" and "Hold On, I'm Coming" for Sam and Dave; "B-A-B-Y" for Carla Thomas; and "I Had a Dream" for Johnnie Taylor.

Hayes began making his own Stax records in 1967, but made his reputation as a performer in 1969, when he recorded *Hot Buttered Soul.* With long songs (there were only four cuts on the whole album) and elaborate arrangements, the album hit #8 on the pop chart and went gold.

Hayes' biggest commercial triumph came in 1971, when he scored the Gordon Parks film *Shaft.* The double-album soundtrack won an Academy Award (making Hayes the first African-American composer so honored) and it yielded "The Theme From *Shaft,*" which, with its insistent hi-hats, wah-wah guitars, and intoned monologue, hit #1 on the pop chart in 1971, went platinum, won a Grammy, and made Hayes an international superstar. Hayes' later appearance at the Grammy Awards telecast—swathed in silver and chains, bathed in clouds of smoke, and surrounded by beautiful women—was a showstopper. His other pop hits include covers of Burt Bacharach's "Walk On By" (#30 pop, #13 R&B, 1969) and Jimmy Webb's "By the Time I Get to Phoenix" (#37 pop and R&B, 1969), and his own "Never Can Say Goodbye" (#22 pop, #5 R&B, 1971), all on Stax's Enterprise subsidiary.

Hayes's early-'70s concerts featured a 20-piece orchestra, the Isaac Hayes Connection, with the singer wearing tights, cape, gold chains around his bare chest, and dark glasses fronting his shaved head. One performance was documented in the film *Wattstax* (1973).

In 1975, after fighting with Stax over royalties, he signed with ABC Records, setting up his own Hot Buttered Soul (HBS) subsidiary. His first ABC album went gold, but subsequent efforts were ignored in the disco market. In 1976 the bottom fell out of Hayes' career. Six million dollars in debt, he moved from Memphis to Atlanta. In 1978 Wallace Johnson, cofounder of the Holiday Inn chain, became his manager, but by 1980 he was suing Hayes for breach of contract. In the meantime, Hayes was taking steps toward a comeback. In 1977 he recorded a double set, *A Man and a Woman,* with Dionne Warwick, and he cowrote Warwick's 1979 Top 20 pop hit "Déjà Vu." On his own on the Polydor label, he returned to the charts with "Zeke the Freak" (#19 R&B, 1978), "Don't Let Go" (#21 pop, #11 R&B, 1979), and "Do You Wanna Make Love" (#30 R&B, 1979). His duet album with Millie Jackson, *Royal Rappin's* (1979), was popular on the soul chart. In 1986 he scored a Top 10 R&B hit with "Ike's Rap," an antidrug song. In 1994 he signed with Virgin Records.

He began acting in 1974 with *Truck Turner,* a blaxploitation film, which he also produced and scored. Among his other feature-film credits are *It Seemed Like a Good Idea at the Time* (1975), *Escape From New York* (1981), *I'm Gonna Git You Sucka* (1988), *Robin Hood, Men in Tights* (1993), *Posse* (1993), *It Could Happen to You* (1994), and *Reindeer Games* (2000). He has also appeared in several made-for-television films and guest-starred on *The Rockford Files, Miami Vice,* and *The A-Team.* In 1996 Hayes recorded the theme to *Beavis and Butthead Do America,* a film version of the popular MTV animated series. He also cowrote the soundtrack. Around the same time he found success as the distinctive voice of Chef, a libidinous school-cafeteria cook on the gross-out cartoon hit *South Park.* The show, on cable's Comedy Central, also spawned the 1999 movie and soundtrack *South Park: Bigger Longer and Uncut* (#28), a video game, and 1998's multiplatinum *Chef Aid: The South Park Album* (#16), to which Hayes contributed four comic nuggets including "Chocolate Salty Balls (P.S. I Love You)" (#1 U.K.) and "Tonight Is Right for Love," a duet with Meat Loaf. Having become a pop culture icon once again, Hayes began working for 98.7 KISS FM and became the second most popular morning DJ in New York.

Under the official name Nene Katey Ocansey I, Hayes is a member of the Royal Family of Noyami Mantse of the Kabiawe Division of the Ada Traditional Area in Ghana. As an African king, he has worked on improving the Ghanian economy (he is an honorary chief in Nigeria as well). He continues to act, compose, and record. In 1992 Hayes became the spokesperson for the World Literacy Crusade. He also lectures on humanitarian issues both here and in Africa and is the founder of the Isaac Hayes Foundation, which works for increased literacy.

Ofra Haza

Born Nov. 19, 1957 or 1959, Tel Aviv, Israel; died Feb. 23, 2000, Tel Aviv
1987—*Fifty Gates of Wisdom* (Shanachie) 1988—*Shaday* (Sire/Warner Bros.) 1989—*Desert Wind* 1992—*Kirya* (East/West) 1997—*Ofra Haza 1997* (BMG/Ariola).

A striking Sephardic beauty whose voice drew comparisons to both Barbra Streisand and legendary Middle Eastern vocalist Om Kalsoum, Ofra Haza was born to Yemenite Jewish parents in Hatikva, Tel Aviv's hardscrabble ghetto for immigrant Jews from Arab lands. At age 12 she joined the Hatikva theater troupe, with which she recorded (winning Israeli music awards for some albums). After serving two compulsory years in the Israeli army, Haza began her own recording career in 1979 and quickly became a top Israeli pop singer—whose records also sold well in neighboring Arab lands. In 1983 she won second prize in the annual Eurovision Song Contest.

In 1985 Haza returned to her roots by recording *Yemenite Songs*, a collection of ancient melodies she'd learned from her mother, with traditional instrumentation and lyrics from the 16th-century poetry of Yemenite-Jewish rabbi Shalom Shabazi. The album became a surprise world-beat hit in England, where Haza's voice was sampled from the track "Im Nin'alu" by Coldcut, for its hit 12-inch remix of rappers Eric B. and Rakim's "Paid in Full."

Haza's voice was also sampled by M/A/R/R/S in its international dance hit "Pump Up the Volume," only months before she released her first major-label U.S. album, *Shaday* (#130, 1989), a mix of Middle Eastern–inflected dance tracks and conventional Western pop ballads. Its souped-up version of "Im Nin'alu" became a minor U.S. dance hit (and a Top 20 pop hit in the U.K.). *Kirya* (1992) was produced by Don Was, featured guest vocals by Lou Reed and Iggy Pop, and was nominated for a Grammy in the world beat category. In 1992 Haza also recorded the single "Temple of Love," with British alternative-rock band Sisters of Mercy, and guested on Thomas Dolby's album *Astronauts & Heretics*. In 1994 she sang at the Oslo, Norway, Nobel Peace Prize ceremony for Israeli prime minister Yitzhak Rabin and Foreign Minister Shimon Peres, and Palestinian leader Yasser Arafat. The next year, she appeared on Paula Abdul's *Head Over Heels*.

She did not release another album until her self-titled import in 1997, the same year she married businessman Doron Ashkenazi. In 1998 her voice graced two movie soundtracks, *The Governess* and Disney's *Prince of Egypt*. In February, 2000—weeks before she was heard singing "Open Your Heart" on the Madonna tribute album *Virgin Voices vol. 2* (Cleopatra)—Haza suddenly and mysteriously died in a Tel Aviv hospital at age 41 (or 43), of massive internal organ failure, which one Israeli newspaper reported was due to complications from AIDS (neither her family nor her husband commented). Israeli Prime Minister Ehud Barak spoke at her Hatikva funeral.

Lee Hazlewood

Born Barton Lee Hazlewood, July 9, 1929, Mannford, OK
1963—*Trouble Is a Lonesome Town* (Reprise) 1964—*The Not So Very Important People* 1966—*Lee Hazlewood Sings Friday's Child* (Reprise) 1968—*Nancy and Lee* (with Nancy Sinatra); *Nancy and Lee–Encore* (with Nancy Sinatra) (RCA) 1973—*Poet, Fool or Bum* (Capitol) 1975—*A House Safe for Tigers* (CBS) 1976—*20th Century Lee* (RCA) 1977—*Back on the Street Again* (EMI) 1999—*Farmisht, Flatulence, Origami, ARF!! and Me* (Smells Like Records).

Lee Hazlewood's long career includes work as an intriguing songwriter, pop record producer, and baritone singer (most notably in duets with Nancy Sinatra). He was raised in Port Arthur, Texas, and attended Southern Methodist University before being drafted to fight in Korea. Upon his discharge in 1953 he became a country disc jockey in Phoenix. By 1955, he was writing songs and producing an occasional recording session. His major success of the period was Sanford Clark's 1956 hit "The Fool," which he wrote and produced and which sold 800,000 copies. (The song was also a modest hit when covered by the Gallahads that year.)

In 1957 Hazlewood moved to Philadelphia and cofounded Jamie Records (Dick Clark was one of the partners), which he used to launch the career of guitarist Duane Eddy. Over three and a half years, he produced, among others, "Rebel Rouser," "Yep!" and "Forty Miles of Bad Road," which collectively sold about 20 million copies. In the early '60s Hazlewood had a hand in running such minor labels as Trey, East-West, and Gregmark, and in 1965 he produced several hits for Dino, Desi and Billy.

Hazlewood is best known to the public for his work with Nancy Sinatra [see entry]. Besides producing her hits "These Boots Are Made for Walkin' " (#1, 1966) and "Sugar Town" (#5, 1966), Hazlewood dueted with her on "Jackson" (#14, 1967), "Summer Wine" (#49, 1967), "Lady Bird" (#20, 1967), and "Some Velvet Morning" (#26, 1968), all of which he wrote. Many of Hazlewood's sexually charged songs were filled with double entendres, leaving listeners questioning their true meaning. That, along with his extraordinary deep voice, which he used to talk-sing his compositions, inspired post-punk artists who rediscovered his music in the '80s.

In 1967 Hazlewood's own label LHI Records signed Gram Parsons' International Submarine Band, whose 1968 album, *Safe at Home*, was produced by Hazlewood's then-girlfriend Suzi Jane Hokom. By the close of the '60s, Hazlewood was living in Stockholm, Sweden, and alternating between periods of virtual retirement and occasional solo activity in Europe.

In the '80s Hazlewood moved to Phoenix, Arizona, and retired from the music business. He reemerged in 1995, touring hip rock clubs with Nancy Sinatra in support of her comeback album. He discovered he'd become a cult figure among the postpunk cognoscenti, and by the end of the decade many of his early recordings had been reissued by Sonic Youth drummer Steve Shelley's Smells Like Records label. In 1999 the label released Hazlewood's first new recordings in decades, a collection of Tin Pan Alley standards. Telling one interviewer, "I'm happy that Sonic Youth drag along a few other people who like obscure old fucks like me," Hazlewood actually flew to New York to attend a "Loser's Lounge" nightclub tribute to his music.

Jeff Healey Band

Formed 1985, Toronto, Ontario, Can.
Jeff Healey (b. Norman Jeffrey Healey, Mar. 25, 1966, Toronto), gtr., voc.; Joe Rockman (b. Joseph Rockman, Jan. 1, 1957, Toronto), bass; Tom Stephen (b. Thomas Stephen, Feb. 2, 1955, St. John, New Brunswick), drums.
1988—*See the Light* (Arista) 1990—*Hell to Pay* 1992—*Feel This* 1995—*Cover to Cover* 1998—*The Very Best of the Jeff Healey Band* (BMG International, U.K.) 1999—*The Master Hits: The Jeff Healey Band* (Arista Heritage) 2000—*Get Me Some* (Atlantic).

Having lost his sight to eye cancer at a year old, blues-rock guitarist Jeff Healey developed an unconventional lap-top technique that involves using all five fingers for effects and bending strings with his thumb to hit unusual notes.

Healey received his first guitar at the age of three and cut his teeth on country licks. After attending the School for the Blind in Brantford, he registered at a local high school, where he played guitar and trumpet in jazz and concert bands and helped organize a blues-based group called Blues Direction. In 1985 a friend convinced legendary guitarist Albert Collins to let the 19-year-old Healey join him onstage during a Toronto club gig. Impressed, Collins invited the young musician to play with him and guitarist Stevie Ray Vaughan a few nights later. Healey was soon in hot demand for bar appearances.

Needing a band, Healey tapped local drummer Tom Stephen and Stephen's friend, bassist Joe Rockman. The Jeff Healey Band toured Canada for two years before signing with Arista Records in New York. Arista chose veteran Jimmy Iovine to produce the group's first album, just as Iovine was putting together the soundtrack for a film that featured a bar band whose guitarist was blind and played the instrument on his lap. This coincidence was even more uncanny than it might have seemed: The screenwriter for *Road House*, a film starring Patrick Swayze, had conceived the character after seeing Healey perform. The Canadian trio got the movie gig, and 1988's *See the Light* (#22) went platinum, yielding the #5 single "Angel Eyes" in 1989. Despite guest appearances by Mark Knopfler, George Harrison, and Jeff Lynne, 1990's *Hell to Pay* (#27) didn't fare as well. A third album, 1992's *Feel This*, only reached #174, and in 1995 the band released an album of covers.

Meanwhile, Healey, a longtime avid record collector whose vinyl library numbers more than 20,000, had begun hosting a local radio show called *My Kinda Jazz* from his home in Toronto in late 1991. The Canadian Broadcasting Company took the show national soon after, and it has been running on a regular basis since. The band also toured in Europe every summer before returning with *Get Me Some* in 2000.

Heart

Formed 1970, Seattle, WA
Ann Wilson (b. June 19, 1950, San Diego, CA), voc., gtr., flute; Nancy Wilson (b. Mar. 16, 1954, San Francisco, CA), voc., gtr., mandolin; Roger Fisher (b. 1950), gtr.; Howard Leese (b. June 13, 1951), kybds., synth., gtr.); Michael Derosier, drums; Steve Fossen, bass.
1976—*Dreamboat Annie* (Mushroom) 1977—*Little Queen* (Portrait) 1978—*Magazine* (Mushroom); *Dog and Butterfly* (Portrait) (– Fisher) 1980—*Bébé Lé Strange* (Epic); *Greatest Hits Live* 1981—(– Derosier; – Fossen) 1982—*Private Audition* (+ Mark Andes [b. Feb. 19, 1948, Philadelphia, PA], bass; + Denny Carmassi, drums) 1983—*Passionworks* 1985—*Heart* (Capitol) 1987—*Bad Animals* 1990—*Brigade* 1991—*Rock the House Live!* 1993—(– Andes; – Carmassi; + Fernando Saunders [b. Jan. 17, 1954, Detroit, MI], bass; + Denny Fongheiser [b. Apr. 21, 1959, Alameda, CA], drums) *Desire Walks On* 1994—*Heart: 20 Years of Rock & Roll* CD-ROM (Bob Hamilton's Lifework Series) 1995—*The Road Home* 1998—*Greatest Hits* (Sony) 2000—*Greatest Hits 1985–1995* (Capitol).
Nancy Wilson solo: 1999—*Live at McCabe's Guitar Shop* (Epic).
The Lovemongers (Ann Wilson; Nancy Wilson; + Sue Ennis, voc., gtr., kybds.; + Frank Cox, voc., gtr., mandolin, kybds.): 1992—*Battle of Evermore* EP (Capitol) 1997—*Whirlygig* (Will) 1998—*Here Is Christmas* (2B Music).

Hard-rock band Heart, led by singer Ann Wilson and featuring her sister Nancy on guitar, sold millions of records in the late '70s. All but written off by 1985, they then engineered a comeback that saw them surpass their initial success.

The Wilson sisters grew up in Southern California and Taiwan before their Marine Corps captain father retired to the Seattle suburbs. After attending college they returned to Seattle, with Nancy working as a folksinger and Ann joining an all-male local group in 1970 called Heart. (The group was formed in 1963 by Steve Fossen and Roger and Mike Fisher as the Army. They later changed the name to White Heart, shortened to Heart in 1974.) Upon joining, Ann became lead guitarist Mike Fisher's girlfriend, and when Nancy joined in 1974, she became involved with Fisher's brother Roger.

After many one-nighters in the Vancouver area, in 1975 they attracted the attention of Canada's Mushroom label, run by Shelly Siegel. He had them cut *Dreamboat Annie*, which upon release in Canada sold 30,000 copies. In the U.S.

Heart

Siegel released it first in Seattle, where it quickly sold another 25,000. With two hit singles—"Crazy on You" (#35, 1976) and "Magic Man" (#9, 1976)—the album eventually sold over a million copies.

By early 1977, the Wilson sisters had switched to CBS' subsidiary Portrait, a move that resulted in a prolonged legal fight with Siegel. In retaliation he released the partly completed *Magazine* at the same time Portrait released *Little Queen*. A Seattle court ruled that Mushroom had to recall *Magazine* so that the Wilsons could remix several tracks and redo vocals before rereleasing the disc. (The Wilsons had wanted the album taken off the market completely.)

Little Queen, with the hit "Barracuda" (#11, 1977), became Heart's second million-seller; *Magazine* and the double-platinum *Dog and Butterfly* followed suit in 1978. During sessions for *Bébé Lé Strange,* the Wilson-Fisher liaisons ended. Roger Fisher formed his own band in the Seattle area. Howard Leese and Nancy took up the guitar slack, and Nancy Wilson's childhood friend Sue Ennis helped out on song collaborations. The group hit the road for a 77-city tour to support *Bébé,* then returned to make *Private Audition.*

That album and the following year's *Passionworks* (featuring new bassist Mark Andes [Spirit, Jo Jo Gunne, Firefall] and drummer Denny Carmassi [Gamma]) failed to go gold, putting Heart at a career crossroads. But the group's first album for Capitol, simply titled *Heart* (#1, 1985), sold 5 million copies on the strength of four Top 10 hits: "What About Love?" (#10, 1985), "Never" (#4, 1985), "These Dreams" (#1, 1986), and "Nothin' at All" (#10, 1986). In June 1986 Nancy Wilson married journalist, screenwriter, and director Cameron Crowe; she made a cameo appearance in his movie *Fast Times at Ridgemont High. Bad Animals* (#2, 1987), too, contained a chart-topper, in the power ballad "Alone," as well as "Who Will You Run To" (#7, 1987) and "There's the Girl" (#12, 1987). In 1989 Ann Wilson and Cheap Trick's Robin Zander had a #6 hit with their duet, "Surrender to Me." *Brigade* (#3, 1990) became Heart's sixth multiplatinum LP and added three more Top 25 hits to its catalogue.

Following a 1990 tour, the Wilson sisters put together an informal acoustic group called the Lovemongers with Sue Ennis and Frank Cox; a four-song EP that included a version of Led Zeppelin's "Battle of Evermore" came out in late 1992, and the quartet performed several times in the Seattle area. The Lovemongers released a full-length album in 1997. When Heart reemerged with *Desire Walks On* (#48) in 1993, it was without Andes and Carmassi. For the group's subsequent tour, their places were taken by bassist Fernando Saunders and drummer Denny Fongheiser. The band offered live acoustic versions of its best-known songs on 1995's *The Road Home,* which was produced by Led Zeppelin's John Paul Jones. The pared-down format echoed Heart's low profile in the late '90s. Of the two sisters, Nancy has kept busiest, scoring her husband's movies *Jerry Maguire* and *Almost Famous,* and releasing a solo record in 1999. That same year, she and Ann embarked on a tour on their own, the first time they had ever done so.

In addition to their own recording career, the Wilson sisters have played a key role on the Seattle music scene. Among the groups who have recorded at their Bad Animals studio are R.E.M., Pearl Jam, Alice in Chains, and Soundgarden. Heart's *Heart: 20 Years of Rock & Roll* was the first CD-ROM multimedia biography/greatest-hits package ever released.

The Heartbreakers/Johnny Thunders

Formed 1975, New York, NY
Johnny Thunders (b. John Anthony Genzale, July 15, 1952, New York; d. Apr. 23, 1991, New Orleans, LA), gtr., voc.; Walter Lure (b. Apr. 22, 1949, New York), gtr., voc.; Richard Hell (b. Richard Myers, Oct. 2, 1949, Lexington, KY), bass, voc.; Jerry Nolan (b. May 7, 1946, New York; d. Jan. 14, 1992, New York), drums.

1976—(– Hell; + Billy Rath, bass) 1977—*L.A.M.F.* (Track, U.K.) (– Nolan; + Ty Styx, drums) 1979—*Live at Max's Kansas City* (Max's Kansas City/Beggars Banquet, U.K.) 1982—*D.T.K.: Live at the Speakeasy* (Jungle, U.K.) 1984—*Live at the Lyceum Ballroom* (ABC, U.K.); *L.A.M.F. Revisited* (Jungle, U.K.).
Johnny Thunders solo: 1978—*So Alone* (Real) 1983—*New Too Much Junkie Business* (ROIR); *Diary of a Lover* (PVC) 1987—*Stations of the Cross* (ROIR) 2001—*Belfast Nights* (Triple X).

After the original New York Dolls [see entry] broke up, Johnny Thunders—who had been the Dolls' Keith Richards to David Johansen's Mick Jagger—and Jerry Nolan formed the Heartbreakers, first as a trio with former Television bassist Richard Hell, who soon left to lead his own band, the Voidoids. If the New York Dolls were a precursor to punk rock, then the Heartbreakers served as a living bridge to it—updating classic Rolling Stones–style, sneering two-guitar rock in prototypical fast-and-furious style. With Thunders' shambling, drugged-out, foul-mouthed onstage charm, and songs like "Chinese Rocks" and "Too Much Junkie Business" celebrating the heroin-junkie lifestyle, these Heartbreakers could not be confused with Tom Petty's backup band.

The Heartbreakers built a following with a year of East Coast club gigs, but drew no offers from record companies. Sex Pistols impresario Malcolm McLaren, who had been involved in the Dolls' final days, invited the Heartbreakers to tour England, where they joined the Pistols, the Clash, the Damned, and the Slits on the historic 1976 Anarchy Tour. (Jerry Nolan later claimed he and Thunders first introduced Johnny Rotten and other punks to heroin during this time.) Heralded by punk rockers who'd been inspired by the Dolls, the Heartbreakers stayed in England for over a year, recording their debut album, *L.A.M.F.* (from an obscene graffiti used by the teen gangs of which Thunders and Nolan had been members). It was so poorly produced that Nolan quit the band in disgust and formed the short-lived Idols back in New York, while former Clash drummer Terry Chimes took Nolan's place briefly before the Heartbreakers drifted apart in London.

Thunders stayed there, and in 1978 recorded a critically acclaimed solo album, *So Alone,* with backing from Sex Pistols Steve Jones and Paul Cook, Peter Perrett of the Only Ones, Thin Lizzy's Phil Lynott, and ex–Small Faces/Humble Pie guitarist Steve Marriott. The album included a rare glimpse of Thunders' tender side in the classic "You Can't Put Your Arms Around a Memory," as well as nods to his musical roots in girl-group sass ("Great Big Kiss") and surf music (an amphetamine cover of the Chantays' "Pipeline"). Thunders returned to New York in late 1978 for the first of many Heartbreakers reunion/farewell gigs, which was captured on *Live at Max's Kansas City.* In 1980 Thunders formed Gang War with former MC5 guitarist Wayne Kramer, while Lure and Rath started the Heroes with Lure's younger brother Richie (a guitarist in the late-'70s punk band the Erasers). Thunders formed another short-lived band, Cosa Nostra, before reconvening the Heartbreakers again in 1982. By this time Lure was working as a stockbroker. In 1984, with former Generation X guitarist (and future Sigue Sigue Sputnik leader) Tony James, Thunders finally remixed *L.A.M.F.* for *Revisited.* The Heartbreakers (with Nolan) held a final New York City reunion show in 1990. A year later Thunders, just back in the U.S. from a successful tour of Japan, died of a lethal mixture of methadone and alcohol in a New Orleans hotel room.

Heaven 17

Formed 1979, Sheffield, Eng.
Martyn Ware (b. May 19, 1956, Sheffield), synth.; Ian Craig-Marsh, (b. Nov. 11, 1956, Sheffield), synth.; Glenn Gregory (b. May 16, 1958, Sheffield), voc.
1982—*Heaven 17* (Arista) 1983—*The Luxury Gap* 1984—*How Men Are* 1986—*Pleasure One* (Virgin) 1988—*Teddy Bear, Duke & Psycho* 1997—*Bigger Than America* (Eye of the Storm) 1998—*Retox/Detox* (Eagle) 1999—*How Live Is* (Almafame).

Computer-operators-turned-synthesizer-wizards Martyn Ware and Ian Craig-Marsh had worked together in the band Human League before forming the British Electric Foundation, an experimental, dance-oriented production project that worked with a variety of singers and musicians. Heaven 17, a trio consisting of Ware, Craig-Marsh, and singer Glenn Gregory, became the best-known B.E.F. offshoot. Named after a group in Anthony Burgess' novel *A Clockwork Orange,* Heaven 17 faced the same accusations of slickness that met many technopop acts, but the band also won praise for its sophisticated electrofunk arrangements, and for Gregory's singing, which was judged unusually expressive for his genre.

Ware and Craig-Marsh hooked up with ex-photographer Gregory at a drama center in Sheffield. Heaven 17's first single, "(We Don't Need This) Fascist Groove Thang," was released in England in 1981; it became a minor hit there (#45), despite a BBC Radio ban induced by its title. The trio's eponymous debut album followed in 1982, and hit the U.S. charts at #68 the following year. Meanwhile, 1983's *The Luxury Gap* peaked at #4 in the U.K. In 1984 Gregory took part in the star-studded recording sessions for Band Aid's "Do They Know It's Christmas?" single. But despite *How Men Are*'s success in England (#12 U.K., 1984), a commercial foothold eluded Heaven 17 in America, where the group never surpassed the mediocre chart performance of its first album. In 1988, after the release of *Teddy Bear, Duke & Psycho,* Ware and Gregory focused on production projects. By this point Ware had coproduced Tina Turner's 1983 cover of Al Green's "Let's Stay Together" (#26 pop, #6 U.K.)—which featured Gregory on backing vocals—and Terence Trent D'Arby's debut album, *Introducing the Hardline According to Terence Trent D'Arby* (1987). Ware and Craig-Marsh resurrected B.E.F. at large in 1990, and produced a single for the R&B singer Lalah Hathaway in 1991. In 1994 Ware produced Erasure's LP *I Say, I Say, I Say.*

The same year, a remix of the 1983 single "Temptation" was released and sold well worldwide, reminding the public that Heaven 17 still existed (the group had never broken up). Encouraged by the response, the members collaborated on their first album in eight years, *Bigger Than America.* To support the new release, the band embarked on its first tour ever, initially as an opening act for Erasure and then on its own. *Retox/Detox* was a collection of new versions of Heaven 17 songs recorded with '90s electronica artists, while *How Live Is* culled performances from its recent concerts. The group was working on a new studio album in 2000.

Heavy D. and the Boyz

Formed 1984, Mt. Vernon, NY
Heavy D. (b. Dwight Myers, May 24, 1967, Jam.), voc.; Eddie F. (b. Eddie Farrell, Mar. 25, 1968), DJ; G-Whiz (b. Glen Parrish, Oct. 20, 1968, New Rochelle, NY), stylist; Trouble T-Roy (b. Troy Dixon, Oct. 19, 1967; d. July 15, 1990), dancer.
1987—*Living Large* (Uptown/MCA) 1989—*Big Tyme* 1990—(– Trouble T-Roy) 1991—*Peaceful Journey* 1993—*Blue Funk* 1994—*Nuttin' but Love* 1997—*Waterbed Hev* (Uptown/Universal) 1999—*Heavy.*

At first Heavy D. seemed to be a novelty rapper, calling himself the Overweight Lover and giving his songs names like "Chunky But Funky." But his deep, amiable baritone and funky, fluid grooves, often characterized by the Teddy Riley–produced R&B-rap style New Jack Swing, won the approval of critics and serious hip-hop fans alike. In addition to Riley, the group has used a variety of well-known producers, including Erick Sermon, Marley Marl, Gang Starr's DJ Premier, and Heavy D.'s cousin Pete Rock.

Dwight Myers grew up the youngest of six children in a middle-class, Mt. Vernon, New York, home listening to rap on the radio. While still in his teens he won $1,500 in Atlantic City, with which he and Eddie Ferrell bought a computer, which he later traded for a drum machine and started making tapes in Ferrell's basement with friends Glen Parrish and Troy Dixon. The 260-pound, 6-foot-3-inch, light-skinned Myers began calling himself Heavy D.

Heavy D. and the Boyz: G-Whiz, Eddie F., Heavy D.

The rapper's messages could be romantic or tough, but they never celebrated violence like many of his successful contemporaries. In 1987 Heavy D. and the Boyz released *Living Large.* Both their second album, *Big Tyme* (#19 pop, #1 R&B, 1989), and third, *Peaceful Journey* (#21 pop, #5 R&B, 1991), sold platinum. In addition, Heavy D. wrote the theme song for the popular television show *In Living Color.* The group suffered two tragedies between *Big Tyme* and *Peaceful Journey.* In 1989 Heavy D.'s brother, Tony Myers, was gunned down. Then, while on tour in 1990, Trouble T-Roy fell from a ledge to his death during rehearsals. A year later, nine fans were killed and 29 injured during a stampede at a concert organized by Sean Combs at the City College of New York.

The group's string of hit singles, beginning in 1986, include: "Mr. Big Stuff" (#60 R&B, 1986), "Don't You Know" (#12 R&B, 1988), "We Got Our Own Thang" (#10 R&B, 1989), "Somebody for Me" (#8 R&B, 1989), "Gyrlz, They Love Me" (#12 R&B, 1990), "Now That We Found Love" (#11 pop, #5 R&B, 1991) (a rap cover of Third World's 1979 hit), and "Is It Good to You" (#32 pop, #13 R&B, 1991). Singles from 1993's *Blue Funk* (#40 pop, #7 R&B) were not as successful, but the Boyz came back in 1994 with the smash "Got Me Waiting" (#20 pop, #3 R&B), the first single from *Nuttin' but Love.* Both albums went gold.

In the early '90s Heavy D. launched an acting career, worked as a producer, and by 1996 was the president of Uptown Records—making him the first rapper to be simultaneously an active performer and a top label executive. Then, in 1997, Heavy D. left that post and made a surprisingly strong return to the charts with *Waterbed Hev* (#9 pop, #3 R&B, 1997). The single "Big Daddy" reached #18 on the pop chart, and his collaboration with Queen Latifah, "Need Your Love," reached #70. In 1999 *Heavy* had the rapper trading rhymes with such guests as Q-Tip, Cee-Lo of Goodie Mob, and Chico DeBarge. That same year, Heavy D. acted in *Cider House Rules* and appeared with Eddie Murphy and Martin Lawrence in *Life.*

Bobby Hebb

Born July 26, 1941, Nashville, TN
1966—*Sunny* (Philips).

Singer/songwriter Bobby Hebb is best known for the light, sentimental "Sunny" (#2, 1966). He was one of seven children of blind parents who taught him to play the guitar. At age 12, Hebb became one of the first blacks to play the Grand Ole Opry, when country legend Roy Acuff invited him to perform. In the early '60s he moved to Chicago, graduated from a dental technician's course, and took music classes while occasionally accompanying Bo Diddley on the spoons. He studied guitar with Chet Atkins, who helped him break into show business. Hebb eventually met Sylvia Shemwell, with whom he worked as Bobby and Sylvia. He later cut such tunes as "Night Train to Memphis" and "You Broke My Heart and I Broke Your Jaw."

In 1963 Hebb's brother Hal (a member of the Marigolds) was killed in a mugging. Hebb responded with "Sunny." He was unable to sell it to publishers, but in 1966, while recording an album, he cut the song at the end of a session to use up some extra time, and it became a hit. By year's end, Hebb had appeared on several major network television shows and toured the U.S. with the Beatles. (The singer claims to have recommended keyboardist Billy Preston to the Fab Four, after Ringo Starr asked him if he knew of any funky piano players.) Followup hits proved elusive, however. His last two chart appearances came before the year was out, with "A Satisfied Mind" (#39) and "Love Me" (#84).

Hebb had isolated U.K. hits like "Love Love Love" in the early '70s on GRT Records. As the decade progressed he made occasional club appearances in America and got a reworked "Sunny" ("Sunny '76") onto the soul chart but mostly lived a quiet life in a colonial mansion in Salem, Massachusetts.

Hebb claims to have written over 3,000 songs, a third of them published—including material for Percy Sledge, Mary Wells, Marvin Gaye, Billy Preston, Herb Alpert, and Lou Rawls, whose recording of Hebb's "A Natural Man" won a Grammy in 1971. "Sunny" was widely covered as well, showing up on discs by Cher, Georgie Fame, and Gloria Lynne, among others. Hebb now lives in an artists' colony in the small Massachusetts town of Rockport.

Michael Hedges

Born Dec. 31, 1953, Enid, OK; died Dec. 2, 1997, Mendocino, CA
1981—*Breakfast in the Field* (Windham Hill) 1984—*Aerial Boundaries* 1985—*Watching My Life Go By* 1986—*Santabear's First Christmas* 1987—*Live on the Double Planet* 1988—*Strings of Steel* 1989—*The Shape of the Land* 1990—*Taproot* 1994—*The Road to Return* 1996—*Oracle* 1999—*Torched.*

Solo steel-string acoustic guitarist Michael Hedges was by far the most ferocious-sounding artist to record for Windham Hill, the pioneering New Age label. Hedges had the intensity—and some of the techniques—of such acclaimed rock guitarists as Eddie Van Halen.

Hedges began studying piano at age four; after growing up listening to pop and rock music (he's cited the Beatles and Jethro Tull), he took up guitar, flute, clarinet, and cello. He focused on classical guitar at the Peabody Conservatory in Baltimore, then attended Stanford's Center for Computer Research and Musical Acoustics—at both schools, studying by day and playing steel-string acoustic guitar in bars and cafes by night. Windham Hill founder Will Ackerman discovered Hedges performing at the Varsity Theater in Palo Alto. Hedges' all-instrumental debut, *Breakfast in the Field,* won raves from such jazz-rock guitar greats as Larry Coryell. Hedges' style and technique—a combination of unusual tunings, two-handed fretboard tapping, and full-chord hammer-ons and pull-offs, as opposed to the usual single-note variety—produced a harmonically rich and highly percussive sound that made his single guitar sound like a full band. *Aerial Boundaries* was nominated for a Best Instrumental Grammy; the title track was used in some TV commercials.

In 1985 Hedges introduced his vocals (in a jazzy, Joni Mitchell style), flute, synthesizer, and electric bass on the poorly received *Watching My Life Go By,* which featured guest vocals by Bobby McFerrin. That same year he recorded the soundtrack for a children's television special, *Santabear's First Christmas*. Through the late '80s and into the '90s with *Taproot* and *The Road to Return,* Hedges continued to focus on composition and vocals in addition to his remarkable guitar playing. In 1989 he contributed arranging, guitar, and background vocals to two tracks on David Crosby's *Oh Yes I Can.* His 1996 album *Oracle* reaffirmed Hedges' acoustic roots, but a fatal car accident the next year put a premature close to a much-lauded career. *Oracle* won Hedges a posthumous Grammy in 1998, and a final album, *Torched,* followed in 1999.

Richard Hell and the Voidoids

Formed Sep. 1976, New York, NY
Richard Hell (b. Richard Myers, Oct. 2, 1949, Lexington, KY), bass, voc.; Marc Bell (b. July 15, 1956, New York), drums; Robert Quine (b. Dec. 30, 1942, Akron, OH), gtr., voc.; Ivan Julian (b. June 26, 1955, Washington, DC), gtr., voc.
1976—*Richard Hell* EP (Ork) 1977—*Blank Generation* (Sire) 1978—(– Bell; + Jerry Antonius, bass, kybds.; + Frank Mauro, drums) 1980—(– Antonius; – Mauro; + Naux [b. July 20, 1951, San Jose, CA], gtr.; + Fred Maher, drums) 1982—*Destiny Street* (Red Star) 1984—*R.I.P.* (ROIR) 1990—*Funhunt* 1995—*Go Now* EP (Richard Hell with Robert Quine) (Tim/Kerr).
Dim Stars: 1992—*Dim Stars* (Caroline).

Richard Hell led the Voidoids, one of the most harshly uncompromising bands on New York's late-'70s punk scene, playing songs with dissonant, jagged guitar lines and dark, free-association imagery that owed something to both Captain Beefheart and the Velvet Underground. Hell had played with Johnny Thunders' Heartbreakers [see entry] and with the Neon Boys, who later became Television [see entry]. He then formed the Voidoids to perform his own songs. They were regular attractions at the punk showcase CBGB, along with Blondie, the Ramones, and Talking Heads.

Hell's 1977 debut album, *Blank Generation,* provided two anthems for the scene, the title cut and "Love Comes in Spurts." Although Hell performed frequently, he remained obscure outside of New York and London. In 1979 Nick

Lowe produced a single, "The Kid With the Replaceable Head."

In 1982 Hell resurfaced with a new band and an album, *Destiny Street.* (Original Voidoids guitarist Robert Quine, meanwhile, had joined Lou Reed's band for *The Blue Mask.*) Hell also began an acting career, appearing in Susan Seidelman's 1982 film *Smithereens.* He later acted in a 1993 underground film, Rachel Amodeo's *What About Me?.*

By the mid-'80s, Hell had seemingly put music behind him; his writing—nonfiction, fiction, and poetry—was published by a variety of magazines, and he began doing spoken-word performances. *R.I.P.* and *Funhunt* documented live shows and outtakes; *Go Now* consists of Hell, accompanied by Quine, reading extracts from his novel by that name, which was eventually published by Scribner in 1996.

In 1992 Hell joined the Dim Stars, a side project initiated by Sonic Youth's Thurston Moore and Steve Shelley with Gumball's Don Fleming; the group, which played a limited number of gigs, released a triple seven-inch EP and a self-titled album. By 1999, Hell had begun work on a second novel, and his writing appeared in the collection *The Rolling Stone Book of the Beats.* The original Voidoids briefly reassembled in 2000 to record the one-off "Oh," a new studio track released only on the Internet.

Jimi Hendrix

Born Nov. 27, 1942, Seattle, WA; died Sep. 18, 1970, London, Eng.
1967—*Are You Experienced?* (Reprise) 1968—*Axis: Bold as Love; Electric Ladyland* 1969—*Smash Hits* 1970—*Band of Gypsies* (Capitol) 1971—*The Cry of Love* (Reprise); *Rainbow Bridge* 1972—*Hendrix in the West* 1973—*Soundtrack Recordings From the Film, Jimi Hendrix* 1975—*Crash Landing* 1976—*Midnight Lightning* 1978—*The Essential Jimi Hendrix* 1979—*The Essential Jimi Hendrix, vol. 2* 1982—*The Jimi Hendrix Concerts* 1986—*Band of Gypsys 2* (Capitol/EMI) 1988—*Radio One* (Rykodisc) 1990—*Lifelines: The Jimi Hendrix Story* (Reprise); *Hendrix Speaks: The Jimi Hendrix Interviews* (Rhino) 1991—*Stages 1967–70* (Reprise) 1994—*Blues* (MCA) 1995—*Voodoo Soup* 1997—*First Rays of the New Rising Sun* (Experience Hendrix/MCA); *South Saturn Delta* 1998—*BBC Sessions; Experience Hendrix: The Best of Jimi Hendrix* 1999—*Live at the Fillmore East; Live at Woodstock* 2000—*Jimi Hendrix Experience.*

Jimi Hendrix was one of rock's few true originals. He was one of the most innovative and influential rock guitarists of the late '60s and perhaps the most important electric guitarist after Charlie Christian. His influence figures prominently in the playing style of rockers ranging from Robin Trower to Living Colour's Vernon Reid to Stevie Ray Vaughan. A left-hander who took a right-handed Fender Stratocaster and played it upside down, Hendrix pioneered the use of the instrument as an electronic sound source. Players before Hendrix had experimented with feedback and distortion, but he turned those effects and others into a controlled, fluid vocabulary every bit as personal as the blues with which he began. His expressively unconventional, six-string vocabulary has lived on in the work of such guitarists as Adrian Belew, Eddie Van Halen, and Vernon Reid. But while he unleashed noise—and such classic hard-rock riffs as "Purple Haze," "Foxy Lady," and "Crosstown Traffic"—with uncanny mastery, Hendrix also created such tender ballads as "The Wind Cries Mary," the oft-covered "Little Wing," and "Angel," and haunting blues recordings such as "Red House" and "Voodoo Chile." Although Hendrix did not consider himself a good singer, his vocals were nearly as wide-ranging, intimate, and evocative as his guitar playing.

Hendrix's studio craft and his virtuosity with both conventional and unconventional guitar sounds have been widely imitated, and his image as the psychedelic voodoo child conjuring uncontrollable forces is a rock archetype. His songs have inspired several tribute albums, and have been recorded by a jazz group (1989's *Hendrix Project*), the Kronos String Quartet, and avant-garde flutist Robert Dick. Hendrix's musical vision had a profound effect on everyone from Sly Stone to George Clinton—and, through them, Prince—to Miles Davis. His theatrical performing style—full of unmistakably sexual undulations, and such tricks as playing the guitar behind his back (a tradition that went back at least to bluesman T-Bone Walker) and picking it with his teeth—has never quite been equaled. In the decades since Hendrix's death, pop stars from Michael Jackson to Prince have evoked his look and style.

As a teenager, Hendrix taught himself to play guitar by listening to records by blues guitarists Muddy Waters and B.B. King and rockers such as Chuck Berry and Eddie Cochran. He played in high school bands before enlisting in the U.S. Army in 1959. Discharged after parachuting injuries

Jimi Hendrix

in 1961, Hendrix began working under the pseudonym Jimmy James as a pickup guitarist. By 1964, when he moved to New York, he had played behind Sam Cooke, B.B. King, Little Richard, Jackie Wilson, Ike and Tina Turner, and Wilson Pickett. In New York he played the club circuit with King Curtis, the Isley Brothers, John Paul Hammond, and Curtis Knight.

In 1965 Hendrix formed his own band, Jimmy James and the Blue Flames, to play Greenwich Village coffeehouses. Chas Chandler of the Animals took him to London in the autumn of 1966 and arranged for the creation of the Jimi Hendrix Experience, with Englishmen Noel Redding on bass and Mitch Mitchell on drums.

The Experience's first single, "Hey Joe," reached #6 on the U.K. chart early in 1967, followed shortly by "Purple Haze" and its double-platinum debut album, *Are You Experienced?* (#5, 1967). Hendrix fast became the rage of London's pop society. Though word of the Hendrix phenomenon spread through the U.S., he was not seen in America (and no records were released) until June 1967, when, at Paul McCartney's insistence, the Experience appeared at the Monterey Pop Festival. The performance, which Hendrix climaxed by burning his guitar, was filmed for *Monterey Pop.*

Hendrix's next albums were major hits (*Axis: Bold as Love* [#3, 1968], *Electric Ladyland* [#1, 1968]) and he quickly became a superstar. Stories such as one reporting that the Experience was dropped from the bill of a Monkees tour at the insistence of the Daughters of the American Revolution became part of the Hendrix myth, but he considered himself a musician more than a star. Soon after the start of his second American tour, early in 1968, he renounced the extravagances of his stage act and simply performed his music. A hostile reception led him to conclude that his best music came out in the informal settings of studios and clubs, and he began construction of Electric Lady, his own studio in New York.

Hendrix was eager to experiment with musical ideas, and he jammed with John McLaughlin, Larry Coryell, and members of Traffic, among others. Miles Davis admired his inventiveness (and, in fact, planned to record with him), and Bob Dylan—whose "Like a Rolling Stone," "All Along the Watchtower," and "Drifter's Escape" Hendrix recorded—later returned the tribute by performing "All Along the Watchtower" in the Hendrix mode.

As 1968 came to a close, disagreements arose between manager Chas Chandler and co-manager Michael Jeffrey; Jeffrey, who opposed Hendrix's avant-garde leanings, got the upper hand. Hendrix was also under pressure from Black Power advocates to form an all-black group and to play to black audiences. These problems exacerbated already existing tensions within the Experience, and early in 1969 Redding left the group to form Fat Mattress. Hendrix replaced him with an army buddy, Billy Cox. Mitchell stayed on briefly, but by August the Experience was defunct. In summer 1969 the double-platinum *Smash Hits* (#6) was released.

Hendrix appeared at the Woodstock Festival with a large informal ensemble called the Electric Sky Church, and later that year he put together the all-black Band of Gypsys—with Cox and drummer Buddy Miles (Electric Flag), with whom he had played behind Wilson Pickett. The Band of Gypsys' debut concert at New York's Fillmore East on New Year's Eve 1969 provided the recordings for the group's only album during its existence, *Band of Gypsys* (#5, 1970) (a second album of vintage tracks was released in 1986). Hendrix walked offstage in the middle of their Madison Square Garden gig; when he performed again some months later it was with Mitchell and Cox, the group that recorded *The Cry of Love* (#3, 1971), Hendrix's last self-authorized album. With them he played at the Isle of Wight Festival, his last concert, in August 1970. A month later he was dead. The cause of death was given in the coroner's report as inhalation of vomit following barbiturate intoxication. Suicide was not ruled out, but evidence pointed to an accident.

In the years since his death, the Hendrix legend has lived on through various media. Randi Hansen (who appeared in the video for Devo's 1984 cover of "Are You Experienced?") became the best-known of a bunch of full-time Hendrix impersonators, even re-forming the Band of Gypsys with bassist Tony Saunders and Buddy Miles—who, briefly in the late '80s, was replaced by Mitch Mitchell.

Over a dozen books have been written about Hendrix, including tomes by both Redding and Mitchell; the most authoritative bio is generally considered to be David Henderson's *'Scuse Me While I Kiss the Sky.* And virtually every note Hendrix ever allowed to be recorded has been marketed on approximately 100 albums, some of which mine his years as a pickup guitarist, various bootleg and legitimate live concerts and jam sessions, and even interviews and conversations. A controversial series produced by Alan Douglas, who recorded over 1,000 hours of Hendrix alone at the Electric Lady studio in the last year of his life, garnered attention through the mid-'90s. With the consent of the Hendrix estate, Douglas edited the tapes, erased some tracks, and dubbed in others, with mixed results. *Radio One* collected energetic live-in-the-studio performances by Hendrix and the Experience recorded for British radio in 1967.

In 1990 the first of several Hendrix tribute albums, *If Six Was Nine,* was released. Former Free/Bad Company/Firm vocalist Paul Rodgers released another tribute (*The Hendrix Set,* 1993) and appeared on the all-star *Stone Free,* which featured Hendrix covers by musicians ranging from Eric Clapton to Buddy Guy to the Cure to Ice-T to classical violinist Nigel Kennedy.

In 1991 Hendrix's ex-girlfriend Kathy Etchingham, along with Mitch Mitchell and his wife, Dee, began prodding Scotland Yard to reopen an investigation into their friend's death. England's attorney general finally agreed to the request in 1993; in early 1994 Scotland Yard announced it had found no evidence to bother pursuing the case any further. In 1993 an audio-visual exhibit of Hendrix's work called "Jimi Hendrix: On the Road Again" toured college campuses and art galleries in the U.S., to enthusiastic—and predominately young—audiences.

In 1994 a 24-year-old Swede named James Henrik Daniel

Sundquist claimed to have been conceived by the guitarist and Eva Sundquist during a 1969 Stockholm sojourn. Sundquist legally challenged Hendrix's father, James "Al" Hendrix, as the sole heir to the Jimi Hendrix estate, which was estimated to be worth at least $30 million. A year earlier, Al Hendrix, who in the mid-'70s had signed away the rights to portions of his son's work to various international conglomerates, had claimed that he'd been misled. With the financial aid of Paul Allen, the billionaire Hendrix fan who cofounded Microsoft with Bill Gates, he filed a federal lawsuit against those conglomerates and against the holding companies and lawyers connected to the estate. In 1995 he regained complete control of his son's estate, which included Jimi Hendrix's finished and unreleased recordings, as well as his musical compositions. This evolved into a series of CD reissues that were remastered from the original tapes. Having rereleased CDs of the guitarist's entire catalogue, the Hendrix estate, under the Experience Hendrix imprint of MCA, also issued the album on which Hendrix was working at the time of his death, *First Rays of the New Rising Son* (#49, 1997). *South Saturn Delta* (#51, 1997) delved further into the archives. *Experience Hendrix: The Best of Jimi Hendrix* (#133, 1998) followed, as did the double-CD *BBC Sessions* (#50, 1998), the Band of Gypsys–era *Live at the Fillmore East* (#65, 1999), *Live at Woodstock* (#90, 1999), and, in 2000, the four-CD/eight-LP *Jimi Hendrix Experience* box set. Meanwhile Paul Allen amassed his cash to fund a modest Jimi Hendrix museum, which eventually blossomed into the $100 million Experience Music Project. Eight years in the making, the high-tech, interactive rock & roll museum—complete with a Jimi Hendrix Gallery—opened at the Seattle Center in 2000.

Nona Hendryx

Born Oct. 9, ca. 1946, Trenton, NJ
1977—*Nona Hendryx* (Epic) 1983—*Nona* (RCA) 1984—*The Art of Defense* 1985—*The Heat* 1987—*Female Trouble* (EMI) 1989—*SkinDiver* (Private Music) 1992—*You Have to Cry Sometime* (with Billy Vera) (Shanachie) 1999—*Transformation: The Best of Nona Hendryx* (Razor & Tie).

Throughout her nearly 40 years as a performer, Nona Hendryx has established herself as a versatile singer and composer with individual flair, playing girl-group pop, glam funk, hard rock, new wave, and New Age. She joined Patti LaBelle and the Bluebelles with her friend Sarah Dash when she was 16. She stayed with LaBelle and Dash through their transformation into Labelle [see entry] and their breakup in 1977. That year, on her eponymous debut, she established herself as a rocker.

Always known for her wild style, Hendryx quickly fell into New York's new-wave hipoisie, singing backup on Talking Heads' *Remain in Light*, singing on Material's 1981 club hit "Bustin' Out," and forming her own bands Zero Cool and Propaganda. *Nona* was coproduced by Material and featured a lineup including Nile Rodgers, Jamaaladeen Tacuma, and Sly Dunbar. An eclectic and impressive all-female band played on the track "Design for Living": Tina Weymouth (Talking Heads), Nancy Wilson (Heart), Valerie Simpson (Ashford and Simpson), Laurie Anderson, and Gina Schock (Go-Go's). The dance-funk album included the hits "Keep It Confidential" (#22 R&B, 1983) and "Transformation" (#40 R&B, 1983).

Many of the same personnel—with the addition of Afrika Bambaataa—played on *The Art of Defense*, on which the use of three percussionists and three synthesizists indicated Hendryx's interest in a fusion of rhythms and sounds. The album was again coproduced by Material. Producers Bernard Edwards and Arthur Baker brought their dance electronics skills to *The Heat*, which featured Keith Richards on the Grammy-nominated "Rock This House" and "I Sweat (Going Through the Motions)" (#28 R&B, 1984). Hendryx again pursued a mix of styles on *Female Trouble*, which yielded the single "Why Should I Cry?" (#5 R&B, 1987). She changed labels and sound for *SkinDiver*. Coproduced by Private Music founder Peter Baumann (ex–Tangerine Dream), the album was more atmospheric than her previous funk and rock work.

Hendryx has recorded and collaborated with Peter Gabriel, George Clinton, Bernie Worrell, Cameo, Mavis Staples, Bobby Brown, Prince, Garland Jeffreys, and Yoko Ono. She has written songs for Patti LaBelle, Sandra St. Victor, Naomi Campbell, and Lisa Lisa, and produced other artists, including Lisa Lisa. Her music has been used in films including *Perfect* and *Coming to America*. She has also composed for such dance companies as Alvin Ailey and Dance Theatre Workshop.

In 1992 Hendryx and blue-eyed soulman Billy Vera released *You Have to Cry Sometime*, an album consisting mostly of covers, including versions of '60s hits by Marvin Gaye, Solomon Burke, and the Isley Brothers. In 1999 Hendryx produced *Word: Life*, a concert held at New York's Irving Plaza featuring African-American poets and musicians. She also started her own label, Free Records, to issue spoken word and other recordings. In 2000 Hendryx wrote music and lyrics for the theater production of playwright Charles Randolph-Wright's *Blue*, a comedy depicting the foibles of an upscale African-American family.

Don Henley: See the Eagles

Clarence "Frogman" Henry

Born Mar. 19, 1937, Algiers, LA
1961—*You Always Hurt the One You Love* (Argo) 1969—*Is Alive and Well and Living in New Orleans and Still Doing His Thing* (Roulette) 1970—*Bourbon Street, Canal Street* 1979—*New Recordings* 1983—*The Legendary Clarence "Frogman" Henry* 1994—*Ain't Got No Home: The Best of Clarence "Frogman" Henry* (MCA).

"I can sing like a man . . . I can sing like a girl . . . I can sing like a frog," claimed Clarence Henry in his rollicking 1956 Top 10 R&B hit "Ain't Got No Home." And he did—a piercing falsetto shriek and the guttural inhaled style that earned him his nickname. Henry, who'd learned piano and trombone as a child, went on to sing and play piano with Bobby Mitchell's New Orleans R&B band in 1955 and remained a Crescent City favorite after his first hit. In 1961 he scored national pop and R&B hits with the Allen Toussaint–produced ballads "I Don't Know Why I Love You but I Do" (by Bobby Charles) and "You Always Hurt the One You Love." His other chartmaking singles included "Lonely Street" and "On Bended Knee" (1961) and "A Little Too Much" (1962). In the late '60s Henry appeared in a number of rock & roll revival shows, and in the early '70s he was still a popular act in New Orleans clubs. In 1982 "Ain't Got No Home" was featured on the soundtrack of the period film *Diner.* In the early '90s, a ruptured disk nearly ended the Frogman's performing career, but he persevered. In 1994 "I Don't Know Why I Love You, But I Do" was featured on the soundtrack to the hit movie *Forrest Gump;* the soundtrack to the 1996 film *Casino* included "Ain't Got No Home."

Henry Cow/Fred Frith

Formed 1968, Cambridge, Eng.
Fred Frith (b. Feb. 17, 1949, Heathfield, Eng.), gtr., violin, piano; Tim Hodgkinson, kybds., reeds; Chris Cutler, drums, tape effects; John Greaves, bass, piano, voc.; Geoff Leigh, reeds, sax.
1973—*Legend* (Virgin) 1974—(– Leigh; + Lindsay Cooper, bassoon, oboe) *Unrest* (Virgin, U.K.) 1975—*Desperate Straights* (with Slapp Happy); *In Praise of Learning* (with Slapp Happy) (+ Dagmar Krause, voc.) 1976—*Concerts* (Caroline, U.K.) 1978—(– Krause) *Western Culture* (Broadcast, U.K.).
Art Bears: Frith; Cutler; Krause
1978—*Hopes and Fears* (Random Radar) 1979—*Winter Songs* (Recommended) 1981—*The World as It Is Today* (Re, U.K.).
John Greaves/Peter Blegvad: 1977—*Kew. Rhone.* (Virgin).
Fred Frith: 1974—*Guitar Solos* (Caroline, U.K.) 1980—*Gravity* (Ralph) 1981—*Speechless* 1982—*Killing Time* (with Massacre) (OAO/Celluloid); *Live in Japan* (Recommended, Jap.) 1983—*Cheap at Half the Price* (Ralph) 1984—*Learn to Talk* (with Skeleton Crew) (Rift) 1986—*The Country of Blinds* (with Skeleton Crew) 1988—*The Technology of Tears* (SST) 1990—*The Top of His Head* (Crammed, Bel.); *Step Across the Border* (RecRec) 1991—*Guitar Solos Complete* (East Side Digital) 1992—*Helter Skelter* (with François-Michel Pesenti) (RecRec, Swit.) 1994—*Quartets* 1995—*Middle of the Moment* 1996—*Allies* 1997—*Eye to Ear* (Tzadik); *The Previous Evening* (ReR, U.K.); *Etymology* (with Tom Cora) (Rarefaction) 1998—*Pacifica* (Tzadik); *Funny Valentine* (with Massacre) 1999—*Stone, Brick, Glass, Wood, Wire (Graphic Sources 1986–1996)* (Angelica, It.).

Henry Cow's determined, uncompromising eclecticism—its music spans rock, fusion, free improvisation, medieval chamber music, modern-classical, and avant-garde *musique concrète*—and committed socialist politics limited the band's following to a small, dedicated cult. Initially, the group's anticommercial leanings (it was formed the year of the Paris student riots) even kept it from a recording contract. In 1971 Henry Cow played the Glastonbury Festival (a sort of British Woodstock) en route to London to record its critically acclaimed debut LP. In 1973 the group scored an avant-garde British production of Shakespeare's *Tempest,* toured with the German progressive group Faust, and appeared on one side of the out-of-print *Greasy Truckers Live at Dingwall's Dance Hall* LP.

Henry Cow opened for Captain Beefheart on a European tour in 1974 and released its second LP, which included "Bittern Storm Over Ulm," a radical refraction of the Yardbirds' "Got to Hurry." In 1975 the band merged with the mutant cabaret outfit Slapp Happy (Dagmar Krause, Anthony Moore, and Peter Blegvad) for *Desperate Straights,* a collection of shorter songs, and for *In Praise of Learning,* where political lyrics were accompanied by noisy modern-classical music. Slapp Happy subsequently disbanded, and Krause joined Henry Cow.

In 1978, just before the release of Henry Cow's swan song, *Western Culture,* Frith, Blegvad, and Cutler made their first U.S. appearances in New York City. Since then, the remarkably prolific Frith's various projects have included the Art Bears, for which he, Cutler, and Krause recorded dissonant, quirky songs; Massacre, a noisy, rock-flavored power trio with bassist Bill Laswell and drummer Fred Maher; theater scores and the avant-rock band Naked City with John Zorn; the experimental Skeleton Crew, with the late cellist Tom Cora and harpist Zeena Parkins; a stint in Anton Fier's Golden Palominos; guest work with artists like the Residents, Brian Eno, and Swans; and solo work, which sometimes consists of free improvisation on disassembled guitars and various homemade electric instruments. On *Cheap at Half the Price,* he sang for the first time—typically in a peculiar high-pitched tone. Frith began releasing his own albums in 1974, some of which paired him with fellow avant-garde guitarists Hans Reichel, Henry Kaiser, and Derek Bailey. By the early '90s, he was a fixture at New York City's avant-garde haven, the Knitting Factory. European directors Nicolas Humbert and Werner Penzels chose Frith as the subject of their acclaimed 1990 documentary *Step Across the Border.* By the end of the decade, the guitarist was living in Oakland, California, where he taught music composition at Mills College. *Stone, Brick, Glass, Wood, Wire* is a four-CD set.

Blegvad performed in New York in the early '80s with Carla Bley, John Greaves of Henry Cow, and Arto Lindsay; he continued to work into the '90s, as a solo artist and in such groups as the Golden Palominos. Moore recorded more than a half-dozen atonal, poppish solo albums under the name A. or Anthony More. Cutler, Hodgkinson, and Cooper continued to make avant-garde music in Europe. Cutler also runs the influential, multinational Recommended Records.

The Heptones

Formed 1965, Kingston, Jam.
Barry Llewelyn (b. 1947, Jam.), voc.; Earl Morgan (b. 1945, Jam.), voc.; Leroy Sibbles (b. 1949, Jam.), voc.
1970—*On Top* (Studio One); *Black Is Back* 1971—*Freedom*

Line; and Friends, vol. 1 (Joe Gibbs) 1976—*Cool Rasta* (Trojan); *Night Food* (Island) 1977—*Party Time* 1978—*In Love With You* (United Artists); *Better Days* (Third World) 1979—*The Good Life* (Greensleeves) (– Sibbles; + Naggu Morris [b. ca. 1951]) 1981—*Street of Gold* (Park Heights) 1982—*One Step Ahead* (Sonic); *On the Run* (Shanachie) 1995—*Sea of Love* (Heartbeat) 1999—*The Meaning of Life: Best of 1966–1976* (Trojan).

With their lilting rhythms and American-style soul harmony singing, the Heptones were the archetypical rock-steady group. Like the "rude boys" who were their first fans, the band members came from the Kingston slum Trenchtown. Morgan had previously led a group, and in 1965 he formed the new vocal trio with Sibbles, formerly a welder, and Llewelyn, an auto mechanic.

After five unsuccessful singles for Ken Lack's label, Coxsone Dodd released the 45 "Fatty Fatty" on his Studio One label in 1966; although it was banned from Jamaican radio because of its sexual innuendos, "Fatty Fatty" was a huge hit. In Britain it was credited to Ken Boothe (a Studio One singer who had already built a small following in the U.K.); none of the early British releases bore their name. The Heptones were one of Jamaica's most popular groups of the late '60s, hitting with Sibbles songs like "Baby (Be True)," "Why Must I," "Why Did You Leave," and "Cry Baby Cry."

They stayed with Dodd's label until 1970, by which time rock steady was hardening into reggae. Their songs showed reggae's influence mostly in their increasingly political lyrics. Among their hits for producers Joe Gibbs, Geoffrey Chung, and Harry J. were "Young, Gifted and Black" (1970), "Hypocrites" (1971), "Freedom to the People" (1972; used as an anthem by the Jamaican People's National Party in their successful election campaign), a cover of Harold Melvin and the Blue Notes' "I Miss You" (1972), and "Book of Rules" (1973), which was featured in the 1979 film *Rockers*.

In 1973 the Heptones moved to Canada for two years, making Toronto their base for tours in the U.S. and Great Britain. They celebrated their return to Jamaica in 1975 with the chart-topping "Country Boy," and the following year signed their first multinational contract. Their first American-released album, *Night Food*, contained new versions of "Fatty Fatty" and "Book of Rules." *Party Time*, produced by Lee Perry, emphasized the reggae sound.

In 1979 Sibbles left the group to begin a solo career. Morgan and Llewelyn maintained the group with the addition of Naggu Morris. They toured the U.S. in 1982, while Sibbles toured with his own group. Throughout the '80s, both remained popular live draws. Sibbles returned to Jamaica in 1992 with plans to revitalize his recording career, and released *It's Not Over* on the VP label in 1997.

Herman's Hermits

Formed 1963, Manchester, Eng.
Peter "Herman" Noone (b. Nov. 5, 1947, Manchester), voc., piano, gtr.; Karl Green (b. July 31, 1947, Salford, Eng.), gtr., harmonica; Keith Hopwood (b. Oct. 26, 1946, Manchester), gtr.; Derek "Lek" Leckenby (b. May 14, 1945, Leeds, Eng.; d. June 4, 1994, Eng.), gtr.; Barry Whitwam (b. July 21, 1946, Manchester), drums.
1965—*The Best of Herman's Hermits* (MGM) 1966—*Best of, vol. 2* 1968—*Best of, vol. 3*.
Peter Noone and the Tremblers: 1980—*Twice Nightly* (Johnston) 1982—*One of the Glory Boys*.
Peter Noone with Phil Ramone: 1993—*Playback* (Noone/Ramone).

Major stars from the pop side of the British Invasion, Herman's Hermits had 11 Top 10 hits from 1964 through 1967. By the time changing musical trends had reduced the group to a curiosity, it had already sold over 40 million singles and albums worldwide.

Peter Noone studied singing and acting at the Manchester School of Music, and was featured in the early '60s in several plays and on BBC-TV. By 1963, he was playing with the Heartbeats, a local Manchester group that consisted of Karl Green, Keith Hopwood, Derek Leckenby, and Barry Whitwam. The others claimed that Noone, then performing under the name Peter Novak, resembled Sherman of the *Rocky and Bullwinkle* television cartoon series; they then shortened the nickname to Herman.

In early 1964 they attracted the attention of U.K. producer Mickie Most, who released the group's first single, "I'm Into Something Good" (#13), that fall. It spent three weeks at the top of the British chart and sold over a million copies worldwide. In 1965 the Hermits dominated the U.S. chart, placing six singles in the Top 10 and appearing in the Connie Francis teen flick *Where the Boys Meet the Girls*. Herman's Hermits' hits (which actually featured such British sessionmen as future Led Zeppeliners Jimmy Page and John Paul Jones) included "Mrs. Brown You've Got a Lovely Daughter" (#1), "I'm Henry the Eighth, I Am" (#1) (originally written in 1911 for a Cockney comedian), "Can't You Hear My Heartbeat" (#2), "Wonderful World" (#4), "Silhouettes" (#5) (originally recorded by the Rays), "Just a Little Bit Better" (#7) (all in 1965), "Listen People" (#3), "Dandy" (#5) (written by Ray Davies of the Kinks), "A Must to Avoid" (#8), and "Leaning on the Lamp Post" (#9) (all 1966). *The Best of Herman's Hermits* stayed on the album chart 105 weeks. Their last big hit was "There's a Kind of Hush" (#4) b/w "No Milk Today" (#35) in early 1967.

By 1971, the group had disbanded amid legal battles for royalties. The Hermits surfaced a few years later, sans Herman, for an abortive attempt at a comeback with Buddah Records. (Noone rejoined the others briefly in 1973 for some British Invasion Revival shows.)

Initially Noone returned to acting. In 1970 he met David Bowie, who supplied him with his first British solo hit, "Oh You Pretty Things," and played piano on the sessions. Their subsequent collaborations failed, however, as did Noone's other early-'70s releases for Rak Records. Mid-decade, Noone spent three years hosting a mainstream British television series but quit to avoid being pigeonholed as a cabaret performer. He moved to the south of France and cut a few singles that were moderate hits there and in Belgium.

By the late '70s, Noone had taken up part-time residence in L.A., where the thriving club scene induced him to try a comeback with a contemporary rock band, the Tremblers, whose members (guitarist/keyboardist Gregg Inhofer, drummer Robert Williams, guitarist George Conner, and bassist Mark Browne) had played variously with the Pop, Tonio K., Barbra Streisand, and Olivia Newton-John. Their 1980 debut album, *Twice Nightly,* marked Noone's debut as a producer of a record on which he performed. In 1982 he released an LP entitled *One of the Glory Boys* and appeared as Frederic in the Broadway production of *The Pirates of Penzance.* For five years in the '90s he hosted the VH1 program *My Generation.* Leckenby and Whitwam carried on as the Hermits until the former's death in 1994. Whitwam dragged the band's name through the '90s while Noone billed himself as Herman's Hermits Featuring Peter Noone to play the oldies circuit.

Kristen Hersh: See Throwing Muses/Belly

John Hiatt

Born 1952, Indianapolis, IN
1974—*Hangin' Around the Observatory* (Epic) 1975—*Overcoats* 1979—*Slug Line* (MCA) 1980—*Two Bit Monsters* 1982—*All of a Sudden* (Geffen) 1983—*Riding With the King* 1985—*Warming Up to the Ice Age* 1987—*Bring the Family* (A&M) 1988—*Slow Turning* 1990—*Stolen Moments* 1993—*Perfectly Good Guitar* 1994—*Hiatt Comes Alive at Budokan* 1995—*Walk On* (Capitol) 1997—*Little Head* 2000—*Crossing Muddy Waters* (Vanguard).

Singer/songwriter John Hiatt has had his songs covered by Rick Nelson, Dave Edmunds, the Searchers, Three Dog Night, Bonnie Raitt, and others, although his solo career has been only moderately successful.

Hiatt played in various garage bands before leaving his hometown at age 18 in 1970. He was discovered in Nashville by an Epic talent scout and made two quirky albums for the label—*Hangin' Around the Observatory* and *Overcoats*—that drew critical kudos but negligible sales. Without a record contract, Hiatt spent the next few years touring folk clubs as a solo act, before signing with MCA. He released two more records, the more new-wavish *Slug Line* and *Two Bit Monsters,* and received more critical nods, but despite some touring, they failed in the marketplace. Hiatt played and sang on sessions and toured with Ry Cooder, and he appears with Cooder (singing two songs) on the soundtrack to 1982's *The Border.*

Through the first half of the '80s, Hiatt's good-reviews/weak-sales pattern continued; meanwhile, he descended into alcoholism and suffered the suicide of his first wife. Hiatt was dumped by Geffen Records, but then got sober, remarried, and landed a new deal with A&M. He gathered Cooder, bassist Nick Lowe (who had produced some of his Geffen work), and session super-drummer Jim Keltner to record *Bring the Family*—which, with *Slow Turning* and *Stolen Moments,* would comprise Hiatt's "recovery trilogy," which brought him the most glowing reviews of his career, if not much of a rise in sales. Hiatt, Cooder, Lowe, and Keltner also recorded in 1992 under the name Little Village. For *Perfectly Good Guitar,* Hiatt recruited members of such younger bands as Cracker, School of Fish, and Wire Train. After the release of a live album in 1994, Hiatt left A&M for Capitol Records, which released the Grammy-nominated *Walk On* (#48) in 1995 and *Little Head* in 1997. During the next two years, four separate best-of collections were released by the singer's various labels. In late 1999 Hiatt's status as a songwriter's songwriter paid dividends in a new job: hosting the PBS studio concert series *Sessions at West 54th.* He also switched labels again, recording his 2000 release *Crossing Muddy Waters* for the reactivated Vanguard Records.

Dan Hicks and His Hot Licks

Formed 1968, San Francisco, CA
Dan Hicks (b. Dec. 9, 1941, Little Rock, AK), gtr., voc., harmonica, drums; David LaFlamme (b. Apr. 5, 1941, Salt Lake City, UT), violin; Bill Douglas, bass; Mitzy Douglas, voc.; Patti Urban, voc.
1968—(revised lineup: Hicks; Sherry Snow, voc.; Tina Natural (b. Christina Gancher, 1945), voc., celeste, perc.; Jimmie Bassoon, bass; Jon Weber (b. 1947), gtr.; Gary Pozzi, violin) 1969—(– Bassoon; + Jaime Leopold [b. 1947, Portland, OR], fiddle, bass; – Pozzi; + Sid Page [b. 1947, Portland], violin, mandolin) *Original Recordings* (Epic) (– Snow; – Gancher; – Weber; + Nicole Dukes, voc.; + Naomi Eisenberg [b. Brooklyn, NY], voc., violin; + Maryanne Price [b. Providence, RI], voc., cornet; + Bob Scott, drums; – Dukes; – Eisenberg) 1971—*Where's the Money* (Blue Thumb) (+ John Girton [b. Burbank, CA], gtr.) 1972—*Strikin' It Rich* 1973—*Last Train to Hicksville . . . the Home of Happy Feet* 1974—(group disbands) 1991—*The Very Best of Dan Hicks and His Hot Licks* (See for Miles) 1994—*Lost in the Eighties* (Rare Prime Cuts); *At the Boarding House, 1971; Paramount Theater, 1990* 1997—*Return to Hicksville* (Hip-o) 1998—*Early Muses* (Big Beat) 2000—(group re-forms as Dan Hicks and the Hot Licks: Hicks; Page; + various musicians) *Beatin' the Heat* (Hollywood).
Dan Hicks solo: 1978—*It Happened One Bite* (Warner Bros.) 1988—*Mistletoe Jam* (with the Christmas Jug Band) (Relix) 1994—*Shootin' Straight* (On the Spot).

In the late '60s and early '70s Dan Hicks performed his wry, jazzy, ironic, pseudo-nostalgia songs with the Hot Licks, a group modeled on Django Reinhardt's quintet, and the Lickettes, a pair of female vocalists. He grew up in Santa Rosa, California, began playing drums at age 11, and switched to guitar at age 20. In his teens he played in various local folk and jazz bands. He continued drumming while attending

San Francisco State College. Eventually he landed in the original Charlatans, a self-confessed amateur band, with whom he played from 1965 to 1968. During his last six months with the Charlatans, he began playing with his own group (documented on *Early Muses*), including violinist David LaFlamme, who later formed It's a Beautiful Day [see entry].

By early 1968, Hicks' drummerless group, the Hot Licks, was signed to Epic; its only album for the label, *Original Recordings*, flopped. After a series of personnel changes, the band signed to Blue Thumb in 1971. Its three albums for that label—*Where's the Money* (recorded live at L.A.'s Troubadour), *Strikin' It Rich*, and *Last Train to Hicksville* (the first Licks LP with a drummer)—blended the Andrews Sisters, Western swing, ragtime, and jazz. Hicks became known for compositions like "How Can I Miss You (When You Won't Go Away)," "Walkin' One and Only" (which was covered by Maria Muldaur), and "I Scare Myself" (recorded later by Thomas Dolby). Violinist Sid Page (who later played with Sly and the Family Stone) departed after *Last Train*, and by 1974 those particular Hot Licks were no more.

Following the group's breakup, Hicks has been sporadically active in the Bay Area as a solo artist, sometimes billed as Lonesome Dan Hicks. In early 1978 he reemerged with *It Happened One Bite*. He went on to form the Acoustic Warriors, with whom he recorded 1994's live *Shootin' Straight*. He revived the Hot Licks name for a 1991 reunion concert, and again for *Beatin' the Heat*, his star-studded comeback featuring Hot Licks alumnus Page, along with Elvis Costello, Tom Waits, Bette Midler, Brian Setzer, and Rickie Lee Jones.

The Highwaymen: See Johnny Cash; Waylon Jennings; Kris Kristofferson; Willie Nelson

Jessie Hill

Born Dec. 9, 1932, New Orleans, LA; died Sep. 17, 1996, New Orleans
1972—*Naturally* (Blue Thumb) 1978—*Golden Classics* (Collectables).

New Orleans pianist Jessie Hill's moment of national glory came with "Ooh Poo Pah Doo—Parts I & II" (#28, 1960), the first national hit produced by Allen Toussaint. Hill wrote the song, which Toussaint orchestrated with a call-and-response format recalling Ray Charles' "What'd I Say." But Hill was unable to come up with a followup hit. He recorded for Minit through 1963, his most successful effort being "Whip It on Me" (#91, 1960). He then moved to L.A. and fell in with other New Orleans expatriates like Dr. John (who covered Hill's "Qualify" on one of his solo albums). Hill recorded sporadically throughout the decade, culminating in a 1970 album for Blue Thumb. In the early '70s he returned to New Orleans, where he continued to write and perform in nightclubs until his death in 1996. His tunes, which include "Sweet Jelly Roll," "I Got Mine," and "Can't Get Enough," have been recorded by Ike and Tina Turner, and Sonny and Cher, among others.

Lauryn Hill: See the Fugees

Robyn Hitchcock/Soft Boys

Born Mar. 3, 1953, London, Eng.
With the Soft Boys, formed 1976, Cambridge, Eng.: Hitchcock, voc., gtr., bass; Alan Davies, gtr.; Andy Metcalfe, bass; Otis Fagg (b. Morris Windsor), drums.
1977—*Give It to the Soft Boys* EP (Raw, U.K.) (– Davies; + Kimberley Rew [b. Eng.], gtr., voc.) 1979—*A Can of Bees* (Two Crabs, U.K.) (– Metcalfe; + Matthew Seligman, bass) 1980—*Underwater Moonlight* (Armageddon, U.K.) 1981—*Two Halves for the Price of One* 1983—*Invisible Hits* (Glass Fish, U.K.) 1993—*1976–81* (Rykodisc).
With the Egyptians, formed 1984: Hitchcock, voc., gtr.; Andy Metcalfe, bass; Morris Windsor, drums; Roger Jackson, kybds.
1985—*Fegmania!* (Slash); *Gotta Let This Hen Out!* (Relativity) 1986—*Exploding in Silence* EP; *Element of Light* (Glass Fish/Relativity) (– Jackson) 1988—*Globe of Frogs* (A&M) 1989—*Queen Elvis* 1991—*Perspex Island* 1993—*Respect* 1996—*Greatest Hits* (A&M).
Robyn Hitchcock solo: 1981—*Black Snake Diamond Role* (Armageddon, U.K.) 1982—*Groovy Decay* (Albion, U.K.) 1984—*I Often Dream of Trains* (Glass Fish, U.K.) 1986—*Groovy Decoy* (Glass Fish/Relativity); *Invisible Hitchcock* 1990—*Eye* (Twin/Tone) 1995—*Gravy Deco (The Complete Groovy Decay/Decoy Sessions)* (Rhino); *You & Oblivion* 1996—*Moss Elixir* (Warner Bros.) 1997—*Uncorrected Personality Traits* (Rhino) 1998—*Storefront Hitchcock* (Warner Bros.) 1999—*Jewels for Sophia*.

Robyn Hitchcock has the heart of a singer/songwriter but the warped sensibility of a man one step ahead of or behind his time. The former Soft Boy was perhaps the definitive cult artist of the '80s: devoutly followed but little known. Hitchcock was born in an artistic middle-class family in West London. He dropped out of art school and moved to Cambridge in 1974, where he began performing his eccentric folk songs. He played in a number of bands, including Maureen and the Meatpackers, before forming the Soft Boys in 1976 with drummer Morris Windsor, guitarist Alan Davies, and bassist Andy Metcalfe.

After *Give It to the Soft Boys* introduced their demented progressive rock in 1977, the band fired Davies and hired Cambridge guitar wizard Kimberley Rew, later of Katrina and the Waves. The London label Radar briefly signed the Soft Boys but dropped them after the single "(I Want to Be an) Anglepoise Lamp" stiffed. *A Can of Bees* was a bizarre album whose "Hu-man Music" introduced the folk-ballad style that would become one of Hitchcock's strengths.

The Soft Boys worked on an album that the label did not

The Soft Boys: Robyn Hitchcock, Kimberley Rew, Morris Windsor, Matthew Seligman

release (many of its songs were later included on 1983's *Invisible Hits*). In 1979 the band taped an acoustic show that, with its clever covers and Hitchcock's eccentric banter, illustrated why they had a firm live following (the tape was released in 1983 via mail order). Working with a tiny budget and largely using an 8-track recorder, the Soft Boys then recorded the masterful *Underwater Moonlight* (1980).

The Soft Boys toured the U.S. and released *Two Halves for the Price of One*, a collection of live tracks and oddities, before breaking up in 1981. Influenced by the Byrds and Syd Barrett, the Soft Boys were out of sync with the punk rock of their time, although many American bands, including R.E.M. and the Replacements, later claimed them as a major influence. In 1993 Rykodisc released a two-CD retrospective, and in January 1994 the band reunited for a show in London. After Matador reissued *Underwater Moonlight* in early 2001, the band reunited and did a series of well-received concerts in the U.S.

Hitchcock was still finding his voice on his first two solo albums, which he recorded with Matthew Seligman. Seligman then joined the Thompson Twins, and Hitchcock recorded *Groovy Decay* with bassist Sara Lee. (An alternate version of the album, featuring the demos with Seligman, was later released as *Groovy Decoy*.) Hitchcock retired for two years and wrote lyrics for Captain Sensible (the Damned [see entry]). He returned in 1984 with the beautiful, acoustic *I Often Dream of Trains*, on which he finally sustained the combination of sensitivity and imagination that is his forte. That year the Soft Boys' first EP was rereleased as *Wading Through a Ventilator*, inspiring Hitchcock to contact Windsor and Metcalfe (who had also played with XTC and Squeeze), along with keyboardist Roger Jackson, and form the Egyptians.

The Egyptians have had a spotty career, hovering on the edges of artistic and commercial success. *Fegmania!* tracks "Egyptian Cream," "My Wife and My Dead Wife," and "The Man With the Light Bulb Head" were praised for their absurd images and narratives. With fans like R.E.M.'s Peter Buck (who has played with the Egyptians) as boosters, Hitchcock signed to A&M and scored college-radio hits with "Balloon Man" (off *Globe of Frogs*) and "So You Think You're in Love" *(Perspex Island)*. Primarily on the strength of live shows, he has developed a devoted audience in America (he's still largely ignored in his native England). *Respect* (1993) is dedicated to his late father; the album was recorded on the Isle of Wight, where Hitchcock sometimes makes his home. Hitchcock also paints, and many of his albums feature his artwork. In 1995 Rhino began releasing all of Hitchcock's work on CD.

Hitchcock signed with Warner Bros. in 1996 and issued *Moss Elixir*, a spare, mostly acoustic record and his first since disbanding the Egyptians. In 1998 he released *Storefront Hitchcock*. The album was the soundtrack to a concert film of the same name directed by Jonathan Demme. The film was shot in a vacant Manhattan storefront. *Jewels for Sophia* (1999) featured guest appearances from Peter Buck, Grant Lee Phillips, and Young Fresh Fellows Scott McCaughey, Tad Hutchinson, and Kurt Bloch. More of a rock record than its predecessors, the album also evinced disarming sincerity, especially given Hitchcock's typically droll sense of humor.

Hole

Formed 1989, Los Angeles, CA
Courtney Love (b. July 9, 1964, San Francisco, CA), voc. gtr.; Eric Erlandson (b. Jan. 9, 1963, Los Angeles), gtr.; Jill Emery, bass; Caroline Rue, drums.
1991—*Pretty on the Inside* (Caroline) 1992—(– Rue; – Emery; + Patty Schemel [b. Apr. 24, 1967, Seattle, WA], drums; + Kristen Pfaff [b. 1967; d. June 16, 1994], bass) 1994—*Live Through This* (Geffen) (– Pfaff; + Melissa Auf der Maur [b. Mar. 17, 1972, Montreal, Can.], bass) 1998—*Celebrity Skin* (Geffen) 2000—(– Auf der Maur).

In the way that Yoko Ono can never be mentioned without the thought of John Lennon, Courtney Love will be forever tied to Nirvana's Kurt Cobain. Yet Love's confrontational stage presence with her band Hole, as well as her gut-wrenching vocals and powerful punk-pop songcraft, have made her an alternative-rock star in her own right.

Love's father, an early, minor Grateful Dead associate, and mother, a therapist, divorced when she was five. As a child, she lived on a commune in New Zealand with her mother. When she was 12, she did time at an Oregon reformatory after she got caught shoplifting. Dropping in and out of college, and living off a trust fund, Love moved from place to place, working as a stripper in Japan, Alaska, and California, and hanging out with mope-rockers in Liverpool, England. Back in L.A., she became friendly with director Alex Cox and scored small roles in a couple of his films, including *Sid & Nancy.*

By the time Love formed Hole with Eric Erlandson in 1989, she had already appeared as a vocalist in an early incarnation of San Francisco's Faith No More and in the Minneapolis all-girl band, Sugar Baby Doll, with Babes in Toyland's Kat Bjelland and L7's Jennifer Finch.

Hole began garnering the attention of the U.S. underground via the band's incendiary live performances and two early singles, "Dicknail" and "Retard Girl." Sonic Youth's Kim Gordon and Gumball's Don Fleming coproduced the acerbic debut album, *Pretty on the Inside.* These recordings and English tours made Hole the darlings of the U.K. music press. Hole was seemingly put on hold, however, during Love's courtship with and eventual marriage to Cobain (on February 24, 1992). The band, which had been courted by several major labels, signed a lucrative contract with Nirvana's [see entry] label Geffen.

After giving birth to a daughter, Frances Bean Cobain, Love and her husband became involved in a battle with children's services over custody of the baby, due to charges in the press that Love had done heroin during her pregnancy; the couple won the right to keep their baby.

In 1993 Hole began recording *Live Through This* with Erlandson, Patty Schemel, and Kristen Pfaff. One week before its release, Cobain was found dead of a self-inflicted gunshot wound to the head. Amid the tragedy, the album won rave reviews. Tragedy struck again on June 16, 1994, when bassist Pfaff overdosed on heroin. Vowing to keep Hole alive, Love enlisted Canadian bassist Melissa Auf der Maur and the band embarked on a tour, first opening for the Lemonheads, then for Nine Inch Nails. *Live Through This* (#52, 1994) made steady progress in the charts, yielding the singles "Miss World," which got modern-rock radio airplay, and "Doll Parts" (#65, 1994). The album went platinum in 1995, the year Hole toured with the fifth Lollapalooza. *My Body, the Hand Grenade* (1997) was a compilation made by Erlandson of rare and unreleased early material.

In the mid-'90s Love underwent a metamorphosis that made her even more controversial. The baby-doll dresses were replaced with Versace threads, and she began appearing on fashion-magazine covers. Music took a backseat in 1996 and '97, when Love concentrated on her acting career, including a role as a drug addict in Milos Forman's *The People vs. Larry Flint* that earned her a Golden Globe nomination. In 1997 Love fought a high-profile battle against the independent film *Kurt and Courtney,* which suggested she was responsible for Cobain's death, and succeeded in having it banned from that year's Sundance Film Festival. Hole's next album, the Southern California–drenched *Celebrity Skin* (#9, 1998), went platinum and was nominated for three Grammys. Smashing Pumpkin Billy Corgan cowrote five of the songs. A single, the lavish ballad "Malibu," reached #81.

Melissa Auf der Maur left the band in early 2000 and joined Smashing Pumpkins. About the same time, Hole ended its relationship with its record label and began distributing MP3s, videos, and updates through its Web site. Love has become an outspoken defender of Napster and an advocate of artists' rights. In September 2000 Love signed a contract with a publisher for a book of poetry, a lyric book, and an insider's guide to the music business. A few months later she announced she would be recording a punk-rock album with a new band for the independent label Epitaph. Dubbed Bastard, the band was comprised of Hole drummer, Schemel, bassist Gina Crosley, and Veruca Salt guitarist Louise Post. In 2001 Love also began recording the soundtrack to her forthcoming film, *Hello Suckers,* which featured her singing '20s-era standards, backed by a ragtime band.

Billie Holiday

Born Eleanora Fagan, Apr. 7, 1915, Baltimore, MD; died July 17, 1959, New York, NY
1958—*Lady in Satin* (Columbia) 1959—*Last Recording* (Verve) 1972—*God Bless the Child* (Columbia) 1991—*Lady in Autumn: The Best of the Verve Years* (Verve); *The Legacy (1933–1958)* (Columbia); *The Complete Decca Recordings* (GRP) 1993—*The Complete Billie Holiday on Verve (1945–1959)* (Verve).

Billie Holiday—"Lady Day"—is the preeminent female jazz vocalist. From her artistic heyday in the mid-'30s through the following two decades of misfortune and drug addiction, Holiday continually rewrote the rules for jazz singing. Her voice was distinguished neither by power nor tonal beauty but by a superb, unerring ability to improvise melodic lines from the framework of standard songs; to subtly twist rhythm and expertly manipulate melody in order to personalize every song she sang. Revered for the directness and wrenching honesty of her work, Holiday relied on drama rather than sentiment to express the emotional content of her material.

Clarence Holiday, Billie's errant father, was a guitarist for Fletcher Henderson's big band. As a child, Holiday did odd jobs for a local brothel in order to hear recordings of Bessie Smith and Louis Armstrong that were played there. Her parents already split up and her mother impoverished, Holiday's early adolescence turned into a nightmare when, after being raped at age 10, she was accused of being "provocative" and sent to a reformatory.

Holiday moved to New York City in the late '20s, taking any singing jobs she could find around Harlem. Influential talent scout/producer John Hammond heard Holiday in 1933 and set up her first recording session, which included Benny Goodman as one of the supporting musicians. In 1935 Holiday began working with Teddy Wilson, Goodman's featured pianist. For Holiday's recordings Wilson would handpick players from the cream of the prominent big bands; it was at these sessions that Holiday developed her remarkable rapport with Count Basie's brilliant tenor saxophonist Lester Young. These Columbia recordings, which extend into the mid-'40s, are generally considered Holiday's finest work, and include such signature songs as "Miss Brown to You," "He's Funny That Way," "What a Little Moonlight Can Do," and "God Bless the Child" (which she helped to compose).

Holiday joined Count Basie's big band for one year in 1937, signing on next with white clarinetist Artie Shaw's band. Racial restrictions—Holiday wasn't allowed to enter hotels from the same entrance as the rest of the band—revolted her, and she soon quit. Holiday led her own groups until the end of her career.

Holiday's fame blossomed in 1939 during her extended engagement at New York's Café Society, the first interracial nightclub. That year she also recorded (for Commodore Records) "Strange Fruit," a signature ballad about prejudice and lynching in the South. In 1944 Holiday left Columbia to record for Decca. During this time, Holiday's heroin addiction led to several serious legal bouts. She was imprisoned for a year and afterward was prohibited from playing New York nightclubs. Holiday's personal life was also in disarray, owing to her self-destructive attraction to abusive and manipulative men.

Although Holiday's voice was by now worn from years of drugs and drink, her Verve recordings from the '50s capture some of her most moving and nuanced performances. By 1959, Holiday's hard living had caught up to her. On her deathbed, Holiday was arrested for heroin possession in the New York City hospital where she was being treated for kidney disease, and subsequently died.

Jennifer Holliday

Born Oct. 19, 1960, Houston, TX
1983—*Feel My Soul* (Geffen) 1985—*Say You Love Me* 1987—*Get Close to My Love* 1991—*I'm on Your Side* (Arista) 1994—*On & On* (Intersound) 1996—*The Best of Jennifer Holliday* (Geffen).

Jennifer Holliday reached the top of the pop charts via her show-stopping performance in the hit Broadway musical *Dreamgirls*. The R&B-based singer was raised in Houston by her mother, a grade-school teacher. She began singing as a teenager in the Pleasant Grove Baptist Church choir. Her plans to become a lawyer were forever changed when a member of a touring production of *A Chorus Line* saw her in a Houston play and paid for her flight to New York to audition for *Your Arms Too Short to Box With God*. Holliday got the lead.

In 1981 the singer was cast as Effie in *Dreamgirls*, the musical based loosely on the Supremes. (Ex-Supreme Mary Wilson, who maintained that the musical was emotionally if not factually true, titled her subsequent best-selling autobiography *Dreamgirl: My Life as a Supreme*.) Her performance of "And I Am Telling You I'm Not Going" (#22 pop, #1 R&B, 1982) won Holliday a Tony and a Grammy (the single appeared on the *Dreamgirls* soundtrack). Holliday became an overnight sensation, the incredible vocalist with no formal training and a downhome demeanor, the large-bodied, upstart ingenue who had walked out on director Michael Bennett *(Chorus Line)* during rehearsals for *Dreamgirls*. Geffen signed Holliday and in 1983 released *Feel My Soul* (#31), which yielded the hit "I Am Love" (#2 R&B, 1983), as well as the single "Just Let Me Wait" (#24 R&B, 1983).

In 1984 Holliday sang on the Foreigner hit "I Want to Know What Love Is." In 1985 she returned to the stage in *Sing, Mahalia, Sing*. But *Say You Love Me*, released that year, yielded only a few minor R&B hits that failed to cross over to the pop charts (although the album's cover of Duke Ellington's "Come Sunday" did earn Holliday her second Grammy, for best inspirational performance).

Geffen dropped Holliday and Arista signed her. *I'm on Your Side* (#29 R&B, 1991) paired Holliday with established writers (Diane Warren, Angela Bofill, Narada Michael Walden) and producers (Barry Eastmond, Michael Powell), but fared little better than its predecessors, despite Holliday's much-vaunted new svelte image. The title track reached #10 on the R&B chart in 1991.

In 1994 Holliday released a gospel LP on which she openly acknowledged her stylistic debt to Aretha Franklin. Holliday then returned to Broadway, playing the role of the Teen Angel in a 1995 revival of *Grease*, after which she moved to L.A. to pursue a career in television. She has since had a regular part as a gospel singer on *Ally McBeal*. Holliday also released singles in 1999 and 2000; neither fared as well as her early hits.

The Hollies

Formed 1962, Manchester, Eng.
Graham Nash (b. Feb. 2, 1942, Blackpool, Eng.), gtr., voc.; Allan Clarke (b. Apr. 15, 1942, Salford, Eng.), voc.; Anthony Hicks (b. Dec. 16, 1943, Nelson, Eng.), gtr.; Donald Rathbone (b. Eng.), drums; Eric Haydock (b. Feb. 3, 1943, Manchester), bass.
1963—(– Rathbone; + Robert Elliott [b. Dec. 8, 1942, Burnley, Eng.], drums) 1965—*Here I Go Again* (Imperial); *Hear! Here!* 1966—(– Haydock; + Bernard Calvert [b. Sep. 16, 1943, Burnley, Eng.], bass) *Beat Group!*; *Bus Stop* 1967—*Stop, Stop, Stop; The Hollies' Greatest Hits; Evolution* (Epic); *Dear Eloise/King Midas in Reverse* 1968—(– Nash; + Terry Sylvester [b. Jan. 8, 1945, Liverpool, Eng.], gtr., voc.) 1969—*Words and Music by Bob Dylan; He Ain't Heavy, He's My Brother* 1970—*Moving Finger* 1971—(– Clarke; + Mikael Rikfors [b. Swed.], voc.) *Distant Light* 1972—*Romany* 1973—(– Rickfors; + Clarke) 1974—*Hollies* 1975—*Another Night* 1977—*The Hollies/Clarke, Hicks, Sylvester, Calvert, Elliott* (Epic) (– Clarke) 1978—(+ Clarke) *A Crazy Steal* 1981—(– Sylvester; – Calvert) 1983—(band re-forms: Nash; Elliott; Hicks; Clarke) *What Goes Around . . .* (Atlantic) 1993—*30th Anniversary Collection* (EMI).

After the Beatles, the Hollies were the most consistently successful singles band in Britain, and their string of hits extended into the '70s.

The Hollies: Bernie Calvert, Graham Nash, Tony Hicks, Allan Clarke, Bobby Elliott

The group was formed by childhood friends Allan Clarke and Graham Nash, who had worked together as the Two Teens, Ricky and Dane, and the Guytones. They became the Deltas with the addition of Don Rathbone and Eric Haydock, then the Hollies after Tony Hicks joined them. The group was named after Buddy Holly. By late 1963, they had British Top 20 hits with covers of the Coasters' "Searchin' " and Maurice Williams and the Zodiacs' "Stay." Around this time they also wrote a book, *How to Run a Beat Group.*

With Clarke on lead vocals and Nash leading the harmonies, the Hollies had a string of U.K. hits that included "Just One Look," "Here I Go Again," "We're Through" (1964), "Yes I Will," "I'm Alive" (their first British #1), and "Look Through Any Window" (1965). The latter was one of the several singles that entered the U.S. chart, but it wasn't until "Bus Stop" (#5) in 1966 that the group cracked the U.S. Top 10. Over the next several months, their U.S. hits included "Stop Stop Stop" (#7, 1966), "Carrie-Anne" (#9, 1967), "On a Carousel" (#11, 1967), and "Pay You Back With Interest" (#28, 1967).

In the late '60s the Hollies shifted to more experimental rock. The results—*Stop! Stop! Stop!, Evolution, Dear Eloise/ King Midas in Reverse*—didn't establish them as an album group. Nash, one of the group's main writers, quit in late 1968. He was reportedly upset that the band was recording an entire LP of Dylan covers *(Words and Music by Bob Dylan)* and yet had refused to record several of his own songs, including "Marrakesh Express," a hit for his next band, Crosby, Stills and Nash.

The Hollies advertised in British trade papers for Nash's replacement and found Terry Sylvester, who stayed with the group until 1981. In 1970 "He Ain't Heavy, He's My Brother" hit #7, but within a year Clarke was forced out because of personality clashes with other band members. This left Hicks the only original member. Clarke briefly pursued a solo career *(My Real Name Is 'Arold* and *Headroom),* only to rejoin the group in 1973 after his replacement, Swedish vocalist Mikael Rikfors, was fired because his thickly accented lead vocals sounded strange onstage. Rikfors has since had a very successful career in Scandinavia; among the artists who have recorded his compositions are Cyndi Lauper, Richie Havens, and Santana.

The Hollies had their biggest U.S. hit with "Long Cool Woman (in a Black Dress)" (#2, 1972) and hit a second peak with "The Air That I Breathe" (#6, 1974). In 1977 Clarke again quit the band and released another solo LP *(I Wasn't Born Yesterday),* yet returned to the group for *A Crazy Steal.* Epic dropped the Hollies in 1979. Their last group effort was a 1980 British LP entitled *Buddy Holly,* released in conjunction with Paul McCartney's Buddy Holly Week. In 1983 Nash, Clarke, Elliott, and Hicks re-formed to record *What Goes Around . . . ,* which produced a Top 30 version of the Supremes' "Stop! In the Name of Love." Since then, Allan, Hicks, and Elliott have continued to tour, while 1993 saw those three plus Sylvester and original bassist Haydock record two new tracks: "Nothing Else But Love," written by Richard Marx; and Nik Kershaw's "The Woman I Love," a #42 hit in England. The Hollies reunited with Nash again to record a track for a 1996 Buddy Holly tribute album, in which their voices harmonized with a tape of Holly's. "He Ain't Heavy, He's My Brother," reissued in 1988, topped the British chart.

Buddy Holly and the Crickets

Born Charles Hardin Holley, Sep. 7, 1936, Lubbock, TX; died Feb. 3, 1959, near Clear Lake, IA
Crickets: (The Crickets were Buddy Holly's backup group until late 1958, when they went their separate ways. See text. The Crickets remained active following Holly's death.)
Formed ca. 1955, Lubbock, TX: Sonny Curtis (b. May 9, 1937, Meadow, TX), gtr.; Don Guess, bass; Jerry Allison (b. Aug. 31, 1939, Hillsboro, TX), drums.
The Crickets also included, at various times: Niki Sullivan (b. 1939), gtr.; Joe Mauldin, bass; Tommy Allsup, gtr.; Glen Hardin (b. May 18, 1939, Wellington, TX), piano; Jerry Naylor (b. Mar. 6, 1939, Stephenville, TX), voc.; Waylon Jennings (b. June 15, 1937, Littlefield, TX), gtr.
1957—*Chirpin' Crickets* (Brunswick) 1959—*The Buddy Holly Story* (Coral) 1963—*Reminiscing* 1964—*Showcase* 1978—*The Buddy Holly Story* soundtrack (Epic); *20 Golden Greats* (MCA) 1985—*Legend* 1993—*The Buddy Holly Collection.*

Buddy Holly

Buddy Holly was a rock pioneer. He wrote his own material; used the recording studio for doubletracking and other advanced techniques; popularized the two guitars, bass, and drums lineup; and recorded a catalogue of songs that continue to be covered: "Not Fade Away," "Rave On," "That'll Be the Day," and others. His playful, mock-ingenuous singing, with slides between falsetto and regular voice and a trademark "hiccup," has been a major influence on Bob Dylan, Paul McCartney, and numerous imitators. When he died in an airplane crash at 22, he had been recording rock & roll for less than two years.

Holly learned to play the piano, fiddle, and guitar at an early age. He was five when he won $5 for singing "Down the River of Memories" at a local talent show. In the early '50s he formed the country-oriented Western and Bop Band with high school friends Bob Montgomery and Larry Welborn. Between late 1953 and 1955 they performed on local radio station KDAV and recorded demos and garage tapes, several of which were posthumously released as *Holly in the Hills*. By 1956 (after Holly had dropped the *e* from his last name), the group's reputation on the Southwestern country circuit led to a contract to cut country singles in Nashville for Decca. The label didn't think much of Montgomery, who graciously bowed out, insisting that Holly accept the deal. With Sonny Curtis and Bob Guess, Holly cut "Blue Days, Black Nights" b/w "Love Me," billed as Holly and the Two Tunes. Like subsequent pure country releases ("Modern Don Juan," "Midnight Shift," and "Girl On My Mind"), it went unnoticed. One of his last recordings for the label (which Decca refused to release) was "That'll Be the Day," a song that in a later rock version became one of Holly's first hits. During this period, Holly began writing prolifically. Typical of his romantic fare was a song that began as "Cindy Lou" but was changed to "Peggy Sue" at new Cricket Jerry Allison's suggestion. ("Peggy Sue" was the future Mrs. Allison; they've since divorced.) It eventually became one of Holly's biggest hits.

Following the failed sessions with Decca, Holly and his friends returned to Lubbock. In 1956 and 1957 Holly and drummer Allison played as a duo at the Lubbock Youth Center and shared bills with well-known stars as they passed through the area. Once they opened for a young Elvis Presley (Holly later said, "We owe it all to Elvis"), who influenced Holly's move into rock & roll.

On February 25, 1957, Holly and the newly named Crickets drove 90 miles west to producer Norman Petty's studio in Clovis, New Mexico, to cut a demo. Their rocking version of "That'll Be the Day" attracted a contract from the New York–based Coral/Brunswick label, and it rose to #1 by September. As with many of Holly's early hits, producer Petty picked up a cowriter's credit. The song's success prompted the Crickets' first national tour in late 1957. Several promoters (including those at the Apollo Theatre in New York, where Holly and his group became one of the first white acts to appear) were surprised that the group was white.

Under a contractual arrangement worked out by Petty (who quickly became Holly's manager), some discs were credited to the Crickets, while others bore only Holly's name. His first hit under the latter arrangement was "Peggy Sue" (#3, 1957), which also became one of several big hits in England, where he toured to much acclaim in 1958. "Oh, Boy!," released at year's end by the Crickets, hit #10. By 1958, Holly had reached the Top 40 with "Maybe Baby" (#17), "Think It Over" (#27), "Early in the Morning" (#32), and "Rave On" (#37).

In October 1958 Holly left Petty and the Crickets (who continued on their own), moved to Greenwich Village, and married Puerto Rico–born Maria Elena Santiago after having proposed to her on their first date. His split from Petty (who died in 1984) led to legal problems, which tied up his finances and prompted Holly to reluctantly join the Winter Dance Party Tour of the Midwest in early 1959. He also did some recording in New York; many of the tapes were later overdubbed and released posthumously. During that last tour, Holly was supported by ex-Cricket guitarist Tommy Allsup and future country superstar Waylon Jennings (whose first record, "Jolé Blon," Holly produced).

Tired of riding the bus, and in order to get his laundry done, Holly, along with a couple of the tour's other featured performers, the Big Bopper and Ritchie Valens, chartered a private plane after their Clear Lake, Iowa, show to take them to Moorhead, Minnesota. Piloted by Roger Peterson, the small Beechcraft Bonanza took off from the Mason City, Iowa, airport at about 2:00 a.m. on February 3, 1959, and crashed a few minutes later, killing all on board.

Holly's death was marked by the release of "It Doesn't Matter Anymore" (#13, 1959), which topped the U.K. chart for six consecutive weeks. In his wake, Holly left behind enough old demos and uncompleted recordings to fill several posthumous collections. A 1978 feature film, *The Buddy*

Holly Story (starring Gary Busey), revived interest in Holly's life and career.

The Crickets continued on as a group through 1965, with a variety of personnel revolving around Allison, Curtis, and Glen D. Hardin. This lineup had some minor U.S. success but, like Holly, the Crickets were most popular in England, where they had three early-'60s hits—"Love's Made a Fool of You," "Don't Ever Change," and "My Little Girl"—the latter of which was included in the British film *Just for Fun*. The Crickets later costarred with Lesley Gore in *The Girls on the Beach*. As the '60s progressed, the Crickets' activities became more sporadic and included a Holly tribute album recorded with Bobby Vee. It was Vee who had filled Holly's spot on the ill-fated 1959 tour.

In 1973 Hardin left to join Elvis Presley's band (he would later join Emmylou Harris' Hot Band). Around this time the Crickets recorded an album with a lineup that included Allison, Curtis, and English musicians Rick Grech and Albert Lee (another future Hot Band member). Curtis and Mauldin regrouped the original Crickets in 1977 to perform in England for Buddy Holly Week (sponsored by Paul McCartney, who had just purchased the entire Holly song catalogue).

Some of the Crickets have had solo careers. In 1958 Allison released "Real Wild Child" for Coral Records (with Holly on lead guitar) under the nom de disc of Ivan. Curtis, who wrote Holly's "Rock Around With Ollie Vee," went on to write "I Fought the Law" (covered by the Bobby Fuller Four and the Clash), "Walk Right Back" (for the Everly Brothers, for whom Curtis played lead guitar off and on throughout the '60s), and the theme song of *The Mary Tyler Moore Show*. He has made solo albums since 1958 for A&M, Mercury, Coral, Liberty, Imperial, and other labels. By the early '80s, he was still active with Elektra/Asylum, for which he released the single "The Real Buddy Holly Story" as a response to the Hollywood biopic, which he and others criticized as being factually inaccurate.

In 1986 Holly was one of the first inductees into the Rock and Roll Hall of Fame; seven years later he was honored with his own postage stamp. In 1988 the Crickets released a new album, *Three Piece*, on Jerry Allison's Rollercoaster label. Again they played the Buddy Holly Week festival that year; McCartney joined them onstage. In 1989 the musical *Buddy: The Buddy Holly Story* opened on London's West End; it ran on Broadway in 1990, and as of this writing continues its London run. It has starred Brits as well as Americans in the role of Buddy Holly, including U.S. actor Paul Hipp and musician Robert Burke Warren [see the Fleshtones entry]. In 1996 MCA released *Not Fade Away: Remembering Buddy Holly*, featuring contributions from Waylon Jennings, Los Lobos, the Band, the Crickets, and others, as well as a "duet" between Holly and namesake the Hollies. Three years later the Buddy Holly Museum opened in Lubbock.

Holy Modal Rounders

Formed 1963, New York, NY
Peter Stampfel (b. Oct. 29, 1938, Milwaukee, WI), banjo, fiddle, voc.; Steve Weber (b. June 22, 1942, Philadelphia, PA), gtr., voc.
1964—*The Holy Modal Rounders* (Prestige); *Holy Modal Rounders 2* 1967—*Indian War Whoop* (ESP) 1969—*The Moray Eels Eat the Holy Modal Rounders* (Elektra); *Good Taste Is Timeless* (Metromedia) 1972—*Stampfel and Weber* (Fantasy) 1975—*Alleged in Their Own Time* (Rounder) 1976—*Last Round* (Adelphi) 1981—*Goin' Nowhere Fast* (Rounder); *Have Moicy* (as the Unholy Modal Rounders) 1998—*Holy Modal Rounders, 1 & 2* (Fantasy) 1999—*Too Much Fun!*
Peter Stampfel solo: 1986—*Peter Stampfel and the Bottlecaps* (Rounder) 1989—*The People's Republic of Rock 'n' Roll* (Homestead) 1995—*You Must Remember This* (Gert Town) 2001—*I Make a Wish for a Potato.*

The Holy Modal Rounders, a loose group centering on Peter Stampfel and Steve Weber, are gonzo traditionalists who mix old folk and bluegrass tunes with their own bouncy, absurdist free associations. The Rounders' closest brush with commercial success came when their "If You Wanna Be a Bird" appeared on the *Easy Rider* movie soundtrack, but such songs as "Boobs a Lot" and "My Mind Capsized" kept folk rock from taking itself too seriously.

Stampfel was previously with folk groups like MacGrundy's Old Timey Wool Thumpers. He and Weber met in 1963 on the East Coast. They recorded albums for Prestige and then began working with the Fugs [see entry] and contributed to the Fugs' first record on the Broadside label.

In 1965 the groups went their separate ways; Stampfel formed the Moray Eels, and Weber revived the Rounders moniker and added other musicians for the first time (including playwright Sam Shepard, who played drums and wrote songs) for *Indian War Whoop* on ESP. They also scored Shepard's play *Operation Sidewinder*. Around the same time, the group's free-flowing lineup also briefly included Jeff "Skunk" Baxter, later with Steely Dan and the Doobie Brothers.

In the early '70s their *Good Taste Is Timeless*, featuring "Boobs a Lot," got some FM airplay. Shortly thereafter, Fantasy Records released *Stampfel and Weber*, followed in 1975 by a reunion LP, *Alleged in Their Own Time*, on Rounder Records (named in their honor). In late 1981, still folk-cult favorites, Stampfel and Weber did some East Coast dates as a duo to support *Goin' Nowhere Fast*, and Stampfel has continued to appear around New York City with his group, the Bottle Caps. In 1999 the two reunited as Holy Modal Rounders for *Too Much Fun!*

Hoodoo Gurus

Formed 1981, Sydney, Austral.
Dave Faulkner (b. Oct. 2, 1954, Perth, Austral.), voc., gtr.; Brad Shepherd (b. Feb. 1, 1961, Sydney), gtr., voc.; Clyde Bramley, bass; James Baker, drums.
1983—*Stoneage Romeos* (A&M) 1985—(– Baker; + Mark Kingsmill [b. Dec. 4, 1956, Sydney], drums) *Mars Needs Guitars!* (Big Time/Elektra) 1987—*Blow Your Cool!* 1988—

(– Bramley; + Rick Grossman [b. Nov. 2, 1955, Sydney], bass) 1989—*Magnum Cum Louder* (RCA) 1991—*Kinky* 1992—*Electric Soup* 1994—*Crank* (Zoo/BMG) 1996—*Blue Cave.*

Aussie pub rockers the Hoodoo Gurus built their music from the debris of American pop culture—everything from garage-band pop to science-fiction B movies. But while their unique sensibility earned them critical favor and a college-radio following, wide U.S. appeal eluded them.

Le Hoodoo Gurus, as they were originally called, formed in a friend's living room as a five-piece band, including ex-Scientists Rod Radalj and James Baker. Singer Dave Faulkner was the group's sole continuous member; he first came to musical infamy in 1979 with the underground hit "Television Addict" by his Perth band the Victims.

By their debut album the Hoodoos were a four-piece, with Faulkner's wacky pop songs braced by Brad Shepherd's junk-metal guitar. *Stoneage Romeos* (which was dedicated to, among others, Arnold [the Pig] Ziffel from the 1960s TV sitcom *Green Acres*) introduced the band's offbeat take in songs like "(Let's All) Turn On," "I Want You Back," "I Was a Kamikaze Pilot," and "Leilani." The album was a critical and college-radio smash Down Under and well received in America. Shortly after its U.S. release, Mark Kingsmill joined the band. With the first single from *Mars Needs Guitars!*, the Australian Top 20 hit "Bittersweet," Faulkner showed a more sensitive, serious side. But on "Like Wow—Wipeout" the Hoodoo Gurus' sound was reminiscent of '60s garage rockers, while the title track paid homage to their hankering for sci-fi kitsch.

Constant touring brought the Hoodoos to the U.S. and Europe. The Bangles helped them with one of their biggest singles, "What's My Scene," from 1987's *Blow Your Cool!;* the women also sang on the album track "Good Times." On the East Coast, the band became buddies with New York's Fleshtones (who in the '90s would release an album on Faulkner's Australian indie label). Rick Grossman, formerly of the Divinyls, joined in 1988. *Magnum Cum Louder* gave the band three alternative club hits: "Come Anytime," "Another World," and "Baby Can Dance." The album's title ironically addressed the band's reluctant pigeonholing into the college-radio market; the track "Where's That Hit?," ostensibly about baseball, is clearly autobiographical. *Kinky* featured the Hoodoo Gurus' paean to '60s sexuality, "Miss Freelove '69," but the album failed to make a dent on the charts. Three years later, the band resurfaced with *Crank,* released several months earlier in Australia. Produced by Ed Stasium, the hard-rocking album included guest backing vocals from ex-Bangle Vicki Peterson and New York City chanteuse Wendy Wild.

After releasing *Blue Cave* in 1996, the Hoodoos called it quits, but not before embarking on a final Australian tour. Faulkner went on to work on soundtracks and musicals while Grossman started playing with the Ghostwriters.

The Hoodoo Gurus: Dave Faulkner, Brad Shephard, Mark Kingsmill, Rick Grossman

John Lee Hooker

Born Aug. 22, 1917, Vance, MS; died June 21, 2001, Los Altos, CA
1961—*John Lee Hooker Plays and Sings the Blues* (Chess) 1962—*Folklore of John L. Hooker* (Vee Jay) 1966—*It Serves You Right* (Impulse) 1968—*Urban Blues* (Stateside) 1970—*No Friend Around* (Red Lightnin'); *Alone, vol. 1* (Labor) 1971—*Coast to Coast* (United Artists); *Endless Boogie; Hooker 'n' Heat* (with Canned Heat) (Liberty); *Goin' Down Highway 51* (Specialty) 1972—*Boogie Chillen* (Fantasy); *Never Get Out of These Blues Alive* 1974—*Best of* (Crescendo); *Don't Turn Me From Your Door* (Atco) 1975—*John Lee Hooker* (New World) 1978—*The Cream* (Tomato) 1981—*Hooker Alone, vol. 1* (Labor) 1982—*Hooker Alone, vol. 2* 1987—*Jealous* (Pausa); *The Best of John Lee Hooker* (GNP Crescendo) 1989—*The Healer* (Chameleon) 1991—*Mr. Lucky* (Charisma); *The Ultimate Collection 1948–1990* (Rhino) 1992—*Boom Boom* (Charisma) 1993—*John Lee Hooker on Vee-Jay 1955–1958* (Vee-Jay) 1995—*Chill Out* (Pointblank) 1997—*Don't Look Back* 1998—*The Best of Friends.*

Blues musician John Lee Hooker helped define the post–World War II electric blues with his one-chord boogie compositions and his rhythmic electric guitar work. His deep voice was inimitable. Historically, he was one of the great links between the blues and rock & roll.

Hooker was one of 11 children. He sang at church in Clarksdale, Mississippi. His first musical instrument was an inner tube stretched across a barn door. In his adolescence he was taught rudimentary guitar technique by his stepfather, William Moore, who often performed at local fish fries, dances, and other social occasions in the late '20s; another early influence was Blind Lemon Jefferson. In 1931 Hooker went to Memphis, where he worked as an usher at the Daisy Theater on Beale Street. He moved to Cincinnati in 1933 and sang with gospel groups like the Big Six, the Delta Big Four, and the Fairfield Four.

His career eventually took root in Detroit in the late '30s. He began recording in the late '40s. Hooker was exclusively a singles artist for his first few very prolific years. His first release, "Boogie Chillen," issued on the Modern label, was an instant million-seller and a jukebox hit. "I'm in the Mood" sold a million copies in 1951; the blues-record market was soon saturated with Hooker material on myriad labels, often released under such pseudonyms as Birmingham Sam, John Lee Booker, Boogie Man, John Lee Cooker, Delta John, Johnny Lee, Texas Slim, and Johnny Williams. His only pop chart entry was with "Boom Boom" (#60, 1962), later recorded by the Animals. In 1959 he cut his first album for Riverside Records and made his debut performance at the Newport Folk Festival. He toured Europe extensively in the early '60s. In the mid-'60s he toured and recorded frequently with Britain's Groundhogs.

By 1970, Hooker was living in Oakland, California. He teamed up with Canned Heat for *Hooker 'n' Heat* (Liberty), which made inroads on the American charts (#73) and abroad. Charlie Musselwhite and Van Morrison joined Hooker in 1972 for *Never Get Out of These Blues Alive,* the release of which roughly coincided with Fantasy's double-LP *Boogie Chillen,* a compilation of early material and previously unreleased tapes from 1962. Hooker continued to tour and record in the '70s and '80s, often opening for rock acts like Canned Heat and Foghat. In 1980 he appeared in *The Blues Brothers* film.

The late '80s brought a renewal of interest in Hooker. British and American rockers, including the Spencer Davis Group, the J. Geils Band, Canned Heat, and George Thorogood, had covered his songs. He sang the title role on Pete Townshend's 1989 album *The Iron Man,* which was based on a children's book. The same year he joined the Rolling Stones for their concerts in Atlantic City, New Jersey. *The Healer* (#62, 1989), which featured guest appearances by Carlos Santana, Robert Cray, Los Lobos, George Thorogood, Canned Heat, and others, was his biggest commercial success. The album spent 38 weeks on the chart. Hooker earned his first Grammy Award for "I'm in the Mood," the album's duet with Bonnie Raitt. In October 1990 New York's Madison Square Garden hosted an all-star concert celebrating Hooker's music. Raitt, Joe Cocker, Huey Lewis, Ry Cooder, Gregg Allman, Willie Dixon, and others joined the bluesman for the occasion. That year he also joined Miles Davis on the Grammy-nominated movie soundtrack *The Hot Spot.* (Davis reportedly called Hooker "the funkiest man alive, buried up to his neck in mud.")

In 1991 Hooker was inducted into the Rock and Roll Hall of Fame; he was nominated for another Grammy for 1991's *Mr. Lucky,* which featured tracks recorded with the Robert Cray Band, Keith Richards, Ry Cooder, Tom Waits, Van Morrison, Johnny Winter, Carlos Santana, and others. His 1992 release *Boom Boom* featured guest guitar work by ex–Fabulous Thunderbird Jimmie Vaughan and blues great Albert Collins.

In early 1995 Hooker announced that he would lighten his touring schedule. Van Morrison, who played on 1995's *Chill Out,* produced 1997's *Don't Look Back,* which features appearances by both Morrison and Los Lobos. *The Best of Friends* rounds up Hooker's numerous superstar collaborations. The first biography about the bluesman, *Boogie Man,* was published in Europe in 1999, and in America the following year. In 2000 Hooker won a Grammy for lifetime achievement. He died in his sleep at the age of 83.

The Hooters

Formed 1980, Philadelphia, PA
Rob Hyman, voc., kybds.; Eric Bazilian, voc., gtr.; John Lilley, gtr.; Fran Smith Jr., bass, voc.; David Uosikkinen, drums.
1983—*Amore* (Antenna) 1985—*Nervous Night* (Columbia) 1987—*One Way Home* 1989—*Zig Zag* 1993—*Out of Body* (MCA) 1994—*Greatest Hits, I* (Sony International); *Greatest Hits, II; The Hooters Live* (MCA International) 1996—*Hooterization* (Sony/Legacy).
Largo (Hyman; Bazilian; + Rick Chertoff, trumpet, drums, sax, voc., perc.): 1998—*Largo* (Blue Gorilla/Mercury).

The Hooters burst onto the charts in the summer of 1985 with *Nervous Night* and a string of moderate hits—"And We Danced" (#21, 1985), "Day by Day" (#12, 1986), and "Where Do the Children Go" (#38, 1986)—that reflected the group's wide-ranging and diverse musical influences and loves. Blending basic rock & roll instrumentation and themes with folk instrumentation (mandolin, dulcimer, accordion, and the melodica, or "hooter," from which they took the group's name), the Hooters forged a unique sound that, since the late '80s, has found a wider audience overseas than in the U.S.

Rob Hyman and Eric Bazilian were members of Baby Grand, a group that cut two albums for Arista in the late '70s and included future producer Rick Chertoff. When that group broke up, Bazilian and Hyman continued writing and doing session work. They arranged for, played on, and provided backing vocals for Cyndi Lauper's 1983 breakthrough album *She's So Unusual,* for which Hyman cowrote the hit single "Time After Time." Shortly thereafter, the duo rounded out the Hooters with three additional musicians. The band released several independent singles and an album, *Amore,* which sold 100,000 copies.

Their debut for Columbia, *Nervous Night* (#12, 1985), went platinum, and its followup, *One Way Home* (#27, 1987), was certified gold, despite a lack of Top 50 singles. By then the Hooters had topped a number of music-magazine polls as best new group and best new live act, but the commercial momentum soon began to let up. *Zig Zag* missed the Hot 100, although a rendition of the folk classic "500 Miles" (featuring Peter, Paul and Mary, who had recorded the song in the early '60s) went to #97 in 1989.

Around the world, however, it was a far different story. In England "Satellite" from *One Way Home* went to #22; it was also a hit in Germany. The group has also earned gold and platinum albums in Japan, Australia, and several European countries. Bazilian and Hyman have continued to work with a number of artists, including Johnny Clegg and Savuka, Taj Mahal, and Sophie B. Hawkins. Most recently, they cowrote and played on Joan Osbourne's 1995 hit album *Relish,* which included the Bazilian-penned single "One of Us." Osbourne, alongside Lauper, the Chieftains, and members of the Band, also appeared on the 1998 self-titled debut by a Largo, a folkier, more ethereal project led by Bazilian, Hyman, and Chertoff. In 1999 Ricky Martin covered Bazilian and Hyman's "Private Emotion" on his self-titled, breakthrough album.

Hootie & the Blowfish

Formed 1986, Columbia, SC
Darius Rucker (b. 1966, Charleston), voc., gtr.; Mark Ryan (b. 1967, Gaithersburg, MD), gtr.; Dean Felber (b. 1967, Gaithersburg), bass; Jim Sonefeld (b. 1965, Chicago, IL), drums.
1991—*Kootchypop* EP (self-released) 1994—*Cracked Rear View* (Atlantic) 1996—*Fairweather Johnson* 1998—*Musical Chairs* 2000—*Scattered, Smothered & Covered.*
Mark Byan solo: 2000—*30 on the Rail* (Atlantic).

Hootie & the Blowfish's major label debut *Cracked Rear View* was released with little fanfare in the fall of 1994. Prior to its release, the Blowfish were an unassuming if easily likeable college bar band with one self-released EP to their credit. But as soon the album's lead single, "Hold My Hand" (#10), took off, both Hootie and *Cracked Rear View* were well on their way into the record books. By 1995, *Cracked Rear View* was a #1 record, destined to sell 16 million copies and become the second highest-selling debut album in history (behind 1976's *Boston*).

The members of Hootie came together while attending the University of South Carolina in Columbia, South Carolina (frontman Darius Rucker, guitarist Mark Ryan, and bassist Dean Felber hooked up in 1986, with fellow student Jim Sonefeld joining on drums three years later). After adopting the nicknames of a couple of their friends (Hootie, Blowfish), the band commenced playing at bars and frat parties throughout the South and East Coast, eventually building up a following that snatched up some 50,000 copies of their 1991 EP *Kootchypop* and as many T-shirts as the band could print up. Impressed by their grassroots success, Atlantic signed the group a couple of years later. While many critics dismissed the breezily catchy folk-rock songs on *Cracked Rear View,* so far removed from the edgy alt rock and grunge still in vogue at the time, radio listeners and record buyers embraced it wholeheartedly. In addition to "Hold My Hand," the album's hits included "Let Her Cry" (#9), "Only Wanna Be With You" (#6), and "Time" (#14). Rucker, who sang in a deep, warm baritone and stood out by being a black man in a predominately white genre, attracted the most media attention; he was the one many inevitably assumed to be "Hootie," with the rest of the group his backup "Blowfish."

Cracked Rear View was still selling strongly when Hootie & the Blowfish released their followup effort, *Fairweather Johnson,* in the spring of 1996. Although it debuted at #1 and eventually went triple platinum, it was considered a commercial disappointment next to its blockbuster predecessor. The album yielded only two modest hits: "Old Man & Me" (#13) and "Tucker's Town" (#38). *Musical Chairs,* released two years later, debuted and peaked at #4.

In 2000 the band issued *Scattered, Smothered & Covered* (#71), a collection of B sides and cover songs, including their take on Led Zeppelin's "Hey Hey What Can I Do" from 1995's *Encomium: A Tribute to Led Zeppelin.* The year also produced the first Hootie-related solo offering, guitarist Mark Bryan's *30 on the Rail.*

Mary Hopkin

Born May 3, 1950, Pontardawe, South Wales
1969—*Postcard* (Apple) 1971—*Earth Song* 1972—*Those Were the Days* 1979—*Welsh World of Mary Hopkin* (Decca); *Kidnapped* 1995—*Those Were the Days—The Best of Mary Hopkin* (Capitol).

Welsh singer Mary Hopkin was briefly an international star in the late '60s. She began singing at age four and was soon taking voice lessons and singing in the Congregational Tabernacle Choir. Hopkin studied music, art, and English at the local grammar school and continued at Cardiff College of Music and Drama. While a student there, she earned extra money by singing in pubs. When she appeared on the BBC-TV variety show *Opportunity Knocks* in 1968, she was spotted by the model Twiggy, who told Paul McCartney about her. McCartney signed her to Apple and supervised her first sessions, which produced "Those Were the Days" (#2, 1968). The song had already been recorded by the Limeliters, who had adapted it from a Russian folk song called "Darogoi Dlimmoya" (Dear for Me), first recorded in the '20s.

Hopkin was 18 years old when her debut album, *Postcard,* was released. McCartney wrote and produced her second single, "Goodbye" (#13, 1969), which hit #2 on the British chart. She then moved on to work with producer Mickie Most. Hopkin enjoyed lesser hits in the early '70s—including "Temma Harbour," "Que Sera, Sera (Whatever Will Be, Will Be)," "Think About Your Children" (1970), and "Knock Knock Who's There" (1972)—and toured a bit.

As an actress, she costarred in 1969 with Tommy Steele in a pantomime production of *Dick Whittington* at the London Palladium and in 1971 appeared with David Essex in *Cinderella* in Manchester. Around the same time, she married British record producer Tony Visconti and began raising a family. Through the mid-'70s her singing career was limited to occasional backup vocals (as Mary Visconti) for Ralph McTell, David Bowie, and Thin Lizzy. In 1976 "If You Love Me," on Visconti's Good Earth label, hit #32 on the English chart. She starred in a 1980 Christmas production of *Rock Nativity* at the Hexagon Theatre in Reading.

In 1981 she and Visconti broke up, and Hopkin, then a mother of two, returned to music. First she briefly joined a British trio, Sundance; then in 1984 she reemerged as lead singer of a group called Oasis (not the '90s Brit-pop band). Its debut album placed in the U.K. Top 25. She performed with the Chieftains on several occasions in the '90s. In 2000 she collaborated with the U.K. group the Crocketts.

Lightnin' Hopkins

Born Mar. 15, 1912, Centerville, TX; died Jan. 30, 1982, Houston, TX
1959—*Lightnin' Hopkins* (Folkways) 1965—*Down Home Blues* (Prestige) 1968—*Texas Blues Man* (Arhoolie) 1970—*Lightnin', vol. 1* (Poppy) 1972—*Double Blues* (Fantasy); *Lonesome Lightnin'* (Carnival) 1976—*All Them Blues* (DJM) 1989—*Texas Blues* (Arhoolie) 1990—*The Gold Star Sessions, vol. 1; The Gold Star Sessions, vol. 2* 1991—*The Complete Prestige/Bluesville Recordings* (Prestige/Bluesville) 1992—*The Complete Candid Recordings of Lightnin' Hopkins and Otis Spann* (Mosaic).

The most frequently recorded traditional blues artist in history (who, paradoxically, did the bulk of his performing as an impoverished street singer), Sam "Lightnin' " Hopkins was a country-blues stylist whose career spanned more than three decades, even though he did not begin in earnest until he was nearing middle age. His solo style, with its irregular verses and voice-and-guitar call-and-response, has roots in the earliest blues.

Born in a small farming community, Hopkins lived virtually his entire life in the Houston area. He was one of six children (his sister and four brothers were also musicians), and at age eight he debuted on a guitarlike instrument fashioned from a cigar box and chicken wire. Subsequently, his brother Joel "John Henry" Hopkins (later a well-known bluesman in his own right) taught him to play guitar. Hopkins dropped out of school to hobo through Texas, playing informally in the streets and jamming with folk legends like Blind Lemon Jefferson, whom he met in the summer of 1920. As the '30s progressed he supported himself primarily as a farmworker, while playing for tips in Texas bars and nightspots. More than once Hopkins found himself working the Houston County Prison Farm's road gang. After drifting for several years he settled in Houston's Third Ward ghetto after World War II and then rarely left.

In 1946 Hopkins and pianist Wilson "Thunder" Smith went to L.A. and cut some sides for the Aladdin label. While there, he gained his Lightnin' moniker. When little came of the Aladdin sessions, he returned to Houston and, backed only by his own guitar, cut "Short Haired Woman" b/w "Big Mama Jump" in 1947 for Gold Star Records. It sold 40,000 copies; and the followup, "Baby Please Don't Go," doubled that figure, beginning two years of local success.

Over the next few years Hopkins recorded prolifically for several companies based in Houston, L.A., and New York. He insisted upon being paid in cash for each studio take, thereby relinquishing his rights to his material (he rarely received royalties on his massive catalogue of work) and causing confusion in his recording legacy. (A complete Hopkins discography would include efforts for over 20 record companies.) His style and stance are represented on reissues and compilation/anthologies like Tradition's *Autobiography* and *Best,* Arhoolie's *Early Recordings,* Prestige's *Greatest Hits,* and others compiled from his hundreds of sides. Among his many compositions were "December 7, 1941," "Don't Embarrass Me, Baby," "Ball of Twine," "I'm Gonna Meet My Baby Somewhere," and "Little Antoinette."

When Texas blues fell from national favor by the mid-'50s, Hopkins' career nosedived, though he did record and perform in Europe, usually solo; sometimes with a backing ensemble. Reduced once again to Houston street singing (perennially working the Dowling Street area), he was saved by the later folk and blues revival and was rediscovered by musicologist and author Sam Charters *(The Country Blues),* who recorded him for Folkways in 1959. That same year, he played the University of California Folk Festival and in 1960 appeared at Carnegie Hall in a show featuring Joan Baez and Pete Seeger. In 1961 Hopkins toured with Clifton Chenier's band and continued to play regularly at Houston nightspots like Irene's and the Sputnik Bar. A 1967 documentary on the singer, *The Blues of Lightnin' Hopkins,* won the Gold Hugo Award at the Chicago Film festival.

Hopkins performed at folk festivals and in rock venues in the late '60s, but was slowed by an auto crackup in 1970 that put his neck in a protective brace. Nevertheless he continued club work on and off through the '70s. In the early '70s he recorded for the Denver-based Tumbleweed Records. Meanwhile, tapes continued to surface on a variety of labels, and in 1972 he contributed to the soundtrack of the feature film *Sounder.* Hopkins remained sporadically active for the rest of the decade, capping his lengthy career with an appearance at Carnegie Hall in spring 1979. He did little recording in his final years but could be seen prowling the Houston streets in his black Cadillac Coupe de Ville. In 1981 he underwent surgery for cancer of the esophagus, which later proved terminal.

Nicky Hopkins

Born Feb. 24, 1944, London, Eng.; died Sep. 6, 1994, Nashville, TN
1966—*Revolutionary Piano* (Columbia, U.K.) 1973—*The Tin Man Was a Dreamer* 1975—*No More Changes* (Mercury).

Studio keyboardist Nicky Hopkins was in and out of groups in Britain and the U.S. beginning in the '60s; Ray Davies wrote the Kinks' "Session Man" in his honor.

Hopkins began playing the piano at age three and studied at the Royal Academy of Music from 1956 to 1960. He joined Screamin' Lord Sutch's Savages in 1960 and two years later moved to the Cyril Davies R&B All-Stars; the two groups included many musicians who would make their names in the British Invasion and its aftermath. Hopkins left Davies in May 1963 because of illness and began work as a session keyboardist after he emerged from the hospital 19 months later. He recorded with the Rolling Stones, the Beatles, the Who, the Small Faces, the Kinks, and other bands, and in 1968 he joined the Jeff Beck Group, which at the time included Rod Stewart and Ron Wood.

In the late '60s he also recorded with his own short-lived group, Sweet Thursday, which included future Cat Stevens guitarist Alun Davies and Jon Mark of the Mark-Almond Band. But after nine months in the Jeff Beck Group, Hopkins joined the Quicksilver Messenger Service in San Francisco and recorded with it on *Shady Grove*. He also recorded with Steve Miller and the Jefferson Airplane, and appeared with the Airplane at the Woodstock Festival.

In the '70s Hopkins returned to work as a sideman, touring with the Rolling Stones (he appears on "Jumpin' Jack Flash" and "Sympathy for the Devil" and the albums *Let It Bleed, Exile on Main Street,* and *Black and Blue*) in 1972 and sporadically with the Jerry Garcia Band, and backing Graham Parker and others on records. His attempt at a solo career in the mid-'70s was widely ignored. In 1979 he joined the group Night, which had a hit single that year with "Hot Summer Nights," but quit soon after. He then moved to Northern California, where he kept a low profile. He later moved to Nashville, where he died of complications from previous intestinal surgeries.

Bruce Hornsby and the Range

Formed 1984, Los Angeles, CA
Bruce Hornsby (b. Bruce Randall Hornsby, Nov. 23, 1954, Richmond, VA), voc., kybds.; David Mansfield, violin, mandolin, gtr.; George Marinelli Jr., gtr.; Joe Puerta, bass; John Molo, drums.
1986—*The Way It Is* (RCA) 1988—(– Mansfield; + Peter Harris, gtr., mandolin) *Scenes From the Southside* 1990—(– Harris) *A Night on the Town.*
Hornsby solo: 1993—*Harbor Lights* (RCA) 1995—*Hot House* 1998—*Spirit Trail* 2000—*Here Come the Noise Makers.*

Pianist and singer Bruce Hornsby spent years writing and playing for other artists before his own band, the Range, broke through in 1986 with "The Way It Is," an antiracism song that became a #1 pop single. Hornsby's increased visibility made his eclectic, jazz-influenced skills even more highly sought after; numerous and diverse popular acts enlisted his support, solidifying his reputation as a musician's musician. Meanwhile, Hornsby's recordings with the Range, which mixed roots-rock textures with mellow R&B overtones, continued to appeal to a core audience of adult-contemporary and album-oriented rock fans.

Raised in Williamsburg, Virginia, the lanky Hornsby played varsity basketball in high school and dreamed of a professional athletic career. His piano studies sidetracked him, though, and Hornsby wound up studying at Boston's Berklee College of Music, and earning his degree from the University of Miami's School of Music in 1977. In 1980, with a band including his older brother, Bob, and drummer John Molo, Hornsby moved to L.A. There, he and his younger brother, John, were hired as contract writers for 20th Century–Fox. (Hornsby eventually cowrote with his brothers several songs for his albums.) Hornsby also did session work and toured in Sheena Easton's band. By 1984, the Range's original lineup was complete and eager to be signed. At first, though, even the pushing of early supporter Huey Lewis, a big star at the time, proved futile; but then a demo of songs performed acoustically by Hornsby attracted major-label interest.

The Way It Is, fueled by the title track, reached #3 (also #1 Adult Contemporary) and spawned the additional hits "Mandolin Rain" (#4 pop, #1 Adult Contemporary, 1987) and "Every Little Kiss" (#14, 1987). Subsequently, Hornsby and the Range collected a Grammy for Best New Artist. A sophomore album, 1988's *Scenes From the Southside,* reached #5 and yielded the #5 pop single "The Valley Road" (#1 Adult Contemporary) and the #35 followup "Look Out Any Window." Then 1990's *A Night on the Town* peaked at #20 and produced the #18 single "Across the River," which featured Jerry Garcia on guitar.

Meanwhile, Hornsby tickled the ivories on albums by Bob Dylan, Robbie Robertson, Bonnie Raitt, and Squeeze, among others. He cowrote and played on Don Henley's 1989 hit "End of the Innocence," and toured extensively with the Grateful Dead, putting in 18 months with the band after keyboardist Brent Mydland's death in 1990.

In 1993, after disbanding the Range—keeping Molo as his drummer and adding bassist Jimmy Haslip to his core backing band—Hornsby released the solo album *Harbor Lights* (#46), featuring appearances by Raitt, Garcia, Phil Collins, Pat Metheny, and Branford Marsalis. The disc offered "Fields of Gray" (#69), a reflection on Hornsby's new parenthood of twin sons. Two years later he returned with the eclectic *Hot House,* with guest artists Garcia, Metheny, Chaka Khan, and bluegrass banjo virtuoso Béla Fleck. The album produced the upbeat "Walk in the Sun" (#54, 1995). Meanwhile, Hornsby continued playing live, both as a headliner and as a supporting player for friends such as Raitt as well as on the festival circuit. His solo sets were often jazzy and improvisational, and a focus on jams was prominent on the 1998 two-CD studio set *Spirit Trail.* In 1998 longtime drummer Molo tired of Hornsby's intensive touring schedule and took an extensive break from performing.

Johnny Horton

Born Apr. 3, 1925, Los Angeles, CA; died Nov. 5, 1960, Milano, TX
1959—*The Spectacular Johnny Horton* (Columbia) 1960—

Johnny Horton Makes History; Johnny Horton's Greatest Hits 1971—*The World of Johnny Horton* 1989—*American Originals.*

Johnny Horton was one of the first country & western singers to cross over onto the pop chart. His "The Battle of New Orleans" was a #1 hit in 1959.

Sources disagree as to where and when Horton was born (some claim April 30, 1927, or November 30, 1929, and Tyler, Texas, is sometimes stated as his place of birth). His mother taught him to play guitar at an early age, and he later attended Seattle University, where he majored in petroleum engineering and dabbled in songwriting. After traveling around Alaska and Louisiana, he started performing in clubs and on Pasadena radio station KXLA, billed as the Singing Fisherman.

In 1951 Horton moved to Shreveport, Louisiana, where for eight years he was a star attraction on *The Louisiana Hayride* radio show. He began recording in 1951 but had little success until his move to Columbia Records. There his version of Jimmie Driftwood's "Battle of New Orleans" hit in 1959; it was also a hit for Lonnie Donegan in England (#2, 1959). Horton's subsequent hits included "Johnny Reb" (#54, 1959), "Sink the Bismarck" (#3, 1960), and "North to Alaska" (#4, 1960), the title song to a John Wayne film. Around 1960 Horton, an avid believer in the occult, became convinced his death was imminent. He rescheduled engagements frequently, but perhaps not often enough, for while returning home from a performance at the Skyline in Austin he was killed in a car accident. By strange coincidence, the Skyline had been the site of Hank Williams' last performance, and Horton's widow, Billy Jean, had been married to Williams as well.

Hot Chocolate

Formed 1970, London, Eng.
Errol Brown (b. Jam.), voc.; Patrick Olive (b. Grenada), gtr., perc., bass; Larry Ferguson (b. Nassau), kybds.; Harvey Hinsley (b. Mitcham, Eng.), gtr.; Ian King, drums; Tony Wilson (b. Trinidad), bass, voc.
1973—(– King; + Tony Connor [b. Romford, Eng.], drums) 1974—*Cicero Park* (Big Tree) 1975—*Hot Chocolate* (– Wilson) 1976—*Man to Man* 1977—*10 Greatest Hits* 1978—*Every 1's a Winner* (Infinity) 1979—*Going Through the Motions* 1980—*Mystery* (EMI) 1993—*Every 1's a Winner: The Very Best of Hot Chocolate* 1995—*The Rest of, the Best of Hot Chocolate* 2000—*Hot Chocolate Collection.*

This Caribbean-British interracial soul band had '70s hits with social-comment dance tunes. Their biggest one in America was "You Sexy Thing" (#3, 1976), and their "Brother Louie" (a Top 10 hit for them in England in 1973) became a #1 hit for Stories in America the same year. The London-based band got its first contract with the Beatles' Apple label, for which it released a reggae-style version of John Lennon's "Give Peace a Chance" (1970). Hot Chocolate then worked with producer Mickie Most, concentrating on singles. It established itself in the U.K. in the early '70s with moderately successful releases like "Love Is Life" (#6 U.K., 1970) and "I Believe (in Love)" (#8 U.K., 1971). "Emma" (#8 U.S., #3 U.K., 1975) finally broke the group stateside in early 1975, followed by "Disco Queen" (#28, 1975) and "You Sexy Thing."

Errol Brown and Tony Wilson wrote most of Hot Chocolate's songs, and in the early '70s their compositions were covered by Mary Hopkin, Peter Noone (Herman's Hermits), April Wine, and Suzi Quatro. But in 1975 Wilson left the group for a solo career (his solo debut, "I Like Your Style," came out in 1976). Hot Chocolate persevered with 1976's *Man to Man*, which expanded its considerable following in Europe. The group enjoyed moderate U.S. success with "Don't Stop It Now" (#42, 1976), "So You Win Again" (#31, 1977), "Going Through the Motions" (#53, 1979), and "Are You Getting Enough Happiness" (#65, 1982). Brown and company cracked the U.S. Top 10 again in early 1979 with "Every 1's a Winner" (#6).

Hot Chocolate remained popular in the U.K., charting with "Girl Crazy" (#7 U.K., 1982) and "It Started With a Kiss" (#5 U.K., 1982); when Brown quit for a solo career in 1987, the band broke up. Ten years later, Hot Chocolate found itself reheated as "You Sexy Thing" was prominently featured in two hit movies—*Boogie Nights* and *The Full Monty*—and a TV commercial for Burger King.

Hothouse Flowers

Formed 1986, Dublin, Ire.
Liam O'Maonlai (b. Nov. 7, 1964, Dublin), voc., kybds., harmonica; Fiachna O'Braonain (b. Nov. 27, 1965, Dublin), gtr.; Peter O'Toole (b. Apr. 1, 1965, Dublin), bass, bouzouki; Jerry Fehily (b. Aug. 29, 1963, Bishops Town, Ire.), drums; Leo Barnes (b. Oct. 5, 1965, Dublin), sax.
1988—*People* (London) 1990—*Home* 1993—*Songs From the Rain* (PolyGram) 1995—(– Fehily; – Barnes) 1998—*Born* (London, U.K.).

Hothouse Flowers has endeared itself to modern rock fans with a rootsy, passionate pop hybrid incorporating elements of traditional Irish folk music and American blues and gospel. Singer Liam O'Maonlai and guitarist Fiachna O'Braonain met in grade school, started playing together as teenagers, and quit college in 1985 to become the Incomparable Benzini Brothers, an acclaimed street-performance act that, after the addition of a bassist, drummer, and sax player, evolved into Hothouse Flowers. In 1986 the fledgling musicians were spotted on Irish television by U2's Bono, who immediately offered them support.

The following year, Hothouse Flowers released its first single on U2's own label, Mother Records, a feat that attracted the interest of many major record companies. The band soon landed a deal with PolyGram's London label. Its 1988 debut album, *People*, reached the top of the Irish chart within a week and went to #2 in England. In America, though, *People* would reach only #88, and two subsequent albums would make even less of an impression. Its failure to transcend cult status in the U.S. notwithstanding, Hothouse Flowers nevertheless drew critical praise for its warm sound, and particularly for O'Maonlai's raw, soulful vocals, which inspired comparisons to Van Morrison and Bruce Springsteen.

After a long world tour that ended in 1994, the members took a nearly two-year break. During this period, O'Maonlai formed a trio called alt with ex–Split Enz/Crowded House creative force Tim Finn and songwriter Andy White. The trio released an album called *altitude* in 1995, and toured behind it. Meanwhile, O'Braonain and O'Toole recorded and toured with singer Michelle Shocked. When the Hothouse Flowers members got together to discuss the future of the band in late 1995, drummer Fehily and saxophonist Barnes were let go, as the remaining trio decided to experiment with a harder-edged sound. O'Toole switched instruments, from bass to rhythm guitar and mandolin, and the re-formed group released *Born* in Europe in 1998. O'Maonlai planned to record a solo album of traditional Irish music in 2000.

Hot Tuna

Officially split from Jefferson Airplane, 1972
Jorma Kaukonen (b. Dec. 23, 1940, Washington, DC), gtr., voc.; Jack Casady (b. Apr. 13, 1944, Washington, DC), bass.
1970—*Hot Tuna* (RCA) (+ Will Scarlet, harmonica) 1971—*First Pull Up—Then Pull Down* (+ Papa John Creach [b. May 28, 1917, Beaver Falls, PA; d. Feb. 22, 1994, Los Angeles, CA], elec. violin; + Sammy Piazza, drums) 1972—(– Scarlett) *Burgers* (Grunt) 1974—(– Creach) *The Phosphorescent Rat* 1975—(– Piazza; + Bob Steeler, drums) *America's Choice; Yellow Fever* 1976—*Hoppkorv* 1977—(– Steeler) 1978—*Double Dose* (+ Nick Buck, kybds.) 1979—*Final Vinyl* 1984—*Splashdown* (Relix) 1985—*Historic Hot Tuna* 1989—(+ Harvey Sorgan [b. Apr. 16 1957, Rockville Centre, NY], drums) 1990—(+ Michael Falzarano [b. May 22, 1951, Brooklyn, NY], gtr., mandolin, harmonica, voc.); *Pair a Dice Found* (Epic) 1992—(+ Pete Sears [b. May 27, 1948, Bromley, Eng.], kybds.) *Live at Sweetwater* (Relix) 1993—*Live at Sweetwater Two* 1996—*Classic Acoustic; Classic Electric* 1996—*Hot Tuna in a Can* (RCA) 1997—*Splashdown Two* (Relix) 1998—*Live in Japan; The Best of Hot Tuna* (RCA) 1999—*And Furthermore . . .* (Arista).
Jorma Kaukonen solo: 1974—*Quah* (Grunt) 1979—*Jorma* (RCA) 1980—*Barbeque King* 1985—*Too Hot to Handle* (Relix); *Magic* 1995—*Magic Two; The Land of Heroes* (American Heritage/Relix) 1996—*Christmas* 1999—*Too Many Years.*

Jack Casady and Jorma Kaukonen, original recording members of the Jefferson Airplane, grew up together in northwest Washington, DC. After high school Kaukonen headed for the Philippines to join his relocated government-service parents and traveled in the Orient before moving to San Francisco and working as a folkie. He soon fell in with the Airplane and called his old friend Casady, then teaching guitar in Washington. The two stayed with the Airplane until 1972.

By then they had already started Hot Tuna (they originally called the group Hot Shit, but RCA balked), which was intended to operate as a satellite band. Early on, other members of the Airplane played with Tuna, including vocalist Marty Balin and drummers Spencer Dryden and Joey Covington. The group's low-key debut was recorded live at Berkeley's New Orleans House with harmonica player Will Scarlett and Kaukonen on acoustic guitar. Their music eventually became loud and electric.

First Pull Up—Then Pull Down marked the arrival of the middle-aged black violinist Papa John Creach. Born in Pennsylvania in the early part of the century, Creach was 18 when his family moved to Chicago, where he received some classical training and was briefly affiliated with the Illinois Symphony Orchestra. By the late '30s, he had begun two decades of touring the cocktail lounge circuit. After settling in San Francisco in the '60s, he became friends with drummer Joey Covington, who recommended that Tuna get in touch with Creach. Creach was with Hot Tuna from 1971 until 1973. He played concurrently with the Airplane and launched a solo career with his 1971 self-titled Grunt/RCA debut. By the time of 1972's *Filthy,* Creach had formed his own band, Zulu, which he continued after leaving Tuna.

Hot Tuna's first album as a completely autonomous entity was its fourth, *The Phosphorescent Rat.* The group was a commercial oddity; despite the fact that its mid-'70s releases weren't big sellers, it insisted on playing concerts of at least two hours, which necessitated headliner status. In 1978 the group disbanded.

Kaukonen then resumed the solo recording career he had started with 1974's *Quah* (produced by Casady), releasing *Jorma* in 1979. Kaukonen toured solo, while nurturing a fondness for ever-changing hair color and tattoos. He also played briefly in a San Francisco–based new-wave band, Vital Parts. Casady, meanwhile, materialized with white-blonde hair in a new-wave outfit of his own, SVT. In 1984 both musicians reverted: Casady reunited with former Jefferson Airplane singers Marty Balin and Paul Kantner in a group called KBC; while Kaukonen, still flying solo, started playing acoustic blues and folk again. (He later released two more albums, *Too Hot to Handle* and the live *Magic.*) Also that year, Relix Records released *Splashdown,* a Hot Tuna radio performance from 1975.

In 1983 Casady and Kaukonen staged a "temporary reunion," playing some club dates together. The band reformed on a more permanent basis in 1986, adding new member Michael Falzarano, a multi-instrumentalist and singer, in 1990. (Falzarano had previously accompanied Hot Tuna on its 1983 reunion gigs.) That year, a full-fledged tour and new studio album, *Pair a Dice Found,* followed. In 1992 Hot Tuna released *Live at Sweetwater,* featuring guests Pete Sears (formerly of Jefferson Starship), Maria Muldaur, and the Grateful Dead's Bob Weir; *Sweetwater Two* followed the next year. Also in the early '90s, Casady toured with Paul Kantner in Jefferson Starship: The Next Generation, while Kaukonen traveled with Falzarano in a musical aggregation called Kaukarano.

By 1992, keyboardist Sears had joined the band, and Harvey Sorgen had replaced Bob Steeler on drums. This incarnation toured often and released a series of live albums; concurrently, Kaukonen recorded more solo material. In addition, Kaukonen continued to run Fur Peace Ranch Guitar Camp, which he founded with his wife and manager, Vanessa Lillian, in 1989, in the Appalachian Mountains of Ohio. Here he conducted guitar workshops alongside such fellow instructors as band mate Casady (who taught bass), bluesman John Hammond, folk singer Arlo Guthrie, and former *Saturday Night Live* bandleader G.E. Smith.

Son House

Born Eddie House, Mar. 21, 1902, Riverton, MS; died Oct. 19, 1988, Detroit, MI
1965—*Father of the Folk Blues* (Columbia) 1973—*Son House* (Arhoolie) 1979—*The Real Delta Blues* (Blue Goose) 1991—*Delta Blues: The Original Library of Congress Sessions From Field Recordings 1941–1942* (Biograph) 1992—*Father of the Delta Blues: The Complete 1965 Recordings* (Legacy) 1998—*Original Delta Blues.*

Blues vocalist and guitarist Son House—often cited as a major influence by Muddy Waters, Robert Johnson, Bob Dylan, and Bonnie Raitt—was one of the Mississippi Delta bluesmen who laid the groundwork for rock & roll in the years prior to World War II. House was one of the instigators of the regional tendency toward biting guitar sounds, dramatic vocals, and full-tilt rhythm sections.

House was born on a plantation, and by age 15 was delivering sermons in churches in Louisiana and Tennessee. In the early '20s he became pastor of a Baptist church in Lyon, Mississippi. In 1927 he taught himself to play guitar, and from then on he was a fixture on the Delta house-party circuit. Around 1928 he worked as part of Dr. McFadden's Medicine Show, but that career was quickly ended by a stint in the state prison at Parchman, Mississippi. Released in 1929, he moved to Lula, Mississippi, where he came under the tutelage of Delta legend Charley Patton. Through Patton he recorded his first sides for the Paramount label in 1930. House did not record again for 10 years, but he was an active performer, in partnership with Willie Brown, in the rural South. In the early '40s musicologist Alan Lomax, tipped off to House's prodigious talent by Muddy Waters, recorded him for the Library of Congress (in sessions later released commercially on Arhoolie, and in 1991 on Biograph). House moved to Rochester, New York, in 1943, and from then until 1964 he played only occasionally and only locally.

Spurred by the folk-blues revival of the early '60s, House reemerged to much acclaim, attracting a large white audience for the first time in his life. He began recording in earnest, touring the campus and coffeehouse circuits, appearing at folk and blues festivals in the U.S., Canada, and Europe, and performing at rock venues. House was the subject of a 1969 film short, and he appeared in several documentaries and on television before retiring from music in 1974. He lived the rest of his years in Detroit.

The Housemartins: See Fatboy Slim

House of Pain: See Everlast

Cissy Houston

Born Emily Houston, 1933, Newark, NJ
1971—*Cissy Houston* (Janus) 1977—*Cissy Houston* (Private Stock) 1979—*Warning—Danger* (Columbia) 1980—*Step Aside for a Lady* 1992—*I'll Take Care of You* (with Chuck Jackson) (Shanachie) 1995—*Midnight Train to Georgia: The Janus Years* (Ichiban) 1996—*Face to Face* (House of Blues) 1997—*He Leadeth Me.*

Gospel-soul singer Cissy Houston was a member of the '60s soul group the Sweet Inspirations and has since pursued a sporadic solo career (abetted by occasional session work) as she split her time between music and raising a family. She first sang with a family gospel group, the Drinkard Singers, which sometimes included her nieces Dionne and Dee Dee Warwick. The group was well known on the East Coast gospel circuit and recorded for RCA and Savoy.

After quitting the Drinkards, Houston established herself as a pop backup singer in New York. By 1967, she had become lead vocalist in the Sweet Inspirations. "Sweet Inspiration," a gospel-pop single, cracked the Top 20 in early 1968, and they established further credentials with their backup work for Aretha Franklin, Elvis Presley, Neil Diamond, Dusty Springfield, and others. Houston quit the group in 1970 and began recording solo with *Cissy Houston,* which included "Be My Baby" (#92, 1971). Houston was the first to record "Midnight Train to Georgia," which later became a hit single for Gladys Knight. She also toured as part of Dionne Warwick's backup trio, which included Dee Dee Warwick and Darlene Love. Houston devoted the next several years primarily to raising her three children, so her second solo disc was not released until 1977.

Houston has continued to be a popular backup vocalist, notably on Chaka Khan's *Chaka* (1978); Aretha Franklin's *Aretha* (1980), *Love All the Hurt Away* (1981), and *Jump to It* (1982); and Luther Vandross' *Never Too Much* (1981) and *Forever, For Always, For Love* (1982). She hosted a weekly radio broadcast from the New Hope Baptist Church in Newark and played occasional New York club dates with her then-less-famous daughter, Whitney. In 1995 she received the Rhythm & Blues Foundation's Pioneer Award. *Face to Face* (1996) and *He Leadeth Me* (1997) each won a Grammy Award for Best Traditional Soul Gospel Album.

Thelma Houston

Born Mississippi
1971—*Sunshower* (ABC/Dunhill) 1975—*I've Got the Music in*

Me (Sheffield Labs) 1976—*Any Way You Like It* (Tamla) 1977—*The Devil in Me; Thelma and Jerry* (with Jerry Butler) (Motown) 1978—*Ready to Roll* (Tamla); *Two to One* (Motown) 1981—*Superstar Series, vol. 20; Never Gonna Be Another One* (RCA) 1983—*Thelma Houston* (MCA) 1986—*Qualifying Heat* 1990—*Throw You Down* (Reprise) 1991—*The Best of Thelma Houston* (Motown).

Thelma Houston's dramatic, quavering, gospel-based delivery made her one of disco's most distinctive voices. As a youngster in Mississippi she sang in churches before her family moved to California. By the late '60s, she was working Southern California clubs, thereby attracting the attention of the Fifth Dimension's manager, Marc Gordon, who landed her a contract with ABC/Dunhill. Over the next few years, she made pop records with such producers as Jimmy Webb (the critically acclaimed *Sunshower*) and Joe Porter.

Houston's most successful effort from this period was a version of Laura Nyro's "Save the Country" (#74, 1970). Her breakthrough came via Tamla/Motown and the Gamble-Huff disco hit "Don't Leave Me This Way" (#1, 1977). Other efforts for Motown included an appearance on the soundtrack of the Motown-produced film *The Bingo Long Traveling All Stars & Motor Kings* (1976). She has also appeared in the films *Norman . . . Is That You?, Death Scream,* and *The Seventh Dwarf.* In 1977 she joined Jerry Butler for *Thelma and Jerry.* "Saturday Night, Sunday Morning" (#34 pop, #19 R&B, 1979) returned her to the chart as the disco era came to a close. In the '70s and '80s she had modest success on RCA and MCA. "You Used to Hold Me So Tight," peaking at #13 R&B in 1984, was her highest-charting record since 1976. In 1989 she appeared on the soundtrack to the film *Lean on Me.* She continues to perform, and she occasionally sings on compilations and on albums by other artists.

Whitney Houston

Born Aug. 9, 1963, Newark, NJ
1985—*Whitney Houston* (Arista) 1987—*Whitney* 1990—*I'm Your Baby Tonight* 1992—*The Bodyguard* soundtrack 1995—*Waiting to Exhale* soundtrack 1996—*The Preacher's Wife* 1998—*My Love Is Your Love* 2000—*Whitney: The Greatest Hits.*

As the daughter of renowned gospel and soul singer Cissy Houston, and the cousin of Dionne Warwick, Whitney Houston was better connected than most young vocalists when she embarked on a recording career in the mid-'80s. But neither genes nor industry contacts can account for the level of superstardom to which Houston quickly ascended. Blessed with a sublimely creamy, agile voice—and picture-perfect looks to boot—the singer delivered the sort of buoyant dance tunes and smooth, hummable ballads that are equally at home on the pop, R&B, and Adult Contemporary charts. For years critics carped that her supple singing would be better served by more soulful, less commercially ingratiating material; when she finally did emerge with a more urban sound, the media homed in on her increasingly irresponsible personal behavior. But where America's record-buying public was concerned, Houston became a star of the highest order, one whose appeal crossed races, cultures, and generations.

As a child, Houston sang in her family's church choir. At 15 she began performing in her mother's nightclub act. While attending a Catholic high school, the lithe beauty signed with a modeling agency and posed for magazines including *Glamour* and *Vogue.* After graduating, she continued to model and sing, backing up Lou Rawls and Chaka Khan, then at 19 was spotted by Arista president Clive Davis—who had previously steered the careers of Warwick and Houston family friend Aretha Franklin—while giving a showcase in Manhattan. Davis signed Houston, and started choosing songs for her debut album, which featured duets with established stars Teddy Pendergrass (her first hit, "Hold Me") and Jermaine Jackson, and cost Arista an extraordinarily hefty sum of $250,000.

Released in 1985, *Whitney Houston* proved a worthwhile investment, shooting to #1 and generating the smash singles "You Give Good Love" (#3 pop, #1 R&B, 1985), "Saving All My Love for You" (#1 pop, #1 R&B, 1985), "How Will I Know" (#1 pop, #1 R&B, 1985), and "Greatest Love of All" (#1 pop, #3 R&B, 1986). *Whitney* solidified Houston's success, reaching #1 and spawning "I Wanna Dance With Somebody (Who Loves Me)" (#1 pop, #2 R&B, 1987), "Didn't We Almost Have It All" (#1 pop, #2 R&B, 1987), "So Emotional" (#1 pop, #5 R&B, 1987), "Where Do Broken Hearts Go" (#1 pop, #2 R&B, 1988), and "Love Will Save the Day" (#9 pop, #5 R&B, 1988). Also in 1988, Houston recorded "One Moment in Time," NBC-TV's theme song for the Summer Olympics (#5 pop). In 1989 she teamed up with Aretha Franklin on the #5 R&B hit "It Isn't, It Wasn't, It Ain't Never Gonna Be."

In 1990 *I'm Your Baby Tonight*'s title track topped the pop and R&B charts, as did "All the Man That I Need." There were

Whitney Houston

more hits in 1991—"Miracle" (#9 pop, #2 R&B), "My Name Is Not Susan" (#20 pop, #8 R&B), and "I Belong to You" (#10 R&B)—but, peaking at #3, *Baby* proved disappointing after its predecessors. Houston bounced back in a big way, though, with the 1992 film *The Bodyguard,* in which she made her acting debut (as a singing star, opposite Kevin Costner), to mixed reviews and huge box office success. The movie's soundtrack—with six tracks sung by Houston—proved even more successful, hitting #1 and producing a monster single, Houston's cover of Dolly Parton's "I Will Always Love You" (1992), which remained at the top of the chart for an unprecedented 14 weeks, as well as a cover of Chaka Khan's 1978 hit "I'm Every Woman" (#4 pop, #5 R&B, 1993) and "I Have Nothing" (#4 pop, #4 R&B, 1993). In 1992 Houston married singer Bobby Brown [see entry]; their first child, Bobbi Kristina, was born the next year.

Houston's next career move was to attempt to duplicate the success of the movie/soundtrack combination of *The Bodyguard* with 1995's black-female friendship film *Waiting to Exhale,* in which the singer costarred alongside Angela Bassett. The movie was popular with audiences, and resulted in a few more hit singles for Houston, most notably "Exhale (Shoop Shoop)" (#1 pop and R&B) and a duet with CeCe Winans, "Count on Me" (#8 pop, #7 R&B, 1996). In 1996 Houston starred with Denzel Washington and Courtney B. Vance in *The Preacher's Wife,* a box-office disappointment whose soundtrack nevertheless gave her another charting ballad, "I Believe in You and Me" (#4 pop, #4 R&B). She tried the small screen in 1997, producing and playing the Fairy Godmother to Brandy's Cinderella in a *Wonderful World of Disney* remake of *Rodgers and Hammerstein's Cinderella.* In 1998 Houston released her first studio album since 1990, the uncharacteristic *My Love Is Your Love* (#13 pop, #7 R&B). Aside from a handful of ballads, including her Oscar-winning duet with fellow diva Mariah Carey, "When You Believe" (#15 pop, #33 R&B, 1998–99), from *The Prince of Egypt,* and the Diane Warren–penned torch song "I Learned From the Best" (#13 R&B, 1999), the album showcased a new, savvy street credibility that had previously come through only in Houston's later interviews and her private life with Brown. Hip-hop personalities and producers such as Wyclef Jean, Lauryn Hill, Rodney Jerkins, Missy Elliott, and Faith Evans collaborated with the vocalist on various tracks. The public still loved the new Whitney, giving her hits with the sultry "Heartbreak Hotel" (#2 pop, #1 R&B), the kick-him-out anthem "It's Not Right But It's Okay" (#4 pop, #7 R&B, 1999), and the reggae-inflected title track (#4 pop, #2 R&B, 1999).

While Houston was back in the spotlight, reports of her already notorious prima donna behavior became more prevalent in 1999 and 2000: She was often hours late for interviews, photo shoots, and rehearsals; canceled concerts and talk-show appearances; and in what would be the start of a string of tabloid stories questioning her state of mind, dodged arrest for marijuana possession at a Hawaii airport in January 2000 (charges were later dismissed). In the months that followed that incident, Houston was a surprising no-show at her mentor Clive Davis' induction into the Rock and Roll Hall of Fame, and was allegedly booted out of Academy Awards rehearsals for an all-star tribute to Burt Bacharach. Rumors about her tumultuous marriage to Brown resurfaced, particularly when he was briefly imprisoned in mid-2000 for a parole violation. Yet Houston attempted to have the last laugh with a powerful performance at an Arista Records anniversary party that also served as a tribute to Davis, plus the release of a two-disc greatest-hits collection that equally highlighted her ballads and dance-club remixes and featured four new songs, three of which were duets with Deborah Cox, Enrique Iglesias, and George Michael.

Howlin' Wolf

Born Chester Arthur Burnett, June 10, 1910, West Point, MS; died Jan. 10, 1976, Hines, IL
1958—*Howlin' Wolf* (Chess) 1964—*Moaning in the Moonlight* 1965—*Poor Boy* 1966—*Real Folk Blues* 1967—*More Real Blues; Evil; Live and Cookin' at Alice's Revisited* 1971—*The London Sessions* 1986—*His Greatest Sides, vol. 1* (Chess/MCA) 1987—*Cadillac Daddy: Memphis Recordings, 1952* (Rounder) 1991—*The Chess Box* (Chess/MCA) 1997—*His Best (Chess 50th Anniversary Collection).*

Delta bluesman Howlin' Wolf was one of the most influential musicians of the post–World War II era, and his electric Chicago blues—featuring his deep, lupine voice—shaped rock & roll.

Chester Arthur Burnett, named after the 21st president, was raised on a cotton plantation in Ruleville, Mississippi, and learned guitar as a child. In the Mississippi Delta area he began studying with the rural masters, notably guitarist and vocalist Charley Patton, his biggest single influence, and his half sister's husband, harmonica player Sonny Boy Williamson (Rice Miller).

As Howlin' Wolf, he played his first gig in the South on January 15, 1928, and throughout the '30s frequently performed on street corners. He formed his first band, the House Rockers, in Memphis in 1948 with pianist Bill Johnson, lead guitarist Willie Johnson, and drummer Willie Steele. Later personnel included at various times harmonica players James Cotton and Little Junior Parker, pianist Ike Turner, and guitarist Willie Johnson.

In 1951 Turner, a freelance talent scout, had Wolf record for Sam Phillips' Memphis-based Sun Records. Those masters were then leased to Chess Records, and in 1957 one of them, "Moanin' at Midnight," became his first R&B hit. In 1952 Wolf moved to Chicago, where his music was well received. Some consider the recordings he made for Chess during the '50s and '60s his best. Among them were the 1957 R&B hit "Sitting on Top of the World," "Spoonful," "Smokestack Lightnin'," "Little Red Rooster," "I Ain't Superstitious," "Back Door Man," "Killing Floor," and "How Many More Years." His songs, many of them written by Willie Dixon, have been covered by American and English rock acts like the Rolling Stones (with whom Wolf appeared on the *Shindig!* TV show in 1965), Grateful Dead, the Yardbirds, Jeff Beck, the Doors, Cream, the Electric Flag, Little Feat, and Led Zeppelin.

Wolf, who stood an imposing 6-foot-3 and weighed nearly 300 pounds, frequently appeared at blues and rock festivals in the late '60s and early '70s. His 1971 album, *The London Sessions,* featured backup support from Eric Clapton, Ringo Starr, Steve Winwood, and Charlie Watts and Bill Wyman of the Rolling Stones. That same year Wolf received an honorary doctorate from Columbia College in Chicago. He lived the last years of his life in Chicago's crumbling South Side ghetto. He suffered several heart attacks in the early '70s and received kidney dialysis treatment, but he continued to play occasionally; one of his last concerts was in November 1975 at the Chicago Amphitheatre with B.B. King, Bobby "Blue" Bland, and Little Milton. He entered a hospital in mid-December and died at age 65 of complications from kidney disease. Howlin' Wolf was posthumously inducted into the Rock and Roll Hall of Fame in 1991.

The Hues Corporation

Formed 1969, Los Angeles, CA
H. Ann Kelly (b. Hubert Ann Kelly, Apr. 24, 1947, Fairchild, AL), voc.; St. Clair Lee (b. Bernard St. Clair Lee Calhoun Henderson, Apr. 24, 1944, San Francisco, CA), voc.; Fleming Williams (b. Flint, MI), voc.
1974—*Freedom for the Stallion* (RCA) (– Williams;+ Tommy Brown [b. Birmingham, AL], voc.) *Rockin' Soul* 1975—*Love Corporation* (– Brown; + Karl Russell [b. Apr. 10, 1947, Columbia, OH], voc.) 1977—*I Caught Your Act* (Warner/Curb); *Best of the Hues Corporation* (RCA) 1978—*Your Place or Mine* (Warner Bros.).

Disco-soul group the Hues Corporation had its one big hit with "Rock the Boat" (#1, 1974), which sold over 2 million copies. A vocal trio featuring two men and a woman, the Hues took its name from Howard Hughes (changing the spelling to avoid legal problems).

After working the lounge circuit, the group signed with RCA in 1973 and had a minor pop hit with the title track of its debut album, *Freedom for the Stallion.* The Corporation's big success came in mid-1974 with "Rock the Boat." Followups like "Rockin' Soul" (#18, 1974) and "Love Corporation" (#62, 1975), with Tommy Brown in place of Fleming Williams, were modest in comparison. Brown left in 1975; his spot was taken by Karl Russell.

The Hues Corporation made frequent TV appearances in the mid-'70s and also appeared in the film *Blacula.* Longtime vocal arranger and producer Wally Holmes was still on board after the group switched to Warner/Curb Records in 1977 for *I Caught Your Act;* the LP's title track (#92, 1977) was the act's last chart appearance. Russell left the group in 1980 and became an ordained minister in Anniston, Alabama, where he runs Soni Boo Records, a gospel label.

The Human League

Formed 1977, Sheffield, Eng.
Phil Oakey (b. Oct. 2, 1955, Sheffield), voc., synth.; Martyn Ware (b. May 19, 1956, Sheffield), synth.; Ian Craig Marsh (b. Nov. 11, 1956, Sheffield), synth.; Philip Adrian Wright (b. June 30, 1956, Sheffield), stage visuals.
1979—*Reproduction* (Virgin) 1980—*Travelogue* (– Ware; – Marsh; + Ian Burden [b. Dec. 24, 1957, Sheffield], bass, synth.; + Suzanne Sulley [b. Mar. 22, 1963, Sheffield], voc.; + Joanne Catherall [b. Sep. 18, 1962, Sheffield], voc.) 1981—(+ Jo Callis [b. May 2, 1955, Glasgow, Scot.], synth.) 1982—*Dare* (A&M); *Love and Dancing* 1983—*Fascination!* 1984—*Hysteria* 1986—*Crash* 1988—*Greatest Hits* 1990—*Romantic?* 1995—*Octopus* (EastWest) 1998—*The Very Best of the Human League* (Ark 21).
Philip Oakey with Giorgio Moroder: 1985—*Philip Oakey and Giorgio Moroder* (A&M).

Armed with synthesizers and electronic percussion, the Human League became the undisputed leader of the British electropop movement in 1982. The band topped the American chart with the million-selling "Don't You Want Me," taken from *Dare,* its third British album and first U.S. release. Led by Philip Oakey, the League had released its debut album, *Reproduction,* three years earlier. *Travelogue* followed the next year. Both critically acclaimed works featured synthesizer textures reminiscent of Kraftwerk and dark lyrics that Oakey delivered in an ominous voice reminiscent of mid-'70s David Bowie.

Oakey felt the band's heavy reliance on prerecorded tapes in live shows was dishonest, which led to the departures of Martin Ware and Ian Marsh in 1980. The two synthesizists formed the popular Heaven 17 later that year. Meanwhile, Oakey and remaining Human Leaguer Philip Wright recruited bassist/synthesizer player Ian Burden, two female backing singers, and synthesizist Jo Callis, former guitar-playing leader of Scotland's punk-kitsch rockers the Rezillos. Allying itself with producer Martin Rushent (the Stranglers, Buzzcocks), the Human League recorded *Dare,* which quickly brought it fame in England. Coinciding with its subsequent American success, the group toured the States, where audiences got a good taste of U.K. electropop, complete with robotic drum machines.

That the group's songwriters (mainly Oakey, Callis, and Burden) were less than prolific quickly became apparent. *Love and Dancing* reprised instrumental tracks from *Dare,* while *Fascination* contained just five songs. Two of them became hits in 1983: the Motown-ish "Mirror Man" (#30) and "(Keep Feeling) Fascination" (#8), which mimicked the vocal arrangement of Sly and the Family Stone. *Hysteria* introduced a gutsier sound, with Callis playing guitar and Burden thumping an actual bass. "The Lebanon," a powerful guitar-driven track about the strife in that country, was a minor hit at #64.

The following year Oakey recorded an album with disco producer Giorgio Moroder; the Human League's decision to hire modern-funk producers Jimmy Jam and Terry Lewis to helm *Crash* wasn't as surprising as it might seem. The plaintive "Human," a Jam-Lewis composition, hit #1. Curiously, rather than build on its momentum, the Human League all but disappeared until 1990. That year's *Heart Like a Wheel* contained a Top 40 hit in the title track. Oakey and company vanished once again until the 1995 release of the commercially unsuccessful *Octopus*. In the late '90s the band occasionally surfaced to play new-wave revival bills.

Humble Pie

Formed 1969, Essex, Eng.
Steve Marriott (b. Jan. 30, 1947, London, Eng.; d. Apr. 20, 1991, Arkesden, Eng.), gtr., voc., kybds., harmonica; Peter Frampton (b. Apr. 22, 1950, Beckenham, Eng.), gtr., voc.; Greg Ridley (b. Oct. 23, 1947, Carlisle, Eng.), bass, voc.; Jerry Shirley (b. Feb. 4, 1952, Eng.), drums.
1969—*As Safe as Yesterday Is* (Immediate, U.K.); *Town and Country* 1970—*Humble Pie* (A&M) 1971—*Rock On; Performance—Rockin' the Fillmore* (– Frampton; + David "Clem" Clempson [b. Sep. 5, 1949, Eng.], gtr., voc.) 1972—*Smokin'; Lost and Found* 1973—*Eat It* 1974—*Thunder Box* 1975—*Street Rats* (group disbands) 1980—(group re-forms: Marriott; Shirley; + Bobby Tench, voc., gtr.; + Anthony Jones, bass) *On to Victory* (Atco) 1981—*Go for the Throat* 1982—*The Best* (A&M).
Steve Marriott solo: 1976—*Marriott* (A&M) 1981—*Steve Marriott.*

Early-'70s hard-rock band Humble Pie was formed and fronted by the raspy-voiced Steve Marriott, who had left the Small Faces in 1968. He hooked up with ex-Herd guitarist Peter Frampton (whose boyish good looks had already elicited teenybopper acclaim), ex–Spooky Tooth bassist Greg Ridley, and drummer Jerry Shirley. In 1969 the group retired to Marriott's Essex cottage for months of rehearsal. Its first single, "Natural Born Boogie," hit the Top 5 on the U.K. chart. Neither the quartet's debut album, *As Safe as Yesterday Is,* nor the acoustic-oriented *Town and Country* made much of an impact in the U.S. until repackaged as *Lost and Found.*

Humble Pie toured the U.S. for the first time in late 1969 but returned home to find that the Immediate label had gone under. It found a new manager (Dee Anthony) and label (A&M), and its next LP, *Humble Pie,* featured Frampton's melodic acoustic rock. But neither it nor the gutsier *Rock On* provided an American breakthrough. Anthony sent the group to America on a frenzied tour that produced *Performance—Rockin' the Fillmore,* recorded live at New York's Fillmore East in May 1971. Loud and raucous, it went gold. Frampton [see entry] left the group in late 1971.

The loss of the guitarist, combined with the outstanding sales of the rock-and-blues-oriented *Fillmore* album, prompted the group to concentrate on boogie material. *Smokin',* its first album with new guitarist Dave "Clem" Clempson, was the group's most successful, reaching #6. But shortly thereafter Humble Pie's fortunes fell, and in 1975 the members split up.

Shirley formed an L.A. group, Natural Gas, with ex-Badfinger member Joey Molland. Clempson (previously with Colosseum) joined Greenslade before he and Pie bassist Ridley teamed up with former Jeff Beck drummer Cozy Powell to form the short-lived Strange Brew. Clempson has since played with Jack Bruce, among others.

Marriott, meanwhile, led Steve Marriott's All-Stars before participating in a Small Faces reunion in 1976. By 1980, Marriott and Shirley had re-formed Humble Pie with ex–Jeff Beck vocalist Bobby Tench. Their two albums—1980's *On to Victory* and 1981's *Go for the Throat*—were met with limited success. In mid-1981 the group's tour of the U.S. was interrupted when Marriott smashed his hand in a hotel door. In June, having recovered, he had to halt the tour again when he was hospitalized in Dallas with an ulcer. Once again Humble Pie disbanded, with Shirley going on to drum for the hard-rock group Fastway and for a version of Badfinger. Shirley, who had moved to Cleveland and worked as a radio personality, put together a new Humble Pie, which toured in the '90s. In 1991, when Marriott died in a fire in his 16th-century cottage at age 44, he and Peter Frampton were recording together. They completed three songs, which appeared on Frampton's later solo albums.

Alberta Hunter

Born Apr. 1, 1895, Memphis, TN; died Oct. 17, 1984, New York, NY
1961—*Songs We Taught Your Mother* (Prestige/Bluesville) 1978—*Remember My Name* 1980—*Amtrak Blues* (Columbia).

Alberta Hunter sang the blues for over 70 years, and was one of the first black American musicians to tour the world. A spellbinding cabaret singer, Hunter could be both sophisticated and sassy, winking slyly through double entendres or reducing her audience to tears. Among her best-known recordings are "Down Hearted Blues," "A Good Man Is Hard to Find," "My Castle's Rocking," and "You Can't Tell the Difference After Dark." She began singing professionally as a teenager in Chicago. In 1921 Hunter performed and recorded with the Fletcher Henderson orchestra and made her first solo recordings. Upon moving to New York that year, she began recording regularly; she recorded in 1924 with Louis Armstrong's Red Onion Jazz Babies for the Gennett label.

Hunter first performed on Broadway when she replaced Bessie Smith in the musical comedy *How Come* in 1923. By 1925, she was leading her own trio in club work and took it on subsequent national tours. In 1927, billed as "America's Foremost Brown Blues Singer," she played in England, France, and Monaco. She visited Scotland, Egypt, Greece, and the Scandinavian countries in the '30s. Back home, Hunter appeared with Paul Robeson in a 1928 Broadway production of *Showboat* and, beginning in the early '30s, expanded her audience through a featured spot on WABC radio's *Negro Achievement Hour.* By the end of the decade she was regularly featured on several East Coast stations. In the mid-'30s she had one of her most active club periods, playing Harlem's Cotton Club and appearing at Connie's Inn with Louis Armstrong.

Hunter's recording career revitalized alongside the Depression economy, and in the mid-'30s she recorded with the Jack Jackson Orchestra on HMV. She recorded in 1939 with the Charlie Shavers Quartet for Decca and in 1940 with the Eddie Heywood orchestra for Bluebird. She spent most of World War II with the USO touring China, Burma, India, Egypt, and Africa, including a 1945 command performance for General Dwight D. Eisenhower at Frankfurt, Germany. She was given a meritorious service award for her contributions to the war effort.

Hunter returned to New York club work after the war and by the early '50s was recording again. In 1957 she retired from music to work as a nurse, which she did for two decades, with only infrequent returns to performing: some sessions in 1961 and 1962 for the Prestige/Bluesville, Riverside, and Folkways labels.

In 1977, at age 82, Hunter reemerged to establish residency at the Cookery in New York's Greenwich Village. The attendant publicity prompted a Columbia contract. Her wit and style are amply demonstrated in a 1985 video, *Jazz at the Smithsonian*. She died from natural causes.

Ian Hunter

Born June 3, 1946, Shrewsbury, Eng.
1975—*Ian Hunter* (Columbia) 1976—*All-American Alien Boy* 1977—*Overnight Angels* (Columbia, U.K.) 1979—*You're Never Alone With a Schizophrenic* (Chrysalis); *Shades of Ian Hunter* (Columbia) 1980—*Welcome to the Club* (Chrysalis) 1981—*Short Back n' Sides* 1983—*All of the Good Ones Are Taken* (Columbia) 1989—*Y U I Orta* (with Mick Ronson) (Mercury) 1995—*Ian Hunter's Dirty Laundry* (Cleveland International) 1997—*The Artful Dodger* (Citadel, U.K.) 2000—*Once Bitten Twice Shy* (Columbia/Legacy); *Missing in Action.*

The former leader of Mott the Hoople [see entry], singer/songwriter Ian Hunter pursued a moderately successful solo career in the late '70s, but within a few years he had faded from view.

Hunter's family settled in Blackpool but moved frequently. His father, who worked for MI5, the British CIA, was regularly transferred. By the time Hunter was 11 he had attended 17 different schools. His family finally settled in Shrewsbury, where he played with a band called Silence that recorded an unsuccessful album. In 1962 he played harmonica in another amateur band but continued to work day jobs until 1968, when he started playing bass in Germany with Freddie "Fingers" Lee. A few months later he helped launch Mott the Hoople in England.

With its debut album in 1969, Mott the Hoople established itself as Dylan-influenced hard-rockers with "Rock and Roll Queen" and, under the tutelage of David Bowie, became glitter-rock favorites with 1972's *All the Young Dudes* and its title single. During his last days with the group, Hunter wrote the autobiographical *Reflections of a Rock Star,* published in 1977. In late 1974 he left after being hospitalized in New Jersey for physical exhaustion.

Hunter moved to New York and made his self-titled solo debut, which featured ex-Bowie guitarist Mick Ronson, who had played in a late version of Mott. The album produced a British Top 20 hit, "Once Bitten Twice Shy." Hunter toured America and England in late 1975. His next two albums were *All-American Alien Boy* and *Overnight Angels* (which Hunter later called "disgusting"; it wasn't issued in the U.S. until Columbia included it on the retrospective *Shades of Ian Hunter*).

You're Never Alone With a Schizophrenic (#35, 1979), Hunter's successful Chrysalis debut, once again featured Mick Ronson as producer, arranger, and guitarist. By 1980, Hunter had formed his own band, including Ronson, guitarist Tom Morringello, and keyboardists George Meyer and Tom Mandell. He toured that year to promote his live *Welcome to the Club.* Mick Jones of the Clash produced *Short Back n' Sides* in 1981.

Hunter has also produced records, including Ellen Foley's debut album and Generation X's second LP, *Valley of the Dolls.* In addition he wrote Barry Manilow's hit "Ships." After *All the Good Ones Are Taken,* he wasn't heard from again until 1989's *Y U I Orta,* another collaboration with Ronson. It came out months after the American band Great White scored a #5 hit with "Once Bitten Twice Shy." Hunter put in an appearance at the April 1992 AIDS benefit concert honoring the late Freddie Mercury. Guitar great Ronson died of cancer in 1993.

In 1995 Hunter resurfaced in Ian Hunter's Dirty Laundry, a one-off band featuring Glen Matlock (ex–Sex Pistols), Honest John Plain and Darrell Barth (ex-Crybabys), Vom (ex–Doctor and the Medics), and Casino Steel (ex–Hollywood Brats). He was on his own again for 1997's *The Artful Dodger,* which remains unreleased in America. *Once Bitten* is a double-CD of Mott-era material and solo hits. It includes a version of "All the Young Dudes" on which Hunter is backed by Def Leppard.

Ivory Joe Hunter

Born Oct. 10, 1914, Kirbyville, TX; died Nov. 8, 1974, Memphis, TN
1971—*The Return of Ivory Joe Hunter* (Epic); *16 of His Greatest Hits* (King); *Ivory Joe Hunter* (Everest) 1989—*I'm Coming Down With the Blues* (Home Cooking) 1994—*Since I Met You Baby; The Best of Ivory Joe Hunter* (Razor & Tie).

A pop-blues singer, pianist, and songwriter, Ivory Joe Hunter was a popular R&B figure in the '40s and '50s, and one of the first R&B singers to interpret country songs. He started playing the piano in grade school and eventually developed a style influenced by Fats Waller. He worked as program director at KFDM radio in Beaumont, Texas, and made his first recordings in 1933 for the Library of Congress via musicologist Alan Lomax.

Hunter recorded briefly with Johnny Moore's Three Blazers for the Exclusive label. He soon started his own Ivory Records and scored his first regional hit with "Blues at Sunrise." He then left Texas in 1942 for California, where he helped form and recorded for Pacific Records ("Pretty Mama Blues"). With King Records from 1947 to 1950, his R&B hits included "Landlord Blues" and "Guess Who" in 1949, and "I Quit My Pretty Mama" in 1950. Signed to MGM, Hunter released "I Almost Lost My Mind," which hit #1 on the R&B chart and had sold a million copies by the time Pat Boone covered it in 1956. Hunter spent most of the '50s on the R&B chart, first with such MGM releases as "I Need You So" (#2, 1950), and then, after signing with Atlantic in 1954, alongside Ray Charles and Chuck Willis.

Hunter finally reached white listeners with "Since I Met You Baby" (#12, 1956), which got him exposure on the *Ed Sullivan Show.* After "Empty Arms" (1957), "Yes I Want You" (1958), and "City Lights" (1959), Hunter's popularity declined, although he continued to record. In the late '60s he sang country as a revue member of the Grand Ole Opry in Nashville, and he tried a comeback in 1971 when he released *The Return of Ivory Joe Hunter.* In late 1974 Hunter died of cancer in a Memphis hospital. His songs have been covered by Nat "King" Cole, the Five Keys, and Elvis Presley, who cut "My Wish Came True" and "Ain't That Loving You, Baby."

Mississippi John Hurt

Born July 3, 1893, Teoc, MS; died Nov. 2, 1966, Grenada, MS
1966—*Mississippi John Hurt Today* (Vanguard) 1967—*The Immortal Mississippi John Hurt* 1970—*The Best of Mississippi John Hurt* 1972—*Last Sessions.*

Blues singer Mississippi John Hurt was renowned for his fingerpicking and restrained phrasing. He was one of sharecroppers Isom and Mary Hurt's three children, and he lived as a sharecropper most of his life. A frequent singer in local churches, Hurt dropped out of school at age 10 in 1903, by which time he'd taught himself to play a three-finger-picking style of guitar.

Most of Mississippi John Hurt's performances were for audiences in the Avalon, Mississippi, area. Heavily influenced by Jimmie Rodgers, as were many bluesmen of the era, he slowly developed an original country/Delta blues style. In 1928 he was taken to New York and Memphis to cut a few sides for Okeh Records, among them a rendition of the blues standard "Stack-O-Lee." But during the Great Depression, Hurt faded back into rural anonymity until he was rediscovered, at age 70, during the early-'60s folk-blues revival by blues enthusiast Tom Hoskins.

Hurt played at the Newport Folk Festival in 1963, 1964, and 1965; at Carnegie Hall; at rock clubs like the Café Au Go Go in New York; on TV's *Tonight Show* in 1963; and in the 1965 Canadian Broadcasting documentary *This Hour Has Seven Days.* He also reactivated his recording career, cutting several albums, including *Today, The Immortal Mississippi John Hurt,* and *Last Sessions,* which was recorded in a Manhattan hotel in 1966, shortly before his death from a heart attack. Hurt helped popularize such traditional material as "Candy Man Blues" and "C.C. Rider" as well as his own "Coffee Blues" and "Chicken." He was survived by his widow, Jesse, and their 14 children. In 2001 *Avalon Blues: A Tribute to the Music of Mississippi John Hurt* was released. Produced by Peter Case, it featured new recordings of Hurt songs by Lucinda Williams, Steve Earle, John Hiatt, and others.

Hüsker Dü/Grant Hart/Bob Mould/Sugar

Formed 1979, St. Paul, MN
Bob Mould (b. Oct. 16, 1960, Malone, NY), gtr., voc.; Greg Norton (b. Mar. 13, 1959, Rock Island, IL), bass; Grant Hart (b. Grantzberg Vernon Hart, Mar. 18, 1961, St. Paul), drums, voc.
1981—*Land Speed Record* (New Alliance) 1982—*Everything Falls Apart* (Reflex) 1983—*Metal Circus* EP (SST) 1984—*Zen Arcade* 1985—*New Day Rising* 1985—*Flip Your Wig* 1986—*Candy Apple Grey* (Warner Bros.) 1987—*Warehouse: Songs and Stories* 1993—*Everything Falls Apart and More* (Rhino) 1994—*The Living End* (Warner Bros.).
Grant Hart solo: 1988—*2541* EP (SST) 1989—*Intolerance* 1996—*Ecce Homo* (World Service) 1999—*Good News for Modern Man* (Pachyderm).
Grant Hart with Nova Mob: 1991—*Admiral of the Sea* EP (Rough Trade); *The Last Days of Pompeii* 1994—*Nova Mob* (Restless).
Bob Mould solo: 1989—*Workbook* (Virgin) 1990—*Black Sheets of Rain* 1994—*Poison Years* 1995—*Egooveride* EP (Rykodisc) 1996—*Hubcap* 1998—*The Last Dog & Pony Show.*
Bob Mould with Sugar: 1992—*Copper Blue* (Ryko) 1993—*Beaster* EP 1994—*File Under: Easy Listening* 1995—*Besides.*

Hüsker Dü laid the groundwork for the '90s alternative-rock boom when it became one of the first DIY-era American indie bands to land a major-label deal. The Minnesota-based power trio's influential sound expanded the parameters of punk by incorporating hummable pop melodies and introspective lyrics into a thick hardcore foundation.

Bob Mould was born to mom-and-pop grocery store owners in an upstate New York farming town near Lake Placid. In 1978 he moved to St. Paul, Minnesota, to attend Macalester College, where he took urban studies and worked part-time at a record store. It was there that he met Grant Hart, a local drummer who shared his love of punk rock, and Greg Norton, who played bass and listened to jazz. The three began rehearsing together in Norton's basement, naming themselves Hüsker Dü (Swedish for "do you remember?") after a '50s board-game.

In the early '80s the trio signed to SST and released *Land Speed Record,* a milestone of hardcore whose 17 songs clocked in at just over a meteoric 26 minutes. For the next five years, Hüsker Dü—along with Black Flag, Minutemen, R.E.M., and Twin City peers the Replacements—toured almost constantly and released some of the most important albums of the postpunk era. Hüsker Dü hit its artistic peak with 1984's *Zen Arcade,* one of punk's few double-disc clas-

Hüsker Dü: Greg Norton, Grant Hart, Bob Mould

sics, and one of even fewer punk concept albums (it chronicled a boy's passing from adolescence into adulthood).

By 1986, the band was plagued by internal problems, including drug use and a power struggle between songwriters Mould and Hart. On its major-label debut, *Candy Apple Grey,* Mould's lyrics had become more inward-looking than ever, while the rage in Hart's angst-laden rockers had reached the boiling point. Over Warner Bros.' objections, the band followed up with a second double-disc LP, 1987's *Warehouse: Songs and Stories,* with the songwriting split down the middle. On the eve of the group's 1987 tour, Hüsker Dü's young manager, David Savoy, committed suicide. A recording from that tour was released as 1994's *The Living End.*

On January 25, 1988, Bob Mould, having put down drugs and drink, quit the band to pursue a solo career as a post-punk confessional singer/songwriter. Mould's first Virgin album, *Workbook* (#127, 1989), took up from where his more reflective material on *Candy Apple Grey* and *Warehouse* left off. After 1990's *Black Sheets of Rain* (#123), Mould was dropped by Virgin and cofounded a record company, SOL (Singles Only Label). By 1992, he formed a new band, Sugar, and signed to Rykodisc in the U.S. and Creation in the U.K., settling somewhere between the melodic roar of Hüsker Dü and his solo material. Sugar released *Copper Blue* that year and enjoyed the modern-rock hits "Helpless" (#5, 1992) and "If I Can't Change Your Mind." After 1995's *Besides* (#122), a collection of rarities and live cuts, Mould disbanded Sugar and resumed his solo career with the tortured *Hubcap* (#101, 1996), playing all the instruments himself and inscribing it with the words, "This one is for me." His 1998 album *The Last Dog & Pony Show* was named for what he promised would be his final high-decibel rock tour, to be followed thereafter by live acoustic performances.

Bassist Greg Norton left the music business altogether to become a chef when Hüsker Dü dissolved. But Grant Hart immediately returned to SST for the *2541* EP and a 1989 solo album, *Intolerance,* before forming Nova Mob. The new band released two albums, beginning in 1991 with a rock opera called *The Last Days of Pompeii.* Hart broke up Nova Mob three years later and continued his solo career with the live acoustic *Ecce Homo* in 1996 and *Good News for Modern Man* in 1999. He also played keyboards on a track on Patti Smith's *Gung Ho* in 2000.

Janis Ian

Born Janis Eddy Fink, May 7, 1951, New York, NY
1967—*Janis Ian* (Verve Forecast); *For All the Seasons of Your Mind* 1968—*The Secret Life of J. Eddy Fink* 1969—*Who Really Cares* 1971—*Present Company* (Capitol) 1974—*Stars* (Columbia) 1975—*Between the Lines; Aftertones* 1977—*Miracle Row* 1978—*Janis Ian* 1979—*Night Rains* 1980—*Best of Janis Ian* 1981—*Restless Eyes* 1993—*Breaking Silence* (Morgan Creek) 1995—*Revenge* (Beacon) 1997—*Hunger* (Windham Hill) 2000—*God & the FBI.*

Singer/songwriter Janis Ian began her career at 15 with a 1967 hit about interracial romance entitled "Society's Child." After an eight-year slump, she returned to pop radio in 1975 with a platinum LP and Grammy Award–winning single, "At Seventeen."

The daughter of a music teacher, Ian studied piano as a child and began writing songs when she enrolled in Manhattan's High School of Music and Art. There she changed her surname from Fink to Ian (her brother's middle name). The folk journal *Broadside* published her "Hair of Spun Gold" and invited her to perform at a hootenanny at the Village Gate. Ian soon had a contract with Elektra but was dropped when she insisted upon recording her own material; she then signed with Verve.

In 1966 she recorded a song she had written while waiting to see her guidance counselor, "Society's Child (Baby I've Been Thinking)." It was banned by several radio stations and ignored by the rest until conductor Leonard Bernstein featured Ian on his CBS-TV special *Inside Pop: The Rock Revolution,* where she performed the song accompanied by the New York Philharmonic. "Society's Child" became a #14 hit in 1967.

Ian dropped out of high school in her junior year and released her first album. She recorded two more albums for Verve but never produced a followup hit single. She gave away most of her earnings to friends and charities; management and taxes took the rest. Ian retired before she was 20. She moved to Philadelphia and married photojournalist Peter Cunningham. Her marriage lasted only a short while, and Ian returned to recording with the unsuccessful *Present Company.* She moved to California, where she lived alone and continued writing. Her next album, *Stars,* included "Jesse," a #30 hit for Roberta Flack, later covered by Joan Baez on *Diamonds and Rust.*

Ian's most commercially successful year was 1975, when she sold over $5 million worth of records. She released the platinum *Between the Lines,* which included "Watercolors" and "At Seventeen" (#3), the latter of which got her a Grammy for Best Female Vocal. Followups like *Aftertones, Miracle Row, Janis Ian,* and *Night Rains* were less popular. Following a 12-year hiatus from recording, Ian—having revealed her homosexuality—returned to the scene with *Breaking Silence,* whose subdued, folkish songs forthrightly tackled such subjects as battered wives ("His Hands"), eroticism ("Ride Me Like a Wave"), concentration camps ("Tattoo"), and '60s nostalgia ("Guess You Had to Be There"). The lyrics on 1995's *Revenge* dealt with prostitution and homelessness. Following 1997's *Hunger,* Ian successfully underwent surgery to remove a benign liver tumor. Willie Nelson and Chet Atkins assisted her on "Memphis," a track from 2000's *God & the FBI.*

Ian and Sylvia

Formed 1959, Toronto, Can.
Ian Tyson (b. Sep. 25, 1933, Victoria, British Columbia, Can.); Sylvia Tyson (b. Sylvia Fricker, Sep. 19, 1940, Chatham, Ontario, Can.).
1962—*Ian and Sylvia* (Vanguard) 1963—*Four Strong Winds* 1964—*Northern Journey* 1965—*Early Morning Rain* 1966—*Play One More* 1967—*So Much for Dreaming; Ian and Sylvia* (Columbia) 1968—*Nashville* (Vanguard); *Full Circle; The Best of Ian and Sylvia* 1970—*Greatest Hits, vol. 1* 1971—*Greatest Hits, vol. 2* 1972—*You Were on My Mind* (with the Great Speckled Bird) (Columbia) 1973—*The Best of Ian and Sylvia* 1998—*Vanguard Session* (Vanguard).
Ian Tyson solo: 1975—*Ol' Eon* (A&M) 1979—*One Jump Ahead of the Devil* (Boot) 1993—*And Stood There Amazed; I Outgrew the Wagon* (Vanguard) 1994—*Eighteen Inches of Rain; Cowboyography; Old Corrals & Sagebrush & Other Cowboy Culture Classics* 1996—*All the Good 'Uns* 1999—*Lost Herd.*
Sylvia Tyson solo: 1975—*Woman's World* (Capitol) 2000—*River Road and Other Stories* (Outside, Can.).

Canadian folksingers/songwriters Ian and Sylvia were active in the folk revival of the early '60s as performers and composers. By the late '60s, they had turned to country music.

Ian Tyson was raised on a Canadian farm. He traveled much of western Canada working various jobs, including performing in the rodeo, until he was seriously injured at age 19. Shortly after turning 21 and enrolling in the Vancouver School of Art, he started singing in clubs, sometimes as part of a group called the Sensational Stripes. Tyson graduated from art school and moved to Toronto, where he worked days as a commercial artist and, with partner Don Francks, played blues and traditional folk material. He was well known in Canadian music circles by the time he met Sylvia Fricker in 1959.

Fricker's mother was a music teacher, organist, and choir director at their church. Sylvia became involved in the Toronto folk scene after graduating from high school. Within a year of meeting, she and Tyson were performing regularly as a duo.

They moved to New York in the early '60s and began working on the club-and-campus folk circuit. Their first album, recorded in a Masonic temple in Brooklyn, featured traditional songs; their second contained Ian Tyson's best-known song, "Four Strong Winds." Sylvia's "You Were on My Mind" (a 1965 hit for We Five) was on the duo's fourth album, *Northern Journey,* which was released around the time they married in 1964.

As the '60s ended the Tysons moved toward country music and briefly toured and recorded with a C&W band called Great Speckled Bird. Tyson began a solo career with a country single, "Love Can Bless the Soul of Anyone," and later became the host of a music-variety show on Canadian television. He produced Sylvia's solo debut, *Woman's World,* and she began hosting a folk-music show, *Touch the Earth,* on CBC radio. The couple divorced and went their separate ways in 1975.

After settling down on a ranch in the foothills of southern Alberta's Rockies, Ian Tyson began recording albums of cowboy songs in the early '80s, among them *Cowboyography,* which went platinum in Canada (the dates above indicate U.S. releases). Sylvia Tyson continued her solo career and eventually joined the country-folk group Quartette. In 1995 she and Tom Russell coauthored a collection of anecdotes entitled *And Then I Wrote: The Songwriter Speaks.* In 2000 she was performing *River Road and Other Stories,* a one-woman show of monologues and songs, complete with a companion album.

Ice Cube

Born O'Shea Jackson, June 15, 1969, Los Angeles, CA
1990—*AmeriKKKa's Most Wanted* (Priority); *Kill at Will* EP 1991—*Death Certificate* 1992—*The Predator* 1993—*Check Yo Self* EP 1994—*Lethal Injection; Bootlegs & B-Sides; You Know How We Do It* EP; *Bop Gun (One Nation)* EP 1997—*Featuring . . . Ice Cube* 1998—*War & Peace Vol. 1 (The War Disc)* 2000—*War & Peace Vol. 2 (The Peace Disc).*
Westside Connection (with Mack 10 and WC): 1996—*Bow Down* (Priority).

When Ice Cube left the notorious L.A. rap group N.W.A in 1990, he continued writing hard-hitting gangsta rap songs that pushed buttons in the media as well as among parents, politicians, and police. He also embarked on a successful acting career that by the end of the decade had almost eclipsed his musical output.

The son of a strict two-parent home (his mom was a clerk, and dad a groundskeeper at UCLA), South Central L.A. native O'Shea Jackson found success with N.W.A [see entry] after graduating from college in 1988 with a degree in drafting. In 1990 he had a falling out with N.W.A's management and went solo. For his first album, Cube and his group, Da Lench Mob, enlisted Public Enemy's celebrated Bomb Squad production team, whose dense musical collages include artful uses of sampling and turntable manipulation. Released in spring 1990, *AmeriKKKa's Most Wanted* (#19 pop, #6 R&B, 1990) went gold in 10 days and platinum in three months. A sonically forceful, lyrically vicious album, it juxtaposes a barrage of disparaging terms like "bitch" and "ho" with astute, politically charged observations of ghetto life: gang violence, black-on-black killing, abusive police, poverty, drugs, money, and sex roles. Parents and officials immediately criticized Cube for being a bad role model; Cube countered that that was not his responsibility. Even among rock critics who defended his gangsta rap for its realism, he was censured for the brutal track "You Can't Fade Me," in which the song's protagonist fantasizes aborting his girlfriend's pregnancy with a coat hanger.

AmeriKKKa's Most Wanted also introduced Cube's female collaborator, Yo Yo, who on the point-counterpoint track "It's a Man's World" offered a black woman's perspective to counter Cube's male-centric observations. (Ice Cube landed Yo Yo a reported six-figure deal with Atlantic and coproduced her 1991 #5 R&B debut album, *Make Way for the Motherlode.*) For all its unanswered questions and contradictions, *AmeriKKKa's Most Wanted* is considered a rap classic.

With his powerful, rhythmic baritone delivery, Ice Cube has maintained a consistently high standing among critics and fans. Still, after the *Kill at Will* EP (#34 pop, #5 R&B, 1991), he returned with two of his most controversial songs to date on *Death Certificate* (#2 pop, #1 R&B, 1991): "Black Korea," wherein he denigrates Korean market owners, and "No Vaseline," in which he antagonistically refers to N.W.A manager Jerry Heller as a "Jew." The songs led to the first condemnation of an artist in the editor's note of the music trade publication *Billboard.* The album's single, "Steady Mobbin'," reached #67 pop and #30 R&B that year. In December 1992 Ice Cube made history again when *The Predator* debuted at #1 on both the pop album and R&B charts (it sold 1.5 million within a month of release); the album included "It Was a Good Day" (#15 pop, #7 R&B, 1993), a clever ghetto fantasy where everything goes surprisingly right for 24 hours.

By late 1993, *Lethal Injection* reached #5 pop and #1 R&B. Cube didn't release another solo album of new material for several years, though he formed Westside Connection with rappers Mack 10 and WC for a blast of "old-school gangsta hip-hop" entitled *Bow Down* (#2 pop, #1 R&B, 1996). He also wrote and produced Da Lench Mob's *Guerrillas in the Mist.* Cube reunited with ex–band mate Dr. Dre for the single "Natural Born Killaz" (#16 R&B, 1994), but a followup album collaboration to be called *Helter Skelter* did not materialize.

In the early '90s Cube began a second career as an actor and filmmaker, building on a flair for songwriting and rapping that was already richly cinematic. His first film was John Singleton's acclaimed 1991 drama *Boyz N the Hood,* in which Cube portrayed a teenage ex-con in South Central L.A. named Doughboy. He then appeared in 1992's *Trespass* as a thug sidekick to fellow actor/gangsta rapper Ice-T. While appearing in Singleton's *Higher Learning,* the director encouraged Cube to write his own films. In 1995 the rapper appeared in the comedy *Friday,* which he also coscripted with frequent music collaborator DJ Pooh. Ice Cube then wrote, directed, and acted in 1998's *The Players Club.* His Hollywood career has alternated between the popular likes of the horror film *Anaconda* (1997) and critical successes such as the Gulf War satire *Three Kings* (1999). Cube wrote, produced, and starred in slapstick-heavy *Next Friday* in 2000. He stars in *John Carpenter's Ghosts of Mars,* due for release in late 2001.

Converted to the Nation of Islam in 1992, Cube was by the late '90s a dedicated family man, a married father of three. He returned to recording with a two-album project: *War & Peace Vol. 1 (The War Disc)* (#7 pop, #2 R&B, 1998) and *War & Peace Vol. 2 (The Peace Disc),* which also reunited Cube with N.W.A's Dr. Dre and MC Ren on the opening track, "Hell Low." The new albums sold respectably but failed to match the numbers of his early solo career. A new track credited to N.W.A also appeared on the soundtrack to Cube's *Next Friday,* followed by a national arena tour in 2000 with Dre, Ren, Snoop Dogg, and Eminem.

Ice-T

Born Tracy Marrow, b. Feb. 16, 1958, Newark, NJ
1987—*Rhyme Pays* (Sire) 1988—*Power* 1989—*Freedom of Speech . . . Just Watch What You Say* 1991—*O.G. Original Gangster* 1993—*Home Invasion* (Rhyme Syndicate/Priority); *The Classic Collection* (Rhino) 1996—*VI: Return of the Real* (Rhyme Syndicate/Priority) 1999—*Seventh Deadly Sin* (Coroner/Atomic Pop).
With Body Count: 1992—*Body Count* (Sire) 1994—*Born Dead* (Virgin) 1997—*Violent Demise: The Last Days.*

Ice-T was one of the creators of gangsta rap, building a hard-edged West Coast sound rooted in his own experiences hustling on the streets of L.A. But he became hip-hop's most controversial figure in 1992 after coming under fire for "Cop Killer," a song by his thrash-metal side band, Body Count. The lyrics painted a brutal picture of the strife between inner-city police and ghetto youth, and even drew criticism from then-President George Bush. At nearly every turn, Ice-T has been martyred or chastised, managing to offend both the left and right with his provocative words. In the minds of his supporters, Ice-T's violent, often misogynistic tales of mayhem are more sarcastic and even humorous than cynical or gratuitous. With his blunt vocal delivery, narrative-style writing, and mesmerizing B-movie images, Ice-T was one of the earliest West Coast rappers to gain respect among the New York hip-hop set. As an artist, he set the stage for N.W.A, Snoop Dogg, and the Notorious B.I.G. and mingled easily with underground rockers on the first Lollapalooza Tour in 1991. He founded his own Rhyme Syndicate label (distributed by Sire/Warner Bros.) and introduced the likes of Everlast.

Born Tracy Marrow in New Jersey, he was raised by an aunt in L.A. after the death of his parents. Inspired by ghetto novelist/poet Iceberg Slim, he began penning poems while attending Crenshaw High School. At 15 he started hanging out with gang members on the streets of South Central L.A. He was never a gang member himself but spent his days as a young criminal (committing anything from robbery to kidnapping, he later told interviewers) before spending four years in the army. By 1983, he had adopted the name Ice-T (in honor of Iceberg Slim) and recorded a sing-song rap called "The Coldest Rap" over a funky Jimmy Jam–Terry Lewis backing track; the song, for which he received $20, came out on the independent label Saturn. The next year Ice-T landed a regular gig at seminal L.A. rap club the Radio and was asked to appear in the movie *Breakin'* (he also appeared in its sequel).

By the time of his 1987 debut album, *Rhyme Pays*, Ice-T had started incorporating poignant stories about inner-city street life ("6 'n the Mornin'," "Squeeze the Trigger") into his heretofore mostly light, sex-obsessed repertoire. Complaining that the songs glorified sex and violence, Tipper Gore's Parents' Music Resource Center (PMRC) persuaded Sire to attach a warning sticker to the album. Meanwhile, actor/director Dennis Hopper liked Ice-T's tales enough to ask the rapper to pen the title song for his 1988 gang-culture film *Colors*.

Power (#35 pop, #6 R&B, 1988) produced two minor hits, "High Rollers" (#76 R&B) and a personalized take on Curtis Mayfield's "Pusherman," retitled "I'm Your Pusher" (#13 R&B). Continuing to draw fire from cultural watchdog organizations, Ice-T teamed up with former Dead Kennedys frontman Jello Biafra, who'd had an earlier run-in with the PMRC himself, for the sarcastic kick-off track of his subsequent album, *The Iceberg/Freedom of Speech . . . Just Watch What You Say* (#37 pop, #11 R&B, 1989). Although the album was well received, Ice-T later said he had been too preoccupied with the censorship issue. In 1991 Ice-T released his magnum opus, *O.G. Original Gangster* (#15 pop, #9 R&B), a ferocious, 24-track album that chronicled the life of a ghetto tough in songs like "Home of the Bodybag," "Straight Up Nigga," and "Lifestyles of the Rich and Infamous." *O.G.* also introduced his thrash-metal band Body Count on the song of the same name.

Body Count's self-titled debut album came out to little fanfare in 1992. Then a Texas police group noticed a track called "Cop Killer" and threatened to boycott Sire's parent company, Time Warner. Within a year, Ice-T became a household name, appearing on the cover of ROLLING STONE in a police uniform. After initially supporting the artist, Time Warner quickly accepted when the rapper offered to remove "Cop Killer" from the album; the label soon began asking other artists under its umbrella to remove similarly objectionable material. When the company rejected the artwork for Ice-T's next solo album, *Home Invasion*, the rapper elected to be released from his seven-album contract; he left the company in January 1993 with five gold albums. (In 1993 he released *Home Invasion* [#14 pop, #9 R&B], artwork and all, on the independent label Priority.) Warner's decision to let go of Ice-T provided a chilling symbol of how intense corporate fear of rap had become in the wake of "Cop Killer." Body Count (including high school friend Ernie C. on guitar) reemerged with a third album, *Violent Demise: The Last Days*, in 1997 on Virgin Records.

In 1994 Ice-T's autobiography, *The Ice Opinion*, was published by St. Martin's Press. By then, he had begun a successful acting career, appearing in several films, including *New Jack City* (1991), *Ricochet* (1991), *Trespass* (1992), and *Surviving the Game* (1994). He also played an ex-con-turned-crimefighter on the short-lived network TV drama *Players* in 1997. But Ice-T continued to rap, even as his sales noticeably diminished, releasing *VI: Return of the Real* (#89 pop, #19 R&B, 1996) and *Seventh Deadly Sin* (1999).

Icicle Works

Formed 1980, Liverpool, Eng.
Ian McNabb (b. Robert Ian McNabb, Nov. 3, 1960, Liverpool), gtr., voc.; Chris Layne, bass; Chris Sharrock, drums.
1984—*Icicle Works* (Arista) 1985—*The Small Price of a Bicycle* (Chrysalis) (+ Dave Green, kybds.) 1986—*Seven Singles Deep* (Beggars Banquet, U.K.) 1987—*If You Want to Defeat Your Enemy Sing His Song* (Beggars Banquet/RCA) (– Layne; – Sharrock; + Roy Corkhill, bass; + Zak Starkey [b. Sep. 13, 1965, London], drums) 1988—*Blind* (– Green; – Starkey; + Dave Baldwin, kybds.; + Paul Burgess, drums; + Mark Revell, gtr.) 1990—*Permanent Damage* (Epic, U.K.) 1992—*Best of Icicle Works* (Beggars Banquet, U.K.).

Playing poker-faced, neopsychedelic pop rock with jangly guitars, Icicle Works (who took their name from an obscure science-fiction novel) emerged from the postpunk Liverpool scene that produced Echo and the Bunnymen. Icicle Works grew out of such local Liverpool bands as City Limits and Cherry Boys, and scored its first U.K. hit single with "Nirvana" in 1982. The band's debut album charted in the U.S. (#40, 1984) and yielded a Top 40 pop hit in "Whisper to a Scream (Birds Fly)" (#37, 1984). The group's second album was a British hit but failed to make the U.S. chart. In fact, Icicle Works made no further impact in the U.S., save for the news that ex-Beatle Ringo Starr's son, Zak Starkey, joined on drums for 1987's *Blind*.

Icicle Works disbanded in 1990, with bandleader Ian McNabb embarking on a solo career. He released *Truth and Beauty* on the British indie label This Way Up in early 1993, and recorded a second solo album, *Head Like a Rock*, in 1994 in L.A. with American musicians, including Billy Talbot and Ralph Molina of Crazy Horse and legendary Meters drummer Joseph "Zigaboo" Modeliste. That album, and its successor, *Merseybeast*, were both released in 1995. McNabb also performed and recorded with Mike Scott of the Waterboys.

Ides of March

Formed ca. 1964, Berwyn, IL
James Peterik, lead voc., gtr., kybds., sax; Ray Herr, voc., gtr., bass; Larry Millas, gtr., organ, voc.; Bob Bergland, bass, sax; John Larson, trumpet; Chuck Somar, horn; Michael Borch, drums.
1970—*Vehicle* (Warner Bros.) 1971—*Common Bond* 1972—*World Woven* (RCA) 1973—*Midnight Oil* 2000—*Ideology* (Sundazed).

A seven-piece group with horns from the suburbs of Chicago, the Ides of March were often accused of being Blood, Sweat and Tears imitators. Their one big hit, "Vehicle" (#2, 1970), sounded like BS&T, but the Ides of March had actually formed long before Blood, Sweat and Tears (or the Ides' local contemporaries Chicago).

The group members met in elementary school and formed the band while in high school. In the next few years they all enrolled in the same college. The band scored two minor 1966 hits—"You Wouldn't Listen" and "Roller

Coaster"—and faded until 1970, when Peterik's "Vehicle" was released. The record had been certified gold by November 1972, but the Ides proved unable to find a followup hit.

The Ides left Warner Bros. for RCA, to little avail, then disbanded. A mid-'70s attempt to regroup never got off the ground. Peterik returned to the chart over a decade later as a member of Survivor, whose single "Eye of the Tiger" hit #1 in the summer of 1982. He also wrote and cowrote hits for .38 Special. Peterik went solo in 1996 and formed the project World Stage. He collaborated with Brian Wilson on "Dream Angel," which was featured on the ex–Beach Boy's 1998 *Imagination* album. The original Ides reunited in 1990, adding two new musicians to the lineup. Their recent recordings include an EP, a tribute song for the 1998 Chicago Cubs baseball team, and a greatest-hits package featuring new material.

Billy Idol/Generation X

Born William Michael Albert Broad, Nov. 30, 1955, Stanmore, Middlesex, Eng.
With Generation X: formed 1976, London, Eng.: Billy Idol, voc.; Tony James, bass, voc.; Bob Andrews, gtr., voc.; John Towe, drums.
1978—*Generation X* (Chrysalis) 1979—*Valley of the Dolls* 1981—*Kiss Me Deadly; Dancing With Myself* EP 1985—*The Best of Generation X.*
Billy Idol solo: 1981—*Don't Stop* EP 1982—*Billy Idol* (Chrysalis) 1983—*Rebel Yell* 1986—*Whiplash Smile* 1987—*Vital Idol* 1990—*Charmed Life* 1993—*Cyberpunk* 2001—*Greatest Hits.*

From his beginnings as frontman for Generation X, Billy Idol's career has touched on trends from punk to cyberpunk. While his sincerity has sometimes been questioned, with four platinum albums—*Rebel Yell* (#6, 1983), *Whiplash Smile* (#6, 1986), *Vital Idol* (#10, 1987), and *Charmed Life* (#11, 1990)—there is no doubting his success. One of the earliest acts to embrace MTV, Idol became a network fixture in a series of sexually suggestive, bimbo-festooned videos. While widely reviled, the clips fixed Idol's sneering, leather-clad, bad-boy image and made hits of "White Wedding" (#36, 1983), "Rebel Yell" (#46, 1984), "Eyes Without a Face" (#4, 1984), "To Be a Lover" (#6, 1986), "Mony Mony 'Live' " (#1, 1987), and "Cradle of Love" (#2, 1990).

A Beatle-loving child of the '60s, by 1976 William Broad had changed his name to Billy Idol, dyed his hair platinum blond, and begun hanging out at Malcolm McLaren's Sex boutique. He joined Chelsea, an early punk band, that year, leaving two months later with Tony James to form Generation X. Unabashedly commercial, they had a string of British hits in 1977, including "Your Generation," "Ready Steady Go," and "Wild Youth," and were the first punk band to appear on the BBC's *Top of the Pops.*

A second album, *Valley of the Dolls,* produced by Mott the Hoople's Ian Hunter, was not well received, nor was *Kiss Me Deadly.* Idol quit in 1981, but not before releasing an EP *Dancing With Myself.*

Idol, who had spent four years as a child on Long Island, moved to Greenwich Village and signed with Kiss manager Bill Aucoin. He put together a band with guitarist and songwriting partner Steve Stevens plus a group of local musicians and recorded an EP, *Don't Stop* (#71, 1981). Produced by Giorgio Moroder protégé Keith Forsey, it was notable for its cover of Tommy James and the Shondells' 1968 smash "Mony Mony" and a revamped version of "Dancing With Myself," a club hit. On this and subsequent albums Idol and Forsey merged punk's rebel stance with slickly produced metallic rock and an undercurrent of disco dance rhythms.

Idol's image as a lusty bad boy was maintained offstage as well. His tours were infamous for their excesses, and Idol was accused of attempted rape in 1985. In 1990 he was seriously injured in a motorcycle accident in L.A. The accident kept him from playing the part of Tom Baker in Oliver Stone's *The Doors* (1991) (he ended up playing the smaller part of Cat) and delayed the release of *Charmed Life,* his first album of new material in three years and his first without Stevens. *Charmed Life* revived Idol's career, but his brand of misogyny seemed tired. After a three-year hiatus Idol returned with *Cyberpunk* (#48, 1993). Its title, videos, and accompanying computer press release caused many to claim that Idol was once again jumping on a bandwagon, this time that of a punky sci-fi Internet subculture.

The '80s revival found him appearing as himself in the Adam Sandler hit, *The Wedding Singer* (1998). In 2001 he attempted a comeback, appearing on VH1's *Storytellers* and as the subject of *Behind the Music;* he also released *Greatest Hits* (#74, 2001).

Julio Iglesias

Born Julio Jose Iglesias de la Cueva, Sep. 23, 1943, Madrid, Spain
1980—*Hey!* (Columbia) 1981—*From a Child to a Woman* 1982—*Moments* 1983—*In Concert; Julio* 1984—*1100 Bel Air Place* 1985—*Libra* 1988—*Non Stop* 1990—*Starry Night* 1994—*Crazy* 1996—*Tango* 1998—*My Life: The Greatest Hits* 2000—*Noche de Cuatro Lunas.*

From Valentino on, America's infatuation with the image of the Latin lover refuses to die. In the '80s Julio Iglesias slipped effortlessly into the role and for a brief moment it looked like the suave crooner would achieve in America the incredible success that he had enjoyed around the rest of the world.

The man whom the *Guinness Book of World Records* claims has sold more records than any other singer (an estimated 250 million by 2000) originally wanted to be a professional soccer player. When a near-fatal car accident ended that dream in 1962, Iglesias spent his recovery time learning how to play guitar, compose, and sing. Bowing to his father's wishes, Iglesias studied law, but music remained his love. After winning first prize at the 1968 Spanish Song Festival, where he sang his own "La Vida Sigue Igual," Iglesias was signed by Discos Columbia. In the '70s Iglesias became a major MOR star in Europe and Latin America. Often recording versions of his songs in Spanish, French, Italian, German, Portuguese, and English, Iglesias achieved near-global success.

He had his first major English-language hit in 1981 when his version of Cole Porter's "Begin the Beguine" topped the British charts. His U.S. breakthrough came through the unlikely but immensely popular 1984 duet with Willie Nelson, "To All the Girls I've Loved Before" (#5). A duet with Diana Ross, "All of You" (#19), hit later that year. Both tracks appeared on the triple-platinum *1100 Bel Air Place.*

Iglesias' tall, dark, and handsome looks, European charm, and ultrasmooth singing endeared him to a romance-starved audience, but a noticeable difficulty with spoken English hampered his wider appeal. Despite the initial hits and adoring fans, Iglesias could not sustain his stateside recording success. Nevertheless, he has become a perennial live attraction, regularly filling houses from Radio City Music Hall to Vegas, and he continues to sell well. *Starry Night,* featuring his cover of Don McLean's "Vincent," went to #37, while 1994's *Crazy,* featuring guests Dolly Parton and Art Garfunkel, went to #30. *Tango,* his 1996 collection of classic tango songs, peaked at #81, but topped *Billboard*'s Latin 50 chart for 10 weeks. He was knocked off the top by his son Enrique, who later crossed over to top *Billboard*'s Hot 100 chart with 1999's "Bailamos" and 2000's "Be With You." (Another son of Iglesias, Julio Jr., also crossed over to the Hot 100 in 1999).

Iglesias' first major career retrospective, 1998's *My Life: The Greatest Hits,* was a double-disc set that devoted a disc each to both his English and Latin hits. In 2000 he released his 77th album, the Spanish *Noche de Cuatro Lunas,* which found Iglesias contributing his own songs for the first time in nearly two decades.

The Impressions

Formed 1957, Chicago, IL
Curtis Mayfield (b. June 3, 1942, Chicago; d. Dec. 26, 1999, Roswell, GA), voc., gtr.; Jerry Butler (b. Dec. 8, 1939, Sunflower, MS), voc.; Arthur Brooks (b. Chattanooga, TN); Richard Brooks (b. Chattanooga), voc.; Sam Gooden (b. Sep. 2, 1939, Chattanooga), voc.
1958–59—(– Butler; + Fred Cash [b. Oct. 8, 1940, Chattanooga], voc.) 1961—(– A. and R. Brooks) 1963—*The Impressions* (ABC) 1964—*The Never Ending Impressions; Keep On Pushing* 1965—*People Get Ready; Greatest Hits* 1968—*Best of the Impressions; We're a Winner* 1970—(– Mayfield; + Leroy Hutson, voc.) 1973—(– Hutson; + Reggie Torrian, voc.; + Ralph Johnson, voc.) 1974—*Finally Got Myself Together* (Curtom) 1976—*For Your Precious Love* (Vee-Jay); *Originals* (ABC); *The Vintage Years* (Sire) 1979—*Come to My Party* (20th Century–Fox) ca. 1980—(– Johnson; + Nate Evans, voc.) 1981—*Fan the Fire* 1989—*The Impressions' Greatest Hits* (MCA) 1992—*The Young Mods' Forgotten Story* (Curtom); 1992—*Curtis Mayfield and the Impressions: The Anthology 1961–1977* (MCA) 1993—*Their Complete Vee-Jay Recordings* (Vee-Jay) 1997—*The Very Best of the Impressions* (Rhino).

The Impressions' close vocal harmonies and big-band–style horn arrangements were precursors of and a major influence on '60s soul, especially its romantic ballads. The group's original members—Sam Gooden, and brothers Richard and Arthur Brooks—were in a Tennessee group, the Roosters, and made their way to Chicago, where they hooked up with a team of songwriter/producers, Jerry Butler and Curtis Mayfield, of the Northern Jubilee Gospel Singers.

The Impressions' first hit, "For Your Precious Love" (#11, 1958), featured Butler's lead vocals, but within the year he left the group for a solo career (although he continued to work with Mayfield [see entry]). Cash, who had not been in the initial lineup, replaced Butler. After the group's next major hit, "Gypsy Woman" (#20 pop, #2 R&B), in 1961, the Brooks brothers dropped out, leaving the trio of Mayfield, Gooden, and Cash.

Mayfield became the Impressions' leader and, with a distinctly soft yet emotive falsetto, the group's lead vocalist. Under his guidance, the Impressions became one of the era's most popular vocal groups. Their trio vocals were also a major influence on Jamaican pop. Through the '60s, the group had hits with Mayfield's love songs, such as "Talking About My Baby" (#14, 1964), "I'm So Proud" (#14 pop, #14 R&B, 1964), "Woman's Got Soul" (#29 pop, #9 R&B, 1965), and his gospel-tinged message songs, including "Keep On Pushin' " (#10, 1964), "People Get Ready" (#14, 1965), and "Amen" (#7, 1965). Mayfield also kept up an active career as producer, arranger, and songwriter; he left the Impressions in 1970.

Howard University graduate Leroy Hutson took over the group in the early '70s and kept it on the soul chart with "Check Out Your Mind," "(Baby) Turn On to Me," and "Ain't Got Time," among others, before going solo in 1973. Cash and Gooden regrouped with Reggie Torian and Ralph Johnson, and had a Top 20 pop hit (#1 R&B) in 1974 with "Finally Got Myself Together," and they did the soundtrack for the blaxploitation film *Three the Hard Way.* They continued to record for various labels into the '80s, with middling success, although a 1975 single, "First Impressions," hit the U.K. Top 20. In 1983 Butler and Mayfield rejoined the group for a reunion tour, and they performed together intermittently through the years.

The Impressions last recorded with Mayfield shortly before his death in December 1999: a new version of "People Get Ready" for Atlanta's Year 2000 celebration. In 2000 the Impressions received the Rhythm & Blues Foundation's Pioneer Award.

The Incredible String Band

Formed 1965, Glasgow, Scot.
Mike Heron (b. Dec. 12, 1942), voc., gtr., assorted instruments; Robin Williamson (b. Nov. 24, 1943), voc., gtr., assorted instruments; Clive Palmer, banjo.

1966—*The Incredible String Band* (Elektra) (– Palmer) 1967—*The 5000 Spirits or the Layers of the Onion; The Hangman's Beautiful Daughter* (+ Christina "Licorice" McKenzie, violin, assorted instruments; + Rose Simpson, bass) 1968—*Wee Tam; The Big Huge* 1969—*Changing Horses* 1970—*I Looked Up; U; Be Glad for the Song Has No Ending* (Reprise) 1971—(– Simpson; + Malcolm Le Maistre, bass, voc.) 1972—*Liquid Acrobat as Regards the Air* (Elektra); *Earth Span* (Island) 1973—(– McKenzie) *No Ruinous Feud* (+ Gerald Dott, kybds., reeds) 1974—*Hard Rope and Silken Twine* (+ John Gilston, drums; + Graham Forbes, gtr.) 1974—*Seasons They Change* 1997—(group re-forms: Heron; Williamson; Palmer; + Lawson Dando, piano; + Bina Williamson, voc.) *The Chelsea Sessions 1967* (Pig's Whisker, U.K.) 1998—*Bloomsbury 1997* 1999—*At the Pure Fountain.*

A highly eclectic Scottish folk group founded in the mid-'60s, the Incredible String Band had a repertoire of original songs derived from British traditional ballads, Appalachian tunes, Delta blues, Indian ragas, Ethiopian *oud* music, calypso, Gilbert and Sullivan, and international folk styles. Fans of their proto–world music included Led Zeppelin (Robert Plant once credited the group as an inspiration for his band's forays into British folk) and the Rolling Stones (who tried and failed to sign ISB to their Mother Earth label in the late '60s). Though there were other shifting members of the band, ISB was essentially just two Glasgow-born songwriters, Robin Williamson and Mike Heron, who between them played a wide assortment of instruments.

In 1965 Williamson played in a jug-band duo at Glasgow's Incredible Folk Club with its owner Clive Palmer. Heron (who had played in the Edinburgh rock group Rock Bottom and the Deadbeats) joined soon after, and the trio took its name from Palmer's club. After an eponymous debut on Elektra in 1966, Williamson and Palmer traveled in North Africa. Upon their return, Palmer left the group, but the other two kept performing in local clubs. In November 1966 they made their first concert appearance outside Scotland, at London's Royal Albert Hall, with Tom Paxton and Judy Collins on the bill. The two American artists helped spread ISB's reputation in the U.S. (Collins later recorded Williamson's "First Girl I Loved"), and in 1967 its second LP, *The 5000 Spirits or the Layers of the Onion,* was acclaimed on both sides of the Atlantic.

A cult audience developed in the U.S., but in England ISB was a mainstay of the hippie movement. In 1967 the virtuoso multi-instrumentalist duo version of ISB recorded one more LP, *The Hangman's Beautiful Daughter.* Williamson and Heron then added two women: bassist Rose Simpson and Christina McKenzie on violin, kazoo, and other instruments. Their first releases together, the two-disc *Wee Tam* and *The Big Huge,* were viewed by some as indulgent and disappointing, and the band's reputation declined as the '60s ended, though their music became increasingly ambitious. The album *U* was conceived as a loose stage show that played with a mime troupe.

In 1971 Simpson left, replaced by Malcolm Le Maistre in 1972. Gerard Dott, another multi-instrumentalist, replaced McKenzie in 1973. He knew Heron from childhood and had played in a skiffle band with Williamson and Heron. In 1971 the band members were drifting apart, with Heron releasing the solo LP *Smiling Men With Bad Reputations,* Williamson issuing his own LP, *Myrrh,* in 1973. (Both had become Scientologists.) By the time of their last show together in 1974, they had become harder-rocking after adding drummer Gilston and guitarist Forbes. Heron did session work and later formed Mike Heron's Reputation with ex-ISB's Gilston, Forbes, and Le Maistre. Williamson moved to L.A., formed Robin Williamson's Merry Band, and released three LPs of poetry and music and a 1981 solo album on Flying Fish Records.

In the late '90s the Incredible String Band's original members, augmented by new pianist Lawson Dando and Williamson's wife Bina, reunited. The group has toured several times and released several archival and live reunion albums on Palmer's Pig's Whisker label.

Indigo Girls

Formed 1980, Decatur, GA; became Indigo Girls 1983
Amy Ray (b. Apr. 12, 1964, Atlanta, GA) voc., gtr.; Emily Saliers (b. July 22, 1963, New Haven, CT) voc., gtr.
1986—*Indigo Girls* EP (Indigo) 1987—*Strange Fire* 1989—*Indigo Girls* (Epic) 1990—*Nomads Indians Saints* 1991—*Back on the Bus, Y'All* EP 1992—*Rites of Passage* 1994—*Swamp Ophelia* 1995—*1200 Curfews* 1997—*Shaming of the Sun* 1999—*Come On Now Social.*

Blending their voices in powerful harmonies over acoustic guitars, the Indigo Girls have attained a degree of pop success rare for artists so firmly rooted in folk and women's music. Amy Ray's rough alto and moody rock songs provide an edgy balance to Emily Saliers' warm soprano and folkish compositions.

The two childhood friends began making music together while still in high school in suburban Atlanta, calling themselves Saliers and Ray. They continued to perform while attending Emory University, where they changed their name to the Indigo Girls. They released their first independent single, "Crazy Game," in 1985, followed by an EP and a full-length album before signing with Epic. They established a large enough following with their independent releases that they could maintain artistic control in their major-label deal. Members from both R.E.M. and the Hothouse Flowers play on the Grammy-winning, Scott Litt–produced *Indigo Girls.* Although the single "Closer to Fine" was played by MTV, VH1, and some radio stations, constant touring, a supportive press, and devoted fans drove the duo's gold and platinum record sales.

Litt produced *Nomads Indians Saints,* which featured Mary Chapin Carpenter, the Ellen James Society, drummers Kenny Aronoff and Jim Keltner, and bassist Sara Lee, and included the Grammy-nominated single "Hammer and a Nail." *Back on the Bus, Y'All* was a live EP. On *Rites of Passage,* the band experimented with rock noise and Latin and African percussion, working with producer Peter Collins, whose credits include Queensrÿche and Alice Cooper. Guests include the Roches, Jackson Browne, David Crosby, Lisa Germano, and Budgie and Martin McCarrick from Siouxsie and the Banshees. The album (#21, 1992) was nominated for a Grammy. Collins also produced 1994's *Swamp Ophelia* (#9), which featured the duo's first totally electric song, "Touch Me Fall." In addition to including such previous guests as Germano, the Roches, and Lee, *Ophelia* featured Jane Siberry, and ex–Allman Brothers pianist Chuck Leavell.

Alongside their somber spirituals, the Indigo Girls frequently sing about environmentalism, feminism, and other social issues. They have played benefits on behalf of Habitat for Humanity, the Children's Health Fund, and Humanitas, among others. Ray actively supports independent music and is the founder of the Atlanta-based Daemon Records, whose roster has included James Hall, the Ellen James Society, Danielle Howle, the Rock-A-Teens, and Kristen Hall. In 1994 both Ray and Saliers acted in the Herbert Ross film *Boys on the Side.* They also starred in an update of the musical *Jesus Christ Superstar* that cast Ray as Jesus and Saliers as Mary Magdalene.

In 1995 the Indigo Girls released their second live album, *1200 Curfews* (#40). Their next record, *Shaming of the Sun* (#7, 1997), continued the musical experimentation the duo had begun with *Swamp Ophelia,* featuring tape loops and rock guitar solos. It also boasted guest appearances from Dallas Austin and Steve Earle. *Come On Now Social* (1999) grew out of a series of London jam sessions with Ghostland, a band that backed Sinéad O'Connor during the 1998 Lilith Fair Tour. The album included cameos from Meshell Ndegéocello, Joan Osborne, Sheryl Crow, and Luscious Jackson drummer Kate Schellenbach, as well as the broadside "Faye Tucker," a song about Karla Faye Tucker, the first woman executed by the state of Texas since the Civil War.

James Ingram

Born Feb. 17, 1952, Akron, OH
1983—*It's Your Night* (Qwest) 1986—*Never Felt So Good* (Warner Bros.) 1990—*It's Real* 1991—*The Power of Great Music* 1993—*Always You* 1999—*Forever More (Love Songs, Hits & Duets)* (Private Music).

With his smooth, deep voice and ladies' man charm, James Ingram is a true pop singles artist: In the '80s he became a chart-topping, Grammy-winning balladeer mostly on the basis of his collaborations with such artists as Quincy Jones, Patti Austin, and Michael McDonald.

Ingram moved from Akron to L.A. in the mid-'70s with the band Revelation Funk, but the group soon broke up, and he began singing demo tapes for a publishing company. Ray Charles hired Ingram to produce, play keyboards, and write songs for him. Until Quincy Jones heard one of Ingram's tapes and asked him to sing on an album, Ingram hadn't considered himself a vocalist. In 1981 Ingram won a Grammy without having released an album of his own, when he was honored for "One Hundred Ways" (#14, 1981), from Jones' *The Dude.* "Just Once" from that album went to #17. Other collaborations with Jones include "We Are the World," the film *The Color Purple,* and Michael Jackson's album *Thriller* (Ingram cowrote "P.Y.T. [Pretty Young Thing]").

"Baby, Come to Me" (#1, 1982), from Austin's album *Every Home Should Have One,* became the theme for the soap opera *General Hospital.* Ingram's gold 1983 debut album yielded the Grammy-winning "Yah Mo B There," a duet with McDonald. Ingram performed a string of songs for soundtracks, including "How Do You Keep the Music Playing?" (#45, 1983), another duet with Austin, for *Best Friends;* "Somewhere Out There" (#2, 1986), with Linda Ronstadt, for *An American Tail;* and "Better Way" (#66, 1987) for *Beverly Hills Cop II.* But Ingram didn't score a hit on his own until the Thom Bell–produced *It's Real,* which featured "I Don't Have the Heart" (#1, 1990).

Ingram was out of the limelight during the mid-'90s, but returned to the charts in 1998 when he was the featured vocalist on John Tesh's "Give Me Forever (I Do)," a #5 hit of the *Billboard* Hot AC (Adult Contemporary) chart. Ingram and Tesh repeated the formula with "Forever More (I'll Be the One)," which peaked at #12 on the Hot AC chart the following year. Ingram's 1999 best-of album includes the latter hit, plus newly recorded material, along with a version of "My Funny Valentine" set to hip-hop beats.

The Ink Spots

Formed late '20s, Indianapolis, IN
Members have included Jerry Daniels, gtr., voc.; Orville "Hoppy" Jones (b. Feb. 17, 1905, Chicago, IL; d. Oct. 18, 1944, Chicago), voc.; Charles Fuqua (d. 1971), gtr., voc.; Ivory "Deek" Watson (d. 1969), voc.
1936—(– Daniels; + Bill Kenny [b. 1915; d. Mar. 23, 1978], voc.) 1980—*The Best of the Ink Spots* (MCA).

Though the Ink Spots enjoyed their greatest popularity years before rock & roll came into being, their vocal style was a precursor to the smooth doo-wop vocal groups of the '50s, including the Ravens, the Marcels, the Flamingos, the Platters, and others.

The original group was formed when Daniels, Jones, Fuqua, and Watson met in Indianapolis. After moving to New York in the early '30s, they changed their name from King, Jack and the Jesters to the Ink Spots. In 1935 they signed with RCA Victor, then Decca. Soon thereafter, lead singer Jerry Daniels left the group and was replaced by Bill Kenny. In February 1939 the Ink Spots released "If I Didn't Care," their first million-selling record. Subsequent hits included "My Prayer," "Maybe," "We Three," "Whispering Grass," "To Each His Own," and "I Don't Want to Set the World on Fire," a song that was revived in the late '80s for Chanel commercials.

After Hoppy Jones died on October 18, 1944, from what was discovered to have been a brain hemorrhage, internal dissension cast the group's future in doubt. A flurry of personnel changes ensued, leaving Kenny the sole consistent member. Charlie Fuqua (uncle of Harvey Fuqua of the Moonglows and later Motown fame) established his own group of Ink Spots. This group toured the world and was the first black act to play in a number of venues throughout the American South. The Ink Spots had a final #1 hit with "To Each His Own" in 1946. There have been several lineups of Ink Spots through the years, but only the original lineup was inducted into the Rock and Roll Hall of Fame in 1989.

Inspiral Carpets

Formed 1986, Chadderton, Eng.
Stephen Holt (b. Eng.), voc.; Graham Lambert (b. July 10, 1964, Oldham, Eng.), gtr.; Clint Boon (b. June 28, 1959, Oldham), organ; David Swift (b. Eng.), bass; Craig Gill (b. Dec. 5, 1971, Manchester, Eng.), drums.
1988—(– Holt; – Swift; + Thomas Hingley [b. July 9, 1965, Oxford, Eng.], voc.; + Martyn Walsh [b. July 3, 1968, Manchester], bass) 1990—*Life* (Mute) 1991—*The Beast Inside* 1992—*Revenge of the Goldfish* 1994—*Devil Hopping* 1995—*The Singles.*

Inspiral Carpets emerged in the late '80s, with Stone Roses and Happy Mondays, from Manchester, England's pre-rave psychedelic dance-rock scene. Inspiral Carpets were more of a throwback than other bands on the scene, with Clint Boon's reedy Farfisa organ recalling mid-'60s garage rock, and pudding-bowl haircuts defining their look. In England the band managed to balance commercial success with independent-label credibility. In the U.S. it steadily built a core cult through albums on Mute Records (the label that had launched synth-pop bands Depeche Mode and Erasure) and live shows, where Inspiral Carpets (who recorded as live as possible in the studio) proved they could play, and blew some minds with a trippy light show.

The band's swirling, melodic neo-'60s sound was already formed on its first single, 1987's "Plane Crash." Original vocalist Stephen Holt was replaced by Thomas Hingley, whose portentous, Jim Morrison–style vocals evoked Ian McCulloch and Julian Cope, respectively, of early '80s Liverpool neopsychedelic bands Echo and the Bunnymen and Teardrop Explodes. Inspiral Carpets formed its own label, Cow Records, gaining notoriety for its slogan "Cool as Fuck." The band's first album, *Life* (1990), hit #2 in the U.K.; its sophomore effort, 1991's *The Beast Inside,* did nearly as well, charting at #4 U.K. By Inspiral Carpets' third album, *Revenge of the Goldfish* (#17 U.K., 1992), Graham Lambert's guitar—often surf-like in its reverb—had taken on near-equal footing with Boon's organ. After the 1994 release of *Devil Hopping,* the group was dropped by Mute and disbanded. Boon launched his own act, the Clint Boon Experience!, in 1999.

The Intruders

Formed 1960, Philadelphia, PA
Phil Terry (b. Nov. 1, 1943, Philadelphia), voc.; Robert "Big Sonny" Edwards (b. Feb. 22, 1942, Philadelphia), voc.; Samuel "Little Sonny" Brown, voc.; Eugene "Bird" Daughtry (b. Oct. 29, 1939, Kinston, NC; d. Dec. 25, 1994), voc.
1968—*Cowboys to Girls* (Gamble) 1969—*Intruders Greatest Hits* 1973—*Save the Children* 1995—*The Best of the Intruders: Cowboys to Girls* (Legacy).

This vocal quartet was an early project for the production team of Kenny Gamble and Leon Huff. The group's members sang around Philadelphia in the early '60s and recorded one single for the local Gowen Records in 1961. Three years later they met Leon Huff, who produced their single "All the Time" on Musicor Records. By 1966, Huff had teamed with Kenny Gamble to form Gamble Records, and the Intruders became the company's first signing.

The Intruders' first chart single, "(We'll Be) United" (#14 R&B), started a hot streak in 1966. "Devil With an Angel's Smile" hit #26 R&B, also in 1966. "Together" (#9 R&B; later a huge hit for Tierra), "Baby, I'm Lonely" (#9 R&B), and "A Love That's Real" (#35 R&B) in 1967 built the Intruders' and the Gamble and Huff team's national reputation.

The next year was the Intruders' peak, with the million-selling "Cowboys to Girls" (#6 pop, #1 R&B). "Love Is Like a Baseball Game" (#26 pop, #4 R&B, 1968) and "Slow Drag" (#12 R&B, 1969) followed. Gamble and Huff gave them "Sad Girl" (#14 R&B) in 1970 and "When We Get Married" (#8 R&B) and "(Win, Place or Show) She's a Winner" (#12 R&B) in 1972. The Intruders' "I'll Always Love My Mama" (#36 pop, #6 R&B, 1973) was a disco mainstay and a perennial Mother's Day favorite.

In 1975 the Intruders broke up. But in 1984, Eugene Daughtry, who'd been working as a truck driver, assembled a new group with his brother Fred, cousin Al Miller, and Lee Williams. A 1984 single, "Who Do You Love?," made the charts in England.

INXS

Formed 1977, Sydney, Austral.
Garry Gary Beers (b. June 22, 1957, Sydney), bass; Michael Hutchence (b. Jan. 22, 1960, Sydney; d. Nov. 22, 1997, Sydney), voc.; Andrew Farriss (b. Mar. 27, 1959, Perth, Austral.), kybds., gtr.; Jon Farriss (b. Aug. 10, 1961, Perth), drums; Tim Farriss (b. Aug. 16, 1957, Perth), gtr.; Kirk Pengilly (b. July 4, 1958, Sydney), gtr., sax, voc.
1980—*INXS* (Aus. Deluxe) 1981—*Underneath the Colours* 1983—*Shabooh Shoobah* (Atco); *Dekadance* EP 1984—*The Swing* 1985—*Listen Like Thieves* (Atlantic) 1987—*Kick* 1990—*X* 1991—*Live Baby Live* 1992—*Welcome to Wherever You Are* 1993—*Full Moon, Dirty Hearts* 1994—*INXS: The Greatest Hits* 1997—*Elegantly Wasted* (PGD/PolyGram) 2001—*Shine Like It Does: The Anthology (1979–1997)* (Atlantic/Rhino).
Michael Hutchence solo: 2000—*Michael Hutchence* (V2).

INXS: Tim Farriss, Michael Hutchence, Jon Farriss, Garry Gary Beers, Kirk Pengilly, Andrew Farriss

Years before it became fashionable for white artists to mix guitar rock textures with hip-hop beats, INXS emerged from Down Under with a danceable funk-rock fusion that would make the band international stars by the mid-'80s. Adding to the group's commercial appeal was the charisma of its lead singer, Michael Hutchence, who combined Jaggeresque posturing with looks evoking a lankier Jim Morrison; like Morrison, Hutchence would meet an early, tragic death that shocked the world.

INXS began as a family act, originally calling itself the Farriss Brothers. While still in high school, Andrew Farriss and Hutchence—who would become INXS's primary composer and lyricist, respectively—joined forces in a band that also included Garry Beers; around the same time, Tim Farriss and Kirk Pengilly were playing in groups together. The five got together with drummer Jon Farriss in 1977, completing the lineup that would officially become INXS two years later (after Jon graduated high school). At that point, the group relocated from Perth, where Jon went to school, back to Sydney, and began playing pubs in and around the Australian capital. Gigs in other parts of the country followed, leading to an Australasian record contract.

The band soon set its sights on an American audience, signing with Atco Records and embarking on an extensive U.S. tour in support of 1983's *Shabooh Shoobah*. Later that year a studio session with noted funk producer Nile Rodgers resulted in the groove-ridden single "Original Sin," which approached the Top 40 and showed up again on 1984's *The Swing*. But INXS's real breakthrough came with 1985's *Listen Like Thieves,* which went to #11 and produced the #5 single "What You Need" the following year. *Kick* (1987) sent the Aussies into the pop stratosphere, peaking at #3 and yielding four hit singles: the #1 smash "Need You Tonight" and, in 1988, "Devil Inside" (#2), "New Sensation" (#3), and "Never Tear Us Apart" (#7). In the wake of such success, 1990's *X* was, relatively, a mild disappointment, peaking at #5 but spawning just one Top 10 single, "Suicide Blonde" (#9).

INXS nonetheless remained extremely popular, selling out London's Wembley Stadium in 1991 and releasing a live album and video, *Live Baby Live,* while Hutchence remained visible by dating bubblegum singer/actress Kylie Minogue and supermodel Helena Christensen. *Welcome to Wherever You Are* (1992) got positive reviews for its sonic adventurousness, but was again only moderately successful, producing an AOR radio hit with "Beautiful Girl" (#46) in 1993. Later that year, INXS released its tenth album, *Full Moon, Dirty Hearts* (#53), which featured Chrissie Hynde (duetting with Hutchence on the title track) and Ray Charles. In 1994 INXS departed from Atlantic (which released the band's greatest-hits collection that year), joined PolyGram, and embarked on recording a new studio album.

In 1995 Hutchence began a relationship with British talk-show host Paula Yates, the estranged wife of famed Live Aid organizer Bob Geldof. The new couple had a daughter, Heavenly Hiraani Tiger Lily, in 1996, and planned to marry, but their happiness was marred by the paparazzi and Yates' bitter divorce and custody battle over her and Geldof's three daughters. Meanwhile, *Elegantly Wasted* was released in the spring of 1997 and the title track was a mild hit (#13, 1997). While in his hometown of Sydney preparing for INXS' 20th anniversary tour in November 1997, the 37-year-old Hutchence hanged himself in his hotel room in what was widely believed to be a suicide (though one theory that emerged was that his death was an accident resulting from autoerotic asphyxiation). Yates would die of a heroin overdose in September 2000. Geldof would be awarded temporary custody of Hutchence's daughter.

For two years prior to his death, Hutchence had been recording a solo album with producers Andy Gill of Gang of Four and Danny Saber of Black Grape. The self-titled album was released posthumously in 2000, with Hutchence's friend Bono adding vocals to one track. The rest of the band—who had learned of Hutchence's death while waiting for him to show up for rehearsal—surfaced in 2000 as the house band for Broadway composer Tim Rice's *Musical Spectacular,* a brief tour. They were also involved with the making of an Australian television documentary about INXS, an INXS photograph book, and a final album by the band, featuring Hutchence's vocals, all slated for release in 2001.

Iron Butterfly

Formed 1966, San Diego, CA
Doug Ingle (b. Sep. 9, 1946, Omaha, NE), kybds., voc.; Ron Bushy (b. Sep. 23, 1945, Washington, DC), drums, voc.; Jerry Penrod (b. San Diego), bass; Darryl DeLoach (b. San Diego), voc.; Danny Weis (b. San Diego), gtr.
1968—*Heavy* (Atco) (– Penrod; – DeLoach; – Weiss; + Lee

Dorman [b. Sep. 15, 1942, St. Louis, MO], bass, gtr., piano; + Erik Braunn [b. Aug. 11, 1950, Boston, MA], gtr., voc.) *In-A-Gadda-Da-Vida* 1969—*Ball* 1970—*Live* (– Braunn; + Mike Pinera [b. Sep. 29, 1948, Tampa, FL], gtr., voc.; + Larry "Rhino" Reinhardt [b. July 7, 1948, FL], gtr.) 1971—*The Best of Iron Butterfly/Evolution; Metamorphosis* (group disbands) 1974—(group re-forms: Braunn; Bushy; + Phil Kramer [b. July 12, 1952, Youngstown, OH], bass; + Howard Reitzes [b. Mar. 22, 1951, Southgate, CA], kybds., gtr.) 1975—*Sun and Steel* (MCA); *Scorching Beauty* 1993—(group re-forms: Bushy; Pinera; + Dorman, bass; + Derek Hilland, kybds., voc.) *Light and Heavy: The Best of Iron Butterfly* (Rhino).

Now remembered as a passing fancy of the acid-rock era, at its peak Iron Butterfly was considered a leading hard-rock band. During the group's relatively brief lifetime, it sold about 7 million albums; *In-A-Gadda-Da-Vida* sold 4 million copies alone. The album's focal point was the 17-minute title track (featuring a 2½-minute drum solo), which was also something of a catalyst in establishing "progressive" FM radio programming.

"In-A-Gadda-Da-Vida" was written by group leader, organist, and chief vocalist Doug Ingle, whose father was a church organist. Ingle formed his first group at age 16 in San Diego, where he met drummer Ron Bushy, one of four San Diegans to accompany Ingle to L.A. in late 1966.

In L.A., Iron Butterfly worked Bido Lito's and eventually moved to the Galaxy and the Whisky-a-Go-Go. By early 1967, the band had a recording contract. Its debut disc stayed on the charts for nearly a year, partly because of the national exposure the group got as an opening act for the Doors and the Jefferson Airplane. Shortly after the LP was released, three of the original members left, among them Danny Weis, later of Rhinoceros.

With new bassist Lee Dorman and guitarist Erik Braunn, Iron Butterfly recorded *In-A-Gadda-Da-Vida* ("In a Garden of Eden," some suggested), which became Atlantic's then-biggest seller. The album stayed on the chart for 140 weeks, 81 of them in the Top 10. An edited version of the title track hit #30. *Ball* hit #3 and went gold, but subsequent efforts failed.

In late 1969 Braunn left and later formed Flintwhistle with Penrod and DeLoach of the original lineup. He and Dorman also discovered Black Oak Arkansas, whose first album was produced by Dorman and guitarist Mike Pinera (formerly of Blues Image), who replaced Brann in Iron Butterfly. Also joining was Larry "Rhino" Reinhardt (who had been living with Gregg and Duane Allman). *Metamorphosis* followed, but the group broke up after its farewell performance on May 23, 1971.

During Iron Butterfly's career, all six of its albums charted; it toured the U.S. eight times and Europe as well. The group was featured in the film *Savage Seven* (along with Cream), from which came the first of several singles ("Possession" b/w "Unconscious Power"). Yet another, "Easy Rider," was featured in the film of the same name. In the mid-'70s the group was revived by Braunn and Bushy with the inconsequential *Scorching Beauty* and *Sun and Steel;* other lineups have appeared over the years. Pinera went on to play with Cactus and Alice Cooper. In 1973 Dorman formed jazz-rock outfit Captain Beyond.

Iron Maiden

Formed 1976, London, Eng.
Paul Di'anno (b. May 17, 1959, London), voc.; Steve Harris (b. Mar. 12, 1957, London), bass, voc.; Dave Murray (b. Dec. 23, 1958, London), gtr.; Doug Sampson, drums.
1979—(+ Tony Parson, gtr.) 1980—(– Parson; – Sampson; + Dennis Stratton [b. Nov. 9, 1954, London], gtr.; + Clive Burr, drums) *Iron Maiden* (Harvest/Capitol) (– Stratton; + Adrian Smith [b. Feb. 27, 1957, London], gtr.) 1981—*Killers; Maid in Japan* (– Di'anno; + Bruce Dickinson [b. Paul Bruce Dickinson, Aug. 7, 1958, Worksop, Eng.], voc.) 1982—*The Number of the Beast* (– Burr; + Nicko McBrain [b. June 5, 1954], drums) 1983—*Piece of Mind* 1984—*Powerslave* 1985—*Live After Death* 1986—*Somewhere in Time* 1988—*Seventh Son of a Seventh Son* 1990—(– Smith; + Janick Gers, gtr.) *No Prayer for the Dying* (Epic) 1992—*Fear of the Dark* 1993—*A Real Live One* (Capitol); *A Real Dead One; Live at Donnington* (– Dickinson; + Blaze Bayley, voc.) 1995—*The X Factor* (CMC) 1998—*Virtual XI* 1999—*Ed Hunter* (Portrait) (– Bayley; + Dickinson; + Smith) 2000—*Brave New World* (Portrait).
Bruce Dickinson solo: 1990—*Tattooed Millionaire* (Columbia) 1994—*Balls to Picasso* (Mercury) 1996—*Skunkworks* (Raw Power) 1997—*Accident of Birth* (CMC).

Taking its name from the medieval torture device, Iron Maiden was part of England's late-'70s crop of heavy-metal bands that boasted simple guitar riffs, bone-crunching chording, and shrieking vocals.

Formed in 1976 by Steve Harris and Dave Murray, the first incarnation of Iron Maiden was inspired by the do-it-yourself punk ethos, and the group released an EP, *The Soundhouse Tapes,* on its own label, Rock Hard Records. *Iron Maiden,* the band's 1980 Capitol debut album, was pure, unadulterated screaming heavy metal. It went Top 5 in Britain; the following year's *Killers* made #12. America, however, was slower to embrace the denim- and leather-clad group, which distinguished itself from its peers with unusually literate songs (written by Harris) full of hellish imagery ("Children of the Damned"), their themes borrowed from films ("The Number of the Beast," inspired by *The Omen II*) and ancient mythology ("Flight of Icarus"). Maiden was certainly one of the few bands of any genre to employ a mascot, a 10-foot rotting corpse named Eddie.

The Number of the Beast, featuring new vocalist Bruce "Air Raid Siren" Dickinson, topped the LP chart in Britain and initiated a streak of seven consecutive platinum or gold albums in the States, despite virtually no radio or MTV exposure. The followup, 1983's *Piece of Mind,* went to #14; *Somewhere in Time* made #11. Beginning with *Seventh Son of a Seventh Son,* sales began to slip. In 1990 Adrian Smith, who came aboard in 1980, left to form A.S.A.P. with drummer

Zak Starkey, son of Ringo. Janick Gers took his place in time to record *No Prayer for the Dying,* Maiden's last album to go gold in the States. It contained "Bring Your Daughter to the Slaughter," a song originally recorded by Dickinson alone for the *Nightmare on Elm Street, Part 5* soundtrack. Dickinson's version went to #1 in the U.K.

Iron Maiden has weathered its numerous personnel changes without a hitch. By the time of his 1993 exit from Maiden, Dickinson, a top-rated fencer and swordsman, had already published a novel, *The Adventures of Lord Iffy Boatrace,* and released a solo album. He reunited with his old mates in 1999, after the departure of his replacement, Blaze Bayley, formerly of the group Wolfsbane. At the same time Smith returned to the fold. That year's greatest-hits album, *Ed Hunter,* also spawned a namesake Maiden video game. The all-new *Brave New World* (2000) features a three-guitar lineup.

Chris Isaak

Born June 26, 1956, Stockton, CA
1985—*Silvertone* (Warner Bros.) 1987—*Chris Isaak* 1989—*Heart Shaped World* (Reprise) 1993—*San Francisco Days* 1995—*Forever Blue* 1996—*Baja Sessions* 1998—*Speak of the Devil.*

Chris Isaak's pompadoured good looks are something of a throwback to the '50s and early '60s, and so is his music. Isaak's tender, crooning vocal style and his habit of offsetting chugging rockers with haunted ballads of isolation and heartache have invited comparisons to Elvis Presley and Roy Orbison. The singer/songwriter, who has enjoyed good reviews and an enthusiastic cult following since the mid-'80s, scored his breakthrough hit in 1991 with "Wicked Game" (#6 pop).

Isaak didn't embark on a musical career until after graduation from the University of the Pacific with a degree in English and communications arts. (He also boxed for a while, getting his nose broken seven times.) The singer/guitarist moved to San Francisco, where he formed Silvertone, a band that came to the attention of producer Erik Jacobsen, who helped Isaak land a solo contract with Warner Bros. Isaak's 1985 debut album was named after his band, whose members have continued to back him on tour. (A new guitarist, Hershel Yatovitz, was added to the lineup beginning with *Baja Sessions.*)

Despite acclaim from the press and other musicians, Isaak's moody, guitar-driven songs weren't much of a success on radio or MTV. Then in 1990, after his third album, *Heart Shaped World,* had been declared a flop, director David Lynch used an instrumental version of "Wicked Game" on the soundtrack of *Wild at Heart.* The song caught the attention of an Atlanta, Georgia, radio station music director. He tracked down Isaak's original version and, with the support of listeners, soon had it on heavy rotation. Word spread to stations across the country, and the single hit the Top 10 in early 1991. His next album, *San Francisco Days,* reached the Top 40, but no singles charted.

Forever Blue in 1995 featured the mild hit "Somebody's Crying" (#45), and contained another track that would repeat Isaak's breakthrough of having a song from a past release gain renewed life thanks to a movie. "Baby Did a Bad, Bad Thing" was used to atmospheric effect in the coming attraction to Stanley Kubrick's last film, 1999's *Eyes Wide Shut.* In the interim, 1996's *Baja Sessions* included a cover of Orbison's "Only the Lonely," but neither that album nor 1998's *Speak of the Devil* produced any hit singles.

Isaak's classic handsomeness and dry sensibility have also gotten him work as an actor. After earning small parts in two Jonathan Demme films, *Married to the Mob* and *The Silence of the Lambs,* Isaak costarred in Bernardo Bertolucci's *Little Buddha* (1993), and appeared in such other works as Tom Hanks' *That Thing You Do!* (1996) and Hanks' miniseries *From the Earth to the Moon* (1998). He gained more exposure in 2001 playing a somewhat fictionalized version of himself in the Showtime series *The Chris Isaak Show,* which glamorized the lives of Isaak and his band mates.

The Isley Brothers

Formed ca. 1955, Cincinnati, OH
Rudolph Isley (b. Apr. 1, 1939), voc.; Ronald Isley (b. May 21, 1941), lead voc.; O'Kelly Isley (b. Dec. 25, 1937; d. Mar. 31, 1986, Alpine, NJ), voc.; Vernon Isley (d. 1955).
1955—(– V. Isley) 1959—*Shout* (RCA) 1962—*Twist and Shout* (Wand) 1964—*Twisting and Shouting* (United Artists) 1966—*This Old Heart of Mine* (Tamla) 1969—*It's Our Thing* (T-Neck) (+ Ernie Isley [b. Mar. 7, 1952], bass, perc., gtr.; + Marvin Isley [b. Aug. 18, 1953], bass, perc.; + Chris Jasper, kybds., synth.) 1971—*In the Beginning . . . With Jimi Hendrix* 1972—*Brother, Brother, Brother* 1973—*3 + 3; Isleys' Greatest Hits* 1974—*Live It Up* 1975—*The Heat Is On* 1976—*Harvest for the World* 1977—*Go for Your Guns* 1978—*Showdown;* 1979—*Winner Take All* 1980—*Go All the Way* 1981—*Grand Slam* 1983—*Between the Sheets* 1984—(– M. Isley; – E. Isley; – C. Jasper) 1985—*Masterpiece* (Warner Bros.) 1987—*Smooth Sailin'* 1989—*Spend the Night* 1990—(Ronald, Rudolph, Ernie, and Marvin Isley reunite) 1991—*The Isley Brothers Story, vol. 1: The Rockin Years (1959–68)* (Rhino); *The Isley Brothers Story, vol. 2: T-Neck Years (1968–85)* 1992—*Tracks of Life* (Warner Bros.) 1996—*Mission to Please* (T-neck/Island) 1999—*It's Your Thing: The Story of the Isley Brothers* (Sony/Legacy).
Isley, Jasper, Isley: 1985—*Caravan of Love* (Columbia) 1987—*Different Drummer* (CBS Associated).
Chris Jasper solo: 1987—*Superbad* (CBS Associated).
Ernie Isley solo: 1990—*High Wire* (Elektra).

A Cincinnati-born family group, which by now has included two generations of Isleys, the Isley Brothers started out on the black R&B circuit and had occasional pop and AOR successes. The original members (including a fourth brother, Vernon, who died in a 1955 bicycle accident) were encouraged to sing by their father, a professional singer, and their mother, a pianist who accompanied them when they performed in churches before Vernon's death. Tenor Ronnie Isley was soon designated lead vocalist.

In 1957, while still in their teens, Ronald, Rudolph, and O'Kelly (who later dropped the O') went to New York and over the next year recorded several unsuccessful neo-doo-wop tunes (including "The Angels Cried"). While performing at the Howard Theater in Washington, DC, in the summer of 1959, the group was spotted by an RCA executive, who signed the Isleys. Their debut single for the label was "Shout," written in the call-and-response gospel vocal style; it was the first and most successful of the RCA recordings produced for them by Hugo Peretti and Luigi Creatore. "Shout" reached only #47 on the pop chart but became an R&B standard (since covered by such diverse artists as Lulu, Joey Dee and the Starliters, Tom Petty, and the Blues Brothers). It eventually sold over a million copies, and the group earned enough to move the entire family from Cincinnati to New Jersey.

Although the Isleys toured widely, it wasn't until they'd left RCA in 1962 and recorded "Twist and Shout" (originally recorded by the Topnotes, later covered by the Beatles) on Wand Records that they had their next hit; it reached #17. Subsequent releases on Wand and United Artists failed to hit, and the brothers toured on the R&B circuit with their backup band, which included Jimmy James (a.k.a. Jimi Hendrix). Hendrix was with the Isleys for most of 1964 and made his first recordings with them, including several sides for Atlantic and one for the Isleys' T-Neck label ("Testify"). Some of his work with the group was released in 1971 as *In the Beginning*.

In 1965 the Isleys signed to the Motown subsidiary Tamla, but although they worked with Motown's top writing and production team, Holland-Dozier-Holland, only their first single, "This Old Heart of Mine" (#12, 1966) became a pop hit. The song hit #3 in England two years later, after the Isleys had moved there to sustain their career. In 1969 they returned home and began recording for their own label, T-Neck Records. Named after their adopted hometown of Teaneck, New Jersey, the label was a revival of a company started in the early '60s and then abandoned. Their first release, "It's Your Thing" (#2, 1969), became their biggest pop hit, eventually selling over 2 million copies; it won a Grammy for Best R&B Vocal Performance. "It's Your Thing" was written and produced by the Isleys themselves, as were "I Turned You On" (#23, 1969) and "Pop That Thang" (#24, 1972).

In 1969 the Isleys added a second generation: brothers Ernest and Marvin, as well as brother-in-law Chris Jasper and nonrelative drummer Everett Collins. With Ernie's Hendrix-like guitar lines, the group often covered material by rock writers like Stephen Stills—whose "Love the One You're With" was a #18 hit in 1971 for the Isleys—Eric Burdon and War's "Spill the Wine" (#49, 1971), and Bob Dylan's "Lay Lady Lay" (#71, 1971).

"That Lady (Part I)" (#6, 1973), a 2-million-selling single, made *3 + 3* a platinum album. The Isleys' next big pop hit, the gold "Fight the Power (Part I)" (#4, 1975), came from *The Heat Is On*. While the following year's *Harvest for the World* didn't produce any gold singles, it still sold over half a million copies in three days.

In the latter part of the '70s, the Isleys adapted to the disco market. Though their pop hits ended, albums *(Go for Your Guns, Showdown, Winner Take All, Go All the Way, Grand Slam, Between the Sheets)* continued to sell gold or platinum, and they scored a number of R&B #1 hits: "The Pride" (1977), "Take Me to the Next Phase (Part 1)" (1978), "I Wanna Be With You (Part 1)" (1979), and "Don't Say Goodnight" (1980). Their more contemporary-styled R&B hits in the '80s and '90s included "Between the Sheets" (#3 R&B, 1983), "Choosey Lover" (#6 R&B, 1983), "Smooth Sailin' " (#3 R&B, 1986), "Spend the Night (Ce Soir)" (#3 R&B, 1989), "One of a Kind" (#38 R&B, 1990), "Sensitive Lover" (#24 R&B, 1992), "Let's Lay Together" (#24 R&B, 1996), "Floatin' on Your Love" (#14 R&B, 1996), and "Tears" (#12 R&B, 1997). In addition, Ronald Isley enjoyed success outside the group with a pair of duets: "Lay Your Troubles Down" (#10 R&B, 1990, with his future wife Angela Winbush) and a remake of "This Old Heart of Mine" (#10 pop, 1990, with Rod Stewart).

In 1984 Ernie and Marvin Isley and Chris Jasper left to form Isley, Jasper, Isley. They had a #1 R&B hit with "Caravan of Love" in 1985; the song went to #1 in the U.K. in an a cappella cover version by the Housemartins the following year. The trio's other R&B Top 20 hits include "Look the Other Way" (1984), "Insatiable Woman" (1986), "8th Wonder of the World" (1987), and "Givin' You Back the Love" (1987). O'Kelley died of a heart attack in 1986, and not long after, Rudolph left to join the ministry.

The Isley Brothers reunited in 1990. In 1992 they were inducted into the Rock and Roll Hall of Fame. In 1994 they won a copyright infringement suit against Michael Bolton, proving to the court's satisfaction that Bolton's hit "Love Is a Wonderful Thing" was based on their song of the same name. Bolton ignited controversy when, in commenting on the trial's outcome, he suggested that the jury had granted the Isleys a large award because they are black and he is white. The Isley Brothers were awarded 100 percent of the profits from the single and 28 percent of the profits from the album. In 2001 the Isley Brothers, featuring Ronald Isley a.k.a. Mr. Biggs, entered their sixth decade of hitmaking with "Contagious" (#41, pop, #10 R&B).

It's a Beautiful Day

Formed 1968, San Francisco, CA
David LaFlamme (b. Apr. 5, 1941, Salt Lake City, UT), elec. violin, voc.; Linda LaFlamme, kybds.; Val Fuentes (b. Nov. 25, 1947, Chicago, IL), drums; Pattie Santos (b. Nov. 16, 1949, San Francisco; d. Dec. 14, 1989, Healdsburg, CA), voc., perc.; Hal Wagenet (b. Willits, CA), gtr.; Michael Holman (b. Denver, CO), bass.
1968—(– L. La Flamme; + Fred Webb [b. Santa Rosa, CA], kybds.) 1969—*It's a Beautiful Day* (Columbia) 1970—*Marrying Maiden* 1971—(– Holman; + Bill Gregory, gtr.; + Tom Fowler, bass) *Choice Quality Stuff* 1972—*Live at Carnegie Hall* 1973—(– D. LaFlamme; – Fowler; + Graig

Block, violin; + Bud Cockrell, bass) *It's a Beautiful Day . . . Today* 1974—*1001 Nights* (group disbands) 1979—*It's a Beautiful Day.*
David LaFlamme solo: 1977—*White Bird* (Amherst) 1978—*Inside Out.*
Pattie Santos and Bud Cockrell: 1978—*New Beginnings* (A&M).
David and Linda La Flamme: 2000—*Workin' the Gold Mine* (Davlin).

It's a Beautiful Day came to national prominence with its FM standard, "White Bird." The group was led by David LaFlamme, who started playing violin at age five, and later played as soloist with the Utah Symphony. After serving in the army, he moved to California in 1962. Through the '60s he performed several styles of music, including jazz with the John Handy Concert Ensemble. LaFlamme often jammed with several future members of Big Brother and the Holding Company and was part of an early version of Dan Hicks and His Hot Licks.

By the time he formed It's a Beautiful Day on a summer afternoon (hence the group name), LaFlamme was playing jazz, classical, folk, and rock. He played on a specially adapted amplified solid-body five-string violin (the fifth string was a low C, so the instrument's range was as wide as that of a violin and viola combined), and LaFlamme's soloing established the group as a top local draw. Three of the songs on the group's self-titled 1969 debut, including "White Bird," were penned by LaFlamme and his wife, Linda, who left the group shortly thereafter and formed the communal San Francisco band Titus' Mother. *It's a Beautiful Day* stayed on the chart for more than a year and went gold.

In 1970 the group toured England. After several personnel changes, it released *Marrying Maiden.* The LP included "Don and Dewey," a tribute to the '50s duo of the same name and featured the eponymous Don "Sugarcane" Harris. The group disbanded in 1974 after its sixth LP, *1001 Nights,* went largely unnoticed. By that time David LaFlamme had been tossed out by the others, who allegedly felt he took a disproportionate share of royalties. Replacement Graig Block was the grand-nephew of violin virtuoso Jasche Heifetz. LaFlamme later recorded two solo LPs, *White Bird* (1977) and *Inside Out* (1978). Two later band members, Bud Cockrell and David Jenkins, formed Pablo Cruise in 1973. In 1989 Pattie Santos died in a car accident. The remaining original members briefly re-grouped as It's a Beautiful Day and performed in 1998. Aided by IABD drummer Val Fuentes, the LaFlammes released a CD several years later.

Freddie Jackson

Born Freddie Anthony Jackson, Oct. 2, 1958, New York, NY
1985—*Rock Me Tonight* (Capitol) 1986—*Just Like the First Time* 1988—*Don't Let Love Slip Away* 1990—*Do Me Again* 1992—*Time for Love* 1994—*The Greatest Hits of Freddie Jackson; Here It Is* (RCA); *Freddie Jackson at Christmas* 1995—*Private Party* (Street Life) 1998—*Anthology* (RCA) 1999—*Life After 30* (Orpheus).

Freddie Jackson was among the most successful of the new R&B singers to follow in the wake of Luther Vandross. Along with such vocalists as James Ingram and Alexander O'Neal, Jackson came to epitomize the "love man"—the full-throated, neoclassic soul singer whose pleas of love and lust relied on displays of bravura, technique, and openhearted emotion.

Jackson began singing in church while growing up in Harlem. He later held down a day job as a word processor while singing backup vocals at night for such established singers as Evelyn "Champagne" King and Angela Bofill. After singing with the bands Mystic Merlin and LJE, he became so disheartened with the music business that he quit for a year, but upon returning he quickly came to the attention of vocalist Melba Moore. She took Jackson on tour with her as a backup vocalist and featured soloist, exposure that brought his long-awaited recording contract. "Rock Me Tonight (for Old Times Sake)" (#18 pop, #1 R&B) and "You Are My Lady" (#12 pop, #1 R&B), from his 1985 debut album, made him an instant star.

Jackson's first two albums went platinum, and he became a major live act; in 1989 he headlined four nights at Broadway's Lunt-Fontanne Theater. While pop hits tapered off, Jackson scored repeatedly on the R&B charts: "Tasty Love" (#1, 1986), "A Little Bit More" (with Melba Moore) (#1, 1986), "Do Me Again" (#1 1991), and "Main Course" (#2, 1991). In 1994, in hopes of reigniting his chart success, Jackson moved from Capitol to RCA. The anticipated revival not forthcoming, he again withdrew from the spotlight, only to resurface again in early 2000 with *Life After 30*.

Janet Jackson

Born Janet Damita Jackson, May 16, 1966, Gary, IN
1983—*Janet Jackson* (A&M) 1984—*Dream Street* 1986—*Control* 1989—*Janet Jackson's Rhythm Nation 1814* 1993—*janet.* (Virgin) 1995—*Design of a Decade 1986/1996* (A&M) 1997—*The Velvet Rope* (Virgin) 2001—*All for You.*

As the baby of pop music's best-known family, Janet Jackson could have spent her career in the shadow of her eight siblings, particularly brother Michael. Instead, with the help of some savvy creative and professional advisers outside the family, Janet established herself as the preeminent pop-funk diva of the late '80s and early '90s. Her wispy voice was a pale echo of Michael's, but on Janet's albums—and in her videos and live performances, which revealed a crisp, athletic dance technique not unlike her brother's—singing wasn't the point. Her slamming beats, infectious hooks, and impeccable production values were perfectly suited to the breezy zeal with which she declared her social and sexual independence.

As a young child, Jackson was a tomboy who aspired to be a jockey. When she was seven, though, her father, Joseph, encouraged her to join her brothers—by then famous as the Jackson 5—in their music and variety act. (Sister La Toya joined them for several shows in 1974; the following year, La Toya, eldest sister Rebbie, and brother Randy were all in on the act, while brother Jermaine bowed out.) Shows in Las Vegas resulted in a summer-replacement TV show in 1976 (on CBS), which led Janet to roles on the popular sitcoms *Good Times* and *Diff'rent Strokes.*

Next, Jackson secured a contract with A&M Records, and in 1982, while still managed and creatively guided by her father, she released a forgettable debut album, *Janet Jackson.* The album did yield a #6 R&B single, "Young Love." Another TV role, on the series *Fame,* followed, as did another unremarkable album, 1984's *Dream Street,* and another R&B hit, "Don't Stand Another Chance" (#9). Also in 1984, at the age of 18, Jackson defied her family by marrying singer James DeBarge, whose fledgling R&B sibling act DeBarge was being hyped as a successor to the Jacksons. The marriage was annulled after less than a year; but the seeds of Jackson's independence from the family dynasty, and her father in particular, were firmly planted.

Then John McClain, an A&M executive and family friend, suggested that Jackson work with Jimmy Jam and Terry Lewis of the Time. Collaborating with these musician/writer/producers, Jackson recorded her breakthrough album, 1986's *Control,* which topped the pop and R&B album charts and spawned numerous hits: "What Have You Done for Me Lately" (#4 pop, #1 R&B), "Nasty" (#3 pop, #1 R&B), "When I Think of You" (#1 pop, #3 R&B), and, in 1987, "Control" (#5 pop, #1 R&B), "Let's Wait Awhile" (#2 pop, #1 R&B), and "The Pleasure Principle" (#14 pop, #1 R&B). Helping fuel these singles were Jackson's highly energized, elaborately staged videos, most of which featured movie-musical-inspired choreography by Paula Abdul, who was discovered by Jackie Jackson, Abdul's boyfriend during her L.A. Lakers cheerleading days.

Having asserted her adulthood and self-reliance with *Control,* by 1987 Jackson had dismissed her father as manager (as other siblings had done before her) before recording *Rhythm Nation 1814. Control*'s successor dealt with larger social issues, like the need for tolerance, and found Jam and Lewis assuming more of the songwriting duties. (Years later, Jackson would also credit her boyfriend, René Elizondo Jr., for contributing ideas to many of her songs beginning with this album; it was known that he helped choreograph, and eventually directed, some of her videos.) *Rhythm Nation* hit #1 in the pop and R&B categories in 1989, and generated the smash singles "Miss You Much" (#1 pop and R&B) and, in 1990, "Rhythm Nation" (#2 pop, #1 R&B), "Escapade" (#1 pop, #1 R&B), "Alright" (#4 pop, #2 R&B), "Come Back to Me" (#2 pop, #2 R&B), "Black Cat" (#1 pop, #10 R&B), and "Love Will Never Do (Without You)" (#1 pop, #3 R&B). To promote the album, Jackson embarked on her first major tour, which matched the energy and spectacle of her videos.

In 1991 Virgin Records owner Richard Branson lured Jackson away from A&M with a contract worth more than $30 million. Her last original hit with A&M was a 1992 duet with Luther Vandross, "The Best Things in Life Are Free" (#10 pop, #1 R&B), recorded for the soundtrack to the film *Mo' Money.* In 1993 Jackson made her own movie debut as the heroine (opposite rapper Tupac Shakur) of director/screenwriter John Singleton's *Poetic Justice,* for which she received lukewarm reviews but an Oscar nomination for the song "Again."

That same year, Jackson's Virgin album *janet.* shot to the top of the pop and R&B charts, as did the single "That's the Way Love Goes." More Top 10 singles followed, including "If" (#4 pop, #3 R&B, 1993) and "Again" (#1 pop, #7 R&B, 1994). Her new material was just as confrontational, and more aggressively sexual, than her previous work had been; ditto for the accompanying tour, which featured Jackson in midriff-baring costumes, interacting suggestively with male dancers—indeed, more reminiscent of Madonna than Michael. While Janet's once squeaky-clean image wasn't shattered by scandal as her brother's was, it was clear by the early '90s that the littlest Jackson was nobody's baby, and very much her own woman.

Jackson's status as a hitmaker led her to help her brother Michael regain some credibility by collaborating with him on the duet and elaborate video for "Scream" (#5 pop, #2 R&B) in 1995. The same year, she also had a solo hit with "Runaway" (#3 pop, #6 R&B). She'd continue to please her fans with her next album, *The Velvet Rope* (#1 pop, #2 R&B), in 1997. At times still sensual in nature—including a cover of Rod Stewart's seduction song "Tonight's the Night," without a change in the gender of the woman being sung to—much of the album had a melancholy feel and self-doubting lyrics. While doing interviews to promote the album and its tour, Jackson admitted to dealing with depression and long-standing self-esteem issues while working on the album. It did produce its share of hits, including "Got 'Til It's Gone" (#3 R&B, 1997), based around a sample of Joni Mitchell's "Big Yellow Taxi" and featuring the rapper Q-Tip, "Together Again" (#1 pop, #8 R&B, 1997), and "I Get Lonely" (#3 pop, #1 R&B, 1998), featuring the group BLACKstreet. In 1999 she enjoyed a hit with Busta Rhymes, "What's It Gonna Be?!," which hit the top of the R&B singles chart.

But Jackson's life wasn't everything it appeared to be. Fans were surprised when, in 2000, Jackson's longtime creative and romantic partner, Elizondo, filed for divorce from the singer after nine years of marriage. Although Elizondo was seen as a loving, stable presence in Jackson's life, it had not been public knowledge that the couple had ever married. Jackson explained that she'd wanted to protect the union from media scrutiny. Also in 2000 Jackson returned to acting, costarring with multiple versions of Eddie Murphy in *Nutty Professor II: The Klumps,* which featured Jackson's "Doesn't Really Matter" (#5, 2000). In 2001 Jackson released the double-platinum *All for You* (#1, 2001), featuring the #1 title track.

Jermaine Jackson: See the Jackson 5

Joe Jackson

Born David Ian Jackson, Aug. 11, 1954, Burton-on-Trent, Eng.
1979—*Look Sharp* (A&M); *I'm the Man* 1980—*Beat Crazy* 1981—*Joe Jackson's Jumpin' Jive* 1982—*Night and Day* 1983—*Mike's Murder* soundtrack 1984—*Body and Soul* 1986—*Big World* 1987—*Will Power* 1988—*Live 1980/86* 1989—*Blaze of Glory* 1991—*Laughter and Lust* (Virgin) 1994—*Night Music* 1997—*Heaven and Hell* (Sony Classical) 1999—*Symphony No. 1* 2000—*Live in New York: Summer in the City* (Manticore/Sony Classical); *Night and Day II.*

When singer Joe Jackson first emerged at the height of 1979's pop-new-wave explosion, he was frequently compared to Elvis Costello and Graham Parker. Beginning with his third album, however, Jackson shattered his "angry young man" image and released a series of credible forays into reggae and big-band jazz as well as symphonic and other idioms. As Jackson has made abundantly clear in interviews, a number of songs (including "Hit Single" and "Obvious Song"), and his controversial 1984 statement "Video Is Killing Music," he cares little for the trappings or machinations of pop stardom. Like the late Frank Zappa, he considers himself primarily a composer, not a rock star.

Jackson began studying violin at age 11, but after a few years he persuaded his parents to buy him a piano so that he could write songs. He later studied oboe and percussion as well. He received a scholarship to study composition at London's Royal Academy of Music from 1971 to 1974. After graduation he formed a band called Arms and Legs. While working as musical director at the Portsmouth Playboy Club, Jackson produced an LP-length demo of his songs that got him a publishing contract with Albion Music. Soon afterward, A&M producer David Kershenbaum got Jackson a recording contract with his label.

Look Sharp was recorded in a week and a half. The single "Is She Really Going Out With Him?" hit #21, and the album went to #20. *I'm the Man,* released six months later, hit #22. Jackson was quickly labeled a power-pop performer, an image that was changed with the release of *Beat Crazy,* an ominous reggae-inflected LP. Jackson himself produced it, and his group was billed for the first time as the Joe Jackson Band. The LP was less commercially successful (#41), and a three-song EP that included Jackson singing Jimmy Cliff's "The Harder They Come" (available only on British import) got considerably more U.S. airplay.

Within months of the LP's release, Jackson was back in the studio working on *Jumpin' Jive,* a collection of '40s swing tunes, including some by Louis Jordan. A novel idea at the time, *Jumpin' Jive* was fairly popular (#42) but yielded no hit singles, although Jackson toured the U.S. with a big band.

In 1982 Jackson moved to New York to record *Night and Day,* which incorporated hints of salsa, funk, and minimalism; the sleek, jazzish "Steppin' Out" (#6) sold 250,000 copies, and the album went gold. His last Top 40 single to date was "You Can't Get What You Want (Till You Know What You Want)" (#15, 1984), from *Body and Soul.*

In 1986 Jackson recorded *Big World* over three nights before a live audience. Each subsequent album—the autobiographical *Blaze of Glory,* the instrumental *Will Power,* and the acclaimed *Laughter and Lust*—found critical favor but middling commercial success. Though Jackson has proved more popular outside the United States, where his eclecticism, daring, and outspokenness are embraced, he has been living mostly in New York since 1984. The city was the inspiration for a followup to *Night and Day,* 2000's *Night and Day II,* and the setting for a live album featuring covers along with some of Jackson's hits rearranged for piano, bass, and drums.

Beginning with his 1983 appearance on the soundtrack for *Mike's Murder,* Jackson has scored a number of films, including *Tucker* (1988), *Queens Logic* (1990), and *Three of Hearts* (1992). He has also turned toward classical music, composing for and performing with the Tokyo Philharmonic Orchestra (*Shijin No Ie,* 1985), writing classical/pop hybrids (*Night Music,* 1994; *Heaven and Hell,* 1997), and even a full-on symphony (*Symphony No. 1,* 1999). In 1999 Jackson published a memoir, *A Cure for Gravity: A Musical Pilgrimage.*

Mahalia Jackson

Born Oct. 26, 1911, New Orleans, LA; died Jan. 27, 1972, Chicago, IL
1963—*Bless This House* (Columbia); *Mahalia Jackson: Greatest Hits* 1968—*Sings the Best-loved Hymns of Dr. Martin Luther King* 1971—*Sings America's Favorite Hymns* 1972—*The Great Mahalia Jackson* 1976—*How I Got Over* 1991—*Gospels, Spirituals and Hymns* (Legacy/Columbia).

Mahalia Jackson is generally regarded as one of the best and certainly the most popular gospel singers ever. Her forceful, bluesy style was greatly influenced by Ma Rainey and Bessie Smith, though Jackson never sang secular music. Aretha Franklin cites Jackson as her favorite singer.

Jackson and family regularly attended New Orleans' Mount Moriah Baptist Church. Despite her strict religious training, she heard and enjoyed New Orleans' wealth of jazz and blues. She often listened to the music of Smith and Rainey on records. In 1927 she moved to Chicago, where she worked as a domestic and a nurse. In 1935 Jackson made her recording debut after scouts for Decca Records had heard her sing at a funeral. From Decca, Jackson moved to the small Apollo label, where she became a gospel legend. Her recording of "Move On Up" sold more than 2 million copies. In concert Jackson was known to extend it to as long as 25 minutes. Crucial to her popularity was her accompanist, pianist Mildred Palls, whom record executive John Hammond called "the greatest gospel accompanist that ever lived."

In 1954 Jackson signed to Columbia Records, where A&R director Mitch Miller used strings and choirs to back her, increasing her popularity with whites, but inhibiting much of her earlier fire. In 1996 gospel singer Mavis Staples and pianist Lucky Peterson released *Spirituals and Gospel: Dedicated to Mahalia Jackson,* a tribute to their mentor Jackson, who died of heart failure in 1972.

Marlon Jackson: See the Jackson 5

Michael Jackson

Born Aug. 29, 1958, Gary, IN
1971—*Got to Be There* (Motown) 1972—*Ben* 1973—*Music and Me* 1975—*Forever, Michael; The Best of Michael Jackson* 1979—*Off the Wall* (Epic) 1982—*Thriller* 1987—*Bad* 1991—*Dangerous* 1995—*HIStory: Past, Present, and Future, Book I* 1997—*Blood on the Dance Floor: HIStory in the Mix* (Sony).

In the years since Michael Jackson made his first national television appearance with his brothers at the age of 11, he has evolved from a singing and dancing soul music prodigy to the self-proclaimed but widely acknowledged "King of Pop." As a musician, he has ranged from Motown's snappy dance fare and lush ballads to techno-edged New Jack Swing to work that incorporates both funk rhythms and hard-rock guitar. At his early-'80s zenith, riding the crest of his best-selling album, *Thriller,* spotlit in his red zippered jacket and single white sequined glove, he was ubiquitous. A superb businessman, Jackson has exerted unparalleled control over his career and has, in effect, managed himself since he and his brothers (sans Jermaine) left Motown for Epic Records in 1975. As a singer, dancer, and writer, Jackson's talent is unassailable.

With the passage of time, however, and especially since 1993, it is Jackson's personality that has dominated headlines formerly dedicated to his prodigious artistic accomplishments and humanitarian efforts. His charity work was enormous and focused always on his highly publicized identification with children. Infatuated with Peter Pan and E.T., Jackson seemed a kind of childlike extraterrestrial: benign (if in an eerie way), either sexless or sexually ambiguous, neither black nor white. Secluded by his celebrity, he appeared to touch down to earth only on stage or videotape; fanatically private, he generated endless gossip. In 1993, with Jackson facing allegations of child molestation, his career was rocked with scandal as gargantuan as his fame. Not since Shirley Temple has a child star so entranced the American public, and the massive public soul-searching the allegations against Jackson inspired were but one indication of the almost inestimable role he has played in shaping pop culture. Jackson returned to the tabloids in 1994 with the shocking announcement that he had wed Lisa Marie Presley, an act that led to even more speculation about his motives but which undeniably made him, until his divorce two years later, the son-in-law of the late Elvis Presley.

The Jackson 5's lead singer and focal point, Michael became more popular than the group as the '80s began. He had a string of solo hits in the early '70s ("Got to Be There" [#4, 1971]; "Rockin' Robin" [#2, 1972]; "Ben" [#1, 1972]) and played the Scarecrow in the film version of *The Wiz* in 1978. But it was with veteran producer Quincy Jones, whom he met while filming *The Wiz,* that Jackson began his amazing rise. In 1979 the team's *Off the Wall* made him the first solo artist to release four Top 10 hits from a single album. "Don't Stop Till You Get Enough" (#1, 1979), "Rock With You" (#1, 1979), "Off the Wall" (#10, 1980), and "She's Out of My Life" (#10, 1980) presented him as a mature artist whose funk rhythms and pop melodies appealed equally to blacks and whites. In the album's wake, the Jacksons' *Triumph* sold a million copies and prompted a $5.5 million-grossing tour. Even at this early stage, Jackson and his brothers were exploring video, and the short film that accompanied this album's title track was an imaginative, technically advanced effort.

In 1982 Jackson and Jones collaborated on a storytelling record of Steven Spielberg's *E.T.* The album, which was hastily withdrawn from the market due to a legal dispute, is now a prime Jackson collectable. That year, Diana Ross, one of Jackson's mentors, scored a #10 hit with Michael's "Muscles." Jackson had also begun an alliance with Paul McCartney, who had written "Girlfriend" for *Off the Wall.* The two reconvened to cowrite the duet "The Girl Is Mine" (#2, 1982).

It was 1983 that marked Jackson's complete ascension. With Quincy Jones again producing, *Thriller* yielded, in addition to "The Girl Is Mine," two other hit singles by early 1983—"Billie Jean" (#1, 1983) and "Beat It" (#1, 1983) (with a guitar solo delivered gratis by Eddie Van Halen)—and went on to become the best-selling album in history, with over 45 million copies sold worldwide. Charting at #1 in every Western country, it spent a record 37 weeks at U.S. #1. The first album ever to simultaneously head the singles and albums charts for both R&B and pop, it eventually generated an unprecedented seven Top 10 singles, including "P.Y.T. (Pretty Young Thing)" (#10, 1983), "Wanna Be Startin' Somethin' " (#5, 1983), "Human Nature" (#7, 1983), and "Thriller" (#4, 1983). Of its record 12 Grammy nominations, it won eight in 1983, a historical sweep.

Thriller also broke through MTV's de facto color line; where videos by black artists had rarely been shown, Michael's self-choreographed "Beat It," costing $160,000, received extensive play. The "Thriller" video, with a voiceover by horror movie stalwart Vincent Price and state-of-the-art special effects, was directed by John Landis, establishing Jackson's practice of working with notable filmmakers. In May, performing solo and with his brothers on NBC's *25 Years of Motown* special, Michael popularized his distinctive "Moonwalk" dance step, and, in performing "Billie Jean," was the only artist featured on the program whose repertoire included a non-Motown song. Later in 1983, while another duet with McCartney—"Say Say Say" from Paul's *Pipes of Peace*—

topped the charts for six weeks, Jackson announced a $5 million sponsorship deal with Pepsi-Cola.

In 1984, while filming a Pepsi commercial Jackson was seriously injured when a pyrotechnic effect went awry, setting his hair on fire. The singer underwent surgery for scalp burns; he later received facial laser surgery. Rumors about other reconstructive work began shortly before the release of *Thriller* and would build in coming years. Among the procedures he has been rumored to have undergone are facelifts, a purported six nose surgeries, and the lightening of his skin with chemicals (it was also alleged that he took female hormones to maintain his falsetto).

After receiving a Presidential Award from Ronald Reagan in June 1984, Jackson joined his brothers on a supporting tour for the Jacksons' *Victory* (from which Michael's duet with Mick Jagger, "State of Shock," reached #3). The highly publicized tour, which Jackson undertook reluctantly, was plagued by mismanagement (boxing promoter Don King was in charge, much to Jackson's displeasure, and his parents were coproducers), internal strife (at one point, several of the Jackson brothers, their parents, and numerous other parties had each retained their own lawyers), and general mismanagement (the method of selling tickets prompted a public outcry). A disillusioned Jackson donated his revenues to children's charities. Nonetheless, the shows were considered spectacular, brimming with high-tech special effects. Jackson ended the year by receiving a star on the Hollywood Walk of Fame.

In 1985 Jackson cowrote with Lionel Richie "We Are the World," the theme song for USA for Africa. It reached #1 and embellished Michael's reputation as a humanitarian. Jackson's relationship with Paul McCartney soured later that year as, bidding against both McCartney and Yoko Ono, he secured the ATV music publishing catalogue for $47.5 million: among ATV's holdings, more than 250 Lennon/McCartney songs. (Jackson has long been known inside the industry for his almost encyclopedic command of the details of his business dealings.)

Shortly after signing a second contract with Pepsi in 1986 for $15 million, Jackson released *Bad,* the biggest-shipping album of all time, in 1987. Its 17-minute title track video was directed by Martin Scorsese. *Bad* generated five #1s in 1987–88: "Just Can't Stop Loving You," "Bad," "The Way You Make Me Feel," "Man in the Mirror," and "Dirty Diana." The *Bad* tour—over a year long—became the biggest-grossing tour in history and one of the most expensive (Jackson's entourage included 250 people).

With 1988 came Jackson's long-awaited, heavily illustrated, and brief autobiography, *Moonwalk,* in which he claimed that his father, Joseph Jackson, had hit him as a child. Generally, however, the book (edited by Jacqueline Onassis) was considered unrevealing. (A second volume of his writings, *Dancing the Dream,* was published in 1992 to less enthusiastic response.)

By the end of the '80s, Jackson had moved from the Encino, California, family home to Neverland, an estimated $28-million, 2700-acre California ranch complete with ferris wheel, an exotic menagerie, a movie theater, and a security staff of 40. There Jackson—famous for clean-living (he neither smoked, drank, nor used drugs, and was rarely seen in the company of a woman)—hosted an endless series of parties for children, many of them disabled, critically ill, or underprivileged.

His popularity seemingly unassailable, Jackson signed a $28-million deal with L.A. Gear sportswear to be its spokesperson, but the idea proved a failure and Jackson was dropped after one commercial. At the start of the '90s, however, Jackson's popularity was massive enough to land him the biggest contract ever awarded an entertainer. Jackson signed a $65-million deal with Sony Corporation in 1991 that promised him an unprecedented share of the profits from his next six albums, his own record label, a role in developing video software products, and a chance to star in movies. Reportedly he would receive more than $120 million an album if each could match the sales of *Thriller.* Sony reported that it expected revenues of $1 billion from the partnership. By 1991, Jackson's celebrity status was unquestioned—he'd hosted Elizabeth Taylor's eighth wedding at Neverland and been publicly praised by such Hollywood establishment figures as Fred Astaire, Jane Fonda, and Katharine Hepburn—and he seemed unstoppable.

In 1991, at a recording cost of $10 million, *Dangerous* was released. Coproduced by New Jack Swing creator Teddy Riley, the album featured material ("Heal the World," "Who Is It") that recalled his work with Quincy Jones, with whom he had parted ways shortly after *Bad.* Riley, however, toughened and updated Jackson's sound, stripping off some of the smooth studio gloss of his previous works. With the $1.2-million video for the single "Black or White," Jackson demanded that MTV and Black Entertainment Television (BET) announce him as "the King of Pop" (a fact he would later deny in a live televised interview with Oprah Winfrey). Hoping to outdistance *Bad*'s over $20 million in sales, he prepared for a spectacular world tour. Also in 1992, he embarked on a five-nation African tour; there, however, he was widely criticized for his aloof behavior. That same year, with his personal fortune estimated at $200 million, Jackson established the Heal the World Foundation to raise awareness of children-related issues, including abuse.

With 1993 came Jackson's crisis. The year, however, began auspiciously. Appearing in January at the NAACP Image Awards, the American Music Awards, and the pre-Inaugural gala for President Bill Clinton, he also reached 91 million viewers in his half-time performance at Super Bowl XXVII, the most widely viewed—and many said, boring—entertainment event in TV history. And he announced the start of a $1.25 million program to provide drug prevention and counseling services to L.A. children following that city's riots. In a February TV interview with a less than incisive Oprah Winfrey, he revealed that he suffered from vitiligo, a disease he maintained discolored his skin, and that he was a victim of abuse at the hands of his father, Joseph. He tried to dispel such long-standing tabloid rumors as the one that he once tried to buy the bones of the Elephant Man or had slept in a hyperbaric chamber. He also said that he was dating movie actress Brooke Shields, who had been a companion during the *Thriller* period. The interview was one of the most-watched television programs in history. In March he formed Michael Jackson Productions Inc., an independent film company that would give a share of its profits to his Heal the World Foundation. In June he debuted his MJJ/Epic record label, releasing the *Free Willy* soundtrack.

But scandal erupted on August 17 when a Beverly Hills psychiatrist approached the L.A. Police after a 13-year-old patient claimed that Jackson had fondled him. Later, specific charges brought by the boy's father claimed that Jackson had sexually abused the boy at his house earlier in the year. After the father obtained a ruling to deny Jackson contact with the son, the police raided Neverland, seizing videotapes and other possible evidence (nothing incriminating turned up). While traveling to Bangkok for the *Dangerous* tour, Jackson denied the charges, his security consultant maintaining that the boy's father had attempted to extort $20 million to start a production company (he added that Jackson received at least 25 such extortion threats a year). With Pepsi supporting him and his retinue denying a suicide attempt, Jackson turned 35 at the end of August. Shortly thereafter, Jackson canceled his second Singapore show, claiming migraine headaches.

In September Jackson's sister, La Toya, reported that he used to spend the night with young boys in his room, and two former employees, who maintained that Jackson owed them $500,000 in wages, asserted that they'd witnessed Jackson's sexual involvement with several young boys. Jackson then pulled out of a deal to contribute the title track to the movie *Addams Family Values*. After Jackson's alleged victim filed a civil suit for seduction and sex abuse, the singer canceled the rest of the *Dangerous* tour, maintaining that pressure from the charges had left him addicted to painkillers. Pepsi then ended its 10-year partnership with the star. In November five former Neverland guards sued Jackson for firing them, allegedly because they knew about his relationships with minors. Toward the end of the year, business continued, with Sony announcing that *Dangerous* sales had topped 20 million and Jackson signing a $70-million, five-year deal with EMI Music to administer his ATV catalogue. But in December, back in the U.S., Jackson in a four-minute cable TV broadcast confronted his accusers and decried the extensive examination of his body that the police had conducted as part of their investigation.

On January 25, 1994, lawyers for Jackson and the alleged victim announced a private settlement of the boy's case, despite the fact that Jackson resolutely continued to deny wrongdoing. While terms were not disclosed, estimates of Jackson's payment reached as high as $26 million. One day earlier, following a criminal investigation into Jackson's claims that the boy's father was part of an extortion plot against him, the D.A. declined to file charges. The L.A. district attorney also investigated the claims of a second boy that Jackson had shared a bed with him, even while the boy alleged no impropriety on the singer's part. The district attorney, also finding no evidence of wrongdoing, concluded the investigation. In August a statement issued by MJJ Productions verified two months of rumors that Jackson had married 26-year-old Lisa Marie Presley, who had been estranged from her husband, with whom she had two children.

Jackson and his bride appeared on television with Diane Sawyer to discuss the marriage; it would be a short-lived one, as the couple divorced in 1996. Jackson later married Debbie Rowe, a nurse he'd met in the early '80s when undergoing treatment for vitiligo. A boy, Prince, and a girl, Paris, resulted from the union.

In 1995, ushered in with a $30-million marketing campaign, the largest in history, Jackson's *HIStory,* a double-album of hits and new material, was released. Featuring "Scream," a duet with his sister Janet, the album dropped out of the Top 10 after only a few weeks. The song "They Don't Care About Us" including the lyric "Jew me/sue me" provoked charges of anti-Semitism even from such stalwart Jackson supporters as Steven Spielberg. In 1997 a followup, *Blood on the Dance Floor: HIStory in the Mix* (#24), also fared poorly (by Jackson's admittedly remarkable standards).

In 1997 Jackson was found innocent by Milanese authorities of plagiarism for his song "Will You Be There" (from *Dangerous* and used in the film *Free Willy*); Italian singer/songwriter Albano Carrisi had accused Jackson of copying his 1986 song "I Cigni Di Balaka." In 1999, after several appeals courts had continued to rule in Jackson's favor, a criminal court in Rome found Jackson guilty of plagiarism, but the approximately $3,000 fine was suspended. Since then, Jackson's lawyers have appealed the ruling in an attempt to remove the judgment against him. Jackson is slated to star as the famed writer in a film entitled *The Nightmares of Edgar Allan Poe* (the filming has not started as of early 2001), and was reportedly working on a new album. Also, in England, he enjoyed a kind of vicarious revival, with British dance-music artists recording a number of hits featuring Jackson samples.

Millie Jackson

Born 1943, Thompson, GA
1972—*Millie Jackson* (Spring) 1973—*It Hurts So Good* 1974—*Caught Up* 1977—*Feelin' Bitchy* 1978—*Get It Out'cha System* 1979—*A Moment's Pleasure; Royal Rappin's* (with Isaac Hayes) (Polydor); *Live and Uncensored* (Spring) 1980—*For Men Only* (Polydor); *I Had to Say It* 1981—*Just a Lil' Bit Country* 1982—*Live and Outrageous (Rated XXX)* 1986—*An Imitation of Love* (Jive) 1988—*The Tide Is Turning* 1992—*Young Man, Older Woman* 1994—*Rock N' Soul* (Ichiban) 1995—*It's Over!?* 1997—*Totally Unrestricted: The Millie Jackson Anthology* (Rhino).

Soul singer and songwriter Millie Jackson was internationally popular for well over a decade, thanks to live shows that interwove gritty deep-soul singing and raunchy raps. Jackson grew up in Georgia and lived with her grandfather, a preacher, until she ran away at age 14. She came to New York

City and worked as a model, mostly for confession magazines. In 1964, on a bet, she jumped onstage and sang at the Palm Cafe in Harlem. For the rest of the '60s, she worked as a singer around New York. She cut a single in 1969 for MGM, but kept her day job until she signed with Spring Records in 1971.

Jackson had her first soul hit in 1972 with "A Child of God" (#22 R&B), followed by "Ask Me What You Want" (#14 R&B), and "It Hurts So Good" (#3 R&B, 1973), which was included on the soundtrack of *Cleopatra Jones*. Her breakthrough was the 1974 album *Caught Up*, the first recording of her live act. It was a concept album on which Jackson played a wife on one side and the Other Woman on the other; it yielded a hit single, "(If Loving You Is Wrong) I Don't Want to Be Right" (#42 pop, 1974), and went gold. Both *Feelin' Bitchy* and *Get It Out'cha System* went gold, although Jackson's language was often so blunt that she got no airplay. *Feelin' Bitchy* was a gold album. Jackson recorded a duet album, *Royal Rappin's*, with Isaac Hayes in 1979 and continued to play large halls and record regularly into the early '80s, acting as her own manager and coproducer, and with her own publishing company, Double Ak-Shun Music.

Following her 1981 excursion to Nashville for *Just a Lil' Bit Country*, Jackson was absent from the recording scene for almost five years—aside from a noncharting 1985 duet with Elton John, "Act of War" (on his *To Be Continued*). In 1986 she signed a new deal with Jive Records. *An Imitation of Love*, on which Jackson finally ceded production control to others, yielded a Top 10 R&B hit in "Hot! Wild! Unrestricted! Crazy Love!" But her commercial profile never again ascended to its '70s heights; ironically, Jackson—with her soulful vocalizing, insistence on live bands, and practiced stagecraft—found herself displaced by the rap music she'd so vividly presaged. In the mid-'90s Jackson turned the basis of the song "Young Man, Older Woman" into a theatrical musical comedy.

Rebbie Jackson: See the Jackson 5

Wanda Jackson

Born Oct. 20, 1937, Maud, OK
1960—*Rockin' With Wanda* (Capitol) 1966—*Wanda Jackson Sings Country Blues* 1972—*Praise the Lord* 1974—*Country Gospel* (Word) 1979—*Greatest Hits* (Capitol) 1990—*Rockin' in the Country: The Best of Wanda Jackson* (Rhino) 1996—*Vintage Collections* (Capitol).

Wanda Jackson burst on to the predominantly male rockabilly scene in the mid-'50s with a dynamic stage presence, a robust voice, and a gift for songwriting. Dubbed the "Queen of Rockabilly," she has also performed country and gospel songs over the course of her long career.

Growing up in Oklahoma and Bakersfield, California, Jackson first sang professionally at age nine. At 13, she got her own radio program, and soon after she began singing with such country & western stars as Hank Thompson. In 1954 she got a record deal with Decca. A 1955 appearance with Elvis Presley caused Jackson to add rockabilly to her repertoire, when Presley raved that her strong voice was perfect for the style. In 1956 she signed to Capitol and her repertoire became feisty and in your face: "Hot Dog," "Fujiyama Mama," "Mean, Mean Man," and particularly, her biggest hit, "Let's Have a Party" (#37, 1960), which featured backing by Gene Vincent's Blue Caps. By the early '60s, with rockabilly waning, she returned to country, scoring with her self-penned "Right or Wrong" (#29, 1961) and "In the Middle of a Heartache" (#27, 1961). Jackson became very popular overseas ("Fujiyama Mama" was a big hit in Japan), and she has recorded in German, Dutch, and Japanese (phonetically).

In June 1971 she and her husband became born-again Christians, so she began adding gospel songs to her repertoire. In the mid-'90s Jackson toured with Rosie Flores, and found a new generation of fans. She continues to tour throughout the world.

The Jackson 5/The Jacksons/ The Jackson Family

Formed 1967, Gary, IN
Sigmund Esco "Jackie" Jackson (b. May 4, 1951, Gary), voc.; Toriano Adaryll "Tito" Jackson (b. Oct. 15, 1953, Gary), gtr., voc.; Jermaine La Jaune Jackson (b. Dec. 11, 1954, Gary), voc., bass; Marlon David Jackson (b. Mar. 12, 1957, Gary), voc.; Michael Joe Jackson (b. Aug. 29, 1958, Gary), lead voc.
1969—*I Want You Back* (a.k.a. *Diana Ross Presents the Jackson 5*) (Motown) 1970—*ABC; Third Album; Christmas Album* 1971—*Maybe Tomorrow* 1972—*The Jackson 5's Greatest Hits* 1973—*Get It Together* 1974—*Dancing Machine* 1975—(+ Steven Randall "Randy" Jackson [b. Oct. 29, 1961, Gary], voc., kybds.) 1976—*The Jacksons* (Epic) 1977—*Motown Special* (Motown); *Anthology; Goin' Places* (Epic) 1978—*Destiny* 1980—*Triumph* (Epic) 1981—*Live* 1984—*Victory* 1989—*2300 Jackson Street.*
Jermaine Jackson solo: 1972—*Jermaine* (Motown) 1973—*Come Into My Life* 1976—*My Name Is Jermaine* 1977—*Feel the Fire* 1978—*Frontiers* 1980—*Let's Get Serious; Jermaine* 1981—*I Like Your Style* 1982—*Let Me Tickle Your Fancy* 1984—*Jermaine Jackson* (Arista) 1986—*Precious Moments* 1989—*Don't Take It Personal* 1991—*You Said* (La Face/Arista).
Jackie Jackson solo: 1973—*Jackie Jackson* (Motown) 1989—*Be the One* (Polydor).
Marlon Jackson solo: 1987—*Baby Tonight* (Capitol).
Randy Jackson solo, as Randy and the Gypsies: 1989—*Randy & the Gypsies* (A&M); as Randy Jackson's China Rain: 1991—*Bed of Nails.*
As the Jackson Family: ca. 1976—Jackson 5 + Maureen "Rebbie" Jackson (b. May 29, 1950, Gary), voc.; + La Toya Jackson (b. May 29, 1956, Gary), voc.; + Janet Jackson (b. May 16, 1966, Gary), voc.
Rebbie Jackson solo: 1984—*Centipede* (Columbia) 1986—

Reaction 1988—*R U Tuff Enuff* 1998—*Yours Faithfully* (MJJ). La Toya Jackson solo: 1980—*La Toya Jackson* (Polydor) 1981—*My Special Love* 1984—*Heart Don't Lie* (Private I) 1986—*Imagination* 1988—*You're Gonna Get Rocked; La Toya* (Teldec) 1994—*From Nashville to You* (Mar Gor) 1995—*Bad Girl* (Prime Cuts).

Since its national debut in 1969 with "I Want You Back," the Jackson 5 has been the most accomplished, successful black pop soul vocal group and one of the most popular family acts in pop music. Over the group's long and unparalleled career, the Jackson brothers upheld and expanded the R&B/soul vocal traditions of their idols and mentors, evolving from a Temptations-style, closely directed vocal group to a self-contained soul/disco/pop powerhouse. The constant media focus on lead-singing prodigy Michael Jackson [see entry] has overshadowed the contributions of his brothers, especially in the later phase of their career, when they each wrote and produced material on the group's two most acclaimed albums, *Triumph* and *Destiny*.

The group's father, Joseph Jackson, had been a guitarist in a group called the Falcons (not to be confused with the group of "You're So Fine" fame) with his brother and three other men. Shortly after Joseph married Katherine Scruse, their quickly growing family forced him to give up his musical ambitions. Although he worked as a crane operator, he maintained an interest in music, often playing his electric guitar in the house. Katherine often led the children in singing songs, especially harmony-rich country & western standards, which she loved.

Beginning in the early '60s, Tito, Jermaine, and Jackie performed around Gary, Indiana, as the Jackson Family; around 1964 Michael and Marlon joined, and the group became the Jackson 5. Popular in their hometown, in 1968 they cut one unsuccessful single, "Big Boy" b/w "You've Changed." By then the group (which included keyboardist Ronnie Rancifer and drummer Johnny Jackson [no relation]) had been opening shows for such R&B stars as Sam and Dave, the Isley Brothers, the O'Jays, Gladys Knight and the Pips, James Brown, and the Temptations, among others. On weekends, they traveled by van throughout the Midwest, venturing as far from home as Phoenix, Arizona, and Washington, DC. Though numerous Motown performers knew of and worked with the young group, it was probably Bobby Taylor of the Vancouvers and Gladys Knight (not Diana Ross, as label publicity later claimed) who brought them to Berry Gordy Jr.'s attention. Although Gordy did not attend their Motown audition, it was filmed, and within months the Jackson 5 were signed to the label.

The Jacksons: Michael Jackson, Tito Jackson, Randy Jackson, Jackie Jackson, Marlon Jackson

Although Motown would remain a force in black music for several more years, historically speaking, the Jackson 5 was perhaps the last act to benefit from the label's all-encompassing approach to talent development. Newly relocated to L.A., Motown no longer kept a staff of choreographers, etiquette teachers, and coaches. Instead, Berry Gordy entrusted much of the Jackson 5's early training to one of his most recent hirings, Suzanne de Passe. The boys and their father were moved to L.A., where the boys lived with Diana Ross or Berry Gordy. Even from this early point, friction between Gordy and Joseph Jackson over the handling of the Jackson 5 was evident, although Joseph remained, at least nominally, their manager.

In January 1970 "I Want You Back" hit #1 and sold over 2 million copies, becoming the first of a string of 13 Top 20 singles for Motown, including "ABC" (#1, 1970), "The Love You Save" (#1, 1970), "I'll Be There" (#1, 1970, their biggest seller), "Mama's Pearl" (#2, 1971), "Never Can Say Goodbye" (#2, 1971), "Maybe Tomorrow" (#20, 1971), "Sugar Daddy" (#10, 1971), "Little Bitty Pretty One" (#13, 1972), "Lookin' Through the Windows" (#16, 1972), "Corner of the Sky" (#18, 1972), "Dancing Machine" (#2, 1974), and "I Am Love" (#15, 1975). Many of the group's Motown hits were written by "The Corporation" (Freddie Perren, Fonce Mizell, Deke Richards, and Berry Gordy Jr.). The Jackson 5 toured frequently, always tutored and supervised by the Motown staff.

In 1972 the group received a commendation from Congress for its "contributions to American youth." Throughout the '70s and '80s, the Jacksons and their family (which included three sisters: Rebbie, La Toya, and Janet) were considered ideal role models. Prompted by Motown, the national media regularly touted the family's strong religious beliefs (mother Katherine and several of the children, including Michael, were devout Jehovah's Witnesses) and work ethic. In fact, the family was often erroneously depicted as having arisen from the ghetto, a PR fabrication that infuriated the Jackson parents.

The Jackson 5 voiced their animated likenesses for a Saturday morning cartoon series in 1971, and beginning in 1976 all nine siblings starred in *The Jacksons,* a CBS musical-variety program. During that time, the entire clan also appeared in Las Vegas shows that featured the Jackson 5 (now six with the inclusion of youngest son Randy) and their three sisters. Like many young singing acts, the Jacksons had witnessed a decline in record sales through the mid-'70s. They began to outgrow the teen-idol market, and through the decade all of the brothers, except Michael and Randy, married early. While dance music was beginning to dominate black music, Motown stubbornly held the Jackson 5 to its old formula rather than move in the direction of "Dancing Machine" (#2, 1994), for example. Both Joseph and the Jackson brothers believed they would benefit by writing and producing their own records, something Gordy and Motown were notoriously reluctant to permit. In fact, Joseph had overseen the construction of a state-of-the-art recording studio at the family home in Encino, California, to encourage his sons to become more creatively independent.

Like many other Motown artists, the Jackson 5 left the label over artistic control. When the group announced its departure in 1975, the label sued for breach of contract. The $20-million suit was eventually settled in 1980, with the Jacksons paying $600,000 ($100,000 in cash and $500,000 in "other items") and the label retaining all rights to the name the Jackson 5. The move also brought the family's first public rift, as Jermaine refused to leave Motown with his brothers. In 1973 he had married Berry Gordy Jr.'s only daughter, Hazel Joy, in what was then claimed to be one of the most lavish weddings in the history of Hollywood. It was also viewed by some to be the merger of record-business dynasties, but given Joseph Jackson and Berry Gordy's long-running mutual dislike, it never was.

Like Jackie (who released a quickly forgotten LP in 1973) and Michael (whose solo career is recounted in his entry), Jermaine had also tested the waters as a solo act. Although Michael continually overshadowed his siblings, in the group's early years, Jermaine was successfully promoted as a teen idol. His *Jermaine* (#27, 1972) spun off a Top 10 remake of Shep and the Limelites' "Daddy's Home." Subsequent releases on his father-in-law's label did not fare nearly as well until 1980's *Let's Get Serious* (#6 pop, #1 R&B), with its #9 pop, #1 R&B title track. For the next couple of years, Jermaine's singles made a solid showing on the R&B charts (1980's "You're Supposed to Keep Your Love for Me" and "Little Girl, Don't You Worry," and 1981's "You Like Me, Don't You" and "I'm Just Too Shy") but returned to the pop Top 20 with "Let Me Tickle Your Fancy" (#18 pop, #5 R&B, 1982). Shortly thereafter, with the blessings of his father-in-law and with Hazel functioning as his manager, Jermaine moved to Arista, where his eponymously titled 1984 label debut became his first Top 20 LP since 1980 and an R&B #1. Boosted by a string of stylishly crafted videos, "Dynamite" (#15 pop, #8 R&B, 1984) and "Do What You Do" (#13 pop, #14 R&B, 1984) pushed the album to gold. However, Jermaine's later efforts—including a duet with Pia Zadora (with whom he also performed)—flopped, and *Don't Take It Personal,* like his second, third, and fourth Motown albums, did not enter the Top 100. In 1987 Jermaine and Hazel divorced.

Meanwhile, back in March 1976, the remaining five Jackson brothers changed their name to the Jacksons and signed with Epic. Kenny Gamble and Leon Huff produced their first two Epic LPs, *The Jacksons* (featuring "Enjoy Yourself" [#6 pop, #2 R&B, 1976]) and *Goin' Places* (#63, 1977), neither of which the Jackson brothers believed suited them. They began writing their own material, beginning with *Destiny,* which contained "Shake Your Body (Down to the Ground)"; within a few years they were producing most of their own material as well. Except for four singles that failed to crack the Top 40, the Jacksons picked up the streak where they'd left off and the hits kept coming: "Show You the Way to Go" (#28 pop, #6 R&B, 1977), "Blame It on the Boogie" (#54 pop, #3 R&B, 1979), "Shake Your Body (Down to the Ground)" (#7 pop, #3 R&B, 1979), "Lovely One" (#12 pop, #2 R&B, 1980), "Heartbreak Hotel" (sometimes titled "This Place Hotel" and not to be confused with the Elvis Presley hit of the same name) (#22 pop, #2 R&B, 1980). In light of Michael's preeminence, many historians overlook the songwriting contributions of the other brothers, each of whom cowrote at least one of the hits above.

Through 1979 and 1980, Michael's *Off the Wall* dominated the charts. The Jacksons' *Triumph* (#10 pop, #1 R&B, 1980) sold a million copies and prompted a 39-city tour that grossed $5.5 million. Then, as always, the Jackson's live shows garnered outstanding reviews. They were among the first acts to incorporate lavish special effects, and with *Triumph*'s "Can You Feel It," video pioneers of sorts. Although the song was not a hit, a special video produced for it was used to open their concerts. A live LP, *Jacksons Live* (#30 pop, #10 R&B, 1981), documented this period.

Through 1981 and most of 1982 the Jacksons kept a low profile, although with Michael moving increasingly outside his father's managerial control, Joseph turned his attention again to the Jackson sisters, overseeing the production of La Toya's and Janet's first albums. Neither was hugely successful, although each had a share of R&B charting singles: La Toya, with "Stay the Night" (#31 R&B, 1981) and "Bet'cha Gonna Need My Lovin' " (#22 R&B, 1983), and Janet with "Young Love" (#6 R&B, 1982) and "Say You Do" (#15 R&B, 1983). For Janet Jackson [see entry], greater success would come only after she declared her artistic independence from her father with *Control* in 1986. During this time, Joseph also encouraged his eldest, Rebbie, who had married a fellow Jehovah's Witness and seemed an unlikely entertainer, to record. "Centipede" (#24 pop, #4 R&B, 1984) and "Plaything" (#8 R&B, 1988) were her biggest hits. Subsequent singles, including a 1986 duet with Cheap Trick's Robin Zander ("You Send the Rain Away") and rapper Melle Mel ("R U Tuff Enuff"), were quickly forgotten.

The years 1983 and 1984 marked a turning point for all the Jacksons, and beginning with the six brothers' reunion at the *Motown 25* television special taping, the family would dominate the charts and the news for the next 18 months. Interestingly, it was after the brothers' reunion—their first appearance with Jermaine since the 1974 Las Vegas show, after which he announced his decision to stay behind with Motown—that Michael dazzled the audience with his performance of his first single off *Thriller,* "Billie Jean," and unveiled his Moonwalk dance step. Critics agree that was a pivotal moment in Jackson's career, as indeed it was. But it also marked the beginning of the end for the Jackson brothers. By most credible accounts, it was Jermaine, who was always Joseph's favorite son and the most aggressive of the siblings, who pushed hardest for a continuation of the reunion and what would become the Victory Tour. Although the brothers had severed all business ties with Joseph, he and their mother, along with boxing promoter Don King, produced the tour. By the time it opened in Kansas City, on July 6, 1984, the enterprise was awash in so much controversy that Michael pledged all of his proceeds to charity. Nevertheless, the tour became the most widely covered and largest-grossing tour of its time. Given *Thriller*'s massive success, few were surprised to learn that the Victory Tour and album (#4 pop, #3 R&B, 1984) would be Michael's swan song with the group. But Marlon also announced his decision to leave once the tour ended. His "Don't Go" (#2 R&B, 1987) from *Baby Tonight* is his biggest solo hit to date. Although *Victory* sold over 2 million copies, it spawned just one Top 10 hit, "State of Shock" (#3, 1984), a duet between Michael and Mick Jagger. It would be the Jacksons' last Top 10 pop hit.

Ironically, the family's decline began following a 24-month period between January 1983 and December 1984 when Michael had six Top 10 (including two #1) solo hits, Jermaine had two Top 20 pop hits, and Rebbie, Janet, and La Toya were near-constant presences on the R&B chart. But the personal and public turmoil that has marked the family was just beginning. Janet eloped with singer James DeBarge while the rest of the family was traveling with the Victory Tour; La Toya, then Michael, moved out of the family home. For La Toya, whose early ambivalence toward her career is apparent, record sales remain elusive in the U.S., although she has performed throughout the rest of the world, recording albums that range from smutty Euro-disco to faux-country. In the wake of her two appearances in *Playboy* magazine (the first of which, in 1989, became one of the magazine's best-selling issues), her international bestseller *La Toya: Growing Up in the Jackson Family* (in which she accused her father of child abuse), and her now-dissolved marriage to controversial manager Jack Gordon, La Toya became a figure of controversy both inside and outside the family. While her parents and several siblings have been vociferously critical of her, others, including Michael, have pledged their support. Obscured in the public outcry over her book was the fact that in the French edition of her autobiography, Katherine Jackson had written of Joseph beating the children and having extramarital affairs; these passages were deleted from the later U.S. edition. And while several Jackson family members protested the right of any Jackson to reveal family secrets, before and after La Toya's book, several other siblings and even Joseph had floated proposals for their own version of the family saga; only Katherine and Michael (whose *Moonwalk* also alluded to physical abuse) found takers. La Toya appeared publicly with her brothers (except Jermaine) as part of USA for Africa. Having split acrimoniously with Gordon in the mid-'90s, she has since renewed ties with her family.

Other Jacksons made headlines as well. In 1980 Katherine Jackson (accompanied by Janet and Randy) attacked one of Joseph's secretaries in his office with a blunt instrument. No charges were filed. Jermaine's marriage to Hazel Gordy ended, as did Jackie's to his wife Enid (who later accused him of physically attacking her and won a court order barring him from her home); Jackie and Enid divorced in 1986. Randy, who had been nearly killed in a late-'70s car accident that severely damaged his legs, was convicted of physically abusing his wife and his infant daughter in 1991. He pleaded no contest to the battery charge and was to have entered a rehabilitation program. In 1994 Tito's ex-wife Delores, known as Dee Dee, whom he had married in 1972 and with whom he had three children, drowned in a friend's swimming pool.

In the summer of 1989, the Jacksons—by then a quartet of Jackie, Jermaine, Tito, and Randy—released *2300 Jackson Street* (the address of their Gary, Indiana, childhood home) nearly five years after *Victory*. It peaked at a disappointing #59, and its autobiographical title track, which reunited the brothers with Michael and Janet, and a number of nieces and nephews, did not chart. In 1991 Jermaine released "Word to the Badd," a clear attack on Michael, which made headlines but did not become a hit.

The family's plans to open a Jackson family museum in Las Vegas and their mismanaged Jackson Family Honors tribute were overshadowed by the then-pending child-abuse allegations against Michael. The Family Honors program, which aired in February 1994, was plagued by slow ticket sales, allegations of financial improprieties, and a final show that was deemed lackluster. In the mid-'90s sketchy reports of *J5*, a new Jacksons album featuring most of the famous siblings, began to surface. Despite that, no group material has been issued as of mid-2001.

By all indications, with the exception of Michael's and Janet's spectacular careers, the Jackson family's dominance as an entertainment dynasty had come to an end. Unfortunately, their long-held public status as role models and exemplars of conservative family values has also been damaged irrevocably (oddly, in no small part because of the highly rated, family-controlled 1992 made-for-TV account of their early years, which depicted Joseph as violent and demanding). Despite this, the family remains unique in the annals of pop-music history, a phenomenal success story that will surely continue to unfold for years to come.

Mick Jagger: See the Rolling Stones

The Jaggerz/Donnie Iris

Formed 1965, Pittsburgh, PA
Donald Iris (b. Dominic Ierace, 1943, Ellwood City, PA), gtr., voc.; Benny Faiella (b. Eugene Faiella, Beaver Falls, PA), gtr., bass; Thom Davies (b. Duquesne, PA), kybds., trumpet; James Ross

(b. Aliquippa, PA), bass, trombone; William Maybray, bass; James "Pugs" Pugliano, drums.
1969—*Introducing the Jaggerz* (Gamble) 1970—*We Went to Different Schools Together* (Kama Sutra) 1971—(– Ross) 1975—*Come Again* (Wooden Nickel) 1998—(lineup: Faiella; Ross; Pugliano; others) *And the Band Played On . . .* (Jaggerz).
Donnie Iris solo: 1980—*Back on the Streets* (MCA) 1981—*King Cool* 1982—*The High and the Mighty* 1983—*Fortune 410* 1985—*No Muss . . . No Fuss* (HME) 1992—*Footsoldier in the Moonlight* (Seathru) 1999—*Together Alone* (Primary).

Led by frontman/lead vocalist Donnie Iris (credited on the LPs as D. Ierace), the Jaggerz had a #2 1970 single with the million-selling "Rapper." Their debut 45, "Baby I Love You" (Gamble Records), with William Maybray on lead vocals, was a flop. The next year they signed to Kama Sutra and recorded *We Went to Different Schools Together,* which contained "The Rapper." Two subsequent singles, "I Call My Baby Candy" and "What a Bummer," never even reached the Top 70. By then, Iris had left the band to pursue a solo career; the group continued without him and recorded an LP in 1975 for Wooden Nickel Records, but with no success.

Iris worked in a Pittsburgh recording studio and then joined Wild Cherry, which had a platinum single in 1976 with "Play That Funky Music." With ex–Wild Cherry keyboardist Mark Avsec, Iris began composing. Around 1979 he recorded *Back on the Streets* for a Cleveland label, Midwest National. He then formed his own band. MCA later released the LP nationally, and in 1980 Iris' "Ah! Leah!" went to #29. In 1981 Iris, with his band the Cruisers, released *King Cool.* It produced two Top 40 hits, "Love Is Like a Rock" and "My Girl." Iris continues to record and tour; he often performs "The Rapper" in his shows. Jimmy Ross, meanwhile, performed on the oldies circuit as a member of the Skyliners ("Since I Don't Have You"). In 1998 he revived the Jaggerz for a self-released CD with Faiella and Pugliano.

The Jam/Paul Weller/The Style Council

The Jam, formed 1973, Woking, Eng.: Paul Weller (b. May 25, 1958, Woking), gtr., voc.; Bruce Foxton (b. Sep. 1, 1955, Eng.), bass, voc.; Rick Buckler (b. Dec. 6, 1955, Woking), drums, voc.
1977—*In the City* (Polydor); *This Is the Modern World* 1978—*All Mod Cons* 1979—*Setting Sons* 1980—*Sound Affects* 1981—*Absolute Beginners* 1982—*The Gift; Dig the New Breed* 1983—*Snap!* 1991—*Greatest Hits* 1992—*Extras* 1993—*Live Jam* 1996—*The Jam Collection* 1997—*Direction, Recreation, Creation.*
The Style Council, formed 1983, Eng.: Weller; + Mick Talbot, kybds.; + Dee C. Lee, voc.
1983—*Introducing the Style Council* EP (Polydor) 1984—*My Ever Changing Moods* (Geffen) 1985—*Internationalists* 1986—*Home & Abroad* (Polydor) 1987—*The Cost of Loving* 1988—*Confessions of a Pop Group* 1989—*The Singular Adventures of the Style Council (Greatest Hits, vol. 1)* 1994—*Here's Some That Got Away* 1996—*The Style Council Collection.*
Paul Weller solo: 1992—*Paul Weller* (Go! Discs/London) 1993—*Wild Wood* 1995—*Stanley Road* 1997—*Heavy Soul* (Island) 1998—*Modern Classics—The Greatest Hits* 2000—*Heliocentric.*

First with the Jam, then with Style Council and as a solo artist, songwriter/guitarist Paul Weller mined a range of pop styles, from the Jam's punk-colored Mod and Merseybeat, through the Style Council's white soul, to his '90s excursions into folk and psychedelia. While Weller and his groups have enjoyed immense popularity in the U.K., here in the U.S. Weller's work has found a small, devoted following at best.

Though it first came to prominence in London's 1976 punk-rock explosion, the Jam shared only a high-speed, stripped-down approach with its contemporaries. The trio's clothes, haircuts, and tunes reflected an obsession with the mid-'60s Mod style, and some termed the band the new Who. Although Paul Weller's gruffly accented vocals and earnest songs never broke through to American audiences, the Jam became consistent hitmakers in Britain.

Weller, while attending Sheerwater Secondary Modern School in Woking, originally formed a folk duo with guitarist Steve Brooks in 1972. They later formed the Jam with guitarist Dave Waller and drummer Rick Buckler. Waller and Brooks quit in 1974, and bassist Bruce Foxton joined. With Weller's father as manager, they worked on '60s R&B and Mod-rock covers and some originals; in 1976 they made a successful London debut at the 100 Club's first punk extravaganza. Their debut album was a British hit, yielding a Top 40 U.K. single in the title tune (from which the Sex Pistols later used a riff for their "Holiday in the Sun"). *Modern World* followed the same format, but the album was so harshly criticized by the British music press that the highly sensitive Weller nearly broke up the band. That year the Jam also released soul covers of "Back in My Arms Again" and "Sweet Soul Music."

The Jam: Rick Buckler, Paul Weller, Bruce Foxton

Just before the well-received *All Mod Cons* (#6 U.K., 1978), the group released three successful U.K. singles: "News of the World" (#27), a cover of the Kinks' "David Watts" (#25), and "Down in the Tube Station at Midnight" (#15), which revealed a new political commitment. "Tube Station," a protest against Britain's anti-immigrant "Paki-bashing" phenomenon, was banned by the BBC. *Setting Sons* (#137 U.S., #4 U.K., 1979) was a decline-of-the-Empire/class-conflict concept album and yielded the British hit "The Eton Rifles" (#3, 1979); it also included "Heatwave." *Sound Affects* (#2 U.K., 1980) was the Jam's biggest commercial success to date, with a #1 British hit in "Start!" and another minor U.K. hit in the acoustic ballad "That's Entertainment."

The Jam continued making inroads on the American market with *The Gift* (#82 U.S., #1 U.K., 1982) which yielded the Motownish "Town Called Malice." Both *Cons* and *Sons* went gold in England. In 1980 Weller appeared on Peter Gabriel's third solo LP. In October 1982 Weller announced that the group was breaking up: "It really dawned on me how secure the situation was, the fact that we could go on for the next 10 years making records, getting bigger and bigger. . . . That frightened me because I realized we were going to end up . . . like the rest of them." Nonetheless, the group's English fans never gave up, and its last single, "Beat Surrender," came on the chart there at #1 in 1982.

Weller quickly released his first post-Jam efforts as leader of Style Council in 1983. Officially only a duo with Weller and Mick Talbot, Style Council was a bold experiment that Weller later admitted was not entirely successful. Working with a number of guest artists, including Curtis Mayfield, Style Council was conceived as an American '60s-style soul unit with a political point of view. Critics were mixed on how well that goal was met, but U.K. fans were unanimous in their support. Between 1983 and 1988, the group had seven U.K. Top 10 hits: "Speak Like a Child" and "Long Hot Summer" (1983), "My Ever Changing Moods," "Groovin' (You're the Best Thing)" b/w "Big Boss Groove," and "Shout to the Top" (1984), "Walls Come Tumbling Down!" (1985), and "It Didn't Matter" (1987). In contrast, here in the States, the Style Council placed only one Top 30 single, "My Ever Changing Moods" (#29, 1984), and only the album of the same name made the Hot 100, at #56, also in 1984. Facing declining interest, the Style Council disbanded in 1990. In 1986 Weller married fellow Style Council member Dee C. Lee (whom he later divorced), and cowrote and coproduced her group Slam Slam's 1991 album, *Free Your Feelings*.

Weller reemerged with the Paul Weller Movement in early 1991 and released his first, eponymous solo album the following year. His followup, *Wild Wood*, launched Weller on a run of critical and commercial success: The album went to #2 in the U.K. and was nominated for the country's prestigious Mercury Music Prize; its successor, *Stanley Road* (featuring guest appearances by Steve Winwood and Oasis' Noel Gallagher), produced two British Top 10 singles ("The Changing Man," #7, and "You Do Something to Me," #9) and went to #1 in the U.K. The record also won Weller a 1995 BRIT Award for Best Male Artist, which he won again the following year. But despite his continued success in Britain with his next two releases, *Heavy Soul* (#2 U.K.) and the greatest-hits compilation *Modern Classics* (#7 U.K.), Weller failed to make a mark in America. Subsequently, his 2000 release, *Heliocentric*, was released only in the U.K.

Elmore James

Born Elmore Brooks, Jan. 27, 1918, Richland, MS; died May 24, 1963, Chicago, IL
1966—*Blues Masters, vol. 1* (Blue Horizon) 1969—*Whose Muddy Shoes* (Chess) 1970—*Tough* (Blue Horizon) 1971—*The Sky Is Crying* (Sphere Sound); *I Need You* 1973—*Street Talkin'* (Muse) 1976—*Anthology of the Blues: Legend of Elmore James* (Kent); *Anthology of the Blues: Resurrection of Elmore James* 1982—*Red Hot Blues* (Quicksilver) 1989—*The Complete Fire and Enjoy Sessions, Part I* (Collectables); *The Complete Fire and Enjoy Sessions, Part II; The Complete Fire and Enjoy Sessions, Part III; The Complete Fire and Enjoy Sessions, Part IV* 1992—*The Complete Elmore James Story* (Capricorn/Warner Bros.); *Elmore James—King of the Slide Guitar: The Fire/Fury/Enjoy Recordings* (Capricorn) 1994—*The Classic Early Recordings, 1951–1956* (Atomic Beat) 2001—*Shake Your Money Maker: The Best of the Fire Sessions* (Buddah).

One of the most influential postwar urban-blues guitarists, Elmore James was the one Chicago bluesman perhaps most responsible for shaping the styles of slide-guitar playing that translated from blues to rock. His anthems, like "It Hurts Me Too," "Dust My Broom" (by Robert Johnson), "Shake Your Money Maker," and "The Sky Is Crying," have been covered by Eric Clapton, Fleetwood Mac, John Mayall, Savoy Brown, George Thorogood, and others. His influence can most directly be heard in the slide-guitar work of Duane Allman and the Rolling Stones' Brian Jones.

James began picking on a homemade lard-can guitar as a child. By the late '30s, he was working Mississippi taverns with blues legends Robert Johnson and Sonny Boy Williamson (Rice Miller). Between 1943 and 1945 he served in the navy. He began recording in 1951 for the Trumpet label in Jackson, Mississippi. He later moved to Chicago but continued to perform in the South and parts of the Midwest.

It was when he began recording in Chicago that James became one of the first and foremost modernizers of the Delta blues tradition. In 1963, while visiting the home of his cousin Homesick James, a bluesman with whom he'd performed in the '40s, Elmore James suffered a fatal heart attack. His stylistic influence can be traced to bluesmen like J.B. Hutto, B.B. King, Freddie King, Jimmy Reed, and Hound Dog Taylor, as well as rockers like Jimi Hendrix and Johnny Winter. His son, Elmore James Jr., is also a musician.

Etta James

Born Jamesetta Hawkins, Jan. 25, 1938, Los Angeles, CA
1961—*At Last* (Chess); *Second Time Around* 1963—*Etta James; Top Ten; Rocks the House* 1965—*Queen of Soul*

1967—*Call My Name* 1968—*Tell Mama* 1970—*Sings Funk* 1971—*Losers Weepers; Peaches* 1972—*Miss Etta James* (Crown); *Best of; Twist With; Golden Decade* (Chess) 1973—*Etta James* 1974—*Come a Little Closer* 1975—*Etta Is Better Than Evah!* 1978—*Deep in the Night* (Warner Bros.) 1986—*Blues in the Night, vol. 1: The Early Show* (Fantasy); *The Late Show* 1988—*The Sweetest Peaches: The Chess Years, vol. 1 (1960–66)* (Chess/MCA); *The Sweetest Peaches: The Chess Years, vol. 2 (1967–1975); Seven Year Itch* (Island) 1989—*The Gospel Soul of Etta James* (Arrival) 1990—*Stickin' to My Guns* (Mercury) 1992—*The Right Time* (Elektra) 1993—*How Strong Is a Woman: The Island Sessions* (4th & Broadway) 1994—*Mystery Lady: Songs of Billie Holiday* (Private); *Live From San Francisco* 1995—*Time After Time* 1997—*Love's Been Rough on Me* 1998—*Life, Love & the Blues* 1999—*Best of Etta James: The Millennium Collection* (MCA); *Heart of a Woman* (Private) 2000—*The Chess Box* (Chess); *Matriarch of the Blues* (Private).

Soul singer Etta James survived a decade-long heroin addiction to forge a career that has seen her turn out well over a dozen hits and was still going strong with concert appearances past the year 2000. James was still in her early teens and singing with a vocal trio called the Peaches when legendary R&B bandleader Johnny Otis [see entry] discovered her. At Otis' L.A. home, he and Etta cowrote her first hit, "Roll With Me, Henry," an answer to Hank Ballard and the Midnighters' off-color "Work With Me, Annie." Under the title "The Wallflower," "Henry" became a #2 R&B hit in 1955. That year Georgia Gibbs had a #1 pop hit with a mild cover of the tune, called "Dance With Me, Henry." Later, James' version was retitled "Dance With Me, Henry."

Through the mid-'50s James became a mainstay of Otis' revue and scored another R&B hit with "Good Rockin' Daddy" (#12, 1955). In 1960 she moved from Modern to Chess Records' Argo subsidiary, and the R&B hits began coming again: "All I Could Do Was Cry" (#2 R&B), "My Dearest Darling" (#5 R&B), and a duet as Etta and Harvey (with Harvey Fuqua of Harvey and the Moonglows) entitled "If I Can't Have You" (#52 pop, #6 R&B). She also sang background vocals on Chuck Berry's "Almost Grown" and "Back in the U.S.A."

James continued making R&B hits through the early '60s. In 1961 she had more Top 10 R&B hits with "At Last" (#2 R&B) and "Trust in Me" (#4 R&B), and in 1962 with "Something's Got a Hold on Me" (#4 R&B) and "Stop the Wedding" (#6 R&B). In 1963 she hit the pop chart with "Pushover" (#25 pop, #7 R&B), as well as "Pay Back" (#78), "Two Sides to Every Story" (#63), and "Would It Make Any Difference to You" (#64); 1964 brought "Baby, What You Want Me to Do?" (#82) and "Loving You More Every Day" (#65).

In the '60s she developed a heroin addiction that lasted through 1974 and kept her much of the time in L.A.'s Tarzana Psychiatric Hospital. Still, she hit big with "Tell Mama" (#23 pop, #10 R&B, 1967), "Losers Weepers" (#26 R&B, 1970), and "I've Found a Love" (#31 R&B, 1972). Though she has not had any major hit records since ending her heroin addiction, James has remained a popular concert performer. She played the Montreux Jazz Festival in 1977 and opened some dates for the Rolling Stones' 1978 U.S. tour. *Seven Year Itch* was produced by keyboardist Barry Beckett, house keyboardist at Alabama's legendary Muscle Shoals studio, where James had recorded such '60s R&B hits as "I'd Rather Go Blind." She returned to Muscle Shoals to record *The Right Time*, which reunited her with Jerry Wexler (the longtime Aretha Franklin producer, who'd worked on James' *Deep in the Night* album) and included a duet with Steve Winwood; shortly after the album's release, James was inducted into the Rock and Roll Hall of Fame. She won her first Grammy for 1994's *Mystery Lady: The Songs of Billie Holiday*. In 1995 she published her autobiography (cowritten with David Ritz), *Rage to Survive*. James continues to record and perform to an ever-increasing audience and critical acclaim.

Rick James

Born James Johnson, Feb. 1, 1948, Buffalo, NY
1978—*Come Get It* (Gordy) 1979—*Bustin' Out of L Seven; Fire It Up* 1980—*Garden of Love* 1981—*Street Songs* 1982—*Throwin' Down* 1983—*Cold Blooded* 1984—*Reflections* 1985—*Glow* 1986—*The Flag; Greatest Hits* 1988—*Wonderful* (Reprise) 1994—*Bustin' Out* (Motown) 1997—*Urban Rhapsody* (Private I/Mercury).

Singer/songwriter/keyboardist/guitarist Rick James emerged in the late '70s with an energetic blend of blatant come-ons and dance music he called "punk funk." James was expelled from five different schools before leaving Buffalo at 15 to join the U.S. Naval Reserves. Soon after, he went AWOL and ended up in Toronto, where, as Ricky Matthews, he formed and fronted a band called the Mynah Birds, which included Neil Young and Bruce Palmer (later of Buffalo Springfield) and Goldy McJohn (of Steppenwolf). They were signed to Motown and recorded, but nothing was released, and the group soon disbanded. James then worked as a sideman, playing bass with several groups through the '70s, with only minimal success.

In 1978 James re-signed with Motown, this time as a songwriter and producer. That year his solo debut, *Come Get It*, sold a million copies, and "You and I" was a hit (#13 pop, #1 R&B). Subsequent singles—"Mary Jane" (#41 pop, #3 R&B, 1978), "Bustin' Out" (#6 pop, #8 R&B, 1979), "High on Your Love Suite" (#12 R&B, 1979), "Love Gun" (#13 R&B, 1979), "Big Time" (#17 R&B, 1980), "Give It to Me Baby" (#40 pop, #1 R&B, 1981), "Super Freak (Part 1)" (#16 pop, #3 R&B, 1981)—propelled each of his releases, including the uncharacteristically ballad-laden *Garden of Love*, onto the pop chart.

James' stage image—long corn-rowed and beaded hair, elaborate sequined costumes and instruments—and his bass-heavy music have prompted comparisons with Sly Stone and with George Clinton's Parliament-Funkadelic. James has also produced Teena Marie, the Temptations ("Standing on the Top"), and Carl Carlton.

Beginning around 1983, James' career entered a slump,

and although he remained a formidable presence on the R&B chart, none of his releases made the Top 30. His R&B Top 20 singles include "Dance wit' Me (Part 1)" and "Hard to Get" (1982); "Cold Blooded" (#1 R&B), "U Bring the Freak Out," and a duet with Smokey Robinson, "Ebony Eyes" (1983); "17" (1984); "Can't Stop" and "Glow" (1985); and "Sweet Sexy Thing" (1986). In 1983 he unveiled the Mary Jane Girls, a quartet of sexy singers he produced and wrote for. While he had a #3 hit with his "In My House" for the Mary Jane Girls and produced comedian Eddie Murphy's debut album and #2 hit single, "Party All the Time," James' own releases began to fall by the wayside. A #1 R&B song featuring rapper Roxanne Shanté, "Loosey's Rap," failed to make the pop chart at all in 1988, but James returned to the pop chart via MC Hammer's "U Can't Touch This," a 1990 megahit that featured "Super Freak."

James made the news again in 1991 after he and a female companion were arrested and charged with two instances of physically abusing women who refused to join them in group sex. James, who admitted he was a cocaine addict and that the attacks occurred during drug binges, was later convicted of assaulting one of the women. He was sentenced to five years, four months in prison. In a press release issued to coincide with the release of *Bustin' Out,* James commented on the positive aspects of his drug rehabilitation and prison experience, admitting that he had been a drug addict for over 35 years. He also claimed to have written an autobiography, tentatively entitled *Memoirs of a Superfreak.* In 1996 James was released from prison and quickly got to work on the somewhat successful *Urban Rhapsody* (#170 pop, #31 R&B, 1997). He toured in support of *Urban Rhapsody* until November 1998, when he suffered a stroke onstage.

Tommy James and the Shondells

Formed 1960, Niles, MI
Lineup ca. 1965: Tommy James (b. Thomas Gregory Jackson, Apr. 29, 1947, Dayton, OH), voc.; Ronald Rosman (b. Feb. 28, 1945), kybds.; Michael Vale (b. July 17, 1949), bass; Vincent Pietropaoli, drums; George Magura, sax, bass, organ.
1965—(– Pietropaoli; – Magura; + Peter Lucia [b. Feb. 2, 1947], drums; + Eddie Gray [b. Feb. 27, 1948], gtr.) 1966—*Hanky Panky* (Roulette) 1968—*Mony Mony* 1969—*Crimson and Clover* 1969—*The Best of Tommy James and the Shondells* 1989—*Anthology* (Rhino).
Tommy James solo: 1976—*In Touch* (Fantasy) 1977—*Midnight Rider* 1980—*Three Times in Love* (Millennium) 1991—*Tommy James: The Solo Years (1970–1981)* 1995—*A Night in Big City: An Audio-Movie* (Aura).

Tommy James and the Shondells were one of the most consistently successful American pop groups of the late '60s. Group leader and singer James taught himself to play guitar at age nine; four years later he formed the Shondells. The group played locally, and in 1963 recorded a Jeff Barry–Ellie Greenwich song, "Hanky Panky," as a favor for a local disc jockey. In late 1965 a Pittsburgh DJ began playing it, and more than 20,000 copies were sold within a few days. After its national release on Roulette in 1966, it hit #1 and sold a million copies, whereupon James assembled a new cast of Shondells.

Between 1966 and the Shondells' 1970 dissolution, the group amassed 13 other Top 40 hits, among them "I Think We're Alone Now" (#3, 1967), "Mirage" (#10, 1967), "Mony, Mony" (#3, 1968), "Crimson and Clover" (#1, 1969), "Sweet Cherry Wine" (#7, 1969), and "Crystal Blue Persuasion" (#2, 1969). With "Crimson and Clover" (the group's biggest seller at 5.5 million), the Shondells' sound became more psychedelic than bubblegum; James began producing, as well. After the group disbanded, James returned to his home in upstate New York for several months (partially to recuperate from a drug problem) before reemerging in 1970 to produce Alive and Kickin's hit version of his "Tighter, Tighter." He had a #4 hit the following year with "Draggin' the Line." The Shondells, meanwhile, materialized that year as a new group called Hog Heaven, which released one LP on Roulette.

James' subsequent singles failed to crack the Top 30, and solo LPs like *Midnight Rider* (produced by Jeff Barry) never hit. He returned to the chart in 1980, however, with "Three Times in Love" (#19). By that time, it was estimated James had sold over 30 million records. Although the '80s brought him no more hits, covers of Tommy James and the Shondells' songs seemed to be everywhere. Joan Jett took "Crimson and Clover" to #7 in 1982, and in 1987 Billy Idol's version of "Mony Mony" replaced teen singer Tiffany's "I Think We're Alone Now" as the #1 record in the U.S. In the mid-'90s James formed the Aura label, for which he continues to release solo efforts and archival Shondells material.

The James Gang

Formed 1967, Cleveland, OH
Jim Fox, drums; Tom Kriss, bass; Glen Schwartz, gtr.
1969—(– Schwartz; + Joe Walsh [b. Nov. 20, 1947, Wichita, KS], gtr., voc.) *Yer Album* (ABC) (– Kriss; + Dale Peters, bass) 1970—*James Gang Rides Again* 1971—*Thirds; Live in Concert* (– Walsh; + Domenic Troiano [b. ca. 1945, Modugno, It.], gtr.; + Roy Kenner, voc.) 1972—*Straight Shooter; Passin' Through* 1973—*Best of* (– Troiano; + Tommy Bolin [b. 1951, Sioux City, IA; d. Dec. 4, 1976, Miami, FL], gtr.); *Bang* (Atco); *Gold Record* (ABC) 1974—*Miami* (Atco) (– Bolin; – Kenner; group disbands) 1975—(group re-forms: Fox; Peters + Richard Shack, gtr.; + Bubba Keith, gtr., voc.) *Newborn* 1976—*Jesse Come Home* 2000—*Greatest Hits* (MCA).

The James Gang was a favorite American hard-rock band during the early '70s. Founded by drummer Jim Fox, who had played in Cleveland bands since age 14, the group earned a word-of-mouth reputation throughout the Midwest. Glen Schwartz (who left to join Pacific Gas and Electric) was replaced by future Eagle Joe Walsh [see entry], the group's best musician and star attraction. Pete Townshend, a friend of the Gang, arranged for it to open for the Who in Europe in 1971.

Despite a career-long lack of hit singles, the trio's second, third, and fourth LPs all went gold, and it continued to be a major concert draw around the world for a while after Walsh's departure to form Barnstorm. His replacement, Domenic Troiano, left in 1973 to join the Guess Who, and Walsh recommended Tommy Bolin for the part. But Bolin (who had worked with Billy Cobham) contributed to only two LPs—*Miami* and *Bang* (originally titled *James Gang Bang*)—before joining Deep Purple. Vocalist Roy Kenner soon left as well, and in 1974 the group temporarily disbanded, only to re-form a year later with Bubba Keith and Richard Shack. The James Gang never recaptured its early momentum and disbanded for good in 1976.

Jan and Dean

Jan Berry, born Apr. 3, 1941, Los Angeles, CA; Dean Torrence, born Mar. 10, 1941, Los Angeles
1962—*Golden Hits* (Liberty); *Surf City and Other Swingin' Cities* 1963—*Drag City* 1964—*The Little Old Lady From Pasadena* 1965—*Golden Hits, vol. 2; Command Performance/Live in Person* 1966—*Golden Hits, vol. 3* 1971—*Legendary Masters* (United Artists) 1974—*Gotta Take That One Last Ride* 1982—*One Summer Night/Live* (Rhino) 1995—*Teen Suite 1958–1962* (Varése Vintage) 1996—*Golden Summer Days.*

Between their 1958 debut single, "Jennie Lee," and Jan Berry's near-fatal car crash in April 1966, Jan and Dean were the premier surf music duo, charting 13 Top 30 singles and selling over 10 million records worldwide.

The two were friends and football teammates at Emerson Junior High in L.A. They formed a group, the Barons, with drummer Sandy Nelson ("Teen Beat," "Let There Be Drums") and future Beach Boy Bruce Johnston. With a singer named Arnie Ginsburg, they recorded a #8 hit for Arwin Records entitled "Jennie Lee," written about a local stripper. Dean Torrence, who sang lead, was serving in the National Guard when the contracts were signed, so the single was credited to Jan and Arnie.

Once Torrence returned, he and Berry resumed their partnership, Ginsburg joined the army, and Arwin dropped them. Herb Alpert and Lou Adler became their managers and produced "Baby Talk" (#10, 1959) for their small Dore label. Five Top 100 entries on the Dore and Challenge labels preceded the pair's signing with Liberty in 1961. After three minor hits, in 1963 they recorded their only #1, "Surf City," a song cowritten by their friend Brian Wilson. The Beach Boys leader also contributed vocals and worked with Jan and Dean on their debut LP, *Linda Goes Surfin'*; Torrence, uncredited, later sang lead on the Beach Boys' 1966 smash "Barbara Ann." The Beach Boys and Jan and Dean often appeared on each other's records until their record companies objected.

Berry did the bulk of the duo's songwriting, including the soundtrack for a 1964 Fabian beach movie entitled *Ride the Wild Surf.* The pair hosted *The T.A.M.I. Show* that same year. Both continued their educations full-time (Torrence was premed and then an architecture student at UCLA; Berry an art and design student at USC) until they were convinced of their musical success. Their hits included "Heart and Soul" (#25, 1961), "Linda" (#28, 1963), "Honolulu Lulu" (#11, 1963), "Drag City" (#10, 1964), "Dead Man's Curve" (#8, 1964), "The Little Old Lady (From Pasadena)" (#3, 1964), "Ride the Wild Surf" (#16, 1964), "Sidewalk Surfin' " (#25, 1964), "You Really Know How to Hurt a Guy" (#27, 1965), "I Found a Girl" (#30, 1965), and "Popsicle" (#21, 1966).

But by the mid-'60s, their friendship had become strained to the point where they considered breaking up. In April 12, 1966, Berry crashed his Corvette into a parked truck at 65 mph on L.A.'s Whittier Boulevard. His three passengers were killed, and he sustained brain damage so severe that it wasn't until 1973 that he was able to remember an entire song lyric. He is still partially paralyzed and suffers speech difficulties. During the years of recovery, he regularly recorded demos for Lou Adler as therapy. Meanwhile, Torrence had recorded a solo album, *Save for a Rainy Day* (over which Berry was furious), and became head of Kitty Hawk Graphics in Hollywood. Between then and 1981 he won design awards (and one Grammy) for his album covers (among his clients were the Nitty Gritty Dirt Band, the Beach Boys, Nilsson, Steve Martin, Linda Ronstadt, and, of course, Jan and Dean). Berry also recorded on his own, issuing "Mother Earth" and "Don't You Just Know It" in 1972 on his old friend Lou Adler's Ode label.

The pair made a premature and unsuccessful comeback appearance in 1973 (lip synching to prerecorded tracks), but by 1977 they were again performing live on occasion. A television-movie account of their lives entitled *Dead Man's Curve* aired in 1978 on ABC-TV and renewed interested in Jan and Dean. They continue to tour and in 1982 released *One Summer Night—Live.* They later appeared on the *Back to the Beach* soundtrack. As of 1999 the duo still made 40 to 50 public appearances a year.

Jane's Addiction/Porno for Pyros

Formed 1986, Los Angeles, CA
Perry Farrell (b. Perry Bernstein, Mar. 29, 1959, Queens, NY), voc.; Eric Avery (b. Apr. 25, 1965, Los Angeles), bass; David Navarro (b. June 6, 1967, Santa Monica, CA), gtr.; Steve Perkins (b. Sep. 13, 1967, Los Angeles), drums.
1987—*Jane's Addiction* (Triple X) 1988—*Nothing's Shocking* (Warner Bros.) 1990—*Ritual de lo Habitual* 1991—*Live and Rare* (WEA) 1997—*Kettle Whistle* (– Avery; + Flea, bass).
Porno for Pyros, formed 1992, Los Angeles: Farrell, voc.; Perkins, drums; + Peter DiStefano (b. Jul. 10, 1965, Los Angeles), gtr.; Martyn Le Noble (b. Apr. 14, 1969, Vlaardingen, Neth.), bass.
1993—*Porno for Pyros* (Warner Bros.) 1996—*Good God's Urge.*
Perry Farrell with Psi Com: 1994—*Psi Com* (Triple X, reissue).

Deconstruction (Avery; Navarro): 1994—*Deconstruction* (American).
Polar Bear (Avery; Biff Sanders, drums; Thomas Van Wendt, gtr.): 1997—*Polar Bear* EP (Dry Hump).
Perry Farrell solo: 2001—*Song Yet to Be Sung* (Virgin).
Dave Navarro solo: 2001—*Trust No One* (Capitol).

Led by the flamboyant, outspoken Perry Farrell, Jane's Addiction blended elements of art rock, punk, and metal into an ambitious musical juxtaposition of sublime beauty and utter decadence. The group broke up during its peak of popularity in 1991, just after its appearances on the first Lollapalooza Tour (which Farrell organized). Farrell continued chasing his muse in Porno for Pyros.

Perry Bernstein spent the early part of his life working for his jeweler father in New York City's diamond district. When he was still a child, his mother committed suicide (Farrell alluded to this later, on "Then She Died . . ." from *Ritual de lo Habitual,* singing to a friend who has died of an overdose, "Will you say hello to my ma? . . . She was an artist, just as you were"). After her death, the Bernsteins moved to Woodmere, Long Island, and then to Miami.

Bernstein attended college briefly in Oceanside, California, but quit after having a nervous breakdown. He then started lip synching and doing exotic dancing in a Newport Beach nightclub, taking the stage name Perry Farrell by adopting his brother's first name as his last (making a pun on *peripheral*). In 1981 he started the gothlike Psi Com, which released an indie-label EP before breaking up in 1985.

A year later Farrell formed Jane's Addiction, which he named after a prostitute friend who introduced him to band mates Eric Avery and David Navarro. Farrell, reputedly a control freak, became notorious among L.A.'s arty rock scene. Sporting Day-Glo girdles or black vinyl bodysuits, heavy mascara, and neon dreadlocks, he stalked stages singing in his high, mannered voice while the members of his band churned out a foreboding sound often compared to Led Zeppelin. After releasing a self-titled live album on L.A.'s Triple X Records, a major-label bidding war ensued. Warner Bros. won, putting out *Nothing's Shocking* the following year.

In 1990, on the strength of a catchy single and video ("Been Caught Stealing"), *Ritual de lo Habitual* skyrocketed up the charts, peaking at #19. The album made the news when some record chains refused to carry it because of its cover art (it featured Farrell's own nude sculptures). At the band's request, Warners issued the album to some stores in a plain white cover with only the text of the First Amendment printed on it.

That same year, Farrell codirected a film called *Gift,* a free-form creation that included scenes of Jane's Addiction live in Mexico City and a Santeria wedding. Farrell remained in the limelight throughout 1991, when he brought his idea of an alternative-rock traveling circus to life with Lollapalooza, was busted on drug charges in Santa Monica, and brought Jane's Addiction to a close. In 1992 he and drummer Perkins formed Porno for Pyros, which put out its self-titled debut album to cool reception the following year. Porno returned in 1996 with *Good God's Urge* (#20). That same year, Porno guitarist Peter DiStefano was diagnosed with cancer. Though he survived, the band never returned to action.

Navarro and Avery formed the experimental, short-lived Deconstruction in 1993 before Navarro left to join the Red Hot Chili Peppers. The guitarist was in the Chili Peppers long enough to record *One Hot Minute,* a disappointment both commercially and critically. Between bands, Navarro could be heard on a variety of influential albums, including Alanis Morissette's *Jagged Little Pill* and Nine Inch Nails' *Further Down the Spiral.*

Navarro was visible again in 1997, when Farrell unexpectedly reconvened Jane's Addiction for a six-week national tour and the album *Kettle Whistle* (#21), a collection of outtakes, live recordings, and two new tracks. Chili Peppers bassist Flea sat in for Avery, who chose not to return. Avery instead focused on Polar Bear, a collaboration with Biff Sanders of Ethyl Meatplow. Mixing rock with electronic elements and Middle Eastern tempos, Polar Bear released a self-titled EP.

Lollapalooza continued forward, but when Farrell's partners booked mainstream metal band Metallica as the 1996 headliner, he pulled out and immediately created the short-lived ENIT Festival. By 1998, Lollapalooza was shut down indefinitely. Farrell had by then fully embraced the electronic dance movement, and in the late '90s he could be found working the turntables as a DJ in clubs in L.A. and New York. In 1999 he released *Rev,* which collected several Jane's Addiction and Porno for Pyros recordings with two new tracks. Farrell also began work on a solo album featuring such guests as Dave Navarro and Mad Professor. Entitled *Song Yet to Be Sung,* it was released in June 2001 concurrently with Navarro's debut solo album, *Trust No One.*

Japan

Formed 1974, London, Eng.
David Sylvian (b. David Batt, Feb. 23, 1958, London), voc., gtr.; Steve Jansen (b. Steve Batt, Dec. 1, 1959, London), drums; Richard Barbieri (b. Nov. 30, 1958), kybds.; Mick Karn (b. Anthony Michaelides, July 24, 1958, London), sax; Rob Dean, gtr.
1978—*Adolescent Sex* (Hansa, Ger.); *Obscure Alternatives* 1979—*Quiet Life* (Fame) 1980—*Live in Japan* (Hansa, Ger.); *Gentlemen Take Polaroids* (Virgin) 1981—(– Dean) *Tin Drum; Assemblage* (Hansa, Ger.) 1983—*Oil on Canvas* (Virgin) 1984—*Exorcising Ghosts* 1989—*A Souvenir From Japan* (Hansa, Ger.).
Mick Karn solo: 1982—*Titles* (Virgin) 1987—*Dreams of Reason Produce Monsters* 1993—*Bestial Cluster* (CMP).
Rain Tree Crow: 1991—*Rain Tree Crow* (Virgin).
David Sylvian solo: 1984—*Brilliant Trees* (Virgin) 1985—*Alchemy—An Index of Possibilities* (Virgin, U.K.) 1986—*Gone to Earth* (Virgin) 1987—*Secrets of the Beehive* 1988—*Plight & Premonition* (with Holger Czukay) (Venture) 1989—*Weatherbox* (Virgin); *Flux + Mutability* (with Czukay) (Venture)

1991—*Ember Glance: the permanence of memory* 1993—*The First Day* (with Robert Fripp) (Virgin) 1994—*Damage: Live* (with Robert Fripp); *Darshan Remixes* (Alex) 1999—*Dead Bees on a Cake* (Virgin); *Approaching Silence.*

Precursors of England's short-lived New Romantic movement, London's Japan mixed glam theatrics and synthesizer pop with influences as diverse as Erik Satie and Motown to achieve success in the Far East, notoriety at home, and indifference in the U.S.

With his brother Steve on drums, David Sylvian led the quartet, which signed with German label Ariola-Hansen in 1977. Sylvian's Bryan Ferry–style vocals and the band's pop-star glamour marked them as an alternative to punk; their following was largest among Japanese listeners. With industry legend Simon Napier Bell as manager, they switched to Virgin, and their English audience grew. Sylvian began collaborating with Yellow Magic Orchestra's Ryuichi Sakamoto [see entry]; their albums continued to reflect a sometimes baffling stylistic variety, although they gained U.K. Top 20 hits with "Quiet Life," "Ghosts," and a cover of Smokey Robinson and the Miracles' 1967 hit "I Second That Emotion."

Tension between Sylvian and saxophonist Mick Karn caused Japan's breakup in 1982, but its principal members continued recording. Karn alternated between music and sculpture, collaborations, and session work (Midge Ure, Gary Numan, Robert Palmer). He released solo albums and, for a short time, joined Bauhaus' Peter Murphy in the duo Dali's Car. Jansen and Barbieri in 1986 collaborated on an album entitled *Worlds in a Small Room,* then worked briefly together as the Dolphin Brothers.

In 1989 Japan reunited as Rain Tree Crow and subsequently released an album of the same name in 1991. Sylvian soon left to concentrate on his own work. His sound departed further from Japan's; either solo or with Robert Fripp, Bill Nelson, or Can alumnus Holger Czukay, his work verged on New Age ambience. He also eschewed the theatricality that was his former band's trademark. His interest in aesthetics, however, remained. In 1984 he published his first book of photographs, *Perspectives: Polaroids 82/84;* in 1990 his installation of sculpture, sound, and light, *Ember Glance: the permanence of memory,* was staged in Japan.

Jason and the Scorchers

Formed 1981, Nashville, TN
Jason Ringenberg (b. Nov. 22, 1958, Kewanee, IL), voc., gtr., harmonica; Warner Hodges (b. June 4, 1959, Wurtzburg, Ger.), gtr., voc.; Jeff Johnson (b. Dec. 31, 1959, Nashville), bass; Perry Baggs (b. Mar. 22, 1962, Nashville), drums, voc.
1982—*Reckless Country Soul* EP (Praxis) 1983—*Fervor* EP 1985—*Lost & Found* (EMI America) 1986—*Still Standing* (+ Andy York [b. July 28, 1961, Wichita, KS], gtr.; + Ken Fox [b. Feb. 16, 1961, Toronto, Ont., Can.], bass) 1989—*Thunder and Fire* (A&M) 1992—*Essential Jason and the Scorchers, vol. I: Are You Ready for the Country* (EMI) 1995—*A Blazing Grace* (Mammoth) 1996—*Clear and Impetuous Morning* 1998—*Midnight Roads & Stages Seen.*
Jason Ringenberg solo: 1992—*One Foot in the Honky Tonk* (Liberty).

Jason and the Scorchers was one of the hottest live acts among the mid-'80s cow-punk bands. Unlike the majority of groups on the updated country-rock scene, however, Jason and company actually emerged from Nashville, not the West Coast.

Raised on his parents' Sheffield, Illinois, hog farm, Jason Ringenberg sang and played guitar in a number of bluegrass, folk, and country bands during his teens. In 1981 he moved to Nashville, where he met his fellow Scorchers after singer-guitarist Warner Hodges witnessed Ringenberg perform in a chaotic local band opening for Carl Perkins. The following year the group recorded its first EP as Jason and the Nashville Scorchers and toured with R.E.M. While on the road, Ringenberg and R.E.M. singer Michael Stipe collaborated on *Fervor*'s "Both Sides of the Line," and Stipe sang backup vocals on the EP's "Hot Nights in Georgia." The song that most identified the Scorchers' oeuvre, perhaps, was *Fervor*'s Ramones-meets-Southern-rock update of Bob Dylan's "Absolutely Sweet Marie."

Jason and the Scorchers' subsequent albums moved closer to country rock, with Ringenberg's ballads becoming more heartfelt and Hodges' guitar work more Stoneslike. Two later cover songs that further crystalized the band's sound were "Lost Highway" (from *Lost & Found*) and "19th Nervous Breakdown" *(Still Standing).* The band's guitar attack was beefed up for *Thunder and Fire* (1989) with the addition of Andy York. Label problems and a grueling 1990 U.S. tour opening for Dylan hammered the nail in the band's coffin, however. Hodges, York, and Fox joined former Del Lord guitarist Eric Ambel's Roscoe's Gang, and Ringenberg attempted a career as a solo country artist, releasing *One Foot in the Honky Tonk,* a hard-edged traditional C&W release that also failed to attract mainstream country audiences. After EMI issued *Essential Jason and the Scorchers, vol. 1,* consisting of the out-of-print *Fervor* and *Lost & Found,* along with some B sides, the original members regrouped and began performing again in 1994. The band then released *A Blazing Grace* in 1995 and soon entered an Atlanta storefront studio for 1996's *Clear and Impetuous Morning,* which again featured metal-strength riffs amid the C&W. The reinvigorated band then released a two-disc live set, 1998's *Midnight Roads & Stages Seen.* Hometown respect for the Nashville country rockers finally emerged in 2000, when the Country Music Hall of Fame included Scorchers artifacts in the museum's permanent collection.

Jay and the Americans

Formed 1961, Brooklyn, NY
John "Jay" Traynor, lead voc.; Kenny Vance (b. Kenny Rosenberg,

Dec. 9. 1943), voc.; Sandy Deane (b. Sandy Yaguda, Jan. 30, 1943), voc.; Howie Kane (b. Howard Kirshenbaum, June 6, 1942), voc.
1962—(+ Marty Sanders [b. Feb. 28, 1941], voc.; – Traynor; + Jay Black [b. David Blatt, Nov. 2, 1941], lead voc.) 1986—*All-Time Greatest Hits* (Rhino).

Jay and the Americans were a clean-cut vocal group whose '60s hits included four Top 10 entries. The group's first hit, the Leiber and Stoller–produced "She Cried" (#5, 1962), featured the original Jay, John Traynor, on lead vocals. That year, he left the group, and guitarist Marty Sanders invited his songwriting partner, David Blatt, to audition. Blatt adopted the moniker Jay, and the reconstituted group had its first hit with "Only in America" (#25, 1963). The song was originally recorded by the Drifters, but when the group's label decided not to release it, their vocals were erased, and Jay and the Americans' were added to the original tracks. The following year Jay and Americans hit #3 with "Come a Little Bit Closer," and in 1965 the grandiose "Cara Mia" hit #4. This, their best-remembered hit, was revived in the Netherlands in 1980 and reached #1.

In 1965 they released an uptempo cover of "Some Enchanted Evening" (#13) and Neil Diamond's first hit as a songwriter, "Sunday and Me" (#18). It was not until 1969 that they again hit the Top 10, this time with the million-selling cover of the Drifters' 1960 hit "This Magic Moment" (#6).

The group stopped recording in 1970 after hitting the Top 20 for the last time with "Walking in the Rain" (#19). A contractual dispute with United Artists over publishing rights kept the band from recording for a number of years. Jay Black kept the name alive by touring as a rock nostalgia act into the '90s. As a solo artist, he recorded an album in 1975 and later had a minor European hit with "Love Is in the Air" (covered by John Paul Young in the U.S.). Future Steely Dan founders Donald Fagen and Walter Becker were part of the group's backup band in the early '70s, and in 1970 Kenny Vance produced their soundtrack album for *You Got to Walk It Like You Talk It.* Vance also worked as a solo artist, recording his debut album in 1975. Sanders pursued writing, and Deane went into producing. "Looking for an Echo," a nostalgic tribute to doo-wop, was recorded with an ad hoc group that included several Americans and ex-Rascal Eddie Brigati.

The Jayhawks/Golden Smog

Formed 1985, Minneapolis, MN
Mark Olson (b. Sep. 18, 1961, Minneapolis), voc., gtr., harmonica; Gary Louris (b. Mar. 10, 1955, Toledo, OH), voc., gtr.; Marc Pearlman (b. July 29, 1961, St. Petersburg, FL), bass; Norm Rogers, drums.
1986—*The Jayhawks* (Bunkhouse) 1988—(– Rogers; + Thad Spencer, drums) 1989—*Blue Earth* (Twin/Tone) (– Spencer; + Ken Callahan, drums) 1992—*Hollywood Town Hall* (American) 1995—(– Callahan; + Karen Grotberg [b. Mar. 18, 1959], piano, voc.) *Tomorrow the Green Grass* (+ Tim O'Reagan [b. Oct. 1, 1958, Chandler, AZ], drums, voc.; – Olson) 1997—(+ Kraig Johnson [b. May 9, 1965, Minneapolis], gtr., voc.) *Sound of Lies* 2000—*Smile* (Columbia/American) (– Grotberg; + Jen Gunderman [b. Nov. 23, 1969], kybds., voc.).
Mark Olson with the Original Harmony Ridge Creek Dippers: 1997—*The Original Harmony Ridge Creek Dippers* (Creek) 1998—*Pacific Coast Rambler* 1999—*Zola and the Tulip Tree* 2000—*My Own Jo Ellen* (Hightone).
Golden Smog (Louris; Pearlman; Johnson; Jeff Tweedy, gtr., voc.; Murphy, gtr., voc.; Jody Stephens, drums): 1992—*On Golden Smog* (Crackpot) 1995—*Down by the Old Mainstream* (Rykodisc) 1998—*Weird Tales.*

Drawing heavily from templates of the Louvin Brothers and Gram Parsons, the Jayhawks (along with contemporaries Uncle Tupelo and its splinter groups, Wilco and Son Volt) helped usher in the "alt country" or "y'alternative" movement of the '90s. After the departure of founder and cofrontman Mark Olson in 1995, however, the Jayhawks shifted gears and moved toward a more sophisticated pop-rock sound in the vein of fellow Minneapolis cult heroes Big Star.

The Jayhawks came together in 1985 when Olson, a stand-up bass player with the Minneapolis rockabilly act Stagger Lee, recruited drummer Norm Rodgers, bassist Marc Pearlman, and guitarist Steve Retzler to back him up in an ensemble that would allow him to play his own material. Retzler was soon replaced by Gary Louris, a veteran of another local rockabilly band, Safety Last. The Jayhawks' self-titled, self-released debut album earned them a demo deal with A&M in 1988, but the label was uninterested in the results. Rodgers was replaced by Thad Spencer, and Louris—discouraged by the band's prospects and recovering from a serious auto accident—jumped ship. He came back on board after local label Twin/Tone picked up the band on the strength of their A&M demo and released *Blue Earth* in 1989. The album failed to make a commercial impression, but it attracted the attention of producer George Drakoulias, who signed the band to Def American after hearing *Blue Earth* in the background during a phone call with Twin/Tone.

Produced by Drakoulias (and featuring the band's third drummer, Ken Callahan), *Hollywood Town Hall* was released in 1992 to rave reviews. Marked by the shared lead vocals and striking harmonies of Olson and Louris, the album would prove to be an Americana landmark, eventually hailed by ROLLING STONE as one of the essential albums of the decade. The band's first "hit" of note would not come until the followup, 1995's *Tomorrow the Green Grass* (#92), which featured the Louris-sung singles "Blue" and "Bad Time," the latter a Grand Funk Railroad cover. The group now featured piano player Karen Grotberg and drummer Tim O'Reagan, but their future was thrown into question when Olson announced his departure to spend more time with his wife, singer/songwriter Victoria Williams, who suffered from multiple sclerosis. The couple relocated to the desert outside Joshua Tree California, and formed the rootsy folk band Original Harmony Ridge Creekdippers. They self-released three

Creekdippers albums before signing with Hightone Records, which issued *My Own Jo Ellen* in 2000.

With Louris stepping up as frontman and Kraig Johnson, from the Minneapolis band Run Westy Run, joining as an extra guitarist, the Jayhawks carried on with *Sound of Lies* (1997). The album found the band scaling back on the country- and folk-inspired elements of their sound in favor of a more psychedelic pop approach, with darker lyrics and heavier guitar. They continued in this direction for 2000's Bob Ezrin–produced *Smile*. Grotberg left after the recording of the album and was replaced by Jen Gunderman.

Louris, Pearlman, and Johnson also moonlight in Golden Smog, a loose-knit side project that also includes members of Wilco (Jeff Tweedy), Soul Asylum (Dan Murphy), and Big Star (Jody Stephens). The group originated as a novelty cover act (as demonstrated on the 1992 EP *On Golden Smog*), but two subsequent albums of original material established the mercurial unit as a critically well-received touring and recording act in its own right.

Jay-Z

Born Shawn Carter, Dec. 4, 1970, Brooklyn, NY
1996—*Reasonable Doubt* (Roc-A-Fella/Priority) 1997—*In My Lifetime, vol.1* (Roc-A-Fella/Def Jam) 1998—*Volume 2 . . . Hard Knock Life* 1999—*Volume 3 . . . The Life & Times of S. Carter* 2000—*Dynasty: Roc La Familia 2000*.

One of the top hip-hop performers of the late '90s, hardcore rapper Jay-Z grew up in Brooklyn's tough Marcy Projects. (He supposedly took his name from two nearby subway lines.) Like fellow New York rappers DMX and Nas, he achieved broad mainstream acceptance for his unflinching accounts of urban life. After appearing on tracks by Big Jaz and Original Flavor, Jay-Z released his first album, *Reasonable Doubt* (#23 pop, #3 R&B, 1996), which included "Ain't No Nigga" (#50 pop, #17 R&B, 1996) with Foxy Brown. Another single, "Can't Knock the Hustle" (#73 pop, #35 R&B, 1996), featured guest vocals from Mary J. Blige. Unhappy with the album's distribution, Jay-Z formed his own record company, Roc-A-Fella, and signed a deal with Def Jam. *In My Lifetime, vol. 1* (#3 pop, #2 R&B, 1997) was an unqualified success, but 1998's *Volume 2 . . . Hard Knock Life* (#1 pop and R&B, 1998) allowed the rapper to thoroughly dominate the pop charts. Two singles, debuting within a month of each other, did the rest: the jaunty "Can I Get a . . ." (#19 pop, #6 R&B, 1998), from the *Rush Hour* soundtrack, and "Hard Knock Life (Ghetto Anthem)" (#15 pop, #10 R&B, 1998), which used a sample of a children's chorus from *The Original Broadway Cast of "Annie."* The rapper embarked on a hugely successful tour and boosted the careers of such protégés as Ja Rule, Beanie Sigel, and Memphis Bleek. *Volume 2* sold more than 4 million copies and won a Grammy Award for Best Rap Album. The 1999 followup, *Volume 3 . . . The Life & Times of S. Carter* (#1 pop and R&B, 2000), along with two hits—Mariah Carey's #1 pop and R&B "Heartbreaker" (on which he rapped) and "Do It Again (Put Ya Hands Up)" (#17 R&B, 1999)—continued the winning trend. In December 1999 Jay-Z was charged with first-degree assault in the stabbing of record executive Lance "Un" Rivera. A new album, *The Dynasty: Roc La Familia* (#1 pop and R&B, 2001), included the hit "I Just Wanna Love U (Give It 2 Me)" (#11 pop, #1 R&B, 2001).

Jazz Crusaders: See the Crusaders

D.J. Jazzy Jeff and the Fresh Prince: See Will Smith

Wyclef Jean: See the Fugees

Blind Lemon Jefferson

Born ca. July 1897, Couchman, TX; died ca. Dec. 1930, Chicago, IL
1968—*Master of the Blues, vol. 1* (Biograph) 1969—*Blind Lemon Jefferson 1926–1929* 1971—*Master of the Blues, vol. 2* 1971—*Black Snake Moan* (Milestone) 1974—*Blind Lemon Jefferson* 1988—*King of the Country Blues* (Yazoo).

One of the first country bluesmen of the '20s, arguably the most influential, and surely the most commercially popular, singer/guitarist Blind Lemon Jefferson (Lemon was his given first name) influenced other bluesmen like Lightnin' Hopkins, Big Joe Williams, Robert Pete Williams, T-Bone Walker, and B.B. King.

Blind from birth, Jefferson began performing in his early teens on streets and at parties and picnics. He was as much a "songster"—with a repertoire spanning blues, shouts, moans, field hollers, breakdowns, ballads, religious hymns, and prison and work songs—as a bluesman. As a teenager he worked throughout Texas, then hoboed through the South and Southwest, from Georgia to St. Louis, into the early '20s, although Dallas was always his home base. Around 1925 he was signed to Paramount Records, for which he recorded his own distinctive, haunting country blues under his own name, and religious songs under the pseudonym Deacon L.J. Bates. His blues recordings were among the best-selling "race" records of the 1925–30 era.

Jefferson reportedly suffered a heart attack in 1930 in Chicago and was left on the streets to die of exposure just before Christmas. His best-remembered tunes include "Black Snake Moan," "See That My Grave Is Kept Clean," "Long Lonesome Blues," and "Booger Rooger Blues," in which he coined the term "booger rooger" (for a wild party), which later became "boogie-woogie." A 1970 biography, *Blind Lemon Jefferson*, by Bob Groom, was published by Blues World.

The Jefferson Airplane/ Jefferson Starship/Starship

Jefferson Airplane, formed 1965, San Francisco, CA
Marty Balin (b. Martyn Jerel Buchwald, Jan. 30, 1942, Cincinnati, OH), voc.; Paul Kantner (b. Mar. 17, 1941, San Francisco, CA), gtr., voc.; Jorma Kaukonen (b. Dec. 23, 1940, Washington, DC), gtr., voc.; Signe Toly Anderson (b. Sep. 15, 1941, Seattle, WA), voc.; Bob Harvey, bass; Skip Spence (b. Alexander Lee Spence, Apr. 18, 1946, Ontario, Can.; d. Apr. 16, 1999, Santa Cruz, CA), drums.
1965—(– Harvey; + Jack Casady [b. Apr. 13, 1944, Washington, DC], bass) 1966—*Jefferson Airplane Takes Off* (RCA) (– Anderson; + Grace Slick [b. Grace Barnett Wing, Oct. 30, 1939, Chicago, IL], kybds., voc.; – Spence; + Spencer Dryden [b. Apr. 7, 1943, New York, NY], drums) 1967—*Surrealistic Pillow; After Bathing at Baxter's* 1968—*Crown of Creation* 1969—*Bless Its Pointed Little Head; Volunteers* 1970—*The Worst of the Jefferson Airplane* (– Dryden; + Joey Covington, drums) 1971—(– Balin; + Papa John Creach [b. May 28, 1917, Beaver Falls, PA; d. Feb. 22, 1994, Los Angeles, CA], fiddle) *Bark* (Grunt) 1972—(– Covington; + John Barbata, drums) *Long John Silver* (+ David Freiberg [b. Aug. 24, 1938, Boston, MA], voc., bass, gtr., kybds.; – Kaukonen; – Casady) 1973—*Thirty Seconds Over Winterland* 1974—*Early Flight* 1977—*Flight Log* 1987—*2400 Fulton Street—An Anthology* (RCA) 1990—*White Rabbit and Other Hits* 1992—*Jefferson Airplane Loves You.*
As Jefferson Starship: 1974—(Slick; Barbata; Freiberg; Creach; Kantner; + Peter Kangaroo [b. Peter Kaukonen], bass; + Craig Chaquico [b. Sep. 26, 1954, Sacramento, CA], gtr.; – Kangaroo; + Pete Sears [b. Eng.], bass) *Dragon Fly* 1975—(+ Balin) *Red Octopus* (– Creach) 1976—*Spitfire* 1978—*Earth* (– Slick; – Balin) 1979—*Jefferson Starship Gold* (+ Mickey Thomas [b. Dec. 3, 1949, Cairo, GA], voc.; – Barbata; + Aynsley Dunbar [b. Jan. 10, 1946, Liverpool, Eng.], drums) *Freedom at Point Zero* 1981—(+ Slick) *Modern Times* 1982—*Winds of Change* (– Dunbar; + Don Baldwin, drums) 1984—*Nuclear Furniture* (– Kantner; – Freiberg).
As Starship: 1985—*Knee Deep in the Hoopla* (Grunt) (– Sears) 1987—*No Protection* 1988—(– Slick) 1989—*Love Among the Cannibals* (RCA) 1990—(+ Brett Bloomfield, bass; + Mark Morgan, kybds.) (group disbands) 1991—*Greatest Hits (Ten Years and Change, 1979–1991)* (RCA).
Jefferson Airplane re-forms: 1989—(the 1966–1974 lineup: Kantner; Balin; Slick; Casady; Kaukonen) *Jefferson Airplane* (Epic).
As Jefferson Starship ("the Next Generation"): 1992—(Kantner; Casady; Creach; + Tim Gorman, kybds., voc.; + Prairie Prince [b. May 7, 1950, Charlotte, NC], drums, perc.; + Mark "Slick" Aguilar, gtr., voc.; Darby Gould [b. ca. 1965], voc.) 1994—(+ Balin; + Diana Mangano; – Creach) 1995—*Deep Space/Virgin Sky* (Intersound) (– Gorman; – Gould) 1996—(– Cambra; + T Lavitz, kybds.) 1999—*Windows of Heaven* (CMC International); *Greatest Hits—Live at the Fillmore* (– T Lavitz; + Chris Smith [b. 1964, New Haven, CT], kybds.).
Paul Kantner solo: 1970—*Blows Against the Empire* (credited to Paul Kantner/Jefferson Starship) (RCA) 1983—*The Planet Earth Rock and Roll Orchestra.*
Paul Kantner and Grace Slick: 1971—*Sunfighter* (Grunt).
Kantner, Slick, David Freiberg: 1973—*Baron Von Tollbooth and the Chrome Nun* (Grunt).
Grace Slick solo: 1974—*Manhole* (Grunt) 1980—*Dreams* (RCA) 1981—*Welcome to the Wrecking Ball* 1984—*Software.*
Grace Slick and the Great Society: 1970—*Collector's Item From the San Francisco Scene* (Columbia).
Marty Balin solo: 1973—*Bodacious DF* (RCA) 1980—*Rock Justice* (EMI) 1981—*Balin* 1983—*Lucky* 1990—*Balince—A Collection* (Rhino) 1991—*Better Generation* (GWE).
Mickey Thomas solo: 1971—*As Long as You Love Me* (MCA) 1981—*Alive Alone* (Elektra).
Craig Chaquico solo: 1993—*Acoustic Highway* (Higher Octave) 1994—*Acoustic Planet* 1996—*A Thousand Pictures* 1997—*Once in a Blue Universe.*
Papa John Creach solo: 1971—*Papa John Creach* (Grunt) 1972—*Filthy* 1974—*Playing My Fiddle for You* (with Zulu) 1975—*I'm the Fiddle Man* (with Midnight Sun) (Buddha) 1976—*Rock Father* 1992—*Papa Blues* (Bee Bump).
KBC Band: formed 1985 (Kantner; Balin; Casady; + Aguilar, gtr.; + Barry Lowenthal, drums; + Gorman, kybds., voc.; + Keith Crossan, sax): 1986—*KBC Band* (Arista).

Through myriad personnel shifts, including the 1984 departure of founder/guiding light Paul Kantner, several name changes, and its metamorphosis from a group of hippie revolutionaries to MOR pop powerhouse—and back again—the Jefferson Airplane/Starship franchise proved one of the most durable and volatile in rock.

At the start, the Jefferson Airplane epitomized the burgeoning Haight-Ashbury culture and provided its soundtrack. The Airplane established a psychedelic unity with

Jefferson Airplane: Paul Kantner, Grace Slick, Spencer Dryden, Marty Balin, Jorma Kaukonen, Jack Casady

communal vocal harmonies and a synthesis of elements from folk, pop, jazz, blues, and rock. The band got started in 1965 when Marty Balin, formerly with the acoustic group the Town Criers, met Paul Kantner at the Drinking Gourd, a San Francisco club. They were first a folk-rock group, rounded out by Jorma Kaukonen, Skip Spence, Signe Anderson, and Bob Harvey, though Harvey was soon replaced by Jack Casady. Their first major show was on August 13, christening the Matrix Club, which later became the outlet for new S.F. bands. RCA signed them late in the year, and *Jefferson Airplane Takes Off* (#128, 1966) came out in September 1966 and went gold.

Just before the LP came out, in the summer of 1966, Signe Anderson left to have a baby and was replaced by former model Grace Slick. Slick had been a member of the Great Society, a group formed in 1965. The Great Society, which included Grace's husband at the time, Jerry Slick, and her brother-in-law Darby, had completed two LPs for Columbia that weren't released until after Slick became a star with the Airplane. Spence left the Airplane to form Moby Grape and was replaced by a former jazz drummer, Spencer Dryden, completing the Airplane's most inventive lineup.

Slick's vocals were stronger and more expressive than Anderson's; she later claimed that she always tried to imitate the yowl of the lead guitar. She brought with her two former Great Society songs to *Surrealistic Pillow*—"Somebody to Love" (by Darby Slick) and her own "White Rabbit" (which was banned in some areas as a pro-drug song)—both of which became Top 10 singles, and the album (#3, 1967) sold half a million copies. *After Bathing at Baxter's* (#17, 1967) included a nine-minute psychedelic jam-collage, "Spayre Change," and occasioned the group's first battle with RCA over obscene language: The word "shit" was deleted from the lyric sheet. *Baxter's* had no hit singles and didn't sell well, but the Airplane recouped with the gold *Crown of Creation* (#6, 1968), which included Slick's "Lather" and David Crosby's "Triad," a song about a *ménage à trois* that had been rejected by Crosby's current group, the Byrds.

The band's ego conflicts were already beginning, however, as Slick stole media attention from Balin (the band's founder), and the songwriting became increasingly divergent. Live, Slick and Balin traded vocals in battles that became increasingly feverish, and the volatile sound of the band in concert was captured on *Bless Its Pointed Little Head* (#17, 1969). By the time the sextet recorded 1969's *Volunteers,* the Airplane's contract allowed it total "artistic control," which meant that the "Up against the wall, motherfuckers" chorus of "We Can Be Together" appeared intact. The Airplane performed at the Woodstock and Altamont festivals but then had its second major shakeup. Dryden left in 1970 to join the New Riders of the Purple Sage (he was replaced by Joey Covington), and the band stopped touring when Slick became pregnant by Kantner. Anxious to perform, Kaukonen and Casady formed Hot Tuna [see entry] (originally Hot Shit), which later seceded from the Airplane, although, like most band members, they would return.

In the meantime, Kantner and the housebound Slick recorded *Blows Against the Empire* (#20, 1970). Billed as Paul Kantner and Jefferson Starship (the debut of the name), the LP featured Jerry Garcia, David Crosby, Graham Nash, and other friends. It became the first musical work nominated for the science-fiction writers' Hugo Award. At the same time, a greatest-hits package entitled *The Worst of the Jefferson Airplane* (#12, 1970) was released. On January 25, 1971, Slick and Kantner's daughter, China, was born; and that spring, Balin, who had nothing to do with *Blows* and contributed only one cowritten composition to *Volunteers,* left. He formed a short-lived band, Bodacious D.F.

In August the Airplane formed its own label, Grunt, distributed by RCA. The band's reunited effort, *Bark* (#11, 1971), saw them with Covington and all of Hot Tuna, including violinist Papa John Creach, who had first performed with Hot Tuna at a Winterland show in 1970. The band had grown apart, though, and Hot Tuna and Kantner-Slick were each writing for their own offshoot projects. In December 1971 Slick and Kantner released *Sunfighter* (#89, 1971) under both their names, with baby China as cover girl. (China grew up to become an MTV VJ and an actor.)

In July 1972 this version of the Airplane recorded its last studio LP, *Long John Silver* (#20), with some drumming from ex-Turtle John Barbata. In August 1972 at a free concert in New York's Central Park, the band introduced ex–Quicksilver Messenger Service bassist, keyboardist, and vocalist David Freiberg to the ranks. The Airplane unofficially retired at that point. By that September, Casady and Kaukonen had decided to go full-time with Hot Tuna, though they appeared on the live LP *Thirty Seconds Over Winterland* (#52, 1973), which came out in April 1973. Slick, Kantner, and Freiberg recorded *Baron Von Tollbooth and the Chrome Nun* (#120, 1973), one of the band's least popular efforts. Slick's equally disappointing solo debut, *Manhole* (#127), appeared in January 1974. By then, she had developed a serious drinking problem, and the band was hoping that the Tuna players would return. They did not.

Finally, in February 1974 Slick and Kantner formed the Jefferson Starship (no strict relation to the group on *Blows*), with Freiberg, Creach, Barbata, and 19-year-old lead guitarist Craig Chaquico. Chaquico had played with the Grunt band Steelwind with his high school English teacher Jack Traylor and on Slick and Kantner's collaborative LPs beginning with *Sunfighter.* The new group also included Peter Kangaroo (Jorma's brother), though in June he was replaced by Pete Sears, a British sessionman who had played on Rod Stewart's records and had been a member of Copperhead. On *Dragon Fly* (#11, 1974), Balin made a guest appearance on his and Kantner's song "Caroline." The LP went gold.

Balin tentatively rejoined the band in January 1975, and the group's next big breakthrough came with *Red Octopus,* its first #1 LP, hitting that position several times during the year and selling 4 million copies. Balin's ballad "Miracles" was a #3 single. The band was more popular than ever, but in Slick's opinion the music had become bland and corporate, and her rivalry with Balin had not diminished. The group's followup LP, 1976's *Spitfire,* went #3 and platinum, its first album to do so. But after the successful *Earth* (#5, 1978; also platinum), both Slick and Balin left.

By then, Slick and Kantner's romance had ended; in November 1976, she married the band's 24-year-old lighting director, Skip Johnson. Slick's alcoholism forced her to quit the band in the middle of a European tour, leading to a crowd riot in Germany when she did not appear. Her solo albums were neither great critical nor great commercial successes, although throughout the years, her distinctive singing style never changed. In 1980 Balin produced a rock opera entitled *Rock Justice* in San Francisco. Balin did a solo LP of MOR love songs and in 1981 had a hit single with "Hearts."

With its two lead singers gone, the group's future again seemed in question, but in 1979 singer Mickey Thomas, best known as lead vocalist on the Elvin Bishop hit "Fooled Around and Fell in Love," joined, and Barbata was replaced by Aynsley Dunbar, a former Frank Zappa and David Bowie sideman who had just left Journey. The new lineup's *Freedom at Point Zero* (#10, 1979) went gold. The group's momentum ground to a halt in 1980 after Kantner suffered a brain hemorrhage that, despite its severity, left no permanent damage. The next year came *Modern Times* (#26, 1981), which featured Slick on one track; she rejoined the band in February 1981, and the Jefferson Starship again ascended with a string of Top 40 hits: "Be My Lady" (#28, 1982), "Winds of Change" (#38, 1983), and "No Way Out" (#23, 1984).

Professing his disdain for the group's more commercial direction, Kantner left in 1984, taking with him the "Jefferson" of its name. Then known simply as Starship, the group enjoyed even greater commercial success. From the platinum #7 *Knee Deep in the Hoopla* came "We Built This City" (#1, 1985), "Sara" (#1, 1986), and "Tomorrow Doesn't Matter Tonight" (#26, 1986). *No Protection* (#12, 1987) included the group's third #1 hit, 1987's "Nothing's Gonna Stop Us Now," and "It's Not Over ('Til It's Over)" (#9, 1987), which was later adopted as the theme song of Major League Baseball. The last Top 40 single, "It's Not Enough," appeared in 1989. The core trio of Thomas, Chaquico, and Baldwin, abetted by Brett Bloomfield and Mark Morgan, attempted to keep the ship aloft, but in 1990 they called it quits. Thomas formed yet another group, Starship With Mickey Thomas, whose only links to the original dynasty were himself and latecomer Bloomfield.

In the meantime, in 1989 Kantner, Slick, Balin, Casady, and Kaukonen revived the early Jefferson Airplane lineup and released *Jefferson Airplane* (#85, 1989). Before that, Kantner, Balin, and Casady formed the KBC Band; its self-titled LP went to #75 in 1986. With Starship now disbanded, Kantner reclaimed the Jefferson Starship moniker and put together a new lineup in 1991, which included Airplane/Starship stalwarts Casady and Creach as well as Tim Gorman (who had worked with the Who and the Jefferson Airplane), ex-Tube Prairie Prince, ex-KBC member Slick Aguilar, and lead singer Darby Gould, whom Kantner discovered fronting her band World Entertainment War. Gould was joined by vocalist Diana Mangano. The next year, Balin joined. This group, dubbed by Kantner Jefferson Starship—The Next Generation, toured in the early '90s to positive reviews. With Slick (who had by then retired from performing) guesting on several songs, the band recorded the live *Deep Space/Virgin Sky,* which consisted of new material as well as "covers" of classic Airplane and Starship tracks. The band continues to tour regularly; the album *Windows of Heaven* first came out in Germany in 1998 but was remixed for its American release in 1999.

In 2000 Balin, Kantner, and Casady started touring as Jefferson Airplane's Volunteers and were promptly sued by Jefferson Airplane manager and shareholder of Jefferson Airplane Inc., Bill Thompson, for using the name without permission. Adding to the confusion, Mickey Thomas has been touring as Starship Featuring Mickey Thomas since 1992.

Slick has remained true to her vow not to perform anymore and now dedicates herself to painting. Invoking health reasons, she declined to appear with Jefferson Airplane when it performed at its induction into the Rock and Roll Hall of Fame in January 1996 (though she guested on ex–4 Non Blondes singer Linda Perry's album *In Flight* later that same year). In 1998 she published her autobiography, *Somebody to Love?*

Garland Jeffreys

Born ca. 1944, Brooklyn, NY
1969—*Grinder's Switch Featuring Garland Jeffreys* (Vanguard) 1973—*Garland Jeffreys* (Atlantic) 1977—*Ghost Writer* (A&M) 1978—*One-Eyed Jack* 1979—*American Boy and Girl* 1981—*Escape Artist* (Epic); *Rock & Roll Adult* 1983—*Guts for Love* 1991—*Don't Call Me Buckwheat* (RCA) 1992—*Matador and More* (A&M) 1997—*Wildlife Dictionary* (Logic/BMG.).

Garland Jeffreys' urban-romantic lyrics and tough-edged rock & roll gained him a large critical following, though little commercial success in the U.S. Jeffreys, who is part black, part white, and part Puerto Rican, endured growing up mulatto in Sheepshead Bay, Brooklyn. He attended Syracuse University, in part because it was football hero Jim Brown's alma mater. There he befriended Lou Reed and upon graduating in 1965 spent a short while in Florence, Italy, studying Renaissance art. After briefly attending New York's Institute of Fine Arts, he began writing and singing songs.

By 1966, Jeffreys was performing solo in the Lower Manhattan club the Balloon Farm, which also featured musicians such as John Cale, Eric Burdon, and Lou Reed. Jeffreys made his living waiting tables and playing in several small-time bands—Train, Mandoor Beekman, and Romeo—before joining with the Buffalo-area group Raven to form Grinder's Switch in 1969. The band cut only one LP, *Grinder's Switch Featuring Garland Jeffreys,* before breaking up in 1970. Jeffreys resumed his solo career, playing Manhattan clubs and signing with Atlantic in 1973.

His self-titled debut, part of which was recorded in Jamaica, was released that March, and a nonalbum single entitled "Wild in the Streets" became an FM anthem. Critics applauded Jeffreys' emotive voice and tense music, but the single flopped. Frustrated, Jeffreys retired for a while, then returned in 1975 with a single on Arista, "The Disco Kid." Following tours with Jimmy Cliff and Toots and the Maytals,

Jeffreys re-signed with A&M in late 1976 and released *Ghost Writer* the next year. That album was praised for its romantic lyrics and Jeffreys' unique vocals, but neither it nor its two followups sold well.

Jeffreys left A&M after 1979's *American Boy and Girl.* The samba "Matador" went Top 10 in several European countries, winning him a new U.S. deal with Epic, which released *Escape Artist* in 1981. The album included a cover of "96 Tears" and was well received. Jeffreys toured, backed by the Rumour, resulting in a live LP out in late 1981 called *Rock & Roll Adult.* Following the less well-received *Guts for Love,* Jeffreys essentially disappeared from the recording scene for nearly eight years. *Don't Call Me Buckwheat* was a critically acclaimed examination of racial issues.

Waylon Jennings

Born June 15, 1937, Littlefield, TX
1966—*Folk Country* (RCA) 1967—*Love of the Common People* 1969—*Waylon Jennings* (Vocalion) 1970—*The Best of Waylon Jennings* (RCA); *Singer of Sad Songs* 1971—*The Taker/Tulsa* 1972—*Ladies Love Outlaws* 1973—*Lonesome, On'ry & Mean; Honky Tonk Heroes* 1974—*The Ramblin' Man; This Time* 1975—*Dreamin' My Dreams* 1976—*Are You Ready for the Country; Wanted: The Outlaws* (with Willie Nelson, Jessi Colter, and Tompall Glaser); *Waylon Live* 1977—*Ol' Waylon* 1978—*Waylon & Willie* 1979—*Greatest Hits* 1980—*Music Man* 1982—*Black on Black; WWII* (with Willie Nelson) 1986—*Will the Wolf Survive* (MCA) 1988—*Full Circle* 1990—*The Eagle* (Epic) 1992—*Too Dumb for New York City, Too Ugly for L.A.* 1993—*Cowboys, Sisters, Rascals & Dirt* (RCA); *The RCA Years—Only Daddy That'll Walk the Line* 1994—*Waymore's Blues (Part II)* 1996—*Right for the Time* (Justice) 1998—*Closing In on the Fire* (Ark 21) 2000—*Never Say Die Live!* (Sony/Lucky Dog).
With the Highwaymen (Jennings, Willie Nelson, Johnny Cash, and Kris Kristofferson): 1985—*Highwayman* (Columbia) 1990—*Highwayman 2* 1995—*The Road Goes on Forever* (Capitol) 1999—*Highwayman Super Hits* (Sony).

Waylon Jennings, along with Willie Nelson, was one of the founding fathers of the rougher, so-called outlaw country movement that championed honky-tonk country over the string-laden Nashville style.

At age 12, Jennings became one of the youngest disc jockeys in radio, working at a Texas country station. At 22, he moved to Lubbock, where he continued to work as a DJ, and then teamed up with Buddy Holly, who asked him to join his touring band on bass. He toured with Holly in 1959, and Holly produced Jennings' first solo single, "Jolé Blon," on Brunswick Records. Jennings was booked on the charter plane flight in which Holly was killed, but gave his seat to the Big Bopper.

In 1963 Jennings formed his own group, the Waylors, and played a brand of folk country, recording for Trend, J.D.'s (part of Vocalion), Ramco, and A&M. He was signed to RCA by Chet Atkins in 1965, began to play mainstream country, and

Waylon Jennings

had a #23 C&W hit with his version of "MacArthur Park" in 1969, which won Jennings his first Grammy. But in the early '70s, with albums like *Ladies Love Outlaws,* Jennings began to develop a more rebellious style, with a rockier edge, and he was booked into rock venues. The 1976 album *Wanted: The Outlaws,* featuring Waylon, Willie Nelson, Tompall Glaser, and Jennings' wife, Jessi Colter, was the first country LP to be certified platinum. *Ol' Waylon,* the first platinum record by a solo country artist, contained the #1 C&W hit "Luckenbach, Texas." Jennings' duets with Willie Nelson also produced the hits "Good Hearted Woman" and his second Grammy winner, "Mammas Don't Let Your Babies Grow Up to Be Cowboys" (#42 pop, 1978). Both "Luckenbach, Texas" and "Good Hearted Woman" crossed over to #25 on the pop charts. His *Greatest Hits* (1979) sold over 4 million copies (C&W's first quadruple-platinum album) and included the #1 country hit "Amanda." (By the early '80s, Jennings had to his credit five platinum LPs, and four platinum and eight gold singles.)

In 1985 Jennings joined Nelson, Johnny Cash, and Kris Kristofferson as the Highwaymen, releasing three albums. A move to MCA and producer Jimmy Bowen expanded Jennings' musical range, exemplified by his cover of Los Lobos' "Will the Wolf Survive" (#5 C&W, 1986). Jennings had triple-bypass heart surgery in 1988 (Johnny Cash recuperated from his own heart surgery in a room across the hall). In 1991 Jennings' song "The Eagle" became an unofficial anthem for the troops of Operation Desert Storm. His 1994 LP, *Waymore's Blues (Part II),* was produced by Don Was. *Right for the Time,* released two years later on the independent Texas label Justice Records, hit stores at the same time as his acclaimed autobiography, *Waylon,* cowritten with Patti Smith guitarist/rock scribe Lenny Kaye. The same summer found Jennings braving young rock audiences on the Lollapalooza Tour, appearing on three dates right before headliners Soundgarden and Metallica. Two years later he surfaced on another indie, Ark 21, for which he cut *Closing in on the Fire* (#71 C&W). Guests on the album included rockers Sting, Sheryl Crow, and Mark Knopfler, as well as legendary "Country Gentleman" Carl Smith, whom Jennings coaxed out of retirement to sing on one track. The year 2000 found Jennings back on a major label (Sony imprint Lucky Dog), which released *Never Say Die Live.* The live album, featuring a reunion of Jennings' old road band as well as guest peformances by his wife, Jessi Colter, and newfangled Nashville "outlaws" Montgomery Gentry and Travis Tritt, was recorded over two nights in January 2000 at Nashville's historic Ryman Auditorium.

The Jesus and Mary Chain

Formed 1984, East Kilbride, Scot.
William Reid (b. Oct. 28, ca. 1958, Glasgow, Scot.), gtr., voc.; Jim Reid (b. Dec. 29, ca. 1961, Glasgow), gtr., voc.; Douglas Hart, bass; Murray Dalglish, drums.
1984—(– Dalglish; + Bobby Gillespie, drums) 1985—*Psychocandy* (Reprise) (– Gillespie; + John Loder, drums) 1987—(– Loder; + John Moore [b. Dec. 23, 1964, Eng.], drums) *Darklands* (Warner Bros.) 1988—*Barbed Wire Kisses* 1989—(– Moore; numerous lineup changes follow, only the major ones are listed) *Automatic* (+ Richard Thomas, drums; – Hart) 1992—*Honey's Dead* (Def American) 1994—(– Thomas; + Ben Lurie, bass, gtr.; + Steve Monti, drums) *Stoned & Dethroned* (American) 1998—*Munki* (Sub Pop) (– William Reid).

With pretty pop melodies buried deep in feedback and grindingly distorted guitars, the Jesus and Mary Chain became darlings of the mid-'80s British press and a college-radio cult hit in the United States. Their melancholy noise made them one of the most distinctive of the Velvet Underground's many musical progeny and paved the way for critically acclaimed early-'90s noise-guitar bands such as My Bloody Valentine.

Shortly after forming the band just outside Glasgow, Scotland, the Reid brothers moved the Jesus and Mary Chain to London to record their first single, "Upside Down." In late 1984 came the first in an ongoing series of drummer changes (after 1986, the drummers were mostly used for live shows only, not for the albums). Bobby Gillespie, vocalist with another Scottish band, Primal Scream, replaced Dalglish on drums—which consisted of banging out simple time on a snare drum and one tom-tom, much like the Velvet Underground's Maureen Tucker. The Jesus and Mary Chain's early work was sneering, thrashing postpunk, delivered in furious 20-minute sets that sometimes ended with audiences violently annoyed by the brevity of the set, the loud feedback, and/or the Reids' singing with their backs to the crowd. The band accepted the obvious comparison to punk rock but then turned around in fall 1985 and recorded the first of its slow, throbbing noise-pop classics, "Just Like Honey," which was built on the classic Phil Spector drumbeat from "Be My Baby." Gillespie returned to Primal Scream a month before *Psychocandy* was released to enormous critical acclaim in both England and America.

The Jesus and Mary Chain: Ben Lurie, Jim Reid, William Reid

The *Darklands* album was followed by a North American tour during which Jim Reid was arrested for assaulting a male heckler. (Reid was later acquitted by a Toronto court.) In early 1992 the group was banned from the British television show *Top of the Pops* over the lyrics to its single "Reverence," which included such lines as "I wanna die just like Jesus Christ / I wanna die just like J.F.K." That summer the band played the U.S. on the second annual Lollapalooza Tour. *Stoned & Dethroned* (1994) proved a departure for the Reid brothers, with its soft, acoustic sound; the album's first single, "Sometimes Always," featured Mazzy Star's Hope Sandoval. Though the song hinted at a commercial breakthrough, it was four years before another U.S. release. *Munki,* released by Seattle's Sub Pop label, was a flop. William Reid quit the same year, and the group disbanded in 1999. William recorded solo; Jim formed the band Freeheat.

Jesus Jones

Formed 1988, London, Eng.
Mike Edwards (b. June 22, 1964, London), voc., gtr.; Jerry De Borg (b. Oct. 30, 1963, London), gtr.; Barry D (b. Iain Baker, Sep. 29, 1965, Surrey, Eng.), kybds.; Al Jaworski (b. Jan. 31, 1966, Plymouth, Eng.), bass; Gen (b. Simon Matthews, Apr. 23, 1964, Wiltshire, Eng.), drums.

1989—*Liquidizer* (SBK) 1991—*Doubt* 1993—*Perverse* 1998—*Already* (Combustion/EMI) 1998—*Greatest* (EMI, Jap.).

Mixing post–new-wave pop rock with liberal doses of sampling and dance rhythms, Jesus Jones scored a huge 1991 hit with "Right Here, Right Now," a song that marveled at the end of the Soviet empire. Topping the charts on both sides of the Atlantic, "Right Here, Right Now" was used as a campaign theme by presidential candidate Bill Clinton before he adopted Fleetwood Mac's "Don't Stop."

Mike Edwards, Jerry De Borg, Al Jaworski, and Gen had been together in a London band called Camouflage. While vacationing in Spain in 1988, they renamed themselves Jesus Jones, reportedly because they were Brits—"Joneses"—surrounded by people named "Jesus." Iain "Barry D" Baker then joined, and he and Edwards began working on getting new sounds with digital-sampling synthesizers. Influenced by rap, alternative rock, and England's pre-rave acid-house scene, Jesus Jones recorded its debut album in late 1988. It produced a U.K. hit in "Info Freako" (#42, 1989), which failed to chart in America but got some college-radio play. In February 1990 Jesus Jones became one of the first British bands to perform in Romania after the fall of that country's oppressive Ceausescu regime. *Doubt* (#25, 1991) topped America's alternative-rock charts and yielded big hit singles in "Right Here, Right Now" (#2, 1991) and "Real, Real, Real" (#4, 1991). *Perverse* (#59, 1993), however, failed to make much of a splash. After a four-year hiatus, the band changed labels and returned with *Already*, which was released a year later in the U.S.

Jethro Tull

Formed 1967, Blackpool, Eng.
Ian Anderson (b. Aug. 10, 1947, Edinburgh, Scot.), voc., flute, gtr.; Mick Abrahams (b. Apr. 7, 1943, Luton, Eng.), gtr.; Glenn Cornick (b. Apr. 24, 1947, Barrow-in-Furness, Eng.), bass; Clive Bunker (b. Dec. 12, 1946, Blackpool), drums.
1968—(– Abrahams; + Martin Barre [b. Nov. 17, 1946], gtr.) 1969—*This Was* (Reprise); *Stand Up* 1970—*Benefit* (+ John Evan [b. Mar. 28, 1948], kybds.) 1971—(– Cornick; + Jeffrey Hammond-Hammond [b. July 30, 1946], bass) *Aqualung* (– Bunker; + Barriemore Barlow [b. Sep. 10, 1949], drums) 1972—*Thick as a Brick; Living in the Past* (Chrysalis) 1973—*A Passion Play* 1974—*War Child* 1975—*Minstrel in the Gallery* 1976—*M.U.—The Best of Jethro Tull* (– Hammond-Hammond; + John Glascock [b. 1953; d. Nov. 17, 1979, London, Eng.], bass; + David Palmer, kybds.) *Too Old to Rock 'n' Roll* 1977—*Songs From the Wood; Repeat: Best of, vol. 2* 1978—*Heavy Horses; Burstin' Out* (Live) (– Glascock; + Tony Williams, bass) 1979—*Stormwatch* (– Williams; – Evan; – Barlow; + Eddie Jobson [b. Apr. 28, 1955, Eng.], kybds., violin; + Dave Pegg [b. Nov. 2, 1947, Birmingham, Eng.], bass; + Mark Craney [b. Los Angeles, CA], drums) 1980—*"A"* 1981—(– Craney; – Jobson; + Gerry Conway, drums; + Peter-John Vettese, kybds.) 1982—*The Broadsword and the Beast* 1984—*Under Wraps* (– Conway) 1985—*Original Masters (Best of)* 1987—*Crest of a Knave* (– Vettese; + Conway, drums; + Doane Perry, drums) 1988—*20 Years of Jethro Tull* 1989—*Rock Island* (– Conway; + Martin Allcock, kybds.) 1991—*Catfish Rising* (– Vettese; – Allcock; + John "Rabbit" Bundrick, kybds.; + Foss Patterson, kybds.; – Bundrick; – Patterson; – Perry; + Dave Mattacks, drums) 1992—*A Little Light Music* 1992—(– Mattacks; + Perry; + Andy Giddings, kybds.) 1993—*The Best of Jethro Tull; 25th Anniversary Boxed Set* 1995—(– Pegg; + Steve Bailey, bass) *Roots to Branches* 1999—(– Bailey; + Jonathan Noyce, bass) *J-Tull Dot Com* (Fuel/Varèse Sarabande).
Ian Anderson solo: 1983—*Walk Into Light* (Chrysalis) 1995—*Divinities: Twelve Dances With God* (Angel) 2000—*The Secret Language of Birds* (Fuel/Varèse Sarabande).

Named for no apparent reason after an 18th-century British agronomist who invented the machine drill for sowing seed, Jethro Tull has been one of the most commercially successful and eccentric progressive-rock bands. In 1987, two decades after its founding, the band won a Grammy for Best Hard Rock/Metal Performance, Vocal or Instrumental, for *Crest of a Knave*.

Jethro Tull began as a blues-based band with some jazz and classical influences, and was initially proclaimed by the British press in 1968 as "the new Cream." By the early '70s, it had expanded into a full-blown classical-jazz-rock-progressive band and in the late '70s turned toward folkish, mostly acoustic rock, all the while selling millions of albums and selling out worldwide tours. Jethro Tull's driving force is Ian Anderson. With his shaggy mane, full beard, and penchant for traditional tartan-plaid attire, Anderson acquired a reputation as a mad Faginesque character with his Olde English imagery and stage antics like playing the flute or harmonica while hopping up and down on one leg. (He confessed to ROLLING STONE in 1993 that he had only recently learned the correct fingerings.)

Anderson moved to Blackpool as a child and met the future members of Jethro Tull in school. He and members of both early and later Jethro Tull lineups formed the John Evan Band in the mid-'60s, which played in northern England with middling success. In late 1967 the band regrouped as Jethro Tull, adding guitarist Mick Abrahams and drummer Clive Bunker, and Anderson taught himself the flute.

The band had its first big success at the 1968 Sunbury Jazz and Blues Festival in England. Tull recorded its debut, *This Was*, that summer, and by autumn it was high on the LP chart in England. The album was released in the U.S. in 1969, and though it sold only moderately, critics hailed the band. That year the British music weekly *Melody Maker* made Jethro Tull its #2 Band of the Year, after the Beatles (the Rolling Stones were third). Abrahams left after the first LP (Black Sabbath's Tony Iommi briefly replaced him) to form Blodwyn Pig [see entry] and later the Mick Abrahams Band.

Jethro Tull's first U.S. tour in 1969 paved the way for the chart success of *Stand Up* (#20), on which Martin Barre replaced Abrahams. One of the more popular numbers on that album was an Anderson flute instrumental based on a Bach "Bouree." (*This Was* had featured Rahsaan Roland Kirk's "Serenade to a Cuckoo"; Anderson had acquired his trademark flute effects—singing through the flute and flutter-tonguing—from Kirk.) Tull's next LP, *Benefit* (#11, 1970), went gold in the U.S., and the group began selling out 20,000-seat arenas. Cornick left to form Wild Turkey and was replaced by Jeffrey Hammond-Hammond, a childhood buddy of Anderson's who'd been mentioned in several Tull tunes ("A Song for Jeffrey," "Jeffrey Goes to Leicester Square," "For Michael Collins, Jeffrey and Me").

By far the band's most successful record in the United States, *Aqualung* (#7, 1971) was an antichurch/pro-God concept album, which eventually sold over 5 million copies worldwide, yielding FM standards like "Cross-Eyed Mary," "Hymn 43," and "Locomotive Breath." Then Bunker left to form the abortive Jude with ex–Procol Harum Robin Trower, ex–Stone the Crows Jim Dewar, and Frankie Miller. His replacement was Barriemore Barlow, whose superlative technique was put to good use on *Thick as a Brick,* another concept album in which one song stretched over two sides in a themes-and-variations suite, a vague protest against Life Itself. The album reached #1 in the U.S. and went gold. *A Passion Play* (#1, 1973) followed the same format but was even more elaborate; critics soundly thrashed Anderson for his indulgence, resulting in his permanent mistrust of the music press and a two-year touring layoff.

However, the heavily orchestrated *War Child* (#2, 1974) became Tull's next gold LP (the *Living in the Past* compilation, with a hit in its title tune, had also gone gold) and yielded a #12 hit single in "Bungle in the Jungle." *Minstrel in the Gallery* (#7, 1975), Tull's first extended flirtation with Elizabethan folk ideas, went gold, and *M.U.—The Best of Jethro Tull* (#13, 1976) went platinum. Hammond-Hammond then left, replaced by John Glascock. In the title cut of *Too Old to Rock 'n' Roll* (#14, 1976), Anderson turned ironic self-deprecation into self-glorification. *Songs From the Wood* (#8, 1977), with its minor hit single "The Whistler," was Tull's deepest exploration into acoustic folk (Anderson had just produced an LP for Steeleye Span). The band's next two albums continued to merge the rustic with Anderson's tortuously intricate classical/jazz/rock thematics.

During 1978 Glascock's health deteriorated, and he was replaced by Tony Williams. Glascock died in 1979 after undergoing heart surgery, and his replacement was former Fairport Convention member Dave Pegg. Before *"A"* (#30, 1980), Anderson revamped the band to include ex–Roxy Music Eddie Jobson and Mark Craney. The tour supporting *"A"* was documented and incorporated into the long-form video *Slipstream.* Beginning with *The Broadsword and the Beast* (#19, 1982), Anderson cowrote material with Peter Vettese, who had also worked with him on his solo album, *Walk Into Light.* The following year's *Under Wraps* continued to evince the group's new keyboard-dominated sound and, by Tull standards, was a flop, topping at #76.

In 1984 a throat problem forced Anderson to forgo singing for the next three years. By then he had established a profitable business raising salmon in Scotland. The first album he recorded after that involuntary hiatus was *Crest of a Knave* (#32, 1987), the group's first gold album since *Stormwatch* and the recipient of the first-ever Best Hard Rock/Metal Performance Grammy. Many observers felt that given the competition (which included Metallica and AC/DC) and the ill-fitting category, this was one of the more ridiculous awards in Grammy history. Jethro Tull hit the road, but *Rock Island* stalled at #56, and even a return to a more blues-influenced sound could not pull *Catfish Rising* past #88. Interestingly, in the U.K. that album debuted at #1 on both the heavy-metal and folk/roots charts. *A Little Light Music,* a live recording of a stripped-down Tull consisting of only Anderson, Barre, Dave Pegg, with Dave Mattacks on drums, went only to #150.

A silver-anniversary world tour ran from early 1993 to mid-1994. Once it ended, Anderson began work on an album for EMI's classical division, and Martin Barre released his first solo album. Although Jethro Tull is not the commercial force it once was (1999's studio offering, *J-Tull Dot Com,* peaked at only #161), its catalogue still sells phenomenally well, and its best-known songs are staples of AOR and classic-rock radio.

Joan Jett

Born Joan Larkin, Sep. 22, 1960, Philadelphia, PA
1981—*Bad Reputation* (Boardwalk); *I Love Rock 'n' Roll* 1983—*Album* (Blackheart/MCA) 1984—*Glorious Results of a Misspent Youth* 1986—*Good Music* 1988—*Up Your Alley* 1990—*The Hit List* (Blackheart/Epic) 1991—*Notorious* 1994—*Pure and Simple* (Warner Bros.); *Flashback* (Blackheart) 1997—*Fit to Be Tied: Great Hits by Joan Jett* (Mercury/Blackheart) 1999—*Fetish* (Blackheart) 2001—*Unfinished Business* EP.
With Evil Stig: 1995—*Evil Stig* (Blackheart/Warner Bros.).

Singer/guitarist Joan Jett was one of the most surprising success stories of the early '80s. The latter-day leader of the much-maligned all-female teenage hard-rock group the Runaways [see entry], Jett could barely get a U.S. deal for her first solo album at the beginning of 1981. One year later her second solo LP had a #1 single and went Top 5 and platinum.

Jett's family moved to Baltimore when she was in grade school and to Southern California when she was 14. That Christmas she got her first guitar. Her initial and continuing inspiration was the British early-'70s glitter-pop music of T. Rex, Gary Glitter, Slade, David Bowie, and Suzi Quatro, whose tough stance Jett most closely emulated. At 15 she met producer Kim Fowley at Hollywood's Starwood Club and became part of his group, the Runaways. The band gave its last show New Year's Eve 1978 in San Francisco.

In the spring of 1979 Jett was in England trying to get a solo project going. While there she cut three songs with ex–Sex Pistols Paul Cook and Steve Jones, two of which came out as a single in Holland only. Back in L.A., Jett produced the debut album by local punks the Germs and acted in a movie based on the Runaways (with actresses playing the rest of the band) called *We're All Crazy Now* (its title taken from the Slade song). The movie was never released, but while working on it Jett met Kenny Laguna (producer of Jonathan Richman, Greg Kihn, and the Steve Gibbons Band) and Ritchie Cordell (bubblegum legend who cowrote Tommy James and the Shondells' "I Think We're Alone Now" and "Mony Mony").

Jett fell ill and spent six weeks in the hospital suffering from pneumonia and a heart-valve infection. She then assembled a solo debut, with Laguna and Cordell producing, using the Jones-Cook British tracks plus guest musicians Sean Tyla and Blondie's Clem Burke and Frank Infante. As *Joan Jett*, the album came out in Europe only. It was rejected by every major and minor label in the U.S., and finally Laguna put out the LP himself. After much positive U.S. press, the album was picked up by Boardwalk in January 1981 and renamed *Bad Reputation*. But it didn't sell.

After a year of touring with her band the Blackhearts, Jett's second LP, even harder-rocking than the first, came out in December 1981, including a version of "Little Drummer Boy" on the pre-Christmas editions. It immediately bolted up the chart, aided by a remake of a B side by the Arrows, the pop-heavy-metal single "I Love Rock 'n' Roll," which hit #1 in early 1982. Jett reached the Top 20 twice more that year with a pair of covers, Tommy James' "Crimson and Clover" (#7) and Gary Glitter's "Do You Wanna Touch Me (Oh Yeah)" (#20).

The singer/guitarist's popularity has been sporadic ever since. The followup to *I Love Rock 'n' Roll* went gold but contained only the Top 40 "Fake Friends"; by the time of 1988's *Up Your Alley*, Jett's career appeared all but finished. The previous year, her foray into film (*Light of Day*, the story of a struggling rock & roll band, starring Michael J. Fox) had fared poorly at the box office, and even her version of the title song, penned by Bruce Springsteen, failed to break the Top 30. But the platinum *Up Your Alley* put Jett's gritty, unadorned hard rock back on the chart with "I Hate Myself for Loving You" (#8, 1988) and "Little Liar" (#19, 1988). Then came another dry spell, broken only by yet another cover tune: AC/DC's vengeful "Dirty Deeds" (#36, 1990).

In 1992 Jett left Epic Records for Warner Bros. At a time when she was verging on becoming a punk anachronism, she became frequently cited as an archetype of the so-called Riot Grrrl movement of women-led bands. She produced a single for Bikini Kill, whose singer Kathleen Hanna then cowrote four songs on Jett's 1994 LP, *Pure and Simple*. Despite that album's positive reviews, Jett wasn't able to keep the momentum going. She released a live album with the Gits (a punk band whose singer, Mia Zapata, had been murdered) under the moniker Evil Stig and continued to associate with the indie-rock scene, but her own output since *Pure and Simple* has been slim. In addition to a pair of compilations, there have been only 1999's confidential *Fetish* (a mix of old, rare, and new songs) and the 2001 EP *Unfinished Business*, which collects five sports-related songs, including a version of "Love Is All Around" (the theme to *The Mary Tyler Moore Show*).

In 1999 Jett and the Blackhearts performed for allied troops in the Balkans. At the end of 2000 Jett joined the Broadway cast of *The Rocky Horror Show*, playing Columbia and Usherette.

Jewel

Born Jewel Kilcher, May 23, 1974, Payson, UT
1995—*Pieces of You* (Atlantic) 1998—*Spirit* (Atlantic)
1999—*Joy: A Holiday Celebration.*

Atz Kilcher and Lenedra Carroll may not have made much of an impression with the two albums they recorded as a folk duo (1977's *Early Morning Gold* and 1978's *Born and Raised on Alaska Land*), but their daughter, Jewel, would become one of the most successful female solo artists of all time. She was catapulted into the mainstream—and to the forefront of the Lilith Fair pack of new female singer/songwriters—on the strength of a powerfully expressive voice and a debut album, *Pieces of You*, that took about nine months to chart and sold more than 11 million copies.

Jewel (who uses only her first name professionally) was born in Utah, where her father was attending college. Soon after, her parents moved the family back to Homer, Alaska, to live on the 800-acre homestead of her paternal grandfather, a Swiss emigrant who helped draft Alaska's state charter. Their log cabin home had no running water. At the age of six, Jewel began singing with her parents and two brothers in local bars and restaurants. She continued performing with her father after her parents' divorce two years later but moved to Anchorage to be with her mother when she was 15 and then to Michigan to attend the Interlochen Fine Arts Academy, where she studied opera and learned to play guitar. After graduation she rejoined her mother in San Diego, where she began a series of waitress jobs to make rent before deciding to live out of her VW van and concentrate on songwriting. This led to a steady gig at the local Inner-Change Coffeehouse, where Jewel began attracting such a large crowd that she landed a recording contract with Atlantic within five months. She was 19.

Released in February 1995, *Pieces of You* seemed to be dead on arrival. But the label stuck by her, and 14 months of steady touring later, the album's lead single, "Who Will Save Your Soul," began to take off. The song debuted on the singles chart in June 1996 and peaked at #11. A second single, "You Were Meant for Me," went to #2. By the time the third single, "Foolish Games" (also featured on the *Batman & Robin* soundtrack), went to #7, *Pieces of You* had climbed to #4. The album was met with mixed reviews—Jewel herself would later dismiss many of the songs as immature and poorly recorded—but her voice (particularly her knack for both scat singing and yodeling) was widely regarded as a marvel. When *Time* magazine spotlighted the '90s brigade of female singer/songwriters for a 1997 cover story on Sarah McLachlan's successful all-woman Lilith Fair festival tour, it was Jewel's face that adorned the cover, with the headline "Jewel and the Gang."

Released nearly four years after *Pieces of You, Spirit* (1998) debuted at #3 and sold over 4 million copies (as opposed to its 11-million-selling predecessor). The lead single, "Hands," went to #6, but "Down So Long" and "Jupiter (Swallow the Moon)" stalled at #59 and #51, respectively. Jewel's popularity and visibility remained high, however, as evidenced by the success of her 1998 poetry collection, *A Night Without Armor,* which topped the *New York Times* bestseller list.

In 1999 she cofounded (with her mother) her own nonprofit charity organization, Higher Ground for Humanity—intended, according to her Web site, to "inspire positive change on global, community, and individual levels." The same year, she performed both at Woodstock '99 and at the NetAid concert at Giants Stadium in New Jersey, sang two duets with Merle Haggard for his career retrospective, *For the Record: 43 Legendary Hits,* and released the Christmas album *Joy: A Holiday Collection* (#32). She also made her film debut with a starring role in director Ang Lee's Civil War drama, *Ride With the Devil.*

In 2000 Jewel released her second book, *Chasing Down the Dawn,* a collection of journals chronicling both her public and private life. As of this writing, a new album was in the planning stages.

Jodeci

Formed 1988, Charlotte, NC
K-Ci (b. Cedric Hailey, Sep. 2, 1969, Charlotte), voc.; Jo-Jo (b. Joel Hailey, June 10, 1971, Charlotte), voc.; Devante Swing (b. Donald DeGrate, Sep. 29, 1969, Newport News, VA), voc.; Mr. Dalvin (b. Dalvin DeGrate, July 23, 1971, Newport News), voc.
1991—*Forever My Lady* (Uptown/MCA) 1993—*Diary of a Mad Band* 1995—*The Show, the After-Party, the Hotel.*
K-Ci & Jo-Jo: 1997—*Love Always* 1999—*It's Real.*
Dalvin DeGrate: 2000—*Met.A.Mor.Phic* (Maverick).

Jodeci helped lead the first wave of romantically inclined R&B vocal groups who wed neo-doo-wop harmonies to '90s dance rhythms. While at first overshadowed on the pop charts by Boyz II Men and Color Me Badd, Jodeci was enormously popular with black audiences when all three groups emerged in 1991. The group finally claimed a Top 10 pop crossover of its own two years later.

The Hailey and DeGrate brothers met while singing in different Charlotte, North Carolina, church choirs. Taking their group name from a combination of three members' stage names, Jodeci landed a record deal after singing for executives at MCA's Uptown black pop label. The group's debut album, *Forever My Lady* (#18 pop, #1 R&B, 1991), sold more than 2 million copies, yielding hits in "Stay" (#41 pop, #1 R&B, 1991) and the title track (#25 pop, #1 R&B, 1991), which was cowritten and coproduced by Al B. Sure! DeVante Swing reciprocated by cowriting and coproducing Sure!'s album *Private Times and the Whole 9.*

In April 1993 K-Ci and DeVante Swing turned themselves in to Teaneck, New Jersey, police where they were arraigned on charges of aggravated sexual contact and weapons possession; they were subsequently sentenced to probation and community service. Four months later "Lately," from Jodeci's appearance in early 1993 on *Uptown MTV Unplugged,* rose to #4 on the pop chart (#1 R&B). Success followed with the release later that year of *Diary of a Mad Band* (#3 pop, #1 R&B), which featured the singles "Cry for You" (#15 pop, #1 R&B, 1993) and "Feenin' " (#25 pop, #2 R&B, 1994).

The group's next release, 1995's *The Show, the After-Party, the Hotel* (#2 pop, #1 R&B), launched three singles onto the charts: "Freek 'n You" (#14 pop, #3 R&B), "Love U 4 Life" (#31 pop, #8 R&B), and "Get On Up" (#22 pop, #4 R&B). K-Ci scored with a solo single, a remake of Bobby Womack's "If You Think You're Lonely Now" (#17 pop, #11 R&B), from the soundtrack to the 1995 film *Jason's Lyric,* and joined Jo-Jo for "How Could You" (#53 pop, #16 R&B, 1996) from the film *Bulletproof.* The pair was also featured on 2Pac's (Tupac Shakur) #1 hit, 1996's "How Do U Want It." It wasn't long before the brothers cut loose with their own album, 1997's *Love Always* (#6 pop, #2 R&B), which was an attempt to tone down Jodeci's racy lyrical content while focusing more on lush balladry. The singles included "You Bring Me Up" (#26 pop, #7 R&B), "Last Night's Letter" (#46 pop, #15 R&B), "All My Life" (#1 pop and R&B), and "Don't Rush (Take Love Slowly)" (#24 R&B). In 1999 the brothers released a second album, *It's Real.* The following year, Dalvin DeGrate's solo album, *Met.A.Mor.Phic,* was released on Madonna's Maverick label.

Billy Joel

Born William Martin Joel, May 9, 1949, Bronx, NY
1972—*Cold Spring Harbor* (Family/Philips) 1973—*Piano Man* (Columbia) 1974—*Streetlife Serenade* 1976—*Turnstiles* 1977—*The Stranger* 1978—*52nd Street* 1980—*Glass Houses* 1981—*Songs in the Attic* 1982—*The Nylon Curtain* 1983—*An Innocent Man* 1985—*Greatest Hits: vol. I & vol. II* 1986—*The Bridge* 1987—*Концерт In Concert)* 1989—*Storm Front* 1993—*River of Dreams* 1997—*Greatest Hits, vol. III; The Complete Hits Collection 1973–1997* 2000—*2000 Years—The Millennium Concert.*

Beginning as a quintessential confessional singer/songwriter, Billy Joel has gone on to render consistently well-crafted pop. Classically trained, he combines rock attitude with musicianly professionalism. Whether taking the form of rock & roll, new wave, hard-edged dance fare, '60s nostalgia, or political statement, his songs are marked by a melodicism derived ultimately from Tin Pan Alley and Paul McCartney. His forte is the romantic ballad epitomized by his signature tune, "Just the Way You Are." Unlike that of many of his pop-music contemporaries, Joel's work has been perceived as progressing over the years, moving steadily from the purely personal, some would argue sophomoric, concerns of his earliest work to embrace a wider range of styles—particularly with his classical compositions—and subjects. As bard of everyday suburban dream and disappointment, he has achieved a singular voice and status.

When Joel was eight, his father, a German Jew, left the family to live in Vienna, Austria, and divorced Joel's mother. She struggled to support her two children in suburban Hicksville, Long Island, where, as a teenager, Joel ran with a leather-jacketed street gang. He also boxed for three years, breaking his nose in the process.

In the late '60s, after playing in a series of local cover bands, he joined the Long Island group the Hassles, who released two meager-selling records on the United Artists label. He then formed a hard-rock duo, Attila, with Hassles drummer Jonathan Small; Small's wife, Elizabeth Weber, would later wed Joel. Attila's only album also failed. Taking up commercial songwriting, Joel signed with Family Productions in 1971. His solo debut, *Cold Spring Harbor,* demonstrated both his fondness for Long Island and the somber side of his singing/songwriting approach, but because the tapes were inadvertently sped up slightly in production, Joel's voice sounded nasal and unnatural.

Legal and managerial woes precluded an immediate followup, and for six months Joel performed in West Coast piano bars under the name "Bill Martin." These experiences informed his breakthrough, *Piano Man,* yielding hits in the Top 30 title track, the Top 100 "Travelin' Prayer," and "Worse Comes to Worst." His third solo album, another respectable seller, featured "The Entertainer" (#34, 1974). *Turnstiles* came next, and although "New York State of Mind" eventually became a standard, Joel's career appeared to be in a holding pattern. Then came *The Stranger* and a string of hit singles: 1977's "Just the Way You Are" (#3) and 1978's "Movin' Out (Anthony's Song)" (#17), "She's Always a Woman" (#17), and "Only the Good Die Young" (#24). "Just the Way You Are," written for his first wife and then-manager Elizabeth (the couple divorced in 1982), won two Grammys in 1979 and became a popular tune for both weddings and cover versions—by some counts, there have been approximately 200 versions of the song recorded.

More hits followed—from 1978's *52nd Street,* "My Life" (#3, 1978), "Big Shot" (#14, 1979), and "Honesty" (#24, 1979); from 1980's *Glass Houses,* "It's Still Rock and Roll to Me" (#1, 1980) and "You May Be Right" (#7, 1980)—and in 1979 Joel appeared at the Havana Jam Concert in Cuba. In 1981 he released *Songs in the Attic,* a live collection of pre-*Stranger* material; also that year, "Say Goodbye to Hollywood" (later recorded by Ronnie Spector) became a hit. Despite the hits, Joel remained in his most vociferous critics' eyes "a lightweight"; Joel responded publicly by tearing up critical reviews onstage during his concerts.

Critically and musically, the tide seemed to turn for Joel with the socially conscious *The Nylon Curtain,* which showcased his musical skill and pop traditionalist's gift for song structure. That, along with his perseverance and industry, began winning critical converts (in 1992, Joel was inducted into the Songwriters Hall of Fame, followed by induction into the Rock and Roll Hall of Fame in 1999). Featuring "Pressure" (#20, 1982), "Allentown" (#17, 1982), a Reagan-era unemployment lament, and "Goodnight Saigon" (#56, 1983), about Vietnam vets, *The Nylon Curtain* went to #7. Several of Joel's singles were showcased in innovative ("Pressure") and dramatic ("Allentown") music videos that were put into heavy rotation on the then-new MTV. The multiplatinum *An Innocent Man,* a stylistic homage to early '60s AM-radio pop, offered "Tell Her About It" (#1, 1983), "An Innocent Man" (#10, 1983), "The Longest Time" (#14, 1984), "Keeping the Faith" (#18, 1985), and "Uptown Girl" (#3, 1983), a Four Seasons–esque valentine for Christie Brinkley, the model whom Joel would marry in 1985 (the couple divorced in 1994). After a seven-night run at Madison Square Garden in 1984, he released *Greatest Hits: vol. I & vol. II,* his seventh consecutive Top 10 album.

The Bridge (1986) found him duetting on "Baby Grand," with Ray Charles, for whom Joel's and Brinkley's daughter, Alexa Ray, was named. The next year Joel toured the Soviet Union; the live *Концерт* documented the concerts. In 1989 *Storm Front* and its first single, "We Didn't Start the Fire," charted simultaneously at #1; its centerpiece ballad "Shameless" became a hit for Garth Brooks two years later, and its supporting tour saw Yankee Stadium hosting its first rock concert. By this time, Joel had reorganized his band, found new management, and, for longtime producer Phil Ramone, substituted Foreigner guitarist Mick Jones.

With 1993's *River of Dreams,* which also hit #1, Joel's lyrical content, oftentimes topical and acerbic, revealed a more philosophical outlook. With a cover painting by Brinkley, and employing producer Danny Kortchmar (known for his work with James Taylor and Don Henley), *River* featured fellow Long Islander Leslie West (ex-Mountain) on guitar. The album's title track reached #3, and "All About Soul," with guest vocals by the group Color Me Badd, peaked at #29. A tour of the U.S. with fellow piano man Elton John followed in 1994. (The duo would tour internationally in 1998.)

The title of *River of Dreams'* last track, "Famous Last Words," would prove prophetic in terms of the direction Joel's career would take next. In 1997, the year he released another volume of greatest hits (with three new recordings that were all cover songs, an oddity for the prolific songwriter), Joel announced that he was concentrating on composing classical music for the foreseeable future. Still, he didn't disappear from the public eye; he continued to speak about songwriting to aspiring musicians at colleges and performed with his band on tour, culminating in a 1999 New Year's Eve concert at New York's Madison Square Garden, which resulted in a live two-disc set.

Joel's career has been marked by tumultuous business moves—his 1972 relinquishing of publishing rights to Family Productions, his legal battles with Elizabeth, and a $90-million lawsuit Joel filed against his ex-manager and former brother-in-law Frank Weber in 1989 alleging fraud and misappropriation of funds (in 1990 he was awarded $2 million and, in a twist, by 1994 Joel was paying Weber $550,000 and forgiving $600,000 still owed). In September 1992 Joel filed another $90 million lawsuit, this time against former lawyer Allen Grubman, charging fraud, malpractice, and breach of contract (in October 1993 Joel and Grubman announced that litigation had ceased; no news of a financial settlement followed). And, not stopping, Joel also filed sued against his onetime tour manager Rick London (Elizabeth's brother-in-law); Joel then dropped the suit in early 1995. Deeply suspicious of the music business, Joel has fought for lower concert-ticket prices and attacked ticket scalping; he has contributed extensively to philanthropic causes, including many on Long Island.

David Johansen/Buster Poindexter

Born Jan. 9, 1950, Staten Island, NY
1978—*David Johansen* (Blue Sky) 1979—*In Style* 1981—*Here Comes the Night* 1982—*Live It Up* 1984—*Sweet Revenge* (Passport) 1990—*Crucial Music: The David Johansen Collection* (CBS Special Projects) 1993—*The David Johansen Group Live* (Epic) 1995—*From Pumps to Pompadour: The David Johansen Story* (Rhino) 2000—*David Johansen and the Harry Smiths* (Chesky).
As Buster Poindexter: 1987—*Buster Poindexter* (RCA) 1989—*Buster Goes Berserk* 1994—*Buster's Happy Hour* (Forward/Rhino).

A rock & roll chameleon, David Johansen moved from the protopunk leader of the New York Dolls [see entry] to a sincere, soulful solo singer to Buster Poindexter, an ultrasmooth lounge singer. Like the Dolls, his solo albums garnered much critical acclaim but few financial rewards; only as Poindexter was he able to gain popular acclaim.

Growing up, Johansen played in many local bands (including the Vagabond Missionaries and Fast Eddie and the Electric Japs) before forming the Dolls in late 1971. He was the Dolls' rubber-faced, loose-jointed lead singer, a self-mocking showman. In 1975, just as the downtown New York music scene was gathering steam, the Dolls fell apart, and Johansen didn't enter a recording studio again until late 1977, when he recorded his debut solo LP. Dolls guitarist Syl Sylvain toured with Johansen to support the LP, which included several songs the two had written while they were still in the Dolls. *David Johansen* attempted to bring the Dolls' spirit to the masses ("Funky But Chic"). The album bombed commercially (selling only about 68,000 copies), but critics raved about the songwriting and Johansen's streamlined but raw, soulful rock.

Johansen's next two solo LPs saw him making some musical compromises in pursuit of a wider audience. *In Style*, with its thicker, Motown-influenced sound (the Four Tops' Levi Stubbs is one of Johansen's early favorites), solidified Johansen as a critics' pet but sold only a bit better than the debut. *Here Comes the Night* (#160, 1981) attempted a more overt commercial turn, but despite a tour opening for then-hitmaker Pat Benatar, the album still didn't spark much consumer interest. Since all along Johansen had been known for his top-notch live shows, he tried to recoup in 1982 by releasing his first live record, *Live It Up* (#148, 1982). The single, an Animals medley featuring "We Gotta Get Out of This Place," "It's My Life," and "Don't Bring Me Down," was a minor hit. That year, Johansen appeared at Shea Stadium, opening for the Clash and the Who.

Buster Poindexter (a.k.a. David Johansen)

Sweet Revenge was a last-ditch attempt at commercial success, with Johansen rapping and singing over a synthesized dance beat. Its failure caused him to rethink his career, and in 1984 he emerged as the tuxedoed Buster Poindexter (also the name of his music publishing company), playing piano bars with a repertoire that included Tiny Bradshaw and Joe Liggins songs.

Originally a trio, Poindexter's band expanded into the Banshees of Blue, with additional backup singers, guitars, and horns. The first Buster Poindexter album (#90, 1988) included a high-energy cover of the 1984 Caribbean soca hit "Hot Hot Hot" (#45, 1988). Buster's Caribbean success helped Johansen, who had been a member of the Ridiculous Theatrical Company prior to joining the Dolls, in his side career as an actor. He was cast in *Married to the Mob* (1988) and *Scrooged* (1988); as Buster, he appeared on *Saturday Night Live* and *The Tonight Show*. In the fall of 1994 Johansen hosted *Buster's Happy Hour* on VH1.

Johansen's latest incarnation, as blues revivalist, came about by accident. When Allan Pepper, the coowner of the celebrated New York nightclub the Bottom Line, was preparing for the club's 25th anniversary, he asked Johansen to perform but wanted something different than Buster Poindexter. Johansen had rediscovered the blues he listened to as a youth and put together a new act featuring songs by

Muddy Waters, Lightnin' Hopkins, and other rock and blues forefathers. He called the band the Harry Smiths in tribute to the legendary folk-blues archivist who compiled the seminal *Anthology of American Folk Music.* Intended as simply a one-off gig, the response to the show was so enthusiastic that Johansen booked more shows and eventually took the band into the studio.

Elton John

Born Reginald Kenneth Dwight, Mar. 25, 1947, Pinner, Middlesex, Eng.
1970—*Elton John* (Uni) 1971—*Tumbleweed Connection; Friends* (Paramount); *11-17-70* (Uni); *Madman Across the Water* 1972—*Honky Château* 1973—*Don't Shoot Me, I'm Only the Piano Player* (MCA); *Goodbye Yellow Brick Road* 1974—*Caribou; Greatest Hits* 1975—*Empty Sky* (originally released in 1969, U.K. only); *Captain Fantastic and the Brown Dirt Cowboy; Rock of the Westies* 1976—*Here and There; Blue Moves* (MCA/Rocket) 1977—*Greatest Hits, vol. II* (MCA) 1978—*A Single Man* 1979—*The Thom Bell Sessions; Victim of Love* 1980—*21 at 33* 1981—*The Fox* (Geffen) 1982—*Jump Up!* 1983—*Too Low for Zero* 1984—*Breaking Hearts* 1985—*Ice on Fire* 1986—*Leather Jackets* 1987—*Live in Australia* (MCA); *Greatest Hits, vol. III, 1979–1987* (Geffen) 1988—*Reg Strikes Back* (MCA) 1989—*Sleeping With the Past* 1990—*To Be Continued* 1992—*The One; Greatest Hits 1976–86; Rare Masters* (Polydor) 1993—*Duets* (MCA) 1994—*Circle of Life* (Hollywood) 1995—*Made in England* (Rocket/Island) 1996—Love Songs (MCA) 1997—*The Big Picture* (Rocket) 1999—*Aida* (PolyGram) 2000—*The Road to El Dorado* soundtrack (DreamWorks).

For most of the '70s, Elton John and lyricist Bernie Taupin were a virtual hit factory, with 25 Top 40 singles, 16 Top 10, and six #1 hits; 15 of the 19 albums released in the United States during that time went gold or platinum. In the '80s their fortunes declined only slightly. To date, they have achieved more than four dozen Top 40 hits and become one of the most successful songwriting teams in pop history. John's rich tenor and gospel-chorded piano, boosted by aggressive string arrangements, established a musical formula, while he reveled in an extravagant public image. At the start of the '90s John confessed the personal costs of that extravagance—drug abuse, depression, bulimia—and revealed as well his impressive struggles to regain control. Since the late '80s, he has been deeply involved in the fight against AIDS. And while his critical stature has varied over the years, his melodic gifts have proved undeniable. He was inducted into the Rock and Roll Hall of Fame in 1994. In 1998, he became Sir Elton, with Queen Elizabeth dubbing him a knight.

As Reginald Dwight, John won a piano scholarship to the Royal Academy of Music at age 11. Six years later he left school for show business. By day he ran errands for a music publishing company; he divided evenings between a group, Bluesology, and solo gigs at a London hotel bar. Bluesology was then working as a backup band for visiting American soul singers such as Major Lance, and Patti LaBelle and the Blue Belles. In 1966 British R&B singer Long John Baldry hired Bluesology as his band (in 1971 Elton coproduced an album of Baldry's).

Elton John

Responding to an ad in a music trade weekly, Dwight auditioned for Liberty Records with his hotel repertoire. The scouts liked his performance but not his material. (Liberty wasn't his only audition; he was also rejected by King Crimson and Gentle Giant.) Lyricist Bernie Taupin (born May 22, 1950, Sleaford, England) had also replied to the Liberty ad, and one of the scouts gave Dwight a stack of Taupin lyrics. Six months later the two met. By then, Dwight was calling himself Elton John, after John Baldry and Bluesology saxophonist Elton Dean. (Some years later he made Elton Hercules John his legal name; Hercules was a childhood nickname.) John and Taupin took their songs to music publisher Dick James, who hired them as house writers for £10 (about $25) a week, and whose Dick James Music owned all John-Taupin compositions until 1975.

Taupin would write lyrics, sometimes a song an hour, and deliver a bundle to John every few weeks. Without changing a word, and only rarely consulting Taupin, John would fit tunes to the phrases. Arrangements were left to studio producers. For two years they wrote easy-listening tunes for James to peddle to singers; on the side, John recorded current hits for budget labels like Music for Pleasure and Marble Arch.

On the advice of another music publisher, Steve Brown, John and Taupin started writing rockier songs for John to record. The first was the single "I've Been Loving You" (1968), produced by Caleb Quaye, former Bluesology guitarist. In 1969, with Quaye, drummer Roger Pope, and bassist Tony Murray, John recorded another single, "Lady Samantha," and an album, *Empty Sky.* The records didn't sell, and John and Taupin enlisted Gus Dudgeon to produce a followup with Paul Buckmaster as arranger. (Brown continued to advise

John until 1976; Dudgeon produced his records through *Blue Moves* and sporadically in the mid-'80s.) *Elton John* established the formula for subsequent albums: gospel-chorded rockers and poignant ballads.

Uni (later MCA) released *Elton John* (withholding *Empty Sky* until 1975), and John made his historical American debut at the Troubadour in L.A. in August 1970, backed by ex–Spencer Davis Group drummer Nigel Olsson and bassist Dee Murray. (Murray would play with John off and on until his death in 1992 from a stroke suffered during treatment for skin cancer.) Kicking over his piano bench Jerry Lee Lewis–style and performing handstands on the keyboards, John left the critics raving. "Your Song" (#8, 1970) carried the album to the American Top 10. *Tumbleweed Connection*, with extensive FM airplay, sold even faster. By the middle of 1971, two more albums had been released: a live set taped from a WPLJ-FM New York radio broadcast on November 17, 1970, and the soundtrack to the film *Friends*, written three years before. Despite John's public repudiation of it, *Friends* went gold. Elton John was the first act since the Beatles to have four albums in the American Top 10 simultaneously. *Madman Across the Water* (#8) came out in October 1971, and before year's end a Bernie Taupin recitation-and-music album, *Taupin*, was on the market.

Honky Château was the first album credited to the Elton John group: John, Olsson, Murray, and guitarist Davey Johnstone. And with the 1972 release of "Rocket Man" (#6), John began to dominate the Top 10. "Crocodile Rock" was his first #1; "Daniel" and "Goodbye Yellow Brick Road" reached #2. Then came the tidal wave: "Bennie and the Jets" (#1), "Don't Let the Sun Go Down on Me" (#2), "The Bitch Is Back" (#4), a cover of Lennon-McCartney's "Lucy in the Sky With Diamonds" (#1), "Philadelphia Freedom" (#1), "Someone Saved My Life Tonight" (#4), and "Island Girl" (#1). *Honky Château* was the first of seven #1 albums, the most successful being *Goodbye Yellow Brick Road*, which held the #1 spot for eight weeks in late 1973, and a 1974 greatest-hits compilation that held fast at #1 for 10 weeks.

In 1973 John formed his own MCA-distributed label and signed acts—notably Neil Sedaka ("Bad Blood," on which he sang background vocals) and Kiki Dee (with whom he recorded "Don't Go Breaking My Heart" [#1, 1976])—in which he took personal interest. Instead of releasing his own records on Rocket, he opted for $8 million offered by MCA. When the contract was signed in 1974, MCA reportedly took out a $25-million insurance policy on John's life.

That same year, Elton John joined John Lennon in the studio on Lennon's "Whatever Gets You Thru the Night," then recorded "Lucy in the Sky With Diamonds" with Dr. Winston O'Boogie (Lennon) on guitar. Dr. O'Boogie joined Elton John at Madison Square Garden, Thanksgiving Day 1974, to sing both tunes plus "I Saw Her Standing There." It was Lennon's last appearance on any stage and came out on an EP released after his death.

In the mid-'70s John's concerts filled arenas and stadiums worldwide. He was the hottest act in rock & roll. And his extravagances, including a $40,000 collection of custom-designed and determinedly ridiculous eyeglasses and an array of equally outrageous stagewear, seemed positively charming.

After *Captain Fantastic* (1975), the first album ever to enter the charts at #1, John overhauled his band: Johnstone and Ray Cooper were retained, Quaye and Roger Pope returned, and the new bassist was Kenny Passarelli (formerly of Joe Walsh's Barnstorm). James Newton-Howard joined to arrange in the studio and to play keyboards. John introduced the lineup before a crowd of 75,000 in London's Wembley Stadium in the summer of 1975, then recorded *Rock of the Westies;* also that year, he was honored with a star on Hollywood's Walk of Fame. And John appeared as the Pinball Wizard in the Ken Russell film of the Who's *Tommy.* But John's frenetic recording pace had slowed markedly, and he performed less often. A live album, *Here and There,* had been recorded in 1974. John's biggest hit in 1976 was the #1 Kiki Dee duet. A single from the downbeat *Blue Moves* (#3, 1976), "Sorry Seems to Be the Hardest Word," reached #6.

In November 1977 John announced he was retiring from performing. After publishing a book of his poems—*The One Who Writes the Words for Elton John*—in 1976, Taupin began collaborating with others. John secluded himself in any of his three mansions, appearing publicly only to cheer the Watford Football Club, an English soccer team that he later bought. Some speculated that John's retreat from stardom was prompted by adverse reaction to his 1976 admission in ROLLING STONE of his bisexuality.

A Single Man employed a new lyricist, Gary Osborne, but featured no Top 20 singles. In 1979, accompanied by Ray Cooper, John became the first Western pop star to tour the Soviet Union, then mounted a two-man comeback tour of the U.S. in small halls. John returned to the singles chart with "Mama Can't Buy You Love" (#9, 1979), a song from an EP recorded in 1977 with Philadelphia soul producer Thom Bell. A new album, *Victim of Love,* failed to sustain the rally, and by 1980, John and Taupin reunited to write songs for *21 at 33* and *The Fox.* (Taupin put out a solo album, *He Who Rides the Tiger.*) A single, "Little Jeannie," reached #3. An estimated 400,000 fans turned out for a free concert in New York's Central Park in August, later broadcast on HBO. Olsson and Murray were back in the band, and John had just signed a new recording contract. His second Geffen LP—*Jump Up!*—contained "Empty Garden (Hey Hey Johnny)," his tribute to John Lennon, which he performed at his sold-out Madison Square Garden show in August 1982. He was joined on stage by Yoko Ono and Sean Ono Lennon, Elton John's godchild.

In 1983, with a version of "I Guess That's Why They Call It the Blues" (#4), featuring Stevie Wonder on harmonica, Elton had his biggest hit since 1980—and while he wouldn't match his '70s success, he would continue to place in the Top 10 throughout the '80s—"Sad Songs (Say So Much)" (#5, 1984), "Nikita" (#7, 1986), an orchestral version of "Candle in the Wind" (#6, 1987), and "I Don't Wanna Go On With You Like That" (#2, 1988). His highest-charting single was a collaboration with Dionne Warwick, Gladys Knight, and Stevie Wonder on "That's What Friends Are For" (#1, 1985). Credited to

Dionne and Friends, the song raised funds for AIDS research. His albums continued to sell, but of the six released in the latter half of the '80s, only *Reg Strikes Back* (#16, 1988) placed in the Top 20.

And the '80s were years of personal upheaval for John. In 1984 he surprised many by marrying studio engineer Renate Blauel. While the marriage lasted four years, John later maintained that he had realized that he was gay before he married. In 1986 he lost his voice while touring Australia and shortly thereafter underwent throat surgery. John continued recording prolifically, but years of cocaine and alcohol abuse, initiated in earnest around the time of *Rock of the Westies'* 1975 release, were beginning to take their toll. In 1988 he performed five sold-out shows at New York's Madison Square Garden, his final concert—his 26th—breaking the Grateful Dead's career record of 25 sold-out Garden appearances. But that year also marked the end of an era: Netting over $20 million, 2,000 items of John's memorabilia were auctioned off at Sotheby's in London, as John bade symbolic farewell to his excessive, theatrical persona. (Among the items withheld from the auction were the tens of thousands of records John had been carefully collecting and cataloguing throughout his life.) In later interviews, he deemed 1989 the worst period of his life, comparing his mental and physical deterioration to Elvis Presley's last years.

Around that time, he was deeply affected by the plight of Ryan White, an Indiana teenager with AIDS. Along with Michael Jackson, John befriended and supported the boy and his family until White's death in 1990. Confronted by his then-lover, John checked into a Chicago hospital in 1990 to combat his drug abuse, alcoholism, and bulimia. In recovery, he lost weight and underwent hair replacement, and subsequently took up residence in Atlanta, Georgia. In 1992 he established the Elton John AIDS Foundation, intending to direct 90 percent of the funds it raised to direct care, 10 percent to AIDS prevention education. He also announced his intention to donate all future royalties from sales of his singles (beginning with "The One") in the U.S. and U.K. to AIDS research. That year, he released the #8 album *The One*, his highest-charting release since 1976's *Blue Moves*, and John and Taupin signed a music publishing deal with Warner/Chappell Music—an estimated $39-million, 12-year agreement—that would give them the largest cash advance in music publishing history.

In 1992, at the Freddie Mercury Memorial and AIDS Benefit concert at Wembley Stadium, John duetted with Axl Rose on Queen's "Bohemian Rhapsody," a reconciling gesture, given Rose's previously homophobic reputation. He also released *Duets*, a collaboration with 15 artists ranging from Tammy Wynette to RuPaul. He was inducted into the Rock and Roll Hall of Fame in 1994. He collaborated with Tim Rice on music for the animated film *The Lion King*. The soundtrack featured "Can You Feel the Love Tonight," an Academy Award–winner for Best Original Song; the hit also won a Grammy for Best Male Pop Vocal Performance. At the Academy Awards ceremonies, John acknowledged his domestic partner, Canadian filmmaker David Furnish. Furnish, in 1997, made a well-received, candid documentary, *Tantrums and Tiaras*. In 1995 John released *Made in England* (#13, 1995), which featured the hit single "Believe" (#13, 1995). In 1996 Bernie Taupin released the album *Last Stand in Open Country*, with a band of his friends called Farm Dogs.

The year 1997 was a significant one for John personally and professionally. He lost two close friends, designer Gianni Versace and Princess Diana. Upon Diana's death, Bernie Taupin reworked the lyrics of a song originally written about Marilyn Monroe in 1973. The resulting tribute, "Candle in the Wind 1997" b/w "Something About the Way You Look Tonight" (Rocket/A&M), easily became the all-time highest-certified single, with U.S. sales of 11 million in the first month (all proceeds were donated to the Diana, Princess of Wales Memorial Fund). John's accomplishment is particularly stunning when matched against his previous track record. "Candle," his 16th certified single, has outsold all of his other gold and platinum singles combined. The song is not on his 1997 album *The Big Picture*, which was released shortly after the tribute single.

Also in 1997 vestiges of the flamboyant Elton resurfaced as he threw a 50th birthday party, costumed as Louis XIV, for 500 friends (the outfit cost more than $80,000). In 1999 John had a pacemaker installed to overcome a minor heart problem. That year, as well, he collaborated again with Tim Rice, this time on a Broadway musical version of Verdi's opera *Aida*. The pair also collaborated on a DreamWorks animated feature, *The Road to El Dorado*.

John has written and/or performed on countless tracks by other artists. He has played piano on records by Rick Astley, Kevin Ayers, Jon Bon Jovi, Jackson Browne ("Redneck Friend"), Bob Dylan, George Harrison, the Hollies ("He Ain't Heavy, He's My Brother"), Ringo Starr, and Rod Stewart. Among the many records to which he contributed backing vocals are Tom Jones' "Delilah" and "Daughter of Darkness," Olivia Newton-John's "The Rumour," and "Dyin' Ain't Much of a Livin' " from *The Blaze of Glory: Young Guns II*. At the 2001 Grammy Awards show, John duetted with Eminem on the controversial white rapper's "Stan." Gay-rights activists and organizations criticized John for embracing (literally and figuratively) Eminem.

Little Willie John

Born William J. Woods, Nov. 15, 1937, Cullendale, AR; died May 27, 1968, Walla Walla, WA
1956—*Fever* (King) 1970—*Free at Last* 1977—*Little Willie John 1953–1962.*

Little Willie John was part of the same revolutionary generation of gospel-trained soul singers that yielded Sam Cooke, James Brown, and Jackie Wilson. He was 18 when he had his first hit, "All Around the World," and 23 when he made his biggest hit, "Sleep" (#13, 1960). John stood just over five feet (which, combined with his youthfulness, earned him his nickname) and had a voice that was stronger and rougher than Wilson's or Cooke's, and richer and more wide-ranging than Brown's. He was first discovered at a Detroit talent show in 1951 by Johnny Otis, though King Records' Syd Nathan ignored Otis' recommendation and instead signed Hank Ballard, who'd performed at the same show.

For the next few years John occasionally sang with the Duke Ellington and Count Basie orchestras and toured with R&B saxophonist Paul Williams' combo before King finally signed him. He first dented the R&B chart with the Joe Turner–ish big-band rock of "All Around the World." John was the first artist to record the R&B standard "Fever." His version hit the Top 30, but two years later Peggy Lee's went to #8. The song has since been recorded countless times, including in charting versions by the McCoys (1965) and Rita Coolidge (1973). Madonna covered it on *Erotica* in 1992. Through the late '50s he scored other R&B hits with "Talk to Me, Talk to Me," "Let Them Talk" (both ballads), and the James Brown–inspired "Heartbreak." Only "Talk to Me, Talk to Me" and "Sleep" made the pop Top 20. In 1966, by which time his hits had run out, Little Willie John was convicted of manslaughter and sent to prison in Walla Walla, Washington, where he died of a heart attack. Though he is an overlooked figure, his significance is perhaps best indicated by the title of an album by fellow King Records artist James Brown: *Thinking of Little Willie John and a Few Nice Things*. John was posthumously inducted into the Rock and Roll Hall of Fame in 1996.

Linton Kwesi Johnson

Born 1952, Chapelton, Jam.
1978—*Dread Beat an' Blood* (Virgin Frontline) 1979—*Forces of Victory* (Mango) 1980—*Bass Culture; LKJ in Dub* 1984—*Making History; Reggae Greats* 1985—*Linton Kwesi Johnson Live* (Rough Trade); *In Concert With the Dub Band* (Shanachie); *Dub Poetry* (Mango) 1991—*Tings an' Times* (Shanachie) 1994—*In Dub, vol. 2* (LKJ) 1997—*LKJ A Cappella Live* 1998—*Independent/Intavenshan* (Island) 1999—*More Time* (LKJ).

A Jamaican-English intellectual and poet, Linton Kwesi Johnson has earned critical respect and cult-level sales. His songs assault racism with protest verses in Jamaican patois, sung/spoken in a distinctive, deep voice to rock-solid reggae accompaniment.

Living in England since 1963, Johnson has been inspired by the black American scholar W.E.B. Du Bois. He was associated with the Youth League of the British Black Panther Party and, while studying for a sociology degree, started to give poetry readings backed by a group of drummers called Rasta Love (writing with a reggae beat in his head, he called himself a "dub poet").

His first album, *Dread Beat an' Blood,* was the soundtrack to a film about Britain's Jamaican immigrants; the message of the music was in keeping with London's Rock Against Racism movement and Brixton's racial turmoil in the late '70s. *Forces of Victory,* with strong support from bassist/arranger Dennis Bovell, yielded minor underground hits in "Reality Poem" and "Sonny's Lettah," while *LKJ in Dub* was predominantly instrumental. While he continued to record throughout the '80s, Johnson regarded himself primarily as a political activist, working for Race Today, a black political organization, and writing on black affairs for academic and political publications. Between 1985 and 1988 he retired from performing, although his writing, its social consciousness paralleling that of Gil Scott-Heron, continued to influence such poets as Michael Smith and Mutabaruka. Among his influential books are *Voices of the Living and the Dead, Dread Beat and Blood,* and *Inglan Is a Bitch.*

Johnson reactivated his musical career with 1991's studio album, *Tings an' Times;* by this juncture he had become acknowledged, at least in critical circles, as not only a reggae pioneer but a forerunner of the urban poetry of rap.

Robert Johnson

Born May 8, 1911, Hazelhurst, MS; died Aug. 16, 1938, Greenwood, MS
1961—*King of the Delta Blues Singers* (Columbia) 1970—*King of the Delta Blues Singers, vol. 2* 1990—*The Complete Recordings.*

Though a street singer whose repertoire was not limited to the blues, Robert Johnson is among the first and most influential Delta bluesmen, despite his having recording only 29 songs before dying at the age of 27. He is credited with writing blues standards like "Dust My Broom" (which Elmore James made into a postwar electric-blues anthem), "Sweet Home Chicago," "Ramblin' on My Mind," "Crossroads" (covered by Cream), "Love in Vain" and "Stop Breaking Down" (covered by the Rolling Stones), and "Terraplane Blues" (covered by Captain Beefheart and His Magic Band on *Mirror Man*). Equally important, Johnson's persona and his songs introduced a musical and lyrical vocabulary that are the basis of the modern blues and blues-based rock.

Little was known of Johnson's life until Peter Guralnick set out to discover what truth he could about the bluesman; his *Searching for Robert Johnson* (1988) stands as the closest thing to a definitive biography. Johnson was born to Mrs. Julia Dodds, the product of her extramarital relationship with Noah Johnson. As a young boy he lived with his mother and baby sister in a number of homes, including that of a Charles Spencer, who kept two mistresses, one of whom was Johnson's mother, and their children. Johnson's mother left him in Spencer's care until, at age seven or so, Johnson was deemed too disobedient and was returned to his mother and his new stepfather, Willie "Dusty" Willis. He lived with them in Robinsonville, 40 miles south of Memphis, until young manhood.

He began playing the Jew's harp, then the harmonica. Sometime in his teens he began using the surname of Johnson. Poor eyesight and lack of interest in education led him to quit school. Sometime in the late '20s, he picked up the guitar. He was influenced by pioneering Delta bluesmen like

Charley Patton and Willie Brown, as well as any number of journeyman musicians he met.

In 1929, at age 17, he married Virginia Travis; she and their first baby died during childbirth in April 1930. Shortly thereafter Johnson met Son House, who would become an important influence on the young bluesman. It was then that Johnson decided to leave behind the sharecropping life he seemed destined for and take to the road. He returned to his birthplace and there met his mentor, Ike Zinneman, an obscure bluesman. Also in Hazelhurst, he married Calletta Craft, a woman who reportedly worshiped him and allowed him the freedom of spending days and nights in Zinneman's company. The darker, more occult aspects of the Johnson legend first appear here; reputedly, Zinneman learned the blues playing his guitar while sitting atop tombstones. Johnson began writing down his songs, and when not picking cotton, he performed locally in juke joints or on the courthouse steps. Sometime in the early '30s, he left his birthplace for the Mississippi Delta. His wife suffered a breakdown and returned to her home; she died a few years later.

After a brief return to Robinsonville, he settled in Helena, Arkansas, where he met and played with Robert Nighthawk, Elmore James, Honeyboy Edwards, Howlin' Wolf, Calvin Frazier, Memphis Slim, Johnny Shines, Sonny Boy Williamson II, Hacksaw Harney—a virtual who's who of early rural blues. It was at this time that he took up with Estella Coleman and unofficially adopted her son Robert Lockwood Jr., who was to become a respected bluesman himself, using the name Robert Jr. Lockwood. Johnson toured up and down the Mississippi, as far north as New York and Canada. It also was during this time that his stature grew, and he became protective and jealous of his playing style. His repertoire included blues standards, his own compositions, and even such popular tunes of the day as "Yes, Sir, That's My Baby" and "Tumbling Tumbleweeds."

Johnson was always attractive to women; as his prowess grew, he was the object of jealousy, from fellow musicians and jilted boyfriends and husbands. He often claimed that he learned to play guitar from the Devil himself, and many of his recordings evince a haunting, otherworldly inspiration. Over the years, he became erratic, often moody, but always ambitious. For years he had wanted to record, and on November 23, 1936, he finally did. The first song he recorded was "Terraplane Blues." It became a best-selling hit for Vocalion, a Columbia Records specialty label. During his lifetime, over the course of three recording sessions that November, Johnson created what is arguably the most influential single artist's catalogue in rock and blues history: "Kindhearted Woman Blues," "I Believe I'll Dust My Broom," "Sweet Home Chicago," "Rambling on My Mind," "When You've Got a Friend," "Come On in My Kitchen," "Phonograph Blues," "Blues," "They're Red Hot," "Dead Shrimp Blues" (never issued), "Cross Road Blues," "Walking Blues," "Last Fair Deal Gone Down," "Preaching Blues (Up Jumped the Devil)," "If I Had Possession Over Judgment Day," "Stones in My Passway," "I'm a Steady Rollin' Man," "From Four Till Late," "Hellhound on My Trail," "Little Queen of Spades," "Malted Milk," "Drunken Hearted Man," "Me and the Devil Blues," "Stop Breakin' Down," "Traveling Riverside Blues," "Honeymoon Blues," "Love in Vain," and "Milkcow's Calf Blues."

In August 1938 Johnson played the last show of his life. While playing at a roadhouse, he attempted to rekindle a relationship with the owner's wife. Sonny Boy Williamson, who was with him, cautioned him not to drink from an open whiskey bottle he was offered. Johnson refused to heed the warning, and three days later died of strychnine poisoning and pneumonia. He was buried in an unmarked grave.

Despite his comparatively small number of recordings, Johnson has a paramount place in blues history and, though he played acoustically, was a strong influence on such electric bluesmen as Muddy Waters, Elmore James, Johnny Shines, Robert Jr. Lockwood, Robert Nighthawk, and others. There were rumors that Johnson had played electric guitar. Just after his death, producer/manager John Hammond, organizing his first landmark Spirituals to Swing concert, wanted Johnson to perform; unable to locate the late Delta bluesman, Hammond settled for Big Bill Broonzy.

To the surprise of the record industry, the double-CD box set *Robert Johnson: The Complete Recordings* sold over half a million copies and was certified platinum. Over half a century after Johnson's death, the CD package received a Grammy for Best Historical Recording.

George Jones

Born George Glenn Jones, Sep. 12, 1931, Saratoga, TX
1960—*George Jones Sings* (Mercury); *Country Church Time; George Jones Salutes Hank Williams* 1961—*Country and Western Hits* 1964—*George Jones Sings Like the Dickens!* (United Artists) 1965—*George Jones & Gene Pitney* (with Gene Pitney) (Musicor); *The Race Is On* (United Artists) 1969—*I'll Share My World With You* (Musicor) 1971—*We Go Together* (with Tammy Wynette) (Epic) 1979—*My Very Special Guests* 1980—*I Am What I Am* 1981—*Still the Same Ole Me* 1982—*A Taste of Yesterday's Wine* (with Merle Haggard) 1991—*Along Came Jones* (MCA); *The Best of George Jones 1955–1967* (Rhino) 1992—*Walls Can Fall* (MCA) 1993—*High-Tech Redneck* 1994—*Cup of Loneliness: The Classic Mercury Years* (Mercury); *The Bradley Barn Sessions* (MCA) 1994—*The Essential George Jones: The Spirit of Country Music* (Legacy/Epic); *One* (with Tammy Wynette) 1996—*I Lived to Tell It All* 1998—*It Don't Get Any Better Than This* 1999—*The George Jones Collection; Cold Hard Truth* (Asylum); *Live With the Possum.*

George Jones is the king of country singers and a highly acclaimed songwriter. His straightforward aversion to trends and his dark but romantic persona have served him well through nearly five decades of recordings, a highly publicized marriage to and divorce from singer Tammy Wynette, and bouts with addictions and poor health. Though he dominated country radio from the late '50s into the '80s, his more recent recordings have received little airplay. He remains, however, the preeminent country stylist and is so acknowledged by critics and young country stars alike.

Jones grew up the eighth child in a poor Texas family, his father an alcoholic laborer, his mother a church pianist. He came to music early, singing at 9, playing guitar at 11, and writing his first song at 12. Jones ran away from home at age 14; in 1947 he was hired by the duo Eddie and Pearl. A regular radio spot gave Jones his first glimmer of fame and also got him his first endearing nickname, Possum, so dubbed by a disc jockey for Jones' close-set eyes and turned-up nose. By 18 Jones already had a wife, a child, and a broken marriage behind him.

After three years in the Marine Corps, Jones returned to Texas to start his musical career in earnest. He again gained attention while singing on the radio. A Houston producer, H. W. "Pappy" Daily, signed Jones to the Starday label; there, Jones had his first C&W hits, including "Why Baby Why" (# 4, 1955), "You Gotta Be My Baby" (#7, 1956), and "Just One More" (#3, 1956). After Starday merged with the national label Mercury in 1957, Jones began cutting the classic singles that made him famous; among them, 1959's "White Lightning," Jones' first C&W #1 and his only pop hit (#73). Other hits from this period include "Who Shot Sam" (#7, 1959), "The Window Up Above" (#2, 1960), and "Tender Years" (#1, 1961).

Jones' long string of country hits includes "She Thinks I Still Care" (#1, 1962), "You Comb Her Hair" (#5, 1963), "The Race Is On" (#3, 1964), "We Must Have Been Out of Our Minds" (a duet with Melba Montgomery) (#3, 1963), "Walk Through This World With Me" (#1, 1967), "A Good Year for the Roses" (#2, 1970), "The Grand Tour" (#1, 1974), "He Stopped Loving Her Today" (#1, 1980), and "Yesterday's Wine" (with Merle Haggard) (#1 1982). In addition to these and other major sellers were dozens of Top 20 hits. In all, Jones has found himself on the C&W chart—as a solo artist or in duet settings—over 150 times.

But Jones' phenomenal success as an artist ran neck and neck with his increasingly erratic behavior. Jones' excessive drinking, and later drug abuse, caused him to consistently miss shows (giving him the new nickname, No Show Jones), shirk off recording sessions, and behave violently toward wives and friends. In 1969 Jones married country superstar Tammy Wynette. Though their four-year marriage was stormy (Jones was accused of beating her and threatening her with a rifle), the two had chart success together during and after the marriage: "We're Gonna Hold On" (#1, 1973), "Golden Ring" (#1, 1976), "Near You" (#1, 1976), and "Two Story House" (#2, 1980).

Jones turned over a new leaf in his recording career and personal life during the 1980s. Eschewing the overproduced sound that had been cluttering his work, Jones returned to his honky-tonk roots. He sought help for substance abuse, amended his no-show ways, and established a stable fourth marriage. His 1992 single "I Don't Need Your Rockin' Chair" (#34 C&W) featured 10 contemporary country hitmakers, including Garth Brooks, Clint Black, Alan Jackson, and Travis Tritt. In 1994 Jones recorded *The Bradley Barn Sessions,* a series of duets with performers including Trisha Yearwood, Keith Richards, and Mark Knopfler. That fall, Jones underwent triple bypass surgery; upon recovery, he returned to the studio to record *One,* a reunion album with Wynette that the pair supported with a short tour. The following year saw the release of his notoriously self-deprecating, tell-all autobiography, *I Lived to Tell It All.* An album of the same name followed later that year, peaking at #26 on the country chart. In 1998 he began hosting his own variety show on TNN, *The George Jones Show,* which ran for two years.

Jones recorded one more album for MCA in 1998 but asked to be released from the label out of frustration from lack of radio airplay. He was in the finishing stages of recording his debut for Asylum the following year when he drove his sport-utility vehicle into a concrete bridge, landing him in the hospital with damaged lungs and liver. He later pleaded guilty to DWI—his first slip off the wagon in more than a dozen years. He survived the ordeal with a new lease on life, a rush of renewed media interest, and his highest-charting album of the decade, *Cold Hard Truth* (#5 C&W), which featured the single "Choices" (#24 C&W). *Live With the Possum* followed later the same year.

Grace Jones

Born May 19, 1952, Spanishtown, Jam.
1977—*Portfolio* (Island) 1978—*Fame* 1979—*Muse* 1980—*Warm Leatherette* 1981—*Nightclubbing* 1982—*Living My Life* 1985—*Slave to the Rhythm* (Manhattan) 1986—*Island Life* (Island); *Inside Story* (Manhattan) 1989—*Bulletproof Heart* (Capitol) 1993—*Sex Drive* (Island) 1998—*Private Life: The Compass Point Sessions.*

Grace Jones, the provocative 6-foot model-turned-disco-singer, was first mainly a cult artist of the New York gay dance clubs. There she developed a reputation as much for her archly stylish look and S&M-tinged theatrical stage show (she'd enter on a motorcycle and dance with body builders) as for her monotone singing. In 1980, when she followed the dance-club trend to emphasize rock disco, her music won more broad-based support and critical respect.

Jones grew up in Jamaica, where her father was a clergyman influential in local politics (as was his father before him). She moved with her family to Syracuse, New York, when she was 12 and, after attending college, traveled to Manhattan to work for the Wilhelmina Modeling Agency. After a stint of acting, appearing in the film *Gordon's War,* she was far more successful as a model in Paris, posing for the covers of *Vogue, Der Stern,* and *Elle.* Jones wanted to be a singer and while in France did some recording.

In 1977 Jones landed a record deal with Island, with disco mixer Tom Moulton as her producer, and recorded "I Need a Man," a big dance hit that summer. She had other disco hits with "La Vie en Rose" and "Do or Die." Her first three albums catered mainly to the urban dance crowd, receiving little critical attention, but that changed when she began to cover more rock-oriented material on *Warm Leatherette.* Produced

Grace Jones

by Chris Blackwell, the album included versions of the Pretenders' "Private Lives," Roxy Music's "Love Is the Drug," and Tom Petty's "Breakdown." The Sly Dunbar/Robbie Shakespeare–produced *Nightclubbing* (#32, 1981), with a David Bowie/Iggy Pop–penned title track, had her biggest R&B single (#5) with "Pull Up to the Bumper" and was voted Album of the Year by England's *New Musical Express.*

"Nipple to the Bottle" (#17 R&B, 1982) helped *Living My Life* reach #69 in 1983, and Jones scored two more R&B Top 20 singles: "Slave to the Rhythm" (#20 R&B, 1985), from the Trevor Horn–produced album of the same title, and "I'm Not Perfect (But I'm Perfect for You)" (#9 R&B, 1986), from *Inside Story* (which Jones coproduced with Nile Rodgers). Jonathan Elia and Clivilles and Cole (better known for their C + C Music Factory) produced *Bulletproof Heart,* but none of her albums since *Nightclubbing* has entered the U.S. Top 40.

Not surprisingly, Jones has made some memorable film appearances, in *Conan the Destroyer, A View to a Kill,* and *Boomerang.* She has also produced several acclaimed videos, including the Grammy-nominated 1983 long-form program *A One Man Show.* In 1996 she married her former bodyguard, Atila Altaunbay, in Rio de Janeiro during Carnival. *Sex Drive* marked her return to her original label, Island. The title track was a #1 hit on the dance chart. A remix of "Pull Up to the Bumper" appeared on the dance charts in 2000.

Howard Jones

Born John Howard Jones, Feb. 23, 1955, Southampton, Hampshire, Eng.
1984—*Human's Lib* (Elektra) 1985—*Dream Into Action* 1986—*Action Replay* EP; *One to One* 1989—*Cross That Line* 1992—*In the Running* 1993—*The Best of Howard Jones; Working in the Backroom* (Dtox, U.K.) 1995—*Live Acoustic America* (Plump) 1997—*Angels and Lovers* (Pony Canyon In, U.K.) 1998—*People* (Ark 21) 2000—*Perform.00* (Seven Days Music, Ger.); *Pefawm* (Dtox).

With his endearing pop sensibility and canny ear for a melodic hook, Howard Jones was responsible for some of the warmest and most accessible techno pop released in the mid-'80s. Jones wrote lyrics as buoyant as his music, revealing humanist ideals and encouraging positive action and self-esteem. As ROLLING STONE observed, this child of the '60s was "called everything . . . from a synthesized Gilbert O'Sullivan to a high-tech hippie."

Jones began playing piano at the age of seven. As a teenager in Canada (his parents had moved the family) he played organ in a progressive-rock outfit called Warrior. Jones later studied at the Royal Northern School of Music in Manchester, England, but dropped out. He gave piano lessons and ran a produce-delivery business with his wife while performing in several funk and jazz bands. But what finally attracted a record company executive's attention was his one-man show, which featured a drum machine, a sequencer, and polyphonic keyboards. Supplementing the act was a mime named Jed Hoile, who would tour with Jones for years to come.

In the early '80s Jones signed to WEA in Europe and Elektra in the U.S. His 1984 debut album, *Human's Lib* (#59 U.S., #1 U.K.), did well in England and on American college radio, thanks to catchy numbers like "New Song" (#27 U.S., #3 U.K., 1983) and "What Is Love?" (#33 U.S., #2 U.K., 1983). The singer made a bigger splash in the States with *Dream Into Action,* which went to #10 in the U.S. and yielded the lithe, rhythmic single "Things Can Only Get Better" (#5). Jones' most successful song to date is "No One Is to Blame," a wistful ballad from his 1986 EP *Action Replay.* Produced by Phil Collins, "Blame" peaked at #4.

In the Running (1992) was more organic in its musical approach than Jones' previous five releases, emphasizing the singer's piano work and several atypically melancholy songs. The tour supporting the album featured a single percussionist accompanying Jones on piano. *In the Running* sold poorly, though, and Jones' longtime major label declined to renew his contract. Jones established his own label, Dtox, and recorded his next album *(Working in the Backroom)* in his home studio; he sold the album at his concerts. His ingenuity impressed an independent U.K. label, which distributed his live album, 1995's *Live Acoustic America.* After another U.K. disc, Jones signed to the American indie Ark 21, which released *People* in 1998, and participated in the Big Rewind Tour with Culture Club and the Human League the same year.

Jones has maintained the Dtox label and occasionally works with new bands; he coproduced the 1996 debut album for the British group JanuaryLand, as well as a single for the U.K. trio Lovatux in 1998. He has also continued to record his own material: *Perform.00,* featuring reworkings of old songs plus some new ones—including a duet with

Duncan Sheik—was released in a few European countries in 2000. That same year he released a double album *(Pefawm),* also a combination of old and new tracks, via the Internet.

Quincy Jones

Born Mar. 14, 1933, Chicago, IL
1961—*The Quintessence* (MCA/Impulse) 1969—*Walking in Space* (A&M) 1970—*Gula Matari* 1972—*Smackwater Jack* 1973—*You've Got It Bad, Girl* 1974—*Body Heat* 1975—*Mellow Madness* 1976—*I Heard That!* 1977—*Roots* 1978—*Sounds and Stuff Like That* 1981—*The Dude* 1982—*Q; The Best* 1989—*Compact Jazz: Quincy Jones* (Phillips/PolyGram); *Back on the Block* (Qwest) 1993—*Miles & Quincy Live at Montreux* (with Miles Davis) (Warner Bros.) 1995—*Q's Jook Joint* 1999—*From Q, With Love.*

One of the most prolific and successful figures in contemporary pop, Quincy Jones began as a jazz and soul trumpeter, became a bandleader overseas, and returned to America to carve out a long and still-prospering career as a composer, arranger, and producer. His best-known and best-selling work may have been with Michael Jackson, but Jones has worked for hundreds of other successful acts, including Herb Alpert, Louis Armstrong, LaVern Baker, Glen Campbell, Ray Charles, José Feliciano, Roberta Flack, Aretha Franklin, Herbie Hancock, B.B. King, Little Richard, Manhattan Transfer, Johnny Mathis, Frank Sinatra, Billy Preston, Paul Simon, Ringo Starr, George Benson, Bill Withers, James Ingram, the Brothers Johnson, and the Jacksons. Jones has also had a successful career recording under his own name, and has scored over 35 films and composed about a dozen TV-show themes. By the early '90s, he had been nominated for 76 Grammys (the most for any artist) and he had won 26. As one of the first blacks to score films and become a record company executive, he also helped advance the status of African-Americans in the music business.

Jones moved with his family at an early age to Seattle, where he began studying trumpet while in grade school. At 14 he met Ray Charles, and the two formed a band that began playing Seattle soul clubs. While working with Charles, he became an arranger. At age 15 he joined vibraphonist Lionel Hampton's big band and was all set to embark on a European tour when Hampton's wife demanded he be kept off the tour so he could attend school.

Within a year Jones had won a scholarship to Boston's Berklee School of Music, where he took 10 classes a day and earned money by playing in strip joints at night. Word of the young trumpeter's skills got out through the jazz grapevine, and at 17 he was invited to New York by jazz bassist Oscar Pettiford to write two arrangements for an album. Jones received $17 per arrangement. He stayed in New York, relishing the opportunity to hang out with Charlie Parker, Thelonious Monk, and Miles Davis. He began playing at recording sessions and at Manhattan jazz clubs, and eventually rejoined Hampton's orchestra for a European tour. Jones also toured Europe with Dizzy Gillespie. In the mid-'50s he made Paris his home.

In France he became music director for Barclay Records and was staff composer/arranger for Harry Arnold's Swedish All-Stars of Stockholm. He also studied classical composition with Nadia Boulanger, who had once taught Igor Stravinsky. Through the '50s Jones won awards in Europe for his arranging and composing. According to his bio, in the mid-'50s Jones became the first popular conductor/arranger to record with a Fender bass; if true, that's a good example of the way Jones has always kept his ears as open to pop and R&B as to the more sophisticated sounds of jazz. Toward the end of the decade he began leading an 18-piece big band, which was a financial failure. He returned to the States in 1961, $100,000 in debt.

In New York, Jones became a vice president at Mercury Records, making him one of the first blacks to hold such a post. There he produced, arranged, and played on hundreds of sessions, as well as producing 10 gold records for Lesley Gore, including "It's My Party," "Judy's Turn to Cry," and "You Don't Own Me." He won his first Grammys in 1963 for his arrangement of the Count Basie Orchestra's recording of "I Can't Stop Loving You," and in the mid-'60s arranged Frank Sinatra's "Fly Me to the Moon." He stayed with Mercury from 1961 to 1968 and also recorded albums of his own.

In 1965 Jones scored his first film, Sidney Lumet's *The Pawnbroker.* He went on to score or write theme songs for *Mirage, The Slender Thread, Walk Don't Run, In the Heat of the Night, A Dandy in Aspic, In Cold Blood, Enter Laughing, For Love of Ivy,* and *Bob and Carol and Ted and Alice.* Jones received Oscar nominations for his *In Cold Blood* score and for "The Eyes of Love" from *Banning* (1967) and "For Love of Ivy" (1969). He won an Academy Award for his score for *In the Heat of the Night.* He also composed theme music for TV shows, including *Ironside, The Bill Cosby Show,* and *Sanford and Son,* as well as PBS's *Rebop,* and has received several Emmy Awards.

In 1969 Jones signed with A&M Records and began a solo recording career in earnest. *Walking in Space* (#56, 1969) and *Smackwater Jack* (#56, 1971) won Grammys. In 1971 Jones scored the music for the Academy Awards show. By that time he had been married for several years to Peggy Lipton, star of TV's *The Mod Squad.* The couple later divorced. In 1973 he collaborated on Aretha Franklin's *Hey Now Hey* LP and won a Grammy for his single "Summer in the City" from *You've Got It Bad, Girl.* In 1974 his *Body Heat* album made the pop Top 10 and went gold. Later that year he was hospitalized for the first of two severe neural aneurysms.

Jones returned in 1976 with the first of his many protégés, the Brothers Johnson, who had performed on Jones's *Mellow Madness.* He produced and arranged their platinum debut LP, *Look Out for #1.* In 1977 Jones won an Emmy for his score for the TV miniseries *Roots,* and he scored the 1978 film *The Wiz.* It was while working on *The Wiz* that Jones met Michael Jackson. The following year Jones produced and arranged Jackson's multimillion-selling *Off the Wall.*

Jones continued his producing/arranging successes in

the early '80s with Chaka Khan and Rufus, George Benson, and James Ingram. He released another of his hit albums, *The Dude* (#10), in 1981; it was his biggest hit since *Body Heat,* remaining on the chart for over a year and yielding a Top 30 single in a version of Chaz Jankel's "Ai No Corrida." In 1982 Jones produced another Ingram hit, "One Hundred Ways" ("Just Once" had been the first), and won five Grammy Awards, including one for *The Dude.* A compilation album of his solo work, entitled *Q,* was released, and Jones went on to produce Donna Summer's self-titled album that year, as well as Michael Jackson's mega-hit, *Thriller* (Jones also produced Jackson's 1987 album *Bad*).

Through the '80s, Jones moved into film and television production, coproducing Stephen Spielberg's 1985 adaptation of Alice Walker's novel *The Color Purple.* After the 1985 Grammy Awards gala, Jones oversaw the arrangement and production of "We Are the World," the anthem of USA for Africa. His album *Back on the Block* (#9, 1989) found Jones anticipating the early-'90s' "jazz-rap" trend, bringing together such jazz stars as Dizzy Gillespie, Miles Davis, Ella Fitzgerald, and Sarah Vaughan, with rappers Ice-T, Big Daddy Kane, and Melle Mel. The album, which also featured Ray Charles, won a Best Album Grammy in 1990—the same year Jones also won a Grammy Legends Award, and saw the theatrical release of his film biography, *Listen Up: The Lives of Quincy Jones.*

In 1991 Jones became executive producer of the hit NBC-TV comedy show, *Fresh Prince of Bel-Air,* a vehicle for rapper Will Smith of D.J. Jazzy Jeff and the Fresh Prince. Two years later, he launched the glossy hip-hop magazine *Vibe,* and released *Miles and Quincy Live at Montreux*—a document of Miles Davis' final recording, for which Jones conducted the lush Gil Evans charts Davis had first recorded in the late '50s. In 1995 Jones won the Jean Hersholt Humanitarian Award at the Academy Awards. That same year Qwest released *Q's Jook Joint* (#32 pop, #6 R&B, #1 Contemporary Jazz), a selection of contemporary versions of the mogul's older material. This all-star hit celebrated Jones' 50 varied years in the music business. *From Q, With Love* is a two-CD compilation of Jones' production work.

Rickie Lee Jones

Born Nov. 8, 1954, Chicago, IL
1979—*Rickie Lee Jones* (Warner Bros.) 1981—*Pirates* 1983—*Girl at Her Volcano* EP 1984—*The Magazine* 1989—*Flying Cowboys* (Geffen) 1991—*Pop Pop* 1993—*Traffic From Paradise* 1995—*Naked Songs* 1997—*Ghostyhead* 2000—*It's Like This.*

Though Rickie Lee Jones' music is an eccentric mixture of R&B, Beat jazz, and folk, her debut album made her an instant star. The LP quickly went platinum, bolstered by the single "Chuck E's in Love." It would be her only hit single, but Jones kept a solid cult following into the late '90s.

Jones grew up in Phoenix, Arizona; Olympia, Washington; and various cities in California. In 1973, at age 19, she went to L.A., where she worked as a waitress and eventually began performing in small clubs. Much of her act consisted of rhythmic spoken-word monologues. This Beat influence was also a crucial part of her later music and led to her friendship with singer/songwriter Tom Waits. (Jones is pictured on the back of Waits's 1978 *Blue Valentine* LP and sang a Waits song on the *King of Comedy* soundtrack.)

Jones attracted the interest of Warner Bros. Records in late 1978, when her early manager Nick Mathe sent the company a four-song demo she had originally cut under the auspices of A&M. In addition, friend Ivan Ulz sang the song "Easy Money" over the phone to Little Feat's Lowell George, who, after visiting Jones, recorded her song for his *Thanks I'll Eat It Here* solo LP. All this intrigued Warners staff producer Ted Templeman and A&R man Lenny Waronker, who signed her. The latter coproduced her debut with Russ Titleman.

Released in April 1979, "Chuck E's in Love" rose to #4. On the album (# 3, 1979), Jones' voice ranged from a faint moan to a sexy, full-throated roar. Some critics praised her unique song structures with their jazz and show-tune shadings, plus her lyrical "visions," filled with colorful, low-down characters. Others saw her as a pseudo-bohemian. Jones bridled at being frequently compared to Joni Mitchell, citing Laura Nyro and Van Morrison as prime influences.

Her 1981 followup, *Pirates* (#5), used longer and more complex songs about death and transfiguration; it went gold. *Girl at Her Volcano* (#39, 1983) was a 10-inch EP; all but one song were ballad covers. *The Magazine* (#44, 1984) and *Flying Cowboys* (#39, 1989)—the latter produced by Steely Dan's Walter Becker and featuring collaborations with the Scottish band Blue Nile—both sold respectably. The David Was–produced *Pop Pop* (#121)—with jazzmen Charlie Haden and Joe Henderson supporting Jones, as she crooned all ballad covers, ranging from '20s Tin Pan Alley to Jimi Hendrix and Jefferson Airplane—did not fare so well. Jones dueted with John Mellencamp on "Between a Laugh and a Tear" on his 1985 *Scarecrow* album, and in 1989 with Dr. John on the Grammy-winning "Makin' Whoopee," from his *In a Sentimental Mood. Traffic From Paradise* (#111, 1993) featured a cover of David Bowie's "Rebel Rebel," and such guests as David Hidalgo of Los Lobos, Lyle Lovett, Brian Setzer, and acoustic guitar virtuoso Leo Kottke (whose album *Peculiaroso* Jones produced). *Naked Songs* (#121, 1995) documented live performances from an acoustic tour, while 1997's *Ghostyhead* (#159) was a riskier venture: Jones's foray into electronic textures and percussive loops, albeit of a low-key, homegrown variety. For 2000's *It's Like This,* the singer was back on more familiar artistic turf, recording standards and classic rock tunes (Traffic's "The Low Spark of High-Heeled Boys") with guest musicians such as Joe Jackson, Taj Mahal, and Ben Folds.

Tom Jones

Born Thomas Jones Woodward, June 7, 1940, Pontypridd, Wales
1965—*It's Not Unusual* (Parrot); *What's New, Pussycat?; Thunderball* (United Artists) 1966—*A-Tom-Ic Jones* (Parrot)

1967—*Funny Familiar Forgotten Feelings; Thirteen Smash Hits; Green, Green Grass of Home* (PolyGram) 1968—*The Tom Jones Fever Zone* (Parrot); *Help Yourself; Delilah* (PolyGram) 1969—*Tom Jones Live!* (Parrot); *This Is Tom Jones; Live in Las Vegas* (Parrot) 1970—*Tom; I (Who Have Nothing)* 1971—*She's a Lady; Tom Jones Live at Caesar's Palace* 1972—*Close Up* 1973—*The Body and Soul of* 1974—*Somethin' 'bout You Baby I Like* 1975—*Memories Don't Leave Like People Do* 1976—*Say You'll Stay Until Tomorrow* (Epic) 1977—*Tom Jones Greatest Hits* (London); *What a Night* (Epic) 1979—*Rescue Me* (MCA) 1981—*Darlin'* (Mercury) 1983—*Don't Let Our Dreams Die Young* (Polydor) 1984—*Love Is on the Radio* (London) 1985—*Tender Loving Care* (Mercury); *The Country Side of Tom Jones* (London) 1987—*Things That Matter Most to Me* (Mercury) 1988—*Move Closer* (Jive) 1991—*Carrying a Torch* (Chrysalis, U.K.) 1994—*The Lead and How to Swing It* (Interscope) 1997—*Tom Jones Live* (BMG); *I Need Your Lovin'* (32 Jazz) 1999—*Reload* (Gut, U.K.) 2000—*It's Not Unusual* (PolyGram).

While possessing a voice nearly as remarkably expressive as those of the R&B legends he admires, Tom Jones initially achieved more notoriety as a sex symbol than respect as a singer. After a career encompassing '60s pop followed by '70s conquests of country and Las Vegas, Jones made a surprising late-'80s comeback, spearheaded by covers of Prince's "Kiss" (#13, 1987) and EMF's "Unbelievable."

The son of a coal miner, Tom Woodward grew up in a home that had no bath and began singing in church as a child. As a teenager he had problems with drinking and delinquency. By age 16 he had married and was working odd jobs, from carpentry and glove-cutting to construction. A part-time pub singer, he later taught himself drums and played with various local bands before adopting the stage name Tommy Scott and forming the Senators. By 1963, the group had become a popular local attraction, and the following year fellow Welshman Gordon Mills became his manager.

In 1964 Woodward changed his surname to Jones, after the success of the film *Tom Jones,* and the pair went to London, where Jones signed to Decca. After one single flopped, Jones requested a new Mills number, "It's Not Unusual," which had originally been intended for Sandie Shaw. Jones' brassy version was #1 in Britain and Top 10 in America in 1965; later that year came the million-selling followup, the Bacharach-David theme from the film *What's New Pussycat?* In 1967 Jones' version of Porter Wagoner's country tune "Green, Green Grass of Home" (#11) was an international hit. Other hit singles from this period include "Delilah," "Love Me Tonight," and "I'll Never Fall in Love Again" (1969); "Daughter of Darkness," "I (Who Have Nothing)," "Without Love (There Is Nothing)" (1970); and "She's a Lady" (1971).

But more than a pop star, Jones was a phenomenon. The year 1969 saw four of his albums go gold and the debut of his highly rated U.S. television variety series, *This Is Tom Jones.* Among the highlights of the show's two-year run was Jones and guest Janis Joplin bumping and grinding through a duet, much of which was shot from the waist up. Jones' reputation as a sex symbol was further enhanced by a well-publicized affair with the Supremes' Mary Wilson. (As of this writing, Jones, a grandfather, is still wed to his first wife.) Though the hits waned, Jones remained a top draw live, where female fans pelted him with room keys and panties, a form of tribute Jones claims to have since tired of.

While in the early years critics were sometimes less than kind to Jones, he has counted among his admirers Elvis Presley and Paul McCartney, who wrote "The Long and Winding Road" especially for him. His original fans, it seems, never went away, and with "Kiss," "Unbelievable," and a 1993 #1 U.K. hit with the Beatles' "All You Need Is Love," a new, younger audience embraced him as well. His well-received musical series, *The Right Time,* on VH1 and guest shots on several TV shows, including *The Simpsons,* further fueled the early-'90s Tom Jones "revival."

That revival, spearheaded by Mark Woodward, Jones' son and manager, first received a critical imprimatur when Jones recorded the U.K.-only *Carrying the Torch* in collaboration with Van Morrison. He bolstered his new success by appearing in a version of Dylan Thomas' *Under Milkwood,* directed by Anthony Hopkins, singing at Carnegie Hall at a benefit for Sting's Rainforest Foundation, contributing a sly remake of Randy Newman's "You Can Leave Your Hat On" to the hit film *The Full Monty,* and appearing in the Tim Burton movie, *Mars Attacks.* In 1999, signed to the independent U.K. label Gut Records, he released an album of duets with Van Morrison, Natalie Imbruglia, and others. By then his status was assured: A young British band, Space, had recorded a tribute single, "The Ballad of Tom Jones," and the singer had been awarded the honor of the Order of the British Empire.

Janis Joplin

Born Jan. 19, 1943, Port Arthur, TX; died Oct. 4, 1970, Hollywood, CA
1967—*Big Brother and the Holding Company* (Mainstream) 1968—*Cheap Thrills* (Columbia).
Janis Joplin solo: 1969—*I Got Dem Ol' Kozmic Blues Again Mama!* (Columbia) 1971—*Pearl* 1972—*In Concert* 1973—*Greatest Hits* 1974—*Janis* soundtrack 1980—*Anthology* 1982—*Farewell Song* 1993—*Janis* (Sony) 1999—*Box of Pearls: The Janis Joplin Collection.*

Singer Janis Joplin was perhaps the premier blues-influenced singer of the '60s, and certainly one of the biggest female stars of her time. Even before her death, her tough blues-mama image only barely covered her vulnerability. The publicity concerning her sex life and problems with alcohol and drugs made her something of a legend. In recent years, periodic attempts to recast her life and work within the context of feminism have met with mixed results, and of her deceased contemporaries (Jimi Hendrix, Jim Morrison, et al.), she is perhaps the least well known to younger audiences.

Born into a comfortable middle-class family, Joplin was a loner by her early teens, developing a taste for blues and folk music; soon she retreated into poetry and painting. She ran away from home at age 17 and began singing in clubs in

Janis Joplin

Houston and Austin, Texas, to earn money to finance a trip to California. By 1965, she was singing folk and blues in bars in San Francisco and Venice, California; had dropped out of several colleges; and was drawing unemployment checks. She returned to Austin in 1966 to sing in a country & western band, but within a few months a friend of San Francisco impresario Chet Helms told her about a new band, Big Brother and the Holding Company [see entry], which needed a singer in San Francisco. She returned to California and joined Big Brother.

Joplin and Big Brother stopped the show at the 1967 Monterey Pop Festival; Albert Grossman agreed to manage them, and Joplin was on her way to becoming a superstar. After a fairly successful first LP in 1967 with Big Brother, Columbia Records signed the unit; and *Cheap Thrills,* with the hit single "Piece of My Heart" (#12, 1968), became a gold #1 album. Within a year Joplin had come to overshadow her backing band, and she left Big Brother (though she appears, uncredited, on a few tracks on the group's 1971 *Be a Brother* LP), taking only guitarist Sam Andrew with her to form the Kozmic Blues Band.

Joplin toured constantly and made television appearances as a guest with Dick Cavett, Tom Jones, and Ed Sullivan. Finally the *Kozmic Blues* LP appeared, with gutsy blues-rock tracks like "Try (Just a Little Bit Harder)." During this time she became increasingly involved with alcohol and drugs, eventually succumbing to heroin addiction. Yet her life seemed to be taking a turn for the better with the recording of *Pearl.* She was engaged to be married and was pleased with the Full Tilt Boogie Band she'd formed for the *Pearl* album (Pearl was her nickname). On October 4, 1970, her body was found in her room at Hollywood's Landmark Hotel, face down with fresh puncture marks in her arm. The death was ruled an accidental heroin overdose.

The posthumous *Pearl* LP (#1, 1971) yielded her #1 hit version of former lover Kris Kristofferson's "Me and Bobby McGee" and was released with one track, "Buried Alive in the Blues," missing the vocals Joplin didn't live to complete. Several more posthumous collections have been released, as well as the 1974 documentary *Janis.* The 1979 film *The Rose,* starring Bette Midler, was a thinly veiled account of Joplin's career. She has since been the subject of several biographies, including *Love, Janis,* penned by her therapist sister, Laura, and Alice Echols' 1999 work, *Scars of Sweet Paradise.* Joplin's former residence in San Francisco's Haight district was converted into a drug rehab center in 1999.

Louis Jordan

Born Louis Thomas Jordan, July 8, 1908, Brinkley, AR; died Feb. 4, 1975, Los Angeles, CA
1975—*The Best of Louis Jordan* (MCA) 1980—*I Believe in Music* (Classic Jazz) 1992—*Just Say Moe! Mo' of the Best of Louis Jordan* (Rhino) 1999—*Let the Good Times Roll: Anthology 1938–1953* (MCA).

It's impossible to overstate Louis Jordan's importance to popular music, particularly rock & roll. Via his vocal approach, song structures, and lyrics, Jordan was the direct link between rhythm & blues and rock & roll. B.B. King, Ray Charles, and Chuck Berry, among other artists, are specific in their admiration for Jordan, claiming him as an important model for their own music; all have also recorded his songs.

Jordan learned saxophone as a youth in Arkansas. He later toured with the famed Rabbit Foot Minstrels revue, where he played behind such blues legends as Bessie Smith, Ma Rainey, and Ida Cox. Moving to New York in the mid-'30s, Jordan, by now an accomplished jazz alto saxophonist, worked with Clarence Williams and Louis Armstrong before hooking up with drummer Chick Webb's swing band. In addition to playing sax in the horn section, Jordan began singing with the band, mainly on such blues and novelty songs as "Gee, But You're Swell" and "Rusty Hinge."

In 1938 Jordan started his own small group, the Elks Rendez-Vous Band, named for the club where they were playing a long-term engagement. Jordan signed with a major label, Decca, and in 1939 changed the name of the group to the Tympany Five.

From 1941 to 1949 Jordan had a series of hit records that defined his humorous, bluesy, and always musical approach, including "Knock Me a Kiss," "I'm Gonna Move to the Outskirts of Town," "What's the Use of Gettin' Sober (When You're Gonna Get Drunk Again)," "Five Guys Named Moe," "Is You Is or Is You Ain't My Baby," "Caldonia," "Beware," "Choo Choo Cha Boogie," "Saturday Night Fish Fry," and "Let the Good Times Roll." These songs are classic models of "jump style" rhythm & blues; their arrangements drawing from swing and blues, their rocking rhythms pointing toward a new music that was just around the corner. During this period, Jordan performed his songs in a series of short comic films that can be seen as precursors to music videos.

Jordan's hits continued into the early '50s, "Ain't Nobody Here But Us Chickens," "Run Joe," "Early in the Morning," and "School Days" among them. By this time Jordan was not only the most popular figure in the burgeoning R&B market, but also the most influential.

Jordan's importance to rock & roll was made clear by Jordan's Decca producer Milt Gabler. When later producing seminal records by Bill Haley and His Comets, Gabler claimed he fashioned their sound purely after Jordan's earlier sides, particularly in the treatment of the guitars and horns.

Jordan left Decca in 1954, and his popularity almost immediately began to diminish. He recorded and toured heavily throughout the '50s and '60s, but rock & roll, the music he had helped bring into the world, supplanted his sophisticated, smoother style.

Jordan died in 1975 from heart failure. But his music wasn't forgotten. Joe Jackson's 1981 *Jumpin' Jive* paid tribute to Jordan in its song selections and arrangements. In the early '90s, *Five Guys Named Moe*, a revue based on Jordan's music, ran on London's West End and New York's Broadway.

Journey

Formed 1973, San Francisco, CA
Neal Schon (b. 1955, San Mateo, CA), voc., gtr.; Ross Valory (b. 1950, San Francisco), bass; Gregg Rolie (b. 1948), voc., kybds.; Prairie Prince (b. May 7, 1950, Charlotte, NC), drums; George Tickner, gtr.
1974—(– Prince; + Aynsley Dunbar [b. 1946, Liverpool, Eng.], drums) 1975—*Journey* (Columbia) (– Tickner) 1976—*Look Into the Future* 1977—*Next* (+ Robert Fleischman, voc.; – Fleischman; + Steve Perry [b. 1949, Hanford, CA], voc.) 1978—*Infinity* (– Dunbar; + Steve Smith [b. Boston], drums) 1979—*Evolution; In the Beginning* 1980—*Departure* 1981—(– Rolie; + Jonathan Cain, kybds.) *Captured; Escape* 1983—*Frontiers* 1986—(– Smith; – Valory) *Raised on Radio* 1988—*Greatest Hits* 1989—(group disbands) 1992—*Time³* 1996—(group re-forms: Perry; Cain; Schon; Valory; Smith) *Trial by Fire* 1998—(– Perry; – Smith; + Steve Augeri, voc.; + Dean Castronovo, drums) 2001—*Arrival.*
Steve Perry solo: 1984—*Street Talk* (Columbia) 1994—*For the Love of Strange Medicine.*
Neal Schon (with Jan Hammer): 1981—*Untold Passion* (Columbia) 1983—*Here To Stay.*
Jonathan Cain solo: 1994—*Back to the Innocence* (Interscope).

Between their 1975 debut as a predominantly instrumental progressive rock group and their first platinum LP in 1978, Journey underwent format changes that led to their emergence as one of the top American hard-pop bands. Gregg Rolie had cofounded Santana with Carlos Santana and had sung lead on several Santana tunes, including "Evil Ways" and "Black Magic Woman." Neal Schon joined Santana after its second LP, *Abraxas,* when he was 17. The two left Santana in 1972. Rolie and his father opened a restaurant in Seattle, while Schon jammed with other Bay Area musicians.

Former Santana road manager Walter Herbert brought Schon and Rolie together again with ex–Steve Miller bassist Ross Valory, who, along with George Tickner, had played in Frumious Bandersnatch, a Bay Area group Herbert managed. In an impromptu contest on San Francisco station KSAN-FM, listeners were asked to name the band; the winning name was Journey. The group played its first shows with Prairie Prince, who was then drummer with the Tubes. When he decided to stay with the Tubes, British journeyman Aynsley Dunbar, whose earlier associations included John Mayall, Jeff Beck, the Bonzo Dog Band, Mothers of Invention, Lou Reed, and David Bowie, joined. Within a year of its 1974 New Year's Eve debut at San Francisco's Winterland, the group was signed to Columbia. Following Journey's debut LP, on which Rolie did most of the singing, Tickner, tired of touring, left the band. The group's next two albums sold moderately. Herbert, convinced that the group needed a lead singer, hired Robert Fleischman. Meanwhile, Steve Perry, a drummer/singer, had contacted the group several times asking to join. Due to a series of fortuitous events—Perry was recommended to Herbert by a Columbia executive around the time Herbert had decided to fire Fleischman—Perry was in. With *Infinity* (#21, 1978), their fourth LP and the first with Perry, Journey became a top group, as moderately successful singles ("Wheel in the Sky," "Lights") and constant touring made *Infinity* the group's first platinum LP; it eventually sold 3 million copies.

In September 1978, soon after *Infinity*'s success, Dunbar was dismissed from the group for what Herbert termed "incompatibility of the first order." In April 1980 Journey's Nightmare Productions charged that Dunbar had been overpaid more than $60,000 in advances. In May 1980, Nightmare Productions (in which the band members and Herbert owned stock) was sued for $3.25 million by Dunbar, who claimed that he had been "squeezed out" of the group just

Journey: Jonathan Cain, Steve Perry, Neal Schon, Ross Valory, Steve Smith

when the earnings were increasing, and he sued for breach of contract, nonpayment of royalties, and other charges.

Meanwhile, Dunbar (who joined Jefferson Starship) was replaced by Steve Smith, formerly Journey's drum roadie, who had studied at the Berklee School of Music and played with Focus, Jean-Luc Ponty, and Montrose. "Lovin', Touchin', Squeezin' " from *Evolution* (#20, 1979) was Journey's first Top 30 hit; earlier that year "Just the Same Way" had been a moderate success.

In 1980 "Anyway You Want It" from *Departure* (#8, 1980) hit #23. *Departure* became Journey's third consecutive multiplatinum album. Columbia repackaged material from the first three (pre-Perry) LPs as *In the Beginning.* After *Departure,* Rolie tired of touring and left. He was replaced by ex-Babys keyboardist Jonathan Cain, who cowrote Journey's 1981 #4 ballad hit, "Who's Crying Now." In 1981 Schon recorded an LP entitled *Untold Passion* with keyboardist Jan Hammer. *Escape* became the group's first #1 LP. It sold 7 million copies and spawned two other Top 10 hits: "Open Arms" and "Don't Stop Believin'." All of the Perry LPs have been certified platinum, and in late 1982 the group became the first rock band to inspire a video game, Journey—Escape.

Like many other mainstream hard-rock outfits, Journey made the transition to video, and their post-1983 albums continued to sell in the millions. Bolstered by a string of Top 20 hits that included "Separate Ways (Worlds Apart)" (#8, 1983), "Faithfully" (#12, 1983), "Only the Young" (#9, 1985)," "Be Good to Yourself" (#9, 1986), "Suzanne" (#17, 1986), "Girl Can't Help It" (#17, 1986), and "I'll Be Alright Without You" (#14, 1987), *Frontiers* (#2, 1983), *Raised on Radio* (#4, 1986), and *Greatest Hits* (#10, 1988) sold over 10 million copies combined. Steve Perry also launched a successful side solo career and had a #3 hit with 1984's "Oh Sherrie" from his double-platinum *Street Talk* (#12).

The group disbanded after Schon and Cain left in 1989 to join Cain's ex-Babys band mate John Waite in Bad English [see the Babys entry]; in 1991 Valory and Rolie joined the Storm. *Time³* peaked only at #90. In late 1993 the band, minus Perry, reunited at a Bay Area concert honoring Herbert. In 1994 Perry had a hit album with *For the Love of Strange Medicine* (#15, 1994) and a top single, "You Better Wait" (#6, 1994). However, he and Journey resumed activity in 1996, resulting in *Trial by Fire* (#47 pop). The single "When You Love a Woman" hit #1 on the Adult Contemporary chart. Perry departed again and was replaced by sound-alike Steve Augeri for "Remember Me," Journey's contribution to the 1998 *Armageddon* soundtrack. The group, which also sported a new drummer, released *Arrival* in early 2001.

Joy Division/New Order

Joy Division: Formed 1976, Manchester, Eng.
Ian Curtis (b. July 15, 1956, Macclesfield, Eng.; d. May 18, 1980, Macclesfield), voc.; Bernard Sumner (b. Bernard Albrecht, Jan. 4, 1956), gtr.; Peter Hook (b. Feb. 13, 1956, Salford, Eng.), bass; Stephen Morris (b. Oct. 28, 1957, Macclesfield), drums.
1979—*Unknown Pleasures* (Factory, U.K.) 1980—*Closer* 1981—*Still* 1995—*Permanent* (Qwest) 1998—*Heart & Soul* (London).
New Order, formed 1980, Manchester: Hook; Sumner; Morris; + Gillian Gilbert (b. Jan. 27, 1961, Manchester, Eng.), kybds.
1981—*Movement* (Factory, U.K.) 1983—*Power, Corruption and Lies* 1985—*Low-life* (Qwest) 1986—*Brotherhood* 1987—*Substance* 1989—*Technique* 1993—*Republic* 1995—*The Best of.*
Electronic: Sumner; + Johnny Marr (b. John Maher, Oct. 31, 1963, Manchester), gtr.; + Neil Tennant (b. Neil Francis Tennant, July 10, 1954, Brunton Park, Eng.), voc.
1991—*Electronic* (Warner Bros.) 1996—*Raise the Pressure* 1999—*Twisted Tenderness* (Koch).
The Other Two: Gilbert; Morris.
1993—*The Other Two and You* (Qwest) 1999—*Superhighways* (PolyGram).
Revenge: Hook; + David Hicks, gtr.; + Chris Jones, kybds.; + Ashley Taylor, drums; + David Potts, bass.
1990—*One True Passion* (Capitol).
Monaco: Hook; Potts.
1997—*Music for Pleasure* (Polydor).

Until the death of singer Ian Curtis in 1980, Joy Division was one of Britain's most admired and promising postpunk bands. New Order built on that promise, with 1983's "Blue Monday" forging an influential alliance of new wave and dance music.

Joy Division's Velvet Underground–derived drone and Curtis' matter-of-fact, gloomy lyrics scored significant club hits with "She's Lost Control," "Transmission," and "Love Will Tear Us Apart," a British hit single (#13 U.K., 1980). Formed by Hook and Sumner after seeing the Sex Pistols play in Manchester on June 4, 1976, the group took shape after Curtis responded to a "seeking singer" ad posted by the two at the local Virgin record store. Morris joined on drums the following year. The band, naming itself Joy Division after Nazi military prostitute compounds, released a four-song EP, *Ideal for Living,* by year's end.

In April 1978 the band generated a buzz when they performed at a Stiff Records battle of the bands. After turning down deals with Britain's RCA and Radar labels, the group recorded their first album, *Unknown Pleasures,* with producer Martin Hannent. They chose Manchester independent Factory Records to release the album, which was an immediate success in the U.K.

The next year the band's acclaim grew as they toured England and Europe. In March they returned to the studio to record their second album, *Closer.* Curtis, who was responsible for much of the group's dark vision, suffered from epileptic grand mal seizures—occasionally while performing onstage. Having attempted suicide in the past, Curtis hanged himself on May 18, 1980, just prior to the release of *Closer* (Joy Division's most commercially successful album) and the group's first U.S. tour. A collection of demos, outtakes, and live performances, *Still,* was released in 1981.

The remaining members regrouped as New Order and added Morris' girlfriend Gillian Gilbert on keyboards. Like

Joy Division, it has eschewed publicity, with no band photos on album covers, and playing low-key, unemotional concerts. The group's sound—a brighter but still moody version of Joy Division, with Sumner's monotonal yet plaintive vocals at the center—gained it club hits with "Everything's Gone Green" (1981) and "Temptation" (1982).

"Blue Monday" (1983) was New Order's breakthrough. Released only as a 12-inch single, it matched the band's usual emotional chill to a propulsive dance track and reached #5 on the *Billboard* dance chart, selling over 3 million copies worldwide. Sessions with dance producer Arthur Baker followed, producing "Confusion" (1983), another dance-floor favorite, which hit #71 R&B.

The band left Factory Records in 1985, signing with Quincy Jones' new Qwest label. Although *Low-life* (#94, 1985) and *Brotherhood* (#117, 1986) were their first American chart albums, sales were disappointing. *Substance* (#36, 1987), *Technique* (#32, 1989), and the hit single "True Faith" (#32, 1987) turned things around, but the band members turned their backs on stardom, releasing only the British World Cup Soccer theme "World in Motion . . ." (#1 U.K., 1990) before unofficially parting ways to pursue solo projects.

Sumner had the greatest success, teaming with ex-Smiths guitarist Johnny Marr and Pet Shop Boy Neil Tennant on "Getting Away With It" (#38, 1990), featured on *Electronic* (#109, 1991). Bassist Peter Hook's solo project, Revenge, released *One True Passion* (#190, 1990), while Morris and Gilbert wrote British TV themes, eventually releasing an album as the Other Two.

New Order re-formed in 1993, releasing *Republic* (#11), followed by a successful tour of the U.S. But the band members went their own ways after the tour, Sumner continuing with Electronic, Hook exiling himself in Monaco, and Gilbert and Morris (now husband and wife) remaining the Other Two.

Joy Division remained an influence on modern rock, as shown by the continuing interest in their scant output, reissued in *Permanent,* a "greatest hits" collection with several rare and unreleased tracks, and *Heart & Soul,* a four-CD box set that collected their every extant recording. In 1998 New Order performed a hometown reunion show. In the following year, they recorded their first new song in more than six years, "Bruta," for the Leonardo DiCaprio film *The Beach.*

Joy of Cooking

Formed 1967, Berkeley, CA
Terry Garthwaite (b. July 11, 1938, Berkeley), gtr.; Toni Brown (b. Nov. 16, 1938, Madison, WI), voc., piano; Ron Wilson (b. Feb. 5, 1933, San Diego, CA), congas; Fritz Kasten (b. Oct. 19, Des Moines, IA), drums; David Garthwaite (b. CA), bass.
1970—*Joy of Cooking* (Capitol) (– D. Garthwaite; + Jeff Neighbor [b. Mar. 19, 1942, Grand Coulee, WA], bass) *Closer to the Ground* 1972—*Castles* (– Brown) 1990—*Retro Rock #3: The Best of Joy of Cooking* (Capitol).

Joy of Cooking was one of the first rock bands led by women. Though the group lasted over five years, it had only one hit, "Brownsville," from its debut, and a small cult following. Terry Garthwaite began singing and playing guitar in junior high school and made her television debut at 14. A graduate of UC at Berkeley, she met Toni Brown, a creative writing graduate of Bennington College, and together with Garthwaite's brother David, Ron Wilson, and Fritz Kasten, they formed Joy of Cooking, a folk-rock group. Four years later they signed a record deal with Capitol, and "Mockingbird" became an FM staple. After their third LP, Brown left the group, and Garthwaite formed a larger band, which toured and recorded an album that was never released because of contractual problems.

In 1973 Brown and Garthwaite recorded an album entitled *Cross Country.* They have each recorded solo albums and were reunited in 1977 for *The Joy,* which received positive critical reaction but garnered few sales. They have since disbanded; both have recorded solo.

Judas Priest

Formed 1969, Birmingham, Eng.
Kenneth "K.K." Downing (b. Oct. 27, 1951, West Midlands, Eng.), gtr.; Ian Hill (b. Jan. 20, 1952, West Midlands), bass.
1971—(+ Rob Halford [b. Aug. 25, 1951, Birmingham], voc.; + John Hinch, drums) 1974—(+ Glenn Tipton (b. Oct. 25, 1949, West Midlands), gtr.; – Hinch; + Alan Moore, drums) *Rocka Rolla* (Gull) 1976—*Sad Wings of Destiny* 1977—(– Moore; + Simon Phillips, drums) *Sin After Sin* (Columbia) 1978—(– Phillips; + Les Binks, drums) *Stained Class* 1979—*Hell Bent for Leather; Unleashed in the East* (– Binks; + Dave Holland, drums) 1980—*British Steel* 1981—*Point of Entry* 1982—*Screaming for Vengeance* 1984—*Defenders of the Faith* 1986—*Turbo* 1987—*Priest . . . Live* 1988—*Ram It Down* 1989—(– Holland; + Scott Travis, drums) *Painkiller* 1992—(– Halford) 1993—*Metalworks '73–'93* 1995—(+ Tim "Ripper" Owens, voc.) 1997—*Jugulator* (CMC).

Judas Priest, a leather-clad heavy-metal band, was formed by guitarist K.K. Downing and bassist Ian Hill. In 1971 frontman Rob Halford joined (he'd previously worked in theatrical lighting), having met Hill, whom his sister was then dating (and later married). The band didn't get a contract until 1974, just after guitarist Glenn Tipton joined. Its first LP was released that year, but both it and the 1976 followup, *Sad Wings of Destiny,* sold marginally.

The band began to develop a following in England, and in 1977 Priest signed with Columbia, which released *Sin After Sin.* Produced by ex–Deep Purple bassist Roger Glover, *Sin* featured guest drummer Simon Phillips and an unlikely heavy-metal version of Joan Baez's "Diamonds and Rust" similar in style to Nazareth's 1973 treatment of Joni Mitchell's "This Flight Tonight." The group's songs, highlighted by Tipton and Downing's dual lead-guitar attack, were catchier and shorter than most other early-'70s heavy metal, anticipating late-decade acts like Def Leppard.

Stained Class (#173, 1978) featured new drummer Les Binks, replaced with ex-Trapeze member Dave Holland after Priest's live-in-Japan *Unleashed in the East* (#70, 1979). The

Judas Priest: Ian Hill, K.K. Downing, Rob Halford, Glenn Tipton, Dave Holland

live LP included a version of Fleetwood Mac's "Green Manalishi." Over the years Judas Priest became increasingly known for its extravagant live show, which featured Halford, in his trademark S&M gear, thundering onstage on a Harley-Davidson motorcycle. The band's seventh album, 1980's *British Steel* (#34), was its first U.S. Top 40 entry, and a heavy-metal landmark. Concise songs like "Living After Midnight" and "Breaking the Law" mated metal aggression with new-wave melodicism. Both went Top 20 in Britain.

The 1981 followup, *Point of Entry* (#39, 1981), failed to build on the band's momentum, but the platinum *Screaming for Vengeance* (#17, 1982) broke Judas Priest in a big way stateside, and gave the group its closest thing to an American hit single, "You've Got Another Thing Comin' " (#67, 1982). The song's stylish video showed Priest performing on a laser-lit stage while a conservative business type outfitted in a trenchcoat and bowler hat appears to be fleeing some unseen, sinister force. At the clip's end, Tipton and Downing's guitars explode—as does the character's head, literally—leading to a powerful climax.

Vengeance, Defenders of the Faith (#18, 1984), and *Turbo* (#17, 1986) all went platinum, and Priest's mid-'80s success spurred sales of its earlier albums. Through 1990's *Painkiller* (#26, 1990), all but the group's second live LP, released in 1987, had sold more than 500,000 copies apiece. By the late '80s, however, other, younger metal bands began to make inroads on Priest's audience.

In 1986 Judas Priest became the unwitting object of controversy when the parents of two mentally unstable Reno, Nevada, teenagers sued both the group and Columbia Records for $6.2 million, claiming that a song on 1978's *Stained Class* contained subliminal messages that drove their sons to shoot themselves in 1985. One died instantly; the other lived but overdosed fatally on methadone three years later. Priest was acquitted of all charges in the six-week 1990 trial. The gold *Painkiller* came out shortly thereafter.

Halford, who'd relocated to Arizona in the early '80s and then moved to San Diego in 1999, abruptly quit Judas Priest in December 1992 to form his own band, the grungy Fight, which was active in the mid-'90s. (Scott Travis, Priest's drummer since 1990, assisted him but remained in Judas Priest.) Later in the decade, Halford led the industrial Two, which signed to Trent Reznor's nothing label. He also briefly fronted a post-Ozzy Black Sabbath, and collaborated with Pantera. In 1998 he obliterated many a metal stereotype (and confirmed years' worth of rumors) by openly announcing his homosexuality. In 1999 he returned to metal under the name Halford, and parted ways with nothing.

Tipton released a solo album in 1997. The four remaining members of Judas Priest auditioned vocalist Tim "Ripper" Owens, a longtime fan who had fronted a JP tribute act. He joined his idols after singing only a portion of one song. The group's first album sans Halford, *Jugulator,* peaked at #82 in 1997.

The Judds/Wynonna

Formed 1983, Nashville, TN
Naomi Judd (b. Diana Judd, Jan. 11, 1946, Ashland, KY), voc.; Wynonna Judd (b. Christina Ciminella, May 30, 1964, Ashland), voc., gtr.
1984—*The Judds: Wynonna & Naomi* (Curb/RCA); *Why Not Me* 1985—*Rockin' With the Rhythm* 1987—*Heart Land; Christmas Time With the Judds* 1988—*Greatest Hits* 1989—*River of Time* 1990—*Love Can Build a Bridge; Collector's Series* 1991—*Greatest Hits, vol. 2* 1995—*Number One Hits* 2000—*The Judds Reunion.*
Wynonna solo: 1992—*Wynonna* (Curb/MCA) 1993—*Tell Me Why* 1996—*revelations* 1997—*Collection; The Other Side* (Curb/Universal) 2000—*New Day Dawning* (Mercury/Curb).

After rising to fame in the mid-'80s, the Judds remained the most beloved mother-daughter act in country music—in any mass-appeal musical genre, in fact—until chronic hepatitis forced Wynonna Judd's mom, Naomi, to retire in 1991. Though Naomi's age-defying beauty earned much media attention, it was Wynonna's rich, authoritative lead vocals (Naomi usually sang harmony) and her equally confident way with ballads and rootsy rockers that gave the duo musical cachet, and enabled the younger Judd to embark on a successful solo career in the early '90s.

Naomi married at 17, and at 18 gave birth to Christina Ciminella, who later changed her name to Wynonna. (The choice was inspired by a reference in the song "Route 66.") The family moved to L.A. in 1968; two years later Naomi left Wynonna's father, who had by then fathered a second daughter, Ashley (later a successful actress). Eventually, mother and children relocated to Morrill, Kentucky, where, as Naomi struggled to make ends meet, Wynonna discovered the guitar. The Judds then moved back to California; there Naomi earned a nursing degree and spent her off-hours singing with Wynonna. In 1979 they were in the Nashville suburb of Franklin, and Naomi wound up nursing the daughter of a prominent C&W producer, Brent Maher, after the girl was injured in a car accident. After her recovery, Naomi gave Maher a demo tape that she and Wynonna had made; impressed, Maher passed it on to executives at RCA Records' Nashville division, who signed the duo.

Over the next few years, the Judds consistently took their smooth harmonies and old-fashioned but unsentimental songs to the top of the C&W chart. Their #1 C&W singles (later collected on the retrospective *Number One Hits*) included "Mama He's Crazy" (1984), "Why Not Me" (1984), "Girls Night Out" (1985), "Love Is Alive" (1985), "Have Mercy" (1985), "Grandpa (Tell Me 'Bout the Good Old Days)" (1986), "Rockin' With the Rhythm of the Rain" (1986), "Cry Myself to Sleep" (1986), "I Know Where I'm Going" (1987), "Maybe Your Baby's Got the Blues" (1987), "Turn It Loose" (1988), and "Change of Heart" (1988). Other hits included a remake of "Don't Be Cruel" (#10 C&W, 1987), "Give a Little Love" (#2 C&W, 1988), and "One Hundred and Two" (#6 C&W, 1991). In addition, the Judds garnered five Grammy Awards, in the Best Country Vocal Duet category.

After an emotional (and thoroughly publicized) farewell tour in 1991, Wynonna began working on her solo debut. *Wynonna* (1992) won critical raves, topped the C&W chart, and produced three #1 country singles: "She Is His Only Need," "I Saw the Light," and "No One Else on Earth," as well as the #4 single "My Strongest Weakness." *Wynonna* also became a #4 pop album. In 1993 Wynonna joined forces with tour mate and fellow crossover star Clint Black for the single "A Bad Goodbye" (#43 pop, #2 C&W, 1993). Also in 1993, Wynonna released her second solo album, *Tell Me Why* (#5 pop, #1 C&W, 1993), and Naomi published a best-selling memoir, *Love Can Build a Bridge*, which was made into a highly rated TV movie in 1995. Wynonna then reunited with her mother, whose illness was in remission, for a nationally televised performance at the 1994 Super Bowl during half-time.

Later that year, Wynonna announced she was pregnant with her first child by her Nashville businessman boyfriend, Arch Kelley III. The pregnancy prompted the singer to take an 18-month break from touring, though she began recording her album *revelations* (released in 1996). Son Elijah Judd Kelley was born in December 1994; when Wynonna was expecting their second child, she married Kelley, in January 1996. Daughter Grace was born that summer.

Her *revelations* (#9 pop, #2 C&W) contained a nearly eight-minute version of Lynyrd Skynyrd's "Free Bird," as well as the #1 country hit "To Be Loved by You" and the #14 "Heaven Help My Heart." The compilation *Collection* (#72 pop, #9 C&W) followed in 1997, as did *The Other Side* (#38 pop, #5 C&W), with the country singles "When Love Starts Talkin' " (#13 C&W) and "Come Some Rainy Day" (#14 C&W). In 1998 Wynonna's energies were devoted to a messy divorce from Kelley.

In 1999 Naomi, in remission for a few years, started to host a nationally syndicated radio show, *Heart to Heart With Naomi Judd*, from her home in a Nashville suburb. She and Wynonna held a reunion concert in Phoenix on New Year's Eve 1999. (A live recording of highlights was later released.) The concert led to a two-month reunion tour in early 2000, as well as a limited-edition four-song Judds EP packaged with a percentage of Wynonna's 2000 solo album, *New Day Dawning*. Wynonna's album included covers of the Fabulous Thunderbirds' "Tuff Enuff" and Joni Mitchell's "Help Me."

The Jungle Brothers

Formed 1986, Brooklyn, NY
Mike G (b. Michael Small, May 13, 1969, New York, NY), voc.; Afrika Baby Bambaataa (b. Nathaniel Hall, May 22, 1970, New York), voc.; Sammy B (b. Samuel Burwell, Dec. 9, 1967, New York), DJ.
1988—*Straight Out the Jungle* (Idlers/Warlock) 1989—*Done by the Forces of Nature* (Warner Bros.) 1993—(+ Torture [b. Colin Bobb, Oct. 18, 1974, Guyana], voc.) *J. Beez wit the Remedy* 1997—*Raw Deluxe* (Gee Street/V2) (– Burwell) 2000—*V.I.P.*

The Jungle Brothers opened the doors to the '90s jazz-rap trend by blending horns and scat vocals into their early raw, lilting hip-hop style. Often sporting bright African colors, psychedelic beads, and wire-rimmed shades, the group was part of the late-'80s neo-hippie rap collective known as the Native Tongues, along with De La Soul, A Tribe Called Quest, and Queen Latifah.

While attending high school in Brooklyn, Michael Small began a rap group in 1986 with Harlemites Natha-niel Hall and Samuel Burwell. An early demo tape of their music made it into the hands of influential DJ Red Alert, of the New York City radio station WRKS-FM, who helped the JBs land a deal with the independent rap label Idlers Records. The group's first single, "Jim Browski," was popular among the city's hip-hop underground, but it was the B side, "I'll House You," a blend of rap and the house dance-music style, that really turned heads.

The Jungle Brothers signed with Warner Bros. in 1989 and released *Done by the Forces of Nature* (#46 R&B, 1989). They spent the next few years producing such artists as Fishbone and A Tribe Called Quest, and contributed a song to the soundtrack of *Living Large*, a film in which they appeared. Funksters Bootsy Collins, Gary "Mudbone" Cooper, and Bernie Worrell collaborated on the 1993 album *J. Beez wit the Remedy* (#52 R&B), as did outrageous new JB member Torture. The group's music remains influential and critically praised, though commercial success continues to elude them.

The JBs collaborated with reggae singer Luciano on the 1996 single "Who Could It Be?" (#96 R&B). After 1997's *Raw Deluxe* (#37 R&B), Burwell left the group. By now the Jungle Brothers had embraced the U.K. electronic dance scene and enjoyed an underground hit with a remix of their track "Jungle Brother" by the drum-and-bass duo Urban Takeover (made up of Aphrodite and Mickey Finn). The duo was soon invited to appear on Propellerheads' debut album, and they in turn asked that group's Alex Gifford to produce 1999's *V.I.P.*, bathing the album under a layer of drum-and-bass as the Jungle Brothers moved even further away from mainstream rap's tales of guns and money. Now married and with families, the Jungle Brothers doggedly promoted Afrocentrism, spirituality, and good times.

Kaleidoscope/David Lindley

Formed 1966, Berkeley, CA
Fenrus Epp (b. Chester Crill, a.k.a. Max Buda, Templeton Parceley, Connie Crill), violin, kybds., voc.; John Vidican, perc.; Solomon Feldthouse (b. Sulyman Feldthouse), gtr., voc., strings; David Lindley (b. 1944, San Marino, CA), violin, gtr., voc.; Chris Darrow, gtr., voc., violin.
1967—*Side Trips* (Epic) 1968—*A Beacon From Mars* (– Darrow; – Vidican; + Stuart Brotman, bass; + Paul Lagos, drums) 1969—*Kaleidoscope* 1970—(– Brotman; + Ron Johnson, bass; + Jeff Kaplan [d. 1970], gtr., voc.) *Bernice* (Columbia) (– Feldthouse; – Crill; + Richard Aplan, flute (group disbands) 1975—(group re-forms: Feldthouse; Brotman; Lagos; Crill; Darrow) 1976—*When Scopes Collide* (Pacific Arts) 1991—*Greetings From Kartoonistan . . . We Ain't Dead Yet* (Gifthorse/Curb) 1991—*Egyptian Candy: A Collection* (Legacy).
David Lindley solo: 1981—*El Rayo-X* (Elektra) 1982—*Win This Record!* 1988—*Very Greasy.*

Kaleidoscope was known in the late '60s for eclectic albums that drew from bluegrass, blues, Cajun music, Middle Eastern music, and acid rock, using various exotic instruments (e.g., saz, oud). Despite a noteworthy appearance at the 1968 Newport Folk Festival and a live act that included flamenco and belly dancers, Kaleidoscope's early albums, *Sidetrips* and *Beacon From Mars,* were ignored. John Vidican and Chris Darrow were replaced by Paul Lagos and Stuart Brotman, with no resulting rise in popularity for subsequent LPs *Kaleidoscope* and *Bernice.* Shortly after the 1970 drug-related death of guitarist Jeff Kaplan, a recent recruit, the band broke up, although Darrow, Lagos, Brotman, Feldthouse, and Crill reunited in 1975 to record *When Scopes Collide,* with only minor contributions from Lindley (under the name DeParis Letante) and in 1991 for *Greetings From Kartoonistan.*

After he left Kaleidoscope, Darrow recorded solo albums for United Artists and other labels. One of those efforts was created with members of British folk-rockers Fairport Convention. "Max Buda" made a guest appearance on Darrow's 1979 LP, *Fretless.* Since the '70s, Feldthouse has been making jewelry, playing sessions, working as a solo flamenco artist, and participating in the long-running world-music group Sirocco. Brotman became involved with the klezmer revival.

Today Kaleidoscope is remembered primarily as the band led by David Lindley before he hooked up with Jackson Browne and Ry Cooder. In the '80s Lindley also recorded solo LPs. In the early '90s he visited Madagascar, where he recorded and documented music with avant-garde guitarist Henry Kaiser. Later in the decade he collaborated with Jordanian percussionist Hani Naser. By 2000, Lindley was performing with banjo player Wally Ingram.

Kansas

Formed 1970, Topeka, KS
Kerry Livgren (b. Sep. 18, 1949, KS), gtr., kybds., synth.; Steve

Walsh (b. 1951, St. Jospeh, MO), kybds., synth., voc.; Robby Steinhardt (b. 1951, MS), violin, voc.; Richard Williams (b. 1951, KS), gtr.; Phil Ehart (b. 1951, KS), drums; Dave Hope (b. Oct. 7, 1949, KS), bass.
1974—*Kansas* (Kirshner) 1975—*Masque; Song for America* 1976—*Leftoverture* 1977—*Point of Know Return* 1978—*Two for the Show* 1979—*Monolith* 1980—*Audio-Visions* 1981—(– Walsh; + John Elefante [b. 1958, Levittown, NY], voc., kybds.) 1982—*Vinyl Confessions* 1983—*Drastic Measures* (CBS Associated) (group disbands) 1984—*The Best of Kansas* 1986—(group re-forms: Walsh; Ehart; Williams; + Steve Morse [b. July 28, 1954, Hamilton, OH], gtr.; + Billy Greer, bass, gtr.) *Power* (MCA) 1988—(numerous personnel changes follow) *In the Spirit of Things* 1994—*The Kansas Box Set* (Legacy) 1995—*Freaks of Nature* (Intersound) 1997—(+ Steinhardt) 1998—*Always Never the Same* (River North) 1999—(+ Livgren; + Hope) 2000—*Somewhere to Elsewhere* (Magna Carta) (– Livgren; – Hope).
Steve Walsh solo: 1979—*Schemer-Dreamer* (Kirshner).

Although Kansas' ornate and complex rock has been dismissed by critics as a pastiche of early-'70s British progressive rock, some of the band's albums have sold in the millions. For years the group labored through the Midwest, playing clubs and bars, its odd mix of Anglophilia and boogie falling mostly on bewildered ears. The members met while attending high school in Topeka, and after playing in various local groups, Kerry Livgren, Phil Ehart, and Dave Hope formed the first edition of Kansas in 1970. A year later they changed their name to White Clover and added Robby Steinhardt, a classically trained violinist who had played with orchestras in Europe when his father, chairman of the music-history department at the University of Kansas, was there on sabbatical. The group went through numerous personnel changes before Ehart, seeking new ideas, went to England in 1972. On his return four months later, he revived White Clover with Hope, Steinhardt, Richard Williams, and Steve Walsh; Livgren, who became the group's main songwriter, joined soon after, and they reverted to the name Kansas.

The sextet's first album initially sold about 100,000 copies, but constant touring built its following, and Kansas' second and third LPs each sold about 250,000. *Leftoverture* (#5, 1976), which featured "Carry On Wayward Son" (#11, 1977), sold over 3 million copies. The 1977-released *Point of Know Return* (#4) went triple platinum, garnering two hit singles—"Point of Know Return" (#28) and "Dust in the Wind" (#6). *Two for the Show,* a live album (#32, 1978), is also platinum, and *Monolith* (#10, 1979) (Kansas' first self-produced venture) and *Audio-Visions* (#26, 1980) are gold.

In 1980 schisms began to form within the group. Livgren and then Hope became born-again Christians. Livgren cut a solo album, *Seeds of Change,* in 1980, as Walsh had the previous year with *Schemer-Dreamer.* Walsh also sang on ex-Genesis Steve Hackett's solo album, *Please Don't Touch.* By the end of 1981, Walsh had left the group to form a hard-rock quartet called Streets. *Vinyl Confessions,* the first Kansas LP to feature his replacement, John Elefante, went Top 20 and delivered a #17 hit with "Play the Game Tonight." But after one more studio album, *Drastic Measures* (1983), the group disbanded. Livgren and Elefante both went on to find considerable success in contemporary Christian music, the former as an artist, the latter as a producer.

In 1986 Ehart, Williams, and Walsh regrouped, adding the brilliant jazz-fusion guitarist Steve Morse (Dixie Dregs, Steve Morse Band) and bassist Billy Greer, who'd played with Walsh in Streets. Neither of that group's two LPs, *Streets* (1983) and *Crimes in Mind* (1985), had sold well. The revamped Kansas' first album, *Power,* produced the group's fourth, and last, Top 20 hit, "All I Wanted." However, 1988's *In the Spirit of Things* did not find a receptive audience. The followup, *Freaks of Nature,* appeared seven years later. Having splintered 19 years earlier, the original Kansas lineup, augmented by Greer, reconvened for 2000's *Somewhere to Elsewhere.*

Paul Kantner: See Jefferson Airplane

KC and the Sunshine Band

Formed 1973, Florida
Harry Wayne Casey (b. Jan. 31, 1951, Hialeah, FL), voc., kybds.; Richard Finch (b. Jan. 25, 1954, Indianapolis, IN), bass; Jerome Smith (b. June 18, 1953, Miami, FL; d. July 28, 2000, W. Palm Beach, FL), gtr.; Robert Johnson (b. Mar. 21, 1953, Miami), drums; Fermin Coytisolo (b. Dec. 31, 1951, Havana, Cuba), congas; Ronnie Smith (b. 1952, Hialeah), trumpet; Denvil Liptrot, sax; James Weaver, trumpet; Charles Williams (b. Nov. 18, 1954, Rockingham, NC), trombone.
1974—*Do It Good* (T.K.) 1975—*The Sound of Sunshine* (a.k.a. *The Sunshine Band*) 1976—*Part 3; KC and the Sunshine Band* 1977—*I Like to Do It* (President) 1978—*Who Do Ya (Love)* (T.K.) 1979—*Do You Wanna Go Party?* 1980—*Greatest Hits* 1981—*The Painter* (Epic) 1982—*All in a Night's Work* 1989—*The Best of KC and the Sunshine Band* (Rhino) 1993—*Oh Yeah* (ZYX) 1999—*25th Anniversary Edition* (Rhino).
KC solo: 1984—*KC Ten* (Meca).

KC and the Sunshine Band were the most successful promulgators of the boisterous, tropically funky dance music known as the Miami Sound. The Sunshine Band originated in the T.K. Studios in Hialeah, Florida, near Miami. H.W. Casey, a former record retailer, began working in 1973 for Tone Distributors, where he met Richard Finch, a Miami session bassist hired by T.K. as an engineer. The two formed a songwriting partnership and recorded as KC and the Sunshine Junkanoo Band. (Junkanoo is a percussion-oriented pop from the Bahama Islands, characterized by a liberal mix of horns, whistles, and vocal chants.) Their first record, "Blow Your Whistle," reached #27 on R&B chart in 1973, and its followup (as KC and the Sunshine Band), "Sound Your Funky Horn," went to #21 early the next year, persuading T.K. to release an album.

Do It Good was a hit in Europe, and the single "Queen of

Clubs" went to #7 on British chart in 1974 (not placing on American chart until its reissue two years later), when KC and the Sunshine Band toured the U.K. Casey and Finch wrote, arranged, and produced "Rock Your Baby," a #1 hit for George McCrae (who had sung on *Do It Good*) on both pop and R&B charts in 1974, which sold a reported 11 million copies worldwide. The following year KC and the Sunshine Band struck gold with "Get Down Tonight" (#1 pop and R&B).

KC and the Sunshine Band—now expanded to nine members, all black except for Casey and Finch—ruled the charts and the dance floors for the next three years. "That's the Way (I Like It)" and "(Shake, Shake, Shake) Shake Your Booty" reached #1 on the pop chart in 1975 and 1976, respectively. The Sunshine Band became the first act to score four #1 pop singles in one 12-month period since the Beatles in 1964. Three of these were #1 R&B as well. The band's string of hit singles continued with "I'm Your Boogie Man" (#1 pop, #3 R&B, 1977) and "Keep It Comin' Love" (#2 pop, #1 R&B, 1977).

It looked as if the group had come to the end of the string in 1978 with the minor hits "Boogie Shoes" and "It's the Same Old Song," but in 1979 KC and company returned with "Do You Wanna Go Party" (#8 R&B), "Please Don't Go" (#1 pop), and "Yes, I'm Ready," the latter featuring the vocals of Teri De Sario (#2 pop, #20 R&B). In 1984, after Casey had recovered from a serious 1982 car crash, the group hit the Top 20 again with "Give It Up," which went to #1 in the U.K. Casey and Finch were also involved in hitmaking—as songwriters, producers, or both—for Betty Wright (her Grammy-winning "Where Is the Love"), Jimmy "Bo" Horne, Fire (the female vocal group that backed the Sunshine Band on "That's the Way"), and Leif Garrett.

In the early '90s KC revamped his act, releasing a new album and making numerous television and concert appearances, both here and in Europe, where the group always had a strong following. He currently milks the disco revival circuit and is shopping around a new album entitled *Yummy.* Guitarist Jerome Smith was crushed to death in a construction accident.

Ernie K-Doe

Born Ernest Kador Jr., Feb. 22, 1936, New Orleans, LA; died July 5, 2001, New Orleans
1961—*Mother-in-Law* (Minit) 1972—*Ernie K-Doe* (Janus) 1990—*Ain't No Shame in My Game* (Syla) 1993—*I'm Cocky But I'm Good* 1999—*The Best of Ernie K-Doe* (Mardi Gras).

With his national chart-topper "Mother-in-Law," Ernie K-Doe was one of the young black singers whose jaunty beat and rollicking good humor popularized New Orleans R&B in the early '60s. Raised by an aunt in New Orleans, Kador was heavily influenced by gospel. By the time he was 15, he had become a member of the Golden Chain Jubilee Singers and the Zion Travellers. He made his first recording when he was in Chicago visiting his mother in 1953. It was never released. He went on to sing with the Moonglows and the Flamingos, and two years later Kador returned to New Orleans, where he made a name for himself with a vocal group called the Blue Diamonds. By then he had legally changed his name to K-Doe.

An outgoing showman, K-Doe made the Blue Diamonds a favorite act in the Crescent City. After recording with them for Savoy, he cut his first solo record, "Do Baby Do," for Specialty in 1956. He also recorded for Herald before "Hello My Lover," a single for Minit, became a regional hit in 1959. His next hit was "Mother-in-Law," a novelty song produced by Allen Toussaint. The record went to #1 on both the pop and R&B charts in 1961.

He followed "Mother-in-Law" with a handful of singles for Minit, the most successful of which were "Te-Ta-Te-Ta-Ta" (#53 pop, #21 R&B, 1961) and "I Cried My Last Tear" (#69, 1961). He later recorded for Duke, placing "Later for Tomorrow" at #37 on the R&B chart in 1967, and subsequently for Janus. Allen Toussaint produced a couple of K-Doe albums in the early '70s, though K-Doe soon left Toussaint. Into the '90s, he remained active on the New Orleans club circuit and appeared regularly at Delta region music festivals. He died of liver failure at age 65.

Paul Kelly

Born Paul Maurice Kelly, Jan. 13, 1955, Adelaide, Austral.
1987—*Gossip* (A&M) 1988—*Under the Sun* 1989—*So Much Water So Close to Home* 1991—*Comedy* (Doctor Dream) 1994—*Wanted Man* (Vanguard) 1995—*Deeper Water* 1996—*Live at the Continental and the Esplanade* 1998—*Words and Music.*

Paul Kelly has been known to (a relatively small) American audience since 1987, but in his native Australia, this literate songwriter (*So Much Water So Close to Home* takes its title from a Raymond Carver story) has been working since 1977.

Kelly started out as a folksinger, playing Adelaide coffee shops in the mid-'70s. He moved to Melbourne in 1976 and became part of that city's pub scene, playing solo and with the bands High Rise Bombers, the Dots (who released two albums), and, finally, the Coloured Girls. The last of these, taken from a lyric in Lou Reed's "Walk on the Wild Side," were signed by A&M for American distribution. For America the name was changed to Paul Kelly and the Messengers in deference to racial sensitivities; the group (Michael Armiger, bass; Michael Barclay, drums; Pedro Bull, keyboards; Steve Connolly, guitar; and Chris Coyne, sax) adopted that name in Australia by 1989. A&M released the Australian double LP, *Gossip,* in the States as a single album. It mixed writerly craftsmanship with punk passion and was met with critical raves but low sales. Even production by Scott Litt (R.E.M.), brought in for *So Much Water,* could not change matters, and A&M dropped Kelly in 1989. In 1991 he was signed by the independent Doctor Dream label, and released *Comedy.* He moved to folk specialist Vanguard Records for 1994's *Wanted Man,* which found him spanning continents, collaborating with Americans Dr. Dre, members of Was (Not Was) and Bonnie Raitt's backing band, and fellow Australian Nick Cave.

Again, the album was met with critical plaudits and commercial shrugs in America, a fate that met his next two albums.

R. Kelly

Born Robert Kelly, Jan. 8, 1969, Chicago, IL
1992—*Born Into the 90's* (Jive) 1993—*12 Play* 1995—*R. Kelly* 1998—*R.* 2000—*TP-2.Com.*

Raised on Chicago's South Side, R&B vocalist R. Kelly had years of show business experience behind him when his debut album, *Born Into the 90's* (#42 pop, #3 R&B, 1992), was released. A natural musician, he had busked on city streets and won a national talent contest with one of his early groups, MGM, before putting together the group Public Announcement to begin recording in 1991. The singer's often provocative lyrics and blend of hip-hop and funk rhythms, old-school soul, and polished production was instantly successful, laying the platform for a career as a prolific singles artist and an in-demand producer and songwriter for other artists, including Whitney Houston and Boyz II Men.

After the single "She's Got That Vibe" (#7 R&B, 1991), R. Kelly scored two consecutive chart-topping 1992 R&B hits, "Honey Love" and "Slow Dance (Hey Mr. DJ)." All the tunes got pop airplay, but "Dedicated" (#31 pop, #9 R&B, 1993) performed strongest outside the R&B market. The next album, *12 Play* (#2 pop, #1 R&B, 1993), was a major breakthrough, selling more than 5 million copies and firmly establishing Kelly's libidinous persona with the hits "Sex Me (Parts I & II)" (#20 pop, #8 R&B, 1993), "Bump n' Grind" (#1 pop and R&B, 1994), and "Your Body's Callin' " (#13 pop, #2 R&B, 1994). During 1994 Kelly produced the successful debut album by Aaliyah, a teenage Detroit R&B singer. Kelly also wrote and coproduced "You Are Not Alone" for Michael Jackson, which was released in 1995 on *HIStory.*

Kelly's self-titled third album, released late in 1995, toned down the overt sexuality that had become his trademark, due in part to the influence of his friend, the gospel singer Kirk Franklin. The recording topped the pop and R&B charts, sold more than 7 million copies, and produced three #1 R&B singles: "You Remind Me of Something" (#4 pop, 1995), "Down Low (Nobody Has to Know)" (#4 pop, 1996), and "I Can't Sleep Baby (If I)" (#5 pop, 1996). "I Believe I Can Fly" (#2 pop, #1 R&B, 1996), from the *Space Jam* soundtrack, won three Grammy Awards. Kelly's next hit, "Gotham City" (#9 pop and R&B, 1997), was also from a movie, *Batman & Robin.* In late 1998 the two-CD *R.* debuted at #2 (#1 R&B) and sold more than 6 million copies. Following the success of "I'm Your Angel" (#1 pop, #5 R&B, 1998), a duet with Celine Dion, Kelly put six straight singles on the R&B chart during 1999, including "When a Woman's Fed Up" (#22 pop, #5 R&B), "Did You Ever Think" (#27 pop, #8 R&B), and "If I Could Turn Back the Hands of Time" (#12 pop, #5 R&B). He was also featured on Sean Combs' "Satisfy You" (#2 pop, #1 R&B). The next year's *TP-2.Com* topped the charts, despite lukewarm reviews.

Chris Kenner

Born Dec. 25, 1929, Kenner, LA; died Jan. 25, 1976
1963—*Land of a Thousand Dances* (Atlantic) 1987—*I Like It Like That* (Collectables).

New Orleans vocalist Chris Kenner had a hit single in 1961 with "I Like It Like That." But in the record business—and especially the New Orleans music community in which he had been active since the '50s—he was best known for writing hits for Fats Domino, Wilson Pickett, and the Dave Clark Five.

Kenner started his career as a singer with a gospel quartet, the New Orleans Harmonizing Four, in the early '50s and made his first records for the Baton and Imperial labels in 1957. His "Sick and Tired" on Imperial was cut that year, but Fats Domino's cover made #22 in 1958. Kenner remained a local figure, recording for labels like Pontchartrain, until he teamed up with Allen Toussaint, producer for Minit Records' Instant label. "I Like It Like That," their first collaboration, went to #2 on both the R&B and pop charts in 1961. The song returned to the Top 10 four years later in a cover version by the Dave Clark Five. Kenner's classic "Land of 1000 Dances"—which in his 1963 rendition made it to #77—was a #30 hit for Cannibal and the Headhunters in 1965 and a #6 hit for Wilson Pickett in 1966. Two other acts, the Three Midniters and Electric Indian, had modest hits with the song. Kenner's 1964 recording of "Something You Got" was a huge success in New Orleans.

Alcohol addiction plagued Kenner throughout his life, which hit a low with his 1968 conviction for statutory rape. He continued to record with Instant until 1969 and died seven years later of a heart attack.

Kentucky Colonels

Formed 1961, California
Clarence White (b. June 7, 1944, Lewiston, ME; d. July 14, 1973, Palmdale, CA), gtr., voc.; Billy Ray Lathum (b. Jan. 12, 1938), banjo; Roland White (b. Apr. 23, 1938, Madawaska, ME), mandolin, voc.; Roger Bush, bass; LeRoy Mack, Dobro; Bobby Sloane, fiddle.
1963—*New Sounds of Bluegrass America* (Briar) 1964—*Appalachian Swing!* (World Pacific) 1965—(– Sloane; – C. White) 1974—(+ C. White) *Kentucky Colonels* (Rounder) 1975—*Livin' in the Past;* (+ Scotty Stoneman, voc., fiddle) *The Kentucky Colonels With Scotty Stoneman* 1978—*Kentucky Colonels 1966* 1979—*Kentucky Colonels 1965–1967* 1980—*Clarence White and the Kentucky Colonels* 1984—*On Stage* 1988—*1955–1967; The Kentucky Colonels Featuring Clarence White* 1991—*Long Journey Home* (Vanguard).

A seminal bluegrass band, the Kentucky Colonels featured two brothers, the mandolinist Roland White and guitarist Clarence White, who later went on to fame in the last edition of the Byrds.

The Maine-born White brothers had been playing country music since 1954 as the Country Boys (with brother Eric on bass). In 1961 Roger Bush replaced Eric White, and the Kentucky Colonels were formed. The group established itself at folk festivals and throughout the national bluegrass circuit; they performed twice on Andy Griffith's TV show. The group's 1964 masterpiece, *Appalachian Swing!*, was reissued by Rounder in 1993.

In 1965 Clarence White left the group, turning his attention to the electric guitar and quickly becoming a top L.A. sessionman. White joined the Byrds in 1968, staying until the group split up in 1973. Roland White unsuccessfully attempted to revive the Kentucky Colonels after Clarence's departure; Roland later worked with Bill Monroe and Lester Flatt and, in the '70s, Country Gazette.

Following the Byrds' demise, the Kentucky Colonels regrouped with Clarence White for occasional shows. After one of these 1973 performances, in Southern California, Clarence White was killed by a drunk driver while loading his equipment into a van. Roland White has continued to perform on the folk and bluegrass circuit with various aggregations of players.

Doug Kershaw

Born Jan. 24, 1936, Teil Ridge, LA
1969—*The Cajun Way* (Warner Bros.) 1970—*Spanish Moss* 1971—*Doug Kershaw* 1972—*Swamp Grass; Devil's Elbow* 1973—*Douglas James Kershaw* 1974—*Mama Kershaw's Boy* 1975—*Alive and Pickin'* 1976—*The Ragin' Cajun* 1977—*Flip Flop Fly* 1978—*Louisiana Man* 1979—*Louisiana Cajun Country* (Starflite) 1989—*The Best of Doug Kershaw* (Warner Bros.) 1999—*Two Step Fever* (Susie Q); *Diggy Diggy Lo.*

Doug Kershaw is America's best-known Cajun fiddler, though his traditional bayou sound has always been a bit too exotic to secure him a major country or rock audience. He was born on a tiny island in the Gulf of Mexico in a poor French-speaking community and didn't learn English until after he turned eight. His father was an alligator hunter who shot himself through the head when Doug was just seven. The family soon relocated to Lake Arthur, Louisiana, where Doug went to school and practiced on his older brother's fiddle, which he'd first fooled with at age five; he has since taught himself 28 other instruments.

Kershaw played his first date at age eight, at a local bar called the Bucket of Blood, with his mother accompanying him on guitar. He graduated from McNeese State University with a degree in mathematics, and then with two of his brothers he formed the Continental Playboys.

Kershaw was writing by the time he left the bayou at age 18 to try to record in Nashville. Billed as Rusty and Doug (Rusty was his 16-year-old brother), the two recorded for Hickory Records and became regulars on the Grand Ole Opry by 1957. After a stint in the army, Kershaw penned his best-known piece, "Louisiana Man," in 1960, which went to #10 on the country & western chart the next year and became a country standard. Also in 1961 the two hit the C&W list with "Diggy Liggy Lo" (#14), but the brothers had no followup, and they soon broke up.

It wasn't until later in the '60s that Kershaw got beyond his regional reputation. With the help of producer Buddy Killen, he got a contract with Warner Bros., which led to 1969's *The Cajun Way.* His appearance on *The Johnny Cash Show* that summer (on the same program as Bob Dylan) attracted national attention and brought him to the rock circuit. Kershaw was offered a cameo acting role in the "psychedelic western" movie *Zachariah,* and also appeared in *Medicine Ball Caravan* (a rock tour film), *We Have Come for Your Daughters,* and 1978's *Days of Heaven.* In 1999 he was performing 200 concerts a year and planning a chain of restaurants called Doug Kershaw's Cajun Kitchen. He released two new albums, one of which is in French, and was working on his autobiography.

Chaka Khan

Born Yvette Marie Stevens, Mar. 23, 1953, Great Lakes, IL
1978—*Chaka* (Warner Bros.) 1980—*Naughty* 1981—*What 'Cha Gonna Do for Me* 1982—*Echoes of an Era* (Elektra-Musician); *Chaka Khan* (Warner Bros.) 1984—*I Feel for You* 1986—*Destiny* 1988—*CK* 1989—*Life Is a Dance/The Remix Project* 1992—*The Woman I Am* 1996—*Epiphany: The Best of Chaka Khan* (Reprise) 1998—*Come 2 My House* (NPG).
With Rufus: 1973—*Rufus* (ABC) 1974—*Rags to Rufus; Rufusized* 1975—*Rufus Featuring Chaka Khan* 1977—*Ask Rufus* 1978—*Street Player* 1979—*Numbers; Masterjam* (MCA) 1981—*Party 'Til You're Broke; Camouflage* 1983—*Live—Stompin' at the Savoy* (Warner Bros.).

Chaka Khan, lead singer for Rufus and later a solo act, grew up on Chicago's South Side. At age 11 she formed her first band, the Crystalettes, who played the Chicago area. She was also very active at school and became president of the Black Students Union at age 16. At the time, she was also a member of the Afro-Arts Theater, which toured briefly with Mary Wells. A few years later, when Khan was working on the Black Panthers' breakfast program, she took her African name, Chaka, which means "fire."

In 1969 Khan quit school and worked with a band called Lyfe and then the Babysitters, doing endless sets of dance music. In 1972 she teamed up with Kevin Murphy (ex-American Breed) and Andre Fisher to form Rufus. The band went on to earn six gold or platinum LPs before Khan went solo in 1978. Her first album, *Chaka,* was produced by Arif Mardin and featured members of the Average White Band and Rufus guitarist Tony Maiden. It went gold and contained Ashford and Simpson's "I'm Every Woman" (#21, and a 1993 hit for Whitney Houston).

While under contract to do two more LPs with Rufus, with whom she traded barbs in the press, Khan continued to record solo LPs and tour with her own band. In 1979 she sang vocals on Ry Cooder's *Bop Till You Drop,* and in 1982 she recorded live with Rufus at New York's Savoy Theater. She also collaborated with Lenny White, Chick Corea, Freddie Hubbard, Joe Henderson, and Stanley Clarke on an album of jazz standards, *Echoes of an Era.*

Khan's pop career was revived by *I Feel for You* (#14, 1984), which went platinum and yielded a #3 pop hit in the title track, an obscure song written by Prince, from his second album. Khan's version was produced by Quincy Jones, who mixed in rapping by Melle Mel of Grandmaster Flash and the Furious Five, hip-hop turntable scratching, and harmonica flourishes by Stevie Wonder. The track won Khan a Grammy for Best Female R&B Vocal Performance. While she continued to score R&B hits, Khan's subsequent efforts fared disappointingly on the pop charts: *Destiny* reached #67, and *CK* only #125. After that album, Khan moved to Europe, splitting time between homes in England and West Germany. She sang backing vocals on Steve Winwood's hit "Higher Love." In 1990 she won a Grammy for her duet with Ray Charles, "I'll Be Good to You." In 1996 she released a best-of compilation, *Epiphany* (#84 pop, #22 R&B). That year "Missing You," from the soundtrack to the film *Set It Off,* found Khan collaborating with R&B divas Brandy, Tamia, and Gladys Knight for a #25 pop and a #10 R&B single. Allied with Prince's NPG label, Khan returned in 1998, but *Come 2 My House* peaked only at #49 on the R&B chart.

Khan's sister Taka Boom is also a singer, with a recording career of her own; Khan's daughter Milini was a member of the group Pretty in Pink.

Kid Creole and the Coconuts/ Dr. Buzzard's Original Savannah Band

Dr. Buzzard's Original Savannah Band, formed 1974, New York, NY
August Darnell (b. Thomas August Darnell Browder, Aug. 12, 1950, Bronx, NY), voc., bass, gtr.; "Sugar-Coated" Andy Hernandez (a.k.a Coati Mundi, b. Jan. 3, 1953, New York), vibraphone, voc.; Stony Browder Jr. (b. 1949, Bronx), gtr., kybds; Cory Daye (b. Apr. 25, 1952, Bronx), voc.; Mickey Sevilla (b. 1953, P.R.), drums.
1976—*Dr. Buzzard's Original Savannah Band* (RCA) 1978—*Dr. Buzzard's Original Savannah Band Meets King Penett* 1980—*James Monroe H.S. Presents Dr. Buzzard's Original Savannah Band Goes to Washington* (Elektra).
Kid Creole and the Coconuts, formed 1980, New York, NY: Original lineup: Darnell; Hernandez; Fonda Rae, voc.; Lourdes Cotto, voc.; Brooksie Wells, voc.; Franz Krauns, gtr.; Andrew Lloyd, perc.; Winston Grennan, drums; Peter Schott, kybds.
1980—*Off the Coast of Me* (Ze/Antilles) 1981—*Fresh Fruit in Foreign Places* (Sire) 1982—*Wise Guy* 1983—*Doppelganger* 1985—*In Praise of Older Women and Other Crimes* 1987—*I, Too, Have Seen the Woods* 1990—(+ Daye, voc.) *Private Waters in the Great Divide* (Columbia) 1991—*You Shoulda Told Me You Were . . .* 1992—*Kid Creole Redux* (Sire) 1995—*To Travel Sideways* (Hot Productions); *Kiss Me Before the Light Changes* 1999—*The Conquest of You* (SPV, Ger.).

August Darnell built an entire career on an ahead-of-its-time mixture of different sounds he called "mulatto music," a combination of Latin, Caribbean, and disco rhythms with big band, swing, and pop show tunes.

The son of a Dominican father and French-Canadian mother, Darnell grew up in the Bronx, where in 1965 he formed the rock band the In-Laws with his brother, Stony Browder Jr. By 1976, they had formed Dr. Buzzard's Original Savannah Band, enlisting Browder's girlfriend, Cory Daye, as vocalist. That year "Cherchez la Femme" became a hit in New York discos and eventually reached #31 R&B and #27 pop. Later albums had trouble finding success on increasingly segmented radio playlists; by 1980 the Savannah Band had all but collapsed.

Darnell had originally envisioned Kid Creole and the Coconuts as a side project while Browder put together a new Savannah Band. He had produced albums for Machine and James Chance, and signed a deal with Ze Records in 1980. Taking Hernandez along as co-composer and arranger, Darnell saw Kid Creole as representative of modern America, embodying all races and cultures. He also insisted that the band was small enough to tour, something the string- and horn-laden Savannah band could not do. Onstage, band members assumed fictitious identities, sported costumes, and were part of a choreographed and elaborately produced show.

Kid Creole and the Coconuts' debut album, *Off the Coast of Me,* and its followup, *Fresh Fruit in Foreign Places* (#180, 1981), told the story of Mimi, a tale conceived along the lines of a Latin/Caribbean *Odyssey,* with the music reflecting each stop of Mimi's travels. With former Savannah Band member Gichy Dan providing rapping narratives, the band performed the albums' material at New York's Public Theater.

Signs of fracture surfaced with *Wise Guy* (#145, 1982; a.k.a *Tropical Gangsters* in Europe). Originally conceived as a Darnell solo project, it became a Kid Creole album at the request of Warner Bros. executives. The album gave the band its only U.S. chart single, "I'm a Wonderful Thing, Baby" (#44 R&B, 1982). Kid Creole albums became Darnell albums in all but name, with the band a loose amalgamation of musicians and singers.

More popular in England, where they had three Top 10 hits in 1982 ("I'm a Wonderful Thing, Baby" [#4], "Stool Pigeon" [#7], "Annie, I'm Not Your Daddy" [#2]), Darnell and his crew began to tour Europe extensively, appearing at the Montreux Jazz Festival and performing for the United Nations in Geneva. In the States, they were seen in the 1984 movie *Against All Odds* and provided the music for the Francis Ford Coppola segment of *New York Stories* (1989). Darnell also wrote the score for Eric Overmyer's off-Broadway musical *In a Pig's Valise* in 1987.

Darnell recorded three more Kid Creole albums for Sire before he moved the band to Columbia Records in 1990. Their Columbia debut, *Private Waters in the Great Divide,* featured "The Sex of It," a song written and produced by Prince.

Most of Kid Creole's activity (such as it was) in the '90s took place in Europe and especially Japan, where the band remained popular. From 1997 through 1999, Darnell starred in the retro musical *Oh! What a Night* in various locations around England, concluding with a London run in fall 1999; he has also begun to sing in Las Vegas. Meanwhile, Coati Mundi regularly appears in New York with his Rhumbaphonic Orchestra.

Kid Frost

Born Arturo Molina Jr., May 31, 1962, Los Angeles, CA
1990—*Hispanic Causing Panic* (Virgin) 1992—*East Side Story.*

Kid Frost uses hip-hop to raise Chicano consciousness, rapping in Spanish and English about life in East L.A. The son of a musically minded career military man, Frost was raised on bases in Guam and Germany. Exposed to Latin music at home, he began playing guitar, keyboards, and drums. When his family returned to East L.A., he discovered the rough urban life he documents in his songs.

Frost made a critical splash with his debut, *Hispanic Causing Panic* (#67 pop, #45 R&B, 1990), whose anthemic single "La Raza" (#42, 1990) heralded a new era of Latin rap. On the track "Come Together," Frost rapped about the importance of uniting rather than fighting. He practiced what he preached by founding Latin Alliance, a coalition of Hispanic rappers, in 1989. The 1991 Virgin album *Latin Alliance* featured Frost and Cuban-born Mellow Man Ace rapping with War on "Low Rider."

East Side Story (#73 pop, #54 R&B, 1992) paints blunt pictures of urban life. The single "No Sunshine," an update of the classic Bill Withers tune, was featured as the chilling backdrop to *American Me,* Edward James Olmos' film about prison life. The album includes cameos by Main Source and Boo-Yaa T.R.I.B.E. Frost follows up his messages by playing benefits for Rock the Vote and supporting antigang activities. In 1992 he rapped on "City of Fallen Angels," a record raising funds for relief efforts after the L.A. riots. He also appeared on a 1997 single by Domino. Excluding a few live appearances, he has remained fairly quiet through early 2001.

Kid 'n Play

Formed ca. 1988, E. Elmhurst, Queens, NY
Kid (b. Christopher Reid, Apr. 5, 1964, Bronx, NY), voc.; Play (b. Christopher Martin, July 10, 1962, Queens), voc.
1988—*2 Hype* (Select) 1990—*Kid 'n Play's Funhouse*
1991—*Face the Nation.*

Kid 'n Play, best known for their rap and dance performances in the *House Party* movies of the early '90s, represented hip-hop's wholesome, middle-class, television-friendly image in much the same way as D.J. Jazzy Jeff and the Fresh Prince. With his freckles and seven-inch-high vertical hairstyle, Kid, the son of a black social worker father and white teacher mother, was at one time one of the most recognizable faces in rap. His sidekick Play, child of an ex-con-turned-minister father and church secretary mother, sported a cleaner-cut look with his neatly trimmed mustache and wacky, self-designed clothes.

Formed in the same Queens neighborhood that spawned turntable king Eric B., of Eric B. and Rakim, as well as rap producer Hurby "Luv Bug" Azor, the duo initially called themselves Fresh Force. Azor, the producer of hitmakers Salt-n-Pepa, became their manager and signed them to his own Select label. Kid 'n Play's early singles provided an upbeat alternative to New York's harder-edged hip-hop. Their first hit, "Rollin' With Kid 'n Play" (#11 R&B, 1989), was fun and catchy. The duo followed up with several moderate hits including "2 Hype" (#46 R&B, 1989), "Fun House (The House We Dance In)" (#27 R&B, 1990), and "Ain't Gonna Hurt Nobody" (#51 pop, #26 R&B, 1991).

After *2 Hype,* with its expanded palette of go go and house styles, sold nearly a million copies, hitting the Top 10 on the R&B albums chart, the success threatened Kid 'n Play's street credibility; they were accused in some circles of selling out. The group's complete crossover into the pop mainstream came in 1990 when they appeared in Reginald and Warrington Hudlin's surprise hit movie *House Party,* with a performance that drew comparisons to Abbott and Costello. By 1994, Kid 'n Play had returned to the silver screen three times, in *House Party 2* (1991), *Class Act* (1992), and *House Party 3* (1994), and starred in their own Saturday morning cartoon series, *Kid 'n Play.*

The partnership soon dissolved, and by 1996, Martin (a.k.a. Play) had squandered his hip-hop fortune, divorced actress Shari Headly *(Coming to America),* and contemplated suicide. But he recovered from his depression to write, direct, and perform a play loosely based on those experiences, *Radio Live: The House Party With a Purpose.* While Martin has expressed hope in reuniting with his former partner, both worked mainly as actors in subsequent years: Reid (a.k.a. Kid) in a 1999 TV movie, *Border Line;* that same year, Martin appeared in a stage play, *Rapp's City,* codirected by Cheryl "Salt" James of Salt-n-Pepa.

Kid Rock

Born Robert James Ritchie, Jan. 15, 1971, Romeo, MI
1990—*Grits Sandwiches for Breakfast* (Jive) 1993—*The Polyfuze Method* (Continuum) 1994—*Fire It Up* EP (Top Dog/Continuum) 1996—*Early Mornin' Stoned Pimp* (Top Dog)
1998—*Devil Without a Cause* (Top Dog/Lava/Atlantic)
2000—*The History of Rock.*

After spending a decade toiling in obscurity and releasing a handful of albums that went nowhere, Kid Rock—Detroit's self-proclaimed "American Bad Ass"—spiked the title track of his fourth album, 1998's *Devil Without a Cause,* with a bold declaration: "I'm going platinum!" With the white trash rap/rock anthem "Bawitdaba" and a star-making performance at Woodstock '99, he delivered on his promise. By the end of 2000, *Devil Without a Cause* was closing in on U.S. sales of 6 million.

Kid Rock was born Robert James Ritchie in Romeo, Michigan, a small, rural town north of the Detroit metro area, where his father owned a Lincoln-Mercury dealership. While growing up, Ritchie frequently clashed with his father, whom he blamed for being a workaholic, resulting in Ritchie's leaving home on multiple occasions as a teenager. He experimented with drugs and occasionally sold crack for spending money, but his primary focus was music. Though raised on his parent's classic rock & roll albums (Creedence Clearwater Revival, Bob Seger, etc.), Ritchie was just as taken with rap and hip-hop. He formed his own break-dance crew, the Furious Funkers, and refined his scratching skills. Before long, he was DJ'ing and rapping at clubs and parties throughout the Detroit area, slowly building a reputation that led to a deal with Jive Records.

His 1990 debut, *Grits Sandwiches for Breakfast,* netted Kid Rock an opening spot on an Ice Cube tour and sparked controversy when the FCC threatened to fine a college radio station $23,750 for playing the album's homage to oral sex, "Yo-Da-Lin in the Valley." The fine was eventually dropped, and so was Kid Rock; *Grits Sandwiches* failed to sell enough to hold Jive's interest. He then signed to the indie label Continuum, which released 1993's *The Polyfuze Method* and the 1994 heavy metal–leaning EP, *Fire It Up.* Both failed to reach an audience beyond his local Detroit following. Undaunted, Kid Rock borrowed $8,500 from his father to set up his own label, Top Dog, and self-release his third full-album, *Early Mornin' Stoned Pimp,* in 1996. The album sold enough for Kid Rock to attract the attention of Atlantic Records.

Devil Without a Cause (#4, 1999) was slow out of the gate but began a steady climb up the *Billboard* Top 200 as rock radio and MTV picked up on the album's hybrid rap/metal singles "I Am the Bullgod" (#31 Mainstream Rock) and "Bawitdaba" (#10 Modern Rock). A third single, "Cowboy" (which threw dirty Southern rock and country elements into the mix), went to #5 on the Modern Rock chart and #82 on the Hot 100. In 1999—10 years after his debut album—Kid Rock was nominated for a Best New Artist Grammy (he lost to Christina Aguilera).

The History of Rock (#2, 2000) featured remixed and rerecorded versions of tracks culled from his pre-Atlantic career and a couple of new tracks. He also announced plans to issue various projects by members of his Twisted Brown Trucker Band on his Atlantic-distributed Top Dog label, beginning with *Double Wide* (2000) by his DJ, Uncle Kracker. An album was also planned for his sidekick, Joe C. (born Joseph Calleja), but the diminutive 26-year-old rapper—who suffered from the digestive disorder celiac disease—died in his sleep on November 16, 2000.

Johnny Kidd and the Pirates

Formed 1959, England
Best known and longest-lived lineup: Johnny Kidd (b. Frederick Heath, Dec. 23, 1939, London, Eng.; d. Oct. 7, 1966, Eng.), voc.; Mick Green, gtr.; Johnny Spence, bass; Frank Farley, drums.
1978—*Best of Johnny Kidd and the Pirates* (EMI); *Out of Their Skulls* (Warner Bros.) 1979—*Skull Wars.*

Singer Johnny Kidd is best remembered as coauthor of the rock classic "Shakin' All Over," a tune covered by many bands, including the Guess Who and the Who. Although Kidd and the Pirates never gained a commercial foothold in the U.S., in his homeland Kidd is revered, and his band, the Pirates, is recognized as one of the first hard-rocking bands England produced before 1962, and a prototype for the heavy-metal guitar trios it predated by nearly a decade.

Kidd and the Pirates were primarily a singles and live concert act. Onstage, Kidd wore black leather and an eyepatch. Their first hit was Kidd's 1959 "Please Don't Touch," which hit #25 in the U.K. A year later "Shakin' All Over," epitomizing Kidd's intense, Gene Vincent–inspired hard-rockabilly approach, was a #1 hit. "You Got What It Takes" (#25) and "Restless" (#22) were other 1960 successes, but the band didn't hit again until 1963's "I'll Never Get Over You," which went to #4. "Hungry for Love," which got as high as #20 that year, was the band's last commercial gasp, as the Merseybeat explosion put it permanently out of the limelight.

In April 1966 Kidd, depressed over his declining fortunes, disbanded the group, only to return a month later with a new lineup that included Nick Simper (later of Deep Purple). That fall Kidd died in a car crash. In 1976 Mick Green (who'd played with Billy J. Kramer and the Dakotas, and the Cliff Bennett Band) re-formed the original Pirates with Spence and Farley. This revived lineup stayed together and recorded four U.K. albums before they broke up in 1982. By then Green was a well-established guitar hero.

Greg Kihn Band/Greg Kihn

Formed 1975, Berkeley, CA
Original lineup: Greg Kihn (b. 1952, Baltimore, MD), voc., gtr.; Robbie Dunbar, gtr.; Larry Lynch, drums, voc.; Steve Wright, bass, voc.
1976—*Greg Kihn* (Beserkley) (– Dunbar; + Dave Carpender, gtr.) 1977—*Greg Kihn Again* 1978—*Next of Kihn* 1979—*With the Naked Eye* 1980—*Glass House Rock* (+ Gary Phillips, kybds.) 1981—*Rockihnroll* 1982—*Kihntinued* (– Carpender; + Greg Douglass, gtr.) 1983—*Kihnspiracy* 1984—*Kihntagious* (EMI/Beserkley) 1985—*Citizen Kihn* (EMI) 1986—*Love and Rock and Roll* 1989—*Kihnsolidation: The Best of Greg Kihn* 1994—*Mutiny* (Clean Cuts/Rounder) 1996—*Horror Show* 2000—*All the Right Reasons* (U.K.).

Greg Kihn's band—a power-pop outfit influenced by the Yardbirds, the Beau Brummels, and Bruce Springsteen, among others—began as one of the four original acts on the Beserkley label of Berkeley, California. Kihn first came to Berkeley from Baltimore in late 1974 and wound up contributing two solo songs to the 1975 anthology *Beserkley Chartbusters, vol. 1.* He also sang backup vocals on Jonathan Richman's "Roadrunner."

At the time, Kihn used Earth Quake as his support band, and his first album, in 1976, featured guitarist Robbie Dunbar from the group (Dunbar's brother Tommy was in the Rubinoos, another Beserkley act), plus bassist Steve Wright and Lynch. Kihn added Dave Carpender to replace Dunbar in early 1976. The band's second album was harder rocking than the first and included a reworking of Springsteen's "For You"; Springsteen later adapted Kihn's arrangement for his own live shows.

The band's next few albums began to sell (about 125,000 copies each), and it built a following in the Bay Area. But Kihn never developed more than a cult following until *Rockihnroll's* "The Breakup Song (They Don't Write 'Em)" reached #15 in 1981. Keyboardist Gary Phillips, who joined in time for that album, had previously worked in Earth Quake and Copperhead, with ex-Quicksilver guitarist John Cipollina.

"Jeopardy" and its popular video brought Kihn to the Top 5 in 1983 and *Kihnspiracy* to #15. *Kihntagious* peaked at #121 the following year. His last hit was "Lucky" (#30) in 1985. While Kihn has not repeated that chart success, he has continued to release a number of albums under his own name. He writes and edits a fan newsletter called *Rocklife* and has written a number of novels, including *The Real Reason English Rock Stars Love America,* which he plans to serialize on the Internet. The critically acclaimed *Mutiny* featured Kihn in an acoustic setting performing songs by Elliott Murphy, the Temptations, and Bob Dylan, among others. *Horror Show* coincided with the 1996 publication of Kihn's gore novel of the same name. He has also worked as a morning radio personality in San Jose.

Killing Joke

Formed 1978, London, Eng.
Jaz Coleman (b. Feb. 26, 1960, Cheltenham, Eng.), voc., kybds.; Geordie (b. K. Walker, Dec. 18, 1958, Newcastle-upon-Tyne, Eng.), gtr.; Youth (b. Martin Glover, Dec. 27, 1960, Africa), bass; Paul Ferguson (b. Mar. 31, 1958, High Wycombe, Eng.), drums.
1980—*Killing Joke* (EG) 1981—*What's This For . . . !* 1982—*Revelations; Ha! Killing Joke Live* EP (– Geordie; – Youth; + Paul Raven, bass) 1983—*Fire Dances* 1985—*Night Time* 1987—*Brighter Than a Thousand Suns* 1988—*Outside the Gate* (– Ferguson; + Geordie, gtr.; + Martin Atkins [b. Aug. 3, 1959, Coventry, Eng.], drums) 1990—*Extremities, Dirt, & Various Repressed Emotions* (Noise/RCA) 1994—(– Atkins; + Youth) *Pandemonium* (Big Life/Zoo) 1996—*Democracy.*

Known for its loud, energetic stage performances—with frontman Jaz Coleman wearing warpaint and shaking maniacally—England's Killing Joke initially tried to bridge the seemingly disparate styles of punk rock and disco with a big dance beat and noisy, abrasive guitars. In this regard the band was similar to Public Image Ltd., and in fact in its late-'80s incarnation Killing Joke included ex-PiL drummer Martin Atkins. The band was also known for sometimes savage lyrics and often sardonic and controversial record-sleeve art and posters. Killing Joke was banned from performing a Glasgow, Scotland, gig after a 1980 concert poster depicted Pope Pius XII appearing to bless two columns of Nazi brownshirts.

Jaz Coleman, reportedly of Egyptian descent, first began working with ex–Matt Stagger Band drummer Paul Ferguson; Youth, who had played with the Rage at the seminal London punk club the Vortex, and guitarist Geordie soon joined. Their first single, "Wardance," found careening punkish energy and stomping metallic mass colliding over a martial rhythm. Legendary British radio DJ John Peel, who was so impressed by "Wardance" he said it had to be someone famous recording under an assumed name, gave it intense play. The walloping tribal rhythms of such early Killing Joke singles as "Psyche" and "Follow the Leader" landed the group on *Billboard*'s disco chart.

Coleman's occult obsessions led the band to disintegrate after its third album; he fled to Iceland in anticipation of the apocalypse. Youth followed, then returned to England to work with Ferguson on a new band called Brilliant. But then Ferguson went to Iceland too, taking new bassist Paul Raven with him. The revamped Killing Joke returned to England and recorded more conventional albums, lacking the ominous power of its earlier work. Geordie rejoined for the *Extremities* album, a return to noisy avant-dance form. After a four-year hiatus, Killing Joke came back as a three-piece—Coleman, Geordie, and original bassist Youth—releasing the harshly metallic album *Pandemonium.* In fall 1994 the trio embarked on a world tour. Coleman also devoted his energies to classical music, becoming a composer-in-residence for the New Zealand Symphony Orchestra, while Youth found a parallel career remixing dance tracks. The band released *Democracy* in 1996, which took an expectedly bitter view of politics.

Albert King

Born Albert Nelson, Apr. 25, 1923, Indianola, MS; died Dec. 21, 1992, Memphis, TN
1962—*The Big Blues* (King) 1967—*Born Under a Bad Sign* (Stax) 1968—*King of the Blues Guitar* (Atlantic) 1972—*I'll Play the Blues for You* (Stax) 1975—*Truckload of Lovin'* (Utopia) 1977—*The Pinch* (Stax) 1979—*Chronicle; New Orleans Heat* (Tomato) 1982—*Albert King Masterworks* (Atlantic/Deluxe) 1986—*The Best of Albert King* (Stax/Fantasy) 1989—*Let's Have a Natural Ball* (Modern Blues) 1990—*Wednesday Night in San Francisco (Live at the Fillmore)* (Stax/Fantasy); *Thursday Night in San Francisco (Live at the Fillmore)* 1999—*The King* (Charly).

Albert King's mammoth physical presence—he weighed more than 250 pounds and stood 6-foot-4—was reflected in his harsh, imposing vocals and biting, influential blues style.

He bought his first guitar for $1.25 sometime around 1931

(he later played a left-handed Gibson Flying V), and his first inspiration was T-Bone Walker. For a long while he had to work nonmusic jobs to survive (including bulldozer operator and mechanic), but in the late '40s King settled in Osceola, Arkansas, and worked local gigs with the In the Groove Boys. He then migrated north, where he played drums for Jimmy Reed and also sang and played guitar on his own singles, including "Lonesome in My Bedroom" and "Bad Luck Blues" for the Parrot label in 1953.

King then moved to St. Louis and formed another band, but he didn't record again until 1959, when he signed to the local Bobbin label. He worked for several small companies in the early '60s, including King Records, which released his 1961 hit "Don't Throw Your Love on Me Too Strong" (#14 R&B). But King's real break came in 1966, when he signed to Stax. Using the label's famed Memphis sidemen, he cut some of his best-known works, including "Laundromat Blues" (1966) and his album *Born Under a Bad Sign,* made with Booker T. and the MG's in 1967. King began to break through to white audiences: He appeared at the first Fillmore East show on March 8, 1968, with Tim Buckley and Big Brother and the Holding Company, and also played at the hall's closing on June 27, 1971. (A live album, *Live Wire/Blues Power,* had been recorded at Fillmore West.)

In November 1969 King played with the St. Louis Symphony Orchestra, forming what was termed "an 87-piece blues band." Over the years his songs have been covered by Free, John Mayall, the Electric Flag, and others. He toured more than ever in the '70s, though he left Stax in 1974. King signed to Utopia in 1976 and to Tomato in 1978, charting some minor R&B singles. In 1990 he made a guest appearance on guitarist Gary Moore's *Still Got the Blues,* and he continued to perform until his death from a heart attack at age 69. At King's funeral, Joe Walsh—just one of many six-string disciples—paid tribute with a slide-guitar rendition of "Amazing Grace."

B.B. King

Born Riley B. King, Sep. 16, 1925, Itta Bena, MS
1965—*Live at the Regal* (ABC) 1968—*B.B. King Story* (Blue Horizon) 1969—*B.B. King Story, vol. 2; Live and Well* (Bluesway); *Completely Well* 1970—*Indianola Mississippi Seeds* (ABC) 1971—*Live in Cook County Jail; Live at the Regal* 1973—*The Best of B.B. King* 1974—*Together for the First Time . . . Live* (with Bobby "Blue" Bland) (MCA) 1975—*Lucille Talks Back* (ABC) 1976—*B.B. King Anthology; Together Again . . . Live* (with Bobby "Blue" Bland) (MCA) 1977—*Kingsize* (ABC); *Lucille* 1978—*Midnight Believer* 1979—*Take It Home* 1981—*There Must Be a Better World Somewhere* (MCA) 1983—*Blues 'n' Jazz* 1985—*Six Silver Strings* 1986—*The Best of B.B. King, vol. 1* (MCA) 1988—*Do the Boogie! B.B. King's Early 50s Classics* (Virgin) 1989—*King of the Blues* (MCA) 1990—*Live at San Quentin* 1991—*There Is Always One More Time; Live at the Apollo* (GRP) 1993—*Blues Summit* (MCA); *My Sweet Little Angel* (Virgin) 1995—*Heart & Soul* 1996—*How Blue Can You Get?: Classic Live Performances 1964 to 1994* (MCA) 1997—*Deuces Wild* 1999—*Let the Good Times Roll: The Music of Louis Jordan; Blues on the Bayou* 2000—*Riding With the King* (with Eric Clapton) (Reprise).

B.B. King is universally recognized as the leading exponent of modern blues. Playing his trademark Gibson guitar, which he refers to affectionately as Lucille, King's voice-like string bends and left-hand vibrato have influenced numerous rock guitarists, including Eric Clapton, Mike Bloomfield, and David Gilmour of Pink Floyd, as well as modern blues players such as Buddy Guy. An eight-time Grammy winner, King has received virtually every music award, including the Grammy for Lifetime Achievement in 1987.

King picked cotton as a youth. In the '40s he played on the streets of Indianola before moving on to perform professionally in Memphis around 1949. As a young musician, he studied recordings by both blues and jazz guitarists, including T-Bone Walker, Charlie Christian, and Django Reinhardt.

In the early '50s King was a disc jockey on the Memphis black station WDIA, where he was dubbed the "Beale Street Blues Boy." Eventually, Blues Boy was shortened to B.B., and the nickname stuck. The radio show and performances in Memphis with friends Johnny Ace and Bobby "Blue" Bland built King's strong local reputation. One of his first recordings, "Three O'Clock Blues" (#1 R&B), for the RPM label, was a national success in 1951. During the '50s, King was a consistent record seller and concert attraction.

King's *Live at the Regal* is considered one of the definitive blues albums. The mid-'60s blues revival introduced him to white audiences, and by 1966 he was appearing regularly on rock concert circuits and receiving airplay on progressive

B.B. King

rock radio. He continued to have hits on the soul chart ("Paying the Cost to Be the Boss," #10 R&B, 1968) and always maintained a solid black following. *Live and Well* was a notable album, featuring "Why I Sing the Blues" (#13 R&B, 1969) and King's only pop Top 20 single, "The Thrill Is Gone" (#15 pop, #3 R&B, 1970).

In the '70s King also recorded albums with longtime friend and onetime chauffeur Bobby Bland: the gold *Together for the First Time . . . Live* (1974) and *Together Again . . . Live* (1976). Stevie Wonder produced King's "To Know You Is to Love You." In 1982 King recorded a live album with the Crusaders.

King's tours have taken him to Russia (1979), South America (1980), and to dozens of prisons. In 1981 *There Must Be a Better World Somewhere* won a Grammy Award; he won another in 1990 for *Live at San Quentin.* He was inducted into the Blues Foundation Hall of Fame in 1984, and the Rock and Roll Hall of Fame in 1987. In 1990 he received the Songwriters Hall of Fame Lifetime Achievement Award. In May 1991, he opened B.B. King's Blues Club in Memphis. A second one opened in New York City in 2000.

In 1989 he sang and played with U2 on "When Love Comes to Town," from their *Rattle and Hum.* The four-disc box set released that same year, *King of the Blues,* begins with King's career-starting single "Miss Martha King," originally released on Bullet in 1949. For *Blues Summit,* King was joined by such fellow bluesmen as John Lee Hooker, Lowell Fulson, and Robert Cray.

King once said he aspired to be an "ambassador of the blues," and by the '90s he seemed to have attained just that iconic status. In 1995 he received the Kennedy Center Honors. The next year saw the publicatioin of his award-winning autobiography, *Blues' All Around Me* (coauthored with David Ritz). In 2000 the double-platinum *Riding With the King* (with Eric Clapton) topped *Billboard's* Top Blues Albums chart, which it has remained on for more than a year as of this writing.

Ben E. King

Born Benjamin Earl Nelson, Sep. 28, 1938, Henderson, NC
1961—*Spanish Harlem* (Atco) 1964—*Ben E. King's Greatest Hits* (Atlantic) 1975—*Supernatural Thing; Ben E. King Story* 1976—*I Had a Love* 1977—*Benny and Us* (with the Average White Band) (Atco) 1978—*Let Me Live in Your Life* (Atlantic) 1981—*Street Tough* 1987—*The Ultimate Collection: Ben E. King* 1993—*Anthology* (Atlantic/Atco) 1999—*Shades of Blue* (Half Note).

Ben E. King's smooth tenor earned him a reputation as a romantic R&B singer for a career that has spanned more than 30 years. He hit a commercial peak as lead vocalist for the late-period Drifters and as a solo artist in the early '60s.

King sang in church choirs in North Carolina, and when his family moved to Harlem he formed his first group while attending James Fenimore Cooper Junior High. It was called the Four B's, as all members' names started with B. In the mid-'50s King tried out unsuccessfully for the Moonglows, but by 1956 he had joined a professional band, the Five Crowns, whose manager supposedly found the 18-year-old King through a chance meeting. King toured with the band, which included Bobby Hendricks, who left to become lead singer for the Drifters in early 1958.

The Five Crowns made 11 records between 1952 and 1958, none of them hits, but in 1959 the Drifters' manager, George Treadwell (who owned the name but was deserted by the original band), thought the Crowns were good enough to become his "new Drifters." The new group immediately hit it big with "There Goes My Baby" (#2 pop, #1 R&B, 1959), sung and cowritten by King, and reputedly the first R&B hit to use strings. King sang lead on two other gold singles for the band (all produced by Jerry Leiber and Mike Stoller), including their biggest pop smash and only #1, "Save the Last Dance for Me" (1960). He also sang on the standard "This Magic Moment" (#16 pop, #4 R&B, 1960).

In mid-winter 1960 King went solo and had a #10 pop, #15 R&B hit in 1961 (supervised by Phil Spector) with "Spanish Harlem," a song Spector wrote with Jerry Leiber. King followed it with another Top 10 the same year, the stark self-penned "Stand by Me" (#4 pop, #10 R&B). In 1962 he hit with "Don't Play That Song" (#11 pop, #2 R&B). After that King fared better on the R&B chart than the pop chart, though his 1963 hit "I (Who Have Nothing)" (#29 pop, #16 R&B) became a top seller for Tom Jones in 1970. By the end of 1963, King's career had slowed; though he often played in Europe, he was largely out of the spotlight until 1975, when he re-signed with his old label, Atlantic, and had an immediate hit with "Supernatural Thing, Part 1" (#5). In 1977 he collaborated with longtime admirers the Average White Band on *Benny and Us* (with two R&B Top 30 hits, "Get It Up" and "A Star in the Ghetto"), while continuing with several solo hits, including 1980's "Music Trance" (#29 R&B).

King's career was revived in 1986 when "Stand by Me" became a Top 10 hit a second time after it was featured in the Rob Reiner film of the same name, costarring teenage actor River Phoenix. Another song of King's—a remake of the Monotones' "Book of Love," recorded with Bo Diddley and Doug Lazy—made it into a movie, 1991's *The Book of Love.* He continues to tour and record.

Carole King

Born Carole Klein, Feb. 9, 1942, Brooklyn, NY
1968—*Now That Everything's Been Said* (with the City) (Ode) 1970—*Carole King: Writer* 1971—*Tapestry; Music* 1972—*Rhymes and Reasons* 1973—*Fantasy* 1974—*Wrap Around Joy* 1975—*Really Rosie* 1976—*Thoroughbred* 1977—*Simple Things* (Capitol) 1978—*Welcome Home* (Avatar); *Her Greatest Hits* (Ode) 1979—*Touch the Sky* (Capitol) 1980—*Pearls: Songs of Goffin and King* 1982—*One to One* (Atlantic) 1983—*Speeding Time* 1989—*City Streets* (Capitol) 1993—*Colour of Your Dreams* (King's X/Rhythm Safari) 1994—*Carole*

King: In Concert; Time Gone By 1996—*The Carnegie Hall Concert: June 18, 1971* (Sony/Legacy).

Singer/songwriter Carole King has had two outstanding careers. Throughout the '60s she was one of pop's most prolific songwriters, writing the music to songs like the Shirelles' "Will You Love Me Tomorrow?" and the Drifters' "Up on the Roof," with most lyrics by her first husband, Gerry Goffin. Then in 1971 her multimillion-selling *Tapestry* helped popularize the '70s pop-rock singer/songwriter genre.

King began playing piano at age four; in high school she started her first band, the Co-sines. While attending Queens College in 1958 she met Gerry Goffin, and the two became cowriters. King had written some early singles like "Goin' Wild" and "Baby Sittin,' " but they went nowhere. Neil Sedaka had a hit dedicated to her in October 1959 called "Oh! Carol," but her reply song, "Oh! Neil," stiffed.

In 1961 she and Goffin cowrote "Will You Love Me Tomorrow?," a #1 hit for the Shirelles, and the song has been covered countless times since. The two young writers, like Sedaka, Cynthia Weil, and Barry Mann, wrote their songs for Don Kirshner and Al Nevins' Aldon Music in Brill Building cubicles. They wrote over 100 hits in a range of rock styles, including "Wasn't Born to Follow" (the Byrds), "Chains" (the Cookies), "Don't Bring Me Down" (the Animals), and "I'm Into Something Good" (Herman's Hermits). In 1962 the King-Goffin team wrote, arranged, conducted, and produced the song "The Loco-Motion" for their 17-year-old babysitter, Little Eva (Boyd) [see entry], and it went #1 that summer. That year King made a brief foray into solo recording, but her only hit single at the time was "It Might as Well Rain Until September" (#22).

In the mid-'60s Goffin, King, and columnist Al Aronowitz tried to launch their own label, Tomorrow Records. It failed, but one band they produced, the Myddle Class, included bass player Charles Larkey, who became King's second husband after she divorced Goffin and moved to L.A. with her two children, Sherry and Louise (who launched a recording career of her own at age 19 in 1979 with *Kid Blue*).

In 1968 King formed a group called the City, with Larkey and guitarist Danny Kortchmar, who had both previously played on three Fugs albums. They also knew each other from the New York club circuit, where the Myddle Class had played with Kortchmar's band the Flying Machine, which also included vocalist James Taylor. The City never toured because of King's stage fright, though they did make one unsuccessful LP on Ode Records, *Now That Everything's Been Said.* The LP later yielded hits for Blood, Sweat and Tears ("Hi-De-Ho") and James Taylor ("You've Got a Friend," which also appeared on King's *Tapestry*). Taylor encouraged King to write her own lyrics and finally record solo again, resulting in 1970's *Writer,* with a backup band that included Kortchmar and others (who later recorded two Atlantic albums under the name Jo Mama). King toured with Jo Mama and Taylor, and they all worked on the 1971 critical and commercial windfall, *Tapestry,* which had two hit singles ("It's Too Late," #1, 1971; "So Far Away," #14, 1971), won four Grammys, went #1, and stayed on the chart for nearly six years. It remains a solid catalogue performer and has now sold 22 million copies.

King's early-'70s LPs went gold and Top 10 (*Music* and *Wrap Around Joy* both hit #1), and in late 1974 she had a #2 hit with "Jazzman" from *Wrap Around Joy.* In 1975 King wrote the music for a children's program, *Really Rosie,* and began to write with Goffin again. She switched to Capitol Records in late 1976, and her first album for the new label, *Simple Things* (#17, 1977), went gold. She began touring with a band called Navarro, introduced to her by Dan Fogelberg, and married her collaborator at the time, Rick Evers, who died of a heroin overdose in 1978.

By then her albums were selling modestly, though she did better with her 1980 *Pearls* LP (#44), which featured King's versions of some of her best-known '60s collaborations with Goffin, such as "One Fine Day" (#12, 1980) and "Hey Girl." King hasn't had a Top 40 hit since, and she has considerably slowed down her recording and touring schedules. In 1989 Eric Clapton guested on the title single from *City Streets.* Her 1993 album *Colour of Your Dreams* was released on her own King's X label and included Guns n' Roses guitarist Slash on the track "Hold Out for Love." For *Carole King: In Concert,* the 1990 Rock and Roll Hall of Fame inductee was supported by an eight-piece band that included her daughter Sherry Goffin on background vocals. In 1994 she made her Broadway acting debut when she took over Petula Clark's role in *Bloodbrothers.*

Involved in environmental issues since the '80s, the songwriter was honored at the 1999 star-studded event Carole King: Making Music With Friends—A Concert for Our Children, Our Health, and Our Planet. The following year, she was a guest on fellow Brill Building songwriter Barry Mann's album *Soul & Inspiration.*

King's music remains an essential part of America's pop consciousness. In 1993 the off-Broadway revue *Tapestry: The Music of Carole King* evoked the songwriter's biggest hits. A tribute album, 1995's *Tapestry Revisited,* featured singers such as Celine Dion, Faith Hill, Rod Stewart, and Richard Marx performing songs from King's enduring 1971 record.

Earl King

Born Earl Silas Johnson, Feb. 7, 1934, New Orleans, LA
1978—*New Orleans Rock 'n' Roll* (Sonet); *Earl King* (Vivid) 1986—*Glazed* (with Roomful of Blues) (Black Top) 1990—*Sexual Telepathy* 1994—*Hard River to Cross* 1997—*New Orleans Street Talkin'* 2001—*King of New Orleans* (Uni/Fuel 2000).

Along with Robert Parker, Irma Thomas, and Lee Dorsey, Earl King is one of New Orleans' major R&B singers. King's father was a blues pianist who died when King was a child. Young Earl King started his career as a gospel singer around 1950 and learned to play guitar and sing the blues a few years later. He sang with pianist Huey "Piano" Smith until 1953, when he recorded his first solo work for Savoy under the name Earl Johnson. In 1954 King was signed by Art Rupe to Specialty Records and had a regional hit that year with "A Mother's Love."

His touring group was then called Earl King and the Kings (they also recorded separately for Specialty), but in 1955 King signed with Johnny Vincent's new Ace label. He immediately scored his biggest hit, "Those Lonely, Lonely Nights." It sold 250,000 copies without ever entering the national chart. The song, a two-chord slow ballad, was a major influence on all future Louisiana swamp rock, paving the way for people like Dr. John, who later covered King's "Let's Make a Better World" on *Destively Bonnaroo.* Later in 1955 "Don't Take It So Hard" went to #13 R&B.

King had some local hits in 1958, like "Well-O Well-O Well-O Baby." He worked for Rex Records in 1959 with then staff sessionman Mac Rebennack (later known as Dr. John). That year he also sold 80,000 copies of "Everybody Has to Cry Sometime" under the pseudonym Handsome Earl. His first release for Imperial in 1960 was the savage "Come On," later covered by Jimi Hendrix, and his biggest hit for the label was a #17 R&B hit in 1962, "Always a First Time." King's witty "Trick Bag" (an archetypal piece of New Orleans funk later covered by Robert Palmer) was later redone by the Meters in 1976 with King sitting in. In the mid-'60s he worked as a session musician for Motown, where he recorded several unreleased sides. He then returned to New Orleans, where he played with Professor Longhair, cutting one of the Professor's best-known songs, "Big Chief." King recorded for many obscure labels in the '60s while also continuing on the New Orleans scene as a songwriter (for the Dixie Cups, Lee Dorsey, the Meters, Fats Domino, and Professor Longhair, among others) and producer.

During the '70s and early '80s he performed almost every year at the New Orleans Jazz and Heritage Festival. In 1986 *Glazed* was nominated for the Best Contemporary Blues Album Grammy.

Evelyn "Champagne" King

Born June 29, 1960, Bronx, NY
1977—*Smooth Talk* (RCA) 1979—*Music Box* 1980—*Call on Me* 1981—*I'm in Love* 1982—*Get Loose* 1983—*Face to Face* 1985—*Long Time Coming* 1988—*Flirt* (EMI Manhattan) 1989—*Girl Next Door* (EMI America) 1993—*Love Come Down—The Best of Evelyn "Champagne" King* 1995—*I'll Keep a Light On* (Expansion, U.K.).

Pop-soul singer Evelyn "Champagne" King was 17 when she hit it big with the single "Shame" (#9 pop, #7 R&B), a sexy song that was part of disco's domination of the charts in 1978. The publicity fable goes that King, who grew up in Philadelphia, was working nights as a cleaning lady at Philadelphia International Studios when staff producer Theodore Life overheard her quietly crooning Sam Cooke's "A Change Is Gonna Come." He immediately offered to produce her, resulting in 1977's *Smooth Talk* (#14, 1978), which included "Shame" and "I Don't Know If It's Right" (#23 pop, #7 R&B). The album and both singles went gold, as did her next album, *Music Box.* In 1981 King had her first #1 R&B hit with "I'm in Love" (#40 pop), followed by a second R&B #1, "Love Come Down" (#17 pop). Her other R&B hit singles include "Betcha She Don't Love You" (#2 R&B, 1982), "Shake Down" (#12 R&B, 1984), "Your Personal Touch" (#9 R&B, 1985), "Flirt" (#3 R&B, 1988), "Kisses Don't Lie" (#17 R&B, 1988), and "Hold On to What You've Got" (#8 R&B, 1988). She continues to perform on the international disco revival and soul circuits.

Freddie King

Born Freddie Christian, Sep. 3, 1934, Gilmer, TX; died Dec. 28, 1976, Dallas, TX
1970—*My Feeling for the Blues* (Cotillion) 1971—*Gettin' Ready . . .* (Shelter) 1972—*Texas Cannonball* (A&M) 1973—*Woman Across the River* (Shelter) 1974—*Burglar* (RSO) 1975—*The Best of Freddie King* (Shelter); *Larger Than Life* (RSO) 1976—*Best of Freddie King* (Island) 1977—*Original Hits* (Starday/King); *(1934–1976)* (RSO) 1989—*Just Pickin'* (Modern Blues).

Freddie King, a pioneering modern blues guitarist, was a major influence on rock guitarists, especially in the British blues boom of the '60s. Growing up in Texas, King heard the recordings of Arthur Crudup, Big Bill Broonzy, Blind Lemon Jefferson, and Lightnin' Hopkins, but he later described his guitar style as a cross between Muddy Waters, T-Bone Walker, and B.B. King (no relation); a mixture of country and urban blues. When he was 16, his family moved to Chicago, where he would sneak into blues clubs to jam with Muddy Waters' band. He also played with Memphis Slim, LaVern Baker, Willie Dixon, and others before recording his first solo record in 1956.

In 1960 King joined the Federal label and had several big R&B hits, including "Hideaway" and "Have You Ever Loved a Woman?" (later covered on *Layla* by Eric Clapton, a longtime admirer). Federal released 77 songs by King, including 30 instrumentals, in the next six years. But by 1966 King was without a contract, living as a semi-obscure legend in Texas.

Meanwhile, his songs were being covered in England by bands like Chicken Shack and John Mayall, and he eventually took advantage of the blues revival, playing some shows in England. That led to a 1968 contract with Cotillion and two albums produced by King Curtis. He then signed to Leon Russell's Shelter label, released three albums, and did enough full-time concert-hall touring to earn him a more mainstream white rock audience—the largest following of his career. In 1974 King switched to RSO and cut *Burglar* in England with help from Eric Clapton; he followed it up with *Larger Than Life* in 1975. The next year, three days after a Christmas-night show in Dallas, King died of heart failure, a bloodclot, and internal bleeding from ulcers.

King Crimson

Formed 1969, England
Robert Fripp (b. May 16, 1946, Wimbourne, Eng.), gtr., Mellotron; Greg Lake (b. Nov. 10, 1948, Bournemouth, Eng.), bass, voc.; Ian McDonald (b. June 25, 1946, London, Eng.), kybds., sax, flute, voc.; Michael Giles (b. 1942, Bournemouth), drums; Pete Sinfield (b. Eng.), lyrics, light show.
1969—*In the Court of the Crimson King* (Atlantic) (– McDonald; – Giles; – Lake) 1970—*In the Wake of Poseidon* (+ Gordon Haskell [b. Eng.], voc., bass; + Andy McCulloch [b. Eng.], drums; + Mel Collins [b. Eng.], sax, flute, Mellotron) 1971—*Lizard* (– Haskell; – McCulloch; + Boz Burrell [b. Raymond Burrell, ca. 1946, Lincoln, Eng.], bass, voc.; + Ian Wallace [b. Sep. 29, 1946, Bury, Eng.], drums; – Sinfield) 1972—*Islands; Earthbound* (Editions U.K., U.K.) (– Burrell; – Wallace; – Collins; + Bill Bruford [b. May 17, 1949, London], drums; + Jamie Muir [b. Eng.], perc.; + John Wetton [b. July 12, 1949, Derby, Eng.], bass, voc.; + David Cross [b. 1948, Plymouth, Eng.], violin, kybds.; Robert Palmer-Jones [b. Eng.], lyrics) 1973—*Larks' Tongues in Aspic* (Atlantic) (– Muir) 1974—*Starless and Bible Black; Red* (– Cross; group disbands) 1975—*USA* 1981—(group re-forms: Fripp; Bruford; + Adrian Belew [b. Robert Steven Belew, Dec. 23, 1949, Covington, KY], gtr., voc.; + Tony Levin [b. Anthony Levin, June 6, 1946, Boston, MA], bass, Chapman Stick) *Discipline* (Warner Bros.) 1982—*Beat* 1984—*Three of a Perfect Pair* 1991—*Frame by Frame* (EG/Caroline); *The Essential King Crimson* (Caroline) 1992—*The Great Deceiver: Live 1973–74* 1993—*The Concise King Crimson* (Caroline); *The Abbreviated King Crimson* 1994—(+ Pat Mastelotto, drums; + Trey Gunn, gtr., Chapman Stick) *VROOOM* EP (Discipline) 1995—*Thrak* (Virgin); *B'Boom* (Discipline) 1996—*THRaKaTTaK; Schizoid Man* EP (Alex) 1997—*Epitaph* (Discipline) 1998—*The Night Watch; Absent Lovers: Live in Montreal 1984* 1999—*Cirkus* (Caroline); *The Deception of the Thrush* (Discipline); *The ProjeKcts* (– Bruford; – Levin) 2000—*The ConstruKCtion of Light* (Virgin).

The eerie, portentous sound of early King Crimson set the tone for British art rock. But by the time the group's Mellotron-heavy sound and psychedelic lyrics had turned into lucrative clichés, leader Robert Fripp had long since shifted the group's style toward music that was far more eccentric, complex, and dissonant.

The original Crimson's roots went back to 1967, when the Bournemouth trio Giles, Giles and Fripp began making whimsical pop, which resulted in one British-only album in 1968 called *The Cheerful Insanity of Giles, Giles and Fripp.* (For a short time Judy Dyble, early Fairport Convention vocalist, also sang with them.) The band broke up in November 1968, and while bassist Peter Giles went on to become a solicitor's clerk, Fripp and drummer Mike Giles formed Crimson with ex-Gods bassist Greg Lake and their old associate Ian McDonald, who introduced them to lyricist Pete Sinfield. Sinfield also worked the band's psychedelic light show.

Crimson made its debut at the London Speakeasy on April 9, 1969, and on July 5 the group played to 650,000 people at the Rolling Stones' free Hyde Park concert. In October *In the Court of the Crimson King,* with music by McDonald and Fripp, was released, and endorsed by Pete Townshend as "an uncanny masterpiece." But the group soon began an endless series of personnel changes, with only Fripp remaining through it all. On the band's debut U.S. tour, Giles and McDonald left, the latter in a band-control squabble. The two recorded a Crimson sound-alike album, *McDonald and Giles,* in 1970. During the sessions for Crimson's second album, Greg Lake also left, to form Emerson, Lake and Palmer. He'd met Emerson, then with the Nice, during Crimson's disastrous U.S. tour. Crimson might have ended there if Fripp had accepted offers to replace Pete Banks in Yes or to join Aynsley Dunbar in Blue Whale. Instead he brought in Gordon Haskell to complete the vocals on the second album (Elton John had also tried out), got old friend Pete Giles for a brief stint on bass, persuaded brother Mike to do "guest drumming," and pulled in some other friends, including future member Mel Collins, to finish it up. Fripp's guitar style was already distinctive; he used classical-guitar technique to create angular, sustained, screaming phrases on his Gibson, and he usually performed seated.

In late 1970 Fripp formed a new Crimson with Collins, Haskell, Sinfield, and drummer Andrew McCulloch (later of Greenslade). Jon Anderson of Yes did a guest vocal on the resulting *Lizard.* Two days after the album was finished, the band fell apart. One vocalist who tried out for the next Crimson was Roxy Music's Bryan Ferry, but Fripp opted for singer Boz Burrell, whom he taught to play bass. The band, rounded out by Collins and drummer Ian Wallace, recorded the subdued *Islands* in 1971 and, like the first group, fell apart on its U.S. tour. (Burrell later joined Bad Company.) Even the longstanding Pete Sinfield left this time; he recorded a solo LP and produced the debut Roxy Music album. The *Islands*-period band did manage to release a poorly recorded live document of its U.S. tour, *Earthbound,* released in the U.K. only.

Fripp emerged in 1972 with his most forward-looking and brashest Crimson, including Bill Bruford (who left the far more successful Yes to join), John Wetton (of Family), new lyricist Robert Palmer-Jones, David Cross, and Jamie Muir (who left for a Buddhist monastery after *Larks' Tongues in Aspic*). This lineup specialized in brainy, Gothic metal and jagged, dissonant free improvisation, and drew critical comparisons to Captain Beefheart's Magic Band and, thanks to Cross' electric violin, the Mahavishnu Orchestra. Cross also left after the followup, *Starless and Bible Black,* but he did play with the band until its last tour, culminating in a final show in New York's Central Park on July 1, 1974. A live LP from that date and *Red,* recorded with Cross as a "guest" member in late summer 1974, were both released after the disbanding. Ian MacDonald was about to rejoin the band and did play on *Red* (he joined Foreigner in 1976).

But as artistically successful as *Red* was, Fripp came to hate the entire art-rock movement (which was at its commercial peak), along with the mechanics of the music business itself (which he termed "vampiric"), and so he officially ended the band on September 28. On October 18, 1974, Fripp stated, "King Crimson is completely over. For ever and ever."

Fripp decided to work as a "small, mobile, intelligent, self-sufficient unit," in contrast to the overgrown "dinosaur" bands he'd come to loathe. Using the echo-delay tape system devised by Brian Eno for 1973's *No Pussyfooting*, which he dubbed "Frippertronics," Fripp played solo concerts, slowly building minimalist chords with the notes on tape. He produced and played on Daryl Hall's first solo album, *Sacred Songs*, and two albums by the Roches, and added guitar lines to albums by Eno, David Bowie, Peter Gabriel, Talking Heads, and Blondie. In 1980 he returned to group performing with the short-lived League of Gentlemen (the name of one of Fripp's earliest amateur bands), which also featured former XTC keyboardist Barry Andrews, and which added a danceable rock beat to Fripp's intricate, repeating guitar lines; League bassist Sara Lee went on to join Gang of Four.

In 1981 Fripp revived King Crimson as a quartet that he had been planning to call Discipline, including session bassist Tony Levin (who had toured with Peter Gabriel), guitarist Adrian Belew (ex-Zappa, ex-Bowie, ex–Talking Heads), and Bruford. The new band drew on minimalism, African and Far Eastern polyrhythms, and the angularity of the final Crimson of the '70s. The group toured the U.S. and Europe to wide acclaim, but disbanded after recording its third album, *Three of a Perfect Pair.*

In 1994 Fripp—after recording and touring the previous year with ex-Japan vocalist David Sylvian—announced yet another re-formation of King Crimson. Calling the new lineup a double trio, he enlisted two drummers, Bruford and David Sylvian's drummer Pat Mastelotto. Also in the band: Belew, Levin, and Chapman Stick (a 12-string instrument combining elements of bass and guitar) player Trey Gunn (who'd been a student in one of Fripp's "Guitar Craft" seminars, and had played on the 1991 album *Kneeling at the Shrine* by Fripp and his wife Toyah Wilcox's band, Sunday All Over the World). This lineup debuted with the EP, *VROOOM*, on Fripp's own independent Discipline Records.

In 1997, after extensive touring for *Thrak*, the band "fractalized" (as Fripp put it) into four subgroups called "Projekcts," which were recorded on *Deception of the Thrush* and *The ProjeKcts;* the techno-groove-jam Projekct 2 (Fripp, Gunn, and Belew on electronic drums only) also released its own *Space Groove* album on Discipline. Partly to counter bootleggers, Fripp released a steady stream of new and old Crimson live recordings: *Epitaph* featured the original 1969 lineup, *Night Watch* the 1972–74 edition, and *Cirkus* collected live recordings spanning the band's entire career (he also released "Collectors Club" concert recordings of lineups throughout Crimson history, by mail-order only, through the Discipline Web site). With Bruford and Levin sitting out [see Bruford entry], Crimson returned as a quartet on *ConstruKCtion of Light.*

King Curtis

Born Curtis Ousley, Feb. 7, 1934, Fort Worth, TX; died Aug. 13, 1971, New York, NY

1967—*Live at Small's Paradise* (Atco) 1968—*Best of King Curtis; Blues at Montreux* (Atlantic) 1971—*Live at Fillmore West* (Atco) 1988—*Soul Twist* (Collectables) 1989—*The Best of King Curtis* 1994—*Instant Soul: The Legendary King Curtis* (Razor & Tie).

Saxophonist King Curtis, a definitive R&B session soloist and bandleader (of the Kingpins), was a favorite of pop, rock, soul, and jazz performers, especially after his famous tenor sax solo on the Coasters' 1957 hit "Yakety-Yak."

An adopted child, Curtis was first influenced by fellow Southwesterners T-Bone Walker and Buster Smith, plus such jazz saxophonists as Lester Young and Louis Jordan. He got his first sax at age 12, played in several high school bands, and turned down several college scholarships to tour with Lionel Hampton's band.

Curtis arrived in New York in 1952 and was discovered by a record company scout who found him session work. He went on to back more than 125 performers, including the Shirelles, Wilson Pickett, Sam and Dave, Eric Clapton, the Allman Brothers, and Delaney and Bonnie. In addition, Curtis made his own records, beginning in the late '50s. "Soul Twist," on the small Enjoy label, topped the R&B chart (#17 pop, 1962). He later signed with Capitol and then in 1965 with Atco. His first release for that label was an instrumental version of "Spanish Harlem."

Curtis played on several of Aretha Franklin's records, including "Bridge Over Troubled Water," and was appointed her musical director just before he died. (He assembled the band that graced a number of her most famous records: Richard Tee, Cornell Dupree, Jerry Jemmott, and Bernard Purdie.) The saxophonist also produced or coproduced albums by Roberta Flack, Delaney and Bonnie, Donny Hathaway, Freddie King, and Sam Moore of Sam and Dave. One of his last recording sessions was for John Lennon's *Imagine*. He was stabbed to death outside his home on New York's West 86th Street after he asked two men who were shooting drugs to move off his steps. In 2000 Curtis was inducted into the Rock and Roll Hall of Fame.

King Floyd

Born Feb. 13, 1945, New Orleans, LA
1971—*King Floyd* (Cotillion) 1975—*Well Done* (Chimneyville) 1977—*Body English* 1994—*Choice Cuts* (Malaco) 2000—*Old Skool Funk.*

Soul-funk singer King Floyd began his career at age 12 in New Orleans. He began recording for the local Uptown label in 1964, and two years later he moved to Pulsar, where he enjoyed further regional success. By the time he released his biggest hit, the self-penned slow and sassy (with reggae overtones) "Groove Me" (#6, 1971), he was working under the guidance of another New Orleans veteran, Wardell Queezergue, at the Malaco studios in Jackson, Mississippi. He made other isolated appearances on the pop chart in the early '70s with songs like "Baby Let Me Kiss You" (#29, 1971) and

"Woman Don't Go Astray" (#53, 1972). Floyd remains active in New Orleans and does session work.

The Kingsmen

Formed 1958, Portland, OR
Lynn Easton, voc., sax; Jack Ely, gtr., voc.; Mike Mitchell, gtr.; Bob Nordby, gtr., bass.
1962—(+ Don Gallucci, organ; + Gary Abbott, drums)
1963—(– Ely; – Nordby; – Gallucci; – Abbot; + Norm Sundholm, bass, voc.; + Dick Peterson, drums, voc.; + Barry Curtis, organ, voc.; numerous personnel changes follow) *The Kingsmen in Person* (Wand) 1964—*The Kingsmen, vol. 2* 1965—*The Kingsmen, vol. 3; The Kingsmen on Campus* 1966—*15 Great Hits* 1985—*The Best of the Kingsmen* (Rhino).

Well before the '90s grunge onslaught, the Northwest was a particularly fertile breeding ground for raunchy rock & roll in the early '60s. Paul Revere and the Raiders became the area's most successful group, but the most famous song—indeed one of the best known and most notorious songs in the history of rock & roll—was "Louie Louie." Though the Raiders cut their version in 1963, it was the Kingsmen who had the hit.

"Louie Louie," first recorded by its composer, Richard Berry, in 1956, is marked by a three-chord progression simple enough to endear it to every last fratband. The Kingsmen's version (#2, 1963), recorded for $50, stood out thanks to co-founder Jack Ely, who garbled his words to the extent that no one knew exactly what he was singing. By educated guesses it was obscene enough to be banned by many radio stations and to spark an FCC investigation. The Kingsmen, however, always maintained that they had said nothing lewd. The story behind the song was chronicled in a 1993 book, *Louie Louie,* by Dave Marsh.

Two more hits followed—"Money" (#16, 1964) and "The Jolly Green Giant" (#4, 1965)—before the band first went on hiatus in 1967. Guitarist Mike Mitchell fronted the Kingsmen when they signed a contract with Capitol in 1973, which ultimately went nowhere. With Dick Peterson and Barry Curtis in the group since 1963, the quintet has continued to perform into 2001. On November 9, 1998, 10 of the band's past and present members won a five-year court battle over 30 years of back royalties for "Louie Louie," when the Supreme Court declined to hear an appeal of an earlier 1995 decision granting the Kingsmen back royalties.

Kingston Trio

Formed 1957, San Francisco, CA
Bob Shane (b. Feb. 1, 1934, Hilo, HI), various string instruments, voc.; Nick Reynolds (b. July 27, 1933, San Diego, CA), various string instruments, voc.; Dave Guard, (b. Nov. 19, 1934, Honolulu, HI; d. Mar. 22, 1991, Rollinsford, NH), various string instruments, voc.
1958—*The Kingston Trio* (Capitol) 1959—*From the Hungry i; The Kingston Trio at Large; Here We Go Again!* 1960—*Sold Out; String Along; Stereo Concert* 1961—*Make Way!; Goin' Places; Close-up* (– Guard; + John Stewart [b. Sep. 5, 1939, San Diego], gtr., voc.) 1962—*College Concert; Best of the Kingston Trio; Something Special; New Frontier* 1963—*The Kingston Trio #16; Sunny Side!* 1964—*Time to Think; Back in Town* 1965—*Best of the Kingston Trio, vol. 2* 1967—(– Stewart; – Reynolds) 1973—(as the New Kingston Trio: Shane, + Roger Gamble [d. 1985], various string instruments, voc.; + George Grove [b. Oct. 9, 1947, Hickory, NC], various string instruments, voc.) 1985—(– Gamble; + Bob Haworth [b. Oct. 9, 1946, Spokane, WA], various string instruments, voc.) 1988—(– Haworth; + Reynolds) 1990—*Capitol Collectors Series* 1995—*The Capitol Years* 1999—(– Reynolds; + Haworth).

The Kingston Trio was a clean-cut, more commercial alternative to the left-tinged folksingers of the late '50s. Inspired by Woody Guthrie and the Weavers, the trio scored its only #1 hit in 1958 with "Tom Dooley," a song based on a 19th-century folk tune, "Tom Dula." Until the emergence of Peter, Paul and Mary, Nick Reynolds, Bob Shane, and Dave Guard were the country's preeminent folksingers: Five of their first six albums reached #1, and every one of the trio's first 17 LPs, through 1963, made the Top 20.

In 1961 John Stewart replaced Guard, who went on to form the Whiskeyhill Singers. The group attempted to broaden its repertoire from traditional American and English folk songs to include contemporary protest songs, such as its 1962 single, "Where Have All the Flowers Gone" (#21). Nevertheless, the Kingston Trio's popularity waned, and by 1967 both Reynolds and Stewart had left (the latter for a solo career). They were replaced by Roger Gamble and George Grove in 1973, when Shane re-formed the group as the New Kingston Trio and began touring again. A 1982 PBS TV special hosted by Tom Smothers brought together all six Kingston Trio members for the first time. Gamble was replaced after he suffered a sudden, fatal heart attack in 1985. Guard died of cancer in 1991. Reynolds, who'd re-joined the trio in the '80s, retired in 1999. The group—founding member Shane with Grove and Haworth—continues to tour and record.

King's X

Formed 1980, Springfield, MO
Jerry Gaskill (b. Dec. 27, 1957, Bridgeton, NJ), drums; Doug Pinnick (b. Sep. 3, 1950, Joliet, IL), bass, voc.; Ty Tabor (b. Sep. 17, 1961, Jackson, MO), gtr., voc.
1988—*Out of the Silent Planet* (Megaforce) 1989—*Gretchen Goes to Nebraska* 1990—*Faith Hope Love by King's X*
1992—*King's X* (Atlantic) 1994—*Dogman* 1996—*Ear Candy*
1997—*Best of King's X* 1998—*Tape Head* (Metal Blade)
2000—*Please Come Home . . . Mr. Bulbous.*
Ty Tabor solo: 1998—*Moonflower Lane* (Metal Blade)
Platypus (Ty Tabor): 1999—*When Pus Comes to Shove* (Velvel)
2000—*Ice Cycles* (InsideOut).

Poundhound (Doug Pinnick): 1998—*Massive Grooves From the Electric Church of Psychofunkadelic Grungelism Rock Music* (Metal Blade).
Supershine (Doug Pinnick): 2000—*Supershine* (Metal Blade).

Seeing themselves more as a band of Christians than as a Christian-rock band, the biracial King's X (bassist/vocalist Doug Pinnick is black) laces powerful, pop-laden heavy metal with spiritual messages.

All three members had previously been involved in Christian music: Doug Pinnick and Jerry Gaskill met playing in the popular Christian-rock group Petra and later backed Christian rocker Phil Keaggy; Ty Tabor played bluegrass in his family's band. Tybor met Gaskill at Springfield's Evangel College, and in 1980 they formed the Edge. (A fourth member, Dan McCollom, was recruited but left the band early on.)

After touring for five years, they moved to Houston, lured by promises of financial backing. That deal collapsed, but the band met Sam Taylor (formerly with ZZ Top's management), who produced them, managed them, and rechristened them King's X, after a band he had liked in high school.

Their first two albums, *Out of the Silent Planet* and *Gretchen Goes to Nebraska,* went nowhere, even though critics and other musicians took note of their structurally complex songs and tight harmonies. *Faith Hope Love by King's X* (#85, 1990), powered by the single "It's Love," finally brought the band into the Top 100. In 1991 they contributed "Junior's Gone Wild" to the *Bill and Ted's Bogus Journey* soundtrack. The next year they released their first major-label album, the self-titled *King's X* (#138), which proved to be a commercial disappointment. In 1994 King's X played the Woodstock Festival and released a new album, *Dogman.* After another studio album, *Ear Candy,* and a compilation, King's X was dropped by Atlantic and signed with independent label Metal Blade, on which it released two more albums of its lyrical prog metal, *Tape Head* and *Please Come Home . . . Mr. Bulbous.* The band unveiled a goofy streak with *Tape Head*'s "Walter Bela Farkas (Live Peace in New York)," in which guest Wally Farkas did his best to emulate Yoko Ono's most extreme vocal stylings.

In addition to King's X, Tabor and Pinnick have recently developed busy solo careers. Tabor wrote, produced, and played most of the instruments on 1998's *Moonflower Lane;* he then recorded two albums with Platypus. Not to be left behind, Pinnick handled most of the creative duties (with a bit of help from King's X's Gaskill) in Poundhound then Supershine, each of which has released an album.

The Kinks

Formed 1963, London, Eng.
Ray Davies (b. June 21, 1944, London), gtr., voc.; Dave Davies (b. Feb. 3, 1947, London), gtr., voc.; Mick Avory (b. Feb. 15, 1944, London), drums; Pete Quaife (b. Dec. 27, 1943, Tavistock, Eng.), bass.
1964—*You Really Got Me* (Reprise) 1965—*Kinks-Size; Kinda Kinks* 1966—*Kinks Kinkdom; The Kinks Kontroversy; The Kinks Greatest Hits!; Face to Face* 1967—*Something Else; Live at the Kelvin Hall* 1968—*(The Kinks Are) The Village Green Preservation Society* (– Quaife; + John Dalton, bass); *Arthur, or the Decline and Fall of the British Empire* 1970—*Lola Versus Powerman and the Moneygoround, Part One* 1971—(+ John Gosling, kybds.) *Muswell Hillbillies* (RCA) 1972—*The Kinks Kronikles* (Reprise); *Everybody's in Show-Biz* (RCA) 1973—*Preservation Act 1* 1974—*Preservation Act 2* 1975—*The Kinks Present a Soap Opera; The Kinks Present Schoolboys in Disgrace* 1976—(– Dalton; + Andy Pyle, bass) 1977—*Sleepwalker* (Arista) 1978—*Misfits* (– Pyle; – Gosling; + Jim Rodford [b. July 7, 1945, St. Alban's, Eng.], bass, voc.; + Gordon Edwards, kybds.; – Edwards) 1979—*Low Budget* (+ Ian Gibbons, kybds., voc.) 1980—*One for the Road* 1981—*Give the People What They Want* 1983—*State of Confusion* 1984—(– Avory; + Bob Henrit [b. May 2, 1945, Eng.], drums) *Word of Mouth* 1986—*Come Dancing With the Kinks; Father Christmas; Think Visual* (MCA) 1988—*Live: The Road* (London) (– Gibbons) 1989—*U.K. Jive* (+ Mark Haley, kybds.) 1993—*Phobia* (Columbia) 1995—*Tired of Waiting for You* (Rhino) 1996—*To the Bone* (Guardian).
Dave Davies solo: 1980—*AFL1-3603* (RCA) 1981—*Glamour* 1983—*Chosen People* (Warner Bros.) 1987—*The Album That Never Was* (PRT) 1998—*Unfinished Business: Dave Davies Kronikles 1964–1998* (Essential) 2000—*Live at the Bottom Line* (Koch International).
Ray Davies solo: 1998—*The Storyteller* (Capitol).

The Kinks were part of the British Invasion, and their early hits, "You Really Got Me" and "All Day and All of the Night," paved the way for the power chords of the next decade's hard rock. But most of leader Ray Davies' songs have been elegies for the beleaguered British middle class, scenarios for rock theater, and tales of show-business survival. After their first burst of popularity, the Kinks became a cult band in the mid-'70s until, buoyed by the new wave's rediscovery of the Davies catalogue, they returned to arenas in the '80s. In the '90s brothers Dave and Ray established more separate identities while the Kinks' reputation remained secure.

Ray Davies was attending art school when he joined his younger brother Dave's band, the Ravens, in 1963. In short order Ray took over the group—renamed the Kinks—retaining bassist Pete Quaife and recruiting Mick Avory to play drums. With this lineup they released a pair of unsuccessful singles before recording "You Really Got Me," a #1 hit in England that reached #7 in the U.S. in 1964. The following year "All Day and All of the Night" and "Tired of Waiting for You" both reached the Top 10 in the U.S. and set a pattern for future releases of alternating tough rockers ("Who'll Be the Next in Line") and ballads ("Set Me Free").

In 1966 the Kinks released two singles of pointed satire, "A Well Respected Man" (#13) and "Dedicated Follower of Fashion" (#36), indicating the personal turn Ray Davies' songs were taking. Their next album, *The Kinks Kontroversy,* though containing another hard-rock 45, "Till the End of the Day" (#50) was increasingly introspective, with songs like

The Kinks: (top) Dave Davies, Mick Avory, (bottom) Peter Quaife, Ray Davies

"I'm on an Island." Also that year, an appearance on the American TV show *Hullabaloo* resulted in a problem with the American Federation of Musicians that wasn't resolved until 1969 and prevented the group from touring the U.S. for some time. "Sunny Afternoon" (#14, 1966) from *Face to Face* was their last hit of that period.

During their years of U.S. exile, Ray Davies composed the first of many concept albums, *(The Kinks Are) The Village Green Preservation Society* (1968), an LP of nostalgia for all the quaint English customs (such as virginity) that other bands were rebelling against. Dave Davies, who had been writing the occasional song for the Kinks almost from the beginning, had a "solo" hit in England with "Death of a Clown," actually a Kinks song that he wrote and sang. More of Dave's singles followed ("Susannah's Still Alive," "Lincoln County"), none of which repeated the success of "Clown." A planned solo album was recorded but released much later, in 1987, as *The Album That Never Was.* The Kinks' next LP, *Arthur, or the Decline and Fall of the British Empire,* was, with the Who's *Tommy,* an early rock opera written for a British TV show that never aired.

The Kinks' next concept album, *Lola Versus Powerman and the Moneygoround, Part One* (#35, 1970), was built around the story of trying to get a hit record. "Lola," undoubtedly the first rock hit about a transvestite, reached #9. *Lola* was the group's first Top 40 LP since 1966's *The Kinks Greatest Hits* (#9).

The group then left Reprise for RCA, continuing to work on concept pieces, once again without hits. Nevertheless it acquired a reputation as a cheerfully boozy live band; Kinks performances were known for messy musicianship and onstage arguments between Ray and Dave Davies, while Ray clowned with limp wrists and sprayed beer at the audience. This was chronicled on *Everybody's in Show-Biz* (#70, 1972), a double album split between Ray Davies' first road songs and a loose live set.

Concept albums became soundtracks for theatrical presentations starring the Kinks in the next years. *Preservation Acts 1* and *2, Soap Opera* (#51, 1975), and *Schoolboys in Disgrace* (#45, 1975) were all composed for the stage, complete with extra horn players and singers. For all of the elaborate shows, though, the albums weren't selling.

The Kinks left RCA and concept albums behind in 1976, and 1977's *Sleepwalker* hit #21 with its title track (#48). They finally scored a hit in 1978 with "A Rock 'n' Roll Fantasy" (#30, 1978), off *Misfits* (#40, 1978). *Low Budget* (#11, 1979), aided by another successful 45, "(Wish I Could Fly Like) Superman" (#41, 1979), became the Kinks' first gold record since the Reprise greatest-hits collection of their early singles.

In the meantime, new groups began rediscovering the Kinks' catalogue, notably Van Halen ("You Really Got Me") and the Pretenders ("Stop Your Sobbing"). The group, which had tightened up considerably onstage with the addition of former Argent bassist Jim Rodford in 1978, responded with *One for the Road* (#14, 1980), a double live album that was accompanied by one of the first full-length rock videos. It, too, went gold, as did *Give the People What They Want* (#15, 1981).

Over the years, Ray Davies has also produced two albums by Claire Hamill (for his ill-fated Konk Records), worked with Tom Robinson, and scored the films *The Virgin Soldiers* and *Percy.* Dave Davies finally came out with a solo album, *AFL1-3603,* in 1980, followed by *Glamour* in 1981 and *Chosen People* in 1983; all featured Dave on most of the instruments and achieved modest success.

Thanks in part to some beautifully produced videos, the Kinks' third wind continued with *State of Confusion* (#12, 1983), which gave the group its first Top 10 hit since "Lola": the delightfully nostalgic "Come Dancing" (#6, 1983). A wistful ballad, "Don't Forget to Dance," cracked the Top 30 later in the year. Other mid-'80s activities included *Return to Waterloo* (1985), a film Ray Davies wrote and directed, incorporating Kinks music; and Ray having a daughter, Natalie, with Chrissie Hynde of the Pretenders in 1983. The relationship ended the following year. In 1986 Ray also acted in the film *Absolute Beginners.*

Beginning with *Word of Mouth* (#57, 1984), the Kinks once again fell on hard times. None of the band's subsequent albums sold well. But the Kinks, with ex-Argent drummer Bob Henrit in place of Avory, remain a touring attraction. In 1993 the group undertook its first U.S. tour in more than three years to promote *Phobia.* The album's first single, "Hatred (A Duet)," poked fun at the long-standing filial antagonism between Ray and Dave Davies that has led both brothers to quit the band on more than one occasion. Despite the sibling rivalry and sagging record sales, these 1990 Rock and Roll Hall of Fame inductees endure with dignity and wit. In 1992 Ray directed a documentary on the making of the Charles Mingus tribute album, *Weird Nightmare.*

The band's 1996 release, *To the Bone*, was a live-in-the-studio rerecording of many of their hits. In 1995 Ray Davies' "unauthorized autobiography" *X-Ray* was published in the U.S. He then did some shows performing a spoken word/unplugged piece called *20th Century Man*, for which he read sections of his book and sang Kinks songs. By that time, the band's reputation was enjoying another revival, as contemporary British stars Blur and Oasis acknowledged their debt to the Kinks. And in the U.S., Velvel Records initiated a 15-album reissue series of the group's classic recordings. Dave published *Kink*, his own autobiography, in 1997, a recounting of his early debauchery and current interest in metaphysics. Also in the '90s he provided the musical score for John Carpenter's *Village of the Damned* and toured with a band called Dave Davies Kink Kronikles. In 2000 Ray Davies' first collection of short stories, *Waterloo Sunset: Stories*, was published.

Kiss

Formed 1972, New York, NY
Gene Simmons (b. Chaim Whitz, changed to Gene Klein, Aug. 25, 1949, Haifa, Israel), bass, voc.; Paul Stanley (b. Stanley Eisen, Jan. 20, 1950, Queens, NY), gtr., voc.; Peter Criss (b. Peter Crisscoula, Dec. 20, 1947, Brooklyn, NY), drums, voc.; Ace Frehley (b. Paul Frehley, Apr. 27, 1951, Bronx, NY), gtr.
1974—*Kiss* (Casablanca); *Hotter Than Hell* 1975—*Dressed to Kill; Alive* 1976—*Destroyer; Kiss—The Originals; Rock and Roll Over* 1977—*Love Gun; Alive 2* 1978—*Double Platinum* 1979—*Dynasty* 1980—*Unmasked* (– Criss; + Eric Carr [b. July 12, 1950, Brooklyn; d. Nov. 24, 1991, New York], drums) 1981—*Music From "The Elder"* 1982—(– Frehley; + Vinnie Vincent, gtr.) *Creatures of the Night* (Mercury) 1983—*Lick It Up* 1984—(– Vincent; + Mark St. John, gtr.) *Animalize* 1985—(– St. John; + Bruce Kulick, gtr.) *Asylum* 1987—*Crazy Nights* 1988—*Smashes, Thrashes and Hits* 1989—*Hot in the Shade* 1991—(– Carr; + Eric Singer, drums) 1992—*Revenge* 1993—*Alive III* 1996—(– Kulick; – Singer; + Frehley; + Criss) *Unplugged; You Wanted the Best You Got the Best!!* 1997—*Greatest Kiss* (– Frehley; – Criss; + Kulick; + Singer) *Carnival of Souls* (– Kulick; – Singer; + Frehley; + Criss) 1998—*Psycho-Circus* 2001—(– Criss; + Singer).
Paul Stanley solo: 1978—*Paul Stanley* (Casablanca).
Gene Simmons solo: 1978—*Gene Simmons* (Casablanca).
Ace Frehley solo: 1978—*Ace Frehley* (Casablanca) 1987—*Frehley's Comet* (Megaforce) 1988—*Live + 1; Second Sighting* 1989—*Trouble Walkin'*.
Peter Criss solo: 1978—*Peter Criss* (Casablanca) 1993—*Criss* (Tony Nicole Tony).

Kiss may have been one of the biggest-selling acts of the '70s, but it will always be known, above all else, as the band without a face. Until 1983, when the group removed its distinctive comic-book makeup, the four members' faces supposedly had never been photographed (although pictures of them applying their makeup for an early photo session ran in *Creem* magazine in the early '80s). Theatrics and basic hard rock have been Kiss' main calling card. The quartet formed in the heyday of glitter and rock theater, and it set out to define, at first, evil cartoon-character personas, highlighted by Gene Simmons' bass-playing, fire-breathing, (stage) blood-spewing ghoul.

The group was founded by Simmons and Stanley, who met in a band in 1970. They found Criss through his ad in Rolling Stone. After rehearsing as a trio, the group took out an ad in the *Village Voice* for a guitarist with "flash and balls" and discovered Ace Frehley. At the time, they were all working dead-end jobs, with the exception of Simmons, who taught school at P.S. 75 in Manhattan. Their visual image and game plan were in place from the start. After a few New York shows, Kiss met independent television director Bill Aucoin, who helped the group get a deal with Casablanca Records.

The critics hissed at the anonymous heavy-metal thud rock on the band's first three albums and howled at its mock-threatening image. Nonetheless, Kiss hit it off with its fans (the Kiss Army) from the very start. After some hard financial times (an entire 1975 tour was reportedly financed on Aucoin's American Express card), the band took off with *Alive* (#9, 1975), which contained the Top 20 hit "Rock and Roll All Nite."

In 1976 the band's sound and image shifted toward not necessarily softer but certainly more commercial fare, beginning with Criss' ballad "Beth" (#7, 1976), a million-seller that he wrote for his wife, Lydia. Accordingly, Kiss' audience grew from mostly male adolescent heavy-metal fans to include more teenyboppers. As the group racked up more and more platinum records—six between 1976 and 1979—it became increasingly less threatening. Young fans were frequently photographed wearing the makeup of their favorite Kiss member.

On June 28, 1977, Marvel Comics published a Kiss comic book. The red ink used supposedly contained a small amount of blood from the band members themselves. It sold over 400,000 copies. In the fall of 1978 NBC broadcast a feature-length animated cartoon entitled *Kiss Meets the Phantom of the Park*, and Marvel issued a second Kiss comic. But the

Kiss: Gene Simmons, Paul Stanley, Peter Criss, Ace Frehley

group's popularity was beginning to wane. Four simultaneously released solo LPs sold poorly—Frehley's was most popular—although the group had several hit singles, including the disco-metal oddity "I Was Made for Loving You" (#16, 1979). In 1980 Criss left for a solo career. He was replaced by Eric Carr, who drummed into the '90s but died of cancer at age 41. The group then briefly changed its image, abandoning the comic-book characters for a New Romantic–influenced look. *Music From "The Elder,"* an overambitious concept album, featured songs cowritten by Lou Reed and was the group's first album not to go gold. Kiss quickly reverted to its ghoul makeup and primitive hard-rock music, and *Creatures of the Night* eventually sold 500,000 copies and was certified gold.

What to do? Change image again. *Lick It Up* (#24, 1983) depicted the group (now with Vinnie Vincent in place of Frehley) without its makeup and sparked a commercial resurgence. By the early '90s, Kiss had sold more than 70 million albums. And as proof that in rock & roll anyone can become a legend if he sticks around long enough, 1994 saw the release of *Kiss My Ass,* on which artists as diverse as Garth Brooks, Lenny Kravitz, and Anthrax recorded their favorite Kiss songs as a tribute to the band critics loved to hate.

The success of the album anticipated the 1996 reunion of the original Kiss for the taping of MTV's *Unplugged* (#15, 1996), which in turn led to a full-on reunion tour—the year's highest-grossing concert attraction—complete with makeup, stage blood, and pyrotechnics. With *Carnival of Souls* (#27, 1997) already recorded, Kulick and Singer left and the recombinant Kiss released *Psycho-Circus* (#3, 1998), feeding interest in what the band claimed was a 2000 farewell tour. Whether or not Kiss is kaput, the band's legacy is ensured by the savvy merchandising of its instantly recognizable, cartoonish image, which has inspired pinball games, plastic action figures and comic book spinoffs. Meanwhile, Simmons has enjoyed a long-term second career playing movie villains. He appeared, with the original band, in the 1999 film *Detroit Rock City,* a teen comedy about the misadventures of a Kiss fan (Edward Furlong) en route to a big Detroit show. As of this writing, Simmons was penning his autobiography, tentatively entitled *KISS and Make Up,* and the "farewell tour" was rolling on through 2001.

The KLF

Formed 1987, England
Bill Drummond (b. William Butterworth, Apr. 29, 1953, S.A.), synth, samplers; Jimi Cauty (b. James Cauty, 1956, Devon, Eng.), gtr.
1990—*Chill Out* (WaxTrax, U.K.) 1991—*The White Room* (Arista).

Britain's mysterious, mischievous KLF made post-hip-hop, rave-influenced, psychedelic trance-dance music that one critic described as "dance music for the home." Its name stood for "Kopyright Liberation Front"; the group's stated mission was to see if sampling would hold up in a court of law.

Bill Drummond had played in the new-wave band Big in Japan (with Holly Johnson, later of Frankie Goes to Hollywood); ran Liverpool's Zoo Records and managed its two top acts, Echo and the Bunnymen and Teardrop Explodes; and was an A&R executive with WEA Records when he signed ex–Zodiac Mindwarp guitarist Jimi Cauty's band, Brilliant (whose only album flopped). Drummond and Cauty recorded dance singles under the names Disco 2000, Space, and Justified Ancients of Mu Mu—often shortened to "Jams." The Jams album *1987 (What the Fuck's Going On)* drew a quick lawsuit from Abba, whose "Dancing Queen" was heavily sampled on it (as were the Beatles, Led Zeppelin, and others). It was immediately recalled, and reissued—with all unauthorized samples edited out—as an extended single, "The Jams 45 Edits EP." (Authorized samples were used in the followup single, "Who Killed the Jams?")

As the Timelords, Drummond and Cauty combined a hip-hop version of Gary Glitter's "Rock and Roll Part 2" with the theme of the popular British science-fiction TV show *Dr. Who;* the resulting "Doctoring the Tardis" topped the U.K. chart in 1988. Cauty and Drummond then became KLF, and recorded *Chill Out,* which reflected the near–New Age work Cauty had begun doing with the Orb [see entry].

Drummond and Cauty scored an international dance hit with "What Time Is Love?" (#57, 1991) from the group's first U.S. album, *The White Room* (#39, 1991). It also contained the smash pop hit "3 A.M. Eternal" (#5, 1991), which was accompanied by a music video showing the group clad in robes and hoods, moving in formation as if enacting some strange, cultish ritual. In 1992 the KLF had another hit with "Justified and Ancient," a surreal feature for country-music queen Tammy Wynette, who gamely wore a skintight, turquoise mermaid dress for the video. The song reached #11 on the pop chart—higher than Wynette's 1968 classic "Stand by Your Man."

Drummond and Cauty broke up the KLF in late 1992 but continued working as conceptual pranksters "The K Foundation." In 1993 they announced that they'd recorded a "world anthem"—"Que Sera Sera" redone as "K Sera Sera" with the Red Army Choir—but refused to release it until world peace was achieved.

The Knack

Formed 1978, Los Angeles, CA
Doug Fieger (b. Aug. 20, Detroit, MI), gtr., voc.; Berton Averre (b. Dec. 13, Van Nuys, CA), gtr.; Bruce Gary (b. Apr. 7, 1952, Burbank, CA), drums; Prescott Niles (b. May 2, New York, NY), bass.
1979—*Get the Knack* (Capitol) 1980—*. . . but the Little Girls Understand* 1981—*Round Trip* (group disbands) 1991—(group re-forms: Fieger; Averre; Niles; + Billy Ward, drums) *Serious Fun* (Charisma) (– Ward) 1998—(+ Terry Bozzio

[b. Dec. 27, 1950, San Francisco, CA], drums) *Proof: The Very Best of the Knack* (Rhino); *Zoom.*
Doug Fieger solo: 2000—*First Things First* (Zen).

In the summer of 1979 the Knack enjoyed one of the biggest commercial debuts in rock history. Its first album, recorded in 11 days for a mere $18,000, went gold in 13 days, platinum in seven weeks, and eventually sold 5 million copies worldwide. The single "My Sharona" sold 10 million copies. However, the group quickly suffered an equally intense backlash. With its Beatles-like packaging (the back cover of *Get the Knack* imitated *A Hard Day's Night*), plus what critics saw as contrived pop innocence and sexist lyrics, the band members were labeled cynical fakes—an accusation heightened by their refusal to do interviews. In the wake of the Knack's success, scores of "innocent pop" L.A. bands were signed. A "Knuke the Knack" movement arose in the more radical quarters of the very same L.A. club scene where the band had begun.

Songwriters Doug Fieger met Berton Averre in California when he moved there from Detroit in 1971 with his band Sky, which made two LPs for RCA. During the mid-'70s Fieger and Averre began writing together, and after working abroad, Fieger moved back to L.A., where he, Averre, and Bruce Gary teamed up with Prescott Niles to form the Knack.

The Knack played the Southern California club circuit for seven months, resulting in 13 labels wanting to sign the band. Capitol won out, and the Knack's debut, produced by Mike Chapman (who did many of the successful pop–new wave LPs of that year, including Blondie's), was released by June 1979 with the #1 single "My Sharona." The critical backlash and the lack of individual image caught up with the Knack commercially, though, and its followup album sold a comparatively disappointing 600,000 copies. The band members began to argue constantly, their third LP, *Round Trip* (#93, 1981), barely broke the Top 100, and following an unsuccessful 1981 tour they disbanded.

Averre, Gary, and Niles continued as the Game briefly before going on to back up others: Gary drummed behind Bob Dylan, Jack Bruce, and Bette Midler; Averre, too, played with the Divine Miss M., while Niles toured with Josie ("Johnny, Are You Queer?") Cotton. They regrouped again in the mid-'80s as the Front, with actor Steven Bauer on vocals. Fieger, meanwhile, founded Doug Fieger's Taking Chances, which went nowhere. In 1987 Niles, Averre, and a newly sober Fieger got back together, with drummer Bill Ward. A 1991 album, *Serious Fun,* did not chart, and the Knack members went their separate ways again. Fieger, in addition to playing a small role on the hit TV series *Roseanne,* recorded a solo album produced by Don Was. In 1994 the Knack began touring again after "My Sharona" found a new audience through its inclusion in the *Reality Bites* soundtrack. Ex–Missing Persons/Frank Zappa drummer Terry Bozzio replaced Ward on 1998's *Zoom,* which failed to cause much of a commercial stir. As of this writing, the original lineup was still touring.

Gladys Knight and the Pips

Formed 1952, Atlanta, GA
Gladys Knight (b. May 28, 1944, Atlanta), voc.; Merald "Bubba" Knight (b. Sep. 4, 1942, Atlanta), voc.; Brenda Knight, voc.; William Guest (b. June 2, 1941, Atlanta), voc.; Eleanor Guest, voc. (b. 1940; d. 1997, Atlanta).
1957—(– B. Knight; – E. Guest; + Edward Patten [b. Aug. 2, 1939, Atlanta], voc.; + Langston George, voc.) 1962—(– George) 1967—*Everybody Needs Love* (Motown) 1968—*Feelin' Bluesy; Silk 'n' Soul* 1969—*Nitty Gritty* 1970—*Greatest Hits* (Soul) 1971—*If I Were Your Woman* 1972—*Neither One of Us* 1973—*Imagination* (Buddah) 1974—*Anthology* (Tamla); *Claudine* soundtrack (Buddah); *I Feel a Song* 1975—*2nd Anniversary; The Best of Gladys Knight and the Pips* 1976—*Gladys Knight and the Pips' Greatest Hits* 1980—*About Love* (Columbia) 1982—*Touch* 1983—*Visions* 1985—*Life* 1987—*All Our Love* (MCA) 1990—*Soul Survivors: The Best of Gladys Knight and the Pips* (Rhino) 1997—*The Ultimate Collection* (Motown).
Gladys Knight solo: 1991—*Good Woman* (MCA) 1994—*Just for You* 1998—*Many Different Roads* 2001—*At Last.*

Gladys Knight and the Pips rose to prominence on the Motown label in the late '60s, but their popularity peaked after they moved to Buddah in 1973. The group is a family, the members of which were all born in Atlanta, where Gladys' parents sang in church choirs. As a child, she herself sang with the Mount Mariah Baptist Church choir, and toured Southern churches with the Morris Brown Choir before she was five. At seven she won a grand prize on the *Ted Mack Original Amateur Hour,* which led to several TV appearances. The Pips were formed in 1952 at Gladys' older brother Merald's birthday party, when, to entertain the family, Gladys arranged an impromptu singing group, including Merald, sister Brenda, and cousins William and Eleanor Guest. Cousin James Woods urged them to go pro; they adopted his nickname, "Pip."

They toured nationally with Jackie Wilson and Sam Cooke before Gladys was 13, but their 1957 recording debut with Brunswick went nowhere; Eleanor and Brenda left to get married, and were replaced by cousin Edward Patten and Langston George. This configuration, with Gladys' grainy alto still up front, recorded its first R&B Top 20 hit in 1961, the Johnny Otis–penned "Every Beat of My Heart." George left after two more singles ("Letter Full of Tears" went Top 5), and the group became a quartet.

The group faltered in the early '60s. In 1962 Gladys had a baby, and the Pips did studio backups; even after they reunited they were still known only to R&B fans. They had no connection to the mass audience until the mid-'60s, when they were a guest act on the Motown touring revue. Signed to Motown, their cover of "Heard It Through the Grapevine" became a #2 smash in 1967. They also scored with "The End of the Road" (#15), "Friendship Train" (#17), and "If I Were Your Woman" (#9).

Just as "Neither One of Us" (#2) was mounting the chart, the group decided to leave Motown in 1973, citing lack of

Gladys Knight and the Pips: Edward Patten, Merald "Bubba" Knight, William Guest, Gladys Knight

label support. Their first LP for Buddah, *Imagination* (#9, 1973), made the move worthwhile. It was their biggest seller, going gold and yielding three gold singles: "Midnight Train to Georgia" (#1, 1973), "I've Got to Use My Imagination" (#4, 1974), and "Best Thing That Ever Happened to Me" (#3, 1974). In 1973 the group won two Grammys: Best Pop Vocal Performance by a Duo, Group or Chorus for "Neither One of Us" and Best R&B Vocal Performance by a Duo, Group or Chorus for "Midnight Train to Georgia." Motown continued to release albums by the group after it had left; the group claims it has never received royalties from these or "Neither One of Us."

The hits continued with "The Way We Were"/"Try to Remember" (#11, 1975), and the band did the movie soundtrack to *Claudine* with Curtis Mayfield in 1974, which included the single "On and On" (#5, 1974). Gladys made her acting debut in 1976 in a film with the unlikely subject of love set among the Alaskan oil fields, called *Pipe Dreams;* in 1985 she also costarred in the short-lived TV series *Charlie and Co.* In 1977, because of legal proceedings involving the band's attempted switch of labels to Columbia, plus an old unsettled suit by Motown, Gladys was not allowed to record with the Pips on LP for three years (though they did sing together live).

In the meantime, the group's popularity waned. Gladys recorded a solo LP, and the Pips did two albums for Casablanca, finally reuniting in 1980 on Columbia with *About Love,* produced by Ashford and Simpson, yielding the #3 R&B hit "Landlord." *Visions* also had hit singles, "Save the Overtime (for Me)" (#66 pop, #1 R&B, 1983) and "You're Number One (In My Book)" (#5 R&B, 1983). "Love Overboard" (#13 pop, #1 R&B, 1987), from *All Our Love* (#39, 1987), won the group a Grammy in 1988 for Best R&B Performance by a Duo or Group with Vocal. Another single from that album, "Lovin' on Next to Nothin' " went to #3 R&B the following year.

Gladys Knight's *Good Woman* (#45 pop, #1 R&B, 1991) featured many of her own songs. In the accompanying press release, the group was described as "suspended." Knight's solo hits include "It's Gonna Take All Our Love" (#29 R&B, 1988), "License to Kill" (from the James Bond film) (#69 R&B, 1989), "Men" (#2 R&B, 1991), "Where Would I Be" (#66 R&B, 1992), and "Next Time" (#30 R&B, 1995). She also won a Grammy in 1986 for the AIDS-benefit record "That's What Friends Are For," which she recorded with Dionne Warwick, Stevie Wonder, and Elton John. In 1996 she collaborated with R&B divas Brandy, Tamia, and Chaka Khan on "Missing You" (#25 pop, #10 R&B) for the soundtrack to *Set It Off.* Following her 1997 divorce from her third husband, motivational speaker Les Brown, Knight became a Mormon. *Many Different Roads* was her first inspirational album. In the late '90s she had a recurring role on TV's *The Jamie Foxx Show.* Her autobiography, *Between Each Line of Pain and Glory: My Life Story,* came out in 1997.

Kool and the Gang

Formed 1964, Jersey City, NJ
Robert "Kool" Bell (b. Oct. 8, 1950, Youngstown, OH), voc., bass; Ronald Bell (b. Nov. 1, 1951, Youngstown), tenor sax; Dennis "Dee Tee" Thomas (b. Feb. 9, 1951, Jersey City), sax, flute; Claydes Smith (b. Sep. 6, 1948, Jersey City), lead gtr.; Robert "Spike" Mickens (b. Jersey City), trumpet; Rickey Westfield (b. Jersey City), kybds.; George "Funky" Brown (b. Jan. 5, 1949, Jersey City), drums.
1971—*Live at the Sex Machine* (De-Lite); *The Best of Kool and the Gang; Music Is the Message* 1972—*Live at P.J.'s; Good Times* 1973—*Wild and Peaceful; Kool Jazz* 1974—*Light of Worlds* 1975—*Kool and the Gang Greatest Hits!; Spirit of the Boogie* (Polydor) 1976—(+ Clifford Adams [b. Oct. 8, 1952, NJ], trombone) *Love and Understanding; Open Sesame* 1977—*The Force* (– Westfield) 1978—*Kool and the Gang Spin Their Top Hits; Everybody's Dancin'* 1979—(+ James "J.T." Taylor [b. Aug. 16, 1953, SC], voc.) *Ladies Night* 1980—*Celebrate!* (Mercury) (+ Curtis Williams [b. Dec. 11, 1962, Buffalo, NY], kybds.; + Michael Ray [b. Dec. 24, 1962, NJ], trumpet, voc.) 1981—*Something Special* 1982—*As One* 1983—*In the Heart* 1984—*Emergency* 1986—*Forever* (Mercury) 1988—*Everything's Kool and the Gang: Greatest Hits and More* 1989—(– Taylor; + Skip Martin, voc.; + Odeon Mays, voc.; + Gary Brown, voc.) *Sweat* 1993—*The Best of Kool and the Gang, 1969–1976; Unite* (JRS) 1995—(various lineup changes; + Taylor) 1996—*State of Affairs* (Curb).
J.T. Taylor solo: 1989—*Master of the Game* (MCA) 1991—*Feel the Need* 1993—*Baby, I'm Back* 2000—*A Brand New Me* (Taylor Made).

In the '70s and '80s Kool and the Gang enjoyed many platinum hits with their horn-driven funky dance and pop music, but they started out in the mid-'60s playing jazz. They began as the Jazziacs, formed while they were all attending Lincoln High School in Jersey City (except guitarist Smith). Leader Robert "Kool" Bell's father used to room with Thelonious Monk, whose music, along with Miles Davis' and John Coltrane's, offered early influences, as did Pharoah Sanders and Leon Thomas, who sometimes showed up at the band's local jam sessions. The group went through several name changes, including the Soul Town Review and the New Dimensions, before becoming Kool and the Gang in 1968. They shifted to more accessible funk R&B, and their eponymous debut single in 1969 reached #19 on the R&B chart.

Kool and the Gang's sound—designed by the group's musical director, Ronald Bell—was highlighted by chunky guitar fills, staccato horn blasts, and group "party" vocal chants. Several modest dance hits, like "Funky Man" (#16 R&B, 1970) and "Love the Life You Live" (#31 R&B, 1972), led to their massive breakthrough in 1973 with three top singles on one gold album, *Wild and Peaceful* (#30, 1973), including "Funky Stuff" (#29 pop, #5 R&B, 1973), "Jungle Boogie" (#4 pop, 1974; #2 R&B, 1973), and "Hollywood Swinging" (#6, 1974). Other hit singles include "Higher Plane" (#1 R&B, 1974), "Rhyme Tyme People" (#3 R&B, 1974), "Spirit of the Boogie" (#1 R&B, 1975), "Caribbean Festival" (#8 R&B, 1975), "Love and Understanding (Come Together)" (#8 R&B, 1976), and "Open Sesame—Part 1" (#6 R&B, 1976). Their dance style anticipated disco, but they were temporarily shoved in the background by the trend, though they got a minor pop hit with "Open Sesame," which appeared on the next year's *Saturday Night Fever* soundtrack. Some of their music in the mid-'70s reflected their "spiritual phase"—several members are devout Muslims. In the late '80s Ronald Bell changed his name to Khalis Bayyan, and Robert Bell became Amir Bayyan.

In 1978 the band got new management and a full-fledged lead singer who could handle ballads. Tenor James Taylor (no relation to the pop-folk singer) fronted the band on 1979's *Ladies Night* (#13) and with the help of coproducer Eumir Deodato, it hit the pop Top 10 (#1 R&B) with the title track. The single went gold, the album, platinum. In 1980 Kool and the Gang released "Too Hot" (#5 pop, #3 R&B, 1980), and "Celebration" (#1 pop, #1 R&B, 1980), which went platinum and became a theme song for the return of the U.S. hostages from Iran, not to mention a standard of wedding bands everywhere. The *Celebrate!* (#10) LP also went platinum, as did *Something Special* (#12, 1981), yielding the hits "Take My Heart (You Can Have It If You Want It)" (#17 pop, #1 R&B, 1981), "Steppin' Out" (#12 R&B, 1982), "Get Down on It" (#10 pop, #4 R&B, 1982), "Big Fun" (#21 pop, #6 R&B, 1982), and "Let's Go Dancin' (Ooh La, La, La)" (#30 pop, #7 R&B, 1982).

Kool and the Gang's popularity continued through the '80s, but many of their biggest hits—"Joanna" (#29, 1983) and "Tonight" (#13 pop, #7 R&B, 1984) from *In the Heart* (#29, 1983) and "Fresh" (#9 pop, #1 R&B, 1984), "Cherish" (#2 pop, #1 R&B, 1985), and "Emergency" (#18 pop, #7 R&B, 1985) from the platinum *Emergency* (#13, 1984)—were softer ballads. Other hits include "Victory" (#10 pop, #2 R&B, 1986), "Stone Love" (#10 pop, #4 R&B, 1987), and "Holiday" (#9 R&B, 1987). Taylor left the group in 1989 and released his solo debut that year. His biggest hit single to date is "All I Want Is Forever," a #2 R&B duet with Regina Belle from the film *Tap* (1989).

The group's first album without Taylor, *Sweat*, did not make a great commercial impression, peaking on the R&B albums chart at #52. The group's more recent singles include "Rags to Riches" (#38 R&B, 1988), "Raindrops" (#27 R&B, 1989), and "Never Give Up" (#74 R&B, 1989). Taylor returned in time for 1996's *State of Affairs*, but chart success eluded the album. That didn't matter; Kool and the Gang's music lives on in the samples and tributes of contemporary rappers such as Sean Combs, Coolio, and Will Smith. The group (sans J.T. Taylor) continues to tour.

Kool Moe Dee

Born Mohandas DeWese, Aug. 8, New York, NY
1986—*Kool Moe Dee* (Rooftop-Jive) 1987—*How Ya Like Me Now* 1989—*Knowledge Is King* (Jive-RCA) 1990—*African Pride* EP (Jive) 1991—*Funke Funke Wisdom* 1993—*Greatest Hits* 1994—*Interlude* (Easylee).

Kool Moe Dee is one of rap's more eloquent practitioners of braggadocio. Having discovered the joys of making rhymes via Dr. Seuss' *How the Grinch Stole Christmas* and heavyweight champ Muhammad Ali's boasting, the young Mohandas DeWese was poised to join New York's burgeoning late-'70s rap scene. When the Treacherous Three, a hip-hop trio he belonged to, split up, he continued on his own, releasing the musically spare *Kool Moe Dee*. The album became an instant classic of rap's so-called old-school style and contained the minor pop hit "Go See the Doctor" (#89, 1987). The title track of the platinum *How Ya Like Me Now* (#35, 1987) put Kool Moe Dee into a blistering feud with L.L. Cool J (he claimed Cool J ripped off his style). A temporary truce was called in 1990 when the two shook hands backstage at Harlem's Apollo Theatre. "How Ya Like Me Now" reached #22 on the R&B chart in late 1987, but it took 1988's "Wild, Wild West" (#4, R&B) to get Kool Moe Dee into the Top 10. His *Funke Funke Wisdom* was a critical disappointment, though it spawned the single "How Kool Can One Blackman Be?" (#49 R&B, 1991). In 1992 the IRS auctioned Kool Moe Dee's Mercedes-Benz for $20,300 and the proceeds were credited toward the $180,000 in back taxes he owed. In 1993 a greatest-hits album was released. The next year Dee reunited with the Treacherous Three for a guest-laden LP entitled *Old School Flava*. Singed to DJ Easy Lee's label, he also released his most recent solo album, *Interlude*. In 1999 "Wild Wild West" climbed to #1 on the pop chart (#3 R&B), when Will Smith, Dru Hill, and Dee himself remade the song, which served as the title track to the movie in which Smith starred that year.

Al Kooper

Born Feb. 5, 1944, Brooklyn, NY
1969—*I Stand Alone* (Columbia); *You Never Know Who Your Friends Are* 1970—*Kooper Session* (with Shuggie Otis); *Easy Does It* 1971—*Landlord* soundtrack (United Artists); *New York*

City (Columbia) 1972—*A Possible Projection of the Future/ Childhood's End; Naked Songs* 1975—*Unclaimed Freight—Al's Big Deal* 1976—*Act Like Nothing's Wrong* (United Artists) 1982—*Championship Wrestling* (Columbia) 1994—*Rekooperation* (MusicMasters) 1995—*Soul of a Man: Al Kooper Live.*
With Mike Bloomfield and Stephen Stills: 1968—*Super Session* (Columbia).
With Mike Bloomfield: 1969—*The Live Adventures of Mike Bloomfield and Al Kooper* (Columbia).

Al Kooper played a major role in the blues rock of the '60s. He originated what has become commonly known as the "Dylanesque organ" with his work on *Highway 61 Revisited,* helped popularize the blues with the Blues Project, and put together Blood, Sweat and Tears, which began the big-band jazz-rock trend that influenced bands like Chicago. He also discovered Lynyrd Skynyrd and the Tubes.

Kooper, who prefers to play piano or guitar, turned professional at age 15, when he joined the Royal Teens after they had a #3 hit in 1958 with "Short Shorts." He left the band in the late '50s, turned to writing and session work, and studied for a year at the University of Bridgeport. In 1965 he cowrote a #1 hit for Gary Lewis and the Playboys, "This Diamond Ring." That same year, producer Tom Wilson gave Kooper a job playing organ on Dylan's single "Like a Rolling Stone" and later on *Highway 61 Revisited.* Kooper also backed Dylan at his 1965 Newport Folk Festival appearance and worked on *Blonde on Blonde* and, later, *New Morning.*

In 1965 Kooper and Steve Katz formed the Blues Project [see entry], and in 1967 they founded Blood, Sweat and Tears [see entry]. Kooper picked the band members and produced their 1968 debut, *Child Is Father to the Man,* but he left before the band's big commercial success to work as a Columbia staff producer and record several collaborative LPs. The first was 1968's *Super Session* with guitarists Mike Bloomfield (whom he met during the Dylan sessions) and Stephen Stills. That album became one of the year's bestsellers. Kooper again collaborated with Bloomfield in 1969 for a live LP. He went on to record several solo albums, which received less attention than his collaborations or the albums he'd done session work on (e.g., the Rolling Stones' *Let It Bleed* and Jimi Hendrix's *Electric Ladyland*).

By the '70s, Kooper had become known more as a producer than as a musician. He oversaw the first three Lynyrd Skynyrd records, the Tubes' 1975 debut, and Nils Lofgren's *Cry Tough.* In 1976 he cut his first solo LP in three years and published an autobiography, *Backstage Passes.* On St. Patrick's Day 1981 he performed in New York City in a Blues Project reunion, and later that year he toured with Bob Dylan. Kooper celebrated his 50th birthday with a Bottom Line show in 1994, a year that saw the release of his first album in 12 years, *Rekooperation.* In between he toured as part of Joe Walsh's band in 1991, played keyboards on a 1990 Byrds session, produced the 1991 LP *Scapegoats* by Green on Red, and scored a short-lived TV series, *Crime Story.* In 1995 he coproduced *For the Love of Harry,* an album that paid tribute to Harry Nilsson. In 1997 Kooper began teaching at Boston's Berklee College of Music. He gave up the post in 2000, when he moved to upstate New York to care for his mother. In 1998 he published a book of his music memoirs, *Backstage Passes and Backstabbing Bastards.*

Korn

Formed 1993, Huntington Beach, CA
Jonathan Davis (b. Jonathan Houseman Davis, Jan. 18, 1971, Bakersfield, CA), voc.; Brian "Head" Welch, (b. Brian Phillip Welch, June 19, 1970, Torrance, CA), gtr.; James "Munky" Shaffer, (b. June 6, 1970, Rosedale, CA), gtr.; Reggie "Fieldy" Arvizu (b. Reginald Arvizu, Nov. 2, 1969), bass; David Silveria, (b. Sep. 1970, Bakersfield), drums.
1994—*Korn* (Immortal/Epic) 1996—*Life Is Peachy* 1998—*Follow the Leader* 1999—*Issues.*

If point of impact of the early-'90s grunge explosion can be traced to Nirvana's *Nevermind,* the full commercial arrival of rap-metal can be pinpointed to August 1998—the month Korn's aptly titled third album, *Follow the Leader,* debuted at #1. Rage Against the Machine had reached that landmark two years earlier, but *Follow the Leader* opened the floodgates; subsequent releases by Korn and fellow rock rappers Limp Bizkit (and to a lesser extent Papa Roach) would all either bow at #1 or entrench themselves in the Top 10 for weeks and months on end well into the turn of the 21st century.

Korn came together in 1993, when mortuary assistant Jonathan Davis, who sang in a band called Sex Art, was invited to join a metal group called Creep. All hailing from Bakersfield, California, its members—Brian "Head" Welch, James "Munky" Shaffer, Reggie "Fieldy" Arvizu, and David Silveria—originally had recorded an album under the moniker L.A.P.D. With Davis handling lead vocals and primary songwriting duties, the band renamed itself Korn and relocated to Orange County's Huntington Beach. A deal with Epic imprint Immortal followed, resulting in the group's self-titled debut released in the fall of 1994.

MTV and radio largely ignored the album, but relentless touring and a rabid fan base (via gigs and the Internet) eventually pushed sales past the 2-million mark. The followup, 1996's *Life Is Peachy,* debuted at #3 and also went double platinum. The album also gave the band its first taste of MTV rotation with the video for "A.D.I.D.A.S." and a headlining slot on the Lollapalooza festival tour.

By the time the quadruple-platinum *Follow the Leader* (#1, 1998) hit stores two years later, Korn didn't need invitations to join other festival tours—it headlined its own: Its inaugural Family Values Tour also featured the German industrial band Rammstein, Orgy, Ice Cube, and Limp Bizkit, who garnered a record deal thanks to Korn's support. The special-effects-laden video for the album's "Freak on a Leash" helped Korn win its first Grammy. Released in November 1999, Korn's *Issues* also debuted at #1 (selling nearly 600,000 copies its first week in stores) and went triple platinum. The band premiered the album in its entirety with a special concert at New York's famed Apollo Theatre in Harlem.

Alexis Korner

Born Alexis Koerner, Apr. 19, 1928, Paris, Fr.; died Jan. 1, 1984, London, Eng.
1969—*Alexis Korner's All Stars Blues Incorporated* (Transatlantic) 1970—*The New Church* (Metronome) 1972—*Accidentally Born in New Orleans* (Warner Bros.); *Bootleg Him!* 1974—*Snape Live on Tour* (Brain) 1975—*Get Off My Cloud* (Columbia) 1978—*Just Easy* (Intercord) 1979—*Me* (Jeton).

Alexis Korner is better known for the musicians he discovered than for the music they made in his bands. His group Blues Inc., formed in 1961, was a major factor in the '60s blues revival in England and America.

Educated throughout Europe, Korner was already 34 years old and a veteran of a dozen years in jazz and skiffle groups when he formed Blues Inc. with Charlie Watts (later a Rolling Stone), Cyril Davies, and Dick Heckstall-Smith (later of John Mayall's Bluesbreakers and Colosseum). Among the dozens of musicians to woodshed with Blues Inc. before Korner broke up the group in 1967 were Mick Jagger; Cream's Ginger Baker and Jack Bruce; Hughie Flint (later with Mayall, then McGuinness-Flint); Danny Thompson, John Renbourn, and Terry Cox (all future Pentangle); Graham Bond; and Long John Baldry. Between Blues Inc. and his next band, New Church, with Danish singer Peter Thorup, Korner worked with pre–Led Zeppelin Robert Plant, Humble Pie's Steve Marriott, and Andy Fraser, who later formed Free with assistance from Korner that included suggesting the group's name and arranging for its debut performance.

New Church had a sizable European following, but it wasn't until 1971 and CCS (the Collective Consciousness Society), a 25-member–plus group assembled by noted British pop producer Mickie Most and fronted by Korner and Thorup, that he had his first chart entry, at the age of 43: "Whole Lotta Love." That same year Korner appeared on B.B. King's *In London* LP, Korner's first American record. He and Thorup toured the U.S. the next year, opening for King Crimson. By tour's end Mel Collins, Ian Wallace, and Boz Burrell (later of Bad Company) had quit Crimson and formed Snape with Korner and Thorup. They recorded the album *Accidentally Born in New Orleans* around the same time that *Bootleg Him!*, a retrospective of Korner's work, was finally released in America.

In England Korner had his own popular BBC Radio 1 program. At the time of his death from lung cancer, he was working on a 13-part TV series chronicling the history of rock & roll.

Leo Kottke

Born Sep. 11, 1945, Athens, GA
1969—*Twelve String Blues* (Oblivion) 1970—*Circle 'Round the Sun* (Symposium) 1971—*Mudlark* (Capitol) 1972—*Six and Twelve-String Guitar* (Takoma); *Greenhouse* (Capitol) 1973—*My Feet Are Smiling; Ice Water* 1974—*Dreams and All That Stuff* 1975—*Chewing Pine* 1976—*Leo Kottke 1971–1976—Did You Hear Me?; Leo Kottke* (Chrysalis) 1978—*Burnt Lips* 1979—*Balance* 1980—*Live in Europe* 1982—*Guitar Music* 1983—*Time Step* 1986—*A Shout Towards Noon* (Private Music) 1988—*Regards From Chuck Pink* 1989—*My Father's Face* 1990—*That's What* 1991—*Great Big Boy; Essential Leo Kottke* (Chrysalis) 1993—*Peculiaroso* (Private Music) 1997—*Standing in My Shoes* 2000—*One Guitar, No Vocals*.

Leo Kottke's propulsive fingerpicked guitar instrumentals and (to a lesser extent) his gallows-humor lyrics have garnered him a solid cult following. He grew up in 12 different states and tried playing violin and trombone. While living in Muskogee, Oklahoma, a cherry bomb planted by a neighborhood kid in a bush exploded, permanently impairing young Kottke's hearing in his left ear. Later, during a brief stint in the Naval Reserve, his right ear was damaged by firing practice. After the navy, Kottke went to St. Cloud State College in Minnesota, but after three years he dropped out and began hitchhiking around and practicing the guitar, which he'd been playing since he was 11.

Kottke's first LP, *Twelve String Blues*, was a 1969 set at the Scholar Coffee House in Minneapolis. He sent tapes to guitarist John Fahey, who signed him to his own Takoma label and introduced him to manager/producer Denny Bruce (who had played drums for the early Mothers of Invention). Kottke's one album for Takoma, *Six and Twelve-String Guitar*, was a collection of solo instrumentals that eventually sold 400,000 copies; in its liner notes, Kottke described his voice as "geese farts on a muggy day." He signed with Capitol and put out six albums, using bass and drums as studio backup and introducing his vocals, which weren't so bad. He appeared on the soundtrack of Terence Malick's 1978 film *Days of Heaven*. *Guitar Music* was his first all-instrumental LP since his Takoma album; *Time Step* was produced by T Bone Burnett and included guest vocals by Emmylou Harris. Kottke continues to tour as a soloist and in 1993 released *Peculiaroso*, produced by Rickie Lee Jones. The David Z–produced *Standing in My Shoes* followed in 1997. *One Guitar, No Vocals* includes new material as well as reinterpretations of older pieces.

Kraftwerk

Formed 1970, Dusseldorf, W. Ger.
Ralf Hütter (b. 1946, Krefeld, Ger.), voc., electronics, organ; Florian Schneider-Esleben (b. 1947, Dusseldorf), voc., electronics, woodwinds; Klaus Dinger, drums; Thomas Homann, gtr., bass.
1970—*Kraftwerk* (Philips, Ger.) (– Homann; + Michael Rother, gtr.; + Eberhardt Krahnemann, bass) 1972—(– Krahnemann; – Hütter) (+ Hütter) *Kraftwerk 2* 1973—(– Dinger; – Rother) *Ralf and Florian* (Vertigo, U.K.) 1974—(+ Klaus Roeder, violin, kybds.; + Wolfgang Flür, electronic perc.) *Autobahn* 1975—(– Roeder; + Karl Bartos, kybds., voc.) *Radio-Activity* (Capitol) 1977—*Trans-Europe Express* 1978—*The Man-Machine* 1981—*Computer World* (Warner Bros.) 1986—*Electric Cafe* (EMI) 1990—(– Flür; – Bartos; + Fritz Hijbert, electronic perc.) 1991—*The Mix* (Elektra).

Kraftwerk's robotic, repetitive, all-electronic music influenced virtually every synthesizer band that followed in its wake. In the mid-'70s the German group literally invented the man-machine sound and image. In 1970 Ralf Hütter and Florian Schneider-Esleben, who had met studying classical music at the Dusseldorf Conservatory, founded Kling-Klang Studio. Their first recorded appearance together is on 1970's *Tone Float,* the debut by a psychedelic kraut-rock quintet called Organisation. After leaving that group, Hütter and Schneider took the name Kraftwerk ("power plant") and began experimenting with integrating mechanized sounds from everyday life into music. Following numerous lineup changes, during which two members defected to form the influential kraut-rock band Neu!, Kraftwerk was reduced to a duo. After *Ralf and Florian* (not released in the U.S. until 1975), the pair added Klaus Roeder and Wolfgang Flür.

They found immediate success with their first U.S. release, *Autobahn,* which went Top 5. The requisite hit was an edited version of the 22-minute minimalist title track about a monotonous journey along the famed German–Austrian superhighway. Kraftwerk's next two LPs were paeans to such other modern-world wonders as the radio *(Radio-Activity)* and the train *(Trans-Europe Express).* David Bowie cited Ralf and Florian as an influence for his *Low* and *"Heroes"* albums. (There is some evidence that Bowie's "V-2 Schneider" is a tribute.) Kraftwerk confirmed its cold, conceptualist image with "Trans-Europe Express" and "Showroom Dummies," both of which became late-'70s disco hits. In 1977 the group toured the U.S. playing electronic instruments and dressed in mannequin outfits. The members later threatened to tour by sending over robots in lieu of themselves while they rested in their studio.

The Man-Machine featured more accessible music. Kraftwerk then disappeared for three years, not emerging until 1981 with the pop-oriented *Computer World* (#72, 1981), which stayed on the U.S. chart for 42 weeks and produced a #1 U.K. single, "The Model." Meanwhile, the "Trans-Europe Express" melody and the rhythm of "Numbers" made their way into rap, on Afrika Bambaataa's "Planet Rock." After 1986's *Electric Cafe,* Kraftwerk kept a relatively low profile, releasing only a best-of, *The Mix.*

Thanks to the flood of new techno, ambient, and experimental electronic sounds, in the '90s a new set of fans embraced Kraftwerk's catalogue and its ideas. The band headlined the U.K.'s Tribal Gathering concert in 1997 and has played select live dates, festivals, and raves. In 1999 the world exhibition organization Expo 2000 commissioned Kraftwerk to record "Expo 2000," the event's theme song. It doubled as a single.

Billy J. Kramer and the Dakotas

Formed 1963, Liverpool, Eng.
Billy J. Kramer (b. William Howard Ashton, Aug. 19, 1943, Bootle, Eng.), voc.; Tony Mansfield (b. May 28, 1943, Salford, Eng.), drums; Mike Maxfield (b. Feb. 23, 1944, Manchester, Eng.), gtr.; Robin Macdonald (b. July 18, 1943, Nairn, Scot.), gtr.; Raymond Jones (b. Oct. 20, 1939, Oldham, Eng.; d. Jan. 20, 2000), bass.
1964—*Little Children* (Imperial) N.A.—*The Best of Billy J. Kramer and the Dakotas* (Capitol).

Billy J. Kramer was the type of crooner that dominated the British pop chart until the Beatles changed the rules. Ironically he owed his fleeting fame largely *to* the Beatles: He shared their manager, Brian Epstein; their label, EMI-Parlophone; and their producer, George Martin. And two of his biggest hits were written by John Lennon and Paul McCartney.

Liverpudlian William Ashton had already adopted his stage name, Billy J. Kramer, by 1963, when he and his group, the Coasters, were spotted by Brian Epstein. Epstein set Kramer up with a Manchester combo, the Dakotas, and the Beatles' songwriters, John Lennon and Paul McCartney. "Do You Want to Know a Secret?" was his first success, in 1963, followed by "Bad to Me," a hit on both sides of the Atlantic (#9 U.S.). (Kramer later recalled how he'd learned "Do You Want to Know a Secret?" from a crude demo tape John Lennon had recorded in a bathroom.) The singer's biggest non–Lennon/McCartney number was "Little Children" (#7, 1964). His last hit came in 1965 with "Trains and Boats and Planes" (#47, 1965). Soon after, Brian Epstein began devoting more attention to the Beatles, and the Dakotas split up. Kramer continued performing on the cabaret circuit until the mid-'70s, when he unsuccessfully attempted a comeback. Between 1973 and 1983 he released 11 singles on seven different U.K. labels. In 1984 Kramer relocated to Long Island, and he continues to perform on the oldies circuit.

Alison Krauss

Born July 23, 1971, Champaign, IL
1987—*Too Late to Cry* (Rounder) 1989—*Two Highways* (with Union Station) 1990—*I've Got That Old Feeling* 1992—*Every Time You Say Goodbye* (with Union Station) 1994—*I Know Who Holds Tomorrow* (with the Cox Family) 1995—*Now That I've Found You: A Collection* 1997—*So Long So Wrong* (with Union Station) 1999—*Forget About It.*

Blessed with an angelic voice and virtuosic fiddling skills, bluegrass propagator Alison Krauss has already accrued more honors than most artists receive in a lifetime. By age 22, she had won two Grammys, been inducted into the Grand Ole Opry, and recorded with some of the best-known artists in country music. She also boasts noteworthy record production skills and fronts Union Station, an acclaimed bluegrass outfit.

Krauss displayed her musical aptitude at an early age. When she was 5 she started taking classical violin lessons in her hometown of Champaign, Illinois, and by age 12 had become the state fiddling champion. She had discovered bluegrass at age 8, and at 14 joined Union Station, a local bluegrass band. That year the group, billed as Alison Krauss and Union Station, mesmerized a throng at the Newport Folk Festival, garnering the young fiddler a recording contract with Rounder Records. Her first solo effort, *Too Late to Cry,* was augmented by bluegrass legends Jerry Douglas (Dobro), Sam Bush (mandolin), and Tony Trischka (banjo).

Two years later, Krauss' bandleading skills were showcased on *Two Highways,* her first album with Union Station. In 1990 *I've Got That Old Feeling,* a solo effort (her contract allows her to alternate solo albums and albums with Union Station), won Krauss her first Grammy for Best Bluegrass Album, and in 1992 she received another for *Every Time You Say Goodbye.* That July she was the first bluegrass artist in 29 years to join the Grand Ole Opry, and that year she was named Female Vocalist of the Year by the International Bluegrass Music Association (IBMA), who also awarded her its Album of the Year award for *Every Time You Say Goodbye.*

In 1994 she produced and collaborated on the Cox Family's bluegrass/gospel album *I Know Who Holds Tomorrow.* In 1995 the fiddler confirmed her appeal to a wider audience than bluegrass usually gets when her cover of "When You Say Nothing at All" (#53 pop, #3 C&W)—which appeared first on a Keith Whitley tribute album, then on the Krauss collection *Now That I've Found You* (#13 pop, #2 C&W)—became a hit. Proving that this success was no fluke, Krauss charted yet again with her next studio albums, *So Long So Wrong* (#4 C&W, 1997; Grammy for Best Bluegrass Album) and *Forget About It* (#60 pop, #5 C&W, 1999). In 2000 she headlined Rounder's 30th-anniversary show in New York.

In addition to her own work, Krauss has played on sessions with such diverse artists as Vince Gill, Michael McDonald, Dolly Parton, Phish, and Kenny Rogers—whose "Buy Me a Rose" (#1 C&W, 2000) became Krauss' first time at the top of the charts; she contributed guest vocals. In classic bluegrass style, she continues to combine influences, melding the traditional with the new, thus solidifying her niche as one of the foremost ambassadors of the genre.

Lenny Kravitz

Born Leonard Albert Kravitz, May 26, 1964, New York, NY
1989—*Let Love Rule* (Virgin) 1991—*Mama Said* 1993—*Are You Gonna Go My Way* 1995—*Circus* 1998—5 2000—*Greatest Hits* (EMD/Virgin).

Lenny Kravitz survived the ridicule of being called "Mr. (Lisa) Bonet" and the scorn of critics who accused him of being a derivative neohippie to forge a successful career making anachronistic, soul-inflected, '60s-style rock for the '90s.

The only child of white TV news producer Sy Kravitz and black actress Roxie Roker (of TV's *The Jeffersons*), Kravitz spent the first 10 years of his life in Manhattan, then moved with his family to L.A., where his first musical experience came in the California Boys Choir. He taught himself guitar, bass, piano, and drums. Kravitz attended the exclusive Beverly Hills High School (classmates included Saul Hudson, later Slash, and Maria McKee), where he adopted the David Bowie–inspired, wild-party persona Romeo Blue. In 1985

Lenny Kravitz

Kravitz met actress Lisa Bonet of TV's *The Cosby Show.* They were married in 1987 and had one daughter, Zoe, before separating in 1991; their divorce became final two years later.

Let Love Rule displayed Kravitz's voice, which sounded uncannily like Elvis Costello's, and his retro-rock style, which sounded uncannily like all sorts of people—the Beatles, Bob Dylan, Jimi Hendrix. While reviews were mixed, the album sold fairly well (#61, 1989), and the title track reached #89 in 1990.

In 1990 Kravitz shared writing and producing chores with Madonna on her "Justify My Love." A year later Prince discovery Ingrid Chavez (who costarred in his *Graffiti Bridge*) sued, claiming she had cowritten the song with Kravitz. He admitted to having worked with Chavez, but maintained that they had agreed to keep her role in writing the song "private." The matter was eventually settled out of court. The rhythm track, meanwhile, had been sampled from a Public Enemy song.

In January 1991, as tensions in the Persian Gulf mounted, Kravitz hastily recorded an all-star cover of John Lennon's "Give Peace a Chance" (#54), with guitar work by Slash and vocal and video appearances by over two dozen other artists, including Yoko Ono, Sean Lennon, Bonnie Raitt, Peter Gabriel, Run-D.M.C., L.L. Cool J, and the Red Hot Chili Peppers.

Mama Said (#39, 1991) sold better than its predecessor, with the polished, Curtis Mayfield–style "It Ain't Over Til It's Over" hitting #2, his highest-charting single to date. In 1993 Kravitz released *Are You Gonna Go My Way* (#12). The hard-rocking, extremely Hendrixesque title track was nominated for two 1994 Grammys. Two years later, *Circus* (#10, 1995) reflected the singer's reportedly newfound focus on Christianity, with such tracks as "God" and "The Resurrection." Meanwhile, Kravitz suffered the death of his mother that December. The performer joined the 1996 summer H.O.R.D.E. Tour, and in 1998 released *5* (#36, 1998), whose hit "Fly Away" (#12 pop, 1998) won a Grammy Award and received extensive exposure from usage in television commercials. A cover version of the Guess Who's 1970 hit "American Woman," included on the *Austin Powers: The Spy Who Shagged Me* soundtrack, reached #49 in 1999. His next move was a heavily hyped, triple-platinum *Greatest Hits* (#2, 2000) and the #4 album track "Again."

Kris Kross

Formed 1991, Atlanta, GA
Mack Daddy (b. Chris Kelly, Aug. 11, 1978, Englewood, NJ), voc.; Daddy Mack (b. Chris Smith, Jan. 10, 1979, Atlanta), voc.
1992—*Totally Krossed Out* (Ruffhouse/Columbia) 1993—*Da Bomb* 1996—*Young, Rich & Dangerous.*

Wearing their clothes backward and rapping in prepubescent squeaks, the members of Kris Kross were a teenybopper, hip-hop sensation in the early '90s. The two Chrises were discovered by producer Jermaine Dupri while he was shopping at an Atlanta mall. He groomed and coached them for a year—dressing them in baggy, backward gear—and wrote songs for their multiplatinum debut, *Totally Krossed Out* (#1 pop, #1 R&B, 1992). The duo called themselves the Mack Daddy (Kelly) and Daddy Mack (Smith) and rapped about missing the school bus and sneaking into clubs. Propelled by the multiplatinum single "Jump" (#1, 1992), which sampled the Jackson 5's "I Want You Back," and "Warm It Up" (#13 pop, 1993), Kris Kross became international stars. They toured Europe opening for Michael Jackson and appeared in the film *Who's the Man?* as well as on a score of TV shows.

By their second album, the boys' voices had begun to deepen, and they accordingly tried to evince a more hardcore attitude, rapping like young gangstas. Whereas Dupri wrote their debut, Kelly contributed some lyrics on *Da Bomb* (#13 pop, #2 R&B, 1993). Several songs featured dancehall rhythms, with reggae rapper Supercat guesting on "Alright" (#19 pop, #8 R&B, 1993). That single and "I'm Real" (#84 pop, #45 R&B, 1993) garnered some chart success. The pair continued to mature on 1996's *Young, Rich & Dangerous* (#15 pop, #2 R&B), which boasted a collaboration with Da Brat, Mr. Black, and Aaliyah entitled "Live and Die for Hip Hop" (#72 pop, #36 R&B). The Chrises have long since disappeared from hip-hop, but "Jump" endures as an anthem at professional basketball games.

Kris Kristofferson

Born June 22, 1937, Brownsville, TX
1970—*Kristofferson* (Monument) 1971—*Me and Bobby McGee; Cisco Pete* (Columbia); *The Silver-Tongued Devil and I* (Monument) 1972—*Josie; Border Lord; Jesus Was a Capricorn* 1973—*Why Me?* 1974—*Spooky Lady's Sideshow* 1975—*Who's to Bless and Who's to Blame* 1976—*Surreal Thing; A Star Is Born* soundtrack (Columbia) 1977—*Songs of Kristofferson* 1978—*Easter Island* 1979—*Shake Hands With the Devil* 1980—*Help Me Make It Through the Night; To the Bone* 1981—*Nobody Loves Anybody Anymore* 1986—*Repossessed* 1990—*Third World Warrior* (Mercury) 1991—*Singer/Songwriter* (Columbia Legacy) 1995—*A Moment of Forever* (Justice) 1999—*The Austin Sessions* (Atlantic).
With Rita Coolidge: 1973—*Full Moon* (A&M) 1974—*Breakaway* (Monument) 1978—*Natural Act* (A&M).
With Willie Nelson: 1984—*Music From SongWriter* soundtrack (Columbia); *How Do You Feel About Foolin' Around.*
With the Highwaymen (Willie Nelson, Johnny Cash, and Waylon Jennings): 1985—*Highwayman* (Columbia) 1990—*Highwayman 2* 1995—*The Road Goes On Forever* (Capitol) 1999—*Highwayman Super Hits* (Sony).
With Waylon Jennings, Willie Nelson, and Billy Joe Shaver: 2000—*Honky Tonk Heroes* (Pedernales/FreeFalls).

Kris Kristofferson finished out the '70s as a movie star, but several of his songs—"Sunday Morning Coming Down," "Me and Bobby McGee," and "Help Me Make It Through the Night"—have become country-rock standards. In the early '70s their boozy romanticism helped define "outlaw" country.

After receiving a Ph.D. from Pomona College, Kristofferson went to Oxford University on a Rhodes scholarship in 1958. He first wanted to be a novelist, but he was also writing songs; he changed his name to Kris Carson and was signed by Tommy Steele's manager. In 1960 he joined the army, but five years later, when he was about to accept a job teaching English at West Point, he decided instead to invest all his time in songwriting once again, encouraged by a meeting with his idol, Johnny Cash. He moved to Nashville in 1965 and tried to pitch his songs while working as a night janitor at the Columbia studios, cleaning ashtrays at the same time Bob Dylan was recording *Blonde on Blonde* there. (Billy Swan, Kristofferson's future guitarist, later worked the same job.)

His break finally came in 1969, when Johnny Cash gave Kristofferson's song "Me and Bobby McGee" to Roger Miller, who made it a hit on the country chart. Kristofferson appeared on Cash's TV show, and Cash had a hit with "Sunday Morning" in 1969. In March 1971, Janis Joplin's version of "Bobby McGee" went to #1, and about the same time Sammi Smith had a #8 pop hit with "Help Me Make It Through the Night." Kristofferson's own recording debut was released in June 1970. His commercial potential caught up to his critical success on 1971's *The Silver-Tongued Devil and I,* which went gold. The next year's *Border Lord* was panned, and from then on his recording career declined. Meanwhile, he made his film debut in 1972's *Cisco Pike* and two years later appeared in *Pat Garrett and Billy the Kid,* a film in which his second wife, Rita Coolidge, also appeared. They were married in 1973; they had met two years earlier. From there, Kristofferson established himself as an actor in *Alice Doesn't*

Live Here Anymore, The Sailor Who Fell From Grace With the Sea, Semi-Tough, Convoy, and a remake of *A Star Is Born* with Barbra Streisand.

Kristofferson had a 20-year drinking problem, which he finally kicked in the late '70s. He toured and recorded throughout the '70s, sometimes with Coolidge until their marriage dissolved in December 1979. Since 1980 Kristofferson has appeared in well over a dozen films, including features such as *Heaven's Gate* (1980), *Rollover* (1981), *Trouble in Mind* (1985), and 1984's *SongWriter,* in which he costarred with fellow "outlaw" Willie Nelson. He has also costarred in numerous made-for-TV movies and miniseries. In 1994 he costarred in *Sodbusters,* and the following year played a murderous sheriff in director John Sayles' *Lone Star.* His other '90s films include Sayles' *Limbo, Payback* (with Mel Gibson), and *A Soldier's Daughter Never Cries.*

Kristofferson is known for his outspoken leftist political views, which, he claims, led to his break from his longtime label, Columbia, in the late '80s. To date, all of his major country hits have been collaborative efforts with Nelson, Johnny Cash, and Waylon Jennings in the country supergroup the Highwaymen: 1985's "Highwayman" (#1 C&W), "Desperadoes Waiting for a Train" (#15 C&W), and 1990's "Silver Stallion" (#25 C&W). Meanwhile, Kristofferson's solo output has slowed considerably in the last decade. After 1990's politically themed *Third World Warrior,* it would be five years before he resurfaced with the Don Was–produced *A Moment of Forever* on the independent Justice label. *The Austin Sessions,* released by Atlantic in 1999, was comprised of newly recorded versions of Kristofferson's best-known songs with guests including Steve Earle, Jackson Browne, and Vince Gill.

KRS-ONE/Boogie Down Productions

Formed 1986, Bronx, NY
KRS-ONE (b. Lawrence "Kris" Parker, 1966, Bronx), voc.; Scott LaRock (b. Scott Sterling, Bronx; d. Aug. 25, 1987, Bronx), DJ.
Boogie Down Productions: 1987—*Criminal Minded* (B Boy) (– LaRock; + Kenny Parker [b. Bronx], DJ) 1988—*By All Means Necessary* (Jive) 1989—*Ghetto Music: The Blueprint of Hip Hop* 1990—*Edutainment* 1991—*Ya Know the Rules* EP; *Live Hardcore Worldwide: Paris, London, & NYC* 1992—*Sex and Violence.*
KRS-ONE solo: 1993—*Return of the Boom Bap* (Jive) 1995—*KRS-ONE* 1997—*I Got Next* 2000—*A Retrospective: Dedicated to Scott LaRock* 2001—*Sneak Attack* (In the Paint/Front Page/KOCH).

Beginning as a pioneering gangsta rap group, Boogie Down Productions (BDP) had become the hip-hop vehicle for rapper Kris "KRS-ONE" Parker's philosophical proselytizing by the time of 1990's *Edutainment.* Parker had embarked on an ambitious antiviolence crusade after his partner, DJ Scott LaRock, was gunned down in 1987 while trying to break up a street fight. Still, it is Boogie Down Production's blend of hip-hop with reggae dancehall and rock influences that sets the group apart from other message-oriented rappers.

Growing up on welfare in Brooklyn and the Bronx, Kris Parker was introduced to rap music through his mother's collection of discs, including some by the Treacherous Three and Grandmaster Flash. Parker ran away from home at 13 and began living on the streets. During the day he would read about philosophy and religion at the library, and at night he'd practice his rapping at the homeless shelters where he lived. At 17 he got his GED.

While staying at the Franklin Armory Shelter in the Bronx, Parker met social worker Scott Sterling, known on weekends as DJ Scott LaRock. The two formed BDP and released *Criminal Minded* on the independent B Boy record label in 1987. The album's smooth grooves and hard rhymes foreshadowed gangsta rap. In August that year LaRock was killed.

Parker kept going with his brother Kenny, releasing *By All Means Necessary* (#75 pop, #18 R&B, 1988) the following year. The album introduced the rapper's "edutainment" style of rap in songs such as "My Philosophy" and "Stop the Violence," the latter of which Parker turned into a movement in 1989 to help curb black-on-black violence. BDP's albums sold relatively well. Both *Ghetto Music* (#36 pop, #7 R&B, 1989) and *Edutainment* (#32 pop, #9 R&B, 1990) went gold and continued Parker's message of antiviolence. Although *Live Hardcore Worldwide* failed to make it onto the pop chart, *Sex and Violence* reached #42 (#20 R&B, 1992). *Return of the Boom Bap,* KRS-ONE's solo debut, reached #37 (#5 R&B, 1993), while the commercial success of *KRS-ONE* (#19 pop, #2 R&B, 1995) and *I Got Next* (#3 pop, #2 R&B, 1997) bolstered BDP/KRS's fan base.

By the late '80s, Parker had begun doing college lecture tours wherein he would touch on a range of topics including Afrocentrism, religion, politics, violence, and his own revisionist views of American history. In 1991 he organized a group of artists including Chuck D., L.L. Cool J, Queen Latifah, British folkie Billy Bragg, and R.E.M.'s Michael Stipe for the consciousness-raising compilation *H.E.A.L. (Human Education Against Lies): Civilization Vs. Technology.* Toward the end of the '90s KRS began erecting the Temple of Hiphop—an organization dedicated to the teaching of hiphop history—and became a mentor/tutor at Harlem's Riverside Church.

In 2000 KRS-ONE bought out of his contract with Jive and began putting together material for *Sneak Attack,* his first studio album in four years.

Fela Anikulapo Kuti/Femi Kuti

Fela Kuti (b. Fela Ransome Kuti, Oct. 15, 1938, Abeokuta, Nigeria; d. Aug. 2, 1997, Lagos, Nigeria), voc., sax, kybds.
1970—*Fela's London Scene* (Makossa) 1971—*Fela With Ginger Baker Live; Open and Close* (EMI) 1972—*Shakara* 1973—*Afrodisiac; Gentleman* (Creole) 1975—*He Miss Road* (EMI); *Question Jam Answer* (Makossa); *Expensive Shit; Roforofo Fight; Mr. Follow-Follow* (Phonodisc); *Confusion* (Polydor); *Monkey Banana* (Coconut) 1976—*Upside Down* (London); *Na Poi; Yellow Fever; Kalakuta Show* (Makossa) 1977—*Zombie*

(Mercury); *Fear Not for Man* (Decca); *J.J.D. (Johnny Just Drop); Stalemate; Opposite People; Sorrow Tears and Blood* (Kalakuta) 1979—*Coffin for Head of State* (Makossa); *V.I.P.: Vagabonds in Power; Unknown Soldier* (Phonodisc) 1980—*Fela and Roy Ayers: Music of Many Colors; Authority Stealing* (Polydor); *I.T.T. (International Thief)* 1981—*Black President* (Arista, U.K.); *Original Sufferhead* 1982—*Unnecessary Begging* (Makossa); *Alagbon Close* 1983—*Perambulator* (Lagos International) 1984—*Live in Amsterdam* (EMI, Fr.) 1985—*Army Arrangement* (Celluloid); *Shuffering and Shmiling; No Agreement* 1987—*Teacher Don't Teach Me Nonsense* (Mercury) 1988—*I Go Shout Plenty* 1989—*Beasts of No Nation* (Shanachie) 1990—*Odoo* 1992—*Black Man's Cry: Classic Fela* 1993—*The '69 Los Angeles Sessions* (Stern's Africa) 1999—*Underground System; Live* (Shanachie); *The Best of Fela Kuti: The Black President* (Universal).
Femi Kuti (b. Olufemi Anikulapo Kuti, June 16, 1962, London, Eng.), voc., sax: 1995—*Femi Kuti* (Tabu) 1996—*Femi Kuti & Positive Force* (Melodie) 1999—*Shoki Shoki* (Barclay Fr.); *Shoki Remixed.*

Fela Anikulapo Kuti was the leading exponent—and arguably the originator—of afro-beat, an urban West African dance-while-you-protest style that modernized traditional Yoruba music (call-and-response chanting over polyrhythmic drumming) with repeated R&B-style horn figures and funk-styled guitar chords. Keyboardist, saxophonist, vocalist, composer, and bandleader, he was also one of the most politically outspoken figures in international pop.

Fela Kuti was the son of Funmilayo Kuti, a woman well known in Nigeria as a feminist and labor organizer; she exerted early and lasting influence on Fela, although his youthful interests were more musical than political. In 1959 he went to England to study at the Trinity College of Music, and he began playing piano in jazz, R&B, and rock bands with African, British, and American musicians, among them Ginger Baker of Cream. He also took up the alto saxophone.

Returning to Nigeria in the mid-'60s, he formed a band that was successful enough to afford a move en masse to the U.S. in 1969. Alternating between New York and L.A., the band made virtually no impression on American audiences, but influenced by American black militants, Fela returned to Nigeria in 1970 with new ideas about the role of the musician in political change.

He formed a new band, Africa 70 (also spelled Afrika 70), an ensemble of 20 instrumentalists, singers, and dancers, and began making albums that showed the influences of James Brown and Sly and the Family Stone. He set up a communal estate for the band and their families on the outskirts of Lagos, eventually building a hospital and a recording studio on its grounds (the latter with the help of Ginger Baker, who lived in Nigeria for much of the '70s). The site became a meeting place for West African radical artists, writers, and activists and the object of harassment by Nigeria's military junta. Fela's songs were highly critical of government corruption, police brutality, and the greed of foreign investors. Nigerian hits (most of his releases) such as "Zombie" and "Monkey Banana" openly mocked the authorities.

After Fela and associates were jailed and beaten by police on a number of occasions, he declared his property the independent Kalakuta Republic. On February 18, 1977, presumably in reaction to that act of treason, 1,000 armed soldiers attacked Kalakuta. In a full day of fighting, Kalakutans were raped, wounded, and arrested, and the settlement was burned. Fela's mother later died from injuries she suffered in the attack. After being released from jail, Fela and his followers exiled themselves to Ghana for a year. There he married his 27 female singers and dancers, giving him 28 wives.

On his return to Nigeria, Fela rebuilt Kalakuta but was banned from giving concerts, which previously had drawn as many as 100,000 fans to each. So, for the first time since 1970, he took his show abroad, traveling through Germany, Italy, and France with his entourage of 70. Back in Nigeria in 1979, he formed a political party, Movement of the People, and ran for the presidency of Nigeria that year until election authorities banned him from the campaign. In 1983 Fela's band, now known as Egypt 80, was joined for an African tour by American jazz trumpeter Lester Bowie, of the Art Ensemble of Chicago (he plays on *Perambulator* and *Fear Not for Man*).

Fela had promised to run again for Nigeria's presidency in 1983, but a military government returned to power that year, and in September 1984, as he was about to depart for an international tour, Fela was arrested at Lagos Airport and sentenced to five years in jail for currency smuggling. During his incarceration, his son Femi, who had played sax in the band for several years, took over leadership of Egypt 80, and New York avant-funk bassist and producer Bill Laswell (Material, Time Zone) finished production of material that became *Army Arrangement,* bringing in P-Funk keyboardist Bernie Worrell and other musicians to play over Fela's tapes. Meanwhile, Amnesty International took up Fela's cause and, after another change in Nigeria's government, worldwide publicity led to Fela's release in July 1985. He was immediately flown to appear at the final show of Amnesty International's Conspiracy of Hope Tour in New Jersey. There, looking frail, he played piano with Rubén Blades and percussion with the Neville Brothers.

A year later, a much stronger Fela and Egypt 80 finally toured the U.S., to sizable audiences and great critical acclaim; they returned in 1989 with reggae singer Jimmy Cliff and African reggae star Lucky Dube. In March 1993 Fela was jailed once again in Lagos, on a murder charge stemming from the beating death of a worker at Fela's home. The charge was eventually dropped.

Fela's mammoth recorded output dropped off considerably in the '90s, and in retrospect it may have been due to failing health; he succumbed to AIDS-related heart failure in 1997. Femi, who'd already recorded with some Egypt 80 members, began his own career, leading his band Positive Force with the critically acclaimed *Shoki Shoki.* His afrobeat was far less political than his father's, but his hit single "Beng Beng Beng" was still banned by the Nigerian government for its sexual content. While rappers Q-Tip and Mos Def sampled Fela's music, Femi collaborated with the Roots for one track on *Shoki Shoki,* and appeared on rapper Common's *Like Water for Chocolate.* Fela's former drummer Tony Allen also released the critically acclaimed *Black Voices* in 1999.

Jim Kweskin Jug Band

Formed 1963
Jim Kweskin (b. July 18, 1940, Stamford, CT), gtr., voc.; Bill Keith, pedal steel gtr., banjo; Mel Lyman (b. Melvin Lyman, Mar. 24, 1938, Eureka, CA; d. Apr. 1978, Boston, MA), harmonica, banjo; Fritz Richmond, jug, washtub bass; Richard Greene, fiddle; Maria D'Amato Muldaur (b. Maria Grazia Rosa Domenica D'Amato, Sep. 12, 1943, New York, NY), voc., kazoo, tambourine; Geoff Muldaur (b. 1945, Pelham, NY), gtr., voc.
1968—*The Best of the Jim Kweskin Jug Band* (Vanguard) 1970—*Greatest Hits* 1998—*Acoustic Swing & Jug.*

The Jim Kweskin Jug Band was a slaphappy answer to the earnestness of the "folk revival" as typified by Peter, Paul and Mary. The members rarely wrote their own material but specialized in uncovering folk, blues, jazz, and novelty tunes of the past and remaking them in their raucous acoustic style. Kweskin was merely the nominal leader of the ever-shifting aggregation; Geoff Muldaur was more likely to be heard on lead vocals and guitar. Maria D'Amato, who would later wed Muldaur and have a successful duo and solo career under her married name, also sang and played fiddle, although the latter instrument would eventually be manned by future Blues Project/Seatrain virtuoso Richard Greene. Fritz Richmond blew jug and became a virtuoso on washtub bass.

One of the later additions to the band was harmonica player Mel Lyman. Lyman, a self-styled prophet and authoritarian religious leader, split up the group in 1967. Kweskin became a disciple; the others went solo or faded into obscurity. Lyman's followers maintain that he died in 1978 after a long illness, though there are no existing funeral records or death certificates pertaining to the event. They deny rumors that he is still living or that he fled to Europe. Kweskin's solo work includes *Jim Kweskin's America* (1971), *Jim Kweskin Lives Again* (1978), and *Swing on a Star* (1980). In the '90s Kweskin performed with his group, Jim Kweskin and Samoa with the Swinging Tenants. A newly formed Jim Kweskin Jug Band playing the group's old repertoire hit the Northeast club circuit in 2001.

Patti LaBelle

Born Patricia Louise Holt, Oct. 4, 1944, Philadelphia, PA
1977—*Patti LaBelle* (Epic) 1978—*Tasty* 1979—*It's Alright With Me* 1980—*Released* 1981—*Best of/The Spirit's in It* (Philadelphia International) 1983—*I'm in Love Again* 1985—*Patti* 1986—*The Winner in You* (MCA) 1989—*Be Yourself* 1990—*This Christmas* 1991—*Burnin'; Wishing You a Merry Christmas* (Hits of Sugarhill) 1992—*Live!* (MCA) 1994—*Gems; Flame* 1996—*Greatest Hits* 1998—*Live! One Night Only* 1999—*Best of Patti LaBelle: 20th Century Masters* 2000—*When a Woman Loves.*

Following the 1976 breakup of Labelle, the group she'd founded 15 years before, Patti LaBelle embarked on a solo career. It took her nearly a decade to achieve massive success; during that time she established herself as a soul diva noteworthy for her three-octave contralto and theatrical stage presence.

LaBelle, whose self-titled debut featured the kind of sassy funk and yearning ballads she'd been singing for years, continued releasing credible albums while initiating an acting career. In 1982 she costarred with Al Green in the Broadway revival of *Your Arms Too Short to Box With God* and then went on to play a blues singer in the movie *A Soldier's Story* and star in the Truman Capote/Harold Arlen musical *House of Flowers.* On television, she appeared in the Emmy-winning *Motown Salutes the Apollo* and *Sisters in the Name of Love* as well as the sitcoms *A Different World* and *Out All Night.*

On her albums, she became known primarily for duets with performers ranging from her ex-Labelle band mates Nona Hendryx and Sarah Dash to Gladys Knight, Michael Bolton, Bobby Womack, and Grover Washington Jr. "New Attitude," from the *Beverly Hills Cop* soundtrack, gained her a #17 hit in 1985; her biggest success came with *Winner in You* and its duet with Michael McDonald, "On My Own" (#1, 1986).

In 1992 winning a Grammy for Best Female R&B Vocal Performance for *Burnin'*, LaBelle lists among her many other awards the Martin Luther King Lifetime Achievement Award and the Ebony Achievement Award; twice she has been the recipient of the NAACP Entertainer of the Year Award. Her appearance in the 1985 Live Aid telecast underscored the charitable interests she continues to promote: She has served as spokeswoman for the National Cancer Institute (all three of her sisters died from the disease) and national chairwoman of the Black Health Research Foundation, and has worked for AIDS awareness.

In 1996 her autobiography, *Don't Block the Blessings: Revelations of a Lifetime,* became a bestseller. She followed it with a 1999 cookbook, *LaBelle Cuisine: Recipes to Sing About* and in 2001 *Patti's Pearls: Lessons in Living Genuinely, Joyfully, Generously.* She has also produced a line of designer cosmetics. Music, however, remains paramount for LaBelle: In 2000 she released *When a Woman Loves,* a concept album about the female perspective on romance, with songs by Diane Warren.

Labelle

Formed as Patti LaBelle and the Blue Belles, 1961, Philadelphia, PA
Patti LaBelle (b. Patricia Louise Holt, Oct. 4, 1944, Philadelphia), voc.; Nona Hendryx (b. Aug. 18, 1945, Trenton, NJ), voc.; Sarah Dash (b. May 24, 1942, Trenton), voc.; Cindy Birdsong (b. Dec. 15, 1939, Camden, NJ), voc.
1967—(– Birdsong) *Dreamer* (Atlantic) 1971—(group was renamed Labelle) *Labelle* (Warner Bros.); *Gonna Take a Miracle* (with Laura Nyro) (Columbia) 1972—*Moonshadow* (Warner Bros.) 1973—*Pressure Cookin'* (RCA) 1974—*Nightbirds* (Epic) 1975—*Phoenix* 1976—*Chameleon.*
Patti LaBelle solo: see entry.
Nona Hendryx solo: see entry.
Sarah Dash solo: 1979—*Sarah Dash* (Kirshner) 1985—*You're All I Need* (Capitol).

In its 16 years together, Labelle developed from a fairly conventional '60s girl group—replete with sequined gowns, bouffants, and polished choreography—into a band with a unique, space-queen look, an idealistic political consciousness, and an individual gospel-tinged, funky rock & roll sound. They began as Patti LaBelle and the Blue Belles, bringing together LaBelle and Cindy Birdsong from the Ordettes with Nona Hendryx and Sarah Dash from the Del Capris. Their 1962 single "I Sold My Heart to the Junkman" became a #15 hit, followed by versions of "Danny Boy" (#76, 1964) and "You'll Never Walk Alone" (#34, 1964).

The Blue Belles became a trio in 1967 when Birdsong left to replace Florence Ballard in the Supremes. Although they were hugely popular at the Apollo Theatre and on the soul circuit, they were mismanaged. In 1970 Britisher Vicki Wickham (who knew the Blue Belles from their mid-'60s appearance on the English TV show *Ready Steady Go,* which she produced) became their manager, revamping their image and leading them toward more contemporary rock. She also encouraged Hendryx to contribute more of her own songs.

In 1971, after Wickham rechristened the group Labelle, it released an eponymous debut on Warner Bros. and toured the U.S. with the Who. That same year the band collaborated with Laura Nyro on *Gonna Take a Miracle,* a collection of '50s and '60s soul and doo-wop remakes. In 1973 Labelle, at a headline Bottom Line show, joined the glitter trend, debuting its soon-to-be-famous lamé space-cadet suits. In 1974 it became the first black act ever to play New York's Metropolitan Opera House; there it introduced what was to become its only million-selling hit, "Lady Marmalade" (#1, 1975), a shouter about a Creole hooker. The single, written by Bob Crewe, Allen Toussaint, and Kenny Nolan, highlighted its *Nightbirds* LP, produced by Toussaint in New Orleans.

Labelle: Nona Hendryx, Patti LaBelle, Sarah Dash

Since Hendryx and Patti LaBelle had basic musical differences, Labelle broke up in 1976. Sarah Dash played small clubs and began recording solo albums in 1979. She continues to work as a background singer for various artists, including Keith Richards, the Rolling Stones, LaBelle, and Hendryx. The three were reunited on "Release Yourself," from LaBelle's 1991 solo album *Burnin'.*

Ladysmith Black Mambazo

Formed 1964, Ladysmith, S.A.
Joseph Shabalala (b. Aug. 28, 1940, S.A.), voc.; Headman Shabalala (b. Oct. 9, 1945, S.A.; d. Dec. 11, 1991, S.A.), voc.; Jockey Shabalala (b. Nov. 4, 1944, S.A.), voc.; Ben Shabalala (b. Nov. 30, 1957, S.A.), voc.; Albert Mazibuko (b. Apr. 16, 1948, S.A.), voc.; Abednego Mazibuko (b. Mar. 12, 1954, S.A.), voc.; Russel Mthembu (b. Mar. 12, 1947, S.A.), voc.; Inos Phungula (b. Mar. 31, 1945, S.A.), voc.; Jabulani Dubazana (b. Apr. 25, 1954, S.A.), voc.; Geophrey Mdletshe (b. Jan. 23, 1960, S.A.), voc.
1984—*Induku Zethu* (Shanachie) 1985—*Ulwandle Oluncgwele* 1986—*Inala* 1987—*Shaka Zulu* (Warner Bros.) 1988—*Umthombo Wamanzi* (Shanachie); *Journey of Dreams* (Warner Bros.) 1989—*How the Leopard Got His Spots* (with Danny Glover) (Windham Hill) 1990—*Classic Tracks* (Shanachie); *Two Worlds One Heart* (Warner Bros.) 1991—(– H. Shabalala) 1992—*Best of Ladysmith Black Mambazo* (Shanachie) 1994—*Liph' Iqiniso; Gift of the Tortoise* (Warner Bros.); *Inkanyezi Nezazi* (Flame Tree) 1996—*Thuthukani Ngoxolo* (Shanachie) 1997—*Heavenly* 1998—*Vol. 2: Best of Ladysmith* 1999—*In Harmony: Live at the Royal Albert Hall.*

Through its participation in Paul Simon's 1986 *Graceland* album and 1987 tour, Ladysmith Black Mambazo became the most well-known African group in the Western world. Before then, it spent two decades becoming one of the best-selling groups in South Africa. Formed by Joseph Shabalala with his family and friends in the town of Ladysmith, LBM is a Zulu *mbube* choir who plays a rhythmic a cappella music alternately called *mbaqanga, Iscathamiya,* or "township jive." Iscathamiya was born in the mines of South Africa, where black laborers, living in camps far from home, developed a style of competitive singing and dancing to pass the time. The workers brought the contests, called *Cothoza Mfana,* back to the townships with them.

Ladysmith Black Mambazo

Joseph went to Durban and sang in bands before returning to Ladysmith to form his own group, with his brothers Headman and Jockey Shabalala (Ben joined later) and his cousins Albert and Abednego Mazibuko. Soon Ladysmith Black Mambazo was the champion of Cothoza Mfana. It got its first recording contract in 1970 and has released more than 30 albums in South Africa, some of which Shanachie rereleased in America (U.S. release dates are listed in discography, above). LBM sang on two of *Graceland*'s tracks, "Diamonds on the Soles of Her Shoes" and "Homeless," and subsequently toured with Simon, also appearing with him on a Showtime TV special and *Saturday Night Live.*

This fame garnered the group its own deal with Warner. Its 1987 album, *Shaka Zulu,* produced by Simon and sung partly in English, won a Grammy. *Journey of Dreams* includes a Simon-arranged version of "Amazing Grace." *How the Leopard Got His Spots* is a Rudyard Kipling tale narrated by Danny Glover. On *Two Worlds One Heart,* the group collaborated with George Clinton.

Ladysmith also contributed songs to the soundtracks for *Coming to America* and *Dry White Season,* played on harpist Andreas Vollenweider's album *Book of Roses,* were featured in Michael Jackson's *Moonwalker* video, have been regular guests on *Sesame Street,* and appeared in an award-winning 7-Up commercial. In 1992 the band toured South Africa with Simon; the following year it performed as the chorus in *The Song of Jacob Zulu,* a Steppenwolf Theatre Company production that played on Broadway at New York's Plymouth Theatre. The music won a Drama Desk Award.

Ladysmith Black Mambazo's world fame did not protect it from the brutal injustices of its homeland's political system, however. In December 1991 Headman Shabalala was shot along a highway near Durban; a white security guard was convicted of manslaughter.

LBM collaborated with Dolly Parton, Bonnie Raitt, Phoebe Snow, and Lou Rawls on its 1997 album *Heavenly,* a record that featured a mix of American and Zulu spirituals, as well as instrumental accompaniment. In 1998 the U.K. division of Heinz used "The Star and the Wise Man," a song from Ladysmith's *Inkanyezi Nezazi* album (1994), in a series of TV ads marketing soups, baked beans, and spaghetti. The song became a Top 20 single in England. On October 7, 1998, the group's longtime producer West Nkosi, a prime mover on the South African music scene since the '60s, died after sustaining injuries in a car wreck.

Greg Lake: See Emerson, Lake and Palmer

Major Lance

Born Apr. 4, 1941, Chicago, IL; died Sep. 3, 1994, Decatur, GA
1963—*The Monkey Time* (Okeh) 1976—*Um, Um, Um, Um, Um, Um/The Best of Major Lance* (Epic) 1977—*Live at the Torch* (Contempo) 1978—*Now Arriving* (Tamla) 1995—*Everybody Loves a Good Time! The Best of Major Lance* (Legacy) 2000—*The Very Best of Major Lance.*

With Curtis Mayfield writing his material and Carl Davis producing, soul vocalist Major Lance enjoyed many hits in the early '60s and helped establish what became known as the Chicago soul sound, along with the Impressions, Jerry Butler, Gene Chandler, and others. Lance had spent some time as a professional boxer, and he recorded for Mercury before meeting Mayfield and signing with Okeh, Columbia's revitalized "race" label. After hearing the song "The Monkey

Time," which Mayfield had written for Lance, Okeh president Carl Davis hired Mayfield as staff producer and Lance as a singer.

Mayfield and Lance's first release, "Delilah" (1962), was a flop. But the followup, "The Monkey Time," shot to #8 in September 1963 and helped kick off a dance trend called the Monkey. The song's orchestral sound (arranged by Johnny Pate) was adapted by Okeh as a "Chicago style" and can be heard on Mayfield's later recordings with the Impressions. Lance's highest-charting pop hit, "Um, Um, Um, Um, Um, Um," hit #5 in February 1964 (the song was also the first major British hit for Wayne Fontana and the Mindbenders the same year).

Although Lance's pop hits ceased soon after, he had several minor R&B chart successes through 1970. He switched to Carl Davis' Dakar Records in 1968 and then to Mayfield's Curtom label. In 1972 Lance recorded for Volt, and in 1974 he signed to Playboy Records, where he rerecorded "Um, Um, Um . . ." with little success. In 1982 eight of Lance's songs were included on the Epic compilation *Okeh Soul;* prior to its release Lance had emerged from a prison stay for a 1978 cocaine-selling conviction. He died of heart disease at age 55 in 1994.

Jonny Lang

Born Jon Gordon Langseth, Jan. 29, 1981, Fargo, ND
1995—(As Kid Jonny Lang and the Big Bang) *Smokin'* (Oarfin) 1997—*Lie to Me* (A&M) 1998—*Wander This World.*

Although he was only 16 when his major-label debut, 1997's *Lie to Me,* was released, blues guitarist Jonny Lang got a relatively late start as teen prodigies go. He began playing saxophone at 11 but did not pick up guitar until he was 13, shortly after his father, a former drummer, took him to see a local Fargo, North Dakota, act, the Bad Medicine Blues Band. Lang began taking lessons from the band's guitarist, Ted Larsen, and within months was fronting the group (renamed Kid Jonny Lang and the Big Bang). After a move to Minneapolis and the independent release of the band's *Smokin'* in 1995, Lang was signed as a solo artist to A&M the following year. Released on the eve of his 16th birthday, *Lie to Me* debuted at #1 on *Billboard*'s New Artist Chart and earned Lang opening spots on tours with Aerosmith, the Rolling Stones, and B.B. King, as well as a cameo alongside Wilson Pickett in the movie *Blues Brothers 2000.* Though often lumped alongside fellow young guitar slingers Kenny Wayne Shepherd and Derek Trucks, Lang distinguishes himself by handling his own vocals. Featuring songs ranging from 12-bar blues to soul to funk, *Wander This World* (#28, 1998) was as much a showcase for his voice as it was his guitar playing. In 1999, shortly before embarking on a tour with Jeff Beck, Lang performed at Mick Jagger's 56th birthday party in France and alongside B.B. King for President Clinton at a PBS-filmed blues extravaganza on the White House lawn. His third A&M album was slated for release in 2001.

k.d. lang

Born Kathryn Dawn Lang, Nov. 2, 1961, Consort, Alberta, Can.
1984—*A Truly Western Experience* (Bumstead) 1987—*Angel With a Lariat* (Sire) 1988—*Shadowland* 1989—*Absolute Torch and Twang* 1992—*Ingénue* 1993—*Even Cowgirls Get the Blues* soundtrack 1995—*All You Can Eat* (Warner Bros.) 1997—*Drag* 2000—*Invincible Summer.*

Because of her androgynous aesthetic, outspoken political views, and proud lesbianism, k.d. lang has frequently been attacked by conservatives, but she's come out smelling like a rose. The "cowgirl from Calgary" claimed three Grammys, including Best Female Pop Vocal Performance in 1992.

Despite her sometimes campy approach to country & western music—she used to perform in rhinestone-studded garb and cat's-eye glasses—lang is an authentic country girl, raised in an isolated rural town. She began singing at age five, and by her teen years was performing at weddings. She grew up listening to classical music and rock, discovering country when she played a Patsy Cline–type character in a play at Red Deer College. In 1982 she answered an ad in an Edmonton newspaper placed by a Western swing band. She and the band, the Reclines, toured Canada for two years.

Her first album was released by an Edmonton indie, to little notice. It was her live shows, where lang could outkitsch Minnie Pearl and out-emote Barbra Streisand, that drew the attention of Sire Records head Seymour Stein. Once lang was signed, her more serious side came across, and she toned down her crazy stage act. *Angel With a Lariat,* recorded with the Reclines and produced by Dave Edmunds, was accordingly rocking.

In 1987 lang did a remake of "Crying" with Roy Orbison. Although the single sold 50,000 copies in the U.S., radio play eluded lang, who was considered too weird for country stations, and too country for rock stations. Perhaps to prove her authenticity, *Shadowland* (1988) paid homage to the genre's leading ladies. The album was produced by former Cline mentor Owen Bradley and included guest appearances by Loretta Lynn, Kitty Wells, and Brenda Lee. On 1989's *Absolute Torch and Twang,* lang mixed her crooning (particularly on the magnificent "Pullin' Back the Reins") and honky-tonk sides ("Three Days"). The album won her a 1989 Grammy for Best Female Country Vocal Performance.

In 1990 lang filmed a commercial for the "Meat Stinks" campaign of People for the Ethical Treatment of Animals. Although the spot never aired, *Entertainment Tonight* ran a story on it. Stations in the cattle-producing Midwest boycotted lang (not that they played her music much before), her mother was swamped with hate mail, and the sign honoring her in her hometown was defaced with the words "Eat Beef Dyke." Lang's career proved surprisingly immune to such controversies: *Ingénue*'s smoldering pop went double platinum and garnered lang one Grammy and five nominations.

Interviewed for the gay magazine *The Advocate* in 1992, lang, who had been out to anyone paying attention since she was a teen, officially proclaimed her homosexuality. Far from ruining her career, the announcement seemed to fan the fires of media interest: In 1993 *New York* magazine dubbed her the icon of "Lesbian Chic," and in photographer Herb Ritts' send-up of a Norman Rockwell illustration, a *Vanity Fair* cover showed her reclining in a barber's chair, clutching and pretending to be shaved by scantily clad model Cindy Crawford. That year lang wrote the soundtrack for *Even Cowgirls Get the Blues*. She starred in the 1991 Percy Adlon film *Salmonberries* and has stated that she plans to continue pursuing an acting career.

All You Can Eat (#37, 1995) found lang leaving country music behind altogether and reinventing herself yet again, this time as a sultry dance-pop diva. *Drag* (#29, 1997), a concept album produced by Craig Street (Cassandra Wilson), used smoking as a metaphor for love and addiction and featured mostly torchy ballads. Included on the record were covers of Peggy Lee's "Don't Smoke in Bed" and the Les Paul and Mary Ford hit "Smoke Rings." lang's wry remake of the Steve Miller Band's "The Joker" was the album's first single.

In 1997 lang performed the song "Surrender" for the closing credits of the James Bond movie *Tomorrow Never Dies*. She also did more acting, appearing in the TV sitcom *Dharma and Greg* and playing a feminist film director in the made-for-TV movie *Mario Puzo's The Last Don*. In 2000 lang released *Invincible Summer*, a collection of Brazilian surf pop produced by Madonna cohort Damian LeGassick. Also in that year, she appeared in the thriller *Eye of the Beholder*.

Daniel Lanois

Born Sep. 19, 1951, Hull, Quebec, Can.
1989—*Acadie* (Opal/Warner Bros.) 1993—*For the Beauty of Wynona* (Warner Bros.).

Called "the most important record producer to emerge in the '80s" by Rolling Stone, Daniel Lanois has drawn kudos for his work with U2, Peter Gabriel, and Bob Dylan. Like his sometime-collaborator Brian Eno, Lanois has shown a flair for delicate, atmospheric touches, both in producing material for other musicians and in his own projects as a composer and recording artist. Stressing emotional vibrancy over the technical aspects of making albums, Lanois has recorded in such unlikely settings as castles, dairy barns, and a former porn theater in his efforts to elicit honest, spontaneous performances. The results of this visceral approach have ranged from the soaring intensity of Lanois' Grammy-winning coproduction (with Eno) of U2's *The Joshua Tree* to the moody, understated passion of his own solo efforts.

Lanois' French-Canadian parents were both musically inclined: His mother sang, and his father (and grandfather) played fiddle. When they separated in 1963, Lanois moved with his mother to a suburb of English-speaking Hamilton, Ontario, where he learned to play guitar and began playing gigs with various Canadian artists. In 1970 Lanois set up a home studio with his brother Robert; 10 years later, after working with numerous local musicians, they opened Grant Avenue Studio in Hamilton.

Lanois' break came in 1979 when Eno, who was beginning to pioneer his starkly dreamy "ambient music," did some recording at his studio. The chemistry between Eno and Lanois in their instrumental experiments came to commercial fruition when Eno was tapped to produce an album for U2. For that effort, 1984's *The Unforgettable Fire*, Eno enlisted Lanois as coproducer. The results impressed another pop star, Peter Gabriel, who asked Lanois to coproduce his soundtrack to the 1984 film *Birdy*. Gabriel and Lanois again shared production credit for 1986's *So* and 1992's *Us*, Gabriel's most successful albums. Lanois continued to work with U2 as well, coproducing 1987's *The Joshua Tree* with Eno, served as principal producer for 1991's *Achtung Baby*, which earned him another Grammy, and teamed up with Eno again to coproduce the band's Grammy-winning 2000 release *All That You Can't Leave Behind*. In addition, Lanois earned praise for coproducing, with Robbie Robertson, the singer's eponymous solo debut in 1987, and for his work at the boards on Bob Dylan's *Oh Mercy* (1989) and *Time Out of Mind* (1997); the Neville Brothers' *Yellow Moon* (1989); Luscious Jackson's *Fever in Fever Out* (1996); and for streamlining the efforts of country artists Emmylou Harris (1995's *Wrecking Ball*) and Willie Nelson (1998's *Teatro*). In 1989 Lanois released *Acadie*, his debut as a singer/songwriter. The album was received enthusiastically by critics, as was its 1993 successor, *For the Beauty of Wynona*. So far, though, the quirky radiance of Lanois' songs hasn't proved as accessible to pop fans as the work of his celebrated clients. Still, he continues to impress his peers and has crossed over to film work, scoring the soundtracks to Billy Bob Thornton's *Sling Blade* (1996) and *All the Pretty Horses* (2000), and participating as part of the Million Dollar Hotel Band, along with Bono and Eno, for the soundtrack to the Bono-cowritten, Wim Wenders–directed movie *The Million Dollar Hotel* (2000).

Bill Laswell/Material

Born Feb. 12, 1955, Salem, IL
1983—*Baselines* (Celluloid/Elektra/Musician) 1988—*Hear No Evil* (Venture/Virgin) 1994—*Axiom Ambient: Lost in the Translation; Psychonavigation* (Subharmonic) 1995—*Cymatic Scan; Bass Terror* (Sub Rosa); *Silent Recoil* (Low) 1996—*Second Nature* (Subharmonic); *Sacred System, Chapter One: Book of Entrance* (ROIR); *Oscillations* (Subharmonic); *Outland, vol. 2* (EFA); *Psychonavigation, vol. 2; Dark Massive/Disengage: Ambient Compendium* (Cleopatra); *Equations of Eternity* (WordSound) 1997—*City of Light* (Sub Rosa); *Dub Meltdown* (WordSound); *Sacred System, Chapter 2* (Roir); *Ambience Dub, vol. 1* (APC); *Ambience Dub, vol. 2* 1998—*Oscillations, vol. 2: Advanced Drum'n'Bass* (Sub Rosa); *Outland, vol. 3* (EFA); *Equations of Eternity, vol. 2: Veve* (WordSound); *Nagual Suite* (RCA); *Jazzonia* (Douglas); *Divination: Sacrifice* (Meta); *Dreams of Freedom: Ambient Translations of Bob Marley in Dub* (Axiom/Island); *Panthalassa: The Music of Miles Davis, 1969–1974* (Columbia) 1999—*Dark Side of the Moog 7* (EFA); *Boniche Dub* (APC); *Invisible Design* (Tzadik); *Psychonavigation, vol. 4* (EFA); *Rasa: Serene Timeless Joy* (Meta); *Imaginary Cuba*

(RCA); *Broken Vessels* (Velvel); *Panthalassa: The Remixes* (Columbia) 2000—*Permutation* (ION); *Emerald Aether: Shape Shifting* (Shanachie); *Dub Chamber 3* (Roir); *Outland, vol. 4* (EFA); *Moog 6* (Fax World); *Lo-Def Pressure* (Sub Rosa).
With Material, formed 1979, New York, NY:
Laswell, bass; Michael Beinhorn, kybds.; Fred Maher, drums. 1979—*Temporary Music 1* EP (Zu) 1981—*Temporary Music 2* EP (Red Music U.K.); *Busting Out* EP (ZE-Island); *Memory Serves* (Celluloid/Elektra/Musician) 1982—(– Maher; + Nicky Skopelitis [b. Jan. 19, 1960, New York], gtr.) *One Down* (Celluloid/Elektra) 1986—*Red Tracks* (Red) 1989—(– Beinhorn) *Seven Souls* (Virgin) 1991—*The Third Power* (Axiom) 1994—*Hallucination Engine*.
With Praxis: 1984—*Praxis* EP (Celluloid) 1992—*Transmutation* (Axiom).

Bassist and producer Bill Laswell is a rampant musical cross-pollinator and conceptualist, forging new directions for the fusion of jazz, rock, and funk. Laswell grew up in Detroit, where he played in funk bands. He moved to New York in 1978 and formed Material, originally to back Daevid Allen (Gong) on a U.S. tour. The group soon became a floating vehicle for musical experimentation.

The original incarnation of Material was based around the rhythm section of Laswell, Michael Beinhorn, and Fred Maher. They recorded a few EPs, including the club single "Busting Out" with Nona Hendryx [see entry] singing, and the album *Memory Serves*, which featured Sonny Sharrock, Fred Frith, George Lewis, and Henry Threadgill. Minus Maher but plus guitarist Nicky Skopelitis, Material recorded the funky *One Down*, again featuring Hendryx and Frith as well as Archie Shepp, Nile Rodgers, Oliver Lake, and Whitney Houston. *Red Tracks* compiled the Temporary Music EPs. Beinhorn departed in 1989, going on to produce such artists as Soundgarden.

On *Seven Souls*, Material explored Arabic music, featuring guests Fahiem Dandan, Simon Shaheen, and L. Shankar, as well as beat author William Burroughs. Laswell produced rather than played on *The Third Power*, which featured Bootsy Collins, the Jungle Brothers, Bernie Worrell, Sly Dunbar, and Robbie Shakespeare (Laswell produced Sly and Robbie's solo albums). On *Hallucination Engine*, Material explored ambient music; the single "Mantra" was remixed by British ambient artists the Orb. Laswell's collaborators included Wayne Shorter, Shaheen, Worrell, Collins, Dunbar, Burroughs, and Shankar.

Laswell's work outside of Material has been equally varied and fruitful. In 1982 he formed Massacre with Frith and Maher, releasing the album *Killing Time*. That year he also played bass on Laurie Anderson's "Mr. Heartbreak." Laswell's first solo album features key players of the downtown New York music scene of the '80s, including cowriter Beinhorn, Martin Bisi, Ronald Shannon Jackson, Ralph Carney, and Daniel Ponce. The album was released by Celluloid, a label Laswell helped form and run.

In 1983 Laswell cowrote and produced Herbie Hancock's hit "Rockit" and won a Grammy for a track on Hancock's following album, *Sound-System*. In 1984 Laswell produced the single "World Destruction," featuring Afrika Bambaataa and Johnny Lydon. Calling himself Praxis, Laswell experimented with hip-hop and a drum machine on a 1984 EP, and played with Bootsy Collins and guitarist Buckethead on a 1992 album. His 1988 solo album, *Hear No Evil*, features violinist Shankar and Skopelitis. Laswell has played with numerous other acts, including the Golden Palominos, Last Exit, Brian Eno, David Byrne, Peter Gabriel, Fab Five Freddy, John Zorn, and Peter Brötzmann. He has produced such artists as Mick Jagger, Yellowman, Motörhead, Iggy Pop, and the Ramones.

In 1988 Laswell formed Axiom Records in a partnership with Island Records. There he has continued to be a post-modern Renaissance man, releasing (out-of-this-) world music, experimental jazz, and mutant rock. In 1990 he established Greenpoint Studio. He traveled to the remote village of Jajouka, Morocco, in 1991 to record Bachir Attar and the Master Musicians of Jajouka, released on Axiom as *Apocalypse Across the Sky* (1992).

The second half of the '90s found Laswell more prodigious than ever, releasing between five and nine albums per year. *Panthalassa: The Music of Miles Davis, 1969–1974* (1998) subjects recordings from Davis' jazz-rock fusion and hard-funk phases to electronic reconstruction. Laswell did much the same thing with the work of reggae legend Bob Marley on *Dreams of Freedom* (1998), and with Cuban and Irish music on *Imaginary Cuba* (1999) and *Emerald Aether* (2000), respectively.

Cyndi Lauper

Born Cynthia Anne Stephanie Lauper, June 22, 1953, New York, NY
1983—*She's So Unusual* (Portrait) 1986—*True Colors* 1989—*A Night to Remember* (Epic) 1993—*Hat Full of Stars* 1995—*12 Deadly Cyns and Then Some* (Epic) 1997—*Sisters of Avalon* (Sony) 1998—*Merry Christmas . . . Have A Nice Life!*

With her little-girl voice, thrift-store style, and art-school training, Cyndi Lauper was one of the earliest female icons to harness MTV's influence and become a pop star. Her debut album was the first in history by a woman to have four Top 5 singles; led by "Girls Just Want to Have Fun," it also won her the unlikely title of "Woman of the Year" from *Ms.* magazine.

Lauper was raised in Brooklyn and Queens by her waitress mother, a life she paid homage to when her mother starred in the video for "Girls." After dropping out of high school and spending a few years "finding herself," Lauper sang for cover bands on Long Island. She almost ruined her voice and sought training from Katherine Agresta, an opera singer and rock & roll vocal coach. She then spent four years singing and writing songs for Blue Angel, a rootsy rock band whose strong New York following never translated into sales for their eponymous 1980 Polydor album.

Lauper filed for bankruptcy after Blue Angel split, and for a while sang in a Japanese restaurant dressed like a geisha until her manager and boyfriend David Wolff landed her a deal with the CBS imprint Portrait. *She's So Unusual* (#4, 1983) became an international hit, eventually selling more than 5 million records in the U.S. alone, led by "Girls" (#2, 1983), "All Through the Night" (#5, 1984), "She Bop" (#3, 1984), and "Time After Time" (#1, 1984). The album, produced by Rick Chertoff and featuring Rob Hyman and Eric Bazilian of the Philadelphia band the Hooters [see entry], won Lauper a Grammy and put the singer on the brink of superstardom. On *The Tonight Show,* the rainbow-haired singer with the Betty Boop voice claimed that professional wrestler Captain Lou Albano was her mentor and had taught her the keys to fame: politeness, etiquette, and grooming.

Lauper was never able to match the success of her debut, although 1986's *True Colors*' title track went to #1 and featured "Change of Heart" (#3, 1986) and a cover of Marvin Gaye's "What's Going On" (#12, 1987). In 1985 she had a #10 hit with "The Goonies 'R' Good Enough," from the film *The Goonies.* (Lauper's own ventures into acting have proved ill-fated: One movie never made it out of the studio, and 1988's *Vibes* and 1993's *Life With Mikey* flopped.)

A Night to Remember was trashed by critics and stalled at #37 on the pop chart; it contained one hit, "I Drove All Night" (#6, 1989). In 1990 she ended her personal and professional relationship with Wolff; the following year she married actor David Thornton, with Little Richard presiding.

She returned in 1993 with *Hat Full of Stars* (#112), reasserting control over her career (coproducing and cowriting all tracks) and proving to critics that she had grown with the times. The album deals with such issues as racism, backstreet abortions, and incest; collaborators include Mary Chapin Carpenter, Junior Vasquez, and her old friends the Hooters. The album faltered commercially, however, yielding no hit singles.

In 1994 Lauper made a comeback of sorts in the U.K. with the release of the anthology *12 Deadly Cyns and Then Some,* which reached #2, and "Hey Now (Girls Just Want to Have Fun)," a remix of her first hit, which topped the singles chart. Despite the remix's appearance in the movie *To Wong Foo, Thanks for Everything, Julie Newmar,* the album fared less well when later issued in the U.S. (#81 pop, 1995). Its followup, *Sisters of Avalon* (#188 pop, 1997), Lauper's first album of new material in four years, also went nowhere.

Lead Belly

Born Huddie Ledbetter, ca. 1885, Mooringsport, LA; died Dec. 6, 1949, New York, NY

1953—*Lead Belly's Last Sessions, vol. 1* (Folkways); *Lead Belly's Last Sessions, vol. 2* 1968—*Leadbelly Sings Folk Songs* 1969—*Leadbelly* (Capitol) 1973—*Leadbelly* (Fantasy) 1989—*Alabama Bound* (RCA); *Bourgeois Blues* (Collectables) 1991—*King of the Twelve-String Guitar* (Columbia/Legacy); *Midnight Special* (Rounder); *Gwine Dig a Hole to Put the Devil In; Let It Shine on Me* 1994—*The Titanic; Nobody Knows the Trouble I've Seen; Go Down Old Hannah* 1996—*Where Did You Sleep Last Night* (Folkways) 1997—*Bourgeois Blues.*

Lead Belly (sometimes spelled "Leadbelly"), the self-styled "king of the 12-string guitar," was one of the modern world's prime links to rural traditions. He helped inspire the folk and blues revivals of the '50s and '60s.

Lead Belly grew up in Louisiana and Texas, where his family moved when he was five. He was eight when he started playing the Cajun accordion (windjammer). According to Lead Belly, at age seven he broke up arguments between his parents by hitting his father in the head with a poker and threatening him with a shotgun. Traveling around in his early teens, the singer picked up music that dated back to slave days, and by the time he was 17 he was playing guitar—first an 8-string and then the 12-string. At 18 he was forced to leave his home after he impregnated the same girl twice without marrying her. He went to West Texas to pick cotton and began playing with his friend and mentor Blind Lemon Jefferson in Dallas.

But Lead Belly's troubles followed him, and he spent a year in prison on the Harrison County chain gang for assaulting a woman. He escaped and adopted the name Walter Boyd. When he was 33 he shot and killed a man in an argument over a woman, and on June 7, 1918, he received a 30-year sentence. Five years later, however, Lead Belly wrote a song begging Texas governor Pat Neff for a pardon; in 1925 Neff complied. Lead Belly's hollering style reflected his hard years in prison, and it wasn't long before he was back behind bars—for attempted murder—at Louisiana's Angola penitentiary. It was there that folklorists John A. and Alan Lomax discovered him in 1933 while recording music for the Library of Congress. The Lomaxes recorded the incarcerated Lead Belly singing an updated version of the song that had charmed Pat Neff. This time Governor O.K. Allen heard it and, likewise, let Lead Belly out of prison in 1934.

Upon his release, the Lomaxes brought him to New York. They published a book about him in 1936, and he recorded his best-known songs: "The Rock Island Line," "The Midnight Special," and "Goodnight Irene." Whether Lead Belly wrote, adapted, or simply remembered the songs and copyrighted them for himself is unknown, though it is certain that he was the first to bring them to the public. In 1939 Lead Belly landed in jail yet again (New York's Rikers Island) and served two years for assault. But all of this only enhanced his legend. While in New York he played with Pete Seeger, Woody Guthrie, and Sonny Terry and later toured the East Coast.

Ironically, six months after the singer died of Lou Gehrig's disease in 1949, his "Goodnight Irene" became a folk hit for the Weavers. There were many repackagings of his work in the late '60s to early '70s, and in 1976 a film about his life, directed by Gordon Parks, was released.

Led Zeppelin

Formed 1968, England
Jimmy Page (b. James Patrick Page, Jan. 9, 1944, Heston, Eng.), gtr.; John Paul Jones (b. John Baldwin, Jan. 3, 1946,

Sidcup, Eng.), bass, kybds.; Robert Plant (b. Aug. 20, 1948, Bromwich, Eng.), voc.; John "Bonzo" Bonham (b. John Henry Bonham, May 31, 1948, Redditch, Eng.; d. Sep. 25, 1980, Windsor, Eng.), drums.
1969—*Led Zeppelin* (Atlantic); *Led Zeppelin II* 1970—*Led Zeppelin III* 1971—*Untitled* (known as *Runes* or *Zoso*) 1973—*Houses of the Holy* 1975—*Physical Graffiti* (Swan Song/Atlantic) 1976—*Presence; The Song Remains the Same* 1979—*In Through the Out Door* 1982—*Coda* 1990—*Led Zeppelin* (Atlantic) 1992—*Remasters* 1993—*Led Zeppelin—Boxed Set 2; Led Zeppelin—The Complete Studio Recordings* 1997—*The BBC Sessions* 1999—*Early Days: The Best of Led Zeppelin, vol. 1* 2000—*Latter Days: The Best of Led Zeppelin, vol. 2.*

It wasn't just Led Zeppelin's thunderous volume, sledgehammer beat, and edge-of-mayhem arrangements that made it the most influential and successful heavy-metal pioneer, it was the band's finesse. Like its ancestors the Yardbirds [see entry], Zeppelin used a guitar style that drew heavily on the blues; its early repertoire included remakes of songs by Howlin' Wolf, Albert King, and Willie Dixon (who later won a sizable settlement from the band in a suit in which he alleged copyright infringement; see his entry for details). But Jimmy Page blessed the group with a unique understanding of the guitar and the recording studio as electronic instruments, and of rock as sculptured sound; like Jimi Hendrix, Page had a reason for every bit of distortion, feedback, reverberation, and out-and-out noise that he incorporated. Few of the many acts that try to imitate Led Zeppelin can make the same claim.

Page and Robert Plant were grounded also in British folk music and fascinated by mythology, Middle Earth fantasy, and the occult, as became increasingly evident from the band's later albums (the fourth LP's title is comprised of four runic characters). A song that builds from a folk-baroque acoustic setting to screaming heavy metal, "Stairway to Heaven," fittingly became the best-known Led Zeppelin song and a staple of FM airplay, although like most of the group's "hits," it was never released as a single. Though critically derided more often than not, Led Zeppelin was unquestionably one of the most enduring bands in rock history, with U.S. sales of more than 100 million records.

When the Yardbirds fell apart in the summer of 1968, Page was left with rights to the group's name and a string of concert obligations. He enlisted John Paul Jones, who had done session work with the Rolling Stones, Herman's Hermits, Lulu, Dusty Springfield, and Shirley Bassey. Page and Jones had first met, jammed together, and discussed forming a group when both were hired to back Donovan on his *Hurdy Gurdy Man* LP. Page had hoped to complete the group with drummer B.J. Wilson of Procol Harum and singer Terry Reid. Neither was available, but Reid recommended Plant, who in turn suggested Bonham, drummer for his old Birmingham group, Band of Joy. The four first played together as the session group behind P.J. Proby on his *Three Week Hero*. In October 1968 they embarked on a tour of Scandinavia under the name the New Yardbirds. Upon their return to England they recorded their debut album in 30 hours.

Adopting the name Led Zeppelin (allegedly coined by Keith Moon), they toured the U.S. in early 1969, opening for Vanilla Fudge. Their first album was released in February; within two months it had reached *Billboard*'s Top 10. *Led Zeppelin II* reached #1 two months after its release, and since then every album of new material has gone platinum; five of the group's LPs have reached #1. After touring almost incessantly during its first two years together, Zeppelin began limiting its appearances to alternating years. The band's 1973 U.S. tour broke box-office records throughout the country (many of which had been set by the Beatles), and by 1975 its immense ticket and album sales had made Led Zeppelin the most popular rock & roll group in the world. In 1974 the quartet established its own label, Swan Song. The label's first release was *Physical Graffiti* (#1, 1975), the band's first double-album set, which sold 4 million copies.

On August 4, 1975, Plant and his family were seriously injured in a car crash while vacationing on the Greek island of Rhodes. As a result, the group toured even less frequently. That and speculation among fans that supernatural forces may have come into play also heightened the Zeppelin mystique. (Plant believed in psychic phenomena, and Page, whose interest in the occult was well known, once resided in Boleskine House, the former home of infamous satanist Aleister Crowley.)

In 1976 Led Zeppelin released *Presence*, a 4-million seller.

Led Zeppelin: Jimmy Page, John Bonham, Robert Plant, John Paul Jones

The group had just embarked on its U.S. tour when Plant's six-year-old son, Karac, died suddenly of a viral infection. The remainder of the tour was canceled, and the group took off the next year and a half. In late 1978 Plant, Page, Jones, and Bonham began work on *In Through the Out Door,* their last group effort. They had completed a brief European tour and were beginning to rehearse for a U.S. tour when, on September 25, 1980, Bonham died at Page's home of what was described as asphyxiation; he had inhaled his own vomit after having consumed alcohol and fallen asleep. On December 4, 1980, Page, Plant, and Jones released a cryptic statement to the effect that they could no longer continue as they were. Soon thereafter it was rumored that Plant and Page were going to form a band called XYZ (ex-Yes and Zeppelin) with Alan White and Chris Squire of Yes; the group never materialized. In 1982 Zeppelin released *Coda* (#6, 1982), a collection of early recordings and outtakes.

Plant and Page each pursued solo careers [see entries]. Jones released a soundtrack album, *Scream for Help,* in 1986, and has worked in production. The remaining members of Zeppelin have reunited three times. They played in 1985 at Live Aid (with Phil Collins and Tony Thompson on drums), and in May 1988 (with John Bonham's son, Jason, on drums) at the Atlantic Records 40th-anniversary celebration at New York's Madison Square Garden. They also performed at Jason Bonham's wedding. Zeppelin's concert movie, *The Song Remains the Same* (originally released in 1976), is still a staple of midnight shows around the country, and Zeppelin tunes like "Stairway to Heaven," "Kashmir," "Communication Breakdown," "Whole Lotta Love," and "No Quarter" are still in heavy rotation on classic-rock radio playlists. In 1990 a St. Petersburg, Florida, station kicked off its all-Zeppelin format by playing "Stairway to Heaven" for 24 hours straight. (Less than two weeks later, the station had expanded its playlist to include Pink Floyd.)

In fall 1994 Page and Plant participated in the *No Quarter* album, which they followed up with a new 1998 studio effort, *Walking Into Clarksdale.* Jones, who was not invited to join them, was by then working and touring with Diamanda Galás, with whom he recorded 1994's *The Sporting Life.* In 1997 a live-in-the-studio collection of Zeppelin's BBC radio sessions peaked at #12 and went platinum. In 1999 the recording industry announced that the band was only the third act in music history to achieve four or more diamond-certified albums, signifying sales of 10 million copies.

Albert Lee

Born Dec. 21, 1943, Leominster, Eng.
1979—*Hiding* (A&M) 1982—*Albert Lee* 1986—*Speechless* (MCA) 1987—*Gagged but Not Bound* 2000—*Con Sabor Latino* (WEA Latina).

British guitarist Albert Lee has earned a strong reputation as a sideman for Jackson Browne, Dave Edmunds, Joan Armatrading, Joe Cocker, Eric Clapton, Emmylou Harris, Rodney Crowell, and others. Beyond his adaptability, he is one of the few English guitarists more interested in country music than in blues. Lee began playing piano at age seven, emulating Jerry Lee Lewis. But by 16 he had switched to guitar. In 1964 he joined Chris Farlowe's backup group, the Thunderbirds, which also included Carl Palmer. The Thunderbirds were a popular R&B outfit in England, and Jimmy Page and Steve Howe have cited Lee's work as an early influence. In 1968 the band dissolved. Lee joined Country Fever and later formed the country-influenced Heads, Hands and Feet. After three albums, that band folded, and Lee went on to play on Jerry Lee Lewis' *The Session* LP.

In 1973 Lee joined Rick Grech with the Crickets, still singing Buddy Holly's tunes; a year later he was in L.A. doing session work, including a stint with Don Everly. He joined Joe Cocker for his 1974 tour of Australia and New Zealand, and A&M offered Lee a solo contract in 1975. Before he got around to finishing an album, though, Lee joined Emmylou Harris' Hot Band. He stayed in Harris' band for two years and left in 1978 to finally record his solo album but continued to play on Harris' records as well.

Instead of touring to support his own album, Lee took to the road in 1979 as part of Eric Clapton's band. He played on Clapton's live LP *Just One Night* (1980) and on his studio albums, *Another Ticket* (1981) and *Money and Cigarettes* (1983). Between tours with Clapton, he finished a second solo album. He has also toured with the Everly Brothers, among others.

Alvin Lee: See Ten Years After

Arthur Lee: See Love

Brenda Lee

Born Brenda Mae Tarpley, Dec. 11, 1944, Atlanta, GA
1960—*Brenda Lee* (Decca); *This Is . . . Brenda* 1961—*Emotions; All the Way* 1962—*Sincerely; Brenda, That's All* 1963—*All Alone Am I; Let Me Sing* 1965—*Too Many Rivers* 1966—*10 Golden Years* 1975—*Brenda Lee Now* (MCA) 1976—*L.A. Sessions* 1980—*Take Me Back; Even Better* 1991—*The Brenda Lee Anthology, vol. 1 1956–1961; The Brenda Lee Anthology, vol. 2 1962–1980* 1999—*Rockin' Around the Christmas Tree* (Decca).

Singer Brenda Lee's decade-spanning recording career began when she was only 12; by the time she was 16, her single "Rockin' Around the Christmas Tree" (#14, 1960) became an international hit. By age seven Lee was singing on radio and TV shows in Atlanta. Her father died when she was eight, and her income helped support the family. In 1956 she met Red Foley's manager, Dub Albritten. He booked her on shows with Foley, which led to national TV exposure. On July 30 of that year Lee entered a Nashville studio with Owen Bradley (producer of Patsy Cline and later Loretta Lynn) and recorded "Rockin' Around the Christmas Tree." Lee soon toured Europe, where, to appease French promoters who had thought she was an adult, Albritten spread the rumor that she was a 32-year-old midget.

Back in the U.S., Lee next recorded some of her biggest hits: "Sweet Nothings" (#4, 1960), "I'm Sorry" (#1, 1960), "I Want to Be Wanted" (#1, 1960), and many other early-'60s Top 10s. She soon became known as "Little Miss Dynamite," and by the time she was 21 she had cut 256 sides for Decca Records.

In the '70s Lee's hits were on the country chart rather than the pop chart. She scored with "If This Is Our Last Time" (#30 C&W, 1971), "Nobody Wins" (#3 C&W, 1973), and three Top 10s in 1974. She continued to record country hits while also doing a syndicated Nashville interview show. Lee had a small acting role in *Smokey and the Bandit 2,* and she sang the title song of Neil Simon's *Only When I Laugh.* In 1988 she joined Loretta Lynn and Kitty Wells as guests on k.d. lang's *Shadowland* album, produced by Owen Bradley. Lee remains an active live performer on the oldies and country circuits. *Rockin' Around the Christmas Tree,* a 1999 compilation, boasts three new tracks.

In 1984 Lee received a Governors Award from the National Academy of Recording Arts and Sciences, the organization that awards the Grammy. She has also received numerous other distinctions. Her lifetime record sales are estimated at over 100 million copies.

Peggy Lee

Born Norma Deloris Egstrom, May 6, 1920, Jamestown, ND
1957—*The Man I Love* (Capitol) 1969—*Is That All There Is?* 1980—*The Best of Peggy Lee* (MCA) 1990—*Capitol Collectors Series: The Early Years; The Peggy Lee Songbook: There'll Be Another Spring* (Musicmasters) 1992—*Moments Like This* (Chesky) 1998—*Miss Peggy Lee* (Capitol) 1999—*The Complete Recordings 1941–1947* (Columbia/Legacy).

Peggy Lee's subdued singing style, which embraces jazz, blues, Latin, swing, and pop, first came to public attention in her work with Benny Goodman's orchestra, especially in 1943, when she released the hit "Why Don't You Do Right?" Lee's mother died when she was 4, and she began working on a farm by 11 and singing professionally at 14, first at a Fargo, North Dakota, radio station and later at a Palm Springs hotel, where she met Goodman.

After her hit with Goodman's band, she married the group's guitarist, David Barbour, and retired for several years to have a child before she and Barbour began writing new material together, with Peggy usually providing the lyrics. Lee was one of the forerunners of the rock trend that encouraged singers to write their own material, and with Barbour she wrote, among others, "I Don't Know Enough About You," "Mañana," and "It's a Good Day." She has also collaborated with Sonny Burke, Duke Ellington, Quincy Jones, Johnny Mandel, and Dave Grusin. Lee's hit most covered by rock performers is "Fever" (#8, 1958).

She was one of the first old-guard performers to recognize the Beatles' talents, and as a "reward," Paul McCartney later wrote "Let's Love" for her, which became the title of her Atlantic debut in 1974. In 1969 she had one of her biggest hits with Leiber and Stoller's "Is That All There Is?," arranged by Randy Newman.

Lee appeared in three films, making her debut in 1951's *Mr. Music,* followed by a remake of *The Jazz Singer* with Danny Thomas (1953), and *Pete Kelly's Blues* (1955), for which she was nominated for an Academy Award. In 1955 she cowrote songs and voiced the character Peg in Disney's animated feature film *Lady and the Tramp.* She also cowrote with Victor Young and sang the title songs of the films *Johnny Guitar* and *Tom Thumb.*

Although she suffered bouts of poor health, she continued to perform and record new studio albums into the '90s. In 1983 she mounted a short-lived one-woman Broadway show entitled *Peg.* Her autobiography, *Miss Peggy Lee,* was published in 1989, and was a bestseller in the U.K. She has received numerous awards throughout her career, and was a founding artist of the John F. Kennedy Center for the Performing Arts. In 1994 she received the Society of Singers' Lifetime Achievement Award. Declining health, including two strokes, kept her out of the public eye in the late '90s, though numerous retrospectives have allowed her legacy to endure.

The Left Banke

Formed 1965, New York, NY
Steve Martin, voc.; Tom Finn, bass; Jeff Winfield, gtr.; George Cameron, drums; Michael Brown (b. Michael Lookofsky, Apr. 25, 1949, Brooklyn, NY), organ, piano, harpsichord.
1967—*Walk Away Renee/Pretty Ballerina* (Smash) (– Winfield; + Rick Brand, gtr.; – Brown) 1969—*The Left Banke Too* 1986—*Strangers on a Train* (Camerica) 1992—*There's Gonna Be a Storm: The Complete Recordings, 1966–1969* (Mercury).

Left Banke leader Michael Brown began studying piano and harpsichord when he was eight. At 16 he wrote "Walk Away Renee." Two years later, in 1966, his band, the Left Banke, released the song as its first single, and it became a #5 hit. The followup, "Pretty Ballerina" (#15, 1967), was similar to "Renee" in its classical-tinged melody, choirboy vocals, and strings-and-harpsichord accompaniment (then dubbed baroque rock). After composing the bulk of the material for the Left Banke's debut LP and a second album, Brown left the group. The Left Banke continued unsuccessfully without him, breaking up in 1969.

Brown's next band, Montage, was not particularly successful, and he then formed Stories with vocalist Ian Lloyd but left before its big 1973 hit, "Brother Louie" (written by members of Hot Chocolate). Brown then worked for a while as an A&R man for Mercury Records.

In 1976 he formed the Beckies, who lasted long enough to record a single LP for Sire. Since then Brown has remained mostly out of sight, surfacing briefly as a sideman with New York singer Lisa Burns. "Walk Away Renee" was covered by the Four Tops in 1968 and was once again a smash. Martin, Finn, and Cameron regrouped without Brown in 1978 for an album released eight years later on the independent Camerica label, *Strangers on a Train.*

Lemonheads

Formed 1986, Boston, MA
Evan Dando (b. Mar. 4, 1967, Boston), voc., gtr., drums; Ben Deily, voc., gtr., drums; Jesse Peretz, bass.
1986—*Laughing All the Way to the Cleaners* EP (Huh-Bag) (+ Doug Trachten, drums) 1987—*Hate Your Friends* (Taang!) (– Trachten; + John Strohm, gtr.) 1988—*Creator* 1989—*Create Your Friends* (– Strohm); *Lick* (– Deily; – Peretz; + David William Ryan [b. Oct. 20, 1964, IN], drums) 1990—*Lovey* (Atlantic) 1991—*Favorite Spanish Dishes* (– Peretz; + Juliana Hatfield [b. July 27, 1967, Wicasset, ME], bass) 1992—*It's a Shame About Ray* (– Hatfield; + Nick Dalton [b. Nov. 14, 1964, Austral.], bass) 1993—*Come On Feel the Lemonheads* 1996—*Car Button Cloth* (TAG/Atlantic) (+ Bill Gibson, bass; + Murph [b. Emmett Patrick Murphy], drums).

Lemonheads started out as a democratic pop-punk band in the style of Hüsker Dü and the Replacements, but evolved into a vehicle for singer/songwriter Evan Dando's catchy postpunk pop songs. By the early '90s, Dando's music, together with his cover-boy good looks, had won the band a succession of magazine spreads.

Born to progressive parents—his mother had been a model, his father an attorney—Evan Dando grew up in Boston's North Shore. Among his parents, two sisters, and a brother, the music around the house ranged from Steely Dan and the Motown roster to Neil Young and Black Sabbath. When he was 12, Dando's parents split up, and he shut down emotionally. He became fascinated by Charles Manson, and years before Guns n' Roses sparked controversy by covering a Manson song, Lemonheads included the mass murderer's ballad "Home" on *Creator.*

While still in high school, Dando and friends Ben Deily and Jesse Peretz (son of *New Republic* editor in chief Marty Peretz) formed the Whelps. Before recording the first EP, the group became the Lemonheads, named for the popular Midwestern candy. At the time, Dando played drums. On the strength of their initial 7-inch EP, the Lemonheads signed with the independent Taang! label and put out *Hate Your Friends, Creator,* and *Lick.* But a power struggle began to erode the Dando-Deily relationship, resulting in a temporary breakup during which Dando played with Juliana Hatfield's [see entry] Blake Babies. When Dando rejoined on guitar, Deily departed.

The group signed with Atlantic after its cover of Suzanne Vega's "Luka" became popular on college radio. By that time, the Lemonheads had become Dando's band, and in 1991 Peretz quit to become a successful video director for the likes of the Foo Fighters, the Breeders, and the Lemonheads. Their first successful album for the major label was *It's a Shame About Ray* (#68), on which Hatfield repaid Dando by filling in on bass (onetime roommates, the two were rumored to be romantically involved, though both denied it). After the group's cover of Simon and Garfunkel's "Mrs. Robinson" became an MTV hit, Atlantic reissued *It's a Shame . . .* with that song tacked on the end. While earning new fans, Dando's side career as a teen-idol cover boy earned some underground backlash, including a fanzine called *Die! Evan! Die!* As usual, Dando seemed amused. Like much of the band's work, *Come On Feel the Lemonheads* (#56, 1993)—notable for a guest appearance by former Flying Burrito Brothers pedal steel guitarist Sneaky Pete Kleinow—garnered more press coverage (particularly after Dando spoke openly about his drug use and was frequently seen with Courtney Love) than sales. In 1994 Dando began touring acoustically with English drummer/singer/songwriter Epic Soundtracks (Swell Maps, Jacobites, These Immortal Souls), with whom he'd collaborated on songwriting.

By 1996, what had become severe drug abuse for Dando (sampling heroin, speed, ecstasy, acid, etc.) was overcome in time for *Car Button Cloth,* recorded with a new lineup that included former Dinosaur Jr drummer Murph, and ex–Eastern Dark bassist Bill Gibson. Dando also dabbled as an actor, appearing in *Reality Bites* and *Heavy.* And by 2000, the singer traveled to Australia to record an album of country cover songs, with plans to record another of solo pop tunes.

John Lennon and Yoko Ono

John Lennon, born John Winston Lennon, Oct. 9, 1940, Liverpool, Eng.; d. Dec. 8, 1980, New York, NY; Yoko Ono, born Feb. 18, 1933, Tokyo, Japan.
John Lennon and Yoko Ono: 1968—*Unfinished Music No. 1: Two Virgins* (Apple) 1969—*Unfinished Music No. 2: Life With the Lions* (Zapple); *Wedding Album* (Apple); *Live Peace in Toronto, 1969* (with the Plastic Ono Band) 1972—*Some Time in New York City* 1980—*Double Fantasy* (Geffen) 1982—*The John Lennon Collection* 1984—*Milk and Honey* (Polydor) 1986—*Live in New York City* (Capitol).
John Lennon solo: 1970—*John Lennon/Plastic Ono Band* (Apple) 1971—*Imagine* 1973—*Mind Games* 1974—*Walls and Bridges* 1975—*Rock 'n' Roll; Shaved Fish* 1982—*John Lennon Collection* 1986—*John Lennon Live in New York City* (Capitol/EMI); *Menlove Avenue* (Capitol) 1988—*Imagine: John Lennon* 1990—*Lennon* (EMI) 1998—*Anthology* (Capitol); *Lennon Legend: The Very Best of John Lennon* (Apple); *Wonsaponatime* (Capitol).
Yoko Ono solo: 1970—*Yoko Ono/Plastic Ono Band* (Apple) 1971—*Fly* 1973—*Approximately Infinite Universe; Feeling the Space* 1981—*Season of Glass* (Geffen) 1982—*It's Alright (I See Rainbows)* (Polydor) 1985—*Starpeace* 1992—*Onobox* (Rykodisc); *Walking on Thin Ice* 1994—*New York Rock* original cast recording (EMI) 1996—*Rising* (Capitol).

John Lennon was the Beatles' most committed rock & roller, their social conscience, and their slyest verbal wit. After the group's breakup, he and his second wife, Yoko Ono, carried on intertwined solo careers. Ono's early albums presaged

Yoko Ono and John Lennon

the elastic, screechy vocal style of late-'70s new-wavers like the B-52's and Lene Lovich. L7 and Babes in Toyland have also been influenced by and benefited from Ono's attitudinal, emotionally trailblazing work. Lennon strove to break taboos and to be ruthlessly, publicly honest. When he was murdered on December 8, 1980, he and Ono seemed on the verge of a new, more optimistic phase. In the years since Lennon's death, many critics and music historians have revised their view of Ono to recognize her contributions as a pioneering woman rock musician and avant-garde artist.

Like the other three Beatles, Lennon was born to a working-class family in Liverpool. His parents, Julia and Fred, separated before he was two (Lennon saw his father only twice in the next 20 years), and Lennon went to live with his mother's sister, Mimi Smith; when Lennon was 17 his mother was killed by a bus. He attended Liverpool's Dovedale Primary School and later the Quarry Bank High School, which supplied the name for his first band, a skiffle group called the Quarrymen, which he started in 1955. In the summer of 1956 he met Paul McCartney, and they began writing songs together and forming groups, the last of which was the Beatles. In 1994 a tape of John and the Quarrymen performing two songs, made July 6, 1957, the day he met McCartney, came to light. Recorded by Bob Molyneux, then a member of the church's youth club, it was auctioned at Sotheby's that September, fetching $122,900 from EMI. On the tape, Lennon sings "Puttin' on the Style," then a #1 hit for skiffle king Lonnie Donegan, and "Baby Let's Play House," the Arthur "Hard Rock" Gunter song that had been recorded by Elvis Presley and a line of which ("I'd rather see you dead, little girl, than to be with another man") Lennon later used in the Beatles' "Run for Your Life."

Just before the Beatles' official breakup in 1970 (Lennon had wanted to quit the band earlier), Lennon began his solo career, more than half of which consisted of collaborations with Ono.

Ono was raised in Tokyo in a wealthy Japanese banking family. She was an excellent student (in 1952 she became the first woman admitted to study philosophy at Japan's Gakushuin University) and moved to the U.S. in 1953 to study at Sarah Lawrence College. After dropping out, she became involved in the Fluxus movement, led by New York conceptual artists including George Maciunas, La Monte Young, Diane Wakoski, and Walter De Maria. During the early '60s Ono's works (many of which were conceptual pieces, some involving audience participation) were exhibited and/or performed at the Village Gate, Carnegie Recital Hall, and numerous New York galleries. In the mid-'60s she lectured at Wesleyan College and had exhibitions in Japan and London, where she met Lennon in 1966 at the Indica Gallery.

The two began corresponding, and in September 1967 Lennon sponsored Ono's "Half Wind Show" at London's Lisson Gallery. In May 1968 Ono visited Lennon at his home in Weybridge, and that night they recorded the tapes that would later be released as *Two Virgins*. (The nude cover shots, taken by Lennon with an automatic camera, were photographed then as well.) Lennon soon separated from his wife, Cynthia (with whom he had one child, Julian, in 1964); they were divorced that November. Lennon and Ono became constant companions.

Frustrated by his role with the Beatles, Lennon, with Ono, got a chance to explore avant-garde art, music, and film. While he regarded his relationship with Ono as the most important thing in his life, the couple's inseparability and Ono's influence over Lennon would be a source of great tension among the Beatles, then in their last days.

Three days after Lennon's divorce, he and Ono released *Two Virgins,* which, because of the full-frontal nude photos of the couple on the jacket, was the subject of much controversy; the LP was shipped in a plain brown wrapper. On March 20, 1969, Lennon and Ono were married in Gibraltar; for their honeymoon, they held their first "Bed-in for Peace," in the presidential suite of the Amsterdam Hilton. The peace movement was the first of several political causes the couple would take up over the years, but it was the one that generated the most publicity. On April 22, Lennon changed his middle name from Winston to Ono. In May they attempted to continue their bed-in in the United States, but when U.S. authorities forbade them to enter the country because of their arrest on drug charges in October 1968, the bed-in resumed in Montreal. That May, in their suite at the Queen Elizabeth Hotel, they recorded "Give Peace a Chance"; background chanters included Timothy Leary, Tommy Smothers, and numerous Hare Krishnas. Soon afterward "The Ballad of John and Yoko" (#8, 1969) was released under the Beatles' name, though only Lennon and McCartney appear on the record.

In September, Lennon, Ono, and the Plastic Ono Band (which included Eric Clapton, Alan White, and Klaus Voormann) performed live in Toronto at a Rock 'n' Roll Revival show. The appearance, which was later released as *Live Peace in Toronto, 1969,* was Lennon's first performance before a live concert audience in three years. Less than a month later he announced to the Beatles that he was quitting the group, but it was agreed among them that no public announcement would be made until after pending lawsuits involving Apple and manager Allen Klein were resolved. In October the Plastic Ono Band released "Cold Turkey" (#30, 1969), which the Beatles had declined to record, and the next month Lennon returned his M.B.E. medal to the Queen. In a letter to the Queen, Lennon cited Britain's involvement in Biafra and support of the U.S. in Vietnam and—jokingly—the poor chart showing of "Cold Turkey" as reasons for the return.

The Lennons continued their peace campaign with speeches to the press; "War Is Over! If You Want It" billboards erected on December 15 in 12 cities around the world, including New York, Hollywood, London, and Toronto; and plans for a peace festival in Toronto. When the festival plans deteriorated, Lennon turned his attention to recording "Instant Karma!" which was produced by Phil Spector, who was then also editing hours of tapes into the album that would be the Beatles' last official release, *Let It Be*. In late February 1970 Lennon disavowed any connection with the peace festival, and the event was abandoned. In April, McCartney—in a move that Lennon felt was an act of betrayal—announced his departure from the Beatles and released a solo LP. From this point on (if not earlier), Ono replaced McCartney as Lennon's main collaborator. The Beatles were no more.

At the time, much attention was focused on Ono's alleged role in the band's end. An *Esquire* magazine piece racistly entitled "John Rennon's Excrusive Gloupie" was an extreme example of the decidedly antiwoman, anti-Asian backlash against Ono that she and Lennon endured for years to come. As Ono told Lennon biographer Jon Wiener in a late 1983 interview for his book *Come Together: John Lennon in His Time*, "When John I were first together he got lots of threatening letters: 'That Oriental will slit your throat while you're sleeping.' The Western hero had been seized by an Eastern demon."

In late 1970 Lennon and Ono released their *Plastic Ono Band* solo LPs. Generally, Ono's '70s LPs were regarded as highly adventurous works and were thus never as popular as Lennon's. Lennon's contained "Mother," which, along with other songs, was his most personal and, some felt, disturbing work—the direct result of his and Ono's primal scream therapy with Dr. Arthur Janov. In March 1971 "Power to the People" hit #11, and that September, Lennon's solo LP *Imagine* was released; it went to #1 a month later. By late 1971 Lennon and Ono had resumed their political activities, drawn to leftist political figures like Abbie Hoffman and Jerry Rubin. Their involvement was reflected on *Some Time in New York City* (recorded with Elephant's Memory), which included Lennon's most overtly political releases (his and Ono's "Woman Is the Nigger of the World" and Ono's "Sisters, O Sisters"). The album sold poorly, reaching only #48.

Over the next two years Lennon released *Mind Games* (#9) and *Walls and Bridges* (#1), which yielded his only solo #1 hit, "Whatever Gets You Thru the Night," recorded with Elton John. On November 28, 1974, Lennon made his last public appearance, at John's Madison Square Garden concert. The two performed three songs: "Whatever Gets You Thru the Night," "I Saw Her Standing There," and "Lucy in the Sky With Diamonds," released on an EP after Lennon's death. Next came *Rock 'n' Roll*, a collection of Lennon's versions of '50s and early-'60s rock classics like "Be-Bop-a-Lula." The release was preceded by a bootleg copy, produced by Morris Levy, over which Lennon successfully sued Levy. *Rock 'n' Roll* (#6, 1975) would be Lennon's last solo release except for *Shaved Fish*, a greatest-hits compilation.

Meanwhile, Lennon's energies were increasingly directed toward his legal battle with the U.S. Immigration Department, which sought his deportation on the grounds of his previous drug arrest and involvement with the American radical left. On October 7, 1975, the U.S. Court of Appeals overturned the deportation order; in 1976 Lennon received permanent resident status. On October 9, 1975, Lennon's 35th birthday, Ono gave birth to Sean Ono Lennon. Beginning in 1975, Lennon devoted his full attention to his new son and his marriage, which had survived an 18-month separation from October 1973 to March 1975. For the next five years, he lived at home in nearly total seclusion, taking care of Sean while Ono ran the couple's financial affairs. Not until the publication of a full-page newspaper ad in May 1979 explaining his and Ono's activities did Lennon even hint at a possible return to recording.

In September 1980 he and Ono signed a contract with the newly formed Geffen Records, and on November 15 they released *Double Fantasy* (#1, 1980). A series of revealing interviews were published, "(Just Like) Starting Over" hit #1, and there was talk of a possible world tour.

But on December 8, 1980, Lennon, returning with Ono to their Dakota apartment on New York City's Upper West Side, was shot seven times by Mark David Chapman, a 25-year-old drifter and Beatles fan to whom Lennon had given an autograph a few hours earlier. Lennon was pronounced dead on arrival at Roosevelt Hospital. At Ono's request, on December 14 a 10-minute silent vigil was held at 2 p.m. EST in which millions around the world participated. Lennon's remains were cremated in Hartsdale, New York. At the time of his death, Lennon was holding in his hand a tape of Ono's "Walking on Thin Ice."

Two other singles from *Double Fantasy* were hits: "Woman" (#2, 1981) and "Watching the Wheels" (#10, 1981). *Double Fantasy* won a Grammy for Album of the Year (1981). Three months after the assassination, Ono released *Season of Glass*, an LP that deals with Lennon's death (his cracked and bloodstained eyeglasses are shown on the front jacket), although many of the songs were written before his shooting. *Season of Glass* is the best known of Ono's solo LPs; it was the first to receive attention outside avant-garde and critical circles.

In 1982 Ono left Geffen for Polydor, where she released *It's Alright, Milk and Honey* (which featured six songs by Ono and six by Lennon), and *Starpeace*. During the Starpeace Tour, Ono performed behind the Iron Curtain, in Budapest, Hungary, but the tour was not as warmly received elsewhere. None of these albums was particularly successful commercially, but in the wake of renewed appreciation for Ono's work, Rykodisc issued the six-CD box set *Onobox* in 1992 and five years later reissued on CD the entire Ono catalogue. In 1984 a number of artists, including Rosanne Cash, Harry Nilsson, Elvis Costello, Roberta Flack, and Sean Lennon (in his recording debut), participated in *Every Man Has a Woman Who Loves Him,* a collection of Ono songs. Following a 1989 retrospective at New York's Whitney Museum, Ono's artwork found a new audience and has since been shown continuously throughout the world. In 1994 she wrote a rock opera entitled *New York Rock,* which ran off-Broadway for two weeks to largely positive reviews. Clearly autobiographical, the play was a love story featuring songs from every phase of her recording career.

In addition to pursuing her own projects, Ono has maintained careful watch over the Lennon legacy. In the mid-'80s she opened the Lennon archives to Andrew Solt and David Wolper for their 1988 film biography *Imagine* (Ono and Solt's documentary on the making of the album *Imagine, Gimme Some Truth,* was released in 2000). Coming as it did just a few months after the publication of Albert Goldman's scurrilous *The Lives of John Lennon,* some observers saw *Imagine* as a piece of spin control. In fact, however, it had been in the works for more than five years by then. Ono's decision not to sue Goldman (she stated that her lawyers warned that legal action would only bring more attention to the discredited tome) was in itself controversial. Paul McCartney urged a public boycott of the Goldman book, which was almost universally reviled. Shortly after its publication, Sean asked to study abroad, and Ono accompanied him to Geneva, where they took up residence for a few years. On September 30, 1988, a week before *Imagine*'s release, John Lennon received his star on the Hollywood Walk of Fame. It is located near the Capitol Records building.

On March 21, 1984, Ono, Sean Lennon, and Julian Lennon were present as New York City Mayor Ed Koch officially opened Strawberry Fields, a triangular section of Central Park dedicated to John's memory and filled with plants, rocks, and other objects that Ono had solicited from heads of state around the world. In 2000 there were a number of events commemorating Lennon's 60th birthday and the 20th anniversary of his death, including a major exhibition on Lennon and his work at the Rock and Roll Hall of Fame & Museum.

Julian Lennon

Born John Charles Julian Lennon, Apr. 8, 1963, Liverpool, Eng.
1984—*Valotte* (Atlantic) 1986—*The Secret Value of Daydreaming* 1989—*Mr. Jordan* 1991—*Help Yourself* 1999—*Photograph Smile* (Fuel).

John Lennon's only child by his first wife, Cynthia Powell, Julian Lennon already had a small niche in rock history (Paul McCartney wrote "Hey Jude" about him) before he released *Valotte,* the debut album that was his biggest hit to date.

While growing up, Julian wasn't close to John, who divorced Cynthia in 1968 and then relocated to New York with Yoko Ono. Despite his father's wealth, Julian lived a typical middle-class life with his mother. Clearly, however, the younger Lennon's musical sensibilities were shaped by his father's music and that of the Beatles, as well as David Bowie, Steely Dan, and the Police. After his father was murdered in December 1980, Lennon spent some time haunting London nightclubs before deciding to put his long-harbored musical ambitions to the test.

He hooked up with Atlantic Records and veteran producer Phil Ramone (Billy Joel, Paul Simon). In 1985 *Valotte* (named for the French château where it was recorded) yielded the hit singles "Valotte" (#9), "Too Late for Goodbyes" (#5), and "Say You're Wrong" (#21). Critics and listeners noted Lennon's uncanny physical and vocal resemblance to his father, but they also praised the young songwriter and multi-instrumentalist (guitar, keyboards, percussion) for his moodily insinuating melodies. He even earned a Grammy nomination for Best New Artist of 1985. Unfortunately, 1986's *The Secret Value of Daydreaming* wasn't as well received, and 1989's *Mr. Jordan* and 1991's *Help Yourself* were all but ignored.

Frustrated, Lennon decided to take a break from the music industry, opting to break ties with Atlantic and spend several years traveling and dabbling in other creative pursuits, such as painting, photography, cooking, and acting. He resurfaced to cowrite a song for the 1995 movie *Mr. Holland's Opus* (whose soundtrack also contains a couple of John's songs), as well as file a lawsuit against Yoko Ono for a share of his late father's copyrights. The two reached an out-of-court financial settlement in 1996, although around that time, he had to buy some of John's memorabilia in order to have personal mementos of his father. On occasion, he has since been openly critical about Ono's handling of the elder Lennon's estate, specifically her decision to authorize his artwork to be reprinted on such items as neckties and mugs. His comeback album, *Photograph Smile* was originally released in Europe on the label he had formed, Music from Another Room, before being issued in the States in 1999.

Sean Lennon

Born Oct. 9, 1975, New York, NY
1998—*Into the Sun* (Grand Royal).

The son of John Lennon and Yoko Ono, Sean Lennon blends the pop craft of his father's music with the avant-garde inventiveness of his mother's to create his own experimental, alternative-rock vision. The songs on his debut album, *Into the Sun,* incorporate Eastern music, bossa nova, jazz, pop, hard rock, and country, as well as the kitchen-sink, cut-and-paste techniques of fellow contemporary artists Stereolab, Beck, and the Beastie Boys.

When Lennon was born, his famous father had taken time off from his own music to raise his son while Ono handled the family's business affairs. After the elder Lennon was shot to death outside the family's Dakota apartment building on Manhattan's Upper West Side in 1980, Sean was suddenly thrust into the public eye. Almost immediately afterward, he was shielded from the media, and later attended boarding schools in Switzerland. Lennon reemerged in 1991, when he appeared as a pianist on friend Lenny Kravitz's album *Mama Said*. Lennon briefly attended Columbia University in the early '90s but dropped out as his interest turned to New York's indie-rock scene.

In the mid-'90s, Lennon encouraged his mother to begin performing again, and the two formed the noise-rock group IMA. The band performed around New York and became the basis of Ono's 1995 album *Rising*. It was during this period that Lennon began dating Yuka Honda, the keyboard player for the experimental East Village duo Cibo Matto [see entry]. Lennon appeared on Cibo Matto's 1997 album *Super Relax*, eventually becoming the group's permanent bassist.

Through his association with Honda, Lennon met the Beastie Boys, who had signed Cibo Matto to their Grand Royal label. Beastie Boy Adam Yauch liked Lennon's solo music and asked if he wanted to record an album for the label. When *Into the Sun* was released in the spring of 1998, critics lauded the album for its ambitiousness. Partly due to Lennon's association with the hip indie-rock scene, he has been able to elude the comparisons to his father that dogged the pop career of his half brother, Julian, a decade earlier. *Into the Sun* was a modest seller, reaching only #153 on *Billboard*'s album chart.

Annie Lennox: See Eurythmics

The Lettermen

Formed 1960, Los Angeles, CA
Tony Butala (b. Nov. 20, 1940, Sharon, PA), voc.; Bob Engemann (b. Feb. 19, 1936, Highland Park, MI), voc.; Jim Pike (b. Nov. 6, 1938, St. Louis, MO), voc.
1966—*The Best of the Lettermen* (Capitol) 1967—*The Lettermen!!! . . . and "Live!"* (– Engemann; + Gary Pike, voc.); *Goin' Out of My Head* 1969—*Hurt So Bad* (– J. Pike; + Doug Curran, voc.; numerous personnel changes follow) 1974—*All-Time Greatest Hits* 1981—(lineup: Butala; Donovan Scott Tea, voc.; Mark Preston, voc.; Donnie Pike, voc.) 1986—(lineup: Butala; Pike; Tea; Robert Poynton, voc.) 2001—(lineup: Butala; Tea; Darren Dowler, voc.).

The Lettermen have been harmonizing pop songs for more than 40 years. Personnel have changed, their repertoire has been revamped with the times, and their hits are long behind them, but they continue. Original members Tony Butala, Bob Engemann, and Jim Pike all had a measure of music-business experience, in guises ranging from the Mitchell Boys Choir to Stan Kenton, when they formed the Lettermen in 1960. They were hired by George Burns and Jack Benny to open their live shows. A brief tenure with Warner Bros. Records followed before the Lettermen signed with Capitol in 1961. Their first single for the label, "The Way You Look Tonight," went gold; in 1962 "When I Fall in Love" and "Come Back Silly Girl" were Top 20 hits. Their albums of that period always made the Top 100; four were certified gold. They have grossed over $25 million in sales for Capitol Records. As tastes in music changed, the Lettermen adapted their smooth voices to the latest trend: folk revival when they started out, electric guitars in the mid-'60s, even disco and new wave in later years.

In 1967 they went through their first shift in personnel. Engemann was replaced by Gary Pike (Jim's brother), without any affect on their hitmaking abilities; they scored one of their biggest successes that year with a medley of "Goin' Out of My Head" and "Can't Take My Eyes Off of You." "Hurt So Bad" (#12, 1969) was their last gold record, though the trio continued releasing records on Capitol throughout the '70s. The Lettermen also branched into commercials, earning a Golden Globe Award for a Pan-Am ad. In 1982 they left Capitol for the Applause label. Still overseen by Butala, the group has not charted an LP since 1974, but it continues to record new material and tour successfully.

Levert/Gerald Levert

Formed 1982, Cleveland, OH
Gerald Levert (b. July 13, 1966, Canton, OH), voc.; Sean Levert (b. Sep. 28, 1968, Cleveland), voc.; Marc Gordon (b. Sep. 8, 1964), kybds., voc.
1986—*Bloodline* (Atlantic) 1987—*The Big Throwdown* 1988—*Just Coolin'* 1990—*Rope a Dope Style* 1993—*For Real Tho'* 1997—*The Whole Scenario* 2001—*The Best of Levert* (Rhino).
Gerald Levert solo: 1991—*Private Line* (EastWest) 1994—*Groove On* 1998—*Love & Consequences* 2000—*G* (Elektra).
Gerald Levert and Eddie Levert: 1995—*Father & Son* (EastWest).
Gerald Levert with LSG: 1997—*Levert, Sweat, Gill* (EastWest).
Sean Levert solo: 1995—*The Other Side* (Atlantic).

With keyboardist/vocalist Marc Gordon, singing brothers Gerald and Sean Levert—sons of the O'Jays' Eddie Levert Sr.—formed a trio that adapted the smooth, soulful harmonies of the O'Jays, Spinners, and other leading '70s R&B groups to a progressively aggressive funky and hip-hop–driven musical style.

The Levert siblings hooked up with Gordon while in their midteens. After practicing at the Leverts' home studio, the threesome began performing in Ohio clubs. An independently released single, "I'm Still," became popular in the Baltimore/Washington, DC, region, attracting the interest of Atlantic Records. Levert's debut album, *Bloodline*, yielded the #1 R&B hit "(Pop, Pop, Pop, Pop) Goes My Mind." The following year *The Big Throwdown* (#32 pop, #3 R&B, 1987) produced the R&B singles "Casanova" (#5 pop, #1 R&B, 1987), "My Forever Love" (#2 R&B, 1987), and "Sweet Sensation" (#4 R&B, 1988). In 1988 the band again topped the R&B singles chart with "Addicted to You," from the film soundtrack *Coming to America*.

Also in 1988 Gerald Levert and Gordon formed Trevel

Productions, a writing and producing team that worked with such artists as the O'Jays, Anita Baker, Men at Large, Teddy Pendergrass, and Miki Howard, whose hit "That's What Love Is" (#4 R&B, 1988) featured Gerald on vocals. Levert's 1988 album, *Just Coolin'* (#79 pop, #6 R&B), was produced by Trevel and generated another #1 R&B single with the title song, featuring rapper Heavy D. "Gotta Get the Money" reached #4. *Rope a Dope Style* (#9 R&B, 1990) spawned hits with the title track (#7 R&B, 1990), "All Season" (#4 R&B, 1990), and "Baby I'm Ready" (#1 R&B, 1991). Gerald's solo album, *Private Line*, peaked at #2 R&B and included the singles "School Me" (#3 R&B, 1992), "Can You Handle It" (#9 R&B, 1992), and "Baby Hold On to Me" (#1 R&B, 1992), the latter a duet between Gerald and his father. After the release of Gerald's second solo effort, *Groove On* (#2 R&B) in 1994, Gerald and Eddie recorded an album of duets, 1995's *Father & Son* (#20 pop, #2 R&B). The same year, Sean released his solo recording, *The Other Side* (#22 R&B).

While the group Levert still released one more album (1997's *Whole Scenario*, #10 R&B), Gerald was increasingly pursuing other endeavors. Also in 1997, he released an album with another group, LSG, comprised of himself and fellow R&B crooners Keith Sweat and Johnny Gill (ex–New Edition). The supergroup toured in 1998; by this time, it had become apparent that Levert the group would not continue. Gerald released another solo album, *Love & Consequences*, in 1998 and toured with Patti LaBelle the following year. He also dabbled in acting, appearing on the sitcom *The Jamie Foxx Show*, and formed a label, United Sound Records, to sign new talent. In 2000 he released a solo album on Elektra, titled simply *G*.

Furry Lewis

Born Mar. 6, 1893, Greenwood, MS; died Sep. 14, 1981, Memphis, TN
1969—*Presenting the Country Blues* (Blue Horizon) 1970—*In Memphis* (Matchbox) 1971—*Furry Lewis* (Xtra); *& Fred McDowell* (Biograph); *Furry Lewis Band* (Folkways) 2001—*Take Your Time* (with Lee Baker Jr.) (Adelphi).

Legendary Memphis bluesman Walter "Furry" Lewis is thought by some to be the first guitarist to play with a bottleneck, a technique later used by Robert Johnson, Bukka White, and Johnny Shines. (Earlier musicians had achieved a similar effect using a knife across the strings.) The son of a Mississippi sharecropper, Lewis moved from his birthplace to Memphis in 1899 and, while still in school, began playing guitar in local bands with W.C. Handy, Will Shade, and the Memphis Jug Band. He was a teen when he began performing on Beale Street.

Lewis toured the country in medicine shows and also played the jukes with Memphis Minnie and Blind Lemon Jefferson as early as 1906 and straight through the '20s. In 1916 he lost a leg in a railroad accident; it was replaced by a wooden stump. In 1927 he and Jim Jackson auditioned for the Vocalion label in Chicago. The next year his first recordings, including "Good Looking Girl Blues," "John Henry," and "Billy Lyons and Stack O'Lee," were released.

His singing style was a kind of talking blues, but the market for that music died in the Depression, and Furry spent the next 44 years supporting himself as a street cleaner. He did some performing by night, but he didn't record again until the late '50s, when Sam Charters recorded him for Prestige. Later recordings for Biograph, Folkways, Adelphi, and Rounder never earned enough for Lewis to quit the sanitation department. He did play many blues and folk festivals in the '60s and '70s and recorded with Bukka White, though his best shot at fame came in the early '70s, when he toured with Don Nix and the Alabama State Troopers and appeared on a Leon Russell television special.

In 1975 the Rolling Stones invited him along as their opening act in Memphis, and after a meeting with him, Joni Mitchell wrote "Furry Sings the Blues," which appeared on her *Hejira* album. Lewis also appeared on *The Tonight Show* and in two films, Burt Reynolds' *W.W. and the Dixie Dance King*, and *This Is Elvis*. He died of heart failure at age 88.

Gary Lewis and the Playboys

Formed 1964, Los Angeles, CA
Most popular lineup: Gary Lewis (b. Gary Levitch, July 31, 1945, Los Angeles), drums, voc.; Al Ramsey (b. July 27, 1943, NJ), gtr.; John R. West (b. July 31, 1939, Uhrichsville, OH), gtr.; David Walkes (b. May 12, 1943, Montgomery, AL), kybds.; David Costell (b. Mar. 15, 1944, Pittsburgh, PA), bass.
1965—*This Diamond Ring* (Liberty) 1966—*Golden Greats* 1968—*More Golden Greats*.

With seven consecutive Top 10 singles in 1965 and 1966, and over 7.5 million records sold, Gary Lewis was certainly one of the most successful Hollywood offspring turned rock & roller. Lewis was drafted in 1966, and since his 1969 army discharge, he has attempted several comebacks. The eldest son of comedian Jerry Lewis started playing drums at age 14; four years later he formed the Playboys. They became a regular fixture at Disneyland, and producer Snuff Garrett signed them to Liberty in 1964. With Leon Russell's arrangements and Al Kooper as cowriter, the Playboys scored a #1 hit their first time out with "This Diamond Ring."

Russell also worked on the subsequent singles: "Count Me In" (#2, 1965), "Save Your Heart for Me" (#2, 1965), "Everybody Loves a Clown" (#4, 1965), "She's Just My Style" (#3, 1966), "Sure Gonna Miss Her" (#9, 1966), and "Green Grass" (#8, 1966).

The group appeared in *A Swingin' Summer* (1965) and *Out of Sight* (1966). The Playboys' popularity had waned just slightly when Lewis was drafted, and upon his discharge he re-formed the group with other musicians. Though Lewis would score two more chart singles, he would never again have a Top 10 hit, despite an attempt to update his image from teenage pop star to "sensitive" singer/songwriter. His career was further complicated by drug problems and a divorce. Lewis performs regularly on the oldies circuit with the

Playboys, who now consist of Rich Spina, Billy Sullivan, John Dean, and Michael Hadak.

Huey Lewis and the News

Formed 1979, Marin County, CA
Huey Lewis (b. Hugh Cregg III, July 5, 1950, New York, NY), voc., harmonica; Chris Hayes (b. Nov. 24, 1957, CA), gtr.; Mario Cipollina (b. Nov. 10, 1954, CA), bass; Bill Gibson (b. Nov. 13, 1951, CA), drums; Sean Hopper (b. Mar. 31, 1953, CA), kybds.; Johnny Colla (b. July 2, 1952, CA), sax, gtr.
1980—*Huey Lewis and the News* (Chrysalis) 1982—*Picture This* 1983—*Sports* 1986—*Fore!* 1988—*Small World* 1991—*Hard at Play* (EMI) 1994—*Four Chords and Several Years Ago* (Elektra) 1996—(– Cipollina; + John Pierce, bass) *Time Flies . . . the Best of Huey Lewis and the News.*

One of the most commercially successful American bands of the early to mid-'80s, Huey Lewis and the News have released 17 Top 40 singles and sold over 12 million albums' worth of conservative, straight-ahead rock & roll. While critics derided the group for its bland predictability, fans were drawn to lead singer Huey Lewis and the band's fun-time persona and its radio-friendly sound.

The group traces its roots to the Bay Area, where Lewis and future News member Sean Hopper founded a country-rock group called Clover. Contrary to popular misconception, the entire band did not back Elvis Costello on his debut album; only Hopper did. The group had a U.K. record deal, and its first single, "Chicken Funk," was produced by Nick Lowe, but neither of its albums made much of an impression. Another Clover member, John McFee, quit to join the Doobie Brothers, and the group soon disbanded. Back in California, Lewis formed American Express. Among the members were ex-Soundhole Johnny Colla, Bill Gibson, and Mario Cipollina (the brother of Quicksilver Messenger Service's John Cipollina). In 1980 the group signed with Chrysalis, which requested a name change. Later that year Huey Lewis and the News' self-titled debut LP came and went without making a nick on the chart.

Early 1982 saw the release of the group's breakthrough album, *Picture This* (#13, 1982), which took off on the strength of the Mutt Lange–penned "Do You Believe in Love" (#7, 1982), followed by "Hope You Love Me Like You Say You Do" (#36, 1982). The group's second release, the 7-million-selling *Sports* (#1, 1983), stayed on the chart over three years. Boosted by a series of tongue-in-cheek videos that showcased Lewis' movie-star good looks, this album spun off five Top 20 hits, including four Top 10s: "Heart and Soul" (#8, 1983), "I Want a New Drug" (#6, 1984), "The Heart of Rock & Roll" (#6, 1984), and "If This Is It" (#6, 1984). Late in 1984 Lewis brought suit against Ray Parker Jr., alleging that the latter's hit "Ghostbusters" was a plagiarization of "I Want a New Drug." The case was later settled out of court. The next year brought the group's first #1 single, "The Power of Love," from the hit movie *Back to the Future.*

Three years elapsed between the release of *Sports* and *Fore!* (#1, 1986), which sold 3 million copies. From it came five more hits: "Stuck With You" (#1, 1986), "Hip to Be Square" (#3, 1986), Bruce Hornsby's "Jacob's Ladder" (#1, 1987), "I Know What I Like" (#9, 1987), and "Doing It All for My Baby" (#6, 1987). Around this time Lewis had helped Hornsby secure a record deal, and Lewis wrote several songs on his debut album.

The News' next release, *Small World* (#11, 1988), marked a change in direction, and while critics were not impressed, there were two hits: "Perfect World" (#3, 1988) and "Small World" (#25, 1988). *Hard at Play* (#27, 1991) was the first of the group's LPs since their debut to chart outside the Top 20; its only hit was "Couple Days Off" (#11, 1991). *Four Chords and Several Years Ago* (#55, 1994) is a collection of R&B and rock remakes. Lewis made his screen-acting debut in Robert Altman's 1994 film *Short Cuts;* he later appeared alongside Gwyneth Paltrow in 2000's *Duets.*

Jerry Lee Lewis

Born Sep. 29, 1935, Ferriday, LA
1958—*Jerry Lee Lewis* (Sun) 1964—*The Greatest Live Show on Earth* (Smash); *Live at the Star Club Hamburg* (Philips) 1968—*Another Place, Another Time* (Smash) 1969—*Jerry Lee Lewis' Original Golden Hits, vol. 1* (Sun); *Jerry Lee Lewis' Original Golden Hits, vol. 2* 1970—*A Taste of Country; Sunday Down South; Ole Tyme Country Music; There Must Be More to Love Than This* (Mercury) 1971—*Original Golden Hits, vol. 3* (Sun); *Monsters* 1973—*The Session* (Mercury) 1978—*Best of Jerry Lee Lewis, vol. 2* (Mercury) 1980—*Killer Country* (Elektra) 1982—*The Best of Jerry Lee Lewis (Featuring 39 and Holding)* 1984—*18 Original Sun Greatest Hits* (Rhino) 1985—*Milestones* 1986—*Twenty Classic Jerry Lee Lewis Hits* (Original Sound) 1987—*Rare and Rockin'* (Sun) 1989—*Rare Tracks* (Rhino); *Classic Jerry Lee Lewis* (Bear Family, Ger.) 1994—*All Killer, No Filler!* (Rhino) 1995—*Young Blood* (Sire); *Killer Country* (Mercury).

Though he had only three Top 10 hits in the first, purely rock & roll phase of his career, many critics believe Jerry Lee Lewis was as talented a '50s rocker as Sun labelmate Elvis Presley. Some also believe he could have made it just as big commercially if his piano-slamming musical style was not so relentlessly wild, his persona not so threateningly hard-edged.

Lewis' first musical influences were eclectic. His parents, who were poor, spun swing and Al Jolson records. But his earliest big influence was country star Jimmie Rodgers. In his early teens he absorbed both the softer country style of Gene Autry and the more rocking music of local black clubs, along with the gospel hymns of the local Assembly of God church. Lewis first played his aunt's piano at age eight and made his public debut in 1949 at age 14, sitting in with a local C&W band in a Ford dealership parking lot. When he was 15 Lewis went to a fundamentalist Bible school in Waxahachie, Texas, from which he was soon expelled. He has often said that rock & roll is the Devil's music.

Jerry Lee Lewis

In 1956 Lewis headed for Memphis (financed by his father) to audition for Sam Phillips' Sun Records. Phillips' assistant, Jack Clement, was impressed with Lewis' piano style but suggested he play more rock & roll, in a style similar to Elvis Presley's. (Presley had recently switched from Sun to RCA.) Lewis' debut single, "Crazy Arms" (previously a country hit for Ray Price), did well regionally, but it was the followup, 1957's "Whole Lotta Shakin' Going On" (#3), that finally broke through. The song first sold 100,000 copies in the South; after Lewis' appearance on Steve Allen's TV show, it sold over 6 million copies nationally. "Great Balls of Fire" (#2, 1957) sold more than 5 million copies and was followed by more than a half million in sales for "Breathless" (#7, 1958) and "High School Confidential" (#21, 1958), the title theme song of a movie in which Lewis also appeared. Both "Whole Lotta Shakin' " and "Great Balls" were in the pop, country, and R&B Top 5 simultaneously, "Shakin' " at #3 pop, and #1 R&B and C&W, and "Great Balls" at #2 pop, #3 R&B, and #1 C&W. Lewis' high school nickname was the "Killer," and it stuck with him as he established a reputation as a tough, rowdy performer with a flamboyant piano style that used careening glissandos, pounding chords, and bench-toppling acrobatics.

Lewis' career slammed to a stop, though, after he married his 13-year-old third cousin, Myra Gale Brown, in December 1957. (She was his third wife; at age 16 he had wed a 17-year-old, and soon after that ended, he got caught in a shotgun marriage.) The marriage lasted 13 years, but at the time, Lewis was condemned by the church in the U.S. and hounded by the British press on a 1958 tour. His career ran dry for nearly a decade. He had a modest 1961 hit with "What'd I Say," but in 1963 he left Sun for Smash/Mercury. He toured relentlessly, playing clubs, billing his act as "the greatest show on earth." On the way, he developed a drinking problem. In 1968 he played Iago in a rock-musical version of Shakespeare's *Othello* called *Catch My Soul.*

Eventually, Lewis and his producer, Jerry Kennedy, decided to abandon rock & roll for country music. In 1968 Lewis had the first of many Top 10 country hits with "Another Place, Another Time," followed by "What Made Milwaukee Famous (Made a Loser Out of Me)." Between then and the early '80s he had more than 30 big country hits, including "To Make Love Sweeter for You" (#1 C&W, 1968), "There Must Be More to Love Than This" (#1 C&W, 1971), "Would You Take Another Chance on Me" (#1 C&W, 1971), "Chantilly Lace" (#1 C&W, 1972), "Middle Age Crazy" (#4 C&W, 1977), and "Thirty-nine and Holding" (#4 C&W, 1981). Subsequent singles were minor C&W hits, none charting higher than #43.

In 1973 Lewis released *The Session,* a return-to-rock album recorded in London with a host of top British musicians, including Peter Frampton, Alvin Lee, Klaus Voormann, and Rory Gallagher, redoing oldies. It resulted in some pop chart success with "Drinkin' Wine Spo Dee Odee," an R&B song he'd performed at his public debut in 1949. In 1978 Lewis signed with Elektra and enjoyed some FM radio play with "Rockin' My Life Away." He also continued to tour, performing all the styles of his career: rock, country, gospel, blues, spirituals, and more. In 1981 Lewis played a German concert with fellow Sun alumni Johnny Cash and Carl Perkins. The show was released as an album called *Survivors* in 1982. On June 30, 1981, Lewis was hospitalized in Memphis with hemorrhaging from a perforated stomach ulcer. After two operations, he was given a 50-50 chance of survival; four months later he was back on tour. He appeared on the 1982 Grammy Awards telecast with his cousin Mickey Gilley; another cousin is TV evangelist Jimmy Swaggart.

Lewis' personal life has been marked by tragedy and controversy. In 1973 Jerry Lee Lewis Jr., who played drums in his father's band, was killed in an automobile accident. (Lewis' brother had died when hit by a car when Jerry was two.) His other son, Steve Allen (named after the talk-show host), drowned in 1962 at age three. In September 1976 Lewis accidently shot his bassist in the chest.

In 1982 his estranged fourth wife, Jaren Gunn Lewis, also drowned in a pool under mysterious circumstances shortly before their divorce settlement. His fifth wife, Shawn Stephens Lewis, was found dead in their home 77 days after their wedding. Although investigative pieces, including one in ROLLING STONE, exposed discrepancies in Lewis' and various local law-enforcement officials' accounts of the incident and flaws in the investigation, no charges were ever brought against Lewis. Despite the presence of blood at the couple's home, on Lewis, and on his wife's body, investigators did not even test to determine whose blood it was. A private and illegal (since it was conducted out of state) autopsy performed by the same coroner who determined that Elvis Presley had succumbed to cardiac arrhythmia declared Shawn Lewis was determined to have died from pulmonary edema. Even after published reports established problems with the investigation, the case was not reopened. Jerry Lee Lewis remarried again, taking his sixth wife. She later gave birth to Jerry Lee Lewis III, Lewis' only surviving son (he also had a daughter with Myra).

In recent years, Lewis has been plagued by serious health problems and battles with the IRS. He was treated at the Betty Ford Clinic for addiction to painkillers. His health has been poor and record sales have dropped off. He last came to widespread public attention in 1989, when the biographical film *Great Balls of Fire,* starring Dennis Quaid as Lewis, was released. Lewis was among the first 10 inductees into the Rock and Roll Hall of Fame in 1986. In 1995 he finally released a new album, *Young Blood.* He continues to gig sporadically. In 1999 he performed in Baltimore, Maryland, at the Smithsonian Institution's bash celebrating the 300th anniversary of the piano.

Ramsey Lewis

Born May 27, 1935, Chicago, IL
1956—*Ramsey Lewis and His Gentlemen of Swing* (Argo) 1958—*Down to Earth* (EmArcy) 1959—*An Hour With the Ramsey Lewis Trio* (Argo) 1960—*Stretchin' Out; Ramsey Lewis Trio in Chicago* 1961—*More Music from the Soil; Never on Sunday* 1962—*Country Meets the Blues; Bossa Nova; Sound of Spring* 1963—*Pot Luck; Barefoot Sunday Blues* 1964—*The Ramsey Lewis Trio at the Bohemian Caverns; You Better Believe Me; Bach to the Blues* 1965—*The In Crowd* (Cadet); *Choice! The Best of The Ramsey Lewis Trio* 1966—*Wade in the Water* (Chess); *Movie Album; The Groover* (Cadet); *Hang On Ramsey!; Swingin'* 1967—*Goin' Latin; Dancing in the Street* 1968—*Maiden Voyage; Ramsey Lewis Trio; Up Pops Ramsey* 1969—*Mother Nature's Son; Solid Ivory; Another Voyage; Piano Player* (Chess) 1970—*Them Changes* (Cadet) 1971—*Back to the Roots* 1973—*Funky Serenity* (Columbia); *Ramsey Lewis' Newly Recorded All-Time, Non-Stop Golden Hits* 1974—*Solar Wind* 1975—*Sun Goddess; Don't It Feel Good; Live in Tokyo* (Cadet) 1976—*Salongo* (Columbia) 1977—*Love Notes; Tequila Mockingbird* 1978—*Legacy* 1979—*Ramsey* (CBS); 1980—Routes (Columbia) 1981—*Blues for the Night Owl; 3 Piece Suite* 1982—*Live at the Savoy; Chance Encounter* 1983—*Reunion; Les Fleurs* 1984—*The Two of Us* (with Nancy Wilson) 1985—*Fantasy* 1987—*Keys to the City* 1988—*We Meet Again* (with Billy Taylor) (CBS); *A Classic Encounter With the Philharmonic Orchestra* 1989—*Urban Renewal* (Columbia) 1992—*Ivory Pyramid* (GRP) 1993—*Sky Islands* 1995—*Between the Keys* 1998—*Dance of the Soul* 1999—*Appassionata* (Narada); *Eye on You* (Columbia); *Encore! Ramsey Lewis Trio in Tokyo* (Chess) 2000—*Urban Nights III* (Narada).

Keyboardist Ramsey Lewis has had much commercial success with pop-jazz instrumentals, particularly in the mid-'60s, when his remakes of current hits—Dobie Gray's "The 'In' Crowd," the McCoys' "Hang On Sloopy"—went Top 20. Releasing consistently well-crafted albums, Lewis has maintained a solid career.

Lewis studied classical piano at the Chicago College of Music and De Paul University. He began playing professionally at age 16 with the Clefs, a group that included bassist Eldee Young and drummer Isaac Red Holt, with whom he formed the Ramsey Lewis Trio in 1956. In 1965 the Trio won a Grammy for "The 'In' Crowd" (#5, 1965) ("Hang On Sloopy" [#11, 1965] won a Grammy in 1973 after being rereleased on *Golden Hits*). Besides the Trio's albums, Lewis played with Max Roach, Sonny Stitt, and Clark Terry. In 1965 the Trio broke up. His former sidemen founded Young-Holt Unlimited and scored a #3 hit with "Soulful Strut" in 1969. In 1966 Lewis' new trio, drummer Maurice White, later of Earth, Wind & Fire, and Cleveland Eaton on bass scored another hit with "Wade in the Water" (#19) and Lewis received another Grammy for "Hold It Right There."

Lewis enjoyed much success through the mid-'70s, and his *Sun Goddess* (#12, 1975), produced by White, went gold. In the '80s he explored new settings: *Keys to the City* juxtaposes piano with synth; *Classic Encounter* features the Philharmonic Orchestra. He also duetted with jazz pianist Billy Taylor and singer Nancy Wilson. In 1990 Lewis began cohosting a jazz radio show in Chicago; shortly thereafter he became a host for a BET jazz program. In the '90s he produced music for commercials with his son Kevyn and was appointed Art Tatum Professor in Jazz Studies at Chicago's Roosevelt University.

Smiley Lewis

Born Overton Amos Lemons, July 5, 1920, Union, LA; died Oct. 7, 1966, New Orleans, LA
1970—*Shame Shame Shame* (Liberty) 1978—*I Hear You Knocking* (United Artists); *The Bells Are Ringing.*

Singer/guitarist/pianist Smiley Lewis was a major New Orleans R&B performer, though his best songs became pop hits only for other people. His parents moved to New Orleans from his small-town birthplace when he was 11, and he began recording there in 1947 for Deluxe Records under the name Smiling Lewis. The best-loved work of this gravel-voiced singer came during his 1950–60 period, when he was produced by Dave Bartholomew, yielding such songs as "Shame Shame Shame" and two R&B hits, "The Bells Are Ringing" (#10, 1952) and "I Hear You Knocking" (#2, 1955), which featured a classic piano intro from Huey Smith. A few months later, Lewis' version of "Knocking" was eclipsed by Gale Storm's #2 pop hit cover. The song was revived 15 years later by Dave Edmunds, who made it a hit again. Another of Lewis' tunes, "One Night (of Sin)," was cleaned up and changed to "One Night (of Love)" and became a hit for Elvis Presley in 1958.

Beginning in 1961, Lewis recorded for Okeh, then Dot and Loma Records (at the last, produced by Allen Toussaint), and he worked until his death in 1966 of stomach cancer.

Gordon Lightfoot

Born Nov. 17, 1938, Orillia, Ont., Can.
1966—*Lightfoot* (United Artists) 1968—*The Way I Feel; Did She Mention My Name?* 1969—*Back Here on Earth; Early Lightfoot; Sunday Concert* 1970—*Sit Down Young Stranger* (Reprise); *If You Could Read My Mind* 1971—*Summer Side of Life* 1972—*Don Quixote; Old Dan's Records* 1973—*Sundown* 1974—*The Very Best of Gordon Lightfoot* (United Artists) 1975—*Cold on the Shoulder* (Reprise); *Gord's Gold* 1976—*Early Morning Rain; Summertime Dream* 1978—*Endless Wire* (Warner Bros.) 1980—*Dream Street Rose* 1982—*Shadows* 1983—*Salute* 1986—*East of Midnight* 1988—*Gord's Gold, vol. 2* 1993—*Waiting for You* (Reprise) 1998—*A Painter Passing Through* 1999—*Songbook* (Rhino).

One of the most successful Canadian singer/songwriters, baritone Gordon Lightfoot was inspired to write his own songs by writers like Bob Dylan, Tom Paxton, and Phil Ochs in the early '60s. Prior to that he played piano, worked summers in his father's laundry, and then immigrated to L.A. in 1958 to attend now defunct Westlake College. There he studied orchestration but soon returned to Toronto, where he worked as an arranger and producer of commercial jingles until 1960. Encouraged by Pete Seeger and friends Ian and Sylvia, he then switched to guitar and, along with his studio work, began playing folk music at local coffeehouses.

Lightfoot soon developed his own identity with countryish material like his debut Canadian hit, "Remember Me." Ian and Sylvia added two of his folky numbers to their stage show, "For Lovin' Me" and "Early Morning Rain," and introduced Lightfoot to their manager, Albert Grossman, who promptly gave both songs to his other clients Peter, Paul and Mary. The trio made "For Lovin' Me" a #30 U.S. hit in 1965.

On his own, Lightfoot began releasing solo albums in 1966, the first six on United Artists. Each sold between 150,000 and 200,000 copies. In 1969 he switched to Reprise, and his label debut, *Sit Down Young Stranger,* sold 750,000 copies with the help of his first U.S. hit, "If You Could Read My Mind" (#5, 1971). Many other artists, including Bob Dylan, Jerry Lee Lewis, Johnny Cash, Elvis Presley, Barbra Streisand, and Judy Collins, continued to cover his songs.

Lightfoot's popularity peaked in the mid-'70s with a #1 gold LP and single in 1974, both called Sundown. He hit #2 with "The Wreck of the Edmund Fitzgerald" (about an ore vessel that sank on Lake Superior), released on the *Summertime Dream* LP in May 1976. Although he didn't release an album of new material between 1986 and 1993, Lightfoot toured regularly. He still commands a loyal following, particularly in his homeland. In November 1997 he received that country's highest official honor, the Order of Canada citation, for his efforts in spreading Canadian culture.

Lil' Kim

Born Kimberly Denise Jones, July 11, 1975, Brooklyn, NY
1996—*Hard Core* (Atlantic) 2000—*The Notorious K.I.M.*

Lil' Kim took female MCing to its raunchiest, loudest, most empowering extent. By depicting the lewdest of female-dominated sexual fantasies—a role reversal in the sometimes misogynistic pop-music world—she redefined hip-hop feminism.

Lil' Kim grew up on the same block as the Notorious B.I.G. [see entry] in the Bedford-Stuyvesant section of Brooklyn. After leaving home at 15 and resorting to drug dealing, she was convinced by her close friend and future boyfriend B.I.G. to give up dealing for rapping. In 1995 B.I.G. enlisted Lil' Kim as the sole woman in the Junior M.A.F.I.A. (Masters At Finding Intelligent Attitudes), a collective of Brooklyn-based MCs. The group's first and only album, *Conspiracy* (#8 pop, #2 R&B, 1995), introduced Lil' Kim's nasty-as-I-wanna-be attitude to a mass audience and generated the hits "Player's Anthem" (#13 pop, #7 R&B, 1995) and "Get Money" (#17 pop, #4 R&B, 1996). In 1996 Atlantic released Lil' Kim's solo debut, *Hard Core* (#11 pop, #3 R&B, 1996), which features tracks produced by Sean Combs and others. "No Time" (#18 pop, #9 R&B, 1996), featuring a rap by Sean Combs, held the top spot on the rap singles chart for 11 consecutive weeks.

Four days after "No Time" was certified gold, B.I.G. was murdered. Lil' Kim then joined Sean Combs on 1998's Bad Boy Tour, and appeared on recordings by Jay-Z, Missy Elliott, and Mobb Deep. *The Notorious K.I.M.* (#4 pop, #1 R&B, 2000) features "Hold On," a tribute to Notorious B.I.G.

Limp Bizkit

Formed 1994, Jacksonville, FL
Fred Durst (b. William Fredrick Durst, Aug. 20, 1971, Jacksonville), voc.; Wes Borland (b. Wesley Scott Borland, Feb. 7, 1975, Nashville, TN), gtr.; John Otto (b. ca. 1978), drums; Sam Rivers (b. Sep. 21, 1977, Jacksonville), bass.
1995—(+ DJ Lethal [b. Leor DiMant, Dec. 18, 1972, Latvia], turntables) 1997—*Three Dollar Bill, Y'all$* (Flip/Interscope) 1999—*Significant Other* 2000—*Chocolate Starfish and the Hot Dog Flavored Water.*
Wes Borland with Bigdumbface: 2001—*Duke Lion Fights the Terror!!* (Interscope).

While Rage Against the Machine and Korn first took the rap-rock genre into Top 10 territory, Limp Bizkit carried it into the record books. Highlighted by the call-and-response anthem "Nookie," the band's second album, *Significant Other,* knocked the Backstreet Boys' blockbuster *Millennium* off the top of the charts in 1999, and 2000's *Chocolate Starfish and the Hot Dog Flavored Water* debuted at #1 and became the year's fastest-selling rock album.

While growing up in Gastonia, North Carolina, frontman Fred Durst embraced both punk and rap, splitting his leisure time between skateboarding and break dancing. After high school, he did a short stint in the navy (he received a medical discharge after injuring his wrist in a skateboarding accident) and settled in Jacksonville, Florida, where he worked as a tattoo artist. Forming Limp Bizkit in 1994, Durst enlisted guitarist Wes Borland, drummer John Otto, and bassist Sam

Rivers. The following year, former House of Pain turntablist DJ Lethal joined the fold (having met the band when Limp Bizkit opened a House of Pain show). The band's fate was sealed when Durst tattooed the members of Korn [see entry] and afterward gave them a demo tape; Korn passed it along to people in the music industry, and by 1997, Limp Bizkit had landed a deal with Flip/Interscope.

The band's first album, *Three Dollar Bill, Y'all$* (#22, 1997) attracted controversy early on when the story broke that Interscope had bought advertising time from a Portland, Oregon, radio station to play the single "Counterfeit" 50 times. Limp Bizkit weathered the payola storm and saw its rap/metal cover of George Michael's "Faith" become a Modern Rock hit. During its concert performances that year, the band would emerge onstage at the beginning of each show from a giant toilet. By the time *Significant Other* bowed at the top of the chart in late 1999, Limp Bizkit had become a rock superstar, headlining its own tour and garnering a prime slot at the ill-fated Woodstock '99 (where the band's performance of "Break Stuff" would be cited by many as initiating the mayhem and hooliganism that ultimately brought the three-day festival down in flames).

The controversial Woodstock appearance did little to slow Limp Bizkit down, however. Durst, who made no secret of his ambition to be an industry power player as well as a rock star, was given his own Flawless imprint by Interscope and was appointed senior vice president of A&R. During the summer of 2000, Limp Bizkit went against the grain of the music industry by aligning itself with the controversial online song-trading software company Napster by participating in a free-admission tour with Cypress Hill (Napster picked up the bill). The band's third album, *Chocolate Starfish and the Hot Dog Flavored Water,* debuted at #1 in October 2000, selling more than a million copies its first week in stores. Earlier that year, the band also had scored another Modern Rock hit with the *Mission: Impossible-2* soundtrack offering, "Take a Look Around." In 2001 guitarist Borland branched out with the side-project band Bigdumbface.

David Lindley: see Kaleidoscope

Arto Lindsay: See DNA

Lipps, Inc.

Formed 1977, Minneapolis, MN
Steven Greenberg (b. Oct. 24, 1950, St. Paul, MN), kybds., synth., bass, drums, perc., voc.; Cynthia Johnson (b. Apr. 6, 1956, St. Paul), voc.; David Rivkin, gtr.; Tom Riopelle, gtr.; Terry Grant, bass; Ivan Rafowitz, kybds.
1980—*Mouth to Mouth* (Casablanca); *Pucker Up* 1981—*Designer Music.*

Lipps, Inc. (pronounced "lip-sync") burst out of Minnesota's Twin Cities in 1980, the same year that Prince began his ascent to superstardom with *Dirty Mind.* Where Prince launched a career by bridging rock, pop, and funk to form the Minneapolis Sound, Lipps, Inc. had only one big hit—the instant classic "Funkytown" (#1 pop, #2 R&B, 1980), an extended dance track that seamlessly melded percolating synth pop (complete with electronic vocals), slashing funk guitar, disco strings, and the gospelish vocals of Cynthia Johnson over a relentless big beat.

A studio-bound unit, Lipps, Inc. was the brainchild of composer/producer/multi-instrumentalist Steven Greenberg. Johnson had been Minnesota's Miss Black U.S.A. contestant in 1976. Aside from "Funkytown," *Mouth to Mouth* (#5, 1980) also produced a minor hit in "Rock It" (#64 pop, #85 R&B, 1980). The prompt followup album *Pucker Up* (#63, 1980) yielded only "How Long" (#29 R&B, 1980). Lipps, Inc. scored minor hits with the subsequent singles "Hold Me Down" (#70 R&B, 1981) and "Addicted to the Night" (#78, 1983), then, following several lineup changes, disbanded. A decade later, Greenberg surfaced as the founder of October Records; in 1998 he produced a quickly forgotten movie entitled *Funkytown.* Johnson kept working on the Minneapolis music scene, leading an all-female funk band, Kat Klub, and eventually becoming a jazz singer. As David Z, guitarist David Rivkin would go on to become one of Prince's sound engineers (his brother Bobby was Prince's first drummer); he is currently a well-known producer, based in Nashville.

Mance Lipscomb

Born Apr. 9, 1895, Navasota, TX; died Jan. 30, 1976, Navasota
1962—*Mance Lipscomb, Texas Songster* (Arhoolie) 1964—*Mance Lipscomb, Texas Songster, vol. 2* 1966—*Mance Lipscomb, Texas Songster, vol. 3* 1968—*Mance Lipscomb, Texas Songster, vol. 4* 1970—*Mance Lipscomb, Texas Songster, vol. 5; Trouble in Mind* (Reprise) 1994—*Texas Blues Guitar* (Arhoolie).

Discovered during the early-'60s folk-blues boom, singer/guitarist/fiddler Mance Lipscomb is generally considered a Texas country-blues great, an artistic descendant of Blind Lemon Jefferson and compatriot of Lightnin' Hopkins. Actually, though, Lipscomb was a bluesman and more: a songster and minstrel who performed ballads, reels, shouts, and breakdowns as well as blues. Though he didn't record until age 65, his influence has been noted in the work of Bob Dylan, Janis Joplin, and the Grateful Dead, among others.

Lipscomb learned to play fiddle from his father, an emancipated slave turned professional musician, and played with him around the Navasota-Brazos area until 1911. Between shows Lipscomb taught himself guitar and worked the fields. Before 1956 he played only for small gatherings of friends and coworkers at picnics or dances. He moved to Houston in 1956, and in 1960 was discovered by Chris Strachwitz, a folk-music archivist and founder of Arhoolie Records, who brought tapes of his music to various members of the folk-blues community. Lipscomb played several folk festivals and was recorded by Arhoolie. He continued recording and performing until 1974, when heart disease forced him to retire. Lipscomb also appeared in several documentary films:

The Blues (1962), *The Blues Accordin' to Lightnin' Hopkins* (1968), Les Blank's *Blues Like Showers of Rain* (1970), *A Well Spent Life* (1971), and *Out of the Blacks Into the Blues* (1972).

Lisa Lisa and Cult Jam

Formed 1984, New York, NY
Lisa Lisa (b. Lisa Velez, Jan. 15, 1967, New York), voc.; Spanador (b. Alex Mosely, 1962, New York), gtr.; Mike Hughes (b. 1963, New York), drums.
1985—*Lisa Lisa & Cult Jam With Full Force* (Columbia) 1987—*Spanish Fly* 1989—*Straight to the Sky* 1991—*Straight Outta Hell's Kitchen* 1997—*Super Hits*.
Lisa Lisa solo: 1994—*LL77* (Pendulum/ERG).

Lisa Lisa and Cult Jam come from the same New York dance-music scene that produced Madonna, but their Latin roots are authentic rather than appropriated. Lisa Velez grew up in New York's Hell's Kitchen, the youngest of 10 children. She began singing in church at age nine, and in high school was involved in musical theater. She met percussionist Mike Hughes in 1983 at the Fun House, a downtown New York club where Velez hung out because she heard Madonna was discovered there.

Hughes and Spanador had been working with the Brooklyn group and production team Full Force, which was looking for a female singer with a girlish voice for a song it had written. Taking the name Lisa Lisa, patterned after Full Force's U.T.F.O. hit "Roxanne, Roxanne," the singer and her new band and producers scored an underground dance smash with "I Wonder If I Take You Home" (#34 pop, #6 R&B, 1985). The song was first released on the 1984 *Breakdancing* compilation, then as a single in 1985. Their platinum debut album, *Lisa Lisa & Cult Jam With Full Force* (#52, 1985), featured the hit and a number of other dance tracks, including "All Cried Out" (#8 pop, #3 R&B, 1986).

Featuring a larger variety of sounds, including dance, funk, salsa, and doo-wop, the platinum *Spanish Fly* (#7, 1987) was an even bigger hit, yielding the singles "Head to Toe" (#1 pop, #1 R&B, 1987), "Lost in Emotion" (#1 pop, #1 R&B, 1987), "Someone to Love Me for Me" (#7 R&B, 1987), and "Everything Will B-Fine" (#9 R&B, 1988). Lisa Lisa and Cult Jam opened for David Bowie that year and toured the world as a headlining act.

The group's success began to stall with their third album, *Straight to the Sky*, which featured only the minor hit "Little Jackie Wants to Be a Star" (#29, 1989). Lisa Lisa, Cult Jam, and Full Force tried to recapture their dance/pop success by bringing in C + C Music Factory's David Cole and Robert Clivilles to produce one side of *Straight Outta Hell's Kitchen;* until then, Full Force had been the band's sole producers, songwriters, arrangers, and managers. But the album's one hit, "Let the Beat Hit 'Em" (#37 pop, #1 R&B, 1991), failed to cross over in a big way to the pop audience.

Velez subsequently parted ways with her band, producers/managers, and label. In December 1993 Pendulum/ERG released Lisa Lisa's solo debut, "Skip to My Lu" (#38 R&B); an album, *LL77*, followed in January 1994. Success as a solo artist nevertheless eluded Valez as *LL77* failed to break into *Billboard*'s Top 100 album chart. The singer approached everyone from Sean Combs to Michael Jackson about putting out a followup album, but she couldn't get a record deal. In 1997 she took her act to the stage, starring in *Barrio Babies*, a musical about young Latinos trying to make it in Hollywood.

Velez has used her fame to try to be a positive role model for urban youth. She has participated in campaigns to increase AIDS awareness and to fight illiteracy, drug abuse, and teen suicide.

Little Anthony and the Imperials

Formed 1957, New York, NY
Anthony Gourdine (b. Jerome Anthony Gourdine, Jan. 8, 1940, New York), lead voc.; Ernest Wright Jr. (b. Aug. 24, 1941, Brooklyn, NY), second tenor; Clarence Collins (b. Mar. 17, 1941, Brooklyn), baritone; Tracy Lord, first tenor; Glouster "Nat" Rogers, bass.
1961—(– Lord; – Rogers; + Sammy Strain [b. Dec. 9, 1941], first tenor; – Gourdine; + George Kerr, lead) 1963—(group reunites: Gourdine; Strain; Wright; Collins) 1964—*I'm on the Outside Lookin' In* (DCP) 1965—*Goin' Out of My Head* (Veep) Early '70s—(– Wright; + Kenny Seymour) 1974—(– Seymour; + Bobby Wade, voc.) *On a New Street* (Avco) 1989—*Best of Little Anthony and the Imperials* (Rhino) 1992—(group reunites: Gourdine; Strain; Collins; Wright).
Little Anthony solo: 1980—*Daylight* (MCA/Songbird).

Little Anthony and the Imperials are considered one of the best late-'50s doo-wop groups. Their first and biggest hit was the million-selling "Tears on My Pillow" (#4, 1958). Lead singer Anthony Gourdine began his career with the Duponts, a band of Brooklyn singers who cut two singles in 1955 on the Winley and Royal Roost labels. He then formed the Chesters, who cut one song under that name in 1957 on Apollo and then were renamed the Imperials by their new label, End. The Little Anthony moniker for the then 5-foot-4 (he is now 5-foot-10) singer was added by Alan Freed and first turned up on later pressings of "Tears on My Pillow." The group had another hit in 1960, "Shimmy, Shimmy, Ko-ko Bop" (#24), then broke up. Little Anthony was idle until 1963, after the group had re-formed minus Lord and Rogers, and having added Sammy Strain. This lineup had consistent chart success with "Goin' Out of My Head" (#6, 1964) (written by Teddy Randazzo, formerly of the Three Chuckles), "Hurt So Bad" (#9, 1965), and "Take Me Back" (#16, 1965).

After that the Imperials had no more major chart action but continued recording on Veep from 1966 to 1968, United Artists (1969 to 1970), and on Avco in 1974, which yielded the #25 soul hit "I'm Falling in Love With You." Little Anthony played solo on the Las Vegas circuit in the early '70s and, after a slow period later in the decade, became a born-again Christian. He signed a solo deal in 1980 with MCA/Songbird and released *Daylight*, produced by B.J. Thomas. Gourdine spent much of the '80s and early '90s playing supper clubs as well. Strain later joined the O'Jays, and the remaining Imperials, with a few lineup changes, continued to tour as well.

In 1992 Gourdine, Wright, Collins, and Strain reunited for a Madison Square Garden oldies show. What was supposed to have been a onetime event grew into a permanent re-formation (which Strain left the O'Jays to participate in) that officially began on Valentine's Day 1993. They appeared on a television special celebrating *American Bandstand*'s 40th anniversary. The Imperials continued to perform into 2000.

Little Eva

Born Eva Narcissus Boyd, June 29, 1945, Bell Haven, NC
1962—*LIllloco-Motion* (Dimension) 1988—*The Best of Little Eva* (Murray Hill) 1989—*Back on Track* (Malibu).

Perhaps no baby-sitter in history ever got a bigger break than Eva Boyd, who, the story goes, at age 17 was baby-sitting for songwriters Carole King and Gerry Goffin. They asked her to record a tune they'd just written called "The Loco-Motion." The song borrowed its arrangement from the Marvelettes' "Please Mr. Postman." With the Cookies ("Chains") as backup singers, plus the powerhouse voice of the newly named Little Eva, the record went to #1 on the pop and R&B charts in 1962. Eva had another danceable followup with "Keep Your Hands off My Baby" (#12 pop, #6 R&B, 1962), and in 1963 she scored a Top 20 with "Let's Turkey Trot" (#20 pop, #16 R&B), all recorded for Dimension. Eva also recorded "Swingin' on a Star" (#38, 1963), a duet with Big Dee Irwin, formerly of the Pastels.

Eva's sister Idalia also recorded with the label, earning only one minor hit, "Hoola Hooping." Eva cut a few more records for other labels, including Spring and Amy, but never re-created her original overnight success. Disenchanted with the music business, she retired in the early '70s, but in the '90s began performing live again on the oldies circuit.

Little Feat

Formed 1969, Los Angeles, CA
Lowell George (b. 1945; d. June 29, 1979, Arlington, VA), voc., gtr., slide gtr., harmonica; Bill Payne (b. Mar. 12, 1949, Waco, TX), kybds., voc.; Richard Hayward, drums; Roy Estrada, bass, voc.
1971—*Little Feat* (Warner Bros.) 1972—*Sailin' Shoes* (– Estrada; + Kenny Gradney [b. New Orleans, LA], bass; + Paul Barrere [b. July 3, 1948, Burbank, CA], gtr., voc.; + Sam Clayton, congas) 1973—*Dixie Chicken* 1974—*Feats Don't Fail Me Now* 1975—*The Last Record Album* 1977—*Time Loves a Hero* 1978—*Waiting for Columbus* 1979—*Down on the Farm* (– George) (group disbands) 1981—*Hoy-Hoy!* 1988—(group re-forms: Barrere; Payne; Hayward; Clayton; Gradney; + Craig Fuller, voc., gtr.; + Fred Tackett, gtr., trumpet) *Let It Roll* 1990—*Representing the Mambo* 1991—*Shake Me Up* (Morgan Creek) 1994—(– Fuller; + Shaun Murphy, voc.) 1995—*Ain't Had Enough Fun* (Zoo) 1996—*Live From Neon Park* 1998—*Under the Radar* (CMC International) 2000—*Chinese Work Songs; Hotcakes and Outtakes: 30 Years of Little Feat* (Rhino).
Lowell George solo: 1979—*Thanks I'll Eat It Here* (Warner Bros.).
Paul Barrere solo: 1983—*On My Own Two Feet* (Atlantic) 1984—*Real Lies* 1995—*If the Phone Don't Ring* (Zoo).

Little Feat mixed every strain of Southern music—blues, country, gospel, rockabilly, boogie, New Orleans R&B, and Memphis funk—with surreal lyrics and a sense of absurdity and professionalism that could only have come from Southern California. Despite this, Little Feat had two gold albums; the live *Waiting for Columbus* went platinum. And Little Feat enjoyed a strong cult following and became one of California's most influential bands of the '70s.

The band was formed by Lowell George and Roy Estrada, both former Mothers of Invention members; Richie Hayward, ex-Fraternity of Man (of "Don't Bogart That Joint" on the *Easy Rider* soundtrack); and classically trained pianist Bill Payne. George's bluesy vocals and slide guitar dominated the sound of the band, and his playful songwriting set its tone; although he could write conventional country-rock songs like "Willin' " (which appeared on the first two Feat albums and has been covered by Linda Ronstadt, Commander Cody, and others), he reveled in wordplay and non sequiturs. As a child, George appeared on TV's *Ted Mack's Original Amateur Hour*, playing a harmonica duet with his brother Hampton; he played flute in the Hollywood High School orchestra and, later, oboe and baritone saxophone in Frank Sinatra recording sessions. In 1965 he started a folk-rock group, the Factory, which Hayward joined after answering an ad. The Factory recorded for Uni Records. When it broke up, George became rhythm guitarist in Frank Zappa's Mothers of Invention and was with a short-lived Standells (of "Dirty Water" fame) reunion before starting Little Feat.

After "Easy to Slip" from *Sailin' Shoes* failed to hit, Little Feat went through one of its many breakups, and the first (prior to its 1988 re-formation) to result in personnel changes. Estrada went into computer programming, though he briefly rejoined Zappa a few years later. He was replaced by two New Orleans musicians, Kenny Gradney and Sam Clayton, along with guitarist Paul Barrere.

The Little Feat of *Dixie Chicken* was slightly less raucous and more funky; the group toured with New Orleans songwriter Allen Toussaint, whose "On Your Way Down" appeared on *Dixie Chicken*. For the rest of the decade, Little Feat established itself as a touring band, particularly on the East Coast and in the South. The group also became a mainstay of the L.A. music community; Payne, especially, did a lot of session work. The band kept an erratic recording schedule, partly because it was frequently breaking up, and partly because George, who had become Feat's producer, had trouble making final decisions; song titles and lyrics would often appear on album covers but not on the LPs themselves.

Beginning with *The Last Record Album*, Barrere and Payne (usually as collaborators) began to take on a larger share of the songwriting, moving the band toward jazz rock. George produced an album by the Grateful Dead *(Shakedown Street)* and announced periodically that he was working on a solo album. When *Thanks I'll Eat It Here* (originally the projected title of *Sailin' Shoes*) finally appeared in 1979, George announced Little Feat's breakup and went on tour with his own band; in the middle of the tour, he died, apparently of a heart attack. Little Feat finished *Down on the Farm* and disbanded; *Hoy-Hoy!* compiled live tracks and alternate takes.

After George's death, Hayward toured with Joan Armatrading and recorded and toured with Robert Plant. Payne returned to studio work and occasional tours, including one with James Taylor. In 1983 and 1984 Barrere released solo albums (reissued on one CD in 1995) and toured with his own band.

Barrere, Payne, Hayward, Gradney, and Clayton reformed Little Feat in 1988, with guitarists Fred Tackett (an L.A. sessionman who'd appeared on some earlier Feat albums) and Craig Fuller (formerly with country-rock band Pure Prairie League). *Let It Roll* (#36, 1988) went gold; *Representing the Mambo* (#45, 1990) didn't, and *Shake Me Up* reached only #126. Fuller was replaced by Shaun Murphy, the band's first female member, in 1994.

Little Feat may not make the headlines anymore, but it continues to tour regularly and has gained a healthy following among admirers of new jam bands. It returned the favor by covering Phish's "Sample in a Jar" on 2000's *Chinese Work Songs. Hotcakes and Outtakes* is a four-CD set covering the band's entire career and including demos from the Lowell George era.

Little Milton

Born James Milton Campbell Jr., Sep. 7, 1934, Inverness, MS
1969—*Grits Ain't Groceries* (Checker) 1972—*Little Milton Greatest Hits* (Chess); *Walking the Back Streets* (Stax) 1974—*Golden Decade* (Phonogram); *Blues 'n' Soul* (Stax); *Montreux Festival; Tin Pan Alley* 1976—*Blues Masters* (Chess) 1983—*Age Ain't Nothin' but a Number* (MCA) 1984—*Playing for Keeps* (Malaco) 1985—*I Will Survive* 1986—*Annie Mae's Cafe* 1987—*Movin' to the Country* 1988—*Back to Back* 1990—*Too Much Pain* 1991—*Reality* 1992—*Strugglin' Lady* 1994—*I'm a Gambler* 1995—*Live at Westville Prison* (Delmark); *Greatest Hits* (Malaco) 1996—*Cheatin' Habit* 1997—*Greatest Hits* (Chess) 1998—*For Real* (Malaco) 1999—*Welcome to Little Milton.*

Through a career that spans more than five decades, veteran blues singer/guitarist Little Milton has emerged as a blues master. The son of Delta sharecroppers, he took up guitar at the age of 12, his love of music inspired by the Grand Ole Opry radio broadcasts as well as blues and gospel. (He considers T-Bone Walker his most important influence.) At 15 he left home to play with Eddie Kusick, Rice Miller (Sonny Boy Williamson), and Willie Love. In 1953 he was signed to Sun Records, where he recorded with Ike Turner (later of Ike and Tina fame). Milton soon moved on to other labels, including Meteor in 1957 and St. Louis' Bobbin, which he cofounded, in 1958.

His single "I'm a Lonely Man" caught the attention of Leonard Chess, who signed him to Checker in 1961. There he had his first real success with "So Mean to Me" (#14 R&B, 1962). In 1965 he went all the way to #1 R&B with "We're Gonna Make It," a #25 pop hit. His gospel-soulful vocals were reminiscent of Bobby Bland, yet still distinctive, earning him another top hit that year with "Who's Cheating Who?" (#43 pop, #4 R&B). Some of his Checker hits were arranged by Donny Hathaway. In 1967 he had a #7 R&B hit with "Feel So Bad."

Milton had many other Checker hits (five R&B Top 20 singles in 1969 alone) before going to Memphis in 1971 to sign with Stax. He enjoyed R&B hits with that label as well, including "That's What Love Will Make You Do" (#9, 1972), and released one of his best-known singles, "Walkin' the Back Streets and Cryin'." He also performed in the 1973 film *Wattstax*.

After leaving Stax in 1976, Milton produced LPs for the Glades label in Miami and continued to tour. He experienced a career resurgence after signing to Malaco in 1984. In 1988 he received the W.C. Handy Blues Entertainer of the Year Award and was inducted into the Blues Hall of Fame. He received the Pioneer Award from the Rhythm & Blues Foundation in 1997. *For Real* and *Cheatin' Habit* were Top 15 blues LP hits. *Welcome to Little Milton,* his 1999 album that featured such guest artists as Lucinda Williams, Dave Alvin, Delbert McClinton, and Gov't Mule, among others, earned a Grammy nomination for Best Contemporary Blues Album. He continues to tour extensively.

Little Richard

Born Richard Wayne Penniman, Dec. 5, 1932, Macon, GA
1959—*His Biggest Hits* (Specialty); *Little Richard's Grooviest 17 Original Hits* 1965—*King of Gospel Songs* (Mercury); *Little Richard's Greatest Hits Recorded Live* (Okeh) 1975—*The Very Best of Little Richard* (United Artists) 1985—*Essential* (Specialty); *18 Greatest Hits* (Rhino) 1988—*Shut Up! A Collection of Rare Tracks* 1989—*The Specialty Box Set* (Specialty) 1990—*The Specialty Sessions* 1991—*The Georgia Peach* 1992—*Shake It All About* (Walt Disney) 1996—*Shag On Down by the Union Hall* (Specialty).

Pounding the piano and howling lyrics in a wild falsetto, Little Richard—the so-called Quasar of Rock—became a seminal figure in the birth of rock & roll. His no-holds-barred style, mascara-coated eyelashes, and high—almost effeminate—pompadour were exotic and in many ways personified the new music's gleeful sexuality and spirit of rebellion. In his own way—and as he is wont to exclaim to anyone in earshot—he is the king of rock & roll.

One of 12 children, Penniman grew up in a devout Seventh-Day Adventist family; his two uncles and a grandfather were preachers, though his father sold bootleg whiskey. The young Penniman sang gospel and learned piano at a local church. But his parents never encouraged his musical interests, and at age 13 Penniman was ejected from their house. (In a 1982 televised interview, he claimed it was because of his homosexuality.) He moved in with a white family, Ann and Johnny Johnson, who ran Macon's Tick Tock Club. There Richard first performed.

In 1951 Penniman won a contract with RCA after playing at an Atlanta radio audition. His recordings during the next two years were fairly conventional jump blues, like "Every Hour" and "Get Rich Quick," neither of which made any commercial impression. In 1952 he moved to Houston, where he recorded for Don Robey's Peacock label. Initially he recorded with the backup groups the Deuces of Rhythm and the Tempo Toppers, though in 1955 he switched to fronting the Johnny Otis Orchestra for four sides. He toured small black nightclubs, performing mostly blues; his rock numbers were not well received.

Down on his luck, he sent a demo tape to Art Rupe of Specialty Records in L.A., who, as luck would have it, had been looking for a hard-edged voice like Penniman's to front some New Orleans musicians. Rupe signed on "Bumps" Blackwell as the producer and, with a Crescent City rhythm section, Little Richard entered the studio on September 14, 1955. One of the songs he cut was an old between-song filler piece called "Tutti Frutti" (with lyrics cleaned up by New Orleans writer Dorothy La Bostrie; one original line was "Tutti Frutti, good booty/If it don't fit, don't force it, you can grease it, make it easy"). Richard's whooping, shouting vocals, sexy-dumb lyrics, and wild piano banging on "Tutti Frutti" set the style for his future hits. The single sold to both black and white fans—over 3 million copies by 1968—and its influence was incalculable. Out of Richard's approximately 36 sides for Specialty, seven were gold: "Tutti Frutti" (#17), "Long Tall Sally" (#6), "Rip It Up" (#17) in 1956; "Lucille" (#21), "Jenny, Jenny" (#10), and "Keep a Knockin' " (#8) in 1957; and "Good Golly, Miss Molly" (#10, 1958). Penniman also appeared in three early rock & roll movies: *Don't Knock the Rock* (1956), *The Girl Can't Help It*—in which his salacious reading of the title song is a revelation—(1956), and *Mister Rock 'n' Roll* (1957).

But in 1957, at the height of his success, Little Richard suddenly quit his rock career after a tour of Australia. He claimed that a vision of the apocalypse came to him in a dream, and that he saw his own damnation. In his authorized biography he tells a story of a plane flight during which the overheated engines appeared in the darkness of night to be on fire. He prayed to God and promised that if the plane landed safely he would change his ways. A few days later, while performing outdoors, he caught a glimpse of the Russian satellite *Sputnik,* and days after that, a plane he was scheduled to have flown in crashed. Interpreting these incidents as divine signs that he should change his ways, Richard entered Oakwood College in Huntsville, Alabama, where he received a B.A. and was purportedly ordained a minister in the Seventh-Day Adventist Church. (Richard has since claimed that he was never a minister.) Specialty tried to keep his conversion a secret, issuing the hit "Keep a Knockin'," pieced together from half-finished sessions. In 1959 he recorded his first religious album, *God Is Real,* which was reissued.

Little Richard

Little Richard did not return to rock until 1964. After a failed attempt to gain a major audience on the evangelical circuit with his gospel recordings, he tried to resurrect his rock following with the anachronistic and unsuccessful "Bama Lama Bama Loo" on Specialty in 1964. The world was already switching its attention to the newer sounds of the Beatles. (Ironically, Little Richard was one of Paul McCartney's idols.) Through the years, Little Richard mounted many unsuccessful comeback attempts on Vee-Jay, Modern, Okeh, and Brunswick.

His best shot came in the early '70s, when he got a contract with Reprise and recorded three R&B/rock LPs—*The Rill Thing, King of Rock 'n' Roll,* and *Second Coming*—which garnered some fair critical notices and led to some recording sessions with Delaney and Bonnie and Canned Heat. Richard did some late-night talk shows and club dates during the early '70s, but by the decade's close, he was again stressing his attachment to the church, preaching and singing gospel, and renouncing rock & roll, drugs, and his own homosexuality. Over the years, he has alluded to having embraced heterosexuality, but in 2000 he probably described his past most accurately when he told the *Los Angeles Times,* "I was what you called back in that day a freak. I was flamboyant in every direction. I'm glad I'm able to look back on it and say, 'Thank you, Lord,' and go on."

The year 1984 saw the publication of *The Life and Times of Little Richard,* an authorized biography by Charles White. Incredibly frank, the book got plenty of attention for its juicy anecdotes (including a threesome with a stripper and Buddy Holly, and a mid-'70s bout with drug addiction) and guilt-ridden accounts of his battle to tame his sexuality. "Homosexuality is contagious," he is quoted as having saying. "It's not something you're born with." The book ends with a chapter-long sermon from Richard. Later he claimed that in some portions of the book he had been misquoted. He shares the copyright with Charles White and his longtime manager Robert "Bumps" Blackwell.

But one can never count Little Richard out of the spotlight for long, and in 1985—at nearly age 60—he launched a formidable comeback with a featured role in the hit film, *Down and Out in Beverly Hills;* he also appeared in *Why Do Fools Fall in Love* and *Last Action Hero.* He made guest appearances on such popular television series as *Miami Vice, Martin,* and *Full House* and has been a pitchman in commercials for a number of companies, including Taco Bell, McDonald's, and Charlie perfume. He contributed backing vocals to the U2–B.B. King hit "When Love Comes to Town," and duetted with Elton John on the latter's *Duets* and Tanya Tucker on *Rhythm, Country & Blues* ("Somethin' Else").

In a development that surely would surprise his first-generation fans, Little Richard has had his greatest latter-day recording success with a new generation: their grandchildren. After recording a rock-rap version of "Itsy Bitsy Spider" for the all-star Pediatric Aids Foundation benefit album *For Our Children,* Richard recorded *Shake It All About.* It included children's standards, such as "On Top of Old Smokey," and his own "Keep a Knockin' " (complete with him yelling "Shut up!" to his background chorus of kids). He also appears on *Kermit Unpigged* (1994) and in Shelley Duvall's award-winning children's video, *Mother Goose Rock 'n' Rhyme.* He also sang the theme song to the PBS children's program, *The Magic School Bus.*

On into the 21st century, Little Richard remains one of the most recognized and quotable celebrities in the world. His life story was the subject of a made-for-TV movie in 2000, starring the actor Leon. The apparently ageless (and vegetarian) Richard continues to tour, his spirit and passion for the music—and himself—undiminished. As he announced from a stage shortly after his 66th birthday, "I'm still beautiful. I'm not conceited—I'm convinced!"

Little Richard was among the first 10 inductees into the Rock and Roll Hall of Fame in 1986. In 1993 he received a Lifetime Achievement Award from the National Academy of Recording Arts and Sciences. He performed at Bill Clinton's presidential inaugural in 1992. In his hometown of Macon he has been honored with a street bearing his name, Little Richard Penniman Boulevard. He has also received the Rhythm & Blues Foundation's Pioneer Award.

Little River Band

Formed 1975, Melbourne, Austral.
Beeb Birtles (b. Gerard Bertelkamp, Nov. 28, 1948, Amsterdam, Neth.), gtr.; Graham Goble (b. May 15, 1947, Austral.), gtr.; Glenn Shorrock (b. June 30, 1944, Chatham, Eng.), lead voc.; Roger McLachlan (b. N.Z.), bass; Derek Pellicci (b. Eng.), drums; Rick Formosa (b. Sep. 1, 1954, Rome, It.), gtr.
1975—*Little River Band* (Harvest) 1976—*After Hours* 1977—(– Formosa; – McLachlan; + David Briggs, gtr., voc.; + George McArdle, bass) *Diamantina Cocktail* 1978—*Sleeper Catcher* 1979—*First Under the Wire* (– McArdle) 1980—*Backstage Pass* (+ Wayne Nelson, voc. bass) 1981—*Time Exposure* 1982—*Greatest Hits* (– Briggs; + Steve Housden [b. Sep. 21, 1951, Bedford, Eng.], gtr.; + John Farnham [b. Eng.], voc.; – Shorrock) 1983—*The Net* 1985—(– Pellicci; + Steven Prestwich, drums; + David Hirschfelder, kybds.) *Playing to Win* 1986—*No Reins* 1988—(– Farnham; – Hirschfelder; – Prestwich; + Shorrock; + Pellicci) 1988—*Monsoon* (MCA) 1990—*Get Lucky* (MCA/Curb) 1991—*Worldwide Love* (Curb) 1994—*Reminiscing—The 20th Anniversary Collection* (Rhino) 2000—*Where We Started From* (self-released, Austral.) (lineup: Housden; Nelson; + Kevin Murphy, drums; + Greg Hind, gtr.; + Glenn Reither, kybds.)

Australia's Little River Band has enjoyed numerous hits in America with its vocal-harmony country pop. The band began in 1975 from the ashes of a CSN&Y-type group called Mississippi. Though LRB formed in Australia, only Graham Goble was born there. Glenn Shorrock, born in England, moved to Australia as a teenager and was part of one of the country's most successful '60s teenybop bands, the Twilights. At the same time, Beeb Birtles played in the successful Aussie band Zoot, which used to dress entirely in pink and also included Rick Springfield. As a teenager, Rick Formosa was invited to join the Edgar Winter Group, but his parents made him turn down the offer.

In 1972 Shorrock moved back to England, joined the classical-rock band Esperanto, and later did studio sessions with Cliff Richard. There, in 1975, he met Birtles, Goble, and Pellicci, who'd just broken up Mississippi. The four agreed to form a new band (taking their name from a road sign) back in Melbourne, eventually with McLachlan (bass) and Formosa (guitar). They signed with Capitol and in 1976 released their eponymous debut, which included the #28 U.S. hit "It's a Long Way There." Before the first U.S. tour that same year, Formosa and McLachlan left.

The band's next American record was a best-of from two Australian LPs. Titled *Diamantina Cocktail,* it included the breakthrough hit "Help Is on Its Way" (#14, 1977). LRB also scored big with "Reminiscing" (#3, 1978) and "Lady" (#10, 1979). In late 1979 "Lonesome Loser" (#6, 1979) and "Cool Change" (#10, 1979) drove *First Under the Wire* into platinum sales. McArdle left after a 1979 U.S. tour, gave away all his money, and moved into Australia's Blue Mountains for a three-year Bible-study course.

In 1980 the band released a double live album, then added American bassist Wayne Nelson. The band scored another Top 10 single in 1981 with "The Night Owls" (#6) from *Time Exposure,* produced by George Martin. Other hits from that album were "Take It Easy on Me" (#10) and "Man on Your Mind" (#14).

Briggs left, then Shorrock pursued a solo career. John Farnham, a singer from Adelaide, replaced Shorrock, and numerous personnel changes followed. Farnham left for a very successful solo career in Australia, then Shorrock returned. Working again with Boylan, they recorded their first MCA LP, *Monsoon.*

As of this writing, three of their LPs are platinum, including the double-platinum *Greatest Hits,* and two others gold. Though Little River Band had eight entries in *Billboard* magazine's list of the 50 all-time biggest Australian hits in the U.S., the band has yet to repeat its earlier success. Still, despite numerous changes in personnel, the band still tours regularly and in 2000 self-released its first studio album in more than a decade.

Little Walter

Born Marion Walter Jacobs, May 1, 1930, Marksville, LA; died Feb. 15, 1968, Chicago, IL
1963—*The Best of Little Walter* (Chess) 1969—*Hate to See You Go* 1972—*Blues Boss Harmonica* 1974—*Confessin' the Blues* 1986—*Blues World of Little Walter* (Delmark) 1989—*The Best of Little Walter, vol. 2* (Chess) 1993—*The Essential Little Walter.*

Whether or not Little Walter was actually the first person to amplify the harmonica, as has been claimed, he was a pioneer in using the microphone to bring out the moaning, echoing, and hornlike sounds that are basic to modern blues harmonica. Walter Jacobs began playing the harmonica as a child in the South, and he attracted the attention of Muddy Waters, with whom he often recorded and toured in the late '50s. When the blues scene centralized in Chicago and went electric in the '50s, with Waters as one of its stars, Walter moved north. He joined Waters' band and started releasing his own records. The instrumental "Juke" was a #1 R&B hit in 1952, one of the biggest hits of any Delta-Chicago bluesman.

Throughout the '50s Little Walter placed records in the R&B Top 10: "Sad Hours," "Blues With a Feeling," "Mean Old World," "You Better Watch Yourself," "You're So Fine," "Key to the Highway," and his other #1 record, "My Babe." He toured with the Aces, formerly Junior Wells' band, breaking out of the blues circuit to play Harlem's Apollo Theatre and other large venues. And though he never made the pop chart, his reputation and influence were widespread, especially in England, where a generation of harmonica players learned from his records and from his disciple Cyril Davies. Walter, who possessed a volcanic temper and a fondness for drink, died from head injuries suffered in a Chicago street fight.

Live

Formed 1985, York, PA
Edward Kowalczyk (b. July 16, 1971, York), voc., gtr.; Chad Taylor (b. Nov. 24, 1970, Owings Mills, MD), gtr.; Patrick Dahlheimer (b. May 30, 1971, York), bass; Chad Gracey (b. July 23, 1971, York), drums.
1991—*Four Songs* EP (Radioactive); *Mental Jewelry* 1994—*Throwing Copper* 1997—*Secret Samadhi* 1999—*The Distance to Here.*

Characterized by an earnest approach to anthemic rock and a spiritual zeal reminiscent of *Joshua Tree*–era U2, Live climbed from modest Modern Rock success to the mainstream on the strength of its 1994 breakthrough album, the 6-million-selling *Throwing Copper.*

Edward Kowalczyk, Chad Taylor, Patrick Dahlheimer, and Chad Gracey came together for a middle-school talent show in the Pennsylvania blue-collar town of York. The group remained together throughout high school, going through a handful of band names and new-wave covers before settling on the moniker Public Affection and recording a self-released cassette of originals, *The Death of a Dictionary,* in 1989. Frequent trips into New York to play at CBGB helped net the band a deal with Radioactive Records in 1991. With the new name Live, the band entered the studio with former Talking Heads keyboardist Jerry Harrison that year and began recording the EP *Four Songs.* The single "Operation Spirit (The Tyranny of Tradition)" went to #9 on the Modern Rock chart and paved the way for the band's Harrison-produced, full-length debut, 1991's *Mental Jewelry* (#73). The album's lyrics, penned by Kowalczyk, were heavily inspired by Indian guru Jiddu Krishnamurti.

Fueled by heavy touring (including billing at Woodstock '94 and Peter Gabriel's WOMAD tour) and a string of hit singles ("I Alone," "All Over You," and the #1 Modern Rock hits "Selling the Drama" and "Lightning Crashes"), *Throwing Copper* went to #1 in 1994. The momentum continued long enough to help 1997's *Secret Samadhi* (coproduced by the band and Jay Healy) debut at #1. Deriving its name from a state of Hindu meditation, the album spawned four Modern Rock hit singles, but failed to match its predecessor's success, with sales topping off at 2 million. Harrison came back on board as coproducer for 1999's *The Distance to Here,* which debuted at #4 and featured the #78 single "The Dolphin's Cry."

Living Colour

Formed 1983, Brooklyn, NY
William Calhoun (b. July 22, 1964, Brooklyn), drums; Corey Glover (b. Nov. 6, 1964, Brooklyn), voc.; Vernon Reid (b. Aug. 22, 1958, London, Eng.), gtr.; Muzz Skillings (b. Manuel Skillings, Jan. 6, 1960, Queens, NY), bass.
1988—*Vivid* (Epic) 1990—*Time's Up* 1992—(– Skillings, + Doug Wimbish [b. Sep. 22, 1956, Hartford, CT], bass) 1993—*Stain* 1995—*Pride* 1998—*Super Hits.*
Vernon Reid solo: 1996—*Mistaken Identity* (Sony).
Corey Glover solo: 1998—*Hymns* (LaFace).

A black band playing rock, Living Colour has used the platform of rock stardom to advocate a political agenda of self-reliance and self-knowledge. As spearheads of New York's Black Rock Coalition, they put their philosophy into action, advancing the cause of other African-American rock bands. Their energetic, rhythmically complex, and harmonically sophisticated music—which draws equally from Jimi Hendrix, Led Zeppelin, and post–*Bitches Brew* Miles Davis—was accessible enough to yield charting singles, including "Cult of Personality" (#13, 1989) and "Glamour Boys" (#31, 1989).

Vernon Reid had already gained fame as a guitarist in Ronald Shannon Jackson's Decoding Society and Defunkt before he formed Living Colour in 1983. (The group's name is taken from the old NBC preprogram announcement, "The following program is brought to you in . . ."). Originally a side project with a revolving cast of musicians, the lineup solidified in 1985 when Corey Glover, who met Reid in 1982, rejoined the band after acting in *Platoon.* Black Rock Coalition events brought Reid in contact with Berklee College of Music graduate Calhoun and Skillings, who had played with Harry Belafonte.

Mick Jagger heard Living Colour at CBGB in 1987 and offered to finance a demo. The two songs he produced, "Which Way to America?" and "Glamour Boys," helped garner the band a contract with Epic, and appeared, remixed, on its debut, *Vivid* (#6, 1988). While critically lauded, the album languished until the video for "Cult" appeared on MTV. The politically charged single became a gold record and earned the group an MTV Video Music Award for Best New Artist.

The band opened up for the Stones on 1989's Steel Wheels Tour, and Reid played on Keith Richards' *Talk Is Cheap.* This activity did not detract from Living Colour. *Time's Up* (#13, 1990), which includes guests Little Richard, Mick Jagger, and Queen Latifah, received an even better critical reception than their debut, and, like *Vivid,* won the Best Hard Rock Performance Grammy.

Tensions began to rise in 1991. With no new album forthcoming, Epic released *Biscuits* (#110, 1991), an EP of outtakes, live performances, and covers. Reid and Glover played in a side project, Nightshade, and in early 1992 Skillings left the band. He was replaced by Sugar Hill session bassist and George Clinton veteran Doug Wimbish. The new band coproduced *Stain* (#26, 1993), which focused less on political issues and more on interpersonal relationships in such songs as "Bi" and "Mind Your Own Business." In early 1995 the band announced it had broken up.

Living Colour: Doug Wimbish, Vernon Reid, Corey Glover, William Calhoun

Of all of the band's members, Reid has had the most active, versatile career. The year following Living Colour's breakup, he released a solo album, *Mistaken Identity,* on which he enrolled jazz legend Teo Macero and hip-hop studio whiz Prince Paul as coproducers, and which featured guest turns by clarinetist Don Byron and turntablist DJ Logic. Reid continues to play regularly in New York, popping up in unexpected corners: He wrote a score for the dance performance *Jazz Train* in 1998, and appeared in the Brooklyn Academy of Music's tributes to Prince and Jimi Hendrix in 1999 and 2000. Reid enjoys experimenting with various musical partners, and often explores his avant tendencies in combos such as Guitar Oblique (with fellow guitarists Elliott Sharp and David Torn), Masque, and My Science Project.

As for Glover, he settled on a more traditional funk-and-soul style on 1998's *Hymns,* which he cowrote with the Family Stand's Peter Lord and V. Jeffery Smith. At the end of 2000, Living Colour reunited for a surprise show in New York.

L.L. Cool J

Born James Todd Smith, Jan. 14, 1968, Queens, NY
1985—*Radio* (Def Jam/Columbia) 1987—*Bigger and Deffer* 1989—*Walking With a Panther* 1990—*Mama Said Knock You Out* 1993—*14 Shots to the Dome* 1995—*Mr. Smith* 1996—*All World: Greatest Hits* 1997—*Phenomenon.*

Ever since he had his first hit single at age 16, L.L. Cool J has been one of rap's brightest artists, propelled by both his willingness to stay street and his desire to be a pop icon. L.L.'s parents divorced when he was four, and he was raised by his grandparents in Queens. He began rapping when he was nine; his grandfather bought him a DJ system when he was 11. He made tapes in his basement, which he sent to record companies, including Def Jam, then being formed by Rick Rubin and Russell Simmons. In 1984 "I Need a Beat" became Def Jam's first release; it sold 100,000 copies, and L.L. dropped out of high school.

Radio (#6 R&B, 1985) was the first Def Jam album. The platinum disc was considered groundbreaking for L.L.'s arrangement of raps into song structures, with verses and choruses. The album included the anthem "I Can't Live Without My Radio" (#15 R&B, 1985), which L.L. performed during his cameo in the movie *Krush Groove. Bigger and Deffer* (#3, 1987), produced by L.L. and the L.A. Posse, lived up to its title, going double platinum with the singles "I Need Love" (#14 pop, #1 R&B, 1987) and "I'm Bad" (#4 R&B, 1987). The former, a ballad, clinched L.L.'s image as a heartthrob. His name stands for Ladies Love Cool James; *Playgirl* magazine named him one of the 10 sexiest men in rock.

In 1988 L.L. had a minor hit with "Going Back to Cali" (#31 pop, #12 R&B) from the *Less Than Zero* soundtrack. He headlined a Def Jam tour and played a Just Say No Foundation antidrug concert at Radio City Music Hall. Some rap fans felt L.L. sold out on *Walking With a Panther* (#6 pop, #1 R&B, 1989), which yielded the single "I'm That Type of Guy" (#15 pop, #7 R&B, 1989). He was booed at an Apollo show; L.L. himself has said he was out of touch with the rap constituency at that time.

He came back swinging with the Grammy-winning *Mama Said Knock You Out* (#16 pop, #2 R&B, 1990), a tough, compelling album coproduced with Marley Marl that is L.L.'s biggest-selling record to date. L.L.'s comeback was kicked off by "The Boomin' System" (#48 pop, #6 R&B, 1990), followed by "Around the Way Girl" (#9, 1990) and "Mama Said Knock You Out" (#17 pop, #12 R&B, 1991). In May 1991 he was the first rap artist to perform on MTV's *Unplugged.* On *14 Shots to the Dome* (#5 pop, #1 R&B, 1993), L.L. seemed confused about his strategy again; he stuck with the past by working with Marl but tried to update his credibility with some gangsta poses. None of the album's four singles made it into the Top 20.

Aiming for an impact outside the rap world, L.L. appeared in the films *The Hard Way* (1991) and *Toys* (1992) and performed at the 1993 presidential inauguration. In addition, concerned with children's welfare, he taped a radio commercial for a "Stay in School" literacy campaign and founded the Camp Cool J Foundation and Youth Enterprises, a program for urban youth.

In 1995 L.L. starred in *In the House,* a network-TV sitcom that ran for three seasons. He also recorded *Mr. Smith* (#20 pop, #4 R&B), a multiplatinum album that produced three Top 10 singles. "Hey Lover" (#3 pop, #3 R&B, 1995), which featured the group Boyz II Men on backing vocals, won the MC a Grammy for Best Rap Solo Performance in 1996. *Phenomenon* (#7 pop, #4 R&B, 1997), a semiconfessional album, yielded three more hit singles; the record was released in conjunction with the publication of the L.L.'s autobiography, *I Make My Own Rules.* Since then the rapper has focused on acting, appearing in several feature films, notably Oliver Stone's *Any Given Sunday.*

Richard Lloyd: See Television

Nils Lofgren

Born June 21, 1951, Chicago, IL
With Grin: 1971—*Grin* (Spindizzy) 1972—*1 + 1; All Out* 1973—*Gone Crazy* (A&M) 1985—*Best of Grin* (Epic) 1999—*The Very Best of Grin* (Columbia).
Nils Lofgren solo: 1975—*Nils Lofgren* (A&M) 1976—*Cry Tough* 1977—*I Came to Dance; Night After Night* 1979—*Nils* 1981—*Night Fades Away* (Backstreet) 1983—*Wonderland* 1985—*Flip* (Columbia); *The Best of Nils Lofgren* (A&M) 1989—*Classics Volume 13* 1991—*Silver Lining* (Rykodisc) 1992—*Crooked Line* 1995—*Damaged Goods* (Pure) 1997—*Code of the Road: Greatest Hits Live* (The Right Stuff) 1998—*Acoustic Live.*

Pop-rock singer, songwriter, and guitarist Nils Lofgren was the leader of Grin and later led his own bands before joining Bruce Springsteen's E Street Band in the '80s. Lofgren moved with his parents to Maryland, near Washington, DC, as a child, and there he began playing accordion at age five and studied jazz and classical music before turning to rock at 15. He formed Grin in 1969 with bassist Bob Gordon and drummer Bob Berberich (later adding younger brother Tom on second guitar). The group's local reputation attracted Neil Young and Danny Whitten of Crazy Horse, whom Nils met while they were touring through Maryland. At age 17 Lofgren played piano and sang on Young's 1970 LP *After the Goldrush,* and the next year he did a guest spot on Crazy Horse's debut LP, to which he also contributed two songs.

Instead of staying with Young or Crazy Horse, Lofgren used the credits to help him get a record contract for Grin. The trio signed to Spindizzy (a Columbia subsidiary), and its 1971 debut was critically praised for its tuneful ballads and tight melodic rockers, as was the followup, *1 + 1,* which included "White Lies." The single never passed #75, though, and Grin's tours failed to attract large audiences. In 1973 Young again asked Lofgren to take time out from Grin to join him for the Tonight's the Night Tour. Lofgren agreed and later played on the 1975 album of the same name. In 1973 Grin signed with A&M, but *Gone Crazy* was not well received. That and the group's financial problems caused it to disband in mid-1974. Later that year, when Mick Taylor left the Stones, Lofgren was briefly rumored as a replacement.

Lofgren signed with A&M and debuted in 1975 with the acclaimed *Nils Lofgren.* In 1976 he followed it with *Cry Tough,* produced by Al Kooper. He began to build a following, largely on the strength of live shows. *Nils* included three songs Lofgren had cowritten with Lou Reed. (A different three written by the two appear on Reed's *Bells* LP.) In 1980 Lofgren signed with Backstreet Records, which issued *Night Fades Away.*

After joining Neil Young for his 1983 *Trans* tour, Lofgren replaced Little Steven Van Zandt in Bruce Springsteen's E Street Band in 1984. He stayed until Springsteen stopped working with that group in 1991, then joined the 2000 reunion tour. Springsteen made a guest appearance on Lofgren's *Silver Lining* (#153, 1991), which was recorded for the tiny independent Towebell label, and picked up for distribution by a bigger indie, Rykodisc.

Lofgren continues to record and tour, but his solo activities have a much lower profile than his work in the E Street Band.

Kenny Loggins

Born Jan. 7, 1948, Everett, WA
1977—*Celebrate Me Home* (Columbia) 1978—*Nightwatch* 1979—*Keep the Fire* 1980—*Alive* 1982—*High Adventure*

1985—*Vox Humana* 1988—*Back to Avalon* 1991—*Leap of Faith* 1993—*Outside: From the Redwoods* 1994—*Return to Pooh Corner* 1997—*Yesterday, Today, Tomorrow: The Greatest Hits of Kenny Loggins; The Unimaginable Life* 1998—*December* 2000—*More Songs From Pooh Corner* (Sony/Wonder).

Singer/songwriter Kenny Loggins has been successful as half of the duo Loggins and Messina, a gentle-rocking solo artist, and a writer and performer of hit soundtrack tunes. He began playing guitar while in the seventh grade of a parochial school in Alhambre, California, where his family settled after living in Detroit and Seattle. In college Loggins joined a folk group, but by the late '60s he had turned to rock, first in Gator Creek and then in Second Helping. In 1969 he left Second Helping and worked for $100 a week as a songwriter for ABC Records' publishing outlet, Wingate Music. Around this time, he toured with the remnants of the Electric Prunes.

Back in L.A., Loggins met Jim Ibbotson of the Nitty Gritty Dirt Band. Ibbotson and the band decided to record four of Loggins' songs on their *Uncle Charlie and His Dog Teddy;* one of them, "House at Pooh Corner," was a minor hit. In 1970 Don Ellis, an A&R staffer at Columbia and a close family friend, introduced Loggins to ex-Poco Jim Messina, who was looking for acts to produce. Clive Davis signed Loggins to the label, and the singer spent the year working up material with Messina, leading to their informal joint debut. Their union would last five years and yield seven successful albums before the split in late 1976 [see Loggins and Messina].

In 1977 Loggins released his solo debut, the platinum *Celebrate Me Home* (#27, 1977). He continued in the same pop-rock style with 1978's *Nightwatch* (#7), which also sold over a million copies and included the #5 single "Whenever I Call You 'Friend' " (cowritten with Melissa Manchester and featuring a vocal by Stevie Nicks). *Keep the Fire* (#16, 1979) boasted "This Is It" (#11, 1979). Loggins cowrote the Doobie Brothers' 1979 hit "What a Fool Believes."

He had a hit in 1980 with "I'm Alright" (#7), the theme song from the movie comedy *Caddyshack*. More hits from other films followed through the '80s: "Footloose" (#1, 1984) and "I'm Free (Heaven Help the Man)" (#22, 1984) from *Footloose;* "Danger Zone" (#2, 1986) from *Top Gun;* "Meet Me Halfway" (#11, 1987) from *Over the Top;* and "Nobody's Fool" (#8, 1988) from *Caddyshack II*. For the relatively less successful *Leap of Faith* (#71, 1991) and *Return to Pooh Corner* (#65, 1994), the singer/songwriter drew heavily on his personal life; the former addressed his divorce from his wife, Eva, while the latter contained songs and lullabies he'd sung to his four children.

After a short break and a greatest-hits collection (#39, 1997), Loggins returned with *The Unimaginable Life*, another confessional album that this time addressed in unflinchingly personal detail his life with new wife, Julia (with whom he also coauthored a companion book of the same title). While the album peaked at #107, Loggins scored another Adult Contemporary hit with "For the First Time" from the film *One Fine Day*. He concluded the '90s with a Christmas record, *December*, and another album of children's music, *More Songs From Pooh Corner*.

Loggins and Messina

Kenny Loggins, born Jan. 7, 1948, Everett, WA; Jim Messina, born Dec. 5, 1947, Maywood, CA
1972—*Kenny Loggins With Jim Messina Sittin' In* (Columbia); *Loggins and Messina* 1973—*Full Sail* 1974—*On Stage; Motherlode* 1975—*So Fine* 1976—*Native Sons; The Best of Friends* 1977—*Finale* 1980—*Best Of.*
Kenny Loggins solo: see entry.
Jim Messina solo: 1979—*Oasis* (Columbia) 1981—*Messina* (Warner Bros.).

The highly successful Loggins and Messina partnership began by accident. Ex-Poco and Buffalo Springfield guitarist Jim Messina agreed to produce Kenny Loggins' solo album, but during the recording sessions the two discovered their styles complemented each other and decided to form a band, which scored a string of country-pop hits.

Messina was raised in Harlingen, Texas, and began playing guitar at age five. He was 12 when his parents moved to California. After graduating from high school in 1965, Messina began doing studio work at Harmony Recorders Audio Sound, Wally Heider, and Sunset Sound, where in late 1967 he met the Buffalo Springfield while that group was recording its second LP, *Buffalo Springfield Again*. He wound up producing and playing bass on the group's final LP, *Last Time Around*, and then formed Poco with fellow ex-Springfield Richie Furay. After two years and three albums, he left Poco in November 1970 to become an independent producer for Columbia; his first project was to be Kenny Loggins.

Their live debut at the Troubadour in Los Angeles was billed as the Kenny Loggins Band with Jim Messina. Loggins and Messina's 1972 debut album billed them as *Kenny Loggins With Jim Messina Sittin' In*. The debut album took a slow climb up the chart but eventually went platinum, aided by one of its tunes, "Danny's Song," which became a Top 10 hit for Anne Murray. It also included the light Caribbean-pop FM radio favorite "Vahevala."

The duo's second LP was its first equal billing and gave Loggins and Messina the hit singles "Your Mama Don't Dance" (#4, 1972) and "Thinking of You" (#18, 1973). The album went platinum, as did the followup, *Full Sail*. Although generally dismissed by critics, Loggins and Messina continued to sell more gold and platinum records. Their reworking of '50s hits, *So Fine*, sold disappointingly, and even though their final and seventh LP, *Native Sons*, went gold, they broke up in November 1976. A best-of *(The Best of Friends)* and a second live LP *(Finale)* were released after the split. Loggins, who went on to a hugely popular solo career, claims his and Messina's partnership was an informal union (each was contracted separately to Columbia), and they always thought each LP would be their last together. Messina's solo efforts met with far less acclaim that did his ex-partner's. In 1989 he rejoined Poco for the successful reunion album *Legacy.*

London Suede

Formed Oct. 1989, London, Eng.
Brett Anderson (b. Sep. 29, 1967, Haywards Heath, Eng.), voc., gtr.; Bernard Butler, gtr.; Matt Osman (b. Oct. 9, 1967, Welwyn Garden City, Eng.), bass; Justine Frischmann (b. Sep. 16, 1969, London), gtr.; Mike Joyce (b. June 1, 1963, Manchester, Eng.), drums; Simon Gilbert (b. May 23, 1965, Stratford-upon-Avon, Eng.), drums.
1991—(– Joyce) 1992—(– Frischmann) 1993—*Suede* (Nude/Columbia) 1994—*Dog Man Star; Stay Together* EP (– Butler; + Richard Oakes [b. Oct. 1, 1976, Perivale, Eng.], gtr.) 1996—*Coming Up* (+ Neil Codling [b. Dec. 5, 1973, Stratford-upon-Avon], kybds.) 1997—*Sci-Fi Lullabies* 1999—*Head Music* 2000—*Sessions CD.*
Bernard Butler solo: 1995—*The Sound of McAlmont-Butler* (Hut) 1998—*People Move On* (Creation/Columbia) 2000—*Friends & Lovers.*

Suede helped create the '90s Brit-pop movement with a melodic, guitar-heavy sound, conquering the U.K. charts while paving the way for greater international success by the likes of Oasis and Blur. Initially centered around the songwriting team of Brett Anderson and Bernard Butler, Suede drew attention for both its glam-influenced sound and a sexually provocative, androgynous image.

Schoolmates Anderson and Matt Osman formed the band Geoff in 1985 and recorded two demos before leaving for university studies in London. The pair reunited a few years later to form the short-lived band Suave & Elegant before placing an ad seeking a guitarist in *New Musical Express.* Bernard Butler responded and became a songwriting partner with Anderson. They called the new band Suede, named after the Morrissey song "Suedehead." A variety of musicians came and went, including drummer Mike Joyce (formerly of the Smiths). Justine Frischmann briefly joined before leaving in 1992 to form Elastica [see entry].

Following the debut singles "The Drowners" (#49 U.K., 1993) and "Metal Mickey" (#17 U.K., 1993), Suede's self-titled debut album was an immediate hit in Britain, reaching #1. The album also spawned the single "Animal Nitrate" (#7 U.K., 1993), but the band was unable to significantly crack the American market. Even worse, the band was forced to call itself London Suede in America, where an obscure Maryland-based lounge singer calling herself Suede had filed a lawsuit. Anderson and Butler's relationship disintegrated during the making of the followup, *Dog Man Star.* Butler quit shortly after it was finished and was replaced by 17-year-old Richard Oakes.

Dog Man Star was a commercial disappointment, but Butler enjoyed a U.K. Top 10 single, "Yes," with soul singer David McAlmont. Suede resurfaced in 1996 with *Coming Up* (#1 U.K.), but the album wasn't released in the U.S. for nearly a year. *Head Music* followed in 1999. Butler released a solo debut, *People Move On,* in 1998. *Friends & Lovers* followed in 2000.

Lone Justice/Maria McKee

Formed 1983, Los Angeles, CA
Maria McKee (b. Aug. 17, 1964, Los Angeles), voc., gtr.; Ryan Hedgecock (b. Feb. 27, 1961, Los Angeles), gtr., voc.; Marvin Etzioni (b. Apr. 18, 1956, New York, NY), bass, voc.; Don Heffington (b. Dec. 20, 1950, Los Angeles), drums.
1985—*Lone Justice* (Geffen) 1986—(– Etzioni; – Heffington; + Shayne Fontayne, gtr.; + Gregg Sutton, bass; + Rudy Richman, drums; + Bruce Brody [b. Dec. 11, 1950], kybds.) *Shelter* (– Hedgecock) 1999—*This World Is Not My Home.*
Maria McKee solo: 1989—*Maria McKee* (Geffen) 1993—*You Gotta Sin to Get Saved* 1996—*Life Is Sweet*
Marvin Etzioni solo: 1992—*The Mandolin Man* (Restless) 1993—*Bone* 1994—*Weapons of the Spirit.*
Ryan Hedgecock solo: 1992—*Echo Park* (Yellow Moon, U.K.).
Hedgecock with Parlor James: 1996—*Dreadful Sorry* EP (Discovery) 1998—*Old Dreams* (Sire).

An exponent of L.A.'s thriving early-'80s club scene, Lone Justice won critical kudos—and the admiration of some of rock's biggest names—with its self-titled 1985 debut album. Produced by Jimmy Iovine, *Lone Justice* folded country and gospel inflections into spirited, rootsy rock arrangements. Singer Maria McKee was born into a musical family; her half brother was Bryan MacLean of the '60s band Love. Her mighty soprano is texturally evocative of such greats as Aretha Franklin, Janis Joplin, and Dolly Parton, and her authoritative delivery inspired comparisons to other rock & soul luminaries—among them Bruce Springsteen and Bob Dylan, who were both Lone Justice fans. So was Tom Petty, who lent the group a song for its first album, and U2, on whose 1985 tour Lone Justice was an opening act.

The band was formed by McKee and Hedgecock, who initially began performing as an acoustic duo. With the addition of a rhythm section, the band went electric, began attracting attention on the L.A. club circuit, and signed a deal with Geffen. Though *Lone Justice* garnered raves, it proved a commercial disappointment. Dissension grew within the band, particularly after Iovine, who had become the group's manager, downplayed the other members' contributions in favor of McKee's. By the second album, 1986's *Shelter,* there was an all-new lineup, save for McKee and, on acoustic guitar, Hedgecock, who left soon after the LP's release. The title ballad, cowritten by McKee and Springsteen's E Street Band guitarist Little Steven Van Zandt, who also coproduced the album, hit the Top 50 (#47), but by then the band had thrown in the towel.

McKee continued working with keyboardist Bruce Brody and released an eponymous solo debut in 1989, on which Brody, Robbie Robertson, Richard Thompson, and Marc Ribot participated as musicians and/or songwriters. (Most of the album's songs were written or cowritten by McKee, who had contributed or collaborated on a fair amount of Lone

Justice's material.) For her second album, McKee reunited with Lone Justice's original rhythm section and enlisted Jayhawks guitarists/vocalists Mark Olson and Gary Louris. The singer then took a turn in an unexpected direction for her third solo album, 1996's *Life Is Sweet*: Rather than relying on her tried-but-true country-rock sound, she played lead guitar and explored alternative-rock territory. McKee resurfaced in 2001 on the *Songcatcher* soundtrack singing traditional country folk.

As for the other members of Lone Justice, Etzioni released a trio of solo albums and produced discs for such bands as Counting Crows and Toad the Wet Sprocket. Hedgecock recorded the LP *Echo Park* for a British label, formed Parlor James with Amy Allison (the daughter of jazz musician Mose Allison), and joined Allison's other band, the Maudlins. Heffington contributed drums to recordings by the Jayhawks, Victoria Williams, and Lucinda Williams. Fontayne joined Springsteen's band in 1992, during the Boss' non–E Street Band period.

This World Is Not My Home (1999) is a Lone Justice retrospective with nine previously unreleased tracks.

Long Ryders

Formed in 1982, Los Angeles, CA
Sid Griffin (b. Sep. 18, 1955, Louisville, KY), gtr. and other stringed instruments, voc.; Stephen McCarthy (b. Feb. 12, 1958, Richmond, VA), gtr., voc.; Greg Sowders (b. Mar. 17, 1960, La Jolla, CA), drums; Tom Stevens (b. Sep. 17, 1956, Elkhart, IN), bass.
1983—*10-5-60* EP (PVC) 1984—*Native Sons* (Frontier) 1985—*State of Our Union* (Island) 1987—*Two Fisted Tales* 1989—*Metallic B.O.* cassette (Long Ryders Fan Club) 1995—*BBC Radio 1 Live Concert* (Windsong) 1998—*Long Ryders Anthology* (PolyGram).
Sid Griffin solo: 1997—*Little Victories* (Country-Town).
Coal Porters (with Griffin): 1991—*Rebels Without Applause* (Zuma) 1994—*Land of Hope and Crosby* (Temple Bar) 1995—*Los London*.
Western Electric (with Griffin): 2000—*Western Electric* (Gadfly).
Gutterball (with McCarthy): 1993—*Gutterball* (Mute) 1995—*Weasel* (Break Out).

Blending punk attitude with late-'60s country-rock instrumentation, the Long Ryders were principal exponents of the mid-'80s L.A. underground pop style known as cow punk.

Leader Sid Griffin left his native Kentucky for L.A. after reading about punk rock in a magazine. Inspired by his hero, the late Gram Parsons, he also wound up rediscovering the country music of his youth. In 1982 he formed Long Ryders with fellow displaced Southerner Stephen McCarthy. After a disappointing first EP, the band released the well-received *Native Sons* (featuring guest vocals by ex-Byrd Gene Clark). Long Ryders' Island output sold poorly and received lukewarm critical response. Unhappy with the way the label had promoted them, the band members called it quits after 1987's *Two Fisted Tales*.

Griffin, who relocated to London, eventually formed another country-rock band, the Coal Porters. In 1997 he released a solo album, *Little Victories*, which included appearances by Billy Bragg, Steve Wynn, and Griffin's wife, former Dream Academy singer Kate St. John. McCarthy, moving back to his native Richmond, Virginia, teamed up with ex-members of the Silos, Dream Syndicate, and House of Freaks and formed the off-the-cuff outfit Gutterball, which released a self-titled album on Mute Records in 1993.

Griffin authored *Gram Parsons: A Musical Biography*, published by a small press in 1985. By 1997 he was working on both a biography of Gene Clark of the Byrds and a "funny pop" autobiography. Griffin continued to explore his Parsons obsession as both a music journalist and musician; he has appeared on two Parsons tribute albums to date. He reemerged in 2000 with a new band called Western Electric. On a self-titled debut album that same year, Griffin's new project remained typically hook-filled and earthy, but with such added postmodern elements as electronic beats and dreamy lap steel guitar that brought the music surprisingly close to trip-hop.

Loose Ends

Formed ca. 1981, London, Eng.
Carl McIntosh, bass, gtr., voc.; Jane Eugene, voc.; Steve Nichol, trumpet, kybds.
1984—*A Little Spice* (Virgin, U.K.) 1985—*So Where Are You* 1986—*Zagora* 1988—*The Real Chuckeeboo* (MCA) 1990—(– Eugene; – Nichol; + Linda Carriere; + Sunay Suleyman) *Look How Long*.

During its heyday in the latter half of the '80s, the British trio Loose Ends enjoyed success in two separate capacities: first, as a pop-funk outfit whose catchy output did well on the American R&B charts; then as songwriter/producers and remixers for other R&B acts. Trumpeter and keyboardist Steve Nichol was already a working studio musician, with the Jam's album *The Gift* among his credits, when he met singer Jane Eugene at the Guildhall School of Music and Drama. The two hooked up with Carl McIntosh, a session bassist who also sang and played guitar, to complete Loose Ends' lineup, and were signed by Virgin Records' U.K. division in the early '80s. (Their recordings would be distributed in the U.S. by MCA.)

After becoming a fixture on England's funk scene with a couple of danceable singles, the band released its debut album, *A Little Spice* (#46 U.K., 1984); the album reached #46 in the States upon release the following year. Also in 1985, Loose Ends hit the top of the R&B singles chart with "Hangin' on a String (Contemplating)," a track featured on its second LP, *So Where Are You* (#13 U.K.). Over the next few years, the group continued making albums and scored R&B smashes like "Slow Down" (#1, 1986) and "Watching You" (#2, 1988). Meanwhile, its members wrote and produced material for pop-soul artists like Juliet Roberts, Five Star, and Cheryl Lynn, and also worked as remixers. In 1990 a new incarnation of Loose Ends, in which Eugene and Nichol were replaced by Linda Carriere and Sunay Suleyman, released the #10 R&B single "Don't Be a Fool," followed by the LP *Look How Long* (#124 pop, #28 R&B). The album generated the moderate R&B hit "Cheap Talk" (#28, 1991).

Jennifer Lopez

Born July 24, 1970, Bronx, NY
1999—*On the 6* (Work/Epic) 2001—*J.Lo.*

An actress and dancer whose break came when in 1990 she was hired as one of the gyrating "Fly Girls" on the black-oriented comedy series *In Living Color,* Bronx-born Jennifer Lopez already had a successful movie career—starring in such films as *Money Train* (1995), *Selena* (1997), and *Out of Sight* (1998)—when she recorded her debut album *On the 6* (#8 pop, #8 R&B, 1999). The release of the dance-oriented album with tracks produced by, among others, Emilio Estefan and Lopez's future boyfriend, Sean Combs, was well timed to join a wave of Latin pop artists, such as Ricky Martin and Enrique Iglesias, crossing over to the mainstream. Driven by videos that emphasized Lopez's choreographic moves and sex appeal, the album charted for 42 weeks, with hit singles in "If You Had My Love" (#1 pop, #6 R&B, 1999) and "Waiting for Tonight" (#8 pop, 1999). Lopez's pop success boosted her profile on the big screen, where she appeared in the thriller *The Cell* (2000) and the romantic comedy *The Wedding Planner* (2001); she ranks as the highest-paid Latina actress in Hollywood history. Her relationship with Combs made tabloid fodder, and in December 1999 she was held for questioning after fleeing a New York nightclub shooting with Combs and his protégé Shyne, though no charges were pressed against Lopez. As the case was going to court (and before Combs' acquittal), the couple's breakup was announced and Lopez's second album, *J.Lo,* was released, entering the charts at #1, with the lead-off single, "Love Don't Cost a Thing" (#3, 2001).

Lords of the New Church: See the Dead Boys

Los Bravos

Formed 1965, Spain
Michael Kogel (b. Apr. 25, 1945, Berlin, Ger.), lead voc., gtr.; Manuel Fernandez (b. Sep. 29, 1943, Seville, Spain), kybds.; Miguel Vicens Danus (b. June 21, 1944, Palma de Mallorca, Spain), bass; Pablo Sanllehi, a.k.a. Pablo Gomez (b. Nov. 5, 1943, Barcelona, Spain), drums; Antonio Martinez (b. Oct. 3, 1945, Madrid, Spain), gtr.
1966—*Black Is Black* (Press).

Los Bravos became the first Spanish rock band to have an international hit single when "Black Is Black" reached #4 in 1966. A combination of local bands Mike and the Runaways (who had several hits in Spain during the early '60s) and Los Sonor, they were signed to British Decca after Decca's Spanish representative sent one of the group's singles to producer Ivor Raymonde. Though Los Bravos never matched the sales of "Black Is Black," "Going Nowhere" and "Bring a Little Lovin' " were minor successes in 1966 and 1968 respectively, and "I Don't Care" climbed to #16 on the British chart in 1966. By the end of the decade their popularity was confined to Spain. In 1972 Kogel had a minor hit single, "Louisiana," under the name Mike Kennedy.

Los Lobos

Formed 1973, East Los Angeles, CA
Cesar Rosas (b. Sep. 26, 1954, Hermosillo, Mex.), gtr., voc.; David Hidalgo (b. Oct. 6, 1954, Los Angeles), voc., gtr., accordion, violin, banjo, piano, perc.; Luis "Louie" Perez (b. Jan. 29, 1953, Los Angeles), drums, voc., gtr., perc.; Conrad R. Lozano (b. Mar. 21, 1951, Los Angeles), bass, *guitarron*, voc.
1978—*Los Lobos del Este de Los Angeles: Just Another Band From East L.A.* (New Vista) 1983—*. . . And a Time to Dance* EP (Slash) 1984—(+ Steve Berlin [b. Sep. 14, 1955, Philadelphia, PA], sax, flute, kybds., harmonica, melodica) *How Will the Wolf Survive?* (Slash/Warner Bros.) 1987—*La Bamba* soundtrack; *By the Light of the Moon* 1988—*La Pistola y el Corazón* 1990—*The Neighborhood* 1992—*Kiko* 1993—*Just Another Band From East L.A.: A Collection* 1996—*Colossal Head* 1999—*This Time* (Hollywood) 2000—*El Cancionero—Mas y Mas: A History of the Band From East L.A.* (Rhino).
Cesar Rosas solo: 1999—*Soul Disguise* (Rykodisc).
Rosas and Hidalgo with Los Super Seven: 1998—*Los Super Seven* (RCA); *Canto* (Sony/Legacy).
Hidalgo and Perez with Latin Playboys: 1994—*Latin Playboys* (Slash/Warner Bros.) 1999—*Dose* (Atlantic).
Hidalgo with Houndog: 1999—*Houndog* (Columbia/Legacy).

For nearly three decades Los Lobos have been exploring the artistic and commercial possibilities of American biculturalism, moving back and forth between their Chicano roots and their love of American rock. Although the band first gained fame as part of the early-'80s roots-rock revival, they don't so much strip music down as mix it up, playing norteño, blues, country, Tex-Mex, ballads, folk, and rock.

Los Lobos have been guests on albums by Ry Cooder, Elvis Costello, Fabulous Thunderbirds, Roomful of Blues, and Paul Simon. Their music has been used in the films *La Bamba, Eating Raoul, The Mambo Kings, Alamo Bay,* and *Chan Is Missing.*

Cesar Rosas, Conrad Lozano, David Hidalgo, and Louie Perez have known one another since they were adolescents in East L.A. They formed Los Lobos (Spanish for "the Wolves") to play weddings and bars in their neighborhood. Although they had previously played in rock and Top 40 bands, together they decided to experiment with acoustic folk instruments and explore their Mexican heritage, playing

Los Lobos: David Hidalgo, Louie Perez, Steve Berlin, Conrad Lozano, Cesar Rosas

norteño and *conjunto* music on instruments including the *guitarron* and *bajo sexto.* Los Lobos got their first full-time gig in 1978, playing at a Mexican restaurant in Orange County. That year they also released their debut album, *Just Another Band From East L.A.*.

Eventually, Los Lobos' experimentation led them back to electric instruments. They played one of their last acoustic shows opening for Public Image Ltd. at the Olympic Auditorium in L.A. in 1980, where they were booed by the audience. Nonetheless inspired by punk's energy, Hidalgo and Perez began writing songs and playing Hollywood clubs. The Blasters became fans and urged Slash to sign Los Lobos.

. . . And a Time to Dance was produced by T Bone Burnett and Blasters saxman Steve Berlin. Its divergent collection of dance songs included the 70-year-old Mexican Revolution song "Anselma," which won a Grammy in 1983 for Best Mexican-American Performance. Berlin joined Los Lobos for *Will the Wolf Survive?* a much praised album whose title track later became a country hit for Waylon Jennings. On *By the Light of the Moon,* coproduced by Burnett, Los Lobos wrote political songs about life in the barrio.

In 1987 Los Lobos recorded several Ritchie Valens songs for the *La Bamba* soundtrack (#1, 1987). Though the success of the title track (#1, 1987) and "Come On, Let's Go" (#21, 1987) suddenly lifted Los Lobos out of their bar-band, critics'-fave status, they took a noncommercial detour with *La Pistola y el Corazón,* featuring the traditional Mexican music they had played throughout the '70s.

On *The Neighborhood,* they returned to more rocking material, working with John Hiatt, the Band's Levon Helm, and drummer Jim Keltner. The album's title paid homage to the deep connections the band still feels to East L.A. In 1991 Hidalgo and Perez wrote songs with the Band for that group's reunion album. The material inspired *Kiko,* an evocative, avant-Latin-pop album produced by Mitchell Froom. In 1993 Slash released a 20-year-anniversary retrospective of Los Lobos songs; *Just Another Band From East L.A.: A Collection* includes material from the band's debut LP, rare B sides, and live tracks, as well as the band's hits.

Latin Playboys (1994), a self-titled album by an ad hoc group consisting of Hidalgo, Perez, Froom, and Tchad Blake, was a cross between the music of Los Lobos and Captain Beefheart. The muscular funk rock of Los Lobos' next album, *Colossal Head* (#81 pop, 1996), split the difference between *Kiko* and *Latin Playboys.*

In 1998 Rosas and Hidalgo released *Los Super Seven* as part of a loose-knit Latin supergroup of the same name that included Freddy Fender, Joe Ely, and accordionist ace Flaco Jiménez, among others. A followup was released in 2001, which included vocalists Raul Malo of the Mavericks and Caetano Veloso. In 1999 Rosas released *Soul Disguise,* a gritty, R&B-inflected solo record. For his part, Hidalgo teamed up with ex–Canned Heat guitarist Mike Halby as Houndog for a self-titled blues album. After this rash of side projects, Los Lobos returned to the studio to make *This Time,* the final installment in a trilogy of heady, groove-rich albums (including *Kiko* and *Colossal Head*) exploring Mexican folklore and mysticism. In 2001 Los Lobos was the recipient of the Billboard Century Award.

Lounge Lizards

Formed 1979, New York, NY
John Lurie (b. Dec. 14, 1952, Minneapolis, MN), sax; Evan Lurie (b. Sep. 28, 1954), piano; Arto Lindsay (b. May 28, 1953, Richmond, VA), gtr.; Anton Fier (b. June 20, 1956, Cleveland, OH), drums; Steve Piccolo, bass.
1981—*The Lounge Lizards* (EG) 1983—(– Lindsay; – Piccolo; – Fier; + Peter Zummo, trombone; + Tony Garnier, bass; + Doug E. Bowne, drums) *Lounge Lizards—Live at the Drunken Boat* (Europa) 1984—(– Zummo; – Garnier; + Roy Nathanson, sax; + Curtis Fowlkes, trombone; + Marc Ribot, gtr., trumpet; + Erik Sanko [b. Sep. 27, 1963, New York], bass) 1985—*Live 79/81 ROIR Sessions* cassette (ROIR) 1986—*Live in Tokyo—Big Heart* (Island) 1987—(+ E.J. Rodriguez, perc.) *No Pain for Cakes* 1989—*Voice of Chunk* (Lagarto) 1991—(– Evan Lurie; – Nathanson; – Fowlkes; – Ribot; – Rodriguez; – Sanko; – Bowne; + Michael Blake [b. Montreal, Can.], sax; + Steven Bernstein [b. Oct. 8, 1961, Washington, DC], trumpet, cornet; + Jane Scarpantoni [b. Oct. 4, 1960, Nyack, NY], cello; + Bryan Carrott, vibes, marimba, tympani; + Michele Navazio [b. Mar. 10, 1960, Elgin, IL], gtr.; + Billy Martin [b. Oct. 3, 1963, New York], perc.; + Oren Bloedow, bass; + G. Calvin Weston [b. June 6, 1959, Philadelphia, PA], drums) *Lounge Lizards—Berlin 1991 Part 1* (Verabra, Ger.) 1992—*Lounge Lizards—Live in Berlin 1991, vol. 2* 1993—(– Carrott; – Bloedow; + Sanko; + Dave Tronzo [b. Dec. 13, 1957, Rochester, NY], slide gtr.; + Danny Blume, gtr.,; + John Medeski, piano, organ) 1998—*Queen of All Ears* (Strange & Beautiful).
With Teo Macero and London Philharmonic Orchestra: 1984—*Fusion* (Europa).
John Lurie solo: 1986—*Stranger Than Paradise/The Resurrection of Albert Ayler* (Enigma) 1987—*Down by Law/*

Variety (Intuition/Capitol) 1989—*Mystery Train* (RCA) 1998—*Fishing With John* 1999—*African Swim & Manny & Lo* 2000—*The Legendary Marvin Pontiac: Greatest Hits* (Strange and Beautiful).
John Lurie National Orchestra: 1993—*Men With Sticks* (Crammed Disc).
Evan Lurie solo: 1990—*Selling Water by the Side of the River* (Island).

The Lounge Lizards became a hip downtown New York band in the '80s by playing "fake jazz," music based more on the feel of jazz than the structures. The group started as a one-time gig playing songs John Lurie had written for a movie. Their punk-lounge act went over big, though, and the Lizards have taken themselves and their music increasingly seriously over the years.

The initial band, featuring brothers John and Evan Lurie, noise guitarist Arto Lindsay, former Feelies drummer Anton Fier, and bassist Steve Piccolo, was half a rock band. That lineup played on the Lizards' debut and the ROIR live cassette released in 1985, with guitarists Dana Vlcek and Danny Rosen playing on some tracks on the latter. Lindsay and Fier left to form Ambitious Lovers and Golden Palominos respectively, and the Lizards replaced them with more conventional jazz players. The group became popular in Europe, where it recorded several live albums and where some of its LPs were released before American labels caught on.

Island signed the Lizards in 1986. Lurie's vocals were featured for the first time on *No Pain for Cakes*. After two albums, Lurie became frustrated with the record company and released *Voice of Chunk* on his own label, via mail order, with ads placed in magazines and on TV. The venture lost money, and that lineup of the group broke up soon after. Lurie re-formed the Lizards for more tours and the Berlin live albums. The Lounge Lizards continued to be popular in New York and Europe into the mid-'90s.

John Lurie has also been a successful artist outside the Lizards. He performed solo at Carnegie Hall in 1980 and in 1982 was a featured soloist with the Quebec Symphony Orchestra. In 1991 he composed string quartets for the Kronos Quartet and in 1992 composed and performed a string quartet for the Balanescu Quartet. In 1991–92 he toured Europe with the John Lurie National Orchestra. He has composed and recorded several soundtracks for filmmaker Jim Jarmusch, including *Stranger Than Paradise* (the album includes a composition for the Albert Ayler dance company), *Down by Law* (the soundtrack is backed with *Variety,* the score for a Betty Gordon film), and *Mystery Train;* other Lounge Lizards also played on these albums. In addition, Lurie acted in *Stranger Than Paradise; Down by Law; Wild at Heart; Paris, Texas;* and *The Last Temptation of Christ.* From 1990 to 1992 he created a pilot for a cable television series, *Fishing With John,* on which he took guests to unique fishing spots, such as Tom Waits to Jamaica and Dennis Hopper to Thailand.

After years of legal and management problems, Lurie launched his own Strange and Beautiful label, on which the Lizards released *Queen of All Ears* in 1998. The same year, Lurie also issued the soundtrack to his series of nature-show spoofs, *Fishing With John.* In 2000 he put out a wickedly funny solo album under the name of Marvin Pontiac, a fictional alter ego born to a West African father and a white Jewish mother from New Rochelle, New York, a pedigree that fairly sums up the scope of Lurie's visionary music.

Evan Lurie released solo albums in Belgium in 1985 and 1989. On *Selling Water by the Side of the River,* he is joined by a violinist and a *bandoneon* player.

Courtney Love: See Hole

Darlene Love

Born Darlene Wright, July 26, 1938 or 1941, Los Angeles, CA
1984—*Live* (Rhino) 1988—*Paint Another Picture* (Columbia) 1992—*The Best of Darlene Love* (Abkco); *Bringing It Home* (with Lani Groves) (Shanachie) 1998—*Unconditional Love* (Harmony).

As one of Phil Spector's handpicked early-'60s girl-group singers, Darlene Love sang some lead vocals with the Crystals, Bob B. Soxx and the Blue Jeans, and also had hits under her own name.

Darlene Wright started singing in 1958 with an L.A. vocal group called the Blossoms. (Her sister Edna later sang with the Honey Cone, which hit big in 1971 with the #1 "Want Ads.") The Blossoms recorded without success as a foursome for Capitol Records between 1958 and 1960, and then as a trio for Challenge and Okeh. They also did backup singing on the L.A. session circuit, supporting Bobby "Boris" Pickett ("Monster Mash"), James Darren ("Goodbye Cruel World"), Bobby Day ("Rockin' Robin"), and many others.

When Love came to Spector's attention, he had her and the Blossoms sing "He's a Rebel," which went #1 in 1962. The producer had originally intended the Gene Pitney composition for the Crystals, and in fact put *their* name on the record, though they didn't sing a note. Love also sang lead on "He's Sure the Boy I Love" (#11, 1963), also falsely credited to the Crystals, and in the short-lived vocal trio Bob B. Soxx and the Blue Jeans, who had a hit with "Zip-a-Dee Doo-Dah" (#8 pop, #7 R&B, 1963), from the Walt Disney movie *Song of the South.* All of these recordings were on Spector's Philles label.

Love went on to record six Philles singles under her own name, including "Wait Till My Bobby Gets Home" (#26, 1963), "(Today I Met) The Boy I'm Gonna Marry" (#39, 1963), and "A Fine Fine Boy" (#53, 1963). She also appears on Phil Spector's classic Christmas album. Love continued to sing with the Blossoms throughout the '60s. They were regulars on *Shindig* and toured with Elvis Presley in the early '70s. Love then sang backup for Dionne Warwick for 10 years, beginning in 1971.

In the '80s the singer branched out into acting, appearing in the *Lethal Weapon* films and the Broadway show *Leader of the Pack.* She also recorded two solo albums.

Long respected as one of the top vocalists in pop music, Love finally received long-overdue recognition in 1993, when a show based on her career, *Portrait of a Singer*, opened in January at New York's Bottom Line club. Love performed weekly in the long-running show. In 1996 she participated in the revue *20th-Century Pop* with Merry Clayton and Marianne Faithfull. She continues to perform around the country, garnering critical praise for her annual holiday show, *Love for the Holidays*.

In 1993 Love sued Phil Spector for back royalties; in 1997 a New York Supreme Court jury ruled in her favor but, because of the statute of limitations in New York State, awarded her only $263,500 for royalties going back to 1987. In 1998 the singer published her autobiography, *My Name Is Love*, and released a gospel album, *Unconditional Love*.

Monie Love

Born Simone Johnson, July 2, 1970, London, Eng.
1990—*Down to Earth* (Warner Bros.) 1993—*In a Word or 2*.

Born in England but raised partly in Brooklyn, rapper Monie Love has bridged musical and geographical gaps with help from influential friends the world over. She began rapping at 14, when she set her poems to music. Love had her first success in London's dance clubs with her second single, "Grandpa's Party," a tribute to Afrika Bambaataa. In 1988 she met stateside Bambaataa boosters the Jungle Brothers, becoming their European road manager. (She raps on their second album.) Later that year she came to New York and joined the Native Tongues group of rappers, whose ranks include De La Soul and Queen Latifah.

Love first came to fame in the U.S. rapping with Latifah on "Ladies First," the track from Latifah's debut album that heralded a new wave of "womanist" hip-hop artists. She also guested on the single "Buddy" from De La Soul's groundbreaking *3 Feet High and Rising*. Her own albums have fused rap with house music, to somewhat mixed results. Three tracks on *Down to Earth*, including the singles "It's a Shame (My Sister)" (#26 pop, #8 R&B, 1991), a remake of the Spinners' 1970 hit, and "Monie in the Middle," were produced by the Fine Young Cannibals' Andy Cox and David Steele, while the Jungle Brothers' Afrika Baby Bambaataa produced six songs. The album reflected the positive political consciousness and psychedelic sense of humor of the Native Tongues school.

In between albums, Love had her first baby, and the featured cut off 1993's *In a Word or 2* (#75 R&B) was "Born 2 B.R.E.E.D." (#56 R&B). It and one other track were produced by Prince. The album challenged the conservative "family values" agenda articulated the previous year by U.S. Vice President Dan Quayle and offered words of encouragement to young blacks. The track "Bullets Carry No Names" was cowritten by Ice-T.

Love's third album for Warner was shelved after her A&R rep left the label. In order to pay the bills—the rapper subsequently had a second daughter—she landed a radio show on New York's Hot 97 R&B station. Love also cohosted MTV's *Lip Service*. Meanwhile, she was without a record deal until she signed with the U.K.-based Relentless label, on which she released a single, "Slice of Da Pie," in 2000. An album featuring guest appearances by the Roots and members of the Native Tongues collective was in the works as of mid-2001.

Love/Arthur Lee

Formed 1965, Los Angeles, CA
Arthur Lee (b. Arthur Porter Taylor, Mar. 7, 1945, Memphis, TN), gtr., voc.; Bryan MacLean (b. Sep. 25, 1946, Los Angeles; d. Dec. 25, 1999, Los Angeles), gtr., voc.; John Echols (b. 1945, Memphis), lead gtr.; Ken Forssi (b. 1943, Cleveland, OH; d. Jan. 5, 1998), bass; Don Conka, drums.
1965—(– Conka; + Alban "Snoopy" Pfisterer [b. 1947, Switz.], drums) 1966—*Love* (Elektra) (+ Michael Stuart, drums; + Tjay Cantrelli, horns; Pfisterer switches to kybds.) 1967—*Da Capo* (– Pfisterer; – Cantrelli) 1968—*Forever Changes* (– MacLean; – Echols; – Forssi; – Stuart; + Frank Fayad, bass; + George Suranovitch, drums; + Jay Donnellan, gtr.) 1969—*Four Sail; Out Here* (Blue Thumb) (– Donnellan; + Gary Rowles, gtr.) 1970—*False Start* 1974—(group re-forms: Lee; + Melvan Whittington, lead gtr.; + John Sterling, rhythm gtr.; + Sherwood Akuna, bass; + Joe Blocker, drums; + Herman McCormick, congas) *Reel to Real* (RSO) 1975—(group disbands; periodic reunions follow) 1980—*Best of Love* (Rhino) 1982—*Love Live; Studio/Live* (MCA) 1992—*Arthur Lee and Love* (New Rose, Fr.) 1995—*Love Story 1966–1972* (Rhino).
Arthur Lee solo: 1972—*Vindicator* (A&M) 1981—*Arthur Lee* (Rhino).
Bryan MacLean solo: 1997—*IfYouBelieveIn* (Sundazed) 2000—*Candy's Waltz*.

Love, headed by singer/guitarist Arthur Lee, was a seminal '60s L.A. band, emerging from the Sunset Strip at the same time as the Byrds, Buffalo Springfield, the Doors, and the Mamas and the Papas. The group started out playing a Byrds-influenced folk rock but later covered many styles, including bluesy R&B, pop, and hard rock.

Lee moved from his Memphis birthplace to L.A. with his family when he was five. By age 17 he was playing in local bands, including Arthur Lee and the LAGs (styled after Booker T. and the MG's). The band, which included later Love member John Echols, cut one single for Capitol, an instrumental, "The Ninth Wave." Love was formed with unknown musicians: MacLean had been a roadie for the Byrds, and Forssi had played with the Surfaris after their hits faded. Lee originally called the group the Grass Roots, but changed it, since the name was already taken by another soon-to-be-well-known band.

Love's first album was hailed by critics as a classic in the new folk-rock style and sold 150,000 copies. Its 1966 single "My Little Red Book" (penned by Burt Bacharach and Hal David) was a minor hit. The band's second album, *Da Capo*, featured some topically druggy lyrics, jazz touches, and a few personnel changes. The album was another groundbreaker, featuring one of the first side-long cuts in rock, the 20-minute-long "Revelation." The album also included the

Top 40 hit "7 and 7 Is." *Forever Changes*, however, is considered by many to be Love's best, its answer to *Sgt. Pepper*, with orchestral touches, including horn and string arrangements, and a psychedelic feel that influenced many of the early-'80s neopsychedelic British bands such as the Monochrome Set, the Teardrop Explodes, and Echo and the Bunnymen.

In 1968 Lee reorganized the group (members of the first edition later claimed excessive drug use had driven the band apart; MacLean said he nearly overdosed on heroin, then joined a Christian ministry and suffered a nervous breakdown) and hired a new band of three, plus four sessionmen to help out in the studio on *Four Sail* and *Out Here;* he briefly renamed himself Arthurly. Love next toured England (the band seldom left L.A.), and Lee recorded a full LP with Jimi Hendrix. The album was buried in legal problems, though one track, "The Everlasting First," turned up on *False Start* in 1970. In 1971 Lee dismissed his band.

Lee was supposed to have recorded a solo album for Columbia, but his debut wound up on A&M in 1972, the hard-rocking *Vindicator*, credited to Arthur Lee and Band Aid. Like later Love LPs, the record didn't sell well. In 1973 he planned to make another solo album with Paul Rothchild's new Buffalo Records, but the label folded before the LP was released. In 1974 Lee came back on RSO with an all-new Love, but the music disappointed many and included three remakes of old Love cuts. His next effort was a solo EP in 1977 on Da Capo Records. In 1979 he toured locally with MacLean (whose sister Maria McKee would emerge in the '80s with the country-rock band Lone Justice) and another incarnation of Love, and in 1980 Rhino Records put out *Best of Love*, a compilation of '60s tracks. In 1981 the label issued a new Arthur Lee solo LP, his first in seven years. In 1994 Lee, backed by members of the New York–area punk band Das Damen, toured clubs under the Love banner, to ecstatic reaction from audiences and critics, who urged reappraisal of his oeuvre as the missing link between the Byrds and the Doors. That comeback was cut short in 1996 when Lee—who had had several run-ins with the law over the years—was sentenced to 8 to 12 years in prison for illegal possession of a firearm after pointing a pistol at a neighbor.

Forssi died of brain cancer in early 1998. MacLean remained in the Christian ministry and returned to making music. He died of a heart attack on Christmas Day, 1999, without having completed an album. *IfYouBelieveIn* (1997) and *Candy's Waltz* (2000) are two collections of demos and solo recordings spanning the '60s through the '80s.

Love and Rockets: See Bauhaus

Loverboy

Formed 1979, Calgary, Can.
Paul Dean (b. Feb. 19, 1946, Can.), gtr.; Mike Reno, voc.; Doug Johnson, kybds.; Matt Frenette, drums; Scott Smith (b. Feb. 13, 1955; d. Nov. 30, 2000, near San Francisco, CA), bass.
1980—*Loverboy* (Columbia) 1981—*Get Lucky* 1983—*Keep It Up* 1985—*Lovin' Every Minute of It* 1987—*Wildside* 1988—(group disbands) 1989—*Big Ones* 1993—(group re-forms: Dean; Reno; Johnson; Frenette; Smith) 1994—*Loverboy Classics* 1997—*VI* (CMC) 2000—(– Smith).
Paul Dean solo: 1989—*Hard Core* (Columbia).

Paul Dean had been involved with 13 unsuccessful Canadian bands (including Streetheart) before meeting Mike Reno, himself a veteran of many groups, having recorded with Moxy. They teamed up originally to work as a studio-based duo a la Steely Dan. But when record-company interest hinged on their forming a band, they held auditions. Doug Johnson, Matt Frenette, and Scott Smith were chosen, and the quintet was named Loverboy (Coverboy was also under consideration). Their modernized, new-wave-tinged hard rock became the surprise hit of 1981 as, buoyed by the group's incessant touring, their self-titled debut album went double platinum and hatched two successful singles: "Turn Me Loose" (#35, 1981) and "The Kid Is Hot Tonite" (#55, 1981). Their second album, *Get Lucky*, featuring the hits "Working for the Weekend" (#29, 1981) and "When It's Over" (#26, 1982), went multiplatinum, as did 1983's *Keep It Up*. In 1984 lead singer Reno had a hit with "Almost Paradise . . . Love Theme From *Footloose*," a duet with Ann Wilson of Heart (#7). *Lovin' Every Minute of It*, the band's last platinum effort to date, featured the Top 10 singles "Lovin' Every Minute of It" and "This Could Be the Night." *Wildside* didn't reach the Top 40, and *Big Ones* just scraped in at #189. Loverboy disbanded in spring 1988, but after playing together in what was to have been a one-time-only appearance, the members regrouped. A fall 1993 tour with the re-formed April Wine was followed by an 80-date U.S. tour in summer 1994. They continued to perform through the '90s, releasing the all-new *VI*. The *Loverboy Classics* anthology even went gold in 1998. The band was devastated in late 2000 when bassist Scott Smith drowned after a wave swept him out of his sailboat. As of early 2001 the quartet planned to carry on despite the tragedy.

Lyle Lovett

Born Nov. 1, 1957, Klein, TX
1986—*Lyle Lovett* (MCA/Curb) 1988—*Pontiac* 1989—*Lyle Lovett and His Large Band* 1992—*Joshua Judges Ruth* 1994—*I Love Everybody* 1996—*The Road to Ensenada* 1998—*Step Inside This House* 1999—*Live in Texas.*

Lyle Lovett's songs coolly confront the cynical, sometimes violent and misogynistic side of romance. Originally marketed as a country singer (and garnering a number of C&W hits), Lovett has taken his increasingly eclectic, sly music (and increasingly pronounced Eraserhead-style pompadour) well beyond Nashville to a wider audience and an acting career.

Born into a small town that has become a large Houston suburb, Lovett attended Texas A&M University in the mid-'70s. He started performing at coffeehouses and continued

Lyle Lovett

to play in Europe, where he traveled while a graduate student. Originally doing covers, he later wrote his own songs because he felt he "was never a good enough singer to do Merle Haggard."

His career did not take off until he returned to the States in 1984. Nanci Griffith (whom Lovett met in college when he interviewed her for the school paper) covered his "If I Were the Woman You Wanted" on *Once in a Very Blue Moon* in 1984. He sang on that album and her next, *Last of the True Believers;* Lacy J. Dalton recorded his "Closing Time." Through singer Guy Clark (a Lovett idol), MCA's Tony Brown received a demo of Lovett's songs in 1984; Brown signed Lovett and produced his first three albums. While ostensibly a country album, *Lyle Lovett* features undercurrents of folk, rock, and jazz. Despite its lack of standard Nashville fare, the LP yielded four C&W hits: "Farther Down the Line" (#21 C&W, 1986), "Cowboy Man" (#10 C&W, 1986), "God Will" (#18 C&W, 1987), and "Why I Don't Know" (#15 C&W, 1987).

Lovett's subsequent albums became progressively more eclectic. The bluesy *Pontiac* (#117 pop, #12 C&W, 1988) included "Give Back My Heart" (#13 C&W, 1987), "She's No Lady" (#17 C&W, 1988), and "I Loved You Yesterday" (#24 C&W, 1988), and Lovett toured Europe backed by only his guitar and a cellist. With *Lyle Lovett and His Large Band,* he did a 180-degree turn, augmenting his sound with horns and strings. The tuxedoed singer pictured on the cover showed just how far Lovett had moved from country, and the music matched his new urbane image, with jazzy arrangements and snatches of standards. A #10 C&W album, *Large Band* lacked hit singles ("I Married Her Just Because She Looks Like You" reached only #45 C&W) but brought Lovett to the attention of pop audiences (#62 pop) and helped him earn a Grammy Award for Best Male Country Vocal Performance in 1989. *Large Band* also contained his gender-bending version of Tammy Wynette's "Stand by Your Man," later used to great effect in the 1992 film *The Crying Game.*

Joshua Judges Ruth (#57 pop, 1992), which didn't make the country chart, was recorded in L.A. with Little Feat producer George Massenburg, taking Lovett further afield. The songs added heavy doses of gospel and pop, and Lovett became a featured artist on VH1. L.A. seems to have agreed with Lovett: He has acted in several films, including four directed by Robert Altman, and appeared in episodes of the TV sitcoms *Mad About You* and *Dharma and Greg.* Lovett married actress Julia Roberts in 1993; the couple divorced in 1995.

In 1994 Lovett released *I Love Everybody* (#26), an album consisting entirely of songs he had written before he launched his recording career. *The Road to Ensenada* (#24 pop, #4 C&W) marked Lovett's return to the country chart. The record featured guest appearances from Jackson Browne, Shawn Colvin, and Randy Newman, and won a Grammy for Best Country Album. *Step Inside This House* (#55 pop, #9 C&W) found Lovett covering the songs of such fellow Texans as Guy Clark, Townes Van Zandt, and Willis Alan Ramsey, songwriters who had a formative influence on Lovett. *Live in Texas* was culled from dates that Lovett played in Austin and San Antonio with his Large Band in 1995.

Lene Lovich

Born Lili Marlene Premilovich, Mar. 30, 1949, Detroit, MI
1979—*Stateless* (Stiff/Epic) 1980—*Flex* 1981—*New Toy* EP 1982—*No Man's Land* 1990—*March* (Pathfinder).

Though she had hit singles in England and Europe, Lene Lovich has yet to reach the American singles chart. Her new-wave-era, Slavic-milkmaid getup, and ululating vocals were distinctive, to say the least, and they fit the oddball lyrics and pop hooks devised by Lovich and cowriter and future husband Les Chappell.

Lovich was born in Detroit and moved to England when she was 13. After studying sculpture at London's Central School of Art, she took part in experimental theater, worked as a go-go dancer, played all manner of music, and became interested in dream images (inspiring her to visit Salvador Dalí). She and Chappell joined the soul-funk band the Diversions in 1975, with whom they recorded an album for Polydor that was never released. While still with the group, Lovich recorded the Lovich-Chappell composition "Happy Christmas." In 1978 author and disc jockey Charlie Gillett introduced Lovich to Stiff Records' president, Dave Robinson. A few months later, Stiff issued her version of Tommy James and the Shondells' "I Think We're Alone Now" and put her on the Be Stiff Tour '78 with Rachel Sweet, the Records, Wreckless Eric, Mickey Jupp, and Jona Lewie.

After American record companies refused her debut LP (as well as those by most other Be Stiff artists), the tour came to New York; Epic Records became interested. In summer 1979, almost a year after its release in the U.K., *Stateless* came out in the U.S. In England, "Lucky Number" and "Say When" (written by James O'Neill of Fingerprintz) had become hit records, as did "Bird Song," the first single from *Flex,* released in 1980. "New Toy," the title track of Lovich's six-song mini-LP of 1981, was another British success that failed to crack the U.S. chart, although it was a rock-disco favorite (its writer, Thomas Dolby, subsequently started a successful solo career). In 1982 she found herself without a record label.

Lovich also costarred with Herman Brood and Nina Hagen in the 1979 film *Cha-Cha,* played the lead in the French television film *Rock,* and assumed the title role in the 1983 London stage play *Mata Hari,* which she cowrote.

Since the mid-'80s she has been actively involved in the animal-rights movement. In 1988 she received a Humanitarian Award from People for the Ethical Treatment of Animals (PETA). She wrote and recorded "Rage" with Erasure; the song appeared on the animal-rights benefit album *Tame Yourself.* Lovich has also written for opera (*The Collector,* with Cerrone) and recorded Peter Hammil and Judge Smith's opera, *Fall of the House of Usher.* Shortly after the release of 1990's *March,* her label folded. As of the mid-'90s she was working on a novel.

Lovin' Spoonful

Formed 1965, New York, NY
John Sebastian (b. Mar. 17, 1944, New York), gtr., Autoharp, harmonica, lead voc.; Steve Boone (b. Sep. 23, 1943, Camp Lejeune, NC), bass; Zal Yanovsky (b. Dec. 19, 1944, Toronto, Can.), lead gtr., voc.; Joe Butler (b. Jan. 19, 1943, New York), drums.
1965—*Do You Believe in Magic* (Kama Sutra) 1966—*Daydream; Hums of the Lovin' Spoonful* 1967—*The Best of the Lovin' Spoonful* (– Yanovsky; + Jerry Yester, gtr.) 1968—(– Sebastian; group disbands) 1990—*Anthology* (Rhino) 1999—*Live at the Hotel Seville* (Varèse Vintage) 2000—*Greatest Hits* (Buddha).

Electrified jug band the Lovin' Spoonful had two years as New York's leading folk rockers. Its sound was dubbed "good-time music," and when the good times stopped in 1967 after publicity about the arrest of Steve Boone and Zal Yanovsky for drugs, so did the quartet's hits.

John Sebastian and Yanovsky founded the Spoonful; they had been members of the Mugwumps with future Mamas and Papas Cass Elliot and Denny Doherty (as immortalized in the Mamas and Papas' "Creeque Alley"). The group's first single, Sebastian's "Do You Believe in Magic," went Top 10 in 1965, as did its followup, "You Didn't Have to Be So Nice," in early 1966. More hits followed in 1966 and 1967: "Daydream" (#2), "Did You Ever Have to Make Up Your Mind?" (#2), "Summer in the City" (the Spoonful's lone #1), "Rain on the Roof" (#10), "Darling Be Home Soon" (#15), "Nashville Cats" (#8), and "Six O'Clock" (#18). During its peak period, the Spoonful made three albums and also provided the soundtracks to Francis Ford Coppola's *You're a Big Boy Now* and Woody Allen's *What's Up, Tiger Lily?*

But that ended after Boone and Yanovsky reportedly set up someone they knew in a drug bust in May 1966. Apparently, both Boone and Yanovsky were arrested in Berkeley, California, for possession of marijuana, and, in exchange for the police department not prosecuting, the two introduced an undercover narcotics agent to an acquaintance who purchased drugs, resulting in the acquaintance's arrest. The ensuing publicity created a public outcry calling for a boycott of their records and concerts. Yanovsky left the group in June 1967. He was replaced by Jerry Yester, the former producer of the Association, which included his brother Jim Yester. Though the hits didn't stop altogether ("She Is Still a Mystery," #27, 1967), the Spoonful's popularity was waning. After one LP without Yanovsky, *Everything Playing,* Sebastian, who wrote and sang most of the songs, left to start his solo career [see entry].

The group broke up in 1968. Butler formed a new Lovin' Spoonful and put out an album, *Revelation: Revolution '69,* with no success. The drummer then took up acting, appearing in several Broadway plays *(Hair, Mahogany)* and films *(Born to Win, One Trick Pony),* and also worked as a Hollywood sound editor and sound-effects man. Yester recorded *Farewell Aldebaran* with his wife, Judy Henske (coproduced by Yanovsky), and formed the band Rosebud, which made one album. He has continued to work as a producer, credited on Tom Waits' first album. Yanovsky returned to Canada and opened a restaurant in Kingston, Ontario, Chez Piggy, while Boone ran a recording studio on a 135-foot houseboat that he docked in Baltimore's Inner Harbor. Little Feat, Bonnie Raitt, Emmylou Harris, and Ricky Skaggs all recorded there; in 1977, it sank.

The original Lovin' Spoonful reunited in 1980 to perform "Do You Believe in Magic" in Paul Simon's film *One Trick Pony.* In 1991, Boone, Butler, and Yester began touring as the Lovin' Spoonful, with drummer John Marrella and keyboardist/guitarist Lena Yester, Jerry's daughter. In 2000 the group was inducted into the Rock and Roll Hall of Fame. Boone has also been attempting to launch a new band called Forq.

Nick Lowe

Born Mar. 24, 1949, Walton-on-Thames, Eng.
1978—*Pure Pop for Now People* (Columbia) 1979—*Labour of Lust* 1982—*Nick the Knife* 1983—*The Abominable Showman* 1984—*Nick Lowe and His Cowboy Outfit* 1985—*The Rose of England* 1988—*Pinker and Prouder Than Previous* 1989—*Basher: The Best of Nick Lowe* 1990—*Party of One* (Reprise/Warner Bros.) 1994—*The Impossible Bird* (Upstart) 1998—*Dig My Mood* 1999—*Nick Lowe: The Doings (The Solo Years)* (Edsel, U.K.) 2001—*The Convincer* (Yep Roc).

With Little Village (Lowe; John Hiatt; Jim Keltner; Ry Cooder): 1992—*Little Village* (Reprise).

For over 30 years, singer, songwriter, and producer Nick Lowe has created a body of work that includes boozy, good-time British pub rock, sharp satire, and introspective contemporary American country. The son of a Royal Air Force officer, Lowe grew up in England and the Mideast. His first band, Kippington Lodge, eventually became Brinsley Schwarz [see entry], for which Lowe did much of the songwriting. When Brinsley Schwarz broke up in 1975, Lowe began writing more openly sardonic pop songs while performing with Rockpile [see entry] and producing. Releasing singles under a variety of names, Lowe was honing his broad ironic streak and his unapologetic talent for lifting other people's hooks. For "Bay City Rollers, We Love You" and "Rollers Show," Lowe recorded as the Tartan Horde ("Rollers Show" later turned up on *Pure Pop*). "Let's Go to the Disco" was supposedly by the Disco Bros. In 1976 Lowe cofounded Stiff Records with Dave Edmunds [see entry] and manager Jake Rivera. The label's first release was Lowe's 45 "So It Goes" b/w "Heart of the City"; he also recorded "I Love My Label." In the next year, working as staff producer, he oversaw records by Elvis Costello *(My Aim Is True, This Year's Model, Armed Forces, Get Happy),* Mickey Jupp (whose "Switchboard Susan" Lowe covered on *Labour of Lust*), the Damned, Wreckless Eric, and Alberto y Los Trios Paranoias, as well as two records of his own. These included the EP *Bowi* (an "answer" to David Bowie's LP *Low),* which featured a version of Sandy Posey's "Born a Woman," and "Marie Provost," later on *Pure Pop.*

In late 1977 Lowe and Costello left Stiff to join label cofounder Jake Riviera's new venture, Radar Records. He had his first British hit with "I Love the Sound of Breaking Glass," which was included on that year's LP *Pure Pop* (*Jesus of Cool* in the U.K.). *Labour of Lust,* though billed as a solo album, was really the work of Rockpile. It yielded Lowe's only American Top 40 single, "Cruel to Be Kind" (#12, 1979). His next charting single was "I Knew the Bride (When She Used to Rock and Roll)" (#77, 1985), with backing from Huey Lewis and the News.

Lowe remained an active producer, working on a number of Costello's albums, several LPs by Graham Parker and the Rumour (including *Howlin' Wind*), one by Dr. Feelgood, and the Pretenders' debut single, "Stop Your Sobbing," in addition to his then-wife Carlene Carter's *Musical Shapes* and *Blue Nun,* and a session with her stepfather, Johnny Cash, who performed Lowe's "Without Love" (off *Labour of Lust*).

In 1981 Rockpile disbanded, and Lowe resumed his solo career, releasing *Nick the Knife* and returning to the road with a band alternately known as the Chaps and Noise to Go that included former Rumour guitarist Martin Belmont, ex-Ace/Squeeze pianist Paul Carrack (for whom Lowe produced a solo album), and Lowe playing rhythm guitar instead of bass. Among Lowe's '80s production credits are two later Elvis Costello albums (*Trust* and *Blood and Chocolate,* which he coproduced), the Fabulous Thunderbirds' *T-Bird Rhythm,* and John Hiatt's *Riding With the King.* In 1990 he and Carter, who had married on August 18, 1979, divorced.

During the late '80s Lowe suffered from what he described as a deep depression for about two years. He has also suffered from alcoholism. Feeling overlooked and unable to see a future for the music he loved, he considered retiring from music. Riviera and Costello urged him to get back to work. He worked with Hiatt on his *Bring the Family* (1987), and out of that project grew Little Village, a band made up of Lowe, Hiatt, Jim Keltner, and Ry Cooder, whose self-titled album came out in 1992. Also around that time Lowe began working in Costello's band and undertook a solo acoustic tour in England.

In 1990 Lowe landed a new solo deal with Warner/Reprise, and old cohort Dave Edmunds (with whom Lowe has had an up-and-down relationship through the years) produced *Party of One,* which included the amusing single "All Men Are Liars," with a verse rhyming "Rick Astley" with "ghastly." In 1994 Lowe played bass on Elvis Costello's *Brutal Youth,* and around the same time, songwriting royalties for Curtis Stigers' version of "(What's So Funny 'Bout) Peace, Love, and Understanding?" on the record-breaking *The Bodyguard* soundtrack earned Lowe more than $1 million. Dropped by Warners, Lowe moved to the indies for his next release. Critically acclaimed, country-tinged *The Impossible Bird* contained Lowe's "The Beast in Me," which he wrote for his former father-in-law Johnny Cash, who made it the centerpiece of his masterful, 1994 Grammy-winning *American Recordings,* and featured ex–Commander Cody guitarist Bill Kirchen. *Dig My Mood* was also well received and combined his usual pop rock with jazz touches. *The Convincer* displayed a range of styles, including R&B, country, jazz, and pop.

L7

Formed 1985, Los Angeles, CA
Suzi Gardner (b. Aug. 1, 1960, Altus, OK), gtr., voc.; Jennifer Finch (b. Aug. 5, 1966, Los Angeles), bass, voc.; Donita Sparks (b. Apr. 8, 1963, Chicago, IL), gtr., voc.; Roy Koutsky, drums.
1987—*L7* (Epitaph) 1990—(– Koutsky, + Demetra "Dee" Plakas [b. Nov. 9, 1960, Chicago], drums) *Smell the Magic* EP (Sub Pop) 1992—*Bricks Are Heavy* (Slash) 1994—*Hungry for Stink* 1996—(– Finch; + Gail Greenwood, bass) 1997—*The Beauty Process: Triple Platinum* (Warner Bros.) 1998—*Omaha to Osaka* (Man's Ruin) 1999—(– Greenwood; + Janis Tanaka, bass) *Slap-Happy* (Wax Tadpole/Bong Load).

L7 brings a sense of outrage and outrageousness to the normally muddied world of grunge. Although the four women despise being identified by gender, they were nonetheless leaders in the early-'90s resurgence of women rockers. The band helped found Rock for Choice, an organization that hosts fund-raising concerts to support the cause of reproductive rights. In 1992 L7 seemed to challenge the masculine clichés of rock quite literally when Sparks pulled a

L7: Donita Sparks, Suzi Gardner, Jennifer Finch, Dee Plakas

tampon from her vagina and threw it into the crowd at England's mammoth Reading Festival.

L7 (the name comes from the slang for "square") built its following through independent releases and frequent tours of Europe and the States. It went through a series of drummers, some of them male, before settling on Plakas. A single for Sub Pop's singles club and an EP for the label, with the catchy, anthemic "Shove," made it one of Hollywood's hottest underground bands. *Bricks Are Heavy,* featuring the popular alternative track "Pretend We're Dead," was produced by Butch Vig on the heels of his success with Nirvana's *Nevermind.* In 1994 L7 performed in the John Waters film *Serial Mom,* and won more fans via Lollapalooza appearances and the release of its highly praised album *Hungry for Stink.*

As intimated by its wry title, hopes were high for L7's 1997 followup, *The Beauty Process: Triple Platinum* (#172 pop). Yet despite production assistance from Rob Cavallo (Green Day), wider success eluded the group. After Warner Bros. dropped the band from its roster, L7 put out a live album, *Omaha to Osaka,* on the independent Man's Ruin imprint. Then it started its own Wax Tadpole label, through which it released *Slap-Happy* in 1999. The album found the group in fine form, its crunching riffs and biting humor fully intact. *The Beauty Process,* a video documentary about the band produced and directed by ex-Nirvana bassist Krist Novoselic, followed later in the year.

Lulu

Born Marie McDonald McLaughlin Lawrie, Nov. 3, 1948, Glasgow, Scot.
1967—*To Sir With Love* (Epic) 1971—*New Routes* (Atco) 1979—*Don't Take Love for Granted* (Rocket) 1981—*Lulu* (Alfa) 1994—*Independence* (SBK).

At age 18 Lulu recorded "To Sir With Love," the title theme from the movie in which she costarred with Sidney Poitier. It quickly went to #1 in the U.S., becoming the first hit by an artist from the U.K. to hit the top of the U.S. chart without ever entering the British chart. This success led her to much work on TV and on the cabaret circuit. Before recording this pop ballad, however, she and her band, the Luvvers, had hit the British Top 10 with a cover of the Isley Brothers' hit "Shout." (Lulu's version hit #94 in the U.S. Top 100 in 1964 and #96 as a reissue in 1967 at the height of her U.S. popularity.)

Marie Lawrie made her show-business debut at age nine singing at Bridgeton Public Hall and soon began appearing regularly with a local accordion band. At age 14 she began singing weekend gigs in Glasgow clubs and by 15 was a regular in that area with her group the Glen Eagles. In 1964 her group was renamed Lulu and the Luvvers and hit the chart with "Shout."

In 1966 Lulu went solo (and became the first British female act to perform behind the Iron Curtain, in Poland), and in 1967 she hit the British Top 10 again with Neil Diamond's "The Boat That I Row." That year her performance in *To Sir With Love* garnered raves. In the late '60s Lulu worked as both a TV personality and a recording artist, and in 1969 she married Bee Gee Maurice Gibb (they divorced in 1973). With the production team of Jerry Wexler, Tom Dowd, and Arif Mardin, she recorded *New Routes* at Muscle Shoals in 1970, from which sprang the U.S. Top 30 hit "Oh Me, Oh My, I'm a Fool for You, Baby."

In the early '70s Lulu toured throughout the world, headlining in such places as Las Vegas and Berlin, and had her own prime-time BBC-TV weekly music series. She was absent from the U.K. chart until 1974, when she again hit the Top 10 with the David Bowie–arranged cover of his "The Man Who Sold the World," and from the U.S. chart until 1981, when she hit with "I Could Never Miss You (More Than I Do)" (#18) and "If I Were You" (#44). Except for a remake of "Shout," a U.K. Top 10 hit in 1986, she did not record again until 1993's *Independence,* a dance-oriented work. The title cut was a U.K. Top 20 hit and a dance hit here. Other successful singles include a duet with Bobby Womack, "I'm Back for More," and a U.K. #1 cover of Dan Hartman's "Relight My Fire." She has also begun writing songs; she cowrote Tina Turner's "I Don't Wanna Fight." As of 2000, she continued to act, perform, and occasionally record.

Luna

Formed 1991, New York, NY
Dean Wareham (b. Aug. 1, 1963, Wellingston, N.Z.), voc., gtr.; Justin Harwood (b. July 6, 1965, Taradale, N.Z.), bass; Stanley Demeski (b. ca. 1960), drums
1992—*Lunapark* (Elektra) 1993—*Slide* EP 1994—*Bewitched*

(+ Sean A. Eden [b. Mar. 5, 1965, London, Ont., Can.], gtr., voc.) 1995—*Penthouse* 1996—*Luna* EP (– Demeski; + Lee Wall [b. Apr. 23, 1968, Winston-Salem, NC], drums) 1997—*Pup Tent* 1999—*The Days of Our Nights* (Jericho/Sire) 2001—*Live* (Arena Rock).
Dean Wareham solo: 1991—*Anaesthesia* EP (No. 6 Records).

After the breakup of the acclaimed indie band Galaxie 500, New Zealand–born singer/guitarist Dean Wareham formed Luna 2 in 1991. The new band, which also included Chills bassist Justin Harwood and ex-Feelies drummer Stanley Demeski, later trimmed the name to Luna and signed to Elektra Records, debuting with *Lunapark*. Like Galaxie 500, Luna was in the mold of New York's Velvet Underground/Television school, with moody, minimalist rock and imagistic, literate wordplay. The result could often be understated, though the band kicked up the beat on tour. On *Bewitched*, Luna added second guitarist Sean A. Eden. The album also featured a guest appearance by Sterling Morrison of the Velvet Underground. Luna continued that trend by inviting Television's Tom Verlaine, as well as Stereolab's Laetitia Sadier, to appear on 1995's *Penthouse*. That album's cover of Serge Gainsbourg's "Bonnie and Clyde" was a particular crowd pleaser. By now Luna enjoyed a strong following and regular critical support, albeit without attaining any chart action. Just prior to the scheduled release of *The Days of Our Nights*, though, Luna was dropped from Elektra. Six months later, independent Jericho Records released the 1999 album, which closed with an arch cover of Guns n' Roses' "Sweet Child O' Mine." The band's first live album was issued on another indie label in 2001.

Lydia Lunch

Born Lydia Koch, June 2, 1959, Rochester, NY
1980—*Queen of Siam* (Ze) 1981—*Eight-Eyed Spy* (Fetish); *Pre-Teenage Jesus* EP (Ze); *13.13* (Ruby) 1982—*The Agony Is the Ecstasy* EP (with the Birthday Party) (4AD) 1985—*The Uncensored Lydia Lunch* cassette (Widowspeak) 1987—*Honeymoon in Red* (with Rowland S. Howard) 1988—*Stinkfist* EP (with Clint Ruin); *The Crumb* EP (with Thurston Moore) 1989—*Naked in Garden Hills* (with Harry Crews); *Drowning in Limbo* 1991—*Shotgun Wedding* (with Rowland S. Howard) (Triple X) 1993—*Crimes Against Nature* 1995—*Rude Hieroglyphics* (with Exene Cervenkova) (Rykodisc) 1996—*Universal Infiltrators* (Atavistic) 1998—*Matrikamantra; Widowspeak* (WMC/Pilot).

At 16, Lydia Lunch was one of New York's first "no wave" artists with her band Teenage Jesus and the Jerks. Working with a variety of bassists, Lunch (vocals and guitar)—alternately shrieking and chanting in a monotone—and Bradly Field ("drum") recorded two singles (later collected on a 12-inch), four cuts for Brian Eno's *No New York* compilation, and an EP (pre–Teenage Jesus) featuring original member James Chance (then Siegfried) [see entry] on saxophone before he left the band to form the Contortions. A side project of the period was Beirut Slump, whose lone 45 included sometime-Jerk Jim Sclavunos on bass and filmmaker Vivienne Dick on violin. Lunch also starred in three of Dick's movies, as well as in Beth and Scott B's *Black Box*, *The Offenders*, and, in 1982, *Vortex* (which debuted at the New York Film Festival).

In 1980 Lunch left no wave behind and recorded *Queen of Siam* with the aid of ex-Contortions/John Cale bassist George Scott (a.k.a. Jack Ruby), saxophonist Pat Irwin, ex-Voidoid and Teenage Jesus producer Robert Quine on guitar, and big-band arranger Billy Ver Planck, the composer of the theme to *The Flintstones*. Concurrently, Lunch, Scott, Irwin, Sclavunos (on drums), and guitarist Michael Paumgardhen started the bluesy Eight-Eyed Spy. Scott's death from a heroin overdose in 1980 kept Eight-Eyed Spy from making a full studio LP, though a combination of live performances and studio work with Irwin on bass filled a posthumous cassette and an album.

With the end of Eight-Eyed Spy, Irwin concentrated on his instrumental group, the Raybeats (he later became a touring member of the B-52's), while Sclavunos and Paumgardhen joined Lunch's Devil Dogs. But turnover in personnel and a repertoire of cover songs kept that group from recording. Instead, Lunch moved to California and started 13.13. The lineup of the group was fluid (one version included three members of early L.A. punk rockers the Weirdos). In 1982 Lunch appeared on an EP, *The Agony Is the Ecstasy*, with the Birthday Party. Also that year Lunch collaborated with X's Exene Cervenkova on a book of poetry entitled *Adulterers Anonymous*. The mid-'80s saw Lunch concentrating more on her highly confrontational spoken-word performances. She founded Widowspeak Productions in 1984 to release her own and others' work. Lunch also began a collaboration with notorious underground filmmaker Richard Kern, starring in his films *The Right Side of My Brain* (with Henry Rollins) and *Fingered*.

Other collaborations were musical: She recorded with ex–Birthday Party guitarist Rowland S. Howard, including 1987's *Honeymoon in Red* and 1991's *Shotgun Wedding*, and on a 1988 EP, *Stinkfist*, with Jim Thirlwell, a.k.a. Foetus, a.k.a. Clint Ruin. Also in 1988 she formed the combo Harry Crews with Sonic Youth bassist/vocalist Kim Gordon and recorded *The Crumb* with Sonic Youth's Thurston Moore. With Exene Cervenkova, she recorded *Rude Hieroglyphics*, a mix of songs and spoken-word tracks, in 1995.

In 1993 Lunch taught a visiting-artists workshop for the San Francisco Art Institute's performance/video department. That year Triple X released a three-CD box set, *Crimes Against Nature*, of Lunch's spoken-word performances. In 1997 Lunch's novel *Paradoxia* was published; her writing has appeared in several other books, including *The Rolling Stone Book of the Beats* (1999) and *Men's Journal: The Great Life* (2000). Lunch's photography has also been anthologized and exhibited, and she contributed a track, "Gloomy Sunday," to 1999's *The Blair Witch Project* soundtrack.

John Lurie: See Lounge Lizards

Frankie Lymon and the Teenagers

Formed 1955, New York, NY
Frankie Lymon (b. Sep. 30, 1942, New York; d. Feb. 28, 1968, New York), lead voc.; Sherman Garnes (b. June 8, 1940, New York; d. 1978), bass voc.; Joe Negroni (b. Sep. 9, 1940, New York; d. 1977), baritone voc.; Herman Santiago (b. Feb. 18, 1941, New York), first tenor voc.; Jimmy Merchant (b. Feb. 10, 1940, New York), second tenor voc.
1956—*The Teenagers Featuring Frankie Lymon* (Gee)
1986—*Frankie Lymon and the Teenagers: For Collectors Only* (Murray Hill) 1989—*The Best of Frankie Lymon and the Teenagers* (Rhino) 1998—*The Very Best of Frankie Lymon and the Teenagers.*

When he was 13, Frankie Lymon had a #1 R&B record (#6 pop and #1 U.K.) with "Why Do Fools Fall in Love?" At 18 his career was over; eight years later he died of a heroin overdose. He was the first young black teen idol and an inspiration to countless young singers, including Ronnie Spector, Garland Jeffreys, Marvin Gaye, Michael Jackson, and Diana Ross, whose cover of "Fools" was a Top 10 hit in 1981. More than 25 years after his death, the two surviving Teenagers, Herman Santiago and Jimmy Merchant, made music-business and legal history when a federal court recognized them as the authors of the song and awarded them back royalties estimated in the millions.

The rags-to-riches-to-rags story began in New York, where Lymon and the Teenagers were school friends who sang on street corners. The Teenagers were originally a quartet, known first as the Ermines, then the Coupe de Villes. They discovered Lymon, who had sung in his father's gospel group, the Harlemaires, and he joined the group, which then became the Premiers. In 1955 Richard Barrett of the Valentines heard them perform on a street corner outside his window and arranged for the group to be signed by the record label his group recorded for, Gee. Label executives were impressed by the group with Santiago singing lead, but when it came time to record a song Santiago and Merchant cowrote, "Why Do Fools Fall in Love?," Lymon stepped in since Santiago had a cold. The song, credited to Lymon and producer George Goldner, was their first record. By then they were known as Frankie Lymon and the Teenagers.

Lymon's boyish soprano became the group's trademark, and the group's clean-cut, innocent image was embraced by the public and the record industry at a time when Congress was beginning to investigate payola. Smiling and neatly attired in letter sweaters and loose, sharply creased trousers, Frankie Lymon and the Teenagers were a crossover smash. "Fools" was one of four Top 20 R&B songs off the Teenagers' debut album; the others were "I Promise to Remember" (#10, 1956), "I Want You to Be My Girl" (#13 pop, #3 R&B, 1956), and "The ABC's of Love" (#14 R&B, 1956). The LP also included "I'm Not a Juvenile Delinquent," which the group sang in the 1956 Alan Freed film *Rock, Rock, Rock.* A year later, after appearing in another Freed movie, *Mr. Rock and Roll,* and making a successful tour of the U.K., Lymon left the group for a solo career.

The Teenagers continued without him, with a string of less charismatic lead singers, but nothing hit. After reuniting with Lymon briefly in 1965, the group called it quits for many years. By then Lymon, too, had fallen on hard times, mostly due to his worsening drug addiction. His first 45, "Goody Goody," was a modest hit (#20 pop, 1957); subsequent records were outright flops. A comeback attempt in 1960 with Bobby Day's "Little Bitty Pretty One" hit #58. His handlers had tried a number of new stylistic approaches for Lymon, whose natural change in voice was less appealing. But Lymon's problems ran much deeper. In the '60s he was arrested for drug possession and claimed in an *Ebony* magazine profile to have been a pimp at the height of the Teenagers' success. He had left the army, married a schoolteacher named Emira Eagle, and was playing the lounge at an Augusta, Georgia, Howard Johnson's when he got a brief job in New York. Just a few days after returning to his hometown, he was found dead of a heroin overdose. In the '70s Garnes died of a heart attack, and Negroni passed away after a cerebral hemorrhage. Merchant became a cabdriver.

In 1981, to commemorate the silver anniversary of "Fools," Santiago and Merchant recruited Pearl McKinnon and Eric Ward. There were a few more personnel changes in the revived Teenagers. One latter-day edition included Jimmy Castor [see entry] (who understudied for Frankie Lymon at the group's height), Tony Sal (ex–Ronnie and the Daytonas and the Jimmy Castor Bunch), and New York City oldies radio disc jockey Bobby Jay.

In the meantime, "Why Do Fools Fall in Love?" had proven its durability, becoming a hit record again for the Happenings in 1967, being featured on the hit *American Graffiti* soundtrack, and being covered many times. In 1984 Frankie Lymon's widow filed for a renewal of her late husband's copyright on the song, only to discover that it had become the property of unscrupulous record executive Morris Levy. A lawsuit was then filed in federal court, charging that Levy and Goldner had fraudulently represented themselves as the coauthors of a song written by Frankie Lymon. With millions in back royalties at stake, Levy recalled a woman, Elizabeth Waters, who had contacted him several years before, claiming she had been married to Lymon in the '60s (Waters, it was later discovered, was legally married to another man when she married Lymon). Levy also tracked down another woman who claimed to have been married to Lymon, Zola Taylor, a former singer with the Platters. (She could produce no wedding license for the nuptials that allegedly occurred in Tijuana.) It was later revealed that Levy had promised both women financial compensation in return for their disputing Emira Lymon's claim of widowhood, and it worked. Waters won the case around the same time Levy was sentenced to 10 years in federal prison for extortion in another case. An appellate court reversed the decision, deeming Emira to be Lymon's legal widow.

But the twists and turns did not end there. Merchant and Santiago pressed their own case, claiming they were the true authors of the song and, thus, the rightful recipients of any royalties due. Although their case appeared weakened by the years that had elapsed, in 1992 a federal court proclaimed Jimmy Merchant and Herman Santiago—not Lymon, Goldner, or Levy, by then all deceased—the song's authors and rightful copyright owners. The two Teenagers had successfully argued that they were tricked out of the royalties, then intimidated (through a 1969 death threat) into silence. In most such cases, the plaintiffs never see justice; at best, royalties are awarded going back the previous three years. For Merchant and Santiago, though, the judge ruled in their favor and went even further, awarding royalties back to 1969. Unfortunately, the decision was overturned on appeal; the Teenagers lost again.

In 1993 the band was inducted into the Rock and Roll Hall of Fame. Actor Larenz Tate portrayed Lymon in the 1998 biopic *Why Do Fools Fall in Love*. Santiago has publicly questioned the factual accuracy of certain passages of the film.

Barbara Lynn

Born Barbara Lynn Ozen, Jan. 16, 1942, Beaumont, TX
1976—*Here Is Barbara Lynn* (Oval) 1988—*You Don't Have to Go* (Ichiban) 1993—*You'll Lose a Good Thing* (Sounds of the Fifties, Neth.) 1994—*So Good* (Bullseye Blues) 2000—*Hot Night Tonight* (Antone's).

Barbara Lynn is an East Texas R&B singer (and left-handed guitar player) with a bluesy voice and a casual, low-key style. Her first and biggest hit, the New Orleans–style standard "You'll Lose a Good Thing" (#8 pop, #1 R&B, 1962), was written by the 16-year-old Lynn as a poem. She was discovered singing blues in Louisiana clubs by musician/arranger Huey P. Meaux, who subsequently produced all her records. Most of her early hits—including "You're Gonna Need Me" (#13 R&B, 1963) and "It's Better to Have It" (#26 R&B, 1965)—were recorded in Cosimo Matassa's New Orleans studio but were released by Philadelphia-based Jamie Records.

In 1966 Lynn signed to Meaux's Tribe label but recorded no hits. In 1968 she went to Atlantic, hitting with "This Is the Thanks I Get" (#39 R&B, 1968) and "(Until Then) I'll Suffer" (#31 R&B, 1971). The Rolling Stones covered her "Oh! Baby (We Got a Good Thing Goin')" on *Rolling Stones Now!* Recording-wise, little was heard from Lynn through the '80s except for a single LP from Ichiban. Six years later *So Good* was released to critical acclaim. The followup, 2000's *Hot Night Tonight*, features appearances by Ivan Neville, Bernard Fowler, and Daryl Jones.

Loretta Lynn

Born Loretta Webb, Apr. 14, 1935, Butcher Hollow, KY
1966—*Don't Come Home a' Drinkin'* (Decca) 1968—*Greatest Hits* 1970—*Coal Miner's Daughter* 1972—*Lead Me On* (with Conway Twitty) 1974—*Greatest Hits, vol. 2* (MCA) 1975—*Back to the Country; Home* 1976—*When the Tingle Becomes a Chill; Somebody Somewhere* 1977—*I Remember Patsy; Out of My Head and Back in My Bed* 1979—*We've Come a Long Way, Baby* 1980—*Loretta; Lookin' Good* 1981—*Two's a Party* (with Conway Twitty) 1982—*I Lie; Making Love From Memory* 1983—*Lyin', Cheatin', Woman Chasin', Honky Tonkin', Whiskey Drinkin' You* 1985—*Just a Woman* 1988—*Who Was That Stranger* 1991—*The Country Music Hall of Fame: Loretta Lynn* 1992—*The Old Rugged Cross* 1993—*Honky Tonk Angels* (with Dolly Parton and Tammy Wynette) (Columbia) 1994—*Honky Tonk Girl: The Loretta Lynn Collection* (MCA) 1995—*An Evening With Loretta Lynn* (Musketeer) 2000—*Still Country* (Audium).

Country singer and songwriter Loretta Lynn grew up in the remote, poverty-stricken town of Butcher Hollow, Kentucky. Named after Loretta Young, Lynn didn't do much singing in her early youth. Instead, after one month of dating, she was married at age 13 to Mooney (Moonshine) Lynn (he was 19), who took her 3,000 miles away to Custer, Washington, where he worked in logging camps. Lynn became a mother at 14 and had four children in her first four years of marriage; she was a grandmother at 29. Besides taking care of the kids, taking in other people's laundry, and occasionally making extra money by picking strawberries with migrant workers, Lynn began writing songs on her Sears Roebuck guitar. Her husband encouraged her to go public and became her manager, lining up shows at local bars and clubs. At age 27 Lynn cut a record for the California Zero label, "I'm a Honky Tonk Girl," which she and Mooney promoted themselves by visiting radio stations around the country. They worked their way to Nashville, and the song eventually became a #14 hit on the C&W national chart.

Loretta Lynn

Once in Nashville, Lynn persuaded Ott Devine, manager of the Grand Ole Opry, to book her, and she first appeared there in October 1960. An appearance with Buck Owens led to a contract with Decca, for whom she's made more than 50 records over a period of 30 years. Her first Decca hit, produced by Owen Bradley in 1962, was called "Success" (#6 C&W). Since then she has had 16 #1 C&W hits, including the standards, "Don't Come Home a' Drinkin' (With Lovin' on Your Mind)" (1966), "Fist City" (1968), "Woman of the World (Leave My World Alone)" (1969), and the autobiographical "Coal Miner's Daughter" (1970). Also in 1970 she began touring regularly with Conway Twitty, with whom she had a number of #1 C&W hits, including 1971's "After the Fire Is Gone" and "Lead Me On," followed by "Louisiana Woman, Mississippi Man" (1973), "As Soon As I Hang Up the Phone" (1974), and "Feelins' " (1975). Lynn was the first woman to win the Entertainer of the Year Award from the Country Music Association, in 1972. Her self-penned controversial hit "The Pill" (#70 pop, #5 C&W, 1975) was seen by some as a down-home feminist classic, while "One's on the Way" (#1 C&W, 1971) celebrated motherhood.

Her later hits included the C&W #1 singles "Rated 'X' " (1972), "Love Is the Foundation" (1973), "Trouble in Paradise" (1974), "Somebody Somewhere (Don't Know What He's Missin' Tonight)" (1976), "She's Got You" (1977), "Out of My Head and Back in My Bed" (1977), as well as other C&W Top 20 hits, such as "When the Tingle Becomes a Chill" (1975), "We've Come a Long Way, Baby," "I Can't Feel You Anymore" (1979), and "I Lie" (1982).

In 1976 Lynn (with *New York Times* reporter George Vecsey) wrote her autobiography, *Coal Miner's Daughter,* and it became one of the 10 biggest-selling books of that year. In 1980 a movie based on Lynn's autobiography and starring Sissy Spacek came out, to much acclaim. (Spacek, who sang Lynn's songs in the film, won the Best Actress Oscar for her performance.) Lynn herself has dabbled in acting, making guest appearances on *Fantasy Island* and *The Dukes of Hazzard,* as well as *The Muppet Show.*

Although Lynn's recording career slowed to a halt in the late '80s (1988's *Who Was That Stranger* would be her last solo album for a dozen years), she remained one of country music's most popular and well-loved stars. She was inducted into the Country Music Hall of Fame in 1988 and presented with the Pioneer Award at the 1995 Academy of Country Music Awards. *Honky Tonk Girl: The Loretta Lynn Collection,* a career-spanning three-disc box set, was released in 1994. She joined Dolly Parton and Tammy Wynette to record 1993's *Honky Tonk Angels* album, but she spent much of the first half of the '90s nursing her ailing husband, Mooney, who passed away in 1996 from diabetes complications. They had been married 48 years. In September 2000, her 40th anniversary as a performer, Lynn returned with the Randy Scruggs–produced *Still Country* on the independent Audium label. The album featured two new songs of her own, including her tribute to Mooney, "I Can't Hear the Music." She planned to publish her second autobiography in 2001.

Lynyrd Skynyrd

Formed 1966, Jacksonville, FL
Ronnie Van Zant (b. Jan. 15, 1949; d. Oct. 20, 1977, Gillsburg, MS), voc.; Gary Rossington, gtr.; Allen Collins (b. ca. 1952; d. Jan. 23, 1990, Jacksonville), gtr.; Billy Powell, kybds.; Leon Wilkeson (d. July 27, 2001, Ponte Vedra Beach, FL), bass; Bob Burns, drums.
1973—(+ Ed King, gtr.) *Pronounced Leh-Nerd Skin-Nerd* (MCA) 1974—*Second Helping* (– Burns; + Artimus Pyle [b. Spartanburg, SC], drums) 1975—(– King) *Nuthin' Fancy* 1976—*Gimme Back My Bullets* (+ Steve Gaines [b. Seneca, MO; d. Oct. 20, 1977, Gillsburg, MS], gtr.) *One More From the Road* 1977—*Street Survivors* 1978—*Skynyrd's First . . . And Last* 1979—*Gold and Platinum* 1987—*Legend* 1988—*Southern by the Grace of God/Lynyrd Skynyrd Tribute Tour—1987* 1991—(group re-forms: Rossington; Pyle; Wilkeson; King; Powell; + Johnny Van-Zant, voc.; + Randall Hall, gtr.; + Custer, drums) *Lynyrd Skynyrd 1991* (Atlantic) 1993—*The Last Rebel* 1994—*Endangered Species* (Capricorn) 1996—(– King; + Rickey Medlocke, gtr.; + Hughie Thomasson, gtr.) *Freebird . . . The Movie* (MCA) 1997—*Twenty* (CMC International) 1998—*Lyve* 1999—*Edge of Forever* 2000—*Then and Now.*
Johnny Van-Zant solo: 1980—*No More Dirty Deals* (Polydor) 1981—*Round Two* 1982—*The Last of the Wild Ones* 1985—*Van-Zant* (Geffen) 1990—*Brickyard Road* (Atlantic).

Lynyrd Skynyrd was the most critically lauded and commercially successful of the Allman Brothers–influenced Southern bands. When it first rose to prominence in 1973, the group epitomized regional pride that stressed cocky, boisterous hard rock, as opposed to the Allmans' open-ended blues. When the band broke up in 1977 after a plane crash killed Ronnie Van Zant and newcomer Steve Gaines and backup singer Cassie Gaines, Southern rock suffered a tremendous loss.

The nucleus of what would become Lynyrd Skynyrd first met in high school in their hometown, Jacksonville, Florida. Van Zant, Allen Collins, and Gary Rossington formed the band My Backyard in 1965, eventually joined by Leon Wilkeson and Billy Powell. Their later name immortalized a gym teacher, Leonard Skinner, who was known to punish students who had long hair.

The band, with original drummer Bob Burns, was playing in Atlanta at a bar called Funocchio's in 1972, when it was spotted by Al Kooper, who was on a tour with Badfinger and also scouting bands for MCA's new Sounds of the South label. Kooper signed Skynyrd and produced its 1973 debut, *Pronounced Leh-Nerd Skin-Nerd,* adding session guitarist Ed King (late of Strawberry Alarm Clock). The group's initial hook was its three-guitar attack, topping the Allmans' trademark two-guitar leads. Skynyrd first got major FM airplay with the lengthy "Freebird." What had been written as a tribute to Duane Allman eventually became an anthem for Skynyrd fans and—when revived, without lyrics, by the Rossington Collins Band in 1980—a tribute to Van Zant.

The band hooked up with the Who's *Quadrophenia* tour

Lynyrd Skynyrd: Leon Wilkeson, Allen Collins, Ronnie Van Zant, Gary Rossington, Artimus Pyle, Steve Gaines, Billy Powell

in 1973 and acquired a reputation as a live act. Its 1974 followup LP, the multiplatinum *Second Helping,* also produced by Kooper, reached #12. It included another instant Southern standard, "Sweet Home Alabama" (#8, 1974), a reply to Neil Young's "Alabama" and "Southern Man." But Van Zant often wore a Neil Young T-shirt, and Young later offered the band several songs to record, though they never made it to vinyl.

In December 1974 Artimus Pyle joined as a replacement for Burns; King quit a month later. The band's third record went to #9, but 1976's *Gimme Back My Bullets,* produced by Tom Dowd, sold somewhat less. Skynyrd regrouped in October 1976 with the double live *One More From the Road* (recorded at Atlanta's Fox Theater), which went to #9, sold triple platinum, and featured new third guitarist Steve Gaines, plus a trio of female backup singers, including Gaines' sister Cassie. The band became one of the biggest U.S. concert draws.

Street Survivors, its sixth LP, was released three days before the plane crash of October 20, 1977. Skynyrd was traveling in a privately chartered plane between shows in Greenville, South Carolina, and Baton Rouge, Louisiana, when it crashed just outside Gillsburg, Mississippi, killing three members. The rest escaped with injuries. Fuel shortage was a possible cause of the crash, although by the next year a lawsuit filed against the airplane company faulted the plane's personnel and its mechanical integrity. Ironically, the cover of the band's last LP pictures the members standing in flames and included an order form for a "Lynyrd Skynyrd survival kit." There was also a Van Zant composition about death called "That Smell." The LP cover was changed shortly after the accident, and the album (#5, 1977) went on to become one of Skynyrd's biggest sellers. The next year *Skynyrd's First . . . and Last* was released, consisting of previously unavailable early band recordings from 1970 to 1972 (the band had planned on releasing it before the accident). It went platinum, and in 1980 MCA released a best-of called *Gold and Platinum.*

That same year a new band emerged from Lynyrd Skynyrd's ashes. The Rossington-Collins Band [see entry] featured three of the surviving members plus female lead singer Dale Krantz. Artimus Pyle, meanwhile, began touring with his Artimus Pyle Band in 1982.

In 1986 tragedy struck again when Allen Collins crashed his car, killing his girlfriend and leaving him paralyzed from the waist down. Four years later he died of respiratory failure due to pneumonia at age 37. To mark the 10th anniversary of the fatal plane crash, in 1987 Rossington, Powell, Wilkeson, and King put Lynyrd Skynyrd back together, along with guitarist Randall Hall and Johnny Van-Zant (the only one of the brothers who hyphenates his surname) on lead vocals. The younger brother of Ronnie and Donnie (.38 Special) was a marginally successful solo artist, releasing five albums from 1980 through 1990. Dale Krantz, by then Dale Krantz Rossington, sang backup for a 32-date Skynyrd reunion tour, which was chronicled on the following year's double live album, *Southern by the Grace of God/Lynyrd Skynyrd Tribute Tour—1987.*

In 1991 the same group (minus Pyle, and with "Custer" on drums) released a new LP, *Lynyrd Skynyrd 1991.* Both it and 1993's *The Last Rebel* carried on Skynyrd's musical tradition and were well received. The band signed with Southern-rock stronghold Capricorn Records and released the one-off acoustic *Endangered Species* in 1994. Guitarist King left the band shortly after, and new guitarists Rickey Medlocke (formerly of Blackfoot) and Hughie Thomasson (formerly of the Outlaws) were hired as full-time members. The 1996 concert documentary *Freebird . . . The Movie* captured the original band in its prime, on celluloid and an MCA soundtrack. The group's next albums were released on North Carolina–based CMC International, a label that established a solid market niche reviving the careers of slumping arena-rock acts. Sure enough, a 1997 *Behind the Music* special on VH1 aired while the band was in midtour supporting the album *Twenty* (#97, 1997), which marked the 20th anniversary of the fatal, fateful plane crash. Wilkeson died of natural causes in July 2001.

Kirsty MacColl

Born Oct. 10, 1959, London, Eng.; died Dec. 18, 2000, Cozumel, Mex.
1981—*Desperate Character* (Polydor) 1989—*Kite* (Charisma) 1991—*Electric Landlady* 1993—*Titanic Days* (I.R.S.) 1995—*Galore* 2000—*What Do Pretty Girls Do?* (Hux); *Tropical Brainstorm* (V2, U.K.).

Kirsty MacColl's simultaneously witty and affecting songs and crystalline voice won her a large following in Britain, where "There's a Guy Works Down the Chip Shop Swears He's Elvis" (#14 U.K., 1981) and "Walking Down Madison" (#23 U.K., 1991) were Top 40 hits. American listeners have mostly heard Kirsty's vocals on records by the Rolling Stones, the Smiths, Talking Heads, Billy Bragg, and Van Morrison. Her duet with the Pogues' Shane McGowan, "Fairytale of New York" (#2 U.K., 1987), was one of the most successful Christmas singles ever released in Britain.

The daughter of English folk-music legend Ewen MacColl (who, among other things, wrote "The First Time Ever I Saw Your Face"), Kirsty signed with Stiff Records at age 16. Her 1979 debut single, "They Don't Know," failed to make a dent but became a hit (#8 U.S., 1984; #2 U.K., 1983) for Tracey Ullman in 1984. "Chip Shop" and *Desperate Character* (1981) showcased her talent as a rueful *pasticheur,* deftly mixing country, rockabilly, and pop influences. A second album recorded for Polydor in 1983 was rejected and never released.

In 1984 she married producer Steve Lillywhite (Simple Minds, Rolling Stones, U2, Talking Heads). Their first collaboration was a cover of Billy Bragg's "A New England" (#7 U.K., 1985). Lillywhite produced MacColl's first American releases, *Kite* (1989) and *Electric Landlady* (1991). Collaborating with guitarists Johnny Marr (the Smiths), Mark E. Nevin (Fairground Attraction), and Marshall Crenshaw, the albums reflect her social concerns, attacking Margaret Thatcher, shallow pop stars, and the dichotomy between rich and poor. (She also hosted an environmental special on the BBC.) Musically the songs range from dance and rap inflections ("Walking Down Madison") to samba ("My Affair") and include cover versions (the Kinks' "Days" [#12 U.K., 1989]) and original takes on '60s pop (her "He Never Mentioned Love"). MacColl's 1993 album, *Titanic Days,* featured "Can't Stop Killing You" and "Angel," which received U.S. Modern Rock–radio airplay.

The liner notes of the 1995 compilation *Galore* featured testimonies in the form of eulogies from the likes of Bono (who called her "Noelle Coward"), Morrissey, and David Byrne, all praising MacColl as one of the finest British songwriters. MacColl, who'd separated from Lillywhite in 1994 (they divorced in 1997), remained below the radar in the second part of the '90s, sticking to guest appearances on records (most notably Billy Bragg's). She resurfaced in 2000 with *Tropical Brainstorm,* her first album of new material in seven years. Inspired by trips to Cuba and Brazil, it saw the perennially British MacColl winningly try her hand at Latin-American rhythms. Later that year, she released *What Do Pretty Girls Do?*—a collection of BBC radio sessions recorded between 1989 and 1995. She was struck by a boat and killed while scuba diving with her two sons in Mexico. She was 41.

Lonnie Mack

Born Lonnie McIntosh, July 18, 1941, Harrison, IN
1963—*The Wham of That Memphis Man!* (Fraternity) 1969—*Glad I'm in the Band* (Elektra); *Whatever's Right* 1970—*For Collectors Only* 1971—*The Hills of Indiana* 1977—*Home at Last* (Capitol); *Lonnie Mack and Pismo* 1985—*Strike Like Lightning* (Alligator) 1986—*Second Sight* 1988—*Roadhouses & Dance Halls* (Epic) 1990—*Live! Attack of the Killer V* (Alligator); *Dueling Banjos* (QCA) 1998—*South* (Mack's Flying V); *Live at Coco's* 1999—*Direct Hits and Close Calls; The Pressure's All Mine.*

A pioneering rock & roller, Lonnie Mack utilized the whammy bar of his Gibson Flying V to achieve an enormously influential rockabilly sound. Learning guitar at age five, he attended closely to Chet Atkins' and Merle Travis' thumb-and-fingerpicking approach. Les Paul was also an early idol, and Mack's guitar was the highlight of his first group, Lonnie and the Twilighters, as well as the subsequent Troy Seals Band, for whom he played lead.

Going solo in 1961, Mack released an instrumental version of Chuck Berry's "Memphis" that charted at #5. Feeding his guitar through a Leslie cabinet usually employed by organists, he trademarked his distinctive "twangy" sound. A followup, "Wham!," entered the Top 30, and a debut album, *The Wham of That Memphis Man!,* became a roots classic. While overshadowed by his playing, Mack's R&B–influenced singing also drew notice.

An occasional session player for James Brown, Freddie King, and most notably the Doors *(Morrison Hotel),* Mack put out three albums on Elektra at the turn of the decade. *Glad I'm in the Band, Whatever's Right,* and the country-inflected *Hills of Indiana* were more critical than commercial successes, and in 1971, having assumed cult status among musicians, Mack retreated for six years. Surfacing in 1977 with *Lonnie Mack and Pismo* and the acoustic-driven *Home at Last,* he returned to strength with 1985's *Strike Like Lightning,* produced by longtime fan Stevie Ray Vaughan.

Second Sight, Roadhouses & Dance Halls, and *Live! Attack of the Killer V* confirmed his comeback. Concentrating on blues and the country and gospel roots that formed him, his later work displays, with renewed vitality, his rich, vibrato guitar tone. He continues to tour, and in the late '90s began releasing, on his own Mack's Flying V label, a series of Internet-available albums.

Madness

Formed 1978, London, Eng.
Lee Thompson (b. Oct. 5, 1957, London), sax; Chris Foreman (b. Aug. 8, 1958, London), gtr.; Mike Barson (b. Apr. 21, 1958, London), kybds.; Dan Woodgate (b. Oct. 19, 1960, London), drums; Mark Bedford (b. Aug. 24, 1961, London), bass; Graham "Suggs" McPherson (b. Jan. 13, 1961, Hastings, Eng.), voc.; Chas Smash (b. Carl Smyth, Jan. 14, 1959), MC, steps, trumpet.
1979—*One Step Beyond* (Stiff) 1980—*Absolutely* 1981—*7* 1983—*Madness* (Geffen) (– Barson) 1984—*Keep Moving* 1985—*Mad Not Mad* 1986—(group disbands) 1988—(group re-forms as the Madness: Foreman; Thompson; Smyth; McPherson; + Jerry Dammers [b. Gerald Dankin, May 22, 1954, India], kybds.; + Steve Nieve, kybds.; + Bruce Thomas, bass) 1992—*Divine Madness* (Virgin) 1997—*Total Madness . . . The Very Best of Madness* (Geffen) 1999—(group re-forms: Thompson; Forman; Barson; Woodgate; Bedford; McPherson; Smyth) *Universal Madness: Live in Los Angeles* (Golden Voice); *Wonderful* (Virgin, U.K.).

Madness first came to prominence in 1978, along with the Specials, in the forefront of Great Britain's ska revival. (Ska was a prereggae Jamaican dance rhythm popular in the '60s.) In time Madness became a vaudevillian pop group, matching its self-proclaimed "nutty sound" to soul, R&B, and music-hall music as well as ska and becoming a top singles band in Britain. Lee Thompson, Mike Barson, and Chris Foreman had been together since 1976 in the band Morris and the Minors. As group membership varied, Chas Smash and future Madness manager John Hassler auditioned as replacements without success; by 1978 Graham McPherson, Dan Woodgate, and Mark Bedford had all joined the group, now known as the Invaders. That year they changed their name to Madness, after a favorite Prince Buster ska song.

In 1979 the Specials' 2-Tone label released "The Prince," dedicated to Prince Buster. When it reached #16 on the British chart, Madness signed with Stiff. Chas Smash joined as emcee and dancer, and Madness recorded *One Step Beyond.* The title cut became a Top 10 British single, and the album stayed in the British charts for most of a year, peaking at #2. *Absolutely,* with the single "Baggy Trousers" (#3 U.K., 1980) (a Madness onstage trademark), peaked at #2 U.K., as Madness began to broaden its style, becoming spokesmen for Cockney youth. Other U.K. Top 10 singles from that period included "My Girl," "Work Rest and Play," "Embarrassment," "The Return of the Los Palmas Seven," "Grey Day," and "Shut Up."

In 1981 Madness made a film about starting a group, *Take It or Leave It,* playing itself. The British album *7* included two more U.K. hits, "It Must Be Love" and "Cardiac Arrest," and Madness' first #1 British single, "House of Fun," which brought the LP to #5. Through late 1983 the group's further Top 10 U.K. singles were "Driving in My Car" (1982), "Our House" (1982), "Tomorrow's (Just Another Day)" (1983), "Wings of a Dove" (1983), and "The Sun and the Rain" (1983).

But U.S. response to Madness was confined to concert audiences. *Rise and Fall* and *Complete Madness,* the latter a greatest-hits collection released simultaneously with a videocassette, were not released on a U.S. label, although they were bestsellers in Britain and Europe. Despite the popularity of *Madness* (#41, 1983), which included a number of previous British hits from 1981–82, here in the U.S. the group slid back into obscurity. From that album, Madness saw its only U.S. Top 10 hit with "Our House" (#7, 1983). Despite a handful of lively and amusing videos, including "House of Fun," and another minor hit, "It Must Be Love" (#33, 1983), Madness' next album, *Keep Moving,* peaked at #109.

At home, however, Madness continued its winning streak with several more hits, among them "Michael Caine" (#11, 1984), "Yesterday's Men" (#18, 1985), and "(Waiting for) The Ghost Train" (#18, 1986). In the fall of 1986 the group disbanded, although several members returned as the Madness with an unsuccessful album, *The Madness,* that was not released here and was largely ignored at home. Its single, "I Pronounce You," was a minor U.K. hit, then that group broke up as well. Thompson and Foreman continued for one album as the Nutty Boys. Woodgate later joined Voice of the Beehive. McPherson went into management before releasing a solo album, *The Lone Ranger,* in 1995, and Smyth became an A&R man for Go! Discs Records. From 1992–96 the group gave a nod to the American Woodstock when it reunited each year for "Madstock" in London's Finsbury Park. Members reunited again in 1998 for a stateside tour, recording a live album during their L.A. date that they issued the following year. That same year, Madness released its first album of original material in more than a decade, *Wonderful;* a U.K.-only recording, the album produced the #10 British single "Lovestruck."

Madonna

Born Madonna Louise Ciccone, Aug. 16, 1958, Bay City, MI
1983—*Madonna* (Sire) 1984—*Like a Virgin* 1986—*True Blue* 1987—*Who's That Girl; You Can Dance* 1989—*Like a Prayer* 1990—*I'm Breathless; The Immaculate Collection* 1992—*Erotica* (Maverick) 1994—*Bedtime Stories* 1995—*Something to Remember* 1996—*Evita* (Warner Bros.) 1998—*Ray of Light* (Maverick) 2000—*Music.*

Madonna is the most media-savvy American pop star since Bob Dylan and the most consistently controversial one since Elvis Presley. In the minds of her supporters, her sassy approach to dance music and in-your-face videos gave feminism a much-needed makeover throughout the '80s, smashing sexual boundaries, redefining the nature of eroticism, and challenging social and religious mores. To her detractors, she merely reinforced the notion of "woman as plaything," turning the clock back on conventional feminism two decades. One thing is rarely disputed: At nearly every turn, she has maintained firm control over her career and image.

Born in Bay City, Michigan, Madonna Ciccone was one of six children. Her mother died when Madonna was six, leaving her father, a Chrysler/General Dynamics engineer, to raise the family. She began studying dance at 14 and, after graduating from high school in 1976, continued her dance studies at the University of Michigan in Ann Arbor. She moved to New York in 1978, where she studied briefly with the Alvin Ailey dance troupe.

Madonna

Her first crack at pop music came when a boyfriend let her sing and play drums in his band, the Breakfast Club. While in the band, she landed a brief job as backup singer and dancer with disco star Patrick ("Born to Be Alive") Hernandez. In 1981 she quit the Breakfast Club and started writing songs with a former boyfriend from her college years, Steven Bray. The two gained attention in the trendy New York club Danceteria, where the DJ, Mark Kamins, played her tapes; it was Kamins who took Madonna's demo to Sire Records and produced her first club hit, 1982's "Everybody." After a 12-inch single, "Burning Up"/"Physical Attraction," hit #3 on the dance chart in early 1983, she began recording her first album with the high-profile DJ John "Jellybean" Benitez, with whom she became romantically involved. A few months later Sire released her self-titled debut, which peaked at #8. It spawned "Holiday," a single that crossed over from nightclubs to radio, eventually topping out at #16 on the pop chart by the following year.

Madonna enlisted manager Freddie DeMann, who had guided Michael Jackson from the Jacksons' late-'70s slump through *Thriller.* DeMann soon had Madonna making history with a couple of titillating videos. In March 1984 "Borderline" (#10), with its video celebrating interracial love, was released; it was followed by "Lucky Star" (#4), whose video offered provocative glimpses of the star's navel. Public opinion was—and would remain—split. Most critics initially dismissed Madonna as a prefab disco prima donna offering style over substance; a few, however, saw something different and hailed her as a strong new female voice, BOY TOY belt and all. *Madonna* (#8, 1983) sold more than 5 million copies.

In late 1984 the Nile Rodgers–produced *Like a Virgin* (#1, 1984), with its #1 title song, shot to the Top 10 upon its release; it eventually sold more than 10 million copies. Doubtless inspired by her indisputable videogenic presence, DeMann had negotiated movie deals for Madonna (before her stardom, she had already acted in the low-budget indie film *A Certain Sacrifice*), landing her a small part as a nightclub singer in *Vision Quest* and the title role in *Desperately Seeking Susan*. Throughout 1985 Madonna was ubiquitous, appearing in both movies, with hit songs on three albums. By March, "Crazy for You" (#1), from the *Vision Quest* soundtrack, and "Material Girl" (#2), from *Like a Virgin*, were in the Top 5 simultaneously. Her other hits were *Virgin*'s "Angel" (#5) and "Dress You Up" (#5), and the club smash "Into the Groove," from the *Susan* soundtrack. Her Virgin Tour was the hot ticket during the first half of the year.

Also in 1985 Madonna married actor Sean Penn, with whom she appeared in the critical and commercial flop *Shanghai Surprise* (a film produced by ex-Beatle George Harrison). Then she hit the pop world with a musical left hook: "Papa Don't Preach" (#1, 1986). The initial single from the 7-million seller *True Blue* (#1, 1986) drew criticism for its message that young unwed women should keep their babies. As the lyrical content of Madonna's songs deepened, critical acceptance of her began to grow. Her subsequent 1986 hits were "True Blue" (#3) and "Open Your Heart" (#1), followed in 1987 by "La Isla Bonita" (#4). Another ill-advised acting venture, 1987's *Who's That Girl*, was tied into a #1, platinum album of the same name, which included the hit title song (#1) and "Causing a Commotion" (#2). In 1988 she appeared in David Mamet's Broadway production *Speed the Plow*. The next year she and Penn divorced.

She returned to music in 1989 with *Like a Prayer* (#1), and the title song's video—complete with burning crosses and an eroticized black Jesus—launched Madonna's biggest and costliest controversy thus far. Released in March, it was censured by the Vatican, and the public response prompted Pepsi-Cola to cancel the singer's lucrative endorsement deal. Despite that, "Like a Prayer" debuted at #1. The international controversy only raised the singer's profile. *Like a Prayer* spawned four other Top 20 hits: "Express Yourself" (#2), "Cherish" (#2), "Oh Father" (#20), and "Keep It Together" (#8).

Madonna hit her megastar stride in 1990, when she appeared as Breathless Mahoney with then-boyfriend Warren Beatty in *Dick Tracy*; its soundtrack, *I'm Breathless* (#2, 1990), bore hits in "Hanky Panky" (#10) and the nonmovie double-platinum single "Vogue" (#1), which honored and revived the popular gay dance craze. In 1991 she scored hits with "Rescue Me" (#9) and "Justify My Love" (#1); the video for the latter fanned the flames of controversy yet again with its explicit depiction of various forms of sexual expression. She then oversaw the film *Truth or Dare*, a documentary of her Blond Ambition Tour dressed up to look like D.A. Pennebaker's Dylan movie, *Don't Look Back*. Madonna also became one of the first pop stars to speak out about AIDS and help raise money for research.

The singer affirmed her business acumen in 1992 when she signed a seven-year, $60-million deal with Time Warner, guaranteeing release of all albums, films, and books under her Maverick production corporation. Her first Maverick project was a highly controversial 128-page coffee-table photo book, *Sex*, which had Madonna posing nude and wearing S&M gear. *Sex* was followed by the mostly panned erotic film thriller *Body of Evidence* and the album *Erotica*, which peaked at #2 and produced Top 5 hits in 1992: the title track (#3, 1992) and "Deeper and Deeper" (#7). "Bad Girl" (#36) and "Rain" (#14) were both Top 40 hits in 1993. By then, Maverick was releasing work by other artists, including hip-hop chanteuse Meshell Ndegéocello, and Madonna embarked on her worldwide Girlie Show Tour, which drew a mixed critical reaction. An appearance on *The Late Show With David Letterman* returned Madonna to the headlines in spring 1994, when, using an abundance of profanities, she engaged in a verbal sparring match with the comedian. She also returned to the pop chart that year with the #2 single "I'll Remember," from the 1994 film *With Honors*. Her late-1994 album, *Bedtime Stories* (#3), presented a fairly traditional R&B sound and yielded the hit singles "Secret" (#4, 1994) and "Take a Bow" (#1, 1995). The title track (#42) was cowritten by Björk. Madonna then released the compilation *Something to Remember* (#6, 1995), which gathered the singer's ballads with three new songs. She soon won the lead role in a film version of Andrew Lloyd Webber's *Evita*, a musical based on the life of Argentina's Evita Perón. *Evita* earned Madonna favorable reviews and spawned the hit singles "Don't Cry for Me Argentina" (#8) and "You Must Love Me" (#18).

Despite her chameleon inclinations, Madonna stayed consistently within the dance world during the '90s. Her only foray into rock came in a duet with brother-in-law Joe Henry on 1996's *Sweet Relief II: Gravity of a Situation* benefit album. She gave birth to daughter Lourdes in October 1996; the father was personal trainer Carlos Leon.

Madonna assumed an active role at the increasingly successful Maverick, personally approving every act signed, including the chart-topping Alanis Morissette [see entry]. In 1998 Madonna released the soul-searching *Ray of Light* (#2, 1998), an album produced by William Orbit that explored the new sounds of drum and bass, trip-hop, and other forms of electronic dance music. It spawned the hit singles "Frozen" (#2), "Ray of Light" (#5), and "The Power of Good-Bye" (#11). Madonna then recorded a dance version of Don McLean's "American Pie" (#29, 2000) for the soundtrack of her film *The Next Best Thing*. Her collaboration with Orbit continued on 2000's *Music* (#1, 2000), which also featured production by French dance artist Mirwais Ahmadzai. Singles from *Music* included "Music" (#1, 2000) and "Don't Tell Me" (#4, 2000). She gave birth to a son, Rocco, in 2000, and in 2001 she married Rocco's father, British director Guy Ritchie *(Lock, Stock and Two Smoking Barrels; Snatch)*.

Magazine

Formed 1977, Manchester, Eng.
Howard Devoto, voc.; John McGeoch (b. May 28, 1955, Strathclyde, Scot.), gtr., sax; Dave Formula, kybds.; Barry Adamson (b. June 1, 1958, Manchester), bass; Martin Jackson, drums.
1978—*Real Life* (Virgin) (– Jackson; + John Doyle, drums)
1979—*Secondhand Daylight* (– McGeoch; + Robin Simon, gtr.)

1980—*The Correct Use of Soap; Play* (Live) 1981—*Magic, Murder and the Weather* (I.R.S.) (group disbands) 1982—*After the Fact* 1987—*Rays and Hail, 1978–1981* (Virgin) 1991—*Scree: Rarities 1978–1981* (Blue Plate) 2000—*. . . Magazine (Maybe It's Right to Be Nervous Now)* (Virgin, U.K.).
Howard Devoto solo: 1983—*Jerky Versions of the Dream* (I.R.S.).
Luxuria (Devoto and Noko): 1988—*Unanswerable Lust* (Beggars Banquet) 1990—*Beast Box.*
Visage, formed 1978: Steve Strange (b. Steve Harrington, May 28, 1959, Wales), voc.; Midge Ure (b. James Ure, Oct. 10, 1953, Glasgow, Scot.), gtr.; Billy Currie (b. Apr. 1, 1952), violin; Formula; McGeoch; Adamson; Rusty Egan (b. Sep. 19, 1957), drums.
1980—*Visage* (Polydor) 1982—*The Anvil* 1983—*Fade to Grey—The Singles Collection* 1984—*Beat Boy.*
Barry Adamson solo: 1989—*Moss Side Story* (Mute) 1991—*Delusion* soundtrack 1992—*Soul Murder* 1993—*The Negro Inside Me* EP 1996—*Oedipus Schmoedipus* 1998—*As Above, So Below* 1999—*The Murky World of Barry Adamson.*

Howard Devoto formed Magazine after leaving the seminal Manchester punk band, the Buzzcocks [see entry]. The band first came to prominence with a critically acclaimed British hit single, "Shot by Both Sides," which shared its guitar line with a Buzzcocks tune "Lipstick" (both cowritten by Devoto and Buzzcock Pete Shelley). From there, though, the band's sound became more chilly and ponderous, rounding off its punky edges with Dave Formula's adept art-rockish keyboard hooks and fills. The second album was much smoother than the first, and *Soap* was an extremely polished bid for a wider commercial market, something the band might have actually earned had it not broken up after recording only one more LP. Devoto's solo *Jerky Versions of the Dream* offered up a more idiosyncratic musical outlook; his later project, Luxuria, verged on pretension.

Formula, McGeoch, and Adamson participated in Visage, the definitive new-romantic band formed by vocalist Steve Strange. Although Visage had four U.K. Top 20 hits ("Fade to Grey," "Mind of a Toy," "Damned Don't Cry," and "Night Train"), most of the members had commitments elsewhere. McGeogh went on to play with Siouxsie and the Banshees. Midge Ure and Billy Currie were in Ultravox [see entry]. Adamson joined Nick Cave's Bad Seeds [see entry], but left in 1987 for a solo career that started off with three "faux soundtracks"—modern takes on John Barry and Bernard Herrmann—for movies that exist only in his imagination. Starting with 1998's *As Above, So Below,* Adamson began singing more on his records, as well as using contemporary dance grooves. He also contributed music to the theatrical films *Delusion* (1990), *Gas Food Lodging* (1992) and *Lost Highway* (1997).

Taj Mahal

Born Henry Saint Clair Fredericks, May 17, 1942, New York, NY
1968—*Taj Mahal* (Columbia); *The Natch'l Blues* 1969—*Giant Step/De Ole Folks at Home* 1971—*The Real Thing; Happy Just to Be Like I Am* (Mobile Fidelity) 1972—*Recycling the Blues (and Other Related Stuff)* 1973—*Sounder* (Columbia); *Oooh So Good 'n' Blues* 1974—*Mo' Roots* 1975—*Music Keeps Me Together* 1976—*Satisfied 'n' Tickled Too; Anthology, vol. 1* 1977—*Music Fuh Ya' (Musica Para Tu)* (Warner Bros.); *Brothers* 1978—*Evolution (the Most Recent)* 1979—*Taj Mahal and International Rhythm Band Live* (Crystal Clear) 1980—*Taj Mahal and International Rhythm Band* (Magnet); *Going Home* (Columbia) 1981—*The Best of Taj Mahal; Live* (Magnet) 1987—*Taj* (Gramavision); *Live and Direct* (Laserlight) 1988—*Shake Sugaree* (Music for Little People) 1991—*Mule Bone* (Gramavision); *Like Never Before* (Private); *Don't Call Us* (Atlantic) 1992—*Taj's Blues* (Columbia/Legacy) 1993—*World Music* (Columbia); *Dancing the Blues* (Private) 1994—*Taj Mahal 1980* (Just a Memory) 1995—*Mumatz Mahal* (Waterlily Acoustic) 1996—*Live at Ronnie Scott's* (DRG); *Phantom Blues* (Private) 1997—*Señor Blues* (Private); *Shakin' a Tailfeather* (Rhino) 1998—*Sacred Island* (Private); *In Progress and Motion (1965–1998)* (Columbia/Legacy) 1999—*Kulanjan* (Hannibal); *Blue Light Boogie* (Private) 2000—*Shoutin' in Key* (Hannibal); *Big Blues: Live at Ronnie Scott's* (Castle); *Best of Taj Mahal: The Private Years* (Private).

Taj Mahal began developing his archival interest in the roots of black American and Caribbean music while studying at the University of Massachusetts in the early '60s. His family had moved to Springfield, Massachusetts, from Brooklyn when he was young; although his parents were musical (his father a noted jazz arranger and pianist), young Fredericks first sought a college degree in animal husbandry. At the same time, he became a member of the Pioneer Valley Folklore Society and studied the ethnomusicology of rural black styles.

After receiving his B.A., he played blues in Boston folk clubs before moving to Santa Monica, California, and, in 1965, forming a blues-rock band with Ry Cooder and future Spirit drummer Ed Cassidy called the Rising Sons. They signed with Columbia but broke up before recording. Columbia offered the singer—whose moniker, "Taj Mahal," had appeared to him in a dream—a solo deal, and his debut, introducing guitarist Jesse Ed Davis, was released in early 1967. His early albums, including *Giant Step/De Ole Folks at Home* and *The Real Thing,* were blues records laced with ragtime. On later albums he explored calypso and reggae. Live, he's worked solo, accompanying himself with piano, guitar, bass, and harmonica, and he's also appeared with bigger bands; one featured four tubas, another included steel drums. The Pointer Sisters backed him up on some recordings in their early days.

Mahal penned the music for the 1972 film *Sounder* (in which he had a small acting role); he has since written scores for *Sounder II* and *Brothers,* for television shows, and for 1991's Broadway production of *Mule Bone,* by Langston Hughes and Zora Neale Hurston. In 1974 he played bass with the short-lived Great American Music Band, with David Grisman and violinist Richard Greene. He has continued to record extensively. Among the highlights of his later work are the Grammy-winning *Señor Blues, Sacred Island,* which incorporates Hawaiian influences, and *Kulanjan,* which explores his West African heritage. *Shoutin' in Key* (2000) won the Best Contemporary Blues Grammy.

Mahavishnu Orchestra/John McLaughlin

Formed 1971, New York, NY
Original lineup: John McLaughlin (b. Jan. 4, 1942, Yorkshire, Eng.), gtr.; Rick Laird (b. Feb. 5, 1941, Dublin, Ire.), bass; Jerry Goodman, violin; Billy Cobham (b. May 16, 1944, Panama), drums; Jan Hammer (b. Apr. 17, 1948, Prague, Czech.), kybds.
1971—*The Inner Mounting Flame* (Columbia) 1972—*Birds of Fire* 1973—*Between Nothingness and Eternity* 1974—(– Laird; – Goodman; – Cobham; – Hammer; + Jean-Luc Ponty [b. Sep. 29, 1942, Avranches, Fr.], violin; Gayle Moran, kybds., voc.; Ralphe Armstrong, bass; Narada Michael Walden [b. Apr. 23, 1952, Kalamazoo, MI], drums) *Apocalypse* 1975—*Visions of the Emerald Beyond* (– Moran; – Ponty; + Stu Goldberg, kybds.) 1976—*Inner Worlds; In Retrospect* (Polydor) 1980—*Best of the Mahavishnu Orchestra* 1984—(– Armstrong; – Walden; + Bill Evans, sax; Jonas Hellborg [b. ca. 1958, Swe.], bass; + Cobham, drums; Danny Gottlieb [b. Apr. 18, 1953, New York], perc.; Mitch Forman, kybds.) *Mahavishnu* (Warner Bros.) 1987—(– Forman; – Cobham; + Jim Beard, kybds.) *Adventures in Radioland* (Verve) 1999—*The Lost Trident Sessions* (Columbia).
John McLaughlin solo: 1969—*Extrapolation* (Polydor) 1970—*Devotion* (Douglas) 1971—*My Goal's Beyond* 1972—*Love, Devotion and Surrender* (with Carlos Santana) (Columbia) 1978—*Johnny McLaughlin, Electric Guitarist* 1979—*Electric Dreams* (with One Truth Band) 1980—*The Best of John McLaughlin* 1981—*Friday Night in San Francisco* (with Al DiMeola and Paco De Lucia); *Belo Horizonte* (Warner Bros.) 1983—*Passion, Grace and Fire* (with DiMeola, De Lucia) (Columbia); *Music Spoken Here* (Warner) 1990—*Mediterranean Concerto* (ECM); *Live at the Royal Festival Hall* (Uni/Verve) 1991—*The Best of McLaughlin* (Columbia) 1992—*Que Alegria* (Verve) 1993—*Time Remembered: Plays Bill Evans; Free Spirits Featuring John McLaughlin: Tokyo Live* 1995—*After the Rain* (with Free Spirits); *The Promise* 1996—*This Is Jazz, vol. 17* (Sony) 1997—*The Heart of Things* (Verve) 2000—*Live in Paris* (with the Heart of Things).
Shakti: 1976—*Shakti With John McLaughlin* (Columbia) 1977—*A Handful of Beauty; Natural Elements; The Best of Shakti* (Moment) 1999—*Remember Shakti* (Verve).

The original Mahavishnu Orchestra was the apotheosis of the career of guitar virtuoso John McLaughlin. Prior to its formation in 1971, McLaughlin made his name in England with numerous local blues bands, notably the groups of Graham Bond and Brian Auger. He moved to America in the late '60s and became a guitarist in demand, recording six albums between 1969 and 1971, split between the early jazz-rock fusions of Miles Davis and Tony Williams' Lifetime.

In the meantime, having recorded *Extrapolation* with jazz musicians in England, McLaughlin cut his second solo LP, *Devotion,* with Jimi Hendrix's Band of Gypsies rhythm section: drummer Buddy Miles and bassist Billy Cox and Lifetime organist Larry Young. McLaughlin recruited rock studio drummer Billy Cobham (who had played with the progressive, horn-laden band Dreams and with Davis) and violinist Jerry Goodman (a veteran of the classical-influenced Flock) for his third solo album, 1971's *My Goal's Beyond,* which also featured an Indian tabla player, Badal Roy. Next he founded the Mahavishnu Orchestra by adding European jazz-oriented players Rick Laird (onetime bassist with Buddy Rich) and keyboardist Jan Hammer (who had played with Elvin Jones and Sarah Vaughan). Mahavishnu was a name given McLaughlin by his guru, Sri Chinmoy, and for a time the guitarist billed himself as Mahavishnu John McLaughlin.

To Miles Davis' fusion of jazz and rock, McLaughlin added his own synthesis of East and West, mixing the stop-and-start melodies and rhythms of Indian ragas with the force of rock and the improvisational options of jazz. The Mahavishnu Orchestra was an immediate sensation, opening a whole new era of jazz-rock fusion, although even those players who could match McLaughlin's speed couldn't approach his lyricism. The Mahavishnu Orchestra's second album, *Birds of Fire* (#15, 1973), hit the Top 20. But conflicts within the group—especially over composer credit, most of which was claimed by McLaughlin—broke up the first Mahavishnu Orchestra after its third album, a live recording.

McLaughlin recorded *Love, Devotion and Surrender* (#14, 1973) with fellow Sri Chinmoy disciple Carlos Santana, and retained the Mahavishnu Orchestra name for a variety of groups, including one with drummer Narada Michael Walden (later a successful R&B producer and songwriter) and keyboardist Gayle Moran (later of Return to Forever). *Apocalypse* (#43, 1974) involved the London Symphony Orchestra and former Beatles producer George Martin. None of the later Mahavishnu Orchestras got the same commercial and critical response as the first one.

In 1976 McLaughlin, no longer affiliated with Sri Chinmoy, gave up both the name Mahavishnu and the group name Mahavishnu Orchestra. He formed an acoustic group, Shakti, with whom he recorded three albums even closer in style to Indian ragas than the Orchestra had been. After a collaboration with ex–Return to Forever guitarist Al DiMeola, he formed a new electric group, the One Truth Band, with whom he recorded and toured. McLaughlin then moved from New York to Paris and has continued to record with European musicians.

The other original Orchestra members have continued to record and perform. Laird played around New York with numerous jazz and rock groups before devoting himself to photography; after a 1974 collaboration with Hammer, *Like Children,* Goodman apparently dropped out of the music business, resurfacing in the late '80s as a New Age artist. Hammer has recorded frequently on his own, with Jeff Beck, and in 1982 with Journey's Neal Schon; he has his own Red Gate Studio. Hammer's "Miami Vice Theme" was a major hit single (#1, 1985). And Cobham has recorded and performed with a new jazz-rock band nearly every year, also touring with Grateful Dead guitarist Bob Weir's Bobby and the Midnites.

From 1984 to 1986 McLaughlin re-formed the Mahavishnu Orchestra with an entirely different lineup, including drummer Danny Gottlieb, keyboardist Mitch Forman, and saxophonist Bill Evans, who had previously worked with Miles Davis.

Although never entirely forsaking electric music, McLaughlin tended thereafter to concentrate on the acoustic guitar. During the late '80s he occasionally toured as a duo with virtuoso bassist Jonas Hellborg, and then formed a trio with percussionist Trilok Gurtu and bassist Kai Eckhardt. McLaughlin also performed orchestral works *(Mediterranean Concerto)* and appeared on the soundtrack of the 1986 jazz film *Round Midnight.*

McLaughlin performed with Miles Davis as part of a 1991 Davis career retrospective that took place just months prior to the trumpeter's death (McLaughlin had earlier guested on Davis' *You're Under Arrest* and *Aura*). In 1993 McLaughlin collaborated with a European classical guitar quintet to produce a tribute to the late jazz pianist and composer Bill Evans, an important influence for McLaughlin. The next year McLaughlin—back on electric guitar—teamed up with organist Joey DeFrancesco and drummer Dennis Chambers to form the Free Spirits. Among his other projects in the '90s were a collaboration with Free Spirits and legendary jazz drummer Elvin Jones, the forming of a new ensemble, the Heart of Things, and a revival of Shakti. In 2000, rediscovered music by the original Mahavishnu Orchestra was released.

Mahogany Rush/Frank Marino and Mahogany Rush

Formed 1971, Montreal, Can.
Original lineup: Frank Marino (b. Francesco Antonio Marino, Nov. 20, 1954, Montreal), gtr., voc.; Paul Harwood (b. Feb. 30, 1953, Montreal), bass; Jimmy Ayoub (b. Dec. 7, 1941, Honolulu, HI), drums.
1971—*Maxoom* (Kot'ai) 1973—*Child of the Novelty* (20th Century–Fox) 1975—*Strange Universe* 1976—*Mahogany Rush IV* (Columbia) 1977—*World Anthem* 1978—*Mahogany Rush Live* 1979—*Tales of the Unexpected* 1980—(+ Vince Marino, gtr.) *What's Next* 1982—(– Ayoub; + Timm Biery, drums) 1986—(– Harwood; + Peter Dowse, bass) 1987—*Full Circle* (Maze) 1989—*Frank Marino and Mahogany Rush: Double Live* 1990—*From the Hip* (Vision) (– V. Marino) 1991—(– Biery; + Dave Goode, drums) 1996—*Dragonfly: The Best of Frank Marino and Mahogany Rush* (Razor & Tie) 2000—(+ Mick Layne, gtr., kybds.) *Eye of the Storm* (Justin Time).

The long-running supernatural explanation of how guitarist Frank Marino came by his flashy, effects-laden playing style entered into rock legend because it was patently absurd. Today it ranks as an untruth that refuses to die, despite Marino's many vehement denials. For the record, then, here's the gist of the old story. Allegedly, a teenage Marino was in a Montreal hospital recovering from illness, drug overdose, or an auto accident when he lapsed into a deep coma. Upon awakening several days later, Marino claimed he'd been visited by the spirit of Jimi Hendrix. Although a nonmusician (some sources say he could play drums and guitar), Marino picked up the guitar and began playing a lot like Jerry Garcia and Hendrix. In recent years, Marino has disavowed the story altogether.

Whatever happened, Marino, then just 17, found a bassist and drummer, and Mahogany Rush was born. The recorded evidence of *Maxoom* (rereleased in the mid-'70s by 20th Century–Fox) shows a competent heavy-metal guitarist with an intense Hendrix fetish. Marino slowed the pace a bit for *Novelty,* which concentrated more on actual songs, and has since diversified his guitar style a bit in a jazz-rock fusion direction. By the late '70s, the band was billed as Frank Marino and Mahogany Rush. For years, Marino endured critical barbs and moderate records sales (though 1983's "Strange Dreams" got some AOR airplay) at best. Through the '80s, however, he continued to tour and record intermittently for small labels, all the while building a cult among the burgeoning metal contingent. In 2000 he resurfaced and returned to performing after an eight-year hiatus. Die-hard fans hailed *Eye of the Storm* as a return to form. Founding Mahogany Rush bassist Paul Harwood went on to play the blues in Big Bat and the Amazing Bluestones.

The Main Ingredient

Formed 1964, New York, NY
Enrique Antonio "Tony" Silvester (b. Oct. 7, 1941, Colon, Panama), voc.; Luther Simmons Jr. (b. Sep. 9, 1942, New York), voc.; Don McPherson (b. July 9, 1941, Indianapolis, IN; d. July 4, 1971), voc.
mid-'60s—(+ Cuba Gooding [b. Apr. 27, 1944, New York], voc.) ca. 1965—(– Gooding) 1970—*The Main Ingredient L.T.D.* (RCA) 1971—(– McPherson; + Gooding) *Tasteful Soul; Black Seeds* 1972—*Bitter Sweet* (RCA) 1973—*Afrodisiac; Greatest Hits* (+ Carl Tompkins [b. Petersburg, VA], voc.; – Silvester) 1974—*Euphrates River* 1975—*Rolling Down a Mountainside* 1976—*Spinning Around; Shame on the World* (group disbands) 1977—*Music Maximus* (group re-forms: Silvester; Simmons; Gooding) 1980—*Ready for Love* 1981—*I Only Have Eyes for You* 1986—(– Simmons; + Jerome Jackson, voc.) 1996—*A Quiet Storm* (RCA) 2000—(lineup: Gooding; + George Staley Sr., voc.; + Larry Moore, voc.).
Cuba Gooding solo: 1978—*The First Cuba Gooding Album* (Motown) 1979—*Love Dancer.*

In 1971 the Main Ingredient was a smooth black vocal trio on the rise. After years of struggle, it had placed three singles in a row on the R&B chart—"You've Been My Inspiration" (#25, 1970), "I'm So Proud" (#13, 1970), and "Spinning Around" (#7, 1971)—when lead singer Don McPherson died of leukemia. With his replacement, Cuba Gooding (who had been in the group in the '60s but quit to attend college), the group went on to its greatest success.

McPherson, Luther Simmons Jr., Gooding, and Tony Silvester formed the Poets in the early '60s and were signed to Mike Stoller and Jerry Leiber's Red Bird label in 1965. Their one chart record for that label was "Merry Christmas Baby." In 1967 they left Red Bird for RCA, renaming themselves the Insiders. But their luck did not improve until they changed their name again. "You've Been My Inspiration" followed soon after.

After McPherson's death, the Main Ingredient moved toward pop. "Black Seed Keep on Growing" was another soul hit, reaching #15 in 1971, after which the trio finally had its first pop hit, "Everybody Plays the Fool" (#3 pop, #2 R&B, 1972). (In 1993 the song was covered by Aaron Neville.) More pop hits followed in 1974—"Just Don't Want to Be Lonely" (#10 pop, #8 R&B) and "Happiness Is Just Around the Bend" (#35 pop, #7 R&B)—as well as four more Top 40 R&B records before the Main Ingredient broke up in 1976: "You've Got to Take It" (#18) and "You Can Call Me Rover" (#34) in 1973, and "Rolling Down a Mountainside" (#7) and "Shame on the World" (#20) in 1975. Gooding's brief solo career proved disappointing. Silvester, however, became a successful producer of artists including Sister Sledge, Ben E. King, and Bette Midler. Simmons became a stockbroker. In 1980 a reunion as the Main Ingredient featuring Cuba Gooding yielded the R&B chart single "Think Positive" (#69). In 1986 "Do Me Right" also peaked at #69 R&B. The trio continues to perform, with Gooding as the sole holdover from the old days. His son, Cuba Gooding Jr., became a successful actor whose credits include *Boyz N the Hood, Pearl Harbor,* and an Oscar-winning role in *Jerry Maguire.*

Malo

Formed 1971, San Francisco, CA
Original lineup: Jorge Santana (b. June 13, 1954, Jalisco, Mex.), gtr.; Arcelio Garcia Jr. (b. May 7, 1946, Manati, P.R.), voc., perc.; Abel Zarate (b. Dec. 2, 1952, Manila, Philippines), gtr., voc.; Roy Murray, trumpet, trombone, flute, sax; Pablo Tellez (b. July 2, 1951, Granada, Nicaragua), bass; Rich Spremich (b. July 2, 1951, San Francisco), drums; Richard Kermode (b. Oct. 5, 1946, Lovell, WY), kybds.; Luis Gasca (b. Mar. 23, 1940, Houston, TX), trumpet, fluegelhorn.
1972—*Malo* (Warner Bros.); *Dos* 1973—*Evolution* 1974—*Ascension* (group disbands) 1981—(group re-forms: Garcia; + numerous others) 1991—*The Best of Malo* (GNP Crescendo) 1995—*Señorita.*

Like Carlos Santana, brother Jorge formed his own Latin-rock band, Malo (Spanish for "bad"). Reinforcing the Santana connection, two of Carlos' percussionists, Coke Escovedo and Victor Pontoja, guested on Malo's debut LP, which spent a number of weeks in the Top 15 and yielded the band's one hit, "Suavecito" (#18, 1972).

Many of Malo's members were veterans of the San Francisco scene, either with rock bands or with Latin bands from the Mission District. Richard Kermode and Luis Gasca had played together in Janis Joplin's Kozmic Blues Band; Gasca's jazz credentials include stints with Count Basie, Woody Herman, and Mongo Santamaria. *Dos* and *Evolution* both had minor success on the album chart; *Ascension* fared worse, and the band broke up. Gasca has recorded pop-jazz albums for Fantasy Records. Singer Arcelio Garcia fronted several new versions of Malo in the '80s and '90s.

The Mamas and the Papas

Formed 1965, New York, NY
John Phillips (b. Aug. 30, 1935, Parris Island, SC; d. Mar. 18, 2001, Los Angeles, CA), voc., gtr.; Dennis Doherty (b. Nov. 29, 1941, Halifax, Nova Scotia, Can.), voc.; Michelle Phillips (b. Holly Michelle Gilliam, Apr. 6, 1944, Long Beach, CA), voc.; Cass Elliot (b. Sep. 19, 1943, Baltimore, MD; d. July 29, 1974, London, Eng.), voc.
1966—*If You Can Believe Your Eyes and Ears* (Dunhill); *The Mamas and the Papas* 1967—*Deliver* 1968—*Farewell to the First Golden Era; The Papas and the Mamas* (group disbands) 1969—*16 of Their Greatest Hits* 1971—(group re-forms) *People Like Us* (group disbands) 1973—*Golden Hits* 1981—(group re-forms: J. Phillips; Doherty; + Mackenzie Phillips, voc.; + Elaine "Spanky" McFarlane [b. June 19, 1942, Peoria, IL], voc.; Doherty carries on with various lineups) 1998—*Greatest Hits* (MCA).

Although the Mamas and the Papas made their commercial impact with airy California folk pop and were on the scene as L.A. went psychedelic, they were a product of the Greenwich Village folk community. John Phillips had been active in New York since 1957; he had previously attended George Washington University and, for three months, the U.S. Naval Academy. In 1962 he met and married Holly Michelle Gilliam, who had come to New York to be a model; she began singing with his group, the Journeymen.

Denny Doherty had been a member of the Halifax Three, which, after two albums for Epic, included future Lovin' Spoonful member Zal Yanovsky. Doherty and Zanovsky joined Cass Elliot and her first husband, Jim Hendricks, to form Cass Elliot and the Big Three. The group changed its name to the Mugwumps and went electric, with Art Stokes on drums and John Sebastian on harmonica. The Mugwumps recorded one album—not released until 1967—and broke up. Sebastian and Yanovsky formed the Lovin' Spoonful; Elliot fronted a jazz trio; and Doherty joined John and Michelle Phillips as the New Journeymen.

To rehearse, the New Journeymen went to St. Thomas in the Virgin Islands; Elliot joined them and worked on the island as a waitress, then moved to California with her husband. The New Journeymen relocated to California, where they stayed with Elliot and Hendricks, and Elliot officially joined the group. They recorded backing vocals for a Barry McGuire record, then got their own contract as the Mamas and the Papas.

In 1966 and 1967 they had six Top 5 hits—"California

The Mamas and the Papas: John Phillips, Cass Elliott, Denny Doherty, Michelle Phillips

Dreamin' " (#4), "Monday, Monday" (#1), "I Saw Her Again" (#5), "Words of Love" (#5), "Dedicated to the One I Love" (#2), and the autobiographical "Creeque Alley" (#5, 1967)—and four gold albums. John Phillips also wrote a signature song of the flower-power era, "San Francisco (Be Sure to Wear Flowers in Your Hair)" (#4, 1967), which was recorded by Scott McKenzie, an ex-Journeyman. The quartet also appeared at the 1967 Monterey Pop Festival, which John Phillips helped finance.

By 1968, though, the group was falling apart and decided to disband. John and Michelle Phillips had marriage problems; John made a solo LP, *The Wolf King of L.A.*, and then coproduced (with Lou Adler) Robert Altman's 1970 film *Brewster McCloud*. Michelle Phillips appeared in *The Last Movie* with Dennis Hopper, to whom she was later married for eight days. John and Michelle Phillips divorced in 1970. But the band had other, legal problems. Dunhill and group members sued each other for breach of contract (excluding Elliot, who continued to record for the label on her own) and for fraudulent withholding of royalties, respectively. In 1971 the group made what it later admitted was a poor reunion album, *People Like Us*. Cass Elliot continued her solo career until her death from a heart attack in 1974.

Doherty recorded two solo albums but with little success. Michelle Phillips' acting career began to pick up with films like *Dillinger* and Ken Russell's 1976 movie bio of Rudolph Valentino, in which she costarred with Rudolf Nureyev. In 1977 she recorded a solo LP for A&M, *Victim of Romance*. She found greater fame on TV, as a cast member of the popular evening soap *Knots Landing*.

John Phillips had become idle by the mid-'70s, reportedly living off his $100,000-a-year royalties from songs like "California Dreamin'." By 1975 he had stopped work altogether. He was arrested by federal narcotics agents on July 31, 1980. Phillips' eight-year, $15,000-fine sentence was reduced to 30 days. Phillips cleaned up, as did his daughter, actress Mackenzie Phillips *(One Day at a Time)*. The two appeared on numerous television programs and lectured around the country. The pair also decided to revive the Mamas and the Papas. John Phillips contacted Doherty (who by then was hosting a popular television show in Nova Scotia) and filled out the new foursome with Elaine "Spanky" McFarlane, from Spanky and Our Gang [see entry]. John Phillips, who cowrote the Beach Boys' 1988 #1 smash "Kokomo," is also the father of singer Chynna Phillips, formerly of Wilson Phillips. By the mid-'90s Doherty was the sole remnant of the original group.

In 2000, two years after the Mamas and the Papas were inducted into the Rock and Roll Hall of Fame, various newspapers reported that Fox had secured the rights to create a feature film about the '60s quartet. In 2001 Phillips completed recording a solo album, *Phillips 66;* two days later he entered the hospital, where he died of heart failure on March 18.

Melissa Manchester

Born Feb. 15, 1951, Bronx, NY
1973—*Home to Myself* (Bell); *Bright Eyes* 1975—*Melissa* (Arista) 1976—*Help Is on the Way; Better Days and Happy Endings* 1977—*Singin'...* 1978—*Don't Cry Out Loud* 1979—*Melissa Manchester* 1980—*For the Working Girl* 1982—*Hey Ricky* 1983—*Greatest Hits; Emergency* 1985—*Mathematics* (MCA) 1989—*Tribute* (Mika) 1995—*If My Heart Had Wings* (Atlantic); *Melissa Manchester Performs Pocahontas* (Dove Audio) 1997—*The Essence of Melissa Manchester* (Arista) 1998—*Joy* (Angel).

Melissa Manchester is a singer and sometime songwriter in the Peter Allen/Carole Bayer Sager/Barry Manilow MOR axis. A member of a musical family (her father was a bassoonist with the Metropolitan Opera), she began singing jingles at age 15. She attended the High School of Performing Arts in the late '60s while working as a staff writer at Chappell Music. Upon graduation she entered New York University and enrolled in a songwriting seminar taught by Paul Simon. She then played clubs in Manhattan, where she was discovered by Bette Midler and her accompanist, Barry Manilow. They hired her as a backup singer (Harlette) in 1971.

Six months later Manchester got a record contract of her own. Her 1973 debut, *Home to Myself*, featured many songs cowritten by Carole Bayer Sager. In 1975 her third LP, *Melissa*, yielded her first hit, "Midnight Blue." She didn't have a really big followup until her version of Peter Allen/Carole

Bayer Sager's song "Don't Cry Out Loud," which went to #10 in 1979. She cowrote Kenny Loggins' smash duet with Stevie Nicks, "Whenever I Call You 'Friend.' "

In 1980 Manchester became the first performer to have recorded two of the movie themes nominated for an Academy Award, "Ice Castles" and "The Promise." In 1982 she had her biggest hit with "You Should Hear How She Talks About You" (#5) from *Hey Ricky,* which netted her the Grammy for Best Female Vocal Performance. Through the '80s Manchester recorded sporadically. Her *Tribute* is a collection of standards, such as "Over the Rainbow" and "La Vie en Rose." She has branched into acting, appearing in Bette Midler's film *For the Boys* and portraying the title character's mother in the television series *Blossom.* Her recent recordings consist primarily of holiday music. In the late '90s she joined Peabo Bryson and Roberta Flack on the *Colors of Christmas* album and subsequent tour. She also starred in the touring revue *Andrew Lloyd Webber—Music of the Night.*

Mandrill

Formed 1968, New York, NY
Original lineup: Lou Wilson (b. Panama), trumpet, congas, voc.; Ric Wilson (b. Panama), sax, voc.; Carlos Wilson (b. Panama), trombone, flute, gtr., perc., voc.; Omar Mesa (b. Havana, Cuba), gtr., voc.; Bundie Cenac (b. St. Lucia), bass, voc.; Claude Cave, kybds., vibraphone, voc.; Charlie Padro, drums, voc.
1971—*Mandrill* (Polydor) (– Cenac; + Fudgie Kae, bass) 1972—*Mandrill Is* (– Padro; + Neftali Santiago, drums) 1973—*Composite Truth; Just Outside of Town* (– Mesa; + Doug Rodrigues, gtr.) 1974—*Mandrilland* 1975—*Best of Mandrill* (– Kae; + Brian Allsop, bass, voc.; – Santiago; + Andre Locke [b. Brooklyn, NY], drums, voc.; – Rodrigues; + Tommy Trujillo, gtr., voc.) *Solid* (United Artists) (+ Wilfredo Wilson [b. Panama], voc., perc., bass) *Beast From the East* 1977— (– Locke; + Santiago; – Allsop; – Trujillo; + Juaquin Jessup, gtr., perc., voc.) *We Are One* (Arista) 1978—(– Santiago; Jessup; + David Conley [b. Dec. 27, 1953, Newark, NJ], bass) *New Worlds* 1980—*Getting in the Mood* 1988—*The Best of Mandrill* (Polydor).

Emerging from the tough Bedford-Stuyvesant area of Brooklyn, Mandrill played a mixed urban brew encompassing elements of Santana-tinged Latin rock, Chambers Brothers–style soul, and horn-driven rock. The band was founded by the Wilson brothers, all of whom spent their childhoods in Panama. After attending college for various amounts of time (Ric got a medical degree from Harvard), Ric, Lou, and Carlos began jamming together with other musicians, eventually settling on a seven-member lineup. Their debut LP became a big breakout on rock FM radio as well as black stations, aided by the eponymous title song, selling 150,000 copies in the New York area alone. The band's biggest hits were on the soul chart, peaking with 1973's "Fencewalk" at #19. Also that year, Mandrill played with Duke Ellington at the Newport Jazz Festival. Altogether, Mandrill recorded five albums for Polydor, but in January 1975 the group switched to United Artists, moved to L.A., and went through some major personnel changes, all the while retaining the three Wilsons and original member Cave.

For *Beast From the East,* the youngest and fourth Wilson brother, Wilfredo, joined the fold as singer/percussionist. The band did well on concert tours but still didn't break big, and in 1977 it switched to Arista after contributing to the soundtrack of Muhammad Ali's film biography, *The Greatest.* Mandrill's biggest hit was "Too Late" (#37 R&B, 1978). The group continues to perform in New York.

Chuck Mangione

Born Nov. 29, 1940, Rochester, NY
1960—*The Jazz Brothers* (Milestone) 1961—*Hey Baby!* (Original Jazz); *Spring Fever* 1962—*Recuerdo* (Jazzland) 1970—*Friends and Love . . . A Chuck Mangione Concert* (Mercury) 1971—*Together* 1972—*The Chuck Mangione Quartet; Alive!* 1973—*Land of Make Believe* 1975—*Chase the Clouds Away* (A&M) 1976— *Bellavia; Main Squeeze* 1977—*Feels So Good* 1978—*An Evening of Magic: Chuck Mangione Live at the Hollywood Bowl; Children of Sanchez; The Best of Chuck Mangione* (Mercury) 1979—*Fun and Games* (A&M) 1980—*Tarantella* 1982—*Love Notes* (Columbia); *Classics of Modern Jazz, vol. 6* (A&M) 1983—*Journey to a Rainbow* (Columbia) 1984—*Disguise* 1986—*Save Tonight for Me* 1987—*Live at the Village Gate* (Feels So Good); *The Best of Chuck Mangione* 1988—*Eyes of the Veiled Temptress* (Columbia) 1991—*Encore: Mangione Concerts* (Mercury) 1992—*Compact Jazz: Chuck Mangione* (Verve) 1995—*Live at the Village Gate, vol. 2* (Pro Arte) 1996—*Greatest Hits* (Feels So Good); *Boys From Rochester* 1999—*The Feeling's Back* (Chesky) 2000—*Everything for Love.*

By selling a million copies of his instrumental "Feels So Good" in 1978, flügelhornist Chuck Mangione established himself as a pop-jazz star. While never recapturing commercially that late-'70s peak, he can be seen as a precursor of such later purveyors of soothing sounds as Kenny G and John Tesh.

Mangione grew up in a musical family, and big-jazz names passing through Rochester were entertained and fed in the Mangione household. He took up piano at age eight, trumpet two years later. In 1960, with his brother Gap on piano, he formed the Jazz Brothers quintet. After they disbanded in 1965, he performed with Art Blakey and the Jazz Messengers and in trumpeter Maynard Ferguson's band.

Recording on his own, Mangione moved away from jazz's complexities to write and arrange instrumentals for a small group, often backed by strings or full orchestra. He recorded the *Friends and Love* double album with the Rochester Philharmonic. He won his first Grammy (Best Instrumental Composition, 1976) for "Bellavia."

Feels So Good went gold in February 1978; by April of that year it was platinum, and eventually sold more than 2 million copies. "Chase the Clouds Away" was played as background music by ABC-TV during telecasts of the 1976

Olympics. In 1980 Mangione was commissioned by ABC Sports to write music for the Winter Olympics (which made up *Fun and Games*), and his Olympic music won an Emmy that year for Music Composition/Direction. Mangione won another Grammy (Best Pop Instrumental Performance, 1978) for *Children of Sanchez,* a score for a film based on the Oscar Lewis book. In December 1980, Mangione held a massive benefit concert in his hometown for victims of a recent earthquake in Italy; Dizzy Gillespie, Chick Corea, and Steve Gadd were among those present.

Switching to CBS in 1982, Mangione began working with such outside producers as Eumir Deodato and Thom Bell in the mid-'80s. His albums, beginning to employ synthesizers but otherwise still featuring melodic pop jazz, continued to sell respectably, and he toured often, occasionally appearing in concert with symphony orchestras. In the late '80s he reunited with the Jazz Brothers for an American tour.

At the end of the decade, Mangione took an extended, three-year hiatus from music before setting out on the road again with most of the original musicians from the *Feels So Good* album. In the late '90s he began doing voice-over acting in the Fox television series *King of the Hill,* playing himself as a character.

The Manhattans

Formed 1961, Jersey City, NJ
George "Smitty" Smith (d. 1971), lead voc.; Winfred "Blue" Lovett (b. Nov. 16, 1943, NJ), bass voc.; Edward "Sonny" Bivins (b. Jan. 15, 1942, NJ), tenor voc.; Kenneth Kelley (b. Jan. 9, 1943, NJ), second tenor voc.; Richard Taylor (d. Dec. 7, 1987), baritone voc.
1966—*Dedicated* (Carnival) 1967—*For You and Yours* 1968—*With These Hands* (King/Deluxe) 1969—*Million to One* 1970—(+ Gerald Alston [b. Nov. 8, 1942], tenor voc.) 1971—(– Smith) 1972—*There's No Me Without You* (Columbia) 1974—*That's How Much I Love You* 1976—*The Manhattans* 1977—*It Feels So Good* (– Taylor) 1978—*There's No Good in Goodbye* 1979—*Love Talk* 1980—*After Midnight* 1981—*Black Tie; Follow Your Heart* (Solid Smoke) 1983—*Forever by Your Side* (Columbia) 1985—*Too Hot to Stop It* 1986—*Back to Basics* 1988—(– Alston; + Roger Harris) 1989—*Sweet Talk* (Vally Vue) (group disbands) 1993—(group re-forms: Alston; Lovett; + Troy May, voc.; + David Tyson, voc.) 1995—*The Best of the Manhattans—Kiss and Say Goodnight* (Columbia/Legacy).

Steadfast practitioners of a suave, soul-ballad harmony style rooted in doo-wop, anchored by the recitations of "Blue" Lovett, the Manhattans have never maintained mass popularity despite a long string of hits.

Winfred Lovett and Kenneth Kelley had sung in rival Jersey City doo-wop groups; Richard Taylor met Edward Bivins during an air force hitch in Germany in the late '50s. Returning to the New York area, Taylor and Bivins united with Lovett, Kelley, and Smith to form Ronnie and the Manhattans, who recorded several unsuccessful singles, one for Bobby Robinson's Enjoy Records. The Manhattans finally got their break when Barbara Brown, a singer with Joe Evans' Newark-based Carnival Records, retired from recording; she recommended the Manhattans to Evans, who caught them at Harlem's Apollo Theatre and signed them.

After several unsuccessful singles, the group hit big in 1965 with Lovett's tune "I Wanna Be (Your Everything)," which sold 500,000 copies and made the R&B Top 20. (Bivins and Taylor also wrote songs for the group.) In the next two years the Manhattans followed with a string of transitional doo-wop/soul hits like "Searchin' for My Baby," "Follow Your Heart," "Baby I Need You," and "Can I," all of which made the R&B Top 30. In 1968 the group signed with King subsidiary Deluxe, for which it had only minor successes like "If My Heart Could Speak" and "From Atlanta to Goodbye."

In 1971 the group was dealt a seemingly crushing blow when Smith died of spinal meningitis. However, a replacement, Gerald Alston, was discovered in North Carolina, and with a signing to Columbia in 1972, the Manhattans continued to release romantic soul hits. Among those that made the R&B Top 10 were "There's No Me Without You" (1973), "Don't Take Your Love From Me" (1974), "Hurt" (1975), the R&B and pop #1 "Kiss and Say Goodbye" (1976), "I Kinda Miss You" (1976), "It Feels So Good (to Be Loved So Bad)" (1977), "Am I Losing You" (the only one that did not enter the pop chart, 1978), and "Shining Star" (#5 pop, #4 R&B, 1980). By then the Manhattans had been together nearly 20 years. Taylor left in 1977 to pursue his religious interests; he converted to Islam. Alston enjoyed a solo career but returned to the group for its 1993 reunion to commemorate its 30th anniversary.

Bivins leads a latter-day lineup that still records and performs. Regina Belle, who has since gone on to a successful solo career, briefly sang with the group in the mid-'80s.

The Manhattan Transfer

Formed 1969, New York, NY
Tim Hauser (b. Dec. 12, 1941, Troy, NY), voc., gtr., banjo; Pat Rosalia, tambourine, voc.; Erin Dickens, gtr., tambourine, voc.; Gene Pistilli, gtr., voc.; Marty Nelson, gtr., clarinet, piano.
Sometime after 1969—(– Rosalia; – Dickens; – Nelson; – Pistilli) 1972—(+ Alan Paul [b. Nov. 23, 1949, Newark, NJ), voc.; + Janis Siegel [b. July 23, 1952, Brooklyn, NY], voc.; + Laurel Massé [b. ca. 1954], voc.) 1975—*Jukin'* (Capitol, recorded before 1972 with original lineup); *The Manhattan Transfer* (Atlantic) 1976—*Coming Out* 1978—*Pastiche; Live* 1979—(– Massé; + Cheryl Bentyne [b. Jan. 17, 1954, Mount Vernon, WA], voc.) 1980—*Extensions* 1981—*Mecca for Moderns; The Best of the Manhattan Transfer* 1983—*Bodies and Souls* 1984—*Bop Doo-Wopp* 1985—*Vocalese* 1987—*Live; Brasil* 1991—*The Off-Beat of Avenues* (Columbia) 1992—*The Christmas Album; Anthology* (Rhino) 1994—*The Manhattan Transfer Meets Tubby the Tuba* (Summit) 1995—*Tonin'* (Atlantic) 1997—*Swing* 2000—*The Spirit of St. Louis.*
Janis Siegel solo: 1982—*Experiment in White* (Atlantic)

1987—*At Home* 1989—*Short Stories* (with Fred Hersch) 1995—*Slow Hot Wind* (with Fred Hersch) (Varèse Sarabande) 1999—*The Tender Trap* (Monarch).

The Manhattan Transfer is a four-part vocal harmony group that began as a nostalgia act and has since recorded and performed in an array of styles including swing, doo-wop, jazz scat, Latin, and pop. Unlike many pop groups, however, Manhattan Transfer's eclectic approach has served it well: The group has won 10 Grammy Awards, is a perennial winner of annual jazz polls, and is a strong concert draw around the world.

Manhattan Transfer first formed in 1969 as a Jim Kweskin Jug Band–style good-time group and signed to Capitol. It took its name from a novel by John Dos Passos about New York in the '20s. The quartet soon broke up, though, and the only remaining member was Tim Hauser. (Also in that early incarnation was Gene Pistilli, who had written "Sunday Will Never Be the Same" with Terry Cashman for Spanky and Our Gang.)

The new Manhattan Transfer formed in 1972 and soon became popular on New York's cabaret circuit. Hauser had sung in doo-wop groups as a youth, around 1958 with the Criterions in high school and later with the Viscounts, who had a hit with "Harlem Nocturne." Later he played in a folk band with Jim Croce. Alan Paul was a child actor who had appeared in road companies of *Oliver* and *Grease*, in movies *(The Pawnbroker)* and TV commercials. Janis Siegel had recorded with the Young Generation, a group produced by Leiber and Stoller and at one time groomed to be the next Shangri-Las, and in a folk group called Laurel Canyon. With fourth member Laurel Massé they released their Atlantic debut in 1975 (containing "Operator," a #22 hit) and immediately got a summer network-TV replacement series, which lasted three weeks in August. But even with the nostalgia trend of the time, the band didn't sell in this country, though it had a #1 hit in England and France with "Chanson d'Amour."

In 1979, after being injured in an automobile accident, Massé left and was replaced by Cheryl Bentyne, daughter of a swing musician. The band had begun to modernize its look—shifting from tuxedos to a new-wave/Deco combination—and broadened its audience with the release of *Extensions*, from which "Twilight Zone/Twilight Tones" became a modest hit (#30, 1980). That album also included the group's version of "Birdland," for which it was awarded its first Grammy. In mid-1981 the Manhattan Transfer had a Top 10 hit with a remake of the old Ad Libs song "Boy From New York City." That song won a Grammy for Best Pop Vocal Performance by a Duo or Group With Vocal, while "Until I Met You (Corner Pocket)" from the same album got the Grammy for Best Jazz Performance, Duo or Group. The following year, Manhattan Transfer's version of "Route 66" won another Grammy, and the year after that, "Why Not!" continued the streak. In late 1983 "Spice of Life," from *Bodies and Souls*, hit #40. Although conventional hit singles are rare for this group, their work is a staple of easy-listening and jazz-radio formats.

With Jon Hendricks, of the team Lambert, Hendricks, and Ross, the group essayed the jazz vocal style known as vocalese, where lyrics are added to what were originally instrumental jazz pieces. The resulting *Vocalese* garnered 12 Grammy nominations (only Michael Jackson's *Thriller* got more) and won two (the group got one and the album's arrangers got the other). The next album, *Brasil*, which featured songs by Gilberto Gil and Milton Nascimento, among others, was awarded the Grammy for Best Pop Performance by a Duo or Group With Vocal.

With *The Off-Beat of Avenues*, the quartet moved to Columbia Records and, for the first time, wrote or cowrote and produced most of the work. After releasing a Christmas album, the group returned to Atlantic Records with 1995's *Tonin'*, an album focused on '50s and early '60s pop and loaded with guests such as Bette Midler, Phil Collins, and Chaka Khan. The group returned to its jazz inspiration for its subsequent releases, 1997's *Swing* and 2000's *Spirit of St. Louis*, dedicated to the music of Louis Armstrong.

Barry Manilow

Born Barry Alan Pinkus, June 17, 1946, Brooklyn, NY
1972—*Barry Manilow* (Bell) 1973—*Barry Manilow II* 1975—*Tryin' to Get the Feeling* (Arista) 1977—*This One's for You; Barry Manilow Live* 1978—*Even Now* 1979—*Barry Manilow's Greatest Hits; One Voice* 1980—*Barry* 1981—*If I Should Love Again* 1982—*Oh, Julie!; Here Comes the Night* 1983—*Greatest Hits, vol. 2* 1984—*2:00 A.M. Paradise Cafe* 1985—*The Manilow Collections—Twenty Classic Hits; Manilow* (RCA) 1987—*Swing Street* (Arista) 1989—*Barry Manilow* 1990—*Live on Broadway; Because It's Christmas* 1991—*Showstoppers* 1992—*The Complete Collection and Then Some . . .* 1994—*Singing With the Big Bands* 1996—*Summer of '78* 1998—*Manilow Sings Sinatra.*

Pop singer/songwriter Barry Manilow has sold nearly 60 million records worldwide. In 1977 his unabashedly romantic (verging on mawkish) pop gave him five albums on the charts simultaneously, a record surpassed by only Frank Sinatra and Johnny Mathis. He has since focused his attention on a wide range of genres, including Broadway show tunes and traditional jazz.

When Manilow was seven he picked up his first instrument, the accordion. He later attended New York College of Music and the Juilliard School of Music. He also worked in the CBS mailroom, and there, at 18, he met a director who encouraged him to do some musical arranging. Soon after, Manilow wrote an off-Broadway musical adaptation of *The Drunkard*, which had a long run. In 1967 he became musical director of the CBS-TV series *Callback* and later did conducting and arranging for Ed Sullivan productions. He also played in a cabaret-act duo, and in spring 1972, while filling in as house pianist at New York's Continental Baths, he met Bette Midler and soon became her musical director, arranger, and pianist. He coproduced and arranged her 1972 Grammy-winning debut and her 1973 followup. During this time he wrote commercial jingles for Dr Pepper, Band-Aids, and State Farm Insurance, among others (contrary to popular lore, he did not write, although he sang, McDonald's "You Deserve a Break Today").

Manilow landed a solo deal with Bell (later Arista) in 1972 but first toured with Midler as a featured performer before releasing his debut LP in 1972 and doing his own road show in 1974. His second LP came out in 1973, and in only nine weeks his cover of "Mandy" went to #1 in January of 1975. Hits like "Could It Be Magic" (#6, 1975), "It's a Miracle" (#12, 1975), Beach Boy Bruce Johnston's "I Write the Songs" (#1, 1976), and "Trying to Get the Feeling" (#10, 1976) followed. His debut album went platinum, and over the years a dozen more followed suit, including the multiplatinum *Barry Manilow Live, Even Now,* and *Greatest Hits*. His regular coproducer was ex-Archie Ron Dante up until his 10th LP in 1981.

Manilow won an Emmy for one of his TV specials, a special Tony for a Broadway concert, and a Grammy in 1979. In 1980 he produced Dionne Warwick's platinum comeback LP, which contained the hit "I'll Never Love This Way Again." In early 1982 he hit the Top 20 with "The Old Songs" and later had a lesser hit with a remake of the Four Seasons' "Let's Hang On." He continued scoring gold albums through the '80s. *2:00 A.M. Paradise Cafe* (#28, 1984) and *Swing Street* found Manilow moving from schmaltzy pop to a more jazz-oriented sound (he was joined on the albums by such singers and musicians as Mel Tormé, Sarah Vaughan, and Gerry Mulligan).

In 1984 Manilow scored music to words by the great lyricist Johnny Mercer, for the song "When October Goes"; Mercer's widow had found a trunk full of unpublished lyrics and offered them to Manilow. Manilow eventually scored and produced an album full of Mercer lyrics, 1991's *With My Lover Beside Me,* sung by Nancy Wilson. That same year saw Manilow release *Showstoppers,* a collection of Broadway show tunes on which he was joined by such stage singers as Barbara Cook, Michael Crawford, and Hinton Battle. In 1988 Manilow produced a song, "Perfect Isn't Easy," featuring Midler's voice for the animated Disney movie *Oliver and Company.*

In 1994 *Barry Manilow's Copacabana—The Musical* premiered in London (it would tour the U.S. in 2000–2001). *Harmony,* a musical for which he wrote the score, opened at California's La Jolla Playhouse in 1997. He also scored two animated features, *Thumbelina* (1994) and *The Pebble and the Penguin* (1995). With Manilow busy working for the stage and screen, his last two studio recordings have been made up mostly of covers—'70s hits for *Summer of '78* and songs popularized by Frank Sinatra for *Manilow Sings Sinatra.* Manilow's autobiography, *Sweet Life: Adventures on the Way to Paradise,* was published in 1987.

Aimee Mann/'Til Tuesday

Born Sep. 8, 1960, Richmond, VA, voc., bass
1993—*Whatever* (Imago) 1995—*I'm With Stupid* (Geffen) 1999—*Music From the Motion Picture "Magnolia"* (Reprise) 2000—*Bachelor No. 2* EP (SuperEgo).
With 'Til Tuesday, formed 1982, Boston, MA: Robert Holmes (b. Mar. 31, 1959, Hampton, Eng.), gtr.; Joey Pesce (b. Apr. 14, 1962, Bronx, NY), kybds.; Michael Hausman (b. June 12, 1960, Philadelphia, PA), drums: 1985—*Voices Carry* (Epic) 1986—*Welcome Home* (– Pesce; + Clayton Scobel, gtr.; + Jon Brion, gtr.; + Michael Montes, kybds.) 1988—*Everything's Different Now.*

Singer/songwriter Aimee Mann's career offers a classic case study in troubled relations between an artist and her record labels, and a testimony to creative perseverance over the long haul. Picking up her brother's guitar during recovery from a childhood illness, Mann first learned music through the songbooks of Neil Young and Elton John. After high school, she moved to Boston to attend the Berklee College of Music, where she switched from vocal studies to learning the bass.

She joined a local postpunk band, the Young Snakes, and in 1982 formed 'Til Tuesday with English guitarist Robert Holmes, drummer Michael Hausman, whom she'd met at Berklee and with whom she lived for a few years, and keyboardist Joey Pesce. The group won a battle-of-the-bands contest sponsored by a Boston radio station, which led to a record deal. The band's debut, *Voices Carry* (#19, 1985), became a major breakthrough thanks to the success of the pop-rock hit "Voices Carry" (#8, 1985), whose popular video depicts Mann dramatically breaking free of an abusive and controlling lover. 'Til Tuesday's second album, *Welcome Home* (#49, 1986), spawned only minor hits in "What About Love" (#49, 1986) and "Coming Up Close" (#59, 1987). Mann was winning attention as a songwriter, however, and won a fan and friend in Elvis Costello, who cowrote one song with her for *Everything's Different Now,* which sold poorly (#124, 1988) and failed to produce a hit single.

'Til Tuesday broke up, and it was five years before Mann freed herself from the group's Epic contract and reemerged with the very Beatlesque *Whatever,* a critically acclaimed moderate seller. The release of Mann's second album, *I'm With Stupid,* was delayed when her label (Imago) went out of business. The singer balked at an offer by Warner Bros. to release the effort and eventually signed with Geffen, which released it in 1995. Two years later, Mann married fellow singer/songwriter Michael Penn [see entry], whom she would later join in a fancifully themed Acoustic Vaudeville Tour, complete with a standup comic.

Mann's troubles with the record industry continued, however, when Geffen was absorbed by Interscope in 1999. She was dropped by the label but acquired the rights to her unreleased material. Meanwhile, her friendship with filmmaker Paul Thomas Anderson (for whom Penn had scored the movies *Hard Eight* and *Boogie Nights*) led to her songs being used extensively in his 1999 film *Magnolia,* which the director has said was inspired by Mann's music. In early 2000 Mann released the long-delayed *Bachelor No. 2,* which had first seen light as a limited-edition EP sold by the singer on a summer acoustic tour, on her own SuperEgo label.

Manfred Mann

Formed 1964, England
Manfred Mann (b. Michael Lubowitz, Oct. 21, 1940, Johannesburg, S.A.), kybds.; Paul Jones (b. Paul Pond, Feb. 24, 1942, Portsmouth, Eng.), voc., harmonica; Mike Hugg (b. Aug. 11, 1942, Andover, Eng.), drums; Michael Vickers (b. Apr. 18, 1941, Southampton, Eng.), gtr.; Tom McGuinness (b. Dec. 2, 1941, London, Eng.), bass.
1964—*The Manfred Mann Album* (Ascot); *The Five Faces of Manfred Mann; Mann Made* 1965—*My Little Red Book of Winners* (– Vickers; + Jack Bruce [b. May 14, 1943, Lanarkshire, Scot.], bass) *Mann Made Hits* 1966—*Pretty Flamingo* (United Artists); *Greatest Hits* (Capitol) (– Bruce; – Jones) 1967—*Up the Junction* (Fontana) (+ Klaus Voormann [b. Apr. 29, 1942, Berlin, Ger.], bass; + Michael D'Abo [b. 1944, Bethworth, Eng.], voc., gtr., flute) 1968—*The Mighty Quinn* (Mercury) 1992—*The Best of Manfred Mann: The Definitive Collection* (EMI).
Manfred Mann's Earth Band, formed 1971, Eng.: Mann; + Mick Rogers, voc., gtr.; + Colin Pattenden, bass; + Chris Slade, drums.
1972—*Manfred Mann's Earth Band* (Polydor); *Glorified, Magnified* 1973—*Get Your Rocks Off* (a.k.a. *Messin'*) 1974—*Solar Fire; The Good Earth* (Warner Bros.) 1975—*Nightingales and Bombers* (+ Chris Thompson, gtr., voc.; + Dave Flett, gtr.; + Pat King, bass; – Flett; + Steve Waller, gtr.; - Waller; +John Lingwood, drums) 1976—*The Roaring Silence* 1977—*Watch* 1979—*Angel Station* 1980—*Chance* 1984—*Somewhere in Afrika* (Arista) 1991—*Plains Music* (Rhythm Safari/Priority).
Michael D'Abo solo: 1970—*D'Abo* (MCA) 1972—*Down at Rachel's Place* (A&M) 1974—*Broken Rainbows* 1976—*Smith and D'Abo* (Columbia, U.K.).

Although led by two trained musicians who shared a measure of disdain for pop music, Manfred Mann scored an impressive 16 British hit singles during the '60s, many of which were American successes as well, including the #1 record "Do Wah Diddy Diddy" in 1964. Mann himself later moved into jazz rock and AOR.

Manfred Mann and Mike Hugg formed the eight-man Mann-Hugg Blues Brothers in 1962, playing blues and jazz. The following year they pared the group down to a quintet with a new name, Manfred Mann. At this point, they turned to pop-oriented rock & roll. Their first two singles ("Why Should We Not?" and "Cock-a-Hoop") were not especially successful, but their third, "5-4-3-2-1," became their first hit, its popularity aided by its adoption as the theme song of the British rock television program *Ready Steady Go* (Manfred Mann's "Hubble Bubble Toil and Trouble" became the show's theme song later on.) The hits came rapidly after that: "Do Wah Diddy Diddy" (#1, 1964), "Come Tomorrow" (#50, 1965), and "Pretty Flamingo" (#29, 1966).

In 1965 Vickers quit the band and was replaced briefly by Jack Bruce, who left six months later to form Cream. Bruce was replaced by *Revolver* jacket artist Klaus Voormann. Later Paul Jones quit as well to concentrate on acting and a solo recording career. He had two British hits, "High Time" and "I've Been a Bad Bad Boy," from the 1967 film *Privilege*, in which he starred, playing a pop idol. He was replaced by Mike D'Abo.

Fluctuating personnel had less discernible effect on the group's continued chart success than its leader's growing ambivalence. British hits those years included "Semi-Detached Suburban Mr. James," "Ha! Ha! Said the Clown," "My Name Is Jack," and their international hit cover of Bob Dylan's "The Mighty Quinn" (#10, 1968). After scoring the film *Up the Junction* in 1967, Mann and Hugg broke up the band and formed the more ambitious Manfred Mann's Chapter Three, complete with a five-man horn section, while McGuinness joined ex–John Mayall drummer Hughie Flint to form McGuinness Flint. Chapter Three recorded a pair of albums (*Chapter Three*, 1969; *Chapter Three, Volume 2*, 1970) before Mann and Hugg parted company, Hugg to compose soundtracks (some believe he alone was responsible for *Up the Junction*) and Mann to launch Manfred Mann's Earth Band.

The Earth Band was designed to show off the group's virtuosity in a heavy-rock format. Upon its formation in 1971, the group toured extensively, building an audience until in 1977 its version of Bruce Springsteen's "Blinded by the Light" became a #1 single. In 1973 the Earth Band had a British hit with "Joybringer," based on a tune from Gustav Holst's *The Planets*. In five more years of recording, Mann and company were not able to repeat the feat, even when they tried another Springsteen composition, "Spirit in the Night," although it did go to #40. *Somewhere in Afrika* (#40, 1984) was the highest-charting of Mann's U.S.-released albums since the gold *The Roaring Silence* (#10, 1976). "Runner" (#22, 1984) from *Somewhere* was Mann's last hit in the U.S.

Onetime lead singer Michael D'Abo, who sang lead on "Mighty Quinn," pursued an uneven solo career. He was far more successful as a songwriter; among his compositions are "Build Me Up Buttercup" (cowritten with Tony McCaulay and recorded by the Foundations) and "Handbags and Gladrags" (Rod Stewart). *Smith and D'Abo* is a collaborative effort with former Dave Clark Five lead singer Mike Smith. His daughter, Olivia D'Abo, is an actress. She played Kevin Arnold's older sister on *The Wonder Years*.

Minus Mann himself and augmented by a new rhythm section, Jones, D'Abo, McGuinness, Hugg, and Vickers reunited several times in the '90s as the Manfreds.

Marilyn Manson

Formed Marilyn Manson and the Spooky Kids, 1989, Tampa Bay, FL
Marilyn Manson (b. Brian Hugh Warner, Jan. 5, 1969, Canton, OH), voc.; Gidget Gein, bass; Daisy Berkowitz (b. Scott Mitchell Putesky, Apr. 28, 1968, East Orange, NJ), gtr.; Madonna Wayne Gacy (b. Stephen Bier Jr., Mar. 6), kybds.; Sara Lee Lucas (b. Fred Streithorst II), drums.

1993—(– Gein; + Twiggy Ramirez [b. Jeordie White, June 20, 1972, NJ], bass) 1994—*Portrait of an American Family* (Nothing/Interscope) 1995—(– Lucas; + Ginger Fish [b. Kenny Wilson, Sep. 28], drums) *Smells Like Children* EP 1996—(– Berkowitz; + Zim Zum [b. Mike Linton, June 25], gtr.) *Antichrist Superstar* 1997—*Remix & Repent* EP 1998—(– Zim Zum; + John 5 [b. John Lowery], gtr.) *Mechanical Animals* 1999—*The Last Tour on Earth* 2000—*Holy Wood (In the Shadow of the Valley of Death).*

Drawing inspiration from Alice Cooper, Ozzy Osbourne, David Bowie, the occult, and, by his own admission, the King James Bible, Marilyn Manson established himself in the '90s as one of the most vilified agent provocateurs in rock history. Predictably, the more parental groups, politicians, and religious advocates protested his music and stage antics, the more Manson emerged as a martyr in the war against censorship. Charismatic and outspoken in interviews, he defended himself as a result of, rather than a cause of, a corrupt society.

Manson was born and raised Brian Hugh Warner in a middle-class family in Canton, Ohio. He was close to his parents but chafed at the ideologies and rules he had to contend with at the private Christian school he attended. Seduced by the rock albums he was exposed to in school (during lectures about the alleged evil messages embedded in the music), he took to rebellion and got himself expelled. After finishing high school at a public school, he moved to South Florida with his family, where he formed Marilyn Manson and the Spooky Kids in 1989 after a short stint at rock journalism. Each member of the group adopted a stage name patterned after Manson's—the name of a female icon (Marilyn Monroe, Madonna) crossed with a serial killer's (Charles Manson, John Wayne Gacy). The band released a series of self-produced cassettes and developed enough of a reputation on the hard-rock scene to attract the attention of Nine Inch Nails frontman Trent Reznor, who signed them to his Interscope imprint, Nothing Records, in 1993. The following year, Reznor produced the group's industrial-metal debut album, *Portrait of an American Family,* and took the band on tour with Nine Inch Nails.

During the group's first tour, Manson wasted little time in securing his status as a nightmare to the Christian right, exposing himself and feigning (or not) sexual acts with other band members onstage (he was arrested after one concert in Florida). He was made a "reverend" of the Church of Satan by founder Anton LaVey, though Manson would later note that he was no more a practicing Satanist than he was a practicing Christian, as he was baptized.

Nonetheless, the controversy—and a radio hit with a hard-rock cover of the Eurythmics' "Sweet Dreams (Are Made of This)"—pushed the 1995 EP *Smells Like Children* to #31 and gold sales status; it later went platinum. With the prophetically titled *Antichrist Superstar* (#3, 1996), Manson became a superstar. A brutally aggressive concept album about a nihilistic rock god, it spawned a stage show in which Manson stood at a podium and ripped pages out of a Bible. Fueled by rumors (all false) that the shows also involved animal sacrifices, bestiality, and rape, activist groups across America lobbied with varying degrees of success to ban the group's performances. In the midst of all the furor, Manson released his autobiography, *The Long Hard Road out of Hell* (with rock critic Neil Strauss), in 1997, along with the *Remix & Repent* EP (#102).

For *Mechanical Animals* (#1, 1998), Manson adopted the persona of an androgynous, Ziggy Stardust–style glam rocker, Omega. In interviews, he explained that *Antichrist Superstar* and *Mechanical Animals* were both part of a pseudoautobiographical trilogy, told in reverse order—with *Mechanical Animals* intended as a satire in which the protagonist's revolution becomes "sold out." The album went platinum like *Antichrist Superstar* before it, but the accompanying tour was derailed when Manson's music was blamed, along with violent video games, as a negative influence on the two teenage boys responsible for the Columbine High School massacre in April 1999. Manson canceled several concert dates in light of the tragedy but vehemently distanced himself from the tragedy, decrying the killings as well as allegations that his or anybody else's music was in any way responsible for the killers' actions.

After a live album, *The Last Tour on Earth* (#82, 1999), Manson returned in 2000 with the final part of his trilogy, *Holy Wood (In the Shadow of the Valley of Death)* (#13). Telling the story of the future antichrist superstar's origins before his corruption, the album ditched the glam-rock sound of *Mechanical Animals* for a return to heavy, industrialized goth rock. The same year, he launched his own label, Post Human Records, with electronic hard-rock act Godhead his first signing. Manson planned to publish a novel based on his album trilogy in 2001.

Phil Manzanera: See Roxy Music

Teena Marie

Born Mary Christine Brockert, Mar. 5, 1956, Santa Monica, CA 1979—*Wild and Peaceful* (Gordy) 1980—*Lady T; Irons in the Fire* 1981—*It Must Be Magic* 1983—*Robbery* (Epic) 1984—*Starchild* 1986—*Emerald City* 1988—*Naked to the World* 1990—*Ivory* 1994—*Passion Play* (Sara) 1997—*Lovergirl: The Teena Marie Story* (Sony/Columbia/Legacy) 2000—*Black Rain* (Sara).

Before Mariah Carey and Lisa Stansfield hit the R&B chart in the early '90s, Teena Marie distinguished herself as a white singer worthy of the support of such soul-music icons as Rick James and Motown Records. Granted, when Motown released Marie's debut album (on its Gordy label), the record company suspiciously saw fit not to put her photo on the cover. But in 1985, when Marie's single "Lovergirl" hit #4 on the pop chart (and #9 on R&B), an accompanying video got enough airplay to ensure that the attractive singer's face—which, in fact, could have been mistaken for that of a light-skinned black woman—was as accessible as her lithely soulful voice and sultry, jazz-tinged funk-pop songs.

One of six children born to music-loving parents, Mary Christine Brockert began singing professionally at the age of eight, performing at weddings and appearing on TV commercials, using her nickname from early on. Teena Marie also started writing songs on the family piano. Following a year at Santa Monica College, where she studied English, the singer was tapped by Motown chairman Berry Gordy Jr. for a TV project that was eventually shelved. Gordy signed her in 1977, though, and shortly thereafter, James overheard her singing in a recording studio and decided to produce her first album, *Wild and Peaceful,* which spawned the R&B hit "I'm a Sucker for Your Love" (#8, 1979). Marie continued her associations with James and Gordy for the next couple of years, touring with the former (and coyly evading speculation that they were lovers, although they were) and yielding successful R&B singles like "I Need Your Lovin' " (#9, 1980) and "Square Biz" (#3, 1981) for the latter.

In 1981, the year her fourth Motown album was released, Marie was nominated for a Grammy for Best Female R&B Vocal Performance, one of only a few white performers to earn an honor in an R&B category. The same year, though, she sued the company for nonpayment of royalties. She was freed from her contract, awarded a cash settlement, and set a precedent with what became known as the "Teena Marie Law," which protects the rights of recording artists by forbidding a record company to hold an artist under contract if it refuses to release the artist's recordings. The singer was picked up by Epic Records; her second Epic album, *Starchild,* included "Lovergirl," her only Top 20 pop single to date. On the R&B chart Marie remained a viable presence into the late '80s, scoring the hits "Ooo La La La" (#1, 1988) and "Work It" (#10, 1988).

In the early '90s, Marie devoted herself to caring for her newborn daughter, Alia. When Epic dropped her, she started her own label, Sara, on which she released 1994's *Passion Play.* She went back on the road, first as part of Funkfest '95 with Cameo and the Gap Band, then on another funk/R&B revival tour, this one formed by comedian Sinbad and also featuring Earth, Wind & Fire. Marie released another album, *Black Rain,* on her label in 2000.

Mark-Almond Band

Formed 1970, London, Eng.
Jon Mark (b. Cornwall, Eng.), gtrs., voc., perc.; Johnny Almond (b. July 20, 1946, Enfield, Eng.), voc., sax, flute, vibes, congas, oboe; Rodger Sutton (b. Eng.), bass, cello; Tommy Eyre (b. Sheffield, Eng.), piano, organ, gtr.
1971—*Mark-Almond* (Blue Thumb) (+ Dannie Richmond, perc.) 1972—*Mark-Almond 2* (+ Ken Craddock, kybds.; + Colin Gibson, bass) *Rising* (Columbia) 1973—(– Craddock; – Gibson) *Mark-Almond 73* (– Sutton; – Eyre; + Geoff Condon, horns; + Alun Davies, gtr.; + Wolfgang Melz, bass; + Bobby Torres, perc.) (group disbands) 1975—(Mark and Almond reunite) 1976—*To the Heart* (ABC) 1978—*Other People's Rooms* (A&M).

In 1970 Jon Mark and Johnny Almond, two longtime British sessionmen, left John Mayall's Bluesbreakers to form a band that combined mellow jazz and folk.

Before joining Mayall, Mark had coproduced Marianne Faithfull's early albums with Mick Jagger, and later spent two years writing for Faithfull and accompanying her on the road. He also toured with folksinger Alun Davies (later guitarist for Cat Stevens), and from there the two formed a short-lived band called Sweet Thursday, with Nicky Hopkins, Brian Odgers, and Harvey Burns. Though their sole LP on Tetragrammaton was released the day the company folded, "Gilbert Street" became an FM hit in the U.S.

Almond had worked in Zoot Money's Big Roll Band, the Alan Price Set, and his own Johnny Almond's Music Machine, which recorded two solo LPs for Deram in England. Both he and Mark joined Mayall in 1967 (they appear on *Turning Point*), but after a second LP with him, *Empty Rooms,* the two formed the Mark-Almond Band with Tommy Eyre (who'd backed Joe Cocker, Juicy Lucy, and Aynsley Dunbar) and Rodger Sutton, formerly of Jody Grind. The Mark-Almond Band's debut contained the FM hit "The City," an 11-minute jam. An audience began to grow, especially for the group's tours, which featured long instrumental forays. With their second LP, Mark and Almond added guest drummer Dannie Richmond, who'd long been associated with jazz bassist Charles Mingus. Mark-Almond was briefly a seven-piece band, for its *73* album, before disbanding. Mark lost a finger in an accident that year, but came out with a solo LP, *Songs for a Friend,* in 1975.

Later that year he and Almond reunited to record *To the Heart.* They still hadn't found a major audience, but they got another deal on A&M in 1978, resulting in *Other People's Rooms,* which included a new version of "The City." They really were no longer a group (the album was recorded with all studio musicians besides the two principals) and called it quits for good soon after.

The Mar-Keys

Formed 1957, Memphis, TN
Original lineup: Terry Johnson, drums; Steve Cropper (b. Oct. 21, 1941, Willow Springs, MO), gtr.; Donald "Duck" Dunn (b. Nov. 24, 1941, Memphis), bass; Jerry Lee "Smoochie" Smith, piano; Charles "Packy" Axton (b. Feb. 17, 1941; d. Jan. 1976), sax; Don Nix (b. Sep. 27, 1941, Memphis), sax; Wayne Jackson, trumpet; Charlie Freeman (b. Memphis; d. Jan. 31, 1973, Memphis), gtr.
1961—*Mar-Keys* (Atlantic) 1965—*The Great Memphis Sound.*

Though they had just one Top 10 single, the Mar-Keys were among those most responsible for the development of the Memphis sound of the '60s, the hallmark of the influential Stax-Volt label. Guitarist Steve Cropper formed the band in 1957, when he was just 16, as a quartet. By the early '60s they had added horns and keyboards and were backing up Satellite Records (later Stax-Volt) soul stars Rufus and Carla Thomas. They also began releasing their own singles and albums of instrumentals, scoring a Top 10 hit and a gold record in 1961 with their first 45, "Last Night." In later years, after much shifting of personnel, the name Mar-Keys was quietly retired, but various band members remained active. Cropper and Dunn had many hits as half of Booker T. and the MG's [see entry]. Onetime Mar-Key Don Nix went on to a modestly successful solo career and also played with Delaney and Bonnie and Leon Russell, while Jackson joined the Memphis Horns, and Freeman, the Dixie Flyers.

Marky Mark and the Funky Bunch

Formed 1991, Boston, MA
Marky Mark (b. Mark Wahlberg, June 5, 1971, Dorchester, MA), voc.; Scott Ross (b. Apr. 6, 1969, Boston), dancer; Hector Barrons (b. May 14, 1967, Boston), dancer; Terry Yancy (b. Sep. 11, 1969, Boston), DJ.
1991—*Music for the People* (Interscope) 1992—*You Gotta Believe.*

The younger brother of New Kids on the Block's Donnie Wahlberg, Marky Mark was, after Vanilla Ice, rap's second Great White Hope. By the late '90s he had made a successful transition to respected actor.

Marky had a rough upbringing in the lower-class Boston suburb of Dorchester. He discovered hip-hop in the late '80s and, between doing jail time for knocking an Asian-American unconscious with his beer in 1988 and a 1990 arrest for assault, he began weight lifting, taught himself to rap, and practiced break dancing with his brother Donnie.

In 1990 Marky recorded a demo with his brother, and just a year later, he and the Funky Bunch emerged with "Good Vibrations." The record incorporated and credited an old disco hit by Loleatta Holloway (who was featured in the video between shots of Marky lifting weights and rolling around in bed with a pretty girl) and hit #1 in 1991. Its followup, "Wildside" (#10, 1991), was based on and credited Lou Reed's classic "Walk on the Wild Side." Marky's debut album, *Music for the People* (#21, 1991), went platinum. After his rise to fame, publicity got out about his previous violent racial incidents with black and Asian-American youths. Antidefamation groups protested, pressuring Marky to tape antiracism public service announcements.

By the end of 1992, Marky's pumped-up pectorals were omnipresent in magazines and on billboards, through his endorsement of fashion designer Calvin Klein's underwear. But *You Gotta Believe* (#67, 1992) quickly fell off the charts, yielding only one minor hit single in the title track (#49, 1992). In August 1992 Marky and a bodyguard were charged with assaulting a man at a Dorchester tennis court (the case was eventually dismissed by the court). In October 1993 Marky released a home-video workout tape.

Greater things were in store, however, outside the music business. Reverting to his given name, Mark Wahlberg, the rapper/model won the male lead in *Boogie Nights,* the 1997 movie drama loosely based on the life of superendowed '70s porn star John Holmes. Roles followed in the high-profile films *Three Kings* (1999) and *The Perfect Storm* (2000).

Bob Marley and the Wailers

The Wailers, formed 1963, Jamaica
Bob Marley (b. Robert Nesta Marley, Apr. 6, 1945, St. Ann's Parish, Jam.; d. May 11, 1981, Miami, FL), voc., gtr.; Peter Tosh (b. Winston Hubert Macintosh, Oct. 9, 1944, Westmoreland, Jam.; d. Sep. 11, 1987, Barbican, St. Andrew, Jam.), voc., gtr.; Bunny Livingstone (b. Neville Livingstone O'Reilly, Apr. 10, 1947, Kingston, Jam.), voc., perc.; Beverly Kelso, voc.; Junior Braithwaite, voc.
1965—(– Kelso; – Braithwaite) 1969—(+ Aston Francis "Family Man" Barrett [b. Nov. 22, 1946, Kingston], bass; + Carlton Lloyd "Carly" Barrett [b. Dec. 17, 1950, Kingston; d. Apr. 17, 1987, Kingston], drums) 1973—*Catch a Fire* (Island) (+ Earl "Wire" Lindo [b. Jan. 7, 1953, Kingston], kybds.); *Burnin'* (– Tosh; – Livingstone).
As Bob Marley and the Wailers: 1974—(+ Bernard "Touter" Harvey [b. Jam.], kybds.; + Al Anderson [b. Montclair, NJ], gtr.; + the I-Threes [Rita Marley, Marcia Griffiths, Judy Mowatt, all b. Jam.], voc.; + Alvin "Seeco" Patterson [b. Jam.], perc.; + Tyrone Downie [b. Jam.], kybds.; + Julian "Junior" Marvin [b. U.S.], gtr.; + Lee Jaffe, harmonica) *Natty Dread* (Island) (– Marvin; – Jaffe; – Lindo; + Earl "Chinna" Smith, gtr.) 1975—*Live* (– Downie; + Donald Kinsey [b. May 12, 1953, Gary, IN]) 1976—*Rastaman Vibration* (– Kinsey; – Smith; – Harvey; – Anderson; + Marvin; + Downie) 1977—*Exodus* (– Downie) 1978—*Kaya* (+ Lindo; + Anderson; + Downie) *Babylon by Bus* 1979—*Survival* 1980—*Uprising* 1983—*Confrontation* 1984—*Legend* 1991—*Talkin' Blues* (Tuff Gong) 1992—*Songs of Freedom* (Island) 1995—*Natural Mystic* 1999—*Chant Down Babylon.*

Tremendously popular in their native Jamaica, where Bob Marley was regarded as a national hero, the Wailers were also reggae music's most effective international emissaries. Marley's songs of determination, rebellion, and faith found an audience all over the world.

Marley left his rural home for the slums of Kingston at age 14. When he was 17, Jimmy Cliff [see entry] introduced him to Leslie Kong, who produced Marley's first single, "Judge Not," and several other obscure sides. In 1963, with the guidance of Jamaican pop veteran Joe Higgs, Marley formed the Wailers, a vocal quintet, with Peter Tosh, Bunny Livingstone, Junior Braithwaite, and Beverly Kelso. Their first single for producer Coxsone Dodd, "Simmer Down," was one of the biggest Jamaican hits of 1964, and the Wailers remained on Dodd's Studio One and Coxsone labels for three years, hitting with "Love and Affection."

When Braithwaite and Kelso left the group around 1965, the Wailers continued as a trio, Marley, Tosh, and Livingstone trading leads. In spite of the popularity of singles like "Rude Boy," the artists received few or no royalties, and in 1966 they disbanded. Marley spent most of the following year working in a factory in Newark, Delaware (where his mother had

Bob Marley

moved in 1963). Upon his return to Jamaica, the Wailers reunited and recorded, with little success, for Dodd and other producers. During this period, the Wailers devoted themselves to the religious sect of Rastafari.

In 1969 they began their three-year association with Lee "Scratch" Perry, who directed them to play their own instruments and expanded their lineup to include Aston and Carlton Barrett, formerly the rhythm section of Perry's studio band, the Upsetters. Some of the records they made with Perry—like "Trenchtown Rock"—were locally very popular, but so precarious was the Jamaican record industry that the group seemed no closer than before to establishing steady careers. It formed an independent record company, Tuff Gong, in 1971, but the venture foundered when Livingstone was jailed and Marley got caught in a contract commitment to American pop singer Johnny Nash [see entry], who took him to Sweden to write a film score (and later had moderate hits with two Marley compositions, "Guava Jelly" and "Stir It Up").

In 1972 Chris Blackwell—who had released "Judge Not" in England in 1963—signed the Wailers to Island Records and advanced them the money to record themselves in Jamaica. *Catch a Fire* was their first album marketed outside Jamaica, which featured several uncredited performances such as Muscles Shoals' guitarist Wayne Perkins playing lead on "Concrete Jungle" and "Stir It Up." (They continued to release Jamaica-only singles on Tuff Gong.) Their recognition abroad was abetted by Eric Clapton's hit version of "I Shot the Sheriff," a song from their second Island album. They made their first overseas tour in 1973, but before the end of the year, Tosh and Livingstone (who later adopted the surname Wailer) left for solo careers [see entries].

Marley expanded the instrumental section of the group and brought in a female vocal trio, the I-Threes, which included his wife, Rita. Now called Bob Marley and the Wailers, they toured Europe, Africa, and the Americas, building especially strong followings in the U.K., Scandinavia, and Africa. They had U.K. Top 40 hits with "No Woman No Cry" (1975), "Exodus" (1977), "Waiting in Vain" (1977), and "Satisfy My Soul" (1978); and British Top 10 hits with "Jamming" (1977), "Punky Reggae Party" (1977), and "Is This Love" (1978).

In the U.S., only "Roots, Rock, Reggae" made the pop chart (#51, 1976), while "Could You Be Loved" placed on the soul charts (#56 R&B, 1980), but the group attracted an ever larger audience: *Rastaman Vibration* went to #8 pop and *Exodus* hit #20. In Jamaica the Wailers reached unprecedented levels of popularity and influence, and Marley's pronouncements on public issues were accorded the attention usually reserved for political or religious leaders. In 1976 he was wounded in an assassination attempt.

A 1980 tour of the U.S. was canceled when Marley collapsed while jogging in New York's Central Park. It was discovered that he had developed brain, lung, and liver cancer; it killed him eight months later. In 1987 both Peter Tosh and longtime Marley drummer Carlton Barrett were murdered in Jamaica during separate incidents. Rita Marley continues to tour, record, and run the Tuff Gong studios and record company.

Marley was a pioneer not only because he singlehandedly brought reggae to the world, but because his passionate, socially observant music has become a yardstick against which all reggae will forever be measured.

Ziggy Marley and the Melody Makers

Formed 1979, Kingston, Jam.
David "Ziggy" Marley (b. Oct. 17, 1968, Kingston) voc., gtr., kybds.; Stephen Marley (b. Apr. 20, 1972, Wilmington, DE), voc., gtr., perc., DJ; Cedella Marley (b. Aug. 23, 1967, Kingston), voc.; Sharon Marley Prendergast (b. Nov. 23, 1964, Kingston), voc.
1985—*Play the Game Right* (EMI America) 1986—*Hey World!* 1988—*The Best of Ziggy Marley and the Melody Makers; Conscious Party* (Virgin) 1989—*One Bright Day* 1991—*Jahmekya* 1993—*Joy and Blues* 1995—*Free Like We Want 2 B* (Elektra) 1997—*The Best Of (1988–1993)* (Virgin); *Fallen Is Babylon* (Elektra) 1999—*Spirit of Music Chant* 2000—*Live: vol. 1.*

As the eldest son of international reggae stars Bob and Rita Marley, Ziggy Marley was a natural choice to fill the vacuum left by his father's death in 1981. He has been burdened with the double expectations of carrying on reggae's traditions and Rastafarian proselytizing while expanding the music to a new, younger audience. After a rocky start, though, he has generally succeeded, receiving Grammys for both *Conscious Party* and *One Bright Day*.

Taught guitar and drums by his father, Marley started sitting in on the Wailers' recording sessions from age 10; in 1979 an already ailing Bob Marley brought Ziggy, along with sister Cedella, brother Stephen, and half sister Sharon, into the studio to record a single, "Children Playing in the Streets." Called the Melody Makers, the group started playing at family events, gaining notice with an appearance at their father's state funeral in 1981.

Signed by EMI America, the band recorded two albums that veered toward the pop side of reggae. This, combined with Ziggy's preternatural resemblance, both physically and vocally, to his father, caused him to be dubbed, derisively, "Marley lite." Low sales and the fact that EMI wanted to market Ziggy as a solo act moved the band to Virgin Records.

The changes on *Conscious Party* (#23 pop, #26 R&B, 1988) went deeper than a new label. Recorded for the first time outside Kingston, with new producers (Talking Heads' Chris Frantz and Tina Weymouth), the album was well received both commercially and critically, yielding the hit "Tomorrow People" (#39, 1988). *One Bright Day* (#26 pop, #43 R&B, 1989) continued this growth, while *Jahmekya* (#63, 1991) and *Joy and Blues* (#178 pop, #75 R&B, 1993) added modern dance-hall and rock sounds to the mix.

Ziggy has continued the Marley tradition of political activism, becoming a Goodwill Youth Ambassador for the United Nations and winning an NAACP Image Award. He also started the Ghetto Youth United record label in Kingston to record the next generation of reggae music. In 1994 the band switched labels to Elektra and began putting together material for 1995's *Free Like We Want 2 B* (#170). *Fallen Is Babylon* (1997) highlights the increasing songwriting ability of Stephen, who wrote three songs and cowrote four. Stephen also oversaw the recording of the Bob Marley tribute album by various artists, *Chant Down Babylon* (#60 pop, #21 R&B, 1999). The album put a hip-hop spin on Bob Marley standards by combining Bob's original vocals with vocals by contemporary artists such as Lauryn Hill, Busta Rhymes, Erykah Badu, and the Roots. *Spirit of Music*, which was produced by Don Was and features an appearance by Taj Mahal, saw the Melody Makers go in a folkier, more soulful direction.

Branford Marsalis

Born Aug. 26, 1960, New Orleans, LA
1984—*Scenes in the City* (Columbia) 1986—*Royal Garden Blues; Romances for Saxophone* 1987—*Renaissance* 1988—*Random Abstract* 1989—*Trio Jeepy* 1990—*Crazy People Music; Music From Mo' Better Blues* (Sony) 1991—*The Beautyful Ones Are Not Yet Born* (Columbia) 1992—*I Heard You Twice the First Time* 1993—*Bloomington* 1994—*Buckshot LeFonque* 1996—*Dark Keys* 1997—*Music Evolution* (with Buckshot LeFonque) 1999—*Requiem* (Sony).

Where his trumpet-playing younger brother Wynton Marsalis [see entry] represents a strict allegiance to the orthodoxies of the jazz tradition, saxophonist Branford Marsalis openly embraces pop culture while simultaneously maintaining a reputation as a serious jazz musician.

Marsalis grew up in New Orleans; his father, Ellis, is a renowned jazz educator and pianist. As teenagers Branford and Wynton played together in funk bands; while Wynton later disavowed these early experiences, Branford never lost his youthful taste for R&B and rock music. Becoming more committed to jazz, Branford enrolled in Boston's Berklee College of Music. After short stints with the Lionel Hampton Orchestra and Clark Terry's band, Branford joined Wynton in drummer Art Blakey's Jazz Messengers. Starting out on alto saxophone but soon switching to tenor sax, Marsalis was quickly recognized as one of the most proficient of the new traditionalists—young players who were reinvestigating the hard-bop and modal-jazz styles of the '60s.

In 1981 Branford joined Wynton's band and subsequently appeared on his first five recordings, playing both tenor and soprano saxophones. Four years later Branford shocked the jazz world by leaving Wynton's band (by then the most popular in jazz) to record and tour with Sting. From that point on, Marsalis had few qualms crossing the boundaries of musical genre and celebrity. With Sting, Marsalis recorded *The Dream of the Blue Turtles* (1985) and . . . *Nothing Like the Sun* (1987); he also appeared in Sting's rock documentary *Bring on the Night*.

Marsalis started his own quartet in 1986, playing uncompromising jazz much as he had in Wynton's band. Like Wynton, Branford has also made classical recordings. Another Marsalis brother, Delfeayo (a trumpet player), produces most of Branford's records.

Outside projects would find Branford all over the pop-music map: guesting on records by Public Enemy, the Grateful Dead, the Neville Brothers, Tina Turner, and Bruce Hornsby. In 1994 Marsalis continued his exploration of musical genres with *Buckshot LeFonque*, a hip-hop project with Gang Starr's DJ Premier, whom Marsalis had worked with on the soundtrack for Spike Lee's *Mo' Better Blues*. That year also he won, with Bruce Hornsby, a Grammy for Best Pop Instrumental Performance for the tune "Barcelona Mona."

As an actor, Marsalis can be seen in the films *School Daze* and *Throw Momma From the Train*. In 1992 Marsalis became the musical director for *The Tonight Show* and second banana for host Jay Leno, instantly making him the most widely recognized living jazz musician in the world. Disaffected with playing "straight man" to Leno's humor, however, Marsalis left in 1995.

More recently, his projects have continued to reflect his diversity; he released a followup to the highly successful *Buckshot LeFonque* in 1997, and in 1999 one of his most highly regarded jazz albums, a tribute to his longtime keyboard ally, the late Kenny Kirkland.

Wynton Marsalis

Born Oct. 18, 1961, New Orleans, LA
1980—*All American Hero* (Who's Who in Jazz); *Wynton* 1982—*Wynton Marsalis* (Columbia) 1983—*Think of One . . .* 1984—*Hot House Flowers; English Chamber Orchestra* (CBS) 1985—*Black Codes from the Underground* (Columbia) 1986—*J Mood* 1987—*Carnaval; Marsalis Standard Time, vol. 1* 1988—*The Wynton Marsalis Quartet Live at Blues Alley; Baroque Music for Trumpets* (CBS) 1989—*The Majesty of the Blues;* (Columbia) *Crescent City Christmas Card; Quiet City* 1990—

Standard Time, vol. 3: Resolution of Romance; Original Soundtrack from "Tune in Tomorrow"; Trumpet Concertos; 24 (Sony) 1991—*Standard Time, vol. 2: Intimacy Calling* (Columbia); *Thick in the South: Soul Gestures in Southern Blue, vol. 1; Uptown Ruler: Soul Gestures in Southern Blue, vol. 2; Levee Low Moan: Soul Gestures in Southern Blue, vol. 3* 1992—*Blue Interlude* 1993—*Citi Movement* 1994—*In This House, On This Morning* 1995—*Joe Cool's Blues* (Columbia); *Live in Swing Town* (Jazz Door) 1995—*Blakey's Messengers, vol. 1; Blakey's Messengers, vol. 2; Blakey's Theme* (Westwind) 1996—*Live at Bubba's* (Jazz World); *In Gabriel's Garden* (Columbia) 1997—*Jump Start and Jazz* 1998—*The Midnight Blues: Standard Time, vol. 5; One by One* (Delta) 1999—*Marsalis Plays Monk: Standard Time, vol. 4* (Columbia); *A Fiddler's Tale* (Sony); *At the Octoroon Balls; Big Train* (Columbia); *Sweet Release and Ghost Story* (Sony); *Mr. Jelly Lord; Standard Time, vol. 6* (Columbia); *Reeltime* (Sony Classical) 2000—*Portrait of Wynton Marsalis* (CBS); *The London Concert* (Sony Classical); *The Marciac Suite* (Columbia).

Wynton Marsalis is the most important figure in the current-day jazz renaissance. Marsalis galvanized a stagnant musical scene in the early '80s with his spectacular trumpet playing and has since championed America's cultural commitment to jazz.

Marsalis hails from a family steeped in jazz [see Branford Marsalis entry]. By his early teenage years, Marsalis already showed prodigious talent on the trumpet. While studying classical music at school—he was a featured guest soloist with the New Orleans Philharmonic at 14—Marsalis also played funk gigs with Branford and became interested in jazz. In 1979 Marsalis accepted an invitation to attend the Berkshire Music Center at Tanglewood; that fall he was awarded a full scholarship to New York's Juilliard School of Music. By the summer of 1980, Marsalis was already sitting in with drummer Art Blakey's Jazz Messengers. Over the next two years he would play in Blakey's band and Herbie Hancock's V.S.O.P. quartet.

His jazz and classical credentials in order at age 20, Marsalis was given major-label contracts to record in both genres. He formed a quartet, including Branford on saxophones, playing modal hard bop in a style associated with Miles Davis' groups of the mid-'60s. Marsalis took any opportunity to slam the commerciality of electric fusion—as well as pop—exalting instead the purity of acoustic jazz. Marsalis' musical prowess and sartorial splendor excited a wide crop of younger jazzmen, who sprang up unexpectedly in the mid-'80s.

The combination of Marsalis' talent, virulent outspokenness, and support of his powerful record company made him a star overnight. He won jazz and classical Grammys in 1983, and has won 10 altogether. After Branford left his band in 1985, Wynton began delving deeper into the jazz tradition. Greater echoes of Louis Armstrong and Duke Ellington were to be heard in his work; by *The Majesty of the Blues* (1989), Marsalis was exploring his New Orleans roots, mixing earthy, pre-swing jazz with modernistic elements derived from John Coltrane and Miles Davis. *Blue Interlude* and *Citi Movement* found him experimenting with long-form compositions.

In 1988 Marsalis helped develop the jazz program at Lincoln Center and was appointed its artistic director. In the early '90s he began scoring for dance, collaborating with noted choreographers Garth Fagan, Peter Martins, and Twyla Tharp. In 1997, for his jazz opera *Blood on the Fields*, Marsalis became the first nonclassical artist to win a Pulitzer Prize for composition. In 1999 in an endeavor he entitled "Swinging Into the 21st," he released an astonishing 15 CDs, from live recordings to ballet. He has also written two books, *Marsalis on Music* and *Sweet Swing Blues on the Road*.

Marshall Tucker Band

Formed 1971, Spartanburg, SC
Toy Caldwell (b. 1948; d. Feb. 23, 1994, Moore, SC), lead gtr., steel gtr., voc.; George McCorkle, rhythm gtr.; Doug Gray (b. May 2, 1948, Spartanburg), lead voc.; Paul Riddle, drums; Jerry Eubanks (b. Mar. 9, 1950, Spartanburg), alto sax, flute, organ, piano, voc.; Tommy Caldwell (b. 1950; d. Apr. 28, 1980, Spartanburg), bass, voc.
1973—*The Marshall Tucker Band* (Capricorn) 1974—*A New Life; Where We All Belong* 1975—*Searchin' for a Rainbow* 1976—*Long Hard Ride* 1977—*Carolina Dreams* 1978—*Together Forever; Greatest Hits* 1979—*Running Like the Wind* (Warner Bros.) 1980—*Tenth* (– Tommy Caldwell; + Franklin Wilkie, bass) 1981—*Dedicated* 1982—*Tuckerized* 1983—*Just Us* (– Toy Caldwell; – Riddle; – McCorkle; – Wilkie; + Rusty Milner [b. June 2, 1958, Spartanburg], gtr.; + Tim Lawter [b. Dec. 10, 1958, Spartanburg], bass, gtr.) 1988—*Still Holdin' On* (Mercury) 1990—*Southern Spirit* (Cabin Fever Music) 1992—*Still Smokin'* 1993—*Walk Outside the Lines* 1995—*The Best of the Marshall Tucker Band—The Capricorn Years* (Era/K-Tel) 1996—*Country Tucker* 1997—*M.T. Blues* 1998—*Face Down in the Blues* 1999—*Gospel.*
Toy Caldwell solo: 1992—*Toy Caldwell* (Cabin Fever Music).

The Marshall Tucker Band tempered Southern rock with pop, country, ballad, and even MOR "jazz" influences. The band centered on the Caldwell brothers, who, like all the original band members, were born and grew up in Spartanburg, South Carolina. As a teen, Toy Caldwell first worked in a rock & roll outfit, the Rants, which included George McCorkle on rhythm guitar. At the same time, brother Tommy played with Doug Gray in the New Generation. Both groups toured the club circuit until 1966, when they were all drafted into the army. After their discharge four years later, Toy wrote "Can't You See," which later became the Marshall Tucker Band's first U.S. single and a Top 5 country hit for Waylon Jennings in 1976. But first he formed the Toy Factory, with Gray and Jerry Eubanks, a band that lasted almost two years, until 1971, when McCorkle, Paul Riddle, and Tommy Caldwell joined to form the Marshall Tucker Band, named after the piano tuner who owned their rehearsal hall.

Their self-titled debut was released in March 1973, and

they were openers on the Allman Brothers' tour; by 1974 they were headliners. The band's songs received much FM airplay, especially "Take the Highway," "24 Hours at a Time," and "Fire on the Mountain." MTB's debut went gold, followed by five other gold records and one platinum—*Carolina Dreams*—which included "Heard It in a Love Song" (#14, 1977). On January 20, 1977, the band, along with Sea Level, played at the inauguration of President Jimmy Carter. In 1979 the group signed to Warner Bros. for *Running Like the Wind.*

On April 28, 1980, Tommy Caldwell died from injuries sustained in an automobile accident six days earlier. Only a month before, another brother, Tim, had died in a car accident. The band's LP in memory of Tommy, released one year later, was called *Dedicated.* Franklin Wilkie, who'd played with Toy and McCorkle in the Rants, took over on bass. He had also played in the Toy Factory but, instead of joining the initial Marshall Tucker Band, played for six years with Garfeel Ruff, which recorded two albums for Capitol.

In 1983 Toy Caldwell, McCorkle, and Riddle, weary of the road, sold their interest in the group to Gray and Eubanks. Along with guitarist Rusty Milner and bassist Tim Lawter, both Spartanburg natives, they have continued to tour and record with a succession of musicians. Its *Still Smokin'* and *Walk Outside the Lines* LPs showed the band leaning more in a country direction, with several singles making the country Top 100. The band then added another variation to its Southern-rock format: *M.T. Blues* collected blues-inflected numbers from its catalogue and the positive reception it got led to the recording of the studio album *Face Down in the Blues* in 1998. The following year it released a spiritual album, simply titled *Gospel.*

On February 23, 1994, Toy Caldwell died in his sleep of a heart attack at age 45, two years after having released a solo album. As of early 2001, Marshall Tucker included Gray (the only original member left), Milner, Lawter, guitarist Stuart Swanlund, drummer B.B. Borden, and flute/sax player Clay Cook.

Martha and the Vandellas/ Martha Reeves

Formed 1962, Detroit, MI
Martha Reeves (b. July 18, 1941, Detroit), lead voc.; Annette Beard, voc.; Rosalind Ashford (b. Sep. 2, 1943, Detroit), voc.
1963—*Come and Get These Memories* (Gordy); *Heat Wave* (– Beard; + Betty Kelly [b. Sep. 16, 1944, Detroit], voc.) 1965—*Dance Party* 1966—*Greatest Hits; Watchout!* 1967—*Live!* (– Kelly; + Lois Reeves, voc.) 1968—*Ridin' High* 1969—(– Ashford; + Sandra Tilley [d. 1981], voc.) *Sugar n' Spice* 1970—*Natural Resources* 1972—*Black Magic* 1974—*Anthology* 1980—*Motown Superstar Series, vol. 11* (Motown) 1986—*Compact Command Performance* 1993—*Live Wire!: The Singles, 1962–1972; Motown Legends* 1998—*The Ultimate Collection.*
Martha Reeves solo: 1974—*Produced by Richard Perry* (MCA) 1976—*The Rest of My Life* (Arista) 1978—*We Meet Again* (Fantasy) 1980—*Gotta Keep Moving.*

Driven by Martha Reeves' soulful, brassy lead vocals, the Vandellas became Motown's earthier, more aggressive "girl group" alternative to the Supremes. Their biggest hits, like "Dancing in the Street" and "Heat Wave," are among the most popular dance records of the '60s.

Reeves, Beard, and Ashford sang as the Del-Phis in high school and cut one single on Check-Mate Records, a subsidiary of Chess. Reeves had also sung professionally under the stage name Martha LaVaille. In 1961 Reeves got a job at Motown in the A&R department as secretary to Motown A&R director William "Mickey" Stevenson. One day Motown head Berry Gordy Jr. needed background singers in short order for a session; Reeves and her friends were called in. They sang behind Marvin Gaye on "Stubborn Kind of Fellow" and "Hitch Hike" before recording "I'll Have to Let Him Go" as Martha and the Vandellas, taking their new name from Detroit's Van Dyke Street and Reeves' favorite singer, Della Reese.

Their first hit, a beat ballad called "Come and Get These Memories" (#29 pop, #6 R&B, 1963), was followed by two explosive Holland-Dozier-Holland dance records: "Heat Wave" (#4 pop, #1 R&B, 1963) and "Quicksand" (#8 pop, 1963). After being turned down by Kim Weston, "Dancing in the Street" (cowritten by Weston's husband, Mickey Stevenson, and Marvin Gaye) was given to Martha and the Vandellas; they turned it into their biggest hit (#2 pop, 1964). Their other big hits included "Nowhere to Run" (#8 pop, #5 R&B, 1965) and "I'm Ready for Love" (#9 pop, #2 R&B, 1966). "Jimmy Mack" (#10 pop, #1 R&B, 1967) and "Honey Chile" (#11 pop, #5 R&B, 1967) were the last Holland-Dozier-Holland compositions they recorded, and were their last big hits.

By 1967 the group was billed as Martha Reeves and the Vandellas. Annette Beard retired in 1963 and was replaced by former Velvelette Betty Kelly; when Kelly left four years later, Reeves' younger sister Lois took her place. Rosalind Ashford quit the group in 1969 and was replaced by another ex-Velvelette, Sandra Tilley (who had also been one of the Orlons of "South Street" fame). Tilley died during surgery for a brain tumor in 1981. The group broke up in 1973 after giving a farewell performance on December 21, 1972, at Detroit's Cobo Hall. Lois Reeves went on to work with Al Green.

As recounted in her 1994 autobiography, *Dancing in the Street* (cowritten with Mark Bego), Reeves believed that her group's success was undermined by Motown and Berry Gordy Jr.'s obsession with the Supremes. For example, "Jimmy Mack" was held back from release for two years because it sounded too much like the Supremes' then-current singles. The Vandellas and the Supremes' rivalry extended beyond the charts; between Diana Ross and Reeves, it was sometimes personal. A strong personality, Reeves clashed with Gordy, often demanding answers to business questions most other Motown artists didn't ask until years after they left the label. Struggling to maintain a hectic schedule of recording and performing, Reeves became addicted to a range of psychoactive prescription drugs, exacerbating emotional problems that culminated in at least two nervous breakdowns and a period of institutionalization. She has lived drug-free since 1977. In 1989 she, Beard, and Ashford sued Motown for back royalties.

In 1974 Reeves signed with MCA. Her solo debut, produced by Richard Perry, contained a minor hit in "Power of Love." Although that album, as well as her subsequent solo releases, have been critically acclaimed, she never attained the success she had enjoyed with the Vandellas. She continues to tour and record; sometimes the Vandellas consist of her sisters Lois and Delphine. On special occasions, she performs with Beard and Ashford. In 1995 Kate Pierson and Fred Schneider of the B-52's inducted the trio into the Rock and Roll Hall of Fame.

Ricky Martin

Born Enrique Martin Morales IV, Dec. 24, 1971, San Juan, P.R.
1991—*Ricky Martin* (Sony Discos) 1993—*Me Amaras* 1995—*A Medio Vivir* 1998—*Vuelve* 1999—*Ricky Martin* (C2/Columbia) 2000—*Sound Loaded* (Columbia).

Out of the Latin pop singers that seduced America in 1999—Marc Anthony, Enrique Iglesias, and Jennifer Lopez, to name a few—Ricky Martin emerged as the most successful. By the end of the year, his good looks and inescapable "Livin' la Vida Loca" had propelled Martin—already a huge hit in the rest of the world—to megastar status in the States.

Singing and acting since he was six years old, Martin joined Puerto Rico's premier boy band, Menudo, in 1984. The singer left the band five years later, having reached the maximum age allowed for Menudo members. (To keep its perenially young image, the band dictated that no boy in its rotating lineup could be over the age of 16.) By 1994, Martin had relocated to California and landed a part on the soap opera *General Hospital,* followed by a 1996 stint on Broadway in *Les Misérables.* Meanwhile, beginning in 1991, Martin released four Spanish-language albums, all of which sold well. His fourth, *Vuelve,* went to #1 on the Latin chart and yielded the 1998 World Cup anthem, "La Copa de la Vida (The Cup of Life)," which topped the singles charts in more than 30 countries and, having sold 11 million copies internationally, is the biggest-selling single in the history of Columbia Records. In 1999 Martin gained widespread exposure in the U.S. via an incendiary performance at the Grammy Awards ceremony, at which he also received a Grammy for Best Latin Pop Performance. His first English-language album, *Ricky Martin* (#1, 1999) followed; its kickoff single, "Livin' la Vida Loca," sat at #1 for five weeks and became the fourth biggest-selling single in the history of the Hot 100. Martin released *Sound Loaded* (#4) at the end of 2000, which yielded only one hit single, "She Bangs" (#12, 2000). A duet with Christina Aguilera, "Nobody Wants to Be Lonely" (#43, 2001), was a moderate hit.

John Martyn

Born 1948, Glasgow, Scot.
1968—*London Conversation* (Island); *The Tumbler* 1970—*The Road to Ruin; Stormbringer* (Warner Bros.) 1971—*Bless the Weather* (Island) 1973—*Solid Air; Inside Out* 1975—*Sunday's Child; Live at Leeds* 1977—*So Far, So Good; One World* 1980—*Grace and Danger* (Antilles) 1981—*Glorious Fool* (Duke) 1982—*Well Kept Secret* (Duke/Atlantic) 1983—*Philentropy* (Body Swerve) 1984—*Sapphire* (Island) 1986—*Piece by Piece; Foundations; BBC Radio I Live in Concert* (BBC Prod., U.K.) 1990—*The Apprentice* (Off Beat) 1991—*Cooltide* 1993—*No Little Boy* (Mesa Blue Moon); *Couldn't Love You More* 1994—*Sweet Little Mysteries: The Island Anthology* (Island) 1996—*And* (Go! Discs) 1998—*Live* (Resurgent); *The Church With One Bell* (Thirsty Ear); *Live at Bristo* (Blueprint) 1999—*Dirty Down and Live: Shaw Theatre London, 1990* 2000—*Glasgow Walker.*

Though never a commercial success, John Martyn's eccentric brand of folk—elliptical songwriting, intimately bluesy singing, heavily jazz-flavored music—has held steady appeal for critics and fans. Signed as Island's first white solo artist, Martyn, as early as 1968's *The Tumbler,* caused something of a stir in British folk circles by working with jazz reedman Harold McNair. *Bless the Weather* fully extended the jazz tendencies, while *Inside Out* and *Solid Air* (its title track a eulogy for Martyn's friend, musician Nick Drake) found him using hypnotically repeated melodies and echoplexed acoustic guitar. With his wife, Beverly, Martyn produced two other jazz-inflected discs, *Stormbringer* and *The Road to Ruin.*

One World introduced a new ethno-eclecticism; Martyn had spent time in Jamaica with reggae producers Lee Perry and Jack Ruby. In 1980, after a three-year absence due to substance abuse, Martyn delivered a critical breakthrough with *Grace and Danger,* featuring the percussion, vocals, and production of longtime fan Phil Collins. *Glorious Fool,* featuring Eric Clapton; *Well Kept Secret;* the live *Philentropy;* and *Sapphire* (its relative ebullience a tribute to Martyn's new marriage) continued the progression—traces of folk influence remained, but his sound now had greater mainstream pull. In the late '80s Martyn's alcohol problems resurfaced; he reemerged strongly, however, with *The Apprentice* and *Cooltide.* He began recording for U.S. independent Mesa Blue Moon in 1993. After a three-year hiatus in the mid-'90s, he returned with *And,* which forefronted jazz and trip-hop influences, followed by a set of cover songs, *The Church With One Bell.* In 2000 he reached a new audience by contributing a song to the soundtrack of the film *The Talented Mr. Ripley.*

The Marvelettes

Formed 1960, Inkster, MI
Gladys Horton (b. 1944); Katherine Anderson (b. 1944), voc.; Georgia Dobbins (a.k.a. Georgeanna, a.k.a. Tillman, b. 1944;

d. Jan. 6, 1980, Detroit, MI), voc.; Juanita Cowart (b. 1944), voc.; Wanda Young (b. 1944), voc.
1961—*Please Mr. Postman* (Tamla); *The Marvelettes Sing; Playboy* 1963—(– Dobbins; – Cowart) *Marvelous Marvelettes* 1966—*Marvelettes Greatest Hits* 1967—*Marvelettes* 1968—*Sophisticated Soul* 1969—(– Horton; + Anne Bogan, voc.; – Young) *In Full Bloom* 1970—*Return of the Marvelettes* 1975—*Anthology* (Motown) 1986—*Compact Command Performance* 1998—*The Ultimate Collection.*

Among Motown's female vocal groups, the Marvelettes were the only one whose early sound was pure girl group: girlish and sweet as opposed to sophisticated (like the Supremes) or soulful (like Martha Reeves and the Vandellas). The original Marvelettes were founded by Gladys Horton, a 15-year-old high school student who, together with four girlfriends from Inkster High School, decided to enter a school talent contest. The acts who placed first through third were allowed to audition for Motown talent scouts; the Marvels, as they were then called, came in fourth (though members have since claimed first). Nonetheless, they did audition for a Motown scout, who advised them to develop original material. Dobbins rewrote "Please Mr. Postman," a song a neighbor named William Garrett (who happened to be a mail carrier) gave her. "Postman"—which features Marvin Gaye on drums—has the distinction of being not only the Marvelettes' debut recording and their first and biggest hit, but Motown's first #1 pop record. The song stayed on the chart for almost six months.

The next year proved their most successful, with "Playboy" (#7 pop, #4 R&B), "Beechwood 4-5789" (#17 pop, #7 R&B), "Someday, Someway" (#9 R&B), and "Strange I Know" (#10 R&B). "Too Many Fish in the Sea" (#25 pop, #15 R&B), "I'll Keep Holding On" (#11 R&B), and "Danger Heartbreak Dead Ahead" (#11 R&B) were their 1965 hits. In 1963 both Dobbins and Cowart quit the group due to the strain of touring. Florence Ballard of the Supremes occasionally subbed on tours. Thereafter, the Marvelettes continued as a trio.

Many Motown historians assert that the Marvelettes were not as well promoted as some of the label's other female acts, specifically the Supremes and the Vandellas. Ironically, in 1963 the trio refused to record a Holland-Dozier-Holland song entitled "Baby Love." When recorded by the Supremes, "Baby Love" turned out to be one of 1964's biggest hits and one of Motown's best sellers and the first of that group's string of a dozen #1 hits.

Over the next two years, the Marvelettes, with Wanda Young Rogers (she married Miracle Bobby Rogers; they've since divorced), regained the pop chart with three of Smokey Robinson's most notable productions: "Don't Mess With Bill" (#7 pop, #3 R&B, 1966), "The Hunter Gets Captured by the Game" (#13 pop, #2 R&B, 1967), and "My Baby Must Be a Magician" (#17 pop, 1968; #8 R&B, 1967). Robinson's "Here I Am Baby" (#14 R&B, 1968) and Ashford and Simpson's "Destination: Anywhere" (#28 R&B) marked the end of the Marvelettes' most lucrative years. Interestingly, while most Motown groups duplicated their success in the U.K., the Marvelettes had just one Top 20 hit there, Van McCoy's airy ballad "When You're Young and in Love." By this time Horton (who along with Young had been a lead singer) had left, and the numerous personnel changes that followed reduced the group to nothing more than a name.

In 1980 Dobbins, who had married the Contours' Billy Gordon, died in her mother's Detroit home of sickle-cell anemia. Wanda Young Rogers has continued to work on and off with lineups of the Marvelettes, and several members have recorded for the British Motorcity label. A group, now featuring Horton and Young as sometime "special guests," continues to perform.

Richard Marx

Born Richard Noel Marx, Sep. 16, 1963, Chicago, IL
1987—*Richard Marx* (EMI/Manhattan) 1989—*Repeat Offender* 1991—*Rush Street* (Capitol) 1994—*Paid Vacation* 1997—*Flesh and Bone; Greatest Hits* 2000—*Days of Avalon* (Signal 21).

The son of a jingle-composing father and a jingle-singing mother, it was perhaps inevitable that Richard Marx would create '70s-style hook-filled pop. With his good looks, nice-guy image, and gift for catchy melodies, Marx became a sizable MTV star in the late '80s.

After accompanying his parents to recording studios, Marx began singing on commercial jingles himself at age five. As a teenager he began writing songs, and at age 18, through a series of acquaintances, he managed to get a demo to Lionel Richie, then a member of the Commodores. Richie encouraged Marx to come to L.A.; there he sang backup on such Richie solo hits as "All Night Long (All Night)" and "Running With the Night," and wrote songs with Kenny Rogers ("What About Me") and for Chicago. After writing a song for *Staying Alive,* the John Travolta sequel to *Saturday Night Fever,* he met the female lead, Cynthia Rhodes (best known for her dancing in Toto's "Rosanna" video), whom he would marry in 1989.

After five years of trying, Marx finally landed his own deal and promptly produced an eponymous double-platinum debut album (#8, 1987) that yielded four hit singles: the Eagles-like "Don't Mean Nothing" (#3, 1987), with slide guitar from ex-Eagle Joe Walsh; "Should've Known Better" (#3, 1987), with backing vocals by ex-Tube Fee Waybill and ex-Eagle Timothy B. Schmit; "Endless Summer Nights" (#2, 1988); and "Hold On to the Nights" (#1, 1988). The triple-platinum *Repeat Offender* produced such hits as "Satisfied" (#1, 1989), "Right Here Waiting" (#1, 1989), "Angelia" (#4, 1989), "Too Late to Say Goodbye" (#12, 1990), and "Children of the Night" (#13, 1990). The latter celebrated, and raised some funds for, the L.A. organization of the same name, which aided teen prostitutes and runaway children.

Rush Street (#35, 1991) was promoted with a publicity-stunt tour in which Marx played five coast-to-coast concerts—at airports in Baltimore, New York, Cleveland, Chicago, and L.A.—in 24 hours; its hit singles included

"Keep Coming Back" (#12, 1991), "Hazard" (#9, 1992), and "Take This Heart" (#20, 1992). He returned in 1994 with *Paid Vacation* (#37, 1994). The R&B–flavored *Flesh and Bone* followed three years later, charting with the single "Until I Find You Again" (#42, 1997) and featuring guest vocalists Luther Vandross and Randy Jackson. Marx also dueted with Donna Lewis on "At the Beginning" (#45, 1997), from the soundtrack to the animated film *Anastasia*. Marx switched labels for his next release, 2000's *Days of Avalon*.

Dave Mason

Born May 10, 1946, Worcester, Eng.
1970—*Alone Together* (Blue Thumb) 1971—*Dave Mason and Cass Elliot* 1972—*Headkeeper; Dave Mason Is Alive!* 1973—*It's Like You Never Left* (Columbia); *The Best of Dave Mason* (Blue Thumb); *Dave Mason* (Columbia) 1975—*Split Coconut* 1976—*Certified Live* 1977—*Let It Flow* 1978—*Mariposa de Oro* 1980—*Old Crest on a New Wave* 1988—*Two Hearts* (MCA/Voyager) 1999—*Ultimate Collection* (Hip-O/Universal); *Live: 40,000 Headmen Tour* (with Jim Capaldi) (Receiver, U.K.) 2000—*Super Hits* (Columbia).

Singer, songwriter, and guitarist Dave Mason has gone from being an integral early member of the acclaimed British jazz-pop band Traffic, to a top-selling solo act, to performing beer commercials when his solo albums were faltering, to briefly joining Fleetwood Mac.

By the mid-'60s, Mason was working in a band with drummer Jim Capaldi. In 1967 the pair met Steve Winwood, and they formed Traffic [see entry]. Mason's songwriting gave the band its first big commercial successes in the U.K. with "Hole in My Shoe," "You Can All Join In," and "Feelin' Alright" (later a Top 40 hit for Joe Cocker). However, Mason's pop-rock sensibility clashed with Winwood's jazz/blues leanings, and Mason was in and out of the band frequently, finally leaving for good in late 1968. He coproduced (with Jim Miller) the debut LP by the British band Family [see entry], *Music in a Doll's House*, then formed a short-lived band with Capaldi, Traffic reedman Chris Wood, and keyboardist Wynder K. Frog.

Having met seminal country-rocker Gram Parsons while touring with Traffic, Mason went to L.A. There Parsons introduced him to Delaney and Bonnie Bramlett, and he joined their Friends Tour of 1969, much of which was shared with Eric Clapton and Blind Faith (which included Winwood). Back in L.A., Mason recorded *Alone Together* (#22, 1970) with Capaldi, Leon Russell, Rita Coolidge, Delaney and Bonnie, and others. The LP stayed on the album chart over six months and went gold. The opening track, "Only You Know and I Know," was a #42 single for Mason in 1970; Delaney and Bonnie's version hit #20. Mason toured the U.S. much of the year, taking time off in June to play a London show with Clapton's Derek and the Dominos at their Lyceum debut.

In the summer of 1970 Mason renewed an old acquaintance with Mama Cass Elliot, forming a duo act that debuted at L.A.'s Hollywood Bowl that September, and recording a poorly received LP together. When the partnership dissolved, Mason briefly returned to England to guest with Traffic for a tour that resulted in the live LP *Welcome to the Canteen*, and he played on George Harrison's *All Things Must Pass*.

From that point on, Mason's solo career was erratic, though many of his subsequent LPs sold well. *Headkeeper* was half new material, half live renditions of earlier songs, while *Is Alive* was all of the latter. *Best of* furthered the apparent holding pattern, though *It's Like You Never Left* (#50, 1973), with support from Graham Nash and Stevie Wonder, and later albums saw Mason recoup somewhat. *Dave Mason* (#25, 1974) and *Split Coconut* (#27, 1975) were the two highest-charting albums after his solo debut. He had his biggest solo hit in 1977, when "We Just Disagree," from *Let It Flow* (#37, 1977), reached #12. By late 1981 Mason could be heard singing radio commercials for Miller Beer.

Since 1983 he has continued to tour with his band, but his chart success has been spotty at best. In early 1994 it was announced that he had joined Fleetwood Mac [see entry]; he toured with the band that summer, then played on its 1995 release *Time*. Mason resumed his solo career in 1996. In 1999 he toured with Capaldi, with whom he released a live album.

Massive Attack

Formed 1987, Bristol, Eng.
Daddy G (b. Grant Marshall, Dec. 18, 1959, Bristol), voc., prod.; 3-D (b. Robert Del Naja, Jan. 21, 1965, Brighton, Eng.), voc., prod.; Mushroom (b. Andrew Vowles, ca. 1968), prod.
1991—*Blue Lines* (Virgin) 1994—*Protection* 1995—*No Protection: Massive Attack vs. Mad Professor* (Circa) 1998—*Mezzanine* (Virgin); *Singles 90/98* (– Mushroom).

With their roots in the Bristol, England, club scene of the early '80s, the members of Massive Attack originated trip-hop, one of the most influential sounds of the '90s, combining the rhythmic urgency of hip-hop, the freewheeling samples of the DJ's craft, soul-rich melodies, and dub-reggae's hefty, intoxicating bottom end. The group began in 1983 as a loose collective of singers, rappers, DJs, and producers that staged parties under the name the Wild Bunch. Included in its ranks were Mushroom (Andrew Vowles) and Daddy G (Grant Marshall), as well as Nellee Hooper (later of Soul II Soul, and a producer for Madonna, Björk, and others), and Tricky [see entry]. The Wild Bunch released a 1986 cover of Burt Bacharach's "The Look of Love," which became a European dance-club sensation, just as legal authorities began to clamp down on the Bristol party circuit. In 1987 graffiti artist 3-D (Robert Del Naja) joined Daddy G and Mushroom to form Massive Attack. A series of singles led to the 1991 release of *Blue Lines*, which featured an array of vocalists—including Shara Nelson, Tricky, and reggae singer Horace Andy—and promoted a somnambulatory beat that ran counter to the hyped-up dance rhythms of techno. On its 1994 followup, *Protection*, the group enlisted Everything But the Girl vocalist Tracey Thorn, who lent a jazzier feel and contributed songs, with additional vocals from Andy, Tricky, and Nigerian singer Nicolette. The next year saw the release of *No Protection: Massive Attack vs. Mad Professor,* a radical remix of *Protection* in league with the antic British reggae producer. Three years later, the group followed with *Mezzanine* (#60, pop), with guest vocalists Andy, Elizabeth Fraser of the Cocteau Twins, and Sara Jay. The same year, an 11-CD box set, *Singles 90/98,* compiled remixes of a career's worth of singles. Mushroom left to pursue a solo career. As of 2001, the remaining duo was back in the studio, preparing a new album.

Master P

Born Percy Miller, Apr. 29, 1970, New Orleans, LA
1991—*Get Away Clean* (In a Minute) 1992—*Mama's Bad Boy; The Ghetto's Tryin' to Kill Me* (No Limit) 1995—*99 Ways to Die* 1996—*Ice Cream Man* 1997—*Ghetto D* 1998—*MP Da Last Don* 1999—*Only God Can Judge Me* 2000—*Ghetto Postage.*

Epitomizing the rapper as self-made mogul, Master P came out of seemingly nowhere—which, in hip-hop terms, was New Orleans—in the early '90s. He subsequently created his own sprawling, family-based roster of gangsta rap and R&B acts, whose recordings were churned out at a feverish pace on his independent label, No Limit. Though best known for the signature groan of his 1998 platinum hit "Make 'Em Say Uhh!" (#16 pop, #18 R&B), P won at least as much attention as a businessman. An entrepreneur with interests in films, toys, clothing, and sports management, P made the cover of *Fortune* magazine in 1999 as one of the richest Americans under age 40, ranking #28 with a net worth of $361 million.

Raised by his grandmother in the notoriously tough Calliope projects in New Orlean's Third Ward, P—born Percy Miller—was exposed to the street life he would later draw on in his music. In 1988 his brother Kevin was shot to death in a drug-related incident. He moved to Richmond, California, where his mother lived, and opened the No Limit record store with $10,000 from a malpractice settlement after the death of his grandfather. He released two unnoticed albums in the '90s. Convinced of the strong market for gangsta rap, P moved back to New Orleans, where he founded No Limit as a label and in 1992 released *The Ghetto's Tryin' to Kill Me,* the first of scores of unapologetically hard-core, funk-driven underground rap albums to be recorded for his imprint. In addition to his own albums—*99 Ways to Die* (#41 R&B, 1995); the gold *Ice Cream Man* (#26 pop, #3 R&B, 1996); the double-platinum *Ghetto D* (#1 pop, #1 R&B, 1997); the quadruple-platinum *MP Da Last Don* (#1 pop, #1 R&B, 1998); *Only God Can Judge Me* (#2 pop, #1 R&B, 1999); and *Ghetto Postage* (#26 pop, #2 R&B, 2000)—P recorded three albums with the trio Tru (featuring his younger brothers, also No Limit solo artists, Silkk the Shocker and C-Murder): *True* (#25 R&B, 1995), *Tru 2 Da Game* (#8 pop, #2 R&B, 1995), and *Da Crime Family* (#5 pop, #2 R&B, 1999). P also oversaw recordings from Snoop Dogg, Mystikal, Mia X and Fiend, and others. Between occasional efforts to initiate a second career as a pro-

Master P

fessional basketball player (he had won a sports scholarship to the University of Houston prior to starting his recording career) and negotiating the NFL contract of Heisman Trophy winner Ricky Williams, P also directed the semiautobiographical, straight-to-video release *I'm Bout It* (1997) and produced the theatrical releases *I Got the Hook Up* (1998) and *Foolish* (1999) with comedian Eddie Griffin. Other productions include the straight-to-video action dramas *Da Game of Life* (1998) and *Da Last Don* (1998).

matchbox twenty (originally matchbox 20)

Formed 1995, Orlando, FL
Rob Thomas (b. Feb. 14, 1972, Ger.), voc.; Kyle Cook (b. Aug. 29, 1975, IN), gtr., voc.; Adam Gaynor (b. Nov. 26, 1963), gtr., voc.; Brian Yale (b. Oct. 24, 1968), bass; Paul Doucette (b. Aug. 22, 1972, Pittsburgh, PA), drums.
1996—*Yourself or Someone Like You* (Lava/Atlantic) 2000—*mad season by matchbox twenty.*

Sturdy if unassuming musicianship, relentless touring, and the radio-ready songs of lead singer Rob Thomas made matchbox twenty a surprise success in the late '90s. Its 1996 debut album, *Yourself or Someone Like You,* had gone platinum 10 times over by 2000.

Dividing his youth between Florida and South Carolina before dropping out of high school to sing in bands throughout the Southeast, Rob Thomas began playing in Orlando with bassist Brian Yale and drummer Paul Doucette. The three left the band Tabitha's Secret to form matchbox 20 with guitarists Kyle Cook and Adam Gaynor. Enlisting Collective Soul producer and keyboardist Matt Serletic to produce their demos, they crafted guitar rock that fused a '90s grunge edge with a '70s stadium-rock accessibility.

Signed in 1996, the band released a debut that took a while to catch on but, boosted by heavy MTV rotation, stayed on the charts for nearly two years. *Yourself or Someone Like You,* filled with such crowd-pleasing singles as "Push," "3 A.M.," " Real World" (#38, 1998) and "Back 2 Good" (#29, 1998) found the band becoming a favorite among those alternative-rock fans who responded to a more commercial version of a sound that crossed the styles of such predecessors as R.E.M. and Pearl Jam.

The lyrics to "Push"—"I wanna push you around"—provoked the ire of women's advocacy groups, and the band was sued in 1998 by ex-members of Tabitha's Secret for a share of song profits, but in general matchbox 20 kept a fairly low profile for so successful an outfit. By 1998, it had been voted Best New Band in the ROLLING STONE annual readers poll, opened for the Rolling Stones' *Bridges to Babylon* Tour in Texas, and had amassed a strong following in North America and in Australia and New Zealand. That year also it contributed, along with artists like Elton John and Jewel, to *Legacy: A Tribute to Fleetwood Mac's Rumours,* and Thomas was featured in *People* magazine's "50 Most Beautiful People in the World" issue.

In 1999 "Smooth," sung and cowritten by Thomas, was featured as the lead single for Carlos Santana's phenomenally successful *Supernatural;* as a result, Thomas was named BMI's Pop Songwriter of the Year in 1999, and won three Grammy Awards in 2000 for Song of the Year, Record of the Year, and Best Pop Collaboration With Vocals.

In 2000 the quintet released its eagerly anticipated sophomore effort, *mad season by matchbox twenty* (#3). The album featured a slight name change (from matchbox "20" to "twenty") and music that again asserted Thomas' gift for penning hook-laden singles.

Material: See Bill Laswell

Johnny Mathis

Born John Royce Mathis, Sep. 30, 1935, San Francisco, CA
1957—*Warm* (Columbia) 1958—*Merry Christmas; Swing Softly; Open Fire, Two Guitars* 1959—*Heavenly; Faithfully* 1963—*Johnny's Newest Hits* 1975—*Feelings* 1978—*You Light Up My Life; That's What Friends Are For* (with Deniece Williams) 1981—*The First 25 Years—The Silver Anniversary Album* 1984—*Live* 1986—*The Hollywood Musicals* 1993—*How Do You Keep the Music Playing?; The Music of Johnny Mathis: A Personal Collection* 1996—*All About Love* 1998—*Because You Loved Me: Songs of Diane Warren* 2000—*Mathis on Broadway.*

Johnny Mathis' smooth ballad singing and distinctive, nasal tenor voice have made him, by some people's figures, the second most consistently charted album artist in popular music, just after Frank Sinatra. He is said to have become one of America's first black millionaires. His *Greatest Hits* album from 1958 spent 490 weeks—nine and a half years—on the chart.

Mathis' parents worked as domestics for a San Francisco millionaire. At 13 Johnny took professional opera lessons, though his early goal was to become a physical education teacher. (In 1956, while attending San Francisco State College, he was invited to the Olympic track trials held in Berkeley.) Singing in a jam session at San Francisco's 440 Club, Mathis was discovered by Columbia Records executive George Avakian, who sent him to New York to record. His first recordings were jazz influenced, but Columbia A&R head Mitch Miller told him to switch to pop ballads.

His first hit came just one year later in July 1957, "Wonderful Wonderful" (#14), followed by "It's Not for Me to Say" (#5) and his big #1 in November, "Chances Are." Most of Mathis' big hits, including "The Twelfth of Never" (#9, 1957), "Misty" (#12, 1959), and "What Will Mary Say" (#9, 1963), were in the late '50s and early '60s, though his albums sold consistently well thereafter (always at least 250,000 copies, as he covered whatever MOR songs were hits at the time). He captured younger ears and hearts with his 1978 duet with Deniece Williams, "Too Much, Too Little, Too Late," which soared to #1 on both soul and pop charts (he and Williams also recorded "Without Us," used as the theme for the TV show *Family Ties*). He made some unsuccessful stabs at rock and postdisco dance recordings before returning to his trademark romantic pop balladry in the late '80s. The compilation *A Personal Collection* included a Mathis duet with Barbra Streisand, who had long cited him as a favorite and chief influence, on a medley from *West Side Story.*

Into the '90s, Mathis was still headlining Atlantic City and Las Vegas resorts—even selling out three shows at New York's Carnegie Hall in October 1993—entrancing sold-out crowds of middle-aged people, many of whom had shared their first kiss, or conceived their children, to the (recorded) sound of his voice.

Dave Matthews Band

Formed 1991, Charlottesville, VA
Dave Matthews (b. Jan. 9, 1967, Johannesburg, S.A.), voc., gtr.; Boyd Tinsley (b. May 16, 1964, Charlottesville), violin; LeRoi Moore (b. Sep. 7, 1961, Durham, NC), reeds; Peter Griesar (b. Mar. 19, 1969, New York, NY), kybds.; Stefan Lessard (b. June 4, 1974, Anaheim, CA), bass; Carter Beauford (b. Nov. 2, 1958, Charlottesville), drums.
1993—(- Griesar) *Remember Two Things* (Bama Rags) 1994—*Under the Table and Dreaming* (RCA) 1996—*Crash* 1997—*Live at Red Rocks 8.15.95* (Bama Rags/RCA) 1998—*Before These Crowded Streets* (RCA) 1999—*Listener Supported* (Bama Rags/RCA) 2001—*Everyday* (RCA).
Dave Matthews and Tim Reynolds (b. Dec. 15, 1957, Weisbaden, Ger., gtr.): 1999—*Live at Luther College.*

The Dave Matthews Band emblazoned the '90s with its hybrid of jazz, folk, and world music. By the end of the decade, Matthews' introspective lyrics and distinctive vocal timbre resonated through capacity stadiums across the U.S., as the

DMB (an acronym used by avid followers) achieved an arena-rock magnitude equal to that of the Rolling Stones, Led Zeppelin, and the Grateful Dead.

The son of a physicist father and an architect mother, Matthews spent his formative years in Johannesburg, South Africa, and Westchester County, New York. After being drafted by the South African military to fight in favor of an apartheid political system at the age of 18, Matthews retreated with his family to the U.S. for good and soon ended up in Charlottesville, Virginia. There he began writing songs on his acoustic guitar during the day and working as a bartender at Miller's—Charlottesville's premier bar for local musicians—by night. Matthews eventually began jamming with top-notch players who frequently gigged at Miller's: guru trumpeter John D'earth, fusion drummer Carter Beauford, and reeds player LeRoi Moore. By spring 1991, the Dave Matthews Band played its first concert at a rooftop party in Charlottesville with its soon-to-be permanent lineup: Beauford, Moore, virtuosic violinist Boyd Tinsley, and bassist Stefan Lessard.

In the tradition of the Grateful Dead and Phish, the Dave Matthews Band built up a fan base by allowing fans to record and circulate tapes of the band's performances. Fan favorites like "Ants Marching" and "Tripping Billies" were revamped nightly as the band opened up ample musical space for improvisation. The band's first record, 1993's *Remember Two Things,* was an indie success on the college charts and eventually went gold. RCA signed the band and released *Under the Table and Dreaming* (#11, 1994), which yielded the hits "What Would You Say," "Ants Marching," and "Satellite." Within a year, *Under the Table and Dreaming* went four times platinum.

After playing on the jam-band-friendly H.O.R.D.E. summer tour with Blues Traveler and the Allman Brothers and headlining a few national tours, the Dave Matthews Band recorded 1996's *Crash,* which debuted at #2 on the pop albums chart. Matthews and brethren then proceeded to generate a string of live recordings as a way of celebrating the band's live aesthetic. *Live at Red Rocks 8.15.95* (#3, 1997), *Live at Luther College* (#2, 1999) (recorded on one of Matthews' acoustic-only tours with guitarist and longtime collaborator Tim Reynolds), and *Listener Supported* (#15, 1999) all document Matthews' commitment to his ever-swelling, increasingly diversified fan base. Meanwhile, 1998's studio album, *Before These Crowded Streets,* a series of solemn narratives about a tormented man's yearnings for his lover, debuted at the #1 spot on the pop albums chart. The dawning of the new millennium saw Matthews pick up an electric guitar for the first time on a studio recording. Produced and cowritten by Quincy Jones apprentice Glen Ballard, the uncharacteristically gritty *Everyday* (#1, 2001) signifies the DMB's evolution into a world-class rock band without conceptual boundaries.

Iain Matthews

Born Ian Matthew MacDonald, June 16, 1946, Lincolnshire, Eng.
1970—*Matthews Southern Comfort* (Uni); *Second Spring* (Decca); *Later That Same Year* (MCA); *If You Saw Thro' My Eyes* (Vertigo); *Tigers Will Survive* 1973—*Valley Hi* (Elektra) 1974—*Some Days You Eat the Bear . . . and Some Days the Bear Eats You; Journeys From Gospel Oak* (Mooncrest) 1976—*Go for Broke* (Columbia) 1977—*Hit and Run* 1978—*Stealin' Home* (Mushroom) 1979—*Siamese Friends* 1980—*Spot of Interference* (RSO) 1988—*Walking a Changing Line—The Songs of Jules Shear* (Windham Hill) 1990—*Pure and Crooked Gold* (Gold Castle) 1992—*Best of Matthews Southern Comfort* (MCA) 1993—*The Soul of Many Places* (Elektra); *The Skeleton Keys* (Mesa/Blue Moon) 1994—*The Dark Ride* (Watermelon) 1996—*God Looked Down* 1998—*Excerpts from Swine Lake* (Blue Rose, Ger.) 2000—*A Tiniest Wham.*
With Hamilton Pool: 1995—*Return to Zero* (Watermelon).
With Elliott Murphy: 2001—*La Terre Commune* (Eminent).

A founding member of the seminal British folk-rock band Fairport Convention [see entry], Matthews left that band in 1969 after its second LP. (He used his middle name for a surname to avoid confusion with King Crimson's Ian McDonald; in the past Matthews has spelled his first name as "Ian"). He formed his own group, Matthews Southern Comfort, which hit with a cover of Joni Mitchell's "Woodstock" (#23 U.S., #1 U.K., 1971). In addition to Matthews' songwriting, vocals, and guitar, the ensemble also featured pedal steel guitarist Gordon Huntley, who went on to play on Rod Stewart's solo album *Never a Dull Moment.* Matthews left Southern Comfort in late 1970 for a solo career; in 1972 he formed Plainsong, which recorded *In Search of Amelia Earhart* (Elektra) before disbanding. He moved to California and continued recording solo albums.

Despite the Fairport association, Matthews has never considered himself a folkie; his first band, Pyramid, was a surf group. Yet he did record *Siamese Friends,* an album of traditional music. Still, most of his efforts feature country-flavored pop that's suited to his high tenor voice. He had a hit in 1979 with "Shake It" (#13). In the late '70s he moved to Seattle, where he formed the band Hi-Fi with David Surkamp, former vocalist with St. Louis progressive rockers Pavlov's Dog. Hi-Fi released a live EP *(Hi-Fi Demonstration Record)* for First American–SP&S. Matthews worked as a talent scout for Island Music and Windham Hill from 1983 to 1988. In 1988 the singer/guitarist recorded *Walking a Changing Line,* Windham Hill's first all-vocal album. Now a resident of Austin, Texas, he remains as active and as eclectic as ever. He regrouped Plainsong for a string of '90s albums, commencing with 1992's *Dark Side of the Room.* The band dissolved again in 2000. Matthews' 1993 solo effort, *The Skeleton Keys,* was his first album to contain all original material.

The Mavericks

Formed 1989, Miami, FL
Raul Malo (b. Raul Martinez, Aug. 7, 1965, Miami), voc., gtr.; Robert Reynolds (b. Apr. 30, 1962, Kansas City, MO), bass; Paul

Deakin (b. Sep. 2, 1959, Plainsville, OH), drums; Ben Peeler, gtr., lap steel, mandolin, banjo.
1990—*The Mavericks* (Y&T) 1991—(– Peeler; + David Lee Holt, gtr.) 1992—*From Hell to Paradise* (MCA) 1994—(– Holt; + Nick Kane [b. Nicholas James Kane, Aug. 21, 1954, Jerusalem, GA], gtr.) *What a Crying Shame* 1995—*Music for All Occasions* 1998—*Trampoline* 1999—*Super Colossal Smash Hits of the 90s: The Best of the Mavericks* (Mercury).

The Mavericks started out playing honky-tonk in Miami bars, only to develop an expansive mix of country, rock & roll, Cuban, and lounge music that would dazzle and, later, bewilder the Nashville establishment. It would also win the band quite a few rock and pop fans in the process.

The group coalesced when bass player Robert Reynolds convinced longtime pal Paul Deakin, a drummer with both a degree in jazz and local punk cred, to start a country band with him. The plan was for Reynolds to play rhythm guitar and sing, but the arrival of Raul Malo, the Mavericks' original bassist, soon changed that. The son of Cuban expatriates, Malo proved himself to be an emotive crooner in the Roy Orbison mold; it wasn't long before he was fronting the band.

In 1990, with lead guitarist Ben Peeler on board, the Mavericks released their self-titled debut album on the local Y&T label. Major-label country-record execs soon got wind of the project and flew the group to Nashville to play a high-profile showcase, at which MCA offered the Mavericks a contract. In 1992, with David Lee Holt replacing Peeler, the band recorded *From Hell to Paradise*. The album consisted mostly of Malo's socially conscious originals, including the hard-hitting title track, the saga of his aunt's flight from Cuba to Miami to escape Castro's rule. The record's first single, a turbo-charged cover of Hank Williams' "Hey Good Lookin'," dented the country Top 100 (#74 C&W, 1992).

Looking for a hit, the Mavericks eschewed message songs for crisp, radio-ready fare on 1994's *What a Crying Shame* (#54 pop, #6 C&W). The group also substituted guitarist Nick Kane for Holt. Both moves paid off when the album yielded a pair of Top 20 country singles, "There Goes My Heart" (#20 C&W, 1994) and "O What a Thrill" (#18 C&W, 1994), the latter written by singer/songwriter Jesse Winchester. Adding keyboardist sideman Jerry Dale McFadden and graduating to headliner status along the way, the group toured hard behind the album, which eventually went platinum. In 1994 Reynolds married country hitmaker Trisha Yearwood; the couple would later divorce.

The Mavericks' next album, *Music for All Occasions* (#58 pop, #9 C&W, 1995), veered hard into lounge-music territory. It also drew mixed reviews, its detractors dismissing the record as retro kitsch. Nevertheless, the album went gold and produced three more hit singles, including "Here Comes the Rain" (#22 C&W, 1995) and "All You Ever Do Is Bring Me Down" (#13 C&W, 1996). The former won the group a Grammy in 1996. The album also attracted trendy audiences who were popularizing the '50s exotica of Esquivel and Martin Denny.

Trampoline (#96 pop, #9 C&W, 1998), recorded live in a converted Nashville church, proved to be the Mavericks' most ambitious album to date. A kaleidoscopic record that encompassed all of the band's influences and then some, the album was hailed as a triumph by critics and fans but didn't fare as well commercially as the group's previous two releases, causing the Mavericks and MCA to part company. Guitarist Nick Kane put out a solo album in 1999, while Reynolds and McFadden released a 2000 album as part of Swag, a supergroup of sorts featuring Tom Petersson of Cheap Trick and Ken Coomer of Wilco. Malo participated in the Latin supergroup Los Super Seven, with members of Los Lobos, Caetano Veloso, and Susana Baca, which released *Canto* in 2001. Later that year he began recording his first solo album.

Maxwell

Born May 23, 1973, Brooklyn, NY
1996—*Maxwell's Urban Hang Suite* (Columbia) 1997—*MTV Unplugged* 1998—*Embrya.*

Maxwell emerged as one of the few artists in the '90s to put the Motown feel back into R&B. The son of a West Indian mother and Puerto Rican father, the Brooklyn native began playing music around the age of 16. After borrowing a Casio keyboard from a friend, Maxwell (his record-label publicist refuses to divulge his birth name) soon became obsessed with writing music. In the early '90s he built up a small following by performing at various Manhattan clubs and handing out tapes to friends and acquaintances.

In 1994 Maxwell signed a deal with Columbia, which released his debut, *Maxwell's Urban Hang Suite* (#45 pop, #8 R&B, 1996), a collection of soulful compositions packed with romantic imagery and lulling rhythms. "Ascension (Don't Ever Wonder)" (#36 pop, #8 R&B, 1996), the album's first single, and "Sumthin' Sumthin' " (#23 R&B, 1997) took Maxwell's seductive voice to a broad audience. His *MTV Unplugged* special, which turned into a seven-song album (#53 pop, #15 R&B, 1997), demonstrated Maxwell's Marvin Gaye–like ability to captivate a live audience with smooth vocals, sensual looks, and a formidable backing band. *Embrya* (#3 pop, #2 R&B, 1998) enjoyed even more commercial success, solidifying Maxwell's star status. In 1999 his "Fortunate" (#4 pop, #1 R&B) was featured on the movie soundtrack *Life*.

John Mayall/John Mayall's Bluesbreakers

John Mayall, born Nov. 29, 1933, Macclesfield, Eng.
The Bluesbreakers, formed 1963, London, Eng.:
Mayall, kybds., harmonica, voc., gtr.; Davy Graham, gtr.; John McVie (b. Nov. 26, 1945, London), bass; Peter Ward, drums; – Graham; + Bernie Watson, gtr.
1964—(+ Hughie Flint, drums; – Watson; + Roger Dean, gtr.)
1965—*John Mayall Plays John Mayall* (Decca, U.K.) (– Dean;

+ Eric Clapton [b. Mar. 30, 1945, Ripley, Eng.], gtr.; – Clapton; + various musicians on gtr., including Peter Green [b. Oct. 29, 1946, London], gtr.; – McVie; + Jack Bruce [b. May 14, 1943, Glasgow, Scot.]; + Clapton; – Bruce; + McVie) 1966—*Bluesbreakers—John Mayall With Eric Clapton* (London) (– Clapton; – Flint; + Aynsley Dunbar [b. Jan. 10, 1946, Lancaster, Eng.], drums) 1967—*A Hard Road* (– Dunbar; + Mick Fleetwood [b. June 24, 1947, Redruth, Eng.], drums; – Fleetwood; – Green; + Mick Taylor [b. Jan. 17, 1948, Welwyn Garden City, Eng.]; + Keef Hartley [b. Mar. 8, 1944, Preston, Eng.], drums; + Chris Mercer, sax; + Rip Kant, sax; – Kant); *Crusade; The Blues Alone* (+ Henry Lowther, trumpet; + Dick Heckstall-Smith [b. Sep. 26, 1934, Ludlow, Eng.], sax; – McVie; + Paul Williams, bass; – Williams; + Keith Tillman, bass) 1968—*Diary of a Band, vol. 1; Diary of a Band, vol. 2* (– Tillman; + Andy Fraser [b. Aug. 7, 1952, London], bass; – Fraser; + Tony Reeves, bass; – Hartley) *Bare Wires* (+ Jon Hiseman [b. June 21, 1944, London], drums; – Mercer; – Lowther; – Hiseman; – Heckstall-Smith; + Colin Allen, drums; – Reeves; + Steve Thompson, bass); *Blues From Laurel Canyon* 1969—(– Taylor; – Allen; + Jon Mark [b. Cornwall, Eng.], gtr.; + Johnny Almond [b. July 20, 1946, Enfield, Eng.], sax) *Looking Back; Turning Point* 1970—*Empty Rooms* (Polydor) (– Mark; – Almond; + Harvey Mandel [b. Mar. 11, 1945, Detroit, MI], gtr.; – Thompson; + Alex Dmochowski; – Dmochowski; + Larry Taylor, bass; + Don "Sugarcane" Harris [b. June 18, 1938, Pasadena, CA; d. Nov. 30, 1999, Los Angeles, CA], violin); *USA Union* 1971—(+ Clapton; + M. Taylor; + Hartley) *Back to the Roots* (– Clapton; – M. Taylor; – Hartley) *Thru the Years* (London) (– Mandel; – Harris; + Jimmy McCulloch [b. 1953, Glasgow; d. Sep. 27, 1979, London], gtr.) *Memories* (Polydor) (– McCulloch; + Freddy Robinson, gtr.; + Blue Mitchell, trumpet; + Ron Selico, bass; + Clifford Solomon, saxes; – Selico; + Hartley) 1972—*Jazz-Blues Fusion* (+ Victor Gaskin, bass; + Fred Jackson, baritone and tenor saxes; + Charles Owens, tenor and soprano flute; + Ernie Watts, tenor sax; – Solomon; + Red Holloway, flute, saxes) *Moving On* 1973—*The Best of John Mayall* (+ D. Harris; – Jackson; – Owens; – Watts) *Ten Years Are Gone* 1975—(– Mitchell; – Robinson; + Hightide Harris, bass, gtr.; – D. Harris; – Hartley; + Randy Resnick, gtr.; + Soko Richardson, drums) *The Latest Edition* (– H. Harris; – Resnick; + L. Taylor; – Holloway; + D. Harris; + Dee McKinnie [b. 1950], voc.; + Rick Vito [b. Oct. 13, 1949, Darby, MA], gtr.; + Jay Spell, kybds.) *New Year, New Band, New Company* (Blue Thumb); *Notice to Appear* 1976—*A Banquet in Blues* (ABC) 1977—(– McKinnie; – S. Richardson; – Vito; – D. Harris; + Holloway; + Gary Rowles, gtr.; + Frank Wilson, drums; + Warren Bryant, perc.; + Pepper Watkins, voc.; + Patty Smith, voc.) *Lots of People* (– Holloway; – Rowles; – Spell; – L. Taylor; – Wilson; – Bryant; – Watkins; – P. Smith; + James Quill Smith, gtr.; + Steve Thompson, bass; + S. Richardson, drums) *A Hard Core Package* 1978—*The Last of the British Blues* (group disbands; *Bottom Line* features nonband musicians) 1979—*Bottom Line* (DJM) (+ J. Smith; + Vito, gtr.; + Chris Cameron, piano, clarinet; + Christian Mostert, soprano and tenor saxes, flutes; + Angus Thomas, bass; + Ruben Alvarez, drums; + Maggie Parker, voc.); *No More Interviews* 1980—(– Vito; – Cameron; – Mostert; – Thomas; – Alvarez; + Kevin McCormick, bass; + S. Richardson, drums) *Road Show Blues* ca. 1981—(– McCormick; – J. Smith; – S. Richardson; – Parker; + Don McMinn, gtr.; + Bobby Manuel, gtr.; + Jeff Davis, bass; + Mike Gardner, drums) 1982—(Bluesbreakers reunion lineup: Mayall; McVie; Mick Taylor; Colin Allen) (group disbands) ca. 1984—(lineup: Mayall; Coco Montoya, gtr.; Kal David, gtr.; Willie McNeil, drums; Walter Trout, gtr.; Bobby Haynes, bass) 1985—(– David; – McNeil; + Joe Yuele [b. Jan. 26, 1951, Haverhill, MA], drums) 1986—*Behind the Iron Curtain* (GNP Crescendo) 1987—*The Power of the Blues* (Entente, Ger.) 1988—*Chicago Line* (Island); *Archives to Eighties: Featuring Eric Clapton and Mick Taylor* (Polydor); *Primal Solos* (PolyGram) 1990—(– Haynes; + Freebo, bass; – Trout) *A Sense of Place* (Island) 1991—(– Freebo; + Rick Cortes, bass) 1992—*John Mayall: London Blues, 1964–1969* (PolyGram); *John Mayall: Room to Move, 1969–1974* 1993—*Wake Up Call* (Silvertone) 1994—*The 1982 Reunion Concert* (with the 1982 reunion lineup above) (Repertoire); *Cross Country Blues* (with 1980 and 1984 lineups above) (One Way) (– Montoya; + Buddy Whittington [b. Dec. 28, 1956, Fort Worth, TX], gtr.) 1995—*Spinning Coin* (Silvertone) 1995—(– Cortes; + John Paulus, bass]) 1997—*Blues for the Lost Days* 1998—*As It All Began: The Best of John Mayall and the Bluesbreakers* (PolyGram); *Drivin' On: The ABC Years 1975–1982* (MCA) 1999—*Padlock on the Blues* (Padlock) (– Paulus; + Greg Rzab, bass) 2000—*Live at the Marquee 1965* (Spitfire) (– Rzab; + Hank Van Sickle [b. Pittsburgh, PA], bass) 2001—*Along for the Ride* (Eagle/Red Ink).

The father of the British blues movement, John Mayall has also been its hardiest perennial, taking the phrase "back to the roots" with more dogged seriousness than most. He's been one of the most famous talent scouts in rock music, having discovered many musicians—Eric Clapton, Mick Taylor, Jack Bruce, Keef Hartley, Aynsley Dunbar, Jon Mark, John Almond, Jon Hiseman, Peter Green, Mick Fleetwood, and John McVie—who went on to significant careers of their own. He was also something of an iconoclast: He formed his first band when he was nearly 30, and in the late '60s, when hyperamplification was the rage, Mayall veered toward a subdued acoustic sound. As of this writing, despite closing in on the age of 70, Mayall continues to tour and record.

Mayall began playing guitar and ukulele at age 12; by 14 he was playing boogie-woogie piano as well. After graduating from Manchester Junior School of Art in 1949, he worked briefly as a window dresser. In 1955 he formed his first group, the Powerhouse Four. At age 18 Mayall entered the British army; upon his discharge he returned to art school. After graduating from art school in 1959 he became a successful typographer and graphic artist (he later designed many of his album covers). In 1962 he formed the Blues Syndicate; he moved to London in 1963.

John Mayall and the Bluesbreakers' debut LP was recorded live in December 1964 and originally released only in England. By the time of the second Bluesbreakers LP (the

John Mayall

first released in the U.S.), Mayall had been playing music for nearly 20 years. In 1965 Clapton was on guitar, and Jack Bruce had replaced McVie. Decca dropped the group, and around this time Mayall recorded a single, "I'm Your Witchdoctor" (produced by Jimmy Page), for Immediate. Clapton had left the group shortly before, and McVie returned in 1966 to join Green on guitar and Hughie Flint (later with McGuinness Flint) on drums. In the meantime, *Bluesbreakers—John Mayall With Eric Clapton* became Mayall's first major hit. Green, McVie, and Mick Fleetwood left after 1967 to form Fleetwood Mac, and Mick Taylor (later of the Rolling Stones) came in on guitar that year; at age 16 bassist Andy Fraser (later with Free) joined in 1968; in the early '70s so did guitarists Harvey Mandel (later with Canned Heat, among others) and Rick Vito (later of Fleetwood Mac). In addition, many other musicians have rehearsed, performed, or recorded with Mayall without officially becoming part of any of his numerous lineups. Mayall never seemed perturbed by the many personnel changes; in fact, he often encouraged his musicians to leave for greater fame and wealth.

Virtually all of Mayall's albums of this period were critically acclaimed and, for blues records, commercially successful as well. *Bluesbreakers—John Mayall With Eric Clapton* and *A Hard Road* were Top 10 albums in the U.K. *Crusade,* another U.K. Top 10 LP, introduced 18-year-old Mick Taylor, drummer Keef Hartley (who, like Mayall, had an intense interest in Native American culture), and horn arrangements played by noted British jazz-rock sessionmen like Chris Mercer and Dick Heckstall-Smith. On *Blues Alone* Mayall played all the instruments except drums (handled again by Hartley). *Bare Wires* (#3 U.K.) made a transition from blues to progressive jazz rock; Heckstall-Smith and Hiseman left after this album to form the jazz-rock band Colosseum. It was the first Mayall album to enter the U.S. chart, peaking at #59.

After he had become known in the U.S., Mayall bought a house in the L.A. area and recorded *Blues From Laurel Canyon* (#68, 1969). *Turning Point* (#32, 1969), Mayall's only gold LP, was all acoustic, with no drums; it featured Jon Mark's acoustic rhythm guitar and Johnny Almond's reed arsenal, and included one of Mayall's most popular tunes, "Room to Move." Mayall hit a commercial peak stateside with *Diary of a Band,* a two-volume collection of recordings by previous Bluesbreaker lineups. It was followed by his highest-charting album to date, *USA Union* (#22, 1970), which included future Mayall stalwarts Larry Taylor, Harvey Mandel, and Don "Sugarcane" Harris. Like a number of Mayall's band members, these three would drift in and out of the lineup for years to come. *Back to the Roots* (#52, 1971) featured a onetime lineup that included Mayall's latest band plus Mick Taylor, Eric Clapton, Johnny Almond, and Keef Hartley. (In 1988 Mayall, who was never satisfied with the sound of this album, discovered, restored, and remixed the original tapes, rerecording most of the drum parts with then-current Bluesbreaker drummer Joe Yuele and his own vocal and instrumental tracks. The result, *Archives to Eighties,* contains 13 of *Back to the Roots'* 18 tracks and is considered not only a successful restoration but one of Mayall's most important '80s releases.)

Mayall shifted focus for *Jazz-Blues Fusion* (#64, 1972), which featured jazz trumpeter Blue Mitchell. Mitchell, as well as tenor saxophonist Ernie Watts, and an extensive horn and reeds section appeared on *Moving On.* Mayall's music, with the exception of "Room to Move," got little stateside airplay even during his early-'70s heyday. By the mid-'70s, Mayall's star had faded somewhat, as had his voice—hence the addition of female singer Dee McKinnie on *New Year, New Band, New Company. Notice to Appear,* produced by New Orleans songwriter Allen Toussaint, won little success commercially or critically. *A Banquet in Blues* and *Lots of People* continued this trend. Still, Mayall kept recording. He lost virtually everything he owned, including the original artwork for some of his album covers, which he designed, and a priceless collection of pornography (some dating back to the Victorian era), when his California home was destroyed by fire in 1979. That year also saw the dissolution of another Bluesbreakers lineup. Mayall then recorded *The Bottom Line,* essentially a solo album that featured Cornell Dupree, Steve Jordan, Paul Shaffer, Michael and Randy Brecker, Lee Ritenour, Jeff Porcaro, and Cheryl Lynn among its many guest musicians. Both it and *No More Interviews* (the first album to feature Mayall's wife, singer/songwriter Maggie Parker, on vocals—they married in 1982) represented a return to form.

In early 1982, Mayall, McVie, and Taylor staged a Bluesbreakers reunion, playing a short series of dates in America and Australia. A live album of the reunion concerts was recorded but not released, due to lack of record-company interest. It finally saw the light of day in 1994 under the title *The 1982 Reunion Concert.*

Following *Road Show Blues,* Mayall ceased recording for the next five years, devoting his time to live performances in and around California. In 1984 he assembled the core of one of his most stable lineups, featuring guitarist Coco Montoya (who would remain for a decade) and bassist Bobby Haynes. His next live release, *Behind the Iron Curtain,* neither returned him to the charts nor incited great critical enthusiasm. Yet he retained a following strong enough to support several tours of the U.S. and Europe and, unlike many blues purists of his generation, survived to catch the next blues-revival wave in the late '80s.

By the early '90s Mayall seemed to have come full circle: His 1993 album *Wake Up Call,* which features guest artists Albert Collins, Mick Taylor, Mavis Staples, and Buddy Guy, was one of five nominated for a Best Contemporary Blues Album Grammy. *Padlock on the Blues* featured guest appearances by John Lee Hooker and Ernie Watts. Though the basic lineup has been unusually stable the past decade, the Bluesbreakers have moved on. Longtime guitarist Coco Montoya began a successful solo career, and bassist Greg Rzab joined the Black Crowes and Jimmy Page in summer 2000. Typically, Mayall (who neither smokes nor drinks and never did drugs) began the new century—at age 66—still on the road, traveling the world, about 100 days a year.

Curtis Mayfield

Born June 3, 1942, Chicago, IL; died Dec. 26, 1999, Roswell, GA
1970—*Curtis* (Curtom) 1971—*Curtis/Live!; Roots* 1972—*Superfly* 1973—*His Early Years With the Impressions* (ABC) 1974—*Sweet Exorcist* (Curtom) 1975—*America Today* 1976—*Give, Get, Take and Have* 1977—*Never Say You Can't Survive* 1978—*Do It All Night* 1979—*Heartbeat* (RSO) 1980—*Something to Believe In* 1981—*Love Is the Place* (Boardwalk) 1982—*Honesty* 1985—*We Come in Peace With a Message of Love* (CRC) 1988—*Live in Europe* (Ichiban) 1990—*Take It to the Streets* (Curtom) 1996—*New World Order* (Warner); *People Get Ready! The Curtis Mayfield Story* (Rhino) 1997—*The Very Best of Curtis Mayfield* (Castle).

Curtis Mayfield was a driving force in black music from the early '60s through the mid-'70s, as a singer, writer, producer, and label owner.

Mayfield began singing with gospel groups such as the Northern Jubilee Singers, who were part of his grandmother's Traveling Soul Spiritualist Church. He met lifelong friend and collaborator Jerry Butler [see entry] at a gospel function, and they went on to form the Impressions [see entry], a rhythm & blues vocal group, in 1957. In 1958 they, along with Sam Gooden and Richard and Arthur Brooks, recorded "For Your Precious Love" on Vee-Jay Records. Butler's cool baritone dominated the record, and he left to pursue a solo career. Mayfield and Butler teamed up again in 1960, with Butler singing and Mayfield writing and playing guitar on "He Will Break Your Heart" (#7 pop, #1 R&B). A re-formed Impressions with Mayfield, Gooden, and Fred Cash signed with ABC-Paramount and scored with Mayfield's flamenco-styled "Gypsy Woman" (#20 pop, #2 R&B).

Mayfield then entered a prolific period during which his writing and singing would come to define the Chicago sound, which rivaled Motown in the early and mid-'60s. With the Impressions, Mayfield produced, wrote, and sang lead on numerous hits; some included uplifting civil-rights-movement messages. "It's All Right" (#4 pop, #1 R&B) in 1963; "I'm So Proud" (#14 pop), "Keep On Pushing" (#10 pop), and "Amen" (#7 pop, #17 R&B) in 1964; "People Get Ready" (#14 pop, #3 R&B) in 1965; and "We're a Winner" (#14 pop, #1 R&B) in 1968 reflect the quality of Mayfield's work.

Meanwhile, as the staff producer for Columbia-distributed Okeh Records, Mayfield wrote memorable music for Major Lance—"The Monkey Time" (#8 pop, #4 R&B) and "Um, Um, Um, Um, Um, Um" (#5 pop)—and for Gene Chandler: "Just Be True" (#19 pop) and "Nothing Can Stop Me" (#18 pop, #3 R&B). On his own Windy C and Mayfield labels, he produced hits with the Five Stairsteps and Cubie, "World of Fantasy" (#12 R&B), and the Fascinations, "Girls Are Out to Get You" (#13 R&B), respectively.

In the late '60s Mayfield started his third company, Curtom, this one distributed by Buddah Records. During the '70s Curtom moved from Buddah to Warner Bros. to RSO Records for distribution. In 1970 Mayfield also made a major career move, leaving the Impressions to go solo, though he continued to direct the group's career through the decade.

Solo albums—*Curtis* (#19), *Curtis/Live!* (#21), and *Roots* (#40) all sold well, establishing Mayfield as a solo performer. But it was his soundtrack to the blaxploitation film *Superfly* that is generally considered his masterpiece—an eerie yet danceable blend of Mayfield's knowing falsetto with Latin percussion and predisco rhythm guitars. The 4-million-

Curtis Mayfield

selling album (#1, 1972) included two gold singles, "Superfly" (#8 pop, #5 R&B) and "Freddie's Dead" (#4 pop, #2 R&B); it sold an additional million copies as a tape. It foreshadowed Mayfield's continued involvement with film in the '70s. He scored *Claudine,* writing the Gladys Knight and the Pips' single "On and On" in 1974; *Let's Do It Again,* which featured the Staples Singers on the title song in 1975; and *Sparkle* with Aretha Franklin in 1976. Two years later Mayfield and Franklin would team again for *Almighty Fire.* In 1977 Mayfield would both score and act in the low-budget prison drama *Short Eyes,* a critical success.

As a solo artist, Mayfield continued to score with "Future Shock" (#11 R&B, 1973), "If I Were Only a Child Again" (#22 R&B, 1973), "Can't Say Nothin' " (#16 R&B, 1973), "Kung Fu" (#3 R&B, 1974), "So in Love" (#9 R&B, 1975), "Only You Babe" (#8 R&B, 1976), and two duets with Linda Clifford: "Between You Baby and Me" (#14 R&B, 1979) and "Love's Sweet Sensation" (#34 R&B, 1980).

In 1980 Mayfield, who by then had moved with his family (including six children) from Chicago to Atlanta, signed with Boardwalk Records and enjoyed a popular album and singles with *Love Is the Place* and "She Don't Let Nobody (But Me)" (#15 R&B) and "Toot 'n' Toot 'n' Toot" (#2 R&B). Mayfield rejoined the Impressions for a 1983 reunion tour. Mayfield's recording career hit a wall when Boardwalk went bankrupt, but he formed his own CRC label to release 1985's *We Come in Peace With a Message of Love,* which went unnoticed, as did his 1990 album for the revived Curtom label (distributed by Atlanta's Ichiban). Mayfield continued touring, however, and was especially popular in England, where the band the Blow Monkeys recorded a duet with him in 1987, "(Celebrate) The Day After You."

In 1990 Mayfield scored the dud movie *Return of Superfly;* the music was released on an album, *Superfly 1990,* on which Mayfield collaborated with rapper Ice-T—one of several '90s stars, such as Arrested Development and Lenny Kravitz, to cite Mayfield's influence. On August 14, 1990, while Mayfield was performing an outdoor concert in Brooklyn, New York, a lighting rig fell atop him, leaving him permanently paralyzed from the neck down. Mayfield and the Impressions were subsequently inducted into the Rock and Roll Hall of Fame, and a lavish and emotional tribute was paid to Mayfield at the 1994 Grammy Awards gala.

In 1994 Shanachie Records released an all-star Mayfield-tribute album entitled *People Get Ready,* which featured Delbert McClinton, Jerry Butler, Bunny Wailer, and Huey Lewis and the News. Another tribute, *A Tribute to Curtis Mayfield,* included Eric Clapton, Elton John, Bruce Springsteen, Gladys Knight, and Jerry Butler, among others. The enduring appeal of Mayfield's songs is evidenced in the wide range of artists who have recorded them: Deniece Williams ("I'm So Proud"), UB40 ("I Gotta Keep Moving"), David Allan Coe ("For Your Precious Love"), Rod Stewart and Jeff Beck ("People Get Ready"), and En Vogue ("Giving Him Something He Can Feel").

In 1996 Mayfield released his last album, *New World Order,* which included guest appearances by Aretha Franklin and Mavis Staples. Considerably weakened by his quadriplegia, Mayfield was forced to record some of his vocals one line at a time. (This is because the diaphragm, which is crucial to vocal control, was rendered paralyzed by Mayfield's spinal cord injury.) The record was warmly greeted. Unfortunately, complications from diabetes, which had resulted in the amputation of a leg in 1998, led to his death at age 57 in 1999. Just prior to his death, he and the Impressions had recorded their part of an all-star version of "People Get Ready" for the Atlanta's Year 2000 celebration. In 2000 Mayfield was posthumously inducted into the Songwriters' Hall of Fame and, with the Impressions, he received the Rhythm & Blues Foundation's Pioneer Award.

Paul McCartney

Born James Paul McCartney, June 18, 1942, Liverpool, Eng. 1967—*The Family Way* soundtrack (London Records) 1970—*McCartney* (Apple) 1971—*Ram* (credited to Paul and Linda McCartney) 1980—*McCartney II* (Columbia) 1982—*Tug of War* 1983—*Pipes of Peace* 1984—*Give My Regards to Broad Street* 1986—*Press to Play* (Capitol) 1987—*All the Best!* 1989—*Flowers in the Dirt* 1990—*Tripping the Live Fantastic; Tripping the Live Fantastic—Highlights!* 1991—*Unplugged; CHOBA B CCCP—The Russian Album; Liverpool Oratorio* (EMI Classics) 1993—*Off the Ground; Paul Is Live* 1997—*Flaming Pie; Paul McCartney's Standing Stone* (EMI Classics) 1999—*Run Devil Run.*

Wings, formed 1971: P. McCartney; Linda McCartney (b. Linda Louise Eastman, Sep. 24, 1941, Scarsdale, NY; d. Apr. 17, 1998, Santa Barbara, CA), kybds., voc.; Denny Laine (b. Brian Hines, Oct. 29, 1944, Eng.), gtr., kybds., voc.; Denny Seiwell, drums.

1971—*Wild Life* (Apple) 1972—(+ Henry McCullough [b. Scot.], gtr.) 1973—*Red Rose Speedway* (– McCullough; – Seiwell); *Band on the Run* 1974—(+ Jimmy McCulloch [b. June 4, 1952, Glasgow, Scot.; d. Sep. 27, 1979, London, Eng.], gtr.; + Geoff Britton, drums; – Britton; + Joe English [b. Feb. 7, 1949, Rochester, NY], drums) 1975—*Venus and Mars* (Capitol) 1976—*Wings at the Speed of Sound; Wings Over America* (– English; – McCulloch) 1978—*London Town; Wings Greatest* (+ Steve Holly, drums; + Laurence Juber, gtr., voc.) 1979—*Back to the Egg* (Columbia) 2001—*Wingspan (Hits & History)* (Capitol).

The Fireman (McCartney; Youth [b. Dec. 27, 1960]) 1994—*Strawberries Oceans Ships Forest* (Capitol) 1998—*Rushes.*

Paul McCartney's gift for light-pop songwriting has made him the most commercially successful ex-Beatle and one of the most successful songwriters of the century. He answered his critics in 1976 with the single "Silly Love Songs," one of many post-Beatles hits. If, as some critics maintain, his solo work hasn't measured up to the standards of his collaborations with John Lennon, McCartney has still shown a consistent talent for writing songs that are tuneful and popular. McCartney was also the only ex-Beatle to form a permanent working band; Wings, which he led from 1971 to 1981, recorded for more years than the Beatles. Sir Paul is the only ex-Beatle to date to have been knighted.

Paul McCartney grew up in working-class Liverpool. His father, James, led the Jim Mac Jazz Band in the 1920s. A few months after his mother, Mary, died of breast cancer in 1956, Paul bought his first guitar and learned to play. In June 1956 he met Lennon and asked to join his band, the Quarrymen; McCartney's rendition of Eddie Cochran's "Twenty Flight Rock" at a subsequent audition won him entry.

In 1963 McCartney met Jane Asher, to whom he addressed many of his best-known love songs, and on Christmas Day 1967, at a McCartney family party, he announced their engagement. But by July 1968 the engagement was off. Soon after, he met American photographer Linda Eastman, whom he married on March 12, 1969.

In April 1970, only two weeks before the scheduled release of the Beatles' *Let It Be*, McCartney released his first nonsoundtrack solo album—a one-man-studio-band LP recorded in Campbelltown, England, in late 1969. The double-platinum *McCartney* (#1, 1970) had a pronounced homemade quality; it was spare and sounded almost unfinished, but it also contained "Maybe I'm Amazed," which became an international hit and McCartney's first post-Beatles pop standard (the Beatles had only recently disbanded as the tune became a hit). The winsome, homespun-ditty motif continued with *Ram* (#2, 1971), credited to Paul and Linda McCartney. It also inspired Lennon's "How Do You Sleep?"—a vicious, thinly veiled attack on McCartney. Meanwhile, *Ram* yielded two major hit singles in "Another Day" (#5, 1971) and "Uncle Albert/Admiral Halsey," which made #1 in America.

Later in 1971 McCartney formed Wings, which was intended as a recording and touring outfit. Along with Linda, Wings featured American session drummer Denny Seiwell and ex–Moody Blues guitarist Denny Laine. Wings' *Wild Life*, with Linda McCartney on keyboards and backup vocals, sold only moderately, failing to yield a hit single. In 1972 ex–Grease Band guitarist Henry McCullough joined.

Paul McCartney

McCartney spent 1972 releasing several singles, including "Give Ireland Back to the Irish" (#16 U.K.) (rush-released after the January 1972 "Bloody Sunday" incident in which British soldiers killed 13 Irish civilians in Londonderry, Ireland; the song was banned by the BBC), "Mary Had a Little Lamb" (#9, U.K., #28 U.S.) (yes, the nursery rhyme), and the hard-rocking, mildly salacious "Hi Hi Hi." Only the latter was a major U.S. hit, going to #10 in 1973.

Red Rose Speedway (#1, 1973), the next Wings album, yielded a #1 hit single in the U.S. with the heavily orchestrated ballad "My Love." Also in 1973, McCartney was arrested and then released on a drug charge, and he did his own television special, which received mixed reviews in both the U.S. and the U.K. Later Wings made its first tour of Britain and recorded the title theme song for the James Bond film *Live and Let Die*, which went to #2 in the U.S. Laine released a solo LP, *Ahh Laine*.

After Wings' U.K. tour, Seiwell and Henry McCullough left the group. Denny Laine accompanied Paul and Linda to Nigeria to record *Band on the Run*. While each of the previous Wings albums had ended up going gold, *Band on the Run* (#1, 1974) went triple platinum in short order and yielded two Top 10 hit singles—"Helen Wheels" (#10, 1973) and "Jet" (#7, 1974)—and the bouncy title track minisuite (#11, 1974). It also included McCartney's answer to Lennon's "How Do You Sleep?" in "Let Me Roll It," and featured a cover photo of McCartney accompanied by such celebrities as film actors James Coburn and Christopher Lee.

McCartney formed a new Wings, recruiting guitarist Jimmy McCulloch from Thunderclap Newman and Stone the Crows, and drummer Geoff Britton, a British karate expert. They recorded "Junior's Farm" (#3, 1974) in Nashville in 1974 and, later that year, went to New Orleans (where they found new drummer Joe English) to record *Venus and Mars*, which yielded several hit singles (including the #1 "Listen to What the Man Said") and went platinum. *At the Speed of Sound* found McCartney giving his band members a chance to compose and sing much of the material, but McCartney's own contributions were almost all hits. Two went gold: "Silly Love Songs" (#1, 1976) and "Let 'Em In" (#3, 1976). Shortly after the album's release, Wings completed a world tour that had begun in Britain on September 9, 1975, and ended on October 21, 1976. The *Over America* triple-record live album was recorded on that tour.

In 1977 McCartney, under the pseudonym Percy Thrillington, recorded an obscure, all-instrumental version of *Ram* and produced Denny Laine's *Holly Days*, a solo album of Buddy Holly songs. A live "Maybe I'm Amazed" hit #10 in 1977. That year saw the release of the McCartney-Laine "Mull of Kintyre," based on a Scottish folk song, which became the first single ever to sell 2 million copies in Britain and was a minor hit in the U.S. as well. It was McCartney's first British #1 single since he'd left the Beatles. Later that year, under the name Susie and the Red Stripes, McCartney and Wings had another minor hit single in the reggae-inflected "Seaside Woman."

After *London Town*, which yielded another #1, "With a

Little Luck," Jimmy McCulloch departed for the re-formed Small Faces. *Back to the Egg* failed to yield a hit and sold unspectacularly. In January 1980 McCartney was arrested for possession of marijuana in Tokyo at the beginning of a Japanese tour, jailed for 10 days, then freed and not prosecuted. Soon after, he and Wings embarked on a British tour, after which drummer English left. McCartney then organized all-star benefit concerts for the people of Kampuchea and released *McCartney II* (#3, 1980), his first one-man-band album since his solo debut. It contained the #1 hit "Coming Up."

In April 1981 Denny Laine announced he was leaving Wings, the reason being McCartney's reluctance to tour because of the death threats he was receiving in the wake of John Lennon's murder. McCartney continued with the well-received *Tug of War,* a solo album featuring a host of guest performers (Laine, ex-Beatle Ringo Starr, Beatles producer George Martin), most notably Stevie Wonder, who sang with McCartney on the #1 hit single "Ebony and Ivory." *Tug* also yielded a #10 hit in "Take It Away." McCartney sang on Michael Jackson's "The Girl Is Mine," a Top 10 hit in 1983. Jackson returned the favor by singing on *Pipes of Peace*'s "Say Say Say," which topped the chart later that same year.

Embittered by the 1967 sale of publishing rights to his and John Lennon's Beatles songs to British film producer Lew Grade—a sale made while the Beatles were in India with Maharishi Mahesh Yogi—McCartney has invested extensively in pop-song copyrights over the years. Among his holdings are the entire Buddy Holly catalogue, "On Wisconsin," and "Autumn Leaves." However, shortly after "Say Say Say" was a hit, McCartney advised Michael Jackson to invest in music publishing—and Jackson later bought the Northern Songs catalogue, which included all of the Beatles songs McCartney had written with Lennon. McCartney never hid his anger at the move, especially when Jackson began licensing Beatles tunes for television commercials (such as "Revolution," used in a late-'80s Nike sneaker ad). McCartney later told *Musician* magazine that "complications with Yoko" (whose son Sean was a close friend of Jackson's) had prevented him from making a competitive bid for his own songs.

In 1984 McCartney made a dramatic feature film, *Give My Regards to Broad Street,* set within London's music industry, which was roundly panned by critics. Its soundtrack (#21, 1984) consisted largely of rerecorded Beatles and McCartney hits; the album went gold, and one new track, the ballad "No More Lonely Nights," became a #6 pop hit. He scored a #7 pop hit in 1985 with the theme song to the comedy film *Spies Like Us. Press to Play* (#30, 1986), found McCartney collaborating with ex-10cc Eric Stewart; the album's only hit was "Press" (#21, 1986). In 1988, as a sort of glasnost gesture, McCartney released an album of rock oldies exclusively on the Soviet Melodiya label under the title *CHOBA B CCCP* ("Back in the USSR," roughly translated). For *Flowers in the Dirt* (#21, 1989), McCartney collaborated on some songs with Elvis Costello (McCartney also cowrote and played on a couple of tracks on Costello's *Spike,* including "Veronica"). The album yielded a hit in "My Brave Face" (#25, 1989), but McCartney was reportedly quite disappointed that the album failed to chart higher, despite a 1989 world tour (with a band featuring ex-Pretenders guitarist Robbie McIntosh and ex–Average White Band bassist Hamish Stuart) that was documented on *Tripping the Live Fantastic* (#26, 1990).

In early 1991 McCartney became one of the first major artists to release an album from his appearance on MTV's *Unplugged* acoustic showcase; *Unplugged (The Official Bootleg)* hit #14. Later that year McCartney released *CHOBA B CCCP* in the U.S. (where it reached only #109) and unveiled his first classical work, *Liverpool Oratorio* (#177, 1991), which failed to impress classical critics. McCartney returned to pop with *Off the Ground;* the album entered the chart at #17 but dropped quickly and failed to yield a hit single. His New World tour fared better, and resulted in another live album, *Paul Is Live* (#78, 1993). In April 1993 McCartney was joined onstage by Starr for "Hey Jude" at an all-star Earth Day concert in Los Angeles.

In 1994 McCartney quietly assumed the pseudonym the Fireman and released *Strawberries Oceans Ships Forest,* a techno-dance collaboration with ambient producer Youth (a second Fireman album, *Rushes,* would follow in 1998). Executed with far less stealth was the massive *Beatles Anthology* project, in which he reunited with George Harrison and Ringo Starr for a documentary miniseries and three double albums of demos and live rarities (all three topped the U.S. chart). *Anthology 1* and *2* each included a "new" Beatles track ("Free as a Bird," #6, 1995, and "Real Love," #11, 1996, respectively), which were built upon John Lennon demo recordings.

McCartney was knighted by the Queen of England in 1997. Later that year he released *Flaming Pie* (#2) (the title a reference to a joke Lennon told about how the Beatles got their name), which featured guest appearances by Starr, George Martin, Steve Miller, Jeff Lynne, and McCartney's son, James, on guitar. He closed out the year by releasing his second classical piece, *Standing Stone* (#194).

On April 17, 1998, McCartney lost the love of his life when Linda succumbed to breast cancer. Except for the 10 days he spent in jail in Japan, the couple had never been apart. Though her musical talent was often questioned by critics, Linda found great success in other endeavors: as an animal-rights activist, photographer, vegetarian cookbook author, and vegan frozen-foods entrepreneur. The couple had four children: Heather (from Linda's previous marriage), Mary, Stella, and James. After a year of mourning, McCartney went back into Abbey Road studio with a new band (including Pink Floyd's David Gilmour and Deep Purple's Ian Paice) and began recording the vintage rock & roll covers (and three new originals) that made up *Run Devil Run* (#27, 1999). He celebrated its release with a one-off gig at Liverpool's Cavern Club on December 14, 1999, which was broadcast over the Internet to an audience of more than 3 million. Earlier that year he was inducted into the Rock and Roll Hall of Fame as a solo artist.

The year 2000 saw the release of *A Garland for Linda* (#7

Classical), a benefit album of modern classical pieces, including McCartney's own "Nova." A new solo album of original material was planned for release by year's end.

Delbert McClinton

Born Nov. 4, 1940, Lubbock, TX
1972—*Delbert and Glen* (Clean) 1973—*Subject to Change* 1975—*Victim of Life's Circumstances* (ABC) 1976—*Genuine Cowhide* 1977—*Love Rustler* 1978—*Second Wind* (Capricorn); *Very Early Delbert McClinton* (Le Cam) 1979—*Keeper of the Flame* (Capricorn) 1980—*The Jealous Kind* (Capitol) 1981—*Plain From the Heart* 1989—*Live From Austin* (Alligator) 1990—*I'm With You* (Curb) 1991—*Best of Delbert McClinton* 1992—*Never Been Rocked Enough* 1993—*Delbert McClinton* 1994—*Honky Tonkin' Blues* (MCA) 1997—*One of the Fortunate Few* (Rising Tide) 1999—*The Ultimate Collection* (Hip-o) 2001—*Nothing Personal* (New West).

Delbert McClinton has been singing R&B, blues, rockabilly, and country for 35 years, starting on the Texas honky-tonk circuit. In the late '50s McClinton's Straitjackets were the house band and one of the few white acts at Jacks, a Fort Worth club where they backed up Howlin' Wolf, Lightnin' Hopkins, and Big Joe Turner. McClinton's first record, a cover of Sonny Boy Williamson's "Wake Up Baby," released in 1960, was the first white single played on Fort Worth's KNOK.

Inspired by bluesman Jimmy Reed, McClinton switched from guitar to harmonica, and in the early '60s, when he toured England with Bruce Channel (he'd played on Channel's #1 1962 hit "Hey Baby"), he taught some harp licks to John Lennon, who was playing in a then-unknown opening act, the Beatles. In 1964 and 1965 he had a group called the Ron Dels, who were shunted around to three labels, though one song ("If You Really Want Me To, I'll Go") did reach the Hot 100 in 1965.

McClinton spent the late '60s on the local Texas bar circuit, until he and Glen Clark formed Delbert and Glen, a duo that cut two LPs for Atlantic's Clean subsidiary in 1972 and 1973. He didn't get a solo contract until 1975, and his subsequent albums on ABC won critical kudos but sold poorly. In 1978 he recorded two discs for Capricorn just before the label folded; his composition "Two More Bottles of Wine" later became a #1 country hit for Emmylou Harris, and the Blues Brothers recorded his "B Movie Boxcar Blues." His next record, *The Jealous Kind,* recorded with some Muscle Shoals musicians, turned his luck around, earning McClinton his own Top 40 hit, "Giving It Up for Your Love" (#8, 1980).

Since then, McClinton has retained a strong following, having released several more albums. In 1992 he won a Grammy for his duet with Bonnie Raitt, "Good Man, Good Woman," and in 1993 another duet, with Tanya Tucker, entitled "Tell Me About It" was nominated for Best Country Collaboration With Vocals. His *Live From Austin* was also nominated for a Best Contemporary Blues Grammy. After several years of silence he returned with *One of the Fortunate Few.* Since the early '90s he's also hosted and booked Delbert McClinton & Friends Sandy Beach Cruises, in which 1,000 fans pack a Caribbean cruise ship and enjoy a week of nonstop concerts performed by dozens of musicians.

Delbert McClinton

Van McCoy

Born Jan. 6, 1944, Washington, DC; died July 6, 1979, Englewood, NJ
1975—*Disco Baby* (Avco) 1976—*The Hustle* (H&L) 1978—*My Favorite Fantasy* (MCA) 1979—*Lonely Dancer; Sweet Rhythm* (H&L).

Throughout the '60s and '70s, Van McCoy was primarily a songwriter and producer for artists like Aretha Franklin, Gladys Knight and the Pips, Peaches and Herb, and Melba Moore. He had one of disco's biggest hits with his own 1975 instrumental single "The Hustle" (#1 pop, #1 R&B).

McCoy studied piano from age four, and a year later he and his older brother Norman, a violinist, began performing at Washington teas as the McCoy Brothers. He wrote his first song at age 12, and while studying psychology at Howard University, he began singing with the Starlighters, a group that cut a few locally released records. During his second year at Howard, he moved to Philadelphia and started a record label with his uncle.

McCoy then began writing and producing hits for Ruby and the Romantics, Gladys Knight, Barbara Lewis, and others. He recorded an album on Columbia, then in 1968 formed his own record production and music publishing company with Joe Cobb. In 1973 he and Charles Kipps established White House Productions, renamed McCoy-Kipps Productions in 1976. Other popular singles by McCoy include "Change With the Times" (#46 pop, #6 R&B, 1975) and "Party" (#69 pop, #20 R&B, 1976). He died of a heart attack in 1979.

Ian McCulloch: See Echo and the Bunnymen

Michael McDonald

Born Feb. 12, 1952, St. Louis, MO
1982—*If That's What It Takes* (Warner Bros.) 1985—*No Lookin' Back* 1990—*Take It to Heart* (Reprise) 1993—*Blink of an Eye* 2000—*Blue Obsession* (Ramp).

In the latter half of the '70s, as singer and keyboardist for the Doobie Brothers, onetime Steely Dan member Michael McDonald helped redefine the sound of what had once been a straight-ahead rock & roll band. McDonald's soulful, falsetto-happy vocals and gospel-influenced instrumental technique guided the Doobies into mellow R&B territory. After that group disbanded in 1982, the singer/songwriter embarked on a solo career that took him even further in that direction. On his own, and in duets with several leading R&B artists, McDonald established a smooth, light, jazz-inflected style that appealed to fans of adult contemporary music. He also garnered a few major pop singles and earned the respect of critics and the R&B community.

Before the Doobies' breakup, McDonald sang backup on one of Christopher Cross' big hits, 1980's "Ride Like the Wind" (#2). McDonald released his first solo album, *If That's What It Takes,* two years later. The album went to #6 and spawned the single "I Keep Forgettin' (Every Time You're Near)" (#4 pop, #7 R&B, 1982). The following year he teamed up with James Ingram on "Yah Mo B There" (#19 pop, #5 R&B, 1984). *No Lookin' Back* featured a slightly harder-edged sound than its predecessor. The album peaked at #45, and its title track went to #34, both in 1985.

In 1986 another duet with a contemporary soul icon proved McDonald's biggest hit to date: "On My Own," a lovelorn ballad that paired him with Patti LaBelle, was a #1 smash. McDonald entered the Top 10 again later that year with "Sweet Freedom" (#7), the theme song for the film comedy *Running Scared.* McDonald didn't release another studio album until 1990, though, and that effort, *Take It to Heart,* only made it to #110. In 1992 the singer enjoyed a slight commercial rebound, and a considerable artistic coup, when Aretha Franklin featured him on her 1992 R&B hit, "Ever Changing Times" (#19). Also that year, McDonald reconciled with the driving forces behind Steely Dan, Donald Fagen and Walter Becker, in the New York Rock and Soul Revue, a recording and touring collective that also included Boz Scaggs, Phoebe Snow, and Chuck Brown. In 1993 McDonald released his fourth solo album, *Blink of an Eye,* a commercial flop.

In 1995 McDonald joined the Doobie Brothers for a reunion tour; the same year, he sought creative inspiration by moving with his wife and two children from Southern California to Nashville. He continued to tour solo and recorded an album that would have been released in 1997 had he and his record label, Reprise, not parted ways. McDonald returned to the spotlight in 1999, performing a song ("Eyes of a Child") on the soundtrack to the animated movie *South Park: Bigger, Longer and Uncut.* Around the same time, he formed an independent label, Ramp Records, with producer Chris Pelonis and actor Jeff Bridges (who is also a musician). With three more tracks added since the '97 sessions, McDonald's *Blue Obsession* was Ramp's first release, in 2000. The same year, the singer was honored with the Yamaha Lifetime Achievement Award and tribute concert, where he performed with the Doobie Brothers, among others.

Mississippi Fred McDowell

Born Jan. 12, 1904, Rossville, TN; died July 3, 1972, Memphis, TN
1969—*I Don't Play No Rock 'n' Roll* (Capitol) 1972—*Mississippi Fred McDowell 1904–1972* (Just Sunshine) 1973—*Keep Your Lamp Trimmed and Burning* (Arhoolie) 1989—*Shake 'Em On Down* (Tomato) 1993—*The Train I Ride* (New Rose) 1995—*Live at the Mayfair Hotel* (American).

Although Mississippi Fred McDowell didn't make his first recording until the age of 55, he proved to be among the most influential of blues singers/guitarists on rock & roll, particularly with singer/guitarist Bonnie Raitt, who brought him on her early tours and recorded his songs. McDowell made dozens of records but is probably best known as the composer of "You Got to Move," covered by the Rolling Stones on *Sticky Fingers.*

McDowell taught himself the guitar as a teenager and played locally in Tennessee while working as a farmer. In 1926 he moved to Memphis to become a professional musician, which he gave up for farming again in 1940, when he relocated to Como, Mississippi. His recording career began in 1959, at which point he began devoting more and more time to music. He made records, frequently with his wife, Annie Mae, and played at all the major folk and blues festivals of the '60s. With the increased attention paid by rock & rollers to bluesmen, he appeared at a number of rock festivals as well. In addition to his many records, McDowell was captured in nearly a half-dozen films, including *The Blues Maker* (1968) and *Fred McDowell* (1969). He died of abdominal ulcers in 1972.

Reba McEntire

Born Reba Nell McEntire, Mar. 28, 1955, Chockie, OK
1980—*Feel the Fire* (Mercury) 1981—*Heart to Heart* 1982—*Unlimited* 1983—*Behind the Scenes* 1984—*Just a Little Love* 1985—*The Best of Reba McEntire; Have I Got a Deal for You* (MCA) 1986—*Whoever's in New England; What Am I Gonna Do About You; Reba Nell McEntire* (Mercury) 1987—*The Last One to Know* (MCA); *Reba McEntire's Greatest Hits; Merry Christmas to You* 1988—*Reba* 1989—*Sweet Sixteen; Reba Live* 1990—*Rumor Has It* 1991—*For My Broken Heart* 1992—*It's Your Call* 1993—*Greatest Hits,*

vol. 2 1994—*Read My Mind* 1995—*Starting Over* 1996—*What if It's You* 1998—*If You See Him* 1999—*The Secret of Giving: A Christmas Collection; So Good Together.*

A feisty redhead with a thick Oklahoma accent, Reba McEntire parlayed a strong, pure voice and a penchant for singing songs about ordinary women—and the extraordinary demands that life places on them—into country-music superstardom. She is one of the best-selling female country artists of all time, yet still remains accessible enough for her fans to refer to her simply as Reba. McEntire's unaffected, strikingly emotional delivery invited a few comparisons to her idol Patsy Cline; and like Cline, McEntire made news outside the C&W arena as the result of a plane crash: In 1991 eight members of her band were killed when a twin-engine jet bound for a show in Texas slammed into the side of a mountain. (The musicians included Jim Hammon, Paula Kaye Evans, Michael Thomas, Terry Jackson, Joey Cigainero, Tony Saputo, and Chris Austin, as well as band manager, Kirk Cappello.) The tragedy occurred the same year that McEntire released *For My Broken Heart,* her most consistently grim album (and one of her biggest commercial successes).

McEntire's father was a steer roper on the rodeo circuit. During high school, the singer competed at rodeos as a barrel racer, and played nightclubs with her siblings as the Singing McEntires. She eventually went to college and planned to become a teacher, but a gig singing the national anthem at the National Rodeo Finals resulted in a contract with Mercury Records. Her first Top 10 C&W hit came in 1980—four years after signing—with "(You Lift Me) Up to Heaven" (#8). A steady stream of country hits followed: "Today All Over Again" (#5, 1981), "I'm Not That Lonely Yet" (#3, 1982), "Can't Even Get the Blues" (#1, 1982), "You're the First Time I've Thought About Leaving" (#1, 1983), "Why Do We Want (What We Know We Can't Have)" (#7, 1983), and "Just a Little Love" (#5, 1984).

But it was in the latter half of the 1980s, after she switched to MCA Records, that McEntire's star really rose. Her string of Top 3 C&W albums began with 1986's *Whoever's in New England* (#1) and continued with *What Am I Gonna Do About You* (#1, 1986), *Greatest Hits* (#2, 1987), *The Last One to Know* (#3, 1987), *Reba* (#1, 1988), *Sweet Sixteen* (#1, 1989), *Reba Live* (#2, 1989), *Rumor Has It* (#2, 1990), *For My Broken Heart* (#3, 1991), *It's Your Call* (#1, 1992), *Greatest Hits, vol. 2* (#2, 1993), *Read My Mind* (#2, 1994), *Starting Over* (#1, 1995), *What If It's You* (#1, 1996), and *If You See Him* (#2, 1998). (*If You See Him* also went to #8 on the pop-album chart in 1998.) McEntire racked up an equally impressive list of top country singles, including "How Blue" (#1, 1984), "Somebody Should Leave" (#1, 1985),"Whoever's in New England" (#1, 1986), "Little Rock" (#1, 1986), "What Am I Gonna Do About You" (#1, 1986), "One Promise Too Late" (#1, 1987), "The Last One to Know" (#1, 1987), "Love Will Find Its Way to You" (#1, 1988), "I Know How He Feels" (#1, 1988), "New Fool at an Old Game" (#1, 1988), "Cathy's Clown" (#1, 1989), "Walk On" (#2, 1990), "You Lie" (#1, 1990), "Rumor Has It" (#3, 1990), "Fallin' Out of Love" (#2, 1991), "For My Broken Heart" (#1, 1991), "Is There Life Out There" (#1, 1992), "The Greatest Man I Never Knew" (#3, 1992), "Does He Love You" (#1, 1993), "Till You Love Me" (#2, 1994), "The Heart Is a Lonely Hunter" (#1, 1995), "And Still" (#2, 1995), "The Fear of Being Alone" (#2, 1996), "How Was I to Know" (#1, 1996), "I'd Rather Ride Around With You" (#2, 1997), and "If You See Him/If You See Her," a collaboration with Brooks & Dunn (#1, 1998).

McEntire is also known as a strong businesswoman; she and her second husband, Narvel Blackstock—her band's steel guitarist, who became her road manager—ran Starstruck Entertainment, a company that handled song publishing and managing other acts. McEntire branched out into acting in 1989 with a role in the cult horror flick *Tremors*. She also costarred in the Kenny Rogers' TV movie *The Gambler,* as well as a few telefilms based on her own songs. In 1994 McEntire published her autobiography, *Reba: My Story* (written with Tom Carter), which spent 15 weeks on the *New York Times* bestseller list. That same year, her album *Read My Mind* reached #2 on the country chart. She continued to release a new album almost every year in the late 1990s, and two in 1999, one a Christmas collection. In 1999 McEntire also published a second book, *Comfort From a Country Quilt: Finding New Inspiration and Strength From Old-Fashioned Values,* reflections on her life, particularly being a mother to her then-nine-year-old son, Shelby. In addition, she went on the road with *The Singer's Diary,* a musical play about her life and career from 1974 to 1991 (with McEntire playing herself) that ended with a concert. In March 2001 she returned to feature-film acting in *One Night at McCool's,* with Michael Douglas and Paul Reiser. She became a hit on Broadway that year as well, starring in *Annie Get Your Gun.*

McFadden and Whitehead

Gene McFadden, born 1949, Philadelphia, PA; John Whitehead, born 1948, Philadelphia
1979—*McFadden and Whitehead* (Philadelphia International) 1980—*I Heard It in a Love Song*
John Whitehead solo: 1988—*I Need Money Bad* (Mercury).

Gene McFadden and John Whitehead are prolific songwriters who contributed greatly to the success of Kenny Gamble and Leon Huff's Philadelphia International Records.

The duo's career began when both belonged to a vocal group called the Epsilons. They worked with many of the Stax stars, including Otis Redding, and sang background vocals on Arthur Conley's "Sweet Soul Music." Later the group's name was changed to Talk of the Town. Frustrated by their lack of success as performers, McFadden and Whitehead turned to songwriting. During their tenure as staff writers for PIR, they wrote "Bad Luck," "Where Are All My Friends," and "Wake Up Everybody" for Harold Melvin and the Blue Notes (all with arranger Vic Carstarphen); "Backstabbers" (Whitehead with Gamble and Huff) for the O'Jays; and "I'll Always Love My Mama" (Whitehead, Carstarphen, Huff) for the Intruders.

In 1979 they recorded one of that summer's most popular

singles, "Ain't No Stoppin' Us Now" (#13 pop, #1 R&B). In the early '80s the duo produced records for Teddy Pendergrass, Melba Moore, and others. They each took a turn at recording solo albums. Whitehead was convicted in the '80s of tax evasion. He had a minor R&B hit in 1988 with "I Need Money Bad." As of 2000 the pair was together again, working on new material for the Philly Sounds label.

Bobby McFerrin

Born Mar. 11, 1950, New York, NY
1982—*Bobby McFerrin* (Elektra/Musician) 1984—*The Voice* 1986—*Spontaneous Inventions* (Blue Note) 1988—*Simple Pleasures* (EMI-Manhattan) 1990—*Medicine Music* 1992—*Hush* (with Yo-Yo Ma) (Sony Masterworks); *Play* (with Chick Corea) (Blue Note) 1995—*Paper Music* (with the St. Paul Chamber Orchestra) (Sony Classical) 1996—*Bang!Zoom* (Blue Note); *The Mozart Sessions* (with Chick Corea and the St. Paul Chamber Orchestra) (Sony Classical); *The Best of Bobby McFerrin* (Blue Note) 1997—*Circlesongs* (Sony Classical).

A human one-man band, vocalist Bobby McFerrin is one of the most unique talents in the history of America's performing arts. McFerrin has developed a virtuosic ability to vocally produce musical sounds and tones that can replicate virtually any instrument—a miracle of technique and musical knowledge balanced by a zany wit and nerve.

Both of McFerrin's parents were opera singers; his father dubbed Sidney Poitier's singing in the 1959 film version of *Porgy and Bess*. McFerrin studied piano rather than voice, attending Juilliard and Sacramento State College. He had been playing piano for University of Utah dance workshops when he decided to change musical direction. While singing in journeyman bands, McFerrin came to the attention of noted jazz vocalist Jon Hendricks, who recruited him for his own group. McFerrin's next break came when comedian Bill Cosby caught him performing with Hendricks' group in a San Francisco club. Cosby got McFerrin booked at the prestigious Playboy Jazz Festival in 1980. After his triumphant appearance at the 1981 Kool Jazz Festival in New York, McFerrin was signed by Elektra.

McFerrin had no intention of being a traditional jazz singer. He performed alone, using his multitextured voice while rhythmically beating his body to simulate full-band accompaniment. Standard jazz fare was also avoided; McFerrin took on James Brown's "I Feel Good," the Beatles' "Blackbird," Cream's "Sunshine of Your Love," and funky tunes like his original "I'm My Own Walkman"; all manner of classical, jazz, and pop strains would routinely arise during his free-form performances.

In 1988 McFerrin had a fluke hit single with "Don't Worry Be Happy" (#1), a Reagan-era piece of gloss with a video that helped to cement McFerrin's lovable madcap image. By the late '80s McFerrin was ubiquitous—recording with jazz musicians (Chick Corea) and classical players (Yo-Yo Ma), and singing *The Cosby Show* theme and on TV commercials. In 1993 he was a featured performer at the White House jazz picnic, a sure sign, along with the 10 Grammy Awards he'd earned over the years, of his mainstream appeal.

In 1994 McFerrin's career took a new turn when he was appointed creative chair of the St. Paul Chamber Orchestra—he would serve as conductor and develop educational programs. He has continued to release albums ranging from classical music to jazz to pop.

MC5

Formed 1965, Lincoln Park, MI
Rob Tyner (b. Robert Derminer, Dec. 12, 1944; d. Sep. 17, 1991, Royal Oak, MI), voc.; Wayne Kramer (b. Apr. 30, 1948, Detroit, MI), gtr.; Fred "Sonic" Smith (b. WV; d. Nov. 4, 1994, Detroit), gtr.; Michael Davis, bass; Dennis Thompson, drums.
1969—*Kick Out the Jams* (Elektra) 1970—*Back in the USA* (Atlantic) 1971—*High Time* 1983—*Babes in Arms* cassette (ROIR) 2000—*The Big Bang!: Best of the MC5* (Rhino).
Wayne Kramer solo: 1995—*The Hard Stuff* (Epitaph) 1996—*Dangerous Madness* 1997—*Citizen Wayne* 1998—*LLMF (Live Like a Mutherfucker).*

Some called the MC5 (for "Motor City Five," after their home base) the first '70s band of the '60s. The group's loud, hard, fast sound and violently antiestablishment ideology almost precisely prefigured much of punk rock. There was, however, one crucial difference: The MC5 truly believed in the power of rock & roll to change the world.

The band first formed in high school and came to prominence in 1967–68 as the figureheads (or "house band") of John Sinclair's radical White Panther Party. At concerts and happenings the band caused a sensation by wearing American flags and screaming revolutionary slogans laced with profanities. In 1968 the MC5 went with Sinclair to Chicago to play while the Democratic Convention was under way. Its debut LP (#30, 1969), recorded live in 1968, captured the band in typical raw, revved-up, radical form, and embroiled Elektra Records in controversy over the title tune's loud-

The MC5: Fred "Sonic" Smith, Michael Davis, Dennis Thompson, Wayne Kramer, Rob Tyner

and-clear shout "Kick out the jams, motherfuckers!" Some stores refused to stock the album; in response, the MC5 took out strongly worded ads in underground papers and, to Elektra's further distress, plastered one offending store's windows with Elektra stationery on which was scrawled, "Fuck you." Elektra and the MC5 parted company shortly thereafter, but not before the band had cut another version of "Kick Out the Jams," with "brothers and sisters" substituted for the offending expletive. (It was available as a single and on some subsequent issues of the album, against the band's wishes.)

When Sinclair went to jail on a marijuana charge, the MC5 was left with neither a manager nor a label. Atlantic signed the group, and its debut was produced by rock critic Jon Landau. *Back in the USA* was hailed by critics as one of the greatest hard-rock albums of all time. Record sales were almost nil, however, and never improved. Dropped by Atlantic, the band went to England but soon fell apart, with Michael Davis and Dennis Thompson the first to leave.

Rob Tyner had some success as a songwriter and photographer; he died of a heart attack in 1991. (The remaining members reunited to play a benefit concert for Tyner's family.) Davis went on to form the Ann Arbor band Destroy All Monsters, with ex-Stooge Ron Ashton; Thompson struggled with abortive solo ventures; and in the late '70s Smith formed the Sonic Rendezvous Band, which toured Europe with Iggy Pop and recorded one single. Remaining in the Detroit area, in 1980 he married Patti Smith, with whom he had two children; in November 1994 he died from heart failure.

In the mid-'70s Wayne Kramer pled guilty to a cocaine-dealing charge and spent two years in prison, where he played music with jazz trumpeter Red Rodney. Upon his release, Kramer formed a short partnership with ex–New York Doll and ex-Heartbreaker Johnny Thunders (Gang War), was featured guitarist with Motor City funksters Was (Not Was) (Kramer played the psychedelic guitar on the single "Wheel Me Out"), released two singles, and led his own band, Air Raid. In 1994 Kramer signed with punk label Epitaph and recorded the first of several solo albums featuring his crunchy hard rock and lyrics reflecting on social and political issues. *The Hard Stuff* (1995) included guest spots from members of Bad Religion and Suicidal Tendencies. Kramer continues to tour, usually backed by a rhythm section, and occasionally does spoken-word performances. In 2001 he formed his own label, MuscleTone Records, and played in the loose-knit band the Racketeers.

Kate and Anna McGarrigle

Kate McGarrigle, born 1946, Montreal, Can.; Anna McGarrigle, born 1944, Montreal
1976—*Kate and Anna McGarrigle* (Warner Bros.) 1977—*Dancer With Bruised Knees* 1978—*Pronto Monto* 1980—*French Record* (Hannibal) 1983—*Love Over and Over* (Polydor) 1990—*Heartbeats Accelerating* (Private Music) 1996—*Matapedia* (Hannibal) 1998—*The McGarrigle Hour.*

The McGarrigle sisters' songs bring together a wide range of folk and pop styles, from Stephen Foster parlor songs to Celtic traditional songs to Cajun fiddling to gospel to pop standards. Although their wry, generally unsentimental songs have been best known in the U.S. as covers (by Linda Ronstadt, Maria Muldaur, and others), they have had hits in Canada and Europe, especially with songs recorded in French.

The McGarrigles grew up in Montreal and are bilingual. In the mid-'60s they were half of the Mountain City Four, whose other members (Chaim Tannenbaum and Dane Lanken) continue to perform and record with them. While Anna was studying at Montreal's Ecole des Beaux Arts and Kate was attending McGill University, the National Film Board of Canada commissioned the Mountain City Four to score a film, *Helicopter Canada.*

Kate performed around New York in the '60s, sometimes as a duo with Roma Baran (who later produced Laurie Anderson), and both sisters wrote songs. Anna's first effort, "Heart Like a Wheel," was used in the soundtrack of *Play It as It Lays* and became the title tune of the double-platinum Linda Ronstadt album; Ronstadt has also covered Kate's "(Talk to Me of) Mendocino" and "You Tell Me That I'm Falling Down." Maria Muldaur covered Kate's "The Work Song" and Anna's "Cool River."

Kate married New York singer/songwriter Loudon Wainwright III, and her song "Come a Long Way" appeared on Wainwright's *Attempted Moustache,* which also included Kate's backup vocals; Kate and Anna both sang on Wainwright's *Unrequited.* Shortly after the birth of their son, Rufus—who would later embark on his own career as a singer/songwriter—the marriage broke up.

The McGarrigles' songwriting brought them a contract on their own, but their high, reedy voices and homey arrangements were not well received by U.S. radio programmers despite critics' raves. The McGarrigles toured infrequently; their U.S. tour after their debut LP consisted of two weeks of Massachusetts dates. After *Pronto Monto,* an attempt to make more conventional-sounding folk pop, the McGarrigles were dropped by Warner Bros. Kate appeared on an album by Albion Country Band, a Fairport Convention offshoot. The McGarrigles reemerged with a Canadian bestseller, *French Record,* a compilation of material in French from previous albums and new French songs. *Love Over and Over,* a return to their original style, was the occasion for a U.S. tour. After headlining the Newport Folk Festival in 1992, the sisters toured the U.K. and Europe for two years before releasing 1996's *Matapedia.* Their first album in six years, the record included the Emmylou Harris collaboration "Goin' Back to Harlan," which the three had recorded a year earlier for Harris' *Wrecking Ball.* Harris reappeared on *The McGarrigle Hour,* which featured singers such as Linda Ronstadt and several McGarrigle family members—sister Jane; Kate's ex, Loudon Wainwright; their son, Rufus Wainwright; and Anna's husband, Dane Lanken, among others—performing songs by the likes of Irving Berlin, as well as McGarrigle originals. In 2001 the McGarrigles' vocals were featured on Nick Cave's *No More Shall We Part.*

Roger McGuinn: See the Byrds

Barry McGuire

Born Oct. 15, 1935, Oklahoma City, OK
1965—*Eve of Destruction* (Dunhill) 1966—*This Precious Time* 1968—*The World's Last Private Citizen.*

Singer/songwriter Barry McGuire's first and last hit was his debut solo record, the prototypical protest song "Eve of Destruction." The Bob Dylan–style folk-rock tune made #1 in 1965, although some stations banned it because of its pessimistic lyrics. It also inspired an answer record, "Dawn of Correction."

Before "Eve," McGuire had been with the New Christy Minstrels and had been the featured vocalist on their 1963 hit "Green Green." He was further credited with helping to launch the career of the Mamas and the Papas, for which he was thanked with a mention in "Creeque Alley." In the '70s McGuire had his own dawn of redemption: After a decade of drug addiction, he became a born-again Christian and sold hundreds of thousands of Christian pop records. In the mid-'80s he moved to New Zealand but continues to perform and record.

Sarah McLachlan

Born Jan. 28, 1968, Halifax, Nova Scotia, Can.
1988—*Touch* (Nettwerk) 1991—*Solace* (Arista) 1993—*Fumbling Towards Ecstasy* 1994—*The Freedom Sessions* 1996—*Rarities, B-Sides and Other Stuff* (Nettwerk) 1997—*Surfacing* (Arista) 1999—*Mirrorball.*

Canadian singer/songwriter Sarah McLachlan rose to international prominence during the mid-'90s, thanks to her expressive voice and a series of increasingly mature albums. Toward the end of the decade, her solo career became somewhat overshadowed by the Lilith Fair, the unexpectedly successful summer touring festival that McLachlan founded to showcase women musicians. McLachlan was raised by her adoptive parents in Halifax, Nova Scotia, where she took piano, guitar, and voice lessons as a child. While fronting a new-wave band called October Game at age 17, she was offered the chance to record a demo as a solo artist for Canada's Nettwerk label. Her parents balked at the idea, so she refused. But when the label extended a better offer two years later, after McLachlan had finished her first year of art college, she accepted and moved to Nettwerk's home in Vancouver, British Columbia, where she still resides.

In 1988 Nettwerk put out McLachlan's debut, *Touch,* which went gold in Canada and was released worldwide the next year. Her followup and first recording for Arista, *Solace,* showed an increased maturity in her songwriting and foreshadowed the lyrical depth she would exhibit on 1993's *Fumbling Towards Ecstasy.* Inspired in part by a trip the singer took to Cambodia and Thailand, and the suffering she witnessed there, *Fumbling* saw McLachlan extending the subject matter of her lyrics beyond her previous topics of love and romantic relationships. The album, which yielded the hit singles "Possession" (#73, 1994) and "Good Enough" (#77, 1994), went triple platinum and gained McLachlan a wide fan base. Her next recording, 1997's *Surfacing,* extended her previous success: It went to #2, produced three hit singles ("Adia," [#3]; "Angel," [#4]; and "Building a Mystery," [#13]), and won McLachlan two Grammy Awards, for Best Female Pop Vocal Performance and Best Pop Instrumental Performance. The album eventually sold more than 7 million copies.

In 1997 McLachlan launched the Lilith Fair, which she founded in defiance of numerous promoters' insistence that a tour featuring more than one woman would never sell. In addition to the headlining McLachlan, the fair's bill included Tracy Chapman, Jewel, Joan Osborne, and Paula Cole and became the summer's top-grossing tour, outselling the more established (and male-dominated) Lollapalooza and H.O.R.D.E. festivals. Lilith Fair diversified its lineup during the next two years, showcasing musicians such as Erykah Badu, Bonnie Raitt, Missy Elliott, Luscious Jackson, the Dixie Chicks, and the Pretenders. Sticking to her resolution to keep the festival to a three-year run, McLachlan headed up the final Lilith Fair in 1999. In June of that year she released the triple-platinum live album *Mirrorball* (#3, 1999), for which she won the Grammy for Best Female Pop Vocal Performance in 2000.

Maria McKee: See Lone Justice

Malcolm McLaren

Born Jan. 22, 1946, London, Eng.
1983—*Duck Rock; D'Ya Like Scratchin'* (Island) 1984—*Would Ya Like More Scratchin'; Fans* 1985—*Swamp Thing* 1989—*Waltz Darling* (Epic) 1990—*Round the Outside! Round the Outside!* (Atlantic) 1994—*Paris* (V2) 1996—*The Largest Movie House in Paris* (Noi) 1998—*Buffalo Gals Back to Skool* (Priority); *World Famous Supreme Team Show* (Atlantic).

Whether considered a postmodern genius or a posturing charlatan, Malcolm McLaren is one of the postpunk era's most provocative characters.

McLaren spent the '60s in various art schools before becoming entranced with the Internationale Situationist, a Marxist/Dadaist faction who had stirred up trouble during the 1968 Paris student protests. In 1969 radical fashion designer Vivienne Westwood came into McLaren's life, prompting McLaren's involvement with youth culture. (The couple have a child, Joseph.)

By the early '70s McLaren was operating the clothing store Let It Rock, which catered to the neo-'50s Teddy Boy style. There he met the seminal glam-punk band, the New York Dolls [see entry], then on a British tour. Becoming their manager in 1974, he relocated to New York. Setting the pattern for McLaren's future managerial endeavors, the relationship with the Dolls was short-lived. Back in London, McLaren opened another clothing store, Sex, specializing in S&M fashion. Picking from the store's rebellious, underclass clientele, McLaren formed the Sex Pistols [see entry], a prefab band, to help play out his anarchist fantasies. McLaren's brilliant manipulation of record companies and the media, as well as the band itself, is legendary.

After the Pistols' breakup following their disastrous 1978 U.S. tour, McLaren devised Bow Wow Wow [see entry]. Although McLaren fostered the careers of both Adam Ant [see entry] and Boy George [see Culture Club entry], bowing out before either reached fame, he never aligned himself fully with another group or singer again.

For his next project McLaren merged indigenous music from around the world with contemporary black dance music, transforming himself into a brilliant synthesist in the eyes of some, a cultural imperialist in others'. *Duck Rock* features "Buffalo Girls" (#9 U.K., 1982) and "Double Dutch" (#3 U.K., 1983), unique pastiches that draw together hip-hop, Southern folk music, and African tribal rhythms. *Fans* was even more outrageous, combining rap and hip-hop with opera fragments, as in the single "Madam Butterfly" (#13 U.K., 1984). *Waltz Darling*, credited to Malcolm McLaren and the Bootzilla Orchestra, teamed Bootsy Collins and Jeff Beck with a symphony orchestra for another skewed mélange of high-, mid-, and low-brow culture.

With visions of subverting the film world, McLaren spent four unproductive years in Hollywood. He tried to develop projects with Steven Spielberg and had a highly publicized affair with actress/model Lauren Hutton. By the early '90s McLaren had quit California and returned to Europe. In 1993 he released *Paris*, featuring film icon Catherine Deneuve; four years later he worked on the hip-hop album *Buffalo Gals Back to Skool*, wrote ancient Greek music for an NBC made-for-TV movie of *The Odyssey*, wrote a film musical treatment of the life of Christian Dior, and began a stage adaption of his own life story. In 1998 he created and managed a Chinese girl group, Jungk, and was commissioned to write his autobiography. In 1999 he ran for mayor of London, proposing to legalize brothels and marijuana. He aborted the bid in summer 2000.

John McLaughlin: See Mahavishnu Orchestra

Don McLean

Born Oct. 2, 1945, New Rochelle, NY
1970—*Tapestry* (United Artists) 1971—*American Pie* 1972—*Don McLean* 1973—*Playin' Favorites* 1974—*Homeless Brother* 1976—*Solo* 1977—*Prime Time* (Arista) 1980—*Chain Lightning* (Millennium) 1981—*Believers* 1983—*Dominion* 1986—*Greatest Hits Then & Now* (Capitol) 1987—*Love Tracks* 1990—*For the Memories, vols. 1 & 2* (Gold Castle) 1992—*Classics* (Curb) 1995—*River of Love.*

Though he had occasional subsequent hits, singer/songwriter Don McLean is chiefly remembered for his #1 single of 1972, "American Pie," an 8½-minute saga inspired by the death of Buddy Holly. The song propelled his second album to #1 and obscured McLean's folksinging past and future for many years.

Before his sudden fame, McLean had earned a small following for his work with Pete Seeger on the sloop *Clearwater*, which sailed up and down the Hudson River on ecology campaigns. Perry Como turned one of the songs from McLean's debut album, "And I Love You So," into an international hit, and songwriters Norman Gimbel and Charles Fox made McLean the subject of "Killing Me Softly With His Song," Roberta Flack's Grammy Award–winning single of 1973. But even as *American Pie* yielded a second hit, the ballad "Vincent" (#12) (played daily at Amsterdam's Van Gogh Museum), McLean's smash success proved unrepeatable, and he spent a period of several years refusing to play "American Pie" and letting his career wind down.

McLean's albums for his new label, Millennium, started selling, and in 1981 he had a few hits: a remake of Roy Orbison's "Crying" (#5), his own "Castles in the Air" (#36), and "Since I Don't Have You" (#23). The rest of the decade found McLean bouncing from one style to another: *Dominion* was recorded live with an orchestra and rock backing band; *Greatest Hits Then & Now* was half new songs, half rerecorded, best-of material; *Love Tracks* was a straight-ahead country album; and *For the Memories* was covers of songs by composers ranging from Irving Berlin, George Gershwin, and Cole Porter, to Hank Williams, Willie Nelson, and Leiber and Stoller. In 1995 McLean released *River of Love*, his first new studio album in years. In 2000 Madonna had a hit with a cover of "American Pie," which appeared in the film *The Next Best Thing*.

Grant McLennan: See the Go-Betweens

MC Lyte

Born Lana Moorer, Oct. 11, 1971, Queens, NY
1988—*Lyte as a Rock* (First Priority/Atlantic) 1989—*Eyes on This* 1991—*Act Like You Know* 1993—*Ain't No Other* 1996—*Bad as I Wanna B* (EastWest) 1998—*Seven & Seven.*

MC Lyte is one of rap's steadiest-hitting and most respected female stars, known for her street-smart sensibility. Lyte grew up in Brooklyn, where she began rapping at age 12. When she was 16, her father started First Priority records and released Lyte's debut single, "I Cram to Understand U (Sam)," a clever rap about a boyfriend whose "other woman" turns out to be crack. The family act continued when Lyte's brothers Milk and Gizmo of Audio Two produced *Lyte as a Rock*. The narrative songs with minimal beats included "10% Dis" and "Paper Thin."

Lyte continued to write songs that were strong on content in *Eyes on This*, including the singles "Cha Cha Cha,"

"Cappuccino," and "Stop, Look, Listen." "I'm Not Having It" was used in a TV commercial about AIDS, an issue Lyte has frequently spoken out about. In 1990 she became the first rapper to play Carnegie Hall when she performed at an AIDS benefit. She has recorded public service announcements for Musicians for Life and visited schools for the Stop the Violence movement.

On *Act Like You Know* Lyte called in a variety of producers to add new touches of soul and R&B to her sound. The single "When in Love" (#14 R&B, 1991) was produced by Wolf and Epic, who had created huge hits for Bell Biv DeVoe. The album also included the rap hits "Poor Georgie" (#83 pop, #11 R&B, 1992) and "Eyes Are the Soul" (#84 R&B, 1992). Lyte fans protested that the rapper had softened her tough street style, and after *Act Like You Know* was only mildly popular compared with gangsta rap's gangbuster sales, Lyte went "hard" again on *Ain't No Other* (#90 pop, #16 R&B, 1993). The album opens with a bragging boost from KRS-ONE and features the single "Ruffneck," (#35 pop, #10 R&B, 1993) produced by Wreckx-N-Effect, a paean to criminally minded homeboys. The album also includes "Steady Fucking," a biting response to disses made by Roxanne Shanté. The album purposely avoided message songs; Lyte told interviewers she thought her audience was tired of hearing preaching and teaching.

MC Lyte started a management company in the early '90s, Duke Da Moon, with fellow female rappers Lin Que and Kink Easy, both of whom perform on "Hard Copy" from *Ain't No Other*. In 1996 Lyte released "Keep On, Keepin' On" (#10 pop, #3 R&B), a gold single featuring the female R&B quartet Xscape that appeared in the movie *Sunset Park*. *Bad as I Wanna B* (#59 pop, #11 R&B, 1996) charted two other singles, notably "Cold Rock a Party" (#11 pop, #5 R&B). In 1997 the rapper also acted in *An Alan Smithee Film—Burn Hollywood Burn,* a movie satirizing show business. Her costars included Whoopi Goldberg and Sylvester Stallone. Lyte's 1998 album, *Seven & Seven* (#71 R&B), didn't fare as well as its predecessors, despite the presence of guest producers Missy Elliott and L.L. Cool J.

James McMurtry

Born Mar. 18, 1962, Fort Worth, TX
1989—*Too Long in the Wasteland* (Columbia) 1992—*Candyland* 1995—*Where'd You Hide the Body?* 1997—*It Had to Happen* (Sugar Hill) 1998—*Walk Between the Raindrops.*

The son of noted novelist and screenwriter Larry McMurtry, singer/songwriter James McMurtry has drawn praise for his own terse, gritty character sketches. The elder McMurtry gave his son his first guitar when he was seven: James' mother—an English professor who divorced his father while James was a toddler—taught him his first chords. Later, as a student at the University of Arizona, James McMurtry began playing and singing at a local cafe.

He eventually returned to Texas, where he tended bar in San Antonio while continuing to perform. Then his father, who was scripting a film called *Falling From Grace,* passed a copy of McMurtry's demo tape on to the movie's director and star, John Mellencamp. Impressed by McMurtry's rootsy folk-rock songs, Mellencamp helped the young singer land a record contract and coproduced his 1989 debut album, *Too Long in the Wasteland,* with Michael Wanchic, a member of Mellencamp's band. McMurtry also appeared on the soundtrack to *Falling From Grace,* as part of a group called Buzzin' Cousins, whose other members were Mellencamp, John Prine, Joe Ely, and Dwight Yoakam. (The Cousins contributed the track "Sweet Suzanne.") In 1992 McMurtry released *Candyland,* produced by Wanchic, with Mellencamp as executive producer. The ambitious *Where'd You Hide the Body?* was released with a video of short film interpretations of each song, produced with film students from California State and the University of Southern California. Guitarist Charlie Sexton played on *It Had to Happen* and *Walk Between the Raindrops.*

Big Jay McNeely

Born Cecil James McNeely, Apr. 29, 1927, Los Angeles, CA
1956—*Big "J" in 3-D* (Federal) 1963—*Big Jay McNeeley Live at Cisco's* (Warner Bros.); *Big Jay McNeely Selections* (Savoy) 1989—*Swingin' Cuts* (Collectables) 1993—*Live at Birdland 1957* 2000—*Central Avenue Confidential* (Atomic Theory).

One of the original honking rock & roll tenor saxophonists, Big Jay McNeely was famed for his playing-on-his-back acrobatics and his raw, hard-swinging playing, both of which influenced subsequent rock guitarists such as Dick Dale and Jimi Hendrix. Billed as the King of the Honkers, McNeely had his first hits in 1949, with "Deacon's Hop" (#1 R&B) and "Wild Wig" (#12 R&B). His best-known composition is "There Is Something on Your Mind," a #5 R&B hit (#44 pop) in 1959 when sung by his own band's vocalist, Haywood "Little Sonny" Warner; New Orleans singer Bobby Marchan had an even bigger hit with "There Is Something on Your Mind, Part 2" the next year (#1 R&B, #31 pop). The song has since been recorded by Gene Vincent, King Curtis, B.B. King, and Etta James.

McNeely retired from music for 20 years, during which time he worked for the post office in L.A. He returned to performing in 1983 and, unlike many of his contemporaries, is doing very well. He continues to tour and to record with blues and rockabilly bands, mostly in Europe and Australia. According to Jim Dawson, the author of *Nervous Man Nervous: Big Jay McNeely and the Rise of the Honking Tenor Sax,* McNeely earned more from performing in the '90s than at any other time in his career. He continues to perform.

Clyde McPhatter: See the Drifters

Christine McVie; John McVie: See Fleetwood Mac

Meat Loaf

Born Marvin Lee Aday, Sep. 27, 1947, Dallas, TX
1971—*Stoney and Meat Loaf* (Rare Earth) 1977—*Bat out of Hell* (Cleveland International) 1981—*Dead Ringer* 1983—*Midnight at the Lost and Found* 1984—*Hits out of Hell; Bad Attitude* 1986—*Blind Before I Stop* 1987—*Meat Loaf Live* 1993—*Bat out of Hell II: Back Into Hell* (MCA) 1995—*Welcome to the Neighborhood* 1998—*The Very Best of Meat Loaf* (Epic) 1999—*VH1 Storytellers* (Beyond).

Bat out of Hell (#14, 1977) made Meat Loaf rock's first 250-pound-plus superstar since Leslie West. One of the biggest-selling LPs of the '70s, *Bat* has sold over 13 million copies in the U.S. Within a few years of its release, however, Meat Loaf all but disappeared from the U.S. music scene, only to reemerge again in 1993 with an album more successful than *Bat*.

It's unclear exactly when and how Marvin Lee Aday became Meat Loaf, but by 1966, when he moved from his native Texas to California, he'd formed a band alternately known as Meat Loaf Soul and Popcorn Blizzard, which, until its breakup in 1969, had opened shows for the Who, Iggy Pop and the Stooges, Johnny and Edgar Winter, and Ted Nugent. He then auditioned for and got a part in a West Coast production of *Hair* and traveled with the show to the East Coast and then to Detroit, where he hooked up with a singer named Stoney to record the unsuccessful LP *Stoney and Meat Loaf*—rereleased in 1979 as *Meat Loaf (Featuring Stoney)*. Meat Loaf went to New York to appear in the off-Broadway gospel musical *Rainbow in New York* in 1973, and then successfully auditioned for *More Than You Deserve*, written by Jim Steinman.

Steinman, a New Yorker who'd spent his early teen years in California, had studied classical piano. Later he wrote a play called *Dream Engine* in New York. Meanwhile, Meat Loaf had played Eddie in the hugely successful cult film *The Rocky Horror Picture Show* and sung lead vocals on one side of Ted Nugent's platinum LP *Free for All*. After meeting at *More Than You Deserve* auditions, Meat Loaf and Steinman toured with the National Lampoon Road Show; then Steinman wrote a musical called *Never Land* (a *Peter Pan* update), from which would come much of the material for *Bat out of Hell*. (*Never Land* was produced in 1977 at Washington's Kennedy Center.) Meat Loaf and Steinman rehearsed for a full year before Todd Rundgren, an early supporter of the project, agreed to produce them.

At first, *Bat*, with its highly theatrical, bombastically orchestrated teen drama, sold well only in New York and Cleveland. Then Meat Loaf hit the road with a seven-piece band that included singer Karla DeVito in the role Ellen Foley had played on the LP's "Paradise by the Dashboard Light" (which also included a cameo by New York Yankees former shortstop and announcer Phil Rizzuto). The LP was platinum by the end of the year, with the hit singles "Paradise by the Dashboard Light" (#39), "Two out of Three Ain't Bad" (#11), and "You Took the Words Right out of My Mouth" (#39).

Meat Loaf appeared in the films *Americathon* (1979) and *Roadie* (1980). In 1981 Steinman released his own Rundgren-produced solo LP, *Bad for Good*. Still the world awaited *Bat*'s sequel. Stories circulated that Meat Loaf had been coaxed to sing on *Bad for Good* but couldn't or wouldn't because of a variety of physical and emotional problems. Finally, toward the end of 1981, *Dead Ringer* (#45, 1981) was released to meager response. Meanwhile, Steinman initiated lawsuits against Epic and Meat Loaf. *Midnight at the Lost and Found* had no Steinman material and included a few songs cowritten by "M. Lee Aday." Meat Loaf eventually declared bankruptcy and underwent physical and psychological therapy to get his voice back. He somehow managed to keep making records, which went virtually unnoticed in the U.S., though he remained a concert draw in England.

In 1993 Meat Loaf—back with Steinman—reemerged with *Bat out of Hell II: Back Into Hell*, unabashedly picking up, in sound and story, right where "Mr. Loaf" (as the *New York Times* called him) had left off with *Bat out of Hell*. The comeback album sold even faster than the original, entering the chart at #25 and eventually hitting #1, selling 10 million copies within three months worldwide, and yielding a hit single in "I'd Do Anything for Love (But I Won't Do That")". In January 1994 that song won Meat Loaf his first Grammy, in the category of Best Male Rock Vocal Performance. Meat Loaf also mounted a Broadway/arena-rock tour reminiscent of days of yore, with his entrance heralded by bombastic power chords interrupting a string quartet, which opened the shows playing a medley of his early hits. This renewed popularity led to prestigious engagements, such as a duet with Luciano Pavarotti at a benefit concert for the children of Bosnia in 1995.

Despite this success, Steinman and Meat Loaf parted ways once again. Although it featured contributions from the likes of Diane Warren, who penned the single "I'd Lie for You (and That's the Truth)" (#13, 1995), *Welcome to the Neighborhood* (#17, 1995) quickly sank from the chart and the following tour did not do well; the singer was then dropped by MCA. In the mid-'90s his former label, Cleveland International, and Sony became involved in several lawsuits concerning claimed underpayment of royalties for *Bat out of Hell*. The cases were settled out of court for an undisclosed amount in 1998.

Without a label, Meat Loaf once again turned to acting, appearing in *Crazy in Alabama* and *Fight Club*, both in 1999. That same year he released the live *VH1 Storytellers*, along with an autobiography, *To Hell and Back*.

Meat Puppets

Formed in 1980, Phoenix, AZ
Curt Kirkwood (b. Jan. 10, 1959), gtr., voc.; Cris Kirkwood (b. Oct. 22, 1960, Amarillo, TX), bass, voc.; Derrick Bostrom (b. June 23, 1960, Phoenix), drums.
1981—*In a Car* EP (World Imitation) 1982—*Meat Puppets*

(SST) 1983—*Meat Puppets II* 1985—*Up on the Sun* 1986—*Out My Way* EP 1987—*Mirage; Huevos* 1989—*Monsters* 1990—*No Strings Attached* 1991—*Forbidden Places* (London) 1994—*Too High to Die* 1995—*No Joke!* 1999—*You Love Me* EP; *Live in Montana* (Rykodisc) (– Cris Kirkwood; – Bostrom; + Shandon Sahm, drums; + Kyle Ellison, gtr.; + Andrew Duplantis, bass).

Meat Puppets started out as an engagingly incompetent, country-tinged thrash trio. By its third full-length album, however, the band had developed a signature sound that pitted the deconstructionist attitude of American hardcore against the carefree spirit of the Grateful Dead.

Brothers Curt and Cris Kirkwood grew up in Phoenix, Arizona, where they attended a Jesuit prep school and played in various mainstream-oriented rock bands. Not interested in continuing their educations, the two formed Meat Puppets along with local drummer Derrick Bostrom. In the beginning the group was so intent on playing a rough and spontaneous style of music that they refused even to rehearse.

In 1981 the Puppets released *In a Car,* an EP of earsplitting avant rock boasting five songs in five minutes. The trio's irreverence so impressed Black Flag guitarist Greg Ginn that he signed the Puppets to his influential SST label and released the band's noisy, experimental debut LP later the following year (and reissued *In a Car* in 1985).

The Kirkwoods took a radically different approach on the influential *Meat Puppets II,* delivering a set of ragged, out-of-tune country-punk songs that hinted at their future desert-breeze-style sound. Growing more professional with each subsequent release, the psychedelic/country/punk/folk on *Up on the Sun* came out to flattering reviews in 1985.

In 1990, on the strength of *Huevos* and *Monsters,* as well as Curt Kirkwood's continually improving Jerry Garcia–style fretwork, the band signed to London Records, releasing *Forbidden Places* the next year. (*No Strings Attached* is a retrospective of Meat Puppets' SST work.) Kurt Cobain, a longtime Meat Puppets fan, invited the Kirkwoods to join Nirvana in its December 1993 *Unplugged* performance, where Cobain sang three songs from *Meat Puppets II.* The exposure helped push the Puppets' *Too High to Die* to #62 the following year, and earned them an alternative radio hit with "Backwater." But the band could not maintain that popularity with 1995's *No Joke!* (#183).

Subsequent years were largely inactive. Cris Kirkwood fell into severe drug abuse (his wife died of an overdose), and he officially left the band. Bostrom also left, though he remained active in Rykodisc's 1999 reissues of the Meat Puppets' SST catalogue and the band's Web site. By 1998, Curt Kirkwood had relocated to Austin and recruited new members into the Puppets: drummer Shandon Sahm (the son of Doug Sahm), sometime Butthole Surfer guitarist Kyle Ellison, and bassist Andrew Duplantis. In 2000 the band signed to Breaking Records, an Atlantic imprint owned by Hootie & the Blowfish.

Megadeth

Formed 1983, Los Angeles, CA
Dave Mustaine (b. Sep. 13, 1961, La Mesa, CA), gtr., voc.; David Ellefson (b. Nov. 12, 1964, MN), bass; Chris Poland, gtr.; Gars Samuelson (b. 1958; d. July 14, 1999, Orange City, FL), drums.
1985—*Killing Is My Business . . . and Business Is Good* (Combat) 1986—*Peace Sells . . . But Who's Buying?* (Capitol) (– Poland; – Samuelson; + Jeff Young, gtr.; + Chuck Behler, drums) 1988—*So Far, So Good . . . So What?* (– Young; – Behler; + Marty Friedman [b. Dec. 8, 1962, Washington, DC], gtr.; + Nick Menza [b. July 23, 1964, Ger.], drums) 1990—*Rust in Peace* 1992—*Countdown to Extinction* 1994—*Youthanasia* 1995—*Hidden Treasures* 1997—*Cryptic Writings* 1999—*Risk* (– Menza; + Jimmy DeGrasso [b. Mar. 16, 1963, PA], drums) 2000—*Capitol Punishment: The Megadeath Years* (– Friedman; + Al Pitrelli [b. Sept. 26, 1962, NY], gtr.).

When guitarist Dave Mustaine was booted out of Metallica early in its career, he formed Megadeth, which continued his former group's thrash-metal style with even more speed and intensity.

Mustaine was seven when his parents divorced, and his family wound up living in poverty in the Southern California suburbs. During his teens, Mustaine's mother was often away, leaving him with his sisters; he told a journalist that a brother-in-law once punched him in the face for listening to Judas Priest. Mustaine's revenge was to join a heavy-metal band, and in 1981 he became a founding member of Metallica [see entry], from which he was fired two years later in a power struggle over leadership and allegations of his drug use. Mustaine, whose reputation for outspokenness and mood swings is notorious, formed Megadeth that same year with Minnesota native Dave Ellefson.

Mustaine and Ellefson hoped to create a jazz-oriented progressive strain of heavy metal based on chops as much as emotional aggression. Megadeth's first album, *Killing Is My*

Megadeath: Nick Menza, Dave Mustaine, Marty Friedman, David Ellefson

Business . . . and Business Is Good, succeeded in that regard and garnered mainly positive reviews, even from critics normally hostile to heavy metal. Mustaine's drug use, meanwhile, deepened with his discovery of heroin. Still, the band's subsequent albums, *Peace Sells . . . But Who's Buying?* (#76, 1986) and *So Far, So Good . . . So What?* (#28, 1988), continued in its celebrated lightning-speed, chops-heavy style.

In 1990 Mustaine was arrested for impaired driving and went into a 12-step program for his drug and alcohol problems. The same year, Megadeth released *Rust in Peace,* which reached #23. Mustaine's former band, meanwhile, paved the way for thrash metal when its self-titled album of 1991 skyrocketed to the top of the charts; Megadeth followed in Metallica's footsteps the next year with *Countdown to Extinction,* which went to #2.

Offstage, Mustaine continued getting into trouble: In 1993 Megadeth was dumped from its opening spot on Aerosmith's tour when that group tired of Mustaine's misbehavior. Megadeth returned in 1994 with *Youthansia* (the album's press release was written by novelist Dean Koontz), which debuted at #4. That same year, Mustaine slipped back into drug use briefly during a tour, but has since returned to sobriety, claiming even to refuse nitrous oxide while in the dentist's chair.

Before recording 1997's *Cryptic Writings* (#10), Mustaine started work on a degree in business management at the University of Phoenix and began mastering Web design. He put those new skills to work when his company designed the Web site for Alice Cooper's theme restaurant, Alice Cooper'stown.

Megadeth's lineup changes continued, as former Suicidal Tendencies drummer Jimmy DeGrasso joined in time for 1999's *Risk.* That album's title and revamped sound were inspired by published comments from Metallica's Lars Ulrich suggesting that Megadeth take more musical risks. The subsequent album incorporated surprising industrial and Middle Eastern flavors along the edges.

The Mekons

Formed May 1977, Leeds, Eng.
Jon Langford (b. Oct. 11, 1957, Newport, S. Wales), voc., gtr., drums; Tom Greenhalgh (b. Nov. 4, 1956, Stockholm), voc., gtr.
1979—*The Quality of Mercy Is Not Strnen* (Virgin, U.K.) 1980—*The Mekons* (Red Rhino, U.K.) 1982—*It Falleth Like Gentle Rain From Heaven—The Mekons Story* (CNT, U.K.) 1983—*The English Dancing Master* EP 1985—(+ Sally Timms [b. Nov. 29, 1959, Leeds], voc.; + Lu Knee (a.k.a. Lu Edmunds), bass; + Steve Goulding, drums; + Susie Honeyman, violin) *Fear and Whiskey* (Sin, U.K.) 1986—*Crime and Punishment* EP; *The Edge of the World; Slightly South of the Border* EP 1987—*Honky Tonkin'* (Twin/Tone) 1988—*So Good It Hurts* 1989—*Original Sin; The Mekons Rock 'n' Roll* (A&M) 1990—*F.U.N. '90* EP; *New York* (ROIR) 1991—*The Curse of the Mekons* (Blast First, U.K.) 1992—*Wicked Midnite* EP (Loud) 1993—(+ Sarah Corina, bass) *I ❤ Mekons* (Quarterstick) 1994—*Retreat From Memphis* 1995—*United* 1996—*Pussy, King of the Pirates* (with Kathy Acker) 1998—*Me* 2000—*Journey to the End of the Night.*
Waco Brothers (with Langford and Goulding): 1995—*To the Last Dead Cowboy* (Bloodshot) 1997—*Cowboy in Flames; Do You Think About Me?* 1999—*Waco World* 2000—*Electric Waco Chair.*
Jon Langford solo: 1998—*Skull Orchard* (Sugar Free).
Sally Timms: 1995—*To the Land of Milk and Honey* (Feel Good All Over) 1999—*Cowboy Sally's Twilight Laments . . . For Lost Buckaroos* (Bloodshot).

Intensely independent, idealistic yet cynical, the Mekons are one of the longest-lasting combos of the British punk era. Their music has gone from dissonant, minimal art punk, to danceable, dub-heavy electronics, to ragged country, sensitive folk, and anthemic rock & roll. (Space does not permit a full accounting of all the group members' various solo and outside projects.) A postpunk cottage industry—and favorite among rock critics—the Mekons never attained more than a cult following. The group's bad luck with record labels and staunchly leftist politics are legendary.

Tom Greenhalgh and Jon Langford were Leeds art students when the Sex Pistols came through town in 1976. Inspired by the group's amateurish playing, Greenhalgh, who knew only two chords, formed the Mekons (named for a green-headed alien in a '50s comic strip, *Dan Dare, Space Pilot of the Future*). Within months, future guitarist Jon Langford joined on drums, the two emerging as a band alongside their more political Leeds University brethren, the Gang of Four.

After a single, "Never Been in a Riot" (a witty reply to the Clash's "White Riot"), the band signed with Virgin and released *The Quality of Mercy Is Not Strnen,* a humorous, intelligent, but utterly inept collection of noisy punk. In a move that would repeat itself throughout the Mekons' career, Virgin dropped the band midway through recording of their second album. When some of the members bowed out, the group developed a revolving-door membership, with Greenhalgh and Langford the only constants.

The band released *Devils Rats and Piggies a Special Message From Godzilla* (later known simply as *The Mekons*) on the U.K. independent label Red Rhino. After a 1980 European tour and two subsequent New Year's Eve shows in New York with hometown friends Gang of Four, the Mekons nearly called it quits. (Langford formed a side band, Three Johns, which put out 13 albums over the next seven years.) In 1982 the group compiled a hodgepodge of old and new material for *The Mekons Story,* released on yet another U.K. indie, CNT. With renewed vigor, they returned to the studio and recorded the country-tinged *English Dancing Master.*

In the two years that lapsed between albums, Sally Timms, a Leeds native who had sung with the band in the past, joined, followed by ex-Rumour drummer Steve Goulding, bassist Lu Knee (a.k.a. Lu Edmonds), and classically trained violinist Susie Honeyman. In 1985 the group released the celebrated *Fear and Whiskey* (issued in the U.S. in 1989 as

The Mekons: Sally Timms, Jon Langford, Susie Honeyman, Tom Greenhalgh

Original Sin), revealing an interest in rough-hewn country music that would later flourish in '90s solo projects by Timms and Langford (with the twangy Waco Brothers). By then, the Mekons had evolved a distinct, though highly eclectic, sound. Their mid- to late-'80s Sin and Twin/Tone albums were generally well received, but the Mekons became most loved for their raucous live shows.

In 1989 the Mekons signed with A&M and released their most critically acclaimed album, *The Mekons Rock 'n' Roll*, a collection of heartfelt rockers with a healthy dose of skepticism. But more major-label troubles were around the corner. After the bizarre, sparse, dance-oriented *F.U.N. '90*—which contained a crude recording of the late rock critic Lester Bangs singing behind a dub-heavy track—the Mekons asked to be released from A&M, citing insufficient financial support. A&M said no, then refused to release the group's followup album. In 1991 the aptly named *Curse of the Mekons* appeared on U.K. label Blast First, but A&M retained the American rights. The album, which Langford has called one of the Mekons' best, was not released in the U.S. until 2001.

More problems arose in 1992 when a WEA subsidiary, Loud Records, signed the Mekons but promptly suffered financial troubles, which led to their sitting on the group's next album, a collection of Mekons-style love songs called *I ❤ Mekons*, for nearly a year. The group finally released the record on the independent Quarterstick label in 1993; the following year, it put out *Retreat From Memphis*.

Throughout their career, the Mekons' core membership of Langford and Greenhalgh (and later Timms and Honeyman) has been joined by a host of musicians, including founding members Kevin Lycett (guitar) and Mark White (vocals), as well as ex–Pretty Thing Dick Taylor (guitar), Brendan Crocker (guitar), Rico Bell (accordion), Sarah Corina (bass), among others. And by the late '90s, much of the band had relocated to Chicago, finding champions at such local indie labels as Quarterstick and Bloodshot.

In 1996 "Mekons United," a traveling multimedia art exhibition celebrating their work in recorded sounds and visual arts, toured museums in the U.S. (In subsequent years, Langford would enjoy solo exhibitions of his paintings.) An accompanying book and CD, the mostly electronic *United*, were also released. That same year, the band collaborated with author Kathy Acker on a performance-art piece, *Pussy, King of the Pirates*, which toured live and was released on CD. The Mekons' hunger for new sounds and styles blossomed further on 1998's *Me*, which mixed guitars, strings, and traditional Arabic instruments with synthesizers and experiments in dub and drum loops. The folk-soul blend *Journey to the End of the Night* emerged in 2000.

Melanie

Born Melanie Safka, Feb. 3, 1947, Queens, NY
1969—*Born to Be* (Buddah); *Melanie* 1970—*Candles in the Rain; Leftover Wine* 1971—*The Good Book; Gather Me* (Neighborhood) 1972—*Four Sides of Melanie* (Buddah); *Stoneground Words* (Neighborhood) 1973—*At Carnegie Hall* 1974—*Madrugada; As I See It Now* 1975—*Sunset and Other Beginnings* 1976—*Photograph* (Atlantic) 1978—*Phonogenic—Not Just Another Pretty Face* (Midsong) 1979—*Ballroom Streets* (RCA) 1982—*Arabesque* (Blanche) 1985—*Am I Real or What* (Amherst) 1990—*The Best of Melanie* (Rhino) 1991—*Precious Cargo* (Precious Cargo) 1993—*Freedom Knows My Name* (Lonestar) 1997—*Low Country; Antlers* 1999—*Beautiful People: The Greatest Hits of Melanie* (Buddha) 2000—*Melanie Recorded Live @ Borders* (DES).

Singer/songwriter Melanie caught the last upsurge of hippie innocence in songs like "Lay Down (Candles in the Rain)" and "Beautiful People." While she sold over 22 million records around the world, her childlike demeanor, cracked voice, and naive lyrics made her a novelty act before her time.

Melanie Safka's family moved to Boston and then to Long Branch, New Jersey, when she was a teenager. After high school she studied at the American Academy of Dramatic Arts. Soon after she signed a song-publishing agreement with her future producer and husband, Peter Schekeryk. In 1967 she won a recording contract with Columbia Records, which released her single "Beautiful People." When the record did not sell, Columbia dropped her and she returned to the local folk clubs until 1969, when a single from *Born to Be*, "What Have They Done to My Song, Ma," hit in France.

In August 1969 Melanie appeared at Woodstock, which inspired her to write "Lay Down (Candles in the Rain)." Released in spring 1970, it became a #6 single, and the *Candles in the Rain* LP went gold. From then on, it became a ritual for her loyal fans to light candles at her shows. In summer 1970 "Peace Will Come (According to Plan)" hit #32, and she made a live album, *Leftover Wine*. That fall, the New Seekers had a smash hit with their version of "What Have They Done to My Song, Ma."

In 1971 Melanie and her husband formed their own record company, Neighborhood, and the singer immediately had her biggest success, the #1 "Brand New Key," which sold over 3 million copies. Another single off the LP, "Ring the Living Bell," hit the Top 40. *Gather Me* went gold. That same year, she performed and toured the world as a spokesperson for UNICEF.

After that, her records stopped selling, and in 1975 Neighborhood folded. She was signed by Atlantic Records, and her label debut, *Photograph,* was coproduced by company president Ahmet Ertegun and Schekeryk. In 1978 she recorded for Midsong, and the next year released *Ballroom Streets* on RCA. In 1989 Melanie won an Emmy for "The First Time I Loved Forever," her song for the TV show *Beauty and the Beast.* She toured Europe and continued recording for small and import labels in the '90s. As of 2001 she had 33 albums to her name. The mother of three has also performed at several Woodstock anniversary concerts and at various humanitarian events. Her daughters sing as a duo called Safka.

John Mellencamp

Born Oct. 7, 1951, Seymour, IN
1976—*Chestnut Street Incident* (Mainman/MCA) 1978—*A Biography* (Riva) 1979—*John Cougar* 1980—*Nothin' Matters and What If It Did* 1982—*American Fool* 1983—*Uh-huh* 1985—*Scarecrow* 1987—*The Lonesome Jubilee* (Mercury) 1989—*Big Daddy* 1991—*Whenever We Wanted* 1993—*Human Wheels* 1994—*Dance Naked* 1996—*Mr. Happy Go Lucky* 1997—*The Best That I Could Do (1978–1988)* 1998—*John Mellencamp* (Columbia) 1999—*Rough Harvest* (Mercury).

Singer/songwriter John Mellencamp became one of 1982's biggest stars when his fifth LP, *American Fool,* went to #1, sold over 5 million copies, and yielded two hit singles, "Hurts So Good" (#2) and "Jack and Diane" (#1). More important, perhaps, has been Mellencamp's evolution from a Springsteen-style hard-rock stylist into what one critic called a "renaissance rocker." From *American Fool* on, Mellencamp's critical stock rose even as record sales leveled off.

Mellencamp was born with a form of spina bifida, a potentially crippling neural tube defect that required surgery and a lengthy hospitalization. Coddled by his mother and encouraged by his father to excel, Mellencamp grew into a self-proclaimed rebel. At 17 he eloped with his pregnant girlfriend, Priscilla Esterline, and began attending community college and working a series of blue-collar jobs. He had written a number of songs before he moved to New York at age 24 to begin a music career. There he met David Bowie's manager, Tony DeFries, who christened Mellencamp Johnny Cougar, helped him get what has been reported as a $1 million deal with the Mainman label, and oversaw the recording of his debut, *Chestnut Street Incident.* The LP, which consisted of cover tunes, failed to hit, and MCA dropped Mellencamp, who, it has been reported, was not even aware that he had "adopted" the Cougar stage name until he saw his album cover. That and several other early experiences in the music business, no doubt, contributed to the sometimes jaundiced view of show business that Mellencamp has expressed repeatedly through the years.

Four years later he signed (to his dismay, as John Cougar) with Riva Records and, working with Rod Stewart's manager, Billy Gaff, recorded two more LPs, the latter of which, *John Cougar* (#64, 1979), contained "I Need a Lover." Previously a radio hit for Pat Benatar, "I Need a Lover" was a #28 hit for Mellencamp in the U.S. and went to #1 in Australia. *Nothin' Matters* (#37, 1980), produced by Steve Cropper, sold 900,000 copies and contained the hits "This Time" (#27, 1980) and "Ain't Even Done With the Night" (#17, 1981). Cougar divorced his first wife in 1981, and that year married Vicky Granucci. (They would later divorce.)

Two years later came Mellencamp's commercial breakthrough, *American Fool* (#1, 1982). The videos for its hit singles—the Grammy-winning "Hurts So Good" (#2, 1982), "Jack and Diane" (#1, 1982), and "Hand to Hold On To" (#19, 1982)—quickly became MTV staples, and Cougar toured as an opening act for Heart. The next year's *Uh-Huh* (#9, 1983) came out with *American Fool* still on the charts and included "Crumblin' Down" (#9, 1983), "Pink Houses" (#8, 1983), and "Authority Song" (#15, 1984). That year Mellencamp, who had incorporated "Mellencamp" into his stage name, embarked on his first headlining tour. With *Scarecrow* (#2, 1985) Mellencamp stayed the hard-rock course, producing another string of hits: "Lonely Ol' Night" (#6, 1985), "Small Town" (#6, 1985), "R.O.C.K. in the U.S.A." (#2, 1986), "Rain on the Scarecrow" (#21, 1986), and "Rumbleseat" (#28, 1986).

In 1985 Mellencamp, with Willie Nelson and Neil Young, was a co-organizer of Farm Aid. He appeared at Farm Aid concerts I through VI. Over the years, he has also given concerts to call attention to the American farmer's plight, and in 1987 he testified before a congressional subcommittee on the issue. In addition he has been an outspoken critic of beer- and cigarette-company sponsorship of concert tours and refuses to allow his music to be used in commercials.

Mellencamp's style took a dramatic turn with *The Lonesome Jubilee* (#6, 1987), which blended traditional American folk instrumentation (for example, Lisa Germano's violin and accordions) in a number of songs that lamented rather than celebrated contemporary Middle America. Its hits were "Paper in Fire" (#9, 1987), "Cherry Bomb" (#8, 1987), and "Check It Out" (#14, 1988). His next albums, more deeply introspective in some ways, each sold about a million copies, but the hits were fewer and farther between than in previous years. *Big Daddy* (#7, 1989) included the somewhat cynical semiautobiographical "Pop Singer" (#15, 1989), and *Whenever We Wanted* (#17, 1991)—his first album as John Mellencamp, rather than John Cougar Mellencamp—featured "Get a Leg Up" (#14, 1991) and "Again Tonight" (#36, 1992). The "Get a Leg Up" video featured model Elaine Irwin, who became his third wife. *Human Wheels* (#7, 1993) yielded no major hit singles. *Dance Naked* (#13, 1994) featured the #3 hit cover of Van Morrison's "Wild Night," a duet with singer/bassist Meshell Ndegéocello. Mellencamp's plans to embark on a large 1994 North American tour were scuttled after he was diagnosed with a heart condition. Although initial reports described Mellencamp's problem as an arterial blockage, he later admitted that he had suffered a heart attack.

As if to comment on his brush with mortality, Mellencamp titled his next album *Mr. Happy Go Lucky* (#9, 1996) and sought out dance-mix specialist Junior Vasquez to put an urban spin on his signature heartland sound. Tony Toni Toné bassist Raphael Saadiq and North Mississippi diddley-bow player Lonnie Pitchford were among guest performers. "Key West Intermezzo (I Saw You First)" (#14, 1996) was a hit, and a second single, "Just Another Day," reached #46. Not all was happy-go-lucky, however, as Mellencamp terminated his relationship with his label the following year. Though he owed PolyGram/Mercury five albums, he was free to sign with Columbia after signing off on *The Best That I Could Do: 1978–1988* (#33, 1997), a hits collection, and the acoustic *Rough Harvest* (#99, 1999). His emancipatory release was called *John Mellencamp* (#41, 1998), and featured guest appearances by ex–Guns n' Roses guitarist Izzy Stradlin and drummer Stan Lynch of Tom Petty and the Heartbreakers.

Mellencamp has produced or coproduced all of his own albums, as well as Mitch Ryder's *Never Kick a Sleeping Dog* (1983), James McMurtry's *Too Long in the Wasteland* (1989), and the soundtrack from *Falling From Grace* (1992), the film in which he made his acting and directorial debut. Written by Larry McMurtry (James' father, of *Lonesome Dove* fame), *Falling From Grace* garnered mixed reviews, but some praised Mellencamp's direction. In the '90s Mellencamp has also exhibited his paintings throughout the country, including in the *Twice Gifted* show. His work also appears in the book *Musicians as Artists*. He received the Billboard Century Award in 2001.

Harold Melvin and the Blue Notes

Formed 1955, Philadelphia, PA
Harold Melvin (b. June 25, 1939, Philadelphia; d. Mar. 24, 1997, Mount Airy, PA), voc.; Bernard Wilson, voc.; Jesse Gillis Jr., voc.; Franklin Peaker, voc.; Roosevelt Brodie, voc. ca. 1960—(Melvin; Wilson; + John Atkins, voc.; + Lawrence Brown, voc.)
ca. 1970—(Melvin; Lawrence Brown, voc.; Lloyd Parks, voc.; Bernard Wilson, voc.; + Teddy Pendergrass [b. Mar. 26, 1950, Philadelphia], drums, then voc.).
1972—*Harold Melvin and the Blue Notes* (Philadelphia International) 1973—*I Miss You; Black and Blue* (– Parks; + Jerry Cummings, voc.) 1975—*To Be True; Wake Up Everybody* (– Pendergrass; + David Ebo, voc.) 1976—*All Their Greatest Hits* 1977—*Reaching for the World* (ABC) (+ Dwight Johnson, bass/baritone voc.; + Bill Spratley, baritone voc.) 1980—*The Blue Album* (Source) 1981—*All Things Happen in Time* (MCA) 1981 on—(various personnel) 1995—*If You Don't Know Me by Now: The Best of Harold Melvin and the Blue Notes* (Legacy/Epic).

Although formed in 1955, this Philadelphia-based vocal group did not attain widespread popularity until the mid-'70s, with Teddy Pendergrass [see entry] as lead singer. Harold Melvin founded the Blue Notes as an old-style doo-wop group with three other singers and Bernard Wilson, the only other member who would remain through most of its many incarnations. Melvin was not a great lead singer, but he was a highly disciplined leader who designed the group's precision choreography, an upscale "tie and tails" look, and a broad repertoire that made the group as popular in Atlantic City pimp bars as in Miami hotel showrooms.

The first Blue Notes recorded its first single, "If You Love Me," for Josie but disbanded soon after, leaving Melvin and Wilson to regroup with new lead John Atkins and Lawrence Brown. After years in the '60s on the chitlin' circuit, they were signed to the William Morris Agency on the recommendation of Martha Reeves. They frequently appeared in supper clubs in Las Vegas, Lake Tahoe, Reno, and Miami Beach.

Around the time Atkins left, Pendergrass joined. He had been drumming in a faux Cadillacs group when Melvin, who had fired his entire band, hired the whole group to back the Blue Notes. Pendergrass, an excellent drummer, moved up to the lead spot after another of dozens of personnel shifts. Although Melvin and the Blue Notes was a Philly fixture, the city's leading producers, Kenny Gamble and Leon Huff, had no interest in the group until they caught a live show with Pendergrass up front. Soon, the group was signed to the mighty Philadelphia International Records and, along with the O'Jays, became one of the first groups associated with the Sound of Philadelphia.

From 1972 until Pendergrass left in October 1975 to pursue a solo career, Harold Melvin and the Blue Notes had three #1 R&B singles: "If You Don't Know Me by Now" (#3 pop, 1972), "The Love I Lost" (#7 pop, 1973), and "Wake Up Everybody" (#12 pop, 1976). Other hits included "I Miss You" (#58 pop, #7 R&B, 1972), "Satisfaction Guaranteed" (#58 pop, #6 R&B, 1974), "Where Are All My Friends" (#8 R&B, 1974), "Bad Luck" (#15 pop, #4 R&B, 1975), "Tell the World How I Feel About 'Cha Baby" (#7 R&B, 1976), and "Hope That We Can Be Together Soon" (#42 pop, 1975) (featuring Sharon Paige).

As Pendergrass' star rose, friction increased between Melvin and him (in part, because many people assumed that Teddy was Harold). A compromise in billing was struck, with "featuring Teddy Pendergrass" added to the group's name. Following Pendergrass' departure for a hugely successful solo career, Melvin brought in lead singer David Ebo, and the group signed to ABC. Although the Blue Notes' label debut, "Reaching for the World," hit #6 on the R&B chart, subsequent releases failed to match their mid-'70s success. In 1979 they switched to Source Records, where "Prayin' " was a moderate R&B hit (#18).

Their last charting single was 1984's "I Really Love You." The group continued to tour, with an ever-changing lineup. At various times throughout the Blue Notes' career, members have included Bunny Sigler and Billy Paul [see entry]. Melvin suffered strokes in July and November 1996 and another shortly before his death in March 1997.

Memphis Slim

Born Peter Chatman, Sep. 3, 1915, Memphis, TN; died Feb. 24, 1988, Paris, Fr.
1973—*Legacy of the Blues* (GNP/Crescendo) 1975—*Rock Me Baby* (Black Lion) 1976—*Chicago Boogie* 1978—*Boogie Woogie* (Festival) 1993—*Memphis Slim at the Gate of Horn* (Vee-Jay) 1995—*Chicago Blues Masters, vol. 1* (with Muddy Waters) (Capitol) 1997—*The Bluebird Recordings 1940–1941* (RCA).

Blues singer and barrelhouse pianist Memphis Slim was perhaps the first bluesman to leave America for Europe and become a star there. He is also the composer of "Every Day (I Have the Blues)," which became a big-band standard when sung by Joe Williams with Count Basie's orchestra.

Having taught himself the piano and learned from such Memphis greats as Speckled Red and Roosevelt Sykes, Slim went to Chicago in 1939, where he met Big Bill Broonzy. Though Broonzy told Slim that he had talent but lacked an original style, by 1940 Slim had become Broonzy's accompanist, a job he held until the late '40s. Slim led his own groups as a singer/pianist on the late-'40s blues circuit and had a minor R&B hit in the early '50s with his own "Beer Drinkin' Woman." With the folk boom of the late '50s and early '60s, Slim's popularity was renewed, and he played for large white audiences for the first time. His band at that time included the Chicago bassist/composer Willie Dixon. In 1959 Slim earned a standing ovation at the Newport Folk Festival and, shortly thereafter, shared the bill at New York City's Village Gate with Pete Seeger. At this time, he recorded for Folkways, but his recorded legacy may be found on dozens of albums from many labels.

In 1960 Memphis Slim first toured Europe and was well enough received that he went back again in 1962, doing especially well at his French debut. After an Israeli tour in 1963, he made Paris his home. He became a celebrity, a star performer at major music halls in England and all over the Continent, and he was an often-seen face on French TV. Though his later recordings failed to recapture the raw energy of his classic '50s small-group recordings, Memphis Slim recorded with a number of British, American, and European jazz and rock musicians, including Alexis Korner (Slim occasionally toured England in the early '60s with Korner and Cyril Davies), Alex Harvey, and others. He died of kidney failure in 1968.

Men at Work

Formed 1979, Melbourne, Austral.
Colin Hay (b. June 29, 1953, Scot.), voc., gtr.; Ron Strykert (b. Aug. 18, 1957, Austral.), gtr., voc.; Jerry Speiser (b. Austral.), drums, voc.; Greg Ham (b. Sep. 27, 1953, Austral.), sax, flute, voc., kybds.; John Rees (b. Austral.), bass, voc.
1982—*Business as Usual* (Columbia) 1983—*Cargo* 1984—(– Speiser; – Rees) 1985—*Two Hearts* (group disbands) 1996—(group re-forms: Ham; Hay; + various new personnel) *Contraband* 1998—*Brazil.*
Colin Hay solo: 1987—*Looking for Jack* (Columbia) 1990—*Wayfaring Sons* (MCA) 1992—*Peaks and Valleys* 1994—*Topanga* (Lazy Eye, Austral.) 1998—*Transcendental Highway.*

Australia's Men at Work were one of the most successful rock groups of 1982 and won that year's Grammy for Best New Artist. Its American debut, *Business as Usual,* broke the Monkees' 1966 record for the longest run at #1 for a debut LP (15 weeks) and included two #1 singles, "Who Can It Be Now?" and "Down Under."

Colin Hay, the group's lead singer and main songwriter, moved with his family to Australia from Scotland at age 14. The group, several members of which had played together in other aggregations, became a regular Australian pub band, first gaining a following at the Cricketer's Arms Hotel bar. By the time Men at Work signed with Australian Columbia, the band had a national following and was the highest-paid unrecorded band in the country. The band's debut LP, when released in its homeland, stayed at #1 for 10 weeks, beating the record previously held by Split Enz's *True Colours.* In the U.S., *Business as Usual* sold 5 million copies and spent nearly two years on the album chart. In its videos for "Who Can It Be Now?" and the exotic "Down Under," the band established a zany persona right out of *A Hard Day's Night,* while Hay's reedy voice drew comparisons to Sting.

Cargo, issued in April 1983, had been finished since the previous summer but was held for release because of the debut's phenomenal success. It debuted in the Top 30 with *Business* still in the Top 5, and within weeks, both albums were in the Top 10. Men at Work's second effort was also enormously successful, going double platinum and spawning the hits "Overkill" (#3, 1983), "It's a Mistake" (#6, 1983), and "Dr. Heckyll and Mr. Jive" (#28, 1983).

But while their records were scaling the charts, Men at Work were at one another's throats, arguing over management and songwriting. Drummer Jerry Speiser and bassist John Rees left in 1984. In 1985, following the release of the gold *Two Hearts,* Hay, guitarist Ron Strykert, and keyboardist/saxophonist Greg Ham called it quits. Hay released several solo albums, but by then American audiences had lost interest. He subsequently became an actor and was living in California by the mid-'90s. To coincide with the 1996 release of a Men at Work retrospective, he revived the band with the help of Ham. In 1998 they toured the world and issued *Brazil,* a collection of live hits taped in South America.

Natalie Merchant

Born Oct. 26, 1963, Jamestown, NY
1995—*Tigerlily* (Elektra) 1998—*Ophelia* 1999—*Live in Concert.*

Natalie Merchant grew up the daughter of Sicilian working-class parents in economically depressed Jamestown, New York. While still living at home and attending a local community college, she joined 10,000 Maniacs [see entry] at age 17. She won a huge following as the band's lead vocalist, onstage focal point, and frequent songwriter. In 1992, during preproduction for that year's *Our Time in Eden,* she told her band mates she'd be leaving the group, but stayed with them long enough to tour behind the album and make an appearance on *MTV Unplugged* (released on album in 1993).

Merchant financed and produced the recording of her solo debut, *Tigerlily* (#13, 1995), which she cut live in the studio with a three-piece band. An unmitigated success, the subdued, languid-sounding album spawned several hit singles, including "Carnival" (#10, 1995), "Wonder" (#20, 1995), and "Jealousy" (#23, 1996). Her next effort, the lush, dirgelike *Ophelia* (#8, 1998), had an accompanying long-form video directed by ROLLING STONE art director Fred Woodward and chief photographer Mark Seliger. With a nod to artist Cindy Sherman, the 22-minute film depicted Merchant in a number of guises ranging from circus queen to nun to sufragette, among others. The album's only single to receive much airplay was "Kind & Generous."

In 1999 Merchant contributed guest vocals to Billy Bragg's Woody Guthrie project, *Mermaid Avenue, vol. 2,* which was released in 2000 and featured new music set to Guthrie lyrics. Merchant's June 13, 1999, appearance at New York's Neil Simon Theater was documented on *Live in Concert* (#82, 1999).

The Merseybeats

Formed 1963, Liverpool, Eng.
Tony Crane, gtr., voc.; Aaron Williams, gtr., voc.; Bill Kinsley, bass, voc.; John Banks, drums.
1964—*The Merseybeats* (Fontana) (– Kinsley; + John Gustafson, bass); *England's Best Sellers* (Arc Int'l).

Taking their name from the label given to Liverpool's British Invasion bands, the Merseybeats first scored U.K. hits with ballads, starting with covers of the Shirelles' "It's Love That Really Counts" (#24, 1963) and Dusty Springfield's "Wishin' and Hopin' " (#13, 1964). Their next, and biggest, British hit came with Peter Lee Stirling's "I Think of You" (#5, 1964), followed by "Don't Turn Around" (#13, 1964) and "Last Night" (#40, 1964).

In 1964 they were joined by bassist John Gustafson (later briefly with Roxy Music) from another local hitmaking unit, the Big Three. The band broke up in 1966, but Tony Crane and Billy Kinsley continued as the Merseys, scoring their biggest hit with "Sorrow" (#4 U.K., 1966), later covered by David Bowie. After a few more English hits, "I Love You, Yes I Do" (#22 U.K., 1965) and "I Stand Accused" (#38 U.K., 1966), the Merseys broke up. Crane and Kinsley continue to tour in England with a reconfigured lineup.

Metallica

Formed 1981, Los Angeles, CA
James Alan Hetfield (b. Aug. 3, 1963, Los Angeles), gtr., voc.; Ron McGovney, bass; Dave Mustaine (b. Sep. 13, 1961, La Mesa, CA), gtr.; Lars Ulrich (b. Dec. 26, 1963, Gentofte, Den.), drums
1982—(– McGovney; + Clifford Lee Burton [b. Feb. 10, 1962; d. Sep. 27, 1986, Swed.], bass) 1983—(– Mustaine; + Kirk Hammett [b. Nov. 18, 1962, San Francisco, CA], gtr.) *Kill 'Em All* (Megaforce) 1984—*Ride the Lightning* (Megaforce/Elektra) 1985—*Whiplash* EP (Megaforce) 1986—*Master of Puppets* (Elektra) (– Burton; + Jason Newsted [b. Mar. 4, 1963, Battle Creek, MI], bass) 1987—*The $5.98 EP Garage Days Re-Revisited* 1988—*. . . And Justice for All* 1991—*Metallica* 1993—*Live Shit: Binge & Purge* 1996—*Load* 1997—*ReLoad* 1998—*Garage Inc.* 1999—*S&M* 2001—(– Newsted).

In the '80s—when big hair and small ideas dominated heavy metal—Metallica's dense blend of brains and brawn gave the genre a much-needed charge. By 1991, fans had responded to Metallica's message in droves, buying 6 million copies of the group's fifth full-length album—*Metallica*—and elevating its previous LPs to platinum. In the process, grim-faced guitarist/singer James Hetfield became not only a hero for the nation's largest fraternity of misfits—suburban metalheads—but also a critically respected songwriter and bandleader. Metallica ended the decade as the biggest-selling rock act of the '90s.

Hetfield and Lars Ulrich came from different worlds to form Metallica in the L.A. suburbs in 1981. Hetfield, whose father was owner of a trucking company and mother a light-opera singer, was raised in a strict Christian Science home; Ulrich, a recently transplanted Dane, had intended to become a professional tennis player like his father, Torben Ulrich. What the two teenagers shared was an interest in the gritty music of U.K. hard rockers Motörhead. Adding guitarist Dave Mustaine and bassist Ron McGovney, the band started writing songs and recording demo tapes. Metallica's lineup solidified after Clifford Lee Burton replaced McGovney in 1982, and the Bay Area guitarist Kirk Hammett replaced Mustaine the following year. Mustaine, who was booted out for excessive substance abuse, went on to form Megadeth [see entry].

After gaining a solid cult following among fans who could not identify with contemporary pretty-boy pop-metal combos such as Van Halen and Bon Jovi, Metallica became known for its sophisticated, often complex song structures and serious lyrics that reflected teen obsessions with anger, despair, fear, and death. In sharp contrast to those of other death-obsessed metal bands, Metallica's lyrics pose deeper questions about justice and retribution, drug addiction, mental illness, and political violence. The group's debut album, *Kill 'Em All,* is an anarchic catharsis of gloom, with songs like "No Remorse" decrying the insanity of war and "Seek and Destroy" looking at mindless street violence. (Rereleased in 1986, the album went to #155.) On subsequent albums, the subject matter alternated between the political *(. . . And Justice for All)* and the personal *(Metallica).*

In 1986 Metallica's tour bus skidded off an icy road in Sweden, killing bassist Burton. The surviving members took some time off before regrouping with ex–Flotsam and Jetsam bassist Jason Newsted. Newsted's more solid playing style brought a thicker, tighter sound, which contributed to the group's massive success in the late '80s and early '90s. On August 8, 1992, the band experienced another near-tragedy when their pyrotechnics went awry during an ill-fated performance with Guns n' Roses (it was the same night of G n' R's notorious riot show) at Montreal's Olympic Stadium; Hetfield wound up walking into a wall of flames and suffering serious burns, but recovered fully.

Metallica had developed its following without the benefit of radio play, so it came as a bit of a surprise when *Master of Puppets* reached #29 in 1986. The followup EP, *Garage Days Re-Revisited,* a collection of covers of songs by various punk and metal bands including Killing Joke and the Misfits, made it to #28. Metallica's first Top 10 album was . . . *And Justice for All,* which reached #6 in 1988 with its single "One," breaking in to the Top 40 at #35. Its striking video included clips from the 1971 antiwar film adaptation of Dalton Trumbo's *Johnny Got His Gun,* the tale of a faceless quadruple-amputee World War I veteran. After a three-year hiatus, the much-anticipated *Metallica* (a.k.a. the Black Album) entered the charts at #1. The album contained a string of hits, including "Enter Sandman" (#16), "The Unforgiven" (#35), and "Nothing Else Matters" (#34). Metallica's first official live album, *Live Shit* (#26, 1993), was recorded in 1993 over five shows in Mexico City.

In 1994 Metallica sued its longtime label, Elektra, seeking escape from a contract that locked the band in to a modest 14 percent royalty rate. The suit was settled out of court, and the band re-signed with the label. By then, Metallica recognized the changes on the rock landscape epitomized by Nirvana, and in 1996 the band fully stepped away from its early lyrics of blood and guts and explored some nonmetal influences for an updated, almost alternative-leaning sound on *Load* (#1). The album continued the band's string of hits with "Until It Sleeps" (#10), "Hero of the Day" (#60), and "King Nothing" (#90). Metallica also sought to change its image: Band members cut their hair, and the abstract album cover by controversial photographer Andres Serrano (famous for his work *Piss Christ*) depicted a mixture of blood and semen. Not all fans were pleased.

More confusion followed when Metallica headlined the alternative rock-themed Lollapalooza Tour in 1996. That year, the band also made a surprise stop at the Whisky-a-Go-Go in Hollywood for the 50th birthday party of Lemmy of Motörhead, appearing at the club all dressed like the metal veteran and performing a full set of Motörhead songs. In 1997 Metallica finished songs left over from the *Load* sessions for the heavier *ReLoad* (#1), which included vocals by Marianne Faithfull on "The Memory Remains" (#28). The album also contained "The Unforgiven II" (#59). The next year, Metallica combined the original *Garage Days Revisited* EP with 11 new covers and various B sides for the two-disc set *Garage Inc.* (#2). A live collaboration with the San Francisco Symphony (arranged and conducted by Michael Kamen) was recorded for 1999's *S&M.*

In 2000 Metallica led a battle over the rights of recording artists against Napster, a popular music file-sharing Web site where fans could download music (including Metallica's) for free. Metallica not only responded with copyright infringement suits against Napster but demanded that the estimated 335,000 Napster users who had ever downloaded a Metallica track be permanently barred from the service. To critics it was a confounding strategy that inevitably targeted some of the band's most rabid followers. Despite a fan backlash, the controversy failed to derail that year's successful stadium tour with Korn and Kid Rock. In January 2001 Newsted left Metallica on good terms; the band has vowed to carry on a with a replacement.

The Meters

Formed 1967, New Orleans, LA
Art Neville (b. Arthur Lanon Neville, 1938, New Orleans), kybds., voc.; Leo Nocentelli, gtr., voc.; Joseph "Zigaboo" Modeliste, drums, voc.; George Porter Jr., bass, voc.
1969—*The Meters* (Josie) 1970—*Look-Ka Py Py; Struttin'* 1972—*Cabbage Alley* (Reprise) 1974—*Rejuvenation; Cissy Strut* (Island) 1975—(+ Cyril Neville [b. 1950, New Orleans], perc., voc.) *Fire on the Bayou* (Reprise) 1976—*Trick Bag* 1977—*New Directions* (Warner Bros.) (group disbands) 1990—(group re-forms: A. Neville; Nocentelli; Porter Jr.; + Russell Batiste, drums) *Good Old Funky Music* (Rounder) 1991—*Funky Miracle* (Charly) 1992—*The Meters Jam; Uptown Rulers: The Meters Live on the Queen Mary* (Rhino) 1995—(– Nocentelli; + Brian Stoltz, gtr.) *Funkify Your Life: The Meters Anthology* 1997—*The Very Best of the Meters.*

The Meters were better known—and better paid—as New Orleans' finest backup band than as a self-contained feature act. Their lean, peppery R&B gave a funky flavor to recordings by out-of-towners like Paul McCartney and Labelle, but on their own, their rhythms were too tricky, their vocals too understated, and their sound altogether too spare to reach a broad audience.

When Art Neville formed the group in 1967, he had been a prominent musician in New Orleans for almost 15 years. He was still in high school when, leading the Hawketts, he cut the 1954 Chess single "Mardi Gras Mambo," which made them a popular regional act and is still pressed every year for Mardi Gras. He had put out a handful of regional hits as a soloist—"Cha Dooky Doo" and "Ooh-Whee Baby" on Specialty in the late '50s, and "All These Things" on Instant in 1962—before he formed Art Neville and the Sounds with his brothers Charles and Aaron as singers, guitarist Leo Nocentelli, bassist George Porter, and drummer Ziggy Modeliste around 1966. They played local clubs until producer Allen Toussaint and his business partner Marshall Sehorn hired them, minus Charles and Aaron, to be the house rhythm section for their Sansu Enterprises in 1968. As such, they backed Lee Dorsey, Chris Kenner, Earl King, Betty Harris, and Toussaint himself on stage and in the studio in the late '60s and early '70s.

Concurrently, the quartet performed on its own as the Meters. Their popularity was not limited to New Orleans, and their hits—mostly dance instrumentals—included "Sophisticated Cissy" (#34 pop, #7 R&B, 1969), "Cissy Strut" (#23 pop, #4 R&B, 1969), "Look-Ka Py Py" (#11 R&B, 1969), and "Chicken Strut" (#11 R&B, 1970).

In 1972 the Meters signed with Reprise Records, retaining Toussaint as their producer and Sehorn as manager. The major label did not bring about a commercial breakthrough—in fact, the moderate hits gave way to minor hits—but the Meters were widely heard, if not recognized, on albums by Dr. John, Robert Palmer, Jess Roden, Labelle, King Biscuit Boy, and Paul McCartney and Wings. They backed Dr. John on tours in 1973 and King Biscuit Boy in 1974, and opened shows for the Rolling Stones on the Stones' 1975 American and 1976 European tours.

In 1975 the Meters joined George and Amos Landry—members of a Mardi Gras ceremonial "black Indian tribe," the Wild Tchoupitoulas, and uncle and cousin, respectively, to Neville—to record *The Wild Tchoupitoulas* (Island, 1976). Aaron, Charles, Art, and Cyril Neville contributed vocals to the sessions, reuniting the Neville Sounds for the occasion. Shortly before that album's release, Cyril joined the Meters. A year later, the group cut ties with Toussaint and Sehorn, complaining that it was denied artistic control. For *New Directions,* the Meters teamed with San Francisco producer Dave Rubinson, but that album was not to their satisfaction either, and in 1977, when Toussaint and Sehorn claimed the Meters name, the band broke up. Art and Cyril joined Aaron and Charles as the Neville Brothers, while the other band members found freelance work in New Orleans. Modeliste drummed for Keith Richards and Ron Wood on their New Barbarians tour in 1979.

The Meters re-formed in 1990 with drummer Russell Batiste taking over for Modeliste, who had moved to L.A. and become a session player. In 1994 founding member Nocentelli left the band, reportedly because of disagreements with Art Neville over whether or not the band should be compensated for samples lifted from their back catalogue by contemporary hip-hop groups. Brian Stoltz, who replaced Nocentelli, had played with the Neville Brothers. The Meters continue to tour. In 1995 Rhino released *Funkify Your Life,* a two-CD compilation of the group's early Josie and Warner Bros. sides. In November 2000 Porter, Neville, Nocentelli, and Modeliste reunited for a one-night-only concert in San Francisco, marking the first time in 20 years that the quartet all shared the same stage.

Pat Metheny

Born Aug. 12, 1954, Lee's Summit, MO
1975—*Bright Size Life* (ECM) 1977—*Watercolors* 1978—*Pat Metheny Group* 1979—*New Chautauqua* 1980—*American Garage; 80/81* 1981—*As Falls Wichita, So Falls Wichita Falls* (with Lyle Mays) 1982—*Offramp* 1983—*Travels; Rejoicing* (with Charlie Haden and Billy Higgins) 1984—*First Circle; ECM Works* 1985—*The Falcon and the Snowman* soundtrack (EMI America) 1986—*Song X* (with Ornette Coleman) (Geffen) 1987—*Still Life (Talking)* 1988—*ECM Works II* (ECM) 1989—*Letter From Home* (Geffen) 1990—*Question and Answer* (with Dave Holland and Roy Haynes) 1992—*Secret Story* 1993—*The Road to You: Recorded Live in Europe* 1994—*Zero Tolerance for Silence* 1995—*We Live Here* 1996—*Sign of Four* (Knitting Factory); *Quartet* (Geffen) 1997—*Beyond the Missouri Sky, A Map of the World* (with Charlie Haden) (Uni Verve); *Imaginary Day* (Warner Bros.); *Jim Hall/Pat Metheny* (Telarc) 1998—*Passagio Per Il Paradiso* (Geffen International) 1999—*All the Things You Are* (Fruit Tree); *A Map of the World* (Warner Bros.) 2000—*Trio 99>00.*

Practically overnight in the late '70s, Pat Metheny became one of the most influential voices in contemporary jazz guitar. His chiming guitar work, rooted in bop but tinged with country and occasional rock overtones, insistent yet ethereal, signaled a visionary talent on the instrument. A 13-time Grammy winner, Metheny has managed to be commercially successful while pursuing an artistic vision that encompasses a wide range of jazz styles.

Metheny began seriously delving into jazz and the guitar at age 14; within two years he was working professionally in Kansas City. After a stint at the University of Miami, Metheny was invited by the vibist and bandleader Gary Burton—who had heard him earlier at a Wichita jazz festival—to teach at Boston's Berklee College of Music, the nation's premier jazz school. Metheny then joined Burton's band, at times playing an electric 12-string guitar—an instrument almost unheard of in jazz.

After playing with Burton, Metheny put together his own group; among the musicians was keyboardist Lyle Mays, a mainstay of Metheny's bands ever since. Before the band recorded 1978's *Pat Metheny Group,* Metheny had already released *Bright Size Life* (1975) and *Watercolors* (1977). On the latter two albums, he was accompanied by drummer Bob Moses and bassist Jaco Pastorius, whom he'd met in Miami in the mid-'70s. Pastorius and Metheny also toured together in 1979 as part of Joni Mitchell's band. (Some of those performances were recorded for Mitchell's album *Shadows and Light.*)

With the success of *New Chautaqua* (#44, 1979), *American Garage* (#53, 1979), and *As Falls Wichita, So Falls Wichita Falls* (#50, 1981), Metheny made deeper inroads into the pop market and became the most influential jazz-guitar stylist since John McLaughlin. Although his own group used the instrumentation of a typical rock band by employing electric bass and keyboards (including synthesizers), Metheny kept his hand in more traditional jazz contexts as well. The album *80/81* found him recording with two Ornette Coleman sidemen, bassist Charlie Haden and tenor saxophonist Dewey Redman; 1984's *Rejoicing* was a trio session with Haden and drummer Billy Higgins; *Question and Answer* (1990) featured bassist Dave Holland and drummer Roy Haynes. In 1986 Metheny shared a recording with one of his heroes, Ornette Coleman, on *Song X,* a highly praised collaboration.

Metheny's score for John Schlesinger's 1985 film, *The*

Falcon and the Snowman, featured "This Is Not America" (#32, 1985), cocomposed and sung by David Bowie. *Still Life (Talking)* (#86, 1987), Metheny's first solo album for Geffen, went gold. By the mid-'80s, Metheny had become seriously interested in both advanced technologies—experimented widely with synthesizers and guitar effects and designs that included a 42-stringed instrument—and world music. He began exploring Brazilian and African music and expanded his groups to include percussionists and a singer. Metheny also guested on recordings by Brazilian singer/songwriter Milton Nascimento. In the early '90s, Metheny toured and recorded with saxophonist Joshua Redman. Among the highlights of his work since have been an impressionistic collaboration with Haden, *Beyond the Missouri Sky,* a lush, pastoral work that marked Metheny's return to film scoring, and *Trio 99>00,* another fine trio outing, this time with bassist Larry Grenadier and drummer Bill Stewart. Despite changes in format and sound, Metheny's acclaim and popularity have remained consistent.

MFSB

Formed early '70s, Philadelphia, PA
1973—*MFSB* (Philadelphia International); *MFSB: Love Is the Message* 1974—*TSOP* (TSOP) 1975—*Universal Love* (Philadelphia International) 1976—*Philadelphia Freedom; Summertime* 1977—*The End of Phase I* 1978—*MFSB and Gamble Huff Orchestra* (TSOP) 1980—*Mysteries of the World* 1995—*The Best of MFSB: Love Is the Message* (Legacy) 1999—*Deep Grooves.*

MFSB (Mother, Father, Sister, Brother) was the nickname for the crew of studio musicians who played on most of the "Sound of Philadelphia" records released by Kenny Gamble and Leon Huff's Philadelphia International Records in the early '70s. Many of these musicians appeared on Cliff Nobles' popular dance tune "The Horse" (#2 pop and R&B) in 1968. Under the MFSB title, they had a #1 pop and R&B single, "TSOP (The Sound of Philadelphia)," in 1974. For many years, that Kenny Gamble–Leon Huff composition was the theme for the syndicated music show *Soul Train.* Many MFSB members also appeared on Salsoul Orchestra recordings. Although personnel changed frequently in the later years, musicians on MFSB's most popular early LPs included Ron Kersey and Kenny Gamble (keyboards); Norman Harris, Roland Chambers, and Bobby Eli (guitars); Lenny Pakula (organ); Zach Zachery (sax); Ronnie Baker (bass); Vince Montana (vibes); Earl Young (drums); Larry Washington (percussion); and Don Renaldo (conductor).

George Michael

Born Georgios Kyriacos Panayiotou, June 25, 1963, London, Eng.
1987—*Faith* (Columbia) 1990—*Listen Without Prejudice vol. 1* 1996—*Older* (DreamWorks) 1998—*Ladies & Gentlemen: The Best of George Michael* (Epic) 1999—*Songs From the Last Century* (Virgin).
With Queen and Lisa Stansfield: 1993—*Five Live* EP (Hollywood).

Few could have guessed that the transition from teenybopper idol to serious singer/songwriter would go as smoothly as it did for George Michael, who became famous as half of the British pop duo Wham! [see entry] before ascending to pop superstardom with his solo debut, *Faith.* Whereas in Wham! Michael used his cherubic good looks and uncanny knack for a melodic hook to create ingratiating but disposable pop, his solo work reveals an earnest effort to achieve deeper musical and emotional resonance. His radiant ballads, insidious dance tracks, and blue-eyed soul singing established him as a top artist. His popularity never waned in the U.K.—all of his albums have reached either #1 or #2 on the album charts there—but subsequent efforts have been able to match his early solo successes in the U.S.

Michael's first post-Wham! outing was "I Knew You Were Waiting (for Me)," a duet with Aretha Franklin that hit #1 in 1987 and earned Michael a Grammy for Best R&B Performance by a Duo. Shortly afterward, Michael released the funky first single off of *Faith,* "I Want Your Sex," which, bolstered by a sexy video, quickly soared to #2. The album would eventually spin off four #1 hits: "Faith" (1987), the shimmering "Father Figure" (1988), the romantic ballad "One More Try" (1988), and "Monkey" (1988). "Kissing a Fool" hit #5, further boosting the 14 million–selling *Faith,* 1988's smash album and Grammy winner for Album of the Year.

In his videos and media appearances, Michael cultivated a sex-symbol image, albeit a more rugged—leather, chin stubble, sneer—and mature one than he had nurtured in Wham! But with the release of his second solo effort, *Listen Without Prejudice vol. 1,* in 1990, Michael surprised fans and industry insiders by shunning the press and saying that he wouldn't make videos. The album peaked at #2 nonetheless, and there was a chart-topping hit, the somber "Praying for Time" (#1, 1990). The danceable second single, "Freedom 90"—whose lyrics spelled out Michael's decision to abandon his rock-star persona—went to #8 (1990) and was made into a video, albeit without Michael's presence. (Instead, a bevy of supermodels lip-synched his vocals.) In late 1991 Michael was back on the charts with a #1 version of Elton John's "Don't Let the Sun Go Down on Me," recorded live with John.

A year later, Michael announced that he would take legal action to terminate his contract with Sony Music, the corporation that took over his label, Columbia Records. He charged that Sony, still wishing to package Michael as a sex symbol, lacked respect for his artistic expression and that it only halfheartedly supported his projects benefiting AIDS research and prevention, among them his duet with Elton John and his three-track contribution to a compilation album called *Red Hot + Dance.* In 1993, Sony grudgingly granted Hollywood Records permission to release *Five Live,* an EP of two cover songs performed by Michael on his 1991–92 tour and three from his appearance at the Freddie Mercury tribute concert in 1992, during which he sang Queen songs with surviving members of that band. All proceeds from the record went to the Phoenix Trust, an AIDS charity set up in Mercury's memory.

In June 1994 a London court rejected Michael's claim that his contract with Sony amounted to "restraint of trade" and upheld the $12 million contract the singer had signed with the company in 1988. At the time, Michael owed the label six more albums on a contract that could run to 2003. Two months later, Michael filed an appeal of the verdict. As the legal battle continued, Michael was unable to release new product. Under a special arrangement, however, Michael performed his song "Jesus to a Child" on television as part of an annual appeal to raise funds for needy children. After hearing the six-minute song, listeners pledged $32,000 to the charity.

In 1995, though Michael lost the appeal he filed, he signed new contracts with DreamWorks in the U.S. and Virgin in the rest of the world. He released his first album of new material in six years, *Older,* in 1996 (#6), featuring "Jesus to a Child" (#7) and the dance track "Fastlove" (#8), but the release sold just 900,000 copies in the U.S.

Michael's profile was heightened again in 1998, but for a more notorious reason: In April of that year, he was arrested for lewd conduct in the men's room of a public park in Beverly Hills. Speculation arose regarding the nature of the "lewd conduct," and before Michael could become the target of international crude jokes, he took control of the matter and outed himself as homosexual on CNN. Though the court fined him and ordered him to perform community service, he seemed somewhat relieved to reveal the truth to the media and his fans. That fall, he even set the scene for his video for "Outside" (one of two new songs from *Ladies & Gentlemen: The Best of George Michael*) in a public restroom; it featured dancing men dressed in leather and male actors portraying police officers kissing. Unfortunately, this was no joke to Michael's real-life arresting officer, who filed a lawsuit against him, claiming slander; the judge dismissed the case.

In late 1999 Michael put the embarrassing events of the previous year behind him with the release of *Songs From the Last Century,* an album of cover songs coproduced by Phil Ramone (Billy Joel) that ran the gamut from the Depression-era "Brother Can You Spare a Dime" to the Police's "Roxanne." In 2000 Michael participated in Equality Rocks, a concert in Washington, DC, organized by the Human Rights Campaign that highlighted the issue of gay rights.

Lee Michaels

Born Nov. 24, 1945, Los Angeles, CA
1968—*Carnival of Life* (A&M) 1969—*Recital; Lee Michaels* 1970—*Barrel* 1971—*5th* 1972—*Life; Space and First Takes* 1973—*Nice Day for Something* (Columbia) 1974—*Tailface* 1975—*Saturn Rings* (ABC) 1992—*The Lee Michaels Collection* (Rhino).

Screaming himself hoarse, pounding his overamped Hammond organ, and backed only by an enormous drummer called Frosty, Lee Michaels made his name as one of the original hard rockers—and surely the first, perhaps the only, to play hard rock on a keyboard rather than a guitar. His 1971 hit "Do You Know What I Mean?" stands as the classic example of Michaels' unique sound.

Though he concentrated on this heavy-keyboard approach during much of his career, Michaels could also play sax, accordion, trombone, and guitar. He'd started out as a lounge pianist in Fresno in the mid-'60s, with aspirations to be a jazz/blues horn player. Instead, he joined his first band, the Sentinels, in 1965. After the Sentinels disbanded, Michaels and the band's drummer, John Barbata (later with the Turtles and Jefferson Starship), joined a Bay Area band led by Joel Scott Hill. However, Michaels, inspired by a Jefferson Airplane show, soon left to pursue his own sound. He assembled a five-piece band named for himself, and recorded his debut LP.

After another change of heart—and much experimentation with organs and amplifiers—Michaels dismissed his band. Though the public responded favorably to his one-man-band debut, *Recital,* his greatest success resulted from collaborations with Frosty (Bartholomew Eugene Smith-Frost). About six and a half hours' worth of jamming resulted in *Lee Michaels,* his most successful LP to that time. Michaels and Frosty toured as a duo, selling out major halls across the U.S. Michaels' third LP yielded "Heighty Hi" and a cover of the blues standard "Stormy Monday," both of which received substantial FM-radio airplay. Frosty then left to form his own band, Sweathog.

Michaels kept at it and had his only hits in 1971 with "Do You Know What I Mean?" (#6) and "Can I Get a Witness?" (#39); the album on which they appeared, *5th,* went Top 20. *Space and First Takes* featured drummer Keith Knudsen, who later left Michaels to join the Doobie Brothers, at which point Michaels retired for an extended holiday in Hawaii to "sit under a tree." He reunited with Frosty for *Tailface,* but with his successes apparently behind him, Michaels again retired after *Saturn Rings.*

Mickey and Sylvia

Mickey Baker (b. McHouston Baker, Oct. 15, 1925, Louisville, KY), gtr., voc.; Sylvia Robinson (b. Sylvia Vanderpool, Mar. 6, 1936, New York, NY), voc., gtr.
1989—*Love Is Strange and Other Hits* (RCA).

In 1954, Mickey Baker, a blues guitarist who had recorded as a solo act, met vocalist Sylvia Vanderpool. He gave her guitar lessons, and from this evolved a partnership that in 1956 produced the million-selling hit "Love Is Strange" (#11 pop, #2 R&B). The pair had two more hits—"There Oughta Be a Law" (#46 pop, #15 R&B, 1957) and "Baby You're So Fine" (#52 pop, #27 R&B, 1961)—before breaking up in 1961 when Mickey moved to Europe. (They reunited briefly in 1965 to perform a few gigs.) Later, Mickey wrote several guitar instruction books, including the bestseller *Jazz Guitar.*

In 1956 Sylvia had married Joe Robinson, and more than a decade later the couple founded All Platinum Records and All Platinum Studios. As a producer, Sylvia's credits range from the 1961 Ike and Tina Turner hit "It's Gonna Work Out Fine" (on which she also played guitar) to the Moments' 1970 gold single "Love on a Two-Way Street" (which she cowrote) and Shirley and Company's 1976 disco hit "Shame, Shame, Shame" (which she wrote).

In 1973 Sylvia returned to the chart with "Pillow Talk" (#3 pop, #1 R&B) on her own Vibration label. She also continued to hit the R&B chart through 1978, notably with "Sweet Stuff" (#16, 1974) and "Automatic Lover" (#43, 1978). In the late '70s Sylvia revived the ailing All Platinum label by renaming it Sugar Hill and putting together a group of rap vocalists, the Sugar Hill Gang, which had a smash hit with "Rapper's Delight" (#26 pop, #4 R&B, 1979). She went on to sign and produce other top rap acts such as Grandmaster Flash and the Furious Five and the Funky Four Plus One.

Bette Midler

Born Dec. 1, 1945, Paterson, NJ
1972—*The Divine Miss M* (Atlantic) 1973—*Bette Midler* 1974—*Songs for the New Depression* 1977—*Broken Blossom; Live at Last* 1979—*Thighs and Whispers; The Rose* soundtrack 1980—*Divine Madness* 1983—*No Frills* 1985—*Mud Will Be Flung Tonight!* 1989—*Beaches* soundtrack 1990—*Some People's Lives* 1991—*For the Boys* soundtrack 1993—*Gypsy* soundtrack 1995—*Bette of Roses* 1997—*Experience the Divine* 1998—*Bathhouse Betty* (Warner Bros.) 2000—*Bette.*

Early on, singer Bette Midler's sexpot camp image—trash with flash—proved as important to her success as did her singing. Over the next three decades, Midler survived several career setbacks, but she turned in a series of acclaimed film performances and returned to the top of the charts in 1989 with "Wind Beneath My Wings." And while her later hits tend toward MOR-ish sentimentality, her record-breaking 1993 concert tour and her 1999 Divine Miss Millennium Tour proved that the Divine Miss M had lost none of her humor or charm. She is, as one critic wrote, "Sophie Tucker, Ethel Merman, and Judy Garland rolled into one furiously energetic package."

Midler was born in New Jersey but raised in Hawaii. From an early age, she took an interest in acting (her mother named her after Bette Davis), and in high school Midler worked in theater and sang in a female folk trio called the Pieridine Three. In 1965 she had a bit part as a missionary's wife in the film *Hawaii,* after which she left for L.A.; she later moved to New York. There (in between odd jobs like go-go dancing in a New Jersey bar), Midler got parts in several Tom Eyen off-Broadway productions, followed by a three-year run in Broadway's *Fiddler on the Roof,* during which she eventually moved from the chorus to the featured part of Tzeitel. In 1971 she played the double role of Mrs. Walker and the Acid Queen in the Seattle Opera Association's production of *Tommy.*

Around 1970 Midler decided to concentrate on singing and was soon performing at the Continental Baths, a gay men's club in New York City. There she developed her campy comedy routines and a broad musical repertoire that included Andrews Sisters takeoffs, blues, show tunes, and '60s girl-group numbers. Her piano accompanist was Barry Manilow. She quickly became a cult item and soon an aboveground sensation on major TV talk shows. Her debut LP, *The Divine Miss M,* went gold and won her the Grammy for Best New Artist. She appeared on the cover of *Newsweek* and had a #8 hit with a remake of the Andrews Sisters' "Boogie Woogie Bugle Boy" in 1973.

Sales after the second LP dropped off sharply, though she always retained a loyal concert following. In 1979, Midler starred in *The Rose,* a film loosely based on the life of Janis Joplin. Her performance earned her an Oscar nomination. The soundtrack LP went platinum in 1980, aided by the Top 10 title song. Later in the year, a Midler concert film and soundtrack entitled *Divine Madness* were released. Her humorous memoirs of her first world tour, *A View From a Broad,* hit the bestseller list that year as well. Her next literary effort was a children's book entitled *The Saga of Baby Divine,* which was published in 1983.

Midler's career slump began in 1982 with her next feature film, the ironically titled *Jinxed.* A critical and commercial bomb, the comedy was released amid rampant rumors of disagreements between Midler and her costars and director. Her reputation was damaged, seemingly irreparably, and she suffered a nervous breakdown. In later interviews she openly discussed that painful period as one of heavy drinking and deep depression. In 1984, after a brief courtship, she married Martin von Haselberg, a commodities trader and performance artist who was part of a duo known as the Kipper Kids. Soon thereafter, Midler began to turn her career around with a series of comedies for the Walt Disney Studio–Touchstone Pictures: *Down and Out in Beverly Hills* and *Ruthless People* (both 1986), *Outrageous Fortune* (1987), and *Big Business* (1988), in which she and Lily Tomlin each played dual roles as two sets of twin sisters. She returned to drama with *Beaches,* a sentimental paean to women's friendship that spawned a multiplatinum #2 soundtrack album and the #1 Grammy-winning single "Wind Beneath My Wings."

In 1991 Midler costarred with Woody Allen in *Scenes From a Mall* and later that year starred in *Stella.* Also in 1991 another multiplatinum album, *Some People's Lives,* produced the #2 Grammy-awarded ballad "From a Distance." The song got a lot of play during the Gulf War. She received her second Oscar nomination for *For the Boys,* a musical that follows a USO entertainer and her partner (played by James Caan) through three wars. The movie was not a commercial success but garnered favorable reviews, and the soundtrack went gold. The film was in the news again when comedienne Martha Raye charged that details of the film's story line were derived from an outline of Raye's own life story, a treatment for which Raye claimed that Midler had seen. The charges were dismissed on February 23, 1994, because the judge ruled there was no basis for the suit.

In 1992 Midler won an Emmy for singing several sentimental songs (including one she'd written entitled "Dear Mr. Carson," described as "a love letter from America's women") to Johnny Carson on one of the last *Tonight Show* broadcasts. Midler's 1993 tour, Experience the Divine, showed her in top form. She delivered an over-the-top reading of Mama Rose in a made-for-television version of *Gypsy* that same year, and also starred in the feature film *Hocus Pocus*. She returned to recording in 1995 with the release of the ballad-heavy *Bette of Roses;* she also did a cameo in the movie *Get Shorty* the same year. Midler's most successful movie comeback came in 1996, though, when she costarred with Diane Keaton and Goldie Hawn as a spurned ex-wife in *The First Wives Club*. She followed it up with the romantic comedy *That Old Feeling* in 1997, the same year she filmed a concert special for HBO. Called *Diva Las Vegas,* the concert won Midler a Best Performance Emmy. Perhaps inspired by that musical success, Midler recorded another album, *Bathhouse Betty,* in 1998. The title and much of the disc's content harkened back to Midler's early days working at the Continental Baths and her old bawdy style. (It also included a ballad more typical of her latter-day chart popularity, "My One True Friend," which was used over the end credits of the Meryl Streep film *One True Thing*.) Midler got back to her show-business roots even further by embarking on a small-scale tour of dance clubs in support of the album.

Throughout the '90s, Midler also got heavily involved with charity work, lending her name, time, and financial support to causes such as AIDS, voter registration, and, most notably, restoring parks and highways in New York City. She toured on a larger scale in 1999 and continued her acting career with back-to-back flops in early 2000: the feature films *Isn't She Great* (in which she played *Valley of the Dolls* author Jacqueline Susann) and *Drowning Mona* (in which her title character is killed off early in the movie). More promising were her efforts in late 2000; a role in the Mel Gibson–Helen Hunt movie *What Women Want* and her own sitcom, *Bette*, on CBS, which ran for one season. In the latter, Midler played a slightly fictionalized version of herself, a well-known actress/singer.

Midnight Oil

Formed 1976, Sydney, Austral.
Peter Garrett (b. Apr. 16, 1953, Sydney), voc.; Rob Hirst (b. Sep. 3, 1955, Sydney), drums, voc.; Jim Moginie (b. May 18, 1956, Sydney), gtr., kybds.; Martin Rotsey (b. Feb. 19, 1956, Sydney), gtr; Andrew "Bear" James, bass.
1978—*Midnight Oil* (Powderworks) 1979—*Head Injuries* 1980—(– James; + Peter Gifford, bass) *Bird Noises* EP 1981—*Place Without a Postcard* 1983—*10, 9, 8, 7, 6, 5, 4, 3, 2, 1* (Columbia) 1984—*Red Sails in the Sunset* 1985—*Species Deceases* EP 1987—*Diesel and Dust* 1990—(– Gifford; + Dwayne "Bones" Hillman [b. May 7, 1958, N.Z.], bass) *Blue Sky Mining* 1992—*Scream in Blue Live* 1993—*Earth and Sun and Moon* 1996—*Breathe* (Sony/Work) 1997—*20,000 Watt R.S.L.—The Collection* (Columbia) 1998—*Redneck Wonderland* 2000—*The Real Thing* (Sony).

Midnight Oil holds the distinction of being the only known rock band whose lead singer ran for a seat on the Australian senate (in 1984, on a Nuclear Disarmament Party ticket). In fact, frontman Peter Garrett—he of the shaved head and somewhat forbidding stature—and his band mates have never been shy about sharing their social and political convictions. Such concerns have often been at the fore of the Oils' lean, driving guitar rock, whether they're addressing the evils of nationalism gone amok or the dangers of dissing Mother Nature. Moreover, the band's dedication to political and environmental causes has extended beyond its songs; having formed alliances with organizations ranging from Greenpeace to the Tibet Council, Midnight Oil has endorsed these projects—through benefit concerts and general outspokenness—with an ardor that's made the efforts of many other socially conscious artists pale in comparison.

Drummer Rob Hirst and guitarists Martin Rotsey and Jim Moginie first played together as the Farm, touring Sydney's northern coast, before recruiting Garrett, then a law student, through a newspaper ad in the mid-'70s. (Garrett received his degree in 1977 but never practiced.) In 1976, adding bassist Andrew "Bear" James to the lineup, the band became Midnight Oil and quickly developed an avid following for its live shows. Record companies were unsure of Garrett's market potential, however, and so after numerous rejections, the Oils formed their own independent label, Powderworks. (The group's indie releases were later reissued by Columbia in the U.S.) The band promoted its eponymous debut album (recorded in 10 days) with concerts benefiting Greenpeace, the anti–uranium mining movement, and Save the Whales. A second album, *Head Injuries,* went gold in Australia.

Midnight Oil's star rose further, domestically at least, with its major-label debut album, *10, 9, 8, 7, 6, 5, 4, 3, 2, 1,* which remained in the Australian Top 40 for two years. Meanwhile, the Oils continued to work benefit concerts, including several on behalf of nuclear disarmament, into its hectic touring schedule. The Oils finally enjoyed their international breakthrough when 1987's *Diesel and Dust* reached #21 in the U.S. and yielded the #17 pop single "Beds Are Burning," an angry wake-up call about the plight of aboriginal Australians—a prominent theme on the album and in the band's work at large—and their biggest hit to date.

Blue Sky Mining followed its predecessor to the upper reaches of the American LP chart (#20), but its most successful single, "Blue Sky Mine," peaked at #47. Shortly after its release, the Oils staged a concert outside the Exxon building in Manhattan to express their disgust over the Exxon *Valdez* oil spill in Alaska. (A video of the performance, *Black Rain Falls,* was released to raise funds for Greenpeace.) A subsequent live album, *Scream in Blue Live* (#141, 1992), and another two studio efforts, *Earth and Sun and Moon* (#49, 1993) and the uncharacteristically nonpolitical *Breathe* (1996), proved commercially disappointing. However, a 1997 greatest-hits collection, *20,000 Watt R.S.L.*, debuted at #1 on the Australian album chart. Perhaps inspired by this success and fueled by Garrett's new position as president of the Australian Conservation Foundation—in part leading to him being named an Official Living Treasure by the Australian National Trust—the band's next album, 1998's *Redneck Wonderland*, was angrier in tone, attacking widespread conservatism. The band released *The Real Thing* in 2000, around the same time they performed at the closing ceremony of the Summer Olympic Games in Sydney.

Drummer Hirst, also a songwriter, released two albums in Australia with his side project, Ghostwriters, a duo with Rick Grossman of Hoodoo Gurus, in the '90s.

Mighty Clouds of Joy

Formed ca. 1955, Los Angeles, CA
Joe Ligon (b. Oct. 11, 1936, Troy, AL), voc.; Johnny Martin (b. Los Angeles; d. 1987), voc.; Elmo Franklin (b. Oct. 8, 1936, FL), voc.; Ermant Franklin, voc.; Richard Wallace (b. June 9, 1940, TX), voc., bass; Jimmy Jones, voc.; David Walker, voc.
ca. 1960—(+ Leon Polk, voc.) 1962—*Live at the Music Hall* (Peacock) 1964—*Presenting: The Untouchables* 1966—*Sing Songs of Rev. Julius Cheeks and the Nightingales* 1968—*Live! At the Apollo* ca. 1960s—(– Polk; – Jones) 1972—*A Bright Side* 1973—*Best of Mighty Clouds of Joy* 1974—*It's Time* (ABC/Dunhill) 1975—*Kickin'* (ABC) 1977—*Truth Is the Power* 1978—*Live and Direct; The Very Best of the Mighty Clouds of Joy* 1979—*Changing Times* (Epic) ca. late 1970s—(– Ermant Franklin) Early 1980s—(+ Paul Beasly, voc.; + Johnny Valentine [b. July 3, 1962, Newark, NJ], drums, voc.) 1980—*Cloudburst* (Myrrh) 1982—*Request Line* (ABC); *Miracle Man* (Myrrh); *Mighty Clouds Alive* 1983—*Sing and Shout* 1987—(– Beasly; + Michael Cook, voc.; – Martin) *Catching On* (Word) 1989—*Night Song* 1991—(lineup: Ligon; Wallace; Elmo Franklin; Cook; Michael McCowin [b. Oct. 18, 1959, Dallas, TX], voc.) *Pray for Me* 1993—*Memory Lane (Best of)* (– Cook; + Wilbert Williams [b. Apr. 26, 1959, Sanfred, NC], voc.) 1996—*Power* (Intersound) 1997—*Live in Charleston* 1999—*It Was You* (CGI-Platinum) 1999—(lineup: Ligon; Wallace; McCowin; Valentine; + Ron Staples, voc., bass) 2000—(– Cook; – Cowin; + Tim Woodson, voc.) 2001—(– Woodson; + Cook).

One of the top contemporary gospel vocal units, and one of the very few to attempt a pop/soul crossover, the Mighty Clouds of Joy have won three Grammy awards: Best Gospel Performance, Traditional for *Live and Direct* (1978) and *Changing Times* (1979) and Best Traditional Soul Gospel Album for *Pray for Me* (1991). Through their long career, they have shared the stage with artists as diverse as Earth, Wind & Fire, the Rolling Stones, the Reverend James Cleveland, Paul Simon, Marvin Gaye, Aretha Franklin, and Andrae Crouch. Incorporating choreography, a colorful wardrobe (as opposed to the traditional black of other gospel acts), and R&B/soul instrumentation such as drums, electric keyboards, and electric guitars (the above chronology does not include all musicians), the Mighty Clouds of Joy have been among the more progressive and most popular of modern gospel groups. Their latter-day repertoire has incorporated the Isley Brothers' "Shout" and the O'Jays' "Love Train" alongside more traditional gospel fare.

The core original members—Joe Ligon, Johnny Martin, Elmo Franklin, Ermant Franklin, Richard Wallace, Jimmy Jones, and David Walker—first got together in high school in L.A. Later members would include Leon Polk and Paul Beasly from the Gospel Keynotes. As of mid-2001, Ligon and Wallace are the sole original members remaining in the group, though Elmo Franklin was with the lineup through the '90s. Lead singer Joe Ligon, whose father sang in a quartet, was heavily influenced by the gritty, grunting style of the Reverend Julius Cheeks of the Sensational Nightingales (as was Wilson Pickett) and the sermons of the Reverend C.L. Franklin (Aretha's father).

In 1959 the group signed to Houston, Texas–based Peacock, home of such gospel giants as the Dixie Hummingbirds and the Nightingales. There they recorded their first gospel hit, "Steal Away to Jesus." Toward the end of their Peacock label days, critics began comparing the Clouds' high-harmony sound to that of Curtis Mayfield and the Impressions, although overall their approach was rawer.

Throughout their long career, the Mighty Clouds have worked with a number of pop producers. In 1974 they recorded *It's Time* with backing from members of Philadelphia International's house band, MFSB, and production by Kenny Gamble and Leon Huff. The Grammy-winning *Changing Times* was produced by Frank Wilson, whose earlier writing and production credits at Motown included the Supremes' "Up the Ladder to the Roof" and the Four Tops' "Still Water Love." Wilson also produced *Night Song*. The Mighty Clouds' Top 10 R&B hits include "Ride the Mighty High" and "Time." In 1980 they moved to ABC's Christian-oriented Myrrh label, and *Cloudburst* was produced by Earth, Wind & Fire's Al McKay. Freddie Perren, another Motown producer/writer, was responsible for *Sing and Shout*.

The group performed with Paul Simon during his 1993 monthlong series of shows in New York City. They continue to tour the world and record—their latest release, *It Was You*, was nominated for a Grammy in the Best Traditional Soul Gospel Album category.

The Mighty Diamonds

Formed 1973, Kingston, Jam.
Donald "Tabby" Shaw (b. Oct. 7, 1955, Kingston), lead voc.; Lloyd "Judge" Ferguson (b. Aug. 28, 1949, Kingston), harmony voc.; Fitzroy "Bunny" Simpson (b. May 10, 1951, Kingston), harmony voc.
1976—*Right Time* (Virgin) 1977—*Ice on Fire* 1978—*Planet Earth; Stand Up* (Channel One) 1979—*Deeper Roots* (Front Line/Virgin) 1980—*Tell Me What's Wrong* (J&J) 1981—

Indestructible (Alligator) 1982—*Reggae Street* (Shanachie) 1988—*Get Ready* (Rohit); *Never Get Weary* (Live & Learn) 1989—*Ready for the World* (Shamar) 1993—*Paint It Red* (RAS Records) 1994—*Speak the Truth* 1995—*Need a Roof* (Channel One) 1997—*Deeper Roots Plus Dub* (Caroline) 1999—*Right Time Come* (NYC Music); *Heads of Government* (Penthouse).

One of the young reggae vocal trios modeled on the original Wailers, the Heptones, and others of the late '60s and early '70s, the Mighty Diamonds became one of the most popular reggae groups of the second generation by setting their incisive, militant lyrics in close, soft-toned harmonies and languorous rhythms. They had their first hit in Jamaica in 1974 with "Shame and Pride." Two more hits that year showed the range of their material: "Jah Jah Bless the Dreadlocks" was based on Rastafarian chants, while "Let's Put It All Together" was a reggae version of the Stylistics' hit. (American soul music has been an essential element of virtually every Diamonds song.)

By the end of 1975, Jamaican hits like "Right Time," "Have Mercy," and "I Need a Roof" had been picked up by reggae fans in England, and in 1976, the group was signed to Virgin Records, which released its first album in the U.K. and the U.S. later that year. The year 1976 saw the Diamonds' first visit to America; they toured with Toots and the Maytals. They made a name for themselves as entertaining showmen with their comic stage patter and occasional soul ballads.

But in spite of their Americanisms (*Ice on Fire* was produced by New Orleans R&B veterans Allen Toussaint and Marshall Sehorn), the Mighty Diamonds were no more able to break into the American pop market than others among their Jamaican compatriots. In Jamaica, on the other hand, they continued to score big hits—among them "Tamarind Farm" in 1979 and "Wise Son" (#1) in 1980. "Pass the Kouchie," a hymn to marijuana, was banned by the Jamaican government, but when released as "Pass the Knowledge," it also went to #1 (1981). (Another version of this song, "Pass the Dutchie," was a hit for Musical Youth in late 1982.)

Although styles gave way to dancehall in the late '80s, the Mighty Diamonds remained steadfast reggae traditionalists. The group recorded frequently throughout the next decade and was a popular draw on the reggae concert circuit.

Mike + the Mechanics: See Genesis

Amos Milburn

Born Apr. 1, 1927, Houston, TX; died Jan. 3, 1980, Houston
1963—*The Return of the Blues Boss* (Motown) 2001—*The Best of Amos Milburn* (Capitol).

Amos Milburn was one of rhythm & blues' most consistent-selling vocalists from the mid-'40s into the '50s. He signed with L.A.-based Aladdin Records in 1946 and the next year had a million-seller with "Chicken Shack Boogie." Subsequently, Milburn would top the R&B chart with songs about alcohol: "Bad Bad Whiskey" (#1 R&B, 1950), "One Scotch, One Bourbon, One Beer" (#2 R&B, 1953), "Thinking and Drinking" (#8, 1952), and "Let Me Go Home, Whiskey" (#3, 1953). "One Scotch," also sung by John Lee Hooker was revived by George Thorogood and the Destroyers in the late '70s. Milburn recorded for various labels, including Motown and Ace, until a stroke in the late '60s left him partially paralyzed.

Buddy Miles

Born Sep. 5, 1946, Omaha, NE
With the Buddy Miles Express: 1968—*Expressway to Your Skull* (Mercury) 1969—*Electric Church* 1994—*Hell and Back* (Rykodisc).
With the Buddy Miles Band: 1970—*Them Changes; We Got to Live Together* 1971—*Message to the People; Live* 1972—*Carlos Santana and Buddy Miles Live* (Columbia).
Solo: 1973—*Chapter VII* (Columbia); *Booger Bear* 1974—*All the Faces of Buddy Miles* 1975—*More Miles Per Gallon* (Casablanca) 1976—*Bicentennial Gathering of the Tribes* (with Dickey Betts) 1997—*The Very Best of Buddy Miles* (Mercury/Universal) 1998—*Miles Away From Home* (Hip-O/Universal).
With the Buddy Miles Regiment: 1981—*Sneak Attack* (Atlantic).
With the California Raisins: 1987—*The California Raisins Sings the Hits* (Priority) 1988—*Sweet, Delicious & Marvelous; Christmas With the California Raisins.*
With Hardware: 1994—*Third Eye Open* (Rykodisc).

Buddy Miles' long and interesting career spans over four decades and includes stints as a Jimi Hendrix sideman and bandmember as well as a lead vocal spot for the popular Claymation "group" the California Raisins. Though best known as a singer/drummer, he also plays guitar a la Hendrix, left-handed and upside down.

By the time he was 12, Miles was drumming in his father's jazz group, the Bebops. Approximately three years later, he began working with a number of groups, including the Delfonics, the Ink Spots, and Ruby and the Romantics. He also had played on the session that produced the Jaynetts' 1963 hit "Sally Go 'Round the Roses." Miles was playing in Wilson Pickett's backup band in 1967 when guitarist Mike Bloomfield spotted him at a Brooklyn Murray the K show and invited him to join the Electric Flag. Miles appears on that group's *A Long Time Coming* (1968), *The Electric Flag* (1969), and *The Band Kept On Playing* (1974).

In 1968 Miles formed his Buddy Miles Express from the ruins of Electric Flag; the Express (which featured guitarist Jim McCarty, later with Cactus) peppered Miles' mélange of hard rock and soul with brassy horn charts. Then and since, too, Miles played drums on many other artists' records, including an early John McLaughlin album, *Devotion,* Jimi Hendrix's *Electric Ladyland,* and Muddy Waters' *Fathers and Sons.* Over the years, he recorded two albums with Carlos

Santana (1972's *Miles/Santana Live* and 1987's *Freedom*) as well.

The Express came to a halt when Miles joined Hendrix and bassist Billy Cox in what was probably the first black rock group, Hendrix's Band of Gypsies. It was a brief alliance, but it produced the acclaimed *Band of Gypsies*, a live album recorded on New Year's Eve 1969. It included versions of Miles' "Them Changes" and "We Gotta Live Together." Just 10 months later Hendrix died in London, and Miles re-formed the Buddy Miles Express, which included Cox. It was this group that had a minor hit with "Them Changes."

Though Miles would remain prodigiously active for some time, "Them Changes" was his last fling at the pop charts under his own name. In 1974 he joined the reunited Electric Flag for a comeback that dissolved before the end of the year. Beginning in 1978, he served a jail term for grand theft; he had left famous tailor Nudie's store without paying for some merchandise. He was also convicted of auto theft. While doing his time, Miles formed bands at both the California Institution for Men at Chino and San Quentin.

It would seem that Miles' career was all but finished, but shortly after his release from prison in 1985, Miles recorded "I Heard It Through the Grapevine" for a producer friend. The track found its way to an advertising firm then "casting" the voices for its California Raisins commercials. Miles went on to voice the "lead" Claymation Raisin for the Cleo-winning series of ads and sang on the dried fruits' three LPs, which included the platinum *The California Raisins Sing the Hit Songs*, produced by Ross Vanelli. In 1992 Miles formed Hardware, a trio that includes guitarist Steve Salas and bass player Bootsy Collins. Into the new millennium, he continued to tour across the globe with a rotating backing band.

Steve Miller Band

Formed 1966, San Francisco, CA
Steve Miller (b. Oct. 5, 1943, Milwaukee, WI), gtr., voc.; James "Curly" Cooke, gtr., voc.; Lonnie Turner (b. Feb. 24, 1947, Berkeley, CA), bass; Tim Davis, drums.
1967—(+ Boz Scaggs [b. June 8, 1944, OH], gtr., voc.; + Jim Peterman, kybds., voc.; – Cooke) 1968—*Children of the Future; Sailor* (Capitol) (– Scaggs; – Peterman; + Ben Sidran, kybds.) 1969—*Brave New World; Your Saving Grace* (– Turner; – Sidran; + Bobby Winkelman, gtr., bass, voc.) 1970—*Number 5* 1971—(– Davis; – Winkelman; + Ross Valory [b. 1950, San Francisco], bass; + Jack King, drums; + Dickie Thompson, kybds.; + Gerald Johnson, bass) *Rock Love* 1972—(– Valory; + Sidran; + Roger Clark, perc.) *Recall the Beginning . . . A Journey From Eden; Anthology* (– Johnson) 1973—(+ Turner; – Jack King; + John King, drums) *The Joker* (– John King; – Sidran) 1976—(+ Gary Mallaber [b. Oct. 11, 1946, Buffalo, NY], drums) *Fly Like an Eagle* 1977—(+ Byron Allred, kybds.; + David Denny, gtr.; + Greg Douglas, gtr.) *Book of Dreams* 1978—*Greatest Hits 1974–78* 1981—(– Denny; – Douglas; + Johnson) *Circle of Love* (+ Kenny Lee Lewis [b. 1954, Pasadena, CA], gtr.; + John Massaro, gtr.) 1982—*Abracadabra* 1983—*Live* 1984—*Italian X-Rays* 1986—*Living in the 20th Century* 1988—(– Mallaber; – Lewis; + Gordon Knudtson, drums; + Billy Peterson, bass) *Born 2B Blue* 1993—*Wide River* (Polydor) 1994—*Steve Miller Band Box Set* (Capitol) 1997—*Greatest Hits 1974–1978* (DCC Gold Disc).

In his long career, Steve Miller has gone from being one of the first young white West Coast blues-rockers to one of the biggest-selling pop-rock artists of the late '70s and early '80s. Although his record sales have slowed considerably since (for his new LPs, that is), this deliberately enigmatic figure remains a fixture on classic-rock radio and the concert trail.

Miller's father was a music-loving pathologist who often brought home guests like Charles Mingus and T-Bone Walker. At age four, Steve met guitarist Les Paul, who taught him some chords and later let him sit in on some Les Paul–Mary Ford studio sessions. At age 12, Miller formed his first blues band, the Marksmen Combo. The band stayed together for five years and included Boz Scaggs, who played off and on with Miller later and has had a prominent career of his own.

At the University of Wisconsin, Miller led one of the first blues-rock bands in town, the Ardells, which included Scaggs, pianist Ben Sidran, and future Cheap Trick manager Ken Adamany. The group later evolved into the Fabulous Knight Trains. Miller left college to go to Denmark, where he studied literature at the University of Copenhagen. He soon grew disillusioned with academia, however, and moved to Chicago, where his interest in blues was rekindled both by the classic black city-blues artists on the South Side and by the new generation of young white blues players that included Mike Bloomfield, Elvin Bishop, and Paul Butterfield. He formed a short-lived band with Barry Goldberg (who went on to join Bloomfield in the Electric Flag), the Goldberg-Miller Blues Band.

In 1966 Miller moved to San Francisco and formed the Steve Miller Blues Band with guitarist James "Curly" Cooke, bassist Lonnie Turner, and drummer Tim Davis. The quartet became a local favorite, playing many free outdoor shows; it also backed Chuck Berry on a live album recorded in 1967 at the Fillmore, and contributed three tunes to the soundtrack of the film *Revolution*. After playing the Monterey Pop Festival in 1967, Miller was approached by Capitol Records. He helped change the economics of rock music by holding out for what was at the time a record-breaking advance payment for a debut LP and a sizable royalty rate. The band's first LP, *Children of the Future*, was recorded in England, with Glyn Johns and the band coproducing. It became an almost instant staple of progressive FM radio, although it failed to yield a hit single. The second LP, *Sailor* (#24, 1968), contained "Livin' in the USA," which grazed the Top 50 and remains a rock-radio classic. By that time, the band had dropped the "Blues" from its name.

Miller's audience expanded with his next several albums: *Brave New World* (#22, 1969), *Your Saving Grace* (#38, 1969), *Number 5* (#23, 1975), and *Rock Love* (#82, 1971). None of these albums produced hit singles, although many of Miller's album tracks continued to get heavy exposure on FM radio, especially "Brave New World," "Space Cowboy," and "My Dark Hour" (on which Paul McCartney plays bass, pseudonymously though transparently credited as Phil Ramon).

In early 1972 Miller broke his neck in an auto accident, but the injury wasn't diagnosed until several weeks later. He then developed hepatitis, which sidelined him through early 1973. Meanwhile, the *Anthology* (#56, 1972) collection was selling well (it eventually went gold in 1977). Miller kept writing tunes while convalescing.

In 1973 *The Joker* (#2) revealed a new Steve Miller. The sound was slick and bouncy; the LP's title song was a #1 single in the U.S. and went gold; the album went platinum. Instead of rushing to capitalize on his breakthrough success, though, Miller took three years to deliver a followup. *Fly Like an Eagle* (#3, 1976) consolidated his newfound popular success and stayed on the chart for nearly two years. "Take the Money and Run" was a #11 single; "Rock'n Me" was a #1 single; the title tune made #2 on the singles chart and also went gold. (In the late '90s it became the theme song for a U.S. Postal Service ad campaign.) The LP and its title track even made the Top 20 on the R&B chart. Through mid-2001, it had sold more than 4 million copies.

Book of Dreams (#2, 1977), like *Eagle*, passed the platinum mark (3 million copies by 2001) and contained three hits: "Jet Airliner" (#8), "Jungle Love" (#23), and "Swingtown" (#17). Those and other Miller favorites appeared on *Greatest Hits 1974–78* (#18, 1978), which has now sold 8 million copies.

In 1978 Miller took a break and moved to a farm in Oregon, where he built a 24-track studio. He did not release another record until 1981's *Circle of Love*, which contained "Heart Like a Wheel" (#24, 1981) (not the Anna McGarrigle song popularized by Linda Ronstadt) and a bizarre side-long track titled "Macho City." The album went merely gold, prompting predictions that Miller's commercial years were behind him. But 1982's *Abracadabra* gave him his third #1 hit in the title track, which was boosted by a catchy video. *Born 2B Blue* (#108, 1988) marked a dramatic shift, featuring jazz standards with Ben Sidran, vibraphonist Milt Jackson, and saxophoist Phil Woods. While it did not sell well, critics were impressed.

With the release of *Wide River* in 1993, the 50-year-old Miller undertook a 50-city tour, during which he played mainly to audiences less than half his age. Miller has not put out any new studio album since, but he remains a strong live draw, playing sets made up mostly of material from his '70s work. The 1997 *Greatest Hits* sold more than 7 million copies.

Milli Vanilli

Formed 1988, Munich, Ger.
Fabrice Morvan (b. May 14, 1966, Guadeloupe, Fr.), alleged voc.; Rob Pilatus (b. June 8, 1965, Ger.; d. Apr. 3, 1998, Frankfurt, Ger.), alleged voc.

1989—*Girl You Know It's True* (Arista) 1990—*The Remix Album.*
As Rob & Fab: 1993—*Rob & Fab* (Taj).

Milli Vanilli's first hit was titled "Girl You Know It's True" (#2, 1989), but by 1990 the Grammy Award–winning duo became synonymous with all that is fake in pop. Not only were they accused of lip-synching their #1 hits—"Baby Don't Forget My Number," "Blame It on the Rain," and "Girl I'm Gonna Miss You" (all 1989)—on television and onstage, but they confessed to not having sung a note on their records, either. The startling admission resulted in broken careers, more than 25 lawsuits, an embarrassed Grammy Award committee, and a deeply chagrined record label.

The story begins when the German-born Pilatus, an out-of-work break dancer and model, met Fabrice Morvan, a Parisian gymnast, in an L.A. disco in 1984. The two frustrated singers returned to Europe to begin a career. Their initial attempt at stardom, a 1986 German release, flopped. Looking for work, they showed up at producer Frankie Farian's Munich studio. Farian, best known for his work with Boney M, had just recorded "Girl You Know It's True" (a song originally recorded by an American band, Numarx) with a musically accomplished but unattractive band. Rob and Fab were pliable and photogenic but untalented. Offering the duo $4,000 each plus royalties, Farian christened them Milli Vanilli, variously defined as Turkish for "positive energy," the name of a Berlin disco, or an homage to British synth-pop band Scritti Politti.

Decked out in bulge-revealing bicycle shorts and shoulder-length dreadlocks, Morvan and Pilatus danced and mouthed the song on European TV, working it into an international hit that crossed the Atlantic when Clive Davis picked it up for his Arista label. An album, *Girl You Know It's True* (#1, 1989), was quickly recorded.

The Milli Vanilli scam began to unravel after Charles Shaw, a U.S. Army veteran who was the actual singer, went public with his story in late 1989. After months of denials, Pilatus, who wanted more money and a chance to sing, confirmed that his and Morvan's sole contribution to Milli Vanilli was visual. The Grammy committee was the first to respond, rescinding the band's Best New Artist Grammy in November. Twenty-seven lawsuits were then filed, charging Arista Records, its parent BMG, and various concert promoters with fraud. The suits were settled in a Chicago court by a decision granting anyone with proof of purchase of *Girl You Know It's True* a rebate of up to $3. More than 80,000 claims had been filed as of 1995.

On November 30, 1991, despondent over his career and the breakup of a romance, Pilatus attempted suicide in L.A. Farian released an album by the "Real Milli Vanilli" in 1991, but without Rob and Fab's visual appeal, it stiffed. Pilatus and Morvan recorded an album, *Rob & Fab*, but lacking Farian's musical gloss, it, too, failed.

Morvan dealt with his fall from grace as best he could; he relocated to L.A. and took a series of low-profile jobs (including one with Berlitz) while continuing to work on a solo career. He returned to performing as a solo act in late 1997, and his work as a singer and a songwriter received some mildly favorable reviews.

Pilatus, on the other hand, never recovered from the Milli Vanilli fiasco and developed severe drug problems. In 1996 a judge ordered him to enter an L.A. rehabilitation program after he pleaded guilty in three assault cases. During that period, Pilatus made another suicide attempt, ingesting alcohol and pills, slitting his wrists, and threatening to jump from a ninth-floor window. Pilatus died of a heart attack in a Frankfurt hotel room in 1998.

Stephanie Mills

Born Mar. 22, 1957, Queens, NY
1973—*Movin' in the Right Direction* (Paramount) 1976—*For the First Time* (Motown) 1979—*What Cha Gonna Do With My Lovin'* (20th Century) 1980—*Sweet Sensation* 1981—*Stephanie* 1982—*Tantalizingly Hot* (Casablanca) 1983—*Merciless* 1984—*I've Got the Cure* 1985—*Stephanie Mills* (MCA) 1987—*If I Were Your Woman* 1989—*Home* 1991—*Christmas* 1992—*Something Real* 1995—*The Best of Stephanie Mills* (Mercury); *Personal Inspirations* (Gospocentric) 1996—*Greatest Hits* (MCA).

Stephanie Mills was still a teenager when her starring role in the original Broadway production of *The Wiz* catapulted her to fame and paved the way for a recording career that would find her bubbly, lyric soprano gracing several popular R&B singles. Like many R&B artists, the petite Mills got her start singing in church, at Baptist services in Brooklyn, New York. At only nine years old, she won the prestigious talent competition at Harlem's Apollo Theatre. Appearances with the Isley Brothers and the Spinners followed, as did an album on Paramount Records and a role in the Broadway play *Maggie Flynn*.

In 1975 Mills won the part of Dorothy in the all-black musical-theater adaptation of *The Wizard of Oz*. The show was a smash, and Motown Records founder Berry Gordy Jr. took an interest in its star. (Ironically, Gordy's most famous protégée, Diana Ross, usurped the role of Dorothy in the film version of *The Wiz*.) Mills' Motown debut, *For the First Time*, was produced and written by noted hitmakers Burt Bacharach and Hal David. Nonetheless, it proved a commercial disappointment, and Motown dropped Mills. The young singer bounced right back, though, signing with 20th Century Records and, in 1979, enjoying her first R&B hit, "What Cha Gonna Do With My Lovin' " (#8). The following year, Mills scored an even bigger R&B single, the #3 "Sweet Sensation," and landed a #6 pop hit with "Never Knew Love Like This Before" (#12, R&B). In 1981, Mills again reached #3 on the R&B chart with "Two Hearts," a duet with Teddy Pendergrass.

After switching over to Casablanca Records, Mills generated just one R&B Top 10 single between 1982 and 1985, "The Medicine Song" (#8). Meanwhile, her 1980 marriage to Shalamar's Jeffrey Daniels—the first of three failed marriages for Mills—quickly soured. The latter half of the decade was more fortuitous: Mills topped the R&B singles chart in 1986 with "I Have Learned to Respect the Power of Love" and repeated this achievement twice the next year, with "I Feel Good All Over" and "(You're Puttin') A Rush on Me." Another song, "Secret Lady," reached #7. In the early '90s Mills became Dorothy again in a touring company of *The Wiz*. In 1992 she released *Something Real*, which yielded one moderately successful R&B single, "All Day, All Night" (#20, 1993).

Professional hardship was to follow, however; in 1993, Mills parted ways with her longtime label, MCA, and sued her business manager for misappropriation of funds. She returned to her roots with a gospel album, *Personal Inspirations*, in 1995. After taking some time off to concentrate on her third marriage, to Detroit radio station program director Mike Saunders, Mills returned to musical theater. She appeared in a Detroit holiday production of Langston Hughes' *Black Nativity*, led by her *Wiz* director, George Faison, in 1995; costarred with Teddy Pendergrass in a touring revival of *Your Arms Too Short to Box With God* in 1996; and was featured on the Chicago stage in *Ragtime* in 1999.

Garnet Mimms and the Enchanters

Formed 1963, Philadelphia, PA
Garnet Mimms (b. Garrett Mimms, Nov. 26, 1937, Ashland, WV), voc.; Sam Bell (b. Philadelphia), voc.; Charles Boyer (b. NC), voc.; Zola Pearnell (b. Philadelphia), voc.
1963—*Cry Baby* (United Artists) 1964—(– the Enchanters) *As Long as I Have You* 1966—*I'll Take Good Care of You* 1973—*Remember* EP 1977—*Garnet Mimms Has It All* (Arista).

Five of the songs Garnet Mimms recorded are better known through the versions by his fan Janis Joplin: "Cry Baby," "My Baby," "Try (Just a Little Bit Harder)," "Piece of My Heart," and "Get It While You Can." In 1962 Mimms was a promising but unsuccessful singer who had recently abandoned his R&B group, the Gainors. The Enchanters were ex-Gainor Sam Bell and Charles Boyer and Zola Pearnell, the latter two veteran gospel singers and songwriters. Philadelphia producer Jerry Ragavoy gave them their 1963 million-selling hit, "Cry Baby" (#4 pop, #1 R&B), a gritty James Brown–styled gospel-soul frenzy featuring Mimms screaming the title phrase over and over. The tune was written by Ragavoy (a.k.a. Norman Meade) and producer Bert Berns (a.k.a. Bert Russell), a co-owner of Bang Records. With the exception of "Maybe" (by Richard Barrett), Ragavoy cowrote the other three songs covered by Joplin as well.

Within a year, Mimms and the Enchanters (which were in fact an ever-changing roster of female session singers that at times included Dionne and Dee Dee Warwick and Cissy Houston) had three more hits: "For Your Precious Love" (#26, 1963), "Baby Don't You Weep" (#30, 1963), and "A Quiet Place" (#78, 1964). In 1964 Ragavoy split Mimms from the Enchanters. The latter went more or less ignored, but Mimms himself had hits with "Tell Me Baby" (#69), "One Girl" (#67), and "Look Away" (#73) (later covered by Manfred Mann and the Spencer Davis Group) in 1964; "A Little Bit of Soap" (#95, 1965), and "I'll Take Good Care of You" (#30 pop, #15 R&B) in 1966.

For the next several years, Mimms continued to record,

with spotty success. A 1974 project with members of the group Brass Construction, for instance, went nowhere. In 1977 Mimms, backed by his new group, the Truckin' Co., had a minor hit in both the U.S. and the U.K. with "What It Is" from the album *Garnet Mimms Has It All.* Mimms has since become a born-again Christian. Howard Tate, who had been one of the Gainors, had a hit with "Get It While You Can," one of Mimms' unsuccessful singles.

The Mindbenders: See Wayne Fontana and the Mindbenders

Ministry

Formed 1981, Chicago, IL
Al Jourgensen (a.k.a. Hypo Luxa, b. Allen Jourgensen, Oct. 9, 1958, Havana, Cuba), voc., gtr.; Lamont Welton, bass; Stevo, drums.
1981—*Cold Life* EP (Wax Trax!) 1982—(– Welton; – Stevo; + Stephen George, drums) 1983—*With Sympathy* (Arista) 1986—(– George) *Twitch* (Sire) (+ Paul Barker [a.k.a. Hermes Pan, b. Feb. 8, 1950, Palo Alto, CA], bass, programming; William Rieflin [b. Sep. 30, 1960, Seattle, WA], drums; Roland Barker [b. June 30, 1957, Mountainview, CA], kybds.) 1987—*Twelve Inch Singles* (Wax Trax!) 1988—*The Land of Rape and Honey* (Sire) 1989—*A Mind Is a Terrible Thing to Taste* (+ Mike Scaccia [b. June 14, 1965, Babylon, NY], gtr.) 1990—*In Case You Didn't Feel Like Showing Up (Live)* 1992—*Psalm 69: The Way to Succeed and the Way to Suck Eggs* (– Rieflin; – Scaccia; + Louis Svitek, gtr.; + Duane Buford, programmer; + Rey Washam, drums) 1996—*Filth Pig* 1999—*Dark Side of the Spoon* (Warner Bros.) 2000—*Live Psalm 69 Tour* (Ipecac Records).

Ministry began as a fairly faceless dance combo derivative of the early '80s British synth-pop groups. But by the band's second full-length album, frontman Al Jourgensen had started pitting the abrasive sounds of such avant-industrial pioneers as Cabaret Voltaire, Einstürzende Neubauten, and Front 242 against a full-bodied guitar assault. By the early '90s, Ministry's signature art-damaged metal had sparked an ear-bleeding sensation, and Jourgensen was being hailed as the Phil Spector of industrial disco.

After discovering punk rock at a late-'70s Ramones show, Jourgensen moved to Chicago and formed Ministry. The group put out a few singles and an EP on the local independent label Wax Trax! before signing with Arista in 1982. When the label attempted to mold Jourgensen into an American version of England's Howard Jones, the singer/guitarist put up a fight and was dropped. Three years later, a regrouped Ministry surfaced on Sire, where, in an unusual arrangement, the group was not required to submit demo tapes to keep the company abreast of its progress. After the release of *Twitch,* Jourgensen and new partner Paul Barker began perfecting Ministry's self-described "aggro" sound: angry, shouted vocals and samples over a thick wall of guitar.

Ministry's tour for its second full-length Sire album, *The Land of Rape and Honey,* featured a virtual who's who of abrasive alternative rock: Nine Inch Nails' Trent Reznor, Fini Tribe's Chris Connelly, Skinny Puppy's Ogre, Jesus Lizard's David Yow, former PiL/Killing Joke drummer Martin Atkins, and others. Connelly returned as guest vocalist on *A Mind Is a Terrible Thing to Taste* and the 1990 live album *In Case You Didn't Feel Like Showing Up.* Meanwhile, Jourgensen and Barker had become figureheads of a sort of Chicago/Wax Trax! musical mafia, producing offshoot projects such as Revolting Cocks (basically Ministry with Chris Connelly as lead vocalist), 1,000 Homo DJs, Acid Horse, Pailhead, Pigface, and Lard, among others.

In 1992 Ministry ascended to new heights with *Psalm 69: The Way to Succeed and the Way to Suck Eggs.* The album shipped at 350,000 copies (nearly 100,000 more than any previous release) and entered the charts at #27. It received glowing reviews, even from critics who had heretofore shunned the arty industrial genre. The single "Jesus Built My Hotrod" featured guest vocals by Butthole Surfer Gibby Haynes. Ministry's newfound success was cemented when the group appeared on the 1992 Lollapalooza Tour. Fans would have a long wait between albums, however. Jourgensen spent the next few years surviving two near-fatal car crashes, a divorce, the death of friend River Phoenix, and a 1993 move to Austin, Texas, where he was convicted of drug possession. Still, in Austin, Ministry built a studio and began work on a followup to *Psalm 69.* But technical problems nearly led to a band breakup. Jourgensen returned to Chicago, where the album was finally completed. The result was *Filth Pig,* which reached #19 on the pop album chart. Among the tracks was a brooding, grinding version of Bob Dylan's "Lay Lady Lay."

Ministry released *Dark Side of the Spoon* in 1999, stretching beyond industrial boundaries by incorporating acoustic instruments (including banjos, sitars, and zithers) into its usual chaotic musical fabric. The band also stirred controversy when Kmart refused to carry the album, citing cover art that showed the backside of a nude, overweight woman wearing a dunce cap and standing before a blackboard that read "I will be God." The band toured in 1999, though Jourgensen suggested Ministry would release just one more album before disbanding. Meanwhile, he formed another of his many side projects, Buck Satan and the 666 Shooters, a country band.

Mink DeVille/Willy DeVille

Formed 1974, San Francisco, CA
Willy DeVille (b. William Boray, Aug. 27, 1953, New York, NY), voc., gtr., harp; Louis X. Erlanger, gtr., voc.; Bobby Leonards, kybds.; Ruben Siguenza, bass; T.R. "Manfred" Allen, drums.
1977—*Cabretta* (Capitol) 1978—*Return to Magenta* (– Leonards; – Siguenza; – Allen) 1980—*Le Chat Bleu*

(– Erlanger; + Rick Borgia, gtr.; + Kenny Margolis, accordion, kybds.; + Joey Vasta, bass; + Thommy Price, drums; + Louis Cortelezzi, horns) 1981—*Coup de Grâce* (Atlantic) 1983—*Where Angels Fear to Tread* 1985—*Sportin' Life.*
Willy DeVille solo: 1986—*Miracle* (A&M) 1990—*Victory Mixture* 1994—*Backstreets of Desire* (Forward/Rhino) 1996—*Loup Garou* (Discovery) 1999—*Horse of a Different Color* (East West, Fr.).

Although Mink DeVille emerged from New York's late-'70s punk-rock scene, its music was romantic R&B. After the band appeared on the 1976 *Live From CBGB* compilation LP, it was signed by Capitol. The core of the band had been formed in San Francisco, where leader Willy DeVille had traveled after a 1971 trip to London from his Lower East Side home. There he met Ruben Siguenza and Tom Allen, and the three began playing leather bars and lounges under names like Lazy Eights and Billy DeSade and the Marquis. After reading about the Ramones and CBGB in a music magazine, the three of them formed Mink DeVille.

The band's debut LP was produced by Jack Nitzsche and was a critical success, yielding a U.K. Top 20 hit single in "Spanish Stroll." In 1979 Willy DeVille moved to Paris to record *Le Chat Bleu,* firing most of his band in the process. When Capitol heard the tapes of the new LP—replete with accordion-backed traditional French and Cajun-style romantic ballads—it delayed the album's U.S. release for nearly a year, prompting DeVille to sign with Atlantic.

DeVille made his Atlantic debut with *Coup de Grâce.* Both *Where Angels Fear to Tread* and *Sportin' Life* were well received by critics here but little known to listeners. DeVille disbanded the group after *Sportin' Life.* Like many artists before him, he found a much more enthusiastic audience in France, where he lived for a while and still maintains a home.

Mark Knopfler produced *Miracle,* which included "Storybook Love," a song nominated for an Oscar after it was included on the *The Princess Bride* soundtrack. On *Victory Mixture,* DeVille paid tribute to New Orleans, another of his several current "hometowns." He continued to explore classic R&B, Cajun, and rockabilly styles on *Loup-Garou* (1996), which included a duet with Brenda Lee on "You'll Never Know." Despite a positive critical response to that album in the U.S., DeVille's followup, *Horse of a Different Color* (1999), was an import.

Minor Threat: See Fugazi

Minutemen/fIREHOSE

Minutemen, formed 1979, San Pedro, CA
D. Boon (b. Dennes Dale Boon, Apr. 1, 1958; d. Dec. 22, 1985, AZ), gtr., voc.; Mike Watt (b. Dec. 20, 1957, Portsmouth, VA), bass, voc.; Frank Toche, drums.
1980—(– Toche; + George Hurley [b. Sep. 4, 1958, Brockton, MA], drums) *Paranoid Time* EP (SST) 1981—*The Punch Line* 1982—*Bean-Spill* EP (Thermidor) 1983—*What Makes a Man Start Fires?* (SST); *Buzz or Howl Under the Influence of Heat* 1984—*Double Nickels on the Dime; The Politics of Time* (New Alliance) 1985—*Tour-Spiel* EP (Reflex); *My First Bells 1980–1983* cassette; *Project: Mersh* EP; *3-Way Tie (for Last)* 1987—*Ballot Result; Post-Mersh, vol. 1; Post-Mersh, vol. 2* 1989—*Post-Mersh, vol. 3* 1998—*Introducing the Minutemen.*
fIREHOSE, formed 1986, San Pedro, CA:
Watt; Hurley; eD fROMOHIO (b. Ed Crawford, Jan. 26, 1962, Stubenville, OH], gtr., voc.).
1986—*Ragin', Full-On* (SST) 1987—*if'n* 1989—*fROMOHIO* 1991—*flyin' the flannel* (Columbia) 1992—*The Live Totem Pole* EP; *The Red & the Black* EP 1993—*Mr. Machinery Operator.*
Mike Watt solo: 1995—*Ball-Hog or Tugboat?* (Columbia) 1997—*Contemplating the Engine Room* (Sony).

The Minutemen were one of the most adventurous hardcore punk bands, taking the music to places no one expected it could go—into funk, free jazz, even folk. Fiercely independent and to the far left politically, the trailblazing power trio delivered brief, angular blasts of formless music at breakneck speeds, though with a gutsy, unaffected groove.

Mike Watt and D. Boon were childhood friends in the blue-collar town of San Pedro, California, when they formed the Reactionaries, a fairly conventional rock four-piece. With the rise of punk in the late '70s, they renamed themselves the Minutemen (for the new brevity of their songs and the ironic right-wing reference). In honor of his hometown, Watt spray-painted "Pedro" on the body of his bass.

Minutemen were the second band (behind Black Flag) to release a record on the seminal South Bay independent punk label SST in 1980: *Paranoid Time,* an EP of short songs and free-form political rants Watt dubbed "spiels." With 1981's *The Punch Line,* the Minutemen locked in to their signature groove and gained a strong following on the L.A. punk scene. *Bean-Spill* is a whiplash five-song EP with a six-minute running time. The trio ventured into free-jazz territory on *What Makes a Man Start Fires?* and *Buzz or Howl,* its music and politics taking on a near-poetic elegance in tunes like "Bob Dylan Wrote Propaganda Songs" and "I Felt Like a Gringo." The 45-song *Double Nickels on the Dime* (trucker lingo for 55 mph on Interstate 10) is one of punk's few double-record sets, and stands with Hüsker Dü's *Zen Arcade* as an American punk classic.

In 1985 the Minutemen released two albums of longer, more accessible songs—*Project Mersh* (a sarcastic play on the word commercial) and *3-Way Tie (for Last)*—that included cover versions (Steppenwolf's "Hey Lawdy Mama" and Creedence Clearwater Revival's "Have You Ever Seen the Rain") and the most structured original compositions of their career. That year, they toured behind R.E.M.

In December 1985, at the height of the trio's career, Boon died in a van accident in the Arizona desert following a gig. Watt and Hurley planned to throw in the towel, but re-formed as fIREHOSE when an enthusiastic Minutemen fan, 19-year-old Ed Crawford, called from Ohio and asked to step in on guitar. fIREHOSE continued in the Minutemen vein, but with longer songs and a more folky feel (courtesy of Crawford). (Watt and his wife, former Black Flag bassist Kira Roessler, also formed the part-time double-bass duo, Dos, whose two albums, *Dos* [1986] and *Numero Dos* [1989], came out on New Alliance.) After the band released three independent albums, Columbia signed fIREHOSE and released *flyin' the flannel, The Live Totem Pole* EP, and the J Mascis–produced *Mr. Machinery Operator.* Then, on February 12, 1994, fIREHOSE played a final, unadvertised gig before a small, devoted crowd back where the whole thing started—in downtown San Pedro.

By June 1994, Mike Watt, who had played with Saccharine Trust in the mid- to late-'80s, had begun work on a solo album with help from Eddie Vedder (Pearl Jam), Thurston Moore (Sonic Youth), Frank Black (Pixies), Dave Grohl (Nirvana, Foo Fighters), the Beastie Boys, Chris Cornell (Soundgarden), Henry Rollins, and nearly 50 other musicians. Released as *Ball Hog or Tugboat?* (#129, 1995), the album spawned a Modern Rock radio hit in "Against the 70's" (sung by Vedder). A subsequent Watt solo tour featured an all-star backing band (again including Vedder and Grohl). Watt then appeared on Porno for Pyros' *Good God's Urge* and toured as a member of the band. In 1997 he released a "punk-rock opera" called *Contemplating the Engine Room,* recorded with drummer Steve Hodges and guitarist Nels Cline, who played one of Boon's old guitars on a track. For the first time, Watt handled all of the singing on the album, which was dedicated to his late father and Boon.

That same year, Watt joined Cline, keyboardist Money Mark (Beastie Boys), and Stephen Perkins (Jane's Addiction, Porno for Pyros) in a new improvisational band called Banyan. Watt toured with a new backing band, Pair of Pliers in 1999, but was sidelined by a serious intestinal illness. He returned to the road the next year with his own band and with J Mascis & the Fog. By now, George Hurley was playing as part of Red Krayola, with Mayo Thompson (Pere Ubu) and David Grubbs (Gastr del Sol).

Missing Persons

Formed 1980, Los Angeles, CA
Dale Bozzio (b. Dale Consalvi, Mar. 2, 1955, Boston, MA), voc.; Warren Cuccurullo (b. Dec. 8, 1956), gtr.; Chuck Wild, kybds.; Patrick O'Hearn (b. ca. 1956), bass; Terry Bozzio (b. Dec. 27, 1950, San Francisco, CA), drums.
1982—*Missing Persons* EP (Capitol); *Spring Session M* 1984—*Rhyme & Reason* 1986—*Color in Your Life* 1987—*The Best of Missing Persons* (Capitol/EMI) 1999—*Late Nights, Early Days* (Sumthing Distribution).

Missing Persons is one of several early MTV new-wave bands remembered as much for its look as its songs. The focus of attention was vocalist Dale Bozzio, a former Boston-area Playboy Bunny with a hiccupy, Lene Lovich–like voice and a futuristic camp/sci-fi look that featured peekaboo plastic outfits (including Plexiglass-bowl bras) and hot-pink hair.

Terry Bozzio was playing drums with Frank Zappa when he first met Dale Consalvi, who'd come to Hollywood to pursue acting, in an L.A. recording studio. Though Bozzio soon after toured with U.K., the pair eventually formed Missing Persons in 1980, the year after they married. They enlisted guitarist Warren Cuccurullo and bassist Patrick O'Hearn, who had also played in Zappa's band, and Chuck Wild, a classically trained keyboardist.

Missing Persons' eponymous debut EP, recorded in 1981 and reissued by Capitol (#46, 1982), contained what would be their two biggest hits, "Words" (#42, 1982) and "Destination Unknown" (#42, 1982), which set pop-rock melodies and Dale's squeaky voice against electronic textures. Both songs were also included on the group's first and most successful album, *Spring Session M* (#17, 1982), the title an anagram for the band's name. *Rhyme & Reason* (#43, 1984) produced only a minor hit in "Give" (#67, 1984), and when *Color in Your Life* stiffed (#86, 1986, no hit singles), the group broke up, as did the Bozzios' marriage. Dale remarried twice, released one quick-vanishing solo album on Prince's Paisley Park label, and finally settled back in the Boston area to raise two children. Terry Bozzio spent three years working with Jeff Beck (he appears on Beck's 1989 *Guitar Shop* album), then gave drum clinics and classes around the world. Cuccurullo joined Duran Duran in 1990, O'Hearn made a series of successful instrumental New Age albums, and Wild wrote scores for film and TV; among his credits is the final season of the *Max Headroom* show.

Nostalgia for '80s pop, fueled by soundtracks for such films as *The Wedding Singer,* brought Missing Persons back together in the late '90s, and the band toured with contemporaries Wang Chung and A Flock of Seagulls. *Late Nights, Early Days,* featuring live recordings from 1981, was released in 1999. In mid-2001 all original members of Missing Persons reunited to play a handful of shows in Southern California. Plans were in the works for a full-scale tour, followed by a new recording.

Mission of Burma

Formed 1979, Boston, MA
Clint Conley (b. May 16, 1955, Indianapolis, IN), bass, voc.; Roger Miller (b. Feb. 24, 1952, Ann Arbor, MI), gtr., voc.; Martin Swope (b. June 1, 1955, Ann Arbor), tapes; Pete Prescott (b. Oct. 26, 1957, Nantucket Island, MA), drums.
1981—*Signals, Calls, and Marches* EP (Ace of Hearts) 1982—*VS.* 1985—*The Horrible Truth About Burma* 1987—*Mission of Burma* EP (Taang!); *Forget* 1988—*Mission of Burma* (Rykodisc).

Mission of Burma combined the smarts of progressive and art rock with the energy of punk, virtually inventing the shimmering, noisy-but-melodic wall-of-guitar sound adopted by such postpunk bands as Hüsker Dü. The band remained relatively unknown outside of the Northeast during its early '80s heyday and split up before making its biggest impact on American independent rock.

The classically trained Roger Miller grew up in Ann Arbor, Michigan, where he would often see his favorite local bands, the Stooges and MC5. By 1978, tired of the Detroit-area music scene, he moved to Boston. There he joined Clint Conley in Moving Parts, which splintered into Mission of Burma, with local drummer Pete Prescott and Martin Swope, a Michigan friend of Miller's who created the band's behind-the-scenes tape effects. The first of Burma's legendary, loud gigs was in February 1979.

Mission of Burma's debut recording was the tuneful 1980 single "Academy Fight Song," which became a postpunk classic and was covered by R.E.M. in 1989. *Signals, Calls, and Marches* contained another postpunk staple, "That's When I Reach for My Revolver." Burma hit its artistic peak on the 1982 LP *VS.* The title of the posthumous live album, *The Horrible Truth About Burma,* refers to Miller's increasing problem with tinnitus, a hearing disorder that forced Burma into early retirement in 1983. (The Taang! releases include outtakes, and the Rykodisc collection combines the first two albums with selected live and unreleased tracks.)

Miller continued making music but focused on quieter solo projects, mainly such avant-garde groups as the Binary System and his and Swope's Birdsongs of the Mesozoic. He also created soundtrack music as part of the Alloy Orchestra. Prescott formed the Volcano Suns, and Conley temporarily dropped out of music to become a TV producer. Meanwhile, Mission of Burma's influence continued, evidenced by Moby's cover of the band's "That's When I Reach for My Revolver" on his 1997 *Animal Rights* album. The former collaborators always dismissed speculation on a Burma reunion, though in 1998, Miller performed reworked Burma material with the Saturnalia String Trio. In 2000 Mission of Burma finally performed a brief, unexpected reunion of sorts in a Boston club when Miller played keyboards and cornet with the Peer Group, a band that included Prescott and Conley.

Joni Mitchell

Born Roberta Joan Anderson, Nov. 7, 1943, Fort Macleod, Can. 1968—*Joni Mitchell* (Reprise) 1969—*Clouds* 1970—*Ladies of the Canyon* 1971—*Blue* 1972—*For the Roses* (Asylum) 1974—*Court and Spark; Miles of Aisles* 1975—*The Hissing of Summer Lawns* 1976—*Hejira* 1977—*Don Juan's Reckless Daughter* 1979—*Mingus* 1980—*Shadows and Light* 1982—*Wild Things Run Fast* (Geffen) 1985—*Dog Eat Dog* 1988—*Chalk Mark in a Rain Storm* 1991—*Night Ride Home* 1994—*Turbulent Indigo* (Reprise) 1996—*Hits; Misses* 1998—*Taming the Tiger* 2000—*Both Sides Now.*

One of the most respected singer/songwriters in music, Joni Mitchell is also one of rock's most daring and uncompromising innovators. Her career has ranged from late-'60s and early-'70s popularity with confessional folk-pop songs to her current exalted cult status via a series of jazz-inflected experiments that presaged the multicultural and world-music experiments of Paul Simon, Peter Gabriel, and Sting by more than a decade. Through the '80s and '90s, Mitchell's influence could be seen in a range of artists beyond the legion of female—and male—singer/songwriters who claim her. Prince, Jimmy Page, Robert Plant, Janet Jackson, John Mellencamp, Donna Summer, Cassandra Wilson, and a host of jazz musicians acknowledge her. Several of Mitchell's early compositions became famous in versions recorded by others—Crosby, Stills and Nash's "Woodstock," for example—but her own ululating vocals and open-tuned guitar continue to inspire imitators. In more recent years, younger female jazz-influenced singers have attempted to emulate her smoke-burnished voice and distinctive delivery. Her sound and her style, however, remain uniquely her own.

An only child, Roberta Anderson grew up in Saskatoon, Canada. At age nine she was stricken with polio. Defying doctors' predictions that she would never walk again, she recovered after spending nights in the children's ward singing at the top of her lungs. Throughout her childhood, she was involved in art and music, and she taught herself to play guitar from a Pete Seeger instruction book. When she enrolled at the Alberta College of Art in Calgary, she took a ukulele with her and began playing folk music.

She soon moved to Toronto, where she began performing on the local folk scene and gave birth to a baby girl. The social stigma of being an unwed mother was so intense that Mitchell did not even tell her parents. Without money, a job, or even a home, she entered into what she later termed "a marriage of convenience" to folksinger Chuck Mitchell in 1965. They moved together to Detroit, where Mitchell felt she had no option but to place her daughter, named Kelly Dale Anderson, up for adoption. She and Chuck Mitchell soon divorced; he continues to perform.

Mitchell became a critical sensation on Detroit's folk scene, and her notices led to a series of successful engagements in New York. There, in 1967, she was signed by Reprise Records. In late 1968 Judy Collins had a smash hit with Mitchell's "Both Sides Now." (In 1991 Carly Simon turned the song's lyrics into a children's book.) Collins also recorded Mitchell's "Michael From the Mountains" on her *Wildflowers* album; the British folk-rock band Fairport Convention recorded Mitchell's "Eastern Rain"; and Tom Rush recorded "The Circle Game." Thanks to this indirect success, Mitchell's debut LP—coproduced by David Crosby—sold fairly well. *Clouds* (#31, 1969) sold better; *Ladies of the Canyon* (#27, 1970) went platinum and yielded a minor hit single: "Big Yellow Taxi" (#67, 1970) (which Janet Jackson sampled nearly 30 years later in her hit "Got 'Til It's Gone").

Mitchell's next platinum album was the critically acclaimed *Blue* (#15, 1971), which featured "Carey," "My Old Man," and "The Last Time I Saw Richard." That album included contributions from musician friends like James Taylor (purportedly the subject of "Blue" and, from *For the Roses,* "See You Sometime"). *For the Roses* (#11, 1972) went gold and contained another minor hit single, the countryish "You Turn Me On (I'm a Radio)" (#25, 1972). The highest-charting album of Mitchell's long career remains 1974's *Court and Spark* (#2), which yielded the hit single "Help Me" (#7, 1974). By this time, Mitchell's sound had grown from simple, unadorned acoustic guitar and voice into a sophisticated continental-pop blend replete with horns, keyboards, and complex backing vocal arrangements performed by Mitchell

Joni Mitchell

herself. *Court and Spark* pointed to Mitchell's future direction with its version of Annie Ross' jazz-jive "Twisted," Mitchell's first recorded cover.

For the live *Miles of Aisles* (#2, 1974) album, Mitchell was accompanied by the jazz-fusion band L.A. Express (which included Tom Scott, who had figured prominently on *Court*). *The Hissing of Summer Lawns* (#4, 1975) was complex and sophisticated; it fared poorly critically. Yet that album is today cited as influential by jazz artists and singers (particularly such tracks as "Edith and the Kingpin" and "Shades of Scarlet Conquering"). In any case, *Hissing* was a commercial hit, and years later critical opinion has been revised to acknowledge its bold experiments ("The Jungle Line" was probably the first pop record to use Burundi drums). It also contained her cooler but no less cutting observations on the music industry's conflict between business and art ("The Boho Dance"), a theme that would become increasingly prominent in both Mitchell's art and interviews. *Hejira* (#13, 1976), though smoother and more spare instrumentally, was another commercial success that baffled many critics. To a greater degree than any of her previous works, this album tackled issues of commitment and freedom from a uniquely feminine perspective. In 1976 Mitchell appeared at the Band's San Francisco farewell concert and in the filmed documentary of that event, *The Last Waltz*.

In light of her previous two albums, the double-album *Don Juan's Reckless Daughter* (#25, 1977) was a logical if mysterious next step. Some critics felt that her lyrics had grown more convoluted and vague; indeed, Mitchell was using song structures far more ambitious and rich than the straight singer/songwriter confessional mode. Still, contrary to the then-prevailing view, *Don Juan's Reckless Daughter* was not all wild experimentation; in fact, half of its tracks (for example, "Talk to Me," "Off Night Backstreet," "Jericho") might have worked on any previous Mitchell album. But with jazz musicians Larry Carlton and Wayne Shorter, augmented by a group of Latin percussionists (including Airto), Mitchell scouted new musical territory in "The Tenth World" and the side-long "Paprika Plains." Perhaps indirectly, *Don Juan* led to Mitchell's most daring and most controversial project, her work with jazz bassist and composer Charles Mingus. Then dying of amyotrophic lateral sclerosis (Lou Gehrig's disease), Mingus invited Mitchell to collaborate with him. She set lyrics to some of the last melodies Mingus wrote, composed the rest of the material herself, and released *Mingus* not long after the bassist's death. It received mixed reviews but went to #17, an incredibly high chart position for a jazz album and a testament to Mitchell's fans' enduring interest in her work. The live album *Shadows and Light* (#38, 1980), which featured a band including Jaco Pastorius of Weather Report, jazz-rock guitarist Pat Metheny, and the a cappella vocal group the Persuasions, also met mixed reviews.

Years later, Mitchell repeatedly and adamantly expressed no regrets about the rocky course she set. "I would do it all over again in a minute for the musical education," she told ROLLING STONE. In 1982 Mitchell released her first album for Geffen, *Wild Things Run Fast* (#25, 1982), a more pop-oriented album that featured a cover of Elvis Presley's "(You're So Square) Baby I Don't Care" (#47, 1982). That year she married her bassist, Larry Klein. (They divorced in 1992 but have continued to work together.)

With *Dog Eat Dog* (#63, 1985), Mitchell's work showed a new emphasis on social commentary. Coproduced by Thomas Dolby, the album featured appearances by Michael McDonald ("Good Friends") and actor Rod Steiger (as a money-grubbing evangelist on "Tax Free"). *Chalk Mark in a Rainstorm* (#45, 1988)—with a guest roster that included Peter Gabriel ("My Secret Place"), Willie Nelson, Tom Petty, and Billy Idol ("Dancin' Clown")—was hailed by some critics as a return to form. Others, however, found it bland. Throughout the '80s Mitchell all but abandoned the concert stage. Her hastily arranged acoustic set at the 1986 Amnesty International benefit (she was a last-minute substitute for Pete Townshend) was cut short when the crowd, obviously unfamiliar with her work, booed her.

Mitchell experienced a resurgence of sorts with the '90s, due to a confluence of events: a trio of albums generally considered among her best, her finding and reestablishing a relationship with the daughter she had given up for adoption, and a flurry of industry accolades and honors. Fans and critics swooned over *Night Ride Home* (#41, 1991), an album of readily accessible albeit sophisticated jazz-tinged pop. Three years later, *Turbulent Indigo* (#47, 1994) was released to glowing critical response and a Best Pop Album Grammy. While promoting that album, Mitchell disclosed that she was suffering from post-polio syndrome, a neurological condition related to her childhood bout with the disease that made it difficult for her to perform. Because her repertoire includes more than 50 different tunings, Mitchell was considering quitting the stage until she obtained a Roland VG-8 computerized guitar that eliminates the need for retuning.

In 1995 Mitchell became the fourth artist to receive *Billboard*'s Century Award (previous recipients were George Harrison, Billy Joel, and Buddy Guy). It would seem that the award was made for Mitchell, since it recognizes artists who have not been accorded the acknowledgement they deserve. Two years later, Mitchell was reunited with her daughter, Kilauren Gibb, and a grandson. Though Mitchell had been quietly seeking her daughter and had written, however obliquely, of the matter in several songs (*Blue*'s "Little Green" and *Wild Things*' "Chinese Café"), Kilauren began to suspect the connection when she received some basic information about her biological parents that seemed to match information posted on a Joni Mitchell fan Web page. Mitchell skipped her 1997 induction into the Rock and Roll Hall of Fame because she wanted to spend more time with her newly discovered family on her first Mother's Day.

Taming the Tiger (#75, 1998) was another critical triumph, followed in 2000 by a concept collection of standards concerning romance, *Both Sides Now* (#66, 2000). Using orchestral and big-band backing, Mitchell tackled such classics as "At Last," "Stormy Weather," "You're My Thrill," and "You've Changed," with two of her older songs, "Both Sides Now" and "A Case of You." *Both Sides Now* received the Best Traditional Pop Vocal Album Grammy.

In the late '90s, Mitchell began appearing on television occasionally and performing in concert. In 1998 she undertook a limited tour with Bob Dylan, and in 2000 she toured to promote *Both Sides Now*. That spring, TNT presented "An All Star Tribute to Joni Mitchell," on which k.d. lang, Cassandra Wilson, Elton John, Richard Thompson, James Taylor, Wynonna, and others performed her music.

Mitchell has produced or coproduced each of her albums since her debut and has maintained control of her master recordings and her publishing from the beginning of her career. An accomplished painter and photographer, she created the art for each of her album covers, and her artwork has been exhibited throughout the world. Her first major career retrospective, *Voices—The Work of Joni Mitchell,* opened at the Mendel Art Gallery in Saskatoon in June 2000.

Willie Mitchell

Born Jan. 3, 1928, Ashland, MS
1968—*Live* (Hi); *Soul Serenade; Solid Soul* 1969—*On Top* 1970—*Robbin's Nest* 1971—*Hold It* 1973—*The Many Moods of Willie Mitchell* 1977—*Best of Willie Mitchell* 1986—*That Driving Beat* 1999—*Soul Serenade: The Best of Willie Mitchell* (Hi/The Right Stuff).

Although he reached the R&B Top 40 repeatedly during the '60s as a bandleader, Willie Mitchell really made his mark in the music business as vice president of Hi Records, where he helped fashion modern Memphis soul.

Mitchell studied trumpet in high school and performed in dance bands before forming his first group in 1954. By the end of the decade, that group had become the house band at the Home of the Blues label, where it also began recording its own instrumentals. Mitchell became a well-known studio musician and arranger; he worked with Charlie Rich, the Bill Black Combo, and Ace Cannon, among others. Mitchell signed with Hi in 1961, and started slowly with "20-75" and "Percolatin' " in 1964 before scoring his first R&B hit, "Buster Browne" (#29), in 1965. It was followed by the R&B hits "Bad Eye" (#23, 1966), "Soul Serenade" (#10, 1968), "Prayer Meetin' " (#23, 1968), "30-60-90" (#31, 1969), and "My Babe" (#37, 1969). Mitchell also began producing singers, including O.V. Wright, Syl Johnson, and Otis Clay, but he never stopped playing—that's his trumpet solo on B.J. Thomas' breakthrough hit, "Raindrops Keep Falling on My Head."

After the death of Hi president Joe Cuoghi around 1964, Mitchell took on more production and administrative duties for the label, and in 1969 he abandoned what remained of his own recording career to produce his discovery, Al Green. Mitchell's first two 1970 hits as a producer were Green's "I Can't Get Next to You" and Ann Peebles' "Part Time Love." Through the decade, his success was uninterrupted. He oversaw all of the recordings that established Al Green high among the most influential singers of the '70s, and produced others, including Ann Peebles on "I Can't Stand the Rain," in the soul style he and Green pioneered.

Mitchell worked with Al Green again in the '80s on *He Is the Light* and *Going Away*. Among the many other artists he has produced are Ike and Tina Turner, Rufus Thomas, Bobby Bland, and Paul Butterfield. In 1994 he opened his Willie Mitchell's Rhythm & Blues Club, on Beale Street, in Memphis. (Interestingly, the same location previously housed Jerry Lee Lewis' the Spot.)

Moby

Born Richard Melville Hall, Sep. 11, 1965, New York, NY
1992—*Moby* (Instinct); *Ambient* 1993—*Early Underground; Move* EP (Elektra) 1995—*Everything Is Wrong* 1996—*Rare: The Collected B-sides 1989–1993* (Instinct); *Animal Rights* (Elektra) 1997—*I Like to Score* 1999—*Play* (V2) 2000—*Mobysongs 1993–1998* (Elektra).

Often tagged the king of techno—as well as the first face of techno—Moby is notable among the hordes of anonymous DJs merely because he has stepped out from behind his turntable to seek the attention typically awarded only to rock stars. Yet his music—a symphonic combination of disco beats, punk-rock speed, and anthemic lyrics—withstands the focus. Conveniently, Richard Melville Hall's nickname, given to him as a child (in reference to his great-great-great-uncle Herman Melville's *Moby Dick*), fits perfectly with the pseudonyms of other techno artists like Aphex Twin, the Orb, and the Prodigy. But Moby's devout spirituality, veganism, and abstinence from alcohol and drugs are a departure from the typically bacchanalian rave scene.

Moby grew up in Darien, Connecticut, where, while in high school, he formed his first band, the Vatican Commandos, a hardcore punk outfit for which he played guitar. After dropping out of college (where he studied religion and phi-

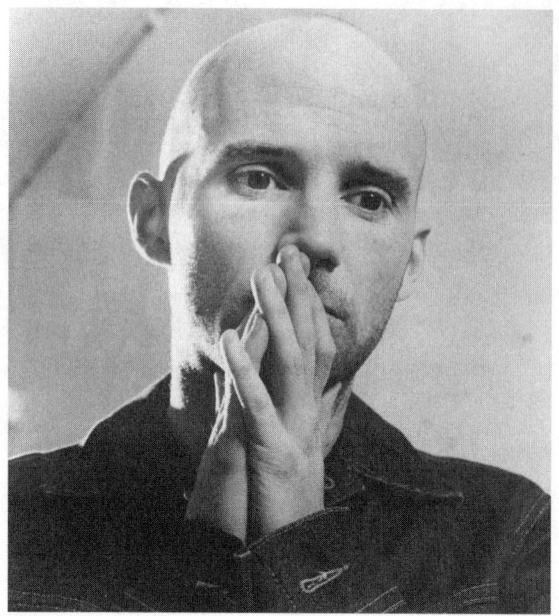

Moby

losophy), he moved to New York and started hanging out in dance clubs and DJing. By 1990, he had released some singles and EPs for the underground dance label Instinct; these included "Go," which set the *Twin Peaks* TV show theme to a frantic dance beat and went to #10 in the U.K. in 1991. This led to some remix projects (Michael Jackson, Depeche Mode, Pet Shop Boys, Brian Eno, and the B-52's) and a record deal with Elektra.

With the release of 1995's *Everything Is Wrong*, Moby stretched the techno sound; the album contains the expected high-BPM tracks yet also features a bluesy punk song ("What Love") and the metallish "All That I Need." For its release party, Moby actually performed some of the songs on acoustic guitar.

That affinity for guitar was prophetic; Moby's 1996 followup *Animal Rights* revealed his passion for punk and hardcore—he even did a cover of Mission of Burma's "That's When I Reach for My Revolver." The album drew mixed reviews, however, and many dance-music fans felt abandoned by one of their gurus. Meanwhile, Moby continued to work on film scores, and he released a compilation of his movie tunes entitled *I Like to Score*.

With 1999's *Play* (#45, 2000), a party-pleaser that also ingeniously pushed musical boundaries with its combinations of electronica and old blues and gospel recordings, Moby managed to capture both critical acclaim (two Grammy nominations and top honors in the 1999 *Village Voice* critics poll) and legions of new fans (the album went double platinum in 2000 and sold more than 3 million copies worldwide). Suddenly, Moby's music was heard in countless movie trailers, TV shows, and commercials, while the man himself became an unlikely poster boy for Calvin Klein. His former label, Elektra, tried to cash in on Moby's new fame with the compilation *Mobysongs 1993–1998*, a survey of his earlier work. "South Side" (#14, 2001) featured Gwen Stefani.

Moby Grape

Formed 1966, San Francisco, CA
Skip Spence (b. Alexander Spence, Apr. 18, 1946, Windsor, Can.; d. Apr. 16, 1999, Santa Cruz, CA), gtr.; Peter Lewis (b. July 15, 1945, Los Angeles, CA), gtr.; Jerry Miller (b. July 10, 1943, Tacoma, WA), gtr.; Bob Mosley (b. Dec. 4, 1942, Paradise Valley, CA), bass; Don Stevenson (b. Oct. 15, 1942, Seattle, WA), drums.
1967—*Moby Grape* (Columbia) 1968—*Wow* (– Spence) 1969—*Moby Grape '69; Truly Fine Citizen* (group remains active with numerous names and personnel changes) 1971—*20 Granite Creek* (Reprise) 1978—*Live Grape* (Escape) 1983—*Moby Grape '83* (San Francisco Sound) 1993—*Vintage: The Best of Moby Grape* (Sony/Legacy).
Skip Spence solo: 1969—*Oar* (Columbia).
Bob Mosley solo: 1972—*Bob Mosley* (Reprise) 1986—*Wine & Roses* EP (Niteshift) 1989—(as Mosley Grape) *Live at Indigo Ranch* (San Francisco Sound) 1999—*Never Dreamed* (Taxim, Ger.).
Jerry Miller Band: 1995—*Life Is Like That* (Messaround).
Peter Lewis solo: 1995—*Peter Lewis* (Taxim, Ger.).

Of the many groups to emerge from San Francisco in the late '60s, Moby Grape stood out as the band that most preferred structured songs to free-form jamming and the one that mixed L.A. folk rock with San Francisco's standard psychedelia. But it was never able to capitalize on its potential, partly because of hype from Columbia Records that threatened to bury its debut album. Moby Grape grew out of Northern California's Frantics, which included Jerry Miller, Bob Mosley, and Don Stevenson. Mosley met Peter Lewis (son of actress Loretta Young), who had recently abandoned Peter and the Wolves for solo work; Skip Spence was a guitarist who had played drums with the Jefferson Airplane and cowritten several songs ("My Best Friend," "Blues From an Airplane") that appeared on the Airplane's early albums.

Released in June 1967, *Moby Grape* became infamous at once when Columbia chose to release eight of its 13 cuts simultaneously on 45s, confusing radio DJs. Only the frenetic "Omaha" charted. The record also came with a poster of the band and a front-cover photograph that featured Stevenson with his middle finger extended (later airbrushed out). Amid the furor, the actual music was virtually ignored.

Moby Grape's second album, *Wow*, was similarly derailed by gimmickry; it contained a track that could be played only at 78 rpm and a "bonus" LP, *Grape Jam*, that included Al Kooper and Mike Bloomfield. Moby Grape then disbanded but re-formed as a quartet soon after, without Spence, and commemorated the event with *Moby Grape '69*. This set a pattern of breakup, re-formation, album, breakup that continues until this day. Before 1995, the members were legally forbidden from using the name Moby Grape; over the years they came up with such imaginative permutations as Maby Grope, Mosley Grape, the Melvilles (as in Herman Melville, author of *Moby Dick*), and the Legendary Grape. Miller, Lewis, Mosley, and Stevenson carried the project into the early '90s. Mosley, who was homeless in the middle of the decade, was occasionally gone. A 1998 tour featured Miller, Lewis, and Mosley but not Stevenson.

Absent from these reunions was Spence, a diagnosed paranoid schizophrenic who showed signs of mental illness during the Moby Grape's original run. On tour, he once broke into Stevenson's room, claiming that voices had told him the drummer was possessed by the devil; by 1968, he'd been committed to New York's Bellevue Hospital. In 1991, while a resident of a residential-care house in San Jose, California, he contributed a song, "All My Life I Love You," to a cassette by Miller, Stevenson, Mosley, Lewis, and two new musicians. This '90s version of Moby Grape opened shows for another reunited California band, the Doobie Brothers (whom Spence allegedly named). In 1993 Spence joined the other original members onstage for a Bay Area gig. That year's release of a CD retrospective, *Vintage*, brought this now-revered Moby Grape more attention than it ever received during its lifetime.

Spence's stark, darkly eccentric 1969 solo release, *Oar*, became a sought-after item in the late '90s. Shortly after the performer's death in 1999, Birdman Records issued *More Oar: A Tribute to Alexander "Skip" Spence*, a song-for-song cover of the album featuring acts ranging from Beck to Tom Waits to Mudhoney. The original LP was reissued with 10 bonus tracks that year as well.

Modern English

Formed 1979, Colchester, Eng.
Robbie Grey, voc., gtr.; Gary McDowell, gtr., voc.; Stephen Walker, kybds.; Mick Conroy, bass, gtr., voc.; Richard Brown, drums.
1980—*Mesh and Lace* (4AD) 1983—*After the Snow* (Sire) 1984—*Ricochet Days* (– Walker; – Brown; + Aaron Davidson, kybds., gtr., voc.) 1986—*Stop Start* 1990—*Pillow Lips* (TVT) 1996—*Everything Is Mad* (Imago).

This British postpunk pop-rock band scored a minor MTV-era hit with "I Melt With You" (#78, 1983), a mix of pounding drums, jangling guitars, and a prominent synthesizer riff, which was much more upbeat and romantic than the songs on Modern English's bleak, Joy Division–inspired debut album. The single was from *After the Snow* (#70, 1983), which was in fact the band's best-selling album. Modern English's only subsequent U.S. chart entry was "Hands Across the Sea" (#91, 1984) from *Ricochet Days* (#93, 1984). *Stop Start* failed to crack the Top 100, as did *Pillow Lips*, recorded after a four-year hiatus. The band then split apart as Grey took a three-year break. He re-formed the group in 1995 and released another album, *Everything Is Mad*, the following year.

Molly Hatchet

Formed 1975, Jacksonville, FL
Dave Hlubek (b. 1952, Jacksonville), gtr.; Duane Roland (b. Dec. 3, 1952, Jeffersonville, IN), gtr.; Steve Holland (b. 1954, Dothan, AL), gtr.; Danny Joe Brown (b. 1951, Jacksonville), voc.; Banner Thomas, bass; Bruce Crump, drums.
1978—*Molly Hatchet* (Epic) 1979—*Flirtin' With Disaster* 1980—*Beatin' the Odds* (– Brown; + Jimmy Farrar [b. La Grange, GA], voc.) 1981—*Take No Prisoners* (– Farrar; + Brown) 1982—(– Thomas; – Crump; + Barry Borden [b. May 12, 1954, Atlanta, GA], drums; + Riff West [b. Apr. 3, 1950, Orlando, FL], bass) 1983—*No Guts . . . No Glory* 1984—(– Holland; – Borden; + John Galvin, kybds.; + Crump) *The Deed Is Done* 1985—*Double Trouble Live* 1987—(– Hlubek; + Bobby Ingram, gtr.) 1989—*Lightning Strikes Twice* (Capitol) (numerous personnel changes follow) 1996—(– Brown; + Phil McCormack, voc.) *Devil's Canyon* (CBH, Ger.) 1998—*Silent Reign of Heroes* (CMC); *Super Hits* (Epic/Legacy) 2001—*Kingdom of XII* (CMC).
Danny Joe Brown solo: 1981—*Danny Joe Brown and the Danny Joe Brown Band* (Epic).

Molly Hatchet is a guitar-heavy Southern-blues-boogie and heavy-metal band from Jacksonville, Florida, home of Lynyrd Skynyrd, Grinderswitch, Blackfoot, and .38 Special. Ronnie Van Zant, lead singer of Lynyrd Skynyrd, planned to produce Hatchet shortly after it formed, but died in a 1977 plane crash.

The group's debut LP went platinum; its second, double platinum. All the while, Molly Hatchet (its name taken from Hatchet Molly, a legendary Southern prostitute who allegedly lured men to her lair, where she castrated and mutilated them) toured as steadily as any working band, often playing more than 250 dates per year. The group also established an image as gun-toting, hard-drinking rowdies. Worn out from the road, vocalist Danny Joe Brown left in early 1980; the following year he released a solo LP. Along with new vocalist Jimmy Farrar, Molly Hatchet added a horn section (from Tower of Power) for the first time on *Take No Prisoners*. Farrar then left for a solo career, and Brown rejoined. The group's 1985 live album featured a version of Lynyrd Skynyrd's "Freebird," in tribute to their original mentor. Molly Hatchet continued to tour into the '90s. With the 1996 departure of Brown, a diabetic whose health had been worsening, the band pressed on, relieved of any original members and led by '80s holdovers Bobby Ingram and John Galvin.

The Moments/Ray, Goodman, and Brown

The Moments, formed mid-'60s, Hackensack, NJ
Mark Greene, lead voc.; John Morgan, voc.; Richie Horsely, voc.
1969—(– Greene; – Horsely; + William Brown [b. June 30, 1946, Perth Amboy, NJ], voc.; + Al Goodman [b. Mar. 31, 1947, Jackson, MS], voc.; – Morgan; + Johnny Moore, voc.) 1970—(– Moore; + Harry Ray [b. Dec. 15, 1946, Hackensack;

d. Oct. 1, 1992], voc.) 1984—*The Moments' Greatest Hits* (Chess/MCA).
As Ray, Goodman, and Brown: 1980—*Ray, Goodman and Brown* (Polydor); *Ray, Goodman and Brown II* 1992—(– Ray; + Kevin Owens, voc.).

The Moments were a trio that recorded numerous hits for New Jersey–based All Platinum Records' Stang label. The original Moments, featuring Mark Greene's falsetto, charted with "Not on the Outside" (#57 pop, #13 R&B) in 1968. After a series of personnel changes, a new group of Moments—Billy Brown, Al Goodman, and Johnny Morgan—had a million-selling single with "Love on a Two-Way Street" (#3 pop, #1 R&B) in 1970.

After Harry Ray replaced Morgan, the group maintained its popularity with black audiences. The Moments had another big hit with 1974's "Sexy Mama" (#17 pop, #3 R&B). A legal battle with All Platinum (owned by Joe and Sylvia Robinson, she of Mickey and Sylvia fame) in the mid-'70s left the group idle for two and a half years. It resurfaced in 1979 as Ray, Goodman, and Brown on the Polydor label and had hits with "Special Lady" (#5 pop, #1 R&B, 1980), "Happy Anniversary" (#16 R&B, 1980), and "Take It to the Limit" (#8 R&B, 1989). They also provided backing vocals for a pair of Millie Jackson LPs. Ray died of a stroke in 1992. Assisted by Kevin Owens, Goodman and Brown continued to perform into 2000.

Eddie Money

Born Edward Mahoney, Mar. 21, 1949, Brooklyn, NY
1977—*Eddie Money* (Columbia) 1978—*Life for the Taking* 1980—*Playing for Keeps* 1982—*No Control* 1983—*Where's the Party?* 1986—*Can't Hold Back* 1988—*Nothing to Lose* 1989—*Greatest Hits: Sound of Money* 1991—*Right Here* 1992—*Unplug It In EP* 1995—*Love and Money* (Wolfgang) 1997—*Shakin' With the Money Man* (CMC) 1999—*Ready Eddie.*

Eddie Money is a rough-voiced rock singer whose self-titled debut album contained two hit singles, "Baby, Hold On" (#11, 1978) and "Two Tickets to Paradise" (#22, 1978). The son of a New York City policeman, Edward Mahoney seemed destined to follow in his father's footsteps, and he attended the New York Police Academy. But at night he moonlighted in a rock & roll band as Eddie Money. Deciding that he loved rock more than police work, the singer quit the academy and moved to Berkeley, California, where he sang at Bay Area bars. Promoter Bill Graham signed on as Money's manager and negotiated his contract with Columbia Records.

A familiar face in the early days of MTV, Money maintained a low profile for about three years before releasing *Can't Hold Back;* during that time he was working to overcome a drug problem. That album became the biggest of his career, going platinum on the strength of a #4 duet with Ronnie Spector, "Take Me Home Tonight." He continued through the '80s with fairly consistent success. His other Top 30 hits include "Maybe I'm a Fool" (#22, 1979), "Think I'm in Love" (#16, 1982), "I Wanna Go Back" (#14, 1987), "Endless Nights" (#21, 1987), "Walk on Water" (#9, 1988), "The Love in Your Eyes" (#24, 1989), and "Peace in Our Time" (#11, 1990). Signed to CMC International in the late '90s, he continues to draw on the rock nostalgia circuit.

Monica

Born Monica Arnold, Oct. 24, 1980, Atlanta, GA
1995—*Miss Thang* (Rowdy/Arista) 1998—*The Boy Is Mine* (Arista).

One of the most popular of a new breed of young vocalists to emerge from the Atlanta urban music scene in the '90s, Monica became a chart-topping R&B star before her 15th birthday. Raised in the Atlanta suburb of College Park, the singer was touring with a gospel choir, Charles Thompson and the Majestics, when she was 10, and frequently participated in local talent showcases. It was at one of these events that she was discovered by producer Dallas Austin, who headed the Atlanta-based Rowdy label. In 1995 her debut, *Miss Thang* (#36 pop, #7 R&B, 1995) was released, and Monica enjoyed a string of hit singles: "Don't Take It Personal (Just One of Dem Days)" (#2 pop, #1 R&B, 1995), "Before You Walk Out of My Life" (#7 pop, #1 R&B, 1995), "Like This and Like That" (#4 R&B, 1995), "Why I Love You So Much" (#9 pop, #3 R&B, 1996), and the Diane Warren tune "For You I Will" (#4 pop, #2 R&B, 1997), from the *Space Jam* soundtrack. By the time her next album, *The Boy Is Mine* (#8 pop, #2 R&B, 1998), was released, Monica had graduated early from high school (with a 4.0 average) and parlayed her tall, elegant looks into a modeling contract and an acting career. The leadoff single "The Boy Is Mine" (#1 pop, #1 R&B, 1998), a duet with another youthful diva, Brandy, became the third-highest-selling single in the history of the Hot 100, according to *Billboard.* Two other hits followed: "The First Night" (#1 pop, #1 R&B, 1998) and "Angel of Mine" (#1 pop, 1998; #2 R&B, 1999).

Monica

The Monkees

Formed 1965, Los Angeles, CA
David Jones (b. Dec. 30, 1945, Manchester, Eng.), voc.; Michael Nesmith (b. Dec. 30, 1942, Houston, TX), gtr., voc.; Peter Tork (b. Feb. 13, 1944, Washington, DC), bass, voc.; Mickey Dolenz (b. Mar. 8, 1945, Tarzana, CA), drums, voc.
1966—*The Monkees* (Colgems) 1967—*More of the Monkees; Headquarters; Pisces, Aquarius, Capricorn and Jones Ltd.* 1968—*The Birds, the Bees and the Monkees; Head* soundtrack 1969—(– Tork) *Instant Replay* (group disbands) 1976—*Greatest Hits* (Arista) 1986—(group re-forms: Jones; Tork; Dolenz) *Then and Now . . . The Best of the Monkees* 1987—*Pool It!* (Rhino) 1996—(+ Nesmith) *Justus.*

The Monkees were the first, and arguably the best, of the prefabricated '60s and '70s pop groups (others include the Partridge Family and the Archies). Manufactured by TV executives to capitalize on the success of the Beatles, they were hard to take seriously. But thanks in large part to the songwriting of Neil Diamond, Tommy Boyce and Bobby Hart, and their own Mike Nesmith, the Monkees made some exceptionally good pop records, such as "I'm a Believer," "(I'm Not Your) Steppin' Stone," and "Pleasant Valley Sunday."

Davy Jones had been a stage actor and a racehorse jockey in Britain; Mickey Dolenz, whose father had starred in several films, became a child actor at age 10 in various TV shows (including NBC's *Circus Boy*) under the name Mickey Braddock; Michael Nesmith and Peter Tork had worked as musicians before becoming Monkees. The group was formed for a TV comedy series dreamed up by Columbia Pictures executives, specifically inspired by the Beatles' film *A Hard Day's Night.* Some 500 candidates auditioned for the show in fall 1965; among those rejected were Stephen Stills and Danny Hutton (who went on to Three Dog Night). The Monkees were chosen for their personalities and photogenic capacities, not for musical ability.

In the beginning, they sang but did not play any instruments, leaving that to L.A. studio players, and on the TV show they only mimed playing as they lip synched. The show first aired in September 1966 and became an immediate success. That same year, the Monkees' debut LP went gold and yielded three Top 20 gold singles: "I'm a Believer" (by Neil Diamond), "Last Train to Clarksville," and "Steppin' Stone." The first two hit #1.

The "nonmusician" Monkees frantically learned instruments so they could tour and at least appear competent. They succeeded at this, though they certainly couldn't reproduce their records' studio sound live. With hordes of screaming teens attending every show, though, it didn't matter much anyway. This, combined with Colgems' (a Don Kirshner company) refusal to reveal the truth about the Monkees' lack of playing ability, rankled Nesmith in particular. After intergroup arguments about what to do, Nesmith told a 1967 New York press conference, "There comes a time when you have to draw the line as a man. We're being passed off as something we aren't. We all play instruments, but we didn't on any of our records. Furthermore, our record company doesn't want us to and won't let us." *Look* magazine ran the story, prompting a heated meeting between group members and Screen Gems, during which Nesmith nearly came to blows with an executive when told he could be legally suspended from the band. Eventually the band got its wish, and the hits kept on coming: Diamond's "Little Bit Me, Little Bit You" (#2), Gerry Goffin and Carole King's "Pleasant Valley Sunday" (#3), and John Stewart's "Daydream Believer" (#1) in 1967; "Valleri" (#3) in 1968. The LPs *Headquarters; Pisces, Aquarius . . . ;* and *Birds, Bees . . .* all went gold.

The Monkees: Peter Tork, Mickey Dolenz, Davy Jones, Mike Nesmith

The group staged successful worldwide tours in 1967 and 1968. In 1967 in London, Dolenz brought Jimi Hendrix to the band's attention, and the Monkees invited him to open their summer U.S. tour. The group's audience didn't know what to make of Hendrix, still unknown in America at the time, and booed him; he quit the tour after two weeks.

The TV show was canceled in late 1968, after which Tork left the band, while the other three continued for another year and a half. The Monkees' 1968 film *Head,* written by series producer Bob Rafelson and Jack Nicholson, initially struck most as a surrealistic extension of the television show's wacky humor. Featuring cameo appearances by Victor Mature, Annette Funicello, Sonny Liston, and Frank Zappa, and some of the group's more adventurous music, *Head* was a box-office flop. Decades later, however, it stands as a pioneering effort in long-form music video.

Mike Nesmith [see entry] went on to have a fairly prolific and successful career as a country-rock songwriter (he wrote "Different Drum," a 1968 hit for Linda Ronstadt's group the Stone Poneys), singer, and producer, and an early rock-video maker *(Popclips);* Jones and Dolenz reunited with Boyce and Hart for a 1976 LP. Tork and his band the New Monks conducted small-scale tours in the early '80s.

In 1986 the Monkees enjoyed a major revival in popularity that pulled six of their old LPs onto the chart. MTV rebroadcast the television series, beginning in March 1987. A new best-of, *Then and Now,* went platinum, and "That Was Then, This Is Now," one of three new tracks recorded by Jones, Dolenz, and Tork, hit #20. The trio toured that summer and came out with a new album, *Pool It!,* the following year. Nesmith had no interest in becoming a Monkee again, but did join the other three onstage in July 1989, one day before the band was awarded a star on Hollywood's Walk of Fame. Both Jones, who tours tirelessly on his own, and Dolenz, a successful producer of commercials, wrote books about their experiences as Monkees. Dolenz's *I'm a Believer* (coauthored with Mark Bego) was published in 1994.

Surprisingly, Nesmith returned for the Monkees' 1996 studio album, *Justus,* which coincided with Rhino Records' complete 21-volume video anthology of the television show. The group's *Greatest Hits* collection went gold in 2000. That year, the VH1 cable music network aired *Daydream Believers,* an original movie about the quartet.

Bill Monroe

Born Sep. 13, 1911, Rosine, KY; died Sep. 9, 1996, Springfield, TN
1962—*Bluegrass Ramble* (MCA) 1963—*Bluegrass Special* 1965—*Bluegrass Instrumentals* 1969—*Voice From on High* 1970—*Kentucky Bluegrass* 1972—*Uncle Pen* 1973—*Bean Blossom* 1984—*Columbia Historic Edition* (Columbia) 1986—*Stars of the Bluegrass Hall of Fame* (MCA) 1987—*Bluegrass '87* 1988—*Southern Flavor* 1989—*Live at the Opry—Celebrating 50 Years at the Grand Ole Opry* 1991—*Cryin' Holy Unto the Lord; Mule Skinner Blues* (RCA) 1994—*The Music of Bill Monroe, 1936–1994* (MCA).
With the Monroe Brothers: 2000—*The Monroe Brothers vol. 1: What Would You Give in Exchange for Your Soul?* (Rounder) 2001—*The Monroe Brothers vol. 2: Just a Song of Old Kentucky.*

Few practitioners of American music have had as profound an impact on their particular idiom as Bill Monroe, "the Father of Bluegrass." With a career that spanned six decades, he was almost single-handedly responsible for amalgamating elements of blues, gospel, jazz, country, and Celtic folk into the string-driven hybrid we now call bluegrass, named after Monroe's seminal group, the Blue Grass Boys.

The youngest of eight children, Monroe grew up in rural Kentucky and was exposed to music at an early age. His mother sang and played several instruments, while his uncle was a talented fiddler. Since his older brothers already played fiddle and guitar, the nine-year-old Bill decided to take up the mandolin.

When he was 18, Bill moved to East Chicago, Indiana, where he began paying his musical dues. Five years later, he joined his brother Charlie in Charlotte, North Carolina, where they became popular purveyors of traditional blues and gospel. Beginning in 1936, the Monroe Brothers recorded some 60 songs for RCA showcasing their mandolin/guitar configuration and intertwining vocal harmonies. Two years later, the duo split, and Bill formed the Kentuckians, soon renamed the Blue Grass Boys in honor of Monroe's beloved "bluegrass state" of Kentucky.

In October 1939, Monroe and his group joined the Grand Ole Opry in Nashville and toured with the Opry's road show. Meanwhile, the Blue Grass Boys became a veritable training ground and revolving door for Monroe's talented musical apprentices. (Over 100 musicians have claimed membership in the ensemble over the years.) In 1946 Monroe assembled his most legendary cast of Blue Grass Boys: Lester Flatt (guitar and vocals), Earl Scruggs (banjo), Chubby Wise (fiddle), and Howard Watts (bass). It was with this stellar outfit that Monroe would forge the classic bluegrass sound: high vocal harmonies, extemporaneous mandolin licks, solidly rhythmic guitar and banjo, sinewy fiddle bursts, and jazzy bass runs. The quintet recorded such classic Monroe originals as "Kentucky Waltz" (#3 C&W, 1946), "Footprints in the Snow" (#5 C&W, 1946), "Blue Moon of Kentucky" (1947) (covered in 1955 by Elvis Presley), and "Wicked Path of Sin" (#13 C&W, 1948). When Flatt and Scruggs departed in late 1948, Monroe continued his chart success. All told, Monroe had nine Top 30 country hits between 1946 and 1959.

Monroe was elected to the Country Music Hall of Fame in 1970 but did not rest on his laurels. The 1986 album *Stars of the Bluegrass Hall of Fame* features Monroe with some famous protégés: Ralph Stanley, Mac Wiseman, and the Seldom Scene, among others. That same year, the U.S. Senate passed a resolution that recognized Monroe's "many contributions to American culture," and in 1988 *Southern Flavor* won the first ever Grammy for bluegrass music. Monroe also received the Academy of Recording Arts and Sciences' Lifetime Achievement Award in 1993. The following year he was showcased in *High Lonesome,* a critically acclaimed film documentary chronicling the history of bluegrass music. Though he suffered from several health problems, Monroe continued to perform into his 80s. A debilitating stroke in early 1996 led to his death on September 9 of that year. He was inducted as a pioneer into the Rock and Roll Hall of Fame in 1997. Produced by Monroe protégé Ricky Skaggs, a 2000 Monroe tribute album, *Big Mon,* with performances by artists including Dwight Yoakam, Dolly Parton, and John Fogerty, was nominated for a Grammy in 2001.

Montrose

Formed 1974, California
Ronnie Montrose (b. Nov. 29, 1947, CO), gtr.; Sammy Hagar (b. Oct. 13, 1947, Monterey, CA), voc.; Bill Church, bass; Denny Carmassi, drums.
1973—*Montrose* (Warner Bros.) 1974—(– Church; + Alan Fitzgerald, bass, kybds.) *Paper Money* 1975—(– Hagar; + Bob James, voc.; + Jim Alcivar, kybds.) *Warner Bros. Presents Montrose* 1976—(+ Randy Jo Hobbs, bass) *Jump On It* (group disbands) 1987—(group re-forms: Montrose; + Johnny Edwards, voc.; + James Kottack, drums; + Glen Letsch, bass) *Mean* (Enigma) 1994—*Music From Here* (Fearless Urge).

Ronnie Montrose solo: 1978—*Open Fire* (Warner Bros.) 1983—*Territory* 1988—*The Speed of Sound* 1990—*The Diva Station* 1991—*Mutatis Mutandis* (I.R.S.) 1996—*Mr. Bones* (Sega) 1999—*Bearings* (RoMoCo).
With Gamma: 1979—*Gamma 1* (Elektra) 1980—*Gamma 2* 1982—*Gamma 3* 1992—*The Best of Gamma* (GNP Crescendo).

Ronnie Montrose's heavy-metal power bands seem at odds with the delicate acoustic and restrained electric guitar he lent to Van Morrison's *Tupelo Honey* and *St. Dominic's Preview* LPs. After playing in local bands in Colorado, Montrose went to California around 1970. There he played on sessions for Beaver and Krause, the Beau Brummels, Gary Wright, Kathi McDonald, and Dan Hartman, as well as for Morrison. In 1972 he played with Boz Scaggs before joining the Edgar Winter Band, and in 1973 Montrose turned down an offer to be Mott the Hoople's lead guitarist. Instead, he formed his own band.

Montrose's debut album, despite no singles, went platinum. Lead vocalist Sammy Hagar left for a solo career after Montrose's second LP; by 1978 ex-Montrose members Church, Fitzgerald, and Carmassi had joined Hagar. Carmassi later joined Heart, Coverdale/Page, and Ted Nugent. In the early '80s Montrose was leading another band, Gamma, which released three albums before breaking up. He then briefly revived Montrose, which released *Mean* in 1987, before reverting to solo work again. Among the lineup for *Mean* were future Kingdom Come drummer James Kottak and future Foreigner singer Johnny Edwards. The group dissolved again, and Ronnie Montrose continued to record solo. His recent work tends toward jazz rock. In 1996 he completed the soundtrack to the video game *Mr. Bones*. *Bearings* is an acoustic work.

Moody Blues

Formed 1964, Birmingham, Eng.
Denny Laine (b. Brian Hines, Oct. 29, 1944, Jersey, Eng.), gtr., voc.; Mike Pinder (b. Dec. 27, 1941, Birmingham), kybds., voc.; Ray Thomas (b. Dec. 29, 1941, Stourport-on-Severn, Eng.), flute, voc.; Clint Warwick (b. Clinton Eccles, June 25, 1939, Birmingham), bass; Graeme Edge (b. Mar. 30, 1941, Rochester, Eng.), drums.
1965—*Go Now—Moody Blues #1* (London) 1966—*The Magnificent Moodies* (Decca, U.K.) (– Warwick; – Laine; + Justin Hayward [b. David Justin Hayward, Oct. 14, 1946, Swindon, Eng.], gtr., voc.; + John Lodge [b. July 20, 1945, Birmingham], bass, voc.) *Days of Future Passed* (Deram) 1968—*In Search of the Lost Chord* 1969—*On the Threshold of a Dream; To Our Children's Children's Children* (Threshold) 1970—*A Question of Balance; In the Beginning* (Deram) 1971—*Every Good Boy Deserves Favour* (Threshold) 1972—*Seventh Sojourn* 1974—*This Is the Moody Blues* 1977—*The Moody Blues Caught Live + 5* (London) 1978—*Octave* (– Pinder; + Patrick Moraz [b. June 24, 1948, Morges, Switz.], kybds.) 1981—*Long Distance Voyager* (Threshold) 1983—*The Present* 1985—*Voices in the Sky/The Best of the Moody Blues* 1986—*The Other Side of Life* 1988—*Sur la Mer* (Polydor) 1989—*Legend of a Band: Greatest Hits 1967–1988* (Threshold) 1991—*Keys of the Kingdom* (Polydor) 1992—(– Moraz) 1993—*A Night at Red Rocks With the Colorado Symphony Orchestra* (Polydor) 1994—*Time Traveller* (Polydor/Threshold) 1999—*Strange Times* (Universal).
Justin Hayward solo: 1977—*Songwriter* (Deram) 1980—*Night Flight* 1985—*Moving Mountains* (Threshold) 1989—*Classic Blue* 1997—*View From the Hill*.
John Lodge solo: 1977—*Natural Avenue* (London).
Hayward and Lodge: 1975—*Blue Jays* (Threshold).
Graeme Edge Band featuring Adrian Gurvitz: 1975—*Kick Off Your Muddy Boots* (Threshold) 1977—*Paradise Ballroom* (London).
Ray Thomas solo: 1975—*From Mighty Oaks* (Threshold) 1976—*Hopes Wishes and Dreams*.
Mike Pinder solo: 1976—*The Promise* (Threshold) 1994—*Off the Shelf* (One Step) 1995—*A Planet With One Mind* 1996—*A People With One Heart* 2000—*An Earth With One Spirit*.
Patrick Moraz solo: 1983—*Music for Piano and Drums* (Editions E.G.) 1986—*Flags* 1995—*Windows of Time* (Hot Records).

Though their first hit single, "Go Now" (#10, 1965), was a classic Merseybeat ballad, the Moody Blues were best known as one of rock's first classical-pomp groups. Since then, the Moodies have made regular forays back onto the hit-singles chart and remain a perennial arena-filling live attraction. Well into their fourth decade (with the core quartet of Ray Thomas, Justin Hayward, John Lodge, and Graeme Edge intact since 1967), the Moody Blues have proved impervious to the long-prevalent critical view that their music is bombastic and pretentious. The Moody Blues were among the first groups to make extensive use of the Mellotron and the flute. Their early psychedelic-influenced works were highly evocative, and their sometimes obtuse lyrics (as in "Nights in White Satin") have been thought by fans to possess a deeper meaning.

Before becoming the Moody Blues, all of the band members had worked in various local Birmingham blues and R&B bands: Ray Thomas and Mike Pinder played with the rockabilly-inspired El Riot and the Rebels (who often opened for the Beatles in England in the mid-'60s) and later the R&B-style Krew Cats, who were popular in Hamburg, Germany. Meanwhile, Denny Laine was fronting Denny Laine and the Diplomats (which included future Electric Light Orchestra drummer Bev Bevan), and Graeme Edge had been in a series of groups, the most recent being Gerry Levene and the Avengers (which included future ELO member and Move leader Roy Wood). Clint Warwick had belonged to the Rainbows. A number of misconceptions regarding the group's name have endured, but they chose Moody Blues to have the word "Blues" in it and because Mike Pinder's favorite song was Duke Ellington's "Mood Indigo."

Initially a blues-influenced band, the Moody Blues began playing in spring 1964, by which time Laine and Pinder were

The Moody Blues: Justin Hayward, Ray Thomas, Patrick Moraz, Graeme Edge, John Lodge

writing songs while the group was performing a catalogue of Motown, James Brown, and American blues songs. The group also backed a long list of American blues musicians, including Little Walter Jacobs and Sonny Boy Williamson (Rice Miller), on their U.K. tours. The Moodies' second single, "Go Now," was a cover of a little-known R&B song. It went to #1 in the U.K. and #10 in the U.S. in 1965. Subsequent singles did not fare as well, and the group was living near poverty. Warwick tired of the situation and left; Laine followed months later. (In the '70s, Laine would join Paul McCartney's Wings.) John Lodge, who'd played with Thomas in bands before the Moody Blues, replaced Laine. When Eric Burdon, who had collected a bag of letters in response to an ad he'd placed to find musicians for a new Animals lineup, invited Thomas to pore through them for the Moody Blues, the first he chose was from Justin Hayward. Hayward had worked in a number of bands and just recorded a solo single, produced by Lonnie Donegan, that went nowhere. In September 1966 he was hired.

That same year the Moody Blues signed a new recording contract, with Deram. After a few more unnoticed singles, at the behest of the label, the group was to record a rock version of Dvorak's *Symphony No. 9*. Were it not for their purchase of a Mellotron (a keyboard instrument that reproduces the sounds of violins, flutes, choirs, and so forth, through tapes) in 1967, the Moody Blues might never have been heard from again. But with the Mellotron (and, occasionally, actual orchestras) providing grandiose symphonic accompaniment, the Moodies' material had changed to cosmic lyrics set to heavily orchestrated pop tunes and extended suites. The week's studio time Deram granted them for the Dvorak project was used instead to record *Days of Future Passed*. With the Hayward-penned hit single "Tuesday Afternoon" (#24, 1968), the platinum *Days of Future Passed* went to #27 in the U.K. (where "Nights in White Satin" was the hit single) and #3 in the U.S., where it remained on the chart over two years. That LP—credited as having been recorded with a group of musicians billed as the (nonexistent) London Festival Orchestra—kept returning to the album chart as late as 1973. Hayward's "Nights in White Satin" has had an interesting chart history, hitting #19 in 1967 in the U.K., then returning to the chart two more times in the next dozen years (#9 U.K., 1972; #14 U.K., 1979). Here in the U.S., "Nights" was not a hit until 1972, when it reached #2.

Though the Moody Blues concentrated on writing musically ambitious and lyrically profound songs, they were still capable of turning out crowd-pleasing singles, such as "Question" (#21, 1970), "The Story in Your Eyes" (#23, 1971), "Isn't Life Strange?" (#29, 1972), and "I'm Just a Singer (In a Rock and Roll Band)" (#12, 1973). Their albums of this period all went gold: *In Search of the Lost Chord* (#23, 1968), *On the Threshold of a Dream* (#20, 1969), *To Our Children's Children's Children* (#14, 1970), *A Question of Balance* (#3, 1970), *Every Good Boy Deserves Favour* (#2, 1971), and *Seventh Sojourn* (#1, 1972). In addition to their widely played hit singles, the Moody Blues also had an album-track catalogue of songs that received heavy exposure on FM radio: "The Story in Your Eyes," "Ride My See Saw," "Higher and Higher," and "Legend of a Mind." In 1969 the band established its own label, Threshold, as a Decca subsidiary.

After *Seventh Sojourn*, the Moody Blues took a lengthy sabbatical, during which time all five members pursued solo and collaborative projects. Graeme Edge recorded two albums with guitarist/keyboardist/vocalist Adrian Gurvitz; Lodge and Hayward recorded *Blue Jays*, a sort of Moody Blues continuation, then put out records individually; Thomas issued *From Mighty Oaks*; and Pinder followed with *The Promise*. In the late '80s Hayward's *Classic Blue* found him singing "MacArthur Park" and "Stairway to Heaven," among other hits, with backing by the London Symphony Orchestra. Of his solo efforts, only *Blue Jays* was a Top 30 album.

In 1978 the Moody Blues regrouped for the platinum *Octave* (#13)—which included "Steppin' in a Slide Zone" (#39, 1978)—though on a subsequent U.S. tour, Pinder was replaced by ex-Refugee, ex-Yes keyboardist Patrick Moraz. Pinder has since continued to compose and record, although his releases have been rare. With Moraz, the band recorded *Voyager*, which hit #1 and boasted the hit singles "Gemini Dream" (#12) and "The Voice" (#15). Critically regarded as outmoded, the Moody Blues soldiered on. Except for 1983's Top 30 single "Sitting at the Wheel," the Moody Blues were absent from the singles chart until "Your Wildest Dreams" (#9, 1986), a nostalgic song accompanied by a sentimental and at times humorously self-deprecating video. The album it came from, *The Other Side of Life*, went to #9, and two years later, "I Know You're Out There Somewhere" (#30, 1988), from *Sur la Mer* (#38, 1988), was another hit. *Keys of the Kingdom* (#94, 1991) proved the group's lowest-charting album of new material, yet the Moody Blues were able to mount a successful tour. Around that time, Moraz left the group. In 1992 the Moody Blues celebrated the silver anniversary of *Days of Future Passed* with a tour featuring a full orchestra. A show at Colorado's majestic Red Rocks amphitheater was recorded for an album and filmed for a video documentary that was later shown on PBS. In 1999 they released *Strange Times,* their first album of new music in eight years and first attempt at producing themselves.

The Moonglows/Harvey Fuqua

Formed 1950, Cleveland, OH
Bobby Lester (b. Jan. 13, 1930, Louisville, KY; d. Oct. 15, 1980, Louisville), voc.; Harvey Fuqua (b. July 27, 1929, Chicago, IL), voc.; Alexander "Peter" Graves (b. Apr. 17, 1939, AL), voc.; Prentiss Barnes (b. 1921, Magnolia, MS). voc.; Billy Johnson (b. Aug. 1929, d. Apr. 29, 1987), gtr.
1959—*Look, It's the Moonglows* (Chess) 1962—*The Best of Bobby Lester and the Moonglows* 1964—*The Moonglows* 1972—*The Return of the Moonglows* (RCA) 1984—*Their Greatest Hits* (Chess) 1991—*Sincerely* (Huub) 1992—*On Stage* 1996—*Rare Acapella Recordings* (Starr Digital) 2000—*Harvey & the Moonglows 2000* (Resurging Artists).

Influenced by the classic black pop vocal stylings of the Ink Spots and the Mills Brothers, doo-wop quartet the Moonglows in turn influenced virtually every succeeding black male R&B vocal group.

In the early '50s Louisville, Kentucky, baritone Harvey Fuqua and tenor Bobby Lester sang together on street corners and in local talent shows before Fuqua relocated to Cleveland; he and his wife left Louisville after a fire in which the couple's two children and her mother were killed. In Ohio, Fuqua formed a jazz-oriented vocal trio, the Crazy Sounds, and enlisted Lester as a fourth member to join himself, tenor Peter Graves, and bass Prentiss Barnes. Legendary Cleveland DJ Alan Freed, host of *The Moondog Rock 'n' Roll Party* radio show, discovered the group, signed them first to his Champagne Records label and then to Chance and Chess Records in Chicago. The group, which Freed redubbed the Moonglows, also starred in two of Freed's seminal rock & roll movies, 1956's *Rock, Rock, Rock,* and 1957's *Mister Rock and Roll.* Written by Fuqua but partially credited to Freed, "Sincerely," the Moonglows' first Chess single, soared to #1 on the R&B chart in 1955; it reached #20 on the pop chart while a glossy version by the McGuire Sisters went to #1. In 1956 "See Saw" became a #6 R&B, #25 pop hit; the next year, "Please Send Me Someone to Love" also placed in the pop chart. By 1958, with guitarist Billy Johnson on board and the group's name now Harvey and the Moonglows, "Ten Commandments of Love" went to #22 pop.

On their recordings, Lester and Fuqua alternated singing lead. Tension between the two led to the group breaking up in 1959. Lester moved to Chicago and opened a nightclub, and Fuqua moved to Detroit, where in 1960 he launched what would be a long and successful career in artist development. He formed two Detroit labels, Harvey and Tri-Phi, and worked as producer and talent scout for Motown. (He also married Berry Gordy's sister Gwendolyn.) Among his discoveries were Marvin Gaye (whom Fuqua featured in the short-lived New Moonglows), the Spinners, and the Dells. Among his Motown productions were the Supremes' "Someday We'll Be Together," Stevie Wonder's "Yester-Me, Yester-You, Yesterday," and a number of duets by Marvin Gaye and Tammi Terrell.

In the mid-'70s, after a brief Moonglows reunion and the release of a single, "Sincerely, '72," Fuqua made a foray into disco with his protégé Sylvester. In 1982 he produced Marvin Gaye's last studio album, *Midnight Love.*

The Moonglows were inducted into the Rock and Roll Hall of Fame in 2000; that year also saw the release of *Harvey & the Moonglows 2000* on Fuqua's own Resurging Artist Records. Since the '90s, Fuqua has been a trustee for the Rhythm & Blues Foundation, an organization that helps R&B veterans receive songwriting and performance credit, financial assistance, and medical treatment. He continues to perform.

Alanis Morissette

Born June 1, 1974, Ottawa, Can.
1991—*Alanis* (MCA Canada) 1992—*Now Is the Time* 1995—*Jagged Little Pill* (Maverick) 1998—*Supposed Former Infatuation Junkie* 1999—*MTV Unplugged.*

Alanis Morissette pulled off one of the most successful second acts in rock history in the summer of 1995, when the former teen dance-pop star reinvented herself as the undisputed queen of alt-rock angst with *Jagged Little Pill* and its vitriolic lead single, "You Oughta Know." The album went on

Alanis Morissette

to sell 16 million copies in the U.S., surpassing the record for a female solo artist previously set by her label boss, Madonna.

Morissette (along with a twin brother) was born in 1974 to a couple of educators in Ottawa, Ontario. She showed an early interest in performing; she began piano lessons at age six, penned her first song at nine, and landed an acting gig on the Nickelodeon children's television series *You Can't Do That on Televison* at age 10. In 1987 she used part of her TV earnings to finance a self-released single, "Fate Stay With Me," which in turn led to a publishing deal and her signing to MCA Canada.

Although both *Alanis* (1991) and *Now Is the Time* (1992) sold well enough to make Morissette a moderately successful pop star in Canada (where she was given a Juno Award for Most Promising Female Artist in 1992), neither album made any impact south of the border. A fortuitous move to L.A. in 1994, however, led the 20-year-old singer to Glen Ballard, a producer/songwriter who had honed his craft working under Quincy Jones and writing and producing hits for Michael Jackson ("Man in the Mirror") and Wilson Phillips. Together, Morissette and Ballard quickly hammered out the aggressive rock songs that would become *Jagged Little Pill.* Their demos landed Morissette a new record deal with Madonna's Warner Bros. subsidiary, Maverick Records.

Released in June 1995, *Jagged Little Pill* (#1) spawned a handful of Modern Rock and crossover pop hits, beginning with the bitter breakup rant, "You Oughta Know" (#13, 1995), and continuing with "Hand in My Pocket" (#15, 1995), "All I Really Want" (#65, 1995), "Ironic" (#4, 1996), and "You Learn" (#6, 1996). *Pill* would also earn Morissette four Grammy Awards, including Album of the Year. By the time she released 1998's decidedly lower-key, Eastern-music-inspired *Supposed Former Infatuation Junkie* (#1), *Jagged Little Pill* had sold close to 28 million copies worldwide.

Inevitably, given the runaway success of its predecessor, *Supposed Former Infatuation Junkie* (coproduced by Morissette and Ballard) was judged a commercial disappointment despite domestic sales of 3 million. Nevertheless, the album's "Thank U" climbed to #17, while "Uninvited," plucked from the 1998 soundtrack to the Nicolas Cage movie *City of Angels,* earned Morissette two more Grammys (including Best Rock Song).

In 1999 Morissette embarked on a co-headlining tour with fellow alt-rock singer/songwriter Tori Amos, and attracted some controversy by playing the role of God in the Kevin Smith comedy *Dogma.* Meanwhile, sales of her live *MTV Unplugged* set topped off at half a million, and the album peaked at #63. Morissette was scheduled to deliver a new studio album—her first self-produced effort—by the end of 2001.

Morphine

Formed 1990, Cambridge, MA
Mark Sandman (b. 1952; d. July 3, 1999, Rome, It.), bass, voc., kybds., gtr.; Dana Colley, sax, voc.; Jerome Dupree, drums.
1992—(– Dupree; + Billy Conway, drums) *Good* (Accurate/Distortion) 1993—*Cure for Pain* (Rykodisc) 1995—*Yes* 1997—*Like Swimming* (DreamWorks); *B-Sides and Otherwise* (Rykodisc) 2000—*The Night* (DreamWorks).

Arising from the local Boston combos Treat Her Right and Three Colors, Morphine floored critics and amazed a devoted cult of fans throughout the '90s. The trio immediately distinguished itself with its cool, peculiar musical approach, which shunned guitar in favor of frontman Mark Sandman's distorted two-string slide bass and Dana Colley's ferocious, jazz-tinged sax. The bizarrely bluesy, out-of-nowhere debut, *Good,* made inroads on American college radio and seemed like a promising start.

Signed to the larger Rykodisc label and rounded out by new, extraordinarily skillful drummer Billy Conway, the members of Morphine became press darlings and alternative-rock notables with 1993's *Cure for Pain,* which featured such memorably lusty tracks as "Thursday" and "Candy." The combination of Sandman's detached, ironic mutter and bleary-eyed, darkly sexual imagery had grown just as compelling as his self-described, minimalist "low-rock." The album sold over 300,000 copies on the strength of nonstop touring and the appearance of several of its tunes in the hit independent film *Spanking the Monkey.* Morphine also attracted a substantial European following; the three-piece played the Montreaux Jazz Festival in 1995. *Yes* (#101, 1995) and its single "Honey White" repeated the successful formula.

Making the leap to the major label DreamWorks but keeping its idiosyncratic tendencies intact, the band unveiled *Like Swimming* (#67, 1997). Morphine came to a sudden and unfortunate end, however, when Sandman died of a heart attack during a 1999 concert in Italy. Colley and Conway recruited many of the departed bassist's friends (including original Morphine drummer Jerome Dupree) and toured as the nine-piece Orchestra Morphine in tribute to their former cohort. *The Night,* recorded prior to Sandman's passing, finds guitar, keyboards, and backing vocals creeping into the group's formerly bare-bones rumble.

Van Morrison

Born George Ivan Morrison, Aug. 31, 1945, Belfast, N. Ire.
1965—*Them* (Parrot); *Them Again* 1967—*Blowin' Your Mind* (Bang) 1968—*Astral Weeks* (Warner Bros.) 1970—*Moondance; His Band and the Street Choir* 1971—*Tupelo Honey* 1972—*St. Dominic's Preview* 1973—*Hard Nose the Highway* 1974—*It's Too Late to Stop Now; Veedon Fleece; T.B. Sheets* (Bang) 1977—*This Is Where I Came In; A Period of Transition* (Warner Bros.) 1978—*Wavelength* 1979—*Into the Music* 1980—*Common One* 1982—*Beautiful Vision* 1983—*Inarticulate Speech of the Heart* 1985—*A Sense of Wonder* (Mercury); *Live at the Grand Opera House, Belfast* 1986—*No Guru, No Method, No Teacher* 1987—*Poetic*

Champions Compose 1989—*Avalon Sunset* 1990—*Enlightenment; The Best of Van Morrison* (Polydor) 1991—*Bang Masters* (Epic); *Hymns to the Silence* (Polydor) 1993—*The Best of Van Morrison, vol. 2; Too Long in Exile* 1994—*A Night in San Francisco* 1995—*Days Like This* 1996—*How Long Has This Been Going On* (Verve); *Songs of Mose Allison: Tell Me Something* (PolyGram) 1997—*The Healing Game* (Polydor) 1998—*The Philosopher's Stone* 1999—*Back on Top* (Pointblank/Virgin) 2000—*The Skiffle Sessions: Live in Belfast, 1998.*
With the Chieftains: 1988—*Irish Heartbeat* (Mercury).
With Linda Gail Lewis: 2000—*You Win Again* (Pointblank/Virgin).

Part Celtic bard, part soulster, and part ecstatically scatting mystical visionary, Van Morrison is a painfully introverted figure who rarely gives interviews and is often at a loss to explain his own lyrics. In the studio, he can sing like a soul man getting the spirit; onstage, however, his brilliance can be undercut by whim or temper, and he has upon occasion alienated audiences by rushing through songs and remaining aloof between them. Nonetheless, his influence among rock singer/songwriters is unrivaled by any living artist outside of that other prickly legend, Bob Dylan. Echoes of Morrison's rugged literateness and his gruff, feverishly emotive vocal style can be heard in latter-day icons ranging from Bruce Springsteen to Elvis Costello, while the Irish artist's own restless muse has kept him prolific and engaging through the '90s.

Morrison's mother sang at social gatherings, and his father collected classic blues and jazz records. He learned guitar, saxophone, and harmonica while in school, and was playing with Belfast blues, jazz, and rock bands by his midteens. At 15, he quit school, joined an R&B band called the Monarchs, and toured Europe with them as saxophonist. While in Germany, a film director offered Morrison a role in a movie as a jazz saxophonist. The project was dropped, and Morrison returned to Belfast and opened an R&B club in the Maritime Hotel. He recruited some friends to form Them, which became an immediate local sensation as the club's house band.

Them recorded two singles in late 1964: "Don't Start Crying Now" (a local hit) and Big Joe Williams' "Baby Please Don't Go" (which made the British Top 10 in early 1965). After the latter's success, the band moved to London and hooked up with producer Bert Berns. They recorded Berns' "Here Comes the Night," which went to #2 in the U.K. and made the Top 30 in the U.S. Them's next two singles, "Gloria" (by Morrison) and "Mystic Eyes," were minor U.S. hits; "Gloria" was later covered by the Shadows of Knight (who took the song to #10 in 1966) and Patti Smith. Them's lineup underwent constant changes, and Berns brought in sessionmen, including Jimmy Page, for their albums. After a mostly unsuccessful U.S. tour in 1966, the group returned to England. Morrison disbanded Them, which soon re-formed with Ken McDowell as vocalist.

Morrison, meanwhile, grew frustrated by music-business manipulations (Them had wrongly been given a rough-kids image by their company), stopped performing, and moved back to Belfast. Meanwhile, Bert Berns (a.k.a. B. Russell) formed Bang Records in New York, and sent Morrison a plane ticket and an invitation to record four singles for his new label. One of them, "Brown Eyed Girl," reached #10 in the U.S. in 1967. Morrison toured America but was again disgruntled when Berns released the other singles—which Morrison considered demos—as *Blowin' Your Mind.*

Van Morrison

After Berns died of a sudden heart attack in December 1967, Morrison undertook an East Coast tour and wrote material for his next album. Warner Bros. president Joe Smith signed him in early 1968, and Morrison went into a New York studio that summer with numerous jazz musicians. In 48 hours he cut one of rock's least classifiable, most enduring albums, *Astral Weeks,* the first manifestation of Morrison's Irish-romantic mysticism. Though most of its cuts were meandering and impressionistic, with folky guitars over jazzy rhythms topped by Morrison's soul-styled vocals, critics raved; the album is still considered one of Morrison's richest, most powerful efforts.

His next album, *Moondance* (#29, 1970), traded the jazz-and-strings sound of *Astral Weeks* for a horn-section R&B bounce. The title tune and "Come Running" were chart singles, the latter in 1970 (#39), the former not until late 1977. The fittingly titled "Into the Mystic" became a minor hit for Johnny Rivers, while "Caravan" became an FM radio favorite. It was the first Morrison album to chart in the Top 100, and it eventually went platinum. *His Band and the Street Choir* (#32, 1970) yielded two uptempo R&B-flavored Top 40 hits in "Domino" (#9, 1970) and "Blue Money" (#23, 1971). By this time, Morrison had moved to Marin County, California, and married a woman who called herself Janet Planet.

Tupelo Honey (#27, 1971) reflected his new domestic contentment. It yielded a hit in "Wild Night" (#28) and went gold, thanks to progressive FM radio, which latched on to the lyrical title tune (featuring Modern Jazz Quartet drummer

Connie Kay). *St. Dominic's Preview* (#15, 1972) included the minor hit single "Jackie Wilson Said" (#61) and contained two extended journeys into the mystic: "Listen to the Lion" and "Almost Independence Day." In 1972 Morrison guested on the John Lee Hooker–Charlie Musselwhite album *Never Get Out of These Blues Alive*.

By the time of *Hard Nose the Highway* (#27, 1973), Morrison had formed the 11-piece Caledonia Soul Orchestra, which was featured on the live LP *It's Too Late to Stop Now*. In 1973, though, Morrison suddenly divorced Janet Planet, disbanded the Caledonia Soul Orchestra, and returned to Belfast for the first time since 1966. There he began writing material for *Veedon Fleece* (#53, 1974).

Morrison took three years to produce a followup. He reportedly began sessions for an album four different times (one with jazz-funk band the Crusaders), but completed none. By 1976, he was living in California again. Late that year he appeared at the Band's farewell concert and in Martin Scorsese's film of the event, *The Last Waltz*. Finally, in 1977 came *A Period of Transition* (#43, 1977), which featured short jazz and R&B-oriented tunes and backup by pianist Mac "Dr. John" Rebennack. For *Wavelength* (#28, 1978), Morrison took on concert promoter Bill Graham as manager (they split in 1981); the album sold fairly well. Still, Morrison's chronic stage fright continued to plague him. At a 1979 show at New York's Palladium, he stormed off the stage midset without a word and didn't return.

The more serene *Into the Music* (#43, 1979) implied that Morrison had become a born-again Christian, and *Common One* (#73, 1980) delved more into extended mysticism. *Beautiful Vision* (#44, 1982) was more varied and concise, and it generated, as usual, sizable critical acclaim and respectable sales. It also included "Cleaning Windows," which contained references to such Morrison inspirations as Lead Belly, bluesmen Blind Lemon Jefferson, Sonny Terry, Brownie McGhee, and Muddy Waters, as well as Beat author Jack Kerouac and country singer Jimmie Rodgers. *Inarticulate Speech of the Heart* (#116, 1983) offered "special thanks" to L. Ron Hubbard, founder of the Church of Scientology.

With *A Sense of Wonder* (#61, 1985), Morrison continued on his spiritual journey and drew further on literary influences, incorporating the work of a favorite poet, William Blake, on the track "Let the Slave." Meanwhile, Morrison rediscovered his ethnic roots and wanderlust, leaving his California home to travel nomadlike through Dublin, Belfast, and London. On *No Guru, No Method, No Teacher* (#70, 1986), the singer shared this sense of rebirth, while the album's title sneered at critics who had tried to pigeonhole his religious beliefs.

Morrison delved deeper into Celtic imagery with *Poetic Champions Compose* (#90, 1987) and collaborated with Ireland's best-loved traditional band, the Chieftains, on *Irish Heartbeat* (#102, 1988). *Avalon Sunset* (#91, 1989) contained "Whenever God Shines His Light on Me," a duet with Cliff Richard that became Morrison's first British Top 20 single since his days with Them, and "Have I Told You Lately That I Love You," which in 1993 became a #5 U.S. hit for Rod Stewart.

Morrison entered the '90s with the nostalgia-drenched *Enlightenment* (#62, 1990), on which he recalled first becoming acquainted with rock & roll and continued to explore the links between spiritual and romantic love. These themes carried over onto the similarly acclaimed double album *Hymns to the Silence* (#99, 1991), while on *Too Long in Exile* (#29, 1993), the singer brought things full circle, covering songs by some of his heroes—including Ray Charles and Sonny Boy Williamson—and duetting with John Lee Hooker on Them's "Gloria," with enough ardor to dispel any suspicions that age had mellowed him. Hooker, in fact, turned up as a surprise guest at some of Morrison's concerts in the early '90s, and Morrison would produce two of Hooker's albums in the late '90s. Morrison's spirited 1993 performances in San Francisco, documented on *A Night in San Francisco* (recorded December 18), were indicative of his renewed vigor onstage. That same year, Morrison was inducted into the Rock and Roll Hall of Fame. A couple of years later, *How Long Has This Been Going On* (1996), a live jazz show recorded with Georgie Fame and Friends at Ronnie Scott's Club in London in 1995 also attested to his renewed energy. Nevertheless, *Days Like This* (#33, 1995) and *The Healing Game* (#32, 1997) were railed by critics as predictable, lackluster performances, especially Morrison's vocals; the former, however, included two duets with his daughter, Shana. Morrison took on an elder-statesman role when the song "Days Like This" was adopted as a peace anthem in Northern Ireland, and he received an Order of the British Empire title in 1996. A prolific artist, he continued his extraordinary output of an album nearly every year, and released *The Philosopher's Stone*, a two-disc set of previously unreleased material, in 1998. *Back on Top*, an album of new material, followed the next year. In 2000 Morrison was inspired by working with other musicians, and he released a concert recording of skiffle tunes performed with Lonnie Donegan, *The Skiffle Sessions: Live in Belfast, 1998*, and *You Win Again*, an album of country, rockabilly, and blues covers performed with singer/pianist Linda Gail Lewis, the sister of Jerry Lee Lewis.

Morrissey: See the Smiths

The Motels

Formed 1971, Berkeley, CA
Martha Davis (b. Jan. 15, 1951, Berkeley), voc.; Dean Chamberlain, gtr.; Lisa Brennis, bass; Chuck Wada, gtr.
1975—(+ Robert Nueman, drums; – Brennis; + Richard D'Andrea, bass) 1977—(– Wada; – Chamberlain; – D'Andrea; + Jeff Jourard, gtr.; – Neuman; + Michael Goodroe, bass; + Marty Jourard, sax, kybds.; + Brian Glascock, drums) 1979—*Motels* (Capitol) 1980—(– J. Jourard; + Tim McGovern, gtr.) *Careful* 1981—(– McGovern; + Guy Perry, gtr.) 1982—*All Four One* 1983—(+ Scott Thurston, gtr., kybds.) *Little Robbers* 1985—*Shock* 1990—*No Vacancy: The Best of the Motels* 2001—*Anthologyland* (Oglio).
Martha Davis solo: 1987—*Policy* (Capitol).

The Motels were one of L.A.'s original new-wave bands and one of its most respected, though it took them a long time to capitalize commercially on either point. After a number of personnel shake-ups and 10 years into their existence, the Motels released their first hit single, "Only the Lonely," and their first hit album, *All Four One*.

Motels singer/songwriter Martha Davis started her first band in 1972. Having married at age 15, she was by then the mother of two daughters. Over four years, the group changed its name from the Warfield Foxes to the Motels, changed its image from a joke to a serious venture, and moved from Berkeley to L.A. Early members Dean Chamberlain (who went on to Code Blue) and Richard D'Andrea (who later played with ex-Blondie Gary Valentine's the Know) left the group. The next version, with Marty Jourard, Michael Goodroe, Brian Glascock (brother of late Jethro Tull bassist John Glascock), and Jourard's brother Jeff, signed to Capitol and recorded *The Motels*. Tim McGovern, once of L.A. power-poppers the Pop, replaced Jourard for *Careful* and a stillborn LP called *Apocalypso*. Capitol rejected the latter. McGovern left the Motels (to reappear with the Burning Sensations); the band rerecorded *Apocalypso*'s songs with studio musicians.

The gambit paid off with "Only the Lonely" (#9, 1982). The band's next album, the gold *Little Robbers*, contained another #9 pop hit, "Suddenly Last Summer." *Shock*, another Top 40 album, included "Shame" (#21, 1985). Davis then discovered she had cancer, which was instrumental in splitting up the Motels. Having recovered successfully, she released a 1987 solo album containing the single "Don't Tell Me the Time." She continues to perform live and recently worked on a children's music project. The two-disc *Anthologyland* contains an odd assortment of Motels demos, alternate versions, and live tracks.

Mother Love Bone: See Pearl Jam

Mothers of Invention: See Frank Zappa

Mötley Crüe

Formed 1981, Los Angeles, CA
Tommy Lee (b. Thomas Lee Bass, Oct. 3, 1962, Athens, Gr.), drums; Mick Mars (b. Bob Deal, Apr. 3, 1956, Huntington, IN), gtr., voc.; Vince Neil (b. Vince Neil Wharton, ca. 1961, Hollywood, CA), voc.; Nikki Sixx (b. Frank Carlton Serafino Ferranno, Dec. 11, 1958, San Jose, CA), bass.
1982—*Too Fast for Love* (Elektra) 1983—*Shout at the Devil* 1985—*Theatre of Pain* 1987—*Girls, Girls, Girls* 1989—*Dr. Feelgood* 1991—*Decade of Decadence—'81–'91* 1992—(– Vince Neil; + John Corabi [b. Apr. 26, 1959, Philadelphia, PA], voc.) 1994—*Mötley Crüe* (Elektra/Asylum) 1996—(– Corabi; + Neil, voc.) 1997—*Generation Swine* 1998—*Greatest Hits* (Motley Records/Beyond) 1999—*Supersonic and Demonic Relics* (Beyond); *Live Entertainment or Death* 2000—(– Lee; + Randy Castillo [b. Dec. 18, 1961, Albuquerque, NM], drums) *New Tattoo*.
Vince Neil solo: 1993—*Exposed* (Elektra).
Union (John Corabi): 1998—*Union* (Mayhem) 2000—*The Blue Room* (Spitfire).
Methods of Mayhem (Tommy Lee): 1999—*Methods of Mayhem* (MCA).

The poster boys for '80s hair-metal, Mötley Crüe parlayed an image of fast-living, hard-driving postadolescent reprobates and fast, pummeling songs into platinum-level heavy-metal superstardom, topping the charts with *Dr. Feelgood* (#1, 1989) and coming close with *Theatre of Pain* (#6, 1985), *Girls, Girls, Girls* (#2, 1987), and a greatest-hits collection, *Decade of Decadence—'81–'91* (#2, 1991).

Nikki Sixx was a member of the locally successful L.A. metal band London when he decided to form his own band. Tommy Lee came aboard as drummer, and they decided to call themselves Christmas. Guitarist Mick Mars was discovered through a classified ad reading "LOUD RUDE AGGRESSIVE GUITARIST AVAILABLE." That he used the same hair dye as Sixx cemented the relationship. Vocalist Vince Neil was plucked from a Cheap Trick cover band. Mars came up with the new, strangely umlauted name. Their eponymous, independently released debut was picked up by Elektra and retitled *Too Fast for Love* (#77, 1983).

Shout at the Devil (#17, 1983), with its canny hints of Satanism, followed, but the band did not catch on in a big way until *Theatre of Pain* (#6, 1985). Fueled by a cover of Brownsville Station's anthemic "Smokin' in the Boys Room" (#16, 1985) and "Home Sweet Home" (#89, 1985), considered to be the first "power ballad" played on MTV, the album sold over 2 million copies.

For all the album sales, Crüe was known as a live band, playing a rock version of a Vegas review, a leering embrace of all things hedonistic, with elaborate sets and lighting, revolving drum sets, pyrotechnics, and dancing girls. Still, *Girls, Girls, Girls* (#2, 1987) and *Dr. Feelgood* (#1, 1989) continued the band's streak of platinum albums, selling 2 million and 4 million copies respectively. *Decade of Decadence—'81–'91* (#2, 1991) included new material, such as their misguided cover of the Sex Pistols' "Anarchy in the U.K."

Mötley Crüe lived the rock & roll lifestyle to the fullest, with celebrity marriages—Tommy Lee to *Dynasty* and *Melrose Place* star Heather Locklear from 1986 to 1994, then to *Baywatch* bombshell Pamela Anderson in 1995 (they divorced in 1998 and reunited in 1999 only to split again), and Nikki Sixx to former Prince protégée Vanity in 1987—substance abuse, and scrapes with the law. Sixx spent over a year addicted to heroin. In 1986 Neil was convicted of vehicular manslaughter, the result of a 1984 drunken accident that killed Hanoi Rocks drummer Nicholas Dingley and seriously injured two others. He served 20 days in jail, performed 200 hours of community service, and was assessed $2.6 million in damages. (Tragedy would touch Neil again in 1994 when his four-year-old daughter Skylar died of a rare childhood cancer.)

In 1992 Neil was replaced by John Corabi; he filed a

$5 million wrongful termination suit, then formed the Vince Neil Band, which included ex–Billy Idol sidekick guitarist Steve Stevens, bassist Robbie Crane, drummer Vik Foxx, and guitarist Dave Marshall, and released *Exposed* (#13, 1993). Meanwhile, Mötley Crüe's first album with Corabi at the mike (#7, 1994) was also the band's first one to be certified only gold. Corabi was fired in 1996 (and later joined Union with ex-Kiss guitarist Bruce Kulick) so that Neil could rejoin the Crüe fold. The reunion album, *Generation Swine* (#4, 1997), attempted to explore grunge and industrial sounds, but despite the band covering itself ("Shout at the Devil '97"), its constituency didn't bite, and the record quickly fell off the chart. *Greatest Hits* (#25, 1998) and *Live Entertainment or Death* (#133, 1999) continued Mötley Crüe's commercial skid. Shortly after completing the subsequent tour, drummer Lee spent four months in jail for assaulting his then-wife, Pamela. Upon being released, Lee left the band and formed Methods of Mayhem, in which he played guitar and sang. He was replaced in Mötley Crüe by former Ozzy Osbourne drummer Randy Castillo. The new lineup returned to its original hard-rock formula on *New Tattoo* (#41, 2000), but the album was received tepidly.

Motörhead

Formed 1975, England
Lemmy Kilmister (b. Ian Kilmister, Dec. 24, 1945, Stoke-on-Trent, Eng.), bass, voc.; Eddie Clark, gtr.; Phil "Philthy Animal" Taylor (b. Sep. 21, 1954, Chesterfield, Eng.), drums.
1977—*Motörhead* (Chiswick, U.K.) 1979—*Overkill* (Bronze, U.K.); *Bomber* 1980—*Ace of Spades* (Mercury) 1981—*No Sleep Till Hammersmith* 1982—*Iron Fist* (– Clark; + Brian Robertson [b. Glasgow, Scot.], gtr.) 1983—*Another Perfect Day* (– Robertson; – Taylor; + Phil Campbell [b. May 7, 1961, Pontypridd, Wales], gtr.; + "Wurzel" [b. Oct. 23, 1949, Cheltenham, Eng.], gtr.; + Pete Gill, drums) 1984—*No Remorse* (Bronze) 1986—*Orgasmatron* (GWR/Profile) 1987—*Rock 'n' Roll* 1988—*No Sleep at All* (Enigma) 1990—*The Birthday Party* (GWR) 1991—*1916* (WTG) (– Gill; + Taylor, drums; – Taylor; + Mikkey Dee [b. Oct. 31, 1963, Olundby, Swed.], drums) 1993—*March or Die* 1994—*Bastards* (Motörhead/ZYX) 1995—(+ Campbell) *Sacrifice* (CMC International) (– Wurzel) 1996—*Overnight Sensation* 1998—*Snake Bite Love* 1999—*Everything Louder Than Everyone Else* 2000—*We Are Motörhead; The Best of Motörhead.*

Known to produce no less than 126 decibels in its live shows, England's Motörhead is easily one of the world's loudest rock & roll bands. The heavy-metal group's raunchy leather-biker image underlined its fascination with violence, as did such album titles as *Overkill, Bomber,* and *Iron Fist.* Motörhead's hard-and-fast sound prefigured the thrash and speed-metal genres of the late '80s and '90s, and the group was cited as an influence by Guns n' Roses (who had Motörhead open on their 1992 U.S. tour) and Metallica.

Bassist/vocalist Lemmy Kilmister, formerly with progressive British rockers Hawkwind [see entry], put together Motörhead in 1975, and the group released its self-titled debut album in 1977, in the middle of the punk boom. After establishing itself on the British chart with two subsequent albums, the band recorded *Ace of Spades,* its official American debut. Motörhead has yet to make a significant dent in the American chart, but it is a huge concert draw in the U.K. and has steadily built a cult following in the U.S.

With the balladic title track of *1916,* Motörhead began breaking out of its trademark bludgeoning sound; the trend continued on *Bastards* (Kilmister originally intended to call the group Bastard) with "Lost in the Ozone" and "Don't Let Daddy Kiss Me," a song about incest from a little girl's point of view.

Onetime Motörhead guitarist "Fast" Eddie Clarke went on to form Fastway with ex–Humble Pie Jerry Shirley. He was briefly replaced in Motörhead by ex–Thin Lizzy Brian Robertson, before Wurzel and Phil Campbell (who has also variously gone by the names Wizzo, Zoom, and Wizzo von Wizzo) settled the lineup through the '80s. Wurzel left after the recording of *Sacrifice,* and the band's lineup settled down to a three-piece again.

The Motors

Formed 1977, England
Nick Garvey, voc., gtr., bass; Andy McMaster, voc., kybds., bass; Bram Tchaikovsky (b. Peter Bramall), gtr., voc.; Ricky Slaughter, drums, voc.
1977—*The Motors I* (Virgin) 1978—*Approved by the Motors* (– Tchaikovsky; – Slaughter) 1980—*Tenement Steps.*

The Motors' two songwriters, Nick Garvey and Andy McMaster, met in Ducks Deluxe, a British pub-rock band. Garvey joined Ducks in its early stages in December 1972, after working as road manager for the Flamin' Groovies. The Scottish McMaster had been involved in rock since the mid-'60s, playing for a while with the Stoics, which included Frankie Miller, and he'd also written a successful record of children's songs. He joined Ducks just before its second and final record, *Taxi to the Terminal Zone.* After the group broke up, Garvey switched from bass to guitar and formed the Snakes, while McMaster worked for a music publisher.

In early 1977 the two began collaborating on songs, soon recruiting ex-Snakes drummer Ricky Slaughter and guitarist Bram Tchaikovsky. Their debut, highlighted by Garvey and McMaster's dual lead vocals, boasted the British hit single "Dancing the Night Away." After the British success of "Airport" (from *Approved by the Motors*), Garvey and McMaster decided to fire the rest of the band and go on as a studio twosome with revolving musicians. Tchaikovsky went on to record four solo albums; Garvey produced his debut, 1979's *Strange Man, Changed Man,* which contained the Top 40 hit "Girl of My Dreams." The two Motors decided to forgo touring, and they released *Tenement Steps* (produced by Jimmy Iovine) in 1980. The LP featured the minor hit "Love and

Loneliness," with Rockpile's Terry Williams on drums and ex-Man Martin Ace on bass.

Mott the Hoople

Formed 1968, Hereford, Eng.
Stan Tippens (b. Eng.), lead voc.; Mick Ralphs (b. Mar. 31, 1948, Hereford), gtr., voc.; Overend Pete Watts (b. May 13, 1947, Birmingham, Eng.), bass; Dale "Buffin" Griffin (b. Oct. 24, 1948, Ross-on-Wye, Eng.), drums; Verden Allen (b. May 26, 1944, Hereford), organ.
1969—(– Tippens; + Ian Hunter [b. June 3, 1946, Shrewsbury, Eng.], piano, gtr., lead voc.) *Mott the Hoople* (Atlantic) 1970—*Mad Shadows* 1971—*Wildlife* 1972—*Brain Capers; Rock 'n' Roll Queen; All the Young Dudes* (Columbia) 1973—(– Allen) *Mott* (– Ralphs; + Morgan Fisher, kybds.; + Ariel Bender, a.k.a. Luther James Grosvenor [b. Dec. 23, 1949, Evesham, Eng.], gtr.) 1974—*The Hoople; Mott the Hoople Live* (– Bender; + Mick Ronson [b. ca. 1946, Hull, Eng.; d. Apr. 30, 1993, London, Eng.], gtr.; – Hunter; – Ronson) 1975—(name changed to Mott; + Ray Major, gtr.; + Nigel Benjamin, voc.) *Drive On* 1976—*Shouting and Pointing; Greatest Hits* 1993—*The Ballad of Mott: A Retrospective* 1994—*Backsliding Fearlessly: The Early Years* (Rhino).
British Lions (Watts; Griffin; Fisher; Major; + John Fiddler, voc.): 1978—*British Lions* (RSO).

Mott the Hoople started out as an uneven, hard-rock Dylanesque curiosity but ended as a glitter-age group. Mott also gave rise to the solo career of songwriter Ian Hunter [see entry]. The group began in the late '60s, when Mick Ralphs, Verden Allen, Overend Pete Watts, and Dale Griffin began playing around Hereford, England, in a group called Silence. They got a record contract in early 1969 and went to London with vocalist Stan Tippens to record under producer Guy Stevens, who renamed the band Mott the Hoople after a 1967 novel by Willard Manus. Tippens was replaced by Ian Hunter in July. (Tippens subsequently became the band's road manager and later worked for the Pretenders.)

The group recorded its eponymous debut album in August 1969, and it garnered much curious attention for Hunter's Dylan-like rasp and the odd choice of covers, such as Sonny Bono's "Laugh at Me." *Mad Shadows* was moodier and poorly received, and the country-oriented *Wildlife* did not fare well either.

Yet even though its records didn't sell, Mott became a big live attraction in England. In July 1971, the group caused a mini-riot at London's Albert Hall, which factored into the hall management's decision to ban rock completely. After the release of *Brain Capers,* the group was ready to disband, but then David Bowie stepped in to give it a focused glam-rock image and a breakthrough single.

He first offered "Suffragette City," but the band wanted "Drive In Saturday," which Bowie refused to give up. Luckily, Mott accepted his offer of a third song, "All the Young Dudes." Bowie produced the LP of the same name, and Mott had a top British single with "Dudes." The song became a signature piece for glitter rock and a gay anthem—something it took the all-straight band a while to get used to. "All the Young Dudes" went to #37 in the U.S.

The group's followup album, 1973's *Mott,* was its masterpiece—a self-produced effort that featured the British hit singles "Honaloochie Boogie" and "All the Way From Memphis." It was also a concept album about the fight for, and mistrust of, success, highlighted by the autobiographical "Ballad of Mott the Hoople." Around this time, Hunter's *Diary of a Rock Star* was published in England.

Despite its success, the band began to fall apart. Allen left because the group rarely recorded his songs. Ralphs quit because he was upset by Allen's leaving and irked that one of his songs for Mott, "Can't Get Enough," was beyond the singing range of either himself or Hunter. (The song was a Top 5 hit the following year for Ralphs' next band, Bad Company [see entry].) Hunter and company filled the guitar gap with Luther Grosvenor—formerly with Spooky Tooth and Stealer's Wheel—who changed his name to Ariel Bender upon joining. The *Live* album was taken from shows in London in November 1973 and in New York in May 1974.

The band had just begun to sell well in the States when another falling-out occurred. Late in 1974, Mick Ronson [see entry] replaced Bender. By the end of the year, Hunter and Ronson had split together, and Mott the Hoople was no more. Hunter had a solo deal with Columbia, but his first tour, billed as the Hunter-Ronson Band, was a disaster, with a disillusioned band playing to half-filled houses. Meanwhile, Watts, Griffin, and Fisher, joined by Ray Major and Nigel Benjamin, carried on as Mott. They released two undistinguished albums, after which Benjamin left, and the band fell apart again. Undaunted, the remaining members added a new lead singer, ex–Medicine Head John Fiddler, and continued for two years under the name British Lions. After Allen had left Mott back in 1973, he formed Cheeks with future Pretenders James Honeyman-Scott and Martin Chambers. The group toured through 1976 but never recorded. Ronson died of cancer.

Bob Mould: See Hüsker Dü

Mountain

Formed 1969, New York, NY
Felix Pappalardi (b. 1939, Bronx, NY; d. Apr. 17, 1983, New York), bass, voc.; Leslie West (b. Leslie Weinstein, Oct. 22, 1945, Queens, NY), gtr., voc.; N.D. Smart, drums.
1969—*Leslie West—Mountain* (Leslie West solo) (Windfall) 1970—(– Smart; + Corky Laing [b. Apr. 26, 1948, Montreal, Can.], drums; + Steve Knight, organ) *Mountain Climbing* 1971—*Nantucket Sleighride; Flowers of Evil* 1972—*Mountain Live (The Road Goes On Forever)* (group disbands) 1973—*Best of* (Columbia) 1974—(group re-forms: West; Pappalardi; + Alan Schwartzberg, drums; + Bob Mann, kybds.) *Twin Peaks* (– Schwartzberg; – Mann; + Laing) *Avalanche* (group disbands)

1985—(group re-forms: West, Laing, + Mark Clarke, bass) 1986—*Go for Your Life* (Scotti Bros.) 1995—*Over the Top* (Legacy).
Leslie West solo: 1975—*The Great Fatsby* (Phantom) 1994—*Dodgin' the Dirt* (Blues Bureau International).

Cream pioneered the power-trio format; Mountain capitalized on it. The trio was formed in 1969 by Cream's producer, Felix Pappalardi, and 250-pound ex-Vagrant guitarist Leslie West.

The Vagrants had been Long Island legends but never could expand their appeal as had local predecessors the Young Rascals. Although the release of the Vagrants' single "Respect" preceded Aretha Franklin's, the group was buried when Franklin's rendition came out soon after. Atco turned to Pappalardi to record the group's fourth single, but it was another flop. When the fifth attempt proved no better, the band broke up.

West set to recording a solo album, produced by Pappalardi. The result, *Leslie West—Mountain,* inspired the two to form Mountain, with N.D. Smart held over from the *Mountain* LP, and the addition of Steve Knight. Mountain proved akin to a cruder, louder version of Cream. Propelled by the momentum of West's solo album and Pappalardi's production credentials, success was nearly instantaneous. The band's fourth live performance was at the Woodstock festival. Smart was then replaced by Corky Laing, who handled drumming chores on Mountain's debut album, *Mountain Climbing* (#17, 1970), which went gold and yielded the #21 hit "Mississippi Queen."

Nantucket Sleighride earned the group another gold album in 1971. But the formula began to wear thin, and after one more studio album and a live LP, Pappalardi decided to return to production. Knight disappeared along the way as well, and ex-Cream bassist Jack Bruce joined what was thereafter known as West, Bruce and Laing. That group recorded three LPs for Columbia. *Why Dontcha* (1972) and *Whatever Turns You On* (1973) were moderately successful. After the second LP, the group disbanded; a live LP, *Live 'n' Kickin',* followed.

In the ensuing years, West and Laing periodically resurrected the Mountain moniker, sometimes with Pappalardi (who'd suffered hearing loss from the group's thundering volume and had to semiretire from live work), sometimes not. They have also appeared in the New York metropolitan area billed as the New Mountain. West has performed with his group, the Leslie West Band, as well. In 1982 Laing formed the Mix, and from 1986 to 1989, he led a blues band that featured guest stars Mick Taylor and Lester Chambers. Since 1989, Laing has been vice president of A&R for PolyGram Records.

In 1983 Pappalardi was shot dead by his wife and songwriting collaborator, Gail Collins. Two years later West, Laing, and bassist Mark Clarke issued *Go for Your Life,* which featured concise hard-rocking numbers and a noticeably svelte (well, maybe not *svelte*) West. Today, the guitarist pops up from time to time on shock jock Howard Stern's radio show. In the '90s Laing and West compiled Mountain's silver-anniversary retrospective, *Over the Top,* which included three new songs.

The Move/Roy Wood

Formed 1966, Birmingham, Eng.
Roy Wood (b. Ulysses Adrian Wood, Nov. 8, 1946, Birmingham), gtr., voc.; Bev Bevan (b. Nov. 25, 1944, Birmingham), drums, voc.; Carl Wayne (b. Aug. 18, 1944, Moseley, Eng.), voc.; Trevor Burton (b. Mar. 9, 1944, Aston, Eng.), gtr., bass, voc.; Chris "Ace" Kefford (b. Dec. 10, 1946, Moseley), bass, voc.
1968—*The Move* (Regal Zonophone, U.K.) (– Kefford) 1969—(– Burton; + Rick Price [b. June 10, 1944, Birmingham], bass, voc.) 1970—*Shazam* (A&M) (– Wayne; + Jeff Lynne [b. Dec. 30, 1947, Birmingham], gtr., kybds, voc.) 1971—*Looking On* (Capitol) (– Price) *Message From the Country* 1972—(group disbands; becomes Electric Light Orchestra) *Split Ends* (United Artists) 1974—*The Best of the Move* (A&M) 1979—*Shines On.*
Roy Wood solo: 1973—*Boulders* (United Artists); *Wizzard's Brew* (Harvest) 1974—*See My Baby Jive; Introducing Eddie and the Falcons* (Warner Bros.) 1975—*Mustard* (Jet) 1977—*Super Active Wizzo* (Warner Bros.) 1979—*On the Road Again.*

The Move's half-ironic pop made the group popular in Britain in the late '60s, but it was virtually unknown in America until its final days, when its energies were concentrated on a transformation into the Electric Light Orchestra [see entry]. With Roy Wood's songwriting, the Move was a remarkably versatile group, sending pop singles to the top of the English chart while its albums featured extended forays into all manners of folk rock, heavy metal, and psychedelia.

The Move started in 1966, when five of Birmingham's top musicians left their respective cover bands—Wood from Mike Sheridan and the Nightriders; Trevor Burton from the Mayfair Set; and Carl Wayne, Bev Bevan, and Ace Kefford from Carl Wayne and the Vikings—for a greater challenge. Wood's compositions acknowledged British trends, notably the psychedelic movement, as well as classical music: The band's debut single, "Night of Fear," was based on the *1812 Overture;* it hit #2 on the U.K. chart in early 1967.

With the aid of crafty manager Tony Secunda (who died in 1995), the Move achieved almost instant notoriety. Its stage act climaxed with the destruction of television sets and automobiles with axes, and a publicity mailing for a 1967 45, "Flowers in the Rain," depicted Prime Minister Harold Wilson in bed with his secretary. This latter stunt resulted in a lawsuit and the band's loss of royalties, which would have been considerable: The single reached #2 on the British chart. The Move's first and only English #1 was the lush "Blackberry Way."

Even within the group, the Move's image was divided. Carl Wayne was an aspiring balladeer who eventually left the group for a cabaret and TV career; Trevor Burton and Chris Kefford were rock & rollers. Kefford quit first, not to be heard from again, and Burton followed in 1969. He stayed active for a while as a member of the Uglys (with future ELO member

Richard Tandy), the Balls (with Steve Gibbons and former Moody Blue Denny Laine, later of Wings), and, in the late '70s, the Steve Gibbons Band.

With Rick Price on bass, the Move recorded *Shazam,* an album of six cuts in six different styles interspersed with man-on-the-street interviews. The album was calculated to combat the group's British bubblegum image. The British group Amen Corner turned the opening track, "Hello Susie," into a Top 5 U.K. hit in mid-1969. Soon after *Shazam*'s release, Wayne left. His place was taken by Jeff Lynne, who had replaced Wood in the Nightriders as they were renamed the Idle Race. (The Idle Race enjoyed modest British popularity, due in part to the Wood composition "Here We Go Round the Lemon Tree.") After 1971's *Looking On,* which included the Move's sixth Top 10 British hit, a throbbingly heavy number titled "Brontosaurus," the band announced a planned metamorphosis into the Electric Light Orchestra, incorporating classical-music instrumentation such as cello and violin.

But there were to be more Move records: an adventurous LP, *Message From the Country,* and a series of commercial singles (collected on *Split Ends*). In the meantime, Price had left the band; he had become superfluous once the group abandoned the stage. While the Move put out its last contract-fulfilling singles in 1971 and 1972 (including Lynne's rousing "Do Ya," a minor hit for the Move, later a much greater one for ELO), the recording of the first Electric Light Orchestra album was under way. On its release in summer 1972, the Move was finished. No sooner had ELO officially begun, however, than Wood quit, abandoning classical rock for '50s-influenced rock & roll. In the '70s and '80s, he released albums on his own and with his group Wizzard. Although little known in the U.S., he continued to have success at home: two Phil Spector–esque singles, "See My Baby Jive" and "Angel Fingers," topped the chart there in 1973.

Alison Moyet/Yaz

Born Genevieve Alison-Jane Moyet, June 18, 1961, Billericay, Essex, Eng.
With Yaz (Moyet, voc.; Vince Clarke [b. July 3, 1960, South Woodford, Eng.], kybds): 1982—*Upstairs at Eric's* (Sire) 1983—*You and Me Both* 1999—*The Best of Yaz* (Reprise).
Alison Moyet solo: 1984—*Alf* (Columbia) 1987—*Raindancing* 1991—*Hoodoo* 1993—*Essex* 1995—*Singles* (Sony).

Alison Moyet rose to fame in her native England in the early '80s as half of the short-lived but influential technopop duo Yazoo (known as Yaz in the U.S.). While her partner, ex–Depeche Mode songwriter Vince Clarke, crafted electronic-based arrangements, cowriter Moyet's earthy, soulful alto lent heart to the material—as Annie Lennox's mezzo did to Eurythmics' music. Unlike Eurythmics, Yaz didn't enjoy commercial success in the U.S., though the duo's sultry, rhythmically compelling style—and particularly Moyet's voice—was admired by fans of progressive pop. The pair's debut, *Upstairs at Eric's,* featured the new-wave dance-club hits "Don't Go," "Only You," and "Situation." When Yaz split up after *You and Me Both,* Clarke went on to form the Assembly and, later, Erasure [see entry]. Moyet, meanwhile, embarked on a solo career that garnered more widespread recognition in the U.K. than it did stateside.

As a teenager in the late '70s, Moyet was drawn to punk's energy, but she soon realized that her warm voice was better suited to R&B. She sang with a couple of pub bands before hooking up with Clarke. After Yaz disbanded, Moyet continued offsetting synth-laden orchestration with a sensuous, bluesy vocal technique. Her solo debut, *Alf,* sold more than 1.5 million copies in England alone and went Top 10 all over Europe and in Australia. *Raindancing* (1987) was also well received by fans, entering the British charts at #2.

Moyet was not satisfied with the production, promotion, or marketing of either album, however. After taking a few years off, the singer rebounded in 1991 with *Hoodoo.* A denser, more stylistically diverse album—and to Moyet and critics, a more successful one, too—it sold fewer copies than any of her previous efforts, although the first single from the album, "It Won't Be Long," received a Grammy nomination in the Best Female Rock Vocal category. *Essex* wasn't the commercial breakthrough that Moyet may have hoped for, either, but the album did garner some very favorable reviews. The year 1995 saw the release of Moyet's greatest-hits collection, *Singles,* which entered the U.K. charts at #1 and eventually went double platinum there. The following year she contributed vocals to the Tricky album *Nearly God,* released in the U.K. In 1999—more than 15 years after the duo's demise—*The Best of Yaz* was released, and a new remix of "Situation" hit #1 on the Hot Dance Music/Club Play chart in the U.S.

Mudhoney

Formed 1988, Seattle, WA
Mark Arm (b. Feb. 21, 1962, CA), voc, gtr.; Dan Peters (b. Aug. 18, 1967, Seattle), drums; Steve Turner (b. Mar. 28, 1965, Houston, TX), gtr.; Matt Lukin (b. Aug. 16, 1964, Aberdeen, WA), bass.
1988—*Superfuzz Bigmuff* EP (Sub Pop) 1989—*Mudhoney* 1990—*Boiled Beef & Rotting Teeth* 1991—*Every Good Boy Deserves Fudge* 1992—*Piece of Cake* (Reprise) 1993—*Blinding Sun* EP; *Five Dollar Bob's Mock Cooter Stew* EP 1995—*My Brother the Cow* 1998—*Tomorrow Hit Today* 2000—*March to Fuzz* (Sub Pop).

Mudhoney was one of the leading players in the early-'90s Seattle scene. Named for a Russ Meyer film, the band formed after Mark Arm and Steve Turner left Green River, the prototypical Northwest-sound band whose members also went on to form Mother Love Bone and Pearl Jam. Arm and Turner joined with Matt Lukin, who had been fired by sludge progenitors the Melvins, and Dan Peters, who briefly played with Nirvana and the Screaming Trees. With their big distorted-guitar sound (their debut was named after an effects pedal), '70s hard-rock homages, and twisted, ironic take on rockism, Mudhoney's early records defined grunge. Their

"Touch Me I'm Sick" single was parodied as "Touch Me I'm Dick" in the movie *Singles*, and the Matt Dillon character in that film was rumored to be modeled after Arm.

Before Nirvana came along, Mudhoney was Sub Pop's biggest-selling band. The group was especially popular in England, where it first toured with Sonic Youth in 1989 and was supported by influential DJ John Peel. The members are faithful to the indie aesthetic, recording *Every Good Boy Deserves Fudge* and *Piece of Cake* at Conrad Uno's Egg Studio (first on 8-track, then progressing to 16) and releasing numerous one-off projects, including a 1989 single on which they and Sonic Youth covered each other and a similar 1994 single with Texas singer/songwriter Jimmie Dale Gilmore. Financial problems at Sub Pop drove the quartet to a major label. Still, Mudhoney refused to be serious on *Piece of Cake;* one track featured Lukin making fart sounds.

My Brother the Cow (1995) found Mudhoney, a band whose music had long relied on riffs and clever turns of phrase, making great strides in the songwriting department and earning widespread critical acclaim. If anything, *Tomorrow Hit Today* (1998) featured even stronger material; produced by legendary Memphis producer Jim Dickinson, it also boasted tighter playing and a cleaner sound. Lukin left the band in 1999 (the bass player was immortalized in Pearl Jam's "Lukin"), leaving the remaining members of the group dubbed "the grandfathers of grunge" and contemplating whether or not to soldier on as a trio.

Geoff and Maria Muldaur

Geoff Muldaur (b. 1945, Pelham, NY), gtr., voc.; Maria Muldaur (b. Maria Grazia Rosa Domenica d'Amato, Sep. 12, 1943, New York, NY), voc., violin.

Geoff and Maria Muldaur: 1969—*Pottery Pie* (Reprise) 1972—*Sweet Potatoes* (Warner Bros.).

Geoff Muldaur solo: 1964—*Geoff Muldaur* (Prestige) 1965—*Sleepy Man Blues* 1975—*Is Having a Wonderful Time* (Reprise) 1976—*Motion* 1978—*Geoff Muldaur and Amos Garrett* (with Amos Garrett) (Flying Fish) 1979—*Blues Boy* 1986—*I Ain't Drunk* (Hannibal) 1998—*Secret Handshake* (Hightone) 2000—*Password*.

Maria Muldaur solo: 1972—*Mud Acres* (Rounder) 1973—*Maria Muldaur* (Reprise) 1974—*Waitress in a Donut Shop* 1976—*Sweet Harmony* 1978—*Southern Winds* (Warner Bros.) 1979—*Open Your Eyes* 1980—*Gospel Nights* (Takoma) 1982—*There Is a Love* (Myrrh) 1983—*Sweet and Low* (Tudor) 1985—*Transblucency* (Uptown) 1991—*On the Sunny Side* (Music for Little People) 1993—*Louisiana Love Call* (Black Top) 1994—*Meet Me at Midnite* 1995—*Jazzabelle* (Stony Plain) 1996—*Fanning the Flames* (Telarc) 1998—*Southland of the Heart; Swingin' in the Rain* (Rhino) 1999—*Meet Me Where They Play the Blues* (Telarc) 2000—*Maria Muldaur's Music for Lovers*.

The Muldaurs, who married in the mid-'60s and divorced in 1972, both graduated from the early-'60s folk scene, Geoff with Jim Kweskin's Jug Band, Maria with the Even Dozen Jug Band (which included John Sebastian, Stefan Grossman, Steve Katz, and Joshua Rifkin) and the Kweskin band. They have recorded solo and together. Maria's career has been far more commercially successful.

The two married while they were both with Kweskin's Jug Band. Geoff Muldaur had made a couple of rather obscure albums that demonstrated his attraction to folk blues, vintage jazz, gospel, and country music. Maria D'Amato, in the meantime, had grown up in Greenwich Village, listening to blues and big-band music. In high school she formed an all-girl Everly Brothers–inspired group, the Cameos, and then the Cashmeres, who were offered a recording contract that her mother forbade her to sign because Maria was still a minor. She gravitated to the Village folk scene with the Even Dozen Jug Band, then joined Kweskin, where she sang the blues and Leiber and Stoller—and married Geoff.

Their two duo LPs were eclectic and folksy to the point of sounding homemade ("Produced by Nobody," proclaimed the *Sweet Potatoes* sleeve), and both featured the guitar of Amos Garrett, with whom both Muldaurs would remain associated. In 1973 Geoff moved to Woodstock and worked with Paul Butterfield's Better Days band.

Maria began her own career in 1973 with her enormously successful debut LP, which featured a wide range of material contributed by such artists as Dolly Parton, Dan Hicks, Dr. John, Kate McGarrigle, and Wendy Waldman. "Midnight at the Oasis" was a Top 10 single from the album, and the LP eventually sold gold. Her second album featured horn arrangements by Benny Carter and contained the hit "I'm a Woman" (#12, 1975). The failure of her third album to sell well, despite continuing critical acclaim, left her disillusioned. Geoff, in the meantime, released elaborately produced solo albums on Reprise and folksier ones on Flying Fish. Maria continued to record solo, albeit more and more sporadically. In 1978 she guested on Elvin Bishop's *Hog Heaven* LP. By 1980, she was a born-again Christian, and within a year had released a gospel album.

Through the remainder of the '80s and '90s, Maria recorded in a range of styles. *Transbluecency* was a critically lauded pop-jazz effort, while *Louisiana Love Call* featured Amos Garrett as well as Charles and Aaron Neville, Dr. John, and other New Orleans–based musicians. *On the Sunny Side* is a children's record; *Swingin' in the Rain* contains '30s and '40s big-band songs arranged for kids. Maria has also acted *(Pump Boys and Dinettes; The Pirates of Penzance)*.

After a long hiatus, Geoff appeared on the 1993 self-titled debut by Jenni Muldaur, his daughter with Maria. Having become a record producer and an Emmy-winning composer for television and film, he returned to the studio in the late '90s with the roots-flavored *Secret Handshake*. He has continued to record and perform as a bluesy solo artist.

Mungo Jerry

Formed 1969, London, Eng.

Ray Dorset (b. Mar. 21, 1946, Ashford, Eng.), gtr., voc.; Colin

Earl (b. May 6, 1942, Hampton Ct., Eng.), piano; Paul King (b. Jan. 9, 1948, Dagenham, Eng.), banjo, gtr., jug; Mike Cole, string bass.
1970—*Mungo Jerry* (Janus); *Memoirs of a Stockbroker; In the Summertime* (Pye) 1975—*Mungo Jerry* 1978—*Ray Dorset and Mungo Jerry* (Polydor).

Mungo Jerry was a British quartet of skiffle revivalists (skiffle was roughly the English equivalent of jug-band music) that had a novelty hit in 1970 with "In the Summertime," a #3 single (#1 in England) that earned the group a gold record in the U.S and eventually sold 6 million copies worldwide.

Prior to 1970, the band had been known as the Good Earth, and if the name change helped it achieve its hit, it never did the trick again in the U.S. However, Mungo Jerry did have an impressive list of Top 40 successes in Britain: "Baby Jump," "Alright, Alright," "You Don't Have to Be in the Army to Fight the War," "Lady Rose," "Open Up," "Wild Love," and "Longlegged Woman Dressed in Black."

Michael Martin Murphey

Born Mar. 14, 1945, Dallas, TX
1972—*Geronimo's Cadillac* (A&M) 1973—*Cosmic Cowboy Souvenir* 1974—*Michael Murphey* (Epic) 1975—*Blue Sky Night Thunder; Swans Against the Sun* 1976—*Flowing Free Forever* 1978—*Lone Wolf* 1979—*Peaks, Valleys, Honky-Tonks and Alleys* 1982—*Michael Martin Murphey* (Liberty) 1983—*The Heart Never Lies* 1986—*Tonight We Ride* 1988—*River of Time* 1989—*Land of Enchantment* (Warner Bros.) 1990—*Cowboy Songs I* 1991—*Cowboy Christmas—Cowboy Songs II* 1993—*Cowboy Songs III—Rhymes of the Renegades; Wide Open Country* 1995—*America's Horses; Sagebrush Symphony* 1997—*Horse Legends* 1998—*Cowboy Songs IV* (Valley Entertainment) 1999—*Acoustic Christmas Carols.*

One of the original "cosmic cowboys" of country rock, Michael Murphey started out as one of the leaders of the late-'60s–to–mid-'70s Austin, Texas, "progressive country" music scene. Before he became a musician, Murphey had been intent on joining the Southern Baptist ministry and had studied Greek at North Texas State University and creative writing at UCLA. After working as a staff songwriter at Screen Gems (the Monkees' "What Am I Doing Hangin' 'Round") for five years in the late '60s and a brief stint with the Lewis and Clarke Expedition, Murphey began performing solo. Producer Bob Johnston signed him to A&M and produced Murphey's debut LP in Nashville.

The title tune of his debut made #37 on the singles chart and was covered by Hoyt Axton, Cher, Claire Hamill, and others. He smoothed out his style for his biggest hit, 1975's "Wildfire" (#3). In 1980 his "Cherokee Fiddle" was featured on the *Urban Cowboy* film soundtrack; he also appeared in the film *Take This Job and Shove It*. Also that year, Murphey wrote the screenplay for and appeared in *Hard Country*.

In 1982 he had a Top 20 pop hit with "What's Forever For?" (#1 C&W). His other country hits include "Still Taking Chances" (#3 C&W, 1982), "Love Affairs" (#11 C&W, 1983), "Don't Count the Rainy Days" (#9 C&W, 1983), "Will It Be Love by Morning" (#7 C&W, 1984), "What She Wants" (#8 C&W, 1984), "Carolina in the Pines" (#9 C&W, 1985), "A Face in the Crowd"—a duet with Holly Dunn—(#4 C&W, 1987), "A Long Line of Love" (#1 C&W, 1987), "I'm Gonna Miss You, Girl" (#3 C&W, 1987), "Talkin' to the Wrong Man"—a duet with Murphey's son, Ryan—(#4 C&W, 1988), "From the Word Go" (#3 C&W, 1988), and "Never Givin' Up On Love" (#9 C&W, 1989), from the film *Pink Cadillac*. Among the artists who have covered Murphey's material are John Denver ("Boy From the Country"), the Nitty Gritty Dirt Band ("Cosmic Cowboy"), Kenny Rogers ("Ballad of Calico"), and Jerry Jeff Walker ("Backslider's Wine"). He continues to tour approximately 150 days a year.

In 1990 Murphey released an album of cowboy songs and continued to make records in that vein, albeit with a decidedly easy-listening bent, throughout the decade. Among the highlights from these albums is Murphey's duet with Johnny Cash on "Tennessee Stud" (from *Horse Legends*). Murphey's move in this direction was a natural outgrowth of his role as a promoter of WestFest, the annual traveling celebration of the Western history, art, and culture that he founded in 1986.

Elliott Murphy

Born Mar. 16, 1949, Garden City, NY
1973—*Aquashow* (Polydor) 1974—*Lost Generation* (RCA) 1976—*Night Lights* 1977—*Just a Story From America* (Columbia) 1981—*Affairs* (Courtesan) 1982—*Murph the Surf* 1984—*Party Girls/Broken Poets* (WEA International) 1985—*Après le Deluge* (EMIS) 1987—*Milwaukee* (New Rose) 1988—*Change Will Come* 1989—*Live Hot Point* 1990—*12* 1991—*If Poets Were King* EP 1992—*Diamonds by the Yard* (Razor & Tie); *Paris/New York* (New Rose) 1993—*Unreal City* (Razor & Tie) 1996—*Selling the Gold* (DejaDisc) 1999—*Beauregard* (Koch) 2000—*April—A Live Album* (Last Call, Fr.). With Iain Matthews: 2001—*La Terre Commune* (Eminent).

Singer/songwriter Elliott Murphy's 1973 debut was hailed as "the best Dylan since 1968," and over the years Murphy has developed a following in both the U.S. (where he was born and raised, in Garden City, an upper-middle-class Long Island suburb) and Europe, where he now lives. His father owned the Aqua Show in Queens, near the World's Fair grounds, where big-band acts like Duke Ellington would perform. Murphy began playing guitar at age 12, and by age 13 he had formed his first band. In 1966 his group, the Rapscallions, won a New York State battle of the bands.

Murphy then moved to Europe, where he sang in the streets and, in 1971, had a bit part in Fellini's *Roma*. With his brother Matthew he traveled Europe, busking. He returned to New York, where, during the early '70s, he was a regular in New York's Mercer Arts Center scene with the New York Dolls, Patti Smith, and others, and performed with his band Elliott Murphy's Aquashow. He was discovered by critic Paul

Nelson, and though his band's *Aquashow* LP was widely acclaimed, commercial success eluded him in America. Some of his best-known songs, such as "Drive All Night" and "The Last of the Rock Stars," received exposure on FM radio. His only hits have been in Europe.

In 1981 Murphy formed his own label, Courtesan, and began writing short stories and a novel. Over the years his work has appeared in *Spin* and in Rolling Stone, for which he conducted major interviews with Tom Waits and Keith Richards; he also penned the liner notes for *1969: Velvet Underground Live.* His novel, *Cold and Electric,* was published in France in the late '80s around the time he moved to Paris, where he still resides with his wife and son.

Murphy's work still garners critical acclaim. *Party Girls/Broken Poets,* for example, won the 1984 New York Music Award for Album of the Year despite never having been released in the United States, and in 1996 longtime admirer Bruce Springsteen joined Murphy for a duet on *Selling the Gold*'s "Everything I Do (Leads Me Back to You)." In 2001 Murphy released *La Terre Commune,* a collaboration with Fairport Convention founding member Iain Matthews.

Peter Murphy: See Bauhaus

Anne Murray

Born Morna Anne Murray, June 20, 1945, Springhill, Can.
1970—*Snowbird* (Capitol) 1973—*Danny's Song* 1974—*Country; Love Song* 1976—*Keeping in Touch* 1978—*Let's Keep It That Way* 1979—*New Kind of Feeling* 1980—*Anne Murray's Greatest Hits* 1981—*Where Do You Go When You Dream* 1984—*Heart Over Mind* 1986—*Something to Talk About* 1987—*Harmony; Country Hits; Songs of the Heart* 1988—*As I Am* 1989—*Anne Murray Christmas; Love Songs; Greatest Hits, vol. 2* 1990—*You Will* 1991—*Yes I Do* 1992—*Fifteen of the Best* 1993—*Croonin'* 1994—*Now & Forever* 1996—*Anne Murray* 1999—*What a Wonderful World—26 Inspirational Classics* (Straightway/Sparrow).

Anne Murray, the MOR country-pop singer, was the first female Canadian vocalist to earn a gold record in the U.S. (Joni Mitchell was second, with *Ladies of the Canyon.*) Born and raised in a coal-mining town, Murray was always interested in singing. While attending the University of New Brunswick in the mid-'60s, she auditioned unsuccessfully for the Halifax TV show *Sing Along Jubilee;* two years later she was hired for the station's summer series. She taught physical education on Prince Edward Island but also sang in small clubs and sometimes on another Canadian show, *Let's Go,* spurred on by Brian Ahern (her first producer) and Bill Langstroth (who became her husband; they have two children).

In the late '60s, Murray recorded her first LP for the small Canadian label Arc, which led to a deal with Capitol of Canada. She debuted in America in mid-1970 with the gold *Snowbird* LP and its title-song single (#8), which later in the year became the first 45 by a Canadian female to go gold. Murray began to appear regularly on Glen Campbell's U.S. TV show, and toured and recorded the LP *Anne Murray/Glen Campbell* with him in 1971. Still, she didn't have another major American hit until March 1973 and her Top 10 cover of Kenny Loggins' "Danny's Song." Other hit singles include a cover of Lennon and McCartney's "You Won't See Me" (#8, 1974), "Love Song" (#12, 1975), and "I Just Fall in Love Again" (#12, 1979).

After taking three years off to raise her family, Murray came back in January 1978 with the platinum *Let's Keep It That Way,* her biggest success ever, bolstered by the #1 pop, #4 country, gold ballad "You Needed Me" and the Top 5 country hit "Walk Right Back." *New Kind of Feeling* also went platinum, as did *Greatest Hits* and *Christmas Wishes.* As far as the U.S. pop singles charts go, Murray's big streak ended then, but she's enjoyed ongoing success in country. "A Little Good News" (#1 C&W, 1983) won her the Grammy for Best Female Country Vocal Performance in 1983; it was also the Country Music Awards' single of the year. In 1985 her duet with Dave Loggins (of "Please Come to Boston" fame), "Nobody Loves Me Like You Do," was another #1 country hit and country-music award winner. Among her other country hit singles are "Just Another Woman in Love" (#1 C&W, 1984), "Time Don't Run Out on Me" (#2 C&W 1985), "I Don't Think I'm Ready for You" (#7 C&W, 1985), "Now and Forever (You and Me)" (#1 C&W 1986), "Feed This Fire" (#5 C&W, 1990), and a duet with Kenny Rogers, "If I Ever Fall in Love Again" (#28 C&W, 1989). *What a Wonderful World* (1999) found her trying to crack the devotional-music market.

In her native Canada, Murray was named Country Female Vocalist of the Year every year from 1979 to 1986. She continues to tour and to record, having sold over 40 million albums worldwide.

My Bloody Valentine

Formed 1984, Dublin, Ire.
Kevin Patrick Shields (b. May 21, 1963, Queens, NY), gtr., voc.; Colm Michael O'Ciosoig (b. Oct. 31, 1964, Dublin), drums; Dave Conway (b. Dublin), voc.; Tina (b. Dublin), kybds.
1985—*This Is Your Bloody Valentine* EP (Tycoon; Ger. Dossier, 1988) (+ Deborah Ann Googe [b. Oct. 24, 1962, Somerset, Eng.], bass) 1986—*Geek* EP (Fever) *The New Record by My Bloody Valentine* EP (Kaleidoscope Sound) 1987—*Sunny Sundae Smile* EP (Lazy); *Strawberry Wine* EP; *Ecstasy* EP [– Conway; – Tina; + Bilinda Jayne Butcher [b. Sep. 16, 1961, London, Eng.], gtr., voc.) 1988—*My Bloody Valentine Isn't Anything* (Creation, U.K.) 1990—*Tremolo* EP (Creation, U.K.) 1991—*Loveless.*

The original My Bloody Valentine sounded nothing like the post-1988 model, which introduced a groundbreaking studio concoction of discordant guitar and effects and fragile melodies, kicking off Britain's late-'80s dream-pop scene.

After moving from New York to Ireland at age six, Kevin Shields befriended Colm O'Ciosoig, who shared his obsession with pop music. In 1984 the two formed My Bloody Valentine, named for a B movie, with singer Dave Conway. It wasn't until 1988's *Isn't Anything,* however, that MBV locked into its unusual, influential sound, inspired equally by the churning guitars of the Jesus and Mary Chain, the melodic sense of the Cocteau Twins, and the dissonance of Sonic Youth. (All of their U.K. releases from 1988 were subsequently released in the U.S.) Sire signed MBV that same year, but it took a full three years for the band to complete its full-length magnum opus, *Loveless,* which cost a reported $500,000 and nearly sunk its British label. (The LP reached only #24 in the U.K. and didn't chart in the States.) The band's approach onstage—motionless and reserved—popularized the phrase "shoe gazers" to describe their (and those who followed in their footsteps) passive, introspective demeanors.

My Bloody Valentine has yet to return after the deeply influential *Loveless.* After moving to Island Records, plans for a followup were reportedly hobbled by technical problems. Nevertheless, up through the late '90s, Shields promised that another album was imminent. By then, though, bassist Deborah Ann Googe had joined former Stereolab keyboardist Katharine Gifford in Snowpony, which released *The Slow Motion World of Snowpony* in 1998. O'Ciosoig joind Clear Spot. And Shields occasionally appeared on records by the likes of J Mascis and Dinosaur Jr and Experimental Audio Research before finally joining Primal Scream on tour in 2000 as a result of coproducing that group's *XTRMNTR* album.

Nas

Born Nasir Ben Olu Dara Jones, ca. 1973, Brooklyn, NY
1994—*Illmatic* (Columbia) 1996—*It Was Written* 1999—*I Am . . . ; Nastradamus.*

One of the more distinctive rap artists to emerge in the mid-'90s, Nas put an emphasis on gritty, poetic storytelling. His dense, percussive mixes, which didn't preclude savvy pop moves, won him both commercial success and critical support. The son of masterful jazz cornetist and songwriter Olu Dara, with whom he has sometimes recorded, Nas was raised in the Queensbridge Houses, a massive Queens housing project that hip-hop pioneers Marley Marl and MC Shan also called home. As a child, he wrote short stories about his life in the projects and conceived his own comic books and screenplays, taking inspiration from the films of Martin Scorsese and George Lucas. He got his break as a rapper when MC Serch (formerly of the group 3rd Bass) picked his tune "Halftime" for inclusion on the soundtrack to the independent film *Zebrahead* (1992). A deal with Columbia followed, and in 1994 Nas released his debut album, *Illmatic* (#12 pop, #2 R&B, 1994). Two years later, the followup *It Was Written* (#1 pop and R&B, 1996), featuring collaborations with Dr. Dre, DJ Premier, and Havoc of Mobb Deep, premiered at the top of the charts and went double platinum. Nas charted highest with the singles "Street Dreams" (#22 pop, #18 R&B, 1996) and "Head Over Heels" (#35 pop, #17 R&B, 1997), on which he guested with Allure. In 1998 he starred in *Belly,* a gangsta-rap drama from video director Hype Williams. During 1999 he released two albums. *I Am . . .* (#1 pop and R&B, 1999) charted highest, fueled by the singles "Nas Is Like" (#86 pop, #30 R&B, 1999) and "Hate Me Now" (#62 pop, #18 R&B, 1999), a duet with Sean Combs. The latter tune featured a sample from Carl Orff's *Carmina Burana* and achieved notoriety when Combs was arrested for allegedly beating Nas' manager, Steve Stoute, over a scene in the song's video in which Combs is depicted nailed to a cross. The video was revised, Combs paid Stoute $50,000, and charges were dropped. After appearing as a guest on Missy "Misdemeanor" Elliott's "Hot Boyz" (#5 pop, #1 R&B, 1999), Nas released *Nastradamus* (#7 pop, #2 R&B, 1999).

Graham Nash: See Crosby, Stills, Nash and Young; the Hollies

Johnny Nash

Born Aug. 19, 1940, Houston, TX
1972—*I Can See Clearly Now* (Epic) 1973—*My Merry-Go-Round* 1974—*Celebrate Life* 1979—*Let's Go Dancing* 1993—*The Reggae Collection.*

Johnny Nash was one of the first performers to bring reggae to the attention of the American public, doing so with the self-penned "I Can See Clearly Now," a #1 hit in 1972. He also recorded Bob Marley's first U.S. hit song in 1973 with a cover of Marley's "Stir It Up" (#12). Though many believed him to be Jamaican, Nash actually grew up in Texas and had been recording since 1957. He began singing gospel in a Baptist church and by 13 was on the Houston TV show *Matinee,* breaking the era's local-television color bar. He sang C&W as well as pop, easy-listening soul, and calypso. In 1956 Arthur Godfrey gave him a spot on his TV show, where Nash performed for the next seven years.

Nash began his recording career in 1957 for ABC-Paramount with "A Teenager Sings the Blues." His first chart single was "A Very Special Love" (#23, 1958), which was followed by "The Teen Commandments," sung with Paul Anka and George Hamilton IV (#29, 1959). In the early '60s, he recorded unsuccessfully for Warner Bros. (1962–63), Groove, and Argo (1964). Still, his compositions did well for others: like "What Kind of Love Is This," for instance, became a Top 20 hit for Joey Dee in 1962. In the late '60s Nash began recording at Byron Lee's studio in Jamaica and went on to build his own studio there. He formed his own labels, Joda and Jad, before hitting the chart again with the reggae "Hold Me Tight," a Top 5 pop hit in 1968. Around this time he had more hits in England, including a reggae cover of Sam Cooke's "Cupid" in 1969. Nash also began to star in films, such as *Take a Giant Step,* Sweden's *Love Is Not a Game* (1974), and *Key Witness.* In 1971, while living in England, he signed to Epic, leading to his "I Can See Clearly Now" peak in 1972. After 1973's "Stir It Up" (a hit in England back in 1971), Nash had no more big American hits, though he maintained his popularity in England with covers of Little Anthony and the Imperials' "Tears on My Pillow" (#1 U.K., 1975) and Sam Cooke's "(What a) Wonderful World" (#25 U.K., 1976).

Naughty by Nature

Formed 1986, East Orange, NJ
Treach (b. Anthony Criss, Dec. 2, 1970, East Orange), voc.; Vinnie (b. Vincent Brown, Sep. 17, 1970, East Orange), voc.; Kay Gee (b. Kier Gist, Sep. 15, 1969, East Orange), DJ.
1991—*Naughty by Nature* (Tommy Boy) 1993—*19NaughtyIII* 1995—*Poverty's Paradise* 1999—*Nature's Finest; 19Naughty9: Nature's Fury* (Arista).

The rap trio Naughty by Nature came out of nowhere in summer 1991 with its massive hit "O.P.P." (#6 pop, #5 R&B), a cheating anthem for the hip-hop '90s. Ironically, the group originally had recorded the track in 1989 but was unable to find anyone interested in releasing it until NBN met rapper Queen Latifah at a party. Latifah signed the group to her Flavor Unit Management company and brought it to Tommy Boy. "O.P.P.," with its call-and-response chorus of " 'Ya down wit' O.P.P.?/Yeah, you know me!,' " sold more than 2 million copies and was nominated for a Grammy. The key to the song's success was its juxtaposition of a rough ghetto rap by Treach (short for "the treacherous MC") with the pop pep of samples from the Jackson 5's "ABC." The song also teased the censors: Treach's rap says the title stands for "Other People's Property," but the lyrics also indicate the final P means "pussy." The second single from *Naughty by Nature* (#16, 1991), "Ghetto Bastard," was retitled "Everything's Gonna Be Alright" for radio. Naughty by Nature also performed the single "Ghetto Anthem" from the *Juice* soundtrack.

The group returned to the top of the charts with *19NaughtyIII* (#3 pop, #1 R&B, 1993) and the single "Hip Hop Hooray" (#8 pop, #1 R&B, 1993). The song's video was directed by Spike Lee, and the group performed the hit in the movie *Who's the Man?* The album featured Vinnie's raps more than their debut had, but Treach's rhyming style continued to get lavish praise from critics and other rappers.

Poverty's Paradise (#3 pop, #1 R&B, 1995), another mix of head-bobbers and message raps, produced two more big singles. "Feel Me Flow" (#17 pop, #17 R&B) was built upon a sample of the Meters' "Find Yourself," "Craziest" (#51 pop, #27 R&B) upon a sample of Charles Wright's "That's All That Matters Baby." *Poverty's Paradise* won a Grammy for Best Rap Album. In 1997 NBN released "Mourn You Til I Join You" (#51 pop, #24 R&B), a tribute to the late Tupac Shakur. *19Naughty9: Nature's Fury* (#22 pop, #9 R&B, 1999) included "Jamboree," a single featuring the female R&B duo Zhane that reached the Top 10 on both the pop and R&B charts. In 1999 Treach married Sandra "Pepa" Denton of the female rap trio Salt-N-Pepa.

Nazareth

Formed 1968, Dunfermline, Scot.
Dan McCafferty (b. William McCafferty, Oct. 14, 1946, Dunfermline), voc., bagpipes; Manny Charlton, gtr.; Darrell Sweet (b. May 16, 1947, Bournemouth, Eng.; d. Apr. 30, 1999, New Albany, IN), drums; Pete Agnew (b. Sep. 14, 1946, Dunfermline), bass, voc.
1971—*Nazareth* (Warner Bros.) 1972—*Exercises* 1973—*Razamanaz* (A&M); *Loud 'n' Proud* 1974—*Rampant* 1975—*Hair of the Dog* 1976—*Close Enough for Rock 'n' Roll; Play 'n' the Game* 1977—*Hot Tracks; Expect No Mercy* 1978—(+ Zal Cleminson [b. May 4, 1949, Glasgow, Scot.], gtr.) *No Mean City* 1980—*Malice in Wonderland* (– Cleminson) 1981—*The Fool Circle* (+ Billy Rankin, gtr.; + John Locke [b. Sep. 25, 1943, Los Angeles, CA], kybds.) *S'Naz* 1982—*2XS* (– Locke) 1983—*Sound Elixir* (MCA) (– Rankin) 1988—*Classics* 1989—(– Charlton; + Rankin) 1993—*No Jive* (Griffin) 1995—(– Rankin; + Jimmy Murrison [b. Nov. 8, 1964], gtr., voc.; + Ronnie Leahy [b. Apr. 10, 1947, kybds., piano) 1999—*Boogoaloo* (CMC) (– Sweet; + Lee Agnew [b. 1971], drums, voc.).
Dan McCafferty solo: 1975—*Dan McCafferty* (A&M).

Nazareth is a hard-rocking (sometimes heavy-metal) group from Scotland whose major distinguishing feature, besides its Rod Stewart-ish lead singer, Dan McCafferty, has been its penchant for inventively arranged, pile-driving versions of quieter songs by writers like Joni Mitchell, Woody Guthrie, Tim Rose, and Bob Dylan. The members met in Dunfermline in the semipro band the Shadettes, which included McCafferty, Pete Agnew, and Darrell Sweet. When Manny Charlton joined in 1968, they changed their name to Nazareth (inspired by the first line of the Band's "The Weight") and got their first record contract in 1971. The quartet's first two LPs were generally ignored, but for 1973's *Razamanaz,* it switched to A&M and got Roger Glover (ex–Deep Purple bassist) to produce. Nazareth had its first British hits that year: "Broken Down Angel" (#9) and "Bad Bad Boy" (#10). *Loud 'n' Proud* yielded a brutal version of Joni Mitchell's "This Flight Tonight," which hit big in the U.K. and got some FM airplay in the U.S. It also included a nine-minute metallic rendition of Dylan's "The Ballad of Hollis Brown." The LP established Nazareth in Europe and Canada, where it has had many gold and platinum records.

The group's only U.S. hit was "Love Hurts" (#8, 1976), a song written by Boudleaux Bryant for the Everly Brothers that had been a hit for Jim Capaldi in England. Also that year, Nazareth reached #14 in England with "My White Bicycle," originally a psychedelia-period song from Tomorrow (a band that included future Yes guitarist Steve Howe). Vocalist McCafferty released a solo LP in 1975; meanwhile, Nazareth kept its lineup intact until 1978, when it added second guitarist Zal Cleminson, who had spent five years with the Sensational Alex Harvey Band and also played on McCafferty's solo LP. Cleminson appeared only on *No Mean City* and *Malice in Wonderland.* By 1981, the group was back to a foursome, but it expanded to a sextet the following year with the additions of former Spirit keyboardist John Locke and guitarist Billy Rankin. *Malice in Wonderland* and *Fool Circle* were produced by ex–Steely Dan and Doobie Brother Jeff Baxter. (Nazareth's previous five LPs had been produced by Charlton, taking over for Glover, who had produced *Razamanaz, Loud 'n' Proud,* and *Rampant.*)

By the mid-'80s, Nazareth was without a U.S. record label, but the band continued to issue albums regularly in Canada and Europe. In 1993, 10 years after its last American release, Nazareth brought out *No Jive.* One again the group was a foursome, but with Rankin in place of the talented Charlton, who'd left in 1990 to pursue production work. Following further lineup changes and the all-new *Booglaloo,* founding drummer Sweet suffered a fatal heart attack during a 1999 American tour. Rankin and Charlton have also recorded solo for small and import labels.

The Nazz

Formed 1967, Philadelphia, PA
Todd Rundgren (b. June 22, 1948, Upper Darby, PA), gtr., voc.; Stewkey (b. Robert Antoni, Nov. 17, 1947, Newport, RI), kybds., lead voc.; Thom Mooney (b. Jan. 5, 1948, Altoona, PA), drums; Carson G. Van Osten (b. Sep. 24, 1946, Cinnaminson, NJ), bass.
1968—*Nazz* (SGC) 1969—*Nazz Nazz* 1970—*Nazz 3.*

The Nazz, Todd Rundgren's first recording band, was a power-pop quartet from Philadelphia. Rundgren and Carson Van Osten came from Woody's Truck Stop (a Philly blues band), Thom Mooney was from the Munchkins, and Stewkey had previously been with Elizabeth—all local groups. The foursome made its live debut in July 1967, opening for the Doors at Philadelphia's Town Hall, and by the following February had a record contract. Its debut LP, *Nazz,* showcased Rundgren as the group's chief writer, though Stewkey handled lead vocals. The material, influenced by the Beatles and the early Who, included the hard-rocking "Open My Eyes" and "Hello It's Me," which later appeared on Rundgren's *Something/Anything* solo LP in 1972. The band got good press and began turning up in the teen magazines. But problems set in with its second LP, *Nazz Nazz:* There were ego conflicts (Rundgren and Mooney fought the most), and the album, originally planned as a double LP called *Fungo Bat,* was split by management into 1969's *Nazz Nazz* and 1970's *Nazz 3.* The tracks on the latter LP originally featured Rundgren's lead vocals, but these were erased and Stewkey's put on instead. Before *Nazz 3* came out, Rundgren and Van Osten quit. Stewkey and Mooney kept a version of the Nazz going until mid-1970. Mooney then left for California and later played with the Curtis Brothers and Tattoo, with ex-Raspberry Wally Bryson. He was also in Bob Welch's power trio, Paris. Van Osten became an animation artist; Rundgren became a successful producer and solo artist; Stewkey joined a band with future Cheap Trickster Rick Nielsen called Fuse, which recorded one LP for Epic. Mooney also joined Fuse for a while but left before it became Sick Man of Europe, which eventually included Tom Petersson, also later of Cheap Trick. One bootleg disc of theirs surfaced, *Retrospective Foresight,* which included, besides some originals, several Nazz outtakes from various incarnations.

The Nazz: Todd Rundgren, Thom Mooney, Stewkey, Carson G. Van Osten

Meshell Ndegéocello

Born Michelle Johnson, Aug. 29, 1968, Berlin, Ger.
1993—*Plantation Lullabies* (Maverick) 1996—*Peace Beyond Passion* 1999—*Bitter.*

In the tradition of Gil Scott-Heron and Public Enemy, Meshell Ndegéocello's music asserts and embodies black power. Add to this racial insurgency her outspokenness about her own bisexuality, and bassist/songwriter Ndegéocello was one of the most politically forthright artists of the '90s.

Ndegéocello's parents—a devout mother and saxophone-playing father—would have a direct impact on her music. Growing up in the Washington, DC, area, Ndegéocello, who at the time was still going by her birth name Michelle Johnson, exposed herself to African music, jazz, and go-go. After spending limited time in music programs at the Duke Ellington School of the Arts and Howard University, Ndegéocello became pregnant and fled to New York in fear of her parents' reaction. In 1988 she gave birth to her son, Askia, and renamed herself Meshell Ndegéocello (the surname is Swahili for "free like a bird").

Following an unsuccessful audition as bassist for Living Colour and time spent with the activist band Women in Love, Ndegéocello signed with Maverick and in 1993 released *Plantation Lullabies* (#166 pop, #35 R&B, 1994). Mostly conceived in her Harlem studio, *Plantation Lullabies* details Ndegéocello's internal and external battles with homophobia, racism, drug addiction, and ghetto life. The songs "Dred Loc" (#86 R&B, 1993) and "If That's Your Boyfriend (He Wasn't Last Night)" (#73 pop, #23 R&B, 1994), both tales of sexual experiences with men, introduced the androgynously attractive Ndegéocello as an urban philosopher with an artful message of feminism and sexual liberation.

"Wild Night," a 1994 duet with John Mellencamp, brought Ndegéocello's baritone vocals and funky bass lines to a wider audience and peaked at #3 on the pop chart. Her 1996 followup, *Peace Beyond Passion* (#63 pop, #15 R&B, 1996), brims with soulful funkiness and religious myth. From "Leviticus: Faggot," a tale about parents repudiating their homosexual son, to the spoken words of "Make Me Wanna Holler," *Peace Beyond Passion* paints a portrait of Ndegéocello as a renaissance woman—a spiritual-minded singer, poet, rapper, and multi-instrumentalist. Her third album, *Bitter* (#105 pop, #40 R&B, 1999), veers away from some of the acrid realities of her first two efforts to reveal a more delicate, solemn side.

Meshell Ndegéocello

Youssou N'Dour

Born Oct. 1, 1959, Dakar, Senegal
1986—*Nelson Mandela* (Polydor) 1987—*Inedits 84085* (Celluloid) 1988—*Immigres* (Virgin) 1989—*The Lion* 1990—*Set* 1992—*Eyes Open* (40 Acres and a Mule/Columbia) 1994—*The Guide (Wommat)* (Chaos/Columbia) 2000—*Joko* (Sony).

A "world beat" or "Afro-pop" pioneer, Youssou N'Dour began catching on with European and American audiences in the late '80s with his brand of *mbalax*—traditional Senegalese percussion-based music—that the singer combined with pop strings and jazz chord changes, funky horns, and Islamic-inflected vocals.

Born into a family of griots (storyteller/historians) and musicians, N'Dour grew up in cosmopolitan Dakar, listening to West African music, reggae, and R&B. By his mid-teens, he was already the chief vocalist for the Star Band, Senegal's top pop outfit, and he formed his own band, Etoile de Dakar, in 1979. Eventually changing their name to Le Super Etoile and becoming African superstars (N'Dour set up his own production company and opened a nightclub), the 10-piece band began performing in London and Paris in the early '80s.

Riveted by N'Dour during a 1984 concert in London, world-music enthusiast Peter Gabriel traveled to Senegal to meet him. Subsequent N'Dour appearances in 1986 on Gabriel's *So*, Paul Simon's *Graceland*, and on a Gabriel world tour drew notice from Western record companies; 1986's *Nelson Mandela* introduced N'Dour to worldwide audiences. Appearing in 1988 as part of Amnesty International's Human Rights Now! Tour alongside Sting and Bruce Springsteen increased his exposure; he also recorded with Harry Belafonte and Ryuichi Sakamoto.

To critics who have accused N'Dour, or at least his record companies, of diluting the distinctively Senegalese energy of his music on *The Lion*, *Set*, and, to a lesser degree, *Eyes Open*, N'Dour replies that he no longer considers himself exclusively an African artist. Indeed, his 1994 LP, *The Guide*, featured Branford Marsalis and Neneh Cherry as guests and sold more than 1 million copies internationally. N'Dour's duet with Cherry, "7 Seconds," also became a major European hit. But then, seemingly on the verge of attaining global reach akin to that of Bob Marley, N'Dour surprised pundits and retreated to Dakar.

There, using Gabriel's Real World complex in England as his model, N'Dour began building up his entertainment empire. Most notably, he formed his own record label and started releasing roots-oriented music (his own recordings and those of other artists) to African audiences. N'Dour didn't resurface in international circles until he and Axelle Red performed his "La Cour Des Grands" at the 1998 soccer World Cup. In 2000 N'Dour released *Joko,* his first album geared toward the global market in six years. An expansive collection that ranges from reggae to rap, the record includes collaborations with Sting, Gabriel, and former Fugees mainstay Wyclef Jean.

Fred Neil

Born 1937, St. Petersburg, FL; died July 7, 2001, Summerland Key, FL
1964—*Hootenanny Live at the Bitter End* (FM); *World of Folk Music; Tear Down the Walls* 1966—*Fred Neil* (Capitol) 1967—*Bleecker and Macdougal* (Elektra) 1969—*Everybody's Talkin'* (Capitol) 1970—*Little Bit of Rain* (Elektra); *The Other Side of This Life* (Capitol) 1971—*Sessions* 1999—*The Many Sides of Fred Neil* (Collectors' Choice).

Although songwriter Fred Neil did not record a new album or tour for 30 years prior to his death, and even at the peak of his career, he kept a low profile, his honey-laden baritone, 12-string guitar playing, and introspective songwriting (particularly his "Everybody's Talkin' ") made him a cult figure among folk-rock aficionados.

While still in his teens, Neil performed at the Grand Ole Opry. In the late '50s, he moved to New York, and Buddy Holly recorded a number of his tunes, including "Come Back Baby." The flipside to Roy Orbison's hit "Cry" was a cover of Neil's "Candy Man" (#25, 1961). Neil became part of the Greenwich Village folk scene, where his songwriting and his mastery of 12-string guitar made him a leading figure. His earliest recordings featured backing by John Sebastian and Felix Pappalardi, but none of his albums sold well. He spent long hours in the studio rerecording tracks with legendary producer Nik Venet. (*Other Side of This Life* features Gram Parsons on a track.) Neil's biggest hit, and the song for which he is best known, is Harry Nilsson's cover of his "Everybody's Talkin' "(#6, 1969), from the *Midnight Cowboy* soundtrack.

After moving to Coconut Grove, Florida, Neil, who had developed a heroin problem, became a recluse. On Earth Day 1970, Neil established the Dolphin Project with partner Richard O'Barry. The few performances he gave over the years since were local benefit concerts for the Coconut Grove–based organization.

For such an obscure figure, Neil's impact on other singer/songwriters has been widespread: His songs have been covered by the Lovin' Spoonful, José Feliciano, It's a Beautiful Day, the Youngbloods, Eric Burdon and the Animals, Dion, Stevie Wonder, Johnny Mathis, Neil Diamond, Richie Havens, and Linda Ronstadt, among many others. Billy Bragg's version of Neil's "The Dolphin Song" (earlier recorded by Tim Buckley), was a U.K. hit in 1992. He was found dead at his Florida home in 2001.

Vince Neil: See Mötley Crüe

Rick Nelson

Born Eric Hilliard Nelson, May 8, 1940, Teaneck, NJ; died Dec. 31, 1985, DeKalb, TX
1957—*Ricky* (Imperial) 1958—*Ricky Nelson* 1959—*Ricky Sings Again; Songs by Ricky* 1960—*More Songs by Ricky* 1961—*Ricky Is 21* 1962—*Album Seven by Rick* 1963—*Best Sellers by Ricky Nelson; For Your Sweet Love* (Decca) 1964—*Rick Nelson Sings "For You"* 1966—*Bright Lights & Country Music* 1967—*Country Fever* 1968—*Another Side of Rick* 1969—*Perspective* 1970—*Rick Nelson in Concert; Rick Sings Nelson* 1971—*Rudy the Fifth* 1972—*Garden Party* 1974—*Windfall* (MCA) 1977—*Intakes* (Epic) 1981—*Playing to Win* (Capitol) 1986—*Memphis Sessions* (Epic) 1990—*Ricky Nelson, vol. 1: The Legendary Masters Series* (EMI) 1991—*The Best of Rick Nelson, vol. 2* 1993—*Stay Young: The Epic Recordings* (Epic) 1995—*1969–1976* (Edsel) 1996—*Rockin' With Ricky* (Ace) 1999—*25 Greatest Hits* (EMI); *Anthology* (BGO) 2000—*The Best of Ricky Nelson* (Castle); *Legacy* (Capitol).

When singer Rick Nelson was posthumously inducted into the Rock and Roll Hall of Fame in 1987, ROLLING STONE publisher and Hall of Fame cofounder Jann Wenner noted "the critical myopia that dogged [Nelson's] career." Indeed, Rick, or Ricky, as he was known early on, launched his career from a position of privilege: his family's popular weekly television series, *The Adventures of Ozzie and Harriet.* Nelson was wealthy, handsome, a household name, and an American teen idol long before he ever cut a record. In nearly every regard, he would seem the antithesis of the early rockers who made the music he first loved and recorded, rockabilly, and far removed from the late-'60s environment that nurtured early country rock, of which he was at the vanguard. And yet musicians as diverse as Eric Andersen and John Fogerty, and even some of his own heroes, including Carl Perkins and Scotty Moore, admired and respected Nelson.

Nelson's father was a famous bandleader and his mother a singer and actress who had been famous since the early '30s. In 1949, Rick and his older brother David began playing themselves on their parents' popular radio comedy series, *The Adventures of Ozzie and Harriet,* which went to TV three years later. From his first appearance, the impish, wisecracking Rick became the program's most popular character. His trademark line, "I don't mess around, boy," became a national catchphrase with prepubescent viewers. Not surprisingly, when Ricky began singing on the show in 1957, he had a massive audience. According to Nelson, he had no musical ambitions until a girlfriend said she was in love with Elvis Presley. He retorted that he too was cutting a record—which in reality he had no plans to do—and then did.

His first hit was a cover of Fats Domino's "I'm Walkin' "; it went to #4 in 1959 and sold a million records after Nelson performed it on TV. The flip side, "A Teenager's Romance," hit #2. Between then and 1961, Nelson had more than two dozen pop hits, several of them double-sided, including the rockabilly "Be-Bop Baby" (#3, 1957), "Stood Up" (#2, 1958) b/w "Waitin' in School" (#18, 1958), "Believe What You Say"

Rick Nelson

(#4, 1958) b/w "My Bucket's Got a Hole in It" (#12, 1958), "Lonesome Town" (#7, 1958) b/w "I Got a Feeling" (#10, 1958), "It's Late" (#9, 1959) b/w "Never Be Anyone Else but You" (#6, 1959), "Just a Little Too Much" (#9, 1959). He also hit with ballads, such as "Poor Little Fool" (#1, 1958), Baker Knight's "Lonesome Town," "Sweeter Than You" (#9, 1959), and "Travelin' Man" (#1, 1961) and its B side, the Gene Pitney–penned "Hello Mary Lou" (#9, 1961). Some of Nelson's early hits, including "Waitin'," "Believe What You Say," and "It's Late," were penned by Dorsey and/or Johnny Burnette [see entries]. For seven years, Nelson's backup band featured James Burton, who later became Presley's lead guitarist.

In 1962, Nelson had three more Top 10 hits ("Young World," the autobiographical "Teenage Idol," and "It's Up to You"), and another in 1964, "For You." By then he had married Kris Harmon, another product of a show-business family, and become the father of the first of his four children, daughter Tracy. Twins Matthew and Gunnar [see entry on Nelson] and a third son, Sam, followed shortly. As of 1964, Nelson's hit-making days were behind him, and after the family's show was canceled in 1966, he found himself at loose ends. Late that year he appeared, costarring with Joanie Summers (of "Johnny Get Angry" fame), in a little-seen, sophisticated rock satire entitled *On the Flip Side.* Nelson's fame also brought him numerous film offers, but unlike many other teen idols, from the beginning he eschewed the typical teen fare for more acclaimed parts such as his role in Howard Hawks' classic *Rio Bravo* (1959), which costarred John Wayne and Dean Martin, and *The Wackiest Ship in the Army* (1960), with Jack Lemmon.

Nelson continued to record (he'd signed a 20-year contract in 1963) but, as he later admitted, without enthusiasm until he began recording in a style that would soon become known as country rock. On *Bright Lights & Country Music* and *Country Fever,* Nelson covered material by Doug Kershaw, Willie Nelson, Hank Williams, and Bob Dylan, as well as contributed his own "Alone." Hanging out at the L.A. country-rock bastion the Troubadour, Nelson recruited ex-Poco bassist Randy Meisner and began forming the Stone Canyon Band, which at various times would also include Dennis Larden of Every Mother's Son; Richie Hayward, briefly on leave from Little Feat; Tom Brumley of Buck Owens' Buckaroos; Steve Love, later with Roger McGuinn and the New Riders of the Purple Sage; and Steve Duncan, later of the Desert Rose Band. With this group, he scored a minor commercial comeback with a cover of Dylan's "She Belongs to Me" (#33, 1969). A double live album recorded at the Troubadour in 1970, *Rick Nelson in Concert,* marked a crucial turning point for Nelson. With songs by Dylan, Tim Hardin, and Eric Andersen (who supplied the liner notes), it put to rest the charge that he was a talentless teen idol and garnered unanimous rave reviews.

His next success rose out of failure. In October 1971, when Nelson and his band appeared at a rock & roll revival at New York's Madison Square Garden, the audience booed his long-hair look and new material, particularly a version of the Rolling Stones' "Honky Tonk Women." Just a few months later, however, on a tour of England (his first, despite having had 19 Top 40 hits there), fans, including Elton John and Cliff Richard, turned out in droves and, more important to Nelson, fully accepted his new direction. Out of these experiences, he wrote his last million-seller (his first in over a decade) and his personal anthem, "Garden Party." It hit #6, went gold in 1972, and pushed the album of the same name to #32 (Nelson's best album-chart showing since 1964).

Followup albums didn't catch on, and by the mid-'70s, Nelson had lost his MCA contract. He released an album on Epic in 1977, then moved to Capitol for *Playin' to Win.* For a while, it was rumored that another fan, Paul McCartney, planned to produce Nelson, but nothing came of it. Partially because he so loved performing and partially due to an expensive and protracted divorce from his wife, Nelson found himself on the road an average of 250 nights a year through the late '70s and early '80s. When he sang in "Garden Party" "If memories are all I'd sing / I'd rather drive a truck," he meant it, even turning down a long-term million-dollar-plus offer (arranged by Elvis Presley's manager, Colonel Tom Parker) to play Las Vegas at a point when he was deeply in debt. In September 1984 he was invited, along with John Fogerty, the Judds, and Dave Edmunds, among others, to join in the finale of a Sun Records reunion album that featured Nelson's early idols Johnny Cash, Roy Orbison, Carl Perkins, and Jerry Lee Lewis. (The album documenting the event, *Interviews From "The Class of '55" Recording Sessions,* won a Grammy in 1986 for Best Spoken Word or Nonmusical Recording; it was Nelson's only Grammy.)

By 1985, Nelson had assembled a new, young band: bassist Pat Woodward, drummer Ricky Intveld, keyboardist Andy Chapin (who'd worked with Steppenwolf and the Association), and lead guitarist Bobby Neal, whom Nelson had met on an earlier recording date in Memphis. (The resulting

Memphis Sessions, a collection of rockabilly covers, was released posthumously.) That August, a live documentary of Nelson was taped during a tour on which he opened for Fats Domino and was backed by the Jordanaires. He signed a new deal with Curb/MCA and, on December 26, completed recording Buddy Holly's "True Love Ways" for his upcoming album. He closed his last performance four days later with Holly's "Rave On."

On December 31, 1985, en route to a New Year's Eve show in Dallas, Texas, Nelson's DC-3 (which had previously been owned by Jerry Lee Lewis) caught on fire and crashed in a field near DeKalb, Texas. Early press reports erroneously suggested that drug use, namely freebasing cocaine, might have played a role in the crash that killed Rick, his band, and his fiancée, Helen Blair (the pilot and copilot survived). In fact, the National Transportation Safety Board's 1987 report determined that the fire began in a malfunctioning gas heater. Nelson was buried in L.A.'s Forest Lawn Cemetery.

In the years immediately following Rick Nelson's death, many other artists paid tribute to him: Bob Dylan included "Lonesome Town" in his 1986 concerts, and newer artists, including Jimmie Dale Gilmore, Dwight Yoakam, and Chris Isaak, have cited his influence. Sons Matthew and Gunnar, now known professionally as Nelson, regularly perform their father's hits, particularly "Garden Party" and "Lonesome Town," in concert. The enduring appeal of "America's favorite family" made A&E's *Biography* broadcast of *Ozzie & Harriet: The Adventures of America's Favorite Family* one of the series' highest-rated programs ever.

Sandy Nelson

Born Sander L. Nelson, Dec. 1, 1938, Santa Monica, CA
1961—*Let There Be Drums* (Imperial) 1962—*Drums Are My Beat!; Golden Hits.*

Sandy Nelson scored several hits in the late '50s and early '60s with his rocking guitar-and-drum-based instrumentals, most notably 1959's "Teen Beat" (#4). Nelson was friends with Jan and Dean, Nancy Sinatra, and Phil Spector when they were all in high school. His first band was Kip Tyler and the Flips, which at one point included future Beach Boy Bruce Johnston on piano. That band recorded for Ebb and Challenge records. Nelson later played on the Teddy Bears' gold "To Know Him Is to Love Him" (he also toured with them) and also drummed on Gene Vincent's 1959 *Crazy Times* LP before recording "Teen Beat" for the small Original Sound label. The song went gold, and Nelson was quickly signed by Imperial Records. His second hit, however, didn't come until 1961, with "Let There Be Drums" (#7).

Just before he cut that record, Nelson lost his left foot in a car accident—but it didn't affect his drumming. He later hit with "Drums Are My Beat" (#29, 1962) and a "Teen Beat" update inventively titled "Teen Beat '65" (#44, 1964). He continued to record, with only minor success, through the mid-'70s.

Tracy Nelson

Born Dec. 27, 1944, Madison, WI
1965—*Deep Are the Roots* (Prestige) 1968—*Living With the Animals* (Mercury) 1969—*Make a Joyful Noise; Mother Earth Presents Tracy Nelson Country* 1970—*Satisfied* 1971—*Bring Me Home* (Reprise) 1973—*A Poor Man's Paradise* (Columbia) 1974—*Tracy Nelson* (Atlantic) 1975—*Sweet Soul Music* (MCA) 1976—*Time Is on My Side* 1978—*Homemade Songs* (Flying Fish) 1980—*Doin' It My Way* (Adelphi) 1993—*In the Here and Now* (Rounder) 1995—*I Feel So Good* 1996—*Move On* 2001—*Ebony & Irony* (Eclectic/CMD).
With Marcia Ball and Irma Thomas: 1998—*Sing It!* (Rounder).

Tracy Nelson was long considered one of the strongest female singers in rock—especially during her time with Mother Earth during the late '60s, when she was sometimes compared to Janis Joplin. But she soon edged away from Mother Earth's R&B gospel and began stressing country when the band moved to Nashville. One of her songs, "Down So Low," has been covered by Linda Ronstadt and many other singers.

Growing up in Wisconsin, Nelson began playing piano at age five, guitar at 13. She also sang in the church choir. She played coffeehouses while attending the University of Wisconsin and also during that period formed her first band, the Fabulous Imitations, which was followed by the White Trash Blues Band, which lasted two weeks. She recorded her first solo LP around this time, too, the blues-influenced *Deep Are the Roots* on Prestige, with harmonica player Charlie Musselwhite and other Chicago blues musicians backing her. In 1966 Nelson moved to San Francisco, and in July of that year she formed Mother Earth (named after a Memphis Slim blues song). Its critically respected debut, *Living With the Animals,* included backup by Elvin Bishop and Mark Naftalin of the Paul Butterfield Blues Band. In 1969 the group moved to a farm outside Nashville, and its music became increasingly country oriented (as evidenced on *Mother Earth Presents Tracy Nelson Country*). After *Bring Me Home,* the band went through many personnel changes; the only member to stick with Nelson through them was guitarist John "Toad" Andrews. In 1973 the band (by now billed as Tracy Nelson/Mother Earth) released *A Poor Man's Paradise,* and in 1974 Nelson recorded her self-titled solo Atlantic debut. The album included a duet with Willie Nelson, "After the Fire Is Gone," which was nominated for a Grammy. In 1975 she signed with MCA, and in the late '70s she recorded albums for the independent Flying Fish and Adelphi labels. *Homemade Songs* included a duet with Carlene Carter. Comfortable playing Nashville clubs, Nelson vanished from the recording scene for over a decade before reemerging with 1993's critically acclaimed *In the Here and Now,* recorded in Nashville with such guest artists as Musselwhite and New Orleans R&B singer Irma Thomas, to whom she had dedicated her 1976 album *Time Is on My Side.* The '90s saw Nelson return to blues and R&B, a move culminating in 1998's *Sing It!,* a collaboration with Thomas and pianist Marcia Ball.

Willie Nelson

Born Apr. 30, 1933, Abbott, TX
1962—*. . . And Then I Wrote* (Liberty) 1963—*Here's Willie Nelson* 1967—*Make Way for . . .* (RCA); *The Party's Over* 1968—*Texas in My Soul; Good Times* 1971—*Willie Nelson and Family; Yesterday's Wine* 1972—*The Willie Way* 1974—*Phases and Stages* (Atlantic) 1975—*What Can You Do to Me* (RCA); *Red Headed Stranger* (Columbia) 1976—*The Sound in Your Mind; Troublemaker; Wanted! The Outlaws* (with Waylon Jennings, Tompall Glaser, Jessi Colter) (RCA); *Live* 1977—*To Lefty From Willie* (Columbia) 1978—*Waylon and Willie* (with Waylon Jennings) (RCA); *Stardust* (Columbia) 1979—*Willie and Family Live; Pretty Paper; . . . Sings Kristofferson; Sweet Memories* (RCA); *One for the Road* (with Leon Russell) (Columbia) 1980—*San Antonio Rose* (with Ray Price); *Honeysuckle Rose* soundtrack 1981—*Somewhere Over the Rainbow; Willie Nelson's Greatest Hits and Some That Will Be* 1982—*Always on My Mind; Pancho and Lefty* (with Merle Haggard); *Waylon and Willie: WWII* (with Waylon Jennings); *In the Jailhouse Now* (with Webb Pierce) 1983—*Tougher Than Leather; Without a Song* 1984—*City of New Orleans; Angel Eyes; Music From Songwriter* (with Kris Kristofferson); *Funny How Time Slips Away* (with Faron Young) 1985—*Half Nelson; Me and Paul; Brand on My Heart* (with Hank Snow) 1986—*Partners; The Promiseland* |1987—*Island in the Sea* 1988—*What a Wonderful World; All-Time Greatest Hits, vol. 1* (RCA) 1989—*A Horse Called Music* (Columbia) 1990—*Nite Life: Greatest Hits and Rare Tracks 1959–71* (Rhino); *Born for Trouble* (Columbia) 1991—*Who Will Buy My Memories?* (Sony Music Special Products); *Clean Shirt* (with Waylon Jennings) (Epic) 1993—*Across the Borderline* (Columbia) 1994—*Moonlight Becomes You* (Justice) 1995—*Healing Hands of Time* (Liberty); *Willie Nelson: A Classic and Unreleased Collection* (Rhino) 1996—*Spirit* (Island) 1998—*Teatro* 1999—*Night and Day* (Free Falls) 2000—*Me and the Drummer* (with the Offenders) (Luck); *Milk Cow Blues* (Island); *Willie Nelson Live at the Grapevine Opry* (Great Music).
With the Highwaymen (Johnny Cash, Waylon Jennings, and Kris Kristofferson): 1985—*Highwayman* (Columbia) 1990—*Highwayman II* 1995—*The Road Goes On Forever* (Capitol) 1999—*Highwaymen Super Hits* (Sony).

One of country & western's most popular, prolific, and distinctive singer/songwriters, Willie Nelson started out as a songwriter without much of a solo singing career and eventually became a star singer mostly covering pop and C&W standards. His dry, wry voice and plaintive, understated delivery helped him transcend country to reach wider pop audiences. In the '70s he spearheaded "outlaw" country—the non-Nashville alliance between "redneck" country musicians and "hippie" rock musicians—and helped establish Austin, Texas, as a country-rock capital. His grizzled face brought him film roles in *Electric Horseman, Honeysuckle Rose, Barbarossa,* and 1984's *Songwriter,* in which he costarred with Kris Kristofferson (who, a year later, would join Nelson, Johnny Cash, and Waylon Jennings on the first Highwaymen project). His problems with the Internal Revenue Service, as well as his leisure-time marijuana use, made Nelson an "outlaw" for real—and a counterculture style hero to many, long after the counterculture had gone back underground.

Nelson was raised by his grandparents and worked cotton fields until he was 10, when he began playing guitar in local German and Czech polka bands. He joined the air force, after which he attended Baylor University in Waco, Texas. Before dropping out, he sold Bibles and encyclopedias door-to-door, worked as a disc jockey and musician, and taught Sunday school. While teaching Sunday school in Fort Worth, Nelson was also playing honky-tonk clubs on Saturday nights; when his parishioners demanded he choose between the church and music, he chose the latter. He played bars around the country, taught guitar, and wrote songs.

With the $50 he earned from his first published song, "Family Bible," Nelson went to Nashville, where songwriter Hank Cochran got him a publishing contract. Nelson wrote pop and C&W hits for many artists: "Night Life" for Rusty Draper, "Funny How Time Slips Away" for Jimmy Elledge and Johnny Tillotson, "Crazy" for Patsy Cline, "Hello Walls" for Faron Young, "Wake Me When It's Over" for Andy Williams, and "Pretty Paper" for Roy Orbison. Eventually, he had a recording contract of his own, but his weathered tenor and his taste for sparse backup were considered uncommercial.

When his Nashville home burned down around 1970, Nelson moved back to Texas, continuing to record, write, and perform. In 1972 he held his first annual Fourth of July picnic with young and old rock and country musicians in Dripping Springs, Texas—an event that would soon become a local institution. The Fourth of July was named Willie Nelson Day by the Texas Senate in 1975. In Austin, Nelson also began to clarify his own ideas on country music, simultaneously reclaiming traditions of honky-tonk, Western swing, and early country music and giving the songs a starker, more modern

Willie Nelson

outlook. *Phases and Stages,* a concept album produced by Arif Mardin, introduced Nelson's mature style, and 1975's *Red Headed Stranger,* a "country opera," made his music a commercial success. With a hit remake of Fred Rose's "Blue Eyes Crying in the Rain" (originally recorded by Roy Acuff in the '40s), the album went gold. In 1975 Nelson shared the *Outlaws* compilation LP with Waylon Jennings, Tompall Glaser, and Jessi Colter, three other country musicians ignored by the Nashville establishment; it was the first platinum country LP.

Nelson and his band, which included his older sister Bobbie on piano, toured constantly through the '70s and were a major concert attraction through the South and West before the rest of the country caught on. But by the end of the decade, Nelson was an established star. *Willie and Family Live* (1978) went double platinum.

Meanwhile, Nelson's songwriting tapered off; he did an album-length tribute to Kris Kristofferson and made duet albums with George Jones, Merle Haggard, and Ray Price. The 4 million–seller *Stardust,* produced by Memphis veteran Booker T. Jones, was an album of old pop standards. For *Honeysuckle Rose,* Nelson wrote one new song, "On the Road Again," that became a #1 country single and a #20 pop hit. In the '80s Nelson had multiplatinum albums with *Always on My Mind* and *Greatest Hits* while maintaining his prolific output of music and films. The first Highwaymen collaboration with Kristofferson, Jennings, and Johnny Cash (#35, 1985) went gold—as did the 1985 *Half Nelson,* though it reached only #178 on the pop albums chart. In 1984 Nelson dueted with Julio Iglesias on the #5 pop hit "To All the Girls I've Loved Before"; in 1985 he helped launch the first Farm Aid concert for America's embattled family farmers. Along with Neil Young and John Mellencamp, he has helped organize each succeeding Farm Aid benefit show.

Since the early '70s, even while performing in Las Vegas (as he did in the late '70s), Nelson has sported his standard attire: long hair and beard, headband, jeans, T-shirt, and running shoes. The latter four items were nearly the only possessions he had left after the IRS investigated him and in 1990 slapped him with a $16.7 million bill. Nelson was forced to auction off almost all of his possessions in 1991 (most of them reportedly bought by friends who vowed to return them to Nelson once he regained financial stability). To help raise desperately needed capital, Nelson sold *Who'll Buy My Memories?* (subtitled *The IRS Tapes*) direct through an 800 telephone number. Nelson and the IRS eventually agreed to a $9 million settlement, and the singer sued the accounting firm of Price Waterhouse, claiming it had mismanaged his finances. More money came in through Nelson's appearances in TV and radio ads for Taco Bell.

In 1993 Nelson recorded the acclaimed *Across the Borderline,* on which such in-demand rock pros as producer Don Was (who'd recently rescued Bonnie Raitt and the B-52's from commercial oblivion) and mixer Bob Clearmountain recorded Nelson duetting with Bonnie Raitt, Sinéad O'Connor, and Bob Dylan, on tunes by Dylan, Paul Simon, Peter Gabriel, John Hiatt, and Lyle Lovett. Nelson followed that up with *Moonlight Becomes You,* a *Stardust*-style album of old pop standards that began with a "hidden" track in which Nelson told listeners that the album was on independent Justice Records because no major label would gamble on releasing such a record. Be that as it may, Nelson moved to Liberty for his next recording, 1995's *Healing Hands of Time,* another set of pop standards. The following year, he became the first country performer to sign with Island Records, and he released the self-penned, self-produced *Spirit;* he followed that with the critically acclaimed *Teatro* (#104, 1998), a collaboration with producer Daniel Lanois. Eclectic as always, Nelson then released a jazzy collection of instrumentals (1999's *Night and Day*) before seguing into his first blues record (2000's *Milk Cow Blues*), on which he revisited some of his older songs. His long-delayed reggae album, on which he has been working on and off since 1996 with producer Don Was, is now scheduled for a 2001 release. Nelson was inducted in the Country Music Hall of Fame in 1993.

Nelson

Formed 1988, Los Angeles, CA
Matthew Nelson (b. Matthew Gray Nelson, Sep. 20, 1967, Los Angeles), voc., bass; Gunnar Nelson (b. Gunnar Eric Nelson, Sep. 20, 1967, Los Angeles), voc., gtr.; Brett Garsed (b. Apr. 20, 1963, Victoria, Austral.), lead gtr.; Joey Cathcart (b. June 29, 1967, San Fernando Valley, CA), rhythm gtr.; Paul Mirkovich (b. Mar. 20, 1963, Studio City, CA), kybds.; Bobby Rock (b. July 13, 1963, Houston, TX), drums.
1990—*After the Rain* (DGC/Geffen) 1995—*Because They Can* 1998—*Imaginator* (Varèse).

Identical twin sons of the late rock star Rick Nelson, Gunnar and Matthew Nelson were among a string of successful second-generation rock acts to emerge in the late '80s (e.g., Julian Lennon, Ziggy Marley, and Wilson Phillips). The Nelson twins, though, are the only ones whose family's show-business legacy spans four generations. With their waist-length blond hair and videogenic good looks, Gunnar and Matthew were pop-star naturals, and Nelson's melodic, neo-'70s AOR-rock—echoing Boston, Foreigner, and Heart—found a wide audience.

Gunnar and Matthew grew up in a typical latter-day Hollywood home, a far cry from the '50s idyll that their paternal grandparents Ozzie and Harriet Nelson depicted on their long-running TV series *The Adventures of Ozzie and Harriet.* In fact, father Rick, Ozzie and Harriet's boy, was often on tour, while his wife, Kris Harmon (sister of actor Mark Harmon and actress Kelly Harmon), became an alcoholic and later a drug abuser. After their parents separated bitterly in 1977 amid mutual charges of infidelity and substance abuse, the twins stayed first with their mother, then—on their 18th birthday in 1985—moved in with Rick, who'd whetted their musical appetites by taking them backstage, on tour, and to recording studios when he could. Three months later, on New Year's Eve, 1985, Rick was killed in a plane crash en route to a concert. Gunnar and Matthew had planned to accompany their

London M25, the circular highway on which ravers traveled to their late-night destinations. In the early to mid-'90s, the two revolutionized the mainstream perception of dance music by releasing full-length cohesive albums (instead of a string of singles) and by re-creating their music live rather than performing prerecorded songs.

The Hartnolls grew up in West Kent, a rural suburb of London. There they spent their youth listening to punk, electropop, and their father's film soundtracks. Electropop in particular inspired them to buy a drum machine and, later, some synthesizers; by 1988, Paul had recorded two electro pieces, which he sold to British label Ffrr. Their first collaborative effort as Orbital, "Chime," appeared the next year. With its undeniable beat and exuberant, chiming synth notes, the single went to #17 in the U.K. in 1990 and is still regarded as a classic dance track. It also secured the brothers a slot on the British TV show *Top of the Pops,* during which they played their single while wearing T-shirts emblazoned with anti–poll tax slogans. A live version of "Chime" (#73 U.K., 1991) reappeared on Orbital's untitled full-length debut, widely referred to as the Green Album in reference to its jacket color. Essentially a collection of unrelated songs, the release was a less comprehensive effort than its followup, the similarly untitled Brown Album. As the record, also known as *Orbital 2,* went to #28 in the U.K., the brothers played 1994's rock-centric Woodstock 2 and the second stage of England's equally rock-oriented Glastonbury Festival. Their Glastonbury performance was so successful that the Hartnolls were asked to play the festival's main stage the following year.

While Orbital's first full-lengths were rooted in acid house, 1994's *Snivilisation* was a darker, more challenging effort that debuted in the U.K. at #4. The album had a political slant as well, attacking the country's antirave Criminal Justice Bill. Also containing its share of political platforms (this time advocating energy conservation), 1996's *In Sides* debuted at #5 in the U.K., while its 28-minute single "The Box" went to #11. Its successor, 1999's *The Middle of Nowhere,* was slighted by critics but went Top 5 in the U.K. and was the first Orbital album to crack the Top 200 in the States. Orbital's next projects included recording the "Beached" single with Angelo Badalamenti (#36 U.K., 2000) and remixing techno godfathers Kraftwerk in 2000.

Orchestral Manoeuvres in the Dark/OMD

Formed 1978, London, Eng.
Andy McCluskey (b. June 24, 1959, Heswall, Eng.), synth., kybds., electronics, voc.; Paul Humphreys (b. Feb. 27, 1960, London), synth., kybds., electronics, voc.; David Hughes, bass, kybds.; Malcolm Holmes, drums.
1980—*Orchestral Manoeuvres in the Dark* (Dindisc/Virgin); *Organisation* (– Hughes; + Martin Cooper, kybds., sax) 1981—*Architecture and Morality* (Virgin/Epic) 1983—*Dazzle Ships* 1984—*Junk Culture* (Virgin/A&M) (+ Neil Weir, horns; + Graham Weir, horns) 1985—*Crush* 1986—*The Pacific Age* (– N. Weir; – G. Weir) 1988—*In the Dark/The Best of OMD* 1989—(group disbands) 1991—(group re-forms: McCluskey, synth., bass, voc.) *Sugar Tax* (Virgin) (+ Nigel Ipinson [b. 1970, Eng.], kybds.; + Phil Coxon [b. 1959, Eng.], kybds.; + Stuart Kershaw, drums) 1993—*Liberator* 1996—*Universal.*

One of England's longest-running and poppiest postpunk electropop bands, Orchestral Manoeuvres in the Dark was originally formed by Paul Humphreys and Andy McCluskey, two Kraftwerk fans who had first had a duo called VCL XI in 1976, then joined such little-known larger groups as Hitlers Underpantz and the Id. In 1978 they adopted the name Orchestral Manoeuvres in the Dark, recording and performing with 4-track tapes they made and played back on a tape deck they called "Winston."

In June 1979, the trendy Manchester label Factory released the duo's debut single, "Electricity," a classic piece of hooky, percolating synth pop. It was a Top 40 British hit and got significant play in American new-wave clubs. Humphreys and McCluskey soon replaced their rhythm-box percussion with a live rhythm section (drummer Malcolm Holmes had been in the Id). The 1980 single "Enola Gay" (named for the plane that dropped the first atomic bomb on Japan), with a somewhat richer sound and more romantic feel than "Electricity," was a Top 10 British hit and got more play on America's burgeoning new-wave club and radio circuit.

The critically acclaimed *Architecture and Morality* barely charted in the U.S. (#144, 1982), and *Dazzle Ships* and *Junk Culture* were critically derided as overly indulgent, but OMD made a comeback with *Crush* (#38, 1985), which added the Weir brothers' horn section and yielded the group's first U.S. hit singles, "So in Love" (#26, 1985) and "Secret" (#63, 1985). OMD scored its biggest hit with "If You Leave" (#4, 1986), from the teen-romance movie *Pretty in Pink. The Pacific Age* (#47, 1986) yielded a hit single in "(Forever) Live and Die" (#19, 1986), and the best-of *In the Dark* (#46, 1988) produced a hit in the new track "Dreaming" (#16, 1988). The band then broke up, with Humphreys leaving McCluskey to form Listening Pool. McCluskey restarted OMD in 1991 and recorded *Sugar Tax,* which failed to chart—though it sold 2 million copies worldwide—followed by the less successful *Liberator.* A subsequent album, *Universal,* was released in 1996.

The Orioles

Formed 1946, Baltimore, MD
Sonny Til (b. Earlington Tilghman, Aug. 18, 1925; d. Dec. 9, 1981), lead voc.; George Nelson (d. ca. 1959), lead and baritone voc.; Alexander Sharp (d. ca. 1970s), tenor voc.; Johnny Reed, bass voc.; Tommy Gaither (d. 1950), gtr.
1950—(– Gaither; + Ralph Williams, gtr., baritone voc.) 1953—(– Nelson; + Gregory Carol; + Charlie Hayes)

N.A.—*Greatest Hits* (Collectable) 1981—*Sonny Til and the Orioles Visit Manhattan Circa 1950s* (Collectables).

The Orioles are cited by many rock historians as the first rhythm & blues vocal group and a harbinger of the '50s doo-wop sound. As teens, they were known as the Vibranaires. A local saleslady/songwriter, Deborah Chessler, managed the group and landed them a spot on Arthur Godfrey's *Talent Scouts* television program in 1948. They lost, but became regulars on Godfrey's national broadcast.

The group joined Natural Records in 1948, and then changed its name to the Orioles. Contrary to popular misconception, the group did not name itself for the baseball team. The Orioles made the R&B chart with several singles, including "It's Too Soon to Know" (#13 pop, #1 R&B, 1948)—the first stylistically black, or, to use the industry term of the time, "race," record to place that high on the pop chart. Their later hits include "Lonely Christmas" (#8 R&B, 1949) and "Tell Me So" (#1 R&B, 1949). The latter is considered most significant because it used "a wordless falsetto doing a kind of obbligato to the lead vocal," according to critic/disc jockey Barry Hansen. This technique would later be a staple of doo-wop vocals. Other R&B hits followed: "A Kiss and a Rose" (#12 R&B, 1949), "Forgive and Forget" (#5 R&B, 1949), and "What Are You Doing New Year's Eve" (#9 R&B, 1949). In 1950 Gaither was killed in an automobile accident that seriously injured Nelson and Reed. "Pal of Mine" is a tribute to Gaither.

Nelson quit, and two new members made the group a quintet. This lineup recorded "Crying in the Chapel" (#11 pop, #1 R&B, 1953), which was one of the first R&B songs to cross over to the pop market and a #3 hit for Elvis Presley in 1965. Its followup, "In the Mission of St. Augustine," was the Orioles' last hit. The original Orioles disbanded in 1954, though over the years various groups have performed and recorded under the name. The year Sonny Til died, 1981, saw the release of *Sonny Til and the Orioles Visit Manhattan Circa 1950s,* which contained new versions of doo-wop oldies. By then only Reed and Williams of the original lineup were still alive. The group was inducted into the Rock and Roll Hall of Fame in 1995.

Tony Orlando and Dawn

Formed 1970, New York, NY
Tony Orlando (b. Michael Anthony Orlando Cassavitis, Apr. 3, 1944, New York), voc.; Telma Louise Hopkins (b. Oct. 28, 1948, Louisville, KY), voc.; Joyce Elaine Vincent-Wilson (b. Dec. 14, 1946, Detroit, MI), voc.
1970—*Candida* (Bell) 1973—*Tuneweaving* 1974—*Prime Time* 1975—*Tony Orlando and Dawn/Greatest Hits* (Arista) 1998—*The Definitive Collection.*

Tony Orlando and Dawn had many MOR hits in the early '70s, including "Tie a Yellow Ribbon 'Round the Ole Oak Tree," the largest-selling single of 1973. In 1981 it became something of a theme song for the return of U.S. hostages from Iran; the yellow ribbon has become a national symbol for any homecoming, whether from a war or a kidnapping.

At age 16 Orlando auditioned for producer Don Kirshner, who teamed him up with songwriter Carole King. Kirshner produced and King wrote Orlando's first hits, all in 1961: "Halfway to Paradise" (#39), "Bless You" (#15), and "Happy Times (Are Here to Stay)" (#82). In a short while, though, Orlando stopped singing, in part because Kirshner sold his company to Screen Gems, which was more interested in publishing than recording. For a while, Orlando worked in promotion, and in 1967 he became manager of April-Blackwood Music, the publishing arm of Columbia Records.

In early 1970 Bell Records producer Hank Medress (a former member of the Tokens) asked Orlando to sing lead over a demo he had received from Telma Louise Hopkins and Joyce Elaine Vincent, a duo calling itself Dawn. The two Detroit-based singers had previously backed Johnnie Taylor, Edwin Starr, Freda Payne, Frijid Pink, and others. Hopkins had also been part of Isaac Hayes' Hot Buttered Soul and later sang on "Shaft." Orlando's voice was dubbed over the original, and "Candida" shot to #3 in 1970. (Supposedly, he didn't meet Dawn until after it hit.) An alternate account claims that Orlando recorded both "Candida" and its followup, "Knock Three Times" with session singers and that Hopkins and Vincent were not hired until after these were hits.

Orlando kept his day job until after their second single, "Knock Three Times," hit #1 in 1971. Then he signed with Bell, and the group (then called Dawn, featuring Tony Orlando) finally started touring in September 1971. In 1973 they returned to the charts with the #1 hit "Tie a Yellow Ribbon 'Round the Ole Oak Tree." Other hits included "Say, Has Anybody Seen My Sweet Gypsy Rose?" (#3, 1973), "Steppin' Out (Gonna Boogie Tonight)" (#7, 1974), and "He Don't Love You (Like I Love You)" (#1, 1975).

After that, their hits stopped, though the group still played many concert dates and hosted a musical-variety television series that ran intermittently for two and a half years on CBS. In July 1977, during a show in Massachusetts, Orlando shocked Dawn and the audience by announcing his retirement and claiming that he was giving up show business for Jesus Christ. Orlando's decision followed the death of his sister and suicide of comedian Freddie Prinze, a close friend. Orlando also had a cocaine problem and suffered from manic depression. In November 1977 he made a solo comeback, playing Las Vegas, and later signed with Casablanca, though only one chart hit, "Sweets for My Sweet" (#54, 1979), followed. He appeared on Broadway in *Barnum* in 1980. The two women worked unsuccessfully as Dawn. Hopkins later went into acting; she has appeared on television's *Bosom Buddies, Gimme a Break,* and *Family Matters.*

Beginning in the late '80s, Orlando cohosted Jerry Lewis' Labor Day Telethon to benefit the Muscular Dystrophy Association. In 1988 Orlando, Hopkins, and Vincent-Wilson briefly re-formed Dawn. In the early '90s Orlando relocated to Branson, Missouri, where he performs regularly at his Tony Orlando Yellow Ribbon Music Theater.

Orleans

Formed 1972, New York, NY
Lance Hoppen (b. 1954, Bayshore, NY), bass; Wells Kelly (d. Oct. 30, 1984, London, Eng.), organ, voc., drums; Larry Hoppen, voc., kybds., gtr.; Jerry Marotta, drums, perc.; John Hall (b. Oct. 25, 1947, Baltimore, MD), gtr., voc.
1973—*Orleans* (ABC) 1974—*Let There Be Music* (Asylum) 1976—*Waking and Dreaming* 1977—(– Hall; – Marotta; + Bob Leinbach, kybds., voc.; + R.A. Martin, kybds., voc.) 1979—*Forever* (Infinity) 1982—*One of a Kind* (Radio/Atlantic) 1990—*Still the One* (Elektra); *Orleans Live* (Major) 1996—*Ride* (Dinosaur Entertainment) 1997—*Dance With Me: The Best of Orleans* (Elektra/Rhino).
John Hall solo: 1970—*Action* (CBS) 1978—*John Hall* (Asylum) 1979—*Power* (Columbia) 1981—*All of the Above* (EMI America) 1983—*Search Party* 1992—*On a Distant Star* (Pioneer, Jap.) 1998—*Recovered* (Siren Song).

Orleans had a few pop hits in the mid-'70s written by leader/guitarist John Hall and his wife, Johanna. The group was founded by John Hall (among whose songwriting credits is Janis Joplin's "Half Moon"), Larry Hoppen, and Wells Kelly. Larry's brother Lance joined later in the year. Through the next year they became a popular East Coast club attraction. They signed with ABC in 1973 and cut their eponymous debut with producers Barry Beckett and Roger Hawkins at Alabama's Muscle Shoals studio.

In 1974 Orleans recorded a self-produced album at Bearsville studio, but ABC rejected it and dropped the group from the roster. Elektra-Asylum picked up Orleans and released its Chuck Plotkin–produced *Let There Be Music* (#33, 1975) late in the year. "Dance With Me" (#6, 1975) was the group's first big hit. *Waking and Dreaming* (#30, 1976) contained "Still the One" (#5), which the ABC television network used as its theme song for the year.

In 1977 Hall left to begin a solo career. He signed to Elektra Records and soon became a spokesman for the anti–nuclear power movement, playing a key role in organizing MUSE (Musicians United for Safe Energy) and writing its anthem, "Power."

Orleans continued on through various personnel changes and in 1979 had a #11 hit with "Love Takes Time" from *Forever* (#76, 1979). By this time, the band had moved to MCA's Infinity label, which in 1980 went bankrupt. The group stayed together and appeared in clubs through 1981, and in 1982 released *One of a Kind*. In 1984 Wells Kelly died in London after choking on his own vomit as a result of heroin and cocaine intoxication. The band kept on going with the three early members and various guest drummers—four different ones appear on the 1996 album *Ride*.

Beth Orton

Born Dec. 14, 1970, East Dereham, Norfolk, Eng.
1996—*Trailer Park* (Heavenly, U.K.) 1997—*Best Bit* EP 1999—*Central Reservation* (Deconstruction/Arista).

Beth Orton first grabbed attention with a sly mixture of acoustic folk and trip-hop beats backing her haunted and soulful lyrics. Though her second album was a step toward more traditional folk, Orton's passionate, if understated, music has been hailed as setting the trend for a new generation of singer/songwriters.

Orton, whose father died when she was 11, was raised with two older brothers in Norfolk, England, by her mother, a writer and activist for improved child-care laws. In the mid-'80s the family moved to London, where Orton studied acting and eventually joined a traveling theater company. Involved in London's dance-music scene, Orton met producer William Orbit, who was so taken by Orton's speaking voice that he invited her to record in his studio. As a duo called Spill, Orton and Orbit recorded a cover of John Martyn's "Don't Wanna Know About Evil" and released *SuperPinkyMandy* in Japan.

After guesting on a variety of albums—including the Chemical Brothers' *Exit Planet Dust*—Orton spent three and a half months meditating at a Buddhist monastery in Thailand. She returned to find various record companies interested in her music. The downbeat folk and modern textures of her solo debut, *Trailer Park*, earned wide acclaim and sales of 300,000 copies worldwide. For 1999's *Central Reservation* (#110), Orton dropped many of the overt techno beats, moving toward a folkier sound. Ben Harper played guitar on the album, which was coproduced by David Roback of Mazzy Star.

Ben Orr: See the Cars

Jeffrey Osborne

Born Mar. 9, 1948, Providence, RI
1982—*Jeffrey Osborne* (A&M) 1983—*Stay With Me Tonight* 1984—*Don't Stop* 1986—*Emotional* 1988—*One Love–One Dream* 1990—*Only Human* (Arista) 1997—*Something Warm for Christmas* (Modern) 1999—*Ultimate Collection* (Hip-O) 2000—*That's for Sure* (Private).

Singer/songwriter Jeffrey Osborne's soulful baritone and romantic R&B ballads were first heard in the '70s, when he fronted the group L.T.D. (Love, Togetherness, Devotion) and later in his highly successful solo work.

He grew up in New England, one of 12 children of an accomplished amateur trumpeter father. Learning the trumpet and then drums at an early age, Osborne played in bands throughout high school before signing on as drummer for the Greensboro, North Carolina–based L.T.D. at age 22 in 1970. Formerly the backup band for Sam and Dave, the 10-piece horn-driven outfit encouraged Osborne's singing, and on their six albums and such hits as "Love Ballad" (#20, 1976) and "(Every Time I Turn Around) Back in Love Again" (#4, 1977), he displayed the influence of Motown, Johnny Mathis, and Sarah Vaughan.

After a decade with L.T.D., Osborne went solo, enlisting

veteran jazz-rock fusion keyboardist George Duke as producer. With "On the Wings of Love" from his self-titled debut scoring #29 in 1982, Osborne blueprinted the glossy soul-music approach that would become his mainstay. In 1986 his "You Should Be Mine (The Woo Woo Song)" reached #13; a year later, his Burt Bacharach–written duet with Dionne Warwick, "Love Power," became a #12 hit. He recorded "She's on the Left," a #1 R&B (#48 pop, 1988). Since then, while his singing style has provoked comparisons to Teddy Pendergrass and Luther Vandross, he has yet to deliver on the potential for first-rank stardom he displayed with L.T.D. His self-produced 2000 release, *That's for Sure*, found him in fine ballad style.

Joan Osborne

Born July 8, 1962, Anchorage, KY
1991—*Soul Show* (Womanly Hips Music) 1993—*Blue Million Miles* EP 1995—*Relish* (Blue Gorilla/Mercury) 1996—*Early Recordings* 2000—*Righteous Love* (Interscope).

Born and raised outside of Louisville, Kentucky, Joan Osborne moved to New York in the mid-'80s to study film at New York University. She shifted to music after being coaxed by friends to sing an old gospel standard at a jam session at a local club. Proving a natural at blues belting in the style of Etta James and Janis Joplin, she returned the following week and was soon performing with her own band.

After two releases on her own Womanly Hips label (the live *Soul Show* and the EP *Blue Million Miles*), Osborne began writing songs with producer Rick Chertoff and former Hooters members Eric Bazilian and Rob Hyman in 1993. The results became *Relish* (#9, 1995), which was released on Chertoff's Mercury-distributed Blue Gorilla label. "One of Us," a Bazilian song imagining God as "a slob like one of us," climbed to #4. The album went triple platinum and was nominated for seven Grammys in 1996. (It won none.)

Apart from the *Early Recordings* (1996) compilation, Osborne would take five years to release her followup to *Relish*, in part because Mercury dropped her after rejecting the album she turned in. In the interim, she toured with Sarah McLachlan's Lilith Fair festival, studied Qawwali singing with Nusrat Fateh Ali Khan in Pakistan, and recorded a duet of "Chimes of Freedom" with Bob Dylan for the TV miniseries *The '60s*. The time off the radio took its toll, however; when Osborne returned with the Mitchell Froom–produced *Righteous Love* (on new label Interscope) in 2000, it peaked at #90. Concurrent with the album's release, Osborne launched her online women's interest magazine, *Heroine Magazine*.

Ozzy Osbourne

Born John Osbourne, Dec. 3, 1948, Birmingham, Eng.
1980—*Blizzard of Ozz* (Jet) 1981—*Diary of a Madman* 1982—*Speak of the Devil* 1983—*Bark at the Moon* (CBS Associated) 1986—*The Ultimate Sin* 1987—*Tribute* 1988—*No Rest for the Wicked* 1990—*Just Say Ozzy* 1991—*No More Tears* (Epic) 1993—*Live & Loud* 1995—*Ozzmosis* 1997—*The OzzFest, vol. 1: Live* (Red Ant); *The Ozzman Cometh*.
With Black Sabbath: see entry.

Onetime lead singer with Black Sabbath [see entry], Ozzy Osbourne traded on his former band's legacy of loud hard rock and mystical/occult trappings, and his own propensity for grossly outrageous acts, to become one of heavy metal's best-loved and most successful frontmen.

"I'm not a musician," Osbourne once claimed, "I'm a ham." In 1981, at an L.A. meeting of Columbia Records executives, Ozzy bit the head off a live dove; a few months later he bit the head off a bat tossed to him by a fan at a Des Moines concert. (Osborne claims to have thought it was a rubber toy.) The latter incident resulted in the singer receiving a series of rabies shots.

Osbourne has said there was "a lot of insanity" in his family; that he'd made several suicide attempts, as early as age 14, "just to see what it would feel like"; that at one point he and Black Sabbath drummer Bill Ward took acid every day for two years; and that his last months with Black Sabbath in 1978 were "very unhappy. I got very drunk and very stoned every single day."

Osbourne's first two solo LPs went double platinum, and in 1981 "You Can't Kill Rock 'n' Roll" garnered heavy FM-AOR airplay. Then, on March 19, 1982, near Orlando, Florida, Ozzy's tour plane, which was buzzing his tour bus, crashed. Osbourne and most of his band were in the bus and unhurt, but his guitarist, Randy Rhoads; hairdresser Rachel Youngblood; and pilot/bus driver Andrew Aycock were all in the plane, and all were killed. Rhoads was replaced within a few weeks by Brad (Night Ranger) Gillis, and the show went on. Later that year, Osbourne married his manager, Sharon Arden. He also recorded a live album, *Speak of the Devil*, at the Ritz in New York. Each of his succeeding albums, except for the 1990 *Just Say Ozzy*, went at least platinum (*Bark at the Moon* and *No More Tears* went double platinum). *Tribute* (#6, 1987) included live recordings featuring Randy Rhoads, from 1981.

For Osbourne, 1986 was particularly eventful: In April he was fined several thousand dollars by the New Jersey Meadowlands after his fans trashed the arena during a concert; that summer, he made his movie debut as an antirock minister in the horror film *Trick or Treat*; and toward the end of the year, he disappeared for three weeks—eventually turning up at California's Betty Ford Clinic, where he'd checked in to battle his alcoholism.

A favorite whipping boy of the religious right, Osbourne was the target of an antirock sermon delivered in early 1990 by New York City's John Cardinal O'Connor. Between 1985 and 1990, Osbourne was sued by three different sets of parents (two from Georgia, one from California), all claiming his song "Suicide Solution," from *Blizzard of Ozz*, had induced their sons to commit suicide. (Lamenting the death of AC/DC's Bon Scott, the song is clearly antialcohol and antisuicide.) Osbourne prevailed in every suit.

In 1991 Osbourne announced his No More Tours Tour to

support *No More Tears*—an alleged farewell jaunt, during which he broke a foot while jumping around onstage in Chicago and later caused a near-riot in Irvine, California, when he invited his audience onstage. (That show, billed as a benefit to fund replacement of Randy Rhoads' graffiti-covered tombstone, broke even once Osbourne paid damages to the venue.) In October 1992 the tour brought Osbourne to San Antonio, Texas—the first time he'd played there since February 1982, when he'd been banned from the city for urinating on the Alamo. (Osbourne has also been banned, for various reasons and lengths of time, from Boston, Baton Rouge, Corpus Christi, Las Vegas, and Philadelphia.) Osbourne's two tour-ending shows in Costa Mesa, California, were opened by Black Sabbath—with Judas Priest's Rob Halford replacing Sabbath singer Ronnie James Dio, who refused to open for his predecessor. Osbourne did a four-song miniset with Sabbath at the final show. The tour produced the *Live & Loud* album, which earned Osbourne his first Grammy nomination, for Best Metal Performance for the track "I Don't Wanna Change the World."

Only weeks after the tour ended, Osbourne's publicists said he might indeed tour again, but not as a solo act. Alleged financial bickering scuttled subsequent negotiations for a 1993 Ozzy-Sabbath reunion tour. In spring 1994 he recorded a version of Sabbath's "Iron Man"—originally recorded when he was still in the band—with Irish band Therapy? for the Sabbath tribute album *Nativity in Black*. His next album was *Ozzmosis*, which sold 3 million copies and hit #4 in 1995. With the subsequent tour a major success, Osbourne in 1996 launched Ozzfest, a heavy rock–themed package tour that grew into one of the top summer concert attractions of the late '90s and helped to boost the careers of acts such as Marilyn Manson and Pantera. An album, *The OzzFest, Vol. 1: Live* documented the tour's inaugural dates. By 1997, the event prompted a Black Sabbath reunion. A double CD, *Reunion*, was released the next year, and the group headlined a 1999 tour to promote it.

Osibisa

Formed 1969, London, Eng.
Teddy Osei (b. Ghana), saxes, flute, voc.; Sol Amarfio (b. Ghana), perc.; Mac Tontoh (b. Ghana), trumpet; Robert Bailey (b. Trinidad), kybds., drums; Wendell Richardson (b. Antigua), gtr., voc.; Spartacus R. (b. Grenada), bass; Loughty Lasisi Amao (b. Nigeria), saxes.
1970—*Osibisa* (Decca) 1972—*Woyaya* 1973—*Heads* (– Amao; + Kofi Ayivor [b. Ghana], drums; – R.; + Jean Dikota Mandengue [b. Cameroon], bass; – Richardson; + Gordon Hunte [b. Guyana], gtr., voc.); *Superfly TNT* (Buddah) (– Hunte) *Happy Children* (Warner Bros.) 1974—(+ Kiki Gyan [b. Ghana], kybds.; + Paul Golly [b. Cameroon], gtr.) *Osibirock* 1975—(+ Richardson; + Mike Odumusu [b. Lagos, Nigeria], bass; + Kof Ayivor, perc., voc.) 1976—*Welcome Home* (Antilles) (– Golly; – Gyan; – Richardson) *Ojah Awake* 1977—(– Bailey; + Richardson) *Black Magic Night* (group disbands) 1980—(group re-forms: Osei; Amarfio; Tontoh; numerous personnel changes follow) *Mystic Nights* (Calibre, U.K.) 1995—*Unleashed* (Red Steel, U.K.) 1997—*Monsore* 1999—*The Best of Osibisa* (Cleopatra) 2000—*Aka Kakra* (Red Steel, U.K.).

Osibisa was by no means the first band to play a cross between Western pop and African traditional music, but it was the first to become more popular in the West than in Africa. The band was made up of both African and Caribbean musicians.

Teddy Osei's career began over a decade before he formed Osibisa in England; in the late '50s and early '60s, he played sax with a highlife band, the Comets, in Kumasi, Ghana. In 1962 he went to England on a Ghanaian government scholarship to study at the London College of Music. He led a number of bands in London, among them Cat's Paw in the late '60s; that band included Ghanaian younger brother Mac Tontoh's longtime friend Sol Amarfio, with whom Osei recorded a film soundtrack in London in 1969. They formed a quartet with Nigerian drummer Remi Kabaka, until Kabaka joined Ginger Baker's Air Force.

By 1970, West Indians Wendell Richardson and Robert Bailey had joined, and they named themselves with the West African Akan word for a certain dance rhythm. Spartacus R., a West Indian, and Loughty Amao, a West African, joined in time to record a demo tape that BBC radio aired before record companies heard it. The music was an original fusion of polyrhythmic African percussion, rock guitar, keyboard riffs, and R&B-style horn charts; songs were in Akan and in English.

After a series of London club dates, Osibisa signed with Decca. The group's debut album, produced by Tony Visconti, made the U.K. Top 10 and the U.S. Top 60. In the next year, Osibisa toured Europe, North America, and Africa, and in the following year traveled to the Orient and Australia. Everywhere, the colorfully costumed band appeared on television; in Great Britain, the BBC devoted a special to Osibisa. Its music was further spread by the soundtrack to *Superfly TNT* and by Art Garfunkel's 1973 cover of Amarfio's "Woyaya."

By 1973, when Osibisa signed with Warner Bros., half of the original group had left. Richardson sat in for Paul Kossoff on Free's 1973 U.S. tour, then made a solo album, *Pieces of a Jigsaw*, before rejoining Osibisa in 1975. In 1976, after moving to Island Records' Antilles label, the group had its biggest hit, "Sunshine Day" (#17 U.K.), from *Welcome Home*, but the members disbanded the following year. In 1980 Osei, Amarfio, and Tontoh reunited for *Mystic Nights*, made with session musicians. Osibisa continued to tour internationally.

The Osmonds/Donny Osmond/ Marie Osmond

Formed 1957, Ogden, UT
Alan Osmond (b. June 22, 1949, Ogden), voc., gtr.; Wayne Osmond (b. Aug. 28, 1951, Ogden), voc., gtr., sax, banjo, bass, drums; Merrill Osmond (b. Apr. 30, 1953, Ogden), voc., bass; Jay Osmond (b. Mar. 2, 1955, Ogden), drums; Donny Osmond

(b. Donald Clark Osmond, Dec. 9, 1957, Ogden), voc., kybds.; Marie Osmond (b. Oct. 13, 1959, Ogden), voc.; Jimmy Osmond (b. Apr. 16, 1963, Canoga Park, CA), voc., drums.
The Osmonds: 1971—*The Osmonds* (MGM); *Homemade* 1972—*Phase-III; The Osmonds "Live"; Crazy Horses* 1973—*The Plan* 1974—*Love Me for a Reason* 1975—*The Proud One; Around the World Live in Concert* 1976—*Brainstorm* (Polydor); *The Osmond Christmas Album* 1977—*The Osmonds' Greatest Hits* 2000—*All Time Greatest Hits of the Osmonds* (WEA/Atlantic/Curb).
The Osmond Brothers (Alan, Wayne, Jay, and Merrill): 1992—*Greatest Hits* (Curb).
Donny Osmond solo: 1971—*The Donny Osmond Album* (MGM); *To You With Love, Donny* 1972—*Portrait of Donny; My Best to You* 1973—*Alone Together* 1976—*Disco Train* 1977—*Donald Clark Osmond* 1989—*Donny Osmond* (Capitol) 1990—*Eyes Don't Lie* 1992—*The Greatest Hits* (Curb) 1995—*Donny Osmond: Twenty-five Hits* (Curb) 1997—*Four* EP (Nightstar); *Christmas at Home* (Legacy) 2001—*This Is the Moment* (Decca Broadway).
Marie Osmond solo: 1973—*Paper Roses* (MGM) 1974—*In My Little Corner of the World* 1975—*Who's Sorry Now* 1977—*This Is the Way That I Feel* 1985—*There's No Stopping Your Heart* (Curb) 1986—*I Only Wanted You* 1988—*All in Love* 1989—*Steppin' Stone* 1990—*The Best of Marie Osmond* 1995—*Marie Osmond: Twenty-five Hits* (Curb).
Donny and Marie: 1973—*I'm Leaving It All Up to You* (MGM) 1976—*Donny & Marie—Featuring Songs From Their Television Show* (Polydor); *Donny & Marie—New Season* 1978—*Goin' Coconuts*.
The Osmonds Second Generation (Alan's eight sons, Merrill's daughter Heather, and, to quote their press release, "many of the other Osmond children"): 1992—*Second Generation* (Curb).
The Osmond Boys (Osmond Brothers' sons): 1990—*Osmond Boys* (Curb).

The Osmonds are the longest-running—not to mention the largest—family dynasty in show business. Beginning in 1962, when brothers Alan, Wayne, Merrill, and Jay got their first professional break, until the present, few years have passed without at least one Osmond on the charts, the television, or the stage. In 1972 alone, the Osmonds received more gold records in a single year than any other group in history, including the Beatles. Between January 24, 1971, and November 6, 1978, the RIAA certified a total of 23 gold discs recorded either by the Osmonds or by Donny and Marie Osmond as solo acts or as a duo: five LPs and three singles by the Osmonds; four LPs and five singles by Donny; one single by Marie; and four LPs and one single by Donny and Marie. But their recording success, coming as it did nearly 15 years after the group formed, proved anything but a fluke. And although at one time or another various Osmond family members seemed down for the count careerwise, they never fail to rebound. In addition to the Osmond Brothers (which also now includes Jimmy), Donny Osmond, and Marie Osmond, the family has produced a second generation of performers destined to carry the Osmond name into the sixth decade.

All of the Osmond progeny were taught music by their parents, George and Olive, and raised in a strict Church of Jesus Christ of Latter-day Saints (LDS, or Mormon) environment. They began singing religious and barbershop-quartet songs with their parents. Alan, Wayne, and Merrill, later joined by Jay, originally began performing locally to earn money to finance the two-year religious missions the boys planned to serve after completing high school. Their mastery of barbershop harmony impressed even professional singers. Their big break came when in 1962 the Osmond Brothers (at the time, Alan, Jay, Merrill, and Wayne) went to Disneyland wearing identical suits and were invited to perform by the house barbershop quartet. They made their national television debut on "Disneyland After Dark," a taped musical segment shown occasionally on *Walt Disney's Wonderful World of Color*. On the recommendation of his father, Jay, Andy Williams auditioned them and invited them on to his TV variety series, where they were regulars from 1962 to 1971 (Donny joined in 1963). During their tenure with Williams, they performed every type of music imaginable, often in intricately choreographed numbers involving everything from tap dancing to roller-skating. So well rehearsed were they that they became known throughout the industry as "the one-take Osmonds." In the mid-'60s, the five Osmonds also did TV shows with Jerry Lewis and toured with Pat Boone and Phyllis Diller.

By the time the boys began recording, they'd all learned to play instruments and, through diligent touring, had become a mammoth MOR attraction, performing in top theaters as well as in hotel showrooms throughout the country, including in Las Vegas. As successful as they were, the older brothers, led by Alan, loved rock & roll and were intent on changing with the times, even though this posed a major career risk. In 1970 producer Mike Curb teamed the group with Fame Studios producer Rick Hall, known for his work with Aretha Franklin, Wilson Pickett, and other soul giants. In Muscle Shoals, Alabama, he produced the first in a string of hits, including their gold debut effort, the Jacksons-style "One Bad Apple" (#1, 1971). The group was criticized in some quarters for "imitating" the Jacksons; ironically, Jackson patriarch Joseph had his children study the Osmonds on the Williams show in their preprofessional days. Other 1971 hit singles for the Osmonds included "Double Lovin' " (#14), "I Can't Stop" (#96), and the million-selling "Yo-Yo" (#3). The Osmonds' record company then decided to cash in on young Donny's popularity with preadolescent girls and, against the wishes of Donny and his brothers, began recording him as a solo artist. Donny's million-selling debut single, "Sweet and Innocent" (#7) set the pattern for bubblegum success. Donny's solo singles were not only teenybopper fodder, but—unlike the hits of his teen-magazine "rival" David Cassidy—they were teenybopper classics of an earlier era. Donny hit gold again with "Go Away Little Girl" (#1). The year 1972 brought more hits: Donny's "Hey Girl/I Knew You When" (#9) and the Osmonds' hard-rocking original "Down by the Lazy River" (#4) both went gold. The Osmonds had further hits with "Hold Her Tight" (#14, 1972) and "Goin'

Home" (#36, 1973). Donny hit with the singles "Puppy Love" (#3), "Why" (#13), and "Too Young" (#13) in 1972, and "The Twelfth of Never" (#8, 1973) and "A Million to One/Young Love" (#23, 1973). Four of their albums—*Osmonds, Phase-III, The Osmonds "Live,"* and *Crazy Horses*—were Top 20 and, along with *Homemade* (#22, 1971), gold.

While their success was indisputable, critics had a field day trashing their wholesome, "unhip" image. To their credit, the group remained true to their religious and personal values, and were not shy about discussing their beliefs, though they did not proselytize. Interestingly, in most other parts of the world in the early to mid-'70s, the Osmonds were considered a bona fide rock band, far better known for the heavy-metal crunch of "Crazy Horses" than Donny's bubblegum hits. In England, particularly, "Osmond mania" reached Fab Four proportions with fans overrunning Heathrow Airport to greet the boys. In France, where "Crazy Horses" was a major hit, their audience comprised hippies and bikers.

In 1973 the brothers released *The Plan* (#58, 1973), their first of six albums not to go gold. The group's pet project, this concept album explains man's spiritual evolution from an LDS perspective (although anyone unfamiliar with LDS beliefs would not discern that). Delivered to select FM stations without the group identified, *The Plan* did receive some airplay—until programmers realized it was an Osmonds album. After *Love Me for a Reason* (#47, 1974), none of the group's albums cracked the Top 100 again.

In 1973 Marie, who had toured and performed with her brothers sporadically through the years (she made her television debut on *The Andy Williams Show* at age four), made her recording debut with the #1 country & western hit "Paper Roses" (#5 pop, 1973). Little Jimmy Osmond began recording, too. His debut LP and single, "Long Haired Lover From Liverpool," made the U.S. Top 40 in 1972 and topped the U.K. chart for six weeks. But he was most successful in the foreign market, particularly in Japan, where he was known affectionately as "Jimmy Boy" and later had his own television series. By the early '90s, Jimmy (who was doing his own business tax returns before he was old enough to drive) had become the family's business mastermind with a financial empire built on savvy real estate investments and events production.

Following a guest-host stint on Mike Douglas' show, Donny and Marie were offered their own weekly musical variety series by ABC. Reluctantly, they agreed, in part because the family viewed the series as a way to get away from the near-constant touring that had dominated their lives (the entire family traveled together) for the past decade. Donny and Marie were just 18 and 16 respectively when *The Donny and Marie Show* debuted in test episode in November 1975. Though the pair was out front, it was a very much a family effort, with various brothers producing, directing, and overseeing the music. To do so, they put their music career on hold with, it turned out, disastrous results. Partway through the show's three-year run, the family decided to relocate back to Utah. There they invested their considerable fortune in a state-of-the-art television and recording studio, from which the show was produced. When the series was canceled after three years, the studio failed to bring in the projected business. That and other business mishaps resulted in the family losing literally everything they had. (Some estimates place losses as high as $70 million.) Though because of the way the business partnership was structured, individual family members were personally liable for debts, father George Osmond flatly refused to consider declaring bankruptcy, which he considered dishonorable. Instead, the family hit the road.

Through the '80s, Marie emerged as the star of the family. She continued her success on the country charts with a number of hits, including the C&W #1 singles "Meet Me in Montana" (a duet with Dan Seals, 1985), "There's No Stopping Your Heart" (1985), and "You're Still New to Me" (a duet with Paul Davis, 1986). In the mid-'90s, she toured in *The Sound of Music*, and made her Broadway debut in *The King and I*.

Meanwhile, Donny's career was in a nosedive. In March 1982 he appeared on Broadway in George M. Cohan's musical *Little Johnny Jones*, which closed on opening night. He headed his own production company for a number of years before returning to recording in the late '80s. Peter Gabriel invited Osmond to record in his Bath, England, studio and helped him secure a deal with Virgin (U.K.). Released in 1988, *Donny Osmond* (#54, 1989) looked like a flop. Donny was ready to start a home-security business in Utah when a program director at New York's WPLJ started playing "Soldier of Love" without identifying the singer. After several weeks of suspense, the "mystery artist" was revealed, and the single hit #2 in 1989. Other charting singles from that album were "Sacred Emotion" (#13, 1989) and "Hold On" (#73, 1989). *Eyes Don't Lie* didn't make the Hot 100, but it contained "My Love Is a Fire" (#21, 1990). Osmond, by then anxious to shirk his old teenybopper image, surprised many people by speaking out against the PMRC in 1985 and gently mocking his old image in the video for Jeff Beck's "Ambitious." In 1992 he joined a Canadian company of *Joseph and the Amazing Technicolor Dreamcoat* in the title role. Over his six years in the role, the production broke records in several cites. Ten years after "Soldier of Love," Donny was back. During that time, however, he began experiencing severe panic attacks that nearly ended his career, and he was diagnosed with social phobia. Since going public with this, in 1998, he has worked to raise awareness about anxiety disorders.

The Osmond Brothers, sans Donny and plus Jimmy, turned to country music, with instant success. They were named *Billboard*'s top new singles group in 1982, after "I Think About Your Lovin' " (#17 C&W, 1982) put them back on the chart (until 1986, they would chart 10 more C&W singles). In Branson, Missouri, they own, operate, and perform at the Osmond Family Theater, one of the town's top attractions. Alan, who has multiple sclerosis, speaks about the disorder and has written children's books. Wayne was cured of brain cancer in the mid-'90s.

The family founded the Osmond Foundation for the deaf (two of the group's older brothers, Virl and Tom, were born deaf). In the early '80s, the foundation was expanded and is affiliated with the Children's Miracle Network Telethon, which was cofounded by Marie and actor John Schneider and raises money for children's hospitals.

In 1998 Donny and Marie returned to television with their syndicated talk show, *Donny & Marie.* Produced by Dick Clark, the series fared better than many competitors but ran for only two seasons. In the summer of 1999, Marie experienced severe postpartum depression following the birth of her seventh child. In 1999 Donny published his best-selling autobiography, *Life Is Just What You Make It: My Story So Far* (cowritten with Patricia Romanowski). In 2001 the family authorized a made-for-television movie of their rock & roll era, *The Osmonds,* which further revealed the triumphs and tragedies of a family that has seen more of both than most. In her 2001 best-selling autobiography, *Behind the Smile,* Marie revealed that she had been sexually abused as a child (by someone outside her family) and discussed her bouts with postpartum depression.

In 2000 Donny played Joseph in the David Mallett–directed video version of *Dreamcoat,* costarring Sir Richard Attenborough and Joan Collins. Also that year he duetted with housewife-turned-pop-star Suzy K on her hit "Now I Know." The following year, he released his collection of Broadway and pop standards, *This Is the Moment.* It debuted at #10 in the U.K. and peaked at #64 in the U.S.

Johnny Otis

Born John Veliotes, Dec. 8, 1921, Vallejo, CA
1969—*Cold Shot* (Kent) 1970—*Cuttin' Up* (Epic) 1971—*Live at Monterey; The Original Johnny Otis Show* (Savoy) 1981—*The New Johnny Otis Show* (Alligator) 1989—*The Capitol Years* (Capitol) 1993—*Spirit of the Black Territory Bands* (Johnny Otis and His Orchestra) (Arhoolie) 1995—*Too Late to Holler* (Night Train/City Hall) 1997—*Johnny Otis R&B Dance Party, vol. 1* (J&T) 1998—*Johnny Otis Blues and Swing Dance Party, vol. 1* 1999—*Blues, Bounce, Beat, Boogie, Bebop and Ballads* (Blue Boar); *The Complete Savoy Recordings* (Savoy) 2000—*Cold Shot* (J&T).

As a talent scout and bandleader, Johnny Otis was a central figure in the development of rhythm & blues and rock & roll in the early '50s. He was born of Greek-American parents, but from his childhood, he lived among blacks and in fact considered himself black. As he later wrote in his autobiography, *Listen to the Lambs,* "I did not become black because I was attracted to Negro music. My attitude was formed long before I moved into the music field."

In his Berkeley neighborhood, Otis became interested in blues, gospel, and swing, and in his teens became an accomplished drummer, dropping out of high school to play in the Bay Area and tour the Southwest with various swing bands. In 1941 he married his wife, Phyllis, a black woman; they had five children. By the mid-'40s Otis had his own big band, but when the big-band format lost popularity, he stripped his crew down to a nine-piece group with small horn and rhythm sections, which became a standard rhythm & blues lineup. In 1945 he had his first regional hit with a version of "Harlem Nocturne." That year he also played drums on Johnny Moore's Three Blazers hit "Drifting Blues." In 1951 he discovered a group called the Royals (that would later be known as Hank Ballard and the Midnighters). In 1948 Otis and a partner, Bardu Ali, opened a popular Watts nightclub, the Barrelhouse Club. It closed in the early '50s after Otis made a series of R&B hits featuring singers he had discovered in L.A.: Little Esther Phillips, Mel Walker, and the Robins, who would later become known nationally as the Coasters.

"Double Crossing Blues" (#1 R&B), "Mistrustin' Blues" (#1 R&B), "Deceivin' Blues" (#4 R&B), "Dreamin' Blues" (#8 R&B), "Wedding Boogie" (#6 R&B), "Far Away Christmas Blues" (#4 pop, #6 R&B), and "Rockin' Blues" (#21 pop, #2 R&B) were all hits in 1950. In 1952 "Sunset to Dawn," sung by Mel Walker, was a #10 R&B hit. From 1950 to 1954, the Johnny Otis Rhythm and Blues Caravan touring revue traveled across the U.S. with then-unknown performers including Hank Ballard, Little Willie John, Big Mama Thornton, and Jackie Wilson. Otis heard Jerry Leiber and Mike Stoller's "Hound Dog," and he produced Thornton's version of it. "Every Beat of My Heart," written by Otis in the early '50s, became Gladys Knight and the Pips' first hit in 1961 and has been covered regularly ever since.

In 1954 Otis quit the road for a DJ spot at L.A.'s KFOX, later landing a television show in the late '50s. But he hadn't given up music, and in 1958 he had his biggest hit with the Bo Diddley–style "Willie and the Hand Jive" (#9 pop, #5 R&B). For most of the '60s, Otis' musical career was dormant, though he was very active in the civil-rights movement and politics. His mid-'60s book, *Listen to the Lambs,* concerned the 1965 Watts riot and also told the story of his life.

With his guitarist son Johnny Otis Jr., or "Shuggie," Johnny Otis returned to recording with *Cold Shot* (1969), *Cuttin' Up* (1970), and *The Johnny Otis Show Live at Monterey* (1971), a double album reuniting his old band and singers. Otis recorded a number of early R&B artists for his Blues Spectrum label, including Louis Jordan, Charles Brown, Big Joe Turner, Eddie "Cleanhead" Vinson, Clarence "Gatemouth" Brown, and himself. In 1978 Otis became an ordained minister and founded the nondenominational Landmark Community Church in L.A. He is also an accomplished painter, author, and sculptor. His 1993 *Spirit of the Black Territory Bands* featured a '40s-style big band. For a time he performed in his Johnny Otis Cabaret in California, which has since closed. In 1994 he was inducted into the Rock and Roll Hall of Fame. He continues to tour, and he remains a presence on the radio. As of 2000 he was teaching a course about African-American music at the University of California at Berkeley.

Shuggie Otis

Born Johnny Otis Jr., Nov. 30, 1953, Los Angeles, CA
1969—*Kooper Session: Al Kooper Introduces Shuggie Otis* (Columbia) 1970—*Here Comes Shuggie Otis* (Epic) 1971—

Freedom Flight 1975—*Inspiration Information; Preston Love's Omaha Bar-B-Q* (Kent); *Shuggie's Boogie: Shuggie Otis Plays the Blues* (Epic/Legacy).

Johnny Otis' son Shuggie was a prodigy, playing bass professionally with a jazz band in San Diego at 12 and joining his father's band as guitarist and doing session work on guitar, bass, organ, piano, and harmonica by 13. *Cold Shot,* which featured Shuggie on guitar, brought him to the attention of Al Kooper, who teamed up with Shuggie for the loose jam of *Kooper Session.* The younger Otis played bass on Frank Zappa's *Hot Rats* and guitar on violinist Sugarcane Harris' first solo LP. After three more albums he retired in 1975 at age 22; in 1977 his "Strawberry Letter 23" was a Top 5 hit for the Brothers Johnson. An appearance on *The New Johnny Otis Show* in 1981 was his first recording in several years, aside from session work on his father's Blues Spectrum label. He and his brother Nick, a drummer, still play in their father's band. Shuggie Otis' '90s backing band, the Otis Connection, also features Nick, as well as Shuggie's son, Lucky. In 2001 a repackaged version of *Inspiration Information* (released by David Byrne's Luaka Bop label) spurred a rediscovery of Otis.

John Otway

Born Oct. 2, 1952, Aylesbury, Eng.
1977—*John Otway + Wild Willy Barrett* (Polydor, U.K.) *1978—Deep and Meaningless* 1979—*Where Did I Go Right?* 1980—*Way and Bar; Deep Thought* (Stiff) 1982—*All Balls and No Willy* 1989—*The Wimp and the Wild* 1995—*Premature Adulation* (Amazing Feet).

One of the great eccentric footnotes to rock history, John Otway's only hit came on his 1977 single, "(Cor Baby, That's) Really Free" (#27 U.K.). He has spent the rest of his career trying to replicate that success with a combination of constant touring in England, lunatic, hyperactive performances, and a series of ever more bizarre publicity stunts. The Who's Pete Townshend signed Otway and partner Wild Willy Barrett to Track Records in 1974 and produced two flop singles. Otway was signed by Polydor during the punk explosion of 1977, even though his sound was closer to pub rock. The label suggested he recut "Cor Baby" in a more anarchic style, and Otway had "the Hit." His followup, "Geneve," a ballad recorded with an orchestra, puzzled his fans and disappeared without a trace, as did his three Polydor albums. When the label dropped him, Otway staged "Polython," a benefit concert that raised £1,500 for his former employers. He moved on to Stiff in 1980. To promote his cover of Gene Pitney's "The Man Who Shot Liberty Valence," the label pressed three copies without Otway's vocal; he would personally visit the homes of fans who bought the instrumental versions and add the vocal "live." After two albums Stiff, too, dropped him. Undeterred by his lack of success, Otway plowed on. He "signed" Warner Bros. as his record label in 1986, sending them a £200 advance and releasing "Jerusalem" with a counterfeit Warner label. Warners eventually released a legitimate version of the single, which sold about 50 copies. In 1990 he wrote an autobiography, *Cor Baby, It's Really Me (Rock and Roll's Greatest Failure).* It sold more copies than any of his records. In 1995 Otway released his first album of new material in 12 years, *Premature Adulation.* Four years later, Otway received unexpected vindication when BBC listeners placed his song "Beware of the Flowers Cause I'm Sure They're Going to Get You Yeh"—the B side of his sole hit—seventh in a poll to find the nation's favorite lyrics. He finished ahead of Leonard Cohen, Paul Simon, and Bob Dylan. Otway remains active; by 1999, he estimated he had played more than 3,000 shows.

OutKast

Formed 1993, Atlanta, GA
Dré (b. Andre Lauren Benjamin, May 27, 1975, Atlanta), voc.; Big Boi (b. Antwan Andre Patton, Feb. 1, 1975, Savannah, GA), voc.
1994—*Southernplayalisticadillacmuzik* (LaFace) 1996—*ATLiens* 1998—*Aquemini* 2000—*Stankonia.*

Inspired by the Afrocentric psychedelics of George Clinton and Sly Stone, OutKast created an idiosyncratic sound blending funk and Southern bump. Dré and Big Boi met during the 10th grade at Tri-Cities High School in Atlanta. Shortly before Big Boi graduated (Dré dropped out during his junior year to focus on music), OutKast signed with LaFace as the label's first rap act and began working on its debut album *Southernplayalisticadillacmuzik* (#20 pop, #3 R&B, 1994). The album's first single, "Player's Ball" (#37 pop, #12 R&B, 1994), went gold and helped put Atlanta on the map as a hip-hop city.

The group's sophomore effort, *ATLiens* (#2 pop, 1996), yielded the catchy "Elevators (me & you)" (#12 pop, #5 R&B, 1996) and peaked at #1 on the R&B albums chart. The

OutKast

Grammy-nominated *Aquemini* (#2 pop, #2 R&B, 1998) distinguished Dré and Big Boi as capable producers/songwriters, and featured funk forefather George Clinton on the song "Synthesizer." Another *Aquemini* track, "Rosa Parks" (#55 pop, #19 R&B, 1999), spawned some legal controversy when the civil-rights heroine sued OutKast for using her name to promote their music (the suit was dismissed in 1999). In 2000 OutKast released *Stankonia* (#2 pop and R&B), its most critically acclaimed album. *Stankonia*'s "Ms. Jackson" was inspired by Dré's breakup with his longtime girlfriend, singer Erykah Badu.

The Outlaws

Formed 1974, Tampa, FL
Hughie Thomasson, gtr., voc.; Billy Jones (d. Feb 4, 1995, Spring Hill, FL), gtr., voc.; Henry Paul, gtr., voc.; Frank O'Keefe (d. Feb 26, 1995, Clearwater, FL), bass; Monte Yoho, drums.
1975—*The Outlaws* (Arista) 1976—*Lady in Waiting* 1977—(– O'Keefe; – Paul; + Harvey Dalton Arnold, bass; + David Dix, drums) *Hurry Sundown* 1978—(+ Freddie Salem, gtr., voc.) *Bring It Back Alive; Playin' to Win* 1979—(– Salem) *In the Eye of the Storm* (– Arnold; + Rick Cua, bass, voc.) 1980—*Ghost Riders in the Sky* (– Yoho) 1981—(– Jones) 1982—*Los Hombres Malo* (group disbands); *Greatest Hits of the Outlaws/High Tides Forever* 1983—(group re-forms: Paul; Thomasson; + Chris Hicks, gtr., voc.; + Barry Borden, bass; + Jeff Howell, drums) 1986—*Soldiers of Fortune* (Pasha) (– Paul) 1993—*Hittin' the Road* (Blues Bureau International) 1994—*Diablo Canyon* (Blues Bureau International/Relativity) 1995—(– Jones; – O'Keefe) 1996—*The Best of the Outlaws: Green Grass and High Tides* (Arista).
Henry Paul Band: 1979—*Grey Ghost* (Atlantic) 1980—*Feel the Heat* 1981—*Anytime* 1982—*Henry Paul.*

Tampa's Outlaws built a solid audience by merging Eagles-style country rock and vocal harmonies (Eagles' producer Bill Szymczyk produced *Hurry Sundown*) and Allman Brothers–style twin-guitar Southern rock. The Outlaws were managed by Alan Walden, who felt it an impropriety to enter a business relationship with his brother Phil, who ran Capricorn; the Outlaws became Clive Davis' first Arista signing. Their name notwithstanding, the Outlaws were considerably smoother-sounding than fellow Southern rockers Molly Hatchet and .38 Special, with whom they shared an initial audience and touring circuit. The Outlaws appeared sporadically on the pop chart with "There Goes Another Love Song" (#34, 1975), two minor hits, and "(Ghost) Riders in the Sky" (#31, 1980). Henry Paul led his own band after leaving the Outlaws in 1977, but in 1983 he rejoined the group. *Ghost Riders, Bring It Back Alive,* and *Outlaws* all went gold. In 1993 Paul formed Blackhawk. In 1994 the Outlaws mounted the Southern Spirit package tour with the Marshall Tucker Band and .38 Special. Jones and O'Keefe died within weeks of one another in 1995. Guitarist Hughie Thomasson has been active in the latter-day version of Lynyrd Skynyrd. Former guitarist Freddie Salem opened a club in his native Akron, Ohio.

Buck Owens

Born Alvis Edgar Owens Jr., Aug. 12, 1929, Sherman, TX
1961—*Under Your Spell Again* (Capitol) 1963—*On the Bandstand* 1964—*Best of Buck Owens; Together Again* 1965—*I've Got a Tiger by the Tail* 1966—*Dust on Mother's Bible; The Carnegie Hall Concert* 1967—*Buck Owens and His Buckaroos in Japan; Your Tender Loving Care* 1968—*The Best of Buck Owens, vol. 2* 1972—*Too Old to Cut the Mustard* 1976—*Buck 'Em!* (Warner Bros.) 1979—*Our Old Mansion* 1981—*Love Don't Make the Bars* (Capitol) 1988—*Hot Dog!; Buck Owens and the Buckaroos Live at Carnegie Hall* (Country Music Foundation) 1990—*All-Time Greatest Hits, vol. 1* (Curb) 1992—*The Buck Owens Collection 1959–1990* (Rhino).

Chief purveyor, along with Merle Haggard, of the honky-tonk music dubbed the Bakersfield Sound (after his California home base), Buck Owens was a top-selling country artist in the '60s and cohost of the country comedy television show *Hee Haw* from 1969 to 1986. Emerging from semiretirement in 1987, he gained a new audience with longtime fan and neotraditionalist Dwight Yoakam when the pair released a Top 10 country single, "The Streets of Bakersfield."

Owens nicknamed himself Buck after a favorite mule when he was just three. His farming family settled in Arizona in the '30s. At 16, he was married and an accomplished guitarist; he moved to Bakersfield at age 21. As a session player in nearby L.A., he worked with Gene Vincent, Sonny James, and Stan Freberg. He formed the Schoolhouse Playboys in 1951 and recorded rockabilly using the name Corky Jones.

Signed to Capitol, he released under his own name the #4 hit "Under Your Spell Again" in 1959; its success kicked off an astonishing run of 75 charting country singles that continued into the early '80s (42 made the Top 10; 20 reached #1). Among his #1 sellers, delivered in an appealing, almost pleading tenor voice and backed by his crack band the Buckaroos, were 1963's "Act Naturally" (covered later by the Beatles), "I've Got a Tiger by the Tail" (1965), "Waitin' in Your Welfare Line" (1966), and "Open Up Your Heart" (1966). Resisting the string-laden, pop-oriented productions of contemporary Nashville, the Buckaroos favored a rootsy style confined to drums, pedal steel, two guitars, and the occasional fiddle; Owens' 1969 version of Chuck Berry's "Johnny B. Goode" revealed his rockabilly beginnings and the populist sympathies of the Bakersfield Sound. His songs have been covered by artists as diverse as Ray Charles ("Crying Time") and Emmylou Harris ("Together Again"), and Owens himself has released over 100 albums.

By his own account overexposed during his 16 years with the hugely popular but critically derided *Hee Haw,* Owens spent the latter '70s in semiretirement. During that time, he mourned the loss of Buckaroos guitarist Don Rich, who was killed in a 1974 motorcycle wreck. He concentrated on his business affairs, which included running several radio stations and a recording studio, until Dwight Yoakam encouraged him in the late '80s to return to active performing. The resulting albums, 1988's *Hot Dog!* and a box set, 1992's *The Buck Owens Collection 1959–1990,* revived interest in Owens, an interest confirmed in 1996 by his induction into the Country Music Hall of Fame and the Nashville Songwriters Hall of Fame. Around that time, he opened the $8 million Crystal Palace, a nightclub-museum in Bakersfield. The business venture proved successful, adding to his reported $100 million fortune. Owens joined Yoakam again in 2000, singing on tracks on Yoakam's *Tomorrow's Sounds Today.*

Ozark Mountain Daredevils

Formed 1971, Springfield, MO
John Dillon (b. Feb. 6, 1947, Stuttgart, AR), gtr., dulcimer, mandolin, Autoharp, piano; Steve Cash (b. May 5, 1946, Springfield), voc., harmonica; Randle Chowning (b. 1950), gtr., mandolin, harmonica, voc.; Michael "Supe" Granda (b. Dec. 24, 1950, St. Louis, MO), bass, voc.; Buddy Brayfield (b. 1951), piano; Larry Lee (b. 1947, Springfield), drums, voc., gtr., piano.
1973—*Ozark Mountain Daredevils* (A&M) 1974—*It'll Shine When It Shines* 1975—*The Car Over the Lake* 1976—(– Chowning; + Rune Walle [b. Nor.], gtr., banjo) *Men From Earth* 1977—(– Brayfield; + Ruell Chapell, kybds., voc.; + Jerry Mills, mandolin; + Steve Canaday [d. Sep. 25, 1999], gtr., drums, voc.) 1978—*Don't Look Down; It's Alive* 1980—*Ozark Mountain Daredevils* (Columbia) 1983—*Best Of* (A&M) 1985—*The Lost Cabin Sessions* (Sounds Great) 1994—(lineup: Cash; Dillon; Granda; + Bill Brown [b. Mar. 21, 1960, NC] gtr., voc.; + Ron Gremp [b. June 22, 1955, St. Louis], drums) 1997—*Archive Alive!* (Archive Recordings); *13* (New Era).
Supe and the Sandwiches (with Michael Granda): 1997—*The Springfield Chronicles* (Missouri Mule Music).
The Garbonzos (with Michael Granda): 1998—*Eat Our Beans* (Missouri Mule Music).

Growing out of a Springfield assemblage called Cosmic Corncob and His Amazing Mountain Daredevils, this unusually eclectic country-rock unit first came to national attention with "If You Wanna Get to Heaven" (#25, 1974). Mixing Appalachian and hillbilly string music with Southern boogie and country pop, the Ozark Mountain Daredevils released three fairly successful albums. Their 1973 eponyomously titled debut went gold and peaked at #26. *It'll Shine When It Shines,* which included "Jackie Blue" (#3, 1975), was their highest-charting album, at #19.

The group's hold on the pop chart slipped after that, however. Chowning left in 1976 for a solo career. As of early 2001, Cash, Dillon, and Granda (with additional members) continue to perform throughout the U.S.; they released a new studio album, *13,* in 1997. Starting in the '80s, Granda—now based in Nashville—developed his solo work, participating in groups such as the Dog People, Supe and the Sandwiches, and the Garbonzos. Latter-day drummer Steve Canaday died in a plane crash.

Augustus Pablo

Born Horace Swaby, ca. 1953, Kingston, Jam.; died May 18, 1999, Kingston
1972—*This Is Augustus Pablo* (Kaya) 1974—*King Tubby Meets Rockers Uptown* (Clocktower) 1975—*Ital Dub* (Trojan) 1977—*Pablo Nuh Jester* (City Line) 1978—*East of the River Nile* (Rockers International/Message) 1979—*Original Rockers* (Greensleeves) 1980—*Rockers Meets King Tubby Inna Fire House* (Shanachie) 1982—*Earth's Rightful Ruler* (Rockers International) 1983—*King David's Melody* (Alligator) 1986—*Rising Sun* (Shanachie) 1988—*Rockers Comes East; Eastman Dub* (Greensleeves) 1989—*Rockers Story* (Ras) 1990—*Blowing With the Wind* (Shanachie) 1991—*Pablo Meets Mr. Bassie; Rockers International Showcase* (Rykodisc); *One Step Dub* (Greensleeves); *Live in Tokyo Japan* (Rockers International) 1992—*Authentic Golden Melodies* 1993—*Presents Rockers Dub Store 90s* 1994—*Heartical Chart* (Ras); *Presents Cultural Showcase* 1995—*Classic Rockers* (Island) 1996—*King Selassie I Calling* (Message) 1997—*In Roots Vibes* (Lagoon); *Presents DJs From the 70s & 80s* (Big Cat) 1998—*The Red Sea* (Aquarius) 1999—*Valley of Jehosophat* (Ras); *Pablo & Friends* 2000—*The Great Pablo* (Music Club).

Dub producer, composer, arranger, keyboardist, Augustus Pablo is one of the most distinguished names in reggae. He was equally renowned as the foremost exponent of the melodica, which has been used by numerous reggae artists as well as by Joe Jackson, the Clash, Gang of Four, and Cyndi Lauper's onetime backing band, the Hooters.

While still calling himself Horace Swaby, Pablo taught himself piano at Kingston College School and played organ at the local church. One day, he borrowed a melodica from a girlfriend and became fascinated by it. Bob Marley took young Swaby into his Kingston studios, where in 1969–70 Swaby contributed melodica lines to Lee Perry–produced Wailers tracks such as "Sun Is Shining," "Kaya," and "Memphis." Pablo has also led backing bands for Jimmy Cliff and Burning Spear and was at one time a member of Sly Dunbar's Skin, Flesh and Bones Band.

In 1971 producer Herman Chin-Loy gave Pablo his *nom de disc,* and the following year Pablo had his first hit single, "Java," which established his distinctive sound: Reggae rhythms supporting sinuous minor-key melodica and organ lines, and exotic modalities that Pablo termed "Far Eastern." He had reportedly claimed the influence of Modern Jazz Quartet vibraphonist Milt Jackson.

Around 1973, Pablo came under the sway of King Tubby, who with Lee Perry was one of the first dub producers. Pablo's *King Tubby Meets Rockers Uptown* is a landmark of dub; tunes are remixed almost beyond recognition. Pablo's most formidable trait was his unique (within dub) focus on melody; he made a long-running practice of dubbing such pop tunes as "Fiddler on the Roof" (in both *Uptown*'s "Say So" and *East of the River Nile*'s "Jah Light"), "Old Man River" (*This Is Augustus Pablo*'s "Jah Rock"), Rod McKuen's "Jean" (*Pablo Nuh Jester*'s "Fat Jean"), and Bill Withers' "Ain't No Sunshine" (*Original Rockers*' "Thunder Clap"), as well as following standard dub practice revamping reggae hits (including Marley's "Dem Belly Full" as "Pablo Meets Mr. Bassie," on the album of the same name).

Pablo's penchant for melodicism, and the near–New Age pastoral lyricism of his arrangements, set him further and further apart from the reggae mainstream through the '80s and '90s. Only on *Rockers Comes East* did Pablo flirt with the synth-heavy computer-rhythm sound that had come to dominate dub. On his next album, 1990's *Blowing With the Wind,* he returned to his trademark plaintive riffs, mellow grooves, and melodica/string-synth/vibraphone colorations. Pablo normally spent most of his time seeking inspiration in the remote hillsides outside of Kingston. In 1985 he played a rare U.S. concert at the Kitchen in New York City, and he undertook his only full-scale U.S. tour a year later. *Valley of Jehosophat* would be his last new studio album: Within weeks of its release, Pablo died of complications from the degenerative nerve disorder myasthenia gravis. Obituaries noted his influence on such trip-hop units as England's Massive Attack.

Pablo Cruise

Formed 1973, San Francisco, CA
Dave Jenkins (b. FL), gtr., bass, voc.; Cory Lerios (b. CA), kybds., voc.; Bud Cockrell (b. MS), bass, voc.; Steve Price (b. CA), drums.
1975—*Pablo Cruise* (A&M) 1976—*Life Line* 1977—*A Place in the Sun* (– Cockrell; + Bruce Day [b. CA], bass, voc.) 1978—*Worlds Away* 1980—*Part of the Game* (– Day; + John Pierce, bass, voc.; + Angelo Rossi, gtr., voc.) 1981—*Reflector* (– Price; + David Perper, drums, voc.; – Rossi; + Stef Birnbaum, gtr.) 1983—*Out of Our Hands* 1984—(group disbands) 1988—*Classics, vol. 26* 1997—(group re-forms: Jenkins; Cockrell; + James Henry, perc.; + Billy Johnson, drums; + Kincaid Miller, kybds.).

A band with a string of tunes that have become favorites on AM and FM radio and TV, Pablo Cruise exemplified the wholesome, ultrasmooth California sound. Indeed, its music has been called "music to watch sports by," and Pablo Cruise songs have been used as soundtracks for ABC's *Wide World of Sports,* CBS's *Sports Spectacular,* and NBC's *Sportsworld,* as well as for a surfing documentary called *Free Ride.* The band has also contributed to the soundtracks of the films *An Unmarried Woman* and *Dreamer.*

Pablo Cruise comes by its California heritage honestly. Dave Jenkins, Cory Lerios, and Steve Price were formerly with Stoneground, while Bud Cockrell came from It's a Beautiful Day. When Cockrell left to pursue a musical career with his wife, Pattie Santos (ex–It's a Beautiful Day), he was replaced by Bruce Day, formerly of Santana. (Santos died in a car accident in December 1989 at age 40.) The band first drew attention for such instrumentals as "Ocean Breeze" (from its debut LP) and "Zero to Sixty in Five" (from *Life Line*), both of which became FM-radio favorites. The band's first big hit was "Whatcha Gonna Do?" (#6, 1977), but Pablo Cruise really made it with *Worlds Away,* which contained three hit singles: "Love Will Find a Way" (#6, 1978), "Don't Want to Live Without It" (#21, 1978), and "I Go to Rio" (#46, 1979). The LP sold a million copies within a year of its release, as did *A Place in the Sun.* In 1981 Pablo Cruise scored again with its final hit, "Cool Love." The group disbanded in 1984, and Jenkins went on to join ex–Creedence Clearwater Revival Stu Cook and two ex–Doobie Brothers, John McFee and Keith Knudsen, in Southern Pacific. Around 1997, Cockrell and Jenkins re-formed Pablo Cruise with new members. The group continues to perform.

Jimmy Page

Born Jan. 9, 1944, Heston, Eng.
1982—*Death Wish II* soundtrack (Swan Song) 1988—*Outrider* (Geffen) 1993—*Coverdale/Page* 1994—*No Quarter; Jimmy Page and Robert Plant Unledded* (Atlantic) 1998—*Walking Into Clarksdale* (with Robert Plant) 2000—*Live at the Greek* (with the Black Crowes) (TVT)
With the Firm (Page, gtr.; Paul Rodgers [b. Dec. 17, 1949, Middleborough, Eng.], voc.; Chris Slade, drums; Tony Franklyn, bass): 1985—*The Firm* (Atlantic) 1986—*Mean Business.*

One of rock's most important and influential guitar players, writers, and producers, Jimmy Page has alternated between solo projects and collaborations with other superstars since the demise of Led Zeppelin [see entry] in 1980. But surpassed by new trends and technology, Page's later work has been as bound to classic rock as his legendary past accomplishments. In 1994 he rejoined vocalist Robert Plant to perform Zeppelin songs, along with new compositions, for an MTV *Unplugged* performance, entitled *Unledded,* and an album, *No Quarter.*

After Zeppelin drummer John Bonham's death, Page didn't touch a guitar for nine months. His first collaborative project after that, with Yes' Chris Squire and Alan White, never made it out of the studio. His soundtrack for the film *Death Wish II* is a predominantly instrumental album that at points found him playing fitfully with synthesizers. A 1983–84 ARMS benefit tour brought Page to the concert stage for the first time since 1980. He also contributed to former band mate Robert Plant's first solo album, *Pictures at 11,* in 1982.

Two years later Page founded the Firm with former Free and Bad Company vocalist Paul Rodgers. Page once referred to the band as a vehicle to show people he wasn't the drug user oft rumored. In the fall of 1984, however, he was arrested for possession of cocaine, his second offense, and his personal life continued to remain shrouded in mystery, colored by rumors of an interest in the occult and a period of heroin addiction.

The Firm released two albums and toured once, to lukewarm critical and mixed fan response. Then, because he wanted to "avoid routine," Page released his first nonsoundtrack studio album, *Outrider* (#26, 1988), which featured vocals by John Miles, Chris Farlowe, and Plant. *Outrider* earned Page a Grammy nomination for best rock instrumental and sent him on his first solo tour. For his next album, Page paired up with former Deep Purple and Whitesnake vocalist David Coverdale, whose similarities to Rodgers and Plant have provoked the ex-Zep singer to call him "David Coverversion." The Page-Coverdale collaboration is a solid if somewhat generic contribution to the hard rock Page pioneered (the album peaked at #5 in 1993).

Page and Plant put their differences aside in 1994 when they reunited to record a new album, *No Quarter,* in Wales, Morocco, and London, where *Unledded,* the MTV *Unplugged* special, was taped. A mix of Led Zep and new songs, the album featured musicians from Marrakech, India, and Egypt. Page and Plant embarked on a 1995 tour to promote the album.

In 1998 Page and Plant released *Walking Into Clarksdale,* the first album of new material they had recorded together in two decades. "Most High," a single, recalled Zep's hypnotic "Kashmir," but the album (its title an allusion to the cradle of the Delta blues) was more wistful than bombastic. Page was also featured on Sean Combs' "Come With Me," a song from the movie *Godzilla* that set rap lyrics to the melody from "Kashmir." In 1999 Page toured with the Black Crowes, performing a mix of Zep and Crowes material, as well as old blues covers. *Live at the Greek,* a tour document, came out in 2000.

Robert Palmer

Born Robert Alan Palmer, Jan. 19, 1949, Batley, Eng.
1974—*Sneakin' Sally Through the Alley* (Island) 1975—*Pressure Drop* 1976—*Some People Can Do What They Like* 1978—*Double Fun* 1979—*Secrets* 1980—*Clues* 1982—*Maybe It's Live* 1983—*Pride* 1985—*Riptide* 1988—*Heavy Nova* (EMI Manhattan) 1989—*"Addictions" vol. 1* (Island) 1990—*Don't Explain* (EMI) 1992—*Ridin' High; "Addictions" vol. 2* (Island) 1994—*Honey; The Very Best of Robert Palmer* (EMI) 1999—*Rhythm & Blues* (Pyramid/Rhino); *Disturbing Behavior* (EMI).

During the first part of his recording career, white soul singer Robert Palmer was equally renowned for his taste in rock and R&B cover songs as for his impeccably tailored suits. By the mid-'80s, however, Palmer had achieved mainstream stardom through a series of records that pitted his cool, understated vocals against smooth, catchy pop songs or overtly hard rockers.

Palmer spent most of his childhood on the island of Malta. Back in Britain as a teenager, he first sang in the band Mandrake Paddle Steamer, then went professional with the Alan Bown Set in 1968. The next year, he joined Dada, which changed its name to Vinegar Joe, releasing three albums (*Vinegar Joe* and *Rock 'n' Roll Gypsies,* both 1972, and *Six Star General,* 1973). When the band broke up, Palmer went solo.

Sneakin' Sally Through the Alley featured backup and songs by members of Little Feat and the Meters; the title track was by Allen Toussaint. Little Feat also had a hand in *Pressure Drop,* featuring the Toots and the Maytals' title cut and Palmer's own "Give Me an Inch." After making *Some People Can Do What They Like,* Palmer moved to Nassau, Bahamas. He had his first U.S. hit with ex-Free Andy Fraser's "Every Kinda People" (#16, 1978) from *Double Fun,* it was followed by Moon Martin's "Bad Case of Loving You (Doctor, Doctor)" (#14, 1979) from *Secrets,* the first album Palmer produced himself.

Clues, with a band including Chris Frantz (Talking Heads) and Gary Numan and material by Numan, found Palmer, on such cuts as "Johnny and Mary" and "Looking for Clues," moving into smooth synthesizer-driven pop. He followed his first Top 20 British hit, "Some Guys Have All the Luck," with *Maybe It's Live.*

Palmer's profile was raised considerably by his 1985 tenure in Power Station, a group consisting of Duran Duran's John Taylor and Andy Taylor and Chic's Tony Thompson. "Bang a Gong" and "Some Like It Hot" (#6, 1985) saw him rocking out more than before; unwilling to tour with the band, however, he soon departed.

The sleek rock he'd debuted with Power Station fostered his breakthrough, *Riptide.* "Addicted to Love" (#1, 1986) and "I Didn't Mean to Turn You On" (#2, 1986) were guitar-powered confections with instant mainstream appeal; boosted by videos featuring deadpan elegant models mimicking the role of backup band, they established Palmer as an ironic sex symbol, an MTV-era Cary Grant.

Moving with his family to Switzerland, Palmer contributed to the film *Sweet Lies* before releasing *Heavy Nova* and its hits, "Simply Irresistible" (#2, 1988) and "Early in the Morning" (#19, 1988). Its styles ranging from bossa nova to '40s-style balladeering, the album also demonstrated Palmer's continuing eclecticism. A collaboration with UB40 on Bob Dylan's "I'll Be Your Baby Tonight" enlivened *Don't Explain,* and on *Ridin' High,* Palmer turned in a credible collection of Tin Pan Alley and cabaret standards. The world beat–influenced *Honey* was inspired by Palmer's fondness for the great African singer King Sunny Ade. Palmer then reunited with John Taylor in a version of Power Station for 1996's *Living in Fear.* In 1999 he returned to soul music with *Rhythm & Blues,* an album on which he played virtually all the instruments.

Charlie Parker

Born Charles Christopher Parker, Aug. 29, 1920, Kansas City, KS; died Mar. 12, 1955, New York, NY
1953—*The Greatest Jazz Concert Ever* (Fantasy) 1978—*The Complete Savoy Studio Sessions* (Savoy) 1988—*Bird: The Complete Charlie Parker on Verve* (Verve); *Bebop & Bird, vol. 1* (Rhino); *Bebop & Bird, vol. 2* 1989—*The Legendary Dial Masters, vols. I & II* (Stash) 1995—*Bird With Strings: The Master Takes* (Verve) 1997—*Yardbird Suite: The Ultimate Charlie Parker Collection* (Rhino).

Alto saxophonist Charlie Parker was the most important figure in bebop, the musical form that revolutionized jazz in the mid-'40s. Also known as "Bird" or "Yardbird" (the stories vary as to how the nicknames came to be), Parker's innovative conceptions of jazz harmony and rhythm, along with an incredible command of his instrument, made him the most venerated musician of his time and a legend before his untimely death at age 35.

Born in the right time and the right place, Parker grew up listening to the great bands and soloists who made Kansas City, Missouri, their stomping ground in the early '30s. Hearing tenor saxophonist Lester Young with Count Basie's band inspired the precocious Parker, who had begun playing saxophone at age 11. By 17, after intensive practice, Parker had honed his skills and found work with the Kansas City band of Buster Smith, an altoist who exerted a strong influence on Parker's playing.

In 1938 and 1939, Parker spent time in New York, where he got to observe advanced musicians such as pianist Art Tatum and further define his burgeoning style. In 1940 Parker returned to Kansas City and joined Jay McShann's big band, with which he did his first recordings. Parker stayed with McShann for two years, but the lure of New York, with its coterie of forward-thinking musicians, proved too strong.

Due to a musicians' union strike that lasted for the next few years, Parker's rapid growth went undocumented. In 1943 Parker played in pianist Earl Hines' band and then in an offshoot band led by Hines' singer Billy Eckstine. Both of these bands were important proto-bop bands whose players were on the cusp of jazz's next wave. During this time, Parker was also attending the monumental Harlem jam sessions led by pianist Thelonious Monk and drummer Kenny Clarke, where seeds of bop's development were also being sown.

The breakthrough came in 1945 when Parker, alongside trumpeter Dizzy Gillespie—the only other player in the same virtuosic league as Parker—made a series of recordings that included "Shaw 'Nuff," "Salt Peanuts," and "Hot House" and defined the new music. A session under Parker's leadership soon after produced "Now's the Time," "Billie's Bounce," and "Koko." Bebop was a whole new ball game: The harmonies were more complex, the rhythms varied and unpredictable, the tempos ultrafast. Seemingly overnight, jazz went from dance-oriented music to art music designed for listening only.

Parker and Gillespie, whose band had been the rage in New York, headed for California in late 1945 for what turned out to be a disastrous sojourn. Bebop was unpopular with the West Coast public, Parker and Gillespie quarreled, and Parker slid full force into a drug problem that had plagued him since his teens. By July 1946, Parker had suffered a mental collapse and was institutionalized at the Camarillo State Hospital for seven months.

On his release, Parker was again at the top of his form, cutting more brilliant sides that included "A Night in Tunisia," "Relaxing at Camarillo," "Ornithology," and "Yardbird Suite," before heading back to New York. There, he put together a first-rate band with drummer Max Roach and trumpeter Miles Davis, whose recordings for Dial are among Parker's greatest work. By this time, Parker was the most acclaimed and influential jazz musician alive. Over the next few years, though, Parker's exceptional music contrasted with the downward swing of his personal life; heroin addiction and alcoholism destroyed whatever semblance of order Parker tried to impose on his life. In 1949 Parker made a triumphant tour of Europe; in New York, a popular nightclub, Birdland, was named in his honor.

Throughout the '50s, Parker continued making exceptional music with his own groups, on tour with Jazz at the Philharmonic, as a solo performer, and at occasional reunions with Dizzy Gillespie, who had gone on to become a star; but his behavior became increasingly erratic. In 1954, following the death of Parker's daughter Chan, the bottom fell out of his life. His excessive behavior mangled an all-star performance at Birdland in early 1955, leading him to be banned from the club. Depressed and in ill health, Parker took refuge at the New York apartment of jazz patron Baroness Nica de Konigswarter. While watching TV there, Parker died of a hemorrhage related to pneumonia.

Graham Parker

Born Nov. 18, 1950, London, Eng.
1976—*Howlin' Wind* (Mercury); *Heat Treatment* 1977—*The Pink Parker* (Vertigo/Mercury); *Stick to Me* (Mercury) 1978—*The Parkerilla* 1979—*Squeezing Out Sparks* (Arista) 1980—*The Up Escalator* 1982—*Another Grey Area* 1983—*The Real Macaw* 1985—*Steady Nerves* (Elektra) 1988—*The Mona Lisa's Sister* (RCA) 1989—*Human Soul; Live! Alone in America* 1991—*Struck by Lightning* 1992—*Burning Questions* (Capitol) 1993—*Passion Is No Ordinary Word: The Graham Parker Anthology (1976–1991)* (Rhino) 1995—*12 Haunted Episodes* (Razor & Tie) 1996—*Acid Bubblegum* 1997—*The Last Rock N Roll Tour* 1999—*Loose Monkeys: Spare Tracks and Lost Demos* (UpYours/Razor & Tie).

One of the most critically acclaimed graduates of the mid-'70s British pub-rock scene, singer/songwriter Graham Parker was compared to Bob Dylan and Bruce Springsteen for the best of his angry, eloquent songs. Yet the commercial success he always seemed to deserve remained, for the most part, just outside his grasp.

Until 1975, Parker lived off a succession of odd jobs, including gas-station attendant and breeder of mice and guinea pigs for a scientific institute. He had also spent time in a cover band playing in Gibraltar and Morocco in the late '60s.

In 1975 Dave Robinson (who would found Stiff Records in 1977) heard some Parker demos and became his manager, backing him with a band of pub-rock veterans: The Rumour [see entry] included guitarist Brinsley Schwarz and keyboardist Bob Andrews from the band Brinsley Schwarz [see entry] (which also included Nick Lowe, who produced Parker's first and third LPs), guitarist Martin Belmont from Ducks Deluxe, bassist Andrew Bodnar, and drummer Steve Goulding from Bontemps Roulez. Parker's first two LPs with the Rumour won mammoth critical acclaim but sold barely respectably in the U.S.

Parker had many run-ins with his label, Mercury, accusing it of poor distribution and promotion that resulted in the mediocre sales (*Heat Treatment* did best, selling some 60,000 copies and peaking at #169). *Stick to Me* (#125, 1977), which had to be quickly rerecorded after the original tapes were mangled, sold about as much, though Parker's club audiences had grown, thanks to the emergence of punk. In 1978 Parker rushed out the live *Parkerilla* (#149, 1978), reportedly in order to escape his Mercury contract. Parker wrote the scathing "Mercury Poisoning" about the label's alleged incompetence; it was released as the B side of a promotional 45 by his new label, Arista, and did not turn up on album until the 1993 *Anthology.*

Arista signed Parker after an intense music-industry bidding war. His first Arista LP, *Squeezing Out Sparks* (#40, 1979), stands as probably his finest artistic and commercial achievement; it made the Top 40, with "Local Girls" and "Passion Is No Ordinary Word" garnering heavy FM-radio play. Parker's star continued to rise with a live cover of the Jackson 5's "I Want You Back" (never included on an album until *Anthology*) that was widely played on college radio. But Parker was unable to consolidate that incipient success. *The Up Escalator* (#40, 1980; produced by Jimmy Iovine) and *Another Grey Area* (#51, 1982; produced by Jack Douglas) met with mixed response and unexceptional sales; and by then the Rumour had released a couple of LPs on its own. Various studio musicians and others, including Nicky Hopkins and Hugh McCracken, backed up Parker. Bruce Springsteen sang on *Escalator*'s "Endless Night." Various Rumour members, meanwhile, worked with Nick Lowe and Garland Jeffreys.

Parker had a minor hit single with "Wake Up Next to You" (#39, 1985), but since then, only 1985's *Steady Nerves* (#57) and 1988's *The Mona Lisa's Sister* (#77) made the Top 100. His subsequent albums have all received favorable notices: *12 Haunted Episodes,* the first of his recordings on U.S. independent Razor & Tie, is a lovely, primarily acoustic set; *Acid Bubblegum* found Parker in his more rocking, angry guise: Following its release, he played a slew of fiery live shows, backed by the spirited young punk-pop band the Figgs. *Loose Monkeys* was initially available only on the Internet. Since 1988, Parker has been living in the Woodstock, New York, area, where he began devoting some of his time to prose writing (contributing to *Rolling Stone's Alt-Rock-a-Rama* [1996] and *The Rolling Stone Book of the Beats* [1999]) and doing spoken-word performances. Parker's first work of fiction, *Carp Fishing on Valium,* was published by St. Martin's Press in 2000.

Junior Parker

Born Herman Parker, Mar. 3, 1927, West Memphis, AR; died Nov. 18, 1971, Blue Island, IL
1960—*Driving* (Duke) 1961—*Blues Consolidated* 1964—*Junior Parker* (Bluesway) 1967—*Like It Is* (Mercury) 1970—*Outside Man* (Capitol) 1972—*Blue Shadows Falling* (Groove Merchant); *Good Things Don't Happen Everyday* 1973—*You Don't Have to Be Black . . .* (People); *The Best of Junior Parker* (MCA) 1974—*Love Ain't Nothing but Business* 1976—*Love My Baby* EP (Charly) 1978—*Legendary Sun Performers* 1992—*Junior's Blues: The Duke Recordings, vol. 1* (MCA).

A highly respected blues vocalist and harmonica player, Junior Parker may be best known as the author of Elvis Presley's 1955 classic "Mystery Train." But Parker had a long, noteworthy career of his own, which included stints with blues performers like Sonny Boy Williamson II, Howlin' Wolf, B.B. King, and Johnny Ace.

Parker's career began in 1948 at a Sonny Boy Williamson show, where Parker responded to Williamson's request for a harmonica player from the audience; Parker ended up playing with Williamson for the rest of his tour and leading the band when Williamson had solo commitments. In 1949 Parker played with Howlin' Wolf and, two years later, after Wolf had temporarily retired, took over that band, which also included pianist Ike Turner and guitarist M.T. Murphy. Parker then moved to Memphis and joined the Beale Streeters, which also included B.B. King, Bobby Bland, Johnny Ace, and Rosco Gordon. In 1952 Parker formed his own band, the Blue Flames, with whom he made his first recordings for Modern. He then moved to Sun Records, where he had a massive hit, "Feelin' Good," in 1953. His second Sun release, "Mystery Train," was a minor hit; Presley had much more success with it. In 1954 Parker began a four-year association with Houston's Duke Records.

In 1953 Parker had joined the Johnny Ace Revue, which also included Big Mama Thornton. When Ace died (losing a game of Russian roulette) in 1954, Parker took over the Revue, renaming it Blues Consolidated, and toured with it through 1961. He also toured with Bobby Bland and Joe Hinton.

Among Parker's many R&B hits were "Next Time You See Me" (#7, 1957), "Driving Wheel" (#5, 1961), "In the Dark" (#7, 1961), and "Annie Get Your Yo-Yo" (#6, 1962). Some of his

Junior Parker

better-known earlier performances were "Mother-in-Law Blues" and "Barefoot Rock." On some of these early recordings, Parker's guitarist, Pat Hare, can be heard experimenting with unusually uptempo driving rhythms and distorted solos. As late as 1971, Parker was still having minor R&B hits, among them "Ain't Gon' Be No Cutting Loose" and "Drowning on Dry Land," and had recorded for Blue Rock, Minit, and Capitol. His death came after surgery for a brain tumor.

Maceo Parker

Born Feb. 14, 1943, Kinston, NC
1970—*Doing Their Own Thing* (House of the Fox) 1974—*Us* (People) 1975—*Funky Music Machine* (El Cello) 1990—*For All the King's Men* (4th and Broadway); *Pee Wee, Fred & Maceo* (Gramavision); *Roots Revisited* (Verve) 1991—*Mo' Roots* 1993—*Life on Planet Groove; Southern Exposure* (RCA/Novus) 1998—*Funk Overload* (What Are?) 2000—*Dial M-A-C-E-O.*

If only for his soulful work with James Brown, saxophonist Maceo Parker's place in R&B history is secure. Parker began his musical career playing tenor saxophone in local bands in his native North Carolina; early groups included the Junior Blue Notes, which Parker formed in elementary school with his brothers, trombonist Kellis and drummer Melvin.

In 1962 James Brown heard Melvin at a club and offered him an open invitation to join his band. Two years later, when he approached Brown to take him up on his offer, Melvin brought along Maceo, and Brown hired them both. During his tenure with Brown, Parker—who played tenor and baritone saxophones—became one of the band's chief soloists. Brown's cry, "Maceo, blow your horn" would be the prelude for Parker's funky statements.

Parker left Brown's band in 1970 and worked in a series of groups including Maceo and the Macks, Maceo and All the King's Men, and Fred Wesley and the JB's. When Parker rejoined Brown in 1973, he switched to alto saxophone. Although Parker freelanced throughout the next 20 years with George Clinton's P-Funk conglomerations and Bootsy's Rubber Band, his main gig was with Brown. When Brown was imprisoned in 1993, Parker struck out on his own to remarkable acclaim. His first two solo recordings on Verve reached #1 on the jazz chart. Parker found that he had achieved near-legendary stature: New bands including Deee-Lite, 10,000 Maniacs, De La Soul, and Living Colour used him on their recordings, and rappers continuously sampled his work with Brown. In 1998 he returned to funkier fare after his Verve jazz excursions, collaborating with Prince and Ani DiFranco and featuring his son Corey Parker as resident rapper in his band.

Van Dyke Parks

Born Jan. 3, 1943, Hattiesburg, MI
1968—*Song Cycle* (Warner Bros.) 1972—*Discover America* 1975—*The Clang of the Yankee Reaper* 1984—*Jump!* 1989—*Tokyo Rose* 1998—*Moonlighting: Live at the Ash Grove.*
Brian Wilson and Van Dyke Parks: 1995—*Orange Crate Art* (Warner Bros.).

Even by Hollywood standards, Van Dyke Parks is an oddball. His specialty—in his over two decades in the music business as songwriter, lyricist, arranger, and producer—is dense aural and verbal montages, which are most easily sampled in his lyrics for the Beach Boys' "Heroes and Villains" or "Surf's Up."

Parks moved with his family to Hollywood at age 13 and became a child actor while studying classical piano and composition. In the early '60s, he reportedly signed with a major studio to write soundtracks. Instead, he began writing his own songs, one of which, "High Coin," has become a folk-rock standard and was covered by Bobby Vee, Harper's Bizarre, and the Charlatans (San Francisco), among others. In the mid-'60s, he produced such hits as the Mojo Men's cover of Stephen Stills' "Sit Down I Think I Love You" and Harper's Bizarre's cover of Cole Porter's "Anything Goes."

In 1966 Parks began collaborating with Brian Wilson of the Beach Boys on the never-released *Smile* LP; some of the songs appeared on later Beach Boys albums. He also produced Judy Collins, Randy Newman, Ry Cooder, Phil Ochs, Arlo Guthrie, and others, becoming something of an L.A. local legend for his mysterious, meticulous methods. His first solo LP, an ambitious and eclectic project four years in the making, earned him the reputation of "the first art rocker."

Parks was made director of audiovisual services for Warner Bros. in 1970, a post he quit a year later. He also played keyboards on sessions with Judy Collins and with the Byrds (on "5D [Fifth Dimension]"), and in the score for Robert Altman's *Popeye*, in which he briefly appeared onscreen. His two other solo LPs showcased his love of calypso music; both featured the Esso Trinidad Steel Band. He has also scored *Goin' South* and *The Two Jakes*. Neither *Jump!*, which was centered around the fictional character of Uncle Remus, nor *Tokyo Rose*, an examination of U.S.-Japanese relations, sparked much interest. Although his records never sold very well when originally issued, they were all rereleased on CD in 1990.

Then, in 1995, nearly 30 years after their ill-fated collaborations on *Smile*, Parks and Wilson started working together again on an album entitled *Orange Crate Art*. Wilson provided all lead and most backing vocals for the dozen new songs (mostly about California and its mythological appeal) that Parks wrote, arranged, and produced. Critics were generally enthusiastic about the album's nostalgic pop, but there was little commercial interest.

Parliament: See George Clinton

Alan Parsons

Born 1949
Alan Parsons Project, formed 1975, London, Eng.

1976—*Tales of Mystery and Imagination—Edgar Allan Poe* (Arista) 1977—*I Robot* 1978—*Pyramid* 1979—*Eve* 1980—*The Turn of a Friendly Card* 1982—*Eye in the Sky* 1983—*The Best of the Alan Parsons Project* 1984—*Ammonia Avenue* 1985—*Vulture Culture* 1986—*Stereotomy* 1987—*Gaudi* 1992—*Try Anything Once* 1996—*On Air* (River North) 1999—*The Time Machine* (Miramar).

Alan Parsons is mainly a producer/engineer. He worked on the Beatles' *Abbey Road* and Paul McCartney's *Wildlife* and *Red Rose Speedway.* He also produced Pink Floyd's *The Dark Side of the Moon* and Al Stewart's *Time Passages.* He plays keyboards and sometimes sings with the Alan Parsons Project, a loose collection of English session players interpreting Parsons' and lyricist/manager Eric Woolfson's arty, highly synthesized and orchestrated concepts.

Vocalists on his LPs have included Arthur Brown, Steve Harley of Cockney Rebel, Allan Clarke of the Hollies, and ex-Zombie Colin Blunstone. *I Robot, Card* (about a gambling obsession), and *Eye* all went platinum. These and Parsons' other LPs have yielded an array of hits: "Games People Play" (#16, 1980), "Time" (#15, 1981), "Eye in the Sky" (#3, 1982), and "Don't Answer Me" (#15, 1984) all went Top 20. Following the gold *Ammonia Avenue,* the group's releases have been of more interest to die-hard fans than to casual listeners. The "Project" was dropped from the ensemble's name for 1992's *Try Anything Once.* The following year, Parsons produced an album by Yes with the London Philharmonic Orchestra. He embarked on his first-ever tours in 1994 and 1995. Released in 1996, *On Air* is a concept work about flying that features Christopher Cross and Eric Stewart of 10cc. In 1999 comedian Mike Myers dubbed his villain's death ray "The Alan Parsons Project" in the hit comedy *Austin Powers: The Spy Who Shagged Me;* flattered, Parsons sampled the movie's dialog on his H.G. Wells–inspired album *The Time Machine.*

Gram Parsons

Born Ingram Cecil Connor III, Nov. 5, 1946, Winter Haven, FL; died Sep. 19, 1973, Joshua Tree, CA
1973—*GP* (Reprise) 1974—*Grievous Angel* 1976—*Sleepless Nights* (A&M) 1979—*Gram Parsons: The Early Years 1963–1965* (Sierra/Briar) 1982—*Gram Parsons and the Fallen Angels—Live 1973* (Sierra) 2000—*Another Side of This Life* (Sundazed) 2001—*Sacred Hearts & Fallen Angels: The Gram Parsons Anthology* (Rhino).
With the International Submarine Band: 1968—*Safe at Home* (LHI).
With the Flying Burrito Brothers: see entry.

Georgia-bred singer/songwriter Gram Parsons brought traditional country music to the rock & roll audience. With his wracked, emotive vocals and his compelling C&W songcraft, he was a major influence on a variety of artists ranging from Emmylou Harris to Keith Richards to Elvis Costello. Though he hated the term "country rock" and the kind of music the term came to define, Parsons undoubtedly pioneered the genre, via his groups the International Submarine Band and the Flying Burrito Brothers, one album with the Byrds, and his solo recordings. Though none of the bands he started or the albums he made was ever commercially successful, he has achieved near-mythic status since his 1973 death at age 26. In the '90s his work continues to be embraced by a new generation of artists, many of them alt-country artists and alt-rockers.

Ingram Cecil Connor spent much of his childhood in Waycross, Georgia. The son of a Florida citrus heiress and a Tennessee-born World War II vet named Coon Dog Connor, he grew up in the lap of luxury. At age nine, he learned to play the piano, but his main musical inspiration was seeing Elvis Presley perform that year at his local auditorium. By age 12, he'd begun playing guitar. At that point, however, his life was shattered by the suicide of his father.

The family moved to his maternal grandparents' mansion in Winter Haven, Florida; the next year, his mother married Robert Parsons, who adopted Gram and legally changed his surname to Parsons. At age 14, Parsons began playing in a succession of local rock & roll bands as well as in folk groups. In 1964 his group the Shilohs made some recordings and performed throughout the Southeast. The next year, on the day Parsons graduated from high school, his mother died of alcohol poisoning. Parsons left Florida that fall for Harvard, where he spent more time playing music than studying. After one semester, he dropped out and moved from Cambridge to the Bronx with his new group, the International Submarine Band. In 1966, with a repertoire of traditional country and R&B-tinged songs, the band played a few shows in New York, then relocated to L.A. after recording an unsuccessful single for Columbia. There, the band got a cameo role in Roger Corman's *The Trip,* but by the time Parsons recorded the ISB album *Safe at Home* (for Lee Hazlewood's LHI label), the band had broken up, and Parsons made the album primarily with session players. Soon after its release, Parsons met Chris Hillman and through him joined the Byrds [see entry]. The Byrds' *Sweetheart of the Rodeo* included two Parsons songs, "Hickory Wind" (cowritten with Bob Buchanan) and "One Hundred Years From Now." (Parsons' lead vocals on several songs were not released until 1990, on the Byrds box set.)

After just three months in the Byrds, Parsons quit in summer 1968, refusing to join the band's tour of South Africa, reportedly because of his opposition to apartheid. In late 1968 he and Hillman (who also left the Byrds) formed the Flying Burrito Brothers [see entry]. Parsons played a strong role on the Burritos' first LP, but left the band in April 1970, just before *Burritos Deluxe* came out.

In 1970 Parsons, after recovering from injuries sustained in a motorcycle accident, recorded some tracks with producer Terry Melcher that were never released. He spent the next two years indulging in the rock & roll lifestyle, including a stint at his friend Keith Richards' French villa during the recording of the Stones' *Exile on Main Street.* Parsons did not record again until his 1973 solo debut *GP,* which featured Emmylou Harris [see entry] (who'd been discovered by Hillman) and backing by Rick Grech (ex–Blind Faith and Family); a friend from his Cambridge days, Barry Tashian (of Barry and the Remains fame); and three members of Elvis Presley's touring band, Glen D. Hardin, James Burton, and Ronnie Tutt.

Following a brief tour with his band, the Fallen Angels, Parsons returned to the studio to record *Grievous Angel.* It had just been completed when, in September 1973, Parsons overdosed on a combination of morphine and tequila while relaxing at a favorite desert retreat near the Joshua Tree National Monument. He was pronounced dead after being rushed to the Yucca Valley Hospital. A few days later, his coffin, en route to New Orleans for burial, was stolen by his friend and road manager Phil Kaufman and taken back to Joshua Tree and set afire. It was later revealed that Parsons had expressed a wish for his ashes to be scattered at Joshua Tree in the event of his death.

Parsons' legacy lived on as Emmylou Harris toured with his old band and covered and popularized his material, as did many others, including Costello on his country LP, *Almost Blue.* Costello also wrote liner notes for a 1982 British compilation of Parsons' work. Bernie Leadon's song "My Man," from the Eagles' 1974 *On the Border,* was a tribute to Parsons, and a song Richie Furay wrote about him in 1969, "Crazy Eyes," was the title track of a 1973 Poco LP.

In 1979 Sierra/Briar Records released an album of early Parsons material with the Shilohs; a live recording of a Fallen Angels gig was released by the label four years later. In 2000 Sundazed issued Parsons' 1965–66 solo acoustic demos, which included an early version of "Brass Buttons," a song that had been recorded by Parsons' Florida buddy Jim Carlton. *The Gram Parsons Notebook,* also released in 2000, featured bluegrass-style songs composed of music set to Parsons' lyrics found in one of his journals by former ISB member John Nuese.

Tribute albums have also kept Parsons' songs alive. In 1993 Rhino issued *Conmemorativo: A Tribute to Gram Parsons,* with his songs covered by the Mekons, Uncle Tupelo, Bob Mould, Peter Buck (R.E.M.), Peter Holsapple, Susan Cowsill, Steve Wynn, and others. Emmylou Harris was the executive producer of the 1999 tribute album *Return of the Grievous Angel* (Almo Sounds) featuring, among others, Lucinda Williams, Steve Earle, and Harris duets with Chrissie Hynde, Beck, and Sheryl Crow. A performance by many of the album's contributors was televised on the PBS program *Sessions at West 54th Street* in 1999.

Dolly Parton

Born Jan. 19, 1946, Sevierville, TN
1969—*Just the Two of Us* (with Porter Wagoner) (RCA) 1970—*The Best of Dolly Parton* 1971—*Joshua* 1973—*My Tennessee Mountain Home* 1974—*Love Is Like a Butterfly* 1975—*The Bargain Store; Best of Dolly Parton; Dolly* 1976—*All I Can Do* 1977—*New Harvest . . . First Gathering; Here You Come Again* 1978—*In the Beginning* (Monument); *Heartbreaker* (RCA) 1979—*Great Balls of Fire* 1980—*9 to 5 and Odd Jobs* 1982—*Heartbreak Express; Greatest Hits* 1983—*Burlap and Satin* 1984—*The Great Pretender; Once Upon a Christmas* (with Kenny Rogers) 1987—*Trio* (with Linda Ronstadt and Emmylou Harris) (Warner Bros.); *Rainbow* (Columbia) 1989—*White Limozeen* 1991—*Eagle When She Flies* 1992—*Straight Talk* (Hollywood) 1993—*Slow Dancing With the Moon* (Columbia); *Honky Tonk Angels* (with Loretta Lynn and Tammy Wynette) 1994—*Heartsongs: Live From Home* (Blue Eye) 1995—*Something Special* (Columbia) 1996—*I Will Always Love You and Other Greatest Hits; Treasures* (Riding Tide) 1998—*Hungry Again* (Decca) 1999—*Trio II* (with Linda Ronstadt and Emmylou Harris) (Asylum); *The Grass Is Blue* (Sugar Hill) 2001—*Little Sparrow.*

Dolly Parton's girlish soprano and songs about old-time virtues made her a major country star in the early '70s. Later in that decade, she wooed the pop audience and became a household name, her playful, self-deprecating comments about her blond sex-bomb image winning hearts as her finely crafted country-pop singles yielded a succession of more than 20 C&W #1 hits. Parton wrote many of her own hits, either alone or in collaboration with Bill Owens. Among the songs she's written is "I Will Always Love You," a #1 country hit for Parton in 1974 and 1982 that sold over 4 million copies in 1992 for Whitney Houston.

Parton grew up poor on a farm in the foothills of Tennessee's Smoky Mountains, the fourth of 12 children born to a farming couple. Her sister Stella later became a singer as well, and five other siblings have worked as professional musicians. Parton sang in church as a girl, and at age 10 appeared on the Cass Walker TV show in Knoxville with members of her grade school class. She became a regular on

Dolly Parton

Walker's radio show, where she performed until age 18. Parton appeared at the Grand Ole Opry at age 12, and her first single, "Puppy Love," was released by the blues-oriented Louisiana label Goldband.

One day after graduating high school, in 1964, she moved to Nashville and signed with Monument. Her first day in town, she met Carl Dean, whom she married two years later. Early recordings, in a rock vein, were not successful. Her big break came with "Dumb Blonde," a minor hit that peaked at #24 on the country chart. In 1967 she joined singer Porter Wagoner's syndicated country-music show, and "Miss Dolly," as she was called, became very popular with viewers. She signed to RCA, and the duo had many country hits, including "Just Someone I Used to Know" (1969) and "Daddy Was an Old Time Preacher Man" (1970). While with Wagoner, she charted over a dozen solo country & western hits, including "Joshua" (#1, 1970) and "Coat of Many Colors" (#4, 1971).

In 1974 Parton left Wagoner completely, having released *Jolene*, the title track of which became her second #1 country hit and a minor pop crossover. Other singers began to take an interest in her work. Linda Ronstadt covered "I Will Always Love You" (which Parton wrote about leaving Porter Wagoner) in 1975 on *Prisoner in Disguise*, Emmylou Harris sang "Coat of Many Colors" that same year, and Maria Muldaur covered "My Tennessee Mountain Home" on her first record. The covers encouraged Parton to bring her country to the pop market, which she did with *New Harvest*. The LP was more rock-oriented and included a version of "Higher and Higher." She also broke away from the country circuit to play rock clubs.

Parton's first major pop single was "Here You Come Again," which went gold and hit #3 in early 1978. The LP of the same name went platinum. She also hit the pop Top 20 that year with "Two Doors Down." Parton had successfully crossed over; "Baby, I'm Burnin' " (#25, 1978) even had some success in discos. Other #1 C&W hits of that time include "You're the Only One" (1979), "Starting Over Again" (1980), and "Old Flames Can't Hold a Candle to You" (1980). By 1980, Parton was a regular headliner in Las Vegas, and that year she earned an Oscar nomination for her film debut in *9 to 5* (costarring Jane Fonda and Lily Tomlin). Parton's recording of the title theme was a #1 hit in pop and country. In 1982 she costarred with Burt Reynolds in *The Best Little Whorehouse in Texas*. Her other film credits include *Rhinestone* (with Sylvester Stallone, 1984), *Steel Magnolias* (with Julia Roberts and Shirley MacLaine, 1989), *Straight Talk* (with James Woods, 1992), the made-for-television *Wild Texas Wind* (with Gary Busey, 1992), and *The Beverly Hillbillies* (1993). In 1976 she hosted a syndicated music show, *Dolly*; her 1987 prime-time variety show of the same name on ABC did not fare as well and was canceled after one season.

Immediately before the release of *Rhinestone Cowboy*, Parton began a difficult period plagued by health problems. Through the '80s she continued to score C&W #1 hits with "But You Know I Love You" (1981), "I Will Always Love You" (1982), the Bee Gees–written and –produced duet with Kenny Rogers, "Islands in the Stream" (1983), "Tennessee Homesick Blues" (1984), "Real Love" (another duet with Rogers, 1985), "Think About Love" (1985), "Why'd You Come in Here Lookin' Like That" (1989), "Yellow Roses" (1989), and "Rockin' Years" (1991), a duet with Ricky Van Shelton.

Parton's most successful album of the period was *Trio*, a collection of traditional country songs performed with Emmylou Harris and Linda Ronstadt. In 1987 it won a Grammy for Best Country Album by a Duo or Group with Vocal. In 1999 the long-awaited followup, *Trio II*, was released. It featured a Grammy-winning (Best Country Collaboration With Vocals) cover of Neil Young's "After the Gold Rush." In 1993 Parton teamed with Loretta Lynn and Tammy Wynette for *Honky Tonk Angels*, an album featuring the songs of country singers such as Patsy Cline and Kitty Wells (who appears on the title track).

In 1986 Parton opened Dollywood, a Smoky Mountain theme park. She has also established the Dolly Parton Wellness and Rehabilitation Center of Sevier County Medical Center as well as the Dollywood Foundation, which works to lower the high school–dropout rate in her home county. In 1994 she released her autobiography, *Dolly: My Life and Unfinished Business*. In 1996 Parton picked up her eighth career Country Music Association Award, for Vocal Event of the Year, for a new version of "I Will Always Love You" (#15 C&W, 1995) recorded with Vince Gill for a greatest-hits set. After 1996's *Treasures*, an album of covers, Parton moved to Decca and recorded *Hungry Again*, a rootsy collection of self-penned songs that kicked off what many critics viewed as an artistic reawakening for the veteran performer. In 1994 she was inducted into the Country Music Hall of Fame and cut her first bluegrass album, *The Grass Is Blue*, for the independent Sugar Hill label. The set featured an all-star band of bluegrass pros (including mandolin ace Sam Bush and Dobro player Jerry Douglas, among others) and went on to win Parton Album of the Year at the International Bluegrass Music Awards and a pair of Grammy nominations. She followed it in 2001 with a second bluegrass effort, *Little Sparrow*, which in addition to several new originals featured such left-field covers as Cole Porter's "I Get a Kick Out of You" and Collective Soul's gospel-rock anthem "Shine."

The Partridge Family

Formed 1970, Los Angeles, CA
David Cassidy (b. Apr. 12, 1950, New York, NY), voc., gtr.; Shirley Jones (b. Mar. 31, 1934, Charleron, PA), voc.; studio musicians.
1970—*The Partridge Family Album* 1971—*Up to Date; The Partridge Family Sound Magazine* 1972—*The Partridge Family Shopping Bag; The Partridge Family at Home With Their Greatest Hits* 1989—*The Partridge Family Lunchbox/Greatest Hits* (Arista).

The Partridge Family, featuring teen idol David Cassidy, was more a marketing idea than a band. Their music was plugged on *The Partridge Family* TV series, which was about a family as traveling pop band (based loosely on the

Cowsills), though only two of the actors actually sang on the group's many hit singles. The two real voices were Cassidy (who also played some guitar) and his stepmother, Shirley Jones, a veteran lead in many musicals, including *The Music Man, Carousel,* and *Oklahoma!*

Rounding out the family on the TV show were Danny Bonaduce, Brian Foster, Suzanne Crough, and ex-model Susan Dey. The show premiered on ABC on September 25, 1970, and weeks later the group's first single, "I Think I Love You," rose to #1 and went on to sell 4 million copies. Their debut, *The Partridge Family Album* (#4, 1970), went gold, and within 12 months, the group had two more gold LPs (the total eventually would reach five), both in the Top 10. Cassidy (who played Keith Partridge) sang lead, and, by 1972, he'd begun to tour and record solo as well as with "the band." Under the Partridge Family name came three more 1971 hits: "Doesn't Somebody Want to Be Wanted" (#6), "I'll Meet You Halfway" (#9), and "I Woke Up in Love This Morning" (#13). They had three more Top 40 hits, two in 1972 and then, the next year, "Looking Through the Eyes of Love" (#39).

But the Partridge Family's popularity had waned by that time, and in 1974 the show ended. Cassidy went on to a solo career [see separate entry]. Dey continued acting; she appeared in several films, including *Echo Park* (with Tom Hulce), and became a regular on the popular television series *L.A. Law.* Bonaduce has had a checkered career, marked by run-ins with the law over drugs, several stints as a disc jockey, and a number of publicity stunts, one of which was a boxing match with fellow ex–teen idol Donny Osmond.

Jaco Pastorius: See Weather Report

Charley Patton

Born Apr. 1891, Bolton, MS; died Apr. 28, 1934, Indianola, MS
1988—*Founder of the Delta Blues* (Yazoo) 1991—*King of the Delta Blues* 1992—*Charley Patton: The Complete Recorded Works* (Peavine).

Gruff-voiced Charley Patton was an early Delta-blues singer of mythic status. In his day the most popular bluesman in Mississippi, Patton also recorded ballads and religious and ragtime songs. His acoustic guitar technique and his bottleneck slide playing—its rhythmic complexity influenced by West African drumming—his refusal to be confined to standard 12-bar blues patterns, and the emotional intensity of his songs made him a signal figure of the Delta blues, capable of both furthering the form and transcending it.

Remaining in the Mississippi Delta (the northwest corner of the state) until his death at age 43, Patton began recording for Paramount in 1929; by that time, he'd already been a popular live performer among both black and white audiences for at least 15 years. "Pony Blues," "Tom Rushen Blues," and "Moon Going Down" are representative of a vast repertoire that influenced Howlin' Wolf, Big Joe Williams, and Son House. House, however, was also among a sizable camp who derided Patton for "clownish" behavior, a charge refuted musically, at least, by the social consciousness evident in "Down the Dirt Road Blues" and its attack on racism and by the fervor of Patton's religious recordings. Clearly, Patton was an outsized figure, given to his own myth making, but the thematic breadth of his songs (from tales of lust and cocaine use to political observation and finely detailed reportage) qualified him as a poetic representative of a complex Southern rural world. He died in 1934 from a chronic heart condition.

Billy Paul

Born Paul Williams, Dec. 1, 1934, Philadelphia, PA
1970—*Ebony Woman* (Philadelphia International) 1971—*Going East* 1972—*360 Degrees of Billy Paul* 1973—*Feelin' Good at the Cadillac Club; War of the Gods* 1974—*Live in Europe* 1975—*Got My Head on Straight; When Love Is New* 1976—*Let 'Em In* 1977—*Only the Strong Survive* 1979—*First Class* 1983—*Billy Paul's Greatest Hits* 1985—*Lately* (Total Experience) 1988—*Wide Open* (Ichiban) 1999—*Me and Mrs. Jones: The Best of Billy Paul* (Epic/Legacy) 2000—*Live World Tour 1999* (Philly Sounds).

The success of singer Billy Paul's #1 pop and R&B hit "Me and Mrs. Jones" in 1972 helped establish Kenny Gamble and Leon Huff's then-young Philadelphia International Records and brought Paul's jazzy, unpredictable singing to its widest audience.

Paul first appeared in public at age 11, when, encouraged by friend Bill Cosby, he sang on Philadelphia radio station WPEN. As a teen, Paul had extensive musical training (Temple University, West Philadelphia Music School, Granoff Music School) and had sung with the Flamingos and the Blue Notes. He recorded as a jazz singer for Jubilee Records. One evening in the late '60s, Paul met Gamble at Philadelphia's Cadillac Club. Paul would record for Gamble's ill-fated Neptune Records before working with him again at Philadelphia International. "Mrs. Jones," written and produced by Gamble and Huff, is regarded as one of their classic records.

Though Paul's later releases never matched "Mrs. Jones," he had several soul hits through 1980, including "Am I Black Enough for You" (#29 R&B) in 1973, "Thanks for Saving My Life" (#9 R&B) in 1974, and "Let's Make a Baby" (#18 R&B) in 1976. Signed to the Philly Sounds label in 2000, he remains an active performer.

Les Paul

Born Lester Polfus, Jan. 9, 1915, Waukesha, WI
1955—*Les and Mary* (with Mary Ford) (Capitol); *The New Sound; Bye Bye Blues* 1956—*The Hit Makers* 1959—*Lover's Luau* (Columbia) 1965—*The Fabulous Les Paul and Mary Ford* 1968—*Guitar Artistry* (with the Les Paul Trio); *Les Paul Now* (London) 1976—*Chester and Lester* (with Chet Atkins) (RCA)

1978—*Guitar Monsters* (with Chet Atkins) 1986—*Feedback* (with the Les Paul Trio) (Circle) 1991—*Les Paul: The Legend and the Legacy* (Capitol); *Les Paul Trio* (LaserLight) 1992—*The Best of the Capitol Masters* (with Mary Ford).

Though he had a long and successful pop-jazz career, both with and without singer Mary Ford (born Colleen Summer, July 7, 1928, Pasadena, California; died September 30, 1977), guitarist Les Paul is of paramount importance to rock & roll as the creator of the solid-body electric guitar and as a pioneer in modern recording techniques such as electronic echo and studio multitracking.

Having learned harmonica, guitar, and banjo by age 13, Paul was playing with midwestern semipro country & western bands. He moved to Chicago in his late teens and became a regular on WLS. He then concentrated on performing for a few years before taking over the house band at WJJD in 1934, and he later became something of a hillbilly star under the pseudonyms Hot Rod Red and, later, Rhubarb Red. He formed the Les Paul Trio—which included Chet Atkins' brother Jimmy on rhythm guitar and vocals and Ernie Newton on bass—in 1936, and with them moved to New York in 1937. They became regulars on bandleader Fred Waring's NBC radio show and stayed with Waring's Pennsylvanians orchestra for five years.

Around this time, Paul began seriously thinking about revolutionizing the guitar. He had become interested in electronics at age 12, when he built a crystal radio set. He built his first guitar pickup from ham radio headphone parts in 1934, and by 1941 he had built the first prototypical solid-body electric guitar, a four-foot wooden board with strings, pickup, and a plug, which he called the "Log" and still uses to test against other guitars.

Meanwhile, in New York, Paul's musical aspirations moved toward jazz. He jammed informally with such greats as Art Tatum, Louis Armstrong, Ben Webster, and others, including electric (hollow-body) guitarist Charlie Christian. Paul left Waring in 1941, spent a year as music director for two Chicago radio stations, and moved to L.A. In 1942, he was drafted and worked for the Armed Forces Radio Service, playing behind Bing Crosby, Rudy Vallee, Johnny Mercer, Kate Smith, and others. Upon his discharge in 1943, he worked as a staff musician for NBC radio in L.A. He backed Bing Crosby with his trio and toured with the Andrews Sisters. With Crosby's encouragement, Paul built his first recording studio in his L.A. garage in 1945. There he began to pioneer such now-standard recording techniques as close microphone positioning ("close-miking"), echo delay, and multitracking. In 1948 he broke his right elbow in an auto accident and had it reset at a special angle so he could still play guitar.

In the late '40s, Paul met and married singer Mary Ford, and they began recording together—unsuccessfully at first—for Decca and Columbia. After moving to Capitol, they had a long string of hits, including "Mockin' Bird Hill" (#3, 1951), "How High the Moon" (#1, 1951), "The World Is Waiting for the Sunrise" (#3, 1951), and "Vaya Con Dios" (#1, 1953). These recordings—among the earliest multitracked pop songs—featured Ford's voice answering Paul's "talking" guitar. Paul also had some instrumental hits on his own: "Nola" (#9, 1950), "Whispering" (#7, 1951), "Tiger Rag" (#6, 1952), and "Meet Mister Callaghan" (#5, 1952). The couple's hits—individual and otherwise—stopped in 1961; two years later Paul and Ford were divorced. Ford died of diabetes in 1977.

By that time, Paul's interests had shifted to experimenting and innovating. He built the Les Paul Recording Guitar in the early '50s and used it on his own recordings, not allowing Gibson to market that model until 1971. Since they were first marketed in May 1952, Les Paul Gibsons have been known for their "hot" pickups, "fatter" tone, and sustaining capacity, as compared to the twangier electric guitars of Leo Fender.

In the early '50s, Paul built the first 8-track tape recorder, which helped pioneer multitrack recording, and he invented "sound-on-sound" recording, which has since become known as overdubbing. His other inventions include the floating bridge pickup, the electrodynamic pickup (both patented), the dual-pickup guitar, the 14-fret guitar, and various types of electronic transducers used both in guitars and recording studios.

In 1974 Paul returned to music making, and three years later had a hit LP in the Grammy-winning *Chester and Lester,* a collaboration with country guitarist Chet Atkins. A 1980 documentary, *The Wizard of Waukesha,* opened and closed with scenes of Les Paul in the late '70s, still playing guitar, demonstrating his latest invention: a little box called the "Les Paulverizer," a device that could record, play back, and allow the musician to talk to anyone onstage, and which made his guitar sound like something that had inhaled laughing gas.

Paul has remained active, recording with Al DiMeola (on the latter's *Splendido Hotel*) and Manhattan Transfer's Janice Siegel (with whom he recorded her version of "How High the Moon" for her solo LP *Experiments in Light*). In 1988 Paul was inducted into the Rock and Roll Hall of Fame. From 1984 until 1996, Paul continued to appear once a week at Fat Tuesday's in New York; he eventually moved his weekly gig to the Iridium club near Lincoln Center, where he continues to play. Slowed only slightly by arthritis, he remains an American institution. In 2001 he received a Grammy for his technical achievements.

Pavement

Formed 1988, Stockton, CA
Stephen Malkmus (a.k.a. SM, b. ca. 1966, Santa Monica, CA), gtr., voc., kybds., bass, perc.; Scott Kannberg (a.k.a. Spiral Stairs, b. Stockton), gtr., voc., kybds., perc., trombone.
1989—(+ Gary Young, drums) 1990—(+ Rob Chamberlain, gtr., voc.; + Bob Nastanovich [b. Rochester, NY], perc., kybds., voc.) (– Chamberlain) 1991—(+ Mark Ibold [b. Cincinnati, OH], bass, voc., kybds.) 1992—*Slanted and Enchanted* (Matador); *Watery, Domestic* EP 1993—*Westing (by Musket and Sextant)* (Drag City) (– Young; + Steve West [b. Richmond,

VA], drums) 1994—*Crooked Rain, Crooked Rain* (Matador) 1995—*Wowee Zowee!* 1996—*Pacific Trim* EP 1997—*Brighten the Corners* 1999—*Terror Twilight.*
Gary Young solo: 1995—*Hospital* (Big Cat).
Marble Valley (Steve West solo): 1997—*Sauckiehall Street* (Echostatic) 2000—*Sunset Sprinkler.*
Stephen Malkmus solo: 2001—*Stephen Malkmus* (Matador).

Mixing cacophony and elegant pop, Pavement was arguably the most popular and influential "lo-fi" indie-rock band of the '90s. By the time of its breakup in 2000, the group had worked with big-name producers and traded detuned guitars and sci-fi sound effects for low-key sophistication. Pavement began in late 1988/early 1989, when primary songwriter Stephen Malkmus and longtime friend Scott Kannberg decided to self-release a single. The resulting 7-inch, *Slay Tracks: (1933–1969),* cost $800 and received favorable notice in the alternative press. Augmented by 40-ish ex-hippie Gary Young, who owned the studio where they recorded, they continued to churn out smartly barbed 7-inch and 10-inch EPs for the Drag City label, which compiled these efforts as *Westing (by Musket and Sextant).*

In 1991 the trio completed *Slanted and Enchanted,* which sold over 100,000 copies and appeared on many critics' 1992 top 10 lists. Mark Ibold, bassist for New York noisemongers the Dustdevils, and Bob Nastanovich, a college chum of Malkmus, joined the bicoastal crew in time for its initial tours, although they weren't integrated into the studio lineup until the sessions for *Crooked Rain, Crooked Rain.* Pavement's early, sloppy performances often found Young on top of the drum kit rather than behind it. In 1993 he was replaced by Steve West.

Riding a wave of ecstatic press and still signed to indie powerhouse Matador Records, Pavement unveiled the more listener-friendly but still experimental *Crooked Rain* (#121, 1994), which yielded the catchy single "Cut Your Hair." But the quirks of the sprawling, wildly varied followup, *Wowee Zowee!* (#117, 1995), irked new fans who were expecting hook-filled consistency.

Produced by Mitch Easter, *Brighten the Corners* (#70, 1997) was the first largely subdued Pavement album. *Terror Twilight* (#95, 1999), overseen by Nigel Godrich (Radiohead, Beck), slides further into maturity with hints of country and '70s soft rock. Malkmus' cryptic lyrics and nasal, wavering voice remain the only links with the past.

Throughout the '90s, Malkmus, Nastanovich, and West backed poet/guitarist David Berman in the Silver Jews. Malkmus and the Seattle indie band Silkworm also recorded as the Crust Brothers. Ibold sat in with Free Kitten, a band led by Sonic Youth's Kim Gordon and ex–Pussy Galore guitarist Julia Cafritz. Young, who reunited with Pavement as a guest on a 1999 single, released a loopy 1995 solo album. Using the name Marble Valley, West completed two fractured works of his own. In early 2001, several months after Pavement announced its dissolution, Matador issued Malkmus' solo debut.

Tom Paxton

Born Oct. 31, 1937, Chicago, IL
1962—*I'm the Man Who Built the Bridges* (Gaslight) 1964—*Ramblin' Boy* (Elektra) 1965—*Ain't That News* 1966—*Outward Bound* 1967—*Morning Again* 1969—*The Things I Notice Now; Tom Paxton 6* 1970—*The Compleat Tom Paxton* 1971—*How Come the Sun* (Reprise) 1972—*Peace Will Come* 1973—*New Songs for Old Friends* 1975—*Something in My Life* (Private Stock) 1977—*New Songs From the Briar Patch* (Vanguard) 1978—*Heroes* 1979—*Up & Up* (Mountain Railroad/Flying Fish) 1980—*The Paxton Report* 1983—*Bulletin* (Hogeye) 1984—*Even a Gray Day* (Flying Fish); *The Marvellous Toy & Other Gallimaufry* (Cherry Lane/Alcazar) 1986—*One Million Lawyers and Other Disasters* (Flying Fish); *A Paxton Primer* (Pax); *A Folk Song Festival* 1987—*And Loving You* (Flying Fish); *Balloon-alloon-alloon* (Pax) 1988—*Politics* (Flying Fish); *A Child's Christmas* (Pax) 1989—*The Very Best of Tom Paxton* (Flying Fish) 1990—*A Car Full of Songs* (Pax) 1991—*Peanut Butter Pie; It Ain't Easy* (Flying Fish) 1992—*Suzy Is a Rocker* (Sony Kids' Music) 1994—*Wearing the Time* (Sugar Hill) 1996—*Live for the Record* 1999—*I Can't Help Wonder Where I'm Bound: The Best of Tom Paxton* (Rhino) 2001—*Tom Paxton Live From Mountain Stage* (Blue Plate).

Singer/songwriter Tom Paxton and his topical songs first came to prominence along with performers such as Bob Dylan, Phil Ochs, and Joan Baez during the early-'60s Greenwich Village folk revival. Through a career that now spans over 40 years, he has continued to release albums and tour.

Paxton was raised in Oklahoma (his parents moved there when he was 10) and studied drama at the University of Oklahoma. He began writing songs, and after graduating in 1959 with a BFA, he joined the army. He later moved to New York, where he played the folk circuit. The Gaslight Club issued his first (now out-of-print) album, but his first national major release wasn't until early 1964's *Ramblin' Boy.*

Paxton's albums mixed increasingly topical political songs (like "What Did You Learn in School Today," "Talking Vietnam Pot Luck Blues," and, later, "Talking Watergate") with occasional love songs (like "The Last Thing on My Mind") and children's songs. He recorded seven albums for Elektra and then switched to Reprise in 1971, when he moved to England and recorded three LPs, including *New Songs for Old Friends,* produced by Tony Visconti and featuring Ralph McTell on guitar.

Paxton's compositions are more popularly known in versions performed by others. Peter, Paul and Mary covered "Going to the Zoo" and were among the many who covered "The Last Thing on My Mind"; John Denver did "Forest Lawn" and "Whose Garden Was This?"; other songs have been covered by Judy Collins, the Kingston Trio, and the Weavers. Paxton continues to command a loyal following and has expanded into writing music and books for children. He has written 14 children's books (published by Morrow Junior Books) and released the acclaimed children's albums *The Marvellous Toy & Other Gallimaufry, Balloon-alloon-alloon, A Child's Christmas, A Car Full of Songs, Peanut But-*

ter Pie, and *Suzy Is a Rocker,* most on his own Pax label. He has hosted two series for BBC Radio, *Tom Paxton's America* and *Tom Paxton: Still Ramblin'.*

Freda Payne

Born Sep. 19, 1945, Detroit, MI
1972—*The Best of Freda Payne* (Invictus) 1991—*Greatest Hits* (HDH).

Soul singer Freda Payne's greatest recording success came at Invictus Records in the early '70s under the guidance of its owner/producers Lamont Dozier and Eddie and Brian Holland.

Payne's parents envisioned a career in the performing arts for both Freda and her sister Scherrie (who later joined a latter-day version of the Supremes). Both studied voice and piano as children at the Detroit Institute of Musical Arts; both later studied ballet. At 18, Payne moved to New York. Her best gig in the next two years was a stint in the chorus of a Pearl Bailey show. In 1965 she served as the understudy for Leslie Uggams in the Broadway musical *Hallelujah, Baby!* There she met Quincy Jones, with whom she toured. For the rest of the '60s, she worked as a jazz singer, performing with the top big bands, including Duke Ellington's.

After Eddie Holland left Motown, he persuaded Payne to join his new label and sing pop music. In 1970 and 1971, the Holland-Dozier-Holland production team furnished Payne with some neo-Motown music that would include two gold singles, "Band of Gold" (#3 pop, #20 R&B, 1970) and "Bring the Boys Home" (#12 pop, #3 R&B, 1971). The latter was one of the era's rare black anti-Vietnam songs. Other popular Payne records of the period were "Deeper and Deeper" (#24 pop, #9 R&B, 1970), "Cherish What Is Dear to You (While It's Near to You)" (#99 pop, #11 R&B, 1971), and "You Brought the Joy" (#52 pop, #21 R&B, 1971).

Subsequently, Payne recorded for ABC and Capitol Records. In the early '80s Payne hosted the syndicated television talk show *For You Black Woman,* and she continues to perform as a singer.

Peaches and Herb

Formed 1965
Herb Fame (b. Herbert Feemster, 1942, Washington, DC), voc.; Francine Barker (b. Francine Hurd, 1947, Washington, DC), voc.
1967—*Let's Fall in Love* (Date) 1968—*Greatest Hits* (– Barker; + Marlene Mack [b. 1945, VA], voc.) 1969— (– Mack; + Barker) 1977—(– Barker; + Linda Green [b. Washington, DC], voc.) 1978—*2 Hot!* (Polydor) 1979—*Twice the Fire* 1980—*Worth the Wait* 1981—*Sayin' Something!* 1983—*Remember* (Columbia) (– Green) 1992—(+ Patrice Hawthorne, voc.) 1996—*Love Is Strange: The Best of Peaches and Herb* (Epic/Legacy).

The Peaches and Herb story is a tale of four women, two careers, and one Herb. The original team of Francine Barker and Herb Fame formed in 1965 at the urging of producer Van McCoy. At the time, Barker was lead singer of a female vocal group, the Sweet Things, and Fame was a solo act on Date Records. The Sweet Things and Fame met while on tour together. McCoy suggested that Barker and Fame form the duo, which he then produced.

The B side of their first single, "Let's Fall in Love" (#21 pop, #11 R&B), began a series of hits from 1967 to 1969 on Date: "Close Your Eyes" (#8 pop, #4 R&B), "For Your Love" (#20 pop, #10 R&B), and "Love Is Strange" (#13 pop, #16 R&B) in 1967; "United" (#46 pop, #11 R&B) in 1968; and "When He Touches Me" (#49 pop, #10 R&B) in 1969.

Marlene Mack filled in for Barker for one year, but by the time Barker returned, the duo's hits had stopped. After signing with Columbia in 1970, they suffered another dry spell and eventually quit the record business. During the '70s, Fame was a DC police officer. For a time in the mid-'70s, he and Barker released singles on their own BS label in Washington. In 1977, though, Fame found a new Peaches, Linda Green, and returned full-time to music. After a brief tenure with MCA Records, they signed to Polydor, where their "Shake Your Groove Thing" (#5 pop, #4 R&B, 1978) and the ballad "Reunited" (#1 pop, #1 R&B, 1979)—both from the platinum *2 Hot!* (#2 pop, #1 R&B)—were Herb's biggest hits yet. Through the early '80s, the duo released over a half dozen more charting singles, including "We've Got Love" (#44 pop, #25 R&B, 1979), "I Pledge My Love" (#19 pop, #37 R&B, 1979), and, most recently, "Remember" (#35 R&B, 1983). Herb found yet another Peaches in 1992 and began performing more dance-oriented material.

Pearl Jam

Formed 1990, Seattle, WA
Jeff Ament (b. Mar. 10, 1963, Big Sandy, MT), bass; Stone Gossard (b. July 20, 1966, Seattle), gtr.; Dave Krusen, drums; Mike McCready (b. Apr. 5, 1965, Seattle), gtr.; Eddie Vedder (b. Dec. 23, 1964, Chicago, IL), voc.
1991—*Ten* (Epic) (– Krusen; + Dave Abbruzzese [b. May 17, 1968], drums) 1993—*Vs* 1994—*Vitalogy* (– Abbruzzese; + Jack Irons, drums) 1996—*No Code* 1998—*Yield;* (– Irons; + Matt Cameron [b. Nov. 28, 1962, San Diego, CA], drums) *Live on Two Legs* 2000—*Binaural.*
Mother Love Bone: (Ament; Gossard; + Bruce Fairweather, gtr.; + Andrew Wood [d. Mar. 19, 1990, Seattle], voc.; + Greg Gilmore, drums) 1990—*Apple* (Polydor).
Temple of the Dog (Ament; Gossard; McCready; Cameron; + Chris Cornell [b. July 20, 1964, Seattle], voc.): 1991—*Temple of the Dog* (A&M).
Mad Season (McCready; + Layne Staley [b. Aug. 22, 1967, Bellevue, WA], voc.; + Barrett Martin, drums; + John "Baker" Saunders, bass): 1995—*Above* (Columbia).
The Rockfords (McCready; + Carrie Akre, voc.; + Chris Friel, drums; + Danny Newcomb, gtr.; + Rick Friel, bass): 2000—*The Rockfords* (Epic).
Brad (Gossard; + Shawn Smith, kybds., voc.; + Regan Hagar,

drums; + Jeremy Toback, bass, voc.): 1993—*Shame* (Epic) 1997—*Interiors*.
Three Fish (Ament; + Robbi Robb, voc.; + Richard Stuverud, drums): 1996—*Three Fish* (Epic) 1999—*The Quiet Table*.

Though it was responsible for popularizing the Seattle sound and style known as "grunge," Pearl Jam proved to be more than a flash-in-the-pan by expanding on its initial solid, guitar-heavy Led Zeppelin–influenced songs and by making good use of charismatic Eddie Vedder's impassioned vocals. Leaping from obscurity to superstardom, the band sold over 15 million copies of its first two albums. After a couple of years during which it got mired in high-profile controversies, Pearl Jam recovered and firmly established itself as a durable band working in a classic-rock mode.

Pearl Jam's roots in the Seattle scene go deep: In the mid-'80s, Jeff Ament and Stone Gossard were members of the seminal Seattle band Green River, which split in 1987. Half the band formed Mudhoney [see entry], while Gossard and Ament joined singer Andrew Wood in Mother Love Bone. One of the earliest Seattle bands to sign with a major label, Mother Love Bone seemed on the verge of breaking big when Wood died of a heroin overdose in 1990. Mercury Records wanted Gossard and Ament (with Bruce Fairweather on guitar and drummer Greg Gilmore) to record with a new singer, but the band declined. (Gossard, Ament, McCready, and Vedder, along with Soundgarden's Chris Cornell and Matt Cameron, recorded *Temple of the Dog* [#5, 1992], a memorial to Wood, in 1990.)

Gossard and Ament, along with Seattle veteran Mike McCready, started work on a demo tape in late 1990. They asked former Red Hot Chili Peppers drummer Jack Irons to join, giving him a copy of the tape. Irons was involved with his own band but passed the demo on to a singer he knew in San Diego, Eddie Vedder. Vedder immediately wrote lyrics to the songs and mailed back a tape that included his vocals; he was invited up to Seattle.

With the addition of drummer Dave Krusen, the new band was complete. They called themselves Mookie Blaylock, for the basketball player, but changed the name to Pearl Jam, after a psychedelic confection made by Vedder's half–Native American great-grandmother, Pearl. (The band did not forget Blaylock: Their debut album, *Ten* [#2, 1992], was named for his uniform number.) On the strength of its Mother Love Bone connections and a growing national interest in the Seattle scene, Pearl Jam was signed by Epic Records in early 1991. Krusen left the band after the sessions for *Ten;* he was replaced by Matt Chamberlain on tour, with Dave Abbruzzese filling the drum chair in the fall of 1991.

The band toured extensively, headlining small halls and opening for the Red Hot Chili Peppers, Neil Young, and U2. They headlined the 1992 Lollapalooza Tour and opened for Keith Richards on New Year's Eve 1992. Vedder, Gossard, and Ament took time out to play Matt Dillon's backing band, Citizen Dick, in the 1992 Seattle-based movie *Singles*.

Although Pearl Jam was originally marketed as an "alternative" band, its connection to classic rock of the '60s and '70s soon became apparent. Vedder filled in for Jim Morrison at the Doors reunion for the 1993 Rock and Roll Hall of Fame induction ceremonies; he also took part in concerts honoring Bob Dylan and Pete Townshend. The band backed Neil Young on "Rockin' in the Free World" at the 1993 MTV Video Music Awards.

It was apparent, though, that Vedder was having trouble coping with the demands of stardom: He would show up for photo sessions wearing a mask, and he was surly and uncommunicative in interviews. There were reports that he performed drunk, and in 1993 he was arrested in New Orleans for public drunkenness and disturbing the peace after a barroom brawl. None of this detracted from the band's popularity—*Vs.* (#1, 1993), its second album, sold a record-setting 1.3 million copies in its first 13 days of release.

Pearl Jam then canceled a summer tour when, in a public dispute over service charges against Ticketmaster, it couldn't keep admission prices as low as it wanted; band members also testified against Ticketmaster before Congress. That fight ultimately ended in retreat for Pearl Jam. The band did not make any videos to promote *Vs.* Instead, it went back into the studio and recorded its third album, *Vitalogy.* The vinyl version was released two weeks before the CD and cassette, debuting on the charts at #55—the first album to appear on *Billboard*'s album chart solely on the basis of vinyl sales since the proliferation of the CD in the mid-'90s. Once the CD arrived in stores, *Vitalogy* zoomed to #1.

The following year, Pearl Jam backed Neil Young on his *Mirror Ball* album. The band also appeared at Young's Bridge School Benefit concert (one of several it has done over the years) as part of its increasing involvement in political activism and various charities. Indeed, over the years, Pearl Jam has supported such causes as Kosovar refugees, women's self-defense, opposition to the death penalty, and Ralph Nader's 2000 presidential campaign.

Though Pearl Jam was at the peak of its popularity in the mid-'90s, it also went through some rocky times. The holder of the drumming seat changed again as Abbruzzese was replaced by Jack Irons. The band's attempt to experiment with its sound, 1996's *No Code* (#1, 1996), met with tepid response. Despite its initial success, the album dropped out of the Top 20 within two months.

The band retreated to safer ground. *Yield* (#2, 1998) was straightforward hard rock and was accompanied by the band's first music video since *Ten*'s "Jeremy." Pearl Jam also returned to playing mainstream arenas (many of them selling their tickets through Ticketmaster) in the summer; drummer Matt Cameron became a permanent addition that summer as well. The band members, especially Vedder, even started to look as if they were finally becoming comfortable with their status as rock stars. The group had also become strong enough to overcome a tragic accident—nine fans were crushed and suffocated during Pearl Jam's set at the Roskilde, Denmark, festival on June 30, 2000. Initially held "morally responsible" by the Danish police, the group was later cleared of all blame.

In many ways, Pearl Jam continues to defy expectations. For instance, it still plays exclusive shows for its fan-club members, who also receive limited-edition Christmas singles—one of them turning into the surprise hit "Last Kiss" (#2, 1999) when it got a wider release. And in September 2000, the band made history by self-releasing 25 live double albums in one week, and by having five of them enter the *Billboard* 200 simultaneously: *16/6/00: Spodek, Katowice, Poland* (#103); *22/6/00: Fila Forum Arena, Milan, Italy* (#125); *20/6/00: Arena di Verona, Verona, Italy* (#134); *30/5/00: Wembley Arena, London, England* (#137); and *26/6/00: Sporthalle, Hamburg, Germany* (#175). Pearl Jam continued to release documents of its 2000 tour, reaching a total of 72 sets by mid-2001. The one triple CD, *11/6/00: Seattle, Washington,* was the most popular, entering the chart at #98.

Ann Peebles

Born Apr. 27, 1947, East St. Louis, MO
1971—*Part Time Love* (Hi) 1972—*Straight From the Heart* 1974—*I Can't Stand the Rain* 1976—*Tellin' It* 1978—*If This Is Heaven* 1992—*Full Time Love* (Bullseye Blues) 1996—*Fill This World With Love.*

Soul singer Ann Peebles is best known for her 1973 hit "I Can't Stand the Rain," but her grainy Memphis-style soul singing has influenced such stars as Bonnie Raitt. Peebles began performing at age eight when she joined the Peebles Choir, a gospel group founded by her great-grandfather. After graduating from high school, she started working St. Louis nightclubs. In 1969 producer Willie Mitchell signed her to his Memphis-based Hi Records, where she worked with the same session band that Al Green used. Her first single, "Walk Away," hit #22, and later hits like "Part Time Love" (#7 R&B), "I Pity the Fool" (#18 R&B), and "Breaking Up Somebody's Home" (#13 R&B) sold well, particularly in the South.

"I Can't Stand the Rain" (#38 pop, #6 R&B) was written by Peebles and her husband, Don Bryant. " 'Rain' is the greatest record I've heard in two years," said John Lennon at the time of its release. The song has been covered by numerous performers ranging from rock bands to disco divas. It was later included in the film *The Commitments* (1991). Peebles continued recording through the late '70s, after which she and her husband basically left the music business to raise their family and run a home preschool program for children. The pair also remained active on the Memphis gospel scene. In 1992 Peebles returned to recording with her first record in a decade and a half, *Full Time Love.* The 1996 followup, *Fill This World With Love,* features Mavis Staples and Shirley Brown.

Teddy Pendergrass

Born Mar. 26, 1950, Philadelphia, PA
1977—*Teddy Pendergrass* (Philadelphia International) 1978—*Life Is a Song Worth Singing* 1979—*Teddy; Teddy Live! Coast to Coast* 1980—*TP* 1981—*It's Time for Love* 1982—*This One's for You* 1983—*Heaven Only Knows* 1984—*Greatest Hits; Love Language* (Asylum) 1985—*Workin' It Back* 1988—*Joy* (Elektra) 1990—*Truly Blessed* 1993—*A Little More Magic* 1997—*Greatest* Hits (Philadelphia International); *You and I* (Surefire) 1998—*This Christmas (I'd Rather Have Love)* 2001—*Greatest Slow Jams* (EMD/Right Stuff).

Teddy Pendergrass is a singular voice in R&B. His gospel-influenced, sensual style is an oft-cited influence on contemporary male vocalists, and his early solo efforts placed him alongside Marvin Gaye and Al Green among the most influential singers of the era. Despite a 1982 car accident that left him partially paralyzed, Pendergrass has continued recording, writing, and garnering Grammy nominations. Already a star as lead vocalist of Harold Melvin and the Blue Notes [see entry], Pendergrass launched a solo career in 1976 that achieved R&B-to-pop crossover success at a time when the charts were becoming increasingly segregated. He also became the first black male vocalist to have four consecutive studio albums certified platinum.

The seventh and only surviving son of a deeply religious mother, Pendergrass attended a Pentecostal church seven days a week, where he sang. Though he received a calling to minister as a child, he was never ordained. His father, who had abandoned the family a month before Pendergrass' birth, was murdered 12 years later. Although Pendergrass' mother forbade him to listen to secular music, he was exposed to it on the streets of North Philadelphia, where he lived just blocks from the legendary Uptown Theater. Working with his mother at Sciolla's, a popular South Philly nightclub, Pendergrass got his first glimpse of show business close-up, watching acts like Chubby Checker. It is also where he taught himself to play the drums.

Pendergrass sang with informal groups in his teens and hit the road at 18 as a drummer with Little Royal, an R&B performer who claimed to be James Brown's brother. Afterward,

Teddy Pendergrass

Pendergrass returned to Philadelphia, where he joined the backup band for an imposter group claiming to be the Cadillacs (of "Speedoo" fame). When Harold Melvin tapped the group to replace a recently dissolved Blue Notes lineup, Pendergrass came along. Sometime around 1970, Melvin promoted him to the lead-vocalist spot. A contract with Kenny Gamble and Leon Huff's Philadelphia International followed, and the group became one of the top vocal groups of the mid-'70s.

In fall 1975 Pendergrass quit the Blue Notes. Working with manager Shep Gordon (Blondie, Alice Cooper), Pendergrass was positioned to cross over beyond the R&B market. With the release of his solo debut, he was marketed as a sex symbol and became known to his fans as Teddy Bear. "I Don't Love You Anymore" (#41 pop, #5 R&B, 1977) was the single from that platinum album (#17 pop, #5 R&B). His next LP, *Life Is a Song Worth Singing* (#11 pop, #1 R&B, 1978), was highlighted by the seductive "Close the Door" (#25 pop, #1 R&B, 1978), a steamy tale continued the next summer with "Turn Off the Lights" (#48 pop, #2 R&B) from *Teddy* (#5 pop, #1 R&B, 1979).

Backed by his Teddy Bear Orchestra, Pendergrass in concert fueled a reaction among female fans much like that of his idol, Jackie Wilson. "For Women Only" concerts were instituted, with ladies given stuffed teddy bears to fondle and chocolate teddy bear lollipops to lick during the show. Some of the excitement was captured in the gold *Teddy Live! Coast to Coast* (#33 pop, #5 R&B, 1979). Pendergrass' image as a confident (some would say arrogant) playboy fit offstage as well (to wit, a Main Line mansion, a collection of luxury cars, and a brief affair with Marvin Gaye's wife, Jan). Nonetheless, he turned down the heat on *TP* (#14 pop, #3 R&B, 1980), which featured the old-school soul classic "Love TKO" (#44 pop, #2 R&B, 1980) and a duet with Stephanie Mills on "Feel the Fire." They also collaborated on the single "Two Hearts" (#40 pop, #2 R&B, 1981). *It's Time for Love* (#19 pop, #6 R&B, 1981) included "You're My Latest, My Greatest Inspiration" (#43 pop, #4 R&B, 1981) and went gold. Pendergrass made his film debut in *Soup for One*. He also sang one song, "Dream Girl," on the Chic-produced soundtrack.

On March 18, 1982, Pendergrass' spinal cord was severely injured when his Rolls-Royce smashed into a highway divider and then a tree on a winding road outside Philadelphia. A faulty electrical system that rendered the power steering inoperable was later determined to be the cause of the crash. Pendergrass was paralyzed from the chest down and left with only limited use of arms. After months of physical therapy, he returned home to discover that Philadelphia International and CBS had no interest in continuing with him. (Two albums, *This One's for You* [#59 pop, #6 R&B, 1982] and *Heaven Only Knows* [#123 pop, #9 R&B, 1983], were compiled from the vaults.) Based on a demo of "You're My Choice (Choose Me)" (in a finished version, a #15 R&B hit in 1984) produced by Luther Vandross, Elektra/Asylum's Bob Krasnow gambled on Pendergrass. The first album, *Love Language* (#38 pop, #4 R&B, 1984), included his comeback hit—and Whitney Houston's first big hit—in "Hold Me" (#46 pop, #5 R&B, 1984). Pendergrass' video for the semi-autobiographical "In My Time" showed him singing in his wheelchair. Though Pendergrass had to undergo grueling physical therapy to regain his vocal strength, he persevered. In the years since the accident, Pendergrass has survived addictions to cocaine and alcohol, several life-threatening complications, a second car accident that resulted in a potentially fatal injury to his liver, and, at one point, a desire to commit suicide.

Pendergrass returned to the stage at 1985's Live Aid, performing "Reach Out and Touch (Somebody's Hand)" with his friends Nickolas Ashford and Valerie Simpson. Though his recording schedule was sporadic and his personal appearances extremely limited, his albums consistently hit the R&B Top 20: *Workin' It Back* (#96 pop, #6 R&B, 1985), *Joy* (#54 pop, #2 R&B, 1988), *Truly Blessed* (#49 pop, #4 R&B, 1991), and *A Little More Magic* (#92 pop, #13 R&B, 1993). His biggest hits from this period include "Love 4/2" (#6 R&B, 1986), "Joy" (#77 pop, #1 R&B, 1988), the Grammy-nominated "Make It With You" (#23 R&B, 1990) (from the Elektra tribute collection *Rubaiyat—Elektra's 40th Anniversary*), "It Should've Been You" (#1 R&B, 1991), the Grammy-nominated, Gerald Levert–written and –produced "Voodoo" (#25 R&B, 1993), and "Believe in Love" (#105 pop, #14 R&B, 1994). In an attempt to exert more control over his career, Pendergrass began writing some of his material and executive producing his albums, beginning with *Workin'*.

In 1996 he toured for the first time since his accident, with a 20th-anniversary revival of Vinnette Carroll's *Your Arms Too Short to Box With God*, for which Carroll wrote him a special part. The show and Pendergrass received rave reviews in all 22 cities they visited. The show's climax was him singing his own "Truly Blessed," an autobiographical song that also provided the title for his 1998 autobiography (cowritten with Patricia Romanowski). An activist for the rights of the disabled, Pendergrass in 1998 founded the Teddy Pendergrass Education/Occupation Alliance for the Disabled. In 2000 he performed the Blue Notes' inspirational "Wake Up Everybody" at the Republican National Convention. In 2001 he returned to the concert stage.

The Penguins

Formed 1954, Los Angeles, CA
Cleveland Duncan (b. July 23, 1935, Los Angeles), lead voc.; Curtis Williams (b. 1935), tenor voc.; Dexter Tisby (b. 1936), voc.; Bruce Tate (b. 1935), tenor voc.
1955—(– Tate; + Randolph Jones, baritone voc.) 1957—*The Cool, Cool Penguins* (Dootone) 1993—*The Authentic Golden Hits of the Penguins* (Juke Box Treasures).

After attracting a strong local following in the early '50s, the Penguins scored a big hit with a song written either by Curtis Williams and Jesse Belvin or by Belvin alone (sources vary), "Earth Angel." The song was #8 pop, #1 R&B in 1954, and has since sold an estimated 10 million copies. Unfortunately, the Crew-Cuts covered that same song a year later and made it a bigger pop hit (something they'd earlier done with the Chords' "Sh-Boom").

The Penguins switched from Dootone to Mercury (they were part of a package signing engineered by manager Buck Ram that also included the Platters) to Atlantic Records, never achieving followup success commensurate with their one and only hit. After one release for Atlantic and one for Sun State Records, they returned to California nearly broke and split up. Lead singer Duncan re-formed the band several times. In 1963 they recorded a song written for them by Frank Zappa and Ray Collins (later of the Mothers of Invention), "Memories of El Monte." When it failed to hit, Tisby and some latter-day members joined the Coasters. Tisby eventually moved to Hawaii. For decades the Penguins, lead by sole surviving original member Duncan, have made steady appearances at '50s revival concerts. As of 1998 Duncan was still performing.

Michael Penn

Born Aug. 1, 1958, New York, NY
1989—*March* (RCA) 1992—*Free-for-All* 1997—*Resigned* (57/Epic) 2000—*MP4: Days Since a Lost Time Accident* (Sony/Epic).

The older brother of actor Sean Penn, Michael Penn gained some fame and success in his own right with his Beatlesque debut album, *March,* which earned him Best New Artist MTV Video Music Award (1990) and spawned a hit single in "No Myth" (#13, 1990).

The son of actor/director Leo Penn and actress Eileen Ryan, Penn (whose other brother Christopher also became a movie actor) was born in New York's Greenwich Village in 1958 and moved with his family to L.A. a year later. Penn grew up listening to the Beatles, and, by junior high, he had learned guitar and played in a band covering hits by David Bowie, Cream, and the Rolling Stones.

At Santa Monica High School, Penn began writing what he would later call "earnest, downbeat" songs. In the early '80s he formed a band called Doll Congress, which, despite having enough of a local following to open once for R.E.M., did not work often enough to support Penn, whose odd jobs included appearing as an extra on TV's *St. Elsewhere.* A year after he left the group, Penn performed on a 1987 episode of *Saturday Night Live* that his brother Sean hosted. Penn later said the experience made him very nervous, but he subsequently hooked up with Doll Congress keyboardist Patrick Warren and began work on the songs that would make up *March.*

March garnered critical raves for its thoughtful folk pop, and sparked by the success of the "No Myth" single and video, it sold well, too (#31, 1989). One of the most intriguing things about the album was Warren's extensive and resourceful use of the Chamberlin, an antiquated keyboard quite similar to the proto-sampling Mellotron in that each key activates a tape recording of a note played by an actual instrument (violin, flute, oboe, etc.). The album yielded another, lesser hit single in "This & That" (#53, 1990). Penn's followup album, *Free-for-All,* while similar in sound to *March,* fared far worse commercially, reaching only as high as #160 in just two weeks on the chart. Penn took five years to return with *Resigned,* which he recorded for Pearl Jam producer Brendan O'Brien's Atlanta-based 57 Records imprint. It was a big year for Penn, who also married singer/songwriter Aimee Mann and formed an important alliance with filmmaker Paul Thomas Anderson, through which he wrote music for the films *Hard Eight* and *Boogie Nights.* In 2000 Penn released his fourth album, *MP4: Days Since a Lost Time Accident,* and he joined Mann on an offbeat Acoustic Vaudeville tour.

Pentangle/Bert Jansch/John Renbourn

Formed 1967, England
Bert Jansch (b. Nov. 3, 1943, Glasgow, Scot.), gtr., voc.; John Renbourn (b. Aug. 8, 1944, London, Eng.), gtr.; Jacqui McShee (b. Dec. 25, 1943, London), voc.; Danny Thompson (b. Apr. 1939, Devon, Eng.), bass; Terry Cox (b. Buckinghamshire, Eng.), drums, perc.
1968—*The Pentangle* (Reprise) 1969—*Sweet Child* 1970—*Basket of Light* 1971—*Cruel Sister; Reflection* 1972—*Solomon's Seal* 1973—*Pentangling* (group disbands) 1975—*Collection* 1978—*Anthology* 1981—*Heartbreak* (Hannibal) 1983—(group re-forms) 1985—*Open the Door* (Varrick) 1986—*In the Round* (– Renbourn; – Thompson; + Mike Piggott, gtr.; + Nigel Portman-Smith [b. Feb. 7, 1950, Sheffield, Eng.], bass, kybds.) 1989—*A Maid That's Deep in Love* (Shanachie); *So Early in the Spring* (Green Linnet) 1990—(lineup: Jansch; McShee; Portman-Smith; + Gerry Conway [b. Sep. 11, 1947, Norfolk, Eng.], drums; + Peter Kirtley [b. Sep. 26, 1945, Hebburn-on-Tyne, Eng.], gtr., voc.) 1991—*Think of Tomorrow* 1992—*Early Classics* (Shanachie) 1993—*One More Road* (Permanent, U.K.).
Bert Jansch solo: 1968—*Birthday Blues* (Reprise) 1969—*Stepping Stones* (Vanguard) 1970—*Jack Orion* 1971—*Rosemary Lane* (Reprise) 1973—*Moonshine* 1977—*A Rare Conundrum* (Kicking Mule) 1980—*13 Down* 1981—*Heartbreak* (Hannibal) 1990—*Sketches* (Temple) 1991—*The Ornament Tree* (Gold Castle) 1992—*The Best of Bert Jansch* (Shanachie) 1993—*Three Chord Trick* (Virgin, U.K.) 1995—*When the Circus Comes to Town* (Cooking Vinyl, U.K.) 1998—*Toy Balloon* 2000—*Crimson Moon* (Castle).
John Renbourn solo: 1969—*Sir John—A Lot of Merre Englandes Musik Thynge and Ye Grene Knyghte* (Reprise) 1970—*The Lady and the Unicorn* 1972—*John Renbourn; Faro Annie* 1976—*The Hermit* (Transatlantic, U.K.) 1979—*The Black Balloon* (Kicking Mule) 1980—*The Enchanted Garden* 1986—*The Nine Maidens* (Flying Fish) 1988—*Ship of Fools* 1993—*Wheel of Fortune* (with Robin Williamson) 1998—*Traveler's Prayer* (Shanachie).
John Renbourn Group: 1977—*Maid in Bedlam.*
Bert Jansch and John Renbourn: 1992—*After the Dance* (Shanachie).

Jacqui McShee solo: 1995—*About Thyme* (with Gerry Conway and Spencer Cozens) (GJS, U.K.) 2000—*Passe Avant* (as Jacqui McShee's Pentangle) (Park, U.K.).

With the virtuoso acoustic guitars of Bert Jansch and John Renbourn, folksinger Jacqui McShee, and the jazz-based rhythm section of Danny Thompson and Terry Cox (ex-Alexis Korner Blues Band), Pentangle achieved solid cult status with a unique repertoire that included traditional English folk songs, jazz, blues, and occasional originals, all intricately arranged. It rarely used amplification until the muted electric guitars of *Cruel Sister*. Pentangle's debut LP did fairly well on the U.K. chart; the rest achieved modest U.S. and U.K. success.

Upon the group's breakup in 1973, Thompson worked with Nick Drake and John Martyn, while Jansch and Renbourn reunited (they'd made a duo LP, *Bert and John*, in 1966) for tours and LPs. Renbourn had begun making solo LPs while with Pentangle, and he has over a dozen of his own records out and has recorded a number of albums with Stefan Grossman. McShee joined John Renbourn's band from 1974 to 1981. In 1983 the original lineup re-formed solely for *Open the Door*, but a newer lineup that included cofounders Jansch and McShee continued until the mid-'90s. The current band is essentially an extension of McShee's solo career. Danny Thompson toured with Richard Thompson in a quartet that included Pete Zorn and former Fairport Convention and Jethro Tull member Dave Pegg.

Pere Ubu

Formed 1975, Cleveland, OH

David Thomas (a.k.a. Crocus Behemoth, b. June 14, 1953), voc.; Tom Herman (b. Apr. 19, 1949), gtr.; Peter Laughner (b. ca. 1953; d. June 22, 1977), gtr.; Tim Wright, bass; Allen Ravenstine (b. May 9, 1950), synth.; Scott Krauss (b. Nov. 19, 1950), drums.

1976—(– Laughner; – Wright; + Tony Maimone [b. Sep. 27, 1952, Cleveland], bass) 1978—*The Modern Dance* (Blank/Mercury); *Datapanik in the Year Zero* EP (Radar, U.K.); *Dub Housing* (Chrysalis) 1979—*New Picnic Time* (– Herman; + Mayo Thompson [b. Feb. 26, 1944], gtr., voc.) 1980—*The Art of Walking* (Rough Trade) 1981—*390° of Simulated Stereo Ubu Live, vol. 1* (– Krauss; + Anton Fier [b. June 20, 1956, Cleveland], drums) 1982—*Song of the Bailing Man* (group disbands) 1985—*Terminal Tower: An Archival Collection* (Twin/Tone) 1987—(group re-forms: Thomas; Ravenstine; Maimone; Krauss; + Jim Jones [b. Mar. 12, 1950], gtr.; + Chris Cutler [b. Jan. 4, 1947], drums) 1988—*The Tenement Year* (Enigma) 1989—*Cloudland* (Mercury); *One Man Drives While the Other Man Screams* (Rough Trade) 1990—(– Ravenstine; + Eric Drew Feldman [b. Apr. 16, 1955], synth.; – Cutler) 1991—*Worlds in Collision* (Mercury) 1992—(– Feldman) 1993—*Story of My Life* (Imago) (+ Garo Yellin, electric cello; – Maimone; – Yellin; + Robert Wheeler, kybds.; – Krauss; + Scott Benedict, drums) 1994—(+ Michele Temple, bass) 1995—*Raygun Suitcase* (Cooking Vinyl) (– Benedict; + Scott Mehlman, drums; – Jones); *The Hearpen Singles* (Tim/Kerr) 1996—*Datapanik in the Year Zero* (DGC) 1997—(+ Jones) 1998—(– Jones; + Wayne Kramer, gtr.) *Pennsylvania* (Tim/Kerr) 1999—(– Kramer) *Apocalypse Now* (Thirsty Ear).

David Thomas solo: 1981—*The Sound of the Sand and Other Songs of the Pedestrians* (Rough Trade) 1982—*Vocal Performances* EP 1983—*Variations on a Theme; Winter Comes Home* (Re Records) 1985—*More Places Forever* (Rough Trade/Twin/Tone); *Monster Walks the Winter Lake* 1987—*Blame the Messenger* (Rough Trade) 1996—*Erewhon* (Tim/Kerr) 1997—*David Thomas, Monster* 1999—*Mirror Man* (Thirsty Ear) 2000—*Bay City* 2001—*Surf's Up*.

Pere Ubu's music is a unique mixture of control and anarchy, incorporating driving rock, synthesized "found" sounds, falling-apart song structures, and David Thomas' careening vocals and wide-eyed lyrics.

Founding members Thomas and Laughner, both rock journalists (Laughner with *Creem*), named the band after the hero of *Ubu Roi*, a play by French absurdist Alfred Jarry. Ubu was part of the fertile Ohio rock scene that also fostered Tin Huey and Devo. Their first single, "30 Seconds Over Tokyo" b/w "Heart of Darkness," was released independently in 1975 on Hearthan and reissued on *Datapanik*. In early 1976 the initial lineup recorded another two-sided single, "Final Solution" b/w "Cloud 149," traveled to New York several times, and disbanded. In July they regrouped as the quintet that recorded their first three albums. Tim Wright moved to New York and joined the no-wave band DNA. In 1977 Laughner died of alcohol and drug abuse.

Though it sold only 15,000 copies in the U.S., *The Modern Dance* influenced an entire school of postpunk bands, including R.E.M., Hüsker Dü, and the Pixies. By touring the U.S. and, in 1978, England, Pere Ubu became well known on

Pere Ubu: Scott Krauss, Jim Jones, David Thomas, Tony Maimone

the burgeoning new-wave circuit and particularly popular in England. After their British shows, they signed with Chrysalis and released *Dub Housing*, whose dark, surreal atmosphere made it a classic underground rock album.

Herman left for solo work in 1979, making an album with some Cleveland avant-punk cohorts *(Frontier Justice)* before moving to Houston. He was replaced by Mayo Thompson, formerly of the Texas psychedelic band Red Crayola, with whom Pere Ubu recorded *The Art of Walking*. Ubu members also appeared on Crayola's *Soldier Talk*. Artistic and personal squabbles broke up the band again in early 1982, with Maimone and Krauss leaving to form their own group, Home and Garden.

In 1981 Thomas, an avowed Jehovah's Witness, recorded *The Sound of the Sand*, the first of two solo albums with British folk-rock guitarist Richard Thompson. He did a few solo concerts in 1982 backed only by prerecorded tapes and Tin Huey saxophonist Ralph Carney. By 1984, Thomas had moved to England, though he would eventually commute to Cleveland for frequent musical collaborations. The personnel on Thomas' 1987 album, *Blame the Messenger*, became the re-formed Pere Ubu of *The Tenement Year*, which included a two-drum lineup featuring Krauss, again, and British prog-rocker Chris Cutler, of Henry Cow and the Art Bears.

Longtime keyboardist Allen Ravenstine left Ubu after 1989's near-pop album, *Cloudland*, to become a Northwest Airlines pilot. He was replaced by Captain Beefheart sideman Eric Drew Feldman on the even more commercial-sounding *Worlds in Collision*, produced by Gil Norton (Pixies). Feldman left to join ex-Pixies leader Charles Thompson (a.k.a. Frank Black). In 1993 Pere Ubu recorded *Story of My Life*, initially titled *Johnny Rivers Live at the Whisky A Go Go*, with its most stripped-down lineup yet. The record failed again to attract mainstream interest, despite rave reviews. *Raygun Suitcase* followed two years later to an identical fate. One sign of the band's continued influence was the 1996 release of *Datapanik in the Year Zero*, a five-disc retrospective. (Three years later, Thomas' solo work would get similar treatment on the five-disc *David Thomas, Monster*.) In 1998 Thomas staged *Disastrodome*, a theatrical/musical performance/lecture, in London and New York. That same year, guitarist Tom Herman recorded with Pere Ubu for the first time in two decades on the acclaimed *Pennsylvania*. It was followed a year later by the live *Apocalypse Now*. David Thomas & the Pale Orchestra released *Mirror Man* in 1999 and featured such guests as Linda Thompson and Peter Hammill.

Carl Perkins

Born Apr. 9, 1932, Tiptonville, TN; died Jan. 19, 1998, Jackson, TN

1958—*Dance Album of Carl Perkins* (Sun); *Whole Lotta Shakin'* (Columbia) 1969—*Carl Perkins' Greatest Hits; Carl Perkins on Top* 1970—*Boppin' the Blues* (with NRBQ) 1973—*My Kind of Country* (Mercury) 1982—*The Survivors* (with Johnny Cash and Jerry Lee Lewis) (Columbia) 1985—*Carl Perkins* (Dot) 1986—*Original Sun Greatest Hits* (Rhino); *Up Through the Years, 1954–1957* (Bear Family); *The Class of '55* (with Johnny Cash, Roy Orbison, Jerry Lee Lewis) (America) 1989—*Born to Rock* (Universal/MCA); *Honky Tonk Gal: Rare and Unissued Sun Masters* (Rounder) 1990—*The Million Dollar Quartet* (with Elvis Presley, Jerry Lee Lewis, and Johnny Cash) (BMG); *Classic Carl Perkins* (Bear Family); *Jive After Five: The Best of Carl Perkins (1958–1978)* (Rhino) 1991—*The Dollie Masters: Country Boy's Dream* (Bear Family) 1992—*Restless: The Columbia Recordings* (Columbia Legacy); *Friends, Family, and Legends* (Platinum); *706 Reunion* (with Scotty Moore) (Belle Meade) 1993—*Carl Perkins & Sons* (BMG); *Take Me Back; Disciple in Blue Suede Shoes* 1996—*Go, Cat, Go!* (Dinosaur).

One of the architects of rock & roll, Carl Perkins is best known as the writer and original singer of the rockabilly anthem "Blue Suede Shoes" (#2, 1956). Along with Jerry Lee Lewis, Johnny Cash, and Elvis Presley, Perkins was one of the seminal rockabilly artists on Sam Phillips' Sun label, but a series of bad breaks, followed by personal problems, undermined his solo career. Despite that, Perkins persevered, creating a body of work that has been both critically acclaimed and extremely influential on songwriters, guitar players, and singers alike.

Perkins grew up poor in a sharecropping family that picked cotton in various northwestern Tennessee fields around Tiptonville. Perkins was first put to work at age six, and it was in the fields that he first heard gospel songs. At night, he heard hillbilly country and Delta blues over the family radio. An older, black field hand befriended Perkins and taught him to play guitar; by age 10 Perkins was entertaining his classmates. He made his radio debut with his school band, singing "Home on the Range."

He kicked off his musical career in the mid-'40s, performing at local dances with his brothers Jay and Clayton as the Perkins Brothers Band. In 1953 drummer W.S. "Fluke" Holland joined. The next year, after hearing Presley's debut Sun single, "Blue Moon of Kentucky" (a Bill Monroe song Perkins and his group had been playing since 1949), Perkins and his brothers drove to Memphis to audition for Phillips. Shortly thereafter, they signed to the label and released Perkins' first single, "Movie Magg" (a song Perkins wrote at age 13) b/w "Turn Around." In early 1955 came "Let the Jukebox Keep On Playing" b/w "Gone Gone Gone." Perkins' biggest hit came in late 1956. "Blue Suede Shoes" was an instant smash and made Perkins the first white country artist to cross over to the R&B chart as well. A country, pop, and R&B hit, "Blue Suede Shoes" alternated with Elvis Presley's first post-Sun single, "Heartbreak Hotel," for the top spots on national and regional charts. (Shortly thereafter, Presley issued his "Blue Suede Shoes"; over time, Perkins' original sold more copies.)

Perkins was at the height of his career when tragedy struck. He and his group were driving to New York to appear on Perry Como's television program when their driver fell asleep at the wheel, causing the car to hit the back of a truck before plunging into water. The driver was killed, and Carl and his brother Jay were seriously injured. Although Perkins

Carl Perkins

was back on the road in about a month, Jay never fully recovered and was later diagnosed with a brain tumor, from which he died in 1958. Years later, Perkins admitted that he used his brother's death as a reason to drink. A quiet, self-effacing man, Perkins later observed, "I felt out of place when 'Blue Suede Shoes' was Number One. I stood on the Steel Pier in 1956 in Atlantic City . . . and the Goodyear blimp flew over with my name in big lights. And I stood there and shook and actually cried. That should have been something that would elevate a guy to say, 'Well, I've made it.' But it put fear in me."

In early 1958 Perkins moved to Columbia Records, where he recorded several more minor rockabilly hits, but by the early '60s, he'd hit a low point. On a British tour in 1964, Perkins was surprised to learn that the Beatles admired him and that George Harrison taught himself to play guitar by copying Perkins' records. Perkins became friendly with the Beatles and oversaw the sessions where they recorded five of his songs—"Matchbox," "Honey Don't," "Your True Love," "Blue Suede Shoes," and "Everybody's Trying to Be My Baby." Rick Nelson, Johnny Burnette, and Patsy Cline, among others, also covered his songs. Like many other rockabilly artists, Perkins turned to country material as the rockabilly trend died, and by 1965 he was part of Johnny Cash's touring troupe. In 1968 he wrote the huge hit for Cash, "Daddy Sang Bass" (#1, 1969). When Cash got his national television show in 1969, Perkins became a regular guest, and he toured and recorded with Cash as well.

As a solo artist, Perkins cut some country records and recorded an album with NRBQ. After the Cash show ended, he toured as Johnny's guitarist until 1975. He then formed the C.P. Express with his sons Greg and Stan, and started his own label, Suede, on which he released two albums (*The Carl Perkins Show* and *Carl Perkins Live at Austin City Limits*). In late 1978 Perkins released a basic rock & roll LP called *Ol' Blue Suede's Back,* which sold 100,000 copies in England. In 1981 he did some sessions for Paul McCartney's *Tug of War;* in early 1982, an album entitled *Survivors,* recorded live in Germany with Jerry Lee Lewis and Johnny Cash, was released. Three years later Lewis, Cash, and Orbison were reunited for *The Class of '55,* a special event that included such Perkins disciples as John Fogerty and Rick Nelson.

Through the years, Perkins continued to record and write. He cowrote the Judds' 1989 hit "Let Me Tell You About Love," on which he played lead guitar. In 1992 Dolly Parton had a C&W hit with a song Perkins wrote for her, "Silver and Gold." In 1992 Perkins was diagnosed with throat cancer; following treatment, he was declared cancer-free a year later, and kept writing and recording. He owned two Jackson, Tennessee, restaurants; one, Suede's, is filled with his career memorabilia. In 1981 he founded the Carl Perkins Center for the Prevention of Child Abuse. He was inducted into the Rock and Roll Hall of Fame in 1987. Perkins' 1996 album, *Go, Cat, Go!* featured Willie Nelson, John Fogerty, Paul Simon, and Tom Petty. His authorized biography, *Go, Cat, Go! The Life and Times of Carl Perkins, the King of Rockabilly,* by David McGee, was published in 1994. Perkins suffered a series of strokes and died in 1998.

Joe Perry Project: See Aerosmith

Lee "Scratch" Perry

Born Rainford Hugh Perry, Mar. 20, 1936, Hanover, Jam.
1971—*Africa Blood* (Trojan) 1975—*Scratch on the Wire* (Island) 1976—*Super Ape* (Mango); *Roast Fish, Collie Weed and Corn Bread* (Lion of Judah) 1977—*Double Seven* (Trojan); *Return of the Super Ape* (Mango) 1979—*Cloak and Dagger* (Black Art) 1980—*The Return of Pipecock Jackson* 1981—*The Upsetter Collection* (Trojan) 1982—*Scratch and Co.: Chapter One* (Clocktower); *Mystic Miracle Star* (Heartbeat) 1984—*History, Mystery and Prophecy* (Mango); *Reggae Greats* 1985—*The Upsetter Box* (Trojan) 1986—*Battle of Armagideon* 1987—*Time Boom X De Devil Dead* (On-U Sound) 1988—*Satan Kicked the Bucket* (Bullwackies); *Some of the Best* (Heartbeat) 1989—*All the Hits* (Rohit); *Chicken Scratch* (Heartbeat) 1990—*Build the Ark* (Trojan); *From the Secret Laboratory* (Mango); *Message From Yard* (Rohit); *Lee Scratch Perry Meets Bullwackie in Satan's Dub Cassette* (ROIR); *Version Like Rain* (Trojan) 1991—*Lord God Muzick* (Heartbeat) 1992—*The Upsetter & the Beat; Soundzs From the Hot Line* 1993—*Black Ark in Dub* (Lagoon); *Heavy Manners: Reggae's Best* 1994—*Smokin'* (VP); *In Dub Confrontation, vol. 1* (Lagoon); *News Flash* 1995—*Quest* (Clocktower); *Larks From the Ark* (Nectar Masters); *Stay Red* (Lagoon Reggae); *Scratch the Upsetter Again* (Trojan); *Experryments at the Grassroots of Dub* (RAS); *Super Ape Inna Jungle; The Upsetter Shop* (Heartbeat); *In Dub Confrontation, vol. 2* (Lagoon); *Kung Fu Meets the Dragon; Glory Dub* 1996—*Who Put the Voodoo 'Pon Reggae; Words of My Mouth* (Trojan); *Introducing Lee Perry* (Lagoon); *Reminah Dub* (Original Music); *The Best of Lee Perry* (Upsetter); *The Great Lee*

Perry the King of Dub (Graylan); *The Upsetter Presenting Dub* (Rhino); *Voodooism* (Pressure Sounds) 1997—*Arkology* (Island); *Technomajikal* (ROIR); *Upsetter in Dub* (Heartbeat) 1998—*Live at Maritime Hall* (Maritime Hall); *Dry Acid 1968–1969* (Trojan); *Dub Fire* (RAS); *Archive* (Rialto) 1999—*Lick Shot* (X-ploit); *The Upsetter Shop, vol. 2: 1969–1973* (Heartbeat); *Chapter Two of Words* (Trojan) 2000—*Lost Treasures of the Ark* (Orchard); *Ultimate Collection* (Hip-O); *Upsetter: Essential Madness* (Metro Music); *On the Wire* (Trojan).
Lee Perry and Friends: 1988—*Give Me Power* (Trojan) 1989—*Open the Gate; Shocks of Mighty 1969–1974* (Attack); *Mystic Warrior Dub* (Ariwa) 1990—*Public Jestering* 1995—*Black Ark Experyments* (RAS).
As Jah Lion: 1976—*Colombia Colly* (Mango).
Lee "Scratch" Perry and Mad Professor: 1989—*Mystic Warrior* (RAS) 2000—*Lee Perry Meets Mad Professor* (Orange Street).

Working under many names—as well as in many capacities: disc jockey, producer, record businessman, songwriter, singer—Lee Perry has been a guiding force in the development of reggae. In addition to his own trailblazing music, he has produced hits for the Wailers, Junior Byles, Max Romeo, the Heptones, Gregory Isaacs, Junior Murvin, and the Clash. Known for his bizarre behavior and stream-of-consciousness interviews, he often dons costumes and headdresses made of found objects such as feathers, toys, playing cards, and coins.

He began his career in his teens as Little Lee Perry, a DJ for Coxsone Dodd's Downbeat Sound System. When he made his recording debut with "The Chicken Scratch" on Dodd's Studio One label in the early '60s, he became known as Scratch Perry. For most of the '60s, he worked at Studio One as A&R director and producer of Jamaican hits for Justin Hines, Delroy Wilson, and Shenley Dufus, among others; he also recorded his own material like "Trials and Crosses" and "Doctor Dick."

In 1968 Perry left Dodd and worked briefly—as producer and performer—with Joe Gibbs, Byron Lee, and Clancy Eccles. With the success of Perry's first independent release, an instrumental called "The Upsetter," he acquired another sobriquet—the Upsetter. He named his label Upsetter and his studio band the Upsetters. That same year, 1968, he had a hit with "People Funny Boy," billing himself as Lee "King" Perry. An unusually slow song for its time, "People Funny Boy" was one of the first real reggae hits. Most of Perry's late-'60s hits, like "Clint Eastwood," "Live Injection," and "Return of Django" (#5 U.K., 1969), were instrumentals that set his spaghetti Western–style themes in reggae as dry, spacious, and ominous as the western desert.

In 1969 Perry began working with the Wailers. During the next three years, he oversaw their transformation from a ska vocal trio into a full-fledged five-piece reggae band—with bassist Aston "Family Man" Barrett and his drummer brother Carlton from the Upsetters—that would become the most acclaimed Jamaican group in the world. "Duppy Conqueror," "Small Axe," "Kaya," and "Sun Is Shining" were some of the Wailers' songs Perry wrote. The Wailers began producing themselves for their own label in 1971 but were reunited with Perry for occasional sessions in the late '70s.

Signed to Island in 1973, Perry and his Upsetters maintained a rocky relationship with the company on and off for several years. In 1974 he built his Black Ark Studio in the backyard of his Kingston home. Perry was one of the pioneers of the reggae instrumental studio art known as dubbing—reworking a taped track by removing some parts and exaggerating others. His use of technology such as drum machines and phase shifters gave his mixes a cutting-edge sound that had a profound influence on dub and, later, dancehall. His work in the '70s with toasters like U-Roy, Prince Jazzbo, I-Roy, Big Youth, and Dennis Alcapone established him in the forefront of toasters' dub; he would make hit after hit from the same rhythm track until the tape wore out. Perry recorded his own toasting under the pseudonym of Jah Lion. He also recorded as Pipecock Jackson and under his own name. His most popular releases in the '70s, "Station Underground News" and "Roast Fish and Corn Bread," were vocals.

Perry reportedly torched his studio in 1980 and began traveling. His musical output became more eccentric and experimental, though it remained highly respected by critics. He lived in Amsterdam in the mid-'80s, and then in London. In 1990 Perry moved to Switzerland, only occasionally returning to Jamaica, where he eventually abandoned plans to rebuild his historic Black Ark Studio. In 1997 Perry's public profile rose with the release of *Arkology*, a three-disc anthology. That same year the Beastie Boys invited him to appear at the Tibetan Freedom Concert in New York (where he appeared in a football helmet covered with small mirrors), followed by an extensive U.S. tour with sometime collaborator Neal "the Mad Professor" Fraser. By now he was acknowledged as a key influence on '90s trip-hop and electronic dance music. In 2000 he released the recently completed *On the Wire*—an album begun a decade earlier, before Perry disappeared to Switzerland with the tapes—to more critical acclaim.

The Persuasions

Formed 1962, Brooklyn, NY
Jerry Lawson (b. Jan. 23, 1944, Fort Lauderdale, FL), lead voc.; Jayotis Washington (b. May 12, 1941, Detroit, MI), tenor voc.; Joseph "Jesse" Russell (b. Sep. 25, 1939, Henderson, NC), tenor voc.; Herbert "Toubo" Rhoad (b. Oct. 1, 1944, Bamberg County, SC; d. Dec. 8, 1988), baritone voc.; Jimmy "Bro" Hayes (b. Nov. 12, 1943, Hopewell, VA), bass voc.
1968—*A Cappella* (Straight) 1971—*We Came to Play* (Capitol) 1972—*Street Corner Symphony; Spread the Word* 1973—*We Still Ain't Got No Band* (MCA) 1974—*More Than Before* (A&M); *I Just Want to Sing With My Friends* (– Washington; + Willie Daniels) 1977—*Chirpin'* (Elektra) (– Daniels; + Washington) 1979—*Comin' at Ya* (Flying Fish) 1983—*Good News* (Rounder) 1986—*No Frills* 1988—*Live at the Whispering Gallery* (– Rhoad) 1993—*Toubo's Song* (Hammer N' Nails) 1994—

Right Around the Corner (Bullseye Blues) 1996—*Sincerely* 1997—*You're All I Want for Christmas; Man Oh Man* (Capitol) 1999—*On the Good Ship Lollipop (Music for Little People)* 2000—*Sunday Morning Soul* (Bullseye Blues); *Frankly A Cappella: The Persuasions Sing Zappa!* (Earthbeat!/Rhino); *Might As Well: The Persuasions Sing Grateful Dead* (Grateful Dead/Arista).

Since 1962, the Persuasions' unique brand of a cappella has made them a popular live attraction and sought-after as backup singers. Tenors Jesse Russell and Jayotis Washington, baritones Toubo Rhoad and Jerry Lawson, and nonpareil bass Jimmy Hayes started the group in Brooklyn, where all had migrated. Each had sung with gospel and secular vocal groups, and from the beginning the Persuasions have mixed doo-wop, soul, and pop into their repertoire.

The Persuasions' first recording was a single on Minit/United Artist Records in 1966. The following year they were taped at a Jersey City performance by doo-wop fan David Dashev, who got the tape to Frank Zappa, who released it as *A Cappella* in 1968 on his Straight Records. When Warner Bros. purchased Straight, label executives wanted to record the Persuasions with a band, but the group refused. From 1971 to 1973 the Persuasions made three records for Capitol. With MCA Records in 1973, they cut one album, *We Still Ain't Got No Band*. The following year Washington left the group and was replaced by Willie Daniels; Daniels left in 1977, and Washington returned that year.

Two mid-'70s albums with A&M, *More Than Before* and *I Just Want to Sing With My Friends,* included instrumental backing and resulted in two singles making the lower end of the R&B chart: "I Really Got It Bad for You" in 1974 and "One Thing on My Mind" in 1975. From 1974 on, the Persuasions worked steadily as guest vocalists behind Stevie Wonder, Phoebe Snow, Ellen McIlwaine, Don McLean, and others. They cut the critically acclaimed *Chirpin'* for Elektra in 1977, with Dashev producing. After backing Joni Mitchell on a 1979–80 tour, the Persuasions were featured on her *Shadows and Light* live album, including the single "Why Do Fools Fall in Love?" With Rhoad's death in 1988, the group became a quartet. It was featured prominently in Spike Lee's 1990 television special *Do It A Cappella* and on the accompanying album. In the mid-'90s director Fred Parnes completed the acclaimed film *Spread the Word: The Persuasions Sing A Cappella.* Extant for over 35 years, the vocal ensemble tours and records frequently. Recently the Persuasions issued an album of kids' music (1999's *On the Good Ship Lollipop*) and tributes to Zappa and the Grateful Dead (2000's *Frankly A Cappella* and *Might As Well*).

Pet Shop Boys

Formed Aug. 1981, London, Eng.
Neil Tennant (b. Neil Francis Tennant, July 10, 1954, North Shields, Northumberland, Eng.), voc.; Chris Lowe (b. Christopher Sean Lowe, Oct. 4, 1959, Blackpool, Lancashire, Eng.), kybds.

1986—*Please* (EMI); *Disco* 1987—*Actually* 1988—*Introspective* 1990—*Behavior* 1991—*Discography* 1993—*Very* 1994—*Disco 2* 1995—*Alternative* 1996—*Bilingual* (Atlantic) 1999—*Nightlife* (Parlophone/Sire).

Like the Monty Python comedy troupe, the duo Pet Shop Boys could have been conceived only by the English. Less a band per se than a musical vehicle for wry, cheeky commentary on pop culture, Pet Shop Boys—singer Neil Tennant and keyboardist Chris Lowe—won kudos for their clever, danceable synth pop and deadpan ballads, which were as tender as they were irreverent.

Lowe was an architecture student and Tennant a journalist when they met in 1981 in an electronics shop and discovered they shared a passion for synthesizers and dance music. As a youth, Tennant had been active in theater and had sung and played guitar in a band called Dust; Lowe had studied piano and trombone and had played the latter in a dance-standard band. Calling themselves Pet Shop Boys, a name taken from friends who actually worked in a pet shop, Tennant and Lowe began writing songs together. In 1983 Tennant, then an editor at the British pop music journal *Smash Hits,* hooked up with producer Bobby "O" Orlando while on business in New York. Orlando worked on an early version of the Boys' first single, "West End Girls."

In 1985 the finished mix of "West End Girls" shot to #1 in numerous countries, including the U.S., where Pet Shop Boys' debut album, *Please,* peaked at #7. *Please* also spawned the pop hit "Opportunities (Let's Make Lots of Money)" (#10). An album of dance remixes, *Disco,* followed in 1986. In 1987 Boys scored another three Top 10 singles in America: "It's a Sin" (#9); "What Have I Done to Deserve This?" (#2), a duet between Tennant and his favorite female singer, Dusty Springfield; and a remake of an Elvis standard made a hit years later by Willie Nelson, "Always on My Mind" (#4).

In the summer of 1988 Pet Shop Boys released the documentary film *It Couldn't Happen Here.* After putting out another album that year, *Introspective,* the duo produced Liza Minnelli's 1989 album, *Results,* which featured a high-tech rendition of Stephen Sondheim's "Losing My Mind." Later that year Tennant cowrote and sang on "Getting Away With It," the debut single by Electronic, a group formed by New Order's Bernard Sumner and ex-Smiths guitarist Johnny Marr.

Pet Shop Boys have continued to reap acclaim with the albums *Behavior* (#45, 1990) and *Very* (#20, 1993). In 1991, on the heels of a well-received single seguing U2's "Where the Streets Have No Name" with Frankie Valli's "Can't Take My Eyes Off of You," they released *Discography,* a singles compilation. Following the pair's production of Boy George's single "The Crying Game" in 1992, *Very* included a remake of the Village People's "Go West," the once-triumphant song now sounding like an elegy for AIDS victims. The next two years saw repackaged releases: 1994's *Disco 2* was a dance remix album, while 1995's *Alternative* was a collection of B sides. The duo's next new studio release, 1996's *Bilingual,* explored Latin rhythms; it was not particularly successful or popular. But 1999's *Nightlife* (#84, 1999), backed by the Boys' first U.S. tour in eight years—and boasting an elaborate set and costumes—was a hit with the dance-club crowd, thanks to the pulsating #1 Club Play hit "New York City Boy" (#53, 1999). The album also included the straightforwardly named "You Only Tell Me You Love Me When You're Drunk" and a duet with Kylie Minogue, "In Denial," the latter from a set of songs Tennant and Lowe were writing for a stage musical about gay club life. Also in 1999, Tennant and Lowe sued conservative British author Roger Scruton for libel, based on the writer's implication in his book *An Intelligent Person's Guide to Culture* that the Pet Shop Boys' recordings owed more to technology in the studio than any creativity on the members' part. The Boys won an undisclosed sum in the suit.

Pete Rock and C.L. Smooth

Formed 1984, Mount Vernon, NY
Pete Rock (b. Peter Phillips, June 21, 1970, Mount Vernon), voc.; C.L. Smooth (b. Corey Penn, Oct. 8, 1968, New Rochelle, NY), DJ.
1992—*Mecca & the Soul Brother* (Elektra) 1994—*The Main Ingredient.*
Pete Rock solo: 1998—*Soul Survivor* (Loud/RCA).

Pete Rock and C.L. Smooth are rappers well respected for both their own work and Rock's production of other rap acts. The duo met in their teens in "money-earnin' " Mount Vernon, home of such hip-hop stars as Al B. Sure! and Heavy D. They began recording raps on Rock's cassette player after school, until Eddie F., the most popular local DJ and a budding producer, brought them to his 12-track. Eddie put Rock and Smooth on a remix of Johnny Gill's gold single "Rub U the Right Way," which eventually landed them their first gig outside their neighborhood, in Madison Square Garden with Gill.

Mecca & the Soul Brother (#43 pop, #7 R&B, 1992) was praised for its honest stories of urban romance and living and for Rock's mix of jazz, R&B, and reggae. "They Reminisce Over You (T.R.O.Y.)" (#58 pop, #10 R&B, 1992) was a #1 rap hit. *The Main Ingredient* followed two years later (#51 pop, #9 R&B, 1994), after which the duo called it quits. Rock has produced records by Kid n' Play, Shabba Ranks, and Heavy D and remixed singles for Public Enemy, Naughty by Nature, and Run-D.M.C. *Soul Survivor* (#39 pop, #7 R&B, 1998), Rock's solo debut, features guest appearances by members of the Wu-Tang Clan and the Roots, as well as C.L. Smooth. In 1999 the MC rapped on "World Renown," a single by Norwegian producer Tommy Tee.

Peter and Gordon

Formed 1963, London, Eng.
Peter Asher (b. June 22, 1944, London), voc., gtr.; Gordon Waller (b. June 4, 1945, Braemar, Scot.), voc., gtr.
1964—*A World Without Love* (Capitol) 1965—*Peter and Gordon; True Love Ways* 1966—*The Best of Peter and Gordon* 1967—*Lady Godiva.*

Peter and Gordon were an enormously successful British pop/folk team in the mid-'60s. After their breakup, Gordon all but vanished into obscurity, but Peter Asher has kept his name in the limelight as a manager/producer of Linda Ronstadt, James Taylor, 10,000 Maniacs, and others.

Both Peter and Gordon came from upper-middle-class families and were products of private schools, the two meeting at Westminster School for Boys in London. They worked together as a campus duo, in an Everly Brothers vein, and decided to try the London club scene. Because of their school's 9 P.M. dorm curfew, they had to sneak over a 12-foot spiked fence to do it, which they managed successfully for about a year. Eventually they left school to concentrate on music, recording demos and making the record-company rounds.

Asher and Waller landed a contract in 1963 and within a year had their first and biggest hit, "World Without Love," written by Paul McCartney, who at the time was courting Asher's sister Jane. The tune went to #1 in the U.S. and the U.K. in 1964.

Between 1964 and 1967 the duo had a string of hit singles that included: "Nobody I Know" (#12) and "I Don't Want to See You Again" (#16) in 1964; Del Shannon's "I Go to Pieces" (#9), Buddy Holly's "True Love Ways" (#14), and "To Know You Is to Love You" (#24) in 1965; and "Woman" (#14) and "Lady Godiva" (#6) in 1966.

In 1968 the duo broke up, and Asher became A&R head of the Beatles' Apple label, where he signed and produced James Taylor before moving to the United States. From the early '70s on, Asher's client roster has included Taylor, Linda Ronstadt, Carole King, Joni Mitchell, Randy Newman, and Warren Zevon, as well as such newer artists as John Wesley Harding, Iris DeMent, and Mary's Danish. In 1989 he won a Grammy for Producer of the Year for his work on Ronstadt's *Cry Like a Rainstorm, Howl Like the Wind.*

Peter, Paul and Mary

Formed 1961, New York, NY
Peter Yarrow (b. May 31, 1938, New York), voc., gtr.; Noel Paul Stookey (b. Nov. 30, 1937, Baltimore, MD), voc., gtr.; Mary Travers (b. Nov. 7, 1937, Louisville, KY), voc.
1962—*Peter, Paul and Mary* (Warner Bros.) 1963—*Peter, Paul and Mary—Moving; Peter, Paul and Mary—In the Wind* 1964—*Peter, Paul and Mary in Concert* 1965—*A Song Will Rise; See What Tomorrow Brings* 1966—*The Peter, Paul and Mary Album* 1967—*Album 1700* 1968—*Late Again* 1969—*Peter, Paul & Mommy* 1970—*Ten Years Together* 1978—*Reunion* 1986—*No Easy Walk to Freedom* (Gold Castle) 1988—*A Holiday Celebration* 1990—*Flowers and Stones* 1993—*Peter, Paul & Mommy, Too* (Warner Bros.) 1995—*LifeLines* 1996—*LifeLines Live* 1998—*Around the Campfire* 1999—*Songs of Conscience & Concern—A Retrospective Collection.*

Peter Yarrow solo: 1972—*Peter* (Warner Bros.).
Paul Stookey solo: 1971—*Paul and* (Warner Bros.).
Mary Travers solo: 1971—*Mary* (Warner Bros.) 1972—*Morning Glory* 1973—*All My Choices* 1974—*Circles* 1978—*It's in Everyone of Us* (Chrysalis).

Peter, Paul and Mary became the most popular acoustic folk group of the '60s. They were also the first to bring commercial success to Bob Dylan, by covering his "Blowin' in the Wind," a #2 hit in August 1963.

The trio met while each was working in Greenwich Village and were encouraged by manager Albert Grossman to join forces in 1961. Yarrow had had some success as a solo folk artist. After graduating in psychology from Cornell, he toured locally and appeared on the CBS special *Folk Sound U.S.A.* in May 1960. Grossman spotted Yarrow there and arranged for him to perform at the Newport Folk Festival and make a national tour. Stookey was a stand-up comic in Greenwich Village and previously had led a high school rock & roll group.

Mary Travers, who grew up in Greenwich Village, had sung in school choruses and folk groups. She sang in the chorus of a 1957 Broadway flop called *The Next President* with Mort Sahl. In 1961 she met Stookey, who encouraged her to sing again, and Grossman decided she was right to round out the trio. They rehearsed for seven months, with Milt Okun crafting their arrangements. Soon after they played a special engagement at New York's Bitter End, they signed with Warner Bros. Records.

The group's debut LP spent seven weeks at #1 in 1962, and two songs from it, "Lemon Tree" (#35) and Pete Seeger's "If I Had a Hammer" (#10), cracked the Top 40. The latter helped bring folk and protest consciousness to the mainstream. The album remained on the Hot 100 Albums chart for three and a half years. They often toured college campuses and played at rallies. As always, they were deeply involved in the issues they sang about. They marched with Dr. Martin Luther King Jr., and in 1969 Yarrow helped organize the March on Washington.

After "Blowin' in the Wind" reached #2, the trio's cover of Dylan's "Don't Think Twice It's Alright" hit #9 in October 1963. In May of that year "Puff the Magic Dragon" (#2) stirred some controversy, since it was interpreted by some as a drug song. In fact it was just one of their many children's songs. (They released a whole LP of these in 1969 called *Peter, Paul & Mommy.*) Peter, Paul and Mary were also known for covering songs by soon-to-be-famous singer/songwriters, including John Denver ("Leaving on a Jet Plane," a #1 smash in 1969) and Gordon Lightfoot ("For Lovin' Me," a Top 30 single in 1965, and "Early Morning Rain"). Their other hits singles were "I Dig Rock and Roll Music" (#9, 1967) and "Day Is Done" (#21, 1969).

The group decided to break up in 1970 and released a best-of collection that May. It was their 10th album (out of 11) to make the Top 20. They each pursued solo careers, with considerably less artistic and commercial success. Stookey's records (as Noel Paul Stookey) reflected his Christian religious convictions. His best-known solo song was "Wedding Song (There Is Love)" (#24, 1971), written for Yarrow's marriage. Yarrow also coproduced and wrote Mary MacGregor's 1977 #1 hit "Torn Between Two Lovers." He formed a group called the Bodyworks Band, with which he performs and records Christian-oriented music. In 1970 Yarrow was convicted of "taking immoral liberties" with a female minor; in 1981 he was granted a full presidential pardon by Jimmy Carter. Travers hosted a radio talk show for a while and later a BBC television series.

The trio reunited occasionally in the '70s, at benefits such as the 1972 George McGovern campaign fund-raiser, which also brought back Simon and Garfunkel, and Mike Nichols and Elaine May. In 1978 they re-formed; they released a new LP and toured nationally. Their music continues to reflect contemporary political and social concerns, from civil war ("El Salvador") and apartheid ("No Easy Walk to Freedom") to AIDS ("Home Is Where the Heart Is"). They have starred in four PBS specials, including one to accompany the release of their second children's album, *Peter, Paul & Mommy, Too* and one centered around the *LifeLines* album, which featured guests such as Emmylou Harris, Judy Collins, John Sebastian, and B.B. King. *Around the Campfire* (1998) was a collection of folk classics, while *Songs of Conscience & Concern* (1999) was a retrospective focusing on the band's lesser-known material. In 2000 they embarked on a 40th-anniversary tour across North America.

Ray Peterson

Born Apr. 23, 1939, Denton, TX
1960—*Tell Laura I Love Her* (RCA Victor).

A late-'50s singer with a 4½-octave voice, Ray Peterson specialized in ballads like "The Wonder of You" (a hit for Elvis Presley in 1970) and the classic death-rock song "Tell Laura I Love Her," in which the hero dies in a stock-car race he'd entered hoping to win the $1,000 prize so that he could buy his girlfriend a wedding ring.

Peterson began singing while a polio patient in Warm Springs Foundation Hospital in Texas, to amuse the other patients. He started performing in local clubs and eventually moved to L.A., where he was signed by Stan Shulman of RCA Records. His first record was 1958's "Let's Try Romance," followed by "Tail Light," a cover of the R&B standard "Fever," and the hard-rocking "Shirley Purley," none of which made the chart.

Peterson's first hit was "The Wonder of You" (#25, 1959) written by Baker Knight, composer of numerous hits for Rick Nelson. He followed with "Tell Laura I Love Her" (#7, 1960), by Ellie Greenwich and Jeff Barry; the Phil Spector–produced "Corinna, Corinna" (#9, 1961); "Missing You" (#29, 1961); and "I Could Have Loved You So Well" (#57, 1962) by Gerry Goffin and Barry Mann. In 1961 Peterson formed his own label, Dunes, which released all records after and including "Corinna, Corinna," and to which he signed Curtis Lee ("Pretty Little Angel Eyes"). After some more discs for MGM failed, Peterson briefly tried a career as a country singer. He continues to record and perform.

Tom Petty and the Heartbreakers

Formed 1975, Los Angeles, CA
Tom Petty (b. Oct. 20, 1950, Gainesville, FL), voc., gtr.; Mike Campbell (b. Feb. 1, 1954, Gainesville), gtr.; Benmont Tench (b. Sep. 7, 1954, Gainesville), kybds.; Ron Blair (b. Sep. 16, 1952, Macon, GA), bass; Stan Lynch (b. May 21, 1955, Gainesville), drums.
1976—*Tom Petty and the Heartbreakers* (Shelter) 1978—*You're Gonna Get It* 1979—*Damn the Torpedoes* (Backstreet) 1981—*Hard Promises* 1982—(– Blair; + Howie Epstein [b. July 21, 1955], bass) *Long After Dark* 1985—*Southern Accents* (MCA); *Pack Up the Plantation* 1987—*Let Me Up (I've Had Enough)* 1991—*Into the Great Wide Open* 1993—*Greatest Hits* 1994—(– Lynch) 1995—*Playback* 1996—*Songs and Music From "She's the One"* (Warner Bros.) 1999—*Echo* 2001—*Tom Petty and the Heartbreakers Anthology: Through the Years* (Universal).
Tom Petty solo: 1989—*Full Moon Fever* (MCA) 1994—*Wildflowers* (Warner Bros.).

Tom Petty

In the '70s Tom Petty came up with a distillate of FM radio '60s rock—chiming Byrds guitars, Rolling Stones rhythms, and a slurred version of Bob Dylan/Roger McGuinn vocals. First penning tales of outcasts and long-suffering lovers, he broadened his thematic range to encompass musings on his Southern heritage and to propagate a very American individualism. The Heartbreakers evolved into a classic rock & roll band, and Petty's invitation in the '80s to join Dylan, Roy Orbison, George Harrison, and Jeff Lynne in the side-project supergroup the Traveling Wilburys confirmed his stature.

Petty, the son of a Florida insurance salesman, quit high school at 17 to join one of the state's top bands, Mudcrutch, with future Heartbreakers Mike Campbell and Benmont Tench. In the early '70s they sent Petty to L.A. to seek a record contract; Denny Cordell's Shelter Records (co-owned with Leon Russell) delivered.

The group disbanded soon after moving to L.A., and while Cordell offered to record Petty solo, nothing happened until 1975, when Petty heard a demo that Campbell and Tench were working on with Ron Blair and Stan Lynch. The quintet became the Heartbreakers, inherited Petty's Shelter contract, and released a self-titled debut in 1976. At first it sold poorly.

Then the Heartbreakers toured England, opening for Nils Lofgren. Within weeks, they were headlining and the album was on the British charts. ABC then rereleased "Breakdown" in the U.S., and the single cracked the Top 40 nearly a year after its initial release. Another song, the very Byrdsy "American Girl," was recorded by ex-Byrd Roger McGuinn. The band's second album boasted the singles "Listen to Her Heart" (#59, 1978) and "I Need to Know" (#41, 1978).

Just as the Heartbreakers' career was taking off, a legal battle arose when Petty tried to renegotiate his contract after MCA bought ABC; by mid-1979 he'd filed for bankruptcy. After nine months of litigation, Petty signed to Backstreet Records, a new MCA affiliate. His triumphant return, *Damn the Torpedoes,* hit #2, selling over 2.5 million copies, and established Petty as a star. And his singles placed higher: "Don't Do Me Like That" (#10, 1979) and "Refugee" (#15, 1980).

In 1981 Petty again got into another record-company hassle by challenging MCA's intention to issue *Hard Promises* with a $9.98 list price. After he threatened to withhold the LP—or entitle it *$8.98* and organize fan protest letters—the album came out at $8.98. *Hard Promises* went on to platinum status, with the #19 hit "The Waiting."

Petty had a #3 1981 hit in "Stop Draggin' My Heart Around," a duet with Stevie Nicks off her solo *Bella Donna,* on which the Heartbreakers also appeared. Also in 1981, he produced Del Shannon's comeback, *Drop Down and Get Me.* In 1982 "You Got Lucky" (#20) from *Long After Dark,* reiterated the veteran strengths of the Heartbreakers, but with Ron Blair departing, they underwent the novelty of a personnel change (ex–John Hiatt sideman Howie Epstein joined on bass). Three years in the making, *Southern Accents* was hard going; frustrated during its mixing, Petty punched a wall and broke his left hand. The album, coproduced by Eurythmics' Dave Stewart, found Petty achieving a new lyrical maturity and, with "Don't Come Around Here No More," scoring a #13 hit.

In 1986, right before Petty and the Heartbreakers embarked upon a world tour with Dylan, Petty's house burned down (arson was suspected). His wife and two daughters escaped, but most of his belongings were destroyed. Nineteen eighty-seven's *Let Me Up (I've Had Enough)* hit #20 and was certified gold, a relatively disappointing showing in view of the group's '80s success. Respite came with the 1988 release of the Traveling Wilburys [see entry] debut; working with former ELO founder/guitarist and fellow Wilbury Jeff Lynne, Petty released the masterful solo album *Full Moon Fever*. Its "Free Fallin' " (#7, 1989) gave him a revitalizing hit.

With most of the Heartbreakers playing on *Fever*, Petty retained band loyalty, and it paid off on *Into the Great Wide Open*, a fine collection coproduced with Lynne. In the interim Petty had released a second Wilburys album (1990's *Volume 3*), and his band had begun establishing themselves as sidemen, with Campbell working on Roy Orbison's *Mystery Girl*, cowriting Don Henley's "The Boys of Summer" and, with Lynch, contributing to Henley's *The End of the Innocence*. Meanwhile, Tench worked with such acts as U2 and Elvis Costello, and Epstein produced his girlfriend Carlene Carter's 1990 LP *I Fell in Love*.

Petty's record-business controversies continued, however, with the surprise 1992 revelation that he had signed a secret $20 million, six-album deal with Warner Bros. in 1989. Reportedly he had kept the contract secret to avoid the ire of MCA, to which he owed two more albums at the time. In an unrelated dispute, in 1993 he was vindicated by the U.S. Supreme Court when they let stand a lower court's finding that Petty's "Runnin' Down a Dream" did not infringe the copyright to an earlier piece written by songwriter/plaintiff Martin Allen Fine.

A year after a #5 *Greatest Hits* album in 1993, drummer Stan Lynch, who had been working as a songwriter and/or producer with the re-formed Eagles, Leonard Cohen, Don Henley, and the Mavericks, departed the band. Petty returned in 1994 with a second solo album, *Wildflowers*, which, again, featured most of the Heartbreakers. That year also saw the release of a Petty tribute album, *You Got Lucky*.

In 1996 Petty and the Heartbreakers reunited and recorded songs for Ed Burns' film *She's the One*; they also served as "backup band" on Johnny Cash's *Unchained*. That year, Petty and his wife ended their two-decade-long marriage, an event that purportedly added to the darker tone of 1999's masterful *Echo* (#10). In 1997 Petty had acted in the Kevin Costner movie, *The Postman*, but by 1999, his emphasis was squarely on music. In typical Petty fashion, *Echo*'s first single, "Free Girl Now," was offered on the MP3 format, which Internet users could download free (for two days, before his label requested that he remove it); the band also refused to increase ticket prices for the *Echo* tour.

Liz Phair

Born Elizabeth Clark Phair, Apr. 17, 1967, New Haven, CT
1993—*Exile in Guyville* (Matador) 1994—*Whip-Smart* 1995—*Juvenalia* EP 1998—*Whitechocolatespaceegg*.

Liz Phair, the in-your-face indie sweetheart, sent up "Guyville" (i.e., the male-dominated alternative-music scene dubbed as such by Chicago rockers Urge Overkill) in her debut, *Exile in Guyville*—a song-by-song response to the Stones' *Exile on Main Street*. The album drove home the point that gender has nothing to do with whether or not an artist can rock with intelligence and sexual savvy.

Raised in a wealthy suburb of Chicago, Phair studied art at Oberlin College, where she was constantly experimenting with songwriting. A friend, guitarist Chris Brokaw, later of the band Come, prodded Phair to make a tape of her songs, which resulted in her signing to Matador and recording *Guyville*. Her followup, *Whip-Smart* (#27, 1994), revealed itself to be a more introspective album—although her melting pot of punk, folk, and pop doesn't hide her frank, often sexual lyrics. The boldness and self-assurance Phair portrayed on her albums was not so apparent during her solo concerts, however, at which Phair suffered from stage fright. She took a break in 1995, marrying Jim Staskausas, a Chicago film editor who worked on her videos. She released the *Juvenalia* EP that summer, which featured material from her homemade "Girlysound" tapes. During 1996, she began recording a new album with producer Scott Litt, shelved the project, and gave birth to a son. Working with *Guyville* and *Whip-Smart* producer Brad Wood, she later returned to the studio, releasing *Whitechocolatespaceegg* (#35) in 1998. Phair explained that the title came from a dream she had while she was pregnant. Though toned down from the postfeminist friskiness of her earlier albums, the songs candidly explored themes of domestic tension and parenthood. She toured that summer as part of Lilith Fair, and launched a full-scale band tour later in the year.

Little Esther Phillips

Born Esther Mae Jones, Dec. 23, 1935, Galveston, TX; died Aug. 7, 1984, Torrance, CA
1970—*Burnin'* (Atlantic) 1972—*From a Whisper to a Scream* (Kudu); *Alone Again (Naturally)* 1973—*Black Eyed Blues* 1974—*Performance* 1975—*What a Difference a Day Makes* 1976—*For All We Know; Confessin' the Blues* (Atlantic); *Capricorn Princess* (Kudu) 1977—*You've Come a Long Way Baby* (Mercury) 1978—*All About Esther* 1979—*Here's Esther . . . Are You Ready* 1986—*A Way to Say Goodbye* (Muse) 1990—*The Best of Esther Phillips* (Columbia) 1997—*The Best of Esther Phillips (1962–1970)* (Rhino).

Throughout her long career, singer Esther Phillips covered blues, rhythm & blues, and jazz, each in her own earthy style.

As a child in Texas, Phillips sang in churches before her family moved to L.A. in the late '40s. At 13 she won a talent show at L.A.'s Barrelhouse Club, run by R&B impresario Johnny Otis. For the next three years, she recorded with Otis' orchestra as Little Esther Phillips and built a national following among black record buyers. Two duets with another Otis discovery, Mel Walker, resulted in the Top 10 R&B hits "Cupid's Boogie" (#2 R&B, 1950) and "Ring-a-Ding-Doo" (#8 R&B, 1952). As a solo singer, Phillips had a #1 R&B hit with "Double Crossing Blues" in 1950.

Because of illness, she retired in 1954 and settled in Houston. She returned to music in the early '60s with New York's Lenox Records and in 1962 enjoyed international success with "Release Me" (#8 pop, #1 R&B), a reworking of a country hit. A 1963 duet with Big Al Downing on "You Never Miss Your Water (Until Your Well Runs Dry)" is well remembered, though it was not a hit at the time. She signed with Atlantic in the mid-'60s and had success with a cover of the Beatles' "And I Love Her," done as "And I Love Him" (#11 R&B).

In the late '60s Phillips' recordings suffered as she battled a heroin addiction at Synanon, a treatment center. In 1971 she signed with Kudu Records, where she cut a series of bluesy jazz albums. Her chilling interpretation of Gil Scott-Heron's antidrug "Home Is Where the Hatred Is" (#40 R&B) is considered by many to be one of her finest efforts. "I Never Found a Man (To Love Me Like You Do)" (#17 R&B) in 1972 showed that Phillips still had commercial appeal. This fact was further demonstrated by her 1975 disco hit "What a Difference a Day Makes" (#20 pop, #10 R&B, #6 U.K.). In 1981 an album on Mercury Records was produced by jazz trumpeter Benny Golson. In 1982 she duetted with Swamp Dogg on one song from his *I'm Not Selling Out, I'm Buying In.*

Plagued for years by declining health and substance-abuse problems, Phillips died of kidney and liver failure.

Sam Phillips

Born Leslie Phillips, June 28, 1962, East Hollywood, CA
1983—*Beyond Saturday Night* (Word/Myrrh) 1984—*Dancing With Danger* 1985—*Black and White in a Grey World* 1987—*The Turning* 1988—*The Indescribable Wow* 1991—*Cruel Inventions* (Virgin) 1994—*Martinis and Bikinis* 1996—*Omnipop (It's Only a Flesh Wound Lambchop)* 1999—*Zero Zero Zero* 2001—*Fan Dance* (Nonesuch).

Sam Phillips has had two recording careers. The first, under her real name Leslie Phillips, was as an in-demand contemporary Christian singer/songwriter whose four albums for the Word/Myrrh label, beginning with 1984's *Beyond Saturday Night,* averaged sales of 200,000 copies each. But after the release of 1987's *The Turning,* which was produced by her future husband, T Bone Burnett, Phillips turned her back on the born-again gospel music scene, changed her professional name to Sam (a nickname since childhood), and forged a career as a critically acclaimed secular performer.

Raised in Glendale, California, Phillips turned to the church out of an early interest in philosophy and spirituality. After earning accolades for her Christian rock, however, she began to feel restrained by the genre, frustrated by what she perceived to be its right-wing agenda. She continued to explore spiritual metamorphosis in her secular albums, but she also ventured into themes of sexuality and personal relationships, her lyrics often marked by a wry sense of humor reminiscent of Randy Newman. Beginning with her first album for Virgin, 1988's *The Indescribable Wow,* she also revealed a strong affinity for Beatlesque pop melodies, while the Grammy-nominated *Martinis and Bikinis* (#182, 1994) and 1996's more experimental *Omnipop (It's Only a Flesh Wound Lambchop)* also displayed elements of baroque, lounge, and psychedelia. *Zero Zero Zero* (1999) was an anthology of her Virgin recordings, highlighted by rerecordings and new songs. Burnett, whom she married in 1989, has produced all of her albums since *The Turning.*

In 1995 Phillips ventured into a third career, film, when she played a murderous mute terrorist in *Die Hard With a Vengeance.* Her first album of new material in five years, *Fan Dance* (also a Burnett collaboration), was another eloquent, lovely effort and her first for the Nonesuch label.

Phish

Formed 1983, Burlington, VT
Trey Anastasio (b. Sep. 30, 1964, Fort Worth, TX), gtr., voc.; Jon Fishman (b. Feb. 19, 1965, Philadelphia, PA), drums, voc.; Mike Gordon (b. June 3, 1965, Boston, MA), bass, voc.; Jeff Holdsworth (b. Nov. 14, 1963), gtr.
1985—(+ Page McConnell [b. May 17, 1963, PA], kybds., voc.) 1986—(- Holdsworth) 1988—*Junta* (Phish) 1990—*Lawn Boy* (Absolute A-Go-Go) 1992—*A Picture of Nectar* (Elektra) 1993—*Rift* 1994—*Hoist* 1995—*A Live One* 1996—*Billy Breathes* 1997—*Slip, Stitch & Pass* (Elektra/Asylum) 1998—*The Story of the Ghost; Phish (The White Tape)* (Phish) 1999—*Hampton Comes Alive* (Elektra/Asylum) 2000—*Farmhouse; The Siket Disc.*
With Dude of Life: 1994—*Crimes of the Mind* (Elektra).
Trey Anastasio solo: 1996—*Surrender to the Air* (Elektra) 1998—*One Man's Trash* (Phish) 2000—*Trampled by Lambs & Pecked by Doves* (with Tom Marshall).

To its fans, Phish is not just a band—it's a way of life. Although the group's studio efforts sell well enough, occasionally making high chart debuts, Phish is primarily a live phenomenon. Like thousands of Deadheads before them, Phish fans loyally follow the group from city to city, trade bootleg tapes with the band's blessings, and feverishly debate the merits of past set lists (Phish never plays the same set twice). By nurturing this grass-roots following, Phish bypassed commercial radio and evolved over the course of a decade into one of—if not *the*—hottest live attractions in America.

The band first came together in drummer Jon Fishman's dorm room at the University of Vermont. Fellow students Trey Anastasio and Jeff Holdsworth brought their guitars by to jam, and they were later joined by bassist Mike Gordon, who answered a bulletin-board ad posted by Anastasio. Fan Page McConnell, a student at Goddard College, joined as a keyboardist in 1985, and Holdsworth left the following year. Early performances around this time also featured percussionist Marc Daubert, as well as occasional appearances by the enigmatic singer Dude of Life (with whom the band would later record the album *Crimes of the Mind*). In 1988 Phish recorded its first album, *Junta,* which was sold as a cassette at gigs. By the time the band released its second album, *Lawn Boy* (1990), on the independent label Absolute A-Go-Go, Phish's growing fan base had begun to establish a presence on the fledgling Internet at Phish.Net. Elektra signed the group a year later and released *A Picture of Nectar* in 1992, followed by reissues of *Lawn Boy* and *Junta*.

Beginning with 1993's *Rift* (#51), the band's popularity began to translate into chart success. The following year's *Hoist,* which spawned Phish's only video (for "Down With Disease"), went to #34, followed by 1995's double disc *A Live One* (#18), *Billy Breathes* (#7, 1996), the live *Slip, Stitch & Pass* (#17, 1997), *The Story of the Ghost* (#8, 1998), the sprawling, six-disc *Hampton Comes Alive* (#120, 1999), and *Farmhouse* (#12, 2000). But it was live, not on disc, that Phish defined itself throughout the decade. In addition to the band's trademark marathon improvisational jams (drawing equally from jazz, rock, and country), fans could count on such weird variables as Fishman's vacuum-cleaner solos and the band's penchant for oddball covers; in 1994 Phish began a semiannual tradition of performing an entire classic album live on Halloween as a "musical costume" (ranging from the Beatles' White Album to the Who's *Quadrophenia* and Talking Heads' *Remain in Light*). In 1997 the band's weekend festival, the Great Went, held in Limestone, Maine, drew an audience of 62,000. The following year's Lemonwheel Festival, also in Limestone, drew a comparable crowd. Phish ended the '90s playing for 75,000 fans at a two-night millennial concert at Florida's Big Cypress Seminole Indian Reservation.

After touring in support of 2000's *Farmhouse,* Phish announced an indefinite hiatus. Fans were left with Elektra's official release of *The Siket Disc,* a collection of studio outtakes, along with the feature-length documentary *Bittersweet Motel* and periodic updates on its Web site about such band member side projects as Gordon's experimental film *Outside Out* and *Trampled by Lambs & Pecked by Doves,* an album by Anastasio and Phish lyricist Tom Marshall. Other rarities offered for sale online included *The White Tape,* a collection of early 4-track demos recorded in 1984.

Phranc

Born Susan Gottlieb, Aug. 28, 1957, Santa Monica, CA
1985—*Folksinger* (Rhino) 1989—*I Enjoy Being a Girl* (Island) 1991—*Positively Phranc* 1995—*Goofyfoot* EP (Kill Rock Stars) 1998—*Milkman* (Phancy).

Phranc calls herself the "all-American Jewish lesbian folksinger" and composes music in the traditional '60s protest style of Phil Ochs, Tom Paxton, and Joan Baez. The daughter of an insurance salesman and dental hygienist, Susan Gottlieb knew early on that she was different from her friends. By 1974, she had found refuge in the local lesbian-feminist community; the following year she changed her name to Phranc, dropped out of Venice High School, and got a buzz-cut flattop.

Musically influenced by her cantor grandfather, Phranc started singing at gay coffeehouses, and by the late '70s discovered L.A.'s burgeoning punk-rock scene. By 1980, after playing in three punk bands, including Catholic Discipline, she had tired of the music's misogyny and Nazi iconography and had written "Take Off Your Swastika" (which would show up later on 1989's *I Enjoy Being a Girl*); she played the song at a punk show one night on her acoustic guitar so that members of the mosh pit could hear the words. Phranc decided then to return to folk music for good. Unlike most folkies, however, she has performed on bills with bands ranging from Dead Kennedys to Morrissey.

Phranc's unflinching treatment of her sexuality, as well as other aspects of her personal life and politics, has undoubtedly kept her music from gaining a wider audience. Although *Folksinger* was well received critically, it remained a cult item. In 1989 Island signed Phranc but never quite figured out how to market her. The label released 1989's *I Enjoy Being a Girl,* rereleased *Folksinger* in 1990, and then dropped her after the release of 1991's *Positively Phranc.*

Undaunted, she turned her energies toward visual art, earning exhibitions in New York and L.A. Her next musical project came in 1992: a swaggering impersonation of Neil Diamond, complete with blow-dried wig and glittering threads, calling the act "Hot August Phranc." In 1995 Phranc released the surf-themed *Goofyfoot,* and included deadpan covers of Bobbie Gentry's "Ode to Billy Joe" and Herman's Hermits' "Mrs. Brown, You've Got a Lovely Daughter." Her self-released *Milkman,* produced by Warren A. Bruleigh (Violent Femmes), was her first full-length album in seven years. The 1998 release collected minimalist songs rooted in the folk tradition, with lyrics of humor and loss, partly inspired by the murder of her brother.

Bobby "Boris" Pickett

Born Feb. 11, 1938, Somerville, MA
1962—*The Original Monster Mash* (Garpax).

Bobby "Boris" Pickett's ticket to fame was an ability to imitate monster-movie star Boris Karloff, something he put to good use on the novelty hit "Monster Mash," a #1 in 1962.

After three years in the Signal Corps in Korea, Pickett had drifted to Hollywood, where he attempted to establish himself as a comedian and actor. He appeared in 1967's *It's a Bikini World,* and he later appeared in a number of television episodes (on *Bonanza, The Beverly Hillbillies,* and *Petticoat Junction*), on television commercials, and in a few movies *(The Baby Maker).* After joining a singing group called the Cordials, he and group member Leonard Capizzi wrote "Monster Mash." Gary Paxton—Flip of Skip and Flip fame and the lead singer on the Hollywood Argyles' novelty hit "Alley Oop"—released it on his own Garpax label. There were a few less-successful followups: "Monster's Holiday" (#30, 1962), "Monster Motion" (1963), and "Graduation Day" (#88, 1963). His backup group, the Crypt-Kickers, included Leon Russell and Paxton.

He continued to work as an actor and has since written screenplays, but "Monster Mash" has proven the hit that will not die. A Halloween tradition now, it was revived in 1973, and hit #3 in the U.K. and #10 in the U.S. In the mid-'80s Pickett recorded a "Monster Rap" that got some airplay. According to an interview from that period, Pickett claimed to have last performed "Monster Mash" in a Sunset Strip club backed by none other than the then-unknown Van Halen. He continues to creep around on the oldies circuit.

Wilson Pickett

Born Mar. 18, 1941, Prattville, AL
1965—*In the Midnight Hour* (Atlantic) 1966—*The Exciting Wilson Pickett* 1967—*The Wicked Pickett; The Sound of Wilson Pickett; The Best of Wilson Pickett* 1968—*I'm in Love; The Midnight Mover* 1969—*Hey Jude* 1970—*Right On* 1971—*Don't Knock My Love* 1973—*Mr. Magic Man* (RCA) 1974—*Tonight I'm My Biggest Audience; Miz Lenas Boy* 1977—*Join Me and Let's Be Free* 1978—*A Funky Situation* (Big Tree) 1979—*I Want You* (EMI) 1981—*The Right Track* 1987—*American Soul Man* (Motown) 1992—*A Man and a Half: The Best of Wilson Pickett* (Rhino/Atlantic) 1993—*The Very Best of Wilson Pickett* (Rhino) 1999—*It's Harder Now* (Bullseye Blues & Jazz).

Singer Wilson Pickett applied his rough, swaggering, sexy, "wicked" style to a series of stripped-down soul classics to create one of the most enduring soul legacies.

After his family migrated from Alabama to Detroit in 1955, young Pickett formed a gospel group, the Violinaires (which included Eddie Floyd and Sir Mack Rice), who were popular in local churches. In 1959 he was recruited by the R&B vocal group the Falcons. He wrote and sang lead on the Falcons' "I Found a Love" (#6 R&B, 1962). Falcons producer Robert Bateman suggested he go solo, and Pickett signed with Lloyd Price's Double L Records in 1963 and had hits with two of his songs, "If You Need Me" (#30 R&B) and "It's Too Late" (#17 R&B).

In 1964 Pickett signed with Atlantic. Following two unsuccessful singles, Atlantic executive/producer Jerry Wexler took Pickett to Memphis, where he recorded with Booker T. and the MG's. "In the Midnight Hour" (#21, 1965), credited to Pickett and guitarist/producer Steve Cropper, was a major breakthrough. Recording in a similar style with musicians in Memphis, Muscle Shoals, and Miami, Pickett had a long series of R&B hits that occasionally crossed over to pop, including "634-5789" (#13 pop, #1 R&B) and "Land of 1,000 Dances" (#6 pop, #1 R&B) in 1966; "Funky Broadway" (#8 pop, #1 R&B) in 1967; "I'm a Midnight Mover" (#6 R&B) in 1968; and the tribute record "Cole, Cooke, and Redding" (#61 pop, #4 R&B) in 1970.

Later that year he recorded in Philadelphia with the Gamble and Huff production team, scoring with "Engine Number 9" (#14 pop, #3 R&B, 1970) and "Don't Let the Green Grass Fool You" (#17 pop, #2 R&B, 1971). Pickett's last three Atlantic hits were "Don't Knock My Love" (#13 pop, #1 R&B, 1971), "Call My Name, I'll Be There" (#10 R&B, 1971), and "Fire and Water" (#24 pop, #2 R&B, 1972). In March 1971 Pickett headlined a tour of American and African musicians in Ghana. The resulting film and album, *Soul to Soul,* featured Pickett prominently.

Pickett signed to RCA Records in 1973, followed by stints recording for Wicked (his own label), Big Tree, and EMI-America, but none of his later releases proved as popular. In the '80s he joined Don Covay, Joe Tex, and other '60s soul legends in the Soul Clan. In 1991 he was inducted into the Rock and Roll Hall of Fame, and in 1998 he appeared in the film *Blues Brothers 2000.* Though he continued to tour, he was rarely in the news except for items concerning minor skirmishes with the law. Twelve years would pass before his next album of new material, 1999's *It's Harder Now* (with liner notes stating that it was recorded "by actual musicians in real time without click tracks . . . samples, loops, or digital instruments").

Pink Floyd

Formed 1965, London, Eng.
Syd Barrett (b. Roger Keith Barrett, Jan. 6, 1946, Cambridge, Eng.), gtr., voc.; Richard Wright (b. July 28, 1945, London), kybds., voc.; Roger Waters (b. Sep. 6, 1944, Surrey, Eng.), bass, voc.; Nick Mason (b. Jan. 27, 1945, Birmingham, Eng.), drums.
1967—*The Piper at the Gates of Dawn* (Tower) 1968—(+ David Gilmour [b. Mar. 6, 1944, Cambridge], gtr., voc.) *A Saucerful of Secrets* (Harvest); *Tonight Let's All Make Love in London* soundtrack (Instant Analysis) 1969—(– Barrett) *More* soundtrack (Harvest); *Ummagumma* 1970—*Atom Heart Mother; Zabriskie Point* soundtrack (MGM) 1971—*Meddle* (Harvest); *Relics* 1972—*Music From La Vallee: Obscured by Clouds* soundtrack 1973—*Dark Side of the Moon; A Nice Pair* (reissue of first two LPs) 1975—*Wish You Were Here* (Columbia) 1977—*Animals* 1979—*The Wall* 1981—*A Collection of Great Dance Songs* 1982—(– Wright) 1983—*The Final Cut; Works* (Capitol) 1984—(– Waters) 1987—(+ Wright) *A Momentary Lapse of Reason* 1988—*Delicate Sound of Thunder* 1992—*Shine On* (Columbia) 1994—*The Division Bell* 1995—*P.U.L.S.E.; Box 1975–1988* (CBS) 2000—*Is There Anybody Out There?; The Wall: Live* (Sony).
Roger Waters solo: 1984—*The Pros and Cons of Hitch Hiking* (Columbia) 1987—*Radio K.A.O.S.* 1990—*The Wall—Live in Berlin* (Mercury) 1992—*Amused to Death* (Columbia).
David Gilmour solo: 1978—*David Gilmour* (Columbia) 1984—*About Face.*
Richard Wright solo: 1978—*Wet Dream* (EMI/Harvest) 1984—*Identity.*
Nick Mason solo: 1981—*Nick Mason's Fictitious Sports* (Columbia) 1985—*Profiles.*
Syd Barrett solo: see entry.

With the release of 1973's *The Dark Side of the Moon,* Pink Floyd abruptly went from a moderately successful acid-rock band to one of pop music's biggest acts. The recording, in fact, remained on *Billboard*'s Top 200 album chart longer than any other release in history. Along with 1979's *The Wall,* it established the band as purveyors of a distinctively dark vision. Experimenting with concept albums and studio technology and breaking free of conventional pop-song formats, Pink

Floyd prefigured the progressive rock of the '70s and ambient music of the '80s.

As early as 1964, Pink Floyd's original members, except Syd Barrett, were together studying architecture at London's Regent Street Polytechnic School. With Barrett, an art student who coined the name the Pink Floyd Sound after a favorite blues record by Pink Anderson and Floyd Council, they began playing R&B-based material for schoolmates. By 1967 they had developed an unmistakably psychedelic sound; long, loud suitelike compositions that touched on hard rock, blues, country, folk, electronic, and quasi-classical music. Adding a slide-and-light show, one of the first in British rock, they became a sensation among London's underground as a featured attraction at the UFO Club. Barrett, who was responsible for most of the band's early material, had a knack for composing singles-length bits of psychedelia, and Pink Floyd had British hits with two of them in 1967: "Arnold Layne" (#20 U.K.), the tale of a transvestite, and "See Emily Play" (#60 U.K.). The latter, however, was the last hit single they would have for over a decade; space-epic titles like "Astronomy Domine" and "Interstellar Overdrive" were more typical.

In 1968 Barrett [see entry], allegedly because of an excess of LSD experimentation, began to exhibit ever more strange and erratic behavior. David Gilmour joined to help with the guitar work. Barrett appeared on only one track of *Secrets,* "Jugband Music," which aptly summed up his mental state: "I'm most obliged to you for making it clear / That I'm not really here." Without Barrett to create concise psychedelic singles, the band concentrated on wider-ranging psychedelic epics.

From 1969 to 1972 Pink Floyd made several film soundtracks—the most dramatic being *Zabriskie Point,* in which Michelangelo Antonioni's closing sequence of explosions was complemented by Floyd's "Careful With That Axe, Eugene"—and began using its "azimuth coordinated sound system" in concert, a sophisticated 360-degree P.A. With *Atom Heart Mother,* they topped the British chart in 1970; stateside success, however, still eluded them.

Their breakthrough came in 1973 with *The Dark Side of the Moon.* The themes were unremittingly bleak—alienation, paranoia, schizophrenia—and the music was at once sterile and doomy. Taped voices mumbling ominous asides (something the band had used before) surfaced at key moments. Yielding a surprise American hit in "Money," (#13, 1973), the album went on to mammoth long-running sales success. Ultimately remaining on the *Billboard* Top 200 album chart for 741 weeks, *Dark Side* showcased the talents of Pink Floyd's chief members: Waters' lyrics, Gilmour's guitar. The two would continue to dominate the band but soon furiously contend against each other.

Pink Floyd: Rick Wright, David Gilmour, Nick Mason, Roger Waters

The group's subsequent albums explored the same territory, with Waters' songs growing ever more bitter. *Wish You Were Here* (#1, 1975) was dedicated to Barrett and elegized him with "Shine On You Crazy Diamond." *The Wall,* Waters' finest moment, topped the U.S. chart for 15 weeks, while its nihilistic hit, "Another Brick in the Wall," was banned by the BBC and in 1980 became the band's only #1 American single. Meanwhile Pink Floyd's stage shows had become increasingly elaborate. For the *Dark Side* and *Wish* tours, there were slide/light shows and animated films, plus a giant inflated jet that crashed into the stage; for *Animals,* huge inflated pigs hovered over the stadiums; for *The Wall* (due to enormous expense, performed 29 times only in New York, L.A., and London) there was that, plus an actual wall built, brick by brick, across the stage, eventually obscuring the band from audience view. Shortly thereafter, Wright left, due to conflict with Waters.

With *The Final Cut* (#6, 1983), subtitled *A Requiem for the Postwar Dream,* Waters penned his darkest work yet. It also marked the effective end of the original Pink Floyd, with Waters bitterly departing, and Gilmour and Mason cementing their alliance. (Two films related to the original band—minus Barrett—have been made: the documentary *Pink Floyd Live at Pompeii* [1971] and *The Wall* [1982]. The latter featured stunning animation by Gerald Scarfe—Bob Geldof starred in the live-action sequences—and illustrated music from Pink Floyd's LP of the same name. The first remains a cult movie; the second was a massive commercial success.)

In 1978, with Gilmour's *David Gilmour* and Wright's *Wet Dream,* Pink Floyd's members had started releasing solo albums. Mason had begun a sideline career as a producer in 1974 with Robert Wyatt; ultimately his very diverse roster included Gong, Carla Bley, the Damned, and Steve Hillage. Solo work continued into the '80s: In 1984 came Waters' *The Pros and Cons of Hitch Hiking,* Wright's *Identity,* and Gilmour's *About Face* (with lyrical contributions by Pete Townshend). A year later Mason released *Profiles.* Concurrently, Gilmour played sessions with Bryan Ferry, Grace Jones, and Arcadia; in 1986 he formed David Gilmour & Friends with Bad Company's Mick Ralphs.

In 1986 Waters brought suit against Gilmour and Mason, asking the court to dissolve the trio's partnership and to block them from using the name Pink Floyd. A year later Waters lost his suit, and the other members, as Pink Floyd, released *Momentary Lapse of Reason* (#3, 1987). As Waters put out his own *Radio K.A.O.S.,* the others launched a Pink

Floyd tour that grossed nearly $30 million. (Though Wright was included on the tour and album, he wasn't legally considered an official band member but a salaried employee.) With the live *Delicate Sound of Thunder,* Gilmour, Mason, and Wright again billed themselves as Pink Floyd and went on to more successful touring, including a gig performed in Venice aboard a giant barge, which was televised worldwide.

In 1990 Waters presented an all-star cast, including Sinéad O'Connor, Joni Mitchell, and Van Morrison, in a version of *The Wall* performed at the site of the Berlin Wall (chronicled in *The Wall—Live in Berlin*). Two years later he released the dour *Amused to Death.*

With Wright rejoining Gilmour and Mason as a full band member, Pink Floyd garnered immediate success with *The Division Bell* in 1994. Named after the bell in the British House of Commons that summons members to parliamentary debate, the album featured songs written by Gilmour in collaboration with his ex-journalist girlfriend Polly Samson. Two weeks after its release, *The Division Bell* shot to #1 on the album chart, and in late spring the band embarked on an elaborate American tour. *P.U.L.S.E.* (#1, 1995) documented the '94 tour, including a live performance of *Dark Side of the Moon* in its entirety. In 1996 Pink Floyd was inducted into the Rock and Roll Hall of Fame. Still antagonistic with his former band mates, Waters didn't attend the ceremonies. After a successful solo tour in 1999, he embarked upon writing a modern opera about the French Revolution, recording with an 80-piece orchestra and 100-member choir.

In the interim, *Dark Side of the Moon* had taken on yet new life, when certain Pink Floyd fans began playing the album while watching *The Wizard of Oz* and noting how the 1973 album seemed to provide an uncannily appropriate soundtrack to the 1939 film. The band itself denied that it had intended any sort of parallel between its music and the movie, but rumors persisted of an eerie connection between the two. Pink Floyd also entered the new millennium by releasing a live version, from 1980, of *The Wall,* in double-CD format, with a lavishly illustrated history.

Gene Pitney

Born Feb. 17, 1941, Hartford, CT
1962—*The Many Sides of Gene Pitney* (Musicor); *Only Love Can Break a Heart* 1963—*World-Wide Winners* 1964—*Gene Pitney's Big Sixteen; It Hurts to Be in Love* 1965—*Famous Country Duets* (with George Jones); *George Jones and Gene Pitney* (with George Jones); *Looking Through the Eyes of Love* 1966—*Big Sixteen, vol. 3* 1968—*Double Gold: The Best of Gene Pitney* 1969—*Sings Bacharach* 1987—*The Gene Pitney Anthology, 1961–1968* (Rhino); *Anthology* 1988—*Gene Pitney; Gene Pitney, vol. 2* 1995—*Gene Pitney: The Great Recordings* (Tomato).

Gene Pitney's long and varied career includes over 20 chart-making singles and just as many albums, spanning rock, pop ballads, and Italian-flavored country novelties, as well as work and friendship with Phil Spector, the Rolling Stones, and country singer George Jones. Best known for singing pop covers, Pitney also wrote many tunes himself. His biggest hits include "Town Without Pity" (#13, 1962), "(The Man Who Shot) Liberty Valance" (#4, 1962), "Only Love Can Break a Heart" (#2, 1962), "Half Heaven–Half Heartache" (#12, 1963), "Mecca" (#12, 1963), "It Hurts to Be in Love" (#7, 1964), and "I'm Gonna Be Strong" (#9, 1964).

Pitney studied piano, guitar, and drums while at Rockville High School in Connecticut, and by the time he graduated he'd already written and published some songs. He dropped out of the University of Connecticut and for a time enrolled in Ward's Electronic School. He began performing as the male half of the duo Jamie and Jane, then as a singer/songwriter under the name Billy Brian. By 1961 he had written "Hello Mary Lou" for Rick Nelson. In 1962 he wrote "He's a Rebel" for the Crystals and became friends with producer Phil Spector. He also wrote for Roy Orbison and Tommy Edwards.

Yearning for a hit of his own, Pitney locked himself in a studio in 1961, played and overdubbed every instrument, and multitracked his vocals. The result was his first hit, "(I Wanna) Love My Life Away" (#39, 1961). This attracted the attention of the songwriting team of Burt Bacharach and Hal David, who cowrote "Only Love Can Break a Heart," "(The Man Who Shot) Liberty Valance," and "24 Hours From Tulsa" for him. Pitney's label, Musicor, was primarily involved in country & western music, and Pitney began recording material in that vein, including an album of duets with George Jones.

In 1964 Pitney's publicist, Andrew Loog Oldham, introduced him to the Rolling Stones, whom Oldham produced. He recorded the Jagger-Richards composition "That Girl Belongs to Yesterday" and with Phil Spector sat in on one of their 1964 recording sessions.

Though he was much more popular in England than in America, Pitney remained a prolific recording artist, putting out numerous albums per year in the mid-'60s. At that time, in response to his tremendous popularity in Italy, he began recording albums of country tunes sung in Italian. His last U.S. chart appearance was in 1969, and he continued to hit the U.K. chart until 1974.

Since the mid-'70s, Pitney has toured the U.S. infrequently but continued to work elsewhere in the world. He has recorded in Italian, Spanish, and German. In 1988 a remake of "Something's Gotten Hold of My Heart," recorded with Marc Almond, went to #1 in the U.K. Five years later, Pitney finally returned to the U.S. concert stage for the first time in nearly two decades with a sold-out appearance at Carnegie Hall. Pitney divides his time between touring (largely overseas) and managing his sizable business empire, which includes the Crystal Lake Beach and Boat Club in Connecticut, where he slung hamburgers as a teen.

Pixies/The Breeders/Frank Black

Formed 1986, Boston, MA
Black Francis (b. Charles Michael Kitteridge Thompson IV, Apr. 1965, Long Beach, CA), gtr., voc.; Joey Santiago (b. June 10,

1965, Manila, Philippines), gtr.; Kim Deal (b. June 10, 1961, Dayton, OH), bass, voc.; David Lovering (b. Dec. 6, 1961, Boston), drums.
1987—*Come On Pilgrim* EP (4AD) 1988—*Surfer Rosa* 1989—*Doolittle* (4AD/Elektra) 1990—*Bossanova* 1991—*Trompe le Monde* 1997—*Death to the Pixies: 1987–1991* 1998—*Pixies at the BBC.*
Kim Deal with the Breeders, formed 1990: Deal; Tanya Donelly (b. July 14, 1967, Newport, RI) (see Throwing Muses entry), gtr., voc.; Josephine Wiggs (b. Brighton, Eng.), bass, cello, voc.; Shannon Doughton (a.k.a. Mike Hunt, b. Britt Walford, Louisville, KY), drums
1990—*Pod* (4AD/Elektra) 1992—(+ Kelley Deal [b. June 10, 1961, Dayton], gtr., voc.) *Safari* EP 1993—(– Donelly; – Walford; + James Macpherson [b. June 23, 1966, OH], drums) *Last Splash.*
Kim Deal with the Amps: 1995—*Pacer* (Elektra).
Black Francis, as Frank Black, solo: 1993—*Frank Black* (4AD/Elektra) 1994—*Teenager of the Year* 1996—*The Cult of Ray* (American).
As Frank Black and the Catholics: 1998—*Frank Black and the Catholics* (SpinArt) 1999—*Pistolero* 2001—*Dog in the Sand* (What Are Records?).

With seductive pop melodies, distorted surf riffs, extraterrestrial lyrics, a mysterious Latin flavor, and leader Black Francis' deranged shrieks, the Pixies came off like Beach Boys on acid. Quintessential college rockers, the Pixies fared particularly well in England, where they attracted an impressive following and scored minor aboveground hits with singles such as "Monkey Gone to Heaven" and "Velouria"; in the U.S. they remained primarily critics' darlings and a major influence on such bands as Nirvana. When the quartet split up in 1992, bassist Kim Deal went on to greater popular success with the Breeders.

Charles Michael Kitteridge Thompson IV got his first taste of pop music–making as an adolescent living in the L.A. suburbs and messing around with instruments in the garage. However, when his Pentecostal mother and stepfather moved the family to New England, rock & roll slipped to the back burner. It wasn't until the mid-'80s—six months into his stint as a U. Mass exchange student in Puerto Rico—that the astronomy-obsessed Thompson gave himself a choice: He would either go to New Zealand to see Halley's comet or form a band.

In 1986 Thompson returned to Boston and recruited former college roommate Joey Santiago, who came from one of the wealthiest families in the Philippines, to play guitar. Naming themselves Pixies in Panoply, they took out a newspaper ad for a bassist interested in Hüsker Dü and Peter, Paul and Mary. Ohio native Kim Deal—a onetime biochemist (analyzing blood, no less)—responded and brought along her drummer friend David Lovering. On the advice of his biological father, a biker and bar owner, Thompson adopted the stage name Black Francis.

The Pixies released their debut EP on England's arty 4AD label in 1987 and followed the next year with the full-length *Surfer Rosa.* After much domestic college-radio play and critical raves, the band signed with Elektra in 1989 and released the landmark *Doolittle* (#98; #8 U.K.). But there was turmoil within the band, caused by Deal's increasing unhappiness with Thompson's creative dominance. The followup albums *Bossanova* and *Trompe le Monde* included no songs written by Deal. During a break in 1990, Deal formed the Breeders along with Throwing Muses guitarist Tanya Donelly and released the critically acclaimed *Pod* back-to-back with the Pixies' *Bossanova.*

For his first solo album under new pseudonym Frank Black, Thompson recruited Santiago, members of Pere Ubu, and various session players. The album found the eccentric songwriter moving closer than ever toward Brian Wilson territory, even doing an edgy, if respectful cover of Wilson's *Pet Sounds* classic, "Hang Onto Your Ego." While promoting the album, Thompson casually indicated to interviewers that the Pixies were over—before informing the rest of the band. For his third album, 1996's *The Cult of Ray* (#127), Thompson signed to producer Rick Rubin's American Recordings. The album sold fewer than his previous solo records, and when American began reorganizing, Thompson and a followup album already recorded were left in limbo. He finally left American and returned in 1998 with *Frank Black and the Catholics,* released on the small indie label SpinArt. Thompson continued to record and tour, seemingly at peace with his diminishing profile and life as a cult figure.

In 1995 Santiago and Lovering formed the short-lived Martinis. And the Breeders' second full-length album, *Last Splash* (#33, 1994)—recorded without Donelly, who left to form Belly—was a critical smash, spawning the single "Cannonball" (#44, 1994). A music video of the song directed by Spike Jonze and Sonic Youth's Kim Gordon became an MTV staple. Deal was joined in the newest lineup of the group by twin sister, Kelley, who was in an early teenage acoustic folk version of the Breeders. But the band's momentum was stalled when Kelley was busted for heroin and sent to rehab. After her release, she recorded a 1996 solo album as the Kelley Deal 6000 called *Go to the Sugar Altar.*

Meanwhile, Kim Deal had begun working on what was originally to be a solo album. Instead, she released the 33-minute *Pacer* in 1995 as part of a band called the Amps. Drummer Jim Macpherson was the only other holdover from the Breeders, as Deal recruited two players from Dayton, Ohio, into the Amps. Two years later, the same musicians toured as the Breeders.

Robert Plant

Born Aug. 20, 1948, Bromwich, Eng.
1982—*Pictures at 11* (Swan Song) 1983—*The Principle of Moments* (Es Paranza) 1985—*Shaken 'n' Stirred* 1988—*Now and Zen* 1990—*Manic Nirvana* 1993—*Fate of Nations.*
With the Honeydrippers: 1984—*Volume One* (Es Paranza).
With Jimmy Page: 1994—*No Quarter: Jimmy Page and Robert Plant Unledded* (Atlantic) 1998—*Walking Into Clarksdale.*

Since Led Zeppelin's breakup in December 1980 (following the September 1980 death of drummer John Bonham), singer Robert Plant consistently refused to rest on past laurels. Instead, he has produced a series of progressive albums that have been critical and commercial successes. In the '80s and '90s, he has been musically more interested in hip-hop, punk, and world musics than the heavy metal or classic rock of Zeppelin imitators. In 1994, however, after repeatedly blocking any long-term Led Zeppelin reunions, Plant joined Page to perform Led Zep songs, along with new compositions, for an MTV *Unplugged* performance, entitled *Unledded,* and album, *No Quarter.*

Plant's first returns to music after Zeppelin drummer John Bonham's death were jam sessions with a group of local R&B musicians called the Honeydrippers. He produced and wrote *Pictures at 11* (#5, 1982) with Robbie Blunt on guitar, Paul Martinez on bass, and Jezz Woodruffe on keyboards. *The Principle of Moments* (#8, 1983) was the first release by Plant's Atlantic-distributed label, Es Paranza. Its music ranged from the artsy "Big Log" (#20, 1983) to the more traditional "In the Mood" (#39, 1983). In 1983 Plant went on his first solo tour.

In 1985 Plant undertook a couple of side projects: the Crawling King Snakes with Phil Collins, who recorded a cut for the *Porky's Revenge* soundtrack; and a Honeydrippers EP. The latter, which reunited Plant with Zeppelin guitarist Jimmy Page (and included Jeff Beck and Nile Rodgers), went Top 5 and produced hits with the string-drenched ballad "Sea of Love" (#3, 1984) and "Rockin' at Midnight" (#25, 1985). He and Page also played live with John Paul Jones at 1985's Live Aid benefit concert. On *Shaken 'n' Stirred* (#20, 1985) Plant experimented with hip-hop motifs, synthesizers, and intricate rhythms supplied by Little Feat drummer Richie Hayward. The album was strikingly noncommercial, though it did yield the minor hit "Little by Little" (#36, 1985). Plant broke up his band after a subsequent tour. Listening to a pile of demo tapes, he discovered keyboardist Phil Johnstone, with whom he has collaborated since. Johnstone and Plant cowrote seven of the nine songs on the platinum *Now and Zen* (#6, 1988), which featured guitarist Doug Boyle, bassist Charlie Jones, and drummer Chris Blackwell. The album was widely acclaimed for its mix of old and new: "Tall Cool One" (#25, 1988) featured a solo from Page and samples of old Zeppelin songs. The track was partially a response to the Beastie Boys' heavy reliance on a sample of Led Zeppelin's "The Ocean" for their song "She's Crafty." "Tall Cool One" was later used in a Coke commercial.

Plant contributed the song "The Only One" to Page's 1988 *Outrider* album. In 1989 he recorded "Smoke on the Water" with Ian Gillan, Brian May, and Bruce Dickinson to benefit victims of a massive earthquake in Armenia. Plant worked with the same crew from *Zen* on *Manic Nirvana* (#13, 1990), which, though well received critically, went only gold. On *Fate of Nations* he "went back to the misty mountains," as he put it, playing folksy songs influenced by his rediscovery of '60s West Coast groups like Moby Grape. Plant continued to work with Johnstone and Jones and added guitarists Kevin Scott MacMichael (Cutting Crew) and Francis Dunnery (It Bites). The album featured appearances by classical violinist Nigel Kennedy, Clannad singer Maire Brennan, and guitarist Richard Thompson. The first single was a cover of Tim Hardin's folk-rock classic "If I Were a Carpenter."

No Quarter illustrated Plant's interest in Arabic music, with two (of three) new songs recorded in Marrakech, Morocco, backed by Gnaoui musicians. Other world musicians guested on the album, including Indian ghazal singer Najma Akhtar on a new version of "The Battle of Evermore." In 1995 Plant joined Page in a tour to support the album. In 1997 Plant's Es Paranza imprint released a tribute album to the late Rainer Ptacek, a Czechoslovakian musician who contributed to *Fate of Nations.* The following year Plant teamed up with the Flaming Lips for a track on another tribute record, this one to former Moby Grape guitarist Alexander "Skip" Spence [see Moby Grape entry]. In 1998 Page and Plant released *Walking Into Clarksdale,* the first album of new material they had recorded together in two decades. "Most High," a single, recalled Zep's hypnotic "Kashmir," but the album (its title an allusion to the cradle of the Delta blues) was more wistful than bombastic.

The Plasmatics

Formed 1978, New York, NY
Wendy Orleans Williams (b. 1951, Rochester, NY; d. Apr. 6, 1998, Storrs, CT), voc., chainsaw, machine gun; Richard Stotts, gtr.; Chosei Funahara, bass; Wes Beech, gtr.; Stu Deutsch, drums.
1980—(– Funahara; + Jean Beauvoir, bass) 1981—*New Hope for the Wretched* (Stiff); *Beyond the Valley of 1984* (– Deutsch; – Beauvoir); *Metal Priestess* EP 1982—*Coup d'Etat* (Capitol).
Wendy O. Williams solo: 1984—*W.O.W.* (Passport) 1986—*Kommander of Kaos* (Gigausus) 1987—*Maggots: The Record* (Profile).
Ultrafly and the Hometown Girls: 1988—*Deffest! And Baddest!* (Deffest Disc/Profile).
Jean Beauvoir solo: 1986—*Drums Along the Mohawk* (Columbia) 1988—*Jacknifed.*

The original Plasmatics were a sex-and-violence-touting heavy-metal band that debuted in the New York punk clubs in 1978. They were fronted by barely dressed ex–topless dancer Wendy O. Williams (W.O.W. for short), whose early act included smashing televisions with a sledgehammer, blowing up Cadillac Coup de Villes, cutting guitars in half with a chain saw, and singing.

Essentially, the band was the brainchild of manager Rod Swenson, a Yale graduate with a master's degree in fine arts. During the '70s he came to New York, dubbed himself Captain Kink, and began producing and promoting live sex shows. One of his stars was Williams (who was raised on a farm in upstate New York and ran away at 16). After his work in porn, Swenson did videos for Patti Smith and the Ramones, which inspired him to start a band, with Williams fingering herself and demolishing things up front, backed by a guitarist (Richard Stotts) with a blue Mohawk cut who wore a nurse's uniform and sometimes a tutu, plus other visual gimmicks. The band's music was all fast and loud, and the lyrics were about murder, sex, and fast food.

The Plasmatics debuted at CBGB on July 26, 1978, and immediately got lots of coverage for their antics. An audience began to grow, especially in England, where they stressed their connection to heavy metal. Williams kept up her stunts, as on September 12, 1980, when she jumped out of a brakeless car just before it plunged into the Hudson River. The band's debut album sold marginally, as did their followup, *Beyond the Valley of 1984.* On January 18, 1981, Williams was arrested on obscenity charges in Milwaukee and on similar charges in Cleveland the next day. She and Swenson were also charged with resisting arrest and disorderly conduct after an altercation with the police, which landed both in a Milwaukee hospital. They later sued and lost their case. In 1982 the band signed with Capitol. Beauvoir joined Little Steven and the Disciples of Soul in 1982. Neither of his solo albums did well commercially.

Williams continued to tour and record, at times with a Plasmatics lineup. She briefly led Ultrafly and the Hometown Girls, an ill-advised attempt at rap. A fitness buff, health-food enthusiast, vegetarian, and animal-rights activist, she also pursued an acting career in film (*Reform School Girls,* 1986) and on television (*McGyver,* 1990). In 1991 she and Swenson moved to Storrs, Connecticut. Seven years later, Williams committed suicide by shooting herself in the head. Swenson said that his companion had been depressed for some time. She reportedly felt "past her peak" and found it "difficult to lead a normal life." Stotts went on to form the Richie Stotts Experience.

The Platters

Formed 1953, Los Angeles, CA
Tony Williams (b. Apr. 15, 1928, Roselle, NJ; d. Aug. 14, 1992), lead voc.; David Lynch (b. 1929, St. Louis, MO; d. Jan. 2, 1981), tenor voc.; Herbert Reed (b. 1931, Kansas City, MO), bass voc.; Alex Hodge, baritone voc.
1954—(+ Zola Taylor [b. 1934], contralto voc.) 1955—(– Hodge; + Paul Robi [b. 1931, New Orleans, LA; d. Feb. 1, 1989], voc.) 1960—*Encore of Golden Hits* (Mercury) 1961—(– Williams; + Sonny Turner [b. ca. 1939, Cleveland, OH], voc.) 1962—(– Robi; – Taylor; + Nate Nelson [b. Apr. 10, 1932, New York, NY; d. June 1, 1984], voc.); + Sandra Dawn [b. New York], voc.) 1965—(original lineup disbands) 1986—*Anthology (1955–1967)* (Rhino) 1991—*The Very Best of the Platters* (Mercury); *The Magic Touch: An Anthology.*

During the Platters' peak years (1955 to 1960), they were led by Tony Williams and enjoyed a series of massive crossover hits that made them the preeminent black vocal group of the time.

Original members Williams, David Lynch, Alex Hodge, and Herb Reed were signed by manager Buck Ram to Federal Records in 1953. After some of the group's unsuccessful efforts, Ram replaced Hodge with Paul Robi and added Zola Taylor, who belonged to Shirley Gunter and the Queens (a group fronted by the sister of Cornel Gunter, of the Flairs and the Coasters). The Platters' seventh Federal single, "Only You," was their first regional hit. Along with another vocal group Ram managed, the Penguins, they were signed in a package deal to Mercury.

At Mercury they became one of the nation's top vocal groups and a major nightclub attraction. A new version of "Only You" (#5) along with "The Great Pretender," which hit #1 in February 1956, made 1955 a breakthrough year. In 1956 they appeared in two rock films, *The Girl Can't Help It* and *Rock Around the Clock.*

Other major hits for the Platters were "The Magic Touch" (#4 pop and R&B), "My Prayer" (#1 pop, #2 R&B), "You'll Never Know" (#11 pop, #9 R&B) in 1956; "I'm Sorry" (#23 pop, #15 R&B) in 1957; "Twilight Time" (#1 pop and R&B) and "Smoke Gets in Your Eyes" (#1 pop, #3 R&B) in 1958; and "Enchanted" (#12 pop, #9 R&B) in 1959. The Platters were very popular in England and in Australia, where virtually all of these singles were hits as well, and "Smoke" went to #1.

In the summer of 1959, the group suffered a setback in popularity after the four male members were arrested in Cincinnati and accused of having had sexual relations with four female minors, among them, three white girls. Although the men were acquitted, public reaction to the incident led some radio stations to pull their latest single, "Where," off the air.

The Platters' last Top 10 single was 1960's "Harbor Lights," although they had several more Top 40 singles, including "If I Didn't Care" in 1961. Williams went solo and was replaced as lead singer by Sonny Turner in 1961, but Mercury continued to release old Williams-led singles through 1964. Off the charts from 1961 to 1966, the Platters changed lineup in 1962, with Sandra Dawn replacing Taylor and Nate Nelson taking Robi's spot. At the Musicor label they had a limited comeback with "I Love You 1000 Times" (#31 pop, #6 R&B, 1966) and "With This Ring" (#14 pop, #12 R&B, 1967).

There followed wholesale personnel changes and releases on United Artists before a return to Mercury in 1974. Williams and Ram battled in court during the '70s over the rights to the Platters' name; Ram won the case. There have been numerous groups of Platters performing through the years with little or no relation to the original combo. As of 2000, Herb Reed, the sole active member of the first lineup, was leading the only official version of the group, whose name and trademark he had been granted. Zola Taylor made news in the late '80s, when she was one of three women claiming to have been Frankie Lymon's widow. The Platters were inducted into the Rock and Roll Hall of Fame in 1990.

Plimsouls: See Peter Case

P.M. Dawn

Formed 1989, Jersey City, NJ
Prince Be "the Nocturnal" (b. Attrell Cordes, May 19, 1970,

Jersey City), voc.; DJ Minutemix a.k.a. "J.C. the Eternal" (b. Jarrett Cordes, July 17, 1971, Jersey City), DJ.
1991—*Of the Heart, of the Soul and of the Cross: The Utopian Experience* (Gee Street/Island) 1993—*The Bliss Album . . . ? (Vibrations of Love & Anger & the Ponderance of Life & Existence)* 1995—*Jesus Wept (Vibrations of Love & Anger & the Ponderance of Life & Existence)* 1998—*Dearest Christian, I'm So Very Sorry for Bringing You Here, Love, Dad* 2000—*The Best of P.M. Dawn.*

P.M. Dawn was the most pop-oriented, psychedelic, and (with Arrested Development) popular of the wave of early '90s "alternative rap" groups. An unlikely synthesis of Brian Wilson and De La Soul—of lushly harmonized, vocal-dominated pop melodicism and exotically eclectic, flower-powered hip-hop—P.M. Dawn's critically acclaimed debut album *Of the Heart, of the Soul and of the Cross* found rotund, introspective vocalist and songwriter Prince Be singing (both leads and layered harmonies) as often as rapping, with equal aplomb.

Attrell and Jarrett Cordes' stepfather, a percussionist with Kool and the Gang, set Attrell's mystical course early by giving him a Donovan album. The brothers' tastes broadened through discarded 45s their garbageman uncle brought them. After graduating from high school, they became Prince Be and DJ Minutemix of P.M. Dawn (inspired by the scripture "in the darkest hour comes the light"). Tiny Warlock Records released their first single, "Ode to a Forgetful Mind," which found some success in England, where Gee Street Records signed the group.

P.M. Dawn went to London to record *Of the Heart . . .* (#48, 1991), on which Prince Be sang "Reality Used to Be a Friend of Mine" and rapped about reincarnation in "Even After I Die"; there were also a Delta blues slide-guitar break, a quote from the Beatles' "Baby You're a Rich Man," and samples of Dr. John, Chick Corea, Hugh Masekela, and the Doobie Brothers (P.M. Dawn once described themselves not as rappers or pop-rappers, but as "sampling artists"). The album yielded pop hits in "Set Adrift on Memory Bliss" (#1, 1991), built on a sample of Spandau Ballet's "True," and "Paper Doll" (#28, 1992).

In January 1992 hard-core rapper KRS-ONE, a founder of the Stop the Violence movement, jumped onstage to attack (but not seriously harm) P.M. Dawn at a New York City show. It was retaliation for Prince Be's late-1991 comment to a magazine that "KRS-ONE says he wants to be a teacher, but a teacher of what?" Nine months later P.M. Dawn hit with "I'd Die Without You" (#3, 1992), a romantic ballad from the soundtrack of the Eddie Murphy movie *Boomerang. The Bliss Album . . . ?* (#30, 1993), which included Boy George's guest vocals on "More Than Likely" and a cover of the Beatles' "Norwegian Wood," produced the hit single "Looking Through Patient Eyes" (#6, 1993). Prince Be did production and remix work for fashion model Naomi Campbell's short-lived attempt at a recording career. P.M. Dawn's music grew ever gentler and more lushly pop, but sales steadily decreased. *Jesus Wept* (#119), which Prince Be called a "gospel record," failed to make the R&B charts, as did its singles "Downtown Venus" (#48), based on a sample of Deep Purple's "Hush," and "Sometimes I Miss You So Much" (#95); *Dearest Christian* (the title addressed to Prince Be's son) failed to chart altogether, though "I Had No Right" was a minor hit (#44 pop, #82 R&B).

Poco

Formed 1968, Los Angeles, CA
Richie Furay (b. May 9, 1944, Yellow Springs, OH), gtr., voc.; Jim Messina (b. Oct. 30, 1947, Harlingen, TX), gtr., voc., bass; Rusty Young (b. Feb. 23, 1946, Denver, CO), pedal steel gtr., Dobro, voc.; George Grantham (b. Jan. 20, 1947, Cordell, OK), drums, voc.; Randy Meisner (b. Mar. 8, 1946, Scottsbluff, NE), bass, voc.
1969—*Pickin' Up the Pieces* (Epic) (– Meisner) 1970—(+ Timothy B. Schmit [b. Timothy Bruce Schmit, Oct. 30, 1947, Sacramento, CA], bass, voc., gtr.) *Poco* 1971—(– Messina; + Paul Cotton [b. Feb. 26, 1945, AL], gtr., voc.) *Deliverin'; From the Inside* 1972—*A Good Feeling to Know* 1973—*Crazy Eyes* (– Furay) 1974—*Seven; Cantamos* 1975—(+ Al Garth, banjo, fiddle, sax) *Head Over Heels* (ABC); *The Very Best of Poco* (Epic) 1976—*Live; Rose of Cimarron* (ABC) (– Garth) 1977—*Indian Summer* (– Schmit; – Grantham; + Steve Chapman [b. Nov. 14, 1949, London, Eng.], drums; + Charlie Harrison [b. Apr. 8, 1953, Tamworth, Eng.], bass) 1978—*Legend* 1980—(+ Kim Bullard [b. May 6, 1955, Atlanta, GA], kybds.) *Under the Gun* (MCA) 1981—*Blue and Gray* 1982—*Cowboys and Englishmen; Ghost Town* (Atlantic) (– Harrison) 1984—*Inamorata* (– Bullard; + Grantham; + Jack Sundrud [b. Sep. 7, 1949, Crookston, MN], bass, voc.]) 1989—(original quintet re-forms) *Legacy* (RCA); *Crazy Loving: The Best of Poco 1975–1982* (MCA) 1990—*Poco: The Forgotten Trail* (Epic/Legacy) (– Furay; + Sundrud) 1992—(– Meisner; – Messina; – Grantham; – Sundrud; + Cotton; + Richard Neville [b. Dec. 1, 1952, Oklahoma, TX], bass, voc.; + Tim Smith, drums, voc.) 2000—(– Neville; – Smith; + Grantham; + Sundrud).

Country-rock band Poco started out in August 1968 with great commercial promise. Founders Richie Furay and Jim Messina were from Buffalo Springfield [see entry], and the L.A. country-rock scene was just beginning to peak. But despite steady sales, Poco never quite reached a mass audience. Rusty Young met Furay and Messina when he played pedal steel guitar on sessions for Buffalo Springfield's "Kind Woman." Young was asked to join another L.A. country-rock band, the Flying Burrito Brothers, but he chose to be in Poco. George Grantham had been a bandmate of Young's in Boenzee Cryque, a Colorado band that went to L.A., where it broke up. And Randy Meisner came from a rival Colorado band, the Poor. Furay also auditioned Gregg Allman (then with the Allman Joys) for the band, but it didn't work out.

The new group originally called itself Pogo, but Walt Kelly, the creator of the comic strip, sued, and the members changed the name to Poco. Within a month, Meisner quit (he soon joined Rick Nelson's Stone Canyon Band, then Linda Ronstadt, and then the Eagles in 1971). Several record companies considered signing Poco following its live L.A. debut in November 1968 at the Troubadour. Furay's Springfield contract with Atlantic complicated matters, but Poco was allowed to sign with Epic after the label traded Graham Nash to Atlantic (to form Crosby, Stills and Nash) in exchange for Poco.

Pickin' Up the Pieces sold over 100,000 copies. Following Meisner's departure, the band continued as a quartet until February 1970, when Tim B. Schmit (a veteran of local folk, surf, and pop groups) joined. Schmit had originally auditioned for Poco in 1968 but lost out to Meisner. This new five-member Poco recorded *Poco* and the live *Deliverin'* before Messina quit, claiming he was tired of touring. The guitarist/producer soon teamed up with Kenny Loggins [see entry].

Messina's replacement was Paul Cotton, former lead guitarist in a Buffalo Springfield–type band, the Illinois Speed Press. This lineup lasted for three LPs. In 1973, just after recording *Crazy Eyes,* Furay, frustrated with the band's poor financial prospects, left to form a quasi-supergroup, the Souther-Hillman-Furay Band, which disbanded after two LPs. He then pursued a commercially unrewarding solo career before turning his full attention to religion.

Furay's departure was expected to be fatal, but Poco's next four albums as a quartet through 1977 sold somewhat better than previous efforts. During these years, the Eagles [see entry] dominated the field that Poco was expected to mine; and in 1977, after Meisner left the Eagles, Schmit replaced him. Drummer Grantham also quit, in January 1978.

With lone original member Young plus Cotton at the helm, the band finally hit in early 1979 with its 14th LP, *Legend* (#14). Poco now included an English rhythm section, Steve Chapman and Charlie Harrison (who'd played together for eight years with Leo Sayer and Al Stewart), plus keyboardist Kim Bullard, who'd backed Crosby, Stills and Nash. The new lineup hit #17 with "Crazy Love" and then had a Top 20 hit later that year with "Heart of the Night."

Poco's commercial success was brief, however, with subsequent albums returning to the band's previous level of sales. In 1989 the original group re-formed for an album, *Legacy,* which produced two Top 40 hits: "Call It Love" (#18) and "Nothin' to Hide" (#39), the latter cowritten and produced by Poco admirer Richard Marx. The group toured in 1990, but tensions soon arose between Furay, by then a minister in Boulder, Colorado, and the others. He soon left Poco, which has since continued to tour, revolving around Young and Cotton. Original drummer Grantham and mid-'80s era bassist Jack Sundrud returned in 2000. Many of Poco's members past and present have released solo albums and worked as session players.

The Pogues

Formed 1982, London, Eng.
James Fearnley (b. Oct. 9, 1954, Worsley, Eng.) accordion; Jeremy "Jem" Max Finer (b. July 25, 1955, Stoke-on-Trent, Eng.), banjo, gtr.; Shane MacGowan (b. Shane Patrick Lysaght MacGowan, Dec. 25, 1957, Kent, Ire.), voc.; Cait O'Riordan (b. Jan. 4, 1965, Nigeria), bass; Peter "Spider" Stacy (b. Dec. 14, 1958, London), whistle, voc.; Andrew Rankin (b. Nov. 13, 1953, London), drums.
1984—*Red Roses for Me* (Stiff) 1985—(+ Philip Chevron [b. Jun. 17, 1957, Dublin, Ire.], gtr.) *Rum, Sodomy & the Lash* 1986—(– O'Riordan; + Darryl Hunt [b. May 4, 1950, Nottingham, Eng.], bass; + Terry Woods [b. Dec. 4, 1947, Dublin], banjo) *Poguetry in Motion* EP 1988—*If I Should Fall From Grace With God* (Island) 1989—*Peace and Love* 1990—*Hell's Ditch* 1991—*Essential Pogues* (– MacGowan; + Joe Strummer [b. John Mellor, Aug. 21, 1952, Ankara, Turkey], voc.) 1992—(– Strummer) 1993—*Waiting for Herb* (Chameleon) 1994—(– Woods; – Fearnley; + James McNally, accordion, whistle, piano) 1995—*Pogue Mahone* (WEA).
Shane MacGowan and the Popes: 1995—*The Snake* (ZTT Warner Bros.) 1997—*Crock of Gold* (ZTT, U.K.).

The musical equivalent of a pub crawl, the Pogues have staggered through a career that combines the instrumentation and tunes of traditional Irish music with the energy and attitude of punk. The band was formed in 1982 when Shane MacGowan, then a member of a north London punk band called the Nipple Erectors—later shortened to the Nips—saw Spider Stacy playing tin whistle in a London tube station. They hit it off and, along with Nip Jim Fearnley on guitar, began to perform traditional Irish tunes in London's streets and pubs. Calling themselves Pogue Mahone (Gaelic for "kiss my ass"), they recruited Finer, Ranken, and O'Riordan and added MacGowan's earthy, Joycean original songs to their repertoire. The sextet garnered a reputation as a drunkenly raucous live act, and in 1984 released a single, "Dark Streets of London," on their own, eponymous label. Their reputation increased when they were hired as the opening act on the Clash's 1984 tour. (Some of the Clash's political fury rubbed off, as the Pogues became vehemently anti-Thatcher.) They signed with Stiff Records that year, and released *Red Roses for Me.*

Rum, Sodomy & the Lash was produced by Elvis Costello, who married O'Riordan after she left the band. By then, the band had expanded to an octet. The Pogues did not record again until 1988. In the interim they appeared in Alex Cox's film *Straight to Hell* (1987) and moved to Island Records. Their initial release for the label, the Steve Lillywhite–produced *If I Should Fall From Grace With God* (#88, 1988), included the #2 U.K. hit, "Fairytale of New York," featuring singer/songwriter Kirsty MacColl (the daughter of songwriter/playwright Ewan MacColl and then the wife of Lillywhite). The three Lillywhite-produced albums expanded the group's musical palette, adding Middle Eastern sounds on "Turkish Song of the Damned" from *God* and jazz stylings on *Peace and Love* (1989).

Finer and Stacy began to take on additional singing and writing chores as MacGowan's drinking (he claimed not to have spent a day completely sober since he was 14) began to interfere with his musical duties. He missed a series of 1988 U.S. dates opening for Bob Dylan, and by 1991 he had become so unreliable he was asked to leave the band. He was replaced by former Clash singer Joe Strummer (who had produced 1990's *Hell's Ditch*). Strummer left in 1992, and Spider Stacy took over the vocals on 1993's *Waiting for Herb*. In 1994 MacGowan resurfaced, performing with a new band, the Popes, for the first time on St. Patrick's Day at a London club. That year the group recorded its first album, *The Snake*, filled with dark new songs by MacGowan. MacGowan toured to support its U.S. release in 1995, the same year the Pogues released its final album, *Pogue Mahone*, before disbanding in 1996.

Buster Poindexter: See David Johansen

The Pointer Sisters

Formed 1971, Oakland, CA
Ruth Pointer (b. Mar. 19, 1946, Oakland), voc.; Anita Pointer (b. Jan. 23, 1948, Oakland), voc.; Bonnie Pointer (b. July 11, 1950, East Oakland, CA), voc.; June Pointer (b. Nov. 30, 1954, Oakland), voc.
1973—*The Pointer Sisters* (Blue Thumb) 1974—*That's a Plenty; Live at the Opera House* 1975—*Steppin'* 1978—(– Bonnie) *Energy* (Planet) 1980—*Special Things* 1981—*Black & White* 1982—*So Excited!* 1983—*Break Out* 1985—*Contact* (RCA) 1986—*Hot Together* 1988—*Serious Slammin'* 1989—*Greatest Hits* 1990—*Right Rhythm* (Motown) 1994—*Only Sisters Can Do That* (SBK) 1996—*Fire: The Very Best of the Pointer Sisters* (RCA) 1997—*Yes We Can: The Best of Blue Thumb Recordings* (Hip-O).
Bonnie Pointer solo: 1978—*Bonnie Pointer* (Motown) 1979—*Bonnie Pointer II* 1984—*The Price Is Right* (Private).
Anita Pointer solo: 1987—*Love for What It Is* (RCA).

The Oakland-born Pointer sisters are a vocal group whose repertoire spans pop, jazz, country, and R&B, and has evoked comparisons to the Supremes and the Andrews Sisters. Their biggest hits—which didn't come until the '80s—are soulful, high-powered pop. Both of the Pointer parents were ministers at the West Oakland Church of God. Singing in church was the sisters' only performing experience until Bonnie and June began singing in San Francisco clubs in 1969 as Pointers, a Pair. Anita joined them, and eventually San Francisco producer David Rubinson hired them as background vocalists on several records. In 1971 Bill Graham became their manager. From 1971 to 1973 the trio sang behind Elvin Bishop, Taj Mahal, Tower of Power, Dave Mason, Sylvester, Boz Scaggs, and Esther Phillips.

When the Pointers backed Elvin Bishop at L.A.'s Whisky-a-Go-Go, Atlantic executive Jerry Wexler signed them. Two singles were cut with R&B veteran Wardell Quezergue; one, "Don't Try to Take the Fifth," was unsuccessfully released in 1972. That year, Ruth left her job as a keypunch operator to join her sisters. Rubinson helped the Pointers get out of contracts with Graham and Atlantic and signed them to ABC's Blue Thumb label.

In 1973 their self-titled debut, featuring Allen Toussaint's "Yes We Can Can" (#11 pop, #12 R&B) and Willie Dixon's "Wang Dang Doodle" (#61 pop, #24 R&B), brought national recognition. The sisters' neo-nostalgic penchant for '40s clothes, plus their wide repertoire, landed them on a number of national television variety shows. On tour they became the first black women to play Nashville's Grand Ole Opry and the first pop act to perform at San Francisco's Opera House. In 1974 PBS filmed a documentary on the Pointer family.

That year "Fairytale," written by Anita and Bonnie Pointer, went to #13 on the pop chart (#37 C&W) and won a Grammy as Best Country Single of 1974. The sisters' first two LPs went gold. The next year brought a #1 R&B hit, "How Long (Betcha' Got a Chick on the Side)" (#20 pop). But between 1975 and 1977, June suffered a nervous breakdown, the group filed a lawsuit against ABC/Blue Thumb for back royalties, Bonnie wanted to go solo, and the Pointer Sisters were still being identified (and categorized) as a nostalgia group.

In 1978 Bonnie signed a solo contract with Motown. She had top charting records there in 1978—"Free Me From My Freedom/Tie Me to a Tree (Handcuff Me)" (#58 pop, #10 R&B)—and in 1979, with "Heaven Must Have Sent You" (#11 pop, #52 R&B). She did not have another release until 1984, in part due to legal battles with Motown.

Her sisters signed with producer Richard Perry's Planet Records, where they enjoyed steady pop success. A cover of Bruce Springsteen's "Fire" (#2 pop, #14 R&B, 1979) started a string continued by Toussaint's "Happiness" (#30 pop, #20 R&B, 1979), "He's So Shy" (#3 pop, #10 R&B), and "Could I Be Dreaming" (#52 pop, #22 R&B) in 1980; "Slow Hand" (#2 pop, #7 R&B) in 1981; and "Should I Do It" (#13 pop), "American Music" (#16 pop, #23 R&B), and "I'm So Excited" (#30 pop, #42 R&B) in 1982.

The following year's Top 10, double-platinum *Break Out* (#8 pop, #6 R&B, 1983) featured "Automatic" (#5 pop, #2 R&B, 1984), "Jump (for My Love)" (#3 pop, #3 R&B, 1984), a remixed version of "I'm So Excited" (#9, 1984), and "Neutron Dance" (#6 pop, #13 R&B, 1984). The platinum *Contact* (#24 pop, #11 R&B, 1985) included "Dare Me" (#11 pop, #6 R&B, 1985). The trio's following albums did not fare as well, and the group took time off before releasing their 1994 SBK label debut. Unfortunately, the sisters were released from their record contract in the mid-'90s. In 1996 they joined the national tour of

The Pointer Sisters: Ruth Pointer, Anita Pointer, June Pointer

Ain't Misbehavin', a revue based on Fats Waller's life. But June missed a lot of performances, and the tour had to be cut short; she was eventually asked to leave the group in late 1999 with the stipulation that she could return only if she gave up drugs. Eventually, in mid-2000, she entered a rehab program and was treated for addiction to crack and Xanax. As of this writing, the sisters were supposed to perform together again.

Poison

Formed 1982, Harrisburg, PA
Bret Michaels (b. Bret Michael Sychak, Mar. 15, 1963, Harrisburg), voc., gtr.; Matt Smith (b. PA), gtr.; Bobby Dall (b. Robert Kuykendall, Nov. 2, 1963, Miami, FL), bass, voc.; Rikki Rockett (b. Richard Ream, Aug. 8, 1961, Mechanicsburg, PA), drums.
1985—(– Smith; + C.C. DeVille [b. Bruce Anthony Johannesson, May 14, 1962, Brooklyn, NY], gtr., voc.) 1986—*Look What the Cat Dragged In* (Enigma/Capitol) 1988—*Open Up and Say . . . Ahh!* 1990—*Flesh & Blood* 1991—*Swallow This Live* (Capitol) (– DeVille; + Richie Kotzen [b. Feb. 3, 1970, Reading, PA], gtr.) 1993—*Native Tongue* (– Kotzen; + Blues Saraceno [b. Oct. 17, 1971], gtr.) 1996—*Greatest Hits 1986–1996* (– Saraceno) 1999—(+ DeVille) 2000—*Crack a Smile . . . And More!; Power to the People* (Cyanide Music).

One of the most successful pop-metal groups of the late '80s, Poison paved the way for less-energetic and less-glam-styled bands like Warrant and Winger. The band began in central Pennsylvania, where Bret Michaels (a diabetic, as he would reveal after Poison's rise to fame) and Rikki Rockett formed Paris with guitarist Matt Smith and bassist Bobby Dall. They drove to Hollywood and became Poison. Smith was replaced by the flamboyant C.C. DeVille, a veteran of many New York and L.A. hard-rock bands (including Roxx Regime, which became born-again metal band Stryper after he left).

Poison's popularity on the L.A. metal-club circuit led to a record deal, and the group's debut album, *Look What the Cat Dragged In* (#3, 1986), sold 3 million copies, thanks to such hits as "Talk Dirty to Me" (#9, 1987), "I Want Action" (#50, 1987), and the ballad "I Won't Forget You" (#13, 1987). *Open Up and Say . . . Ahh!* (#2, 1988) yielded "Nothin' But a Good Time" (#6, 1988), "Fallen Angel" (#12, 1988), the ballad "Every Rose Has Its Thorn" (#1, 1988), and a cover of Loggins and Messina's "Your Mama Don't Dance" (#10, 1989). *Flesh & Blood* (#2, 1990) produced the hits "Unskinny Bop" (#3, 1990), "Something to Believe In" (#4, 1990), "Life Goes On" (#35, 1991), and "Ride the Wind" (#38, 1991). In late 1990 Michaels cowrote and produced his girlfriend Susie Hatton's debut album, while DeVille guested on Warrant's hit single "Cherry Pie."

Swallow This Live (#51, 1991) signaled Poison's decline. In late 1991 Michaels warned DeVille and Dall, through the metal press, to stop doing so many drugs or be fired. In 1992 DeVille was replaced by Richie Kotzen, who debuted on *Native Tongue,* which entered *Billboard*'s pop albums chart at #16 in early March 1993, but dropped off the chart three months later, yielding only the minor hit single "Stand" (#50, 1993). By year's end, Kotzen was replaced by 21-year-old Blues Saraceno. Poison's next studio album, *Crack a Smile,* was to have been released in 1996, but was shelved by Capitol for four years. Saraceno split, and the band became inactive as Michaels focused on efforts for a production company he shared with actor Charlie Sheen. By 1999, however, DeVille had rejoined the group and Poison was back on the road. A new release, *Power to the People,* compiled recent live performances and new studio tracks, including DeVille's debut as a lead vocalist, "I Hate Every Bone in Your Body But Mine."

The Police

Formed 1977, England
Stewart Copeland (b. Stewart Armstrong Copeland, July 16, 1952, Alexandria, VA), drums; Sting (b. Gordon Matthew Sumner, Oct. 2, 1951, Wallsend, Newcastle, Eng.), bass, voc., sax, kybds.; Andy Summers (b. Dec. 31, 1942, Blackpool, Eng.), gtr.
1978—*Outlandos d'Amour* (A&M) 1979—*Reggatta de Blanc* 1980—*Zenyatta Mondatta* 1981—*Ghost in the Machine* 1983—*Synchronicity* 1986—*Every Breath You Take: The Singles* 1993—*Message in a Box: The Complete Recordings* 1995—*The Police Live!* 1997—*The Very Best of Sting and the Police.*
As Strontium 90, with Mike Howlett: 1997—*Police Academy* (Ark 21).
Stewart Copeland solo: 1980—*Klark Kent* EP (I.R.S.) 1983—*Rumble Fish: The Original Motion Picture Soundtrack* (A&M) 1985—*The Rhythmatist* (A&M) 1990—*Noah's Ark* (Lightyear).
Copeland with Animal Logic: 1989—*Animal Logic* (I.R.S.) 1991—*Animal Logic II.*
Andy Summers solo: 1982—*I Advance Masked* (with Robert Fripp) (A&M) 1984—*Bewitched* (with Robert Fripp) 1987—*XYZ* (MCA) 1988—*Mysterious Barricades* (Private Music) 1989—*The Golden Wire* 1990—*Charming Snakes* 1991—*World Gone Strange* 1993—*Invisible Threads* (with John Etheridge) (Mesa Blue Moon) 1996—*Synaesthesia* (CMP, Ger.) 1997—*The Last Dance of Mr. X* (RCA) 1998—*Retrospective* (Windham Hill); *Strings of Desire* (with Victor Biglione) (RCA) 1999—*Green Chimneys: The Music of Thelonious Monk* 2000—*Peggy's Blue Skylight.*

The Police's canny, forward-looking combination of pop hooks, exotic rhythms, blond good looks, adventurous management, and good timing won the trio a mass following in America and around the world. Its distinctive sound—songs centered on Sting's bass patterns and high, wailing vocals, with Summers' atmospheric guitar, and Copeland's intricate drumming—was among the most influential approaches since punk. While the Police seemed at first to be a white reggae band, it later incorporated ideas from funk, minimalism, Arab, Indian, and African music. But as the chief singer, songwriter, and bassist, Sting began harboring solo ambi-

The Police: Sting, Andy Summers, Stewart Copeland

tions, which led to the band's untimely demise in 1984, following its fifth and most successful album, *Synchronicity*.

Sting, who got his nom de fame because of a yellow-and-black jersey he often wore as a young musician, had been a teacher, ditchdigger, and civil servant and had worked with several jazz combos in Newcastle, England, including Last Exit, before he met American drummer Stewart Copeland at a local jazz club. Copeland, the son of a jazz-loving CIA agent and an archaeologist with an appreciation for classical music, had grown up in the Middle East, attended college in California, moved to England in 1975, and joined the English progressive-rock group Curved Air.

After Curved Air broke up in 1976, Copeland formed the Police with Sting and guitarist Henri Padovani in 1977, replacing Padovani with Summers after some months of club dates. (The new trio played for several months with bassist Mike Howlett, who went on to become a record producer, in a group called Strontium 90.) Summers had played with numerous groups since the mid-'60s, including Eric Burdon and the Animals, the Kevin Ayers Band, the Zoot Money Big Roll Band, and Neil Sedaka; he had also studied classical guitar in California.

From the start, the Police distinguished itself for its maverick business practices. Before recording anything, the threesome portrayed a bleached-blond punk-rock band in a chewing-gum TV commercial—a move that drew the scorn of Britain's punks. But in punk style, the group's first single, "Fall Out" (with Padovani), was homemade and frenzied. Released in 1978 by Illegal Records Syndicate (I.R.S.)—an independent label founded by Stewart Copeland and his brother Miles (also the group's manager)—"Fall Out" sold about 70,000 copies in the U.K.

The following year, the Police signed with A&M, negotiating a unique contract that awarded the group a higher-than-standard royalty rate instead of a large advance. The Police's next unorthodox move was to tour America before releasing any records there. Through Frontier Booking International (FBI)—Stewart's brother Ian Copeland's agency—the band borrowed equipment, rented a van, and traveled cross-country to play club dates, sowing the seeds of a following that would make its first U.S. release, "Roxanne," a moderate hit (#32, 1979; it was already a British hit).

Both *Outlandos d'Amour* and *Reggatta de Blanc* entered the U.S. Top 30, while in the U.K. "Message in a Bottle" and "Walking on the Moon" went to the top of the singles chart. A 1980 world tour took the Police to Hong Kong, Thailand, India, Egypt, Greece, and Mexico—countries that rarely receive foreign entertainers. *Zenyatta Mondatta* (#5, 1980), which contained "De Do Do Do, De Da Da Da" (#10, 1980) and "Don't Stand So Close to Me" (#10, 1981), was the group's first U.S. platinum album. It was followed by a second million-seller, *Ghost in the Machine* (#2, 1981), which secured the Police among the big hitmakers of the decade with "Every Little Thing She Does Is Magic" (#3, 1981).

Meanwhile, the three musicians worked on various outside projects. Sting embarked on a film career, acting in *Quadrophenia* (1979), *Radio On* (1979), and *Brimstone and Treacle* (1982), which he also scored; and performing solo in *The Secret Policeman's Other Ball* (1982). Summers collaborated with Robert Fripp on two albums. Copeland recorded with Peter Gabriel, released a solo EP as Klark Kent, and composed the soundtrack for Francis Ford Coppola's movie *Rumble Fish* (1983).

The three regrouped for 1983's chart-topping *Synchronicity*, which spawned the monster hit "Every Breath You Take" (#1, 1983), and also produced "Synchronicity II" (#16, 1983), "King of Pain," (#3, 1983), and "Wrapped Around Your Finger" (#8, 1984). After a triumphant world tour, it was announced that the Police would take a "sabbatical" to devote time to individual pursuits; but in 1985, as Sting released a successful solo album and started touring with a new band, it became clear that the singer had no plans to reunite with Copeland and Summers. In later years, interviews revealed a playful but real tension between Sting and Copeland, causing speculation that this interaction may have played a part in the group's end as well.

Still, fans were hopeful when the group played together at several shows on Amnesty International's Conspiracy of Hope Tour in 1986. That year also brought a Police greatest-hits compilation that was supposed to include new tracks but didn't, largely because Sting wouldn't write any. Instead the trio included "Don't Stand So Close to Me '86," a subpar new version of the original hit, which peaked at #46. (Several remixes were intended, but a freak polo accident prevented Copeland from drumming.) It was the Police's last recording to date. The trio re-formed in front of an exclusive audience to perform at Sting's wedding to Trudie Styler in 1992 and sat for its first joint interview in 15 years in 1999. The group was the subject of a few tribute albums—two reggae and one rock *en Español*—in the late '90s. Meanwhile, Sting lent his most famous Police compositions, "Every Breath You Take" and "Roxanne," to rap producer/mogul Sean Combs for sampling and a remix, respectively, in 1997.

Copeland and Summers have enjoyed more modest solo success, at least commercially, than Sting [see entry]. In 1985 Copeland released *The Rhythmatist,* an album documenting his experiments collaborating with African folk percussionists. More film scores followed, as well: Oliver Stone's *Wall Street* and *Talk Radio* and numerous others. The drummer also composed themes for television series, including *The Equalizer* (an instrumental album called *The Equalizer and Other Cliff Hangers* was released in 1988; it is now out of print), and released two albums with another rock band, Animal Logic, formed with jazz bassist Stanley Clarke and singer Deborah Holland. Then, after composing *King Lear* for the San Francisco Ballet, he presented his first opera, *Holy Blood and Crescent Moon,* in 1989; a second, *Horse Opera,* followed in 1993, with a mini-opera based on the Edgar Allan Poe short story "The Cask of Amontillado" presented in 1994. Also in '94, Copeland coordinated a tour of international percussion groups. Copeland is responsible for the eclectic, atmospheric music featured in the best-selling Spyro the Dragon videogame series.

Summers' post-Police career, while less varied, has been distinguished by adventurous rock, jazz, and fusion albums, both alone and in collaboration with such respected musicians as Fripp and British jazz guitarist John Etheridge. His 1999 solo release *Green Chimneys: The Music of Thelonious Monk* featured Sting on vocals of the track "Round Midnight." Also in '99, Summers participated in a cross-cultural songwriting exchange workshop in Cuba.

Jean-Luc Ponty

Born Sep. 29, 1942, Avranches, Fr.
1967—*Sunday Walk* (MPS) 1968—*More Than Meets the Ear* (World Pacific Jazz) 1969—*Electric Connection; Live at Donte's; The Jean-Luc Experience* 1970—*Astorama* (Far East) 1972—*New Violin Summit* (MPS); *Open Strings; Live in Montreux* (Inner City) 1973—*Ponty/Grappelli* (with Stephane Grappelli) (America) 1975—*Upon the Wings of Music* (Atlantic) 1976—*Aurora; Imaginary Voyage* 1977—*Enigmatic Ocean* 1978—*Cosmic Messenger* 1979—*A Taste for Passion; Live* 1980—*Civilized Evil* 1981—*Mystical Adventures* 1983—*Individual Choice* 1984—*Open Mind* 1985—*Fables* 1987—*The Gift of Time* (Columbia) 1989—*Storytelling* 1991—*Tchokola* (Epic) 1992—*Puss in Boots* (with Tracey Ullman) (Rabbit Ears/BMG) 1993—*No Absolute Time* (Atlantic); *Jean-Luc Ponty With the George Duke Trio* (One Way) 1995—*The Rite of Strings* (with Stanley Clarke and Al DiMeola) (EMD/I.R.S./Gai Saber) 1997—*Live at Chene Park* (Atlantic) 2000—*The Very Best of Jean-Luc Ponty* (Rhino).

Commercially successful jazz-rock-fusion violinist/composer Jean-Luc Ponty draws on both classical technique and sophisticated technology. He has played both acoustic and electric violin with Frank Zappa, the Mahavishnu Orchestra, Elton John, and his own bands. His solo records have featured both jazz stalwarts (Chick Corea and George Benson) and pop players (Ray Parker Jr. and Patrice Rushen). He has also worked on occasion with jazz violinists Stephane Grappelli and Stuff Smith.

Ponty's father, a music teacher, gave him his first violin at age three, and the boy's classical studies began at age five. Ponty left school at 13 to study violin on his own, practicing six hours a day, and at 15 entered the Conservatoire National Supérieur de Musique de Paris, graduating two years later at the head of his class. At age 18 he joined the Concerts Lamoureux Symphony Orchestra for three years. In 1964 he gave up the classics for jazz and played at the Antibes Jazz Festival the next year. He has since played several times at most of the major jazz festivals, including Newport, Montreux, and Monterey.

Ponty first visited the U.S. in 1967, when he took part in a violin summit at the Monterey Jazz Festival. In 1969, after having toured Europe for three years, he moved to America to play with the George Duke Trio. He returned to Europe in 1971 and formed the Jean-Luc Ponty Experience with guitarist Philip Catherine. Before leaving America, though, he had played on Zappa's *Hot Rats* and also recorded *King Kong,* an album of Zappa compositions (because of legal problems, Zappa did not get production credit).

Back in France, Ponty met Elton John and contributed violin work to the singer's *Honky Chateau.* In 1973 he came back to America, where he spent a year with Zappa's Mothers of Invention, followed by a year with the Mahavishnu Orchestra before forming his own band and recording a string of commercially successful jazz-rock-fusion albums. From 1971 to 1979, he consistently won the violin category in *Down Beat*'s critics and readers polls.

In the '80s Ponty began composing on synthesizers; *Fables* featured groundbreaking work on the Synclavier, an electronic keyboard that interfaces with a computer. He toured extensively, playing both a traditional Barcus-Berry open-bodied violin and a Zeta electronic model, and performed his original compositions with both the Montreal Symphony and the New Japan Philharmonic. *Tchokola* (1991), with its complex West African–based rhythms and an African band, was a marked departure from Ponty's usual sound. In the '90s, he continued recording—his music, with such rare exceptions as *Rite of Strings* with bassist Stanley Clarke and guitarist Al DiMeola, taking a New Age turn.

Iggy Pop/Iggy and the Stooges

Born James Jewel Osterberg, Apr. 21, 1947, Ypsilanti, MI
The Stooges, formed 1967, Ann Arbor, MI
Iggy Pop, voc.; Ron Asheton (b. ca. 1948, Ann Arbor), gtr.; Dave Alexander, bass; Scott Asheton (b. ca. 1950, Ann Arbor), drums.
1969—*The Stooges* (Elektra) 1970—*Fun House* (– Alexander; + James Williamson [b. Birmingham, MI], gtr.; Ron Asheton switches to bass) 1971—(group disbands) 1972—(group re-forms: Iggy; Ron Asheton, bass; Scott Asheton; Williamson) 1973—*Raw Power* (Columbia) (+ Scott Thurston, bass, kybds.)

1974—(group disbands) 1976—*Metallic K.O.* (Skydog) 1978—*Kill City* (Bomp) 2000—*1970: The Complete Fun House Sessions* (Handmade/Rhino).
Iggy Pop solo: 1977—*The Idiot* (RCA); *Lust for Life* 1978—*TV Eye* 1979—*New Values* (Arista) 1980—*Soldier* 1981—*Party* 1982—*Zombie Birdhouse* (Animal) 1984—*Choice Cuts* (RCA) 1986—*Blah Blah Blah* (A&M) 1988—*Instinct* 1990—*Brick by Brick* (Virgin) 1993—*American Caesar* 1996—*Naughty Little Doggie* (Virgin) 1999—*Avenue B* 2000—*The Heritage Collection* (Arista) 2001—*Beat 'Em Up* (Virgin).

With his outrageous, cathartic, and at times dangerous stage antics, and the relentless rock & roll that accompanied them, Iggy Pop prefigured both '70s punk and '90s grunge. With his persona as that of the eternal misfit, saboteur of all convention, Pop has parlayed twisted social commentary, an affecting if limited vocal style, and unlikely survival smarts into a long career characterized by scant commercial success, sizable critical notice, and a fanatic cult.

Raised in a trailer park, James Osterberg played drums as a teen in a local garage band, the Iguanas. He dropped out of the University of Michigan in 1966 and went to Chicago, where he listened to urban blues on the South Side. He returned to Detroit as Iggy Stooge and, inspired by a Doors concert, formed the Stooges. They debuted on Halloween 1967 in Ann Arbor and were appropriately frightening onstage: Iggy contorting his shirtless torso, letting out primal screams, rubbing peanut butter and raw steaks over his body, gouging his skin with broken glass, diving into the crowd, all while the Stooges played raw, basic rock. Some thought the band the embodiment and the future of rock; others were appalled that they were so unrepentantly primitive.

Elektra, the Doors' label, signed them in 1968. Though a decade later their first two albums would be hailed as seminal punk, they sold only moderately upon release. The band went through various personnel changes following the 1970 album *Fun House*, eventually breaking up, with Iggy retiring for over a year to kick a heroin addiction. Around this time, he ran into David Bowie, who resolved to resurrect Iggy's career. Bowie regrouped some of the Stooges and produced *Raw Power*, a critical success.

A dispute with Bowie's manager Tony DeFries forced Iggy and the re-formed Stooges onto the road without a manager. Through 1973 there was a return to drug addiction, and by the next year the band imploded. Iggy spent 1974–75 in L.A., trying to solve assorted legal problems. He committed himself to an L.A. mental hospital and was visited by Bowie (whose "Jean Genie" on the 1973 *Aladdin Sane* is said to be about Iggy). In 1976 Bowie took Iggy with him on his European tour, after which they settled in Berlin for three years. Concurrently, Bowie produced Pop's *The Idiot* and *Lust for Life*, meditations on modern malaise that benefitted from Bowie's professionalism; other albums of this period, like *Metallic K.O.* and *Kill City*, were semi-bootleg issues of older Stooges-era material.

In 1977 Iggy toured the U.S. with Bowie (unannounced) playing keyboards; Blondie was their opening act. Signing to Arista in the late '70s, Iggy released *New Values*, an album of trenchant rock; his other Arista work, however, suggested the beginnings of self-parody and sold dismally. Publishing his autobiography, *I Need More*, and signing with Blondie guitarist Chris Stein's Animal label in 1982, he put out another strong collection, *Zombie Birdhouse*. Yet only when "China Girl," cowritten by Pop and David Bowie, appeared on the latter's 1983 *Let's Dance* and became a hit for Bowie did Iggy achieve a measure of financial stability and mainstream interest.

With Bowie producing and ex–Sex Pistol Steve Jones on guitar, *Blah Blah Blah* showed Iggy attempting his most accessible music; peaking at #75, it fared nearly as well as *The Idiot* (#72, 1977), but alienated some of his hard-core following. Beginning in the mid-'80s, Pop began accepting character roles in movies (*Sid and Nancy*, *The Color of Money*, *Cry-Baby*, the kids movie *Snow Day*, and *Dead Man*); he was sought after as punk's elder statesman, even though Iggy's outrageousness by then was less a daily reality than a determined role. Married in 1984 and a proponent of at least his version of domestic bliss, Iggy reserved his animal spirits for recording. *Instinct* was Pop at his most metallic; *Brick by Brick* had him trying again for accessibility and duetting with Kate Pierson of the B-52's ("Candy"). Lauded by critics, *American Caesar* was his return to raw form, helped out with guest vocals on two tracks by one of his chief successors, Henry Rollins. If anything, *Naughty Little Doggie* rocked harder, and by the mid-'90s Pop enjoyed genuine cult-legend status. He was invoked as muse/hero in Irvine Welsh's *Trainspotting* and Danny Boyle's film of that novel (which used "Lust for Life" on its soundtrack); filmmaker Todd Haynes patterned *Velvet Goldmine* on the Pop-Bowie relationship and Bowie; and in 1997 Joan Jett and the Blackhearts and the Red Hot Chili Peppers were featured on *We*

Iggy Pop

Will Fall: The Iggy Pop Tribute. Pop ended the century with *Avenue B,* a dark, string-laden work, influenced by his fondness for Frank Sinatra. Musings on turning 50 and the fallout from his recent divorce, the album was his most introspective to date.

Portishead

Formed 1994, Bristol, Eng.
Geoff Barrow (b. Dec. 9, 1971, Southmead, Eng.), kybds.; Beth Gibbons (b. Jan. 4, 1965, Keynsham, Eng.), voc.; Adrian Utley (b. Apr. 27, 1957, Northampton, Eng.), gtr.; Dave McDonald (b. June 18, 1964, Southmead), eng.
1994—*Dummy* (Go! Discs, U.K.) 1997—*Portishead* (London) 1998—*Glory Times* (Go! Discs, U.K.); *PNYC* (London).

Vocalist Beth Gibbons and keyboardist Geoff Barrow first met in a job-retraining program offered by the unemployment office in Bristol, England. Gibbons, who came from Devon, was a veteran of numerous local bands, and Barrow, who hailed from nearby Portishead, had already accumulated studio experience as a teenager, working on vocalist Neneh Cherry's *Homebrew,* producing a track for fellow Bristol artist Tricky, and remixing tracks for Primal Scream, Paul Weller, and Depeche Mode. Along with guitarist Adrian Utley and sound engineer Dave McDonald, Barrow and Gibbons began collaborating on new music, using odd and elaborate recording techniques, sampling bits of spy-movie soundtracks, and employing a Theremin, the electronic instrument responsible for the eerie whine in vintage sci-fi movies and the Beach Boys' "Good Vibrations." The band's first effort was a short film, *To Kill a Dead Man,* which Barrow and Gibbons wrote and performed in. The project and its unusual soundtrack won record-label attention. The group signed to the U.K. label Go! Discs, which released 1994's *Dummy,* whose unanticipated success in England popularized the style dubbed "trip-hop," an atmospheric, nearly narcotic sound, mixing hip-hop beats with the downtempo undertow of dub reggae, oddly skewed samples, and the studio experimentation of electronic music, and was first realized by the Bristol group Massive Attack. Portishead added a fixation with James Bond–ish movie soundtracks, a jazzier flow, and Gibbons' sexily mournful vocals. Released on London Records in the U.S. the next year, the album became an underground sensation, reaching #79 and selling more than 150,000 copies after a video for the single "Sour Times (Nobody Loves Me)" (#53, 1995) garnered frequent airing on MTV.

It took two more years for the group to release its followup, *Portishead* (#21, 1997), which found Barrow striving to move beyond the sound that had become widely emulated, even on TV commercials. Portishead's next release was an album of remixes, *Glory Times,* followed by the live album, *PNYC* (#155, 1998), recorded at New York's Roseland Ballroom.

Porno for Pyros: See Jane's Addiction

Power Station: See Duran Duran; Robert Palmer

Prefab Sprout

Formed 1982, England
Paddy McAloon (b. June 7, 1957, Durham, Eng.), voc., gtr.; Martin McAloon (b. Jan. 4, 1962, Durham), bass; Wendy Smith (b. May 31, 1963, Durham), voc., gtr.; Michael Salmon, drums.
1984—*Swoon* (Kitchenware/Epic) (– Salmon; + Neil Conti [b. Feb. 12, 1959, London, Eng.], drums) 1985—*Two Wheels Good* (a.k.a. *Steve McQueen)* 1988—*From Langley Park to Memphis* 1989—*Protest Songs* 1990—*Jordan: The Comeback* (Epic) 1992—*A Life of Surprises: The Best of Prefab Sprout* 1997—*Andromeda Heights* (Kitchenware/Columbia, U.K.).

Singer and tunesmith Paddy McAloon, the driving force behind Prefab Sprout, has been praised as an heir to the richly melodic, tenderly lyrical tradition of pop songwriting embodied by artists like Paul McCartney, Brian Wilson, and Marvin Gaye. Although grand-scale commercial success has eluded the band, Prefab Sprout is appreciated, especially in England, for its delicate but lush postmodern pop, which incorporates subtle jazz inflections (a la Steely Dan), and for the quirky literateness of McAloon's lyrics, which have paid homage to American cultural icons such as Elvis Presley and Jesse James.

While growing up in rural England, McAloon and his brother Martin listened to records by the Beatles and the Who, and to contemporary American standards by Burt Bacharach and Jimmy Webb. In 1982 a single released independently by the siblings as Prefab Sprout, "Lions in My Own Garden (Exit Someone)," caught the attention of record-store manager Keith Armstrong, who signed them to his Kitchenware Records. Then the McAloons enlisted Wendy Smith, an early fan with a breathy soprano voice, and Armstrong struck a deal with Epic Records. The band's debut album, *Swoon,* which debuted in the U.K. Top 20, caught the attention of electro-pop musician/producer Thomas Dolby, who produced *Two Wheels Good* (released as *Steve McQueen* outside the U.S.), hailed by American and British critics as one of the year's best albums.

From Langley Park to Memphis produced a European pop hit with "The King of Rock 'n' Roll," which rose to #7 in the U.K. The album also featured guest appearances by Stevie Wonder and Pete Townshend. *Jordan: The Comeback* got good notices but made little impact on the charts. The band disappeared for much of the '90s, while Paddy McAloon married and had children, wrote mammoth conceptual scores that he didn't record (one ongoing project, started in 1991, is called *Earth: The Story So Far*), and eventually composed songs for other artists (Cher, Jimmy Nail). Meanwhile, Conti did session work, while Martin McAloon and Smith pursued new careers in music education. After a touch of renewed national recognition with a 1997 song,

"Where the Heart Is," which served as the theme to a British television series, Paddy McAloon gathered the band (sans Smith, who had recently given birth) for a rare tour throughout the U.K. in 2000. Around this time, Paddy McAloon was also preparing to release a largely instrumental album with some spoken-word interludes, called *I Trawl the Megahertz.*

Elvis Presley

Born Elvis Aron Presley, Jan. 8, 1935, East Tupelo, MS; died Aug. 16, 1977, Memphis, TN
1956—*Elvis Presley* (RCA); *Elvis* 1957—*Elvis' Christmas Album* 1958—*Elvis' Golden Records, vol. 1* 1959—*For LP Fans Only; A Date With Elvis* 1960—*50,000,000 Elvis Fans Can't Be Wrong: Elvis' Golden Records, vol. 2; Elvis Is Back; His Hand in Mine* 1961—*Something for Everybody* 1962—*Pot Luck* 1963—*Elvis' Golden Records, vol. 3* 1965—*Elvis for Everyone!* 1967—*How Great Thou Art* 1968—*Elvis TV* special soundtrack; *Elvis' Golden Records, vol. 4* 1969—*From Elvis in Memphis; From Memphis to Vegas/From Vegas to Memphis* 1970—*Back in Memphis; That's the Way It Is; On Stage—February 1970; Elvis in Person at the International Hotel, Las Vegas, Nevada; World Wide 50 Gold Award Hits, vol. 1, no. 1; World Wide 50 Gold Award Hits, vol. 1, no. 2; World Wide 50 Gold Award Hits, vol. 1, no. 3; World Wide 50 Gold Award Hits, vol. 1, no. 4* 1971—*Love Letters From Elvis; Elvis Country; Elvis Sings the Wonderful World of Christmas* 1972—*Burning Love; He Touched Me; As Recorded at Madison Square Garden; Elvis Now* 1973—*Separate Ways; Aloha From Hawaii via Satellite* 1974—*Elvis—A Legendary Performer, vol. 1* 1975—*Promised Land; Today* 1976—*Elvis—A Legendary Performer, vol. 2; From Elvis Presley Boulevard, Memphis, Tennessee* 1977—*Welcome to My World; Moody Blue; Elvis in Concert* 1978—*Elvis—A Legendary Performer, vol. 3; He Walks Beside Me* 1980—*Elvis Aron Presley* 1981—*This Is Elvis* soundtrack 1982—*Elvis: The Hillbilly Cat* (The Music Works); *Elvis: The First Live Recordings; Memories of Christmas* (RCA) 1983—*Elvis—A Legendary Performer, vol. 4* 1984—*Rocker; Elvis' Gold Records, vol. 5; Elvis—A Golden Celebration* 1985—*Reconsider Baby; A Valentine Gift for You; Always on My Mind* 1986—*Return of the Rocker* 1987—*The Complete Sun Sessions; The Number One Hits; The Memphis Record* 1988—*Essential Elvis; Stereo '57 (Essential Elvis, vol. 2); 50 World Wide Gold Award Hits, vol. 1, pt. 1; 50 World Wide Gold Award Hits, vol. 1, pt. 2; The Top Ten Hits; Elvis in Nashville; The Alternate Aloha* 1989—*Known Only to Him: Elvis Gospel, 1957–1971* 1990—*The Million Dollar Quartet* (with Johnny Cash, Jerry Lee Lewis, and Carl Perkins); *The Great Performances* 1991—*The Essential Elvis, vol. 3; Collector's Gold; Elvis Presley Sings Leiber and Stoller* 1992—*Elvis—The King of Rock 'n' Roll—The Complete 50's Masters* 1994—*From Nashville to Memphis: The Essential 60's Masters I* 1995—*Command Performances: The Essential 60's Masters II; Walk a Mile in My Shoes: The Essential 70's Masters III* 1996—*Essential Elvis, vol. 4: A Hundred Years From Now; Great Country Songs* 1997—*Greatest Jukebox Hits; Elvis Platinum: A Life in Music; An Afternoon in the Garden* 1998—*A Touch of Platinum; A Touch of Platinum, vol. 2; Essential Elvis, vol. 5: Rhythm and Country* 1999—*Sunrise; Artist of the Century* 2000—*Elvis Presley, Such a Night: The Stellar Nashville Sessions, 1960–1964* 2001—*The Blue Suede Shoes Collection; Elvis: Live in Las Vegas.*

Simply put, Elvis Presley was the first real rock & roll star. A white Southerner singing blues laced with country, and country tinged with gospel, he brought together American music from both sides of the color line and performed it with a natural hip-swiveling sexuality that made him a teen idol and a role model for generations of cool rebels. He was repeatedly dismissed as vulgar, incompetent, and a bad influence, but the force of his music and his image was no mere merchandising feat. Presley signaled to mainstream culture that it was time to let go. Today, over 20 years after his death, Presley's image and influence remain undiminished. While certainly other artists preceded him and he by no means "invented" rock & roll, he is indisputably its king.

As a recording artist, Presley's accomplishments are unparalleled. He is believed to have sold over 1 billion records worldwide, about 40 percent of those outside the U.S. The RIAA has awarded Presley the largest number of gold, platinum, and multiplatinum certifications of any artist in history; as of early 2001, 131. His chart performance, as tracked by *Billboard,* is also unmatched, with 149 charting pop singles: 114 Top 40, 40 Top 10, and 18 #1s.

Presley was the son of Gladys and Vernon Presley, a sewing-machine operator and a truck driver. Elvis' twin brother, Jesse Garon, was stillborn, and Presley grew up an only child. When he was three, his father served an eight-month prison term for writing bad checks, and afterward Vernon Presley's employment was erratic, keeping the family just above the poverty level. The Presleys attended the First

Elvis Presley

Assembly of God Church, and its Pentecostal services always included singing.

In 1945 Presley won second prize at the Mississippi-Alabama Fair and Dairy Show for his rendition of Red Foley's "Old Shep." The following January he received a guitar for his birthday. In 1948 the family moved to Memphis, and while attending L.C. Humes High School there, Presley spent much of his spare time hanging around the black section of town, especially on Beale Street, where bluesmen like Furry Lewis and B.B. King performed.

Upon graduation in June 1953, Presley worked at the Precision Tool Company and then drove a truck for Crown Electric. He planned to become a truck driver and had begun to wear his long hair pompadoured, the current truck-driver style. That summer he recorded "My Happiness" and "That's When Your Heartaches Begin" at the Memphis Recording Service, a sideline Sam Phillips had established in his Sun Records studios where anyone could record a 10-inch acetate for four dollars.

Presley was reportedly curious to know what he sounded like and gravely disappointed by what he heard. But he returned to the Recording Service again on January 4, 1954, and recorded "Casual Love Affair" and "I'll Never Stand in Your Way." This time he met Phillips, who called him later that spring to rerecord a song that Phillips had received on a demo, "Without You." Despite numerous takes, Presley failed miserably and at Phillips' request just began singing songs in the studio. Phillips then began to believe that he had finally found what he had been looking for: "a white man with the Negro sound and the Negro feel."

Phillips enlisted lead guitarist Scotty Moore and bassist Bill Black, both of whom were then playing country & western music in Doug Poindexter's Starlight Wranglers. Though some sources cite the date of their first meeting as July 4, 1954, the three had actually rehearsed for several months, and on July 5, 1954, they recorded three songs: "I Love You Because," "Blue Moon of Kentucky," and what would become Presley's debut, Arthur "Big Boy" Crudup's "That's All Right."

Two days later Memphis disc jockey Dewey Phillips (no relation to Sam) played the song on his *Red Hot and Blue* show on radio station WHBQ. Audience response was overwhelming, and that night Presley came to the studio for his first interview. Scotty Moore became Presley's manager, and "That's All Right" b/w "Blue Moon of Kentucky" became his first local hit. After playing local shows, Presley made his first—and last—appearance at the Grand Ole Opry on September 25. Legend has it that after his performance he was advised by the Opry's talent coordinator to go back to driving trucks.

By October Presley had debuted on *The Louisiana Hayride,* a popular radio program on which he appeared regularly through 1955. He made his television debut on a local television version of *Hayride* in March 1955. Meanwhile, "Good Rockin' Tonight" b/w "I Don't Care if the Sun Don't Shine" were hits in the Memphis area.

In early 1955 Moore stopped managing Presley, although he would continue to play in Presley's band for several years. Presley's new manager was Memphis disc jockey Bob Neal. Colonel Thomas Parker first entered Presley's career when he helped Neal make some tour arrangements. Presley, still considered a country act, continued to perform locally, and in April he traveled to New York City, where he auditioned unsuccessfully for Arthur Godfrey's *Talent Scouts* program. But on May 13 his performance in Jacksonville, Florida, started a riot, Presley's first. "Baby, Let's Play House" b/w "I'm Left, You're Right, She's Gone" was released and hit #10 on the national C&W chart in July.

That September, Presley had his first #1 country record, a version of Junior Parker's "Mystery Train" b/w "I Forgot to Remember to Forget." By this time Colonel Parker, despite Presley's agreement with Neal, had become increasingly involved in his career. When RCA purchased Presley's contract from Sun for a then unheard-of $35,000, Hill and Range, a music publisher with which Parker had some connections, purchased Sam Phillips' Hi-Lo Music for another $15,000. In addition, Presley received a $5,000 advance, with which he bought his mother a pink Cadillac. (It remains among his possessions preserved at Graceland.)

Presley became a national star in 1956. He and Parker traveled to Nashville, where Presley cut his first records for RCA (including "I Got a Woman," "Heartbreak Hotel," and "I Was the One"), and on January 28, 1956, the singer made his national television debut on the Dorsey Brothers' *Stage Show,* followed by six consecutive appearances. In March, Parker signed Presley to a managerial agreement for which he would receive 25 percent of Presley's earnings. The contract would last through Presley's lifetime and beyond.

Presley performed on the Milton Berle, Steve Allen, and Ed Sullivan television shows. The Colonel arranged Presley's debut at the New Frontier Hotel in Las Vegas that April, but the two-week engagement was canceled after one week due to poor audience response. In August he began filming his first movie, *Love Me Tender,* which was released three months later and recouped its $1 million cost in three days. Elvis' hit singles that year were all certified gold; they included "Heartbreak Hotel" (#1), "I Was the One" (#19), "Blue Suede Shoes" (#20), "I Want You, I Need You, I Love You" (#1), "Hound Dog" (#1), "My Baby Left Me" (#31), "Don't Be Cruel" (#1), "Love Me Tender" (#1), "Anyway You Want Me (That's How I Will Be)" (#20), "Love Me" (#2), and "When My Blue Moon Turns to Gold" (#19). By early 1957 he was the idol of millions of teens and the perfect target for the wrath of critics, teachers, clergy, and even other entertainers (including many country performers), all of whom saw his style as too suggestive; he was nicknamed Elvis the Pelvis by one writer. Presley repeatedly claimed not to understand what all the criticism was about. On January 6, when Presley made his last of three appearances on Ed Sullivan's show, he was shown only from the waist up.

In March 1957 Presley purchased Graceland, a former church that had been converted into a 23-room mansion; the next month "All Shook Up" began an eight-week run at #1. It was preceded in 1957 by "Poor Boy" (#24), "Too Much" (#1), and "Playing for Keeps" (#21). Presley's next single was his first gospel release, "(There'll Be) Peace in the Valley (for Me)"; it went to #25.

Presley was also the first rock star to cross over into films with consistent commercial, if not critical, success. His second film, *Loving You,* was released in July 1957, and "(Let Me Be Your) Teddy Bear" from its soundtrack hit #1 on the pop, country, and R&B charts, as did "All Shook Up," and "Jailhouse Rock," the title song from Presley's next movie, which featured Leiber and Stoller songs. Other hit singles from 1957 were "Loving You" (#20) and "Treat Me Nice" (#18).

That December he received his draft notice but was granted a 60-day deferment to complete filming *King Creole,* a drama based on the novel *A Stone for Danny Fisher,* costarring Carolyn Jones and Walter Matthau. These first four feature films are considered his best. Early in the game, Presley truly intended to be taken seriously as an actor. Unfortunately, once he left the service, the choice of roles was left entirely up to Colonel Parker, and the results were rarely satisfactory for either the audience or Presley. However, since Presley would not tour again until the early '70s, it was through the films that most fans saw him. Despite anything that might be said of these films, that reason alone accounts for their massive success.

On March 24, 1958, Presley entered the army. The preceding months brought two hits: "Don't" (#1, 1958) and "I Beg of You" (#8, 1958). He took leave a few months later to be with his mother; Gladys Presley died the day after his arrival home in Memphis, on August 14, 1958. In later interviews Presley would call her death the great tragedy of his life. In the years since his death, much has been written about his relationship with his mother and her impact on him. She was without question the most important person in his life. At her funeral, he cried out, "You know how much I lived my whole life just for you," words that were both true in the moment and prophetic, for the absence of Gladys, and his love for her, seemed to have never really left his mind. He was shipped to Bremerhaven, West Germany, and in January 1960 was promoted to sergeant. He was discharged in March.

Colonel Parker, meanwhile, had continued to release singles Presley had recorded before his departure, ensuring that while Elvis was gone, he would not be forgotten. And he wasn't. He scored a number of hits in absentia, including "Wear My Ring Around Your Neck" (#2, 1958), "Don'tcha Think It's Time" (#15, 1958), "Hard Headed Woman" (#1, 1958), "Don't Ask Me Why" (#25, 1958), "One Night" (#4, 1958), "I Got Stung" (#8, 1958), "(Now and Then There's) A Fool Such as I" (#2, 1959), "I Need Your Love Tonight" (#4, 1959), "A Big Hunk o' Love" (#1, 1959), and "My Wish Came True" (#12, 1959). In 1958 alone, Presley earned over $2 million. Shortly after his return to civilian life in March 1960, he recorded his first stereo record, "Stuck on You" (#1), and later that month he taped a TV program with Frank Sinatra, *The Frank Sinatra–Timex Special.*

In July, Presley's father remarried. Vernon Presley's second wife, Davada "Dee" Stanley, and her three sons would later write *Elvis: We Love You Tender,* one of dozens of insiders' tell-all biographies that were published following his death. Also at this time, Presley gathered more closely around him the friends, employees, and hangers-on who would become known as the Memphis Mafia and would accompany him almost constantly until his death. Presley's world became increasingly insular.

The films *G.I. Blues* and *Flaming Star* were released in 1960, and "It's Now or Never" hit #1 in both the U.K. and the U.S. Presley had five #1 U.S. hits: "Stuck on You," "It's Now or Never," "Are You Lonesome Tonight" (1960); "Surrender" (1961); and "Good Luck Charm" (1962). Other Top 10 singles included "I Feel So Bad" (#5, 1961), "Little Sister" (#5, 1961), "(Marie's the Name) His Latest Flame" (#4, 1961), "Can't Help Falling in Love" (#2, 1961), "She's Not You" (#5, 1962), "Return to Sender" (#2, 1962), "(You're the) Devil in Disguise" (#3, 1963), and "Bossa Nova Baby" (#8, 1963). Meanwhile, over Christmas 1960, Priscilla Beaulieu, the teenage daughter of an army officer whom Presley had met in Germany, visited Graceland. In early 1961 she moved in to live, it was said, under the supervision of Presley's father and stepmother. Interestingly, the press largely went along with the spin Colonel Parker put on the story, and few seemed troubled that the King of Rock & Roll shared his domain with his teenage girlfriend.

After a live performance on March 25, 1961, at a benefit for the USS *Arizona,* Presley left the concert stage. He spent the next eight years making B movies: *Wild in the Country; Blue Hawaii* (1961); *Follow That Dream; Kid Galahad; Girls! Girls! Girls!* (1962); *It Happened at the World's Fair; Fun in Acapulco* (1963); *Kissin' Cousins; Viva Las Vegas; Roustabout* (1964); *Girl Happy; Tickle Me; Harum Scarum* (1965); *Frankie and Johnny; Paradise, Hawaiian Style; Spinout* (1966); *Easy Come, Easy Go; Double Trouble; Clambake* (1967); *Stay Away Joe; Speedway; Live a Little, Love a Little* (1968); *Charro!; The Trouble With Girls (and How to Get Into It); Change of Habit* (1969). With a few exceptions, the soundtrack music was indisputably poor. But by the mid-'60s, Presley was earning $1 million per movie plus a large percentage of the gross. Most of the movies had a concurrently released soundtrack LP. Four of them hit #1 *(Loving You, G.I. Blues, Blue Hawaii, Roustabout),* and an additional seven were Top 10. Presley often made his displeasure with these films known to friends and associates, but Colonel Parker would not relent in his insistence that his sole client stick with a winning formula. Years later, in 1974, Parker's shortsightedness as a manager resulted in his refusing Barbra Streisand's offer to have Presley costar with her in what became a hit remake of *A Star Is Born.* Parker felt Streisand didn't deserve equal billing with Presley.

Meanwhile, the younger rock audience heard Presley disciples like the Beatles more often than they heard Presley himself. But Presley did not disappear, and he was not, like most American rockers, swept away by the British Invasion, though the Top 10 became increasingly beyond his reach, with only "Crying in the Chapel" (which he recorded in 1960) at #3 (1965) making the cut. Presley turned increasingly inward, focusing on his family. On May 1, 1967, Presley and Priscilla were wed in Las Vegas; on February 1, 1968, their only child, Lisa Marie, was born. Fearing he had been forgotten, Presley made a last-gasp bid to regain his footing. He defied Colonel Parker and followed the advice of director Steve Binder for his "comeback" television special. (Parker had wanted it to be a Christmas show.) Over the summer Presley taped the surprisingly raw, powerful *Elvis* television special that was broadcast on December 3 to high ratings. Its soundtrack reached #8. It included his first performance before an audience in over seven years (though many portions were taped without an audience). It also spun off his first Top 15 hit single since 1965, the socially conscious "If I Can Dream" (#12, 1968). The importance of this moment in Presley's life cannot be overestimated. Years later, the '68 comeback special still stands as one of the most powerful performances in rock history.

With that success behind him, Presley turned to performing in Las Vegas. His monthlong debut at the International Hotel in Las Vegas began on July 26, 1969, and set the course for all of Presley's future performances. His fee for the four weeks was over $1 million. Riding the crest of his comeback, Presley released a series of top singles, including "In the Ghetto" (#3, 1969), "Suspicious Minds" (#1, 1969, and his first chart-topper since early 1962), "Don't Cry Daddy" (#6, 1969), and "The Wonder of You" (#9, 1970). He toured the country annually, selling out showrooms, auditoriums, and arenas, frequently breaking box-office records. Until his death, he performed a total of nearly 1,100 concerts. There were two on-tour documentaries released, *Elvis: That's the Way It Is* (1970) and *Elvis on Tour* (1972), the latter of which won the Golden Globe Award for Best Documentary.

Presley was honored with countless Elvis Presley Days in cities around the country, and the U.S. Jaycees named him one of the 10 most outstanding young men of America in 1970. His birthplace in Tupelo was opened to the public, and on January 18, 1972, the portion of Highway 51 South that runs in front of Graceland was renamed Elvis Presley Boulevard. That October, Presley had his last Top 10 hit when "Burning Love" hit #2.

Meanwhile, Presley's personal life became the subject of countless tabloid headlines. Priscilla, from whom Presley had been separated since February 1972, refused to return to Graceland, and on his birthday in 1973 he filed for divorce. Less than a week later the TV special *Elvis: Aloha From Hawaii* was broadcast via satellite to over a billion viewers in 40 countries, an indication of his international appeal, although (with the exception of three dates in Canada in 1957 and an impromptu performance while on leave in Paris in 1959) Presley never performed outside the U.S. The special's soundtrack album became his last #1 album, in 1973.

Outwardly, Presley appeared to have been granted a second chance. He was more popular than ever, and the fan worship that would blossom into one of the biggest personality cults in modern history was taking hold. Offstage, however, Presley was plagued by self-doubt, poor management, and a basic dissatisfaction with his life. He repeatedly threatened to quit show business, but debts and his financial obligations to his large extended family, employees, and assorted hangers-on made that impossible. Unbeknownst to the public until after his death, Presley turned to drugs. Soon after he left the army, he became increasingly wary of the public and would often rent whole movie theaters and amusement parks to visit at night. By the late '60s, he was nearly a total recluse. Among the many books written about Presley by those who knew him, Priscilla's account, *Elvis and Me*, goes so far as to suggest that he might have suffered a nervous breakdown. Although it now seems clear that Presley was taking drugs—namely amphetamines—while in the service (and perhaps even before), his abuse of prescription drugs, including barbiturates, tranquilizers, and amphetamines, increased during the last years of his life. Several painful physical conditions may have initiated this trend. Ironically, he remained devoutly spiritual, never drank alcohol, and publicly denounced the use of recreational drugs. In one of his few unplanned excursions from Graceland, he actually showed up at the White House in 1970 to meet President Richard M. Nixon and received an honorary Drug Enforcement Administration agent's badge. Days later he was given a special tour of FBI headquarters, where, according to FBI files made public after Presley's death, the singer offered to provide information on persons he believed were a bad influence on American youth.

Toward the end of his life, however, his onstage presence began to deteriorate. He would babble incoherently and rip his pants, having grown quite obese, and on at least one occasion he collapsed. Despite his clearly worsening health, he maintained a frantic tour schedule. This was due to the fact that in 1973 Colonel Parker had negotiated a complex deal whereby Presley sold back to RCA the rights to many of his masters in exchange for a lump-sum payment of which only $2.8 million came to him. Essentially, after 1973 Parker was earning nearly 50 percent commission (as opposed to the 10 percent industry standard). Worse, however, Presley was not earning any more royalties on sides recorded before 1973, although they continued to sell in the millions year after year. Parker's need to satisfy personal gambling debts was said to be the reason for the self-serving deal. On top of it all, Presley opposed tax shelters on principle; he naively relied on his father for business advice; and he gave away expensive gifts and cash heedlessly. The result, by the mid-'70s, was near-certain financial disaster.

Presley's last live performance was on June 25, 1977, in Indianapolis. He was reportedly horrified at the impending publication of *Elvis: What Happened?*, the tell-all written by three of his ex-bodyguards and Memphis mafiosi that was the first printed account of his drug abuse and obsession with firearms, to name just two headline-grabbing revelations. The book came out on August 12. On August 16, 1977—the day before his next scheduled concert—Presley was discovered by his girlfriend Ginger Alden dead in his bathroom at Graceland. Although his death was at first attributed to congestive heart failure (an autopsy also revealed advanced arteriosclerosis and an enlarged liver), later investigation revealed evidence that drug abuse may have been at least part of the cause of death. Because the family was allowed to keep the official autopsy report private, additional speculation regarding contributing factors in Presley's death has run wild. Through the years, several insiders have insisted that he was suffering from bone cancer, to name just one unsubstantiated claim. In September 1979 Presley's private physician, Dr. George Nichopoulos, was charged by the Tennessee Board of Medical Examiners with "indiscriminately prescribing 5,300 pills and vials for Elvis in the seven months before his death." He was later acquitted.

Thousands gathered at Graceland, where Presley lay in state before he was buried in a mausoleum at Forest Hill Cemetery in Memphis. After attempts were made to break into the mausoleum, Presley's body and that of his mother were moved to the Meditation Garden behind Graceland. Nearly two years later, his father, Vernon, died and was also buried there. With Vernon dead, all of Presley's estate passed on to Lisa Marie.

Court battles over the estate ended in June 1983 after 21 months of litigation with a settlement that ended four lawsuits. One of the terms of the agreement called for Parker to turn over most of his interest in Presley's audio and video recordings to RCA and the Presley family in return for a large monetary settlement. Lisa Marie's court-appointed guardian ad litem, Blanchard Tual, wrote in his report on Presley's financial affairs that Parker had "handled affairs not in Elvis' but in his own best interest." Parker died of a stroke in February 1997 at the age of 87. Priscilla Presley assumed control of the estate and through a number of business moves made the Presley estate many times more valuable than it had ever been during Elvis' lifetime. The cornerstone of the Elvis Presley Enterprises, Inc. (EPE) financial empire is the Tennessee state law Priscilla Presley pushed for that guarantees to heirs the commercial rights to a deceased celebrity's image and likeness. As a result, the name Elvis Presley is, technically speaking, a trademark, and anyone selling Presley-related merchandise in the U.S. must pay EPE an advance fee plus a royalty on every item sold.

Claiming the funds were needed to maintain the property (the estate was valued at only $5 million in 1979 and the costs to maintain Graceland are estimated at nearly half a million dollars annually), Priscilla Presley opened Graceland to the public in the fall of 1982. Although it is not preserved in exactly the way Elvis Presley left it, and the second floor, where his bedroom is located, remains off-limits to the public, millions have come from all over the world to pay homage to the King of Rock & Roll. In 1991 Graceland was added to the National Register of Historic Places. At last count, 700,000 people visit Graceland annually. In the mid-'90s, the Presley estate was estimated to have been worth over $100 million. At the turn of the century, it was estimated that the presence of Graceland was responsible for bringing $100 million into the local Memphis economy. The Elvis Presley Charitable Foundation was created in 1985 by Elvis Presley Enterprises to support various causes. In 2000 ground was broken for Presley Place in Memphis, which will provide a year of free housing, child care, job training, and other services for homeless families.

Presley's sole heir, Lisa Marie, married a fellow Scientology follower, Danny Keough, in 1988. They had two children: Danielle and Benjamin Storm. In 1993 they were divorced, and in May 1994 she married Michael Jackson. They divorced in 1996, after 18 months of marriage.

To date, over 300 books about Elvis Presley have been published in the United States alone. His enduring power as a cultural force is beyond the scope of this book, but it has been examined in a number of works by authors including Dave Marsh, Greil Marcus, and Peter Guralnick, to name a few. Guralnick's award-winning two-volume biography—*Last Train to Memphis: The Rise of Elvis Presley* (1994) and *Careless Love: The Unmaking of Elvis Presley* (1999)—is perhaps the closest to a definitive account as we will ever have. In 1986 Presley was among the first 10 performers inducted into the Rock and Roll Hall of Fame.

Billy Preston

Born Sep. 9, 1946, Houston, TX
1965—*The Wildest Organ in Town* (Vee-Jay) 1966—*Most Exciting Organ Ever* 1969—*That's the Way God Planned It* (Apple); *Encouraging Words* 1971—*I Wrote a Simple Song* (A&M) 1972—*Music Is My Life* 1973—*Everybody Likes Some Kind of Music* 1974—*The Kids and Me* 1975—*It's My Pleasure* 1976—*Billy Preston* 1977—*A Whole New Thing* 1980—*Late at Night* (Motown) 1981—*Billy Preston and Syreeta* (with Syreeta Wright) 1982—*Best of Billy Preston* (A&M) 1995—*Minister of Music* (Pepperco Music Group) 1996—*Words and Music* (with Edna Tatum) 2000—*Ultimate Collection* (Hip-O/Universal).

Though keyboardist/vocalist Billy Preston has recorded prolifically since he was a teenager, he may be best known for his performances as a sideman for Little Richard, Ray Charles, the Beatles, and the Rolling Stones. Preston's family moved to L.A. when he was two years old. At age 12 he had a cameo part in a film about W.C. Handy, *St. Louis Blues,* playing the composer as a child. Little Richard heard him in 1962 and invited him to appear on a European tour. There, backing Richard, Preston met Sam Cooke (who signed him to his SAR label) and the Beatles. After Cooke's death Preston moved to Vee-Jay records, where he cut an instrumental gospel album, *The Most Exciting Organ Ever,* his first charting record.

Preston was playing in the house band of the television show *Shindig* when Ray Charles recruited him for his band. George Harrison spotted Preston on a BBC Ray Charles special and contacted him. Subsequently he was signed to the Beatles' Apple Records, where he cut two Harrison-produced albums, *That's the Way God Planned It* (whose title cut was a minor hit and which hit #127 on rerelease in 1972) and *Encouraging Words.* Preston also became a valuable sideman for the Beatles, appearing on "Get Back" and "Let It Be." Following the Beatles' breakup, he performed on Harrison's *All Things Must Pass* and at the Concert for Bangla Desh in 1971.

Preston had several hits on A&M Records in the early '70s, including the instrumental "Outa-Space" (#2 pop, #1 R&B) in 1972; "Will It Go Round in Circles" (#1 pop, #10 R&B) and "Space Race" (#4 pop, #1 R&B) in 1973; and "Nothing From Nothing" (#1 pop, #8 R&B) in 1974. Each single went gold, and "Outa-Space" won a Grammy as Best Pop Instrumental Performance. In 1975 Preston wrote what became Joe Cocker's biggest solo hit, "You Are So Beautiful." That same year Preston was featured on the Rolling Stones' tour; he had previously recorded with them *(Goats Head Soup, It's Only Rock 'n Roll, Sticky Fingers, Exile on Main Street),* and he later appeared on *Black and Blue* and *Love You Live.*

Preston was active as a session musician through the late '70s and into the '80s, though his solo career declined. In 1979 he reached the Top 5 with "With You I'm Born Again," a duet with Syreeta Wright. Preston toured with Ringo Starr in 1989 and recorded for the U.K. Motorcity label in the early '90s, but he could not restart his career. In 1992 he pleaded no contest to charges of assault and possession of cocaine and was sentenced to prison and drug treatment, followed by house arrest and probation. (He later admitted that his addiction to alcohol and crack cocaine had been going on for nearly 30 years.) Preston released two gospels albums in the mid-'90s. In 1997 he was arrested for cocaine possession, accused of violating his probation, and sentenced to three years in prison. The following year he and his ex-manager were indicted in an alleged insurance-fraud conspiracy. Preston pleaded guilty and agreed to testify against the other defendants, including his former manager; he received one year in jail, which ran concurrently with his other sentence. Upon his release from prison, Preston resumed live performance.

The Pretenders

Formed 1978, London, Eng.
Chrissie Hynde (b. Sep. 7, 1951, Akron, OH), voc., gtr.; Pete Farndon (b. 1953, Hereford, Eng.; d. Apr. 14, 1983, London), bass; James Honeyman-Scott (b. Nov. 4, 1957, Hereford; d. June 16, 1982), gtr.; Martin Chambers (b. 1952, Hereford), drums.
1980—*The Pretenders* (Sire) 1981—*Extended Play* EP; *The Pretenders II* 1982—(– Farndon; – Honeyman-Scott) 1983—(+ Robbie McIntosh, gtr.; + Malcolm Foster, bass) 1984—*Learning to Crawl* 1986—(– Chambers; – Foster; + T. M. Stevens, bass; + Blair Cunningham, drums) *Get Close* 1987—*The Singles* (– McIntosh) 1990—(+ Billy Bremner [b. 1947, Scot.], gtr.; + Dominic Miller, gtr.; John McKenzie, bass) *Packed!* 1993—(+ Chambers; + Adam Seymour, gtr.; + Andy Hobson, bass) 1994—*Last of the Independents* 1995—*The Isle of View* (Warner Bros.) 1999—*¡Viva El Amor!*.

The Pretenders, originally three Englishmen and an American woman, emerged at the close of the '70s as one of the new wave's most commercially successful groups. Its focal point was Chrissie Hynde, the band's songwriter, lead singer, and rhythm guitarist, whose tough songs and stage persona put feminist self-assertion into her own distinctive hard rock.

A single gig with an Akron band, Sat. Sun. Mat. (which included Mark Mothersbaugh, later of Devo), was Hynde's sole performing experience when, after three years of studying art at Kent State University, she left (with money earned as a waitress) for the rocker's life in London in 1974. She began writing savagely satiric reviews for *New Musical Express;* but after playing cover girl for a story on Brian Eno, she moved to France to form a band. When nothing materialized, she returned to Akron, where she joined Jack Rabbit; it broke up, and Hynde returned to France and then to England by 1976, as punk rock was burgeoning. She tried to enlist a young guitarist, Mick Jones, into her would-be group, but Jones committed himself to another new group, the Clash.

She was then hired by punk fashion entrepreneur and Sex Pistols manager Malcolm McLaren (in whose boutique, Sex, Hynde had worked when she'd first come to London) to play guitar in Masters of the Backside. After months of rehearsal, she was dismissed; the group turned into the Damned. Hynde played guitar or sang backup behind Johnny Moped, Chris Spedding, Johnny Thunders (the New York Dolls, the Heartbreakers), and Nick Lowe. With these contacts and a growing repertoire of original songs, she recorded a demo tape. Dave Hill, founder of Real Records, became her manager and advanced her the money to audition and hire a band.

Bassist Pete Farndon had recently returned to England from Australia, where he had played for two years with a popular Aussie group, the Bushwackers. He called James Honeyman-Scott, who had toured with several bands, notably Cheeks, a group led by ex–Mott the Hoople keyboardist Verdon Allen. Honeyman-Scott joined Hynde, Farndon, and drummer Gerry Mackleduff to record two Hynde compositions—"Precious" and "The Wait"—and a 1964 number penned by Ray Davies of the Kinks, "Stop Your Sobbing." Nick Lowe pegged "Stop Your Sobbing" b/w "The Wait" for a hit and offered to produce a single, which he did in one day in the fall of 1978. The next day, the Pretenders left for Paris for its debut gig and a weeklong club engagement.

Mackleduff was replaced by Cheeks' former drummer, Martin Chambers, then working as a drummer and driving instructor in London. In January 1979 "Stop Your Sobbing" was released in Britain. Soon it was in the Top 30. The followup, "Kid," written by Hynde and produced by Chris Thomas, did well, too. By spring, the Pretenders were selling out performances all over the U.K. In May the band began work on an album, with Thomas producing. *The Pretenders,* released worldwide in January 1980, was universally lauded. "Brass in Pocket" hit #1 in the U.K. and Australia and reached #14 in the U.S. After whipping off another single, "Talk of the Town," for the British market, Hynde brought her band stateside, where its album was rising to #9.

It took the band over a year and a half to produce a followup, although a five-song EP was issued in the interim. Finally, in August 1981 *Pretenders II* (#10) was released to mixed reviews. It included another tune by Ray Davies, "I Go

The Pretenders: Pete Farndon, Chrissie Hynde, Martin Chambers, James Honeyman-Scott

to Sleep," and Hynde showed up so frequently on the Kinks tour that summer that her relationship with Ray Davies soon became public knowledge. (The two never married but had a daughter, Natalie, in 1983.) A 1981 tour of the U.S. was postponed when, in October, Chambers badly injured his hand; the eventual tour was the last time the original Pretenders played together.

Farndon was booted from the group on June 14, 1982; two days later Honeyman-Scott died of a drug overdose. Farndon himself would die of a drug overdose the following April. Surviving members Hynde and Chambers recorded the gorgeous, wistful "Back on the Chain Gang" (dedicated to Honeyman-Scott) with ex-Rockpile guitarist Billy Bremner and Big Country bassist Tony Butler; it hit #5 in 1983. The intro to its flip side, "My City Was Gone" (also featuring Bremner), later became the theme song of Rush Limbaugh's radio program.

Another year passed, however, before the release of the aptly titled *Learning to Crawl,* which introduced new members Robbie McIntosh and Malcolm Foster. The album (#5, 1984) went platinum and spawned hits in "Middle of the Road" (#19, 1984) and "Show Me" (#28, 1984). In May 1984 Hynde married Jim Kerr, lead singer of Simple Minds; the two had a daughter but soon split up. Hynde got married again in 1997, to Colombian sculptor Lucho Brieva.

Since 1986's *Get Close,* the Pretenders have consisted mostly of Hynde and a succession of musicians, with spotty results. "Don't Get Me Wrong" (#10, 1986) was the group's last Top 10 hit. McIntosh went on to play and record with Paul McCartney; former Smiths guitarist Johnny Marr stepped in for the band's remaining tour dates. For *Last of the Independents* (#41, 1994), the band's first album in four years, Chambers came back on board, joined by Adam Seymour, formerly of the Katydids, and ex-Primitives bassist Andy Hobson. The album spawned a Top 40 single in the ballad "I'll Stand by You," and the lineup remained intact for the acoustic live album, *The Isle of View* (#100, 1995) and 1999's *¡Viva El Amor!* (which also featured Hynde's hero Jeff Beck on the track "Legalize Me"). *¡Viva El Amor!*'s cover photo, featuring Hynde holding her fist in the air in the fashion of a classic Colombian propaganda poster, was taken by Linda McCartney a month before her death.

Although the long waits between LPs have dulled her group's once shining commercial career, Hynde remains an influential performer and songwriter. Her performances with the Pretenders on the 1999 Lilith Fair were regarded by many critics as the highlight of the woman-centric festival tour. Hynde is also an outspoken crusader for People for the Ethical Treatment of Animals. In March 2000 she was arrested on felony charges of third-degree criminal mischief in New York for destroying an estimated $1,000 worth of merchandise during a protest of what she termed "black-market" leather from India at a Gap clothing store (a charge the Gap disputes). Manhattan Criminal Court adjourned the case "in contemplation of dismissal," contingent upon Hynde's staying out of trouble for six months.

Lloyd Price

Born Mar. 9, 1933, Kenner, LA
1972—*To the Roots and Back* (GSF) 1986—*Lloyd Price* (Specialty); *Personality Plus; Walkin' the Track* 1990—*Greatest Hits* (Curb) 1991—*Lawdy!* (Specialty) 1993—*Lloyd Price, vol. 2: Heavy Dreams* 1994—*Lloyd Price Sings His Big Ten* (Capitol/Curb) 1998—*Body With Nobody* (KJAC).

Singer/songwriter Lloyd Price was a major figure in the early years of New Orleans rock & roll. "Lawdy Miss Clawdy" (1952), written by Price as a commercial jingle for a local radio station, was a #1 R&B hit. In the next two years, Price had several Top 10 R&B singles, "Oooh-Oooh-Oooh" (#5), "Restless Heart" (#8), and "Ain't It a Shame" (#7), before serving in Korea from 1954 to 1956. Upon his discharge, he relocated to Washington, DC. There he started KRC (Kent Record Company), one of the first black-owned labels, and recorded "Just Because." (He also started one of the first black-owned publishing companies, Lloyd & Logan Music.) Determined not to relinquish creative or financial control of his work, Price was ahead of his time in leasing his recordings to record labels to distribute as opposed to being under contract to a label. Leased to ABC-Paramount in 1957, "Just Because" reached pop #29 and R&B #3. Two years later came Price's greatest success, "Stagger Lee" (#1 pop and R&B, 1958), a reworking of the New Orleans folk song "Stagolee" (also known as "Stack-o-Lee"). The song—a tale of betrayal and violence—had been recorded in various versions dating back to the '20s.

Price's subsequent ABC recordings shifted from the rocking New Orleans style to a mainstream pop sound, as reflected by "Personality" (#2 pop, #1 R&B), "I'm Gonna Get Married" (#3 pop, #1 R&B), "Where Were You (On Our Wedding Day)" (#23 pop), "Come Into My Heart" (#2 R&B), in 1959; "Lady Luck" (#14 pop, #3 R&B) and "Question" (#19 pop, #5 R&B) in 1960. Price was an enterprising businessman during the '60s, operating the Double L and Turntable labels and a New York nightclub called the Turntable. In 1969, after his partner, Harold Logan, was murdered in the Double L offices, Price briefly quit the music business. In 1972, around the same time he left the country for Nigeria, he released a new album, *To the Roots and Back.* In Africa he worked with Don King in promoting music events and the legendary 1974 "Rumble in the Jungle" heavyweight-title bout between Muhammad Ali and George Foreman, later commemorated in the documentary film *When We Were Kings*. He returned to the States in the '80s but performed rarely. In the '90s he began performing again, reactivated his Lloyd & Logan Music, and built a multitrack studio near his home in Westchester, New York. In 1998 he released *Body With Nobody*, his first new album in 26 years, which included hip-hop–flavored versions of "Personality" and "Stagger Lee."

Price received the Pioneer Award from the Rhythm & Blues Foundation in 1994. He was inducted into the Rock and Roll Hall of Fame in 1998.

Maxi Priest

Born Max Alfred Elliott, June 10, 1960, London, Eng.
1985—*You're Safe* (Virgin, U.K.) 1986—*Intentions* 1987—*Maxi* (Virgin) 1990—*Bonafide* (Charisma) 1991—*Best of Me* 1992—*Fe Real* 1996—*Man With the Fun* (Virgin) 1999—*CombiNation.*

Maxi Priest is a soulful British reggae singer who in the late '80s and early '90s managed to win over both Jamaican musical purists and American pop radio. The son of a factory worker, Priest grew up in Southeast London. Reggae was in his genes: He is the nephew of genre pioneer Jacob Miller. Priest entered the music world through carpentry. Having built his own studio at 14, he subsequently left school and began constructing sound systems for London's Saxon International. Soon he was DJ'ing for Saxon's mobile reggae–music stations himself.

Priest's first single, "Hey Little Girl," went to #8 on the British reggae charts in 1983 and became a #1 hit in Jamaica. Virgin signed the artist and released two albums in England before Priest's U.S. debut. The record company showed marketing savvy by convincing Priest to cover Cat Stevens' "Wild World" (#25, 1988) on *Maxi;* with reggae stalwarts Sly and Robbie providing rhythms, the album also appealed to longtime reggae fans.

Priest made his first visit to reggae's home, Jamaica, for the recording of *Bonafide*. With producers including Soul II Soul, dancehall star Gussie Clarke, and Dunbar, the album covered a range of reggae styles. The single "Close to You" (#1, 1990) was Priest's biggest hit. *Best of Me* compiled Priest's singles. In 1991 the singer was featured on Shabba Ranks' "Housecall (Your Body Can't Lie to Me)" (#4 R&B) and Roberta Flack's "Set the Night to Music" (#45 R&B).

Priest's 1992 album *Fe Real* (#46 R&B) yielded two more singles, but only "Groovin' in the Midnight" (#26 R&B) was a chart success. After undergoing contractual problems and a change of labels, Priest returned with *Man With the Fun* (#108 pop, #43 R&B) in 1996. "That Girl," a collaboration with reggae star Shaggy that sampled Booker T. and the MG's' "Green Onions," crossed over to the pop singles charts (#20 pop, #34 R&B). In 1999 Priest released *CombiNation,* a ballad-heavy album that includes a cover of Stevie Wonder's "Golden Lady."

Primus

Formed 1984, San Francisco, CA
Tim "Herb" Alexander (b. Apr. 10, 1965, Cherry Point, NC), drums; Les Claypool (b. Sep. 29, 1963, Richmond, CA), bass, voc.; Todd Huth (b. Mar. 13, 1963, San Leandro, CA), gtr.
1989—(– Huth; + Larry LaLonde [b. Sep. 12, 1968, Richmond, gtr.]) *Suck on This* (Prawn Song) 1990—*Frizzle Fry* (Caroline) 1991—*Sailing the Seas of Cheese* (Interscope) 1992—*Miscellaneous Debris* EP 1993—*Pork Soda* 1995—*Tales From the Punchbowl* 1996—(– Alexander; + Brian "Brain" Mantia, drums) 1997—*Brown Album* 1998—*Rhinoplasty* 2000—*Antipop.*
Sausage (Claypool, bass, voc.; Huth, gtr.; Jay Lane [b. Dec. 15, 1964, San Francisco], drums): 1994—*Riddles Are Abound Tonight* (Interscope).
Les Claypool and the Holy Mackerel: 1996—*Highball With the Devil* (Interscope).
Frog Brigade (Claypool; Huth; Lane; Jeff Chimenti, kybds.; Skerik, sax; Eenor, gtr.): 2001—*Live Frogs: Set 1* (Prawn Song).

A stark amalgam of spacy rhythms, roiling bass, angular guitar, cartoony vocals mixed with sea chanteys, a shot of surreal humor, and a piscene obsession, Primus is one of the leading lights of the alternative scene. The peak of the group's popularity came when it headlined the 1993 Lollapalooza Tour and entered the charts at #7 with its fourth album, *Pork Soda* (#7, 1993). It remains a bridge between the punk, progressive, and jam scenes.

Originally called Primate, the band was the brainchild of bassist Les Claypool (who once auditioned for Metallica and was turned down after attempting to lead them in an Isley Brothers tune), along with guitarist Todd Huth and a drum machine. Alexander was discovered through an ad. Huth left in 1989, replaced by LaLonde, who had played with Claypool in an earlier band, Blind Illusion.

Claypool's father lent the band $1,000 in 1989 to release

Primus: Tim Alexander, Les Claypool, Larry LaLonde

the live *Suck on This.* Caroline reissued the album and released their next, *Frizzle Fry.* They signed with Interscope after owner Ted Fields took them on a fishing trip. *Sailing the Seas of Cheese* (#116, 1993), their major-label debut, has sold over 700,000 copies to date, and the band expanded its audience after opening for Jane's Addiction, Public Enemy, Anthrax, and for U2 on the Zoo TV Tour, setting the foundation for the platinum success of *Pork Soda.* Primus' next release, *Tales From the Punchbowl* (#8, 1995), was almost as popular, benefiting from the impact of the single "Wynona's Big Brown Beaver," which was nominated for a Grammy for Best Hard Rock Performance. Further albums did not fare as well: *Brown Album* (#21, 1997) was the first record with longtime friend and new drummer Brian "Brain" Mantia, while *Rhinoplasty* (#106, 1998) was a collection of covers and two live original songs. The band recorded the theme to the *South Park* animated series in 1998.

In 1999 Primus showed its reach by playing on both Ozzfest (headlined by Black Sabbath) and the Family Values Tour (headlined by Korn and Limp Bizkit), and by releasing *Antipop* (#44), which featured an array of guest players and producers such as Tom Waits, the Police's Stewart Copeland, Metallica's James Hetfield, and Rage Against the Machine's Tom Morello. Despite the group's decreasing chart presence, it remains an extremely popular live band.

In addition to Primus, Claypool has been involved in several side projects. In 1994 he hooked up with old band mate guitarist Huth and drummer Jay Lane to record *Riddles Are Abound Tonight,* which included some of their pre-Primus songs. Abetted by guest musicians, Claypool played most of the instruments on Holy Mackerel's 1996 album *Highball With the Devil.* Frog Brigade, which performs covers and songs by Sausage and Holy Mackerel, is mostly a live outfit. In 2000 Claypool also started performing with Stewart Copeland and Phish's guitarist Trey Anastasio under the name Oysterhead.

Prince

Born Prince Rogers Nelson, June 7, 1958, Minneapolis, MN
1978—*For You* (Warner Bros.) 1979—*Prince* 1980—*Dirty Mind* 1981—*Controversy* 1982—*1999* 1984—*Purple Rain* 1985—*Around the World in a Day* (Paisley Park) 1986—*Parade (Music From the Motion Picture "Under the Cherry Moon")* 1987—*Sign 'O' the Times* 1988—*Lovesexy* 1989—*Batman* (Warner Bros.) 1990—*Graffiti Bridge* (Paisley Park) 1991—*Diamonds and Pearls* 1992—*The Symbol Album* 1993—*The Hits/The B-Sides; The Hits; The Hits 2* 1994—*Come* (Warner Bros.); *The Black Album* 1995—*The Gold Experience* 1996—*Girl 6* soundtrack; *Chaos and Disorder; Emancipation* (NPG/EMI) 1998—*Crystal Ball; Newpower Soul* 1999—*The Vault—Old Friends 4 Sale* (Warner Bros.); *Rave Un2 the Joy Fantastic* (Arista).

One of the most flamboyant, controversial, influential, and popular artists of the '80s, Prince is also one of the least predictable and most mysterious. At a time when comparable megastars such as Michael Jackson, Madonna, and Janet Jackson were delivering an album every three years or so, Prince remained prolific to an almost self-destructive degree—and was given to wayward, self-indulgent career moves (even declaring in the '90s a name change to an unpronounceable symbol) that could alienate even his most ardent supporters. Yet his taut, keyboard-dominated Minneapolis Sound—a hybrid of rock, pop, and funk, with blatantly sexual lyrics—not only influenced his fellow Minneapolis artists the Time and Janet Jackson's producers (and ex-Time members) Jimmy Jam and Terry Lewis, but also impacted much of '80s dance-pop music. And Michael, Madonna, and Janet were comparable to Prince only in terms of star power. None could match the formidable breadth of his talents, which included not just singing and dancing but also composing, producing, and playing instruments (not to mention directing videos and, however ineffectively, movies). In fact, Prince played all the instruments on his first five albums, and has produced himself since signing with Warner Bros. at age 21.

Under the name "Prince Rogers," Prince's father John Nelson was the leader of a Minneapolis-area jazz band, in which his mother was the vocalist. Prince started playing piano at age 7, guitar at 13, and drums at 14, all self-taught. By age 14 he was in a band called Grand Central, which later became Champagne. Four years later, a demo tape he made with engineer Chris Moon reached local businessman Owen Husney. In 1978 Husney negotiated Prince's contract with Warner Bros.

"Soft and Wet" (#92 pop, #12 R&B, 1978) from *For You* introduced his erotic approach, while "I Wanna Be Your Lover" (#11 pop, #1 R&B) and "Why You Wanna Treat Me So Bad?" (#13 R&B) from *Prince* (#22, 1979) suggested his musical range. *Dirty Mind* (#45, 1980)—a loose concept album including songs such as "Head," about oral sex, and "Sister," about incest—established Prince's libidinous image once and for all. One of its few songs that wasn't too obscene for airplay, "Uptown," went to #5 R&B, while "When You Were Mine" became Prince's most widely covered song and a minor comeback hit for Mitch Ryder in 1983 (it was later covered by Cyndi Lauper, among others, as well).

Controversy (#21, 1981) had two hits, the title cut (#70 pop, #3 R&B, 1981) and "Let's Work" (#9 R&B, 1982). *Prince, Dirty Mind,* and *Controversy* all eventually went platinum. For his second album, Prince had formed a racially and sexually mixed touring band that included childhood friend Andre (Anderson) Cymone on bass, Dez Dickerson on guitar, keyboardists Gayle Chapman and Matt Fink, and drummer Bobby "Z" Rivkin. By the *Dirty Mind* tour, Chapman had been replaced by Lisa Coleman. In concert Prince would sometimes strip down to black bikini underpants or finish the set doing "pushups" on a brass bed.

A double album, *1999* (#9, 1982), went platinum, bolstered by the Top 10 singles "Little Red Corvette" (#6, 1983) and "Delirious" (#8, 1983), and the title track (#12, 1982). "Little Red Corvette" was also among the first videos by a black performer to be played regularly on MTV.

Prince "discovered" another Minneapolis band, the Time, whose first two albums went gold (the third went platinum);

Prince

in turn, the Time supplied backup for Vanity 6, a female trio that had a club hit with "Nasty Girl" (Vanity would leave Prince's fold in 1983 to launch an unsuccessful solo career). Prince denied that he was the "Jamie Starr" who produced albums by the Time and Vanity 6. He did take both bands on tour with him, however. After the tour, Dez Dickerson left Prince's band to launch an abortive solo career; he would be replaced by Wendy Melvoin.

Prince vaulted to superstardom in 1984 with *Purple Rain,* a seemingly autobiographical movie set in the Minneapolis club scene and costarring the Time and Apollonia 6 (Patricia "Apollonia" Kotero having replaced Vanity). It was an enormous hit, as was the soundtrack album, which spent 24 weeks atop the chart and sold over 10 million copies, yielding hit singles in "When Doves Cry" (#1, 1984), "Let's Go Crazy" (#1, 1984), "Purple Rain" (#2, 1984), "I Would Die 4 U" (#8, 1984), and "Take Me With U" (#25, 1985). The album marked the first time in his career that Prince had recorded with, and credited, his backing band, which he named the Revolution. The opening act on Prince's 1984 tour was another of his female protégées, Latin percussionist Sheila E. [see entry], the daughter of Santana percussionist Pete Escovedo, who hailed from Oakland, California, and whose album *The Glamorous Life* Prince had produced that year.

At the 1985 Grammy Awards, Prince won Best Group Rock Vocal for "Purple Rain" and R&B Song of the Year for "I Feel for You" (actually from *Prince,* and a hit cover for Chaka Khan in 1984). After the gala, Prince—who for all his sexual exhibitionism onstage was painfully shy offstage—declined an offer to take part in the all-star recording session for "We Are the World" (he later donated the track "4 the Tears in Your Eyes" to the USA for Africa album). That, and his fey demeanor at the 1985 Academy Awards show, where he won a Best Original Score Oscar for *Purple Rain,* were the first signals of Prince's personal eccentricities to his newfound mass audience. In 1985 Prince also wrote Sheena Easton's suggestive hit single "Sugar Walls," under the pseudonym "Alexander Nevermind." And Tipper Gore credited allusions to masturbation in the *Purple Rain* track "Darling Nikki" with inspiring her to form the Parents Music Resource Center and to launch the Senate hearings on offensive rock lyrics, which led to the record industry's "voluntary" album-stickering policy.

Prince followed up *Purple Rain* with the psychedelic *Around the World in a Day,* which topped the chart for three straight weeks but was considered a critical and commercial disappointment. Prince reportedly had to be persuaded to release singles from it, but the album did yield hits in the Beatlesque "Raspberry Beret" (#2, 1985) and the funky "Pop Life" (#7, 1985). Upon the album's release Prince's management announced his retirement from live performance (which would last for two years), and the opening of his own studio and record label, both named Paisley Park—after a track on the new album (which also included a spiritual epic, "The Ladder," which Prince wrote with his previously estranged father). Paisley Park recording acts included the Family (fronted by Wendy Melvoin's twin sister, Susannah), Mazarati (led by Cymone's replacement, Brown Mark), Madhouse (a jazz-funk band led by Prince's sax player Eric Leeds), and Jill Jones (who'd appeared, draped around Lisa Coleman, in the "1999" video). None of them ever had a hit, although the Family's Prince-penned "Nothing Compares 2 U" would later be a massive hit for Sinéad O'Connor.

In spring 1986 Prince was back atop the pop singles chart with "Kiss," a stripped-down return to his funk roots. It would be heard (briefly) in Prince's next movie, *Under the Cherry Moon,* a romantic trifle shot on the French Riviera, with Prince replacing music video auteur Mary Lambert (Madonna's "Like a Virgin," among others) as director midway through production. The film bombed with critics and moviegoers; its soundtrack album *Parade* (#3, 1986) yielded two minor hit singles in "Mountains" (#23, 1986) and "Anotherloverholenyohead" (#63, 1986). On July 1, 1986, Prince played an impromptu live set following the world premiere of *Cherry Moon* in Sheridan, Wyoming (where the winner of an MTV movie-premiere contest lived).

In 1987 Prince fired the Revolution (Wendy and Lisa [see entry] would go on to record as a duo, scoring a minor hit single with "Waterfall") and, retaining only Matt Fink, replaced them with a new, unnamed band featuring Sheila E. on drums. They debuted with the double-album *Sign 'O' the Times* (#6, 1987), widely hailed by critics as a return to form. It yielded hit singles in the stark title track (#3, 1987), the funky Sheena Easton duet "U Got the Look" (#2, 1987), and the poppy "I Could Never Take the Place of Your Man" (#10, 1987). Prince toured Europe with a theatrically choreographed show, but rather than touring the U.S. released a film of a concert shot in Rotterdam, Holland.

In late 1987 rumors circulated of a new Prince project, *The Black Album,* said to consist of musically and lyrically raw funk tracks. It was not officially released until late 1994, but until then it became one of the most bootlegged LPs in pop history (tapes were stolen from Warner's German pressing plant). His next official release was the mild *Lovesexy* (#11, 1988), which got lackluster reviews and yielded only one hit, "Alphabet Street" (#8, 1988), but did prompt Prince's first U.S. tour in four years, performed on a rotating stage that Prince entered in a pink Cadillac.

In 1989 Prince had his first chart-topping album in four years with his soundtrack for director Tim Burton's big-budget film *Batman;* "Batdance" was Prince's first #1 since "Kiss." His half-sister Lorna Nelson lost a lawsuit claiming he'd stolen her lyrics for "U Got the Look." Two months after the release of his *Batman* album, Prince—who'd already written and produced an album for Paisley Park signee Mavis Staples and undertaken productions for the Time's Morris Day and Jerome Benton and *Batman* star Kim Basinger—released *Graffiti Bridge,* a film that seemed to be a delayed sequel to *Purple Rain,* again pitting Prince against the Time on the Minneapolis club scene. Prince's love interest was played by Ingrid Chavez, who would gain greater fame for helping Lenny Kravitz write Madonna's hit "Justify My Love" (though she'd have to sue Kravitz to get a composing credit). The movie was another critical and commercial disaster; the soundtrack album (#6, 1990) yielded the hit "Thieves in the Temple" (#6, 1990) and Tevin Campbell's Prince-penned "Round and Round" (#12, 1991).

In January 1991, at his recently opened Glam Slam nightclub in Minneapolis, Prince unveiled a new band, the New Power Generation, who would not tour the U.S. until 1993. The band included an unimpressive rapping dancer (Anthony "Tony M" Mosely), in Prince's first nod to hip-hop, which had claimed a significant share of his black-pop audience and with which he never seemed comfortable musically. The following month Prince was sued for severance pay and punitive damages by his ex-managers, Robert Cavallo, Joseph Ruffalo, and Steven Fargnoli, whom Prince had fired in 1988. Eight months later he released his fifth album in five years, *Diamonds and Pearls* (#3, 1991), which spawned Top 10 hits in the lascivious "Gett Off" (#21, 1991), "Cream" (#1, 1991), and the title track (#3, 1992). Warner Bros. made Prince a vice president when he re-signed with the label in 1992. His next album (#5, 1992) was titled after an unpronounceable merger of the male and female gender symbols; its hit singles included "7" (#8, 1992), "My Name Is Prince" (#36, 1992), and the profane "Sexy M.F." (#66, 1992). Prince produced an album for yet another female protégée, Carmen Electra, and New York's Joffrey Ballet announced that it was choreographing a four-part ballet to Prince's music, called *Billboards* (it would premiere at the University of Iowa in October 1993).

In September 1993 Prince pulled the most eccentric move of his career, changing his name to the unpronounceable symbol with which he'd titled his last album. "Symbol Man," "Glyph," or "the artist formerly known as Prince"—shortened to the Artist—as he was now known, suffered widespread ridicule—followed by a business setback in February 1994, when Warner Bros. dropped its distribution deal with Paisley Park Records, effectively putting the label out of business. Two weeks later the Artist released a new single, "The Most Beautiful Girl in the World" (#3 pop, #2 R&B), not on Warners but on independent Bellmark Records, which had had a huge hit the previous summer with Tag Team's "Whoomp! There It Is"; Warners said it allowed this "experiment" at the Artist's request but would release his future product.

Come (#15 pop, #2 R&B) released later that year, was credited to "Prince (1958–1993)," and spawned two singles drawn from the label's backlog of Prince recordings: "Letitgo" (#31 pop, #10 R&B) and "Space" (#71 R&B). The legit *Black Album* (#47 pop, #18 R&B) was finally released two weeks before Christmas. As his relationship with the label continued to wane, the Artist began appearing with the word *slave* scrawled on his cheek. Warners released four more albums: *The Gold Experience* (#6 pop, #2 R&B, 1995), which scored a hit in "I Hate U" (#12 pop, #3 R&B) but was more notorious for the racy track "P Control"; the soundtrack to Spike Lee's movie *Girl 6* (#75 pop, #15 R&B, 1996); and *Chaos and Disorder* (#26 pop, 1996). (The archival *The Vault—Old Friends 4 Sale* was released in 1999.) Meanwhile, the Artist issued the triple-CD set *Emancipation* (#2 R&B, 1996) on his own New Power Generation (NPG) label, which was distributed through Capitol/EMI. The album went double platinum, and a remake of the Stylistics' 1972 hit "Betcha by Golly Wow" reached #10 on the R&B chart. The Artist also wed Mayte García, a 22-year-old dancer and vocalist in his band. Their son reportedly died of a rare disorder called Pfeiffer's Syndrome shortly after birth in November 1996. Culling tracks from his archives, the Artist put out the four-CD compilaton *Crystal Ball* (#62 pop, #59 R&B) in 1998, which he packaged in a clear plastic ball and marketed through his Web site by offering a fifth bonus disc. It sold 250,000 copies. Five months later came the more conventionally conceived single album, *Newpower Soul* (#22 pop, #9 R&B).

As the millennium loomed, so did the Warners rerelease of "1999" (#45 R&B, 1999) and the Artist's own *1999 (The New Master)* EP. That fall, *Rave Un2 the Joy Fantastic* (#18 pop, #8 R&B, 1999) was released through a licensing arrangement with Arista. (Stating his displeasure with Arista's marketing of the album, the Artist would later declare his intention to release a new version through his Web site called *Rave In2 the Joy Fantastic.*) The album, which was produced by "Prince," featured guest appearances by folk-rock singer Ani DiFranco and rapper Chuck D—among others—both performers whom the Artist admired for distributing their music independently. With the expiration of his Warner/Chappell publishing contract on December 31, 1999, the Artist announced the following May that he was reclaiming his given name.

John Prine

Born Oct. 10, 1946, Maywood, IL
1971—*John Prine* (Atlantic) 1972—*Diamonds in the Rough*

1973—*Sweet Revenge* 1975—*Common Sense* 1976—*Prime Prine—The Best of John Prine* 1978—*Bruised Orange* (Asylum) 1979—*Pink Cadillac* 1980—*Storm Windows* 1984—*Aimless Love* (Oh Boy) 1986—*German Afternoons* 1988—*John Prine Live* 1991—*The Missing Years* 1993—*Great Days: The John Prine Anthology* (Rhino) 1995—*Lost Dogs & Mixed Blessings* (Oh Boy) 1997—*Live on Tour* 1999—*In Spite of Ourselves* 2000—*Souvenirs.*

John Prine is a critically acclaimed singer/songwriter who has gone from solo acoustic folk to hard country to rockabilly to soft rock, all the while maintaining his hardheaded vision of white proletarian America.

Prine learned guitar from his father and played the Chicago coffeehouse circuit while working at the post office. With his friend and sometime production cohort Steve Goodman, Prine graduated from the Chicago folk scene. Paul Anka liked some of Prine's Hank Williams–influenced songs and was instrumental in landing him a recording contract. In 1971 Prine went to Memphis and cut his debut. That LP's most notable song may have been "Sam Stone," a bleak portrait of a drug-addicted Vietnam veteran, which aptly demonstrated Prine's laconic, drawling delivery.

Though his own commercial success was meager, other artists began recording his songs: the Everly Brothers did "Paradise," and both Joan Baez and Bette Midler recorded "Hello in There." *Common Sense* saw Prine shocking his folk audience by using hard-rock rhythms and a guttural singing style. *Bruised Orange*, produced by Goodman, returned Prine to the acoustic format of *Diamonds in the Rough*, while *Pink Cadillac* was an electric rockabilly album produced by Sam Phillips and his son Knox at Sun Studios.

Prine formed his own label, Oh Boy Records, in 1983. His second album for the label, the countryish *German Afternoons*, earned a Grammy Award nomination for Best Contemporary Folk Recording. After releasing his first live album in 1988, Prine won the Best Contemporary Folk Grammy for *The Missing Years*, which was produced by Howie Epstein of Tom Petty's Heartbreakers, and had guest appearances by Petty, Bruce Springsteen, and Bonnie Raitt (who had been singing Prine's "Angel From Montgomery" in concert for years).

After starting to record *In Spite of Ourselves* in 1997, he discovered a cancerous growth on his neck. In 1998 George Strait got a #1 C&W hit with one of Prine's compositions, "I Just Want to Dance With You"; the ensuing financial windfall helped Prine pay his medical bills. He beat the cancer and, after an interruption of nearly two years, resumed work on the album. In a premiere for Prine, *In Spite of Ourselves* (#21 C&W, 1999) was made up of covers (save for the title song) and each track was a duet with a different female singer—guests included Emmylou Harris, Iris DeMent, Lucinda Williams, Patty Loveless, and Melba Montgomery. In 2000 Prine covered himself with *Souvenirs*, on which he offered new studio recordings of some of his classic material.

Prine made his movie acting debut with a small role in John Mellencamp's 1992 *Falling From Grace*, then appeared in Billy Bob Thornton's *Daddy and Them* (slated for a 2001 release). He retains a cult following for his down-to-earth, unadorned insights.

P.J. Proby

Born James Marcus Smith, Nov. 6, 1938, Houston, TX
1964—*I Am P.J. Proby* (Liberty) 1965—*P.J. Proby; P.J. Proby's in Town; Somewhere* 1967—*Enigma; Phenomenon* 1968—*What's Wrong With My World; Believe It or Not* 1969—*Three Week Hero* 1996—*EP Collection* (See for Miles).

P.J. Proby is a Presleyesque singer who was always more popular in England than in his native America, though even there, his chart appearances became increasingly rare after 1968. Proby's big break came when British TV producer Jack Good brought him to the U.K. for a Beatles special in 1964; he hit with the Good-produced "Hold Me" (#70 U.S., #3 U.K.), a frantic revival of a 1939 ballad. Prior to that, Proby had been living in Hollywood, doing odd jobs, playing bit parts in films, and recording demos like "Jet Powers." After "Hold Me," followups failed to generate comparable success, and he switched styles; he began singing melodramatic versions of tunes from the Broadway musical *West Side Story*, for example.

Proby toured England in 1965 with Cilla Black but was expelled from the country later that year after a series of incidents in which he split his velvet trousers onstage. In 1967 his tour choreographer was future Runaways Svengali Kim Fowley. That year he had his biggest U.S. hit with "Niki Hoeky" (#23). By 1968, though, Proby was bankrupt. He was lured back to England by Good in 1971 to appear in *Catch My Soul*, a rock adaptation of *Othello*. Proby also played the older Elvis Presley in the West End musical *Elvis* in 1977. After years as a steady-drawing revival act in England, Proby unexpectedly teamed up with the Dutch classical-rock band Focus in 1978 for the *Focus con Proby* LP. In the '80s he recorded for the British label Savoy and did songs inspired by the Sex Pistols and David Bowie's *"Heroes."* By the late '90s, many of his original albums had been reissued on CD by the tiny label See for Miles.

Procol Harum

Formed 1966, London, Eng.
Gary Brooker (b. May 29, 1945, Eng.), piano, voc.; Keith Reid (b. ca. 1948), lyrics; Matthew Fisher (b. Mar. 7, 1946, Eng.), organ; Ray Royer (b. Oct. 8, 1945, Eng.), gtr.; Dave Knights (b. June 28, 1945, Eng.), bass; Bobby Harrison (b. June 28, 1943, Eng.), drums.
1967—(– Royer; – Harrison; + Robin Trower [b. Mar. 9, 1945, London], gtr.; + B.J. Wilson [b. Barrie James Wilson, Mar. 18, 1947, Eng.; d. Oct. 8, 1990], drums) *Procol Harum* (Deram) 1968—*Shine On Brightly* (A&M) 1969—*A Salty Dog* 1970—(– Fisher; – Knights; + Chris Copping [b. Aug. 29, 1945, Eng.], bass, organ) *Home* 1971—*Broken Barricades* (– Trower; + Dave Ball [b. Mar. 30, 1950], gtr.; + Alan Cartwright [b. Oct. 10, 1945], bass) 1972—*Live in Concert* (– Ball; + Mick

Grabham, gtr.) 1973—*Grand Hotel* (Chrysalis) 1974—*Exotic Birds and Fruit* 1975—*Procol Ninth* 1976—(– Cartwright; + Pete Solley, organ; Copping switches to bass) 1977—*Something Magic* (group disbands) 1991—(group re-forms: Brooker; Trower; Fisher; Reid; + Dave Bronze, bass; + Mark Brzezicki, drums) *The Prodigal Stranger* (Zoo) 1995—*The Long Goodbye* (RCA Victor) 2000—*BBC Live in Concert* (Fuel 2000).
Gary Brooker solo: 1979—*No More Fear of Flying* (Chrysalis) 1982—*Lead Me to the Water* (Mercury) 1984—*Echoes in the Night*.
Matthew Fisher solo: 1973—*Journeys End* (RCA) 1980—*Matthew Fisher* (A&M).

With the 1967 worldwide smash "A Whiter Shade of Pale"—a combination of mystical lyrics, a somber tempo, and an organ line lifted directly from Bach's *Suite No. 3 in D major*—Procol Harum established itself, along with the Moody Blues, as an early British "classical rock" band. Though the band never matched that spectacular success, "A Whiter Shade of Pale" has outlasted the Summer of Love. It has sold over 6 million copies worldwide and has been covered in soul, jazz, and country versions.

The band—whose only other U.S. hit was an orchestrated 1972 reworking of 1967's "Conquistador"—included only one member with classical training: Matthew Fisher, who studied at the Guildhall School of Music. Procol Harum actually began as an R&B band, the Paramounts (Gary Brooker, Robin Trower, Chris Copping, and B.J. Wilson), in London's Southend section in 1963. The Paramounts made several singles, but only a cover of "Little Bitty Pretty One" achieved any local success, and they broke up in 1966.

Later that year Brooker met lyricist Keith Reid (who was always listed as a full-fledged band member on the group's albums), and they formed a band—with Fisher, Ray Royer, Dave Knights, and Bobby Harrison—to record their songs. The name Procol Harum allegedly came from the name of a friend's cat (they often jokingly referred to themselves as the "Purple Horrors"); roughly translated from Latin, it means "beyond these things." The original Procol Harum ended up recording only one single, the crucial "A Whiter Shade of Pale" (on which sessionman Bill Eyden replaced Harrison).

In the wake of the single's success (repeated to a somewhat lesser degree in the U.K. by "Homburg" in mid-1967), Royer and Harrison were replaced by Trower and Wilson, and this lineup recorded the first three Procol Harum albums.

In late 1969 Fisher and Knights departed (Fisher has since recorded solo albums) and were replaced by Copping. *Home* saw Trower leading the band in a harder-rocking direction. The same held true for *Broken Barricades*, but the guitarist's Jimi Hendrix–inspired hard-rock leanings were never fully integrated and seemed at odds with the band's stately pace and Reid's existential-visionary lyrics. Trower left in July 1971. He went on to form the short-lived Jude with British R&B singer Frankie Miller and then the highly successful Robin Trower Band, a Hendrixian power trio, whose 1973 debut, *Twice Removed From Yesterday*, was produced by Fisher.

With new guitarist Dave Ball, Copping concentrating on organ, and new bassist Alan Cartwright, the band recorded *Live in Concert* (#5, 1972) with the Edmonton Symphony Orchestra and the Da Camera Singers. The success of the symphonic "Conquistador" remake caused a minor resurgence in sales, on which the group failed to capitalize with *Grand Hotel* (#21, 1973), a mélange of orchestral epics and harder-rocking tunes. By the time of *Hotel*, Ball had left to form Bedlam and was replaced by ex-Cochise guitarist Mick Grabham. Two more albums, *Exotic Birds and Fruit* and *Procol Ninth*, went nowhere. After a two-year hiatus, the band tried one last time with *Something Magic*—produced by Jerry Leiber and Mike Stoller—then broke up for good. After another two years, during which he played in the 1979 Concerts for Kampuchea, Brooker made a solo album, *No More Fear of Flying*, which was both a critical and commercial disappointment. In 1981 he played piano on Eric Clapton's LP *Another Ticket*, and in 1982 and 1984 he released two more solo records.

In 1991, two years after the death of B.J. Wilson, Brooker, Fisher, Reid, and Trower reunited to record *The Prodigal Stranger*. With Geoff Whitehorn in place of Trower, and bassist Dave Bronze and Big Country drummer Mark Brzezicki, they toured and continue to perform occasionally. Brooker also toured with the Prague Symphony. In 1995 the band released *The Long Goodbye*, which featured old songs rearranged for orchestra and guest Tom Jones on one song. *BBC Live in Concert* came out in 2000 but is a 1974 recording.

Prodigy

Formed 1990, London, Eng.
Liam Howlett (b. Aug. 21, 1971, Braintree, Eng.), instruments; Keith Flint (b. Mar. 27 or Sep. 17, 1969, London), voc.; Leeroy Thornhill (b. Oct. 7 or 8, 1969, Barking, Eng.), dancer; Maxim Reality (b. Keith "Keeti" Palmer, Mar. 21, 1967, Peterborough, Eng.), voc.
1991—*What Evil Lurks* EP (XL, U.K.) 1992—*The Prodigy Experience* (Elektra) 1994—*Music for the Jilted Generation* (Mute) 1997—*The Fat of the Land* (Maverick) 1999—*The Dirtchamber Sessions, vol. 1* (XL/Beggars Banquet) 2000—(– Thornhill) 2001—*Always Outnumbered, Never Outgunned*.
Maxim solo: 2000—*Hell's Kitchen* (XL, U.K.).
Leeroy Thornhill solo as Flightcrank: 2000—*Twisted* EP (Copasetik).

With the help of well-chosen samples, Prodigy took electronica-driven studio wizardry and successfully mixed it with rock's trademark sense of aggression and showmanship. Born outside London, Liam Howlett was first attracted to two-tone ska. He was in the hip-hop group Cut to Kill for a while, then discovered acid house in the late '80s, which is when he started both DJ'ing in clubs and producing home recordings. Keith Flint and Leeroy Thornhill heard Howlett spin and offered to dance at his gigs—and thus Prodigy was born in 1990. Prodigy honed its live skills by adding reggae vocalist Maxim Reality (who usually goes simply by Maxim), building upon the larger-than-life presence of Flint (who sported multiple body piercings and multicolored hair), and touring constantly—a rare occurrence for a club-bred act. One of Howlett's self-releases, the EP *What Evil Lurks,* was reissued by XL in 1991. The next single, "Charly," based on a cartoon sample, was a surprise Top 10 hit in the U.K. By 1992, Prodigy had enough singles to collect them on *The Prodigy Experience,* which went gold in England but bombed so badly in the U.S. that the band was dropped by its American label, Elektra. In 1994 *Music for the Jilted Generation* entered the U.K. chart at #1. Its aggressive mix of samples and break beats was also nominated for the Mercury Prize. The album did not fare as well in the U.S., peaking at #198.

Prodigy finally got its first chart-topping song in the U.K. with "Firestarter." Originally released in March 1996, it boasted lead vocals by Flint and samples of the Breeders and the Art of Noise. This success led to a bidding war in the U.S.; the group signed to Maverick. "Firestarter" (#30, 1997) became Prodigy's breakthrough single in the U.S. *The Fat of the Land* was released seven months afterward, but the band had kept the momentum going and, fueled by gigantic hype, the album entered the chart at #1 in the U.S. and 23 other countries; it went on to sell 2.3 million copies. In America, Prodigy became many rock fans' point of entry into dance music, offering an immediately identifiable frontman in Flint, rocklike energy and volume, sampled guitar riffs, and even a cover of L7's "Fuel My Fire." "Smack My Bitch Up" (#89, 1997), which sampled cult hip-hop band Ultramagnetic MC's, was widely criticized for being misogynistic. The group succumbed to Wal-Mart's demand that the title be bleeped on pressings sold by the chain.

For all intents and purposes Howlett *is* Prodigy; he's the only member of the band contracted to a label, and though it was credited as "Prodigy Present," *The Dirtchamber Sessions Volume 1* actually was a mix CD by Howlett, who put it together as both a tribute to artists who had influenced him, from Grandmaster Flash to Jane's Addiction, and as a tip of the hat to electronica contemporaries such as Fatboy Slim and the Chemical Brothers. In April 2000, with Prodigy back in the studio working on *Always Outnumbered, Never Outgunned,* Thornhill left to pursue a solo career as Flightcrank. That same year, Maxim released a solo album.

Professor Longhair

Born Henry Roeland Byrd, Dec. 19, 1918, Bogalusa, LA; died Jan. 30, 1980, New Orleans, LA
1972—*New Orleans Piano* (Atlantic) 1975—*Rock 'n' Roll Gumbo* (Barclay) 1978—*Live on the Queen Mary* (Harvest) 1980—*Crawfish Fiesta* (Alligator) 1981—*Mardi Gras in New Orleans* (Nighthawk) 1982—*The Last Mardi Gras* (Atlantic) 1987—*Houseparty New Orleans Style* (Rounder) 1989—*New Orleans Piano (Blues Originals, vol. 2)* (Atlantic) 1993—*'Fess: The Professor Longhair Anthology* (Rhino).

Professor Longhair originated one of the classic styles of rock & roll piano playing, a New Orleans potpourri—ragtime, jazz, Delta blues, zydeco, West Indian, and Afro-Cuban dances—distilled into boogie-woogie bass lines in the left hand and rolling arpeggios in the right. It was the style popularized by Fats Domino, Huey "Piano" Smith, Allen Toussaint, Dr. John, and scores of others.

Henry Byrd first played piano when, as a boy, he discovered an abandoned upright in a New Orleans alley. Recalling everything he'd heard while dancing for tips outside nightclubs and behind parade bands, he taught himself to play. It was not until he was 30, however, that he began to work professionally as a musician; before then he'd had stints as a prizefighter, a gambler, and a vaudeville dancer. In 1949 he formed a quintet called Professor Longhair and His Shuffling Hungarians, which included Robert Parker on tenor sax, and recorded four songs—"She Ain't Got No Hair," "Mardi Gras in New Orleans," "Professor Longhair's Boogie," and "Bye Bye Baby"—on the Star Talent label.

The following year, the Professor was signed to Mercury and rerecorded "She Ain't Got No Hair" under the title "Baldhead," which reached #5 on *Billboard*'s R&B chart. Longhair later recorded on over a dozen labels, while a combination of poor health and mismanagement kept his career from being established. He received virtually nothing for "Go to the Mardi Gras," his 1959 remake of his own "Mardi Gras in New Orleans," which became a theme song of the annual carnival. Although "Big Chief" was a modest hit in the Louisiana area for him and Earl King in 1964, he soon after left the music business and took up manual labor to support himself and his family.

In 1971 Longhair was rediscovered by talent scouts for the New Orleans Jazz and Heritage Festival; thereafter he performed at every New Orleans Festival until his death and appeared on the 1976 live Festival album. His comeback also took him to the Newport Folk Festival in 1973 and to several festivals in Europe. In the last decade of his life, Atlantic released a collection of his vintage recordings, and he put out three newly recorded albums. Shortly before his death from a heart attack, he was engaged to tour with the Clash. In 1991 he was inducted into the Rock and Roll Hall of Fame.

Psychedelic Furs

Formed 1978, London, Eng.
Richard Butler (b. June 5, 1956, Kingston-upon-Thames, Eng.), voc.; Tim Butler (b. Dec. 7, 1958, Eng.), bass; Duncan Kilburn (b. Eng.), sax; Roger Morris (b. Eng.), gtr.
1978—(+ John Ashton [b. Nov. 30, 1957, Eng.], gtr.) 1979—(+ Vince Ely [b. Eng.], drums) 1980—*The Psychedelic Furs* (Columbia) 1981—*Talk, Talk, Talk* (– Kilburn; – Morris) 1982—*Forever Now* (– Ely; + Phil Calvert, drums) 1984—*Mirror Moves* (– Calvert; + Paul Garisto, drums) 1987—*Midnight to Midnight* (– Garisto; + Ely; + Mars Williams, gtr.; + Joe McGinty, kybds.) 1988—*All of This and Nothing* 1989—*Book of Days* (+ Knox Chandler, gtr., cello) 1990—

(– Ely; + Don Yallech, drums) 1991—*World Outside* (group disbands) 1994—*Here Came the Psychedelic Furs: B-Sides & Lost Grooves* (Legacy) 1996—*In the Pink* (Sony Special Products) 1997—*Should God Forget: A Retrospective* (Columbia) 2001—*Greatest Hits* (Legacy).
Love Spit Love, formed 1991: R. Butler; T. Butler; Richard Fortus, gtr.; Frank Ferrer, drums.
1994—*Love Spit Love* (Imago) 1997—*Trysome Eatone* (Maverick).

Though their name sounded psychedelic, the Furs' sound was very much a product of punk. Ironically, the group would become most closely associated with its very unpunklike "Pretty in Pink." The group began in early 1978 when leader, vocalist, and songwriter Richard Butler joined with his younger brother Tim, Duncan Kilburn, and Roger Morris. They decided on the name because it would stand out from all the S&M-named bands of the time and pay homage to their psychedelic-era idols like the Doors, the early Stooges, and the Velvet Underground.

Richard Butler had previously been an art student in college, but around his graduation he decided to pursue music, although he knew little about playing. In November 1978 John Ashton joined on second guitar, and in spring 1979 they added drummer Vince Ely. The band's early dirges (which it describes as "beautiful chaos") were played by BBC disc jockey John Peel, which led to the Furs' signing with Columbia. Their debut was produced by Steve Lillywhite and Howard Thompson, with two tracks on the U.S. version produced by Martin Hannett. Though well received, it sold only moderately, as did their 1981 followup, *Talk, Talk, Talk* (#89), despite its clearer lyrics and production (this time all by Lillywhite). The album is notable for containing the original version of "Pretty in Pink."

Despite significant MTV exposure and a high profile with college-radio audiences, the Psychedelic Furs sold only moderately here and at home. The group's third album, the gold *Forever Now* (#61, 1982), was produced by Todd Rundgren and featured brass and strings; it included the Furs' first U.S. hit, "Love My Way" (#44, 1983). *Mirror Moves* (#43, 1984) featured "Heaven," a U.K. Top 30 single, and the group mounted a large international tour.

Around this time director John Hughes informed the group that he'd written a movie script based on "Pretty in Pink." The Psychedelic Furs' rerecorded version of the 1981 album track hit #41 and was included on the career retrospective *All of This and Nothing* (#102, 1988) and the *Pretty in Pink* soundtrack. Previous to this, the group released its highest-charting LP, *Midnight to Midnight* (#29, 1987), featuring "Heartbreak Beat" (#27, 1987), its sole Top 30 U.S. single. Throughout the Psychedelic Furs' history, members have come and gone, with the Butler brothers and John Ashton the constants. Neither of the group's last two studio albums—*Book of Days* and *World Outside*—improved its fortunes, and in 1991 the Psychedelic Furs broke up.

Richard Butler, with brother Tim, started a new group, Love Spit Love. The group's debut album spent one week on the chart, at #195; the single, "Am I Wrong," peaked at #83 in 1994. Its second release, *Trysome Eatone*, followed three years later. In 2000 the Psychedelic Furs reunited for a summer tour before releasing a greatest-hits collection in 2001.

Psychic TV

Formed 1981, London, Eng.
Genesis P-Orridge (b. Neil Megson, May 22, 1949, Manchester, Eng.).
1988—*Allegory and Self* (Revolver) 1990—*Towards Thee Infinite Beat* (Wax Trax!); *Beyond Thee Infinite Beat* 1994—*Hex Sex: The Singles, pt. 1; Pagan Day* (Cleopatra) 1995—*Godstar: The Singles, pt. 2* 1996—*Trip Reset* 1998—*Origin of the Species* (Invisible) 1999—*"Origin of the Species" Volume Too!; Best Ov Time's Up* (Cleopatra).

Confrontational, mercurial, veering from the unlistenable to achingly pretty pop, the self-proclaimed "Temple ov Psychick Youth," Psychic TV has a mission: to provide "the most important work . . . in the popular medium." Their albums, mixtures of dada, pop, and spoken word, embrace everything from side-long excursions into white noise to wispy tunes to ethnic music to found-sound collages.

It all makes sense when you discover the "collective" is led by Genesis P-Orridge, a founding member (along with Chris Carter, Cosey Fanni Tutti, and Peter Christopherson) of Throbbing Gristle. Schooled in the same situationist thought and theories of media manipulation Malcolm McLaren used to promote the Sex Pistols, Throbbing Gristle was more a group of performance artists than a pop band in their four-year existence (1975–1979). Drawing on William Burroughs and Philip K. Dick, they viewed the world as a dysfunctional, postindustrial wasteland, and their confrontational music and multimedia performances were designed to shake listeners from their acquiescence.

Psychic TV continued Throbbing Gristle's musical and media guerrilla tactics. Originally P-Orridge With Peter Christopherson, P-Orridge then insisted the band was a collective with no set lineup. Some members (P-Orridge's wife at the time, Paula Brooking, John Gosling, and Richard Daws among them) remained through many of the band's numerous metamorphoses. While only a few Psychic TV albums have been issued in the U.S., the band's output was steady. In the mid-'80s for instance, they announced that they would release 23 live albums, one a month, on the 23rd of each month. Though they didn't quite make it, the 14 albums they managed (most of which came out in 1987) were enough to put them in the *Guinness Book of World Records*. *Allegory and Self* (1988), their first American release, contains Psychic TV's 1986 minor British hit, "Godstar" (#67 U.K.), a pop song about Brian Jones. But soon afterward, P-Orridge changed tactics. Exposed to house records in 1986, he became enamored of dance music, and with the albums *Towards the Infinite Beat* and *Beyond* . . . he moved into the realm of techno and rave, extended grooves with a noise overlay, accompanied in concert by video and slide shows. Often credited as introducing the term "acid house" in England, P-Orridge also released the influential *Jack the Tab* compilation, which actually consisted of him and collaborators such as Dave Ball (ex–Soft Cell) and Larry Thrasher under various pseudonyms. This late-'80s output was later collected on both *Origin of the Species* two-CD sets.

In 1992 P-Orridge's Brighton house was raided by the British authorities after a television show alleged that he was involved in a Satanic cult—an allegation based on what turned out to be nothing more than an old Psychic TV video. P-Orridge moved to the U.S., where he has been living ever since. In the mid-'90s he launched events titled "Transmedia Evenings," which consisted of multimedia collages and spoken word, with Thrasher. P-Orridge ended Psychic TV in 1996 and now concentrates on two projects, Splinter Test (with Thrasher) and Thee Majesty (with various collaborators). In 1995 he was badly injured after trying to escape a fire in producer Rick Rubin's studio; he was awarded close to $2 million in damages in 1998.

Public Enemy

Formed 1982, Garden City, NY
Chuck D (b. Carlton Ridenhour, Aug. 1, 1960, NY), voc.; Flavor Flav (b. William Drayton, Mar. 16, 1959, NY), voc.; Terminator X (b. Norman Lee Rogers, Aug. 25, 1966, NY), DJ; Professor Griff (b. Richard Griffin), minister of information.
1987—*Yo! Bum Rush the Show* (Def Jam) 1988—*It Takes a Nation of Millions to Hold Us Back* 1990—*Fear of a Black Planet* 1991—*Apocalypse 91 . . . The Enemy Strikes Back* 1992—*Greatest Misses* 1994—*Muse Sick-N-Hour Mess Age* 1998—*He Got Game* 1999—*There's a Poison Goin' On* (Atomic Pop).
Chuck D solo: 1996—*The Autobiography of Mistachuck* (Mercury).
Professor Griff solo: 1990—*Pawns in the Game* (Luke Records) 1991—*Kao's II Wiz*7*Dome* 1992—*Disturb N tha Peace* 1998—*Blood of the Profit* (Blackheart).
Terminator X solo: 1991—*Terminator X and the Valley of the Jeep Beets* (RAL) 1994—*Terminator X and the Godfathers of Threatt: Super Bad.*
Chuck D and Professor Griff with Confrontation Camp: 2001—*Objects in the Mirror Are Closer Than They Appear* (Artemis).

Arguably the most important and politically controversial group of its time, Public Enemy introduced a hard, intense, hip-hop sound and vocal delivery that changed the course of rap and influenced a generation of artists. The group's inventive production team, the Bomb Squad, tailored a unique, noisy, layered avant-garde-inspired pop sound that incorporated sirens, skittering turntable scratches, and cleverly juxtaposed musical and spoken samples. PE's songs were characterized by lead rapper Chuck D's politically charged rhymes delivered in a booming, authoritarian voice, and his sidekick/jester, Flavor Flav, who broke in with taunts, teases, and questions.

The members of Public Enemy came together at Adelphi University on Long Island, where Carlton Ridenhour studied graphic design and worked at student radio station WBAU. There he met Hank Shocklee (future brainchild of the Bomb Squad) and Bill Stephney (future Def Jam executive), with whom he struck up a friendship, talking philosophy, politics, and hip-hop late into the night. After rapping over a track Shocklee had created, "Public Enemy No. 1," Ridenhour started appearing regularly on Stephney's radio show as Chuckie D. Def Jam cofounder Rick Rubin heard a tape of the rap and started calling Ridenhour.

At first the rapper shunned Rubin, feeling he was too old to begin a career as an entertainer. But he eventually came up with an elaborate plan that involved Shocklee as producer, Stephney as marketer, and DJ Norman Rogers on the turntables. He recruited his Nation of Islam cohort Richard Griffin to coordinate the group's backup dancers, the Security of the First World (S1W), whose members carried fake Uzis and did stiff, martial-arts moves as a parody of Motown-era dancers. Ridenhour enrolled his old friend William Drayton, who as Flavor Flav would act as a foil to Chuck D's more sober character.

Calling themselves "prophets of rage," Public Enemy released their debut album, *Yo!, Bum Rush the Show,* in 1987. A more sophisticated version of early East Coast gangsta rappers like Boogie Down Productions or Schoolly D, the group at first went nearly unnoticed except by hip-hop insiders and New York critics. The second album, *It Takes a Nation of Millions to Hold Us Back,* took the pop world by storm. Reaching #42 (#1 R&B, 1988), it was immediately hailed as hip-hop's masterpiece and eventually sold a million copies. *Nation* contained the minor hit "Bring the Noise" (#56 R&B, 1988), which foreshadowed PE's knack for controversy, with Chuck D calling Black Muslim leader Louis Farrakhan a prophet. Having referred to rap as "CNN for black culture," he castigates white-controlled media in "Don't Believe the Hype" (#18 R&B, 1988).

In May 1989, just after the group did "Fight the Power" (#20 R&B, 1989), the theme song for Spike Lee's film *Do the Right Thing,* Professor Griff, who had previously made racist comments onstage, dropped a verbal bomb. In an interview with the *Washington Times,* he said Jews are responsible for "the majority of wickedness that goes on across the globe." PE leader Chuck D responded indecisively, first firing Griff, then reinstating him, then temporarily disbanding the group. When Griff then attacked his band mates in another interview, he was dismissed permanently. Chuck D responded to the fiasco by writing "Welcome to the Terrordome" (#15 R&B, 1990), a ferociously noisy track in which the rapper asserts, "they got me like Jesus." That lyric fanned the coals of controversy yet again, with Chuck D himself being branded an anti-Semite.

PE followed with its first Top 10 album, *Fear of a Black Planet* (#10 pop, #3 R&B, 1990), which explored the nature of white racism in songs like "Burn Hollywood Burn" and "911 Is a Joke" (#15 R&B, 1990), and called on African-Americans to unite in "Brothers Gonna Work It Out" (#20 R&B, 1990) and "War at 33⅓." By the end of 1990, DJ Terminator X had left for a solo career, followed by the exits of Bomb Squad members Shocklee and Stephney. But Public Enemy's momentum only accelerated. Upon its release in 1991, *Apocalypse 91* shot to #4 (#1 R&B), spawning the hits "Can't Truss It" (#50 pop, #9 R&B, 1991) and "Shut Em Down" (#26 R&B, 1992). *Greatest Misses* reached #13 (#10 R&B) in 1992 and was criticized for its unexciting remixes. The same year, Public Enemy teamed up with thrash-metal band Anthrax for a successful update of "Bring the Noise" and a joint tour. They also opened for U2's Zoo TV Tour.

PE returned in 1994 with *Muse Sick-N-Hour Mess Age*, which included lyrics critical of the fast-rising gangsta-rap genre and its frequent glorification of violence, drugs, and money. But, like those of other older rap artists, the album debuted fairly high on the chart only to quickly fall in sales (#14 pop, #4 R&B, 1994).

Beginning in 1991, Flavor Flav had some run-ins with the law. He was convicted of assaulting his girlfriend and served a 20-day jail sentence. In 1993 he was charged with attempted murder when he allegedly shot at a neighbor in a domestic squabble; he chose to undergo drug rehabilitation, and the charges were dropped.

By 1996, Chuck D founded the Sony-supported Slam Jamz rap label, created the Rapp Style clothing company, and released his first solo album, *The Autobiography of Mistachuck*. The following year he published a book, *Fight the Power: Rap, Race and Reality*, and soon reconvened the original lineup of Public Enemy to record the soundtrack album to Lee's 1998 film *He Got Game*. The project brought the group renewed visibility: The album reached #26 (#10 R&B), while the title track hit #78 on the R&B singles chart and won regular rotation on MTV. Chuck D closed the '90s as a typically outspoken champion of Internet distribution of music, even making Public Enemy's 1999 album *There's a Poison Goin' On* available first as a low-cost download. Chuck D and Professor Griff's rock-rap side project, Confrontation Camp, toured and released one album in 2000.

Public Image, Ltd. (PiL)

Formed 1978, England
John Lydon (a.k.a. Johnny Rotten, b. Jan. 31, 1956, Eng.), voc.; Keith Levene (b. Eng.), gtr., electronics; Jah Wobble (b. John Wordle, a.k.a. Dan MacArthur, Eng.), bass; Jim Walker (b. Can.), drums; Jeanette Lee, videos; Dave Crowe, business, finances.
1978—*First Issue* (Virgin, U.K.) 1979—(– Walker; + Richard Dudanski, drums; – Dudanski; + Martin Atkins [b. Aug. 3, 1959, Coventry, Eng.], drums) 1980—*Second Edition* (Island); *Paris au Printemps* (Virgin) (– Atkins; – Wobble) 1981—(– Crowe) *Flowers of Romance* (Warner Bros.) (– Lee) 1983—*Live in Tokyo* (Elektra) (– Levene) 1984—*This Is What You Want . . . This Is What You Get* 1986—*Album* (a.k.a. *Cassette*, a.k.a. *Compact Disc*) 1987—*Happy?* (Virgin) 1989—*9* 1990—*The Greatest Hits, So Far* 1992—*That What Is Not* 1999—*Plastic Box*.
John Lydon solo: 1997—*Psycho's Path* (Virgin).

Public Image arose from the ashes of the Sex Pistols, the group's original intent as much a reaction to that band as the Pistols were to '70s rock & roll before them. Former head Pistol Johnny Rotten took back his real name, John Lydon, after the last Sex Pistols show on January 14, 1978. He conceived Public Image as a group organization to create "anti–rock 'n' roll" to embody what the more conventionally rock-rooted Pistols only sang about. Lydon teamed up with Keith Levene, who was an early member of the Clash and also a classically trained guitarist and pianist, plus novice bassist Jah Wobble and drummer Jim Walker, from the Canadian group the Furys. Their original name was Carnivorous Buttock Flies, but they quickly changed to PiL (for Public Image, Limited, the "Limited," since they professed to see themselves as a company rather than a rock band). Financial advisor Dave Crowe was credited as a band member.

PiL made their live debut in London on Christmas Day, 1978, just before their first LP, *First Issue*, came out. It was not released in the U.S., and its slow, embittered songs got mostly negative reviews. Yet it soared to the top of the British charts. Critics caught on with 1979's *Metal Box*, initially released in England in a limited edition of 50,000 incorporating three 12-inch 45-rpm EPs squeezed into a film canister. It came out the next year in the U.S. as *Second Edition* (#171, 1980), a conventional double LP, to almost universal critical acclaim. *Second Edition* was characterized by a uniquely droning sound with prominent dublike bass, neo-psychedelic guitar from Levene, oddly danceable rhythms, and haunting echoed vocals. Levene's dissonant guitar influenced a whole range of bands, from Killing Joke and U2 to Gang of Four. The band toured the U.S. in spring 1980 with new drummer Martin Atkins. At the end of the tour in June, Atkins was fired (he later recorded as Brian Brain and formed Pigface, a veritable industrial supergroup); a few weeks later Wobble was fired as well. Wobble had released two solo LPs during his time in the band, and group members charged he had used some PiL backing tracks on these without permission.

Later in 1980, a live LP from the band's Paris show the previous January, called *Paris au Printemps*, was issued in Europe only. In spring 1981 *The Flowers of Romance*, named for late Sex Pistol Sid Vicious' first band, was released. Atkins as drummer-for-hire played on three tracks, with Levene and Lydon handling the rest. It was a stark, mostly percussion- and vocals-oriented record with some Middle-Eastern vocal influences. Its major connection to rock & roll may have been its audacity.

In May 1981 Lydon and Levene, filling in for Bow Wow Wow, played New York's Ritz. Performing behind a video screen with a hired rhythm section, with Lee on hand to tape the proceedings (the images were projected onto the screen), the band jammed as Lydon and Levene taunted the sold-out crowd. They were pelted with beer bottles as a riot ensued. In 1983, during the recording of *This Is What You Want . . .*, Levene acrimoniously left PiL. His guitar parts were erased; Levene released his version of the album independently as *Commercial Zone*. Lydon found himself with a club hit via "This Is Not a Love Song" and recruited a faceless backup band. From this point on, PiL was a de facto John Lydon solo project. In the recording studio he worked with such veterans as producer/bassist Bill Laswell, guitarist Nicky Skopelitis, and drummer Tony Williams. Enlisting producer Gary Langan on *Happy?* (#169, 1987) and Stephen Hague on *9* (#106, 1989), Lydon assembled dance music that rarely reached the bilious passion of early PiL. Backed by a revolving cast of usually uncredited musicians, he became the type of "entertainer" he claimed to detest. Lydon reclaimed the "Rotten" moniker on *Happy?* In 1993, working with the techno production team Leftfield, he released a dance track, "Open Up," in the U.K. His autobiography, *Rotten: No Irish—No Blacks—No Dogs* (written with Keith and Kent Zimmerman), was published in 1994.

In 1996 Lydon joined the original members of the Sex Pistols for a 20th-anniversary reunion tour, which was documented on the release *Filthy Lucre Live*, and the following year he released *Psycho's Path*, a solo disc recorded under his own name. He also enjoyed a stint as a video personality, hosting *Rotten Television* on VH1 in 2000.

Gary Puckett and the Union Gap

Formed 1967, San Diego, CA
Gary Puckett (b. Oct. 17, 1942, Hibbing, MN), voc.; Dwight Bement (b. Dec. 1945, San Diego), sax; Kerry Chater (b. Aug. 7, 1945, Vancouver, Can.), bass; Gary Withem (b. Aug. 22, 1946, San Diego), piano; Paul Wheatbread (b. Feb. 8, 1946, San Diego), drums.
1968—*Woman, Woman* (Columbia); *Young Girl; Incredible* 1970—*Greatest Hits.*

Gary Puckett and the Union Gap had four gold pop-soul soundalike hits within a year, beginning in late 1967 with "Woman, Woman" (#4).

The band formed in January 1967 in San Diego, where all the members had gone to school. They played the local circuit as the Outcasts but then took the name Union Gap from a small town in Washington state near where Puckett grew up. The only member with prior professional experience was Paul Wheatbread, who, after attending San Diego's Mesa College, became a regular on Dick Clark's *Where the Action Is*. He had played with the Turtles, the Mamas and the Papas, Paul Revere and the Raiders, and Otis Redding.

The Union Gap's visual gimmick was to appear in blue-and-gold Civil War uniforms. After "Woman, Woman" the band hit #2 with both "Young Girl" and "Lady Willpower" in 1968. Next came "Over You" (#7, 1968). "Young Girl," a British #1, became a hit (#6) a second time in England in 1974. All the Union Gap albums were produced by Jerry Fuller, author of "Young Girl," "Lady Willpower," and in 1961, Rick Nelson's #1 hit "Travelin' Man." But after 1969's "Don't Give In to Him" (#15) and "This Girl Is a Woman Now" (#9), the group's hits faded, and it disbanded in 1971.

Kerry Chater, who had written many Union Gap songs, penned tunes for Cass Elliot, Charlie Rich, and Bobby Darin. He also did backup vocals for Sonny and Cher and *The Tonight Show* and recorded two solo LPs for Warner Bros.: *Party Time Love* and *Love on a Shoestring* (1978). Puckett pursued a solo career without success. In the mid-'80s he hit the nostalgia circuit with the Turtles in 1984 and the Monkees two years later. He still tours and writes songs with his brother David, and in 1992 he released a solo LP in Germany, *Love Me Tonight*. Puckett and his band continue to tour worldwide, performing more than 150 shows a year.

Pulp

Formed Arabacus Pulp, 1978, Sheffield, Eng.
Jarvis Cocker (b. Sep. 19, 1963, Sheffield), voc., gtr.; Peter Dalton, gtr.; David Lockwood, bass; Mark Swift, drums. 1978—(– Lockwood; + Phillip Thompson, bass) 1980—(– Swift; + Jimmy Sellars, drums) 1981—(– Sellars; + Wayne Furniss, drums; – Thompson; + Jamie Pinchbeck, bass) 1982—(– Pinchbeck; + Peter Boam, bass; – Dalton; + Simon Hinkler, kybds.; + David Hinkler, kybds., trombone; + Barry Thompson, clarinet, flute) *It* (Red Rhino) 1984—(+ Russell Senior [b. May 18, 1961, Sheffield], gtr., violin; – Furniss; + Magnus Doyle, drums; – Boam; + Peter Mansell, bass; – Simon Hinkler; – David Hinkler; – Thompson) 1985—(+ Candida Doyle [b. Aug. 8, 1963, Belfast, N. Ire.], kybds.) 1987—*Freaks* (Fire Records) (– Doyle; + Nick Banks [b. July 28, 1965, Rotherham, Eng.], drums; – Mansell; + Steven Havenhand, bass; – Havenhand; + Anthony Genn, bass) 1988—(– Genn; + Steve Mackey [b. Nov. 10, 1966, Sheffield], bass) 1992—*Separations* 1993—*PulpIntro* (Island) 1994—*His 'N' Hers; Masters of the Universe* (Fire) 1995—(+ Mark Webber [b. Sep. 14, 1970, Chesterfield, Eng.], gtr.) *Different Class* (Island) 1997—(– Senior) 1998—*This Is Hardcore; Countdown—1992–1983* (Velvel).

With coy, lanky frontman Jarvis Cocker remaining the sole constant member through a series of shifting lineups, Sheffield, England's Pulp labored for more than a decade in obscurity before peeking into the British pop mainstream with their 1994 major-label debut, *His 'N' Hers*. The following year's *Different Class* catapulted the band to headlining status at England's massive Glastonbury festival and established Cocker as English music-press royalty.

At age 15, Cocker formed Pulp (originally called Arabacus Pulp) in 1978 with a trio of school friends. After a handful of personnel changes (and abbreviating the band name), the group recorded a demo that landed it a John Peel radio session in 1981. A nearly entirely new lineup was in place by the time Pulp recorded its first album—the quiet, primarily acoustic *It*—the following year. The group's second album, 1987's *Freaks*, was with two new members, guitarist/violinist Russell Senior and keyboardist Candida Doyle, who would stay on board with Cocker for at least a decade. *Separations* was recorded in 1989 but not released until July 1992; by then Pulp had moved to Sheffield indie label Gift and issued "O.U. (Gone, Gone)," the first of several Gift singles. With these releases, coupled with its first tour, Pulp finally started to attract major label interest, leading to its signing with Island Records in 1993. Island collected the Gift recordings onto the *PulpIntro* compilation and followed it a month later with the single "Lipgloss," which went to #50 in the U.K. The song was featured on 1994's *His 'N' Hers,* which went to #9 on the British album chart and was nominated for the U.K.'s distinguished Mercury Prize for music. It didn't win, but Pulp's fortunes had clearly taken a turn for the better. Propelled by the #2 U.K. disco-rock single "Common People"—a sly, danceable commentary on social-class disparity later voted the best song of the '90s in a BBC/*London Times* poll—*Different Class* (1995) debuted at #1 on the British album chart. Pulp held its own against Oasis and Blur in the Brit-pop frenzy of the summer of 1995, landing a headlining spot at the Glastonbury Festival as a last-minute replacement for the Stone Roses and garnering significant tabloid coverage due to drug references in the controversial U.K. #2 single "Sorted for E's & Wizz." Cocker received even more coverage for his stunt at the 1996 BRIT Awards, in which he ran onstage to mock a messianic theatrical performance by Michael Jackson featuring children. A scuffle with one of Jackson's bodyguards (and allegations that one of the children on stage was hurt in the confusion) led to Cocker's being apprehended by police for questioning, but all charges were eventually dropped. Later that year, *Different Class* was awarded the Mercury Prize. In 1998, a year after the departure of Russell Senior from the band, Pulp returned with *This Is Hardcore.* It didn't spawn as many hit singles as *Different Class,* but debuted at the top of the U.K. chart and went to #114 in the U.S., where Pulp had slowly developed a cult following and rave reviews in the wake of its mid-'90s U.K. success.

James and Bobby Purify

James Purify, born May 12, 1944, Pensacola, FL; Bobby Purify, born Robert Lee Dickey, Sep. 2, 1939, Tallahassee, FL
1988—*100% Purified Soul* (Bell).

James and Bobby Purify's 1966 debut, "I'm Your Puppet," was laid-back soul that charmed both black and white audiences, reaching #6 pop and #5 R&B. These cousins, who had been singing together just over a year before "Puppet," had previously been members of a Florida band called the Dothan Sextet. They subsequently charted with "Shake a Tail Feather" (#25 pop, #15 R&B), "I Take What I Want" (#41 pop, #23 R&B), and "Let Love Come Between Us" (#23 pop, #18 R&B) in 1967.

In 1970 Bobby quit the act, and Ben Moore became James' new partner. This duo had a hit in the mid-'70s in the U.K. with a remake of "I'm Your Puppet," but the duo did little after 1974's "Do Your Thing" (#30 R&B).

Pylon

Formed 1979, Athens, GA
Vanessa Briscoe Hay (b. Vanessa Briscoe, a.k.a. Vanessa Ellison, Oct. 18, 1955, Atlanta, GA), voc.; Randy Bewley (b. Randall Bewley, July 1955, Sarasota, FL), gtr.; Michael Lachowski (b. Aug. 21, 1956, Portsmouth, VA), bass; Curtis Crowe (b. June 2, 1956, Atlanta), drums.
1980—*Gyrate* (DB); *Pylon!!* EP (Armageddon, U.K.) 1983—*Chomp* (DB) 1988—*Hits* 1990—*Chain* (Sky).

The hardest-hitting proponents of the Athens new-wave sound, Pylon hails from the same fertile college-town scene that produced the B-52's and R.E.M. Like an apolitical answer to England's Gang of Four, Pylon played a brutally physical, stripped-down form of funk rock, with silence and subtraction used to dramatic effect, as in dub reggae.

Pylon's members came together while studying art at the University of Georgia in Athens. Their first single, "Cool" b/w "Dub," made an immediate impact on new-wave rock-club dance floors. After the well-received *Gyrate,* they released another powerful double-A-side single, "Crazy" b/w "M-Train." *Chomp* included more college/alternative radio staples, in "Beep" and "Yo-Yo." Vanessa Briscoe (originally known as Vanessa Ellison) then married Bob Hay, who played in another Athens band, the Squalls.

Pylon disbanded by mutual agreement in 1984 (footage of the band appeared in the 1987 documentary film *Athens, Georgia: Inside/Out*). R.E.M. covered "Crazy" on its *Dead Letter Office.* In 1988 Pylon reunited and spent two years touring before recording *Chain,* which was released on the heels of the *Hits* collection. The new album found the group pursuing the same old danceable, muscular minimalism.

Suzi Quatro

Born Suzi Quatrocchio, June 3, 1950, Detroit, MI
1973—*Suzi Quatro* (Bell) 1974—*Quatro* 1975—*Your Mama Won't Like Me* (Arista) 1977—*Aggro Phobia* (RAK) 1978—*If You Knew Suzi* (RSO) 1980—*Greatest Hits; Rock Hard* (Dreamland) 1996—*The Wild One: Classic Quatro* (Razor & Tie).

Suzi Quatro was a pioneer female rocker who got a lot of attention in her early-'70s heyday with her leather look and British glitter hard-pop sound. Fronting her own band and playing hard, sexual music, she was the prototype and idol of Joan Jett.

Born to a musical family (her father was a semipro jazz bandleader), Quatro began playing bongos at age eight in her father's jazz trio. Her sister Patti later played with the all-female Fanny for a while, and brother Michael released several "Jam Band" LPs in the mid-'70s. In 1965 Suzi quit high school and formed her first band with sisters Patti, Nancy, and Arlene, an all-girl unit called Suzi Soul (her stage name) and the Pleasure Seekers.

The group did some dates entertaining troops in Vietnam, and by the end of the '60s it had changed its name to Cradle. Producer Mickie Most (Donovan, Jeff Beck, the Animals) saw Cradle in Detroit, and after the group disbanded in 1970, Suzi Quatro took up Most's offer to come to England and sign with his RAK Records. She wrote her own debut single, 1972's "Rolling Stone," but it didn't sell, so Most linked her up with the highly commercial Nicky Chinn–Mike Chapman songwriting/producing team, who gave her a string of British hits in the bubblegum/hard-rock vein of Slade, T. Rex, and Gary Glitter.

"Can the Can" (#1 U.K., over 2 million sold), "Daytona Demon" (#14 U.K.), and "48 Crash" (#3 U.K.) all hit in England in 1973, as did "Devil's Gate Drive" (#1 U.K., a million-seller) and "The Wild One" (#7 U.K.) in 1974. Quatro stressed her tough image ("She hasn't owned a dress in years," claimed her bio). In 1974 Quatro tried to repeat her European triumph in the U.S. with tours that year and the next, opening for Alice Cooper. But despite heavy media coverage, commercial success was not forthcoming. "All Shook Up" and "Can the Can" were minor hits in the U.S., but during her time stateside she soon lost her British fans.

In 1977 Quatro began appearing on the hugely popular U.S. TV show *Happy Days* as the one-season semiregular Leather Tuscadero, who fronted the hard-rock band Leather and the Suedes. She got a new record deal with RSO and released *If You Knew Suzi* (still produced by Chapman), which yielded the hit "Stumblin' In" (#4, 1979), a duet with singer Chris Norman. She signed with Chapman's label Dreamland in 1980 and had a minor U.S. hit, "Lipstick" (#51, 1981).

Quatro quit touring in 1982 to have a daughter, and in the years since she's found success in TV and the stage: She hosted a British TV show called *Gas* in 1983; she later starred in *Annie Get Your Gun* in London's West End; and in 1991 she portrayed actress Tallulah Bankhead in a U.K. musical, *Tallulah Who?* In 1999 she was hosting *Rockin' With Suzi Q,* a one-hour program on the BBC's Radio 2. That year she also returned to performing and began writing music in a somewhat mellower, more contemporary style. Quatro has been married since the mid-'70s to Len Tuckey, her longtime guitarist and a former member of the group the Nashville Teens ("Tobacco Road").

Queen

Formed 1971, England
Freddie Mercury (b. Farroukh Bulsara, Sep. 5, 1946, Zanzibar; d. Nov. 24, 1991, London, Eng.), voc., piano; Brian May (b. July 19, 1947, London), gtr.; John Deacon (b. Aug. 19, 1951, Leicester, Eng.), bass; Roger Meddows-Taylor (b. July 26, 1949, Norfolk, Eng.), drums.
1973—*Queen* (Elektra) 1974—*Queen II; Sheer Heart Attack* 1975—*A Night at the Opera* 1976—*A Day at the Races* 1977—*News of the World* 1978—*Jazz* 1979—*Live Killers* 1980—*The Game; Flash Gordon* soundtrack 1981—*Greatest Hits* 1982—*Hot Space* 1984—*The Works* (Capitol) 1986—*A Kind of Magic* 1989—*The Miracle* 1991—*Innuendo* (Hollywood) (– Mercury) 1992—*Classic Queen; Live at Wembley '86; Greatest Hits; Five Live* EP (with George Michael and Lisa Stansfield) 1995—*Queen at the BBC; Made in Heaven* 1998—*The Crown Jewels.*
Freddie Mercury solo: 1985—*Mr. Bad Guy* (Columbia) 1987—*Barcelona* (with Montserrat Caballe) (Hollywood) 1992—*The Great Pretender.*
Brian May solo: 1983—*Star Fleet Project* (Capitol) 1993—*Back to the Light* (Hollywood) 1998—*Another World.*
Roger Taylor solo: 1981—*Fun in Space* (Elektra) 1984—*Strange Frontier* (Capitol) 1994—*Happiness?* (Parlophone, U.K.) 1998—*Electric Fire.*

The enormously popular British band Queen epitomized pomp rock, with elaborate stage setups, smoke bombs, flashpots, lead singer Freddie Mercury's half-martial, half-coy preening onstage, and highly produced, much-overdubbed music on record. Queen can be traced back to 1967, when Brian May and Roger Taylor joined singer Tim Staffell in a group called Smile. Staffell soon left to go solo, and the remaining two Smiles teamed up with Freddie Mercury (from a group called Wreckage) and later John Deacon. They played very few gigs at the start, avoiding the club circuit and rehearsing for two years while they all remained in college. (May began work on a Ph.D. in astronomy; Taylor has a degree in biology; Deacon, a degree in electronics; and Mercury had one in illustration and design.) They began touring in 1973, when their debut album was released. After a second LP, the band made its U.S. tour debut, opening for Mott the Hoople.

Queen's sound combined showy glam rock, heavy metal, and intricate vocal harmonies produced by multitracking Mercury's voice. May's guitar was also thickly overdubbed; *A Night at the Opera* included "God Save the Queen" rendered as a chorale of lead guitar lines. (Until 1980's *The Game*, the quartet's albums boasted that "no synths" were used.) Queen's third LP, *Sheer Heart Attack*, featured "Killer Queen," its first U.S. Top 20 hit. The LP also became its first U.S. gold.

Queen: Roger Taylor, Freddie Mercury, Brian May, John Deacon

Heavy-metal fans loved Queen (despite Freddie Mercury's onstage pseudo-dramatics, which had more to do with his admitted influence Liza Minnelli than with Robert Plant), and the band's audience grew with its breakthrough LP, *A Night at the Opera*. It contained the six-minute gold "Bohemian Rhapsody" (#2, 1976), which featured a Mercury solo episode of "mama mia" with dozens of vocal tracks. "Bohemian Rhapsody" stayed at #1 in England for nine weeks, breaking the record Paul Anka had held since 1957 for his "Diana." The promotional video produced for it was one of the first nonperformance, conceptual rock videos.

Queen has had eight gold and six platinum records; through the mid-'80s only its second LP and the 1980 soundtrack to the film *Flash Gordon* failed to sell so impressively. The group's U.S. Top 40 singles include "Killer Queen" (#12), 1975; "Bohemian Rhapsody" (#9), "You're My Best Friend" (#16), "Somebody to Love" (#13), 1976; "We Are the Champions" b/w "We Will Rock You" (#4), 1977; "Fat Bottomed Girls" b/w "Bicycle Race" (#24), for which the group staged an all-female nude bicycle race, 1978; "Crazy Little Thing Called Love" (#1), 1979; "Another One Bites the Dust" (#1), 1980; "Under Pressure" with David Bowie (#29), 1981; "Body Language" (#11), 1982; and "Radio Ga-Ga" (#16), 1984. At first their hits were marchlike hard rock, but in the late '70s the group began to branch out; its two biggest hits were the rockabilly-style "Crazy Little Thing Called Love" and the disco-style "Another One Bites the Dust," a close relative of Chic's "Good Times," that went to #1 pop and R&B.

In 1981 Taylor released a solo album, *Fun in Space*, and later in the year the band recorded with an outsider for the first time, writing and singing with David Bowie on "Under Pressure," included on both their platinum *Greatest Hits* and

Hot Space. One side of *Hot Space* was typically bombastic rock, while the other contained funk followups to "Another One Bites the Dust." Fans were relatively cool to *Hot Space;* it did not go platinum. Queen's next LP, *The Works* (#23, 1984), marked a return to hard-rock form. It contained the nostalgic "Radio Ga-Ga."

Queen ceased to be a commercial force in the States; its next two LPs didn't even go gold. Yet all over the world the group retained its regal status. The gold *Innuendo,* which went to #30 here, shot to #1 in Britain in early 1991. By then rumors were rampant that Mercury was ill with AIDS, something the group continually denied. That November he released a statement from his deathbed confirming the stories; just two days later he died of the disease in his London mansion at age 45.

On April 20, 1992, the surviving members of Queen were joined by a host of stars—including Elton John, Axl Rose, David Bowie, Def Leppard, and many other admirers—for a memorial concert held at Wembley Stadium that was broadcast to a worldwide audience of more than 1 billion. Ironically, around the time of the Wembley concert, Queen was enjoying its greatest American popularity in years, thanks to the memorable scene from the movie *Wayne's World,* in which main characters Wayne (Mike Myers) and Garth (Dana Carvey) and buddies sing along to "Bohemian Rhapsody" as it blares on the car radio. The rereleased single soared to #2.

A posthumous Mercury solo album was released in 1992. May continues to record solo and with the Brian May Band. Roger Taylor recorded three albums with a sideline band, the Cross, which began in 1987; he eventually resumed his solo career. In 1995 Queen finally completed its swan song *Made in Heaven* (#58), which features vocals recorded by Mercury during the last year of his life. In 1996 a statue of the singer was unveiled in Montreux, Switzerland. Queen was inducted into the Rock and Roll Hall of Fame in 2001.

Queen Latifah

Born Dana Owens, Mar. 18, 1970, Newark, NJ
1989—*All Hail the Queen* (Tommy Boy) 1991—*Nature of a Sista'* 1993—*Black Reign* (Motown) 1998—*Order in the Court.*

Queen Latifah was not the first strong female rapper, but she was the first, on the heels of Public Enemy's black nationalism and in the company of her Afrocentric Native Tongues movement, to add a pro-woman activist stance to hip-hop's agenda, clearing a space for women with her declaration of "Ladies First."

Latifah (the word is Arabic for "delicate and sensitive") grew up in middle-class East Orange, New Jersey, where she was a high-school basketball star. She began her hip-hop career as a human beat-box in a group called Ladies Fresh. She then recorded tracks with her friend Mark the 45 King, who gave the demos to Fab Five Freddy, who passed them on to Tommy Boy. *All Hail the Queen* was a minor record saleswise, but its impact was profound, primarily because of "Ladies First," a proud track in which Latifah supported girl love by rapping with Monie Love. De La Soul and KRS-ONE also appeared on the album. Latifah was nominated for a Grammy and named best female rapper of the year by ROLLING STONE in 1990. An informed and articulate commentator on hip-hop and youth cultures in general, La Queen became a media darling.

Latifah broke through to a larger pop audience by rapping on David Bowie's remake of "Fame" and singing with Troop and Levert on a cover of the O'Jays' "For the Love of Money," from the *New Jack City* soundtrack (#12 R&B, 1992). On *Nature of a Sista'* she moved away from her role as rap spokesperson and into more personal, soulful arenas. She wasn't surrendering—"Latifah's Had It Up 2 Here" (#13 R&B, 1992) was the opening track—but she had had "Nuff of the Ruff Stuff." She sang on a number of tracks, used live instruments, and expanded upon the house and dance rhythms she'd used on her debut, to best effect on the single "Fly Girl" (#16, 1992), which she sang with male crooners Simple Pleasure.

Latifah moved to Motown for her third and first gold-selling album, *Black Reign* (#15 R&B, 1994), which yielded the hits "U.N.I.T.Y." (#23 pop, #7 R&B, 1994) and "Just Another Day" (#37 R&B, 1994). "U.N.I.T.Y." also won her a Grammy for Best Rap Performance in 1994. *Black Reign* was dedicated to her brother, a police officer who had died the previous year in a motorcycle accident. (Latifah herself belongs to a cycle club.) Her increased popularity was aided by her starring role in *Living Single.* The highly rated TV sitcom has been criticized, though, for lampooning African-American lives.

Latifah has reinvested her earnings, buying a video store and starting a management and production company, Flavor Unit, whose clients include Naughty by Nature, SWV, OutKast, and L.L. Cool J. In addition to *Living Single,* which is now in syndication, Latifah has appeared in the films *Jungle Fever, Juice,* and *House Party 2* and on the TV show *The Fresh Prince of Bel-Air.* Latifah's movie roles grew more ambitious with *Living Out Loud, Sphere,* and *Set It Off,* the last of which found her playing a lesbian bank robber.

The legal troubles depicted in *Set It Off* took on real-life proportions when Latifah was arrested on weapons and marijuana charges (later dropped) after being stopped for speeding in 1996. However, she bounced back with *Order in the Court* (#95 pop, #16 R&B, 1998), an album filled with positive messages bolstered by coproducers Pras of the Fugees [see entry] and Kay Gee of Naughty by Nature [see entry]. Latifah also toured as part of the 1998 Lilith Fair lineup.

In 1999 La Queen published *Ladies First: Revelations of a Strong Woman,* a book on self-esteem based on her life experiences cowritten with music journalist Karen Hunter. The rapper also began hosting *Queen Latifah,* a daytime talk show that explores social and interpersonal issues and attracts some 2 million viewers.

Queensrÿche

Formed 1981, Bellevue, WA
Chris DeGarmo (b. June 14, 1963, Wenatchee, WA), gtr.; Eddie Jackson (b. Jan. 29, 1961, Robstown, TX), bass; Scott Rockenfield (b. June 15, 1963, Seattle, WA), drums; Geoff Tate (b. Jan. 14, 1959, Stuttgart, Ger.), voc.; Michael Wilton (b. Feb. 23, 1962, San Francisco, CA), gtr.
1983—*Queensrÿche* (EMI) 1984—*The Warning* 1986—*Rage for Order* 1988—*Operation: Mindcrime* (EMI Manhattan) 1990—*Empire* (EMI) 1991—*Operation: Livecrime* 1994—*Promised Land* 1997—*Hear in the Now Frontier* (Capitol) 1998—(– DeGarmo; + Kelly Gray [b. June 20, 1963, Seattle] gtr.) 1999—*Q2k* (Atlantic) 2000—*Queensrÿche: Greatest Hits* (Virgin).

For almost a decade, Queensrÿche was a hard-working band whose art-metal albums won it more respect than sales. But *Empire* (#7, 1990) and its Top 10 hit single "Silent Lucidity" (#9, 1991) launched the group into international stardom.

The band was formed in 1981 in the Seattle suburb of Bellevue, Washington, by Chris DeGarmo and Michael Wilton. Sick of playing in cover bands, the two high school friends recruited fellow bar-band veterans Geoff Tate and Eddie Jackson. They avoided the local club scene, opting instead for extended rehearsals, culminating in the release of the self-financed EP, *Queen of the Reich* in 1983. It sold more than 20,000 copies and led to the band's signing with EMI. *Queensrÿche* (#81, 1983), the quintet's major label debut, was an expanded version of the EP.

The Warning (#61, 1984) and *Rage for Order* (#47, 1986) were supported by tours opening for Kiss, Bon Jovi, and Metallica. *Operation: Mindcrime* (#50, 1988), a concept album depicting a nightmarish future of drugs and media manipulation, brought Queensrÿche some critical plaudits. *Empire*, a more song-oriented mix of rockers and ballads, was languishing in the lower reaches of the album chart until MTV started running the video for "Silent Lucidity." The heavy exposure (at one point the video ran about 44 times a week) pushed the album to double-platinum status, with "Silent Lucidity" named *Billboard*'s most popular rock song in 1991.

The band toured extensively to support its newfound popularity, joining the Monsters of Rock Tour in 1991. Queensrÿche also released *Operation: Livecrime* (#38, 1991), an album and video recapping the elaborate stage show that accompanied the *Operation: Mindcrime* song cycle in concert. Four years after *Empire*—and after including an original song, "Real World," on the soundtrack to the 1993 Arnold Schwarzenegger movie *Last Action Hero*—Queensrÿche returned with *Promised Land*, debuting at #3 and containing the moderately successful single "I Am I." The band's next effort, 1997's *Hear in the Now Frontier*, debuted at #19 on the pop album chart. However, the original lineup would undergo an abrupt change in 1998 when guitarist and frequent songwriter DeGarmo left the group, causing harsh feelings between him and the longtime friends in the band. DeGarmo was replaced by Kelly Gray, known for producing Seattle band Candlebox's debut album and who was already set to coproduce Queensrÿche's next disc; Tate had played with Gray years before in a pre-Queensrÿche group. *Q2k* was released in 1999, but fans of the band's distinctive art-metal sound were confused by the generic raw edges to these songs, resulting in disappointing sales. A greatest-hits collection followed in 2000.

? [Question Mark] and the Mysterians

Formed 1962, Flint, MI
Question Mark (b. 1945, Mex.), voc.; Robert Martinez, drums; Larry Borjas, gtr. Later members included: Robert Lee Balderrama (b. 1950, Mex.), gtr.; Frankie Rodriguez Jr. (b. Mar. 9, 1951, Crystal City, TX), kybds.; Francisco Lugo (b. Mar. 15, 1947, Welasco, TX), bass; Edward Serrato (b. 1947, Mex.), drums.
1966—*96 Tears* (Cameo); *Action* 1985—*The Dallas Reunion Tapes: 96 Tears Forever* (ROIR) 1997—*96 Tears Revisited* (Collectables) 1998—*Do You Feel It Baby?* (Norton) 1999—*More Action* (Cavestomp!).

Question Mark and the Mysterians' one song of consequence was a 1966 #1 hit that epitomized a classic rock & roll sound. The unforgettable "96 Tears" featured leader ?'s gruff vocals and a now-famous organ line played on a Vox Continental, not, as legend has it, on a Farfisa.

The band's quick rise and fall were mirrored in the mystery surrounding its personnel. The leader was never photographed without sunglasses; he legally changed his name to simply "?". (The song is credited to Rudy Martinez, though ? has refused to say whether that's his name, and he has never revealed his background. Some believe that Martinez is a name he invented in order to collect royalties.)

What *is* known is that most of the band members were born in Mexico and later moved to Detroit. Two of the original players, Robert Martinez and Larry Borjas, went into the army before the Mysterians' big success. The group became local favorites in the Detroit area, and "96 Tears" was the first cut for a small Flint, Michigan, record company. It became the most requested song on Flint's WTAC and Detroit's KCLW, which led to a national deal with Cameo Records. The song went on to sell over a million copies. Later in the year the Mysterians hit #22 with "I Need Somebody," but their followups flopped, and by 1968 they'd called it quits. Mel Schacher, who became the bassist with Grand Funk Railroad, played in a later version of the combo.

In 1981, ? and the Mysterians made a low-level comeback. They toured and played oldies plus new material. The same year, Garland Jeffreys released a minor hit version of the old smash ("96 Tears" had become very popular in new-wave circles in the late '70s, seen as an early punk nugget). Joe "King" Carrasco also performed it live in 1980; in fact, he built his entire sound around the tinny-organ style that ? had helped pioneer. The Mysterians went on hiatus again in 1984.

In 1997, ?, drummer Robert Martinez, bassist Big Frank

Lugo, guitarist Robert Balderrama, and organist Little Frank Rodriguez Jr. made their first New York appearance at that year's Cavestomp! Festival. Following an avalanche of press and the release of 1998's live *Do You Feel It Baby?,* the Mysterians issued the double-CD *More Action,* their first studio album in 33 years. Like the new wavers before them, a whole new generation of alternative, neo-garage, and indie rockers connected with "96 Tears," both in concert and via the new record's Spanish version of the song.

Quicksilver Messenger Service

Formed 1965, San Francisco, CA
Gary Duncan (b. Sep. 4, 1946, San Diego, CA), gtr., voc.; John Cipollina (b. Aug. 24, 1943, Berkeley, CA; d. May 29, 1989, Greenbrae, CA), gtr.; David Freiberg (b. Aug. 24, 1938, Boston, MA), bass, voc.; Greg Elmore (b. Sep. 4, 1946, San Diego), drums; Jim Murray, voc., harmonica.
1967—(– Murray) 1968—*Quicksilver Messenger Service* (Capitol) 1969—*Happy Trails* (– Duncan; + Nicky Hopkins [b. Feb. 24, 1944, London, Eng.; d. Sep. 6, 1994, Nashville, TN], kybds.) *Shady Grove* 1970—(+ Duncan; + Dino Valenti [b. Chester Powers, Nov. 7, 1943, New York, NY; d. Nov. 16, 1994, Santa Rosa, CA], voc., gtr.) *Just for Love* (– Hopkins) 1971—(+ Mark Naftalin, piano) *What About Me* (– Cipollina; – Freiberg; + Mark Ryan, bass; – Naftalin; + Chuck Steales, organ) *Quicksilver* 1972—*Comin' Thru* 1973—*Anthology* (lineup: Valenti; Duncan; Elmore; + others) 1975—*Solid Silver* (group disbands) 1987—(group re-forms: Duncan; + Sammy Piazza, drums; + W. Michael Lewis, kybds.) *Peace by Piece* 1991—*Sons of Mercury: The Best of Quicksilver Messenger Service, 1968–1975* (Rhino) 1996—(lineup: Duncan; Lewis; + others) *Shape Shifter* (Pymander) 1997—*Live at Fieldstone* (Pymander/Captain Trip).

Quicksilver Messenger Service was one of the vintage acid-rock San Francisco bands of the late '60s. Its early shows and albums (featuring the heavily tremoloed guitar work of John Cipollina, plus that of second guitarist Gary Duncan) contributed some of the best-remembered instrumental jam music of the period. But as the '60s ended, Quicksilver's popularity waned, and it never achieved the national popularity of its San Francisco contemporaries, Jefferson Airplane and the Grateful Dead.

The group formed in 1965 with Gary Duncan, John Cipollina (whose godfather was classical pianist Jose Iturbi), David Freiberg, Greg Elmore, and Jim Murray. Its original guitarist was to have been Dino Valenti (a Greenwich Village folksinger and, under the name "Chester A. Powers," writer of "Hey Joe" and the Youngbloods' hit "Get Together"). But Valenti was arrested on a drug charge and jailed for 18 months.

In December 1965 the quintet began playing the local circuit, but soon after, Murray left to study the sitar. Quicksilver recorded its debut as a quartet in December 1967, and it came out in May 1968, featuring jams like the 12-minute "The Fool." The band also provided two songs for the soundtrack of *Revolution,* out that year, and in late 1968 QMS recorded its part-live second LP, *Happy Trails,* the group's only gold album. In January 1969 Valenti got Duncan to move to New York and form a group with him; British session keyboardist Nicky Hopkins took Duncan's place and was prominently featured on *Shady Grove.*

In early 1970 Duncan returned, bringing Valenti with him. Valenti finally joined Quicksilver three years late (though his "Dino's Song" appears on the debut LP). The new sextet issued *Just for Love,* and "Fresh Air" received substantial FM airplay, helping to make the LP one of its biggest sellers (#27, 1970).

Hopkins left just before the release of *What About Me,* and some of the tracks featured his replacement, Mark Naftalin, formerly of the Paul Butterfield Blues Band. Cipollina also left around this time; he later formed Copperhead with early Quicksilverite Jim Murray. During 1971 Freiberg left. That year he was jailed for marijuana possession; in 1972 he began a 12-year hitch with Jefferson Airplane/Starship. The remaining Quicksilver threesome—Duncan, Elmore, and Valenti—produced two more LPs, *Quicksilver* and *Comin' Thru,* with Mark Ryan (bass) and keyboardist Chuck Steales, but these sparked little public interest. Though the band didn't break up, it was virtually inactive from 1972 to 1975. That year, Valenti, Duncan, and Elmore recorded *Solid Silver* with bassist Skip Olsen and keyboardist W. Michael Lewis (and with Cipollina and Freiberg making cameos). Quicksilver then disbanded.

Duncan put together another configuration in 1987 to record *Peace by Piece,* but the LP went nowhere, and Quicksilver called it a day once again. John Cipollina, whose younger brother Mario found fame in the '80s as bassist for Huey Lewis and the News, continued to perform with a variety of bands, including the Welsh group Man and the Dinosaurs. A longtime sufferer of severe emphysema, he died in 1989 at age 45. Duncan returned again in the mid-'90s with another incarnation of Quicksilver. Valenti died in 1994 following surgery.

Quiet Riot

Formed 1975, Burbank, CA
Kevin DuBrow (b. Oct. 29, 1955, Los Angeles, CA), voc.; Randy Rhoads (b. Dec. 6, 1956, Burbank; d. Mar. 19, 1982, Lakeland, FL), gtr.; Kelly Garni (b. Oct. 29, 1957, N. Hollywood, CA), bass; Drew Forsyth (b. May 14, 1956, Hollywood, CA), drums.
1977—*Quiet Riot* (CBS/Sony, Jap.) (– Garni; + Carlos Cavazo [b. July 8, 1957, Atlanta, GA], gtr.) 1978—*Quiet Riot II* (– Rhoads; + Rudy Sarzo [b. Nov. 9, 1952, Havana, Cuba], bass; – Forsyth; + Frankie Banali [b. Nov. 14, 1953, Queens, NY], drums) 1983—*Metal Health* (Pasha/CBS) 1984—*Condition Critical* (– Sarzo; + Chuck Wright, bass) 1986—*QR III* (– Wright; + Paul Shortino, voc.; + Sean McNabb, bass) 1987—(– DuBrow) *Wild Young and Crazee* (group disbands) 1988—*Quiet Riot* 1990—(group re-forms: DuBrow; Cavazo;

+ Kenny Hillary, bass; + Bobby Rondinelli, drums) 1993—*The Randy Rhoads Years* (Rhino) 1995—*Down to the Bone* (Kamikaze) 1999—(– Hillary; – Rondinelli; + Sarzo; + Banali) *Alive and Well* (Cleopatra).

Heavy-metal band Quiet Riot was a bigger attraction on the mid-'70s Hollywood club scene than Van Halen and the Knack, yet both of them were signed to major-label recording deals before Quiet Riot. The original lineup recorded two now-out-of-print albums released only in Japan (selections from which were reissued as *The Randy Rhoads Years*), before its breakup was precipitated by the departure of guitarist Rhoads for Ozzy Osbourne's band. Rhoads died in a 1982 Florida plane crash a week before he was due to join the re-formed Quiet Riot in the studio.

The new Quiet Riot's first U.S. album, *Metal Health* (#1, 1983), became the highest-charting debut ever by an American metal band, thanks largely to heavy MTV play of the video for the Slade remake "Cum On Feel the Noize" (#5, 1983). The album yielded a second hit in "Bang Your Head (Mental Health)" (#31, 1983). *Condition Critical* (#15, 1984) fared worse, as did its second Slade-cover single, "Mama Weer All Crazee Now" (#51, 1984). *QR III* (#31, 1986) failed to produce a hit single.

In 1987 the band fired DuBrow, branding him an out-of-control egomaniac in an unusually harsh press release. After one eponymous album (#119, 1988), the new lineup disbanded. In 1990 DuBrow reunited with guitarist Carlos Cavazo to form Heat, which they soon renamed Quiet Riot for club tours. The re-formed group has remained a live attraction, while recording *Down to the Bone* (1995) and *Alive and Well* (1999).

Radiohead

Formed 1987, Oxford, Eng.
Thom Yorke (b. Oct. 7, 1968, Wellingborough, Eng.), voc., gtr.; Jonny Greenwood (b. Nov. 5, 1971, Oxford), gtr., kybds.; Colin Greenwood (b. June 26, 1969, Oxford), bass; Ed O'Brien (b. Apr. 15, 1968, Oxford), gtr., voc.; Phil Selway (b. May 23, 1967, Hemingford Grey, Eng.), drums.
1993—*Pablo Honey* (Capitol) 1995—*The Bends* 1997—*OK Computer* 2000—*Kid A* 2001—*Amnesiac.*

Radiohead emerged from the fading '90s Brit-pop invasion with a sound that was moody, melodic, and explosive, with roots planted firmly in both alternative culture and the art-rock legacy of such classic rockers as Pink Floyd. With the release of 1997's *OK Computer,* Radiohead was among the most closely watched bands of the decade, drawing on influences as varied as Queen, R.E.M., and Miles Davis. The Oxford musicians were embraced as saviors of modern guitar rock, only to resurface in 2000 with a new sound heavy with electronics, minimal vocals, and few guitars.

Singer/guitarist Thom Yorke first turned to music while growing up in Scotland and Oxford, England. Born with his left eye closed and paralyzed, Yorke endured five corrective surgeries before age six. He learned guitar while unhappy at boarding school, where he met bassist Colin Greenwood. The two formed a punk band called TNT. In 1987 they joined friends Ed O'Brien (guitar) and Phil Selway (drums) in a new band called On a Friday. Colin's younger brother, Jonny, was soon recruited on guitar. The band dissolved as members scattered to different universities. The quintet regrouped in 1991 as Radiohead, a name taken from a Talking Heads song.

Radiohead quickly built a following on the Oxford club scene, and soon drew record-company interest from London. The band signed to U.K. label Parlophone within a year, and in 1992 toured England and began recording a debut album, *Pablo Honey* (#32, 1993), released on Capitol in the U.S. That collection included "Creep" (#34), an intense anthem of self-loathing that blended Yorke's alternately anguished and gentle vocals ("I wish I was special . . . but I'm a creep") with Jonny Greenwood's raw spasms of guitar. It was a hit in both the U.S. and England, but Radiohead was labeled a one-hit wonder by critics. The band responded two years later with *The Bends* (#88), which demonstrated a growing musical scope and explored deeper levels of alienation on the songs "Fake Plastic Trees" and "High and Dry" (#78). Sales were significantly less than for the debut, but critics began to reassess the band.

With *OK Computer* (#21, 1997), coproduced by the band and Nigel Godrich (an engineer on *The Bends*), the band enjoyed wide acclaim. Though Yorke and the band denied any coherent theme to the album, various tracks—including "Karma Police" and "Paranoid Android"—examined encroaching technology and millennial anxiety. *OK Computer* topped many of that year's critics polls and won the Best Alternative Music Grammy. Though the album enjoyed no Top 40 singles, Radiohead built a committed following through incessant touring. (The '97–'98 tour was later depicted as a dehumanizing exercise in boredom and fatigue in *Meeting People Is Easy,* director Grant Gee's downbeat 1999 documentary.)

The members of Radiohead continued to work and reside in Oxford. While fans waited three years for a followup to *OK Computer,* a wave of Radiohead-influenced guitar bands (Travis, Coldplay) began to enjoy chart success in England and the U.S.—which made the long-awaited release of *Kid A* (#1, 2000) and the band's new electronic and ambient leanings more surprising. Recorded during sessions with Godrich, *Kid A* sent guitars deep into the background while exploring long instrumental passages and sometimes incoherent vocals. The album won mostly positive, if sometimes puzzled critical notices and a second Best Alternative Music Album Grammy. The band released no singles from the album and played few shows. A second album featuring some tracks from the same sessions, *Amnesiac,* debuted at #2 in June 2001.

Gerry Rafferty

Born Apr. 16, 1947, Paisley, Scot.
1971—*Can I Have My Money Back?* (Transatlantic) 1974—*Revisited* 1978—*City to City* (United Artists) 1979—*Night Owl* 1980—*Snakes and Ladders* 1991—*Right On Down the Line: Best of Gerry Rafferty* (EMI) 1992—*On a Wing and a Prayer* (Avalanche) 1994—*Over My Head* 2000—*Another World* (Icon, U.K.).

Though he had recorded a well-received 1971 solo album, it wasn't until five years after his former band, Stealers Wheel [see entry], had a hit with "Stuck in the Middle With You" that singer/songwriter Gerry Rafferty came into his own as a solo act. Previous to that, he was a member of the Fifth Column and then half of a Scottish folk duo called the Humblebums, with Billy Connolly. He began his solo career in 1971.

In 1978 his "Baker Street" was a huge international hit—it reached #2 in the U.S.—and the LP it came from, *City to City,* went platinum and topped the album chart. It also included the #12 hit "Right Down the Line." This success came after three years of post–Stealers Wheel management/record-label problems. Rafferty, who rarely performs live and then only in England and Europe, has never repeated that degree of success, although the gold *Night Owl* contained two hits, "Days Gone Down (Still Got the Light in Your Eyes)" (#17, 1979) and "Get It Right Next Time" (#21, 1979). He produced the Proclaimers' 1987 U.K. hit "Letter From America." He continues to perform and record.

Rage Against the Machine

Formed 1991, Orange County, CA
Zack de la Rocha (b. Jan. 12, 1970, Long Beach, CA), voc.; Tom Morello (b. May 30, 1964, New York, NY), gtr.; Tim Commerford (b. Torrance, CA), bass; Brad Wilk (b. Sep. 5, 1968, Portland, OR), drums.
1992—*Rage Against the Machine* (Epic) 1996—*Evil Empire* 1999—*The Battle of Los Angeles* 2000—*Renegades* (– de la Rocha).

As well known for its activism as for its music, Rage Against the Machine nonetheless helped lay the groundwork for the aggression-fueled rock-and-rap genre, which, in the hands of acts like Korn and Limp Bizkit, would come to rival both teen pop and hip-hop on the mainstream charts by the late '90s. Frontman Zack de la Rocha brought the rap with his verbal flow and politically charged lyrics; the rest of the guys brought the rock with an emphasis on Tom Morello's mix of punk-metal riffs and experimental guitar sounds.

Both de la Rocha and Morello were born into activist families. De la Rocha, who grew up in suburban Irvine, California, and East L.A., is the son of a painter, Beto, who devoted his work to Chicano causes; Harlem-born Morello's parents were an African rebel-turned-diplomat and a white civil-rights activist. Morello graduated from Harvard with a social studies degree and moved to California, where he found a kindred political spirit in de la Rocha. With drummer Brad Wilk and bassist Tim Commerford (a friend of de la Rocha's since grade school), they formed Rage Against the Machine in 1991 and released a self-produced 12-song cassette the following year, which quickly won them a deal with Epic. The band did not sign until it was assured full creative control.

Rage Against the Machine (#45, 1993) landed the group a spot on the Lollapalooza Tour and spawned the MTV video "Freedom," with which the band hoped to raise support for imprisoned American-Indian activist Leonard Peltier. Other

Rage Against the Machine: Brad Wilk, Tim Commerford, Zach de la Rocha, Tom Morello

causes championed by the band over the course of their career have included death-row inmate Mumia Abu-Jamal's fight for a new trial, the plight of sweatshop workers, and the Zapatista freedom fighters in Chiapas, Mexico. Critics would often question whether or not the band's message was getting through to the majority of their fans, but the success of RATM's second album, *Evil Empire* (#1, 1996), proved that the music, at least, was connecting with a sizable audience. The audience was still in force three years later, with *The Battle of Los Angeles* debuting at #1 and the single "Guerilla Radio" reaching #69 in 1999.

The year 2000 proved to be an eventful and tumultuous one for the band. A Rhyme and Reason coheadlining tour with the Beastie Boys (in the tradition of RATM's 1997 jaunt with the Wu-Tang Clan) was scrapped due to an injury in the Beastie Boys camp, but a free concert outside the Democratic National Convention in L.A. protesting the two-party political system went off without a hitch—until a handful of protesters began a small riot with police, following the band's set. Less than a month later, Commerford was arrested and charged with assault and resisting arrest after he scaled a stage prop during the MTV Video Music Awards (both charges were dropped when he pleaded guilty to disorderly conduct). In October, shortly after the recording of the Rick Rubin–produced covers album *Renegades* (#14, 2000), de la Rocha announced his sudden departure from the group, citing a communication breakdown. He diverted his attention to the recording of his debut solo album, while the remaining members of the group vowed to continue with a new singer. A live album recorded with de la Rocha at the same time as *Renegades* was tentatively scheduled for a 2001 release. In 2001 the band went into the studio with former Soundgarden frontman Chris Cornell. It was reported that Rage members had formed a new band with Cornell, which would be getting a new name.

Rainbow: See Ritchie Blackmore

The Raincoats

Formed 1977, London, Eng.
Gina Birch (b. ca. 1956, Eng.), voc., bass; Ana Da Silva (b. ca. 1949, Portugal), voc., gtr.; Ross Crichton, gtr.; Nick Turner, drums.
1977—(– Crichton; – Turner; + Kate Korus, gtr.; + Richard Dudanski, drums) 1978—(– Korus; + Jeremie Frank, gtr.) 1979—(– Frank; + Vicky Aspinall [b. ca. 1956, Eng.], voc., violin, gtr., kybds.; – Dudanski; + Palmolive, drums) *The Raincoats* (Rough Trade, U.K.) 1980—(– Palmolive; + Ingrid Weiss [b. ca. 1961, Eng.], drums) 1981—*Odyshape* (– Weiss; + Dudanski; + Charles Hayward, drums, perc.; + Paddy O'Connell, bass, gtr., sax) 1983—*The Kitchen Tapes* (ROIR) 1984—*Moving* (Rough Trade, U.K.) (+ Derek Goddard, perc.) (group disbands) 1994—(group re-forms: Da Silva; Birch; + Anne Wood, violin; + Steve Shelley [b. June 23, 1962, Midland, MI], drums) 1995—*Extended Play* EP (Smells Like Records) (– Shelley; + Heather Dunn, bass, drums) 1996—*Looking in the Shadows* (DGC).

The Raincoats took a feminist approach to the "anyone can play" ethos of British punk, and in the process evolved musically—from the abrasive amateurism of their debut album, through the awkwardly graceful, folkish delicacy of *Odyshape*, to the ethno-funk inflections of *Moving*. The group also won critical acclaim for resolutely refusing to live out any of the traditional rock-woman stereotypes. Missing-in-action for a decade, the Raincoats returned in 1994—after being invoked as an inspiration by Nirvana's Kurt Cobain—to performance and recording.

After playing their first gig in 1978, opening for the punk band Chelsea in London, the Raincoats became an all-girl group in 1979 with the addition of classically trained violinist Vicky Aspinall (the only Raincoat with any musical training) and ex-Slits drummer Palmolive. This lineup recorded the Raincoats' first single, 1979's "Fairytale in the Supermarket," and the group's crude-sounding debut album. Palmolive left to follow spiritual pursuits in India (she eventually settled in Massachusetts as a born-again Christian). She was replaced by Ingrid Weiss, who shared drumming duties on *Odyshape* with assorted males, including former Raincoat Richard Dudanski (who'd also played with Public Image, Ltd.) and ex–Soft Machine Robert Wyatt. The Raincoats took a more deliberate and open-ended approach on *Odyshape;* their harmony vocals evoked traditional part- and round-singing, while Aspinall's violin recalled John Cale's viola with the Velvet Underground.

The Kitchen Tapes was recorded in 1982 on a U.S. tour. The same lineup recorded many of the same songs on *Moving*, acclaimed as the group's most confident-sounding effort yet. But the band broke up after its release. In February 1994 Cobain encouraged his band's label, DGC, to issue all three Raincoats albums in the U.S. A month later Da Silva and Birch (with Sonic Youth's Steve Shelley on drums) reunited the Raincoats for an East Coast tour of the U.S. (performing in New York City the night Cobain's suicide was announced). That summer, the Raincoats also released *Extended Play*, an EP of songs broadcast live on BBC Radio 1, DJ John Peel's show, in April 1994. The band's surprising renaissance was capped by *Looking in the Shadows*.

Bonnie Raitt

Born Nov. 8, 1949, Burbank, CA
1971—*Bonnie Raitt* (Warner Bros.) 1972—*Give It Up* 1973—*Takin' My Time* 1974—*Streetlights* 1975—*Home Plate* 1977—*Sweet Forgiveness* 1979—*The Glow* 1982—*Green Light* 1986—*Nine Lives* 1989—*Nick of Time* (Capitol) 1990—*The Bonnie Raitt Collection* (Warner Bros.) 1991—*Luck of the Draw* (Capitol) 1994—*Longing in Their Hearts* 1995—*Road Tested* 1998—*Fundamental.*

Bonnie Raitt

Singer/guitarist Bonnie Raitt's music incorporates blues, R&B, pop, and folk. Though her albums always had sold respectably (averaging several hundred thousand copies) and she had been a headliner since the mid-'70s, it was not until 1989's *Nick of Time* that she achieved the great commercial success critics had been predicting since she debuted in 1971.

The daughter of Broadway singer John Raitt (star of *The Pajama Game* and *Carousel*), Bonnie Raitt started playing guitar at age 12 and was immediately attracted to the blues. In 1967 she left her L.A. home to enter Radcliffe, but she dropped out after two years and began playing the local folk and blues clubs. Dick Waterman, longtime blues aficionado and manager, signed her, and soon she was performing with Howlin' Wolf, Sippie Wallace, Mississippi Fred McDowell, and other blues legends. Her reputation in Boston and Philadelphia led to a record contract with Warner Bros.

Raitt's early albums were critically acclaimed for her singing and guitar playing (she is one of the few women who play bottleneck) as well as her choice of material, which often included blues as well as pop and folk songs. Most of Raitt's repertoire consists of covers, and she has gone out of her way to credit her sources, often touring with them as opening acts. Her sixth album, *Sweet Forgiveness* (#25, 1977), went gold and yielded a hit cover version of Del Shannon's "Runaway" (#57, 1977). *The Glow* (featuring her first original tunes since three on *Give It Up*) (#30, 1979) was produced by Peter Asher, but it did not sell as well as its predecessor.

A Quaker, Raitt has played literally hundreds of benefits over the course of her career. She was a founder of M.U.S.E. (Musicians United for Safe Energy), which in September 1979 held a massive concert at Madison Square Garden, with other stars like Jackson Browne, James Taylor, and the Doobie Brothers. It was later commemorated on a three-LP set. In 1982 she released her eighth LP, *Green Light* (#38, 1982), a harder-rocking effort aided by her backup band, the Bump Band, which included veteran keyboardist Ian MacLagan (of the Faces and the Stones; Raitt's longtime bassist and tuba-player, Freebo, remained a constant sideman through her various backup bands). They toured with Raitt in mid-1982, greeted by the usual critical acclaim. Her work also appeared on the platinum 1980 *Urban Cowboy* soundtrack, with the country song "Don't It Make You Wanna Dance."

When *Nine Lives* (#115, 1986) flopped, Raitt lost her deal with Warner Bros. Prince reportedly produced an album's worth of tracks with her, but they were never released. Instead, Raitt reemerged in 1989 on Capitol with her Don Was–produced breakthrough album *Nick of Time*, which smoothed out her rough bluesy edges yet avoided crass commercialism. It topped the charts, sold 4 million copies, and won an Album of the Year Grammy (one of four awards won by a thunderstruck Raitt at the 1990 gala; one was for her duet with Delbert McClinton, "Good Man, Good Woman"). The pattern held with *Luck of the Draw* (#2, 1991), another Was production, which included the hit singles "Something to Talk About" (#5, 1991) and "I Can't Make You Love Me" (#18, 1991). It sold over 4 million copies and netted three more Grammys, for Album of the Year, Best Female Rock Vocal, and Best Pop Vocal Performance. Raitt earned another in 1990, for Best Traditional Blues Recording, for "In the Mood," a duet with John Lee Hooker on his album *The Healer*. Her former label Warner Bros. capitalized on Raitt's high profile by releasing *The Bonnie Raitt Collection* (#61, 1990), which included live duets with Sippie Wallace and John Prine.

In April 1991 Raitt married actor Michael O'Keefe (they divorced in 1999). Raitt also cofounded the Rhythm & Blues Foundation, dedicated to raising awareness and money for influential musical pioneers left impoverished in their old age by unfair record deals and lack of health insurance. Raitt once again found success working with producer Don Was, as 1994's *Longing in Their Hearts* topped the chart and went platinum shortly after its release; it sold over 2 million copies. It included "Love Sneakin' Up on You" (#19, 1994) and "You" (#92, 1994). Around this time, Raitt had a hit with "You Got It" (#33, 1995) from the film *Boys on the Side*, and a minor hit with "Rock Steady"(#73, 1995), a duet with Bryan Adams. *Road Tested* (#44, 1995) is a live album. In 1995 Raitt became the first woman guitarist to have a guitar named for her. All royalties from the sale of Fender's Bonnie Raitt Signature Series Stratocaster go to programs to teach inner-city girls to play guitar.

Her next effort, *Fundamental* (#17, 1998), produced by Mitchell Froom and Tchad Blake, was a less polished collection that some viewed as a return to the fine roots- and blues-based work of her earlier, hitless days. Raitt called 1982's *Green Light* the album's "true predecessor." Inducted into the Rock and Roll Hall of Fame in 2000, Raitt continues to perform for and speak out on a wide range of issues, including nuclear power, reproductive freedom, and the environment.

The Ramones

Formed 1974, New York, NY
Joey Ramone (b. Jeffrey Hyman, May 19, 1951; d. Apr. 15, 2001, New York), voc.; Johnny Ramone (b. John Cummings, Oct. 8, 1951, Long Island, NY), gtr.; Dee Dee Ramone (b. Douglas Colvin, Sep. 18, 1952, VA), bass; Tommy Ramone (b. Tom Erdelyi, Jan. 29, 1952, Budapest, Hungary), drums.
1976—*Ramones* (Sire) 1977—*Ramones Leave Home; Rocket to Russia* (– Tommy Ramone; + Marky Ramone [b. Marc Bell, July 15, 1956, New York], drums) 1978—*Road to Ruin* 1979—*It's Alive* 1980—*End of the Century* 1981—*Pleasant Dreams* 1983—*Subterranean Jungle* (– Marky Ramone; + Richie Ramone [b. Richard Reinhardt, a.k.a. Richie Beau], drums) 1984—*Too Tough to Die* 1986—*Animal Boy* 1987—*Halfway to Sanity* (– Richie Ramone; + Marky Ramone, drums) 1988—*Ramones Mania* 1989—*Brain Drain* (– Dee Dee Ramone; + C.J. Ramone [b. Christopher Joseph Ward, Oct. 8, 1965, Long Island], bass) 1990—*All the Stuff (and More) vol. 1* (Sire) 1991—*All the Stuff (and More), vol. 2; Loco Live* 1992—*Mondo Bizarro* (Radioactive) 1994—*Acid Eaters* 1995—*Adios Amigos* 1996—*Greatest Hits Live* (MCA) 1997—*We're Outta Here!* (Radioactive) 1999—*Hey! Ho! Let's Go: The Anthology* (Rhino).
Dee Dee Ramone: 1995—*I Hate Freaks Like You* (World Service) 1997—*Zonked!!* (Other People's Music) 2000—*Greatest and Latest* (Conspiracy).
Marky Ramone: 1997—*Marky Ramone and the Intruders* (Thirsty Ear) 1999—*Answer to Your Problems?* (Zoer).

In the mid-'70s the Ramones shaped the sound of punk rock in New York with simple, fast songs, deadpan lyrics, no solos, and an impenetrable wall of guitar chords. Twenty years later, with virtually all of their peers either retired or having moved on to forms other than punk, Joey and Johnny Ramone, the band's core, continued adamantly to parlay the same determinedly basic sound. The cultural importance of the group became most apparent in 2001, when leader Joey Ramone was eulogized not only in the rock press but the *New York Times* and other general media.

The group formed in 1974 after the foursome graduated or left high school in Forest Hills, New York. The original lineup featured Joey on drums, Dee Dee sharing guitar with Johnny, and Tommy as manager, but they soon settled on their recording setup. Their name and pseudonym came via

The Ramones: Johnny Ramone, Joey Ramone, Marky Ramone, Dee Dee Ramone

Paul McCartney, who had briefly called himself Paul Ramon back when the Beatles were the Silver Beatles. The Ramones gravitated toward the burgeoning scene at CBGB, where their 20-minute sets of rapid-fire, under-two-and-a-half-minute songs earned them a recording contract before any of their contemporaries except Patti Smith.

In 1976 *Ramones* was a definitive punk statement, with songs like "Beat on the Brat," "Blitzkrieg Bop," and "Now I Wanna Sniff Some Glue"—14 of them, clocking in at under 30 minutes. The group traveled to England in 1976, giving the nascent British punk scene the same boost they had provided to New Yorkers. Before the year was out, *Ramones Leave Home* had been released. As throughout its career, the band toured almost incessantly.

With their next two singles, the group began to soften their sound slightly. "Sheena Is a Punk Rocker" and "Rockaway Beach" made explicit their debt to '60s AM hit styles such as bubblegum and surf music, and both made the lower reaches of the Top 100. They were included on *Rocket to Russia,* which also contained their first ballad, "Here Today, Gone Tomorrow." At this point Tommy quit the group, preferring his behind-the-scenes activity as coproducer, "disguised" as T. Erdelyi (his real name).

His replacement was Marc Bell, henceforth dubbed Marky Ramone. He was formerly one of Richard Hell's Voidoids and before that a member of Dust, who recorded a pair of albums during the '60s. His first LP with the Ramones, *Road to Ruin,* was their first to contain only 12 songs and their first to last longer than half an hour. Despite their glossiest production yet, featuring acoustic guitars and real solos, its two singles, "Don't Come Close" and a version of the Searchers' "Needles and Pins," failed to capture a mass audience. Neither did their starring role in Roger Corman's 1979 movie *Rock 'n' Roll High School.*

As the 1980s began, the Ramones tried working with noted pop producers Phil Spector *(End of the Century)* and 10cc's Graham Gouldman *(Pleasant Dreams),* but commercial success remained elusive. After *Subterranean Jungle,* Marky Ramone departed, to be replaced by ex-Velveteens Richard Beau. As Richie Ramone, the drummer played on four albums, before Marky returned in 1987. *Too Tough to Die*, with Eurythmic Dave Stewart producing the pop single "Howling at the Moon," recaptured some of their '70s energy, and "Bonzo Goes to Bitburg" off *Animal Boy* offered cutting political satire. However, the remainder of the decade too often found them parodying their earlier strengths.

In 1989 the Ramones gained their widest exposure with the title track to the soundtrack for Stephen King's *Pet Sematary*, but also underwent their most significant internal shift. Dee Dee departed, first to record, as Dee Dee King, a rap album, *Standing in the Spotlight*, and then to form the rock group Chinese Dragons. His post-Ramones career included publishing the autobiography *Poisoned Heart: Surviving the Ramones* and, in the late '90s, playing with his wife, Barbara, and Marky Ramone in the Ramones spinoff unit, the Ramainz. A heroin addict and substance abuser for 14 years, Dee Dee had been the Ramones' truest punk (going solo, he also joined AA); his departure signaled the end of an era, if not a style. AWOL from the marines at the time he enlisted in the band, C.J. Ramone infused youthful energy—he was 14 years younger than Joey and Johnny—but the band's sound remained the same.

Mondo Bizarro, with a guest appearance by Living Colour guitarist Vernon Reid and songs that attacked both drugs and the PMRC's Tipper Gore, ushered the band into the '90s, their influence by then apparent in such rowdy outfits as Guns n' Roses and the Beastie Boys. In 1994 they persevered with *Acid Eaters*, a tribute to '60s idols like the Animals and Rolling Stones. With Joey sober since the start of the decade and Marky in recovery from alcoholism, they continued their relentless touring for two more years until their final show in August 1996. Marky formed Marky Ramone and the Intruders and has released two albums to date. Joey went on to manage the Independents, a horror-punk-ska band, to act in the indie film *Final Rinse*, and, in 1999, to coproduce a Ronnie Spector EP, *She Talks to Rainbows*. In 2001 he announced he had been diagnosed with lymphoma six years earlier and was undergoing treatment for the disease. He died that year. Little Steven Van Zandt presided over an all-star party on what would have been Joey's 50th birthday, a month after his death. The U.S. Congress proclaimed May 19, 2001, Joey Ramone Day.

Rancid

Formed Nov. 1991, Berkeley, CA
Tim Armstrong (b. Nov. 25), gtr., voc.; Matt Freeman (b. Apr. 23, 1966, Albany, CA), bass; Brett Reed (b. July 12), drums.
1993—*Rancid* (Epitaph) 1994—(+ Lars Fredericksen [b. Aug. 31, Campbell, CA], gtr.) *Let's Go* 1995—*. . . And Out Come the Wolves* 1998—*Life Won't Wait* 2000—*Rancid.*

Spawned from the same Bay Area latter-day hardcore punk scene as Green Day, and likewise heavily influenced by the Clash, Rancid achieved mainstream success while unabashedly celebrating the blue-collar ethic and hyper-aesthetic of classic punk—complete with Mohawks and jumpy rhythms inspired by ska music. The band came together in 1991 when guitarist Tim Armstrong was recovering from alcoholism. As part of his therapy, he started Rancid with bassist and childhood friend Matt Freeman. The pair had previously played together in Operation Ivy—a late-'80s ska-punk outfit that had been a staple of Gilman Street, the legendary East Bay punk club that also fostered Green Day—and the Dance Hall Crashers. Brett Reed, another Gilman Street regular, joined on drums, and the group released a five-song EP in 1992. Its self-titled debut album came out the next year on California punk stronghold Epitaph Records. Guitarist Lars Fredericksen, a former member of U.K. Subs, joined in time to record the band's breakthrough release *Let's Go* (#97 pop, 1995), which went gold. A major label bidding war erupted, and by year's end the group was contemplating a $1.5 million offer from Epic Records.

Rancid opted to stay with Epitaph, and released . . . *And Out Come the Wolves* (#45 pop, 1995), with two singles, "Time Bomb" (#48, 1995) and "Ruby Soho" (#63, 1995), getting heavy airplay on modern rock stations. Three years later, *Life Won't Wait* (#35 pop, 1998) was Rancid's most ambitious effort, as the group expanded its range to include doo-wop harmonies, soul, and rockabilly elements, and feature such guests as Buju Banton and Dicky Barrett of the Mighty Mighty Bosstones. Going back to its punk roots for its second self-titled release in 2000, Rancid capped a rags-to-riches decade with a loud-fast-rules rejoinder to its unexpected success.

Rank and File/Alejandro Escovedo

Formed 1981, New York, NY
Chip Kinman (b. Oct. 4, 1957, Edenton, NC), voc., gtr., harmonica; Tony Kinman (b. Apr. 3, 1956, Quantico, VA), voc., bass; Alejandro Escovedo (b. Jan. 10, 1946, San Antonio, TX), voc., gtr.; Slim Evans (b. Jim Evans), drums.
1982—*Sundown* (Slash–Warner Bros.) 1983—(– Escovedo; – Evans) 1984—*Long Gone Dead* 1987—*Rank and File* (Rhino).
Alejandro Escovedo solo: 1992—*Gravity* (Watermelon) 1993—*Thirteen Years* 1994—*The End* EP; *Hard Road* (with True Believers) 1996—*With These Hands* (Rykodisc) 1997—*The Pawn Shop Years* (with Buick MacKane) 1998—*More Miles Than Money: Live 1994–1996* (Bloodshot) 1999—*Bourbonitis Blues* 2001—*A Man Under the Influence.*

Rank and File mixed energetic power pop with a country twang, kicking off the early-'80s musical hybrid called cow punk. Army-brat brothers Tony and Chip Kinman spent part of their childhoods living in North Carolina, where they were surrounded by country music. By the time they reached the West Coast in the late '70s, the brothers had discovered punk and formed the Dils, whose politically charged "I Hate the Rich" and "Class War" are considered unsung classics of West Coast punk. In 1981 Chip Kinman teamed up with former Nuns guitarist Alejandro Escovedo in New York to form

Rank and File. (The Dils and Nuns had played together in San Francisco, and there Tony Kinman and Escovedo had performed with a loose-knit group they dubbed Rank and File.) Tony joined soon after, the band dropped its rhythm section, and the three moved to Austin in 1982. There, they recruited drummer Slim Evans.

After initial cries of "sellout" from devoted Dils fans, Rank and File released *Sundown* to overwhelming critical praise for songs such as "Coyote," about the mistreatment of illegal aliens, and the poppy "Amanda Ruth." The Kinmans' grittier side was compared to Johnny Cash, while their harmonies were likened to the Everly Brothers. Amid dissension, Escovedo and Evans left, and the Kinmans relocated to L.A. Recorded with session players, *Long Gone Dead* received a lukewarm reception. The group's nontwangy Rhino album passed nearly unnoticed in 1987.

In 1986 Escovedo—whose extended family includes Santana percussionist Pete Escovedo and Pete's daughter, former Prince percussionist Sheila E.—formed True Believers with his brother Javier. The band released its critically acclaimed but commercially disappointing self-titled album, produced by Memphis sessionman Jim Dickinson (Big Star, Replacements), on Rounder-EMI. Six years later Escovedo kicked off a solo career with the critical hit *Gravity*, which expressed his grief over the suicide of his second wife—and the mother of two of his children. It was followed in 1994 by *Thirteen Years*. While he also performed with the Alejandro Escovedo Orchestra, the rock band Buick MacKane, and with the Setters (which included Walter Salas-Humara of the Silos), Escovedo won the most acclaim for his solo work. His 1996 album *With These Hands* included an appearance by Willie Nelson (on "Nickel and a Spoon") and featured several members of Escovedo's extended family, including Sheila E. The music set a mix of country, hard rock, and Latin rhythms against lyrics that explored family values. The more raucous *Bourbonitis Blues* followed in 1999. *A Man Under the Influence* (2001) was produced by Chris Stamey (dB's).

The Kinmans continued together as the avant-rock duo Blackbird, blending their clean harmonies and melodies with a cruder industrial sound. Between 1988 and 1993 the duo released three self-titled albums: The first two, unofficially called "the red one" and "the black one," came out on Iloki; the third, called "the orange one," was released by Scotti Brothers. The Kinmans also dabbled in a band called Cowboy Nation (*Journey Out of Time*, 2000), which returned the brothers to the rootsy C&W of that beloved first Rank and File album.

Shabba Ranks

Born Rexton Rawlston Fernando Gordon, Jan. 17, 1966, Saint Ann's Parish, Jam.
1991—*As Raw as Ever* (Epic) 1992—*Rough & Ready, vol. I; X-Tra Naked* 1993—*Rough & Ready, vol. II* 1995—*A Mi Shabba* 1999—*Shabba Ranks and Friends.*

With his deep, gruff voice and lyrics and image based firmly in "slackness" (overt sexuality), Shabba Ranks became the biggest-selling and highest-profile star of "dancehall," the reggae subgenre marked by fast rhythms and fast-talking vocals. Dancehall began in the late '60s, is credited with anticipating and influencing rap (original Bronx rap DJ Kool Herc was an emigrant from Jamaica), and gained an international audience after rap's ascendence in the late '80s.

Like Bob Marley, Ranks emerged from Saint Ann's Parish and the Trenchtown ghetto. Influenced by such "toasters" (reggae's version of rappers) as Josey Wales and Yellowman, he began performing in Kingston in 1980 and soon was recording Jamaican hit singles with such leading record producers as King Jammy and Bobby Digital. His 1989 "Wicked in Bed" caught on with Caribbean-music fans in America and Britain, and in 1991 he was featured on Scritti Politti's cover of the Beatles' "She's a Woman," a U.K. Top 20 hit that paved the way for a major label deal with Epic Records. *As Raw as Ever* (#89 pop, #1 R&B, 1991), yielded hits in "Housecall (Your Body Can't Lie to Me)" (#37 pop, #4 R&B, 1991), a duet with reggae crooner Maxi Priest, and "The Jam" (#52 R&B, 1992), a duet with rapper KRS-ONE. The album won 1991's Best Reggae Album Grammy, making Ranks the first dancehall artist so honored. Epic then released *Rough and Ready, Volume I* (#78, 1992), a collection of Ranks' Jamaican hits that yielded a hit single in "Mr. Loverman" (#40 pop, #2 R&B, 1992).

X-tra Naked (#64, 1992) produced another big hit in "Slow and Sexy" (#33 pop, #4 R&B, 1992), a duet with Johnny Gill; the album also included duets with rappers Queen Latifah and Chubb Rock. Ranks then guested on Eddie Murphy's *Love's Alright* and appeared in Murphy's video for "I Was King." In December 1992, however, Ranks told a British TV show that he agreed with dancehall star Buju Banton's controversial track "Boom Bye Bye," which advocated the killing of gay men. "If you forfeit the laws of God Almighty," declared Ranks, "you deserve crucifixion." Resulting protests by gay-rights groups led *The Tonight Show* to cancel Ranks' scheduled appearance in March 1993. Ranks subsequently said he regretted his remarks and that he did not "approve of any act of violence against homosexuals or any other human beings."

Whether or not the controversy impacted album sales, *A Mi Shabba*, released in 1995, failed to chart as highly as its predecessors, reaching #133. Its singles, "Let's Get It On" (#81 pop, #27 R&B) and "Shine Eye Gal" (#57 R&B), fared better. The 1999 package *Shabba Ranks and Friends* compiled the best of Ranks' hit collaborations.

Rare Earth

Formed 1969, Detroit, MI
Gil Bridges, flute, sax, perc., voc.; Pete Rivera (a.k.a. Peter Hoorelbeke), drums, voc.; John Persh, bass, trombone, voc.; Rob Richards, gtr., voc.; Kenny James, kybds.
1969—*Get Ready* (Rare Earth) 1970—*Ecology* (– Richards;

+ Ray Monette, gtr.; – James; + Mark Olson, kybds.; + Ed Guzman [b. ca. 1944; d. July 29, 1993], perc.) *One World* 1971—*In Concert* (– Persh; + Mike Urso, bass, voc.) 1973—*Willie Remembers; Ma* (– Rivera) 1975—*Back to Earth* (numerous personnel changes ever since) 1976—*Midnight Lady* 1977—*Rare Earth* (Prodigal) 1978—*Band Together; Grand Slam* 1993—*A Different World* (Koch).

Hard-rockers Rare Earth enjoyed several major hits with Motown Records in the early '70s and was reportedly the first white act signed to the black-owned company. Founding members Pete Rivera, John Persh, and Gil Bridges grew up in Detroit listening to and playing Motown hits in local bars as the Sunliners. In 1969 they became Rare Earth and added three new members. With the aid of Motown session guitarist Dennis Coffey they attracted the company's attention and in 1969 were signed to a Motown subsidiary renamed Rare Earth.

The group's first album, *Get Ready* (#12), was quite successful; and the title cut, a reworking of the Temptations' hit, was a #4 single. *Ecology* and *One World* in 1970 spawned "(I Know) I'm Losing You," another Temptations remake (#7 pop, #20 R&B), "Born to Wander" (#17 pop, #48 R&B), "I Just Want to Celebrate" (#7 pop, #30 R&B), and "Hey, Big Brother" (#19 pop, #48 R&B). Much of the group's material was produced by Motown staff producer Norman Whitfield.

After this peak period, the band continued with Motown until it released *Rare Earth* on Prodigal Records in 1977. Rare Earth, with Gil Bridges and Ray Monette still remaining from the early lineup, continues today. The group released an album in 1993, when the band was especially popular in Germany. In the mid-'90s original drummer Pete Rivera played with the Classic Rock All Stars, which featured Spencer Davis and members of Iron Butterfly and Sugarloaf.

The Rascals/The Young Rascals

Formed 1965, New York, NY
Felix Cavaliere (b. Nov. 29, 1944, Pelham, NY), voc., kybds.; Eddie Brigati (b. Oct. 22, 1946, New York), voc.; Gene Cornish (b. May 14, 1945, Ottawa, Can.), gtr.; Dino Danelli (b. July 23, 1945, New York), drums.
1966—*The Young Rascals* (Atlantic) 1967—*Collections; Groovin'* 1968—*Once Upon a Dream; Time Peace; Freedom Suite* 1969—*See* 1970—*Search and Nearness* 1971—(– Brigati; – Cornish; + Buzzy Feiten [b. New York], gtr.; + Robert Popwell [b. Daytona, FL], bass; + Ann Sutton [b. Pittsburgh, PA], voc.) *Peaceful World* (Columbia) 1972—*The Island of Real* 1992—*The Rascals Anthology (1965–1972)* (Rhino).
Felix Cavaliere solo: 1974—*Felix Cavaliere* (Bearsville) 1975—*Destiny* 1976—*Treasure* (Epic) 1980—*Castles in the Air* 1994—*Dreams in Motion* (Karambolage).
Eddie Brigati solo (with David Brigati): 1976—*Brigati* (Elektra).

The term "blue-eyed soul" was allegedly coined for the Rascals (although none of them had blue eyes), whose approximation of mid-'60s black pop crossed the color line.

The Rascals: Felix Cavaliere, Gene Cornish, Eddie Brigati, Dino Danelli

Dino Danelli began his career as a teenage jazz drummer (he played with Lionel Hampton's band) but switched to R&B while working in New Orleans, and he returned to New York to accompany such R&B acts as Little Willie John. There he met Eddie Brigati, a pickup singer on the local R&B circuit.

Felix Cavaliere had studied classical piano before becoming the only white member of the Stereos, a group based in his suburban hometown. While a student at Syracuse University, he formed a doo-wop group, the Escorts. After leaving school, Cavaliere moved to New York City, where he met Danelli, and the two migrated to Las Vegas to try their luck with a casino house band. On their return to New York, Cavaliere joined Joey Dee and the Starliters (sometimes spelled Starlighters), which included Brigati and Gene Cornish.

The Rascals came together in 1964 after Cavaliere, Brigati, and Cornish left Dee and formed a quartet with Danelli. In February 1965 they began gigging in New Jersey and on Long Island. By year's end, they had changed their name to the Young Rascals (after the old television series) and released their first Atlantic single, "I Ain't Gonna Eat Out My Heart Anymore" (#52, 1965), sung by Brigati. The group took a turn when Cavaliere sang the followup, "Good Lovin' " (#1, 1966), one of the year's biggest hits. In the following two years, the group had nine more Top 20 hits, including "You Better Run" (#20, 1966), "(I've Been) Lonely Too Long" (#16, 1967), "Groovin' " (#1, 1967), and "A Girl Like You" (#10, 1967), most of them Cavaliere-Brigati compositions.

Established hitmakers, the group tried to get serious in 1967, dropping the "Young" from its name and the Edwardian knickers from its onstage wardrobe. With *Freedom Suite*, the Rascals' music took on elements of jazz, but the quartet continued to score with "How Can I Be Sure" (#4, 1967), "A Beautiful Morning" (#3, 1968), and "People Got to Be Free" (#1, 1968). Cavaliere and Brigati wrote the latter song shortly after the 1968 assassinations of Martin Luther King Jr. and Robert F. Kennedy. Though they never brandished their politics like some bands, the Rascals truly lived theirs, demanding that a black act appear on the bill at each of its concerts. The principled stand cost them dates in the South.

The Rascals never had another Top 20 hit after "People Got to Be Free." With *Search and Nearness,* their songs made room for lengthy instrumental tracks by jazzmen like Ron Carter, Hubert Laws, and Joe Farrell. Record sales and concert attendance plummeted. In 1971 they signed to Columbia, but Brigati and Cornish left before their label debut. Filling their shoes were Buzzy Feiten (Butterfield Blues Band), fresh from sessions for Bob Dylan's *New Morning;* Robert Popwell, whose session credits included work for Dylan, Aretha Franklin, Eddie Floyd, and Tim Hardin; and Ann Sutton, who had sung with various soul and jazz groups in Philadelphia. The band broke up in the early '70s.

Brigati recorded an album with his brother David in 1976; Cornish and Danelli started a group called Bulldog and later were part of Fotomaker with former Raspberries guitarist Wally Bryson. Feiten joined Neil Larsen in a duo in 1980. Cavaliere has continued as a solo artist and as a producer (Laura Nyro, Deadly Nightshade). In 1994 producer Don Was' Karambolage released the singer's first new album in nearly a decade and a half. Around the same time, Cavaliere also played keyboards for Ringo Starr's All-Starr Band. In 1982 Danelli joined Steve Van Zandt's Little Steven and the Disciples of Soul. He, Cornish, and Cavaliere reunited in 1988 for a U.S. tour, but the following year Danelli and Cornish sued Cavaliere to prevent him from using the Rascals name. In a Solomon-like ruling, a judge allowed Cornish and Danelli to call themselves the New Rascals, and for Cavaliere to advertise himself as "formerly of the Young Rascals." In 1991 Eddie and David Brigati were featured on *The New York Rock and Soul Revue,* an all-star live album spearheaded by Steely Dan cofounder Donald Fagen. In 1997 the original Rascals were inducted into the Rock and Roll Hall of Fame.

The Raspberries/Eric Carmen

Formed 1970, Cleveland, OH
Eric Carmen (b. Aug. 11, 1949, Cleveland), voc., bass, gtr.; Wally Bryson (b. July 18, 1949, Gastonia, NC), gtr.; Jim Bonfanti (b. Dec. 17, 1948, Windber, PA), drums; Dave Smalley (b. July 10, 1949, Oil City, PA), bass, gtr.
1972—*Raspberries* (Capitol); *Fresh* 1973—*Side 3* (– Bonfanti; – Smalley; + Michael McBride, drums; + Scott McCarl, bass) 1974—*Starting Over* 1991—*Collectors Series* 2000—*Refreshed* EP (Legendstar).
Eric Carmen solo: 1975—*Eric Carmen* (Arista) 1977—*Boats Against the Current* 1978—*Change of Heart* 1980—*Tonight You're Mine* 1985—*Eric Carmen* (Geffen) 1988—*The Best of Eric Carmen* (Arista) 2000—*I Was Born to Love You* (Pyramid).

The Raspberries, with their Beatles-like harmonies, Mod-influenced suits, and power pop, seemed very out of place when they first recorded in 1972, partly because the general trend in America at the time was toward longer FM-oriented tracks.

The Raspberries: Jim Bonfanti, Wally Bryson, Eric Carmen, Dave Smalley

The band formed in Cleveland in 1970 from several local groups. Jim Bonfanti had drummed on the Outsiders' 1966 hit "Time Won't Let Me." He was later in the Mods with Dave Smalley and Wally Bryson, who changed their name to the Choir. They became the most popular band in Cleveland, with a minor 1967 hit, "It's Cold Outside." Eric Carmen, who can both croon sensuously and scream rock & roll like Paul McCartney, joined the local Cyrus Erie as lead singer, and Bryson left the Choir to join Carmen's band. They recorded a few unnoticed singles for Epic; Carmen then recorded with a band called the Quick before going solo, writing and recording "Light the Way," later covered by Oliver.

At the turn of the decade, Carmen, Bryson, Bonfanti, and Smalley finally united in the Raspberries. In mid-1971 their demos attracted the attention of future producer Jimmy Ienner, who got them a contract with Capitol. Their debut LP had a raspberry-scented scratch-and-sniff sticker on the cover. The second single, "Go All the Way," hit #5 and sold more than 1.3 million copies. The second LP included "I Want to Be With You" (#16, 1972) and "Let's Pretend" (#35, 1973). Carmen wrote and sang most of the hits, many of which (including the three listed above) were paeans to making out.

During the recording of *Side 3,* internal problems developed. Bonfanti and Smalley resisted the group's teenybopper image, and by the end of the year they'd left, forming Dynamite with two ex-members of Freeport, another Cleveland band. They were replaced by Michael McBride, who had played in Cyrus Erie with Carmen, and Scott McCarl, who had sent an audition tape to Ienner. The new foursome released its fourth and final LP, *Starting Over,* a concept album about stardom that many critics called the best LP of 1974. Although the single "Overnight Sensation (Hit Record)" reached #18, the album flopped, and the band quit in frustration.

Carmen went on to an intermittently successful solo career as a pop balladeer. His first solo LP contained three hits:

"Sunrise" (#34, 1976), "Never Gonna Fall in Love Again" (#11, 1976), and "All by Myself" (#2, 1976), the latter of which incorporated a Rachmaninoff melody, as did several other songs by the classically trained pianist/guitarist. Carmen had only one more Top 20 hit over the next 10 years ("Change of Heart," #19, 1978) but did compose "That's Rock 'n' Roll" (#3, 1977) and "Hey Deanie" (#7, 1977), both smashes for teen heartthrob Shaun Cassidy, and "Almost Paradise (Love Theme from *Footloose*)," a Top 10 hit for Loverboy's Mike Reno and Heart's Ann Wilson in 1984. Three years later another film, *Dirty Dancing*, gave Carmen his own hit with "Hungry Eyes" (#4, 1987). A followup, "Make Me Lose Control" soared to #3 the following spring, but no new albums appeared between 1985 and 2000's *I Was Born to Love You*. In the interim Celine Dion's version of Carmen's "All by Myself," became an international megasmash in 1996. Also in 2000 Carmen toured with Ringo Starr's All-Starr Band while Raspberries Bryson, Smalley, and McCarl regrouped and recorded a new EP, *Refreshed*.

Ratt

Formed 1981, Los Angeles, CA
Bobby Blotzer (b. Oct. 22, 1958), drums; Robbin Crosby, gtr.; Juan Croucier (b. Aug. 22, 1959), bass; Warren De Martini (b. Apr. 10, 1963), gtr.; Stephen Pearcy (b. July 3, 1956), voc.
1983—*Ratt* (Time Coast) 1984—*Out of the Cellar* (Atlantic) 1985—*Invasion of Your Privacy* 1986—*Dancin' Undercover* 1988—*Reach for the Sky* 1990—*Detonator* 1991—*Ratt & Roll 8191* 1997—*Collage* (D-Rock) 1999—(– Croucier; + Robbie Crane, bass) *Ratt* (Portrait) 2000—(– Pearcy; + Jizzy Pearl, voc.; + John Corabi, gtr.).

One of the most popular L.A. '80s metal bands, Ratt concentrated mostly on the music, a standard-issue combination of Zeppelin and Aerosmith. Four out of seven albums went platinum, with two cracking the Top 10: *Out of the Cellar* (#7, 1984) and *Invasion of Your Privacy* (#7, 1985).

Ratt began in 1981 with friends Robbin Crosby and Stephen Pearcy. They met Warren De Martini on the club scene. After seeing drummer Bobby Blotzer on MTV, they tracked him down; Blotzer brought along Juan Croucier. Their friendship with Mötley Crüe helped them to secure a contract with Atlantic; the label signed them after an executive saw a live show. *Out of the Cellar*, their debut for Atlantic, contained "Round and Round," the #12 hit that became an MTV staple (featuring a cameo appearance by comedian Milton Berle in full drag).

Ratt remained popular for the length of its career. For 1990's *Detonator* (#23) the group collaborated with songwriter-for-hire Desmond Child. Stephen Pearcy's departure in 1992, for the usual "artistic differences," marked the end of the band—for a time. With "hair metal" becoming a viable nostalgia act in the late '90s, Pearcy and De Martini got Ratt back together. Two new albums, *Collage* (1997) and *Ratt* (#169, 1999), didn't do well, and Ratt resorted to touring on retro bills with fellow metallers Poison. In January 2000 Pearcy quit the band again; he was replaced by ex–Love/Hate and L.A. Guns singer Jizzy Pearl. Later that year, ex–Mötley Crüe guitarist John Corabi joined the band.

Genya Ravan

Born Goldie Zelkowitz, 1942, Lodz, Pol.
1972—*Genya Ravan With Baby* (Columbia) 1973—*They Love Me/They Love Me Not* (Dunhill) 1974—*Goldie Zelkowitz* (Janus) 1978—*Urban Desire* (20th Century–Fox) 1979—*And I Mean It*.

During her two decades as a rock musician, Genya Ravan led one of the first self-contained all-female bands, sang hits for Ten Wheel Drive, and later became the first female producer hired by a major record label.

Growing up in the Jewish ghetto on New York's Lower East Side, young Goldie Zelkowitz developed an interest in R&B. She ran with a teenage gang and dropped out of high school for a musical career, which began in a Brooklyn lounge when she walked onstage and began singing with Richard Perry's band, the Escorts, who made her their lead singer. She sang their version of "Somewhere" from *West Side Story*; the record never charted nationally but made #1 in Detroit.

In 1962 she formed Goldie and the Gingerbreads, probably the first girl group in which all the women played their own instruments. They stayed together until 1967, achieving their biggest successes in England, where they eventually relocated and later toured with the Rolling Stones, the Yardbirds, Manfred Mann, and the Kinks.

In 1969 Zelkowitz changed her name to Genya Ravan and formed Ten Wheel Drive ("Morning Much Better," #74, 1970), an otherwise all-male jazz-blues band with a five-piece horn section in the mold of Blood, Sweat and Tears. She left in 1971 to form her own band, Baby, which toured with Sly and the Family Stone and backed up Ravan on her first solo album. At that time most of her material was written by Baby's guitarist, Mitch Styles, formerly of Diamond Reo.

In 1975 Ravan became the first woman producer hired by a major label when RCA had her produce cabaret act Gretchen Cryer and Nancy Ford (who wrote the feminist musical *I'm Getting My Act Together and Taking It on the Road*) and the debut album by Rosie (who later joined the Harlettes). A little over a year later, Ravan formed the short-lived Taxi. She also produced demos for CBGB owner Hilly Kristal, including the Shirts, a popular band at the club, as well as the debut LP by the Dead Boys, *Young, Loud and Snotty*. She later sang on Blue Öyster Cult's *Mirrors* LP and produced material by ex-Ronette Ronnie Spector. Lou Reed guested on *Urban Desire*, Ian Hunter on *And I Mean It*; both albums stuck to her hard-nosed rock vein, with many songs written by Ravan. In 1980 Ravan formed her own label, Polish Records. She appeared on *The Warriors* soundtrack. She is currently head of production and promotion for CBGB's in-house record label. In 1997 Goldie and the Gingerbreads performed a 30-year reunion show honoring the release of *The Rolling Stone Book of Women in Rock.*

Johnnie Ray

Born Jan. 10, 1927, Dallas, OR; died Feb. 24, 1990, Los Angeles, CA
1952—*Johnnie Ray* (Columbia) 1957—*The Big Beat* 1978—*Johnnie Ray—An American Legend* 1997—*High Drama: The Real Johnnie Ray* (Legacy).

Though he had started to go deaf as a youngster, Johnnie Ray still managed to become one of America's most popular male vocalists of the early and mid-'50s, with a dozen gold records. He left home for Hollywood, then ended up in Detroit in 1951. There he met blues singer LaVern Baker and her manager, Al Green (not the Memphis soul singer), who helped Ray work on his music. He was discovered by Detroit disc jockey Robin Seymour, and in 1951 he signed to Columbia's Okeh subsidiary. That year his "Whiskey and Gin" was a minor hit in the Midwest.

Ray went to New York, where, with Mitch Miller producing and the Four Lads backing, he recorded "Cry," a #1 ballad in 1952. Because he was so emotional during his performances, Ray is frequently cited as the first popular singer to break with the cool, professional stance of earlier pop crooners like Perry Como. Among critics' nicknames for him was Prince of Wails. Through the early to mid-'50s Ray had many pop hits, including "Please Mr. Sun," a cover of the Drifters' "Such a Night," "Just Walking in the Rain," "Yes Tonight, Josephine," and "You Don't Owe Me a Thing."

Although Ray's chart success ended in the U.S. nearly as quickly as it began, he was extremely popular in the U.K., where he made 29 chart appearances in the Top 40, as opposed to four here, between 1952 and 1960. He also recorded three duets with Doris Day that charted there. In the following years, Ray popped up occasionally as an oldies act both on TV and in concerts. He died of liver failure. Even in death, Ray was not forgotten by his British fans: Morrissey often wore a hearing aid onstage in an unusual tribute to Ray, and the opening line of Dexy's Midnight Runners' #1 1984 hit, "Come On Eileen," mentions him.

Mac Rebennack: See Dr. John

Redbone

Formed 1968, Los Angeles, CA
Lolly Vegas (b. Fresno, CA), gtr., lead voc.; Pat Vegas (b. Fresno), bass, voc.; Anthony Bellamy (b. Los Angeles), gtr.; Peter De Poe (a.k.a. Last Walking Bear, b. Neah Bay Reservation, WA), drums.
1970—*Redbone* (Epic); *Potlatch* 1971—*Message From a Drum* 1973—*Wovoka* 1974—(– De Poe; + Butch Rillera, drums) *Beaded Dreams Through Turquoise Eyes* 1975—*Come and Get Your Redbone* 1978—*Cycles* (RCA) 1994—*Redbone: Live* (Avenue/Rhino) 1996—*Golden Classics* (Collectables).

Redbone consisted of four American Indians (the band's name is a derogatory Cajun slang term for *half-breed*) who sometimes wore traditional dress onstage and played "swamp rock" (popularized by Creedence Clearwater) with some funk influences. "Come and Get Your Love," highlighted by Lolly Vegas' lead vocals, was its only major hit (#5, 1974).

The band formed in California in 1968. The members had all grown up poor in migrant camps. In the mid-'60s brothers Pat and Lolly Vegas (the latter became Redbone's leader) played in a band on TV's *Shindig.* They also did West Coast session work, backing Odetta and John Lee Hooker, and wrote "Niki Hoeky," which became a hit for P.J. Proby (#23, 1967).

Anthony Bellamy used to play flamenco guitar at his parents' restaurant and later performed with local L.A. rock & roll bands; Peter De Poe was a ceremonial drummer on the reservation where he was born. The band united on the L.A. club circuit, got a deal with Epic, and released its debut in January 1970, including its own version of "Niki Hoeky."

Redbone's albums never sold well, and while the group did have some catchy, soulful rock tracks like 1971's "Maggie" (#45) and 1972's Top 25 hit "Witch Queen of New Orleans," it later explored more traditional Indian roots music. By the late '70s Redbone had faded. The group continues to tour, however, and in 1994 released a live album recorded in 1977.

Otis Redding

Born Sep. 9, 1941, Dawson, GA; died Dec. 10, 1967, Madison, WI
1964—*Pain in My Heart* (Atco) 1965—*The Great Otis Redding Sings Soul Ballads* (Volt); *Otis Blue/Otis Redding Sings Soul* 1966—*Complete and Unbelievable . . . The Otis Redding Dictionary of Soul; The Soul Album* 1967—*Otis Redding Live in Europe; King and Queen* (with Carla Thomas) (Stax); *History of Otis Redding* (Volt) 1968—*The Dock of the Bay; The Immortal Otis Redding* (Atco); *Otis Redding in Person at the Whisky-a-Go-Go* 1969—*Love Man* 1970—*Tell the Truth* (Atco); *Otis Redding/Jimi Hendrix Experience* (Reprise) 1982—*Otis Redding Recorded Live* (Atlantic) 1987—*The Otis Redding Story* 1992—*Remember Me* (Stax); *The Very Best of Otis Redding* (Rhino) 1993—*Good to Me: Live at the Whisky a-Go-Go, vol. 2* (Stax); *Otis! The Definitive Otis Redding* (Rhino/Atlantic) 1995—*The Very Best of Otis Redding, vol. 2.*

Otis Redding's grainy voice and galvanizing stage shows made him one of the greatest male soul singers of the '60s. At the time of his death, he was making his first significant impact on the pop audience after years as a favorite among blacks.

In his youth, Redding was influenced by both Little

Richard and Sam Cooke, and early in his career he was a member of Little Richard's backing band, the Upsetters. In the late '50s, he met Johnny Jenkins, a local guitarist, who invited him to join his group, the Pinetoppers, who were managed by Phil Walden. Feeling that he'd gone as far as he could go in Macon, Redding moved to L.A. in 1960. There he cut a handful of singles, including the Little Richard–esque "Gamma Lamma." Upon returning to Macon in 1961, he recorded "Shout Bamalama" and garnered some local attention.

After taking odd jobs around the South, Redding worked as a chauffeur and was working again with Jenkins when the guitarist landed a contract with Atlantic. One day in October 1962, when it seemed that Jenkins' session wasn't going anywhere, Redding hastily recorded his own ballad, "These Arms of Mine." He had accompanied Jenkins to the session with the intent of getting a chance to record. By 1963, "These Arms of Mine" had become Redding's first hit. It hit #20 on the R&B chart and established Redding as a recording artist. But it was his impassioned performances on the so-called chitlin' circuit that made him, next to James Brown, the most popular black entertainer of the mid-'60s.

Redding wrote many of his own hits, including "Mr. Pitiful" (#41 pop, #10 R&B, 1965), "Fa-Fa-Fa-Fa-Fa (Sad Song)" (#29 pop, #12 R&B, 1966), and "(Sittin' on) The Dock of the Bay" (#1 pop, #1 R&B, 1968), all co-credited to Stax session guitarist Steve Cropper; "I've Been Loving You Too Long" (#21 pop, #2 R&B, 1965), with Jerry Butler; "Respect" (#35 pop, #4 R&B, 1965), "I Can't Turn You Loose" (#11 R&B, 1965), and "My Lover's Prayer" (#61 pop, #10 R&B, 1966). He also had hits with the Rolling Stones' "Satisfaction" (#31 pop, #4 R&B, 1966) and Sam Cooke's "Shake" (#47 pop, #16 R&B, 1967). Among his LPs, *Dictionary of Soul* is considered one of the best examples of the Memphis soul sound.

Otis Redding

Redding also played an important role in the careers of other singers. In 1967 he cut a duet album with Carla Thomas, *King and Queen,* which had a hit in "Tramp" (#26 pop, #2 R&B). Redding produced his protégé Arthur Conley's tribute "Sweet Soul Music" (#2 pop and R&B) in 1967—an adaptation of Sam Cooke's "Yeah Man"—which became a soul standard. Redding also established his own label, Jotis, and was planning to get more deeply involved in talent management, development, and production.

Redding's appearance at the Monterey Pop Festival in 1967 introduced the singer to white rock fans. His intense performance (captured in the film *Monterey Pop* and on the LP *Otis Redding/Jimi Hendrix*) was enthusiastically received. As a gesture of thanks, Redding and Steve Cropper wrote "(Sittin' on) The Dock of the Bay." It was recorded on December 6, 1967, at the end of a long session. The whistling at the end came about, Cropper claims, because Redding forgot a vocal fadeout he had rehearsed before. It would become his biggest hit, yet Redding never lived to see its release.

On December 10, 1967, his chartered plane crashed into a Wisconsin lake, killing Redding and four members of his backup band, the Bar-Kays. In early 1968 "The Dock of the Bay" hit #1 on both the pop and R&B charts. Fourteen years later his two sons and a nephew formed their own group, called the Reddings, and covered "The Dock of the Bay" (#55 pop, #21 R&B). Otis Redding was inducted into the Rock and Roll Hall of Fame in 1989 by Little Richard.

Helen Reddy

Born Oct. 25, 1941, Melbourne, Austral.
1971—*I Don't Know How to Love Him* (Capitol); *Helen Reddy* 1972—*I Am Woman* 1973—*Long Hard Climb* 1974—*Love Song for Jeffrey; Free and Easy* 1975—*No Way to Treat a Lady; Helen Reddy's Greatest Hits* 1976—*Music, Music* 1977—*Ear Candy; Pete's Dragon* soundtrack 1978—*We'll Sing in the Sunshine; Live in London* 1979—*Reddy* 1980—*Take What You Find* 1981—*Play Me Out* (MCA) 1983—*Imagination* 1987—*Helen Reddy Greatest Hits (and More)* (Capitol) 1990—*Feel So Young* (Helen Reddy, Inc.) 1997—*When I Dream* (Varèse Vintage) 1998—*Center Stage; I Am Woman: The Essential Helen Reddy* (Razor & Tie).

Among her many hits, singer Helen Reddy will no doubt be best remembered as the composer and singer of "I Am Woman," which went to #1 and won a Grammy in 1972. Reddy began performing at the age of four at the Tivoli Theatre in Perth, Australia, and she toured much of that country with her show-business parents. She left boarding school at age 15 to work with a road show, acting as well as singing. She eventually landed her own Australian TV show, *Helen Reddy Sings,* and in 1966 she won a trip to New York in the Australian Bandstand International contest, sponsored by Philips-Mercury Records.

Reddy had little success in New York, but she did meet Jeff Wald, an agent with the William Morris talent agency, whom she married a year later. (They divorced in the early '80s; in 1983 she married Milton Ruth.) In 1970 Wald arranged for her to perform on *The Tonight Show,* and within a year Reddy had her first hit, a version of "I Don't Know How to Love Him" (#13, 1971) from the Broadway rock musical *Jesus Christ Superstar.*

Reddy's other hits included "Peaceful" (#12), "Delta Dawn" (#1), and "Leave Me Alone" (#3), in 1973; "Keep On Singing" (#15), "You and Me Against the World" (#9), and "Angie Baby" (#1), in 1974; "Emotion" (#22), "Bluebird" (#35), and "Ain't No Way to Treat a Lady" (#8), in 1975; "I Can't Hear You No More" (#29) in 1976; and "You're My World" (#18) in 1977. In 1973 she had her own summer-replacement variety show on NBC, and for most of the rest of the '70s she was a hostess on NBC's late-night rock-variety show *The Midnight Special.*

By then her run at the Top 40 had ended. She did some acting, appearing in *Airport 1975* (1974), the Disney children's film *Pete's Dragon* (1977), and *Sgt. Pepper's Lonely Hearts Club Band* (1978). In the mid-'70s she served as Commissioner of Parks and Recreation for her adopted home state of California. More recently she has returned to the theater, notably on Broadway and in the West End of London in the hit musical *Blood Brothers.* She is one of the foremost interpreters of English playwright Willy Russell, having appeared in four productions of his one-woman show, *Shirley Valentine.* In 2000 she guest-starred in the CBS television series *Diagnosis Murder. Center Stage,* a collection of showtunes, was her first album of completely new material in 15 years.

Red Hot Chili Peppers

Formed 1983, Hollywood, CA
Flea (b. Michael Balzary, Oct. 16, 1962, Melbourne, Austral.), bass; Jack Irons (b. July 18, 1962, Los Angeles, CA), drums; Anthony Kiedis (b. Nov. 1, 1962, Grand Rapids, MI), voc.; Hillel Slovak (b. Apr. 13, 1962, Haifa, Israel; d. June 25, 1988, Los Angeles), gtr.
1983—(– Slovak; – Irons; + Jack Sherman, gtr.; + Cliff Martinez, drums) 1984—*The Red Hot Chili Peppers* (EMI America) 1985—(– Sherman; – Martinez; + Slovak; + Irons) *Freaky Styley* 1987—*The Uplift Mofo Party Plan* 1988—(– Slovak; – Irons; + Blackbyrd McKnight, gtr.; + D.H. Peligro, drums) 1989—(– McKnight; – Peligro; + John Frusciante [b. Mar. 5, 1970, New York, NY], gtr.; + Chad Smith [b. Oct. 25, 1962, St. Paul, MN], drums) *Mother's Milk* 1991—*BloodSugarSexMagik* (Warner Bros.) 1992—*What Hits!?* (EMI America) (– Frusciante; + Arik Marshall [b. Feb. 13, 1967, Los Angeles], gtr.) 1993—(– Marshall; + Jesse Tobias, gtr; – Tobias; + Dave Navarro [b. June 7, 1967, Santa Monica, CA], gtr.) 1994—*One Hot Minute* (Warner Bros.) 1998—(– Navarro; + Frusciante) 1999—*Californication.*
John Frusciante solo: 1994—*Niandra La 'Des and Usually Just a T-Shirt* (American) 2001—*To Record Only Water for Ten Days* (Warner Bros.).

A potent combination of L.A. skateboard cool, tattoos, thrash, and funk, the Red Hot Chili Peppers overcame personal problems to emerge as one of the early '90s premier bands with 1991's *BloodSugarSexMagik* (#3) and "Under the Bridge" (#2). Their over-the-top performances and a sometimes excessive obsession with sex have inspired accusations of both sexism and criminal behavior.

After meeting at L.A.'s Fairfax High, Flea, Slovak, and Irons, with Kiedis as MC, formed the band Anthem School. Kiedis, the son of actor and Sunset Strip personality Blackie Dammett, already had show-biz experience after playing Sylvester Stallone's son in the 1976 film *F.I.S.T.* Flea, an Australian-born, New York–raised musical prodigy, departed to join the L.A. punk band Fear, as well as act in Penelope Spheeris' *Suburbia* (1983). (He later appeared in such films as Gus Van Sant's *My Own Private Idaho* [1992] and Joel and Ethan Coen's *The Big Lebowski* [1998]; he also voices the character Donny in Nickelodeon's animated series *The Wild Thornberries.*) Irons and the Israeli-born Slovak then formed What Is This?

In 1983 the Chilis played their first show, an impromptu one-song jam at an L.A. club. The group went over well enough to be asked back (for two songs) and soon became a popular Hollywood club attraction. The band's self-titled debut—with Flea, Kiedis, Cliff Martinez, and Jack Sherman (What Is This? had other contractual obligations)—was produced by Gang of Four guitarist Andy Gill. The album stiffed; Irons and Slovak returned, and the band took to the road, sometimes appearing onstage wearing only strategically placed tube socks.

Freaky Styley (1985), produced by George Clinton and with guest appearances by funk horn players Maceo Parker and Fred Wesley, improved matters musically if not commercially. More rock-oriented, *The Uplift Mofo Party Plan* (#148, 1987) sold better, and contained the band's signature tune, "Party on Your Pussy." Any optimism was shattered by the 1988 death of guitarist Hillel Slovak from a heroin overdose. Disturbed by Slovak's death and Kiedis' heroin addiction, Irons quit. An interim band with P-Funk guitarist Blackbyrd McKnight and Dead Kennedys drummer D.H. Peligro did not take hold. Kiedis recruited a Chili Peppers fan, guitarist John Frusciante, and auditions brought Chad Smith. This version of the band recorded *Mother's Milk* (#52, 1989). With videos for "Knock Me Down" and their cover of Stevie Wonder's "Higher Ground" on MTV, it looked like the Peppers were about to break through.

The band's lifestyle came under some attack, though, with Kiedis convicted in 1989 of indecent exposure and sexual battery in an incident following a concert in Virginia. The next year during a taping of an *MTV Spring Break* special in Florida, Flea and Smith jumped offstage, with Flea grabbing a woman and carrying her on his shoulders, and Smith spanking her. The two were charged, and Flea was found guilty of battery, disorderly conduct, and solicitation to commit an unnatural and lascivious act; Smith was found guilty of battery.

The Chili Peppers' next album, *BloodSugarSexMagik,* produced by Rick Rubin, was written and recorded in a mansion the band claimed was haunted. It sold over 4 million copies, leading to their headlining Lollapalooza in 1992. Just prior to the tour, John Frusciante left the band and was replaced by Arik Marshall. Marshall lasted only a year and, after many auditions and one false start with Jesse Tobias, was replaced by former Jane's Addiction guitarist Dave Navarro. The 1995 release *One Hot Minute* (#4) went platinum, but failed to generate the excitement of *BloodSugar,* precipitating a fallow phase in the band's career. Flea joined Navarro for a 1997 reunion tour of Jane's Addiction, and Navarro and Kiedis slipped back into old drug habits. Navarro quit the group in 1998 to pursue solo ambitions, casting the future of the band in doubt. Instead of breaking up, however, the Chili Peppers invited Frusciante to return, the guitarist having recovered from a severe drug addiction. The subsequent album, *Californication* (#3, 1999), was a commercial and critical triumph, with a hit single in "Scar Tissue" (#9, 1999) and a major tour that included a fateful show at Woodstock '99, where the group had the dubious distinction of performing as a fiery melee erupted.

Redman

Born Reggie Noble, Apr. 17, 1974, Newark, NJ
1992—*Whut? Thee Album* (RAL) 1994—*Dare Iz a Darkside* 1996—*Muddy Waters* (Def Jam) 1998—*Doc's Da Name* 2001—*Malpractice.*
Method Man & Redman: 1999—*Blackout!* (Def Jam).

Redman is one of the most respected lyricists in '90s hip-hop. He grew up in a rough corner of Jersey City, New Jersey, where his mother first bought him a pair of turntables at age 10. He earned his Redman moniker the following year, when his face turned red after being hit with a snowball. By 16 he switched from DJ to rapper and soon attracted the attention of EPMD mastermind Erick Sermon. After Redman's mother kicked him out for selling drugs, he moved in with Sermon and stayed for two years. During that time Redman appeared on EPMD recordings and became a member of Sermon's "Hit Squad" collective.

Whut? Thee Album (#49, 1992), coproduced by Sermon, included the rap hit "Blow Your Mind." *Dare Iz a Darkside* (#13) followed in 1994. The next year he collaborated with Method Man (of the Wu-Tang Clan) on "How High" (#13) from *The Show* soundtrack album, followed by a joint appearance on Redman's *Muddy Waters* (#12, 1996). It was the beginning of what would become a regular partnership. Redman's *Doc's Da Name 2000* (#11) was released in 1998. The next year, Redman and Method Man teamed up for an entire album, *Blackout!* (#3), with tracks produced by Sermon and Wu-Tang leader, RZA. Also in 1999 Redman guested on Limp Bizkit's "N 2 gether Now" (#73).

Jerry Reed

Born Jerry Hubbard, Mar. 20, 1937, Atlanta, GA
1971—*When You're Hot, You're Hot* (RCA) 1972—*The Best of Jerry Reed* 1976—*Both Barrels* 1977—*East Bound and Down* 1983—*The Bird* 1985—*Collector's Series* 1986—*Lookin' at You* (Capitol) 1995—*The Essential Jerry Reed* (RCA) 1996—*Flyin' High* (Southern Tracks) 1999—*Pickin'.*

Jerry Reed is known mostly among musicians for his fast-pickin' guitar style, and among the masses for his jokey, C&W-to-pop hits of the early '70s. He got a record contract with Capitol in 1955 at age 18. He had been playing in bands since his early teens and had worked in a cotton mill. Initially Reed got attention as a songwriter, especially with "Crazy Legs" (which Gene Vincent recorded in 1956) and some covers by Brenda Lee.

From 1959 to 1961 Reed served in the army, and upon his release he moved to Nashville, where he had two minor hits on Columbia, "Hully Gully Guitars" and "Goodnight Irene." Reed worked primarily as a session guitarist until 1965, when he signed to RCA. Elvis Presley began to record Reed's work, giving him his first pop chart exposure with 1968's "Guitar Man" (which became Reed's nickname; it was also a hit for Reed the year before). Presley also cut Reed's "U.S. Male."

The guitarist's albums began to place on the C&W chart, and in 1970 he had his first gold single with his pop crossover debut, "Amos Moses," a swamp-rock song (#8 pop, #16 C&W). He became a household name with regular appearances on *Glen Campbell's Goodtime Hour* (1970–72). In 1971 he had a Top 10 pop and #1 C&W hit with the novelty number "When You're Hot, You're Hot," which also won a Grammy. In 1973 he again hit #1 with "Lord, Mr. Ford." Reed also won critical acclaim and a Grammy for a duet LP with Chet Atkins, *Me and Jerry.* In 1982 he had a #1 C&W hit with "She Got the Goldmine (I Got the Shaft)."

He branched out into acting in the mid-'70s with Southern roles, first in 1975's *W.W. and the Dixie Dance Kings,* and then in *Gator* (1976), both with Burt Reynolds. Next he costarred in the popular Reynolds *Smokey and the Bandit* series, consisting of three feature films released between 1977 and 1983. In the meantime, Reed continued his television career, as host of *The Jerry Reed When You're Hot You're Hot Hour* (1972), as a regular on *Dean Martin Presents Music Country* (1973), playing a detective on *Nashville 99* (1977), and starring in the action-adventure series *Concrete Cowboys* (1981). In 1998 he enjoyed a role in *The Waterboy,* the fifth highest-grossing film of that year. He also collaborated with Waylon Jennings, Bobby Bare, and Mel Tillis on the *Old Dogs* album. *Pickin',* released the following year, contains five instrumentals and five vocal tracks.

Jimmy Reed

Born Sep. 6, 1925, Dunleith, MS; died Aug. 29, 1976, Oakland, CA

1957—*I'm Jimmy Reed* (Vee-Jay) 1961—*Jimmy Reed at Carnegie Hall* 1974—*The Best of Jimmy Reed* (Crescendo) 1988—*Bright Lights, Big City* (Chameleon) 1994—*The Classic Recordings* (Tomato) 1997—*Lost in the Shuffle* (32 Records) 1998—*Cry Before I Go* (Drive Archive).

Jimmy Reed, one of the most influential blues harpists and performers, was also the composer of such standards as "Big Boss Man," "Honest I Do," "Bright Lights, Big City," and "Baby, What You Want Me to Do."

The son of a sharecropper, Reed began performing in the Chicago area in the late '40s to early '50s, and in 1953 he signed with Vee-Jay Records. His first big hit was "You Don't Have to Go" (#9 R&B) in 1955. The next year he scored with "Ain't That Lovin' You Baby" (#7 R&B). Between 1956 and 1961 he had 11 more Top 20 R&B hits, including "Honest I Do" (#10, 1957) and "Baby, What You Want Me to Do" (#10, 1960), both of which crossed over to Top 40 pop success.

Reed's work has been covered by many others, including Elvis Presley ("Baby, What You Want Me to Do"), Van Morrison and Them ("Bright Lights, Big City"), Pretty Things ("Big Boss Man"), the Rolling Stones, and Aretha Franklin, both of whom do versions of "Honest I Do."

He died at age 50 following an epileptic seizure. In 1988 his widow and their eight children filed a multimillion-dollar lawsuit against Arc Music, claiming that neither Reed nor his wife had sufficient education to comprehend a deal he signed in 1967, releasing all the rights to his songs for a flat fee of $10,000. As part of the settlement, both parties agreed not to divulge its terms.

Lou Reed

Born Lewis Alan Reed, Mar. 2, 1942, Brooklyn, NY
1972—*Lou Reed* (RCA); *Transformer* 1973—*Berlin* 1974—*Rock 'n' Roll Animal; Sally Can't Dance* 1975—*Lou Reed Live; Metal Machine Music* 1976—*Coney Island Baby; Rock and Roll Heart* (Arista) 1977—*Walk on the Wild Side* (RCA) 1978—*Street Hassle* (Arista); *Live: Take No Prisoners* 1979—*The Bells* 1980—*Growing Up in Public; Rock and Roll Diary* 1982—*The Blue Mask* (RCA); *I Can't Stand It* 1983—*Legendary Hearts* 1984—*New Sensations; Live in Italy* 1985—*City Lights: Classic Performances* (Arista) 1986—*Mistrial* (RCA) 1989—*New York* (Sire); *Retro* (RCA) 1992—*Magic and Loss* (Sire); *Between Thought and Expression: The Lou Reed Anthology* (RCA) 1996—*Set the Twilight Reeling* (Reprise) 1998—*Perfect Night Live in London* 1999—*The Definitive Collection* (Arista) 2000—*Ecstasy* (Reprise).
With John Cale: 1990—*Songs for Drella* (Sire).

As the lead singer and songwriter of the Velvet Underground in the late '60s, Lou Reed was responsible for a body of work that was alienated from the prevailing optimism of the day and was passionately bleak, and which remains highly influential today. He is often referred to as the godfather of punk. His solo recording career, beginning in 1972, has been more idiosyncratic and marked by sudden turnabouts in image and sound, from self-consciously commercial product to white noise to unpredictable folk rock.

Lou Reed

Before the formation of the Velvet Underground [see entry] in 1965, Reed grew up in Freeport, Long Island, then attended Syracuse University, studying poetry (under Delmore Schwartz, to whom Reed dedicated a song on the first Velvet Underground LP) and journalism. Reed's poems were published in *Fusion* magazine. (In 1977 he earned an award from the Coordinating Council of Literary Magazines for his poem "The Slide" and in 1992 was awarded France's Order of Arts and Letters.) After leaving Syracuse, Reed returned to New York City and worked for Pickwick Records, taking part in the studio group that recorded various Reed-penned songs, released by the Beachnuts and the Roughnecks. During this period, he met the musicians with whom he would subsequently form the Velvet Underground. With two of them he formed a band called the Primitives, which became the Warlocks and made one record.

Reed's 1970 departure from the Velvet Underground was bitter; he did not even stay to complete their fourth album, *Loaded,* though songs from that project ("Sweet Jane" and "Rock & Roll") would become permanent fixtures of his live show and reputation. He became a virtual recluse for nearly two years, until moving to England and beginning a solo career in 1971. *Transformer* (#29, 1972) was his pop breakthrough. Produced by Velvet Underground fan David Bowie, it yielded Reed's only Top 20 hit to date, "Walk on the Wild Side," an ode to the denizens of Andy Warhol's '60s films. With Bowie's aid, Reed made the transition to the glitter rock of the period, camping up his presumed homosexuality with bleached-blond hair and black fingernail polish. Typically, the next record, *Berlin,* was as grim in tone as *Transformer* had been playful.

Reed's recordings have continued to be unpredictable. A pair of live albums drawn from the same set of concerts (including the gold *Rock 'n' Roll Animal,* #45, 1974) featured streamlined heavy-metal versions of Velvet Underground material, while a later tour would pander to theatrics: Reed, for example, pretended to shoot up while performing the song "Heroin." *Sally Can't Dance* reached the Top 10 and was repudiated by Reed almost on release. After another live LP, he followed with *Metal Machine Music,* four sides of grating instrumental noise, alternately considered high art worthy of RCA's classical division and a gambit to get off the label.

Reed moved to Arista in 1976 and at first made impeccably produced, harrowing music like the title cut of *Street Hassle* (#89, 1978). He then entered a relatively peaceful phase, typified by album titles like *Rock and Roll Heart* and *Growing Up in Public.* He married Sylvia Morales on Valentine's Day 1980, and his songs about the seamy side of life began to appear alongside paeans to suburban life—"I'm an average guy," he sang on *The Blue Mask.*

In the mid-'80s Reed gained more of the spotlight when a number of postpunk bands, including R.E.M., U2, and Sonic Youth, began singing his praises and vocally claiming inspiration by the Velvet Underground. The second creative wind that began with the alternately hopeful and frightening *Blue Mask* continued with the more accessible *New Sensations* (#56, 1984) and *Mistrial* (#47, 1986). Reed then moved to Sire, where he hit an artistic plateau with *New York, Songs for Drella,* and *Magic and Loss.* A brutal song cycle about urban decay, 1989's *New York* was his first Top 40 album since *Sally Can't Dance.*

In 1989 Reed played guitar on former Velvet Underground drummer Maureen "Moe" Tucker's solo album, *Life in Exile After Abdication.* The same year, he reunited with another fellow VU mate, John Cale, for a work-in-progress performance of *Songs for Drella,* a pop requiem the two wrote for their late friend and mentor, Andy Warhol, who had died three years earlier; in 1990 an album and video were released. The Velvet Underground reunited in 1993 for some well-received European dates, but again broke up bitterly before their planned U.S. performances (reportedly because Reed insisted on producing the album of the band's upcoming MTV *Unplugged* appearance, which was subsequently canceled). The band reunited once more in 1996, after the death of member Sterling Morrison, to be inducted into the Rock and Roll Hall of Fame and perform a tribute song to the late guitarist.

Reed's 1992 album *Magic and Loss* (#80, 1992), a somber meditation on the process and pain of aging and death, inspired by the cancer deaths of two friends (including songwriter Doc Pomus), was considered his most inspired work since *The Blue Mask.* The same year, RCA released a box set of Reed's music, *Between Thought and Expression,* which followed a 1991 book of selected Reed lyrics of the same name.

Throughout the '80s and into the '90s, Reed showed a newfound political-activist side, appearing at the 1985 Farm Aid benefit concert, the 1986 Amnesty International Tour, and contributing to the Artists United Against Apartheid *Sun City* record. In 1993 he performed at an inaugural event honoring the home state of former Vice President Al Gore. Reed had also moved into acting—in the 1980 movie *One Trick Pony* and advertisements for Honda scooters, which used "Walk on the Wild Side," and Wim Wenders' 1993 film, *Faraway, So Close.*

Over the years Reed has found affinity with some of rock & roll's romantics and mythologists: Bruce Springsteen appeared uncredited on 1978's *Street Hassle,* and Reed inducted Dion into the Rock and Roll Hall of Fame; he also cowrote songs for Kiss and Nils Lofgren. Reed's sidemen have included Jack Bruce (ex-Cream) and jazz trumpeter Don Cherry; for *The Blue Mask* and *Legendary Hearts,* he toured with an acclaimed band that included ex-Voidoids Robert Quine on guitar and Fred Maher on drums, and ex–Jean-Luc Ponty bassist Fernando Saunders; and for *New York* and the *Magic and Loss* tour, he brought along R&B crooner Little Jimmy Scott as a backup vocalist. Split from his wife Sylvia by 1994, Reed was frequently in the company of avant-garde performance artist Laurie Anderson, with whom he began improvising instrumental pieces at home.

Anderson served as an emotional influence on 1996's *Set the Twilight Reeling* (#110), an album that mixed romance and nostalgia amid Reed's darker interests. That same year, Reed collaborated with theatrical director Robert Wilson on the production of *Time Rocker;* they collaborated again in 2000 on *Poe-try,* based on the works of Edgar Allen Poe.

After another wait of four years between studio albums, Reed returned in 2000 with *Ecstasy,* which continued his commitment to minimalist rock & roll with thoughtful, if sometimes confrontational lyrics on dreams, desire, and despair. Anderson performed electric violin on two tracks, and guitarist Mike Rathke joined Reed for the raw, droning guitar pattern of the 18-minute "Like a Possum." Reed also published *Pass Thru Fire—The Collected Lyrics.*

Martha Reeves: See Martha and the Vandellas

R.E.M.

Formed 1980, Athens, GA
Michael Stipe (b. John Michael Stipe, Jan. 4, 1960, Decatur, GA), voc.; Peter Buck (b. Peter Lawrence Buck, Dec. 6, 1956, Berkeley, CA), gtr.; Mike Mills (b. Michael Edward Mills, Dec. 17, 1958, Orange, CA), bass, voc.; Bill Berry (b. William Thomas Berry, July 31, 1958, Duluth, MN), drums.
1982—*Chronic Town* EP (I.R.S.) 1983—*Murmur* 1984—*Reckoning* 1985—*Fables of the Reconstruction* 1986—*Lifes Rich Pageant* 1987—*Document; Dead Letter Office* 1988—*Eponymous; Green* (Warner Bros.) 1991—*Out of Time* 1992—*Automatic for the People* 1994—*Monster* 1996—

New Adventures in Hi-Fi (Warner Bros.) 1997—(– Berry) 1998—*Up* 2001—*Reveal.*

The most popular college-rock band of the '80s, R.E.M. underwent a steady, decade-long rise from underground heroes to bona fide superstars. The quartet's arty mix of punk energy, folky instrumental textures, muffled vocals, and introspective, often oblique lyrics influenced a generation of alternative-rock bands. By the time of its $10 million, five-record deal with Warner Bros. in 1988, the band had gone from playing hole-in-the-wall pizza parlors to major arenas.

Army brat Michael Stipe was an introverted child who spent much of his time hanging out with sisters Lynda and Cyndy. By 1975, he had begun reading articles about Patti Smith and the burgeoning New York punk scene, and while in high school in St. Louis, he joined a short-lived punk-rock cover band. In 1978 Stipe enrolled at the University of Georgia at Athens, where he majored in painting and photography. While shopping at the local Wuxtry record shop, he met store manager Peter Buck, a native Californian and avid pop fan who shared Stipe's interest in adventurous music. Deciding to form a band, within a year, they connected with fellow students Bill Berry and Mike Mills, childhood friends from nearby Macon who had played together in various Southern rock groups. In April 1980 the four formed R.E.M. (named for the dream state "rapid eye movement") and began rehearsing in a converted church. In July the group played their first out-of-state gig in Chapel Hill, North Carolina, where they met future manager Jefferson Holt.

Though influenced by punk and the DIY aesthetic, R.E.M. developed its own energetic folk-rock style over the next year. Buck's chiming, Byrds-like guitar, together with Stipe's cryptic vocals, became the group's signature sound. In 1981 the group recorded a demo tape of original music at Mitch Easter's Drive-In Studio in Winston-Salem, North Carolina. Two songs from those sessions, "Radio Free Europe" and "Sitting Still," were released as a 7-inch single in July on the homegrown Hib-Tone label. The driving "Radio Free Europe" attracted positive notices, and in October the band returned to Easter's studio to record its first EP. R.E.M. signed with I.R.S. in 1982 and released *Chronic Town* to overwhelming critical praise.

The band's first full-length album, *Murmur* (#36, 1983), was an instant classic, containing everything its supporters had hoped for: more layers of ringing guitar, more passionately vague vocals, more atmospheric melodies, and more seductive pop hooks. It also included a new, tighter version of "Radio Free Europe." The followup, *Reckoning,* failed to break new ground but managed to reach #27, spawning the minor hit "So. Central Rain (I'm Sorry)" and garnering favorable reviews. The group enlisted London-based folk producer Joe Boyd (Fairport Convention, Richard Thompson) for *Fables of the Reconstruction* (#28, 1985), which featured a hazy, psychedelic musical setting. *Lifes Rich Pageant* (#21, 1986) took that experiment further, but with more of a sheen, courtesy of producer Don Gehman (John Mellencamp), who encouraged

R.E.M.: Bill Berry, Peter Buck, Michael Stipe, Mike Mills

Stipe to sing more clearly; its single was "Fall on Me," whose video was directed by Stipe. R.E.M.'s first major hit, "The One I Love" (#9, 1987), from the band's first Top 10 album, *Document* (#10, 1987), was a song of betrayal that was almost universally misinterpreted as a love song. The band's major-label debut, *Green* (#12, 1988), yielded a hit single, "Stand" (#6, 1988), that was the simplest, most hummable song of R.E.M.'s career; the album's other single, "Pop Song 89" (#86, 1988), was a minor hit that made fun of the music business. *Dead Letter Office* (#52, 1987) is a collection of B sides and outtakes, and *Eponymous* (#44, 1988) is a greatest-hits album. Following *Green,* R.E.M. went on a touring hiatus.

It took three years for the band to return with the highly anticipated *Out of Time,* which rocketed to #1, went quadruple platinum, and included "Losing My Religion" (#4, 1991) and "Shiny Happy People" (#10, 1991). The video for the former was banned in Ireland for allegedly homoerotic imagery; the latter was a duet with Kate Pierson of the B-52's. *Out of Time* also featured an expanded instrumental palette of horns and mandolins. The somber *Automatic for the People* (#2, 1992) featured string arrangements by former Led Zeppelin bassist John Paul Jones. Its hits were "Drive" (#28, 1992), "Man on the Moon" (#30, 1993), and "Everybody Hurts" (#29, 1993).

During the latter part of the '80s, R.E.M. became activists, inviting Greenpeace to set up booths at concerts and becoming involved in local Athens politics. On his own, Stipe spoke out on such issues as the environment, animal rights, and the plight of the homeless. He also ushered other artists into the public eye, including folk painter the Rev. Howard Finster, filmmaker Jim McKay (with whom he set up the film company C-00, noted for its series of public-service announcements), and edgy artist Vic Chesnutt [see entry]. Stipe also worked with rapper KRS-ONE of Boogie Down

Productions and Natalie Merchant of 10,000 Maniacs. Meanwhile, Buck produced music by such artists as Kevn Kinney of Drivin' N' Cryin' and Charlie Pickett. In 1990 Buck, Berry, Mills, and singer/songwriter Warren Zevon formed a side band, Hindu Love Gods, which put out a self-titled album on Giant-Reprise.

R.E.M. returned with *Monster* (#1, 1994), which combined rockers featuring heavily reverbed guitars (including that of Sonic Youth's Thurston Moore on one track) and distorted or almost glam-sounding vocals, as well as the band's more traditional-sounding fare. Its first single, "What's the Frequency, Kenneth?" reached only #21, while "Bang and Blame" reached #19 and "Strange Currencies" hit #47. Soon after, the band commenced its first world tour in five years. Within two months, Berry suffered a double brain aneurysm onstage in Switzerland and underwent emergency surgery. He recovered, and the tour resumed two months later, but more medical emergencies interrupted the tour when Mills needed abdominal surgery and Stipe had surgery for a hernia. Two weeks after the tour ended, Buck came down with pneumonia.

In 1996 *New Adventures in Hi-Fi* (#2) was released and R.E.M. re-signed with Warner Bros. for a reported $80 million. But the new album, recorded largely on the road during sound checks, was considered a commercial disappointment. In 1997 Berry left the band after 17 years. R.E.M. chose to continue and released the moody *Up* (#3, 1998), recorded with drummers Barrett Martin (Screaming Trees) and Joey Waronker (Beck), along with '70s drum machines, sequencers, and tape loops.

By now Stipe was exploring work as a filmmaker, having already appeared as a '40s hermit in the 1996 film *Color of a Brisk and Leaping Day*. He then formed a production company, Single Cell Pictures, which enjoyed a critical success in 1999 with the surreal *Being John Malkovich*. Stipe released a book of photographs taken of Patti Smith on tour, while Buck began recording with an improvisational side project called Tuatara. In 1999 R.E.M. recorded the score to the Andy Kaufman biopic *Man on the Moon*, a title taken from the band's own tribute song to the late comedian. The movie soundtrack included a sequel to the original song, "The Great Beyond." The next year R.E.M. traveled to Vancouver to begin work on a new album, *Reveal*, which debuted at #6 in 2001.

The Remains/Barry and the Remains

Formed 1964, Boston, MA
Barry Tashian (b. Aug. 5, 1945, Oak Park, IL), gtr., voc.; Bill Briggs (b. Mar. 19, 1945, Battle Creek, MI), kybds., voc.; Vern Miller (b. Jan. 31, 1945, Orange, NJ), bass, voc.; Chip Damiani (b. Rudolph A. Damiani II, June 16, 1945, Waterbury, CT), drums.
1966—(– Damiani, + N.D. Smart II, drums) *The Remains* (Epic) 1967—(group disbands) 1998—(original group re-forms) 2000—*The Remains* EP (Sundazed).

Formed by Barry Tashian along with fellow Boston University students, the Remains gained a loyal Boston following on the strength of live shows, local hits, and one classic mid-'60s garage-punk single, "Don't Look Back" (no relation to the Dylan film). They soon relocated to New York City. In 1965 they opened local concerts by the Rolling Stones, and in 1966 they opened for the Beatles on that group's last U.S. tour. But after no followup hits materialized, the Remains broke up in 1967.

"Don't Look Back" is included on the *Nuggets* collection. Tashian briefly regrouped the band in the mid-'70s. He later backed Gram Parsons, then joined Emmylou Harris' band. In the '90s he performed and recorded in a country duo with his wife, Holly. He also wrote *Ticket to Ride*, a memoir about the Beatles final tour. The Remains reunited in 1998, for the Purple Weekend, a mod festival in Leon, Spain. That same year they played New York's Cavestomp! extravaganza. In 2000 they continued to perform and recorded new material in Nashville.

Renaissance

Formed 1969, Surrey, Eng.
Keith Relf (b. Mar. 23, 1943, Richmond, Eng.; d. May 14, 1976, Eng.), voc., gtr.; Jim McCarty (b. July 25, 1943, Eng.), drums; Jane Relf (b. Eng.), voc.; John Hawken (b. Eng.), kybds.; Louis Cennamo, bass.
1969—*Renaissance* (Elektra) 1970—(numerous early lineup changes; – K. Relf; – McCarty; – J. Relf; – Cennamo; – Hawken; + Rob Hendry, gtr.) 1971—(+ Jon Camp, bass; + John Tout, kybds.; + Terry Sullivan, perc.; + Annie Haslam, voc.) 1972—*Prologue* (Capitol) (– Hendry; + Michael Dunford, gtr.) 1973—*Ashes Are Burning* 1974—*Turn of the Cards* (Sire) 1975—*Scheherazade and Other Stories* 1976—*Live at Carnegie Hall* 1977—*Novella* 1978—*A Song for All Seasons* 1979—*Azure d'Or* 1980—(– Sullivan; – Tout; + Peter Gosling, kybds.; + Peter Barron, drums; numerous lineup changes follow) 1981—*Camera Camera* (I.R.S.) 1983—*Time-Line* 1987—(group disbands) 1990—*Tale of 1001 Nights, vol. I* (Sire); *Tale of 1001 Nights, vol. II* 1998—(group re-forms: Haslam; Dunford; Tout; Sullivan) 2000—*Tuscany* (Toshiba, Jap.).
Annie Haslam solo: 1977—*Annie in Wonderland* (Sire) 1985—*Still Life* (Ratpack) 1989—*Annie Haslam* (Epic) 1995—*Blessing in Disguise* (One Way) 1997—*Live Under Brazilian Skies* (White Dove) 2000—*The Dawn of Ananda; It Snows in Heaven Too*.
Illusion: (J. Relf; K. Relf; McCarty; Hawken; Cennamo) 1976—(– K. Relf) 1977—*Out of the Mist* (Island) 1978—*Illusions*.

Though Keith Relf and Jim McCarty founded Renaissance shortly after leaving the Yardbirds, their reign did not last long, and the incarnation that came to some prominence in the U.S. in the mid-'70s included neither of them. In 1969 Relf and McCarty joined Relf's sister Jane and John Hawken (ex–Nashville Teens, later with Strawbs) to form an eclectic band fusing folk, jazz, and classical influences with rock. An eponymous LP on Elektra was released later in the year, but both Relf and McCarty quickly became dissatisfied with the venture. Relf and Louis Cennamo moved on to head a harder-rocking band called Armageddon. (Just before Relf's death, he, Jane, and Hawken were forming Illusion, a group not unlike the original Renaissance. After Relf's death the group continued and recorded for Island.)

By the group's 1972 release, *Prologue*, all of the members had changed, though Keith Relf and McCarty had remained involved with Renaissance's songwriting and business affairs. The album had a pop-classical, self-consciously refined art-rock feel highlighted by John Tout's piano and Annie Haslam's clear, high-flying soprano. The lyricist was British poet Betty Thatcher, who wrote the lyrics to fit Michael Dunford's sheet music, which she would receive by mail.

Prologue got lots of U.S. FM airplay, and the group developed a strong following, particularly in New York. Before the followup, *Ashes Are Burning* (#171, 1973), Rob Hendry left and was replaced by songwriter/guitarist Dunford. With *Turn of the Cards* (#94, 1974), Renaissance switched to Sire, and its next LP (*Scheherazade* [#48, 1975]) featured an entire suite complete with a full orchestra. An orchestra also played on the well-received live LP, recorded on the East Coast. Though the group was making less frequent visits to the U.S. and U.K. charts, it remained a successful concert draw in Brazil, Germany, and Japan. Haslam recorded the solo *Annie in Wonderland* (1977), produced by Roy Wood, formerly of the Move and the Electric Light Orchestra. In the '80s Haslam, Camp, and Dunford (along with two new members) cut *Camera Camera* and *Time-Line* for I.R.S. Haslam, Gosling, and Dunford also formed the studio group Nevada.

In 1997 Dunford debuted his theatrical adaptation of *Scheherazade*. As of 2000, most of Renaissance's members still performed and recorded solo, with Haslam being the most active. In 2000 a reunited band issued a Japanese studio album, which coincided with numerous live archival releases. Roy Wood appeared as a guest on the record.

John Renbourn: See Pentangle

REO Speedwagon

Formed 1968, Champaign, IL

Terry Luttrell, voc.; Greg Philbin, bass; Gary Richrath (b. Oct. 18, 1949, Peoria, IL), gtrs.; Neal Doughty (b. July 29, 1946, Evanston, IL), kybds.; Alan Gratzer (b. Nov. 9, 1948, Syracuse, NY), drums.

1971—*REO Speedwagon* (Epic) (– Luttrell; + Kevin Cronin [b. Oct. 6, 1951, Evanston], voc.) 1972—*REO TWO* (– Cronin; + Michael Murphy, voc.) 1973—*Ridin' the Storm Out* 1974—*Lost in a Dream* 1975—*This Time We Mean It* (– Murphy; + Cronin) 1976—*REO* (– Philbin; + Bruce Hall [b. May 3, 1953, Champaign], bass) 1977—*You Get What You Play For* 1978—*You Can Tune a Piano, But You Can't Tuna Fish* 1979—*Nine Lives* 1980—*A Decade of Rock 'n' Roll; Hi-Infidelity* 1982—*Good Trouble* 1984—*Wheels Are Turnin'* 1987—*Life as We Know It* 1988—*The Hits* (– Gratzer; + Graham Lear, drums) 1990—(– Richrath; – Lear; + Bryan Hitt, drums; + Dave Amato, gtr.; + Jesse Harms, kybds.) *The Earth, a Small Man, His Dog and a Chicken* 1991—(– Harms) *The Second Decade of Rock & Roll* 1996—*Building the Bridge* (Castle) 1999—*The Ballads* (Epic/Legacy).

After more than a decade of touring and nine middling albums, this Midwestern journeyman hard-pop quintet sold over 7 million copies of *Hi-Infidelity*. REO Speedwagon (named after a high-speed fire engine) was formed by Neal Doughty and Alan Gratzer while both were students at the University of Illinois in 1968. They became a popular local club attraction. Irving Azoff, who later managed the Eagles and Steely Dan, handled the group in the early '70s, getting it dates opening for other popular Midwestern acts like Bob Seger and Kansas. REO and Azoff severed their relationship in 1977.

Throughout the early '70s, REO Speedwagon's records sold unspectacularly as the group continued to tour. REO went through relatively few personnel changes, the most significant being vocalist Kevin Cronin's departure in 1972 for a solo career; replacement Michael Murphy handled the singing on REO's third, fourth, and fifth LPs. Cronin then returned in 1975; his songwriting and singing would be crucial to the band's ascendance.

REO was the quintet's least successful LP, but its seventh and eighth—the live *You Get What You Play For* and *You Can Tune a Piano, But You Can't Tuna Fish*—were breakthroughs. With Cronin and Gary Richrath coproducing, REO began to develop a more distinctive sound, a mix of rock riffs and pop hooks. *Tuna* contained the band's first chart single, "Roll With the Changes" (#58, 1978), and was its first to sell a million copies. *Nine Lives* in 1979 continued in this pop-rock direction.

Hi-Infidelity in 1980 was a phenomenally successful album, climbing to #1 on the *Billboard* chart three separate times. Four of its singles made the Top 40: "Keep On Lovin' You" (#1, 1980), "Take It on the Run" (#5, 1981), "Don't Let Him Go" (#24, 1981), and "In Your Letter" (#20, 1981). The first two were heavy ballads, a style the group would rely upon from then on. *Good Trouble* (#7, 1982) was a relative disappointment, though it did contain the Top 10 single "Keep the Fire Burnin'."

REO took a two-year sabbatical before coming out with the double platinum *Wheels Are Turnin'* (#7, 1984), which gave the band its second #1: "Can't Fight This Feeling," a strongly melodic ballad. The band placed five more singles in the Top 20 through 1988, but its record sales gradually slackened. When Richrath—one of the band's main writers and a fiery guitar player—left in 1990, not long after drummer Gratzer's departure, REO's ability to carry on appeared in jeopardy. But Cronin, Doughty, and Bruce Hall (a member since 1976) are still at it, with ex–Ted Nugent sideman Dave Amato on guitar and drummer Bryan Hitt, formerly of Wang Chung. In the Midwest especially, REO can still draw crowds. *Building the Bridge* (1996), however, failed to chart. In 1998 REO Speedwagon's attorneys issued a cease-and-desist letter to Royalty Records, home of the punk act REO Speedealer, which subsequently truncated its name to "Speedealer" to avoid confusion.

The Replacements

Formed 1980, Minneapolis, MN
Paul Westerberg (b. Dec. 31, 1959, Minneapolis), voc., gtr., kybds.; Bob Stinson (b. Dec. 17, 1959, Mound, MN; d. Feb. 15, 1995, Minneapolis), gtr.; Tommy Stinson (b. Oct. 6, 1966, San Diego, CA), bass; Chris Mars (b. Apr. 26, 1961, Minneapolis), drums.
1981—*Sorry Ma, Forgot to Take Out the Trash* (Twin/Tone)
1982—*The Replacements Stink* EP 1983—*Hootenanny*
1984—*Let It Be* 1985—*The Shit Hits the Fans; Tim* (Sire)
1987—(– Bob Stinson) *Pleased to Meet Me* (+ Slim Dunlap [b. Robert Dunlap, Aug. 14, 1951, Plainview, MN], gtr.)
1989—*Don't Tell a Soul* 1990—*All Shook Down* (– Mars; + Steve Foley, drums) 1997—*All for Nothing—Nothing for All* (Reprise).
Chris Mars solo: 1992—*Horseshoes and Hand Grenades* (Smash) 1993—*75% Less Fat* 1995—*Tenterhooks* (Bar/None) 1996—*Anonymous Botch.*
Slim Dunlap solo: 1993—*The Old New Me* (Twin/Tone) 1996—*Times Like This* (Restless).
Tommy Stinson (with Bash & Pop): 1993—*Friday Night Is Killing Me* (Sire).
Tommy Stinson (with Perfect): 1996—*When Squirrels Play Chicken* EP (Medium Cool/Restless).
Paul Westerberg solo: 1993—*14 Songs* (Sire) 1996—*Eventually* (Reprise) 1999—*Suicaine Gratification* (Capitol).
Paul Westerberg as Grandpaboy: 1997—*Grandpaboy* EP (Soundproof/Monolyth).

In the '80s the Replacements' blend of punk guitar and pop melodies garnered critical acclaim but little commercial success. Hailing from the Minneapolis home base of acts as diverse as Hüsker Dü and Prince, the quartet was seen by its fans as generational spokesmen; Paul Westerberg's angst-ridden confessional songs cast him as a postpunk Bob Dylan and would influence such '90s stars as the Goo Goo Dolls.

The son of a Cadillac salesman, Westerberg was refused his high-school diploma for failing to show up at graduation. After taking odd jobs as a steel-mill worker and a janitor, he formed the Impediments with drummer Chris Mars, guitarist Bob Stinson, and Stinson's 12-year-old bass-playing brother, Tommy. Inspired by Westerberg's love for the Sex Pistols, the band—renaming itself the Replacements after being banned from a club for rowdy behavior—developed a raucous, drunken stage act: Bob Stinson sometimes performed in underwear or a dress, and the set list ranged from covers of Kiss and Cher to Westerberg's originals. Discovered by Peter Jesperson, cofounder of Twin/Tone Records, they signed with the indie label in 1980 and, gaining a following that nicknamed them the 'Mats (for "placemats"), they put out albums that progressed from the punk assault of their first two releases to the country-tinged *Hootenanny* to *Let It Be,* a collection that placed them at the forefront of alternative-rock bands.

Notorious for their alcoholic self-destructiveness and wildly uneven concerts but celebrated for Westerberg's hook-laden and painfully honest songs, the Replacements hovered on the verge of mainstream acceptance. But even their major-label signing to Sire in 1987 didn't alter their underdog status. While *Tim* reflected the band's increasingly skillful musicianship and Westerberg's stylistic range, exhaustion began setting in. Bob Stinson was fired for excessive drinking in 1987, and *Pleased to Meet Me* was recorded as a trio. Guitarist Slim Dunlap joined in time for *Don't Tell a Soul,* which again delighted reviewers and even produced a single that cracked the Top 100 ("I'll Be You," #51, 1989) but sold only around 300,000 copies. The band's swan song, *All*

The Replacements: Tommy Stinson, Chris Mars, Slim Dunlap, Paul Westerberg

Shook Down, was a Replacements record in name only; fighting what he perceived as Westerberg's dictatorial control, Mars eventually departed (Steve Foley of the Minneapolis band Things Fall Down replaced him for a subsequent tour), and the album was basically a Westerberg solo project with the other Replacements employed as occasional sidemen. Again failing to break into the mainstream, the Replacements broke up in 1991, just short of the '90s alternative explosion they helped inspire. A 1997 retrospective, the two-disc *All for Nothing—Nothing for All* (#143), gathered albums tracks, B sides, and rarities from the Sire years.

Contributing to the popular soundtrack to *Singles,* director Cameron Crowe's 1992 movie about the nascent Seattle music scene, Westerberg finally enjoyed a measure of success; in 1993 he released a solo debut, *14 Songs* (#44, 1993), to mixed reviews. *Eventually* (#50) followed in 1996, with the introspective track "Good Day" inspired by the drug-overdose death of Bob Stinson in early 1995. After returning from a tour in '96, Westerberg was treated for depression. He left Reprise in 1997 and recorded a single and EP under the name Grandpaboy that briefly returned the singer/songwriter to an edgier, rocking sound. Westerberg then signed to Capitol for 1999's *Suicaine Gratification* (#104), earning his best reviews since the Replacements for more songs of intense introspection, but unspectacular sales.

The other Replacements also put out albums whose sound didn't depart greatly from their former band's. Both Dunlap and Mars released critically lauded discs. Tommy Stinson formed Bash & Pop, which released *Friday Night Is Killing Me* on Sire in 1993. That band eventually evolved into Perfect and recorded an EP, *When Squirrels Play Chicken,* in 1996 for Restless Records. A followup album was recorded, but Restless chose not to release it. Within a year, Stinson astonished 'Mats followers by joining the new lineup of Guns n' Roses [see entry]. He worked alongside Axl Rose on that band's long-delayed *Chinese Democracy* album and first appeared onstage with GNR after midnight at a 2001 New Year's Eve show in Las Vegas. As of mid-2001, Westerberg was reportedly finishing another solo album.

The Residents

Formed 1970, San Francisco, CA
1974—*Meet the Residents* (Ralph) 1976—*Third Reich n' Roll* 1977—*Fingerprince* 1978—*Not Available; Duck Stab/Buster & Glen* 1979—*Eskimo; Diskomo* EP; *Nibbles* (Virgin) 1980—*Commercial Album* (Ralph) 1981—*Mark of the Mole* 1982—*The Tunes of Two Cities* 1983—*Intermission* EP; *Residue of the Residents* 1984—*George & James; Whatever Happened to Vileness Fats?* 1985—*The Census Taker* (Episode); *The Big Bubble* (Black Shroud-Ralph) 1986—*Heaven?* (Rykodisc); *Hell!; Stars and Hank Forever!* (Ralph); *13th Anniversary Show—Live in Japan* 1987—*For Elsie* (Cryptic); *God in Three Persons* (Rykodisc) 1988—*The Mole Show Live in Holland* (East Side Digital); *Holy Kiss of Flesh* 1989—*The King and Eye* 1990—*Cube-E Live in Holland* (Enigma-Restless) 1991—*Freak Show* (Official Product) 1992—*Our Finest Flowers* (Ralph-ESD) 1994—*Gingerbread Man* 1996—*Have a Bad Day* 1997—*Our Tired, Our Poor, Our Huddled Masses* (Rykodisc) 1998—*Wormwood* (Ralph-ESD) 2000—*Roadworms.*
With Renaldo and the Loaf: 1983—*Title in Limbo* (Ralph).

The Residents have never identified themselves by name, nor have they ever appeared in photos without some kind of mask (usually giant eyeballs with top hats). Until 1982 they had given only one public concert—1976 at Berkeley, California—where they appeared wrapped in mummylike coverings and played behind an opaque screen. The Residents have made several surrealistic short films, which, like their albums, cryptically elaborate a deliberately perverse antipop vision.

About all that is known is that there are four of them, and that they emigrated from northern Louisiana to San Francisco in the early '70s. The Residents' longtime spokesmen are Hardy Fox and Homer Flynn. The band was named when Warner Bros. sent back an anonymous tape to "Residents" at their return address. On record they use a broad sonic palette, encompassing acoustic chamberlike instrumentation, tonal and atonal quasi-jazz, electronics, noise distortion, and intentionally whiny-nasal vocals. Until the mid-'70s, their albums were available only on the mail-order Ralph label.

The jacket of their debut album originally featured a grotesque dadaesque parody of *Meet the Beatles.* Threatened with legal action, the Residents changed it to depict Beatle-suited figures with crawfish heads and Beatle-like names (i.e., "Paul McCrawfish," "Ringo Starrfish"). The 1976 followup, *Third Reich n' Roll,* depicted *American Bandstand* host Dick Clark as Hitler. *Not Available* features modern-classical suites; *Eskimo* purports to be an Arctic cultural documentary with its otherworldly windswept sounds and native Eskimo chants; and *Commercial Album* fits 40 songs lasting a minute or less each onto one LP.

In October 1982 the Residents played five shows in San Francisco and L.A. Adhering to their "Theory of Obscurity," they were veiled and behind screens throughout the multimedia show, which included props and dancers enacting the "Mark of the Mole" storyline. The story became part of a Mole trilogy that included *Mark of the Mole, The Tunes of Two Cities,* and *The Residents Mole Show.* Meanwhile, the Residents and Ralph Records became embroiled in an internal conflict that led to the group's label hopping in the latter part of the decade.

The Residents issued a steady stream of albums through the '80s, including their American Composer Series (*George & James,* a collection of George Gershwin and James Brown, and *Stars and Hank Forever!,* a tribute to John Philip Sousa and Hank Williams); *God in Three Persons,* an hour-long piece about sexual compulsion and violence; and *The King and Eye* and *Cube-E: The History of American Music in 3 E-Z Pieces,* which focus on Elvis Presley and the collapse of American pop. They spent most of 1986 touring Japan, Australia, Europe, and the United States, and in 1989 took their multimedia *Cube-E* stage show (again with dancers and props) all over the world. At a mid-'80s tour stop in L.A., one of the band's eyeball heads was stolen from backstage, leading one member to switch to a menacing black skull mask. The weirdness continued.

The Residents issued a hodgepodge of recycled, unreleased, and live material in the '80s: *Whatever Happened to Vileness Fats?* revives an abandoned 1972 video project; *Residue* is a rarities collection; and *Heaven?* and *Hell!* compile previously released material. *Freak Show* is a surreal musical comparison of the Residents' own strange performances with circus freak shows. In 1994 they released the album as an interactive CD-ROM. A survey of the mysterious quartet's long career was released in 1997 as *Our Tired, Our Poor, Our Huddled Masses.* The band reemerged the following year to explore skewed biblical themes with *Wormwood,* and in 1999 toured for the first time in nearly a decade.

Paul Revere and the Raiders

Formed 1958, Portland, OR
Paul Revere (b. Jan. 7, 1938, Harvard, NE), kybds., bass; Mark Lindsay (b. Mark Allan Lindsay, Mar. 9, 1942, Eugene, OR), voc., sax, perc.; William Hibbard, bass; David Bell, drums; Robert White, gtr.; Richard White, gtr.
1958—(numerous lineups based around Revere and Lindsay; only the major ones are listed) 1962—(+ Michael "Smitty" Smith [b. Michael Leroy Smith, Portland; d. Mar. 6, 2001, Kona, HI], drums, gtr., organ) 1963—(+ Drake Levin [b. Drake Maxwell Levinshefski, Chicago, IL], gtr.; + Charlie Coe [b. Charles Franklin Coe, Nov. 19, 1944, Portland], bass, gtr., piano, violin, sax; – Coe) 1965—(+ Phil "Fang" Volk [b. Phillip Edward Volk, Portland], bass, gtr., piano) *Here They Come* (Columbia) 1966—*Just Like Us!* (– Levin; + Jim "Harpo" Valley [b. James George Valley, Tacoma, WA], gtr., piano) *Midnight Ride; The Spirit of '67* 1967—(– Volk; – Smith; – Valley; + Coe; + Joe Correro Jr. [b. Nov. 19, 1946, Greenwood, MI], drums; + Freddy Weller [b. Wilton Frederick Weller, Sep. 9, 1947, Atlanta, GA], gtr.) *Greatest Hits; Revolution* 1968—(– Coe; + Keith Allison [b. Sydney Keith Allison, Coleman, TX], bass, gtr., harmonica, kybds., trombone) 1971—*Indian Reservation* (– Correro; + Smith; + Omar Martinez [b. Havana, Cuba], drums, perc., gtr., voc.; + Robert Wooley [b. Coral Gables, FL], kybds., bass) 1972—(– Smith) 1973—(– Weller; + Doug Heath [b. Douglas Robert Heath, Sioux City, IA], gtr., piano, drums) 1975—(– Lindsay; – Allison; + Ron Foos [b. Ronald Andrew Foos, Dec. 25, Seattle, WA], bass, gtr., drums) 1976—*The British Are Coming* (20th Century) 1977—(– Wooley; group disbands) 1978—(group re-forms) 1980—(+ Daniel Krause [b. Watertown, WI], kybds., trumpet) 1983—(+ Carl Driggs [b. Carlos Driggs, Havana], voc., drums, piano, gtr.) *Paul Revere Rides Again* (Hitbound) 1990—*The Legend of Paul Revere* 2000—*Time Flies When You're Having Fun* (Rock n' Roll).
Mark Lindsay solo: 1970—*Arizona* (Columbia); *Silverbird* 1971—*You've Got a Friend* 1996—*Video Dreams* (Lalala).

Paul Revere and the Raiders emerged from the rock & roll scene of the Northwest to become national pop successes, trading on the enormous teenybopper appeal of ponytailed lead singer Mark Lindsay. The Raiders began in 1959 as the Downbeats, a raunchy rock & roll band. Lindsay, who worked as a delivery boy at Revere's drive-in restaurant, played saxophone and sang on raucous, honking numbers like their first record, "Like, Long Hair" (1961), an independent single heard in Portland, Oregon, and nowhere else. They changed their name in mid-1962 and started wearing pseudo–Revolutionary War costumes. Columbia signed the group after hearing an unsolicited tape, and in mid-1963 the Raiders' version of "Louie Louie" was released. Though once again popular in the Northwest, their version was beaten out across America by the Kingsmen's hit. Sometime in 1964 Lindsay left the band; in early 1965 the Raiders moved to California and began to focus on a cleaner, more pop-oriented sound. Lindsay returned shortly thereafter.

"Steppin' Out" was their first national hit single (#46, 1965), aided by the band's prominence on Dick Clark's daily television rock program, *Where the Action Is.* By 1967, the group was known as Paul Revere and the Raiders, featuring Mark Lindsay, which served as acknowledgment that Lindsay was cowriting most of their hits.

The group's singles during these years included "Just Like Me" (#11, 1965), "Kicks" (#4, 1966), "Hungry" (#6, 1966), "The Great Airplane Strike" (#20, 1966), "Good Thing" (#4, 1966), "Ups and Downs" (#22, 1967), and "Him or Me—What's It Gonna Be?" (#5, 1967). Despite the success, the lineup fluctuated constantly. Drake Levin was drafted in 1966 and was replaced by Jim Valley. When Levin returned from the army, he, Michael Smith, and Phil Volk formed Brotherhood, while Valley left for a solo career. Replacements included Freddy Weller (1967–73), destined for a highly successful solo career as a country singer; and Keith Allison (1968–75), a minor teen idol in his own right, mainly thanks to his many appearances as a regular on *Action.*

In 1969 Lindsay began to make solo records in addition to his work with the Raiders. Their success ended early in the '70s after Lindsay's "Arizona" (#10, 1970) and the band's "Indian Reservation" (#1, 1971). Lindsay quit the group in 1975, though he did rejoin Revere the following year to capitalize on America's bicentennial, with a tour and album. Since then he worked briefly in A&R, then forged a successful career singing commercials. He continues to tour the nostalgia circuit. Revere, meanwhile, gigs constantly. As of 2000 his band of Raiders included longtime drummer Omar Martinez, guitarist Doug Heath, bassist Ron Foos, singer Carl Driggs, and keyboardist Daniel Krause, many of whom have been with him since the '70s. In 1985 the group returned to TV on a summer series, *Rock 'N Roll Summer Action,* on ABC.

Busta Rhymes

Born Trevor Smith Jr., May 20, 1972, Brooklyn, NY
1996—*The Coming* (Elektra) 1997—*When Disaster Strikes*

1998—*E.L.E.: Extinction Level Event (The Final World Front)* 2000—*Anarchy.*

Busta Rhymes possesses one of the most recognizable vocal timbres in rap music. His West Indian–tinged lyrical flow, psychedelic garb, and endearing rambunctiousness helped turn Rhymes into a rap superhero, an urban warrior straight out of the P-Funk tradition.

The son of Jamaican immigrant, Seventh-Day Adventist parents, Rhymes got his start with the Leaders of the New School, whose debut, *A Future Without a Past . . .* (#53 R&B, 1991), received some critical acclaim, especially when the boyish anthem "Case of the P.T.A." became popular on the radio and *Yo! MTV Raps*. Rhymes' appearance on 1992's "Scenario" (#57 pop, #42 R&B), a collaborative effort between A Tribe Called Quest and the Leaders of the New School, garnered more praise from fans and critics, motivating Rhymes to go solo. But he stayed on board for the group's second and final album, *T.I.M.E.: The Inner Mind's Eye—The Endless Dispute With Reality* (#66 pop, #15 R&B, 1993).

Though professionally prospering, Rhymes suffered personal tragedy in 1992 when his son was born prematurely and died. This loss seemed to haunt Rhymes' music—each of his four albums mix murky prophesies of the apocalypse with bass-bumping party jams. *The Coming* (#6 pop, #1 R&B, 1996), Rhymes' highly anticipated solo effort, turned the Brooklyn native into an instant hip-hop luminary. "Woo Hah!! Got You All in Check" (#8 pop, #6 R&B, 1996) and "It's a Party" (#52 pop, #27 R&B, 1996) became club staples, and Rhymes soon began touring with such acts as De La Soul and Puff Daddy and the Family. *When Disaster Strikes . . .* (#3 pop, #1 R&B, 1997), *E.L.E.* (#12 pop, #2 R&B, 1999), and *Anarchy* (#4 pop, #1 R&B, 2000), bound together by the Armageddon motif, yielded hits like "Put Your Hands Where My Eyes Could See" (#2 R&B, 1997), "Dangerous" (#9 pop, #4 R&B, 1998), "Turn It Up [Remix]/Fire It Up" (#10 pop, #7 R&B, 1998), and "What's It Gonna Be?!" (#3 pop, #1 R&B, 1999). Rhymes also made cameo appearances on a number of other artists' '90s hip-hop records.

Busta Rhymes

Tutored by renowned video director Hype Williams, Rhymes codirected or directed many of his own videos, always adding his kaleidoscopic Afrocentricism. As an actor, Rhymes has appeared in a couple of John Singleton films: 1995's *Higher Learning*, which also featured rapper Ice Cube, and the 2000 remake of *Shaft*.

Charlie Rich

Born Dec. 14, 1932, Colt, AZ; died July 25, 1995, Hammond, LA
1969—*Lonely Weekends* (Sun) 1973—*Behind Closed Doors* (Epic) 1974—*There Won't Be Anymore* (RCA); *Very Special Love Songs* (Epic); *The Silver Fox* 1976—*Greatest Hits; Silver Linings* 1992—*Pictures and Paintings* (Sire) 1997—*Feel Like Going Home: The Essential Charlie Rich* (Legacy) 2000—*Love Songs* (Columbia).

One of the original Sun rockabilly artists, gray-haired Charlie Rich (known as the "Silver Fox") is a country-and-blues singer, songwriter, and pianist. His career was fitfully successful until his MOR country and pop crossover singles "Behind Closed Doors" and "The Most Beautiful Girl" hit in 1973.

Rich grew up listening to gospel music and learned piano from his missionary Baptist mother; he also sang in the church choir. In high school he met the woman whom he married upon graduation, and who later became his songwriting partner, Margaret Ann Rich. Rich played in dance bands and jazz combos, then spent a year studying music at Arkansas University in 1950.

He joined the air force in 1951, and while stationed in Oklahoma formed his own jazz unit and then a pop band, the Velvetones, who had their own local television show. Though Rich felt he should restrict music to weekends and support his family by farming, his wife pushed his musical aspirations and eventually got him signed to Sun Records. There he wrote songs and played sessions for Johnny Cash, Roy Orbison, and others. His third solo single, "Lonely Weekends," was a #22 hit in 1960.

Rich went to Mercury's Smash subsidiary in 1965, when "Mohair Sam" became his next Top 40 hit. He went to RCA in 1967, achieving a minor hit with "Big Boss Man," then went to Hi and finally Epic. At Epic Rich teamed with Nashville producer Billy Sherrill.

Things finally clicked when Rich covered Kenny O'Dell's "Behind Closed Doors," which went gold and reached #15 in 1973. Later that year "The Most Beautiful Girl" (by Sherrill, Norro Wilson, and Rory Bourke) hit #1; it, too, earned a gold record. The *Behind Closed Doors* LP went platinum. His subsequent Top 40 singles include "There Won't Be Anymore" (#18), "A Very Special Love Song" (#11), and "I Love My Friend" (#24) in 1974, and "Every Time You Touch Me (I Get High)" (#19, 1975). In 1978 Rich appeared in the Clint Eastwood film *Every Which Way But Loose*. His 1992 album, *Pic-*

tures and Paintings, showed his eclecticism, including covers of Duke Ellington's "Mood Indigo" and the gospel standard "I Feel Like Going Home." Rich died in 1995, suffering a blood clot in his lungs.

Cliff Richard

Born Harry Rodger Webb, Oct. 14, 1940, Lucknow, India
1960—*Cliff Sings* (ABC) 1961—*Listen to Cliff* 1962—*It's Wonderful to Be Young* (Dot) 1963—*Hits From the Soundtrack of "Summer Holiday"* (Epic) 1964—*It's All in the Game; Cliff Richard in Spain* 1965—*Swinger's Paradise* soundtrack 1970—*His Land; Good News* (Word) 1976—*I'm Nearly Famous* (Rocket) 1977—*Every Face Tells a Story* 1978—*Green Light* 1979—*We Don't Talk Anymore* (EMI America) 1980—*I'm No Hero* 1981—*Wired for Sound* 1982—*Now You See Me, Now You Don't* 1983—*Give a Little Bit More* 1987—*Always Guaranteed* (Striped Horse) 1988—*Carols* (Word) 1989—*Songs of Life: Mission 89* 1994—*The Collection* (Razor & Tie).

Over a career that spans four decades, Cliff Richard far exceeded his early billing as Britain's answer to Elvis Presley. Since 1958, he has appeared on the U.K. charts for a greater number of weeks than any other artist. His track record in the U.S.—a relatively paltry nine Top 40 singles—doesn't even begin to hint at his massive popularity at home, where he has charted a record 107 Top 40 singles, among them 61 Top 10 hits and 14 Number Ones.

Harry Webb's parents were British subjects in India—his father born in Burma, his mother in India—who didn't see England until 1947. Cliff Richard learned guitar and sang with skiffle bands near his Herefordshire home, and he formed a short-lived vocal group, the Quintones, with one other boy and three girls in 1957. He next joined the Dick Teague Skiffle Group, and worked for a short time as a credit-control clerk in a factory.

In 1958 he put together a backup band, the Drifters, and changed his name to Cliff Richard for the Drifters' first demo, "Lawdy Miss Clawdy." Late that summer the group's first release, "Move It," went to #2, and after a single television appearance and a tour, British teens embraced Richard as their first homegrown rock idol. Richard followed up with two #1s, 1959's "Living Doll" and "Travellin' Light." That year he also appeared in two films, *A Serious Charge* (a.k.a. *Immoral Charge*) and *A Touch of Hell,* and the next year, *Expresso Bongo.* Later movies would include *The Young Ones* (1961), *Summer Holiday* (1963), and *Wonderful Life* (1964). Through these and a near-constant chart presence, Richard quickly became a leading teen idol, not only at home but in Australia, Germany, and elsewhere. His U.K. Top 10 hits of the period included "High Class Baby" (1958); "Travellin' Light," "Mean Streak," and "Living Doll" (1959); "Voice in the Wilderness," "Fall in Love With You," "Please Don't Tease," "Nine Times Out of Ten," and "I Love You" (1960); "Theme for a Dream," "Gee Whiz It's You," "A Girl Like You," and "When the Girl in Your Arms Is the Girl in Your Heart" (1961); "The Young Ones," "I'm Looking Out the Window" b/w "Do You Wanna Dance," "It'll Be Me," and "The Next Time" b/w "Bachelor Boy" (1962); "Summer Holiday," "Lucky Lips," "It's All in the Game," "Don't Talk to Him" (1963); "I'm the Lonely One," "Constantly," "On the Beach," "The Twelfth of Never," "I Could Easily Fall" (1964); "The Minute You're Gone," and "Wind Me Up (Let Me Go)" (1965).

The Shadows [see entry] had a few instrumental hits in England, and those singles often battled on the charts with the recordings made by the band with Richard. Meanwhile, only two of Richard's myriad early U.K. smashes made it into the U.S. Top 40: "Living Doll" (#30, 1959) and "It's All in the Game" (#25, 1964). After that, it would be another dozen years before he had his next U.S. hit. At home, however, he was among the very few young pop artists of his generation to weather and survive the rise of the British Invasion. Richard's long-held clean-cut image solidified with his announcement (at a 1966 Billy Graham crusade) that he had embraced Christianity; widespread popularity with older listeners placed Richard firmly in the British entertainment firmament. Nonetheless, fans panicked at the suggestion that he might abandon his career altogether.

As it turned out, they worried needlessly. Richard never left the charts (in fact, his first hit of 1966 was a Mick Jagger–Keith Richards song, "Blue Turns to Grey"). Although his forays into the Top 10 became less frequent, he remained a near-constant chart presence. He began recording a series of gospel albums *(Good News, About That Man, His Land, Help It Along, Small Corners, Walking in the Light, It's a Small World, Hymns and Inspirational Songs, Carols, Songs of Life: Mission 89)* and releasing an occasional Christmas single. Richard, who claims not to proselytize, also made a series of statements condemning premarital sex, drugs, and sundry attitudes and behaviors associated with rock stardom. In 1968 he parted with his longtime backup group the Shadows; they have since reunited on several occasions.

Richard enjoyed a handful of Top 10 British singles through the late '60s—"Visions" and "Time Drags By" (1966), "In the Country," "It's All Over," "The Day I Met Marie," and "All My Love" (1967), but his biggest hit of that era was "Congratulations," a Eurovision Song Contest contender that went to #1 in England and almost everywhere else in the world except the U.S., where it stalled at #99. He continued to release hit singles at home, among them "Goodbye Sam, Hello Samantha" (1970) and "Power to All Our Friends" (1973).

In 1976 "Devil Woman" became a Top 10 hit in the U.S., beginning an unprecedented run of hits that included "We Don't Talk Anymore," a #1 hit in the U.K. (his 10th) that went into the U.S. Top 10 in 1979. The following year he toured America for the first time since 1963. He was also named an officer of the Order of the British Empire (like the Beatles in 1965). In 1981 Richard's autobiography, *Which One's Cliff?,* was published; he claimed not to have slept with a woman in more than 16 years and also denied that he was homosexual. His other '80s U.S. hits included "Carrie" (#34, 1980), "Dreaming" (#10, 1980), "A Little in Love" (#17, 1981), a cover of Shep and the Limelites' "Daddy's Home" (#23, 1982), and "Suddenly" (#20, 1980), a duet with Olivia Newton-John from the film *Xanadu.*

Back at home, though, Richard remained nearly as popular as ever, and his silver show-business anniversary brought several more U.K. hits, including a duet with Phil Everly, "She Means Nothing to Me," and a six-week sold-out run at a London theater. The following year's duet with Janet Jackson, "Two to the Power of Love" (which appears on her solo album *Dream Street*) was not a hit. He has made a number of appearances on behalf of various charities, and his annual gospel concerts have become something of an institution. In 1986 he starred in the Dave Clark musical *Time,* from which he had several more U.K. hits, including the Stevie Wonder–produced "She's So Beautiful" and "Time" (#17 U.K., 1985). Also early that year he recorded a #1 U.K. version of his 1959 hit "Living Doll" with cast members of the British sitcom *The Young Ones* (named for the Richard hit of the same name); proceeds went to charity. With David Cassidy taking his place in *Time* in early 1987, Richard made a stellar return to the charts with *Always Guaranteed,* boasting two U.K. Top 10 singles, "My Pretty One" and "Some People." His 1988 Christmas single, "Mistletoe and Wine," became the biggest selling single of the year in the U.K. At year's end Richard claimed the #1 single, album, and video there. In 1989 his *Stronger* (including the Stock/Aitken/Waterman single "I Just Don't Have the Heart") joined *Always Guaranteed* as the two best-selling albums of his career. Later that year, his duet with Van Morrison, "Whenever God Shines His Light," hit the Top 20, while a rerecording of "Do They Know It's Christmas" (recorded with an assemblage known as Band Aid II) went to #1.

Richard kicked off his 50th-birthday year with a series of sold-out concerts, the most ambitious of which included a full-stage re-creation of the old British TV rock show on which he was given his first break, *Oh Boy!* He closed 1990 with the #1 U.K. Christmas song, "Saviour's Day." His 1993 *The Album* went to #1 almost immediately. He was knighted in 1995 for his services to charity. That year, he also released a British album, *Songs From "Heathcliff,"* from the namesake theatrical production in which he appeared. In 1998 and 1999 Richard remained popular enough to sell out a run of 32 40th anniversary concerts at the Royal Albert Hall. He also released the U.K. album *As Real as I Wanna Be.* His single "The Millennium Prayer" reached #1 U.K. in 1999.

Keith Richards: See the Rolling Stones

Lionel Richie: See the Commodores

Jonathan Richman/Modern Lovers

Jonathan Richman, born 1951, Boston, MA
1976—*Modern Lovers* (Beserkley) 1977—*Jonathan Richman and the Modern Lovers; Rock & Roll With the Modern Lovers; Modern Lovers Live* 1979—*Back in Your Life* 1983—*Jonathan Sings!* (Sire) 1985—*Rockin' and Romance* (Twin/Tone) 1986—*It's Time for Jonathan Richman and the Modern Lovers* (Upside) 1987—*The Beserkley Years: The Best of Modern Lovers* (Beserkley/Rhino) 1988—*Modern Lovers 88* (Rounder) 1989—*Jonathan Richman* 1990—*Jonathan Goes Country* 1993—*Jonathan, Te Vas a Emocionar!* 1995—*You Must Ask the Heart* 1996—*Surrender to Jonathan* (Vapor) 1998—*I'm So Confused.*

Jonathan Richman is easily one of rock's quirkiest figures. He dreams up songs like "I'm a Little Aeroplane" or "Ice Cream Man," and croons them in a heartfelt tone of boyish wonder. Those neo-nursery rhymes are far removed from the singer/songwriter/guitarist's early days with the original, garage-rock incarnation of the Modern Lovers, the group he formed in New England.

The Lovers—who also featured Jerry Harrison and Dave Robinson, who later joined the Talking Heads and the Cars, respectively—were inspired by the Velvet Underground and wrote songs like "Roadrunner," "Pablo Picasso," and "Hospital." But Richman's tolerance for loud music decreased, and he began to tone down the Modern Lovers; when David Robinson's drum kit was reduced to a single snare drum covered with a towel, he quit. The group also had run-ins with its record company, Warner Bros., and disbanded in 1972. Richman formed a new, completely acoustic Modern Lovers (with guitarist Leroy Radcliffe, bassist Greg "Curly" Kerenan, and drummer D. Sharp), and went on to cut a series of albums for the independent Beserkley label (including the 1976 release *Modern Lovers,* an anthology of Warner demos from the early '70s).

In 1977 Richman's instrumental tune "Egyptian Reggae"—taken from *Rock & Roll with the Modern Lovers*—became a hit in England, Holland, and Germany, where he enjoys large cult followings. In 1978 Richman broke up the acoustic Modern Lovers and became a solo act. A period of self-imposed obscurity in New England was broken in 1980, when Richman began touring fairly regularly. He continues to play frequently, usually backed by ex–Giant Sand drummer Tommy Larkins.

In 1993 he demonstrated his growing interest in Latin culture by recording *Jonathan, Te Vas a Emocionar!* entirely in Spanish. In 1996 he signed to Neil Young's Vapor label, which issued *Surrender to Jonathan.* The album featured a new version of "Egyptian Reggae," song titles like "I Was Dancing in the Lesbian Bar," and bigger, busier arrangements. Richman, whose '90s cult grew thanks to his appearances on NBC's *Late Night With Conan O' Brien,* also made a cameo in the Farrelly Brothers' 1996 comedy *Kingpin.* He played a loopy singing narrator in their next film, 1998's blockbuster *There's Something About Mary.* Several of his tunes appeared on the soundtrack. Ric Ocasek produced Richman's next studio effort, 1999's *I'm So Confused.* While Jonathan Richman has yet to achieve mass acceptance, he is notable for his sheer unpredictability and artistic risk-taking.

Righteous Brothers

Formed 1962, Los Angeles, CA
Bill Medley, (b. Sep. 19, 1940, Santa Ana, CA); Bobby Hatfield (b. Aug. 10, 1940, Beaver Dam, WI).
1964—*Right Now!* (Moonglow); *Some Blue-Eyed Soul* 1965—*You've Lost That Lovin' Feelin'* (Philles); *Just Once in My Life; Back to Back* 1966—*Soul and Inspiration* (Verve) 1967—*Greatest Hits* (Verve) 1969—*Greatest Hits, vol. 2* 1974—*Give It to the People* (Haven) 1989—*Anthology (1962–1974)* (Rhino) 1990—*Best of the Righteous Brothers* (Curb) 1991—*Reunion.*
Bill Medley solo: 1971—*A Song for You* (A&M) 1973—*Smile* 1978—*Another Beginning* (United Artists) 1980—*Sweet Thunder* (Liberty) 1982—*Right Here and Now* (Planet) 1984—*I Still Do* (RCA) 1985—*Still Hung Up on You* 1991—*Blue-Eyed Singer* (Curb) 1993—*Going Home* (Essential) 1996—*Christmas Memories* (Rocktopia) 1997—*Almost Home.*

Bill Medley and Bobby Hatfield's close-harmony ballads came to exemplify so-called blue-eyed (i.e., white) soul. Medley and Hatfield met when both were performing with the Paramours; they broke off to form a duo in 1962. They became the Righteous Brothers reportedly after a black fan referred to them as "righteous," a popular slang term at the time. In 1963 they had a hit on Moonglow Records with "Little Latin Lupe Lu" (#49).

Phil Spector signed them to his Philles Records in 1964. There they cut "You've Lost That Lovin' Feelin'." The Barry Mann–Cynthia Weil–Phil Spector song went to #1 pop, #3 R&B, and was successfully revived by Hall and Oates in 1980. Spector had other significant hits with the Righteous Brothers—"Unchained Melody" (#4 pop, #3 R&B, 1965), "Ebb Tide" (#5, 1965), and "Just Once in My Life" (#9, 1965)—before the duo moved to Verve Records in 1966. That year a Mann-Weil song, "(You're My) Soul and Inspiration," went to #1 pop, #13 R&B for Medley and Hatfield. In that time, the duo was also a regular act on the weekly rock TV show *Shindig!*

In 1968 the Brothers broke up, and Medley recorded solo. Hatfield kept the duo's name and performed with Jimmy Walker. That year Medley had two minor chart singles on his own, "Brown Eyed Woman" (#43) and "Peace Brother Peace" (#48), on MGM Records.

In 1974 Medley and Hatfield reunited to record a tribute to dead rock stars, "Rock and Roll Heaven" (#3), and scored two more hits: "Give It to the People" (#20) and "Dream On" (#32). Medley then retired for five years following the 1976 murder of his first wife, Karen. The duo did appear on an *American Bandstand* anniversary television special in 1981, where they performed a substantially reworked version of "Rock and Roll Heaven" as a tribute to John Lennon. Medley signed with Planet Records in 1982 and released *Right Here and Now,* produced by Richard Perry and featuring a title track by Barry Mann and Cynthia Weil. In 1983 Medley and Hatfield toured together again, as they have continued to do on and off through the years.

The duo returned to the charts in 1990 when "Unchained Melody" found a new audience through its inclusion in the *Ghost* soundtrack; the song went platinum in rerelease. In 1987 Medley's *Dirty Dancing* duet with Jennifer Warnes, "(I've Had) The Time of My Life," won a Grammy and went to #1. In 1993 Medley recorded a new version of "(You're My) Soul and Inspiration" with singer Darlene Love, who, in 1966, had sung background vocals on the Righteous Brothers' original version of the hit. The 1990 Curb anthology was certified platinum.

Billy Lee Riley

Born Oct. 5, 1933, Pocahontas, AR
1977—*Billy Lee Riley* EP (Charly) 1978—*Legendary Sun Performers; Sun Sounds Special* 1994—*Blue Collar Blues* (Hightone) 1997—*Hot Damn!* (Capricorn) 2000—*Shade Tree Blues* (Sun-Up).

Billy Lee Riley is arguably among the most important of the original rockabillies, an artist whose behind-the-scenes contributions as a Sun Records sessionman and unique recording legacy have earned him the respect of self-proclaimed fans such as Bob Dylan.

The son of a sharecropper, Riley learned to play guitar from the black farmworkers he grew up among. An adept multi-instrumentalist on guitar, harmonica, piano, and drums, Riley first recorded as a solo artist for a local Memphis label in 1955. Impressed, Sun Studios owner Sam Phillips signed Riley, and by 1955 he was playing behind label mates Jerry Lee Lewis, Johnny Cash, Roy Orbison, Charlie Rich, and Bill Justis. With guitarist Roland Janes and drummer J.M. Van Eaton, Riley cut a string of rockabilly sides that were simply unlike anything anyone had ever heard before: "Red Hot" and "Flying Saucer Rock 'n' Roll." The former featured what at the time were daring lyrics ("my gal is red hot / your gal ain't doodly squat!"), while in the latter Riley breathlessly enthused about an encounter with little green men who brought "rock & roll all the way from Mars." (Both tunes were revived in 1978 by Robert Gordon and Link Wray.)

The success of "Flying Saucer" gave Riley a brief solo career—Van Eaton and Janes became the Little Green Men—but despite his good looks and wild stage moves, he was soon back in the Sun studio band. In 1962 Riley moved to L.A., where he worked steadily as a session musician on recordings by Herb Alpert, Dean Martin, the Beach Boys, Rick Nelson, Pearl Bailey, and many others. By the early '70s, he had tired of music and quit to begin his own construction and decorating business back in his native Arkansas. Word of his 1979 performance in Memphis spread through rockabilly circles worldwide, and before long Riley was back out on the road throughout Europe and England, where rockabilly commands a large, loyal following.

Although Riley released albums overseas through the years, no new material was issued in the U.S. until 1994's *Blue Collar Blues.* The critically acclaimed collection was recorded in the old Sun studios and brought together Riley with Van Eaton and Janes, as well as saxophonist Ace Cannon. *Hot Damn!* (1997) and *Shade Tree Blues* (2000) were rootsier, bluesier affairs.

Jeannie C. Riley

Born Jeanne Carolyn Stephenson, Oct. 19, 1945, Anson, TX
1968—*Harper Valley PTA* (Plantation) 1969—*Yearbooks and Yesterdays; Things Go Better With Love* 1970—*Country Girl; Generation Gap* 1991—*Here's Jeannie C.* (Playback) 1995—*Praise Him.*

In 1968 Jeannie C. Riley was working as a secretary in Nashville, still trying to get her career as a country singer off the ground. Everything changed when her recording of "Harper Valley PTA" hit #1 on both the pop and country charts, selling 5.5 million copies globally, though in the long run it did more for its author, Tom T. Hall, than it did for Riley. She did, however, win that year's Grammy for Best Female Country Vocal Performance.

Subsequent singles—"The Girl Most Likely," "There Never Was a Time," and "Good Enough to Be Your Wife"—hit the country & western Top 10, but reached only the lower regions of the pop chart. She had C&W hits through 1974. "Harper Valley PTA," on the other hand, made an impression so lasting that it inspired a film and a short-lived spinoff TV series, starring Barbara Eden, 13 years after its release. The success took its toll on Riley personally, and divorce from her childhood-sweetheart husband, Mickey Riley, as well as problems with alcohol followed. In 1976 Riley reemerged, remarried to Mickey and born again. She has continued to record religious material. In 1986 she released "Return to Harper Valley."

Teddy Riley: See Guy

Minnie Riperton

Born Nov. 8, 1947, Chicago, IL; died July 12, 1979, Los Angeles, CA
1970—*Come to My Garden* (Janus) 1974—*Perfect Angel* (Epic) 1975—*Adventures in Paradise* 1977—*Stay in Love* 1979—*Minnie* (Capitol) 1980—*Love Lives Forever* 1997—*Her Chess Years* (Chess).
With Rotary Connection: 1968—*Rotary Connection* (Cadet Concept); *Aladdin; Peace* 1969—*Songs* 1970—*Dinner Music* 1971—*Hey Love.*

Singer Minnie Riperton's angelic five-octave voice made her one of pop's most distinctive singers. After studying opera as a child, Riperton decided she wanted a career in pop music when she reached her teens. She got a job as a receptionist at Chess Records. There she joined a vocal group called the Gems, who sang backup behind Fontella Bass, Etta James, and other Chess acts. In 1967 she sang with a black psychedelic pop band, Rotary Connection, that cut six albums. "Amen" from their 1967 debut album was an FM staple for many years, as was their version of the Rolling Stones' "Ruby Tuesday."

Riperton left the Rotary Connection in 1970 and that year recorded an unsuccessful solo album for Janus, *Come to My Garden.* She sang with Stevie Wonder's backup band Wonderlove before signing with Epic Records in 1974. *Perfect Angel,* which featured two tracks coproduced by Wonder, was her most successful album. It was certified gold and contained Wonder's "Lovin' You" (#1 pop, #3 R&B, 1975). In 1976 Riperton underwent a mastectomy and then became a spokeswoman for the American Cancer Society. Two years later she moved to Capitol Records, where she recorded her last album, *Minnie.* Her condition gradually worsened, and she died of cancer in L.A. *Love Lives Forever* is a posthumous collection consisting of previously unreleased vocal tracks with completely new backing.

Johnny Rivers

Born John Ramistella, Nov. 7, 1942, New York, NY
1964—*Johnny Rivers at the Whisky a Go Go* (Imperial); *Here We a Go Go Again!* 1965—*Meanwhile Back at the Whisky a Go Go* 1966—*Johnny Rivers' Golden Hits* 1967—*Changes; Rewind* 1968—*Realization* 1969—*A Touch of Gold* 1970—*Slim Slo Slider* 1972—*L.A. Reggae* (United Artists) 1973—*Homegrown* 1974—*Last Boogie in Paris* 1978—*Outside Help* (Soul City) 1980—*Borrowed Time* (RSO) 1991—*Johnny Rivers: Anthology (1964–1977)* (Rhino) 1998—*Last Train to Memphis* (Soul City).

In addition to Johnny Rivers' major achievements behind the scenes (discovering talent like the Fifth Dimension and Jimmy Webb, bringing together top studio musicians as a regular band), his own records have sold over 30 million copies. John Ramistella's family moved to Baton Rouge, Louisiana, when he was a small child. He began playing guitar at age eight, and by 13 had joined bands. On a summer trip to New York he met disc jockey Alan Freed, who changed Ramistella to Rivers and got him a contract with Gone Records. Nothing happened, though, and Rivers concentrated on songwriting in New York and L.A. One song, "I'll Make Believe," was recorded by Rick Nelson.

In 1963 Rivers landed a gig at the new Whisky-a-Go-Go on the Sunset Strip. He soon became the club's regular star attraction and, drawing a star-packed audience, made the Whisky L.A.'s hippest nightspot. Rivers' 1964 debut Imperial LP, *Johnny Rivers at the Whisky a Go Go* (#12, 1964), yielded the #2 hit "Memphis." He recorded other live Whisky LPs over the years. His hits throughout the '60s were usually covers and included "Seventh Son" (#7, 1965), a songwriting collaboration with Lou Adler entitled "Poor Side of Town" (#1, 1966), "Secret Agent Man" (#3, 1966), and two Motown covers, "Baby I Need Your Lovin' " (#3, 1967) and "The Tracks of My Tears" (#10, 1967). He covered Van Morrison's "Into the Mystic" in 1970.

In 1966 Rivers was approached by manager Marc Gordon

with a group called the Hi-Fis, previously the Versatiles. Rivers liked them, renamed them the Fifth Dimension, signed them to his newly established record company, Soul City, and linked the group with his friend, songwriter Jimmy Webb. Rivers played guitar on the Fifth Dimension's records and organized a regular band of studio musicians, including Hal Blaine (drums), Larry Knechtel (keyboards), and Joe Osborn (bass).

He continued to enjoy chart success as a performer in the '70s with a remake of Huey "Piano" Smith's '50s hit "Rockin' Pneumonia and the Boogie Woogie Flu" (#6, 1972) and the gold "Swayin' to the Music (Slow Dancin')" (#10, 1977). In 1975 he coaxed Brian Wilson out of retirement to do backups on his version of the Beach Boys' "Help Me Rhonda" (#22). Through the years, Rivers has successfully run his own song-publishing business and record company. He continues to perform. On Soul City Records, he released the all-new *Last Train to Memphis* in 1998.

Rob Base & D.J. E-Z Rock

Formed 1982, New York, NY
Rob Base (b. Robert Ginyard, May 18, 1967, New York), voc.; D.J. E-Z Rock (b. Rodney Bryce, June 29, 1967, New York), DJ.
1988—*It Takes Two* (Profile) 1994—*Break of Dawn* (Funky Base).
Rob Base solo: 1989—*The Incredible Base* (Profile).

Robert Ginyard and Rodney "Skip" Bryce began their career together in Harlem in a fifth-grade rap group called Sureshot Seven. Eventually the group boiled down to the two of them, and as Rob Base & D.J. E-Z Rock, they recorded a couple of singles that failed to hit. Then their track "It Takes Two" (#36 pop, #17 R&B) became a hit the summer of 1988, rising from the underground to pop radio. The song succeeded on the basis of Base's smooth, easy rap and particularly its simple yet memorable backing track; it featured samples of Lyn Collins' 1972 single "Think (About It)" and Strafe's club hit "Set It Off."

It Takes Two (#31, 1988) went platinum and included "Get on the Dance Floor" and "Joy and Pain." The latter featured vocals by young soul singer Omar Chandler and was lyrically based on an old hit by Maze, whose Frankie Beverly sued Base and E-Z Rock for copyright infringement.

Base went solo for a while on the gold-selling *The Incredible Base* (#50 pop, #20 R&B, 1989). The track "Rumors" addressed several false stories circulating about Base—that he'd fathered illegitimate kids and that he'd died from smoking crack, among others. The duo reunited for 1994's *Break of Dawn,* released on their own Funky Base label. Base and E-Z Rock have since embarked on a couple of nationwide tours and put out a pair of singles, including "Diamonds" (2000), on the New York–based Rampage label.

Robbie Robertson: See the Band

The Robins: See the Coasters

Smokey Robinson and the Miracles/ The Miracles

Formed 1957, Detroit, MI
William "Smokey" Robinson (b. Feb. 19, 1940, Detroit), lead voc.; Ronnie White (b. Apr. 5, 1939, Detroit; d. Aug. 26, 1995, Detroit), baritone voc.; Bobby Rogers (b. Feb. 19, 1940, Detroit), tenor voc.; Warren "Pete" Moore (b. Nov. 19, 1939, Detroit), bass voc.; Claudette Rogers Robinson (b. 1942), voc.
1961—*Hi, We're the Miracles* (Tamla) 1962—*Cookin' With the Miracles; I'll Try Something New* 1963—*The Fabulous Miracles; Recorded Live: On Stage; Christmas With the Miracles; The Miracles Doin' Mickey's Monkey* 1965—*Greatest Hits From the Beginning* (Tamla); *Going to a Go-Go* 1966—*Away We a Go-Go* 1967—*Smokey Robinson and the Miracles Make It Happen* 1968—*Smokey Robinson and the Miracles Greatest Hits, vol. 2; Special Occasion* 1969—*Time Out for Smokey Robinson and the Miracles; Four in Blue* 1970—*What Love Has Joined Together; A Pocket Full of Miracles; The Season for Miracles* 1971—*One Dozen Roses* 1974—*Anthology* (Motown) 1994—*Smokey Robinson and the Miracles: The 35th Anniversary Collection.*
As the Miracles (without Robinson): 1972—*Flying High Together* (Tamala) (– Robinson; + William Griffin [b. Aug. 15, 1950, Detroit], lead voc.) 1973—*Renaissance* 1974—*Do It Baby!* 1975—*City of Angels* 1976—*The Power of Music* 1977—(– W. Griffin; + Donald Griffin, lead voc.) *Greatest Hits; Love Crazy* (Columbia); *The Miracles* 1998—*The Ultimate Collection* (Motown).
Smokey Robinson solo: 1973—*Smokey* (Tamla) 1974—*Pure Smokey* 1975—*A Quiet Storm* 1976—*Smokey's Family Robinson* 1977—*Deep in My Soul* 1978—*Love Breeze; Smokin'* 1979—*Where There's Smoke* 1981—*Being With You* 1982—*Touch the Sky* 1983—*Blame It on Love and All the Great Hits* 1987—*One Heartbeat* (Motown) 1990—*Love, Smokey* 1991—*Double Good Everything* (SBK) 1999—*Intimate.*

Soon after his debut with the Miracles, Smokey Robinson became known as one of the premier songwriter/singers in pop music. Bob Dylan called him "America's greatest living poet," and in 1987 ABC's Martin Fry sang that "Everything's good in the world tonight / When Smokey sings," and few would disagree with either. As a writer of love songs, Robinson is peerless: From the straightforward, timeless "My Girl" to the elaborately constructed, metaphor-driven "The Hunter Gets Captured by the Game," "Let Me Be the Time (on the Clock of Your Heart)," and "The Way You Do the Things You Do," he explored every aspect of romantic love. Whether making an elegant declaration of passion ("More Love"), pleading forgiveness ("Ooh Baby Baby"), or musing at love's paradoxical nature ("Ain't That Peculiar," "Choosey Beggar"), Robinson's best songs showed a rare mastery of the pop form. His delicate yet emotionally powerful falsetto is among the most romantic in pop.

In addition, Smokey Robinson made major contributions to the success of Motown, a fact acknowledged by label founder Berry Gordy Jr., when he surprised the singer with a corporate–vice president title in 1961. In addition to providing the label with 27 Top 40 hits with the Miracles, he also wrote, cowrote, or produced some of Motown's biggest hits (the Temptations' "My Girl," Mary Wells' hits) as well as some of its lesser known but more adventurous releases (like the Four Tops' "Still Water [Love]," the Supremes' "Floy Joy").

Robinson founded the Miracles—all Detroit-born—while attending that city's Northern High School. As the Matadors, they played locally, usually performing Robinson originals. In 1957 they met Berry Gordy Jr. while they were auditioning for Jackie Wilson's manager. Gordy, who had written songs for Wilson, was impressed not only by their presentation but by Smokey's prodigious songwriting. "Got a Job," an answer to the #1 hit "Get a Job" by the Silhouettes, attracted local attention in 1958. In 1959 "Bad Girl" was distributed locally by Motown and nationally by Chicago's Chess Records. It hit #93 on the pop chart and convinced Berry Gordy Jr. to expand his fledgling record company into one that would produce and distribute its own product rather than creating records to lease out to others. In 1960 "Shop Around" established both the group and the company when it went to #1 R&B, #2 pop. Its B side was the oft-covered soul ballad "Who's Lovin' You." This marked the beginning of Smokey and Gordy's relationship. According to one Motown history, when Gordy met Smokey, the young songwriter had hundreds of finished and unfinished song lyrics in notebooks, and it was Gordy who trained him to distinguish which were the best among them.

Throughout the '60s, Robinson wrote songs for and produced many other Motown acts, including the Marvelettes ("Don't Mess with Bill," "The Hunter Gets Captured by the Game," and "My Baby Must Be a Magician"); Marvin Gaye ("I'll Be Doggone," with Warren Moore and Marvin Tarplin; "Ain't That Peculiar," with Moore); Mary Wells ("My Guy," "The One Who Really Loves You," and "You Beat Me to the Punch," with Ronald White); and the Temptations ("Get Ready," "Don't Look Back," and "My Girl," with White; "The Way You Do the Things You Do," with Bobby Rogers; "It's Growing," with Moore).

Smokey Robinson and the Miracles: Pete Moore, Ronnie White, Smokey Robinson, Bobby Rogers

Though the Miracles made numerous uptempo singles such as "Mickey's Monkey" (#8 pop, #3 R&B) in 1963 and "Going to a Go-Go" (#11 pop, #2 R&B) in 1966, they are best known for their ballads, including "You've Really Got a Hold on Me" (#8 pop, #1 R&B, 1963), "Ooo Baby Baby" (#16 pop, #4 R&B, 1965), "The Tracks of My Tears" (#16 pop, #2 R&B, 1965), "More Love" (#23 pop, #5 R&B, 1967—by which time they had become Smokey Robinson and the Miracles), "I Second That Emotion" (#4 pop, #1 R&B, 1967), and "Baby, Baby Don't Cry" (#8 pop, #3 R&B, 1969). Their last big hit together was the uptempo "The Tears of a Clown," a #1 hit on both the R&B and pop charts, and in England, in 1970. A great deal of their work in these years featured Marv Tarplin on guitar; he even appeared on a few album covers as if he were a Miracle.

In 1972 Robinson left the group to record on his own and to spend more time with his wife, Claudette (Bobby Rogers' sister, and a Miracle until 1964, though she continued to sing on the group's records). Claudette had toured with the group until a series of miscarriages forced her off the road in the mid-'60s. Robinson wrote "More Love" for Claudette after one of their babies was lost. Their first child, Berry William (named after Gordy), was born in 1968; their daughter Tamla (named for the label) followed. The couple divorced in 1985.

Robinson continued in his duties as a Motown vice president. He also worked frequently with Tarplin, who, after a few years with the Miracles, rejoined Robinson. *A Quiet Storm* (1975) is regarded as his best early solo album. (Its title was eventually used to name a smooth subgenre of modern R&B that developed in the 1990s.) While Smokey has always been a popular concert attraction, his record sales during the '70s fluctuated. It wasn't until 1979's "Cruisin' " (#4 pop, #4 R&B) that Robinson again enjoyed mass success. His #1 R&B single "Being With You" (#2 pop) in 1981 continued his performing comeback, but in the ensuing years, he has placed just two more singles in the pop Top 10 (1987's "Just to See Her" and "One Heartbeat") and one LP in the Top 40 (*One Heartbeat,* which is gold). Despite rampant defections from the label through the '70s and '80s, Robinson did not leave Motown until 1990 (he had resigned his vice presidency there in 1988). He returned to the label in the late '90s and released *Intimate* (#134 pop, #28 R&B, 1999). In his 1989 autobiography, *Smokey: Inside My Life* (cowritten with David Ritz), Robinson openly discussed his marital infidelities and a mid-'80s addiction to cocaine.

Among the artists who have covered Robinson's songs are the Beatles ("You've Really Got a Hold on Me"), the Rolling Stones ("Going to a Go-Go"), Terence Trent D'Arby ("Who's Lovin' You"), Johnny Rivers ("The Tracks of My Tears"), Blondie ("The Hunter Gets Captured by the Game"), Linda Ronstadt ("Ooo Baby Baby," "The Tracks of My Tears"), Kim Carnes ("More Love"), Rare Earth ("Get Ready"), the English Beat ("The Tears of a Clown"), Rita Coolidge ("The Way You Do the Things You Do"), and Luther Vandross ("Since I Lost My Baby"). He has received the Grammys' Living Legend Award and was inducted into the Rock and Roll Hall of Fame with the Miracles in 1987. In 1999 he received a Grammy Lifetime Achievement Award. The following year he became the host of *Intimate With Smokey Robinson,* a two-hour program of love songs and call-ins on the L.A. oldies station Mega 92.3.

After Robinson made his final concert appearance with the group in July 1972, the Miracles continued with lead vocalist Billy Griffin. While they kept charting through 1978, only three singles had significant chart status: "Do It Baby" (#13 pop, #14 R&B) and "Don't Cha Love It" (#4 R&B) in 1974, and their early-1976 #1 pop hit "Love Machine (Part 1)" (#5 R&B). Billy Griffin was replaced by his brother Donald, but the Miracles disbanded in the late '70s. They have reappeared in concert and on records, sometimes including Claudette Robinson. White died of leukemia in 1995.

The Tom Robinson Band/Sector 27

Formed 1977, England
Tom Robinson (b. ca. 1951, Cambridge, Eng.), bass, voc.; Danny Kustow, gtr., voc.; Mark Ambler, organ, piano; Brian "Dolphin" Taylor, drums.
1978—*Power in the Darkness* (Harvest) (– Taylor; – Ambler; + Nick Plytas, kybds.; – Plytas; + Ian "Quince" Parker, kybds.; + Preston Heyman [b. U.S.], drums) 1979—*TRB Two* (group disbands).
Sector 27, formed late 1979: Robinson, voc., gtr.; Jo Burt, bass; Stevie B., gtr.; Derek Quinton, drums, perc.
1980—*Sector 27* (I.R.S.) (group disbands).
Tom Robinson solo: 1982—*North by Northwest* (I.R.S.) 1984—*Hope and Glory* (Geffen, U.K.) 1994—*Love Over Rage* (Scarface) 1996—*Having It Both Ways* (Cooking Vinyl, U.K.).

Singer/songwriter Tom Robinson—one of rock's first openly gay performers—is also noteworthy for using his records to treat his sexual preference as a political issue (e.g., his song "Glad to Be Gay"). He first attracted public attention during the early days of British punk in 1977. The Tom Robinson Band, like the early Clash, played rousing battle-cry rock & roll.

Robinson claimed he was first drawn to rock & roll as an angry counterpoint to his father's love of classical music. At 17 Robinson was shipped off to Finchden Manor, a home for "maladjusted boys." In his six years there, he met guitarist Danny Kustow, and the two became friendly. He left for London in 1973, and there formed Cafe Society, a cabaret, folk-harmony band, with two old friends, Herewood Kaye and Raphael Doyle. Ray Davies signed them to his Konk label in 1973 and produced their one album in 1975. (Robinson and Davies had a falling out, later obliquely chronicled in "Don't Take No for an Answer" on TRB's debut.)

In 1976 Robinson left Cafe Society, and he formed the Tom Robinson Band in January 1977. In October TRB's "2-4-6-8-Motorway" went to #5 in the U.K. The band became press darlings in England, especially after the *Rising Free* EP in early 1978, which included "Glad to Be Gay." That press attention was soon repeated in the U.S., leading to the release of the band's American debut, *Power in the Darkness.* "Glad to Be Gay" got nearly as much radio play on the big-city U.S. stations as "2-4-6-8-Motorway." Robinson also plugged Rock Against Racism on the back of the album cover and included the New York and L.A. gay switchboard numbers on the inner sleeve of the U.S. version.

The band went through some personnel changes before its second LP, which was produced by Todd Rundgren. Despite several U.S. tours, neither LP sold well. The album was poorly received in England also, and Robinson began to feel that TRB's style was no longer fresh, so he broke up the group in July 1979. Earlier that year, Robinson had written a few songs with Elton John, including one for Gay Pride Week. A collaboration with Peter Gabriel, "Bully for You," appeared on *TRB Two* and was a minor hit in England.

Robinson's new band, Sector 27, appeared later in the year, influenced by the harsher wave of postpunk groups like Gang of Four, early XTC, and the Cure. Robinson toured England and then the U.S. in summer 1980. The self-titled LP got good reviews but failed to sell, and Sector 27 fell apart. Robinson moved to Berlin, Germany, working with alternative-cabaret and theater groups. In mid-1982 he resurfaced with a solo record, *North by Northwest.* A 1983 single, "War Baby," cracked the U.K. Top 10. Robinson's subsequent releases were U.K.-only. *Hope and Glory* yielded a minor U.K. hit in a cover of Steely Dan's "Rikki Don't Lose That Number." Robinson regrouped the original TRB for two mid-'80s English albums that sold unexceptionally and were dismissed by U.K. critics as nostalgia-mongering.

He continued performing into the '90s, and released *Love Over Rage,* his first U.S. album in a decade. Although he still identifies himself as gay, he also publicly revealed that he has a relationship with a woman, with whom he has a son. The U.K.-only *Having It Both Ways* contains the memorable track "The Artist Formerly Known as Gay." In 1997 Robinson formed his own Castaway Northwest Records, which reissued his back catalogue. He has also done extensive radio work; in the '90s he was the host of *Locker Room,* a BBC program about men. In 1997 he won a Sony Radio Award for the BBC GLR program *You've Got to Hide Your Love Away.* He remains highly outspoken on a range of issues, including gay rights, AIDS, and the treatment of Native Americans.

The Roches

Formed 1976, New York, NY
Maggie Roche (b. Oct. 26, 1951, Detroit, MI), voc., gtr.; Terre Roche (b. Apr. 10, 1953, New York), voc., gtr.
1975—*Seductive Reasoning* (Columbia) 1976—(+ Suzzy Roche [b. Sep. 29, 1956, Bronxville, NY], voc., gtr. 1979—*The Roches* (Warner Bros.) 1980—*Nurds* 1982—*Keep On Doing* 1985—*Another World* 1987—*No Trespassing* (Rhino) 1989—*Speak* (MCA) 1990—*We Three Kings* (MCA/Paradox) 1992—*A Dove* (MCA) 1994—*Will You Be My Friend?* (Baby Boom) 1995—*Can We Go Home Now?* (Rykodisc).

Suzzy Roche solo: 1997—*Holy Smokes* (Redhouse) 2000—*Songs From an Unmarried Housewife and Mother, Greenwich Village, USA*.
Terre Roche solo: 1998—*The Sound of a Tree Falling* (Earth Rock Wreckerds).

By the time their critically acclaimed debut album as a three-piece band was released, the Roche sisters had been singing together for years. Maggie and Terre had previously recorded as a duo; the trio lineup had performed in New York clubs. With Suzzy's sweet-and-sour voice, Terre's pliant upper register, and Maggie's near baritone, they came out of New York's folk, feminist, and bohemian traditions, mingling barbershop quartet, Irish traditional, Andrews Sisters, doo-wop, and other vocal-group styles in songs—mostly by Maggie—full of wordplay and unexpected twists. Onstage the sisters invariably wore an eccentric array of thrift-shop clothes and sporting gear.

Maggie and Terre began singing professionally in the late '60s. Maggie dropped out of Bard College and Terre left high school in order to accommodate tour schedules. In 1970 they met Paul Simon, and in 1972 they sang backup harmonies on his *There Goes Rhymin' Simon*. Simon's lawyer got the duo a contract with Columbia, which resulted in *Seductive Reasoning*, an album that went largely unnoticed. Maggie and Terre retreated to a friend's temple in Hammond, Louisiana, but eventually drifted back north, performing again for the first time in June 1976 at the Women's Music Festival in Champaign, Illinois. Within a few months Suzzy, who'd been attending the State University of New York in Purchase, joined them, and they became fixtures in Greenwich Village folk clubs.

After amassing local critical raves, they recorded together under the eye of producer Robert Fripp. *The Roches* sold 200,000 copies and contained "The Married Men" (later covered by Phoebe Snow) but failed to yield a hit. Terre sang on Fripp's 1979 solo LP *Exposure*, and the trio sang backup for Loudon Wainwright III's "Golfin' Blues." In 1980, augmented with the rhythm section of ex-Television bassist Fred Smith and Patti Smith drummer Jay Dee Daugherty, they recorded *Nurds*. In mid-1982 Fripp produced their third album, *Keep On Doing*, a primarily acoustic album that nevertheless featured members of King Crimson. *Another World* used a full rock-styled sound, but again failed to sell well.

The Roches then moved to MCA, where *Speak* was another commercial failure. *We Three Kings* was a Christmas album, while *A Dove* returned to the trio's typically playful, audaciously harmonized tunes (including "The Ing Song," every word of which ends in "ing"). The children's record *Will You Be My Friend?* was released independently.

The Roches have also written and recorded music for various theater and television shows, and such films as *Crossing Delancey* and the animated feature *The Land Before Time II*. They also appeared on albums by the Indigo Girls, Was (Not Was), and country singer Kathy Mattea. Steven Spielberg used the siblings to voice animated cockroach sisters in his '90s cartoon TV series *Tiny Toons*.

After the 1995 release of *Can We Go Home Now?*, the Roches split up. Suzzy went solo and released two albums. Terre formed a 12-piece band called Terre Roche and Her Mood Swings, which included her soul mate, Gary Dial, on piano. She self-released her solo debut in 1998. As of 2001 she was spending most of her time teaching music to beginners in New York.

Rockpile

Formed 1976, London, Eng.
Dave Edmunds (b. Apr. 15, 1944, Cardiff, Wales), voc., gtr.; Nick Lowe (b. Mar. 25, 1949, Woodbridge, Eng.), voc., bass; Terry Williams (b. 1948), drums; Billy Bremner (b. 1947, Scot.), gtr., voc.
1980—*Seconds of Pleasure* (Columbia).
Dave Edmunds solo: see entry.
Nick Lowe solo: see entry.
Billy Bremner solo: 1984—*Bash* (Arista, U.K.)

Though it recorded only one album under the name Rockpile, this band had made four previous U.S. tours, and its members had appeared on most solo LPs by the group's best-known members: Nick Lowe [see entry] (who specializes in ironic pop) and Dave Edmunds [see entry] (known for his revitalized rockabilly).

Ex–Love Sculpture guitarist Edmunds called his first solo album *Rockpile* (1972), and his band, which toured to support that album, was also christened Rockpile, though the only member of the more recent group was drummer Terry Williams, who'd filled in on one of Love Sculpture's U.S. tours. Williams had also played with Deke Leonard and Martin Ace, whom he later joined in Man.

This initial Rockpile helped kick off England's pub-rock movement, which included other no-frills groups like Ducks Deluxe and Brinsley Schwarz. Nick Lowe of the Schwarz band met Williams and Edmunds on the pub circuit, and Edmunds produced the final Brinsley LP in 1974. On Edmunds'

Rockpile: Terry Williams, Nick Lowe, Dave Edmunds, Billy Bremner

next solo LP, 1975's *Subtle As a Flying Mallet,* Lowe played and contributed songs.

In mid-1976 Rockpile solidified its new lineup for a brief American tour with Bad Company, rounded out by Billy Bremner, a sessionman who'd backed everyone from Duane Eddy to Lulu. The group's sets offered a furiously paced mixture of Lowe's tuneful ditties and Edmunds' more rocking outbursts. In 1980 the band's two leaders were both signed to the same label, and Rockpile released its one and only LP (#27), which included an EP of Lowe and Edmunds duetting on Everly Brothers tunes. Rockpile toured the U.S. that winter, but in February of 1981 it had a bitter split. Edmunds and Lowe resumed their recording and production careers, while Williams went on to play with Dire Straits. In 1982 Bremner was a temporary replacement for the late James Honeyman-Scott in the Pretenders, but he then rejoined Edmunds' band. Most recently he has become a Nashville session musician. On his *Nick the Knife,* Lowe took a shot at Edmunds in "Stick It Where the Sun Don't Shine," but the two ended their estrangement in the late '80s, and Edmunds produced Lowe's *Pinker and Prouder Than Previous* and *Party of One.*

Jimmie Rodgers

Born Sep. 8, 1897, Meridian, MS; died May 26, 1933, New York, NY
1962—*Country Music Hall of Fame* (RCA) 1965—*Best of the Legendary Jimmie Rodgers* 1975—*My Rough and Rowdy Ways* 1978—*A Legendary Performer* (RCA) 1991—*First Sessions, 1927–1928* (Rounder); *The Early Years, 1928–1929; On the Way Up, 1929; Riding High, 1929–1930; America's Blue Yodeler, 1930–1931; Down the Old Road, 1931–1932; No Hard Times, 1932; Last Sessions, 1933.*

Though his recording career only lasted seven years (from 1927 until his death in 1933), Jimmie Rodgers established himself as the father of modern country music, mixing black blues with folk and traditional hillbilly country.

Rodgers first played the guitar and banjo while working as a water carrier on the M&O Railroad, where he picked up blues influences from black fellow laborers. He later worked as a brakeman until ill health forced him to quit in 1925. (He always had health problems; his mother died of TB when he was four.)

Rodgers had long been an amateur performer, but following his forced retirement he pursued music full-time, becoming a blackface performer in a medicine show. In 1926 he appeared as a yodeler and later that year formed his own band, the Jimmie Rodgers Entertainers. The group soon split. Rodgers got a solo contract with Victor Records and released "The Soldier's Sweetheart" and "Sleep Baby Sleep" in 1927, around the same time the Carter Family made its recording debut. His song "Blue Yodel" became a million-seller, making Rodgers the first country superstar. "Brakeman's Blues" also sold a million, and in 1929 he made the movie short *The Singing Brakeman;* its title became his nickname.

Even during the Depression, Rodgers' records sold well, but his health was deteriorating. Though he was critically ill and had to cancel shows, he continued to record up until his death. His final song, "Fifteen Years Ago Today," was completed the same day he hemorrhaged and lapsed into a coma. The next day he died. In 1961 Rodgers, along with Frank Rose and Hank Williams, became one of the first persons elected to the Country Music Hall of Fame.

Nile Rodgers: See Chic

Tommy Roe

Born May 9, 1942, Atlanta, GA
1962—*Sheila* (ABC-Paramount) 1966—*Sweet Pea* 1969—*Dizzy* (ABC); *12 in a Roe/A Collection of Tommy Roe's Greatest Hits* 1970—*We Can Make Music.*

At the peak of his career, in the late '60s, singer/songwriter Tommy Roe could do no wrong. He had two #1 records, "Sheila" in 1962 and "Dizzy" in 1969, and also scored big with "Sweet Pea" (#8, 1966), "Hooray for Hazel" (#6, 1966), and "Jam Up and Jelly Tight" (#8, 1969). Even a version of Lloyd Price's hit from 1959, "Stagger Lee," reached the Top 30.

At the age of 16 Roe was living in Atlanta, leading his own group, the Satins. In 1960 he recorded one of his own songs, a bald rewrite of Buddy Holly's "Peggy Sue," called "Sheila." Two years later Roe was signed to ABC. His first single there seemed destined for failure until disc jockeys flipped over "Save Your Kisses" and found "Sheila" (in its second version), which became a huge success.

Followup records didn't fare so well. But Roe was doing much better in England, where he relocated for a while in the '60s. Today he continues to perform, alternating between the oldies circuit and country shows.

Kenny Rogers

Born Aug. 21, 1938, Houston, TX
Kenny Rogers and the First Edition: 1967—*The First Edition* (Reprise); *The First Edition's Second* 1969—*The First Edition's '69; Ruby, Don't Take Your Love to Town* 1970—*Something's Burning; Tell It All Brother* 1971—*Kenny Rogers and the First Edition's Greatest Hits; Transition* 1972—*The Ballad of Calico; Backroads* (Jolly Rogers) 1973—*Monumental; Rollin'.*
Kenny Rogers solo: 1974—*Love Lifted Me* (United Artists) 1975—*Kenny Rogers* 1976—*Daytime Friends* 1978—*The Gambler; Ten Years of Gold* 1979—*Kenny* 1980—*Gideon* 1981—*Share Your Love* (Liberty); *Christmas* 1982—*Love Will Turn You Around* 1983—*We've Got Tonight; Eyes That See in the Dark* (RCA); *Twenty Greatest Hits* (Liberty) 1984—*What About Me?; Once Upon a Christmas* (with Dolly Parton) (RCA) 1985—*Heart of the Matter* 1986—*They Don't Make Them Like They Used To* 1987—*I Prefer the Moonlight* 1988—*Greatest Hits* 1989—*Something Inside So Strong* (Reprise);

Christmas in America 1990—*Love Is Strange* 1992—*20 Great Years; Back Home Again* 1993—*If Only My Heart Had a Voice* (Giant) 1994—*Timepiece* (Atlantic) 1996—*Vote for Love* (Q); *The Gift* (Magnatone) 1997—*Across My Heart* 1998—*Christmas From the Heart* (Dreamcatcher) 1999—*She Rides Wild Horses; Through the Years* (Capitol).

Though often dismissed by critics, Kenny Rogers has had well over 40 years of success with folk pop (with the New Christy Minstrels), mild psychedelia and country rock (with the First Edition), and country-pop ballads (as a solo act).

Rogers began singing in a high-school band, the Scholars, who had a regional Texas hit with "That Crazy Feeling." At the University of Houston, he joined a jazz group, the Bobby Doyle Trio, as a vocalist and recorded with it for Columbia. He then joined the New Christy Minstrels [see entry] in 1966.

The First Edition was formed by ex-Minstrels in 1967 and included Mike Settle, Mickey Jones, Terry Williams, and Thelma Camacho. The group made its debut at Ledbetter's in L.A., a club owned by another ex-Minstrel, Randy Sparks. There, the group was brought to the attention of musician/comedian Tommy Smothers, who put Rogers and the First Edition on his popular TV show in January 1968. This led to a Reprise contract, and the act had its first hit just a month later with the quasi-psychedelic "Just Dropped In (To See What Condition My Condition Was In)" (#5). Subsequent hits were in a more countryish vein, like "Ruby, Don't Take Your Love to Town" and the Kingston Trio's "Reuben James" (#26), both in 1969. More hits followed, including the harder-rocking "Something's Burning" (#11) and the gospelish "Tell It All Brother" (#17) in 1970. From 1971 to 1973 the First Edition had its own syndicated TV show, *Rollin' on the River.*

After the breakup of the First Edition, Rogers switched to an MOR-country style and chalked up a string of big hits like "Lucille" (#5, 1977), "The Gambler" (#16, 1979), "Don't Fall in Love With a Dreamer" (#4, 1980; a duet with Kim Carnes), Lionel Richie's "Lady" (his first #1 hit), "I Don't Need You" (#3), "Through the Years" (#13, 1982), "Love Will Turn You Around" (#13, 1982), "We've Got Tonight" (with Sheena Easton) (#6, 1983), "Islands in the Stream" (with Dolly Parton) (#1, 1983), and "What About Me?" (with Kim Carnes and James Ingram) (#15, 1984).

Between 1977 and 1979 alone, Rogers sold over $100 million worth of records, and he soon became a household name. Through the mid-'80s, Rogers' record sales cooled somewhat, although he continued to score C&W hits with "Crazy" (#1 C&W, 1984), "Morning Desire" (#1 C&W, 1985), "Tomb of the Unknown Soldier" (#1 C&W, 1986), "Twenty Years Ago" (#2 C&W, 1986), "I Prefer the Moonlight" (#2 C&W, 1987), and "The Factory" (#6 C&W, 1988), among others. *Love Will Turn You Around* and *We've Got Tonight* went gold; the Barry Gibb–produced *Eyes That See in the Dark, Twenty Greatest Hits,* and *What About Me?* were all certified platinum, and *Once Upon a Christmas* sold 2 million copies, but *Something Inside So Strong* did not even make the Top 100 albums chart.

By then Rogers had branched out into other areas with comparable success. In 1980 he began his acting career, starring in a TV movie entitled, *The Gambler,* based on his 1979 hit. Since then, he has starred in four more films in the same series, two movie-of-the-week productions as the detective MacShayne, and in the feature film *Six Pack* (1982). Since 1979 he has also starred or costarred in over a dozen television specials. He has published several books of his photography, opened a rotisserie-chicken fast-food franchise, and hosted a series of documentaries on the Old West for the Arts and Entertainment Network. He participated in USA for Africa and, with his manager, Ken Kragen, was a principal leader of the charity effort Hands Across America in 1986.

By the late '90s, Rogers had formed his own label, Dreamcatcher Entertainment. His 1999 album *She Rides Wild Horses,* which peaked at #6 C&W, marked his highest chart debut in 15 years. The singles "Buy Me a Rose" (#1 C&W, 2000) and "The Greatest" (#26 C&W, 1999) were successful as well.

The Rolling Stones

Formed 1962, London, Eng.
Mick Jagger (b. Michael Phillip Jagger, July 26, 1943, Dartford, Eng.), voc.; Keith Richards (b. Dec. 18, 1943, Dartford), gtr., voc.; Brian Jones (b. Lewis Brian Hopkins-Jones, Feb. 28, 1942, Cheltenham, Eng.; d. July 3, 1969, London), gtr.; Bill Wyman (b. William Perks, Oct. 24, 1936, London), bass; Charlie Watts (b. June 2, 1941, Islington, Eng.), drums.
1964—*England's Newest Hitmakers/The Rolling Stones* (London); *12 X 5* 1965—*The Rolling Stones, Now!; Out of Our Heads; December's Children* 1966—*Big Hits (High Tide and Green Grass); Aftermath; Got Live If You Want It* 1967—*Between the Buttons; Flowers; Their Satanic Majesties Request* 1968—*Beggars Banquet* 1969—(– Jones; + Mick Taylor [b. Jan. 17, 1948, Hertfordshire, Eng.], gtr.) *Through the Past Darkly; Let It Bleed* 1970—*Get Yer Ya-Ya's Out!* 1971—*Sticky Fingers* (Rolling Stones/Atlantic); *Hot Rocks* (London) 1972—*Exile on Main Street* (Rolling Stones/Atlantic); *More Hot Rocks: Big Hits and Fazed Cookies* (London) 1973—*Goats Head Soup* (Rolling Stones/Atlantic) 1974—*It's Only Rock n' Roll* 1975—*Metamorphosis* (Abkco); *Made in the Shade* (Rolling Stones/Atlantic) (– Taylor; + Ron Wood [b. June 1, 1947, Hillingdon, Eng.], gtr., voc.) 1976—*Black and Blue* 1977—*Love You Live* 1978—*Some Girls* 1980—*Emotional Rescue* 1981—*Sucking in the Seventies; Tattoo You* 1982—*Still Life* 1983—*Undercover* (Columbia) 1984—*Rewind (1971–1984)* 1986—*Dirty Work* (Rolling Stone/CBS) 1989—*Singles Collection—The London Years* (Abkco); *Steel Wheels* (Rolling Stones/CBS) 1991—*Flashpoint* 1992—(– Wyman) 1994—(+ Darryl Jones, bass) *Voodoo Lounge* (Virgin) 1995—*Stripped* 1996—*Rock & Roll Circus* 1997—*Bridges to Babylon* 1998—*No Security.*
Mick Jagger solo: 1984—*She's the Boss* (Atlantic) 1987—*Primitive Cool* 1993—*Wandering Spirit.*

Keith Richards solo: 1988—*Talk Is Cheap* (Virgin) 1991—*Live at the Hollywood Palladium* 1992—*Main Offender.*
Bill Wyman solo: 1974—*Monkey Grip* (Rolling Stones) 1976—*Stone Alone* 1998—*Bill Wyman and the Rhythm Kings* (Velvel); *Struttin' Our Stuff* 1999—*Anyway the Wind Blows.*
Charlie Watts Orchestra: 1986—*Live at Fulham Town Hall* (Columbia).
Charlie Watts solo: 1991—*From One Charlie* (Continuum) 1992—*A Tribute to Charlie Parker With Strings* 1993—*Warm and Tender* 1996—*Long Ago and Far Away* (Virgin) 2000—*Charlie Watts/Jim Keltner Project* (Higher Octave).
Ron Wood solo: 1974—*I've Got My Own Album to Do* (Warner Bros.) 1975—*Now Look* 1979—*Gimme Some Neck* (Columbia) 1981—*1234* 1992—*Slide on This* (Continuum).
Mick Taylor solo: 1979—*Mick Taylor* (Columbia) 1990—*Stranger in This Town* (Maze Music) 1991—*Too Hot for Snakes* (with Carla Olson) (Razor & Tie) 1995—*Coastin' Home* (Shattered) 2000—*A Stone's Throw* (Cannonball).
Willie and the Poor Boys (Wyman, Watts, Jimmy Page, Paul Rodgers, Kenney Jones, Andy Fairweather-Low): 1985—*Willie and the Poor Boys* (Passport) 1994—*Tear It Up* (Blind Pig).

The Rolling Stones began calling themselves the "World's Greatest Rock & Roll Band" in the late '60s, and few disputed the claim. The Stones' music, based on Chicago blues, has continued to sound vital through the decades, and the Stones' attitude of flippant defiance, now aged into wry bemusement, has come to seem as important as their music.

In the 1964 British Invasion they were promoted as bad boys, but what began as a gimmick has stuck as an indelible image, and not just because of incidents like Brian Jones' mysterious death in 1969 and a violent murder during their set at Altamont later that year. In their music, the Stones pioneered British rock's tone of ironic detachment and wrote about offhand brutality, sex as power, and other taboos. In those days, Mick Jagger was branded a "Lucifer" figure, thanks to songs like "Sympathy for the Devil." In the '80s the Stones lost their dangerous aura while still seeming "bad"—they've become icons of an elegantly debauched, world-weary decadence. But Jagger remains the most self-consciously assured appropriator of black performers' up-front sexuality; Keith Richards' Chuck Berry–derived riffing defines rock rhythm guitar (not to mention rock guitar rhythm); the stalwart rhythm section of Bill Wyman and Charlie Watts holds its own; and Jagger and Richards continue to add to what is arguably one of the most significant oeuvres in rock history.

Jagger and Richards first met at Dartford Maypole County Primary School. When they ran into each other 10 years later in 1960, they were both avid fans of blues and American R&B, and they found they had a mutual friend in guitarist Dick Taylor, a fellow student of Richards' at Sidcup Art School. Jagger was attending the London School of Economics and playing in Little Boy Blue and the Blue Boys with Taylor. Richards joined the band as second guitarist; soon afterward, he was expelled from Dartford Technical College for truancy.

The Rolling Stones: Charlie Watts, Bill Wyman, Mick Taylor, Keith Richards, Mick Jagger

Meanwhile, Brian Jones had begun skipping school in Cheltenham to practice bebop alto sax and clarinet. By the time he was 16, he had fathered two illegitimate children and run off briefly to Scandinavia, where he began playing guitar. Back in Cheltenham he joined the Ramrods, then drifted to London with his girlfriend and one of his children. He began playing with Alexis Korner's Blues, Inc., then decided to start his own band; a want ad attracted pianist Ian Stewart (b. 1938; d. December 12, 1985).

As Elmo Lewis, Jones began working at the Ealing Blues Club, where he ran into a later, loosely knit version of Blues, Inc., which at the time included drummer Charlie Watts. Jagger and Richards began jamming with Blues, Inc., and while Jagger, Richards, and Jones began to practice on their own, Jagger became the featured singer with Blues, Inc.

Jones, Jagger, and Richards shared a tiny, cheap London apartment, and with drummer Tony Chapman they cut a demo tape, which was rejected by EMI. Taylor left to attend the Royal College of Art; he eventually formed the Pretty Things. Ian Stewart's job with a chemical company kept the rest of the group from starving. By the time Taylor left, they began to call themselves the Rolling Stones, after a Muddy Waters song.

On July 12, 1962, the Rolling Stones—Jagger, Richards, Jones, a returned Dick Taylor on bass, and Mick Avory, later of the Kinks, on drums—played their first show at the Marquee. Avory and Taylor were replaced by Tony Chapman and Bill Wyman, from the Cliftons. Chapman didn't work out, and the band spent months recruiting a cautious Charlie Watts, who worked for an advertising agency and had left Blues, Inc. when its schedule got too busy. In January 1963 Watts completed the band.

Local entrepreneur Giorgio Gomelsky booked the Stones at his Crawdaddy Club for an eight-month, highly successful residency. He was also their unofficial manager until Andrew Loog Oldham, with financing from Eric Easton, signed them as clients. By then the Beatles were a British sensation, and

Oldham decided to promote the Stones as their nasty opposites. He eased out the mild-mannered Stewart, who subsequently became a Stones roadie and frequent session and tour pianist.

In June 1963 the Stones released their first single, Chuck Berry's "Come On." After the band played on the British TV rock show *Thank Your Lucky Stars,* its producer reportedly told Oldham to get rid of "that vile-looking singer with the tire-tread lips." The single reached #21 on the British chart. The Stones also appeared at the first annual National Jazz and Blues Festival in London's borough of Richmond and in September were part of a package tour with the Everly Brothers, Bo Diddley, and Little Richard. In December 1963 the Stones' second single, "I Wanna Be Your Man" (written by John Lennon and Paul McCartney), made the British Top 15. In January 1964 the Stones did their first headlining British tour, with the Ronettes, and released a version of Buddy Holly's "Not Fade Away," which made #3.

"Not Fade Away" also made the U.S. singles chart (#48). By this time the band had become a sensation in Britain, with the press gleefully reporting that band members had been seen urinating in public. In April 1964 their first album was released in the U.K., and two months later they made their first American tour. Their cover of the Bobby Womack/Valentinos song "It's All Over Now" was a British #1, their first. Their June American tour was a smashing success; in Chicago, where they'd stopped off to record the *Five by Five* EP at the Chess Records studio, riots broke out when the band tried to give a press conference. The Stones' version of the blues standard "Little Red Rooster," which had become another U.K. #1, was banned in the U.S. because of its "objectionable" lyrics.

Jagger and Richards had now begun composing their own tunes (at first using the "Nanker Phelge" pseudonym for group compositions). Their "Tell Me (You're Coming Back to Me)" was the group's first U.S. Top 40 hit, in August. The followup, a nonoriginal, "Time Is on My Side," made #6 in November. From that point on, all but a handful of Stones hits were Jagger-Richards compositions.

In January 1965 their "The Last Time" became another U.K. #1 and cracked the U.S. Top 10 in the spring. The band's next single, "(I Can't Get No) Satisfaction," reigned at #1 for four weeks that summer and remains perhaps the most famous song in its remarkable canon. Jagger and Richards continued to write hits with increasingly sophisticated lyrics: "Get Off My Cloud" (#1, 1965), "As Tears Go By" (#6, 1965), "19th Nervous Breakdown" (#2, 1966), "Mother's Little Helper" (#8, 1966), "Have You Seen Your Mother, Baby, Standing in the Shadow?" (#9, 1966).

Aftermath, the first Stones LP of all original material, came out in 1966, though its impact was minimized by the simultaneous release of the Beatles' *Revolver* and Bob Dylan's *Blonde on Blonde.* The Middle Eastern–tinged "Paint It, Black" (1966) and the ballad "Ruby Tuesday" (1967), were both U.S. #1 hits.

In January 1967 the Stones caused another sensation when they performed "Let's Spend the Night Together" ("Ruby Tuesday" 's B side) on *The Ed Sullivan Show.* Jagger mumbled the title lines after threats of censorship (some claimed that the line was censored; others that Jagger actually sang "Let's spend some *time* together"; Jagger later said, "When it came to that line, I sang mumble"). In February Jagger and Richards were arrested on drug-possession charges in Britain; in May, Brian Jones, too, was arrested. The heavy jail sentences they received were eventually suspended on appeal. The Stones temporarily withdrew from public appearances; Jagger and his girlfriend, singer Marianne Faithfull, went to India with the Beatles to meet the Maharishi Mahesh Yogi. The Stones' next single release didn't appear until the fall: the #14 "Dandelion." Its B side, "We Love You" (#50), on which John Lennon and Paul McCartney sang backup vocals, was intended as a thank-you to fans.

In December came *Their Satanic Majesties Request,* the Stones' psychedelic answer record to the Beatles' *Sgt. Pepper*—and an ambitious mess. By the time the album's lone single, "She's a Rainbow" had become a #25 hit, Allen Klein had become the group's manager.

May 1968 saw the release of "Jumpin' Jack Flash," a #3 hit, and a return to basic rock & roll. After five months of delay provoked by controversial album-sleeve photos, the eclectic *Beggars Banquet* was released and was hailed by critics as the band's finest achievement. On June 9, 1969, Brian Jones, the Stones' most musically adventurous member, who had lent sitar, dulcimer, and, on "Under My Thumb," marimba to the band's sound, and who had been in Morocco recording nomadic Joujouka musicians, left the band with this explanation: "I no longer see eye-to-eye with the others over the discs we are cutting." Within a week he was replaced by ex–John Mayall guitarist Mick Taylor. Jones announced that he would form his own band, but on July 3, 1969, he was found dead in his swimming pool; the coroner's report cited "death by misadventure." Jones, beset by drug problems—and the realization that the band now belonged squarely to Jagger and Richards—had barely participated in the *Beggars Banquet* sessions.

At an outdoor concert in London's Hyde Park a few days after Jones' death, Jagger read an excerpt from the poet Shelley and released thousands of butterflies over the park. On July 11, the day after Jones was buried, the Stones released "Honky Tonk Women," another #1, and another Stones classic. By this time, every Stones album went gold in short order, and *Let It Bleed* (a sardonic reply to the Beatles' soon-to-be-released *Let It Be*) was no exception. "Gimme Shelter" received constant airplay. Jones appeared on most of the album's tracks, though Taylor also made his first on-disc appearances.

After going to Australia to star in the film *Ned Kelly,* Jagger rejoined the band for the start of its hugely successful 1969 American tour, the band's first U.S. trip in three years. But the Stones' Satanic image came to haunt them at a free thank-you-America concert at California's Altamont Speedway. In the darkness just in front of the stage, a young black man, Meredith Hunter, was stabbed to death by members of the Hell's Angels motorcycle gang, whom the Stones—on advice of the Grateful Dead—had hired to provide security for the event. The incident was captured on film by the Maysles brothers in their feature-length documentary *Gimme Shelter.* Public outcry that "Sympathy for the Devil" (which they had performed earlier in the show; they were playing "Under My Thumb" when the murder occurred) had in some way incited the violence led the Stones to drop the tune from their stage shows for the next six years.

After another spell of inactivity, the *Get Yer Ya-Ya's Out!* live album was released in the fall of 1970 and went platinum. That same year the Stones formed their own Rolling Stones Records, an Atlantic subsidiary. The band's first album for its own label, *Sticky Fingers* (#1, 1971)—which introduced their Andy Warhol–designed lips-and-lolling-tongue logo—yielded hits in "Brown Sugar" (#1, 1971) and "Wild Horses" (#28, 1971). Jagger, who had starred in Nicolas Roeg's 1970 *Performance* (the soundtrack of which contained "Memo From Turner"), married Nicaraguan fashion model Bianca Perez Morena de Macias, and the pair became international jet-set favorites. Though many interpreted Jagger's acceptance into high society as yet another sign that rock was dead, or that at least the Stones had lost their spark, *Exile on Main Street* (#1, 1972), a double album, was another critically acclaimed hit, yielding "Tumbling Dice" (#7) and "Happy" (#22). By this time the Stones were touring the U.S. once every three years; their 1972 extravaganza, like those in 1975, 1978, and 1981, was a sold-out affair.

Goats Head Soup (#1, 1973) was termed the band's worst effort since *Satanic Majesties* by critics, yet it contained hits in "Angie" (#1, 1973) and "(Doo Doo Doo Doo Doo) Heartbreaker" (#15, 1974). *It's Only Rock n' Roll* (#1, 1974) yielded Top 20 hits in the title tune and a cover of the Temptations' "Ain't Too Proud to Beg." Mick Taylor left the band after that album; and after trying out scores of sessionmen (many of whom showed up on the next LP, 1976's *Black and Blue*), the Stones settled on Ron Wood, then still nominally committed to Rod Stewart and the Faces (who disbanded soon after Wood joined the Stones officially in 1976). In 1979 Richards and Wood, with Meters drummer Ziggy Modeliste and fusion bassist Stanley Clarke, toured as the New Barbarians.

Black and Blue was the Stones' fifth consecutive LP of new material to top the album chart, though it contained only one hit single, the #10 "Fool to Cry." Wyman, who had released a 1974 solo album, *Monkey Grip* (the first Stone to do so), recorded another, *Stone Alone.* Jagger guested on "I Can Feel the Fire" on Wood's solo first LP, *I've Got My Own Album to Do.* Wood has since recorded several more albums, and while none were commercial hits (*Gimme Some Neck* peaked at #45 in 1979), his work was generally well received.

The ethnic-stereotype lyrics of the title song from *Some Girls* (#1, 1978) provoked public protest (the last outcry had been in 1976 over *Black and Blue*'s battered-woman advertising campaign). Aside from the disco crossover "Miss You" (#1), the music was bare-bones rock & roll—in response, some speculated, to the punk movement's claims that the band was too old and too affluent to rock anymore.

Richards and his longtime common-law wife, Anita Pallenburg, were arrested in March 1977 in Canada for heroin possession—jeopardizing the band's future—but he subsequently kicked his habit and in 1978 was given a suspended sentence.

In 1981 *Tattoo You* was #1 for nine weeks (1980's *Emotional Rescue* also went to #1) and produced the hits "Start Me Up" (#2, 1981) and "Waiting on a Friend" (#13, 1981), the latter featuring jazz great Sonny Rollins on tenor saxophone. The 1981 tour spawned an album, *Still Life,* and a movie, *Let's Spend the Night Together* (directed by Hal Ashby), which grossed $50 million.

Through the '80s the group became more an institution than an influential force. Nevertheless, both *Undercover* (#4, 1983) and *Dirty Work* (#4, 1986) were certifiable hits despite not topping the chart, as every new studio album had done in the decade before. Each album produced only one Top 20 hit, "Undercover of the Night" (#9, 1983) and "Harlem Shuffle" (#5, 1986), the latter a remake of a minor 1964 hit by Bob and Earl.

Jagger and Richards grew estranged from each other, and the band would not record for three years. Jagger released his first solo album, the platinum *She's the Boss,* in 1984. His second, 1987's *Primitive Cool,* didn't even break the Top 40. Richards, who'd long declared he would never undertake a solo album (and who resented Jagger's making music outside the band), countered in 1988 with the gold *Talk Is Cheap,* backed up by the X-Pensive Winos: guitarist Waddy Wachtel and the rhythm section of Steve Jordan and Charley Drayton.

The two Stones sniped at each other in the press and in song: Richards' album track "You Don't Move Me" was directed at his longtime partner. Nevertheless, shortly before the Rolling Stones were inducted into the Rock and Roll Hall of Fame, in January 1989 the two traveled to Barbados to begin writing songs for a new Stones album. *Steel Wheels* (#3, 1989) showed the group spinning its wheels musically, and were it not for the band's first American tour in eight years, it is doubtful the LP would have sold anywhere near its 2 million copies. But the 50-date tour, which reportedly grossed $140 million, was an artistic triumph. As the group's fifth live album, *Flashpoint* (#16, 1991), demonstrated, never had the Stones sounded so cohesive onstage.

Bill Wyman announced his long-rumored decision to leave the group after 30 years, in late 1992. "I was quite happy to stop after that," the 56-year-old bassist told a British TV show. The announcement helped deflect attention from Wyman's love life: In 1989 he married model Mandy Smith, who was just 13½ when the two began dating. The couple divorced in 1990, the same year that Mick Jagger finally married his longtime lover, Jerry Hall. (Jagger and Hall would later split up.)

The early '90s were a time for solo albums from Richards—*Live at the Hollywood Palladium* and *Main Offender* (#99, 1992)—and Jagger's *Wandering Spirit* (#11, 1993). Neither sold spectacularly; apparently fans are most interested in Jagger and Richards when they work together. Wood released *Slide on This,* his first solo album in over a decade, and Watts pursued his real love, jazz, with the Charlie Watts Orchestra.

In 1994 Jagger, Richards, Watts, and Wood, along with bassist Darryl Jones (whose credits include working with Miles Davis and Sting) released the critically well-received *Voodoo Lounge* (#2, 1994) and embarked on a major tour that proved one of the highest-grossing of the year, earning a reported $295 million. *Voodoo Lounge* brought the Stones their first competitive Grammy, 1994's Best Rock Album award. *Voodoo Lounge* was also the group's first release under its new multimillion-dollar, three-album deal with Virgin Records, which included granting Virgin the rights to some choice albums from the Stones' back catalogue, including *Exile on Main Street, Sticky Fingers,* and *Some Girls.* After having languished in storage for nearly three decades, the Rolling Stones' *Rock & Roll Circus* concert film and soundtrack was released in 1996, which featured the Stones in the era of *Beggars Banquet,* and other rock luminaries—the Who, Jethro Tull, John Lennon and Yoko Ono, Eric Clapton, Taj Mahal, and more—as well as various acrobats, fire-eaters, and other circus artists who performed routines between songs.

Meanwhile, back to their standard time lapse of three years between tours, the Stones released *Bridges to Babylon* (#3, 1997, their 19th platinum LP) and launched yet another lavish, sold-out worldwide tour, where they played two-hour concerts consisting of only a few songs off the new album and lots of hits. Corporate sponsorship was particularly intense: long-distance carrier Sprint, for example, paying $4 million to print its company logo on tickets and stage banners. In 1998 the Stones released the obligatory tour album, *No Security.*

In 1997 Richards coproduced and played on *Wingless Angels,* an album of Rastafarian spirituals; guested, with Elvis Presley guitarist Scotty Moore, on *All the King's Men,* a tribute to Presley; and with the rest of the Stones, played on B.B. King's *Deuces Wild.* Assembling the roots-rock band the Rhythm Kings, with Peter Frampton and Georgie Fame sitting in, Bill Wyman put out three albums in the late '90s. Watts continued his jazz excursions with 1996's orchestral offering, *Long Ago and Far Away,* and then forayed into world beat with a 2000 collaboration with veteran session drummer Jim Keltner. Mick Taylor's recording career revived, as the ex-Stone put out Stonesy releases with Carla Olson.

In 2000 "Satisfaction" topped a VH1 Poll of 100 Greatest Rock Songs. Jagger gained more attention in the social columns. In 1998 29-year-old Brazilian model Luciana Gimenez Morad claimed that she was pregnant with his child; Jagger disagreed. Jerry Hall filed for divorce. Jagger, despite the couple's four children, maintained that their Hindu nuptials did not constitute a legal marriage. When Morad's child was born, DNA tests concluded that Jagger was indeed the boy's father.

Henry Rollins: See Black Flag

The Romantics

Formed 1977, Detroit, MI
Wally Palmar (b. Apr. 27, 1953, Hamtramck, MI), gtr., voc.; Mike Skill (b. July 16, 1952, Buffalo, NY), gtr., voc.; Richard Cole, bass, voc.; Jimmy Marinos, drums, voc.
1980—*The Romantics* (Nemperor); *National Breakout* 1981—(– Skill; + Cos Canter [b. July, 25, 1954, Havana, Cuba], gtr.) *Strictly Personal* 1983—*In Heat* (– Marinos) 1985—*Rhythm Romance* (+ Skill, bass) 1990—*What I Like About You (and Other Romantic Hits)* (Epic Associated) 1996—*Breakout* (Sony); *In Concert* (King Biscuit) 1998—*Super Hits* (Sony).

With their matching suits—usually red, purple, or pink leather—and sprightly Merseybeat sound, the Romantics were one of the relatively few power-pop bands to make the national charts. They hit the Top 10 in 1983 with "Talking in Your Sleep" (#3, 1983), but are probably better known for the power-pop anthem "What I Like About You" (#49, 1980), which has been licensed for use in advertisements for, among others, Budweiser beer and Home Box Office.

Formed on Valentine's Day 1977 (hence the name), the Romantics played East Coast clubs and later that year released "Little White Lies" b/w "I Can't Tell You Anything" on their own Spider Records. Their pop sound attracted rock critic Greg Shaw to sign them to his Bomp! label, which released "Tell It to Carrie" in 1978.

They signed with Nemperor Records in 1979, and released their eponymous debut (#61) the next year. After two more albums in the pop vein (*National Breakout* [#176, 1980], *Strictly Personal* [#182, 1981]) stiffed, the Romantics mutated into a more commercial, arena-rock band on *In Heat* (#14, 1983), which contained "Talking in Your Sleep." That year, drummer Jimmy Marinos, who sang lead on "What I Like About You," left.

The Romantics soldiered on, with drummer David Patratos, then ex-Blondie Clem Burke, taking Marinos' place. In 1987 the Romantics discovered that their songs were being licensed for commercials by their managers without the band's permission. They spent several years in litigation over publishing royalties and licensing fees, finally gaining back

The Romantics

their rights in 1995. Though the Romantics continue to play around, 1996's *In Concert* actually was recorded in 1983 and features Marinos.

Romeo Void

Formed 1979, San Francisco, CA
Debora Iyall (b. Apr. 29, 1954), voc.; Frank Zincavage, bass; Peter Woods, gtr.; Jay Derrah, drums; Ben Bossi, sax.
1980—(– Derrah; + John Stench [b. John Haines], drums)
1981—*It's a Condition* (415) (– Stench; + Larry Carter, drums)
1982—*Never Say Never* EP; *Benefactor* (415/Columbia)
1983—(– Carter; + Aaron Smith, drums) 1984—*Instincts*
1992—*Warm, in Your Coat* (Columbia/Legacy).
Debora Iyall solo: 1986—*Strange Language* (415/Columbia).

Debora Iyall's sung-spoken songs for Romeo Void explore the empty consequences of love over a solid postpunk dance beat. The critically acclaimed band was formed in San Francisco in 1979, with most members coming from an art-school background.

Iyall, a Cowlitz Indian, wanted to become a poet as a teenager growing up in Fresno. In 1977, while studying at the San Francisco Art Institute, she sang with a '60s-style pop-revival band, the Mummers and the Poppers, and later met Frank Zincavage, a sculpture student. They formed Romeo Void with other locals Jay Derrah, Peter Woods (both from the M&Ps), and later Ben Bossi. Their debut, *It's a Condition,* featuring "Myself to Myself," received massive critical praise. Playing drums on the LP was John Stench of Pearl Harbour and the Explosions, taking over for Derrah; a number of drummers went through the group. Iyall's tough, unsentimental stance on love was compared to Pretender Chrissie Hynde's, and her sexy deadpan-to-pouty voice also drew attention on the band's 1981 EP *Never Say Never,* coproduced by Ric Ocasek of the Cars. *Benefactor,* including "Never Say Never," was a dance-floor favorite. *Instincts* produced the group's only hit, "A Girl in Trouble (Is a Temporary Thing)" (#35, 1984).

Romeo Void disbanded in 1985, and Iyall released a solo album the following year. The band regrouped and performed in 1993. Iyall has also written poetry and short stories and been published in literary journals and anthologies. In the late '90s she comprised the singing and lyric-writing half of the duo Knife in Water. As of 2000 she was living in the high desert of Southern California.

The Ronettes/Ronnie Spector

Formed 1959, New York, NY
Veronica Bennett (later Ronnie Spector, b. Aug. 10, 1943, New York), voc.; Estelle Bennett (b. July 22, 1944, New York), voc.; Nedra Talley (b. Jan. 27, 1946, New York), voc.
1964—*Presenting the Fabulous Ronettes Featuring Veronica* (Philles) 1992—*The Best of the Ronettes* (Abkco).
Ronnie Spector solo: 1980—*Siren* (Polish) 1987—*Unfinished Business* (Columbia) 1995—*Dangerous: 1976–1987* (Raven, Austral.) 1999—*She Talks to Rainbows* EP (Kill Rock Stars).

In their towering black beehive hairdos and dark eye makeup, the Ronettes were a classic mid-'60s girl group with a sultry twist: vulnerable but tough, sexy but sweet. They were the first bad girls of rock, a racially undefinable (the Bennetts' mother was black and Native American; their father was white) trio that became producer Phil Spector's most successful act.

All three Ronettes are related: Talley is the cousin of the two Bennett sisters. The trio began singing together as the Darling Sisters. By 1961, they had become featured dancers and vocalists at the Peppermint Lounge, performing a song-and-dance routine inspired by Hank Ballard and Chubby Checker's "Twist." They later appeared with New York City disc jockey Murray the K's rock shows and recorded in 1961 and 1962 for Colpix as Ronnie and the Relatives, then the Ronettes.

Spector signed them to his Philles label in 1963. Smitten with Ronnie, he attempted to sign her as a solo artist, but when the group refused to be broken up, he signed them all. Initially the trio provided background vocals for other Spector productions, including records by Darlene Love and Bob B. Soxx and the Blue Jeans. (Earlier in their career, the Ronettes backed up Little Eva, Del Shannon, Bobby Rydell, and Joey Dee, among others.) His first Wall of Sound productions for them were "Baby I Love You" and a song he cowrote with Ellie Greenwich and Jeff Barry, "Be My Baby." That fall it hit #2 and sold over a million copies.

The Ronettes had other, less successful hits: "Baby I Love You" (#24, 1963), "(The Best Part of) Breakin' Up" (#39, 1964), "Walking in the Rain" (#23, 1964), "Do I Love You?" (#34, 1964), "Is This What I Get for Lovin' You?" (#75, 1965), and "I Can Hear Music" (#100, 1966). In 1964 Spector began managing the group as well, and throughout the group's career Spector's possessiveness and jealousy created problems. For example, when they were set to open for the Beatles on their 1966 U.S. tour, he kept Ronnie at home and had another cousin of hers take her place on the road. By then, the group was near to breaking up. Talley married a New York City radio station–programming director, and Estelle married producer Teddy Vann.

In 1966 Ronnie Bennett married Phil Spector. According to her autobiography, *Be My Baby,* Spector virtually held her prisoner in their L.A. mansion. They separated in 1973 and divorced in 1974, by which time Ronnie Spector had developed a serious drinking problem that would last several more years. Although Spector had recorded her for A&M in 1969 ("You Came, You Saw, You Conquered") and Apple in 1971 ("Try Some, Buy Some," coproduced with George Harrison), her first solo releases went unnoticed. Ronnie Spector began her long comeback with a 1973 appearance at a rock-revival show with two new Ronettes; she then released two singles on Buddah.

Through the '70s she later pursued a solo career, inspired by the fact that many notable musicians (including Billy Joel, who wrote "Say Goodbye to Hollywood" for her, and Bruce Springsteen) cited her as an influence. In 1977 Little Steven van Zandt produced her version of "Say Goodbye to Hollywood" (with backing by the E Street Band), but it never charted. She sang on Southside Johnny's debut LP and then cut a solo album in 1980 entitled *Siren*, produced by Genya Ravan. Ronnie Spector's biggest commercial break came in 1986 when her duet with Eddie Money, "Take Me Home Tonight," the chorus of which reprised "Be My Baby," hit #4 and became an oft-seen video. In 1986 her autobiography, *Be My Baby* (written with Vince Waldron) was published. Through the '80s she also performed as one of the "legendary ladies of rock," along with Martha Reeves, Lesley Gore, Mary Wilson, and others.

Remarried and living in Connecticut with her husband and two sons, Spector returned to recording in the late '90s. She began touring on punk and indie-rock bills. The hard-edged, guitar-based *She Talks to Rainbows* features songs written by Joey Ramone (the EP's coproducer, with whom she also sings a duet), Brian Wilson, and Johnny Thunders. In 2000 a Manhattan judge ordered Phil Spector to pay $2.6 million, most of it in back royalties, to Ronnie Spector and her fellow Ronettes.

Mick Ronson

Born ca. 1946, Hull, Eng.; died Apr. 30, 1993, London, Eng.
1974—*Slaughter on Tenth Avenue* (RCA) 1975—*Play Don't Worry* 1989—*Y U I ORTA* (with Ian Hunter) (Mercury) 1994—*Heaven 'n Hull* (Epic Associated) 2001—*Indian Summer* (Pilot).

After having played sessions with pop producer Michael Chapman and David Bowie–producer Gus Dudgeon, Mick Ronson came to attention as the guitarist for Bowie's early-'70s Spiders From Mars backing band. Upon Bowie's temporary retirement from performing in 1973, Ronson launched an unsuccessful solo career. He joined Mott the Hoople in its last days, then continued a partnership with Mott's Ian Hunter in both the Hunter-Ronson Band and on Hunter's solo LPs. In late 1975 Ronson was a surprise member of Bob Dylan's Rolling Thunder Revue. He later went on to help produce Roger McGuinn's *Cardiff Rose* (1976), David Johansen's *In Style* (1979), and Morrisey's *Your Arsenal* (1992), as well as several Ian Hunter LPs.

In 1991, having learned he had liver cancer, the guitarist began recording a new solo album. Friends such as Hunter, David Bowie, John Mellencamp, Chrissie Hynde, and Def Leppard's Joe Elliott lent their voices to *Heaven 'n Hull*, which was released a year after Ronson's death at age 46.

Linda Ronstadt

Born July 15, 1946, Tucson, AZ
1969—*Hand Sown . . . Home Grown* (Capitol) 1970—*Silk Purse* 1972—*Linda Ronstadt* 1973—*Don't Cry Now* (Asylum) 1974—*Different Drum* (Capitol); *Heart Like a Wheel* 1975—*Prisoner in Disguise* (Asylum) 1976—*Hasten Down the Wind; Greatest Hits* 1977—*Simple Dreams* 1978—*Living in the U.S.A.* 1980—*Mad Love; Greatest Hits, vol. 2* 1982—*Get Closer* 1983—*What's New?* 1984—*Lush Life* 1986—*Sentimental Reasons* 1987—*Canciones de Mi Padre* (Elektra); *Trio* (with Dolly Parton and Emmylou Harris) (Warner Bros.) 1989—*Cry Like a Rainstorm, Howl Like the Wind* (Elektra) 1991—*Mas Canciones* 1992—*Frenesi* 1993—*Winter Light* 1995—*Feels Like Home* 1996—*Dedicated to the One I Love* 1998—*We Ran* 1999—*Trio II* (with Dolly Parton and Emmylou Harris) (Asylum); *Western Wall: The Tucson Session* (with Emmylou Harris); *The Linda Ronstadt Box Set* (Elektra) 2000—*A Merry Little Christmas*.

During a recording career spanning four decades, Linda Ronstadt has covered much of America's popular and folk music and appealed to a mass audience that, but for her, might never have heard the work of Buddy Holly, Chuck Berry, or Elvis Costello, not to mention the older pop standards and traditional Mexican songs she sang later in her career.

Ronstadt is half Mexican, half German. She grew up singing Hank Williams and Elvis Presley favorites with her siblings and Mexican folk songs with her father, who played his guitar. While in high school, Linda performed around Tucson with her brother and sister. Local guitarist Bob Kimmel invited her to go with him to L.A. She declined the invitation until after a semester at the University of Arizona, but by the end of 1964 she was in L.A., where she joined the Stone Poneys, a folk group with Kimmel and guitarist Kenny Edwards.

The trio landed a gig at the Troubadour, where promoter Herb Cohen offered Ronstadt a solo management contract. She refused the offer out of loyalty to the trio and doubts about going it alone (earlier, the three had turned down Mercury's offer to make them into a surf-music group to be called the Signets). But when the Stone Poneys failed to attract further interest, they split up, and Ronstadt signed with Cohen, whom she later persuaded to manage the trio.

Cohen got the Stone Poneys a recording contract with Capitol in 1966 and hired Nick Venet to produce three albums. The first was a failed attempt to present the Poneys as a sort of Hollywood Peter, Paul and Mary. The second included one number on which L.A. session musicians backed Ronstadt—"Different Drum," written by Mike Nesmith of the Monkees—which was a Top 20 hit in 1967. It induced Capitol to send the Stone Poneys on tour as an opening act, but Edwards soon quit. (He was reunited with Ronstadt in 1974 and was her bassist for the following five years.) Kimmel and Ronstadt stayed together for a while, using pickup musicians for another tour and recording a few tracks for the third album, but soon Kimmel dropped out, leaving Ronstadt with a contractual obligation to finish, using session musicians. It sold so poorly that it wasn't until *Heart Like a Wheel* went gold seven years later that Ronstadt began to collect royalties.

Solo, Ronstadt floundered for most of the next five years.

Linda Ronstadt

She went through a succession of managers, producers, and backup musicians (including in the last category the four original Eagles). Onstage she was often devastatingly timid, and in the studio her voice was undermined by inappropriate material and arrangements. She attracted brief notice as a country singer—playing the Grand Ole Opry in Nashville, making TV appearances on *The Johnny Cash Show* and a Glen Campbell special—and reached the Top 30 in 1970 with "Long, Long Time" off *Silk Purse*. But by the end of 1972 she was in debt and paying commissions to two managers: Cohen (who still owned her contract) and John Boylan, her current producer. *Don't Cry Now,* her first album on Asylum (although it turned out she owed another to Capitol), was predictably bogged down and unfinished in the studio.

The catalyst to Ronstadt's popularity and acclaim was Peter Asher. A former half of the British pop duo Peter and Gordon, he had gone from performing in the mid-'60s to producing and managing. Under Asher's direction, *Don't Cry Now* was completed after a year in the works, $150,000, and three producers. Despite its flaws, the album sparked Ronstadt's career and prompted Capitol to market a collection of her early songs under the title *Different Drum*.

With Asher as producer and manager, Ronstadt made *Heart Like a Wheel,* which established her best-selling mix of oldies covers and contemporary songs. In addition to astute song choices, high standards of studio craft became Ronstadt and Asher's trademarks. Released shortly before Christmas 1974, *Heart Like a Wheel* reached #1 the following spring and eventually sold 2 million copies. "You're No Good" rocked to #1 on the pop singles chart while its flip side, Hank Williams' "I Can't Help It If I'm Still in Love With You," hit #2 C&W, and won the Grammy for Best Female Country Vocal Performance that year. "When Will I Be Loved" went #2 pop, #1 C&W. Although still hampered by stage fright, Ronstadt became a popular concert attraction and something of a sex symbol.

With a 1976 tour of Europe—her first outside the U.S.—she extended her popularity to the world market. *Heart Like a Wheel* was the first of 17 gold or platinum albums. She won a second Grammy in 1976. Her albums retained a California sensibility with songs by J.D. Souther and Warren Zevon, but she also expanded her repertoire to R&B (the Holland-Dozier-Holland Motown classic "Heat Wave," a couple by Smokey Robinson), show tunes (Hammerstein-Romberg's "When I Grow Too Old to Dream"), traditional folk ballads ("I Never Will Marry," "Old Paint"), reggae (Jimmy Cliff's "Many Rivers to Cross"), and even cocky rock & roll (Jagger-Richards' "Tumbling Dice"). Her hit covers of Buddy Holly ("That'll Be the Day" and "It's So Easy") brought his music to a new audience.

Ronstadt's success gave a substantial boost to other female performers. She was the first to record songs by Karla Bonoff. Maria Muldaur, Wendy Waldman, Emmylou Harris, and Dolly Parton are a few of the female singers who have harmonized with Ronstadt in the studio and onstage; and she was instrumental in the careers of Valerie Carter and Nicolette Larson. With these women, Ronstadt formed tight friendships and a sort of professional support system. (In 1987 she, Parton, and Harris released the platinum *Trio,* a project 10 years in the making.)

By decade's end, Ronstadt was at the height of her popularity; both *Simple Dreams* (1977) and *Living in the U.S.A.* (1978) hit #1. She was also highly visible as the constant companion of California Governor Jerry Brown, with whom she shared the cover of *Time*. Ronstadt's *Mad Love* (#3, 1980) included new-wave rock. Working with a self-styled L.A. new-wave group, the Cretones, she put three songs by group member Mark Goldenberg alongside three by Elvis Costello (whose "Alison" she had covered on her previous album). The response from Ronstadt's audience was decidedly mixed, but "How Do I Make You" went Top 10, as did a remake of Little Anthony and the Imperials' "Hurt So Bad."

Rather than return to the studio, Ronstadt tried something new—the role of Mabel in Gilbert and Sullivan's 19th-century light opera *The Pirates of Penzance*. Ronstadt performed at Central Park's Delacorte Theater in New York City through the summer of 1980 and later appeared in the film version. A subsequent attempt at opera in a production of *La Bohème* was less well received by critics.

In 1982 she released *Get Closer* (#31), her least successful LP of new material in 10 years. Ronstadt then took a stylistic right turn, and she became among the first rock artists to tackle American pop standards. Lavishly orchestrated by veteran arranger Nelson Riddle, the triple-platinum *What's New* (#3, 1983), platinum *Lush Life* (#13, 1984), and gold *Sentimental Reasons* (#46, 1986) were critically acclaimed and introduced baby boomers to such prerock classics as "Someone to Watch Over Me" and "When I Fall in Love."

In 1987 Ronstadt and James Ingram topped the charts with the romantic ballad "Somewhere Out There" from the animated film *An American Tale*, and she made another commercially successful stylistic leap with the all-Spanish *Canciones de Mi Padre* ("Songs of My Father"), which went platinum though reaching only #42 on the chart. Later that year, the *Trio* album with Parton and Harris hit #6 on the chart and also went platinum (it won a Grammy for Best Country Vocal Duo/Group in 1988). *Cry Like a Rainstorm, Howl Like the Wind* (#7, 1989), went double platinum and contained two Grammy award–winning (for Best Pop Performance Duo/Group) ballads sung with Aaron Neville: "Don't Know Much" (#2, 1989) and "All My Life" (#11, 1990). However, two more Spanish-language albums, *Mas Canciones* and *Frenesi,* met with middling sales. Ronstadt returned to English-language recording with 1993's *Winter Light,* which she produced herself with George Massenburg (her first pop solo album in 20 years that Peter Asher did not produce). *Feels Like Home* (#75, 1995) was originally conceived as a followup to *Trio,* but Parton had to withdraw because of scheduling problems. The album included more country-rock sounds but had disappointing sales. That same year Ronstadt sang on a recording of Randy Newman's musical *Faust. Dedicated to the One I Love* (#78, 1996) was a collection of lullabies, but buyers stayed away from *We Ran* (#160, 1998), a return to more pop fare.

The long-in-the-making *Trio II* (#62 pop, #4 C&W) finally came out in 1999, followed a few months later by a duet album with Harris, *Western Wall: The Tucson Sessions* (#73 pop, #6 C&W). Harris and the reluctant Ronstadt, who had not been on the road since 1995, then embarked on a tour. In addition to her well-known dislike for public performances, Ronstadt revealed that she was afflicted with Hashimoto's disease, an autoimmune disorder the side effects of which include a loss of energy; she prefers staying home in Tucson, where she moved back in the early '90s to raise her two adopted children.

The Roots

Formed 1987, Philadelphia, PA
Black Thought (b. Tarik Trotter, Oct. 3, 1973, Philadelphia), voc.; ?uestlove (b. Ahmir Khalib Thompson, Jan. 20, 1971), drums; Josh Abrams, bass; Scott Storch, kybds.
1993—*Organix* (Remedy/Cargo); (– Abrams; + Leonard Nelson Hubbard [b. Feb. 12, 1965, Philadelphia], bass) 1994— (+ Malik B. [b. Abdul Malik Bassett-Smart, Philadelphia], voc.) 1995—(+ Rahzel [b. Rozell Brown, Bronx, NY], voc.) *do you want more?!!!??!* (DGC) 1996—(– Storch; + Kamal [b. James Gray, Apr. 20, 1976, Philadelphia], kybds.; + Scratch [b. Kyle Jones, Aug. 29, 1972, Camden, NJ], voc.) *illadelph halflife* 1999—*things fall apart* (MCA); *The Roots Come Alive.*
Rahzel solo: 1999—*Make the Music 2000* (MCA).
Black Thought solo: 2001—*Hardware* (MCA).
Philadelphia Experiment (?uestlove; Christian McBride, bass; Uri Caine, kybds.): 2001—*The Philadelphia Experiment* (Ropeadope).

Integrating live instrumentation, vocal percussion, and old-school sensibility, the Roots created a unique sound within hip-hop. By touring up to 250 nights a year, the Roots slowly built a following in a fashion similar to the road work of the Grateful Dead, Phish, and the Dave Matthews Band, in which the group also revamped and improvised songs nightly. The group's innovative and fresh recordings document its vision of rap music with no boundaries.

The Roots formed in 1987 when vocalist Black Thought befriended drummer ?uestlove at Philadelphia's High School for Creative Performing Arts. The two began covering hip-hop classics, with Black Thought rapping over ?uestlove's drum beats. The duo eventually added a keyboardist and bassist and recorded *Organix,* an underground album that presages the jazzy, free-form aesthetic the Roots would later perfect. Geffen soon caught wind of the band's increasing following and released *do you want more?!!!??!* (#104 pop, #22 R&B, 1995), which includes concert staples like "Proceed" (#79 R&B, 1995), "Distortion to Static" (#96 R&B, 1994), and "Essaywhuman?!!!??!" Opening concerts for the Beastie Boys and performing on Lollapalooza's second stage added to the Roots' following with an alt-rock audience, while *do you want more?!!!??!* failed to make a big impact in hip-hop circles.

The second album, *illadelph halflife* (#21 pop, #4 R&B, 1996), with its harder edge, tighter beats, and appearances by notables Q-Tip, D'Angelo, Cassandra Wilson, and Common, became an instant success in the hip-hop community. "Clones" (#62 R&B, 1996) and "Push Up Ya Lighter" illustrate the Roots' rawer, streetwise side; conversely, the melodic "One Shine" and "What They Do" (#34 pop, #21 R&B, 1996) emit pure soul. In 1999 the Roots achieved its biggest critical and commercial success yet with *things fall apart* (#4 pop, #2 R&B), which yielded the Grammy award–winning single, "You Got Me" (#39 pop, #11 R&B), a love song featuring vocals by Erykah Badu [see entry]. Later the same year, *The Roots Come Alive* (#50 pop, #12 R&B), documented the band's renowned live performances. At a typical Roots concert, the band cycles through past and present rap standards, performs long instrumentals, and shows off the vocal talents of world-class beat boxers Rahzel and Scratch.

Both Black Thought (who acted in the 2001 indie film *Brooklyn Babylon*) and Rahzel went on to record solo albums, while ?uestlove made significant contributions to albums by Erykah Badu, D'Angelo, and Zack de la Rocha.

Diana Ross

Born Mar. 26, 1944, Detroit, MI
1970—*Diana Ross* (Motown); *Everything Is Everything* 1971—*Surrender* 1972—*Lady Sings the Blues* soundtrack 1973—*Touch Me in the Morning; Diana and Marvin* (with Marvin Gaye); *The Last Time I Saw Him* 1975—*Mahogany* soundtrack 1976—*Diana Ross; Greatest Hits* 1977—*An Evening With Diana Ross; Baby, It's Me* 1978—*The Wiz* soundtrack; *Ross* 1979—*The Boss* 1980—*Diana; It's My Turn* 1981—*To Love Again; Why Do Fools Fall in Love?* (RCA) 1982—*Silk Electric* 1983—*Diana Ross Anthology* (Motown); *Ross* (RCA) 1984—

Swept Away 1985—*Eaten Alive* 1987—*Red Hot Rhythm and Blues* 1989—*Workin' Overtime* (Motown) 1991—*The Force Behind the Power* 1994—*Forever Diana* 1995—*Take Me Higher* 1999—*Every Day Is a New Day.*

Diana Ross' tender, cooing voice brought her to prominence as the lead singer of the Supremes in the '60s. Upon leaving the Supremes [see entry] in January 1970, she established herself as a star of records, stage, television, and screen. Through the '70s and '80s she showed remarkable resilience, consistently rebounding from career setbacks, and remained without question the biggest female pop star of that era.

Ross' career shift was carefully planned by Motown president Berry Gordy Jr. and was foreshadowed when in the late '60s he changed the group's name from simply the Supremes to Diana Ross and the Supremes. By the time she did leave the group, she was clearly positioned as its star. Her initial solo recordings were produced by the husband-and-wife team of Nick Ashford and Valerie Simpson. "Reach Out and Touch (Somebody's Hand)" in 1970 (#20 pop, #7 R&B) was her first solo single. Her next release, a new version of the Marvin Gaye–Tammi Terrell hit "Ain't No Mountain High Enough" (by Ashford and Simpson), reached #1 pop and R&B. The following year, however, she faltered, releasing singles, none of which was a major hit. At that time, most of her attention was taken up with a television special and preparations for playing Billie Holiday in the first Motown film production, *Lady Sings the Blues.* The 1972 film was a commercial success, spawning a #1 soundtrack of Ross singing Holiday ("Good Morning Heartache") and garnering Ross an Oscar nomination for Best Actress.

The title songs from her next two albums, *Touch Me in the Morning* (#5, 1973) and *Last Time I Saw Him* (#52, 1973), were both Top 20 pop singles, the former hitting #1. In 1973 she recorded an album of duets with Marvin Gaye, *Diana and Marvin* (#26, 1973). Her next film, *Mahogany,* directed by Berry Gordy and costarring Billy Dee Williams and Anthony Perkins, failed to match either the commercial or artistic accomplishments of *Lady.* The soundtrack, however, did have the MOR ballad "Do You Know Where You're Going To" (#1 pop, #14 R&B, 1976). Her *Diana Ross* (#5, 1976) was highlighted by "Love Hangover," a ballad-cum-disco dance song that went #1 on both the pop and R&B charts.

As the star of Motown's misconceived film version of the Broadway musical *The Wiz,* Ross took a tremendous risk by insisting that she play the role of Dorothy (originated on Broadway by a much younger Stephanie Mills). Not only was she clearly too old for the part, but the heavy-handed production (costarring Nipsey Russell, Michael Jackson, and Richard Pryor) was a critical and commercial bomb and a rude awakening for Motown. Her 1977 *Baby, It's Me,* produced by Richard Perry, sold disappointingly, as did *Ross* in 1978.

She returned to Ashford and Simpson for 1979's *The Boss* (#14) and was rewarded with her best sales in years. The title song (#19 pop, #10 R&B) reestablished Ross as a pop presence. *Diana* updated her approach. Produced by Nile Rodgers and Bernard Edwards of Chic, the 1980 platinum album went to #1 R&B, #2 pop, and boasted two big singles, "Upside Down" (#1 pop, R&B) and "I'm Coming Out" (#5 pop, #6 R&B). In 1981 Ross duetted with Commodores lead singer Lionel Richie on the #1 theme from the film *Endless Love.* It was the year's most popular single, selling well over 2 million copies, but it proved to be her last hit for Motown.

In 1981 she ended her 20-year tenure with the company and signed with RCA Records. That fall she released her self-produced *Why Do Fools Fall in Love?* (#15, platinum) and had a hit with the title cut, a remake of the Frankie Lymon and the Teenagers hit, and in 1982 with "Mirror, Mirror." In 1982 Ross released her second RCA LP, *Silk Electric,* which featured the #10 single (#4 R&B) "Muscles" (written and produced by Michael Jackson). Her next few years with RCA were fruitful: *Swept Away,* with a Top 20 title track written and produced by Daryl Hall, went gold. "All of You," a duet with Julio Iglesias, was another hit that year. With "Missing You"—a ballad dedicated to Marvin Gaye, but in the video for the song, Ross sang to old footage of Florence Ballard, her mother, Gaye, and Temptation Paul Williams—Ross scored her last Top 10 (#1 R&B) pop hit in 1985. *Eaten Alive*'s title track, with Michael Jackson on backing vocals, hit #10 on the R&B chart but stalled at #77 pop. Ross' biggest successes, like "Missing You," seemed to hark back to her days with Motown. In 1986 the Bee Gees–written and –produced "Chain Reaction" gave Ross a minor hit here, yet in England this affectionate re-creation of the Supremes/Holland-Dozier-Holland style went to #1. Her final RCA album, *Red, Hot Rhythm and Blues,* peaked at #73 with no charting pop singles.

Ross took some time off from her career. In 1985 she married Arne Naess, a Norwegian businessman, and had two sons, Ross and Evan. They separated in 1999 and divorced. She also has three daughters—Rhonda, Tracee, and Chudney—from her first marriage to entertainment manager Robert Silberstein. (In his 1994 autobiography, *To Be Loved,* Berry Gordy wrote of being Rhonda's true biological father.) They married in 1971 and divorced five years later.

After leaving Motown, Ross began to exert greater control over her career with, some have observed, less than desirable results. As an artist and celebrity, Ross' public image was tarnished by two 1983 incidents. The first was her onstage display of temper against ex-Supreme Mary Wilson during the taping of the *Motown 25* special. Ross' reputation as a high-handed diva was already well established, and the incident, coupled with speculation as to how much of the hit play *Dreamgirls* was based on the Supremes story, only solidified that image. The second incident, in which she argued, unconvincingly, that two concerts she gave in Central Park didn't generate sufficient profits to provide her promised $250,000 donation toward a new playground proved equally embarrassing. After the first night's show was rained out, the park was heavily damaged as the crowd of 350,000 retreated from the storm. By the evening's end, 84 people had been arrested after a wild rampage in which a large number of concertgoers and others in the area surrounding the park were attacked and/or robbed. The entire incident left a bitter taste, and although Ross returned a second night to perform, she didn't deliver the funds until after Mayor Ed Koch criticized her publicly over the next five months. Unfortunately, the groundbreaking for the park coincided with the publication of Mary Wilson's *Dreamgirl: My Life as a Supreme*, which some regarded as highly critical of Ross.

In early 1989 Ross left RCA and returned to Motown, where she became a corporate officer and part owner. Despite a rush of publicity and her continued strong concert-ticket sales, she could not regain a foothold on the pop chart. Neither the heavily publicized *Workin' Overtime* nor *The Force Behind the Power* got into the Top 100 albums chart.

In 1994 a four-CD retrospective box set, *Forever Diana*, which Ross oversaw and delivered complete to Motown, was withdrawn from the market for poor sound quality. Earlier that year her long-awaited autobiography (which, unlike most celebrities, she insisted on writing without professional assistance), *Secrets of a Sparrow*, was published to poor reviews and disappointing sales. The following year's *Take Me Higher* (#114 pop, #38 R&B, 1995) had a minimal impact on the chart.

Through her various production companies, Ross has produced a number of television specials and made-for-TV movies, including a film biography of Josephine Baker, in which she played the title role; 1994's *Out of Darkness*, where she played a paranoid schizophrenic; and 1999's *Double Platinum*. Music from the latter movie was actually included on Ross' 1999 album *Every Day Is a New Day*, but even that example of synergy did not help the record, which peaked at #108 (#47 R&B) despite "Not Over You Yet" hitting the Top 10 in England. In April 2000 the singer was the subject of a television special, *VH1 Divas 2000: A Tribute to Diana Ross*, that also starred Faith Hill, Donna Summer, and Mariah Carey, but later that same year an acrimonious (Wilson declined to participate) Supremes reunion tour had to be cut short because of underwhelming ticket sales (see the Supremes entry for a fuller account).

Regardless of her career's ups and downs, Ross' stature among her fans and her power to draw attention to her endeavors is undiminished. She will always be the "first lady of Motown," the label's biggest and perhaps most important star and one of the top entertainers of her generation.

The Rossington-Collins Band

Formed 1979, Jacksonville, FL
Gary Rossington, gtr.; Allen Collins (b. ca. 1952; d. Jan. 23, 1990, Jacksonville), gtr.; Billy Powell, kybds.; Leon Wilkeson (d. July 27, 2001, Ponte Vedra Beach, FL), bass; Barry Harwood (b. GA), gtr., voc.; Derek Hess, drums; Dale Krantz (b. IN), lead voc.
1980—*Anytime, Anyplace, Anywhere* (MCA) 1981—*This Is the Way.*
The Rossington Band: 1988—*Love Your Man* (MCA).

The Rossington-Collins Band was formed by four of the five surviving members of Lynyrd Skynyrd. Nearly two years after the 1977 plane crash that killed Skynyrd lead singer Ronnie Van Zant, guitarist Steve Gaines, and backup vocalist Cassie Gaines, Jacksonville natives Gary Rossington, Allen Collins, Billy Powell, and Leon Wilkeson—all of whom had been injured in the crash—decided to regroup. Of the surviving Skynyrds, only drummer Artimus Pyle declined to join the new band. (He went on to form his own five-piece Artimus Pyle Band in 1979 with members of the Marshall Tucker Band producing.)

Rossington-Collins solidified in late 1979. Female vocalist Dale Krantz, who sang in church gospels as a child, had played with Leon Russell in L.A. after graduating college and in 1977 joined Ronnie Van Zant's brother Donnie's .38 Special as a backup singer. Her hoarse vocals and tough persona surprised many and delighted critics. The group also included Barry Harwood, who completed the three-guitar lineup (in the Skynyrd tradition). He also came from Jacksonville, had done session work with Joe South and Melanie, and had played on three Skynyrd LPs. The last member was Derek Hess, also from Jacksonville, who had played in some local bands with Harwood.

The group's self-produced debut, *Anytime, Anyplace, Anywhere*, came out in June 1980 and went gold. Soon after the LP's release, Collins' wife, Katy, died. RCB dedicated its second album, *This Is the Way*, to her. Though the group seemed to have a promising future, it disbanded in 1983. Collins formed the Allen Collins Band with Powell, Wilkeson, Harwood, and Hess. Paralyzed in a 1986 car accident, he died in 1990. Krantz and Rossington married and started their own group in the late '80s. In 1991 Rossington, Powell, Wilkeson, and former Lynyrd Skynyrd guitarist Ed King put together a new version of Skynyrd, with Johnny Van Zant on lead vocals. Dale Krantz sang backup.

David Lee Roth: See Van Halen

Roxette

Formed 1986, Sweden
Marie Fredriksson (b. May 30, 1958, Östra Ljungby, Swe.), voc.; Per Gessle (b. Jan. 12, 1959, Halmstad, Swe.), gtr., voc.
1986—*Pearls of Passion* (EMI, Swe.) 1988—*Look Sharp!* (EMI) 1991—*Joyride* 1992—*Tourism* 1994—*Crash! Boom! Bang!* 1996—*Baladas en Español* 1999—*Stars* EP (EMI, Swe.); *Have a Nice Day* (Roxette Recordings/EMI, Swe.) 2000—*Don't Bore Us, Get to the Chorus* (Edel America).
Per Gessle solo: 1997—*The World According to Per Gessle* (Fundamental/EMI, Swe.).

In the late '80s and early '90s, a bunch of catchy, well-executed singles made the duo Roxette Sweden's most successful musical export since Abba. Like Abba, singer Marie Fredriksson and songwriter, rhythm guitarist, and vocalist Per Gessle specialized in glossy, guilty-pleasure pop. Gessle had fronted a popular Swedish band, Gyllene Tider, and Fredriksson had embarked on a solo career before the two joined forces in the mid-'80s. From the start, they set their sights on the English-speaking market that is essential to international stardom, writing and recording in English.

Their plan paid off in 1989, when Roxette's second album, 1988's *Look Sharp!,* made a big splash in the U.S., generating the #1 pop singles "The Look" and "Listen to Your Heart" and the #2 hit "Dangerous." In 1990 Fredriksson and Gessle again topped the singles chart with the ballad "It Must Have Been Love," featured on the soundtrack to the film *Pretty Woman.* The following year, Roxette released *Joyride,* which spawned another #1 hit with the title track; another cut, "Fading Like a Flower (Every Time You Leave)," went to #2. At this point the pair was so popular in their native land that the Swedish government issued a postage stamp with their likenesses. Also in 1991 the duo began its first worldwide tour, enlisting support from the same group of musicians who had played on their albums. But a fourth album, 1992's *Tourism,* produced no major hits. The next year, Roxette appeared on another movie soundtrack, *Super Mario Bros.,* with the song "Almost Unreal."

When 1994's *Crash! Boom! Bang!* proved to be more popular everywhere but the U.S., Roxette's 1995 tour skipped North America altogether, instead concentrating on such exotic locales as Moscow, South Africa, and Beijing, making it the first Western pop act to perform in China since Wham! a decade earlier. Similarly, a greatest-hits collection, the coyly titled *Don't Bore Us, Get to the Chorus,* was released worldwide except for the U.S. in 1995. (It was released in the U.S. five years later.) The duo rerecorded several of its hits in Spanish for *Baladas en Español* in 1997. Also that year, Gessle released his first solo album recorded in English. (Both Gessle and Fredriksson had previously released solo efforts in Swedish.) After some time off to devote to their families, Roxette returned with an LP and an EP in Sweden in 1999, and began work on *Room Service,* scheduled for release in 2001.

Roxy Music/Bryan Ferry

Formed 1971, London, Eng.
Bryan Ferry (b. Sep. 26, 1945, Washington, Eng.), voc., kybds.; Graham Simpson, bass; Brian Eno (b. Brian Peter George St. John le Baptiste de la Salle Eno, May 15, 1948, Woodbridge, Eng.), synth., treatments; Andy Mackay (b. July 23, 1946, Eng.), sax, oboe; Dexter Lloyd, drums; Roger Bunn, gtr.
1971—(– Lloyd; – Bunn; + Paul Thompson [b. May 13, 1951, Jarrow, Eng.], drums; + David O'List [b. Eng.], gtr.) 1972—(– O'List; + Phil Manzanera [b. Philip Targett-Adams, Jan. 31, 1951, London], gtr.) *Roxy Music* (Atco) (– Simpson; + Rik Kenton [b. Oct. 31, 1945, Eng.], bass; – Kenton; + John Porter, bass; – Porter; + Sal Maida, bass) 1973—*For Your Pleasure* (– Eno; + Eddie Jobson [b. Apr. 28, 1955, Billingham, Eng.], violin, synth.; – Maida; + John Gustafson, bass) 1974—*Stranded; Country Life* 1975—(– Gustafson; + John Wetton [b. 1949, Derby, Eng.], bass) *Siren* (– Wetton; + Gustafson) 1976—(– Gustafson; + Rick Wills, bass) *Viva!* 1977—*Greatest Hits* 1978—(– Jobson; + Gary Tibbs, bass; + David Skinner, kybds.; + Paul Carrack [b. Apr. 22, 1951, Sheffield, Eng.], kybds.; + Alan Spenner, bass) 1979—*Manifesto* 1980—(– Thompson; + Andy Newmark, drums; – Carrack) *Flesh + Blood* 1982—*Avalon* (Warner Bros.) 1983—*The High Road* EP 1989—*Street Life: 20 Great Hits* (Reprise) 1990—*Heart Still Beating* (Warner Bros.) 1995—*More Than This: The Best of Bryan Ferry and Roxy Music* (Virgin) 2001—*The Best of Roxy Music.*
Bryan Ferry solo: 1973—*These Foolish Things* (Atlantic) 1974—*Another Time, Another Place* 1976—*Let's Stick Together* 1977—*In Your Mind* 1978—*The Bride Stripped Bare* 1985—*Boys and Girls* (Warner Bros.) 1987—*Bête Noire* (Reprise) 1993—*Taxi* 1994—*Mamouna* 1999—*As Time Goes By* (Virgin) 2000—*Slave to Love.*
Phil Manzanera solo: 1975—*Diamond Head* (Atco) 1978—*K-Scope* (EG-Polydor) 1982—*Primitive Guitars* (Editions EG) 1987—*Guitarissimo '75–'82* 1991—*Mato Grosso* (with Sergio Dias) (Black Sun) 1995—*The Manzanera Collection* (Caroline) 1999—*Vozero* (Expression).
Andy Mackay solo (with the Players): 1989—*Christmas* (Rykodisc).
Manzanera and Mackay: 1988—*Crack the Whip* (Relativity) 1989—*Up in Smoke.*
Manzanera and Quiet Sun: 1975—*Mainstream* (Antilles).
Manzanera and 801: 1976—*801 Live* (EG-Polydor).
Manzanera and John Wetton: 1987—*Wetton/Manzanera* (Geffen).

Roxy Music defined the tone of '70s art rock by coupling Bryan Ferry's elegant, wistful romantic irony with initially anarchic and later subdued, lush rock. The band was never as popular in America as it was in Europe, perhaps because its detachment and understatement baffled American tastes. But Ferry's witty hoping-against-hopelessness persona and Brian Eno's happy amateurism filtered into the late-'70s new wave while Roxy Music itself was in suspension.

Ferry and bassist Graham Simpson began searching for band mates around November 1970. Ferry, who would write almost all of Roxy's songs, is the son of a coal miner. He attended the University of Newcastle, where he studied art for three years with pop-conceptual artist Richard Hamilton. At school he sang in a more rock-oriented band, the Banshees, before joining an R&B band called the Gas Board with Simpson. He also taught art.

In January 1971 Andy Mackay joined the fledgling band; he had played oboe as a teenager with the London Symphony Orchestra and saxophone at Reading University. Mackay brought Eno with him. The earliest lineup also included classical percussionist Dexter Lloyd, who left by June, and guitarist Roger Bunn, who soon returned to session work. Drummer Paul Thompson had played with a local band, Smokestack, and guitarist Davy O'List had been with the Nice. O'List left after five months and was replaced by Phil Manzanera from the experimental band Quiet Sun.

Then Simpson decided to give up music, and Roxy Music recorded its debut album with Rik Kenton. They would never

Roxy Music: Andy Mackay, Bryan Ferry, Eddie Jobson, Rick Wills, Phil Manzanera, Paul Thompson

have a full member on bass. The group's debut album, produced by King Crimson lyricist Peter Sinfield, went Top 10 in England in 1972, and "Virginia Plain" went to #4 in Britain, where Roxy Music's '50s-style retro-chic costumes fit in with the glam-rock fad, although its music was far more sophisticatedly primitive. In addition, Ferry's lyrics ranged from deliriously campy to acutely sensitive, and his '50s-greaser-cum-suave-matinee-idol good looks seemed incongruous at the time. This was most apparent when Roxy Music served as opening act for Jethro Tull on a December 1972 U.S. arena tour.

The second Roxy Music album, *For Your Pleasure,* met with a similar reaction; its strangeness was popular in Britain and ignored in America. In July 1973 Eno [see entry] left for a solo career—perhaps inevitably, since he was a songwriter himself, and Roxy Music was Ferry's outlet. Ferry cut his first solo album in 1973, *These Foolish Things.* While treating Lesley Gore and Bob Dylan songs with equal camp disengagement, Ferry also showed a deep affection for pop tradition, which would continue throughout his solo career.

Teenage multi-instrumentalist Eddie Jobson, formerly with Curved Air, replaced Eno for *Stranded,* which also included writing credits for Manzanera and Mackay. With Eno gone, the music now focused on Ferry's singing rather than the band's counterpoint. *Country Life,* also released in 1974, was Roxy's first U.S. success; it went to #37, although its cover, with a glimpse of pubic hair through panties, was banned in some record stores, covered with an opaque wrapper elsewhere, and finally replaced with an inoffensive forest photo.

Roxy toured the U.S. in 1975 with bassist John Wetton, formerly of King Crimson and Family, and later with Uriah Heep, U.K., and Asia. After its most singlemindedly danceable record, *Siren*—which included Roxy's first U.S. hit single, "Love Is the Drug" (#30, 1976)—the group took what it described as an indefinite "rest," leaving the live LP *Viva!* and *Greatest Hits* in its wake.

Ferry's fourth solo album, *In Your Mind* (1977), was the occasion for a world tour with Roxy's Manzanera, Wetton, and Thompson providing backup. For 1978's *The Bride Stripped Bare,* Ferry recorded with L.A. sessionmen and several Roxy regulars. Mackay released solo albums and wrote music for the British TV series *Rock Follies,* while Manzanera recorded and toured briefly with a band called 801, featuring Eno; he also re-formed Quiet Sun for a short time and played sessions for John Cale, Eno, Nico, and others.

In 1978 Roxy Music reunited for *Manifesto,* minus Jobson, who had joined U.K.; the keyboardist later recorded with Frank Zappa and Jethro Tull. *Manifesto* (#23, 1979) (which includes "Dance Away" and "Angel Eyes") became Roxy's highest-charting U.S. album ever. The group embarked on a world tour with guest keyboardist Paul Carrack (formerly of Ace, and later with Squeeze, Nick Lowe, and Mike + the Mechanics) and two bassists, including Gary Tibbs, formerly of the Vibrators and later of Adam and the Ants. Just prior to that tour, Thompson broke his thumb in a motorcycle accident and left the band.

For 1980's *Flesh + Blood* Roxy Music was down to a threesome—Ferry, Manzanera, and Mackay—plus sessionmen. Though their most subdued album, it set Ferry's new (seemingly) heartfelt romantic longing against simpler but richer melodies and signaled a new direction. *Flesh + Blood* became the group's second #1 album in England (after *Stranded*) and went to #35 in the U.S. *Avalon* (#53, 1982) continued in the same vein and yielded the Top 10 British hit "More Than This." It was the group's only LP to sell a million copies in America. The next year Roxy Music toured the U.S. as an eight-piece band plus three backup singers, concurrent with a live EP called *The High Road* (which includes a version of John Lennon's "Jealous Guy," a #1 U.K. shortly after the ex-Beatle's murder). *Heart Still Beating* documents a 1982 French concert.

Given the '80s popularity of such clearly Roxy-influenced acts as the Cars, ABC, and Duran Duran, Ferry and the band's mix of outrageous humor ("In Every Dream Home a Heartache," a love song to an inflatable doll; "Do the Strand"), tongue-in-cheek cool, and exceptional musicianship, their lack of a wider U.S. audience is baffling. Roxy's early music videos, rarely seen in this country outside new-wave rock clubs, were as stylish as its album covers, and as artists' visual presentations became increasingly important, it would seem that Roxy's chance had come.

Since the breakup, Ferry's sporadic recorded output has maintained the sleek, meticulously produced sound of *Avalon. Boys and Girls* eventually went gold. "Kiss and Tell," a track off 1987's *Bête Noir,* became his only Top 40 U.S. hit after it was featured in the movie *Bright Lights, Big City,* starring Michael J. Fox. In 1976 Ferry had been romantically involved with *Siren*'s cover girl, model Jerry Hall; she left him for Mick Jagger. In 1982 he married socialite Lucy Helmore, who'd recently graced the picture sleeve of the "Avalon" 45, a #13 U.K. hit. At the time of 1993's *Taxi,* another interpretive album (produced by, of all people, Robin Trower), Ferry hinted that a Roxy Music reunion might happen. Eight years later, in spring 2001, Ferry, Manzanera, and MacKay, along with Paul Thompson, Chris Spedding, and others, launched an international 30th anniversary tour.

Mackay and Manzanera's first post-Roxy venture was a group called the Explorers; they've also recorded as a duo and, separately, with others, such as John Wetton (Manzanera) and with an instrumental band called the Players (Mackay).

Ferry's 1994 solo album, *Mamouna,* marked a reunion of sorts, with Manzanera, Mackay, and Eno all contributing to the project. The record didn't fair well commercially, although that wasn't the case with "Dance With Life (Brilliant Light)," Ferry's cut on the soundtrack to the movie *Phenomenon;* the single received airplay on a number of Adult Contemporary radio stations. The Grammy-nominated *As Time Goes By* (1999) was a mostly acoustic affair consisting of faithful, reverent covers of prewar pop standards, including songs by George Gershwin, Kurt Weill, and Cole Porter.

Rufus: See Chaka Khan

The Rumour

Formed 1975, England
Bob Andrews (b. June 20, 1949), kybds., voc.; Stephen Goulding, drums; Andrew Bodnar, bass; Brinsley Schwarz, gtr., voc.; Martin Belmont, gtr.
1977—*Max* (Mercury) 1979—*Frogs, Sprouts, Clogs and Krauts* (Stiff) 1980—(– Andrews) 1981—*Purity of Essence* (Hannibal).

The Rumour, five veterans of England's pub-rock scene of the early '70s, is best known as Graham Parker's backup band on his first six LPs. But the group has also recorded its own albums. In addition, it has backed and produced other performers.

The Rumour was first heard from in 1976 on Parker's *Howlin' Wind.* Bob Andrews and Brinsley Schwarz came from the group Brinsley Schwarz (as did the LP's producer, Nick Lowe); Martin Belmont was originally in Ducks Deluxe; Andrew Bodnar and Stephen Goulding were the former rhythm section of Bontemps Roulee.

While working with Parker, members of the Rumour played on Lowe's *Pure Pop for Now People* and on debut LPs by Rachel Sweet and Carlene Carter (the latter produced by Andrews and Schwarz); and they recorded the albums *Max* (in reply to Fleetwood Mac's *Rumours*) and *Frogs . . .*

Andrews left the group in 1980, with the band continuing as a four-piece and recording *Purity of Essence.* The Rumour left Graham Parker a year later to back up Garland Jeffreys on tour (Goulding and Bodnar had played on Jeffreys' 1981 album *Escape Artist*). Belmont went on to record and tour with Nick Lowe. Bodnar has played on Parker's records since the mid-'80s; Schwarz, too, has graced several Parker LPs. Goulding joined the Mekons.

The Runaways

Formed 1975, Los Angeles, CA
Joan Jett (b. Sep. 22, 1960, Philadelphia, PA), gtr., voc.; Sandy West (b. 1960), drums; Micki Steele (b. Michael Steele, June 2, 1954), bass, voc.; – Steele; + Cherie Currie (b. 1960, Los Angeles), lead voc.; + Lita Ford (b. Sep. 23, 1959, London, Eng.), gtr.; + Jackie Fox (b. 1960), bass.
1976—*The Runaways* (Mercury) 1977—*Queens of Noise* (– Fox; – Currie; + Vicki Blue, bass); *Waitin' for the Night* 1981—*Little Lost Girls* (Rhino) 1982—*Best of the Runaways.*

The Runaways were an all-female hard-rock band who suffered from hype, manipulation, and being slightly ahead of their time. Formed on the Sunset Strip in late 1975 by Kim Fowley, they were presented as five hot, tough high-school-age girls out for sex and fun (a fairly novel idea in prepunk days). But with their musical deficiencies, the stigma of Fowley-as-Svengali, and a blatantly sexual presentation—lead singer Cherie Currie wore lingerie onstage—they often seemed more like tease objects than real musicians.

The group started when Fowley met 13-year-old lyricist Kari Krome at a party. He liked her three-minute lyrics about sex, and when she suggested girls a few years older than herself to play her songs, Fowley was interested. First they got Krome's acquaintance Joan Jett and then, through some local ads, Micki Steele and Sandy West. They were going to be a threesome, but after Steele left, Lita Ford, Cherie Currie, and Jackie Fox joined. Only Ford had been in a band before.

The Runaways signed to Mercury, and their Alice Cooper–influenced debut (with much material cowritten by Fowley) came out in May 1976 to universal pans and snickers. Their only real audience was in Japan, where they earned three gold records for their debut and for *Queens of Noise* (for which Currie and Jett split lead vocals) and *Live in Japan.* But after some internal conflict, Currie and Fox left in mid-1977. Jett, who already did most of the writing by that time, took over the lead. Vickie Blue was added on bass. Currie went on to become an actress, costarring with Jodie Foster in *Foxes* (1980), and then appearing in a succession of straight-to-video titles such as *Parasite* (1982) and *Rich Girl* (1991). She later recorded an LP with her sister Marie entitled *Messin' With the Boys.*

The Runaways' *Waitin' for the Night* did no better than its predecessors. The band turned in good performances as U.S. openers for the Ramones' 1978 tour, but they played their final show that year on New Year's Eve. Jett felt that their last LP, *And Now the Runaways!* (out in Europe only; released in the U.S. as *Little Lost Girls* in 1981), was too heavy metal, and so at the start of 1979 she quit, and the group died. Afterward Jett took part in a B movie based loosely on the group, entitled *We're All Crazy Now,* after the Slade song.

Both Jett and Ford went on to successful solo careers [see entries]. Micki—now known as Michael—Steele, meanwhile, joined the poppier Bangles in 1983. Jett paid homage to her former band by reviving its "Cherry Bomb" on her 1984 album *Glorious Results of a Misspent Youth.* The following year Kim Fowley put together a new Runaways with fresh recruits. After one album, 1987's *Young and Fast,* they broke up. Various aggregations of original members have reunited for performances over the years.

Todd Rundgren/Utopia

Born June 22, 1948, Upper Darby, PA
1970—*Runt* (Bearsville) 1971—*Runt: The Ballad of Todd Rundgren* 1972—*Something/Anything?* 1973—*A Wizard/ A True Star* 1974—*Todd* 1975—*Initiation* 1976—*Faithful* 1978—*Hermit of Mink Hollow; Back to the Bars* 1981—*Healing* 1983—*The Ever Popular Tortured Artist Effect* 1985—*A Cappella* (Warner Bros.) 1989—*Nearly Human; Anthology* (Rhino) 1991—*2nd Wind* (Warner Bros.) 1993—*No World Order* (Forward/Rhino) 1995—*The Individualist* (Digital Entertainment) 1997—*With a Twist . . .* (Guardian/ Angel); *The Very Best of Todd Rundgren* (Rhino) 2000—*One Long Year* (Artemis).
Utopia, formed 1974: Rundgren, gtr., voc.; Mark "Moogy" Klingman, kybds.; Ralph Shuckett, kybds.; Roger "M. Frog" Powell, synth.; John Siegler, bass; John "Willie" Wilcox, drums; Kevin Elliman, perc.
1974—*Todd Rundgren's Utopia* (Bearsville) 1975—*Another Live* 1976—(– Klingman; – Shuckett; – Siegler; – Elliman; + Kasim Sulton, bass) 1977—*RA; Oops, Wrong Planet* 1980—*Adventures in Utopia; Deface the Music* 1982—*Swing to the Right; Utopia* (Network) 1984—*Oblivion* (Passport) 1985—*POV* 1989—*Anthology* (Rhino) 1993—*Utopia Redux '92: Live in Japan.*

An eclectically accomplished musician and studio virtuoso, Todd Rundgren has been recording for more than three decades. His musical career has gone from simple pop that never brought the success some critics felt he deserved (only one gold LP, *Something/Anything?*) to the more complex progressive rock of Utopia, which did gain Rundgren a devoted cult following. Through it all, this multi-instrumentalist has maintained a prolific sideline career as a producer; he must also be regarded as a pioneer of rock video, interactive CD, and Web-based music.

Rundgren began playing in a high-school band, Money, then went on to play with Woody's Truckstop in the mid-'60s (a tape recording of the latter makes a brief appearance on *Something/Anything?*). In 1967 he formed the Nazz [see entry], which, contrary to then-prevailing West Coast psychedelic trends, tried to replicate the look of Swinging London in its clothes, Mod haircuts, and Beatles-ish pop sound. In some ways the Nazz was ahead of its time, especially in terms of Rundgren's studio facility and the band's musical sophistication. But the quartet remained a local Philadelphia phenomenon, with one minor hit single, the original version of "Hello It's Me." The Nazz broke up in 1969, at which point Rundgren formed the studio band Runt and hit the Top 20 in 1971 with the single "We Gotta Get You a Woman."

By this time Rundgren had become associated with manager Albert Grossman, who let him produce for his new Bearsville label. By 1972 Rundgren had taken over production of Badfinger's *Straight Up* LP from George Harrison (who was involved with his Bangla Desh concerts) and had engineered the Band's *Stage Fright* and Jesse Winchester's self-titled 1971 LP, as well as produced records by the Hello People, bluesman James Cotton, the Paul Butterfield Blues Band, and Halfnelson (who later became Sparks). In 1973 he would produce the New York Dolls' debut LP, Grand Funk Railroad's *We're an American Band,* and Fanny's *Mother's Pride.*

For many, *Something/Anything?* (#29, 1972) is the high-water mark of Rundgren's solo career. On it he played nearly all the instruments, overdubbed scores of vocals, and managed to cover pop bases from Motown to Hendrix, from the Beach Boys to the Beatles. The album yielded hit singles in "I Saw the Light" (#16, 1972) and "Hello It's Me" (#5, 1973).

A Wizard/A True Star (#86, 1973), while in much the same vein, was more of a critical than commercial success. However, Rundgren's cult following was growing. In *Wizard*'s liner notes he asked fans to send their names to him for inclusion in a poster to be contained in his next LP. As promised, 1974's *Todd* included that poster—with some 10,000 names printed on it in tiny type.

That same year Rundgren unveiled his cosmic/symphonic progressive-rock band Utopia, which gradually expanded his following to mammoth proportions. Utopia was a more democratic band, in which Rundgren shared songwriting and lead vocals with other members (from 1977 on: Roger Powell, Kasim Sulton, and Willie Wilcox). In the mid-'70s Utopia played bombastic suites with "cosmic" lyrics and used pyramids as a backdrop, but in the '80s it returned to Beatles/new wave–style pop (*Faithful* [#54, 1976]). Despite some excellent music, the quartet never placed a single in the Top 40 or saw any of its 11 albums go gold. One of their songs, "Love Is the Answer," was a 1979 Top 10 hit for England Dan and John Ford Coley.

In 1975 Rundgren produced Gong guitarist Steve Hillage's *L,* on which Utopia played backup. A trip to the Middle East in 1978 led Rundgren to a brief flirtation with Sufism; that same year *Hermit of Mink Hollow* (#36, 1978) produced his first hit single in several years in "Can We Still Be Friends?" (a minor hit for Robert Palmer a year later). Rundgren also produced Meat Loaf's monstrously successful *Bat Out of Hell.* In 1979 alone he produced Tom Robinson's *TRB Two,* the Tubes' *Remote Control,* and Patti Smith's *Wave;* in 1980 he produced Shaun Cassidy's *Wasp.*

By that time Rundgren had taken a strong interest in the emerging field of rock video. By 1981 he had built his own computer-video studio in Woodstock, New York, and was making technically advanced surrealistic videotapes. In 1982 Rundgren embarked on a one-man tour, playing sets that were solo-acoustic as well as those in which he was backed by taped band arrangements, with his computer-graphic videos being shown also. He still concentrated on production (with the Psychedelic Furs, among others) and video art.

Utopia took an indefinite sabbatical in 1985. Sulton, in addition to recording on his own, has played with Joan Jett,

Hall and Oates, Patty Smyth, and Cheap Trick. Powell, designer of a shoulder-strap keyboard called the Powell Probe, now engineers software for a computer-graphics firm, while Wilcox writes and produces. In 1992 the four reunited for a tour of Japan, captured on *Utopia Redux '92*.

The following year Rundgren went back out on the road as a high-tech one-man band to perform his unique new album *No World Order*. The world's first interactive music-only CD (available on Philips), it allowed listeners to reshape the 10 songs into an infinite number of versions. To hear the same version of a song twice, Rundgren claimed, users would have to play the disc 24 hours a day, seven days a week "well into the next millennium." Continuing in a similar vein, he then released *The Individualist*, an enhanced CD which paired each song with its lyrics, graphics, and video. At about that time he came up with the monicker TR-i (Todd Rundgren–interactive), to be used for his multimedia work. In typical fashion, though, his next move was to rerecord several of his old songs in bossa-nova arrangements on 1997's *With a Twist . . .* (which also featured Utopia bassist Sulton). That same year he was one of the few Westerners invited to play the Shanghai Festival.

Consistently fascinated with new technological developments, Rundgren created PatroNet, a Web-based service in which subscribers could purchase new songs after paying a yearly fee, in 1998. The 2000 release *One Long Year* collected some of the songs sold through PatroNet. That year he embarked on a tour in which he performed material from his entire catalogue in a power-trio formation that also included Sulton and drummer Trey Sabatelli.

Run-D.M.C.

Formed 1981, Hollis, Queens, NY
Run (b. Joseph Simmons, Nov. 14, 1964), voc.; D.M.C. (b. Darryl McDaniels, May 31, 1964), voc.; Jam Master Jay (b. Jason Mizell, Jan. 21, 1965), turntables, programming.
1984—*Run-D.M.C.* (Profile) 1985—*King of Rock* 1986—*Raising Hell* 1988—*Tougher Than Leather* 1990—*Back From Hell* 1991—*Together Forever: Greatest Hits 1983–1991* 1993—*Down With the King* 2001—*Crown Royal* (Arista).

Run-D.M.C. took hardcore hip-hop from an underground street sensation to a pop-culture phenomenon. Although earlier artists, such as Grandmaster Flash and the Sugar Hill Gang, made rap's initial strides on the airwaves, it was Run-D.M.C. that introduced hats, gold chains, and untied sneakers to youth culture's most stubborn demographic group: white, male, suburban rock fans. In the process, the trio helped change the course of popular music, paving the way for rap's second generation.

The members of Run-D.M.C. grew up together in the middle-class New York neighborhood of Hollis, Queens. By the time Joey Simmons reached his teens, his older brother Russell was becoming a major figure in the burgeoning rap scene, establishing Rush Productions and later cofounding the trailblazing rap label Def Jam along with his white partner Rick Rubin. With Russell's help and encouragement, Joey and Darryl McDaniels started rapping together in the Simmons home.

Upon graduating high school in 1982, the two recruited their old basketball buddy, Jay Mizell, to back them on turntables. Run-D.M.C.'s first single was the groundbreaking 1983 anthem "It's Like That" b/w "Sucker M.C.'s" (#15 R&B); it was followed the same year by "Hard Times" b/w "Jam-Master Jay" (#11 R&B). The songs' sparse music and booming vocal delivery was informed as much by rock as by the pseudo-jazz of earlier recorded rap songs. Moreover, the first single introduced Simmons and McDaniels' unconventional vocal style. Rather than trade off on the verses, they finished each other's lines. The group followed up with a string of R&B chart hits, including "Rock Box" (#22, 1984), "30 Days" (#16, 1984), "King of Rock" (#14, 1985), "You Talk Too Much" (#19, 1985), and "Can You Rock It Like This" (#19, 1985). In 1985 Run-D.M.C. starred in the movie *Krush Groove* alongside Kurtis Blow, the Fat Boys, and the Beastie Boys.

Run-D.M.C.'s third album, 1986's *Raising Hell* (#3 pop, #1 R&B, 1986), confirmed the group's self-professed "King of Rock" status. In a clever marketing scheme, Rick Rubin teamed Run-D.M.C. with Steven Tyler and Joe Perry of then-fading pop-metal band Aerosmith for a remake of the latter's 1976 hit "Walk This Way." The song sent suburban metalheads jumping for their air guitars, as it reached #4 on *Billboard*'s pop chart (#8 R&B), while helping to reinvigorate Aerosmith's career. Other singles from *Raising Hell* included "My Adidas" (#5, 1986), which won the group a corporate sponsorship, "You Be Illin' " (#29 pop, #12 R&B, 1986), and "It's Tricky" (#57 pop, #21 R&B, 1987).

Run-D.M.C. began its decline after 1988's *Tougher Than Leather*, putting out albums but barely making it into the Top 100. *Tougher Than Leather*, though it reached #9 on the pop-album chart and went platinum, was a critical failure, and the film of the same name was a box-office bomb. *Back From Hell* was the group's first album not to go gold; by then, McDaniels and Simmons were recovering from drug and alcohol problems, as well as a rape charge (later dropped) against the latter. In 1993 Run-D.M.C. bounced back with their cleaned-up, Christian-themed seventh album, *Down With the King*, which entered the R&B chart at #1 (#7 pop) and sold nearly 500,000 copies. By 1995 McDaniels was a deacon in his church and Simmons an ordained minister. Simmons also founded a gospel label, REV RUN Records and wrote a self-help book, *It's Like That: The Way to Spiritual Abundance*. Run-D.M.C. continued to tour throughout the '90s and enjoyed an international hit single via Jason Nevins' 1998 remix of "It's Like That." In 2001 Arista released the group's album *Crown Royal* (#37), which featured contributions from Kid Rock, Fred Durst, Method Man, Nas, and Sugar Ray.

RuPaul

Born RuPaul Andre Charles, Nov. 17, 1960, San Diego, CA
1993—*Supermodel of the World* (Tommy Boy) 1996—*Foxy Lady* (Rhino) 1997—*Ho Ho Ho*.

Pop-culture mini-phenomenon RuPaul became nearly ubiquitous in the '90s entertainment media as a black drag queen singing neo-disco and propagating a philosophy that combined self-help assertiveness, a genial attack on convention, and a Warholian emphasis on marketing and self-promotion.

In the early '80s, RuPaul was a fixture of Atlanta's art scene and sang in various comedy, cabaret, and/or rock groups (notably RuPaul and the U-Hauls and Wee Wee Pole) until he moved to New York in the late '80s. There, taken up by denizens of the fashionable demimonde, the 6-foot-7-inch (in heels) personality eventually signed with Tommy Boy. Off his debut album, "Supermodel (You Better Work)" was a video-channel and dance-club hit (#45 pop), and RuPaul began appearing regularly on the talk-show circuit. In 1993 his career began taking off: He recorded a duet version of Elton John's "Don't Go Breaking My Heart" for John's *Duets* album, contributed vocals to the *Addams Family Values* soundtrack, released a Christmas single ("Little Drummer Boy") from a cable television special, *RuPaul's Christmas Ball*, and landed a part in the Spike Lee film, *Crooklyn*.

In 1995 RuPaul penned an autobiography, *Lettin' It All Hang Out*. The year before, he became spokesmodel for Canadian Make-Up Art Cosmetics (MAC), the first drag queen ever to represent a cosmetics company. In 1996 he hosted a late-night talk/variety show on VH1. His screen credits include *The Brady Bunch* and *A Very Brady Sequel*.

Tom Rush

Born Feb. 8, 1941, Portsmouth, NH
1962—*Tom Rush: Live at the Unicorn* (Lycornu) 1963—*Got a Mind to Ramble* (Prestige); *Blues Songs and Ballads* 1965—*Blues and Folk* (Transatlantic); *Tom Rush* (Elektra) 1966—*Take a Little Walk With Me* 1968—*The Circle Game* 1970—*Tom Rush* (Columbia); *Wrong End of the Rainbow; Classic Rush* (Elektra) 1971—*Merrimack County* 1974—*Ladies Love Outlaws* 1975—*The Best of Tom Rush* (Columbia) 1982—*Tom Rush: New Year* (Night Light) 1984—*Tom Rush: Late Night Radio* 1993—*Tom Rush: Work in Progress* 1999—*The Very Best of Tom Rush: No Regrets* (Legacy).

Singer and occasional songwriter Tom Rush came to prominence while working the Cambridge, Massachusetts, coffeehouse circuit (he holds a B.A. from Harvard) in the early '60s. He was eclectic from the beginning, experimenting with blues, jazz, classical arrangements, and electric instrumentation.

The Circle Game, one of pop's first concept albums, yielded Rush's two best-known performances: his own "No Regrets" and the album's title cut, written by Joni Mitchell. Rush was performing songs by Mitchell, Jackson Browne, and James Taylor before any of them were well known. The latter singer has cited Rush as a prime influence on his work. *Merrimack County* presaged a two-year period of self-imposed retirement, broken only by the more commercial *Ladies Love Outlaws*. In 1980 he founded Maple Hill Productions, through which he arranged a series of concerts under the name Club 47 (after the famous Cambridge coffeehouse where Rush, Dylan, Baez, and other seminal folk artists began) to introduce modern folk artists. He also started his own mail-order record label, Night Light Recordings. He continues to write and record; he tours regularly. He is also deeply involved in the wildlife protection organization, the Wolf Fund. He currently hosts his own shows at Boston's Club Passim (formerly the famed Club 47).

Rush

Formed 1969, Toronto, Can.
Alex Lifeson (b. Alex Zivojinovich, Aug. 27, 1953, Surnie, B.C., Can.), gtr.; Geddy Lee (b. Gary Lee Weinrib, July 29, 1953, Toronto), voc., bass, gtr., kybds.; John Rutsey, drums.
1974—*Rush* (Moon/Mercury) (– Rutsey; + Neil Peart [b. Sep. 12, 1952, Hamilton, Ont., Can.], drums) 1975—*Fly by Night; Caress of Steel* 1976—*2112; All the World's a Stage* 1977—*A Farewell to Kings* 1978—*Hemispheres* 1980—*Permanent Waves* 1981—*Moving Pictures; Exit . . . Stage Left* 1982—*Signals* 1984—*Grace Under Pressure* 1985—*Power Windows* 1987—*Hold Your Fire* 1989—*A Show of Hands; Presto* (Atlantic) 1990—*Chronicles* (Mercury) 1991—*Roll the Bones* (Atlantic) 1993—*Counterparts* 1996—*Test for Echo* 1998—*Different Stages—Live.*
Geddy Lee solo: 2000—*My Favorite Headache* (Atlantic).
Victor (Alex Lifeson solo): 1996—*Victor* (Atlantic).

Since the release of its 1976 breakthrough, *2112*, this Canadian, progressive power trio has released nothing but gold or platinum albums. Rush's early critics cited vintage Yes when they first heard singer Geddy Lee's high-pitched vocals, Alex Lifeson's major-chord guitar heroics, and Neil Peart's heavy but adroit drumming. Instruments wrapped themselves around intricate, often epic-length musical structures that carried Peart's apocalyptic lyrics. The band has since won respect as an inventive thinking-person's hard-rock unit. Virtuoso instrumentalists, the three regularly place high in the readers polls of musicians' magazines.

Rush's initial success was based on diligent touring, as the group established itself first in Canada and the northern U.S., then gradually expanded its following despite limited airplay. The futuristic concept album *2112* (#61, 1976), made Rush into a late-'70s force to be reckoned with. But *Permanent Waves* (#4, 1980) caused the trio's popularity to soar. The album, Rush's eighth, marked something of a departure with its shorter compositions, which characterized the band's work into the '90s. The platinum *Signals* (#10, 1982) introduced a refined sound: shimmering guitar similar to the Police's Andy Summers', warm synthesizer backdrops, and, most notably, relatively subdued vocals from Lee, who now sang in a lower (and far more listenable) register. That remained the blueprint for Rush's music throughout the '80s and early '90s. Each of Rush's five albums through 1985's *Power Windows* sold at least 1 million copies, with *Moving Pictures* (#3, 1981) moving over 4 million units. While Rush remained the antithesis of a singles band, *Signals* produced an actual hit, "New World Man" (#21, 1982).

The group lowered its profile somewhat later in the decade, scaling back on touring. Yet the titles from 1987's *Hold Your Fire* through 1998's *Different Stages—Live* (#35) still sold either gold or platinum. *Counterpoints* (#2, 1993) recalled Rush's earlier, earthier sound, with Lifeson once again the instrumental focus. The band then went on an 18-month hiatus. Peart worked on a tribute album to drummer Buddy Rich. With guest help from Primus' Les Claypool, Lifeson made an album under the name Victor. Nevertheless, Rush's next studio offering, *Test for Echo,* leaped to #5 in 1996. In 1998 the trio went on sabbatical again. A devastated Peart had lost his 19-year-old daughter in an auto accident, when his wife Jacqueline died of cancer about a year later. The drummer coped with his grief by riding his motorcycle from Alaska to Mexico. During this period, Lee recorded his solo debut, 2000's *My Favorite Headache.* In 2001 the trio reconvened to begin work on a new album due out in 2002.

The Canadian trio has altered more than just its music over the years. Once perceived as a rather dour bunch (due largely to Peart's often weighty lyrics), Rush has long since revealed a sly sense of humor. In 1982 Lee sang on the Top 20 hit "Take Off" by Bob and Doug McKenzie, the Canadian-bumpkin satire by Dave Thomas and Rick Moranis of the Canada-based TV comedy show *SCTV.* Another *SCTV* character, Joe Flaherty's Count Floyd, introduced the group via video on its 1984 tour. Rush often takes the stage to such prerecorded self-deprecating bits as the Three Stooges theme or Pavement's "Stereo."

Jimmy Rushing

Born Aug. 26, 1903, Oklahoma City, OK; died June 8, 1972, New York, NY
1978—*The Essential Jimmy Rushing* (Vanguard) 1980—*Mister Five by Five* (Columbia) 1988—*The You and Me That Used to Be* (RCA) 1999—*Oh Love* (Vanguard).

Known as "Mr. Five by Five" for his short and wide physique, Jimmy Rushing was arguably the best male blues-based vocalist of the swing era, during which he was a featured attraction with Count Basie's orchestra (1935–50). His tenor voice and his phrasing easily fit jazz, blues, pop, and shouting R&B.

Born to musical parents, Rushing studied violin, piano, and theory as a child, and he sang in church, school glee clubs, and opera-hall pageants. As a teenager he hoboed through the Midwest before moving to California, where he occasionally sang with Jelly Roll Morton and worked solo as a barroom singer/pianist. In the late '20s he was with the seminal Kansas City swing band Walter Page's Blue Devils; and from 1929 to 1935 he was a vocalist with another important early Kansas City big band, Bennie Moten's Kansas City Orchestra.

Rushing then worked with Count Basie, often sharing the microphone with Billie Holiday. In 1946 he recorded with Johnny Otis, and in the early '50s he led his own septet at New York's Savoy Ballroom. He had a resurgence in popularity in the late '50s, and in 1964 he toured Australia and Japan with Eddie Condon's All Stars. He also toured with Benny Goodman's orchestra, appeared on several TV specials, and in 1969 had a singing and acting role in the Gordon Parks film *The Learning Tree.* In 1972 he died from leukemia. Rushing was an immensely influential vocalist for generations of blues, jazz, R&B, pop, and rock singers, and his performances are available on a number of albums under both his own and Basie's names.

Leon Russell

Born Claude Russell Bridges, Apr. 2, 1941, Lawton, OK
1968—*Asylum Choir: Looking Inside* (Smash) 1970—*Leon Russell* (A&M/Shelter) 1971—*Asylum Choir II* (Shelter); *Leon Russell and the Shelter People* 1972—*Carny* 1973—*Leon Live; Hank Wilson's Back* 1974—*Stop All That Jazz* 1975—*Will o' the Wisp; Live in Japan* 1976—*Wedding Album* (with Mary Russell) (Paradise); *Best of Leon Russell* (Shelter) 1977—*Make Love to the Music* (with Mary Russell) (Paradise) 1978—*Americana* 1979—*Willie and Leon* (with Willie Nelson) (Columbia); *Live and Love* (Paradise) 1981—*Leon Russell and New Grass Revival Live* (Warner Bros.) 1984—*Solid State* (Paradise); *Hank Wilson, vol. II* 1992—*Anything Can Happen* (Virgin) 1997—*Retrospective* (Shelter/The Right Stuff) 1998—*Hank Wilson, vol. III—Legend in My Time* (Ark 21) 1999—*Face in the Crowd* (Sagestone).

Leon Russell is perhaps best known as one of the first super-sessionmen, having worked for everyone from Jerry Lee Lewis and Phil Spector to Joe Cocker, Bob Dylan, and the Rolling Stones. He has also maintained a solo career as a countryish blues-gospel performer.

A multi-instrumentalist, Russell studied classical piano from ages 3 to 13. At 14 he learned trumpet and formed his own band in Tulsa (where he grew up) and lied about his age to land a job at a Tulsa nightclub, where he played with Ronnie Hawkins and the Hawks (who later became the Band). Soon after, Jerry Lee Lewis took Russell's band on tour. In 1958 Russell moved to L.A., where he learned guitar from Rick Nelson–sideman James Burton and did studio work with Dorsey Burnette, Glen Campbell, and others. Russell played on nearly all of Phil Spector's hit sessions. He also played on Bob Lind's "Elusive Butterfly," Herb Alpert's "A Taste of Honey," and the Byrds' "Mr. Tambourine Man." In the mid-'60s he arranged some hit records by Gary Lewis and the Playboys, including the gold "This Diamond Ring." He became a close friend of Delaney and Bonnie Bramlett and in 1967 built his own studio. He occasionally appeared on the TV rock show *Shindig!* in the Shindogs band. He also played on Gene Clark's 1967 album, and arranged Harper's Bizarre's 1967 *Feelin' Groovy* LP.

In 1968 Russell teamed up with guitarist Marc Benno to make the critically acclaimed but commercially unsuccessful *Asylum Choir* LP. He then went on the road with Delaney and Bonnie's Friends tour, during which time Joe Cocker recorded Russell's "Delta Lady" at Russell's studio, where Booker T. (of MG's fame) was also working. In 1969 Russell and A&M producer Denny Cordell founded Shelter Records. The following year Russell organized the backing band for Cocker's Mad Dogs and Englishmen Tour, an event and film that eventually made him as much of a star as Cocker. When Mercury seemed reluctant to release the second *Asylum Choir* LP, Russell bought the master tapes and released them himself on Shelter. He played piano on Bob Dylan's "Watching the River Flow" and "When I Paint My Masterpiece" and played at George Harrison's Concert for Bangla Desh in 1971.

From then on, Russell devoted his energies to his solo career, though he toured with the Rolling Stones in the early '70s. He also helped out his wife, singer Mary McCreary, who appeared with him on *Wedding Album* and released her own *Butterflies in Heaven* LP on Shelter in 1973. His first U.K. solo tour, in 1970, found him backed by the ex-Cocker Grease Band. That year he also played on Dave Mason's *Alone Together* LP. In fall 1970 Russell hosted a highly praised hour-long music special on public TV station WNET in New York. *Leon Russell and the Shelter People* (#17, 1971) went gold, while *Carny* (#2, 1972) also went gold on the strength of its Top 20 single "Tight Rope." *Leon Live* went gold as well, and in 1976 Russell's "This Masquerade" (as performed by George Benson) won a Grammy.

After that, Russell returned to his southwestern roots, recording and performing with Willie Nelson and leading a bluegrass band, the New Grass Revival. In recent years, Russell's recordings have been few. Bruce Hornsby produced Russell's long-awaited major-label "comeback" album, *Anything Can Happen,* which failed to spark much interest. After another long period of silence, the songwriter returned in 1998 with the traditional, country-minded *Hank Wilson, vol. III.* The followup, *Face in the Crowd,* is a bluesier affair.

Bobby Rydell

Born Robert Ridarelli, Apr. 26, 1942, Philadelphia, PA
1961—*Bobby's Biggest Hits* (Cameo) 1962—*Biggest Hits, vol. 2* 2000—*Now and Then* (R.D.R.) 2001—*The Complete Bobby Rydell* (Capitol).

In the late '50s and early '60s, there was a preponderance of clean-cut American boys smoothing out the threatening rock & roll beat. The most successful of these was Pat Boone, but the center for this sound was Philadelphia, home of Dick Clark's *American Bandstand,* Frankie Avalon, Fabian, and Bobby Rydell.

Unlike many of the others, who were literally no more than pretty faces, Rydell was a genuine musician. He began playing drums at the age of six and was a nightclub attraction at seven. At nine he entered Paul Whiteman's local *Teen Club* amateur TV show and remained as a regular for three years (Whiteman shortened Ridarelli's surname to Rydell). In 1957 Rydell became the drummer for local rock & roll combo Rocco and His Saints (who also featured Frankie Avalon on trumpet), but he soon struck out on his own. Three major labels turned him down, and Rydell's first two singles for his manager Frankie Day's label flopped. He recorded three more failed singles for Cameo-Parkway.

In 1959 "Kissin' Time" became a #11 hit, launching a four-year period in which Rydell scored 19 Top 30 smashes, including "Volare" (#4), "Sway" (#14), "Swingin' School" (#5), and "Wild One" (#2), all in 1960, and "Forget Him" (#4, 1964). Beatlemania ended his career, as presaged by the film *Bye Bye Birdie,* in which he appeared as Hugo Peabody. Although his hitmaking days are behind him, Rydell continues to perform around the world. Since 1985, he has toured with Fabian and Avalon as one of the Golden Boys of Bandstand. *Now and Then,* issued in 2000 and partly comprising remakes of old hits, was Rydell's first album of new recordings in over two decades.

Mitch Ryder and the Detroit Wheels

Formed 1965, Detroit, MI
Mitch Ryder (b. William Levise Jr., Feb. 26, 1945, Hamtramck, MI), voc.; James McCarty (b. 1947), gtr.; Joseph Kubert (b. 1947; d. 1991), gtr.; Earl Elliot (b. 1947), bass; Johnny "Bee" Badanjek (b. 1948), drums.
Mitch Ryder and the Detroit Wheels: 1966—*Jenny Take a Ride* (New Voice); *Breakout* 1967—*Sock It to Me* 1987—*Greatest Hits* (Roulette) 1989—*Rev Up: The Best of Mitch Ryder and the Detroit Wheels* (Rhino).
Mitch Ryder solo: 1967—*All Mitch Ryder Hits* (New Voice); *All the Heavy Hits* (Crewe); *What Now My Love?* (Dynavoice) 1968—*Mitch Ryder Sings the Hits* (New Voice) 1969—*The Detroit Memphis Experiment* (Dot) 1978—*How I Spent My Vacation* (Seeds and Stems) 1979—*Naked but Not Dead* 1981—*Live Talkies* (Line, Ger.); *Got Change for a Million* 1982—*Smart Ass* 1983—*Never Kick a Sleeping Dog* (Riva) 1986—*In the China Shop* (Line, Ger.) 1988—*Red Blood, White Mink* 1990—*The Beautiful Toulang Sunset* 1992—*La Gash* 1994—*Rite of Passage* 1998—*Monkey Island.*
With Detroit: 1971—*Detroit* (Paramount).

Mitch Ryder is a white soul shouter from Detroit who reached his peak of popularity in the late '60s while fronting the Detroit Wheels. His career began well before that, though. Ryder, who was born in the Polish Detroit enclave of Hamtramck and whose father sang in a big band, had sung with local combos the Tempest and the Peps before forming Billy Lee and the Rivieras. In 1965 their stage act (opening for the Dave Clark Five) caught the attention of Four Seasons–producer Bob Crewe, who signed them and gave Ryder the name he became famous with (supposedly picked out of a phone book) and rechristened the Rivieras the Detroit Wheels.

Their first single combined Little Richard's "Jenny Jenny" and Chuck Willis' "C.C. Rider" into "Jenny Take a Ride," which became a #10 hit in 1966, inspiring followup medleys "Devil With a Blue Dress On" and "Good Golly Miss

Molly" (#4, 1966) and "Too Many Fish in the Sea" and "Three Little Fishes" (#24, 1967). Ryder's next big hit came with the hard-rocking "Sock It to Me Baby" (#6, 1967), which was banned in some markets for allegedly being too suggestive.

At the peak of the group's success, Ryder—under the guidance of Crewe—split from the Detroit Wheels. Former Wheels Rusty Day and Jim McCarty went on to form Cactus with Tim Bogert and Carmine Appice, late of Vanilla Fudge; McCarty then joined the Rockets (with Wheels drummer Johnny Badanjek), who had a #30 hit in 1979, "Oh Well."

Ryder's first attempt at a solo career met with less success, though "What Now My Love" (#30, 1967) became his sixth (and last) Top 40 hit. In 1970 he and Badanjek formed a new seven-piece group known simply as Detroit. Its one album, released in 1971, contained a classic reworking of Lou Reed and the Velvet Underground's "Rock and Roll."

By 1973 Ryder had quit music and moved to Denver. He made a comeback in the late '70s with several albums, all containing his own songs, a few of which alluded to homosexual experiences. In 1983, two years after Bruce Springsteen helped to revive the career of his idol Gary "U.S." Bonds, longtime Ryder fan John Cougar Mellencamp produced the singer's major-label comeback, *Never Kick a Sleeping Dog*. It produced a minor hit in "When You Were Mine," written by Prince, and also contained a duet with Marianne Faithfull.

Since then, Ryder has continued to tour and record, particularly in Germany, where he is revered and has released many albums. In 2000 J-Bird Records issued many of these works in America. Ryder was in the news in 1994, when his song "Mercy," from *Rite of Passage*, was revealed to be a tribute to Dr. Jack Kevorkian. Johnny Badanjek, after a stint in the late '70s and '80s with the Rockets, was back with his old boss before playing with the Romantics and his own group, the Notorious Johnnies. Joseph Kubert died of liver cancer in 1991.

Sade

Born Helen Folasade Adu, Jan. 16, 1959, Ibadan, Nigeria
1985—*Diamond Life* (Portrait); *Promise* 1988—*Stronger Than Pride* (Epic) 1992—*Love Deluxe* 1994—*The Best of Sade* 2000—*Lovers Rock.*

Although Sade is officially a group, for all intents and purposes vocalist Sade (pronounced "shar-day" or "shah-day") *is* Sade. Born in Nigeria, where her Nigerian father was an economics professor and her English mother a nurse, Sade Adu (her stage name) was educated in London. After studying fashion design, and later modeling briefly, Sade landed a spot as backup singer with the British R&B band Pride. There she formed a writing partnership with Pride's guitarist/saxophonist Stewart Matthewman; together, backed by Pride's rhythm section, they began doing their own sets at Pride gigs. Sade's elegant, exotic look and the cool, jazz-inflected approach of her low-keyed singing immediately garnered her considerable attention. In 1983 Sade and Matthewman split from Pride along with keyboardist Andrew Hale, bassist Paul Denman, and drummer Paul Cooke and formed Sade; they got a record deal late that year.

Although Sade's 1984 debut, *Diamond Life,* with its single "Your Love Is King," quickly became a hit in Britain, the album wasn't released in the U.S. until 1985. Propelled by the bossa nova–tinged "Smooth Operator" (#5), *Diamond Life* (#5, 1985) rose to the Top 10; its popularity set the stage for the influx of "Quiet Storm" vocalists spearheaded by Anita Baker among others. *Diamond Life* featured strong original

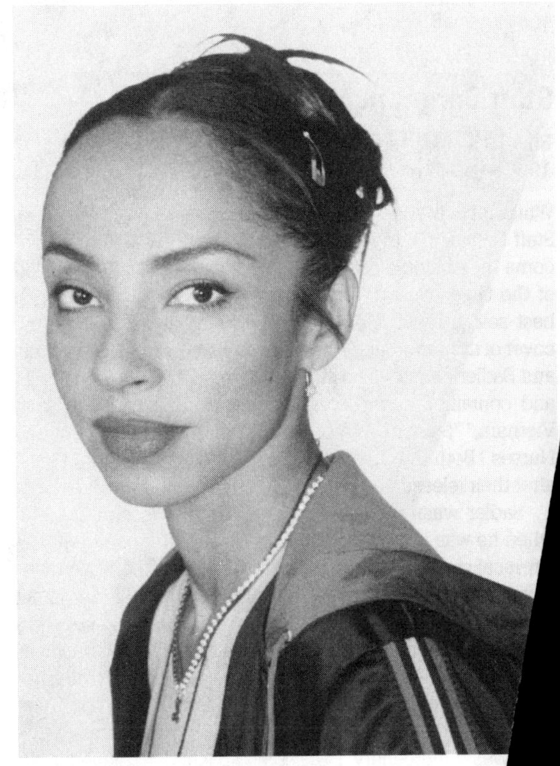

Sade

material by Sade and Matthewman including "Hang On to Your Love," and "When Am I Going to Make a Living" as well as an imaginative remake of Timmy Thomas' 1971 hit "Why Can't We Live Together."

Diamond Life had international sales of over 6 million copies, becoming one of the top-selling debut recordings of the '80s and the best-selling debut ever by a British female vocalist. In 1985 her stature as a major pop star was confirmed when Sade appeared at Wembley Stadium as part of Live Aid.

At the end of the year, *Promise* was released; the album went to #1 in the U.S. spawning the hits "The Sweetest Taboo" (#3) and "Never as Good as the First Time" (#8). Sade had a small part in the 1986 Julien Temple film *Absolute Beginners* and appears on its soundtrack.

Critics faulted 1988's *Stronger Than Pride* (#7) for musical sameness and emotional distance. Four years passed before the release of *Love Deluxe* (#3), whose brisk sales proved that Sade hadn't lost her appeal. An American tour to promote the release was also well received. Sade followed it with a best-of collection and an interactive CD-ROM and retreated to her home in Jamaica to have a baby in 1995. The following year, Matthewman, Denman, and Hale assumed the name Sweetback and released an album of the same name, calling in guest vocalists Maxwell and Amel Larrieux of Groove Theory.

Sade left Jamaica for London in 1997 and returned to the public scene in 2000 with the release of *Lovers Rock* (#3), which again found her teamed with Hale, Denman, and Matthewman.

Staff Sergeant Barry Sadler

orn 1940, NM; died Nov. 5, 1989, TN
'66—*Ballads of the Green Berets* (RCA); *The "A" Team.*

'e recuperating from a leg wound suffered in Vietnam, Sergeant Barry Sadler began writing what would be- the #1 single of 1966, the patriotic novelty "The Ballad Green Berets." The song, inspired by Robin Moore's ing book *The Green Berets* (Sadler's face is on the 1e paperback edition), was written by Moore (lyrics) (music). The similarly named LP also went to #1 ned such Sadler compositions as "Letter From 'aigon," "Trooper's Lament," and "Salute to the the single and the LP were certified gold soon se.

't heard from again until December 1978, volved in a Nashville shooting incident that ter Lee Bellamy, 51, dead. The fracas was woman; no charges were filed against Sadler was involved in another shooting s, though the victim—an ex–business killed. Sadler, in fact, justified his inno- , "I'm a Green Beret. If I'd shot him, e a series of adventure novels; the Ie also established a trust fund for

In 1988 Sadler was shot in the head during a robbery attempt while he was entering a cab in Guatemala. Exactly what he was doing there remains a bit of a mystery. He claimed to have been there training anti-Communist contras; others have disputed that. He suffered some degree of brain damage, and as a result of the shooting was left with some paralysis as well; he died of heart failure the following year at age 49.

Doug Sahm/Sir Douglas Quintet

Born Nov. 6, 1941, San Antonio, TX; died Nov. 18, 1999, Taos, NM
1971—*The Return of Doug Saldaña* (Philips) 1973—*Doug Sahm and Band* (Atlantic); *Texas Tornado* 1974—*Groovers Paradise* (Warner Bros.) 1976—*Texas Rock for Country Rollers* (ABC/Dot) 1980—*Hell of a Spell* (Takoma) 1988—*Juke Box Music* (Antone's) 1992—*The Best of Doug Sahm and Friends: Atlantic Sessions* (Rhino) 1995—*The Last Real Texas Blues Band* (Antone's) 1998—*"S.D.Q. '98"* (Watermelon) 2000—*San Antonio Rock: The Harlem Recordings 1957–1961* (Norton); *The Return of Wayne Douglas* (Tornado).
With Sir Douglas Quintet, formed 1964, San Antonio, TX: Original lineup: Sahm, gtr., voc.; Augie Meyers (b. May 31, 1940, San Antonio), kybds.; Francisco Moran (b. Aug. 13, 1946), sax; Harvey Kagan (b. Apr. 18, 1946), bass; Johnny Perez (b. Nov. 8, 1942), drums.
1965—*Best of Sir Douglas Quintet* (Tribe) 1966—*The Sir Douglas Quintet Is Back!* 1968—*Honkey Blues* (Smash) 1969—*Mendocino* 1970—*Together After Five; 1 + 1 + 1 = 4* (Philips) 1971—*Rough Edges* (Mercury) 1981—*Border Wave* (Takoma) 1994—(group re-forms: Sahm, gtr., voc.; Meyers, kybds., voc.; Shawn Sahm, gtr.; John Jorgenson, gtr.; Speedy Sparks, bass; Neal Walker, bass; Doug Clifford, drums; Shandon Sahm, drums) *Day Dreaming at Midnight* (Elektra).
With the Texas Tornados: see entry.

"Mendocino" and "She's About a Mover" were Doug Sahm and the Sir Douglas Quintet's commercial peaks, but those singles were only part of Doug Sahm's long, varied career. The energetic guitarist, singer, and songwriter dug into all American musics, helping to create the Tex-Mex sound in the '60s, and also drawing upon and playing such sounds as blues, country, folk, rock, Western swing, and jazz.

Sahm grew up in San Antonio, Texas, where he absorbed the strains of music (live and on his father's 78s) that would show up in his own musical gumbo: T-Bone Walker, Guitar Slim, Hank Williams, Lefty Frizzell, Jimmie Rodgers, and Bob Wills, as well as the polkas of Mexican *conjunto* bands. At five, he began learning to play mandolin, fiddle, and acoustic and steel guitar. By age six, he was singing on the radio, billed as Little Doug Sahm. His first Little Doug record was "A Real American Joe," in 1955. Soon after, he formed a rock & roll band and had local hits while still in high school, beginning with "Crazy Daisy" in 1958. (These early recordings have been anthologized on the 2000 Norton set.)

In 1960 Sahm met keyboardist Augie Meyers, and eventually the two teamed up with producer Huey P. Meaux, who urged them to go for a Beatles sound and look to capitalize on the British Invasion. Sahm complied with "She's About a Mover," and with Meyers on Vox organ and the English-sounding name bestowed by Meaux, Sir Douglas Quintet was on its way, filled out by three Mexican-Americans on sax, bass, and drums. "She's About a Mover," featuring a recurring organ line reminiscent of *conjunto* accordion, went into the Top 20, spurring a wave of Tex-Mex hits (by Sam the Sham and ? and the Mysterians). (Sundazed reissued the SDQ's first two albums in 2000.)

When Sahm was arrested for marijuana possession, the group, minus Meyers, moved to San Francisco, where the blues revival and psychedelia had taken hold. A shifting Quintet played loose-limbed blues at the Avalon Ballroom and other such venues; Meyers rejoined in 1968, and the group cut its last big hit, "Mendocino" (#27, 1969). The Quintet's albums grew more experimental and spacier, and didn't sell. Sahm produced albums by bluesman Junior Parker and early Tejano group Louie and the Lovers.

In 1971 Sahm returned to Texas to cut an album of San Antonio barroom honky-tonk, under the name Doug Saldaña, temporarily giving up the Sir Douglas moniker. His first solo album featured Dr. John, *conjunto* accordionist Flaco Jiménez, jazz saxophonist David "Fathead" Newman, and Bob Dylan, who wrote the country-flavored "Wallflower" for Sahm. Mercury capitalized on Sahm's expected stardom with *Rough Edges,* a collection of Quintet outtakes, but Doug Sahm and Band never caught on.

Relocated to Austin, Texas, Sahm continued to record through the '70s under his own name, as the Sir Douglas Band (1973) and as Sir Douglas and the Texas Tornados (1976) with his mixture of Texans, Mexicans, and Californians. *Groovers Paradise* featured Creedence Clearwater's rhythm section, Stu Cook and Doug Clifford. By the late '70s, Sahm had become a leader of Austin's "cosmic cowboy" scene centered around the Armadillo World Headquarters. Meanwhile, new-wave bands—particularly Elvis Costello and the Attractions—were rediscovering the organ-pumping sound of Tex-Mex.

As the '80s began, Sahm resurrected the Quintet with Meyers and Perez to make *Border Wave,* and he toured with them in a band that also included his son Shawn on guitar. The Quintet periodically re-formed throughout the decade, and in 1990 Sahm brought back the Texas Tornados [see entry] moniker for a critically acclaimed and commercially successful collaboration with Meyers, Jiménez, and country star Freddy Fender [see entry]. Sahm re-formed the Quintet yet again in 1994, reuniting with Meyers and ex-Creedence drummer Clifford, and including sons Shawn (who cowrote three songs with his dad for *Day Dreaming at Midnight*) and Shandon, who was then drumming with the Texas hard-rock band Pariah.

The last few years of Sahm's life found him in a flurry of musical activity. In addition to performances with the Tornados and the reconstituted SDQ, he made a 1995 blues album, covering songs by his heroes and joined by musicians such as tenor saxman Rocky Morales, with whom he'd played since childhood. (Sahm's heartfelt notes to the album read like the autobiography of a life lived in music.) In 1998 a musical collaboration with Austin roots-rock band the Gourds was featured on *"S.D.Q. '98."* It also included "Get a Life," Sahm's paean to his beloved hometown, and recordings made with Morales, Meyers, and the SDQ. Just prior to his sudden death of a heart attack in another of his favorite places (Taos), Sahm recorded an album of classic C&W, *The Return of Wayne Douglas.* Featuring ex–Commander Cody guitarist Bill Kirchen, the album consisted of Sahm's old and new country compositions including his kiss-off to the sanitized music coming out of Nashville in the '90s, "Oh No, Not Another One," and, seemingly, his farewell, "Beautiful Texas Sunshine."

Buffy Sainte-Marie

Born Feb. 20, 1941, Saskatchewan, Can.
1964—*It's My Way* (Vanguard) 1965—*Many a Mile* 1966—*Little Wheel Spin and Spin* 1967—*Fire, Fleet and Candlelight* 1968—*I'm Gonna Be a Country Girl Again* 1969—*Illuminations* 1970—*The Best of Buffy Sainte-Marie* 1971—*She Used to Wanna Be a Ballerina; The Best of Buffy Sainte-Marie, vol. 2* 1972—*Moon Shot* 1973—*Quiet Places* 1974—*Native North American Child; Buffy* (MCA) 1975—*Changing Woman* 1976—*Sweet America* (ABC) 1992—*Coincidence and Likely Stories* (Ensign/Chrysalis) 1996—*Up Where We Belong* (Angel).

Born of Cree Indian parents and adopted by a white family as an infant, Buffy Sainte-Marie is one of the most famous Native-American artists in pop music. Her unique vibratoed vocal delivery made her records something of an acquired taste. However, she is best known for the versions of her songs made hits by others artists—including "Until It's Time for You to Go," "The Universal Soldier," "Cod'ine," and "Up Where We Belong," the latter of which she cowrote—and for decades of activism on behalf of Native Americans.

Sainte-Marie was discovered singing in a New York coffeehouse by Vanguard producer Maynard Soloman. Her debut LP contained the protest song "The Universal Soldier," which became a classic of the genre, mainly through well-known cover versions, including those by Donovan and Glen Campbell. Elvis Presley had a Top 40 hit in 1972 (#5 U.K.) with her "Until It's Time for You to Go." Though she began as a solo folksinger, Sainte-Marie infused rock, classical, orchestral, and Native-American styles into her albums. *She Used to Wanna Be a Ballerina* featured backing by Ry Cooder and Neil Young and Crazy Horse. She composed the title song for *Soldier Blue* and scored several other films including *Stripper, Where the Spirit Lives,* and *Attla.* She also sang in the movies *Strawberry Statement* and *Performance.*

Sainte-Marie won an Oscar for "Up Where We Belong," which she cowrote with the arranger, composer, and producer Jack Nietzsche, and Will Jennings. The song was a #1 1982 hit for Joe Cocker and Jennifer Warnes. From 1976 to 1981 she was a familiar face to viewers of *Sesame Street.* Following *Sweet America,* Sainte-Marie did not record again for another 15 years until *Coincidence and Likely Stories.* During that time, she continued working on behalf of Native Americans, giving benefit concerts, speaking, and founding the Nihewan Foundation for Native North American scholarships. She acted in the 1994 film *The Broken Chain.* She was instrumental in founding the Juno Awards' category Music of Aboriginal Canada. Her 1996 album and video *Up Where We Belong* won both a Genie and a Juno in Canada, beating out the likes of Celine Dion and Alanis Morissette. In 1997 Sainte-Marie, who holds a degree in philosophy, a teacher's degree, and a Ph.D. in fine arts, was named an Officer in the Order of Canada, which is the highest civilian honor that country may bestow.

The Saints

Formed 1975, Brisbane, Austral.
Chris Bailey (b. Nov. 29, 1958, Kenya), voc., gtr.; Ed Kuepper, gtr.; Kym Bradshaw, bass; Ivor Hay, drums.
1977—(– Bradshaw; + Alisdair Ward, bass) *(I'm) Stranded* (Sire) 1978—*Eternally Yours* 1979—*Prehistoric Sounds* (Harvest, Austral.) (– Kuepper) 1987—(– Ward; – Hay; + Archie Larizza, bass; + Baz Francis, gtr.; + Iain Shedden, drums; + Joe Chiofalo, kybds.) *All Fools Day* (TVT) 1988—*Prodigal Son* 1995—*The Most Primitive Band in the World* (Restless) 1997—*Howling* (Amsterdamned/Triple X) 1998—*Everybody Knows the Monkey.*
The Aints: 1995—*Shelflife Unlimited: The Best of the Aints* (Restless).
Ed Kuepper solo: 1994—*Character Assassination* (Restless); *The Butterfly Net.*

The first Australian punk band to gain renown in Britain and the U.S., the Saints are best remembered for their debut single, a frantic buzz-saw of sound, "(I'm) Stranded." Formed by Chris Bailey, the Saints recorded "Stranded" on their own label in 1976. After a rave review in the British music weekly *Sounds,* they were signed by EMI. Lead guitarist Ed Kuepper left in 1978 (he later formed the Laughing Clowns), and the band's focus changed to a more traditional, R&B-inflected rock & roll. In 1979 the Saints broke up, but Bailey kept the name, releasing several albums as the Saints and two solo records on French and British labels. The original Saints, minus Kuepper, re-formed in 1984. In 1987 Bailey fired the band. That year, recording with a new lineup, the Saints had their first American release *(All Fools Day)* in nine years. In 1990 Kuepper formed the Aints to protest Bailey's continuing use of the Saints name and material; he also maintained a thriving solo career, releasing an uninterrupted stream of albums. Most of them came out on Australia's Hot Records, though a few, including the anthology *The Butterfly Net,* had a U.S. release.

In 1995 Restless released *The Most Primitive Band in the World,* a series of live tracks recorded by the Saints in 1974. Meanwhile, after another hiatus, Bailey got himself some backing musicians, called them the Saints, and released *Howling,* a return to the band's original no-nonsense rock & roll, which featured a collaboration with ex–Concrete Blonde Johnette Napolitano.

Ryuichi Sakamoto

Born Jan. 17, 1952, Tokyo, Jap.
1978—*Thousand Knives of Asia* (Denon) 1980—*B-2 Unit* (Alfa-Island) 1981—*Left Handed Dream* (Epic) 1983—*Coda* (London); *Merry Christmas Mr. Lawrence* soundtrack (MCA) 1985—*Esperanto* (Midi, Jap.); *Futurista* 1986—*Media Bahn Live; Illustrated Musical Encyclopedia; Piano One* (Private Music) 1988—*No Boundaries* (Columbia); *Neo Geo* (Epic); *The Last Emperor* soundtrack (with David Byrne and Cong Su) (Virgin Movie Music) 1989—*Playing the Orchestra* (Virgin); *Gruppo Musicale* 1990—*Beauty; The Handmaid's Tale* soundtrack (GNP-Crescendo) 1991—*Peachboy* (Windham Hill) 1992—*Heartbeat* (Virgin); *High Heels* (Antilles) 1994—*Hard Revenge* (For Life/Gut); *Sweet Revenge* (Elektra); *Soundbytes* (Mesa/Bluemoon) 1995—*Smoochy* (For Life/Gut) 1996—*1996; Snooty* 1998—*Discord* (Sony Classical) 2000—*BTTB; Cinemage* (Sony).

Ryuichi Sakamoto emerged in the '80s with "Neo Geo," a high-tech style of world music that fuses Asian and Western classical elements with other global sounds. Founder of Yellow Magic Orchestra, a technopop trio, the composer, producer, and actor went on to make influential film scores and pop works.

Taking up piano at age three, Sakamoto played in jazz bands in high school; his cosmopolitan upbringing exposed him to Beethoven, the Beatles, and John Cage, as well as to the films of Pier Paolo Pasolini and Jean-Luc Godard. After

Ryuichi Sakamoto

studying electronic music at the University of Art of Tokyo, he founded Yellow Magic Orchestra in 1978. Their single, "Computer Game (Theme From *The Invaders*)," became a 1980 Top 20 U.K. hit; with two Japanese Top 10 albums, the trio, known for a robotic theatricality indebted to Kraftwerk, were hugely popular at home.

During Y.M.O.'s five-year career, Sakamoto released two solo albums; his subsequent work took a genre-crossing approach. Characterized by perfectionist zeal (*Illustrated Musical Encyclopedia,* with Thomas Dolby, took 20 months to record), his output features diverse guests (Iggy Pop, Bootsy Collins, and Tony Williams on *Neo Geo*) and wide range (with David Sylvian and Ingrid Chavez, 1992's *Heartbeat* incorporates Russian rap, New York dance music, and African rhythms).

Acting with David Bowie in the film *Merry Christmas, Mr. Lawrence,* Sakamoto also penned its score; his collaboration with David Byrne and Chinese musician Cong Su on *The Last Emperor* earned an Oscar. Sakamoto's other projects include music for performance artist Molissa Fenley *(Esperanto);* the score for Pedro Almodóvar's *High Heels;* a piece for the 1992 Olympics; and *Beauty,* an album featuring his English-singing debut and contributions by Brian Wilson, Robbie Robertson, Arto Lindsay, Youssou N'Dour, and Sakamoto's wife, Akiko Yano. Sakamoto's 1994 album *Sweet Revenge* featured guests Holly Johnson (Frankie Goes to Hollywood) and Roddy Frame (Aztec Camera).

In 1993 Sakamoto briefly reunited Yellow Magic Orchestra; 1995's *Smoochy* offered a musical portrait of Rio de Janeiro; *1996* was classically influenced, with brilliant arrangements of piano and strings. Among subsequent works, *Discord* featured a 70-piece orchestra, electronics, and spoken word, and *BTTB (Back to the Basics)* was a stunning solo piano work.

Salt-n-Pepa

Formed 1985, Queens, NY
Cheryl "Salt" James (b. Mar. 8, ca. 1964, Brooklyn, NY), voc.; Sandy "Pepa" Denton (b. Nov. 9, ca. 1961, Kingston, Jam.), voc.; Pamela Greene, DJ.
1986—*Hot, Cool and Vicious* (Next Plateau) 1988—(– Greene; + Deidre "Dee Dee" "Spinderella" Roper [b. Aug. 3, New York, NY], DJ) *A Salt With a Deadly Pepa* 1990—*Blacks' Magic* 1991—*A Blitz of Salt-n-Pepa Hits* 1993—*Very Necessary* (Next Plateau/London) 1997—*Brand New* (Red Ant/London).

Salt-n-Pepa was one of the first rap groups to cross over to the pop charts and one of the few in which the rappers and their DJ were women. They were the first female rappers to have as many as three platinum albums. Cheryl "Salt" James and Sandy "Pepa" Denton were working at Sears when coworker Hurby "Luv Bug" Azor (James' boyfriend) asked them to rap on a project for his audio-production class at New York City's Center for Media Arts. The song, "The Show Stoppa," was an answer to Doug E. Fresh and Slick Rick's "The Show." It was released as a single by Pop Art Records, credited to the band Super Nature, and became a minor hit, reaching #46 on the R&B chart.

Now calling themselves Salt-n-Pepa, after a line in "The Show Stoppa," the duo signed with the rap independent Next Plateau. Azor, who became their manager, produced *Hot, Cool and Vicious* and is credited on the album with writing all the songs, although the rappers have said they contributed lyrics. Three of the platinum album's singles, "Chick on the Side," "My Mike Sounds Nice," and "Tramp," charted moderately on the R&B chart. But then Cameron Paul, a DJ at San Francisco station KMEL, remixed "Push It" (the flip side of "Tramp"); after its release, it peaked on the pop chart at #19 in 1988. "Push It" was nominated for a Grammy in 1988, but Salt-n-Pepa and other rappers boycotted the ceremony when the rap awards were not presented in the telecast. In June that year the group played Freedomfest: Nelson Mandela's 70th Birthday Celebration at London's Wembley Stadium.

Azor also produced *A Salt With a Deadly Pepa,* a solid if not earthshaking followup (though the record eventually went gold). The album includes "Shake Your Thang," a reworking of the Isley Brothers' "It's Your Thang" (performed with DC go-go band EU) and a cover of "Twist and Shout," as well as "Get Up Everybody (Get Up)" and a remix of "Let the Rhythm Run," their contribution to the *Colors* soundtrack. Unfortunately, plans to record with Joan Jett, a la Run-D.M.C. and Aerosmith's collaboration, didn't pan out. *A Blitz of Salt-n-Pepa Hits* featured dance remixes of the band's hits.

The platinum-selling *Blacks' Magic* (#38 pop, #15 R&B, 1990) was a huge success for Salt-n-Pepa artistically and commercially. The group, which had been accused by some rap fans of selling out, paid tribute to Afrocentricity in the album's title and cover art. Alongside Azor and guest producer Steevee-O, Salt produced or coproduced four tracks, and DJ Spinderella produced one. One Salt cut, "Expression" (#26, 1990), went gold before it even entered the Hot 100, thanks to eight weeks at the top of the rap chart. The album also included the hit "Let's Talk About Sex" (#13, 1991), which Salt-n-Pepa rerecorded in 1993 as "Let's Talk About AIDS" for a campaign to educate women about safe sex. That year the band played at the President Clinton's Inaugural Youth Ball, where they met their fan Chelsea Clinton.

Salt-n-Pepa had been having increasing disagreements with Next Plateau and Azor, with whom James was no longer romantically linked. The group demanded larger financial and creative roles in their career and, over Azor's objections, signed with London/PolyGram. Salt-n-Pepa then set much of the creative direction on the popular *Very Necessary* (#4 pop, #6 R&B, 1993), which showcased the women as sophisticated but tough rap divas. On songs like "Shoop" (#4 pop, #3 R&B, 1993) and "Whatta Man" (#3 pop and R&B, 1994), which featured En Vogue on the chorus, the group reveled in their sexuality. The album, which has sold 5 million copies to date, ends with a public-service announcement about AIDS performed by a group of young actors from Boston.

Salt and Pepa both have had film deals. The group performed the song "Start Me Up" in 1992's *Stay Tuned* (the soundtrack was released by Morgan Creek), and Salt also starred in *Who's the Man?* the next year. In 1995 Salt-n-Pepa were awarded the Best Rap Performance Grammy for "None of Your Business" (#32 pop, #57 R&B, 1994).

The group also signed with MCA in 1995, a deal that enabled them to form their own imprint, Jireh Records. The women later dissolved the partnership, citing creative differences, before releasing *Brand New* (#37 pop, #16 R&B) on Red Ant/London in 1997. The album, most of it written and produced in Salt's basement, featured guest performances by Sheryl Crow, Queen Latifah, and Naughty by Nature's Treach (whom Denton married in 1999). *Brand New* produced two moderately successful singles and found the women, all of whom had children by this point, talking less about sex and more about issues such as domestic violence and discrimination. The record received mixed reviews, but Salt-n-Pepa's return to the limelight landed the group their own Cover Girl makeup commercial and a spot on the cover of ROLLING STONE.

Sam and Dave

Samuel Moore, b. Oct. 12, 1935, Miami, FL; David Prater, b. May 9, 1937, Ocilla, GA; d. Apr. 9, 1988, GA
1966—*Sam and Dave* (Roulette); *Hold On I'm Comin'* (Stax); *Double Dynamite* 1967—*Soul Men* 1968—*I Thank You* (Atlantic) 1969—*The Best of Sam and Dave* 1975—*Back Atcha* (United Artists) 1993—*Sweat 'n' Soul Anthology (1965–1971)* (Rhino) 1995—*The Very Best of Sam and Dave.*

Sam Moore and Dave Prater's string of soul and pop hits made them the '60s' most successful black vocal duo. Both had grown up singing in church, and each was a regular solo performer in Southern clubs before they met in 1961 at Miami's King of Hearts club: Moore was emceeing an amateur-night show, and when Prater forgot the words to a Jackie Wilson song, "Doggin' Around," Moore coached him the rest of the way. The pair became a popular club attraction in the Miami area and soon signed to Roulette. They moved to Atlantic in 1965, though executive Jerry Wexler arranged for their records to be recorded at and released by Stax Records. At Stax, Sam and Dave quickly became the favorite foils of the production/songwriting team of Isaac Hayes and David Porter. Their first single, "You Don't Know Like I Know" (#7 R&B), in 1966, began a string of high-powered soul hits. Later in 1966 "Hold On! I'm a Comin' " went to #1 on the R&B chart (#21 pop), while "Said I Wasn't Gonna Tell Nobody" (#8 R&B) and "You Got Me Hummin' " (#7 R&B) rounded out a successful year. In 1967 Sam and Dave (nicknamed "Double Dynamite") gained their widest exposure with "When Something Is Wrong With My Baby" (#2 R&B) and the epochal "Soul Man" (#2 pop, #1 R&B). The next year they scored their last major hit, "I Thank You" (#9 pop, #4 R&B).

The duo's frantic live show was one of pop music's most exciting, yet offstage Moore and Prater barely spoke to each other. After breaking up in 1970, they reunited several times. In 1979 the Blues Brothers' success with "Soul Man" rekindled interest in them, and the duo received bookings at many clubs nationwide. But they split up for good after a New Year's Eve 1981 show at San Francisco's Old Waldorf. Prater then took to the road with another Sam: vocalist Sam Daniels.

In a 1983 interview with the *Los Angeles Herald Examiner,* Moore admitted that he had been a drug addict for 12 years and that the main reason for his feud with his ex-partner was that he'd "lost respect" for him after Prater shot his own wife during a 1968 domestic dispute. Prater escaped prosecution in that instance, but in 1987 he was arrested for selling crack to an undercover cop and sentenced to three years' probation. He died the following year in a car accident. Moore contributed vocals to Bruce Springsteen's *Human Touch* LP in 1992, the same year Sam and Dave were inducted into the Rock and Roll Hall of Fame. Moore continues to perform; he published *Sam and Dave: An Oral History* in 1998. That year he also appeared in the comedy sequel *Blues Brothers 2000.*

Richie Sambora: See Bon Jovi

Sam the Sham and the Pharaohs

Formed early '60s, Texas
Sam the Sham (b. Domingo Samudio, 1940, Dallas, TX), voc., organ; David Martin, bass; Ray Stinnet, gtr.; Jerry Patterson, drums; Butch Gibson, sax.
1965—*Wooly Bully* (MGM) 1966—*Li'l Red Riding Hood* 1970—*Sam, Hard and Heavy* (Atlantic) 1985—*Pharaohization: The Best of Sam the Sham and the Pharaohs* (Rhino).

Sam the Sham and his turban-clad Pharaohs achieved brief but massive success in the mid-'60s with their rollicking Tex-Mex rock & roll. Following the moderately successful independent single "Haunted House," the band moved to MGM, where its second record, "Wooly Bully," sold 3 million copies in 1965, rising to #2.

For the next two years the Pharaohs continued to rack up hit singles: "Juju Hand" (#22, 1965), "Ring Dang Doo" (#33, 1965), the million-selling "Li'l Red Riding Hood" (#2, 1966), and its followup, "The Hair on My Chinny Chin-Chin" (#22, 1966), among them. In 1967 Sam broke up the group and went solo, reverting to his given name, Domingo Samudio.

Though his years of stardom were behind him, he won a Grammy Award in 1970 for his liner notes to the LP *Sam, Hard and Heavy,* which featured the work of a session guitarist named Duane Allman. Samudio resurfaced in 1982, donating two original songs, sung in Spanish, to the soundtrack of *The Border.* Later on he became a street preacher in Memphis. "Wooly Bully," still a bar-band standard, was covered in 1981 by Joan Jett. As of 1995 Samudio worked for a federal institution as a nondenominational Bible teacher in English and Spanish. He performed occasionally, mixing his classics with gospel songs.

David Sanborn

Born July 30, 1945, Tampa, FL
1975—*Taking Off* (Warner) 1976—*Sanborn* 1978—*Heart to Heart* 1979—*Hideaway* 1981—*Voyeur* 1982—*As We Speak* 1983—*Backstreet* 1984—*Straight to the Heart* 1987—*A Change of Heart* 1988—*Close-Up* (Reprise) 1991—*Another Hand* (Elektra) 1992—*Upfront* 1994—*Hearsay* 1995—*Pearls* 1996—*Songs From the Night Before* 1999—*Inside* (Elektra/Asylum).

Alto saxophonist David Sanborn has one of the most recognizable instrumental voices in pop music. As a child Sanborn suffered from polio and breathing ailments, neither of which discouraged his early interest in the saxophone. After moving to St. Louis, the teenage Sanborn began playing with local R&B and jazz musicians.

In 1967 Sanborn joined the Paul Butterfield Blues Band; he played with the group at Woodstock and can be heard on *In My Own Dream, The Resurrection of Pig Boy Crabshaw,* and *Live.* Leaving Butterfield, Sanborn played in the bands of a number of top musicians including Stevie Wonder, joining him for the 1972 Rolling Stones tour for which Wonder was an opening act. (Sanborn can also be heard on Wonder's *Talking Book.*)

When Sanborn went freelance, he became the originator of the ubiquitous saxophone sound of the '70s. His classic work on James Taylor's "How Sweet It Is to Be Loved by You" and David Bowie's "Young Americans" exemplifies the mixture of Hank Crawford–influenced R&B finesse and bold, rock-oriented grit that has become Sanborn's calling card. Sanborn could also be heard on recordings by the Eagles, Bruce Springsteen, Paul Simon, and the Rolling Stones.

Sanborn's own recording career began in 1975 and has thrived since. (He has four gold records, one platinum, and a Grammy for *Voyeur.*) From 1988 to 1990, Sanborn hosted the innovative television show *Night Music,* which presented a widely eclectic blend of artists.

In the '90s Sanborn gained greater respect among the jazz and avant-garde music community: His *Another Hand* (1991) featured noted jazzmen Bill Frisell and Charlie Haden; Sanborn also recorded with avant-garde saxophonist Tim Berne, and in 1995 released *Pearls,* with an orchestra arranged by Johnny Mandel. Sanborn remains in the public eye through his frequent guest appearances with Paul Shaffer's band on *The Late Show With David Letterman.* He has also hosted music-related television programs.

Santana/Carlos Santana

Formed 1967, San Francisco, CA
Original lineup: Carlos Santana (b. July 20, 1947, Autlán de Navarro, Mex.), gtr., voc., perc.; Gregg Rolie (b. June 17, 1947, Seattle, WA), kybds., voc.; David Brown (b. Feb. 15, 1947, NY; d. Sep. 2000), bass; Michael Shrieve (b. July 6, 1949, San Francisco), drums; Mike Carabello (b. Nov. 18, 1947, San Francisco), perc.; José Chepito Areas (b. July 25, 1946, Leon, Nicaragua), perc.
1969—*Santana* (Columbia) 1970—*Abraxas* 1971—(+ Neal Schon [b. ca. 1955], gtr.; + Coke Escovedo, perc.) *Santana III* (– Brown; + Tom Rutley, bass) 1972—*Caravanserai* 1973—*Welcome* 1974—*Greatest Hits; Borboletta* 1975—*Lotus* 1976—*Amigos; Festival* 1977—*Moonflower* 1978—*Inner Secrets* 1979—*Marathon* 1981—*Zebop!* 1982—*Shangó* 1985—*Beyond Appearances* 1987—*Freedom* 1988—*Viva Santana!* 1990—*Spirits Dancing in the Flesh* 1992—*Milagro* (Polydor) 1993—*Sacred Fire—Live in South America* 1995—*Dance of the Rainbow Serpent* (Legacy) 1997—*Live at the Fillmore—1968* 1998—*Best of Santana* (Columbia) 1999—*Supernatural* (Arista).
Carlos Santana solo: 1972—*Carlos Santana and Buddy Miles! Live!* (Columbia) 1973—*Love, Devotion, Surrender* (with John McLaughlin) 1974—*Illuminations* (with Turiya Alice Coltrane) 1979—*Oneness/Silver Dreams—Golden Reality* 1980—*Swing of Delight* 1983—*Havana Moon* 1987—*Blues for Salvador* 1994—*Santana Brothers* (with Jorge Santana and Carlos Hernandez) (Island).

Through a long, erratic career laden with personnel changes, the group Santana has maintained popularity and critical respect with what was in the beginning an innovative fusion of rock, fiery Afro-Latin polyrhythms, and contrasting cool, low-key vocals. In time, group leader/guitarist Carlos Santana was drawn to jazz-rock fusion and worked outside the band with John McLaughlin, Stanley Clarke, and others. Though the mid-'70s saw Santana becoming involved in spiritual mysticism (he affixed "Devadip" before his name), by the decade's end the band was back in hard-driving rhythmic form and chalked up several hit dance singles. The group continued to perform off and on into the '90s; in 1994 Santana appeared at Woodstock '94, one of three acts who had previously performed at the original '69 festival that were asked to return to the 25th anniversary concert. Five years later, Clive Davis signed the band to Arista Records and, by teaming Santana with a varied host of current hitmakers (including Wyclef Jean and Rob Thomas of Matchbox Twenty), orchestrated one of the most phenomenal comeback success stories in rock & roll history.

Carlos Santana is a fourth-generation musician and the son of a violinist father who played mariachi music. His father tried for many years to teach him violin, but at age eight, Santana discovered the guitar and started listening to the electric blues of B.B. King and John Lee Hooker. In 1955 the family moved from the small village of Autlán de Navarro to Tijuana, where Santana began playing guitar in nightclubs. During his teens, the family moved to San Francisco. It was there, working as a dishwasher, that he formed his own band.

The band evolved in San Francisco's Latin district from jam sessions among Santana, David Brown, and Gregg Rolie.

With original drummer Rod Harper and rhythm guitarist Tom Frazer, they became the Santana Blues Band. Though the soft-spoken Santana felt uncomfortable as leader, he lent his name to the group because the local musicians' union required that each band have a designated leader. The group's 1968 debut at San Francisco's Fillmore West (by which time it had become known simply as Santana) received a standing ovation; its local popularity led to a spot at Woodstock, where it stopped the show. The instrumental "Soul Sacrifice," featuring Michael Shrieve's drum solo, is one of the high points of the *Woodstock* soundtrack album.

Santana's overwhelming success at the festival led to a deal with Columbia, and within a few weeks of its late-summer 1969 release, its debut LP was #4 and eventually went double platinum. That album's "Evil Ways" was a Top 10 single in early 1970. *Abraxas,* released later that year, sold 4 million copies and lodged at #1 on the album chart for six weeks; *Santana III,* the first to feature 16-year-old second guitarist Neal Schon, topped the chart for five weeks in late 1971. *Abraxas* yielded hits such as "Black Magic Woman" (#4, 1970), previously recorded by Fleetwood Mac, and veteran salsa bandleader Tito Puente's "Oye Como Va" (#13, 1971), while *Santana III* contained "Everybody's Everything" (#12, 1971) and "No One to Depend On" (#36, 1972).

Caravanserai went platinum; *Welcome,* gold. Both LPs saw Santana's music stretching out into jazzier directions, and the band's personnel changed considerably with every album. Neal Schon and keyboardist Gregg Rolie went on to found Journey; Shrieve played various sessions, including Stomu Yamashta's *Go* series, and later formed Automatic Man and Novo Combo.

In 1972 Carlos Santana made his first recording outside the band, a live album with Buddy Miles. Though dismissed by critics, it, too, sold well, eventually going platinum. The fusion supersession *Love, Devotion, Surrender* found the guitarist playing with John McLaughlin, Jan Hammer, and Billy Cobham of the Mahavishnu Orchestra; Stanley Clarke of Return to Forever; and Larry Young of the Tony Williams Lifetime.

In 1974 Santana collaborated with Alice Coltrane and ex–Miles Davis jazz bassist David Holland, among others, for the string-dominated *Illuminations;* it didn't sell as well as *Love, Devotion, Surrender,* which had gone gold. *Borboletta* featured contributions from Clarke and Brazilian musicians Airto Moreira and Flora Purim. *Lotus* stands out in Santana's mid-'70s period; the three-record set was recorded in Japan and long unavailable in America except as a costly import.

By the late '70s, Santana had tightened up his band into a funkier direction, and enjoyed a hit single with a cover of the Zombies' mid-'60s hit "She's Not There" (#27, 1977), featuring singer Greg Walker. After two more jazz-fusion solo LPs, *Oneness* and *The Swing of Delight*—the latter featuring such fusion stars and former Miles Davis sidemen as Herbie Hancock, Tony Williams, Ron Carter, and Weather Report reedman Wayne Shorter—the Santana band's *Zebop!* became a big seller on the strength of "Winning" (#17, 1981), written by ex-Argent guitarist Russ Ballard; the following year's *Shangó* added another Top 20 hit, "Hold On," with a lead vocal by Alex Ligertwood. *Havana Moon* featured guests Willie Nelson and the Texas blues band the Fabulous Thunderbirds.

Santana appeared at Live Aid in 1985. To celebrate its 20th anniversary the next year, the band played a special San Francisco performance that featured all previous Santana members. *Freedom* reunited Carlos Santana with Buddy Miles, who contributed vocals. The title track of Carlos Santana's sixth solo recording, *Blues for Salvador,* won a 1988 Grammy for Best Rock Instrumental Performance. An acclaimed career retrospective box set, *Viva! Santana,* was released in 1988. Carlos Santana hooked up with saxophonist Wayne Shorter for a 1988 summer tour.

Spirits Dancing in the Flesh (1990) featured guest appearances by Bobby Womack and Living Colour guitarist Vernon Reid, who played on "Jin-Go-Lo-Ba," a reworking of "Jingo," a Santana favorite from the first album. In 1992, after a 20-year association with Columbia Records, Santana moved to PolyGram, appearing first on Polydor, then on Island. *Sacred Fire—Live in South America* attested to the band's tremendous popularity in Latin America. Carlos Santana announced plans in 1993 to start his own specialty label, Guts and Grace, to release jazz, world music, and selections from his extensive private collection of live-performance recordings, including artists as diverse as Jimi Hendrix, Marvin Gaye, Bob Marley, and Stevie Ray Vaughan. Along with a box set *(Dance of the Rainbow Serpent),* Legacy released a live show from the Fillmore featuring the original Santana lineup. That lineup was inducted into the Rock and Roll Hall of Fame in 1998, but Santana's long career was still a year shy of its pinnacle.

Although Santana maintained a core classic-rock audience that supported him on the road, it had been nearly two decades since his last radio hit. In interviews, Santana spoke of an angel, Metatron, who had told him that he was destined to spread the positive message of music to younger listeners through the radio. In late 1997 he signed to Arista, thus reuniting with label head Clive Davis, who had signed Santana to Columbia 30 years earlier. Their goal was to marry Santana's signature instrumental sound with contemporary voices in an attempt to connect with a modern audience. The band's last studio album, 1992's *Milagro,* had failed to crack the Top 100, but Davis boldly talked about producing an album that would outsell the quadruple-platinum *Abraxas.* It proved to be an understatement. With guest performers and writers Wyclef Jean, Dave Matthews, Lauryn Hill, Rob Thomas, Everlast, Eagle-Eye Cherry, and Eric Clapton on board, *Supernatural* (#1, 1999) sold more than 10 million copies within a year of its release (21 million worldwide), far eclipsing *Abraxas* as the best-selling album of Santana's career and putting the 50-something guitarist in the unlikely company of teen chart-toppers 'N Sync and the Backstreet Boys. The lead single, "Smooth" (cowritten and sung by Thomas), spent 12 consecutive weeks at #1. The album went on to earn nine Grammys, including Album, Song, and Record of the Year (for "Smooth"). In the wake of the awards and heavy media interest, *Supernatural* continued to spin off successful singles, with the Wyclef Jean–produced "Maria, Maria" reaching #1.

Joe Satriani

Born July 15, 1957, Carle Place, NY
1984—*Joe Satriani* EP (Rubina) 1986—*Not of This Earth* (Relativity) 1987—*Surfing With the Alien* 1988—*Dreaming #11* EP 1989—*Flying in a Blue Dream* 1992—*The Extremist* 1993—*Time Machine* 1995—*Joe Satriani* 1998—*Crystal Planet* (Epic) 2000—*Engines of Creation* (Sony).
With Eric Johnson and Steve Vai: 1997—*G3 Live in Concert* (Epic).

A rock guitarist of dazzling technical proficiency, Joe Satriani spent years as a relatively unknown working musician before a tour with Mick Jagger heightened interest in his own recording career. Satriani, who also played piano and drums while growing up, became fascinated with the guitar after listening to Jimi Hendrix, whose death inspired the young musician to devote himself to music. Satriani practiced along to blues and classic-rock records, and learned some music theory in school. He quickly became proficient enough to teach the instrument; among his early students were Steve Vai, now a fellow guitar hero, as well as future members of Metallica, Primus, Counting Crows, and Third Eye Blind. Satriani also played in bands and took lessons with the influential bebop jazz pianist Lennie Tristano.

After a stint with a pop band called the Squares, Satriani made his recording debut in 1984 with a self-titled instrumental EP. A couple of instrumental albums followed, selling respectably for their genre. In the late '80s, after Satriani had toured alone and with Greg Kihn, a tip from Vai landed him on the road with Jagger. The exposure helped propel to platinum status Satriani's album *Surfing With the Alien* (#29, 1987), which became the first instrumental LP to enter the Top 40 since 1980 and the first of eight times that the guitarist was nominated for the Best Rock Instrumental Performance Grammy. Satriani's 1989 effort, *Flying in a Blue Dream,* reached #23; 1992's *The Extremist* shot to #22. In 1993 Satriani released the double-CD *Time Machine,* a collection of out-of-print and previously unreleased recordings and new tracks. He followed up this release with a stint as Ritchie Blackmore's replacement on a Deep Purple tour in 1994.

Satriani's 1995 self-titled album was produced by Glyn Johns, who had worked with such notable artists as the Beatles, the Rolling Stones, the Who, Led Zeppelin, and the Eagles. The following year, Satriani toured with fellow guitar virtuosos Vai and Eric Johnson on the G3 tour; the trio released a live album in 1997. His next solo album, 1998's *Crystal Planet,* contained songs named by his then-five-year-old son (such titles included "A Piece of Liquid" and "Psycho Monkey"). *Engines of Creation,* produced by Trevor Horn (Art of Noise, Yes, Seal) and released in 2000, explored Satriani's admiration of techno.

Savage Garden

Formed 1994, Brisbane, Austral.
Darren Hayes (b. May 8, 1972, Brisbane), voc.; Daniel Jones (b. July 22, 1973, Essex, Eng.), kybds., gtr.
1997—*Savage Garden* (Columbia) 1999—*Affirmation* (Sony).

Darren Hayes and Daniel Jones of the Australian pop duo Savage Garden came together in 1993 when Haynes joined Jones' Brisbane-based cover band. After a year and a half, the pair began collaborating on original songs and submitting demos under the name Crush. They secured an independent deal in their homeland, changed their name to Savage Garden, and saw their self-titled debut album top the Australian charts in 1997 before being picked up by Columbia for export later the same year.

Although supplemented by extra musicians both in the studio and onstage, together Hayes and Jones cowrite and arrange all their songs, with Hayes assuming frontman duties—over-the-top costume changes included—during the band's live performances. The group's sound—lush, melodic love songs and catchy pop rock reminiscent of '80s hit duos like Wham! and Roxette—seemed out of place in the hip-hop and alternative-rock climate of the late '90s, but it connected with both Adult Contemporary fans and boy-band-hungry young teens. Propelled by the uptempo lead single "I Want You" (#4, 1997), *Savage Garden* sold 12 million copies worldwide, peaking at #4 and spinning off the additional hits "Truly Madly Deeply" (#1, 1997) and "To the Moon and Back" (#24, 1998). After contributing "The Animal Song" (#19, 1999) to the soundtrack for *The Other Sister,* Savage Garden issued *Affirmation* (#6, 1999), which yielded their second U.S. #1 single, "I Knew I Loved You."

Savoy Brown

Formed 1966, London, Eng.
Kim Simmonds (b. 1947, Wales), gtr., voc.; Bruce Portius, voc.; Martin Stone, gtr.; Ray Chappell, bass; Leo Mannings, drums; Bob Hall, kybds.
1967—*Shake Down* (Decca, U.K.) 1968—(– Portius; – Chappell; – Mannings; + Chris Youlden, voc.; + "Lonesome" Dave Peverett, gtr.; + Rivers Jobe, bass; + Roger Earl, drums) *Getting to the Point* (Parrot) 1969—(– Hall; – Jobe; + Tone Stevens, bass) *Blue Matter; A Step Further* 1970—*Raw Sienna* (– Youlden) *Looking In* 1971—(– Peverett; – Stevens; – Earl; + Paul Raymond, kybds.; + Dave Walker, voc.; + Dave Bidwell, drums; + Andy Pyle, bass; – Pyle; + Andy Silvester, bass) *Street Corner Talking* 1972—*Hellbound Train* (– Silvester; + Pyle, bass; – Walker) *Lion's Share* (– Bidwell; + Jackie Lynton, voc.; + Ron Berg, drums) 1973—*Jack the Toad* 1974—(– Berg; – Raymond; – Lynton; + Eric Dillon, drums; + Stan Webb, gtr., voc.; + Miller Anderson, gtr., voc.; + Jimmy Leverton, bass) *Boogie Brothers* (London) 1975—(– Webb; – Dillon; – Anderson; + Ian Ellis, bass; + Tom Farnell, drums) *Wire Fire* 1976—*Skin 'n' Bone* 1978—*Savage Return* 1981—*Rock 'N' Roll Warriors* (Town House) (numerous personnel changes follow)

1983—*Live in Central Park* (Relix) 1984—*Slow Train* 1988—*Make Me Sweat* (GNP Crescendo) 1989—*Kings of Boogie* 1990—*Live and Kickin'* 1992—*Let It Ride* (Roadhouse) 1994—*Bring It Home* (Viceroy) 1995—*The Savoy Brown Collection* (Mercury Chronicles) 1999—*The Blues Keep Me Holding On* (Mystic).
Kim Simmonds solo: 1997—*Solitaire* (Blue Wave).

This workmanlike blues-rock band became a favorite with American audiences while never achieving widespread popularity at home in Britain. Though Savoy Brown never had a hit single, its albums sold respectably, thanks to dogged touring. The only constant in the band's membership was guitarist Kim Simmonds, who ruled the group with an iron hand and hired and fired members regularly.

Savoy Brown was formed originally as the Savoy Brown Blues Band. In 1968 drummer Bill Bruford (Yes, King Crimson, U.K.) joined them for about a week before moving on to Yes. As the British blues boom wound down in the early '70s, Savoy Brown edged toward a more hard-rock boogie style. Around this time, it also began to concentrate almost exclusively on the U.S., where Simmonds later relocated. In 1971 Dave Peverett, Roger Earl, and Tone Stevens left the band to form another rock-boogie outfit, Foghat. Over the years, Simmonds re-formed the band, drawing on personnel from such British blues bands as Chicken Shack (Walker, Raymond, Silvester, Bidwell, Webb) and the Keef Hartley Band (Anderson).

In 1973 Simmonds announced that Savoy Brown was no more, but the following year he formed yet another version. This group was also known (parenthetically) as the Boogie Brothers, and lasted for only one album. Simmonds continues to tour and record with Savoy Brown. In 1997 he released his first solo album, the acoustic *Solitaire*.

Leo Sayer

Born Gerard Hugh Sayer, May 21, 1948, Shoreham-by-Sea, Eng.
1973—*Silverbird* (Warner Bros.) 1974—*Just a Boy* 1975—*Another Year* 1976—*Endless Flight* 1977—*Thunder in My Heart* 1978—*Leo Sayer* 1979—*The Very Best of; Here* 1980—*Living in a Fantasy; World Radio* 1990—*Cool Touch* (EMI, U.K.) 1993—*Leo Sayer: All the Best* (Chrysalis).

Singer/songwriter Leo Sayer has enjoyed sporadic American success, and at one point, in 1977, he had three Top 40 singles and a platinum album.

While attending Worthington Art College, Sayer formed his first band, Terraplane Blues. He later moved to London and headed a group called Patches. Sayer then began writing songs with David Courtney. Courtney linked the group up with singer/actor Adam Faith, who became its manager. After Patches' debut single sold only 55 copies, Sayer decided to go solo. Faith's wife, Jackie, renamed him Leo, thinking he looked like a lion.

Faith and Courtney produced the debut Sayer LP, *Silverbird*, at Roger Daltrey's studio in Sussex, with Sayer writing the words and Courtney the music. Daltrey liked their songs so much he recorded his debut solo with all material written by the two unknowns, making their "Giving It All Away" a #5 British hit in early 1973. *Silverbird* came out a short time later, and in keeping with the glitter trend, the cover featured Sayer in a Pierrot clown costume (which he also wore live). The LP established Sayer as a big British star in his own right and yielded the #2 English hit "The Show Must Go On."

For *Just a Boy*, Sayer gave up the clown image, which had been ridiculed in the U.S. The album became a British gold LP and featured his first U.S. hit single, "Long Tall Glasses" (#9, 1975). He split with Courtney, who wanted to go solo (he later reunited with Sayer for *Here*). On *Another Year* Sayer wrote the songs with Frank Farrell. The single "Moonlighting" went to #2 in the U.K. but was ignored in the U.S.

Sayer next linked up with Richard Perry, who suggested more covers and new songwriting alliances for 1976's *Endless Flight*. *Flight* was Sayer's platinum U.S. breakthrough, and yielded three hit singles: "You Make Me Feel Like Dancing" (#1, 1976), "When I Need You" (#1, 1977), and "How Much Love" (#17, 1977). *Thunder in My Heart* went gold in the U.K. but flopped in the U.S. Soon his British audience dwindled as well. Though Sayer produced some respectable surface pop in this period, he did not return to the U.S. chart until late 1980, with a #2 cover of Bobby Vee's "More Than I Can Say." He enjoyed several more hits in the U.K. and even had his own television series there, but by decade's end, he had no record deal. His 1990 U.K. "comeback" album, *Cool Touch*, failed to restore his career. However, the late '90s saw him playing universities and disco revivals throughout the U.K.

Boz Scaggs

Born William Royce Scaggs, June 8, 1944, OH
1965—*Boz* (Polydor, U.K.) 1969—*Boz Scaggs* (Atlantic) 1971—*Moments* (Columbia); *Boz Scaggs and His Band* 1972—*My Time* 1974—*Slow Dancer* 1976—*Silk Degrees* 1977—*Down Two, Then Left* 1980—*Middle Man; Hits!* 1988—*Other Roads* 1994—*Some Change* (Virgin) 1997—*Come On Home*.

After over a decade of trying to make it as a solo act, singer/songwriter Boz Scaggs hit with a 5-million-seller, *Silk Degrees*.

Scaggs grew up in Oklahoma and Texas, and while at St. Mark's Preparatory School in Dallas he met Steve Miller. He joined Miller's band, the Marksmen, as lead vocalist while Miller taught him guitar. Scaggs followed Miller to the University of Wisconsin, where they played together in a blues-rock band known as the Ardells or the Fabulous Knight Trains. Returning to Texas in 1963, Scaggs joined an R&B band, the Wigs. The next year, Scaggs and two of the Wigs—John Andrews and Bob Arthur—went to England. Finding little success, they broke up (most of the Wigs eventually forming Mother Earth), while Scaggs roved Europe as a street singer, recording his debut LP in Stockholm. He returned to the U.S. in 1967 and moved to San Francisco. There he reunited with Steve Miller for two albums with the Steve Miller Band: *Children of the Future* and *Sailor*.

Jann Wenner, editor and publisher of ROLLING STONE, helped arrange for Scaggs' U.S. solo debut with Atlantic, *Boz Scaggs*. It was released to some critical acclaim but scant profits. The album gained most of its fame from the tune "Loan Me a Dime," which featured a memorable Duane Allman guitar solo; bluesman Fenton Robinson later successfully sued for composer credit on the song. Scaggs' second and third U.S. LPs were produced by Glyn Johns. On *My Time* he dispensed with a backing band in favor of studio musicians. Also at this time his vocals began to show more of a soul influence. This became even more pronounced on *Slow Dancer*, produced by ex-Motown producer Johnny Bristol, which was again critically hailed but not commercially successful.

Then came 1976's *Silk Degrees*, with its #3 hit, "Lowdown," and other smashes like "Lido Shuffle" (#11, 1977). His studio band for much of the '70s included the nucleus of what became Toto. Though Scaggs has never quite matched that success, *Middle Man* yielded minor hits with "Breakdown Dead Ahead" (#15, 1980) and "Jo Jo" (#17, 1980). Scaggs also appeared on the soundtrack of the film *Urban Cowboy* (1980). In San Francisco Scaggs became known for his annual black-tie concerts on New Year's Eve.

Scaggs' 1994 Virgin Records debut, *Some Change*, was his second album in 14 years. The preceding release, *Other Roads* (#47, 1988), yielded the hit "Heart of Mine" (#35, 1988). During the mid-'80s he opened a restaurant and rock club, Slim's, in San Francisco. Save for a lone 1988 album, Scaggs didn't fully begin to return to music until he appeared as part of Donald Fagen's New York Rock and Soul Revue in 1991. *Some Change* (#91, 1994) was produced by former Beach Boys drummer and Bonnie Raitt band member Ricky Fataar. Its 1997 followup, *Come On Home*, peaked at #94.

Schoolly D

Born Jesse B. Weaver, June 22, 1966, Philadelphia, PA
1986—*Schoolly D* (Schoolly D) 1987—*Saturday Night—the Album; The Adventures of Schoolly D* (Rykodisc) 1988—*Smoke Some Kill* (Jive) 1989—*Am I Black Enough for You?* 1991—*How a Black Man Feels* (Capitol) 1994—*Welcome to America* (Ruffhouse/Columbia) 1995—*The Jive Collection Series, vol. 3* (Jive); *Reservoir Dog* (Contract/PSK) 1996—*Gangster's Story* (CTRA).

On his first album, Schoolly D pioneered gangsta rap with his chilling, unsentimental descriptions of urban violence. His debut featured "PSK—What Does It Mean?," a song about the Philly gang Parkside Killers, as well as the anthem "I Don't Like Rock 'n' Roll." He released his first two albums himself, then signed with Jive, which rereleased *Saturday Night*. *The Adventures of Schoolly D* contains material from the rapper's first albums with a bonus track.

Critics embraced Schoolly D's early work for its raw, journalistic outlook on what would become such familiar gangsta themes as sex and violence. The musical settings were provided by DJ Code Money. On *Am I Black Enough for You?* the rapper tackled the issues of black nationalism and pride. His 1994 release, *Welcome to America*, featured Schoolly D backed by a band, including veteran session player and coproducer Mike Tyler and ex–Urge Overkill bassist Chuck Treece. The album also introduced rapper Cheese.

Reservoir Dog was a leaner-sounding affair, mostly just samples, keys, and a drum machine; it also found Schoolly softening his thuggish persona a bit. The rapper released another album, *Gangster's Story*, in 1996, but apart from being sampled on the Chemical Brothers' single "Block Rockin' Beats," he hasn't been heard from much since.

Scorpions

Formed 1971, Hannover, Ger.
Lothar Heimberg, bass; Klaus Meine (b. May, 25, 1948, Hannover), voc.; Jurgen Rosenthal, drums; Michel Schenker (b. Jan. 10, 1955, Savstedt, Ger.), gtr.; Rudolf Schenker (b. Aug. 31, 1948, Hildesheim, Ger.), gtr.
1972—*Lonesome Crow* (Brain) 1973—(– Rosenthal; – Heimberg; – M. Schenker; + Francis Buchholz [b. Jan. 19, 1950, Hannover], bass; + Wolfgang Dziony, drums; + Ulrich Roth [b. Dec. 18, 1955], gtr.) 1974—*Fly to the Rainbow* (RCA) 1975—*In Trance; Virgin Killer* 1976—(– Dziony; + Rudy Lenners, drums) 1977—(– Lenners; + Herman Rarebell [b. Nov. 18, 1949, Monaco], drums) *Taken by Force* 1978—*Tokyo Tapes* (– Roth; + Matthias Jabs [b. Oct. 25, 1956, Hannover], gtr.; + M. Schenker, gtr.; – Jabs; + Jabs) 1979—*Lovedrive* (Mercury); *Best of Scorpions* (RCA) (– M. Schenker) 1980—*Animal Magnetism* (Mercury) 1982—*Blackout* 1984—*Love at First Sting; Best of Scorpions, vol. 2* (RCA) 1985—*World Wide Live* (Mercury) 1988—*Savage Amusement* 1989—*Best of Rockers 'n' Ballads* 1991—*Crazy World* 1992—(– Buchholz; + Ralph Rieckermann [b. Aug. 8, 1962, Lübeck, Ger.], bass) 1993—*Face the Heat* 1995—*Live Bites (1988–1995)* 1996—(– Rarebell; + Curt Cress, drums) *Pure Instinct* (Atlantic) 1997—*Deadly Sting: The Mercury Years* 1999—(– Cress; + James Kottack [b. Dec. 26, 1962, Louisville, CA], drums) *Eye II Eye* (Koch) 2000—*Moment of Glory* (EMI).

The most popular rock band to come out of Germany, Scorpions broke out as a leading heavy-metal band in the mid-'80s, with three Top 10 LPs: *Blackout* (#10, 1982), *Love at First Sting* (#6, 1984), and *Savage Amusement* (#5, 1988).

Originally formed in 1965 as a pop band by Rudolf Schenker, they broke up and re-formed in 1971 as a hard-rock outfit, featuring Rudolf's brother Michel on guitar. After the 1972 debut, *Lonesome Crow*, Michel left to join UFO (changing the spelling of his name to Michael in the process). Scorpions' five albums for RCA, while popular in Europe, did not crack the American charts, partly, the band later contended, because the label prohibited them from touring stateside. (Ironically, Scorpions' forte is live performance, as was later evinced in their appearances at the US Festival in 1985 and as part of 1990's Monsters of Rock Tour.)

Matters changed with *Lovedrive* (#55, 1979), their first record for Mercury and the first to chart in the U.S. With Michael Schenker back on guitar, the band seemed to come alive. But Schenker left again, unable to keep up with the band's brutal touring schedule, and young Matthias Jabs (who had been hired before Michael returned, then fired, then rehired) took his place. Michael has since led the Michael Schenker Group, and worked with groups named the McAuley Schenker Group and Schenker/McAuley.

Blackout (#10, 1982), Scorpions' first album to go platinum, contained their first modestly successful single, "No One Like You" (#65, 1982), followed in 1984 with "Rock You Like a Hurricane" (#25) from the double-platinum *Love at First Sting* (#6). In 1988 Scorpions toured the Soviet Union, the first heavy metal band to do so. They returned in 1989, with Bon Jovi and Ozzy Osbourne, for the Moscow Music Peace Festival. A ballad, "Wind of Change" (#4, 1991), written about their Russian experiences, included on 1990's *Crazy World* (#21), was released in a Russian version, and won the group an audience with then–Soviet premier Mikhail Gorbachev. In 1992 bassist Buchholz, who also handled some of the band's business matters, left the group in a storm of controversy.

The band confronted the problems arising from Germany's reunification in the songs "Alien Nation," "Unholy Alliance," and "Ship of Fools" on 1993's *Face the Heat* (#24). Drummer Herman Rarebell left the band and was replaced by Curt Cress on *Pure Instinct* (#99, 1996), an album that failed to make much of a dent on the U.S. chart; Cress was replaced by James Kottack (ex–Kingdom Come) on the subsequent tour. On 1999's *Eye II Eye* Scorpions attempted to update their sound by enrolling Peter Wolf as producer and including quasi–dance numbers.

But this was nothing compared to what the German veterans came up with next. On *Moment of Glory* the band, echoing Metallica's collaboration with the San Francisco Symphony on the *S&M* album, hooked up with the Berlin Philharmonic to rerecord some of their old hits (with "Rock You Like a Hurricane" becoming "Hurricane 2000") along with three new songs, including one penned by Diane Warren. Scorpions and the Philharmonic performed live together at the Hannover World Expo in June 2000.

Tom Scott

Born May 19, 1948, Los Angeles, CA
1967—*Honeysuckle Breeze* (Impulse) 1968—*Rural Still Life* 1971—*Great Scott* (A&M) 1974—*Tom Scott and the L.A. Express* (Ode) 1975—*Tom Cat; New York Connection* 1977—*Blow It Out* (Columbia) 1978—*Intimate Strangers* 1979—*Street Beat* 1980—*The Best of Tom Scott* 1981—*Apple Juice* 1982—*Desire* (Elektra/Musician) 1987—*Streamlines* (GRP) 1989—*Flashpoint* (with Eric Gale, others) 1990—*Them Changes* 1991—*Keep This Love Alive* 1992—*Born Again* (with Randy Brecker, Kenny Kirkland, others) 1994—*Reed My Lips; Night Creatures* 1996—*Bluestreak* 1998—*Priceless Jazz* 1999—*Smokin' Section* (Windham Hill).

Though he was known in jazz circles since the late '60s, saxophonist Tom Scott didn't become widely recognized in pop until the mid-'70s for studio work with Carole King, Joni Mitchell, Steely Dan, Blondie ("Rapture"), Paul McCartney, Barbra Streisand, and countless others.

Scott's mother was a classical pianist and his father a film and television theme composer (of, among many others, the themes to *The Twilight Zone* and *Dragnet*). At eight he took up the clarinet, but switched to baritone sax in junior high. He left college after one semester in 1966 and started playing the L.A. clubs with Don Ellis' band and then Roger Kellaway's quartet. His work with Oliver Nelson's band led to a contract with Impulse, which released his first solo album, *Honeysuckle Breeze*. He recorded another LP for Impulse, 1968's *Rural Still Life*, and then two for Flying Dutchman. He also did sessions, playing on *Phil Ochs Greatest Hits* in 1970, and began composing TV scores, first for *Dan August* in 1969. (He later wrote the themes for *Starsky and Hutch, The Streets of San Francisco, Family Ties, Square Pegs,* and many more. He has also done movie scores for *Stir Crazy, Neighbors, Soul Man,* and others.)

In 1971 Scott got a contract with A&M, and on his first LP for the label, *Great Scott,* he did a version of Joni Mitchell's "Woodstock" that so impressed Mitchell that she invited him to play on her *For the Roses* (1972). After that LP, Scott began to develop a band, an informal, ever-shifting group that became the L.A. Express, a pop-jazz band. Ode Records released *Tom Scott and the L.A. Express,* which got more attention than usual, especially after he was featured on Carole King's tour and soloed on her 1974 #2 single "Jazzman."

A new Express played on Joni Mitchell's *Court and Spark* and on her live *Miles of Aisles*. Scott disbanded the L.A. Express in the mid-'70s. He later toured with George Harrison and Ravi Shankar and added sax to Wings' hit "Listen to What the Man Said." In 1978 Scott recorded an album with Billy Cobham, Alphonso Johnson, and Steve Kahn called *Alivemutherfoya.* He has also recorded as part of the New York Connection (with Eric Gale, Richard Tee, and Bob James).

In 1987 Scott signed to GRP, where he released a series of respected albums and led the GRP All-Star Big Band, which tours and records. He was musical director for the ill-fated *Pat Sajak Show. Reed My Lips* (1994) featured such heavyweight players as Grover Washington Jr., Eric Gale, and Robben Ford. Scott reunited with the L.A. Express for 1996's *Bluestreak*.

Gil Scott-Heron

Born Apr. 1, 1949, Chicago, IL
With Brian Jackson: 1970—*Small Talk at 125th and Lenox* (Flying Dutchman); *Free Will* 1973—*Pieces of a Man*

1974—The Revolution Will Not Be Televised; Winter in America (Strata/East) 1975—*The First Minute of a New Day* (Arista); *From South Africa to South Carolina* 1976—*It's Your World* 1977—*Bridges.*
Solo: 1978—*Secrets; The Mind of Gil Scott-Heron* 1980—*1980; Real Eyes* 1981—*Reflections* 1982—*Moving Target* 1984—*The Best of Gil Scott-Heron* 1994—*Spirits* (TVT) 1999—*Evolution & Flashback: The Very Best of Gil Scott-Heron* (RCA).

Writer-turned-singer Gil Scott-Heron stresses his literate, politically conscious lyrics as much as his funk and jazz-based music. His oeuvre has been cited as an influence on some schools of rap as well as on the burgeoning spoken-word movement of the '90s.

Scott-Heron's mother was a librarian (his father, a pro soccer player), and Scott-Heron wrote detective stories as an early teen. At 19 he published his first novel, *The Vulture,* followed by a book of rap verse called *Small Talk at 125th and Lenox* and a second novel, *The Nigger Factory.* Scott-Heron believed he could reach more people through music, so he began to collaborate with a friend from Pennsylvania's Lincoln University, Brian Jackson. They each played piano, and at first Jackson wrote music to Scott-Heron's words, but soon they began to collaborate on the music.

The two cut three LPs for Flying Dutchman, first a mostly verbal version of his verse, *Small Talk,* followed by two more musical albums, *Pieces of a Man,* which included the militant poem "The Revolution Will Not Be Televised" (also popularized by Labelle on its *Pressure Cookin'* LP), and *Free Will.* In 1974 the two became the first signing to the new Arista label; the following year they released *The First Minute of a New Day.* It was also the debut of Scott-Heron and Jackson's jazzy backup group, the Midnight Band.

The followup, 1975's *From South Africa to South Carolina,* included the R&B hit "Johannesburg" (#29 R&B, 1975). Scott-Heron began writing on his own, without Jackson, in the late '70s. His first single after going solo, "Angel Dust," reached #15 on the R&B charts in 1978.

Over the years Scott-Heron's music generally has gotten good reviews, though some critics have considered his lyrics didactic. He appeared at the antinuclear MUSE benefit at Madison Square Garden in September 1979, where he performed his own atomic warning, "We Almost Lost Detroit." He also recorded "Shut 'Um Down" (#68 R&B, 1980) on the same subject.

In 1985 Scott-Heron was featured on the all-star anti-apartheid record *Sun City,* and continued touring with his own band, the Amnesia Express. By then, the influence of Scott-Heron's work had begun to surface in rap. Public Enemy's 1991 "1 Million Bottlebags" updated Scott-Heron's 1974 "The Bottle" (a minor R&B hit [#98] in 1977). But although his work is regarded as a precursor of rap, Scott-Heron didn't jump on the bandwagon. "It's something that's aimed at the kids," Scott-Heron said. "I have kids, so I listen to it. But I would say it's not aimed at me. I still listen to the jazz station."

He toured throughout the '80s and ended a 10-year hiatus from recording new material with 1994's *Spirits.* Among the album's new songs was "Message to the Messengers," in which he took gangsta rappers to task for straying from the course with their violent lyrics. By decade's end he was at work on a new album and was looking for a publisher for a new book, *The Last Holiday,* about Martin Luther King Day. In 1998 *The First Minute of a New Day, Winter in America,* and *From South Africa to South Carolina* were all reissued on CD for the first time with bonus material on Rumal-Gia, Scott-Heron's imprint on TVT Records; *It's Your World* and *The Mind of Gil Scott-Heron* followed in 2000.

Screaming Trees

Formed 1984, Ellensburg, WA
Mark Lanegan (b. Nov. 25, 1964, Ellensburg), voc.; Van Conner (b. Mar. 17, 1967, Apple Valley, CA), bass; Gary Lee Conner (b. Aug. 22, 1962, Ft. Irwin, CA), gtr.; Mark Pickerel, drums.
1985—*Other Worlds* EP (Velvetone) 1986—*Clairvoyance* 1987—*Even If and Especially When* (SST) 1988—*Invisible Lantern* 1989—*Buzz Factory; Changes Come* double EP (Sub Pop); *Something About Today* EP (Epic) 1991—*Uncle Anesthesia* (– Pickerel; + Barrett Martin [b. Apr. 14, 1967, Olympia, WA], drums) *Anthology* (SST) 1992—*Sweet Oblivion* (Epic) 1993—*Time Is of the Essence* EP 1996—*Dust.*
Mark Lanegan solo: 1990—*The Winding Sheet* (Sub Pop) 1994—*Whiskey for the Holy Ghost* 1998—*Scraps at Midnight* 1999—*I'll Take Care of You* 2001—*Field Songs.*

Screaming Trees are a psychedelic-tinged postpunk band from the rural Pacific Northwest formed by 300-pound brothers Van and Gary Lee Conner. Sons of video-store owners in Ellensburg, Washington, the Conners formed Screaming Trees along with friend Mark Lanegan out of a collective love of both hard rock and punk. The group's SST output is rawer and grungier than its Epic releases, although its Doors-like groove has remained a constant.

The Trees have a reputation for boozing and fighting, often breaking up and regrouping over the years. Lanegan's role as the band's creative center was frequently hobbled by heroin addiction and other drug use; he was arrested in San Francisco in 1997 for allegedly trying to buy crack (charges were later dropped). Each member has done side projects: Lanegan began his singer/songwriter solo career with *The Winding Sheet* (1990), which included a rendition of Leadbelly's "Where Did You Sleep Last Night?" with accompaniment by Nirvana's Kurt Cobain and Krist Novoselic, who would later record their own version; Lee Conner formed the Purple Outside in 1990 and put out *Mystery Lane* on New Alliance; and Van Conner (who went on hiatus in 1991 to tour with Dinosaur Jr) formed Solomon Grundy, which released a self-titled album on New Alliance in 1990.

In 1990 the Trees signed with Epic. The band's first full-length album for the label was 1991's *Uncle Anesthesia,* coproduced by Chris Cornell of Soundgarden. By the end of 1992, following the massive success of fellow Washingtonians Nirvana and Pearl Jam, the Trees' second full-length Epic release, *Sweet Oblivion*, began to garner a fair amount of mainstream exposure via MTV's "grunge-mania," helping the album to sales of more than 300,000. The band also gained new listeners with the hit "Nearly Lost You" through their appearance on the platinum soundtrack to Cameron Crowe's 1992 film *Singles*.

The band reconvened in two L.A. studios in 1995 to record *Dust* (#134, 1996), which included the single "All I Know." A critical success, the album reflected the darkness and melancholy that had descended on Seattle with the recent deaths of Cobain, Hole bassist Kristin Pfaff, and singer Mia Zapata (who was brutally raped and murdered). Sales were disappointing, however, and after appearing on the 1996 Lollapalooza Tour, the band again dissolved. Lanegan relocated to Southern California and focused on two more solo projects, *Scraps at Midnight* and *I'll Take Care of You*. Drummer Barrett Martin, meanwhile, joined Mad Season with Mike McCready (Pearl Jam) and Layne Staley (Alice in Chains) to record *Above* (#24, 1995); he also performed percussion duties on R.E.M.'s *Up* in 1998, and joined guitarist Peter Buck in the instrumental band Tuatara. In June 2000 the Screaming Trees performed at the opening of Seattle's Experience Music Project and then promptly broke up, apparently for good.

Seal

Born Sealhenry Olumide Samuel, Feb. 19, 1963, London, Eng.
1991—*Seal* (Sire/Warner Bros.) 1994—*Seal* 1998—*Human Being*.

Though his first recording success came through England's house-music scene, Seal's critically acclaimed debut album presented him as a somewhat mystically inclined singer/songwriter mixing elements of folk, soul, pop, and rock. The son of Nigerian and Brazilian parents who separated when he was a toddler, Sealhenry Samuel earned a degree in architecture, designed leather clothes, and worked in electrical engineering and other odd jobs before he began singing in London pubs. A funk band called Push invited him along on a tour of Japan, after which he joined a blues band in Thailand, then spent several months traveling alone through India.

Seal returned to England and happened to meet house/techno producer Adamski, on whose U.K. dance hit "Killer" Seal wrote lyrics and sang. That led to a deal for Seal himself, whose debut album was produced by ex-Buggle Trevor Horn (ABC, Art of Noise). *Seal* (#24, 1991) yielded a Top 10 pop hit in "Crazy" (#7, 1991), the video for which showed off Seal's distinctive facial scars (the result of a skin ailment). The rerecorded "Killer" was only a minor hit (#100, 1991). In 1993 he joined Jeff Beck on "Manic Depression," for the Jimi Hendrix all-star tribute album *Stone Free*. The next year Seal released his second album, again self-titled and produced by Trevor Horn. Despite the early success of the single "A Prayer for the Dying" (#21, 1994), the record got a second life when "Kiss From a Rose" (#1, 1995) was included on the *Batman Forever* soundtrack. It charted as a single a year after Seal's album had come out, and went on to win Grammys for Best Song, Best Record, and Male Pop Vocal of the Year.

After contributing a cover of Steve Miller's "Fly Like an Eagle" to the *Space Jam* soundtrack (#10, 1996), Seal teamed up with Horn once again on his third album, *Human Being* (#22, 1998).

Seals and Crofts

Formed 1969, California
Jim Seals (b. Oct. 17, 1941, Sidney, TX), gtr., sax, fiddle, voc.; Dash Crofts (b. Darrell Crofts, Aug. 14, 1940, Cisco, TX), drums, voc., mandolin, kybds., gtr.
1970—*Seals and Crofts* (TA); *Down Home* 1971—*Year of Sunday* (Warner Bros.) 1972—*Summer Breeze* 1973—*Diamond Girl* 1974—*Unborn Child* 1975—*I'll Play for You; Greatest Hits* 1976—*Get Closer; Sudan Village* 1977—*One on One* 1978—*Takin' It Easy* 1979—*The Seals and Crofts Collection* (K-Tel) 1980—*The Longest Road* (Warner Bros.).
Dash Crofts solo: 2000—*Today* (Nuance).

Jim Seals and Dash Crofts were a commercially successful soft-rock pop duo through the '70s. Both were born in small Texas towns and met when Crofts was a teenage drummer for a local band. Later Seals joined a local band called Dean Beard and the Crew Cuts; later Crofts came aboard that outfit, and, to make a long, complicated story short, by mid-1958 both were touring with the Champs, then riding the success of their huge #1 Latin-rock instrumental hit "Tequila." The pair later moved to L.A., where both worked as session musicians and tried to make a go of their own recording careers. In 1965 Seals and Crofts (who spent two years in the service and then returned to the Champs upon being discharged in 1964), left the Champs. Two groups, the Mushrooms and the Dawnbreakers, failed. But out of the latter, first Crofts (who married fellow Dawnbreaker Billie Lee Day) and then Seals were introduced to the Bahá'í faith.

In 1969 Seals and Crofts decided to try it as a duo. They signed to Talent Associates and released two largely ignored LPs before signing to Warner Bros. in 1971. Their first album for their new label also bombed, but their second, *Summer Breeze*, went to #7 in 1972 on the strength of its #6 title tune and "Hummingbird" (#20, 1972). *Diamond Girl* (#4, 1973), spun off two more hits, "Diamond Girl" (#6, 1973) and "We May Never Pass This Way (Again)" (#21, 1973). Seals and Crofts, though devout followers of their chosen faith, did not proselytize directly, but they insisted on a clause in their contracts stating that they be given time after each concert to speak to interested fans about Bahá'í. Crofts' wife's sister wrote a poem after viewing a documentary on abortion. Seals wrote the music, and in 1974 the duo released "Unborn Child," an antiabortion song written from the fetus' point of view ("Momma, don't!"). Seals and Crofts, ignoring Warner Bros.' advice, also chose to title the album *Unborn Child* (#14, 1974). A critical and commercial flop, "Unborn Child" rose only as high as #66 and prompted pro-choice demonstrations at many of their shows.

Over a year later they returned with "I'll Play for You" (#18, 1975), from *I'll Play for You* (#30, 1975). The following year's *Get Closer* (#37, 1976), featuring "Get Closer" (#6, 1976), was Seals and Crofts' last Top 40 LP. Carolyn Willis, formerly of Bob B. Soxx and the Blue Jeans and Honey Cone, was featured on that album and its live followup, *Sudan Village* (#73, 1976). The pair sang music for a Robby Benson film, *One on One*, from which "My Fair Share" went to #28 in 1977. *Takin' It Easy* (#78, 1978) included their last Top 20 single, "You're the Love" (#18, 1978). Their final studio effort, *The Longest Road*, didn't even crack the album chart; Chick Corea and Stanley Clarke guest on it.

Warner Bros. dropped the duo soon after that, but by then, as both have indicated in recent years, it didn't really matter to them. Except for a short 1991–1992 reunion tour and a number of appearances together at Bahá'í-related gatherings, the two have not played together. Crofts lived in Mexico, then Australia, then Nashville. Seals has lived on a coffee farm in Costa Rica since 1980. Dan Seals, Jimmy's younger brother, recorded in the '70s as England Dan and John Ford Coley. More recently, he has had a string of country hit singles. In 1997 rapper Busta Rhymes sampled "Sweet Green Fields" from Seals and Crofts' *Get Closer*. Crofts completed a solo album, complete with new Adult Contemporary versions of the duo's old material, in 1998; originally a limited edition, it was widely released in 2000.

The Searchers

Formed 1961, Liverpool, Eng.
John McNally (b. Aug. 30, 1941, Liverpool), gtr., voc.; Mike Pender (b. Michael Prendergast, Mar. 3, 1942, Liverpool), gtr., voc.; Tony Jackson (b. July 16, 1940, Liverpool), bass, voc.; Chris Curtis (b. Aug. 26, 1942, Oldham, Eng.), drums, voc.
1964—*Meet the Searchers* (Kapp); *Hear! Hear!* (Mercury); *This Is Us* (Kapp) (– Jackson; + Frank Allen [b. Dec. 14, 1943, Hayes, Eng.], bass, voc.) 1965—*The New Searchers LP; The Searchers No. 4* 1966—(– Curtis; + John Blunt [b. Mar. 28, 1947, London, Eng.], drums, voc.) 1969—(– Blunt; + Billy Adamson, drums) 1972—*Second Take* (RCA) 1980—*The Searchers* (Sire) 1981—*Love's Melodies* 1985—(– Pender; + Spencer James [b. Spencer Frederick James, 1953, Eng.], gtr., voc.) 1988—*Greatest Hits* (Rhino) 1998—(– Adamson; + Eddie Rothe [b. Walter Edgar Rothe, Buckingham, Eng.], drums).

The Searchers were one of the best of the Liverpool pop bands to emerge in the wake of the Beatles. Their sound matched their clean-cut looks: pretty, gentle, with perfect close-harmony vocals and ringing guitar lines that presaged the Byrds.

The Searchers, originally formed to back up British singer Johnny Sandon, took their name from the John Ford–John Wayne film. They went to Hamburg, Germany, to play the Star Club after the Beatles' success there, and then returned to Liverpool. A&R man Tony Hatch offered them a recording contract after they had established a residency at Liverpool's Iron Door club. Their first U.K. hit came in 1963 with their cover of the Drifters' "Sweets for My Sweet." "Needles and Pins," written by Sonny Bono and Jack Nitzsche, was #1 in Britain in 1964 (#13 U.S.); it eventually sold over a million copies.

The Searchers toured America, Australia, and New Zealand that year. Their only subsequent U.S. Top 20 hits were "Don't Throw Your Love Away" (#16, 1964) and "Love Potion Number 9" (#3, 1965). In Britain their Top 20 success continued through 1965, with "Sugar and Spice" (1963); "Someday We're Gonna Love Again," "When You Walk in the Room," and "What Have They Done to the Rain" (1964); and "Goodbye My Love" and "He's Got No Love" (1965). They then became stalwart club and cabaret performers for many years before resurfacing on Sire in 1979. In the wake of new wave, both *The Searchers* and *Love's Melodies* sounded entirely contemporary (containing songs by Tom Petty, Will Birch and John Wicks of the Records, and Alex Chilton) and elicited glowing reviews. Neither sold well, however, and so the group returned to the touring circuit. Cofounder Pender left in 1985 to form his own live act, Mike Pender's Searchers. Longtime drummer Billy Adamson left the remaining Searchers in 1998, but otherwise, the band has been traveling the world with few changes.

Sebadoh/Sentridoh/The Folk Implosion

Formed ca. 1986, Westfield, MA
Louis K. Barlow (b. July 17, 1966, Dayton, OH), voc., gtr., bass; Eric Gaffney, drums.
1989—*The Freed Man* (Homestead) 1990—*Weed Forestin; The Freed Weed* 1991—(+ Jason Lowenstein [b. July 20, 1971, Boston, MA], voc., bass, gtr.) *III* 1992—(+ Bob Fay, drums) *Smash Your Head on the Punk Rock* (Sub Pop) 1993—*Bubble & Scrape* 1994—*Bakesale* (– Gaffney) 1996—*Harmacy* 1997—(– Fay; + Russell Pollard [b. June 12, 1975, CA], drums) 1999—*The Sebadoh.*
Lou Barlow with Sentridoh: 1994—*Winning Losers* (Smells Like Records) 1995—*Losing Losers* (Shrimper); *Lou Barlow and His Acoustic Sentridoh* (Smells Like Records).
Lou Barlow with the Folk Implosion: 1994—*Take a Look Inside* (Communion) 1997—*Dare to Be Surprised* 1999—*One Part Lullaby* (Interscope) 2000—*Ep* EP (Communion).

The master of lo-fi and one of underground rock's most venerated songwriters, Lou Barlow has demonstrated a flair for confessional folk rock buried under various degrees of feedback and white noise. His bands—Sebadoh, the Folk Implosion, and the mostly solo Sentridoh—represent a commitment to the indie aesthetic that has made Barlow a college radio hero alongside the likes of Pavement and Guided by Voices.

Barlow grew up in Jackson, Michigan, before his father's job transferred the family to Massachusetts. At age 13 Barlow was drawn to the raw emotion of the hardcore punk bands Minor Threat, Dead Kennedys, and Black Flag, which he discovered on college radio. He soon formed the punk band Deep Wound with J Mascis. That partnership evolved into the band Dinosaur Jr [see entry] in the mid-'80s. Barlow originally formed Sebadoh with drummer Eric Gaffney as a side project, but it quickly became full-time when Barlow was fired from Dinosaur Jr in 1989 after Mascis hit him with a guitar during a Connecticut performance. Sebadoh's earliest recordings were bedroom tapes of Barlow's edgy folk rock and Gaffney's noisier experiments, initially released in cassette form, before signing to Homestead Records. The label collected those early cassette releases onto the 1989 CD *The Freed Weed.*

Bassist Jason Loewenstein (Dissident Voices) was recruited into the band, but differing styles caused tensions between Barlow and Gaffney. Sebadoh signed to Sub Pop in 1992, and Gaffney quit the band three times in the next year. He left permanently after 1994's *Bakesale,* and was replaced by Bob Fay. *Harmacy* (#126, 1996) presented a notably cleaner sound, and included strings on the song "Willing to Wait." It was the second Sebadoh album with Barlow fully in charge, though Loewenstein wrote half the songs. The year after the release of *The Sebadoh* (#197, 1999), the band was dropped by Sub Pop.

Barlow also released several albums with Sentridoh and the hip-hop informed Folk Implosion, a collaboration with singer/songwriter John Davis. With the Folk Implosion, Barlow and Davis wrote songs for the film soundtrack to 1995's *Kids,* and enjoyed an unexpected lo-fi Top 40 hit in "Natural One" (#29, 1995).

John Sebastian

Born Mar. 17, 1944, New York, NY
1970—*John B. Sebastian* (MGM); *John Sebastian Live* 1971—*Cheapo-Cheapo Productions Presents the Real Live John Sebastian* (Reprise); *The Four of Us* 1974—*The Tarzana Kid* 1976—*Welcome Back* 1989—*The Best of John Sebastian* (Rhino) 1993—*Tar Beach* (Shanachie) 1996—*I Want My Roots* (Music Masters) 1999—*Chasin' Gus's Ghost* (Hollywood).

John Sebastian's solo career took off almost immediately after breaking up his old group, the Lovin' Spoonful [see entry]. He appeared in an unscheduled set at Woodstock and captured the audience with songs like "I Had a Dream" and a persona that was the epitome of the tie-dyed hippie.

John B. Sebastian, his first solo album, featured "I Had a Dream," as well as a remake of the Spoonful's "You're a Big Boy Now," and though it produced no hit singles, it went to #20 and became the best-selling album of Sebastian's solo career. *Cheapo-Cheapo Productions Presents the Real Live John Sebastian* was meant to counter an unauthorized live set released and quickly deleted by his old label, MGM, and it relied largely on previously recorded material. Sebastian worked with Little Feat's Lowell George on *Tarzana Kid* (which included their joint composition "Face of Appalachia"). Sebastian's fortunes were temporarily reversed with his first hit single in close to 10 years, "Welcome Back" (#1, 1976), the title song of the TV show *Welcome Back, Kotter,* which outsold the Spoonful's best-selling single by nearly two-to-one, and was the second-best-selling single of 1976.

Though Sebastian then vanished from the recording scene for over 15 years, he remained active: touring, both solo and as opening act or accompanist to acts as diverse as NRBQ, Sha Na Na, Tom Petty, Graham Parker, Willie Dixon, and Les Paul; appearing on TV shows, and writing music for the *Care Bears* show; and writing a children's book, *J.B.'s Harmonica.* Sebastian declined to take part in a 1992 Lovin' Spoonful reunion. In 1994 he formed the J-Band, a touring jug band, who appeared on Garrison Keillor's popular radio show, *The Prairie Home Companion,* and on *Late Night With Conan O'Brien.*

Jon Secada

Born Juan Secada, Oct. 4, 1962, Havana, Cuba
1992—*Jon Secada* (SBK) 1994—*Heart, Soul & a Voice* 1997—*Secada* (SBK/EMI) 2000—*Better Part of Me* (Sony).

Jon Secada's debut album, released in both English and Spanish, charted in the Top 20, a victory both for the artist and for the Latin sound—a mixture of romantic ballads and dance pop—he helped bring into the mainstream.

Secada emigrated from Cuba with his parents as a child and grew up in Hialeah, Florida, where he later worked in his family's diner before earning a master's degree in jazz at the University of Miami. There he met two future members of Gloria Estefan and the Miami Sound Machine. Shopping his Stevie Wonder–influenced material to Estefan's husband and manager, Emilio, he broke into the music business by cowriting six songs for Estefan's *Into the Light,* including two 1991 #1 hits, "Coming Out of the Dark" and "Can't Forget You."

After touring with Estefan as backup vocalist, he released his first album. While his label, SBK, planned that he record only in English, he convinced the company to release two songs in Spanish. When both hit #1 on the Latin chart, he redid the entire album in a Spanish version, *Otro Día Mas Sin Verte;* it went on to win a Grammy for Best Latin Pop Album in 1992. (Secada has since continued to release his albums in English and Spanish versions.) *Jon Secada* (#15, 1992), with its four Top 40 singles, "Just Another Day," "Do You Believe in Us," "Angel," and "I'm Free," sold 4 million copies worldwide; all four were #1 Latin hits as well. A genuine Latin music star who also duetted with Frank Sinatra on the latter's *Duets II,* Secada in the '90s began penning songs for up-and-comers Ricky Martin and Jennifer Lopez.

Neil Sedaka

Born Mar. 13, 1939, Brooklyn, NY
1962—*Neil Sedaka Sings His Greatest Hits* (RCA) 1974—

Sedaka's Back (MCA/Rocket) 1975—*The Hungry Years* 1976—*Steppin' Out* 1977—*A Song* (Elektra) 1980—*In the Pocket* 1981—*Now* 1986—*Me and My Friends* (Polydor) 1994—*Laughter in the Rain—The Best of Neil Sedaka 1974–1980* (Varèse Vintage) 1998—*Tales of Love and Other Passions* (Artful).

Neil Sedaka began in the late '50s as a writer of hit songs, became a hitmaking performer himself, then returned to songwriting until the early '70s, when Elton John helped him resume a singing career that briefly propelled him back into the spotlight.

As a teenager, Sedaka was selected by Arthur Rubinstein to play on a show on New York City's classical music station, WQXR. By that time, he had become strongly attracted to popular music as well, and he began writing songs at age 13 to lyrics by his high school friend Howard Greenfield. He formed a backing band, the Tokens [see entry], who later had a hit of their own, "The Lion Sleeps Tonight."

While on a two-year scholarship to New York's Juilliard School of Music, Sedaka sold his first tune, "Stupid Cupid," a hit for Connie Francis in 1958, as was his "Where the Boys Are" (which Francis sang in the hit teen movie of the same title) in 1961. He also sold Sedaka-Greenfield songs to Jerry Wexler at Atlantic Records, who placed them with R&B singer LaVern Baker and Clyde McPhatter. On the advice of Doc Pomus, Sedaka signed up with Al Nevins and Don Kirshner's Aldon Publishing. They felt Sedaka's own high-pitched voice was worth consideration and got him signed with RCA as a singer. In 1959 he had two hits, "The Diary" (#14) and "I Go Ape" (#42). More Sedaka-Greenfield hits followed: "Oh! Carol" (#9) in 1959; "Stairway to Heaven" (#9) in 1960; "Calendar Girl" (#4), "Little Devil" (#11), and "Happy Birthday, Sweet Sixteen" (#6) in 1961; "Breaking Up Is Hard to Do" (#1) and "Next Door to an Angel" (#5) in 1962. Sedaka also played a part in music-video history with the film for "Calendar Girl," today being counted among the first conceptual promotional clips.

Sedaka's performing career slowed in 1963. However, through the '60s and early '70s he and Greenfield continued to write hits for others, including the Fifth Dimension's "Workin' on a Groovy Thing," Tom Jones' "Puppet Man," and Davy Jones' "Rainy Jane." Greenfield, in the meantime, had also found success collaborating with Carole King; together they wrote "Crying in the Rain" for the Everly Brothers. Sedaka and Greenfield split up in 1973, after Sedaka had begun a performing comeback in England. After Sedaka made three LPs in Britain with Graham Gouldman of 10cc coproducing, Elton John helped him get back onto the U.S. chart, first by reissuing cuts from the three British LPs on one U.S. package *(Sedaka's Back)*, then by having him record for his Rocket label. *Sedaka's Back* (#23, 1974) and *The Hungry Years* (#16, 1975) both went gold. "Laughter in the Rain" was a #1 hit for Sedaka in 1974, and his "Love Will Keep Us Together" (cowritten with Greenfield) was a #1 smash for the Captain and Tennille, winning a 1975 Grammy as Record of the Year.

Sedaka's second recording streak culminated with the #1 hit "Bad Blood" (1975), which featured John on backing vocals; a bluesy reworking of "Breaking Up Is Hard to Do" (#8, 1976); and "Love in the Shadows" (#16, 1976). Since then Sedaka and Greenfield have collaborated regularly. Sedaka has become a successful MOR ballad singer and has made numerous TV and concert appearances; he remains a familiar face on the nostalgia circuit. In 1980 he and his daughter Dara recorded "Should've Never Let You Go," which reached #19 on the pop chart.

The Seeds

Formed 1965, Los Angeles, CA
Sky Saxon (b. Richard Marsh, ca. 1946, Salt Lake City, UT), voc., bass, harmonica; Jan Savage, gtr.; Daryl Hooper, kybds.; Rick Andridge, drums.
1966—*The Seeds* (GNP Crescendo); *Web of Sound* 1967—*Future* 1968—*Raw and Alive: Merlin's Music Box* 1969—*A Full Spoon of Seedy Blues* 1977—*Fallin' Off the Edge* 1993—*Travel With Your Mind.*

On the cusp of the early-to-mid-'60s garage-rock boom and the mid-to-late-'60s flower-power era came the Seeds. Their Top 40 hit of 1967, "Pushin' Too Hard," matched their scruffy looks with a nasty, threatening drive and ominous lyrics. This product of the L.A. teen scene had a few more minor hits—"Mr. Farmer," "Can't Seem to Make You Mine," and "Thousand Shadows"—later that year; all were very much in the vein of "Pushin'," though their sound gradually became more psychedelic. The group disbanded in 1969.

After making records with the legendary religious cult-psych ensemble Ya Ho Wa 13 (a.k.a. Father Yod and the Spirit of '76), lead singer Sky Saxon—sometimes rechristened Sky Sunlight—attempted several comebacks fronting a number of bands. He has released numerous solo albums. In the mid-'80s, ROLLING STONE magazine tracked him down at home in Kailua, Hawaii, where he claimed to be living with two common-law wives and five kids, and praying to dogs, since, as he explained, "God is dog spelled backwards." Former Seeds guitarist Jan Savage joined the L.A. Police Department.

After several years of playing with L.A. punk musicians (including members of the Dream Syndicate and Redd Kross) Saxon reunited the original Seeds for a tour in 1989. In the late '90s he made another resurgence, having become an icon to the international psychedelic underground. In 1998 he was backed by ?'s Mysterians at New York's Cavestomp! Festival. The following year the Seeds announced news of a forthcoming album.

Pete Seeger

Born May 3, 1919, New York, NY
1941—*Talking Union and Other Union Songs* (Folkways) 1943—*Songs of the Civil War, vol. 1* 1950—*Darling Corey* 1951—*Lonesome Valley* 1953—*American Folksongs for*

Children 1955—*Bantu Choral Folk Songs* (Folkways) 1957–62—*American Favorite Ballads, vols. 1 to 5* 1958—*Pete Seeger and Sonny Terry at Carnegie Hall* (with Sonny Terry) 1960—*Pete Seeger With Memphis Slim and Willie Dixon at the Village Gate* (with Memphis Slim and Willie Dixon); *American History in Ballad and Song, vol. 1* (Folkways) 1961—*American History in Ballad and Song, vol. 2* 1963—*We Shall Overcome* (Columbia) 1964—*Songs of Struggle and Protest, 1930–1950* (Folkways) 1965—*WNEW's Songs of Selma* 1966—*Dangerous Songs?* (Columbia) 1967—*Pete Seeger Sings Woody Guthrie* (Folkways); *Pete Seeger's Greatest Hits* (Columbia); *Waist Deep in the Big Muddy and Other Love Songs* 1969—*Young vs. Old* 1972—*The World of Pete Seeger* 1975—*Pete Seeger and Arlo Guthrie in Concert Together* (with Arlo Guthrie) (Warner Bros.) 1978—*The Essential Pete Seeger* (Vanguard) 1982—*Precious Friend: Arlo Guthrie and Pete Seeger* (with Arlo Guthrie) (Warner Bros.) 1989—*We Shall Overcome: The Complete Carnegie Hall Concert* (Columbia) 1990—*Children's Concert at Town Hall* 1996—*Pete* (Living Music) 1997—*The Best of Pete Seeger* (Vanguard) 1998—*If I Had a Hammer: Songs of Hope and Struggle* (Smithsonian/Folkways); *Headlines and Footnotes: A Collection of Topical Songs.*

Pete Seeger is unquestionably the foremost contemporary popularizer of American folk music. From his pop-folk successes with the Weavers in the late '40s, through the '50s, when he was blacklisted by the government, through the '60s, when he became a cultural hero through his outspoken commitment to the antiwar and civil rights struggles, until now, Seeger has remained an indomitable, resourceful, and charming performer. He wrote a number of folk standards—including "If I Had a Hammer" (with Lee Hays) and "Where Have All the Flowers Gone?"—and has preserved and given exposure to thousands of other songs.

Seeger's interest in music began early. His father, Charles Seeger, was a musicologist, and his mother a violin teacher; both were on the faculty of the Juilliard School of Music. He had learned banjo, ukulele, and guitar by his teens, when he developed an interest in America's folk-music legacy at age 16, after attending a folk festival in North Carolina. He began working with noted folk archivist and field recorder Alan Lomax before traveling around the country, absorbing rural music. He attended Harvard University and served in the army in World War II. In the '40s Seeger became a friend and singing associate of Woody Guthrie before forming the Weavers [see entry], an enormously popular folk quartet that popularized such folk chestnuts as "On Top of Old Smokey" and Lead Belly's "Goodnight Irene."

In the '50s Seeger's sympathies with humanitarian socialism led him to be blacklisted by the House UnAmerican Activities Committee; still Seeger continued to perform wherever he could. He recorded for Folkways and signed with John Hammond and Columbia Records in the early '60s. As always, Seeger did more than just perform. A gifted storyteller and music historian, he brought to his audiences not just the songs but the stories of the people who wrote and first sang them. In his 1993 autobiography, *Where Have All the Flowers Gone,* for example, Seeger writes of "Wimoweh": "Please don't sing it the way the American pop record had it: 'In the jungle . . . , etc.' This trivializes a song of great historical importance."

With the arrival of the Vietnam War protests, Seeger was rediscovered by a younger audience. In 1965 the Byrds had a #1 hit with Seeger's "Turn! Turn! Turn!," a Biblical passage set to music. From the mid '70s on, Seeger has worked regularly with Woody Guthrie's son Arlo. He has crusaded for ecology with the sloop *Clearwater,* giving concerts along the Hudson River. In 1994 he received the Presidential Medal of the Arts, as well as a Kennedy Award. He was inducted into the Rock and Roll Hall of Fame as an early influence in 1996. *Pete,* released later that year, was his first new studio album in 17 years. It featured everything from traditional ballads to gospel to a community chorus to an activist rap. Seeger has toured and sung around the world. His music instructional books and records inspired generations of self-taught musicians and folksingers (including Joni Mitchell).

Seeger's half sister, Peggy, is also an accomplished folk musician and songwriter. In addition to her feminist anthem "Gonna Be an Engineer," Peggy also wrote with her husband, Ewan MacColl. In the '50s she moved to England, where she joined a folk group called the Ramblers, with Alan Lomax, Shirley Collins, and MacColl (writer of "The First Time Ever I Saw Your Face"). A British citizen, Peggy Seeger continues to tour and record. Half brother Mike Seeger, also a musician, was a member of the New Lost City Ramblers and an important part of the folk revival of the '60s.

Bob Seger

Born May 6, 1945, Dearborn, MI
1969—*Ramblin' Gamblin' Man* (Capitol); *Noah* 1970—*Mongrel* 1971—*Brand New Morning* 1972—*Smokin' O.P.'s* (Palladium) 1973—*Back in '72* 1974—*Seven* (Capitol) 1975—*Beautiful Loser* (Capitol) 1976—*Live Bullet; Night Moves* 1978—*Stranger in Town* (Capitol) 1980—*Against the Wind* 1981—*Nine Tonight* 1983—*The Distance* 1986—*Like a Rock* 1991—*The Fire Inside* 1994—*Greatest Hits* 1995—*It's a Mystery.*

For years, singer/songwriter Bob Seger remained a local Michigan rock hero. His music brought together Detroit's two legacies—hard rock and soul—while a series of bad breaks denied him the nationwide audience critics thought his hard-driving workingman's rock deserved. But he came into his own in 1976 with the gold *Live Bullet* and platinum *Night Moves* LPs.

Seger's father had been a big-band leader who quit music to work in a factory, then left the family when Seger was 12, leaving the boy to live in near-poverty with his mother and brother. (His father died in a fire in 1968.) In 1961 Seger led a three-piece band, the Decibels, then joined another local Michigan band, the Town Criers, before going on

Bob Seger

to Doug Brown's Omens. Seger recorded "East Side Story" with members of the Town Criers and the Omens; the tune had previously been a failure for the Underdogs, who included Michael and Suzi Quatro and future Eagle Glenn Frey, but Seger's version was a local hit in 1966. He later produced Frey's first solo single, "Such a Lonely Child."

In the late '60s Seger had strong followings in the Midwest and Florida as well as more big local hits, such as "Nutbush City Limits," "Ramblin' Gamblin' Man," and, most notably, "Heavy Music," which had begun climbing the national chart before dropping when Seger's record company, Cameo, folded. He also recorded an answer record to Staff Sergeant Barry Sadler's "The Ballad of the Green Berets"—"Ballad of the Yellow Beret," for Are You Kidding Me Records in 1966—but when legal action was threatened, the label withdrew the 45.

Seger signed with Capitol in 1969. Despite having his first national hit in early 1969 with a rereleased "Ramblin' Gamblin Man" (#17), he left music later that year to go back to college. By 1970, though, he was back on the road with a group called Teegarden and Van Winkle, a partnership resulting in 1972's *Smokin' O.P.'s,* his first for his own label, Palladium. *Back in '72,* partly recorded at Muscle Shoals and including J.J. Cale backing on some cuts, was yet another commercial failure, as was *Seven,* which yielded the failed single "Get Out of Denver" (later covered by Dave Edmunds).

After moving back to Capitol, things slowly began to click with *Beautiful Loser,* which introduced Seger's own backup unit, the Silver Bullet Band (Drew Abbott, guitar; Robyn Robbins, keyboards; Alto Reed, sax; Chris Campbell, bass; Charlie Allen Martin, drums), and included another local Detroit hit, "Katmandu." The *Live Bullet* double album, recorded in Detroit, stayed on the U.S. chart for over three years and eventually went quadruple platinum.

The 5-million-seller *Night Moves* established Seger on ballads (the hit title tune, #8, 1977; "Mainstreet," #24, 1977) as well as hard rock ("Rock and Roll Never Forgets," #41, 1977). *Stranger in Town* yielded four major hits: "Still the Same" (#4), "Hollywood Nights" (#12), and "We've Got Tonite" (#13) in 1978, and "Old Time Rock & Roll" (#28) in 1979. By the time of the 4-million-selling *Against the Wind* (1980), Seger's only #1 LP, his singles had become almost exclusively ballads: "Fire Lake" (#6), "Against the Wind" (#5), and "You'll Accomp'ny Me" (#14). Only "Horizontal Bop" (#42), from that album, was uptempo. The singer's second live LP, *Nine Tonight,* became his fifth consecutive multiplatinum release.

But beginning with 1982's *The Distance,* Seger's sales began to taper off (his taking three- and five-year sabbaticals between records certainly was a factor), although that album and the two to follow, *Like a Rock* and *The Fire Inside,* each sold a million copies. *The Distance* also signaled the gradual revamping of the Silver Bullet Band. Guitarist Drew Abbott quit in anger after Seger began using session musicians such as pianist Roy Bittan from Bruce Springsteen's E Street Band and guitarist Waddy Wachtel. The band has shed members ever since, with only bassist Chris Campbell remaining. Former Grand Funk keyboardist Craig Frost came aboard in 1980 and on *Like a Rock* cowrote two songs with Seger, who also provided a home, briefly, to ex-GFR drummer Don Brewer.

Seger contributed the song "Understanding" to the soundtrack of the film *Teachers* in 1984; it went Top 20. "Shakedown," from 1987's *Beverly Hills Cop II,* topped the chart. The Keith Forsey tune had been offered first to Seger's pal Glenn Frey, but he contracted laryngitis and couldn't record it. *The Fire Inside* (1991), coproduced by Don Was, gave Seger only one hit, "Real Love" (#24). *Greatest Hits* went double platinum, peaked at #8, and spent 99 weeks on the album chart in 1994 and 1995. The all-new *It's a Mystery* peaked at #27 though it produced no hit singles.

The Seldom Scene

Formed 1971, Arlington, VA
John Duffey (b. Mar. 4, 1934, Washington, DC; d. Dec. 10, 1996, Arlington), mandolin; Mike Auldridge (b. Dec. 30, 1938, Washington, DC), Dobro; Ben Eldridge (b. Aug. 15, 1938, VA), banjo; John Starling (b. Mar. 26, 1940, Durham, NC), gtr., voc.; Tom Grey, bass.
1972—*Act One* (Rebel) 1973—*Act Two; Act Three* 1974—*Old Train* 1975—*Recorded Live at the Cellar Door* 1976—*The New Seldom Scene Album* 1977—(– Starling; + Phil Rosenthal, gtr., voc.) 1978—*Baptizing* 1979—*Act Four* (Sugar Hill) 1981—*After Midnight* 1983—*. . . At the Scene* 1986—(– Rosenthal; – Gray; + Lou Reid, gtr., voc., mandolin; + T. Michael Coleman [b. Jan. 13, 1951, Leaksville, NC], bass, voc.) *The Best of the Seldom Scene, vol. 1* (Rebel) 1988—*A Change of Scenery* (Sugar Hill) 1990—*Scenic Roots* 1992—*Scene 20: 20th Anniversary Concert* 1993—(– Reid;

+ Starling; – Starling) 1994—*Like We Used to Be* (+ Lawrence "Moondi" Klein [b. Mar. 13, 1963, Port Jefferson, NY], gtr., voc.) 1995—(– Auldridge; – Klein; – Coleman; + Fred Travers, Dobro; + Dudley Connell, gtr., voc.; + Ronnie Simpkins, bass) 1996—*Dream Scene* (– Duffey; + Reid) 2000—*Scene It All.*

For more than 30 years the Seldom Scene has been making vital bluegrass music while adhering to the "new grass" ethos, a genre that combines the instrumentation and style of bluegrass with material most often performed by rock and/or folk musicians. Founded by John Duffey, "the father of modern bluegrass," the group's unique approach has enabled it to balance tradition and innovation without alienating advocates of either camp. The Seldom Scene's "new grass" roots come honestly: Both Duffey and original bass player Tom Grey were members of the first progressive bluegrass outfit, the Country Gentlemen, formed in 1957. Like the Scene, they covered contemporary country, pop, and folk tunes in addition to bluegrass standards.

The Seldom Scene has recorded with some of the biggest names in contemporary country music, and has simultaneously acquired a reputation as a powerful, spontaneous live ensemble. Guest fiddler Ricky Skaggs graces *Act Three*, and *The New Seldom Scene Album* features Linda Ronstadt on vocals. *Old Train* includes both Skaggs and Ronstadt, as the band runs through its trademark concoction of traditional and new material. *Scene 20* chronicles two nights of performance at the band's second home, the Birchmere club in Alexandria, Virginia. Completely free of overdubs, this album includes all eight Seldom Scene members up to that point, and Emmylou Harris contributes lead vocals to the bittersweet "Satan's Jeweled Crown."

In 1994 the Seldom Scene released *Like We Used to Be*, which marked the return of guitarist/vocalist John Starling, who departed again before the album was released. Taking his place was Moondi Klein, who moved to Washington, DC, in 1984, harboring aspirations of joining the Seldom Scene, with whom he had been enamored since discovering bluegrass music at age 14.

In 1995 three members of the band, including Klein and founding Dobro player Mike Auldridge, defected to concentrate on Chesepeake, the side project they had formed a couple of years earlier. The remaining Scenesters plus three new recruits recorded 1995's *Dream Scene*, which was Duffey's last album with the band. He died of a heart attack in late 1996. Lou Reid, who had played with the Seldom Scene in the late '80s and early '90s, returned to the fold. Original banjoist Ben Eldridge and the others released the surprisingly faithful, less slick *Scene It All* in 2000.

The Selecter

Formed 1979, Coventry, Eng.
Noel Davies, gtr.; Charley Anderson, bass; Pauline Black, voc.; Charley "H" Bembridge, drums; Compton Amanor, gtr.; Arthur "Gaps" Hendrickson, voc.; Desmond Brown, kybds.
1980—*Too Much Pressure* (Chrysalis) 1981—*Celebrate the Bullet* (group disbands) 1992—*Out in the Streets* (Triple X) (group re-forms: Davies; Black; + Perry Melius, drums; + Martin Stewart, kybds.; + Nick Welsh, bass) 1993—*Madness* EP 1994—*The Happy Album* 1995—*Hairspray* 1996—*Back Out on the Streets* 1997—*The Very Best of the Selecter* 1999—*Cruel Brittania* (Snapper Music, U.K.); *Perform the Trojan Songbook* (Receiver, U.K.).

Along with the Specials, Madness, and the English Beat, the Selecter was one of the main bands in the ska-influenced trend that broke big in England in 1979. Like the other bands in this "movement," the Selecter used the old Mod two-tone fashion style as a visual aid. Its music was an upbeat blend of ska (quicker and less brooding than reggae, which also influenced the group's music), rock, and soul, with socially conscious lyrics, backed up by the band's own racially and sexually integrated lineup.

Like the Specials, the members of the Selecter all hailed from the industrial city of Coventry, about 80 miles northwest of London. Noel Davies had written a song called "The Selecter" that he tried to sell to various companies, without success. Davies and the Specials financed their own label, 2-Tone, and issued a single, "Gangsters" b/w "The Selecter," with Davies playing guitar. The single went British Top 10 in 1979, and Davies formed a band.

Charley Anderson, Charley Bembridge, Arthur Hendrickson, and Compton Amanor had been playing in the Coventry roots-reggae band Hard Top 22; the band was completed with Pauline Black and Desmond Brown, who were working in another local rock-reggae outfit. Their 2-Tone label went on to become one of England's most successful independent record companies, and the band's 1980 debut, *Too Much Pressure*, came out in America on Chrysalis. Highlighted by Black's lead vocals, the sound was fast-paced and politically

The Selecter: Charley Anderson, Noel Davies, Charley Bembridge, Compton Amanor, Pauline Black, Desmond Brown, Arthur "Gaps" Hendrickson

charged. It was the rage for a short while in England (the single "Three Minute Hero" went Top 10 there), but it did not go over in America despite positive press and a strong summer tour. In 1981 the Selecter released a second album, *Celebrate the Bullet*; and was featured in the film and soundtrack to *Dance Craze*, chronicling all the 2-Tone bands, but broke up later that year.

Black released a British single, "Pirates of the Airwaves," that year, but soon left the music business to concentrate on acting, appearing on the British children's show *Hold Tight*. In 1992 she again joined forces with Davies in a re-formed Selecter, featuring members of the band Bad Manners. They toured to support *Out in the Streets* (1992), a greatest-hits collection, and returned to the studio in 1993 to record the *Madness* EP with ska legend Prince Buster. The band continues to tour and record regularly. One of its latest releases, *Perform the Trojan Songbook*, is a collection of classic reggae and ska songs.

Brian Setzer/The Brian Setzer Orchestra

Born Apr. 11, 1959, New York, NY
Brian Setzer solo: 1986—*The Knife Feels Like Justice* (EMI America) 1988—*Live Nude Guitars* (EMI Manhattan).
Brian Setzer Orchestra, formed 1992, Los Angeles, CA: Setzer, voc., gtr.; numerous other musicians.
1994—*The Brian Setzer Orchestra* (Hollywood) 1996—*Guitar Slinger* (Interscope) 1998—*The Dirty Boogie* (Interscope) 2000—*Vavoom!*
Brian Setzer's 68 Comeback Special, formed 2000: Setzer; Bernie Dresel, drums; Mark Winchester, bass.
2001—*Ignition!* (Surfdog).

When the neo-swing movement spread from L.A. cocktail lounges into the American mainstream on the heels of the 1996 movie *Swingers*, Brian Setzer was ready for it. In 1992 the former Stray Cats guitarist, who had seen two solo albums and a Stray Cats reunion fail to make an impression, hit upon the novel idea of marrying his electric guitar with a big band orchestra. The Brian Setzer Orchestra's self-titled 1994 debut sold modestly, as did *Guitar Slinger*, their 1996 followup. By the time of 1998's *Dirty Boogie*, however, Setzer found himself at the forefront of a nationwide swing revival. The album featured a duet with No Doubt's Gwen Stefani on the Elvis Presley/Ann-Margret classic "You're the Boss," but the track that proved the strongest selling point was a cover of Louis Prima's 1956 hit "Jump Jive an' Wail" (#94)—thanks in part to the simultaneous use of the original in a popular Gap TV ad. The album climbed to #9, was certified double platinum, and won two Grammys, for Best Pop Performance Duo/Group (for "Jump Jive an' Wail") and Best Pop Instrumental Performance (a cover of Santo and Johnny's #1 instrumental hit "Sleepwalk"). The inevitable wane of the swing fad cooled the sales of *Vavoom!* (#62, 2000), but the instrumental track "Caravan" won the group another Grammy. In the midst of touring behind the album, Setzer road-tested a new rockabilly trio, Brian Setzer's '68 Comeback Special, featuring the Orchestra's rhythm section, drummer Bernie Dresel, and bassist Mark Winchester. An album by the trio, *Ignition!*, was released in summer 2001.

The Sex Pistols

Formed 1975, London, Eng.
Johnny Rotten (b. John Lydon, Jan. 31, 1956, London), voc.; Steve Jones (b. Sep. 3, 1955, London), gtr.; Glen Matlock (b. London), bass; Paul Cook (b. July 20, 1956, London), drums.
1977—(– Matlock; + Sid Vicious [b. John Simon Richie, May 10, 1957, London; d. Feb. 2, 1979, New York, NY], bass) *Never Mind the Bollocks, Here's the Sex Pistols* (Warner Bros.)
1980—*The Great Rock 'n' Roll Swindle* (Virgin) 1996—*Filthy Lucre Live*.

Unabashedly crude, intensely emotional, calculated either to exhilarate or to offend, the Sex Pistols' music and stance were in direct opposition to the star trappings and complacency that, by the mid-'70s, had rendered rock & roll irrelevant to the common bloke. Over the course of their short, turbulent existence, the group released a single studio album that changed, if not the history of rock, at least its course. While the Sex Pistols were not the first punk rockers (that distinction probably goes to the Stooges), they were the most widely known and at least, to appearances, the most threatening. *Never Mind the Bollocks, Here's the Sex Pistols* unquestionably ranks as one of the most important rock & roll records ever, its sound a raw, snarling, yet mesmerizing rejection of and challenge to not only rock & roll music and culture but a modern world that offered, as Rotten sang in "God Save the Queen," "no future." Whether the Pistols were simply a sophisticated hype run amok or the true voice of their generation has been widely debated, yet, oddly, that neither matters nor explains how they came to spark and personify one of the few truly critical moments in pop culture—the rise of punk.

The Sex Pistols were the brainchild of young entrepreneur Malcolm McLaren [see entry]. The owner of a London clothes boutique, Sex, which specialized in "anti-fashion," McLaren had conceived the idea of a rock & roll act that would challenge every established notion of propriety when, in 1975, he found himself managing the New York Dolls in their final months as a group. A part-time employee of Sex, Glen Matlock, played bass with Paul Cook and Steve Jones; he let McLaren know they were looking for a singer. McLaren approached 19-year-old John Lydon, whom he had seen hanging around the jukebox at Sex and who was known mainly for his rudeness.

Lydon had never sung before, but he accepted the invitation and thoroughly impressed the others with his scabrous charisma. McLaren had found his act; he named the group the Sex Pistols. Allegedly, Lydon's disregard for personal hygiene prompted Jones to dub him Johnny Rotten. Ten minutes into their first gig at a suburban art school dance on November 6, 1975, the school's social programmer literally pulled the plug. In the early months of 1976, McLaren's carefully cultivated word-of-mouth about the Sex Pistols made the band the leader of the nascent punk movement. Their gigs inspired the formation of the Clash, Buzzcocks, X-Ray Spex, Joy Division, Siouxsie and the Banshees, and countless other rebel groups in the second half of the '70s.

The press and the record industry ignored the Sex Pistols at first, but by the end of the summer the uproar—both acclamatory and denunciatory—was too loud to be ignored. In November EMI outbid Polydor with a recording contract worth £40,000. The Sex Pistols' first single, "Anarchy in the U.K.," was released in December. That month the band used the word "fucker" in a nationally televised interview; the consequent outrage led promoters and local authorities to cancel all but five of the dates scheduled on the group's national tour and EMI to withdraw "Anarchy in the U.K."—#38 on the U.K. chart in January 1977—from circulation and to terminate its contract with the Sex Pistols.

In March Matlock left to form the Rich Kids and was replaced by John Richie, a previously nonmusical friend of Rotten, who named him Sid Vicious. That same month A&M signed the Pistols for £150,000; just a week later the company fired them for a balance payment of £75,000. In May Virgin signed the Pistols and released their second record, "God Save the Queen," timed to coincide with the Queen's Silver Jubilee that June. The song was immediately banned from airplay in England. Nonetheless it was a top-selling single (cited as a blank at the #2 position on official charts, listed as #1 on independent charts).

When no British hall would book the Pistols, the group went abroad—to the Continent in July and to the U.S. in December, by which time the debut album had been released. In America the band found itself the object of a little adulation, considerable hostility, but mostly uncomprehending curiosity, which turned to scoffing when the group made only halfhearted attempts to live up to its reputation for savagery. Rotten was characteristically critical of the sensationalism and opportunism that had been attached to the Pistols (for which he blamed McLaren), and on January 14, 1978, immediately after a concert in San Francisco, he announced the breakup of the group.

Jones and Cook remained active in the punk movement and formed the Professionals; Jones materialized in the mid-'80s in Chequered Past, featuring former Blondie rhythm section Nigel Harrison and Clem Burke, ex–Iggy Pop sideman Tony Sales, and singer Michael des Barres. Vicious initiated a haphazard solo career, which ended when he was imprisoned in New York on charges of stabbing his girlfriend Nancy Spungen to death in their Chelsea Hotel room. He died of a heroin overdose while out on bail before he could be tried.

Dismissing the Sex Pistols as "a farce" and reverting to his given name, Lydon formed Public Image, Ltd. [see entry]. In 1986 the surviving members of the group and Vicious' mother won a lawsuit against McLaren, charging he had tied up their royalties in two management companies. The plaintiffs were later awarded approximately $1.44 million. That same year, the critically acclaimed Alex Cox film *Sid and Nancy* was released.

In 1996 all four original members reunited to embark on a world tour, including Europe, North and South America, Japan, and Australia, dubbed the Filthy Lucre Tour. The Sex Pistols, uncharacteristically "professional" onstage, nonetheless attacked the old repertoire with a fury. *Filthy Lucre Live*, which documented the re-formed band's London performance, was released in the States in time for the tour's U.S. arrival. In 2000 Julien Temple's *The Filth and the Fury* documentary on the Pistols included some of the footage originally released as *The Great Rock 'n' Roll Swindle* in 1980.

Charlie Sexton

Born Aug. 11, 1968, San Antonio, TX
1985—*Pictures for Pleasure* (MCA) 1989—*Charlie Sexton*
1995—*Under the Wishing Tree* (with the Charlie Sexton Sextet).
With Arc Angels (Sexton, gtr., voc.; Chris Layton [b. Nov. 16, 1955, Corpus Christi, TX], drums; Tommy Shannon [b. Apr. 18, 1948, Tucson, AZ], bass; Doyle Bramhall II [b. Dec. 24, 1968, Dallas, TX], gtr., voc.): 1992—*Arc Angels* (DGC).
Doyle Bramhall II solo: 1996—*Doyle Bramhall II* (Geffen)
1999—*Jellycream* (RCA).

Charlie Sexton's precocious guitar skills earned him a record contract at the age of 15, but it was his high cheekbones and skinny, vaguely androgynous sensuality that won the singer and musician heavy rotation on MTV two years later, when his 1985 debut album and single hit the pop chart. Alas, a teen idol's reign is usually short-lived; and so in the early '90s, after a disappointing sophomore effort, Sexton resurfaced as one-fourth of Arc Angels, a roots-rock outfit that made a bid for the sort of artistic credibility that he had aspired to as a child prodigy. By 1994, the Arc Angels had disbanded, and Sexton was recording a new album with a different band.

The guitarist was born to hippie teenage parents (his mother was 16 when Sexton was born; his father served time in prison when Sexton was a young child). Sexton's prodigious behavior began when he picked up a guitar at the age of four, encouraged by his blues-and-rockabilly-loving mother. (Younger brother Will fronts the band Will and the Kill.) By the time he was 10 the fledgling musician was sitting in on club gigs around Austin, Texas; about a year later he met Joe Ely, who enlisted him for a six-week tour. Sexton left home to live in Austin full-time when he was just 12; by 13 he was playing professionally. He played in various other bands before being signed by MCA Records. Session work with Keith Richards and Ron Wood, Bob Dylan, and Don Henley followed before the teenager's first album, *Pictures for Pleasure*, was released and shot to #15, spawning the #17 single "Beat's So Lonely." Sexton's low, throaty vocals and buoyantly disposable hard-rock songs evoked shades of Billy Idol, another videogenic bad boy whose star was then falling fast. As for Sexton, his self-titled second album peaked at #104, then quickly disappeared.

In 1990, while working on material for a comeback effort at the Austin Rehearsal Complex (ARC), Sexton encountered drummer Chris Layton and bassist Tommy Shannon, the rhythm section of Stevie Ray Vaughan's band Double Trouble, and singer/guitarist Doyle Bramhall II (the son of drummer Doyle Bramhall, who had played with Vaughan's brother Jimmie in the Fabulous Thunderbirds). The musicians clicked immediately, and became the group Arc Angels shortly afterward, following Stevie Ray's death in a 1990 helicopter crash. Their eponymous 1992 debut album was predictably a gritty, bluesy, album-rock-oriented affair, and was produced by Little Steven Van Zandt; *Arc Angels* (#126, 1992) garnered critical acclaim, if not commercial success. The group broke up soon after, partly amid Bramhall's growing dependence on heroin. (After the band's demise, Bramhall successfully completed a rehab program.)

In 1994 Sexton hooked up with a new band—bassist George Reiff, keyboardist Michael Ramos, and drummer Rafael Gayol (the latter two from the band BoDeans)—and recorded *Under the Wishing Tree*, released in 1995 and credited to the Charlie Sexton Sextet. More musically diverse and lyrically personal than his previous work, the album was well received critically but wasn't a popular hit. Sexton began recording an album with his brother for A&M Records in 1998, but when the record label was acquired by Seagram, the project was dropped. With bassist Shannon and drummer Layton fresh from the disbanded Storyville and Bramhall working on his second solo album, the Arc Angels briefly reunited for a club tour in 1999. Bramhall went on to tour with Roger Waters later that year. Sexton joined Bob Dylan's band around the same time. In 2001 he coproduced Lucinda Williams' *Essence*.

The Shadows

Formed 1958 as the Drifters, London, Eng.
Hank B. Marvin (b. Oct. 28, 1941, Newcastle, Eng.), gtr., voc.; Bruce Welch (b. Nov. 2, 1941, Bognor Regis, Eng.), gtr., voc.; Ian Samwell, bass; Terry Smart, drums; Ken Payne, gtr.
Early years—(– Samwell; + Jet Harris [b. July 6, 1939], bass; – Smart; + Tony Meehan [b. Mar. 2, 1942, London], drums; – Meehan; + Brian Bennett [b. Feb. 9, 1940, London], drums) 1962—*The Shadows* (Columbia, U.K.) (– Harris; – Bennett; + "Licorice" Locking, bass) 1963—*Greatest Hits* (– Locking; + John Rostill [b. June 16, 1942, Birmingham, Eng.; d. Nov. 26, 1973], bass) 1965—*More Hits* 1968—(– Welch; + Adam Hawkshaw, gtr., voc.) 1972—(– Hawkshaw; + Welch; + John Farrar, bass, gtr., voc.) 1973—*Specs Appeal* (EMI) 1976—*Rarities* 1977—*The Best of the Shadows; 20 Golden Greats* 1996—*Shadows Are Go!* (Scamp).

While still backing British teen idol Cliff Richard in the late '50s, the Shadows began to branch out into a successful instrumental-rock career of their own, which made ever-bespectacled lead guitarist Hank B. Marvin one of the most influential British rock guitarists.

Marvin, whose twanging guitar leads were the group's hallmark, took up banjo and guitar as a youth, and by 14 he and schoolmate Bruce Welch were playing together in skiffle groups. They moved to London's Soho section, and after a few months of living in poverty, they joined Richard's touring band, which already included Terry Smart and Ian Samwell (the latter wrote Richard's first hit, "Move It").

The group was originally called the Drifters, but changed its name to the Shadows to avoid confusion with the American vocal group. They stayed with Richard through 1968, despite their own long string of hits. They appeared with Richard in films like *Expresso Bongo, The Young Ones, Summer Holiday,* and *Finders Keepers,* and despite several personnel changes, they always maintained their trademark sound. Their first single, 1959's "Feelin' Fine," wasn't a hit, but their fourth, 1960's "Apache," was a long-running #1 in the U.K. In 1981 it was revived in a rap-funk version by the Sugar Hill Gang.

Most of their 20-plus followup hits—"F.B.I.," "Kon Tiki," "Atlantis," "Frightened City" (1961); "Shindig" (1963); "Don't Make My Baby Blue" (1965)—were instrumentals and were mainly U.K. successes, including 13 Top 10 hits. In 1962 Tony Meehan and Jet Harris performed as a duo and had three 1963 hits in Britain: "Diamonds" (#1), "Scarlet O'Hara" (#2), and "Applejack" (#4). After Harris was involved in a car crash, Meehan returned to songwriting and production work.

Welch finally quit in 1968, precipitating the first of several Shadows breakups. Within two years, though, he and Marvin were back together with Bennett and Australian guitarist John Farrar. They recorded two LPs as Marvin, Welch and Farrar. Ex-bassist Rostill had gone on to play with Tom Jones, record a few solo singles, and write tunes for Engelbert Humperdinck, the Family Dogg, and others, and was fatally electrocuted by his guitar in 1973.

Meanwhile, the Shadows had split up again in 1969—when Welch fell ill—and they re-formed several times through the '70s. The title of 1973's *Specs Appeal* referred to Marvin's glasses. In 1977 the *20 Golden Greats* album was #1 in Britain, and the Shadows re-formed again to tour by popular demand. They have regrouped several times over the years. In 1986 Marvin appeared on a remake of "Living Doll" that Cliff Richard recorded with the cast of the popular British comedy *The Young Ones*.

Bennett, Welch, Farrar, and Marvin have done session and production work; Welch has worked with Cliff Richard and Farrar with Olivia Newton-John; Meehan has become a successful producer and arranger. The group last placed an album in the U.K. Top 10 in the mid-'80s. In 1983 the Shadows received the Ivor Novello Award for their contribution to British music. In 1990 Bennett retired from the group. Marvin, who has had a prickly relationship with Welch, pursued solo projects. Bennett and Marvin have also toured with their sons.

The Shaggs

Formed 1967, Fremont, NH
Betty Wiggin (b. Dec. 24, 1950, Exeter, NH), voc., gtr.; Dorothy "Dot" Wiggin (b. Mar. 21, 1948, Portsmouth, NH), gtr., voc.; Helen Wiggin (b. Dec. 17, 1946, Kittery, ME), drums.
1969—*Philosophy of the World* (Third World) 1982—*Shaggs' Own Thing* (Red Rooster) 1988—*The Shaggs* (Rounder).

Three self-taught sisters raised in a remote area of New England, the Shaggs formed (at their disciplinarian father's bidding) one of the first all-girl bands who played their own instruments and wrote and sang their own songs—making music that was so primitively quirky it spawned a cult following among NRBQ and other rock cognoscenti and future fans of punk rock including Kurt Cobain.

Textile worker Austin Wiggin Jr. got instruments for his three young daughters, Dot, Helen, and Betty, and insisted they form a band, even though the girls exhibited no musical talent. After woodshedding for less than a year, and inspired by their favorite group, Herman's Hermits, the sisters entered a Massachusetts recording studio to record their homegrown songs, about such topics as their cat Foot Foot, their parents, and the idea that the grass is always greener on the other side. The result, as described by Irwin Chusid, who featured the band in his book *Songs in the Key of Z*: "Hacked-at chords, missed downbeats, out-of-socket transitions, blown accents, and accidental convergences abound. The sisters' arrangements are so uncoordinated they seem to be riffing off their genetic code." Local label Third World pressed 1,000 copies of *Philosophy of the World*. The album was sold locally at weekly Saturday night Shaggs gigs at the Fremont Town Hall, which the girls dutifully played to please their father. Younger sister Rachel sometimes joined in on bass. When Dad died in 1975, the sisters put away their instruments for nearly 25 years.

Meanwhile, the album fell into the hands of outsider music buffs, like NRBQ keyboardist Terry Adams, who arranged for its national release in 1980, and Frank Zappa, who named it in a *Playboy* survey as his third favorite album of all time. In 1982 NRBQ's Red Rooster label released slightly more accomplished, later recordings, *Shaggs' Own Thing*.

Still, the story of the Shaggs was shrouded in mystery until 1999, when a *New Yorker* writer tracked the sisters down for a comprehensive profile. In November 1999 Dot and Betty performed in a New York nightclub with a stand-in drummer (sister Helen suffers from depression and couldn't make the gig), and the sisters have since sold their life-story movie rights to Artisan Entertainment. Over the years, the Shaggs' recordings have been available in various formats, combinations, and sequencing, and in 1999 RCA reissued on CD an exact replica of the original *Philosophy* (with the same cover, liner notes, and sequencing).

Tupac Shakur/2Pac

Born Lesane Parish Crooks, changed to Tupac Amaru Shakur, June 16, 1971, Brooklyn, NY; died Sep. 13, 1996, Las Vegas, NV

1991—*2Pacalypse Now* (Interscope) 1993—*Strictly 4 My N.I.G.G.A.Z.* 1995—*Me Against the World; So Many Tears* EP 1996—*All Eyez on Me* (Death Row); *The Don Killuminati: The 7 Day Theory* (as Makaveli) 1997—*R U Still Down? (Remember Me)* (Amaru/Jive) 1998—*In His Own Words* (Mecca); *Greatest Hits* (Interscope) 2001—*Until the End of Time*.

Tupac + Outlawz: 1999—*Still I Rise* (Interscope).
2Pac with Thug Life: 1994—*Volume 1* (Interscope).

Tupac Shakur (a.k.a. 2Pac) was among the most dynamic, influential, and self-destructive rappers of the '90s. And true to his appropriately titled 1995 chart-topping album, *Me Against the World*, he attempted to define himself as a performer amidst numerous criminal charges and convictions. His husky voice described the rapper's stark contradictions, preaching misogyny and strong women, street wisdom and the violence of his "thug life"—words he had tattooed across his torso. The critical and commercial success of his music (as well as an acclaimed acting career) was continually overshadowed by his legal entanglements, which began only after he became a recording artist. In the life of this alternately acclaimed and vilified gangsta rapper, art and reality became tragically blurred, culminating in his 1996 murder in Las Vegas.

Shakur was the son of Black Panther Party members Billy Garland and Afeni Shakur (Shakur is Arabic for "thankful to God"), who was in jail (and later acquitted) on bombing charges while pregnant with him. Sometime after his birth, he was named Tupac Amaru, for an Incan chief whose name translates as "shining serpent." Shakur spent his earliest years in the Bronx and Harlem, and at age 13 made his acting debut in a production of *A Raisin in the Sun* at an Apollo Theatre benefit for Jesse Jackson's 1984 presidential campaign. He spent the rest of his childhood moving around the country with his mother. He attended the Baltimore School of the Arts before dropping out and settling, at the age of 17, in Marin County, California. The rapper then successfully auditioned to become a dancer and roadie for the rap group Digital Underground [see entry] and simultaneously worked relentlessly on his own material. He appeared on that group's *This Is an E.P. Release* EP (1990) and *Sons of the P* (1991). In 1991 he signed with Interscope and released the album *2pacalypse Now* (#64 pop, #13 R&B, 1992), a musical mixture of inner-city portraiture and messages of racial strength. An underground hit, the album spawned the single "Brenda's Got a Baby" (#23 R&B).

Shakur also became a successful actor in the early '90s, appearing in Ernest Dickerson's *Juice* (1992) and *Above the Rim* (1994), and giving a critically acclaimed performance opposite Janet Jackson in John Singleton's *Poetic Justice* (1993). Despite a promising start and wide praise for his performances, the rest of his film work was far less acclaimed; he ended his acting career as James Belushi's sidekick in the mostly ignored *Gang Related*.

Shakur's second album, *Strictly 4 My N.I.G.G.A.Z.* (#24 pop, #4 R&B, 1993), yielded the hits "I Get Around" (#11 pop, #5 R&B, 1993) and "Keep Ya Head Up" (#12 pop, #7 R&B, 1993). He also released an album as part of the short-lived Thug Life group in 1994.

Even longer than Shakur's hit list, though, was his police blotter. In 1992 the rapper was arrested after a six-year-old California boy was killed by a stray bullet discharged during a scuffle between Shakur and two others. (A lawsuit filed by the boy's family was later settled out of court.) He was then charged in Atlanta with shooting two off-duty police officers in October 1993. Charges in both cases were dismissed. The following month Shakur and two members of his entourage were charged with sexual abuse following an incident in a New York luxury hotel. In early 1994 he was found guilty of assault on *Menace II Society* codirector Allen Hughes and served 15 days in jail. By the end of the year, the rapper was found guilty of the sexual assault only a day after being shot by muggers in the lobby of a New York recording studio. He was later sentenced to one and half to four and a half years in prison. While his 1995 album *Me Against the World* (#1 pop, #1 R&B) headed to the top of the charts, Shakur headed for prison. Shakur became the first artist to reach #1 on the *Billboard* charts while serving a prison sentence. The hit single "Dear Mama" (#9 pop, #3 R&B) suggested a depth of feeling that led some critics to reassess the rapper and his work.

By now Shakur was a lightning rod for a highly publicized West Coast vs. East Coast hip-hop feud. Shakur was released after serving just eight months of his sentence, the result of a parole arrangement and a $1.4 million bond paid by Death Row label CEO Marion "Suge" Knight. The rapper signed with Death Row in late 1995, soon releasing the dark, two-disc *All Eyez on Me* (#1 pop, #1 R&B, 1996). On the album, Shakur attacked his enemies with furious threats of violence, while speaking of his own early death as inevitable. The album also included "How Do You Want It" (#1 pop, #1 R&B), "California Love" (#6 pop) (with Dr. Dre and Roger Troutman), and "Hit 'Em Up," on which Shakur claimed to have slept with the Notorious B.I.G.'s wife, singer Faith Evans.

Then, on September 7, Shakur was shot near the Las Vegas Strip while riding in the passenger seat of Knight's BMW. The shooting came about two hours after a scuffle that involved Shakur and Knight in the lobby of the MGM Grand Hotel (an incident that ultimately led to Knight, 31, being handed a nine-year prison sentence for violating his parole). Six days later Shakur died from his injuries. He was 25. No arrests were ever made. In addition, despite calls within the hip-hop community to halt the violence, the Notorious B.I.G. was killed in a similar fashion six months later.

Like Elvis Presley and Jimi Hendrix before him, Shakur was soon the subject of a flood of posthumous album releases and rumors that he faked his death. The first release was *The Don Killuminati: The 7 Day Theory* (#1 pop, 1 R&B, 1996), released under the pseudonym Makaveli. It was followed by *R U Still Down? (Remember Me)* (#2 pop, #1 R&B, 1997), released on Amaru/Jive, an imprint headed by his mother. In 1997 his estate began a war of lawsuits against Death Row, complaining of $150 million in unpaid royalties, demanding the return of more than 150 unreleased master recordings, and a voiding of the rapper's contract with the label. A 1998 settlement awarded the tapes to Shakur's estate, which sanctioned the release that year of *Greatest Hits* (#3 pop, #1 R&B); it includes "Unconditional Love" (#73 R&B, 1998) and "Changes" (#32 pop, #12 R&B, 1999). "Do for Love" (#21 pop, #10 R&B, 1998) appears on *R U Still Down?* In 2001 the fourth posthumous collection, *Until the End of Time*, debuted at #1.

Shalamar

Formed 1977, Los Angeles, CA
Jeffrey Daniels (b. Aug. 24, 1957, Los Angeles), voc.; Jody Watley (b. Jan. 30, 1961, Chicago, IL), voc.; Howard Hewett (b. Oct. 1, 1957, Akron, OH), voc.
1978—*Disco Gardens* (Solar) 1979—*Big Fun* 1981—*Three for Love; Go for It* 1982—*Friends* 1983—*The Look* 1984—*Heart Break* (– Daniels; – Watley; + Delisa Davis, voc.; + Micki Free, voc.) 1985—(– Hewett; + Sidney Justin, voc.) 1987—*Circumstantial Evidence* 1990—*Wake Up.*
Howard Hewett solo: 1986—*I Commit to Love* (Elektra) 1988—*Forever and Ever* 1990—*Howard Hewett* 1995—*It's Time* (Caliber).
Jody Watley solo: see entry.

This good-looking vocal trio was comprised of black teen idols from the late '70s and early '80s; each pursued a successful solo career after leaving the group. The original Shalamar was made up of several L.A. session singers convened in 1977 by concert promoter Dick Griffey to record a medley of Motown dance hits, "Uptown Festival" (#25 pop, #10 R&B, 1977). With producer Leon Sylvers III, they had a dance hit with "Take That to the Bank" (#11 R&B, 1978), a lively number that was the model for other hits on Griffey's new Solar ("Sound of Los Angeles Records") label.

For a touring group, Griffey recruited Jeffrey Daniels and Jody Watley, two dancers from *Soul Train*, the television show hosted and produced by his friend and sometime business partner Don Cornelius. Howard Hewett joined after the original third member, Gerald Brown, left. "The Second Time Around" (#8 pop, #1 R&B, 1979) established them as stars; they followed up with "Right in the Socket" (#22 R&B, 1980), "Full of Fire" (#24 R&B, 1980), and "Make That Move" (#6 R&B, 1981).

Adding to their teen appeal was a real-life love triangle between Daniels, Watley, and singer Stephanie Mills. The two Shalamar singers had been childhood sweethearts, but after meeting Mills in New York, Daniels married the Broadway star; less than a year later, they were divorced—all of which was dramatically reported in teen magazines. In 1981 Shalamar released "This Is for the Lover in You" (#17 R&B, 1981) and "Sweeter as the Days Go By" (#19 R&B, 1981). The group's last two big hits were "Dead Giveaway" (#22 pop, #10 R&B, 1983) and "Dancing in the Sheets" (#17 pop, #18 R&B, 1984), the latter from the hit movie *Footloose* soundtrack.

Watley [see entry] left to pursue her solo ambitions. Daniels also quit. He moved to England, where he hosted that country's version of *Soul Train;* he also appeared in the West End production of *Starlight Express*. Hewett, the remaining member of the most successful lineup, left in 1985. His R&B hit singles include "I'm for Real" (#2 R&B, 1986), "Stay" (#8 R&B, 1986), "I Commit to Love" (#12 R&B, 1987),

"Strange Relationship" (#9, 1988), and "Show Me" (#2 R&B, 1990). In 1989 he married actress Nia Peeples. The new version of Shalamar placed a number of singles on the R&B chart, including "Games" (#11 R&B, 1987).

Sha Na Na

Formed 1969, New York, NY
Original lineup: Johnny Contardo, voc.; Scott Powell, voc; Frederick Dennis "Denny" Greene, voc.; Don York, voc.; Bruce Clarke, bass; John "Jocko" Marcellino, drums; Ritchie Joffe, voc.; Elliot Cahn, gtr.; Henry Gross, gtr.; Chris Donald, gtr.; Screamin' Scott Simon, piano, bass; John "Bowzer" Baumann, piano, voc.; Lennie Baker (b. Apr. 18, 1946, Whitman, MA), sax.
1969—*Rock & Roll Is Here to Stay* (Kama Sutra) 1971—*Sha Na Na* 1972—*The Night Is Still Young* 1973—*The Golden Age of Rock 'n' Roll; From the Streets of New York* 1974—*Hot Sox* 1975—*Sha Na Now* 1976—*Best of Sha Na Na* 1990—*34th & Vine* (Gold Castle) 1993—*The Sha Na Na 25th Anniversary Collection* (Laurie) 1999—*Rock 'n' Roll Dance Party* (The Gold Label).

Sha Na Na were forerunners of the '50s revival craze that eventually spawned television shows like *Happy Days* and the movie *Grease.* They began while students at Columbia University, making frequent appearances at the Fillmore East. Lennie Baker, who had played saxophone on '50s hits, was their claim to authenticity. Their big break was a booking at the Woodstock festival in 1969. The band's humor, choreography, and '50s costuming caught on. Though the band was never particularly successful on record, Sha Na Na became a popular live attraction, first on the rock & roll circuit, later in nightclubs. Their popularity reached unprecedented heights starting in 1977, when they began a syndicated TV show, which ran until 1981 and was shown around the world. They also appeared in the movie *Grease* (1978).

Over the years, personnel has been fluid, the most notable change being the departure of original guitarist Henry Gross in 1970 for a solo career, which was highlighted by the 1976 hit single "Shannon." John "Bowzer" Baumann went into television, cohosting a local L.A. morning show in the '80s. Screamin' Scott Simon cowrote "Sandy," which became a hit for John Travolta from the *Grease* soundtrack. Simon has also released solo albums.

As of 1994 Sha Na Na—with Jocko Marcellino, Donny York, Lennie Baker, and Screamin' Scott from the original lineup—made an appearance at the Woodstock '69 Reunion in Bethel, New York, and, the year before that, a two-week stint in the entertainment capital of the heartland, Branson, Missouri. Latterday members include Reggie De Leon, an actor and choreographer and furniture designer who appeared in *Stayin' Alive* and *White Men Can't Jump,* among other films; Chico Ryan, who had belonged to the Happenings and later toured with the Comets; Rob MacKenzie; Jimmy Wall; and Lisa, the group's first "greaserette."

In 1998 Sha Na Na celebrated its 30th anniversary, which loosely coincided with the 20th anniversary of *Grease.* Longtime member Ryan (b. David-Allan Ryan, Apr. 9, 1948, Arlington, MA), who spent 25 years with the ensemble, died shortly thereafter on July 26, 1998, in Boston. As of 2000 the group still performed over 100 nights per year, and Jocko, Donny, and Screamin' Scott remained in the lineup. The greasers still maintain a high profile at corporate, casino, fair and festival, and performing arts venues.

The Shangri-Las

Formed 1964, Queens, NY
Mary Ann Ganser (b. ca. 1948; d. 1971, NY), voc.; Marge Ganser, voc. (b. ca. 1948; d. Jul. 28, 1996); Liz (Betty) Weiss, voc.; Mary Weiss, voc.
1964—*Leader of the Pack* (Red Bird) 1965—*Shangri-Las '65* 1966—*I Can Never Go Home Anymore; Golden Hits* (Mercury) 1976—*Remember (Walking in the Sand)* EP (Charly, U.K.) 1996—*The Best of the Shangri-Las* (Mercury Chronicles).

Of the early-'60s girl vocal groups who rose meteorically to fame and disappeared nearly as quickly, one of the few white units was the Shangri-Las: two sets of sisters (the Gansers were twins) who first started singing together at Andrew Jackson High School in Queens. Their stock in trade was the teen-angst-ridden mini-melodramas written for them by George Morton, sometimes abetted by Jeff Barry and Ellie Greenwich.

In early 1964 they attracted the attention of writer/producer George "Shadow" Morton, who got the new Red Bird label (for which he was a producer) off the ground with the first Shangri-Las hit, his "Remember (Walkin' in the Sand)" (#5, 1964). A few months later, they recorded the motorcycle-gang melodrama "Leader of the Pack"—a typically showy Morton production complete with sound effects and talk-over sections—which was #1. A death-rock classic, "Leader of the Pack" showcased Mary Weiss' emotional, often overwrought delivery, which so perfectly suited the stories of teen runaways, parental death, and good teens gone bad that followed. Their other hits included "Maybe" (#91) and "Give Him a Great Big Kiss" (#18) in 1964; "Out in the Streets" (#53), "Give Us Your Blessings" (#29), "Right Now and Not Later" (#99), and "I Can Never Go Home Anymore" (#6) in 1965; and "Long Live Our Love" (#33), "He Cried" (#65, a remake of Jay and the Americans' "She Cried"), and "Past, Present and Future" (#59) in 1966.

The group, despite several in-and-out personnel shifts (Liz left early on, and the group remained a trio), was a top concert attraction in the U.S. and the U.K. in those years. But by the late '60s, a morass of legal entanglements, poor chart showings, and a low royalty rate on their biggest hits conspired to bring the Shangri-Las to an end. All four married. Mary Ann Ganser died of encephalitis in 1971. In 1989 the three surviving Shangri-Las reunited for the first time in over 20 years; they occasionally performed in the '90s. Marge Ganser succumbed to breast cancer in 1996. She was 48.

Del Shannon

Born Charles Westover, Dec. 30, 1939, Coopersville, MI; died Feb. 8, 1990, Santa Clarita, CA
1961—*Runaway* (Big Top) 1963—*Little Town Flirt* 1965—*Handy Man* (Amy); *Sings Hank Williams; 1,661 Seconds* 1966—*This Is My Bag* (Liberty); *Total Commitment* 1967—*Best of* (Dot) 1968—*Further Adventures of Charles Westover* 1970—*Del Shannon Sings* (Post) 1973—*Live in England* (United Artists); *Best of* (Polydor) 1975—*Vintage Years* (Sire) 1981—*Drop Down and Get Me* (Elektra) 1990—*Greatest Hits* (Bug/Rhino) 1991—*Rock On!* (Gone Gator/MCA).

With hit songs like "Runaway" and "Hats Off to Larry," Del Shannon was one of the few early rockers who wrote his own material and held his own through the British Invasion. Shannon was 14 when he learned guitar and began performing in school shows. After graduating high school, he took his stage name from those of a friend (Mark Shannon) and his boss's car (a Cadillac Coupe de Ville). In early 1960 a Grand Rapids area disc jockey passed live tapes of Shannon on to manager/publishers Harry Balk and Irving Micahnik, who then signed Shannon to Detroit's Big Top label. Big Top sent him to New York to record, but not much came of it.

On a second trip to New York, Shannon recorded "Runaway," which—with its galloping beat, Max Crook's protosynthesizer Musitron solo, and Shannon's nearly hiccuping falsetto vocals—went to #1 in 1961. He followed up with "Hats Off to Larry" (#5), "So Long Baby" (#28) and "Hey! Little Girl" (#38) in 1961; and "Little Town Flirt" (#12) in 1962. He first toured England in 1962 and the next year met the Beatles there. His version of Lennon-McCartney's "From Me to You" made Shannon the first American to cover a Beatles tune.

In 1963 Shannon had legal problems with Balk and Micahnik; the action instituted that year dragged on for the next decade. Still, he had more hits with "Keep Searchin' (We'll Follow the Sun)" (#9, 1964) and "Stranger in Town" (#30) in 1965. That year Peter and Gordon recorded Shannon's "I Go to Pieces." In 1966 Shannon signed to Liberty, where producer Snuff Garrett and arranger Leon Russell tried to mold him into a teen idol. When Tommy Boyce asked Shannon to record "Action," the theme for the TV rock show *Where the Action Is,* Shannon turned him down and gave the song instead to Freddy Cannon. The *Total Commitment* LP, belying its title, was almost all covers. In England in 1967, Shannon recorded an album with Andrew Loog Oldham called *Home and Away* (Nicky Hopkins and John Paul Jones played on it).

With his career on the wane, Shannon left Liberty in 1969 and concentrated on production work. He arranged the 1969 hit "Baby It's You" by Smith and produced Brian Hyland's 1970 hit "Gypsy Woman." In England he recorded tracks with Jeff Lynne of the Electric Light Orchestra (including "Cry Baby Cry"). In 1974 Dave Edmunds produced Shannon's "And the Music Plays On." The next year, Shannon signed to Island and released a cover of the Zombies hit "Tell Her No." During 1976 and 1977, Shannon suffered from alcoholism,

Del Shannon

but beginning in 1979 he returned to music. He recorded material under the production supervision of longtime fan Tom Petty, with Petty's band the Heartbreakers backing him. The album included "Sea of Love," which hit #33 in early 1982.

Through the remainder of the decade Shannon continued to perform, although he was financially secure. He was reportedly suffering from depression and had been highly agitated after 15 days on Prozac when he committed suicide by shooting himself in the head. Shannon's wife contends that her husband's suicide was a direct result of the Prozac, a claim the drug's manufacturer denies. Del Shannon was inducted into the Rock and Roll Hall of Fame in 1999.

Roxanne Shanté

Born Lolita Shanté Gooden, Mar. 8, 1970, New York, NY
1989—*Bad Sister* (Cold Chillin') 1992—*The Bitch Is Back* (Livin' Large) 1995—*Greatest Hits* (Cold Chillin').

Roxanne Shanté was one of the first women to directly challenge sexism in rap. At age 14 she recorded "Roxanne's Revenge" (#22 R&B, 1985), an answer to the popular U.T.F.O. song "Roxanne, Roxanne," which dissed women who ignored the band's advances. "Revenge," produced by Shanté's neighbor in the Queensbridge projects, Marley Marl, became an underground hit even before it was pressed to vinyl and kicked off a slew of answer records. U.T.F.O. themselves tried to clarify their position by recording with a woman they dubbed "the Real Roxanne." The group also forced Marl and Shanté to rerecord "Revenge," which sampled an original U.T.F.O. riff. Ultimately, Shanté's tough, street-smart style bested all other Roxannes.

Shanté followed her success with more Marl-produced singles. "Queen of Rox (Shanté Rox On)" was her summation of the "perils of Roxanne," while the lyrics to "Have a Nice Day" and "Go on Girl" were written by Big Daddy Kane. In

1988 she recorded "Loosey's Rap" (#1 R&B, 1988) with Rick James. Shanté toured extensively, then had a baby. She finally recorded an album in 1989; *Bad Sister* (#52 R&B, 1989) showed Shanté was a formidable rapper with a dirty mouth; tracks like "Knockin' Hiney" and "Feelin' Kinda Horny" followed the tradition of her hero, Millie Jackson. On her second album Shanté dropped the name Roxanne. *The Bitch Is Back* (#82 R&B, 1992) featured a variety of producers, including Kool G Rap, The Large Professor, and Grandmaster Flash, but failed to make much of a commercial impact.

In 1995 Shanté performed as part of Old School Throwdown III, a multi-act revue featuring hip-hop pioneers hosted by radio station Hot 97 at New York City's Paramount Theater. That same year she released a greatest-hits album, including the new single "Queen Pin." In 1996 she put out another single, "Bite This," a collaboration with rapper Craig G.

Billy Joe Shaver

Born Aug. 16, 1939, Corsicana, TX
1973—*Old Five and Dimers Like Me* (Monument) 1976—*When I Get My Wings* (Capricorn) 1977—*Gypsy Boy* 1981—*I'm Just an Old Chunk of Coal . . . But I'm Gonna Be a Diamond Someday* (Columbia) 1982—*Billy Joe Shaver* 1987—*Salt of the Earth* 1995—*Restless Wind: The Legendary Billy Joe Shaver 1973–1987* (Razor & Tie).
As Shaver (with Eddy Shaver [b. John Edwin Shaver, June 20, 1962, Waco, TX; d. Dec. 31, 2000, Waco], gtr.): 1993—*Tramp on Your Street* (Zoo/Praxis) 1995—*Unshaven: Live at Smith's Olde Bar* 1996—*Highway of Life* (Justice) 1998—*Victory* (New West) 1999—*Electric Shaver* 2001—*The Earth Rolls On.*
With Willie Nelson, Waylon Jennings, and Kris Kristofferson: 1999—*Honky Tonk Heroes* (Pedernales/FreeFalls).
Eddy Shaver solo: 1996—*Baptism of Fire* (Dixie Frog, Can.).

When Waylon Jennings kick-started the "outlaw" country movement of the '70s with his 1973 album *Honky Tonk Heroes,* he didn't do it alone. Every song but one on the album was penned by Billy Joe Shaver, a fellow Texan who focused on songwriting after a stint in the Navy and working a series of manual labor jobs, including an ill-fated tenure at a sawmill that claimed half the fingers on his right hand. Shaver's songs on Jennings' *Honky Tonk Heroes,* and his own, Kris Kristofferson–produced debut, *Old Five and Dimers Like Me* (also released in 1973), established him as a cult hero and one of the most respected song poets of the Lone Star State. Although he has never enjoyed commercial success on the level of Jennings or Willie Nelson, Shaver's hardscrabble and almost exclusively autobiographical songs have been covered by such artists as Kristofferson, Johnny Cash, Elvis Presley, John Anderson, and Patty Loveless.

Beginning in 1976, Shaver's road band featured his gifted guitarist son Eddy, who cut his first session with his father at age 12 and was on the road with him by age 14. After Eddy coproduced his father's 1987 set *Salt of the Earth,* the pair began touring and recording together under the band name Shaver. Their 1993 Shaver debut, *Tramp on Your Street,* showcased Eddy's classic hard rock– and blues-inspired electric guitar heroics and was widely regarded as one of the strongest albums of Billy Joe's career. Producer Brendan O'Brien (Pearl Jam) captured their high-octane live show on 1995's *Unshaven,* while 1998's *Victory,* named after Billy Joe's mother, focused on Billy Joe's gospel songs and his son's acoustic slide and finger-picking skills. The following year's *Electric Shaver* marked a return to the band's more familiar roadhouse roar, but on the morning of December 31, 2000, Eddy Shaver overdosed on heroin in a motel room. *The Earth Rolls On,* finished shortly before his death, was released in the spring of 2001.

Jules Shear

Born Jules Mark Shear, Apr. 7, 1952, Pittsburgh, PA
1983—*Watch Dog* (EMI America); *Jules* EP 1985—*The Eternal Return* 1987—*Demo-Itis* (Enigma) 1989—*The Third Party* (I.R.S.) 1992—*The Great Puzzle* (Polydor) 1993—*Horse of a Different Color: The Jules Shear Collection 1976–1989* (Razor & Tie) 1994—*Healing Bones* (Polydor) 1998—*Between Us* (High Street) 2000—*Allow Me* (Zoë/Rounder).
With Funky Kings: 1976—*Funky Kings* (Arista).
With Jules and the Polar Bears: 1978—*Got No Breeding* (Columbia) 1979—*Fenetiks* 1996—*Bad for Business* (Columbia Legacy).
With Reckless Sleepers: 1988—*Big Boss Sounds* (I.R.S.).

A prolific songwriter and recording artist, Jules Shear is widely respected by critics and musicians for his glowing melodies and wry, insightful lyrics. Both with bands and on his own, Shear has produced smart, graceful music that has inspired comparisons to guitar pop heroes from the Byrds to Elvis Costello. Commercial success has nonetheless eluded the singer, whose songs have thus far only become pop hits when covered by other artists: Cyndi Lauper took his "All Through the Night" to #5 in 1984, and in 1986 the Bangles reached #10 with another wistful Shear ballad, "If She Knew What She Wants."

Shear began writing songs as a teenager, and his career epiphany came while visiting music clubs during a trip to L.A. after his junior year of college. Rather than return to school, he lingered in the city, and in 1976 formed the band Funky Kings with two older minstrels, Jack Tempchin and Richard Stekol. The trio released one album before Shear left to form Jules and the Polar Bears, whose albums of buoyant rock received excellent reviews.

Shear disbanded the Polar Bears in 1980 (the band's third album was finally released in 1996) and relocated to Boston, where he embarked on a solo career, releasing several acclaimed albums. During this time he became romantically involved with Aimee Mann; their breakup was the topic of much of Mann's final 'Til Tuesday album. In 1986 Shear formed the band Reckless Sleepers with the Cars' guitarist Elliot Easton and two studio veterans. The band quickly split up, due to Shear's dissatisfaction with its hard-rock approach, but reemerged minus Easton (and plus session guitarist Jimmy Vivino) in 1988, with *Big Boss Sounds*. Shear went his own way again for 1989's *The Third Party,* which set his Dylanesque vocals against stark guitar work by the Church's Marty Willson-Piper. Shear's wife at the time, Pal Shazar, contributed vocals to the title track of his 1992 solo effort, *The Great Puzzle,* which he recorded in Woodstock, New York, where he had moved from Boston. Shear also helped conceive MTV's popular *Unplugged* series, which he hosted from 1989 until 1991.

Shear's 1998 effort, *Between Us,* was a melancholy collection of duets mostly reflecting on his separation from Shazar. Shear's duet partners included Carole King, Paula Cole, Rosanne Cash, Curtis Stigers, and Shears' own brother, Rob. The tone of *Allow Me,* released two years later, was more upbeat. Guest vocalists on this album included Vicki Peterson of the Bangles.

Duncan Sheik

Born Nov. 18, 1969, Montclair, NJ
1996—*Duncan Sheik* (Atlantic) 1998—*Humming* 2001—*Phantom Moon* (Nonesuch).

Duncan Sheik's postalternative brand of singer/songwriter music is inspired more by the ambient-based sounds of the Cocteau Twins and Brian Eno and the late English bard Nick Drake than by '70s Southern California icons like Jackson Browne and Joni Mitchell. And Sheik's big break came in a very '90s way: "Barely Breathing" (#18 pop, 1996), from his self-titled debut album, appeared in the hit TV series *ER*.

Duncan Sheik

Raised in New Jersey and South Carolina, Sheik learned to play piano before he was five years old. He eventually picked up the guitar, and by the '80s was playing in cover bands. During the early '90s, he attended Brown University, where he studied semiotics, played in a band with fellow singer/songwriter Lisa Loeb, and recorded a demo track with Tracee Ellis Ross, the daughter of Diana Ross.

In 1992 Tracee Ross delivered the track she had recorded with Sheik to her mother's entertainment lawyer; within six months Sheik had a solo record deal with Atlantic. After moving to L.A. Sheik appeared on a 1993 album by His Boy Elroy, on Epic Records. He recorded his Atlantic debut in France with producer Rupert Hine (Howard Jones, Tina Turner). For his second solo album, the more personal *Humming,* Sheik traveled to El Cortijo, Spain, where he recorded again with Hine. In 2001 he released the atmospheric *Phantom Moon* on Nonesuch.

Pete Shelley: See the Buzzcocks

Shep and the Limelites

Formed 1961, Queens, NY
James "Shep" Sheppard (b. ca. 1936, Queens; d. Jan. 24, 1970, Long Island, NY), voc.; Clarence Bassett, voc.; Charles Baskerville, voc.

As lead singer of the Heartbeats, James Sheppard wrote and recorded "A Thousand Miles Away," which, though it only hit #5 on the R&B chart and #53 on the pop chart, remains one of the best-remembered doo-wop ballads of the era. The group was also notable among its doo-wop contemporaries for being a trio, as opposed to the more common quartet and quintet lineups.

In 1961 he formed Shep and the Limelites and hit big with "Daddy's Home" (#2 pop, #4 R&B). Over the next year and a half, they hit the Hot 100 with five more entries, but none went higher than #42. Interestingly, they formed a song cycle, detailing the ongoing relationship and lives of the characters in the first hit. And so it was followed by "Three Steps From the Altar," "Our Anniversary," "What Did Daddy Do," and "Remember Baby." The group disbanded after a final single in 1967, "I'm a Hurting Inside."

Sheppard was found dead in 1970 in his automobile on the Long Island Expressway after having been robbed and beaten. In 1982, with "A Thousand Miles Away" featured on the soundtrack of *Diner,* Sheppard's Limelites played some doo-wop revival concerts at places like New York's Bottom Line.

Bobby Sherman

Born July 18, 1943, Santa Monica, CA
1969—*Bobby Sherman* (Metromedia) 1970—*Here Comes Bobby; With Love, Bobby* 1971—*Portrait of Bobby; Getting Together* 1972—*Bobby Sherman's Greatest Hits* 1991—

The Very Best of Bobby Sherman (Restless); *The Bobby Sherman Christmas Album.*

Bobby Sherman was a teenybopper heartthrob who had talent. Besides singing and acting, Sherman also played guitar, piano, trumpet, trombone, French horn, drums, and sitar. He'd begun performing in school, but rather than going into show business, he first entered college in California to major in psychology. He later told an interviewer, "I gave up psychology because I realized I was a schizo and belonged in show business with the rest of them." Actually he was disovered by an agent and cast in the television series *Shindig!* where he was a regular from 1964 to 1966. Sherman began writing tunes and making record company rounds, eventually getting some work as a record producer, but none of his early singles clicked.

After *Shindig!* was canceled, Sherman went on to star in the ABC series *Here Come the Brides.* His first hit was 1969's "Little Woman," which made #3 and earned a gold record, and the hits kept coming: "La La La (If I Had You)" (#9, 1969), "Easy Come, Easy Go" (#9, 1970), "Hey, Mister Sun" (#24, 1970), "Julie, Do Ya Love Me" (#5, 1970), "Cried Like a Baby" (#16, 1971), and "The Drum" (#29, 1971). After that, Sherman's record sales fell off. His last bubblegum single was 1972's "Together Again," a tie-in to a failed *Partridge Family* spinoff series. Before and since, Sherman made a number of television guest appearances, on *The Monkees, The Love Boat, Emergency, Fantasy Island, Lobo, Murder, She Wrote,* and *The Mod Squad.* He was also in the 1983 film *Get Crazy.*

As of 2001 Sherman worked as a certified EMT (emergency medical technician), a technical reserve officer with the L.A. Police Department, and a reserve deputy sheriff in San Bernardino County. He also served as a medical training officer at the L.A. Police Academy. In addition, he has sometimes worked as a producer, guest star, director, and composer, primarily for television. His autobiography, *Bobby Sherman: Remembering You,* was published in 1996. He toured the nostalgia circuit in the late '90s.

Shinehead

Born Edmund Carl Aiken, Apr. 10, 1962, London, Eng.
1986—*Rough and Rugged* (African Love Music) 1988—*Unity* (Elektra) 1990—*The Real Rock* 1992—*Sidewalk University* 1995—*Toddin'* 1999—*Praises* (VP).

Shinehead was one of the first artists to fuse reggae and rap styles. He grew up in Jamaica and moved to the Bronx as a teen. After his mom gave him a microphone, he quit college to pursue his love of music. He began toasting in 1982 with the Downbeat International mobile sound system and was a member of the early-'80s African Love Soundsystem. Shinehead's first single was a reggae version of Michael Jackson's "Billie Jean," released in 1984.

Shinehead's debut album was issued on producer Claude Evans' label, African Love Music. It introduced the roots-rock rapper's unique and often wacky style. The track "Who the Cap Fits," based on a Bob Marley tune, was picked up by New York radio stations and became an underground hit. Elektra signed Shinehead and released *Unity,* which includes remixes of some tracks from *Rough and Rugged.* Run-D.M.C.'s Jam Master Jay produced three cuts. The title track, based on the Beatles' "Come Together," calls for rappers to join together and stop dissing each other. The album features Jamaican session band Roots Radics.

On *The Real Rock,* Shinehead shows off his knack for mimicry and odd inspiration with versions of songs by Sly and the Family Stone, Frank Sinatra, and the Everly Brothers. Shinehead continued to offer positive messages, and with his band No Offense Crew, had a strong live following. On *Sidewalk University* Shinehead covers Sting, Paul McCartney, and Stevie Wonder. The single "Try My Love" was a modest hit. In the summer of 1993 Shinehead headlined the Reggae Sunsplash Tour.

Commercial success nevertheless eluded the singer, prompting Elektra to drop him after the release of *Toddin'* (1995). However, Shinehead continued to tour and play festivals; he also won DJ of the Year honors at the inaugural Tamika Reggae Awards held at Manhattan's Lincoln Center in 1998. *Praises,* a 1999 album that included "Collie Weed," a reworking of Seals and Crofts' "Summer Breeze," found Shinehead back in the studio with Jamaica's Roots Radics. He also appeared on one track on Fatboy Slim's [see entry] 2000 album, *The Fatboy Slim/Norman Cook Collection.*

The Shirelles

Formed 1958, Passaic, NJ
Shirley Owens Alston (b. June 10, 1941, Passaic), lead voc.; Addie "Micki" Harris (b. Jan. 22, 1940, Passaic; d. June 10, 1982, Los Angeles, CA), voc.; Doris Coley Kenner (b. Doris Coley, Aug. 2, 1941, Goldsboro, NC; d. Feb. 4, 2000, Sacramento, CA), voc.; Beverly Lee (b. Aug. 3, 1941, Passaic), voc.
1961—*Tonight's the Night* (Scepter); *The Shirelles Sing* 1962—*Baby It's You; Greatest Hits* 1964—*Foolish Little Girl* 1972—*The Shirelles* (RCA) 1982—(– Harris; + Louie Bethune, voc.) 1986—*Anthology* (Rhino) 1995—*The World's Greatest Girl Group.*

One of the first of the late-'50s and early-'60s girl groups and among the few to write their own hits, the Shirelles were also one of the most enduring. The four girls began singing together at school shows and parties. A classmate, Mary Jane Greenberg, heard them singing one of their compositions, "I Met Him on a Sunday." Mary Jane convinced them to bring the song to her mother, Florence, who was in the music business. The Shirelles auditioned in Florence Greenberg's living room and were signed to Greenberg's Tiara label. In early 1958 "I Met Him on a Sunday" had garnered so much airplay that Decca Records bought it; it was on the pop chart for over two months, reaching #49. Greenberg formed her own independent Scepter Records and in 1959 she released the Shirelles' cover of the Five Royales' "Dedicated to the One I

Love." Without a national distributor, the disc only reached #83 on the pop chart. In 1960 the Shirelles scored with "Tonight's the Night" (#39 pop, #14 R&B), a song cowritten by lead vocalist Shirley Owens and produced by her cowriter, Luther Dixon, formerly of the Four Buddies.

Within a year, the Shirelles had their first #1 pop hit (#2 R&B) with the Carole King–Gerry Goffin composition "Will You Love Me Tomorrow?" Scepter rereleased "Dedicated to the One I Love," and it joined "Will You" in the Top 10 for a while early in 1961.

The Shirelles became regulars on disc jockey Murray the K's Brooklyn all-star rock shows. In mid-1961 "Mama Said" (by Dixon and W. Denson) reached #4 pop, #2 R&B, and early in 1962 "Baby It's You" (by Burt Bacharach, Hal David, and Barney Williams) went to #8 pop, #3 R&B. A few months later, "Soldier Boy," a first take recorded initially as album filler, became their second #1 pop single (#3 R&B) and their biggest seller. Then Dixon (who had cowritten "Soldier Boy") left Scepter, precipitating the Shirelles' decline, although their first post-Dixon single, "Foolish Little Girl," went to #4 pop, #9 R&B in 1963.

In 1963 the Beatles covered the Shirelles' "Baby It's You" and "Boys" on their first U.K. LP. The Shirelles continued to perform and record, finally breaking up in the late '60s, then re-forming, sometimes with different members, in the early '70s to play revival concerts. Their later career was no doubt stymied by a contractual provision that prohibited any member who left the group from ever using the Shirelles name.

In 1994, at a Rhythm & Blues Foundation awards ceremony, the three surviving members sang together for the first time in 19 years. Addie Harris had died in 1982 of a heart attack. Shortly thereafter, the remaining original members reunited, sang on a Dionne Warwick album, and began performing again in various reunited permutations. In 1996 they were inducted into the Rock and Roll Hall of Fame. Doris Coley (by then, Doris Kenner-Jackson) died of breast cancer in 2000.

Shirley and Lee/Shirley and Company

Shirley Goodman (b.Shirley Pixley, June 19, 1936, New Orleans, LA), voc.; Leonard Lee (b. June 29, 1935; d. Oct. 23, 1976, New Orleans), voc.
Shirley and Lee: 1960—*Let the Good Times Roll* (Warwick) 1990—*Shirley and Lee* (EMI).
Shirley and Company: 1975—*Shame, Shame, Shame* (Vibration).

Shirley and Lee, who recorded "Let the Good Times Roll" in 1956, were known as "the sweethearts of the blues." Many of their records were supposed to tell the continuing story of their on-again/off-again romance. Long after the duo had gone their separate ways and had stopped making New Orleans R&B hits, Shirley resurfaced in 1975 with the disco hit "Shame, Shame, Shame" (#12 pop, #1 R&B).

Shirley Goodman and Leonard Lee were discovered by New Orleans studio owner Cosimo Matassa when 30 local children, including Shirley and Lee, collected nickels to make a two-dollar demo record of "I'm Gone" at Matassa's studio. Matassa dispatched Eddie Mesner of Aladdin Records to track down the teenaged Shirley and Lee, and they rerecorded "I'm Gone" with ace New Orleans producer Dave Bartholomew. The tune was a #2 R&B hit in 1952. Their lovestory songs were minor early-'50s R&B hits, but the big hit was "Let the Good Times Roll," a #2 R&B hit that also did well on the pop chart (#20) in 1956 and eventually sold over a million copies. Despite Shirley's unique quavery soprano, the duo didn't catch on with white audiences—and their only followup was "I Feel Good" (#38 pop, #5 R&B, 1956).

In 1960 they began recording for Warwick and had three Top 100 hits, including a 1960 remake of "Let the Good Times Roll" (#48). They split up in 1963, and Shirley briefly worked with West Coast singer Jesse Hill (of "Ooh Poo Pah Doo" fame) as Shirley and Jesse. She later did sessions for New Orleans–based performers like Harold Battiste and Dr. John. Lee recorded a few singles as Leonard Lee for Imperial and Broadside in the mid-'60s. In 1972 the pair reunited for one of Richard Nader's Rock & Roll Revival shows.

In 1975 Shirley teamed up with an anonymous crew of studio musicians to record the smash hit "Shame, Shame, Shame," one of the first disco songs. It was cowritten and produced by Sylvia Robinson of Mickey and Sylvia.

Michelle Shocked

Born Michelle Johnston, Feb. 24, 1962, Dallas, TX
1986—*The Texas Campfire Tapes* (Cooking Vinyl/Mercury) 1988—*Short Sharp Shocked* (Mercury) 1989—*Captain Swing* 1992—*Arkansas Traveler* 1994—*Kind-Hearted Woman* (self-released) 1996—*Mercury Poise: 1988–1995* (Polygram); *Kind-Hearted Woman* (Private Music; rerecorded and rereleased version of 1994 album); *Artists Make Lousy Slaves* (self-released) 1998—*Good News.*

Michelle Shocked's music is as unique and well-traveled as its bohemian author: a downhome hobo and squatter whose albums have shown her adept at bluegrass, rock, punk, soul, and country. Shocked grew up on various army bases until she was 14, when her stepfather retired to the small East Texas town of Gilmer. She ran away from home at 16, and in 1979 moved to Dallas to live with her father, a hippie-ish schoolteacher who had introduced Shocked to music in previous summers by taking her to bluegrass festivals and backporch picking sessions.

Shocked attended the University of Texas in Austin for a couple years, but quit and moved to San Francisco, where she became involved in hardcore punk and squatter activism. After returning to Austin in 1983, her mother, a fundamentalist member of the Church of Jesus Christ of Latter-Day Saints (a Mormon), had Shocked committed to a psychiatric hospital for a month, until the insurance ran out. Homeless, Shocked was institutionalized again and jailed a few times for political protests; during one of these experiences she decided to change her name. She lived in New York in the mid-'80s, becoming active in the squatter and "antifolk" movements of Manhattan's Lower East Side. After Ronald Reagan was reelected in 1984, Shocked moved to Amsterdam, although the experience of being raped in Europe ruptured her expatriate dreams.

In May 1986 she returned to Texas and volunteered at the Kerrville Folk Festival. Pete Lawrence, an English producer and label owner, overheard her playing for friends around a campfire and recorded Shocked on a Sony Walkman. He released the recording, crickets chirping in the background and all, and *The Texas Campfire Tapes* went to #1 on the U.K. indie chart. The avowed anarchist suddenly had multinational corporations offering her six-figure contracts; Shocked reputedly turned down a percentage of PolyGram's advance offer in a bid for artistic control.

She had to fight for that control, however. When the label sent her to Dwight Yoakam producer Pete Anderson to produce her first album, Shocked read him a protest statement before she would proceed. He eventually convinced her of his integrity, and in two weeks they recorded *Short Sharp Shocked,* a brilliantly catchy album that got critical raves and some radio play with "When I Grow Up" and "Anchorage." The album showed Shocked was not just a folky but a skilled songwriter with serious rock and pop potential (as well as the ability to play hardcore, on one track with punk band M.D.C.). With an ode to slain graffiti artist Michael Stewart and a cover featuring a photo of Shocked in the stranglehold of a San Francisco riot police officer, Shocked also got her political say.

Anderson returned to produce *Captain Swing,* but the album, which was R&B-oriented, was less well received. Some critics knocked Shocked for shying away from politics, although the album was named after a 19th-century term for industrial sabotage, and the first track was "God Is a Real Estate Developer."

On *Arkansas Traveler* Shocked indulged her wanderlust, recording different tracks in different cities with favorite artists, including Pops Staples, Levon Helm, Red Clay Ramblers, Taj Mahal, Don Was, Hothouse Flowers, Uncle Tupelo, Clarence "Gatemouth" Brown, Doc Watson, and Alison Krauss. She said the album completed a trilogy of tributes to her influences: Texas songwriters and honky-tonk on *Short Sharp Shocked,* jump blues and swing on *Captain Swing,* and fiddle tunes on *Arkansas Traveler.* The album included her own compositions as well as versions of classic minstrel songs and a Woody Guthrie tune. Her attempt to make a political comment on minstrelsy's role in American music by posing in blackface on the album cover, however, was stopped by her record company.

Stating in 1993 that "I am taking responsibility for my own creativity," Shocked began making moves to leave Mercury. Early the next year, she fired her manager and sued the label for failing to honor the creative control clause of her contract. She then recorded and self-released the album *Kind-Hearted Woman,* which was available for sale only at her performances. Shocked settled her lawsuit with Mercury out of court (the suit cited the 13th Amendment abolishing slavery). She got in one last dig, though, by titling her 1996 anthology *Mercury Poise,* a nod to "Mercury Poisoning," Graham Parker's spleen-venting 1978 rant against the label. The compilation also featured three new songs, including "The Quality of Mercy," which first appeared on the *Dead Man Walking* soundtrack.

In 1996 Shocked signed a deal with Private Music, which rereleased *Kind-Hearted Woman* after the singer rerecorded some of its tracks with producer Bones Howe. *Artists Make Lousy Slaves* (1996) and *Good News* (1998) were both DIY projects Shocked sold at her shows.

Wayne Shorter: See Weather Report

Shriekback

Formed 1981, London, Eng.
Dave Allen (b. Dec. 23, 1955, Cambria, Eng.), bass; Barry Andrews (b. Sep. 12, 1956, Lambeth, Eng.), voc., kybds.; Martyn Barker (b. Sep. 9, 1959, Merseyside, Eng.), drums; Carl Marsh, gtr., voc.
1982—*Tench* EP (Y America) 1983—*Care* (Warner Bros.) 1984—*Jam Science* (Arista, U.K.) 1985—*Oil and Gold* (Island) (– Marsh; + Mike Cozzi [b. Nov. 27, 1960, Usk, Wales], gtr.) 1986—*Big Night Music* (– Allen; + Doug Wimbish [b. Sep. 22, 1956, Hartford, CT], bass) 1988—*Go Bang!* 1990—*The Dancing Years* 1992—(– Wimbish; + Allen) *Sacred City* (World Domination) 1994—*Natural History* (Castle) 2000—*Naked Apes & Pond Life* (Mushroom, U.K.); *Best of Shriekback: The Y Record Years* (Castle).

With the pedigree of Gang of Four bassist Dave Allen and XTC singer/keyboard player Barry Andrews, Shriekback plays smart, tuneful funk. But with a career marred by personnel and record company problems, the band has never gathered the momentum necessary for wider popularity. Andrews and Allen joined forces when they found themselves without bands in summer 1981. Adding guitarist/vocalist Carl Marsh and a drum machine, they recorded *Tench* for the independent Y America label in 1982. With Martyn Barker aboard on drums, next year's *Care* (#188) was picked up by Warner Bros., which quickly dropped it. The band's next album, 1984's *Jam Science,* was released by Arista in Europe and the U.K. only. It was notable for its slicker sound, buttressed by synthesized strings and female backing vocals. Next on Island Records, Shriekback's *Oil and Gold,* released in America, had a harsher, rockier sound; although it contained the club favorite "Nemesis," the album did not chart, and Marsh left after its release. He was briefly replaced by former Voidoid Ivan Julian. Following the release of the dark, piano-based *Big Night Music* (#145, 1987), Dave Allen left to form King Swamp, leaving Andrews the lone original member. Doug Wimbish, later of Living Colour, took his place, while Mike Cozzi took on guitar chores. This band appears on the playful, kinetic *Go Bang!* (#169, 1988).

Shriekback disbanded in 1989. Drummer Martyn Barker joined Allen in King Swamp, while Andrews formed Illuminati. Soon after, Allen went on to start Low Pop Suicide. In 1992 Shriekback reunited, with Allen joining Andrews and

Barker, and released *Sacred City* on Allen's World Domination label. Busy with the label, upon which he released his first solo album, *The Elastic Purejoy*, Allen departed Shriekback in 1994. The band carried on, however, touring Europe and attempting to sign to a new label.

The Silos

Formed 1985, New York, NY
Bob Rupe (b. Sep. 16, 1956, MI), gtr., voc.; Walter Salas-Humara (b. June 21, 1961, New York), gtr., voc.; Mary Rowell (b. Sep. 6, 1958, Newport, VT), violin.
1985—*About Her Steps* (Record Collect) 1987—*Cuba* 1990—(– Rowell) *The Silos* (RCA) 1992—(– Rupe; + Rowell) *Hasta La Victoria* (Normal Records, Ger.) 1994—*Susan Across the Ocean* (Watermelon) 1997—*Long Green Boat* (Last Call) 1998—*Heater* (Checkered Past).
Walter Salas-Humara solo: 1988—*Lagartija* (Record Collect) 1995—*Radar* (Watermelon).
Walter Salas-Humara with the Setters: 1993—*The Setters* (Million Miles, Ger.).

The Silos were created by Walter Salas-Humara and Bob Rupe, and included violinist Mary Rowell and a revolving group of backing musicians. The group's rough-hewn, unaffected, but catchy take on folk rock made them critical favorites in the mid-'80s. Recording and distributing their first two albums themselves, the Silos evinced a commercial independence and a stripped-down aesthetic that blazed the trail for later "alternative" bands.

In the early '80s Salas-Humara led the Vulgar Boatmen in Gainesville, Florida, while Rupe was part of Fort Lauderdale's Bobs. Although they knew each other in Florida, they did not form the Silos until they had separately moved to New York within six months of each other.

To help secure gigs for their band, Salas-Humara and Rupe recorded *About Her Steps,* pressing 1,000 copies on their own Record Collect label. The album was reviewed both in the States and the U.K., garnering comparisons to the Velvet Underground, the Byrds, and R.E.M. In 1989 RCA signed the band. By the time their major-label debut was released in 1990, their A&R person had left the label, the album languished, and the group was eventually dropped.

Salas-Humara and Rupe parted ways in 1991. Salas-Humara kept the Silos name, continuing to perform and record with Rowell and assorted musicians; Rupe played briefly with Gutterball, appearing on the group's eponymously titled album in 1993. Rupe played bass for Cracker [see entry] on their 1994 tour and later joined the group. In addition to recording the solo effort *Lagartija,* Salas-Humara joined Austin, Texas, residents Alejandro Escovedo (Rank & File, True Believers) and Michael Hall (Wild Seeds) in a side project called the Setters, issuing a self-titled album.

In 1994 the Silos released *Susan Across the Ocean,* a more rock-leaning effort that included covers of Jonathan Richman's "I'm Straight" and Lucinda Williams' "Change the Locks." The record was dedicated to Manuel Verzosa, a singer/guitarist on the album who died in an auto accident just prior to its release. Salas-Humara followed *Susan* with another solo album, a noisy, discordant record called *Radar. Heater,* a 1998 project released under the Silos moniker, veered even further away from conventional guitar rock, incorporating beats and loops into the band's otherwise rootsy approach.

Carly Simon

Born June 25, 1945, New York, NY
1971—*Carly Simon* (Elektra); *Anticipation* 1972—*No Secrets* 1973—*Hotcakes* 1974—*Playing Possum* 1975—*Best of Carly Simon* 1976—*Another Passenger* 1978—*Boys in the Trees* 1979—*Spy* 1980—*Come Upstairs* (Warner Bros.) 1981—*Torch* 1983—*Hello, Big Man* 1985—*Spoiled Girl* 1986—*Heartburn* soundtrack (Arista) 1987—*Coming Around Again* 1988—*Working Girl* soundtrack 1989—*Greatest Hits Live* 1990—*My Romance; Have You Seen Me Lately?; Postcards From the Edge* soundtrack 1992—*This Is My Life* soundtrack (Qwest) 1994—*Letters Never Sent* (Arista) 1995—*Clouds in My Coffee 1965–1995* 1997—*Film Noir* 2000—*The Bedroom Tapes.*

Singer/songwriter/composer Carly Simon was born into an affluent, musical family. Her father, a cofounder of Simon & Schuster publishers, played classical piano in his spare time; one sister, Lucy, is a folksinger and composer (she wrote the score for the musical *The Secret Garden*); another, Joanna, is an opera singer.

Simon left Sarah Lawrence College to work as a folk duo with Lucy. They played New York clubs as the Simon Sisters, breaking up when Lucy got married. The Simon Sisters cut an LP for Kapp and had a minor hit in 1964 with "Winken, Blinken and Nod." Carly continued as a solo act and in 1966 began recording material for a solo debut album with sessionmen including Robbie Robertson, Rick Danko, and Richard Manuel (of the Band), Al Kooper, and Mike Bloomfield. One of the tracks to be included was a version of Eric Von Schmidt's "Baby Let Me Follow You Down," with lyrics rewritten for Simon by Bob Dylan. After the project was abandoned, Simon kept a low profile for the rest of the decade.

She reemerged in 1970 with a single from her debut LP, "That's the Way I've Always Heard It Should Be" (#10, 1971), one of many songwriting collaborations with film critic Jacob Brackman. In late 1971 the title cut of her second LP, *Anticipation* (produced by ex-Yardbird Paul Samwell-Smith), was a #13 hit, and the album was also a bestseller, helping her to win that year's Best New Artist Grammy. Her later hits included the mammoth smash "You're So Vain" (#1, 1972), allegedly inspired by and sung to either Warren Beatty or Mick Jagger (who appears on it as a backup vocalist). *No Secrets* (#1, 1972) went gold later that year; it is her most successful album to date.

On November 3, 1972, she married James Taylor, and in 1974 their duet cover of "Mockingbird" hit #5; the album it came from, *Hotcakes,* went gold. *Playing Possum* would be her last Top 10 album for a few years. Among her Top 30 hits of the mid-'70s were "The Right Thing to Do" (1973) and "I Haven't Got Time for the Pain" (1974). Simon came back strongly in 1977, with the theme song from the James Bond movie *The Spy Who Loved Me*, "Nobody Does It Better," which went to #2, and next year's "You Belong to Me" (#6), which she cowrote with Michael McDonald. *Boys in the Trees*, which included "You Belong," was the last Top 10 and first platinum album of her career. She and Taylor's duet of the Everly Brothers' hit "Devoted to You" went to #36, and her biggest singles of the time were "Jesse" (#11, 1980) and "Why" (#10 U.K, 1982).

With the '80s Simon changed direction, recording 1981's *Torch* (#50), her first collection of pop standards, featuring songs by Hoagy Carmichael, Rodgers and Hart, and others. (She followed it up with two more albums of standards, 1990's *My Romance* [#46] and 1997's *Film Noir* [#84].) In 1981 she also filed for divorce from Taylor (it was finalized in 1983); they have two children, Sally and Ben, who have pursued music as adults. Simon's legendary stage fright, which had caused her to cancel a tour in support of *Come Upstairs*, and a series of interesting but less than stellar singles (such as "Tired of Being Blonde") followed.

Simon's efforts as a composer for film paid off immediately, however, as "Coming Around Again" (from the 1987 film *Heartburn*) became a Top 20 single and "Let the River Run" (from 1988's *Working Girl*) garnered her an Oscar for Best Original Song. She also composed music for the film *Postcards From the Edge*, including "Have You Seen Me Lately?" In the late '80s she also surmounted her stage fright with a live concert on Martha's Vineyard, which was filmed for a popular HBO special, "Carly in Concert—Coming Around Again," and recorded for her gold 1988 LP *Greatest Hits Live*. In 1995 she went on her first major tour since 1981, and even played in New York's Grand Central Terminal. Like the Martha's Vineyard show, the performance was taped for cable (Lifetime Network).

In 1997 Simon was diagnosed with breast cancer. After undergoing a mastectomy and rounds of chemotherapy, she wrote and recorded *The Bedroom Tapes*, her first album of original material in six years, at her home in Martha's Vineyard. Continuing her tradition of autobiographical, introspective songwriting, she dealt with her illness on songs such as "Scar."

Over the past decade, Simon has also successfully diversified her career. In 1993 her opera for young people, *Romulus Hunt*, debuted at the Metropolitan Opera and the Kennedy Center for the Performing Arts. She has written five children's books: *Amy the Dancing Bear, The Boy of the Bells, The Fisherman's Song, The Nighttime Chauffeur*, and *Midnight Farm*. She also set nursery rhymes to music on *Mother Goose's Basket Full of Rhymes* (2000).

Paul Simon

Born Oct. 13, 1941, Newark, NJ
1965—*The Paul Simon Song Book* (CBS, U.K.) 1972—*Paul Simon* (Warner Bros.) 1973—*There Goes Rhymin' Simon* 1974—*Live Rhymin'* 1975—*Still Crazy After All These Years* 1977—*Greatest Hits, Etc.* 1980—*One Trick Pony* 1983—*Hearts and Bones* 1986—*Graceland* 1988—*Negotiations and Love Songs 1971–1986* 1990—*The Rhythm of the Saints* 1991—*Paul Simon's Concert in the Park* 1993—*1964/1993* 1997—*Songs From "The Capeman"* 2000—*You're the One*.

After the 1970 breakup of Simon and Garfunkel [see entry], Paul Simon went on confirm his stature as a first-rate songwriter and performer. His terse, exquisitely crafted songs have drawn on early rock & roll (particularly doo-wop), reggae, salsa, jazz, gospel, blues, New Orleans, and African and South American music, in some cases presaging the conscious blending of world music into mainstream pop by over a decade. In an unassuming, distinctive tenor, Simon has sung of matters personal and universal with attitudes ranging from the whimsical to the reverent. Simon stands apart from most folk-based singer/songwriters of his generation in that he has created a wide-ranging body of work in which the purely musical vocabulary—of style, instrumentation, and sounds—is as evocative and as expressive as his lyrics.

Simon had recorded solo in England between Simon and Garfunkel's first and second albums. On his first album after their breakup, *Paul Simon* (#4, 1972), he began working from a broader stylistic palette and playing with such celebrated artists as jazz violinist Stephane Grappelli; the first single, "Mother and Child Reunion" (#4, 1972) was cut in Jamaica; and "Me and Julio Down by the Schoolyard" (#22, 1972) showed a clear urban Latin influence. Although Simon had ventured outside the classic folk-rock idioms with Garfunkel ("Cecilia," "El Condor Paso"), as a solo artist he pursued these new directions in earnest while returning to such American genres as gospel on *There Goes Rhymin' Simon* (#2, 1973); "Loves Me Like a Rock" (#2) featured the venerable Dixie Hummingbirds on backup. That album also included "Kodachrome" (#2, 1973) and went on to sell 2 million copies. The next year's *Live Rhymin'* (#33, 1974) featured the Dixie Hummingbirds and the Peruvian folk group Urubama.

Despite their sometimes rocky relationship, Simon and Garfunkel never completely severed ties. They performed at a George McGovern fund-raiser in 1972 and Garfunkel was a frequent guest at Simon's concerts. In 1975 they collaborated on their first record since 1970's *Bridge Over Troubled Water*, the single "My Little Town" (#9), which turned up on both Garfunkel's *Breakaway* and Simon's *Still Crazy After All These Years* (#1, 1975). The latter, purportedly about the dissolution of Simon's first marriage, generated the hits "Gone at Last" (#23) (a duet with Phoebe Snow) and "50 Ways to Leave Your Lover" (#1), and won a Grammy for Best Album of 1975.

Next Simon played a small nonsinging part in Woody Allen's *Annie Hall* in 1977, and started working in television, hosting *Saturday Night Live* and his own special. His *Greatest Hits* (#18, 1977) yielded the 1977 #5 hit "Slip Slidin' Away." In 1980 Simon starred in *One Trick Pony*, for which he wrote the screenplay and soundtrack. The story of a journeyman rock & roller, *Pony* received mixed reviews and flopped at the box office, although the salsa-influenced "Late in the Evening" became a #6 hit. In 1981 Simon reunited with Garfunkel again in Central Park; the concert was documented on a live album.

A year later, the pair toured together, intending to collaborate in the studio. When those plans fell through, Simon released *Hearts and Bones* (#35, 1983), the least commercially and critically successful work of his career to date. Including a collaboration with composer Philip Glass, the album failed commercially, and with the end of his second marriage, to actress Carrie Fisher, Simon reached a personal and professional low point.

Seeking inspiration, Simon traveled to South Africa in 1985 to explore its indigenous music, which he had been studying. After participating in the recording of "We Are the World," the all-star anthem for the USA for Africa hunger relief project, he began recording in Johannesburg. He emerged with *Graceland*, a dazzling collection influenced by South African dance music and featuring the vocal group Ladysmith Black Mambazo (for whom he'd later produce two albums), the Everly Brothers, and Los Lobos. *Graceland* scored #3 in 1987—a whimsical single, "You Can Call Me Al," reached #44 (and #23 in rerelease in 1987)—and won a 1988 Grammy for Album of the Year.

Recording in South Africa caused Simon to be blacklisted by the United Nations and the African National Congress (ANC) and to be picketed in concert by antiapartheid protestors. To his credit, Simon spoke at public gatherings, where he addressed his critics face to face and defended his actions, insisting that his motives in breaking the boycott on recording in South Africa were musical, not political. The UN and the ANC dropped their bans in early 1987 after Simon wrote the UN pledging to abide by the terms of their South African boycott. Simon then released a best-selling home video of the Graceland concert in Zimbabwe.

In 1990 *The Rhythm of the Saints*, incorporating strains of West African, Brazilian, and zydeco music, reached #4, and Simon and Garfunkel were inducted into the Rock and Roll Hall of Fame. The next year, Simon hosted a free Central Park concert (at which Garfunkel was pointedly asked not to appear) that drew an estimated 750,000 people. In 1992 Simon married Edie Brickell [see entry], then the lead singer for the New Bohemians; he coproduced his wife's first solo album in 1994.

Simon performed a series of 16 concerts at the Paramount in New York City in the fall of 1993. A retrospective of his career, the concert event also included a reunion with Garfunkel. Over the years, Simon's charitable and social work has involved fundraising for Amazonian rain forest preservation, New York's homeless, and South African children. For his humanitarian efforts, the United Negro College Fund accorded him its highest honor in 1989.

In 1997 Simon won an Emmy for a televised concert special ("Paul Simon Special"), received critical praise for the three-CD Simon and Garfunkel retrospective, *Old Friends*, and collaborated with Nobel Prize–winning author Derek Walcott on a Broadway musical. The show, *The Capeman*, based on the true-life story of a young Puerto Rican immigrant sent to jail for the murders of two Manhattan teens, failed financially. However, it received a Tony Award nomination for Best Original Score written for Theater, and its accompanying CD was warmly received.

In 1999 Simon toured with Bob Dylan; the former rivals were recognized as the premier American songwriters to have emerged from the '60s. The following year, Simon released *You're the One*, a solid set of songs with no overarching conceptual framework. In 2001 he was inducted into the Rock and Roll Hall of Fame as a solo artist.

Simon and Garfunkel

Paul Simon (b. Oct. 13, 1941, Newark, NJ), gtr., voc.; Arthur Garfunkel (b. Nov. 5, 1941, New York, NY), voc.
1964—*Wednesday Morning, 3 A.M.* (Columbia) 1966—*Sounds of Silence; Parsley, Sage, Rosemary and Thyme* 1968—*Bookends; The Graduate* soundtrack 1970—*Bridge Over Troubled Water* 1972—*Greatest Hits* 1982—*The Concert in Central Park* 1997—*Old Friends.*

When they were in the sixth grade together in Forest Hills, New York, Paul Simon and Art Garfunkel found they could harmonize. The first songs they sang together were doo-wop hits, but soon they were singing their own songs. One of those was "Hey, Schoolgirl," which the duo recorded in 1957. An agent of Big Records present at the session signed them on the spot. Calling themselves Tom and Jerry ("Tom Graph" and "Jerry Landis"), they had a Top 50 hit with "Hey, Schoolgirl" and appeared on *American Bandstand*. (In a 1984 *Playboy* interview Simon asserted that the record company agent used payola to get the record played.) Garfunkel estimates the record sold 150,000 copies. When a few followups flopped, Tom and Jerry split up. When they met again in 1962, Garfunkel was studying architecture after trying to record as Arty Garr, and Simon was studying English literature but devoting most of his time to writing and selling his songs. In 1964 Simon, who had just dropped out of law school and quit his job as a song peddler for a music publishing company, took one of his originals to Columbia Records producer Tom Wilson. Wilson bought the song and signed the Everly Brothers–influenced duo.

Wednesday Morning, 3 A.M.—a set that combined traditional folk songs with Simon's originals and Dylan anthems like "The Times They Are A-Changin'," performed only by the two singers accompanied by Simon's acoustic guitar—was lost in the glut of early Dylan imitations. Simon went to work the folk circuit in London, where in May 1965 he recorded a solo album. Several months later, he was performing around England and the Continent when he received the news that one of the songs on *Wednesday Morning*—"The Sounds of Silence"—was the #1 single in the United States. It was not quite the song Simon and Garfunkel had recorded. Wilson (who had played a part in electrifying Dylan's music) had added electric guitars, bass, and drums to the original track. The remixed single was at the vanguard of "folk rock." Simon

Art Garfunkel and Paul Simon

returned to hit the college circuit with Garfunkel and to record a second duo album. Along with the redubbed "Sounds of Silence," the album of that name comprised folk-rock remakes of many of the songs from Simon's U.K. solo album. The production was elaborate, an appropriate setting for Simon's self-consciously poetic songs and Garfunkel's angelic voice, and Simon and Garfunkel turned out to be acceptable to both teenagers (who found them relevant) and adults (who found them intelligent). In 1966 they placed four singles and three albums in the Top 30 (the revived *Wednesday Morning, Sounds of Silence,* and *Parsley, Sage, Rosemary and Thyme*). "Homeward Bound" (#5), "I Am a Rock" (#3), and "Sounds of Silence" (#1) reached the Top 5. Simon was not a prolific writer—most of the material on the first three Simon and Garfunkel albums had been composed between 1962 and 1965—and once *Parsley, Sage* was completed, the duo's output slowed considerably. They released only two singles in 1967: "At the Zoo" (#16) and "Fakin' It" (#23). Simon was developing the more colloquial, less literary style he would bring to his later solo work; the first sign of it was the elliptical "Mrs. Robinson," composed for the soundtrack of *The Graduate.* The film and the soundtrack album were followed within two months by *Bookends;* "Mrs. Robinson" hit #1 in June 1968, *Bookends* soon afterward.

Simon and Garfunkel produced *Bookends* with engineer Roy Halee, who had worked on every Simon and Garfunkel session. (With *Parsley, Sage,* Halee had taken a major role in the arranging; it was Columbia's first album recorded on eight tracks.) "The Boxer" (#7), Simon and Garfunkel's only release in 1969, was Columbia's first song recorded on 16 tracks.

Bridge Over Troubled Water took almost two years to make, as the duo began to pursue their individual projects. They often worked separately in the studio, and as their music became more complex they performed less often on stage; their only appearance in 1969 was on their own network television special. Around this period, Garfunkel's acting career began with a role in *Catch-22.* Soon after the record's release, Simon and Garfunkel staged a brief but very successful tour, which quieted rumors about a breakup, but by the time Garfunkel's second movie, *Carnal Knowledge,* and Simon's 1972 solo album came out, it was clear that their individual solo careers [see entries] were taking precedence. The two left their joint career at its peak, though both have said that their initial intention was not to break up permanently but just take a break from each other. After reaching #1 in spring 1970, *Bridge Over Troubled Water* rode the charts for over a year and a half (spending 10 weeks at the top), eventually selling over 13 million copies worldwide. The LP yielded three hit singles—the title song (a #1 hit, the biggest seller of their career), "Cecilia" (#4), and "El Condor Pasa" (#18)—and won six Grammys. In 1977 it was given the British Britannia Award as Best International Pop Album of the past 25 years, and the title song received the equivalent award as a single. To date the duo has sold more than 20 million albums in the U.S. alone.

Since 1970 the Forest Hills classmates have gotten together on a few notable occasions. The first was a benefit concert for presidential candidate George McGovern at Madison Square Garden, New York, in June 1972. (That occasion also saw the reunions of Peter, Paul and Mary and the comedy team of Mike Nichols and Elaine May.) In 1975 Simon and Garfunkel had a Top 10 hit single with "My Little Town," a song Simon wrote for Garfunkel and sang with him, which appeared on solo LPs by both. Garfunkel joined Simon to perform a selection of their old hits on Simon's 1977 television special, and the two got together again the next year in a studio with James Taylor to record a trio rendition of Sam Cooke's "(What a) Wonderful World." On September 19, 1981, Simon and Garfunkel gave a free concert for an estimated 500,000 fans in New York's Central Park, and in 1982, a double album, *The Concert in Central Park,* went platinum, peaking at #6. They embarked on an extended tour and began recording what was to have been a new Simon and Garfunkel album. Unable to resolve their creative differences, the two abandoned the project, and the material was released on the Paul Simon solo LP *Hearts and Bones.*

The pair performed several shows for charitable causes in the early '90s, and in 1993 a smash 21-date sold-out run at the Paramount Theater in New York City, followed by a tour of the Far East. Though, technically speaking, these shows were not Simon and Garfunkel concerts (they performed together only in the first and last of the show's four segments; the balance was dedicated to Simon's solo work), fans seemed to feel otherwise. Whether for its exquisite craftsmanship or place as a musical-cultural touchstone, or both, the music Simon and Garfunkel created and recorded seems destined to endure. The two were inducted into the Rock and Roll Hall of Fame in 1990. The 1997 box set *Old*

Friends includes remastered hits ("Sounds of Silence," "Bridge Over Troubled Water"), previously unreleased live performances ("Bye, Bye Love"), and demos.

Nina Simone

Born Eunice Waymon, Feb. 21, 1933, Tryon, NC
1957—*Little Girl Blue* (Bethlehem); *Nina Simone and Her Friends* 1959—*The Amazing Nina Simone* (Colpix); *Nina Simone at Town Hall* 1960—*Nina Simone at Newport* 1962—*Nina Simone at the Village Gate; Nina Simone Sings Ellington* 1963—*Nina Simone at Carnegie Hall* 1964—*Nina Simone in Concert* (Phillips); *Broadway.Blues.Ballads.* 1965—*I Put a Spell on You; Pastel Blues* 1966—*Let It All Out; Wild Is the Wind* 1967—*Silk & Soul* (RCA) 1969—*'Nuff Said* 1970—*Black Gold* 1971—*Here Comes the Sun* 1972—*Emergency Ward* 1974—*It Is Finished* 1978—*Baltimore* (CTI) 1982—*Fodder on My Wings* (PolyGram) 1985—*Nina's Back* (VPI) 1987—*Let It Be Me* (Verve) 1988—*Don't Let Me Be Misunderstood* (Mercury) 1991—*The Blues* (Novus/RCA) 1993—*The Essential Nina Simone* (RCA); *A Single Woman* (Elektra) 1994—*The Tomato Collection* (Tomato); *The Essential Nina Simone, vol. 2* (RCA) 1995—*After Hours* (Verve) 1996—*Anthology: The Colpix Years* (Rhino) 1997—*The Ultimate Nina Simone* (Verve); *Saga of the Good Life and Hard Times* (RCA) 1999—*The Very Best of Nina Simone* 2000—*Quiet Now: Night Song* (Verve); *Nina Simone's Finest Hour.*

Singer Nina Simone's music has gone from gospel to jazz to pop to R&B and blues to a raging black protest that moved her off the supper-club circuit and into political rallies and soul concerts. Known since the late '50s as the "High Priestess of Soul," she enjoyed a renaissance in her sixth decade with the publication of her autobiography and the exposure given her music in a popular American film. Taking her stage name from French actress Simone Signoret, she epitomizes the soul diva.

Simone began singing in church and taught herself piano and organ by the time she was seven. She took classical keyboard lessons and attended New York's Juilliard School of Music, then began playing East Coast clubs and concerts. Her first hit was a 1959 gold record of Gershwin's "I Loves You, Porgy."

In the '60s she moved toward R&B, recording Screamin' Jay Hawkins' "I Put a Spell on You" and "Don't Let Me Be Misunderstood" (a subsequent hit for the Animals). This led to sizable popularity in England, where she had hits with "Ain't Got No—I Got Life" (from *Hair*) in 1968 and the Bee Gees' "To Love Somebody" in 1969.

By then she had become a black-power activist (her first protest song, "Mississippi Goddam," mourned the death of slain civil rights leader Medgar Evers), and politically oriented tracks like "Four Women" (on an out-of-print Philips album) alienated her white audience. She became even more intense and unpredictable in concert, and despite continuing critical acclaim, she gradually lost her commercial standing. Financially, she fell upon hard times, and she divorced her manager/husband (her first marriage had also failed). In 1974 Simone quit the music business.

Leaving the States, Simone took up residence in Switzerland, Liberia, Barbados, France, and the U.K. in the mid-'70s. By 1978, however, she had returned to music, releasing *Baltimore* and touring the U.S. again. While the early '80s were a fallow period, Simone experienced a comeback in 1987 when a television commercial for Chanel No. 5 perfume used her early recording "My Baby Just Cares for Me." Her candid 1991 autobiography, *I Put a Spell on You,* and an appearance on Pete Townshend's *Iron Man* boosted her revival. In 1993, with her music featured in the film *Point of No Return* and with a new studio album, *A Single Woman,* Simone gained a new audience for her fiercely elegant fare. In 1995 Simone was ordered to pay a $4,600 fine for shooting at two teenaged boys whom she maintained were disturbing her peace while she was gardening; that year also, she was fined $5,000 for leaving the scene of a car accident that had occurred in 1993. The '90s concluded, however, on a happier note, as her music was presented again in a number of well-crafted anthologies.

Simple Minds

Formed 1978, Glasgow, Scot.
Jim Kerr (b. July 9, 1959, Glasgow), voc.; Charlie Burchill (b. Nov. 27, 1959, Glasgow), gtr., kybds.; Duncan Barnwell, gtr.; Mick McNeil (b. July 20, 1958, Glasgow), kybds.; Tony Donald, bass; Brian McGee, drums.
1978—(– Barnwell; – Donald; + Derek Forbes [b. June 22, 1956, Glasgow], bass) 1979—*Life in a Day* (Zoom, U.K.) 1980—*Real to Real Cacophony; Empires and Dance* (– McGee; + Kenny Hyslop [b. Feb. 14, 1951, Helensburgh, Scot.], drums; – Hyslop; + Mike Ogletree, drums) 1981—*Sons and Fascination/Sister Feelings Call* (Virgin, U.K.) 1982—*New Gold Dream (81-82-83-84)* (A&M); *Themes for Great Cities* (Stiff) (– Ogletree; + Mel Gaynor [b. May 29, 1959, Glasgow], drums); *Celebration* (Virgin) 1984—*Sparkle in the Rain* (A&M) (– Forbes; + John Giblin, bass; + Robin Clark, voc.; + Sue Hadjopoulos, perc.) 1985—*Once Upon a Time* 1987—*Simple Minds Live: In the City of Light* 1989—*Street Fighting Years* (– Clark; – Hadjopoulos; – McNeil; + Peter Vitesse, kybds.) 1991—*Real Life* 1993—*Glittering Prize* (– Vitesse) 1995—*Good News From the Next World* (Virgin).

Scotland's Simple Minds found some success in the latter half of the '80s with a synth-based, epic-pop sound. The band grew out of the Glasgow punk outfit Johnny and the Self-Abusers, which included childhood buddies Jim Kerr and Charlie Burchill. Simple Minds began playing an ambitious postpunk art rock, influenced by Roxy Music and David Bowie and veering from pop songs *(Life in a Day)* to harsher, more experimental sounds *(Real to Real Cacophony)* to cool, aloof Eurodisco *(Empires and Dance)*.

While Simple Minds became critical favorites with the British music press, the band did not attract a significant U.S. following until *New Gold Dream,* which had a warmer musical feel and more positive lyrics, including much religious imagery. It became the group's first American chart album (#69, 1983), and included "Promised You a Miracle" (the only track on which second drummer Kenny Hyslop ever played), which got frequent play on college radio and in rock discos. The videos for that track, and for "Someone Somewhere in Summertime," were also played on MTV.

Sparkle in the Rain (#64, 1984) united Simple Minds with U2 producer Steve Lillywhite, but failed to spawn a U.S. chart single. The band toured with the Pretenders, and in June 1984, Kerr married Pretender Chrissie Hynde in New York's Central Park. They had a daughter, Yasmin, in 1985, before divorcing a few years later. Simple Minds finally achieved their long-predicted U.S. breakthrough with "Don't You (Forget About Me)" (#1, 1985), from the soundtrack of *The Breakfast Club*. The song was written by producer/composer Keith Forsey (*Flashdance*, Billy Idol) and Steve Schiff; Bryan Ferry had turned down the song, and Simple Minds were originally against the idea of recording or releasing it. "Don't You" did not appear on the album *Once Upon a Time* (#10, 1985), which yielded hits of its own in "Alive & Kicking" (#3, 1985), "Sanctify Yourself" (#14, 1986), and "All the Things She Said" (#28, 1986).

Simple Minds were unable to further that commercial success with the concert album *Live in the City of Light* (#96, 1987) and the politically oriented *Street Fighting Years* (#70, 1989). *Real Life* (#74, 1991) returned to the grand-scale sound and more personal lyrics, and spawned a modest U.S. hit single in "See the Lights" (#40, 1991). Kerr married British actress Patsy Kensit in 1992 (the pair divorced four years later). The band's 1993 effort, *Glittering Prize*, was a commercial bomb. Its 1995 album (its first on new label Virgin) *Good News From the Next World* (#87, 1995), was only moderately successful.

Simply Red

Formed 1984, England
Mick Hucknall (b. Michael James Hucknall, June 8, 1960, Manchester, Eng.), voc.
1985—(+ Sylvan Richardson, gtr.; Fritz McIntyre [b. Sep. 2, 1956, Birmingham, Eng.], kybds.; Tony Bowers [b. Oct. 31, 1952], bass; Chris Joyce [b. Oct. 11, 1957, Manchester], drums; Tim Kellett [b. July 23, 1964, Knaresborough, Eng.], horns, kybds.) *Picture Book* (Elektra) 1987—*Men and Women* 1989—(– Richardson; + Aziz Ibrahim, gtr.; + Ian Kirkham [b. Mar. 9], sax) *A New Flame* 1991—(– Ibrahim; – Bowers; – Joyce; + Heitor T.P. [b. Brazil], gtr.; + Shaun Ward, bass; + Gota Yashiki [b. Feb. 26], drums) *Stars* (EastWest) 1995—(– Ward) *Life* 1998—(– T.P.; + Tim Vine [b. Feb. 7], kybds.; + Kenji "Suzuki" Jammer [b. Sep. 18], gtr.; + Mark Jaimes [b. Mar. 30], gtr.; + John Johnson [b. Jan. 21], trombone) *Blue* (Elektra/Asylum) 1999—(+ Wayne Stobbard [b. Dec. 8], bass; + Kevin Robinson [b. Nov. 8], trumpet; + Chris De Margary [b. Sep. 9], sax, flute) *Love and the Russian Winter*.

One of several mellow, blue-eyed soul acts from the U.K., Simply Red distinguished itself from the lot by virtue of its lead singer and primary songwriter, Mick Hucknall. In addition to his striking physical appearance—a shock of red curls atop a visage evoking a young Mickey Rooney—Hucknall boasted a shivery, keening countertenor that drew the attention, and praise, of critics. For some, however, Hucknall's distinctive voice couldn't compensate for the often effete arrangements that characterized Simply Red's hybrid of R&B and Adult Contemporary pop.

As a working-class Manchester lad, Hucknall led a punk-influenced band called the Frantic Elevators in the late '70s and early '80s. Then, yearning to play the pop and soul music that was closer to his heart, the singer put together the short-lived first incarnation of Simply Red. Once that lineup dissolved, Hucknall recruited bassist Tony Bowers, drummer Chris Joyce, and trumpeter/synth player Tim Kellett from another Manchester band, Durutti Column. Adding gospel pianist Fritz McIntyre, Hucknall finally secured the band he wanted. In the years to come, it became clearer that the overriding decisions of Simply Red were Hucknall's to make, as he contracted out musicians for hire rather than treating them as equal partners in a band. In 1985 Simply Red signed to Elektra, releasing that year their first single, "Money$ Too Tight to Mention" (#13 U.K.), and debut album, *Picture Book* (featuring classically trained guitarist Sylvan Richardson, who joined the band after the single's release). It wasn't until 1986, though, that *Book*'s kickoff single, a wistful ballad called "Holding Back the Years," shot to #2 in England—and #1 in the U.S.

Simply Red was received less enthusiastically by American fans over the next few years. (In the U.K., the album *Men and Women* reached #2; and two 1987 singles, "The Right Thing" and a cover of Cole Porter's "Ev'ry Time We Say Goodbye," hit #11.) The group rebounded in 1989, though, with a remake of Harold Melvin and the Blue Notes' "If You Don't Know Me by Now" (#1 U.S., #2 U.K.). A fourth album, *Stars*, topped the British chart—in fact, it became one of the biggest sellers of all time in the U.K.—but stalled at #76 in the U.S. The 1995 followup, *Life*, provided a #1 single, "Fairground," in England, but again, peaked at only #75 in the States. Around this time, Hucknall and his then-manager, Elliot Rashman, formed Blood and Fire, a music label that reissued reggae albums on CD. The group's popularity continued to surge in Europe when its song "We're in This Together" was designated the official theme of Euro '96, the European soccer championships hosted by England that year. Two other albums, 1998's *Blue* and 1999's *Love and the Russian Winter*, played respectfully in Europe but were largely ignored in the U.S.

Hucknall also enjoyed celebrity status in Britain, becoming vocally political in support of Prime Minister Tony Blair, as well as being pictured in the tabloids with numerous women over the years, including singer Kim Wilde, tennis player Stefi Graff, actresses Catherine Zeta-Jones and Brigitte Nielsen, and model Helena Christensen.

Frank Sinatra

Born Francis Albert Sinatra, Dec. 12, 1915, Hoboken, NJ; died May 14, 1998, Los Angeles, CA
1940—*The Song Is You* (RCA) 1944—*Swing and Dance With Frank Sinatra* (Columbia) 1948—*The Voice of Frank Sinatra* (CBS) 1949—*Frankly Sentimental* (Columbia) 1950—*Songs by Sinatra* (CBS) 1954—*Songs for Young Lovers* (Capitol) 1955—*Swing Easy; In the Wee Small Hours; Frankie* (Columbia) 1956—*Songs for Swingin' Lovers!* (Capitol) 1957—*Close to You; A Swingin' Affair!; Where Are You?* 1958—*Come Fly With Me; Only the Lonely* 1959—*Come Dance With Me!; Look to Your Heart; No One Cares* 1960—*Nice 'n' Easy;* 1961—*Sinatra's Swingin' Session!!!; All the Way; Ring-a-Ding Ding!* (Reprise); *Sinatra Swings; Come Swing With Me* (Capitol); *I Remember Tommy* (Reprise) 1962—*Sinatra and Strings; Point of No Return* (Capitol); *Sinatra Sings of Love & Things; Sinatra and Swingin' Brass* (Reprise) 1963—*Sinatra-Basie; The Concert Sinatra; Tell Her You Love Her* (Capitol); *Sinatra's Sinatra* (Reprise); 1964—*It Might as Well Be Swing* (with Count Basie) (Reprise); *Softly, As I Leave You* 1965—*The Selected Cole Porter* (Capitol); *Sinatra '65* (Reprise); *September of My Years; A Man and His Music; My Kind of Broadway* 1966—*Forever Frank* (Capitol); *Moonlight Sinatra* (Reprise); *Strangers in the Night; Sinatra at the Sands; That's Life* 1967—*Francis Albert Sinatra & Antonio Carlos Jobim; Francis A. and Edward K.* (with Duke Ellington) 1968—*Frank Sinatra's Greatest Hits!; Cycles* 1969—*My Way; A Man Alone & Other Songs of Rod McKuen* 1970—*Watertown* 1971—*Sinatra & Company* 1972—*Frank Sinatra's Greatest Hits, vol. 2* 1973—*Ol' Blue Eyes Is Back* 1974—*Some Nice Things I've Missed; Sinatra—The Main Event/Live* 1980—*Trilogy: Past, Present, Future* 1981—*She Shot Me Down* 1982—*The Dorsey/Sinatra Sessions 1940–1942 (vols. 1, 2, and 3)* (RCA) 1984—*L.A. Is My Lady* (Qwest) 1990—*The Capitol Years (discs 1, 2, and 3)* (Capitol); *The Reprise Collection* (Reprise) 1993—*Duets* (Capitol) 1994—*Duets II* 1996—*Everything Happens to Me* (Reprise) 2000—*Classic Sinatra* (Capitol).

Baritone Frank Sinatra was indisputably the 20th century's greatest singer of popular song. Though influenced by Bing Crosby's crooning, and by learning from trombonist Tommy Dorsey's breath control and blues singer Billie Holiday's rhythmic swing, Sinatra mainstreamed the concept of singing colloquially, treating lyrics as personal statements and handling melodies with the ease of a jazz improviser. His best work is standards—Cole Porter, Irving Berlin, Jerome Kern, and the Gershwins—but Sinatra, despite his 1957 denunciation of rock & roll as degenerate, has recorded songs by the likes of Stevie Wonder, George Harrison, Jimmy Webb, and Billy Joel. Not only did his freely interpretive approach pave the way for the idiosyncrasies of rock singing, but with his character a mix of tough-guy cool and romantic vulnerability, he became the first true pop idol, a superstar who through his music established a persona audiences found compelling and true.

Sinatra, an only child of a family with Sicilian roots, grew up in Hoboken, and sang in the glee club of Demarest High School. His break came in 1937, when he and three instrumentalists, billed as the Hoboken Four, won on the *Major Bowes Original Amateur Hour*. After some touring, the group disbanded.

Harry James signed Sinatra to sing with his orchestra, and on July 13, 1939, two weeks after his debut as a big-band vocalist at the Hippodrome Theatre in Baltimore, Sinatra cut his first disc, "From the Bottom of My Heart," with the orchestra. Of the 10 sides he recorded with them, the biggest seller, "All or Nothing at All," sold just over 8,000 copies upon release. In 1943 it was rereleased and became the first of Sinatra's many million-sellers, hitting #2 on the chart.

In 1940 Tommy Dorsey's lead singer, Jack Leonard, quit and Sinatra began a two-year stay with the trombonist. During those years, the band consistently hit the Top 10 (15 entries in 1940–41, including their first, the #1 hit "I'll Never Smile Again"). His radio work with Dorsey was the springboard for Sinatra's solo career. During the war years, Sinatra, married at the time to his childhood sweetheart, Nancy, sang love songs to his mostly female audiences, notably on Lucky Strike's *Hit Parade* and at New York's original Paramount Theatre. Between 1943 and 1946 he had 17 Top 10 chart singles, and earned the sobriquets "The Voice" and "The Sultan of Swoon." With the GIs back in the U.S., public taste shifted away from these songs, and Sinatra's popularity waned. At Columbia, producer Mitch Miller burdened Sinatra with novelty songs (washboard accompaniment on one, barking dogs on another), and his sales slipped to an average of 30,000 per record. In the early '50s, he was dropped by Columbia and by his talent agent and lost his MGM motion picture contract. To regain his popularity, he begged to be cast as Maggio in the film *From Here to Eternity*. His first nonsinging role, it won him a 1953 Oscar and a return to the limelight. (His film debut had been with the Tommy Dorsey Orchestra in 1941's *Las Vegas Nights*.)

The fledgling Capitol Records signed him in 1953 and, with ex-Dorsey trombonist and arranger Nelson Riddle, Sinatra moved into the next phase of his recording career with a new emphasis: saloon ballads and sophisticated swing tunes. With Capitol, he concentrated on albums, although he again charted in the singles Top 10, notably with "Young at Heart" (#2, 1954), "Learnin' the Blues" (#1, 1955), "Hey! Jealous Lover" (#3, 1956), "All the Way" (#2, 1957), and "Witchcraft" (#6, 1958). His best albums of the period were arranged by Riddle, Billy May, or Gordon Jenkins.

Through the early '50s, during which he was married to film actress Ava Gardner, having left Nancy in 1950, Sinatra became a movie star. He won especially high praise for his portrayal of a drug addict in *The Man With the Golden Arm* (1955). Beginning in 1959, two years after he divorced Gardner, his singles failed to hit the Top 30, and in 1961 Sinatra left Capitol to establish his own company, Reprise. (In 1963 he sold Reprise to Warner Bros. and became a vice president and consultant of Warner Bros. Picture Corp.)

Sinatra decided to try again to become a Top 40 singles artist. "The Second Time Around" hit #50 in 1961; subsequent releases charted lower. But in the mid-'60s he recouped. He was the triumphant headliner of the final evening of the 1965 Newport Jazz Festival in a 20-song set accompanied by Count Basie's orchestra, conducted by Quincy Jones. His 1965 Thanksgiving TV special, *Frank Sinatra: A Man and His Music*, a review of his 25-year career, won an Emmy and set the precedent for numerous other TV specials, including one each in the next four years. That year he also picked up a Grammy Lifetime Achievement Award. In 1966–67 he charted three of his biggest Top 10 hits: "Strangers in the Night" (#1, 1966), "That's Life" (#4, 1966), and a duet with daughter Nancy, "Somethin' Stupid" (#1, 1967).

In the '60s he made his Las Vegas debut at the Sands and continued for years as a main attraction at Caesars Palace. Leader of the notorious "Rat Pack," including Sammy Davis Jr., Dean Martin, Peter Lawford, and Joey Bishop, he came to epitomize the hard-drinking, blonde-chasing swinger; a stout Democrat who'd named his son after Franklin D. Roosevelt, he also strongly supported John F. Kennedy's presidential bid. Married from 1966 to 1968 to actress Mia Farrow, he began reconciling with youth culture, covering songs, with indifferent success, by younger writers. In 1968 he recorded "My Way," a French song to which Paul Anka wrote new English lyrics. A modest U.S. hit (#27), it was an overwhelming smash in the U.K., staying in the Top 50 an unprecedented 122 weeks. (Sex Pistol Sid Vicious later recorded a sarcastic version.)

In 1970 Sinatra announced his retirement and was honored with a gala farewell on June 13, 1971, at the L.A. Music Center. He reversed that decision in 1973 with the release of *Ol' Blue Eyes Is Back* (#13), a TV special of the same name, and a performance at the Nixon White House (over the years, Sinatra's politics had become markedly conservative; in 1985, he would produce Ronald Reagan's inaugural gala). In 1974 he mounted an eight-city, 13-date sold-out U.S. tour and performed in Japan and Australia. In Australia he aggravated the paparazzi with his antijournalist harangues: Through the years he referred to the males as parasites, and the females as everything from "a buck-and-a-half hooker" to "two-dollar broads." Married to Zeppo Marx's widow, Barbara, in 1976, however, he appeared to mellow somewhat. In the mid-'70s Sinatra's career slowed down, but in mid-1980, after a five-year recording hiatus, he released *Trilogy* (#17),which included a version of "Theme From *New York, New York*" (#32) that the city fervently adopted.

In the '80s Sinatra continued to perform sold-out concerts in major halls, to star in movies and TV specials, and to spark controversy for his business and political associations. (His 1972 appearances before the House Select Committee on Crime investigating criminal infiltration into horse racing were front-page news.) With 1981's *She Shot Me Down* (#52) and 1984's *L.A. Is My Lady* (#58) he appeared to have ended his recording career. In 1985, he was accorded the Presidential Medal of Freedom, the nation's highest civilian award.

In 1993, however, he enjoyed a renaissance with *Duets* debuting at #2. Featuring top singers—among them Aretha Franklin, Bono, Tony Bennett, Liza Minnelli, and Luther Vandross (some recording their parts via telephone)—it gained Sinatra new young fans. Still touring, with the aid of TelePrompTers, at 78, he collapsed onstage in Virginia in 1994 but soon recovered; days earlier, when presented with a special "Legend" award at the Grammy Awards ceremony—with an over-the-top intro by Bono—he had waxed so emotional that his own handlers requested that television cameras cut away from his acceptance speech. Rumors abounded about Sinatra's health, but he insisted on resuming his tour. By year's end, the sequel *Duets II* was issued, featuring Chrissie Hynde, Linda Ronstadt, and Willie Nelson, among others.

A 1983 honoree at the Kennedy Center Honors, Sinatra was involved for many years in charitable work, particularly in fundraising for multiple sclerosis, chronically ill children, and awareness of child abuse.

Frank Sinatra died of a heart attack on May 14, 1998, in L.A. That year, his FBI dossier, 1,275 pages covering 50 years of surveillance, was released. The document revealed no shocking secrets.

Nancy Sinatra

Born June 8, 1940, Jersey City, NJ
1966—*Boots* (Reprise) 1968—*Nancy and Lee* (with Lee Hazlewood) 1970—*Greatest Hits* 1972—*Nancy and Lee—Encore* (RCA) 1987—*Boots: Nancy Sinatra's All-Time Hits (1966–1970)* (with Lee Hazlewood) (Rhino) 1989—*Fairy Tales and Fantasies: The Best of Nancy & Lee* (with Lee Hazlewood) 1995—*One More Time* (Cougar) 1999—*You Go Go Girl* (Varèse Sarabande).

Frank Sinatra's daughter Nancy recorded a slew of '60s hits, including the sassy "These Boots Are Made for Walkin' " and "How Does That Grab You, Darlin'?" as well as collaborating on several more-obtuse, intriguing compositions, such as "Some Velvet Morning" and "Sand," with producer Lee Hazlewood. Her attitude-laced vocal style and go-go boots fashion sense inspired such postpunk femmes as Sonic Youth's Kim Gordon and the Breeders' Kim Deal.

At an early age Nancy Sinatra began studying dance, acting, singing, and piano. She made her national TV debut in 1960, in a Timex special featuring her father and Elvis Presley, in his first television appearance since leaving the army. She dropped out of the University of Southern California in 1960 after marrying singer/actor Tommy Sands, and did not resume her career until they divorced in 1965.

Her first few, girly-voiced singles, "Like I Do," "Tonight You Belong to Me," and "Think of Me," were hits in England, Europe, and South Africa, but were ignored in the U.S. Then in 1966 she began working with songwriter/producer Lee Hazlewood [see entry] and arranger Billy Strange, who urged her to go for a saucier, lower-register vocal style. Voila, she had her first #1 hit with the million-selling "Boots" soon after. She followed it up with the gold "Sugar Town" b/w "Summer Wine" (#5, 1966). In 1967 Sinatra and Hazlewood hit with the honey 'n' vinegar duet "Jackson" (#14), also a smash for

Johnny Cash and June Carter Cash. Nancy's title tune for the James Bond film *You Only Live Twice* reached #44 the same year, and her 1967 duet with her father, "Somethin' Stupid," took her back to the top of the chart. She also appeared in films, including *The Wild Angels* with Peter Fonda and *Speedway* with Presley.

After the hits quit coming in 1968, Sinatra retired from the entertainment business. Her moody duet with Hazlewood, "Some Velvet Morning," was revived by postpunk icons Lydia Lunch and Rowland S. Howard in the '80s, around the time Sinatra recorded a little-known album with Mel Tillis. Then, in 1995, Sinatra resurfaced, releasing a new album on the tiny Cougar label, posing in *Playboy,* and, with Hazlewood and a band, touring hip rock clubs. Her liner notes to the new recording explained she wanted to sing songs like those she'd done with Hazlewood: "tough and gentle, nasty and sweet, experienced and innocent," and during her comeback interviews she expressed great admiration for Hole's Courtney Love.

Siouxsie and the Banshees

Formed Sep. 1976, London, Eng.
Siouxsie Sioux (b. Susan Dallion, May 27, 1957, London), voc.; Sid Vicious (b. John Simon Ritchie, May 10, 1957, London; d. Feb. 2, 1979, New York, NY), drums; Steve Severin (b. Sep. 25, 1959, London), bass; Marco Pirroni (b. Apr. 27, 1959, London), gtr.
1977—(– Vicious; – Pirroni; + Kenny Morris, drums; + Peter Fenton, gtr; – Fenton; + John McKay, gtr.) 1978—*The Scream* (Polydor) 1979—*Join Hands* (– Morris; + Budgie [b. Peter Clark, Aug. 21, 1957, St. Helens, Eng.], drums; – McKay; + Robert Smith, gtr.) 1980—(– Smith; + John McGeoch, gtr.) *Kaleidoscope* (PVC) 1981—*Ju Ju; Once Upon a Time/The Singles* 1982—*A Kiss in the Dreamhouse* (Polydor) 1983—(– McGeoch; + Smith, gtr.) *Nocturne* (Geffen) 1984—*Hyaena* (– Smith; + John Valentine Carruthers, gtr.) 1986—*Tinderbox* 1987—*Through the Looking Glass* (– Carruthers; + Jon Klein [b. May 9, Bristol, Eng.], gtr.; + Martin McCarrick [b. July 29, London], cello, kybds.) 1988—*Peepshow* 1991—*The Peel Sessions* (Strange Fruit/Dutch East India Trading); *Superstition* (Geffen) 1992—*Twice Upon a Time/The Singles* 1995—*The Rapture.*
The Creatures with Siouxsie Sioux: 1983—*Feast* (Wonderland, U.K.) 1989—*Boomerang* (Geffen) 1999—*Anima Animus* (Instinct); *Hybrids* 2000—*U.S. Retrace.*

As leader of Siouxsie and the Banshees, Siouxsie Sioux has gone from punk-rock fan to seminal punk rocker to elder stateswoman. Outlasting most of their contemporaries, the Banshees have moved from an abrasive, art-punk sound into the mainstream, gaining a Top 40 hit with 1991's "Kiss Them for Me" (#23).

The Banshees grew out of the Bromley Contingent, a group of Sex Pistols fans; Sid Vicious, later a Pistol himself, played drums for their debut performance (which consisted of just one song, an elongated version of "The Lord's Prayer") at the 100 Club's 1976 punk festival. By the time their debut single, "Hong Kong Garden," and the album *The Scream* came out, only Siouxsie and Steve Severin remained from the original lineup (Marco Pirroni went on to join Adam and the Ants). Cure leader Robert Smith joined the band for a 1979 tour, and former Sex Pistol guitarist Steve Jones helped out on *Kaleidoscope;* Magazine's John McGeoch joined the band shortly before its first American tour in 1980. After appearing on two albums *(Ju Ju* and *A Kiss in the Dreamhouse),* McGeoch left in 1982. Smith rejoined the Banshees for a live album, *Nocturne,* and in the studio for *Hyaena* (#157, 1984).

With Smith on board, the band's musical palette widened, adding symphonic elements and a cover of the Beatles' "Dear Prudence" (#3 U.K., 1983). But Smith found playing in two bands wearying and left in 1984. Sioux broke her kneecap onstage in 1985, and the band laid low the remainder of the year. It returned with new guitarist John Valentine Carruthers and *Tinderbox* (#88, 1986), the group's first U.S. Top 100 album. Carruthers left after *Through the Looking Glass* (#188, 1987), an album of cover versions.

Peepshow (#68, 1988), with new members Jon Klein (ex-Specimen) and Martin McCarrick, moved the Banshees in the direction of a techno/dance groove, giving the band its first U.S. chart single: "Peek-a-Boo" (#53, 1988). In 1991 the Banshees were invited by Perry Farrell to perform on the first-ever Lollapalooza Tour. Released in conjuction with the tour, *Superstition* (#65) was the Banshees' best-selling album. In 1993 Siouxsie and Budgie (who had married in 1991) moved to the South of France, and there they began working on *The Rapture* (1995) with coproducer John Cale. That moody album turned out to be the Banshees' last as Sioux and Budgie decided to end the band's run in 1996 to concentrate instead on the Creatures.

Sioux and Budgie started the Creatures, essentially a percussion and voice setup, as a side project in 1981, scoring an early hit with the single "Right Now" (#14 U.K., 1983). They've since released three full-length albums as well as *Hybrids,* a collection of remixes that solidified the Creatures' strong dance-floor appeal. In 1998 the band toured with John Cale, with all three principals taking turns in the spotlight and collaborating on several songs.

Sir Douglas Quintet: See Doug Sahm

Sister Sledge

Formed late '50s, Philadelphia, PA
Debra Sledge (b. 1955), voc.; Joni Sledge (b. 1957), voc.; Kim Sledge (b. 1958), voc.; Kathy Sledge (b. 1959), voc.
1975—*Circle of Love* (Atco) 1979—*We Are Family* (Cotillion) 1980—*Love Somebody Today* 1981—*All American Girls* 1983—*Bet Cha Say That to All the Girls* 1985—*When the Boys Meet the Girls* (Atlantic) 1992—*The Best of Sister Sledge (1973–1985)* (– Kathy Sledge) 1998—*African Eyes* (Farenheit).

This vocal quartet of Philadelphia-born sisters enjoyed considerable success as the '70s ended.

The Sledge sisters made their performing debut at Philadelphia's Second Macedonia Church in the late '50s. Their parents had both been entertainers, and their grandmother Viola Williams was an opera singer. Before they attended elementary school, the four girls entertained at parties as Mrs. Williams' Grandchildren.

In 1971 they recorded "Time Will Tell" for the Money label. It was produced by Marty Bryant and the band Slim and the Boys, the team behind the Stylistics' first hit. While attending college they worked as background singers on several Kenny Gamble and Leon Huff productions, and in 1973 they were signed to Atlantic Records. All four have since graduated from Temple University.

From 1973 to 1978, Sister Sledge recorded in New York and Philadelphia without any significant success. It wasn't until the gold *We Are Family* in 1979, written and produced by Nile Rodgers and Bernard Edwards of Chic, that they became a chart presence. "He's the Greatest Dancer" (#9 pop, #1 R&B) and "We Are Family" (#2 pop, #1 R&B) were dance hits. The latter became the theme song of the Pittsburgh Pirates, the 1979 World Series champions, and later the anthem of gays marching on Washington, DC, that year. In 1981 (the year they began producing their own records) the quartet recorded "He's Just a Runaway," a tribute to the late Bob Marley. The next year, Sister Sledge had a hit with a cover of the Mary Wells oldie "My Guy." Although the group had no further pop hits in the U.S., they had a #1 U.K. hit, "Frankie," in 1985. After that, Kathy sought a solo career, and found some success in Europe in the early '90s. The remaining Sisters continued without her for 1998's *African Eyes*.

The Sisters of Mercy

Formed 1980, Leeds, Eng.
Andrew Eldritch (b. Andrew Taylor, May 10, 1959, Ely, Eng.), voc., gtr., bass, machines; Ben Gunn (b. Benjamin Matthews), gtr.; Craig Adams (b. Apr. 4, 1962, Leeds), bass; Gary Marx (b. Mark Pearman), gtr.
1982—*Alice* EP (Brain Eater) 1983—*The Reptile House* EP 1984—(– Gunn; + Wayne Hussey [b. Jerry Wayne Hussey, May 26, 1958, Bristol, Eng.], gtr.) *Body and Soul* EP (WEA) 1985—*First and Last and Always* (Elektra) 1987—(– Hussey; – Adams; – Marx; + Patricia Morrison, bass) *Floodland* 1990—(– Morrison; + Tony James [b. ca. 1956], bass; + Andreas Bruhn [b. Nov. 5, 1967, Hamburg, Ger.], gtr.; + Tim Bricheno [b. July 6, 1963, Huddersfield, Eng.], gtr.) *Vision Thing* 1992—*Some Girls Wander by Mistake* (Mute) (– James; – Bruhn; – Bricheno) 1993—(+ Adam Pearson [b. Mar. 3, 1964, Coventry, Eng.], gtr.) *A Slight Case of Overbombing: Greatest Hits, vol. 1* (Elektra) 1996—(+ Chris Sheehan [b. N.Z.], gtr.; + Mike Varjak [b. Belgrade, Serbia], gtr.)

The Sisters of Mercy, progenitors of England's "goth," or "gothic," postpunk subgenre, play a darkly psychedelic, danceable music that feasts on what bandleader Andrew Eldritch considers the "corpse of rock & roll." Sisters were formed by Eldritch and Gary Marx as a studio project: a metal band with a drum machine, Doktor Avalanche. After one year and one single released on their Merciful Release label, the Sisters (named after an order of nuns) added Ben Gunn and Craig Adams so they could play live shows. Gunn left the band after its first U.S. tour, in 1983, and was replaced by former Dead or Alive guitarist Wayne Hussey.

After a string of singles and EPs established a strong Sisters following in England, WEA signed the band worldwide. By this time, Sisters had added dance and pop elements to their heavy sound, and *First and Last and Always*, produced by Dave Allen (the Cure), reached the U.K. Top 20. The band was having internal problems, however, and Marx left to form the group Ghost Dance. In typically macabre fashion, the Sisters played a June 1985 concert dubbed "Altamont: A Festival of Remembrance." Shortly afterward, Hussey and Adams left to form the Mission (U.K.). Eldritch, who had been having health problems, moved to Hamburg. Embroiled in a legal fight with his former band mates, he released the EP *Gift* in 1986 under the name Sisterhood, partly to preempt Hussey and Adams from using that name. *Gift* featured tape collages, a cameo by American Alan Vega (Suicide), and another American, ex–Gun Club bassist Patricia Morrison.

Morrison remained Eldritch's sole band mate on *Floodland*, whose single "This Corrosion" became popular among American alternative rockers. Meat Loaf collaborator Jim Steinman produced two album tracks. Morrison left, and Eldritch replaced her with the controversial Tony James, former Generation X bassist and Sigue Sigue Sputnik mastermind. The Sisters continued their transatlantic success with *Vision Thing*, a powerful and pointed commentary on life under Bush and Thatcher. The album, featuring new members Andreas Bruhn and Tim Bricheno and guest appearances by John Perry (Only Ones), yielded the singles "Vision Thing" and "More." In summer 1991 the Sisters, joined by ex-B.A.D. keyboardist Dan Donovan, led a tour of outdoor theaters with Public Enemy, Gang of Four, Warrior Soul, and Young Black Teenagers.

Feuds with their record company kept the Sisters out of the recording studio until they extricated themselves from their contract in 1998. Meanwhile, a side project of Eldritch's called Gangwar released a number of brooding tracks on a 1996 compilation album they split with U.K. synth-pop band James Ray's Performance. The Sisters continue to be a big concert draw among goth fans, even though Eldritch now claims no connection with the goth movement. *Some Girls Wander by Mistake* (1992) and *A Slight Case of Overbombing* (1993) are compilations of previously released material.

Ricky Skaggs

Born July 18, 1954, Cordell, KY
1979—*Sweet Temptation* (Sugar Hill) 1981—*Waitin' for the Sun to Shine* (Epic) 1982—*Highways & Heartaches* 1983—

Don't Cheat in Our Hometown 1984—*Country Boy* 1985—*Favorite Country Songs; Live in London* 1986—*Love's Gonna Get Ya!* 1988—*Comin' Home to Stay* 1989—*Kentucky Thunder* 1991—*My Father's Son* 1993—*Super Hits* 1995—*Solid Ground* (Atlantic) 1997—*Life Is a Journey; Bluegrass Rules!* (Skaggs Family Records) 1999—*Ancient Tones; Soldier of the Cross* 2000—*Big Mon: The Songs of Bill Monroe; 16 Biggest Hits.*

From bluegrass to the top of the country charts and back again, it would be impossible to imagine Nashville without Ricky Skaggs. His work with Emmylou Harris was instrumental in bringing country music back from the slick, overproduced sound that dominated Nashville in the '70s. As a solo artist, Skaggs has had 18 Top 10 C&W singles, with 10 reaching #1, and two #2, including "Uncle Pen" (#1, 1984), the first bluegrass recording to top the country charts since 1963. Skaggs has scored eight C&W Top 20 albums, including three #1s (*Highways & Heartaches* [#61 pop, 1982], *Don't Cheat in Our Hometown*, and *Country Boy* [#180 pop, 1984]). A virtuoso multi-instrumentalist (on guitar, mandolin, banjo, and fiddle), he was named to the Grand Ole Opry in 1982, at the time the youngest performer to receive that honor.

Born into a musical family (his construction worker father played church meeting halls, his mother was a gospel singer and songwriter), Skaggs taught himself mandolin at age five. He also made his first public appearance that year, playing "Ruby" at a Bill Monroe concert. By the late '60s, he started performing with Keith Whitley. When bluegrass legend Ralph Stanley was late for a show in 1970, the promoter asked Skaggs and Whitley, who were in the audience, to fill in. Stanley, who walked in while they were playing, was sufficiently impressed to add them to his band.

Tired of life on the road, Skaggs quit in 1972 and moved to Washington, DC, where he worked for the Virginia Electric and Power company until 1974, when he joined the Country Gentlemen. He played with J.D. Crowe and the New South before forming his own band, Boone Creek, in 1975. He met Emmylou Harris at a party, and when Rodney Crowell left her Hot Band in 1978, she asked Skaggs to replace him. He played on her albums *Blue Kentucky Girl* (1980), *Light of the Stable* (1981), and was musical director and arranger for *Roses in the Snow* (1980). Skaggs recorded a solo album, *Sweet Temptation* (1979), for Sugar Hill, a small North Carolina label, moved to Nashville in 1980, and signed to Epic, who released *Waitin' for the Sun to Shine* (#77 pop, #2 C&W, 1982), which proved there was still an audience for traditional country music. Subsequent albums add some rock touches but never stray far from Skaggs' country roots.

In 1981 Skaggs married Sharon White, one half of the Whites. They recorded a #10 C&W duet in 1987, "Love Can't Ever Get Any Better Than This." He has also dueted with Ray Charles on "Friendship" (1984), and performed with and produced albums for the Bellamy Brothers, Johnny Cash, Rodney Crowell, Exile, Dolly Parton, and Jesse Winchester. In 1994, as "hat acts" flourished in Nashville, Skaggs' contract with Epic ended and he signed with Atlantic, for which he released *Solid Ground* (#72 C&W, 1996) and *Life Is a Journey* (1997), all the while continuing to perform at bluegrass concerts and festivals.

While Skaggs had enormous popular success during the '80s, culminating with his being named Entertainer of the Year by the Country Music Association in 1985, he didn't fare as well in the following decade, finding himself at odds with a Nashville that was producing increasingly pop-ish music. While his last album for Atlantic flopped, the defiantly titled *Bluegrass Rules!* (#45 C&W, 1997), initially released as a side project on the guitarist's own label, Skaggs Family Records, turned into a surprise commercial success and won a Grammy for Best Bluegrass Album in 1999. This prompted Skaggs to leave Atlantic and return to his musical roots. (Using the label as a new creative outlet, he also spearheaded 2000's *Big Mon: The Songs of Bill Monroe*, a tribute to the bluegrass legend.)

In 1999 Skaggs, an openly Christian performer who had won several Dove Awards in the past, released his first gospel album, *Soldier of the Cross* (#65 C&W, 1999).

The Skatalites

Formed 1963, Kingston, Jam.
Don Drummond (b. 1943; d. May 6, 1969), trombone; Rico Rodriguez, trombone; Baba Brooks, trumpet; Johnny "Dizzy" Moore, fluegelhorn, trumpet; Raymond Harper, trumpet; Bobby Ellis, trumpet; Lester Sterling, alto sax; Karl Bryan, alto sax; Roland Alphonso (b. 1936; d. Nov. 20, 1998), tenor sax; Tommy McCook (b. Mar. 4, 1927, Kingston; d. May 5, 1998), trumpet, tenor sax; Ernest Ranglin, gtr.; Jah Jerry (b. Jerome Hines), gtr.; Lloyd Brevette, bass; Jackie Mittoo (b. 1948, Jam.; d. 1988), kybds.; Theophilus Beckford, kybds.; Gladstone Anderson, kybds.; Lloyd Knibb, bass, perc.; Drumbago, drums; Hugh Malcolm, drums.
1963—*Ska Authentic* (Studio One) 1975—*Legendary Skatalites* (Top Ranking) 1977—*African Roots* (United Artists) 1984—*Scattered Lights* (Alligator) 1986—*Stretching Out* cassette (ROIR) 1993—*Skavoovee* (Shanachie) 1994—*Hi-Bop Ska* 1996—*Greetings From Skamania; Foundation Ska* (Heartbeat) 1998—*Ball of Fire* (Island/PolyGram).

From 1963 to 1967 the Skatalites played on nearly every session recorded in Jamaica. Leader Don Drummond virtually invented ska, and the ranks of his band were filled with stars of that and later eras. The band was a major inspiration for the British 2-Tone movement in the late '70s. Drummond was a music teacher at a Catholic boys' school in West Kingston when he formed his band; some members had been his students. With varying numbers according to the demands of the session, they recorded for all of the Jamaican producers, but especially for Coxsone Dodd at his Studio One. They backed Eric Morris, the Charms, Justin Hines, Derrick Morgan, the Maytals, the Wailers, and the Heptones. They issued instrumental records from their sessions as well, scoring Jamaican hits with "Ball o' Fire," "Independent Anniversary Ska," "Confucius," and "Dick Tracy."

One of the first Jamaican acts signed to Island Records and marketed in the U.K., they made the British Top 40 with "Guns of Navarone" in 1967. They also recorded, in various aggregations, as the Don Drummond All Stars, Roland Al and the Soul Brothers, Tommy McCook and the Supersonics, the Baba Brooks Band, the Karl Bryan Orchestra, Jackie Mittoo and the Soul Vendors, Drumbago's All Stars, Sir Coxsone's All Stars, and Roland Alphonso's Alley Cats.

By 1967, the Skatalites were no longer recording under that name, although most of the members were active in Jamaican music until the '80s. Some moved to England, where, like Ernest Ranglin, they maintained careers as session musicians or, like Rico Rodriguez, they began making solo records. Drummond, who had won international jazz trombonist awards, died in 1969 after years of steadily worsening mental illness. In 1975 Tommy McCook, Roland Alphonso, Lloyd Knibb, and Lester Sterling briefly reunited as the Skatalites under Lloyd Brevette's leadership.

The punky ska played by 2-Tone bands like the Specials and Madness in the late '70s and early '80s revived interest in the Skatalites. Rico Rodriguez played on the Specials debut album in 1979 (they also covered "Navarone" in concert). In 1988 the group, now led by Tommy McCook, toured the U.S. *Skavoovee* was released in 1993, supported by a tour that featured latter-day 2-Tone–style bands Special Beat, the Selecter (which had just re-formed), and the New York City–based Toasters. *Hi-Bop Ska* underlined the connections between ska and jazz, and featured Lester Bowie as a guest.

Despite undergoing a triple bypass in 1994, McCook helmed the 1996 studio album *Greetings From Skamania;* he was to die of heart failure in 1998. *Ball of Fire* featured new recordings of some of the Skatalites' old hits; the band at that time included founding members Brevette, Sterling, Alphonso, and Knibb.

Skid Row

Formed 1986, New Jersey
Matt Fallon, voc.; Dave "Snake" Sabo, gtr.; Scotti Hill, gtr.; Rachel Bolan, bass; Rob Affuso, drums.
1987—(– Fallon; + Sebastian Bach [b. Sebastian Bierk, Apr. 3, 1968, Bahamas], voc.) 1989—*Skid Row* (Atlantic) 1991—*Slave to the Grind* 1992—*B-Sides Ourselves* EP 1995—*Subhuman Race* 1998—*Forty Seasons: The Best of Skid Row.*
Sebastian Bach solo: 1999—*Bring 'Em Bach Alive* (Spitfire).

New Jersey–based hard-rock band Skid Row included Bon Jovi's original guitarist, Dave "Snake" Sabo. That connection came in handy when Bon Jovi's management signed Skid Row and offered it the opening-act slot on Bon Jovi's 1989 U.S. tour—where audiences discovered the wild, anything-goes stage persona of pretty-boy frontman Sebastian Bach. Bach would later publicly criticize Jon Bon Jovi for taking a chunk of Skid Row's publishing royalties in exchange for his early support.

The band's debut album (#6, 1989) sold 4 million copies, thanks to the Bon Jovi connection, heavy MTV play of the video for the anthemic "Youth Gone Wild," and the unexpected success of the singles "18 and Life" (#4, 1989) and the power ballad "I Remember You" (#6, 1989). Skid Row also contributed a cover of the Sex Pistols' "Holidays in the Sun" to the 1989 metal all-star album *Stairway to Heaven, Highway to Hell.*

Bach then began courting controversy in earnest. At a December 27, 1989, concert in Springfield, Massachusetts, he was hit in the head with a bottle thrown by a fan. Bach hurled the bottle back into the crowd—hitting an innocent girl in the face—then leapt into the throng and pummeled someone who may or may not have tossed the bottle. Bach faced four assault charges and one count of mayhem. He did no jail time but spent three years on probation and paid an undisclosed settlement to the girl he injured, as well as giving her a personal apology (she'd also endured the taunts of schoolmates angry that she'd "made trouble" for Bach).

About the same time, Bach was pictured in a metal magazine wearing a T-shirt that read AIDS KILLS FAGS DEAD (a parody of an insecticide slogan). Asked by MTV News about the shirt, Bach laughingly said, "I do not condone, comprehend, or understand homosexuality in any way, shape, form, or size." In the face of mounting public outrage, Bach stated that he had friends who were gay and that he disapproved of gay bashing.

Slave to the Grind took a harder-edged and punkier approach than the first album, and yielded no hit singles. Though it entered the chart at #1, the album fell before too long, and sold only a quarter the copies of its predecessor. The five-song EP *B-Sides Ourselves* included Skid Row's covers of Jimi Hendrix's "Little Wing" and the Ramones' "Psychotherapy." The band's subsequent 1995 release, *Subhuman Race,* reached #35 but only charted for nine weeks, performing poorly in the post-Nirvana rock market. Bach was jettisoned the following year, and launched a solo career that included *Bring 'Em Bach Alive*—Japanese concert recordings of old Skid Row hits, plus more recent studio tracks—and a side project with former Breeders guitarist Kelley Deal and Smashing Pumpkins drummer Jimmy Chamberlin called the Last Hard Men. By 2000, Bach was appearing on Broadway in *Jekyll & Hyde,* and Skid Row guitarist Dave Sabo had plans to record with a new band, Ozone Monday.

Slade

Formed 1968, Wolverhampton, Eng.
Noddy Holder (b. Neville Holder, June 15, 1950, Walshall, Eng.), gtr., voc.; Dave Hill (b. Apr. 4, 1952, Fleet Castle, Eng.), gtr.; Jimmy Lea (b. June 14, 1952, Wolverhampton), bass, piano, violin; Don Powell (b. Sep. 10, 1950, Bilston, Eng.), drums.
1969—*Beginnings* (Fontana) 1970—*Play It Loud* (Cotillion) 1972—*Slade Alive* (Polydor); *Slayed* 1973—*Sladest* (Reprise) 1974—*Old, New, Borrowed and Blue* (Polydor) 1975—*In Flame* (Warner Bros.) 1977—*Whatever Happened to Slade?* (Polydor, U.K.) 1984—*Keep Your Hands Off My Power Supply* (CBS) 1985—*Rogues Gallery* 1986—*You Boyz Make Big*

Noyz 1992—(group disbands) 1993—(group re-forms as Slade II: Hill; Powell; + Steve Whalley, gtr., voc.; + Trevor Holliday, bass, voc.) 2000—(– Holliday; + Dave Glover, bass, voc.).

Distinguished by Noddy Holder's harsh screaming, a crudely thunderous rhythm section and song titles that recast the English language ("Gudbuy T'Jane," "Cum On Feel the Noize," "Skweeze Me Pleeze Me"), Slade breathed life into early-'70s hard rock. Within a decade, the group's influence could be seen in newer artists, including Quiet Riot (whose first hit was a cover of "Cum On Feel the Noize" and who covered "Mama Weer All Crazee Now" on its second album), Joan Jett, and any number of glitter-influenced rockers.

Hailing from Wolverhampton, an industrial city near Birmingham, the quartet started as the In Betweens. They changed their name to Ambrose Slade and were spotted one night by Chas Chandler, the former Animal and former manager/producer of Jimi Hendrix. Chandler dropped the Ambrose and became the group's manager and producer, giving them their first British hit in 1971, a cover of Little Richard's "Get Down and Get With It," followed by the #1 record "Coz I Love You."

The key to Slade's primitive attack was Chandler's live-in-the-studio production. Appearing onstage at first with closely cropped haircuts, blue jeans, suspenders, and construction boots—trademarks of England's working-class skinhead movement—Slade was as noisy as the Who and generated an unrestrained "Slademania." Fans stomped, clapped, rushed the stage, fainted, and tossed bras and panties onstage. Slade gradually switched its visual image, becoming one of rock's most gaudily outfitted groups. The four rockers dressed in the unlikely combination of silver sci-fi gear and high-fashion platform boots.

Slade's hits from this period included "Take Me Bak 'Ome" (#1 U.K., 1972), "Mama Weer All Crazee Now" (#1 U.K., 1972), "Gudbuy T'Jane" (#2 U.K., 1972), and "Cum On Feel the Noize" (#1 U.K., 1973), which were generally ignored in the U.S. In 1974 Slade starred in the film *Flame*, in which the members appeared as rock stars on the way to the top. At the same time, Slade's popularity was slipping, with decreasing sales of albums such as *Slade in Flame*, which underlined the group's maturing hard-rock style. Slade carried on, seemingly unable to regain the momentum of its peak period, when it sold more than 10 million records worldwide. In 1981 the group had a British hit with "Lock Up Your Daughters," then in 1983, on the heels of the Quiet Riot hit cover, the group rebounded in the U.K. with "My Oh My," which went to #2. "Run Runaway," from *Keep Your Hands Off My Power Supply*, became Slade's highest-charting single in the U.S., topping at #20. After a few more moderately successful releases in its homeland, Slade split up in 1992. Guitarist Dave Hill, drummer Don Powell, and two new recruits have soldiered on in the U.K. as Slade II. Holder produced the female metal band Girlschool's 1983 album, *Play Dirty*. He finished a witty book, *Who's Crazee Now?*, in 1999 and he occasionally works as an actor. Holder and former Slade bassist Jimmy Lea have also recorded solo.

Slayer

Formed 1982, Los Angeles, CA
Tom Araya (b. June 6, 1961, Chile), bass, voc.; Jeff Hanneman (b. Jan. 31, 1964, Los Angeles), gtr.; Kerry King (b. June 3, 1964, Huntington Park, CA), gtr.; Dave Lombardo (b. Feb. 16, 1965), drums.
1983—*Show No Mercy* (Metal Blade) 1985—*Hell Awaits* 1986—*Reign in Blood* (Def Jam) 1988—*South of Heaven* 1990—*Seasons in the Abyss* (Def American) 1991—*Decade of Aggression Live* 1992—(– Lombardo, + Paul Bostaph [b. Mar. 4, 1965, Hayward, CA], drums) 1994—*Divine Intervention* (American) 1996—*Undisputed Attitude* 1998—*Diabolus in Musica.*

If Slayer did not exist, the tabloid press would invent it: Loud, aggressive, and violent, its songs touch on sadism, Satanism, Nazi death camps, and serial killers. Its music was prominently featured in 1987's troubled-teen film *River's Edge*. A 1988 concert in New York's Felt Forum had to be stopped when fans rampaged, tearing up seats and pelting the stage with debris. And all five teens featured on the "Kids Who Kill" episode of *Geraldo* cited Slayer as one of their favorite bands.

Slayer began in 1982 as part of L.A.'s Huntington Beach head-banging scene. Originally a cover band, by 1983 the band had written "Aggressive Perfector," which appeared on Metal Blade Records' *Metal Massacre III* compilation. Metal Blade also released Slayer's next two albums, *Show No Mercy* and *Hell Awaits*. The group's brutal songs and malevolent obsessions increased its local reputation, but it was unable to garner national attention until Rick Rubin signed the band to his Def Jam label in 1986. Slayer became something of a cause célèbre that year when Columbia (Def Jam's distributor) refused to release *Reign in Blood*, citing references to Nazi physician/torturer Joseph Mengele in the song "Angel of Death," among other offenses. Geffen quickly picked up the album, which became the band's first to chart, peaking at #94.

Starting with the group's followup, *South of Heaven* (#57, 1988), bassist/vocalist Tom Araya became the main songwriter, and Slayer's music and subject matter turned slightly more mainstream, with riffs and melodies replacing drones. The lyrics focused on more earthbound subjects: "Death Skin Mask" from *Seasons in the Abyss* (#40, 1990) was inspired by serial killer Ed Gein.

In 1991 Slayer celebrated its first 10 years together by releasing *Decade of Aggression Live* (#55) and holding down one third of the Clash of the Titans Tour along with Megadeth and Anthrax. The band returned in 1994 with *Divine Intervention* (#8, 1994), its most successful album to date.

Picking up where 1993's "Disorder" (a medley of Exploited songs done in collaboration with Ice-T for the *Judg-*

Slayer: Tom Araya, Paul Bostaph, Kerry King, Jeff Hanneman

ment Night soundtrack) had left off, Slayer released *Undisputed Attitude* (#34, 1996). It featured only one new Slayer track, concentrating instead on a variety of punk covers by the likes of T.S.O.L., Minor Threat, and Verbal Abuse. Bostaph was replaced by ex-Testament drummer John Dette for the following tour, but came back to play on *Diabolus in Musica* (#31, 1998), on which Slayer returned to its usual gruesome lyrical content set to speed metal. In 2000 the band joined the inaugural Tattoo the Earth Tour, reaffirming its status as a grand elder of the metal scene.

Sleater-Kinney

Formed 1994, Olympia, WA
Carrie Brownstein (b. Sep. 27, 1974, Seattle, WA), gtr., voc.;
Corin Tucker (b. Nov. 9, 1972, State College, PA), voc., gtr.;
Lora McFarlane (b. Austral.), drums.
1995—*Sleater-Kinney* (Kill Rock Stars) (– McFarlane; + Toni Gogin, drums) 1996—(– Gogin) *Call the Doctor;* (+ Janet Weiss [b. Sep. 24, 1965, Hollywood, CA], drums, voc.)
1997—*Dig Me Out* 1999—*The Hot Rock* 2000—*All Hands on the Bad One.*
Corin Tucker with Heavens to Betsy: 1994—*Calculated* (Kill Rock Stars).
Corin Tucker with Cadallaca: 1998—*Introducing Cadallaca* (K Records) 2000—*Out West* EP (Kill Rock Stars).
Carrie Brownstein with Excuse 17: 1995—*Excuse Seventeen* (Chainsaw); *Such Friends Are Dangerous* (Kill Rock Stars).

Sleater-Kinney was among the most critically acclaimed bands of the '90s, emerging in the final days of the riot-grrrl movement to fuse radical feminism with challenging, fiery punk. The all-female trio also became dynamic leaders of an alternative-rock movement that had otherwise lost its way in the post-Nirvana years. The band is mostly unknown to the mainstream and has shown little interest in recording for a major label. But for Sleater-Kinney rock & roll is more about empowerment and community than stardom.

Singer/guitarists Corin Tucker and Carrie Brownstein met as students in the early '90s at Evergreen State College in Olympia, Washington. Inspired by Bikini Kill and other riot grrrls, both were already in bands (Tucker in Heavens to Betsy, Brownstein in Excuse 17). The two began writing songs together, were lovers for a time, and with drummer Lora McFarlane founded Sleater-Kinney—named for an Olympia freeway off-ramp. The band's self-titled debut in 1995 introduced a sound that was fast and raw. Tucker's searing wail was set against the band's minimalist rock (just drums and two guitars), with lyrics that confronted sexual abuse and inequality while rebelling against the sexist traditions of rock & roll. On 1996's *Call the Doctor,* Sleater-Kinney claimed its own piece of the rock tradition with the ironic "I Wanna Be Your Joey Ramone." Critics took notice, voting the album among the best of that year.

McFarlane quit in 1995. Her permanent replacement was Janet Weiss (Quasi, Elliott Smith, Motorgoat), who first appeared on 1997's *Dig Me Out* and then 1999's *The Hot Rock* (#181), both critically acclaimed releases. That was followed the next year by *All Hands on the Bad One,* which welded clean pop hooks onto the Sleater-Kinney punk sound, bemoaning the corporate raiding of punk culture on "#1 Must Have" and celebrating the need to rock amid continued sexism on "The Ballad of a Ladyman." Tucker introduced a side project in 1998 called Cadallaca (with Sarah Dougher), featuring a sound similar to, though looser than Sleater-Kinney. Weiss continued to record and tour with Quasi (a collaboration with ex-husband Sam Coomes). And later in 2000 Sleater-Kinney appeared on a new Go-Betweens [see entry] album, *The Friends of Rachel Worth,* that Australian band's first recording in a dozen years.

Percy Sledge

Born Nov. 25, 1940, Leighton, AL
1966—*When a Man Loves a Woman* (Atlantic); *Warm and Tender Soul* 1967—*The Percy Sledge Way* 1968—*Take Time to Know Her* 1969—*The Best of Percy Sledge* 1974—*I'll Be Your Everything* (Capricorn) 1987—*When a Man Loves a Woman (The Ultimate Collection)* (Atlantic) 1992—*It Tears Me Up: The Best of Percy Sledge* (Atlantic) 1995—*Blue Night* (Pointblank/Virgin).

In the mid-'60s singer Percy Sledge was performing throughout Mississippi and Alabama as a member of the Esquires Combo. His career took a dramatic turn for the better in 1966, when he quit to go solo and scored a #1 pop and R&B hit with his debut single, "When a Man Loves a Woman." Sledge remained a popular singer through the end of the decade, working in the same intense balladeering style of "When a Man."

His successes included "Warm and Tender Love" (#17 pop, #5 R&B) and "It Tears Me Up" (#20 pop, #7 R&B) in 1966; "Out of Left Field" (#25 R&B) in 1967; "Sudden Stop" (#41 R&B) in 1968; "Any Day Now" (#35 R&B) in 1969; and especially "Take Time to Know Her" (#11 pop, #6 R&B) in 1968. Sledge's career stalled in the '70s, save for a brief resurgence with the R&B hits "Sunshine" (#89 R&B, 1973) and "I'll Be Your Everything" (#15 R&B, 1974).

Sledge's career faded somewhat after that, although he continued to tour the U.S., England, Japan, and the U.K. through the rest of that decade and into the '80s. The use of "When a Man Loves a Woman" in the 1987 hit film *Platoon* sparked a resurgence for Sledge, and that year the song was rereleased in the U.K., where it went to #2. In 1989 he won the Rhythm & Blues Foundation's Career Achievement Award. He continues to perform, playing over 100 dates a year. As of this writing, he lives in Baton Rouge, Louisiana. In 1994 he was sentenced to five years' probation afer being convicted of tax evasion.

Grace Slick: See the Jefferson Airplane

Slick Rick

Born Ricky Walters, Jan. 14, 1965, London, Eng.
1989—*The Great Adventures of Slick Rick* (Def Jam) 1991—*The Ruler's Back* 1994—*Behind Bars* 1999—*The Art of Storytelling.*

Sporting a black patch over an eye blinded by broken glass as a youth, Slick Rick epitomized a pre-gangsta version of ghetto cool that made him a million-selling star but also proved his downfall when a jail term derailed his career. Ricky Walters moved to the Bronx as a teenager and attended New York's prestigious High School of Music and Art. As MC Ricky D. he joined with human beat-box Doug E. Fresh and the Get Fresh Crew [see entry]; his singsong voice with its odd accent was featured on their 1985 hit "La-Di-Da-Di" b/w "The Show."

Splitting from Fresh, Walters hooked up with rap impresario Russell Simmons and disappeared for three years, amid much rumor. He reemerged with the phenomenal *The Great Adventures of Slick Rick* (#31 pop, #1 R&B, 1989), which went on to sell more than a million copies. The album, produced by Jam-Master Jay, Hank Shocklee, Eric Sadler, and Walters, featured "Teenage Love" (#16 R&B, 1988), "Children's Story" (#5 R&B, 1989), and the infamous misogynist rap "Treat Her Like a Prostitute." Rick was also featured on Al B. Sure!'s single "If I'm Not Your Lover" (#2 R&B, 1989).

On July 3, 1990, Walters was arrested for shooting his cousin, who had allegedly embezzled money from him, and another passenger in his cousin's car. In 1991 he was given a sentence of 3 to 10 years for attempted murder. While out on bail before sentencing, Walters recorded *The Ruler's Back* (#29 pop, #18 R&B, 1991), a powerfully ominous record. While in a work-release program, he released *Behind Bars* (#51 pop, #11 R&B, 1994). Interviews with the rapper from inside prison also opened and closed the 1995 hip-hop documentary *The Show.*

Walters finished serving his sentence in 1996, after which he appeared on a number of hit singles by other acts, most notably Montell Jordan's "I Like" (#28 pop, #11 R&B, 1996). Rick finally released an album of his own, *The Art of Storytelling* (#8 pop, #1 R&B), in 1999. The project featured some of the biggest names in rap, everyone from Snoop Dogg and OutKast to Raekwon from the Wu-Tang Clan. It also saw Rick abandoning his thug stance and, on one track, extolling the virtues of monogamy.

The Slits

Formed 1976, London, Eng.
Ari Up (b. Ariana Forster, 1962, Munich, Ger.), voc.; Kate Korus, gtr.; Suzi Gutsy, bass; Palmolive (b. Paloma Romero, 1955, Spain), drums.
1977—(– Korus; – Gutsy; + Tessa Pollit, bass; + Viv Albertine [b. 1955, Fr.], gtr.) 1978—(– Palmolive; + Budgie [b. Aug. 21, 1957, St. Helens, Eng.], drums) *Cut* (Island/Antilles) 1981—*Return of the Giant Slits* (CBS) 1989—*The Peel Sessions* (Dutch East India) 1997—*In the Beginning* (Cleopatra).

British punk rock's first all-female band of any consequence, the Slits knew nothing about how to play their instruments yet began jamming together anyway—just like many of their male counterparts. Before the band had played a gig, bassist Suzi Gutsy left to join Flicks and guitarist Kate Korus left to form the Modettes (whose "White Mice" was a club favorite and whose cover of the Stones' "Paint It Black" was a minor U.K. hit [#42, 1980]). The Slits made their stage debut in London, opening for the Clash, in March 1977 with new guitarist Viv Albertine and bassist Tessa Pollit, both from Flowers of Romance, Sid Vicious' pre–Sex Pistols backing band.

Lead singer Ari Up was 14 years old at the time of the first Slits show, so the band's ability to perform was somewhat limited. Still, the Slits opened for the Clash on its 1977 "White Riot" tour, with Ari Up making a fashion statement by wearing her panties over her black pants, and leaving numerous combs stuck in her dreads. The Slits did not get a record deal until 1979, by which time original drummer Palmolive had left to help form the Raincoats [see entry], and the Slits had evolved into a white-reggae group. With guest drummer Budgie (formerly with Big in Japan and soon to join Siouxsie and the Banshees) and reggae producer Dennis Bovell, the Slits recorded the dub-influenced *Cut;* new-wave discos in the U.S. gave some play to the frolicsome track "Typical Girls." Demonstrating the neo-tribalism they were affecting at the time, the three Slits wore nothing but thongs and mud for the *Cut* album cover photo. For a subsequent U.S. tour, Budgie was replaced by Bruce Smith, of British avant-jazz-rock band the Pop Group, and the band was filled out by British avant-gardist Steve Beresford on keyboards, trumpet, and miscellaneous toy instruments. The Slits broke up at the end of 1981, which saw a second album, *Return of the Giant Slits,* further emphasizing the group's interest in dark, dubby textures. Up then joined the New Age Steppers, an experimental funk and reggae outfit guided by producer Adrian Sherwood. (Ari's stepfather is Johnny Rotten, whom her mother Nora started dating around the time the Slits first formed and subsequently married.)

Philip (P.F.) Sloan

Born 1946, Los Angeles, CA
1965—*Songs of Our Time* (Dunhill) 1966—*12 More Times* 1968—*Measure of Pleasure* (Atco) 1972—*Raised on Records* (Epic, U.K.) 1993—*P. F. Sloan Anthology* (One Way) 1997—*(Still on the) Eve of Destruction* (All the Best).
With the Fantastic Baggies: *Tell 'Em I'm Surfin'* (Imperial).

Though he had his own career as a Dylan-styled singer/songwriter, P.F. Sloan is best known for his songwriting, particularly Barry McGuire's 1965 smash "Eve of Destruction." Prior to "Eve," Sloan and his partner Steve Barri had written surf-rock hits, and even recorded a few of them disguised as the Fantastic Baggies on the album *Tell 'Em I'm Surfin'*.

In the years that followed, Sloan and Barri worked extensively with the Grass Roots, provided the Turtles with a hit record, "You Baby," and wrote songs for the Searchers, Herman's Hermits, and many others. Because of the groups he was involved with, Sloan's work tended to be dismissed—a situation addressed by Jimmy Webb in his song "P.F. Sloan." Barri remains active as a pop-rock producer. Shortly before his death, ex–Washington Square Bruce Jay Paskow produced an album for Sloan and played guitar in the band that backed the singer for a showcase performance in L.A. in late 1993. Initially issued in Japan, 1997's *(Still on the) Eve of Destruction* was Sloan's first new album in over 20 years.

Sly and Robbie

Formed 1975, Kingston, Jam.
Sly "Drumbar" Dunbar (b. Lowell Fillmore Dunbar, May 10, 1952, Kingston), drums; Robbie "Basspeare" Shakespeare (b. Sep. 27, 1953, Kingston), bass.
1981—*Sly and Robbie Present Taxi* (Mango); *60s, 70s, 80s* 1982—*Sly-Go-Ville* 1983—*Crucial Reggae Driven by Sly and Robbie* 1985—*A Dub Experience; Reggae Greats; Language Barrier* (Island) 1987—*Rhythm Killers* 1988—*The Summit* (RAS) 1989—*Silent Assassin* (Island) 1990—*Two Rhythms Clash* (RAS) 1998—*Friends* (EastWest) 1999—*Drum & Bass Strip to the Bone by Howie B* (Palm Pictures).

Sly Dunbar and Robbie Shakespeare began their careers as teenage session musicians. They teamed up to become one of Jamaica's most celebrated rhythm sections and continued their partnership as bandleaders, producers, and record businessmen.

Dunbar started out in the Yardbrooms, a reggae band of the late '60s that nurtured several of Jamaica's leading instrumentalists. In the early '70s Dunbar was with Skin, Flesh and Bones, who recorded their own records and backed various singers.

Shakespeare studied with Aston "Family Man" Barrett (bassist with the Upsetters, who went on to join the Wailers) and played sessions for Burning Spear, Bunny Wailer, and others. He first played with Dunbar behind Peter Tosh in 1975, and the following year—after Dunbar had returned from touring the U.K. with the Mighty Diamonds—the two formed the Revolutionaires, a leading dub band of the '70s. Concurrently until 1979, Dunbar and Shakespeare led Peter Tosh's band, Word, Sound and Power, in the studio and on tours of North America and Europe. Their sound exemplified the "rockers' riddims" of late-'70s reggae. (Shakespeare played a cameo role in *Rockers,* the 1977 film inspired by that sound.)

In 1978 they set up their own record company, Taxi Productions, formed the Taxi All-Stars from the ashes of the Revolutionaires and Word, Sound and Power, and began working as producers. Taxi's first release was Black Uhuru's "Observe Life." It was followed by numerous albums for Black Uhuru, for established artists like Gregory Isaacs, Max Romeo, Prince Far-I, and Dennis Brown, and for such newer acts as the Tamlins, the Wailing Souls, Jimmy Riley, and General Echo. Their immediately recognizable sound is marked by Robbie's thundering in-the-pocket bass and Sly's innovative use of synthesized drums. In addition, Sly and Robbie (as they are invariably billed) issued their own duo and solo recordings on Taxi. In 1980 they entered into a worldwide distribution agreement with Island Records. Their early-'80s U.S. releases are anthologies of Taxi artists. In the early '80s they worked with such reggae veterans as Jimmy Cliff, Desmond Dekker, and the Paragons, and regularly took their "riddims" on the road with Black Uhuru. They have also worked with artists not usually associated with reggae: Ian Dury, Joan Armatrading, Grace Jones, Manu Dibango, Robert Palmer, Joe Cocker, and even Serge Gainsbourg. Bob Dylan used them as the rhythm section on his 1983 album *Infidels;* Mick Jagger employed them for his 1985 solo debut, *She's the Boss*.

On their own, Sly and Robbie hooked up with avant-funk bassist/producer Bill Laswell for 1985's *Language Barrier,* featuring guest appearances by Afrika Bambaataa and Bob Dylan. Laswell also produced *Rhythm Killers,* which included contributions from Bootsy Collins and dancehall star Shinehead. Collaborating with rappers KRS-ONE, Queen Latifah, and Young MC, Sly and Robbie produced the dub-rap hybrid, *Silent Assassin*. Sly and Robbie also produced Maxi Priest's 1988 U.K. #5 hit "Wild World" (a cover of the Cat Stevens' song) and Chaka Demus and Pliers' 1993 Top 10 U.K. single "Tease Me."

In 1998 the duo recorded *Friends,* an album that featured many of the artists they'd worked with over the years—Keith Richards appeared on a dancehall cover of "(I Can't Get No) Satisfaction," for instance. The following year, they teamed up with producer and remixer Howie B, head of the Pussyfoot label and better known for his work with Tricky and Björk. In keeping with their taste for experimentation, Sly and Robbie performed live in the studio while B simultaneously edited and remixed the tracks.

Sly and the Family Stone

Formed 1967, San Francisco, CA
Original lineup: Sly Stone (b. Sylvester Stewart, Mar. 15, 1944, Dallas, TX), gtr., kybds., voc.; Freddie Stone (b. Fred Stewart, June 5, 1946, Dallas), gtr., voc.; Larry Graham Jr. (b. Aug. 14, 1946, Beaumont, TX), bass, voc.; Cynthia Robinson (b. Jan. 12, 1946, Sacramento, CA), trumpet; Greg Errico (b. Sep. 1, 1946, San Francisco), drums; Rosie Stone (b. Mar. 21, 1945, Vallejo, CA), piano; Jerry Martini (b. Oct. 1, 1943, CO), sax.
1967—*A Whole New Thing* (Epic) 1968—*Dance to the Music; Life* 1969—*Stand* 1970—*Greatest Hits* 1971—*There's a Riot Goin' On* 1973—*Fresh* 1974—*Small Talk* 1975—*High Energy* (reissue of *A Whole New Thing* and *Dance to the Music*); *High on You* 1976—*Heard Ya Missed Me, Well I'm Back* 1979—*Back on the Right Track* (Warner Bros.) 1983—*Ain't But the One Way.*

In the late '60s Sly and the Family Stone fused black rhythms and a psychedelic sensibility into a new pop/soul/rock hybrid that drew both white and black audiences. The Family Stone's music predated disco and inspired the many black self-contained bands that emerged in the '70s; along with James Brown, the Family Stone virtually invented '70s funk, and their impact has proven lasting and widespread. Motown producer Norman Whitfield, for example, patterned that label's forays into harder-driving, socially relevant material (such as the Temptations' "Runaway Child" and "Ball of Confusion") on Sly's work. The pioneering precedent of Sly Stone's racial, sexual, and stylistic mix had an undeniably major influence on Prince and Rick James in the '80s, and the male-female vocal interplay of Human League's "Fascination," for example, can be traced back to any of a number of the group's hits. In the '90s he was paid homage by Earth, Wind & Fire on their *Heritage* album, and in a hit cover of "Everyday People" by rap group Arrested Development.

Sylvester Stewart's family moved from Texas to the San Francisco area in the '50s. At age four, he began singing gospel music and at age 16 made a local hit, "Long Time Away." Stewart studied trumpet, music theory, and composition at Vallejo Junior College and while in school became active on the Bay Area music scene. With his brother, Fred, he formed several short-lived groups, like the Stewart Bros. He was a disc jockey at soul station KSOL, and at Autumn Records he produced records by the Beau Brummels, Bobby Freeman, the Mojo Men, and Grace Slick's first band, the Great Society. He later worked for KDIA.

In 1966 Sly formed a short-lived group called the Stoners, which included female trumpeter Cynthia Robinson. With her he started his next band, Sly and the Family Stone. Sly, Robinson, and Fred Stewart were joined by Larry Graham [see separate entry], Greg Errico, and Jerry Martini, all of whom had studied music and worked in numerous amateur groups. Rosie Stone joined the group soon after. Working around the Bay Area in 1967, this multiracial band made a strong impression. They recorded their debut single, "I Ain't Got Nobody" b/w "I Can't Turn You Loose," on the local Loadstone label.

The Family Stone's debut LP, *A Whole New Thing,* flopped. Its followup, *Dance to the Music,* included the hit title cut (#8 pop, #9 R&B). *Life* sold fewer copies than their previous albums, but their next release, a double-sided single, "Everyday People" b/w "Sing a Simple Song," was #1 on both the R&B and pop charts. *Stand* mixed hard-edged politics with the Family's ecstatic dance music. It rose to #13 on the pop chart and contained Sly standards like the title song, "Don't Call Me Nigger Whitey," "Sex Machine," "Somebody's Watching You," and "I Want to Take You Higher" (#3 pop, #24 R&B). Fiery versions of "Dance to the Music" and "Higher," heard on the Woodstock soundtrack album, established the Family Stone as one of the finest live bands of the late '60s.

Singles like "Hot Fun in the Summertime" (#2 pop, #3 R&B) and "Thank You Falettinme Be Mice Elf Agin" b/w "Everybody Is a Star" (#1 pop and R&B), were the band's commercial peak, and the success of *Greatest Hits* (#2 pop) reflected their immense popularity. The smooth post–doo-wop/pop/soul of "Hot Fun" and the eerie funk of "Thank You" demonstrated the band's considerable range. By this time, *Stand* had been on the charts for more than 80 weeks, and most of the Family's Top 10 singles had gone gold, as had most of their post–*Dance to the Music* LPs. Jazz trumpeter Miles Davis, who'd been flummoxing critics with electrified "fusion" albums, did it again when he named Sly Stone and Jimi Hendrix as his favorite musicians.

After 1970 Sly became somewhat notorious for arriving late for or missing concerts, and it was generally known that he was suffering from drug problems. The group's turning point came in 1971, when *There's a Riot Goin' On* went to #1. Its darkly understated sound, violent imagery, and controversial militant stance were a sharp contrast to the optimism of earlier works. From that album came "Family Affair" (#1 pop and R&B), Sly's last across-the-board hit.

By 1972, the Family Stone was growing restless. Key members Larry Graham and drummer Greg Errico left and were replaced by Rusty Allen and Andy Newmark. From *Fresh,* "If You Want Me to Stay" (#12 pop, #3 R&B) did fairly well, and a blues version of "Que Sera Sera" got some airplay, particularly when rumors of a romance between Sly and Doris Day emerged. *Small Talk* fared moderately well. It took advertising of Sly's public wedding ceremony to Kathy Silva at Madison Square Garden in 1974 to sell it out. "I Get High on You" (#3 R&B) did respectably, but subsequent albums failed.

Meanwhile, disco had emerged, and in 1979 Epic issued *Ten Years Too Soon,* a compilation album on which the quirky original rhythm tracks were erased and a disco beat dubbed in. By the mid '70s, stories of drug problems and arrests were part of the Sly Stone legacy. By 1979, he was with Warner Bros., attempting to make the comeback many observers felt would be as natural as James Brown's, given the current interest in and popularity of funk. In 1981, having been cited as a major influence by George Clinton, he appeared on Funkadelic's *Electric Spanking of War Babies.* He toured with Clinton's P-Funk All-Stars, on his own, and with Bobby Womack in the early '80s. In 1983 Sly was arrested for cocaine possession and entered a rehabilitation program a year later.

In 1986 Stone guested on ex-Time guitarist Jesse Johnson's minor hit "Crazay," which led to a deal with A&M Records. A 1987 single, "Eek-a-Bo-Static," failed to chart; that same year Stone duetted with ex-Motel Martha Davis on "Love & Affection," for the soundtrack of the movie *Soul Man.* Sly's stalled-out career stopped dead for a time when he was jailed in 1987 for cocaine possession. In 1993 Sly and the Family Stone was inducted into the Rock and Roll Hall of Fame. Stone has reportedly been working on a new album since 1995, but as of early 2001 no material has surfaced.

The Small Faces/The Faces

The Small Faces: formed 1965, London, Eng.
Steve Marriott (b. Jan. 30, 1947, London; d. Apr. 20, 1991, Arkesden, Eng.), gtr., voc.; Jimmy Winston (b. James Langwith, Apr. 20, 1945, Eng.), kybds.; Ronnie Lane (b. Apr. 1, 1946, London; d. June 4, 1997, Trinidad, CO), bass; Kenney Jones (b. Sep. 16, 1948, London), drums.
1965—(– Winston; + Ian McLagan [b. May 12, 1945, Hounslown, Eng.], kybds.) 1966—*The Small Faces* (Decca) 1967—*From the Beginning* 1968—*Ogden's Nut Gone Flake* (Immediate) (– Marriott) 1969—*Autumn Stone* (name changed to Faces; new personnel, see below) 1970—*In Memoriam* 1975—*The Vintage Years* (Sire) 1991—*There Are But Four Small Faces* (Immediate) 1992—*All or Nothing* (Sony).
The Faces, formed 1969, London: Lane; McLagan; Jones; + Rod Stewart (b. Jan. 10, 1945, London), voc.; + Ron Wood (b. June 1, 1947, Hillingdon, Eng.), gtr., voc.
1970—*First Step* (Warner Bros.) 1971—*Long Player; A Nod Is as Good as a Wink to a Blind Horse* 1973—*Ooh La La* (– Lane; + Tetsu Yamauchi [b. Oct. 21, 1947, Fukuola, Jap.], bass) 1974—*Overture/Coast to Coast (Mercury)* 1975—(– Stewart) 1976—(– Wood; group disbands) 1978—*Snakes and Ladders: The Best of the Faces* (Warner Bros.).
Ronnie Lane solo: 1974—*Anymore for Anymore* (with Slim Chance) (GM) 1975—*Ronnie Lane's Slim Chance* (with Slim Chance) (A&M) 1976—*One for the Road* (Island; U.K.); *Mahoney's Last Stand* (with Ron Wood) (Atco) 1977—*Rough Mix* (with Pete Townshend) (MCA) 1980—*See Me* (Gem, U.K.).
Ian McLagan solo: 1979—*Troublemaker* (Mercury) 1981—*Bump in the Night.*

The Small Faces got their name for two reasons: They were small, under five-feet-six-inches tall, and they were "faces," as in the Who's "I'm the Face," a declaration of Mod-era hipness. When the Small Faces first hit the British singles charts in 1965 with "Whatcha Gonna Do About It?" (recorded six weeks after their formation), they were seen by British youth as East London's answer to West London's Who. Led by Steve Marriott, the Small Faces became as big an attraction in Britain for their Mod clothing as for their basic, raw R&B-inspired music.

Marriott, a former child actor, formed the band with Ronnie Lane, who had already played with several local bands and was writing his own tunes. McLagan was recruited when original keyboardist, Jimmy Winston, left immediately after the Faces' first hit single. Rounding out the lineup was drummer Kenney Jones, who had studied drums but had never played with a professional band. Though Marriott has said that he could barely play guitar at the time, he and Lane began writing songs together. After attracting a following with fevered London club performances and the success of their first single, the Small Faces were signed to Andrew Loog Oldham's Immediate label and appeared frequently in

The Small Faces: Steve Marriott, Jimmy Winston, Kenney Jones, Ronnie Lane

the U.K. Top 10 for the next few years with 1966's "Sha La La La Lee," "Hey Girl," "All or Nothing," and "My Mind's Eye"; 1967's "Itchycoo Park" and "Tin Soldier"; and 1968's "Lazy Sunday." The only one of their early hits to gain any attention in America was "Itchycoo Park" (#16, 1967), a piece of psychedelia that featured one of the earliest uses of studio "phase-shifting" production.

By 1968, the band was becoming frustrated with its image as a singles band. That changed somewhat in 1968, when they released the concept album *Ogden's Nut Gone Flake*. Still, internal tensions grew, and in 1969 Marriott left to form Humble Pie [see entry]. It seemed a crucial blow at the time, but with the addition of ex–Jeff Beck Group members Rod Stewart and Ronnie Wood the Faces were Small no more. (Literally. Each of the two new members stood a head taller than the remaining, formerly Small, Faces.) The original Small Faces band later reunited, minus Lane and with the addition of Jimmy McCulloch and Rick Wills.

From 1969 to 1975 the Faces worked in the lucrative shadow of Stewart's solo career. Loose and boozy onstage and good-timey on record, the Faces made several arena-circuit U.S. tours playing material from Stewart's solo albums as well as the hits he sang with the group—"Stay With Me" (#17, 1971) and "Cindy Incidentally" (#48, 1973)—while enjoying as wild a lifestyle as possible.

In 1973 Ronnie Lane, an original Small Face, quit and was replaced by ex-Free bassist Tetsu Yamauchi. Lane then started a traveling rock circus, complete with jugglers and fire eaters, called the Passing Show, and recorded four albums with Slim Chance; he also made *Rough Mix* with Pete Townshend of the Who in 1977. In the late '70s Lane was debilitated by multiple sclerosis.

Meanwhile the Faces were slowly dissolving. Wood officially joined the Rolling Stones in 1976 (after having played on their 1975 tour), and McLagan regularly participated in Stones tours and such projects as the New Barbarians; he also records solo albums and has become a sought-after session hand. Jones, who reunited with the original Small Faces in 1977–78, replaced Keith Moon in the Who in 1978. He formed the Law with Paul Rodgers in the early '90s. Lane moved to the United States. In 1983 he appeared at the ARMS (Action Research Multiple Sclerosis) concerts, which featured Ronnie Wood, Charlie Watts, Jeff Beck, Jimmy Page, Steve Winwood, and others. He died in 1997, ending his long battle with multiple sclerosis. Marriott died in a 1991 fire in his home. At the time of his death, he was discussing the possible re-formation of Humble Pie.

Smash Mouth

Formed 1994, San Jose, CA
Steve Harwell (b. Steven Scott Harwell, Jan. 9, 1967, Santa Clara, CA), voc.; Greg Camp (b. Gregory Dean Camp, Apr. 2, 1967, West Covina, CA), gtr.; Paul DeLisle (b. Paul Gerald DeLisle, June 13, 1963, Exeter, Ont., Can.), bass; Kevin Coleman (b. Kevin John Coleman, Oct. 21, 1965, San Jose), drums.
1997—*Fush Yu Mang* (Interscope) 1999—*Astro Lounge* (– Coleman); *The East Bay Sessions* (Break Through) 2000—(+ Michael Urbano, drums).

San Jose's Smash Mouth was pegged as a one-hit wonder when it scored a #1 Modern Rock hit in 1997 with "Walkin' on the Sun," an unabashedly retro rocker that seemed part novelty surf-rock number and part loving homage to the Zombies. Two years later, it proved its staying power by delivering a second radio and video smash with "All Star."

Frontman Steve Harwell, a former rapper with the group F.O.S. (Freedom of Speech), and childhood friend Kevin Coleman hooked up with guitarist Greg Camp and began writing songs together in 1994. With bassist Paul DeLisle on board, the band started playing around the Bay Area and L.A. and landed one song, "Nervous in the Alley," on regular rotation on San Jose station KOME in April 1996. Further exposure at the station's annual summer festival helped spark major label interest, leading to a deal with Interscope in 1997 just in time to release its debut album, *Fush Yu Mang* (the name came from an Al Pacino slur in *Scarface*). The album climbed to #19 and went double platinum behind "Walkin' on the Sun," and a second retro-leaning single, a cover of War's "Why Can't We Be Friends?" The followup album, *Astro Lounge* (#6, 1999), fared even better—selling 3 million copies and yielding the #4 hit "All Star."

At the beginning of the band's 1999 tour in support of *Astro Lounge*, Coleman left due to back problems and was eventually replaced on drums by Michael Urbano. Smash Mouth was slated to release its third album (not counting 1999's early-recordings collection, *The East Bay Sessions*), in 2001.

Smashing Pumpkins

Formed 1989, Chicago, IL
Billy Corgan (b. Mar. 17, 1967, Chicago), gtr., voc.; James Iha (b. Mar. 26, 1968, Elk Grove, IL), gtr.; D'Arcy Wretzky (b. May 1, 1968, South Haven, MI), bass; Jimmy Chamberlin (b. June 10, 1964, Joliet, IL), drums.
1991—*Gish* (Caroline) 1993—*Siamese Dreams* (Virgin) 1994—*Pisces Iscariot* 1995—*Mellon Collie and the Infinite Sadness* 1996—(– Chamberlin) *The Aeroplane Flies High* 1998—*Adore* 1999—(+ Chamberlin; – Wretzky) 2000—*MACHINA/the machines of god* (+ Melissa Auf der Maur [b. Mar. 17, 1972, Montreal, Can.], bass).
James Iha solo: 1998—*Let It Come Down* (Virgin).

Smashing Pumpkins' music is distinguished from most other grunge rock in its incorporation of the high production values, ornate arrangements, and melodicism of such '70s bands as Boston and ELO.

Corgan, whose father is a guitarist, grew up in a Chicago suburb and moved to Florida at age 19 as leader of a goth band, the Marked. Returning home, he formed Smashing Pumpkins, at first simply a duo (Wretzky, Corgan, and a drum machine). A local-label single, "I Am One," led to the release of "Tristessa" on Sub Pop; in 1991, the band's debut album, with Butch Vig producing, became a college-radio favorite, eventually going gold in 1994. The major-label followup fared even better, debuting at #10 in 1993 and making the group alternative-rock stars.

Emphasizing both the virtuosic interplay of Corgan and Jimmy Chamberlin and Corgan's confessional lyrics, the Pumpkins employed a Mellotron, strings, and multiple guitar parts on *Siamese Dreams*, and continued to edge closer to progressive rock than to punk or grunge. *Pisces Iscariot* (1994) is a compilation of earlier recordings. Corgan indulged his prog-rock jones full-on with *Mellon Collie and the Infinite Sadness* (#1, 1995), a double-disc set that spawned a handful of hit singles, including "1979" (#12, 1996). *The Aeroplane Flies High* (#42, 1996) was a 33-song box set compiling *Mellon Collie*'s singles along with B sides and cover songs.

During a 1996 summer tour, Chamberlin and touring keyboardist Jonathan Melvoin both overdosed on heroin at the same time; Melvoin died and Chamberlin was arrested and subsequently fired. Filter's Matt Walker filled his seat for the remainder of the tour, but the band's quietly intimate next album, *Adore* (#2, 1998), was recorded using session percussionists and drum machines. A theater tour promoting the album raised more than $2.7 million for various charities, but when *Adore* stalled at platinum it was considered a commercial failure in the wake of the band's previous sales. Chamberlin was brought back on board in 1999, and *MACHINA/the machines of god* (#3, 2000) represented a return to hook-laden guitar rock. Wretzky quit shortly before the album's release, and was replaced for the ensuing tour by Melissa Auf der Maur of Hole. Sales of *MACHINA* proved no better than *Adore*'s, and during a radio interview on May 23, 2000, Corgan announced that the band would break up at the end of the year.

As the Pumpkins finished their tour commitments through the end of 2000, Corgan revealed plans for one final album of unreleased material from the band. He also hinted at a solo career, an avenue James Iha had already tested via *Let It Come Down* (#64), his 1998 album of singer/songwriter–style love songs. The Smashing Pumpkins officially broke up on December 2, 2000, following a four-hour-long show at Chicago's Cabaret Metro, where the band had debuted in October 1988. In early 2001 the band offered the album *Machina/Friends and Enemies of Modern Music* on its official Web site.

Bessie Smith

Born Apr. 15, 1894, Chattanooga, TN; died Sep. 26, 1937, Clarksdale, MI

1970—*Any Woman's Blues* 1971—*The World's Greatest Blues Singer* (Columbia); *Empty Bed Blues; The Empress* 1972—*Nobody's Blues But Mine* 1989—*Bessie Smith—The Collection* 1991—*The Complete Recordings, vol. 1; The Complete Recordings, vol. 2* 1992—*The Complete Recordings, vol. 3* 1993—*The Complete Recordings, vol. 4* 1996—*The Complete Recordings, vol. 5.*

Bessie Smith is generally considered the greatest and most influential American woman blues singer. She was also the preeminent black performer of her time, a singer/dancer/actress whose later performances (in which she was billed as the Queen of All Torch Singers) revealed a stylistic versatility that promised continued success in other genres, including swing. It is, however, her blues recordings upon which her legend rests and her influence has spread, speaking powerfully and eloquently of satisfaction and defeat, hope and despair.

Smith came by her intimate acquaintance with hard times honestly. One of seven children born to a poor family, she had seen both her parents and two siblings buried before she reached the age of nine. Like many poor black youngsters of her time, she saw little opportunity, and so at age 16 she joined her older brother Clarence in the Moses Stokes Company, one of many traveling vaudeville-type shows popular then. It was while working with this show that Smith first met her mentor and stylistic predecessor, Gertrude "Ma" Rainey. While the literature is rich with accounts of Rainey kidnapping Smith or the pair's alleged rivalry, in fact they were friends.

Smith left the Stokes company within a year of joining and began to perform as a solo act or with any of a number of other touring groups. After working a successful duo act with singer Hazel Greene, Smith began pursuing her solo career in earnest. Details of her life during World War I are sketchy. It is known that she married Earl Love; she later claimed he died in the war. In the early '20s she moved north, to Philadelphia, where she married Jack Gee, in June 1923. Around that same time Columbia Records released her first and most successful record, "Gulf Coast Blues" b/w "Down Hearted Blues." Selling over 780,000 copies within six months, the record launched not only Smith but Columbia's soon burgeoning "race" records division.

For the rest of the decade Smith toured the country, often in a luxurious, custom-designed railway car. The feisty yet insecure Smith's own life was as passionate and tumultuous as some of her darker recordings. Smith had a violent temper and an appetite for extramarital liaisons (with men and women) and liquor. Chris Albertson's acclaimed biography *Bessie* includes dozens of anecdotes, including one of her beating her husband's mistress unconscious on a Harlem street. Yet her stubborn independence served her well; once in North Carolina when she learned that a group of Ku Klux Klansmen were standing outside her show tent and beginning to pull up stakes, she charged outside and shouted, "You just pick up them sheets and run!" And they did.

Smith recorded 160 songs for Columbia, many of which she wrote or cowrote. Among the musicians she recorded with were Louis Armstrong, who joined her on the 1925 classic "Saint Louis Blues," and Fletcher Henderson. In 1929 she starred and sang in a 17-minute short film entitled *St. Louis Blues,* in which she played a woman wronged by a two-timing lover. It is the only extant footage of Smith. That same year, the stock market crash and the rise of "talkies" sent the black vaudeville circuit reeling. The show business milieu in which Smith had thrived was dying. Columbia reduced her recording fee from $200 a side to $125; by 1931 she had no recording contract at all.

Smith revamped her style and her repertoire, trading her traditional feathered and beaded costumes for elegantly understated gowns and pearls. Contemporary standards, like "Tea for Two" and "Smoke Gets in Your Eyes," were part of her show. She had last recorded in 1933, but in 1937 there were plans for new recording sessions and talk of her appearing in a film. Smith seemed on the verge of a commercial comeback when she was critically injured in a Mississippi car accident. Erroneous reports that Smith died because she was refused treatment at a white hospital endured for decades, thanks in part to popular works of literature, such as Edward Albee's play *The Death of Bessie Smith* and various writings about Smith and her music. In fact, Smith was severely injured when the car in which she was riding hit a parked truck on a darkened road. Her injuries included a nearly severed arm and internal damage to the chest and head. Despite being transported to the local black hospital, where her arm was amputated and she was transfused, Smith died within hours. Smith's funeral was among the most lavish and well attended of its time. In Philadelphia an estimated 10,000 mourners paid tribute to the singer as she lay in state; 7,000 stood outside as her gold-trimmed metallic, velvet-lined coffin was placed in the hearse. Despite her costly funeral, Smith's grave remained unmarked for over 30 years. Janis Joplin and Juanita Green, a woman who had worked for Smith, paid for the stone, which was unveiled in August 1970. It read: "The Greatest Blues Singer in the World Will Never Stop Singing."

Elliott Smith

Born Steven Paul Smith, Aug. 6, 1969, Omaha, NE
1994—*Roman Candle* (Cavity Search) 1995—*Elliott Smith* (Kill Rock Stars) 1997—*Either/Or; Good Will Hunting* soundtrack (Capitol) 1998—*XO* (DreamWorks) 2000—*Figure 8.*
With Heatmiser: 1993—*Dead Air* (Frontier) 1994—*Cop and Speeder* 1996—*Mic City Sons* (Caroline).

After years of playing on the indie circuit, both as a solo artist and as the cofrontman for the Portland, Oregon–based distorted-guitar rock band Heatmiser, Elliott Smith suddenly found himself in the national and worldwide spotlight in 1998 when his song "Miss Misery," from the soundtrack to Gus Van Sant's film *Good Will Hunting,* was nominated for an Academy Award. Smith lost to Celine Dion's inescapable *Titanic* theme, "My Heart Will Go On," but came away from the experience with a major label recording deal with DreamWorks Records (which had signed him shortly before the Oscar telecast).

Smith spent the bulk of his early childhood with his mother and stepfather in Dallas, Texas, before moving to Portland, Oregon, to live with his father as a teenager. After attending college in New Hampshire (where he studied political philosophy), Smith returned to Portland and began playing with Heatmiser. The band recorded three albums, beginning with 1993's *Dead Air,* while Smith simultaneously recorded as a solo artist. His three sparsely recorded, mostly acoustic independent albums, 1994's *Roman Candle,* 1995's *Elliott Smith,* and 1997's *Either/Or,* established Smith as an introspective singer/songwriter in the Nick Drake vein, but with a particular knack for disarmingly catchy, Beatlesque melodies. His six songs featured on the *Good Will Hunting* soundtrack (#91, 1998) continued in this direction, but both his 1998 DreamWorks debut, *XO* (#104), and its followup, *Figure 8* (#99, 2000), expanded on his patented brand of melodic gloom pop, as Smith began experimenting with densely layered studio soundscapes reminiscent of *Sgt. Pepper's Lonely Hearts Club Band* and the Beach Boys' *Pet Sounds.*

Huey "Piano" Smith

Born Jan. 26, 1934, New Orleans, LA
1959—*Havin' a Good Time* (Ace) 1961—*For Dancing* 1962—*'Twas the Night Before Christmas* 1963—*Rock 'n' Roll Revival* 1978—*Rockin' Pneumonia.*

New Orleans R&B pianist Huey Smith, together with his vocal group, the Clowns, recorded some of the R&B classics of the '50s. Smith began playing professionally at age 15 with Guitar Slim. In the early '50s, after a stint with Earl King, he played sessions for Lloyd Price, Smiley Lewis, and Little Richard. Meanwhile, he began writing songs and recording for Savoy. A weak singer, he was unsuccessful as a soloist. Consequently, he recruited the Clowns, originally Junior Gordon, Dave Dixon, and Roland Cook. When he signed with Ace they included Bobby Marchan, "Scarface" John Williams, and James Black. They had their first hit: "Rockin' Pneumonia and the Boogie Woogie Flu" (#52 pop, #9 R&B, 1957). A gold record, it was followed by the even bigger "Don't You Just Know It" (#9 pop, #4 R&B, 1958), with Gerri Hall, Eugene Francis, and Billy Roosevelt singing behind Marchan.

Famous for their stage shenanigans and comic dancing, Smith and the Clowns were a popular live attraction throughout the U.S., but they had no more big hits after "Don't You Just Know It." Their best known record is probably one not credited to the group: Frankie Ford's 1959 hit "Sea Cruise," with Ford's vocals over a Clowns backup. The Clowns' own "Don't You Know Yockomo" reached #56 in 1959 before Marchan left the Clowns—to be replaced by Curley Moore—and Smith moved to Imperial. He returned to Ace with "Pop-Eye" (#51 pop, 1962) before the Clowns broke up.

Smith continued to work through the rest of the decade, but his success was local at best. He formed his own label, Pity-Pat, and recorded as the Hueys and Shindig Smith and the Soulshakers. In the early '70s he retired from show business to become a Jehovah's Witness. He made a rare appearance in 2000 when he was honored at the Rhythm & Blues Foundation Pioneer Awards.

Kendra Smith: See the Dream Syndicate

Patti Smith

Born Dec. 30, 1946, Chicago, IL
1975—*Horses* (Arista) 1976—*Radio Ethiopia* 1978—*Easter* 1979—*Wave* 1988—*Dream of Life* 1996—*Gone Again* 1997—*Peace and Noise* 2000—*Gung Ho.*

In the early '70s, painter-turned-poet and sometime playwright (*Cowboy Mouth,* with Sam Shepard) Patti Smith began to set her poems to the electric guitar backup of erstwhile rock writer Lenny Kaye. By the end of the decade, she had proved remarkably influential, releasing what may be the first punk-rock record (the independent 1974 single "Hey Joe" b/w "Piss Factory") and claiming the rock-musician-as-shaman role previously reserved by males. After a nine-year hiatus, Smith returned to recording with the 1988 album *Dream of Life,* the work of a more mellow, but still rebellious songwriter. Another eight years would pass before her second artistic comeback, marked by a trio of acclaimed albums released in quick succession, which found her fighting her way out of a period of intense personal grief stemming from the loss of several of the most important people in her life.

Smith, who grew up in Pitman, New Jersey, first began performing her poetry backed by Kaye and pianist Richard Sohl in 1971. Along with Television, she helped put New York's punk-rock landmark CBGB on the map. As her music grew toward rock & roll, she enlisted Ivan Kral on guitar and Jay Dee Daugherty on drums. This lineup recorded *Horses* (#47, 1975), produced by John Cale, an original mixture of exhortatory rock & roll ("Gloria," "Land of 1000 Dances"), Smith's poetry, vocal mannerisms inspired by Mick Jagger and Jim Morrison, and the band's energetically rudimentary playing. Aerosmith producer Jack Douglas oversaw the Patti Smith Group's second album, *Radio Ethiopia* (#122, 1976), and the result was a more bombastic guitar-heavy record, tempered by the title cut, the height of Smith's improvised free rock.

A fall from a Florida stage hospitalized Smith with neck injuries in early 1977, during which time she wrote her fourth book of poetry, *Babel* (*Seventh Heaven, Witt,* and *Kodak* preceding it). When she was able to perform again, the result was her first Top 20 LP, *Easter* (#20, 1978), produced by Jimmy Iovine, and her only hit single, "Because the Night" (#13, 1978), written by Bruce Springsteen and revised by Smith. She then began her withdrawal from rock & roll—*Wave* (#18, 1979) was overtly religious. Soon after its release, Smith moved to Detroit to live with her new husband, ex-MC5 guitarist Fred "Sonic" Smith, and except for rare local appearances, dropped out of the music scene altogether. She and Smith, who died in late 1994, had two children together.

After the breakup of the Patti Smith Group, Sohl remained close to Smith, and Daugherty played with a variety of people, from folkies like the Roches and Willie Nile to Tom Verlaine, the Waterboys, and the Church. Ivan Kral put in a stint with Iggy Pop (on the LP *Soldier*). Lenny Kaye led several bands, beginning with the Lenny Kaye Connection, and produced such artists as Suzanne Vega.

In 1988 Smith's comeback album, *Dream of Life* (#65), featured her husband (who coproduced the album with Iovine), Daugherty, and Sohl. Its songs included a call-to-arms, "People Have the Power," which got some radio airplay, as well as lullabies for her children. Smith did not tour behind the album, but five years later, on a hot summer night in 1993, she made a rare appearance at Central Park's Summerstage, reading her poetry (including "Piss Factory") and singing a few songs a cappella. She dedicated her performance to two close friends who'd recently died, photographer Robert Mapplethorpe and Richard Sohl. In 1994 W.W. Norton published a book of Smith's poetry, *Early Work: 1970–1979.* She was also at work on a new album, but withdrew from it when her husband died of a heart attack at age 45. A month later, her younger brother (and former road manager), Todd, also died of a heart attack.

Determined to carry on as a tribute to the encouragement her husband and brother had shown her before their passing, Smith performed a string of opening dates with Bob Dylan in late 1995 and issued the intensely personal *Gone Again* in 1996. The album—which featured Kaye, Daugherty, and new band members Tony Shanahan on bass and Oliver Ray on guitar as well as Jeff Buckley, John Cale, and Television's Tom Verlaine—offered a potent mix of songs about mourning and rebirth, reflecting Smith's belief that the beauty of life survives death. Highlights included the title track and the rocker "Summer Cannibals," both cowritten with her husband, and "About a Boy," a bittersweet paean to the late Kurt Cobain of Nirvana. The same year saw the release of *The Coral Sea,* her epic prose poem dedicated to Mapplethorpe, as well as her vocal turn on the song "New Test Leper" from R.E.M.'s *New Adventures in Hi-Fi.*

Armed with the basic guitar chords her husband taught her shortly before his death, Smith continued to write new songs at a steady pace, releasing *Peace and Noise* in 1997 and *Gung Ho* three years later. Both albums found her expanding her focus beyond personal mourning to political reflections on subjects ranging from the Vietnam War to the Heaven's Gate cult and AIDS to American slavery. *Gung Ho* featured guest turns by Michael Stipe and Smith's teenage son Jackson, who played guitar on the song "Persuasion."

In 1998 Doubleday published a comprehensive collection of Smith's lyrics, *Patti Smith Complete: Lyrics, Reflections & Notes for the Future.*

Will Smith/D.J. Jazzy Jeff and the Fresh Prince

Born Willard Christopher Smith Jr., Sep. 25, 1968, Philadelphia, PA
1997—*Big Willie Style* (Columbia) 1999—*Willennium.*
D.J. Jazzy Jeff and the Fresh Prince, formed 1986, Philadelphia, PA: Smith (as Fresh Prince), voc.; Jazzy Jeff (b. Jeff Townes, Jan. 22, 1965, Philadelphia), DJ.
1987—*Rock the House* (Jive/RCA) 1988—*He's the D.J., I'm the Rapper* 1989—*And in This Corner . . .* 1991—*Homebase* 1993—*Code Red* 1998—*Greatest Hits.*

With his clean-cut image and playful, lighthearted approach to rapping, Will "Fresh Prince" Smith had little trouble winning over a multiracial mainstream audience—or parlaying that mass appeal into a successful TV sitcom, *The Fresh Prince of Bel-Air,* and a series of movies that would make him a full-fledged Hollywood star.

Jeff (D.J. Jazzy Jeff) Townes, who began spinning records at age 10, met Smith in 1986. The two joined forces immediately, although their professional future was soon threatened when Smith graduated high school with a scholarship to attend the Massachusetts Institute of Technology. The rapper chose a recording career over MIT, though, and he and Townes released their debut album, *Rock the House* (#83 pop, #24 R&B), in 1987. It included the duo's third single, "Girls Ain't Nothing But Trouble" (#57 pop, #81 R&B, 1988). Its innocence would set the mold for what some critics deemed their "bubblegum rap" style. Their breakthrough came the following year, with the double LP *He's the D.J., I'm the Rapper* (#4 pop, #5 R&B, 1988), one of the first rap albums to go triple platinum. This sophomore effort contained the #12 pop, #10 R&B hit, 1988's "Parents Just Don't Understand," a teenager's lament about, among other things, shopping with Mom. It won the first Grammy offered in the Best Rap Performance category in 1988. The album also featured "A Nightmare on My Street" (#15 pop, #9 R&B, 1988).

In 1991 the duo had its biggest hit with "Summertime," a wistful ode to good times in the 'hood that went to #4 pop, #1 R&B, and earned them another Grammy. It was the first single from *Homebase* (#12 pop, #5 R&B, 1991), which came out the year after the *Fresh Prince* TV show premiered, casting Smith as a Philadelphia homeboy sent to live with wealthy Bel-Air relatives. That show's popularity (it lasted six seasons), as well as Smith's 1993 feature role in the film version of John Guare's dramatic play *Six Degrees of Separation,* seemed to threaten the rapper's musical partnership with Townes. The duo released the commercially disappointing *Code Red* (#64 pop, #39 R&B) in 1993; a greatest-hits compilation was released in 1998, but by that time, Smith was fully ensconced in his new career as a movie star.

After surprising audiences with his dramatic role in *Six Degrees,* Smith proved adept in other genres: buddy-comedy (1995's *Bad Boys* with Martin Lawrence), action-adventure (the 1996 smash *Independence Day*), sci-fi humor (1997's even bigger hit *Men in Black*), conspiracy thriller (1998's *Enemy of the State*), set pieces both wacky (1999's *Wild Wild West*) and pop-spiritual (2000's *The Legend of Bagger Vance*). He played Muhammad Ali in the 2001 bio-pic *Power and Grace.*

Not one to limit his talents, Smith returned to recording with the title song for *Men in Black*—which won a Grammy—followed by his first solo album, *Big Willie Style,* in 1997. (These releases marked the first time Smith recorded under his actual name rather than as the Fresh Prince.) With Townes producing and engineering a handful of tracks, *Big Willie Style* went multiplatinum and to #10 on the pop album chart (#9 R&B), thanks to the hits "Gettin' Jiggy Wit It" (#1 pop, #6 R&B, 1998, and another Grammy winner), "Just the Two of Us," the 1981 Grover Washington Jr.–Bill Withers song remade as a love song to Smith's young son Trey (#20 pop, #17 R&B, 1998), and "Miami" (#17 pop, #73 R&B, 1998). After his 1999 theme song for *Wild Wild West* went to #1 pop and #3 R&B, the double-platinum *Willennium* (#5 pop, #8 R&B, 1999) followed, featuring guest appearances by a posse of harder-edged rappers and R&B singers, including Smith's *Fresh Prince of Bel-Air* costar Tatyana Ali. This album was coproduced by Townes, who had established A Touch of Jazz Studios in Philadelphia, where he worked with artists such as Nuyorican Soul, Kenny Lattimore, and Jill Scott.

Smith also had a side business, Will Smith Enterprises, for which he developed music and TV projects for selective clients, including singer Ali. Although divorced from Trey's mother, Sheree Zampino, Smith appeared in the media as a devoted family man who spoke glowingly of his parents, siblings, son, and eventually, his second wife, actress Jada Pinkett Smith (whom he married New Year's Eve 1997), and the two children he had with her, son Jaden and daughter Willow.

The Smithereens

Formed 1980, Carteret, NJ
Jim Babjak (b. Nov. 17, 1957, Salzburg, Austria), gtr.; Dennis Diken (b. Feb. 25, 1957, Belleville, NJ), drums; Pat DiNizio (b. Oct. 12, 1955, Plainfield, NJ), gtr., voc.; Mike Mesaros (b. Dec. 11, 1957, Trenton, NJ), bass.
1980—*Girls About Town* EP (D-Tone) 1983—*Beauty and Sadness* EP (Little Ricky) 1987—*The Smithereens Live* EP (Restless); *Especially for You* (Enigma) 1988—*Green Thoughts* 1989—*11* (Capitol) 1991—*Blow Up* 1994—*A Date With the Smithereens* (RCA) 1995—*Blown to Smithereens* (Capitol); *Attack of the Smithereens* 1999—*God Save the Smithereens* (Koch).
Pat DiNizio solo: 1997—*Songs and Sounds* (Velvel).

The Smithereens' brand of hard-edged pop songs is reminiscent of the '60s British Invasion, but the mordant sensibility of singer/songwriter Pat DiNizio gives the band a decidedly modern point of view.

The band was formed in 1980 when DiNizio answered an ad placed in a music paper by high-school friends Babjak, Diken, and Mesaros. They released an EP that year, *Girls*

About Town, containing three originals and a cover of the Beach Boys' "Girl Don't Tell Me." Neither that record nor a 1983 release, *Beauty and Sadness,* helped the Smithereens get signed, so they supported themselves playing covers and backing veteran acts the Beau Brummels and Otis Blackwell.

In 1985 DiNizio sent a tape to Enigma Records. The tape, with only the band's name and DiNizio's name and phone number to identify it, fell into the hands of Scott Vanderbilt, who had become a fan while a college DJ. He signed the band and the next year released *Especially for You* (#51), with guest appearances by Marshall Crenshaw (under the name Jerome Jerome) and Suzanne Vega. Its single, "Blood and Roses," was featured in a grade-B slasher film, *Dangerously Close;* the film's production company financed a video, which gained airplay on MTV.

The Smithereens toured extensively; the work paid off with *11* (#41, 1989), their most commercially successful album, and "A Girl Like You" (#38, 1989), the band's only Top 40 single. In 1994 the Smithereens moved to RCA for *A Date With the Smithereens.* The album reunited the band with producer Don Dixon (who produced the group's first two albums) and featured Lou Reed's guitar playing on two songs. The grunge movement of the early- to mid-'90s rendered the Smithereens' power-pop sound dated, and the band followed *Date* with two compilation albums—a best-of collection, *Blown to Smithereens,* and a set of rare tracks, *Attack of the Smithereens.*

In 1997 DiNizio released a solo album, *Songs and Sounds,* in which he expanded on his band's punk-inspired pop by adding a touch of jazz. He regrouped with the Smithereens in 1999, releasing *God Save the Smithereens,* which featured more of the band's familiar catchy pop. In 2000 DiNizio turned his attention to politics, running an unsuccessful campaign in New Jersey for the U.S. Senate as a Reform Party candidate.

The Smiths/Morrissey

Formed 1982, Manchester, Eng.
Morrissey (b. Stephen Patrick Morrissey, May 22, 1959, Manchester), voc.; Johnny Marr (b. John Maher, Oct. 31, 1963, Manchester), gtr.; Mike Joyce (b. June 1, 1963, Manchester), drums; Andy Rourke (b. 1963, Manchester), bass.
1984—*The Smiths* (Sire); *Hatful of Hollow* (Rough Trade, U.K.) 1985—*Meat Is Murder* (Sire) (+ Craig Gannon, gtr.) 1986—*The Queen Is Dead* 1987—(– Gannon) *Louder Than Bombs; Strangeways, Here We Come* 1988—*Rank; Peel Sessions* (Dutch East) 1992—*Best . . . I* (Sire/Reprise); *Best . . . II* 1995—*Singles* (Reprise).
Morrissey: 1988—*Viva Hate* (Sire/Reprise) 1990—*Bona Drag* 1991—*Kill Uncle* 1992—*Your Arsenal* 1994—*Vauxhall and I* 1995—*Southpaw Grammar* (RCA Victor) 1997—*Maladjusted* (PolyGram) 1998—*My Early Burglary Years* (Reprise).

Articulate, broodingly charismatic frontman Morrissey and supple guitarist Johnny Marr made the Smiths one of the most significant English bands of the '80s. An avowed celibate whose lyrics disclosed a sexually ambiguous point of view, Morrissey was given to controversy, whether advocating animal rights or trashing Prime Minister Margaret Thatcher and disco. The band's trancelike, guitar-based music angrily rebutted such British synthesizer pop as the Human League and Thompson Twins.

Morrissey (originally of the Smiths)

Son of a hospital porter and a librarian, Morrissey first expressed himself by writing; unemployed in the late '70s, he wrote a book on James Dean and another on the New York Dolls, whose English fan club he headed. He also played briefly in a band called the Nosebleeds. Veteran of such cult groups as Sister Ray and Freaky Party, Marr first met Morrissey at a 1979 Patti Smith concert, and by 1982 they decided to form a band. The pair eventually enlisted drummer Mike Joyce and bassist Andy Rourke for an eponymous debut that, on U.K. indie label Rough Trade (on Sire in the U.S.), entered the British chart at #2. An earlier single, "Hand in Glove," was then recorded with Morrissey's favorite female singer, '60s British pop idol Sandie Shaw, and scored #27 in the U.K. This coup, along with *The Smiths*' "Heaven Knows I'm Miserable Now" (#10 U.K., 1984), established the band.

The meteoric rise continued with *Meat Is Murder* debuting at #1 on the British chart; the group also caused a stir with Morrissey's stage presence, the singer wearing a garland of gladioli in tribute to Oscar Wilde, a hearing aid in homage to '50s balladeer Johnnie Ray, and a ducktail haircut patterned after English rocker Billy Fury. Some critics sniped that the group's lyrics referred to child molesting, and Morrissey offended others with sharp comments about the all-star Band Aid benefit single for Ethiopian famine relief. His champions, though, hailed his oblique, angst-driven songs as latter-day examples of Ray Davies–styled social commentary. With ex–Aztec Camera guitarist Craig Gannon added, 1986's *The Queen Is Dead* (#2 U.K.) fared handsomely, but a disappointing U.S. tour showed that the Smiths had yet to penetrate the American mainstream. Later that year Johnny Marr was involved in a serious car accident; during his recovery, Gannon was fired. A single, "Sheila Take a Bow," became a Top 10 U.K. hit in mid-1987, but later that year, with Marr deeming their musical approach exhausted, the Smiths disbanded. *Strangeways, Here We Come* and the live *Rank* were released posthumously.

Despite his prolific output—*Viva Hate, Bona Drag, Kill Uncle, Your Arsenal,* and *Vauxhall and I*—Morrissey's solo career hasn't quite matched his success with the Smiths, although the singer has attracted a rabid cult following in the U.S. He released 1995's *Southpaw Grammar* (#66) and 1997's *Maladjusted* (#61) to an ambivalent critical response. (*My Early Burglary Years* was a collection of B sides and rarities.) But a tour in 2000 enjoyed sell-out crowds without a new album or even a record deal.

Besides playing sessions with Bryan Ferry, Talking Heads, the Pet Shop Boys, and Billy Bragg, Marr served for a while with the Pretenders, The The, and Electronic without ever finding a permanent venue. Marr's low profile led to a reputation as British rock's most talented underachiever. But he reemerged in 2000 for the first time at the front of his own band, the Healers, which included former Dub Pistol keyboardist Lee Spender, bassist Alonza Bevan from Kula Shaker, and drummer Zak Starkey (son of Ringo Starr).

Rourke and Joyce played with the Adult Net before backing up Sinéad O'Connor; Joyce eventually joined the reformed Buzzcocks. In 1996 they both sued Marr and Morrissey, complaining over the unequal sharing of Smiths earnings; Rourke settled out of court, but in 1998 Joyce won his case, with a British judge calling Morrissey "devious, truculent, and unreliable." A reunion is not expected.

Patty Smyth/Scandal

Born June 26, 1957, New York, NY
With Scandal, formed 1982, New York: Patty Smyth, voc.; Zack Smith (b. Westport, CT), gtr.; Ivan Elias, bass; Benji King, kybds.; Frankie Larocca, drums.
1982—*Scandal* EP (Columbia) 1984—*The Warrior.*
Patty Smyth solo: 1987—*Never Enough* (Columbia) 1992—*Patty Smyth* (MCA) 1998—*Greatest Hits—Featuring Scandal* (Sony).

Patty Smyth rose to fame as the lead singer of Scandal, a hard-pop outfit that proved the perfect vehicle for Smyth's husky, agile voice and her sexy, tough-girl image. While the band's career was short-lived, Smyth reemerged in the late '80s and early '90s as a successful solo artist. The daughter of a Greenwich Village club-owner mother, Smyth grew up in New York City, and in her teens fronted a band called Patty and the Planets. Supporting herself as a waitress, she hooked up in 1982 with guitarist Zack Smith, Scandal's founder and principal songwriter.

With the support of such singles as "Goodbye to You" (#65, 1982) and "Love's Got a Line on You" (#59, 1983), *Scandal* became the best-selling EP in Columbia Records' history. Smith left the band after its release, but not before cowriting material (with Smyth writing some of the lyrics) for a followup album, *The Warrior* (#17, 1984), which yielded a #7 pop hit with its title track. Scandal split up not long after: Drummer Frankie Larocca became head of A&R at Epic Records. Smyth married punk pioneer Richard Hell; the two had a daughter, Ruby, and later divorced.

In 1987 came Smyth's solo debut, *Never Enough* (#66, 1987), but it wasn't until five years later that, after moving to MCA, the singer reemerged in the Top 10 with "Sometimes Love Just Ain't Enough," a #2 duet ballad with Don Henley featured on her self-titled gold 1992 album. A song she cowrote and performed for the movie *Junior,* "Look What Love Has Done," was nominated for a 1994 Academy Award.

In the latter half of the '90s Smyth began dating tennis-pro-turned-commentator John McEnroe; the couple had a daughter, Anna, in late 1995. Smyth and McEnroe married in 1997, and another daughter, Ava, was born in 1999. While she put her own career on the back burner, Smyth inspired her husband to indulge his own musical aspirations: McEnroe plays guitar in a group called the Johnny Smyth Band. More a hobby than a career change, McEnroe's band plays about 35 gigs a year, and occasionally Smyth joins him onstage to sing.

Snap!

Formed ca. 1989, Pittsburgh, PA
Turbo B. (b. Durron Maurice Butler, Apr. 30, 1967, Pittsburgh), voc.; Penny Ford (b. Nov. 6, 1964, Cincinnati, OH), voc.; Jackie Harris (b. Jacqueline Arlissa Harris, Pittsburgh), voc.
1990—*World Power* (Arista) 1992—(– Ford; + Thea Austin, voc.) *The Madman's Return* 1993—(– Austin; + Niki Haris, voc.) 1994—(– Haris; + Paula Summer [b. Paula Brown], voc.) 1995—*Welcome to Tomorrow* 1997—*Attack! The Best of Snap!, Remixes & All.*
Penny Ford solo: 1993—*Penny Ford* (Columbia).

Created as the project of two German producers, the dance-pop collective Snap! climbed the American chart in 1990 with "The Power," a fierce, relentless track that proved as successful on Top 40 radio as it did in clubs. Like the more visible C + C Music Factory, Snap! was an early-'90s success story manufactured by behind-the-scenes studio wizards but distinguished equally by the sizzling contributions of a succession of female vocalists.

Around 1989, the Frankfurt-based production team (Luca) Anzilotti and (Michael) Muenzing recruited American rapper Turbo B. and soul singer Penny Ford, who had previously been a member of the S.O.S. band. Crediting themselves as Benito Benites and John "Virgo" Garrett III, Anzilotti and Muenzing recorded "The Power," featuring

Turbo B. and Ford as Snap!, for Germany's Logic Records. (Turbo B.'s cousin, singer Jackie Harris, was also credited as a member of Snap!, and filled in for Ford on some early media appearances.) The band was picked up by Arista in 1990, and its single topped the British chart and went almost as far in the U.S. (#2 pop, #4 R&B). Five additional Top 10 hits followed in England, with Ford singing on all of them. Ford then opted for a solo career, so Thea Austin took her place on Snap!'s 1992 sophomore effort, *The Madman's Return*. The album's first single, "Colour of Love," flopped, at which point Turbo B. quit the group, citing creative frustration. But a second single, "Rhythm Is a Dancer," reached #5 on the American pop chart.

Niki Haris, formerly a backup singer for Madonna, replaced Austin for Snap!'s next single, "Exterminate," which entered the U.K. Top 5 in 1993. That same year, Penny Ford released a self-titled album on Columbia, while Anzilotti and Muenzing began work on a third Snap! album with Haris. By the time *Welcome to Tomorrow* was released in 1995, Haris had been replaced by former Paula Abdul backup vocalist Paula Brown (a.k.a. Paula Summer).

Snoop Doggy Dogg/Snoop Dogg

Born Calvin Broadus, Oct. 20, 1972, Long Beach, CA
1993—*Doggystyle* (Death Row) 1996—*Tha Doggfather* 1998—*Da Game Is to Be Sold, Not to Be Told* (No Limit) 1999—*No Limit Top Dogg* 2000—*Dead Man Walkin* (D3/ Death Row); *Tha Last Meal* (No Limit).
With Tha Eastsidaz: 2000—*Snoop Dogg Presents tha Eastsidaz* (Dogg House)

Rapper Snoop Doggy Dogg, with his lazy drawl and gangster persona, became one of the most commercially successful artists in all of rap. Alongside artists like N.W.A, Tupac, and Ice-T, Snoop epitomizes West Coast hip-hop. Debuting in 1992 as a collaborator on Dr. Dre's 1992 multiplatinum *The Chronic*, Snoop followed soon after with the release of *Doggystyle*, which set a new record as the then-biggest selling rap album.

Calvin Broadus (nicknamed Snoop by his mother) was born and raised on the tough streets of Long Beach, California. Shortly after graduating from high school, Snoop was arrested on a cocaine charge; he spent the next three years in and out of jail. In 1990 Snoop began to record underground tapes with a friend, rapper Warren G, who subsequently gave a cassette to his brother, N.W.A's Dr. Dre. Dre was impressed with what he heard, and Dre and Snoop began working together on the single "Deep Cover" for a movie of the same name. By the time Dre started recording *The Chronic*, Snoop was his right-hand man, performing on more than half of the album. Buoyed by the acclaim received for his contributions, Snoop entered the studio to record his own album for Dre's Death Row Records. The result, the Dr. Dre–produced *Doggystyle*, was one of the most anticipated rap records in history. With beats straight out of the P-Funk tradition, songs like "What's My Name?" (#8 pop, #8 R&B, 1993) and "Gin & Juice" (#8 pop, #13 R&B, 1994) became bicoastal party anthems. *Doggystyle* entered the *Billboard* chart at #1 the first week of its release (the first debut album ever to do so).

Despite his success, however, Snoop encountered trouble with the law. In 1993 he was arrested in connection with the murder of a man who the rapper alleged had been stalking him. Together with his bodyguard, who was reported to have fired the gun that killed the man in 1993, Snoop was arraigned to stand trial in L.A. The trial concluded in February 1996 with both Snoop and his bodyguard being acquitted of all charges. In the meantime, the 1994 soundtrack *Murder Was the Case* (#1), from the short film directed by Dr. Dre, featured three Snoop songs, including the title track. In 1996, with Dr. Dre no longer at the controls, Snoop dropped the chart-topping *Tha Doggfather* (#1 pop, #1 R&B).

After the murder of label mate Tupac and the incarceration of Death Row CEO Suge Knight, Snoop dropped the

Snoop Dogg

"Doggy" from his name and moved over to Master P's No Limit imprint. His next two No Limit albums, *Da Game Is to Be Sold, Not to Be Told* (#1 pop, #1 R&B, 1998) and *No Limit Top Dogg* (#2 pop, #1 R&B, 1999), marked Snoop's coming into his own as a producer. He started his own label, Dogg House Records, and oversaw Tha Eastsidaz project. In 2000 Snoop joined forces with Dr. Dre, Eminem, and Ice Cube for the Up In Smoke summer tour, and later released his final album for No Limit, *Last Meal* (#4 pop, #1 R&B). That same year, Death Row released *Dead Man Walkin* (#24 pop, #11 R&B), a collection of material Snoop recorded before he left the label.

Phoebe Snow

Born Phoebe Laub, July 17, 1952, New York, NY
1974—*Phoebe Snow* (Shelter/A&M) 1976—*Second Childhood* (Columbia); *It Looks Like Snow* 1977—*Never Letting Go; Against the Grain* 1981—*Rock Away* (Mirage); *The Best of Phoebe Snow* (Columbia) 1989—*Something Real* (Elektra) 1998—*I Can't Complain* (House of Blues).

With her supple contralto voice, Phoebe Snow burst onto the music scene with an impressive debut LP on Leon Russell's Shelter label that yielded the Top 5 single "Poetry Man."

She had moved with her family from New York to Teaneck, New Jersey, at age three and did not seriously take up music until the late '60s. A shy performer, she began to play Greenwich Village clubs in the early '70s, singing the blues, as well as folk and pop. After her debut LP, she sang with Paul Simon on his hit gospel single "Gone at Last." Her second LP, *Second Childhood* (#13, 1976), included "Two Fisted Love," one of several Snow album tracks that weren't hits per se but were frequently played on FM radio. Her first two albums have been certified gold.

Snow's subsequent albums were not as commercially successful, but she still maintained a small, loyal audience and was by now devoting time to raising her daughter. For years her distinctive voice was often heard on radio and television ads, thanks to a series of commercials for Bloomingdale's, Stouffer's, Salon Selectives, Hallmark, General Foods International, and General Electric. In the early '90s she performed and recorded with Donald Fagen's Rock and Soul Revue. In 1994 she appeared at Woodstock in a gospel group with Mavis Staples, Thelma Houston, and CeCe Peniston.

Social Distortion/Mike Ness

Formed 1979, Fullerton, CA
Mike Ness (b. Apr. 3, 1962, Stoneham, MA), voc., gtr.; Dennis Danell (b. June 24, 1961, Tacoma, WA; d. Feb. 29, 2000, Newport Beach, CA), gtr.; Brent Liles, bass; Derrick O'Brien, drums, voc.
1983—*Mommy's Little Monster* (13th Floor) 1988—(– Liles; – O'Brien; + Chris Reece [b. July 25, San Francisco, CA], drums; + John Maurer [b. July 14, Lynnwood, CA], bass) *Prison Bound* (Restless) 1990—*Social Distortion* (Epic); *Story of My Life . . . and Other Stories* EP 1992—*Somewhere Between Heaven and Hell* 1995—*Mainliner (Wreckage of the Past)* (Time Bomb) 1996—*White Light, White Heat, White Trash* (550 Music/Epic) 1998—*Live at the Roxy* (Time Bomb). Mike Ness solo: 1999—*Cheating at Solitaire* (Time Bomb); *Under the Influences.*

Social Distortion are suburban punk rockers who survived both their genre's burnout and their leader's drug addiction to find belated major-label success. The band was founded by Mike Ness and Dennis Danell, two Orange County schoolmates who had been inspired by the punk scene in nearby L.A. They released their first single, "1945," in 1982. The following album, *Mommy's Little Helper,* introduced Social Distortion's rootsy punk, influenced equally by the Clash and the Rolling Stones. Song titles like "I Just Want to Give You the Creeps" demonstrated their rebels-without-a-cause attitude.

Ness in particular styled himself an outlaw. He was kicked out of his home at 15, subsequently living in shooting galleries, flophouses, and jail. His heroin addiction, fighting, and other self-destructive acts—he fancied himself a sort of Sid Vicious—split the band. Ness and Danell found a new rhythm section, however, and in 1985 Ness quit drugs and alcohol. A tour documentary recorded that year, *Another State of Mind,* captured Social Distortion still in its wild, sordid period.

On the country-influenced *Prison Bound,* Ness reflected on his past. Social Distortion returned to a more punk sound on their eponymous Epic debut, including a hard-rocking version of the Johnny Cash hit "Ring of Fire." The album initially sold more than 250,000 copies (it later went gold) and landed the long-laboring underground band on MTV and a tour with Neil Young. *Somewhere Between Heaven and Hell* was another solid album with a country feel, including the alternative hit "Bad Luck."

After a four-and-a-half-year break from recording, Social Distortion returned with *White Light, White Heat, White Trash* (#27, 1996), an album that included the Top 5 Modern Rock hit "I Was Wrong." The record's title was an allusion to the second Velvet Underground album and to *White Heat,* a 1949 gangster movie starring James Cagney. Frontman Mike Ness released a pair of roots albums in 1999, *Cheating at Solitaire,* which featured guest shots from Bruce Springsteen and Brian Setzer, and *Under the Influences,* a collection of country covers. In 2000 Social Distortion rhythm guitarist Danell died suddenly of a brain aneurysm.

Soft Boys: See Robyn Hitchcock

Soft Cell/Marc Almond

Formed 1980, Leeds, Eng.
Marc Almond (b. Peter Marc Almond, July 9, 1959, Southport, Eng.), voc.; David Ball (b. May 3, 1959, Blackpool, Eng.), synth.
1981—*Non-Stop Erotic Cabaret* (Sire) 1982—*Non-Stop*

Ecstatic Dancing 1983—*The Art of Falling Apart; Soul Inside* EP 1984—*This Last Night in Sodom* 1991—*Memorabilia: The Singles* (Mercury) 1999—*The Twelve Inch Singles* (PolyGram).
Marc Almond solo: 1988—*The Stars We Are* (Some Bizarre/Capitol) 1990—*Enchanted* 1991—*Tenement Symphony* (Sire) 1993—*Twelve Years of Tears* (Sire, U.K.) 1995—*Treasure Box* (EMI, U.K.) 1996—*Fantastic Star* (Mercury, U.K.) 1999—*Open All Night* (Blue Star).
David Ball with the Grid: 1990—*Electric Head* (East West) 1992—*456* (Virgin, U.K.) 1995—*Evolver* (Deconstruction); *Music for Dancing.*

Singer Marc Almond and synthesizer player David Ball were hardly the first British pop musicians to join forces while attending art school. Still, as the technopop duo Soft Cell, they set something of a precedent by adapting a cult soul classic into a cheeky electronic dirge—then having their version of the song, Gloria Jones' "Tainted Love," become 1981's best-selling British single, as well as a #8 pop hit in the U.S. the next year.

A mutual fascination with the U.K. soul scene brought Almond and Ball together, first as collaborators on theatrical music—with Almond writing lyrics to accompany Ball's instrumentals—then as Soft Cell. The band's early shows featured striking visual accompaniment, eventually attracting the attention of a quirky label called Some Bizarre. Released in 1981, the duo's debut single, "Memorabilia," failed to chart; later that year, though, "Tainted Love" generated instant success. Numerous Top 10 singles followed in England, many of them sleazily sensual and all of them distinguished by Almond's rather affected (and often pitch-shy) tenor and Ball's moody synth colorings. By 1983, however, Almond and Ball decided to part company professionally. The aptly titled *This Last Night in Sodom* was released the next year.

By this point, Almond had already formed another band, Marc and the Mambas. The group's two 1983 U.K. albums mixed covers with electrosoul originals and were generally perceived as excessive. In 1984 the singer formed Marc Almond and the Willing Sinners, whose two albums and one EP were stylistically evocative of the Mambas' efforts (and of Soft Cell, for that matter) but somewhat better received. In the late '80s Almond put out a few solo albums, including a Jacques Brel tribute. His first American release was 1988's *The Stars We Are* (#144, 1989), with the minor hit single, "Tears Run Rings" (#67, 1989), followed in 1990 by *Enchanted* and in 1991 by *Tenement Symphony.* Although he lost his U.S. record deal, Almond continued to release albums in the U.K., including the 1993 live recording *Twelve Years of Tears.* Meanwhile, ex–band mate Ball had formed the dance duo the Grid with Richard Norris, exploring techno and house music on several albums (not released in the U.S.) through 1995.

Interest in Almond was piqued in 1999 when he published his autobiography, *Tainted Life.* The book talked about his estrangement from his alcoholic father, his homosexuality, and his onetime addiction to Ecstasy and Valium, which led to a rehab stay in 1995. Also in 1999, Almond started his own label to release his music, Blue Star, which he licenses to other labels for distribution. Blue Star's first album was that year's *Open All Night,* which became his first U.S. release in eight years. The album included a duet, "Threat of Love," with Siouxsie Sioux of Banshees fame. Almond and Ball then began collaborating again. *The Art of Falling Apart* is a reissue of the 1983 LP with bonus tracks; *The Twelve Inch Singles* is a greatest-hits collection. In 1999 Almond published a book of his poetry and prose, *Beautiful Twisted Night.*

Soft Machine/Robert Wyatt

Formed 1966, Canterbury, Eng.
Mike Ratledge, kybds.; Robert Wyatt (b. Robert Ellidge, Bristol, Eng.), drums, voc.; Kevin Ayers (b. Aug. 16, 1945, Herne Bay, Eng.), gtr., voc., bass; Daevid Allen (b. Austral.), gtr., voc.
1967—(– Allen; + Larry Nolan [b. CA], gtr.; – Nolan) 1968—*The Soft Machine* (Probe); (– Ayers; + Hugh Hopper, bass, gtr.) *Volume 2* (Columbia) 1970—(+ Elton Dean, sax; + Marc Charig, trumpet; + Nick Evans, trombone; + Lyn Dobson, flute, sax; + Rob Spall, violin; – Evans) *Third* 1971—(– Charig; – Dobson; – Spall) *Fourth* 1972—(– Wyatt; + Phil Howard, drums; – Howard; + John Marshall, drums) *Fifth* 1973—(– Dean; + Karl Jenkins, sax, kybds.) *Sixth* (– Hopper; + Roy Babbington, bass) *Seventh* 1975—(+ Allan Holdsworth, gtr.) *Bundles* (Harvest) (– Holdsworth) 1976—(– Ratledge; + John Etheridge, gtr.; + Alan Wakeman, sax) *Softs* 1977—*Triple Echo* 1978—(– Babbington; + Steve Cook, bass) *Alive and Well in Paris* 1980—(– Etheridge; – Cook; + Jack Bruce [b. May 14, 1943, Glasgow, Scot.], bass, voc.; + Dick Morisey, sax; + Alan Parker, gtr.) 1981—*Land of Cockayne* (EMI) 1984—(group re-forms: Jenkins; Marshall; + Ray Warleigh, sax; + Dave Macrae, kybds.) 1988—*Live at the Proms 1970* (Reckless, U.K.) 1990—*The Peel Sessions* (Strange Fruit, U.K.) 1991—*As If . . .* (Elite, U.K.) 1995—*The Best of Soft Machine* (See for Miles, U.K.) 1998—*Virtually* (Cuneiform, U.K.) 2000—*Noisette* 2001—*Man in a Deaf Corner (1963–70)* (Mooncrest, U.K.).
Robert Wyatt solo: 1974—*Rock Bottom* (Virgin) 1975—*Ruth Is Stranger Than Richard* 1981—*Nothing Can Stop Us* 1985—*Old Rottenhat* (Gramavision) 1990—*Compilation* 1992—*Dondestan* 1993—*Mid-Eighties* (Rhino) 1994—*Giving Back a Bit—A Little History of* (Virgin, U.K.) 1998—*Shleep* (Thirsty Ear) 1999—*EPs by Robert Wyatt.*

The original Canterbury progressive British rock band (along with Caravan, Gong, Hatfield and the North, National Health, Henry Cow), Soft Machine lasted through seemingly endless personnel changes to become one of Britain's most durable progressive-fusion units. Actually, the original Canterbury band was the Wilde Flowers, who got together at Canterbury's Simon Langton School, where Mike Ratledge, Hugh Hopper, Robert Wyatt, and Caravan's David Sinclair were schoolmates. The Wilde Flowers existed in varying lineups from 1963 to 1965, usually gathering at the home of Wyatt's mother, a writer and disc jockey who introduced her son to modern jazz. (One writer later described a car ride with Wyatt in which he whistled Charlie Parker's "Donna Lee" solo note for note.) Wyatt enrolled in the Canterbury College of Art but dropped out to travel in Europe. There he met beatnik/hippie and fellow avant-gardist Daevid Allen. Hopper soon joined them. Upon their return to Canterbury, they opened up the Wilde Flowers' jazz rock to include more free-form experimentations and "pataphysics," a sort of winsome absurdity derived from French playwright Alfred Jarry.

Ratledge came back to Canterbury next from Oxford University; Hopper went with Sinclair, Pye Hastings, and Richard Coughlan to form another version of the Wilde Flowers, which quickly became Caravan. Ratledge formed Soft Machine with Wyatt, Kevin Ayers, and Allen; they got the name from the William Burroughs novel. After some rehearsal, the band went to London and played with Pink Floyd at the psychedelic UFO club. At this point guitarist Andy Summers (later with the Police) occasionally played with them. In London they met producer Kim Fowley, with whom they recorded two songs, "Feelin' Reelin' Squealin' " and "Love Makes Sweet Music" (reissued on *At the Beginning*); Jimi Hendrix, who was recording "Hey Joe" in the same studio, played some rhythm guitar. The records made little impact in England, and Soft Machine went back to France, settling in St. Tropez, where they soon attracted much notoriety as the center of "happenings" surrounding Alan Zion's production of the Picasso play *Desir Attrape par la Queue*. When they finally returned to Britain late in 1967, Allen had visa problems; he went back to Paris and later founded Gong [see entry]. Soft Machine played some shows as a trio and opened Hendrix's 1968 U.S. tour. (Wyatt painted a suit and tie on his bare torso for the occasion.) In New York they recorded their debut LP with producer Tom Wilson.

After the tour and recording sessions, Soft Machine temporarily disbanded. Ayers went to Ibiza, then Majorca, to write before forming his own band, the Whole World; Ratledge went to London; and Wyatt stayed in the U.S. The record company pressured Wyatt to reassemble the group. Ayers was replaced by Hopper. The new band recorded *Volume Two*, less a concept album than a stream-of-consciousness LP, with 17 tracks bleeding into each other over two sides and jazz influences ranging from cocktail to avant-garde. Toward the end of a long U.K. tour, they added a horn section from Keith Tippett's Centipede Orchestra for *Third*, sax player Elton Dean stayed on to help on *Fourth*, a double LP of four side-long compositions (including Wyatt's magnum opus, "Moon in June"), which again won heavy critical acclaim but sold only moderately.

In 1971 Wyatt began to grow disenchanted with Soft Machine, as the band became more and more formulaic. He left after recording *Fourth* and formed Matching Mole, who recorded two LPs. He went on to have a critically respected career as a solo performer, and was preparing to embark on a Matching Mole reunion when he fell from a fourth-story window. He was left paralyzed from the waist down. With Ratledge's fuzz organ the sole sonic link with the band's past, and Wyatt apparently taking the band's verbal wit with him, Soft Machine gradually devolved into just another jazz-rock fusion band, recruiting members from other such British units as Nucleus (whence came John Jenkins and Karl Marshall). Hopper went on to record solo concept LPs like *1984*. He also formed a band called Isotope, and worked with reedman Elton Dean in Soft Heap. Ayers maintained a respectable solo–singer/songwriter career of his own [see solo entry]. Marshall and Babbington have returned to the jazz and jazz-rock scenes. Ratledge quit Soft Machine in 1976 (replaced by Rick Wakeman's brother Alan), leaving the band with no original members. Jenkins and Marshall continued on through the '90s with a lineup that was still critically respected. When the group finally dissolved, Jenkins became a jingle writer and composer. Marshall played with jazz bassist Eberhard Weber.

In the meantime, Robert Wyatt was becoming a long-established cult artist. His first solo album released after his accident, *Rock Bottom*, was produced by Pink Floyd's Nick Mason; it earned him the prestigious French Prix Charles Cros in 1974. Despite being wheelchair bound, Wyatt continued to tour and to travel, and he has collaborated with a wide range of artists ranging from Everything But the Girl's Ben Watt to Ryuichi Sakamoto. Wyatt has had two U.K. chart singles during his long solo career: a cover of the Monkees' "I'm a Believer" (#29 U.K., 1974) and a rendition of Elvis Costello's antiwar "Shipbuilding" (#35 U.K., 1983). Wyatt's later material, which is clearly political, also includes old folk and protest songs. In the early '80s he recorded the anti-lynching "Strange Fruit" (first popularized by Billie Holiday) and "Caimenera" (better known as "Guantanamera"). In 1998 he resurfaced after a six-year absence and released the widely praised, whimsically challenging *Shleep*, which boasts guest appearances by Brian Eno, Paul Weller, and jazzman Evan Parker. The following year's *EPs* is a historical boxed set of mini-albums.

Son Volt

Formed 1995, St. Louis, MO, and Minneapolis, MN
Jay Farrar (b. Dec. 26, 1966, Belleville, IL), voc., gtr.; Mike Heidorn (b. May 28, 1967, Belleville), drums; Dave Boquist (b. Nov. 21, 1957, Minneapolis), gtr., fiddle, banjo, lap steel; Jim Boquist (b. May 30, 1964, Minneapolis), voc., bass.
1995—*Trace* (Warner Bros.) 1997—*Straightaways*
1998—*Wide Swing Tremolo.*

When Uncle Tupelo [see entry] cofounder Jay Farrar left the Belleville, Illinois, roots-punk combo due to creative differences with partner Jeff Tweedy in 1994, he set out to make music in the rustic, history-conscious vein of predecessors like the Byrds and Flying Burrito Brothers. To that end Farrar formed Son Volt (the group takes its name from Delta bluesman Son House) with former Tupelo drummer and high school pal Mike Heidorn, as well as brothers Jim and Dave Boquist, both of whom were active in Minneapolis' alternative-music scene.

Son Volt's debut album, *Trace* (#166, 1995), was an introspective set of banjo- and fiddle-flecked songs exploring both the heart's longings and the lure of the open road. More muted in tone than *A.M.*, the first release from Wilco (Farrar's former partner Jeff Tweedy's band [see entry]), *Trace* became an instant critical favorite, winding up in the Top 10 of ROLLING STONE's 1995 critics' list. The record, which included a minor hit, the uncharacteristically hard-rocking "Drown," was something of a commercial success as well.

Recorded after the band had spent two years on the road, including appearances at Farm Aid and a slot on the H.O.R.D.E. Tour, *Straightaways* (#44, 1997), was even more laid back than *Trace*. It also didn't fare as well commercially, selling only 95,000 copies. Critics were divided on its merits, some calling it a soporific sequel to *Trace*, others hailing it as a consolidation of that album's virtues. The group's self-produced third album, *Wide Swing Tremolo* (#93, 1998), found Sun Volt cranking up its amps as never before, a sound that harked back to the crunching roots punk of Uncle Tupelo. The record received mixed reviews and didn't sell very well. Rumors began circulating on the Internet toward the end of 1999 that Farrar might be dissolving the band. The fact that he had gone into the studio to demo new songs without the rest of Son Volt, along with reports that Farrar was taking time off to be a father, only heightened speculation.

Sonic Youth

Formed 1981, New York, NY
Kim Gordon (b. Apr. 28, 1953, Rochester, NY), voc., bass, gtr.; Thurston Moore (b. July 25, 1958, Coral Gables, FL), voc., gtr., bass; Richard Edson, drums; Ann DeMarinis, kybds.
1981—(– DeMarinis; + Lee Ranaldo [b. Feb. 3, 1956, Glen Cove, NY], gtr., voc.) 1982—*Sonic Youth* EP (Neutral) (– Edson; + Bob Bert, drums) 1983—(– Bert; + Jim Sclavunos, drums) *Confusion Is Sex* (– Sclavunos; + Bert) *Kill Yr. Idols* EP (Zensor, Ger.) 1984—*Sonic Death: Sonic Youth Live* (Ecstatic Peace) 1985—*Bad Moon Rising* (Homestead); *Death Valley 69* EP (– Bert; + Steve Shelley [b. June 23, 1962, Midland, MI], drums) 1986—*Evol* (SST) 1987—*Sister* 1988—*Master Dik* EP; *Daydream Nation* (Blast First-Enigma) 1990—*Goo* (DGC) 1992—*Dirty* 1994—*Experimental Jet Set, Trash and No Star* 1995—*Washing Machine; Screaming Fields of Sonic Love* 1997—*Anagrama/Improvisation Ajoutee/Tremens/Mieux: De Corrosion* EP (SYR); *Slappkamers Met Slagroom/Stil/Herinneringen* EP 1998—*A Thousand Leaves* (DGC) 1999—*Goodbye 20th Century* (SYR) 2000—*NYC Ghosts & Flowers* (DGC/Interscope).
Sonic Youth with Jim O'Rourke: 1997—*Invito Al Cielo* EP (SYR).
As Ciccone Youth: 1988—*The Whitey Album* (Blast First).
Kim Gordon solo: 2000—*SYR 5* (SYR).
Free Kitten (Gordon with Julie Cafritz): 1994—*Unboxed* (Wiija) 1995—*Nice Ass* (Kill Rock Stars) 1996—*Punk vs. Punk* EP 1997—*Sentimental Education*.
Thurston Moore solo: 1990—*Barefoot in the Head* (Forced) 1995—*Psychic Hearts* (DGC) 1996—*Just Leave Me* (Pure); *Piece for Jetsun Dolma* (Victo) 1997—*Lost to the City* (Intakt) 1999—*Root* (Lo Recordings); *Promise* (with Evan Parker and Walter Prati) (Materiali); *Klangfarbenmelodie . . . And the Colorist Strikes Primitiv* (with Tom Surgal) (Corpus); *In-Store* (with Nels Cline) (Father Yod).
Dim Stars (Moore; Shelley; Richard Hell; Robert Quine; Don Fleming): 1992—*Dim Stars* EP (Ecstatic Peace/Caroline); *Dim Stars* (Caroline).
Lee Ranaldo solo: 1987—*From Here to Infinity* (SST) 1993—*Scriptures of the Golden Eternity* (Father Yod); *Envisioning* (with William Hooker) (Knitting Factory); *East Jesus* (Atavistic) 1996—*Broken Circle* EP (Starlight) 1998—*Amarillo Ramp (For Robert Smithson)* (Starlight); *Clouds* (Victo); *Dirty Windows* (Atavistic).

Sonic Youth is the avatar of noisy, underground guitar rock. After making the transition from uncompromising avant-rockers in the early '80s to indie guitar-pop trailblazers by decade's end, the group became the alternative-music world's brightest beacon. In the '90s Sonic Youth's sound continued to influence younger bands, the most famous evidence being in the grungy, sometimes discordant riffs of Nirvana's "Smells Like Teen Spirit." And if Nirvana's mainstream success briefly suggested crossover potential for Sonic Youth, the band's weakness for wild experimentation never waned.

In the late '70s Thurston Moore, raised in Bethel, Connecticut, and Lee Ranaldo, of New York's Long Island, hit Manhattan just in time for the end of punk rock and its avant-garde cousin, no wave. The two met while performing with

Sonic Youth: Lee Ranaldo, Steve Shelley, Kim Gordon, Thurston Moore

downtown guitar-orchestra composer Glenn Branca, whose extended works featured several guitars playing highly textured, dissonant music. In 1981 Moore formed Sonic Youth with bassist/art-school graduate Kim Gordon (who would marry Moore) and drummer Richard Edson (who later pursued acting and starred in such films as *Stranger Than Paradise* and *Do the Right Thing*). Ranaldo joined before their second gig. The band went through several drummers before locking in with Steve Shelley in 1986.

Sonic Youth's first recordings, released on Branca's Neutral label, mainly consisted of feedback and ringing harmonics, with Gordon or Moore intoning about death, urban decay, and other dreary, no-wave-inspired topics. Moore and Ranaldo became known for propping up a dozen or so guitars behind the band during performances, each tuned unconventionally and some containing objects such as screwdrivers and drumsticks jammed between the strings and fretboards.

With 1985's *Bad Moon Rising*, Sonic Youth hit on a direction that incorporated swirling, Branca-style guitar textures into more traditional pop-based song structures. Critical responses were generally positive, and major labels began knocking at the band's door. But Sonic Youth held out for three more full-length indie-label albums, including the double-length classic *Daydream Nation*, while perfecting its art-pop recipe. (In the meantime they did a tongue-in-cheek tribute to Madonna under the pseudonym Ciccone Youth.)

In 1990 the group's major-label debut, *Goo* (#96), cemented Sonic Youth's stature in the music world and led to an arena tour opening for Neil Young. The move was incongruous but not altogether inappropriate, since both acts worshipped feedback and distortion. (It was also consistent with Sonic Youth's ironic sense of humor.) By the release of *Dirty* (#83, 1992), the former avant-noisemakers were being hailed as the messiahs of modern rock; even *Vanity Fair* profiled Gordon and anointed her the "godmother . . . of alternative rock." In 1994 Sonic Youth released their most popular LP to date, *Experimental Jet Set, Trash and No Star*, which peaked on the U.S. album charts at #34 (and #10 in the U.K.). Later that year, Gordon and Moore had a daughter.

In 1995 Sonic Youth headlined the Lollapalooza Tour, but endured a nightly insult of seeing large numbers of fans leave immediately following the set by support act Hole and celebrity frontwoman Courtney Love. But the tour financed the creation of Sonic Youth's Manhattan studio-workshop. The band earned strong reviews for 1995's *Washing Machine* (#58). By now, Gordon had largely abandoned the bass for guitar. Band members were also exploring a variety of solo projects. Gordon joined Julie Cafritz (of Pussy Galore) in Free Kitten, and Moore released the *Psychic Hearts* album on Geffen in 1995.

Sonic Youth never left the underground, even as it explored more traditional pop structures in the '90s. While remaining on Geffen, in 1997 the band established its own SYR label for a series of experimental and mostly instrumental releases, with tracks stretching beyond 20 minutes. Sonic Youth could appear as animated characters on *The Simpsons* and yet step back into the avant-garde for an acclaimed 1997 performance at New York's Lincoln Center, soon followed by the expansive 74-minute *A Thousand Leaves* album. With 1999's two-disc *Goodbye 20th Century*, the band explored other forms of avant-garde music, tackling compositions by the likes of John Cage and Steve Reich. That same year, a vanload of the band's hot-rodded, one-of-a-kind guitars was stolen at a Southern California tour stop. Sonic Youth had to start again from scratch, which only forced the band into still-further explorations on *NYC Ghosts & Flowers* in 2000.

Sonny and Cher

Salvatore Bono, born Feb. 16, 1935, Detroit, MI; died Jan. 5, 1998, South Lake Tahoe, NV
Cherilyn Sarkasian LaPier, born May 20, 1946, El Centro, CA
1965—*Look at Us* (Atco) 1966—*The Wondrous World of Sonny and Cher* 1967—*In Case You're in Love; Good Times; The Best of Sonny and Cher* 1971—*Sonny & Cher Live* (Kapp) 1972—*All I Ever Need Is You* 1973—*Live in Las Vegas, vol. 2* (MCA); *Mama Was a Rock and Roll Singer, Papa Used to Write All Her Songs* 1974—*Greatest Hits* 1986—*At Their Best* (Pair) 1991—*The Beat Goes On—The Best of Sonny & Cher* (Atlantic) 1993—*I Got You Babe: Rhino Special Editions* (Rhino) 1996—*All I Ever Need Is You: The Kapp/MCA Anthology* (MCA).
Sonny Bono solo: 1967—*Inner Views* (N.A.).
Cher solo: see entry.

Sonny and Cher were a husband-and-wife team who enjoyed a brief period of success as wildly garbed hippie-ish pop singers, followed by a slightly longer stretch when their Vegas-style singing and stand-up comedy found favor with a nationwide TV audience. The partnership ended in divorce, and Cher went on to a solo career as singer, actress, garishly gowned celebrity, and fitness guru.

Bono spent years trying to break into the music business as a songwriter. He'd started writing songs at age seven, and at 12 appeared on the popular music show *Peter Potter's Hit Parade*. In 1957 he placed "High School Dance" on the B side of Larry Williams' "Bony Moronie." When Sonny's tune reached #90 in its own right, he became a staff producer at Specialty, where he also began recording under the name Don Christy. He had no particular success until 1964, when "Needles and Pins," which he cowrote with Jack Nitzsche, became a big hit for the Searchers. By this time, Sonny was working for Phil Spector as writer and backup vocalist. In 1963 he met Cher when she sang backup on some of Spector's sessions.

They married in 1964 and made a couple of unsuccessful singles under various names (Caesar and Cleo) for Vault and Reprise before signing to Atco in 1965. Their first chart entry was the million-seller "I Got You Babe" (#1, 1965). Then came "Baby Don't Go" (#8, 1965), "The Beat Goes On" (#6, 1967) and "solo" hits like Sonny's "Laugh at Me" (#10,

1965) and Cher's "All I Really Wanna Do" (#15, 1965), "Bang Bang (My Baby Shot Me Down)" (#2, 1966), and "You Better Sit Down Kids" (#9, 1967). With the exception of Bob Dylan's "All I Really Wanna Do," Bono wrote and produced all of these records. The pair also made two movies: *Good Times* (1967) and *Chastity* (1969, written by Sonny, starring Cher, named for their daughter). The pop hits slowed at the end of the '60s.

Produced by Snuff Garrett, a pair of Top 10 hits—"All I Ever Need Is You" (#7, 1971) and "A Cowboy's Work Is Never Done" (#8, 1972)—helped Sonny and Cher bounce back in 1971–72. These and a series of successful appearances in Las Vegas and on countless television variety shows led to the TV series—*The Sonny and Cher Comedy Hour* (1971–74) and *The Sonny and Cher Show* (1976–1977)—that made them household names. At that time, however, their marriage was breaking up. During and after the split, both tried solo careers and had solo TV shows. The duo performed their last show as husband and wife at the Houston Astrodome in 1974; they divorced in June 1975. Cher [see solo entry] would be the more successful of the two, however, and Sonny soon abandoned show business.

Beginning in 1983 Bono operated an L.A. restaurant for several years before moving to Palm Springs, where he opened another restaurant and made a successful bid for the mayor's office in 1988. A subsequent run for the U.S. Senate failed. He made occasional forays into performing, costarring in John Waters' *Hairspray* (1988) and making guest appearances on television programs *(The Love Boat, Fantasy Island).* In 1987 Sonny and Cher reunited to perform "I Got You Babe" on *Late Night With David Letterman,* after which Bono seemed visibly moved. In 1991 he wrote *And the Beat Goes On,* which became a regional bestseller in a few markets. In the book, Bono alleged that Cher neglected their daughter, Chastity, and he painted his ex-wife as a cold, calculating careerist. In 1994 Bono, who'd never bothered to register to vote until 1988, was elected to the U.S. House of Representatives, where he proved himself a quick study and became popular with colleagues on both sides of the aisle. He was the second most successful Republican fund raiser after his friend Speaker Newt Gingrich. He was reelected in 1996. Bono made his mark as a supporter of legislation to strengthen copyright laws, among other issues. On other matters (such as same-sex marriage), he was conservative, though when Chastity revealed she was gay, he was initially more accepting and supportive than Cher. (Chastity recounted her life as a gay rights activist and celebrity offspring in her book *Family Outing.*)

Bono died at age 62 of massive head injuries after skiing into a tree at a resort near South Lake Tahoe, Nevada. The death was termed accidental, though in 1998 his widow, Mary (who had assumed his seat in the House following his death), revealed to the *Los Angeles Times* that his longtime dependence on prescription painkillers may have been a contributing factor. She also contended that Bono was insecure, erratic, and subject to mood swings. Cher delivered the eulogy at Sonny's funeral.

S.O.S. Band

Formed 1977, Atlanta, GA
Mary Davis (b. Savannah, GA), voc., kybds.; Jason "TC" Bryant, kybds., voc.; Bruno Speight, gtr., voc.; Billy Ellis, flute; Willie "Sonny" Killebrew, sax; John Simpson, bass, voc.; James Earl Jones III, drums.
1980—*S.O.S.* (Tabu/Columbia) (+ Abdul Raoof, trumpet, voc.) 1981—*Too* (– Jones; + Jerome "JT" Thomas, drums) 1982—*S.O.S. III* 1983—*On the Rise* 1984—*Just the Way You Like It* 1986—*Sands of Time* (– Davis; + Pennye Ford, voc.) 1987—*Diamonds in the Raw* 1988—*The Way You Like It* (CBS Special Prod.) 1991—*One of Many Nights* (A&M).

An Atlanta-based pop-funk outfit, the S.O.S. ("Sounds of Success") Band's eponymous debut album (#12, 1980) spawned the massive late-disco smash "Take Your Time (Do It Right) Part 1" (#3 pop, #1 R&B, 1980), and a lesser dance hit in "S.O.S." (#20 R&B, 1980). But the group's next two albums failed to crack the pop chart; *III,* however, yielded a moderate dance hit in "High Hopes" (#25 R&B, 1982), which was the S.O.S. Band's first collaboration with the writing-producing team of Jimmy Jam and Terry Lewis, then still members of the Prince spin-off band the Time.

In March 1983 Jam and Lewis—during a few days off from a tour by Prince and the Time—flew to Atlanta to produce some S.O.S. Band tracks. Snowed in by a freak storm, the pair missed their next tour date and were promptly fired by Prince. But one of the tracks they were producing, "Just Be Good to Me" (#55 pop, #2 R&B, 1983), reasserted S.O.S. Band's pop status and codified Jam and Lewis' cool, plush, Chic-like sound. They produced half of *On the Rise* (#47, 1983), which also yielded "Tell Me If You Still Care" (#65 pop, #5 R&B, 1983) and "For Your Love" (#34 R&B, 1984), and worked on the group's next two albums. *Just the Way You Like It* (#60, 1984) produced hits in the title track (#60 pop, #6 R&B, 1984) and "No One's Gonna Love You" (#15 R&B, 1984); *Sands of Time* (#44, 1986) contained "The Finest" (#44 pop, #2 R&B, 1986) and "Borrowed Love" (#14 R&B, 1986).

In 1986 Jam and Lewis moved on, and Mary Davis left to launch a solo career; her first album, *Separate Ways* (#82 R&B, 1990) spawned the single "Don't Wear It Out" (#19 R&B, 1990). Davis was replaced by Pennye Ford for *Diamonds in the Raw,* which failed to chart pop but produced the R&B hit "I'm Still Missing Your Love" (#7 R&B, 1989). Though the album didn't chart at all, 1991's *One of Many Nights* yielded the R&B hit "Sometimes I Wonder" (#12 R&B, 1991). Three years later, Davis joined Bryant and Raoof in a new version of the band, which frequently toured as a part of "old school" R&B-themed package shows.

Soul Asylum

Formed 1981, Minneapolis, MN
Dave Pirner (b. Apr. 16, 1964, Green Bay, WI), voc., gtr.; Dan Murphy (b. July 12, 1962, Duluth, MN), voc., gtr.; Karl Mueller

(b. July 27, 1963, Minneapolis), voc., bass; Grant Young (b. Jan. 5, 1964, Iowa City, IA), drums.
1984—*Say What You Will, Clarence . . . Karl Sold the Truck* (Twin/Tone) 1986—*Made to Be Broken; Time's Incinerator* cassette; *While You Were Out* 1988—*Clam Dip & Other Delights* EP; *Hang Time* (Twin/Tone-A&M) 1990—*Soul Asylum and the Horse They Rode In On* 1992—(+ Sterling Campbell, drums) *Grave Dancers Union* (Columbia) 1995—*Let Your Dim Light Shine* 1998—*Candy From a Stranger* (– Campbell) 2000—*Black Gold—The Best of Soul Asylum* (+ Ian Mussington, drums).

Soul Asylum began as a thrashy punk band in the style of hometown peers the Replacements and Hüsker Dü. The group's tireless blend of punk energy, jazzy rhythms, country shadings, and solid songwriting earned it the tag "best live band in America."

In 1981 roommates Karl Mueller and Dan Murphy, 18 and 19 respectively, formed Loud Fast Rules with 17-year-old drummer Dave Pirner. Within three years Pirner had moved to the front, and the group changed its name to Soul Asylum. After the lo-fi *Say What You Will . . .*, produced by Hüsker Dü's Bob Mould, the band locked into its signature song style: loud, anthemic musings on the lives of young misfits.

For the next four years Soul Asylum slogged it out on the independent label Twin/Tone, touring constantly and releasing generally well-received albums. In 1988, the same year the group's Twin/Tone deal was picked up by Herb Alpert's A&M Records, the cover of its album *Clam Dip & Other Delights* featured a send-up of Alpert's own 1965 Tijuana Brass album, *Whipped Cream & Other Delights.* The joke seemed to elicit bad karma for Soul Asylum: Its A&M albums sold poorly even though they were among the group's strongest. After a shakeup at A&M, 1990's *And the Horse They Rode In On* stiffed so badly the band members almost decided to call it quits.

Pirner and Murphy briefly toured the Midwest as an acoustic duo called Murphy and Pirfinkle. Meanwhile Columbia struck a deal with A&M whereby it could release Soul Asylum's next album, and in 1992 the group came back with its biggest success to date. *Grave Dancers Union* (#11) was both a critical and commercial smash, selling a million copies and scoring a #5 hit with "Runaway Train." That song's video also acted as a public service spot by featuring photographs of real teenage runaways, earning endless airplay on MTV. By 1993, Soul Asylum had performed at Bill Clinton's presidential inaugural, and Pirner had begun showing up in the gossip columns because of his relationship with actress Winona Ryder, with whom he appeared in the film *Reality Bites.*

Young was replaced by drummer Sterling Campbell in time for 1995's *Let Your Dim Light Shine* (#6), which produced the hit single "Misery" (#20), but failed to match the popularity of "Runaway Train." In 1998 the band returned with *Candy From a Stranger* (#121), though Campbell soon left, weary of touring. Two years later, Soul Asylum released *Black Gold—The Best of Soul Asylum.*

By now, Pirner had relocated to New Orleans, and he wrote the score to the Kevin Smith film *Chasing Amy.* A Pirner solo album was planned for 2001, though side projects were nothing new to the band. By 1992, Murphy had already joined members of Wilco and the Jayhawks in a country-flavored side project called Golden Smog, which became a serious recording and touring endeavor, along with such lesser-known band projects as Dim Sum and the Three Amigos.

Soul II Soul

Formed 1982, London, Eng.
Jazzie B. (b. Beresford Romeo, Jan. 6, 1963, London), DJ, voc.; Daddae (b. Philip Harvey, Feb. 28, 1964, London), misc.; Nellee Hooper, programming; Caron Wheeler (b. Jan. 19, 1963, London), voc.; Simon Law, kybds.
1989—*Keep On Movin* (Virgin) 1990—(– Wheeler; – Law) *Vol. II—1990—A New Decade* 1992—(– Hooper; + William Mowat [b. May 27, 1954, Stamford, Eng.], kybds.; + Rick Clarke [b. Aug. 17, 1960, London], voc.; + Luis Jordam, perc.; + Kofi Kari Kari [b. Sep. 11, 1962, London], voc.) *Volume III Just Right* 1994—(– Jordam; + Sonya Alphonse [b. Jan. 3, 1975, Wimbledon, Eng.], voc.; + Melissa Bell [b. Mar. 5, 1964, London], voc.; + Vannessa Simon [b. Dec. 7, 1969, Huddersfield, Eng.], backing voc.; + Michael Garnette [b. June 1, 1963, London], kybds.; + Fluxy [b. Oct. 18, 1963, London], drums; + Enyonam Esi Gbesemete [b. Dec. 21, 1969, Ghana], backing voc.; + Julia Payne [b. Apr. 16, 1963, London], backing voc.; + Ingrid Webster [b. May 14, 1964, S.A.], backing voc.; + Damel Carayol [b. Nov. 13, 1956, Gambia], backing voc.; + Lamya Al-Maghairy [b. Oct. 30, 1968, Mombasa, Kenya], voc.; + Mafia [b. Aug. 10, 1962, London], bass) 1995—*Vol. V Believe* 1997—*Time for a Change* (Island) 2000—*Club Mix Hits* (Best Music Int.).

Soul II Soul took its slow-grooving fusion of reggae, soul, and rap, music fused in the clubs of London, and internationalized it with a string of hits and a Marcus Garvey–inspired ideology. Leader Jazzie B. has described the group as more of a concept than a band; Soul II Soul is at once an amorphous collective and Jazzie B.'s solo project. Jazzie B., whose parents are from Antigua, grew up in North London and began working in sound studios at age 11. He and childhood friend Philip "Daddae" Harvey started Soul II Soul as a mobile sound system playing reggae clubs and warehouse parties. At one party in 1985, Soul II Soul rented equipment to Nellee Hooper, formerly of Bristol hip-hop group the Wild Bunch and then Massive Attack. The two argued that night but soon were working together.

Soul II Soul defined late-'80s British club music, and its reputation increased when Jazzie B. and other band associates DJ'd on a British pirate radio station. After a couple of singles failed to hit, Soul II Soul finally struck it big with "Keep On Movin' " (#11 pop, #1 R&B, 1989), a #5 U.K. hit that also found a mass audience in the U.S. The single kicked off the album *Keep On Movin'* (#14 pop, #1 R&B, 1989), called *Club Classics Vol. One* in England, where it was #1. The single and its followup, "Back to Life (However Do You Want Me)" (#4 pop, #1 R&B, 1989), both platinum hits, featured the vocals of longtime studio singer Caron Wheeler. She soon had a falling-out with Soul II Soul and left to pursue a solo career. On the album's third single, "Jazzie's Groove" (#6 R&B, 1989), Jazzie B. articulated his positivist, Afrocentric philosophy: "A happy face, a thumpin' and lovin' bass, for a thumpin' and lovin' race." The album won two Grammys.

Soul II Soul expanded to form an umbrella for a number of enterprises, including a studio, a fashion line, boutiques, and in 1991, the label Funki Dred, originally a joint venture with Motown but now an independent company. In 1990 Hooper and Jazzie B. coproduced Sinéad O'Connor's hit "Nothing Compares 2 U"; they also produced the Chimes, Neneh Cherry, Maxi Priest, and Fine Young Cannibals. As in the past, they used an assortment of singers on *Vol. II—1990—A New Decade* (#21 pop, #14 R&B, 1990), including Victoria Wilson-James on "A Dream's a Dream" (#19 R&B, 1990) and Kym Mazelle on "Missing You" (#29 R&B, 1990) and "Get a Life" (#54 pop, #5 R&B, 1990). The album's assortment of musicians included rapper Fab 5 Freddie and saxophonist Courtney Pine. A world tour for the album featured a fashion show and a 15-piece band. Jazzie B.'s back was injured in a seven-car pileup while on the road in Illinois, however, and Soul II Soul canceled the rest of its American shows.

Wheeler returned to sing on *Volume III Just Right,* an album that featured mostly male vocalists. "Joy" (#14 R&B, 1992) was sung by Richie Stephens, while Kofi Kari Kari handled vocals on "Move Me No Mountain" (#33 R&B, 1992). A whole crew of musicians was on board for 1995's *Vol. V Believe,* which incorporated jungle and other forms of contemporary electronica into Soul II Soul's club sound. The album became a Top 10 hit in the U.K. but had little commercial impact in the States (#67 R&B); its successor, *Time for Change* (1997), didn't chart in the U.S. at all. Over the years, Nellee Hooper has worked with stars ranging from Björk to Madonna and U2.

Soundgarden

Formed 1984, Seattle, WA
Matt Cameron (b. Nov. 28, 1962, San Diego, CA), drums; Chris Cornell (b. July 20, 1964, Seattle), voc.; Kim Thayil (b. Sep. 4, 1960, Seattle), gtr.; Hiro Yamamoto (b. Apr. 13, 1961), bass.
1987—*Screaming Life* EP (Sub Pop) 1988—*Fopp* EP; *Ultramega OK* (SST) 1989—*Louder Than Love* (A&M) (– Yamamoto; + Jason Everman [b. Aug. 16, 1967], bass) 1990—(– Everman; + Ben Shepherd [b. Hunter Shepherd, Sep. 20, 1968, Okinawa, Jap.], bass) 1991—*Badmotorfinger* 1994—*Superunknown* 1996—*Down on the Upside* 1997—*A-Sides.*
Hater (Cameron; Shepherd; + John McBain, gtr.; + Brian Wood, voc.; + John Waterman, bass): 1993—*Hater* (A&M).
Wellwater Conspiracy (Cameron; Shepherd; McBain): 1997—*Declaration of Conformity* (Third Gear) 1999—(– Shepherd) *Brotherhood of Electric: Operational Directions* (Time Bomb).
Chris Cornell solo: 1999—*Euphoria Morning* (A&M).

One of the first bands to come out of the Seattle grunge scene (and one of the earliest to sign with Sub Pop Records), Soundgarden parlayed gloomy metal riffs, surrealistic psychedelia, and punk into platinum with a trilogy of popular albums released in the '90s.

After graduating high school in Illinois in 1981, musicians Kim Thayil and Hiro Yamamoto, as well as fanzine editor (and later Sub Pop founder) Bruce Pavitt, moved to Olympia, Washington, where they planned to attend college. When this did not pan out, the three each ended up in Seattle, attracted by its nascent music scene.

After playing in cover bands, Yamamoto joined his roommate and sometime drummer Chris Cornell in his new band. Thayil signed on, and they called themselves Soundgarden after a noisy pipe sculpture in a Seattle park. The addition of drummer Scott Sundquist in 1985 (he was replaced by Cameron in 1986) freed Cornell to front the band. After contributing two songs to a local compilation, they signed with the new Sub Pop label. Their two EPs, *Screaming Life* (1987) and *Fopp* (1988), attracted major-label interest. But the band decided to stay true to their indie roots, signing to SST for their debut album *Ultramega OK.*

For *Louder Than Love* (#108, 1990), the band signed with A&M. The higher profile of a major label increased sales and helped the band garner a Grammy nomination. Yamamoto left the band in late 1989 to go back to school (in 1994 he joined Truly) and was replaced by Jason Everman, who had previously played with Nirvana. Everman was soon replaced by Hunter "Ben" Shepherd in early 1990.

The sales of *Badmotorfinger* (#39, 1991) were helped by "Outshined" being chosen as an MTV "Buzz Clip" and a spot opening for a Guns n' Roses tour (they were invited by Axl Rose, a longtime fan). In 1991 Cornell and Cameron, along with members of Pearl Jam [see entry] were part of Temple of the Dog, a tribute to the late Mother Love Bone singer Andrew Wood. In 1993, during a break from Soundgarden, Shepherd and Cameron released an album with their side project Hater, a band which also included Andrew Wood's brother Brian. Cameron, Shepherd, and McBain resumed their collaboration in 1997 under the name the Wellwater Conspiracy (in which Cameron and Shepherd were originally billed as Ted Dameron and Zeb, respectively).

Superunknown (1994), debuting at #1, emphasized Cornell's emotional lyrical content and Soundgarden's newfound stylistic flourishes. The album spawned the band's breakthrough track, "Black Hole Sun," which propelled them into the pop mainstream. Cameron even performed the song with the Seattle Symphony and experimental keyboardist Wayne Horvitz. In 1994 "Black Hole Sun" won a Grammy for Best Hard Rock Performance, while another *Superunknown* song, "Spoonman," won for Best Metal Performance.

The musical evolution started on *Superunknown* became even more pronounced on Soundgarden's followup, *Down on the Upside* (#2, 1996). Produced by the band, the album attempted to balance Cornell's trademark tortured lyrics ("Nothing seems to kill me no matter how hard I try"), metal energy, and increasingly complex arrangements and melodies. Despite its initial success with the #1 Modern

Rock hits "Burden in My Hand" and "Blow Up the Outside World," the album wasn't as popular as its predecessor. Subsequent touring was rumored to be rife with the kind of internal tension that had plagued the album's recording.

In April 1997 Soundgarden announced that they were disbanding. Explanations offered at the time included Shepherd's increasingly antagonistic onstage behavior, as well as divergences between Thayil, who wanted to stick to metal, and Cornell, who would have preferred to explore new directions. While Cameron joined fellow grunge survivors Pearl Jam, Cornell released a solo album, *Euphoria Morning* (#38, 1999) in which he was free to display his love for the Beatles and his pop sensibility. In 2001 Cornell began recording with Rage Against the Machine.

Joe South

Born Joe Souther, Feb. 28, 1940, Atlanta, GA
1968—*Introspect* (Capitol) 1969—*Don't It Make You Want to Go Home* 1971—*So the Seeds Are Growing* 1975—*Midnight Rainbows* (Island) 1990—*The Best of Joe South* (Rhino) 1992—*Best of Joe South* (CEMA Special Products).

Joe South was a successful sessionman who went on to become a hit songwriter and performer, crossing over from country to pop in the early '70s.

At age 11, South got his first guitar, and a year later he was appearing regularly on Atlanta country music station WGST. In 1957 he joined the band of Pete Drake, the famed country pedal steel guitar player, and in the early '60s he recorded some unsuccessful solo singles, including "Purple People Eater Meets the Witch Doctor." He also worked for a while as a country disc jockey.

South became a regular session guitarist in Nashville and Muscle Shoals, backing up country artists such as Marty Robbins and Eddy Arnold, in addition to Bob Dylan and Aretha Franklin. He appears on Simon and Garfunkel's "Sounds of Silence." South had also begun to do some songwriting, and in the mid-'60s he wrote hits for the Tams ("Untie Me"), Billy Joe Royal ("Down in the Boondocks"), and early Deep Purple ("Hush").

By 1968, South was recording his own material. *Introspect* at first sold marginally, but when other performers began to cover "Games People Play," Capitol reissued the LP in 1969 under that title. They also released the song as a single, and both album and single went gold. It also won a Grammy as Song of the Year. *So the Seeds Are Growing* included his 1970 hit "Walk a Mile in My Shoes" (#12). His "I Never Promised You a Rose Garden" became an international country and pop hit for Lynn Anderson (#3, 1971).

In 1971 South took time off, in part to recuperate from a hectic schedule and also because of the suicide of his brother Tommy. He lived awhile in the forests of Maui, Hawaii, and did not record again until 1975, when *Midnight Rainbows* was released. A difficult personality, South did not perform for years. In 1994 he played a show in London called *The American South*, where he was showcased along with Allen Toussaint, Guy Clark, Dan Penn, and Vic Chesnutt. "Games People Play" was again a hit in Europe by Jamaican reggae group Inner Circle. Having overcome past problems with a drug dependency, South is now in the music publishing business.

Southside Johnny and the Asbury Jukes

Formed 1974, Asbury Park, NJ
Southside Johnny (b. John Lyon, Dec. 4, 1948, Neptune, NJ), voc., harmonica; Billy Rush (b. Aug. 26, 1952), gtr.; Kevin Kavanaugh (b. Aug. 27, 1951), kybds., voc.; Al Berger (b. Nov. 8, 1949), bass, voc.; Kenny Pentifallo (b. Dec. 30, 1940), drums; Carlo Novi (b. Aug. 7, 1949, Mexico City), tenor sax; Eddie Manion (b. Feb. 28, 1952), baritone sax; Tony Palligrosi (b. May 9, 1954), trumpet; Ricky Gazda (b. June 18, 1952), trumpet; Richie "La Bamba" Rosenberg, trombone.
1976—*I Don't Wanna Go Home* (Epic) 1977—*This Time It's for Real* (– Pentifallo; – Novi) 1978—*Hearts of Stone* (+ Steve Becker, drums; + Joe Gramalin, gtr.) 1979—*The Jukes* (Mercury); *Having a Party With Southside Johnny* 1980—*Love Is a Sacrifice* (– Berger; + Gene Bacia, bass) 1981—*Live/Reach Up and Touch the Sky* 1983—*Trash It Up!* (Mirage) 1984—*In the Heat* 1986—*At Least We Got Shoes* (Atlantic) 1992—*The Best of Southside Johnny* (Epic) 1999—*Messin' With the Blues* (Leroy).
Southside Johnny solo: 1988—*Slow Dance* (Cypress) 1991—*Better Days* (Impact).

Southside Johnny and the Asbury Jukes were an R&B-influenced rock band who graduated from the Asbury Park bar-band scene soon after Bruce Springsteen's massive success.

Johnny Lyon, Springsteen, and Springsteen guitarist Miami Steve Van Zandt played together in the late '60s in Asbury Park groups like the Sundance Blues Band and Dr. Zoom and the Sonic Boom. Lyon got his nickname because he liked blues from the South Side of Chicago. After migrating to Richmond, Virginia, with a band called Studio B, Lyon returned to Asbury Park and formed a duo with Van Zandt called Southside Johnny and the Kid, which became the Bank Street Blues Band with keyboardist Kevin Kavanaugh. In 1974 Van Zandt left again to go on the road with the Dovells (of "Bristol Stomp" fame), whose backing band also included bassist Al Berger. Lyon then joined the Blackberry Booze Band, which included drummer Kenny Pentifallo. With the addition of a horn section, they became the Asbury Jukes. Van Zandt briefly rejoined them before moving on to Springsteen's band. The Jukes became mainstays at Asbury Park's top barroom, the Stone Pony. After Springsteen's successful 1975 U.S. and European tours, Van Zandt became the Jukes' manager/producer and landed them a recording contract. Their debut LP, which included two Springsteen tunes and guest appearances by Ronnie Spector and Lee Dorsey, sold well. *This Time* featured more Van Zandt and Springsteen tunes and included guest shots by members of the Coasters, the Drifters, and the Five Satins. Their third LP, with guest appearances by Van Zandt and E Street Band drummer Max Weinberg, still contained many Van Zandt and

Springsteen titles. On their self-titled fourth LP, the Jukes declared their independence from the Springsteen imprimatur by writing all their own material (Lyon and Rush were the main composers). *The Jukes* went to #48, becoming the highest-charting album of their career. While their albums began to sell less well, they remained a successful touring unit for several more years. Lyon's solo debut, *Better Days* (#96, 1991) reunited him with Van Zandt.

In the summer of 1994 Southside Johnny and the Jukes performed with Bruce Springsteen, Jon Bon Jovi, and others at the 20th-anniversary celebration for the Stone Pony in Asbury Park.

Bob B. Soxx and the Blue Jeans

Formed 1963, New York, NY
Bob B. Soxx (b. Robert Sheen); Darlene Love (b. Darlene Wright, July 26, 1938, Los Angeles, CA); Fanita James.
1963—*Zip-A-Dee Doo-Dah* (Philles).

Out of Phil Spector's Wall of Sound stable came vocal group Bob B. Soxx and the Blue Jeans in 1963, with their only big hit a revamped swinging version of "Zip-A-Dee Doo-Dah" (#8), a tune from the Disney film *Song of the South*. The LP also included covers of tunes like "This Land Is Your Land," "Let the Good Times Roll," and "The White Cliffs of Dover."

Spector had been initially attracted to Robert Sheen (a.k.a. Bob B. Soxx) because his voice reminded him of Clyde McPhatter's. All of the Blue Jeans had been singing since their early teens, and Love and James were both members of another Spector group, the Blossoms. Though they only had three chart hits, the group was a mainstay of the rock-concert circuit between 1963 and 1965. Darlene Love [see entry] went on to have some hits of her own for Spector. James was a backup vocalist for Tom Jones in the early '70s and continued to lead a group of Blossoms through the '80s as well.

Spandau Ballet

Formed 1979, London, Eng.
Tony Hadley (b. June 2, 1960, London), voc., kybds.; Gary Kemp (b. Oct. 16, 1959, London), gtr., kybds.; Martin Kemp (b. Oct. 10, 1961, London), bass; Steve Norman (b. Mar. 25, 1960, London), gtr., sax, perc.; John Keeble (b. July 6, 1959, London), drums.
1981—*Journeys to Glory* (Chrysalis) 1982—*Diamond* 1983—*True* 1984—*Parade* 1985—*The Singles Collection* 1986—*Through the Barricades* (Epic) 1991—*Best of Spandau Ballet* (Chrysalis, U.K.).

British dance-pop band Spandau Ballet was a product of the same fashion-conscious New Romantic scene that produced Duran Duran and Visage, among others. Spandau began as a kilt-clad synth-disco outfit, playing in a handful of ultratrendy London clubs, where genteel kids put off by punk's abrasiveness paraded around in outrageously ornate and fanciful clothes (as opposed to punk style). Spandau Ballet's reputation built so quickly that Island Records chief Chris Blackwell reportedly offered the group a contract the first time he met them, at a London party. The group refused his offer, instead forming its own Reformation label (later licensing its recordings to Chrysalis).

The group's first U.K. hits, "To Cut a Long Story Short" (#5 U.K., 1980) and "Musclebound" (#10 U.K., 1981), also got much play in U.S. clubs, and especially in the New York dance clubs that proliferated in the early '80s. Late 1981 saw Spandau introduce more musical urgency into its postdisco mix, with the soul-inflected "Chant No. 1 (I Don't Need This Pressure On)" (#3 U.K., 1981), which also got heavy U.S. club play.

In 1983 Spandau Ballet surprised critics who'd been dismissing the group as shallow, unmusical fops, with its first U.S. chart album *True* (#19, 1983), and its title single (#4, 1983)—a soulful ballad with the sound and feel of a pop standard. Indeed, nearly a decade later, psychedelic rappers PM Dawn made a sample of "True" the centerpiece of its chart-topping pop hit "Set Adrift on Memory Bliss." *True* also yielded hits in "Gold" (#29, 1983) and "Communication" (#59, 1983), but *Parade* (#50, 1984) spawned only the minor hit "Only When You Leave" (#34, 1984).

No more hits followed, and in 1985 Spandau sued Chrysalis, claiming ineffective promotion had killed its commercial chances in the U.S. The Kemp brothers launched acting careers, to great acclaim, playing real-life British gangsters the Kray twins in the 1990 film *The Krays*, signaling Spandau Ballet's demise later that year. In 1992 Gary Kemp appeared in the film *The Bodyguard*, playing the role of Whitney Houston's manager; the next year, he was featured on the hit U.S. cable-TV comedy series, *The Larry Sanders Show*. In 1998 Martin Kemp joined the cast of the popular British soap opera, *East-Enders*. The following year, the three other former members of the band—Tony Hadley, Steve Norman, and John Keeble—lost a court case against Gary Kemp, who they contended had failed to pay them a promised share of royalties.

The Spaniels

Formed 1952, Gary, IN
James "Pookie" Hudson, lead voc.; Gerald "Bounce" Gregory (b. June 10, 1934, East St. Louis, IL; d. Feb. 12, 1999, Gary), bass voc.; Opal Courtney Jr., baritone voc.; Ernest Warren, tenor voc.; Willis C. Jackson, tenor voc.
1955—(– Courtney; + Cal Carter; – Carter; + James Cochran, baritone voc.; – Warren; – Hudson; – Jackson; + Donald Porter, tenor voc.; + Carl Rainge, lead voc.) 1956—*Goodnight, It's Time to Go* (Vee-Jay) Lineup ca. 1960—(Hudson; Warren; Gregory; + Bill Carey, voc.; + Andy McGruder, voc.; numerous personnel changes follow) 1993—*The Spaniels—Goodnite Sweetheart, Goodnite* (Vee-Jay); (lineup: Hudson; Gregory; Courtney; Jackson; + Billy Shelton, voc.; + Teddy Shelton, voc.) *40th Anniversary* (JLJ).

A mid-'50s doo-wop vocal group, the Spaniels had several big R&B hits but never crossed over into pop-chart success.

They began as street singers in the Gary, Indiana, ghetto, and attracted the attention of local disc jockey Vivian Carter, who became their manager and with James Bracken formed Vee-Jay Records to release their material. The Spaniels' first single was "Baby, It's You," a Top 10 R&B hit in 1953, which established both the band and Vee-Jay Records (whose roster would later include Jimmy Reed and Jerry Butler, among others). In early 1954 their "Goodnite Sweetheart, Goodnite" was a #5 R&B hit (covered on the pop chart by the McGuire Sisters); in 1973 it was used as the closing theme for the film *American Graffiti*. The Spaniels became a top live attraction on the national R&B circuit, but they had undergone many personnel changes beginning in 1955. Through it all, though, the group continued to chart, notably with "You Painted Pictures" (#13 R&B, 1955) and "Everyone's Laughing" (#69 pop, #13 R&B, 1957). The Spaniels began fading in the late '50s, and shortly after "I Know" (#23 R&B, 1960), they broke up again. In 1969 "Pookie" re-formed the Spaniels. They toured the revival circuit and in 1970 released the Spaniels' last charting single, "Fairy Tales" on Lloyd Price's Calla label (#45 R&B).

Hudson and Gerald Gregory occasionally revived the Spaniels throughout the '80s. In 1991 the Smithsonian Institution's Rhythm & Blues Foundation bestowed upon the group its lifetime achievement award. The Spaniels, with several original members intact, released a 40th-anniversary album in 1993. Gregory continued performing with them until mere months before his death in 1999. Hudson continues to carry the torch.

Spanky and Our Gang

Formed 1966, Chicago, IL
Elaine "Spanky" McFarlane (b. June 19, 1942, Peoria, IL), voc.; Nigel Pickering (b. June 15, 1929, Pontiac, MI), bass, gtr., voc.; Oz Bach (b. Paul Bach, 1939, WV; d. Sep. 21, 1998, Asheville, NC), bass, gtr., voc.
1966—(+ Malcolm Hale [b. May 17, 1941, Butte, MT; d. 1968], gtr., voc.) 1967—(+ John Seiter [b. Aug. 17, 1944, St. Louis, MO], drums, voc.) *Spanky and Our Gang* (Mercury) 1968—(– Bach; + Kenny Hodges [b. Jacksonville, FL], gtr., voc., bass; + Lefty Baker [b. Eustace Britchforth, Jan. 7, 1939, Roanoke, VA; d. Aug. 11, 1971], gtr., banjo, voc.) *Like to Get to Know You; Without Rhyme or Reason* (– Hale; group disbands, re-forms with numerous personnel changes) 1969—*Spanky's Greatest Hit(s); Live* 1975—*Change* (Epic).

Along with the Mamas and the Papas, Spanky and Our Gang were part of the late-'60s folk/pop vocal-group movement, with major pop hits like "Sunday Will Never Be the Same" (#9, 1967), "Lazy Day" (#14, 1967), and "Like to Get to Know You" (#17, 1968). In 1982 Spanky joined the re-formed Mamas and the Papas.

Elaine McFarlane had met Mama Cass Elliot in the early '60s and then joined "an electric comedy-jug band," the New Wine Singers, which included Malcolm Hale. "Spanky" met Nigel Pickering, Kenny Hodges, and Lefty Baker while vacationing in Florida. As a quartet they debuted at the Mother Blues club and were an immediate success; they were signed by Chicago-based Mercury Records. Malcolm Hale and John Seiter then joined. They took their name from the *Our Gang* (a.k.a. *Little Rascals*) films.

The Gang began racking up a string of soft-rock/folk-pop hits like "Sunday Will Never Be the Same," "Making Every Minute Count" (#31), and "Lazy Day" in 1967; "Like to Get to Know You" and "Sunday Mornin' " (#30) in 1968. They were often featured on network TV variety shows, though in 1969 their ghetto-consciousness protest song "Give a Damn" was banned on many radio stations. That song was later used in a widely aired public service announcement campaign.

Though Hale had died of cirrhosis in 1968 during the mixing of *Without Rhyme or Reason*, the group retained the rest of the lineup until the hits stopped in 1970. The following year Lefty Baker died of liver complications.

In 1975 McFarlane and Pickering re-formed the band with three new members, playing Texas bars until 1980; McFarlane also appeared on Roger McGuinn's solo debut album. Then came the Mamas and the Papas reunion, with McFarlane even being called "Mama Spanky" by the rest of the group. McFarlane later worked with a new Spanky and Our Gang lineup. She continues to occasionally perform. Original bassist Oz Bach died of lung cancer in 1998.

Sparks

Formed 1971, Los Angeles, CA
Ron Mael (b. Aug. 12, 1948 or 1950, Culver City, CA), kybds.; Russell Mael (b. Oct. 5, 1953 or 1955, Santa Monica, CA), voc.; Earle Mankey, gtr.; Jim Mankey, bass; Harley Feinstein, drums.
1972—*Sparks* (Bearsville); *A Woofer in Tweeter's Clothing* 1974—(– E. Mankey; – J. Mankey; – Feinstein; + Martin Gordon, bass; + Adrian Fisher, gtr.; + Norman "Dinky" Diamond, drums) *Kimono My House* (Island); (– Gordon; – Fisher; + Ian Hampton, bass; + Trevor White, gtr.) *Propaganda* 1975—*Indiscreet* 1976—(– Diamond; – Hampton; – White; + Sal Maida, bass; + Jeff Salen, gtr.; + Hilly Michaels, drums) *Big Beat* (Columbia) 1977—(– Maida; – Salen; – Michaels) *Introducing Sparks* 1979—*Number One in Heaven* (Elektra) 1981—(+ David Kendrick, drums; + Leslie Bohem, bass; + Bob Haag, gtr.) *Whomp That Sucker* (Why-Fi/RCA) 1982—*Angst in My Pants* (Atlantic) 1983—*Sparks in Outer Space* 1984—*Pulling Rabbits Out of a Hat* 1986—(+ John Thomas, kybds.) *Music That You Can Dance To* (Curb/MCA) 1988—(– Kendrick; – Bohem; – Haag) *Interior Design* (Fine Art/Rhino) 1991—*Profile: The Ultimate Sparks Collection* (Rhino) 1995—*Gratuitous Sax and Senseless Violins* (Logic/Arista) 1997—*Plagiarism* (Oglio) 2000—*Balls*.

Sparks' arch combination of witty lyrics with ever-changing pop styles has long perplexed and enticed critics and audiences. Essentially the band is an outlet for the eclectic, eccentric Mael brothers, whose twisted tastes may have been set when they modeled for clothing catalogues as children. The Maels formed the band Halfnelson in the early '70s with friends from UCLA. Halfnelson caught the ear of Todd Rundgren, who got the band signed to Albert Grossman's Bearsville label and produced their first album.

When the eponymous disc failed to sell, the band's manager urged Halfnelson to change its name, and the retitled album was rereleased. The single "Wonder Girl" almost made the Hot 100 (#112, 1972). Sparks' quirky, overwrought art pop fared little better commercially with their second album, *A Woofer in Tweeter's Clothing,* now a cult classic. The Maels relocated to England, where they had found some success on tour, leaving the rest of the band behind. Earle Mankey went on to become a producer and recording artist, while brother Jim helped form Concrete Blonde.

With the assistance of a new band and producer Muff Winwood, Russell's quavering falsetto and Ron's odd lyrics found phenomenal acceptance in England, beginning with 1974's *Kimono My House* (#4 U.K.). Their image—Ron's stiff, nerdy demeanor and signature mustache juxtaposed to Russell's curly mane and beaming androgyny—appealed to British teens. Sparks landed nine U.K. chart hits during this period, starting with "This Town Ain't Big Enough for Both of Us" (#2, 1974), "Amateur Hour" (#7, 1974), and "Never Turn Your Back on Mother Earth" (#13, 1974). After another Top 10 U.K. album, *Propaganda* (#9 U.K., 1974), they began to falter the next year on the Tony Visconti–produced *Indiscreet* (#18 U.K.). In 1976 they returned to the U.S. and recorded *Big Beat* with various players, including Tuff Darts guitarist Jeff Salen. They sang two songs from the album in the film *Rollercoaster.* On the ironically titled *Introducing Sparks,* the Maels recorded with L.A. session players.

Seeking a change, Sparks got Giorgio Moroder to produce *Number One in Heaven.* Although critics derided the band for going disco, the album's dance-synth pop returned the duo to the British charts with three hits, "The Number One Song in Heaven" (#14 U.K., 1979), "Beat the Clock" (#10 U.K., 1979), and "Tryouts for the Human Race" (#45 U.K., 1979). Next, Sparks recorded *Terminal Jive* with Moroder protégé Harold Faltermeyer; although it was never released in the U.S., the album yielded "When I'm With You," a megaseller in France. Sparks adopted the band Bates Motel for its next few albums; Moroder associate and Queen engineer Mack produced 1981's *Whomp That Sucker.* The band divided its time between L.A. and Belgium, where it recorded the self-produced *Sparks in Outer Space.* The album features Sparks fan and Go-Go Jane Wiedlin on two songs, including "Cool Places" (#49, 1983), Sparks' biggest American hit.

After a string of albums that failed to hit in Europe or the U.S., the Maels built a home studio in L.A., where they recorded 1988's *Interior Design.* They also wrote the music for a film by Hong Kong director Tsui Hark. In late 1994 Sparks returned—performing in London and releasing the U.K. album *Gratuitous Sax and Senseless Violins* (the record came out in the States the following year). Two singles from the record, the cheekily titled "When Do I Get to Sing 'My Way' " and "When I Kiss You (I Hear Charlie Parker Playing)," were hits overseas.

Plagiarism (1997) found the brothers paying tribute to themselves with reworked versions of their best-known songs. Producer Tony Visconti was back on board for the club-conscious project, which also included cameos from Erasure, Faith No More, and Jimmy Somerville. *Balls* (2000) consisted of new material but continued in its predecessor's techno vein.

Britney Spears

Born Britney Jean Spears, Dec. 2, 1981, Kentwood, LA
1999—*. . . Baby One More Time* (Jive) 2000—*Oops! . . . I Did It Again.*

Mixing brazen sex-appeal, teenage energy, and radio-ready bubblegum-pop tunes, Britney Spears graduated from the Disney Channel's *Mickey Mouse Club* to the top of the chart.

Born in a small town north of New Orleans, Spears started taking gymnastics lessons after finishing kindergarten. She first auditioned for the Disney Channel's *The New Mickey Mouse Club* at age eight, but she was deemed too young. She went on to make commercials and spend three summers in New York, attending the Professional Performing Arts School; she appeared in the off-Broadway show *Ruthless* in 1991. She was finally accepted on the *The New Mickey Mouse Club,* filming two seasons in 1993–94. Two of her costars on the show were future 'N Sync members Justin Timberlake and JC Chasez. After the cancellation of the show, which had been taping in Orlando, Florida, she went back to her Louisiana home. Through a family friend who was an entertainment lawyer, she auditioned for Jive Records, which signed her; she was 15.

Following in the footsteps of the Backstreet Boys, Spears was sent to Stockholm to record her debut album, *. . . Baby One More Time,* with producers Max Martin and Eric Foster White, a writer who had previously worked with Whitney Houston (one of Spears' acknowledged influences, along with Mariah Carey and Madonna). She prepped the album release by opening for 'N Sync and going on a mall tour of her own, where she performed short sets with backing tapes. Her first single, ". . . Baby One More Time," released in October 1998, debuted at #1, as did the album of the same name, which came out in January 1999. The album also included the singles "Sometimes" (#21, 1999), "(You Drive Me) Crazy" (#10, 1999), and "From the Bottom of My Broken Heart" (#14, 2000). *. . . Baby One More Time* would go on to sell 13 million copies, becoming the best-selling album by a teenage female singer. Spears was nominated for a Grammy as Best New Artist but lost to Christina Aguilera. By then, her public persona was firmly in place, as the singer cultivated sexual allure and youthful innocence—often both at the same time, as in the video for ". . . Baby One More Time," in which she wore a skimpy Catholic school uniform, and in a provocative cover shoot for ROLLING STONE.

Spears confirmed that she was no flash-in-the-pan with

Oops! . . . I Did It Again (#1, 2000), produced by Max Martin and Robert "Mutt" Lange, which sold 1.3 million copies in its first week, on its way to a total of 8 million copies. Singles included the title track (#9, 2000), "Lucky" (#23, 2000), and the gold-selling "Stronger" (#11, 2000). The album explored the same territory of teen romance, though the sexual come-ons were even more obvious. At the same time, the singer, who often discusses her belief in God and her opposition to premarital sex and drugs, was careful to maintain a wholesome image—the lyrics she uses to cover the Rolling Stones' "(I Can't Get No) Satisfaction" deletes a reference to smoking cigarettes. Immediately after the album's release, she embarked on her first headlining tour.

In 2000 Spears cowrote a memoir, *Heart to Heart,* with her mother, Lynne. As of this writing, she was slated to star in her first movie.

The Specials/Fun Boy Three

Formed 1977, Coventry, Eng.
Jerry Dammers (b. Gerald Dankin, May 22, 1954, India), kybds.; Sir Horace Gentleman (b. Horace Panter), bass; Lynval Golding (b. July 24, 1951, Coventry), gtr.; Roddy Radiation (b. Roddy Byers), gtr.; Terry Hall (b. Mar. 19, 1959, Coventry), voc.; Neville Staples, voc., perc.; John Bradbury, drums.
1979—*The Specials* (Chrysalis) 1980—*The Special AKA Live* EP (2-Tone, U.K.); *More Specials* 1981—(group disbands; group re-forms as the Special AKA: Dammers; Bradbury; + Rhoda Dakar, voc.; + Egidio Newton, voc.; + Stan Campbell, voc.; + John Shipley, gtr.; + Gary McManus, bass) 1984—*In the Studio* 1991—*The Singles Collection* 1993—(group re-forms: Staples; Byers; Golding; Panter; + Mark Adams, kybds.; + Aitch Bembridge, drums; + Adam Birch, trombone, trumpet) 1996—*Today's Specials* (Kuff/Virgin) 1998—*Guilty 'Til Proved Innocent!* (Way Cool).
Fun Boy Three (Hall; Staples; Golding): 1982—*The Fun Boy Three* (Chrysalis) 1983—*Waiting* 1984—*The Best of Fun Boy Three.*

The Specials were the prime movers behind England's short-lived two-tone movement of 1979–81, which also included Madness, the Selecter, the English Beat, and several other bands. (The original fans often sported two-tone clothes and the band was racially mixed; ergo the title of the "movement.")

Coming together from mid-1977 to early 1978 in Coventry, the Specials initially played both fast punk and slower roots reggae. But they were unable to bring the two sounds together into a recognizable package, so they reoriented themselves toward ska, an upbeat precursor to reggae that was fashionable in England among Mods and skinheads in the mid-'60s.

By early 1979, after a 1978 tour with the Clash, the Specials cut an independent single, "Gangsters," but for its B side they used a cut by another struggling band, the Selecter. Pressed on the band's 2-Tone label, the single soared to #6 on the British charts. That led to a distribution deal with Chrysalis in June 1979. Soon their 2-Tone label gave British hits to a whole movement of bands—the Selecter, the Beat, and Madness—making it for a while the most successful independent English label since Stiff.

The Specials' debut LP, out in the U.S. in early 1980, was produced by Elvis Costello. Like that of most neo-ska bands, the music was danceable and charged with antiracist sentiment. Most of the music was by leader Jerry Dammers, but it also included the 1967 ska anthem "A Message to You Rudy" (#10 U.K., 1979). The Specials were stars in England, where "Too Much Too Young," a song advocating contraception from their U.K. EP, went to #1. Their other U.K. Top 10 hits were "Rat Race," "Stereotype," and "Do Nothing" (1980). In America, however, the group made little impression, except with critics. Their followup LP confused even the few fans they had here. Released in late 1980, *More Specials* had elements of cocktail jazz, cabaret theatricality, odd pop, and not much ska. In 1981 the Specials, along with several other 2-Tone groups, were featured in a concert movie entitled *Dance Craze,* which was released in the U.K. The 2-Tone label soon fell apart, with the Beat, the Selecter, and Madness all going to other companies. But the Specials hit a poignant high point in England in the summer of 1981 when they released "Ghost Town." It was inspired by the unemployment and racial tensions in England, and its release coincided with black-white riots in Brixton and Liverpool. (Black guitarist Golding was himself a victim of a racial attack, having his throat slashed and requiring 27 stitches.) The single went #1 in England, although it was banned from airplay by the BBC.

Soon after that, though, in October, the band fell apart after vocalists Hall and Staples plus Golding quit to form Fun Boy Three. While that group made no chart impression in the U.S., the trio had a string of Top 20 U.K. pop hits, including "The Lunatics (Have Taken Over the Asylum)" (1981), "The Telephone Always Rings," and "Summertime" (1982), and two Top 10 U.K. singles with Bananarama: "Tunnel of Love" (1983) and "Our Lips Are Sealed" (1983, which Hall cowrote with then-girlfriend Go-Go Jane Wiedlin). In addition, Fun Boy Three also appeared on Bananarama's "It Ain't What You Do, It's the Way That You Do It" (#4 U.K., 1982). Fun Boy Three disbanded in 1983, with Hall going on to form Colourfield and, in 1990, Terry, Blair and Anouchka. He worked with Dave Stewart in Vegas and released a solo album in the U.K.

Roddy Byers fronted a rockabilly group called Roddy Radiation and the Tearjerkers. Panter later joined General Public. Dammers and Bradbury re-formed as the Specials AKA, with a new lineup in late 1981. It was this group—which included Stan Campbell of the Selecter—that recorded "Racist Friend" and "Free Nelson Mandela," a 1984 #9 hit in the U.K. In 1986 Dammers formed Artists Against Apartheid. He would become a key organizer of the Nelson Mandela's 70th Birthday Party concerts in 1988. Later Bradbury, along with Golding and Staples, joined the Special Beat, which was made up of ex-Specials and ex-(English) Beat members. A new version of the Specials, with four original members but notably missing Dammers and Hall, toured in 1994. Having inspired such successful ska-influenced alternative-rock acts as No Doubt, Reel Big Fish, and the Mighty Mighty Bosstones, they released a pair of albums in the mid- to late '90s. In fact members of Rancid, No Doubt, and the Bosstones guested on 1998's *Guilty 'Til Proved Innocent!*

Phil Spector/The Teddy Bears

Born Dec. 25, 1940, Bronx, NY
The Teddy Bears, formed 1958, Los Angeles, CA: Spector, voc.; Marshall Leib, voc.; Annette Kleinbard (a.k.a. Bard), voc.; Harvey Goldstein, voc.
1959—(– Goldstein) *The Teddy Bears Sing!* (Imperial).
Phil Spector as a producer: 1963—*A Christmas Gift to You* (Philles) 1977—*Phil Spector's Greatest Hits* (Warner Bros.) 1991—*Back to Mono* (Abkco).

Over three decades since its heyday, Phil Spector's Wall of Sound still stands as a milestone in recording history. It changed the course of pop-record producing and left some of rock's best-loved music. Spector raised pop production's ambition and sophistication by overdubbing scores of musicians—five or six guitars, three or four pianos, and an army of percussion, including multiple drum kits, castanets, tambourines, bells, and timpani—to create a massive roar. Spector called it "a Wagnerian approach to rock & roll: little symphonies for the kids."

Spector was raised in the Bronx but moved with his mother to L.A. at age 12 after his father died. He began learning guitar and piano while at Fairfax High School, and at 16 played with local jazz combos. In high school, Spector met Marshall Lieb, and in 1957 the two began writing songs. In early 1958, another friend, Annette Kleinbard, joined them to form the trio the Teddy Bears. Spector's choice of a group name was supposedly inspired by Elvis Presley's hit, "(Let Me Be Your) Teddy Bear." In short order they had a Top 10 U.S. and U.K. hit with Spector's first production, "To Know Him Is to Love Him," taken from the inscription on Spector's father's gravestone ("To Know Him Was to Love Him"). The Teddy Bears appeared on national television, but when Spector disagreed with the record company on the group's next release, he moved them to Imperial. There they cut a few singles and *The Teddy Bears Sing!*, which flopped, and soon broke up.

In the fall of 1960 Kleinbard suffered severe facial injuries in a car accident. After recovering, she changed her name to Carol Connors and has written or cowritten a number of hit records, including Billy Preston and Syreeta Wright's "With You I'm Born Again" and "Gonna Fly Now," the theme from the first *Rocky* film. Other films for which she has written music include *Sophie's Choice* and *Rocky III*. Leib became a musician and producer, for, among others, the Everly Brothers. He has also supervised music for a number of feature films.

Spector then enrolled in UCLA, and also worked as a part-time court stenographer. He dropped out and moved back to New York, where he hoped to become a U.N. interpreter in French. But he soon returned to L.A., where he decided to reenter the record business. The 18-year-old Spector approached independent producers Lester Sill and Lee Hazlewood and persuaded them to take him under their wing. At this time, he formed another group, the Spectors Three, but after several flops, they disbanded and Spector concentrated on producing.

In 1960 Sill and Hazlewood sent Spector to New York, where he worked with hitmakers Jerry Leiber and Mike Stoller. With Leiber he cowrote "Spanish Harlem," a mammoth 1960 hit for Ben E. King. Spector also played the guitar break in the Drifters' "On Broadway." He became staff producer for Dunes Records and produced Ray Peterson's "Corinna, Corinna," a Top 10 hit. By this time he was also a freelance producer and A&R man at Atlantic Records as well as an independent producer. He produced Gene Pitney's "Every Breath I Take" and Curtis Lee's "Pretty Little Angel Eyes." Back on the West Coast, the Paris Sisters' "I Love How You Love Me" and the Ducanes' "Little Did I Know" followed. The youthful Spector was becoming an industry sensation.

While these late-1961 hits were still on the charts, Spector returned to New York and with Sill formed Philles (from Phil and Les) Records. He began recording a girl group called the Crystals, who hit in early 1962 with "There's No Other (Like My Baby)." Their next Spector-produced hit, "Uptown," was an even bigger success; and then came "He Hit Me (And It Felt Like a Kiss)," which was banned in some markets because of its lyrics, and the million-selling "He's a Rebel." Spector bought out Sill's part of Philles in late 1962.

At 21, Spector was a millionaire. He began recording on the West Coast, where he crafted his Wall of Sound in earnest, using such sessionmen as guitarists Glen Campbell, Sonny Bono, and Barney Kessel, pianist Leon Russell, and drummer Hal Blaine. Within three years, Spector had 20 consecutive smash hits, including the Crystals' "Da Doo Ron Ron," "Then He Kissed Me," and "He's Sure the Boy That I Love"; the Ronettes' "Be My Baby," "Baby I Love You," "The Best Part of Breaking Up," and "Walking in the Rain"; Darlene Love's "Today I Met the Boy I'm Gonna Marry" and "Wait Till My Bobby Gets Home"; and Bob B. Soxx and the Blue Jeans' "Zip-A-Dee Doo-Dah." The Righteous Brothers' "You've Lost That Lovin' Feeling" sold over 2 million copies. In 1963 Spector made a Christmas album, featuring Darlene Love's "Christmas (Baby Please Come Home)" and the Ronettes' "Santa Claus Is Coming to Town." In a 1964 magazine piece Tom Wolfe profiled Spector, dubbing him "the first tycoon of teen."

By this time, however, Spector had made more enemies than friends in the record business. In 1966 came the turning point, with Ike and Tina Turner's "River Deep—Mountain High." Spector considered it his greatest production to date, but it became a hit only in England. Embittered, Spector went into seclusion for two years, during which time reports of strange, near-psychotic behavior on his part filtered out of his 23-room Hollywood mansion: Spector allegedly mentally abused his wife, Ronnie (formerly of the Ronettes); Spector carried a gun. Except for a cameo appearance as a dope pusher in the film *Easy Rider* and some hits for Sonny Charles and the Checkmates—"Love Is All I Have to Give," "Black Pearl," and "Proud Mary" (the latter employed some 300 musicians)—he remained inactive through the late '60s.

In 1969 Spector was brought in to do a remix on the Beatles' *Let It Be.* He proved he could adapt to more minimal arrangements with Lennon's "Imagine," which he coproduced, and he returned to the Wall of Sound style for George Harrison's *All Things Must Pass* LP. In 1971 Spector oversaw production of Harrison's *The Concert for Bangla Desh* and produced the studio sides of John Lennon and Yoko Ono's *Some Time in New York City.* In 1973 he formed Warner-Spector Records with Warner Bros., but little came of the association. In 1974 and 1975 he survived two near-fatal auto accidents, and in late 1975 formed Spector International, which reissued the *Christmas Album* and *Greatest Hits* packages, and found Spector working with Cher, Dion, Harry Nilsson, Darlene Love, and Spector's latest "discovery," Jerri Bo Keno, still using L.A.'s Gold Star Studios, where he'd made his classics.

Spector's last major productions were Leonard Cohen's *Death of a Ladies' Man* (1977) and the Ramones' *End of the Century* (1980). He was inducted into the Rock and Roll Hall of Fame in 1989. In 1995 he came out of retirement to produce an album by Canadian singer Celine Dion; however, he backed out of the project, citing his disgust with Dion's management team. Later in the decade Spector was the subject of more controversy. He won a 1997 legal battle over the U.K. copyright to the music and lyrics of his first #1 hit, "To Know Him Is to Love Him." In November of that year he referred to the Spice Girls as "the Antichrist" while accepting an honor at a music awards ceremony held by the British magazine *Q.* In 2000 a Manhattan judge ordered Spector to pay $2.6 million, most of it in back royalties, to his ex-wife, Ronnie Spector, and to her former group the Ronettes.

Ronnie Spector: See the Ronettes

Chris Spedding

Born June 17, 1944, Sheffield, Eng.
1970—*Backwood Progression* (Harvest, U.K.) 1972—*The Only Lick I Know* 1976—*Chris Spedding* (RAK) 1977—*Hurt* 1979—*Guitar Graffiti* 1980—*I'm Not Like Everybody Else* 1981—*Friday 13th (Live in NYC)* (Passport) 1986—*Enemy Within* (New Rose, Fr.) 1990—*Cafe Days* (Mobile Fidelity Sound Lab) 1991—*Motorbikin': The Best of Chris Spedding* (EMI, U.K.).

Chris Spedding is one of the most widely experienced session guitarists in rock. He first learned violin as a youngster, but by his early teens gave it up for guitar. He joined a hometown band, the Vulcans, in the late '50s, went with them to London and then joined a country band that toured U.S. Army bases for three years. In 1964 he spent a year on the ship *Himalaya* entertaining passengers; upon his return to London, he worked with ex-Animal Alan Price and ex–Manfred Mann vocalist Paul Jones.

In 1967 he formed Battered Ornaments with Pete Brown, through whom Spedding met ex-Cream bassist Jack Bruce (for whom Brown wrote lyrics). When Battered Ornaments disbanded in 1969, Spedding took his first session job on Bruce's *Songs for a Tailor* LP. He then briefly worked with Ian Carr's jazz-fusion band Nucleus and has since played fusion with Keith Tippett, Mike Westbrook, and Mike Gibbs.

For the next few years, Spedding became one of Britain's busiest session guitarists, working with Lulu, Gilbert O'Sullivan, Dusty Springfield, David Essex, Donovan (he wrote string arrangements on Donovan's *Cosmic Wheels* LP), and John Cale, among many more. During this period he recorded two solo LPs.

In 1972 Spedding and ex-Free bassist Andy Fraser formed the hard-rock band Sharks (which included session bassist Busta Jones, who went on to play with Brian Eno, Talking Heads, and Gang of Four). They made two albums, then broke up in 1974; Spedding worked with Jones on Eno's 1974 *Here Come the Warm Jets.* In 1975 Spedding joined session bassist Dave Cochran and ex–Yes/King Crimson drummer Bill Bruford to form the backing band Trigger for British folk-rock singer/songwriter Roy Harper. Trigger backed Harper on what many consider his best album, *HQ* (reissued as *When an Old Cricketer Leaves the Crease* in the U.S.), and on a 1975 U.K. tour, then disbanded. Spedding then teamed with British pop producer Mickie Most for his next solo album. Spedding's eponymous 1976 solo album yielded the Top 10 U.K. hit "Motorbikin'," and included "Guitar Jamboree," in which Spedding imitated just about every famous rock guitarist in rapid succession. During the '70s, Spedding reportedly turned down an offer to join the Rolling Stones.

Spedding also played sessions with Roxy Music singer Bryan Ferry (on *Let's Stick Together* and *In Your Mind*) and British punk band the Vibrators. He also reportedly played power chords for the first Sex Pistols singles. In 1979 Spedding teamed up with ex–Tuff Darts singer Robert Gordon. In 1980 he played with the New York band the Necessaries, and in 1981 formed a New York trio with Busta Jones and drummer David Van Tieghem, who had worked with minimalist composer Steve Reich and Brian Eno, among others.

Through the '80s and early '90s, he continued doing session work for, among others, Mark Almond (ex–Soft Cell), Marianne Faithfull, Nina Hagen, and Laurie Anderson. He duetted with Chrissie Hynde on the Otis Blackwell tribute album *Brace Yourself.* He has also worked as a record producer, journalist (as music editor of *Details* magazine), and soundtrack composer. He appears in Paul McCartney's *Give My Regards to Broad Street* as a band member. In 1999 he formed a band called 100 Inches. In 2001 he joined Roxy Music's 30th anniversary tour.

The Jon Spencer Blues Explosion

Formed 1991, New York, NY
Jon Spencer, gtr., voc., theremin; Judah Bauer, gtr., harmonica; Russell Simins, drums.

1991—*A Reverse Willie Horton* (Pubic Pop Can) 1992—*The Jon Spencer Blues Explosion* (Caroline); *Crypt Style* (Crypt) 1993—*Extra Width* (Matador) 1994—*Orange* 1995—*Experimental Remixes* EP 1996—*Now I Got Worry* 1998—*Acme* 1999—*Xtra Acme USA.*
Russell Simins solo: 2000—*Public Places* (Grand Royal).

Postmodern smart-ass Jon Spencer first caught the public's eye in the mid-to-late-'80s when he led Pussy Galore, a New-York-by-way-of-Washington, DC, noise band that mixed tuneless garage punk with calculated shock tactics and industrial metal percussion. That group's less severe, later material provided the blueprint for the Blues Explosion's livelier but only vaguely bluesier mix of reverence and cynicism. The trio took shape when Spencer briefly joined the Honeymoon Killers, who included Judah Bauer's roommate Russell Simins.

The Blues Explosion's overlapping first three LPs add up to a thrilling, bass-free blare topped with an affected, attitudinous sneer. The more hi-fi *Extra Width* abandons willful discordance to focus on tight riffs, screaming theremins, and ironic nods to '70s R&B and '90s hip-hop. *Orange* takes the blues deeper into the urban jungle; the stylish, genre-crossing Spencer had become indie rock's answer to the Beastie Boys, whose Mike D., along with Beck, Moby, and members of the Wu-Tang Clan, helped assemble *Experimental Remixes.*

In 1995 Boss Hog, the long-running band led by Spencer and his wife, ex–Pussy Galore/Honeymoon Killers guitarist Cristina Martinez, released an album on Geffen. The following year the Blues Explosion backed real-life Mississippi bluesman R.L. Burnside; Simins concentrated on Butter 08, his side project that included wacky Japanese expats Cibo Matto [see entry]; and Bauer formed the neo-traditional 20 Miles. *Now I Got Worry* sheds some of *Orange*'s slick eclecticism for solid, driving rock & roll. However, 1998's *Acme* renews an interest in studio tinkering. In 2000 the Beasties' Grand Royal label issued Simins' solo debut.

The Spice Girls

Formed 1994, London, Eng.
Ginger Spice (b. Geraldine "Geri" Estelle Halliwell, Aug. 18, 1970, Watford, Eng.), voc.; Posh Spice (b. Victoria Beckham, Apr. 17, 1974, Essex, Eng.), voc.; Scary Spice (b. Melanie "Mel B" Brown, May 29, 1975, Leeds, Eng.), voc.; Sporty Spice (b. Melanie "Mel C" Jayne Chisholm, Jan. 12, 1974, Liverpool, Eng.), voc.; Baby Spice (b. Emma Lee Bunton, Jan. 21, 1976, London), voc.
1996—*Spice* (Virgin) 1997—*Spiceworld* 1998—(– Halliwell) 2000—*Forever.*
Geri Halliwell solo: 1999—*Schizophonic* (Capitol).
Melanie C solo: 1999—*Northern Star* (Virgin).

The Spice Girls fused "girl power," glamour, catchy dance-pop, and zany, Fab Four–style antics to stand not just their native England on its head, but to turn much of the rest of the world upside down as well. The group formed in 1994 when four of its five future members answered an ad seeking "lively girls" for a pop group that father-and-son team Bob and Chris Herbert, manager of the British boy band Take That!, had placed in *The Stage* magazine. All four were hired, along with Michelle Stephenson, to sing in a group called Touch, but the women didn't like the direction the Herberts wanted to take the act, so they opted out of the deal to make a go of it on their own. Meanwhile, they rented a house together, replaced Stephenson (who went off to college) with Emma Bunton, began writing and demoing songs, and rechristened themselves the Spice Girls. They didn't start attracting notice until the spring of 1995 when they hired manager Simon Fuller (Annie Lennox), who helped the group secure a Virgin record deal.

The Spice Girls received their well-known nicknames, based on each member's personality, looks, or interests, from writers at the British teen magazine *Top of the Pops.* The Spice Girls' first single, "Wannabe," an irresistible dance record that promoted sisterhood and featured a playful rap interlude, was an overnight sensation. It was also the first debut single by an all-female group to enter the U.K. charts at #1, where it stayed for seven weeks, before going on to top the charts in 22 other countries, including the U.S. (#1, 1997). *Spice,* the group's first album, a project recorded with studio gurus Richard Stannard, Matt Rowe, and the production duo Absolute, went to #1 in England, and in 1997 became the first debut album by a U.K. act to enter the charts at #1 in the States. In addition to "Wannabe," *Spice* yielded two other Top 10 singles, "Say You'll Be There" (#3, 1997) and "2 Become 1" (#4, 1997). The album, which sold more than 6 million copies in the U.S. and 20 million worldwide, found favor among both critics and fans, giving way to a Spice Girls craze in America. A series of lucrative endorsement deals with companies ranging from Pepsi to Polaroid to Sony Playstation followed.

The late 1997 release of the group's second album, *Spiceworld* (#3), coincided with the opening of the Spice Girls movie of the same name. Both featured the single "Spice Up Your Life" (#18, 1997) and the album shipped an unprecedented 1.4 million copies in the U.K., beating out the record previously held by Frankie Goes to Hollywood's *Welcome to the Pleasuredome.* The group then fired Fuller, known in media circles as "Svengali Spice," and Halliwell assumed managerial duties until her departure in May 1998. (Her solo debut, *Schizophonic* [#42, 1999], made little commercial impact.)

Now a quartet (Halliwell was not replaced), the Spice Girls released their third album, *Forever,* in 2000. The record saw them dispensing with their girlish nicknames and costumes and adopting a more adult image. Yet despite production help from Jimmy Jam and Terry Lewis, the album was, by Spice Girls standards, a commercial failure, selling but a fraction of the copies their first two records did. In November 2000 Chisholm ("Sporty Spice") announced the group would not be touring anymore. All went on to pursue solo projects.

Spinal Tap

Formed 1967, London, Eng. (1978, Los Angeles, CA)
David St. Hubbins (b. Michael McKean, Oct. 17, 1947, New York, NY), gtr., voc.; Nigel Tufnel (b. Christopher Guest, Feb. 5, 1948, New York), gtr., voc.; Derek Smalls (b. Harry Shearer, Dec. 23, 1943, Los Angeles), bass, voc.
1984—*This Is Spinal Tap* (Polydor) 1992—*Break Like the Wind* (MCA).

Probably the funniest inside joke in rock history, Spinal Tap was an ambitious dead-on parody of heavy metal's clichés and excesses, put on by skilled comic actors who wrote and played their own songs, and were big enough fans of the music to satirize it—however brutally—with knowing affection. Indeed, the butts of the joke embraced Spinal Tap, who were invited to take part in such all-star hard-rock projects as the 1986 Hear-N-Aid benefit single, and the 1992 London tribute concert to Queen's Freddie Mercury.

Spinal Tap's principals were old friends and veteran satirists. Harry Shearer and Michael McKean had been in the early-'70s comedy troupe the Credibility Gap; McKean starred as Lenny in the TV show *Laverne and Shirley*, and Shearer was in the 1984–85 cast of TV's *Saturday Night Live*. Also in that cast, Christopher Guest (a schoolmate of McKean's at New York University) had written for the humor magazine *National Lampoon* and won an Emmy for his writing on a Lily Tomlin TV special. Spinal Tap, performing "Rock and Roll Nightmare," debuted in a 1978 ABC-TV comedy special, *The TV Show*, on which Guest, McKean, and Shearer worked with director Rob Reiner. They all began seeking funds for a full-length Spinal Tap film, which took some six years to make.

This Is Spinal Tap was directed in semi-improvised form by Reiner (who appeared in the film as director Marty DiBergi, an obvious takeoff on Martin Scorsese, director of *The Last Waltz*) as a mock-rockumentary of a disastrous U.S. tour. Guest, McKean, and Shearer skewered all aspects of the rock biz, and fomented a long and detailed history of "the loudest band in England," all of whose drummers were cursed to die bizarre, mysterious deaths. Their repertoire featured the near-Kiss of "Tonight I'm Gonna Rock You Tonight," the virtual–Jethro Tull of "Stonehenge" (complete with dancing dwarf Druids), and "Big Bottom," an ode to the female derriere on which Tufnel and St. Hubbins played bass while Smalls played a double-necked bass. Along the way, Tap also spoofed the sounds of the British Invasion ("Gimme Some Money") and psychedelic pop ("[Listen to the] Flower People"), as well as such rock & roll "institutions" as the meddling girlfriend, the sociopathic manager, the Brooklynese publicist (played by Fran Drescher), and the obsequious PR man (played by bandleader Paul Shaffer). Indeed, the film was so sharply understated that some younger moviegoers actually believed they were watching a real film about a real group.

Despite universally glowing reviews and an instant, diehard cult following, neither *This Is Spinal Tap* nor its soundtrack album (#121, 1984) was a commercial smash. Still, the movie inspired a book (1984's *Inside Spinal Tap* by Peter Occhiogrosso), and—after Guest and Shearer did stints in the cast of *Saturday Night Live*—eventual sequels of sorts. *Break Like the Wind* (#61, 1992)—with guests Cher, Jeff Beck, Joe Satriani, and Slash of Guns n' Roses, and such tracks as "Rainy Day Sun," "The Majesty of Rock," and "Bitch School" (its video got MTV airplay)—was followed by the TV special *A Spinal Tap Reunion*, which mixed concert footage (shot before an adoring London audience) and testimonials by such guest stars as Martin Short, Kenny Rogers, Mel Torme, and Guest's wife, Jamie Lee Curtis. The band reunited in 2000 for a handful of shows to promote the DVD release of *This Is Spinal Tap*, with Mick Fleetwood on drums, and again in 2001, when it performed at Carnegie Hall as part of the Toyota Comedy Festival.

Spin Doctors

Formed 1988, New York, NY
Aaron Comess (b. Apr. 24, 1968, AZ), drums; Chris Barron (b. Christopher Barron Gross, Feb. 5, 1968, HI), voc.; Mark Burton White (b. July 7, 1962, NY), bass; Eric Schenkman (b. Dec. 12, 1963, MA), gtr.
1991—*Up for Grabs* EP (Epic); *Pocket Full of Kryptonite* 1992—*Homebelly Groove* 1994—*Turn It Upside Down* (– Schenkman; + Anthony Krizan [b. Aug. 25, 1965, Plainfield, NJ], gtr.) 1996—*You've Got to Believe in Something* (– Krizan) 1999—*Here Comes the Bride* (Uptown/Universal).

Although Spin Doctors are one of a group of early-'90s bands who play improvisational rootsy rock in the tradition of the Grateful Dead, the Doctors first found commercial success with a pop single. Singer/songwriter Chris Barron formed the band Trucking Company in 1989 with Eric Schenkman and John Popper, a friend from high school in Princeton, New Jersey. Popper left to form Blues Traveler [see entry], and Barron and Schenkman formed Spin Doctors with fellow New School of Social Research classmate Aaron Comess. They then recruited Mark White, who had played with Comess in the band Spade. Spin Doctors' first show was at a Columbia University frat house.

The band gigged constantly in the New York area, often playing three sets a night or opening for kindred spirits Blues Traveler. They developed a strong following that soon attracted record company interest. In 1991 Epic signed Spin Doctors and promoted the band on the basis of their shows; the first record was a live EP. *Kryptonite* (#4, 1992) was released in the summer of 1991, but did not take off until a year later, when radio stations and then MTV began playing "Little Miss Can't Be Wrong," a catchy if somewhat misogynist single. (Barron frequently apologized live for the line "Been a whole lot easier since the bitch left town.")

Spin Doctors continued to tour constantly, including playing the H.O.R.D.E. (Horizon of Rock Developing Everywhere) Tour with Blues Traveler, Phish, and Widespread Panic—bands whose hippie-ish energy, extended jams, and untiring gigging led them to be dubbed "the living Dead."

Shows are so crucial to the Spin Doctors' reputation that they encourage concert bootlegs. *Homebelly Groove* is a live album comprising the Doctors' deleted first EP plus extended versions of songs from *Kryptonite. Turn It Upside Down* (#28, 1994), the band's second studio release, was a disappointment both critically and commercially, with no Top 40 singles.

You've Got to Believe in Something (1996) also failed to yield a hit single, but at least it found the Doctors taking some creative risks, as witnessed by the album's unlisted cover of KC and the Sunshine Band's "That's the Way (I Like It)" featuring rapper Biz Markie and actor Tommy Chong. Meanwhile, the Doctors left Epic and signed with Universal, for which they made *Here Comes the Bride* (1999). Unfortunately, the band was unable to tour in support of the record after singer Chris Barron was diagnosed with a rare form of vocal-cord paralysis that left him unable to speak above a whisper. He has since made a full recovery.

The Spinners

Formed 1957, Detroit, MI
Bobbie Smith (b. Apr. 10), tenor voc.; Pervis Jackson (b. May 16), bass voc.; Henry Fambrough (b. May 10), baritone voc.; Billy Henderson (b. Aug. 9), tenor-baritone voc.; George W. Dixon, tenor voc.
1962—(– Dixon; + Edgar "Chico" Edwards, tenor voc.) 1967—*The Original Spinners* (Motown) (– Edwards; + G.C. Cameron, tenor voc.) 1972—(– Cameron; + Phillipe Wynne [b. Apr. 3, 1941; d. July 13, 1984, Oakland, CA], tenor voc.) 1973—*Spinners* (Atlantic) 1974—*Mighty Love; New and Improved Spinners* 1975—*Pick of the Litter; Spinners Live!* 1976—*Happiness Is Being With the Detroit Spinners* 1977—*Yesterday, Today and Tomorrow* (– Wynne; + John Edwards [b. St. Louis, MO], tenor voc.) *Spinners/8* 1978—*The Best of the Spinners; From Here to Eternally* 1979—*Dancin' and Lovin'* 1980—*Love Trippin'* 1981—*Superstar Series, vol. 9* (Motown); *Labor of Love* (Atlantic); *Can't Shake This Feeling* 1983—*Grand Slam* 1989—*Down to Business* (Volt) 1991—*One of a Kind Love Affair—The Anthology* (Atlantic) 1993—*The Very Best of the Spinners* (Rhino) 1999—*At their Best* (Intersound).

The Spinners started as the Domingoes, a group of Ferndale (Detroit) High School students. Around 1961 singer/producer Harvey Fuqua discovered them and began recording the quintet, rechristened the Spinners, on Tri-Phi Records, the label he cofounded with his wife, Berry Gordy's sister, Gwen. The first Spinners single, "That's What Girls Are Made For" (#27 pop, #5 R&B, 1961), featured Bobbie Smith singing lead in a style similar to Fuqua's (not Fuqua himself, as is often reported). The group released a series of singles that didn't click, and a few years later, when Tri-Phi merged with Motown, the Spinners moved to the larger company.

The group was, in some historians' opinion, overlooked at Motown. Although the group had some hits there—"I'll Always Love You" (#8 R&B) in 1965, "Truly Yours" (#16 R&B) in 1966, "We'll Have It Made (#20 R&B) in 1971 and the Stevie Wonder–produced-and-penned "It's a Shame" (#14 pop, #4 R&B) in 1970—the company never considered them a major act. G.C. Cameron was lead singer for much of the late '60s, and Edwards had left. In 1972 the Spinners moved to Atlantic Records and were teamed with Philadelphia producer Thom Bell. Newcomer Phillipe Wynne, who had previously worked in a band with Catfish and Bootsy Collins, was now handling most of the lead vocals, and from 1972 to 1979 the Spinners' close-harmony ballads regularly topped the R&B and pop charts. Their hits included "I'll Be Around" (#3 pop, #1 R&B) and "Could It Be I'm Falling in Love" (#4 pop, #1 R&B), 1972; "One of a Kind (Love Affair)" (#11 pop, #1 R&B) and "Ghetto Child" (#4 R&B), 1973; "Mighty Love, Part 1" (#20 pop, #1 R&B), "I'm Coming Home" (#18 pop, #13 R&B) and, with Dionne Warwick, "Then Came You" (#1 pop, #2 R&B), 1974; "Sadie" (#7 R&B) and "They Just Can't Stop It (the Games People Play)" (#5 pop, #1 R&B), 1975; "Wake Up Susan" (#11 R&B) and "The Rubberband Man" (#2 pop, #1 R&B), 1976; "You're Throwing a Good Love Away" (#5 R&B), 1977; and "If You Wanna Do a Dance" (#17 R&B), 1978. During this time, the Spinners earned five gold albums: *Spinners* (#14, 1973), *Mighty Love* (#16, 1974), *New and Improved* (#9, 1974), *Pick of the Litter* (#8, 1975), and *Happiness Is Being With the Detroit Spinners* (#25, 1976). They were also extremely popular in the U.K., where they were known as the Detroit Spinners to avoid confusion with a British group called the Spinners.

In 1977 Wynne left for a solo career (he also toured with Parliament-Funkadelic) and was replaced by John Edwards. Wynne released several solo albums and had a minor hit with "Wait 'til Tomorrow" in 1983. He died onstage of a heart attack; he was 43.

In 1979 the Spinners returned to the charts with a remake of the Four Seasons' "Working My Way Back to You" (#2 pop, #6 R&B, #1 U.K.). Their "Cupid Medley"—"Cupid/I've Loved You for a Long Time"—was another big hit (#4 pop, #5 R&B, 1980). Subsequent singles hit the R&B chart but none moved into the Top 20. These include "Now That You're Mine Again" and "I Just Want to Fall in Love" (1980), "Yesterday Once More/Nothing Remains the Same," "Long Live Soul Music," "You Go Your Way (I'll Go Mine)" (which was produced by James Mtume and Reggie Lucas), and "Love Connection (Raise the Window Down)" (1981), "Magic in the Moonlight" and "Funny How Time Slips Away" (1982), and "Right or Wrong," at #22 R&B (1984), the group's highest-charting single since 1980's "Cupid" medley. The Spinners continue to tour and record with the same lineup intact since 1977.

Spirit

Formed 1967, Los Angeles, CA
Randy California (b. Randy Craig Wolfe, Feb. 20, 1951, Los Angeles; d. Jan. 2, 1997, Molokai, HI), gtr., voc.; Jay Ferguson (b. John Arden Ferguson, May 10, 1947, Burbank, CA), gtr., kybds., voc.; John Locke (b. Sep. 25, 1943, Los Angeles), kybds., voc., Mark Andes (b. Feb. 19, 1948, Philadelphia, PA), bass, voc.; Ed Cassidy (b. May 4, 1923, Chicago, IL), drums.
1968—*Spirit* (Ode); *The Family That Plays Together* 1969—

Clear Spirit 1970—*The Twelve Dreams of Dr. Sardonicus* (Epic) (– Ferguson; – Andes; – California; + Chris Staehely [b. TX], gtr., voc.; + Al Staehely [b. TX], bass, voc.) 1971—*Feedback* 1973—*The Best of Spirit* 1974—(group re-forms: California; Cassidy; + Barry Keene, bass) 1975—*Spirit of '76* (Mercury) (+ Locke) 1976—*Son of Spirit* (+ Mark Andes; + Matt Andes, gtr.) *Farther Along* 1977—*Future Games (A Magical Kahauna Dream)* (– Locke; – Mark Andes; – Matt Andes; + Larry Knight, bass; various personnel changes ensue) 1978—*Live* (Potato) 1981—*Journey to Potatoland* (Beggar's Banquet/Rhino) 1984—*Spirit of '84* (Mercury) 1989—*Rapture in the Chambers* (I.R.S.) 1990—*Tent of Miracles* (Caroline) 1991—*Time Circle 1968–1972* (Epic/Legacy); *Chronicles* (WERC) 1996—*California Blues*.
Randy California solo: 1972—*Kaptain Kopter and the Fabulous Twirly Birds* (Epic).

Though they did have one hit single, "I Got a Line on You," Spirit were known primarily for their albums: an ambitious, eclectic blend of hard rock, blues, country folk, and prefusion jazz.

Shaven-headed drummer Ed Cassidy met Randy California while he was dating the latter's mother (whom he later married) when Randy was 13. He joined Randy's band, the Red Roosters, which had been formed in 1965 and featured most of the original Spirit lineup. Previously Cassidy had drummed for jazzmen Thelonious Monk, Art Pepper, Cannonball Adderley, and Gerry Mulligan on the West Coast in the mid-'50s, and in the early '60s had formed his own New Jazz Trio. In 1965 he joined Rising Sons with Ry Cooder and Taj Mahal, but was forced to leave the group after injuring his hand during a drum solo.

John Locke, who claimed to be a direct descendant of the British philosopher of the same name, first encountered Cassidy in the New Jazz Trio. At UCLA, he later met Mark Andes and Jay Ferguson, who had grown up together in the San Fernando Valley. Andes' band, the Marksmen, had played sessions with Bobby "Boris" Pickett, among others. Ferguson had met California while with a bluegrass band, the Oat Hill Stump Straddlers. In 1965 Cassidy joined California, Ferguson, and Andes in the Red Roosters, but they broke up in 1966.

In New York City, Cassidy and California played in sessions, and joined numerous bands. Meanwhile, Ferguson formed Western Union with Mark and his brother Matt Andes; the band gained some local popularity before Mark Andes left to briefly join Canned Heat. In late 1966 Cassidy and California returned to the state of California and, with Locke, formed Spirits Rebellious (the name taken from a Kahlil Gibran book), which with the addition of Ferguson and Mark Andes became Spirit.

Their LPs rarely sold better than moderately well, but Spirit were critically well received. Their biggest success critically and commercially was *The Twelve Dreams of Dr. Sardonicus,* the last LP by the original lineup. In mid-1971 Andes and Ferguson left to form Jo Jo Gunne, with Cassidy and Locke bringing in the Staehely brothers from Texas. After recording *Feedback,* however, the two original members quit, leaving the Staehelys to take their own "Spirit" on the road.

Randy California then went to England, where he played sessions with British art-rocker Peter Hammill of Van der Graaf Generator. In late 1971 he began experiencing health problems (a concussion from falling off a horse, and a nervous breakdown), which sidelined him until 1973, when he released a solo LP, *Kaptain Kopter and the Fabulous Twirlybirds.* When California and Cassidy re-formed Spirit in 1974, Chris Staehely went to Jo Jo Gunne.

In 1975 the group played some West Coast reunion dates with Mark Andes, who'd left Jo Jo Gunne and would go on to join Firefall and, later, Heart. Ferguson, in the meantime, had hits on his own ("Thunder Island") and became an active West Coast sessionman and producer. Spirit continued recording and touring. A 1983 reunion resulted in *Spirit of '84.* The group, with Cassidy and California at the helm, has reunited in various configurations over the years. Cassidy has written and published *Ed Cassidy's Musicians' Survival/Resource Manual* (which he sells through ads in music magazines such as *Goldmine*). He has also lectured and given drum seminars.

Spirit came to an end with the 1997 death of California, who drowned while he was pushing his 12-year-old son out of a riptide off the Hawaiian coast. The band completed *California Blues,* a compilation of vintage live material and a dozen new recordings, prior to the incident. Spencer Davis and ex-Doors guitarist Robbie Krieger made cameos on the record, which also marked the return of original keyboardist Locke.

Split Enz/Tim Finn

Formed 1972, Auckland, N.Z.
Tim Finn (b. June 25, 1952, Te Awamutu, N.Z.), voc., piano; Phil Judd, voc., gtr., mandolin; Eddie Rayner, kybds.; Wally Wilkinson, gtr.; Jonathan Michael Chunn, bass; Emlyn Crowther, drums; Noel Crombie, perc., spoons.
1975—*Mental Notes* (Mushroom) 1976—*Second Thoughts* 1977—(– Judd; + Neil Finn [b. May 27, 1958, Te Awamutu], gtr., voc.; – Chunn; – Crowther; + Nigel Griggs [b. Aug. 18, 1949], bass; + Robert Gillie, sax; + Malcolm Green [b. Jan. 25, 1953], drums) *Dizrythmia* (+ Judd; – Judd; – Gillie) 1979—*Frenzy* (– Wilkinson) 1980—*True Colours* (A&M); *Beginning of the Enz* 1981—(– Green) *Waiata* 1982—*Time and Tide* 1984—*Conflicting Emotions* 1987—*History Never Repeats: The Best of Split Enz.*
Tim Finn solo: 1983—*Escapade* (Oz-A&M) 1986—*Big Canoe* (Virgin) 1989—*Tim Finn* (Capitol) 1993—*Before and After* 2000—*Say It Is So* (What Are?).
The Finn Brothers (T. Finn; N. Finn): 1996—*The Finn Brothers* (Discovery).

When the New Zealand band Split Enz began playing in the mid-'70s, it had a lot of trouble being taken seriously because of its weird appearance, complete with glaring clownlike costumes and hairdos that made the members look like parrots. The musicians created an eclectic art-pop amalgam with innovative song structures swinging from ballads to cabaret to heavy pop. They later reemerged with neo-Beatles pop songs and well-made video clips to gain a larger audience. Ultimately, however, Neil Finn (later joined by Tim) found a broader audience with his more orthodox pop rock in Crowded House [see entry].

The band went to Australia in 1975 as a seven-piece outfit and recorded its debut, *Mental Notes,* there in May and June; it was released only in Australia. Split Enz came to the attention of Roxy Music's Phil Manzanera, who produced *Second Thoughts* in England, which was mostly new versions of material from the first record. England became the group's home base. The band went through many personnel changes, including the loss of major songwriter Phil Judd. (The other writer was Tim Finn.) Split Enz's records sold well only in Australia. In 1976 the band toured America, including a date at New York's Bottom Line, opening for Henny Youngman. In January 1977 Chrysalis released its debut U.S. LP, a compilation under the title *Mental Notes.* A year later, Judd briefly rejoined, but he left again, and was replaced by Tim Finn's brother Neil, but the group soon lost its contract. Judd went on to start his own band, the Swingers.

With Tim Finn in charge, Split Enz grew more accessible, grooming itself into a pop band, performing Beatles-influenced songs that, like 10cc's, masked droll undertones with winsome melodies. The band broadened its Australian following, and returned to the U.S. market with *True Colours* in 1980; new anticounterfeiting technology allowed the record to be pressed in laser-etched vinyl with rainbow patterns. "I Got You" gave the band its first taste of U.S. airplay; the single was #1 in Australia for 10 weeks, and the album sold 200,000 copies there.

Split Enz had made rock videos in its early, more eccentric form, and with the advent of cable-cast rock video in the early '80s the combo's latter-day clips received exposure. Even so, the albums sold fewer copies with each release, despite containing pop gems such as "History Never Repeats." The group disbanded in 1985, reuniting four years later in New Zealand. In 1985 Tim Finn married actress Greta Scaachi (they have since split up) and, after a less than stellar solo career, he joined his brother Neil's Crowded House in 1991, only to depart two years later. He briefly played in the band Alt in the mid-'90s. The siblings have also recorded as the Finn Brothers. Split Enz has reunited periodically in New Zealand, with its classic incarnation gigging on New Year's Eve 1999. In 1996 the New Zealand Symphony Orchestra performed a tribute to the band with help from the Finn brothers.

Spooky Tooth

Formed 1967, England
Mike Harrison (b. Sep. 3, 1945, Carlisle, Eng.), voc., kybds.; Gary Wright (b. Apr. 26, 1945, Englewood, NJ), kybds., voc.; Luther Grosvenor (a.k.a. Ariel Bender, b. Dec. 23, 1949, Worcester, Eng.), gtr.; Greg Ridley (b. Oct. 23, 1947, Cumberland, Eng.), bass; Mike Kellie (b. Mar. 24, 1947, Birmingham, Eng.), drums.
1968—*It's All About . . .* (Island, U.K.) 1969—*Spooky Two* (– Ridley; + Andy Leigh, bass); *Ceremony* 1970—(– Wright; + Henry McCullough, gtr.; + Chris Stainton, kybds.; + Alan Spenner, bass) *The Last Puff* 1972—(– Kellie; – McCullough; – Stainton; – Spenner; – Grosvenor; + Mick Jones [b. Dec. 27, 1944, London, Eng.], gtr.; + Chris Stewart, bass; + Bryson Graham, drums) *You Broke My Heart So I Busted Your Jaw* 1973—*Witness* 1974—(– Harrison; – Stewart; + Mike Patto [b. Sep. 22, 1942; d. Mar. 4, 1979, Eng.], kybds., voc.; + Val Burke, bass, voc.) *The Mirror* 1976—*That Was Only Yesterday* (A&M) (group disbands) 1998—(group re-forms: Harrison; Grosvenor; Ridley; Kellie) 1999—*Cross Purpose; The Best of Spooky Tooth: That Was Only Yesterday.*

Though it never had a hit single or a best-selling LP, Spooky Tooth remained a bastion of Britain's hard-rock scene. Gary Wright [see entry] made hits after leaving the band.

Mike Harrison had worked as a clerk before joining the VIPs, which became the group Art in the mid-'60s, with Mike Kellie. Gary Wright had been a child actor (in *Captain Video* and TV commercials) and a psychology student in New Jersey before attending college in Berlin. Spooky Tooth's first two albums, produced by Jimmy Miller, sold respectably in the U.K.; U.S. bassist Greg Ridley left for Humble Pie after the second and was replaced by Andy Leigh for *Ceremony.*

Wright brought in French electronic-music pioneer Pierre Henry to add processed *musique concrète* overdubs. Wright then left to form the short-lived Wonderwheel and reemerged a few years later on his own. Harrison brought in Henry McCullough, Chris Stainton, and Alan Spenner from Joe Cocker's Grease Band for *Last Puff.* Grosvenor left after that LP, later to join Stealers Wheel and Mott the Hoople, and Spooky Tooth entered suspended animation, with Harrison pursuing a short solo career with an LP, *Smokestack Lightning.*

Wright and Harrison re-formed the band in 1972, with future Foreigner [see entry] guitarist Mick Jones. Their next two albums sold fairly well, especially *You Broke My Heart, So I Busted Your Jaw.* Harrison left again to pursue a solo career in 1973; in 1974 Spooky Tooth re-formed yet again, with Mike Patto on vocals and keyboards. (He would work with a few more bands before dying of throat cancer in 1979.) The band broke up again a year later. Kellie, who in 1970 had briefly played with the British supergroup Balls (which also included Denny Laine and Steve Gibbons), resurfaced in the late '70s with the Only Ones. At the end of the '90s, Spooky Tooth's original members, excluding Wright, reunited to record *Cross Purpose.*

Dusty Springfield

Born Mary Isabel Catherine Bernadette O'Brien, Apr. 16, 1939, London, Eng.; died Mar. 2, 1999, Henley-on-Thames, Eng.

1964—*The Dusty Springfield Album* (Philips) 1966—*You Don't Have to Say You Love Me; Golden Hits* 1967—*Look of Love* 1968—*Stay Awhile* (Mercury) 1969—*Dusty in Memphis* (Atlantic) 1970—*A Brand New Me* 1971—*For You, Love, Dusty* (Philips) 1973—*Cameo* (Dunhill) 1978—*It Begins Again* (United Artists) 1979—*Living Without Your Love* 1982—*White Heat* (Casablanca) 1990—*Reputation* 1995—*A Very Fine Love* (Columbia) 1997—*Dusty Springfield Anthology Collection* (Mercury) 1998—*The Very Best of Dusty Springfield.*

Dusty Springfield's husky voice made her one of Britain's best-selling pop-rock singers in the '60s. She and her brother Tom began harmonizing with radio hits as children. Dusty briefly recorded with the Lana Sisters before she and Tom formed a folk trio, the Springfields, with Tim Field. The group, a British equivalent of Peter, Paul and Mary, had U.K. chart hits in 1962–63 with "Island of Dreams" and "Say I Won't Be There," and hit the American Top 20 in 1962 with "Silver Threads and Golden Needles." That year, Field quit, replaced by Mike Hurst (who later produced Cat Stevens), before the trio disbanded. Tom found success as a songwriter for the Seekers, among others.

Springfield continued on her own. In late 1963 she had a British Top 10 hit with "I Only Want to Be With You," which went to #12 in the U.S. in early 1964 and eventually went gold. The tune has since been covered by many other performers. That song was Springfield's first flirtation with Motown-style soul, a sound to which she would often return. She toured the world and had British hits through 1964–65 with Bacharach-David's "I Just Don't Know What to Do With Myself" and "Wishin' and Hopin'," and with Goffin-King's "Some of Your Lovin' " and "Goin' Back." In 1966 "You Don't Have to Say You Love Me" was #1 in the U.K. and #4 in the U.S. She continued to tour extensively and made TV appearances with Tom Jones, Engelbert Humperdinck, and on *The Ed Sullivan Show.* In 1969, with producers Jerry Wexler, Arif Mardin, and Tom Dowd, she recorded *Dusty in Memphis,* which yielded the Top 10 international hit single "Son of a Preacher Man." In 1970 she moved back toward pop with *Brand New Me,* which contained "Land of Make Believe," "Silly Silly Fool," and the title cut. In England her popularity declined, though "How Can I Be Sure," a cover of the Rascals hit, was a 1970 Top 40 hit in the U.K. By then she had scored 17 U.K. and 10 U.S. hit singles.

Between 1971 and 1978 Springfield lived reclusively in America and did not record, except for some backup vocals on Anne Murray's *Together* LP. In 1978 Springfield recorded two comeback albums on the West Coast. The first, *Begins Again,* produced by Roy Thomas Baker (of Queen and Cars fame), fared poorly both critically and commercially; the second, *Living Without Your Love,* produced by David Wolfert, did slightly better. She had a minor 1979 U.K. hit with "Baby Blue," and the following fall she played some New York club dates, her first in eight years.

Springfield's big commercial comeback occurred in 1987, a quarter century after "Silver Threads and Golden Needles," when fan/Pet Shop Boy Neil Tennant invited her to sing on his duo's "What Have I Done to Deserve This?" An international smash, the song hit #2 in the U.S. and in the U.K. She was also featured on the *Scandal* soundtrack, with "Nothing Has Been Proved," and in 1990 *Reputation* was a Top 20 U.K. album. Springfield recorded her 1995 country-tinged album in Nashville. Around that time, she was diagnosed with breast cancer. After a long battle with the disease, she died at her English home in 1999, just prior to her induction into the Rock and Roll Hall of Fame and just two months after receiving an OBE.

Rick Springfield

Born Aug. 23, 1949, Sydney, Austral.
1972—*Beginnings* (Capitol) 1974—*Comic Book Heroes* (Columbia) 1976—*Wait for the Night* (Chelsea) 1981—*Working Class Dog* (RCA) 1982—*Success Hasn't Spoiled Me Yet* 1983—*Living in Oz* 1984—*Hard to Hold* soundtrack; *Beautiful Feelings* (Mercury) 1985—*Tao* (RCA) 1988—*Rock of Life* 1989—*Rick Springfield's Greatest Hits* 1999—*Karma* (Platinum).

Rick Springfield first became a household name as an actor, playing Dr. Noah Drake on the television soap opera *General Hospital.* Later that same year (1981) he became a platinum-selling recording star as well with the #1 single "Jessie's Girl."

Springfield grew up in both Australia and England. He got his first guitar at 13 and formed several bands. He performed his first original material with Zoot, who became a top teen idol band in Australia with a #1 hit, "Speak to the Sky." His remake of "Speak to the Sky" reached the American Top 15 in 1972. Springfield's U.S. label, Capitol, promoted him as a teen star, which got him lots of coverage but kept him from being taken seriously; his next album, *Comic Book Heroes,* also flopped. Legal tangles kept Springfield out of circulation for two years, after which he signed to the small Chelsea label and released *Wait for the Night.* In 1974 he had been originally cast as lead in *The Buddy Holly Story,* but the role went to Gary Busey.

Through the '70s Springfield made guest appearances on *The Six Million Dollar Man* and *Wonder Woman* while still making demos. In early 1980 he signed with RCA. *Working Class Dog,* which contained "Jessie's Girl," was released as Springfield became a regular on *General Hospital.* The album went platinum, as did *Success Hasn't Spoiled Me Yet,* with "I've Done Everything for You" (#8, 1981) and "Don't Talk to Strangers" (#2, 1982), and *Living in Oz* (#12, with the 1983 Top 10 "Affair of the Heart" and Top 20 "Human Touch").

Springfield starred in the critically lambasted *Hard to Hold.* The Top 20 platinum album of the same title included Springfield's last Top 10 hit, "Love Somebody." While the actor's subsequent singles (including "Bruce," about his being mistaken for Bruce Springsteen) all charted in the 20s, fans either didn't warm to his new, more serious direction or simply outgrew him. After a near-fatal motorcycle accident and a prolonged absence, Springfield made a surprise return to the club and casino circuit in 1998. *Karma* marked his first new album in 11 years.

Bruce Springsteen

Born Sep. 23, 1949, Freehold, NJ
1973—*Greetings From Asbury Park, N.J.* (Columbia); *The Wild, the Innocent and the E Street Shuffle* 1975—*Born to Run* 1978—*Darkness on the Edge of Town* 1980—*The River* 1982—*Nebraska* 1984—*Born in the U.S.A.* 1986—*Live, 1975–1985* 1987—*Tunnel of Love* 1992—*Human Touch; Lucky Town* 1995—*Greatest Hits; The Ghost of Tom Joad* 1997—*In Concert/MTV Plugged* 1998—*Tracks* (Sony) 2001—*Bruce Springsteen & the E Street Band: Live in New York City.*

For nearly three decades Bruce Springsteen has been a rock & roll working-class hero: a plainspoken visionary. He is a fervent and sincere romantic whose insights into everyday lives—especially in America's small-town, working-class heartland—have earned comparisons to John Steinbeck and Woody Guthrie. His belief in rock's mythic past and its potential revitalized pop music and made Springsteen a superstar in the '80s. Since then, he has remained true to his artistic calling and shown himself—in rare interviews—to be among the most thoughtful and articulate artists in rock.

Springsteen, of Irish-Italian ancestry, grew up in Freehold, New Jersey, the son of a bus driver and a secretary. He took up the guitar when he was 13 and joined the Castiles a year later. In 1966 the Castiles recorded (but never released) two songs cowritten by Springsteen, and they worked their way up to a string of dates at New York City's Cafe Wha in 1967. During the summer after his graduation from high school, Springsteen was working with Earth, a Cream-style power trio, and hanging out in Asbury Park, New Jersey. He entered Ocean County Community College in the fall, but dropped out when a New York producer promised him a contract; he never saw the producer again.

While in college, he had formed a group with some local musicians, including drummer Vini "Mad Dog" Lopez and keyboardist Danny Federici. Called Child, then Steel Mill, the group worked the Atlantic coast down to Virginia. In summer 1969 Steel Mill visited California (where Springsteen's parents had moved); club dates in San Francisco led to a show at Bill Graham's Fillmore and a contract offer from Graham's Fillmore Records, which Steel Mill turned down because the advance was too small. The band returned east and was joined by an old friend of Springsteen's, Miami Steve Van Zandt, on bass.

Springsteen disbanded Steel Mill in early 1971, intending to put together a band with a brass section and several singers. Meanwhile, he formed Dr. Zoom and the Sonic Boom, which played only three dates. Eventually, the Bruce Springsteen Band was formed with Lopez, Federici, Van Zandt (on guitar), pianist and guitarist David Sancious, bassist Garry Tallent, and a four-piece brass section. After the group's first show, the brass section was dropped and Clarence Clemons, a football-player-turned-tenor-saxophonist (a knee injury aborted his pro career), joined the band. The group didn't last; by autumn 1971 Springsteen was working solo.

Springsteen had auditioned for Laurel Canyon Productions, a.k.a. Mike Appel and Jim Cretecos, who had written a hit for the Partridge Family and produced an album by Sir Lord Baltimore. In May 1972 Springsteen signed a long-term management contract and an agreement giving Laurel Canyon exclusive rights to his songs. Royalty rates effective for five albums were set at a low 3 percent of retail price.

Appel arranged for his new client to audition for John Hammond, who had signed Dylan to Columbia. After hearing Springsteen sing in his office, Hammond set up a showcase for CBS executives at the Gaslight in New York City and supervised a demo session. In June 1972 Columbia president Clive Davis signed a 10-album contract with Appel that gave Laurel Canyon about a 9 percent royalty.

Within the month, Springsteen completed *Greetings From Asbury Park, N.J.* Some of Springsteen's word-crammed songs were set to acoustic singer/songwriter backup, and some to the R&B-inflected rock of the reconstituted Bruce Springsteen Band. Released in January 1973 and touted as one more "new Dylan" effort, *Greetings* initially sold about 25,000 copies, largely to Jersey Shore fans. Springsteen and the band toured the Northeast, playing extended sets that earned him followings in Boston and Philadelphia. A string of dates opening for Chicago, who limited his sets to a half hour, convinced Springsteen not to open for other bands.

With his second album, *The Wild, the Innocent and the E Street Shuffle,* Springsteen and his band integrated lyrics and instrumental passages into long romantic narratives; the average track was over seven minutes. The album sold as poorly as its predecessor, and Springsteen decided to concentrate on his stage show. Replacing Lopez with Ernest "Boom" Carter on drums, he tightened up what became the E Street Band, hired expensive light and sound crews, and rehearsed them to theatrical precision. He made up elaborate stories, often involving band members, to introduce his songs, dramatized the songs as he sang them, and capped his sets with fervently rendered oldies.

In spring 1974 critic Jon Landau saw a Springsteen show in Cambridge, Massachusetts, and wrote in the *Real Paper,* "I saw rock & roll's future and its name is Bruce Springsteen." Columbia used the quote in an ad campaign, and rave reviews of Springsteen concerts and belated notices of *The Wild* began showing up in print. By November 1974, the album had sold 150,000 copies. Springsteen and a revamped E Street Band (pianist Roy Bittan and drummer Max Weinberg replaced Sancious and Carter, who had formed their own fusion group, Tone; Van Zandt joined as second guitarist) were bogged down by an ambitious third album. Landau, who had been visiting the studio with suggestions, became coproducer with Springsteen and Appel (he would later become the singer's manager). Far from toning down Springsteen's histrionics, Landau inflated them with dra-

Bruce Springsteen

matic arrangements. While the album was being mastered, Springsteen wanted to scrap it in favor of a concert album. But that plan was dropped, and in October 1975 *Born to Run* (#3, 1975) was released.

Advance sales put the album on the chart a week before its release date, and it made the Top 10 shortly afterward. Within the month, it hit #3—and gold—while "Born to Run" (#23, 1975) became Springsteen's first hit single. Springsteen embarked on his first national tour. *Time* and *Newsweek* simultaneously ran cover stories on him. Yet Springsteen was still a cult figure—the album didn't stay on the charts long. In spring of 1976 an independent auditor's report called Appel's management "unconscionable exploitation." And when Appel refused permission for Landau to produce the next album, Springsteen sued his manager in July 1976, alleging fraud, undue influence, and breach of trust. Appel's countersuit asked for an injunction to bar Springsteen from working with Landau, which the court granted. Springsteen rejected the producer Appel chose, and the injunction prevented Springsteen from recording until May 1977. An out-of-court settlement gave Springsteen rights to his songs and he was allowed to work with Landau, while his Columbia contract was upgraded. Appel reportedly received a lump-sum settlement.

During the legal imbroglio, Springsteen toured and E Streeters did session work: Bittan with David Bowie and Meat Loaf, Van Zandt produced the debut album by Southside Johnny and the Asbury Jukes, *I Don't Want to Go Home*, which featured several Springsteen compositions. Other Springsteen songs provided hits for the Hollies ("Sandy"), Manfred Mann ("Blinded by the Light," a #1 single in 1977), Robert Gordon ("Fire," later a smash for the Pointer Sisters), and Patti Smith ("Because the Night," to which she contributed some lyrics). And Springsteen continued to write new songs, several of which were chosen for *Darkness on the Edge of Town* (#5, 1978).

Darkness was a dire and powerful album that reflected the troubled period Springsteen had just endured. On tracks like "Badlands," "Promised Land," "Adam Raised a Cain," and the title track, Springsteen sang with choked emotion about working-class problems and the hopes that keep Americans going. The album proved his depth to critics, although it failed to deliver on crossover hopes, yielding only the minor single "Prove It All Night" (#33, 1978).

Work on *The River* began in April 1979 and went on for a year and a half. Springsteen appeared on stage only twice in that period, at the Musicians United for Safe Energy (MUSE) antinuclear benefit concerts in New York, which were filmed as *No Nukes*. Meanwhile, Dave Marsh's best-selling *Born to Run: The Bruce Springsteen Story* was released, spreading the Springsteen legend out in book length. (It was released again in a revised edition, followed by a second Marsh volume, *Glory Days: Bruce Springsteen in the 1980's*, which was published in 1987.)

Coproduced by Springsteen, Landau, and Van Zandt, the double album *The River* (#1, 1980) sold over 2 million copies. A single, "Hungry Heart" (#5, 1980), was Springsteen's first Top 10 hit, followed by "Fade Away" (#20, 1981). *The River* was notable for its shorter, verse-chorus songs that were essentially short stories or character sketches ("Wreck on the Highway," "Independence Day," "Point Blank," "The River"). These four songs especially revealed a sense of resignation, of Springsteen's characters learning to live with what they cannot change.

On the eve of *The River's* release in October 1980, Springsteen kicked off a tour that crisscrossed the United States twice and took him to over 20 European cities; every one of his four-hour shows was sold out. In the fall, he played six benefit concerts in L.A. for Vietnam War veterans. In 1981 Springsteen persuaded Gary "U.S." Bonds (whose "Quarter to Three" was a favorite Springsteen encore) to return to recording, on an album produced by Van Zandt that included Springsteen material. Members of the E Street Band played sessions for Garland Jeffreys, Joan Armatrading, Ian Hunter, and others. Van Zandt continued producing Southside Johnny and the Asbury Jukes, and Bittan produced an album for rock singer Jimmy Mack.

In 1982 Springsteen made *Nebraska* (#3, 1982), a stark album recorded (initially as demo tapes) on a 4-track machine at home. With its tales of losers, desperadoes, and dreamers, the album was Springsteen's folk-song commentary on the social problems of America in the Age of Reagan, and on the nihilism bred by alienation.

After *Nebraska*'s deliberately noncommercial statement, Springsteen decided to head in the other direction and try to bring his message to a mass audience. With the simple, declarative songs on *Born in the U.S.A.* (#1, 1984), Springsteen became a megastar. The album yielded a string of singles—"Dancing in the Dark" (#2, 1984), "Cover Me" (#7, 1984), "Born in the U.S.A." (#9, 1984), "I'm on Fire" (#6, 1985), "Glory Days" (#5, 1985), "I'm Goin' Down" (#9, 1985), and "My Hometown"

(#6, 1985)—and remained in the Top 10 for more than two years. Springsteen made his first videos for the album's singles, including "Dancing in the Dark" directed by Brian De-Palma (the single later won a Grammy). Although on *Born in the U.S.A.,* Springsteen continued to look at the dark side of the American dream, he simplified sentiments and packaged them in an album featuring a U.S. flag on the cover. Not surprisingly, many fans took "Born in the U.S.A." as an upbeat patriotic anthem, although the song was actually about the dead ends hit by a Vietnam vet. Ronald Reagan himself, during the 1984 presidential campaign, tried to coopt Springsteen's vision as his own in one speech. Springsteen attempted to counteract such misinterpretations by meeting with labor, environmental, and civil rights activists in towns he played and mentioning their efforts on stage. Springsteen has always played numerous benefits; in 1985 he sang on USA for Africa's "We Are the World" and on Van Zandt's anti-apartheid project "Sun City." But the Born in the U.S.A. concerts themselves fueled the spectacle of Springsteen's success, with fans waving American flags in sold-out stadiums. The previously scrawny, modest Springsteen had joined the country's mania for pumping iron, and his marathon concerts began to resemble athletic events. Constant touring in 1985 (with Nils Lofgren replacing Van Zandt, who went on to pursue a solo career [see entry], and Patti Scialfa added on vocals) took him to the Far East and Australia for the first time.

The 40-song live album package *Live/1975–85* (#1, 1986) was released partly to counter the flood of bootlegs that had been traded among fans for years. It featured his cover of Edwin Starr's "War" (#8, 1986), a song whose critique he explicitly aimed in concerts at Reagan's militarism.

In 1984 Springsteen met model/actress Julianne Phillips, and the couple married in May 1985. On *Tunnel of Love* (#1, 1987) Springsteen recorded some of his most personal songs—including the Grammy-winning "Tunnel of Love" (#9, 1987), "Brilliant Disguise" (#5, 1987), and "One Step Up" (#13, 1988)—in which he detailed love unraveling. The songs proved to be painfully honest. While he was headlining the 1988 Amnesty International Human Rights Now! Tour, tabloids began reporting that Springsteen and Scialfa were having an affair. In August 1988 Phillips filed for divorce. The couple divorced the next year, and Springsteen married Scialfa in 1991. They moved to L.A. and eventually had three children, Evan James, Jessica Rae, and Sam Ryan.

Springsteen was apparently rethinking his life in general during this period. On the *Tunnel of Love* tour he had tried to shake up the E Street Band's live habits by repositioning them on stage. Still, the large group no longer seemed to be the correct vehicle for his music, and in November 1989 he told them he no longer needed them.

After half a decade's absence Springsteen returned with the simultaneous release of two albums, *Human Touch* (#2, 1992) (coproduced by Bittan, the only E Street Band member on the albums) and *Lucky Town* (#3, 1992). The albums entered the charts at their peak positions, but merely went platinum as opposed to the multiplatinum of his previous three albums. (All of his albums to this point sold platinum.) Springsteen wasn't aiming for the huge success of *Born in the U.S.A.,* but the pop songs of *Human Touch,* which he painstakingly had written over several years, received mixed reviews: Critics generally preferred *Lucky Town*'s ruminations on parenting and adulthood, which revealed new possibilities for a more mature Springsteen.

Springsteen performed on a television program for the first time in 1992, appearing on *Saturday Night Live.* On tour, he recruited a new, younger, and smaller band, but he hadn't quite freed himself from his old, overstated stadium style, and the shows seemed somewhat out of step with the album's more mature tone. For the first time in 15 years, Springsteen played to empty seats. In 1993 Scialfa released her first solo album, *Rumble Doll,* to general critical praise. That year Springsteen wrote and recorded "Streets of Philadelphia" (#9, 1994) for the Jonathan Demme film *Philadelphia;* the song won an Academy Award and four Grammys. *Greatest Hits,* which debuted at #1 on the charts, contained four previously unreleased songs.

In 1995 Springsteen released *The Ghost of Tom Joad,* an austere record in the tradition of *Nebraska* that invoked the populism of Steinbeck and Guthrie and applied it to problems of race and class in America at the end of the 20th century. The album, which Springsteen promoted with his first acoustic solo tour, won a Grammy for Best Contemporary Folk Album, although as of this writing it remains his only album not to go platinum.

After that, Springsteen maintained a low profile until the November 1998 announcement of his induction into the Rock and Roll Hall of Fame. That same week saw the release of *Songs,* a coffee-table book containing his song lyrics, as well as *Tracks* (#27), a career-spanning collection that included 56 unreleased recordings. The album became the first box set ever to debut at #1 on the charts, witnessing to the ongoing relevance of Springsteen's music.

In 1999 Springsteen and the E Street Band reunited for the first time in more than a decade, kicking off their U.S. tour with a record-setting 15 sold-out shows at the Continental Airlines Arena in the group's home state of New Jersey. The band's performances testified to Springsteen's faith in the redemptive power of both rock & roll and the human community. At a show at Madison Square Garden in the spring of 2000, Springsteen also performed "American Skin," a song that explores what happens when that community breaks down—in this case, when New York City police officers shot at West African immigrant Amadou Diallo 41 times while he was reaching for his wallet to show them his ID. Two New York performances were documented on a 2001 live album, which debuted at #5.

Squeeze

Formed 1974, London, Eng.
Chris Difford (b. Apr. 11, 1954, London), gtr., voc.; Glenn Tilbrook (b. Aug. 31, 1957, London), gtr., voc.; Julian "Jools"

Holland, kybds., voc.; Harry Kakoulli, bass; Gilson Lavis (b. June 27, 1951, Bedford, Eng.), drums.
1978—*U.K. Squeeze* (A&M) 1979—(– Kakoulli; + John Bentley [b. Apr. 16, 1951, London], bass) *Cool for Cats; 6 Squeeze Songs Crammed Into One Ten-inch Record* EP 1980—*Argybargy* 1981—(– Holland; + Paul Carrack [b. Apr. 1951, Sheffield, Eng.], kybds., voc.) *East Side Story* 1982—(– Carrack; + Don Snow [a.k.a. Johnny Savannah, b. Jan. 13, 1957, Kenya], kybds., voc.) *Sweets From a Stranger* (group disbands) 1983—*Singles 45's and Under* 1985—(group re-forms: Difford; Tillbrook; Holland; Lavis; + Keith Wilkinson [b. Sep. 24, 1954, Southfield, Eng.], bass, voc.) *Cosi Fan Tutti Frutti* (+ Andy Metcalfe, kybds.) 1987—*Babylon and On* 1989—*Frank* 1990—(– Holland; + Matt Irving, kybds., accordion) *A Round and a Bout* (I.R.S.) (– Irving; – Metcalfe) 1991—*Play* 1993—(– Lavis; + Carrack; + Pete Thomas [b. Aug. 9], drums) *Some Fantastic Place* (A&M) 1994—(– Thomas; + Andy Newmark, drums) 1995—(– Carrack; – Newmark; + Snow; + Kevin Wilkinson, drums) 1996—*Ridiculous* (I.R.S.); *Picadilly Collection* (A&M) 1997—(– Snow; – Keith Wilkinson; – Kevin Wilkinson; + Christopher Holland, kybds.; + Hilaire Penda, bass; + Ashley Soan, drums) 1999—*Domino* (Quixotic London/Valley) (– Difford).
Difford and Tillbrook: 1984—*Difford & Tillbrook* (A&M).
Glenn Tilbrook solo: 2001—*The Incomplete Glenn Tilbrook* (Quixotic).
Jools Holland: 1981—*Jools Holland and His Millionaires* (I.R.S.) 1984—*Jools Holland Meets Rock'a'Boogie Billy* 1990—*World of His Own* 1991—*The Full Compliment* 1993—*The A–Z of the Piano* 1996—*Sex and Jazz and Rock and Roll* (Colisseum, U.K.) 1997—*Lift the Lid* (Coalition, U.K.) 1999—*Hop the Wag*.

Though the band had garnered some critical acclaim and a few minor commercial successes in the late '70s, Squeeze appeared to have broken through in 1981 with *East Side Story*, which yielded a minor U.S. single in "Tempted" and was one of the most highly praised albums of the year. Despite that auspicious beginning (and a Top 20 hit in 1987 with "Hourglass"), the group's commercial fortunes never improved. Bafflingly, while none of its LPs cracked the Top 30 in the U.S., a 1983 "greatest hits" has been certified platinum.

Chris Difford and Glenn Tilbrook had been writing and performing together since 1973, and claim to have written over 1,000 songs to date. With Difford writing the lyrics and Tilbrook penning the music, the pair created a body of smart, poppish but ultimately sophisticated songs. The group was initially formed as Squeeze, but affixed a "U.K." to avoid confusion with a preexisting American band called Tight Squeeze; when the latter disbanded, it went back to Squeeze.

The title tune from *Cool for Cats*, featuring Chris Difford's eccentric guttural vocals, was a #2 U.K. hit and achieved some dance floor success in the U.S.; "Up the Junction" from the same LP fared similarly. *Argy Bargy* yielded "Pulling Mussels (From a Shell)," "Another Nail in My Heart," and "If I Didn't Love You," none hits but all frequently played in new-wave clubs and on new-wave format radio.

In late 1980 Holland left to form his own band, the Millionaires. He was replaced by Paul Carrack, formerly of Ace [see entry]; he'd sung Ace's hit "How Long," which Squeeze included in its live concerts, and sang "Tempted," from the Elvis Costello–coproduced *East Side Story*. Carrack left to join Carlene Carter's band, then to work with her then-husband Nick Lowe's Noise to Go. He was replaced by ex-Sincero Don Snow for *Sweets*, another well-received LP, which yielded FM staples in "Black Coffee in Bed" and "I Can't Hold On." Difford became involved in England's antinuclear movement and wrote what he called the band's "first protest song," "Apple Tree," which was to be included on *Sweets* but, for unknown reasons, was not. That year Difford also cowrote "Boy With a Problem" with Elvis Costello for Costello's *Imperial Bedroom* (Tilbrook had appeared on Costello's *Trust* earlier), and Squeeze played its first Madison Square Garden concert.

In the fall of 1982 the group broke up. Difford and Tilbrook continued to collaborate, and released one eponymously titled album before re-forming the band with Holland, Lavis, and Keith Wilkinson. The resulting *Cosi Fan Tutti Frutti*, another critical hit, topped at #57, and *Babylon and On*, which contained "Hourglass" and "853-5937," stopped at #36. The next two albums did not reach the Top 100. In the meantime, Holland, something of a personality, had hosted a U.K. music show from 1982 to 1987. He then hosted NBC's *Sunday Night*, a unique and respected music performance series not unlike the later *MTV Unplugged*. In England, he has hosted film documentaries, written and starred in a U.K. sitcom about Martians, and hosted the BBC's *Juke Box Jury* and *Later With Jools Holland*. He now plays cool jazz, often backed by a large ensemble.

In 1993, between solo work and stints with Mike + the Mechanics, Carrack returned to Squeeze for *Some Fantastic Place*, which peaked at #182 and produced the single "Everything in the World." More lineup changes ensued for 1996's *Ridiculous* and 1999's *Domino:* Carrack resumed his solo career; drummer Pete Thomas arrived and left to rejoin the Attractions; ex–Roxy Music drummer Andy Newmark came and went; Holland's brother Christopher and ex–Del Amitri drummer Ashley Soan came on board. In 1999 Difford, who had stopped drinking years before, shocked fans by bowing out of the band's American tour, opting not to risk his sobriety. As of 2001, the group's future was in doubt, and Tilbrook released a solo album.

Billy Squier

Born May 12, 1950, Wellesley Hills, MA
1980—*The Tale of the Tape* (Capitol) 1981—*Don't Say No* 1982—*Emotions in Motion* 1984—*Signs of Life* 1986—*Enough Is Enough* 1989—*Hear & Now* 1991—*Creatures of Habit* 1993—*Tell the Truth* 1995—*The Best of Billy Squier: 16 Strokes* 1999—*Happy Blue* (J-Bird).

After more than a decade of performing, heavy-metal guitarist Billy Squier hit it big in 1981 with "The Stroke" and enjoyed a few years of multiplatinum albums.

Squier grew up in an affluent Boston suburb, and after graduating from high school he moved to New York, where he and several friends formed Magic Terry and the Universe. Squier later returned to the Boston area, where he studied at the Berklee School of Music, planning to become a music teacher. But he soon returned to New York where in 1973 he joined the pop group the Sidewinders (he does not appear on their LP). Next he joined Piper, but after two LPs (*Piper* and *Can't Wait*) the group disbanded, and Squier began a solo career.

After his lackluster *The Tale of the Tape* (#169, 1980), Squier came back strong with a #5 LP (*Don't Say No*) and the Top 20 "The Stroke." The album also included "My Kinda Lover" (#45, 1981) and "In the Dark" (#35, 1981) and was eventually certified triple platinum. The next year's *Emotions in Motion* included "Everybody Wants You" (#32, 1982); it sold over 2 million copies, boosted by heavy rotation on MTV. Much to Squier's chagrin, he was embraced as something of a teen idol, an image that was blatantly (even embarrassingly) exploited in the video for "Rock Me Tonite" (#15, 1984). That song, from Squier's last platinum album, *Signs of Life* (#11, 1984), was also his last Top 40 single to date.

Subsequent albums failed to hit: *Enough Is Enough* and *Hear & Now* went Top 70, while *Creatures of Habit* didn't cross into the Hot 100. In 1999 he released the acoustic *Happy Blue*, which boasted a radically different version of "The Stroke."

Squirrel Nut Zippers

Formed 1993, Chapel Hill, NC
Tom Maxwell, gtr., horns, voc.; James Mathus, gtr., piano, voc.; Katharine Whalen, banjo, voc.; Chris Phillips, drums; Ken Mosher, horns, gtr., voc.; Stacy Guess, trumpet; Don Raleigh, bass.
1995—*The Inevitable* (Mammoth) 1996—(+ Andrew Bird, violin; – Guess) *Hot; Sold Out* EP (– Raleigh; + Je Widenhouse, trumpet; + Stu Cole, bass) 1998—*Perennial Favorites; Christmas Caravan* 1999—(– Maxwell; – Mosher; + Tim Smith, sax; + Reese Gray, piano; + David Wright, trombone) 2000—*Bedlam Ballroom.*
Katharine Whalen's Jazz Squad: 1999—*Jazz Squad* (Mammoth).
Tom Maxwell solo: 2000—*Samsara* (Samsara Limited).

The Squirrel Nut Zippers are an aggregation of erstwhile indie rockers who came together around their shared passion for old-time blues, jazz, and string-band music. The last thing they expected was to find themselves at the forefront of a swing revival that would make its way into the cultural mainstream.

The Zippers grew out of a series of potluck dinners–cum–picking sessions held during the summer of 1993 at the Efland, North Carolina, farmhouse of musical and marital partners Jim Mathus and Katharine Whalen. Mathus had been the drummer for a Chapel Hill indie-rock outfit called Metal Flake Mother but wanted to learn to master the country blues he'd heard while growing up in the Mississippi Delta; Whalen loved the jazz singing of Billie Holiday and Chet Baker. Tom Maxwell, Ken Mosher, and Chris Phillips—all regulars at the couple's get-togethers—stirred elements of calypso, hot jazz, and swing into the mix, and it wasn't long before the ensemble was gigging around Chapel Hill.

Naming themselves after Mathus' favorite brand of candy, a chewy, peanut-flavored sweet made by confectioners in Massachusetts, the Zippers released a three-song vinyl EP that included "Roasted Right" on Merge in 1994. The group later signed to another North Carolina–based label, Mammoth, for which they recorded their debut album, *The Inevitable*, in 1995. The record sold moderately well, boosted in part by the inclusion of the song "Anything But Love" on the soundtrack for the movie *Flirting With Disaster*, starring Ben Stiller. But their real commercial breakthrough came with "Hell," a Caribbean-flavored number from their second album, *Hot*, which became a hit on radio and MTV. *Hot* (#27, 1997) eventually went platinum and the Zippers were soon receiving invitations to appear on *A Prairie Home Companion, Late Night With Conan O'Brien*, and *The Late Show With David Letterman*, as well as at the 1996 Summer Olympics. Once the hubbub surrounding "Hell" died down (the band released an EP as a stop-gap measure in 1997), the Zippers returned with *Perennial Favorites* (#18, 1998), which added Klezmer and Western swing to their musical palette. Whalen and Maxwell subsequently released solo albums (Maxwell left the band toward the end of 1998), while the Zippers returned with their fourth full-length record, *Bedlam Ballroom*, in the fall of 2000.

Lisa Stansfield

Born Apr. 11, 1966, Rochdale, Eng.
1989—*Affection* (Arista) 1991—*Real Love* 1993—*So Natural* 1997—*Lisa Stansfield* 1998—*The #1 Remixes* EP.

Lisa Stansfield topped the pop and R&B charts internationally in the early '90s, a rare feat for a white female soul singer from a small town in England. Stansfield started singing in her early teens. Although she had no formal training, she plied her skill arduously at talent contests and social clubs. In the early '80s she hosted the British children's television program *Razzamatazz*. In 1983 she formed the group Blue Zone with former schoolmates Andy Morris and Ian Devaney (her future boyfriend). The trio released several singles and the album *Big Thing* but never broke out of the Manchester club circuit.

In 1989 the British production team Coldcut recorded "People Hold On" with Blue Zone, and the single went to the U.K. Top 20. Arista signed Stansfield as a solo artist, with Morris and Devaney as her composers, musicians, and producers. The platinum *Affection* (#9 pop, #5 R&B, 1990) became an international hit, with the singles "This Is the Right Time" (#21 pop, #13 R&B, 1990), "All Around the World" (#3 pop, #1 R&B, 1990), and "You Can't Deny It" (#14 pop, #1 R&B, 1990). Stansfield broke a color and ocean barrier by topping the U.S. R&B chart three times. In England she won Best British Female Artist at the BRIT Awards in 1991, although she angered organizers by using the show to speak out against the Gulf War.

For *Real Love* (#43 pop, #18 R&B, 1991), Stansfield cut off her trademark spit curl and presented herself as a more serious, mature artist. The singles "Change" (#27, 1991), "All Woman" (#1 R&B, 1992), and "A Little More Love" (#30 R&B, 1992) fared better with R&B and Adult Contemporary audiences than with the pop market. In 1992 she recorded a new version of "All Around the World" with one of her musical influences, Barry White. Stansfield sang Cole Porter's "Down in the Depths" for the AIDS benefit album *Red Hot + Blue*.

So Natural (1993), however, was a commercial and artistic disappointment, a record bloated with ballads that even Stansfield admits were self-indulgent. Its self-titled successor (#55 pop, #30 R&B, 1997) was anything but; galvanized by covers of Barry White's "Never, Never Gonna Give You Up" (#74 pop, #38 R&B) and Phyllis Hyman's "You Know How to Love Me," the album was a soulful return to form. Stansfield then tried her hand at acting, starring in the movie *Swing*, a well-received romantic comedy about a swing band from Liverpool. The picture's 1999 soundtrack album found her reviving "Mack the Knife" and other swing-era standards.

The Staple Singers

Formed 1953, Chicago, IL
Roebuck "Pops" Staples (b. Dec. 28, 1915, Winona, MS; d. Dec. 19, 2000, Dolton, IL), voc., gtr.; Mavis Staples (b. 1940, Chicago), voc.; Cleo Staples (b. 1934, MS), voc.; Pervis Staples (b. 1935, MS), voc.
Mid-'60s—(+ Yvonne Staples [b. 1939, Chicago], voc.)
1968—*Soul Folk in Action* (Stax); *We'll Get Over* 1971—(– P. Staples) *This Time Around; Heavy Makes You Happy* 1972—*Bealtitude: Respect Yourself* 1973—*Be What You Are* 1974—*City in the Sky* 1975—*The Best of the Staple Singers; Great Day* (Milestone) 1976—*Pass It On* (Warner Bros.) 1977—*Family Tree* 1978—*Unlock Your Mind* 1984—*Turning Point* (Private I) 1985—*Chronicle* (Fantasy); *Are You Ready* (Private I) 1991—*Freedom Highway* (Columbia Legacy) 1992—*The Staple Singers* 1999—*Greatest Hits* (Fantasy).
Mavis Staples solo: 1969—*Mavis Staples* (Stax) 1976—*Only for the Lonely* 1977—*A Piece of the Action* (Curtom) 1979—*Oh, What a Feeling* (Warner Bros.) 1989—*Time Waits for No One* (Paisley Park) 1993—*The Voice* 1996—*Spirituals and Gospel: Dedicated to Mahalia Jackson* (with Lucky Peterson) (Gitanes/Verve).
Pops Staples solo: 1992—*Peace to the Neighborhood* (Pointblank/Charisma) 1994—*Father Father*.

First as gospel singers and then as a soul-pop group, the Staples family has maintained a strong following and had several pop and soul hits, usually fronted by Mavis Staples' breathy vocals. The Staples family goes back to Mississippi, where as a young man Roebuck Staples played guitar and sang in local choirs. In the mid-'30s, he and his wife, Oceola, traveled up the Mississippi River to Chicago in search of work, like many of their contemporaries. The Staples had three daughters and a son, each of whom sang from an early age. They put together a family gospel act (which, until the mid-'60s, included all but the youngest daughter, Yvonne) and by the mid-'50s were considered one of the finest vocal groups in the field. The group made its first recording in the early '50s, for Pop Staples' own label, "These Are They" b/w "Faith and Grace," which they sold at concerts. In 1953 they recorded for United, and three years later for Vee-Jay, both Chicago labels, without success. In the early '60s the Staples made their first pop (secular) recordings for Epic, but had no commercial success, although 1967's "Why" snuck onto the lower reaches of the pop chart, and a version of Buffalo Springfield's "For What It's Worth" also charted later that year. Everything changed after they signed to Stax in 1968. Their new material continued to reflect the Staples' commitment to making secular music with a message, but not until 1972's gold *Bealtitude: Respect Yourself* did they make the approach commercial. The Staples' first secular hit was "Heavy Makes You Happy" (#27 pop, #6 R&B); and their next two hits, "Respect Yourself" (#12 pop, #2 R&B) and "I'll Take You There" (#1 pop and R&B), went gold. "If You're Ready (Come Go With Me)" was a #1 R&B hit in 1973. The Staples had succeeded in meshing Memphis soul shuffles with their own messages, and might have continued to release crossover hits were it not for Stax's mid-'70s decline and eventual closing.

Curtis Mayfield's Curtom label was their next home, and in 1974 the Staples had a #1 pop and R&B hit with his "Let's Do It Again" and a #4 hit with "New Orleans," both from the film *Let's Do It Again*. Mayfield also produced two of Mavis' solo albums. A couple of years later, at Warner Bros., the group changed their name to "the Staples" and released two R&B Top 20 singles: "Love Me, Love Me, Love Me" (#11 R&B, 1976) and "Unlock Your Mind" (#16 R&B, 1978). None of their singles charted again until 1984, when three, including a cover of Talking Heads' "Slippery People," appeared. Their last R&B Top 40 single was a 1985 version of "Are You Ready?" The group appeared in 1971's *Soul to Soul*, a documentary of a concert in Ghana, and in *Wattstax* (1973), and *The Last Waltz* (1978). In 1999 the Staple Singers were inducted into the Rock and Roll Hall of Fame.

Mavis Staples also recorded solo, but without comparable success, in part because her own career was frequently suspended due to group obligations. In 1987 Prince signed her to his Paisley Park label, for whom she recorded *Time Waits for No One*, which he coproduced with Al Bell (who had worked with the Staples at Stax). She opened for Prince on the overseas leg of his 1990 tour and appeared on his *Graffiti Bridge*. In addition, she has appeared on records by a range of artists, including Aretha Franklin *(One Lord, One Faith, One Baptism)*, John Mayall, Ray Charles, Kenny Loggins, and Marty Stuart. Pops, who also released solo albums, appears on Mavis' *The Voice*. His 1994 release *Father, Father* won that year's Grammy for Best Contemporary Blues

Album. He died in 2000, after falling in his home and suffering a concussion; he was 85.

Edwin Starr

Born Charles Hatcher, Jan. 21, 1942, Nashville, TN
1968—*Soul Master* (Gordy) 1969—*25 Miles; Just We Two* 1970—*War & Peace* 1971—*Involved* 1974—*Hell Up in Harlem* soundtrack (Tamla) 1976—*Free to Be Myself* (Granite) 1977—*Edwin Starr* (GTO) 1978—*Clean* (20th Century–Fox) 1979—*Happy Radio* 1981—*The Best of Edwin Starr.*

Singer/songwriter Edwin Starr's rough, powerful voice has made him a memorable but erratic hitmaker since the mid-'60s, though he is best known in the United States for his 1970 #1 protest song "War."

Starr sang in high school and began his professional career on Ric-Tic Records, a Detroit-based label that copied the sound of its crosstown rival, Motown, in many of its releases. On Ric-Tic, Starr had hits with his own "Agent Double-O-Soul" (#21 pop, #8 R&B, 1965) and "Stop Her on Sight (S.O.S.)" (#9 R&B, 1966). In 1968 Ric-Tic was purchased by Motown. The gritty Starr-penned "Twenty-five Miles" (#6 pop and R&B, 1969) is regarded as a soul classic. "I'm Still a Strugglin' Man" (#27 R&B) was the followup.

With producer Norman Whitfield, Starr had success in 1970 with two social commentary songs, "War" (#1 pop, #3 R&B) and "Stop the War Now" (#26 pop, #5 R&B). The next year brought "Funky Music Sho Nuff Turns Me On" (#6 R&B). During the late '70s, Starr recorded for 20th Century–Fox Records. His most successful singles of the period were "H.A.P.P.Y. Radio" (#79 pop, #28 R&B, 1979) and "Contact" (#65 pop, #13 R&B, 1979). In 1982 he cut a comical commentary song, "Tired of It," for Montage Records.

Around 1983 Starr moved to England, where, like many other '60s singers, he found a receptive audience. In fact, "H.A.P.P.Y. Radio" and "Contact" had been Top 10 hits there. He has since participated in the Ferry Aid single, "Let It Be" (1987), and recorded with Stock/Aitken/Waterman ("Whatever Makes Our Love Grow"). "It Ain't Fair" reached #56 there in 1985. As of the late '80s, Starr was living in a country manor outside of Birmingham. He owned a rehearsal studio and cafe in Birmingham.

Ringo Starr

Born Richard Starkey Jr., July 7, 1940, Liverpool, Eng.
1970—*Sentimental Journey* (Apple); *Beaucoups of Blues* 1973—*Ringo* 1974—*Goodnight Vienna* 1975—*Blast From Your Past* 1976—*Ringo's Rotogravure* (Atlantic) 1977—*Ringo the 4th* 1978—*Bad Boy* 1981—*Stop and Smell the Roses* (Boardwalk) 1983—*Old Wave* (RCA, Can.) 1989—*Starr Struck: Best of Ringo Starr, vol. 2 (1976–1983)* (Rhino) 1990—*Ringo Starr and His All-Starr Band* (Rykodisc) 1992—*Time Takes Time* (Private Music); *Ringo Starr and His All-Starr Band, vol. 2: Live From Montreux* (Rykodisc) 1998—*Vertical Man* (Mercury); *VH1 Storytellers* 1999—*I Wanna Be Santa Claus* 2001—*The Anthology . . . So Far: Ringo Starr and His All Starr Band* (Kuch).

While some accused Ringo Starr of being a clumsy drummer, many more agreed with George Harrison's assessment: "Ringo's the best backbeat in the business." And while many in the wake of the Beatles' breakup predicted that Starr would be the one without a solo career, he proved them wrong. Not only has he released several LPs (the first came out before the Beatles disbanded) and hit singles, but he's also the only Beatle to establish a film-acting career for himself outside of the band's mid-'60s movies.

Young Richard Starkey's parents had divorced when he was three, and he was raised by his mother and stepfather, a Liverpool house painter his mother married eight years later. By the time he was 13, he'd been in and out of the hospital several times with pleurisy, and once, at age six, with appendicitis. After leaving the hospital in 1955, too old to return to school, he became a messenger boy for British Railways. In 1959, while working as an apprentice engineer, he got his first drum set as a Christmas present, and he joined the Ed Clayton Skiffle Group soon after. By 1961, he was playing drums in Rory Storme's Hurricanes. It was while on tour with that band in Hamburg, Germany, in 1961 that he met John Lennon, Paul McCartney, and George Harrison. A year later, when drummer Pete Best was ousted from the Beatles, Starr agreed to join them. The Ringo stage name came from his penchant for wearing lots of rings.

Beginning with "Boys" on the Beatles' first British album, Starr was given the occasional lead vocal, usually on covers of country tunes such as Carl Perkins' "Honey Don't" and "Matchbox" and Buck Owens' "Act Naturally." Later he sang the lead on "Yellow Submarine" and "With a Little Help From My Friends," songs written for him by Lennon and McCartney. *The Beatles* (the so-called White Album) in 1968 featured Starr's first songwriting credit, "Don't Pass Me By." After appearing in three films with the Beatles, in 1967 Starr made his solo film debut playing a Mexican gardener in the film of Terry Southern's *Candy.* He appeared in *The Magic Christian* (1969, also from a Southern book); in 1970 he costarred with David Essex in *That'll Be the Day;* in 1973 he documented the success of glitter-rock star T. Rex by directing *Born to Boogie;* in 1975 he costarred again with Essex in *Stardust;* and in 1981 he starred in the moderately successful U.S. feature *Caveman* (in April of that year he married his *Caveman* costar Barbara Bach; it was his second marriage).

Starr's solo recording career began in 1970, just prior to the Beatles' breakup, with *Sentimental Journey* (#22, 1970), a collection of Tin Pan Alley standards (allegedly to please his mother) produced by George Martin, with a different arranger for each track. *Beaucoups of Blues* (#65, 1970), released later that year, was a country-music collaboration with guitarist Pete Drake and other Nashville sessionmen. It fared better than its predecessor, but failed to yield a hit. In 1971 Starr appeared on Lennon's *Plastic Ono Band* and Harrison's *All Things Must Pass* LPs, and recorded two hit singles, the hard-rocking "It Don't Come Easy" (#4) and "Back Off Boogaloo" (#9). (Starr later acknowledged that Harrison had cowritten these two songs without being credited.)

Starr appeared at Harrison's Concerts for Bangladesh and in 1972 sat in on Peter Frampton's *Wind of Change* LP. In 1973 he recorded *Ringo* (#2, 1973), with Richard Perry producing. The LP included three Top 10 singles—"Photograph" (#1), "You're Sixteen" (#1), and "Oh My My" (#5)—and featured songs and playing by the other Beatles; Lennon contributed "I'm the Greatest," McCartney "Six O'Clock," and Harrison "Sunshine Life for Me." *Goodnight Vienna* (#8, 1974) yielded hit singles in Hoyt Axton's "No No Song" (#3) and "Only You" (#6). *Blast From Your Past,* a greatest-hits package, went to #30 in 1975. While comanaging a furniture-designing business with his brother in London, Starr in 1975 started his own label, Ring O' Records, and signed to Atlantic. Compared to his previous solo success, his albums for his new label made little impression; *Ringo's Rotogravure,* despite guest appearances by Lennon, McCartney, Eric Clapton, and Peter Frampton, stopped at #28 with one Top 30 single, "Dose of Rock 'n' Roll," and *Ringo the 4th,* at #162, was a flop. *Bad Boy* (#129, 1978) continued the downward spiral.

Starr remained a familiar presence, though. In 1976 he played at the Band's San Francisco farewell concert and appeared in the film of the event, *The Last Waltz.* In 1977 he contributed to an LP by British skiffle pioneer Lonnie Donegan. In late 1981 Starr had a Top 40 hit with "Wrack My Brain," from *Stop and Smell the Roses* (#98, 1981), a tune written and produced by George Harrison. None of his subsequent albums has come near the Top 100.

Old Wave was not released in the U.S. or the U.K., and during this time Starr suffered from myriad problems, foremost among them alcoholism and drug abuse, for which both he and his wife Barbara sought treatment at the Betty Ford Center in 1988. At one point earlier, Starr's drinking had gotten so bad that he went to court to block the release of material he recorded in 1987. In the meantime, Starr became a star of the kiddie set in his portrayal of the miniature conductor and narrator of the acclaimed PBS series *Shining Time Station,* between 1989 and 1991. (Starr had first narrated the British series *Thomas the Tank Engine and Friends* back in 1984.)

Starr has since formed several celebrity configurations of his All-Starr Band. The first, in 1989, featured Levon Helm, Joe Walsh, Clarence Clemons, Rick Danko, Billy Preston, and Dr. John. A 1992 lineup included Ringo's son Zak on drums, Walsh, Timothy B. Schmit, Dave Edmunds, Nils Lofgren, and Todd Rundgren. Later editions have included the Who's John Entwistle, Procol Harum's Gary Brooker, Jack Bruce, Peter Frampton, and Bachman-Turner Overdrive's Randy Bachman. The 1992 release of *Time Takes Time,* coinciding with the silver anniversary of *Sgt. Pepper's Lonely Hearts Club Band,* brought a new flush of publicity for Starr, who often made it amply clear to interviewers that he did not wish to talk about the Beatles.

Though Starr has had little success as a recording artist in the '80s and '90s, he is never long out of view. He appeared in Paul McCartney's *Give My Regards to Broad Street* (1984), a television production of *Alice in Wonderland* (1985), with Zak on the Artists Against Apartheid album and video (1985), with ex–band mate Harrison in the video for "When We Was Fab" (1988), and as himself on *The Simpsons* (1990). In 1994 Starr's first wife, Maureen Cox Starkey Tigrett, died of cancer.

Starr returned to the studio in the late '90s. First he reunited with the other surviving Beatles to record two tracks for the new *Anthology 1* in 1995; he then released *Vertical Man* (#61, 1998), his most successful album in 20 years. Guests ranged from familiar faces like McCartney and Harrison to newcomers Alanis Morissette and Stone Temple Pilots' Scott Weiland, and the songs included a cover of the Beatles' "Love Me Do." The following year Starr recorded his first seasonal album, *I Wanna Be Santa Claus.* In 2001 he hit the road with a new All Starr Band that included Ian Hunter, Sheila E., Greg Lake, Howard Jones, and Roger Hodgson (Supertramp).

Status Quo

Formed 1962, London, Eng.
Francis Rossi (b. May 29, 1949, London), gtr., voc.; Richard Parfitt (b. Rick Harrison, Oct. 12, 1948, Woking, Eng.), gtr., voc.; Alan Lancaster (b. Feb. 7, 1949, London), bass; John Coghlan (b. Sep. 19, 1946, London), drums; Roy Lynes, organ.
1968—*Picturesque Matchstickable Messages* (Pye, U.K.); *Spare Parts* 1969—*Status Quotation* (Marble Arch, U.K.) 1970—*Ma Kelly's Greasy Spoon* (Pye, U.K.) (– Lynes) 1971—*Dog of Two Heads* 1972—*Best of* 1973—*Pile Driver* (A&M) 1974—*Hello; Quo* 1975—*On the Level* 1976—*Status Quo* (Vertigo, U.K.); *Blue for You* 1977—*Live* (Capitol); *Pictures of Matchstick Men* (Hallmark); *Rockin' All Over the World* (Capitol) 1978—*If You Can't Stand the Heat . . .* (Vertigo, U.K.) 1979—*In My Chair* (Mode, Fr.); *Whatever You Want* (Vertigo, U.K.); *Mean Girl* (Mode, Fr.); *Just for the Record* (Pye, U.K.) 1980—*Just Supposin'* (Vertigo, U.K.); *Gold Bars* 1981—*Never Too Late* (– Coghlan; + Pete Kircher, drums) 1982—*Rock 'n' Roll; 1 + 9 + 8 + 2* 1983—*To Be or Not to Be; Back to Back* (– Lancaster; group re-forms: Rossi; Parfitt; + John Edwards, bass; + Jeff Rich, drums; + Andy Bown, kybds.) 1986—*In the Army Now* 1988—*Ain't Complaining* 1989—*Perfect Remedy* 1991—*Rock 'til You Drop* 1994—*Thirsty Work* (Polydor, U.K.) 1996—*Don't Stop* 1998—(– Rich; + Matthew Letley, drums) 1999—*Under the Influence* (Eagle, U.K.) 2000—*Famous in the Last Century* (Universal Music TV, U.K.) (– Bown; + Paul Hirsch, kybds.).

Britain's longest-running hard-rock boogie band, Status Quo has actually had only one U.K. #1 single, "Down Down," in late 1974, and one U.S. hit single, the psychedelic-pop classic "Pictures of Matchstick Men" in 1968 (#12; also a Top 10 U.K. hit).

As schoolmates, the group's members began playing together as the Spectres, who in 1966 recorded two singles for Pye Records. In 1967 they became Traffic Jam and released another single. That year, they changed their name to Status Quo. By 1970, the band had dropped its high-harmony pop style for heavy-metal boogie. Its albums became consistent big sellers in the U.K. Despite touring America in the '70s, the group never broke into the U.S. market.

In England Status Quo released four albums that entered the U.K. chart at #1. Among the band's 45 U.K. charting singles are the Top 5 hits "Caroline" (1973), "Rockin' All Over the World" (1977), "Whatever You Want" (1979), "What You're Proposing" (1980), "Marguerita Time" (1983), "In the Army Now" (1986), "Burning Bridges (On and Off and On Again)" (1988), and "The Anniversary Waltz—Part 1" (1990). This longevity and tenacity have made the musicians legends at home, sort of the Cliff Richard of heavy metal: phenomenally successful but predictable and safe. Despite the expected rounds of personnel changes, Status Quo has remained commercially viable. In a 1993 *Q* magazine interview with Rossi and Parfitt, the pair revealed their unpretentious and very un-rock-star-like charm. Rossi said, "So what if we're boring and only do three chords? There's no point in getting hung up about it," and "As far as I know, our lyrics mean nothing."

Stealers Wheel

Formed 1972, London, Eng.
Gerry Rafferty (b. Apr. 16, 1947, Paisley, Scot.), gtr., voc.; Joe Egan (b. Scot.), kybds., voc.; Rab Noakes, gtr.; Ian Campbell, bass; Roger Brown, drums, voc.
1973—(– Noakes; – Campbell; – Brown; + Paul Pilnick, gtr.; + Tony Williams, bass; + Rod Coombes, drums) *Stealers Wheel* (A&M) 1974—(– Pilnick; – Williams; – Coombes; + Gary Taylor, bass; + Joe Jammer, gtr.; + Andrew Steele, drums) *Ferguslie Park* 1975—(+ Bernie Holland, gtr.; + Dave Wintour, bass) *Right or Wrong* 1976—*Stuck in the Middle With You.*

One of the most critically respected pop groups of the mid-'70s, Stealers Wheel was so ridden with internal turmoil that it was never able to capitalize on its one big hit, "Stuck in the Middle With You," from its Leiber-Stoller-produced debut LP, which made #6 in the U.K. and #2 in the U.S. in 1973.

Gerry Rafferty [see entry] formed the original Stealers Wheel, which never recorded. The band regrouped with Rafferty, Joe Egan, and guitarist Paul Pilnick (formerly of Liverpool band the Big Three; Pilnick later worked with Badger) and drummer Rod Coombes, later of the Strawbs. Stealers Wheel's eponymously titled debut included "Stuck in the Middle With You" and went to #50 in the U.S., but Rafferty had quit before it was released, and only rejoined the band after it had become a hit.

Leiber and Stoller produced *Ferguslie Park*—for which the band included ex–Spooky Tooth guitarist Luther Grosvenor, who would go on to Mott the Hoople—and though the album was again critically acclaimed, it yielded only a Top 30 U.S. single in "Star" and sold poorly. Rafferty and Egan, the obvious nucleus of Stealers Wheel, fell out with Leiber and Stoller before recording a third LP. Mentor Williams produced *Right or Wrong*, but its release was held up for 18 months because of managerial problems, and by the time it came out the public had apparently forgotten Stealers Wheel. Rafferty and Egan were reportedly no longer speaking to each other after the LP's release. Rafferty went on to have a briefly spectacular solo career, while Egan continued to record as well. In 1993 "Stuck in the Middle With You" was resurrected when it was featured in the Quentin Tarantino film *Reservoir Dogs*.

Steeleye Span

Formed 1969, England
Ashley Hutchings (b. Jan. 1945, London, Eng.), bass; Maddy Prior (b. Aug. 14, 1947, Blackpool, Eng.), voc.; Tim Hart (b. Jan. 9, 1948, Lincoln, Eng.), gtr., voc., dulcimer; Gay Woods, voc., concertina; Terry Woods, gtr.
1970—*Hark! The Village Wait* (Chrysalis) (– C. Woods; – T. Woods; + Martin Carthy, gtr.; + Peter Knight, fiddle, mandolin, voc.) 1971—*Please to See the King; Ten Man Mop* (– Hutchings) 1972—(– Carthy; + Rick Kemp [b. Nov. 15, 1941, Little Handford, Eng.], bass, voc.; + Bob Johnson, lead gtr., voc.) *Below the Salt* 1973—*Parcel of Rogues* 1974—(+ Nigel Pegrum, drums) *Now We Are Six* 1975—*Commoner's Crown; All Around My Hat* 1976—*Rocket Cottage* 1977—(+ John Kirkpatrick, voc., accordion; + Carthy) *Storm Force 10; Original Masters* 1978—*Live at Last* (– Knight; – Johnson; group disbands) 1980—(group re-forms: Prior; Hart; Kemp; Johnson; Pegrum; Knight; numerous personnel changes follow) *Sails of Silver* (Takoma) 1986—*Back in Line* (Shanachie) 1989—*Tempted and Tried; Portfolio* 1992—*Tonight's the Night, Live* 1995—(+ Woods) 1996—*Time* 1997—(– Prior) 1999—*Horkstow Grange* (Park).

Steeleye Span was formed with the idea of introducing electric instruments to traditional British folk music—updating mainly 17th- and 18th-century works found in the journals of the English Folk Dance and Song Society.

Founder Ashley Hutchings, formerly bassist for trad-rockers Fairport Convention, left that band after its *Liege and Lief.* Hutchings sought out more purely history-obsessed musicians and came up with two teams: Maddy Prior and Tim Hart (who had performed locally in St. Albans, England, and recorded three traditional albums) plus Gay and Terry Woods (a married couple who were part of the folk-rock group Sweeney's Men). The new fivesome took their name from a character in the Lincolnshire ballad "Horkstow Grange" and recorded *Hark! The Village Wait* in 1970. A few months later the Woodses left, and Hart brought in Martin Carthy, another folk-scene regular, and Peter Knight.

The new lineup recorded two LPs in 1971, *Please to See the King* and *Ten Man Mop,* which included more amplification on their all-traditional pieces. They began to attract attention, especially for Maddy Prior's vocals. The group was appearing in a play written for them called *Carunna,* by Keith

Dewhurst, when Hutchings lost confidence in the project and, in 1971, left to form the very traditional Albion Country Band; Carthy also left. Their replacements were the more rock-oriented Rick Kemp (who had worked with Mike Chapman and spent a week once in King Crimson) and Bob Johnson (who had played in a folk duo with Knight).

This lineup gave Steeleye their first real success. *Below the Salt* in 1972 was their U.S. debut and the Latin a cappella song "Gaudete" became a British hit in 1973. By now, Hart, Carthy, and Prior were doing solo work. In 1973 the band released *Parcel of Rogues,* with its first drummer, ex-Gnidrolog member Nigel Pegrum. He joined full time in 1974, making them a six-piece, inspiring the title of their next LP, *Now We Are Six,* produced by Jethro Tull's Ian Anderson. The band members began to write their own songs and settings for traditional lyrics. Its popularity increased in the U.K. with the gold hit single "Thomas the Rhymer." The LP also featured David Bowie playing sax on "To Know Him Is to Love Him." *Commoner's Crown* in 1975 featured actor Peter Sellers playing ukulele on "New York Girls," and the even more commercial *All Around My Hat* gave them a big British hit with the title track, and also their first U.S. charting. A cult began to grow in America, drawn to the band's live show, which featured Prior's nimble jigs. In 1976 Prior recorded the album *Silly Sisters* with traditional singer June Tabor, and the two toured England. That solo outlet was indicative of the band's splintering, though. After *Rocket Cottage* failed to sell even in England, Knight and Johnson produced a duo album, *The King of Elfland's Daughter.*

In 1977, with the newly rejoined Carthy and Kirkpatrick, Knight and Johnson announced their departure, but first the band gave a farewell concert on March 7, 1978, captured on *Live at Last.* The group has gotten back together several times since with various original members floating in and out of the lineup. Steeleye Span resurfaced with the most popular lineup—Prior and Hart plus Johnson, Kemp, Knight, and Pegrum—on *Sails of Silver.* Prior has continued to record solo, as well. Gay Woods returned before 1996's *Time,* the band's first studio album in seven years. She fronted Steeleye Span on 1999's *Horkstow Grange,* which marked the departure of Prior, the only constant through the previous personnel changes.

Steel Pulse

Formed 1975, Birmingham, Eng.
Selwyn "Bumbo" Brown (b. June 4, 1956, London, Eng.), kybds., voc.; David Hinds (b. June 15, 1956, Birmingham), gtr., voc.; Stephen "Grizzly" Nisbett (b. Mar. 15, 1948, Nevis, West Indies), drums.
1978—*Handsworth Revolution* (Mango) 1979—*Tribute to the Martyrs* 1980—*Reggae Fever* 1982—*True Democracy* (Elektra) 1983—*Earth Crisis* 1984—*Reggae Greats* (Mango) 1986—*Babylon the Bandit* (Elektra) 1988—*State of Emergency* (MCA) 1991—*Victims* 1992—*Rastafari Centennial: Live in Paris—Elysée Montmartre* 1994—*Vex* 1996—*Rastanthology* (Wiseman Doctrine) 1997—*Sound System* (Island) 1997—*Rage and Fury* (Mesa/Blue Moon) 1999—*Living Legacy* (WEA/Lightyear).

Steel Pulse was one of the prime movers in the movement that cross-fertilized reggae rhythms with punk's energy. David Hinds and Selwyn Brown were inspired to start Steel Pulse by listening to Bob Marley and the Wailers' *Catch a Fire.* By 1976, with punk in full swing, the group began to play punk venues such as Manchester's Electric Circus and the Hope and Anchor in London.

Though originally a traditional-sounding reggae unit, the band experimented with lusher production after moving to Elektra in 1982. While Steel Pulse's loose-limbed grooves and the soaring vocals of Hinds and Brown caught most listeners' ears, Steel Pulse's politics have played a large part of its career. The group was among the early leaders of the Rock Against Racism movement in the late '70s; in the late '80s, Hinds joined a million-dollar class-action suit against the New York City Taxi and Limousine Commission after repeatedly being ignored by New York's cab drivers. Steel Pulse's radicalism has not lost them admirers; the band's 1986 album *Babylon the Bandit* won the Best Reggae Album Grammy, and the live *Rastafari Centennial,* widely hailed as a return to form, was nominated for the award in 1992. The following year Steel Pulse performed at Bill Clinton's inauguration, the first reggae band to ever receive such an invitation.

All through the '90s, Steel Pulse continued to craftily court the mainstream while maintaining strong political views—typically, 1997's *Rage and Fury* featured both a cover of Van Morrison's "Brown Eyed Girl" and a guest appearance by Spearhead's activist frontman Michael Franti. *Living Legacy* includes live material recorded between 1996 and 1999.

Steely Dan

Formed 1972, Los Angeles, CA
Walter Becker (b. Feb. 20, 1950, Queens, NY), bass, gtr., voc.; Donald Fagen (b. Jan. 10, 1948, Passaic, NJ), kybds., voc.; Denny Dias, gtr.; Jim Hodder (d. June 5, 1990), drums.
1971—*You Gotta Walk It Like You Talk It* soundtrack (Spark) 1972—(+ David Palmer, kybds., voc.; + Jeffrey "Skunk" Baxter [b. Dec. 13, 1948, Washington, DC], gtr.) *Can't Buy a Thrill* (ABC) 1973—(– Palmer) *Countdown to Ecstasy* 1974—(– Hodder; + Michael McDonald [Feb. 12, 1952, St. Louis, MO], voc., kybds.; + Jeff Porcaro [b. Apr. 1, 1954, CA; d. Aug. 5, 1992, Holden Hills, CA], drums) *Pretzel Logic* 1975—(– Baxter; – McDonald; + various sessionmen, including Elliot Randall, gtr.; Larry Carlton, gtr.; David Paich and Michael Omartian, kybds.; Wilton Felder, bass; Victor Feldman, perc., kybds.) *Katy Lied* 1976—(– Porcaro) *The Royal Scam* 1977—*Aja* 1978—*Greatest Hits* 1979—(– Dias) 1980—*Gaucho* (MCA) 1982—*Steely Dan Gold* 1993—*Citizen Steely Dan 1972–1980* 2000—*Two Against Nature* (Giant).

Donald Fagen solo: 1982—*The Nightfly* (Warner Bros.) 1993—*Kamakiriad* (Reprise).
Donald Fagen with the New York Rock & Soul Revue: 1991—*Live at the Beacon* (Giant).
Walter Becker solo: 1994—*11 Tracks of Whack* (Giant).

Less a band than a concept, Steely Dan was one of the most advanced, successful, and mysterious pop units of the '70s. Combining pop hooks with jazz harmonies, complicated time changes and cryptic, often highly ironic lyrics, the band sounded like no one else. Because of the perfectionism of founders Donald Fagen and Walter Becker, the outfit rarely toured, and toward the end, was composed almost entirely of session musicians, while Becker and Fagen began to play less and less on their own albums. Producer Gary Katz became Steely Dan's "third member," as much because of Becker and Fagen's insistence on pristine sound quality as for Katz's role in forming the band. With Becker and Fagen fronting a version of Steely Dan that toured to great success in 1993, they proved that their long-lived cult was very much alive. And the 2000 release of *Two Against Nature* resurrected the band as a viable recording unit, and also won Steely Dan several Grammy Awards.

Meeting in 1967 at Bard College in upstate New York, Becker and Fagen played in amateur bands, ranging from jazz to rock to pop to progressive rock; one—Bad Rock Group—included future comedian Chevy Chase on drums. Becker and Fagen began composing together and toured from 1970 to 1971 as backing musicians for Jay and the Americans under the pseudonyms Tristan Fabriani (Fagen) and Gustav Mahler (Becker). They also wrote and recorded the album *You Gotta Walk It Like You Talk It,* produced by Kenny Vance of Jay and the Americans. They tried unsuccessfully to start a Long Island band with guitarist Denny Dias, then moved to New York City to sell their tunes to publishers, but had little success aside from placing "I Mean to Shine" on a Barbra Streisand album. They did, however, meet independent producer Gary Katz, who enlisted them at ABC/Dunhill Records in L.A. as staff songwriters as a stipulation to accepting his own contract as a staff producer. It was Katz who hatched the idea for what would become Steely Dan. Steely Dan was the name of a dildo in William Burroughs' *Naked Lunch.*

Steely Dan's debut, *Can't Buy a Thrill* (#17, 1972), yielded two hit singles, "Do It Again" (#6, 1972) and, featuring guitarist Elliot Randall, "Reeling in the Years" (#11, 1973). Hailed by critics, the album sold well. Put off by a singles-oriented audience, as well as inadequate rehearsals, Becker, Fagen, and Katz considered Steely Dan's first tour a total disaster. *Countdown to Ecstasy* (#35, 1973) contained no hit singles—possibly because singer David Palmer had left to form the abortive Big Wha-Koo, forcing Fagen's distinctive vocals to the fore.

On their next effort, Steely Dan was joined by singer/keyboardist Michael McDonald, who sang mostly backup vocals. *Pretzel Logic* (#8, 1974) featured "Rikki Don't Lose That Number" (#4, 1974) and more pronounced jazz leanings; the opening of "Rikki" was a nod to hard-bop pianist Horace Silver, and "Parker's Band" saluted bebop giant Charlie Parker. In 1974 Steely Dan went on their last tour for nearly two decades. Hodder resumed session work; Baxter and then McDonald joined the Doobie Brothers [see entry]; though Dias continued to work with Becker and Fagen for some time, he also returned to playing sessions. Becker and Fagen amassed enormous debts by spending lengthy spells in the studio with high-priced sessionmen. *Katy Lied* (#13, 1975), the first Steely Dan LP by Becker and Fagen plus session players, contained a single that inched into the Top 40, "Black Friday" (#37, 1975), and featured a solo on "Dr. Wu" by jazz alto saxophonist Phil Woods. The DBX noise-reduction system used to enhance the sound malfunctioned, and the album's sleeve contained a lengthy apology from Becker, Fagen, and Katz; still, it sounded cleaner than most contemporary releases. A scheduled tour was scrapped during rehearsals.

The Royal Scam, like most Steely Dan albums, sold well (#15, 1976) and presented some of Becker/Fagen's most mordant lyrics. The seven-song *Aja* (#3, 1977), which included FM favorites like "Peg" (#11, 1977) and "Deacon Blues" (#19, 1978), played by such expert sidemen as the Crusaders, Wayne Shorter, and Lee Ritenour, went Top 5 within three weeks of its release, and became the band's first platinum album. In 1978 jazz bandleader Woody Herman's Thundering Herd Big Band recorded five Becker-Fagen songs, selected by and under the supervision of the duo. A subsequent contractual dispute with MCA (which had absorbed ABC Records) delayed the release of *Gaucho* (#9, 1980), which yielded "Hey Nineteen" (#10, 1980) and featured guitar work by Mark Knopfler and Rick Derringer. Its B side was Steely Dan's only live recording, "Bodhisattva," from the 1974 tour. Also in 1978, Steely Dan's contribution to the movie *FM,* "FM (No Static at All)" (#22), was that soundtrack's highlight. In 1980 Becker suffered a broken leg and other injuries when a car hit him while he was walking in Manhattan.

The following year Becker and Fagen announced that they would go separate ways, though their management denied it would be a permanent separation. In 1982 *Gaucho* won a Grammy for Best Engineered Album, as had *Aja* in 1978. Such passion for sonic detail paid off when, during the '80s and the advent of CDs, Steely Dan's highly crafted catalogue steadily sold. Fagen released his solo *The Nightfly* in 1982 to stellar reviews, then waited until 1993 for the Becker-produced *Kamakiriad.* During that time, Becker produced such artists as Rickie Lee Jones and China Crisis and handled production work for New Age label Windham Hill and jazz label Triloka. After his girlfriend died from a drug overdose (her mother tried to sue Becker, claiming that he had fostered the young woman's drug problem), Becker overcame his own substance-abuse problems.

In the early '90s Becker and Fagen appeared in concert with the New York Rock and Soul Revue alongside Boz Scaggs, Phoebe Snow, and Michael McDonald, documenting the gigs on 1991's *Live at the Beacon.* In 1993, nearly two decades since their last concert, Becker and Fagen headed an 11-piece version of Steely Dan that reprised their works in a

U.S. tour. In 1994 Becker released a critically acclaimed album of his own, *11 Tracks of Whack;* Fagen produced the disc.

In 2000 Steely Dan, with Becker and Fagen coproducing, released their first album of new material in over 20 years, *Two Against Nature.* The record debuted at #6 and won three Grammys, including Album of the Year; its accompanying tour, meanwhile, drew raves. Also that year, Garden Party, an aggregation of smooth-jazz players such as keyboardist Jeff Lorber and saxophonist Dave Koz, put out a Steely Dan tribute album, *No Static at All.* Steely Dan was inducted into the Rock and Roll Hall of Fame in 2001.

Steppenwolf

Formed 1967, Los Angeles, CA
John Kay (b. Joachim F. Krauledat, Apr. 12, 1944, Tilsit, Ger.), gtr., voc.; Michael Monarch (b. July 5, 1950, Los Angeles), gtr.; Goldy McJohn (b. John Goadsby, May 2, 1945), organ; Rushton Moreve (b. ca. 1948, Los Angeles; d. July 1, 1981, Los Angeles), bass; Jerry Edmonton (b. Jerry McCrohan, Oct. 24, 1946, Can.; d. Nov. 28, 1993, near Santa Ynez, CA), drums.
1968—(– Moreve; + John Russell Morgan, bass) *Steppenwolf* (Dunhill); *Steppenwolf the Second* 1969—*Early Steppenwolf* (– Monarch; – Morgan; + Larry Byrom [b. Dec. 27, 1948, U.S.], gtr.; + Nick St. Nicholas [b. Klaus Karl Kassbaum, Sep. 28, 1943, Plön, Ger.], bass) *Steppenwolf at Your Birthday Party* 1970—(– St. Nicholas; + George Biondi [b. Sep. 3, 1945, Brooklyn, NY], bass) *Monster; Steppenwolf Live; Steppenwolf Seven* 1971—*Steppenwolf Gold/Their Greatest Hits* (– Byrom; + Kent Henry, gtr.) *For Ladies Only* 1972—*Rest in Peace* (group disbands) 1973—*16 Greatest Hits* 1974—(group re-forms: Kay; Edmonton; McJohn; Biondi; + Bobby Cochran [b. MN], gtr.) *Slow Flux* (Epic) 1975—(– McJohn; + Andy Chapin [b. Feb. 7, 1952; d. Dec. 31, 1985, DeKalb, TX], kybds.; – Chapin; + Wayne Cook, kybds.) *Hour of the Wolf* (Epic) (group disbands) 1976—*Skullduggery* 1977—*Reborn to Be Wild* 1980—(Kay re-forms Steppenwolf as John Kay and Steppenwolf with new personnel) 1981—*John Kay and Steppenwolf Live in London* (Mercury, Austral.) 1982—*Wolftracks* (Allegiance) 1984—*Paradox* (Attic, Can.) 1987—*Rock & Roll Rebels* (Qwil) 1990—*Rise and Shine* (I.R.S.) 1991—*Born to Be Wild—A Retrospective* (MCA) 1994—*Live at 25* (Era) 1996—*Feed the Fire* (Winter Harvest).
John Kay solo: 1972—*Forgotten Songs and Unsung Heroes* (Dunhill) 1973—*My Sportin' Life* 1978—*All in Good Time* (Mercury) 1987—*Lone Steppenwolf* 1997—*The Lost Heritage Tapes* (Macola).

Though tangentially identified with late-'60s West Coast psychedelia, Steppenwolf's music was uncompromising hard rock, and the term "heavy metal" was popularized in their first hit, "Born to Be Wild."

Leader John Kay, never seen without sunglasses in part due to the fact that he has been legally blind since childhood, escaped from East Germany to West Germany with his war-widowed mother in 1948. Ten years later he emigrated to Canada with his mother and stepfather. A gym teacher who could not pronounce "Joachim" informally rechristened him John; several years later he adopted the Kay surname. In 1963 Kay and his family moved to Buffalo, New York, then to Santa Monica, California, where Kay fell into the burgeoning folk-rock scene and appeared on his first record playing harmonica on a song called "The Frog." He played around the country as a folk singer, and in New York met Jerry Edmonton, of a popular Canadian group called the Sparrows, a group that included Bruce Palmer, who was later replaced by the bass player from Neil Young and Rick James' group the Mynah Birds, Nick St. Nicholas. In 1965 Kay joined the Sparrows, followed by another ex–Mynah Bird, Goldy McJohn. The group toured and recorded (including an early version of Hoyt Axton's "The Pusher") without success and eventually broke up. In 1968 ABC-Dunhill producer Gabriel Mekler encouraged Kay to re-form the group and offered them studio time to make demos. Jerry Edmonton's brother Dennis (a.k.a. Mars Bonfire) offered the group a song he'd written for his solo album, "Born to Be Wild." Opposed to reviving the Sparrow name, the group went with Mekler's suggestion, inspired by the Hermann Hesse novel he had just read: Steppenwolf.

Steppenwolf's hard rock won them favor with local audiences, and *Steppenwolf* (#6, 1968) yielded "Born to Be Wild" (#2, 1968). *The Second* yielded another massive hit single in "Magic Carpet Ride" (#3, 1968), and around the same time, "Born to Be Wild" and "The Pusher" were featured in the film *Easy Rider,* more or less solidifying Steppenwolf's enduring identification as a biker band. *At Your Birthday Party* (#7, 1969) continued the streak with "Rock Me" (from the film *Candy*) (#10, 1969). *Early Steppenwolf* (#29, 1969) consisted of older Steppenwolf demos. Despite having a tough image (Kay was never seen in anything but his shades and tight black leather pants), Steppenwolf, which by 1969 included two members whose families had escaped postwar Germany, was an unabashedly political band. Contrary to a popular rumor, Kay did not run for an L.A. city council seat or any other elected post. However, he was always regarded as a highly articulate and thoughtful spokesperson for his political beliefs, most clearly articulated on the critically blasted concept work *Monster* (#17, 1969). From this album came two singles: "Move Over" (#31, 1969) and the title track (#39, 1970). *Steppenwolf Live* (#7, 1970) contained the group's next-to-last Top 40 single, "Hey Lawdy Mama" (#35, 1970). Although the big hits stopped coming, Steppenwolf remained a popular live act here and abroad, and their later albums—*Steppenwolf 7* (#19, 1970), *Steppenwolf Gold/Their Greatest Hits* (#24, 1971), and *For Ladies Only* (#54, 1971)—fared respectably, despite a lack of focus and a series of personnel changes. In early 1972 the group announced its first breakup. Goldy McJohn formed a group called Damian, and later Manbeast. Edmonton worked with a band called Seven. By the first breakup, Kay had already formed the John Kay Band and recorded his first solo album, *Forgotten Songs and Unsung Heroes.* He had a minor hit single in 1972 with "I'm Movin' On."

Lack of success with their individual projects brought

Kay, Edmonton, and McJohn, along with latterday member George Biondi and Bobby Cochran (nephew of Eddie Cochran, he had worked with the Flying Burrito Brothers and Bob Weir) back together for *Slow Flux* (#47, 1974), which included "Straight Shootin' Woman" (#29, 1974), the group's last Top 40 single. McJohn departed soon after, and Andy Chapin (who would die in the plane crash that killed Rick Nelson) replaced him. When Chapin declined to go on the road, he was replaced by Wayne Cook. This lineup recorded *Hour of the Wolf,* the first album of new material in the group's history not to reach the Hot 100. Dispirited, Steppenwolf broke up again in 1976. Kay continued with a solo career, but reassumed leadership of a new Steppenwolf lineup in 1980. In the years between 1976 and 1980 several former members had toured with unprofessional, bogus versions of the group (Kay and Edmonton owned the name). Since then John Kay and Steppenwolf have recorded regularly and toured North America, Europe, and the Far East. The group has appeared at Farm Aids II and III. In 1989 Kay moved to Tennessee, where he now lives. In 1994 he published his autobiography, cowritten with John Einarson, *Magic Carpet Ride: The Autobiography of John Kay and Steppenwolf.*

Most of the former members of Steppenwolf have remained in the music business. McJohn performed in and around Seattle; St. Nicholas ran a management company and performed Christian rock; Monarch formed Detective and had a country songwriting duo, Stevens and Monarch; Byrom worked as a country sessionman. Rushton Moreve died in a car accident. Jerry Edmonton, who married the widow of former Steppenwolf member Andy Chapin, was also killed in a car wreck.

Stereolab

Formed 1990, London, Eng.
Tim Gane (b. July 12, 1964), gtr., kybds.; Laetitia (Seaya) Sadier (b. May 6, 1968, Fr.), voc., kybds.; Joe Dilworth, drums; Martin Kean, bass; Gina Morris, voc.
1992—*Switched On* (Too Pure); *Peng!; Lo-Fi* EP 1993—(– Dilworth; – Kean; – Morris; + Mary Hansen [b. Brisbane, Austral.], kybds., voc.; + Andy Ramsay, drums; + Sean O'Hagan, gtr.; + Duncan Brown, bass) *The Groop Played "Space Age Batchelor Pad Music"; Jenny Ondioline* EP (Duophonic); *Transient Random-Noise Bursts With Announcements* (Elektra) (– O'Hagan; + Katherine Gifford, kybds.) 1994—*Mars Audiac Quintet* 1995—*Music for the Amorphous Body Study Centre* EP (Duophonic); *Refried Ectoplasm Switched On Vol. II* (Drag City) (– Gifford; + Morgane Lhote, kybds.) 1996—*Emperor Tomato Ketchup* (Elektra) (– Brown; + Richard Harrison, bass) 1997—*Dots and Loops* 1998—*Aluminum Tunes (Switched On Vol. III)* (Drag City) 1999—(– Harrison; + Simon Johns, bass) *Cobra and Phases Group Play Voltage in the Milky Night* (Elektra) 2000—*The First of the Microbe Hunters* EP.

Following in the tradition of '70s kraut-rock bands Faust, Can, and particularly Neu!, England's Stereolab has based its career on the premise that, when it comes to music, less is definitely more. The group's songs stem from a few riffs—played on guitars, vintage Farfisa organs, and Moog synthesizers—repeated over and over. The resulting sound is not only mesmerizing but surprisingly warm and engaging, due in large part to Laetitia Sadier's voice, which sweetly rides atop her band's minimalist musings. The band is also known for its socialist leanings, as Sadier, who sings in both English and her native French and is often backed by longtime band mate Mary Hansen, usually imbues her lyrics with a leftwing political slant.

Stereolab has gone through numerous lineup changes during its prolific career; the only members who have been a constant presence since the band's formation are founders Sadier and Tim Gane. Gane met Sadier in Paris in 1989, at a gig headlined by his band, McCarthy, of whom Sadier was a fan. The two became romantically involved and, after Sadier moved from Paris to London, started Stereolab in 1991. Naming their group after a '50s record label dedicated to the promotion of the hi-fi, the duo released a few singles—some through mail order—of guitar- and vocal-generated droning. Their first three singles are compiled on 1992's *Switched On,* released the same year as their full-length debut, *Peng!* The band went through its first lineup switch prior to the recording of *The Groop Played "Space Age Batchelor Music";* new recruits keyboardist/backing vocalist Mary Hansen and drummer Andy Ramsay have remained part of the group ever since, while guitarist Sean O'Hagan, who also played on the band's first Elektra release, *Transient Random-Noise Bursts With Announcements,* still contributes as a guest collaborator.

In 1994 Stereolab was invited to play Lollapalooza, appearing on the touring festival's second stage. The following year, the group recorded *Music for the Amorphous Body Study Centre;* released on the band's own Duophonic label, the album was designed to accompany an exhibition of work by sculptor Charles Long. As the group moved into the second half of the decade, it started shifting musical directions somewhat, favoring poppier sounds over full-blown drone rock. European prog rock and avant-jazz popped up on its major-label debut, 1996's critically acclaimed *Emperor Tomato Ketchup.* Bossa nova and samba influenced the following year's *Dots and Loops.* Releasing *Cobra and Phases Group Play Voltage in the Milky Night* in 1999, after the birth of Gane and Sadier's first child, Stereolab ushered in 2000 with the EP *The First of the Microbe Hunters.*

Stetsasonic/Prince Paul/Daddy-O

Formed 1981, Brooklyn, NY
Daddy-O (b. Glenn Bolton, Feb. 20, 1961, Brooklyn), voc.; Delite (b. Martin Wright, Nov. 5, 1959, Queens, NY), voc.; Fruitkwan (b. Bobby Simmons, May 7, 1967, Brooklyn), voc.; Wise (b. Leonard Roman, Aug. 20, 1965, Brooklyn), voc., mixer; Prince Paul (b. Paul Huston, Apr. 2, 1967, Long Island, NY), mixer; DBC (b. Marvin Nemley, June 22, 1959), kybds., drums, turntable.

1986—*On Fire* (Tommy Boy) 1988—*Sally* EP; *In Full Gear* 1991—*Blood, Sweat & No Tears.*
Gravediggaz (Prince Paul, Fruitkwan, with RZA and Too Poetic): 1994—*Six Feet Deep* (Gee Street) 1997—*The Pick, the Sickle, & the Shovel* 1998—*Scenes From the Graveyard.*
Prince Paul solo: 1996—*Psychoanalysis: What Is It?!* (Wordsound) 1999—*A Prince Among Thieves* (Tommy Boy).
Handsome Boy Modeling School (Prince Paul with Dan "The Automator" Nakamura): 1999—*So . . . How's Your Girl?* (Tommy Boy).
Daddy-O solo: 1993—*You Can Be a Daddy, But Never a Daddy-O* (Island).

Calling itself "the one and only hip-hop band and the future of soul music," the six-piece Stetsasonic was an ambitious rap group boasting multiple vocalists, live drums, keyboards, and two full-time mixers—the first major hip-hop band to play its own instruments. Rappers Daddy-O and Delite formed the Stetson Brothers, named for the Stetson hat company, in 1982, and began performing at seminal New York hip-hop clubs. By 1984, they'd recruited Wise, Prince Paul, Fruitkwan, and DBC, changed the name to Stetsasonic, and begun work on 1986's *On Fire.* It took two years for the group to follow up with the critically acclaimed *In Full Gear,* which contained its sole hit single, "Sally" (#25 R&B, 1988). Stetsasonic hit its creative peak with *Blood, Sweat & No Tears,* but broke up shortly after its release. Leader Daddy-O continued producing (he mixed a song for rockers Sonic Youth) and released a solo album, *You Can Be a Daddy, But Never a Daddy-O,* in 1993.

Prince Paul went to work as producer of De La Soul during recording of that group's acclaimed 1989 debut, *3 Feet High and Rising,* and two followup albums. He also worked on recordings by Boogie Down Productions, Big Daddy Kane, and MC Lyte. In 1994 he formed the "horror-core" group Gravediggaz with RZA, Too Poetic, and ex-Stetsasonic member Fruitkwan, releasing *Six Feet Deep,* followed in 1997 by *The Pick, the Sickle, & the Shovel.* By then Prince Paul was a leading force in experimental, underground hip-hop, releasing the solo albums *Psychoanalysis: What Is It?!* (1996) and *A Prince Among Thieves* (1999). He also formed Handsome Boy Modeling School with DJ Dan "the Automator" Nakamura, releasing *So . . . How's Your Girl?* in 1999. Both Paul and the Automator then began a collaboration in 2000 with producer Mike Simpson of the Dust Brothers in a new group called the Good, the Bad and the Ugly.

Cat Stevens

Born Steven Demetri Georgiou (a.k.a. Yusef Islam), July 21, 1947, London, Eng.
1967—*Matthew and Son* (Deram) 1968—*New Masters* 1970—*World of* (Decca); *Mona Bone Jakon* (A&M); *Cats Cradle* (London) 1971—*Tea for the Tillerman* (A&M); *Teaser and the Firecat* 1972—*Very Young and Early Songs* (Deram); *Catch Bull at Four* (A&M) 1973—*Foreigner* 1974—*Buddah and the Chocolate Box* 1975—*Numbers; Greatest Hits* 1977—*Izitso* 1978—*Back to Earth* 1984—*Footsteps in the Dark—Greatest Hits, vol. 2* 1988—*Classics, vol. 24* 1995—*The Life of the Last Prophet* (Mountain of Light) (as Yusef Islam) 2000—*A Is for Allah* (as Yusef Islam); *The Very Best of Cat Stevens* (A&M).

Cat Stevens was one of the most successful singer/songwriters of the first half of the '70s, and several of his soft, romantic, and sometimes mystical singles were Top 10 hits. After eight gold albums in a row, his star began to fade, and in the late '70s, following a near-drowning, he converted to Islam, changed his name to Yusef Islam, and dropped out of music.

The son of a Greek father and Swedish mother, Stevens spent his early youth developing a love of Greek folk songs and dances. By the time he entered secondary school, he had also taken an interest in rock & roll and English and American folk music. While attending Hammersmith College in the mid-'60s, he began writing his own songs and performing solo.

In 1966 independent producer Mike Hurst (formerly with the Springfields) produced Stevens' first U.K. hit single, "I Love My Dog." In 1967 "Matthew and Son" went to #2 on the British chart. Meanwhile, Stevens' tunes were British hits for other performers as well. P.P. Arnold hit with "The First Cut Is the Deepest" (later covered by Rod Stewart), the Tremeloes with "Here Comes My Baby." Stevens toured England and Europe, becoming something of a teen idol, and shared bills with Jimi Hendrix and Engelbert Humperdinck, among others.

But Stevens became disenchanted with what he considered the shallowness of his ventures. After his 1968 hit "I'm Gonna Get Me a Gun" (#6 U.K.), he tried to work ambitious classical arrangements into his tunes, to his producers' cha-

Cat Stevens

grin. Stevens' career then came to a standstill when he contracted a near-fatal case of tuberculosis in late 1968 and was confined to a hospital for a year. He took that time to work on his new material, which was unveiled in *Mona Bone Jakon*, a critical success that yielded a British hit single in "Lady D'Arbanville" (#8 U.K., 1970) (purportedly about the actress Patti D'Arbanville). The muted accompaniment was by flutist Peter Gabriel (who would soon find his own fame in Genesis), percussionist Harvey Burns, and perennial Stevens collaborator guitarist Alun Davies.

Stevens' next album, *Tea for the Tillerman*, hit the U.S. Top 10 and stayed on the charts for well over a year, yielding the hit "Wild World." Stevens was now a highly successful concert performer as well. The next album was another hit; *Teaser and the Firecat* went to #3, then gold, and contained the hits "Morning Has Broken" (#6), "Peace Train" (#7), and "Moon Shadow" (#30). Though *Catch Bull at Four* and *Foreigner* were also certified gold, they yielded no big hits. At that time, unbeknownst to many of his fans, Stevens was living in Brazil, donating much of his earnings to charities such as UNESCO. With *Buddah and the Chocolate Box*, featuring "Oh Very Young" (#10), and *Numbers*, Stevens' sales dropped off.

In 1975 Stevens began studying the Koran and later converted to the Muslim religion. In late 1981 the rechristened Stevens announced, "I'm no longer seeking applause and fame," and auctioned off all his material possessions, including his gold records. By then he had married Fouzia Ali; as of the late '80s, they had five children, and he was running a Muslim school outside London. In 1987 10,000 Maniacs covered "Peace Train," and the following year Maxi Priest hit the U.K. Top 10 with a version of "Wild World." What might have grown into a Stevens revival, however, was nipped in 1989, when the media reported that the singer supported Iran's death-sentence condemnation of *Satanic Verses* author Salman Rushdie, whose book had blasphemed the Muslim faith. American radio stations observed an airplay boycott of Stevens' material; 10,000 Maniacs removed "Peace Train" from later pressings of the album on which it appeared.

In the mid-'90s Yusef Islam founded his own label, Mountain of Light, on which he released spoken-word albums. The double-CD *A Is for Allah* contains several songs for children in addition to spoken performances. In 2000 Islam, who has supported humanitarian efforts in Bosnia, oversaw the release of a Cat Stevens retrospective and resurfaced in the music press. He claims to have been unfairly vilified and misquoted about the Rushdie incident.

Al Stewart

Born Sep. 5, 1945, Glasgow, Scot.
1967—*Bedsitter Images* (Columbia, U.K.) 1969—*Love Chronicles* (Epic) 1970—*Zero She Flies* (Columbia, U.K.) 1972—*Orange* 1974—*Past, Present and Future* (Janus) 1975—*Modern Times* 1976—*The Year of the Cat* 1978—*Time Passages* (Arista) 1980—*24 Carrots* 1981—*Indian Summer Live* 1984—*Russians and Americans* (Passport) 1988—*Last Days of the Century* (Enigma) 1992—*Rhymes in Rooms* (Mesa) 1994—*Famous Last Words* 1995—*Between the Wars*.

British folk-rocker Al Stewart sold many records in the late '70s with a sound influenced by mid-period Dylan, and some distinctive name-dropping lyrics that focused on historical themes from Napoleonic invasions to Nostradamus.

Stewart, who moved to Bournemouth with his widowed mother when he was three, first played in rock bands in Bournemouth beginning at age 16. He bought his first guitar from future Police-man Andy Summers and got his first guitar lessons from Robert Fripp. But after hearing Bob Dylan, he started performing his own softer compositions at small London folk clubs in the mid-'60s. Of his first four albums, Columbia allowed only one to be released in the U.S., 1969's *Love Chronicles*. It featured Jimmy Page on guitar and was voted Folk Album of the Year by *Melody Maker*; it included a lengthy, explicit, confessional song about women Stewart had known.

Stewart signed with Janus Records in 1974 and released *Past, Present and Future*. Unlike his four previous LPs (which he's since repudiated) this record traded first-person love songs for historical sagas and received his first American FM airplay.

Modern Times improved the style with catchier melodies and harder-rocking music, helping it to reach the U.S. Top 30. His breakthrough came in late 1976 with the Alan Parsons–produced *The Year of the Cat*. The title single became a Top 10 hit, and the LP went platinum. Stewart then switched to Arista, sparking a complicated lawsuit.

With Parsons again in the studio, *Time Passages* went Top 10 and platinum. Despite two more Top 30 singles, "Song on the Radio" (1979) and "Midnight Rocks" (1980), subsequent LPs were commercial disappointments. Through the '80s, Stewart released only two more albums, though he toured intermittently and apparently devoted a great deal of time to collecting wine (for which he has received numerous awards). *Rhymes in Rooms* is a live recording from 1988. *Famous Last Words* (1993) makes use of traditional folk and classical styles, while *Between the Wars* (1995) draws inspiration from the '20s and '30s.

Billy Stewart

Born Mar. 24, 1937, Washington, DC; died Jan. 17, 1970, NC
1982—*The Greatest* (Chess) 1988—*One More Time* 2000—*The Millennium Collection*.

Billy Stewart qualifies as a unique entry in that he is rock's only high-powered scat man (hence his nickname "Motormouth"), using his outrageous trill to rip the stuffing out of such standards as "Summertime," "Secret Love" and "Every Day I Have the Blues" (#74, 1967).

The son of a piano teacher who had her own gospel group, the Stewart Gospel Singers (Billy was a member during his late teens), he won an amateur contest in Washington with a rendition of "Summertime." This led to club bookings and later to his discovery by Bo Diddley, with whose band he played for two years. Meanwhile he cut his first single, "Billy's Blues (Parts 1 and 2)," and later sang with the Rainbows, who included in their quartet Don Covay.

Stewart then signed with the Okeh label (he is included on 1982's *Okeh Rhythm and Blues* compilation with "Baby, You're My Only Life"). In 1961 he returned to Chess, and in 1966 he hit the Top 100 (his sixth entry) with the scorching version of George Gershwin's "Summertime" (#10), from *Porgy and Bess,* followed that same year by his equally dynamic cover of Fain and Webster's "Secret Love" (#29). Four years later, he and two members of his band were killed when their car plunged into the Neuse River in North Carolina.

Dave Stewart: See Eurythmics

John Stewart

Born Sep. 5, 1939, San Diego, CA
1968—*Signals Through the Glass* (Capitol) 1969—*California Bloodlines* 1970—*Willard* 1971—*The Lonesome Picker Rides Again* (Warner Bros.) 1972—*Sunstorm* 1973—*Cannons in the Rain* (RCA) 1974—*Phoenix Concerts Live* 1975—*Wingless Angels* 1977—*Fire in the Wind* (RSO) 1979—*Bombs Away Dream Babies* 1980—*Dream Babies Go Hollywood; In Concert* (RCA); *Forgotten Songs* 1984—*Centennial* (Homecoming) 1985—*The Last Campaign* 1986—*Secret Tapes '86* 1987—*Trio Years* (with Nick Reynolds); *Punch the Big Guy* (Shanachie) 1991—*Neon Beach, Live 1990* (Homecoming); *Deep in the Noon* 1992—*Bullets in the Hour Glass* (Shanachie) 1993—*Chilly Winds* (Folk Era); *John Stewart: American Originals* (Capitol) 1995—*Airdream Believer* (Shanachie) 1997—*Rough Sketches* (Homecoming) 1999—*John Stewart & Darwin's Army* (Appleseed).

Despite a fairly successful solo career, singer/songwriter John Stewart is probably best remembered as the composer of the Monkees' hit "Daydream Believer" and as a member of the Kingston Trio [see entry].

At Pomona College in the mid-'50s, Frank Zappa taught Stewart the chords to "Streets of Laredo." Stewart went on to form a garage-rock band, the Furies, who recorded a single in the late '50s. Two of Stewart's tunes had been recorded by the Kingston Trio, and when the trio's manager, Frank Werber, told Stewart he was looking for a similar act to sign, Stewart formed the Cumberland Three, which included his former glee-club teacher, Gil Robbins. In July 1961 Stewart replaced Dave Guard in the Kingston Trio, staying on as a salaried member until 1967. Before leaving, Stewart had tried unsuccessfully to form a band with John Phillips (later of the Mamas and the Papas) and Scott McKenzie. He had also formed a short-lived duo with John Denver before either had gained any fame.

"Daydream Believer" (1967) spurred Stewart on to a solo career. His debut LP flopped commercially, but *Bloodlines,* recorded in Nashville, received some critical acclaim and fared slightly better.

Despite his general lack of commercial success, Stewart has maintained pockets of loyal cultists around the country, especially in Phoenix, where his live LP was recorded in 1974. He finally had some success in 1979 with *Bombs Away Dream Babies,* produced by Lindsey Buckingham and featuring Stevie Nicks on backing vocals on the hit single "Gold," which went to #5 in the U.S. Stewart's subsequent Top 40 singles were "Midnight Wind" (#28, 1979), which also featured Buckingham and Nicks, and "Lost Her in the Sun" (#34, 1980). Stewart continues to write, record, and perform. He founded his own label, Homecoming. *Trio Years* features new version of Kingston Trio songs. Some of his '90s work is more electric in its approach.

Rod Stewart

Born Roderick David Stewart, Jan. 10, 1945, London, Eng.
1969—*The Rod Stewart Album* (Mercury) 1970—*Gasoline Alley* 1971—*Every Picture Tells a Story* 1972—*Never a Dull Moment* 1973—*Sing It Again Rod* 1974—*Smiler* 1975—*Atlantic Crossing* (Warner Bros.) 1976—*A Night on the Town; The Best of Rod Stewart* (Mercury) 1977—*The Best of Rod Stewart, vol. 2; Foot Loose and Fancy Free* (Warner Bros.) 1978—*Blondes Have More Fun* 1979—*Greatest Hits* 1980—*Foolish Behaviour* 1981—*Tonight I'm Yours* 1982—*Absolutely Live* 1983—*Body Wishes* 1984—*Camouflage* 1986—*Rod Stewart* 1988—*Out of Order* 1990—*Storyteller: The Complete Anthology: 1964–1990* 1991—*Vagabond Heart* 1992—*The Mercury Anthology* (Polydor) 1993—*Unplugged . . . and Seated* (Warner Bros.); *Vintage* (Polydor) 1995—*A Spanner in the Works* (Warner Bros.) 1996—*If We Fall in Love Tonight* 1998—*When We Were the New Boys* 2001—*Human.*

Gritty-voiced singer and sometime songwriter Rod Stewart earned the tag "vocals extraordinaire" during his first stint with the Jeff Beck Group, and maintained it during his subsequent tenure with the Faces and his commercially more successful solo career. After garnering initial critical acclaim for his unerring choice of cover material, Stewart in the late '70s became known as a jet-setting bon vivant and bottled-blond sex symbol, always a stellar live performer but often indulging in self-parody on his albums. While his later work failed to live up to his early promise, his self-mocking charm and seemingly effortless but heartfelt vocal style have survived. In 1994 he was inducted into the Rock and Roll Hall of Fame.

The son of a Scottish shopkeeper, Stewart was born and raised in London but considers himself a Scot. After a short stint as an apprentice to a pro soccer team, Stewart joined a series of London bands—Jimmy Powell and the Five Dimensions, the Hoochie Coochie Men, Steampacket, and Shotgun Express. In 1967 Jeff Beck enlisted Stewart as vocalist for the Jeff Beck Group. Beck was especially popular in America, where the new group first toured in 1968. Petrified by the first-night audience at New York's Fillmore East, Stewart sang the opening number from backstage. *Truth* (1968) and *Beck-Ola* (1969), established Stewart as a rough-and-ready rock & roll vocal stylist.

In 1969 while still with Beck, Stewart signed a contract with Mercury. His solo debut, *The Rod Stewart Album* (#139, 1969), was recorded with Mick Waller and Ron Wood of the Jeff Beck Group, plus Small Faces keyboardist Ian McLagan and guitarist Martin Quittenton. Stewart's material was a grab bag of gentle folk songs, bawdy drinking songs, a taste of soul, and a couple of barrelhouse rockers. The album sold modestly—Jeff Beck Group fans considered it too subdued—but critics were impressed by Stewart's five original songs. Planning to form a new band with Stewart and the Vanilla Fudge's Tim Bogert and Carmine Appice, Beck disbanded his group. That project finally materialized in 1972, long after Stewart and his buddy Wood had joined the Small Faces, soon redubbed the Faces. Stewart spent the next seven years dividing his time between that band and a solo career, recording a Faces album for each of his own.

In 1970 the Small Faces recorded *First Step,* Stewart recorded *Gasoline Alley* (#27, 1970), and together they toured the United States twice. In the studio with the Faces, Stewart was but one of a quintet of equals merrily banging out rock & roll. On his own, he was different; the moody *Gasoline Alley* amplified his reputation as a sensitive, emotionally compelling singer and storyteller. When *Every Picture Tells a Story* came out in June 1971, the response was swift and strong. In October, the album was simultaneously #1 in America and Britain, the first record to do so. Its first single, "Maggie May," a Stewart-Quittenton song, was the second record to do the same. Before "Maggie May" had faded, Stewart followed up with a gritty version of the Temptations' "(I Know) I'm Losing You" (#24, 1971). *Never a Dull Moment* (#2, 1972), with his own "You Wear It Well" (#13, 1972), was also a hit.

With two gold albums, Stewart's role in the Faces became strained. Late in 1974, Mercury released *Smiler* (#13, 1974), Stewart's last album for the label. Stewart hired veteran American producer Tom Dowd and Muscle Shoals session musicians to record his Warner Bros. debut, *Atlantic Crossing* (#9, 1975). In 1975 he moved to L.A. to escape British income taxes and was soon the toast of the Beverly Hills celebrity set. Stewart retained Dowd and the American studio musicians for the double-platinum *A Night on the Town* (#2, 1976), his first effort to outsell *Every Picture,* largely on the strength of the biggest single of 1976, "Tonight's the Night (Gonna Be Alright)," which topped the U.S. chart for eight weeks.

The Faces had by now fallen apart, and Wood was a full-fledged Rolling Stone. Stewart formed a new, American touring band. The hits kept coming: raunchy rockers like "Hot Legs" (#28, 1978), romantic ballads like "You're in My Heart (The Final Acclaim)" (#4, 1977), and even a #1 disco hit with "Da Ya Think I'm Sexy?" (1979) from the #1 LP *Blondes Have More Fun,* which eventually sold 4 million copies. Of his '80s albums, *Foolish Behavior, Tonight I'm Yours,* and *Out of Order* all went platinum, and Stewart released Top 10 singles throughout the decade, among them, "Passion" (#5, 1980), "Infatuation" (#6, 1984), "My Heart Can't Tell You No" (#4, 1988), and "Downtown Train" (#3, 1989).

Just as his major hits covered the topics of love and sex, Stewart's penchant for youthful blond trophy wives is also well known. After a much publicized liaison with Britt Ekland, Stewart got married for the first time in 1979 to George Hamilton's ex, Alana, with whom he had two children. Following their divorce, Stewart took up with model Kelly Emberg and had a child with her. In 1990 he tied the knot with Australian supermodel Rachel Hunter, with whom he fathered two more kids. That marriage also ended in divorce.

In 1986 Stewart and a re-formed Faces gathered for a performance at a London benefit for Faces' bassist Ronnie Lane, who had developed multiple sclerosis. *Out of Order* (#20, 1989), coproduced by Chic's Bernard Edwards and former Duran Duran guitarist Andy Taylor, was better received than much of his '80s output, boosting a revival in Stewart's critical reputation that blossomed with the 1990 career overview, *Storyteller.* The next year he released *Vagabond Heart* (#10, 1991), his highest charting album since *Blondes.* The #1 single from the movie *The Three Musketeers,* "All for Love" (1994), featured vocals from Bryan Adams, Sting, and Stewart.

Stewart played MTV's *Unplugged* show with Ron Wood joining him, resulting in 1993's multiplatinum *Unplugged . . . and Seated* (#2). That year also, he again rejoined the Faces for a show at the BRIT Awards, at which he received a Lifetime Achievement Award. While Stewart in the '90s sold all his future royalties to a Wall Street firm for $15 million, his commercial success was haphazard. The acoustic-oriented *A Spanner in the Works* (1995) only went gold and didn't yield a Top 40 single, while platinum sales returned with 1996's *If We Fall in Love Tonight* (#19). *When We Were the New Boys,* with edgy fare by Oasis and Primal Scream, was Stewart's self-produced, critically hailed 1998 return to his rocking roots. Soon after, he underwent throat surgery to remove a cancerous nodule on his thyroid gland. "Faith of My Heart" from the *Patch Adams* soundtrack, exemplified his later, smoother style and scored in the Top 10 on Adult Contemporary radio in 1999. His 2001 release, *Human,* a foray into contemporary soul, debuted on the *Billboard* chart at #50.

Stephen Stills: See Buffalo Springfield; Crosby, Stills, Nash and Young

Sting

Born Gordon Matthew Sumner, Oct. 2, 1951, Newcastle-upon-Tyne, Eng.

1985—*The Dream of the Blue Turtles* (A&M) 1986—*Bring On the Night* 1987—*. . . Nothing Like the Sun* 1988—*Nada Como el Sol* EP 1991—*The Soul Cages* 1993—*Ten Summoner's Tales; Demolition Man* soundtrack 1994—*Fields of Gold: The Best of Sting* 1996—*Mercury Falling* 1997—*The Very Best of Sting & the Police* 1999—*Brand New Day* (Interscope).

Having achieved stardom as singer, bassist, and principal songwriter for the Police [see entry], Sting dissolved that band at the peak of its career in the mid-'80s. Sting's solo career is characterized by a restless yen to experiment, and, by pop standards, take risks. He has sought to push the canny musicianship and affinity for exotic musical styles that distinguished his former group in directions that a trio could never have considered. Consequently, some have lamented the absence of the Police's striking economy, just as they've found Sting's literary and historical references pretentious. To his admirers, though, Sting's post-Police projects have ensured his place among the most articulate and intuitive rock musicians of his generation. Sting has recorded more albums as a solo artist than he did with the Police, and his total sales as a solo artist have surpassed that group's total as well.

For his first solo effort, *The Dream of the Blue Turtles* (#2, 1985), Sting enlisted a group of young jazz musicians, including saxophonist Branford Marsalis and Weather Report drummer Omar Hakim. The album was widely viewed as a reclamation of the musical turf Sting had covered while playing in jazz ensembles during his youth. But *Turtles* also drew on elements of classical music, funk, and, perhaps most predictably, reggae. Moreover, the hit songs "If You Love Somebody Set Them Free" (#3, 1985) and "Fortress Around Your Heart" (#8, 1985) were as pop-savvy as any Police singles. The 1986 concert album and documentary *Bring On the Night* featured the players that Sting had assembled for *Turtles* offering live renditions of his new songs, as well as fresh takes on a few Police favorites. *. . . Nothing Like the Sun* (#9, 1987), released shortly after Sting's mother died and dedicated to her, featured a revised, expanded lineup of musicians dominated by Marsalis' saxophone. As on *Turtles,* Sting often played guitar rather than his primary instrument, bass. A moody album full of dense, delicate orchestration, *Sun* spawned only one Top 10 single, the atypically funky "We'll Be Together" (#7, 1987). (The album fared well in South America, though, thanks in part to its various Latin-flavored instrumental touches; hence the EP *Nada Como el Sol,* featuring tracks from *Sun* rendered in Spanish.)

The Soul Cages, inspired by Sting's father's death, was darker still, full of haunted ballads, religious imagery, and traditional English folk flourishes that embellished a newly spare foundation provided by guitarist Dominic Miller, keyboardist David Sancious, drummer Vinnie Colaiuta, and Sting on bass. Again, an anomaly proved the one big hit: the upbeat "All This Time" went to #5. (On that single's strength, the album peaked at #2.) Sting unexpectedly shifted gears for 1993's breezy, buoyant *Ten Summoner's Tales* (#2), which featured the same core of musicians who had appeared on *Cages.* The album went triple platinum, yielding the hits "If I Ever Lose My Faith in You" (#17, 1993) (which also won a Grammy) and "Fields of Gold" (#23, 1993). That same year, Sting shared a #1 megahit single with Bryan Adams and Rod Stewart, "All for Love," from the film *The Three Musketeers.* An anthology, *Fields of Gold,* was released in 1994, featuring two previously unreleased tracks.

Sting released *Mercury Falling* (#5) in 1996; although a few singles were released from the album—notably "Let Your Soul Be Your Pilot" (#86), "You Still Touch Me" (#60), and "I'm So Happy I Can't Stop Crying" (#94)—the album as a whole was more successful than any one song. For the accompanying tour, Sting commuted to his concerts via private jet from one of his three homes so he would have more time to spend with his growing brood, including his sixth child (his fourth with his second wife, film producer Trudie Styler), an infant son. Another greatest-hits compilation was released in 1997, this one combining his solo material with Police hits.

An album of new material, *Brand New Day* (#9, 2000), followed in 1999. The title track was moderately popular on radio, but the song "Desert Rose"—released as a single nearly a year after the album and featuring Arabic backup vocals by Algerian singer Cheb Mami—was a surging success (perhaps helped by its use in a luxury car commercial) reaching #17 and pushing the album to double-platinum status in 2000. Even before the song reached its peak, Mami was snagged as the opening act on Sting's *Brand New Day* tour, giving him Western exposure and allowing him to support Sting on the song during the headliner's set. A critical success, the album also earned two Grammys, for Pop Album of the Year and Best Male Pop Vocal Performance for its title song. With David Hartley, Sting wrote several songs for the 2000 Disney animated children's feature *The Emperor's New Groove.* In the process, he had creative differences with the Disney people, which were captured on film by Styler for the "making-of" documentary *The Sweatbox.*

Equally unpredictable outside the studio, Sting has made numerous film appearances (including *Dune, Stormy Monday, Plenty, Gentlemen Don't Eat Poets,* and *Lock, Stock and Two Smoking Barrels*) and in 1989 starred in a Broadway revival of *The Threepenny Opera.* Four years later he opened a series of stadium shows for the Grateful Dead. What's remained constant is his devotion to human-rights and environmental issues. In the late '80s he not only toured with other stars to benefit Amnesty International, but also helped establish the Rainforest Foundation, and has since crusaded to raise funds and awareness on behalf of the preservation of this endangered Brazilian territory, in part with an annual all-star benefit concert, co-organized by Styler, in New York City.

The Stone Roses

Formed 1985, Manchester, Eng.
Ian George Brown (b. Feb. 20, 1963, Manchester), voc.; John Thomas Squire (b. Nov. 24, 1962, Manchester), gtr.; Andy

Couzens, gtr.; Pete Garner, bass; Reni (b. Alan John Wren, Apr. 10, 1964, Manchester), drums.
1987—(– Couzens; – Garner; + Mani [b. Gary Michael Mountfield, Nov. 16, 1962, Manchester], bass) 1989—*The Stone Roses* (Silvertone) 1995—*Second Coming* (Geffen); *The Complete Stone Roses* (Silvertone) (– Reni; + Robbie Maddix, drums; + Nigel Ippinson, kybds.).

The story of the Stone Roses is one of unfulfilled promise. An overnight success in England with its debut album, the Stone Roses went from playing small clubs in the mid-'80s to massive stadiums by decade's end, with their faces appearing all over the U.K. music papers. The quartet received little more than cursory attention in the U.S., primarily for their role as the most celebrated combo of Manchester's mid-'80s psychedelic rave scene. The Roses' blend of Byrds-like chiming guitars with an updated, Smiths-style pop sensibility garnered critical acclaim. By 1990, however, legal problems had slowed their momentum. After winning freedom from their original label, Silvertone, the Roses landed a reported $4 million deal with Geffen in the U.S., finally returning at the end of 1994 with the disappointing *Second Coming,* before breaking up for good.

Ian Brown, an idealistic blend of beatnik, hippie, anarchist, and punk rocker, came together with self-taught painter John Squire in the early '80s. The two formed a punk band called the Patrol, which became the Stone Roses in 1985. After a couple of singles, the Roses teamed up with producer John Leckie, who helped shape their signature psychedelic pop sound. The group signed with Silvertone in 1988 and put out a single, "Elephant Stone," which reached #8 on the U.K. charts in March 1990. Following the release of their debut album, *The Stone Roses* (#19 U.K., 1989; #86 U.S., 1990), the band had a string of U.K. hits, including "What the World Is Waiting For/Fool's Gold" (#8 U.K., 1989), "Made of Stone" (#20 U.K., 1990), "She Bangs the Drums" (#34 U.K., 1990), "One Love" (#4 U.K., 1990), "I Wanna Be Adored" (#20 U.K., 1991), "Waterfall" (#27 U.K., 1992), and "I Am the Resurrection" (#33 U.K., 1992).

In 1990 members of the band vandalized the offices of Revolver Records after that label reissued old material without their permission. The case got major attention in the U.K. press. Meanwhile, the Roses were back in court later that year when they tried to leave Silvertone for Geffen; the group won the case but lost more career momentum. The band then spent the next two years sporadically recording, slowed during early sessions by drug use. Their comeback album, *Second Coming* (released in England in late 1994), lived up to its name, attracting U.K. media attention and peaking at #4 in England. It failed to ignite wide interest in the U.S (reaching #49), and even at home the Stone Roses were no longer as irresistible. The band's own public arrogance and the arrival of such newer British rock acts as Oasis effectively dimmed whatever appeal remained.

The Stone Roses toured briefly in the U.S. and England, but in 1996 Squire quit the group and reemerged the next year heading the Seahorses. The Stone Roses continued on for another six months but called it quits after a performance at the Reading Festival where Brown appeared visibly drunk. Brown embarked on his own solo career, releasing an album in 1998. The singer then spent two months in a Manchester prison after arguing with a flight attendant. In jail he wrote songs that would be released as 2000's *Golden Greats* album.

Stone Temple Pilots

Formed 1987 (as Mighty Joe Young), San Diego, CA
Scott Weiland (b. Oct. 27, 1967, Santa Cruz, CA), voc.; Dean DeLeo (b. Aug. 23, 1961, NJ), gtr.; Robert DeLeo (b. Feb. 2, 1966, NJ), bass; Eric Kretz (b. June 7, 1966, Santa Cruz), drums.
1992—*Core* (Atlantic) 1994—*Purple* 1996—*Tiny Music . . . Songs From the Vatican Gift Shop* 1999—*No. 4* 2001—*Shangri-La Dee Da.*
Scott Weiland solo: 1998—*12 Bar Blues* (Atlantic).
Talk Show (D. DeLeo; R. DeLeo; Kretz; + Dave Coutts, voc.): 1997—*Talk Show* (Atlantic).

In the wake of the success of the Seattle sound, Stone Temple Pilots emerged in the early '90s with a hard-rock approach that drew heavily on the influence of earlier guitar bands from Led Zeppelin to Blue Cheer. With their debut, *Core,* going platinum shortly after its release, they stirred controversy with "Sex Type Thing," a single about date rape and a stylistic approach that some critics felt drew too heavily on Pearl Jam's. Later, the controversy shifted to frontman Scott Weiland's battle to check a career-threatening heroin addiction.

Having met at a Black Flag concert in the late '80s, singer Weiland and guitarist Robert DeLeo founded Mighty Joe Young to purvey a sound combining heavy-metal–derived guitar with punk brashness; they changed the group's name to Shirley Temple's Pussy before deciding on Stone Temple Pilots. Signing to Atlantic and making the triple-platinum *Core* (#3, 1993) with producer Brendan O'Brien (the Black Crowes, the Red Hot Chili Peppers), they soon gained heavy MTV exposure and, while decrying the "grunge" label, found themselves in the same sales league as Nirvana and Pearl Jam. The single "Plush," which hit #9 on the Modern Rock tracks chart, continued their commercial ascension. Their followup album, *Purple,* debuted at #1 and featured the #1 album rock hits "Vasoline" and "Interstate Love Song." But the band's momentum hit the skids as Weiland fell headlong into a heroin addiction. An arrest in 1995 landed him in rehab for several months and forced the band to cancel a summer tour in support of its third album, the power pop–inspired *Tiny Music . . . Songs From the Vatican Gift Shop* (#4, 1996). They attempted to tour again in fall 1996 and the following spring but had to cancel both times when Weiland relapsed.

While Weiland went in and out of rehab, the rest of the band staved off frustration by recruiting singer Dave Coutts (from the Long Beach, California, band Ten Inch Men) and recording an album as Talk Show. Released in the fall of 1997, it stalled at #131. The following spring, Weiland released his own solo album, *12 Bar Blues* (#42, 1998), but his tour was derailed after a drug arrest (his third) later that year.

STP reconvened in 1999 to record their fourth album, *No.*

4, but by the time of the album's release in October, Weiland was behind bars. He was sentenced to a year in prison in September after surviving a near-fatal overdose—it was his third parole violation following a 1997 conviction in California. He was released in December after serving a little less than half of his sentence. With Weiland determined to stay clean (and free), STP hit the road again in 2000.

Stone the Crows

Formed 1969, Glasgow, Scot.
Maggie Bell (b. Jan. 12, 1945, Scot.), voc.; Les Harvey (b. ca. 1947; d. May 3, 1972, Swansea, Wales), gtr.; Jon McGinnis, kybds.; Jim Dewar (b. Oct. 12, 1946), bass; Colin Allen, drums. 1970—*Stone the Crows* (Polydor); *Ode to John Law* 1971—(– Dewar; – McGinnis; + Steve Thompson, bass; + Ronnie Leahy, kybds.) *Teenage Licks* 1972—(+ Jimmy McCulloch [b. June 4, 1952, Glasgow; d. Sep. 27, 1979, London, Eng.], gtr.) *'Ontinuous Performance.*
Maggie Bell solo: 1973—*Queen of the Night* (Atlantic) 1975—*Suicide Sal* (Swansong).

A Scottish-English soul band, Stone the Crows (the name comes from a Scottish curse meaning "the hell with it") is perhaps most significant for introducing Maggie Bell, a blues singer in the style of Janis Joplin, who went on to a solo career.

Young Maggie Bell had gotten onstage to sing in Glasgow with Alex Harvey (who in the early '70s led the Sensational Alex Harvey Band), earning £2. Harvey introduced her to his brother Les, who was leading the Kinning Park Ramblers. Within a few years Bell and Les Harvey were leading Power, which played clubs and U.S. Army bases in Europe. When Led Zeppelin manager Peter Grant discovered them, he renamed them Stone the Crows. Their first two albums were critically acclaimed but sold few copies.

Jim Dewar eventually left to join ex–Procol Harum guitarist Robin Trower, and Steve Thompson was recruited from John Mayall; with *Teenage Licks* the band seemed on the verge of success. In 1972 Bell won Britain's Top Girl Singer Award for the first of many times, but that year also saw Les Harvey electrocuted by a microphone wire during a show at Swansea University. Jimmy McCulloch came in to finish the sessions for *'Ontinuous,* but the band soon broke up. McCulloch later joined Paul McCartney's Wings and, after that, the re-formed Small Faces; he died of undetermined causes. Bell released several solo LPs. She also did a lot of session work, including Rod Stewart's *Every Picture Tells a Story.* Colin Allen went on to join Focus, and Dewar moved on to Robin Trower's band.

The Stooges: See Iggy Pop

Stories

Formed 1972, New York, NY
Michael Brown (b. Apr. 25, 1949, Brooklyn, NY), kybds., voc.; Steve Love, gtr., voc.; Ian Lloyd (b. Ian Buoncocglio, 1947, Seattle, WA), bass, voc., kybds.; Bryan Madey, drums, voc. 1972—*Stories* (Kama Sutra) 1973—(– Brown; + Kenny Aaronson [b. Apr. 14, 1952, Brooklyn], bass; + Ken Bichel [b. 1945, Detroit, MI], kybds.) *About Us; Traveling Underground* 1974—(– Madey; + Rick Ranno, drums).

Formed by ex–Left Banke mentor Michael Brown, Stories had a #1 hit in 1973 with "Brother Louie." The tune was written by Errol Brown of British soul group Hot Chocolate, who released a competing version of it in 1973.

Brown left before their second LP to become the guiding spirit, writer, and producer of the Beckies (though he never actually performed with them). Bassist Kenny Aaronson went on to work with Hall and Oates, Leslie West, Rick Derringer, Billy Squier, and the supergroup Hagar, Schon, Aaronson, Shrieve. Lloyd pursued a solo career. During a session for one of his albums, musician Mick Jones met fellow sessionman Ian MacDonald, and the pair went on to form Foreigner. Lloyd has since appeared on albums by Foreigner, Peter Frampton, and others. Madey joined the Earl Slick band, and his replacement, Rick Ranno, was later in the group Starz.

The Strangeloves

Formed 1965, Brooklyn, NY
Richard Gottehrer; Robert Feldman; Jerry Goldstein.
1965—*I Want Candy* (Bang).

The Strangeloves' big hit was 1965's "I Want Candy" (#11). The song was treated to some bizarre versions in the early '80s by Lydia Lunch's 8 Eyed Spy and Bow Wow Wow. The Strangeloves were originally a studio-based writer-production trio, and even worked on some outside projects while they were recording their own band. Before they'd taken their name and become a group, they worked for the Angels (creating "My Boyfriend's Back") and the McCoys ("Hang On Sloopy"). Posing as brothers Miles, Niles, and Giles Strange, the three used fake Australian accents and actually convinced everyone they met that they indeed hailed from Down Under. They had two Top 40 followups, "Night Time" (#30, 1966) and "Cara-Lin" (#39, 1965.) After 1966 the band broke up, and each member went back to full-time producing. Richard Gottehrer became a partner in Sire Records in 1970, and along with the two other original Strangeloves recorded unsuccessfully for the label under the name the Strange Brothers Show. In 1976 he produced the debut Blondie LP and in 1981 he coproduced the Go-Go's' first album. Feldman worked with, among others, Jay and the Americans and Johnny Mathis.

The Stranglers

Formed Sep. 1974, Guildford, Eng.
Jet Black (b. Brian Duffy, Aug. 26, 1958, Ilford, Eng.), drums; Jean-Jacques Burnel (b. Feb. 21, 1952, London, Eng.), bass;

Hugh Cornwell (b. Aug. 28, 1949, London), gtr., voc.; Dave Greenfield (b. Mar. 29, 1949, Brighton, Eng.), kybds.
1977—*IV: Rattus Norvegicus* (A&M); *No More Heroes* 1978—*Black and White* 1979—*The Raven* (United Artists, U.K.) 1980—*IV* (I.R.S.) 1981—*The Meninblack* (EMI America); *La Folie* 1982—*Feline* (Epic) 1984—*Aural Sculpture* 1986—*Dreamtime* 1988—*All Live and All of the Night* 1990—*10* (– Cornwell; + John Ellis [b. June 1, 1952, London], gtr.; + Paul Roberts [b. Dec. 31, 1959, London], voc.) 1991—*Greatest Hits 1977–1990* 1993—*Stranglers in the Night* (Viceroy) 1995—(– Tobe; + Black) *About Time* (When?, U.K.) 1997—*Written in Red* 1999—*Coup de Grace* (Festival, U.K.).
Jean-Jacques Burnel solo: 1979—*Euroman Cometh* (United Artists, U.K.) 1988—*Un jour parfait* (Epic, Fr.).
Hugh Cornwell solo: 1979—*Nosferatu* (United Artists, U.K.) 1988—*Wolf* (Virgin) 1999—*Black Hair Black Eyes Black Suit* (Velvel); *First Bus to Babylon* 2000—*Hi Fi* (Koch).

Armed with a nasty misogynist temperament and an aggressive musical attack, the Stranglers are usually classified as a punk band, even though their keyboard-heavy sound—and birth dates—have more in common with rock's previous generation. While never popular in the States, they were hugely successful in the U.K. with 15 Top 40 hits (seven in the Top 10), including "Peaches/Go Buddy Go" (#8 U.K., 1977) and "Golden Brown" (#2 U.K., 1982).

Their background *was* unusual for a punk band: They were formed in 1974 as the Guildford Stranglers by Cornwell, a science teacher; Black, an ice cream salesman and sometimes jazz drummer; and Burnel, an English-born son of French immigrants and a history major. In 1975, calling themselves a "soft-rock group," the trio placed an ad in *Melody Maker* that was answered by Greenfield. After a year of club dates the band, now simply the Stranglers, got its break opening for Patti Smith at London's Roundhouse, followed by a national tour. The exposure led to their signing with United Artists in Britain and A&M in the States.

While Greenfield's swirling keyboards and Cornwell's portentous vocals on *IV Rattus Norvegicus* (#4 U.K., 1977) (the biological name for the Norway rat, the band mascot) and *No More Heroes* (#8 U.K., 1977) left critics comparing the band to the Doors, their attitude placed them squarely in the punk camp: "Peaches" was banned by the BBC for offensive lyrics, and the Greater London Council pulled the plug on a 1977 show when Cornwell appeared on stage in a "Fuck" T-shirt. The entire band was arrested in Nice, France, for inciting a riot when a 1980 concert was canceled.

Failing to make a commercial dent in the U.S., the Stranglers were dropped by A&M after *Black & White*. Their lack of a U.S. label caused *The Raven*, a #4 U.K. hit, to go unreleased stateside until 1986. In 1983, after abortive contracts with two other labels, they signed with Epic. Attempts to soften their sound culminated in *Dreamtime* (#172, 1987), their only U.S. chart album.

Cornwell (who had already recorded solo sets while still in the band) left the Stranglers after *10* and released a handful of albums in the late '80s; some of that material was collected on the American release *Black Hair Black Eyes Black Suit*.

Except for a greatest-hits collection in 1991, nothing was heard from the rest of the band until 1993, when Burnel, Black, and Greenfield were joined by singer Paul Roberts and ex-Vibrators guitarist John Ellis on *Stranglers in the Night* and hit the comeback trail. The band still plays out regularly (even venturing down to a British Army base in the Falklands in 1997) and survived yet another personnel change when Ellis was replaced by Baz Warne in March 2000.

The Strawberry Alarm Clock

Formed 1967, Santa Barbara, CA
Ed King, gtr., voc.; Lee Freeman, gtr., bass, horns, drums, voc.; Mark Weitz, kybds.; Gary Lovetro, bass, voc.; George Bunnel, bass, special effects; Randy Seol, drums, voc.
1967—*Incense and Peppermints* (Uni) 1968—(– Lovetro) *Wake Up, It's Tomorrow; The World in a Sea Shell* 1969—(– Seol; – Bunnel; + Jimmy Pitman, gtr., voc.; + Gene Gunnels, drums) *Good Morning Starshine* 1970—*The Best of the Strawberry Alarm Clock* (– Pitman; – Weitz; + Paul Marshall, gtr., voc.) 1971—*Changes* (Vocalion).

This early psychedelic rock band surfaced in 1967 with the #1 hit and flower-power anthem "Incense and Peppermints." Though it would fade quickly from view, the band was renowned for its psychedelic stage show (drummer Randy Seol played bongos with his hands on fire) and for the presence of two bassists. Guitarist Ed King later resurfaced with Lynyrd Skynyrd.

The group's roots go back to King's early surf-rock group, the Irridescents. Seol broke up his group the Goldtones to join King, Mike Luciano, and Gene Gunnels, and they named themselves Thee Sixpence. They signed to All American Records, where they released "In the Building" b/w "Hey Joe" in spring 1966. Subsequent releases faded quickly. Following a major lineup shift, the group learned that there were two other bands using variations of the "sixpence" name, so in March 1967 the Strawberry Alarm Clock was born.

The singer on the group's biggest hit was not even a band member, but one Greg Munford, the teenage singer of Shapes of Sound and later Crystal Circus. "Incense and Peppermints" was the B side of "The Birdman of Alkatrash," and by the time it was released in April 1967 the group had moved to Uni. Various business problems plagued the band; for example, "Incense and Peppermints" writer Ed King was not properly credited or compensated. Seven months later, the song was at #1 and the album *Incense and Peppermints* on its way to #11. Commercially speaking, it was the group's finest hour, and although another Top 40 hit followed—"Tomorrow" (#23, 1968)—the Strawberry Alarm Clock wound down. Their version of "Good Morning Starshine," from the hit musical *Hair*, was beaten on the charts by a simultaneously released rendition by Oliver. With new member Paul Marshall, King began exploring what we now call Southern rock. The group appeared in Russ Meyer's *Beyond the Valley of the Dolls* (1970), and by late 1971 had disbanded. Shortly before that, however, King met Ronnie Van Zant of Lynyrd Skynyrd. In early 1973 King joined the Southern rock band, first as a bassist then as third lead guitarist.

In the summer of 1982 Lee Freeman happened to spot an ad for Strawberry Alarm Clock at an L.A. nightclub; intrigued, he went in and discovered the ad was a fake, designed to draw in original Alarm Clock members for a reunion. Freeman told ROLLING STONE he planned to assemble most of the original personnel, which he eventually did. This lineup—which included Freeman and King (by then having left Lynyrd Skynyrd and doing session work)—rerecorded "Incense and Peppermints" for a K-Tel album. Freeman then led a lineup of new musicians as the Strawberry Alarm Clock during the '80s.

The Strawbs

Formed as the Strawberry Hill Boys, 1967, Leicester, Eng.
Dave Cousins (b. Jan 7, 1945), voc., gtr., banjo, dulcimer; Tony Hooper, gtr., voc.; Arthur Phillips, mandolin.
1968—(– Phillips; + Ron Chesterman, bass; + Sandy Denny [b. Jan. 6, 1941, Wimbledon, Eng.; d. Apr. 21, 1978, London, Eng.], voc.) 1969—(– Chesterman; – Denny; + Rick Wakeman [b. May 18, 1949, London], kybds.; + John Ford [b. July 1, 1948, London], bass, voc.; + Richard Hudson [b. May 9, 1948, London], drums) *Strawbs* (A&M) 1970—(+ Claire Deniz, cello) *Dragonfly* (– Deniz); *Just a Collection of Antiques and Curios* 1971—*From the Witchwood* 1972—*Grave New World* (– Hooper; – Wakeman; + Dave Lambert [b. Mar. 8, 1949, Hounslow, Eng.], gtr.; + Blue Weaver [b. Mar. 11, 1947, Cardiff, Wales], kybds.) 1973—*Bursting at the Seams; All Our Own Work* (Hallmark) 1974—(– Ford; – Hudson; – Weaver; + John Hawken, kybds.; + Chas Cronk, bass; + Rod Coombes, drums) *Hero and Heroine* (A&M); *By Choice* 1975—*Ghosts* (– Hawken; + John Mealing, kybds.; + Robert Kirby, kybds.) *Nomadness* 1976—*Deep Cuts* (Oyster) 1977—*Burning for You* 1978—(– Coombes; + Tony Fernandez, drums) *Deadlines* (Arista); *The Best of the Strawbs* (A&M) 1983—(group re-forms: Cousins; Hooper; Hudson; + others; numerous lineup changes follow) 1987—*Don't Say Goodbye* (Virgin, Can.) 1991—*Sandy Denny and the Strawbs* (Hannibal); *Ringing Down the Years* (Virgin, Can.) 2000—*The Complete Strawbs* (Witchwood, U.K.).

Through a long career laden with personnel changes, the Strawbs have kept in touch with both their British folk roots and the '70s progressive-rock movement. Dave Cousins, the band's main songwriter, and Tony Hooper formed the Strawberry Hill Boys (named for the London district where they rehearsed) in 1967, singing traditional British and American folk music, then recorded with Sandy Denny (who went on to Fairport Convention) before becoming the Strawbs with the addition of Richard Hudson and John Ford, from Velvet Opera. Their debut LP won great acclaim in British folk circles, but the second, which saw them turning to a keyboard-dominated progressive sound (Nicky Hopkins guested on it), left them between audiences.

Royal Academy of Music graduate Rick Wakeman's classical arpeggios took the band decisively away from folk and into progressive rock. Wakeman left in 1971 to join Yes. His replacement was Blue Weaver, who had played with Andy Fairweather-Low's Amen Corner and, with Dave Mason, had had a minor solo career under the name Wynder K. Frogg. Shortly after Wakeman's departure, internal disagreements among Cousins, Hudson, and Ford led to Cousins' temporary departure, placing the band in limbo in late 1971. Cousins recorded a solo LP, *Two Weeks Last Summer;* Strawbs then regrouped and had their first British hit singles with "Lay Down" in 1972, and in 1973 with Hudson-Ford's "Part of the Union."

After a traumatic 1973 U.S. tour, Hudson and Ford left to work as a team, with three LPs and a 1974 U.S. tour. Weaver also left, and Cousins recruited John Hawken (from Nashville Teens, Vinegar Joe, and Renaissance), Chas Cronk and Rod Coombes (of Stealers Wheel). At this time the band's audience base shifted from the U.K. to the U.S. Though they never became a truly major American attraction, they toured the U.S. constantly and hardly ever played the U.K. After middling success with a series of progressively more commercial late-'70s LPs, the group disbanded. Hudson, Hooper, and Cousins reunited in the '80s and recorded two Canadian studio albums. As of 1998, Cousins, Hudson, Weaver, and Ford remained from the early years. *The Complete Strawbs* (2000) documents a 30th-anniversary tour.

The Stray Cats

Formed 1979, Massapequa, NY
Brian Setzer (b. Apr. 11, 1959, New York, NY), gtr., voc.; Slim Jim Phantom (b. Jim McDonell, 1961), drums; Lee Rocker (b. Lee Drucker, 1961), string bass, voc.
1981—*Stray Cats* (Arista, U.K.) 1982—*Gonna Ball; Built for Speed* (EMI America) 1983—*Rant 'n' Rave With the Stray Cats* 1986—*Rock Therapy* 1989—*Blast Off* 1991—*Let's Go Faster* (Jordan) 1992—*Choo Choo Hot Fish* (JRS/Great Pyramid) 1997—*Runaway Boys: A Retrospective '81–'92)* (EMI America).
Phantom, Rocker, and Slick: 1984—*Phantom, Rocker & Slick* (EMI America) 1985—*Cover Girl.*
Lee Rocker and Big Blue: 1995—*Lee Rocker's Big Blue* (Black Top) 1996—*Atomic Boogie Hour.*
Lee Rocker solo: 1998—*No Cats* (Upright) 1999—*Lee Rocker Live* (J-Bird).

The Stray Cats' cartoonish version of classic '50s rockabilly proved one of the surprise successes of 1982. The group was formed in a Long Island suburb by Brian Setzer (an ex-member of the Bloodless Pharaohs), Slim Jim Phantom, and Lee Rocker (son of clarinetist Stanley Drucker). After playing the Long Island club circuit for several months, the group moved to London with their manager in the summer of 1980.

Although New Romanticism and new wave dominated the British scene, the Stray Cats soon became a popular club act. The group signed with Arista U.K., and Dave Edmunds produced their debut single, "Runaway Boys." Released in England in November 1980, "Runaway Boys" hit the British Top 10, as did their two subsequent singles, "Stray Cat Strut" and "Rock This Town." The Stray Cats opened three dates on the Rolling Stones 1981 North American tour; by that time their debut LP had become a top-selling import in the U.S. Their second LP, *Gonna Ball*, was not as well received as their debut, and by 1982 there were management problems as well. Nonetheless, the group signed to EMI America, which released their U.S. debut, *Built for Speed*, containing material from the two British albums. Within months, the Stray Cats' "Rock This Town" and "Stray Cat Strut" videos were in heavy rotation on MTV; "Rock This Town" was a #9 hit and the album sold over a million copies.

Rant 'n' Rave (#14, 1983) was a more moderate hit, yielding chart singles in "Sexy + 17" (#5, 1983) and "I Won't Stand in Your Way" (#35, 1983). The band then broke up (success "went to our heads," Setzer later said). Lee Rocker and Slim Jim Phantom (by now married to actress Britt Ekland) joined ex–David Bowie guitarist Earl Slick to form Phantom, Rocker and Slick, releasing two albums and appearing in a 1985 Carl Perkins tribute show organized by Edmunds. In addition to his solo career [see entry], Setzer played Eddie Cochran (at the request of Cochran's mother) in the 1987 Ritchie Valens biopic, *La Bamba*. The original Stray Cats re-formed in 1986 for two U.S. albums, neither of which cracked the Top 100, and two more albums on small, independent labels. Lee Rocker has also pursued a solo career, but one that remains rooted in rockabilly and early rock.

Barbra Streisand

Born Barbara Joan Streisand, Apr. 24, 1942, New York, NY
1963—*The Barbra Streisand Album* (Columbia); *The Second Barbra Streisand Album* 1964—*The Third Album; Funny Girl* (Capitol); *People* (Columbia) 1965—*My Name Is Barbra; My Name Is Barbra, Two . . .* 1966—*Je M'appelle Barbra; Color Me Barbra* 1967—*Simply Streisand* 1968—*A Happening in Central Park* 1969—*What About Today?* 1971—*Barbra Streisand's Greatest Hits; The Owl and the Pussycat; Stoney End; Barbra Joan Streisand* 1972—*Live Concert at the Forum* 1973—*Barbra Streisand . . . and Other Musical Instruments* 1974—*The Way We Were; ButterFly* 1975—*Lazy Afternoon; Funny Lady* (Arista) 1976—*Classical Barbra* (Columbia) 1977—*A Star Is Born; Streisand Superman* 1978—*Songbird* 1979—*The Main Event; Wet* 1980—*Guilty* 1981—*Memories* 1983—*Yentl* 1984—*Emotion* 1985—*The Broadway Album* 1987—*One Voice* 1988—*Till I Loved You* 1991—*The Prince of Tides* (Sony/Columbia); *Just for the Record* (Columbia) 1993—*Streisand Sings Harold Arlen* (Sony) 1994—*The Concert* (Sony/Columbia) 1995—*Broadway Collection* (Columbia) 1996—*The Mirror Has Two Faces* 1997—*Higher Ground* (Sony) 1999—*A Love Like Ours* 2000—*Timeless: Live in Concert* (Sony/Columbia).

The top-selling female artist in history, Barbra Streisand has seen more than 30 of her 50 albums achieve gold status; she has sold more than 60 million albums, featuring for the most part the music of Broadway and its derivatives. And with more than 15 films to her credit, she has become emblematic of the consummate entertainer, heir to a show business tradition whose emphasis on sophistication and professionalism hark back to the prerock era. Both for her remarkable singing technique and as a consistent champion of classic American popular song, Streisand stands as one of contemporary music's most significant performers.

Born in Brooklyn, Streisand moved to Manhattan following high school graduation to pursue acting. She began concentrating on singing at the start of the '60s, first in gay clubs and then in Greenwich Village's Bon Soir club. Debuting on Broadway in *I Can Get It for You Wholesale*, she was signed to Columbia; two weeks after her self-titled Grammy-winning album was released in 1963, she was America's best-selling female singer, and her next seven albums entered the Top 5. Starring in 1,350 performances as Fanny Brice in *Funny Girl* consolidated her fame; in 1968 the Hollywood version, Streisand's first film role, earned her an Oscar. A death threat she received as she was about to perform a 1967 concert in Central Park contributed to an increasing anxiety about singing in public, causing her to retire from concert appearances for more than 20 years.

All of Streisand's '60s albums were hugely popular (nine of them charting in the Top 10); all highlighted Tin Pan Alley fare. In the '70s she attempted, with uneven results, the songs of younger writers (Jimmy Webb, Laura Nyro); her first rock & roll album, 1971's *Stoney End* (#10), drew praise, but critics questioned her other work in this vein. In 1977 she teamed with Bee Gee Barry Gibb on the disco *Streisand Superman* (#3); her hitmaking power remained intact ("You Don't Bring Me Flowers" with Neil Diamond, #1, 1978; "No More Tears [Enough Is Enough]" with Donna Summer, #1, 1979).

Streisand continued to make movies—*Hello, Dolly!, The Way We Were, A Star Is Born, The Prince of Tides* (which she also directed), among the more popular—and in 1983, with *Yentl*, an adaptation of a story by Isaac Bashevis Singer, became the first woman to cowrite, direct, produce, and star in a film of her own.

In 1987 she founded the Barbra Streisand Foundation to support liberal political causes, following up on political involvement that had placed her on Richard Nixon's Enemies List, and had drawn her back to live performance for "One Voice," a 1986 Democratic Party fundraiser. Among other examples of her philanthropy are the Streisand Chair in Cardiology at UCLA and the Streisand Chair on Intimacy and Sexuality at USC; she has also been outspoken in support of gay and women's rights and environmentalism.

Her pop icon status assured in the '90s, Streisand was the beneficiary of a tribute of sorts: on *Saturday Night Live*, Mike Myers in drag played Linda Richman, host of the fictional talk show *Coffee Talk*, who as a prototypical Long Island Streisand fan, gushed at every mention of the singer's name.

In 1992 Streisand surprised viewers and *Coffee Talk* guests Madonna and Roseanne Arnold with an unbilled walk-on.

In 1994, with two New Year's performances at the Las Vegas MGM Grand Hotel's Grand Garden, Streisand returned for her first paid concerts in 22 years. With nine metal detectors in place to assuage the performer's concern for personal safety, the highly successful shows previewed her first-ever major tour later that year. The highlights of those performances were documented on *The Concert* (#10, 1994). The next year, she was awarded a Lifetime Achievement Grammy.

As the '90s progressed, Streisand continued to support liberal causes: she sang at Bill Clinton's first inauguration, befriended his mother, Virginia Kelley, and in 1997 released an album of spiritually-oriented material in Kelley's memory. The year before, she had returned to the chart, with "I Finally Found Someone" from her movie *The Mirror Has Two Faces,* peaking at #8. By the end of the decade, Streisand had married actor James Brolin (she was married to actor Elliott Gould from 1963 to 1971; their son, Jason Gould, is also an actor). For 1999 New Years Eve and Day concerts in Las Vegas, she earned a reported $10 million. In July 2000 Streisand announced her farewell from concert performance with shows in L.A. and at Madison Square Garden (for the NYC gigs, VIP tickets cost $2,500, including dinner).

Barrett Strong

Born Feb. 5, 1941, Mississippi
1975—*Stronghold* (Capitol) 1976—*Live and Love* 2001—*Stronghold II* (Boomtown USA/Blaritt).

Barrett Strong's career as a singer/songwriter began on a very promising note with "Money" in 1961, one of Motown founder Berry Gordy's first hits (#23 pop, #2 R&B). It was covered by a wide variety of acts, from the Beatles to the Flying Lizards.

Strong is the cousin of Nolan Strong, of the Detroit vocal group the Diablos. Shortly after "Money," Strong joined Gordy's fledgling recording empire as a performer and a songwriter. But Strong's singing career was soon overshadowed by his songwriting duties, and after 1961 the label released no more of his singles. As a Motown staff writer, he collaborated with Norman Whitfield on some of the songs that revolutionized Motown's sound in the late '60s and early '70s: "I Wish It Would Rain," "Ball of Confusion (That's What the World Is Today)," "Papa Was a Rolling Stone," "Just My Imagination (Running Away With Me)," and "Psychedelic Shack," among others, for the Temptations; "Smiling Faces Sometimes" for the Undisputed Truth; and "War" for Edwin Starr. Among Strong's other songwriting credits is "I Heard It Through the Grapevine," "The End of Our Road," and "How Can I Forget."

In the mid-'70s he tried unsuccessfully to revive his singing career, first on Capitol Records. He currently works as a songwriter and arranger, while signing talent to his label, Blaritt Records. He appeared on the 1992 album *In Their Own Words,* which featured a number of other singer/songwriters. *Stronghold II* was his first full-length release in 25 years.

Stryper

Formed 1983, Orange County, CA
Oz Fox (b. Richard Martinez, June 18, 1961, Whittier, CA), gtr.; Tim Gaines (b. Tim Hagelganz, Dec. 14, 1963, OR), bass; Michael Sweet (b. July 4, 1963, Whittier), voc.; Robert Sweet (b. Mar. 21, 1960, Whittier), drums.
1984—*The Yellow and Black Attack!* (Enigma) 1985—*Soldiers Under Command* 1986—*To Hell With the Devil* 1988—*In God We Trust* 1990—*Against the Law* 1991—*Can't Stop the Rock: The Stryper Collection, 1984–1991* (Hollywood).
Michael Sweet: 1994—*Michael Sweet* (Benson) 1995—*Real* 2000—*Truth* (Restless).

Although its motives have been attacked by both rock critics and Christian evangelist Jimmy Swaggart, Stryper is one of the most successful Christian rock bands, spreading the Word with a slick heavy-metal sound and ending concerts by tossing Bibles into the audience. Their most popular album, *To Hell With the Devil* (#32, 1986), briefly made them platinum-level rock stars.

Brothers Robert and Michael Sweet, inspired by Jimmy Swaggart's evangelical show, were born again in 1975. Robert decided to form a band after seeing Van Halen and being impressed by the show but distressed by the message. In 1983, with his brother on vocals, he recruited bassist Tim Gaines and guitarist Oz Fox. Calling themselves Roxx Regime, they played clubs in Orange County, California, and submitted a demo to Enigma Records. The Sweets' mother persuaded them to perform overtly Christian material, and they changed their name to Stryper after a passage in Isaiah, "With His stripes we are healed." A 1984 mini-LP, *The Yellow and Black Attack!* (named for their trademark yellow-and-black-striped outfits) was followed in 1985 by the gold album *Soldiers Under Command* (#84).

The band reached its commercial peak with the platinum *To Hell With the Devil.* (*Yellow and Black Attack!* was reissued with two extra tracks in 1986, reaching #103.) A slickly produced amalgam of evangelism, power chords, and high-pitched vocals, it reached beyond the narrow Christian audience, yielding a Top 40 hit, "Honestly" (#23, 1987). *In God We Trust* (#32, 1988), a blatant attempt to court pop audiences, was a relative disappointment, reaching only gold status; following 1990's *Against the Law* (#39), the band changed labels, lost the striped outfits, and was back on more typical, secular heavy-metal ground.

In 1992 Michael Sweet left the band to pursue a solo career; in 1995, *Real* was nominated by the Gospel Music Association for a Dove Award for Best Rock Album. After releasing his first two records through a small gospel label, Sweet rejoined the musical mainstream by signing with Restless.

Style Council: See the Jam

The Stylistics

Formed 1968, Philadelphia, PA
Russell Thompkins Jr. (b. Mar. 21, 1951, Philadelphia), lead voc.; Airrion Love (b. Aug. 8, 1949, Philadelphia), tenor voc.; James Smith (b. June 16, 1950, New York, NY), bass voc.; Herbie Murrell (b. Apr. 27, 1949, Lane, SC), baritone voc.;
James Dunn (b. Feb. 4, 1950, Philadelphia), baritone voc.
1971—*The Stylistics* (Avco) 1972—*Round 2: The Stylistics* 1973—*Rockin' Roll Baby* 1974—*Let's Put It All Together; Heavy* 1975—*The Best of the Stylistics; Thank You Baby; You Are Beautiful* 1976—*Fabulous* (Hugo and Luigi); *Wonder Woman* 1978—(– Dunn) 1979—(– Smith) *Love Spell* (Mercury) 1980—*Hurry Up This Way Again* (TSOP) 1986—*All Time Classics* (Amherst); *The Best of the Stylistics (1972–1974); The Best of the Stylistics, vol. 2; Greatest Love Hits* 1992—*Stylistics Christmas; Love Talk* 1996—*Love Is Back in Style* (MRT) (– Thompkins; + Van Fields, voc.; + Harold Brown, voc.).

Led by Russell Thompkins, the Stylistics were leading practitioners of the lush "Philadelphia sound" of the mid-'70s. They came together in 1968, a union of two Philadelphia vocal groups. Herbie Murrell and James Dunn came from the Percussions; Thompkins, Airrion Love, and James Smith joined from the Monarchs. Robert Douglas, a member of their backing band Slim and the Boys, and road manager Marty Bryant wrote "You're a Big Girl Now" for the Stylistics. It began as a hit on the small Sebring Records in the Philadelphia area before being picked up by Avco Records and hitting the national R&B chart at #7.

Philadelphia producer/writer Thom Bell then took control of the Stylistics' music. Collaborating with songwriter Linda Creed (b. ca. 1949; d. April 10, 1986), Bell created "Stop, Look, Listen (to Your Heart)" (#39 pop, #6 R&B) and "You Are Everything" (#9 pop, #10 R&B) in 1971; "Betcha By Golly, Wow" (#3 pop, #2 R&B), "People Make the World Go Round" (#25 pop, #6 R&B), and "I'm Stone in Love With You" (#10 pop, #4 R&B) in 1972; "Break Up to Make Up" (#5 pop and R&B), "You'll Never Get to Heaven" (#23 pop, #8 R&B) and "Rockin' Roll Baby" (#14 pop, #13 R&B) in 1973; and "You Make Me Feel Brand New" (#2 pop, #5 R&B) in 1974.

After the Stylistics' relationship with Bell ended, they began working with Van McCoy [see entry], but the group's record sales in America declined. They remained popular in Europe both on record and in nightclubs throughout the '70s. Among their U.K. hits were three Top 5 singles: "Sing Baby Sing" and "Na Na Is the Saddest Word" (1975), and "Can't Help Falling in Love" (1976). "Can't Give You Anything (But My Love)" (#51 pop, #18 R&B) went to #1 in the U.K. during the summer of 1975.

The group signed to Philadelphia International Records in 1980. By then, Dunn had quit due to health problems and was not replaced, and within a year Smith had left as well. The group remained active in the '80s and '90s as a trio. Thompkins left sometime after 1996's *Love Is Back in Style*.

Styx

Formed 1963, Chicago, IL
James Young (b. Nov. 14, 1949), gtr., voc.; John Curulewski, gtr.; Dennis DeYoung (b. Feb. 18, 1947, Chicago), kybds., voc.; Chuck Panozzo (b. Sep. 20, 1948), bass, voc.; John Panozzo (b. Sep. 20, 1948; d. July 16, 1996, Chicago), drums.
1972—*Styx* (Wooden Nickel) 1973—*Styx II; The Serpent Is Rising* 1974—*Man of Miracles* 1975—*Equinox* (A&M) (– Curulewski; + Tommy Shaw [b. Sep. 11, 1953, Montgomery, AL], gtr., voc.) 1976—*Crystal Ball* 1977—*The Grand Illusion* 1978—*Pieces of Eight* 1979—*Cornerstone* 1981—*Paradise Theatre* 1983—*Kilroy Was Here* 1984—(group disbands) *Caught in Act—Live* 1990—(group re-forms: DeYoung; Young; C. Panozzo; J. Panozzo; + Glen Burtnik, gtr., voc., bass) *Edge of the Century* 1995—(– Burtnik; + Shaw) *Greatest Hits* 1996—(– J. Panozzo; + Todd Sucherman, drums) *Greatest Hits Part 2* 1997—*Return to Paradise* (CMC) 1999—*Brave New World* (– DeYoung; – C. Panozzo; + Burtnik; + Lawrence Gowan, voc., kybds.).
Dennis DeYoung solo: 1984—*Desert Moon* (A&M) 1986—*Back to the World* 1988—*Boomchild* (MCA) 1994—*10 on Broadway* (Atlantic) 1995—*The Hunchback of Notre Dame* (Grand Illusion).
Tommy Shaw solo: 1984—*Girls With Guns* (A&M) 1985—*What If* 1987—*Ambition* (Atlantic) 1998—*7 Deadly Zens* (CMC).

One of the leading exemplars of the FM radio–oriented hard pop known as "pomp rock," Styx also claims the distinction of having been named (in a 1979 Gallup Poll) the most popular rock band among American fans aged 13 to 18. At the height of its commercial powers, Styx released a string of five platinum albums, including the #1 triple-platinum *Paradise Theatre* (1981).

Twins Chuck and John Panozzo, along with Dennis DeYoung and Tom Nardini, worked the Chicago-area bar circuit from 1963 until 1969, when Nardini left the group and the Panozzos and DeYoung entered Chicago State University. There they met John Curulewski, with whom they formed TW4. James Young joined a year later, and they changed their name to Styx (after the river that flows through Hades in Greek mythology).

After incessant touring, their national break came in 1975 with the #6 single "Lady," featuring the blaring vocal triads that are a Styx trademark. From 1977 until their breakup in 1984, every one of their releases sold platinum or better: *The Grand Illusion* (#6, 1977, 3 million sold), *Pieces of Eight* (#6, 1978, 3 million sold), *Cornerstone* (#2, 1979, 2 million sold), *Paradise Theatre*, and *Kilroy Was Here* (#3, 1983, 1 million sold). Their concerts were invariably sold out. Their hit singles included "Come Sail Away" (#8, 1977); "Fooling Yourself (the Angry Young Man)" (#29) and "Blue Collar Man (Long

Nights)" (#21), 1978; "Babe" (#1, 1979); and "The Best of Times" (#3) and "Too Much Time on My Hands" (#9), both 1981.

In 1983 the group toured 3,000-seat halls with a theatrical presentation of *Kilroy Was Here*, an anticensorship concept album that included the hit singles "Mr. Roboto" (#3) and "Don't Let It End" (#6). In 1984 the group members went their separate ways for a while. DeYoung and Shaw, who had written most of Styx's music, each embarked on initially auspicious solo careers. DeYoung's *Desert Moon* (#29, 1984) featured the #10 title single, while Shaw's *Girls With Guns* (#50, 1984) had a #33 title track. Subsequent releases were not as successful, and in 1990 Shaw joined Ted Nugent's Damn Yankees [see entry].

Four members of Styx, with newcomer Glen Burtnik, released the comeback *Edge of the Century* in the fall of 1990. Its "Show Me the Way" (#3, 1990) became something of a theme song during the Gulf War, and "Love at First Sight" was a Top 30 single later that next spring. In 1995 DeYoung played Pilate in the 1995 Broadway revival of *Jesus Christ Superstar*. He later completed his own musical based on *The Hunchback of Notre Dame*.

Shaw returned to the band when he helped rerecord "Lady" for 1995's *Greatest Hits;* Styx's initial label, Wooden Nickel, had refused to license the original version for the A&M compilation. By 1990, drummer John Panozzo had developed a debilitating drinking problem. In 1996 Styx was forced to hire a temporary touring replacement, Todd Sucherman. In July of that year Panozzo died, the result of a gastrointestinal hemorrhage, and Sucherman became a permanent addition. The live *Return to Paradise* was the first-ever gold record for Styx's new label, CMC International. During the sessions for 1999's *Brave New World,* DeYoung developed an acute case of photosensitivity. Styx acrimoniously replaced him for the ensuing tour. Burtnik also returned, this time on bass, to replace Chuck Panozzo, who had also left the band.

Sublime/Long Beach Dub AllStars

Formed 1988, Long Beach, CA
Bradley Nowell (b. Feb. 22, 1968, Long Beach; d. May 25, 1996, San Francisco, CA), voc., gtr; Eric Wilson (b. Feb. 21, 1970, Long Beach), bass; Bud Gaugh (b. Floyd I. Gaugh IV, Oct. 2, 1967, Long Beach), drums.
1992—*40 Oz. to Freedom* (Skunk) 1994—*Robbin' the Hood* 1996—*Sublime* (MCA/Gasoline Alley) 1997—*What I Got . . . The 7 Song EP; Second-Hand Smoke* 1998— *Stand by Your Van—Live in Concert; Acoustic—Bradley Nowell & Friends* 1999—*Greatest Hits.*
Long Beach Dub AllStars, formed 1996, Long Beach, CA: Wilson, bass; Gaugh, drums; Marshall Goodman (b. Jan. 31, 1971, Chicago, IL), turntables, drums, perc.; Richard "RAS-I" Smith (b. Dec. 29, 1970, Long Beach), gtr., voc.; Jack Maness (b. Sep. 10, 1967, St. Louis, MO), kybds., voc.; Opie Ortiz (b. Long Beach), voc.; Timothy Wu (b. Aug. 30, 1976, Long Beach), sax.
1999—*Right Back* (DreamWorks).

When national success finally came to the Long Beach, California, ska-rock band Sublime, it was painfully bittersweet. Frontman Brad Nowell spent eight years of his life in pursuit of rock stardom with the group, relentlessly working the Southern California party and bar scene with bassist Eric Wilson and drummer Bud Gaugh. He saw the band release two moderately successful albums on its own Skunk label before finally securing a long-sought-after major label deal with MCA, but he would never fully realize his dream. On May 25, 1996, three months before Sublime's self-titled MCA debut shipped to stores, Nowell—who had battled a heroin addiction for years—died of an overdose in a San Francisco hotel room. He was 28.

Released 10 weeks after Nowell's funeral, *Sublime* (#25, 1996) steadily went on to become one of the best-selling albums of 1997, spinning off four Modern Rock radio hits and eventually going quintuple platinum. The band's 1992 independent debut, *40 Oz. to Freedom,* also enjoyed a sales spike (going platinum) after being reissued by MCA, while 1997's odds and sods collection, *Second-Hand Smoke,* went to #28. Other vault releases included *Stand by Your Van—Live in Concert* (#49, 1998) and *Acoustic—Bradley Nowell & Friends* (#107, 1998). *Greatest Hits,* issued in late 1999, peaked at #114.

After Nowell's death, Wilson and Gaugh assembled the Long Beach Dub AllStars to perform at a 1996 benefit for Nowell's son, Jakob. Three years later, the group released its debut, *Right Back.*

Sugar: See Hüsker Dü

The Sugar Hill Gang

Formed 1977, New York, NY
Master Gee (b. Guy O'Brien, 1963, New York), voc.; Wonder Mike (b. Michael Wright, 1958, Englewood, NJ), voc.; Big Bank Hank (b. Henry Jackson, 1958, Bronx, NY), voc.
1979—*Rapper's Delight* (Sugarhill) 1981—*The 8th Wonder* 1996—*The Best of Sugarhill Gang* (Rhino) 1999—*Jump On It.*

Before the Sugar Hill Gang's "Rapper's Delight," rap was confined to the clubs and house parties in the New York City area. Following the record's release in the summer of 1979, rap became a part of the pop music vocabulary.

In 1979 Sylvia and Joe Robinson's independent label All Platinum was awash in lawsuits and losing money; the husband-and-wife team (Sylvia had been a hitmaking singer as half of Mickey and Sylvia and as a soloist) expected to quit the record business. At a party for her sister in Harlem, she heard guests chanting rhymes over the instrumental breaks in disco records. Using her son Joey as talent scout, she rounded up three youngsters from the New York area to rap over a rhythm track adapted from Chic's "Good Times," and chartered a new label, Sugarhill, to carry the record, "Rapper's Delight."

According to Sugarhill, the record sold 2 million copies in America. It placed #4 R&B in the U.S., made the Top 5 in the U.K., Israel, and South Africa, among other countries, and went to #1 in Canada. It proved to be the Sugar Hill Gang's only big hit, although "8th Wonder" (#15 R&B, 1981) and "Lover in You" were chart singles. The trio disappeared for most of the '80s, but eventually resurfaced with a few personnel changes (Master Gee was notably absent). The Gang continued performing into the '90s. *Jump On It,* released in 1999, is a winsome album of hip-hop for kids.

Sugar Ray

Formed 1989, as the Shrinky Dinx, Newport Beach, CA
Mark McGrath (b. Mar. 15, 1968), voc., Rodney Sheppard (b. Nov. 25, 1967), gtr., Murphy Karges (b. June 20, 1967), bass, Stan Frazier (b. Apr. 23, 1968), drums.
1995—(+ Craig "DJ Homicide" Bullock [b. Dec. 17, 1970]) *Lemonade and Brownies* (Atlantic) 1997—*Floored* 1999—*14:59*

Riding a wave of Southern California alternative-rock acts that achieved popularity—sometimes fleeting—in the late '90s, Sugar Ray was influenced by a variety of sounds: Red Hot Chili Peppers–style punk-funk, reggae grooves, metal, hip-hop, and a little bit of retro new wave. The group released its debut album *Lemonade and Brownies* in 1995, but constant touring (with Cypress Hill and Korn) failed to generate much interest in it. Sugar Ray was on the verge of disbanding when drummer Stan Frazier came up with music for the Caribbean-flavored song "Fly" [#1 Modern Rock, 1997], which McGrath disliked so intensely that he briefly quit. The singer was talked into rejoining the band, and, borrowing lyrics from the Beatles, Killing Joke, and Gilbert O'Sullivan, created the breakthrough single that drove its next album, *Floored* (#12, 1997), to 2 million in sales. Jokes that Sugar Ray was a one-hit wonder prompted the title of the 1999 album *14:59* (#17, 1999), an allusion to Andy Warhol's comment that "in the future, everyone will be famous for 15 minutes." If the band's time was up, it was going out on a high note. The album matched *Floored* in sales, and produced hit singles in the Motown-inflected reverie "Every Morning" (#3, 1999) and "Someday" (#7, 1999).

Suicide

Formed 1970, New York, NY
Alan Vega (b. Alan Bermowitz), voc.; Martin Rev (b. Martin Reverby), kybds., perc., voc.
1977—*Suicide* (Red Star) 1978—*23 Minutes in Bruxels* (Bronze, U.K.) 1981—*½ Alive* (ROIR) 1986—*Ghost Riders* 1989—*A Way of Life* (Wax Trax) 1992—*Why Be Blue* (Brake Out/Enemy) 1997—*Zero Hour* (Restless).
As Alan Vega and Martin Rev: 1980—*Suicide* (ZE).
Alan Vega solo: 1980—*Alan Vega* (ZE/PVC) 1981—*Collision Drive* (ZE/Celluloid) 1983—*Saturn Strip* (ZE/Elektra) 1985—*Just a Million Dreams* 1990—*Deuce Avenue* (Musidisc, Fr.) 1991—*Power on to Zero Hour* 1993—*New Raceion* 1995—*Dujang Prang* (Thirsty Ear) 1999—*2007* (Double T).
Martin Rev solo: 1980—*Martin Rev* EP (Infidelity) 1985—*Clouds of Glory* (New Rose, Fr.) 1991—*Cheyenne* (Alive) 1996—*See Me Ridin'* (ROIR) 1997—*Marvel* (Daft, Bel.) 2000—*Strangeworld* (Sähkö, Fin.).

When artist/sculptor Alan Vega and keyboardist Martin Rev began performing at New York's Mercer Arts Center (then home to the New York Dolls), they were ahead of their time. Suicide based its music on Rev's repetitive wall-of-noise keyboards (initially a broken Farfisa organ) and pneumatic rhythm machines, with Vega's Presley-ish vocals providing a link to rock & roll tradition. But Vega also brought a form of performance art onstage. He hit himself in the face with his microphone, he whispered and screamed, he strode into the audience seeking to incite involvement or confrontation. Some found Suicide fascinating; others thought them brilliant and important; more seemed to enjoy them as some sort of joke; and most simply hated them.

Suicide opened for the Clash and Elvis Costello on 1978 British tours, where audiences regularly flung beer bottles at the stage, and a few fights broke out. On a limited-edition, European live album (later reissued as a flexi-disc), one can hear audience members grabbing the microphone from the stage and passing it around, hurling epithets at the band the whole time. In 1980 the Cars' Ric Ocasek revealed himself as Suicide's most famous fan. The Cars' *Candy-O* includes a direct allusion to Suicide in "Shoo-Be-Doo." Ocasek got Suicide to open the Cars' 1980 U.S. tour (in L.A. Suicide nearly caused riots, and the concert promoters unsuccessfully tried to have them taken off the bill), included Suicide on a Cars-hosted *Midnight Special,* and produced Suicide's 1980 *Ze* album.

The two got back together again, with Ocasek producing, for 1988's more rhythmic *A Way of Life* and its followup, 1992's *Why Be Blue.* Ironically, the band is now quite revered in Europe. Suicide has become an unmeasurable influence on the industrial dance, noise, techno, ambient, and electronic scenes of the '80s and '90s. The pair's main albums have been reissued on numerous occasions, with scores of bonus tracks. Rev and Vega continue to perform, both together and solo.

Donna Summer

Born Adrian Donna Gaines, Dec. 31, 1948, Boston, MA
1975—*Love to Love You Baby* (Oasis) 1976—*A Love Trilogy; Four Seasons of Love* (Casablanca) 1977—*I Remember Yesterday; Once Upon a Time* 1978—*Live and More* 1979—*Bad Girls; On the Radio: Greatest Hits: vols. I and II* 1980—*Walk Away—Collector's Edition; The Wanderer*

(Geffen) 1982—*Donna Summer* 1983—*She Works Hard for the Money* (Mercury) 1984—*Cats Without Claws* (Geffen) 1987—*All Systems Go* 1989—*Another Place and Time* (Atlantic) 1991—*Mistaken Identity* 1993—*The Donna Summer Anthology* (PolyGram) 1994—*Endless Summer: Donna Summer's Greatest Hits* (Mercury) 1999—*VH1 Presents Live & More: Encore!* (Sony).

Donna Summer was the biggest star to emerge from the mid-'70s disco explosion and went on to pursue a successful pop career. She sang in Boston churches as a child, occasionally as a lead vocalist. In 1967 she made her professional debut at Boston's Psychedelic Supermarket. Later that year, at age 18, she landed a role in the Munich, Germany, production of *Hair.* While in Germany, she married Austrian actor Helmut Sommer, later divorcing him but keeping the Anglicized surname. For a time she sang in a Vienna Folk Opera version of *Porgy and Bess.* Working as a backup singer at Munich's Musicland Studios, Summer met producers Giorgio Moroder and Pete Bellotte. Together the trio created a string of European pop hits for Moroder's Oasis label. In 1975 Moroder licensed Oasis to America's Casablanca Records.

The orgasmic 17-minute title track from *Love to Love You Baby* (#11 pop, #6 R&B, 1975) became a major disco hit, and by year's end had crossed over to pop and R&B charts as well (#2 pop, #3 R&B). Many thought Summer would be a typical one-hit disco act, but Moroder, Bellotte, and Casablanca president Neil Bogart were determined to give her hits and longevity. *A Love Trilogy* (#21 pop, #16 R&B, 1976) solidified her disco following, while *Four Seasons of Love* (#29 pop, #13 R&B, 1976) and "Spring Affair" (#58 pop, #24 R&B) expanded her pop audience.

Donna Summer

With 1977's *I Remember Yesterday* (#18 pop, #11 R&B), Moroder expanded the music's stylistic range. The album yielded the influential synthesizer pop hit "I Feel Love" (#6 pop, #9 R&B). For the disco fairy-tale concept album *Once Upon a Time* (#26 pop, #13 R&B, 1977) Summer contributed lyrics to most of the material. *Live and More* (#1 pop, #4 R&B, 1978) provided Summer with her first pop #1 (#8 R&B), a cover of Jimmy Webb's "MacArthur Park." That year she also appeared in the disco film *Thank God It's Friday.* "Last Dance" (#3 pop, #5 R&B, 1978) from the soundtrack album won two Grammy Awards—one for Summer, one for songwriter Paul Jabara—and an Oscar for Jabara. The double-platinum *Bad Girls* (#1 pop and R&B, 1979) broke down any lingering critical resistance to Summer. "Hot Stuff" (#1 pop, #3 R&B) and the rocking title track (#1 pop and R&B) made her popular with disco, pop, and rock fans. That year, Barbra Streisand duetted with Summer on "No More Tears (Enough Is Enough)" (#1 pop, #20 R&B). Two other crossover hits rounded out Summer's biggest year: "Heaven Knows" (#4 pop, #10 R&B) and "Dim All the Lights" (#2 pop, #13 R&B).

But success also brought problems. In 1980 she sued her manager, Joyce Bogart, and husband Neil for $10 million for mismanagement. She was thus able to end her Casablanca contract and to sign with Geffen Records. *The Wanderer* (#13 pop, #12 R&B, 1980) was her first Geffen release, the title track becoming a strong-selling single (#3 pop, #13 R&B), although the album didn't live up to sales expectations. *The Wanderer* also included Summer's first born-again Christian message song, "I Believe in Jesus." It was around this time that rumors began circulating that Summer had said the emerging AIDS epidemic was God's revenge on homosexuals for living a blasphemous lifestyle; Summer later denied the rumors, but her large gay following dwindled. In 1980 she married Bruce Sudano, lead singer of Brooklyn Dreams, with whom she had recorded "Heaven Knows"; they named their daughter Brook Lyn. *Donna Summer* (#20 pop, #8 R&B) was released in 1982. The Quincy Jones–produced album was a replacement for an LP Giorgio Moroder had produced but Geffen Records had rejected. A track from that unreleased album appears on the *Fast Times at Ridgemont High* soundtrack. She then had her biggest hit album since *Bad Girls* with *She Works Hard for the Money* (#9 pop, #5 R&B, 1983), which yielded a massive hit single in the title track (#3 pop, #1 R&B, 1983), a video for which was played heavily on MTV. The album also contained a more modest hit in the reggae-ish "Unconditional Love" (#43 pop, #9 R&B, 1983), with backing vocals by Britain's Musical Youth. *Cats Without Claws* (#40 pop, #24 R&B, 1984) contained a cover of the Drifters classic "There Goes My Baby" (#21 pop, #20 R&B, 1984); the track "Forgive Me" earned Summer her second Grammy, for Best Inspirational Vocal.

While *All Systems Go* went nowhere (#122 pop, #53 R&B, 1987), yielding only a minor hit single in "Dinner With Gershwin" (#48 pop, #10 R&B, 1987), *Another Place and Time* (#53 pop, #71 R&B, 1989) was produced by the British team of

Stock, Aitken, and Waterman, who'd had synth-driven dance hits with Bananarama and Dead or Alive. They brought Summer back to the Top 10 singles chart with "This Time I Know It's for Real" (#7, 1989). But as the album's followup, *Mistaken Identity*, quickly sank, Summer then embarked on another dry spell. Summer started performing live again in 1996 and that same year she sang a duet on Liza Minnelli's *Gently*. In 1997 "Carry On," a collaboration with Moroder, won a Grammy for Best Dance Recording. In 2000 she was nominated again, this time for "I Will Go With You (Con Te Partiró)" (#79 pop, 1999), off the VH1 special *VH1 Presents Live & More: Encore!* (#43 pop, #33 R&B, 1999).

In 1995 Summer and Sudano moved to Nashville, where they have been writing songs for the likes of Dolly Parton (they cowrote "Starting Over Again") and Reba McEntire. The couple has also been busy working on *Ordinary Girl*, a musical they hope to bring to Broadway.

Andy Summers: See the Police

Sun Ra

Born Herman Blount, May 22, 1914, Birmingham, AL; died May 30, 1993, Birmingham
1956—*Super-Sonic Jazz* (Saturn) 1957—*Sun Song; Sound of Joy* (Delmark) 1958—*Jazz in Silhouette* (Saturn); *Sun Ra and His Solar Arkestra Visit Planet Earth* 1959—*We Travel the Spaceways; The Nubians of Plutonia;* 1960—*Holiday for Soul Dance; Angels and Demons at Play* 1961—*Interstellar Low-Ways; Fate in a Pleasant Mood; The Futuristic Sounds of Sun Ra* (Savoy); *Bad and Beautiful* (Saturn) 1962—*Art Forms of Dimensions Tomorrow; When Sun Comes Out* 1963—*Cosmic Tones for Mental Therapy* 1964—*Other Planes of There* 1965—*The Heliocentric Worlds of Sun Ra, vol. 1* (ESP-Disk); *The Heliocentric Worlds of Sun Ra, vol. 2; The Magic City (Saturn)* 1966—*When Angels Speak of Love; Nothing Is . . .* (ESP-Disk); *Monorails and Satellites* (Saturn) 1967—*Atlantis* 1968—*Pictures of Infinity* (Black Lion); *Outer Spaceways Incorporated; A Black Mass* (Jihad) 1969—*My Brother the Wind, vol. 1* (Saturn) 1970—*My Brother the Wind, vol. 2; It's After the End of the World* (MPS) 1972—*Space Is the Place* (Blue Thumb); *Astro-Black* (Impulse) 1975—*Pathways to Unknown Worlds* 1976—*Live at Montreux* (Saturn); *Cosmos* (Inner City) 1977—*Solo Piano* (IAI); *St. Louis Blues* 1980—*Strange Celestial Road* (Rounder); *Sunrise in Different Dimensions* (Hat Hut) 1983—*Love in Outer Space* (Leo); *Meets Salah Ragab in Egypt* (Praxis) 1984—*Live at Praxis; Cosmo Sun Connection* (Saturn) 1986—*Hours After* (Black Saint) 1987—*Reflections in Blue; A Night in East Berlin* (Leo) 1988—*Live at Pit-Inn, Tokyo* (DIW) 1989—*Out There a Minute* (Blast First); *Blue Delight* (A&M); *Purple Night* 1990—*Mayan Temples* (Black Saint) 1992—*Destination Unknown* (Enja) 1993—*Space Is the Place* soundtrack (Evidence); *Somewhere Else* (Rounder); *Live at the Village Vanguard; Pleiades* (Leo); *Friendly Galaxy* 1994—*Live From Soundscape* (DIW); *Live at Hackney Empire* (Leo) 1995—*Second Star to the Right: A Salute to Walt Disney;* 1996—*Stardust From Tomorrow; The Singles* (Evidence) 1998—*Calling Planet Earth* (Freedom); *Black Myth/Out in Space* (Motor Music) 1999—*A Song for the Sun* (El Ra); *Outer Space Employment Agency: Live at the Ann Arbor Blues & Jazz Festival 1973* (Total Energy); *Life Is Splendid: Live at the Ann Arbor Blues & Jazz Festival 1972; Janus* (1201 Music) 2000—*Standards.*

With his spangly costumes, circus-style multimedia concerts, otherworldly cosmology, and surreal marriage of heady avant-gardism with funky tent-show gospel, Sun Ra was one of the most unique, colorful, and self-determined visionaries in modern popular music. With Miles Davis, he was one of the few authentic jazz figures to exert a wide, discernible influence not just on jazz artists (most explicitly the Art Ensemble of Chicago), but rock and R&B acts too, among them George Clinton, NRBQ, Pink Floyd, and Sonic Youth (for whom Ra opened at New York's Central Park, July 4, 1992). Composer, arranger, bandleader, keyboardist, and philosopher, Ra innovated the use of electronics, Afro-percussive polyrhythms, and collective free improvisation within big-band jazz. Perhaps the first "alternative" artist, he also documented his work through roughly 100 self-produced albums for his own independent El Saturn Research label (many of which went out of print before being reissued on CD by Evidence Music, of Philadelphia, where Ra had been based since the late '60s).

Ra, who claimed to have been born on Saturn and sent to Earth as "an ambassador of the Creator of the Omniverse," was first known on Earth as Herman Blount. Reportedly a musical prodigy, he could instantly play a piano his parents bought for his tenth birthday (or "arrival day" as Ra would call it). Blount studied music in high school under renowned teacher and bandleader John Tuggle "Fess" Whatley and majored in music education at Alabama A&M University. After graduating in the mid-'30s, he led the college band on tour, then played piano in a variety of little-known Southern and Midwestern territory bands—sometimes under the name Sonny Lee—and allegedly backed such blues singers as Wynonie Harris on occasion. By the mid-'40s, he settled in Chicago, playing piano in the band led by his idol, seminal swing arranger Fletcher Henderson; he also worked at Chicago's popular Club DeLisa, arranging scores for floorshows and visiting singers.

Sometime around 1948 Sonny Blount changed the name on his passport to "Le Sony'r Ra" and proclaimed himself "Sun Ra, cosmic messenger." Going against the bebop-combo grain, Ra—though generally regarded as eccentric—slowly built his so-called "Arkestra," attracting a core of talented, dedicated players, some of whom (tenor saxophonist John Gilmore, baritone saxophonist Pat Patrick, and alto saxophonist Marshall Allen) remained with him for decades. The first Arkestras merged Monk's off-center bebop, Ellington's exotic tonal palette, and the earthy punch of Mingus with authoritative world-music elements from Africa, the Caribbean, the Middle East, and the Orient.

In the early '60s the members moved to New York, where

Ornette Coleman, Cecil Taylor, and Albert Ayler were forging the "free jazz" revolution. Ra's controlled use of dissonance, silence, and free-form techniques set him firmly in the jazz avant-garde. From the mid-'60s on, Ra's cult following grew, especially in Europe, as he placed a heavier accent on electronic keyboards (including Moog synthesizer), massed African percussion, and the pageantry of dancers, film projections, and light shows.

The 1974 death of Duke Ellington seemed to inspire Ra to pepper his shows with punk-paced renditions of the classic Ellington and Fletcher Henderson big-band charts of his youth, presaging by several years the rediscovery of tradition by younger avant-garde jazz artists, and making his concerts more accessible. By the '80s, Sun Ra was no longer a leading-edge innovator, but a colorful elder statesman who toured incessantly, often playing rock venues. His final arranging triumph may have been in orchestrating a crowd-pleasing magical mystery tour through jazz history and beyond, from throbbing tribal percussion and roiling full-band noise, to rollicking swing and galvanic neo-gospel chants about outer space.

Despite his declining health, Ra continued performing, albeit in a wheelchair and then playing only skeletal piano. After suffering a third stroke in late 1992, Ra let his band tour without him. He returned to his birthplace, where he succumbed to mounting physical complications eight days after his 79th "arrival day." Under Gilmore's leadership, the band continued playing Ra's music; after the 63-year-old Gilmore died of emphysema in 1995 (the same year that NRBQ, the Residents, and Sonic Youth's Thurston Moore contributed to the Ra tribute album *Wavelength Infinity*), Marshall Allen took over leadership of the Arkestra. Under his direction the band, still represented in stores by myriad CD reissues of long-lost albums, made its first new recording since Ra's death with *A Song for the Sun*.

Supergrass

Formed 1993, Oxford, Eng.
Gaz Coombes (b. Gareth Michael Coombes, Mar. 8, 1976, Oxford), voc., gtr; Mick Quinn (b. Michael Quinn, Dec. 17, 1969, Oxford), bass; Danny Goffey (b. Daniel Goffey, Feb. 7, 1974, Oxford), drums.
1995—*I Should Coco* (Capitol) 1997—*In It for the Money* 1999—*Supergrass* (Island/Def Jam).

Supergrass crafts sunny, uptempo pop with the subversive edge of punk, tapping into the legacies of early Elvis Costello, Small Faces, and the Buzzcocks. Frequently labeled Brit-pop, the band has otherwise largely escaped that genre's public feuds and commercial pressures.

Gaz Coombes and Danny Goffey, ex-members of the Jennifers (a "shoegazing" quartet that released one single in England before disbanding), formed Supergrass with bassist Mick Quinn in 1993. Their first single, "Caught by the Fuzz," released the next year on the indie Backbeat, recounts Coombes' experience as a 15-year-old waiting for his mother to pick him up at jail after being busted for possession. The single attracted the attention of EMI's Parlophone label, which signed the band and reissued the single, which hit #43 on the U.K. chart. Their commercially successful debut album, *I Should Coco* (#1 U.K.) took its title from the cockney expression for "I should think so," and attracted critical acclaim and a cult audience in the U.S., where the album was released on Capitol. *In It for the Money* (#2 U.K.) followed in 1997. Supergrass changed U.S. labels for its self-titled third album (#3 U.K.) to Island/Def Jam. The band's touring lineup usually includes keyboardist Rob Coombes, the singer's brother, who cowrote tracks on the band's last two albums.

Supertramp

Formed 1969, England
Roger Hodgson (b. Mar. 21, 1950, London, Eng.), gtr., voc., bass; Richard Davies (b. July 22, 1944, Eng.), kybds., voc.; Richard Palmer, gtr.; Bob Miller, drums.
1970—*Supertramp* (A&M) (– Palmer; – Miller; + Dave Winthrop [b. Nov. 27, 1948, NJ], sax; + Frank Farrell [b. Birmingham, Eng.], bass; + Kevin Currie [b. Liverpool, Eng.], drums) 1971—*Indelibly Stamped* 1973—*Extremes* soundtrack (Deram) 1974—(– Winthrop; – Farrel; – Currie; + John Anthony Helliwell [b. Feb. 15, 1945, Todmorden, Eng.], sax; + Dougie Thomson [b. Mar. 24, 1951, Glasgow, Scot.], bass; + Bob C. Benberg [b. Robert Siebenberg], drums) *Crime of the Century* (A&M) 1975—*Crisis? What Crisis?* 1977—*Even in the Quietest Moments* 1979—*Breakfast in America* 1980—*Paris* 1982—*". . . famous last words . . ."* 1983—(– Hodgson) 1985—*Brother Where You Bound* 1987—*Free As a Bird; Classics, vol. 9* 1991—*The Very Best of Supertramp* 1997—(lineup: Davies; Helliwell; Benberg; others) *Some Things Never Change* (Chrysalis).
Roger Hodgson solo: 1984—*In the Eye of the Storm* (A&M) 1987—*Hai Hai* 1997—*Rites of Passage* (Unichord, U.K.) 2000—*Open the Door.*

Supertramp began as the wish fulfillment of a millionaire rock fan. By the late '70s, the group's blend of keyboard-heavy progressive rock and immaculate pop had yielded several hit singles and a few platinum LPs.

In the late '60s Dutch millionaire Stanley August Miesegaes heard Rick Davies in a band called the Joint. When that band broke up, Miesegaes offered to bankroll a band if Davies would handle the music. Davies placed classified ads in London newspapers for a band. The first response was from Roger Hodgson, who was to split songwriting and singing with Davies in Supertramp, the name they took from W.H. Davies' 1938 book, *The Autobiography of a Supertramp*. Drummer Bob Miller suffered a nervous breakdown after their first LP's release; he was replaced by Kevin Currie for the next, but like the first, it flopped.

After a disastrous tour, the band (except Davies and Hodgson) broke up. Davies and Hodgson recruited Bob Benberg from pub rockers Bees Make Honey, and John Helliwell and Dougie Thomson from the Alan Bown Set, and A&M sent them to a rehearsal retreat at a seventeenth-century farm. Their next LP, *Crime of the Century,* was the subject of a massive advertising/promotional campaign, and went to #1 in the U.K. but didn't take off commercially in the U.S., though it did sow the seeds of a cult following.

In 1975 the singles "Dreamer" and "Bloody Well Right" from *Crime* achieved some chart success in both the U.K. and the U.S. Supertramp toured the U.S. as a headliner, with A&M giving away most of the tickets. *Crisis?* failed to yield a hit single, but was heavily played on progressive FM radio and solidified the band's audience base, as did *Even in the Quietest Moments* (#16, 1977), which included "Give a Little Bit" (#15, 1977). Supertramp's breakthrough was *Breakfast in America,* a #1 worldwide LP, which eventually sold over 4 million copies in the U.S. and contained hit singles in "The Logical Song" (#6), "Goodbye Stranger" (#15), and "Take the Long Way Home" (#10). The *Paris* live double LP hit #8; and *". . . famous last words . . ."* included another hit, "It's Raining Again" (#11, 1982). In early 1983 Hodgson announced he was leaving the group for a solo career. His first solo release, *In the Eye of the Storm* (#46, 1984), contained his only charting single to date, "Had a Dream (Sleeping With the Enemy)" (#48, 1984). His subsequent work was not as well received.

The group's next album, *Brother Where You Bound* (#21, 1985), contained Supertramp's last charting single to date, "Cannonball" (#28, 1985). Late in 1985 Supertramp embarked on a six-month tour of the United States. Hodgson briefly rejoined to promote the U.K. Top 10 compilation *The Autobiography of Supertramp. Free As a Bird* (1987) missed the Top 100 by one and included a dance hit, "I'm Begging You." In 1997 Davies, Helliwell, and Benberg regrouped Supertramp—minus Hodgson—and, with the aid of studio players, released *Some Things Never Change.*

The Supremes/Diana Ross and the Supremes

Formed 1959, Detroit, MI
As the Primettes: Diana Ross (b. Mar. 26, 1944, Detroit), voc.; Florence Ballard (b. June 30, 1943, Detroit; d. Feb. 22, 1976, Detroit), voc.; Mary Wilson (b. Mar. 6, 1944, Greeneville, MS), voc.; Betty McGlown, voc.
1960—(– McGlown; + Barbara Martin, voc.).
As the Supremes: 1963—(– Martin) *Meet the Supremes* (Motown) 1964—*A Bit of Liverpool; Where Did Our Love Go* 1965—*Sing Country, Western and Pop; More Hits by the Supremes; We Remember Sam Cooke; At the Copa; Merry Christmas* 1966—*I Hear a Symphony; Supremes A Go-Go* 1967—*Sing Holland-Dozier-Holland; Sing Rodgers and Hart.*
As Diana Ross and the Supremes (no personnel change): 1967—*Greatest Hits, vol. 1; Greatest Hits, vol. 2* (– Ballard; + Cindy Birdsong [b. Dec. 15, 1939, Camden, NJ], voc.) 1968—*Reflections; Love Child; Sing and Perform "Funny Girl"; Live at London's Talk of the Town; Join the Temptations* (with the Temptations); *TCB* (with the Temptations) 1969—*Let the Sunshine In; Together* (with the Temptations); *Cream of the Crop; On Broadway* (with the Temptations); *Greatest Hits, vol. 3* 1970—*Farewell* 1974—*Anthology* 1986—*25th Anniversary* 1987—*The Never-Before-Released Masters* 1992—*Every Great #1 Hit* 1995—*The Best of Diana Ross & the Supremes: Anthology* 1997—*The Ultimate Collection.*
As the Supremes (or the "new" Supremes): 1969—(– Ross; + Jean Terrell [b. Nov. 26, ca. 1944, TX], voc.) 1970—*Right On; The Magnificent 7* (with the Four Tops); *New Ways but Love Stays* 1971—*The Return of the Magnificent Seven* (with the Four Tops); *Touch; Dynamite* (with the Four Tops) 1972—*Floy Joy* (– Birdsong; + Lynda Laurence, voc.) *The Supremes Produced and Arranged by Jimmy Webb* 1974—(– Terrell; + Scherrie Payne [b. Nov. 14, 1944], voc.; – Laurence; + Birdsong, voc.) 1975—*The Supremes* 1976—(– Birdsong; + Susaye Greene, voc.) *High Energy; Mary, Scherrie & Susaye* 1977—*At Their Best.*
All lineups: 2000—*The Supremes* (Motown).
Mary Wilson solo: 1979—*Mary Wilson* (Motown).
Scherrie and Susaye: 1979—*Partners* (Motown).
Diana Ross solo: see entry.

With 12 #1 pop singles, numerous gold recordings, sold-out concerts, and regular television appearances, the Supremes were not only the most commercially successful female group of the '60s but among the top 5 pop/rock/soul acts of that decade. Diana Ross, Mary Wilson, and Florence Ballard comprised Motown's flagship group, Berry Gordy Jr.'s black-pop music crossover dream come true that paved the way from rock radio hits and package bus tours to Las Vegas showrooms and Royal Command Performances. At the height of the civil rights movement, they were also embraced by the world as symbols of black achievement and black womanhood. Fronted by Diana Ross during their peak years, they epitomized Holland-Dozier-Holland's classic Motown sound and the label's sophisticated style. Unlike other so-called girl groups, the Supremes had a mature, glamorous demeanor that appealed equally to teens and adults. Beautiful, musically versatile, and unique, the original Supremes were America's sweethearts, setting standards and records that no group has yet equalled.

Diana Ross, Mary Wilson, and Florence Ballard met while each was living in Detroit's Brewster housing project. They began singing together in their teens and in their early years were a quartet, abetted by Betty McGlown and then Barbara Martin. Ballard was the most enthusiastic about pursuing a music career. While still in high school, she and the others became friendly with members of the Primes, a male vocal trio that included future founding Temptations Eddie Kendricks and Paul Williams. That group's manager formed the three girls, along with Williams' girlfriend, McGlown, into a "sister" group and dubbed them the Primettes. Of the three, Ballard, whose soulful style was closer to Aretha Franklin's than Ross', was originally considered the lead singer, although Ross and Wilson both sang lead. They became known locally, and through Ross came to know Smokey Robinson, who arranged their first audition for Gordy. Not yet

The Supremes: Diana Ross, Mary Wilson, Cindy Birdsong

out of high school, the Primettes were deemed too young to be signed, but they continued to hang around Hitsville, where they met other performers and contributed the occasional background vocal to records by other artists, including Mary Wells. In the meantime, they cut a single record for another local label, Lupine. Finally, in January 1961, Gordy signed the group to Motown and suggested that they change their name. Ballard suggested the Supremes.

Gordy groomed all his groups but paid special attention to the Supremes. Years later both Ross and Wilson, like several other Motown acts, would claim that Motown PR exaggerated their alleged impoverished upbringings and state that they had come to the label with their own coordinated stage costumes and choreography (masterminded by Temptation Paul Williams). The girls received instruction in dance, etiquette, and singing and were closely chaperoned. Although rumors of a romance between Gordy and Ross have endured over the years, neither specifically confirmed or denied them until Gordy revealed in his 1994 autobiography, *To Be Loved,* that Ross' eldest daughter, Rhonda, was his. Gordy was especially protective of the group and provided them with support not always offered to all his other acts.

Despite the attention, the group released nine singles that were either moderately successful (such as "Let Me Go the Right Way" and "When the Lovelight Starts Shining Through His Eyes") or flops before the Holland-Dozier-Holland team hit on the dramatic, seductive formula that showcased Ross' distinctive vocal style. Their 10th release, "Where Did Our Love Go," became their first #1 hit in summer 1964, selling over 2 million copies and starting a streak that resulted in two more chart-topping singles before year's end: "Baby Love" and "Come See About Me."

The Supremes' big singles of 1965 were "Stop! In the Name of Love" (#1 pop, #2 R&B), "Back in My Arms Again" (#1 pop and R&B), and "I Hear a Symphony" (#1 pop, #2 R&B). "You Can't Hurry Love" and "You Keep Me Hangin' On" were #1 on both the pop and R&B charts in 1966. "Love Is Here and Now You're Gone" (#1 pop and R&B), "The Happening" (#1 pop, #12 R&B), and "Reflections" (#2 pop, #4 R&B) hit in 1967. During that period the group averaged at least one national television appearance or major concert a week. Not only were the Supremes regular guests on such popular pop shows as *Shindig* and *Hullabaloo,* but on mainstream programs, such as Ed Sullivan's, *The Tonight Show, The Hollywood Palace,* and countless other variety programs where they acquitted themselves in performances with show-business legends like Pearl Bailey and the Andrews Sisters. Early on, Gordy decided that the group's major television appearances would feature their latest hit and a Broadway show tune or standard. They soon became steady headliners at top Vegas venues and supperclubs around the world, including the Copacabana and London's Talk of the Town, and other top Motown acts followed suit. They recorded in several foreign languages and drew huge audiences wherever they appeared. They were also important symbols of black success. As such, they were often seen at Democratic political fund raisers, for President Lyndon Johnson, among others, and were specially invited to attend the funeral of Dr. Martin Luther King Jr. in 1968.

Although the individual group members insisted they were a team, there was no denying that the public saw Ross as the star. Gordy, who had set his sights on moving Motown to L.A. and becoming a movie mogul, laid plans for Ross' eventual solo career. In 1967 "Reflections" was the first single credited to Diana Ross and the Supremes. By then, years of relentless touring and recording had taken their toll. Although both Ross and Wilson always credited Ballard with having founded the group, both later revealed in their respective autobiographies that Ballard's unpredictability, mood swings, and excessive drinking were threatening the group's future. In their and Gordy's defense, Ballard had missed several concert dates and become careless about her appearance and performance. Further, she was embittered by the attention being lavished on Ross, and finally in 1967 either quit or was asked to leave the group.

Although until recently Ballard was portrayed as a victim of Gordy and Ross' ambitions, her story was much more complicated. She left Motown and turned management of her career over to her husband, whose sole experience in the area consisted of being Gordy's chauffeur. Contrary to popular misconception, Ballard did not leave Motown penniless; rather, she received approximately $160,000 but was cheated out of it by her own attorney (who was later disbarred). She recorded an album for ABC that, to date, has not been released, and her two singles releases ("It Doesn't Matter How I Say It" b/w "Goin' Out of My Head" and "Love Ain't Love" b/w "Forever Faithful," both in 1968) failed to chart.

Within a few short years Ballard had three daughters, an unstable marriage, and was suffering from depression, alcoholism, and myriad health problems, including high blood pressure. She lost her home and for a while was separated from her husband and receiving aid for dependent children. Despite a few public appearances, including one that was part of President Richard Nixon's inaugural festivities, she basically gave up singing. Nine years after leaving Motown, she died of cardiac arrest in Detroit at 32. Both Ross and Wilson attended the funeral, presided over by Aretha Franklin's father, the Reverend C.L. Franklin. Among her pallbearers were the Four Tops.

Ballard was replaced by a member of Patti LaBelle and the Blue Belles, Cindy Birdsong. By that point, Holland-Dozier-Holland had left Motown, and while the Supremes continued to have hits with material recorded before the production team's departure, there were signs that in the wake of Aretha Franklin and the rise of soul, their smooth sophistication was becoming passé. "Love Child" (#1 pop, #2 R&B), an uncharacteristically bold song about illegitimacy, was the Supremes' biggest hit of 1968. They continued in the same vein with another slice of ghetto life, "I'm Livin' in Shame" (#10 pop, #8 R&B, 1969). These records were also significant for being the first on which Ross sang with anonymous background singers rather than Birdsong and Wilson. Others included the relatively less popular "The Composer" and "No Matter What Sign You Are." Their other big hits were group duets with the Temptations, with whom they costarred in two highly rated television specials, "T.C.B." (1968) and "G.I.T. on Broadway" (1969). These spun off hit albums and a string of popular singles, including "I'm Gonna Make You Love Me" and "I'll Try Something New."

By early 1969, Ross' future departure was widely rumored, and that November Motown issued the official press release. Speculation as to who would replace her focused on Syreeta Wright, but Gordy gave the spot to Jean Terrell, boxer Ernie Terrell's sister, to whom he'd signed to a solo contract earlier. The year ended with "Someday We'll Be Together" (#1 pop and R&B), a record that featured only one Supreme, Ross. In January 1970 Ross made her farewell appearance at the Frontier Hotel in Las Vegas. The event was documented on the live album *Farewell.* Though Ross went on as a hugely successful solo act [see her entry] her initial efforts were bested on the charts by the so-called "new" Supremes' first releases. Terrell was a stronger, earthier singer, and 1970 brought two Frank Wilson–produced hits: "Up the Ladder to the Roof" (#10 pop, #5 R&B) and "Stoned Love" (#7 pop, #1 R&B). Along with the Four Tops, this new lineup recorded three albums and hit with a powerful version of "River Deep—Mountain High" (#14 pop, #7 R&B, 1970). The progressive psychedelic blues "Nathan Jones" (#16 pop, #8 R&B) was the group's sole hit in 1971. The Smokey Robinson–written and –produced "Floy Joy" (#16 pop, #5 R&B) was considered their best effort of 1972.

By then the Supremes were not the only Motown act to suffer from the company's lack of support. Unlike early Motown artists, however, the newer Supremes, including Terrell, bristled at Gordy's authority and early on (Wilson claims as early as January 1970), he lost interest in the group. Through a series of producers, among them Jimmy Webb and Stevie Wonder (1973's "Bad Weather") and personnel changes that left Wilson the only original and consistent member, the group struggled against Motown's, and eventually the public's, indifference. Interestingly, the latter versions of the group didn't suffer from a lack of talent: Lynda Laurence and Susaye Greene had both been members of Stevie Wonder's group Wonderlove; Greene was a proven songwriter who would later cowrite "I Can't Help It" for Michael Jackson's *Thriller.* Scherrie Payne, sister of Freda, had sung with Holland-Dozier-Holland's group Glass House and was considered a technically gifted vocalist. In 1976 the Greene-Wilson-Payne lineup released the Supremes' last Top 40 single, "I'm Gonna Let My Heart Do the Walking." Wilson, who became the group's leader, decided to pursue a solo career and the last version of the Supremes gave their final farewell performance in London in 1977. Payne and Greene continued briefly as a duo. Birdsong worked as a secretary at Motown, then attempted a solo career. She has since become intensely religious. Terrell and Laurence both retired to marry. They, along with Payne, have performed together in recent years as "Supremes." Rumors that the hit Broadway play *Dreamgirls* was based on the Supremes' story were confirmed with the 1986 publication of Mary Wilson's best-selling autobiography *Dreamgirl: My Life as a Supreme* (cowritten with Arghus Juilliard and Patricia Romanowski). Aside from Ross, Wilson remains the best-known ex-Supreme, and she also authored a sequel recounting the latter-day Supremes, her abusive marriage, and ongoing legal disputes with Motown, *Supreme Faith* (with Romanowski) in 1990.

The first attempt at a Supremes reunion of Ross, Wilson, and Birdsong, occurred at the taping of *Motown 25* in 1983 and ended in embarrassment when Ross pushed Wilson's microphone away from her face. Though the segment was not aired, it was widely reported and seemed to confirm the old image of Ross as the pushy leader. Despite the author's protests to the contrary, Wilson's depiction of Ross further damaged whatever relationship the two might have had.

In 1988, when the Supremes were inducted into the Rock and Roll Hall of Fame, Ross declined to attend, leaving Wilson and Ballard's youngest daughter, Lisa, to accept on behalf of the group. Although Wilson's solo records have not been successful, she continues to perform around the world. In January 1991 Wilson was injured and the youngest of her three children, Pedro Ferrer, was killed in a car accident. In the wake of that accident, she and Ross reconciled. Wilson continues to perform around the world to good reviews; she is also pursuing a degree at New York University.

The Supremes were front-page news again in the spring of 2000, when Ross announced what would become known as the Supremes Return to Love Tour. To the disappointment of fans and critics alike, Ross chose to tour with Payne and Laurence—two Supremes who had not joined the group until after her departure and with whom she had never worked before—after Wilson and Birdsong declined to join her. Though accounts of the negotiations differ in their details, Ross stood to earn an estimated $20 million for the tour, but she and/or her representatives refused to pay Wilson and Birdsong more than $3 million each. Clearly underestimating the public's affection for Wilson and Birdsong and its desire to see a real reunion, Ross forged on with a pretour campaign that included a VH1 *Divas* tribute to her, an hour on *Oprah,* and an interview with Barbara Walters in which she described Wilson as "vindictive" and "angry." While ticket sales were brisk in some cities, most venues did not even sell half their seats, and the tour was canceled midway through. Ross was savaged in the media for what some critics flatly termed egomania. Ironically, the tour's failure reminded anyone who might have forgotten that the Supremes were first, foremost, and always a group of three whose collective magic could not be eclipsed by any individual, not even Ross.

Surface

Formed 1983, West Orange, NJ
David Townsend (b. May 17, 1954, Englewood, CA), gtr., kybds., voc.; David "Pic" Conley (b. Dec. 27, 1953, Newark, NJ), bass, sax, perc., kybds., flute, voc.; Karen Copeland (d. Dec. 5, 1988, NJ), voc.
1984—(– Copeland; + Bernard Jackson [b. July 11, 1959, Stamford, CT], voc.) 1987—*Surface* (Columbia) 1988—*2nd Wave* 1990—*3 Deep* 1991—*The Best of Surface . . . A Nice Time 4 Lovin'* 1994—(– Jackson; – Townsend; + Eric "G. Riff" Moore [b. Aug. 23, 1971, Irvington, NJ], voc.; + Everett "Jam" Benton [b. Sep. 6, 1969, Buffalo, NY], kybds., voc.).
Bernard Jackson solo: 2000—*Bernard Jackson* (Orchard).

Surface is a soul group that scored several hits with its R&B ballads and smooth dance grooves. The band was formed by David Townsend, son of producer/songwriter Ed Townsend and a former member of the Isley Brothers band, and David Conley, who had played with the '70s funk band Mandrill [see entry], with Karen Copeland on vocals. That version of Surface released two singles with mild success. Townsend and Conley then began working with singer/songwriter Bernard Jackson. Surface wrote songs for artists including New Edition, Isaac Hayes, the Jets, Sister Sledge, and Gwen Guthrie and began to record its own material.

Surface's eponymous debut yielded a few hits: "Happy" (#20 pop, #2 R&B, 1987), "Lately" (#8 R&B, 1987), and "Let's Try Again" (#22 R&B, 1987). They avoided sophomore jinx on *2nd Wave,* which included "Shower Me With Your Love" (#5 pop, #1 R&B, 1989). They continued to hit with the R&B market on *3 Deep,* which included "All I Want Is You" (#8 R&B, 1991), featuring backing vocals by Regina Belle, "Never Gonna Let You Down" (#17 pop, #24 R&B, 1991), and "You're the One" (#35 R&B, 1991).

Townsend and Conley produced Aretha Franklin's Grammy-nominated 1991 album *What You See Is What You Sweat.* As of late 1994, Jackson had formed a new group, Townsend was working A&R for a record label, and Conley was managing and producing bands including Tu Luce. Surface has yet to put out another record, but Jackson finally released his self-titled in 2000.

The Surfaris

Formed 1962, Glendora, CA
Pat Connolly (b. 1947), voc., bass; Jim Fuller (b. 1947), gtr.; Bob Berryhill (b. 1947), gtr.; Ron Wilson (b. 1945; d. May 1989), drums; Jim Pash (b. 1949), sax, clarinet, gtr.
1963—*Wipe Out* (Dot); *The Surfaris Play Wipe Out and Others* 1964—*Hit City 64* ca. 1966—(– Berryhill; – Connolly; – Fuller) 1981—*Punkline* (N/A).

The Surfaris rode the wave of the early-'60s surf-music boom, often appearing at Southern California teen dances and beach parties with surf outfits like the Crossfires, who later became the Turtles. The Surfaris had only one big hit record, the 1963 instrumental "Wipe Out," which contained one of rock's first and most influential drum solos. The single hit #2 in 1963 and recharted at #16 in 1966.

It would be the group's only major hit and began life as a throwaway B side, recorded in two quick takes. But while "Wipe Out" would prove to be the Surfaris' ticket to fame, it was also a subject of contention for them. Their debut album, *Wipe Out,* they discovered, contained only two Surfaris tracks: "Wipe Out," and its A side, "Surfer Joe." The rest of the album was recorded by the Challengers, and so it was that group, and not the Surfaris, who received royalties, despite the fact that it was the Surfaris' hit title track that sold it. Then another L.A. group sued the Surfaris, claiming that they were the original and rightful Surfaris. Once all this dust settled, the group began recording again, but there were no further charting singles after "Point Panic" (#49, 1963).

After surf music went out of vogue, the Surfaris followed the folk-rock trend without success. By the mid-'60s, the group was basically disbanded, though Pash kept lineups working for years. The group re-formed on several occasions through the '70s, and in 1981 recorded a new album. Berryhill and Pash have become born-again Christians; Wilson died in poverty; Jim Fuller briefly joined the Seeds. Pash led a group that recorded music for the shortlived *New Gidget* television series in 1986.

"Wipe Out" has been revived countless times, in films (*Back to the Beach,* 1987), commercials (Stri-Dex, Wendy's), and on record (by Herbie Hancock, Dweezil Zappa, Scorpions drummer Herman Rarebell, among many others). In the summer of 1987 the Beach Boys and the Fat Boys had a #12 hit with their remake of the immortal surf classic.

Swamp Dogg

Born Jerry Williams Jr., July 12, 1942, Portsmouth, VA
1970—*Total Destruction to Your Mind* (Canyon) 1971—*Rat On!* (Elektra) 1972—*Cuffed, Collared and Tagged* (Cream) 1973—*Gag a Maggot* (Stone Dogg) 1974—*Have You Heard*

This Story? (Island) 1976—*Swamp Dogg's Greatest Hits* (Stone Dogg) 1977—*Finally Caught Up With Myself* (Musicor); *An Opportunity . . . Not a Bargain!* 1981—*I'm Not Selling Out, I'm Buying In!* (Takoma) 1982—*Best of Swamp Dogg* (Solid Smoke) 1989—*I Called for a Rope and They Threw Me a Rock* (S.D.E.G.) 1991—*Surfin' in Harlem* (Volt) 1995—*Best of 25 Years of Swamp Dogg . . . Or F*** the Bomb, Stop the Drugs* (Pointblank, Virgin) 1996—*Excellent Sides of Swamp Dogg* (S.D.E.G.) 2000—*The Re-Invention of Swamp Dogg; The Little Jerry Williams Anthology a/k/a Swamp Dogg (1954–1969).*

Singer/songwriter/producer Swamp Dogg has had a varied career, during which his work has resulted in hits for other artists but rarely for himself.

Recording at first as "Little Jerry," Jerry Williams began in the '50s as a soul singer. By the middle of the next decade, he had scored a couple of minor hits, "I'm a Lover Man" and "Baby You're My Everything." In 1970 he became chief producer for Wally Roker's Canyon Records, where he was encouraged to stretch out musically, and therefore became Swamp Dogg. Under that name, he released *Total Destruction to Your Mind,* a psychedelically eccentric soul album influenced by Sly and the Family Stone and the Mothers of Invention. "Mama's Baby, Daddy's Maybe" was a minor hit (#33 R&B, 1970), and Swamp Dogg began incorporating touches of bayou style, a la Tony Joe White. Williams then signed with Elektra, but *Rat On!* was a commercial and artistic failure. In 1972 he moved to Cream Records and released *Cuffed, Collared and Tagged,* which included a tribute to Sly Stone called "If It Hadn't Been for Sly" and the John Prine song "Sam Stone." Soon after the album's release, Cream went out of business.

Swamp Dogg (a.k.a. Jerry Williams)

As a producer, Jerry Williams fared better. He wrote Gene Pitney's 1968 hit "She's a Heartbreaker" and produced the Commodores' first single, "I Keep On Dancing," while an Atlantic staff member, and Doris Duke's Top 10 soul hit, "I'm the Other Woman to the Other Woman," in 1970. In 1971 his song "She's All I Got" was a Top 40 pop hit for Freddy North and a #1 country song for Johnny Paycheck. Williams also had soul hits sung by Z.Z. Hill, Irma Thomas, and Charlie Whitehead.

Still Swamp Dogg struggled, although he released several records through the '70s. In the late '80s he formed the S.D.E.G. label and management company, which had a measure of success with the rappers M.C. Breed & DFC, whose self-titled album made the R&B Top 40. Dogg continued to release his own material as well, most notably *The Re-Invention of Swamp Dogg,* a calypso album recorded in Trinidad. The Swamp Dogg sound found new ears as well when Kid Rock, on his multiplatinum *Devil Without a Cause,* sampled Dogg's "I Got One for Ya."

Billy Swan

Born May 12, 1942, Cape Girardeau, MO
1971—*I Can Help* (Columbia) 1975—*Rock 'n' Roll Moon* 1976—*Billy Swan* 1977—*Four* 1978—*You're OK, I'm OK* (A&M) 1978—*Billy Swan at His Best* (Monument) 2000—*Like Elvis Used to Do* (Audium).

Billy Swan, a Nashville journeyman, emerged seemingly from nowhere with one of 1974's biggest hits, the strolling organ-heavy "I Can Help." A #1 on both the pop and country charts, "I Can Help" differed almost completely from Swan's usual output, which leaned toward rockabilly.

Swan had his first success when his song "Lover Please," which he had written at age 16 for his band Mirt Mirley and the Rhythm Steppers, became a nationwide hit in 1962 for Clyde McPhatter. Swan lived off that song's royalties for a time, then moved to Nashville at age 21, where his pursuit of a music career led him to replace Kris Kristofferson as janitor at Columbia's Nashville studios. Within a few years Swan was producing Tony Joe White's first three LPs (including White's hit "Polk Salad Annie"). He also lived for a time in Elvis Presley's uncle's house; in fact, after Presley covered "I Can Help," he gave Swan a pair of his socks.

In 1970 Swan played in Kristofferson's band at the Isle of Wight Festival, and in 1973 he worked with comic country singer and author Kinky Friedman; in 1975 the latter covered "Lover Please" (as did Kristofferson). After the international success of "I Can Help," Swan's debut album yielded a minor U.K. hit in a cover of Otis Blackwell's "Don't Be Cruel." *Rock 'n' Roll Moon,* another critically acclaimed album, contained another minor hit in "Everything's the Same." It was Swan's last pop success, but through 1975 and 1976 he embarked on successful worldwide tours, playing with Nashville session stars like Kenny Buttrey and Charlie McCoy in Paris in 1975, and with Willie Nelson in Britain in 1976. In 1986 he joined with Randy Meisner (ex–Poco and Eagles) and former Bread member James Griffin in Black Tie. The group released *When the Night Falls*. In 2000 Swan released an album of rearranged Elvis Presley covers.

Keith Sweat

Born July 22, 1961, New York, NY
1987—*Make It Last Forever* (Vintertainment/Elektra) 1990—*I'll Give All My Love to You* 1991—*Keep It Comin'* (Elektra) 1994—*Get Up on It* 1996—*Keith Sweat* 1998—*Still in the Game* 2000—*Didn't See Me Coming.*
LSG: 1997—*Levert-Sweat-Gill* (Elektra).

With his good looks and romantic singing style propelled by hard rhythmic tracks, Keith Sweat helped revitalize R&B in the late '80s.

Sweat was born in Harlem, the third of five children, and grew up in projects a few blocks from the Apollo Theatre. He joined his first group at age 15, then became the frontman for Jamilah. After graduating from City College, he worked on Wall Street as a brokerage assistant. He continued to shop his demo around and eventually signed with manager Vincent Davis' Vintertainment label.

Sweat's first single, "I Want Her" (#1 R&B, 1987), produced by Teddy Riley, was the first major New Jack Swing hit, fusing soul and hip-hop. The album, *Make It Last Forever* (#15 pop, 1988; #1 R&B, 1987) was coproduced by Riley and went multiplatinum. It included the singles "Something Just Ain't Right" (#79 pop, #3 R&B, 1988) and "Make It Last Forever" (#59 pop, #2 R&B, 1988), a duet with Jacci McGhee. Sweat continued his pop crossover success on *I'll Give All My Love to You* (#6 pop, #1 R&B, 1990), yielding the hits "Make You Sweat" (#14 pop, #1 R&B, 1990), "I'll Give All My Love to You" (#7 pop, #1 R&B, 1990), and "Merry Go Round" (#2 R&B, 1990), a ballad.

Keith Sweat

Sweat split from Davis and released *Keep It Comin'* (#19 pop, #1 R&B, 1991). The album featured cameos by L.L. Cool J, on "Keep It Comin' " (#17 pop, #1 R&B, 1991), and the Gap Band's Charlie Wilson, as well as the single "Your Love—Part 2" (#71 pop, #4 R&B, 1991). In 1992 Sweat formed Keia Records, a label featuring new R&B and rap acts, that is distributed by Elektra and based in New York and Atlanta. His 1994 album, *Get Up on It* (#8 pop, #1 R&B), yielded such singles as the title track (#69 pop, #12 R&B, 1994), "When I Give My Love (#93 pop, #21 R&B, 1994), and "How Do You Like It?" (#48 pop, #9 R&B, 1994).

Sweat's self-titled followup (#5 pop, #1 R&B, 1996) continued his incredible chart run, producing two more big hits, "Twisted" (#2 pop, #1 R&B, 1996) and "Nobody" (#3 pop, #1 R&B, 1996). In 1997 he teamed up with singers Gerald Levert and Johnny Gill to make *Levert-Sweat-Gill* (#4 pop, #2 R&B). Sweat returned with another solo record, *Still in the Game* (#6 pop, #2 R&B), in 1998, an album of love songs that included the single "Come and Get With Me" (#12 pop, #6 R&B) featuring rapper Snoop Dogg. Peaking at #2, the record was Sweat's first album in a decade not to top the R&B chart.

Matthew Sweet

Born Sidney Matthew Sweet, Oct. 6, 1964, Lincoln, NE
1986—*Inside* (Columbia) 1989—*Earth* (A&M) 1991—*Girlfriend* (Zoo) 1993—*Altered Beast* 1995—*100% Fun* 1997—*Blue Sky on Mars* (Volcano/Zoo) 1999—*In Reverse* (Volcano) 2001—*Time Capsule—1990–2000.*

Matthew Sweet's career has been a kind of Cook's tour of postpunk rock, ranging from Athens, Georgia, to New York to L.A., with *Girlfriend* (#100, 1992), a pristine *Revolver*-meets-Neil-Young amalgam, finally bringing him to the public's attention.

Sweet, a musician in high school, attended the University of Georgia in Athens in 1983 because he was attracted by its music scene. He met Lynda Stipe (sister of R.E.M.'s Michael) there and joined her band, Oh-OK, playing on its Mitch Easter–produced EP, *Furthermore What* (1983). With Oh-OK drummer David Pierce, Sweet formed Buzz of Delight and wrote and produced *Sound Castles* (1984). This EP and a tape of unreleased songs produced by Don Dixon caught the attention of Columbia Records, who brought Sweet to New York and signed him to a solo deal. Settling up north, Sweet recorded *Inside*, playing most of the instruments, backed by a drum machine, and augmented with cameos by Aimee Mann, Chris Stamey (dB's), and Anton Fier. With Fier, Sweet played on the Golden Palominos' *Blast of Silence* (1986), cowriting one song, "Something Becomes Nothing."

Maher coproduced Sweet's next album, *Earth,* with the Blasters' Dave Alvin. Again it was mostly Sweet, with guest appearances by New York guitarists Richard Lloyd (Television) and Robert Quine (Richard Hell, Lou Reed) and singer Kate Pierson (B-52's). Like *Inside,* it generated massive critical admiration but scant sales. Recorded during the breakup of his marriage in 1990, *Girlfriend* (originally titled *Nothing Lasts*) was delayed when Sweet was dropped by A&M. Sweet was about to give up on shopping the tape when Zoo—which had passed on the album—signed him after its president heard the demo playing in a staffer's office. The album marked the first time Sweet had recorded with a "live" band. Its success (over 400,000 copies sold) allowed Sweet to take on other projects, playing on Lloyd Cole's 1990 European solo tour and coproducing Velvet Crush's debut, *In the Presence of Greatness* (1991).

Moving to L.A. in 1992, Sweet used producer Richard Dashut (Fleetwood Mac, Lindsey Buckingham) with Quine and Lloyd, joined by guitarist Ivan Julian, pianist Nicky Hopkins, and drummers Pete Thomas (Elvis Costello), Mick Fleetwood, and Jody Stephens (Big Star) for *Altered Beast* (#75, 1993). Sweet's 1995 release, *100% Fun* (#65), produced by Brendan O'Brien (Pearl Jam, Stone Temple Pilots), again featured guitarists Lloyd and Quine and contained the hit single "Sick of Myself" (#58). Sweet reteamed with producer O'Brien for 1997's *Blue Sky on Mars* (#66), and then hired the team of Jim Scott (Tom Petty), Fred Maher, and longtime Sweet collaborator Greg Leisz to produce 1999's *In Reverse* (#188). Inspired by Phil Spector's production work, the reverb-heavy album featured a cast of 17 backing musicians, including bassist Carol Kaye (the Beach Boys' *Pet Sounds*.)

Rachel Sweet

Born 1963, Akron, OH
1979—*Fool Around* (Stiff/Columbia) 1980—*Protect the Innocent* (Columbia) 1981—*. . . And Then He Kissed Me* 1982—*Blame It on Love* 1992—*Fool Around: The Best of Rachel Sweet* (Rhino).

Rachel Sweet was 18 when rock fans first heard her on Stiff Records' *Akron Compilation,* with a big twangy voice that elicited comparisons to Linda Ronstadt and Brenda Lee. Sweet had begun performing at age five, when she won first prize at an Akron talent contest with a rendition of "I Am a Pretty Little Dutch Girl." She went on to perform in summer stock theater, in TV commercials, and in club shows with Mickey Rooney and Bill Cosby. At age 11, she cut a minor country & western hit single for Derrick Records in Nashville. A few years later, producer Liam Sternberg (a friend of Sweet's father) asked her to sing on a demo of his songs, which he sent to Stiff. Sweet was attending Firestone High School in Akron when "Who Does Lisa Like?" became a minor hit in England and New York. A cover of Carla Thomas' "B-A-B-Y," from Sweet's debut album, also generated some attention, as did her segments in the 1979 Be Stiff Tour and her own tour backed by British band Fingerprintz.

With her second album. Sweet parted ways with Sternberg and Stiff, and has since been searching for a major pop hit. She reached the Top 50 with "Everlasting Love," a duet with teen idol Rex Smith; it appeared on . . . *And Then He Kissed Me.* Sweet herself wrote and produced the album *Blame It on Love,* and in 1982 she worked on a 3-D horror film, *Rock 'n' Roll Hotel.* In 1988 she sang the title song of John Waters' *Hairspray.* She has since appeared on the Comedy Channel and become the voice of the animated Barbie. She continued acting throughout the '90s, notably as a guest on the hit comedy *Seinfeld.*

Sweet

Formed 1968, London, Eng.
Brian Connolly (b. Oct. 5, 1944, Hamilton, Scot.; d. Feb. 10, 1997, Slough, Eng.), voc.; Mick Tucker (b. July 17, 1948, Middlesex, Eng.), voc., drums; Andy Scott (b. July 30, 1949, Wexham, Wales), gtr., kybds., voc.; Steve Priest (b. Feb. 23, 1950, Middlesex), bass, voc., harmonica.
1971—*Funny How Sweet Co-Co Can Be* (RCA) 1972—*Biggest Hits* 1973—*Sweet* (Bell) 1974—*Sweet Fanny Adams* (RCA) 1975—*Desolation Boulevard* (Capitol); *Strung Up* (RCA) 1976—*Give Us a Wink* (Capitol) 1977—*Off the Record* 1978—*Level Headed* (Capitol) (– Connolly; + Gary Moberley, kybds.) *The Sweet* (Camden) 1979—*A Cut Above the Rest* 1980—*Water's Edge* (Capitol) 1982—*Identity Crisis* (Polydor, U.K.) 1990—*Live at the Marquee* (Maze) 1992—*The Best of Sweet* (Capitol).

One of the leading British hard-rock/bubblegum bands in the Chinnichap stable of British writer/producers Nicky Chinn and Mike Chapman, Sweet had hits in the U.K. and later in America as well. The band was originally formed by Brian Connolly and Mick Tucker as Wainwright's Gentlemen in 1968. As Sweet, the band members recorded four unsuccessful singles that flopped before Chinnichap took over in 1971. Sweet's U.K. hits that year included "Co-Co" and "Funny Funny." In 1972 came "Poppa Joe," "Little Willy" (also Top 10 in America in 1973), and "Wig Wam Bam"; and in 1973, "Blockbuster," "Hell Raiser," and "Ballroom Blitz" (Top 10 in the U.S. two years later).

By 1973, the blatant nature of many of Sweet's lyrics and overt stage antics led some British clubs to ban the group. It subsequently tried to abandon its bubblegum image and left inamicably from Chinnichap. The band went on to hit in 1976 in both the U.K. and the U.S. with the Top 10 single "Fox on the Run," but it didn't really change its sound until 1978's *Level Headed* (#52), which yielded the worldwide smash "Love Is Like Oxygen" (#8). A followup entitled "California Nights" was a modest U.S. hit but its last here. Things were not going so well in the U.K. either, and after the disappointment of *Water's Edge,* the group disbanded.

Sweet has returned in various incarnations with different lineups. A club remix of its hits entitled "It's It's the Sweet Mix" was a U.K. hit in 1985, prompting another re-formation, but it was short-lived. Scott toured in the late '80s with the group Paddy Goes to Holyhead. Scott and Tucker re-formed the group for *Live at the Marquee.* Connolly, whose years of hard drinking eventually led to several heart attacks and partial paralysis, continued to perform until his death in 1997.

The Sweet Inspirations

Formed ca. '50s as the Drinkard Sisters, Newark, NJ
Emily "Cissy" Houston, voc.; Sylvia Shemwell (b. Sylvia Guions), voc.; Judy Clay (b. Judy Guions), voc.; Dede Warwick, voc.; Dionne Warwick (b. Dec. 12, 1940, East Orange, NJ), voc.
Ca. mid-'60s (– Dionne Warwick; – Dede Warwick; – Clay; + Estelle Brown, voc.; + Myrna Smith, voc.) 1968—*Sweet Inspirations* (Atlantic); *What the World Needs Now Is Love* 1970—(– Houston) 1994—*The Best of the Sweet Inspirations* (Ichiban).

The Sweet Inspirations trace their beginnings back to the Drinkard Sisters, with Cissy Houston [see entry] and her nieces Dede and Dionne Warwick [see entry], along with the Guions sisters, Judy (later Judy Clay) and Sylvia (later Sylvia Shemwell). They recorded gospel music for RCA before the group disbanded, leaving Houston and Shemwell to round out the group with two new members.

This quartet became renowned throughout the record industry for its fine backing work on hundreds of records, including some by Ronnie Hawkins, William Bell, Solomon Burke, Neil Diamond, Dusty Springfield, and Wilson Pickett. The four women were featured prominently on some of Aretha Franklin's best work. Atlantic Records' Jerry Wexler dubbed them the Sweet Inspirations, and led by Cissy, the group recorded two critically acclaimed albums in 1968, and had a hit single with "Sweet Inspiration" (#18 pop, #5 R&B).

The group continued doing backup work, most notably on Elvis Presley's 1969 hit "Suspicious Minds." The Sweet Inspirations toured with him into the mid-'70s. In 1970 Houston left to join Darlene Love and Dede Warwick as backup singers for Dionne Warwick. The remaining trio continued working, touring with Elvis and, briefly, with Rick Nelson. Former Sweet Inspiration Myrna Smith cowrote the bulk of the material on Beach Boy Carl Wilson's eponymous 1981 solo album. Shemwell, Smith, and Estelle Brown performed together in 1994. They have also reunited for various tributes to Presley.

The Swingin' Blue Jeans

Formed 1959, Liverpool, Eng.
Original lineup: Ray Ennis (b. May 26, 1942, Liverpool), gtr., voc.; Ray Ellis (b. Mar. 8, 1942, Liverpool), gtr.; Les Braid (b. Sep. 15, 1941, Liverpool), bass; Norman Kuhlke (b. June 12, 1942, Liverpool), drums; Paul Moss, banjo (b. Liverpool).
N.A.—(– Moss) 1964—(+ Terry Sylvester [b. Jan. 8, 1945, Liverpool], gtr., voc.) *Hippy Hippy Shake* (Imperial); *Shaking Time* (Llectrola) 1965—*Hey Hey Hey Hey* 1968—(– Sylvester) 1973—(group re-forms; numerous lineup changes follow) 1993—*Hippy Hippy Shake: The Definitive Collection* (EMI Legends).

In 1963, just as England's Merseybeat sound was coming together, the Swingin' Blue Jeans emerged with one of the wildest rock raveups of the era, a cover of Chan Romero's "Hippy Hippy Shake." It went to #2 in the U.K. and #24 in the U.S. The next year, the group's cover of Little Richard's "Good Golly Miss Molly" hit #11, and a version of the Betty Everett hit "You're No Good" (a hit for Linda Ronstadt over a decade later) made it to #3. Though the Swingin' Blue Jeans continued to record and perform, and even re-formed in the early '70s, they would enjoy no further successes. Terry Sylvester later joined the Hollies, replacing Graham Nash. A version of the group, led by guitarist Ray Ennis and bassist Paul Braid, continued to tour in 2001.

Swing Out Sister

Formed 1985, Manchester, Eng.
Corinne Drewery (b. Sep. 21, 1959, Nottingham, Eng.), voc.; Andy Connell (b. July 26, 1961, Manchester), kybds.; Martin Jackson (b. Aug. 30, 1958), drums.
1987—*It's Better to Travel* (Mercury) 1988—(– Jackson) 1989—*Kaleidoscope World* (Fontana/Mercury) 1992—*Get in Touch With Yourself* (Fontana) 1994—*Living Return* (Mercury) 1997—*Shapes and Patterns.*

This British dance-pop band scored right out of the box with its first single, "Breakout" (#6, 1987), a sprightly and melodic showcase for Corinne Drewery's bright vocals. The song's video gently mocked Drewery's background as a fashion designer. Andy Connell had played with Manchester-based avant-fusion band A Certain Ratio, while Martin Jackson had drummed with such bands as Magazine. Jackson left after the #1 U.K. LP *It's Better to Travel* (#40, 1987), which yielded a lesser hit in "Twilight World" (#31, 1987); he contributed drum programming to *Kaleidoscope World* (#61, 1989), which spawned the single "Waiting Game" (#86, 1989). *Get in Touch With Yourself* (#113, 1992) yielded the minor hit single "Am I the Same Girl" (#45, 1992). While the group has sustained its career with popularity in Japan, its presence in America became increasingly scarce. In 1994 it released *Living Return* and in 1997 *Shapes and Patterns,* which featured a cover of Laura Nyro's "Stoned Soul Picnic."

Take 6

Formed 1987, Huntsville, AL
Alvin Chea (b. Nov. 2, 1967, San Francisco, CA), voc.; Mervyn Warren, voc.; David Thomas (b. Oct. 23, 1966, Brooklyn, NY), voc.; Cedric Dent (b. Sep. 24, 1962, Detroit, MI), voc.; Claude V. McKnight III (b. Oct. 2, 1962, Brooklyn), voc.; Mark Kibble (b. Apr. 7, 1964, Bronx, NY), voc.
1988—*Take 6* (Reprise) 1990—*So Much 2 Say* 1991—(– Warren; + Joel Kibble [b. May 16, 1971, Buffalo, NY], voc.) *He Is Christmas* 1994—*Join the Band* 1996—*Brothers* 1998—*So Cool* 1999—*We Wish You a Merry Christmas* 2000—*Tonight: Live.*

Take 6 is an a cappella gospel group that achieved surprising critical and commercial success with their sophisticated, jazz-based arrangements. The group formed in the early '80s at Oakwood College, a Seventh-Day Adventist school. Mark Kibble joined when he heard a quartet singing in a bathroom and added his own improvisation; as the group's primary arranger, he expanded their sound from barbershop quartet to big band, with voices imitating instruments. He also brought in sixth member Mervyn Warren. Originally called Alliance, Take 6 changed their name in 1987 (the same year they signed to Reprise) when they discovered another band with that name.

Their first album contains spirituals and compositions by Kibble and Warren. *Take 6,* featuring "Spread Love," won three Grammys and went gold. *So Much 2 Say* has a larger array of original compositions penned by additional band members. The added variety includes instruments—everyone in the group also plays, and Dent and Warren have done graduate work in music theory—and hip-hop and Latin rhythms. Their second album also went gold and won a Grammy. In 1990 Take 6 performed with k.d. lang [see entry] in the film *Dick Tracy* singing "Ridin' the Rails."

Warren left the band in 1991; he had composed TV theme songs along the way, including the one for *Murphy Brown,* which Take 6 sang. He was replaced by Mark's brother Joel. *He Is Christmas,* which also won a Grammy, is a collection of carols. Take 6 has recorded with Dianne Reeves, Quincy Jones, Joe Sample, Johnny Mathis, and Smokey Robinson. The group's 1994 recording, *Join the Band* (#86 pop, #17 R&B), featured Ray Charles, Stevie Wonder, Queen Latifah, and Herbie Hancock, among others.

Brothers (#71 R&B, 1996) continued in the pop vein of Take 6's most recent work, stressing solo voices over the group's trademark vocal blend. The album, which included a version of Earth, Wind & Fire's "Sing a Song," was a commercial and artistic disappointment. Its 1998 followup, *So Cool* (#92 R&B), found Take 6 once again singing a cappella. It also saw the sextet expanding their sound to include elements of *mbube,* the rhythmic South African vocal style popularized by Ladysmith Black Mambazo. In 2000 Take 6 released their first live album; the set featured a wide range of material culled from a performance at the Blue Note in Tokyo.

Talking Heads

Formed 1975, New York, NY
David Byrne (b. May 14, 1952, Dumbarton, Scot.), voc., gtr.; Tina Weymouth (b. Nov, 22, 1950, Coronado, CA), bass, synth.; Chris Frantz (b. May 8, 1951, Ft. Campbell, KY), drums; Jerry Harrison (b. Feb. 21, 1949, Milwaukee, WI), kybds., gtr.
1977—*77* (Sire) 1978—*More Songs About Buildings and Food* 1979—*Fear of Music* 1980—*Remain in Light* 1982—*The Name of This Band Is Talking Heads* 1983—*Speaking in Tongues* 1984—*Stop Making Sense* 1985—*Little Creatures* 1986—*True Stories* 1988—*Naked* 1992—*Popular Favorites 1976–1992: Sand in the Vaseline* 1996—(– Byrne, as The Heads) *No Talking Just Head* (Radioactive) 1999—*Stop Making Sense* (Special Edition).
Tom Tom Club (Weymouth; Frantz; + others): 1981—*The Tom Tom Club* (Sire) 1983—*Close to the Bone* 1989—*Boom Boom Chi Boom Boom* 1992—*Dark Sneak Love Action* 2000—*The Good the Bad and the Funky* (Rykodisc).
Jerry Harrison solo: 1981—*The Red and the Black* (Sire) 1988—*Casual Gods* 1990—*Walk on Water.*
David Byrne solo: see entry.

Talking Heads was a band of smart, self-conscious white musicians intrigued by the rhythms and spirit of black music. They drew on funk, classical minimalism, and African rock to create some of the most adventurous, original, and danceable music to emerge from new wave—a movement Talking Heads outlasted and transcended in their accomplishment and influence.

David Byrne and Chris Frantz met at the Rhode Island School of Design, where they were part of a quintet called, variously, the Artistics and the Autistics. With Tina Weymouth, Frantz's girlfriend, they shared an apartment in New York and formed Talking Heads as a trio in 1975; they played their first shows at CBGB that June. Their music was never conventional punk rock; it was more delicate and contrapuntal, and their early sets included covers of the '60s bubblegum group the 1910 Fruitgum Company. Jerry Harrison, a Harvard alumnus who had been a Modern Lover with Jonathan Richman until 1974 and had also backed singer/songwriter Elliott Murphy, completed the band in 1977.

Talking Heads toured Europe with the Ramones before recording their first album, and once it was released they began constant touring of the U.S. and Europe. Their first album contained "Psycho Killer," which typecast them as eccentrics, an impression confirmed by Byrne's nervous, wild-eyed stage presence. The album reached the Top 100, and every subsequent album reached the U.S. Top 40.

With *More Songs About Buildings and Food,* Talking Heads began a four-year relationship with producer Brian Eno, an experimentalist who toyed with electronically altered sounds and shared their growing interest in Arabian and African music. *More Songs* included a cover of Al Green's "Take Me to the River," which was the band's first hit (#26, 1978). *Fear of Music* (#21, 1979) was a denser, more ominous record, but its followup, *Remain in Light* (#19, 1980), was an almost complete shift in tone. It used rhythm tracks improvised by Eno and the band in the studio that were layered with vocals and solos, a mixture of African communalism and Western technology (an approach signaled by "I Zimbra," the opening track on *Fear of Music*).

After *Remain in Light,* Talking Heads toured the world with an expanded band: keyboardist Bernie Worrell of Parliament/Funkadelic, guitarist Adrian Belew (who had played with Frank Zappa and David Bowie), bassist Busta Cherry Jones, percussionist Steven Scales, and singers Nona Hendryx (formerly of Labelle) and Dollette McDonald.

Band members then turned to solo projects. Byrne has explored electronics, performance art, and world music, and scored music for films and the stage. Harrison made *The Red and the Black;* and Frantz and Weymouth recorded as the Tom Tom Club, scoring a major disco hit with "Genius of Love," which made the album go platinum. In 1982 the Heads ended their association with Eno; they released a compilation of live performances by all versions of the band and toured the U.S. and Europe as an eight-piece group.

Speaking in Tongues, the first album of new Heads songs in three years, was released in 1983. (A limited edition release of 50,000 copies featured a complex cover designed by artist Robert Rauschenberg. Subsequent copies boasted a simpler design by Byrne.) It was their highest-charting album ever (#15, 1983) and yielded their biggest hit single, "Burning Down the House" (#9, 1983), which was also featured in an eye-catching video that MTV had in heavy rotation. They toured with an expanded band including Alex Weir, a guitarist with the Brothers Johnson. The tour was documented in the acclaimed movie *Stop Making Sense,* directed by Jonathan Demme. The soundtrack (#41, 1984) spent nearly two years on the pop albums chart.

The Heads returned to their core lineup, and simpler song forms, on *Little Creatures* (#20, 1985), which included the Cajun-flavored single "Road to Nowhere" and "Stay Up Late," a sardonic commentary on parenting (which Frantz and Weymouth, by then married, were doing). That album, like its predecessor, went platinum (the only two to do so). In 1986 Byrne directed the feature film *True Stories* (#17), a seemingly sincere look at small-town American eccentrics; the soundtrack album, on which Talking Heads performed straightforward versions of songs sung by various characters in the film, yielded a hit single in "Wild Wild Life" (#25, 1986).

Naked (#19, 1988), produced in Paris by Steve Lillywhite (U2, Simple Minds) and reggae/world-beat keyboardist/producer Wally Badarou, featured guest performances by assorted African and Caribbean musicians living in Paris. After producing the hit album *Conscious Party* for Ziggy Marley and the Melody Makers, Weymouth and Frantz got Byrne, Harrison, and Lou Reed to guest on Tom Tom Club's *Boom Boom Chi Boom Boom,* for a version of the Velvet Underground's "Femme Fatale." In 1990 Tom Tom Club and Harrison's band Casual Gods (which included Alex Weir) toured the U.S. with the Ramones and Blondie singer Deborah Harry.

The long-rumored dissolution of Talking Heads was made official, sort of, in December 1991, when Byrne told the

Los Angeles Times the band was finished. A month later Harrison, Weymouth, and Frantz issued a statement of their disappointment, adding that "Talking Heads *was* a great band." The band's final four new tracks were released as part of the *Popular Favorites* box-set retrospective.

In 1996 Byrne, citing "wrongful use," filed a lawsuit against the members of his former band and Radioactive Records head and former Talking Heads manager Gary Kurfirst to halt the release of a new, Byrne-less album, *No Talking Just Head,* and to prevent the musicians' use of the name "Heads" for a tour. The suit was settled out of court, and plans for both album—with a variety of guest vocalists including XTC's Andy Partridge and former Lone Justice singer Maria McKee—and tour proceeded. All four original members did manage to reteam in 1999 for the release of a 15th-anniversary edition of *Stop Making Sense* (which coincided with the film's release on DVD and a brief theatrical run). And in 2000 the Tom Tom Club was back with a new album, *The Good the Bad and the Funky,* which featured covers of tunes by Lee "Scratch" Perry and Donna Summer.

Tangerine Dream

Formed 1967, Germany
Edgar Froese (b. June 6, 1944, Tilsit, Ger.), synth., kybds., gtr.; Klaus Schulze (b. Aug. 4, 1947, Ger.), synth., kybds.; Konrad Schnitzler, flute.
1970—*Electronic Meditation* (Ohr) 1971—(– Schulze; – Schnitzler; + Christopher Franke [b. Apr. 6, 1953, Berlin, Ger.], synth.; + Steve Shroyder, organ) *Alpha Centauri* 1972—(+ Peter Baumann, synth., kybds., flute) *Zeit* (– Shroyder); *Atem* 1974—*Phaedra* (Virgin) 1975—*Rubycon; Live* 1976—*Atem Alpha Centauri; Richocet; Stratosphere* 1977—*Sorcerer* soundtrack (MCA) 1978—(– Baumann; + Steve Jollife, flute; + Klaus Kreiger, drums) *Cyclone* (Virgin) 1979—*Force Majeure* (+ Johannes Schmoelling, synth., kybds.) 1980—*Tamgram* 1981—*Thief* soundtrack; *Exit* (Elektra) 1984—*Poland* (Relativity) 1985—*Le Parc* 1986—*Legend* (MCA) 1987—*Tyger* (– Franke; + Ralf Wadephal, kybds.) 1988—*Optical Race* (Private Music) (– Schmoelling; + Paul Haslinger, kybds.) 1989—*Lily on the Beach* 1990—*Melrose* 1991—(– Haslinger; + Jerome Froese, kybds.) 1992—*Rockoon* (Miramar) 1993—*Dreaming on Danforth Avenue* (Blue Moon); *220 Volt Live* (Miramar) 1994—*Turn of the Tides* 1995—*Tyranny of Beauty* 1997—*Tournado* (Resurgent) 1999—*Transsiberia* (Tangerine Dream); *Sohoman; Dream Encores; Quinoa; Mars Polaris; Architecture in Motion* (Miramar) 2000—*Great Wall of China* (Tangerine Dream); *Antiques Dreams.*

This German ensemble, its lineup constantly shifting, has been responsible for introducing some of the spaciest exploratory synthesizer music ever. Though many critics have dismissed them as mere self-absorbed post-psychedelic electro-doodlers, others have praised them as sonic painters. Not only did they build up a tenacious European cult following in the '70s but the seven-time Grammy nominees were precursors of both of New Age and ambient-techno music.

They started out as a rock band featuring Edgar Froese (a classical music student, as was Christophe Franke), but as they became increasingly enamored of far-flung improvisations, they abandoned guitars and drums in favor of an almost completely electronic keyboard/synthesizer setup that produced echoing, droning atmospheres rather than conventional songs. Original member Klaus Schulze went on to a career of his own, in much the same musical vein, and mainstay Froese came even further to the fore.

In 1974 the group gained further attention by playing a concert at Rheims cathedral in France, at which some 6,000 fans tried to jam into the 2,000-capacity church to hear Tangerine Dream's always-improvised and often arhythmic, protoplasmic electronics. The next year they went to Britain for the first time, again playing cathedrals wherever possible. The tour was sold out, and featured Michael Hoenig replacing Baumann, who was busy working on his first solo album, *Romance '76.* By that time, Froese had recorded his first solo outing, *Aqua.* Among his other works are *Epsilon in Malaysian Pale, Electronic Dreams, Ages, Macula Transfer, Stunt Man, Pinnacles,* and *Kamikaze 1989.* Baumann later founded the Private Music label.

In the mid-'70s, as they introduced vocals and lyrics (on *Cyclone*) and otherwise continued to gather fans familiar with Pink Floyd and Yes, Tangerine Dream achieved some degree of cult success in the U.S., though never on the scale they enjoyed in England and Europe. Baumann left in 1981 to pursue a solo career, releasing *Repeat Repeat* in 1982, the title cut of which was a minor hit in dance clubs. At the start of the '80s, Tangerine Dream became the first Western band to play East Berlin; they also began experimenting with sampling techniques. Key member Christopher Franke left in 1987 to pursue a solo career, composing film soundtracks and New Age music *(Pacific Coast Highway, The London Concert, New Music for Films).* As a duo consisting of Froese and his son Jerome, Tangerine Dream soldiered on.

Tavares

Formed ca. 1959, New Bedford, MA
Ralph Tavares (b. Dec. 10, 1948), voc.; Arthur "Pooch" Tavares (b. Nov. 12, 1946), voc.; Feliciano "Butch" Tavares (b. May 18, 1953), voc.; Perry Lee "Tiny" Tavares (b. Oct. 24, 1954), voc.; Antone "Chubby" Tavares (b. June 2, 1947), voc.
1974—*Check It Out* (Capitol); *Hard Core Poetry* 1975—*In the City* 1976—*Sky High!* 1977—*Love Storm; The Best of Tavares* 1978—*Future Bound* 1979—*Madam Butterfly* 1980—*Supercharged; Love Uprising* 1981—*Loveline* 1982—*New Directions* (RCA) 1983—(– R. Tavares) 1993—*The Best of Tavares* (Capitol) (– P. Tavares).

Throughout the '70s, the harmonizing Tavares brothers had several R&B and disco hit singles. Their hit version of Hall and Oates' "She's Gone" paved the way for that duo's later success.

The group's grandparents were from the Cape Verde Islands (a Portuguese province in the Atlantic Ocean), and as children the five brothers learned to sing island folk songs and doo-wop favorites from their older brother, John. In 1963 they turned pro as Chubby and the Turnpikes, playing clubs throughout New England. By the time they signed with Capitol in 1973, they had changed their group name to Tavares. Tavares' first album was produced by Johnny Bristol, the second two by the Brian Potter/Dennis Lambert team. The group had hits with two ballads, "Check It Out" (#35 pop, #5 R&B, 1973) and "She's Gone" (#50 pop, #1 R&B, 1974). Ex-Motown producer Freddie Perren took over on *Sky High!*, and the group had the first of a string of pop-disco hits, which include "It Only Takes a Minute" (#10 pop, #1 R&B, 1975), "Heaven Must Be Missing an Angel" (#15 pop, #3 R&B, 1976), and "Whodunit" (#22 pop, #1 R&B, 1977). Major public exposure came when their "More Than a Woman" (#32 pop, #36 R&B) was included on the multimillion-selling *Saturday Night Fever* soundtrack album.

After that, the group had a higher profile on the concert circuit and on the R&B charts than with pop audiences. Their later hits included "Bad Times" (#10 R&B, 1979), "A Penny for Your Thoughts" (#16 R&B, 1982), "Deeper in Love" (#10 R&B, 1983), and "Words and Music" (#29 R&B, 1983). Brother Ralph resigned in 1983; Tiny Tavares followed in the mid-'90s. The remaining members are sporadically active. The original quintet briefly reunited in 1998.

James Taylor

Born Mar. 12, 1948, Boston, MA
1968—*James Taylor* (Apple) 1970—*Sweet Baby James* (Warner Bros.) 1971—*James Taylor and the Original Flying Machine, 1967* (Euphoria 2); *Mud Slide Slim and the Blue Horizon* (Warner Bros.) 1972—*One Man Dog* 1974—*Walking Man* 1975—*Gorilla* 1976—*In the Pocket; Greatest Hits* 1977—*JT* (Columbia) 1979—*Flag* 1981—*Dad Loves His Work* 1985—*That's Why I'm Here* 1988—*Never Die Young* 1991—*New Moon Shine* 1993—*Live* 1994—*Best Live* 1997—*Hourglass* 2000—*Greatest Hits, vol. II.*

James Taylor was the archetypal "sensitive" singer/songwriter of the '70s. His songs, especially his early ones, were tales of inner torment delivered in low-key tunes featuring Taylor's understated tenor and his intricate acoustic guitar accompaniments that drew on folk and jazz. Taylor came across as relaxed, personable, and open; he was imitated by a horde of would-be confessionalists, although his best songs were as artful as they were emotional. They weren't folk songs; they were pop compositions with folk dynamics, and in them Taylor put across more bitterness and resignation than reassurance. As he continued to record, Taylor split his albums between cover singles that were hits ("Handy Man," "You've Got a Friend") and his own songs, maturing into a laid-back artist with a large and devoted following of baby boomers.

Born into a wealthy family, Taylor grew up in Boston. The family subsequently lived in Chapel Hill, North Carolina, where James' father became dean of the medical school of the University of North Carolina, and on Martha's Vineyard off the coast of Cape Cod. Everyone in the family was musical; James initially played the cello. His older brother Alex introduced him to folk and country music, and James soon took up the guitar. When he was 15, summering on Martha's Vineyard, he met another budding guitarist, Danny Kortchmar. Taylor attended high school at a private academy outside Boston. Lonely away from his family, he took off a term in his junior year to return to Chapel Hill, where he played local gigs with Alex's rock band. In 1965 he committed himself to a mental institution—McLean Psychiatric Hospital in Belmont, Massachusetts—to which his sister Kate and brother Livingston would later be admitted. There he began writing songs.

After 10 months, he discharged himself and went to New York, where Kortchmar was putting together the Flying Machine. The group played Greenwich Village coffeehouses and recorded two Taylor originals, "Night Owl" and "Brighten Your Night With My Day," in early 1967 before breaking up. Their demo tape was released as an album after Taylor became popular. One reason for the group's breakup was Taylor's addiction to heroin. In early 1968 he went to England, and in London he recorded a tape of his material and sent it to Peter Asher. As an A&R man for the Beatles' Apple Records, Asher encouraged Paul McCartney to sign him. In mid-1968 Taylor recorded his debut album in London; Asher produced and McCartney and George Harrison sat in on one cut. The LP attracted little attention, and Taylor, still hooked on heroin at the end of the year, returned to America and signed himself into another mental institution. During Taylor's five-month stay, with Apple in disarray, Asher—who became Taylor's producer and manager—negotiated a contract between Taylor and Warner Bros. Before Taylor was released, his solo stage debut at L.A.'s Troubadour had been arranged. From there he went to the Newport Folk Festival, where he met Joni Mitchell (she sang on *Mud Slide Slim*, and he played guitar on her autobiographical *Blue*).

Taylor and Asher rounded up Kortchmar, bassist Lee Sklar, drummer Russ Kunkel, and pianist Carole King to back him on his second album. *Sweet Baby James* attracted little attention initially, but "Fire and Rain" became a #3 hit. *Sweet Baby James* reached the Top 10 in November 1970 and stayed on the LP chart into 1972. Taylor's Apple debut was rereleased, entering the charts in October with the single "Carolina in My Mind." Taylor appeared on a March 1971 cover of *Time* magazine, which hailed his ascent to stardom as a turn toward maturity and restraint in pop music, but at the same time publicized his drug abuses and other skeletons in his and his family's closet. The article also alluded to a possible dynasty of Taylor-made pop stars. Livingston Taylor had launched his singing and songwriting career before his older brother had become famous, but Alex and Kate, while unquestionably musical, found less success.

Within two months of its release, *Mud Slide Slim* was the nation's #2 album. Taylor's version of Carole King's

"You've Got a Friend" hit #1 in 1971, the same year that King's version came out on *Tapestry.* That year Taylor costarred with Dennis Wilson of the Beach Boys in the film *Two-Lane Blacktop.*

Then, almost as suddenly as he had emerged into public attention, he retreated from it. Except for a few benefit concerts for George McGovern's 1972 presidential campaign, Taylor did not perform for another three years. He married Carly Simon in November 1972. Taylor continued to make and sell albums, but he didn't score a Top 10 single between "You've Got a Friend" and 1975. ("Mockingbird," a duet, was released by Simon in 1974.) *One Man Dog* (#4, 1973) contained "Don't Let Me Be Lonely Tonight" (#14, 1973); *Walking Man* (#13, 1974) boasted no hit singles.

A month-long tour in 1974 signaled Taylor's reemergence. He returned to the charts with *Gorilla* (#6, 1975). Taylor's cover of "How Sweet It Is (To Be Loved by You)" hit #5 in 1975. *JT,* including a Top 5 cover of the Jimmy Jones–Otis Blackwell "Handy Man," was Taylor's first release on Columbia. *Greatest Hits* (#23, 1976), for which he rerecorded "Carolina in My Mind" and "Something in the Way She Moves," fulfilled his obligations to Warners. It would go on to sell over 11 million copies. He signed Columbia's lucrative contract before *Hits* was released. The double-platinum *JT* (#4, 1977) also marked Asher's return as producer.

Taylor's albums since *JT* have not quite repeated its success—*Flag* and *Dad Loves His Work* both hit #10—but they have sold consistently. In 1978 he joined Paul Simon and Art Garfunkel on a Top 20 cover of Sam Cooke's "Wonderful World," released by Garfunkel. In 1979 he wrote a couple of songs for a Broadway musical, *Working. Flag* yielded a Top 30 hit with Taylor's typically understated cover of the Brill Building classic "Up on the Roof." Taylor continued to support a variety of causes with benefit concerts. He campaigned for Jimmy Carter in 1976 and for John Anderson in 1980; in 1979 he participated in the MUSE antinuclear rally concerts at Madison Square Garden and appeared in the concert film *No Nukes.*

Taylor's 1981 album, *Dad Loves His Work,* yielded a hit single duet with J.D. Souther, "Her Town Too" (#11), released amid rumors that his marriage to Simon was ending. In 1982 Simon sued Taylor for divorce. From 1982 through 1985 Taylor toured the globe, with a band featuring Little Feat's Bill Payne on piano. *That's Why I'm Here* (#34, 1985), with guests including Joni Mitchell, Don Henley, and Graham Nash, yielded only a minor hit single in a cover of Buddy Holly's "Everyday" (#61, 1985). In December 1985 Taylor wed for the second time, to Kathryn Walker. He continued touring extensively between albums that remained popular—1991's *New Moon Shine* (#37), for instance, sold over a million copies.

The mid-'90s were a time of personal trial for Taylor, who lost his brother Alex to alcoholism in 1994 and divorced Walker in 1996. His first studio album in six years, *Hourglass* (#9, 1997) was yet another platinum success and went on to win the Grammy for Best Pop Album, showing that the singer/songwriter remained impervious to the vagaries of musical trends. Taylor, who has been clean and sober since 1984, married Carolyn Smedvig in 2001. He was inducted into the Rock and Roll Hall of Fame in 2000.

Johnnie Taylor

Born May 5, 1938, Crawsfordsville, AR; died May 31, 2000, Duncanville, TX
1968—*Wanted: One Soul Singer* (Stax) 1969—*Who's Makin' Love; Raw Blues; The Johnnie Taylor Philosophy Continues* 1970—*Johnnie Taylor's Greatest Hits* 1971—*One Step Beyond* 1973—*Taylored in Silk* 1974—*Super Taylor* 1976—*Eargasm* (Columbia) 1977—*Rated Extraordinaire; Chronicle—The 20 Greatest Hits* (Stax) 1978—*Ever Ready* (Columbia); *Disco 9000; The Johnnie Taylor Chronicle* (Stax); *Reflections* (RCA) 1985—*This Is Your Night* (Malaco) 1988—*In Control* 1990—*Crazy for You; Little Bluebird* (Stax) 1991—*I Know It's Wrong, But I . . . Just Can't Do Right* (Malaco) 1992—*The Best of Johnnie Taylor . . . on Malaco, vol. I* 1994—*Real Love* 1996—*Brand New; Good Love!* 1998—*Taylored to Please* 1999—*Gotta Get the Groove Back* 2000—*Lifetime* (Stax).

Johnnie Taylor's gritty soul vocals made him a steady mid-'60s hitmaker and gave him one mammoth disco hit in 1976. Taylor made his recording debut with a Vee-Jay doo-wop group, the Five Echoes, in 1955. In 1957 he became lead singer of the Soul Stirrers, replacing Sam Cooke in the influential gospel quintet. After leaving the Soul Stirrers in 1963, Taylor signed with Cooke's SAR label. Although he abandoned gospel music, songs like "Rome (Wasn't Built in a Day)" reflected his deep religious roots.

Taylor hit his commercial stride after signing with Stax in 1965. Two 1966 releases, "I Had a Dream" (#19 R&B) and "I Got to Love Somebody's Baby" (#15 R&B), were minor hits. With "Who's Making Love" (#5 pop, #1 R&B) in 1968, Taylor replaced the late Otis Redding as Stax's leading male singer. "Take Care of Your Homework" (#20 pop, #2 R&B), "Testify (I Wanna)" (#4 R&B), "I Could Never Be President" (#10 R&B), "Love Bones" (#4 R&B) in 1969; "Steal Away" (#3 R&B), "I Am Somebody, Part II" (#3 R&B) in 1970; and "Jody's Got Your Girl and Gone" (#1 R&B), "Hi-Jackin' Love" (#10 R&B) in 1971 continued the streak. "I Believe in You (You Believe in Me)" (#1 R&B, 1973) and "Cheaper to Keep Her" (#15 pop, #2 R&B, 1973) were his last big hits for Stax.

By 1975 Stax was in turmoil, and its distributor, CBS, took over Taylor's contract. The next year, Taylor's "Disco Lady" (#1 pop and R&B) became the first single ever to be certified platinum. His last Top 40 pop hit was "Somebody's Gettin' It" (#33, 1976), although several of his singles appeared on the R&B chart through 1990. The singer spent most of the '80s and '90s working on a string of well-received albums for the Malaco label. In early 2001, less than a year after his heart attack–related death, Taylor was nominated for a Grammy. His album *Gotta Get the Groove Back* placed in the category of Best Traditional R&B Vocal Album.

Koko Taylor

Born Cora Walton, Sep. 28, 1935, Memphis, TN
1968—*Koko Taylor* 1975—*I Got What It Takes* (Alligator); *Southside Baby* (Black & Blue) 1978—*The Earthshaker* (Alligator) 1981—*From the Heart of a Woman* 1984—*Blues Explosion* (with others) (Atlantic) 1985—*Queen of the Blues* (Alligator) 1987—*Live From Chicago—An Audience With the Queen* 1990—*Jump for Joy* 1991—*What It Takes: The Chess Years* (Chess) 1993—*Force of Nature* (Alligator) 2000—*Royal Blue.*

A mighty-voiced urban blues singer, Koko Taylor is regarded as the contemporary Queen of the Blues. She grew up in Memphis on a sharecropper's farm. She began singing in her local church choir in her teens, but fell under the influence of the blues. At age 18 she and her husband Robert Taylor moved to Chicago, where she began performing with the Buddy Guy/Junior Wells Blues Band. In 1962 Willie Dixon discovered her and arranged for her to begin recording for Chess. He produced her million-selling hit, 1965's "Wang Dang Doodle," as well as other sides. From then through the present, she has toured the U.S., Britain, and Europe extensively.

In 1970 she appeared in the film *The Blues Is Alive and Well in Chicago,* and she played the Montreux Jazz and Blues Festival in 1972 with Muddy Waters. Taylor began recording for Alligator, a Chicago-based independent label specializing in blues, in 1974, and the following year formed her own band, the Blues Machine. She appeared as a singer in David Lynch's film *Wild at Heart* (1990). Of her seven Alligator releases through 1993, five were nominated for Grammy awards; in 1984 *Blues Explosion,* which featured Taylor and Her Blues Machine, Stevie Ray Vaughan and Double Trouble, and others, won the Grammy for Best Traditional Blues Recording. She has received 19 W.C. Handy awards, more than any other female blues artist. In 1996 Taylor married for the second time (she was given away by Buddy Guy). In 1999 she opened the Chicago nightclub Koko Taylor's Celebrity. The uptempo *Royal Blue,* her first album in seven years, features performances by B.B. King, Keb' Mo', and Kenny Wayne Shepherd, along with the Melissa Ethridge–penned single "Bring Me Some Water."

Bram Tchaikovsky: See the Motors

Teardrop Explodes: See Julian Cope

Tears for Fears/Oleta Adams

Formed 1982, Bath, Eng.
Roland Orzabal (b. Aug. 22, 1961, Havant, Eng.), voc., gtr.; Curt Smith (b. June 24, 1961, Bath), bass, voc.
1983—*The Hurting* (Mercury) 1985—*Songs From the Big Chair* 1989—*The Seeds of Love* (Fontana/Mercury) 1992—*Tears Roll Down (Greatest Hits '82–'92)* 1993—(- Smith) *Elemental* (Mercury) 1995—*Raoul and the Kings of Spain* (Epic) 1996—*Saturine Martial & Lunatic* (PolyGram) 2000—*Best of Tears for Fears: The Millennium Collection* (Mercury).
Curt Smith solo: 1993—*Soul on Board* (Mercury) 2000—*Aeroplane* EP (ZeroDisc).
Curt Smith with Mayfield: 1998—*Mayfield* (ZeroDisc).
Oleta Adams (b. ca. 1961, Seattle, WA), backing voc., kybds. 1986–92, solo: 1990—*Circle of One* (Fontana/Mercury) 1993—*Evolution* 1995—*Moving On* 1997—*Come Walk With Me* 1998—*The Very Best of Oleta Adams* (Mercury/PolyGram).

The British pop duo Tears for Fears enjoyed their commercial breakthrough in 1985 with *Songs From the Big Chair,* an album of lush, literate songs that fused Beatlesque melodies with techno-savvy arrangements. Having met as troubled adolescents, band members Roland Orzabal and Curt Smith wrote and sang about the importance of emotional self-awareness and self-expression. Some critics found their songs whiny or precious, but most praised their tender craftsmanship.

Orzabal and Smith became friends while growing up in Bath. Both were from broken homes, and Smith, whose parents had divorced when he was very young, had dabbled in vandalism and petty theft as an adolescent. Orzabal turned to reading instead, and eventually introduced Smith to the writings of psychotherapist Arthur Janov, whose "primal scream" theory stressed that adult neuroses tend to stem from parental abandonment in childhood, and that direct confrontation with these early feelings of loss is emotionally vital. In their late teens Orzabal and Smith formed a power-pop band called Graduate, but dissolved that outfit in the early '80s and focused on exploring Janov's theories—which had also influenced John Lennon—in a musical context.

As Tears for Fears, Orzabal and Smith—with some added help from ex-Graduate keyboardist Ian Stanley—began writing songs and arranging them for synthesizers. A demo of a song called "Pale Shelter" won them a recording contract, and in 1983 their debut album, *The Hurting,* was released, yielding three Top 5 singles in the U.K. But Tears' American breakthrough came with their sophomore effort: *Songs From the Big Chair* topped the pop albums chart here, and scored two #1 singles, "Everybody Wants to Rule the World" and "Shout," as well as the #3 hit "Head Over Heels."

The band took a career risk by waiting four years before releasing a followup to *Songs. The Seeds of Love* reached #8 and yielded a #2 single, "Sowing the Seeds of Love." It also provided a showcase for guest vocalist and rising R&B artist Oleta Adams, whom the duo had heard sing at the Hyatt Regency hotel lounge in Kansas City in 1985. Adams sang backup on the track "Woman in Chains," and her sultry vocals contributed to the new tracks' warmer feel. The singer joined the pair on tour, and Orzabal would go on to coproduce Adams' debut solo album, *Circle of One,* in 1990.

Four years again passed before another Tears for Fears studio album (a hits compilation came out in 1992); and since

Smith left the act in the interim, 1993's *Elemental* (#45) was essentially Roland Orzabal's solo debut. The album, which went gold, generated the single "Break It Down Again" (#25, 1993). That same year, Curt Smith released a solo album, *Soul on Board*, which was largely ignored. By the end of 1994, Orzabal was back in the studio, recording another Tears for Fears LP, *Raoul and the Kings of Spain* (#79, 1995). A rarities collection of the duo's work, *Saturine Martial & Lunatic*, followed in 1996. Meanwhile, Smith formed a band called Mayfield in tribute to namesake Curtis Mayfield; the group released one self-titled album on Smith's own label, Zero-Disc, in 1998.

At this point Orzabal and Smith had not spoken in several years. In 2000 they had dinner with their former manager, still a mutual friend, and soon began cowriting songs again. As of late that year, they were considering recording their efforts and perhaps releasing them as a Tears for Fears project. Yet the two continued with their own careers, with Smith releasing a solo EP in 2000 and Orzabal releasing *Tomcats Screaming Outside* in 2001.

Technotronic

Formed 1989, Aalst, Belgium
Ya Kid K (b. Manuela Barbara Kamosi, Jan. 26, 1972, Kinshasa, Zaire), voc.; Jo Bogaert (b. Thomas de Quincy, May 5, 1956, U.S.), synth.; MC Eric (b. Aug. 19, 1968, Cardiff, Wales), voc.
1989—*Pump Up the Jam: The Album* (SBK) 1995—*Recall*.

An unlikely success story, Technotronic was a Belgian group that brought house music—the impersonal, club-oriented, electronic postdisco dance music pioneered in Chicago—where it never intended to go: to the top of the pop charts. The group included two young African women, one who rapped in English and one who spoke no English and did not even perform on the group's records.

Technotronic began when ex-philosophy teacher and aspiring record producer Joe Bogaert moved from the U.S. to Belgium in the late '80s, aiming to infuse house music with hip-hop. He sent his "new beat" music tapes to prospective rappers, including another transplanted American, MC Eric, and a boyish-looking Zairean girl Ya Kid K, who was with Belgian rap group Fresh Beat Productions. Ya Kid K was featured in "Pump Up the Jam," which became a hit in Europe and then the U.S. (#2, 1989) thanks in large part to its music video, in which Zairean-born fashion model Felly tried to lip-sync rapid-fire lyrics in a language she did not speak. Felly was also featured on the cover of the group's album (#10, 1989), causing futher confusion.

All was cleared up when Ya Kid K and MC Eric took Technotronic on tour, opening shows for DJ Jazzy Jeff and the Fresh Prince, and then for Madonna on her 1990 Blond Ambition Tour. Bogaert later admitted that Felly had been hired purely to give Technotronic "an image." "Get Up! (Before the Night Is Over)" became another dance-to-pop crossover hit (#7, 1990); this time Ya Kid K, who had finally gotten her own management, was featured in the video. Ya Kid K worked with a different Belgian house-music group, Hi Tek 3, to record a solo single, "Spin That Wheel," for SBK's *Teenage Mutant Ninja Turtles* movie soundtrack. Without Ya Kid K, Technotronic released *Body to Body* on a Belgian label in 1991.

In 1992, working with Bogaert and her producer husband Jonathan Kamosi, Ya Kid K recorded the solo album *One World Nation;* it included "Move This," a song from Technotronic's debut album that was released as a single after being featured in a popular Revlon cosmetics commercial starring Cindy Crawford. The 1995 album *Recall* failed to spark a comeback.

Teenage Fanclub

Formed 1989, Glasgow, Scot.
Norman Blake (b. Oct. 20, 1965, Bellshill, Scot.), gtr., voc.; Gerard Love (b. Aug. 31, 1967, Motherwell, Scot.), bass, voc.; Francis McDonald (b. Nov. 21, 1970, Bellshill), drums; Raymond McGinley (b. Jan. 3, 1964, Glasgow), gtr., voc.
1990—(– McDonald, + Brendan O'Hare [b. Jan. 16, 1970, Bellshill], drums) *A Catholic Education* (Matador) 1991—*The King; Bandwagonesque* (DGC) 1993—*Thirteen* 1994—(– O'Hare; + Paul Quinn, drums) 1995—*Grand Prix* 1997—*Songs From Northern Britain* (Creation/Columbia) 2000—*Howdy!* (Columbia).

An alternative to the histrionics of grunge, Teenage Fanclub's witty '60s-flavored pop songs mixed with a modern guitar sound (exemplified by their 1992 Big Star soundalike single, "The Concept") gained it a college-radio following in the U.S and moderate success in the U.K.

Norman Blake and Raymond McGinley were leaders of Glasgow's Boy Hairdressers. They recorded one single, "Golden Shower" (1988), before breaking up, but Blake and McGinley continued working together. With fellow Hairdresser Francis McDonald and new recruit Gerard Love they began writing new songs, recording an entire album's worth of material before performing in public. Francis MacDonald left for another project and Brendan O'Hare, a teenage fan, quit school to replace him. This version of the band recorded *A Catholic Education*. Signed by independent labels Creation in England and Matador in the States, the album emphasized guitars at the expense of songs, but caught the ear of DGC, which bought the band's U.S. contract.

The King, a difficult, noisy album of instrumentals and covers recorded to fulfill Teenage Fanclub's contract with Matador, had a very limited release. Its first DGC album, *Bandwagonesque* (#22 U.K., 1991), produced by Gumball's Don Fleming, showcased the band's songwriting and received critical kudos. An opening slot on Nirvana's 1992 tour brought the group's crowd-pleasing, knockabout performances to a wider audience. The self-produced *Thirteen* (#14 U.K., 1993), like its predecessor, failed to chart in the U.S. The same can be said for the critcally successful *Grand Prix* and *Songs From Northern Britain*, which introduced new drummer Paul Quinn and showed Teenage Fanclub to be tipping its hat to the country-influenced mellowness of the Byrds and Gram Parsons rather than to the deep-fried guitar distortion of the Jesus and Mary Chain or My Bloody Valentine. Blake, Love, and MacDonald appeared to be softening with age, though they still had a knack for writing memorable power-pop hooks.

Television

Formed 1973, New York, NY
Tom Verlaine (b. Thomas Miller, Dec. 13, 1949, Wilmington, DE), gtr., voc.; Richard Lloyd, gtr., voc.; Richard Hell (b. Richard Myers, Oct. 2, 1949, Lexington, KY), bass; Billy Ficca, drums.
1975—(– Hell; + Fred Smith [b. Apr. 10, 1948, New York, bass) 1977—*Marquee Moon* (Elektra) 1978—*Adventure* 1982—*The Blow Up* (ROIR) 1992—*Television* (Capitol).
Tom Verlaine solo: 1980—*Tom Verlaine* (Elektra) 1981—*Dreamtime* (Warner Bros.) 1982—*Words From the Front* 1984—*Cover* 1987—*Flashlight* (Phonogram/I.R.S.) 1990—*The Wonder* 1992—*Warm and Cool* (Rykodisc).
Richard Lloyd solo: 1980—*Alchemy* (Elektra) 1985—*Field of Fire* (Celluloid) 1987—*Real Time* (Celluloid/Grand Slamm) 2001—*The Cover Doesn't Matter* (Upsetter Music).
Richard Hell solo: see entry.

Television appeared at the same time and place as punk rock—in the mid-'70s at CBGB. But while the band's harsh attack and obvious affection for the Velvet Underground linked it to the rest of punk, Television's trademark chiming guitars and the tendency of lead guitarist (and main songwriter) Tom Verlaine and rhythm guitarist Richard Lloyd to spur each other on to long jams evoked such psychedelic-era bands as the Grateful Dead. (Verlaine cited the Rolling Stones, classical composer Maurice Ravel, and jazz musicians Miles Davis and Albert Ayler as influences.) Television had a devout following in New York City and had a major effect on British postpunk rock, but its albums were virtually ignored by the mass market.

Tom Miller (who renamed himself Verlaine after the French Symbolist poet) had dropped out of high school in Wilmington, Delaware, and had left colleges in South Carolina and Pennsylvania before coming to New York in 1968. Richard Hell was a onetime boarding school roommate. With Billy Ficca they formed a short-lived band, the Neon Boys, in 1972. When Lloyd joined in late 1973, they became Television, and were one of the first bands to play at CBGB, along with the Patti Smith Group. (Verlaine and Smith collaborated on a book of poetry, *The Night*.) Hell left in 1975 to form the Heartbreakers [see entry] with ex-New York Doll Johnny Thunders; later he led the Voidoids. Dee Dee Ramone auditioned as bassist, but the gig went to Fred Smith, who had played in the original Blondie. The new lineup played frequently in New York to critical raves and made an independent single, "Little Johnny Jewel."

In late 1974 Brian Eno produced the band's demo recordings (which are still unreleased). Despite a growing cult following, Television didn't release its debut album until 1977. *Marquee Moon* sold poorly, but it made many critics' 10-best lists that year. *Adventure* was softer, more reflective, and restrained than the debut, and sold a bit better. In 1978 Television broke up; four years later the cassette-only live album, *The Blow Up*, was released.

Verlaine released seven solo albums, and though he retained a faithful following, he was still more a critical than commercial success. After recording the score for the film *Love and a .45* in 1994, he continued in that direction. In 1998 he was commissioned to compose original music for a collection of classic silent-film shorts by Man Ray, Fernand Léger, and others, which became the basis for performances—with guitarist Jimmy Ripp—at film festivals and performing arts centers. Lloyd has released several solo albums and in the early '90s recorded with John Doe (of X) and Matthew Sweet. In 1980 Ficca resurfaced with the Waitresses, a New York–Ohio band (led by ex–Tin Huey guitarist Chris Butler) who had a hit with "I Know What Boys Like" in 1981. Smith has played with a number of artists, including the Roches, Willie Nile, the Peregrines, and the Fleshtones, among others, as well as in Verlaine's touring and recording bands, and on Lloyd's solo work.

In 1992 Television reunited to record a self-titled album that, as usual, sold modestly but was well received by critics, who noted admiringly that the band's trademarks—brilliant guitar work, clever songwriting, and *noir*ish lyrics—were all still in evidence. The reunited band did a world tour in 1993. As of 2001, Television continued to play the occasional gig and was reportedly making plans to record.

The Temptations/David Ruffin/ Eddie Kendricks

Formed 1961, Detroit, MI
Otis Williams (b. Otis Miles, Oct. 30, 1941, Texarkana, TX), baritone voc.; Eddie Kendricks (a.k.a. Kendrick, b. Dec. 17, 1939, Union Springs, AL; d. Oct. 5, 1992, Birmingham, AL), tenor voc.; Paul Williams (b. July 2, 1939, Birmingham; d. Aug. 17, 1973, Detroit), voc.; Melvin Franklin (b. David English, Oct. 12, 1942, Montgomery, AL; d. Feb. 23, 1995, Los Angeles, CA), bass voc.; Elbridge Bryant, voc.
1963—(– Bryant; + David Ruffin [b. Davis Eli Ruffin, Jan. 18, 1941, MS; d. June 1, 1991, Philadelphia, PA], tenor voc.) 1964—*Meet the Temptations* (Gordy) 1965—*Temptations Sing Smokey; Temptin' Temptations* 1966—*Gettin' Ready; The Temptations' Greatest Hits* 1967—*Temptations Live!; With a Lot o' Soul; In a Mellow Mood* 1968—*The Temptations Wish It Would Rain; Live at the Copa* (– Ruffin; + Dennis Edwards [b. Feb. 3, 1943, Birmingham], lead voc.) 1969—*Cloud Nine; Puzzle People* 1970—*Psychedelic Shack; Live at London's Talk of the Town; Temptations' Greatest Hits, vol. II; Christmas Card* 1971—*Sky's the Limit* 1972—(– Kendricks; + Ricky Owens, voc.; – Owens; + Damon Harris [b. July 3, 1950, Baltimore, MD], tenor voc.; – P. Williams; + Richard Street [b. Oct. 5, 1942, Detroit], tenor voc.) *Solid Rock; All Directions* 1973—*Masterpiece; Anthology* (Motown); *1990* (Gordy)

1975—*A Song for You; House Party* (– Harris; + Glenn Leonard [b. Washington, DC], tenor voc.) 1976—*Wings of Love; The Temptations Do the Temptations* 1977—(– Edwards; + Louis Price, lead voc.) *Hear to Tempt You* (Atlantic) 1978—*Bare Back* 1979—(– Price; + Edwards) 1980—*Power* (Gordy) 1981—*The Temptations* 1982—(+ Ruffin; + Kendricks) *Reunion* (– Ruffin; – Kendricks) 1983—*Surface Thrills* (– Leonard; + Ron Tyson, tenor voc.) *Back to Basics* (– Edwards; + Ali Ollie Woodson, lead voc.) 1984—*Truly for You* 1985—*Touch Me* 1986—*The Temptations' 25th Anniversary* (Motown); *To Be Continued* (Gordy) (– Woodson; + Edwards) 1987—*Together Again* (Motown) (– Edwards; + Woodson) 1989—*Special* 1990—*Solid Rock* 1991—*Milestone* 1993—*Hum Along and Dance: More of the Best (1963–1974)* (Rhino) (– Street; + Theo Peoples, voc.) 1994—*Emperors of Soul* (Motown) 1995—(– Franklin; + Ray Davis [b. Mar. 29, 1940, Sumter, SC], voc.) *For Lovers Only* 1996—*One by One* (– Davis; + Harry McGilberry Jr. [b. Jan. 19, 1951, Philadelphia], bass voc.; – Woodson) 1997—(+ Terry Weeks [b. Dec. 23, 1963, Bessemer, AL], voc.) 1998—(+ Barrington Henderson [b. June 10, 1956, PA], voc.) *Phoenix Rising; The Ultimate Collection* 2000—*Ear-Resistible* (Interscope).

The Temptations with the Supremes: 1968—*Diana Ross and the Supremes Join the Temptations* (Motown); *TCB* 1969—*Together; On Broadway.*

Eddie Kendricks solo: 1971—*All by Myself* (Tamla) 1972—*People . . . Hold On* 1973—*Eddie Kendricks* 1974—*Boogie Down; For You* 1975—*The Hit Man* 1976—*He's a Friend; Goin' Up in Smoke* 1977—*Slick* 1978—*At His Best; Vintage '78* (Arista) 1981—*Love Keys* (Atlantic) 1998—*Eddie Kendricks: The Ultimate Collection* (Motown).

David Ruffin solo: 1969—*My Whole World Ended* (Motown); *Feelin' Good* 1970—*I Am My Brother's Keeper* (with Jimmy Ruffin) (Soul) 1973—*David Ruffin* (Motown) 1974—*Me 'n' Rock 'n' Roll Are Here to Stay* 1975—*Who Am I?* 1976—*Everything's Coming Up Love* 1977—*In My Stride* 1979—*So Soon We Change* (Warner Bros.) 1980—*Gentleman Ruffin* 1998—*David Ruffin: The Ultimate Collection* (Motown).

David Ruffin and Eddie Kendricks: 1987—*David Ruffin and Eddie Kendricks* (RCA).

Ruffin and Kendricks with Daryl Hall and John Oates: 1985—*Live at the Apollo with David Ruffin and Eddie Kendrick* (RCA).

Dennis Edwards solo: 1984—*Don't Look Any Further* (Gordy) 1985—*Coolin' Out.*

In addition to being the most consistently commercially successful and critically lauded male vocal group in rock history, the Temptations have been charting hits for 40 years. Yet unlike most other living institutions, the Tempts remain a vital, hitmaking group, with the double-platinum *Phoenix Rising* from 1998 living up to its name. In their early "classic" lineup—with alternating lead singers Eddie Kendricks, David Ruffin, and Paul Williams, with Melvin Franklin, and group founder Otis Williams—the Tempts, as they were known, were simply untouchable. Through the years, the group's trademark razor-sharp choreography, finely tuned vocal harmonies, and a number of compelling lead singers (Ruffin, Kendricks, the little known Paul Williams, and later, Dennis Edwards) made them the exemplars of the Motown style. The Temptations have been distinguished among their Motown stable mates (with the exception of the Four Tops) for their ability to move comfortably from smooth pop and standards to provocative, politically charged rock soul, from the Apollo to the Copacabana (and back). Despite personnel changes and conflicts, through countless triumphs and setbacks, the Temptations, with Franklin and Otis Williams at the helm, forged ahead. Today, with Williams the sole surviving original member, the group continues.

The Temptations: Dennis Edwards, Melvin Franklin, Damon Harris, Richard Street, Otis Williams

The Temptations currently hold 13 gold and six platinum albums. The group's chart statistics are unparalleled: between 1964 and 1975 19 Top 20 albums. Over its career, the group has had 37 Top 40 singles (among them 15 Top 10s, including 4 at #1) and 32 R&B Top 10 albums (including 17 at #1).

The original Temptations came together from two struggling vocal groups. Otis Williams (not to be confused with Otis Williams of Charms fame), Elbridge (a.k.a. Al, or El) Bryant, and Melvin Franklin had been in a series of Detroit groups, including Williams' Siberians and Otis Williams and the Distants. Once Franklin, the young bass singer of Detroit's Voice Masters, joined the Distants (which included future Tempt Richard Street) they recorded "Come On" for the local Northern label. Around the time that Williams decided to expand the group, Eddie Kendricks and Paul Williams (no relation to Otis), with Kell Osborne, were working around Detroit as the Primes. Originally from Birmingham, Alabama, this trio was making something of a name for itself in the Motor City. They were doing so well that their manager put together a "sister group," the Primettes, a quartet of young women, three of whom (Diane Ross, Mary Wilson, and Florence Ballard) would later be rechristened the Supremes. Eventually the Primes disbanded, but not before Otis Williams had seen them and been impressed by Kendricks' talent and Paul Williams' knack for creating great choreography.

Kendricks, Paul Williams, Otis Williams, Franklin, and Bryant formed the Elgins in 1961. Later rechristened the Temptations, this lineup recorded two flop singles for the Motown subsidiary label Miracle later that year ("Oh Mother of Mine" b/w "Romance Without Finance" and "Check Yourself" b/w "Your Wonderful Love"). In 1962 they had a #22 R&B single with "Dream Come True" (which featured Berry Gordy's then-wife Raynoma Gordy on harpsichord), but four more flops followed, including "Mind Over Matter" b/w "I'll Love You Til I Die," which Berry Gordy forced them to release under the name the Pirates.

In late 1963, following his violent attack on Paul Williams, Bryant either quit or was fired. Among the singers considered as a replacement were brothers Jimmy and David Ruffin. David, who had created a big impression by jumping onstage with the Tempts unannounced and winning over the crowd, got the spot, and the Temptations' luck changed overnight. They began working with writer/producer Smokey Robinson, whose "The Way You Do the Things You Do" (#11 pop) launched an almost unbroken run of R&B and pop hits that extended into the early '70s. Their 1965 hits included the classic "My Girl" (#1 pop, #1 R&B), "It's Growing" (#18 pop, #3 R&B), "Since I Lost My Baby" (#17 pop, #4 R&B), "My Baby" (#13 pop, #4 R&B), and "Don't Look Back" (#13 pop, #4 R&B). The latter was one of the rare A-side leads by Paul Williams, who would remain the architect of the Temptations' style and sophisticated image.

The next year the hits continued with Robinson's "Get Ready" (#29 pop, #1 R&B), following by the hard soul of producers Norman Whitfield and Brian Holland's "Ain't Too Proud to Beg" (#13 pop, #1 R&B). The first single featured Kendricks on lead, the second Ruffin. From that point on, however, the majority of A sides would feature Ruffin, as did 1966's "Beauty's Only Skin Deep" (#3 pop, #1 R&B) and "(I Know) I'm Losing You" (#8 pop, #1 R&B). Around 1967 Whitfield had become the group's sole producer, moving them more deeply into a rougher-hewn soul style. All the while, however, the group continued to perform and record standards (including Melvin Franklin's longstanding showpiece rendition of "Old Man River"). Other hits from 1967 were "All I Need" (#8 pop, #2 R&B), "You're My Everything" (#6 pop, #3 R&B), and "(Loneliness Made Me Realize) It's You That I Need" (#14 pop, #3 R&B).

The year 1968 brought "I Wish It Would Rain" (#4 pop, #1 R&B), "I Could Never Love Another (After Loving You)" (#13 pop, #1 R&B), and "Please Return Your Love to Me" (#26 pop, #4 R&B). But the most significant event of this period was Ruffin's departure for a solo career. Always a volatile personality, Ruffin had come into the group having enjoyed some limited success as a solo artist. In part, he was dissatisfied with the fact that Motown did not promote him as an individual in the same manner that it was priming Diana Ross as a solo act. Ironically, in terms of stature and image, the Supremes would remain the Temptations' "sister group" in more ways than one. After failing to show up for a concert, the four other members of the group (not Berry Gordy, as has often been reported) fired him.

Initially, Ruffin's departure was viewed as an insurmountable blow. Dennis Edwards (formerly of the Contours) may have lacked some of the vocal polish of his predecessor, but his more aggressive approach perfectly suited the new Sly Stone–influenced, psychedelic soul-rock hybrid Whitfield and the group forged. "Cloud Nine" (#6 pop, #2 R&B) was the first of a series of hits that broached social and political issues (although Motown has long held that "Cloud Nine" contains no allusions to drugs, Gladys Knight and the Pips refused to record it for that reason), and seemed out of character given Motown's traditional conservatism. With "Cloud Nine" and the following hit singles—"Run Away Child, Running Wild" (#6 pop, #1 R&B) and "Don't Let the Joneses Get You Down" (#20 pop, #2 R&B) in 1969; "Psychedelic Shack" (#7 pop, #2 R&B) and "Ball of Confusion (That's What the World Is Today)" (#3 pop, #2 R&B) in 1970—the Tempts became one of the few Motown acts (including Marvin Gaye and Stevie Wonder) who got progressive FM radio airplay. Sandwiched between these releases were singles in the more familiar Tempts style: "I'm Gonna Make You Love Me," a duet with the Supremes recorded before Ruffin's departure (#2 pop and R&B, 1968), the Robinson ballad "I'll Try Something New" (#25 pop, #8 R&B, 1968), and the five-lead workout "I Can't Get Next to You" (#1 pop and R&B, 1969).

The year 1971 began with the last Kendricks-led hit, "Just My Imagination (Running Away With Me)" (#1 pop and R&B), which is perhaps second only to "My Girl" as the group's most beloved song. Kendricks quit to start a fitfully successful solo career. Later that year, Williams also left the group because of poor health. An alcoholic, Paul Williams had been performing with the group but with Richard Street singing his parts from behind the curtain. He remained involved with the group after his official departure, but personal demons and debt drove him to despair. Two years later he was discovered slumped in his parked car just blocks from Motown, dead, presumably from a self-inflicted gunshot wound.

With new replacements Damon Harris (ex-Vibration Ricky Owens was in and out of the group in just weeks and never recorded with them) and Richard Street (most recently of the Monitors), the Temptations continued moving away from ballads with "Superstar (Remember How You Got Where You Are)" (#18 pop, #8 R&B, 1971), "Papa Was a Rollin' Stone" (#1 pop, #5 R&B, 1972), "Masterpiece" (#7 pop, #1 R&B, 1973), "Hey Girl (I Like Your Style)" (#35 pop, #2 R&B, 1973), "The Plastic Man" (#40 pop, #8 R&B, 1973), "Let Your Hair Down" (#27 pop, #1 R&B, 1973), and "Shakey Ground" (#32 pop, #1 R&B, 1975). While the Tempts continued to hit the R&B Top 10 regularly, their singles rarely reached the pop Top 30. Throughout this period, however, they maintained a consistent record as one of the rare Motown groups that sold albums. Through 1976 every album of new material but their debut hit the album Top 40, and 10 were Top 10.

Like many other Motown acts, the Temptations became dissatisfied with the label. Unlike most, however, the Tempts had retained the rights to their name and, by the time they left the label, had succeeded in writing and producing their own commercially overlooked but critically well received LP, *The Temptations Do the Temptations*. It would be their last effort under their original Motown contract. They moved to Atlantic, shortly before which Dennis Edwards left the group for the first of three times. With new singer Louis Price, the Tempts cut two disco-ish albums: *Bare Back* (coproduced by the Holland brothers) and *Hear to Tempt You*. These were unsuccessful, and with Edwards back in Price's place, the group returned to Motown at Berry Gordy's personal request. Gordy cowrote and produced their first hit single in seven years, "Power" (#43 pop, #11 R&B, 1980). The group seemed poised to reclaim its turf, but the Thom Bell–produced *The Temptations* missed the mark. Further releases were halted for the long-awaited Reunion Tour, which in 1982 brought Ruffin and Kendricks back into the fold. This seven-man lineup recorded *Reunion* (#37 pop, #2 R&B, 1982) and embarked on a mini-tour. The album's hit single, "Standing on the Top (Part 1)" (#66 pop, #6 R&B, 1982), was written and produced by Rick James (the Temptations provided background vocals for James' "Super Freak"). The reunion was a fan's dream come true, but talks to make it a permanent venture were scuttled amid intergroup tensions and problems between Kendricks and Ruffin and Motown.

By that point, each of their solo careers had peaked. Ruffin's first single, the urgent "My Whole World Ended (the Moment You Left Me)" (#9 pop, #2 R&B, 1969), was his biggest solo hit. In 1969 he had two other Top 20 R&B singles, "I've Lost Everything I've Ever Loved" (#11) and "I'm So Glad I Fell for You" (#18). Ruffin and his older brother Jimmy (best remembered for 1966's "What Becomes of the Brokenhearted") teamed up for a 1970 album that produced a minor hit in "Stand by Me." David Ruffin soon hit hard times, however. "Walk Away From Love" (#9 pop, #1 R&B, 1975), produced by Van McCoy, was his only other Top 40 hit, though he did reach the R&B Top 10 with "Heavy Love" and "Everything's Coming Up Love" in 1976, and "Break My Heart" in 1979.

After quitting the Tempts, Kendricks moved to the West Coast and began to build a solo career with Motown, which had just relocated there. His early solo recordings (on Tamla) were R&B hits: "It's So Hard for Me to Say Goodbye" and "Can I" (1971), "Eddie's Love" and "If You Let Me" (1972), and "Girl You Need a Change of Mind" and "Darling Come Back Home" (1973). Kendricks' jump to the top of the R&B and pop charts came in 1973 with the falsetto-topped "Keep On Truckin' (Part 1)" (#1 pop and R&B), followed by "Boogie Down" (#2 pop, #1 R&B, 1974). For the next three years Kendricks' songs were regularly in the R&B Top 10: "Son of Sagittarius" (#28 pop, #5 R&B, 1974), "Tell Her Love Has Felt the Need" (#8 R&B, 1974), "One Tear" (#8 R&B, 1974), "Shoeshine Boy" (#18 pop, #1 R&B, 1975), "Get the Cream Off the Top" (#7 R&B, 1975), "Happy" (#8 R&B, 1975), "He's a Friend" (#36 pop, #2 R&B, 1976). In 1977 he signed with Arista. His last single hit for Motown was "Intimate Friends" (#24 R&B, 1978). The move proved to be not as smooth as expected. Kendricks' only big hit for Arista was "Ain't No Smoke Without Fire" (#13 R&B, 1978), and in 1980 he signed with Atlantic.

Both his and Ruffin's careers seemed moribund. Then, in 1985 Daryl Hall and John Oates invited the two onstage for a recorded performance at the newly reopened Apollo Theatre. A Temptations medley reached the Top 20 on the singles chart and revived interest in Kendricks and Ruffin, who later in 1985 lent their voices to the star-studded *Sun City* album by Artists United Against Apartheid. A 1987 album *Ruffin and Kendricks*, spawned a #14 R&B hit, "I Couldn't Believe It."

Kendricks next teamed up with yet another ex-Temptation, Dennis Edwards, for a 1990 single, "Get It While It's Hot," cowritten by Jermaine Jackson. Edwards had some solo success during one of his three hiatuses from the Tempts, including "Don't Look Any Further" (#72 pop, #2 R&B, 1984). Kendricks, Edwards, and Ruffin went on tour together; combined, they'd sung lead on virtually all the Temptations' '60s and '70s hits. In the late '80s, Ruffin, Kendricks, and Edwards began touring with a successful Tribute to the Temptations package tour. (In the mid-'90s, the Tempts sought to prevent Edwards from using the Temptations name [which Otis Williams and Franklin jointly owned]. In 1999 a judge issued a permanent injunction against Edwards, forbidding him to ever use the name in advertising for his performances.)

Things seemed to be looking up, but on June 1, 1991, Ruffin, long plagued by drug addiction (he'd been convicted of cocaine possession in 1988 and entered drug rehab the following year), overdosed on cocaine after visiting a crack house. He lapsed into a coma and when doctors at a Philadelphia hospital failed to revive him, he was pronounced dead. He was 50. Michael Jackson paid for Ruffin's funeral, which was presided over by the Reverend Louis Farrakhan and attended by countless celebrities, among them the surviving original Temptations (Williams, Kendricks, and Franklin), who sang "My Girl." Aretha Franklin and Stevie Wonder also performed.

The following year, Kendricks died of lung cancer at age 52. Again, the surviving Tempts attended his funeral, where Franklin eulogized his former group mate. Later Bobby Womack organized two concerts to raise funds for the singer's survivors.

For the Temptations, however, the years following the reunion were marked by constant international touring and several surprise successes. Following the 1983 Motown 25 segment in which the Tempts and their friends the Four Tops performed a battle of the bands, the two groups took the show on the road. The T'n'T Tour, as it was called, ran for over three years, including a sold-out stint on Broadway, beginning in 1983. They continued cowriting and coproducing much of their more recent material, including 1984's "Treat Her Like a Lady" (#48 pop, #2 R&B), a collaboration between Otis Williams and latter-day member Ali Ollie Woodson. Other '80s singles include "Sail Away" (#54 pop, #13 R&B, 1984), "My Love Is True (Truly for You)" (#14 R&B, 1985), "Do You Really Love Your Baby" (#14 R&B, 1985), "Lady Soul" (#47 pop, #4 R&B, 1986), "I Wonder Who She's Seeing Now" (#3 R&B, 1987), "Look What You Started" (#8 R&B, 1987), "Special" (#10 R&B, 1989), "Soul to Soul" (#12 R&B, 1990), and "The Jones' " (#41 R&B, 1991). Williams penned his autobiography, *Temptations*, in 1988 with Patricia Romanowski. The Temptations were inducted into the Rock and Roll Hall of Fame, by Daryl Hall and John Oates, in 1989.

For the Temptations, the '90s would prove a decade of profound loss and unexpected triumph. Melvin Franklin, who had been in poor health for a number of years due to arthritis, died at age 52 after suffering a heart attack following a brain seizure. At the time, the group was recording a collection of standards, *For Lovers Only;* his last recording was "Life Is But a Dream."

The group's commercial comeback began in the fall of 1998, when NBC aired the two-part miniseries *Temptations*, based on Williams' book of the same name. (The book is slated to be republished in the fall of 2002.) Released about the same time, *Phoenix Rising* (#44 pop, #8 R&B, 1998) and its lead single, "Stay" (#20 pop, #28 R&B, 1998) brought the Tempts to a new generation. Produced by Narada Michael Walden, the album was a major coup for the Tempts, and their first album to be certified platinum. As always, the group continued to tour the world. Its followup, 2000's Grammy-winning *Ear-Resistible*, produced by Gerald Levert and Joe Little III, entered and peaked on the R&B albums chart at #16 (#54 pop).

10cc

Formed 1972, Manchester, Eng.
Eric Stewart (b. Jan. 20, 1945, Manchester), gtr., voc.; Lol Creme (b. Lawrence Creme, Sep. 19, 1947, Manchester), gtr., voc., kybds., bass; Graham Gouldman (b. May 10, 1946, Manchester), gtr., voc., bass, kybds.; Kevin Godley (b. Oct. 7, 1945, Manchester), drums, voc., kybds.
1973—*10cc* (UK) 1974—*Sheet Music* 1975—*The Original Soundtrack* (Mercury); *100cc* (UK) (+ Paul Burgess, drums) 1976—*How Dare You!* (Mercury) 1976—(– Godley; – Creme) 1977—*Deceptive Bends* (+ Rick Fenn, voc., gtr.; + Tony O'Malley, kybds.; + Stuart Tosh, drums, voc., perc.) *10cc Live and Let Live* 1978—*Bloody Tourists* 1979—*Greatest Hits, 1972–1978* 1980—*Look Hear?* (Warner Bros.) 1991—(group re-forms: Gouldman; Stewart; Godley; Creme) 1992—*Meanwhile* (Phonogram, U.K.) (– Godley; – Creme) 1995—*Alive* (Creative Man); *Mirror Mirror* (Critique) 1997—*The Very Best of 10cc* (Mercury Legacy).
Godley and Creme: 1976—*Consequences* (Polydor, U.K.) 1985—*The History Mix, vol. I* (Polydor) 2000—*Freeze Frame* (One Way).
Graham Gouldman solo: 1968—*The Graham Gouldman Thing* (RCA) 1980—*Animalympics* soundtrack (A&M) 1999—*And Another Thing . . .* (For Your Love/Dome, U.K.).

Composed of four prolific singers/players/songwriters, 10cc won critical acclaim for its witty and melodic "art pop." The band began scoring pop hits as it moved closer to the boundary between parody and romantic pop. Graham Gouldman had played with Manchester bands like the Mockingbirds, as well as a later version of Wayne Fontana's Mindbenders. He wrote such mid-'60s British rock hits as "For Your Love," "Heart Full of Soul," and "Evil Hearted You" (recorded by the Yardbirds); "Look Through Any Window" and "Bus Stop" (by the Hollies); and "No Milk Today" (by Herman's Hermits). He had left the Mindbenders in 1968 to go to New York City, where he worked unsuccessfully for bubblegum producers Kasenetz and Katz and released the late-'60s solo LP *The Graham Gouldman Thing*, which was coproduced by John Paul Jones, later of Led Zeppelin.

In 1970 he formed Hotlegs, which included Lol Creme, Kevin Godley, and Eric Stewart. Working out of Strawberry Studios in England, which Stewart partly owned, Hotlegs had a #2 U.K. hit with 1970's "Neanderthal Man." Stewart had also been in the Mindbenders with Gouldman; when Wayne Fontana left the group, Stewart became frontman. Godley and Creme had attended art school together (they designed 10cc's debut album cover) and played together in a few local bands, then played sessions at Strawberry Studios. Like Hotlegs, 10cc would be primarily a studio group (though Hotlegs did tour with the Moody Blues on the heels of its hit single); while fooling around in Strawberry Studios with the Godley-Creme song "Donna," they band transformed it into a sharp-edged satire of late-'50s teen-idol hits and had 10cc's first demo. The tape of "Donna" was taken to British impresario Jonathan King; he claims he rechristened Hotlegs as 10cc (the name supposedly derives from the nine cubic centimeters of semen ejaculated by the average male). Within weeks of its 1972 release, "Donna" was at #2 on the British singles chart. In 1973 came "Rubber Bullets" (#1 U.K.) and "Dean and I" (#10 U.K.), followed by "Wall Street Shuffle" (#10 U.K., 1974), "I'm Not in Love" (#1 U.K., 1975), and "Art for Art's Sake" (#5 U.K., 1975). However, despite critical acclaim, 10cc had no U.S. hit singles, though "Rubber Bullets" became a novelty sensation on FM radio.

That changed with the late-blooming American success of the lush "I'm Not in Love" (#2, 1975). After that hit, Godley and Creme left, to record together and to work on their guitar-modification device, the Gizmo (it clips on over the bridge, and using continuous-motion rotary plectrums, effects infinite sustain and string-section sounds). As a duo Stewart and Gouldman made *Deceptive Bends*, which featured "The Things We Do for Love" (#5, 1977). They then added several new members, including drummer/vocalist Stuart Tosh, formerly of British teenybopper hitmakers Pilot. *Live and Let Live* (#146, 1977) was more or less a flop, but

Bloody Tourists yielded "Dreadlock Holiday" (#44 pop, #1 U.K., 1978).

Godley and Creme continued to record and produce promotional videos for other bands (they refuse to tour); they even had a Top 10 U.K. single in 1982 with "Wedding Bells." Stewart and Gouldman weren't heard from again until 1982's 10cc LP *10 Out of 10* (not released domestically), for which ex–Linda Ronstadt guitarist Andrew Gold [see entry] cowrote and coproduced three songs. 10cc then disbanded, and Gouldman and Gold formed the duo Wax, which had one U.S. hit, "Right Between the Eyes," in 1986. In 1987 "Bridge to Your Heart" went to #12 in England. Gouldman produced the Ramones *(Pleasant Dreams)* and Gilbert O'Sullivan. Stewart has produced other acts and worked with Paul McCartney *(Tug of War)*.

Since 1980 Godley and Creme have become major video auteurs, conceiving and directing a number of popular, groundbreaking clips, including Duran Duran's "Girls on Film," Visage's "Fade to Grey," the Police's "Every Breath You Take," Herbie Hancock's "Rockit," and Elton John's "Kiss the Bride." The duo had a #16 hit with 1985's groundbreaking video "Cry."

10,000 Maniacs

Formed 1981, Jamestown, NY
Natalie Merchant (b. Oct. 26, 1963, Jamestown), voc.; Robert Buck (b. Aug. 1, 1958, Jamestown; d. Dec. 19, 2000, Pittsburgh, PA), gtr.; Dennis Drew (b. Aug. 8, 1957, Buffalo, NY), kybds.; Steven Gustafson (b. Apr. 10, 1957, Madrid, Spain), bass; Jerome Augustyniak (b. Sep. 2, 1958, Lackawana, NY), drums; John Lombardo (b. Sep. 30, 1952, Jamestown), gtr.
1982—*Human Conflict Number Five* EP (Christian Burial Music) 1983—*Secrets of the I Ching* 1985—*The Wishing Chair* (Elektra) (– Lombardo) 1987—*In My Tribe* 1989—*Blind Man's Zoo* 1990—*Hope Chest: The Fredonia Recordings 1982–1983* 1992—*Our Time in Eden* 1994—*MTV Unplugged* (– Merchant; + Mary Ramsey [b. Dec. 31, 1963, Washington, DC], voc., viola, violin; + Lombardo) 1997—*Love Among the Ruins* (Geffen) 1999—*The Earth Pressed Flat* (Bar/None) 2000—(– Buck).
Natalie Merchant solo: see entry.

Without ever scoring a major hit single, 10,000 Maniacs steadily built a considerable audience, through college and alternative radio. The band's sprightly, thoughtful folk rock was dominated by Robert Buck's brightly jangling guitar, Dennis Drew's creamy Hammond organ, and Natalie Merchant's plaintive vocals and bookish, sometimes topical, lyrics. Merchant's decision to quit 10,000 Maniacs following its 1993 tour left the band's future in doubt.

Gustafson, Drew, and Buck first came together through the college scene that spread from Jamestown Community College to the State University of New York (SUNY) at Fredonia. The trio played under such names as Still Life and Burn Victims, then became 10,000 Maniacs (a misreading of the '60s cult gore film title *2,000 Maniacs*). They were soon joined at small-club and party gigs by Merchant, who attended Jamestown CC. *Human Conflict Number Five* and *Secrets of the I Ching* were recorded through a sound-engineering program at SUNY Fredonia. Both records received favorable reviews in the alternative press and some college-radio airplay.

By 1985, 10,000 Maniacs had landed a deal with Elektra. Their major-label debut, *The Wishing Chair,* got glowing reviews from the mainstream music press yet still sold poorly. Lombardo left after an extensive tour; he later formed a duo, John and Mary, with Mary Ramsey, who was destined to replace Merchant in 1994. Elektra assigned veteran L.A. folk-rock producer Peter Asher to oversee the next LP. The combination worked, artistically and commercially, as *In My Tribe* (#37, 1987) yielded the band's first chart singles, "Like the Weather" (#68, 1988) and "What's the Matter Here (#80, 1988)," about child abuse. The group's profile rose higher when it opened on tour for R.E.M.

Asher returned to produce 1989's *Blind Man's Zoo* (#13, 1989), a collection that spanned topics ranging from pregnancy to the colonization of Africa; Merchant wrote "Trouble Me" (#44, 1989) for her father while he was hospitalized. *Hope Chest* (#102, 1990) reissued the band's first two releases. On *Our Time in Eden,* 10,000 Maniacs switched producers from Asher to Paul Fox (Robyn Hitchcock, XTC, the Sugarcubes), expanding its sound dramatically; James Brown hornmen Fred Wesley and Maceo Parker appear on "Few and Far Between." "These Are the Days" (#66, 1992) was a minor hit single. Just after the album was completed, drummer Augustyniak was sidelined with a broken collarbone; ex–E Street Band drummer Max Weinberg sat in. Augustyniak was back on board for the group's performance at MTV's inaugural ball for President Bill Clinton in January 1993. In early August of that year, Merchant announced that she would depart the band for a solo career [see entry]. *MTV Unplugged* was Merchant's recorded swan song with the band, which quickly enlisted sometime backup vocalist Ramsey and reenlisted Lombardo for a new lineup. The 1997 release *Love Among the Ruins,* produced by John Keane (R.E.M., Cowboy Junkies) and Fred Maher, sold 200,000 copies and won the group a Top 40 hit with a remake of Roxy Music's "More Than This" (#25). Two years later, the Maniacs released a roots-oriented lo-fi effort, *The Earth Pressed Flat,* on the independent Bar/None label. In late 2000, however, the band lost another member when founding guitarist Buck died of complications from liver failure.

Ten Years After/Alvin Lee

Formed 1967, Nottingham, Eng.
Alvin Lee (b. Dec. 19, 1944, Nottingham), gtr., voc.; Chick Churchill (b. Jan. 2, 1949, Mold, Wales), kybds.; Leo Lyons (b. Nov. 30, 1943, Bedfordshire, Eng.), bass; Ric Lee (b. Oct. 20, 1945, Cannock, Eng.), drums.
1967—*Ten Years After* (Deram) 1968—*Undead* 1969—*Stonedhenge; Ssssh* 1970—*Cricklewood Green; Watt*

1971—*A Space in Time* (Columbia) 1972—*Alvin Lee & Co.; Rock 'n' Roll Music to the World* 1973—*Recorded Live* 1974—*Positive Vibrations* 1975—*Goin' Home! Their Greatest Hits* 1976—*Anthology* 1977—*Classic Performances* 1981—*Hear Me Calling* (Decca) 1989—*About Time* (Chrysalis) 1991—*Essential Ten Years After.*
Alvin Lee solo: 1973—*On the Road to Freedom* (with Mylon LeFevre) (Columbia) 1974—*In Flight* 1975—*Pump Iron!* 1978—*Rocket Fuel* (with Ten Years Later) (RSO) 1979—*Ride On* (with Ten Years Later) 1980—*Free Fall* (Atlantic) 1986—*Detroit Diesel* (21 Records) 1992—*Zoom* (Domino) 1994—*I Hear You Rockin'* (Viceroy).

Ten Years After was a dependably hard-rocking blues-based band for many years, best remembered for the sped-up blues solos of guitarist Alvin Lee, whose supersonic version of "Goin' Home" was a smash hit at the 1969 Woodstock Festival and in the *Woodstock* film. Alvin Lee and Leo Lyons grew up together in Nottingham. Lee was playing guitar by age 13; and Lyons began performing publicly at age 15. By the early '60s, both were involved in blues groups. Lee performed in a John Lee Hooker show at London's Marquee; Lyons appeared at a Windsor Jazz Festival; both were also studio musicians. They got together in 1964 as Britain's Largest Sounding Trio (with Lyons on drums), which toured England and the Continent and was quite successful in Hamburg. In 1967 Ric Lee (no relation to Alvin) and Chick Churchill joined, completing what was now called Ten Years After.

Alvin Lee's speed made the band a popular concert attraction. Despite a lack of hits, the first few LPs sold well. By 1968 the members of Ten Years After were regulars at New York's The Scene—where they jammed with Jimi Hendrix, Janis Joplin, and Larry Coryell—and at San Francisco's Fillmore West. In Woodstock's wake, the group had several Top 30 LPs: *Ssssh* (#20, 1969), *Cricklewood Green* (#14, 1970), and *Watt* (#21, 1970). *A Space in Time* (#17, 1971) eventually went platinum. By that time the band had chalked up its first hit single, "I'd Love to Change the World," a dreamy song that made the U.S. and U.K. charts in 1971. The group followed with "Baby Won't You Let Me Rock 'n' Roll You" in 1972 and "Choo Choo Mama" in 1973, both minor hit singles.

After *Rock 'n' Roll Music to the World* (#43, 1972), the band took a break from touring. Lee built a studio in his 15th-century Berkshire home and recorded *On the Road to Freedom* with Mylon LeFevre, which also featured guest appearances by Steve Winwood, Jim Capaldi, George Harrison (credited as Harry Georgeson), and Ron Wood. Churchill recorded a solo album, *You and Me.*

In early 1974, with the band's status in doubt, Lee organized a nine-piece band, including reedman Mel Collins and drummer Ian Wallace (both formerly with King Crimson), who played a show at London's Rainbow Theatre before Ten Years After's scheduled appearance. Lee's band was recorded on *Alvin Lee and Company.* Ten Years After did end up playing the Rainbow, and it turned out to be the group's last British concert in the '70s. *Positive Vibrations* (#81, 1974) put an end to the band's recordings until 1989's *About Time* (#120).

Later in 1974, Lee announced plans for a worldwide tour with a cast featuring Collins, Wallace, and keyboardist Ronnie Leahy and bassist Steve Thompson of Stone the Crows. Though Ten Years After seemed officially defunct, its management denied the split. In May 1975 Alvin Lee declared the group to be through and it was announced that Ric Lee had formed his own band. Ten Years After then went out on one more American tour. The demise has never been made official. The original lineup has toured in the '90s.

Lee continued to record with a series of groups, including Ten Years Later (in the late '70s) and the Alvin Lee Band. A later quartet included Mick Taylor, Fuzzy Samuels, and Tom Compton, but their *RX-5* (which was not released in the U.S.) vanished without a trace.

Chick Churchill became a professional manager for Chrysalis Publishing. Leo Lyons produced several mid-'70s albums by British heavy-metal band UFO. Ric Lee formed his own production company.

Tammi Terrell

Born Thomasina Montgomery, Jan. 24, 1946, Philadelphia, PA; died Mar. 16, 1970, Philadelphia
1967—*United* (with Marvin Gaye) (Tamla) 1968—*You're All I Need* (with Marvin Gaye) 1969—*Irresistible Tammi Terrell; Easy* (with Marvin Gaye) 1970—*Greatest Hits* (with Marvin Gaye).

Although Tammi Terrell began recording in 1961, her solo recordings were eclipsed by her immortal duets with Marvin Gaye. Terrell became involved in show business at an early age (her mother was an actress), but nearly gave it up to pursue her education. She was 15 when Luther Dixon discovered her at a talent show, which led to her recording her first single, "If You See Bill," for Scepter/Wand, in 1961. The following year Montgomery, as she was then known, recorded "The Voice of Experience" in 1962. After studying psychology at the University of Pennsylvania, she recorded "I Cried" for James Brown's label. Shortly thereafter, she joined his revue and began what was by all accounts a stormy romantic relationship. She left Brown around 1964, married and divorced (contrary to many sources, her husband was not boxer Ernie Terrell), recorded briefly for Checker, then signed to Motown.

Toward the end of 1965 Terrell's "I Can't Believe You Love Me" made the R&B Top 30. After its followup, "Come On and See Me," failed to make an impression on the pop chart, she was paired with Marvin Gaye for a series of Ashford and Simpson duets: In 1967 "Ain't No Mountain High Enough" (#19 pop, #3 R&B) and "Your Precious Love" (#5 pop, #2 R&B); in 1968 "Ain't Nothing Like the Real Thing" (#8 pop, #1 R&B), "You're All I Need to Get By" (#7 pop, #1 R&B), and "Keep On Lovin' Me Honey" (#24 pop, #11 R&B); in 1969 "Good Lovin' Ain't Easy to Come By" (#30 pop, #11 R&B) and "What You Gave Me" (#6 R&B). "If I Could Build My Whole World Around

You" b/w the Gaye-penned "If This World Were Mine" (#10 pop, #27 R&B) were also released in 1967.

Terrell and Gaye, widely assumed to be lovers, were not. Gaye was married to Anna Gordy, and Terrell was romantically involved with Temptation David Ruffin in what was another tempestuous, at times violent, affair. Gaye, however, felt especially protective toward Terrell. He was deeply affected after she collapsed in his arms onstage during a show in Virginia in 1967. She had long complained of severe migraine headaches, and following her collapse a brain tumor was diagnosed. Terrell retired from the road. Despite eight operations over the next year and a half (resulting in memory problems and partial paralysis), she continued to record with Gaye. Late in his life, Gaye (who was devastated by Terrell's death) revealed that it was not Terrell but Valerie Simpson singing on most of *Easy*, including "Good Lovin' Ain't Easy to Come By" and "What You Gave Me." Previous to that, most believed Simpson stood in for Terrell only on the posthumously released "The Onion Song."

Sonny Terry and Brownie McGhee

Formed 1940
"Sonny" Terry (b. Saunders Terell, Oct. 24, 1911, Greensboro, GA; d. Mar. 11, 1986, Mineola, NY), voc., harmonica; Walter Brown "Brownie" McGhee (b. Nov. 30, 1915, Knoxville, TN; d. Feb. 16, 1996, Oakland, CA), gtr., voc.
1958—*Brownie McGhee and Sonny Terry Sing* (Smithsonian/Folkways) 1960—*Just a Closer Walk With Thee* (Fantasy) 1963—*Live at the 2nd Fret* (Bluesville); *At Sugar Hill* (Fantasy) 1974—*Hometown Blues* (Mainstream) 1978—*Midnight Special* (Fantasy) 1989—*Sonny and Brownie* (A&M) 1991—*Sonny Terry and Brownie McGhee* 1999—*Backwater Blues* (Fantasy).
Brownie McGhee solo: 1958—*Back Country Blues* (Savoy) 1994—*The Complete Brownie McGhee* (Columbia/Legacy).
Sonny Terry solo: 1960—*Sonny's Story* (Bluesville) 1963—*Sonny Is King* 1984—*Whoopin'* (Alligator) 1987—*Sonny Terry* (Collectables) 1991—*The Folkways Years, 1944–1963* (Smithsonian/Folkways).

Sonny Terry and Brownie McGhee were Southern blues musicians with church roots. They paired up in the early '40s and became a popular and influential folk-blues team, despite the fact that both suffered crippling childhood diseases.

Terry was blind, the result of separate childhood accidents in 1922 and 1927. He spent his early years playing harmonica around North Carolina, slowly achieving a wider reputation in the late '30s, thanks to performances with Lead Belly and Blind Boy Fuller.

McGhee contracted polio at the age of four, though he made a substantial recovery that left him only with a limp. His entire family was musical, and he was performing with them by the age of eight. He quit school at 13 to become a full-time musician, and had just begun his recording career when he was introduced to Sonny Terry.

They were a steady duo after that, although they worked apart extensively as well, McGhee under pseudonyms like Spider Sam, Big Tom Collins, Henry Johnson, and Blind Boy Williams. After being discovered by folk revivalists in the '50s, notably Pete Seeger, they went on to perform in clubs, in colleges, and at jazz and blues festivals around the world. They've made dozens of records.

They continued to appear as a duo in the ensuing decades despite the fact they did not get along particularly well. In the early '80s McGhee began touring with his own band. Terry also maintained a solo career until his death in 1986. McGhee died 10 years later; he was 80.

Joe Tex

Born Joseph Arrington Jr., Aug. 8, 1933, Rogers, TX; died Joseph Arrington Hazziez, Aug. 12, 1982, Navasota, TX
1965—*The Best of Joe Tex* (Parrot); *Hold On to What You've Got* (Atlantic); *The New Boss* 1966—*The Love You Save* 1967—*The Best of Joe Tex* 1968—*Live and Lively; Soul Country* 1969—*Buying a Book* 1972—*I Gotcha* (Dial) 1977—*Bumps and Bruises* (Epic) 1978—*Rub Down* 1985—*The Best of Joe Tex* (Atlantic) 1988—*I Believe I'm Gonna Make It: The Best of Joe Tex, 1964–1972* (Rhino) 1991—*Greatest Hits* (Curb/CEMA) 1992—*Show Me: The Hits . . . & More* (Ichiban) 1996—*The Very Best of Joe Tex* (Rhino).

Soul singer Joe Tex recorded in a variety of styles but is best known for his dance hits. Tex first recorded for King from 1955 to 1957, and from 1958 to 1960 for Ace. He was a journeyman performer through most of the early '60s, recording occasionally, but with no success. His first break came in 1961 when James Brown recorded his "Baby You're Right." In 1964 Tex signed to Buddy Killen's Dial Records, a Nashville soul label.

Recordings at what would later become the famous Muscle Shoals studio, Tex broke through in 1965 with "Hold What You've Got" (#5 pop, #2 R&B). Through soul's mid-to-late-'60s heyday, Tex had several big hits, including "I Want to (Do Everything for You)" (#1 R&B), "A Sweet Woman Like You" (#1 R&B), and "The Love You Save" (#10 pop, #2 R&B) in 1965; and the comedic "Skinny Legs and All" (#10 pop, #2 R&B) in 1967.

In 1972 Tex had a big hit with the lecherous "I Gotcha" (#2 pop, #1 R&B). A year later he left Atlantic and through the '70s recorded for numerous companies, although always under the guidance of Buddy Killen. In 1977 Tex had his last major hit, another comedy record, "Ain't Gonna Bump No More (With No Big Fat Woman)" (#12 pop, #7 R&B).

During his later years he had become a Muslim minister and in 1972 adopted the surname Hazziez; he spent most of his time on his farm and was known as a devoted Houston Oilers fan (among his last recordings was a tribute to running back Earl Campbell entitled "Do the Earl Campbell"). In 1981 Tex joined the Soul Clan reunion, which included Wilson Pickett, Don Covay, Solomon Burke, and Ben E. King. Not long after, Tex died of a heart attack on his farm at age 49.

Among the pallbearers at his funeral were Buddy Killen, Wilson Pickett, Ben E. King, Don Covay, and Percy Mayfield.

Texas Tornados

Formed 1989, San Francisco, CA
Freddy Fender (b. Baldemar Huerta, June 4, 1937, San Benito, TX), gtr., voc.; Augie Meyers (b. May 31, 1940, San Antonio, TX), kybds., voc., accordion, bajo sexto; Doug Sahm (b. Nov. 6, 1941, San Antonio; d. Nov. 18, 1999, Taos, NM), gtr., voc.; Flaco Jiménez (b. Mar. 11, 1939, San Antonio), accordion, voc.
1990—*Texas Tornados* (Reprise) 1991—*Zone of Our Own* 1992—*Hangin' On by a Thread* 1996—*4 Aces* 1999—*Live From the Limo, vol. 1.*

The Texas Tornados boasted four legendary Tex-Mex performers: Doug Sahm [see entry] and Augie Meyers were in the Sir Douglas Quintet in the '60s, Freddy Fender [see entry] was originally billed "El Bebop Kid" and "the Mexican Elvis," and Flaco Jiménez has been a star of conjunto music for several decades. Sahm first met Fender in 1959, when both were gigging around San Antonio, and Jiménez played accordion on Sahm's 1973 release, *Doug Sahm and Band;* Sahm's nickname was the Texas Tornado, the title of another 1973 Sahm recording. In 1989 Sahm was booked to play Slim's nightclub in San Francisco and invited Meyers, Jiménez, and Fender to join him. Record companies were immediately interested in their infectious, danceable mix of conjunto, country, polka, and R&B.

Texas Tornados was released in both English and Spanish versions. Although it yielded no single, it sold well and won a Grammy. *Zone of Our Own* mixed English and Spanish (two band members are Hispanic, two white) and was again successful in rock, Latin, and country circles. The title track of *Hangin' On by a Thread* was written for and about the Grateful Dead, a band to whom the Tornados were often compared because of its rootsy sound and intrepid career; the song featured Sahm's son Shawn on guitar. Band members collaborated little on the album's tracks, however, and pursued other musical endeavors until regrouping in 1996 for *4 Aces,* which included the catchy single, "Little Bit Is Better Than Nada." *Live From the Limo* featured country artist Leroy Parnell on slide guitar; following Sahm's sudden death in November 1999, Parnell filled in on some subsequent Tornados dates in Europe. The group later announced it would not continue to perform as the Texas Tornados.

Them

Formed 1963, Belfast, N. Ire.
Original lineup: Billy Harrison, gtr.; Alan Henderson, bass; Ronnie Millings, drums; Eric Wrixen, kybds.; Van Morrison (b. Aug. 21, 1945, Belfast), voc., sax, harmonica.
N.A.—(– Wrixen; – Millings; + Jackie McAuley, kybds.; + Patrick McAuley, drums) 1965—*Angry Young Them* (Decca, U.K.); *Them* (Parrot) 1966—*Them Again* 1972—*Them* 1977—*Story of Them* (London).

In the early days of singer Van Morrison's [see entry] recording and performing career, he was backed by Them, a young Belfast garage band. Morrison and Them had major U.K. hits in 1965 with "Baby Please Don't Go" (#10) and "Here Comes the Night" (#2). Their U.S. hits were "Here Comes the Night" (#24) and "Mystic Eyes" (#33) in 1965; and "Gloria" (#71) in 1966. The latter was beaten on the U.S. chart by the Shadows of Knight's version. Morrison toured Europe and the American West Coast with Them in 1966 (the Doors opened the West Coast shows). When Morrison returned home after the tour, he took a lot of time off before planning his next career move; after a short time, Them disbanded.

During its brief career, its personnel changed often, at various times including guitarist Jimmy Page and keyboardist Peter Bardens (who went on to form Camel). Following Morrison's departure for a solo career and the group's first demise, various members attempted to resurrect the group with negligible success.

These Immortal Souls: See Nick Cave and the Bad Seeds

The The

Formed 1979, London, Eng.
Matt Johnson (b. Aug. 15, 1961, London), voc., kybds.
1983—*Soul Mining* (Epic) 1986—*Infected* 1989—*Mind Bomb* 1993—*Dusk* 1995—*Hanky Panky* 2000—*NakedSelf* (Nothing Records).

The The is the name given to bands led by Matt Johnson, a bald, mercurial, brooding singer/songwriter. While the The's sound has moved from the poppy new-wave dance tracks of *Soul Mining* to the intense bluesy ruminations of *Dusk,* the level of musicianship has remained consistent (over 300 musicians have appeared on the The albums, including Neneh Cherry, Sinéad O'Connor, and the Smiths' Johnny Marr), a testament to Johnson's uncompromising perfectionism.

Johnson was exposed to music while living above his father's pub in London's East End, which was favored by show-business types, and in nightclubs and dancehalls run by an uncle. At age 15 he was hired as tea boy for a small music publisher; by 18 he was assistant engineer at their 8-track studio. A 1979 ad he placed in the *New Musical Express* was answered by synthesist Keith Laws. They played their first gig that May, opening for Scritti Politti, and in 1980 released a single, "Controversial Subject" b/w "Black & White," for 4AD Records.

To satisfy a contractual obligation, Johnson released an album under his own name in 1981, *Burning Blue Soul.* A series of managerial wrangles led to his signing with Epic later that year. An album, *The Pornography of Despair,* was started, delayed, and subsequently abandoned. It took until 1983 for *Soul Mining* to become the The's official debut.

Illness prevented Johnson from recording another album until 1985. *Infected* (#89, 1987), accompanied by an album-length video, expanded the group's cult status. *Mind Bomb* (#138, 1989), a politically charged song cycle, was supported by the The's first tour. *Dusk* (#143, 1993) found Johnson working in a stripped-down acoustic context, reaching new audiences while touring with Depeche Mode. Johnson explored C&W roots music with *Hanky Panky,* an entire album consisting of his versions of Hank Williams songs. Shortly afterward, he moved to New York, working on his subsequent projects there.

In 1997 Johnson recorded an album titled *Gun Sluts* with guitarist Eric Schermerhorn (Iggy Pop), but Epic/Sony found it too experimental and refused to release it—thus making for yet another addition in the Johnson unreleased canon. (The songwriter has announced that he might eventually put the record out on his own label, Lazarus.) History repeated itself with *Gun Sluts*' followup, *NakedSelf,* except this time Johnson left Sony and took the album to Trent Reznor's Nothing Records, which released it in February 2000. But the honeymoon was to be short-lived as Johnson soon became incensed by what he felt were insufficient distribution and promotion efforts on the part of Nothing's parent company, Interscope/Universal. In retaliation, he opted to release free MP3s of *NakedSelf*'s songs on his own Web site.

They Might Be Giants

Formed 1984, Brooklyn, NY
John Flansburgh (b. May 6, 1960, Boston, MA), voc., gtr., drum programming; John Linnell (b. June 12, 1959, New York, NY), voc., kybds., accordion.
1986—*They Might Be Giants* (Bar/None) 1987—*Don't Let's Start* EP 1988—*Lincoln* (Restless/Bar/None) 1990—*Flood* (Elektra) 1991—*Miscellaneous T* (Restless) 1992—*Apollo 18* (Elektra) 1993—(+ Tony Maimone [b. Sep. 27, 1952, Cleveland, OH], bass; + Brian Doherty [b. July 2, 1962, Brooklyn], drums) 1994—*John Henry* 1995—(– Maimone). 1996—(+ Graham Maby, bass; + Eric Schermerhorn, gtr.) *Factory Showroom* 1997—*Then: The Earlier Years* (Restless) 1998—*Severe Tire Damage.*
Linnell solo: 1999—*State Songs* (Rounder/Zoe).

The two Johns who make up They Might Be Giants play songs as infectious and goofy as commercial jingles, yet made endearing by the duo's wacky wordplay and sheer irrepressibility. Theirs is a revenge of the nerds: College radio play and videos that look more geared for the Nickelodeon network than for MTV made them successful alternative artists and garnered them a major-label deal.

The Giants met as tykes in Lincoln, Massachusetts, where they were both from professional, middle-class households. They began writing songs together in high school, although it took them several years to form a band, during which time they both lacklusterly pursued higher ed-

They Might Be Giants: John Linnell and John Flansburgh (with drummer Brian Doherty and bassist Tony Maimone)

ucation, and Linnell played in the Rhode Island new-wave band the Mundanes. In 1981 they moved to Brooklyn together and began recording songs with a drum machine. Naming themselves after a George C. Scott film, they played downtown Manhattan dives and devised an ingenious way to get around dependence on record companies and radio play: Their Dial-a-Song service featured 300 tunes on an answering machine; the line, which only costs a regular toll call, eventually received more than 100 calls a day and as of 2001 remained in operation.

Their 1986 debut became an alternative hit when MTV latched onto the video for "Don't Let's Start." The album showcased the duo's strange wit and coffee-fueled phantasmagoria of musical styles: Song titles include "Youth Culture Killed My Dog" and "I Hope That I Get Old Before I Die." The video for "Ana Ng," from *Lincoln* (#89, 1988), brought them even more popularity. Their major-label debut, *Flood,* continued their MTV-driven success with the singles "Birdhouse in Your Soul" and "Istanbul (Not Constantinople)," but the critics who had adored the band were less pleased with the album's polish. TMBG became particularly popular in England, where the readers of *Q* magazine voted them the best new act of 1990 (although they had been together six years at that point).

The Giants next produced *Apollo 18* (#99, 1992) themselves, once again proving their adeptness at clever gimmicks: The track "Fingertips" was programmed to include 21 refrains that pop up repeatedly when the CD is played on "random" or "shuffle" mode. Touring for the album, the duo played with a band (featuring Pere Ubu bassist Tony Maimone) for the first time. Soon after, Maimone joined as a permanent member, as did drummer Brian Doherty. The band's next album, *John Henry* (#61, 1994), yielded the single "Snail Shell," which received much college-radio airplay.

Factory Showroom (#89 pop, 1996) landed the Giants a slot as the opening act for Hootie and the Blowfish, but the group was unhappy with how Elektra promoted the album and parted company with the label the following year. They put out a pair of compilation albums on the Restless label, including *Severe Tire Damage* (#186 pop, 1998), a collection of concert, radio, and soundcheck recordings. After that, they began releasing and marketing their music on the Internet, where *Long Tall Weekend* (1999) became digital download Web site Emusic's best-selling title to date. Over the years the Giants also have been involved with a number of side projects, notably scoring music for TV and movies, including the opening theme for *Austin Powers: The Spy Who Shagged Me* and the theme and incidental music for the TV sitcom *Malcolm in the Middle.*

Thin Lizzy

Formed 1970, Dublin, Ire.
Philip Lynott (b. Aug. 20, 1951, Dublin; d. Jan. 4, 1986, Dublin), bass, voc.; Brian Downey (b. Jan. 27, 1951, Dublin), drums; Eric Bell (b. Sep. 3, 1947, Belfast, N. Ire.), gtr.
1971—*Thin Lizzy* (Decca) 1972—*Shades of a Blue Orphanage* 1973—*Vagabonds of the Western World* (London) 1974— (– Bell; + Gary Moore [b. Apr. 4, 1952, Belfast, N. Ire.], gtr.; + Andy Gee, gtr.; + John Cann, gtr.; – Gee; – Cann; – Moore; + Brian Robertson [b. Sep. 12, 1956, Glasgow, Scot.], gtr.; + Scott Gorham [b. Mar. 17, 1951, Santa Monica, CA], gtr., voc.) *Night Life* (Mercury) 1975—*Fighting* (Vertigo) 1976—*Jailbreak; Johnny the Fox* 1977—*Bad Reputation* (– Robertson; + Moore; – Moore; + Robertson) 1978—*Live and Dangerous* (Warner Bros.) 1979—*Black Rose/A Rock Legend* (– Robertson; + Moore; – Moore; + Midge Ure [b. James Ure, Oct. 10, 1953, Glasgow], gtr.; – Ure; + Snowy White, gtr., voc.) 1980—*Chinatown* 1982—(– White; + John Sykes, gtr.) *Renegade* (+ Darren Wharton, kybds.) 1983—*Thunder and Lightning* 1984—*Life/Live* 1991—*Dedication: The Very Best of Thin Lizzy* (PolyGram).
Phil Lynott solo: 1980—*Solo in Soho* (Warner Bros.).
Gary Moore solo: 1983—*Corridors of Power* (Mirage) 1984—*Victims of the Future* 1986—*Run for Cover* 1987—*Wild Frontier* (Virgin) 1989—*After the War* 1990—*Still Got the Blues* (Charisma) 1992—*After Hours; The Early Years* (WTG); *Dirty Fingers* (Roadrunner Revisited) 1993—*Blues Alive* (Virgin) 1997—*Dark Days in Paradise* 1998—*Out in the Fields: The Very Best of Gary Moore.*

Fronted by Phil Lynott, a black Irishman, Thin Lizzy was a hard-nosed rock & roll band whose music was mostly distinguished by the strongly masculine-to-macho themes of Lynott's songs, which often celebrated male camaraderie and comic-book heroism. Thin Lizzy's finest hour was unquestionably 1976's *Jailbreak,* whose power chords and R&B undertones established it as a major act in Britain and contained its greatest American success, "The Boys Are Back in Town" (#12).

After being formed in Ireland by Lynott with his boyhood friend, drummer Brian Downey, Thin Lizzy relocated to England in 1971, subsequently scoring a hit single, "Whisky in a Jar" (#6 U.K., 1973). Eric Bell quit the band after the third LP, suffering exhaustion. Indifferent record sales followed until Thin Lizzy released *Jailbreak.* Since that LP, the group continued to record a series of uneven albums (excepting 1978's *Live and Dangerous*) and failed to become a superstar attraction as was once predicted. Lynott, who earned the respect of the new-wave elite in 1978 by forming a spare-time group, the Greedy Bastards, with Rat Scabies of the Damned, released a solo album in 1980, *Solo in Soho,* which sold disappointingly. With Thin Lizzy, Lynott continued his thematic style of songwriting on albums like *Chinatown* and *Renegade,* which also spotlit the twin lead guitar work of Scott Gorham and new member Snowy White, Pink Floyd's ex–stage guitarist.

Through its career, Thin Lizzy released a series of hit singles in the U.K., among them "Don't Believe a Word" (#12 U.K., 1977), "Dancin' in the Moonlight (It's Caught Me in the Spotlight)" (#14 U.K., 1977), "Waiting for an Alibi" (#9 U.K., 1979), "Do Anything You Want to Do" (#14 U.K., 1979), and "Killer on the Loose" (#10 U.K., 1980). Thin Lizzy officially disbanded in 1983.

Lynott published two books of poetry, *Songs for While I'm Away* (1974) and *Philip;* he also continued to make solo LPs and recorded with a new group called Grand Slam. Among his charting singles, the most successful were "Yellow Pearl" (#14 U.K., 1981) and, with Gary Moore, "Out in the Fields" (#5 U.K., 1985). Following a drug overdose, Lynott succumbed to pneumonia and heart failure in early 1986. In May 1986 Thin Lizzy appeared at Self Aid, a Dublin concert, where Bob Geldof stood in for Lynott.

Lynott sang on Moore's U.K. single, 1979's "Parisienne Walkways" (#8 U.K.). Moore also released a number of albums, as a solo artist and with his group G-Force. A leading blues artist in the U.K., Moore has also recorded with Colosseum II, the Greg Lake Band, and BBM (with Jack Bruce and Ginger Baker). His commercial breakthrough was 1990's *Still Got the Blues,* the title track of which hit #97 that year.

13th Floor Elevators: See Roky Erickson

.38 Special

Formed 1975, Jacksonville, FL
Donnie Van Zant, voc.; Don Barnes, gtr., voc.; Jeff Carlisi, gtr.; Ken Lyons, bass; Jack Grondin, drums; Steve Brookins, drums.
1977—*.38 Special* (A&M) 1978—*Special Delivery* 1979— (– Lyons; + Larry Junstrom, bass, gtr.) *Rockin' Into the Night* 1981—*Wild-Eyed Southern Boys* 1982—*Special Forces* 1984—*Tour de Force* 1986—*Strength in Numbers* 1987—

(– Barnes; – Brookins; + Danny Chauncey, gtr., kybds., bass; + Max Carl [b. Max Gronenthal], voc., kybds.) *Flashback* 1989—*Rock & Roll Strategy* 1991—(– Carl; + Barnes; + Scott Hoffman, drums; + Bobby Capps, kybds.) *Bone Against Steel* (Charisma) Mid-'90s—(– Carlisi; – Hoffman; – Grondin; + Greg Morrow, drums) 1997—*Resolution* (Razor & Tie) (– Morrow; + Gary Moffatt, drums) 1999—*Live at Sturgis* (CMC).

Van Zant (D. Van Zant and Johnny Van Zant): 1997—*Brother to Brother* (CMC).

One of the many Southern-rock groups to take its cue from the Allman Brothers Band, .38 Special specializes in blues-based rock & roll that showcases twin lead guitarists and two drummers. Featuring lead vocalist Donnie Van Zant, brother of Lynyrd Skynyrd's Ronnie Van Zant and Johnny Van Zant, .38 Special altered its sound somewhat in the early '80s to accommodate a more melodic approach. This resulted in "Hold On Loosely" (#27, 1981) and the band's first Top 10 single, "Caught Up in You," taken from *Special Forces* (#10, 1982).

The group cut two albums filled with competent Southern rock and toured extensively before racking up a hit album with *Rockin' Into the Night* (#57, 1980), followed by the platinum *Wild-Eyed Southern Boys* (#18, 1981), *Special Forces,* and *Tour de Force* (#22, 1983). Subsequent albums fared respectably; *Strength in Numbers* (#17, 1986) and *Flashback* (#35, 1987) are both gold. In addition, the group had a string of hit singles, including "If I'd Been the One" (#19, 1983), "Back Where You Belong" (#20, 1984), "Teacher Teacher" (#25, 1984), "Like No Other Night" (#14, 1986), and "Second Chance" (#6, 1989). With several original members intact, .38 Special continued to exist into 2000. Donnie Van Zant has also recorded with his brother, Johnny.

Carla Thomas

Born 1942, Memphis, TN
1961—*Gee Whiz* (Atlantic) 1966—*Comfort Me* (Stax); *Carla* 1967—*King and Queen* (with Otis Redding); *Queen Alone* 1969—*The Best of Carla Thomas* (Atlantic) 1971—*Love Means* (Stax) 1986—*Chronicle* (with Rufus Thomas) 1992—*Hidden Gems* 1994—*Sugar.*

Before Aretha Franklin, Carla Thomas was black music's reigning Queen of Soul. Her "Gee Whiz (Look at His Eyes)" in 1961 was, in fact, the first Memphis soul record to make a national impact (#10 pop, #5 R&B); its success resulted in the foundation of Stax Records. The daughter of Memphis music veteran Rufus Thomas, Carla Thomas made her recording debut in 1960, when she duetted with her father on "Cause I Love You" while on summer vacation from college. After "Gee Whiz" succeeded, her education took a backseat to an active performing career.

Throughout the '60s, Thomas was a star member of the Stax roster, scoring with "I'll Bring It Home to You" (#41 pop, #9 R&B) in 1962; "Let Me Be Good to You" (#62 pop, #11 R&B) and "B-A-B-Y" (#14 pop, #3 R&B) in 1966; with Otis Redding on "Tramp" (#26 pop, #2 R&B) and "Knock on Wood" (#30 pop, #8 R&B) and "I'll Always Have Faith in You" (#85 pop, #11 R&B) in 1967; and "I Like What You're Doing to Me," (#9 R&B) in 1969.

After Stax's demise in the mid-'70s, Thomas stopped recording, but still performed on the club circuit. In the late '80s she was an artist-in-residence for the Tennessee Arts Commission, where she worked with young people. She has essentially retired from recording. In 1993 she was given a Pioneer Award from the Rhythm & Blues Foundation.

David Thomas: See Pere Ubu

Rufus Thomas

Born Mar. 26, 1917, Casey, MS
1963—*Walking the Dog* (Stax); *May I Have Your Ticket, Please?* 1970—*Funky Chicken; Rufus Thomas Live/Doing the Push & Pull at P.J.'s* 1972—*Did You Hear Me?* 1973—*Crown Prince of Dance* 1977—*If There Were No Music* (AVI); *Rufus Thomas* EP (Hollywood, U.K.) 1986—*Chronicle* (with Carla Thomas) (Stax) 1988—*That Woman Is Poison* (Alligator) 1992—*Can't Get Away From This Dog* (Stax) 1996—*Blues Thang!* (Sequel) 1997—*The Best of Rufus Thomas: Do the Funky Somethin'* (Rhino) 1999—*Swing Out With Rufus* (High Stacks).

Singer Rufus Thomas has been a fixture on the Memphis music scene since the '40s. He enjoyed his greatest record sales with his mid-'60s and early-'70s dance hits.

While Thomas was attending Memphis' Booker T. Washington High School in the '30s, Professor Nat D. Williams, a history teacher and emcee of a talent show at the Palace Theater, selected him to become his sidekick in a comedy act. Upon graduation from high school, Thomas toured the South with the Rabbit Foot Minstrels, telling jokes, tap dancing, and singing. He performed at tent shows until 1940, when he married. Later that year, he would replace Williams as MC at the Palace talent shows.

When he left the talent shows 11 years later, Thomas worked three other jobs—day worker at a textile plant, MC at a local club and DJing on WDIA, where he befriended another popular disc jockey, B.B. King. During the early '50s he recorded for Sam Phillips and his infant Sun Records. Thomas had his first national hit in 1953 with "Bear Cat" (#3 R&B), an answer record to Big Mama Thornton's "Hound Dog." Rufus and his daughter Carla were early stars of Stax Records. His two 1963 dance hits, "The Dog" (#22 R&B) and "Walking the Dog" (#10 pop, #5 R&B), helped establish that company. In the early '70s, Thomas would have another hot streak with "Do the Funky Chicken" (#28 pop, #5 R&B) and "(Do the) Push and Pull" (#31 pop, #1 R&B) in 1970, and "The Breakdown" (#2 R&B) in 1971. Into the '70s, Thomas worked at WDIA. When Stax went bankrupt, Thomas recorded for a series of labels. He still tours.

Linda Thompson

Born Linda Pettifer, Aug. 23, 1948, Glasgow, Scot.
1985—*One Clear Moment* (Warner Bros.) 1996—*Dreams Fly Away: A History of Linda Thompson* (Hannibal/Rykodisc).

One of the clarion voices of the British folk-rock movement that began in the late '60s, Linda Thompson (born Linda Pettifer, later changed to Peters) won acclaim alongside guitarist husband Richard Thompson [see entry]. Together, the pair recorded a series of powerful, often darkly themed albums between 1974—when Linda first got full billing with her mate on *I Want to See the Bright Lights Tonight*—and 1982, when the couple's rapidly dissolving union was played out as recorded drama on *Shoot Out the Lights*. The couple divorced in 1983, the same year Linda Thompson was named female singer of the year by ROLLING STONE. Two years later, Thompson released a solo album of countryish material, *One Clear Moment,* whose track "Telling Me Lies" was later adapted by Emmylou Harris, Linda Ronstadt, and Dolly Parton on their 1987 *Trio* project. Thompson's songs have also been recorded by Celine Dion, Patti Labelle, and Kenny Rogers, among others. In 1987 work began on a second album, which was never released. (One track, a remake of Richard Thompson's "The Dimming of the Day," surfaced on the 1996 retrospective *Dreams Fly Away.*) Thompson also joined the cast of *The Mysteries,* a trilogy of medieval plays staged by the Royal National Theatre in London. In 1988 Thompson went on hiatus from recording and performing when she was diagnosed with hysterical dysphonia, the medical term for the singer's voice-robbing bouts with anxiety. By 1999, however, she had begun work on a new album built around acoustic folk themes. Recorded in fits and starts, as of mid-2001 it was still incomplete.

Richard Thompson

Born Apr. 3, 1949, London, Eng.
With Linda Thompson (b. Linda Pettifer, Aug. 23, 1948, Glasgow, Scot.), voc.; (R. Thompson, gtr., voc., mandolin, dulcimer).
1974—*I Want to See the Bright Lights Tonight* (Carthage) 1975—*Hokey Pokey; Pour Down Like Silver* 1977—*Almost Live (More or Less)* (Island) 1978—*First Light* (Carthage) 1979—*Sunnyvista* 1982—*Shoot Out the Lights* (Hannibal).
Richard Thompson solo: 1972—*Henry the Human Fly* (Warner Bros.) 1976—*(Guitar, Vocal)* (Carthage) 1981—*Strict Tempo!* 1983—*Hand of Kindness* (Hannibal) 1984—*Small Town Romance* 1985—*Across a Crowded Room* (Polydor) 1986—*Daring Adventures* 1988—*Amnesia* (Capitol) 1991—*Rumor and Sigh* 1993—*Watching the Dark: The History of Richard Thompson* (Rykodisc/Hannibal) 1994—*Mirror Blue* (Capitol) 1996—*You? Me? Us?* 1999—*Mock Tudor.*
With John French, Fred Frith, and Henry Kaiser: 1986—*Live, Love, Larf & Loaf* (Rhino) 1994—*Invisible Means.*
With Danny Thompson: 1997—*Industry* (Rykodisc/Hannibal).

Richard Thompson, a founding member of the British folk-rock group Fairport Convention [see entry], left that band in 1971 for a career that in many ways fulfilled Fairport's goal: to link Celtic folk music to rock. Thompson's gallows-humored, fatalistic songs, whose outlook owes something to his Sufi-Muslim religion, are steeped in the jigs and reels and marches of British folk music, although they are often played on electric instruments.

After leaving Fairport, Thompson first sat in as a guitarist on British folk-rock albums like Mike and Lal Waterson's *Bright Phoebus.* He joined a loose aggregation of Fairport and folk-scene veterans, including drummer Dave Mattacks, singer Sandy Denny, and bassist Ashley Hutchings under the name the Bunch to record an album of pop oldies, *Rock On.* On that album, a friend of Sandy Denny's named Linda Peters (née Pettifer) sang "The Loco-Motion," and she married Thompson soon afterward. Thompson also sat in on Hutchings' first solo project, *Morris On.*

In 1972 Thompson began his solo career with the brilliant, eccentric *Henry the Human Fly,* which juxtaposed Chuck Berry riffs with old-English concertinas on Thompson's original songs. Linda Peters Thompson sang a few backup vocals, but she didn't get full billing until *I Want to See the Bright Lights Tonight,* which was belatedly released in the U.S. as half of the double album *Almost Live (More or Less).* Although Richard Thompson wrote all the duo's material (except for a song on their final album cowritten by Linda), he shared lead vocals with her on the albums they made together, and Linda's emotive mezzo-soprano was widely praised. In 1974 the Thompsons put together an electric band called Sour Grapes, with ex-Fairport guitarist Simon Nicol and a rhythm section, but after a tour opening for Traffic the group broke up. In 1974 the Thompsons converted to Sufism. The pair toured Britain in 1975 with a band that included ex-Fairports Dave Pegg on bass and Dave Mattacks on drums, plus button accordionist John Kirkpatrick. Afterward they retreated to the English countryside to start

Richard Thompson

a Sufi community. They returned in 1978 with *First Light,* which used a U.S. rhythm section. *Strict Tempo!* was an album of instrumentals on which Thompson played all the instruments except percussion (by Mattacks); it included traditional jigs, reels, polkas, and a Duke Ellington tune. He also sat in on the first solo album by David Thomas of Pere Ubu.

Sessions for *Shoot Out the Lights* were originally produced by Gerry Rafferty (Stealer's Wheel, "Baker Street"); unhappy with the results, Thompson shelved the project. Producer Joe Boyd offered to produce the album for his new label, Hannibal. Thompson toured the U.S. as an acoustic solo act before *Shoot Out the Lights* was released, where he met his future wife, concert promoter Nancy Covey. Returning to England, he asked Linda for a divorce. They toured together with a band including Nicol, Mattacks, and bassist Pete Zorn. But the tensions of a disintegrating marriage spilled over to the music, and the pair split acrimoniously. While Linda sought a solo contract, Richard recorded an album of country-and-Celtic-tinged breakup songs, *Hand of Kindness* (#186, 1983). Linda signed with Warner Bros. in 1984, and released an album of edgy, countryish songs [see entry]. It was issued concurrently with Richard's *Across a Crowded Room* (#102, 1985), his first major-label release in seven years.

Thompson recorded at a steady pace throughout the next decade, but his career became a succès d'estime, earning critical raves and low sales. In 1993 Rykodisc released *Watching the Dark,* a three-CD retrospective covering Thompson's career. He's played on albums by artists ranging from Suzanne Vega to Robert Plant. Jo-El Sonnier had a Top 10 C&W hit covering Thompson's "Tear Stained Letter." A tribute album, *Beat the Retreat,* featuring Bonnie Raitt, Los Lobos, R.E.M., Dinosaur Jr, and David Byrne, among other artists, covering Thompson's songs, was released in 1994. The same year Thompson released *Mirror Blue* and joined fellow musicians John French, Fred Frith, and Henry Kaiser to release *Invisible Means,* a sequel of sorts to a quirky 1986 summit of eccentricity, *Live, Love, Larf & Loaf* (which was subsequently reissued in 1996). In 1996 Thompson released *You? Me? Us?,* a Grammy-nominated two-CD set split between electric and acoustic versions of similar material. He then collaborated with bassist Danny Thompson on the 1997 *Industry,* a half-instrumental concept album about the rise and fall of the British industrial complex. The 1999 album *Mock Tudor,* a reflection on Thompson's youth growing up in suburban London, featured his son Teddy Thompson on vocals and guitar. The Thompsons toured together to promote the record, with Teddy joining his father on duets of classic Richard and Linda Thompson songs.

The Thompson Twins

Formed 1977, Chesterfield, Eng.
Tom Bailey (b. Jan. 18, ca. 1954, Halifax, Eng.), voc., kybds.; John Roog, gtr; Pete Dodd, gtr.; Chris Bell, drums.

1981—*A Product of . . .* (T, U.K.) 1982—(+ Alannah Currie [b. Sep. ca. 1957, Auckland, N.Z.], perc., sax, voc.; + Joe Leeway [b. London, Eng.], perc., voc.; + Matthew Seligman, bass) *In the Name of Love* (Arista) (– Roog; – Dodd; – Bell; – Seligman) 1983—*Side Kicks* 1984—*Into the Gap* 1985—*Here's to Future Days* 1986—(– Leeway) 1987—*Close to the Bone* 1988—*The Best of Thompson Twins: Greatest Mixes* 1989—*Big Trash* (Warner Bros./Reprise) 1991—*Queer* (Warner Bros.) 1996—*Greatest Hits* (Arista). Babble: 1994—*The Stone* (Reprise) 1996—*Ether* (Warner Bros.).

Actually a trio—at their peak, anyway—and without a Thompson among them, England's the Thompson Twins hit pay dirt just as new wave was drawing its final breath. With their quirkily videogenic looks and buoyant technopop tunes, Tom Bailey, Alannah Currie, and Joe Leeway were the perfect bunch to usher in the era of Boy George and Duran Duran. Singer/keyboardist/chief songwriter Bailey was an aspiring classical pianist and percussionist/singer Leeway a fledgling actor when they met in 1977, at a teachers' college in Cheshire; but Bailey formed the band's original four-man lineup without Leeway. This incarnation of the Thompson Twins—a name alluding to characters in Hergé's *Tintin* cartoon—played around London and released singles independently before signing with Arista Records in 1981. After the release of their debut album, *A Product of . . . ,* Bailey added Leeway, then a roadie, to the group. Bailey also recruited his girlfriend, Alannah Currie, a former journalist who dabbled in music and flamboyant fashions, and ex–Soft Boys bassist Matthew Seligman.

This seven-piece edition of the Thompsons survived only one album. After *Set* (released in the U.S. as *In the Name of Love*), their manager, another school friend of Bailey and Leeway, fired everyone except those two and Currie. The newly spare Thompsons shot to #2 in the U.K, with their subsequent album, *Quick Step and Side Kick* (*Side Kicks* in the U.S.). Moreover, the album and its successors, *Into the Gap* (#10, 1984) and *Here's to Future Days* (#20, 1985), spawned a chain of hits in England and America: in 1983, "Love on Your Side" (#45 U.S., #9 U.K.), "We Are Detective" (#7 U.K.), "Hold Me Now" (#3 U.S., 1984; #4 U.K.); in 1984, "Doctor Doctor" (#11 U.S., #3 U.K.), "You Take Me Up" (#44 U.S., #2 U.K.); and in 1985, "Lay Your Hands on Me" (#6 U.S.) and "King for a Day" (#8 U.S., 1986; #22 U.K.). In 1986 Leeway left the act; now the Twins were indeed a duo—and a couple. Bailey and Currie, who had initially kept their personal relationship a secret, had a child in 1988. Their professional collaborations proved somewhat less fruitful, their biggest hit to date being 1989's "Sugar Daddy," a #28 single in America.

In 1994 Bailey and Currie—who by now had married, had a second child, and moved to New Zealand—resurfaced in a collective called Babble, whose sound was in the trance-ambient mode. It released *The Stone,* which featured engineer/programmer Keith Fernley (the group's other core member), vocalists Q. Tee and Amy St. Cyr, and computer whiz Charlie Whisker. Babble released a second album, the spiritual *Ether*, in 1996. In the late '90s, Bailey worked as a club DJ and began another career as producer of the New Zealand pop-dance band Stellar*; he won the Top Producer title for the group's debut album at the 2000 New Zealand Music Awards. Meanwhile, Currie is concentrating on the visual art of glass-casting.

Big Mama Thornton

Born Willie Mae Thornton, Dec. 11, 1926, Montgomery, AL; died July 25, 1984, Los Angeles, CA
1966—*In Europe* (Arhoolie) 1967—*Chicago Blues* 1968—*Ball and Chain* 1969—*Stronger Than Dirt* (Mercury) 1971—*She's Back* (Backbeat) 1975—*Jail* (Vanguard); *Sassy Mama* 1978—*Mama's Pride* 1992—*Hound Dog: The Peacock Recordings* (MCA).

A singer/songwriter who also played harmonica and drums, Willie Mae "Big Mama" Thornton was a blues-woman who, in spanning the decades from country to city blues, carried forward the legacy of such seminal blueswomen as Bessie Smith, Ma Rainey, and Memphis Minnie. She was the originator of two songs later made famous by rock & roll superstars: "Hound Dog" (by Elvis Presley), written by Leiber and Stoller, and her own "Ball and Chain" (a hit for Janis Joplin).

Thornton was one of seven children; her father was a minister, her mother a church singer. She became interested in music at an early age and won first prize in a local talent show in her teens. From 1941 to 1948, she toured the South as a singer/dancer/comedienne with Sammy Greene's Hot Harlem Revue. She settled in Houston, Texas, in 1948 and began recording there in 1951. In 1952 she worked with Johnny Otis' band on his Rhythm and Blues Caravan tour, and appeared in package shows with Junior Parker and Johnny Ace during 1953 and 1954. She recorded for small labels like Kent and Baytone.

In 1965 Thornton toured England and Europe with the American Folk Blues Festival, and in 1967 she appeared at one of John Hammond's From Spirituals to Swing concerts at Carnegie Hall, and appeared in the PBS documentary *Black White and Blue.* A year later she appeared at the Monterey Jazz Festival, and in 1969 played the Newport Folk Festival and the Chicago and Ann Arbor Blues festivals. In 1971 she appeared on the Dick Cavett talk show on ABC-TV, and recorded material for the soundtrack of the film *Vanishing Point.* In 1974 she appeared on NBC-TV's rock show *Midnight Special,* and in 1980 appeared on the "Blues Is a Woman" bill with such other veteran blueswomen as Sippie Wallace at the Newport Jazz Festival.

Thornton began recording her later albums with *In Europe. Chicago Blues,* featuring such blues giants as Muddy Waters and Otis Spann, is considered one of her best. *Jail* contains her versions of "Hound Dog" (originally an R&B hit for her in 1953, before Presley's version), "Ball and Chain," and "Little Red Rooster." She died of a heart attack.

George Thorogood and the Destroyers

Formed 1973, Delaware
George Thorogood (b. Feb. 24, 1950, Wilmington, DE), gtr., voc.; Ron Smith, gtr.; Billy Blough, bass; Jeff Simon, drums.
1977—*George Thorogood and the Destroyers* (Rounder) 1978—*Move It On Over* 1979—*Better Than the Rest* (MCA) 1980—(– Smith; + Hank Carter, sax, gtr., kybds., voc.) *More George Thorogood and the Destroyers* (Rounder) 1982—*Bad to the Bone* (EMI America) 1985—(+ Steve Chrismar, gtr.) *Maverick* 1986—*Live* 1988—*Born to Be Bad* (EMI Manhattan) 1991—*Boogie People* (EMI) 1992—*The Baddest of George Thorogood and the Destroyers* 1993—*Haircut* 1995—*Let's Work Together Live* 1997—*Rockin' My Life Away* 1999—*Half a Boy, Half a Man* (CMC).

The son of a white-collar British immigrant and a onetime semipro baseball player, George Thorogood is a spirited re-creator of the driving, raucous urban slide-guitar blues pioneered by Chicago greats like Elmore James.

Thorogood did not become seriously involved with music until 1970, when he saw a show by another blues archivist, John Paul Hammond. Thorogood went to California, where he was soon opening shows for Bonnie Raitt and bluesmen Sonny Terry and Brownie McGhee. In late 1978 Thorogood had a hit single with his raw adaptation of Hank Williams' "Move It On Over," which stayed on the chart into 1978, the first single on the folk-oriented Rounder label. Although Thorogood publicly repudiated *Better Than the Rest,* a demo tape he had signed away, it also charted. In 1981 he and the Destroyers opened several dates on the Rolling Stones' U.S. tour. He and the Detroyers later played gigs in 50 different states over a 50-day period.

Thorogood's big commercial break came in 1982 when "Bad to the Bone," with a video featuring Bo Diddley, got substantial exposure on MTV. The album of the same title, Thorogood's second, went gold, and the group's next three albums—*Maverick, Live, Born to Be Bad*—did likewise, even though none charted higher than #32. In 1985 the group backed Albert Collins at Live Aid. Thorogood is known as much for his tongue-in-cheek lyrics (as in "I Drink Alone") as his bracing guitar work. With few charting singles and a stubborn commitment to straight-ahead blues rock, George Thorogood and the Destroyers have carved out a unique niche. While critics deride the group's now-formulaic approach and record sales have been relatively weak, the group continues to tour and to record. *Rockin' My Life Away* contains two originals but devotes most of its time to songs written by such artists as Elmore James, Merle Haggard, and (somewhat surprisingly) Frank Zappa.

Three Dog Night

Formed 1967, Los Angeles, CA
Danny Hutton (b. Sep. 10, 1946, Buncrana, Ire.), voc.; Chuck Negron (b. Charles Negron, June 8, Bronx, NY), voc.; Cory Wells (b. Feb. 5, 1942, Buffalo, NY), voc.; Mike Allsup (b. Mar. 8, 1947,

Modesto, CA), gtr.; Jimmy Greenspoon (b. Feb. 7, 1948, Los Angeles), kybds.; Joe Schermie (b. Feb. 12, Madison, WI), bass; Floyd Sneed (b. Nov. 22, 1943, Calgary, Can.), drums.
1968—*Three Dog Night* (Dunhill) 1969—*Suitable for Framing; Captured Live at the Forum* 1970—*It Ain't Easy; Naturally* 1971—*Golden Biscuits; Harmony* 1972—*Seven Separate Fools* 1973—(– Schermie, + Jack Ryland, bass; + Skip Konte, kybds.) *Around the World With Three Dog Night* 1973—*Cyan* 1974—*Hard Labor; Joy to the World: Their Greatest Hits* 1975—*Coming Down Your Way* (ABC) 1976—*American Pastime* (– Ryland; – Konte; – Allsup; – Sneed; + Al Ciner, gtr.; + Denny Belfield, bass; + Ron Stockert, kybds.; – Hutton; + Jay Gruska, voc.; group continues with numerous personnel changes) 1983—*The Best of Three Dog Night* (MCA); *It's a Jungle* EP (Passport) 1993—*Celebrate: The Three Dog Night Story, 1965–1975* (MCA).

From the late '60s to early '70s, Three Dog Night was one of the most popular bands in America, with 18 consecutive Top 20 hits (11 of which were Top 10s, including three #1s), seven million-selling singles, and 12 gold LPs—the entire album catalogue up through 1974's *Joy to the World: Their Greatest Hits.* Although the group initially earned critical respect for its innovative interpretations and was a staple of progressive FM-radio playlists, it was later criticized as being crassly commercial. True, Three Dog Night's material was singles-oriented, soul-influenced pop rock, and almost always consisted of covers. But its success was phenomenal. In its favor, however, the group—which chose, arranged, and co-produced its records—provided exposure for songwriters Randy Newman, Elton John and Bernie Taupin, Harry Nilsson, Laura Nyro, Hoyt Axton, Leo Sayer, and others.

The band centered on three lead singers (Cory Wells, Danny Hutton, and Chuck Negron) with four backup musicians (Mike Allsup, Jimmy Greenspoon, Joe Schermie, and Floyd Sneed). Wells knew Hutton from the mid-'60s, when the latter produced Wells' band, the Enemys, for MGM. Hutton, born in Ireland but raised in the U.S., worked as a producer from age 18, and in 1965 he wrote, arranged, and produced as a solo artist the single "Roses and Rainbows" for Hanna-Barbera Records (the cartoon company), which became a small hit. In the fall of that year, he auditioned unsuccessfully for the Monkees. Hutton also recorded for MGM, where he had the minor hit "Big Bright Eyes." It was Hutton who first hit on the three-vocalist-band idea, and he and Wells brought in Negron, who used to sing regularly at the Apollo and had recorded unsuccessfully with Columbia in the mid-'60s. Negron also sang backup on one of Hutton's first singles. (Among others Hutton and Wells considered for the third-vocalist spot were Billy Joe Royal and Crazy Horse founder Danny Whitten.) The trio, renamed Redwood by Brian Wilson, cut two singles with Wilson producing: "Darlin' " and "Time to Get Alone." Neither was ever released, and "Darlin' " later became a hit for the Beach Boys. The trio then moved on to work with Van Dyke Parks, with whom they cut a few demos.

Frustrated by their lack of artistic control, Negron, Hutton, and Wells decided to expand their group to include backing musicians, and by 1968 the lineup was a firm seven-piece. Schermie had been with the Cory Wells Blues Band, which broke up the year before. Sneed had backed José Feliciano, and Greenspoon had done many L.A. sessions. After some initial consultation with Van Dyke Parks and Brian Wilson, Gabriel Mekler, a Hungarian-born classical pianist, who had worked with Steppenwolf, became their producer.

Three Dog Night's 1968 debut, *Three Dog Night* (#11, 1969) contained three singles. First "Nobody" gained initial interest. Its B side was an obscure Lennon-McCartney song previously recorded by Cilla Black, "It's for You." Though never a hit itself, "It's for You" showcased the group's three-part-harmony lead vocals. "Nobody" was followed by the Top 30 cover of Otis Redding's "Try a Little Tenderness." The band's big breakthrough came in 1969 with "One," a Harry Nilsson song that soared to #5 and went gold. *Suitable for Framing* (#16, 1969) charted with "Easy to Be Hard" (#4, 1969) from the rock musical *Hair,* "Eli's Coming" (#10, 1969) by Laura Nyro, and "Lady Samantha," the first stateside success for Elton John and Bernie Taupin. On *It Ain't Easy* (#8, 1970), Three Dog Night covered Randy Newman's "Mama Told Me (Not to Come)" (#1, 1970). In 1971 the band went to #1 with Hoyt Axton's children's song "Joy to the World." Three Dog Night also gave Leo Sayer his first American writing hit by covering "The Show Must Go On" (#14, 1974). The group's other hits include Russ Ballard's song for Argent, "Liar" (#7, 1971), "One Man Band" (#19, 1970), "An Old Fashioned Love Song" (#4, 1971), "Never Been to Spain" (#5, 1972), "Black and White" (#1, 1972), and B.W. Stevenson's "Shambala" (#3, 1973). Three Dog Night sold out shows around the world and in 1972 hosted its own network television special.

By 1974, though, the commercial magic had finally waned. The combo's 13th LP, *Coming Down Your Way* (#70, 1975), was its first not to go gold. In addition, personal friction brewed among the three singers, partly because Negron sang a disproportionate number of the hits; the public saw him as the lead singer. In 1976, after *American Pastime* (#123, 1976), Hutton was replaced by Jay Gruska, and the band got three new musicians, all former members of Rufus—Al Ciner, Denny Belfield, and Ron Stockert. In 1977 Three Dog Night disbanded.

In the late '70s Hutton began managing punk bands, including L.A.'s Fear. He also led a group called the Danny Hutton Hitters, who appeared on the *Pretty in Pink* soundtrack. Wells recorded a pair of solo albums, but only one, 1978's *Touch Me,* was released. Negron also recorded solo in the early '80s. In June 1981 the three original vocalists reunited. Two years later, they released their final record, an EP entitled *It's a Jungle.* Since Negron's departure in the mid-'80s Hutton and Well have toured with other musicians as Three Dog Night. In 1999 Negron published *Three Dog Nightmare,* an autobiography in which he unflinchingly details his descent into and recovery from drug addiction. Throughout the '90s, Three Dog Night's songs have appeared in numerous motion pictures and TV ads.

Throwing Muses/Belly

Formed 1980, Newport, RI
Kristin Hersh (b. Aug. 7, 1966, Atlanta, GA), gtr., voc.; Tanya Donelly (b. July 14, 1966, Newport), gtr., voc.; David Narcizo (b. May 6, 1966, Newport), drums; Elaine Adamedes, bass.
1984—*Throwing Muses* EP (Throwing Muses) 1986—(– Adamedes; + Leslie Langston [b. Apr. 1, 1964, Newport], bass) *Throwing Muses* (4AD, U.K.) 1987—*Chains Changed* EP; *The Fat Skier* EP (Sire) 1988—*House Tornado* 1989—*Hunkpapa* 1991—(– Langston; + Fred Abong, bass) *The Real Ramona* 1992—(– Donelly; – Abong; + Langston) *Red Heaven* 1994—(– Langston; + Bernard Georges [b. Mar. 29, 1965, Gonaive, Haiti], bass) 1995—*University* 1996—*Limbo* (Rykodisc) 1997—*Freeloader* EP 1998—*In a Doghouse*.
Belly, formed 1991, Providence, RI: (Donelly, gtr., voc.; Tom Gorman (b. May 20, 1966, Buffalo, NY), gtr.; Chris Gorman (b. July 29, 1967, Buffalo), drums; Fred Abong, bass.
1993—*Star* (Sire) (– Abong; + Gail Greenwood [b. Mar. 10, 1960, Providence], bass) 1995—*King*.
Kristin Hersh solo: 1994—*Hips and Makers* (Sire) 1998—*Strange Angels* (Rykodisc) 1999—*Sky Motel* (4AD) 2001—Sunny Border Blue.
Tanya Donelly solo: 1997—*Lovesongs for Underdogs* (Reprise).

Throwing Muses pioneered a dense, dreamy, guitar-based sound long before "alternative" was a musical term. Led by singer/songwriter Kristin Hersh and, to a lesser degree, her stepsister Tanya Donelly, they articulated a female vision—intense, meditative, raw—that differed sharply from the videogenic pop of the '80s.

The band was formed by four high school friends in Newport, Rhode Island. After a self-released EP that drew critical praise in Rhode Island and Boston, the Muses changed bassists. They were the first American band signed to London's 4AD label. Their eponymous debut and *Chains Changed* EP, both produced by Gil Norton, were released to gushing attention from the British press.

Their first American releases, however, were too oblique and discordant for tastes here, although the Muses have over the years built a devoted following. As college radio developed into a market segment, the Muses gained greater success with the more melodic *Hunkpapa*. Langston left (she joined Wolfgang Press and returned to record *Red Heaven* with the Muses) and was replaced by Fred Abong. The Muses had a breakthrough on alternative radio with "Counting Backwards" from *The Real Ramona*. Hersh toured America pregnant with her second child, her belly pushing her guitar far in front of her by the final dates.

Donelly developed the side project, the Breeders, with the Pixies' Kim Deal in 1990 [see the Pixies/Breeders entry]. She had contributed one or two songs per album during the Muses' career, and after *Ramona*, decided she needed an outlet for her own tunes. She left the Muses and formed Belly with the brothers Tom and Chris Gorman. The album's poppy, childlike tunes (Donelly calls the songs fairy tales), especially the MTV hit "Feed the Tree," brought Belly more commercial success than the Muses had known. Belly was nominated for a Grammy for Best New Act of 1993. The group released *King* before disbanding in 1996; Donelly's solo debut, *Lovesongs for Underdogs* appeared the following year.

Meanwhile, although the Muses' *Red Heaven* contained several radio-friendly tunes and featured a cameo by Bob Mould (Hüsker Dü, Sugar), it did not get the same support from the record company and radio. Hersh subsequently recorded an acclaimed solo album, *Hips and Makers*, coproduced by Lenny Kaye. It included a cameo from R.E.M.'s Michael Stipe.

With bassist Bernard Georges and founding drummer David Narcizo, Hersh regrouped Throwing Muses in 1994 and recorded the self-produced *University*. Released in early 1995, the album balances streamlined modern rock with experimentation for what is perhaps the band's most accessible effort to date. *Limbo* (1996), a melodic, stripped-down affair, sold poorly; unable to make ends meet touring, the Muses, a band with an indie ethic struggling to make it in the world of corporate rock, called it quits. *In a Doghouse*, a collection of rare early material, appeared in 1998.

Hersh's first solo album after the breakup, *Strange Angels* (1997), was an intimate, acoustic record in much the same vein as *Hips and Makers*. Her next project, available only through her Web site, was a collection of Appalachian folk songs called *Murder, Misery and Then Goodnight*. *Sky Motel* and *Sunny Border Blue* found Hersh returning to the more electric sound of the Muses and playing most of the instruments on the records herself.

Thunderclap Newman

Formed 1969, England
Andy Newman (b. ca. 1943, Eng.), kybds.; Jimmy McCulloch, (b. 1953, Scot.; d. Sep. 27, 1979), gtr.; John "Speedy" Keen (b. Mar. 29, 1945, London, Eng.), voc., drums; and later, Jim Avery (b. Eng.), bass; Jack McCulloch (b. Scot.), drums.
1970—*Hollywood Dream* (Track, U.K.).

Thunderclap Newman was a group haphazardly assembled by Pete Townshend in 1969. The group had one hit, "Something in the Air," and then disbanded. Andy Newman was a 26-year-old eccentric, a barrelhouse jazz pianist who had previously worked as a post office engineer. Townshend first heard a tape of Newman back in 1963. Townshend ran into Jimmy McCulloch during a Who gig where 13-year-old Jimmy's Cowsill-type family opened the show. Townshend knew ex-Mayall roadie "Speedy" Keen from the early Who days; Keen's "Armenia City in the Sky" wound up on *The Who Sell Out*. Townshend made the three members into a regular band and, as producer and bass player (under the pseudonym Bijou Drains), recorded Keen's "Something in the Air." It went to #1 in England, got much FM airplay in America, but only hit #37. It was also used in the films *The Magic Christian* and *Strawberry Statement*. Keen wrote the hit and most of the other material on *Hollywood Dream*.

The band toured England to support the single, with Jim Avery on bass and Jimmy McCulloch's brother Jack on drums (to free Keen for the front vocal spot), but it didn't work out and they disbanded in 1970. Keen went on to make two solo albums, *Previous Convictions* (1973) and *Y'know Wot I Mean?* (1975). Newman had his own solo, *Rainbow*, and then briefly joined ex–Bonzo Dog Band member Roger Spear in Kinetic Wardrobe. McCulloch played with Stone the Crows (with Maggie Bell), John Mayall, and then Paul McCartney's Wings from 1975 until 1978; he died the following year.

Tiffany

Born Tiffany Renee Darwish, Oct. 2, 1971, Norwalk, CA
1987—*Tiffany* (MCA) 1988—*Hold an Old Friend's Hand* 1990—*New Inside* 1996—*Greatest Hits* (Unidisc/Hip-O) 2000—*The Color of Silence* (Eureka).

Tiffany was only 16 when a couple of bubblegum-pop singles took her to the top of the charts. Actually, her 1987 self-titled debut album had been a commercial dud until her manager, George Tobin, helped dream up a marketing ploy that brought her to shopping malls everywhere—literally. Tobin, a music industry veteran, was producing a Smokey Robinson album in his North Hollywood studio when he met Tiffany, who was there making a demo tape. Tiffany, who began singing in public when she was nine, had been performing with country bands, but Tobin believed she could be a hot pop commodity.

It took him three years to land his discovery a major-label contract, with MCA. When the album *Tiffany* proved an equally hard sell, Tobin and a publicist conceived "The Beautiful You: Celebrating the Good Life," a tour that brought Tiffany to teen-infested shopping malls around the country. Tiffany eventually hit #1 on the pop chart—the first album by a teenage girl to do so—as did two of its singles, "Could've Been" and a cover of Tommy James' "I Think We're Alone Now." Another cover, of the Beatles' "I Saw Her Standing There" (substituting the masculine pronoun), went to #7.

Alas, this teen queen's reign would be brief: After "All This Time" (#6, 1988), her sophomore album quickly faded, and a third album was a total flop. In 1988 Tiffany took her mother to court, seeking emancipated-minor status. The settlement stipulated in part that while her mother remained her legal guardian, Tiffany would control her own finances. The same year as her album *New Inside*, Tiffany was the voice of Judy Jetson in *The Jetsons: The Movie*.

In 1992 she married a makeup artist she met on a photo shoot; the couple became the parents of a son, Elijah, later that year. In 1995 Tiffany and her family moved to Nashville, where she hoped to return to singing country music and reinvent her career. By 1997 she was back in L.A. to try pop music again. Inclusion on two compilation albums produced by Cleopatra Records offered interesting exposure: She sang "New Year's Day," backed by industrial band Front Line Assembly, for a 1999 U2 tribute, and "Call Me" for a 2000 Blondie collection. After performing "Key West Intermezzo (I Saw You First)" with John Mellencamp at that year's Farm Aid benefit concert, Tiffany released *The Color of Silence*.

'Til Tuesday: See Aimee Mann

Timbuk 3

Formed 1984, Madison, WI
Pat MacDonald (b. Aug. 6, 1952, Green Bay, WI), voc., gtr., harmonica, bass; Barbara K. MacDonald (b. Oct. 4, 1957, Wausau, WI), voc., gtr., harmonica, violin, mandolin.
1986—*Greetings From Timbuk 3* (I.R.S.) 1988—*Eden Alley* 1989—*Edge of Allegiance* 1991—(+ Wally Ingram [b. Sep. 13, 1962, Beloit, WI], drums; + Courtney Audain [b. Feb. 4, 1960, Trinidad], bass) *Big Shot in the Dark* 1993—*Espace Ornano* (Watermelon) 1995—*A Hundred Lovers* (High Street/Windham Hill).
Pat MacDonald solo: 1997—*Pat MacDonald Sleeps With His Guitar* (Ark 21).

Timbuk 3 is perhaps best remembered as a novelty band, based on its use of a boombox as a rhythm section and its hit single "The Future's So Bright, I Gotta Wear Shades" (#19, 1986). But the MacDonalds are actually talented musicians with serious and often grim viewpoints. "Shades," for example, was about the dangers of yuppie avarice and nuclear technology. Pat and Barbara MacDonald met in Madison, Wisconsin, in 1978 and married five years later. They moved briefly to New York City, then relocated to Austin, Texas, in 1984. Timbuk 3 got a record deal after being featured on a 1985 MTV program about Austin's thriving music scene.

Greetings From Timbuk 3 (#50, 1986), featuring "Shades," introduced the band's musical mix of rock, funk, folk, and country with Pat's often-sarcastic lyrics. Timbuk 3 toured with a boombox playing pretaped rhythm tracks. On *Eden Alley*, Timbuk 3 tried to establish themselves as more serious artists, avoiding novelty hits and weaving a Biblical theme through the album. *Edge of Allegiance* was coproduced by Denardo Coleman, the son of Ornette Coleman, and Jayne Cortez, and featured the satirical "National Holiday." For *Big Shot in the Dark*, the group used a human rhythm section for the first time. *Espace Ornano* was named after the Paris club where it was recorded. *A Hundred Lovers* got some radio airplay with its title track.

In 1997, shortly after the couple dissolved their musical and marital partnership, Pat MacDonald signed with Miles Copeland's Ark 21 label. His wryly titled solo debut, *Pat MacDonald Sleeps With His Guitar*, found him reflecting on recent events in his life with a set of spare, hypnotic songs. Pat also has worked with Aerosmith, singer/songwriter Jill Sobule, and Japanese composer Ryuichi Sakamoto. Barbara is a mainstay of the Austin club scene, performing under the name Barbara K.

The Time

Formed 1981, Minneapolis, MN
Morris Day (b. Springfield, IL, ca. 1958), voc.; Jesse Johnson (b. May 29, 1960, Rock Island, IL), gtr., voc.; Jimmy Jam (b. James Harris III, June 6, 1959, Minneapolis), kybds.; Monte Moir, kybds.; Terry Lewis (b. Nov. 24, 1956, Omaha, NE), bass; Jellybean Johnson, drums.
1981—*The Time* (Warner Bros.) 1982—*What Time Is It?* 1983—(– Jam; – Lewis; – Moir; + Paul "St. Paul" Peterson, kybds., voc.; + Mark Cardenas, kybds.; + Jerry Hubbard, bass; + Jerome Benton, voc., perc.) 1984—*Ice Cream Castle* (group disbands) 1990—(original lineup, + Benton, re-forms) *Pandemonium* (Paisley Park).
Morris Day solo: 1985—*Color of Success* (Warner Bros.) 1988—*Daydreaming* 1992—*Guaranteed.*

After Prince, the Time was the foremost exponent of the funrock hybrid Minneapolis Sound—providing a snappy, crowd-pleasing complement to Prince's more venturesome artistry. The Time was reportedly created by Prince, who put his old friend Morris Day, a onetime band mate in Prince's early group Grand Central, together with members of that band's chief rival on the Minneapolis scene, Flyte Tyme, which had included Jimmy Jam and Terry Lewis, Monte Moir, and Jellybean Johnson. Day, who'd been Grand Central's drummer, replaced Alexander O'Neal [see entry] as Flyte Tyme's vocalist. The Time was completed with the additions of guitarist Jesse Johnson, and Lewis' half-brother Jerome Benton, who became the comic-foil valet to Day's preening-dandy frontman.

The Time's eponymous debut album (#50, 1981) was produced by Prince under the alias "Jamie Starr"; Day's flamboyant act, equal parts swagger and self-mockery, gave the group a cool-yet-comical personality that appealed especially to R&B audiences. Hit singles included "Get It Up" (#6 R&B, 1981), "Cool (Part 1)" (#90 pop, #7 R&B, 1982), and "777-9311" (#88 pop, #2 R&B, 1982). Opening for Prince on his *1999* tour, the Time nearly stole the show with its sharp-dressed choreography and burlesque antics. However, the band's second album, *What Time Is It?* (#104 pop, #26 R&B, 1982), yielded only one minor hit in "The Walk" (#24 R&B, 1982).

In March 1983 Jam and Lewis, moonlighting as freelance producers, were snowed into Atlanta by a freak blizzard while working with the S.O.S. Band. They missed a tour date with Prince, who immediately fired them. Moir left soon after. Jam and Lewis went on to become enormously successful composer/producers for Janet Jackson, among other artists; Moir wrote and produced with their Flyte Tyme Productions and on his own.

The refashioned Time continued on, with a featured role in Prince's breakthrough film *Purple Rain,* which yielded hits for the Time in "Jungle Love" (#20 pop, #6 R&B, 1984) and "The Bird" (#36 pop, #33 R&B, 1985), both of which were included on *Ice Cream Castle* (#24, 1984), the group's first platinum effort. Day and Prince grew apart, however, during the filming of *Purple Rain* and eventually stopped speaking with each other; Day quit the band, followed by Jesse Johnson, and the Time fell apart.

Day released two solo albums, *Color of Success* (#37 pop, #7 R&B, 1985), which yielded "The Oak Tree" (#65 pop, #3 R&B, 1985) and *Daydreaming* (#41 pop, #7 R&B, 1988), which produced the hit "Fishnet" (#23 pop, #1 R&B, 1988). He also acted in the Andrew "Dice" Clay film *Adventures of Ford Fairlane,* and in the shortlived 1990 ABC-TV sitcom *New Attitude.* Johnson, who'd produced some tracks for Janet Jackson before Jam and Lewis made her a megastar, formed the Jesse Johnson Revue, which released three albums; *Shockadelica* (#70 pop, #15 R&B, 1986) featured a duet with Sly Stone on "Crazay" (#53 pop, #2 R&B, 1986).

In 1990 the original Time briefly reunited to appear in Prince's movie *Graffiti Bridge* and to record the album *Pandemonium* (#18 pop, #9 R&B, 1990), which included the hit single "Jerk Out" (#9 pop, #1 R&B, 1990). Day released another solo effort, *Guaranteed,* in 1992, and continued to front the Time, often on summer package tours where the band's catalog of hits remained in demand.

Tiny Tim

Born Herbert Butros Khaury, Apr. 12, 1931, New York, NY; died Nov. 31, 1996, Minneapolis, MN
1968—*God Bless Tiny Tim* (Reprise); *Tiny Tim's Second Album* 1969—*For All My Little Friends* 1996—*Girl* (Rounder); *Tiny Tim's Christmas Album.*

With his strange voice (a trembling falsetto), unique appearance (big nose, stringy hair, and bag-man clothes), and sweet demeanor, Tiny Tim became a highly successful novelty artist in the late '60s to early '70s.

The budding singer had a strong record-collector's interest in the comedic pop of bygone eras, particularly the crooners of the '20s such as Rudy Vallee. He first performed these little-known oldies, accompanying himself on ukulele and using such pseudonyms as Darry Dover and Larry Love, to mostly uninterested audiences in Greenwich Village. By the mid-'60s, Tiny Tim was amassing a cult audience. He played often at Steve Paul's Scene, and eventually got booked on *The Tonight Show,* where he became an instant national celebrity of sorts.

By 1968, rock audiences at such venues as the Fillmores East and West had latched on to Tim's act. Reprise released his first LP in spring 1968. He became a frequent guest on *Laugh-In* as well as on the Carson show. He married 17-year-old Victoria May Budinger (Miss Vicky, as he called her) on the latter program on December 17, 1969. That show was one of the most widely watched television events of the decade. The couple named their daughter Tulip, after Tiny's one major hit, "Tip-Toe Thru' the Tulips With Me" (#17, 1968). Tim and Miss Vicky first filed for divorce in early 1972, at which point he was out of public favor and broke. The divorce was final in 1977.

He continued to perform. In the latter stages of his career he released interesting singles with such titles as "I Saw

Elvis Presley Tiptoeing Through the Tulips" and "The Hicky on Your Neck." His oeuvre also included a cover of AC/DC's "Highway to Hell." In the '80s and '90s Tiny Tim recorded numerous independent and import albums in addition to those listed above. By the mid-'90s he had become a frequent guest on Howard Stern's radio show and on an MTV game show. In 1996 the 64-year-old performer died in the arms of his third wife, Susan, after he had collapsed on the stage of the Minneapolis Women's Club. He had just finished singing "Tip-Toe Thru' the Tulips" at a formal fund-raiser.

TLC

Formed 1991, Atlanta, GA
Tionne "T-Boz" Watkins (b. Apr. 26, 1970, Des Moines, IA), voc.; Lisa "Left Eye" Lopes (b. May 27, 1971, Philadelphia, PA), voc.; Rozonda "Chilli" Thomas (b. Feb. 27, 1971, Atlanta), voc.
1992—*Ooooooohhh . . . On the TLC Tip* (LaFace) 1994—*CrazySexyCool* 1999—*Fanmail.*

One of the most successful R&B groups of the '90s, the "New Jill Swing" trio TLC officially came together after Rozonda "Chilli" Thomas joined Tionne "T-Boz" Watkins and Lisa "Left Eye" Lopes in 1991, replacing a short-term original "C" known as Crystal. Under the management and direction of singer/songwriter/producer Pebbles (née Perri McKissack), the sassy young trio was signed to LaFace Records, the Atlanta-based label cofounded by Pebbles' then-husband (and future Arista President) L.A. Reid. Released in 1992, the group's debut, *Ooooooohhh . . . On the TLC Tip* (#14 pop, #3 R&B) gave TLC its first three of many pop Top 10 hits: "Ain't 2 Proud 2 Beg" (#6 pop, #2 R&B), "Baby-Baby-Baby" (#2 pop, #1 R&B), and "What About Your Friends" (#7 pop, #2 R&B). The women's individual personalities were established early on: T-Boz sang the no-nonsense, tough-girl parts, Chilli the pretty passages, and Left Eye—who earned her moniker by wearing a condom taped over the left lens of her spectacles—brought the rap. Lopes also contributed to the songwriting pool alongside heavyweights Babyface, Dallas Austin, and Jermaine Dupri.

In between *Ooooooohhh* and its followup, TLC remained active by appearing in the movie *House Party 3* and contributing the Prince-penned "Get It Up" (#42 pop, #15 R&B, 1993) to the soundtrack of the Janet Jackson/Tupac Shakur film *Poetic Justice*. Lopes in particular remained in the headlines, thanks to her tumultuous relationship with former Atlanta Falcons player Andre Rison. In 1994 Lopes was sentenced to five years probation for burning Rison's house to the ground after an argument (they later made up). By the time *CrazySexyCool* (#3 pop, #2 R&B) was released later that year, however, the focus was back on TLC's music. Introducing a dramatically sexier and more mature TLC, the album went 11 times platinum and spun off the #1 pop hits "Creep" and "Waterfalls," as well as "Red Light Special" (#2 pop, #3 R&B, 1995) and "Diggin' On You" (#5 pop, #7 R&B, 1995). But in July 1995, in the middle of *CrazySexyCool*'s reign, the group members filed for bankruptcy, claiming they had yet to receive enough money to pay off their debts (particularly Lopes, who owed Lloyd's of London $1.3 million for her damage to her former boyfriend's house).

TLC would wait five years before releasing its next album, but the time away didn't hurt the group's popularity. Released in the spring of 1999, *Fanmail* entered the charts at #1 (beating Eminem's also highly anticipated debut, *The Slim Shady LP* to the top) and dominated the pop and R&B charts for most of the year. The album's hits included "No Scrubs" and "Unpretty," both of which went to #1 on the pop chart. After the album's chart run, however, another long hiatus seemed inevitable, with Lopes and Thomas both working on solo albums by the end of 2000. A greatest-hits album was also rumored, though as of this writing, none of the projects had been released.

Toad the Wet Sprocket

Formed 1986, Santa Barbara, CA
Glen Phillips (b. Dec. 29, 1970), voc., gtr.; Todd Nichols (b. Aug. 10, 1967), gtr.; Dean Dinning (b. June 9, 1967), bass, kybds.; Randy Guss (b. Mar. 7, 1967), drums.
1989—*Bread and Circus* (Columbia) 1990—*Pale* 1991—*Fear* 1994—*Dulcinea* 1995—*In Light Syrup* 1997—*Coil* 1999—*P.S. (A Toad Retrospective).*

Toad the Wet Sprocket, a mellow, artsy pop-rock band that took its name from a Monty Python skit that parodied rock news reports, holds the distinction of being the first group from Santa Barbara, California, to score a major-label record deal. Formed by schoolmates while still in high school, Toad honed its chops at a local bar, playing under names like Three Young Studs and Glen before settling on the Python-inspired moniker. Eventually, a singer from the area asked the band to back him during a recording session, and as a return favor allowed the musicians to cut two of their own songs in his studio. With $650 Toad recorded eight more tracks, making complete what would become its first album.

Duped cassettes of the recording found their way into independent record stores in Santa Barbara, and soon word spread to L.A., where record companies became interested in the group. After being courted by several big labels, Toad decided to sign with Columbia, which rereleased its first album, *Bread and Circus,* late in 1989. By that point the band had almost finished a second album, *Pale*. Columbia's investment showed no real signs of paying off, however, until 1992, when Toad's persistent touring started increasing its college-based following. It was that year that Toad's 1991 album, *Fear,* appeared in the *Billboard* Top 100. *Fear* itself peaked at #49, but the album generated two Top 20 singles, "All I Want" (#15) and "Walk on the Ocean" (#18). *Dulcinea* (#34, 1994) yielded the Top 40 single "Fall Down" (#33, 1994) and the almost–Top 40 hit "Something's Always Wrong" (#41, 1994). A collection of B sides and previously unreleased material, *In Light Syrup* (#37), followed in 1995, giving the members a breather. *Coil* (#19, 1997), featuring the single "Come Down," which reached #13 on the Modern Rock

Tracks chart; that summer, the band participated in the H.O.R.D.E. Tour.

In 1998 the longtime friends concluded that the band was no longer satisfying, and Toad broke up. However, the quartet reunited in the studio to rerecord one track for its 1999 swansong, *P.S. (A Toad Retrospective),* which was mostly a greatest-hits collection. Following the band's breakup, Phillips toured with fellow folk rockers Steve Poltz (the Rugburns), John Doe (X), and Pete Droge in the fall of 1998. He then dabbled in a band called Two Headed Boy. A solo album, *Live at Largo,* was released on the Internet in 2000; he also played solo acoustic dates. Toad guitarist Todd Nichols and bassist/keyboardist Dean Dinning (nephew of Mark Dinning, who had his own hit, "Teen Angel," in 1959) joined forces with Rob Taylor and Erik Herzog to form the band Lapdog. Dinning and Nichols cowrote songs for the band's album, *Near Tonight,* which was self-released in 2000, but Dinning left the group before the album's release; tired of the musician's lifestyle, he pursued voiceover work instead. Drummer Guss became a band manager and played gigs with various other bands as well.

The Tokens

Formed 1958, New York, NY
Best-known lineup: Phil Margo (b. Apr. 1, 1942, Brooklyn, NY), bass voc.; Hank Medress (b. Nov. 19, 1938, Brooklyn), first tenor voc.; Jay Siegel (b. Oct. 20, 1939, Brooklyn), lead baritone voc.; Joseph Venneri (b. 1937, Brooklyn); Mitchel Margo (b. May 25, 1947, Brooklyn), second tenor and baritone voc.
1962—*The Lion Sleeps Tonight* (RCA) 1966—*I Hear Trumpets Blow* (B.T. Puppy) 1967—*Portrait* (Warner Bros.) 1971—*Both Sides Now* (Buddah) 1993—*Oldies Are Now* (B.T. Puppy) 1994—*Wimoweh: The Best of the Tokens* (RCA) 1996—*Esta Noche, El Leon Baila* (B.T. Puppy) 1999—*Unscrewed.*

The Tokens' best-known achievement was their doo-wop-like smash hit "The Lion Sleeps Tonight" (#1, 1961). The song, which is derived from a Zulu folk melody originally titled "Mbube" (which sounded like "wimoweh") was first a hit recording in the '30s in Africa. It was popularized in the '50s by Miriam Makeba, who sang it in Zulu, on Victor Records. This was followed by an English-language rendition by the Weavers entitled "Wimoweh." The Tokens' souped-up English version sold over 3 million copies.

The first version of the Tokens was formed in 1956 by Neil Sedaka and Hank Medress and included Eddie Rabkin and Cynthia Zoliton. The group broke up after recording two Sedaka–Howie Greenfield sides. Medress formed another group, with Jay Siegel, Warren Schwartz, and Fred Kalkstein two years later, but it too dissolved. Medress and Siegel then teamed up with brothers Phil and Mitch Margo. These four formed the group's best-known lineup. Their first single, on Warwick, had been "Tonight I Fell in Love," which sold 700,000 copies in the U.S. and 300,000 in Canada and Europe.

"The Lion Sleeps Tonight" proved a surprise international smash hit, but the later records fell on deaf ears. Shortly after the early 1962 release of the "Lion"-like "B'wa Nina," the band members signed a production/A&R deal with Capitol. Unlike many similar vocal groups, the Tokens had played on and had a hand in producing their own records. They produced the Revlons, among others, but their biggest early production efforts were the Chiffons' "One Fine Day" and "He's So Fine." They also started their own record label, B.T. Puppy Records. Other production credits include the Happenings. Hank Medress produced another version of "Lion Sleeps" for Robert John on Atlantic, which also became a Top 10 smash in 1972. Medress also worked as a staff producer at Bell Records in the early '70s, and teamed up Dawn with Tony Orlando. He has since worked with Buster Poindexter and Dan Hill. Jay Siegel and the Margo brothers became Cross Country and recorded for Atlantic in 1973. In 1981 the best-known lineup reunited for a show at Radio City Music Hall. The group then split up again, with the Margo brothers forming one set of Tokens and Siegel another. Mitch Margo has also been successful as a manager and television producer/writer.

Although the Tokens' record sales never reached earlier levels, they were sought-after background vocalists and have performed on records by Connie Francis, Del Shannon, Bob Dylan, and Keith ("98.6"). Members of the Tokens continued to sing together on occasion, doing commercials for Pan Am ("makes the going great"), Ban, Clairol, Wendy's, Sunkist (the "Good Vibrations" spots), and other products. They have continued to perform and record through the years. They appear on Paul Shaffer's 1989 LP, teaming up with Dion DiMucci, Johnny Maestro, and other early-'60s stars for "When the Radio's On." The use of "The Lion Sleeps Tonight" in the Walt Disney animated feature *The Lion King* (1994) brought the Tokens back into the spotlight. Both Siegel's Tokens and the version led by the Margo brothers and their sons have continued to perform and record.

Tone-Lōc

Born Anthony Terrell Smith, Mar. 3, 1966, Los Angeles, CA
1989—*Lōc-ed After Dark* (Delicious Vinyl) 1991—*Cool Hand Lōc.*

Rap's gravely voiced hedonist Tone-Lōc (the name is short for his street "tag," Tony Loco) made rock history when his *Lōc-ed After Dark* became the first album by a black rap artist to go to #1 on the pop chart, thanks to "Wild Thing" (#2, 1989).

Lōc, the youngest of three children, was raised in a middle-class section of L.A. by his mother (his father died when Lōc was 12). A flirtation with gang life (he was rumored to be a member of the Crips) ended when Lōc was sent to the prestigious Hollywood Professional School. A funk fan too impatient to learn guitar, Lōc was understandably attracted to rap. After junior college he joined a short-lived trio, Triple A. After graduation he sold foreclosed houses, programmed computers, and continued to rap.

His distinctive voice—the result of having his throat

scalded by hot tea and brandy, his mother's cold cure—brought him to the attention of Delicious Vinyl in 1988. An initial single, "On Fire" b/w "I Got It Goin' On," was a local radio hit. His breakthrough came with the followup, "Wild Thing," an infectious paean to the joys of casual sex rapped over a guitar riff sampled from Van Halen's "Jamie's Cryin' " and cowritten by label mate Young MC. (Apparently Young MC became involved after Lōc's rap was rejected by his label as being too obscene.) The song's video, made for about $400, became a staple of MTV, and pushed sales to 2.5 million copies, making it one of the top singles of the '80s. "Funky Cold Medina" (#3), also written by Young MC, followed, also from the debut LP.

It would be three years before the release of Tone-Lōc's next album, *Cool Hand Lōc* (#46 R&B, 1991), which proved a disappointment. In 1995 he was sentenced to anger-management sessions and 100 hours of community service for smashing the windows of a woman's car with a baseball bat in 1993.

Lōc, who had publicly expressed an easygoing, almost casual attitude toward his musical career, has since pursued a respectable acting career. He appeared in the films *Posse, Poetic Justice, Ace Ventura: Pet Detective,* and *Heat,* as well as in the TV series *Roc* and *NewsRadio.* He also does extensive voiceover work, having lent his voice to the animated feature film *Bebe's Kids* and to the children's series *C-Bear and Jamal,* which he also produced. Tone-Lōc still performs his hits.

Tones on Tail: See Bauhaus

Too $hort

Born Todd Anthony Shaw, Apr. 28, 1966, Los Angeles, CA
1987—*Born to Mack* (Dangerous Music) 1988—*Life Is . . . Too $hort* (Jive) 1990—*Short Dog's in the House* 1992—*Shorty the Pimp* 1993—*Get in Where You Fit In* 1995—*Cocktails* 1996—*Gettin' It (Album Number Ten)* 1999—*Can't Stay Away* 2000—*You Nasty.*

Too $hort put Oakland, California, on the hip-hop map with his slow, crude raps and proto-gangster image. The middle-class Todd Shaw re-created himself as a pimp, styled after characters in blaxploitation films and novels. Too $hort, named as a youth for his then-short height, has built up a chart-topping pop career from the very bottom. He began rapping in the early '80s, when he sold homemade tapes on the streets of Oakland. His first three albums were released by the independent label 75 Girls.

After he never got paid for them, he set up his own label and production company in 1987. Along with Too $hort, Dangerous Music has produced discs by Pooh Man, Spice 1, and Ant Banks. Too $hort sold *Born to Mack* out of his trunk, generating enough attention to get signed by Jive; the album subsequently went gold.

Life Is . . . Too $hort (#37, 1989) was released amid phony rumors that Too $hort had died; despite little airplay, the album went platinum, as did its successor, *Short Dog's in the House* (#20, 1990). The latter featured "The Ghetto," a single based on the '70s Donny Hathaway hit "The Ghetto, Part One," as well as "Ain't Nothin' But a Word to Me," a duet with Ice Cube that answered critics who would censor use of the word "bitch" with a series of bleeps. Too $hort became known more and more for his graphically violent and frequently misogynist raps. He developed his mack persona further on *Shorty the Pimp* (#6, 1992), which debuted at #6 on the pop albums chart. *Get In Where You Fit In* (#1 R&B, 1993) debuted even higher at #4. The followup, *Cocktails* (#6 pop, #1 R&B, 1995), continued Too $hort's commercial success. Released the following year, *Gettin' It (Album Number Ten)* (#3 pop, #1 R&B) became Too $hort's sixth album to go platinum. The record's title track featured members of Parliament/Funkadelic.

In 1997 Too $hort turned his attention to the work of other rappers, founding $hort Records and releasing *Nationwide,* a compilation featuring the work of little known MCs from around the U.S. Too $hort also guested on a couple of Scarface's records and released a pair of his own singles, including "Call Me" (#90 pop, #30 R&B, 1997), a duet with rapper Lil' Kim that appeared in the movie *Booty Call. Can't Stay Away* (#5 pop, #1 R&B) and *You Nasty* followed in 1999 and 2000, respectively.

Tool

Formed 1991, Los Angeles, CA
Maynard James Keenan (b. Apr. 17, 1964, Ravenna, OH), voc.; Adam Jones (b. Jan. 15, 1965, Chicago, IL), gtr.; Danny Carey (b. May 10, 1961, MO), drums; Paul D'Amour (b. June 8, 1968, Spokane, WA), bass.
1992—*Opiate* EP (Zoo) 1993—*Undertow* 1996—*Aenima* (Volcano) (– D'Amour; + Justin Chancellor [b. Justin Gunnar Walte Chancellor, Nov. 19, 1971, Eng.], bass) 2001—*Lateralus.*
Maynard James Keenan with A Perfect Circle: 2000—*Mer De Noms* (Virgin).

Emerging in the early '90s, Tool bridged the gap between classic heavy metal and alternative rock, mixing grinding guitars, dark thundering rhythms, and challenging lyrics. The band never appeared in its own videos, which were typically intense and macabre, yet found a large mainstream following with its flair for harsh melody.

Maynard James Keenan was born the only child of a Baptist family near Akron, Ohio. He joined the army in 1982, after spending his youth in Michigan, New Jersey, New York, Oklahoma, Kansas, and Texas. He eventually landed in L.A., where he met guitarist Adam Jones, a sculptor and film special-effects designer who had worked on *Jurassic Park* and *Terminator 2.* With bassist Paul D'Amour and drummer Danny Carey, they formed a band, originally called Toolshed.

Within a year Tool signed with Zoo Entertainment, and in 1992 released an EP, *Opiate.* That was followed a year later with *Undertow* (#50, 1993), which explored themes of inner turmoil with a sound that merged prog rock with punk energy. The album included the Modern Rock radio hits "Sober" and "Prison Sex," a song about child abuse. During the recording of *Aenima* (#2, 1996), D'Amour quit to form a new band, Lusk, and was replaced by Justin Chancellor.

Long periods between albums frequently led to breakup rumors, also fueled by the formation in 2000 of Keenan's band A Perfect Circle, which he refused to call a "side project," and which released *Mer De Noms*. Rumors were put to rest with the release of *Lateralus* in mid-2001.

Toots and the Maytals

Formed 1962, Kingston, Jam.
Frederick "Toots" Hibbert (b. 1946, Maypen, Jam.), lead voc.; Nathaniel "Jerry" Matthias (b. ca. 1945, Jam.), harmony voc.; Ralphus "Raleigh" Gordon (b. ca. 1945, Jam.), harmony voc.
1971—*Monkey Man* (Trojan) 1972—*From the Roots* 1973—*Funky Kingston* 1974—*In the Dark* 1975—*Funky Kingston* (Island) 1976—*Reggae Got Soul* 1978—*The Maytals* (State) 1979—*The Best of Toots and the Maytals* (Trojan); *Pass the Pipe* (Island) 1980—*Just Like That* 1981—*Live!* (– Matthias; – Gordon); *Knock Out!* (Mango) 1984—*Reggae Greats: Toots and the Maytals* 1988—*Toots in Memphis* 1996—*Time Tough: The Anthology* (Island) 1997—*Recoup* (Alla Son) 1998—*Ska Father* (Artists Only!) 2000—*The Very Best of Toots & the Maytals* (Island).

For over three decades, Toots Hibbert's exhoratory vocals and evangelistic stage delivery have charged Jamaican popular music with the fervor of American gospel-rooted soul singers like Otis Redding, Solomon Burke, and Wilson Pickett.

Toots Hibbert spent his first 15 years in a small town in the Jamaican countryside; he left home for Kingston in 1961 and formed a vocal trio with Nathaniel Matthias and Raleigh Gordon. Coxsone Dodd produced their first Jamaican hits—"Hallelujah" (1963) and "Six and Seven Books of Moses" (1963)—when they called themselves the Vikings. They left Dodd for Prince Buster in 1964 and recorded "Little Slea" as the V. Maytals before deciding to work as the Maytals. In the next two years they worked mainly with Byron Lee and his Ska-Kings band. With hits like "If You Act This Way" (1964) and "John and James" (1965), they became a leading group of the ska era.

Toots Hibbert

In 1966 they won the Jamaican Song Festival prize with Hibbert's "Bam Bam." That same year Hibbert was jailed for possession of marijuana. After his release 12 months later, the Maytals recorded "54-46," commemorating his prison experience, for Leslie Kong's Beverley's label. Among the Maytals' other Beverley sides was "Do the Reggay" [*sic*], the 1968 song usually credited with coining the term "reggae."

By that time Kong was releasing Maytals singles in Britain; "Monkey Man" was the first Maytals song to chart overseas (#47 U.K., 1970) (it was covered in 1979 by the Specials on their debut album). Following Kong's death in 1971, the Maytals worked with his former partner Warwick Lynn and established a following.

The 1972 release of *The Harder They Come* introduced the Maytals to the U.S.; the film's soundtrack featured "Sweet and Dandy" and "Pressure Drop." In 1975, now known as Toots and the Maytals, they signed their first major contract with Island Records. Island released *Funky Kingston*—a collection culled from Trojan's *Funky Kingston* and *In the Dark*—which contained the Maytals' unique interpretations of John Denver's "Country Roads," in which "West Virginia" became "West Jamaica." Also in 1975 Toots and the Maytals made their first tour of the U.S., opening shows for the Who. The tour was badly planned, and the Maytals were booed off the stage at many dates. While they remained critical favorites, the Maytals could never match Bob Marley's or Peter Tosh's popularity.

Toots went solo in 1982, although he continued to tour as Toots and the Maytals. In 1988 at Memphis's Ardent recording studio he was accompanied by Sly and Robbie and producer Jim Dickinson (Alex Chilton, Replacements) and recorded a set of Stax/Volt covers, *Toots in Memphis*. In the late '90s, Toots recorded two new studio albums, *Recoup* and *Ska Father*.

The Tornadoes

Formed 1962, London, Eng.
George Bellamy (b. Oct. 8, 1941, Sunderland, Eng.), gtr.; Heinz Burt (b. July 24, 1942, Hargin, Ger.; d. Apr. 7, 2000), gtr.; Alan Caddy (b. Feb. 2, 1940, London), gtr., violin; Clem Cattini (b. Aug. 28, 1939, London), drums; Roger Lavern (b. Roger Jackson, Nov. 11, 1938, Kidderminster, Eng.), kybds.
1963—*Telstar* (London).

The Tornadoes were assembled by British producer/songwriter/entrepreneur Joe Meek in 1962 to back up vocalists who would sing his songs. After working with small-time singers John Leyton and Don Charles, the Tornadoes were hooked up with English teen idol Billy Fury. Later in the year, Meek, inspired by developments in the space program, composed an instrumental for the Tornadoes to record. "Telstar" (the name of the first U.S. communications satellite) became a #1 hit single and eventually sold over 5 million copies around the world. The group had just one other minor success, 1963's "Ride the Wind." They soon broke up. On February 3, 1967, Meek committed suicide. Of the original Tornadoes, George Bellamy and Heinz Burt pursued solo careers; Bellamy later started his own label. Only Clem Cattini, a studio drummer, remains active as a performer.

Tortoise

Formed in 1990, Chicago, IL
Doug McCombs (b. Jan. 9, 1962, Peoria, IL), bass; John Herndon (b. Apr. 8, 1966, Long Island, NY), drums, kybds., vibes; John McEntire (b. Apr. 9, 1970, Portland, OR), drums, vibes; Bundy K. Brown, gtr.; Dan Bitney (b. Oct. 7, 1964, Madison, WI), perc.
1994—*Tortoise* (Thrill Jockey) 1995—*Rhythms, Resolutions & Clusters* 1996—*Millions Now Living Will Never Die* (– Brown; + David Pajo [b. 1970, TX], bass) *A Digest Compendium of the Tortoise's World; Remixed* 1998—*TNT* (– Pajo; + Jeff Parker [b. Apr. 4, 1967, Bridgeport, CT], gtr.) 2001—*Standards.*

Tortoise is an inventive Chicago collective committed to instrumental music rooted in a broad palette of influences: European electronica, dub, modern jazz, Kraut-rock, minimalism, '70s progressive rock, and hip-hop scratching. The result is a sound both atmospheric and challenging, at the forefront of a small experimental movement for which critics provided an oblique name: postrock. The group was founded by bassist Doug McCombs (Eleventh Dream Day) and drummer John Herndon (Poster Children) to explore music that emphasized percussion and bass rhythms over words and guitar solos. They soon drafted other veterans from Chicago's indie rock community: John McEntire (Shrimp Boat; The Sea and Cake), percussionist Dan Bitney, and guitarist Bundy K. Brown.

Calling themselves Tortoise, the band recorded and released several singles in 1993, followed by the self-titled debut album in 1994. Tortoise then recruited indie musicians/producers Steve Albini, Jim O'Rourke, and Brad Wood to remix the tracks for *Rhythms, Resolutions & Clusters.* Live shows were improvisational blends of percussion, guitar, bass, vibes, synthesizers, and samplers, with players constantly swapping instruments mid-song onstage. After another single, 1995's "Gamera," Brown left for other band projects. Bassist David Pajo (Slint) joined in time for 1996's *Millions Now Living Will Never Die,* which included the epic-length track "Djed." For 1998's *TNT,* Tortoise introduced strings and horns for the first time. After Pajo's departure, Tortoise was joined by avant-garde guitarist Jeff Parker, a member of Chicago's Association for the Advancement of Creative Musicians. In 2001 Tortoise released *Standards.*

Peter Tosh

Born Winston Hubert MacIntosh, Oct. 9, 1944, Westmoreland, Jam.; died Sep. 11, 1987, Barbican, St. Andrew, Jam.
1976—*Legalize It* (Columbia) 1977—*Equal Rights* 1978—*Bush Doctor* (Rolling Stones) 1979—*Mystic Man* 1981—*Wanted Dread and Alive* 1983—*Mama Africa* (EMI) 1984—*Captured Live* 1987—*No Nuclear War* 1988—*The Toughest* (Capitol) 1996—*The Best of Peter Tosh: Dread Don't Die* (EMI) 1997—*Honorary Citizen* (Sony) 1999—*Scrolls of the Prophet: The Best of Peter Tosh.*

Peter Tosh first became known (in Jamaica in the early '60s and in Europe and America in the early '70s) as the baritone vocalist of the Wailers. Through his years with the Wailers, however, he also maintained a solo career. From 1964 to 1967 he released numerous singles on Coxsone Dodd's Studio One and Coxsone labels, variously calling himself Peter Macking, Peter MacIntosh, Peter Tosh or—most often—Peter Touch. Among his solo recordings (which often featured Wailers Bob Marley and Bunny Livingston as backup singers) were early versions of "I'm the Toughest" and "400 Years," songs he was later to popularize beyond Jamaica.

Some 1969 sessions with Leslie Kong resulted in British releases on the Bullet and Unity labels, and in 1971 and 1972, recordings cut with Joe Gibbs were released in the U.K. on the Bullet, Punch, and Pressure Beat labels. In 1971 Tosh founded his own Jamaican label, Intel-Diplo H.I.M., on which he began issuing self-produced singles.

After leaving the Wailers in 1973 (complaining that because Marley attracted an undue share of attention overseas, he was relegated to the background), he recorded primarily in Jamaica for Intel-Diplo H.I.M. Tosh shrewdly leased his recordings to foreign companies for world distribution. Columbia got U.S. rights to *Legalize It,* on which Tosh proselytized for the many uses of marijuana, and *Equal Rights,* which contained his perennially popular "Stepping Razor."

In 1978 Mick Jagger and Keith Richards signed Tosh to Rolling Stones Records and sat in on *Bush Doctor,* which featured the Temptations' "Don't Look Back" performed as a duet by Tosh and Jagger (#81). Tosh and his Word, Sound and Power band toured America with the Stones that year, and Jagger joined on his *Saturday Night Live* appearance. He returned to the U.S. regularly. *Mama Africa* included a reggae remake of Chuck Berry's "Johnny B. Goode" (#84, 1983).

Tosh had a history of confrontation with the law. He was jailed for possession of marijuana in the mid-'60s. In 1978, performing for a Kingston crowd of 30,000 that included the Jamaican prime minister, he smoked a "spliff" onstage and berated the prime minister for 30 minutes for not legalizing "ganja." Later that year he was arrested in his studio, taken to a police station, and beaten nearly to death before he was released.

Tosh remained an outspoken figure on the reggae scene. In mid-1987 he released the antiwar album *No Nuclear War.* On September 11, three men armed with 9 mm pistols came to his home and murdered Tosh, local DJ Jeff Dixon, and Tosh's cook "Doc" Brown. Four others, including Tosh's girlfriend, were injured. The motive was officially cited as robbery, but speculation arose that political or personal enmities were involved. Although Dennis Lobban, a street vendor, was arrested and convicted of the murders in 1988, accusations that Tosh was executed refused to die out. A 1993 documentary, *Stepping Razor—Red X* (the "red X" a reference to the mark Tosh claimed was placed after his name on government documents), dramatized these charges.

Toto

Formed 1978, Los Angeles, CA
David Paich (b. June 21, 1954, Los Angeles), kybds., voc.; Steve Lukather (b. Oct. 21, 1957, Los Angeles), gtr., voc.; Bobby Kimball (b. Mar. 29, 1947, Vinton, LA), voc.; Steve Porcaro (b. Sep. 2, 1957, CT), kybds.; David Hungate (b. TX), bass; Jeff Porcaro (b. Apr. 1, 1954, Hartford, CT; d. Aug. 5, 1992, Holden Hills, CA), drums.
1978—*Toto* (Columbia) 1979—*Hydra* 1981—*Turn Back* 1982—*Toto IV* 1984—(– Hungate; + Mike Porcaro [b. May 29, 1955, CT], bass); (– Kimball; + Denis "Fergie" Frederiksen [b. May 15, 1951, Wyoming, MI], voc.) *Isolation; Dune* soundtrack (Polydor) 1986—(– Frederiksen; + Joseph Williams, voc.) *Fahrenheit* (Columbia); *The Seventh One* 1988—(– Williams; – S. Porcaro) 1990—(+ Jean-Michel Byron [b. S. Afr.], voc.) *Past to Present 1977–1990* (– Byron) 1992—(– J. Porcaro) 1993—*Kingdom of Desire* (Relativity) (+ Simon Phillips, drums) 1996—*Tambu* (Sony Legacy) 1998—*Toto XX: 1977–1997* 1999—(+ Kimball) *Mindfields; Livefields.*

A studio band assembled by experienced sessionmen, Toto purvey a smooth, glossy rock sound that netted them several hit singles and best-selling LPs. The group's debut album and the self-produced *Toto IV* were its biggest sellers.

Most of the band members had met around 1972 at Grant High School in Southern California, and they kept meeting on sessions for albums by Steely Dan, Cheap Trick, Pink Floyd, Earth, Wind & Fire, and others. In 1976 Jeff Porcaro, David Hungate, and David Paich performed on Boz Scaggs's *Silk Degrees* LP, for which Paich wrote several songs, including "Lowdown" and "Lido Shuffle."

Toto's debut album sold over 2 million copies by 1979, during which year the band also had a #5 single, "Hold the Line." Both *Hydra* (#37, 1979) and *Turn Back* (#41, 1981) sold moderately, but the big breakthrough came with *Toto IV*, which won the Album of the Year Grammy, sold over 3 million copies, and spun off the group's biggest hits: "Rosanna" (#2, 1982) (written for actress Rosanna Arquette) and "Africa" (#1, 1982), as well as "I Won't Hold You Back" (#10, 1983). The album also earned five additional Grammys, including Record of the Year for "Rosanna."

Subsequent albums did not fare nearly as well; only *Isolation* and *Fahrenheit* cracked the Top 50. Critics derided the group's smooth professionalism, and throughout their years with Toto, group members continued to contribute to others artists' work as studio hands, producers, and writers. They cowrote the Tubes' 1982 Top 40 hit "Talk to You Later." Steve Porcaro cowrote Michael Jackson's "Human Nature." Jeff Porcaro's last studio gigs included drumming on Bruce Springsteen's *Human Touch*. Jeff Porcaro died in 1992 of a heart attack; initial reports stated that it was prompted by an allergic reaction to garden pesticides, but the coroner determined that cocaine use was a contributing factor. Although not released until after Jeff Porcaro's death, *Kingdom of Desire* was the last Toto album on which he performed. Singer Bobby Kimball, who had left Toto in the mid-'80s, rejoined the group at the end of the '90s.

Allen Toussaint

Born Jan. 14, 1938, New Orleans, LA
1958—*The Wild Sounds of New Orleans by Tousan* (RCA) 1971—*Toussaint* (Tiffany) 1972—*Love, Life and Faith* (Reprise) 1975—*Southern Nights* 1978—*Motion* (Warner Bros.) 1991—*The Allen Toussaint Collection* (Reprise) 1996—*Connected* (NYNO).

Singer/pianist/songwriter/arranger/producer Allen Toussaint was as important to the music of New Orleans in the '60s as Dave Bartholomew had been in the '50s. In the '70s, musicians from the rest of the U.S. and abroad came to his city to record with him.

He began playing piano, emulating Professor Longhair, while in grade school. He made his professional debut with the Flamingos when he was in his early teens. In the mid-'50s he began working as a studio keyboardist for Dave Bartholomew (he played piano on some Fats Domino sessions) and with Shirley and Lee. In 1958 he recorded his first solo album, calling himself Tousan. One of his first compositions, "Java," was a hit for Al Hirt in 1964.

When Minit Records was founded in 1960, Toussaint became the label's house songwriter, arranger, and producer for songs like Jessie Hill's "Ooh Poo Pah Doo," Ernie K-Doe's "Mother-in-Law," Chris Kenner's "I Like It Like That," Lee Dorsey's "Ya Ya," Barbara George's "I Know," and records for Aaron Neville, Irma Thomas, Clarence "Frogman" Henry, and Benny Spellman. Toussaint established himself as a hitmaker with the definitive New Orleans sound of the '60s—jaunty dance music characterized by a dialogue of rolling piano licks and horn riffs. His regular studio band included tenor saxophonist Nat Perrilliat, baritone saxophonist Clarence Ford, guitarist Roy Montrell, bassist Peter "Chuck" Badie, and drummers John Boudreaux and James Black.

After producing records for the Instant, Fury, and AFO labels, in 1963 Toussaint went into the army. Even as a serviceman he remained a musician, forming the Stokes to record "Whipped Cream" for Instant; the song became a hit for Herb Alpert and the Tijuana Brass. Discharged from the army in 1965, Toussaint returned to Minit, but the label was sold to Liberty later that year. He and another New Orleans producer, Marshall Sehorn, then founded Sansu Enterprises, which included Marsaint Music Publishers and the Sansu, Amy, and Deesu labels.

In the second half of the '60s, Toussaint wrote and produced hits for Lee Dorsey, Maurice Williams, Ernie K-Doe, Wilbert Harrison, and Sansu's studio band, the Meters. After Sansu opened Sea-Saint Studios in 1972, artists such as Paul Simon, Paul McCartney and Wings, Sandy Denny, and the

Mighty Diamonds recorded there; Toussaint produced sessions by Dr. John, Labelle (including their 1975 bestseller, "Lady Marmalade"), Badger, John Mayall, and Joe Cocker. He was also responsible for the horn arrangements on the Band's 1972 live album, *Rock of Ages,* and the period music for the 1978 soundtrack to Louis Malle's *Pretty Baby.*

Toussaint records his own albums and appears live only occasionally, but his songs have been covered by the Rolling Stones ("Fortune Teller"), Herman's Hermits ("A Certain Girl"), Betty Wright ("Shoorah, Shoorah"), Three Dog Night ("Brickyard Blues"), Frankie Miller ("High Life"), Glen Campbell ("Southern Nights"), the Yardbirds, the Pointer Sisters ("Yes We Can Can"), Maria Muldaur, Little Feat, Boz Scaggs, Bonnie Raitt, Robert Palmer, Ringo Starr, and Warren Zevon. He has also guested on other artists' albums, among them Elvis Costello's *Spike.* He wrote the music for the mid-'80s musical *Stagger Lee.* In 1993 and 1994 Toussaint appeared with a number of other singer-songwriters in a touring show called In Their Own Words. In 1996 he cofounded NYNO Records and released his first new album in nearly two decades. He was inducted into the Rock and Roll Hall of Fame in 1998.

Tower of Power

Formed 1968, Oakland, CA
Lineup, ca. 2001: Emilio Castillo (b. Sep. 24, Detroit, MI), sax, voc.; Stephen "Doc" Kupka (b. Mar. 25), sax, English horn; Francis "Rocco" Prestia (b. Mar. 7), bass, fluegelhorn; Jeff Tamelier, gtr.; Roger Smith, kybds.; Larry Braggs, voc.; Norbert Stachel, sax; Adolpho Acosta, trumpet; Mike Bogart, trumpet; David Garibaldi, drums.
Earlier members include: Lenny Williams (b. Pine Bluff, AK), voc.; Lenny Pickett, sax, flute, piccolo; Mic Gillette, trumpet, trombone, fluegelhorn; Bruce Conte, gtr., voc.; Chester Thompson, kybds., voc.; Brent Byars, congas; Greg Adams, trumpet, voc.; Lee Thornburg, trumpet, fluegelhorn; Nick Milo (b. Oct. 14), kybds.; Russ McKinnon (b. June 24), drums; Carmen Grillo (b. Aug. 8), gtr.; Tom Bowes (b. Oct. 29), voc.; David Mann (b. Aug. 8), tenor sax; Hubert Tubbs, voc.
1971—*East Bay Grease* (San Francisco) 1972—*Bump City* (Warner Bros.) 1973—*Tower of Power* 1974—*Back to Oakland* 1975—*Urban Renewal; In the Slot* 1976—*Live and in Living Color; Ain't Nothin' Stoppin' Us Now* (Columbia) 1978—*We Came to Play* 1979—*Back on the Streets* 1981—*Direct* (Sheffield Labs) 1987—*Power* (Cypress) 1991—*Monster on a Leash* (Epic/Sony) 1993—*TOP* 1995—*Souled Out* 1997—*Rhythm and Business* 1999—*What Is Hip?: Tower of Power Anthology* (Rhino).

This integrated Oakland-based R&B band reached its commercial peak between 1972 and 1975, when Lenny Williams sang lead on its hits "So Very Hard to Go" (#17 pop, #11 R&B, 1973) and "Don't Change Horses (in the Middle of a Stream)" (#26 pop, #22 R&B, 1974).

Emerging from the early-'70s Bay Area club scene, the band made its recording debut with *East Bay Grease* on Bill Graham's San Francisco Records in 1971. The next year, signed to Warner Bros., Tower of Power scored with "You're Still a Young Man" (#29 pop, #24 R&B, 1974), with Rick Stevens as lead vocalist. Williams joined the band for its third album, and continued singing on *Back to Oakland* and *Urban Renewal.* During this period, the band had hits with "So Very Hard to Go" and "What Is Hip?" (#91 pop, #31 R&B). Williams left to sign with ABC as a solo artist; his R&B hits include "Choosing You" (#62) and "Shoo Doo Fu Fu Ooh!" (#31), both 1977. Hubert Tubbs succeeded him and sang lead on "You Ought to Be Having Fun" (#68 pop, #62 R&B) in 1976, when Tower was signed to Columbia.

Throughout the '70s, the Tower of Power's ultraprecise horn section worked as studio musicians on countless other acts' recordings. Among them were Elton John, Elvin Bishop, Santana, and José Feliciano. In 1983 Lenny Pickett was heard in avant-garde music concerts in New York (he now plays with the *Saturday Night Live* band), and keyboardist Chester Thompson joined Santana. The group—whose core membership of founder Emilio Castillo, Steve Kupka, and Rocco Prestia has remained intact through the years—then slid into a difficult period, as members dealt with substance-abuse problems and other pressures. They recorded the direct-to-CD Sheffield Labs album *Direct* and another *Power,* an album that was privately financed and originally released only in Denmark. The group did not disband officially but didn't really begin to come back until after the horn section toured with Huey Lewis and the News during the mid-'80s. (The Tower of Power horns appear on Lewis' *Picture This* and *Fore!*) Soon the rest of the group was traveling, too, joining the horns for Tower of Power midnight shows that occurred after Lewis' gigs.

Although Tower of Power's more recent releases have not been hits, its live shows still draw rave reviews. The horn section often sits in with Paul Shaffer's band on *The Late Show With David Lettermen,* and its latest studio credits include Phish's *Hoist* (1994), Victoria Williams' *Loose* (1994), and Ray Charles' *Strong Love Affair* (1997).

Pete Townshend: See the Who

The Toys

Formed early '60s, Jamaica, NY
June Montiero (b. July 1, 1946, Queens, NY), voc.; Barbara Harris (b. Aug. 18, 1945, Elizabeth, NJ), voc.; Barbara Parritt (b. Oct. 1, 1944, Wilmington, NC), voc.
1966—*The Toys Sing "A Lover's Concerto" and "Attack!"* (DynoVoice).

The Toys were an R&B girl group whose big hit was "A Lover's Concerto," a refashioning of a Bach piece (#2, 1965). The three members met as teenagers at Woodrow Wilson High School in Queens, New York, and continued to sing after their graduation. In 1964 they were signed by the publishing firm Genius Inc., who teamed them with the songwriting duo Sandy Linzer and Denny Rendell. Their big single went #4 R&B, crossed over to pop, and also became a #5 hit in England. During 1965 the song sold over a million copies. The Toys appeared on television rock shows like *Shindig!,* and toured with Gene Pitney. They also appeared in the film *The Girl in Daddy's Bikini.* They had a less successful hit in 1966 with "Attack" (#18). By the next year they were gone from the charts but continued to do session work separately.

Traffic

Formed 1967, England
Steve Winwood (b. May 12, 1948, Birmingham, Eng.), voc., kybds., gtr.; Chris Wood (b. June 24, 1944, Birmingham; d. July 12, 1983, London, Eng.), sax, flute; Dave Mason (b. May 10, 1947, Worcester, Eng.), gtr., voc.; Jim Capaldi (b. Aug. 24, 1944, Evesham, Eng.), drums, voc.
1967—*Mr. Fantasy* (United Artists) (– Mason; + Mason) 1968—*Traffic* (– Mason) 1969—*Last Exit* 1970—*John Barleycorn Must Die* (+ Rick Grech [b. Nov. 1, 1946; d. Mar. 17, 1990, Eng.], bass) 1971—(+ Jim Gordon, drums; + Reebop Kwaku Baah [b. 1944, Lagos, Nigeria; d. 1981], perc.; + D. Mason) *Welcome to the Canteen* (– Mason) *The Low Spark of High-Heeled Boys* (Island) (– Grech; – Gordon; + Roger Hawkins, drums; + David Hood, bass) 1973—*Shoot Out at the Fantasy Factory* 1974—*Traffic on the Road* (Hawkins; – Hood; + Rosco Gee, bass) *When the Eagle Flies* (group disbands) 1975—*Heavy Traffic* (United Artists); *More Heavy Traffic* 1991—*Smiling Phases* (Island) 1994—(group re-forms: Winwood; Capaldi) *Far From Home* (Virgin).

The original Traffic had two phases. At first it was a winsomely psychedelic pop band that blended blues, folk, rock, and R&B and was fronted by Steve Winwood [see entry] and Dave Mason. This group recorded such FM-radio favorites as "Paper Sun" and "You Can All Join In." After Mason left, the band became Steve Winwood's vehicle for longer, moodier excursions that leaned closer to jazz and soul. This group was responsible for "Glad," "Freedom Rider," "Empty Pages," and "Rock & Roll Stew." Traffic was popular in both incarnations.

When the band formed in 1967, Steve Winwood was its best-known member because of his lead vocals with the Spencer Davis Group [see entry]. Winwood left that band to found Traffic. He and his friends Chris Wood, Jim Capaldi, and Dave Mason wrote and rehearsed in a cottage in the English countryside. Traffic's debut LP, *Mr. Fantasy,* contained two British hits, "Paper Sun" and "Hole in My Shoe." But conflicts between Mason's pop style and Winwood's jazz ambitions flared up and in late 1967 Mason split, first joining up with Delaney and Bonnie Bramlett before pursuing a solo career. A 1968 film called *Here We Go Round the Mulberry Bush* contained some of Traffic's music, and the theme song was a minor hit.

Despite differences with Winwood, Mason helped cut *Traffic,* contributing the oft-covered "Feelin' Alright." But by 1968 he had left again. It looked like Traffic was finished in 1969, when Winwood joined Blind Faith [see entry] with Eric Clapton, Ginger Baker, and Rick Grech. However, Blind Faith proved short-lived, and after a stint in Ginger Baker's Air Force in 1970 Winwood began recording his first solo album, the working title of which was *Mad Shadows.* Capaldi and Wood sat in on some sessions, and the LP became Traffic's fifth and most commercially successful album, *John Barleycorn Must Die* (#5, 1970), a gold album and a staple of "progressive" FM radio. The group then added Grech. The next year, before recording *Welcome to the Canteen,* Reebop Kwaku Baah was added on percussion. In addition, that live album featured Jim Gordon augmenting Capaldi on drums and a guest appearance by Mason. Despite the success of the gold album *The Low Spark of High-Heeled Boys* (#7, 1971), Gordon and Grech departed.

Winwood was then stricken with peritonitis, and so the band was temporarily sidelined. Capaldi cut a solo album *(Oh! How We Danced)* in Muscle Shoals, Alabama, and in the process he recruited session players bassist David Hood and drummer Roger Hawkins into the band. They appeared on *Shoot Out at the Fantasy Factory* (#6, 1973) and with another Muscle Shoals musician, keyboardist Barry Beckett, on the live *Traffic on the Road* (#29, 1973). By the sessions for *When the Eagle Flies* (#9, 1974), only the original trio of Winwood, Wood, and Capaldi plus bassist Rosco Gee were left. After that album's release, Winwood and Capaldi started their solo careers in earnest. Gee and Kwaku Baah joined Can [see entry]. Wood died in 1983 in his London apartment after a long illness; Grech died seven years later of kidney and liver failure precipitated by a hemorrhage. Kwaku Baah died of a brain hemorrhage.

Winwood enjoyed the most successful solo career of any of his former band mates. In 1994 he and Capaldi joined forces for what was termed a Traffic reunion (Gee performed in the touring band), and under the group name released the critically well received *Far From Home* (#33, 1994). Shortly thereafter, they returned to their solo endeavors.

The Trammps

Formed mid-'60s, Philadelphia, PA
Lineup ca. early '80s: Earl Young, drums, bass voc.; Jimmy Ellis, lead tenor voc.; Robert Upchurch, baritone voc.; Stanley Wade, bass, tenor voc.; Harold Wade, gtr., tenor voc.
1975—*Trammps* (Golden Fleece); *The Legendary Zing Album* (Buddah) 1976—*Where the Happy People Go* (Atlantic); *Disco Inferno* 1977—*The Trammps III* 1978—*The Best of the Trammps* 1979—*The Whole World's Dancing* 1980—*Slipping Out* 1994—*This Is Where the Happy People Go: The Best of the Trammps* (Rhino).

While the Trammps had their first recording success in 1965 with "Storm Warning," when they were known as the Volcanoes, it was not until a 1975 contract with Atlantic Records, several personnel changes, and the rise of disco that they became a celebrated recording and touring act. Their peak popularity came through the inclusion of their blazing rendition of "Disco Inferno" on the *Saturday Night Fever* soundtrack in 1977.

Basing their vocal style on that of the Coasters (a lead-and-bass vocal combination), the Trammps' earliest success under that name came on the Buddah label with a rendition of "Zing Went the Strings of My Heart" (#17 R&B), featuring Earl Young's bass vocal. Young, a top Philadelphia International session musician and co-owner of the Philadelphia publishing and production company Golden Fleece (with producers Norman Harris and Ronnie Baker) brought the Trammps to that label after their Buddah contract expired. Their association with Golden Fleece yielded an early disco hit, "Love Epidemic" (#75 R&B), in 1973. In 1975 they signed on with Atlantic Records and had the first of a string of hits with the uptempo love plea "Hooked for Life" (#70 R&B), followed by "Hold Back the Night" (#35 pop, #10 R&B, 1975), "That's Where the Happy People Go" (#27 pop, #12 R&B, 1976), and "Disco Inferno" (#11 pop, #9 R&B, 1977). That proved to be their last major hit, and as the disco phase drew to a close, the Trammps faded from sight. In the '90s, a version of the group began touring again.

The Traveling Wilburys

Formed 1988, Los Angeles, CA
Nelson (later Spike) Wilbury (b. George Harrison, Feb. 25, 1943, Liverpool, Eng.), gtr., voc.; Lucky (later Boo) Wilbury (a.k.a. Bob Dylan, b. Robert Allen Zimmerman, May 24, 1941, Duluth, MN), gtr., voc.; Otis (later Clayton) Wilbury (b. Jeff Lynne, Dec. 30, 1947, Birmingham, Eng.), gtr., voc., bass; Charlie T. (later Muddy) Wilbury Jr. (b. Tom Petty, Oct. 20, 1952, Gainesville, FL), gtr., voc.; Lefty Wilbury (b. Roy Orbison, Apr. 23, 1936, Vernon, TX; d. Dec. 6, 1988, Hendersonville, TN), gtr., voc.; Jim Keltner, drums.
1988—*Traveling Wilburys, vol. 1* (Wilbury) (– Orbison) 1990—*Vol. 3.*

With a lineup that included major figures from four decades of rock history, including three indisputable gods (Dylan, Harrison, and Orbison), the Traveling Wilburys were by definition the ultimate supergroup. But their casual good humor and easy rocking style—not to mention their "posing" as a group of brothers—made them the antithesis of a supergroup.

The Traveling Wilburys' roots go back only as far as 1988 or so, when Harrison was setting to work on his next solo album with producer/Beatles fan Jeff Lynne. By chance they happened to find rehearsal space in Bob Dylan's garage, and a series of casual jams with the garage owner, Tom Petty, and Roy Orbison resulted in the new group. Their debut album was a double-platinum smash, going to #3 in late 1988 less on the strength of the minor hit single, "Handle With Care" (#45, 1988), than public interest in the principals. Orbison died suddenly of a heart attack less than one month after *Traveling Wilburys, vol. 1* hit the chart. He was not replaced in the lineup. The group's second album, the playfully titled *Vol. 3* (#11, 1990), was another platinum effort, despite having no hit singles.

[See also individual members' solo entries; the Beatles; Electric Light Orchestra.]

Randy Travis

Born Randy Bruce Traywick, May 4, 1959, Marshville, NC
1982—*Randy Ray Live at the Nashville Palace* (Paula) 1986—*Storms of Life* (Warner Bros.) 1987—*Always and Forever* 1988—*Old 8x10* 1989—*An Old Time Christmas; No Holdin' Back* 1990—*Heroes & Friends* 1991—*High Lonesome* 1992—*Greatest Hits, vol. 1; Greatest Hits, vol. 2* 1993—*Wind in the Wire* 1994—*This Is Me* 1996—*Full Circle* 1998—*You and You Alone* (DreamWorks) 1999—*A Man Ain't Made of Stone.*

With his warm baritone and neotraditional style, Randy Travis dominated country music in the late '80s. In the wake of George Strait, Reba McEntire, and Ricky Skaggs, he found a ready audience for music that eschewed the crossover attempts of '70s country in favor of an approach that recalled Travis' own influences, Hank Williams, Lefty Frizzell, and Ernest Tubb.

Encouraged by his father, a construction company owner, farmer, and sometime musician who hoped his sons would become the next Everly Brothers, Randy Traywick began performing publicly with his brother Ricky at around age 10. Randy's turbulent adolescence—drinking, drugs, and 100-m.p.h. car chases with the police—however, soon sidetracked him.

Lib Hatcher, owner of a Charlotte, North Carolina, country music club, intervened with a judge in one of Randy's court battles; granted custody of the 17-year-old, she began managing him (the two married in 1991). Moving to Nashville in the early '80s, they worked in a nightclub, Hatcher as manager, Traywick as dishwasher, cook, and occasional singer. On the tiny independent Paula Records, as Randy Ray, he released two singles, then recorded the 1982 low-budget album *Randy Ray Live at the Nashville Palace*, which he sold at gigs.

In 1985 the singer finally inked a deal with Warner Bros., changing his name to Randy Travis, after contributing the song "Prairie Rose" to the soundtrack for *Rustler's Rhapsody.* He had also released a single, "On the Other Hand," that had reached #67 on the country chart (in rerelease it hit #1 in 1986).

With *Storms of Life* Travis became the first country performer to sell a million copies of his major-label debut within a year of its release. Joining the Grand Ole Opry and winning a Country Music Association Horizon Award, Travis embarked upon a remarkable run that saw him gain seven #1 country hits in a row (1987's "Forever and Ever, Amen," "I Won't Need You Anymore [Always and Forever]," and "Too Gone Too Long"; 1988's "I Told You So," "Honky Tonk Moon," and "Deeper Than the Holler"; 1989's "Is It Still Over?").

Travis, named Male Vocalist of the Year by the Country Music Association in 1987 and 1988, was at the height of his career (he also won Grammy Awards for Best Male Country Vocal Performance both those years). In 1989 he sustained injuries in a serious car crash but came back with two #1s, "It's Just a Matter of Time" and "Hard Rock Bottom of Your Heart." *Heroes & Friends* included duets with George Jones, Tammy Wynette, B.B. King, and Roy Rogers, among others. *High Lonesome* sold dependably, but at the start of the '90s Travis' hegemony was challenged by up-and-coming "hat acts" such as Garth Brooks and Clint Black, neotraditionalists whose style Travis had helped to pioneer.

Meanwhile, Travis had branched out into acting; since the '80s he has landed roles in numerous TV episodes and movies, including Steven Seagal's *Fire Down Below* and Francis Ford Coppola's *The Rainmaker*. In 1998 Travis signed with the Nashville division of DreamWorks Records to release *You and You Alone* (#49 pop, #7 C&W). The album yielded three Top 10 country singles, including "Spirit of a Boy–Wisdom of a Man," which almost cracked the pop Top 40, stalling at #42.

The Tremeloes

Formed 1959, Dagenham, Eng.
Brian Poole (b. Nov. 3, 1941, Barking, Eng.), voc.; Alan Blakely (b. Apr. 1, 1942; d. June 1, 1996, Bromley, Eng.), rhythm gtr.; Alan Howard, bass; Dave Munden (b. Nov. 2, 1943), drums; Rick Westwood (b. May 7, 1943), lead gtr.
1966—(– Poole; – Howard; + Len "Chip" Hawkes [b. Nov. 2, 1946], bass) 1967—*Here Comes My Baby* (Columbia); *Even the Bad Times Are Good; Suddenly You Love Me* 1968—*58/68 World Explosion* 1974—*Shiner* (DMJ) 1992—*The Best of the Tremeloes* (Rhino).

The Tremeloes began their career as the backup band for British vocalist Brian Poole, and with him had a number of U.K. hit records in 1963 and 1964, including the #1 single "Do You Love Me." When Poole left them in 1966, they brought in Len Hawkes and proceeded to eclipse their former frontman with a trio of British Top 5 hit records: "Silence Is Golden," "Even the Bad Times Are Good," and "Here Comes My Baby," all in 1967. All except the second hit the U.S. Top 20 as well. Even when the hits stopped, the Tremeloes remained a viable nightclub attraction, and they continue to this day, though a car accident forced Hawkes to quit in 1974, and Blakely left on his own the following year. The Tremeloes (with drummer Dave Munden and guitarist Rick Westwood intact) and Poole's solo act are familiar sights on the nostalgia circuit.

T. Rex/Tyrannosaurus Rex/Marc Bolan

Formed 1967, England
Marc Bolan (b. Mark Feld, Sep. 30, 1948, London, Eng.; d. Sep. 16, 1977, London); Steve Peregrin Took (b. Stephen Ross Porter, July 28, 1949; d. Oct. 27, 1980, London).
1968—*My People Were Fair and Had Sky in Their Hair But Now They're Content to Wear Stars on Their Brows* (Regal/Zonophone, U.K.); *Prophets, Seers and Sages, The Angels of the Ages* 1969—(– Took; + Mickey Finn [b. June 3, 1947], gtr., perc.) *Unicorn* (Blue Thumb) 1970—*Beard of Stars* (Regal/Zonophone, U.K.); *T. Rex* (Reprise) 1971—*Electric Warrior* 1972—*The Slider; Tyrannosaurus Rex (A Beginning)* (A&M) 1973—*Tanx* 1974—*Zinc Alloy and the Hidden Riders of Tomorrow* 1975—*Zip Gun Boogie* (EMI, U.K.) 1976—*Futuristic Dragon* 1977—*Dandy in the Underworld* 1998—*T. Rex Unchained: Unreleased Recordings, vols. 1–8* (Mercury).

With his Botticelli face and curls and whimsically glamorous image, Marc Bolan fronted T. Rex, a British group that generated a fan hysteria reminiscent of Beatlemania and produced 11 successive U.K. Top 10 hits between 1970 and 1974. Among these were "Bang a Gong (Get It On)" (#1), "Jeepster" (#2), and "Telegram Sam" (#1). But while T. Rex could not hardly duplicate its British success in America (where its sole major hit was the Top 10 smash "Bang a Gong") the group's heavy guitar sound has had an enduring influence and can be heard in songs such as Love and Rockets' "I'm Alive" and groups like the Soup Dragons.

T. Rex had its beginnings when the group—known as Tyrannosaurus Rex until the 1970 success of "Ride a White Swan"—was formed by Bolan in 1967 with Steve Peregrin (often misspelled Peregrine) Took. A well-known scene-making Mod in the early '60s, Bolan released two singles in the mid-'60s on Decca—"Hippy Gumbo" and "The Wizard"—which failed to establish him as a solo artist. But with the group John's Children, Bolan enjoyed two minor U.K. hits in 1967—"Desdemona" and "Go Go Girl." One year later, Tyrannosaurus Rex recorded its debut album (produced by Tony Visconti), which blended acoustic textures with such instruments as the Chinese gong and talking drums and accented Bolan's lyrics—a blend of myth, fantasy, and magic (others might say utter nonsense). As a British flower-power band, Tyrannosaurus Rex earned a sizable underground following and toured the U.S. in 1969.

The band began to achieve widespread success by embracing a full-blown rock attack on albums like *Electric Warrior* (#32, 1971) (which, like many of the group's hits, included backing vocals by Flo and Eddie). The group's highest-charting U.S. release was *The Slider* (#17, 1972). During the height of T. Rex mania in 1973, Ringo Starr directed a

T. Rex: Mickey Finn and Marc Bolan

documentary on the group's success, *Born to Boogie*. Bolan and the group were at the forefront of the glitter movement, which was far more influential and lasting in their homeland than in the U.S. T. Rex's popularity declined shortly thereafter, and Bolan declared the group extinct in 1975, leaving his wife and exiling himself to America. He returned to England in 1976 and began living with American singer Gloria Jones. Respected by followers of the then burgeoning new-wave scene, Bolan brought the Damned on tour with his newly re-formed T. Rex in 1977 as a support act.

But his solo career never took off in the U.S., partly because of his haphazard personal life. "I was living in a twilight world of drugs, booze, and kinky sex," he told ROLLING STONE. Bolan died in a crash on September 16, 1977, in a car driven by Jones. In 1980 Steve Took died from choking on a cherry while high on morphine. In 2001 Mickey Finn toured with his own "T-Rex."

A Tribe Called Quest

Formed 1988, Queens, NY
Ali (b. Ali Shaheed Muhammad, Aug. 11, 1970, Brooklyn, NY), DJ; Phife (b. Malik Taylor, Apr. 10, 1970, Brooklyn), voc.; Q-Tip (b. Jonathan Davis, Nov. 20, 1970, New York, NY), voc.; Jarobi, voc.
1990—*People's Instinctive Travels and the Paths of Rhythm* (Jive) (– Jarobi) 1991—*The Low End Theory* 1993—*Midnight Marauders* 1996—*Beats, Rhymes and Life* 1998—*The Love Movement* 1999—*The Anthology*.
Q-Tip solo: 1999—*Amplified* (Arista).

Following the lead of De La Soul, their friends and comrades in the "Native Tongues" rap collective, A Tribe Called Quest blazed alternative rap trails with a laid-back, witty, progressive style that paved the way for the "jazz rap" of Digable Planets, Jungle Brothers, and Us3.

Q-Tip, Phife, Ali, and Jarobi met at New York City's Murray Bergtraum High School for Business Careers. Q-Tip's association with De La Soul [see entry] and the Jungle Brothers and a four-song demo led to a 1989 deal with Jive Records. The singles "Description of a Fool" (1989) and "I Left My Wallet in El Segundo" (1990) were followed by their debut album, *People's Instinctive Travels* (#91, 1990), the first rap work to fuse jazz samples with hip-hop structures. A followup, *The Low End Theory* (#45, 1991), had a harder edge and extended the group's jazz leanings, featuring jazz great Ron Carter on upright bass. *Low End*'s "Scenario" was a minor hit (#57, 1991).

In between their albums, Tribe appeared on MTV's *Unplugged;* Q-Tip guest-rapped on Deee-Lite's "Groove Is in the Heart" and on Lenny Kravitz and Sean Lennon's "Give Peace a Chance"; all three Tribe members contributed to the Jungle Brothers' *Straight Out the Jungle* and to De La Soul's "Buddy." In 1993, while Tribe was recording its third album, Ali contributed extensive production work to jazz saxophonist Greg Osby's *3-D Lifestyles*. Released at the end of that year, *Midnight Marauders* (#8 pop, #1 R&B, 1993) yielded

A Tribe Called Quest

"Award Tour" (#47 pop, #27 R&B, 1993), with backing vocals by De La Soul's Trugoy the Dove.

During summer 1994, the group took the hip-hop slot in the Lollapalooza festival, and in 1996 released *Beats, Rhymes and Life* (#1 pop and R&B). Two years later, *The Love Movement* (#3 pop and R&B) proved to be Tribe's finale. Q-Tip pursued a solo career, releasing *Amplified* (#4 R&B) in 1999 and scoring hits with "Vivrant Thing" (#26 pop, #7 R&B) and "Breathe and Stop" (#21 R&B). He also was one of the guest vocalists on Missy "Misdemeanor" Elliott's R&B chart-topper "Hot Boyz."

Tricky

Born Adrian Thaws, Jan. 27, 1968, Bristol, Eng.
1995—*Maxinquaye* (4th & Broadway) 1996—*Nearly God; Pre-Millennium Tension* 1998—*Angels With Dirty Faces* (Island) 1999—*Juxtapose* (PolyGram) 2001—*Mission Accomplished* EP (Epitaph); *Blowback* (Hollywood).

The dark magus of trip-hop—the hybrid genre of subterranean moods merging American hip-hop, Jamaican dub rhythms, and ambient music's otherworldly flow—Tricky hailed from the form's ground zero: Bristol, England. He grew up in Knowle West, a rough-and-tumble part of town, where he was raised by his grandmother and other members of his extended family after his mother died when he was four. Turned onto music after hearing the first Specials album, he eventually joined the Wild Bunch, a local troupe of DJs, rappers, and singers that formed in the early '80s.

He first performed under the name Tricky Kid with Massive Attack [see entry], the group that evolved out of the Wild Bunch, and appeared on its influential 1991 release *Blue Lines*. Tricky contributed to the sequel, 1994's *Protection*, but was already pursuing a solo career before its release, moving to London in 1993 to record a single, "Aftermath," which featured 15-year-old Martina Topley-Bird (who would become Tricky's companion and the mother of his daughter, Maisy). His 1995 debut album *Maxinquaye* (#2 U.K.) was a critics' favorite and a popular success in England, its seductive but overwhelming sense of claustrophobia offset by Tricky's radical reimagining of the rap form (a guitar-driven version of Public Enemy's "Black Steel in the Hour of Chaos," recited by Topley-Bird).

Later that year, Tricky toured the U.S. as an opening act for PJ Harvey, collaborated with horror-core rappers Gravediggaz on *The Hell* EP, and established a production company, Durban Poison. He also was in demand as a remixer, working with Björk (with whom he was romantically linked), Luscious Jackson, and Whale. The 1996 album Nearly God was a collection of collaborations (with Terry Hall, Björk, Alison Moyet, and Neneh Cherry, among others).

Early that year, Tricky moved to New York, where his studio work with underground rappers was documented on the EP *Grassroots*. In November he released his second solo album, *Pre-Millennium Tension*, which reflected an increasingly darker, even paranoid aesthetic. (Touring the U.S. to support the release, Tricky performed with the stage lights extinguished, a shadow illuminated fleetingly.) During 1997 the performer took a supporting role in the comedic sci-fi film *The Fifth Element*. The following year, Tricky released *Angels With Dirty Faces*, and the year after, *Juxtapose*, a joint effort with Cypress Hill's DJ Muggs and DMX producer Grease. In 2001 he released the *Mission Accomplished* EP, followed by *Blowback*, which features Cyndi Lauper, Alanis Morissette, and members of Live and the Red Hot Chili Peppers.

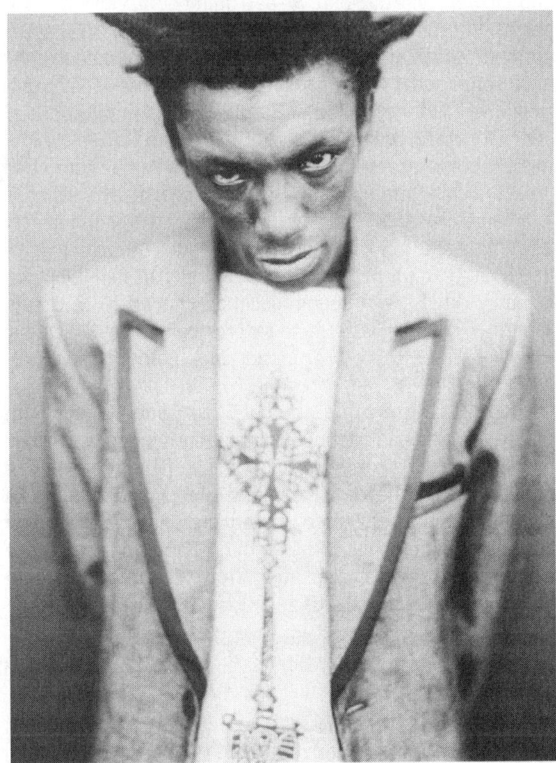

Tricky

Travis Tritt

Born James Travis Tritt, Feb. 9, 1963, Marietta, GA
1990—*Country Club* (Warner Bros.) 1991—*It's All About to Change* 1992—*T-r-o-u-b-l-e; A Travis Tritt Christmas (Loving Time of Year)* 1994—*Ten Feet Tall and Bulletproof* 1995—*Greatest Hits—From the Beginning* 1996—*The Restless Kind* 1998—*No More Looking Over My Shoulder* 2000—*Down the Road I Go* (Columbia); *Super Hits, vol. 2* (Warner Bros.).

Travis Tritt's latter-day outlaw sound has brought him numerous #1 singles, as well as several Top 10 multiplatinum albums on the country charts, some of which have crossed over onto the pop charts. As deeply influenced by Lynyrd Skynyrd and the Allman Brothers as by George Jones and Merle Haggard, this honey-voiced, blue-collar "son of the new South" has scrupulously avoided any identification with Nashville and its "hat acts."

The son of a hardscrabble farmer, Tritt taught himself to play guitar at age eight and wrote his first song at 14. He married at 18 and his wife discouraged his musical career. Tritt worked for a heating and air-conditioning equipment distributor. Neither job nor marriage lasted long. By 1985 Tritt was divorced and performing in Atlanta.

In 1986 he approached a hometown friend working as an Atlanta-based promotion man for Warner Bros. to help produce a demo. Warners signed him, and released *Country Club* (#70 pop, #3 C&W, 1990), with its four C&W Top 40 singles: "Help Me Hold On" (#1, 1990), "I'm Gonna Be Somebody" (#2, 1990), "Put Some Drive in Your Country" (#28, 1990), and "Drift Off to Dream" (#3, 1991).

Tritt's insistance that country music broaden its attraction and open itself to new sounds may have annoyed some purists, but they could not deny his success. *It's All About to Change* (#22 pop, #1 C&W, 1991) featured a duet with Marty Stuart (who joined Tritt on the No Hats Tour in 1992), and the nasty kiss-off waltz "Here's a Quarter (Call Someone Who Cares)" (#2 C&W). Little Feat backed up Tritt on the raucous "Bible Belt." On *T-r-o-u-b-l-e* (#27 pop, #6 C&W, 1992) Tritt was joined by George Jones and Tanya Tucker on backing vocals ("Lord Have Mercy on the Working Man") and Lynyrd Skynyrd's Gary Rossington (who cowrote "Blue Collar Man"). The platinum *Ten Feet Tall and Bulletproof* (#20 pop, #3 C&W, 1994) yielded another #1 country single in "Foolish Pride."

Tritt next collaborated with producer Don Was on the honky-tonk-tinged *The Restless Kind* (#7 C&W, 1996), which spawned a pair of Top 10 country singles. But the album didn't sell as well as its predecessors, and his next release failed to go gold. Tritt, who never left his native Georgia for Nashville, went on a two-year hiatus, parting ways with his record label. In 2000 he came back with his first effort for Columbia, *Down the Road I Go* (#51 pop, #8 C&W), yielding the single, "Best of Intentions" (#48 pop, #20 C&W, 2001).

The Troggs

Formed 1965, Andover, Eng.
Reg Presley (b. Reginald Ball, June 12, 1943, Andover), voc.; Chris Britton (b. June 21, 1945, Watford, Eng.), lead gtr.; Peter Staples (b. May 3, 1944, Andover), bass; Ronnie Bond (b. Ronald Bullis, May 4, 1943, Andover; d. Nov. 13, 1992, Andover), drums.
1966—*Wild Thing* (Fontana) 1967—*Best of the Troggs* 1968—*Love Is All Around* 1969—(group disbands) 1972—(group re-forms: Presley; Bond; + Richard Moore, gtr.; + Tony Murray, bass) 1976—*The Troggs* (Pye) (+ Colin Fletcher, gtr.); *The Original Troggs Tapes* (Private Stock); *Vintage Years* (Sire) N.A.—(– Fletcher; – Moore; – Murray; + Peter Lucas, bass; + Dave Maggs, drums) 1992—*Archeology (1967–1977)* (Mercury) (– Bond) *Athens Andover* (with Peter Buck, Bill Berry, Mike Mills, Peter Holsapple, John Keane) (Rhino).

Though their popularity only lasted a short time, the Troggs were initially one of the most successful mid-'60s British Invasion bands. They're generally known for their 5-million-selling seminal garage-punk hit "Wild Thing" (#1, 1966).

The foursome formed in Hampshire in the mid-'60s, taking its name from the term "troglodyte." "Wild Thing," the Troggs' debut single, was so popular and so frequently covered that it spawned a parody version sung by two people imitating Robert Kennedy and Senator Everett Dirksen. The Troggs' other hits in 1966 were "With a Girl Like You" (#29) and "I Can't Control Myself" (#43).

Their roots-of-power-pop sound, featuring Reg Presley's sometimes innocent, sometimes lecherous vocals, also cracked the Top 10 with "Love Is All Around" (#7, 1968) (revived as a huge U.K. hit for Wet Wet Wet). Though their hits dried up at that point, the Troggs continued to tour Europe. They didn't record, though, for several years.

In 1976 Pye released *The Troggs,* which featured "Summertime," a double-entendre-laden song that also received U.S. FM airplay. That same year, Sire released the *Vintage Years* retrospective, and Private Stock issued the new *Original Troggs Tapes.* The 1980 *Live at Max's Kansas City* included both older hits and newer songs. European albums also appeared. In the early '90s the group recorded *Athens Andover,* a collaboration with members of R.E.M. The Troggs remain perennially popular in Europe, where their music has graced numerous TV commercials. In 1992 the group performed at Sting's wedding. In recent years, Presley has become one of Britain's premier UFO experts.

Robin Trower

Born Mar. 9, 1945, London, Eng.
1973—*Twice Removed From Yesterday* (Chrysalis) 1974—*Bridge of Sighs* 1975—*For Earth Below* 1976—*Robin Trower Live!; Long Misty Days* 1977—*In City Dreams* 1978—*Caravan to Midnight* 1980—*Victims of the Fury* 1981—*B.L.T.* 1982—*Truce* 1983—*Back It Up* 1987—*Passion* (GNP Crescendo) 1988—*Take What You Need* (Atlantic) 1989—*No Stopping Anytime* (Chrysalis) 1990—*In the Line of Fire* (Atlantic) 1991—*Essential* 1994—*20th Century Blues* (V-12) 1997—*Someday Blues* 1999—*This Was Now 74–98; Go My Way.*

In his early years with Procol Harum [see entry], Robin Trower's piercing, distorted guitar sound was more often than not compared to that of Eric Clapton. But on Procol's "Whiskey Train" (on *Home*) and "Song for a Dreamer" (on *Broken Barricades*) Trower exhibited a strong Jimi Hendrix influence; "Song for a Dreamer" was dedicated to Hendrix.

By the time of *Barricades,* it was obvious that Trower's hard-rocking style was at odds with Procol's classical-rock direction, and he left after that album, at first forming the abortive Jude with ex–Jethro Tull drummer Clive Bunker, ex–Stone the Crows bassist Jim Dewar, and Scottish blues singer Frankie Miller. When that venture ran aground, Trower took a year off to re-form a Hendrix-style power trio with Dewar and drummer Reg Isidore. They debuted with 1973's *Twice Removed From Yesterday* (#106, 1973), which was produced by ex-Procol Matthew Fisher.

With *Bridge of Sighs* (#7, 1974) and heavy American touring, Trower came into his own as a guitar hero with U.S. audiences. After that album, Isadore was replaced by Bill Lordan, formerly with Sly and the Family Stone. Meanwhile, Trower took some guitar lessons from another pioneer of electronically modified guitar, Robert Fripp, who had just disbanded King Crimson. *For Earth Below* (#5, 1975) and *Live* (#10, 1976) were top-selling LPs, and through the '70s Trower continued to ably demonstrate his love for Hendrix, usually with solid commercial results. *Long Misty Days* (#24, 1976) and *In City Dreams* (#25, 1977) were both certified gold. *Caravan to Midnight* and *Victims of the Fury* both hit the Top 40.

In 1981 Trower began collaborating with ex-Cream bassist and singer Jack Bruce, for two well-received albums: *B.L.T.* (#37, 1981) (with drummer Jack Lordan) and *Truce* (#109, 1982) (with Reg Isidore in Lordan's place). (*No Stopping Anytime* is a compilation of Trower's recordings with Bruce.) Trower has continued to tour and record, and while his more recent albums have not charted nearly as highly as those of his '70s heyday, he remains a respected guitarist. In the early '90s he appeared on and coproduced with Bryan Ferry the singer's *Taxi* and *Mamouna.* Following the release of two mid-'90s blues homages, Trower returned to full-on rock with 2000's *Go My Way.*

John Trudell

Born Feb. 15, 1946, Omaha, NE
1983—*Tribal Voice* (Peace Company) 1986—*AKA Grafitti Man* 1987—*. . . but This Isn't El Salvador; Heart Jump Bouquet*

1991—*Child's Voice; AKA Grafitti Man* (Rykodisc) 1992—*Fables and Other Realities* (Peace Company) 1994—*Johnny Damas and Me* (Rykodisc) 1999—*Blue Indians* (Dangerous Discs/Inside Recordings).

Native American activist John Trudell writes and performs story songs informed by his political struggle. Growing up on a Santee Sioux reservation, Trudell served as national spokesman for the Indians of All Tribes occupation of Alcatraz Island in 1969. As National Chairman of the American Indian Movement from 1973 to 1979, he was the subject of a 17,000-page FBI file that documented his activities, including his 1979 burning of an American flag in front of the Bureau's Washington headquarters. Shortly thereafter, a fire "of suspicious origin" destroyed Trudell's house on the Shoshone Paiute Indian Reservation in Nevada, killing Trudell's three children, wife, and mother-in-law. In light of the FBI's refusal to investigate the incident, Trudell has consistently maintained government complicity in his family's death.

After publishing a book of poems, *Living in Reality,* in 1982, he began recording home-studio tapes with his friend Jackson Browne. He started by backing his poetry with drums and chanting, but added a rock & roll element when he began collaborating with Kiowa Indian guitarist Jesse Ed Davis (who had played with Browne as well as Bob Dylan, Eric Clapton, and others). Together they recorded *AKA Grafitti Man* (and two other albums), which was released as a mail-order cassette on Trudell's own label and was praised by Bob Dylan as the best album of 1986. Davis died in 1988, but Trudell released an expanded version of *AKA Grafitti Man* on Rykodisc in 1991. His politically charged rock & roll earned strong reviews, and Trudell followed it with his second Rykodisc set, *Johnny Damas and Me,* in 1994. The album examined the theme of women's power and leavened its pop music with Native American chanting. Browne produced Trudell's *Blue Indians* in 1999, which was released on Browne's Dangerous Discs/Inside Recordings label.

John Trudell

In addition to his poetry and music, Trudell has also made forays into acting. He has appeared in the feature films *Thunderheart* (1992) and *Smoke Signals* (1998) as well as the documentary *Incident at Oglala* (1992), all three of which featured American Indian themes.

The Tubes

Formed late '60s, Phoenix, AZ
Fee Waybill (b. John Waldo, Sep. 17, 1948, Omaha, NE), lead voc.; Bill Spooner (b. Apr. 16, 1949, Phoenix), gtr.; Roger Steen (b. Nov. 13, 1949, Pipestone, MN), gtr.; Vince Welnick (b. Feb. 21, 1951, Phoenix), kybds.; Michael Cotten (b. Jan. 25, 1950, Kansas City, MO), kybds.; Prairie Prince (b. May 7, 1950, Charlotte, NC), drums; Rick Anderson (b. Aug. 1, 1947, St. Paul, MN), bass; Re Styles (b. Mar. 3, 1950), voc.
1975—*The Tubes* (A&M) 1976—*Young and Rich* 1977—*Now* 1978—*What Do You Want From Live?* 1979—*Remote Control* 1981—*The Completion Backward Principle* (Capitol); *T.R.A.S.H. (Tubes Rarities and Smash Hits)* (A&M) 1983—*Outside/Inside* (Capitol) 1985—*Love Bomb* (– Waybill) 1992—*The Best of the Tubes* 1993—(lineup: Steen; Prince; Anderson; Waybill; + Gary Cambra [b. Apr. 24, 1957, Walnut Creek, CA], voc., kybds.) 1995—(+ Trey Sabatelli [b. Nov. 3, 1963, Albany, NY], drums) 1996—(+ Dave Medd [b. Sep. 17, Alameda, CA], voc.) *Genius of America* (Popular/Critique) 1999—*Infomercial: How to Be Tubular* (Hux, U.K.); *Dawn of the Tubes* (Phoenix Gems) 2000—*Tubes World Tour 2000* (CMC).

From the mid-'70s through the early '80s, the Tubes' mixture of rock, theater, and satire proved more capable of achieving notoriety than sales. Despite one of the wildest stage shows in the business (verging at times on soft-core pornography) and critical acclaim for their records, their five LPs for A&M were flops (even though the first was produced by Al Kooper and the last by Todd Rundgren). The Tubes came close to scoring hits during this period with a pair of radio staples—the heavy-metal parody "White Punks on Dope" (featuring Waybill in the guise of Quay Lewd) and the mock-girl-group song "Don't Touch Me There."

Bill Spooner, Rick Anderson, and Vince Welnick started embryonic versions of the Tubes in their hometown of Phoenix in the late '60s, though they wouldn't come to be known as the Tubes until they moved to San Francisco in 1972. Early performances were generally reviled, and it took the group three years to build a cult following sufficient to justify a recording contract. But as each LP became another commercial setback, the Tubes began to streamline their act, and by 1980 they were down to six, after experimenting with a propless all-music live show. Many temporary members (not listed above), including several female vocalists, have passed through the ranks since then. When their self-conscious attempt at a hit record, "Don't Want to Wait Anymore," proved successful, the only Tubes present were Waybill and Prince. That song, along with the AOR hit "Talk to You Later," made the Tubes' Capitol debut, *The Completion Backward Principle* (#36, 1981), a big seller. Later that year, the group appeared in the movie *Xanadu*.

In 1983 "She's a Beauty" reached the Top 10, helped by an eye-catching and provocative video that was widely aired on MTV. The album from which it came, *Outside/Inside* (#18, 1983), became the group's best-selling album to date. But the Tubes' luck didn't hold, and two years later, *Love Bomb* (produced by Rundgren) stalled at #87. Waybill showed up on Richard Marx's debut album, and Vince Welnick joined the Grateful Dead, replacing deceased keyboardist Brent Mydland. The group re-formed in the early '90s, touring Europe and the U.S. from 1993 until 1995. After adding another singer and a second drummer, the Tubes recorded their first new studio album in a decade, 1996's *Genius of America*. They have since released several CDs of live and archival material.

Tanya Tucker

Born Oct. 10, 1958, Seminole, TX
1972—*Delta Dawn* (Columbia) 1973—*What's Your Mama's Name* 1974—*Would You Lay With Me (in a Field of Stone)* 1975—*Greatest Hits; Tanya Tucker* (MCA) 1976—*Lovin' and Learnin'; Here's Some Love* 1977—*Ridin' Rainbows; You Are So Beautiful* (Columbia); *Tanya Tucker's Greatest Hits* (MCA) 1978—*TNT* 1980—*Tear Me Apart; Dreamlovers* 1981—*Should I Do It?* 1982—*Live* 1983—*The Best of Tanya Tucker; Changes* (Arista) 1986—*Girls Like Me* (Capitol) 1987—*Love Me Like You Used To* 1988—*Strong Enough to Bend* 1989—*Greatest Hits* 1990—*Tennessee Woman; Greatest Hits Encore* 1991—*Greatest Country Hits* (Curb); *What Do I Do With Me* (Liberty) 1992—*Can't Run From Yourself* 1993—*Greatest Hits 1990–1992; Soon* 1995—*Fire to Fire* 1997—*Complicated* (Capitol).

In the beginning, three things made Tanya Tucker a major country-pop star at age 14: a fine voice, Billy Sherrill's MOR-Nashville production, and an image as a pubescent sexpot. In the years since, she has weathered tabloid accounts of her private life, treatment at the Betty Ford Center in 1989, and a three-year hiatus from recording at the peak of her career to emerge as a mature and extremely popular country star.

Tucker got into music through her construction-worker father, Beau Tucker, who took her to country shows after the family had moved to Wilcox, Arizona, and then to Phoenix. At age 13, she appeared in the film *Jeremiah Johnson*. Her first country hit was 1972's "Delta Dawn," followed by two #1 C&W hits: "What's Your Mama's Name" and "Blood Red and Goin' Down." At age 16 she made the #1 C&W single "Would You Lay With Me (in a Field of Stone)" (#46 pop, 1974).

After she reached the age of consent, Tucker left Columbia and producer Billy Sherrill and signed with MCA. In the late '70s, she briefly tried to become a rock singer, wearing

Tanya Tucker

leather (for *TNT*, at #54 pop, her highest-charting album of the '70s and '80s and gold) and adding fuzz-tone guitars, but she soon retreated into country music. A highly publicized liaison with country-pop crooner Glen Campbell included some duet recordings, but it ended in 1981, and Tucker continued to work the country circuit on her own.

In 1983 she moved to Arista Records; it was an unhappy pairing, and Tucker did not record for the next three years after her initial Arista album. She signed with Capitol Records in 1986 and began a comeback that eclipsed her earlier success. Her #1 C&W hits included "Just Another Love" (1986) and "I Won't Take Less Than Your Love" (1987); other hits were "Highway Robbery" (#2 C&W, 1988), "What Do I Do With Me" (#2 C&W, 1991), "Some Kind of Trouble" (#3 C&W, 1992), "If Your Heart Ain't Busy Tonight" (#4 C&W, 1992), "Two Sparrows in a Hurricane" (#2 C&W, 1992), "It's a Little Too Late" (#2 C&W, 1993), "Tell Me About It," a duet with Delbert McClinton (#4 C&W, 1993), and "Soon" (#2 C&W, 1993). *What Do I Do With Me* (#48 pop, #9 C&W, 1991) was her first platinum album and her biggest crossover success to date. *Can't Run From Yourself* (#51 pop, #12 C&W, 1992) was also certified platinum. With her father functioning as her manager again, Tucker tours heavily. She also appears on *Common Thread*, the Eagles tribute, on *Rhythm Country & Blues*, where she duets with Little Richard on the Eddie Cochran classic "Somethin' Else," and has recorded an as-yet-unreleased duet with Frank Sinatra, "Embraceable

You." Her nonmusical business enterprises include a line of Western wear, salsa, and an exercise video.

In 1997 Tucker published her autobiography, *Nickel Dreams*, a lively account of her life and career that went to #2 on the *New York Times* bestseller list. Tucker also released her 30th album, *Complicated;* a single from the record, "Little Things," reached the country Top 10. In 1998 Tucker sued her record company, Capitol Nashville, claiming that they wouldn't release her from her contract. As of this writing, the case is still pending.

Ike and Tina Turner

Ike Turner, born Izear Luster Turner, Nov. 5, 1931, Clarksdale, MS; Tina Turner, born Anna Mae Bullock, Nov. 26, 1939, Brownsville, TN
1961—*The Soul of Ike & Tina Turner* (Sue) 1962—*Don't Play Me Cheap; It's Gonna Work Out Fine* 1964—*Get It* (Cenco); *Ike & Tina Turner Revue!!!* (Sue) 1965—*Live! The Ike & Tina Turner Show* (Warner Bros.) 1967—*The Ike & Tina Turner Show, vol. II* 1969—*Outta Season* (Blue Thumb); *River Deep—Mountain High* (A&M); *The Hunter* (Blue Thumb) 1970—*Come Together* (Liberty) 1971—*Working Together; Live in Paris; Live at Carnegie Hall/What You Hear Is What You Get* (United Artists); *'Nuff Said* 1972—*Feel Good; Let Me Touch Your Mind* 1973—*Live: The World of Ike & Tina Turner; Nutbush City Limits* 1974—*The Gospel According to Ike & Tina Turner; Sweet Rhode Island Red* 1977—*Delilah's Power* 1985—*Get Back!* (Liberty).
Ike Turner solo: 1972—*Blues Roots* (United Artists) 1973—*Bad Dreams* 1988—*My Blues Country* (Resurgent) 2001—*Here & Now.*
Ike Turner with the Family Vibes: 1971—*Ike Turner Presents: The Family Vibes* (United Artists) 1973—*Confined to Soul.*
Ike and Tina Turner and Homegrown Funk: 1980—*The Edge* (Fantasy).
Tina Turner solo: see entry.

Ike Turner and his wife Tina were first known for their late-'60s and early-'70s recordings and their soul revue. Prior to that, however, Ike was well established as a seminal figure in the early years of rock & roll as both a performer and talent scout. During her tenure with Ike, Tina was one of the most flamboyant, overtly sexual performers in rock. Their recordings rarely captured the intensity of their live performances; in fact, their only gold album and one of their two highest charting is a live album (*Live at Carnegie Hall*, #25, 1970). Beginning in 1976, when Tina snuck out of a hotel and left Ike with just 36 cents in her pocket, she embarked on one of the longest but ultimately most successful comebacks in rock history.

Ike Turner grew up in racist Clarksdale, Mississippi. When he was a child, his father was abducted and beaten by a white man, then died from his injuries after being refused admission to a whites-only hospital. As a child he learned to play piano (from Pinetop Perkins, he claims), and by his teens was leading his own band, which included singer Jackie Brenston. With over 30 members, the group eventually split into two bands—the Top Hatters and Turner's Kings of Rhythm. Turner, who plays a number of instruments, performed uncredited on numerous early R&B and rock & roll tracks. In 1951 he recorded "Rocket '88'" at Sam Phillips' Sun studio in Memphis with lead vocal by saxophonist Jackie Brenston. Unfortunately, Brenston and the Delta Cats, not Ike Turner and the Kings of Rhythm, got the label credit. It became a #1 R&B hit, and over the years it has been frequently cited as the first rock & roll record. Turner went on to become a top session guitarist, talent scout, and producer through the '50s, recording with Junior Parker and Howlin' Wolf, B.B. King, Otis Rush, Roscoe Gordon, Bobby "Blue" Bland, and Johnny Ace.

Turner and his Kings of Rhythm were playing St. Louis nightclubs when he met Anna Mae Bullock. Bullock repeatedly asked Turner if she could sing with his band; he said that she could but never called her to the stage. One night Bullock, who had never sung professionally but had been appearing in talent shows since childhood, simply grabbed the microphone and sang. Soon after, he changed her name to Tina. They eventually married, in Tijuana in 1962, though Ike was still married to another woman at the time. At various times both Ike and Tina have described their marriage as less than ideal.

Even though they were not yet married, they first recorded as Ike and Tina Turner in 1960 after a singer failed to appear for a session. Tina stood in for the missing singer, and the song, "A Fool in Love," became a hit in 1960 (#27 pop, #2 R&B). Ike then developed an entire revue around Tina. Ike later claimed that he patterned her aggressive image after a female Tarzan character he saw in a movie as a child. With

Tina and Ike Turner

nine musicians and three scantily clad female background singers called the Ikettes, the Ike and Tina Turner Revue became a major soul act. In 1961 they charted with "It's Gonna Work Out Fine" (#14 pop. #2 R&B) and "I Idolize You" (#5 R&B). The following year, "Poor Fool" (#38 pop, #4 R&B) and "Tra La La La La" (#9 R&B) were hits. From the mid-'60s on, they were major stars in England, where artists such as the Rolling Stones were unabashed fans. In 1966 Phil Spector recorded them for his last Wall of Sound masterpiece, "River Deep—Mountain High." It went to #3 in England, but did poorly in the U.S. Spector, who believed it to be the finest recording of his career, was so crushed by its disappointing showing that he announced his retirement and went into seclusion. (The Revue also appears in Spector's feature-length concert film, *The Big T.N.T. Show.*)

The Turners continued to make pop hits into the late '60s and opened for the Rolling Stones on their 1969 tour. They were especially successful into the early '70s with steamy covers such as "Come Together" (#57 pop, #21 R&B), "I Want to Take You Higher" (#34 pop, #25 R&B), and "Proud Mary" (#4 pop, #5 R&B), which earned them their only Grammy, for Best R&B Vocal Performance by a Group. Throughout this time, they were also frequent guests on television variety shows. Interestingly, their widespread appeal did not translate into big album sales. The aforementioned *Live at Carnegie Hall* tied *Workin' Together* (1970) for their highest-charting pop album, at #25. Only those and 1969's *Outta Season* made the Top 100 albums chart. The Ikettes (which had numerous personnel changes through the years) had a couple of pop hits on their own: "I'm Blue (The Gong-Gong Song)" (#19, 1962) and "Peaches 'n' Cream" (#36, 1965).

Beginning in 1974, with *Tina Turns the Country On,* Tina began a parallel, initially commercially unsuccessful solo career. After a tumultuous relationship, which she has since described as being marked by physical and emotional abuse, Tina left Ike in 1976 [see solo entry].

Around the time Tina left him, Ike Turner retired to his studio in Inglewood, California, and released two solo LPs. The studio was destroyed by fire in 1982. After 11 arrests on various charges, in 1990 Ike was convicted on several charges, including possessing and transporting cocaine, and sentenced to 18 months in jail. He was in prison when he and Tina were inducted into the Rock and Roll Hall of Fame in January 1991. In September of that year, he was released from jail.

Ike published his autobiography, *Takin' Back My Name* (with an introduction by Little Richard, who claims to have taught Tina how to sing), in 1999. In the book and in numerous interviews he granted through the '90s, he has disputed Tina's account of their marriage and has taken particular issue with how he was depicted in the Disney film based on Tina's autobiography *(I, Tina), What's Love Got to Do With It.* In the late '90s he began writing a column for *Juke Blues* magazine; he performs occasionally and continues to record. In 2001 the release of *Here & Now*, his first album of new material in decades, was marked by numerous live appearances.

Big Joe Turner

Born May 18, 1911, Kansas City, MO; died Nov. 24, 1985, Inglewood, CA
1956—*The Boss of the Blues: Joe Turner Sings Kansas City Jazz* (Atlantic) 1960—*Big Joe Rides Again* 1976—*Nobody in Mind* (Pablo) 1977—*Things That I Used to Do* 1980—*The Midnight Special; The Best of Big Joe Turner* 1981—*Have No Fear Joe Turner Is Here* 1983—*Life Ain't Easy; Blues Train* (Muse) 1984—*Kansas City Here I Come* (Pablo) 1986—*Big Joe Turner Memorial Album: Rhythm & Blues Years* (Atlantic) 1987—*Big Joe Turner: Greatest Hits* 1989—*Flip, Flop & Fly* (Pablo) 1994—*Big, Bad & Blue: The Big Joe Turner Anthology* (Rhino).

Big Joe Turner is indisputably one of rock & roll's forefathers. Songwriter Doc Pomus once remarked of Turner, "Rock & roll would never have happened without him," and many historians agree. Turner was a classic old-style blues shouter whose powerful voice and often playful delivery turned jump-blues staples including "Shake, Rattle and Roll," "Honey Hush," "Sweet Sixteen," "Chains of Love," and "Flip, Flop and Fly" into stepping stones marking the path from the blues to rock & roll. He had been singing for over 20 years when he recorded those songs in the early '50s, and he performed until just months before his death, following years of chronic health problems, at age 74.

Turner got his start as a singing bartender in a Kansas City cabaret in the late '20s. He was already known as one of the most powerful blues singers west of the Mississippi when he teamed up with boogie-woogie pianist Pete Johnson and became one of the originators of "blues shouting." In 1938 talent scout John Hammond brought Turner and Johnson to New York to appear at the Carnegie Hall concert that sparked the boogie-woogie craze of the late '30s and early '40s. As their engagement at Cafe Society—a New York jazz club—extended into a four-year run, boogie-woogie bumped its way into mainstream white pop for the first time. Turner sang jazz-style show blues with pianist Art Tatum, but he also shouted fast boogie-woogie blues with Johnson. The propulsive rhythms and extroverted vocals of songs like "Roll 'Em Pete" showed the stirrings of the rhythm & blues that became popular in the years after World War II.

In 1941 Turner went to Hollywood to appear in Duke Ellington's Jump for Joy Revue. He was based on the West Coast for most of the '40s, joined occasionally by Johnson and pianist Albert Ammons. In 1951 he returned to New York to play the Apollo Theatre with Count Basie. There he met Ahmet Ertegun and Jerry Wexler, who brought him to Atlantic Records, where Ertegun's "Chains of Love" gave him a #2 R&B hit. (Pat Boone had a #10 pop hit with the song five years later.) It was the first of a string of R&B hits on Atlantic between 1951 and 1956, each of which is a rock & roll classic: "Sweet Sixteen" (#4, 1952), "Honey Hush" (#2, 1953), "T.V. Mama" (#9, 1954), "Shake, Rattle and Roll" (#2, 1954, a big hit for Bill Haley later that year in a bowdlerized form), "Flip, Flop and Fly" (#3, 1955), "The Chicken and the Hawk" (#13, 1956), "Corrina, Corrina" (#3, 1956; at #41, his biggest pop hit), and

"Rock a While" (#12, 1956). In addition to Ertegun's songs, his own, and his brother Lou Willie Turner's, he recorded material by Doc Pomus and Leiber and Stoller. The backing musicians on his classic Atlantic R&B sessions included, variously, King Curtis, Mickey Baker, Sam Taylor, Al Sears, Panama Francis, and Choker Campbell.

While he never had the pop success of his imitators, who often cleaned up the sexual metaphors and took some of the energy out of the songs, Turner continued to work through good times and bad. He toured Europe several times in the '50s; and in the '60s and '70s he appeared and recorded with the Johnny Otis Show, Eddie "Lockjaw" Davis, Milt Jackson, Roy Eldridge, Dizzy Gillespie, and Pee Wee Crayton. In 1974 he was featured with Count Basie in *The Last of the Blue Devils,* a film about the Kansas City music scene.

Beginning in the early '80s, Turner suffered from diabetes and arthritis. Later in the decade heart and kidney problems often forced him to walk on crutches, then perform seated. Despite this, his voice never wavered.

Tina Turner

Born Anna Mae Bullock, Nov. 26, 1939, Brownsville, TN
1974—*Tina Turns the Country On* (United Artists)
1975—*Acid Queen* 1978—*Rough* 1979—*Love Explosion*
1984—*Private Dancer* (Capitol) 1986—*Break Every Rule*
1988—*Tina Live in Europe* 1989—*Foreign Affair* 1991—*Simply the Best* 1993—*What's Love Got to Do With It* soundtrack (Virgin) 1994—*The Collected Recordings: Sixties to Nineties* (Capitol) 1996—*Wildest Dreams* (Virgin) 2000—*Twenty Four Seven.*

After a tumultuous relationship, which she has described as being marked by physical and emotional abuse (claims her ex-husband disputes), Tina left Ike Turner in 1976 for what would prove one of the greatest comeback stories in popular music history.

Anna Mae Bullock grew up in Nutbush, Tennessee, the daughter of a black overseer and church deacon father and a part–Native American mother. When she was three, her parents moved away to find better work; grandparents essentially raised Turner and her older sister. Eventually her parents divorced and her mother settled in St. Louis, where Turner moved during high school. It was there that she met Ike Turner at the Club Manhattan. (Her early years with Ike are recounted in that entry.)

Turner had made two solo albums while with Ike. *Acid Queen* (#155, 1975) was named after her memorable role in Ken Russell's film *Tommy.* After leaving Ike in 1976 (they divorced in 1978), Turner got a few bookings but at one point was forced to live on food stamps. A Buddhist since the early '70s, Turner persevered. She recorded two unsuccessful late-'70s albums that were heavy on covers of all genres (from "The Bitch Is Back" to the syrupy "Sometimes When We Touch"). Prior to that, she had placed a cover of Led Zeppelin's "Whole Lotta Love" on the R&B chart, at #61, in 1975. Turner's comeback began in earnest in 1981, when the Rolling Stones offered her a few opening spots on their U.S. tour. Around that time she also opened some shows for Rod Stewart and toured the world. In 1983 she landed a solo deal and by year's end had a U.K. hit with her steamy cover of Al Green's "Let's Stay Together" (#6 U.K.). Her U.S. breakthrough came with *Private Dancer* (#3, 1984), an 11-million-selling international smash that included "Let's Stay Together" (#26 pop, #3 R&B, 1984), "What's Love Got to Do With It" (#1 pop, #2 R&B, 1984), "Better Be Good to Me" (#5 pop, #6 R&B, 1984), and "Private Dancer" (#7 pop, #3 R&B, 1985). Her next two nonalbum songs were from the Mel Gibson film *Mad Max Beyond Thunderdome* (1985), in which Turner costarred as Auntie Entity: "We Don't Need Another Hero (Thunderdome)" (#2 pop, #3 R&B, 1985) and "One of the Living" (#15 pop, #41 R&B, 1985). Turner swept the Grammys in 1984, with "What's Love Got to Do With It" winning Best Female Pop Vocal Performance, and "Better Be Good to Me" taking Best Rock Vocal Performance. "What's Love" was also recognized as Song of the Year and Record of the Year. The following year "One of the Living" won Best Female Rock Performance.

Break Every Rule (#4, 1986), another platinum release, included "Typical Male" (#2 pop, #3 R&B, 1986), "Two People" (#30 pop, #18 R&B, 1986), and "What You Get Is What You See" (#13, 1987). In late 1985 she released a live duet with Bryan Adams, "It's Only Love," which went to #15. Turner, long legendary for her live shows, toured tirelessly. She has always been especially popular in Europe and in England, where *Tina Live in Europe* went to #8 as opposed to #86 in the United States. Despite the relatively disappointing chart showing, *Live in Europe* earned Turner a Best Female Rock Vocal Performance Grammy. She duetted with Mick Jagger at Live Aid in 1985 and is a favorite of British rock stars. Her international tours broke records in many cities. In 1986 Turner took home the Best Female Rock Vocal Performance Grammy for "Back Where You Started."

In 1986 she published her bestselling autobiography, *I, Tina* (cowritten with Kurt Loder), in which she maintained that Ike had been abusing her since the '60s. Her litany of his crimes against her include hitting her, pouring hot coffee on her face, burning her lip with a lighted cigarette, and forcing her to perform while ill and pregnant. She also wrote that she had attempted suicide in 1968.

In 1989 came Turner's first album of new material in over three years, *Foreign Affair* (#31, 1989). Its singles included "The Best" (#15, 1989), with a sax solo by Edgar Winter, and Tony Joe White's "Steamy Windows" (#39, 1990). While it was not her most successful album in the U.S., it outsold *Private Dancer* in the U.K. Also in 1989 Turner celebrated her 50th birthday with a star-studded party that included Mark Knopfler (who wrote "Private Dancer"), Eric Clapton, and other admirers. Turner and Rod Stewart's remake of the Marvin Gaye–Tammi Terrell hit "It Takes Two" went to #5 in the U.K. in 1990. A year later, her greatest-hits package *Simply the Best* went to #1 in the U.K. but didn't clear the Hot 100 albums chart here. In 1992 Turner signed to Virgin.

Turner's autobiography was made into a hit feature film,

What's Love Got to Do With It (1993); the soundtrack (#17, 1993) spawned the hit single "I Don't Wanna Fight" (#9 pop, #51 R&B, 1993), which was cowritten by Steve DuBerry and Lulu.

Dividing her time in the '90s between homes in Zurich, Switzerland, and the South of France, Turner, a Nichiren Shoshu Buddhist for many years, continues to record and tour. In 1996 she released *Wildest Dreams* (#61, 1996), a strong return to form (its 1997 tour was sponsored by Hanes hosiery, in tribute to Turner's famous legs), although only one of its singles, a remake of John Waits' "Missing You" (#84 pop, 1996) made the pop chart. R&B hit singles included "GoldenEye" (the theme from a James Bond thriller that was written for Turner by Bono and the Edge and produced by Nellee Hooper) (#89 R&B, 1995), "Something Beautiful Remains" (#34 R&B, 1996), and the title track, which featured Barry White (#34 R&B). *Twenty Four Seven* (#21 pop, #29 R&B, 2000) entered the charts at #21, the highest chart debut position of her career. In 2000, past age 60, she launched what she announced would be her last stadium tour.

The Turtles/Flo & Eddie

Formed 1962, Westchester, CA
Howard Kaylan (b. Howard Kaplan, June 22, 1947, Bronx, NY), voc.; Mark Volman (b. Apr. 19, 1947, Los Angeles, CA), voc., gtr., sax; Al Nichol (b. Mar. 31, 1946, Winston-Salem, NC), gtr.; Chuck Portz (b. Mar. 28, 1945, Santa Monica, CA), bass; Donald Ray Murray (b. Nov. 8, 1945), drums; Dale Walton, gtr.
Ca. 1963–64—(– Walton; + Tom Stanton, gtr.; – Stanton; + Jim Tucker, gtr.)
1963—*Out of Control* (as the Crossfires) (NA) 1964—(name change to the Turtles) 1965—*It Ain't Me Babe* (White Whale) 1966—*You Baby* 1967—(– Murray; + John Barbata, drums) *Happy Together* (– Portz; + Jim Pons [b. Mar. 14, 1943, Santa Monica], bass; – Tucker) *The Turtles! Golden Hits* (– Barbata; + John Seiter, drums) 1968—*The Turtles Present the Battle of the Bands* 1969—*Turtle Soup* 1970—*More Golden Hits; Wooden Head* 1975—*Happy Together Again* (Sire) 1983—*20 Greatest Hits* (Rhino) 1987—*The Best of the Turtles* 1988—*Turtle Wax: The Best of the Turtles, vol. 2* 1992—*Captured Live* (as the Turtles featuring Flo & Eddie) 1995—*30 Years of Rock 'n' Roll: Happy Together* (LaserLight).
Flo & Eddie: 1972—*The Phlorescent Leech & Eddie* (Reprise) 1973—*Flo & Eddie* 1975—*Illegal, Immoral and Fattening* (Columbia) 1976—*Moving Targets* 1981—*Rock Steady With Flo & Eddie* (Epiphany) 1987—*The Best of Flo & Eddie* (Rhino).

The Turtles were a serious rock band that, through a series of catchy mid- to late-'60s hit singles, was passed off as—and burdened by the image of—happy-go-lucky Top 40 lightweights. Never creatively satisfied with the classic pop material that made them famous, the group (led by vocalists Howard Kaylan and Mark Volman) aspired instead to a more sophisticated Beatlesque style and more socially relevant material. These aspirations—coupled with devastating managerial, financial, and legal problems—broke up the band. Volman, Kaylan, and bassist Jim Pons' subsequent tenure with Frank Zappa, and Volman and Kaylan's duo career as the Phlorescent Leech [Flo] & Eddie, give some indication of the group the Turtles might have been.

The name "Turtles" came from White Whale Records. Prior to the band's signing in 1965, the L.A.-based combo had been known as the Nightriders, and later as the Crossfires. Their local singles during that time were uniformly unsuccessful. Once under contract, they were converted from a surf group (White Whale astutely noting that the trend was on the wane) to folk rock, then in vogue thanks to Bob Dylan, the Byrds, et al. Their debut single, Dylan's "It Ain't Me Babe," went Top 10 in 1965 and launched the band on a brief string of hits: "Let Me Be" (#20, 1965) and "You Baby" (#20, 1966), followed by "Grim Reaper of Love" (#81, 1966) and "Can I Get to Know You Better" (#89, 1966). Each of these showcased the group's trademark sound, a sophisticated pop rock dominated by Kaylan and Volman's distinctive vocals.

The Turtles were not content, however, and were about to break up; but first they released "Happy Together" (#1, 1967), which proved to be their biggest hit, and one of 1967's top 10 records. With their career reinvigorated, "She'd Rather Be With Me" (#3, 1967), "You Know What I Mean" (#12, 1967), and "She's My Girl" (#14, 1967) were followup hits.

Though it included their last two hit 45s—"Elenore" (#6, 1968) and "You Showed Me" (#6, 1969) (one of the first hit singles to feature a Moog synthesizer)—*The Turtles Present the Battle of the Bands* (#128, 1968) was an ambitious reflection of the group's desire to be more than AM-radio fodder. Each song was meant to sound completely different from the others, literally as if performed by a different group. The gatefold sleeve presented the Turtles dressed in 11 guises, including the Crossfires, the country-rock Quad City Ramblers, and the greaser group U.S. Teens featuring Raoul. The next album, *Turtle Soup* (#117, 1969), was produced by the Kinks' Ray Davies when he was at his least commercial. The Turtles played the White House, at the invitation of Tricia Nixon, in May 1969. Their most successful LPs were *Happy Together* (#25, 1967) and *The Turtles! Golden Hits* (#7, 1967).

Unfortunately, around the time "Happy Together" hit, the Turtles became enmeshed in legal battles that would drag on for years to come. Defeated but unbowed, the band split up in mid-1970 but did not quit the business.

Throughout their career, the Turtles had fluid personnel; only lead guitarist Al Nichol was with them from Crossfires to breakup. After some of the original members quit, replacements were found in ex-Leaves (who had one hit with "Hey Joe") bassist Jim Pons and drummer John Barbata. After Barbata quit the group, he drummed with Crosby, Stills, Nash and Young and the Jefferson Starship. Pons stuck with Volman and Kaylan into Zappa's band and the initial Flo & Eddie group. Other temporary Turtles included onetime Monkees producer Chip Douglas (he appeared on "Happy Together") and former Spanky and Our Gang drummer John Seiter.

Prohibited by their record company from using not only the Turtles name but their given names professionally in music, Volman and Kaylan became the Phlorescent Leech [Flo] & Eddie. The duo (with Pons) joined Frank Zappa and contributed to *Chunga's Revenge* (1970), *Live at the Fillmore*

East (1971), the *200 Motels* album and film (1971), and *Just Another Band From L.A.* (which included the Turtles' "Happy Together") (1972). Although they originally used the Phlorescent moniker to avoid contractual problems, the name stuck. Their shows and albums combine straight songs with devastating sendups of rock personalities, genres, and events. They lampooned Pink Floyd's The Wall show with "The Fence," a flimsy bamboo fence over which they tossed cheap inflatable toy animals. Another popular mid-'70s, energy-crisis era routine turned the Village People's "In the Navy" into "In the Gasline." Over the years, no one and nothing—from Kiss to Joni Mitchell, Jim Morrison to Fleetwood Mac, *Flashdance* to the Beastie Boys—has been spared their dead-on, sometimes silly, sendups and satires. As Volman once told Rolling Stone, "We've never catered to the industry we were trying to succeed in."

They briefly gave up touring in 1976 following the accidental death of their guitarist, Philip Reed (he fell from a window, prompting some reports that his death was a suicide), and the untimely death of another close friend, Marc Bolan (T. Rex). Besides several LPs (the second produced by Bob Ezrin), they scored and contributed dialogue to an X-rated animation film called *Dirty Duck*. They have written columns for several publications, including *Creem, Phonograph Record,* and the *L.A. Free Press*. At various times beginning in the mid-'70s they have hosted their own radio program on such stations as L.A.'s KROQ and KMET, New York's WLIR and WXRK, and in syndication. Their instantly recognizable harmonies have graced tracks by Marc Bolan and T. Rex, Stephen Stills, John Lennon and Yoko Ono, Hoyt Axton, Keith Moon, David Cassidy, Alice Cooper, Tonio K., Blondie, the Knack, Sammy Hagar, Burton Cummings, Paul Kantner's Planet Earth Rock & Roll Orchestra, Roger McGuinn, the Psychedelic Furs, Duran Duran, the Ramones, and Bruce Springsteen ("Hungry Heart"), among others.

Beginning in 1980 Flo & Eddie produced and composed a series of popular childrens' records for the *Strawberry Shortcake* and *Care Bears* soundtracks. Kaylan appeared in the film *Get Crazy* (1983). Their annual New Year's Eve shows at New York's the Bottom Line have been a tradition since the '70s.

Volman and Kaylan, as Flo & Eddie, also resurrect the Turtles name for shows. Beginning in the mid-'80s the pair, with a backing band, have appeared with the Turtles, leading the Happy Together Tour, which included other '60s acts. In 1999 Volman received his master's degree in screenwriting. When not touring with Kaylan and the group, Volman teaches college courses on the music business. Pons currently codirects the David Center, a New York–area organization dedicated to helping children with autism.

Shania Twain

Born Eileen Regina Edwards, Aug. 28, 1965, Windsor, Can.
1993—*Shania Twain* (Mercury) 1995—*The Woman in Me* 1997—*Come On Over* 1999—*Come On Over: International Version.*

Within the span of five years Shania Twain went from singing in a resort in the Canadian boondocks to becoming the biggest sensation to hit Nashville since Garth Brooks. Combining glossy pop hooks, arena-rock crunch, and turbocharged twang with MTV-age marketing savvy, Twain has not only sold more records than any female country singer in history but has emerged as an international pop superstar. What makes her transformation all the more remarkable is that she achieved it by overcoming great personal hardship.

Twain grew up poor in the small, rural outpost of Timmins, Ontario, where her birth father walked out on the family before Shania was out of diapers. She started singing early, getting plenty of encouragement from her mother and adoptive father, Jerry Twain, an Ojibway Indian in whose honor she took the name Shania, which is Ojibway for "I'm on my way." By the time Twain was eight, she was performing at social events and talent contests and, after that, on radio, TV, and in bars. Tragedy, however, struck when her mother and stepfather were killed in an auto accident. Forced to put her budding career on hold to care for her four younger brothers, Shania, then 21, took a job singing show tunes, pop, rock, and country hits at a resort in Deerhurst, Ontario. She did that for three years until her brothers were old enough to live on their own. Then in 1991 she moved to Nashville, where she secured a contract with Mercury Records, which released her self-titled debut album (#67 C&W, 1993). Suffering from lackluster material and assembly-line production, it yielded only two minor singles.

Twain's fortune changed when she met hard-rock producer Robert John "Mutt" Lange, who had produced Foreigner, AC/DC, Def Leppard, and other rock bands. Having seen one of Twain's videos, he called to express an interest in collaborating with her. The two subsequently met, married, and embarked on the most successful musical and marital partnership of the '90s. For *The Woman in Me* (#5 pop, #1 C&W, 1995), the couple took Twain originals that Mercury had rejected for her debut, pumped up the volume, and burnished them with a metallic rock and pop sheen. The record also found Twain eschewing the wholesome, demure image she projected on her debut in favor of a bold, sexy new persona. The record produced seven hit singles, including "Any Man of Mine" (#31 pop, #1 C&W, 1995) and "(If You're Not in It for Love) I'm Outta Here" (#74 pop, #1 C&W, 1995). Buoyed by a string of suggestive, midriff-baring videos, as well as Twain's Madonna-like entrepreneurial flair, the album sold in excess of 12 million copies, consolidating the pop-country insurrection started by Garth Brooks, and all without a single tour date to support it.

Critics were divided about Twain's music and image. Nashville boosters claimed that Twain brought country in step with pop, while feminists argued that she was pandering to male libidos to sell records. Fans, however, couldn't get enough, and in 1997 Twain and Lange delivered again with the monumental, defiantly pro-woman *Come On Over* (#2 pop, #1 C&W). The album included a whopping nine hit singles, with "You're Still the One" (#2 pop, #1 C&W, 1998) and "That Don't Impress Me Much" (#7 pop, 1999, #8 C&W, 1998), among others, crossing over into the pop Top 10.

Twain also toured for the first time, playing a string of sold-out dates that were long on bombast and spectacle but likely helped her to secure 1998 Grammy Awards for Best Country Song and Best Female Country Vocal Performance. A perennial Nashville outsider, Twain nevertheless took home Entertainer of the Year honors at the 1999 Country Music Association Awards as well. At sales of 18 million and counting, *Come On Over* has also now become the best-selling album in country music history. A collection of remixes titled *Come On Over: International Version* followed in 1999.

Dwight Twilley

Born June 6, 1952, Tulsa, OK
As the Dwight Twilley Band: 1976—*Sincerely* (Shelter) 1977—*Twilley Don't Mind* (Arista).
Solo: 1979—*Twilley* 1982—*Scuba Divers* (EMI America) 1984—*Jungle* 1986—*Wild Dogs* (CBS) 1993—*The Great Lost Twilley Album* (DCC) 1996—*XXI* (The Right Stuff) 1999—*Tulsa* (Copper); *Between the Cracks, vol. 1* (Not Lame).

Dwight Twilley made a music career out of trying to fuse Elvis Presley's rockabilly with the Beatles' pop, and he never came closer than on his very first single. He and partner Phil Seymour became overnight sensations when "I'm on Fire" came out of nowhere and went Top 20 in 1975. Following that early success, Twilley was bogged down by a split with Seymour, erratic live appearances, and myriad troubles with record companies.

Twilley and collaborator Phil Seymour met when they were 16-year-old Tulsans at a screening of the Beatles' *A Hard Day's Night*. They began playing music together, eventually going to Memphis and doing some recordings at the old Sun studio. They ended up in L.A., and as the Dwight Twilley Band, signed to the shaky Shelter Records. Twilley and Seymour laid down nearly all the parts on their two LPs, *Sincerely* and *Twilley Don't Mind*. Though they were popular with critics, neither album was a commercial success, partially due to Shelter's incompetence; for example, there was no LP to capitalize on the success of "I'm on Fire" for over a year. Seymour left to pursue a solo career in 1978.

Eventually, Twilley freed himself of Shelter and got into a new struggle with his next label, Arista. Following the release of *Twilley* and "Somebody to Love" some months later, Arista rejected his second solo album. After a lengthy battle, Twilley put out *Scuba Divers* on a new label, EMI, in 1982, complete with a redone version of "Somebody to Love." Twilley finally achieved some of the commercial success that had long been predicted for him with "Girls" (#16, 1984) from *Jungle* (#39, 1984).

Meanwhile, after splitting from Twilley, Seymour found some success with a #22 hit in 1981 with "Precious to Me." In addition to recording a couple of solo albums, Seymour worked with a number of other artists, including Del Shannon, and later as a member of the Textones. In 1985 he was diagnosed with lymphoma, which resulted in his death on August 17, 1993, in Tarzana, California, at 41.

Twilley returned somewhat to the limelight in 1992 when his "Why You Wanna Break My Heart" was included on the *Wayne's World* soundtrack, followed by the 1994 publication of his well-received book for divorced fathers, *Questions From Dad*. The latter project led to Twilley receiving an award from the Children's Rights Council. After an earthquake destroyed his L.A. home, Twilley returned to Tulsa, where he recorded his first new album in 13 years. He was joined by original Dwight Twilley Band guitarist Bill Pitcock and other Tulsa-based musicians. *Tulsa* was released on the tiny Copper label in 1999.

Twisted Sister

Formed 1973, Ho-Ho-Kus, NJ
Numerous personnel changes. Best-known lineup: Jay Jay French (b. John French Segall, July 20, 1954, New York, NY), gtr.; Mark "The Animal" Mendoza (b. July 13, 1956, Long Island, NY), bass; Eddie Ojeda (b. Aug. 5, 1954, Bronx, NY), gtr.; A.J. Pero (b. Oct. 14, 1959, New York), drums; Dee Snider (b. Daniel Snider, Mar. 15, 1955, Massapequa, NY), voc.
1982—*Under the Blade* (Secret) 1983—*You Can't Stop Rock and Roll* (Atlantic) 1984—*Stay Hungry* 1985—*Come Out and Play* 1987—(– Pero; + Joe Franco, drums) *Love Is for Suckers* 2000—*Club Daze* (Spitfire).
Widowmaker (Snider; Franco; + Marc Russell, bass; + Al Pitrelli, gtr.): 1992—*Blood and Bullets* (Esquire) 1994—*Stand by for Pain* (Music for Nations).
Dee Snider: 2000—*Never Let the Bastards Wear You Down* (Koch Entertainment).

Twisted Sister's mix of Who-style adolescent rebellion and Alice Cooper makeup was a textbook example of mid- to late-'70s glitter/bar band style. Their 15-year career might read like a thousand others were it not for a single Top 40 hit, "We're Not Gonna Take It" (#21, 1984) and the metal anthem "I Wanna Rock."

Dressed in the most excessive glitter/trash styles, with highly teased hair and lavish eye makeup, Twisted Sister amassed a large following throughout the New York tri-state area but little label interest. Even without a record, Twisted Sister was popular enough to sell out New York City's 3,400-seat Palladium in 1979. They released the independent *Under the Blade* in 1982. After an appearance on the British TV show *The Tube* that year, the group signed with Atlantic.

You Can't Stop Rock and Roll (#130, 1983) sold poorly, and Twisted Sister was relegated to second-division status until they made a splash at an English rock festival. With their reputation as a live band assured, it took the 1984 video for "We're Not Gonna Take It," with lead singer Dee Snider's mad Pierrot image and comically antiestablishment, patricidal storyline, to bring the band to the mainstream, sending the album *Stay Hungry* to #15. For a while Snider was a familiar face, as a regular guest on Howard Stern's radio program, a popular metal-magazine poster boy, and—along with Frank Zappa—as a spokesman against censorship at the Senate subcommittee on communications hearings. In 1987 he wrote (with Philip Bashe) a fairly serious and well-received book of advice for teenagers entitled *Dee Snider's Teenage Survival Guide: How to Be a Legend in Your Own Lunchtime.* Subsequent albums never matched *Stay Hungry*'s popularity, and the band called it quits in 1987.

Unsurprisingly, Snider has remained the most active of Twisted Sister's members. After the band's demise, he formed Desperado, whose album *Bloodied but Unbowed* was supposed to come out on Elektra, but never did; his next band, Widowmaker, released a couple of flop albums. Snider's 2000 solo release *Never Let the Bastards Wear You Down* includes mostly '80s material, along with a cover of AC/DC's "Sin City" by a reunited Twisted Sister. In addition to hosting the syndicated radio show *House of Hair,* Snider also wrote and starred in the 1998 movie *Strangeland,* which featured a character, Captain Howdy, first introduced on Twisted Sister's *Stay Hungry* album.

In 1999 the cosmetics company Urban Decay named one of its colors after Twisted Sister, ensuring that the band would be remembered as one of the brightest footnotes in heavy-metal history. In 2000 group members requested that controversial then–Atlanta Braves pitcher John Rocker cease using their "I Wanna Rock" as his personal theme following his antigay, antiminority comments.

2 Live Crew

Formed 1985, Miami, FL
Luke Skyywalker (b. Luther Campbell, Dec. 22, 1960, Miami), voc.; Fresh Kid Ice (b. Christopher Wong-Won, May 29, Trinidad), voc.; Brother Marquis (b. Mark Ross, Apr. 2, New York, NY), voc.; Mr. Mixx (b. David Hobbs, Sep. 29, CA), DJ.
1986—*The 2 Live Crew Is What We Are* (Luke Skyywalker) 1987—*Move Somethin'* 1989—*As Nasty as They Wanna Be; As Clean as They Wanna Be; Live in Concert* (Effect) 1991—*Sports Weekend (As Nasty as They Wanna Be Part II)* (Luke) (– Ross; – Hobbs; + Verb [b. Larry Dobson], voc.) 1994—*Back at Your Ass for the Nine-4* 1996—(+ Ross; + Hobbs) *Shake a Lil' Somethin'* (Lil' Joe) 1998—*The Real One.*
Luke Featuring the 2 Live Crew: 1990—*Banned in the U.S.A.* (Luke/Atlantic).
Luke solo: 1993—*In the Nude* (Luke) 1994—*Freak for Life 6996* 1996—*Uncle Luke* (Luther Campbell) 1997—*Changin' the Game* (Luke) 2001—*Somethin' Nasty.*

2 Live Crew had been making frankly salacious, but otherwise unexceptional, rap recordings for five years before gaining a national notoriety it otherwise may never have found, thanks to Florida authorities who sought to ban the group's records. 2 Live Crew's 1989 album *As Nasty as They Wanna Be* did, in fact, become the first recording ever declared obscene by an American court of law—even though the group had put a "parental warning" sticker on it and made an edited version, *As Clean as They Wanna Be.* But by March 1993 every obscenity ruling against the group had been overturned.

2 Live Crew founder Luther Campbell claimed to be raised a Catholic, as well as a devoted, community-minded family man; he defended his music as comedy—and indeed, more than any other rap act, 2 Live Crew drew on the black comic tradition of "blue-humored" party records by the likes of Redd Foxx and Richard Pryor, and the risqué '70s work of proto-rapper Blowfly. His first single, "Throw the D," helped launch the booming, bass-heavy Miami Sound in 1984. A year later he formed his label Skyywalker Records (changed to Luke Records after a lawsuit from *Star Wars* creator George Lucas) and 2 Live Crew. The group's second album, *Move Somethin',* caught enough ears to make #68 on the pop chart. But when 1989's *As Nasty as They Wanna Be* (#29, 1989) spawned a hit single in "Me So Horny" (#26, 1989), Jack Thompson—an evangelical Christian attorney from Coral Gables, Florida—launched the legal campaign against Campbell.

In March 1990 a Broward County, Florida, circuit court judge found probable cause that *Nasty* was obscene under state law; sheriff's deputies soon arrested a black record retailer in Fort Lauderdale for selling the album (his conviction was later overturned; a retailer in Huntsville, Alabama, who was also prosecuted for selling the album, was acquitted). Thompson got Florida Governor Robert Martinez to say he thought the album was obscene. Luke Skyywalker Records sued the Broward County sheriff on First Amendment grounds, and the state federal court ruled that there was a prior restraint of free speech, but that the LP was obscene. A week later Campbell and fellow rappers Chris Wong Won and Mark Ross were arrested at a Hollywood, Florida, nightclub, for performing the songs on *Nasty* (which would sell 2 million copies, versus an eighth as many for its *Clean* version).

Later in 1990 the New York–based alternative-rock band Too Much Joy, in a show of solidarity, would be arrested for coming to Hollywood, Florida, and performing covers of *Nasty* songs; the band was ultimately cleared by a jury that deliberated for 13 minutes and then criticized authorities for wasting its time.

Between court appeals, Campbell recorded *Banned in the U.S.A.* (#21, 1990), with a Bruce Springsteen–derived cover and title track (#20, 1990). Capitalizing on the legal furor, Atlantic Records distributed the album. However, 2 Live Crew canceled several fall 1990 shows, as well as a *Banned in the U.S.A.* pay-per-view cable TV special, for lack of demand. On the plus side, Campbell and his cohorts were acquitted of obscenity charges from their nightclub arrest, by a jury that included a 76-year-old woman unfazed by 2 Live Crew's vulgarity, and another woman who wanted to deliver the not-guilty verdict in the form of a rap.

In May 1992 the 11th U.S. Circuit Court of Appeals in Georgia reversed the Florida obscenity ruling against the *Nasty* album; seven months later the U.S. Supreme Court refused to hear an appeal, by which time the original 2 Live Crew had disbanded after releasing *Sports Weekend* (#22, 1991). Meanwhile, Campbell was in more legal trouble over 2 Live Crew's 1989 version of Roy Orbison's classic "Oh, Pretty Woman"—which Campbell and company had changed to be about "big, hairy," "bald-headed," and "two-timin' " women. Orbison's music publisher, the Nashville giant Acuff-Rose, had rebuffed Campbell's request for a license for the song, and sued him upon release of his version, claiming he'd damaged the song's value. Campbell defended his fair-use right to parody. A Nashville court's 1991 ruling against Acuff-Rose was overturned on appeal in 1992, and a year later the U.S. Supreme Court agreed to hear the case. Briefs on behalf of 2 Live Crew were filed by the producers of Home Box Office and political parodist Mark Russell, among others.

Meanwhile, Campbell's Luke Records struck gold in 1993 with the R&B vocal group H-Town, whose debut album, *Fever for Da Flavor* (#16, 1993), yielded a huge hit single in "Knockin' Da Boots" (#3, 1993). In early 1994 the U.S. Supreme Court ruled in favor of Campbell that the Orbison takeoff was a parody. Concurrently, Campbell announced a new 2 Live Crew, and a publishing venture—an adult magazine called *Scandalous*. Campbell continued to pursue entrepreneurial interests—including movie production and Internet sites—and release solo albums throughout the decade, despite losing a $1.6 million lawsuit filed by one of his acts, filing for bankruptcy in 1995, and being investigated by the NCAA for allegedly making payments to members of the University of Miami football team, a charge Campbell denied. Other members of the 2 Live Crew continued to record under the name for Lil' Joe records, owned by Campbell's former attorney, Joe Weinberger, who also acquired the group's back catalogue. In 2001 Campbell claimed his *Somethin' Nasty* would be his last album.

UB40

Formed 1978, Birmingham, Eng.
Astro (b. Terence Wilson, June 24, 1957, Birmingham), voc.; James Brown (b. Nov. 20, 1957, Birmingham), drums; Ali Campbell (b. Feb. 15, 1959, Birmingham), gtr., voc.; Robin Campbell (b. Dec. 25, 1954, Birmingham), gtr., voc.; Earl Falconer (b. Jan. 23, 1959, Birmingham), bass; Norman Hassan (b. Jan. 26, 1958, Birmingham), perc.; Brian Travers (b. Feb. 7, 1959, Birmingham), sax; Mickey Virtue (b. Jan. 19, 1957, Birmingham), kybds.
1980—*Signing Off* (Graduate, U.K.); *The Singles Album* 1981—*Present Arms* (DEP, U.K.); *Present Arms in Dub* 1982—*UB44* 1983—*Live; 1980–1983* (A&M); *Labour of Love* 1984—*Geffrey Morgan* 1985—*The UB40 File* (Graduate, U.K.); *Baggariddim* (DEP, U.K.); *Little Baggariddim* EP (A&M) 1986—*Rat in the Kitchen* 1987—*CCCP: Live in Moscow* 1988—*UB40* 1989—*Labour of Love II* 1993—*Promises and Lies* (Virgin) 1995—*The Best of UB40, vol. 1; The Best of UB40, vol. 2* 1997—*Guns in the Ghetto* 1998—*Presents the Dancehall Album* 1999—*Labour of Love III* 2000—*The Very Best.*

Known in the U.S. for their reggae-inflected covers of Neil Diamond's "Red Red Wine" (#1, 1988) and Elvis Presley's "Can't Help Falling in Love" (#1, 1993), UB40 has had more than 30 singles on the British charts since 1980, becoming one of the best-selling reggae bands in the world.

UB40's multiracial lineup and influences reflect their roots in working-class Birmingham. Originally a gang of layabouts (they took their name from the British unemployment form), they turned to music in early 1978, playing instruments bought with money awarded to singer/guitarist Ali Campbell as compensation for injuries received in a bar fight. Initially so bad they almost broke up, by Christmas they were good enough for Chrissie Hynde to invite them on a Pretenders tour. The band's quickly recorded single "Food for Thought" reached #4 in the U.K. in 1980, and was followed by the albums *Signing Off* (#2 U.K., 1980) and *Present Arms* (#2 U.K., 1981), which included their scathing anti-Thatcher anthem, "One in Ten" (#7 U.K., 1981).

Labour of Love (#14 pop, #1 U.K., 1983), an album of reggae covers that contained "Red Red Wine" (#34 pop, 1984; #1 U.K., 1983) put them in the U.S. chart for the first time. Albums of original material—*Geffrey Morgan* (#60, 1984), *Rat in the Kitchen* (#53, 1986), *UB40* (#44, 1988), and an EP, *Little Baggariddim* (#40, 1985), which included a cover of "I Got You Babe" with Chrissie Hynde (#28, 1985)—sold only respectably in the U.S. In 1988 a Phoenix radio station added "Red Red Wine" to its playlist; other stations followed suit, and the song had a second life as a U.S. megahit, eventually climbing to #1, bringing *Labour of Love* with it to #14. *Labour of Love II* (#30, 1990) was another album of covers and included "The Way You Do the Things You Do" (a 1964 hit by the Temptations), which made it to #6. In 1993 the band released *Promises and Lies* (their second #1 U.K. album), with "Can't Help Falling in Love" and "Higher Ground" (#45, 1993) helping to propel it to #6 on the U.S. albums chart. UB40 never reached these heady heights again in the U.S., with

UB40

1997's *Guns in the Ghetto* peaking at #176. They were also dealt a blow when in 1995 a British judge ruled that the band's 1985 #1 British hit "Don't Break My Heart" had actually been written by Deborah Banks, a Birmingham amateur songwriter, and not by guest UB40 member Javid Khan.

Now better known for their cover versions than for their original material, UB40 continued to pay their respects to reggae with *Presents the Dancehall Album,* a collaboration with top Jamaican singers, and a third installment in the *Labour of Love* series featuring yet more covers of Jamaican classics.

U.K.

Formed 1977, England
Eddie Jobson (b. Apr. 28, 1955, Billingham, Eng.), kybds., violin; John Wetton (b. July 12, 1949, Derby, Eng.), bass, voc.; Allan Holdsworth, gtr.; Bill Bruford (b. May 17, 1948, London, Eng.), drums.
1978—*U.K.* (Polydor) 1979—(– Holdsworth; – Bruford; + Terry Bozzio [b. Dec. 27, 1950, San Francisco, CA], drums) *Danger Money.*

A British art-rock supergroup, U.K. drew together such respected veterans of the progressive-rock genre as Bill Bruford (Yes [see entry], King Crimson [see entry]), John Wetton (King Crimson, Roxy Music [see entry], Uriah Heep [see entry]), Eddie Jobson (Roxy Music), and Allan Holdsworth (Jon Hiseman's Tempest, Tony Williams' Lifetime [see entry], Gong [see entry], Soft Machine [see entry]).

When U.K. was formed, Bruford and Wetton had last worked together in King Crimson; Holdsworth had played on Bruford's first solo album, which was released just prior to U.K.'s formation. U.K. became an immediate hit with progressive-rock fans, and its first album and U.S. tour were financially successful.

As the band featured Jobson's keyboards most prominently, Holdsworth's fluid, jazzy guitar seemed like icing on the cake, and he and Bruford soon left to work together on more jazz-fusion projects. The focus shifted decisively to Jobson as the band became a trio with the addition of drummer Terry Bozzio, fresh from a stint with Frank Zappa's Mothers of Invention. U.K.'s music became simpler and heavier, as Bozzio was less inclined toward dauntingly tricky, cracklingly precise meters than Bruford was. After *Danger Money* had been on the LP charts for a while, U.K. disbanded. Jobson went on to tour with Jethro Tull; Wetton cofounded another art-rock supergroup, Asia [see entry]; Bruford and Holdsworth continued to work together and separately. Bruford resurfaced in 1981 with the re-formed King Crimson, while Holdsworth came back in 1982 with a solo album and a brief low-level U.S. tour, and began working on an album produced by a fan, Eddie Van Halen. Bozzio cofounded Missing Persons [see entry].

James Blood Ulmer

Born Feb. 2, 1942, St. Matthews, SC
1977—*Revealing* (In + Out) 1978—*Tales of Captain Black* (Artists House) 1980—*Are You Glad to Be in America?* (Rough Trade) 1981—*Free Lancing* (Columbia) 1982—*Black Rock* 1983—*Odyssey* 1984—*Part Time* (Rough Trade) 1986—*Phalanx* (DIW); *Live at the Caravan of Dreams* (Caravan of Dreams) 1987—*Original Phalanx* (DIW) *America—Do You Remember the Love?* (Blue Note); *In Touch* (DIW) 1990—*Blues Allnight* (In + Out) 1991—*Black & Blues* (DIW/Columbia) 1993—*Harmolodic Guitar With Strings* (DIW) 1994—*Blues Preacher* (DIW/ Columbia); *Live at the Bayerischer Hof* (In + Out) 1997—*Music Speaks Louder Than Words* (Koch Jazz) 1998—*Forbidden Blues* (DIW).
The Music Revelation Ensemble (Ulmer with David Murray, sax; Amin Ali, bass; Cornell Rochester, drums; Ronald Shannon Jackson, drums).
1980—*Electric Jazz* (DIW); *No Wave* (Moers); *Music Revelation Ensemble* (DIW) 1992—*After Dark* (DIW) 1994—*In the Name of the Music Revelation* (Columbia) 1996—*Knights of Power* (DIW) 1998—*Cross Fire.*

In the early '80s James Blood Ulmer was hailed as the most innovative guitarist of his day. Combining a background of 10 years' hard roadwork on the R&B circuit and a grounding in "harmolodic" theory (harmony-movement-melodic) from its developer Ornette Coleman [see entry], Ulmer's sound has roots in blues, hard rock, and avant-garde jazz.

Prior to *Tales of Captain Black,* his first album as a leader, Ulmer served for four months as the first guitarist for Art Blakey's Jazz Messengers and recorded with jazz organist Larry Young (Khalid Yasim) and tenor saxophonist Joe Henderson; he recorded as well with Coleman in a series of extensive though mostly unreleased sessions (Coleman appears on *Captain Black*). During the '80s Ulmer released more albums (*Are You Glad to Be in America?* introduced his Hendrix-style singing), backed by the cream of the younger jazz players, including drummer Ronald Shannon Jackson (who leads his own band, the Decoding Society) and well-regarded saxophonists Oliver Lake and David Murray. Ulmer's appeal is still largely to the jazz rather than rock audience, despite being picked by Public Image Ltd. to open their first New York concert and being signed in the early '80s to Columbia.

Starting in the late '80s, Ulmer has recorded for smaller labels (Rough Trade, Blue Note) and concentrated on live performances. In concert he usually appears as part of a highly amplified trio or quartet, most notably the Music Revelation Ensemble.

Ultravox

Formed 1973, London, Eng.
John Foxx (b. Dennis Leigh, Chorley, Eng.), voc., synth.; Steve Shears, kybds., voc.; Billy Currie (b. Apr. 1, 1952), kybds., synth., violin; Chris Cross (b. Christopher Allen, July 14, 1952), bass; Warren Cann (b. May 20, 1952, Victoria, Can.), drums.
1977—*Ultravox!* (Island, U.K.) 1978—(– Shears; + Robin Simon, gtr.) *Systems of Romance* (Antilles) 1980—*Three Into One* (Island) (– Foxx; – Simon; + Midge Ure [b. James Ure, Oct. 10, 1953, Glasgow, Scot.], gtr., voc.) 1981—*Vienna* (Chrysalis); *Rage in Eden* 1983—*Quartet* 1984—*Lament; The Collection* 1986—(– Cann; + Mark Brzezicki [b. June 21, 1957], drums) 1990—*U-Vox* (Currie continues with numerous lineup changes).
John Foxx solo: 1981—*John Foxx* (Virgin, Can.).
Midge Ure solo: 1985—*The Gift* (Chrysalis) 1988—*Answers to Nothing* 1991—*Pure* (RCA) 1993—*If I Was: The Very Best of Midge Ure* (Chrysalis) 1996—*Breathe* (RCA).
Billy Currie solo: 1988—*Transportation* (I.R.S./No Speak).

An important precursor of the early-'80s British "electropop" movement, Ultravox was one of the first modern postpunk bands to dispense with guitars in favor of synthesizers.

The band was formed by and around John Foxx, who had become interested in music while dabbling in synthesizers and tapes at school. Foxx went to London in 1974, began writing songs and soon formed Ultravox, who had a minor British hit in 1977 with "My Sex" and made three critically acclaimed albums (the first produced by Brian Eno) before he left to pursue a solo career.

Ultravox regrouped with the addition of Midge Ure, formerly with Scottish popsters Slik and a late version of the ex–Sex Pistol Glen Matlock's Rich Kids. With a more dramatic lead singer and a slightly less foreboding sound, *Vienna* (#3 U.K., 1980) yielded a minor hit single in "Sleepwalk." Its title track hit #2 in the U.K. in 1981. Through its career, Ultravox was far more popular at home than here in the U.S. In addition to *Vienna, Rage in Eden, Quartet, Lament, The Collection,* and *U-Vox* were all U.K. Top 10 albums. The group's U.K. hit singles include "All Stood Still" (#8 U.K., 1981), "Reap the Wild Wind" (#12, 1982), "Hymn" (#11, 1982), "Visions in Blue" (#15, 1983), "Lament" (#22, 1984), and "Love's Great Adventure" (#12, 1984).

Electropopper Gary Numan, among others, has often cited Ultravox's influence on his own work, and Ultravox's Billy Currie toured with Numan. *Three Into One,* a compilation, followed. *Rage in Eden* (like *Systems of Romance* and *Vienna*) was produced by Conny Plank. George Martin produced *Quartet,* which went to #61 and became Ultravox's highest-charting album in the U.S. It included the minor hit single "Reap the Wild Wind" (#71, 1983). None of their other albums, before or since, broke into the Top 100 in the States. The group produced *Lament,* which made little impression stateside. The group's last U.S. release of new material was *U-Vox,* which was issued in the U.K. in 1986, a year before the band went on hiatus. A new Ultravox, led by Currie and various frontmen, released two widely ignored U.K. albums in the mid-'90s.

Several members have gone on to solo careers, most notably Midge Ure. He cowrote Band Aid's "Do They Know It's Christmas?" and is the musical director for the Prince's Trust concerts. His *Answers to Nothing* (#88, 1989) included "Dear God" (#95, 1989). Again, however, Ure's popularity here gives no indication of his success in the U.K., where he had a number of charting singles, including two Top 10s: "No Regrets" (1982) and the U.K. #1 "If I Was" (1985). Billy Currie's first solo album featured guitarist Steve Howe. John Foxx released several solo albums in the '80s, none of which was issued in the U.S. He has also charted a number of singles in England.

Uncle Tupelo

Formed 1987, Belleville, IL
Jeff Tweedy (b. Aug. 25, 1967, Belleville), voc., gtr., bass; Jay Farrar (b. Dec. 26, 1966, Belleville), voc., gtr.; Michael Heidorn (b. May 28, 1967, Belleville), drums.
1990—*No Depression* (Rockville) 1991—*Still Feel Gone* 1992—*March 16–20, 1992* 1993—(– Heidorn; + Ken Coomer, drums; + John Stirratt, bass; + Max Johnston, banjo, fiddle, mandolin, steel gtr.) *Anodyne* (Sire).

Small-town Midwestern high school pals Jeff Tweedy and Jay Farrar began playing together in a band called the Primitives before forming Uncle Tupelo. Mixing noisy punk-influenced guitar and feedback with country-tinged melodic twang, Uncle Tupelo was one of the preeminent roots bands that arose in the heartland in the wake of alternative rock.

After playing the local bar scene for three years, Uncle Tupelo signed with the indie label Rockville, which released

No Depression in 1990; *Still Feel Gone* came out the next year. Its compelling live shows gained the group a following that included college radio listeners. The live-in-the-studio *March 16–20, 1992* included traditional C&W covers and was produced by R.E.M. guitarist Peter Buck. Uncle Tupelo then signed to Sire for the masterful *Anodyne*, which showcased Tweedy and Farrar's harmonies and put the focus on country rock, with multi-instrumentalist Max Johnston adding banjo, mandolin, fiddle, and steel guitar.

Tensions had been building between Tweedy and Farrar, however, and in June 1994 Farrar left the band. Under Tweedy's leadership, Uncle Tupelo transmogrified into Wilco [see entry]. Meanwhile, Farrar formed Son Volt [see entry] with original Tupelo drummer Michael Heidorn, enlisting bassist Jim Boquist and guitarist/fiddler Dave Boquist. Uncle Tupelo's legacy extends well beyond these offshoots, though. Along with fellow punk-bred country rockers the Jayhawks, the group was a catalyst for the grassroots alternative-country movement of the mid-'90s. Uncle Tupelo also gave rise to an online discussion folder dedicated to the group and its music. Named for the title track of the band's debut album (a cover of an old Carter Family song), the folder eventually led to the founding of *No Depression* magazine, which since 1995 has been the principal document of the alt-country movement.

The Undertones/Feargal Sharkey/ That Petrol Emotion

Formed 1975, Derry, N. Ire.
Feargal Sharkey (b. Aug. 13, 1958, Derry), voc.; John O'Neill (b. Aug. 26, 1957, Derry), gtr., voc.; Damian O'Neill (b. Jan. 15, 1961, Belfast, N. Ire.), gtr., voc.; Michael Bradley (b. Aug. 13, 1959, Derry), bass; Billy Doherty (b. July 10, 1958, Larne, N. Ire.), drums.
1979—*The Undertones* (Sire) 1980—*Hypnotised* 1981—*Positive Touch* (EMI/Harvest) 1983—*The Sin of Pride* (Ardeck, U.K.) 1986—*Cher o'Bowlies: Pick of the Undertones* (EMI) 1994—*The Very Best of the Undertones* (Rykodisc).
Feargal Sharkey solo: 1985—*Feargal Sharkey* (Virgin/A&M) 1988—*Wish* (Virgin) 1991—*Songs From the Mardi Gras* (Virgin, U.K.).
That Petrol Emotion, formed 1986: Sean (a.k.a. John) O'Neill; D. O'Neill; + Raymond Gorman (a.k.a. Réamann O'Gormain, b. June 7, 1961, Derry), gtr.; Ciaran McLaughlin (b. Nov. 18, 1962, Derry), drums; Steve Mack (b. May 19, 1963, New York, NY), voc.
1986—*Manic Pop Thrill* (Polydor) 1987—*Babble* 1988—*End of the Millennium Psychosis Blues* (Virgin) 1990—*Chemicrazy* (– S. O'Neill) 1994—*Fireproof*.

Northern Ireland's answer to Manchester, England's Buzzcocks, the Undertones emerged from strife-torn Northern Ireland with a rousing punk-pop sound—delivering teen angst and romance in fast, furious, catchy songs, sung in a distinctive, high-pitched voice by Feargal Sharkey.

The Undertones' first single, "Teenage Kicks" (#31 U.K., 1978), was released on Belfast's Good Vibrations label and received heavy radio play in England from influential DJ John Peel, who called it his favorite record of all time. The band's critically acclaimed debut album (#154, 1980; #13 U.K., 1979) had cover art based on the Who's *My Generation* album. With *Hypnotised* (#6 U.K., 1980) and *Positive Touch* (#17 U.K., 1981), the Undertones slowed the pace and lowered the buzzsaw guitar noise; though their well-crafted pop was praised by critics, both albums failed to chart in the U.S. When the more elaborately produced *Sin of Pride* (#43 U.K., 1983) failed to produce a British hit single, the band broke up.

The Undertones

Sharkey formed the Assembly with keyboardist/composer Vince Clarke (Depeche Mode, Yazoo) to record the 1983 U.K. hit single, "Never Never" (#4), then launched a solo career with the single "Listen to Your Father" (#23 U.K., 1984), on which he was backed by British two-tone band Madness. He released three solo albums between 1985 and 1991, the first of which was produced by Dave Stewart of Eurythmics; his only U.S. charted single, "A Good Heart" (#74, 1986), hit #1 in the U.K.

In 1986 John (now Sean) and Damian O'Neill (now on bass) formed That Petrol Emotion, a critically well-received hard-rock band with some political lyrics and funk and noise elements. The band had only moderate chart success in the U.K. Sean O'Neill departed the band in 1990, and That Petrol Emotion broke up in 1994. The O'Neill brothers joined the other original members of the Undertones—minus Sharkey—for a 2000 reunion.

Underworld

Formed 1988, London, Eng.
Karl Hyde (b. May 10, 1957, Worcestershire, Eng.), voc., gtr.; Rick Smith (b. May 25, 1959, Ammanford, Wales), kybds.; Alfie Thomas, gtr.; Baz Allen, bass; Bryn B. Burrows, drums.
1988—*Underneath the Radar* (Sire) 1989—*Change the Weather* 1990–(group re-forms: Hyde; Smith, kybds., programmer; + Darren Emerson [b. Apr. 30, 1971, Hornchurch, Eng.], DJ, programmer) 1993—*Dubnobasswithmyheadman* (Junior Boys Own) 1996—*Second Toughest in the Infants*

(JBO/Wax Trax!) 1999—*Beaucoup Fish* (V2) 2000—*Everything, Everything* (– Emerson).
Darren Emerson solo: 2000—*Global Underground: Uruguay* (Boxed).

Thanks to its hit single "Born Slippy," Underworld was one of a small group of British electronic artists that achieved mainstream success in America during the mid-'90s. Unlike many of its even more successful contemporaries, however, Underworld did so without the help of rock-styled big-beat anthems (a la the Chemical Brothers) or by essentially transforming itself into a rock band (like Prodigy). Instead, the trio distinguished itself through its hypnotic techno beats and Karl Hyde's stream-of-consciousness lyrics, which the singer appeared to use not for their meaning but for the rhythmic patterns they created.

Underworld's origins stretch back to the early '80s, when Hyde and Rick Smith met while attending Cardiff University in Wales. Their first musical collaboration came with the art-rock band Freur, which had a minor U.K. hit with the 1983 single "Doot Doot." In 1988 they regrouped as Underworld, naming themselves after a film for which they had written the score. This early incarnation of Underworld released two albums of synth pop on Sire (1988's *Underneath the Radar* and 1989's *Change the Weather*) and then disbanded upon returning home from a support slot on the Eurythmics farewell tour.

By then, acid house had caught on in England. Rejuvenated by the change in musical climate, Hyde and Smith re-formed in 1990 with new recruit Darren Emerson, a futures trader and part-time club DJ. The trio released a few singles as Lemon Interrupt on London label Junior Boys Own in 1992; the following year, they returned to the name Underworld and recorded the singles "Rez" and "Mmm Skyscraper I Love You," the latter of which ended up on their 1993 debut, *Dubnobasswithmyheadman*. Critically acclaimed upon its release in Britain, the album was rereleased a year later in the U.S. on the TVT subsidiary Wax Trax! The followup, *Second Toughest in the Infants,* was equally hailed by the press and was nominated for the prestigious Mercury Music Prize in the U.K. Still, Underworld remained more or less unknown outside of certain circles, particularly in the U.S.

All this changed with the single "Born Slippy." Released in the U.K. in 1995 and included on the soundtrack to 1996's hit film *Trainspotting,* the song went to #2 in the U.K. and introduced the Underworld to the American mainstream.

Underworld's third full-length, 1999's *Beaucoup Fish* (#93 pop) failed to garner the critical accolades of its predecessors; nonetheless, it was the first of the group's albums to chart in the U.S. A live Underworld full-length project, *Everything, Everything,* was released in 2000, the same year Emerson left the group to pursue DJing full-time. He released the mix CD *Global Underground: Uruguay* soon after his departure; the remaining two members continued to work on new Underworld material, as well as on their graphic-design company, Tomato.

Uriah Heep

Formed 1970, London, Eng.
David Byron (b. Jan. 29, 1947, Essex, Eng.; d. Feb. 28, 1985), voc.; Mick Box (b. June 8, 1947, London), gtr.; Ken Hensley (b. Aug. 24, 1945, Eng.), kybds., voc.; Paul Newton, bass; Alex Napier, drums.
1970—*Very 'eavy, Very 'umble* (Mercury) 1971—(– Napier; + Keith Baker, drums) *Salisbury* (– Baker; + Lee Kerslake, drums; + Mark Clarke [b. July 25, 1950, Liverpool, Eng.], bass) *Look at Yourself* 1972—(– Newton; – Clarke; + Gary Thain [b. May 15, 1948, Wellington, N.Z.; d. Mar. 19, 1976], bass) *Demons and Wizards; The Magician's Birthday* 1973—*Live* (Warner Bros.); *Sweet Freedom* 1974—*Wonderworld* 1975—(– Thain; + John Wetton [b. July 12, 1949, Derby, Eng.], bass, voc.) *Return to Fantasy; The Best of Uriah Heep* (Mercury) 1976—*High and Mighty* (Warner Bros.) (– Byron; – Wetton; + John Lawton, voc.; + Trevor Bolder [b. June 9, 1950, Hull, Eng.], bass) 1977—*Fire Fly; Innocent Victim* 1978—*Fallen Angel* (– Lawton; + John Sloman, voc.; – Kerslake; + Chris Slade [b. Oct. 30, 1946, drums) 1980—*Conquest* (– Hensley; + Greg Dechert, kybds.) 1981—(group disbands; group re-forms: Box; Kerslake; + Bob Daisley, bass; + Pete Goalby, voc.; + John Sinclair, kybds.) 1982—*Abominog* 1983—*Head First* 1985—*Equator* (CBS) (– Daisley; + Bolder) 1986—(– Goalby; + Bernie Shaw [b. June 15, 1956, Vancouver, Can.], voc.; – Sinclair; + Phil Lanzon [b. Mar. 23, 1950], kybds., voc.) 1988—*Live in Moscow* (Legacy, U.K.) 1989—*Raging Silence* 1991—*Different World* 1995—*Sea of Light* (SPV, U.K.) (+ Lawton; – Lawton) 1998—*Clasic Heep—An Anthology* (Mercury) 1999—*Sonic Origami* (Spitfire).

"If this group makes it, I'll have to commit suicide," wrote one rock critic, expressing the critical consensus on Uriah Heep. This hard-rocking, hard-working group did indeed make it for much of the '70s with a blend of heavy metal and art rock that easily could have been the model for Spinal Tap.

The band's roots were in a London outfit called the Stalkers, which Mick Box joined in 1964. They were later joined by David Byron, who had sung on anonymous hit-cover albums alongside Elton John. Box and Byron then formed Spice with bassist Paul Newton of the Gods (which also included Ken Hensley, formerly with Kit and the Saracens and the Jimmy Brown Sound, and Mick Taylor, the latter going on to John Mayall and the Rolling Stones). Hensley worked briefly with Cliff Bennett's Toe Fat band, then joined Spice, who renamed themselves Uriah Heep after Charles Dickens' conniving paragon of "humility." They cut their hard-rock debut LP, then landed a regular drummer in Keith Baker.

The debut and *Salisbury* (#103, 1971), for which the band was augmented by an orchestra on some cuts, found only minor European success, though Uriah Heep was already an established concert attraction in Britain. *Look at Yourself* (#93, 1971) made the band a success in both the U.S. and U.K., and they consolidated their status with *Demons and Wizards* (#23, 1972), *The Magician's Birthday* (#31, 1972), *Live* (#37, 1973), and *Sweet Freedom* (#33, 1973), which all went gold in Britain and America. Uriah Heep also made the singles chart with "Easy Livin' " (#39, 1972), "Sweet Lorraine" (#91, 1973), "Blind Eye" (#97, 1973), and "Stealin' " (#91, 1973).

In 1974 dissent plagued the band. Bassist Gary Thain suffered a near-fatal electric shock onstage in Dallas, Texas, and later complained that the band was inconsiderate of his physical well-being. Personal problems and drug use furthered Thain's conflicts with the rest of the band, and in early 1975 he was "invited" to leave; he died of a drug overdose a year later. He was replaced by John Wetton, formerly of Family and King Crimson, who stayed with the band for two albums before further internal squabbles resulted in the firing of David Byron in July 1976. Wetton soon left to record a solo album and eventually joined art-rock supergroups U.K. and Asia. Hensley in the meantime had recorded two solo albums, 1973's *Proud Words on a Dusty Shelf* and 1975's *Eager to Please.* With new vocalist John Lawton and bassist Trevor Bolder, from David Bowie's Spiders From Mars band, Uriah Heep continued plowing its heavy-metal furrow for a few more albums. They were a favorite opening act and toured with Jethro Tull, Kiss, Rush, Foreigner, and other top-line arena rockers.

Through the years Uriah Heep has sustained many personnel changes. Among its former members are Chris Slade (who for a time was the drummer in AC/DC and in Jimmy Page's the Firm), and Lee Kerslake and Bob Daisley (both members of Ozzy Osbourne's Blizzard of Oz). The current lineup has remained intact since 1986. The group continues to tour and record, having played 10 sold-out shows in Moscow in 1987. Uriah Heep still keeps a high profle in Europe. On the tour following 1995's *Sea of Light,* the band temporarily reunited with Lawton when vocalist Bernie Shaw developed throat problems.

Usher

Born Usher Raymond, Oct. 14, 1978, Chattanooga, TN
1994—*Usher* (LaFace) 1997—My Way 1999—*Live*
2000—*All About U* 2001—*8701.*

Discovered at an Atlanta talent show, rapper/singer Usher Raymond was signed to R&B powerhouse LaFace Records when he was 14. The gospel-trained performer released his first album *Usher* (#167 pop, #25 R&B) in 1994 and enjoyed success on the R&B charts with "Can U Get Wit It" (#13, 1994) and "Think of You" (#8, 1995). Usher cowrote much of the 5-million-selling followup *My Way* (#4 pop, #1 R&B, 1997), with production by Jermaine Dupri, Babyface, and Sean Combs. The single "You Make Me Wanna" (#2 pop, #1 R&B, 1997) made the vocalist a certified pop star, with "Nice & Slow" (#1 pop and R&B, 1998) and "My Way" (#2 pop, #4 R&B, 1998) confirming his hitmaking prowess. During 1998, Usher made his big-screen debut in the sci-fi spoof *The Faculty,* and went on to roles in the romantic teen comedy *She's All That* and the high-school drama *Light It Up,* as well as a recurring role on *Moesha,* the UPN TV show that featured another young R&B star, Brandy. The 1999 release *Live* (#73 pop, #30 R&B) marked time until Usher could complete his next studio effort, *All About U.* Its single, "Pop Ya Collar," (#60 pop, #25 R&B, 2000) did not fare well commercially. But "U Remind Me," the first single from his 2001 album *8701,* hit #1 pop and R&B.

U.T.F.O.

Formed 1982, Brooklyn, NY
Kangol (b. Shawn Fequiere, Aug. 10, 1966, Brooklyn), voc; Dr. Ice (b. Fred Reeves, Mar. 2, 1966, Brooklyn), voc.; Educated Rapper (b. Jeffrey Campbell, July 4, 1963, Eng.), voc.; Mixmaster Ice (b. Maurice Bailey, Apr. 22, 1965, Brooklyn), DJ.
1985—*U.T.F.O.* (Select) 1986—*Skeezer Pleezer* 1987—*Lethal* 1989—*Doin' It!* 1990—*Bag It and Bone It* (Jive/RCA) 1996—*The Best of U.T.F.O.* (Select).

U.T.F.O. touched a nerve when they released their second rap single, "Roxanne, Roxanne" (#10 R&B, 1985), a dis of a girl who dared to refuse their advances. The hit, produced like all U.T.F.O. records by Full Force, set off numerous response singles, starting with Roxanne Shanté's [see entry] "Roxanne's Revenge" and leading to U.T.F.O.'s own answer, "The Real Roxanne," featuring rapper Joanne Martinez.

Untouchable Force Organization got its first break when they won a break-dancing contest in 1983 at Radio City Music Hall. The Flatbush boys subsequently toured Europe with Whodini (Dr. Ice's older brother was a member of that group), appeared on *The Phil Donahue Show,* and performed at a birthday party for Dustin Hoffman's daughter. *U.T.F.O.* featured both "Roxanne"s plus "Leader of the Pack" (#32 R&B, 1985) and "Fairytale Lover" (#36 R&B, 1985). The group grew musically on *Skeezer Pleezer,* although the album produced no hits, and Educated Rapper, who was battling a drug addiction, didn't perform on it. *Lethal* features a collaboration with thrash-metal band Anthrax and U.T.F.O.'s first foray into gangsta rap. After 1990's *Bag It and Bone It* bombed, U.T.F.O. split up. Kangol produced such artists as Gerardo and Lisa Lisa, and Dr. Ice released a solo album in 1989. In 1995 "Roxanne, Roxanne" was included in a listening booth at the Rock and Roll Hall of Fame & Museum designed to depict the full range of music that constitutes the genre.

Utopia: See Todd Rundgren

U2

Formed 1978, Dublin, Ire.
Bono Vox (b. Paul Hewson, May 10, 1960, Dublin), voc., gtr.; Dave "the Edge" Evans (b. David Evans, Aug. 8, 1961, Barking, Eng.), gtr., kybds., voc.; Adam Clayton (b. Mar. 13, 1960, Oxford, Eng.), bass; Larry Mullen Jr. (b. Oct. 31, 1961, Dublin), drums.
1980—*Boy* (Island) 1981—*October* 1983—*War; Under a*

Blood Red Sky EP 1984—*The Unforgettable Fire* 1985—*Wide Awake in America* EP 1987—*The Joshua Tree* 1988—*Rattle and Hum* 1991—*Achtung Baby* 1993—*Zooropa* 1997—*Pop* (PolyGram) 1998—*The Best of 1980–1990* (Island) 2000—*All That You Can't Leave Behind* (Interscope).
As Passengers, with Brian Eno: 1995—*Original Soundtracks I* (Island/PolyGram).
As U2 as well as the Million Dollar Hotel Band (Bono with Brian Eno and Daniel Lanois): 2000—*The Million Dollar Hotel* soundtrack (Interscope).

U2 began the '80s as a virtually unknown "alternative" group and ended the century as one of the most widely followed rock bands in the world. The Irish rockers were influenced initially by punk's raw energy, but they immediately distinguished themselves from their postpunk peers with a huge, soaring sound—centered on Dave "the Edge" Evans' reverb-laden guitar playing and Paul "Bono" Hewson's sensuous vocals—and songs that tackled social and spiritual matters with an open, tender urgency. U2 shunned the sort of ironic expression and electronic gimmickry that were considered hip in the '80s—until the '90s, that is, when the band began drawing on such elements to reinvigorate and broaden its sound. By 2000's *All That You Can't Leave Behind,* U2 had revived its straight-ahead approach. U2 has maintained not only its massive popularity but also its status as one of the most adventurous and groundbreaking acts in pop music.

The band members began rehearsing together while students at Dublin's Mount Temple High School (the city's only nondenominational school). None was technically proficient at the beginning, but their lack of expertise mothered invention. The Edge's distinctive chordal style, for instance, stemmed largely from the guitarist's inability to play complicated leads, while bassist Adam Clayton and drummer Larry Mullen Jr. provided a rhythm section that was mostly pummeling ardor. The novice musicians quickly developed a following in Ireland and found a manager, Paul McGuinness, who remains with them to this day. They recorded independently before signing to Island Records in 1980.

U2: The Edge, Larry Mullen, Bono, Adam Clayton

U2's 1980 debut album, *Boy,* was produced by Steve Lillywhite. On it, the group earnestly explored adolescent hopes and terrors, rejecting hard rock's earthy egotism and punk's nihilism. Bono, U2's lyricist, was (and still is) a practicing Christian, as were the Edge and Mullen, and on a second LP called *October* (a 1981 Lillywhite production), the singer incorporated imagery evoking their faith. *Boy* and *October* generated the respective singles "I Will Follow" and "Gloria," which got some airplay in the U.S. An American club tour generated further interest, thanks to U2's incendiary live performances.

War cemented U2's reputation as a politically conscious band; among its themes were "the troubles" in Northern Ireland, addressed on the single "Sunday Bloody Sunday." Another single, "New Year's Day," went to #11 in England and #53 in the U.S., while *War* topped the British chart and hit #12 stateside. The group commemorated its 1983 tour with the live EP *Under a Blood Red Sky,* recorded at Red Rocks Amphitheatre in Colorado.

U2's next studio album, 1984's *The Unforgettable Fire,* was the first of several fruitful collaborations with producers Brian Eno and Daniel Lanois. The album generated the group's first American Top 40 single, an ode to American Civil Rights leader Martin Luther King Jr., called "Pride (In the Name of Love)" (#33, 1984). The album hit #12 here, and the Irishmen supported it by headlining arenas around the world. In 1985 U2 was proclaimed "band of the '80s" by Rolling Stone and made a historic appearance at Live Aid. The following year, the group joined Sting, Peter Gabriel, Lou Reed, and others for the Conspiracy of Hope Tour benefiting Amnesty International.

U2 entered the pop stratosphere with 1987's *The Joshua Tree,* a critical and commercial smash that topped the albums chart that year and spawned the #1 hits "With or Without You" and "I Still Haven't Found What I'm Looking For," as well as "Where the Streets Have No Name" (#13, 1987). The LP, which was produced by Eno and Lanois, won the group two Grammys, for Album of the Year and Best Rock Performance. In 1988 U2 wrapped up a triumphant worldwide tour by releasing *Rattle and Hum,* a double album that combined live tracks with new material, and featured guest appearances by Bob Dylan and B.B. King. *Rattle and Hum* seemed bombastic to some critics; an accompanying film documentary also garnered mixed reviews. The LP nonetheless shot to #1, and produced a #3 single, "Desire" (1988). The band's next LP, 1991's *Achtung Baby,* reached #1 and drew rave reviews. The LP marked a stylistic departure, featuring more metallic textures, funkier beats, and intimate, world-weary love songs. Hit singles included "Mysterious Ways" (#9, 1992), "One" (#10, 1992), "Even Better Than the Real Thing" (#32, 1992), and "Who's Gonna Ride Your Wild Horses" (#35, 1992). Another track, "Until the End of the World," was featured in Wim Wenders' 1991 film of the same name. Lanois, who produced *Baby* with support from Eno and Lillywhite, won a Grammy for his work.

In 1992 the band embarked on its Zoo TV Tour, a flashy, multimedia extravaganza that juxtaposed the rugged simplicity of its previous shows. Bono adopted a series of wry guises—the leather-and-shades-sporting Fly, the demonic MacPhisto—that he'd use for encores and, in the Fly's case, press appearances. In 1993, as the tour wound down, the band reentered the studio and made *Zooropa*, a quirky, techno-drunk affair coproduced by Eno, the Edge, and engineer Flood. The album reached #1 but yielded only the minor hit "Stay (Faraway, So Close)" (#61, 1993), which was also on the soundtrack to Wenders' 1993 movie *Faraway, So Close*. Johnny Cash sang lead on the track "The Wanderer." In 1993 the band renewed its contract with Island for an estimated $170 million. U2's contribution to 1995's *Batman Forever* soundtrack, "Hold Me, Thrill Me, Kiss Me, Kill Me," was a Top 20 hit. Also in 1995 the group collaborated with Eno as Passengers on a largely instrumental album called *Original Soundtracks I;* the only track to get attention was "Miss Sarajevo," on which Bono shared vocals with opera singer Luciano Pavarotti. Proceeds from the single's sales went toward war relief in Bosnia. The same year Bono and the Edge cowrote with Irish folk singer Christy Moore a song about the peace process in Ireland, "North and South of the River."

In 1996 Clayton and Mullen recorded a rock version of the "Theme From *Mission: Impossible*" for the film starring Tom Cruise. It went to #7 on the pop chart. The following year saw the release of the electronica-heavy *Pop;* the album debuted at #1 in 27 countries, including the U.S., and garnered hit singles in "Discothèque" (#10, 1997) and "Staring at the Sun" (#26). U2 embarked on its next stage extravaganza, the PopMart Tour, from 1997 to 1998. With a supermarket theme that played upon the concept of commercialism, the tour was even more grandiose than the Zoo TV Tour had been, with immense props that included a giant olive with a 100-foot-long toothpick, a 35-foot-high lemon, and a 100-foot-tall golden arch. At the tour's conclusion, U2 released a greatest-hits compilation with a remixed version of "Sweetest Thing," previously the B side of "Where the Streets Have No Name." This time the song was released as a single (#63, 1998).

Bono returned to political activism in 1999, with much of his focus on fighting world poverty. He met with President Bill Clinton, British Prime Minister Tony Blair, as well as the Pope, as a representative of Jubilee 2000, a nonprofit group devoted to convincing nations to forgive third-world debt in the new millennium. He also cowrote a song, "New Day," with Wyclef Jean of the Fugees [see entry]; the single's proceeds benefited relief efforts in Kosovo and the Wyclef Jean Foundation. The pair performed the song at the United Nations, as well as at NetAid, a concert held simultaneously in London, Geneva, and New Jersey's Giants Stadium, while being simulcast live on the Internet, to benefit several causes, among them third-world debt relief and global poverty.

In early 2000, the Wim Wenders movie *The Million Dollar Hotel,* based on a story co-conceived by Bono, was shown at the Berlin Film Festival and released in many countries. Bono coproduced the film, made a cameo appearance in it, and U2 recorded two new songs for the soundtrack, one of which, "The Ground Beneath Her Feet," was written around lyrics by controversial author Salman Rushdie. In addition, Bono recorded tracks with Lanois and Eno as the Million Dollar Hotel Band. U2 released an album of new material, *All That You Can't Leave Behind* (#3), in late 2000, featuring the single "Beautiful Day" (#40, 2000). Both album and single won Grammys in 2001.

Steve Vai

Born June 6, 1960, Carle Place, NY
1984—*Flex-Able* (Akashic); *Flex-Able Leftovers* (Relativity) 1990—*Passion and Warfare* 1993—*Sex & Religion* 1995—*Alien Love Secrets* 1996—*Fire Garden* (Epic) 1999—*The Ultra Zone* 2000—*The 7th Song: Enchanting Guitar Melodies—Archives, vol. 1.*

Guitarist Steve Vai has led a divided career: While his solo work has been hailed for its nuanced melding of jazz, rock, funk, and classical influences, he also has appeared as a hard-rock guitarslinger for hire on albums by Frank Zappa, David Lee Roth, and Whitesnake.

Like countless other Long Island kids, the 13-year-old Vai picked up a guitar and formed a band. Unlike most, however, he had as a neighbor and guitar teacher Joe Satriani [see entry]. In 1979, when Vai was just 18, Frank Zappa asked him to play lead guitar in his band. Vai appears on numerous Zappa recordings, including *Tinseltown Rebellion* (1981), *You Are What You Is* (1981), *Thing-Fish* (1984), *Them or Us* (1986), and several *Shut Up 'n' Play Yer Guitar* albums, among others.

In 1984 Vai recorded his first solo album, *Flex-Able,* in his home studio. Picked up by Relativity, the record sold close to 250,000 copies without much publicity or airplay. The *Flex-Able Leftovers* EP followed later that same year.

After a short stint in 1985 replacing Yngwie Malmsteen in Alcatrazz, Vai signed on as David Lee Roth's guitar player in 1986 and stayed with him for three years and two albums: *Eat 'Em and Smile* (1986) and *Skyscraper* (1987). He joined Whitesnake for one album, *Slip of the Tongue* (1989). In 1990 he released his third solo album, *Passion and Warfare* (#18). *Sex & Religion* (#48), released in 1993, signaled a move toward pop, with the addition of vocals and a band that included ex–Missing Persons drummer Terry Bozzio. That same year, Vai won a Grammy for Best Rock Instrumental Performance for his work on "Sofa" off the Frank Zappa tribute *Zappa's Universe.*

In 1996 Vai sang lead for the first time on his album *Fire Garden* (#106). That same year, he embarked on the G3 tour with fellow virtuosos Satriani and Eric Johnson. Each guitarist performed solo, then all three would get together and jam; the tour was documented on 1997's *G3: Live in Concert* (#108). Vai continued to experiment on his next solo album, *The Ultra Zone* (#121), on which he married his guitar playing to drum loops and samplers, and even explored dance grooves on tracks like "Voodoo Acid."

Though Vai has slowed down on collaborations to focus on his own music and on Favored Nations, the independent label he launched in February 2000, he still finds time for occasional guest appearances on records such as Al Di Meola's *The Infinite Desire* (1998) and Joe Jackson's *Symphony 1* (1999).

Ritchie Valens

Born Richard Stephen Valenzuela, May 13, 1941, Pacoima, CA; died Feb. 3, 1959, Clear Lake, IA
1959—*Ritchie Valens* (Del-Fi) 1960—*Ritchie Valens in Concert*

at Pacoima Jr. High 1981—*The History of Ritchie Valens* (Del-Fi/Rhino) 1986—*The Best of Ritchie Valens.*

The first of several Latin rockers of the late '50s and early '60s (others included Chan Romero, Chris Montez, Eddie Quinteros, Sunny and the Sunglows, and Cannibal and the Headhunters), Ritchie Valens started playing guitar as a child, and at Pacoima High (near L.A.) he formed his own band, the Silhouettes.

In the spring of 1958 Valens signed with Del-Fi Records and later that year had a Top 50 hit with "Come On, Let's Go," later covered by early-'60s British teen idol Tommy Steele. In early 1959 Valens hit #2 on the chart with his two-sided single "Donna" and "La Bamba," the latter based on a traditional Mexican wedding song. Valens appeared on nationwide TV and in package tours. On one such tour the stars' plane crashed in a snowstorm, killing Valens, Buddy Holly, and the Big Bopper. Valens was only 17. His life story was the basis of the 1987 hit film *La Bamba,* for which Los Lobos performed his music.

Van der Graaf Generator/Peter Hammill

Formed 1967, Manchester, Eng.
Peter Hammill (b. Nov. 5, 1948, London, Eng.), gtr., kybds., voc.; Hugh Banton, kybds.; Chris Judge Smith, drums; Keith Ellis, bass; Guy Evans, drums.
1968—(– Smith) *The Aerosol Grey Machine* (Mercury) 1969—(– Ellis; + Nic Potter, bass; + David Jackson, sax) *The Least We Can Do Is Wave* (Charisma) 1970—*H to He Who Am the Only One* 1971—(– Potter) *Pawn Hearts* 1973—*The Long Hello* 1975—*Godbluff* 1976—*Still Life; World Record* 1977—*The Quiet Zone* 1978—(+ Potter; + Graham Smith, violin) *Vital/Live* 2000—*The Box* (Virgin, U.K.).
Peter Hammill solo: 1972—*Fools Mate* (Charisma); *Chameleon in the Shadows of Night* 1974—*The Silent Corner and the Empty Stage; In Camera* 1975—*Nadir's Big Chance* (as Rikki Nadir) 1977—*Over* 1978—*The Future Now* 1979—*PH 7* 1980—*A Black Box* (Blue Plate) 1981—*Sitting Targets* 1984—*Love Songs* 1986—*Skin* (Enigma); *And Close as This* 1988—*In a Foreign Town* 1990—*Out of Water.*

One of the few top-rank British art-rock bands that never achieved more than cult success in America, Van der Graaf Generator constructed stately sepulchers of Gothic sound with Hugh Banton's churchy Hammond organ and Guy Evans' virtuosic drumming framing the intensely existential verse and tortured vocals of Peter Hammill. Hammill's relentlessly bleak visions were later cited by some members (i.e. Johnny Rotten) of Britain's late-'70s punk-rock movement as their inspiration, and in fact Hammill created a "Rikki Nadir" persona for a solo album that presaged punk.

Van der Graaf Generator formed and split up and reformed several times, usually with the same core personnel, and played only one U.S. concert, in 1976 in New York. Hammill, however, has conducted several solo American tours, selling out club dates.

The band first came together at Manchester University in 1967. Founding member Chris Judge Smith gave the band its name (taken from a device that creates static electricity) but soon left, and the band broke up in late 1968. Hammill recorded material with the Van der Graaf core intended as a solo album, but when the band came back together before its release, *The Aerosol Grey Machine* was issued under Van der Graaf's aegis. Robert Fripp of King Crimson sat in on *H to He.* After the elaborate *Pawn Hearts,* the band broke up again for three years, during which time Hammill pursued his solo career in earnest. Fripp sat in on *Fools Mate* (Hammill returned the favor on Fripp's *Exposure*), ex-Spirit guitarist Randy California on *Silent Corner.*

In 1975, upon the release of the proto-punk *Nadir's Big Chance,* Van der Graaf re-formed again, with a sound that was tighter and more powerful than before. In 1978 Van der Graaf apparently broke up for keeps; Hammill has continued to record solo efforts, remaining a significant cult phenomenon. He continues to tour internationally. Few of his numerous '90s albums have been released domestically.

Luther Vandross

Born Apr. 20, 1951, New York, NY
1981—*Never Too Much* (Epic) 1982—*Forever, for Always, for Love* 1983—*Busy Body* 1985—*The Night I Fell in Love* 1986—*Give Me the Reason* 1988—*Any Love* 1989—*The Best of Luther Vandross, The Best of Love* 1991—*Power of Love* 1993—*Never Let Me Go* (LV/Epic) 1994—*Songs* 1995—*This Is Christmas* 1996—*Your Secret Love* 1997—*One Night With You—The Best of Love, vol. 2* 1998—*I Know* (Virgin).

Luther Vandross emerged from jingles and background singing to become one of the preeminent black male vocalists of the era. With the exception of his solo debut and his post-1994 material, all of his LPs have been certified platinum or double platinum.

Vandross, whose older sister Patricia was a member of the doo-wop group the Crests, began playing piano at age three. In 1972 his song "Everybody Rejoice (A Brand New Day)" was included in the Broadway musical *The Wiz.* Throughout the '70s, Vandross sang on numerous commercials (from ads for the U.S. Army to Burger King). His singing was distinguished by his impeccable phrasing and vocal control. He first came to the attention of the pop world after his friend, guitarist Carlos Alomar, introduced him to David Bowie. Vandross ended up writing ("Fascination") and singing on David Bowie's *Young Americans* (1975) LP; he later toured with Bowie, then recorded and toured with Bette Midler (he appeared on her *Songs for the New Depression*).

He quickly became one of the busiest backing vocalists and arrangers in the business, recording with Ringo Starr, Carly Simon, Donna Summer, Barbra Streisand, and Chaka Khan, among others. During this time Vandross cut two little-noted albums under the name Luther, and sang on "Dance, Dance, Dance (Yowsah, Yowsah, Yowsah)" and "Everybody Dance" for Chic. He continued his highly lucrative jingles career. Following his lead vocal appearances on "Searchin'" and "Glow of Love" (from Change's hit album *Glow of Love*), several labels expressed interest in signing Vandross as a solo act. With the encouragement of his friend Roberta Flack, he invested $25,000 of his own money in two demos: "Never Too Much" and "A House Is Not a Home."

In 1981 he signed with Epic Records, who, on the basis of his demos, granted him full creative control, allowing him to write and produce. *Never Too Much* was a #1 R&B album and the title cut was a #1 R&B single (#33 pop); the album went platinum. Until 1993, each of his albums (with the exception of the #2 R&B *The Best of* and the platinum *Never Let Me Go;* #6 pop, #3 R&B) had topped the R&B chart. *Any Love* and *Power of Love* were also Top 10 pop albums. Other hit LPs include the platinum or multiplatinum *Never Let Me Go* (#6 pop, #3 R&B, 1993), *Songs* (#5 pop, #2 R&B, 1994), and *Your Secret Love* (#9 pop, #2 R&B, 1997); and the gold *This Is Christmas* (#28 pop, #4 R&B, 1995), *One Night With You—The Best of Love, vol. 2* (#44 pop, #17 R&B, 1998), and *I Know* (#26 pop, 1998; #9 R&B, 1999). The latter was Vandross' debut for Virgin Records. He signed to Clive Davis' J Records in late 2000.

His hit singles include "Bad Boy/Having a Party" (#3 R&B, 1982), "I'll Let You Slide" (#9 R&B, 1983), "Superstar/Until You Come Back to Me (That's What I'm Gonna Do)" (#5 R&B, 1984), "'Til My Baby Comes Home" (#4 R&B, 1985), "It's Over Now" (#4 R&B, 1985), "Give Me the Reason" (#3 R&B, 1986), "Stop to Love" (#1 R&B, 1986), a duet with Gregory Hines entitled "There's Nothing Better Than Love" (#1 R&B, 1987), "I Really Didn't Mean It" (#6 R&B, 1987), "Any Love" (#1 R&B, 1988), "She Won't Talk to Me" (#3 R&B, 1988), "For You to Love" (#3 R&B, 1989), "Here and Now" (#6 pop, #1 R&B, 1989), "Treat You Right" (#5 R&B, 1990), "Power of Love/Love Power" (#4 pop, #1 R&B, 1991), "Don't Wanna Be a Fool" (#9 pop, #4 R&B, 1991), "The Rush" (#6 R&B, 1991), the Janet Jackson duet "The Best Things in Life Are Free" (#10 pop, #1 R&B, 1992), "Sometimes It's Only Love" (#9 R&B, 1992), "Little Miracles (Happen Every Day)" (#62 pop, #10 R&B, 1993), "Heaven Knows" (#94 pop, #24 R&B, 1993), "Never Let Me Go" (#31 R&B, 1993), the Mariah Carey duet "Endless Love" (#2 pop, #7 R&B, 1994), "Always and Forever" (#58 pop, #1 R&B, 1994), "Love the One You're With/Going in Circles" (#95 pop, #28 R&B, 1995), "Every Year, Every Christmas" (#32 R&B, 1995), "Your Secret Love" (#52 pop, #5 R&B, 1996), "I Can Make It Better" (#80 pop, #16 R&B, 1996), "When You Call on Me" (#36 R&B, 1997), and "Nights in Harlem" (#29 R&B, 1998).

Throughout his career, he has continued to write and produce for other artists. He produced Aretha Franklin's *Jump to It!* in 1982; the title cut and the album went to #1 on the R&B chart. He also produced Franklin's 1983 *Get It Right*, Cheryl Lynn's 1982 LP *Instant Love*, which contained their duet "If This World Were Mine," a cover of a Marvin Gaye/Tammi Terrell hit, and records for Dionne Warwick, Teddy Pendergrass, and Whitney Houston. In 1993 he made his motion picture debut in Robert Townsend's *Meteor Man*.

Vangelis

Born Evangalos Odyssey Papathanassiou, Mar. 29, 1943, Valos, Gr.

1971—*The Dragon* (Charly, U.K.) 1973—*L'Apocalypse des Animeaux* soundtrack (Polydor) 1974—*Earth* (Vertigo, U.K.) 1975—*Heaven and Hell* (RCA) 1976—*Albedo .39* 1977—*Spiral* 1978—*Beaubourg; Hypothesis* (Affinity); *Best of* (RCA) 1979—*China* (Polydor) 1980—*See You Later* 1981—*The Friends of Mr. Cairo; Chariots of Fire* soundtrack 1982—*Blade Runner* soundtrack 1984—*The Bounty* soundtrack 1985—*Mask* soundtrack 1987—*Opera Sauvage; Ignacio* (Barclay) 1988—*Direct* (Arista) 1989—*Themes* (Polydor) 1991—*The City* (Atlantic) 1992—*1492: Conquest of Paradise* soundtrack 1994—*Blade Runner* soundtrack 1995—*Voices* 1997—*Oceanic* 1998—*El Greco.*

With Aphrodite's Child: 1968—*End of the World/Rain and Tears* (Vertigo, U.K.) 1969—*It's Five O'Clock* 1970—*Aphrodite's Child* (Mercury) 1972—*666—Apocalypse of John* (Vertigo, U.K.) 1975—*The Best of Aphrodite's Child* (Mercury).

Vangelis was in France at the time of the 1968 student riots; unable to return to Greece, he formed a band with Demis Roussos. That band, Aphrodite's Child, released a series of unremarkable progressive-rock albums, and had one European hit single with "Rain and Tears." Roussos went on to become an international MOR singing star. Vangelis turned to a solo career and began composing film scores with *L'Apocalypse des Animeaux*.

In 1974 Vangelis was rumored to be the replacement for Yes's departed keyboard whiz Rick Wakeman. Though he never did join Yes, Vangelis formed a lasting association with Yes singer Jon Anderson, and has worked with him on his solo projects. Vangelis also made albums on his own, such as *Beaubourg*, which were pastiches of electronic music and pop and jazz. Under the name Jon and Vangelis [see Yes entry], he and Anderson had four U.K. chart entries, including two Top 10 hits: "I Hear You Now" (1980) and "I'll Find My Way Home" (1981).

In 1982 Vangelis finally made his commercial breakthrough with the score to the film *Chariots of Fire*. The movie theme was on the singles chart for 15 weeks and went as high as #6, while the score won an Oscar. His followup single, "Titles," failed to match that success, but the *Chariots* theme did inspire numerous soundalikes for American TV commercials.

Vangelis has since scored a number of motion pictures, including *Blade Runner* (1982), *Missing* (1982), *The Bounty* (1984), *Bitter Moon* (1994), and *1492: Conquest of Paradise* (1992). He has also composed music for three Jacques Cousteau documentaries. In 1992 he received the Chevalier Order of Arts and Letters, one of France's most important artistic honors. The 1994 rerelease of *Blade Runner* included never-before-released cuts featuring singers Mary Hopkin, Demis Roussos, and Don Percival.

Van Halen/David Lee Roth

Formed 1974, Pasadena, CA
David Lee Roth (b. Oct. 10, 1955, Bloomington, IN), voc.; Edward Van Halen (b. Jan. 26, 1955, Amsterdam, Neth.), gtr., voc.; Alex Van Halen (b. May 8, 1953, Amsterdam), drums; Michael Anthony (b. June 20, 1954, Chicago, IL), bass.
1978—*Van Halen* (Warner Bros.) 1979—*Van Halen II* 1980—*Women and Children First* 1981—*Fair Warning* 1982—*Diver Down* 1984—*1984* 1985—(– Roth; + Sammy Hagar [b. Oct. 13, 1947, Monterey, CA], voc.) 1986—*5150* 1988—*OU812* 1991—*For Unlawful Carnal Knowledge* 1993—*Van Halen, Live: Right Here, Right Now* 1995—*Balance* 1996—(– Hagar; + Gary Cherone [b. July 26, 1961, Medford, MA], voc.) *Van Halen Best of, vol. 1* 1998—*Van Halen III* 1999—(– Cherone).
David Lee Roth solo: 1985—*Crazy From the Heat* (Warner Bros.) 1986—*Eat 'Em and Smile* 1988—*Skyscraper* 1991—*A Little Ain't Enough* 1994—*Your Filthy Little Mouth* (Reprise) 1997—*The Best* (Rhino) 1998—*DLR Band* (Sumthing Distribution).
Sammy Hagar solo: see entry.

Since their national debut in 1978, Van Halen has become one of the most popular American heavy-metal bands. Initially fronted by the flamboyant and ever-quotable David Lee Roth and always featuring the highly original guitar pyrotechnics of Eddie Van Halen, Van Halen garnered a loyal mass following that held fast after Roth's 1985 departure and beyond.

The Van Halen brothers' father, Jan, was a freelance saxophone and clarinet player who performed styles ranging from big band to classical in the Netherlands. The family arrived in Pasadena "with 15 dollars and a piano," as Eddie once said, in 1967, and Jan washed dishes, then played in wedding bands to support the family. Beginning around age six both Eddie and Alex received piano lessons and extensive classical music training, but once in America they discovered rock & roll. Eddie learned to play drums, and Alex learned to play guitar; eventually they traded instruments and started a band called Mammoth. Roth, the even-then outgoing and outrageous scion of a wealthy family and lead singer of another rival band, Redball Jet, joined them. The bassist and lead singer of another group, Snake, Michael Anthony came aboard shortly thereafter. After learning that there was already another group claiming the name Mammoth, the group considered calling themselves Rat Salade before deciding on Van Halen.

Van Halen played the Pasadena/Santa Barbara bar circuit for more than three years. Its sets initially consisted primarily of cover material ranging from disco to pop, but the band eventually introduced original songs and was soon one of the most popular groups in California, regulars at the Sunset Strip hard-rock club Gazzari's, and an opening act for Santana, Nils Lofgren, UFO, and other established acts. In 1977 Kiss' Gene Simmons spotted Van Halen in L.A.'s Starwood club and financed its demo tape. After seeing the group and upon hearing Simmons' recommendation, Warner Bros. Records' Mo Ostin and staff producer Ted Templeman signed Van Halen. Its self-titled debut album hit #19 and eventually sold more than 6 million copies. The debut single, a pile-driving cover of the Kinks' 1964 hit "You Really Got Me," hit #36. The followup, "Runnin' With the Devil," hit #84.

Van Halen: Alex Van Halen, David Lee Roth, Eddie Van Halen, Michael Anthony

Roth's swaggering good looks and extroverted persona, not to mention pithy statements on the rock & roll lifestyle he claimed to espouse, assured press coverage. But while the mainstream media focused on Roth, musicians and fans were riveted by Eddie Van Halen's guitar mastery and an array of unorthodox techniques that he developed as he taught himself to play: hammer-ons, pull-offs, two-hand tapping, and any combination thereof to produce his unique sound. In addition, the guitarist was also known to build and/or meticulously customize his instruments, using everything from sandpaper to chainsaws to alter the timbre of his instrument and achieve a distinct sound. Long before the group ever recorded, Eddie became a legend among local guitarists eager to learn the secret of his sound. Like countless guitarists before him, from Robert Johnson to Eric Clapton, Eddie began performing with his back to the audience to guard his technique.

Van Halen II, released as new wave began coming to the fore, continued in the group's straight-rock style and featured their first Top 20 single, "Dance the Night Away," as well as the popular "Beautiful Girls." *Women and Children First* spun off the single "And the Cradle Will Rock," a metal showcase that typified the band's dense, loud, crunching style. In 1979 Van Halen launched its second world tour, its first as headliner. Early on, the band embraced its larger-than-life image; for example, tour incidents ranged from Roth's breaking his nose on a lighting rig when jumping onstage to the band trashing its dressing room after a promoter failed to comply with the band's contractual stipulation that the backstage candy dish contain no brown M&Ms. *Fair Warning,* another multiplatinum effort, followed. *Diver Down,* which included a hit cover of Roy Orbison's "Oh, Pretty Woman" (#12, 1982) and a Top 40 version of Martha and the Vandellas' "Dancing in the Street," became the group's highest-charting album to that point, peaking at #3. (In 1981 Eddie married actress Valerie Bertinelli; in 1991 their son, Wolfgang, was born. Three years later, Eddie stopped drinking.)

Van Halen's biggest album with Roth was *1984* (#2, 1984), which contained the #1 hit "Jump" (on which Eddie played synthesizer) as well as "I'll Wait" (#13, 1984), "Panama" (#13, 1984), and "Hot for Teacher" (#56, 1984), all songs supported by popular videos that showcased both Roth's alternately swaggering and clownish persona and Eddie (and the rest of the group's) flashy musicianship. Shortly before *1984*'s release, Eddie Van Halen had composed and played the guitar solo on Michael Jackson's "Beat It," a few bars of heavy metal that many observers believed helped the video land a spot on MTV's then predominantly white playlist. The loquacious Roth and the soft-spoken Eddie had long been considered one of rock's oddest couples. When in 1985 Roth released his four-song EP, *Crazy From the Heat,* and it spun off two hit singles—a cover of the Beach Boys' "California Girls" (#3, 1985) and a medley that paired Al Jolson's "Just a Gigolo" with Louis Prima's "I Ain't Got Nobody" (#12, 1985)—a breakup was widely rumored. The videos for the two songs were hugely popular, and for a time Roth had a film in development (the deal fell through). When Roth delayed recording for Van Halen's seventh album, tensions rose, and Roth left the band. That June, established hard-rock singer Sammy Hagar was named Roth's replacement.

The Hagar era began auspiciously, with the group's next three multiplatinum albums—*5150, OU812,* and *For Unlawful Carnal Knowledge* (or "F.U.C.K.," as it's slyly abbreviated)—hitting #1. Among the hit singles from these records were "Why Can't This Be Love" (#3, 1986), "Dreams" (#22, 1986), "Love Walks In" (#22, 1986), "When It's Love" (#5, 1988), "Finish What You Started" (#13, 1988), and "Feels So Good" (#35, 1989). Van Halen headlined the Monsters of Rock Tour in 1988 and in 1991 bought the Cabo Wabo Cantina, a Cabo San Lucas, Mexico, restaurant and bar. (Hagar later bought out the other members.) The innovative, text-oriented 1992 video for "Right Now" didn't boost the single beyond #55, but it did win MTV's Best Video of the Year award and provided the theme for a round of Pepsi commercials shortly thereafter. The year 1993 saw the release of the band's first live album, *Van Halen Live: Right Here, Right Now* (#5, 1993). *Balance* debuted at #1 in 1995 and sold double-platinum nearly immediately upon its release. It contained one Top 30 hit, "Can't Stop Lovin' You."

Throughout his tenure with Van Halen, Hagar continued to release solo albums [see entry]. While this wasn't considered a problem by the other members, tempers flared in spring 1996, when the band finished the *Balance* tour. Hagar's wife was pregnant and he wanted to take time off; the rest of the group wanted to work on a few new tracks for a greatest-hits compilation, an idea that Hagar was against. Some speculated that Hagar objected because a best-of package would undoubtedly feature songs from the Roth era, songs Hagar had declined to sing in concert. In June of that year, Van Halen claimed that Hagar left the band, while Hagar insisted that he was fired—a difference in opinion that has lasted to this day. The remaining members of Van Halen invited Roth back into the studio with them to record two new tracks for the hits album. That fall, the apparently reunited foursome presented a trophy at the MTV Video Music Awards, and speculation was that Roth was back in the band full-time. Apparently Roth thought so, too, because he was miffed when Eddie, the band's spokesperson, clarified in a press statement that Van Halen's intentions were to include Roth in a couple of new recordings and nothing more. Again, the difference of opinion regarding the group's original intention prevails.

With Hagar gone and Roth out of the picture again, Van Halen hired ex-Extreme [see entry] singer Gary Cherone as its new lead vocalist in November 1996. The choice was initially surprising, because Extreme's biggest hits, "More Than Words" and "Hole Hearted," were ballads, but the bulk of that band's catalogue was hard rock, and the collaboration seemed to reinvigorate Eddie Van Halen. He and Cherone immediately began writing songs together, with Cherone's lyrics inspiring Eddie's music—the first time the group's music wasn't written first. This new incarnation recorded *Van Halen III* (#4, 1998), an album that signaled another Van Halen first: Eddie singing lead on one song. The band toured and the single "Without You" rose to #1 on the Mainstream Rock chart, but CD sales fell quickly. The release sold just 500,000 copies, making it the first Van Halen album not to go at least double platinum. In November 1999 Cherone left the band. He recorded a solo album and returned to a Massachusetts stage production of *Jesus Christ Superstar,* which he starred in after Extreme broke up.

Although the remaining three members of Van Halen are still together, the band's future without a lead singer is uncertain. Meanwhile, Eddie Van Halen, a heavy smoker, participated in what was said to be a clinical trial of preventative treatment for tongue cancer in 2000. In 2001 he revealed that he had been treated for cancer.

Diamond Dave's solo career yielded three platinum albums, with his third and fourth albums, *Eat 'Em and Smile* and *Skyscraper,* both Top 10, featuring the hits "Yankee Rose" (#16, 1986, from *Eat*) and "Just Like Paradise" (#6, 1988, from *Skyscraper*). The band for *Eat 'Em* included bassist Billy Sheehan, guitarist Steve Vai, and drummer Greg Bissonette.

This lineup remained fairly steady for *Skyscraper,* but Sheehan left, and in 1989 Vai began his solo career. *A Little Ain't Enough,* a critical and commercial disappointment despite its Top 20 showing, had no hit singles. In 1991 Roth fired his band and moved to New York City, where in April 1993 he was arrested while purchasing $10's worth of marijuana in Washington Square Park (he received a year's probation). His 1994 release, *Your Filthy Little Mouth,* continued the decline, and a 1998 album credited to the DLR Band fared no better. Even commenting on his low commercial standing, Roth remained quotable as ever and published a breezy, explicit autobiography entitled, *Crazy From the Heat* (with Paul Scanlon), in 1997.

Vanilla Fudge

Formed 1966, New York, NY
Vince Martell (b. Nov. 11, 1945, Bronx, NY), gtr., voc.; Mark Stein (b. Mar. 1947, Bayonne, NJ), kybds., voc.; Tim Bogert (b. Aug. 1944, New York), bass, voc.; Carmine Appice (b. Dec. 15, 1946, Staten Island, NY), drums, voc.
1967—*Vanilla Fudge* (Atco) 1968—*The Beat Goes On; Renaissance* 1969—*Near the Beginning* 1970—*Rock 'n' Roll* 1982—*Greatest Hits* 1984—*Mystery* 1993—*Psychedelic Sundae: The Best of Vanilla Fudge* (Rhino).

One of the first heavy-rock acts, Vanilla Fudge was also a pioneer of the "long version." The band evolved from New York bar bands like the Pigeons and the Vagrants. The Pigeons included Mark Stein (who had played and sung on TV shows as a child and teenager, and who recorded in 1959 for Cameo Records), Tim Bogert, and, eventually, Vince Martell and Carmine Appice.

They named themselves Vanilla Fudge in early 1966 and began practicing their "psychedelic-symphonic rock." They made their New York concert debut July 22, 1967, at the Village Theater with the Byrds and the Seeds. By the end of the year they had signed to Atco Records. Vanilla Fudge's first single was an extended version of the Supremes' "You Keep Me Hangin' On," complete with half-speed tempo, Gothic organ, and quasi-raga guitar. The single was a Top 10 hit, and Vanilla Fudge's debut LP, which contained similarly treated versions of "Eleanor Rigby," "Ticket to Ride," "People Get Ready," and "Bang Bang," went gold. The followup LP sold fairly well but is chiefly remembered as one of the most overreaching concept albums of all time; it purported to be a musical history of the previous 25 years, and included a 12-minute cut that, allegedly, contained the entire history of music.

The third album was even less popular and contained nine minutes of Donovan's "Season of the Witch." The band finally broke up in 1970, after its fifth, least successful album. Appice and Bogert went on to form Cactus; they later teamed up with Jeff Beck in the Beck, Bogert and Appice power trio. Appice became a session drummer; he has backed Rod Stewart, among others. In the mid-'80s he formed his own band, King Kobra; he later performed with Blue Murder. Stein played in the Tommy Bolin Band and toured with Alice Cooper. He also recorded solo for CBS, and has worked on numerous television and radio ads. The band reunited briefly in 1983, resulting in 1984's *Mystery.* Vanilla Fudge toured in 1987; the most recent live date took place in 1988 at the Atlantic Records 40th-anniversary concert at New York's Madison Square Garden.

Dave Van Ronk

Born June 30, 1936, Brooklyn, NY
1959—*Ballads, Blues and a Spiritual* (Folkways) 1960—*Black Mountain Blues* 1962—*Inside Dave Van Ronk* (Prestige) 1963—*Folksinger* 1964—*In the Tradition; Dave Van Ronk and the Ragtime Jug Stompers* (Mercury); *Dave Van Ronk* 1967—*No Dirty Names* (Verve/Folkways) 1968—*Dave Van Ronk and the Hudson Dusters* (Verve) 1974—*Songs for Aging Children* (Cadet) 1976—*Sunday Street* (Philo) 1985—*Going Back to Brooklyn* (Reckless) 1988—*Somebody Else, Not Me* 1990—*Peter and the Wolf* (Alacazam); *Hummin' to Myself* (Gazell) 1991—*The Folkways Years, 1959–61* (Smithsonian Folkways) 1992—*Statesboro Blues* (EPM); *Let No One Deceive You: Songs of Bertolt Brecht* (with Frankie Armstrong) (Flying Fish) 1993—*A Chrestomathy* (Gazell); *A Chrestomathy, vol. 2.* 1994—*To All My Friends in Far-Flung Places* 1995—*From . . . Another Time and Place* (Alcazar).

With his bawdy, gruff yet tender singing style and considerable blues-archivist skills, Dave Van Ronk became one of the most respected members of New York's early-'60s folk boom. Though he's never been a commercial success, he remains influential in folk circles as a performer, historian, and teacher.

Van Ronk grew up in a musical household, surrounded by his grandparents' collection of jazz and ragtime records. His grandfather also played ragtime piano. While in high school in Brooklyn, Van Ronk became avidly interested in traditional jazz and played with New York–area jazz groups upon graduation. After spending eight months at sea with the merchant marines, he returned to New York. Among his first gigs was one in 1957 opening for Odetta, an experience that spurred him on to an in-depth investigation of blues and folk music, resulting in his becoming an avid fan of Josh White. He began performing on the folk circuit.

In 1958 Van Ronk formed a jug band with his friend, frequent collaborator, and fellow archivist Sam Charters and recorded an album for Lyrichord Records. By 1959 he had played folk festivals and been signed to Folkways. While his next few albums for Folkways and Prestige stuck with his folk-blues mode, in 1964 he performed at the Newport Folk Festival with a jazz-flavored jug band; and soon after the festival he formed the Ragtime Jug Stompers, again with Charters.

By this time, Van Ronk had long been a close friend of Bob Dylan, who in the early '60s had frequently stayed at Van Ronk's Greenwich Village apartment. (In May 1974 he appeared with Dylan and others at a New York benefit for

Chilean political prisoners.) At one point early in his career, Van Ronk also turned down manager Albert Grossman's offer of a place in the trio that became Peter, Paul and Mary. He briefly formed a rock-style band, the Hudson Dusters, and tried his hand at acting, but returned to touring.

Unlike many other folk artists of his period, Van Ronk is better known as an interpreter of songs rather than a writer; he was among the first to perform songs by Lightnin' Hopkins, for example, and his repertoire includes songs by writers ranging from Hoagy Carmichael and Louis Jordan to Joni Mitchell and the children's song "Teddy Bears' Picnic." Still living in Greenwich Village, he continues to perform around the world and to teach guitar. His *Fingerpicking Folk, Blues, and Ragtime Guitar,* a six-tape instructional tutorial, is available through Stefan Grossman's Guitar Workshop.

Little Steven Van Zandt

Born Steven Van Zandt, Nov. 22, 1950, Boston, MA
1982—*Men Without Women* (EMI) 1984—*Voice of America* 1987—*Freedom—No Compromise* (Manhattan) 1989—*Revolution* 1999—*Born Again Savage* (Renegade Nation).

In the '80s Steven Van Zandt emerged from stints with fellow New Jersey Shoreans Southside Johnny and Bruce Springsteen to become a political artist. He is best known for putting together the antiapartheid superstar album *Sun City.*

Van Zandt was raised in Middletown, New Jersey, where he formed his first band, the Source, in 1966. In the early '70s he played in a number of groups, including Steel Mill and Southside Johnny's Asbury Jukes, before joining Springsteen's E Street Band as a guitarist in mid-decade. He also continued to work with Southside Johnny, writing songs for and producing the Jukes' first three albums.

In 1982 Van Zandt formed Little Steven and the Disciples of Soul, a 12-piece band including the Asbury Jukes' horn players, former Plasmatics bassist Jean Beauvoir, and ex-Rascals drummer Dino Danelli. Their first album was a solid, rootsy effort that Van Zandt produced under his E Street nickname, "Miami Steve." By his second album, Little Steven had quit Springsteen's group, dropping the "Miami." *Voice of America* showed his newfound commitment to international politics; Black Uhuru later covered the track "Solidarity."

In 1984 Van Zandt made two visits to South Africa, and upon his return, he gathered over 50 performers, including Springsteen, Bob Dylan, Miles Davis, George Clinton, Bonnie Raitt, Lou Reed, and Bono, to form Artists United Against Apartheid. The group recorded Van Zandt's "Sun City." The song grew into an album, coproduced by Arthur Baker, a popular video, and a concert, all of which raised money for antiapartheid efforts. It also refocused public attention on the longstanding cultural boycott against South Africa, which many entertainers had broken by playing the lucrative Vegas-style resort Sun City.

Manhattan, the label that released *Sun City,* signed Van Zandt and released *Freedom—No Compromise,* on which he continued playing protest songs. Springsteen sang on "Native American," and Van Zandt duetted with Ruben Blades on "Bitter Fruit," a song about labor conditions in Central America. None of Van Zandt's solo records has sold well in the U.S., and 1989's *Revolution* produced scarcely a ripple. In 1991 he reunited with Southside Johnny and Springsteen, producing Southside's *Better Days.* The single and video "It's Been a Long Time" featured the three Jerseyites. Van Zandt has also produced a number of other artists, including Gary "U.S." Bonds, Lone Justice, and Ronnie Spector.

Van Zandt spent much of the '90s out of the limelight, but in 1999 landed a role in the popular and critically acclaimed HBO series *The Sopranos,* where he plays the part of Silvio Dante, a Jersey street guy and mob enforcer. Later the same year Van Zandt signed on with Springsteen's reunited E Street Band, with whom he embarked on a year-long world tour. Van Zandt also released *Born Again Savage,* his fifth solo album, in 1999. Initially available only through his Web site, the record features U2's Adam Clayton on bass and Jason Bonham, the son of the late Led Zeppelin drummer John Bonham, on drums. The fifth in a series of concept albums dealing, by turns, with the individual, the family, the state, the economy, and religion, *Born Again Savage* finds Van Zandt exploring various dimensions of human spirituality.

Townes Van Zandt

Born John Townes Van Zandt, Mar. 7, 1944, Fort Worth, TX; died Jan. 1, 1997, Mount Juliet, TN
1967—*First Album* (Poppy/Tomato) 1968—*For the Sake of the Song* 1969—*Our Mother the Mountain* 1970—*Townes Van Zandt* 1971—*Delta Momma Blues* 1972—*High, Low and Inbetween* 1973—*The Late, Great Townes Van Zandt* 1977—*Live at the Old Quarter* 1979—*Flying Shoes* 1987—*At My Window* (Sugar Hill) 1989—*Live and Obscure* 1993—*The Nashville Sessions* (Tomato) 1994—*Road Songs* (Sugar Hill); *No Deeper Blue* 1997—*Rear View Mirror; The Highway Kind* 1999—*A Far Cry From Dead* (Arista/Austin) 2000—*In Pain* (Normal, Ger.).

Townes Van Zandt was a Texas-based singer/songwriter who was content to live the life of a hermetic, legendary folk artist while other performers turned his songs into hits. Van Zandt was born into a wealthy, pedigreed Texas family. His reputation as a rambling man dates back to his childhood, when his family moved frequently. He began playing guitar at 15, after seeing Elvis on TV.

Along with fellow Texas singer/songwriter cult heroes like Guy Clark, Van Zandt began singing folk clubs and juke joints in Houston, branching out into the Southwest circuit. He developed a reputation as a wild man; many of his tunes are drinking songs. His cult following is primarily interested in his somber, poetic, introspective tunes and folksy tales. Van Zandt has frequently been called a more down-home Leonard Cohen.

Van Zandt moved to Nashville the year his first album

came out. He never availed himself of that city's music biz, however, releasing his records on small, poorly distributed labels and allowing his song rights to get hung up in legal quagmires. He moved to Austin, Texas, in the late '70s, just as he was getting his first mainstream exposure with Emmylou Harris' 1977 cover of "Pancho and Lefty," a song he wrote earlier in the decade. Six years later Merle Haggard and Willie Nelson turned the cut into a major country hit with their duet rendition. In 1981 Harris and Don Williams' cover of "If I Needed You" topped the country chart. Van Zandt's songs have also been recorded by Doc Watson and Guy Clark.

Van Zandt returned to Nashville in 1986 and began recording again. *At My Window* was his first album of new material in eight years. He was embraced by a new generation of folk-based artists. Canada's Cowboy Junkies took Van Zandt on tour with them in 1990, and Van Zandt contributed two songs to the Junkies' 1992 album, *Black Eyed Man.* Van Zandt continued to be more interested in writing than recording, allowing his music to be released on disparate labels around the world. *Road Songs,* for example, was released in Europe almost two years prior to its U.S. issue.

Van Zandt began working on a new studio album toward the end of 1996, but didn't live to finish it, dying of a heart attack on January 1, 1997, while recuperating from hip surgery at his home just outside Nashville; he was 52. Guy Clark, Steve Earle, Lyle Lovett, Emmylou Harris, and other friends paid tribute to Van Zandt at a memorial service held in Nashville immediately after his death. Joined by Willie Nelson and Van Zandt's son J.T., much the same group taped a musical tribute to the late singer/songwriter for the PBS music series *Austin City Limits* later in the year. Sugar Hill Records also released a pair of albums at the time of Van Zandt's death: *Rear View Mirror,* a reissue of an acoustic live album that first came out overseas in 1993, and *The Highway Kind,* a collection of more recent recordings. *A Far Cry From Dead* followed in 1999. The album featured studio musicians adding accompaniment to 13 songs Van Zandt had recorded between 1989 and 1991. Two of its tracks were previously unreleased numbers, among them "Sanitarium Blues," a harrowing reflection based on the time Van Zandt spent in a mental hospital as a teenager.

Stevie Ray Vaughan

Born Oct. 3, 1954, Dallas, TX; died Aug. 27, 1990, East Troy, WI

1983—*Texas Flood* (Epic) 1984—*Couldn't Stand the Weather* 1985—*Soul to Soul* 1986—*Live Alive* 1989—*In Step* 1991—*The Sky Is Crying* 1992—*In the Beginning* 1995—*Greatest Hits* 1997—*Live at Carnegie Hall* 1999—*The Real Deal: Greatest Hits, vol. 2* 2000—*Blues at Sunrise; Stevie Ray Vaughan and Double Trouble.*

As the Vaughan Brothers (with Jimmie Vaughan): 1990—*Family Style* (Epic).

Before his untimely death in 1990, guitarist Stevie Ray Vaughan had become the leading figure in the blues-rock revival he spearheaded in the mid-'80s.

Vaughan's first musical inspiration was his older brother Jimmie, a guitarist who later helped form the Fabulous Thunderbirds [see entry]. Together, the brothers immersed themselves in the work of blues guitar greats like B.B. King, Albert King, and Freddie King, and early rock guitarists like Lonnie Mack (whose 1985 comeback, *Strike Like Lightning,* Vaughan would coproduce). By the time he was 14, Vaughan was already playing Dallas blues clubs with a variety of bands including Blackbird, the Shantones, and the Epileptic Marshmallow. Dropping out of high school in 1972, Vaughan relocated to Austin, Texas, the up-and-coming musical haven where his brother had already established himself.

In Austin Vaughan formed the Nightcrawlers and then joined the Cobras for a year. Vaughan's next group was Triple Threat, which included Lou Ann Barton among its five vocalists. After three years with Triple Threat, Vaughan and Barton formed Double Trouble. Barton left to go solo, and Double Trouble reverted to a power trio with Chris Layton on drums and Tommy Shannon, a bassist who had played with Johnny Winter in the late '60s. Vaughan's fluid Hendrix-meets-the-blues-masters guitar playing, his rough-edged vocals, and the trio's live intensity made them local legends. (*In the Beginning* captures a 1980 radio broadcast.)

By 1982 the band's considerable reputation had reached the Rolling Stones, who hired Double Trouble to perform at a private party in New York. That same year, veteran producer Jerry Wexler arranged for Vaughan's band to play the Montreux Jazz Festival—the first time an unsigned, unrecorded group had done so. David Bowie caught the performance and tapped Vaughan to play on his next album. Vaughan's gritty guitar work became one of the unexpected highlights of *Let's Dance.* Legendary talent scout John Hammond became Vaughan's most important mentor, signing Double Trouble to Epic and acting as executive producer for the band's debut, *Texas Flood* (#38, 1983). Vaughan's raw, blues-drenched virtuosity struck a chord with a grass-roots audience. *Couldn't Stand the Weather* (#31, 1984) saw Vaughan pay explicit tribute to Jimi Hendrix with an exact cover of "Voodoo Chile (Slight Return)." In 1985 Vaughan became the first white performer to win the W.C. Handy Blues Foundation's Blues Entertainer of the Year award; that year Vaughan also added keyboardist Reese Wynans to the band.

After collapsing onstage during an English tour, Vaughan sought help to deal with his cocaine and alcohol addictions, entering a treatment center in September 1986. "Wall of Denial" on his 1989 album, *In Step* (#33), addressed his addiction and rehabilitation. In 1987 he made a rare film appearance trading guitar leads on "Pipeline" with surf-guitar king Dick Dale in the Annette Funicello film *Back to the Beach.* A 1989 tour with Jeff Beck attested to Vaughan's renewed strength and continued popularity.

On leaving an East Troy, Wisconsin, theater—following an onstage guitar jam that included Eric Clapton, Jimmie Vaughan, Buddy Guy, Robert Cray, and Jeff Healey—Vaughan was killed in a helicopter crash. By then, Vaughan was firmly established as the era's premier blues-rock performer. Two posthumous releases—*Family Style* (#7, 1990), a collaboration with Jimmie Vaughan, and *The Sky Is Crying*

(#10, 1991)—became Vaughan's best-selling recordings. *Greatest Hits* and *Live at Carnegie Hall* went to #39 and #40, respectively.

In 1995 Jimmie Vaughan organized an all-star tribute concert in Austin featuring Eric Clapton, Buddy Guy, B.B. King and more. *A Tribute to Stevie Ray Vaughan,* released the following year, won a Best Rock Instrumental Grammy for the cut "SRV Shuffle." As a new generation of guitarists (notably Kenny Wayne Shepherd) copped Vaughan's signature style, his catalogue continued to sell more than 800,000 copies a year. Epic/Legacy reissued his first four albums with bonus tracks in 1999, along with *The Real Deal: Greatest Hits, vol. 2,* which entered the charts at #53. *Blues at Sunrise,* a collection of slow blues recordings, was released in 2000 as was the box set *Stevie Ray Vaughan and Double Trouble.*

Bobby Vee

Born Robert Thomas Velline, Apr. 30, 1943, Fargo, ND
1961—*Bobby Vee* (Liberty) 1962—*Bobby Vee Meets the Crickets; Golden Greats* 1963—*The Night Has a Thousand Eyes; Bobby Vee Meets the Ventures* 1967—*Come Back When You Grow Up* 1972—*Robert Thomas Velline* 1975—*The Very Best of Bobby Vee* (United Artists) 1990—*Bobby Vee* (EMI); *U.K. Tour '90* (Rockhouse) 1992—*Last of the Great Rhythm Guitar Players* 1999—*Down the Line.*

One of the longest-lasting teen idols of the early '60s, Bobby Vee got his lucky break when he and his band the Shadows filled in for the late Buddy Holly at a 1958 Mason City, Iowa, concert days after Holly had died in a plane crash. The Shadows (which included Bobby's brother Bill) then managed to get their song "Suzie Baby" recorded locally, and it became a hit. Producer Snuff Garrett signed the band to Liberty Records in 1959, releasing "Suzie Baby" (#77) nationally.

At Liberty, Vee was quickly (and literally) groomed for solo success, under Garrett's supervision. First, Garrett had Vee cover British teen-idol Adam Faith's "What Do You Want?," which flopped at #93 in the spring of 1960. But later that year a cover of the Clovers' R&B hit "Devil or Angel" hit #6 on the U.S. singles chart. "Rubber Ball" (cowritten by Gene Pitney) was a Top 10 hit in the U.S. (#6) and the U.K., and for the next few years the clean-cut Vee, in his high school letter sweater, sang sweetly of the ups and downs of sexless romance from the top of the charts with hits like "Take Good Care of My Baby" (#1) and "Run to Him" (#2) in 1961; "Punish Her" (#20) in 1962; and "The Night Has a Thousand Eyes" (#8) and "Charms" (#13) in 1963.

Vee was just as enormously popular in Britain as in America, and he toured both countries frequently. In the midst of his big-hit years, Vee cut a Buddy Holly tribute album with the Crickets, as well as one other album simply backed by Holly's onetime band. The mid-'60s were fallow years for Vee, but he returned to the charts in 1967 with the million-selling "Come Back When You Grow Up" (#3). In 1972 he recorded an album under his real name, but it did not chart.

In the years since Vee has no further charting singles, but he continues to tour the world (including an annual trip to England, where in 1981 he was awarded a gold album for his *Singles Album*). He resides in Minnesota with his family, and has his own studio and record label, Rockhouse Records. In 1999, with the help of his three sons, Vee celebrated his 40th anniversary in rock & roll by releasing *Down the Line,* another tribute to Holly.

Suzanne Vega

Born Aug. 12, 1959, New York, NY
1985—*Suzanne Vega* (A&M) 1987—*Solitude Standing* 1990—*Days of Open Hand* 1992—*99.9 F°* 1996—*Nine Objects of Desire* 1999—*Best of Suzanne Vega: Tried & True* (PolyGram International, Swe.).

In 1987 a ballad about an abused child, "Luka," proved Suzanne Vega's unlikely ticket to pop stardom, reaching #3 on the singles chart and situating Vega, alongside Tracy Chapman, at the forefront of a new wave of thoughtful, folk-influenced female singer/songwriters. Three years later, Vega's career got another unexpected lift when a pair of enterprising British remixers brought her back into the Top 10 in 1990, with a hip-hop version of her 1987 song "Tom's Diner."

Vega grew up in New York's Spanish Harlem, the eldest of four children. Her Puerto Rican stepfather, a writer and teacher, encouraged Vega's early interest in dance and the guitar. At the High School of Performing Arts, she studied the former and began composing on the latter; at 16 she began playing her songs at Greenwich Village coffeehouses. After graduating, Vega became a literature major at New York's Barnard College while continuing to perform acoustic folk at downtown clubs. In 1983, while supporting herself as a temporary receptionist, she met lawyer Ron Fierstein and musician/producer Steve Addabbo, who were starting their own music promotion company. The fledgling partners began managing Vega, and with their assistance, she landed a contract with A&M Records.

Produced by Addabbo and ex–Patti Smith guitarist Lenny Kaye, Vega's eponymous 1985 debut album, which included "Marlene on the Wall," established her as a critical and cult favorite in the U.S., and reached #11 on the British pop chart. The next year, Vega contributed the song "Left of Center" to the film soundtrack for *Pretty in Pink,* and wrote lyrics for two tracks on Philip Glass' *Songs From Liquid Days.* In 1987 *Solitude Standing* proved her domestic breakthrough album, shooting to #11 (and to #2 in England) with the help of "Luka."

In 1990 Vega's third album, *Days of Open Hand,* peaked at #50 and spawned no hit singles. But that same year, the U.K. sampling/remixing duo DNA added a funky rhythm track to "Tom's Diner," a song from *Solitude Standing,* and released it—without Vega's permission—as a bootleg. Vega and A&M were savvy enough to get rights to the single, which quickly became a club sensation and then a pop hit (#5 U.S., #2 U.K.). In 1991 A&M capitalized further on this success by releasing *Tom's Album,* a collection of reworkings of the song by various artists, including R.E.M.

Perhaps encouraged by this reception, Vega hired noted

keyboardist and producer Mitchell Froom (Elvis Costello, Crowded House, Los Lobos) to incorporate dance and technopop textures on her fourth album. Nonetheless, *99.9 F°* reached only #86, but the recording of this album would change Vega's life; though they weren't involved with each other while working together, six months after wrapping the project, Froom left his wife for Vega, and the two were a secret item while doing interviews for the album in 1992. Their daughter, Ruby, was born in 1994, and the couple married the following year. Froom produced Vega's next album, 1996's *Nine Objects of Desire* (#92), which included the atypically upbeat "No Cheap Thrill" as well as such personal accounts as "Birth-day (Love Made Real)," about giving birth.

Froom became the keyboardist in her band in order to keep the family together while on tour. While this album wasn't a mainstream success either, Vega maintained her fan base, calling for the publication of a book of her lyrics, poems, and essays, entitled *The Passionate Eye: The Collected Writing of Suzanne Vega*, in 1999. Upon its publication, she embarked on a national book tour, reading excerpts and signing autographs. In 2000 she and Froom divorced, and Vega began writing songs about the end of the relationship, singing some of them on tour in Europe. She planned to write enough songs for another album, record them with producer Rupert Hine (Howard Jones, Tina Turner), and release an acoustic-based album in 2001.

Velvet Underground

Formed 1965, New York, NY
Lou Reed (b. Lewis Allen Reed, Mar. 2, 1942, Brooklyn, NY), voc., gtr.; John Cale (b. Dec. 5, 1940, Garnant, Wales), viola, bass, kybds., voc., gtr.; Sterling Morrison (b. Holmes Sterling Morrison Jr., Aug. 29, 1942, Westbury, NY; d. Aug. 30, 1995, Poughkeepsie, NY), bass, gtr.; Angus MacLise (b. Mar. 14, 1938, Bridgeport, CT; d. June 21, 1979, Kathmandu, Nepal), drums, perc.
1965—(– MacLise; + Moe Tucker [b. Maureen Tucker, Aug. 26, 1944, Levittown, NY], drums, voc.) 1966—(+ Nico [b. Christa Päffgen, Oct. 16, 1938, Cologne, Ger.; d. July 18, 1988, Ibiza, Sp.], voc., kybds.) 1967—*The Velvet Underground and Nico* (MGM/Verve) (– Nico) 1968—*White Light/White Heat* (– Cale; + Doug Yule, bass, voc., gtr.) 1969—*The Velvet Underground* (MGM) 1970—(– Tucker; + Billy Yule, drums) *Loaded* (Atlantic) (– Reed; + Walter Powers, bass; – B. Yule; + Tucker) 1971—(– Morrison; + Willie Alexander, gtr., voc.; – Tucker; Yule continues with various lineups) 1972—*Live at Max's Kansas City* (Cotillion) 1973—*Squeeze* (Polydor, U.K.) (group disbands) 1974—*Velvet Underground Live With Lou Reed* (Mercury) 1985—*V.U.* (Verve) 1986—*Another View* 1993—(group re-forms: Reed; Cale; Morrison; Tucker) *Live MCMXCIII* (Sire) 1995—*Peel Slowly and See* (Polydor).

The Velvet Underground never sold many records, but, as many have said, it seems like every one of the group's fans went out and started a band. While their songs were constructed on the same three chords and 4/4 beat employed by most late-'60s rockers, the Velvets were unique in their intentional crudity, in their sense of beauty in ugliness, and in their lyrics. In the age of flower power they spoke in no uncertain terms of social alienation, sexual deviancy, drug addiction, violence, and hopelessness. Both in their sound and in their words, the songs evoked the exhilaration and destructiveness of modern urban life. The group's music and stance were of seminal importance to David Bowie, the New York Dolls, Patti Smith, Mott the Hoople, Roxy Music, the Sex Pistols, R.E.M., Sonic Youth, the Jesus and Mary Chain, Luna, and countless others of the protopunk, punk, and postpunk movements.

In 1964 John Cale [see entry] met Lou Reed [see entry] in New York City. Both had been classically trained—Cale as a violist and theorist, and Reed as a pianist. By the time of their first meeting Cale was engaging in avant-garde experimentation with La Monte Young and Reed was writing poems about down-and-out streetlife. Cale, Reed, Sterling Morrison, and Angus MacLise (the percussionist in Young's ensemble) formed a group that played under various names—the Warlocks, the Primitives, the Falling Spikes—in galleries and at poetry readings around lower Manhattan. As the Primitives, they recorded a series of singles on Pickwick Records, for which Reed had once worked as house songwriter. In 1965 the quartet became known as the Velvet Underground. MacLise, who frowned upon the idea of playing for money, quit prior to the rechristened combo's first paying performance. (A poet and virtuoso percussionist who spent years living in Asia, he died of malnutrition in Nepal in 1979. Archival CDs of his raga-influenced solo work appeared in 1999 and 2000.) Maureen Tucker was enlisted to take his place on a per-diem basis, which became permanent when she constructed her own drum kit out of tambourines and garbage-can lids.

On November 11, 1965, the group played its first gig as the Velvet Underground, opening for the Myddle Class at a high school dance in Summit, New Jersey. Within a few months, Reed, Morrison, Cale, and Tucker had taken up residency at the Cafe Bizarre in Greenwich Village, where they met pop artist Andy Warhol. When they were fired by the Bizarre's management for performing "Black Angel's Death Song" immediately after being told not to, Warhol invited them to perform at showings of his film series, *Cinematique Uptight*. He soon employed them as the aural component of his traveling mixed-media show, the Exploding Plastic Inevitable. For the latter, he augmented the lineup with singer/actress Nico [see entry], to whom he gave equal billing on the Velvets' first album. She sang only three songs on the record, which was recorded in 1966. Two singles—"I'll Be Your Mirror" b/w "All Tomorrow's Parties" and "Sunday Morning" b/w "Femme Fatale"—were released. The LP, which included Reed's "Heroin" and "Venus in Furs" (a song about sado-masochism), appeared nearly a year after its completion. It sported a Warhol cover with a peelable illustration of a banana.

The group had a falling-out with Warhol when it performed in Boston without Nico and the rest of the Inevitable troupe, who arrived late. The Velvets then took on Steve Sesnick as their manager. Without Warhol's name and knack for generating publicity, they faded from public attention. Their following was reduced further with the uncompromisingly noisy *White Light/White Heat,* which they recorded in a single day following a tour of mostly empty theaters. Cale, frequently in a power struggle with Reed, eventually quit. The remaining members enlisted Doug Yule, who had played with a Boston folk-rock Velvets, the Glass Menagerie. The third album, recorded in L.A., was much softer than either of its predecessors. It cost the group all but the most loyal of their following. MGM dropped the band and it was some months before Atlantic became interested.

Upon their return to New York to record in the summer of 1970, the Velvets played a month-long engagement at Max's Kansas City (with Doug's younger brother Billy Yule deputizing for Tucker, who was pregnant). These were the group's first appearances in New York since 1967, and they rekindled some interest. But soon after *Loaded* was finished, Reed, at odds with Sesnick, left the group and moved to England, where he lived for two years before reemerging as a solo performer. Although he denounced *Loaded,* claiming it was remixed after his departure (a charge Yule and Morrison denied), the album introduced "Sweet Jane" and "Rock and Roll."

With Doug Yule now on guitar and new bassist Walter Powers, the Velvet Underground toured the East Coast before Morrison dropped out in 1971 to teach English at the University of Texas in Austin. Tucker left following a tour of the U.K. She moved to Phoenix, Arizona, then to southern Georgia, where she raised a family and in 1980 began recording solo efforts. Yule retained the Velvet Underground name until 1973. Minus any of the principal Velvets, he recorded *Squeeze,* which was released only in Britain.

With the success of Reed's solo career and, to lesser extents, Cale's and Nico's, the Velvet Underground generated more interest in the '70s than it had during its existence. Two live albums were released: 1972's *Live at Max's Kansas City,* recorded the night of Reed's last appearance with the group, and 1974's *The Velvet Underground,* recorded in 1969 in Texas and California.

In 1989 Cale and Reed performed a song cycle written in memory of Andy Warhol, who died in 1988; the work was released on the 1990 album *Songs for Drella.* In June of that year, the best-known lineup of the Velvet Underground (minus Nico, who died in 1988 of head injuries sustained in a cycling accident) reunited onstage at a Warhol tribute in a small town near Paris. Their 10-minute version of the song "Heroin" led to another reunion three years later. With their longstanding differences seemingly resolved (particularly the battling egos of Reed and Cale), the players began rehearsals for several European shows slated for the summer of 1993. Highlights of the tour were documented on a video and album, *Live MCMXCIII.* That fall, however, the band fell apart once more, reportedly due to a spat between Cale and Reed over who would produce the group's upcoming MTV *Unplugged* appearance and album. The members again went their separate ways. All save Reed performed in late 1994, improvising music for the screenings of two silent Warhol films at the Andy Warhol Museum in Pittsburgh. Reed, Cale, and Tucker resumed their solo careers. Morrison, who occasionally performed with Tucker, died of non-Hodgkin's lymphoma in 1995. The following year, the classic lineup was inducted into the Rock and Roll Hall of Fame. The five-CD *Peel Slowly and See* contains the Reed-era albums plus numerous bonus tracks.

The Ventures

Formed 1959, Seattle, WA

Bob Bogle (b. Robert Lenard Bogle Jan. 16, 1934, Wagoner, OK), gtr., bass; Don Wilson (b. Feb. 10, 1933, Tacoma, WA), gtr.; Nokie Edwards (b. Nole Floyd Edwards, May 9, 1939, Lahoma, OK), gtr., bass; Howie Johnston (b. WA; d. 1988), drums.

1960—*Walk Don't Run* (Dolton) 1961—*Another Smash!!; The Ventures; The Colorful Ventures* 1962—(– Johnston; + Mel Taylor [b. Sep. 24, 1933, Brooklyn, NY; d. Aug. 11, 1996, Los Angeles, CA], drums) *Twist With the Ventures; The Ventures' Twist Party, vol. 2; Mashed Potatoes and Gravy; Going to the Ventures Dance Party!;* 1963—*The Ventures Play Telstar; The Lonely Bull; "Surfing"; Let's Go!* 1964—*(The) Ventures in Space; The Fabulous Ventures; Walk, Don't Run, vol. 2* 1965—*The Ventures Knock Me Out!; The Ventures On Stage; The Ventures a Go-Go; Christmas With the Ventures* 1966—*Where the Action Is; The Ventures/Batman Theme; Go With the Ventures; Wild Things!* 1967—(– Edwards; + Gerry McGee [b. Gerald James McGee, Nov. 17, 1937, Eunice, LA], gtr.) *Guitar Freakout; Super Psychedelics; Genius* (Sunset); *Golden Greats by the Ventures* (Liberty) 1969—(+ Johnny Durrill [b. Houston, TX], kybds.) *Hawaii Five-O; Swamp Rock* 1970—*More Golden Greats; The Ventures Tenth Anniversary Album* 1972—(– M. Taylor; – McGee; – Durrill; + Joe Barzle, drums; + Edwards) *Theme From Shaft* (United Artists); *Joy/Ventures Play the Classics* 1979—(– Barzle; + M. Taylor) 1984—(– Edwards; + McGee) 1990—*Walk, Don't Run: The Best of the Ventures* (EMI) 1991—*Greatest Hits* (Curb/Cema) 1996—(– M. Taylor; + Leon Taylor [b. Melvin Leon Taylor, Sep. 23, 1955, Johnson City, TN], drums) 1997—*Wild Again!* (GNP/Crescendo) 1998—*New Depths.*

The Ventures are one of the first, best, most lasting, and influential of instrumental guitar-based rock combos (rivaled only by Britain's Shadows). Their trademark sound—driving mechanical drums, metallic guitars twanging out simple, catchy pop tunes—has filtered down through the years to gain prominence in the sounds of bands like Blondie, the B-52's, the Go-Go's, and others. Often classified as a surf-rock band, the Ventures actually predated surf music and lasted well beyond its early-'60s boom. Some 35 years after their forming, they still play to receptive audiences.

Founding member Bob Bogle had started playing guitar by his teens. In his mid-teens, he supported himself by bringing wet cement to bricklayers, and he moved to Seattle to work. There he met Don Wilson, who had learned piano and trombone as a child, and bass and guitar in the army. By mid 1959 they had begun playing in local clubs. They soon added Nokie Edwards on lead guitar (Bogle switching to bass) and Howie Johnston on drums. They sent their first demo, "Walk Don't Run," to various record labels. When nobody responded, Don Wilson's mother released it as a single on her own Blue Horizon label. It became an instant regional hit in 1960, and in late summer was picked up for distribution by Dolton Records (distributed by Liberty).

In August 1960 "Walk Don't Run" became a #2 hit. The Ventures followed it with a rock version of "Ghost Riders in the Sky," then "Perfidia," "Lullaby of the Leaves," "Diamond Head," and "2,000 Pound Bee," all of which were big hits through the early and mid-'60s.

In 1961 Johnston was hurt in an auto accident and left the group. He was replaced by Mel Taylor. The hits kept on coming, with versions of "Lonely Bull" and "I Walk the Line" in 1963 and a surf remake of "Walk Don't Run" in 1964. For the next few years, their albums still sold and they continued to tour. In 1965 they released what was one of the first instructional records, *Play Guitar With the Ventures.*

In 1967 Edwards was replaced by Gerry McGee, who in 1970 recorded with Delaney and Bonnie Bramlett. In 1972 McGee went solo and Edwards returned. By that time, keyboardist Johnny Durrill had expanded the unit to a quintet, and the Ventures had delved into fuzz-tone and wah-wah guitar modification as well as blues, calypso, and Latin material.

In 1969 they hit the charts again with a version of the theme from the TV show *Hawaii Five-O.* In 1981, Bogle, Wilson, Edwards, and Taylor released a regional West Coast single, "Surfin' and Spyin' " (written by Go-Go Charlotte Caffey), and embarked on successful tours of the U.S. and Japan, where they had long been a star attraction. Bogle, McGee, and Wilson are still active in the group. Mel Taylor died of lung cancer in 1996; just weeks before, he had been on a Japanese tour with the band. His son, Leon, replaced him behind the kit. *Wild Again!* marked the first new Ventures studio album in 15 years. In addition, they have released numerous Japan-only records. Former guitarist Edwards continues to play solo.

Tom Verlaine: See Television

The Verve

Formed 1990, Wigan, Eng.
Richard Ashcroft (b. Sep. 11, 1971, Wigan), voc., gtr.; Nick McCabe (b. Jul. 14, 1971, St. Helens, Eng.), gtr.; Simon Jones (b. Jul. 29, 1972, Liverpool, Eng.), bass; Peter "Sobbo" Salisbury (b. Sep. 24, 1971), drums.
1992—*The Verve* EP (Hut/Caroline) 1993—*A Storm in Heaven* (Vernon Yard/Virgin) 1994—*No Come Down* 1995—*A Northern Soul* 1997—(+ Simon Tong, kybds., gtr.) *Urban Hymns* (Virgin).
Richard Ashcroft solo: 2000—*Alone With Everybody* (Virgin).

School friends Richard Ashcroft, Nick McCabe, Simon Jones, and Peter Salisbury came together as Verve in 1990 in Wigan, England (near Manchester). The group landed a deal with Virgin subsidiary Hut Records in England in 1991, and established its reputation for epic-length, atmospheric guitar jams on a string of early singles like "She's a Superstar," which were collected on the 1992 EP *The Verve.* Its debut album, *A Storm in Heaven* (1993), was met with rave reviews and netted the band a second-stage spot on the 1994 Lollapalooza Tour. The buzz brought it to the attention of jazz label Verve Records, which sued the band for trademark violation and forced it to change its name to the Verve.

Lollapalooza took considerable toll on the group (Ashcroft was hospitalized for exhaustion), and a few weeks after the release of 1995's *A Northern Soul,* he walked. He began work on a solo album with Salisbury, Jones, and childhood friend Simon Tong, but in the eleventh hour McCabe was called in and it became a new Verve album, *Urban Hymns* (1997). The album reached #23 in America on the strength of the #12 single "Bitter Sweet Symphony," which sampled four bars from an instrumental version of the Rolling Stones' "The Last Time." Mick Jagger and Keith Richards were granted all of the publishing rights for the song, and the Verve could not intervene when their publisher sold it to Nike for a commercial; the resulting mainstream exposure helped push the album to platinum status in the States. In the U.K., where the album topped the album chart, the singles "Bitter Sweet Symphony," "The Drugs Don't Work," and "Lucky Man" all hit the U.K. Top 10.

In the wake of its breakthrough success, however, the Verve began to fall apart again. In July of 1998, McCabe announced that he would not tour with the band for the remainder of the year. The group carried on with steel guitarist B.J. Cole, but announced its official breakup the following April. Ashcroft released his debut solo album, *Alone With Everybody* in 2000. The album featured performances by Salisbury, Cole, and Ashcroft's wife, former Spiritualized keyboardist Kate Radley.

The Village People

Formed 1977, New York, NY
Victor Willis, voc.; David Hodo (b. July 7, 1947), voc.; Felipe Rose (b. Jan. 12, 1954), voc., perc.; Randy Jones, voc.; Glenn Hughes (b. July 18, 1950, Bronx, NY; d. Mar. 4, 2001, New York), voc.; Alex Briley (b. Apr. 12, 1951), voc.
1977—*Village People* (Casablanca) 1978—*Macho Men* 1979—(– Willis; + Ray Simpson [b. Jan. 15, 1952, Bronx], voc.) *Cruisin'; Go West* 1980—*Live and Sleazy; Can't Stop the Music* soundtrack (with other artists) 1981—*Renaissance* (RCA) 1982—(– Simpson; + Miles Jay; numerous personnel changes follow) 1982—*Fox on the Box* 1984—*Sex Over the Phone*

The Village People

1988—*Greatest Hits* (Rhino) 1994—(lineup: Rose; Simpson; Hughes; Briley; Hodo; + Jeff Olson [b. Sep. 3, 1952, New York], voc.) 1995—(– Hughes; + Eric Anzalone [b. Dayton, OH], voc).

Under the direction of disco producer Jacques Morali, this campy vocal group had massive late-'70s pop hits with double-entendre-filled songs like "Macho Man" and "Y.M.C.A." In 1977 Morali, with business partners Henri Belolo and Peter Whitehead and lyricist Paul Hurtt, composed self-consciously gay-themed disco songs like "Fire Island" and "San Francisco." With actor/singer Victor Willis handling vocals, the music wowed both gay and straight club audiences. Backed by Casablanca Records president Neil Bogart, Morali formed a group of singer/actors dressed as a cross section of gay stereotypes: a beefy biker, a construction worker, a policeman, an Indian chief, and a cowboy. As Tom Smucker wrote, they "were gay goofs to those who got the joke, and disco novelties to those who didn't."

With major hits like "Macho Man" (#25) in 1978 and "Y.M.C.A." (#2) in 1979, the Village People scored six gold and four platinum records, sold out major concert halls, and appeared on numerous television talk shows. During their first burst of stardom, they reportedly sold over 20 million singles and 18 million albums worldwide. In 1979 Ray Simpson, Valerie Simpson's brother, replaced Willis. By then, however, the group's 15 minutes appeared to have ended. For their 1981 release *Renaissance,* the Village People briefly traded in their old costumes for a fling with a New Romantic wardrobe. They returned to their original style for the foreign-released *Fox in the Box.*

Through the '80s the Village People were all but forgotten in the U.S., but the group maintained a large international following and performed elsewhere. After 1985's "Sex on the Phone" flopped in America and barely cracked the Top 60 in the U.K. (where "Y.M.C.A." reigned as one of that nation's top 25 best-selling records of all time), the act went on hiatus. In the late '80s, Miles Jay, a latter-day Villager, enjoyed minor success as a solo R&B artist. The group proper resurfaced in the '90s featuring Simpson, four original members, and singer Jeff Olson. They now controlled their own careers and toured extensively. Morali died on December 15, 1991, of AIDS-related causes. He was 44. In 1995 ex-heavy metal singer Eric Anzalone became the new Leatherman character, replacing Hughes, who remained involved in the act's business affairs. Hughes, 50, died in 2001 after a long illness and was buried in his biker uniform.

Gene Vincent

Born Vincent Eugene Craddock, Feb. 11, 1935, Norfolk, VA; died Oct. 12, 1971, Los Angeles, CA
1957—*Bluejean Bop!* (Capitol) 1970—*I'm Back and I'm Proud* (Dandelion/Elektra); *If Only You Could See Me Today* (Kama Sutra) 1971—*The Day the World Turned Blue* 1991—*Gene Vincent (Capitol Collectors Series)* (Capitol) 2000—*The Legend at His Best* (Collectables).

One of the first American rockers, Gene Vincent began singing while in the navy in the early '50s. After being discharged in 1955, he performed regularly on live country music radio shows in Norfolk. In 1956 he recorded a demo of a song he and "Sheriff" Tex Davis had written—"Be-Bop-A-Lula"—and sent it to Capitol Records. Capitol heard an Elvis Presley soundalike in his rockabilly stutter-and-hiccup style and signed him to a long-term contract. "Be-Bop-A-Lula," rerecorded by Vincent and his group, the Bluecaps (guitarists Cliff Gallup and Willie Williams, bass player Jack Neal, and drummer Dickie Harrell), in Capitol's imitation–Sam Phillips echo chamber, was a hit nationwide (#7). Vincent's looks—darker, tougher, greasier than Elvis', all blue denim

Gene Vincent and the Blue Caps

and black leather—were featured in the 1956 movie *The Girl Can't Help It* and were imitated widely. Fans even affected his limp, the result of a Navy motorcycle accident that forced him to wear a metal brace on one leg. For several years Gene Vincent and the Bluecaps were among the most popular rock & roll acts in America ("Lotta Lovin' " was a #13 hit in 1957).

When, by the end of the decade, the record industry began to favor cleaned-up, tuned-down pop stars, Vincent went abroad and found huge followings in Australia, Japan, and Europe, wherever "real American rockers" were in demand. He toured England with Eddie Cochran and was critically injured in the car crash that killed Cochran on April 17, 1960. Although Vincent recovered from his injuries, he was devastated by Cochran's death, and his career never regained momentum. Vincent's professional pursuits were no doubt compromised by heavy drinking, mood swings, and erratic behavior; he was married and divorced four times. For most of the '60s he lived in England, where, playing the pub circuit, he retained a small following of latter-day Teddy boys.

A "comeback" album in 1969 failed to attract much attention. Through the years he suffered bouts of disabling pain because of his bad leg; in 1966 doctors suggested amputation, in fact. His fortunes continued to decline, and broke and despondent, he returned to America in September 1971. A month later he tripped in his parents' home and ruptured a stomach ulcer; he died an hour later. "Be-Bop-A-Lula" had, by that time, sold 9 million copies worldwide.

Violent Femmes

Formed 1981, Milwaukee, WI
Gordon Gano (b. June 7, 1963, New York, NY), voc., gtr.; Brian Ritchie (b. Nov. 21, 1960, Milwaukee), bass, voc.; Victor DeLorenzo (b. Oct. 25, 1954, Racine, WI), drums, voc.
1983—*The Violent Femmes* (Slash) 1984—*Hallowed Ground* 1986—*The Blind Leading the Naked* 1988—*3* 1991—*Why Do Birds Sing?* 1993—*Add It Up (1981–1993)* (– DeLorenzo; + Guy Hoffman [b. May 20, 1954, Milwaukee], drums) 1994—*New Times* (Elektra) 1999—*Viva Wisconsin* (Beyond) 2000—*Freak Magnet.*
Gordon Gano solo: 1987—*The Mercy Seat* (Slash).
Brian Ritchie solo: 1987—*The Blend* (SST) 1989—*Sonic Temple & the Court of Babylon* 1990—*I See a Noise* (Dali-Chameleon).
Victor DeLorenzo solo: 1990—*Peter Corey Sent Me* (Dali-Chameleon) 1996—*Pancake Day* (Almo).

Milwaukee's Violent Femmes cornered the market for frantic, angry *acoustic* postpunk folk rock in the early '80s with its landmark self-titled debut and its signature anthems "Blister in the Sun," "Kiss Off" and "Add It Up." The trio—singer/guitarist Gordon Gano, bassist Brian Ritchie, and drummer Victor DeLorenzo—landed its record deal with Slash shortly after being discovered and championed by Pretenders guitarist James Honeyman-Scott. The Violent Femmes remained on the label for nearly a decade, releasing a string of eclectic albums (like 1984's spooky, Appalachian-flavored *Hallowed Ground*) that never achieved mainstream success but fostered a loyal cult and college radio audience (1983's *The Violent Femmes* was finally certified platinum in 1991). The group's highest charting album was 1986's Jerry Harrison–produced *The Blind Leading the Naked* (#84). Like *Hallowed Ground* before it, the album's lyrics strongly reflected Gano's religious upbringing as the son of a Baptist minister.

Each of the members released solo albums; in 1993 DeLorenzo left the Femmes and was replaced by BoDeans veteran Guy Hoffman. The new trio recorded one album for Elektra, 1994's *New Times* (#90), before resurfacing on Beyond five years later for the 1999 live album *Viva Wisconsin.* A new studio effort, *Freak Magnet,* failed to dent the charts in 2000.

Vixen

Formed ca. 1980, Los Angeles, CA
Janet Gardner (b. Mar. 17, 1962, Juneau, AK), gtr., voc.; Jan Kuehnemund, gtr.; Share Pedersen, bass; Roxy Petrucci (b. Mar. 17, 1962, Detroit, MI), drums.
1988—*Vixen* (EMI Manhattan) 1990—*Rev It Up* (EMI) 1998—(– Kuehnemund; + Gina Stile, gtr; – Pedersen; + Maxine Petrucci, bass) *Tangerine* (CMC International) 1999—*The Best of Vixen: Full Throttle* (Razor & Tie/BMG) 2001—(original lineup re-forms: Gardner, Kuehnemund; Petrucci).

An all-female band, Vixen worked in the Bon Jovi/Warrant pop/metal tradition. Roxy Petrucci, the drummer for Madame X, a popular L.A. metal band, formed the group in the early 1980s. Although Vixen found work playing at local clubs and military bases, it went through a number of musicians, including Steve Vai's wife, Pia Koko, on bass. The lineup solidified in 1987, and EMI signed the quartet the following year.

Vixen (#41, 1988), its gold debut, was buttressed by two Top 40 hits: "Cryin' " (#22, 1989) and "Edge of a Broken Heart" (#26, 1988), the latter written, arranged, and produced by Richard Marx. *Rev It Up* (#52, 1990) contained all original material, including the hit "How Much Love" (#44, 1990).

After being dropped by EMI, the band remained inactive until 1998, when they released a new album, *Tangerine,* on which Roxy Petrucci's sister Maxine played bass. Share Pedersen turned up in 1991 on *Contraband,* an LP recorded by other hard-rock musicians, including guitarist Michael Schenker and drummer Bobby Blotzer, then of Ratt.

Bunny Wailer

Born Neville O'Reilly Livingstone, Apr. 10, 1947, Kingston, Jam.
1976—*Blackheart Man* (Island) 1977—*Protest* 1979—*Struggle* (Solomonic) 1980—*Bunny Wailer Sings the Wailers* (Island); *In I Father's House* (Solomonic) 1981—*Rock 'n' Groove; Tribute to the Late Hon. Robert Nesta Marley, O.M.* 1982—*Hook, Line and Sinker* 1983—*Roots, Radics, Rockers, Reggae* (Shanachie) 1986—*Rootsman Skanking* 1987—*Rule Dance Hall; Marketplace* 1988—*Liberation* 1990—*Time Will Tell: A Tribute to Bob Marley; Gumption* 1992—*Dance Massive* 1993—*Just Be Nice* (Ras) 1994—*Crucial* 1995—*Hall of Fame* 1999—*Communication* (Solomonic); *Dubd'sco.*

The last surviving member of the original Wailers, Bunny Livingstone—better known as Bunny Wailer—left the band less than a year after the group made its first tours of the U.K. and the U.S. His aversion to traveling was one reason for his departure. He vowed never to leave Jamaica, but in 1986 he relented, and a sold-out show at New York's Madison Square Garden kicked off a U.S. and European tour. International acclaim accrued to Bob Marley and Peter Tosh (the other original Wailers), while, until the early '80s, Bunny Wailer's following remained small even by Jamaican standards.

In his decade with the Wailers, he was considered the equal of Marley and Tosh as a singer and as a songwriter. "Let Him Go," "Who Feels It," "Jail House," and "Pass It On" are among the songs associated with him. He founded his own record company, Solomonic, in 1972, and recorded his first solo singles—"Life Line," "Bide Up," and "Arab Oil Weapon"—before quitting the Wailers in 1973. Between then and 1976, he retired from the record business and lived in the Jamaican countryside. When he resumed recording, he secured a distribution arrangement with Island Records and released *Blackheart Man* (backed by Marley, Tosh, and the Wailers band) in America and Europe.

Darker and denser than Marley's, less strident than Tosh's, Wailer's music found less acceptance from most quarters, and his records were usually not released in the U.S. Since 1980, as his music has become lighter and more upbeat, he has become a hitmaker in Jamaica. "Ballroom Floor," "Galong So," and "Collie Man" were big hits in 1981, while "Cool Runnings" topped the Jamaican chart that year and "Rock and Groove" followed suit in 1982.

In 1983 he began an association with Shanachie, the label that started releasing his LPs in the U.S. His recent albums, especially *Liberation,* have shown a new musical and political engagement, adding dancehall elements and topical lyrics. In 1990 his tribute to Bob Marley, *Time Will Tell,* won the Grammy for Best Reggae Album. Though he continued to record—including a second Marley tribute released in 1995—Wailer did not tour the U.S. for most of the '90s, paying a 1999 visit with a group that included celebrated guitarist Ernest Ranglin.

Loudon Wainwright III

Born Sep. 5, 1946, Chapel Hill, NC
1970—*Loudon Wainwright III* (Atlantic) 1971—*Album II* 1972—*Album III* (Columbia) 1973—*Attempted Mustache*

1975—*Unrequited* 1976—*T Shirt* (Arista) 1978—*Final Exam* 1980—*A Live One* (Radar) 1983—*Fame and Wealth* (Demon/Rounder) 1985—*I'm Alright* 1986—*More Love Songs* 1989—*Therapy* (Silvertone) 1992—*History* (Virgin) 1993—*Career Moves* 1996—*Grown Man* 1997—*Little Ship* 1999—*Social Studies* (Hannibal/Rykodisc) 2000—*BBC Sessions* (Fuel 2000).

Folksinger/songwriter Loudon Wainwright III, the son of an American writer, has gained considerable critical respect and a modicum of sales for his self-lacerating humor, deadpan irony and often deliberate tastelessness, complemented by a comic rubber-faced stage presence.

Wainwright grew up in New York's Westchester County and Southern California, where his father was the L.A. bureau chief for *Life* magazine. At age 15 Wainwright began attending St. Andrew's School in Delaware (where later the movie *Dead Poets Society* was filmed). There he developed an early interest in folk music. After graduation, he attended Carnegie Mellon University, where he studied acting and directing before dropping out in early 1967 at age 20. In 1968 Wainwright began playing the club and college circuit and attracting a following with his offbeat wit.

His first albums included just vocals and guitar and were simultaneously stark confessionals and a mockery of the whole idea, presenting Wainwright as a sort of insensitive singer/songwriter. With *Album III,* Wainwright mellowed his approach until it resembled slapstick more than anything else, and he crossed over into the pop chart with the Top 20 single "Dead Skunk."

Attempted Mustache played things almost completely for laughs and failed to appreciably increase his sales, but *Unrequited* was received as a welcome return to form. For *T Shirt* and *Final Exam,* Wainwright was backed by a five-piece rock band called Slow Train for such tunes as "Watch Me Rock, I'm Over Thirty." In the early '70s, Wainwright had married Kate McGarrigle of the McGarrigle sisters, and he recorded her song "Come a Long Way." They were separated in 1977 and eventually divorced. They had two children, Martha and Rufus Wainwright, both of whom would later become recording artists.

In 1982 he and Suzzy Roche became the parents of Lucy Roche. Three years later, he moved to England, where he is much more popular than he is here in the States. Richard Thompson coproduced the Grammy-nominated *I'm Alright* with Wainwright. In addition to touring and recording, Wainwright has continued to act, appearing in the Broadway play *Pump Boys and Dinettes* (1982), the TV series *M.A.S.H.,* and the movies *The Slugger's Wife* (1985), *Jacknife* (1989), and *28 Days* (2000). In the U.K., he appeared on the BBC series *The Jasper Carrott Show* as, in the words of his bio, "the resident American wise-guy singer-songwriter." Although his commercial profile in the U.S. has remained low, he is still a critics' favorite, praised for his insightful if sometimes unusual songs. In 1994 Wainwright contributed "The Man Who Couldn't Cry" to Johnny Cash's critically acclaimed LP *American Recordings.* With *Social Studies,* Wainwright focused his satirical wit on such late-'90s phenomena as Y2K paranoia, O.J. Simpson, and the "reunited" Beatles. Many of the songs were originally commissioned by National Public Radio and ABC's *Nightline.*

John Waite: See the Babys

Tom Waits

Born Dec. 7, 1949, Pomona, CA
1973—*Closing Time* (Asylum) 1974—*Heart of Saturday Night* 1975—*Nighthawks at the Diner* 1976—*Small Change* 1977—*Foreign Affairs* 1978—*Blue Valentine* (Elektra) 1980—*Heartattack and Vine* (Asylum) 1983—*Swordfishtrombones* (Island) 1985—*Rain Dogs* 1987—*Frank's Wild Years* 1988—*Big Time* soundtrack 1991—*Night on Earth* soundtrack 1992—*Bone Machine* 1993—*The Black Rider* 1998—*Beautiful Maladies: The Island Years* (Island) 1999—*Mule Variations* (Epitaph).

Singer/songwriter Tom Waits is a one-man beatnik revival. He generally appears with a cap pulled over his brow, a cigarette dangling from his stubbled face, talk-singing and/or mumbling jive in a cancerous growl to the accompaniment of cool saxophone jazz; he also writes romantic ballads, which have been covered by the Eagles, Rickie Lee Jones, and others.

Waits claims he was born in a moving taxi. He grew up in California, where he listened to Bing Crosby, Stephen Foster parlor songs, and George Gershwin. He also developed an intense admiration for, and identification with, such Beat writers as Jack Kerouac and Charles Bukowski. As a teenager, Waits was living out of a car and working as a doorman at the L.A. nightclub the Heritage when he decided he should be performing and began writing songs based on overheard snatches of conversation.

He first played at L.A.'s Troubador club in 1969, and soon moved out of his car and into L.A.'s Tropicana Hotel (a favorite of visiting rock stars). Waits built up a strong cult following as an opening act. Working solo, he merged humorous Beat-influenced free-verse raps with his own compositions. In 1972 he signed to Elektra/Asylum Records, and his debut album was produced by ex–Lovin' Spoonful Jerry Yester. Though the album sold poorly, one of its songs, "Ol' 55," was covered by the Eagles on their *On the Border.* In 1973 Waits toured with a sax-bass-drums trio, often opening for Zappa and the Mothers and usually drawing extremely adverse audience receptions. His second album, produced by Bones Howe, sold a little better than the first.

By 1975 Waits had built a small nationwide cult following and was still opening shows, but he had to cut his trio for financial reasons. Later that year, Waits and Howe assembled a sax-led quartet and an audience to record *Nighthawks at the Diner* (#164, 1975). In 1976 he conducted American and European tours, which were mildly received. In London that year, he composed tunes for his next album, the jazzy *Small*

Change (#89, 1976). *Foreign Affairs* (#113, 1977) contained his duet with Bette Midler, "I Never Talk to Strangers," and on *Blue Valentine* (#181, 1978) Waits introduced electric guitar for the first time.

Waits appeared as a honky-tonk pianist in Sylvester Stallone's film *Paradise Alley,* in 1979. By this time, he was involved with Rickie Lee Jones, whose picture appeared on the back cover of *Valentine.* They broke up in 1980. Waits wrote and recorded the title song for Ralph Waite's 1980 film about skid row, *On the Nickel,* and later recorded two songs for the 1985 documentary on Seattle street kids, *Streetwise,* as well as the soundtrack for Jim Jarmusch's 1992 film *Night on Earth.* In 1982 Waits' soundtrack for Francis Ford Coppola's *One From the Heart* featured him in a number of duets with Crystal Gayle; the soundtrack was nominated for an Academy Award. Coppola cast Waits in several of his films, including *Rumblefish, The Cotton Club, The Outsiders,* and *Bram Stoker's Dracula* (in which Waits delivered a memorable turn as the fly-munching Renfield); he's also acted in the Jarmusch cult film *Down by Law,* the big-budget *Ironweed* with Jack Nicholson and Meryl Streep, and Robert Altman's *Short Cuts.*

Heartattack and Vine (#96, 1980), with Waits playing more electric guitar and an R&B slant to the music, was Waits' best seller since *Small Change,* which gives a good indication of his low commercial profile. Waits then forsook any pretense to accessibility, instead making increasingly harsh and eccentric music. *Swordfishtrombones* (#167, 1983) was an experimental rock work with a surreal range of noisy instrumentation; Waits described it as "a junkyard orchestral deviation," while critics compared it to both Captain Beefheart and Kurt Weill. *Rain Dogs* continued the experimental direction, with Waits often singing through a megaphone; it included "Downtown Train," later a hit for Rod Stewart. (Other artists covering Waits tunes have included Bruce Springsteen with "Jersey Girl," Marianne Faithfull with "Stranger Weather," Bob Seger with "Blind Love" and "New Coat of Paint," and Dion with "Heart of Saturday Night" and "San Diego Serenade"; Canadian vocalist Holly Cole has recorded a complete album of Waits material.) *Frank's Wild Years* was based on songs from a musical play Waits wrote with the woman he married in 1980, playwright and script editor Kathleen Brennan; first staged by Chicago's Steppenwolf Company, it was about a down-and-out lounge singer freezing to death on a park bench, reliving his life in hallucinatory fashion. *Big Time* was the soundtrack of a concert film-with-story that Waits produced himself.

In 1990 Waits won a lawsuit against snack-food giant Frito-Lay, which in 1988 had hired a Waits impersonator to sing a tortilla-chip radio jingle closely modeled on Waits' "Step Right Up" (from *Small Change*). Waits, who had consistently refused to perform in any commercials, won $2.5 million in damages through a decision ultimately upheld by the U.S. Supreme Court.

The clattering *Bone Machine* won a 1992 Grammy Award for Best Alternative Music album. *The Black Rider,* with its demented Weimar-cabaret stylings, was the score from Waits' theatrical collaboration with avant-garde stage designer/director Robert Wilson and author William S. Burroughs. Waits and Wilson collaborated again on a 1993 update of *Alice in Wonderland.* Waits also guested on Bay Area postpunk/fusion band Primus' *Sailing the Seas of Cheese,* and on British composer Gavin Bryars' *Jesus' Blood Never Failed Me Yet,* an unlikely 1994 U.K. hit in which Bryars orchestrated the "found" mumbling of a hymn by a London drunkard.

In 1999 Waits returned to the studio and the concert stage after a long absence. *Mule Variations,* released on the California-based punk label Epitaph, outsold his more recent major-label efforts—and reached #30, his highest-charting album ever—and preceded his first tour in a decade. It also won the Grammy for Best Contemporary Folk Album. The following year, he collaborated with Wilson and Brennan on a Danish production of *Woyzeck.*

Dave Wakeling: See the English Beat

Rick Wakeman: See Yes

The Walker Brothers/Scott Walker

Formed 1964, London, Eng.
Original lineup: John Walker (b. John Maus, Nov. 12, 1943, New York, NY), gtr., voc.; Scott Walker (b. Noel Scott Engel, Jan. 9, 1944, Hamilton, OH), bass, voc., gtr., kybds.; Gary Walker (b. Gary Leeds, Sep. 3, 1944, Glendale, CA), drums, voc.
1965—*The Walker Brothers* (Star Club) 1966—*Portrait* (Philips) 1967—*Images* (Star Club) 1975—*Spotlight On* (Philips); *No Regrets* (GTO) 1976—*Lines* 1978—*Nite Flights* 1995—*Anthology* (One Way).
Scott Walker solo: 1967—*Scott 1* (Fontana, U.K.) 1968—*Scott 2* 1969—*Scott 3; Scott 4* 1970—*Till the Band Comes In* (BGO, U.K.) 1972—*The Moviegoer* (Philips, U.K.) 1973—*Any Day Now; Stretch* (CBS, U.K.) 1974—*We Had It All* 1984—*Climate of the Hunter* (Virgin, U.K.) 1995—*Tilt* (Drag City) 1996—*It's Raining Today: The Scott Walker Story (1967–70)* (Razor & Tie) 1999—*Pola X* soundtrack (Barclay, Fr.).

Though born in America, the Walker Brothers were usually thought of as a British Invasion group because they went to Britain in 1964 after failing to achieve any success in the U.S. In the U.K., pop producer/entrepreneur Jack Good introduced John Maus and Scott Engel to ex–P.J. Proby drummer Gary Leeds and renamed them the Walker Brothers. Within a year, they had a minor British hit, "Love Her," which set their style: dramatic Spectorian arrangements featuring harmony vocals.

In late 1965 they scored their first big international pop hit with "Make It Easy on Yourself," and followed it up in 1966 with "The Sun Ain't Gonna Shine (Anymore)," their biggest American Top 40 hit. The Walkers were teen sensations in

England, but they still couldn't fully crack the American market. They split up after *Images*. Scott Engel (still referring to himself as Scott Walker) enjoyed a somewhat successful solo career in the U.K. In 1975 the original Walkers, with many sessionmen aboard, re-formed. Following one comeback hit in the U.K. with Tom Rush's "No Regrets," they faded from view and resumed their solo projects.

In 1995 Scott Walker returned with his solo album *Tilt*, released on the American indie label Drag City. His sentimental, melancholy pop enjoyed a certain degree of retro-hipness in the '90s. *It's Raining Today* compiles material from his earliest releases.

Jerry Jeff Walker

Born Ronald Clyde, Mar. 16, 1942, Oneonta, NY
1968—*Mr. Bojangles* (Atco) 1969—*Driftin's Way of Life* (Vanguard); *"Five Years Gone"* (Atco) 1970—*Bein' Free* 1972—*Jerry Jeff Walker* (MCA) 1973—*Viva Terlingua* 1974—*Walker's Collectibles* 1975—*Ridin' High* 1976—*It's a Good Night for Singing* 1977—*A Man Must Carry On* 1978—*Contrary to Ordinary; Jerry Jeff* (Elektra) 1979—*Too Old to Change* 1980—*The Best of Jerry Jeff Walker* 1982—*Cowjazz* 1987—*Gypsy Songman* (Tried & True/Rykodisc) 1989—*Live at Gruene Hall* (Rykodisc) 1991—*Great Gonzos* (MCA); *Navajo Rug* (Rykodisc) 1992—*Hill Country Rain* (MCA) 1994—*Viva Luckenbach!* (Rykodisc); *Christmas Gonzo Style* 1995—*Night After Night* (Tried & True) 1996—*Scamp* 1998—*Lonewolf* (Warner Bros.); *Cowboy Boots and Bathin' Suits* (Tried & True) 1999—*Best of the Vanguard Years* (Vanguard); *Gypsy Songman* (Tried & True).

Though he first came to prominence with the psychedelic band Circus Maximus and has long enjoyed a moderately successful solo career as a "cosmic cowboy" in the Austin, Texas, area, Jerry Jeff Walker is best known for writing "Mr. Bojangles," a song covered by artists from Sammy Davis Jr. to the Nitty Gritty Dirt Band. He became attracted to folk music in his youth, and while in his teens he began performing traditional songs in clubs and coffeehouses. He left home in 1959 and became a wandering minstrel, playing the East Coast and more often the West and Southwest and writing. He also worked with guitarist David Bromberg. In Austin, Walker met singer/songwriter Bob Bruno, and together they returned to New York and formed Circus Maximus. The band merged Walker's characteristic country folk with jazz rock and other exotica and became a favorite psychedelic attraction in the Northeast. Their one minor hit was the jazzy "The Wind," which later became a staple of progressive FM radio.

Disputes between Walker and Bruno about musical direction led to a breakup in 1968. New York radio DJ Bob Fass of WBAI-FM taped "Mr. Bojangles" (about an old street dancer Walker had met in a New Orleans jail) during a broadcast by Walker and Bromberg; he aired the much-requested tape, and Walker secured a solo contract.

None of Walker's albums sold well despite the immense popularity of "Mr. Bojangles." Walker then moved to Austin, formed the Four-Man Deaf Cowboy Band, and recorded *Viva Terlingua* in a mobile truck parked in the middle of Luckenbach, Texas. He then formed the Lost Gonzo Band, who recorded an album of their own in 1975 and have toured and recorded with and without him. Walker hosted TNN's *The Texas Connection*. He continues to tour and record regularly.

Jr. Walker and the All Stars

Formed 1964, Detroit, MI
Original lineup: Jr. Walker (b. Oscar G. Mixon, a.k.a. Autry DeWalt Walker III, 1942, Blytheville, AK; d. Nov. 23, 1995, Battle Creek, MI), sax, voc.; Vic Thomas, kybds.; Willie Woods, gtr.; James Graves (d. 1967), drums.
1965—*Shotgun* (Soul) 1966—*Soul Session; Road Runner* 1967—*Jr. Walker and the All Stars Live!* 1969—*Home Cookin'; Jr. Walker and the All Stars Greatest Hits; Gotta Hold On to This Feeling* 1970—*A Gasssss* 1971—*Rainbow Funk; Moody Jr.* 1973—*Peace and Understanding Is Hard to Find* 1974—*Anthology* 1976—*Hot Shot; Sax Appeal; Whopper Bopper Show Stopper* 1978—*. . . Smooth* 1979—*Back Street Boogie* (Whitfield) 1983—*Blow the House Down* (Motown); *The Ultimate Collection.*

Jr. Walker's perky, bluesy tenor sax and raspy voice, backed by his band the All Stars, made him one of Motown's more idiosyncratic performers. In the '70s, studio musicians like Tom Scott and David Sanborn openly imitated Walker's tone and attack.

Walker was a naturally gifted musician, and played both piano and sax as a teen. He worked as a sideman in the late '60s with several R&B bands. With the original All Stars he recorded "Shotgun" (#4 pop, #1 R&B) and started a string of party hits that included "Do the Boomerang" (#10 R&B) and "Shake and Fingerpop" (#7 R&B) in 1965; "How Sweet It Is (to Be Loved by You)" (#18 pop, #3 R&B), "I'm a Road Runner" (#20 pop, #4 R&B) in 1966; "Pucker Up Buttercup" (#3 pop, #11 R&B) and "Come See About Me" (#24 pop, #8 R&B) in 1967; and "Hip City, Part 2" (#7 R&B) in 1968.

With Walker singing more, he enjoyed success with the mellow "What Does It Take (to Win Your Love)" (#4 pop, #1 R&B) and "These Eyes" (#16 pop, #3 R&B) in 1969; "Gotta Hold on to This Feeling" (#21 pop, #2 R&B) and "Do You See My Love (for You Growing)" (#32 pop, #3 R&B) in 1970; and "Walk in the Night" (#46 pop, #10 R&B) in 1972.

Walker continued recording during the '70s, including a stint with ex-Motown producer/writer Norman Whitfield's label, but was never as commercially successful and re-signed with Motown in the early '80s. He played on Foreigner's big 1981 hit "Urgent." He performed into the '90s and died of cancer in 1995.

T-Bone Walker

Born Aaron Thibeaux Walker, May 28, 1910, Linden, TX; died Mar. 16, 1975, Los Angeles, CA

1960—*T-Bone Blues* (Atlantic) 1969—*T-Bone Walker* (Capitol) 1970—*Good Feelin'* (Polydor); *Well Done* (Home Cooking) 1972—*Feelin' the Blues* (B&B) 1973—*Dirty Mistreater* (Bluesway); *I Want a Little Girl* (Delmark) 1990—*The Complete Recordings of T-Bone Walker, 1940–1954* (Mosaic) 1991—*The Complete Imperial Recordings, 1950–1954* (EMI) 1995—*The Complete Capitol/Black & White Recordings* (Capitol) 1996—*Stormy Monday* (LaserLight).

As the first bluesman to exploit the electric guitar, T-Bone Walker stands as an exceptionally important and influential figure. Walker was indispensable to the birth of urban electric blues and its descendants, R&B and rock & roll. His use of finger-vibrato and piercing electric-guitar sustain influenced scores of subsequent blues guitarists such as B.B. King, Freddie King, Buddy Guy, Albert Collins, Albert King, Lowell Fulson, J.B. Hutto, and Otis Rush. Walker's gritty chordal style on fast numbers eventually gave birth to Chuck Berry's archetypal rock guitar riffs.

Born to musical parents (he had a Cherokee Indian grandmother), Aaron Thibeaux Walker moved with his family to Dallas at age two. Through his church choir and street-singing stepfather, Marco Washington, he became interested in music. He acquired the nickname T-Bone early on; it was a corruption of his mother's pet name, T-Bow, from Thibeaux. By the time he was 10, Walker was accompanying his stepfather at drive-in soft drink stands. Soon after he became "lead boy" for the legendary Blind Lemon Jefferson, probably the most popular and influential country bluesman of the '20s. From 1920 through 1923 Walker led Jefferson down Texas streets.

By late 1923, Walker had taught himself guitar and he began entertaining at Dallas parties. He soon was ready to leave home and tour Texas with Dr. Breeding's Big B Tonic Medicine Show. In 1925 he joined blues singer Ida Cox's road show, which toured the South. Back in Dallas in 1929, Walker began recording acoustic country blues as Oak Cliff T-Bone. He continued touring the South and Southwest until 1934, when he moved to the West Coast. A year later, he married a woman named Viola Lee, for whom he wrote his "Viola Lee Blues" (later covered by the Grateful Dead, among others). Over the next decade, Walker worked with both small groups and big bands (from Les Hite's to Fletcher Henderson's), both on the West Coast and on tours through the Midwest and to New York. As early as 1935 he had begun playing primitive electric guitar models, using a sprung-rhythm, single-string lead style derived from Blind Lemon Jefferson's acoustic picking. By the time he first recorded as T-Bone Walker, in 1942, he was quite proficient on the electric guitar and made an instant impression on dozens of other bluesmen. In 1943 he had his biggest blues hit with the immortal "Call It Stormy Monday," which as "Stormy Monday Blues" or just "Stormy Monday" has become one of the most frequently covered blues songs.

Through the '40s and '50s, Walker recorded often and toured frequently (usually with smaller groups). He appeared on TV shows from the '50s through the '70s, toured all over the world, played jazz and blues festivals from Monterey to Montreux and in 1972 appeared in the French film *Jazz Odyssey*. In 1970 Walker won a Grammy for Best Ethnic/Traditional Recording with *Good Feelin'*. He became inactive in 1974, when he was hospitalized with bronchial pneumonia, which felled him a year later.

The Wallflowers

Formed 1990, Los Angeles, CA
Jakob Dylan (b. Dec. 9, 1969, New York, NY), voc., gtr.; Tobi Miller, gtr.; Rami Jaffee (b. Mar. 11, 1969, Los Angeles), kybds.; Barrie Maguire (b. Philadelphia, PA), bass; Peter Yanowitz (b. Sep. 13, 1967, Chicago, IL), drums.
1992—*The Wallflowers* (Virgin) 1993—(– Maguire; + Greg Richling [b. Gregory Martin Richling, Aug. 31, 1970, Los Angeles], bass, voc.) 1994—(– Miller; + Michael Ward [b. Feb. 21, 1967, MN], gtr., voc.; – Yanowitz) 1996—*Bringing Down the Horse* (Interscope) (+ Mario Calire [b. June 25, 1974, Buffalo, NY], drums) 2000—*Breach*.

Fronted by the youngest son of the most revered songwriter in rock, the Wallflowers drew an inordinate amount of press interest upon the release of their self-titled debut in 1992. But Jakob Dylan, determined to establish his own musical legacy rather than submit to profiles seeking insight into his famous father, refused to take the bait. The album sold a modest 40,000 copies, and the band subsequently left the label. Four years later, Dylan returned with a new Wallflowers lineup and stormed the charts on his own terms, landing 1996's *Bringing Down the Horse* in the Top 10 and winning two Grammys with the breakthrough single "One Headlight."

Dylan was born in New York to Bob Dylan and Sara Lowndes, but grew up in L.A., where his family moved when he was three. Although he was exposed to his father's music and the road early on, it wasn't until he saw a Clash concert as a 12-year-old that he felt inspired to ask for his own guitar. After graduating from high school, he briefly attended art school in New York before returning to L.A. to focus on a music career. He formed the Wallflowers in 1990 with a group of school friends, and the band was signed to Virgin Records two years later.

As uncomfortable as Dylan was discussing his father with the press, he was clearly driven by a similar work ethic; despite their debut's lack of commercial success, the Wallflowers toured tirelessly, with Dylan all the while refusing to let his name be featured along with the band's for easy publicity. The tenacity paid off. Weathering a dismissal from Virgin and a series of lineup changes, the group was picked up by Interscope in 1994 and began recording *Bringing Down the Horse* with producer T Bone Burnett. After a slow start, the album began a steady climb up the chart behind the Mainstream Rock radio and video hit "One Headlight" (#1, 1996). That song won the band a Grammy for Best Rock Performance and Dylan one for Best Rock Song in 1997. (That same evening, his father won the Album of the Year award for his *Time Out of Mind*.) The album sold 4 million copies and peaked at #8, spawning the additional Mainstream Rock hits "6th Avenue Heartache" (#10, 1996) and "The Difference" (#3, 1997). In the wake of the album's success, Dylan gradually began to open up to the press, which now sought him out as much as a rock sex symbol as for the connection to his father.

Although it would be another four years before the Wallflowers followed up *Bringing Down the Horse* with a new album, they scored a minor hit with a cover of David Bowie's "Heroes" (#4 Mainstream Rock Track) from the soundtrack to 1998's *Godzilla*. Released in October 2000, their third album, *Breach*, debuted at #13 but failed to match the success of its predecessor. The lead single, "Sleepwalker," reached #73, but the song that attracted the most attention critically was the album track "Hand Me Down," in which Dylan candidly alluded to the struggle of following in his father's formidable footsteps.

Joe Walsh

Born Nov. 20, 1947, Wichita, KS
1972—*Barnstorm* (Dunhill) 1973—*The Smoker You Drink, the Player You Get* 1974—*So What* 1975—*You Can't Argue With a Sick Mind* (ABC) 1978—*But Seriously, Folks* (Asylum); *The Best of Joe Walsh* (ABC) 1981—*There Goes the Neighborhood* (Asylum) 1983—*You Bought It, You Name It* (Full Moon/Warner Bros.) 1985—*The Confessor* 1987—*Got Any Gum?* 1991—*Ordinary Average Guy* (Pyramid/Epic) 1992—*Songs for a Dying Planet* 1994—*Look What I Did: The Joe Walsh Anthology* (MCA) 1997—*Joe Walsh's Greatest Hits: Little Did He Know.*
With Barnstorm: 1972—*Barnstorm* (Dunhill).

Hard-rock guitarist and songwriter Joe Walsh became interested in music through his mother, who played classical piano. His first instruments were the oboe and the clarinet; as a teenager he moved on to bass guitar, but it wasn't until he was a student at Kent State University that he picked up an electric guitar. Walsh went solo after leaving his first major band, the James Gang, in 1971, and later joined the Eagles [see entries]. He added some punch to the Eagles' sound, while his solo albums mixed spacious guitar production with offhandedly cheerful lyrics. Walsh's first solo album, which refined the hard-rock approach of the James Gang with vocal harmonies and more intricate arrangements, sold respectably. *The Smoker You Drink, the Player You Get* (#6, 1973) went gold on the strength of the #23 single "Rocky Mountain Way."

In 1974 Walsh produced and played on Dan Fogelberg's top-selling *Souvenirs* LP, and released his own *So What*. The latter included "Song for Emma," a tribute to his four-year-old daughter, who died in a car accident earlier that year. *So What* (#11, 1975) also featured Walsh's Barnstorm band (his Boulder, Colorado-based group between the James Gang and the Eagles, which had included bassist Kenny Passarelli and drummer Joe Vitale as well as former members of Stephen Stills' Manassas) on only a few cuts, with backing on the rest by J.D. Souther, Dan Fogelberg, and the Eagles. A year later Walsh guested on the first solo album by ex-Spirit Jay Ferguson. For the live *You Can't Argue With a Sick Mind* (#20, 1976), Walsh's band included ex-Beach Boys drummer Ricky Fataar, but by the time of its release Walsh had replaced Bernie Leadon in the Eagles, making his debut with them on *Hotel California*. Walsh continued sporadic solo work, and his platinum *But Seriously, Folks* (#8, 1978) lived up to its title and became a top seller on the strength of the deadpan "Life's Been Good" (#12, 1978), an account of rock-star decadence. In 1979 Walsh further endeared himself to critics and audiences with a semiserious campaign for the presidency. His platform included "Free gas for everyone"; his qualifications, "Has never lied to the American public." The Eagles broke up in 1982 but he rejoined them for their 1994 reunion tour, cheekily titled Hell Freezes Over.

Throughout the '80s Walsh continued to record, although with lessening chart success with each outing. His last Top 40 single was "Life of Illusion" (#34, 1981) from *There Goes the Neighborhood* (#20, 1981). *You Bought It, You Name It* (#48, 1983) and *The Confessor* (#65, 1985) were Walsh's last solo forays into the Hot 100 to date. In 1993 Walsh embarked on his Vote for Me Tour, which, at one point, reunited him with his former James Gang band mates, with whom he'd also appear in several episodes of *The Drew Carey Show* in 1998 and 1999. (They played the other members of Carey's amateur band.) Walsh also performed with Ringo Starr's All-Starr Band in 1992 and guested on Starr's album *Vertical Man* in 1998.

While releasing greatest-hits compilations and touring into the '90s and beyond, Walsh continued to display his irreverent sense of humor; at a 1998 ribbon-cutting ceremony for a new wing of the Rock and Roll Hall of Fame & Museum, for example, he pulled out a chainsaw to cut the ribbon.

War

Formed 1969, Long Beach, CA
Harold Brown (b. Mar. 17, 1946, Long Beach), drums, perc.; Papa Dee Allen (b. Thomas Sylvester Allen, July 19, 1931, Wilmington, DE; d. Aug. 30, 1988, Vallejo, CA), perc., voc.; B.B. Dickerson (b. Aug. 3, 1949, Torrance, CA), bass, voc.; Leroy "Lonnie" Jordan (b. Nov. 21, 1948, San Diego, CA), kybds., voc., bass; Charles Miller (b. June 2, 1939, Olathe, KS; d. June 1980, Los Angeles, CA), reeds, voc.; Lee Oskar (b. Mar. 24, 1948, Copenhagen, Den.), harmonica; Howard Scott (b. Mar. 15, 1946, San Pedro, CA), gtr., voc.
As Eric Burdon and War: 1970—*Eric Burdon Declares "War"* (MGM); *The Black-Man's Burdon* 1976—*Love Is All Around* (ABC).
As War: 1971—*War* (United Artists); *All Day Music* 1972—*The World Is a Ghetto* 1973—*Deliver the Word* 1974—*War Live!* 1975—*Why Can't We Be Friends?* 1976—*War's Greatest Hits* 1977—*Platinum Jazz* (Blue Note); *Galaxy* (MCA) 1978—*Youngblood* soundtrack (United Artists) (+ Alice Tweed Smith, voc.) 1979—(+ Luther Raab, bass) *The Music Band* (MCA)

(– Dickerson; – Miller; + Pat Rizzo, reeds; + Ronnie Hammon, drums) *The Music Band 2* 1982—(– Smith) *Outlaw* (RCA) (– Rizzo) 1983—*Life (Is So Strange)* (– Brown) 1984—(– Rabb; + Ricky Green, bass) 1987—*Best of War . . . and More* (Priority) 1988—(– Allen) 1989—(– Green) 1992—(– Allen; – Oskar) *Rap Declares War* (Avenue) 1993—(+ Brown; + Tetsuya "Tex" Nakamura, harmonica; + Rae Valentine [b. Harold Rae Brown, Jr.], programming; + Kerry Campbell, sax; + Sal Rodriguez, drums, perc., voc.; + Charles Green, sax, flute) 1994—*Peace Sign; War Anthology 1970–1994* 1995—(– Scott; + J. B. Eckl, gtr., voc.) 1996—(– Brown) *The Best of War . . . and More, vol. 2* 1997—*Colección Latina* 1999—(– Campbell; – Green; – Rodriguez; – Eckl; + Fernando Harkless, sax; + Marco Reyes, perc.; + James Backer, gtr.) *Grooves & Messages.*

War's distinctive mix of funk, Latin, and jazz kept the group on the chart for most of the '70s. In 1970 War scored its first hit as ex-Animal Eric Burdon's backup band.

War's roots reach back to 1962, when Harold Brown and Howard Scott cofounded a band called the Creators. Still in high school, the two later met up with Leroy "Lonnie" Johnson and B.B. Dickerson, and in 1965 Charles Miller joined. Through the mid-'60s the Creators worked various L.A. and West Coast clubs, opening for such acts as Ike and Tina Turner. The group came to a temporary halt when Scott was drafted and Dickerson moved to Hawaii. The remaining group members stayed active in music, and at one point found themselves working under the name the Nightshift backing L.A. Rams football star Deacon Jones' ill-fated efforts as a singer. By then percussionist Papa Dee Allen, whose past credits included playing with Dizzy Gillespie, had joined, and the horn section had been expanded.

Around this time the group met Jerry Goldstein, a former member of the Strangeloves ("I Want Candy") and writer and producer for the Angels ("My Boyfriend's Back") and the McCoys ("Hang On Sloopy"). Goldstein, who, as manager, producer, and cowriter, would play a key role in War's success, also knew Eric Burdon [see entry], who was then seriously considering quitting music altogether. After Burdon heard the band, he and his friend, a young Danish harmonica player named Lee Oskar, joined them in a series of rehearsals. The Creators were rechristened War. After just a few dates, Rosen died of a drug overdose, and Dickerson returned.

The band recorded two albums with Burdon (three, if you count *Love Is All Around,* which consists of material recorded in August 1969, several months before sessions for the group's debut album). "Spill the Wine" (#3, 1970) was their biggest hit together; a followup, "They Can't Take Away Our Music," went to #50 in early 1971. War and Burdon were on tour in Europe in the fall of 1970, performing to rave reviews and sold-out halls. Suddenly, shortly after the death of Burdon's friend Jimi Hendrix, the singer abruptly abandoned the group. Left on their own, the members of the band continued to tour and to fulfill their commitments.

War proved itself as a creative force in its own right with *War* (#190, 1971), but its breakthrough came later that year with *All Day Music* (#16, 1971), which featured the hit singles "All Day Music" (#35, 1971) and "Slippin' Into Darkness" (#16 pop, #12 R&B, 1972). From that point, War rolled on through the decade with four Top 10 albums, including the #1 followup, *The World Is a Ghetto.* Hits of the period included "The World Is a Ghetto" (#7 pop, #3 R&B, 1972), "The Cisco Kid" (#2 pop, #5 R&B, 1973), "Gypsy Man" (#8 pop, #6 R&B, 1973), "Me and Baby Brother" (#15 pop, #18 R&B, 1973), "Low Rider" (#7 pop, #1 R&B, 1975), and "Why Can't We Be Friends?" (#6 pop, #9 R&B, 1975). *Deliver the Word* (#6, 1973), *War Live!* (#13, 1974), and *Why Can't We Be Friends?* (#8, 1975) all went gold; *Greatest Hits* (#6, 1976), which included one new song, "Summer" (#7 pop, #4 R&B, 1976), was certified platinum.

Around this time War also worked on movie soundtracks for *Youngblood* and *The River Niger.* Three tracks for *The River Niger* soundtrack and other previously released and unreleased cuts comprised *Platinum Jazz* (#23, 1977), the first platinum album in the history of Blue Note Records. In 1977 War moved to MCA Records, and the title cut from *Galaxy* was a disco hit (#39 pop, #5 R&B, 1978). In 1978 the group suffered its first personnel shift since 1970, when Dickerson left the group during the recording of *The Music Band.* Just two years later, Miller was the victim of a robbery, during which he was murdered. Subsequent albums had neither the commercial nor artistic impact of their early and mid-'70s releases, although the 1982 debut on RCA, *Outlaw,* promised something of a comeback, boasting "You Got the Power" and the title cut, but neither entered the pop Top 40.

Beginning in the mid-'80s, War, buffeted by more personnel changes and their audience's shift to disco, ceased recording and split with Goldstein. But the act never stopped touring. During an opening performance of "Gypsy Man," Allen died onstage of a brain aneurysm; the group has retired the song from its live repertoire. Not long after Allen's passing, War reunited with Goldstein. With several musicians (including Brown's son, Rae Valentine) augmenting the original core membership of Brown, Jordan, and Scott, the band made a triumphant return to recording in 1994 with the acclaimed *Peace Sign* (which featured such guest musicians as Lee Oskar and José Feliciano) and a successful tour. Following more touring and the departures of Brown and Scott, Jordan and War soldiered on and released *Colección Latina,* a 1997 ode to Hispanic culture featuring Feliciano, an acoustic remix of "East L.A.," and a Spanish version of "Low Rider." Meanwhile, Brown and Scott wrote new material with original War chums Dickerson and Oskar. With Goldstein and Jordan in control of War's name, the quartet dubbed itself Guerra ("war" in Spanish) and later, Same Ole Band. Throughout the '90s, War's early work has been sampled or covered on hits by TLC, Janet Jackson, Korn, and Smash Mouth.

Billy Ward and His Dominoes

Formed 1950, New York, NY
Billy Ward (b. Sep. 19, 1921, Los Angeles, CA), voc., piano;

Clyde McPhatter a.k.a. Clyde Ward (b. Nov. 15, 1932, Durham, NC; d. June 13, 1972, New York), voc.; Charlie White (b. 1930, Washington, DC), tenor voc.; Joe Lamont, baritone voc.; Billy Brown, bass voc.
1952—(– White; + James Van Loan, voc.; – Brown; + David McNeil, bass voc.; – McPhatter; + Jackie Wilson (b. June 9, 1934, Detroit, MI; d. Jan. 21, 1984, Mount Holly, NJ), lead voc. 1953—(– McNeil; + Cliff Givens, bass voc.) ca. mid-'50s—(– Lamont; + Milton Merle, baritone voc.) 1957—(– Wilson; + Eugene Mumford [d. 1978], lead voc.) *Billy Ward and the Dominoes* (Federal) 1960—(lineup: Ward; Givens; Merle; + Monroe Powell, lead voc.; + Robbie Robinson, tenor voc.) 1993—*Sixty Minute Men: The Best of Billy Ward and His Dominoes* (Rhino).

This important, popular '50s R&B vocal group is known primarily for having once counted among its members Clyde McPhatter and his replacement, Jackie Wilson. Billy Ward's Dominoes were the first black male vocal group to master both the smooth, sophisticated style of older groups such as the Ravens and the hard-rocking R&B epitomized in their celebratory, double-entendre-filled "Sixty-Minute Man" (1951) and the protosoul classic "Have Mercy Baby" (1952).

Group founder and sole stalwart Ward had begun studying music in L.A. as a child, and at age 14 won a national contest for his composition "Dejection," the award presented by conductor Walter Damrosch. During and after an army stint in the early '40s, Ward became a boxer, and after his discharge he moved east as sports editor and columnist for Transradio Press. He still loved music and was a vocal coach in the Carnegie Hall building. By the late '40s, Ward had his own voice teaching studio on Broadway, and eventually he got the idea to start a singing group with his students. Thus were born the Dominoes.

In 1950 teenage Clyde McPhatter joined as lead tenor, and in 1951 the group had three Top 10 R&B singles: "Do Something for Me" (#6 R&B), "I Am With You" (#8 R&B), and "Sixty-Minute Man" (#17 pop, #1 R&B). Historically "Sixty-Minute Man" broke commercial barriers, for not only was it a wildly successful R&B hit despite (or because of) its ribald content, but it is considered to have been one of, if not the, first R&B record by a black group to make the pop chart as well.

In 1952 their "Have Mercy Baby" was an R&B #1 for several weeks running. They again hit the Top 10 that year with "The Bells" (#3 R&B), "I'd Be Satisfied" (#8 R&B), and "These Foolish Things Remind Me of You" (#5 R&B), McPhatter's last single with the group. He then left to form the Drifters [see entry]. His place was taken by Jackie Wilson [see entry], who sang lead on "Rags to Riches" (#2 R&B, 1953), the group's biggest hit with him. An early-1955 switch to Decca and an emphasis on smooth pop brought the group its biggest pop hit, "St. Therese of the Roses" (#13, 1956), but Wilson departed for a solo career.

With new lead singer Eugene Mumford (previously of the Serenaders and the Larks), the group had several more pop hits, including the biggest of its career, "Star Dust" (#12, 1957), followed by "Deep Purple" (#20, 1957), both on Liberty. Their last charting single was a cover of "Jennie Lee." In 1960 Mumford left to go solo; he later sang with other groups, including versions of the Ink Spots and the Jubilee Four. The group remained popular as a concert attraction into the early '60s.

Jennifer Warnes

Born Jennifer Jean Warnes, Mar. 3, 1947, Seattle, WA
1968—*. . . I Can Remember Everything* (Parrot) 1969—*See Me, Feel Me, Touch Me, Heal Me!* 1972—*Jennifer* (Reprise) 1977—*Jennifer Warnes* (Arista) 1979—*Shot Through the Heart* 1982—*Best of Jennifer Warnes* 1986—*Famous Blue Raincoat* (Cypress) 1992—*The Hunter* (Private); *Just Jennifer* (Deram).

A honey-voiced singer and sometime songwriter, Jennifer Warnes achieved her greatest success with a string of hit movie themes. Warnes' recording of "It Goes Like It Goes," from the 1979 film *Norma Rae,* won an Academy Award. In the 1980s she sang Randy Newman's Oscar-nominated "One More Hour" on the *Ragtime* soundtrack and scored #1 hits with a pair of duets: 1982's "Up Where We Belong," with Joe Cocker, from *An Officer and a Gentleman;* and 1987's "(I've Had) The Time of My Life," with former Righteous Brother Bill Medley, from *Dirty Dancing.* Each duet went to #1 on the pop chart, won an Oscar, and netted a Grammy for Vocal Performance by a Duo or Group.

Warnes toured the L.A. folk circuit in the late '60s, leading to a recording contract with London Records subsidiary Parrot. In 1968, she joined the cast of *The Smothers Brothers Comedy Hour,* and the following year, she performed in the original L.A. production of *Hair.* The Velvet Underground's John Cale produced her *Jennifer* disc for Reprise in 1972, the first release in a series of well-received albums that combined country and folk influences. Warnes also sang backup, both in the studio and on tour, for several artists, including Leonard Cohen, whose songs she would later cover on the acclaimed *Famous Blue Raincoat.* Warnes resurfaced on Arista with 1977's *Jennifer Warnes,* which yielded the #6 pop single "The Right Time of the Night," but movie soundtrack songs sustained her through the next decade. She kept her ties to Medley, with whom she performed at a benefit concert for abused women in 1998.

Dionne Warwick

Born Marie Dionne Warrick, Dec. 12, 1941, East Orange, NJ
1962—*Presenting Dionne Warwick* (Scepter) 1965—*The Sensitive Sound of Dionne Warwick* 1966—*Here I Am* 1967—*Here Where There Is Love; The Windows of the World* 1968—*On Stage and in the Movies; Dionne Warwick's Golden Hits, Part One; Valley of the Dolls* 1969—*Promises, Promises; Soulful; Dionne Warwick's Greatest Motion Picture Hits; Dionne Warwick's Golden Hits, Part Two* 1971—*The Dionne Warwicke*

Story 1972—*Dionne* (Warner Bros.) 1973—*Just Being Myself* 1975—*Then Came You; Track of the Cat* 1977—*A Man and a Woman* (with Isaac Hayes) (Hot Buttered Soul); *Only Love Can Break a Heart* (Musicorp); *Love at First Sight* (Warner Bros.) 1979—*Dionne* (Arista) 1980—*No Night So Long* 1981—*Hot! Live and Otherwise* 1982—*Friends in Love; Heartbreaker* 1983—*How Many Times Can We Say Goodbye* 1985—*Finder of Lost Loves; Friends* 1987—*Reservations for Two* 1989—*The Dionne Warwick Collection/Her All Time Greatest Hits* (Rhino); *Greatest Hits, 1979–1990* (Arista) 1990—*Sings Cole Porter* 1992—*Hidden Gems: The Best of Dionne Warwick, vol. 2* (Rhino) 1993—*Friends Can Be Lovers* (Arista) 1994—*Aquarela do Brasil* 1998—*Dionne Sings Dionne* (River North) 1999—*The Definitive Collection* (Arista).

Since her solo recording debut in 1962, Dionne Warwick has been one of the most successful American pop singers, particularly in the '60s, when she was the voice of songwriters Burt Bacharach and Hal David.

Warwick grew up in a family of gospel singers and received considerable vocal training as a girl, singing with the Drinkard Singers, a group managed by her mother and including her sister Dee Dee. She attended Hartt College of Music in Hartford, Connecticut, and after singing background on some recording sessions, she was signed to Scepter Records in 1962 to work with the production and writing team of Bacharach and David.

"Don't Make Me Over" (#21 pop, #5 R&B) in late 1962 was the first of many Bacharach-David compositions Warwick would record, including "Anyone Who Had a Heart" (#8), 1963; "Walk On By" (#6) and "You'll Never Get to Heaven" (#34), 1964; "Trains and Boats and Planes" (#22 pop, #49 R&B) and "Message to Michael" (#8 pop, #5 R&B), 1966; "I Say a Little Prayer" (#4 pop, #8 R&B) and "Alfie" (#18 pop, #5 R&B), 1967. Over the next two years, she had four huge hits: "(Theme from) Valley of the Dolls" (#2 pop, #13 R&B, 1968), "Do You Know the Way to San Jose" (#10 pop, #23 R&B, 1968), "This Girl's in Love With You" (#7 pop and R&B, 1969), and "I'll Never Fall in Love Again" (#6 pop, #17 R&B, 1970) from the Bacharach-David musical *Promises, Promises.* Of the above songs, only "(Theme from) Valley of the Dolls" was not a Bacharach-David composition. In addition, before 1971 Warwick had 10 more Top 40 hits.

In 1971 Warwick moved to Warner Bros. Records and left Bacharach-David behind. She couldn't duplicate her success, although she worked with a number of fine producer/writers. *Just Being Myself* was written by the Brian Holland and Lamont Dozier team, and *Track of the Cat* by Thom Bell. In 1974 she had a Bell-produced hit, "Then Came You," with the Spinners (#1 pop, #2 R&B). "Once You Hit the Road" (#5 R&B) with Bell did well in 1975. In the early '70s, on the advice of a numerologist, she added an "e" to her surname, but dropped it in 1975. A 1977 live album with Isaac Hayes, *A Man and a Woman,* was well received.

In 1979 she returned to the charts with "I'll Never Love This Way Again" (#5 pop, #18 R&B), produced by Barry Manilow, and "Déjà Vu" (#15 pop, #25 R&B). Manilow also produced her highest-charting album in 10 years, the platinum *Dionne.* In 1982 Bee Gee Barry Gibb coproduced and wrote songs for Warwick's *Heartbreaker* (#25), which hit with the title cut (#10, 1982). Warwick's biggest hit singles of the '80s were all duets: with Johnny Mathis, "Friends in Love" (#38, 1982), with Luther Vandross, "How Many Times Can We Say Goodbye" (#27, 1983), and with Jeffrey Osborne, "Love Power" (#12, 1987). Her biggest hit of the period, however, was "That's What Friends Are For," featuring her with Elton John, Gladys Knight and Stevie Wonder. The proceeds from the Grammy-winning #1 1985 hit went to benefit AIDS research through AMFAR (the American Foundation for AIDS Research). In addition, Warwick has received four other Grammy awards. In 1993 she was reunited with Bacharach and David for "Sunny Weather Lover," which appears on *Friends Can Be Lovers.* That album also contains "Love Will Find a Way," Warwick's duet with her cousin, Whitney Houston. *Dionne Sings Dionne,* issued in 1998, features new renditions of eight Bacharach songs, seven of which boast lyrics by David. In 2000 Warwick toured with Gladys Knight and Randy Crawford.

She has also pursued a range of business interests outside of music, including an interior design firm, a fragrance called Dionne, the Psychic Friends Network, and a television-production company. She is also involved in a number of humanitarian causes.

Dinah Washington

Born Ruth Lee Jones, Aug. 29, 1924, Tuscaloosa, AL; died Dec. 14, 1963, Detroit, MI

1959—*What a Diff'rence a Day Makes!* (Mercury) 1960—*The Two of Us* (with Brook Benton) 1961—*Unforgettable* 1987—*The Complete Dinah Washington on Mercury, vol. 1 1946–1949; The Complete Dinah Washington on Mercury, vol. 2 1950–1952* 1988—*The Complete Dinah Washington on Mercury, vol. 3 1952–1954; The Complete Dinah Washington on Mercury, vol. 4 1954–1956* 1989—*The Complete Dinah Washington on Mercury, vol. 5 1956–1958; The Complete Dinah Washington on Mercury, vol. 6 1958–1960; The Complete Dinah Washington on Mercury, vol. 7 1961* 1993—*First Issue: The Dinah Washington Story (The Original Recordings).*

Dinah Washington was the most popular black female singer of the '50s; her sinuous, nasal, penetrating vocals were marvelously effective on blues, jazz, gospel, or straight pop songs. Growing up in Chicago, she gave gospel recitals on the South Side, accompanying herself on piano. At 15 she secretly entered and won an amateur contest at the Regal Theater and began appearing at local nightclubs. But in 1940 she returned to the church at the urging of Sallie Martin, a powerful figure in the gospel world who helped young Ruth Jones polish her talent.

In 1942 she became immersed in secular music after agent Joe Glaser heard her sing. He suggested she change her name to Dinah Washington and recommended her to Lionel Hampton, with whom she sang from 1943 to 1946. Jazz writer Leonard Feather arranged for her to cut two of his songs for Keynote Records in 1943, "Evil Gal Blues" and "Salty Papa Blues," backed by Hampton's band. During the mid-'50s Washington was known as the "Queen of the Harlem Blues," partially because of her sales consistency, and because her style of blues was much more complex than that of Chicago-area singers. Among her Top 10 R&B hits were "Baby Get Lost" (#1 R&B, 1949), "Trouble in Mind" (#4 R&B, 1952), "What a Diff'rence a Day Makes" (#8 pop, #4 R&B, 1959), and "This Bitter Earth" (#24 pop, #1 R&B, 1960). Also in 1960 Washington cut two popular duets with Brook Benton, "Baby (You've Got What It Takes)" (#5 pop, #1 R&B) and "A Rockin' Good Way" (#7 pop, #1 R&B).

After 18 years with Mercury, Washington went to Roulette Records in 1961. She died in 1963 after consuming weight-reduction pills and alcohol. Thirty years later she was honored with a commemorative postage stamp. In 1993 she was inducted into the Rock and Roll Hall of Fame.

Grover Washington Jr.

Born Dec. 12, 1943, Buffalo, NY; died Dec. 17, 1999, New York, NY
1971—*Inner City Blues* (Kudu) 1972—*All the King's Horses* 1973—*Soul Box* 1975—*Mister Magic; Feels So Good* 1976—*A Secret Place; Soul Box, vol. 2* 1977—*Live at the Bijou* 1978—*Reed Seed* (Motown) 1979—*Paradise* (Elektra); *Skylarkin'* (Motown) 1980—*Winelight* (Elektra); *Baddest* (Motown) 1981—*Come Morning* (Elektra) 1982—*The Best Is Yet to Come* 1984—*Inside Moves* 1985—*Anthology of Grover Washington* 1987—*Strawberry Moon* (Columbia) 1988—*Then and Now* 1989—*Time Out of Mind* 1992—*Next Exit* 1994—*All My Tomorrows* 1996—*Soulful Strut* 1999—*Prime Cuts—The Columbia Years: 1987–1999* 2000—*Aria* (Sony); *Millennium Collection* (Uni/Motown).

Grover Washington Jr.'s recordings, featuring his soulful saxes backed by supple, funky grooves, made him, since the '70s, one of the most commercially viable pop jazzmen.

Starting to play saxophone at age 10, Washington came from a musical family, his father a tenor saxophonist, his mother a choir singer, and his brother a drummer. At 16 he left home to tour with a Columbus, Ohio–based band, the Four Clefs. While in the army from 1965 to 1967, he gigged in Philadelphia with organ trios and rock bands. He also performed in New York with drummer Billy Cobham.

After playing on a number of albums in the early '70s, Washington was signed to Kudu Records by pop-jazz mogul Creed Taylor. *Inner City Blues* introduced his fusion of jazz technique and pop melodicism; his gold *Mister Magic*, arranged by Bob James, established a style that proved successful throughout the '70s and early '80s. This was the first of seven Washington albums of the period to go #1 on the jazz chart and the first to go gold. His best-selling release was the platinum *Winelight*, which contained "Just the Two of Us," featuring Bill Withers' vocal.

Through the '80s, Washington's audience became even more pop oriented; his mellow sound gained exposure on the theme songs for television's *The Cosby Show* and *Moonlighting*. A multi-instrumentalist (tenor, alto, soprano, and baritone saxophone, as well as clarinet, bass, and piano), Washington began working as a producer for jazz group Pieces of a Dream, and producing some of his own albums.

In 1992 Washington again went to #1 on the jazz chart with *Next Exit;* it contained "Summer Chill," cowritten with his son and nominated for a Best R&B Instrumental Grammy Award. In the '90s, he performed at Bill Clinton's inauguration, and alternated acoustic jazz such as *All My Tomorrows*, a stylistic successor to 1988's *Then and Now*, with forays into hip-hop *(Soulful Strut)* and his usual pop-oriented fare. He died from an apparent heart attack in 1999, after taping four tunes for the CBS television show, *The Saturday Early Show*.

Was (Not Was)

Formed ca. 1981, Detroit, MI
Don Was (b. Donald Fagenson, Sep. 13, 1952, Detroit), bass; David Was (b. David Weiss, Oct. 26, 1952, Detroit), sax, flute; Sweet Pea Atkinson (b. Sep. 20, 1945, Oberlin, OH), voc.; Sir Harry Bowens (b. Oct. 8, 1949, Detroit), voc.; Donald Ray Mitchell (b. Apr. 12, 1957, Detroit), voc.
1981—*Was (Not Was)* (Ze/Island) 1983—*Born to Laugh at Tornadoes* (Ze/Geffen) 1988—*What Up, Dog?* (Chrysalis) 1990—*Are You Okay?*
Orquestra Was: 1997—*Forever's a Long, Long Time* (Verve Forecast).

Was (Not Was) unites two studiophiles overflowing with encyclopedic knowledge of pop music, some dyed-in-the-wool R&B singers, and an absurdly eclectic host of outside guests to implode all manner of white and black musical genres.

The Was "brothers" met as children while living in suburban Detroit. Hanging out in the "humor prison"—Weiss' basement—the two spent their adolescence indulging their tilted sensibilities by publishing an alternative newspaper, staging outrageous school productions, and writing songs. Immersed in the local rock and soul scenes that commingled in Detroit, Weiss and Fagenson also dabbled in the radical rock & roll politics of John Sinclair's White Panther party.

Weiss, who plays saxophone and flute, left Detroit for L.A. Fagenson, a bassist, stayed in Detroit eking out a living doing local session work and production. Weiss was writing jazz criticism for the *Los Angles Herald Examiner* but felt unfulfilled musically. The two hometown buddies began a cross-country collaboration; Weiss concocting the surreal lyrics, Fagenson devising the genre-warping music. Taking their name from a word game of Fagenson's son, Was (Not Was) proceeded to collect members of Detroit's pop-rock-funk communities to help them on their first album. Among the groups represented were P-Funk, the MC5, Brownsville Station, and Wild Cherry. The resulting "Out Come the Freaks" and "Tell Me That I'm Dreaming" became dance hits.

Born to Laugh at Tornadoes (#134) upped the eclectic ante even more. Guests included Marshall Crenshaw, Mel Torme, Mitch Ryder, Ozzy Osbourne, Kiss' Vinnie Vincent, and the Knack's Doug Fieger. Critics' darlings but poor sellers, Was (Not Was) was dropped by Geffen. Their next album didn't find them retreating from their now trademark mix-and-match collisions. *What Up, Dog?* (#43) featured Frank Sinatra Jr. on the priceless "Wedding Vows in Vegas" and an Elvis Costello writing collaboration, "Love Can Be Bad Luck." But extra attention was placed on the band's own superlative R&B belters, Sir Harry Bowens and Sweet Pea Atkinson (assisted by Mitchell), whose impassioned vocals helped make "Walk the Dinosaur" a #7 hit.

Are You Okay? (#99) also has its share of unexpected guests (Leonard Cohen, Iggy Pop, the Roches), but the standout track was a remake of the Temptations' 1972 hit "Papa Was a Rollin' Stone" with Bowens and Atkinson singing and G Love E adding a rap that turned the song into a contemporary howl of urban pain. The Was Brothers began to drift apart shortly thereafter, however, and by 1993 Was (Not Was) was no more.

By the late 1980s Don Was had simultaneously established himself among the most in-demand producers in the music industry. His magic touch was best felt on Bonnie Raitt's *Nick of Time* (1989), a project which totally revitalized her career; he was also at the helm for her followup, 1991's *Luck of the Draw.* Was has also produced the B-52's, Iggy Pop, Paula Abdul, and Willie Nelson. Production for Bob Dylan's 1990 *Under the Red Sky* was credited to David and Don Was. In 1994 Don Was produced the Rolling Stones' *Voodoo Lounge,* an endeavor that won him a Grammy and led to two successive Stones albums. He made his film directorial debut in 1995 with the Brian Wilson documentary, *I Just Wasn't Made for These Times.*

In 1997 Don Was rounded up a diverse batch of musicians (including Sweet Pea Atkinson, Merle Haggard, and Herbie Hancock) and issued *Forever's a Long, Long Time* under the banner Orquestra Was. The album set Hank Williams lyrics to R&B arrangements, and the enhanced CD featured a Was-directed/Francis Ford Coppola–produced minimovie starring Atkinson. The following year, Don and David Was reunited to begin working on a new album, but Don's son Tony Fagenson came out of the gate first with the debut album by his own band, Eve 6.

W.A.S.P.

Formed 1984, Los Angeles, CA
Blackie Lawless (b. Steve Duren, Sep. 4, 1954, FL), voc.; Chris Holmes, gtr.; Johnny Rod (b. Dec. 8, 1957, MO), bass, voc.; Randy Piper, gtr., voc.; Tony Richards, drums.
1984—*W.A.S.P.* (Capitol) 1985—*The Last Command* 1986—(– Richards; + Steve Riley, drums, voc.) *Inside the Electric Circus* 1987—(– Riley; + Glen Soderling, drums) *Live . . . In the Raw* 1989—(– Soderling; + Frank Banali [b. Nov. 14, 1953, Queens, NY], drums; + Ken Hensley, kybds.) *The Headless Children* 1991—(– Holmes; – Piper; – Riley; – Hensley; + Stet Howland [b. Aug. 14, 1960, MA], drums) 1992—(+ Bob Kulick, gtr.) *The Crimson Idol* (Capitol/EMI) 1994—*First Blood . . . Last Cuts: Best of W.A.S.P.* 1996—*Still Not Black Enough* (Castle) 1997—(– Kulick; + Holmes, gtr.; + Mike Duda, bass) *K.F.D.* (Raw Power) 1998—*Double Live Assassins* (CMC International) 1999—*Helldorado* 2000—*The Best of the Best, vol. 1, 1984–1999* (Apocalypse M.P.S.); *Sting.*

W.A.S.P. would be just another mildly successful L.A. metal band if not for the attention of the Parents' Music Resource Center. At the 1985 Senate Commerce Committee Hearings they became the prime example of all that was obscene in rock, illustrated with a photo of lead singer Blackie Lawless posed with a buzz saw jutting none-too-subtly between his legs.

Lawless, a nephew of '50s New York Yankee pitcher Ryne Duren, seemed born for this role. A member of the last-ditch version of the New York Dolls, he moved to L.A. in 1976. That year he joined forces with future Mötley Crüe member Nikki Sixx in Sister. He left in 1978 and roamed the L.A. scene until he formed W.A.S.P. with Chris Holmes, the husband of ex-Runaway Lita Ford.

The band became known for their club act, which included crotch rubbings and props such as chainsaws, raw meat, and fake blood. Capitol signed them in 1984 but refused to distribute their initial single, "Animal (Fuck Like a Beast)." The coverage of the Senate hearings boosted the band's notoriety, pushing 1985's *The Last Command* to #49. *The Headless Children* (#48, 1989) tempered the band's usual treatment of sex and violence, becoming their most popular album. In 1991 Lawless introduced a new lineup, and the band became known as Blackie Lawless and W.A.S.P., releasing a concept album titled *The Crimson Idol* in 1993.

Undeterred by the band being dropped from their major label, Lawless has kept W.A.S.P. busy. *Still Not Black Enough* was originally supposed to be a solo album, but Lawless decided to release it under the W.A.S.P. moniker. The following year, Holmes came back into the W.A.S.P. fold. The band has been recording (on small, independent labels) and touring regularly ever since, and its live shows still feature an abundance of gory theatrics.

The Waterboys

Formed Oct. 1982, London, Eng.
Mike Scott (b. Dec. 14, 1958, Edinburgh, Scot.), voc., gtr., kybds.; Anthony Thistlethwaite (b. Aug. 8, 1955, Leicester, Eng.), sax, mandolin, gtr., bass; Kevin Wilkinson (b. Eng.), drums.
1983—*The Waterboys* (Ensign/Chrysalis) (+ Karl Wallinger [b. Oct. 19, 1957, Prestatyn, Wales], kybds.; + Roddy Lorimer [b. Glasgow, Scot.], trumpet) 1984—*A Pagan Place* (– Wilkinson; + Chris Whitten, drums) 1985—*This Is the Sea* (– Wallinger; – Whitten; + Steve Wickham [b. Dublin, Ire.], fiddle;

+ Dave Ruffy [b. Eng.], drums; Guy Chambers [b. Eng.], kybds.; + Marco Weissman, bass) 1986—(– Weissman; – Chambers; – Ruffy; + Trevor Hutchinson [b. Ire.], bass) 1988—(+ Colin Blakey [b. Falkirk, Scot.], flute, whistle, kybds.) *Fisherman's Blues* 1989—(+ Sharon Shannon [b. Ire.], accordion, fiddle; + Ken Blevins, drums; + Noel Bridgeman [b. Dublin, Ire.], drums) 1990—*Room to Roam* (– Wickham; – Blakey; – Shannon; – Bridgeman; – Lorimer; – Blevins) 1991—(– Thistlethwaite; – Hutchinson) *The Best of the Waterboys 1981–1991* 1994—*Dream Harder* (Geffen) 2001—*A Rock in the Weary Land* (RCA, U.K.).
Mike Scott solo: 1995—*Bring 'Em All In* (Chrysalis) 1997—*Still Burning.*

Scottish-born singer/songwriter Mike Scott is the sole constant member of the Waterboys, a group whose sound has changed from dramatic, horn- and keyboard-driven "big music" to folky Irish acoustic songs to guitar-based pop/rock. Throughout, Scott's incisive lyrics have for the most part reflected his interests in spirituality, mysticism, and Celtic poetry. Though quite successful in Britain in the mid-'80s, the Waterboys have yet to find a large audience in the U.S.

Scott, whose mother was an English professor, grew up in a village on the coast of Scotland. In the late '70s he started a fanzine, *Jungleland,* and began playing in punk bands. After studying English and philosophy at Edinburgh University, Scott moved to London with his band, Another Pretty Face. After it broke up, he started the Waterboys (named after a line in "The Kids" from Lou Reed's *Berlin*), recruiting multi-instrumentalist Anthony Thistlethwaite. The two played most of the instruments on 1983's *The Waterboys,* produced by Scott. Keyboardist Karl Wallinger joined for the band's next two recordings, adding his rich keyboard flavorings to Scott's majestic mood-rock. Critics began dubbing the Waterboys' sound "big music" after a song title on *The Pagan Place* (#100 U.K., 1984). *This Is the Sea* (#37 U.K., 1985) proved a fruitful collaboration between Wallinger and Scott, yielding the British hit single, "The Whole of the Moon" (#26 U.K., 1985). (The song returned to #3 on the U.K. chart in 1991, upon rerelease on the #2 charting greatest-hits album.)

Wallinger left the band in 1985 to start his own group, World Party [see entry]. Scott moved from London to Ireland, where he put together a new band, mainly consisting of traditional Irish folk players. Three years later, the lilting, mostly acoustic *Fisherman's Blues* (#13 U.K., 1988) was the result of Scott's new musical environment. *Room to Roam* (#5 U.K, 1990) continued in this direction.

The early '90s found Scott yearning to play electric guitar again. After a change in record labels, Scott relocated once more, this time to New York, without Thistlethwaite and his Irish band mates. *Dream Harder* (#5 U.K., 1993) was recorded with an assortment of session players. It marked a return to electric music, though more stripped-down than the Waterboys' early albums. In 1994 Scott moved back to Britain, living for several months at a spiritual community in Scotland. While there, he recorded his first solo album, *Bring 'Em All In.* Three years later his second solo effort, *Still Burning,* followed. The Waterboy's moniker returned in 2000 when Scott put together a band to play England's Glastonbury Festival. *A Rock in the Weary Land's* release was followed by a Waterboys tour of the States—the band's first in 11 years.

Muddy Waters

Born McKinley Morganfield, Apr. 4, 1915, Rolling Fork, MS; died Apr. 30, 1983, Chicago, IL
1958—*The Best of Muddy Waters* (Chess) 1960—*Muddy Waters at Newport, 1960* 1962—*Fathers and Sons* 1964—*Folk Singer* 1966—*Down on Stovall's Plantation* (Testament) 1968—*Sail On* (Chess) 1971—*They Call Me Muddy Waters* 1972—*The London Sessions* 1973—*Can't Get No Grindin'* 1977—*Hard Again* (Blue Sky) 1978—*I'm Ready* 1979—*Muddy "Mississippi" Waters Live* 1981—*King Bee* 1982—*Rolling Stone* (Chess); *Rare and Unissued* 1989—*Trouble No More (Singles, 1955–1959)* (Chess/MCA); *The Chess Box* 1994—*One More Mile* 1995—*The Chicago Blues Masters, vol. 1* (Capitol) 1996—*Muddy Waters Blues Band featuring Dizzy Gillespie* (LaserLight); *Hoochie Coochie Man.*

Muddy Waters was the leading exponent of Chicago blues in the '50s. With him, the blues came up from the Delta and went electric, and his guitar licks and repertoire have fueled innumerable blues bands. Waters was the son of a farmer and, following his mother's death in 1918, was raised by his grandmother. He picked up his nickname because he fished and played regularly in a muddy creek. He learned to play harmonica, and as a teen he led a band that frequently played Mississippi Delta clubs. His singing was influenced by the style of local bluesman Son House. At 17, Waters began playing guitar by studying Robert Johnson records. In 1940 he traveled to St. Louis and in 1941 joined the Silas Green tent show as a singer and harmonica player. Sometime around 1941–42, Waters was recorded by folk archivists/researchers Alan Lomax and John Work in Mississippi for the Library of Congress.

In 1943 he moved to Chicago, where he found employment in a paper mill. The following year, Waters got an electric guitar and began performing at South Side clubs and rent parties. He cut several sides in 1946 for Columbia's Okeh subsidiary, but none was released until 1981, when they appeared on a Columbia blues reissue, *Okeh Chicago Blues.* In 1946 bluesman Sunnyland Slim helped Waters get signed to Aristocrat Records, where he cut several unsuccessful singles, and Waters continued playing clubs every night and driving a truck six days a week.

In 1948 the Chess brothers changed Aristocrat to Chess. Waters' first single on the new label was "Rollin' Stone," a major blues hit. "I Can't Be Satisfied" and "I Feel Like Going Home" from that year secured his position as a major blues performer. Most of Waters' early recordings featured him on electric guitar, Big Crawford or writer/producer Willie Dixon on bass, and occasionally Little Walter on harmonica. By 1951 he was supported by a complete band with Otis Spann on piano, Little Walter on harmonica, Jimmie Rodgers on second guitar, and Elgin Evans on drums.

"Honey Bee" in 1951; "She Moves Me" (#10 R&B) in 1952; "I'm Your Hoochie Coochie Man" (#8 R&B), "I Just Wanna Make Love to You" (#4 R&B), "I'm Ready" (#5 R&B), and "Got My Mojo Working" in 1954; and "Mannish Boy" (#9 R&B) in 1955 are all regarded as blues classics and have been recorded by numerous rock groups. During the '50s, many of the top Chicago bluesmen passed through Waters' band, including Walter Horton, Junior Wells, Jimmie Rodgers, James Cotton, and Buddy Guy. In addition, Waters was helpful in the early stages of both Howlin' Wolf's and Chuck Berry's careers.

During his peak years as a record seller, most of Waters' sales were confined primarily to the Mississippi Delta, the New Orleans area, and Chicago. But his reputation and music were internationally known, as the attendance at concerts on his 1958 English tour revealed. The Rolling Stones named themselves after his song "Rollin' Stone." After the mid-'50s Waters never had another Top 10 R&B single, but his albums began to reach rock listeners. Into the '60s, Waters appeared at concerts and festivals nationally, such as the 1960 Newport Jazz Festival, where *Muddy Waters at Newport* was cut. In the late '60s and early '70s, he recorded several albums either with rock musicians or in a rock direction, the best of which were *The London Sessions* and *Fathers and Sons,* the latter with many of the players he had influenced, including Mike Bloomfield and Paul Butterfield. In 1971 Waters won the first of several Grammys with *They Call Me Muddy Waters.*

In the early '70s Waters left Chess and sued Chess's publishing arm for back royalties. He signed with Steve Paul's Blue Sky records in 1976, the year he appeared at the Band's farewell concert. Using members of his '50s bands and producer/guitarist Johnny Winter, Waters made three of his best-selling albums, *Hard Again, I'm Ready,* and *King Bee.* Winter and Waters frequently performed together in the '70s and '80s. He last performed publicly at a June 1982 Eric Clapton show. Waters died of a heart attack. In 1987 he was inducted into the Rock and Roll Hall of Fame.

Roger Waters: See Pink Floyd

Jody Watley

Born Jan. 30, 1959, Chicago, IL
1987—*Jody Watley* (MCA) 1988—*Beginnings* (Solar) 1989—*Larger Than Life; You Wanna Dance With Me?* 1991—*Affairs of the Heart* 1993—*Intimacy* 1995—*Affection* (Avitone/Bellmark) 1996—*Greatest Hits* (MCA) 1998—*Flower* (Atlantic).

A leggy dance diva whose minimalist singing and videogenic glamour evoke a more elegant Janet Jackson, Jody Watley was awarded the 1987 Best New Artist Grammy for her eponymous solo debut, which reached #10 in 1987 and yielded two slamming dance-pop singles, "Looking for a New Love" (#2) and "Don't You Want Me" (#6). (Another track, "Some Kind of Lover," went to #10 in 1988.)

The daughter of a minister father and a mother who sang, both of whom had influential friends—the singer Jackie Wilson was her godfather—Watley got her start while still a teenager in the '70s as a dancer on TV's *Soul Train.* She and dance partner Jeffrey Daniels were tapped by producer Don Cornelius to form the dance band Shalamar [see entry]. Little more than a decorative backup singer at first, Watley began writing songs for the band and aspired to sing more, but she was stymied by lead singer Howard Hewett. Artistically frustrated by Hewett, Watley left Shalamar in 1984 and moved to England, where she modeled and did sessions singing, notably on the 1984 Band Aid single "Do They Know It's Christmas?" Back in L.A., she hooked up with former Prince bassist Andre Cymone to cowrite several tracks for *Jody Watley.* Their partnership continued over the next two LPs with solid returns. *Larger Than Life* spawned "Real Love" (#2, 1989), "Everything" (#4, 1989), and, with Erik B. and Rakim, "Friends" (#9, 1989); *Affairs of the Heart* featured a few songs written solely by Watley. Her next album, *Intimacy,* was her least dance-oriented to date—perhaps why it barely reached the Top 40 on the R&B chart, although it was well-received by critics.

In 1995 Watley went through a lot of changes. The public did not discover that she and longtime producer Cymone had been secretly married for years (and they had two children) until the couple divorced. Watley also chose to establish her own label, releasing *Affection* on Avitone (it was distributed by Bellmark); the album included a live, jazzy re-

Jody Watley

make of "Looking for a New Love," and the title track reached #28 on the R&B chart. In 1996, Watley took to the stage as Rizzo in the Broadway revival of *Grease.* Despite her own strong protests that she would not participate in a Shalamar reunion, she was persuaded by Babyface to sing on, "This Is for the Lover in You" (#6 pop, #2 R&B, 1997), with her former band mates, Daniels and Hewett, along with L.L. Cool J, for a Babyface album. That year, Watley also briefly returned to modeling, displaying winter coats for Saks Fifth Avenue. In 1998 Watley did a lot of press in anticipation of her new album, her first with Atlantic; she even posed skimpily clad for a spread in *Playboy.* To her surprise, after releasing a single, "Off the Hook" (#23 R&B, 1998), *Flower*'s release was indefinitely postponed in the U.S. It was, however, released internationally, and Watley played concerts in Europe and Asia. In 2000 Watley performed live with the Nuyorican Soul Orchestra in New York's Central Park and released a dance single, "I Love to Love."

Johnny "Guitar" Watson

Born Feb. 3, 1935, Houston, TX; died May 17, 1996, Yokohama, Jap.
1966—*Bad* (Okeh) 1967—*Two for the Price of One* 1968—*In the Fats Bag* 1973—*Gangster of Love* (Fantasy) 1976—*I Don't Want to Be Alone, Stranger; Captured Live* (DJM); *Ain't That a Bitch* 1977—*A Real Mother for Ya; Funk Beyond the Call of Duty* 1978—*Giant* 1979—*What the Hell Is This* 1980—*Love Jones* 1981—*Johnny "Guitar" Watson and the Family Clone* 1987—*Three Hours Past Midnight* (Ace) 1994—*Bow Wow* (Bellmark) 1999—*The Very Best of Johnny "Guitar" Watson* (Rhino).

Johnny "Guitar" Watson enjoyed great popularity in the mid-'70s with several hit singles and LPs, but his work has been known in blues circles since the '50s. His playing style was influential on Jimi Hendrix, among others, and his "Gangster of Love" was recorded by Steve Miller in 1968.

Watson's father taught him to play piano, and at age 11 his grandmother gave him his grandfather's guitar, which he taught himself to play. He moved to L.A. in 1950, where he began working as a sideman in various bands and recording as a solo artist for Federal Records. Among the bands he played in through the '50s were those led by Amos Milburn, Bumps Blackwell, and Big Jay McNeely. In 1961 he began recording for King. His late-'50s and early-'60s hits include "Three Hours Past Midnight," "Those Lonely Lonely Nights," and "Space Guitar," which was one of the first recorded songs to use reverb and feedback. Through the '60s and '70s, Watson performed around the U.S. and occasionally in Europe. In the early to mid-'60s, he often toured with Larry Williams. Recording for DJM in the mid-'70s, Watson had funk hits with "A Real Mother for Ya" (#41 pop, 1977), "I Don't Wanna Be a Lone Ranger," and "It's Too Late." Later releases on A&M and Mercury were not as well received. He essentially retired in the early '80s but performed occasionally in Europe. After meeting producer Al Bell, he resumed recording. *Bow Wow* and a subsequent series of live gigs marked Watson's tragically short resurgence in 1994. He suffered a fatal heart attack in 1996 during a Japanese tour.

Mike Watt: See Minutemen

Weather Girls

Formed 1982, San Francisco, CA
Martha Wash (b. San Francisco), voc.; Izora Armstead (b. ca. 1943, San Francisco), voc.
1983—*Success* (Columbia) 1985—*Big Girls Don't Cry* 1988—*Weather Girls* 1994—(– Wash; + Dynelle Rhodes, voc.) *Two Tons O' Fun* (Fuel, Ger.).
Martha Wash solo: 1993—*Martha Wash* (RCA) 1998—*The Collection* (Logic/BMG).

Martha Wash and Izora Armstead are gospel-trained disco divas who have tried not to let their extra-large size deter them from pop stardom, whether using it to their advantage—calling themselves Two Tons O' Fun—or fighting sexism and size-ism with lawsuits, as Wash has done.

Both women got their starts singing in church choirs in San Francisco. They first sang together in the gospel group N.O.W. (News of the World). In the late '70s they became backup singers for disco sensation Sylvester as Two Tons O' Fun, releasing a couple albums on the Fantasy label. In 1982 Wash and Armstead teamed with producer and songwriter Paul Jabara to record the single "It's Raining Men" (#46 pop, #34 R&B, 1983). The song became a hit in dance clubs, where it was seized by gay men as an anthem, and was especially big in the U.K. Although the Weather Girls' subsequent albums were praised by critics and the duo continued to have a following, they never repeated their initial success.

In 1990 Wash began singing commercial jingles and working with various groups. She provided the vocals on such dance hits as Black Box's "Everybody, Everybody," and C + C Music Factory's "Gonna Make You Sweat." But because these were groups run by producers who did not deem Wash photogenic, she wasn't credited on the albums and svelte models lip-synched her part in videos. Wash sued the groups and their record companies for fraud, winning a contract with RCA as part of the Black Box settlement.

In 1991 she sang a duet with Luther Vandross, "I Who Have Nothing," on his *Power of Love* album. Wash's solo debut yielded two dance-club hits, "Carry On" and "Give It to You." To support her longtime gay following, Wash has performed numerous AIDS benefits. She rejoined the C + C Music Factory fold [see entry] in 1994, appearing that year on *Anything Goes.* In 1998 Wash released *The Collection,* a career retrospective that offers a sampling of her work with Sylvester, Two Tons O' Fun, Black Box, and C + C Music Factory. The album also contains three new tracks, including "It's Raining Men . . . The Sequel," featuring drag queen RuPaul.

Meanwhile, Armstead and her daughter Dynelle Rhodes

have carried on the Weather Girls name since 1992. The duo has toured abroad extensively and their 1994 album *Two Tons O' Fun* topped the charts in Europe, yielding a pair of hits. Armstead writes much of the group's material, which covers topics ranging from relationships to broader social concerns.

Weather Report

Formed 1970, New York, NY
Josef Zawinul (b. July 7, 1932, Vienna, Austria), kybds., synth.; Wayne Shorter (b. Aug. 25, 1933, Newark, NJ), saxes; Miroslav Vitous (b. Dec. 6, 1947, Prague, Czech.), bass; Alphonse Mouzon (b. Nov. 21, 1948, Charleston, SC), drums; Airto Moreira (b. Aug. 5, 1941, Braz.), perc.
1971—*Weather Report* (Columbia) (– Mouzon; + Eric Gravatt, drums; – Moreira; + Dom Um Romao, perc.) 1972—*I Sing the Body Electric* 1973—*Streetnighter* (– Gravatt; + Ishmael Wilburn, drums; + Alphonso Johnson [b. Feb. 2, 1951, Philadelphia, PA], bass) 1974—*Mysterious Traveller* (– Vitous; – Wilburn; + Alyrio Lima, drums; – Romao; + Ndugu [b. Leon Chancler], perc.) 1975—*Tale Spinnin'* (– Lima; + Chester Thompson, drums; – Ndugu) 1976—*Black Market* (– Johnson; + Jaco Pastorius [b. Dec. 1, 1951, Norristown, PA; d. Sep. 21, 1987, Ft. Lauderdale, FL], bass; – Thompson; + Alejandro Neciosup Acuna, perc.; + Manola Badrena [b. P.R.], perc., voc.) 1977—*Heavy Weather* (– Acuna; – Badrena) 1978—*Mr. Gone* (+ Peter Erskine [b. May 5, 1954, Somers Point, NJ], drums) 1979—*8:30* 1980—*Night Passages* (– Pastorius) 1982— (– Erskine; + Victor Bailey, bass; + Jose Rossy, perc.; + Omar Hakim, drums) 1982—*Weather Report* 1983—*Procession* 1984—*Domino Theory* 1985—*Sportin' Life* 1986— (– Rossy + Mino Cinelu, perc.; + Erskine) *This Is This* 1996—*Birdland* (Sony Legacy); *This Is Jazz, vol. 40: The Jaco Years.*

Between its inception in 1970 and its 1987 breakup, Weather Report was the premier electric jazz ensemble. Born of the Miles Davis groups of the late '60s that also spawned many other fusion bands, Weather Report was one of the very few groups that managed to win commercial success while going its own way. The band's music had the drive of rock, the harmonic sophistication of jazz, the formal ingenuity of classical music, and hints of Brazilian, African, and Asian traditions. The best-known Weather Report tunes, such as "Birdland," sound like electrified global carnivals.

Josef Zawinul and Wayne Shorter were the only constants of Weather Report. The first music Zawinul heard and played was the Gypsy folk music of his family; his first instrument was an accordion. Around the age of 12, when he was living in Nazi-occupied Vienna, he began studying classical piano. In the postwar years, he played jazz at U.S. Army clubs and Viennese cabarets. On the basis of a record he cut in a local studio, he was awarded a scholarship to study at the Berklee College of Music in Boston, and he arrived in the United States in 1959. Three weeks after classes began, he dropped out and went to New York, where he met Shorter.

Shorter had been in the city since 1951, when he entered New York University to study music. After graduating, he played tenor saxophone with Horace Silver before joining Maynard Ferguson's band. Through Shorter, Zawinul began playing with Ferguson as well. Not long after that, however, Shorter moved on to Art Blakey's Jazz Messengers, where he stayed for five years. Zawinul also left Ferguson. He led Dinah Washington's band for over a year and did sessions behind Joe Williams, Yusef Lateef, Ben Webster, and a very young Aretha Franklin. He played the electric piano extensively during nine years in the Cannonball Adderley Quintet, which he joined in 1961, and for whom he wrote "Mercy, Mercy, Mercy."

Shorter joined the Miles Davis Quintet (with keyboardist Herbie Hancock, drummer Tony Williams, and bassist Ron Carter) in 1964. Shorter's work with Davis and on a half-dozen solo albums had established him as one of the outstanding saxophonists of the John Coltrane school, although he later tempered the Coltrane influence with his own lyricism. Shorter was also an outstanding composer; his "Nefertiti" (the title track of a 1967 Miles Davis Quintet album) convinced Zawinul that the two of them should join forces. Meanwhile, Davis decided to experiment with a large electrified ensemble, which Zawinul joined. Zawinul's composition "In a Silent Way" became the title track of the album, recorded in 1968. Zawinul continued to play with Adderley, but he joined the Davis aggregation again in 1969 to record the landmark *Bitches Brew,* to which Zawinul and Shorter contributed compositions.

Shorter left Davis soon after the *Bitches Brew* sessions, and Zawinul left Adderley the following year. Each recorded solo albums before forming a group to experiment with electric jazz. They recruited Czech bassist Miroslav Vitous, who had recently played on a Zawinul date. After studying classical composition at the Prague Conservatory, Vitous—like Zawinul—had come to the U.S. on a scholarship from the Berklee College of Music. His jazz credits included work with Stan Getz, Sonny Rollins, Art Farmer, Herbie Mann, Larry Coryell, and Miles Davis. Clive Davis of Columbia Records reportedly signed the group without even listening to its demo tape. With Brazilian percussionist Airto Moreira and drummer Alphonse Mouzon, Weather Report recorded its highly experimental debut album.

Moreira, who left Weather Report to join Chick Corea, was replaced by another Brazilian, Dom Um Romao, formerly of Sergio Mendes and Brasil '66. Mouzon joined the McCoy Tyner Quartet and was replaced in Weather Report by Tyner's drummer, Eric Gravatt. One side of 1972's *I Sing the Body Electric* was excerpted from a double live album released only in Japan. On the group's third album, *Streetnighter,* Zawinul began using synthesizers as lead instruments and sticking to a funkier beat. *Streetnighter* sold 200,000 copies, quite a number for an album of instrumentals. *Mysterious Traveller* (1974) went further toward dance music with fixed rhythms, riffs, and figures repeated in unison by the bass, saxophone, and synthesizers. *Traveller* introduced bassist Alphonso Johnson, formerly with Chuck Mangione. By *Tale Spinnin',* Johnson had taken over for Vitous.

Tale Spinnin' featured Zawinul's ARP 2600, one of the most advanced of the monophonic synthesizers. On *Black Market,* he introduced the Oberheim polyphonic, and the effect was dramatic. Weather Report's music became almost orchestral in texture. But as Zawinul's arsenal of sounds expanded, Wayne Shorter's role diminished on records, although in Weather Report's concerts he took ample solos. In 1973 Shorter made the album *Native Dancer* with Brazilian songwriter Milton Nascimento.

Black Market included one cut on which the bassist was Jaco Pastorius. Pastorius had introduced himself to Zawinul after a Weather Report concert in Miami in 1975 and given him tapes of his playing. The son of a professional drummer, he had started playing drums at age 13, before taking up the bass. He toured with Wayne Cochran's C.C. Riders for one year and played with Ira Sullivan's big band, the Baker's Dozen, for three. As a freelance bassist in New York and Boston, he worked with Paul Bley and Pat Metheny, and his solo debut album was released concurrently with *Black Market,* introducing his busily contrapuntal fretless bass style. By the *Heavy Weather* sessions, he was a full member of the group, a contributing composer, and coproducer (with Zawinul). While devoting most of his efforts to Weather Report, Pastorius also recorded and toured with Joni Mitchell.

Heavy Weather was Weather Report's most commercially successful album. It sold over 500,000 copies—the first gold album for the group—and Zawinul's "Birdland" was given considerable airplay (a vocal rendition by the Manhattan Transfer was popular three years later).

Mr. Gone (1978) did not depart far from the rich orchestral sound of *Heavy Weather,* but the group no longer included a percussionist. With the addition of drummer Pete Erskine, Weather Report remained a four-piece unit for almost four years. A double album, *8:30,* comprised three sides recorded at two dates at the culmination of the 1979 tour, and one side recorded in Zawinul's home studio. Pastorius left Weather Report in 1982 and formed his own band, Word of Mouth. Tragically, Pastorius's heroin addiction cut his career short; practically penniless, he was beaten to death in 1987.

Procession (1983), with a new lineup, included the first Weather Report song with lyrics (sung by Janis Siegel of Manhattan Transfer). Without the creative three-way Zawinul-Shorter-Pastorius interchange, however, the Weather Report spark fizzled and in 1987 the band broke up.

Shorter formed his own touring groups, which tended toward more traditional jazz forms. Zawinul put together Weather Update, a fusion outfit that featured Erskine and guitarist Steve Khan. Shorter kept a low profile over the next few years. Apart from the heavily arranged *Atlantis* album and brief tours with Carlos Santana and a 1992 all-star Miles Davis tribute band, Shorter was out of the limelight. Ironically, his earlier Davis-era saxophone style and compositional technique had become the most influential sound for a new generation of jazz players. Zawinul continued his forays into neo-fusion with the Zawinul Syndicate, incorporating his continuing interest in world music. In 1996 ex-Miles Davis keyboardist Jason Miles assembled a cast of stellar players for a tribute to the band, *Celebrating the Music of Weather Report,* on Telarc.

The Weavers

Formed 1949, New York, NY
Original lineup: Pete Seeger (b. May 3, 1919, New York), gtr., banjo, voc.; Ronnie Gilbert, voc.; Fred Hellerman (b. May 13, 1927, New York), voc., gtr.; Lee Hays (b. Mar. 14, 1914, Little Rock, AR; d. Aug. 26, 1981, New York), voc., gtr.
1956—*The Weavers at Carnegie Hall* (Vanguard) 1957—*Greatest Hits* 1958—(– Seeger; + Erik Darling [b. Sep. 25, 1933], banjo) *The Weavers on Tour; The Weavers at Home* 1959—*Traveling On With the Weavers* 1961—*The Weavers at Carnegie Hall, vol. 2* 1962—*Almanac* (– Darling; + Frank Hamilton, banjo) 1963—*Reunion at Carnegie Hall, 1963* (group disbands) 1965—*Songbook* 1980—(group re-forms: Seeger; Hays; Hellerman; Gilbert) 1971—*The Weavers' Greatest Hits* 1981—*Together Again* 1987—*Weavers Classics; Reunion at Carnegie Hall, part 2* 1993—*The Weavers: Wasn't That a Time* (Vanguard).

The Weavers were the most important and influential early American folk revivalists, as well as one of the most commercially successful.

The quartet came together, at first informally, in 1948. Hays and Seeger had both been in the Almanac Singers. The Weavers began recording in spring 1950, and with their second single, they had their first big hit: "Tzena, Tzena, Tzena" (#2) backed with Lead Belly's "Goodnight, Irene" (#1). That single alone later went on to sell over 2 million copies, a phenomenal number at that time. Their other hits included "So Long (It's Been Good to Know You)" and "On Top of Old Smoky." In 1952 the group was blacklisted because of some members' leftist political views and associations. They all but disappeared between 1952 and their triumphant Christmas Eve concert at Carnegie Hall in 1955.

Pete Seeger [see entry] left to go solo in 1958 after a dispute with the other members over participating in a cigarette commercial, which he opposed. He was replaced in succession by Erik Darling, Frank Hamilton, and, in 1963, Bernie Krause. A 1963 reunion concert featured all seven Weavers, including Seeger.

The Weavers' legacy heavily influenced the early-'60s folk boom. A number of popular Weavers tunes have made their way onto the pop charts and into the American folk tradition: "Kisses Sweeter Than Wine," "Wimoweh (The Lion Sleeps Tonight)," "If I Had a Hammer," "Guantanamera," and "Turn! Turn! Turn! (To Everything There Is a Season)."

The four original members were reunited in 1981 for a concert that was filmed for the documentary *Wasn't That a Time.* Between reunions, Seeger had gone on to an influential solo career (he was inducted into the Rock and Roll Hall of Fame in 1996). Gilbert has recorded a number of albums, including two with Holly Near (*Lifeline,* 1983; *Singing With You,* 1986) and *Harp* (1985), with Arlo Guthrie and Pete

Seeger. Her solo releases include *The Spirit Is Free* (1985) and *Love Will Find a Way* (1989).

Jimmy Webb

Born Aug. 15, 1946, Elk City, OK
1968—*Jim Webb Sings Jim Webb* (Epic) 1970—*Words and Music* (Reprise) 1971—*And So On* 1972—*Letters* 1974—*Land's End* (Asylum) 1977—*El Mirage* (Atlantic) 1982—*Angel Heart* 1993—*Suspending Disbelief* (Elektra) 1996—*Ten Easy Pieces* (Guardian/Angel).

At age 21, Jimmy Webb was a millionaire, having written such pop hits as Glen Campbell's "By the Time I Get to Phoenix" and the Fifth Dimension's "Up, Up and Away," both of which were Grammy nominees in 1967 for Best Song ("Up, Up and Away" won). Other often-covered Webb songs include "Wichita Lineman," "MacArthur Park," "Galveston," and "The Moon Is a Harsh Mistress."

The son of a Baptist minister, Webb grew up in rural Oklahoma, learning piano and organ. When he moved with his family to San Bernardino, California, in 1964, he was already writing songs. In 1966 he enrolled in San Bernardino Valley College, but dropped out shortly thereafter when his mother died. He moved to L.A. and began making the rounds of the record business. For a time he earned $50 a week working at one recording studio. He also worked for Motown's publishing company, Jobete Music, which in 1965 published Webb's "Honey Come Back." Singer and record executive Johnny Rivers recorded a Webb tune he liked, "By the Time I Get to Phoenix." Though Rivers didn't have a hit with it, he recommended Webb's work to the Fifth Dimension, who had a 1967 hit with "Up, Up and Away." That year Glen Campbell covered "Phoenix." After TWA airlines used "Up, Up and Away" as a commercial theme, Webb formed a company that provided jingles for Chevrolet, Doritos, and Hamm's beer. In 1968 the Brooklyn Bridge hit with Webb's "The Worst That Could Happen." That year Richard Harris (for whom Webb had written the entire LPs *A Tramp Shining* and *The Yard Went On Forever*) scored a #2 pop hit with Webb's melodramatic "MacArthur Park," which was later covered by Waylon Jennings (who won a Grammy with it in 1969), Donna Summer, the Four Tops, and countless others. Glen Campbell had a gold hit with "Wichita Lineman."

Meanwhile, in 1968 Epic had issued an album of Webb singing his own demos, without the artist's consent. Webb had previously made his singing debut with an obscure group called Strawberry Children in 1967, on the single "Love Years Coming." In 1969 he also composed music for the films *Tell Them Willie Boy Is Here* and *How Sweet It Is* and worked on a semiautobiographical Broadway musical, *His Own Dark City*.

Webb's solo concert debut in L.A. in February 1970 was poorly received, despite a capacity audience; none of his solo albums were popular. In 1972 he produced a Supremes album. The next year he had a genuine hit when his "All I Know" was performed by Art Garfunkel (who called Webb "the best songwriter since Paul Simon"). Webb went on to produce Cher's *Stars* LP, a 1975 album by his sister Susan, and a failed Fifth Dimension reunion LP, 1976's *Earthbound*. He began taking three- and four-year intervals between recordings. *El Mirage* was produced by Beatles producer George Martin.

Webb continued writing for films (*Doc*, *The Last Unicorn*, among others) and television (*Amazing Stories*, *Tales From the Crypt*, and *Faerie Tale Theater*). He moved to New York, but his dream of writing musicals for the theater would not be realized. Over a decade passed before he released his critically acclaimed *Suspending Disbelief*, produced by Linda Ronstadt. Two late 1993 New York tribute concerts, featuring Glen Campbell, David Crosby, the Brooklyn Bridge, Art Garfunkel, Michael Feinstein, and Nanci Griffith, drew rave reviews. Webb remade some of his best-loved classics for 1996's *Ten Easy Pieces*. In 1998 he published his first book, *Tunesmith: Inside the Art of Songwriting*.

Bob Weir: See the Grateful Dead

Bob Welch: See Fleetwood Mac

Junior Wells

Born Amos Blackmore, Dec. 9, 1934, Memphis, TN; died Jan. 15, 1998, Chicago, IL
1966—*Hoodoo Man Blues* (Delmark); *It's My Life, Baby* (Vanguard) 1968—*You're Tuff Enough* (Mercury); *Junior Wells Sings at the Golden Bear* (Blue Rock) 1970—*Southside Blues Jam* (Delmark) 1971—*In My Younger Days* (Red Lightning) 1974—*On Tap* (Delmark) 1977—*Blues Hit Big Town* 1993—*Better Off With the Blues* (Telarc) 1996—*Come On in This House* 1997—*Live at Buddy Guy's Legends* 1998—*The Best of the Vanguard Years* (Vanguard).
With Buddy Guy: 1968—*Coming at You* (Vanguard) 1972—*Buddy Guy and Junior Wells Play the Blues* (Atlantic) 1973—*I Was Walking Through the Woods* (Chess) 1979—*Got to Use Your Head* (Blues Ball) 1981—*Alone and Acoustic* (Alligator) 1982—*Drinkin' TNT 'n' Smokin' Dynamite* (Blind Pig) 1993—*Pleading the Blues* (Evidence).

One of the more noted Chicago blues singers and harmonica players, Junior Wells was inspired by the blues harp of Sonny Boy Williamson and Little Walter Jacobs.

Wells began playing harmonica as a child, learning from his neighbor, Junior Parker. He played in the streets of nearby Memphis until, at age 12, he moved from the family farm in Marion, Arkansas, to Chicago. He got his first paying job at age 14. He was just 16 when he first auditioned for Muddy Waters, and in 1952 he replaced Little Walter in Waters' band.

It was with Waters that Wells cut his first solo hit, "Hoodoo Man." Wells's other best-known hit was "Messin' With the Kid," later covered by Rory Gallagher. In 1966 Wells first teamed up with guitarist Buddy Guy, a long-running touring and recording partnership. The pair's 1972 album together, *Play the Blues,* featured guest appearances by Eric Clapton, Dr. John, and the J. Geils Band. In the '70s Guy and Wells opened tour dates for the Rolling Stones. In later years, Wells toured with a large band. He appeared with Van Morrison on six dates of his 1993 U.S. tour. Wells died of lympthatic cancer in 1998. Prior to his passing, he had collaborated with Tracy Chapman and taped a cameo in the film *Blues Brothers 2000.*

Mary Wells

Born Mary Esther Wells, May 13, 1943, Detroit, MI; died July 26, 1992, Los Angeles, CA
1961—*Bye Bye Baby* (Motown) 1962—*The One Who Really Loves You* 1963—*Two Lovers and Other Great Hits; Recorded Live On Stage* 1964—*Mary Wells' Greatest Hits; Together* (with Marvin Gaye); *My Guy* 1965—*Mary Wells Sings Love Songs to the Beatles* (20th Century–Fox) 1966—*The Two Sides of Mary Wells* (Atco) 1981—*In and Out of Love* (Epic) 1990—*Keeping My Mind on Love* (Motorcity, U.K.); *Mary Wells* (Quality) 1995—*You Beat Me to the Punch* (Motown).

Mary Wells was Motown's first big star. At age 16, she met Berry Gordy Jr.'s assistant, Robert Bateman. She had written a song she wanted Jackie Wilson to record and had Bateman introduce her to Gordy, who had been writing material for Wilson. Unable to write her song down, she sang the tune for Gordy. He signed her, and Motown released that song as her debut single, "Bye Bye Baby" (#45 pop, #8 R&B, 1960).

She teamed up with performer/writer/producer Smokey Robinson in 1962, scoring a string of hits including "The One Who Really Loves You" (#8 pop, #2 R&B), "You Beat Me to the Punch" (#9 pop, #1 R&B), and "Two Lovers" (#7 pop, #1 R&B) in 1962; "Laughing Boy" (#15 pop, #6 R&B), "Your Old Stand By" (#40 pop, #3 R&B), and "What's Easy for Two Is So Hard for One" b/w "You Lost the Sweetest Boy" (#22 pop, #8 R&B) in 1963. In 1964 came her biggest Motown hit, "My Guy" (#1 pop). Like her other collaborations with Robinson, it featured Wells' smooth, knowing but coy delivery backed by the producer's understated poppish arrangement. Next came two duets with Marvin Gaye, "What's the Matter With You Baby" (#17 pop) and "Once Upon a Time" (#19 pop). Indisputably the first "first lady of Motown," Wells was the first female singer there to adopt a glamorous stage persona. In 1964, at their request, she opened for the Beatles.

But shortly thereafter Wells made a different kind of Motown history, becoming the first of Gordy's successful artists to sue the label. In the wake of her hits, Wells, encouraged by her husband, songwriter Herman Griffin, sued Motown and won, arguing that the recording contract she signed at age 17 was invalid. Her departure came at the height of her success and was an embarrassment to Gordy, who scrambled to discourage other labels from signing her. In an interesting press release to the music-trade magazines, Motown not only warned that Wells was still under contract to it but bravely predicted that the Supremes would have a #1 single with their forthcoming "Where Did Our Love Go." The rest is history.

Initially, Wells' future looked promising. She received a large contract with 20th Century–Fox, along with promises that she would also be making films, but her releases there went nowhere, and she never appeared in a film. She next signed with Atco in late 1965, where she had the 1966 hit "Dear Lover" (#51 pop, #6 R&B), but none of her subsequent releases was as successful as her Motown recordings. "Dig the Way I Feel" (#35 R&B) on Jubilee in 1969 was a minor hit. She retired from performing and in 1967 married Cecil Womack, with whom she had three children. They divorced in 1977, and Wells began a relationship with Cecil's brother, Curtis Womack, with whom she had another child. She began performing again in the '80s, as renewed interest in Motown created a demand.

In 1987 Wells became one of several ex-Motown artists to begin recording with Ian Levine. She had just finished an album for U.K. release, *Keeping My Mind on Love,* when she discovered she had cancer of the larynx in 1990. A two-pack-a-day smoker, Wells was financially devastated by her illness; she had no health insurance. Many of her friends, including Mary Wilson and Martha Reeves, rallied around her, and several artists, including Rod Stewart, Bruce Springsteen, and Diana Ross, provided financial assistance. One of Wells' last tours found her sharing the bill with ex-Temptations David Ruffin and Eddie Kendricks, who died within 14 months and 3 months of her, respectively.

Wendy and Lisa

Formed 1986, Los Angeles, CA
Wendy Melvoin (b. ca. 1964, Los Angeles), gtr., voc.; Lisa Coleman (b. ca. 1960, Los Angeles), kybds.
1987—*Wendy and Lisa* (Columbia) 1989—*Fruit at the Bottom* 1990—*Eroica* (Virgin) 1991—*Re-Mix-in-a-Carnation.* Girl Bros.: 1998—*Girl Bros.* (Girl Brothers).

Former Prince band mates Wendy and Lisa found a small measure of success on their own with a progressive fusion of pop musical styles. Melvoin and Coleman have known each other since early childhood in L.A., where their fathers were session musicians. Melvoin grew up on jazz; Coleman studied classical piano. Coleman began working with Prince in 1979, first touring with him on the *Dirty Mind* tour. From 1984 to 1986 she and Melvoin played in his band the Revolution, where they arranged songs and string sections. In the film *Purple Rain,* their characters challenged Prince's autocracy.

When Prince broke up the band, the women formed their own group. They played almost all the instruments on *Wendy and Lisa* (#88, 1987) and wrote the songs with coproducer Bobby Z., the Revolution's former drummer. In 1988 they played on Joni Mitchell's *Chalk Mark in a Rainstorm.* On *Fruit at the Bottom* (#119, 1989), the duo added more instrumentalists, including Wendy's twin sister, Susannah (who had fronted the Paisley Park band Family). By *Eroica,* the band was largely a family affair, including Wendy's brother Jonathan on percussion and Coleman's brother David on cello and sister Cole singing. *Eroica* also featured guest vocals by k.d. lang and a song by Michael Penn. The album showed that Wendy and Lisa had musically broken free of Prince; labelwise, they had also liberated themselves from Columbia's expectations of sexy pop hits. *Eroica,* though widely praised by critics for its fusion of funk, rock, jazz, dance, and pop, failed to chart.

Melvoin and Coleman spent much of the '90s composing film scores for movies, including *Dangerous Minds* and *Soul Food.* Individually or as a duo they also played with Seal, Sheryl Crow, and Meshell Ndegéocello. In 1998 they released a self-titled album on the Internet under the name Girl Bros. A probing semi-acoustic affair, the record includes several songs that examine the death of Melvoin's brother Jonathan, a keyboard player who died of an overdose while out touring as a sideman with Smashing Pumpkins [see entry].

Paul Westerberg: See the Replacements

Wham!

Formed 1982, London, Eng.
George Michael (b. Georgios Kyriacos Panayiotou, June 25, 1963, London), voc.; Andrew Ridgeley (b. Jan. 26, 1963, Windlesham, Eng.), gtr.
1983—*Fantastic* (Innervision, U.K.) 1984—*Make It Big* (Columbia) 1986—*Music From the Edge of Heaven* 1997—*The Best of Wham!: If You Were There* (Epic, U.K.).
Andrew Ridgeley solo: 1990—*Son of Albert* (Epic).
George Michael solo: see entry.

Dismissed as a contrived teenybopper act during its mid-'80s reign on the pop chart, the duo Wham! is remembered for its cotton-candy singles, and as singer/songwriter George Michael's [see entry] vehicle to fame. Michael met Wham!'s other half, Andrew Ridgeley, when they were schoolmates in Bushey, a London suburb. In 1979 the two began playing together in a ska-based band, the Executive. When that group dissolved, they wrote songs, made demos, and landed a deal with Innervision Records, a fledgling British label. Wham!'s debut album, *Fantastic,* entered the U.K. chart at #1. Innervision kept most of the royalties, though, and after some legal hassles, the duo switched to Epic.

Their first Epic single, 1984's "Wake Me Up Before You Go Go," premiered at #1 in England; later that year, buoyed by a bouncy video featuring Michael and Ridgeley cavorting in sportswear, it topped the American charts. The ballad "Careless Whisper" also reached #1 in both countries, as did Wham!'s second album, *Make It Big.* The hits "Everything She Wants" (#1), "Freedom" (#3), and "I'm Your Man" (#3) followed in 1985. Meanwhile, critics speculated that Michael, as Wham!'s principal writer and producer, was destined to pursue a career independent of Ridgeley, whose car racing and girl chasing were more conspicuous than his musical contributions. When Wham! did split, in 1986—the year of its third album, *Music From the Edge of Heaven* (#10)—they went out, fittingly, with a bang: a sold-out farewell concert before 72,000 fans at London's Wembley Stadium.

Ridgeley has found little post-Wham! musical success. His 1990 solo album, *Son of Albert* (#130, 1990) bombed in the U.S. and the U.K., producing only one minor U.K. hit, "Shake" (#58 U.K., 1990). After failed turns as an auto racer and a restaurateur, Ridgeley, seemingly content to live on Wham! royalties, put his playboy ways behind him and settled down in an English farmhouse with Bananarama [see entry] singer Keren Woodward and her son, took up surfing, and became an environmental activist for the British lobbying group Surfers Against Sewage.

Whiskeytown

Formed 1994, Raleigh, NC
Ryan Adams (b. Nov. 5, 1974, Jacksonville, NC), voc., gtr., kybds.; Caitlin Cary (b. Oct. 28, 1968, Cleveland, OH), violin, voc.; Phil Wandscher, gtr., voc.; Eric "Skillet" Gilmore, drums; Steve Grothman, bass.
1995—*Angels* EP (Mood Food) 1996—*Faithless Street* 1997—*Rural Free Delivery* (– Gilmore; – Grothman; + Jeff Rice, bass; + Steve Terry, drums) *Stranger's Almanac* (Outpost) 1998—(– Terry; – Wandscher; – Rice; – Grothman; + Gilmore; + Mike Daly [b. Jan. 28, 1972, Roselle Park, NJ], kybds., gtr.; + Brad Rice [b. Aug. 11, 1961, Evansville, IN], gtr., voc.; + Mike Santoro [b. Apr. 8, 1964, Patterson, NJ], bass, voc.; – Santoro; + Ed Crawford, gtr.) 2001—*Pneumonia* (Lost Highway/Mercury).
Ryan Adams solo: 2000—*Heartbreaker* (Bloodshot).

Of all the alt-country bands that emerged in the mid-'90s in the wake of Uncle Tupelo and its splinter groups Wilco and Son Volt, few garnered as much critical praise and cultish fan loyalty as Raleigh, North Carolina's Whiskeytown. Most of the attention drawn to the group was centered on frontman and main songwriter Ryan Adams, who began listening to Gram Parsons and more traditional country artists like George Jones shortly after the breakup of his teenage punk band, Patty Duke Syndrome. In 1994, when Adams was 20, he cofounded Whiskeytown with singer/guitarist Phil Wandscher, fiddler/singer Caitlin Cary, drummer Skillet Gilmore, and bassist Steve Grothman. After releasing the *Angels* EP and the album *Faithless Street* for local indie label Mood Food, the band signed to the Geffen imprint Outpost and in 1997 released *Strangers Almanac,* which yielded the single "Yesterday's News," the band's entrée onto American radio. The mini-album *Rural Free Delivery* was released the same year by their previous label, while Outpost reissued an expanded version of *Faithless Street* in 1998.

Whiskeytown's lineup was notoriously mercurial, but Adams' voice and songs—both frequently compared to

Gram Parsons and Paul Westerberg—kept the group on the Americana radar and netted them invites onto such releases as *The End of Violence* and *Hope Floats* soundtracks and the 1999 Parsons tribute album, *Return of the Grievous Angel*. In 2000, after the group was dropped by Geffen following the label's absorption into Universal, Chicago's independent Bloodshot Records released Adams' first solo album, the mostly well-received *Heartbreaker*. Adams began publicly alluding to Whiskeytown's demise, and not long after *Heartbreaker*'s release, he was signed as a solo artist by a new Mercury Records Americana imprint, Lost Highway. In 2001 it issued a final, previously unreleased Whiskeytown album, *Pneumonia*.

The Whispers

Formed 1962, Los Angeles, CA
Walter Scott (b. Sep. 3, 1943, Fort Worth, TX), voc.; Wallace Scott (b. Sep. 3, 1943, Fort Worth), voc.; Nicholas Caldwell (b. Apr. 5, 1944, Loma Linda, CA); Marcus Hutson (b. Jan. 8, 1943, Los Angeles); Gordy Harmon, voc.
1972—*The Whispers' Love Story* (Janus) 1974—(– Harmon; + Leaveil Degree [b. July 31, 1948, New Orleans, LA], voc.) 1976—*One for the Money* (Soul Train) 1977—*Open Up for Love* 1978—*Headlights* (Solar) 1979—*Whisper in Your Ear; Happy Holidays to You* 1980—*The Whispers; Imagination* 1981—*This Kind of Lovin'* 1982—*The Best of the Whispers; Love Is Where You Find It* 1983—*Love for Love* 1984—*So Good* 1987—*Just Gets Better With Time* 1990—*In the Mood* (Solar/Epic); *More of the Night* (Capitol) 1991—*Somebody Loves You* (Intermedia) 1994—*Christmas Moments* (Capitol) (– Hutson) 1995—*Toast to the Ladies* 1997—*Songbook vol. 1: The Songs of Babyface* (Interscope); *Greatest Hits* (The Right Stuff).

In 1980, after years of minor hits, the Whispers became one of black music's most popular vocal groups, and in 1987, 25 years since they started, the group had its biggest pop hit of all time, "Rock Steady," which was written and produced by L.A. Reid and Babyface.

Twin brothers Walter and Wallace Scott formed the group in L.A. with Nicholas Caldwell, Marcus Hutson, and Gordy Harmon. They cut a few singles in the mid-'60s on the Dore label before they met producer Ron Carson. Carson produced Whispers singles for Canyon/Soul Clock Records, including "Planets of Life," which became a staple of their live show, and their first chart singles, "The Time Will Come" (#17 R&B, 1969) and "Seems Like I Gotta Do Wrong" (#50 pop, #6 R&B, 1970). When Canyon folded, they recorded for Janus, for which they continued with a steady stream of moderate R&B Top 30 hits, including "Your Love Is So Doggone Good" (#19 R&B, 1971) and "I Only Meant to Wet My Feet" (#27 R&B, 1972).

In 1974 they went to Philadelphia to work with producer/guitarist Norman Harris and the MFSB rhythm section. "Bingo" and "A Mother for My Children" did well. By then, Leaveil Degree had replaced Harmon. In the mid-'70s, the band signed with Dick Griffey's Soul Train (later renamed Solar) label and began to climb in popularity, with more R&B hits: "One for the Money (Part I)" (#10 R&B, 1976) and a cover of Bread's "Make It With You" (#10 R&B, 1977). "(Olivia) Lost and Turned Out," a song about prostitution, hit #13 on the R&B chart in the summer of 1978. They followed with "And the Beat Goes On" (#19 pop, #1 R&B, 1980) and "Lady" (#28 pop, #3 R&B, 1980), from 1980's *The Whispers*, "It's a Love Thing" (#28 pop, #2 R&B) in 1981, and "Tonight" (#4 R&B) in 1983.

"Rock Steady" (#7 pop, #1 R&B, 1987) pushed *Just Gets Better With Time* to platinum. Their 1980 album *The Whispers* is also platinum; *Imagination, Love Is Where You Find It*, and *More of the Night* (#8 R&B, 1990) are all gold. Among the Whispers' later hits are "My Heart, Your Heart" (#4 R&B, 1990), "Innocent" (#3 R&B, 1990), and "Is It Good to You" (#7 R&B, 1991). The Scott brothers released a duo album in 1993. The Whispers' mid-'90s singles and albums placed fairly low on the R&B charts until 1997's *Songbook vol. 1*, a record of material by producer Babyface, catapulted the group back to #27 in 1998; the single "My, My, My" hit #1 R&B.

Barry White

Born Sep. 12, 1944, Galveston, TX
1973—*I've Got So Much to Give* (20th Century–Fox); *Stone Gon'* 1974—*Can't Get Enough* 1975—*Just Another Way to Say I Love You; Barry White's Greatest Hits* 1976—*Let the Music Play; Is This Whatcha Wont?* 1977—*Barry White Sings for Someone You Love* 1978—*The Man* 1979—*The Message Is Love* (Unlimited Gold); *I Love to Sing the Songs I Sing* (20th Century–Fox) 1980—*Barry White's Greatest Hits, vol. 2; Sheet Music* (Unlimited Gold) 1981—*Barry and Glodean; Beware!* 1982—*Change* 1983—*Dedicated* 1987—*The Right Night and Barry White* (A&M) 1989—*The Man Is Back!* 1991—*Put Me in Your Mix* 1992—*Just for You* 1994—*The Icon Is Love* 1999—*Staying Power* (Private) 2000—*The Ultimate Collection* (Mercury).
Love Unlimited Orchestra: 1974—*Rhapsody in White* (20th Century–Fox); *Together Brothers* soundtrack; *White Gold* 1975—*Music Maestro Please* 1976—*My Sweet Summer Suite* 1978—*My Musical Bouquet* 1979—*Super Movie Themes, Just a Little Bit Different* 1981—*Let 'Em Dance* (Unlimited Gold); *Welcome Aboard (Presents Mr. Webster Lewis)* 1983—*Rise.*

With his deep, husky voice, lush musical arrangements, and often love-themed songs, singer/songwriter/producer Barry White became a '70s sex symbol (despite his chubby physique). He was also a pioneering producer in disco, who often used large orchestras on his records.

An eight-year-old White made his singing debut in a Galveston church choir. Two years later he was the church organist and part-time choir director. At 16, he joined the Upfronts, an L.A. R&B band, as a singer/pianist. Two years later he helped arrange "The Harlem Shuffle," a minor hit in 1963 for Bob and Earl.

White developed his writing and production skills. In

1966 he went to work as an A&R man for Mustang Records, where he discovered a female vocal trio called Love Unlimited (Diana Taylor, Linda and Glodean James). He produced their gold single, 1972's "Walking in the Rain With the One I Love" (#14 pop, #6 R&B) for Uni Records. In 1973 White signed with 20th Century–Fox Records and made his national recording debut with "I'm Gonna Love You Just a Little More Baby" (#3 pop, #1 R&B), "Never, Never, Gonna Give Ya Up" (#7 pop, #2 R&B), and "I've Got So Much to Give" (#32 pop, #5 R&B). Also that year he started to write for the Love Unlimited Orchestra, with whom he had a string-laden instrumental disco hit, "Love's Theme" (#1 pop, #10 R&B). Love Unlimited's "Under the Influence" was also a big hit. In 1973–74 alone, White wrote, produced, or performed on records whose total sales exceeded over $16 million. Among his gold records are *Rhapsody in White* by the Love Unlimited Orchestra (#8 pop), *Can't Get Enough* (#1 pop), "Can't Get Enough of Your Love, Baby" (#1 pop and R&B), "You're the First, the Last, My Everything" (#2 pop, #1 R&B, 1974); *Just Another Way to Say I Love You* (#17 pop), and *Barry White's Greatest Hits* (#23 pop). In 1977 *Barry White Sings for Someone You Love* (#8 pop) went platinum and "It's Ecstasy When You Lay Down Next to Me" (#4 pop, #1 R&B) went gold. Subsequent R&B hit singles including "Playing Your Game, Baby" (#8 R&B, 1978) and "Your Sweetness Is My Weakness" (#2 R&B, 1978).

By the late '70s, White's appeal was fading, though he scored minor hits with a cover of Billy Joel's "Just the Way You Are" (#44 R&B, 1979) and with the title track from 1982's *Change.* With wife Glodean, White released an album and two minor R&B chart singles, "Didn't We Make It Happen, Baby" (#78 R&B, 1981) and "I Want You" (#79 R&B, 1981). In the late '80s his career experienced something of a resurgence, with "Sho' You Right" (#17 R&B, 1987) and "For Your Love (I'll Do Most Anything)" (#27 R&B, 1987), followed by "The Secret Garden (Sweet Seduction Suite)" (#31 pop, #1 R&B, 1990) from Quincy Jones' *Back on the Block,* "I Wanna Do It Good to You" (#26 R&B, 1990), "When Will I See You Again" (#32 R&B, 1990), and "Put Me in Your Mix" (#2 R&B, 1991). He also appears on Big Daddy Kane's 1991 R&B hit "All of Me." In late 1994 he returned to the top of the R&B chart with "Practice What You Preach" (#18 pop, #1 R&B) from the platinum *The Icon Is Love* (#20 pop, #1 R&B). "Come On" (#87 pop, #12 R&B) followed in 1995. In 1996 White sang on R&B hits by Quincy Jones and Tina Turner. The aptly titled *Staying Power* (#43 pop, #13 R&B) won two R&B Grammys and proved that he hadn't lost his potency in 1999. That same year he published an autobiography, *Love Unlimited.* By mid-2000 he was appearing regularly on the hit television show *Ally McBeal.*

Bukka White

Born Booker T. Washington White, Nov. 12, 1906, Houston, MS; died Feb. 26, 1977, Memphis, TN
1963—*Bukka White* (Sonet) 1964—*Bukka White* (Columbia) 1966—*Memphis Hot Shots* (Blue Horizon) 1969—*Mississippi Blues* (Takoma) 1970—*Big Daddy* (Biograph) 1975—*Sky Songs, vols. 1 and 2* (Arhoolie) 1976—*Legacy of the Blues: Bukka White* (GNP/Crescendo) 1994—*The Complete Bukka White* (Columbia/Legacy); *1963 Isn't 1962* (Genes).

A cousin of blues guitarist B.B. King, Bukka White was, after Robert Johnson, one of the most widely heard Delta bluesmen. White's guitar playing (usually on an acoustic guitar) has influenced B.B. King and many others; his singing has influenced Richie Havens, among others.

White learned guitar as a child from his father, and at age 10 began traveling up and down the Mississippi River as a musician. He also worked as a boxer and a baseball player in the Negro leagues. He began recording in Memphis in 1930 for Victor. In 1937 he recorded his first blues hit, the often-covered "Shake 'Em On Down," for Vocalion in Chicago. But before he could record a followup, he was jailed for two years in Mississippi's Parchman Farm Prison for shooting a man. He was recorded by the Library of Congress while in prison in 1939; pressure from his record company helped win him parole.

Upon his release, White recorded a dozen of his most famous sides for the Okeh label, but he found his rough-hewn country blues were out of style. He labored in obscurity until 1963, when John Fahey heard a recording of his "Aberdeen Mississippi Blues," and, with Ed Denson, tracked White down in Aberdeen, and recorded him for his own Takoma label. The 11 songs recorded then were the first Bukka had committed to tape in 24 years.

By then in his late 50s, White enjoyed a career revival and toured the U.S. and Europe, making occasional film and television appearances. He suffered ill health in the mid-'70s and succumbed to cancer.

Karyn White

Born Karyn Lay Vonne White, Oct. 14, 1965, Los Angeles, CA
1988—*Karyn White* (Warner Bros.) 1991—*Ritual of Love* 1994—*Make Him Do Right.*

In the late '80s Karyn White went from being an accomplished backup singer to topping the charts with her own smooth mix of R&B and pop. As a youth growing up in L.A., White sang in her church choir, which her mother directed; her father was a trumpet player. She entered talent shows and beauty pageants as a teen, and quit the cheerleading squad to save her voice. She sold her first song to a record company at age 17. White fronted the L.A. group Legacy for a while, and toured as a backup singer for R&B vocalist O'Bryan. She did studio session work for such artists as Julio Iglesias, the Commodores, Ray Parker Jr., Bobby Brown, Johnny Gill, Patti LaBelle, Gladys Knight, and Sheena Easton, and cowrote songs for Stephanie Mills and Lace.

In 1986 White had her first hit, singing lead on keyboardist Jeff Lorber's dance hit "Facts of Love" (#27, 1986). The single led to her own deal with Warner Bros. *Karyn White* (#19, 1988) went multiplatinum, led by the L.A. Reid and Babyface–produced "The Way You Love Me" (#7, 1988), the ballad/anthem "Superwoman" (#8, 1989), and "Secret Rendezvous" (#6, 1989). On *Ritual of Love,* Jimmy Jam and Terry Lewis (White's husband) produced and cowrote most of the songs; White coproduced the album and cowrote 10 of 12 tracks. The album yielded the hits "Romantic" (#1, 1991) and "The Way I Feel About You" (#12, 1991). *Make Him Do Right* hit #22 on the R&B album chart.

Tony Joe White

Born July 23, 1943, Oak Grove, LA
1968—*Black and White* (Monument) 1969—*Continued* 1970—*Tony Joe* 1971—*Tony Joe White* (Warner Bros.) 1972—*The Train I'm On* 1973—*Home Made Ice Cream* 1977—*Eyes* (20th Century–Fox); *Tony Joe White* 1980—*Real Thing* (Casablanca) 1983—*Dangerous* (Columbia) 1993—*The Best of Tony Joe White* (Warner Bros.) 2000—*One Hot July* (Hip-O/Mercury).

One of the prime practitioners of the late-'60s country-rock style known as swamp or bayou rock, Tony Joe White was the only one who actually came from the Louisiana bayous and rose to national prominence. White began playing music at age 16 and formed Tony and the Mojos. His next band, Tony and the Twilights, went to Texas, where White remained as a solo singer/songwriter after the group disbanded. He then moved to Nashville, made the rounds of music publishers, and eventually hooked up with Billy Swan, who produced White's first three albums.

White's first two singles, "Georgia Pines" and "Watching the Trains Go By," went unnoticed. "Soul Francisco" was a big European hit in 1967, and White continued to be a major recording and performing star in Europe for the next five years (in 1972 he toured Europe with Creedence Clearwater Revival). In 1969 he hit the Top 10 with the single "Polk Salad Annie," which showcased White's deep, gruff voice and the stylized guitar technique White called "whomper stomper."

Despite frequent TV appearances, it was White's last hit in the U.S. However, several White songs were hits for other artists. Elvis Presley covered "Polk Salad Annie" (as did Tom Jones) and "I've Got a Thing About You Baby." In 1969 Dusty Springfield had a minor hit with White's "Willie and Laura Mae Jones"; and a year later Brook Benton made it to the Top 5 with "A Rainy Night in Georgia." Subsequent hits included Tanya Tucker's "Steamy Windows," and he has also done commercial work for McDonald's and Levi's. Two of his early-'90s albums, *Closer to the Truth* and *Path of a Decent Groove,* were successful in Europe, New Zealand, and Australia. They were not released domestically. He returned with a U.S. release in 2000 that projected a soulful sensuality and showcased White's superb guitar playing.

Whitesnake

Formed 1978, Yorkshire, Eng.
David Coverdale (b. Sep. 21, 1951, Saltburn-by-the-Sea, Eng.), voc.; Micky Moody (b. Aug. 30, 1950, Eng.), gtr.; Bernie Marsden, gtr.; Brian Johnston, kybds.; Neil Murray, bass; David Dowle, drums.
1978—(– Johnston; + Jon Lord [b. June 9, 1941, Leicester, Eng.], kybds.) 1979—(– Dowle; + Ian Paice [b. June 29, 1948, Nottingham, Eng.], drums) 1980—*Ready an' Willing* (Mirage); *Live . . . in the Heart of the City* 1981—*Come an' Get It* 1982—(– Marsden; – Murray; – Paice; + Mel Galley, gtr.; + Colin Hodgkinson [b. Oct. 14, 1945, Eng.], bass; + Cozy Powell [b. Dec. 29, 1947, Cirencester, Eng.; d. Apr. 5, 1998, near Bristol, Eng.], drums) 1983—(– Moody; – Hodgkinson; + John Sykes [b. July 29, 1959, Eng.], gtr.; + Murray) 1984—*Slide It In* (Geffen) (– Lord; – Galley; + Richard Bailey, kybds.) 1985—(– Bailey; – Powell; + Don Airey, kybds.; + Aynsley Dunbar [b. 1946, Liverpool, Eng.], drums) 1987—*Whitesnake* (– Sykes; – Murray; – Dunbar; + Adrian Vandenburg [b. Holland], gtr.; + Vivian Campbell, gtr.; + Rudy Sarzo [b. Nov. 9, 1952, Havana, Cuba], bass; + Tommy Aldridge, drums) 1988—(– Campbell; + Steve Vai [b. June 6, 1960, Carle Place, NY], gtr.) 1989—*Slip of the Tongue* 1994—*Greatest Hits.*

It wasn't just rock critics who derided Whitesnake as a Led Zeppelin rip-off—Led Zep frontman Robert Plant himself once dismissed Whitesnake vocalist and driving force David Coverdale as "David Cover version." With his long blond hair, aristocratic English accent, and relentless sexual double-entendres, Coverdale struck many detractors as the real-life model for David St. Hubbins of mock-metal parody Spinal Tap. Coverdale often had the last laugh, however, scoring pop and metal hits and, eventually, even recording with Plant's erstwhile Led Zep cohort, guitarist Jimmy Page.

Coverdale had been with Deep Purple from 1973 to 1976 [see entry], then recorded two solo albums, *Whitesnake* and *Northwinds;* the former provided a band name when Coverdale formed his own group, recruiting members from Deep Purple, and lesser-known U.K. hard-rock outfits such as Juicy Lucy, Babe Ruth, and Gillan. The band released two Britain-only albums before making its U.S. debut with *Ready an' Willing* (#90, 1980) which yielded a minor hit single in "Fool for Your Loving" (#53, 1980). A steady stream of personnel changes, but no hit singles, followed for the next few years, until the band was signed to the U.S. major label Geffen; despite the lack of a hit, *Slide It In* sold well (#40, 1984) and eventually went double platinum. The arrival of former Thin Lizzy guitarist John Sykes for that album proved crucial, as he helped to write the songs that would put Whitesnake over the top on its next album.

Whitesnake (#2, 1987), which would sell over 8 million copies, featured a chart-topping single in the pop-metal "Here I Go Again," and a #2 single in the power ballad "Is This Love"; the very Zeppelinesque "Still of the Night" was a minor hit (#79, 1987). The band's fortunes were boosted by heavy MTV play of its music videos, which featured Coverdale's buxom girlfriend, B-movie actress Tawny Kitaen, whom he married in 1989. Augmented by the arrival of new guitarist Steve Vai (Frank Zappa, David Lee Roth), *Slip of the Tongue* (#10, 1989) was not as huge as its predecessor, but still successful; hit singles included an updated "Fool for Your Loving" (#37, 1989) and "The Deeper the Love" (#28, 1990). Three years later Coverdale had broken up with Kitaen and hooked up with Page (who had reportedly tried and failed to secure Plant) to record *Coverdale-Page* [see Jimmy Page entry]. After releasing *Greatest Hits*, Coverdale re-formed Whitesnake with Adrian Vandenburg, Rudy Sarzo, Denny Carmassi (drummer for Heart), and Warren De Martini (ex-Ratt guitarist) for a tour in Europe. The group disbanded following a 1997 British farewell tour.

White Zombie/Rob Zombie

Formed 1985, New York, NY
Rob Zombie (b. Rob Cummings, a.k.a. Rob Straker, Jan. 12, 1966, Haverhill, MA), voc.; Sean Yseult (b. 1966), bass; Ena Kostabi, gtr.; Peter Landau, drums.
1985—(– Landau; – Kostabi) 1986—(+ Ivan de Prume [b. Brooklyn, NY], drums; + Tim Jeffs, gtr.; – Jeffs; + Tom Five [b. Tom Guay], gtr.) 1987—*Psycho Head Blowout* EP (Silent Explosion); *Soul-Crusher* 1988—(– Five; + John Ricci, gtr.) 1989—*Make Them Die Slowly* (Caroline) (– Ricci; + Jay "J." Yuenger [b. Chicago, 1967], gtr.) 1992—*La Sexorcisto: Devil Music vol. 1* (Geffen) (– de Prume; + Phil "Philo" Buerstatte [b. 1967, Madison, WI], drums) 1994—(– Buerstatte; + Mark Poland, drums) 1995—(– Poland; + John Tempesta, drums) *Astro-Creep: 2000—Songs of Love, Destruction and Other Synthetic Delusions of the Electric Head* 1996—*Supersexy Swingin' Sounds.*
Rob Zombie solo: 1998—*Hellbilly Deluxe* (Geffen) 1999—*American Made Music to Strip By* (Interscope).

Fusing hardcore, heavy metal, and outsized theatrics, White Zombie celebrated trash culture, incorporating such elements as B-movie humor and true-crime gore. Along the lines of Alice Cooper, GWAR, the Cramps, and Marilyn Manson, they were as much a concept as a band. The group dissolved in late 1998, but frontman Rob Zombie has continued along the same path as a solo artist and horror filmmaker.

Moving to New York City after high school, Rob Cummings met Sean Yseult at art school in 1985. Soon living together, they formed White Zombie, taking the name from a 1932 Bela Lugosi horror film. Their self-produced EP gained them cult fame, as did their album *Soul-Crusher*, and in 1989 Bill Laswell produced *Make Them Die Slowly*.

White Zombie's major-label debut arrived amid personnel changes and notoriety. Televangelists attacked the band's gleefully "satanic" lyrics; Zombie courted controversy by asking convicted mass murderer Charles Manson for permission to use a sample of his voice (he declined, as did horror actor Vincent Price when presented with a similar request). When MTV cartoon characters Beavis and Butt-head praised *La Sexorcisto* (#26, 1993), the album entered the Top 30. The album's "Thunder Kiss '65" was nominated for a Best Hard Rock Performance Grammy, as was "More Human Than Human," from *Astro-Creep: 2000* (#6, 1995). *Supersexy Swingin' Sounds* (#17, 1996) was a collection of *Astro-Creep* remixes featuring contributions by the Dust Brothers and P.M. Dawn.

Zombie released his solo debut, *Hellbilly Deluxe* (#5) in 1998, dissolving White Zombie a couple of weeks after the album's release. That same year, he founded his Zombie A Go-Go record label. *Hellbilly* spawned its own remix followup, *American Made Music to Strip By* in 1999. In between the breakup of White Zombie and the launch of his solo career, Zombie was commissioned to write and direct *The Crow III*. He abandoned the project after two years of rewrites, but in 1999 he designed his own haunted Halloween maze at Universal Studios, Rob Zombie's American Nightmare. A year later he began shooting his directorial debut, *House of 1000 Corpses*, released in 2001.

The Who

Formed 1964, London, Eng.
Peter Dennis Blandford Townshend (b. May 19, 1945, London), gtr., voc.; Roger Harry Daltrey (b. Mar. 1, 1944, London), voc.; John Alec Entwistle (b. Oct. 9, 1944, London), bass, French horn, voc.; Keith John Moon (b. Aug. 23, 1947, London; d. Sep. 7, 1978, London), drums.
1965—*The Who Sings My Generation* (Decca) 1966—*Happy Jack* 1967—*The Who Sell Out* 1968—*Magic Bus—The Who on Tour* 1969—*Tommy* 1970—*Live at Leeds* 1971—*Who's Next; Meaty, Beaty, Big and Bouncy* 1973—*Quadrophenia* (MCA) 1974—*Odds and Sods* 1975—*The Who by Numbers* 1978—*Who Are You* 1979—*The Kids Are Alright* soundtrack (– Moon) *Quadrophenia* soundtrack (Polydor) (+ Kenney Jones [b. Sep. 16, 1948, London], drums) 1981—*Face Dances* (Warner Bros.); *Hooligans* (MCA) 1982—*It's Hard* (Warner Bros.) 1983—*Who's Greatest Hits* (MCA) 1984—*Who's Last* 1985—*Who's Missing* 1987—*Two's Missing* 1988—*Who's Better, Who's Best* 1990—*Join Together* 1994—*The Who: Thirty Years of Maximum R&B* (MCA) 1996—*Live at the Isle of Wight Festival 1970* (Columbia/Legacy); *My Generation: The Very Best of the Who* (MCA) 2000—*The BBC Sessions; 20th Century Masters: The Millennium Collection; The Who Live: The Blues to the Bush/1999* (MusicMaker.com).
Pete Townshend solo: 1972—*Who Came First* (Decca) 1977—*Rough Mix* (with Ronnie Lane) (MCA) 1980—*Empty Glass* (Atco) 1982—*All the Best Cowboys Have Chinese Eyes* 1983—*Scoop* 1985—*White City—A Novel* 1986—*Pete Townshend's Deep End Live!* 1987—*Another Scoop* 1989—*The Iron Man* 1993—*PsychoDerelict* (Atlantic) 1996—*The Best of Pete Townshend: Coolwalkingsmoothtalkingstraight-smokingfirestoking* 1999—*Pete Townshend Live: A Benefit for Maryville Academy* (Platinum) 2000—*Lifehouse Chronicles* (Eelpie); *Lifehouse Elements* (Redline Entertainment).
John Entwistle solo: 1971—*Smash Your Head Against the Wall* (Decca) 1972—*Whistle Rymes* 1973—*John Entwistle's Rigor Mortis Sets In* (Track) 1975—*John Entwistle's Ox: Mad*

Dog 1981—*Too Late the Hero* (Atco) 1996—*The Rock* (Griffin Music); *Thunderfingers: The Best of John Entwistle* (Rhino) 1997—*King Biscuit Flower Hour Presents in Concert* (King Biscuit) 1999—*Left for Live* (J-Bird).
Keith Moon solo: 1975—*Two Sides of the Moon* (MCA).
Roger Daltrey solo: 1973—*Daltrey* (MCA) 1975—*Ride a Rock Horse* 1977—*One of the Boys* 1980—*McVicar* soundtrack (Polydor) 1982—*Best Bits* (MCA) 1985—*Under a Raging Moon* (Atlantic) 1987—*Can't Wait to See the Movie* 1991—*The Best of Rockers and Ballads* (Polydor) 1992—*Rocks in the Head* (Atlantic) 1994—*A Celebration: The Music of Pete Townshend and the Who* (Continuum) 1997—*Martyrs & Madmen: The Best of Roger Daltrey* (Rhino).

In the annals of rock history the Who (like their contemporaries the Rolling Stones and the Beatles) stand alone. Though technically they were Mods and musically self-proclaimed "Maximum R&B," the Who were also the godfathers of punk, the pioneers of the rock opera, and among the first rock groups to integrate (rather than merely fiddle with) synthesizers. The smashed guitars and overturned (or blown up) drum kits they left in their wake fittingly symbolized the violent passions of a band whose distinctive sound was born of the couplings and collisions among Pete Townshend's alternately raging or majestic guitar playing, Keith Moon's nearly anarchic drumming style, John Entwistle's facile, thundering bass lines, and Daltrey's impassioned vocals. The Who would prove a strong influence on such late-'70s groups as the Jam. Ever since guitarist and main songwriter Pete Townshend declared in "My Generation," "Hope I die before I get old," he has been embraced as a spokesman, a role he assumed (he claims) reluctantly. Nonetheless, for the rest of his career with the Who Townshend explored rock's philosophical topography, from the raw rebelliousness of "My Generation" and adolescent angst of "I Can't Explain" to such ambitious, emotionally rich, and beautiful songs as "Love Reign O'er Me."

All four band members grew up around London—Townshend, Daltrey, and Entwistle in the working-class Shepherd's Bush area. Townshend's parents were professional entertainers. He and Entwistle knew each other at school in the late '50s and played in a Dixieland band when they were in their early teens, with Townshend on banjo and Entwistle on trumpet. They played together in a rock band, but Entwistle left in 1962 to join the Detours. That band included Roger Daltrey, a sheet-metal worker. When the Detours needed to replace a rhythm guitarist, Entwistle suggested Townshend, and Daltrey switched from lead guitar to vocals when the original singer, Colin Dawson, left in 1963. Not long after that, drummer Doug Sandom was replaced by Moon, who was then playing in a surf band called the Beachcombers. By early 1964 the group had changed its name to the Who, and not long after, the excitement inspired by Townshend's bashing his guitar out of frustration during a show ensured it would become a part of the act.

Shortly thereafter, the group came under the wing of manager Pete Meaden, who renamed them the High Numbers and gave them a better-dressed Mod image. The High Numbers released an unsuccessful single, "I'm the Face" b/w "Zoot Suit" (both written by Meaden), then got new managers, former small-time film directors Kit Lambert and Chris Stamp. By late 1964 the quartet became the Who again, and with Lambert and Stamp's encouragement they became an even more Mod band, with violent stage shows and a repertoire including blues, James Brown, and Motown covers, solely because their Mod audiences loved that music. In fact, despite the billing, the Who's original songs were anything but classic R&B. The group's demo of "I Can't Explain," with sessionman Jimmy Page adding guitar, brought them to producer Shel Talmy (who had also worked with the Kinks) and got them a record deal. When "I Can't Explain" came out in January 1965, it was ignored until the band appeared on the TV show *Ready, Steady, Go.* Townshend smashed his guitar, Moon overturned his drums, and the song eventually reached #8 in Britain. "Anyway, Anyhow, Anywhere" also reached the British Top 10, followed in November 1965 by "My Generation." It went to #2 in the U.K. but reached only #75 in the U.S. But the Who were already stars in Britain, having established their sound and their personae. Townshend played guitar with full-circle windmilling motions, Daltrey strutted like a bantam fighter, Entwistle (whose occasional songwriting effort revealed a macabre sense of humor) just stood there seemingly unmoved as Moon happily flailed all over his drum kit.

The Who: Roger Daltrey, Pete Townshend, John Entwistle, Keith Moon

After the Who's fourth hit single, "Substitute" (#5 U.K.), Lambert replaced Talmy as producer. Their second album, *A Quick One* (*Happy Jack* in the U.S.; #67, 1967), included a 10-

minute mini-opera as the title track, shortly before the Beatles' concept album *Sgt. Pepper's Lonely Hearts Club Band*. The Who also began to make inroads in the U.S. with "Happy Jack" (#24, 1967) and a tour that included the performance filmed at the Monterey Pop Festival in June.

The Who Sell Out (#48, 1967) featured mock-advertisement songs and genuine jingles from offshore British pirate radio stations; it also contained another mini-opera, "Rael," and a Top 10 hit in England and the U.S., "I Can See for Miles." In October 1968 the band released *Magic Bus* (#39, 1968), a compilation of singles and B sides, while Townshend worked on his 90-minute opus, *Tommy*. The story of a deaf, dumb, and blind boy turned pinball champion/pop idol turned autocratic messianic guru was variously considered both pretentious and profound. Most important, however, *Tommy* was the first successful rock opera. The album hit #4 in the U.S., and its first single, "Pinball Wizard," went to #19. The band would perform *Tommy* a handful of times in its entirety—at London's Coliseum in 1969, at New York City's Metropolitan Opera House on June 6 and 7, 1970, and on some dates during its 1989 reunion tour. Excerpts, including "See Me, Feel Me," "Pinball Wizard," and the instrumental "Underture," were thereafter part of the live show. Troupes mounted productions of it around the world (the Who's performances had been concert versions), and Townshend oversaw a new recording of it in 1972, backed by the London Symphony and featuring Rod Stewart, Steve Winwood, Sandy Denny, Richard Burton, and others. In 1975 Ken Russell directed the controversial high-pop film version, which included Eric Clapton ("Eyesight to the Blind"), Tina Turner ("Acid Queen"), and Elton John ("Pinball Wizard"), as well as Ann-Margret, Oliver Reed, and Jack Nicholson. Moon (as the lecherous Uncle Ernie) and Daltrey (in the lead title role) also appeared in the film.

Bits of *Tommy* turned up on *Live at Leeds* (#4, 1970), a juggernaut live set, which was followed by *Who's Next* (#4, 1971), a staple of FM rock radio. It included Townshend's first experiments with synthesizers—"Baba O'Riley," "Bargain," "Won't Get Fooled Again"—three songs that Townshend originally conceived as part of another rock opera entitled *Lifehouse*. *Meaty, Beaty, Big and Bouncy* (#11, 1971) was followed two years later by the Who's second double-album rock opera, *Quadrophenia* (#2, 1973), a tribute to the tortured inner life of the Mods. It too was a hit and became a movie directed by Franc Roddam in 1979, with Sting of the Police in the wordless role of the bellboy.

While the Who were hugely popular, *Quadrophenia* signaled that Townshend was now a generation older than the fans he had initially spoken for. As he agonized over his role as an elder statesman of rock—as he would do for years to come—the Who released *Odds and Sods* (#15, 1974), a compilation of the previous decade's outtakes. *The Who by Numbers* (#8, 1975) was the result of Townshend's self-appraisal ("However Much I Booze"); it lacked the Who's usual vigor, but yielded a hit single in "Squeeze Box" (#16, 1975). The band could dependably pack arenas wherever it went, but it took some time off the road after *By Numbers*.

The group members—whose personality clashes are almost as legendary as their music—began pursuing more individual projects. Moon released a novelty solo disc, *Two Sides of the Moon*, which featured such guest artists as Ringo Starr, Harry Nilsson, Dick Dale, Joe Walsh, and Flo and Eddie, and Entwistle recorded solo LPs with bands called Ox (with whom he toured in 1975) and Rigor Mortis, and produced four tracks on the debut album by the Fabulous Poodles. Daltrey also recorded solo. His first two efforts are widely considered mediocre, although *Daltrey* boasted the oft-played "Hard Life/Giving It All Away," which, like the rest of the album, was composed by Adam Faith and a then unknown named Leo Sayer. While Daltrey's albums did decently, he had only one Top 40 single here, "Without Your Love," from the *McVicar* soundtrack. The Townshend-penned "After the Fire" received substantial video exposure when released in 1985. Daltrey found considerably more success as an actor. Besides *Tommy*, he has starred in Ken Russell's over-the-top "biography" of composer Franz Liszt, *Lisztomania* (1975) and *McVicar* (1980), the true story of the famous British criminal John McVicar. In the mid-'80s he played the double role of the Dromio twins in a PBS production of Shakespeare's *A Comedy of Errors*. In recent years, he has also appeared on the London stage (*The Beggar's Opera*, 1991) and on British television (*The Little Match Girl*, 1990). In 1999 he played Scrooge in a stage version of Charles Dickens' *A Christmas Carol* in New York City.

In 1970 Townshend contributed four tracks to *Happy Birthday*, a privately released, limited-edition album recorded as a tribute to Townshend's guru, Meher Baba. The following year, *I Am*, a similar limited-edition Baba tribute album, was released. It contained another Townshend track, a nine-minute instrumental version of "Baba O'Riley." As both these records were heavily bootlegged, Townshend's response was to create an "official" version of both albums. The result, *Who Came First* (#69, 1972), was Townshend's first "real" solo album. It included the tracks from *Happy Birthday* and *I Am*, plus new songs, and demos of the Who tracks "Pure and Easy" and "Let's See Action." His second solo release was a collaboration with ex-Faces Ronnie Lane, *Rough Mix* (#45, 1977), which featured a number of FM/AOR radio staples: "Street in the City," "My Baby Gives It Away," and "A Heart to Hang On To."

Meanwhile, punk was burgeoning in Britain, and the Sex Pistols among others were brandishing the Who's old power chords and attitude. Townshend's continuing identity crisis showed up in the title of *Who Are You* (#2, 1978), but the title song became a hit single (#14) that fall, and the album went double platinum. It was the last and highest-charting album by the original band.

The next few years brought tragedy and turmoil, and in a sense, the end of the Who in the death of Keith Moon. Moon always reveled in his reputation as the madman of rock, and his outrageous stunts—onstage and off—were legend. His prodigious drinking and drug abuse (he was once paralyzed for days after accidentally ingesting an elephant tranquilizer) had begun to diminish his playing ability. In 1975 he left England for L.A., where he continued to drink heavily. He returned to England and was trying to kick his alcoholism, but on September 7, 1978, Moon died of an overdose of a sedative, Heminevrin, that had been prescribed to prevent seizures induced by alcohol withdrawal. Although the group continued for another three years, each of the three surviving original members has stated repeatedly that the Who was never the same again.

In 1979 the Who oversaw a concert documentary of their early years, *The Kids Are Alright* (soundtrack, #8, 1979), and worked on the soundtrack version of *Quadrophenia* (#46, 1979), which also included a number of Mod favorites performed by the original artists (such as Booker T. and the MG's' "Green Onions" and James Brown's "Night Train"). Kenney Jones, formerly of the Small Faces, replaced Moon, and session keyboardist John "Rabbit" Bundrick began working with the Who. The new lineup toured, but tragedy struck again when 11 concertgoers were killed—trampled to death or asphyxiated—in a rush for "festival seating" spots at Cincinnati's Riverfront Coliseum on December 3, 1979. The incident occurred before the show, and the group wasn't told of it until afterward.

After 15 years with Decca/MCA, the Who signed a band contract with Warner Bros., and Townshend got a solo deal with Atco. His *Empty Glass* (#5, 1980) included the U.S. Top 10 hit "Let My Love Open the Door" and "Rough Boys," a song long believed to have been an angry reply to a punk musician who had insulted the Who during an interview. Much later, in a 1989 interview with writer Timothy White, Townshend denied that was the case, saying, "It's about homosexuality," and adding that "And I Moved" was as well. Townshend's admission of having "had a gay life," and the statement "I know how it feels to be a woman because I *am* a woman," came as a surprise to many, including his band mates.

In 1981 Townshend performed solo with an acoustic guitar at a benefit for Amnesty International, which was recorded as *The Secret Policeman's Ball*. His falling asleep onstage was the first public sign of his deepening drug addiction. Since the year before, Townshend had been abusing alcohol, cocaine, and freebase cocaine mixed with heroin. He subsequently developed an addiction to Ativan, a tranquilizer he was prescribed during treatment for alcoholism. Ativan combined with freebase and heroin resulted in a highly publicized, near-fatal overdose during which he was rushed to the hospital from a London club. Townshend subsequently underwent electro-acupuncture treatment and cleaned up in 1982.

Amid all this, the revamped Who soldiered on. *Face Dances* (#4, 1981) included the hit single "You Better You Bet" (#18, 1981) and "Don't Let Go the Coat." But Townshend later called the new lineup's debut album a disappointment. One month after *Face Dances* came out, the Who's former producer/manager, Kit Lambert, died after falling down a flight of stairs; he was 45. (Pete Meadon had died three weeks before Moon, in 1978.) Townshend released the wordy *All the Best Cowboys Have Chinese Eyes* (#26, 1982), and soon followed it with the group's *It's Hard* (#8, 1982), an album Daltrey has since been quoted as saying should never have been released. It produced the group's last Top 30 hit to date, "Athena" (#28). The Who then embarked on what they announced would be their last tour, ending with a concert in Toronto on December 17, 1982. Although the group officially broke up in 1982, the quartet reunited to perform several times since, appearing at Live Aid in 1985 and at a U.K. music-awards program in 1988. They celebrated the group's silver anniversary in 1989 with a 43-date U.S. tour which included guest-star-studded performances of *Tommy* in L.A. and New York, and later in London. For this tour Jones was replaced by session drummer Simon Phillips. It was also during this tour that Townshend, whose hearing was extremely damaged from years of listening to loud music through headphones, had to play standing behind a plastic baffle to block the onstage noise.

Townshend also released a number of solo projects throughout the '80s: *Scoop* (#35, 1983) and *Another Scoop* (#198, 1987) collect demo tapes, home recordings, and sundry tracks of historical interest to fans. *White City—A Novel* (#26, 1985) is a concept piece, the soundtrack to a long-form video of the same title and includes "Face the Face"; *The Iron Man: The Musical by Pete Townshend* is the star-studded (Daltrey, Nina Simone, John Lee Hooker) soundtrack to Townshend's rock opera based on a children's story by poet Ted Hughes. *Deep End Live!*, released with an accompanying live video, barely scraped into the Top 100.

Townshend wrote in the liner notes to the 1994 box-set career retrospective *Thirty Years of Maximum R&B*: "I don't like the Who much . . ." Through the years his derisive attitude toward the group has rung false at worst, disingenuous at best. In fact, Townshend's pride (and joy) in performing with the Who was abundantly clear during the band's 2000 tour, when he introduced it—happily—as "the fucking Who."

Despite Townshend's other projects and endeavors, including an editorship with book publisher Faber and Faber and publication of his collected stories, *Horse's Neck* (1985), the Who legacy endures. In 1993 the Broadway production of *Tommy* won five Tony Awards, including one for Townshend for Best Original Score. The next year saw the release of Townshend's *PsychoDerelict* (#118, 1994), a concept album that includes pieces written originally for the *Lifehouse* project. An examination of rock stardom's ravages, *PsychoDerelict* was also performed as a theater piece and filmed (it was subsequently broadcast on PBS). That year he also embarked on his first solo tour with a set list that included a number of Who classics, including "Won't Get Fooled Again." In February 1994 Townshend, Daltrey, and Entwistle reunited for two Carnegie Hall concerts in celebration of Daltrey's 50th birthday. Accompanied by a 65-piece orchestra, the trio was also joined by guest stars including Sinéad O'Connor, Eddie Vedder, and Lou Reed, and the show was filmed for cable television.

Two years later, the group recruited drummer Zak Starkey (son of Ringo Starr) along with a 12-piece backing band and embarked on a series of dates in which they performed the *Quadrophenia* album in its entirety for the first time. Townshend again stuck to rhythm guitar to preserve his hearing (which had been damaged by years of playing amplified lead guitar), leaving lead electric guitar duties to his brother Simon Townshend.

In 1999 Townshend reunited the band again for a charity concert at the House of Blues in Chicago, which led to yet another reunion tour the following year. This time around, however, the Who toured as a quintet—Townshend, Daltrey, Entwistle, Starkey, and John Bundrick on keyboards—with Townshend returning to the electric guitar. The no-nonsense approach resulted in glowing reviews hailing the group's 2000 shows as some of their best in nearly two decades. A live album, *The Who Live: The Blues to the Bush/1999,* was released online via a partnership with MusicMaker.com, and the band even began talking about the possibility of a new studio set in the future. To cap their year, the Who received a Lifetime Achievement Award at the 43rd annual Grammy Awards.

In the midst of all the Who activity in late 1999 and 2000, Townshend returned yet again to his lifelong *Lifehouse* project. The BBC broadcast a *Lifehouse* radio play in December 1999, and in February 2000, Townshend performed the rock opera himself at London's Sadler's Wells Theater. Shortly thereafter he released a six-disc box set, *Lifehouse Chronicles,* on his own Eelpie label via his Web site; a single-disc version, *Lifehouse Elements,* was released in stores by Redline Entertainment. Daltrey, meanwhile, continued planning his own pet project, a film biography of the life of Moon.

Wilco

Formed 1994, St. Louis, MO
Jeff Tweedy (b. Aug. 25, 1967, Belleville, IL), voc., gtr.; Ken Coomer (b. Nov. 5, 1960, Nashville, TN), drums; John Stirratt (b. Nov. 26, 1967, New Orleans, LA), bass, voc.; Max Johnston, gtr., fiddle, mandolin, banjo, voc.
1995—*A.M.* (Reprise) (+ Jay Bennett [b. Nov. 15, 1963, Chicago, IL], gtr., kybds., voc.) 1996—*Being There* (– Johnston; + Bob Egan, gtr., steel gtr.) 1998—(– Egan) 1999—*Summerteeth* 2001—(– Coomer).
Billy Bragg and Wilco: 1998—*Mermaid Avenue* (Elektra) 2000—*Mermaid Avenue vol. II.*

The breakup of the influential, Belleville, Illinois, roots-punk combo Uncle Tupelo [see entry] found Jay Farrar and Jeff Tweedy, the band's principal singer/songwriters, fronting new groups of their own. People expected less from Tweedy than they did from Farrar, who had always been regarded as the more serious artist of the two. It wasn't long, however, before Tweedy's new band Wilco outstripped Farrar's Son Volt [see entry], emerging as one of the few old-school guitar outfits of the late '90s that mattered.

After Farrar walked away from Uncle Tupelo in 1994, Tweedy and the remaining members of the band recorded *A.M.,* joined by Bottle Rockets frontman and former Tupelo roadie Brian Henneman on guitar. The album found Wilco playing scruffy, country-tinged rock that suggested a cross between late-period Replacements and "Wild Horses"–era Rolling Stones. *Being There* (#73, 1996), the band's critically acclaimed followup, saw Tweedy growing leaps and bounds as a songwriter as Wilco moved even further away from the alternative-country of Uncle Tupelo and more in the direction of the tuneful pop-rock of such early '70s bands as Big Star.

Meanwhile, with Tweedy off making a second album with Golden Smog, an alt-country supergroup consisting of members of Soul Asylum and the Jayhawks, the rest of Wilco moonlighted as Courtesy Move. Besides recording several unreleased tracks of their own, the foursome provided backing on albums by singer/songwriters Steve Forbert and Jeff Black. (By this time multi-instrumentalist Bob Egan had replaced Max Johnston, who had left Wilco to play with his sister, Michelle Shocked, and after that, with Freakwater.)

In 1998 Tweedy and company accepted an invitation from British singer/songwriter Billy Bragg to travel to Dublin to set some of Woody Guthrie's unrecorded lyrics to music. The album that resulted, *Mermaid Avenue* (#90, 1998), was by turns funny, sexy, and incisive; testifying to Guthrie's irrepressible spirit and ongoing relevance, it also proved to be the best record that either Bragg or Wilco had ever made. *Summerteeth* (#78, 1999), Wilco's third album, appeared the following year; more pop-leaning than its predecessors, the record was chock-full of bright, buoyant melodies salted with Tweedy's increasingly dark, oblique lyrics. A world tour opening for R.E.M. followed, while 2000 marked the appearance of a second volume of *Mermaid Avenue* that was nearly as luminous as the first.

Deniece Williams

Born June 3, 1951, Gary, IN
1976—*This Is Niecy* (Columbia) 1977—*Songbird* 1978—*That's What Friends Are For* (with Johnny Mathis) 1979—*When Love Comes Calling* (ARC) 1981—*My Melody* 1982—*Niecy* 1983—*I'm So Proud* (Columbia) 1984—*Let's Hear It for the Boy* 1986—*Hot on the Trail; From the Beginning* (Sparrow); *So Glad I Know* 1987—*Water Under the Bridge* (Columbia) 1989—*As Good as It Gets; Special Love* (Capitol/EMI) 1991—*Lullabies to Dreamland* (Word/Epic) 1994—*Greatest Gospel Hits* (Sparrow) 1996—*Love Solves It All* (P.A.R.); *Gonna Take a Miracle: The Best of Deniece Williams* (Columbia/Legacy) 1998—*This Is My Song* (Harmony).

As a child, Deniece Williams sang in gospel choirs, later recording for the local Chicago label, Toddlin' Town. She then turned her attention to a new career in nursing and became a "candy striper." Through a cousin's influence, Williams auditioned for and was recruited by Stevie Wonder to sing in his Wonderlove vocal group. (She toured with Wonder and can be heard on his 1972 LP *Talking Book* and 1976's *Songs in the Key of Life.*) After hearing a demo of her original songs, Earth, Wind & Fire's Maurice White signed Williams to his Kalimba Productions.

This Is Niecy, Williams' first album, spawned the hit "Free" (#25 pop, #2 R&B, 1977). Collaborating in 1978 with singer Johnny Mathis, Williams had a major hit in "Too Much, Too Little, Too Late" (#1 pop, #1 R&B). The same year, the pair followed with a remake of the Marvin Gaye/Tammi Terrell hit "You're All I Need to Get By" (#47 pop, #10 R&B).

In 1982 Williams also scored with a remake of the Royalettes' "It's Gonna Take a Miracle" (#10 pop, #1 R&B), produced by Philly soul auteur Thom Bell. Two years later, "Let's Hear It for the Boy," produced by George Duke and featured in the popular film *Footloose,* charted at #1 pop and R&B. Although it was her last pop smash, Williams continued to have R&B hits including "Never Say Never" (#6, 1987). Williams began recording gospel albums in 1986; one of two she released that year, *So Glad I Know,* won a pair of Grammys.

Since then, Christian music has remained Williams' focus. *Love Solves It All* (1996) leavened the singer's gospel tracks with a pair of R&B singles; 1998's *This Is My Song* was a collection of hymns arranged in an R&B style. In the '90s, Williams also began writing children's books.

Hank Williams

Born Hiram Williams, Sep. 17, 1923, Mount Olive, AL; died Jan. 1, 1953, Oak Hill, WV
1976—*Hank Williams Live at the Grand Old Opry* (MGM) 1985—*Hank Williams: I Ain't Got Nothin' but Time, December 1946–August 1947* (Polydor); *Hank Williams: Lovesick Blues, August 1947–December 1948* 1986—*Hank Williams: Lost Highway, December 1948–March 1949; Hank Williams: I'm So Lonesome I Could Cry, March 1949–August 1949* 1987—*Hank Williams: Long Gone Lonesome Blues, August 1949–December 1950; Hank Williams: Hey Good Lookin', December 1950–July 1951; Hank Williams: Let's Turn Back the Years, July 1951–June 1952; Hank Williams: I Won't Be Home No More, June 1952–September 1952* 1990—*Rare Demos First to Last* (Country Music Foundation) 1991—*The Original Singles Collection* (Polydor) 1998—*The Complete Hank Williams* (Mercury) 2000—*Alone With His Guitar.*

Hank Williams was perhaps the most important country & western performer of his time, and the most influential country artist in the development of rock & roll. His 36 Top 10 C&W hits—including the #1s "Lovesick Blues," "Why Don't You Love Me," "Long Gone Lonesome Blues," "Moanin' the Blues," "Cold, Cold Heart," "Hey, Good Lookin'," "Jambalaya (On the Bayou)," and "I'll Never Get Out of This World Alive"—and magnetic stage presence were instrumental in country music's rise in popularity during his lifetime. ("Kaw-Liga," "Your Cheatin' Heart," and "Take These Chains From My Heart" were posthumous #1 C&W hits in 1953.) But it is as a songwriter that Williams' influence most profoundly changed country music and touched virtually every popular style emanating from it, especially rock & roll. In compositions such as "I'm So Lonesome I Could Cry," for example, Williams expressed intense, personal emotions with country's traditional plainspoken directness, a then revolutionary approach that through the works of George Jones, Willie Nelson, and countless other country artists has come to define the genre. As a singer, Williams mastered a range of styles, from gospel to the pre-rockabilly playfulness of "Hey, Good Lookin'."

Hiram "Hank" Williams was born in a two-room sharecropper's shack in southeastern Alabama. His father was shell-shocked from World War I and committed himself to a veterans' hospital when Hank was seven, leaving Williams' mother to support him and his sister. She played organ in the local Baptist church, where Hank sang in the choir, and she bought him a guitar for $3.50. When he was 11, Williams moved in with relatives in a railroad camp and began frequenting the Saturday-night dances, where he learned about country music and moonshine. The following year, he moved with his family to the larger town of Greenville and began learning blues songs from a black street singer named Rufe "Tee-Tot" Payne. Williams played on streetcorners with Tee-Tot, sold peanuts, and shined shoes.

In 1937 the family moved to Montgomery, Alabama. Hank won an amateur contest by performing his "W.P.A. Blues" and, dubbed the Singing Kid, he secured a twice-weekly radio show on local station WSFA. Soon after, he formed the Drifting Cowboys and began playing the Alabama roadhouse circuit, with his mother as booking agent and driver.

By December 1944, Williams had played nearly every roadhouse in Alabama and had married Audrey Mae Sheppard. Two years later, he signed a songwriting contract with Nashville publishers Acuff-Rose, and he recorded in Nashville on the small Sterling label. Soon after, he got a recording contract with newly formed MGM and began his successful collaboration with producer/arranger Fred Rose. That summer (1948), Williams joined the popular KWKH country music radio program *Louisiana Hayride* in Shreveport. His records started making the C&W charts, and he finally hit big with "Lovesick Blues," which became the #1 country record of 1949.

On June 11, 1949, Williams played at the Grand Ole Opry for the first time and received an unprecedented six encores. His fame grew along with his touring schedule of one-nighters across the country. Besides recording his bluesy C&W records, he also recorded gospel-influenced songs under the name Luke the Drifter. By 1952 his drinking had gotten out of hand, his health had deteriorated, and his marriage ended in divorce. Williams' chronic back problems had resulted in his dependence on painkillers, and in August he was fired from the Grand Ole Opry because of frequent no-shows. Four months later, at the age of 29, he died of a heart attack in the back of his Cadillac en route to a show in Canton, Ohio. (Many years later reports were issued that he actually died in a Knoxville, Tennessee, hotel room after excessive alcohol and drug consumption.)

After his death, Williams' records sold more than ever, and have continued to do so in the nearly 50 years since. His oft-covered catalogue has produced hits for artists ranging from Fats Domino and John Fogerty's Blue Ridge Rangers to Ray Charles and B.J. Thomas and has been the inspiration for a whole new generation of alt-country artists. In the late '90s Mercury Records began reissuing Williams' music on lavish CD sets. The 1998 box set *The Complete Hank Williams* won two Grammys.

Hank Williams Jr.

Born Randall Hank Williams Jr., May 26, 1949, Shreveport, LA
1964—*Your Cheatin' Heart* soundtrack (MGM) 1965—*Father & Son* (with Hank Williams Sr.) 1969—*Live at Cobo Hall, Detroit* 1974—*Living Proof* 1976—*Hank Williams Jr. and Friends; Fourteen Greatest Hits* 1977—*One Night Stands* (Elektra/Curb); *The New South* (Warner Bros./Curb) 1979—*Family Tradition* (Elektra/Curb); *Whiskey Bent and Hell Bound* (Elektra) 1981—*Rowdy; The Pressure Is On* 1983—*Strong Stuff* 1984—*Major Moves* (Warner Bros.) 1985—*Greatest Hits, vol. 2; The Early Years, 1976–78; Five-O* (Warner/Curb) 1986—*Montana Cafe* (Warner Bros.) 1987—*Hank "Live"; Born to Boogie* 1988—*Wild Streak; Standing in the Shadows* (Polydor) 1989—*Greatest Hits, III* (Warner Bros./Curb) 1990—*Lone Wolf; AMERICA (The Way I See It)* 1991—*Pure Hank* 1992—*Maverick* (Curb/Capricorn) 1993—*Out of Left Field* 1995—*Hog Wild* (MCG/Curb) 1996—*A.K.A. Wham Bam Sam; Three Hanks: Men With Broken Hearts* 1999—*Stormy.*

Hank Williams' son has carved out a country-rock career of his own. The young Williams was just three when his father died. He learned to play from his father's friends and associates, who included Jerry Lee Lewis, Johnny Cash, Ray Charles, and Brenda Lee. He changed his name to Hank Williams Jr., and with his mother guiding his career, made his debut at age eight in Swainsboro, Georgia. He made his first appearance at the Grand Ole Opry in 1960 and cut his first record at age 14, "Long Gone Lonesome Blues." His formal concert debut came soon after, at Cobo Hall in Detroit. Williams quit school and began touring, also appearing on TV. At 16, he became the youngest songwriter ever to earn a BMI citation; he also had a #5 C&W hit, "Standing in the Shadows" (1966). On tour, he mainly performed his father's material, with a band called the Cheatin' Hearts. His *Your Cheatin' Heart* soundtrack LP went gold. He later wrote soundtracks for *Time to Sing* and *Kelly's Heroes*. By age 25, he'd been married and divorced twice, and suffered from drug and alcohol problems.

Around 1974 Williams grew disenchanted with Nashville and with living up to his father's legacy. His association with his father endured on record as well: *Fathers & Sons* electronically created "duets" between Williams and his father, and 1969's *Songs My Father Left Me* presented the younger Williams creating melodies to songs for which his father had written lyrics before his death. Hank Williams Jr. temporarily stopped performing. On August 8, 1975, while mountain climbing in Montana, he fell 490 feet, resulting in injuries so severe that his entire face had to be reconstructed surgically.

A year and a half later, he came back in the more rock-oriented "outlaw" mold; fellow "outlaw" Waylon Jennings produced *New South*. In 1979 Williams' autobiography, *Living Proof,* was published by Putnam; it later became a made-for-television film entitled *Living Proof: The Hank Williams Jr. Story* (1983), starring Richard Thomas. He also recorded in the late '60s and '70s as Luke the Drifter Jr. (including two albums in 1969).

Although Williams has had a number of C&W hits through the years, he's a rare presence on the pop charts. In 1981 he had one of his biggest country hits with "All My Rowdy Friends (Have Settled Down)" (#1 C&W). Other hits included a cover of his father's "Honky Tonkin' " (#1 C&W, 1982), "Gonna Go Huntin' Tonight" (#4 C&W, 1983), "Man of Steel" (#3 C&W, 1984), "Attitude Adjustment" (#5, C&W, 1984), "All My Rowdy Friends Are Coming Over Tonight" (#10, C&W, 1984), "I'm for Love" (#1 C&W, 1985), "This Ain't Dallas" (#4 C&W, 1985), "Ain't Misbehavin' " (#1 C&W, 1986), "Country State of Mind' (#2 C&W, 1986), "Mind Your Own Business" (#1 C&W, 1986), "Born to Boogie" (#1 C&W, 1987), "Heaven Can't Be Found" (#4 C&W, 1987), "Young Country" (#2 C&W, 1988), "If the South Woulda Won" (#8 C&W, 1988), the Grammy-winning "There's a Tear in My Beer" (#7 C&W, 1989; an electronically created duet and video using old tapes and footage of his father), "Finders Are Keepers" (#6 C&W, 1989), and "Good Friends, Good Whiskey, Good Lovin' " (#19 C&W, 1990). Hank Williams Jr. also wrote and performed the theme for ABC Television's *Monday Night Football* program. Six albums have been certified platinum, among them: *The Pressure Is On* (#76 pop, 1981), *Hank Williams Jr.'s Greatest Hits* (#107 pop, 1982), *Greatest Hits, vol. 2* (#183 pop, #1 C&W, 1986), *Born to Boogie* (#28 pop, 1987), and *Greatest Hits III* (#61 pop, 1989). He has also charted many #1 C&W LPs, including his 50th album, *Five-O* (1985), and *Wild Streak* (1988). Subsequent releases have made more modest C&W chart showings. *A.K.A. Wham Bam Sam* hit #40 in 1996, while 1999's *Stormy* peaked at #21. Also in 1996 *Men With Broken Hearts,* a project that utilized old recordings of Williams' father along with new recordings of Hank Jr. and his son Hank III, climbed to #29. (Hank III would go on to record as a solo artist, combining twangy C&W with hardcore punk.)

Jerry Williams: See Swamp Dogg

Larry Williams

Born May 10, 1935, New Orleans, LA; died Jan. 2, 1980, Los Angeles, CA
1978—*That Larry Williams* (Fantasy) 1988—*The Best of Larry Williams* (Ace) 1990—*Larry Williams: Bad Boy* (Specialty) 1999—*Bad Boy of Rock 'n' Roll* (Ace).

Larry Williams scored important hits in 1957–58 with "Short Fat Fanny" (#5 pop, #2 R&B), "Bony Moronie" (#14 pop, #9

R&B) (later covered by John Lennon on *Rock 'n' Roll*), and "Dizzy Miss Lizzy" (#69, 1958) (later covered by the Beatles). Their alliterative titles and frantic shouting performances made him a momentary rival to Little Richard.

Little Richard was the star performer of Specialty Records, the label that discovered Williams when he was playing piano on R&B sessions for performers like Lloyd Price, Roy Brown, and Percy Mayfield. Williams' first record for Specialty, a cover of Lloyd Price's "Just Because," was a flop, but was followed by his three big hits of 1957–58. When the hits stopped coming, Williams turned to record production for a time, and then teamed up with Johnny "Guitar" Watson, with whom he recorded several late-'60s R&B hits. He was convicted of and served time for narcotics trafficking in the '60s. His poorly received funk-oriented comeback album for Fantasy in 1978 was his last release. Two years later, he was found dead in his L.A. home, a gunshot wound in his head. The verdict was suicide.

Lucinda Williams

Born Jan. 26, 1953, Lake Charles, LA
1979—*Ramblin' on My Mind* (Folkways) 1980—*Happy Woman Blues* 1988—*Lucinda Williams* (Rough Trade) 1989—*Passionate Kisses* EP 1992—*Sweet Old World* (Chameleon) 1998—*Car Wheels on a Gravel Road* (Mercury) 2001—*Essence* (Lost Highway/Mercury).

Lucinda Williams began her career interpreting country, folk, and blues standards with a cool, almost academic reverence for the music. After a second album of original songs, she seemingly vanished for eight years. In 1988 she returned with a vengeance with *Lucinda Williams,* her highly praised singer/songwriter album that marked a critical turning point in Williams' career. She reached even greater commercial heights with 1998's masterful *Car Wheels on a Gravel Road,* her first gold album.

The daughter of a father who was a poet, college professor, and Hank Williams fan, Williams grew up listening to classic country. She was born in Louisiana, but her family relocated several times during her childhood to spots across the South, as well as Mexico City and Santiago, Chile. At 16, she discovered the writing of Southern novelist Flannery O'Connor, whom she cites as a major influence on her songwriting. Williams attended college for a short time but dropped out in 1971 to devote herself to music.

Folkways signed Williams in 1978 and released her first two albums without fanfare. Between 1980 and 1988 she worked a series of odd jobs, moving in mid-decade from Austin, Texas, to L.A., where she took voice lessons to learn how to sound like Joan Baez, and married and divorced Greg Sowders of the Long Ryders. Much of the biting material on her self-titled comeback album dealt with her marriage.

Rough Trade collapsed in 1991, and Chameleon released her 1992 album *Sweet Old World.* Relocating to Austin, then Nashville, Williams kept busy into the '90s. In 1993 she contributed a track to *Sweet Relief,* the benefit album for singer Victoria Williams (no relation), who suffers from multiple sclerosis, and lent her signature vocals to "Reunion" on Jimmie Dale Gilmore's *Spinning Around the Sun.* Williams' songs have also been covered by others: Patty Loveless scored a Top 10 country hit with "The Night's Too Long," Mary-Chapin Carpenter recorded a Grammy-winning version of her "Passionate Kisses," and Tom Petty's recording of Williams' "Change the Locks" appears on the soundtrack to the 1996 movie *She's the One.*

Lucinda Williams

In 1994, after Chameleon Records became defunct, Williams briefly joined Rick Rubin's American Recordings roster. That deal fell through, and Williams wouldn't put out a new album for another four years. Meanwhile, there was considerable discussion in the press and among fans about the extent to which Williams' perfectionist tendencies might be hindering the record's progress.

The luminous, blues-steeped *Car Wheels on a Gravel Road* (#65, 1998), proved a triumph. The record not only boasted contributions from Emmylou Harris, Steve Earle, and the E Street Band's Roy Bittan, it won Williams widespread critical acclaim, including top honors in the *Village Voice*'s annual critics poll. *Car Wheels* also earned Williams a Grammy for Best Contemporary Folk Album and became the first commercially successful record of her career, going gold within a year of its release. Williams toured extensively after the album came out, both as a headliner and as an opening act for Bob Dylan and Van Morrison. Currently signed to the new subsidiary of Mercury, Lost Highway, Williams released *Essence,* which debuted at #28, in June 2001 to more tempered reviews.

Maurice Williams and the Zodiacs

Formed 1959, Lancaster, SC
Maurice Williams (b. Apr. 26, 1938); Henry Gaston; Wiley

Bennett; Charles Thomas; Little Willie Morrow; Albert Hill; N.A.—(– Hill; – Morrow).

Maurice Williams and the Zodiacs had only one major hit, "Stay." Despite clocking in as the shortest #1 hit single in history, the song has lived up to its title, claiming a place in the Top 40 for three months in 1960 but returning in Top 20 hit versions by Jackson Browne and the Four Seasons and covers by the Hollies, and others. In 1987 it was included in the hit *Dirty Dancing* soundtrack, which also featured the Contours' "Do You Love Me," another example of the Southeast music trend called "beach music," of which Williams' group was a part.

Williams' various groups have contained countless members and worked under many names, beginning with Royal Charms. With another group called the Gladiolas, Williams recorded his "Little Darlin'," an unsuccessful single for them but a hit a couple of years later for the Diamonds. In 1959, following a business dispute, this group lost the rights to the Gladiolas name, and later Williams gathered a new group, which he christened the Zodiacs. This lineup—Henry Gaston, Wiley Bennett, Charles Thomas, and Williams—recorded "Stay" in 1960 with Gaston taking the falsetto break. In the wake of the record's success, the Zodiacs began touring with such established acts as Chuck Berry and James Brown. Subsequent Williams compositions failed to make as big a commercial splash, but locally the Zodiacs were a top draw. Having led a number of Zodiacs lineups in the '70s and '80s, Williams continues to record for the East Coast's beach-music market.

Paul Williams

Born Sep. 19, 1940, Omaha, NE
1970—*Someday Man* (Reprise) 1971—*Just an Old Fashioned Love Song* (A&M) 1973—*Life Goes On* 1974—*Here Comes Inspiration; A Little Bit of Love* 1975—*Phantom of the Paradise* soundtrack; *Ordinary Fool; Bugsy Malone* soundtrack 1977—*Classics* 2001—*Back to Love Again* (Pioneer).

Singer/songwriter Paul Williams started out as a set painter and stunt man in films. In *The Loved One* in 1964, 24-year-old Williams was cast as a 10-year-old child genius. In 1965 he appeared with Marlon Brando in *The Chase*, as another punk kid. While on the set of *The Chase*, Williams first tried his hand at songwriting. He wrote songs with Biff Rose and comedy sketches for Mort Sahl before teaming up in 1967 with lyricist Roger Nichols. Together they wrote such million-selling MOR pop hits as the Carpenters' "We've Only Just Begun" (which started out as a commercial jingle for a bank) and "Rainy Days and Mondays," Helen Reddy's "You and Me Against the World," and Three Dog Night's "Just an Old Fashioned Love Song" and "Out in the Country."

Despite his limited voice, Williams became a successful singer in his own right, and has long been a regular on the talk show and Las Vegas circuits. In 1975 Williams teamed up with lyricist Ken Ascher. A year later, he starred in the title role of the rock film *Phantom of the Paradise*, for which he wrote the soundtrack. The next year, he scored Alan Parker's child-gangster film *Bugsy Malone*. Williams also contributed songs to the Barbra Streisand–Kris Kristofferson remake of *A Star Is Born*, among them his Oscar-winning collaboration with Streisand, "Evergreen." Williams has gone on to write music for a number of other feature films, including *The Muppet Movie* (1980), *The Secret of NIMH* (1982), *The End* (1978), *Rocky IV* (1984), *Ishtar* (1987), and *The Muppet Christmas Carol* (1992).

As an actor Williams has appeared in a number of films, including the three *Smokey and the Bandit* films (1977–1983), *The Doors* (1991), *A Million to Juan* (1994), and *Headless Body in Topless Bar* (1995), and on television (*Picket Fences; Dream On; Walker, Texas Ranger*). In the late-'90s he had a recurring role on the CBS soap opera *The Bold and the Beautiful*. In addition, he does voice-over work.

Following years of cocaine and alcohol abuse, Williams underwent treatment. He not only completed the program but became a licensed drug rehabilitation counselor. *Back to Love Again*, issued in Japan several years before its American release in 2001, was his first studio album since the '70s. It features collaborations with Graham Nash and Richard Carpenter. Paul Williams' brother, Mentor Williams, is a country record producer and writer of a number of well-known songs, including "Drift Away."

The Tony Williams Lifetime

Formed 1969, New York, NY
Tony Williams (b. Dec. 12, 1945, Chicago, IL; d. Feb. 23, 1997, Daly City, CA), drums; John McLaughlin (b. Jan. 4, 1942, Yorkshire, Eng.), gtr.; Larry Young (a.k.a. Khalid Yasun, b. 1940, d. 1978), organ.
1969—*Emergency* (Polydor) (+ Jack Bruce [b. May 14, 1943, Glasgow, Scot.], bass, voc.) 1970—*Turn It Over* 1971—(– McLaughlin; – Bruce; + Ted Dunbar [b. Jan. 17, 1937, Port Arthur, TX], gtr.; + Warren Smith [b. May 14, 1934, Chicago], perc.; + Don Alias, perc.; + Juni Booth, bass) *Ego* (– Young; – Dunbar; – Smith; + Webster Lewis, organ; + David Horowitz, kybds.; + Tequila, gtr., voc.; + Tillmon Williams, tenor sax; + Herb Bushler, bass) 1972—*The Old Bum's Rush* (group disbands) 1975—(group re-forms: Williams; + Allan Holdsworth, gtr.; + Alan Pasqua, kybds.; + Tony Newton, bass, voc.) 1976—*Believe It* (Columbia); *Million Dollar Legs*.
Tony Williams solo: 1962—*Magic Touch of Tony* (Philips) 1964—*Life Time* (Blue Note) 1965—*Spring* 1979—*The Joy of Flying* (Columbia) 1986—*Foreign Intrigue* (Blue Note) 1987—*Civilization* 1988—*Angel Street* 1990—*Native Heart* 1991—*The Story of Neptune* 1992—*Tokyo Live* 1993—*Unmasked* 1996—*Wilderness* (Ark 21) 1998—*Young at Heart* (Sony).

Tony Williams' shifting accents helped define the sound of the Miles Davis [see entry] Quintet of the '60s, a group Williams joined when he was 17. In 1969, after playing with Davis and on numerous Blue Note jazz sessions, he left to form one of the first jazz-rock fusion bands, the Tony Williams Lifetime, with organist Larry Young, guitarist John McLaughlin (who also worked with Davis at the time), and ex-Cream bassist Jack Bruce.

Lifetime played highly complex hard rock, presaging the late-'70s "punk-funk-jazz" of Ornette Coleman and James Blood Ulmer, but after its first two albums the original Lifetime disbanded. Williams freelanced as a jazz drummer and tried making a more conventional funk album, *The Old Bum's Rush,* on which he sang. He joined fellow Davis-quintet veterans under Herbie Hancock's leadership in VSOP, with whom he continued to tour and to record.

In the mid-'70s Williams organized another version of Lifetime, featuring guitarist Allan Holdsworth, formerly of Soft Machine and Gong. Like the first Lifetime, the group was critically acclaimed, but its records sold poorly and it broke up again. Williams' 1979 solo LP featured both fusion players and a duet with avant-garde pianist Cecil Taylor.

In the '80s Williams found new focus by returning to the music of his youth. He formed an acoustic jazz band whose nucleus included acclaimed pianist Mulgrew Miller and trumpeter Wallace Rooney. Williams can be heard on Wynton Marsalis' solo debut recording and also toured with a 1983 band featuring Wynton and Branford Marsalis.

Since 1986's *Foreign Intrigue,* Williams composed the majority of the music for his own band. His expanded work, "Rituals for String Quartet, Piano, Drums and Cymbals," was performed in 1990 with the Kronos Quartet. In 1992 Williams toured with his old Miles Davis band mates Ron Carter, Herbie Hancock, and Wayne Shorter in a tribute to the then recently departed Davis.

Williams then worked in a variety of groups, primarily, after 1995, with his own trio. *Wilderness,* a suite of orchestral works featuring an all-star lineup of Pat Metheny, Stanley Clarke, Herbie Hancock, and Michael Brecker, exemplified the ambition of his later work. He died from a heart attack following a minor gallbladder operation in 1997.

Vanessa Williams

Born Vanessa Lynn Williams, Mar. 18, 1963, Bronx, NY
1988—*The Right Stuff* (Wing/PolyGram) 1991—*The Comfort Zone* 1996—*Star Bright* 1997—*Next* (Mercury) 1998—*Greatest Hits: The First Ten Years* (PolyGram).

Pop music teems with great comebacks, but few are as hard-won or as unexpected as that of singer Vanessa Williams. Raised in a predominantly white suburban community in Westchester, New York, by public-school music teacher parents, Williams studied piano, violin, and French horn as well as classical and jazz dance as a child. She graduated high school with a Presidential Scholarship for drama.

While attending Syracuse University as a musical theater major, she entered the Miss America pageant, in hopes of gaining money and exposure. She won, becoming the first black Miss America in history, but got more exposure than she bargained for when in July 1984 sexually suggestive photographs she had posed for when she was 19 and working for a photographer surfaced in *Penthouse.* The resulting scandal cost her the crown and, it seemed, all hopes of realizing the show-business aspirations that brought her to the pageant in the first place.

Not long after the dust settled, however, Williams landed a few TV appearances and film roles; her image was slowly restored thanks to both her talent and P.R. consultant Ramon Hervey II, whom Williams married in 1987. The same year, she signed a deal with PolyGram's Wing Records; the following year saw the release of her well-received debut album, *The Right Stuff* (#38, 1988), which spawned "Dreamin' " (#8 pop, #1 R&B, 1989). *The Comfort Zone* (#17, 1991) was even more successful: Its Grammy-nominated third single, "Save the Best for Last," went to #1 on the pop, R&B, and Adult Contemporary charts, while "Running Back to You," the title track, and "Work to Do" respectively peaked at #1, #2, and #3, all R&B.

In 1993 Williams scored another pop hit with "Love Is" (#3), a duet with singer Brian McKnight that was featured on a soundtrack to the popular television show *Beverly Hills 90210.* Williams' TV-related credits also include hosting *The Soul of VH1.* Her charity work has ranged from taking part in an East Coast radio station's 1989 "Coats for Kids" campaign to contributing "What Child Is This" to *A Very Special Christmas 2,* an album whose proceeds benefited the Special Olympics. Her public disgrace apparently forgiven if not forgotten, Williams has earned several Grammy nominations and a pair of NAACP Image Awards. She released the 1994 album *The Sweetest Days* (#57 pop, #25 R&B, 1994), which yielded a hit single in the title track (#18 pop, #40 R&B, 1994). In 1995 she got rave reviews for her dance-heavy Broadway debut in *Kiss of the Spider Woman;* the same year, her "Colors of the Wind" (from *Pocahontas*) was an Oscar-winning #4 hit, and she costarred in a TV production of the musical *Bye Bye Birdie.*

In 1996 Williams costarred with action heavyweight Arnold Schwarzenegger in the movie *Eraser* and a Christmas album, *Star Bright,* was released. She and husband Hervey, who by now had three children together, divorced in 1997. The same year, Williams released *Next,* on which she collaborated on some tracks with dance producers Jimmy Jam and Terry Lewis as well as R. Kelly, and set off on her first-ever concert tour, opening for Luther Vandross. She also appeared in the TV miniseries epic *The Odyssey* and starred in the feature film *Soul Food* in 1997. A greatest-hits album was released in 1998, along with the movie *Dance With Me;* Williams also appeared on stage in a limited performance of the '40s musical *St. Louis Woman* in New York City. The entertainer took a slight breather to marry basketball player Rick Fox in 1999 (a daughter was born in 2000), then filmed *Shaft* with Samuel L. Jackson.

Victoria Williams

Born Dec. 23, 1958, Forbing, LA
1987—*Happy Come Home* (Geffen) 1990—*Swing the Statue* (Rough Trade) 1994—*Loose* (Mammoth/Atlantic) 1995—

This Moment: Live in Toronto 1998—*Musings of a Creekdipper* (Atlantic) 2000—*Water to Drink.*

Victoria Williams is one of the most unique singer/songwriters to emerge in the past decade. Yet the audience for her high-pitched warble and whimsical, deeply spiritual blend of folk, rock, country, and gospel was limited until she developed multiple sclerosis (MS) and several of her famous admirers came to her aid. Williams was diagnosed with the degenerative neuromuscular disease while touring with Neil Young in 1992; her lack of health insurance and inability to pay her medical bills motivated Pearl Jam, Soul Asylum, and other artists to record *Sweet Relief,* an album of Williams covers with proceeds going to set up a fund for Williams and other ailing muscians with no resources for health care. The boost not only enabled Williams to get through a rough patch in her life but also led to her record deal with Atlantic.

Williams grew up in a Methodist household in Shreveport, Louisiana, where she soaked up music ranging from folk to blues to black gospel. She later attended Centenary College and played in a bar band with a regional following, but didn't start writing songs until she later took a job in a laundromat at a Colorado resort. In 1979 Williams moved to L.A., where she became a fixture at the Troubadour club's "hoot nights." She moved back to Louisiana for a while, but returned to L.A. in 1984 and began playing with Peter Case [see entry] in a jug-band-style trio called the Incredibly Strung Out Band. The two eventually married and secured solo deals with Geffen (the couple divorced in 1989).

Williams' rootsy 1987 debut *Happy Come Home* featured such players as T Bone Burnett and Bernie Worrell, as well as string arrangements by Van Dyke Parks. The album's overproduction and Geffen's confusion as to how to market the eccentric Williams' idiosyncratic music resulted in its failure to make inroads. For her next release, *Swing the Statue,* Williams moved to punk indie Rough Trade, which went under just as the record was coming out. Williams' diagnosis of MS came shortly thereafter and, with it, the *Sweet Relief* tribute and her Atlantic deal.

Loose (1994) featured guest performances from Tower of Power, Soul Asylum's Dave Pirner, R.E.M.'s Peter Buck and Mike Mills, and Williams' new husband, Mark Olson, then of the Jayhawks [see entry]. Including covers of "What a Wonderful World" (best known for the version by Louis Armstrong) and Spirit's "Nature's Way," *Loose* received radio and video exposure through the single "You R Loved." The live *This Moment* followed in 1995 along with a role in the movie *Even Cowgirls Get the Blues.* In 1998 Williams' *Musings of a Creekdipper* included contributions from Olson, with whom Williams had formed a looseknit combo, the Harmony Ridge Creek Dippers, who also began releasing albums (via its Web site) that the couple recorded at their Joshua Tree home studio. *Water to Drink* (2000) found Williams singing mostly pop standards.

Sonny Boy Williamson

Sonny Boy No. 1: born John Lee Williamson, Mar. 30, 1914, Jackson, TN; died June 1, 1948, Chicago, IL
1959—*Blues in the Mississippi Night* (United Artists) 1964—*Blues Classics by Sonny Boy Williamson* (Blues Classics); *Blues Classics by Sonny Boy Williamson, vol. 2; Blues Classics by Sonny Boy Williamson, vol. 3* 1976—*The Original Sonny Boy Williamson: Southern Blues Classics.*
Sonny Boy No. 2: born Aleck or Alex or Willie "Rice" Miller or Ford, Dec. 5, 1897 or 1899 or 1909, Glendora, MS; died May 25, 1965, Helena, AR
1959—*Down and Out Blues* (Chess) 1962—*Bummer Road* 1963—*Sonny Boy and Memphis Slim* (Vogue) 1964—*Sonny Boy Williamson and the Yardbirds* (with the Yardbirds) (Mercury) 1965—*This Is My Story* (Chess) 1966—*The Real Folk Blues* 1967—*More Real Folk Blues; The Original* (Blues Classics)

Victoria Williams

1973—*In Paris: Sonny Boy Williamson and Memphis Slim* (GNP Crescendo) 1976—*One Way Out* (MCA) 1989—*King Biscuit Time* (Arhoolie) 1992—*Goin' in Your Direction* (Trumpet) 1993—*Sonny Boy Williamson, vol. 1: 1937–1939* (EPM); *Sonny Boy Williamson, vol. 2: 1940–1942* (Alligator) 1993—*The Essential Sonny Boy Williamson* (MCA/Chess) 1995—*In Europe* (Evidence) 1997—*His Best* (Chess).

There were two Sonny Boy Williamsons. The first was John Lee Williamson, who recorded very little and is known mainly as a major influence on such blues-harp giants as Little Walter Jacobs and Junior Wells. The second was Rice Miller, by far the better known.

The first Sonny Boy is acknowledged as the first to play the harmonica as a lead, rather than accompanying, instrument. He is also considered an important and influential singer. Early in his career, he worked with Sleepy John Estes and Homesick James. He moved to Chicago in 1937, where he recorded "Good Morning, Little Schoolgirl" and "Sugar Mama" for RCA/Bluebird and played in a small group featuring Big Bill Broonzy. He was killed in a brutal attack and robbery.

The second Sonny Boy was the author of such blues standards as "One Way Out" (covered by the Allman Brothers Band), "Bye Bye Bird" (covered by the Moody Blues), "Help Me" (covered by Van Morrison), "Eyesight to the Blind" (covered by the Who on *Tommy*), "Fattening Frogs for Snakes," and "Don't Start Me Talking."

Miller—whose name, date of birth, and early life remain something of a mystery—was first noticed in the middle '30s, when he toured under the name Little Boy Blue, playing with Robert Johnson, Elmore James, and others. He first came to prominence, still known as Rice Miller, singing and playing blues harp on the popular radio show *King Biscuit Time,* broadcast from Helena, Arkansas. Miller appropriated the name Sonny Boy Williamson after the show's sponsor asked him to pose as the original Sonny Boy Williamson. The original Sonny Boy did not care to tour the South, and, surprisingly—since the two harmonica players' styles were different—the public accepted Miller as Sonny Boy. Not long after, the original Sonny Boy was murdered, leaving Miller (as many fellow musicians still referred to him) the only Sonny Boy.

Williamson, as he was now known, first recorded in 1951 for the Jackson, Mississippi, Trumpet label. His first hit was his first recording there, "Eyesight to the Blind." That year he also recorded with Elmore James and appears on James' important version of Robert Johnson's "Dust My Broom." At this time Williamson was married to Howlin' Wolf's sister; they soon divorced and he remarried.

In 1955 Williamson moved to Chicago and began recording blues hits for Chess, backed at times by the Muddy Waters band. His ambivalence regarding tour commitments and recording, coupled with a penchant for drinking, gambling, women, and rambling, made him a difficult artist to manage. However, no one he ever recorded for ever got angry enough to stop working with him. Through 1961, Williamson recorded a number of blues hits, including "Don't Start Me to Talkin'," "All My Love in Vain," "Keep It to Yourself," and "Your Funeral and My Trial."

Although by then in his 60s, Williamson never settled down. In 1963 he went to Europe, where he found an appreciative audience. He was especially popular in England, where he caused a sensation in his two-tone suit and bowler hat. In subsequent U.K. tours, he appeared on the British rock TV show *Ready, Steady, Go* and recorded live albums with British Invasion bands the Yardbirds and the Animals. He considered moving to England permanently but instead returned to Mississippi. He later recorded one last session for Chess, then returned to the Delta.

Shortly before his death, Williamson jammed with an early Ronnie Hawkins–led version of the Band, the Hawks, in a juke joint. All through the evening he had been spitting up blood, and some accounts attribute his death to tuberculosis. In fact, he died of a heart attack.

Chuck Willis

Born Jan. 31, 1928, Atlanta, GA; died Apr. 10, 1958, Atlanta
1971—*His Greatest Recordings* (Atlantic) 1980—*Chuck Willis—My Story* (Columbia) 1994—*Let's Jump Tonight! The Best of Chuck Willis, From 1951–56* (Columbia/Legacy) 1998—*The Real Story.*

Chuck Willis was a blues singer/songwriter best remembered as the "King of the Stroll" (although the Diamonds cashed in on the ensuing dance craze with their "The Stroll"). Oft-recorded Willis tunes include "I Feel So Bad" (Foghat, Delbert McClinton, Elvis Presley), "It's Too Late" (Buddy Holly, Otis Redding), and "Hang Up My Rock and Roll Shoes" (the Band, Jerry Lee Lewis).

As a teen, Willis was a popular R&B singer around Atlanta. A local DJ, Zenus "Daddy" Sears, took him to Columbia Records in 1952, where he cut a few minor releases for their Okeh label, including the R&B hits "My Story," a cover of Louis Jordan's "Caldonia," and "You're Still My Baby."

Willis, wearing turbans on stage—at one point he owned 54 of them—was often introduced to audiences as the "Sheik of the Shake." In 1956 Jerry Wexler signed Willis to Atlantic Records, and the next year Willis cut the blues standard "C.C. Rider" (#12 pop, #3 R&B). It was a major hit and established him as the "King of the Stroll." But within the year, Willis died from peritonitis, a complication of surgery for stomach ulcers; he was just 30. Posthumously, "What Am I Living For?" (#9 pop, #3 R&B) became his biggest crossover hit, followed by "Hang Up My Rock and Roll Shoes."

Bob Wills and His Texas Playboys

Formed 1935, Tulsa, OK
Bob Wills (b. Mar. 6, 1905, Limestone, TX; d. May 13, 1975, Fort Worth, TX), voc., fiddle.
1958—*Bob Wills and His Texas Playboys* (MCA) 1963—*Bob*

Wills Sings and Plays (Liberty) 1968—*King of the Western Swing* (MCA) 1969—*The Best of Bob Wills and His Texas Playboys; Living Legend* 1971—*In Person* 1973—*The Bob Wills Anthology* (Columbia); *The Best of Bob Wills* (MCA) 1974—*For the Last Time* (United Artists) 1975—*Fathers and Sons* (Epic); *The Best of Bob Wills, vol. 2* (MCA) 1976—*Remembering . . . The Greatest Hits of Bob Wills* (Columbia); *In Concert* (Capitol) 1977—*24 Great Hits by Bob Wills and His Texas Playboys* (Polydor) 1982—*The Tiffany Transcriptions 1946 & 1947, vol. 1* (Kaleidoscope) 1984—*Best of the Tiffanys: The Tiffany Transcriptions 1946 & 1947, vol. 2; Basin Street Blues: The Tiffany Transcriptions 1946 & 1947, vol. 3* 1985—*You're From Texas: The Tiffany Transcriptions 1946 & 1947, vol. 4* 1986—*The Tiffany Transcriptions 1946 & 1947, vol. 5* 1987—*Sally Grodin: The Tiffany Transcriptions 1946 & 1947, vol. 7; Fiddle* (Country Music Foundation); *The Golden Era* (Columbia); *Columbia Historic Edition* 1988—*More of the Best: The Tiffany Transcriptions 1946 & 1947, vol. 8* (Kaleidoscope) 1990—*In the Mood: The Tiffany Transcriptions 1946 & 1947, vol. 9* 1991—*Anthology, 1935–1973* (Rhino).

Fiddler-bandleader Bob Wills helped change the course of country and pop music in the '30s with his Texas Playboys, a Western swing band numbering anywhere from 13 to 18 members, who fused country & western, pop, blues, and big-band swing. This seminal unit introduced horns, drums, and electric guitars to country music.

The eldest of 10 children born to a fiddle-playing father, Wills moved with his family to Memphis, Texas, in 1913 and began playing fiddle and mandolin in square-dance bands. He moved to Fort Worth in 1929. A year later Wills joined the Light Crust Dough Boys with Milton Brown, and they began recording in 1932. Wills was fired from the band in 1933 for excessive drinking and personality conflicts with leader W. Lee O'Daniel. Wills left with banjoist Johnnie Lee Wills to form the Playboys, and they soon became regulars on radio broadcasts by WACO in Waco, Texas.

They moved to Tulsa, Oklahoma, and became regulars on KVOO. As Bob Wills and His Texas Playboys, they began recording for Brunswick in 1935. In the late '30s Wills's daughter Laura Lee became lead singer with the band; she also wrote songs, and later married Texas Playboys guitarist Dick McBride. In April 1940 they recorded the million-selling "San Antonio Rose" (#11 pop, #3 C&W, 1944), which also became a million-seller for Bing Crosby. Over the years Wills recorded another 22 C&W Top 10 hits, including these #1 singles: "Smoke on the Water" (1945), "Stars and Stripes on Iwo Jima" (1945), "Silver Dew on the Blue Grass Tonight" (1945), "White Cross on Okinawa" (1945), "New Spanish Two Step" (1946), and "Sugar Moon" (1947). Among his other well-known songs were "Faded Love," "Cotton Eyed Joe," "Take Me Back to Tulsa," and "Time Changes Everything."

Wills maintained the Texas Playboys through the early '60s. In 1962 his health began to deteriorate and he suffered a series of heart attacks. In 1968 he was named to the Country Music Hall of Fame. In 1973, during his last recording session, he suffered a stroke from which he never recovered, entering a coma that lasted until his death in 1975. A year later, the Texas Playboys reunited for some memorial concerts. In 1993 Asleep at the Wheel assembled a stellar cast of musicians for *A Tribute to Bob Wills and His Texas Playboys*. Among those participating were Garth Brooks, Merle Haggard, Brooks and Dunn, Willie Nelson, and several former Playboys.

Jackie Wilson

Born June 9, 1934, Detroit, MI; died Jan. 21, 1984, Mount Holly, NJ

1960—*Jackie Sings the Blues* (Brunswick); *My Golden Favorites; My Golden Favorites, vol. 2* 1962—*Jackie Wilson at the Copa* 1963—*Baby Workout* 1965—*Spotlight on Jackie Wilson* 1967—*Whispers* 1972—*Jackie Wilson's Greatest Hits* 1983—*The Jackie Wilson Story* (Epic) 1994—*The Very Best of Jackie Wilson* (Rhino).

Jackie Wilson was one of the premier black vocalists and performers of the late '50s and the '60s. No other singer of his generation so perfectly combined James Brown's rough, sexy style and Sam Cooke's smooth, gospel-polished pop.

Wilson grew up in a rough section of Detroit. In the late '40s, he lied about his age, entered the Golden Gloves, and won in his division. He later quit at his mother's request. He had sung throughout his childhood, and after high school, he began performing in local clubs. He was discovered by Johnny Otis at a talent show in 1951. In 1953 Wilson successfully auditioned for Billy Ward and His Dominoes [see entry], replacing Clyde McPhatter, who had left and formed the

Jackie Wilson

Drifters. Wilson sang lead on "St. Therese of the Roses," the group's second pop Top 20 hit in 1956.

Later that same year Wilson went solo, signing with Brunswick Records. His first single, the sassy " 'Reet Petite" (#62 pop, #11 R&B), written by his friend Berry Gordy Jr., appeared in 1957. In 1958 Wilson began making his mark with "To Be Loved" (#22 pop, #11 R&B) and "Lonely Teardrops" (#7 pop, #1 R&B), two more Gordy tunes. He hit his commercial stride in 1959 with "That's Why (I Love You So)" (#13 pop, #2 R&B), "I'll Be Satisfied" (#20 pop, #6 R&B), "You Better Know It" (#37 pop, #1 R&B), and "Talk That Talk" (#34 pop, #3 R&B). His success continued in 1960 with "Night" b/w "Doggin' Around" (#4 pop, #1 R&B), "All My Love," and "Am I the Man" b/w "Alone at Last" (#8 pop, #10 R&B). His stage show was as athletic as James Brown's, and the sexual hysteria surrounding was unparalleled. In 1961 he was shot and seriously wounded by a female fan in his New York apartment. That year he hit big with "My Empty Arms" (#9 pop, #10 R&B).

With the exception of the frenzied "Baby Workout" (#5 pop, #1 R&B) in 1963, Wilson's next few years yielded few hits. Then in 1966 he was matched with veteran producer Carl Davis, with whom he scored two hits: "Whispers (Gettin' Louder)" (#11 pop, #5 R&B) and "(Your Love Keeps Lifting Me) Higher and Higher" (#6 pop, #1 R&B). Unfortunately, these were Wilson's last great recordings, although he continued to chart singles as a pop-style crooner through 1972. By 1975 he was playing the oldies circuit. On September 25, 1975, at a Dick Clark revue in the Latin Casino in Cherry Hill, New Jersey, he suffered a heart attack onstage while singing "Lonely Teardrops," and was hospitalized and in a coma from which he emerged with significant brain damage. Eight years after the heart attack, Wilson died. He was inducted into the Rock and Roll Hall of Fame in 1987.

Kim Wilson: See the Fabulous Thunderbirds

Wilson Phillips

Formed 1989, Los Angeles, CA
Chynna Phillips (b. Feb. 12, 1968, Los Angeles), voc.; Carnie Wilson (b. Apr. 29, 1968, Los Angeles), voc.; Wendy Wilson (b. Oct. 16, 1969, Los Angeles), voc.
1990—*Wilson Phillips* (SBK) 1992—*Shadows and Light* 2000—*Greatest Hits.*
Carnie and Wendy Wilson: 1993—*Hey Santa!* (SBK) 1997—*The Wilsons.*
Chynna Phillips: *Naked and Sacred* (1995).

Wilson Phillips specialized in rich harmony vocals—no surprise given the group's lineage in two of the most popular pop-rock harmony units of the '60s. Chynna Phillips is the daughter of John and Michelle Phillips of the Mamas and the Papas, and Carnie and Wendy Wilson's father is Brian Wilson, the creative genius of the Beach Boys.

Despite their musical roots, none of the three thought of becoming singers until 1986, when inspired by Band Aid, Live Aid, and USA for Africa, Chynna Phillips first conceived of having famous musicians' children record together for charity. Phillips considered Frank Zappa's daughter Moon Unit, who had scored a left-field hit with "Valley Girl," and Ione Skye, the actress daughter of folksinger Donovan, but she instead turned to her old friends, the Wilson sisters.

From their first rehearsals, the story goes, they found their voices fitting together naturally—Carnie singing low harmony, Wendy singing high parts, and Chynna in between. They decided to work as a group, and briefly considered adding the late Mamas and Papas member Cass Elliot's daughter Owen. The trio polished its sound for two years, working with producer Richard Perry and with songwriter Glenn Ballard (who'd collaborated with Michael Jackson, among others). When music-publishing giant Charles Koppelman launched his SBK Records, Wilson Phillips was among his first signings. With its easy-listening tempos and girlish but rich harmonies, the group's debut album was a massive hit (#2, 1990) that sold over 5 million copies and yielded three #1 singles in "Hold On," "Release Me," and "You're in Love"; "Impulsive" was another big hit (#4, 1990).

In stark contrast, *Shadows and Light* was one of 1992's biggest disappointments: While it reached #4 shortly after its June release and was certified platinum, it failed to yield a hit single. Some observers blamed the album's darker songs—"Flesh and Blood" dealt with the Wilson sisters' troubled relationship with their father, and there was a song about rape—while others blamed a more mature, glamorous image that may have alienated the group's vast teenaged audience. Wilson Phillips canceled a planned summer tour for lack of ticket sales, and spent the rest of 1992 denying breakup rumors. The group disbanded the next year. Separately, Phillips recorded the solo *Naked and Sacred* in 1995, and the Wilson sisters cut a 1993 holiday-themed record, were reunited with their father for the 1995 documentary *I Just Wasn't Made for These Times,* and, in 1997, released the eponymous *The Wilsons.* Carnie also explored other media, launching a short-lived TV talk show in 1995, and, in a dramatic effort to resolve a lifelong struggle with her weight, undergoing gastric bypass surgery in an operation that was cybercast live over the Internet in 1999. In early 2001 the group performed together again at a televised tribute to Brian Wilson, and announced they would be recording a new album.

Jesse Winchester

Born May 17, 1944, Shreveport, LA
1971—*Jesse Winchester* (Ampex) 1972—*Third Down, 110 to Go* (Bearsville) 1974—*Learn to Love It* 1976—*Let the Rough Side Drag* 1977—*Nothin' but a Breeze* 1978—*A Touch on the Rainy Side* 1981—*Talk Memphis* (Bearsville) 1989—*Humor Me* (Sugar Hill) 1999—*Gentleman of Leisure.*

Singer/songwriter Jesse Winchester's early albums were tales of exile from a Southerner who had moved to Canada to avoid the draft. His later work, after he was granted amnesty, has leaned toward easygoing love songs, but Winchester still has a distinctive voice and a style that encompasses acoustic folk and Memphis rockabilly.

Winchester grew up in Memphis and played piano and sang with his church choir. He also learned guitar, and as a teenager he joined various unsuccessful rock bands. In 1967 he went to study in Munich, Germany, and when he found out that his draft notice had arrived at home, he went to Canada, where he's kept a residence ever since.

In 1970 Winchester met Robbie Robertson of the Band, who got him a management contract with Albert Grossman. Robertson produced and played on (with his bandmate Levon Helm) Winchester's debut LP, which included the much-covered songs "Biloxi," "The Brand New Tennessee Waltz," and "Yankee Lady." Todd Rundgren produced part of Winchester's second album (the title refers to Canadian football), and, like the debut, it garnered rave reviews.

Winchester became a Canadian citizen in 1973, and didn't tour the U.S. again until after President Jimmy Carter declared amnesty for draft evaders in 1977. Since then, he has appeared regularly in U.S. clubs, both with a band and as a solo performer. Although his following has never been much more than marginal, he continues to write constantly. In 1999 he emerged from a 12-year recording hiatus with *Gentleman of Leisure,* on which he was aided by guitarist Steve Cropper, the Fairfield Four, and a gospel group.

Winger/Kip Winger

Formed 1986, New York, NY
Kip Winger (b. June 21, 1961, Golden, CO), bass, voc.; Reb Beach (b. Aug. 31, 1963, Baltimore, MD), gtr.; Paul Taylor (b. 1960, San Francisco, CA), gtr., kybds.; Rod Morgenstein (b. Apr. 19, 1957, New York), drums.
1988—*Winger* (Atlantic) 1990—*In the Heart of the Young* (– Taylor; + John Roth [b. May 5, 1967, Springfield, IL], gtr.) 1993—*Pull.*
Kip Winger solo: 1997—*This Conversation Feels Like a Dream* (EMD/Domo) 1999—*Down Incognito* (Cleopatra) 2000—*Songs From the Ocean Floor* (Front, Swe).

Like Poison and Warrant, Winger was a popular light-metal rock group that combined poppy tunes and sex appeal. Hunky lead singer Kip Winger had studied classical piano and guitar with a Juilliard School of Music teacher, and had trained at the Joffrey Ballet School, before meeting Paul Taylor while both were in Alice Cooper's mid-'80s backing band. By 1986 they'd formed a band with drummer Rod Morgenstein, formerly with progressive-fusion band Dixie Dregs, and guitarist Reb Beach, who'd played sessions with Howard Jones, Chaka Khan, and the Bee Gees. The group originally called itself Sahara, but upon learning an L.A. band already had that name, became Winger.

Its debut album (#21, 1988) produced hits in "Seventeen" (#26, 1989) and "Headed for a Heartbreak" (#19, 1989). *In the Heart of the Young* (#15, 1990) had more hits in "Can't Get Enuff" (#42, 1990), "Miles Away" (#12, 1991), and "Easy Come Easy Go" (#41, 1991). Although, thanks to Kip Winger, the band was tremendously videogenic, its appeal quickly waned. Taylor left to pursue songwriting on his own; John Roth joined for *Pull,* a conscious attempt to essay lighter, more melodic songs that bombed, producing no hit singles. After that album's release, Morgenstein left to join the re-formed Dixie Dregs. Kip Winger pursued a solo career, recording *This Conversation Seems Like a Dream* in 1996. His wife, Beatrice, was killed in a car accident later that year. The 1999 release *Down Incognito* was a live acoustic best-of, with a subsequent studio album, *Songs From the Ocean Floor,* a reflection on his wife's death, with appearances by Morgenstein and Beach, and a duet with Moon Unit Zappa.

Wings: See Paul McCartney

Edgar Winter

Born Dec. 28, 1946, Beaumont, TX
1970—*Entrance* (Epic) 1971—*Edgar Winter's White Trash* 1972—*Roadwork* 1973—*They Only Come Out at Night* 1974—*Shock Treatment* 1975—*Jasmine Nightdreams* (Blue Sky); *The Edgar Winter Group With Rick Derringer* 1976—*Together: Live* (with Johnny Winter) 1977—*Recycled* 1979—*Edgar Winter Album* 1981—*Standing on Rock* (Blue Sky) 1989—*Mission Earth* (Rhino) 1990—*Live in Japan* (with Rick Derringer) (Cypress) 1991—*The Edgar Winter Collection* (Rhino) 1994—*Not a Kid Anymore* (Intersound) 1996—*The Real Deal* 1999—*Winter Blues* (Rhino).

Vocalist/keyboardist/saxophonist Edgar Winter is Johnny Winter's younger brother. Edgar was playing in a jazz group around the time that Johnny rose suddenly to fame in the late '60s. Edgar joined his brother's band, playing sax and keyboards, then left to pursue a solo career. [See Johnny's entry for Edgar's early biography.]

On his debut album, Edgar played many instruments himself; though it was critically well received, it sold poorly. For his next two albums, he formed the jazz/R&B horn band White Trash, which became a popular concert attraction (they played the closing night of New York's Fillmore East). Edgar broke the band up, however, and next formed the experimental hard-rock quartet the Edgar Winter Band, which featured bassist-vocalist Dan Hartman and guitarist Ronnie Montrose [see entry]. Their first release was a single, "Hangin' Around," backed by an instrumental called "Frankenstein." An edited "Frankenstein" became the A side of the single; it went to #1 in the U.S. and sold platinum worldwide, as did the Edgar Winter Band's first album, *They Only Come Out at Night* (#3, 1972).

In late 1973, as "Free Ride" (#14, 1973) became another smash hit single, guitarist Rick Derringer [see entry], who'd produced *White Trash* and *They Only,* joined Edgar's band, replacing Jerry Weems, who'd replaced Montrose. They became a major concert attraction, and *Shock Treatment* (#13, 1974), featuring Derringer, sold well. Edgar then recorded a solo LP, *Jasmine Nightdreams* (#69, 1975), but returned to the group for the more rock-oriented *With Rick Derringer* (#124, 1975).

Edgar appears on Johnny Winter's *Johnny Winter* and *Second Winter*, Derringer's *All American Boy* and *Spring Fever*, Dan Hartman's first three solo LPs, and Bette Midler's *Songs for the New Depression*. In 1976 he cut an album of oldies with brother Johnny. He has since released several additional solo works that mix blues and Southern rock. His "Way Down South" appeared on the *My Cousin Vinnie* soundtrack; his music has since been featured in numerous films. In 1990 he teamed up again with Derringer for a world tour that resulted in *Live in Japan*. In 1992 he performed with Johnny at the Ritz in New York; it was the first time the two had shared a stage in 15 years. Gigs supporting 1996's *The Real Deal* were billed as White Trash reunions, as they featured some of the same personnel.

Johnny Winter

Born Feb. 23, 1944, Leland, MS
1968—*The Progressive Blues Experiment* (Imperial) 1969—*Johnny Winter* (Columbia); *The Johnny Winter Story* (GRT) 1970—*Second Winter* (Columbia); *Johnny Winter And* 1971—*Live/Johnny Winter And; About Blues* (Janus); *Early Times* 1973—*Still Alive and Well* (Columbia) 1974—*Saints and Sinners; John Dawson Winter III* (Blue Sky) 1976—*Captured Live; Johnny and Edgar Winter Together* (with Edgar Winter) 1977—*Nothin' but the Blues* 1978—*White, Hot & Blue* 1980—*Raisin' Cain; Johnny Winter Story* 1984—*Guitar Slinger* (Alligator) 1985—*Serious Business* 1986—*Third Degree* 1988—*The Winter of '88* (Voyager) 1991—*Let Me In* (Point Blank/Virgin) 1992—*Hey, Where's Your Brother?* 1993—*Scorchin' Blues* (Columbia/Legacy); *Johnny Winter: A Rock 'n' Roll Collection* (Sony/Legacy) 1994—*White Lightning: Live at the Dallas International Motor Speedway* (Magnum) 1998—*Live in NYC '97* (Virgin).
With Muddy Waters: 1977—*Hard Again* (Blue Sky) 1978—*I'm Ready* 1979—*Muddy "Mississippi" Waters Live; King Bee.*

Johnny Winter came to fame as a much-heralded blues guitarist whose roots-based hard rock was widely popular in the '70s. Late in that decade he reverted to more traditional forms when he backed Muddy Waters in concert and on several recordings. Winter returned from a four-year break to record a series of acclaimed blues records, among them two that were nominated for Grammy awards.

He grew up in Beaumont, Texas, the son of a banjo- and saxophone-playing father and a piano-playing mother. Johnny and his younger brother Edgar—who are both albinos—learned how to play several instruments. The two brothers performed as an Everly Brothers–style duo and even auditioned for *Ted Mack's Original Amateur Hour* when Johnny was just 11. In their teens they formed local rock bands with names like Johnny and the Jammers, the Crystaliers, It and Them, and the Black Plague, playing mainly blues and rock. At age 15, with Johnny and the Jammers, Winter recorded his first record, "School Day Blues," for Dart Records in Houston. After graduating high school, Johnny enrolled in Lamar Technical College but soon dropped out.

Johnny Winter, Randy Hobbs, Richard Hughes

He hitchhiked to Louisiana, where he backed up local blues and rock musicians, and in the early '60s he traveled to Chicago, where he frequented blues clubs. In 1962 Winter played with Mike Bloomfield and Barry Goldberg, among others; they went on to form Electric Flag. Winter eventually returned to Texas, where he played with various journeyman blues bands. After a few years of garnering local raves on the Georgia-Florida circuit, a 1968 ROLLING STONE article, in which Winter was described as a "cross-eyed albino with long fleecy hair, playing some of the gutsiest fluid blues guitar you've ever heard," brought him to national attention. New York club owner Steve Paul read the article and flew out to Texas to sign Winter. Paul installed him as a regular attraction at his New York club, the Scene, and within weeks the guitarist was attracting capacity audiences.

Winter's debut album for Columbia sold well; concurrent with its release came *The Progressive Blues Experiment*, an album of demo tapes he had been peddling around before he got signed. *Second Winter*, recorded in Nashville, won even more ecstatic raves and bigger sales than the debut. The musicians soon assembled a new band (his previous one had been with him since his Texas journeyman days), which included his brother Edgar, guitarist Rick Derringer, bassist Randy Hobbs, and drummer Randy Zehringer from the McCoys, who'd had a massive hit a few years earlier with "Hang On Sloopy." They recorded *And,* after which Bobby Caldwell replaced Zehringer for *And Live.* While both albums were successful, Winter's heavy touring schedule and mounting heroin problem forced him to retire for a time.

He returned in 1973 with the biggest album of his career to date, *Still Alive and Well* (#22, 1973), which featured a song written for him by Mick Jagger and Keith Richards, "Silver Train." Critically, it and *Saints and Sinners* (#42, 1974) are considered Winter's last great, rock-oriented albums. In 1976 he worked with brother Edgar for the first time in several years on *Together* (#89, 1976); by that time, Edgar's popularity had eclipsed Johnny's. For *Nothin' but the Blues,* Winter was joined by Muddy Waters and his band, but the set received only moderate critical reaction and went largely unnoticed. Winter toured and frequently played festivals both solo and as a member of Waters' backing band. He produced and sat in on Waters' LPs *Hard Again, I'm Ready, King Bee,* and *Live. Hard Again* and *Muddy "Mississippi" Waters Live* both won Grammy awards.

Winter eventually took four years off. Like many of his white blues-rock contemporaries, he suddenly found himself out of vogue. The Grammy-nominated *Guitar Slinger* marked his return but in a more blues-roots vein. It, along with *Serious Business* and *Third Degree,* were critically acclaimed. *The Winter of '88* brought Winter back toward rock & roll but nowhere near the popular success he had enjoyed in the '70s. He remains one of the preeminent blues-rockers of his generation.

Steve Winwood

Born May 12, 1948, Birmingham, Eng.
1971—*Winwood* (United Artists) 1977—*Steve Winwood* (Island) 1980—*Arc of a Diver* 1982—*Talking Back to the Night* 1986—*Back in the High Life* 1987—*Chronicles* 1988—*Roll With It* (Virgin) 1990—*Refugees of the Heart* 1995—*The Finer Things* (Island Chronicles) 1997—*Junction 7* (Virgin).

Singer/keyboardist Steve Winwood has found his own hugely successful blend of pop and R&B after years of working with blues, pop, and experimental bands.

Winwood began playing piano as a child, and picked up bass, guitar, and drums as a teenager. At 15 he was a member of his older brother Muff Winwood's jazz band, and a year later the two joined the Spencer Davis Group [see entry]. Stevie Winwood's lead vocals and insistent organ riffs gave the band hits with "Gimme Some Lovin' " and "I'm a Man." At 18, Winwood participated in a studio group, Powerhouse, that included Eric Clapton on guitar; their tracks appeared on *What's Shakin',* an Elektra Records sampler. Winwood then went on to form Traffic [see entry], while Clapton worked with Cream. During Traffic's original on-again, off-again existence (1967–74), Winwood appeared with Clapton in the short-lived supergroup Blind Faith [see entry] and with Ginger Baker's Air Force.

In 1970 Winwood began work on a solo album to be called *Mad Shadows,* but it eventually became the re-formed Traffic's *John Barleycorn Must Die.* After Traffic's *When the Eagle Flies,* Winwood worked with Japanese percussionist Stomu Yamashta and German synthesizer player Klaus Schulze in 1976, resulting in an album, *Go,* and a concert at Royal Albert Hall in London. Winwood's 1977 solo debut, which used a backup band, was a modest success.

But *Arc of a Diver* (#3, 1981), on which Winwood played all the instruments but sang lyrics written by others (including Viv Stanshall of the Bonzo Dog Band and Will Jennings), went platinum, with a Top 10 single, "While You See a Chance" (#7, 1981). *Talking Back to the Night* (#28, 1982), made with the same method, did not fare as well as its predecessor, but four years later the triple-platinum *Back in the High Life* (#3, 1986) took Winwood to the top of the chart with the Grammy-winning "Higher Love" (#1, 1986, which featured Chaka Khan), "Freedom Overspill" (#20, 1986), and the title track (#13, 1987). It remains his most popular album to date. *Chronicles,* a best-of, included a hit in the remixed "Valerie" (#9, 1987), a song originally included on *Talking Back to the Night* that went only to #70 on its initial release.

Winwood's first album for Virgin, *Roll With It* (#1, 1988) was certified double platinum, with another trio of hit singles: "Roll With It" (#1, 1988), "Don't You Know What the Night Can Do?" (#6, 1988), and "Holding On" (#11, 1988). With *Refugees of the Heart* (#27, 1990) Winwood's MOR-ish formula seemed to have worn thin, although "One and Only Man" was a Top 20 hit. In 1994 Winwood rejoined Jim Capaldi in a much-heralded Traffic reunion. *The Finer Things* is a four-disc retrospective. The adult R&B pop of *Junction 7* (#123) failed to generate much excitement.

Wire

Formed 1976, London, Eng.
Colin Newman (b. Sep. 16, 1954, Salisbury, Eng.), gtr., voc.; Bruce Gilbert (b. May 18, 1946, Watford, Eng.), gtr.; Graham Lewis (b. Feb. 2, 1953, Grantham, Eng.), bass, voc.; Robert Gotobed (b. Mark Field, 1951, Leicester, Eng.), drums.
1977—*Pink Flag* (Harvest, U.K.) 1978—*Chairs Missing* 1979—*154* (Warner Bros.) 1981—*Document and Eyewitness* (Rough Trade, U.K.) 1984—*And Here It Is . . . Again . . . Wire* (Sneaky Pete) 1986—*Wire Play Pop* (Pink); *Snakedrill* EP (Mute-Enigma) 1987—*The Ideal Copy; Ahead* EP; *The Peel Sessions* EP (Strange Fruit, U.K.) 1988—*A Bell Is a Cup Until It Is Struck* (Mute-Enigma); *Kidney Bingos* EP (Mute-Restless); *Silk Skin Paws* EP (Mute) 1989—*It's Beginning to and Back Again* (Mute-Enigma); *The Peel Sessions Album* (Strange Fruit, U.K.); *On Returning (1977–1979)* (Restless Retro) 1990—*Manscape* (Mute-Enigma); *Life in the Manscape* EP 1991—*The Drill EP* (Mute-Elektra) 1993—*1985–1990: The A List* 1995—*Behind the Curtain* (EMI) 1996—*Turns & Strokes* (WMO)

1997—*Coatings* 1998—*Dugga Dugga Dugga.*
As Wir: 1991—*The First Letter* (Mute-Elektra).

Wire's art-school approach to punk set the U.K. quartet apart from its brasher contemporaries. Drawing more from avant-garde ideas about minimalism than from stripped-down rock & roll, Wire extracted the essential elements of pop—beat, rhythm, melody—and left it at that. The result was a deceptively simple, unemotional sound whose success rode on the tension between the group's often introspective lyrics, barked vocals, and sparse instrumentation. Despite little attention in the beginning, Wire's first three albums are among the most influential on the postpunk era, cited by Michael Stipe of R.E.M. and Robert Smith of the Cure.

Inspired by the burgeoning U.K. punk scene, and with only rudimentary knowledge of their instruments, South Londoners Colin Newman, Bruce Gilbert, Graham Lewis, and Robert Gotobed came together while attending the same art school. After appearing on an obscure live punk compilation, the band signed with Harvest, a mostly psychedelic/progressive-rock label, in September 1977. Wire's first release, *Pink Flag,* is a crudely produced, 21-track assault of throbbing bass, distortion, and dissonance, but also includes moments of gentle pop elegance. (R.E.M. covered the obscure *Pink Flag* song "Strange" on its first Top 10 album, *Document.*)

Wire stretched out on *Chairs Missing,* with slightly longer songs, more skillful playing, and occasional keyboard brushstrokes (played by producer Mike Thorne). The group expanded its sonic palette yet again on *154,* with added instrumentation and increased attention to production, resulting in a moodier, more sophisticated and textured sound. Its musical evolution complete, the band called it a day in 1980.

Had Wire stopped there, its impact on rock's future would still have been cemented. But in 1986, after five years of posthumous live releases and solo projects—Newman and Gotobed did four albums together under Newman's name; Gilbert and Lewis performed under several names including Dome—the quartet reunited. With an updated experimental synth-pop sound, Wire began churning out a string of albums and toured the U.S. for the first time in 1987. (During that tour, Wire refused to perform its classic early work, and instead had opening act the Ex–Lion Tamers perform the entire *Pink Flag* album.) That same year's *The Ideal Copy* approached the inventiveness of the first three albums, but none of the others were as well received. By 1991's *The Drill* EP, drummer Gotobed had tired of the group's increasing fascination with technology, particularly drum machines. When he left, the group responded by dropping the last letter from its name and releasing 1991's *The First Letter* as Wir before disbanding.

As the band's members explored solo projects (with the exception of Gotobed, who turned to organic farming and worked as a session drummer), the sound of Wire enjoyed an unexpected resurrection in 1995 when the edgy, minimalist riffing of "Three Girl Rhumba" was "borrowed" for Elastica's hit single "Connection." (Elastica paid Wire's song publishers an out-of-court fee.) The band re-formed momentarily in 1996 to play Gilbert's 50th birthday party. Then, in early 2000, Wire reconvened to perform at the Royal Festival Hall in London (after a Dublin warm-up gig). The band continued with a U.S. tour and a setlist that spanned its entire career. Wire also distributed live recordings via the band's Web site.

Bill Withers

Born July 4, 1938, Slab Fork, WV
1971—*Just As I Am* (Sussex) 1972—*Still Bill* 1973—*Bill Withers Live at Carnegie Hall* 1974—*+'Justments* 1975—*The Best of Bill Withers; Making Music* (Columbia) 1976—*Naked & Warm* 1977—*Menagerie; 'Bout Love* 1981—*Bill Withers' Greatest Hits* 1985—*Watching You Watching Me* 1994—*Lean on Me: The Best of Bill Withers* (Columbia/Legacy).

Singer/songwriter Bill Withers recorded a string of understated hits that mixed folk and soul music, including his classic "Lean on Me." He was nearly 30 years old before he sought a career in music. He graduated from high school and worked as a mechanic. In 1967 he moved to L.A. and, while working in an aerospace factory, began recording demos of his songs, which got no response. Withers had just learned how to play guitar, but he was considering giving up songwriting when he met Booker T. Jones in 1970.

Later in 1970 Jones produced and played on Withers' debut LP *Just As I Am* (#39, 1971), using MG's Al Jackson and Donald "Duck" Dunn as well as Stephen Stills, who shared guitar credits with Withers. The album contained the gold single "Ain't No Sunshine," which went to #3 in 1971 and was awarded a Grammy for Best R&B Song. That year Withers made his performing debut in L.A. His followup, "Grandma's Hands" (#42 pop, #18 R&B, 1971) has since been recorded by a number of other singers.

Recorded with members of the Watts 103rd St. Rhythm Band, *Still Bill* (#4, 1972) was even more successful, containing "Lean on Me" (#1 pop and R&B, 1972) and "Use Me" (#2 pop and R&B, 1972). Other hits included "Let Us Love" (#17 R&B, 1972), "Kissing My Love" (#12 R&B, 1973) and "Friend of Mine" (#25 R&B, 1973). The album was certified gold and remains the singer's most successful to date. After two more albums for Sussex, Withers signed with Columbia in 1975, and there he recorded six LPs. *Making Music* (#81, 1975) contained "Make Love to Your Mind" (#10 R&B), and his second gold album, *Menagerie* (#39, 1977), had "Lovely Day" (#30 pop, #6 R&B). But subsequent releases were not nearly as successful as his earlier albums.

He sang on the Crusaders' *Rhapsody in Blues,* then on Grover Washington Jr.'s *Winelight* in 1981. For the latter, he cowrote and sang "Just the Two of Us" (#2 pop, #3 R&B), one of that year's most popular singles. He also recorded a single, "U.S.A." He was basically retired from recording until 1985's *Watching You Watching Me.* He continued to tour occasionally, often with Washington. In the '90s various rappers have sampled Withers' music.

Peter Wolf: See J. Geils Band

Bobby Womack

Born Mar. 4, 1944, Cleveland, OH
1968—*Fly Me to the Moon* (Minit) 1971—*The Womack "Live"* (Liberty) 1971—*Communication* (United Artists) 1972—*Understanding* 1973—*Facts of Life; Across 110th Street* soundtrack (United Artists) 1974—*Lookin' for a Love Again; Bobby Womack's Greatest Hits; I Don't Know What the World's Coming To* 1976—*Safety Zone; BW Goes C&W; Home Is Where the Heart Is* (Columbia); *Pieces* 1979—*Roads of Life* (Arista) 1981—*The Poet* (Beverly Glen) 1984—*The Poet II* 1985—*So Many Rivers* (MCA); *Someday We'll All Be Free* (Beverly Glen) 1986—*Womagic* (MCA) 1987—*The Last Soul Man* 1989—*Save the Children* (with the Womack Brothers) (Solar) 1994—*Resurrection* (Slide/Continuum) 1996—*Only Survivor: The MCA Years* (MCA) 1999—*Traditions* (Capitol); *Back to My Roots.*

As a writer and performer, guitarist Bobby Womack has been one of the most important black musicians of the last 25 years, composing a number of rock and soul standards as well as such diverse songs as Janis Joplin's "Trust Me" and George Benson's hit "Breezin'."

Womack and his four brothers—Cecil, Curtis, Harris, and Friendly Jr.—formed a gospel group, the Womack Brothers, in the late '50s. On the gospel circuit, they met the Soul Stirrers and lead singer Sam Cooke, who later recruited Womack as guitarist for his own pop band. Cooke then signed the Womack Brothers to his Sar label, where, as the Valentinos, they cut two R&B classics, "It's All Over Now" and "Lookin' for a Love" (#8 R&B, 1962). The former would be a major hit for the Rolling Stones, the latter for the J. Geils Band.

After Cooke's death and the Valentinos' breakup, Womack became a top session guitarist, and has played on recordings by Aretha Franklin, King Curtis, Dusty Springfield, and Ray Charles, among others. By then he had married Cooke's widow, Barbara; they divorced in 1970. (Later his brother Cecil would marry Cooke's daughter Linda and form the writing and producing duo of Womack and Womack.) He also continued writing. His "I'm a Midnight Mover" and "I'm in Love" were hits for Wilson Pickett. Womack wrote and played acoustic guitar on Janis Joplin's "Trust Me."

Reviving his solo career in the late '60s, Womack had a few moderate soul hits on the Minit label, but really picked up when he moved to United Artists. His solo career took off in the early '70s with "That's the Way I Feel About 'Cha" (#27 pop, #2 R&B) in 1971; "Woman's Got to Have It" (#1 R&B) and "Harry Hippie" (#8 R&B) in 1972; and "Nobody Wants You When You're Down and Out" (#2 R&B) in 1973. Later R&B hits include "Lookin' for a Love" (#10 pop, #1 R&B, 1974), "You're Welcome, Stop On By" (#5 R&B, 1974), "Check It Out" (#6 R&B, 1975), and "Daylight" (#5, 1976). His albums with Columbia and Arista saw Womack in a commercial decline. According to some sources, Womack, who counted Sly Stone among his closest friends, also had a drug problem. But in

Bobby Womack

1981 he announced he had cleaned up, and he made a tremendous comeback with the #1 R&B LP *The Poet* and a #3 R&B single, "If You Think You're Lonely Now." Later R&B hits include a duet with Patti LaBelle, "Love Has Finally Come at Last" (#3 R&B, 1984) and "I Wish He Didn't Trust Me So Much" (#2 R&B, 1985).

After that, Womack seemed to have disappeared. He appeared with Artists United Against Apartheid, duetted with Mick Jagger on the Rolling Stones' *Dirty Work* ("Going Back to Memphis"), and he reunited with his brothers for *Save the Children,* but he released no new albums for nearly five years. He appeared on Paul Shaffer's *Coast to Coast* and Todd Rundgren's *Nearly Human.* After a period of personal turmoil, Womack reemerged with *Resurrection,* the first album released on Ron Wood's Slide Music label. (Womack had produced Wood's solo debut album in 1974.) It includes guest appearances by Keith Richards, Wood, Charlie Watts, Stevie Wonder, Brian May, and others.

Stevie Wonder

Born Steveland Judkins Morris, May 13, 1950, Saginaw, MI
1962—*Tribute to Uncle Ray* (Motown); *The Jazz Soul of Little Stevie Wonder* 1963—*The 12 Year Old Genius; With a Song in My Heart; Workout, Stevie, Workout* (Tamla); *Little Stevie Wonder* (Motown) 1964—*At the Beach* (Tamla); 1965—*Stevie Wonder* (Motown) 1966—*Up-Tight Everything's Alright; Down to Earth* 1967—*I Was Made to Love Her* 1968—*Greatest Hits; Alfie; For Once in My Life; Eivets Rednow* 1969—*My Cherie Amour;* 1970—*Stevie Wonder Live* (Tamla); *Talk of the Town* (Motown); *Signed Sealed & Delivered* (Tamla) 1971—*Where I'm Coming From; Stevie Wonder's Greatest Hits, vol. 2* 1972—*Music of My Mind; Talking Book* 1973—*Innervisions* 1974—*Fulfillingness' First Finale* 1976—*Songs in the Key of Life;*

Portrait (EMI) 1977—*Looking Back* (Motown) 1979—*Journey Through the Secret Life of Plants* (Tamla) 1980—*Hotter Than July* 1982—*Stevie Wonder's Original Musiquarium I* 1984—*The Woman in Red* soundtrack (Motown) 1985—*In Square Circle* (Tamla) 1987—*Characters* (Motown) 1991—*Music From the Movie Jungle Fever* 1995—*Conversation Peace; Natural Wonder* 1996—*Song Review—Greatest Hits.*

Groomed from an early age for Motown stardom, Stevie Wonder mastered that label's distinctive fusion of pop and soul and then went on to compose far more idiosyncratic music—an ambitious hybrid of sophisticated Tin Pan Alley chord changes and R&B energy, inflected with jazz, reggae, and African rhythms. A synthesizer and studio pioneer, he is one of the few musicians to make records on which he plays virtually all the instruments, and does so with both convincing technique and abandon. A lifelong advocate of nonviolent political change patterned after Martin Luther King Jr. and Mahatma Gandhi, Wonder epitomizes '60s utopianism while remaining resolutely contemporary in his musical experiments.

Stevie Morris' prodigious musical talents were recognized when Ronnie White of the Miracles heard the 10-year-old boy, blind from infancy, playing the harmonica for his children, and introduced him to Berry Gordy Jr. of the Hitsville U.S.A.—soon Motown—organization. Gordy named him Little Stevie Wonder. His third single, "Fingertips (Part 2)" was a #1 pop and R&B hit eight months later. Both on records and in live shows he was featured playing harmonica, drums, piano, and organ, as well as singing—sometimes all in one number.

During his first three years in show business, Wonder was presented as an R&B screamer in the Ray Charles mold; much was made of the fact that both were blind. In 1964 he appeared on the screen in *Muscle Beach Party* and *Bikini Beach*. *Uptight* (#3, 1966) included "I Was Made to Love Her" (#2, 1967), "For Once in My Life" (#2, 1968), and "Shoo-Be-Doo-Be-Doo-Da-Day" (#9, 1968). The Wonder style broadened to include Bob Dylan's "Blowin' in the Wind" (#9, 1966), the optimistic "A Place in the Sun" (#9, 1968), and an instrumental version of Burt Bacharach's "Alfie." In 1969 he hit the upper reaches of the charts with the ballads "My Cherie Amour" (#4) and "Yester-Me, Yester-You, Yesterday" (#7).

As his adolescence came to an end, Wonder took charge of his career. By the time of *Signed Sealed & Delivered* (#25, 1970), he was virtually self-sufficient in the studio, serving as his own producer and arranger, playing most of the instruments himself, and writing material with his wife, Syreeta Wright. In this phase, he scored three more hit singles: "Signed, Sealed, Delivered I'm Yours" (#3, 1970), "Heaven Help Us All" (#9, 1970), and "If You Really Love Me" (#8, 1971).

When he reached his 21st birthday in 1971, he negotiated a new contract with Motown that made him the label's first artist to win complete artistic control (also at 21 he was due the money he had made as a minor; despite earning over $30 million, he received only $1 million). While his singles upheld the company tradition of hook-happy radio fare, they distinguished themselves with such socially conscious subjects as ghetto hardship and political disenfranchisement, especially in evidence in "Living for the City" (#8, 1973). His albums, beginning with *Music of My Mind* (#21, 1972), on which he played most of the instruments, were devoted to his more exotic musical ideas (which incorporated gospel, rock & roll, jazz, and African and Latin rhythms). To his panoply of instruments, he added synthesizers; played with rare invention and funk, they became the signature of his sound.

Wonder's 1972 tour of the United States with the Rolling Stones helped make #1 hits of two singles released within the next year—"Superstition" (written for Jeff Beck) and "You Are the Sunshine of My Life"—from *Talking Book* (#3, 1972). The period was difficult personally for Wonder: In 1972 his marriage to Wright ended after only a year (later, with companion Yolanda Simmons, he had two children, as well as a third child by vocalist Melody McCulley). In 1973 he was in a serious car crash that left him in a coma for four days.

In the four years and three albums following *Talking Book*, Wonder made three more #1 singles ("You Haven't Done Nothin'," "I Wish," and "Sir Duke"), sold millions of each, and received 15 Grammy Awards. *Innervisions* (#4, 1973) also included "Higher Ground" (#4, 1973), while *Fulfillingness' First Finale* (#1, 1974) yielded "Boogie On Reggae Woman" (#3, 1974). His songs were covered widely, and he was an acknowledged influence on musicians from Jeff Beck to George Benson to Bob Marley. Working with B.B. King, the Jacksons, the Supremes, Minnie Ripperton, Rufus, and Syreeta Wright, he established himself as a major songwriter and producer. *Songs in the Key of Life* (#1, 1976) (a double album released after he had signed a $13-million contract

Stevie Wonder

with Motown) was a *tour de force* and topped the charts for 14 weeks.

Journey Through the Secret Life of Plants (#4, 1979) three years in the making, was ostensibly the soundtrack to an unreleased film of the same name. Predominantly instrumental, it failed to catch on in a big way at the time but can be seen as a precursor to New Age music. *Hotter Than July* (#3, 1980) returned to the street-dancing spirit of earlier periods (updated in contemporary idioms such as reggae and rap). It yielded "Master Blaster (Jammin')" (#5, 1980) and Wonder's plea for an international holiday in memory of Martin Luther King Jr., "Happy Birthday." In 1982 fans still waiting for an album of new material were placated with hit singles: "That Girl" (#4), "Do I Do" (#13), "Ebony and Ivory"(#1)—a duet with Paul McCartney—and the greatest-hits package *Musiquarium* (#4, 1982).

The '80s saw Wonder drastically curtailing studio work but continuing to tour (by the end of the decade becoming Motown's first artist to play the Eastern bloc). In 1982, with Bob Dylan and Jackson Browne, he played the "Peace Sunday" antinuclear rally at the Rose Bowl. In 1984 Detroit gave him the key to the city (he later considered a run for mayor of Detroit), and he played harmonica on Elton John's "I Guess That's Why They Call It the Blues." Participating in the recording of USA for Africa's "We Are the World" in 1985, he won that year's Oscar for Best Song for "I Just Called to Say I Love You," (#1, 1984) off *The Woman in Red* (#4, 1984) soundtrack. Dedicating the award to Nelson Mandela, he angered South African radio stations, which then banned all his music.

"Part-Time Lover" (#1, 1985) became the first single simultaneously to top the pop, R&B, Adult Contemporary, and dance/disco charts; its parent album, *In Square Circle*, reached #5 and won the Grammy for Best R&B Male Vocal Performance. Singing with Elton John and Gladys Knight on Dionne Warwick's "That's What Friends Are For" (#1, 1986) gained Wonder another hit, but, deemed relatively lightweight, neither *Characters* (#17, 1987) nor the soundtrack for Spike Lee's *Jungle Fever* (#24, 1991) were greeted with the almost universal acclaim his '70s work had generated.

In 1988 duets with Michael Jackson ("Get It") and Julio Iglesias ("My Love") kept Wonder's name before the public. And, inducted into the Rock and Roll Hall of Fame in 1989 and earning a Lifetime Achievement Grammy, Stevie Wonder continued to enjoy an ultimately unassailable critical reputation even while his recording output was slender. In 1995, four years after receiving the Nelson Mandela Courage Award, he released *Conversation Peace*, an intended epic he'd been working on since the late '80s. Critics greeted the 74-minute long work with mixed reviews but were heartened by his return to recording after an eight-year absence. In 1999 Wonder performed at the halftime show for Super Bowl XXXIII and was among the recipients of the Kennedy Center Honors. He also made a rare hour-long appearance on *Donny & Marie*, where he performed a number of his hits, mostly accompanying himself on keyboards.

Wonder's extensive humanitarian work has concentrated on AIDS awareness; antiapartheid efforts; crusades against drunk driving and drug abuse; and fund-raising for blind and retarded children and the homeless.

Roy Wood: See the Move

World Party

Formed 1986, London, Eng.
Karl Wallinger (b. Oct. 19, 1957, Prestatyn, Wales), voc., kybds., various instr.
1986—*Private Revolution* (Chrysalis) 1990—*Goodbye Jumbo* 1991—*Thank You World* EP 1993—(+ Dave Caitlin-Birch, gtr.; + Chris Sharrock, drums) *Bang!* (– Caitlin-Birch) 1997—*Egyptology* (the Enclave) 2000—*Dumbing Up* (Papillon, U.K.).

Former Waterboys keyboardist Karl Wallinger formed World Party essentially as a solo act, writing and singing all of the songs, arranging and playing most of the instruments, recording and producing himself in his home studio, and generally establishing the "band" as a vehicle for his singular musical vision. A true child of the '60s, Wallinger adapted his infatuation with the Beatles, Jimi Hendrix, and other pop geniuses of that era to fresh, often stunning melodies (accompanied by socially astute lyrics), shimmering guitar-pop textures, and buoyant, often funky rhythms. While this somewhat nostalgic formula engendered much acclaim, World Party's commercial performance generally failed to match its critical success.

Predictably, it was a desire for more creative control that led to Wallinger, once the musical director of the London production of *The Rocky Horror Picture Show*, leaving the Waterboys [see entry]—for all intents and purposes Mike Scott's band—after the release of 1985's *This Is the Sea*, although a song he cowrote entitled "World Party" appeared on that group's 1988 album, *Fisherman's Blues*. In 1987 his first World Party single, the ominous, environmentally conscious "Ship of Fools," went to #27 on the singles chart, becoming the act's biggest hit to date. Its debut album, *Private Revolution*, reached #39, also in 1987. *Goodbye Jumbo* also had its share of ecological references and warnings—and featured a guest vocal by rising star Sinéad O'Connor (as well as appearances by Waterboys Steve Wickham and Anthony Thistlethwaite)—but didn't spawn a Top 40 single, although the track "Way Down Now" was popular in new-wave dance clubs. The album peaked at #73. In promoting *Jumbo* Wallinger toured with two British musicians, guitarist Dave Caitlin-Birch, who had played Paul McCartney in *The Bootleg Beatles* (the British version of the stage show *Beatlemania*) and onetime Lightning Seeds drummer Chris Sharrock, who became Wallinger's core support team, collaborating with him on World Party's next album. (The touring band also included synth player Max Edie, keyboardists Guy Chambers and Ken Campbell, and guitarist Steve McKewan.) That album, *Bang!*, was released in 1993 and reached #2 in the U.K. In the States, however, it only made #126.

Wallinger broke out of his reclusive recording ways in 1994 to act as musical director for the movie *Reality Bites;* he scored the soundtrack to *Clueless* a year later. He released the thoughtful *Egyptology,* featuring Sharrock on drums, in 1997, and he and his touring band went on the road. *Dumbing Up* was released in England in 2000.

Link Wray

Born May 2, 1929, Dunn, NC
1960—*Link Wray and the Wraymen* (Epic) 1963—*Jack the Ripper* (Swan) 1970—*Yesterday-Today* (Record Factory) 1971—*Link Wray* (Polydor) 1973—*There's Good Rockin' Tonight* (Union Pacific) 1976—*Stuck in Gear* (Virgin, U.K.) 1979—*Bullshot* (Charisma/Visa, U.K.) 1980—*Live at the Paradiso* 1992—*Walkin' With Link* (Epic Legacy) 1993—*Rumble! The Best of Link Wray* (Rhino) 1995—*Guitar Preacher: The Polydor Years* (Polydor); *Mr. Guitar* (Norton) 1997—*Shadowman* (Hip-O) 2000—*Barbed Wire* (Ace, U.K.).
With Robert Gordon: 1977—*Robert Gordon With Link Wray* (Private Stock) 1978—*Fresh Fish Special.*

One of the most inflential rock guitarist of the '50s, Link Wray introduced the distorted fuzz-tone guitar sound on his million-selling single "Rumble." For that tune, Wray and his band the Wraymen wanted to approximate the effect of a brawl that took place in a dancehall where they were performing. Wray punctured the speaker in his amplifier with a pencil, which added the crackling, burry fuzz-tone sound to a brooding, ominous mid-tempo riff, anticipating heavy metal by more than a decade.

Wray, who is part Native American, learned bottle-neck guitar as a youth, after moving with family to Arizona. He formed a country band in his late teens with his brothers Doug and Vernon (who sometimes sang under the name Ray Vernon), playing bars, juke joints, and brothels under the name Lucky Wray and the Lazy Pine Wranglers, later the Palomino Ranch Hands. After returning from the Korean War, where he lost a lung to tuberculosis, Wray was advised not to sing. Soon the group became a trio—Wray, Doug Wray on drums, and Shorty Horton on bass, with Vernon Wray producing and occasionally playing rhythm guitar and piano on a few tracks—the Ray Men.

In 1954 Wray recorded "Rumble," cowritten by Wray and local DJ Milt Grant; by 1958 it had sold over a million copies, and it reached #16 that year. By that time Wray had also played on sessions backing his brother Vernon and with Fats Domino and Rick Nelson on Milt Grant's Washington, DC, TV show. In 1959 Wray had another instrumental hit with the rockabilly-style "Raw-Hide" (#23, 1959). Several similar followups failed to hit, however, and by the mid-'60s Wray had retired to a family farm commune in Maryland, where he built a 3-track studio in a shed, playing live only occasionally in local bars. He recorded in his shed quite often, though; word has it that when his backup musicians could not afford drums, Wray had them stomp on the floor and rattle pots, pans, and beer cans instead. Many of Wray's 3-track recordings were issued on the 1971 *Link Wray,* a critically acclaimed LP that sold little and was largely made possible by the acclaim Wray had garnered from rock stars like Pete Townshend of the Who, Jeff Beck and Bob Dylan, and the Kinks.

Wray followed the 1971 LP with several more unsuccessful albums. In 1977 he began working with singer Robert Gordon [see entry], but they parted company a year later, after recording *Fresh Fish Special.* In 1979 Wray recorded *Bullshot,* which was unspectacularly received. Wray has since moved to an island off the coast of Denmark. The 1993 Rhino best-of compiles 20 tracks from the several labels for which he recorded. In 1997 Wray played his first American gigs in 12 years and began performing more frequently in North America. His latest studio releases, *Shadowman* and *Barbed Wire,* are louder and rawer than ever. "Rumble" was used in the '90s films *Pulp Fiction* and *Independence Day.*

Betty Wright

Born Dec. 21, 1953, Miami, FL
1968—*My First Time Around* (Atco) 1972—*I Love the Way You Love* (Alston) 1973—*Hard to Stop* 1974—*Danger: High Voltage* 1976—*Explosion!* 1977—*This Time for Real* 1978—*Live* 1979—*Betty Travelin' in the Wright Circle* 1981—*Betty Wright* (Epic) 1986—*Sevens* (First String) 1988—*Mother Wit* (Ms. B) 1989—*4U2NJOY* 1992—*The Best of Betty Wright* (Rhino) 1994—*B-Attitudes* (Ms. B.).

Betty Wright's fiery soul vocals made her a strong presence on Miami's black music scene of the '70s. She continued to make regular appearances on the R&B chart through the late '80s.

Wright started as a gospel singer with her family group, Echoes of Joy. She turned to R&B at age 13, after being discovered singing along to Billy Stewart's "Summertime" by songwriter/producers Willie Clarke and Clarence Reid. They recorded "Paralyzed," which got some local attention. Two years later, at 14, her "Girls Can't Do What the Guys Do" (#33 pop, #15 R&B) began an association with Miami's T.K. Records stable (including the Alston label) that would continue until that company's demise in the late '70s.

Wright was 18 when her spunky late 1971 hit "Clean Up Woman" (#6 pop, #2 R&B) was certified gold. Her other hits included "Baby Sitter" (#46 pop, #6 R&B, 1972), "Let Me Be Your Lovemaker" (#10 R&B, 1973), and "Where Is the Love" (#15 R&B, 1975), which won a Grammy. In addition to cowriting many of her hits (including the three listed above), she also contributed background vocals to T.K. disco hits by KC and the Sunshine Band and Peter Brown in the '70s.

In 1981 Wright moved to Epic; her first album there included "What Are You Going to Do With It," a collaboration between Wright and Stevie Wonder. Later that summer, she contributed the feisty rap to Richard "Dimples" Fields's "She's Got Papers on Me" that helped make it a major R&B

hit. Her second and last Epic album was produced by Marlon Jackson. She then recorded for the independent First String without success before starting her own Ms. B label. Her last two major R&B chart entries were "No Pain, No Gain" (#14 R&B, 1988) and "From Pain to Joy" (#39 R&B, 1989). She remains musically active, often as a guest vocalist or producer.

Gary Wright

Born Apr. 26, 1943, Creskill, NJ
1970—*Extraction* (A&M) 1971—*Foot Print* 1972—*Ring of Changes* (with Wonderwheel) 1975—*The Dream Weaver* (Warner Bros.); *Light of Smiles* 1977—*Touch and Gone* 1979—*Headin' Home* 1981—*The Right Place* 1988—*Who I Am* 1995—*First Signs of Life* (Worldly) 2000—*Human Love* (Orchard).

Gary Wright, ex-Spooky Tooth member and successful late-'70s solo act, started out as a child actor, debuting on the *Captain Video* TV show in New York at age seven. He also appeared in TV and radio commercials and in the Broadway play *Fanny*, all the while studying piano and organ. He joined various high school rock bands, went to college to study psychology in New York and then to Berlin, Germany.

In Europe, Wright met Mike Harrison, and the two began performing together, leading to the formation of Spooky Tooth [see entry]. When Spooky Tooth temporarily disbanded in 1970, Wright turned to a solo career, forming the band Wonderwheel. His solo work attracted little attention, though, and in 1973 he returned to the re-formed Spooky Tooth. When the band broke up for good in 1974, Wright again embarked on solo ventures, this time with much more success.

The mellow synthesizer-dominated *Dream Weaver* yielded #2 hit singles in the title tune and "My Love Is Alive," and the LP went platinum. No more hit singles were forthcoming, but Wright's subsequent albums won heavy airplay on FM radio. "Dream Weaver" was revived for a new generation, thanks to its inclusion in *Wayne's World*. Subsequent albums, filled with Wright's proto-New Age lyrics, proved less successful. Only *The Light of Smiles* (#23, 1977) and *The Right Place*, which featured Wright's last hit single, "Really Wanna Know You" (#16, 1981) were popular.

O.V. Wright

Born Overton Vertis Wright, Oct. 9, 1939, Leno, TN; died Nov. 16, 1980
1965—*O.V. Wright* (Backbeat) 1966—*Nucleus of Soul* 1970—*Ace of Spades* 1971—*A Nickel and a Nail* 1973—*Memphis Unlimited* 1975—*Into Something I Can't Shake* (Hi) 1978—*The Bottom Line* 1992—*The Soul of O.V. Wright* (Duke-Peacock).

A Memphis soul singer with a dark and moody voice, Wright never attained the level of success some critics believe he deserved. Like many soul singers, he began singing gospel in church as a child. He led a group called the Five Harmonaires, then joined such better known assemblages as the Sunset Travellers, the Spirit of Memphis Quartet, and the Highway QC's. He and Roosevelt Jamison cowrote "That's How Strong My Love Is," which Wright recorded. His commercial frustrations began in 1965, when Otis Redding's version hit before Wright's did.

Wright did have several R&B hits of his own, including "You're Gonna Make Me Cry" (#6 R&B, 1965), "Eight Men, Four Women" (#4 R&B, 1967), "Ace of Spade" (#11 R&B, 1970), "A Nickel and a Nail" (#19 R&B, 1971), and "I'd Rather Be Blind, Crippled and Crazy" (#33 R&B, 1973). But despite high critical praise and the chilling quality of songs like "Ace of Spade," popular acclaim eluded Wright. Although he continued to record through the '70s, he also suffered from drug abuse, which precipitated a fatal heart attack at age 41.

Richard Wright: See Pink Floyd

Syreeta Wright

Born Rita Wright, Pittsburgh, PA
1972—*Syreeta* (Mowest) 1974—*Stevie Wonder Presents Syreeta* 1977—*One to One* (Tamla); *Rich Love, Poor Love* (with G.C. Cameron) (Motown) 1980—*Syreeta* (Tamla) 1981—*Billy Preston and Syreeta* (with Billy Preston) (Motown) 1981—*Set My Love in Motion* (Tamla) 1983—*The Spell*.

As a performer, Syreeta Wright has had only one major hit, a duet with Billy Preston on "With You I'm Born Again" (#4 pop) in 1980. But as a writer she contributed to a number of artists, most significantly to her ex-husband, Stevie Wonder.

She cut a single, "Can't Give Back the Love I Feel for You," in 1968. After it flopped, she worked as a Motown secretary and occasional background singer. She met Wonder and began songwriting as a result. She is the cowriter of such Wonder hits as "Signed, Sealed, Delivered" and "If You Really Love Me." In early 1970, Berry Gordy Jr. wanted Wright to replace Diana Ross in the Supremes, but Mary Wilson refused. Wonder produced Syreeta's first two albums. *Syreeta* and *Stevie Wonder Presents Syreeta*. She married Wonder on September 14, 1970; they divorced 18 months later.

During that period, Wonder first sought and achieved artistic independence from Motown, with one result being some of the most acclaimed work of his career. Wright cowrote songs on Wonder's *Music of My Mind, The Secret Life of Plants,* and *Talking Book*. On the latter she cowrote "Blame It on the Sun" and "Lookin' for Another Pure Love." She continued recording for Motown, but with virtually no chart success until her duet with Billy Preston, "With You I'm Born Again" (#4, 1980). *The Spell*, produced by Jermaine Jackson, did not improve her fortunes, and shortly thereafter she retired from performing. In the late '80s she began recording again for the British Motorcity label. She appeared on

Broadway in a 1995 revival of *Jesus Christ Superstar* in the role of Mary Magdalene.

Wu-Tang Clan

Formed 1990, Staten Island, NY
RZA/Prince Rakeem (b. Robert Diggs, July 5, Brooklyn, NY), voc.; GZA/Genius (b. Gary Grice, Aug. 22, Brooklyn), voc.; Ol' Dirty Bastard (b. Russell Jones, Nov. 15, 1968, Brooklyn), voc.; Inspectah Deck (b. Jason Hunter, July 6, Bronx, NY), voc.; Raekwon (b. Corey Woods, Jan. 20, Brooklyn), voc.; U-God (b. Lamont Hawkins, Nov. 10, Staten Island), voc.; Ghostface Killah (b. Dennis Coles, May 9, 1970, Staten Island), voc.; Method Man (b. Clifford Smith, Mar. 21, 1970, Staten Island, NY), voc.; Masta Killa (b. Elgin Turner, Aug. 18), voc.
1993—*Enter the Wu-Tang (36 Chambers)* (Loud) 1997—*Wu-Tang Forever* 2000—*The W.*
GZA/Genius solo: 1991—*Words From the Genius* (Cold Chillin') 1995—*Liquid Swords* (DGC) 1999—*Beneath the Surface* (MCA).
RZA (with Gravediggaz): 1994—*6 Feet Deep* (Gee Street) 1997—*The Pick, The Sickle and the Shovel.*
RZA solo: 1998—*RZA as Bobby Digital in Stereo* (Gee Street) 1999—*The RZA Hits* (Razor Sharp).
Method Man solo: 1994—*Tical* (Def Jam) 1998—*Tical 2000: Judgement Day.*
Method Man & Redman: 1999—*Blackout!* (Def Jam).
Ol' Dirty Bastard solo: 1995—*Return to the 36 Chambers: The Dirty Version* (Elektra) 1999—*Nigga Please.*
Raekwon solo: 1995—*Only Built 4 Cuban Linx . . .* (Loud) 1999—*Immobilarity.*
Ghostface Killah solo: 1996—*Ironman* (Razor Sharp) 2000—*Supreme Clientele.*
Inspectah Deck solo: 1999—*Uncontrolled Substance* (Loud).
U-God solo: 1999—*Golden Arms Redemption* (Wu Tang/Priority).

The Wu-Tang Clan established a hip-hop empire with street poetics, kung fu mythology, ingenious production and entrepreneurial savvy. The outfit's rugged beats and top-notch MCing have taken the two-turntables-and-a-mike foundation of hip-hop to its grimiest, and arguably most artistic extreme.

A collective of relatives and close friends, the Wu-Tang Clan has its roots in the hostile housing projects of Staten Island, New York (also referred to as Shaolin in Wu lore). Cousins RZA and GZA, the Wu-Tang Clan's forefathers, began collaborating as early as 1976—when RZA was eight years old. As break dancing and freestyle circles sprang up all over New York City, RZA and GZA began writing rhymes and challenging other MCs to battle. During junior high school, RZA befriended Ghostface Killah, U-God, Ol' Dirty Bastard, Method Man, and Raekwon. In 1987, while selling marijuana, RZA purchased a 4-track and began moonlighting as a producer.

Around the time RZA was on trial for attempted murder (in 1992 he was acquitted on the grounds of self-defense), the Wu-Tang Clan recorded its first single "Protect Ya Neck." The group members sold the single to local record stores and radio stations, and it became an underground success. Loud Records soon signed the Wu-Tang Clan to a deal that gave the group members creative control and the freedom to negotiate solo projects with other labels. In 1993 Loud released *Enter the Wu-Tang (36 Chambers)* (#41 pop, #8 R&B), a ghetto narrative filled with martial-arts metaphysics and cryptic instrumentation. Songs like "C.R.E.A.M." (#60 pop, #32 R&B, 1994) and "Can It Be All So Simple" (#82 R&B, 1994) introduced RZA's knack for juxtaposing beats, poignant subject matter, and street vernacular. The video for "Da Mystery of Chessboxin'," depicting hooded swordsmen in black and white masks dueling on a giant chessboard, received frequent airplay on BET's *Rap City* and illustrated the group's mystic philosophies.

In 1994 Method Man's *Tical* (#4 pop, #1 R&B) began a series of Wu solo projects. *Tical,* named after the Wu's slang term for marijuana, spawned the chart-topping remix of "I'll Be There for You/You're All I Need to Get By" (#3 pop, #1 R&B, 1995), a cover of the two Ashford and Simpson classics featuring vocals by Mary J. Blige. Method Man followed up his debut with the equally successful *Tical 2000: Judgement Day* (#2 pop, #1 R&B, 1998) and *Blackout!* (#3 pop, #1 R&B, 1999), the latter a project with buddy Redman. The following Wu solo efforts, mostly produced or coproduced by RZA, also achieved both commercial and critical acclaim: Raekwon's *Only Built 4 Cuban Linx . . .* (#4 pop, #2 R&B, 1995) and *Immobilarity* (#9 pop, #2 R&B 1999); Ol' Dirty Bastard's *Return to the 36 Chambers: The Dirty Version* (#7 pop, #2 R&B, 1995) and *Nigga Please* (#10 pop, #2 R&B, 1999); GZA's *Liquid Swords* (#9 pop, #2 R&B, 1995) and *Beneath the Surface* (#9 pop, #1 R&B, 1999); Ghostface Killah's *Ironman* (#2 pop, #2 R&B, 1996) and *Supreme Clientele* (#7 pop, #2 R&B, 2000); RZA's *RZA as Bobby Digital in Stereo* (#16 pop, #3 R&B, 1998); Inspectah Deck's *Uncontrolled Substance* (#19 pop, #3 R&B, 1999); and U-God's *Golden Arms Redemption* (#58 pop, #15 R&B, 1999). RZA also produced Wu offshoots like Shyheim, GP Wu, Killah Priest, Sunz of Man, Cappadonna, Killarmy, and LA the Darkman, and recorded two albums as a producer/member of the group Gravediggaz.

Amidst all of the prosperity, certain Wu members found themselves in legal trouble. In 1999 Ghostface Killah was sentenced to four to six months in prison for charges stemming from an assault and robbery incident. Ol' Dirty Bastard, who temporarily gave himself the pseudonym Big Baby Jesus, was arrested twice in 1998, once for threatening to kill his ex-girlfriend and once for threatening security guards at a blues club. In January 1999 ODB was arrested for opening fire on police officers (a few weeks later a Brooklyn grand jury declined to indict him), and in March of the same year was arrested for possession of crack cocaine. In November 2000 ODB fled a court-mandated stay at a Pasadena, California, rehab center and was found by law enforcement a few weeks later outside a McDonald's in Philadelphia. In April 2001 he pleaded guilty to the drug charge and faced a two-to-four-year jail term. (In light of the plea, the court ignored his flight from the rehab center.)

Despite all of the legal strife and solo achievements, the Wu-Tang brotherhood remained a unit and recorded two more group albums: *Wu-Tang Forever* (#1 pop, #1 R&B, 1997) and 2000's *The W* (#5 pop, #1 R&B). In 1995 the Wu-Tang Clan launched the lucrative Wu Wear clothing line, and three years later created the video game *Shaolin Style*. In 2000 RZA produced the score to and made a cameo appearance in Jim Jarmusch's *Ghost Dog*, a film about a black samurai who works as a Mafia hitman.

Tammy Wynette

Born Virginia Wynette Pugh, May 5, 1942, Itawamba County, MS; died Apr. 6, 1998, Nashville, TN
1967—*Your Good Girl's Gonna Go Bad* (Epic) 1968—*D-I-V-O-R-C-E* 1969—*Stand by Your Man* 1970—*The First Lady* 1973—*First Songs of the First Lady* 1978—*Womanhood* 1980—*Only Lonely Sometimes* 1981—*You Brought Me Back* 1987—*Higher Ground* 1988—*Anniversary: 20 Years of Hits* 1989—*Next to You* 1990—*Heart Over Mind* 1992—*Tears of Fire: The 25th Anniversary Collection* 1995—*One* (with George Jones) (MCA).
With Dolly Parton and Loretta Lynn: 1993—*Honky Tonk Angels* (Columbia).

Tammy Wynette, whose incredible chart success was matched only by the tumultuous nature of her personal life, is a country music archetype. Between 1967 and 1979 Wynette had 29 Top 10 country hits—20 of which went to #1—and had already been married five times.

Raised by her grandparents on their farm, Wynette paid for music lessons by working the cotton fields. At 17 she married and quickly had three children, one of whom was stricken by spinal meningitis; by 20, she was divorced.

Her dreams of becoming a professional musician put on hold, Wynette got a job as a hairdresser in Birmingham, Alabama. With the tenacity and determination that had served her well throughout her career, Wynette eventually broke into the music industry as a background singer, first on a local TV program, and later on C&W singer Porter Wagoner's TV show. Wynette began making forays into Nashville and in 1967 met producer Billy Sherrill. Their first single together landed on the country charts, "Apartment Number Nine" (#44 C&W, 1966); their next single, 1967's "Your Good Girl's Gonna Go Bad," became a #3 C&W hit.

Two #1 hits quickly followed: "My Elusive Dreams" (with David Houston) and "I Don't Wanna Play House." The year 1968 saw the release of Wynette's classics "D-I-V-O-R-C-E" and "Stand by Your Man," both #1 C&W hits. "Stand by Your Man" (#19 pop) sold more than 2 million copies and became the biggest-selling record by a female singer in country music history. Wynette's recording persona as the long-suffering but loyal wife and mother was now established, and her subsequent hits over the next decade centered around that theme.

In 1968 Wynette married country superstar George Jones. With three #1 hits, the couple had better success as a recording duet than they did as husband and wife; Jones's drinking strained the relationship (he is said to have once chased Wynette around their house with a rifle), causing them to divorce by 1975. They continued to record together, however, with "Golden Ring" and "Near You," hitting #1 on the country chart a year after their separation.

Wynette's chart-topping streak continued throughout the '70s and into the early '80s. Meanwhile, the vicissitudes of her private life were making tabloid headlines: a relationship with Burt Reynolds; a fourth marriage that lasted 44 days; 17 major operations; a fifth marriage; a kidnapping attempt that may have been a publicity stunt; a stint in 1986 at the Betty Ford Clinic to wean her off painkillers; public repudiation by her children; even a minor involvement in the '80s savings and loan scandal.

In 1992 Wynette was back in the national spotlight. "Justified and Ancient"—her collaboration with eccentric Scottish rave act, the KLF—became a freak hit in the U.S. and Britain, giving Wynette her biggest pop success since "Stand by Your Man." Another incident had wider ramifications. In an attempt to publicly defend her husband, then presidential nominee Bill Clinton, against charges of infidelity, Hillary Clinton stated on the news program *60 Minutes* that, "I'm not sitting here like some little woman standing by her man like Tammy Wynette." The country icon demanded a public apology and received one two days later. She teamed with Dolly Parton and Loretta Lynn to record *Honky Tonk Angels* (#6 C&W) in 1993, which spawned the minor hit single "Silver Threads and Golden Needles" (#68 C&W). She also turned in an appearance on Elton John's *Duets* album the same year.

In 1995 Wynette reunited with Jones for the album *One*

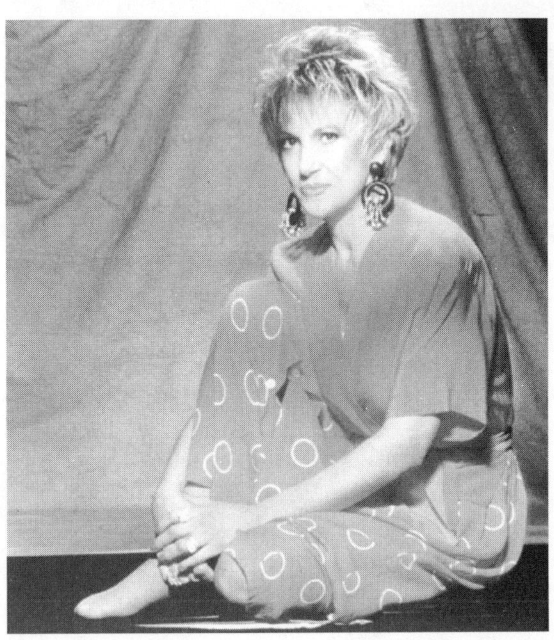

Tammy Wynette

(#117 pop, #12 C&W) and their first performances together in over a decade. The album would be her last; three years later, Wynette died in her sleep at the age of 55. Wynette's final recording, a cover of the Beach Boys' "In My Room" featuring Brian Wilson, surfaced on the tribute album *Tammy Wynette . . . Remembered* (Asylum, 1998). The album featured a host of high-profile artists (including Elton John), but it was quickly overshadowed by a controversial lawsuit concerning the exact cause of Wynette's death. Although her physician determined that Wynette had died of blood clots, and 10 months later the medical examiner disclosed that she had had a terminal illness, three of her daughters filed a wrongful death lawsuit against the doctor and her fifth husband (and manager), George Richey. Wynette had been in poor health for years (including chronic abdominal problems), but her daughters argued that Richey and the physician had enabled their mother's addiction to painkillers and questioned why she was not admitted to a hospital before her death. An autopsy performed a year later determined that Wynette had died of natural causes, but her daughters persisted with their crusade, eventually dropping Richey from the suit but replacing him with the pharmacy that filled her prescriptions. As of this writing, the case remained a subject of hot debate—and considerable sadness—in Nashville.

X

Formed 1977, Los Angeles, CA
John Doe (b. John Duchac, Feb. 25, 1954, Decatur, IL), voc., bass; Exene (b. Christine Cervenkova, Feb. 2, 1956, Chicago, IL), voc.; Billy Zoom (b. Tyson Kindell, Feb. 20, 1948, Savannah, IL), gtr.; Don J. (D.J.) Bonebrake (b. Dec. 8, 1955, Burbank, CA), drums.
1980—*Los Angeles* (Slash) 1981—*Wild Gift* 1982—*Under the Big Black Sun* (Elektra) 1983—*More Fun in the New World* 1985—*Ain't Love Grand* 1987—*See How We Are* (– Zoom; + Dave Alvin [b. Nov. 11, 1955, Los Angeles], gtr.; + Tony Gilkyson, gtr.) 1988—(– Alvin) *Live at the Whisky A Go-Go on the Fabulous Sunset Strip* 1993—*Hey Zeus!* (Mercury) 1995—*Unclogged* (Infidelity) 1997—*Beyond and Back: The X Anthology* (Elektra) 1998—(– Gilkyson; + Zoom).
Exene Cervenkova solo: 1985—*Twin Sisters* (with Wanda Coleman) (Freeway) 1989—*Old Wives' Tales* (Rhino) 1990—*Running Sacred* 1995—*Surface to Air Serpents* (2.13.61).
Cervenkova with Auntie Christ: 1997—*Life Could Be a Dream* (Lookout!).
John Doe solo: 1990—*Meet John Doe* (Geffen).
As the John Doe Thing: 1995—*Kissingsohard* (Rhino/Forward) 1998—*For the Rest of Us* EP (Kill Rock Stars) 2000—*Freedom Is . . .* (SpinArt).

X emerged from the L.A. punk scene as the most critically lauded American band of the early '80s. X helped to vindicate the West Coast scene, which had lagged behind New York and London's early punk and new-wave movements. But while X's music then was properly labeled as punk, the music and lyrics were more sophisticated than the hardcore sound that would later define the genre. And for all the speed and thrust of their playing, X claims roots in rockabilly and old-time country music, which echoes in the vocal harmonies of John Doe and Exene.

The band began in 1977, when John Doe and Billy Zoom met through classified ads in a local publication. Doe's family had moved all around America when he was growing up, and he settled in L.A. in 1976. Zoom had played guitar and sax with Gene Vincent for a while in the '70s and also fronted his own rockabilly band, who had cut several songs. Exene first met Doe at a poetry workshop in Venice, California, and the two soon became lovers and bandmates. The couple, who later married and divorced, also write all the band's lyrics. With D.J. Bonebrake, they began playing at the Masque, Hollywood's seminal punk club. A local following grew quickly, and in 1979, after seeing a performance at the Whisky, ex-Door Ray Manzarek became their producer.

The band's debut LP, *Los Angeles,* out on local Slash Records in 1980, sold over 60,000 copies, an incredible number for a small label, and 1981's *Wild Gift* also eventually sold well. In L.A., they were considered superstars. Their music touched on rockabilly, heavy metal, punk, and country, plus a bit of the Doors with Manzarek's organ and their sped-up version of the Doors' "Soul Kitchen." Both records were highlighted by Exene and Doe's minor-key vocal harmonies and by the incisive lyrics. Both LPs topped critics' year-end best-

X: Billy Zoom, John Doe, Exene, D.J. Bonebrake

of lists; and in 1981 the band was also featured in two concert films: Penelope Spheeris' punk documentary *The Decline of Western Civilization* and *Urgh! A Music War.* In 1981 the band signed with Elektra, which released its third LP, *Under the Big Black Sun.*

Exene continued her work in poetry, doing spoken-word performances, writing a 1982 book of poetry with Lydia Lunch for Grove Press called *Adulterers Anonymous;* and recording a spoken-word album, *Twin Sisters,* with poet Wanda Coleman. John Doe began a side career as an actor, appearing in *Border Radio* (1987), *Slamdance* (1987), *Great Balls of Fire!* (1989), and 1992's *Roadside Prophets* (which costarred Beastie Boy Adam Horovitz). Exene starred in the 1987 film *Salvation!* And in the mid-'80s, Doe and Exene formed the country-folk acoustic band the Knitters, with Blaster Dave Alvin on guitar, for one album, *Poor Little Critter on the Road* (1985), and live performances. However, X itself was about to go through a period of upheaval. Six months before the release of X's next album, Doe and Exene divorced, though they have remained close friends. After 1985's metal-leaning, critically panned *Ain't Love Grand,* Zoom left and eventually quit live performing. He was replaced by guitarists Alvin and Tony Gilkyson. Shortly after recording *See How We Are* (which included the Alvin-penned "4th of July"), Alvin left for a solo career. Both Doe and Exene embarked on solo careers as X began the first of several periods of hiatus. Gilkyson collaborated with Exene on the rootsy *Old Wives' Tales* and *Running Sacred.*

In 1990 X (with Gilkyson) began performing again and three years later released *Hey Zeus!* on a new label, Mercury, and undertook a national tour. Though critically well-received, the band failed to garner much commercial success. Exene continued concentrating on poetry, releasing in 1995 the spoken-word album *Surface to Air Serpents* on Henry Rollins' 2.13.61 label; Doe's second album, *Kissingsohard,* was issued by Rhino the same year. *Unclogged* featured live acoustic versions of 15 years' worth of X songs. Just as the band became active again, Gilkyson quit and X broke up. Doe began focusing more on his acting career, appearing in *Georgia* (1996) and *Boogie Nights* (1997). Playing guitar, Exene formed the punk band Auntie Christ with Bonebrake and Rancid bassist Matt Freeman, releasing *Life Could Be a Dream* in 1997. That same year Elektra issued *Beyond and Back: The X Anthology,* a collection of album tracks, live recordings, and outtakes. Renewed interest in X ultimately led to a reunion with Zoom for several sold-out live shows in 1998. The reunited quartet continued to perform sporadically and recorded (with producer Manzarek) the Doors' "Crystal Ship" for the film soundtrack of *The X-Files: Fight the Future* (1998). The same year Doe released an EP, *For the Rest of Us,* which included "This Loving Thing," a collaboration with Foo Fighter Dave Grohl. *Freedom Is . . .* followed in 2000. In 2001 Zoom (a born-again Christian since the late '70s) was working on a gospel album. He also operates Billy Zoom Music, specializing in amplifier design and repair.

X-Ray Spex

Formed 1977, London, Eng.
Poly Styrene (b. Marion Elliot, ca. 1962, London), voc.; Lora Logic (b. Susan Whitby, ca. 1961, London), sax; Jak Airport (b. Jack Stafford), gtr.; Paul Dean, bass; Chris Chrysler (b. B.P. Hurding), drums.
1978—(– Logic; + Rudi Thompson [b. Steven Rudan], sax) *Germ Free Adolescents* (Blue Plate/EMI) (– Rudan; + Glyn Johns, sax).

X-Ray Spex was one of the few bands in British punk rock's first wave with a memorable female vocalist, in Poly Styrene, who wore exotic clothing and braces on her teeth. Its other female member, saxophonist Lora Logic, would leave before the band made its only album, to lead her own group, Essential Logic.

X-Ray Spex's first hit was 1977's "Oh Bondage, Up Yours!"—a sort of women's lib anthem mixing anguish and wit, which opened memorably with Styrene cooing, "Some people think little girls should be seen and not heard," before screaming out the title. Subsequent singles "The Day the World Turned Dayglo" and "Identity" critiqued the conformity of consumer culture. A year after "Bondage," X-Ray Spex released its only album, *Germ Free Adolescents,* with a title single that was much more polished, melodic, and mellow than "Bondage."

Two months after the album's release, Styrene broke up the band, reportedly claiming to have suffered a nervous breakdown after seeing a UFO. She later joined the Krishna Consciousness movement; X-Ray Spex released one posthumous single, "Highly Inflammable" b/w "Warrior in Woolworths." Styrene left the music business, but returned in 1980, under her given name of Marion Elliot, with the tropically inflected solo album *Translucence.* She released the EP *Gods and Goddesses* in 1986, to little notice. X-Ray Spex reunited in fall 1991 for a "punk nostalgia night" at London's Brixton Academy, also featuring Sham 69, Chelsea, 999, U.K. Subs, and the Lurkers. Another reunion, along wth Lora Logic, took place in late 1996, minus Styrene.

XTC

Formed 1977, Swindon, Eng.
Andy Partridge (b. Dec. 11, 1953, Swindon), gtr., voc., synth.; Colin Moulding (b. Aug. 17, 1955, Swindon), bass, voc.; Terry Chambers (b. July 18, 1955, Swindon), drums; John Perkins (b. Eng.), kybds.; – Perkins; + Barry Andrews (b. Sep. 12, 1956, London, Eng.), kybds.
1978—*White Music* (Virgin, U.K.); *Go 2* (– Andrews; + Dave Gregory [b. Eng.], gtr., synth.) 1979—*Drums and Wires* (Virgin) 1980—*Black Sea* 1982—*English Settlement* (– Chambers) 1984—*Mummer* (Geffen) 1984—*Waxworks: Some Singles 1977–82; The Big Express* 1986—*Skylarking* 1989—*Oranges & Lemons* 1991—*Rag & Bone Buffet* 1992—*Nonsuch* 1997—*Upsy Daisy Assortment* (– Gregory) 1999—*Apple Venus vol. I* (TVT) 2000—*Wasp Star, Apple Venus vol. II.*
As Dukes of Stratosphear: 1985—*25 O'Clock* EP (Virgin, U.K.) 1987—*Psonic Psunspot* (Geffen); *Chips From the Chocolate Fireball.*

Though never earning them sales success, XTC's fastidiously crafted art pop, characterized by innovative rhythms, highly literate lyrics, and sophisticated melodic twists, has provoked critical comparisons to the Beatles and gained them a fanatic cult following.

In 1973 they were known as the Helium Kidz, a New York Dolls–type glitter band that played straightahead rock & roll in their bucolic hometown of Swindon, some 70 miles out of London. The group included XTC's later leader, Andy Partridge, plus second writer Colin Moulding and drummer Terry Chambers. In 1976 they became XTC and reorganized around Partridge's songs—material influenced by the Beatles, Small Faces, and Captain Beefheart.

The band then included John Perkins on keyboards, who was replaced by Barry Andrews (ex-King Crimson) before the foursome recorded their debut, *White Music.* That album, regarded at the time as part of the new wave onslaught, was initially released in England only, as was 1978's *Go 2.* The 1979 U.S. debut, *Drums and Wires,* featured the wry humor of "Making Plans for Nigel." By that album's release, Andrews had left; he later joined Robert Fripp's League of Gentlemen and cofounded Shriekback with Dave Allen of Gang of Four. He was replaced by Dave Gregory.

In late 1980 *Black Sea* entered the U.S. Top 50. Echoing the elegiac Kinks, it was less frenetic than earlier XTC but featured their usual jolting rhythms and strangely perched hooks plus several songs about war. *English Settlement* got rave reviews but didn't sell in America. Faring better in England, it yielded the band's biggest success in "Senses Working Overtime" (#10 U.K., 1982). A double LP in Britain, it had four songs not included on the U.S. edition. The band began a spring U.S. tour, but having collapsed from exhaustion onstage in Paris earlier that year, Partridge then suffered a nervous breakdown in California due to intense stage fright. XTC canceled the tour; Partridge spent the next year as a virtual shut-in, and the group ceased playing live. Chambers then left, and the remaining trio decided to use session drummers from then on.

Mummer and *Big Express* received the usual fine reviews, and a breakthrough came with 1986's *Skylarking.* Produced, to Partridge's initial frustration, by Todd Rundgren, it gained XTC new American listeners when "Dear God," an agnostic anthem originally left off the album, was discovered by a college-radio DJ. *Oranges & Lemons,* 1989's #1 college-radio album of the year, featured a single that finally entered the Top 100 ("The Mayor of Simpleton," #72, 1989)—this despite Partridge's sparring with producer Paul Fox. And while a talent scout for XTC's British label at first rejected almost all of the 32 songs submitted for *Nonsuch,* the band stuck to its guns and again placed at #1 on the college charts.

During the '80s, XTC also fashioned its own alter ego in the Dukes of Stratosphear, releasing clever (at times even hilarious) pseudo-psychedelia that harks back to their primary models. In 1985 the Dukes' *25 O'Clock* sold twice as well as XTC's *Big Express* (1984). *Psonic Psunspot* and the compilation *Chips From the Chocolate Fireball* continued the expert homage/spoof. In addition, Partridge has produced for the Mission U.K., Lilac Time, and other bands and, epitomizing genial English eccentricity, as a hobby has amassed regiments of toy soldiers.

XTC are notorious for their discomfort with the music industry, preferring to concentrate on the music itself. They spent the last half of the '80s in litigation against a former manager, and the bulk of the '90s on recording strike from their record company. By the time they finally found a way out of their contract (yielding a greatest-hits set, *Upsy Daisy Assortment,* in 1997), the group had written enough material for two new albums, *Apple Venus Volume I* and *Wasp Star, Apple Venus Volume II,* both of which were released by the indie label TVT Records.

With *Apple Venus Volume I,* XTC abandoned their traditional sound in favor of lushly orchestrated acoustic songs. Gregory left during the recording of the album for want of more opportunity to play guitar. The album garnered rave reviews, however, and long-suffering XTC fans were rewarded for their patience with the return to form *Wasp Star, Apple Venus Volume II,* which followed a year later.

"Weird Al" Yankovic

Born Alfred Matthew Yankovic, Oct. 23, 1959, Lynwood, CA
1983—*"Weird Al" Yankovic* (Rock 'n' Roll) 1984—*"Weird Al" Yankovic in 3-D* 1985—*Dare to Be Stupid* 1986—*Polka Party!* 1988—*Even Worse* 1989—*UHF/Original Motion Picture Soundtrack and Other Stuff* 1991—*"Weird" Al Yankovic's Greatest Hits* 1992—*Off the Deep End* (Scotti Bros.) 1993—*Alapalooza* 1994—*Permanent Record—Al in the Box* (Way Moby/Volcano) 1996—*Bad Hair Day* (Scotti Bros.) 1999—*Running With Scissors* (Volcano).

A musical parodist in the broad, juvenile yet clever tradition of *Mad* magazine, "Weird Al" Yankovic is known for adding his own gently satirical lyrics to current hit songs. His shaggy, hangdog appearance, affection for slapstick, and amiable willingness to do seemingly anything for a laugh made him a natural for videos. His burlesques of the form and its artistes—especially of Michael Jackson in "Eat It" (from "Beat It") (#12, 1983) and "Fat" (from "Bad") (#99, 1988)—became MTV staples. His medleys of rock tunes given the polka treatment inspired rumors—untrue—that Yankovic was a member of the singing Yankovic family, who made polka and Western swing records in the 1940s. Regardless of his heritage, Yankovic is undoubtedly the most successful comedy recording artist, with more than 11 million albums sold.

Yankovic, a high school valedictorian and architecture student, got his start in 1979, when he sent his "My Bologna"—a parody of the Knack's "My Sharona"—to Dr. Demento, a syndicated radio host specializing in novelty songs and curiosities. Recorded in a bathroom across the hall from his college radio station with only his accordion and vocal, the song was popular enough with Demento's audience for Capitol (the Knack's label) to release it as a single. His next parody, "Another One Rides the Bus" (based on Queen's "Another One Bites the Dust"), became the most requested song in the first decade of the Dr. Demento show.

Yankovic signed with Rock 'n' Roll Records (a CBS subsidiary), which not only gave him access to better recording facilities and the production expertise of Rick Derringer but the financial backing for the video of "Ricky" (#63, 1983). A combination parody of Toni Basil's hit single and video "Mickey" and homage to TV's *I Love Lucy,* "Ricky" was the first of a string of videos that skewered the music, its creators, and its audience, not to mention pop culture in general. While often hilariously hamfisted, Yankovic's takeoffs—such as "I Lost on Jeopardy" (#81, 1984) from *"Weird Al" Yankovic in 3-D* (#81, 1984), which rewrote Greg Kihn's "Jeopardy"; "Like a Surgeon" (#47, 1985), which tackled Madonna's "Like a Virgin," from *Dare to Be Stupid* (#50, 1985)—made their creator and star as much a rock celebrity as his targets. In fact, the longevity of Yankovic's career has surpassed several of the artists' whose songs he has parodied. Nearly half the songs on any of his albums were comedic originals, although only his biggest fans seemed to be aware of "Weird Al" the songwriter. But his lyric rewriting earned him eight Grammy nominations, including two wins.

In 1985 Yankovic released a video collection of his paro-

"Weird Al" Yankovic

dies, *The Compleat Al.* That same year MTV produced an occasional series starring Yankovic as the host of *Al TV,* wherein he spoofed current videos. In 1989 he wrote and starred in the movie *UHF;* costarring a pre–*Seinfeld* Michael Richards, *UHF* did poorly in the theater but later found new life as a cultish video hit.

Polka Party! (#177, 1986), which relied more on music than on videos, stiffed. *Even Worse* (#27, 1988) marked Al's return to rock video, and Michael Jackson. For "Fat," a grossly, literally overinflated Yankovic donned a leather outfit that copied Jackson's on the cover and video of *Bad* down to the last buckle. Jackson not only gave his approval for Yankovic's versions, he lent the subway set used in "Bad" for the "Fat" video.

In 1988 Yankovic collaborated with avant-garde synthesizer artist Wendy Carlos on recorded versions of the classical pieces *Peter and the Wolf* and *Carnival of the Animals Part II.* In 1992 Yankovic turned his eye to another musical trend, grunge, specifically Nirvana. "Smells Like Nirvana" (#35, 1992) took on the Seattle band's image and garbled lyrics, with the accompanying video again using the original set, this time adding cows and Dick Van Patten, while the cover of *Off the Deep End* (#17, 1992) had Yankovic replacing the swimming baby pictured on *Nevermind,* his gaze focused not on a dollar bill but a donut. He also mocked the traveling summer tour Lollapalooza with his 1993 album, *Alapalooza* (#46), which featured "Bedrock Anthem," a combination takeoff of the Red Hot Chili Peppers' "Under the Bridge" and "Give it Away" as well as the classic cartoon series *The Flintstones.* In 1996 he wrote the theme song for the movie satire *Spy Hard,* as well as designed the opening credits and appeared as himself in the film.

The same year, Yankovic released *Bad Hair Day,* which rose to #14 thanks to the success of its first single and video, "Amish Paradise," a takeoff on rapper Coolio's "Gangsta's Paradise" (itself a rewrite of Stevie Wonder's "Pastime Paradise"). The album cover even mimicked the rapper's hairstyle. While Yankovic always prided himself on getting permission to parody, this time there was a miscommunication between the artists' record companies; Yankovic was told Coolio was fine with the idea, but when the album was released, Coolio claimed he never consented. Yankovic sent a letter of apology and vowed not to accept agreement from anyone but the artists themselves.

After being the subject of the Disney Channel mockumentary special *"Weird Al" Yankovic: There's No Going Home* in 1996, the entertainer hosted the *Pee-wee's Playhouse*-esque *Weird Al Show* on CBS' Saturday-morning lineup in 1997 and 1998. He was frustrated by the network's lack of support for his tongue-in-cheek humor, and the show was canceled after one season. Yankovic seemingly disappeared for a time in 1998; when he re-emerged without his trademark mustache and glasses—besides shaving, he'd gotten laser eye surgery—he was unrecognizable. His 1999 release, *Running With Scissors,* peaked at #16, due to the well-timed single "The Saga Begins," a rundown of the current *Star Wars* movie *The Phantom Menace* sung to the tune of Don McLean's "American Pie." Even the official *Star Wars* Web site plugged Yankovic's album, whose release was also timed to the premiere of his *Behind the Music* episode on VH1. In 2000 Yankovic contributed the original "Polkamon" to the soundtrack of the kids' flick *Pokémon 2000: The Movie.*

While Yankovic and his band (bassist Steve Jay, drummer Jon "Bermuda" Schwartz, guitarist Jim West, and keyboardist Ruben Valtierra) are often not taken seriously, they are able to play the original songs they parody note-for-note, both in the studio and on tour, making them a great cover band. Yankovic has also tried his hand at directing music videos, both his own and for other artists, including country comedian Jeff Foxworthy, the Jon Spencer Blues Explosion, Hanson, and the Black Crowes.

The Yardbirds

Formed 1963, London, Eng.
Keith Relf (b. Mar. 22, 1943, London; d. May 14, 1976, Eng.), voc., harmonica; Chris Dreja (b. Nov. 11, 1946, London), gtr., bass; Jim McCarty (b. July 25, 1943, Liverpool, Eng.), drums; Paul Samwell-Smith (b. May 8, 1943, Eng.), bass; Anthony "Top" Topham (b. Eng.), gtr.
1963—(– Topham; + Eric Clapton [b. Mar. 30, 1945, Ripley, Eng.], gtr.) 1965—*For Your Love* (Epic) (– Clapton; + Jeff Beck [b. June 24, 1944, Surrey, Eng.], gtr.) *Having a Rave Up With the Yardbirds* (Epic) 1966—*Over Under Sideways Down; Sonny Boy Williamson and the Yardbirds* (with Sonny Boy Williamson)

The Yardbirds: Chris Dreja, Eric Clapton, Paul Samwell-Smith, Keith Relf, Jim McCarty

(Mercury) (– Samwell-Smith; + Jimmy Page [b. James Patrick Page, Jan. 9, 1944, Heston, Eng.], bass, gtr. ; – Beck) 1967—*Little Games* (Epic); *The Yardbirds' Greatest Hits* 1968—*Live Yardbirds!* (group disbands) 1970—*The Yardbirds/Featuring Performances by Jeff Beck, Eric Clapton, Jimmy Page* 1971—*Live Yardbirds* 1986—*Greatest Hits, vol. 1 (1964–1966)* (Rhino) 1988—*Five Live Yardbirds* (Rhino) 1991—*Vol. 1: Smokestack Lightning* (Sony); *Vol. 2: Blues, Backtracks and Shapes of Things* 1992—(group re-forms: Dreja; McCarty; "Detroit" John Idan, voc., bass, gtr.; Rod Demic, harmonica, bass) *Little Games, Sessions and More* (EMI) 1995—*Clapton's Cradle* (Evidence) 1996—(– Demic; + Ray Major, gtr.; + Laurie Garman, harmonica) 1997—(– Major; – Garman; + Gypie Mayo, gtr.; + Alan Glen, harmonica, perc., voc.) *Live at the BBC* (Warner Bros.).

The Yardbirds virtually wrote the book on guitar-oriented blues-based rock & roll. They were a crucial link between mid-'60s British R&B and late-'60s psychedelia, setting the groundwork for heavy metal. This seminal band spawned three major guitar heroes—Eric Clapton, Jimmy Page, and Jeff Beck—who, with the Yardbirds, pioneered almost every technical six-string innovation of the era, including feedback and fuzz tone.

The Yardbirds formed in June 1963 with Keith Relf, Chris Dreja, Paul Samwell-Smith, Jim McCarty, and guitarist Anthony "Top" Topham, who was replaced in October by Eric Clapton [see entry]. Originally called the Most Blueswailing Yardbirds, the fivesome initially played all strict blues covers of Chess/Checker/Vee-Jay material. They began to attract a large cult audience, especially when they took over the Rolling Stones' residency at the Crawdaddy Club in Richmond. They soon toured Europe with American bluesman Sonny Boy Williamson; a joint LP under both their names was issued in 1965. (It was rereleased in 1975.)

The band's first "solo" album in America was *For Your Love* in August 1965, yielding the hit title track written by Graham Gouldman, later of 10cc. (In the U.K., their first LP was titled *Five Live Yardbirds* and was out in 1964; Rhino reissued it stateside in 1988. The band's British records had different lineups of songs, album titles, and release dates than the U.S. versions.) The Yardbirds' second U.S. LP, *Having a Rave Up,* featured Clapton on only four cuts. He quit in 1965 because he objected to the band's increased pop-commercial direction, namely "For Your Love." In order to stick with purist blues, he joined John Mayall's band. His replacement was Jeff Beck [see entry], and the band soon enjoyed two more hits by Gouldman—"Heart Full of Soul," with its prepsychedelic guitar fuzz licks, and "Evil Hearted You," which charted in the U.K. In 1966 the band had two more hits—"Shapes of Things" (#11) and "Over Under Sideways Down" (#13)—but then Samwell-Smith, who had coproduced the band's records, bowed out to become a producer full-time. He later produced artists including Carly Simon, Cat Stevens, Jethro Tull, and Beverley Craven.

His replacement on bass was Jimmy Page [see entry], who moved to lead guitar as soon as rhythm guitarist Dreja learned bass. For a brief time beginning in the summer of 1966, Page and Beck were co-lead guitarists. (Page was earlier asked to be Clapton's replacement but declined, recommending Beck instead.) This lineup lasted only until November. It can be seen in the rock-club sequence in Michelangelo Antonioni's film *Blow Up,* wherein the Yardbirds perform "Stroll On" (actually a reworking of the Johnny Burnette Trio's "Train Kept A-Rollin' "). Beck had been missing many shows because of illness, and at the end of the year he suffered a full breakdown and left.

The band foundered from there. As a quartet, it released one LP in 1967 called *Little Games,* produced by Mickie Most, but the work was filled with old demos and bad leftover tracks. It came out only in the U.S. More singles were released, but they didn't go far, and in July 1968 the Yardbirds finally broke up. Relf and McCarty formed a folk duo called Together, followed by the classical-rock Renaissance [see entry], and later the heavy Armageddon. Relf died of an electric shock at home on May 14, 1976. Dreja became a photographer; he shot the album-sleeve photos for the first album by Led Zeppelin [see entry], the band Jimmy Page formed first as the New Yardbirds to meet the group's remaining contractual obligations.

Several repackagings of Yardbirds tracks were released through the '80s and '90s. In 1971 the *Live Yardbirds* LP (recorded at New York's Anderson Theater on March 30, 1968) was issued, without the band's consent; the members quickly demanded its removal from the market. It has since become a highly valuable, oft-bootlegged collector's item.

In 1983 McCarty, Dreja, and Samwell-Smith reunited to play the Marquee, and soon formed Box of Frogs with lead vocalist John Fiddler. That band released two albums, only one of which, *Box of Frogs*, was available domestically. In 1989 McCarty joined several other British '60s pop-group members in the British Invasion All-Stars. Most recently he has also been successfully recording new-age music as part of Stairway.

Following the Yardbirds' 1992 induction into the Rock and Roll Hall of Fame, McCarty and Dreja, abetted by ex-members of Mott the Hoople and Dr. Feelgood, began using the band's name on the reunion-tour circuit. However they have yet to record a new studio album. McCarty is also a solo artist.

Trisha Yearwood

Born Patricia Lynn Yearwood, Sep. 19, 1964, Monticello, GA
1991—*Trisha Yearwood* (MCA) 1992—*Hearts in Armor* 1993—*The Song Remembers When* 1994—*The Sweetest Gift* 1995—*Thinkin' About You* 1996—*Everybody Knows* 1997—*Songbook: A Collection of Hits* 1998—*Where Your Road Leads* 2000—*Real Live Woman.*

With a debut that went double-platinum and a powerful voice reminiscent of Linda Ronstadt's, Trisha Yearwood epitomized the early-'90s Nashville artist: grounded in country tradition but reaching an audience raised on '70s pop. Over the past decade, she has released a slew of Top 10 country hits and nine gold or platinum albums.

Moving to Nashville in 1985, Yearwood began singing demos. Garth Brooks enlisted her to sing backup on his debut and to tour with him; through Brooks, she met producer Garth Fundis, who produced *Trisha Yearwood* (#2 C&W, 1991). The album was an instant success, its singles, "She's in Love With the Boy" (#1 C&W, 1991), "Like We Never Had a Broken Heart" (#4 C&W, 1991), "That's What I Like About You" (#8 C&W, 1992), and "The Woman Before Me" (#1 C&W, 1992) helping Yearwood win the Academy of Country Music's Top New Female Vocalist Award in 1992.

Featuring "Wrong Side of Memphis" (#5 C&W, 1992) and a duet with Don Henley, "Walkaway Joe" (#2 C&W, 1993), *Hearts in Armor* (#46 pop, #12 C&W, 1992) consolidated Yearwood's gains. By 1993, she had signed a deal with Revlon to market a perfume called Wild Heart, been featured in the movie *This Thing Called Love*, and been the subject of a biography, *Get Hot or Go Home—Trisha Yearwood: The Making of a Nashville Star* by Lisa Gubernick. *The Song Remembers When* (#40 pop, #6 C&W, 1993), with its accompanying cable-television special and singles "You Say You Will" (#12 C&W, 1993), "Down on My Knees" (#19 C&W, 1993), and the title track (#2 C&W, 1993), continued her rise.

Yearwood has twice won a Best Country Vocal Collaboration Grammy: for her 1994 duet with Aaron Neville on the duet "I Fall to Pieces" and her 1997 duet with Brooks, "In Another's Eyes" (#2 C&W). She has frequently scored hits with songs by women songwriters, including Matraca Berg, Kim Richey, and Bobbie Cryner, among others. She was nominated for an Oscar for the Grammy Award–winning "How Do I Live," featured in the 1997 film *Con Air*. Yearwood had continued to do acting, appearing as a forensic pathologist on the CBS televison series *JAG*. In 2000 *Real Live Woman* debuted at #4 on the country chart; the album featured guest vocals by Emmylou Harris and Jackson Browne.

Yaz: See Allison Moyet; Erasure

Yellow Magic Orchestra: See Ryuichi Sakamoto

Yes

Formed 1968, London, Eng.
Jon Anderson (b. Oct. 25, 1944, Accrington, Eng.), voc., perc.; Peter Banks, gtr., voc; Tony Kaye (b. Jan. 11, 1945, Leicester, Eng.), kybds.; Chris Squire (b. Mar. 4, 1948, London), bass, voc.; Bill Bruford (b. William Scott Bruford, May 17, 1949, Sevenoaks, Eng.), drums.
1969—*Yes* (Atlantic) 1970—*Time and a Word* 1971—(– Banks; + Steve Howe [b. Apr. 8, 1947, London], gtr., voc.) *The Yes Album* (– Kaye; + Rick Wakeman [b. May 18, 1949, London], kybds.) *Fragile* 1972—*Close to the Edge* (– Bruford; + Alan White [b. June 14, 1949, Pelton, Eng.], drums) 1973—*Yessongs; Tales From Topographic Oceans* 1974—(– Wakeman; + Patrick Moraz [b. June 24, 1948, Morges, Switz.], kybds.) *Relayer* 1975—*Yesterdays* 1976—(– Moraz; + Wakeman) 1977—*Going for the One* (Atlantic) 1978—*Tormato* 1980—*Yesshows* (– Anderson; – Wakeman; + Trevor Horn [b. July 15, 1949, Hertfordshire, Eng.], voc.; + Geoffrey Downes [b. Eng.], kybds.) *Drama* 1982—*Classic Yes* 1983—(group re-forms: Anderson; Kaye; Squire; White; + Trevor Rabin [b. Jan. 13, 1954, Johannesburg, S.A.], gtr.) *90125* 1985—*9012Live—The Solos* 1987—*Big Generator* (Atco) 1990—(– Anderson) 1991—(group re-forms: Anderson; Bruford; Wakeman; Howe) *Union* (Arista) 1991—*Yesyears* (Atco) 1993—*Symphonic Music of Yes* (RCA) (group re-forms: Anderson; Kaye; Rabin; Squire; White)

1994—*Talk* (– Kaye; – Rabin; + Howe; + Wakeman; + Billy Sherwood [b. Mar. 14, 1965, Las Vegas, NV], gtr.; + Igor Khoroshev [b. July 14, 1965, Moscow, USSR], piano) 1996—*Keys to Ascension* (CMC International) 1997—*Keys to Ascension, vol. 2* (Cleopatra); *Open Your Eyes* (Beyond Music) 1998—*Something's Coming* (WEA International) 1999—*The Ladder* (Damian) 2000—*House of Yes: Live From the House of Blues* (Beyond Music).
Anderson, Bruford, Wakeman, Howe: 1989—*Anderson, Bruford, Wakeman, Howe* (Arista).
Jon Anderson solo: 1976—*Olias of Sunhillow* (Atlantic) 1980—*Song of Seven* 1982—*Animation* (Mercury) 1988—*In the City of Angels* (Atlantic) 1994—*Deseo* (Windham Hill); *Change We Must* (Angel) 1996—*Toltec* (High Street).
Jon Anderson with Vangelis, as Jon and Vangelis: 1980—*Short Stories* (Mercury) 1982—*The Friends of Mr. Cairo* 1983—*Private Collection* 1984—*The Best of Jon and Vangelis.*
Steve Howe solo: 1975—*Beginnings* (Atlantic) 1979—*Steve Howe Album* 1991—*Turbulence.*
Chris Squire solo: 1975—*Fish Out of Water* (Atlantic).
Rick Wakeman solo: 1973—*The Six Wives of Henry VIII* (A&M) 1974—*Journey to the Centre of the Earth* 1975—*The Myths and Legends of King Arthur; Lisztomania* soundtrack 1976—*No Earthly Connection; White Rock* 1977—*Rick Wakeman's Criminal Record* 1978—*Best Known Works* 1980—*Rhapsodies* 1995—*The Piano Album* (Castle) 1996—*Voyage: The Very Best of Rick Wakeman* (A&M) 1999—*Return to the Centre of the Earth* (EMI).
Bill Bruford solo: [see entry].

One of the most successful progressive-rock bands in history, Yes combined virtuosic musicianship, suitelike neoclassical structures, and three-part high vocal harmonies to form an elaborate whole that most critics called irrelevant high-flown indulgence—and that audiences loved. After undergoing byzantine personnel changes, they updated their sound in the mid-'80s and enjoyed greater commercial success than ever.

Yes was formed after Jon Anderson met Chris Squire at a London music-industry bar in 1968. Anderson had spent the previous 12 years in various bands; Squire, a self-taught bassist, had been in the Syn. With guitarist Peter Banks, keyboardist Tony Kaye, and drummer Bill Bruford [see entry], they formed Yes. One of their first engagements was opening for Cream's London farewell concert in November 1968. The band won instant critical acclaim in Britain, and by the time of their debut album, which mixed originals with covers, were hailed as "the next supergroup." *Time and a Word,* which used an orchestra to flesh out intricately shifting arrangements, was somewhat less well received.

At this point, Yes had yet to break through in America, and Atlantic Records informed them that the next album might be their last. Banks left to form Flash, and new guitarist Steve Howe—formerly of such bands as the Syndicate and Tomorrow—helped make *The Yes Album* (#40, 1971) their breakthrough. With continual FM airplay it went gold.

In 1971 Tony Kaye left to form Badger (he later joined Detective and then Badfinger). His replacement, Rick Wakeman, had garnered acclaim with the Strawbs. *Fragile* (#4, 1972) consolidated the band's success. Highlighted by an edited "Roundabout" (#13, 1972), the album went gold. With *Close to the Edge* (#3, 1972), Yes' ambition attained new heights. Consisting of three extended cuts, with a four-movement title suite, the album too went gold in short order. After recording it, Bruford left to join King Crimson (whose leader, Robert Fripp, had once been approached to replace Peter Banks). His replacement was sessionman Alan White, who had played in John Lennon's Plastic Ono Band.

Yes: Bill Bruford, Rick Wakeman, Chris Squire, Jon Anderson, Steve Howe

The live *Yessongs* (#12, 1973) was followed by the critically derided *Tales From Topographic Oceans* (#6, 1974). The album sold well, however, and the band continued to be a top-drawing live act. But *Tales* brought to a head conflicts between Wakeman, an extroverted meat-eating beer drinker, and the other players, who were sober vegetarians. Wakeman, openly expressing his disillusionment, soon left.

Wakeman's replacement was Patrick Moraz (like Wakeman, classically trained), of progressive-rock band Refugee. He debuted on *Relayer* (#5, 1974), which, like *Close to the Edge,* featured an extended suite and forays into jazz fusion. With the release of *Yesterdays* (#17, 1975), a compilation including tracks from the first two (uncharted) Yes albums, the band took a year off as each member pursued solo projects.

After Yes had made a successful world tour with Moraz, Wakeman rejoined. Both *Going for the One* (#8, 1977) and

Tormato (#10, 1978) returned to shorter, tighter song structures. But though Yes continued to sell albums and fill arenas, its days seemed numbered. Wakeman left again, followed by Anderson, who had written most of Yes' lyrics. Trevor Horn and Geoffrey Downes of the new-wave band the Buggles (who had a hit with "Video Killed the Radio Star" [see entry]) debuted on *Drama* (#18, 1980). Shortly thereafter, Yes broke up.

Howe and Downes then joined with Carl Palmer of Emerson, Lake and Palmer and John Wetton to form the progressive-rock supergroup Asia [see entry], who debuted in 1982 with a massively successful album. Anderson continued to make solo albums. Squire and White planned to start a band called Cinema. But in mid-1983 Anderson, Kaye, Squire, White, and South African guitarist Trevor Rabin re-formed Yes and went on with *90125* (#5, 1983) and its Rabin-penned #1 single, "Owner of a Lonely Heart," both to score the band's highest chart position and to redefine its sound. Largely due to producer Trevor Horn, Yes streamlined its approach, eschewing classical stylings for sonically gorgeous, crafty pop. Rabin's songwriting dominated *The Big Generator* (#15, 1987), after which Anderson quit.

By 1989 the band's personnel squabbles reached new intensity; after a court battle over the group name, Squire, White, Rabin, and Kaye continued as the official Yes, while the warring faction of Anderson, Bruford, Wakeman, and Howe toured and recorded using their surnames. The two camps reconciled on *Union* (#15, 1991), going on to a world tour that, for all the logistical unwieldiness of its eight-player lineup, was a huge commercial success.

In 1993 Anderson, Bruford, and Howe joined the London Philharmonic in a album of symphonic versions of Yes songs. A year later, Yes—this time comprised of the members who'd released *90125*—announced plans to record again, and early 1994 saw the release of *Talk* (#33, 1994). In 1997 the band, with new guitarist Billy Sherwood and additional keyboardist Igor Khoroshev, released two albums in one month, the catchy pop of *Open Your Eyes* and the more typically ambitious *Keys to Ascension, vol. 2.* By this time, Rick Wakeman, while still pursuing a career in Christian music, was back in the Yes fold. *The Ladder* (1999) echoed the progressive-rock melodrama of the band's early heyday.

Dwight Yoakam

Born Oct. 23, 1956, Pikesville, KY
1986—*Guitars, Cadillacs, Etc., Etc.* (Reprise) 1987—*Hillbilly Deluxe* 1988—*Buenas Noches From a Lonely Room* 1989—*Just Lookin' for a Hit* 1990—*If There Was a Way* 1993—*This Time* 1995—*Dwight Live; Gone* 1997—*Under the Covers; Come On Christmas* 1998—*A Long Way Home* 1999—*Last Chance for a Thousand Years—Greatest Hits From the '90s* 2000—*dwightyoakamacoustic.net; Tomorrow's Sounds Today.*

Honey-voiced singer/songwriter Dwight Yoakam can glide from an insinuating croon to a country holler. He set out to revive the honky-tonk tradition pioneered by Merle Haggard, but his highly stylized image and sometimes self-righteous attitude have earned him the disapproval of Nashville's more conservative establishment.

Kentucky-born and Ohio-bred, Yoakam wrote his first song at age 10. By the time he turned 18 he was performing on the Ohio Valley honky-tonk circuit. After attending schools in Ohio and California, Yoakam set out for Nashville, where, by his account, he was rejected for being "too country." (Nashville's *The Tennessean* reported that this rejection consisted of his being passed over at an Opryland audition.)

Inspired by Californian Buck Owens, from Bakersfield, Yoakam relocated in 1978 to neighboring L.A., where he put together the Babylonian Cowboys. Pete Anderson, whose guitar playing, arrangements, and production have been a crucial element in Yoakam's success, joined in 1981.

Gigging in San Fernando Valley honky-tonks, Yoakam and his outfit eventually scored opening slots for bands that were part of L.A.'s burgeoning roots-rock scene, such as the Blasters and Los Lobos. In 1984 Yoakam released an EP, *Guitars, Cadillacs, Etc.,* on his own Oak label. It helped land him a record deal with Reprise's Nashville subsidiary, which re-released it as an album by adding three songs (and a second *Etc.* to its title). Its debut single, a cover of Johnny Horton's "Honky Tonk Man" (#3 C&W, 1986) and title track (#4 C&W, 1986) proved that straight-ahead country music could go platinum.

Dwight Yoakam

A steady stream of country Top 10 singles—a cover of the Elvis hit "Little Sister" (#7 C&W, 1987), "Little Ways" (#8 C&W, 1987), "Please, Please Baby" (#6 C&W, 1987), and "Always Late With Your Kisses" (#9 C&W, 1988), from *Hillbilly Deluxe* (#55 pop, #1 C&W, 1987)—did not change Yoakam's outsider status, though. His trademark look—'50s style fancy embroidered bolero jackets, skintight faded jeans, cowboy boots, and cowboy hat—reflected Yoakam's love for the look as well as the sound of traditional C&W. (In 1990 Yoakam invested in a C&W clothing venture with Manuel, the Western-wear designer who got his start with legendary cowboy couturier Nudie.)

Yoakam's next album, *Buenas Noches From a Lonely Room* (#68 pop, #1 C&W, 1988), yielded the #1 C&W hits "Streets of Bakersfield" (with Buck Owens, whom Yoakam coaxed out of retirement) and "I Sang Dixie." Yoakam sang a duet with k.d. lang—the Flying Burrito Brothers' "Sin City"—on *Just Lookin' for a Hit* (#68 pop, #3 C&W, 1989), and with Patty Loveless on "Send a Message to My Heart" (#47 C&W, 1992), on *If There Was a Way* (#96 pop, #7 C&W, 1990). *Way* also featured the Top 20 C&W singles "You're the One" (#5, 1991), "Nothing's Changed Here" (#15, 1991), and "It Only Hurts When I Cry" (#6, 1992), cowritten with Roger Miller.

In the early '90s, Yoakam made a cameo in the cult film *Red Rock West,* which starred Nicolas Cage, Dennis Hopper, and Lara Flynn Boyle. He also scored the soundtrack for the 1992 film *White Sands* and contributed a version of Elvis's "Suspicious Minds" (#35 C&W, 1992) to *Honeymoon in Vegas* (the soundtrack album hit #4 in 1992). An ill-fated love affair with actress Sharon Stone in 1992 resulted in several emotionally charged compositions on Yoakam's 1993 platinum album *This Time* (#25 pop, #4 C&W, 1993). The album yielded the hits "Ain't That Lonely Yet" (#2 C&W, 1993), which won the Grammy for Best Male Country Performance in 1994, "A Thousand Miles From Nowhere" (#2 C&W, 1993), "Try Not to Look So Pretty," (#14 C&W, 1994), and "Fast as You" (#70 pop, #2 C&W, 1994).

Yoakam has continued to juggle his music-making with his acting. Between 1995 and 1998, he appeared in four films—*The Little Death, Painted Hero, Sling Blade,* and *The Newton Boys*—as well as several television projects. At the same time, he toured and released *Dwight Live* (#56 pop, #8 C&W, 1995), *Gone* (#30 pop, #5 C&W, 1995), *Under the Covers* (#92 pop, #8 C&W, 1997), the holiday collection *Come On Christmas* (#32 C&W, 1997), and *A Long Way Home* (#60 pop, #11 C&W, 1998). None of those albums sold as well as Yoakam's early-'90s work, although *Gone* yielded the #20 country single "Nothing" (1995) and *Home* the #17 country single "Things Change" (1998).

Under the Covers was Yoakam's collection of often radical reinterpretations of songs by an odd assortment of artists including the Clash, the Kinks, Sonny and Cher, and Jimmie Rodgers. The album rendered a minor country hit "Claudette" (1997), a Roy Orbison tune made famous by the Everly Brothers in 1958. In 1999 Yoakam scored his biggest hit in six years, "Crazy Little Thing Called Love" (#64 pop, #12 C&W, 1999), a faithful rendition of Queen's #1 pop hit of 1980. The song was a newly recorded track on the singer's best-of collection, *Last Chance for a Thousand Years* (#80 pop, #10 C&W, 1999).

Yoakam kicked off the new millennium with a back-to-basics collection of acoustic versions of his most popular tunes, *dwightyoakamacoustic.net.* He followed that with *Tomorrow's Sounds Today,* a collection of new songs including more collaborations with Buck Owens and another rock cover (Cheap Trick's "I Want You to Want Me").

Yo La Tengo

Formed 1984, Hoboken, NJ
Ira Kaplan (b. Jan. 7, 1957, NY), voc., gtr.; Georgia Hubley (b. Feb. 9, 1960, NY), voc., drums.
1986—(+ Dave Schramm, gtr.; + Mike Lewis, bass) *Ride the Tiger* (Coyote) 1987—(– Schramm; – Lewis; + Stephan Wichnewski, bass) *New Wave Hot Dogs* 1989—*President Yo La Tengo* (– Wichnewski) 1990—(+ Schramm) *Fakebook* (Bar/None) (– Schramm) 1991—(+ James McNew, bass) 1992—*May I Sing With Me* (Alias) 1993—*Painful* (Matador) 1995—*Electr-O-Pura* 1996—*Genius + Love = Yo La Tengo* 1997—*I Can Hear the Heart Beating as One* 2000—*And Then Nothing Turned Itself Inside-Out.*

The literal and figurative definition of a "critic's band," Yo La Tengo was cofounded by onetime rock scribe (and *Encyclopedia* contributor) Ira Kaplan, who wrote for *New York Rocker* and *The SoHo News* in the early 1980s. His wife and band mate Georgia Hubley, the daughter of Oscar-winning animators *(Mister Magoo),* was raised on Manhattan's Upper West Side. Inspired amateurs whose early albums were tributes to their record collections, guitarist/vocalist Kaplan and drummer/vocalist Hubley emerged in 1984 from the active indie-rock scene that revolved around the Hoboken club Maxwell's. The group, which took for its name what a Spanish-speaking outfielder would yell while awaiting an approaching fly ball ("I've got it!"), has evolved through various lineups and enthusiasms over a nearly two-decade career, displaying both remarkable staying power and impressive artistic growth.

Kaplan and Hubley were joined by a variety of bassists and guitarists prior to recording the 1986 debut album *Ride the Tiger,* a roots-oriented collection that featured guitarist Dave Schramm and bassist Mike Lewis, with production from ex–Mission of Burma bassist Clint Conley. The band's revolving door spun again for the following year's *New Wave Hot Dogs,* with bassist Stephan Wichnewski briefly onboard. Yo La Tengo, whose embrace of both feedback-driven rave-ups and folksier fare have prompted comparisons to the Velvet Underground, made the influence explicit with a version of John Cale and Lou Reed's "It's Alright (The Way That You Live)." *President Yo La Tengo* was produced by guest bassist Gene Holder (of kindred pop spirits the dB's), with Schramm back to play on 1990's *Fakebook,* an acoustic-driven mostly covers album with selections from the Kinks, Gene Clark, the Escorts, and fellow New York rockers The Scene Is Now. Two years later, *May I Sing With Me* marked both a return to the band's noisier instincts and the arrival of new bassist James McNew (ex-Christmas), whose presence formalized Yo La Tengo as a trio.

The 1993 album *Painful* displayed a greater range of tones and textures, as the musicians cultivated their knack for keyboard and guitar-laden atmospherics. They continued in that direction for *Electr-O-Pura,* which mixed clever pop writing and balladry with experimental pieces. The rarities double-disc *Genius + Love = Yo La Tengo* surveyed the band's penchant for quirky cover tunes, collecting tracks from various singles, EPs, and compilations, and boasting a humorous telephone collaboration with Austin, Texas, songwriter/eccentric Daniel Johnston on his song "Speeding Motorcycle." The group also made its big-screen debut portraying "the Factory house band" in the 1996 film *I Shot Andy Warhol. I Can Hear the Heart Beating as One,* from 1997, was a major critical success and became its bestseller, approaching sales of 75,000 copies. Three years later, *And Then Nothing Turned Itself Inside-Out,* was a subdued, lyrical meditation on domestic life that was widely interpreted to be about Kaplan and Hubley's marriage, and featured a cover of George McRae's 1974 disco tune "You Can Have It All."

Jesse Colin Young: See the Youngbloods

Neil Young

Born Nov. 12, 1945, Toronto, Can.
1969—*Neil Young* (Reprise); *Everybody Knows This Is Nowhere* 1970—*After the Gold Rush* 1972—*Harvest; Journey Through the Past* 1973—*Time Fades Away* 1974—*On the Beach* 1975—*Tonight's the Night; Zuma* 1976—*Long May You Run* (with Stephen Stills) 1977—*American Stars 'n Bars* 1978—*Decade; Comes a Time* 1979—*Rust Never Sleeps; Live Rust* 1980—*Hawks and Doves* 1981—*Re•ac•tor* 1982—*Trans* (Geffen) 1983—*Everybody's Rockin'* 1985—*Old Ways* 1986—*Landing on Water* 1987—*Life* 1988—*This Note's for You* (Reprise) 1989—*Freedom; El Dorado* 1990—*Ragged Glory* 1991—*Arc; Weld* 1992—*Harvest Moon* 1993—*Lucky Thirteen: Excursions Into Alien Territory* (Geffen); *Unplugged* (Reprise) 1994—*Sleeps With Angels* 1995—*Mirror Ball* (with Pearl Jam) 1996—*Broken Arrow; Dead Man* soundtrack (Vapor/Warner Bros.) 1997—*Year of the Horse* soundtrack (Warner Bros.) 2000—*Silver & Gold; Road Rock, vol. 1.*

Singer/songwriter Neil Young is sometimes visionary, sometimes flaky, sometimes both at once, but he has never been boring. Indeed, Young has weathered runs of critical and popular ambivalence only to be vindicated by being periodically "rediscovered" by young musicians and fans. He has maintained a large following since the early '70s with music in three basic styles—solo acoustic ballads, sweet country rock, and lumbering garage rock (with some experimental music side trips), all topped by his high voice—and he veers from one to another in unpredictable phases. His subject matter also shifts from personal confessions to allusive stories to bouncy throwaways. A dedicated primitivist, Young is constantly proving that simplicity is not always simple.

Neil Young

As a child, Young moved with his mother to Winnipeg, Canada, after she divorced his father, a well-known sports journalist. He played in several high school rock bands, including the Esquires, the Stardusters, and the Squires. He also began hanging out in local folk clubs, where he met Stephen Stills and Joni Mitchell. Mitchell wrote "The Circle Game" for Young after hearing his "Sugar Mountain." In the mid-'60s Young moved to Toronto, where he began performing solo. In 1966 he and bassist Bruce Palmer joined the Mynah Birds (which included Rick James and had a deal with Motown Records); after that fizzled, he and Palmer drove to L.A. in Young's Pontiac hearse. Young and Palmer ran into Stills and another mutual friend, Richie Furay, out west and formed Buffalo Springfield [see entry], one of the most important of the new folk-country-rock bands, who recorded Young's "Broken Arrow," "I Am a Child," "Mr. Soul," and "Nowadays Clancy Can't Even Sing." But friction developed: Young quit the band, only to rejoin and quit again, and in May 1968, after recording three albums, the band split up.

Young acquired Joni Mitchell's manager, Elliot Roberts, and released his debut solo LP in January 1969, coproduced by Jack Nitzsche. Around the same time Young began jamming with a band called the Rockets, renamed Crazy Horse: drummer Ralph Molina, bassist Billy Talbot, and guitarist Danny Whitten. They backed Young on *Everybody Knows*

This Is Nowhere (#34, 1969), recorded in two weeks. The album includes three of Young's most famous songs: "Cinnamon Girl," "Down by the River," and "Cowgirl in the Sand," which, Young later said, were all written in one day while he was stricken with the flu. The album went gold (and much later, platinum), but Young decided to split his time between Crazy Horse and Crosby, Stills and Nash [see entry], whom he joined in June. In March 1970 his presence was first felt on CSN&Y's *Déjà Vu.*

Young's third solo, the gold (and utterly evocative) *After the Gold Rush* (#8, 1970), included Crazy Horse and 17-year-old guitarist Nils Lofgren. The album yielded the single "Only Love Can Break Your Heart" (#33, 1970), and that plus the CSN&Y album put the spotlight on Young. *Harvest* (#1, 1972), with the #1 single "Heart of Gold," made the singer/songwriter a superstar.

By the release of its live album, *Four Way Street,* in spring 1971, CSN&Y had broken up. In 1972 Young made a *cinema vérité* film, *Journey Through the Past;* the film and its soundtrack were panned by critics. Young confused fans further with *Time Fades Away* (#22, 1973), a rough-hewn live album recorded with the Stray Gators, including Nitzsche (keyboards), Ben Keith (pedal steel guitar), Tim Drummond (bass), and John Barbata (drums). In June 1975 Young released a bleak, ragged album recorded two years earlier, *Tonight's the Night* (#25). The album's dark tone reflected Young's emotional upheaval following the drug deaths of Crazy Horse's Danny Whitten in 1972 and CSN&Y roadie Bruce Berry in 1973. In November Young released the harder-rocking *Zuma* (#25), an emotionally intense work that included the sweeping "Cortez the Killer." Crazy Horse now included Talbot, Molina, and Frank Sampedro (rhythm guitar). In 1976 Young recorded *Long May You Run* (#26) with Stills, which went gold, but he left Stills halfway through a tour.

In June 1977 Young was back on his own with the gold *American Stars 'n Bars* (#21), again a more accessible effort, with Linda Ronstadt doing backup vocals along with newcomer Nicolette Larson. Compiled by Young, *Decade* was a carefully chosen, not entirely hit-centered compilation. *Comes a Time* (#7, 1978) was folkish and went gold.

In fall 1978 Young did an arena tour called Rust Never Sleeps. He played old and new music, performing half the show by himself on piano or guitar, and the other half (which was memorably loud) with Crazy Horse, amid giant mock-ups of microphones and speakers. In June 1979 he released *Rust Never Sleeps* (#8) with songs previewed on the tour, including "Out of the Blue," dedicated to Johnny Rotten and the Sex Pistols. The album also featured "Sedan Delivery" and "Powderfinger," which Young had once offered to Lynyrd Skynyrd, though the band didn't record them. (Back in 1974 Skynyrd had written "Sweet Home Alabama" as an answer to Young's "Southern Man.") In November 1979 Young released the gold *Live Rust* LP (#15), culled from the fall 1978 shows and the soundtrack to a film of the tour (directed by Young) entitled *Rust Never Sleeps.*

The '80s was a particularly strange and erratic decade for Young, even by his own unpredictable standards. Right before presidential election week 1980, he issued *Hawks and Doves* (#30), an enigmatic state-of-the-union address, with one side of odd acoustic pieces and the other of rickety country songs. Exactly one year later he released *Re•ac•tor* (#27), an all-hard-rock LP. In 1982 he moved to Geffen and released *Trans* (#19), which introduced what Young called "Neil 2"; he fed his voice through a computerized Vocoder and sang songs like "Sample and Hold." He toured arenas as a solo performer when the album was released, singing his most-requested songs, covering "backstage" action on a large video screen, and singing along with his Vocoderized video image on songs from *Trans.*

Young's wandering got more extreme with *Everybody's Rockin',* a rockabilly-style album recorded and performed with a group he dubbed the Shocking Pinks. Despite an amusing video for the single "Wonderin'," Young's work started sliding down the charts. *Old Ways* was a country record with guest spots by Willie Nelson and Waylon Jennings. *Landing on Water* used synthesizers on standard rock songs. And *Life* reunited Young with Crazy Horse in lackluster performances. After his disastrous relationship with Geffen—in which he was ultimately slapped with a $3 million suit for making "unrepresentative," noncommercial music—Young returned to his former label for *This Note's for You,* a horn-based R&B album. The video for the title song attacked rockers who allowed their songs to be used in TV ads and was not shown on MTV, although it earned the network's Music Video Award for Best Video of the Year. In 1987, after appearing with his old cohorts in CSN at a Greenpeace benefit, Young rejoined the group briefly for the 1988 CSN&Y album, *American Dream* (#16, 1988). None of Young's '80s albums was particularly well received beyond the artist's loyal core audience, though some—such as *Trans*—had captured critics' interest. Many wrote off his '80s period as typical Neil Young flakiness.

But there were events in Young's personal life that shed light on his increased eccentricity. In 1978 his second son, Ben, was born to his wife, Pegi, with cerebral palsy (in 1972, Young's first son, Zeke, was born to his then-companion, actress Carrie Snodgress, with a milder version of the disorder). Later, in a 1992 interview with *The New York Times,* Young said his '80s output had reflected his frustration with not being able to communicate with Ben: "*Trans* signified the end of one sound and era and the beginning of another era, where I was indecipherable and no one could understand what I was saying."

Young's extramusical activities during the '80s were as unpredictable as the albums. In 1984, to the bewilderment of his fans, he spoke out in favor of conservative Ronald Reagan. He also participated in the 1985 Live Aid benefit and helped organize the subsequent Farm Aid concerts. In 1986 Young and his wife started the Bridge School in San Francisco, a learning center for disabled children. In 1989 a group of alternative rockers, including Sonic Youth, the Pixies, and Dinosaur Jr, contributed to *The Bridge: A Tribute to Neil Young,* whose proceeds went to the school. (Young also organized annual benefit concerts for the school, at which a wide range of artists performed each year.)

Hailed by a new generation of postpunk musicians as the Granddaddy of Grunge, Young had a major comeback beginning in 1989 with *Freedom* (#35), his biggest charter since *Trans.* He introduced its single, "Rockin' in the Free World," in an unbridled, transcendent 1989 performance on *Saturday Night Live* that easily ranks as one of the greatest television moments in rock history. Young then regrouped Crazy Horse for *Ragged Glory* (#31, 1990), a raucous, critically lauded album. With raw, feedback- and distortion-drenched garage rock, the album proved the extent of Young's influence on younger alternative-rock bands such as Dinosaur Jr and Soul Asylum. In 1991 he embraced that new generation of bands by taking noise-rockers Sonic Youth and Social Distortion on the road; the tour was documented on *Weld* (whose 35-minute instrumental companion *Arc* featured extended, noisy feedback jams). Young also began praising rap, particularly the music of Ice-T.

Reuniting him with members of the Stray Gators, *Harvest Moon* (#16, 1992) found Young doing his sentimental acoustic/folk songs again. A sequel to *Harvest,* it was his biggest seller in 13 years. In 1992 Young appeared at the 50th birthday celebration for Bob Dylan, covering Dylan's "Just Like Tom Thumb's Blues" and "All Along the Watchtower." Released in 1993, *Lucky Thirteen* compiles Young's Geffen material, and *Unplugged* documents his live, acoustic performances following the release of *Harvest Moon.*

In 1994 Young contributed the haunting title song to Jonathan Demme's film *Philadelphia,* which was nominated for an Oscar. (Bruce Springsteen's "Streets of Philadelphia" also from the film won.) He also released *Sleeps With Angels* (#9, 1994), his strongest, most consistent, and critically lauded album since *Rust Never Sleeps.*

He was inducted into the Rock and Roll Hall of Fame in 1995 by Eddie Vedder of Pearl Jam, who thanked Young for teaching his band a lot about "dignity, commitment, and playing in the moment." The mutual admiration between the artists resulted in the collaboration *Mirror Ball* (#5, 1995), with Pearl Jam backing Young on his highest-charting album since '72. The next year he was back with Crazy Horse for *Broken Arrow* (#31, 1996). Young recorded a haunting solo electric-guitar score for New York independent filmmaker Jim Jarmusch's 1996 film *Dead Man.* Jarmusch then made a documentary of Young, *Year of the Horse,* released in 1997. Footage from Young and Crazy Horse's 1996 tour is spliced together with older stock from 1976 and 1986; interviews with Young, band members, crew, and associates run throughout. A soundtrack album was also released. Young headlined the H.O.R.D.E. summer festival tour in 1997. In the late '90s, Young, a lifelong model train enthusiast, bought the Lionel Toy Train company, reportedly to delight his son Ben.

In 2000 Young released *Silver & Gold,* a pensive, largely acoustic album featuring drummer Jim Keltner, bassist Donald "Duck" Dunn, Ben Keith on pedal steel and Dobro, and keyboardist Spooner Oldham. Three years in the making, the album was nearly universally hailed. Also that year, *Village Voice* writer Jimmy McDonough filed a $1.8 million suit against Young, alleging that the singer refused to allow publication of a biography written by McDonough that Young originally authorized (as of this writing, the case was still pending). In November 2000, Young released *Road Rock* (#169), a strong live set featuring a duet with Chrissie Hynde on Bob Dylan's "All Along the Watchtower."

Paul Young

Born Jan. 17, 1956, Luton, Eng.
1983—*No Parlez* (Columbia) 1985—*The Secret of Association* 1986—*Between Two Fires* 1990—*Other Voices* 1991—*From Time to Time/The Singles Collection* 1993—*The Crossing* 1995—*Reflections* (Vision Music) 1997—*Love Hurts* (Prime Cuts).

Paul Young is a handsome, blue-eyed soul singer whose massive popularity in his native England has led to the occasional pop hit in the U.S. Young was born in a North London suburb. His first group of note, Streetband, had a novelty hit in the U.K. with "Toast" in 1978. In 1979 Streetband split, and Young and other members formed the eight-piece soul band Q-Tips. The band became popular in England through frequent touring, but its eponymous 1980 album sold poorly.

Young was offered a solo contract by CBS and brought Q-Tips keyboardist Ian Kewley with him. The Royal Family band, along with backup singers the Fabulous Wealthy Tarts, accompanied Young on *No Parlez.* Lushly produced by Laurie Latham, the album was a hit in Europe. It featured a cover of "Wherever I Lay My Hat (That's My Home)," "Come Back and Stay" (#22, 1984), and "Love of the Common People," as well as an unlikely cover of Joy Division's "Love Will Tear Us Apart."

While touring Europe and the U.S., Young strained his voice and was forced to rest. Meanwhile, the Tarts left to pursue their own careers and were replaced by George Chandler, Tony Jackson, and Jimmy Chambers; they hit with a cover of Daryl Hall's "Everytime You Go Away" (#1, 1985). The Latham-produced album included Tom Waits' "Soldier's Things" and "I'm Gonna Tear Your Playhouse Down" (#13, 1985).

Next Young cowrote and coproduced (with Hugh Padgham and Kewley) *Between Two Fires,* which yielded no hits, though. Young took an 18-month hiatus to attend to family, appearing publicly in 1988 to sing at the Nelson Mandela birthday tribute concert in Wembley. He changed direction on *Other Voices,* working with four producers (including Nile Rodgers and Peter Wolf) and such special guests as Chaka Khan, Pink Floyd guitarist David Gilmour, and Stevie Wonder (on harmonica). Young returned to the U.S. charts with the Chi-Lites 1972 hit "Oh Girl" (#8, 1990). The album also featured a version of Free's "A Little Bit of Love." Young's cover of Jimmy Ruffin's 1966 hit "What Becomes of the Brokenhearted" (#22, 1992) was featured in the movie *Fried Green Tomatoes.*

In 1995 Young released *Reflections,* a covers collection

including versions of songs by Aretha Franklin ("Until You Come Back to Me"), Bill Withers ("Ain't No Sunshine"), and the Four Tops ("Reach Out I'll Be There"). The unsuccessful *Love Hurts* (1997) featured updates of hits by Everly Brothers, Joe Tex, and the Temptations.

The Youngbloods/Jesse Colin Young

Formed 1965, Boston, MA
Jesse Colin Young (b. Perry Miller, Nov. 11, 1944, New York, NY), voc., bass, gtr.; Jerry Corbitt (b. Tifton, GA), gtr., voc.; Joe Bauer (b. Sep. 26, 1941, Memphis, TN; d. 1982), drums; Banana (b. Lowell Vincent Levinger, 1946, Cambridge, MA), gtr., kybds.
1967—*The Youngbloods* (RCA); *Earth Music; Two Trips* (Mercury) 1969—*Elephant Mountain* (RCA) (– Corbitt) 1970—*The Best of the Youngbloods; Rock Festival* (Raccoon) 1971—*Ride the Wind; Sunlight* (RCA) (+ Michael Kane, bass) *Good and Dusty* (Raccoon) 1972—*High on a Ridge Top.*
Jesse Colin Young solo: 1964—*The Soul of a City Boy* (Capitol); *Youngblood* (Mercury) 1972—*Together* (Raccoon) 1973—*Song for Juli* (Warner Bros.) 1974—*Light Shine* 1975—*Songbird* 1976—*On the Road* 1977—*Love on the Wing* 1978—*American Dreams* (Elektra) 1982—*The Perfect Stranger* 1987—*The Highway Is for Heroes* (Cypress) 1991—*The Best of Jesse Colin Young: The Solo Years* (Rhino) 1993—*Makin' It Real* (Ridgetop) 1994—*Swept Away* 1995—*Desire.*

The Youngbloods were a folk-rock group led by Jesse Colin Young. Though they had a jazzy, mellow West Coast sound, their roots were in Boston and New York City. Young started out playing the folk circuit in Greenwich Village, where he met Bobby Scott, a composer/singer/pianist who had played with Bobby Darin, among others. Scott financed and produced Young's debut, *The Soul of a City Boy.* Reputedly cut in four hours, the solo LP of Young and acoustic guitar was released on Capitol in 1964. He began to play the Boston clubs and then cut *Youngblood* for Mercury, again with Scott producing, this time with a backup band including friend John Sebastian.

Inspired by the Beatles, Young decided to form a group, beginning with Massachusetts folkie Jerry Corbitt and then adding Joe Bauer and Lowell "Banana" Levinger, the last being the most accomplished musician of the band. In late 1965 the new Youngbloods cut some tracks for Mercury, but these were not released until years later on *Two Trips.* Their official debut was *The Youngbloods,* which included the hits "Grizzly Bear" and "Get Together," written by Dino Valenti, later a singer for Quicksilver Messenger Service. It was first a regional hit, and it didn't take off nationally until it was rereleased two years later in July 1969 after it had been used on a TV public service ad for brotherhood. In 1969 it hit #5 and went gold. RCA later renamed the first album after the single.

The band moved to Marin County, California, in late 1967. Their next two LPs were produced in New York by Felix Pappalardi before they went west. The third, *Elephant Mountain,* was overseen by Charlie Daniels. Corbitt left the band during *Elephant Mountain,* and the Youngbloods continued as a trio, signing to Warner Bros., who gave them their own label, Raccoon, in 1970. RCA began to repackage all their older work, including a best-of that year, also rereleasing for the third time "Darkness Darkness," previously out in August 1968 and March 1969.

The Youngbloods' first two Warners/Raccoon albums were live recordings—*Rock Festival* and *Ride the Wind.* In early 1971, they added bassist Michael Kane, freeing Young to play guitar. The band issued two more LPs—*Good and Dusty* and *High on a Ridge Top*—before disbanding in 1972. Bauer and Banana made solo albums; Corbitt had previously cut two; all of these went nowhere. Bauer, Banana, and Kane briefly united to form the band Noggins, doing one LP, *Crab Tunes,* for Raccoon in 1972. Banana also recorded as Banana and the Bunch, worked with Mimi Fariña, and taught hang gliding. Bauer succumbed to a brain tumor in 1982.

Young was the only musician to successfully carry on. *Together* had the same breezy feel of the Youngbloods, again highlighted by his light, supple vocals. Surviving Youngblood members Banana, Corbitt, and Young reunited first in 1984–85 to tour. Young has continued to perform and record, occasionally with his old band mates. He currently resides on a plantation in Hawaii, where he grows and sells the famed, organic Kona coffee.

Young MC

Born Marvin Young, May 10, 1967, London, Eng.
1989—*Stone Cold Rhymin'* (Delicious Vinyl) 1991—*Brainstorm* (Capitol) 1993—*What's the Flavor?*

Clean-cut, college-educated Young MC was one of the first black rappers to score a Top 10 pop hit, with 1989's "Bust a Move," a credible-sounding, yet catchy and nonthreatening hip-hop track.

Marvin Young's parents, who'd emigrated from Jamaica to England, moved to Hollis, Queens (also home to Run-D.M.C. and L.L. Cool J), when he was two years old. He began writing songs and poems, based on fairy tales and nursery rhymes as a child. He joined protean rap groups in high school and went to the University of Southern California, where he met Michael Ross and Matt Dike, a pair of DJ/producers who co-owned the Delicious Vinyl label. Young recorded a single for the label, "I Let 'Em Know," that found some success in the U.S. and U.K.

In 1989 Young collaborated on lyrics for Tone-Lōc's #2 pop hit "Wild Thing" (the first Top 10 pop hit by a black rapper) and its followup, "Funky Cold Medina." Still at USC, Young recorded his debut album as Young MC, *Stone Cold Rhymin'* (#9, 1989), which included the comical story rap "Principal's Office" (#33, 1989) and "Bust a Move" (#7, 1989), which won the Grammy for Best Rap Performance. Also in 1989 Young appeared on and wrote lyrics for Sly and Robbie's *Silent Assassin.*

He then tried to bolt from Delicious Vinyl, claiming, "On

my album there was stuff I'd never heard before," and that the label kept him from writing soundtrack music for the Eddie Murphy movie *Another 48 HRS.* Delicious Vinyl sued him for breach of contract; the matter was settled out of court in 1991, and Young MC released *Brainstorm* (#66, 1991) on Capitol Records. The album—full of socially responsible tracks like "Use Your Head" and "Keep It in Your Pants"—yielded only the minor hit "That's the Way Love Goes" (#54, 1991). His 1993 album, *What's the Flavor?*, flopped. "Bust a Move" continued to resurface years later, however, covered by *Star Trek* icon William Shatner in one of a series of popular 1999 and 2000 commercials for the Internet bargain-shopping site priceline.com, and featured on the soundtrack for the big-screen football comedy *The Replacements.* By the end of the decade, he was back in the studio, working on new material.

Robin Zander: See Cheap Trick

Zapp/Roger

Formed 1975, Hamilton, OH
Roger "Zapp" Troutman (b. Nov. 29, 1951, Hamilton; d. Apr. 25, 1999), voc., gtr.; Lester Troutman (b. Mar. 3, 1956, Hamilton), drums; Terry Troutman, (b. Apr. 7, 1961, Hamilton), bass; Larry Troutman (b. Aug. 12, 1944, Hamilton; d. Apr. 25, 1999), congas.
1980—*Zapp* (Warner Bros.) 1982—*Zapp II* 1983—*Zapp III* 1985—*The New Zapp IV U* 1989—*Zapp V.*
Roger: 1981—*The Many Facets of Roger* (Warner Bros.) 1984—*The Saga Continues* 1987—*Unlimited!* 1991—*Bridging the Gap* (Reprise).
Zapp & Roger: 1996—*Compilation: Greatest Hits, vol. 2 & More.*

Zapp had a string of post-Parliament funk hits during the '80s, the biggest being "More Bounce to the Ounce—Part I" (#86 pop, #2 R&B, 1980). Though the group's musical foundation was funk, leader Roger Troutman often led Zapp into light jazz or blues. The group spruced up its performances with zany costume changes and quirky vocal effects.

Roger Troutman grew up one of eight children in working-class Hamilton, Ohio. As a child he remembers his parents being unhappy during the week and happy on the weekends, when they would spend time with his aunts and uncles listening to music. Troutman associated music with happiness, and decided to learn to play and sing himself. He began experimenting with a Vocoder, an electronic effect that makes the human voice sound robotic.

In 1975 Troutman and three brothers formed Roger and the Human Body, whose Vocoder-ized funk became their main schtick. The group recorded an independent record, which made its way to Parliament/Funkadelic maestro George Clinton. With Clinton's help, the group landed a deal on Warner Bros., renamed themselves Zapp, and recorded their self-titled debut album with other musicians including Bootsy Collins on guitar.

On the strength of "More Bounce to the Ounce" and "Be Alright" (#26 R&B, 1980), *Zapp* reached #19 on the pop chart in 1980 and went gold. *Zapp II* (#25 pop, 1982) produced the hits "Doo Wah Ditty (Blow That Thing)" (#10 R&B, 1982) and "Dance Floor (Part I)" (#1 R&B, 1982). *Zapp III* (#39 pop, 1983) spawned "I Can Make You Dance (Part I)" (#4 R&B, 1983) and "Heartbreaker" (#15 R&B, 1983). The group returned two years later with *The New Zapp IV U,* scoring a hit with "Computer Love (Part I)" (#8 R&B, 1986). But rap had taken over by mid-decade, and Zapp seemed to get lost in the shuffle; 1989's *Zapp V* charted disappointingly.

In the meantime, Troutman recorded several solo albums in the '80s and into the '90s, under the name Roger, and scored a big hit with 1987's "I Wanna Be Your Man" (#3 pop, #1). He also produced former Zapp backup singer Shirley Murdock's self-titled album, which included the R&B Top 10 single "Go On Without You." Troutman also recorded *Bridging the Gap.*

In 1993 the group—renamed Zapp & Roger—charted

with *All the Greatest Hits* (#39 pop, #9 R&B, 1993), which yielded the hits "Slow and Easy" (#43 pop, #18 R&B, 1993) and "Mega Medley" (#54 pop, #30 R&B, 1993). The recordings of Zapp & Roger were also frequently sampled in the work of such hip-hop acts as Cypress Hill, Snoop Dogg, the Notorious B.I.G., and Ice Cube. In 1996 Troutman guested on Tupac Shakur and Dr. Dre's Top 10 hit "California Love," followed in 1997 by an appearance on the Johnny Gill single "It's Your Body."

The self-described "evangelist of funk" was also a community activist and businessman at home, forming Troutman Enterprises, a construction company involved in building affordable housing for low-income residents in Dayton, Ohio. The company employed unskilled youths who divided their time as construction workers and as members of the latter-day Zapp. But by the mid-'90s, the company sought bankruptcy protection. Then on April 25, 1999, Troutman was found dead from four gunshot wounds in an alley behind his recording studio. The incident was an apparent murder-suicide by older brother and sometime songwriting collaborator Larry Troutman, who was also found dead seven blocks away with a bullet in his head, a revolver by his side.

Frank Zappa/Mothers of Invention

Born Francis Vincent Zappa Jr., Dec. 21, 1940, Baltimore, MD; died Dec. 4, 1993, Los Angeles, CA

Mothers of Invention, formed 1964, Los Angeles: Zappa, voc., gtr., various instruments; Ray Collins, voc.; Dave Coronada, sax; Roy Estrada, bass; Jimmy Carl Black, drums; – Coronada; + Elliot Ingber, gtr.).

1966—*Freak Out!* (Verve) (– Ingber; + Bunk Gardner, sax; + Jim "Motorhead" Sherwood, sax; + Don Preston, kybds.; + Billy Mundi, drums) 1967—*Absolutely Free; We're Only in It for the Money; Lumpy Gravy* (– Mundi) 1968—*Cruising With Ruben & the Jets* 1969—*Uncle Meat* (Bizarre) (+ Lowell George [b. Apr. 13, 1945, Hollywood, CA; d. June 29, 1979, Arlington, VA], gtr.; + Art Tripp III, drums) *Burnt Weeny Sandwich; Weasels Ripped My Flesh* 1970—(group disbands) 1971—(+ Ian Underwood, kybds., reeds; + Howard Kaylan [b. June 22, 1945, New York, NY], voc.; + Mark Volman [b. Apr. 19, 1944, Los Angeles, CA], voc.; + Jim Pons [b. Mar. 14, 1943, Santa Monica, CA], bass) *Fillmore East—June 1971* 1972—*Just Another Band From L.A.; The Grand Wazoo* 1973—*Over-Nite Sensation* (DiscReet).

Frank Zappa: 1969—*Hot Rats* (Bizarre) 1971—*200 Motels* (United Artists) 1972—*Waka/Jawaka* (Bizarre) 1974—*Apostrophe (')* (DiscReet) 1975—*Bongo Fury* (with Captain Beefheart) 1976—*Zoot Allures* (Warner Bros.) 1978—*Studio Tan* (DiscReet) 1979—*Sleep Dirt; Sheik Yerbouti* (Zappa); *Orchestral Favorites* (DiscReet); *Joe's Garage, Act 1* (Zappa); *Joe's Garage, Acts 2 and 3* 1981—*Shut Up 'n Play Yer Guitar* (Barking Pumpkin); *Shut Up 'n Play Yer Guitar Some More; Tinseltown Rebellion* 1982—*Ship Arriving Too Late to Save a Drowning Witch* 1983—*The Man From Utopia; Baby Snakes* 1984—*The Perfect Stranger* (Atlantic); *Francesco Zappa* (Barking Dog); *Them or Us; Thing-Fish* 1985—*Frank Zappa Meets the Mothers of Prevention* 1986—*Jazz From Hell; Broadway the Hard Way* 1988—*Guitar; You Can't Do That on Stage Anymore, vol. 1; You Can't Do That on Stage Anymore, vol. 2* 1989—*You Can't Do That on Stage Anymore, vol. 3* 1991—*The Best Band You Never Heard in Your Life; You Can't Do That on Stage Anymore, vol. 4; Make a Jazz Noise Here; As an Am Zappa* (Rhino); *Trick or Treat; Freaks and Motherfu*#@%!; Piquantique; Saarbrucken 1978; The Ark; 'Tis the Season to Be Jelly; Unmitigated Audacity; Anyway the Wind Blows* 1992—*You Can't Do That on Stage Anymore, vol. 5* (Rykodisc); *Playground Psychotics* (Barking Pumpkin); *At the Circus* (Rhino); *Conceptual Continuity; Disconnected Synapses; Electric Aunt Jemima; Our Man in Nirvana; Swiss Cheese/Fire; Tengo Na Michia Tanta; You Can't Do That on Stage Anymore, vol. 6* (Rykodisc) 1993—*Ahead of Their Time; The Yellow Shark* 1995—*Civilization Phaze III* (Barking Pumpkin); *Does Humor Belong in Music?* (originally released in Europe in 1986) (Rykodisc); *Strictly Commercial: The Best of Frank Zappa* 1996—*The Lost Episodes; Läther* 1997—*Have I Offended Someone?; Strictly Genteel: A Classical Introduction* 1998—*Cheap Thrills; Mystery Disc; Cucamonga* (Del-Fi) 1999—*Zappa on the Road* (Rykodisc); *Son of Cheep Thrills* 2000—*Watermelon in Easter Hay.*

With more than 80 albums to his credit, composer/arranger/guitarist/bandleader Frank Zappa demonstrated a mastery of pop idioms ranging from jazz to rock of every conceivable variety, penned electronic and orchestral works, parlayed controversial satire, and testified in Congress against censorship. As astute an entrepreneur as he was a musician, he was impatient with any division between popular and high art; he combined scatological humor with political wit, required of his players (Little Feat founder Lowell George, guitarists Adrian Belew and Steve Vai, and drummer Terry Bozzio, among them) an intimidating skill, and displayed consistent innovation in instrumental and studio technology.

The eldest of four children of a guitar-playing government scientist, Frank Zappa moved with his family at age 10 to California, eventually settling in Lancaster. Playing in school orchestras and bands, he taught himself a variety of instruments, concentrating on guitar. A collector of '50s rock & roll and R&B singles, he also listened to modern classical composers like Stravinsky and his avowed favorite, Edgard Varèse. In high school he formed the Black-Outs and added country blues to his record collection. He met future collaborator and underground legend Don Van Vliet and allegedly christened him Captain Beefheart. In 1959 he studied music theory at Chaffey College in Alta Loma, California, dropping out after six months.

In 1960 Zappa played cocktail music in lounges and worked on his first recordings and the score for a B movie, *The World's Greatest Sinner.* He also appeared on Steve Allen's TV show, performing a "bicycle concerto" (plucking the spokes, blowing through the handlebars). In 1963 Zappa wrote a score for a Western called *Run Home Slow,* and with the money built a studio in Cucamonga, California. He be-

Frank Zappa

friended future Mothers Ray Collins and Jim "Motorhead" Sherwood, and formed a band with Beefheart called the Soots.

Zappa was charged with conspiracy to commit pornography by the San Bernardino Vice Squad after an undercover policeman requested some sex "party" tapes: Zappa delivered tapes of faked grunting, and served 10 days of a six-month jail sentence. The woman involved was bailed out of jail with royalties from "Memories of El Monte," which Zappa and Collins had written for the doo-wop group the Penguins.

In 1964 Zappa joined the Soul Giants, with Collins (vocals), Dave Coronada (sax), Roy Estrada (bass), and Jimmy Carl Black (drums). Renaming them the Muthers, then the Mothers, he moved the band onto L.A.'s proto-hippie "freak" circuit (Coronada quit, replaced by guitarist Elliot Ingber). The band played clubs for two years, mixing covers with social-protest tunes like "Who Are the Brain Police?" In early 1966 producer Tom Wilson signed them to MGM/Verve and recorded *Freak Out!* MGM, wary of the band's outrageous reputation, forced Zappa to add "of Invention" to the Mothers. Though Zappa advertised the album in underground papers and comics and earned critical respect for the album's obvious musical and lyrical distinction, it ended up losing money.

In 1966, with Ingber departing, eventually to join Captain Beefheart's Magic Band, the Mothers lineup expanded to include saxophonists Bunk Gardner and Motorhead Sherwood, keyboardist Don Preston, and drummer Billy Mundi. Released in 1967, *Absolutely Free* further satirized "straight" America with pointed tunes like "Brown Shoes Don't Make It" and "Plastic People." *We're Only in It for the Money,* a parody of the Beatles' *Sgt. Pepper,* found Zappa savaging hippie pretensions. His montage production techniques—mingling tape edits, noise, recitative, free-form outbursts, and Varèse-like modern classical music with rock—were coming into their own. In 1967 Zappa and the Mothers also recorded *Lumpy Gravy,* with a 50-piece orchestra, including many Mothers, and *Cruising With Ruben & the Jets,* an homage to '50s doo-wop.

Billy Mundi left after *Lumpy Gravy;* by now it was apparent that the Mothers were less a band than a shifting vehicle for Zappa's art. While recording *Money,* Zappa and the group had moved to New York City's Greenwich Village, where they began a six-month residency at the Garrick Theatre. There they pioneered rock theater with a series of often-spontaneous audience-participation skits. While recording *Ruben & the Jets,* the Mothers also began recording *Uncle Meat,* a double album for a never-completed movie. It is the first example of Zappa's trademark complex-meter jazz-rock fusion.

After making *Uncle Meat,* Zappa moved the band back to L.A. and married his second wife, Gail; their four children include daughters Moon Unit and Diva and sons Dweezil and Ahmet Rodan. (Dweezil would become a solo artist in the '80s, then form Shampoohorn with his brother in the '90s; both also became television personalities, as did their sister Moon Unit). In L.A. Zappa moved into movie cowboy Tom Mix's Log Cabin Ranch, where he assembled the increasingly complex *Burnt Weeny Sandwich* and *Weasels Ripped My Flesh.* By this time, the band had come to include second guitarist Lowell George and drummer Art Tripp III.

In late 1968 Zappa and manager Herb Cohen had moved to Warner/Reprise, where they formed their own Straight and Bizarre labels. Zappa recorded such acts as groupie collective the GTO's (Girls Together Outrageously), onetime street-singer Wild Man Fischer, Alice Cooper, and Captain Beefheart (whose *Trout Mask Replica* was one of Zappa's most memorable productions). By the time *Weasels* was released in 1970, Zappa had temporarily disbanded the Mothers because of overwhelming expenses and public apathy. Lowell George and Roy Estrada then founded Little Feat; Art Trip III joined Beefheart (Estrada later joined Beefheart as well); Gardner and Black formed Geronimo Black.

Zappa began composing the soundtrack for *200 Motels.* He also recorded his first solo album, *Hot Rats,* a jazz-rock guitar showcase featuring Beefheart and jazz violinists Jean-Luc Ponty and Don "Sugarcane" Harris. *Hot Rats* was released to great critical acclaim in 1970, as was Ponty's *King Kong,* an album of Zappa compositions (for legal reasons, Zappa's name couldn't be listed as producer and guitarist). In 1970 Zappa also performed the *200 Motels* score with Zubin Mehta and the L.A. Philharmonic at a sold-out L.A. concert. That summer, Zappa re-formed the Mothers, retaining keyboardist/reedman Ian Underwood and adding ex-Turtles Howard Kaylan, Mark Volman (singers then known as the Phlorescent Leech and Eddie), and bassist Jim Pons, along with jazz keyboardist George Duke and British rock drummer Aynsley Dunbar. With this lineup and other session players, Zappa recorded *Waka/Jawaka* and *Chunga's Revenge* as solo albums and the Mothers' *Fillmore East—June 1971* and *Just Another Band From L.A.*

At this point, critics began accusing the Mothers of becoming a cynical, scatological joke, but Zappa displayed no discomfort in portraying two apparently contradictory personae: the raunchy inciter and the serious composer (whose stature in fact would increase over the years, and whose cult always remained intense). In 1971 the *200 Motels* film, featuring Theodore Bikel and Ringo Starr as surrogate Zappas, as well as the Mothers, was released to mixed response. In May 1971 Zappa appeared at one of the last Fillmore East concerts with John Lennon and Yoko Ono; the performance appears on Lennon/Ono's *Some Time in New York City.* As the Mothers personnel began to change more frequently, they embarked on a 1971 tour in which their equipment was destroyed in a fire at Switzerland's Montreux Casino (immortalized in opening act Deep Purple's hit "Smoke on the Water"), and Zappa was injured when a fan pushed him from the stage of London's Rainbow Theatre. A year later the Mothers were banned from Royal Albert Hall for "obscenity."

The Grand Wazoo, with numerous auxiliary players, was a big-band fusion album. And in 1973 Zappa and the Mothers also recorded *Over-Nite Sensation,* on which Zappa simplified his music and kept his lyrics in a scatological-humorous vein, as in "Don't Eat the Yellow Snow" (#86, 1974). Album sales picked up. *Apostrophe (')*—Zappa's highest charting album, at #10—featured an extended jam with ex-Cream bassist Jack Bruce, as well as by-now-typical dirty jokes and satires. The 1975 *Bongo Fury* album reunited Zappa with Beefheart. The latter had fallen out with Zappa after *Trout Mask,* accusing Zappa of marketing him as "a freak."

After producing Grand Funk Railroad's *Good Singin', Good Playin'* in 1976, Zappa filed a lawsuit against Herb Cohen in 1977 and severed ties with Warner Bros., moving to Mercury two years later. There he set up Zappa Records and retired the Mothers name, calling all later groups Zappa. On the new label he released *Sheik Yerbouti* (a pun on KC and the Sunshine Band's "Shake Your Booty"), including the song "Jewish Princess," over which the B'nai B'rith Anti-Defamation League filed a complaint with the FCC against Zappa. That album also yielded a surprise hit single, "Dancin' Fool" (#45, 1979), which lampooned the disco crowd. (*Sheik* peaked at #21 on the albums chart.) *Joe's Garage, Act I,* the first installment of a three-act rock opera, included "Catholic Girls," and Zappa's penchant for barbed attacks continued to infuriate his critics while strengthening his own following.

In 1979 Zappa also released the film *Baby Snakes,* a mélange of concert footage, dressing room slapstick, and clay-figure animation. The late-'70s Zappa bands included guitarist Adrian Belew (who later played with Talking Heads, King Crimson, and David Bowie) and drummer Terry Bozzio (who later with his wife Dale founded Missing Persons). In 1980 Zappa recorded a single, "I Don't Wanna Get Drafted," which Mercury refused to release, prompting him to leave the label and eventually establish his own Barking Pumpkin label.

In 1981 Zappa released his first Barking Pumpkin album; and that year, some ex-Mothers, including Jimmy Carl Black, Don Preston, and Bunk Gardner, united to form the Grandmothers. They toured and recorded, playing all-Zappa material from the Mothers' vintage late-'60s period. That April Zappa produced and hosted a New York City concert of music by Edgard Varèse. He also released a limited edition mail-order-only, three-album series, *Shut Up 'n Play Yer Guitar.*

Zappa parlayed stereotype satire into success once more with "Valley Girl" (#32, 1982) from the *Drowning Witch* album. The song parodied the spoiled daughters of entertainment-industry folk, specifically those in the San Bernardino Valley city of Encino, and featured inspired mimicry by then-14-year-old Moon Unit Zappa. In 1983 Zappa conducted works by Varèse and Anton Webern at San Francisco's War Memorial Opera House.

The '80s saw Zappa consolidating his business affairs; with Gail Zappa in charge, his companies included not only Barking Pumpkin (a mail-order label, distributed by Capitol) but Honker Home Video, Barfko-Swill (for Zappa merchandise), and World's Finest Optional Entertainment Co. (to produce live shows); he also arranged with Rykodisc to rerelease his catalogue on CD. A lifelong free-speech advocate, he testified before a Senate subcommittee in 1985 and assailed the Parents' Music Resource Center (excerpts from the hearings appeared on *Frank Zappa Meets the Mothers of Prevention*); throughout the decade, he also championed voter registration drives. In 1990, at the invitation of Czechoslovakian president Vaclav Havel, a longtime fan, Zappa served for several months as that country's trade, tourism, and cultural liaison to the West. The following year, he considered a run for the U.S. presidency.

Artistically, the '80s were also fertile years for Zappa. Early in the decade, the Berkeley Symphony performed his work; in 1984 conductor/composer Pierre Boulez released *Boulez Conducts Zappa/The Perfect Stranger* (#7, 1984 on the classical chart). In 1988 Zappa undertook a world tour (documented on *Broadway the Hard Way*) and won a Grammy for Best Rock Instrumental for *Jazz From Hell,* an album composed on Synclavier, a highly sophisticated synthesizer that in Zappa found one of its chief devotees. Among his other late-'80s projects were remastering his '60s work for CD and assembling six double-CD sets of live work entitled *You Can't Do That on Stage Anymore*. In 1989 Poseidon Press published his autobiography, *The Real Frank Zappa Book*.

In 1991, in New York City on the eve of a tribute concert entitled "Zappa's Universe," Moon Unit and Dweezil Zappa announced that their father had been diagnosed with prostate cancer. A lifelong teetotaler and abstainer from drugs (Zappa, however, smoked cigarettes and drank coffee incessantly), the composer continued a rigorous work schedule. In 1992 he completed a two-CD sequel to *Lumpy Gravy, Civilization Phaze III* and in 1993 recorded both *The Yellow Shark*, an album of his compositions by the classical group Ensemble Modern, and, also with the Ensemble, an album of Varèse works tentatively entitled *The Rage and the Fury: The Music of Edgard Varèse*. Frank Zappa died on the evening of December 4, 1993, at his L.A. home; he was 52 years old.

He had over the years remixed or remastered all of his recorded output for CD releases; nearly everything has since been rereleased on Rykodisc. He was inducted into the Rock and Roll Hall of Fame in 1995. That year also saw the publication, from St. Martin's Press, of Ben Watson's *Frank Zappa: The Negative Dialectics of Poodle Play*, an exhaustive postmodernist deconstruction/appreciation of the man's music. Four years later, he was remembered, perhaps more fittingly, by an all-Zappa program performed by the Florida Orchestra.

Josef Zawinul: See Weather Report

Warren Zevon

Born Jan. 24, 1947, Chicago, IL
1969—*Wanted—Dead or Alive* (Imperial) 1976—*Warren Zevon* (Asylum) 1978—*Excitable Boy* 1980—*Bad Luck Streak in Dancing School; Stand in the Fire* 1982—*The Envoy* 1987—*A Quiet Normal Life: The Best of Warren Zevon; Sentimental Hygiene* (Virgin) 1989—*Transverse City* 1991—*Mr. Bad Example* (Giant) 1993—*Learning to Flinch* 1995—*Mutineer* 1996—*I'll Sleep When I'm Dead (An Anthology)* (Rhino) 2000—*Life'll Kill Ya* (Artemis).

Singer/songwriter Warren Zevon's ironic tales of physical and psychological mayhem have earned him a cult following and comparisons to figures as diverse as Dorothy Parker, Raymond Chandler, Sam Peckinpah, and Martin Scorsese.

The son of Russian immigrants, Zevon grew up in Arizona and California. He studied music briefly, and after meeting Igor Stravinsky during his junior high school years, Zevon taught himself to play guitar and began writing songs. He played in local bands and at age 16 moved to New York, then to the Bay Area. He wrote songs (including "She Quit Me Man," used in the film *Midnight Cowboy*) and released his debut LP, *Wanted—Dead or Alive*. It was poorly received, and he went to work writing jingles (for Ernest and Julio Gallo wine ads, a famous ketchup, and the Chevrolet Camaro) and as pianist and bandleader for the Everly Brothers shortly before their breakup. Over the next couple of years he continued to work with each brother separately.

In 1976 Linda Ronstadt covered Zevon's "Hasten Down the Wind" on her album of the same title. The next year two more of Zevon's songs appeared on Ronstadt's *Simple Dreams*: "Carmelita" and "Poor Poor Pitiful Me," the latter of which was a hit for Ronstadt in 1978. Zevon, who had been living in Spain, was persuaded by his friend Jackson Browne to return to the U.S. and record. Browne produced *Warren Zevon*, which was released to critical acclaim; he would produce or coproduce all of Zevon's albums through and including *A Quiet Normal Life: The Best of Warren Zevon*.

In 1978 Zevon had a #21 single with "Werewolves of London" from *Excitable Boy* (#8). But his career was temporarily set back by his alcoholism. He did not record for two years, and his live performances were few and erratic. His two 1980 releases, *Bad Luck Streak in Dancing School* (#20) and the live *Stand in the Fire* (#20), represented something of a comeback for Zevon. He announced he had given up alcohol and he released *The Envoy* (#93, 1982), the title track written about U.S. envoy to the Mideast Philip Habib. *Sentimental Hygiene* (#87, 1987) appeared five years later, with backing from members of R.E.M. He also recorded with three-quarters of that group under the name Hindu Love Gods in 1990.

While Zevon continues to be appreciated by critics, his sometimes edgy, satirical work eludes the mass audience. *Transverse City*, a science-fiction–inspired concept album, and *Mr. Bad Example* were not received as warmly as Zevon's earlier work. But starting with his second live album, 1993's *Learning to Flinch*, Zevon bounced back, showing that he retains his unique, original vision and remains a compelling writer and performer. And he also has a circle of dedicated admirers: He was invited to perform "Lawyers, Guns and Money" at Minnesota Governor Jesse Ventura's inauguration party in 1998, and he is a regular guest on *Late Night With David Letterman*, occasionally filling in for bandleader Paul Shaffer. The pared-down *Life'll Kill Ya* (which included a cover of Steve Winwood's "Back in the High Life Again") was released in 2000 to excellent reviews.

In the early '90s, Zevon composed and/or performed a number of theme songs and scores for television series, including *The Drug Wars* (1990), *Tales From the Crypt* (1992), *Route 66* (1993), and *Tekwar* (1993).

The Zombies

Formed 1963, Hertfordshire, Eng.
Colin Blunstone (b. June 24, 1945, Hatfield, Eng.), voc.; Paul Atkinson (b. Mar. 19, 1946, Cuffley, Eng.), gtr.; Rod Argent (b. June 14, 1945, St. Albans, Eng.), kybds., voc.; Hugh Grundy (b. Mar. 6, 1945, Winchester, Eng.), drums; Paul Arnold (b. Eng.), bass.

1964—(– Arnold; + Chris White [b. Mar. 7, 1943, Barnet, Eng.], bass) 1965—*Begins Here* (Decca) 1969—*Odessey and Oracle* (Date) 1973—*Time of the Zombies* (Epic) 1985—*Live on the BBC: 1965–1967* (Rhino) 1990—*Greatest Hits* (Digital Compact Classics) 1998—*Zombie Heaven* (Big Beat, U.K.).

Though the Zombies had several major hits, their career was a frustrating one. Paul Atkinson, Rod Argent, and Hugh Grundy met at St. Albans School, and they soon linked up with Colin Blunstone and bassist Paul Arnold. Six months later Arnold was replaced by Chris White. After winning a rock-band contest held by a local newspaper, they auditioned with British Decca in 1964. That July, the electric-piano-centered "She's Not There" was released; it became a worldwide smash, going to #2 in America. A second single, "Leave Me Be," failed, but "Tell Her No" went Top 10, their last hit for some time. They also contributed songs to the movie *Bunny Lake Is Missing*.

In 1967 they recorded a final LP, *Odessey and Oracle* (the only album the band themselves approve of). They broke up two weeks after it was completed, in December 1967. Columbia staff producer Al Kooper fought to have the album issued; when it was released, in late 1968, it yielded a #1 gold hit in "Time of the Season." The band declined to re-form, although sizable sums were offered to the musicians. Argent already was moving ahead on plans for his eponymous band [see entry] and others were fed up with the music business. Blunstone had first gone back to working in an insurance office, then to working as a singer under the name Neil MacArthur. With that pseudonym he had a 1970 hit with a remake of "She's Not There." He made several, Epic-released solo LPs under his own name, beginning in 1971 with *One Year* (produced by Argent and White). In 1978 the unsuccessful *Never Even Thought* appeared on Elton John's Rocket Records. Blunstone has since formed a group called Keats. He also sang on several records by the Alan Parsons Project.

Atkinson first went into programming computers. He later worked in A&R, first for Columbia in New York, and later at RCA, where he was vice president of West Coast A&R. Grundy also worked in Columbia's A&R department, but in the '80s he ran a horse transport business near London. White cowrote songs and produced records for Argent (for whom he wrote "Hold Your Head Up"). In the '70s he helped discover Dire Straits. Original bassist Arnold became a doctor in Scotland. Epic released a two-record "best-of," *Time of the Zombies*, in 1973. The four-CD *Zombie Heaven* renewed pop fans' interest in the band. By the late '90s, critics often referred to *Odessey and Oracle* as the British equivalent of the Beach Boys' masterpiece *Pet Sounds*. By the decade's end, Argent had finished an album of classical piano and Blunstone had resumed his solo touring after over 20 years. He continues to record on his own as well. The two performed together in New York for the first time in more than 30 years as part of Cave Stomp at the Village Underground nightclub.

John Zorn

Born Sep. 2, 1953, Brooklyn, NY
1980—*Pool* (Parachute) 1981—*Archery* 1983—*Locus Solus* (Tzadik) 1984—*The Big Gundown* (Elektra/Nonesuch); *Ganryu Island* (Tzadik) 1985—*Cobra* (Hat Art); *Voodoo: The Music of Sonny Clark* (Black Saint); *Classic Guide to Strategy* (Tzadik) 1986—*Spillane* (Elektra/Nonesuch) 1987—*News for Lulu* (Hat Hut) 1988—*Spy Vs. Spy: The Music of Ornette Coleman* (Elektra/Nonesuch) 1989—*More News for Lulu* (Hat Hut); *Naked City* (Elektra/Nonesuch) 1991—*Grande Guignol* (Avant, Jap.) 1992—*Filmworks: 1986–1990* (Elektra/Nonesuch); *John Zorn's Cobra Live at the Knitting Factory* (Knitting Factory Works) 1993—*Absinthe* (Avant, Jap.); *Radio; Kristallnacht* (Tzadik) 1994—*John Zorn's Cobra: Tokyo Operation '94* (Avant, Jap.); *Heretic, Jeux Des Dames* 1995—*Film Works, vol. 5: Tears of Ecstasy* (Tzadik); *Nani Nani; The Book of Heads; Elegy; First Recordings 1973; Redbird; New Traditions in East Asian Bar Bands* (Avant) 1996—*Bar Kokhba* (Tzadik) 1997—*Duras: Duchamp* 1998—*Angelus Novus; Circle Maker; Downtown Lullaby* (Depth of Field); *Aporias: Requia for Piano and Orchestra* (Tzadik); *Bribe; Music Romance, vol. 1: Music for Children* 1999—*The String Quartets; Music Romance, vol. 2: Taboo and Exile* 2000—*Lacrosse; Xu Feng; Cartoon S&M.*
With Masada (Zorn; Joey Baron, drums; Greg Cohen, bass; Dave Douglas, trumpet): 1995—*Masada, Vol. 2: Beit* (DIW); *Vol. 3: Gimel; Vol. 5: Hei; Vol. 6: Vay; Live in New York City 1994* (Jazz Door) 1998—*Vol. 9: Tet* (DIW); *Vol. 8: Het; Vol. 10: Yod* 1999—*Vol. 7: Zayin; Vol. 4: Dalet; Live in Jerusalem; Live in Taipei; Live in Middleheim* 2000—*Live in Sevilla 2000; Vol. 1: Alef* (DIW).

Composer, instrumentalist, musical subversist John Zorn was the most important figure to emerge from New York's Downtown avant-garde music scene. Zorn became interested in jazz while briefly attending the liberal Webster College in St. Louis and began studying the alto saxophone.

By the time he returned to his hometown, New York, in 1974, Zorn had already developed his own theories of composition and improvisation, incorporating ideas from traditional and avant-garde strains of jazz, classical, rock, and a panoply of international aesthetics. With his whirlwind energy Zorn became the vortex of the new musical polyglot that was brewing among adventurous players on New York's Lower East Side. His hand in a multitude of projects—from bebop tributes to obscure jazzmen to epic performances of Cobra, which applied rules of game playing to free improvisation—Zorn galvanized the scene.

While Zorn's work is generally released by independent and European labels that cater to the avant-garde, he began recording for Elektra/Nonesuch in the mid-'80s, beginning with *The Big Gundown*, a twisted tribute to cult film composer Ennio Morricone, and *Spillane*, which featured bluesman Albert Collins. Zorn's projects drew upon a pool of like-minded innovators, including guitarist Elliott Sharp, keyboardist Wayne Horvitz, and drummer Bobby Previte.

By the late '80s Zorn was dividing his year between New

York and Tokyo. With Fred Frith, Bill Frisell, and Joey Baron, Zorn formed the band Naked City, which touched on, among myriad musics, his new fascination with thrash rock; Zorn's Spy Vs. Spy band transformed Ornette Coleman's music with its slamming full-force interpretations. In September 1993, in honor of Zorn's 40th birthday, the Knitting Factory (New York's chief downtown avant-garde music club) presented Zorn for a solid month, enabling him to cover a wide if incomplete spectrum of his musical endeavors. The '90s, in fact, found Zorn developing into an incredibly prolific composer. Appointed in 1993 the curator of the Radical New Jewish Culture Festival in New York, throughout the decade Zorn explored his Jewish heritage with two groups: Bar Kokhba and Masada, which combined traditional Jewish and klezmer music with Ornette Coleman–style experimentation. He recorded extensively for DIW, a Japanese jazz label, and for his own labels, Tzadik and Avant, which is a DIW subsidiary.

ZZ Top

Formed 1970, Texas
Billy Gibbons (b. Dec. 16, 1950, Houston, TX), gtr., voc.; Dusty Hill (b. May 19, 1949, Dallas, TX), bass, voc.; Frank Beard (b. June 11, 1949, Houston), drums.
1970—*First Album* (London) 1972—*Rio Grande Mud* 1973—*Tres Hombres* 1975—*Fandango!* 1976—*Tejas* 1977—*Best of ZZ Top* (all reissued on Warner Bros.) 1979—*Deguello* (Warner Bros.) 1981—*El Loco* 1983—*Eliminator* 1985—*Afterburner* 1990—*Recycler* 1992—*Greatest Hits* 1994—*Antenna* (RCA); *One Foot in the Blues* (Warner Bros.) 1996—*Rhythmeen* (RCA) 1999—*XXX.*

ZZ Top began as a rough-and-ready blues-rock power trio from Texas that became a huge mid-'70s concert attraction. Their real commercial peak didn't come, however, until the '80s, when the "Little Ol' Band from Texas" became MTV superstars and sold multiple millions of albums.

ZZ Top was built around guitarist Billy Gibbons, whose career began with the popular Southwestern band Moving Sidewalks, whose "99th Floor" was a regional mid-'60s hit. They opened one night for Jimi Hendrix, and he later mentioned Gibbons on *The Tonight Show* as one of America's best young guitarists. After Moving Sidewalks broke up, Gibbons and manager/producer Bill Ham recruited Frank Beard and Dusty Hill from a Dallas band, American Blues.

Beginning with the release of *First Album* in 1970, ZZ Top has toured constantly, building a national following that has made all the band's albums gold or platinum. A year-long tour in 1976, the Worldwide Texas Tour, was one of the largest-grossing road trips in rock at the time. Onstage with the band were snakes, longhorn cattle, buffalo, cactus, and other Southwestern paraphernalia. The group sold over a million tickets. They didn't record for the next three years, until 1979's *Deguello*. Though ZZ Top's only major hit singles had been *Tres Hombres*' "La Grange" (#41, 1973) and *Fandango!*'s "Tush" (#20, 1975), their albums consistently made the Top 40.

With 1983's *Eliminator,* ZZ Top made a quantum leap from best-kept secret to massive stardom. Thanks to smartly directed video clips for such songs as "Gimme All Your Lovin' " (#37, 1983), "Sharp Dressed Man" (#56, 1983), "Legs" (#8, 1983), and "TV Dinners," Gibbons and Hill, with their long beards (ironically Frank Beard usually wore only a moustache), became MTV icons, as did the cherry red 1933 Ford coupe (restored by Gibbons) that gave the album its name, and which the band drove in the videos. Thanks to this exposure, a whole new audience began buying the band's albums, and *Eliminator* (#9, 1983) eventually sold some 10 million copies, remaining on the chart for over three and a

ZZ Top: Dusty Hill, Frank Beard, Billy Gibbons

half years. "Legs" introduced a pulsating synthesizer beat into ZZ Top's crunching blues-rock riffs.

The trend continued with *Afterburner* (#4, 1985), which contained such video hits as "Rough Boy" (#22, 1985), "Sleeping Bag" (#8, 1985), "Velcro Fly" (#35, 1986), and "Stages" (#21, 1986). The album sold over 3 million copies. After another long world tour, ZZ Top—which had long been based in Houston—announced that, through NASA, it had booked passage as the first lounge band on the space shuttle (though the band has yet to actually fly a mission).

At the peak of its success, ZZ Top still remembered its roots, and launched a fundraising drive to erect a Delta Blues Museum in Clarksdale, Mississippi. At a special ceremony the band unveiled the "Muddywood" guitar, made from a beam taken from the sharecropper's shack in which blues giant Muddy Waters had been raised, and which Gibbons donated to the museum.

ZZ Top appeared to have finally tapped out the motherlode with *Recycler* (#6, 1990), which sold a relatively disappointing 1 million units, and yielded only minor hits in "Doubleback" (#50, 1990) and "Give It Up" (#79, 1990). After Warner Bros. released *Greatest Hits,* ZZ Top left the label and signed a $30 million deal with RCA. The band's first album for the new label, *Antenna,* was named in tribute to rock radio—especially the Mexican border stations of the '50s and '60s that influenced the band. The album entered the chart at #14 but dropped rapidly and failed to yield a hit single. Still, *Antenna* went platinum, proving the band still had a considerable fan base.

But while ZZ Top remains a popular touring attraction, its late-'90s albums have fared poorly on the chart. *Rhythmeen* (#29, 1996) did well enough, but *XXX* (#100, 1999), a mix of live and studio recordings, had dropped out of the *Billboard* Top 200 three months after its release. The band performed at President George W. Bush's inaugural ceremonies in January 2001.

Appendix
Cuts from the Second Edition

Will Ackerman
Barbara Acklin
Faye Adams
Johnny Adams
Marie Adams
Laurel Aitken
Al B. Sure!
Peter Allen
Angel
Angel City/Angels
April Wine
Atlantic Starr
Hoyt Axton
Bees Make Honey
Bill Black Combo
Blackfoot
Black Sheep
Blind Melon
David Blue
The Blues Brothers
Earl Bostic
Brass Construction
Brewer and Shipley
Roy C
The Cadets
The Capris
Carl Carltone
Cerrone
Chase
The Chipmunks
Lloyd Cole
Jessi Colter
Arthur Conley
Cornelius Brothers and Sister Rose
Floyd Cramer
The Crests
The Critters
Julee Cruise
Curved Air
Johnny Cymbal
Cyrkle
Dante and the Evergreens
Bobby Day
The Diamonds
Dick and Deedee
Dino, Desi and Billy
Ral Donner
Ducks Deluxe
Elephant's Memory
Shirley Ellis
An Emotional Fish
Adam Faith
Force M.D.'s
Emile Ford and the Checkmates
Inez and Charlie Foxx
Bobby Freeman
Front 242
Billy Fury
Gene Loves Jezebel
Gerardo
The Golden Palominos
Bobby Goldsboro
The Good Rats
Great White
Boris Grebenshikov
Stefan Grossman
The Groundhogs
GWAR
Johnny Hallyday
Roy Hamilton
The Harptones
Dan Hartman
Jon Hassell
Head, Hands and Feet
Helmet
Eddie Holman
The Honeycombs
The Honey Cone

The House of Love
Engelbert Humperdinck
Brian Hyland
Jellybean
The Jets
Jimmy Jam and Terry Lewis
The Jive Five
Jobriath
Johnny and the Hurricanes
Jo Jo Gunne
Tonio K.
Katrina and the Waves
Eric Kaz
Keith
The Kentucky HeadHunters
Jonathan King
Klaatu
The Knickerbockers
Stacy Lattisaw
Dickey Lee
The Lemon Pipers
Let's Active
Level 42
Bobby Lewis
Linda Lewis
Lindisfarne
Jackie Lomax
John D. Loudermilk
Lush
Yngwie Malmsteen
Material Issue
Kathy Mattea
Ralph McTell
Mel and Tim
Mr. Big
The Muscle Shoals Sound Rhythm Section
Musical Youth
Nektar
Robbie Nevil
Oregon
Gilbert O'Sullivan
Paris
Mica Paris
Ray Parker Jr.
Paul and Paula
Pearl Harbour and the Explosions
Pop Will Eat Itself
Johnny Preston
The Pretty Things
Alan Price
The Proclaimers
Flora Purim
Quarterflash
Eddie Rabbitt
The Ravens
Lou Rawls
Redd Kross
L.A. Reid and Babyface
Rhinoceros
Terry Riley
The Rivingtons
Royal Guardsmen
Royal Teens
Shai
Sigue Sigue Sputnik
Sir Mix-a-Lot
Skinny Puppy
Soul Survivors
The Soup Dragons
Tommy Steele
Stuff
The Sundays
Sutherland Brothers and Quiver
Tackhead
Tesla
3rd Bass
B.J. Thomas
Conway Twitty
The Tymes
UFO
Ugly Kid Joe
Wendy Waldman
Warrant
Ian Whitcomb
White Lion
Chris Whitley
Otis Williams and His Charms
Wreckx-N-Effect
Zebra

About the Contributors

Ann Abel is a former assistant editor of Rolling Stone Press and a freelance writer living in New York.

Steve Appleford is a Los Angeles–based writer and photographer. His work has appeared in a variety of publications, including the *Los Angeles Times*, ROLLING STONE, *Option*, *Spin*, the *Philadelphia Inquirer*, and *Bikini*.

Steve Dollar was chief pop music critic for the *Atlanta Journal-Constitution* for most of the 1990s. He has also written for a variety of publications, including the *Wall Street Journal*, *Newsday*, *Esquire*, *GQ*, *Jazziz*, *Downbeat*, *Salon*, *Spin*, *Request*, and *Stomp and Stammer*. He lives in Brooklyn, New York.

Paul Evans, a contributor to *The ROLLING STONE Album Guide*, *The ROLLING STONE Jazz & Blues Guide*, and the last edition of *The ROLLING STONE Encyclopedia of Rock & Roll*, is a teacher and freelance writer living in Atlanta.

Bill Friskics-Warren is a Nashville-based freelance writer whose work has appeared in the *Nashville Scene*, the *New York Times*, the *Washington Post*, *The Oxford American*, *No Depression*, and the *Journal of Country Music*, among other publications. He is also the coauthor of *Heartaches by the Number*, a critical guide to country music's 500 greatest singles.

Holly George-Warren is the editor or coeditor of numerous books on music, including *The ROLLING STONE Album Guide*, *American Roots Music*, and *The ROLLING STONE Illustrated History of Rock & Roll*. The author of *Shake, Rattle & Roll: The Founders of Rock & Roll*, she also has contributed to *The Encyclopedia of Country Music; Country on Compact Disc; The ROLLING STONE Jazz and Blues Album Guide;* and *Classic Country*, among others. She also has written for numerous publications, including ROLLING STONE, the *New York Times*, the *Village Voice*, the *Journal of Country Music*, *The Oxford American*, *Country Music*, and *No Depression*. In 2001 she received a Grammy nomination (for Best Historical Recording) for coproducing Rhino's five-CD box set *R-E-S-P-E-C-T: A Century of Women in Music*.

Mark Kemp is a former editor of *Option* and former music editor of ROLLING STONE. He has written about music and other topics for a variety of publications. In 1998 he was nominated for a Grammy for his liner notes to the Phil Ochs box set *Farewells & Fantasies*.

Jordan N. Mamone, a former assistant editor of Rolling Stone Press, has contributed to such fine readables as the *New York Press*, *Time Out New York*, *The Met*, *Ego Trip*, *CMJ New Music Report* and *New Music Monthly*, and *Grand Royal*. His liner notes appear on arcane records by YBO² and the Dustdevils. A select few have endured his obnoxious guitar playing for the New York noise-rock trio Alger Hiss.

Steve Mirkin is a Los Angeles–based freelance writer. His work has appeared in ROLLING STONE, *Us*, *Entertainment Weekly*, *Spy*, *Request*, *Option*, and the *New York Times*.

Andrea Odintz has been associated with Rolling Stone Press since 1991, when she was a member of the research staff for *The ROLLING STONE Album Guide* and *The ROLLING STONE Illustrated History of Rock & Roll*. She was a fact-checker for the 1995 edition of *The ROLLING STONE Encyclopedia of Rock & Roll* and later both researched and wrote for *Trouble Girls: The ROLLING STONE Book of Women in Rock*. Her writing has appeared in ROLLING STONE, *TV Guide*, *Total TV*, *The Cable Guide*, *See*, *Yahoo! Internet Life*, *Woman's Day*, *Clarity*, and *American Baby* magazines, as well as on *VH1.com*. Her latest project is raising her son,

Benjamin (with whom she was pregnant while working on this book), with her husband, Jeffrey Cohen, in Queens, New York.

Jon Pareles, a former editor at ROLLING STONE, is the chief popular music critic for the *New York Times.*

Nina Pearlman is a former associate editor of Rolling Stone Press. Her writing has appeared on RollingStone.com as well as in such publications as *Magnet, Alternative Press,* and *The Rocket,* of which she is a former senior editor. She lives in Brooklyn, New York.

Patricia Romanowski, the editor of Rolling Stone Press from 1981 to 1983, is the coauthor of 23 books, including four national bestsellers. Her credits include cowriting the autobiographies of Donny Osmond, Teddy Pendergrass, Annette Funicello, Mary Wilson, and Otis Williams' *Temptations,* on which the Emmy-nominated 1998 miniseries was based. As a coeditor and contributor, she received the ASCAP-Deems Taylor Special Recognition Award for *The New ROLLING STONE Encyclopedia of Rock & Roll.* She is a founding board member of The David Center and co-owner of the OASIS Asperger Syndrome Web site. She is currently pursuing a master's degree in special education of children with autism. She lives with her husband, author Philip Bashe, and their son, Justin, on Long Island.

Michael Shore is editorial director in MTV's production department, where he has also been editorial supervisor at MTV News. He's written *The ROLLING STONE Book of Music Video, Music Video: A Consumer Guide,* and *The History of American Bandstand With Dick Clark,* contributed to previous editions of *The ROLLING STONE Encyclopedia of Rock & Roll* and to *The ROLLING STONE Rock Almanac;* and written for such publications as ROLLING STONE, the *Village Voice, Billboard, Musician, ARTNews, Omni, American Illustrated, Entertainment Weekly, Jazziz,* and the *Soho Weekly News* (R.I.P.), where he worked from 1979 through its demise in 1982. He graduated from Fordham University in 1978.

Andrew Simon is a former editorial assistant of Rolling Stone Press. He has written for *CMJ New Music Monthly, MC², Time Out New York,* RollingStone.com, and SonicNet.com.

Richard Skanse is an Austin, Texas–based freelance writer and former editor and staff writer for *RollingStone.com* in New York. A native of El Paso, Texas, he has written for ROLLING STONE, *Us Weekly, George, Melody Maker,* GetMusic.com, *Performing Songwriter, Texas Music,* and other publications.

Elisabeth Vincentelli is music editor at *Time Out New York.* Her writing has appeared in *Entertainment Weekly,* ROLLING STONE, the *Village Voice, Request, Interview, Newsday,* and *OUT.* She occasionally hosts shows on New York's WFMU. A native of France, she now lives in Brooklyn, New York.

Photo Credits

King Sunny Ade: Adam Scher; Aerosmith: Norman Seeff; Eric Andersen: Unni Askeland; Babes in Toyland: Bill Phelps; Backstreet Boys: Reisig & Taylor; the Beastie Boys: Ari Marcopoulos; Beck: Charlie Gross; Buckwheat Zydeco: Kathy Anderson; Busta Rhymes: Dean Karr; Butthole Surfers: Joseph Cultice; John Cale: Ronn Spencer Archives; Johnny Cash: Martyn Atkins; Cheap Trick: Jim Houghten; Vic Chesnutt: Danny Clinch; Eric Clapton: Kevin Mazur; Leonard Cohen: Scott Newton/Austin City Limits; Albert Collins: Bill Reitzel; Alice Cooper: Randee St. Nicholas; Julian Cope: Ed Sirrs; the Cramps: Lindsay Brice; the Cure: Paul Cox; D'Angelo: Thierry LeGoues; Destiny's Child: Stephen McBride; Ani DiFranco: Albert Sanchez; Digable Planets: Cathrine Wessel; Enya: Simon Fowler; Peter Gabriel: Stephen Lovell Davis; Ben Harper and the Innocent Criminals: Danny Clinch; Gang Starr: Daniel Hastings; Jimmie Dale Gilmore: Scott Newton; Gipsy Kings: Bernard Matussiere; the Go-Go's: Vicki Berndt; Nanci Griffith: Rocky Schenck; Guns n' Roses: Robert John; Buddy Guy: Brad Pines; Emmylou Harris: Brigitte Lacombe; Juliana Hatfield: Andrew Catlin; Heavy D. and the Boyz: Danny Clinch; Soft Boys: Rosalind Kunath; the Hoodoo Gurus: Andrzej Liguz; Hüsker Dü: Daniel Corrigan; INXS: Enrique Badulescu; Waylon Jennings: Frank Ockenfels 3; the Jesus and Mary Chain: Colin Bell; Buster Poindexter: Kate Simon; B.B. King: Kevin Westenberg; Lenny Kravitz: Per Gustafsson; Ladysmith Black Mambazo: Rita Barros; Living Colour: Amy Guip; Los Lobos: Fredrik Nilsen; Lyle Lovett: Michael Wilson; L7: Catalina Leisenring; Loretta Lynn: Peter Nash; Madonna: Patrick DeMarchellier; Master P: Tim Alexander; John Mayall: Richard McLaurin; Delbert McClinton: Jim Herrington; Megadeth: Richard Avedon; the Mekons: Michael Lavine; Moby: Mei Tao; Monica: Courtesy of Arista Records; Alanis Morissette: Michele Laurita; Meshell Ndegéocello: Sheryl Nields; the Neville Brothers: Jeffrey Newberry; Randy Newman: Pamela Springsteen/courtesy of Reprise Records; Trent Reznor: Joseph Cultice; Nirvana: Chris Cuffaro; Nitty Gritty Dirt Band: Butch Adams; N.W.A: Darin Pappas; Oasis: Jill Furmanovsky; OutKast: Michael Lavine; Dolly Parton: Matthew Barnes; Pere Ubu: Carol Kitman; Tom Petty: Robert Sebree; Primus: Andrew McNaughtan; Rage Against the Machine: Danny Clinch; Bonnie Raitt: John Casado; R.E.M.: Keith Carter; the Replacements: Greg Helgeson; Sade: Albert Watson; Ryuichi Sakamoto: Mondino; Duncan Sheik: Julian Broad; Slayer: Ken Schles; Morrissey: Dean Freeman; Snoop Dogg: Michael Miller; Sonic Youth: Enrique Badulescu; Keith Sweat: Gerhard Yurkovic; They Might Be Giants: Michael Halsband; Richard Thompson: Peter Sanders; A Tribe Called Quest: Courtesy of Zomba Recording Corporation; Tricky: Barron Claiborne; John Trudell: Beth Herzhaft; Tanya Tucker: Randee St. Nicholas; UB40: David Schienmann; U2: Anton Corbijn; Lucinda Williams: Alan Messer; Victoria Williams: Chris Strother; "Weird Al" Yankovic: Johnny Buzzerio; Dwight Yoakam: Annalisa.